FEDERAL ESTATE AND GIFT TAXATION

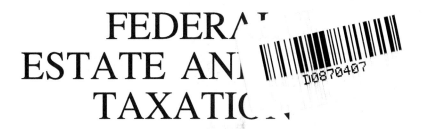

EIGHTH EDITION

RICHARD B. STEPHENS
Late Professor Emeritus
University of Florida

GUY B. MAXFIELD
Professor of Law
New York University

STEPHEN A. LIND
Albert R. Abramson Distinguished
Professor of Law
University of Florida and
Hastings College of the Law

DENNIS A. CALFEE
Professor of Law
University of Florida

ROBERT B. SMITH
Of Counsel, Sutherland, Asbill & Brennan
Atlanta, Georgia

**WARREN
GORHAM
&LAMONT**

A Thomson Company

This book is dedicated to
Richard B. Stephens
Colleague, Coauthor, Mentor, and most importantly, Friend

AUTHORS' NOTE TO THE ABRIDGED STUDENT EDITION

This abridgement of the Eighth Edition of *Federal Estate and Gift Taxation* retains all material of major pedagogical interest but omits those chapters (6 and 7) that are of more interest to the practitioner than to the student. In order to achieve economies necessary to produce a student edition, the original index and tables have been retained rather than revised, despite the dangling cross-references that necessarily result.

Summary of Contents

Table of Contents

PART II   THE ESTATE TAX

2   Imposition of Estate Tax

3   Credits Against Estate Tax

4   The Gross Estate

5   The Taxable Estate

8   Miscellaneous Estate Tax Provisions

PART III   THE GIFT TAX

9   Gift Tax: Determination of Liability

10   Gift Tax: Transfers Subject to Tax

11 Gift Tax Deductions

14 Taxable Amount

15   The Generation-Skipping Transfer Exemption

16   Applicable Rate and Inclusion Ratio

17   Other Definitions and Special Rules

18   Administrative and Miscellaneous Matters

PART I

Overview

An Overview of the Federal Taxes Imposed on Gratuitous Shifting of Interests in Property

¶ 1.01 INTRODUCTION

Squander it! Be not only generous but a spendthrift. That is the way to beat the federal taxes imposed on gratuitous shifting of interests in property. For what one has at death may be subject to the estate tax as it passes to one's survivors; and what is given away during life may not only be subject to the gift tax, but also may be taken into account in computing taxes on one's estate. Even if during life or at death beneficial interests or expectancies in others are created, taxes may be imposed as they accede to enjoyment of those interests. This book is addressed, however, to those who do not heed this advice, to those who do indeed accumulate some wealth and undertake thoughtfully to pass it on to survivors, and to those who assist others in such thoughtful transmission.

The federal statutes imposing taxes on the gratuitous transmission of wealth present a highly intricate body of law. Its complexity is often increased rather than diminished by numerous and sometimes surprising administrative and judicial interpretations of the statute. Logic is an uncertain guide to understanding, except perhaps a kind of sophisticated logic within the matrix of the overall legislative plan. It is therefore risky to generalize about these important federal taxes. At the same time, however, it is not possible to appreciate the function of a cog in this legislative machine without some understanding of its relationship to the other moving parts. Therefore, risky or not, this chapter seeks to provide a panoramic picture of the whole machine. This must be a narrative outline of most of the following chapters, in which a zoom lens is used for close examination.[1]

Can something simple be said about a subject that itself is far from simple?

¶ 1.02 THE ESTATE TAX

[1] Introduction

Since 1916, Congress has imposed a death duty on the transfer of a decedent's taxable estate. A multipurpose graduated rate table is provided,[1] which is used

---

[1] All the footnote references in this chapter are to paragraphs (¶) in subsequent chapters of this book, where general observations made here are presented in detail.

This overview disregards the federal transfer taxation consequences to nonresident noncitizens that are considered in the book. See especially ¶¶ 6.01–6.08 dealing with the federal estate taxation of such persons and ¶¶ 7.01–7.06 dealing with treaties.

[1] See ¶ 2.01[3].

as well in the computation of taxes on lifetime gifts and to a limited extent, on generation-skipping transfers. The lowest rate currently effectively applied to any portion of the taxable estate (after taking account of the unified credit[2] is 41 percent, and the graduated rates range up to a ceiling of 50 percent, which is reached at $2.5 million. The minimum rate is phased up in future years (as the unified credit is increased) and the maximum rate is phased down from the current 50 percent rate to a maximum 45 percent rate in 2007.[3] Intermediate rates apply to incremental amounts between these sums. However, the applicable rates do not depend solely on the taxable estate.

Congress has determined that lifetime gifts after 1976 are to be taken into account in determining estate tax rates. Simply stated, taxable gifts made during life operate to increase the rate of tax on testamentary dispositions of property. Under the partial integration of the estate and gift taxes, a person's lifetime and death transfers are seen as a continuum rather than as separate transactions. This is the reason for the rather involved two-step computation provided in Section 2001(b) of the Code.

The taxable estate is determined by subtracting from the "gross estate"[4] certain "deductions" authorized by the statute. Those concepts, both of which involve some artificiality, are discussed below.

[2] The Gross Estate

[a] Property Owned at Death

Property that a decedent owns at death is obviously subject to the estate tax, and its value enters into the computation of the value of the gross estate.[5] Such property may encompass one's home, bank accounts, and investments; but it also extends to amounts owing to the person as, for example, the principal of a loan one may have made to another during life (plus interest accrued on the loan), salary due from one's employer if not paid at the time of death, and amounts still to be paid for property that the decedent may have sold on a deferred-payment basis during life. Property need not be owned solely by the decedent or owned outright to have an impact on one's gross estate. Thus, one's share of community property or one's interest in property owned as a tenant in common with another, or of a future interest, such as a remainder interest in a trust, or of an undistributed share in a prior decedent's estate, all may have to be valued for inclusion in the value of the gross estate. Even

---

[2] See ¶ 3.02.

[3] See ¶¶ 2.01[3], 3.02.

[4] See ¶ 4.01.

[5] See ¶ 4.05.

property that is subject to a surviving spouse's claim for dower, courtesy, or similar interest does not escape inclusion in the decedent's gross estate.[6] However, property that is subject to a qualified conservation easement is permitted an exclusion from the gross estate.[7]

The question may be raised whether an item of value that in some manner owes its origin to the decedent's death and that is enjoyed thereafter by others must be included. The answer, not anticipated here in detail, will depend upon whether the statute itself provides a special rule for such an item (as it does for the proceeds of insurance on the decedent's life) and, if not, whether it can correctly be said that the decedent had an interest in the item at death. For example, if the decedent had no interest in a worker's compensation award paid to others by reason of the decedent's service-connected death, the amount of the award will not enter into the determination of the decedent's gross estate.

The general principle and subordinate concepts just suggested carry no special surprises. A tax on the transmission of property at death can quite appropriately be measured by the value of property rights that the decedent passes on at the time of death. However, the gross estate for tax purposes is by no means so restricted. Numerous statutory rules pull into the gross estate the value of property in which the decedent had little or no interest at death.

[b] Artificial Aspects of the Gross Estate

[i] Transfers near death. A death duty measured only by what the decedent owned at death could be easily avoided, at least in the usual case in which death is preceded by reminders of mortality. To protect against such avoidance, Congress initially and for many years treated as subject to the death tax the value of property interests that the decedent transferred gratuitously during life in contemplation of death. The fact that at death the decedent had no interest in the property was considered immaterial in taxing these substitutes for testamentary disposition.

After many years, Congress abandoned the awkward subjective contemplation-of-death intent test for includibility, replacing it with an objective nearness-to-death (three-year) test. Under the partially integrated tax system, however, very little additional revenue was generated by including all near-death transfers in the gross estate, usually at a high income tax cost to the government because of the income tax basis provisions. Congress has now limited inclusion of near-death transfers to those certain transfers that have substantial potential for estate tax avoidance.[8]

---

[6] See ¶ 4.06.

[7] See ¶ 4.02[7].

[8] See ¶ 4.07[2].

Of course, a lifetime transfer for full consideration in money or other property carries no threat to the estate tax. So Congress expressly made the near-death rule (as well as the rules relating to transfers with retained interests, to transfers taking effect at death, and to revocable transfers, all discussed here) applicable only to the extent that the lifetime transfer was for less than an adequate and full monetary consideration.[9] A receipt of partial consideration for a lifetime transfer operates to reduce the amount otherwise includible in the gross estate by the amount of the partial consideration received.[10]

A gross-up provision includes gift tax paid on lifetime transfers made within three years of death.[11]

[ii] Transfers with enjoyment retained. The right to enjoy property or to receive the income it produces is one of the attributes of outright ownership, and so is the right to designate which other person shall have such enjoyment or income. Either of these rights may be the only attribute of ownership in which a person is interested for the person's life, if one has had the opportunity to say who shall ultimately receive property in which one once held all the interests. So it might seem that the person could avoid estate taxes by gratuitously transferring property during life, retaining only interests in it or controls over it that expire at death. In such circumstances, there would seem to be no transmission at death subject to estate tax.

However, congressional power to impose a tax carries with it authority to assure that a properly adopted taxing plan will not be thwarted by artful devices. In the enactment of the very first estate tax, Congress required that there be included in the gross estate the value of interests in property transferred during life by the decedent if the nature of the transfer was such that possession or enjoyment of the transferred interest would not take effect until or after the decedent's death. When the Supreme Court gave this seemingly comprehensive language a restrictive reading, Congress more explicitly provided for the estate taxation of lifetime transfers where for one's life (or for some period tied to one's life) the decedent kept enjoyment or control either by means of a retained income interest, the enjoyment of non-income-producing property, or a power to determine who will receive income during one's lifetime.[12] Congress has extended the concept of "enjoyment" to certain transfers with a retention of a right-to-vote stock of a controlled corporation.[13] This is, of course, not to say that one should never make a transfer of the type first suggested in this paragraph, but only that if one does, one continues to be treated as the

---

[9] See ¶¶ 4.07[2][c][i], 4.08[1], 4.09[2], 4.10[2].

[10] See ¶ 4.15[2].

[11] See ¶ 4.07[3].

[12] See ¶ 4.08.

[13] See ¶ 4.08[6][d].

owner of the transferred property for estate tax purposes. It will be interesting
later to examine the height of this and other congressional fences that protect
the estate tax and to consider whether, as viewed by the courts, they are over-
protective. Meanwhile, it should be observed that the rule discussed here applies in an objective way to what was done. In contrast to the now abandoned
contemplation of death provision, it is not at all dependent on the decedent's
motivation for the lifetime transfer. Nor does any three-year or other cutoff period shield such transfers from the tax.

[iii] **Transfers conditioned upon survival.** A third provision artificially
drawing property values into a decedent's gross estate applies where, even
though the decedent has retained no current enjoyment or income rights, nor
any power to confer such enjoyment on another, the decedent has nevertheless
made the transferee's possession or enjoyment of the transferred property conditional upon surviving the decedent.[14] Thus, if *D* places property in a trust
generally for *A*'s benefit but requires the trustee to accumulate the trust income for *D*'s life and to distribute the corpus and accumulated income to *A* or
A's estate only upon *D*'s death, *A* cannot gain either possession or enjoyment
of the property except by surviving *D*. With an important qualification soon to
be mentioned, Congress views such a transfer, taking effect as it does only on
D's death, as essentially a substitute for testamentary disposition of property
and, accordingly, as a transfer that should be subject to the estate tax. This is
so even though an independent trustee may have been appointed and *D* has relinquished both enjoyment and continuing control over the property. In contrast, if the income were to be accumulated for *B*'s life (someone other than
D), perhaps because *B* would support *A* while living, and then corpus and accumulated income were to be paid to *A* at *B*'s death, the statute would not apply. In such circumstances, *A* would get possession and enjoyment when *B*
died, and without regard to whether or not *A* survived *D*.

Actually, a second qualification makes the statute inapplicable even in the
first circumstance mentioned (accumulation for *D*'s life and then distribution
to *A*) unless a further circumstance is supposed. The statute taxes the transferred property only if the decedent transferor has retained a reversionary interest in the property that has a significant value at the time of the decedent's
death. Thus, to bring this supposed transfer within the statute, it might be
amended to say that the income was to be accumulated during *D*'s life and
paid, along with the corpus, to *A* upon *D*'s death, but that if *A* predeceased *D*,
the trust was to terminate and the trust assets were to be returned to *D*. Now,
up to the time of *D*'s death, even though *A* survived *D*, *D* would have a significant chance of getting the property back and both requirements of the statute are met; *A*'s interest is conditional on *D*'s death, and *D* has retained the

---

[14] See ¶ 4.09.

requisite reversionary interest in the property. It should be noted that in such a case the statute taxes the value of the property transferred, not the value of the interest retained by the decedent, and it determines that value as of the date of *D*'s death. Thus, again, ownership of property is artificially attributed to a decedent for purposes of determining the value of *D*'s gross estate.

[iv] **Revocable transfers.** Finally, lifetime gratuitous transfers that are revocable leave the value of the transferred property in the decedent transferor's gross estate.[15] In some settings, this is more a realistic than an artificial concept. Suppose, for example, that *D* places property in a trust, the income to be paid to *A* for life, remainder to *B* or *B*'s estate, but retains the power at any time to revoke the trust and take back the property. Even though the trustee holds legal title to the property and *A* and *B* hold the beneficial interests, the title and beneficial interests both occupy a precarious perch subject to any whim of *D*; thus, it is more realistic to consider *D* the owner of the property. The statute does so. Moreover, even if *D*'s power does not extend to restoring any beneficial rights in *D* (the power reserved might be only to direct the trustee to pay the trust property over to *C*), the statute still applies. And it applies selectively to any interest in the transferred property that was subject to change by *D* at the time of *D*'s death. Thus, if *A*'s income interest was secure but *D* could substitute *C* for *B* as the remainderperson, and if *D* dies before *A*, the value of the remainder interest at the time of *D*'s death would form a part of *D*'s gross estate.

In recent years, the revocable trust (commonly referred to as a living trust) has received some recognition as a device for avoiding probate. It can indeed accomplish that objective, although it is never suggested that a revocable trust can also avoid the estate tax. As far as that exaction is concerned, the settlor's estate is left in the same position as it would have been if the trust had not been established.

The protective estate tax provisions concerning lifetime transfers may often overlap. Obviously, when they do, the gross estate is determined by applying the provision or combination of provisions that yields the largest inclusion in the gross estate.

[v] **Annuities.** Outside the area of lifetime transfers just discussed, Congress has laid down some other express rules for determining whether and to what extent the value of property interests forms a part of a decedent's gross estate. These rules are now considered.

If during one's lifetime a person purchases an annuity solely for the benefit of another, no special statutory rule applies. One has of course made a lifetime transfer, and whether the annuity will have estate tax significance will depend upon whether the transfer falls within the scope of the rules discussed

---

[15] See ¶ 4.10.

earlier. There is no special gross estate rule either, in the case of an annuity purchased after a decedent's death by one's executor in accordance with the terms of the will; funds used for the post-death purchase of an annuity will, however, have had their full estate tax impact as property the decedent owned at death.

A special statutory rule applies to so-called self-and-survivor or joint-and-survivor annuities a decedent purchased for the decedent's benefit and for that of another.[16] Many of these such annuities are various forms of deferred compensation arrangements that are allowed tax relief under the income tax, but not under the estate tax. If the decedent has been receiving, or at least has had a right to receive, payments under the policy at death and payments are to be made to others who survive after the decedent's death, the circumstance may be similar to that in which the decedent made a lifetime transfer of property, retaining enjoyment until death, which, as already explained, renders the decedent's estate taxable. The special rule on annuities taxes the decedent's estate on the value of payments to be made to survivors, but only in an amount commensurate with the decedent's contribution toward the consideration paid for the annuity policy or agreement. For example, if the decedent paid three quarters of the cost of acquisition of the policy, then three quarters of the value of the survivor's rights are taxed in decedent's estate. If the annuitant who dies made no contribution to the cost of acquiring a self-and-survivor or joint-and-survivor policy, no portion of the value of amounts payable to survivors need be included in the decedent's gross estate. Thus, in keeping with the nature of the estate tax, the annuity rule seeks to tax only values that can be said to have been transmitted to others by the decedent.

[vi] Jointly held property. Property that is held jointly by a decedent and others is the subject of specific estate tax legislation applicable to joint bank accounts and other joint tenancies and tenancies by the entirety (not tenancies in common where, as earlier suggested, a decedent's actual interest is taxed) under which the death of one tenant causes that person's full interest in the property to pass to the survivors.[17] Because such property does not pass through the probate estate, laymen are prone to assume that it is not a part of the taxable estate upon death of one of the tenants. An equally erroneous view is that the extent to which such property is taxed at death is invariably measured by the decedent's lifetime interest, i.e., one half the value of the property in the usual joint tenancy. For a long time, Congress has measured the estate tax significance of property owned jointly with survivorship rights by reference to the decedent's contribution to the cost of acquiring the property. Thus, the entire value of the property jointly owned, only a portion of it, or none of

---

[16] See ¶ 4.11.

[17] See ¶ 4.12.

it may be included in the gross estate of the first joint tenant to die: the entire value is included if the tenant furnished all the consideration; none is included if the tenant contributed nothing; and a ratable portion is included if each tenant made a contribution to the acquisition of the property. If joint tenancy property was acquired by gift or bequest from another party (so that no joint tenant contributed to the cost of its acquisition), estate tax recognition is accorded the ratable interests of the joint tenants at their deaths, as if they were equal tenants in common. Interspousal joint tenancies, however, are treated differently; only one half of the value of the property generally is included in the predeceasing spouse's gross estate, regardless of the surviving spouse's proportionate contribution to the cost of the property.[18]

[vii] General powers of appointment. Under time-honored doctrine, a power of appointment over property is not itself property or an interest in property. Thus, if X creates a trust with the income payable to A for life and the remainder payable to B or C, as D may appoint by deed or will, and D dies possessed of the power, D is not deemed to have any "interest" in the trust property. Indeed, on these facts there would seem small reason for taxing D if D never owned the property; and D's rights extend only to preferring one remainderperson over another, and D's estate is not subject to estate tax in this situation. Suppose, however, D could appoint the property to D or could otherwise appoint it less directly for D's own benefit. Such a power then approaches actual ownership of the affected property. In effect, Congress has expressly provided that it shall be treated as ownership for estate tax purposes.[19] Thus, possession of a "general" power of appointment at death is equated with ownership of the affected property. Provisions dealing in this manner with general powers of appointment should not be confused with others that also may rest on some kind of continuing control by the decedent over property. If the property involved is property that the decedent once owned and transferred while retaining certain powers, much less significant control in the decedent at death may leave the value of the property in the decedent's gross estate. Instead, this concerns property that the decedent may never have owned, the decedent's connection with it being only the power of appointment conferred on the decedent by another.

A lifetime exercise (or even a release or lapse) of a "general" power may be accorded the same estate tax treatment as if it were a lifetime transfer of the affected property by the decedent. A lifetime exercise (and sometimes the release or lapse) of a general power is tested for estate tax significance by the nature of the exercise: whether the nature of the mythical transfer by the decedent was such that if the decedent had made an actual transfer of the property,

---

[18] See ¶ 4.12[10].

[19] See ¶ 4.13.

it would be brought into the decedent's gross estate as a lifetime transfer with proscribed interests retained, a transfer conditional upon the decedent's death, or a revocable transfer. As in all these matters, there are details to consider later, but again, the main thrust of the special rule on powers is to equate a general power over property with ownership of the property.

[viii] **Life insurance.** If the decedent owned a policy of insurance on the decedent's life and the proceeds were payable to the decedent's estate, it would probably require no special rule to render the proceeds includible in the decedent's gross estate. Whether that is so or not, the statute expressly taxes the proceeds of insurance on the decedent's life that are "receivable by the executor," and this expression is deemed broad enough to apply if the proceeds may be used for the benefit of the estate.[20]

If, however, the proceeds are payable to others who survive the decedent, a different rule controls. Here, if the decedent at death had no incidents of ownership whatever in the policy (and had transferred no interest in it within three years of death), the proceeds escape taxation in the decedent's estate. Thus, life insurance on the decedent is treated somewhat like any other property that the decedent might own, except that any ownership attribute in the policy in the decedent at the decedent's death taints the entire proceeds for estate tax purposes.[21] This is to some extent so whether the tainting rights or interest was retained by the decedent (even unwittingly) upon a transfer of rights in the policy by the decedent or merely came to the decedent incidentally through the actions of another. A power to change the beneficiaries of a policy, even though the change may not be made directly or indirectly to benefit the decedent, is one among many proscribed incidents of ownership that can cause estate tax liability.

[ix] **Qualifying terminable interest property.** As previously explained, for gross estate inclusion purposes, sometimes a decedent is treated as owning property in which the decedent has no actual interest at all. This will be either property previously owned or, in the case of powers of appointment, property that the decedent had the power to obtain. However, a decedent spouse's gross estate may include property even though the spouse never owned it and could not control its disposition. Its inclusion is required simply because the predeceasing spouse's estate was allowed a marital deduction with respect to the property known as qualifying terminable interest property.[22]

---

[20] See ¶ 4.14[3].

[21] See ¶ 4.14[4].

[22] See ¶¶ 4.16, 5.06[8][d].

[c] Valuation

Every item included within a decedent's gross estate must be valued. The value that must be established for estate tax purposes is generally a fair market value.[23] Essentially, "fair market value" postulates a sale price that would be agreed upon by informed, willing buyers and willing sellers. In some instances, valuation is very nearly automatic. For example, the balance in a checking account is its own expression of value, and securities actively traded on a stock exchange may be valued in accordance with prices paid on the valuation date. At other times, an appraisal is necessary. Who can say at any point in time precisely what the value of 100 acres of unimproved land is, particularly if neither it nor substantially similar land has recently been bought or sold? What is the value of unlisted securities that have not recently been traded? Of stock in a closely held corporation? Of an interest in a partnership? Of a sole proprietorship? Once such interests are initially valued, that valuation may be adjusted for premiums or discounts for such things as control or lack of control over the property or for its lack of marketability.[24] Whatever the difficulties, the statute requires that a value be set for property and property interests that are subject to the estate tax.

All or a part of the decedent's realty may sometimes be valued with reference to its actual use rather than according to its highest or best use. Section 2032A, which attempts to accord tax relief for farms and small businesses, is considered in detail in Chapter 4.[25]

As property values are not static, the other aspect of the valuation question is the time at which, or as of which, evaluation is to be made. The general rule here, which accords with the nature of the tax, is that property is to be valued as of the date of death.[26] There is, however, one surprise under this general rule. Even for property transferred during life, the time of valuation is the same date of death if the value of the property is included in the value of the gross estate because it was the subject of an includible near-death transfer,[27] or because it falls within one of the other rules relating to the artificial gross estate, which were previously discussed here.

The statute provides an elective alternative to the usual date-of-death rule for valuation. In general, all the assets of the estate (not just some) may be valued as of a date six months after death.[28] The alternative, enacted after the great stock market crash of 1929, is a relief provision that takes account of a

---

[23] See ¶ 4.02[2].

[24] See ¶ 4.02[4].

[25] See ¶ 4.04.

[26] See ¶ 4.02[1].

[27] See ¶ 4.07[2].

[28] See ¶ 4.03.

possible hiatus in the value of property that was owned by the decedent. It is obviously harsh to impose taxes at date-of-death values if, even before the estate assets can be marshaled and the taxes paid, the estate has shrunk to a smaller value.

Congress has enacted various provisions dealing with the valuation of property interests.[29] One section provides that the value of an interest subject to a buy-sell agreement or other contract or arrangement is, in general, to be determined without regard to the terms of the agreement.[30] This provision would have the effect of taxing the value of the interest at its full fair market value, even though the interest has to be sold at a lower amount. The section, however, provides an exception if the following three requirements are satisfied: (1) The agreement is a bona fide business arrangement; (2) it is not a device to transfer property to natural objects of one's bounty at a discount price; and (3) its terms are "comparable to similar" arm's-length arrangements.[31] The regulations add a nonfamily arrangement that is treated as satisfying the foregoing exception requirements.[32]

A second section provides that a lapse of a voting right or a liquidation right in a corporate or partnership entity shall be treated either as a transfer includible in the gross estate or as a gift (whichever is applicable) if the holder of such right and family members control the entity immediately before the lapse.[33] The section also disregards an applicable restriction in valuation of an interest in a corporate or partnership entity where there is a transfer of the interest to a family member and family members control the entity.[34] An applicable restriction is not disregarded if the restriction is commercially reasonable and arises out of financing provided by an unrelated party or if it is imposed by federal or state law.[35]

In very broad outline, the foregoing comments suggest the nature of the gross estate for federal estate tax purposes. Congress, of course, does not purport to prohibit any property disposition or arrangement that one may choose to make. The tax may, however, inhibit some arrangements that would otherwise make sense. An arrangement that is expensive taxwise may certainly be the best, but usually not unless the tax cost is understood and weighed along with other considerations in advance.

---

[29] See ¶¶ 19.01, 19.02, 19.03, 19.04, 19.05.

[30] See ¶ 19.04[2].

[31] See ¶ 19.04[3].

[32] See ¶ 19.04[4].

[33] See ¶ 19.05[2].

[34] See ¶ 19.05[3].

[35] See ¶ 19.05[3][b].

[3] Deductions

Authorized deductions must next be considered, for the measure of the tax is the "taxable estate,"[36] a net figure, which is not the "gross estate." Some deductions authorized by the statute rest directly on the notion that the estate tax exaction should be measured by only the net amount that the decedent can pass on at death or, more precisely, the net amount that the decedent is treated as able to pass on, keeping in mind the artificialities involved in the determination of the gross estate. Other deductions are authorized by the statute for policy reasons.

[a] Expenses, Indebtedness, and Taxes

To appropriately reflect the net value that a decedent passes on to others, Congress permits deductions for funeral and administration expenses.[37] Such charges diminish what a decedent can transmit and are appropriately taken into account in measuring the death tax. Some will also see that administration expenses may give rise to income tax deductions as amounts expended for the management or conservation of income-producing property. An estate is an income tax–paying entity that may be entitled to these income tax deductions; and the same deductions may bear on the determination of estate tax liability. Congress imposes some restrictions, rightly or wrongly, on the use of some of these deductions for both purposes. Questions regarding the scope of these restrictions and their propriety may suitably be reserved for later examination.[38]

The claims of one's creditors obviously reduce what may be passed on; and any indebtedness that is a charge on one's property has a like effect, even if the decedent has no personal liability with respect to the debt. Appropriately, Congress permits those obligations to enter into the computation of the net or "taxable" estate.[39]

[b] Losses

Sometimes estate assets are destroyed during the administration of an estate. Where not insured or otherwise compensated for, such casualties do reduce the amount received by beneficiaries; and Congress has permitted such post-death occurrences to be taken into account in determining the net amount that a decedent is seen to transmit in the computation of the taxable estate.[40] It

---

[36] See ¶ 5.02.

[37] See ¶¶ 5.03[2], 5.03[3].

[38] See ¶ 5.03[3][d].

[39] See ¶ 5.03[5].

[40] See ¶ 5.04.

will come to mind, however, that the income tax also allows deductions for casualty losses and again there are restrictions on the use of the deduction for both taxes.[41]

[c] Charitable Deductions

As in the case of the income tax, Congress encourages philanthropy by way of an estate tax charitable deduction.[42] No dollar or percentage limitations are imposed on the amount of testamentary philanthropy that is deductible under the estate tax. However, especially where a decedent seeks to mix private or individual benefits with philanthropy, Congress keeps a tight rein, and detailed requirements of the statute must be carefully observed.[43] To the extent that billions of dollars qualify for income, estate, and gift tax charitable deductions, the government forgoes a share of earnings or other wealth that might increase its tax revenues. A supporting assumption is that but for such beneficences, the government itself would have to expend sums to accomplish the works done by the charitable recipients. However, there are offsetting worries that generate a running criticism of the charitable deduction provisions and sporadic tinkering with their terms.

[d] Marital Deduction

Subject to restrictions that disqualify many "terminable" interests in property, the amount of a bequest or devise to a spouse who survives the decedent is deducted in determining the taxable estate.[44] Although its objective is to allow tax-free interspousal transfers, Congress does impose some limitations on such transfers. In general, transfers of a terminable interest in property do not qualify for the marital deduction if the property will not be potentially taxable either in the surviving spouse's estate or upon an inter vivos transfer by the surviving spouse to a third party. However, there are several exceptions to this terminable interest rule where, in effect, even though an interest is terminable, the government is certain that the property will become taxable either in the surviving spouse's gross estate or upon an inter vivos transfer by the surviving spouse to a third party.[45] The most frequently used terminable interest exception is related to qualifying terminable interest property. Another limitation on tax-free interspousal transfers applies if a surviving spouse is not a citizen of the United States. A marital deduction is denied unless the interspousal trans-

---

[41] See ¶ 5.04[4].

[42] See ¶ 5.05.

[43] See ¶¶ 5.05[4], 5.05[5], 5.05[6], 5.05[7], 5.05[8].

[44] See ¶ 5.06.

[45] See ¶ 5.06[8].

fer occurs through a qualified domestic trust, ensuring the government's collection of revenue.[46]

[e] Family-Owned Business Deduction

Congress has expressed concern that family-owned farms and small businesses may have to be sold to generate funds to pay the federal estate tax and it has enacted several relief provisions to help avoid such consequences.[47] The most recent relief provision is an elective deduction of up to $675,000 for the value of "qualified family-owned business interests" included in a decedent's gross estate. The relief may be a welcome benefit for some estates, but it is not granted without numerous intricate statutory requirements that must be satisfied before the decedent's estate is granted a deduction. Because of an increase in the estate tax unified credit amount in 2004,[48] the deduction expires for the estates of decedents dying after 2003.[49]

[f] State Death Taxes

Commencing in 2005, the state death tax credit[50] is converted from a credit to a deduction, although many of the requirements for the allowance of the credit must still be met to qualify for the deduction.[51]

In summary, the "taxable estate" to which the tax rates are applied is the "gross estate," determined somewhat artificially in the manner indicated earlier, reduced by the amount of deductible funeral and administration expenses, claims and charges against property, casualty losses, charitable bequests, and bequests to the decedent's surviving spouse, a family-owned business deduction, and after 2004, state death taxes paid.

[4] Computation of the Estate Tax

The following steps are taken in the determination of liability for the federal estate tax.[52]

1. Ascertain the total value of the decedent's gross estate.

---

[46] See ¶¶ 5.06[9], 5.07.

[47] See, e.g., ¶¶ 2.02[3][c], 4.04, 5.08.

[48] See ¶ 3.02.

[49] See ¶ 5.08.

[50] See ¶ 3.03.

[51] See ¶ 5.09.

[52] See ¶ 2.01.

2. Ascertain the value of the decedent's taxable estate.
3. Ascertain the amount of the decedent's post-1976 taxable gifts that are not included in the gross estate. Generally, but not always, this figure is the same amount that is reported for such gifts on the decedent's prior gift tax returns.[53]
4. Compute a tentative tax on the aggregate of steps 2 and 3 at the Section 2001(c) rates.
5. From this, subtract the amount of gift tax payable on all post-1976 gifts at the Section 2001(c) rates in effect at the date of the decedent's death.[54] This calculation yields the gross (before credits) estate tax.

Some reflection will reveal that the purpose of this seemingly zigzag plan is to permit post-1976 lifetime gifts not otherwise of estate tax significance to push the taxable estate into the higher brackets of the multipurpose tax rate table.

[5] Credits

The term "gross estate tax" used in the description of the fifth item may be unfortunate. It does not, of course, imply an application of rates to the gross estate; instead, it identifies only a figure for tax liability before taking account of credits that may reduce the amount that must actually be paid. The credits that may be available are discussed in the following paragraphs.

[a] The Unified Credit

Traditionally, Congress has always permitted the tax-free testamentary transmission of some wealth and, even when an estate was large enough to incur some tax, a portion at least of all estates escaped tax. The credit against the tax is subject to a series of transitional rules that currently erase $345,800 of tax, which, assuming no inter vivos taxable gifts, is the amount of tax on a taxable estate of $1 million and that, making the same assumptions, will erase a taxable estate of $3.5 million in the year 2009. The credit not only affects tax liability, but also indirectly affects the requirements for the estate to file an estate tax return.[55]

---

[53] See ¶ 2.01[2][b].
[54] See ¶ 2.01[2].
[55] See ¶ 3.02.

[b] A Credit for State Death Taxes

Subject to sharp restrictions, state estate or inheritance taxes to which a decedent's estate is subject, although paid to the states, have historically been treated as partial payment of federal estate tax liability. In a sense, this is an early adopted revenue-sharing measure that has had the intended effect of inducing all states to impose death taxes, at least up to the amount of the available credit; failing to do so simply means that more of the total tax goes to the federal government, not that total death taxes on the estate are diminished.[56] However, the credit is being phased out over the years 2002 through 2004,[57] and it is converted to a deduction in 2005.[58]

[c] A Credit for Gift Taxes

If the decedent has paid or incurred liability for taxes on lifetime gratuitous transfers made before 1977 but, under the provisions artificially defining the gross estate, the value of the transferred property is included in the measure of the estate tax, the gift tax payment is treated as part payment of the estate tax. This is legislative expression of a congressional objective not to subject a single transfer to the rigors of both the estate and the gift taxes. Both taxes may be imposed on one transfer, but the credit allowed against the estate tax effectively eliminates the double tax aspect of the dual impositions.[59] This credit is of diminishing importance. With respect to post-1976 gifts, the credit is in effect replaced by step 5 in the present computation of the estate tax.

[d] A Credit for Estate Taxes Paid on Property Transmitted to the Decedent by Another Decedent

This credit, like the others, rests on an identifiable hardship that calls loudly for relief. For example, assume A dies, leaving property to B, who dies shortly thereafter, leaving it to C. The estate tax exactions on A's and B's estates, especially if the higher brackets of the graduated rates come into play, might leave relatively little for C. Congress has determined that this type of tax attrition is appropriate only if each decedent enjoys the property for some considerable period. Consequently, if in our example B dies within two years after A, B's "gross estate tax" is determined in the conventional manner, but in determining the "net estate tax payable," B's executor may be able to claim as a credit the entire amount of estate tax paid by A's estate on property that B

---

[56] See ¶ 3.03.
[57] See ¶ 3.03[3][d].
[58] See ¶ 5.09.
[59] See ¶ 3.04.

received from *A*. As the period increases between the death of the decedent and the decedent's benefactor, the hardship of successive estate taxes is considered to diminish; accordingly, Congress provides for a shrinkage of the credit at two-year intervals. When ten years have elapsed between the respective deaths, no credit is allowed.[60]

[e] A Credit for Foreign Death Taxes

The gross estate of a decedent who was a citizen or resident of the United States (this summary discussion does not extend to estates of nonresident noncitizens that, along with a discussion of tax treaties, are the subject of later chapters) includes the value of all the decedent's property wherever situated; some time ago Congress eliminated a provision that had excluded foreign realty. Consequently, portions of an estate may be subject not only to state and federal death duties but to those of foreign countries as well. There is nothing unconstitutional about such multiple exactions, but Congress provides relief from the weight of the foreign exaction that is somewhat more liberal than that provided with respect to death taxes imposed by the states. Again, the relief is in the form of a credit against the federal tax, in this instance for the amount of foreign death taxes paid on property included in the decedent's gross estate. This is an expressed statutory rule not dependent upon conventions or treaties with other countries that often do affect the determination of liability for federal taxes when a taxpayer's interests and activities extend across national boundaries.[61]

[6] Payment of the Estate Tax

The statute fixes the obligation to pay the tax on the "executor," which term, in the case of intestacy, is defined to encompass administrators of the decedent's estate, both de jure and de facto.[62] If required, an estate tax return generally must be filed and the estate taxes paid within nine months of the decedent's death, although in some circumstances both obligations may be extended without a penalty being imposed.[63] However, interest is imposed on any extension of time for payment. The actual burden of the tax generally will fall on the estate subject to probate and upon that portion that is not subject to specific bequests, i.e., the residuary estate. The obligation of the executor to pay

---

[60] See ¶ 3.05.

[61] See ¶ 3.06.

[62] See ¶¶ 2.02, 8.02.

[63] See ¶ 2.02.

does not amount to personal liability of the executor, except in the case of certain improprieties on the executor's part.[64]

Congress could be content with assurances that the tax will be paid without regard to whose purse is actually lightened by the exaction. In general, the primary objective of assuring collection is achieved by authorizing collection out of any property that forms a part of the gross estate. However, the primary burden generally falls on the residuary estate,[65] subject to specific federal statutory rules that may ultimately fasten liability for a share of the tax on recipients of the proceeds of insurance on the decedent's life[66] and property that was subject to a power of appointment in the decedent[67] if, under the artificial gross estate concepts described here, such insurance or appointive property enters into the measurement of the tax. The federal statutes provide a right of recovery in the case of certain property qualifying for the marital deduction[68] and certain property involved in a transfer with a retained income interest or a power to alter the income interest.[69] Beyond this, many states have "apportionment" statutes that often determine the ultimate tax burden.[70]

As an example of their possible application, suppose the decedent held property jointly with a child. If the executor properly pays the estate tax, measured partly by the inclusion of the jointly held property out of the residuary probate estate that does not include that property, should the residuary legatees shoulder the entire tax burden, even though a portion of the property generating the tax went to the child and was not a part of the probate estate? In such circumstances, state statutes may enable the estate to secure contribution for a part of the tax from the recipient of the tainted lifetime gift, thus more equitably "apportioning" the actual tax burden.

¶ 1.03 THE GIFT TAX

[1] Introduction

The gift tax is a junior partner of the estate tax. It is junior in age; after a brief flurry of gift taxation in the 1920s, the present gift tax statute originated in 1932, its date of inception following that of the estate tax by some sixteen

---

[64] See ¶ 8.03.

[65] See ¶ 8.04.

[66] See ¶ 8.05.

[67] See ¶ 8.06.

[68] See ¶ 8.07.

[69] See ¶¶ 4.08, 8.08.

[70] See ¶ 8.04[2].

years. It is no longer junior in stature; apart from exclusions and deductions, its graduated rates, like those of the estate tax, are currently found in the multipurpose rate table. For most of its life, the tax has been imposed on an annual basis, as it is now.[1]

As in the case of the estate tax, the gift tax is an excise, a tax on the transmission of property. Thus, the tax is imposed on the donor and determined with reference to all the donor's gifts;[2] while identification of the donee is required for certain exclusion and deduction purposes, the gift tax is not, like the income tax, a tax on receipts. Nevertheless, a donee may incur liability for the gift tax if the donor does not pay the tax for which the donor is primarily liable.[3]

Because the gift tax and the estate tax are in pari materia, taxing the gratuitous transmission of wealth either during life or at death. Thus, it would be expected, and is the case, that the gift tax is imposed in accordance with graduated rates. In this respect a concern for prior gifts was once a peculiarity of the gift tax. The rates progress in accordance not just with gifts made in the taxable period for which the return is filed, but with reference to all taxable gifts made by the donor since the inception of the gift tax in 1932.[4] The current estate tax computation resembles this more seasoned gift tax device. There still may be substantial advantage in spreading gifts to get the benefit of exclusions that recur annually. However, to the extent that gifts are taxable, the rate of tax generally is the same regardless of whether a very large gift is made all in one year or spread over several years; the accumulative approach of the rate table will produce the same amount of gift tax in either case except in years when there are reductions in the top gift tax rates. Computation is explained at the end of this gift tax summary, but the point will be clearer here if one compares the usual income tax consequences of spreading income over several years.

[2] Transfers Subject to the Gift Tax

The gift tax is, and is intended to be, comprehensive. While limited to transfers of property (no tax is payable on donated services), anything of value may be the subject of a taxable transfer.[5] The tax applies to cash gifts and to those in the form of realty or tangible or intangible personal property. Nor need gifts be made directly; one's payment of one's child's mortgage or interest on the

---

[1] See ¶ 9.02[3].

[2] See ¶ 9.03[3].

[3] See ¶ 9.04[11].

[4] See ¶ 9.03[3].

[5] See ¶ 10.01[3].

mortgage is a gift to the child. Beyond this, any discernible gratuitous shifting of financial advantage from one to another may constitute a gift.

[a] Dominion and Control

A timing question can arise with respect to gifts that take the form of something less than an outright transfer. The key to answering the question of when a gift is made is the determination whether the donor has relinquished dominion and control over the property or property interest transferred.[6] For example, a transfer of property into a trust may constitute a gift. However, if the settlor of the trust retains a right to revoke it, the settlor has not relinquished control over the property and no gift has yet occurred. If the settlor should later relinquish the right to revoke, the transfer would then be complete for gift tax purposes. This suggests two related thoughts. First, the time at which a gift becomes complete determines when it must be reported and gift tax paid. Second, valuation of the gift is to be made at the time the gift becomes complete. Thus, if in the 1980s, *A* placed 100 shares of GE stock in a revocable trust for others and then in the current year relinquished the power of revocation, the gift tax liability on the transfer would be measured not by the lower value of the stock when it was transferred to the trust, but by its much greater value when the gift became complete.[7]

It should not be assumed from the foregoing example that a transfer is incomplete only if the transferor retains a power to take the property back for the transferor's own benefit. It is likewise treated as incomplete if the transferor retains merely the right to shift the interests of others upon whom a financial benefit is only tentatively conferred. However, for gift tax purposes a transfer is deemed complete if the donor retains only a right to alter the time or manner of the enjoyment of the gift by the donee. Also, a transfer is considered complete if the transferor confers control over the property on a third person while relinquishing all control in the transferor.

In this light, it might seem that the gift tax and the estate tax mesh pretty well, and sometimes they do. That is, a transfer may escape the gift tax as not yet complete for the very reason that makes it subject to estate tax when the donor dies. However, it must be stated emphatically that a determination that a particular transfer is subject to estate tax upon the transferor's death is no assurance that the transfer is not subject to gift tax when made.[8] For example, a transfer in trust in which the settlor retains the right to the trust income for life is subject to the gift tax on the remainder, notwithstanding the includibility of the value of the remainder in the settlor's gross estate. Recall, however, that

---

[6] See ¶ 10.01[4].

[7] See ¶ 10.02[1].

[8] See ¶ 10.01[10].

actual estate tax liability will be diminished either by way of credit for gift tax paid or, as it regards post-1976 gifts, by step 5 in the computation of the estate tax.

Of course, for gift tax as well as estate tax purposes, the interest in property that has been gratuitously transferred must be identified. Thus, if our trust settlor provided that upon the settlor's death the trust property was to be paid to unrelated R or R's estate, the gift tax is measured by the value of the remainder interest at the time of the transfer. The life interest retained by the transferor has not been the subject of a gift; and the circumstance is much the same as if a donor owning three acres of land gave away two but kept one.

Other lifetime transfers that are subjected to estate tax because they were intended to take effect only after the transferor's death may likewise be subject to gift tax. For example, if D transfers property to a trust, income to be paid to unrelated B for life and the corpus to be returned to D if living but, if not, remainder to be paid to unrelated R or R's estate, D has made a taxable gift of the value of B's life interest and R's contingent remainder even though, upon D's death survived by B, the value of the remainder would be subjected to estate tax. D has relinquished control of the interests of B and R, even though D has retained an interest in the property that might result in D getting it back while D is alive. The result is not changed if B dies while D is living (so that D does get the property back and R's remainder is wiped out). A snapshot is taken of the circumstances that exist at the time of the transfer; and the photograph is not to be retouched with the aid of hindsight based on subsequent events.

Congress has enacted a series of special gift tax valuation rules to combat perceived weaknesses in the gift tax structure.[9] Under one such rule, concern with donors using the actuarial valuation tables to their benefit in making transfers to family members has caused Congress in such circumstances to conclusively presume that a donor-retained interest in property is valued at zero.[10] Thus, even though only an income interest or a remainder interest is transferred to a family member with the remaining interests in the property retained by the donor, the value of the transferred interest is equal to the full value of the property. The special valuation rule applies even where adequate and full consideration is received for the transferred interest. This special valuation rule plays havoc with some of the long-standing gift tax concepts discussed earlier, although relief is provided when double transfer taxation occurs.[11] Typically, Congress throws in some exceptions to this special valua-

---

[9] See ¶¶ 19.01, 19.02, 19.03, 19.04, 19.05.

[10] See ¶ 19.03[1].

[11] See ¶ 19.03[4][c].

tion rule, including exceptions for qualified personal residence trusts and other qualified retained interests.[12]

A second special valuation of retained interests rule applies where a donor directly or indirectly uses the transfer of a corporate or partnership interest in an attempt to freeze (avoid further appreciation in the value of a retained interest) the value of the donor's gross estate.[13] If a donor transfers an interest in the entity to a family member and retains an interest in which the family members have the discretion as to whether to make distributions to the donor with respect to the retained interest, the discretionary rights are valued at zero, thereby increasing the value of the transferred interest. This rule also applies even though adequate consideration is received for the transferred interest.[14] Again, there are several exceptions to this special valuation rule, and relief provisions come into play if double taxation occurs.[15]

Under general gift tax principles, if one buys property that one requires to be transferred to oneself and another as joint tenants with right of survivorship, one has made a gift to the other of the value of the other's interest (or, stated differently, of the value of the property *less* the value of the interest retained in it by the purchaser). If the property is later sold and the proceeds of sale are divided between them, either joint tenant makes a gift to the other if, in the division, the tenant receives less than the share of the proceeds that represents the value of the tenant's interest in the property at the time of the sale. Thus, in the case of an ordinary joint tenancy created by a purchase funded by one of the two parties, the purchaser who paid for the property would make a gift of one-half its value at the time of the purchase; an equal division of the proceeds at the time of sale would constitute no gift. Similar principles apply to the acquisition of a tenancy by the entirety although, as neither spouse has a right unilaterally to sever the tenancy, the amount of the gift is dependent upon the spouses' relative life expectancies, with the spouse having the greater life expectancy receiving a larger interest in the property.

[b] Consideration

Consideration received for property interests transferred generally plays about the same role in both estate tax and gift tax matters. A transfer for full money value generally is a neutral event for purposes of either tax. If partial consideration is received in the case of a lifetime transfer, the measure of the gift is the amount by which the value of the property transferred exceeds the

---

[12] See ¶ 19.03[3].

[13] See ¶ 19.02.

[14] See ¶ 19.02[2][a][i].

[15] See ¶¶ 19.02[3], 19.02[5][c].

consideration received.[16] In fact, the courts have viewed the statutory expression of this rule as a definition of "gift" for gift tax purposes. In general, a transfer for less than adequate consideration in money's worth is a gift, without regard for showing of donative intent, such as is required to invoke the income tax gift exclusion. The gift tax approach to the matter of consideration should be viewed against the background of the estate tax. In effect, by the gift tax Congress seeks to tax the transfer of property that would otherwise be subject to estate tax when the donor died. To the extent a transferor receives consideration for a transfer, the property potentially subject to estate tax is not diminished; it is more a matter of substitution of one asset for another. No gift tax is needed (and none is imposed) to protect the estate tax in the case of such substitutions; but it will be necessary later to take a close look at what can be treated as consideration for these purposes.[17]

The gift tax statute is far less comprehensive than the estate tax statute in identifying transfers subject to the tax. Consequently, detailed rules in the area have developed largely by way of administrative and judicial decisions in a manner similar to the growth of the common law. Nevertheless, Congress has marked off a few areas for specific legislative treatment. They are briefly noted in following paragraphs [c] through [g].

[c] General Powers of Appointment

As a power of appointment over property is not an interest in property, one who exercises such a power, with the effect that there is a shift in ownership of the property subject to the power, has not made a transfer of the property. Nevertheless, if the power holder had wide discretion as to its exercise, even to the point of using the property directly or indirectly for one's own benefit, one would have something very close to complete ownership of the affected property. Thus, here, as in the case of the estate tax, Congress has by statute essentially equated a general power with ownership. The shifting of property interests, which is occasioned by the exercise (or sometimes the release or lapse) of a general power of appointment, is artificially treated as a transfer of property for gift tax purposes.[18] Whether the constructive transfer constitutes a gift still remains, of course, to be determined under the general principles of the gift tax. For example, one cannot make a gift to oneself; therefore, if a person exercises a power by appointing the subject property to oneself, no gift has occurred, even though the statute expressly treats such an exercise as a "transfer." Again, the result should be viewed against the background of the estate tax. Before exercise, the property was potentially includi-

---

[16] See ¶ 10.02[3].

[17] See ¶¶ 10.02[4], 10.02[5], 10.02[6].

[18] See ¶ 10.04.

ble in the estate of the power holder by reason of the power holder having the general power over the property. After exercise, the property is likewise potentially includible, but now because it is property that the power holder actually owns. There is no policy reason for subjecting the lifetime exercise of the power to the gift tax; and, happily, in some circumstances such as this, the estate and gift taxes do mesh nicely in this respect.

[d] Generation-Skipping Transfer Tax

The third wealth transfer tax is the generation-skipping transfer tax, addressed in more detail later in this chapter. One type of taxable generation-skipping transfer is the inter vivos direct skip. An inter vivos direct skip is also a gift subject to gift tax. To further complicate matters, any generation-skipping transfer tax liability paid with respect to an inter vivos direct skip is treated as an additional gift transfer for gift tax purposes.[19]

[e] Divorce Transfers

Interspousal transfers upon the occasion of a divorce can be within the scope of general gift tax principles; but they may also escape the gift tax under express statutory rules. In general, Congress has said that such transfers in satisfaction of marital rights (and certain support rights of minor children), if made under a written agreement that is entered into not more than one year prior to or two years subsequent to a divorce, shall be treated as made for full consideration, thus avoiding the gift tax.[20]

[f] Disclaimers

Usually, a simple "no, thank you" constitutes a polite rejection of an offer. In the tax area, however, the Service has often asserted that a would-be rejecting transferee of property in effect accepted the property and then also made a transfer of it by way of the transferee's purported rejection. In the case of the gift tax, this can raise the question of whether there were two gifts, or one, or none. Congress has supplied potential donee-donors with a statutory procedure that, if followed, supports a conclusion that no transfer ever occurred.[21] Although the procedure is expressed in the gift tax chapter of the Code, similar problems arising under the estate tax and the tax on generation-skipping transfers are determined according to its terms.[22]

---

[19] See ¶ 10.05.
[20] See ¶ 10.06.
[21] See ¶ 10.07.
[22] See ¶¶ 4.18, 17.04[3].

[g] Qualified Terminable Interest Property

A donor may be treated as owning an interest in property that the donor never owned outright or even had the power to acquire or to dispose of, simply because the donor's spouse was previously allowed a marital deduction for a transfer of the property. Inter vivos actions on the donor's part with respect to the income from the property may trigger a taxable transfer by the donor of the interests other than the donor's own interests for gift tax purposes.[23]

[3] Exclusions

Another gift tax concept, exclusions, plays a significant role in the computation of the gift tax. It can quickly be seen that the gift tax has the capacity to be an atrocious nuisance. Suppose A takes adult child B to dinner the night the first grandchild is born. A makes a gift to B, of course; so must the gift tax be figured more or less along with the state sales tax on the dinner? The next day, A buys a bassinet for the new baby and a week later pays $500 in doctor and hospital bills relating to the birth of the grandchild. Are these gifts subject to tax? Probably not; at this point it might be noted parenthetically that not all payments for the needs and desires of children fall into the gift category at all. A person's discharge of the person's obligation to support another is regarded as beyond the reach of the gift tax statute,[24] despite the otherwise broad meaning accorded the expression "the transfer of property by gift." Thus, looking back, it will be seen that the hypothetical questions raised (transfers to or for the benefit of an *adult* child) were framed so as not to involve the mere discharge of support obligations. What then may remove the transactions from the reach of the gift tax?

Since its inception, the gift tax statute has permitted a donor to make quite substantial tax-free gifts each year. In effect, Congress is saying that birthday, wedding, and other occasional gifts within reasonable limits do not constitute a significant transmission of wealth that would threaten the efficacy of the estate tax, and consequently, such gifts need not be subjected to the gift tax. How generous, then, is this annual exclusion? The answer is: somewhat more generous than its origin and purpose might suggest.

The statute excludes entirely, from the computation of taxable gifts, otherwise taxable transfers by a donor of amounts up to $11,000 to each of any number of donees.[25] This exclusion recurs annually. Thus, there is an $11,000 ($10,000 indexed for inflation after 1998) "annual exclusion." If gifts are made to five donees, the exclusion for the year amounts to $55,000. Five $11,000

---

[23] See ¶ 10.08.

[24] See ¶ 10.02[5].

[25] See ¶ 9.04[1].

gifts can likewise be made the next calendar year, and so on indefinitely, without incurring any gift tax liability. Moreover, the exclusion does not simply eliminate small gifts; it works as well to reduce the significant amount of large gifts. Thus, if *A* gives *B* $100,000 in cash, the "included" gift for the taxable period (the amount taken into account in determining *A*'s taxable gifts) is only $89,000.

The annual exclusion is not available to reduce all manner of gifts; it applies only to gifts of present interests in property. For example, if *D* transfers property in trust, the income to be paid to *B* for life, remainder to *C* or *C*'s estate, *D* has made gifts to both *B* and *C*, each of whom receives a beneficial interest in the trust property. Does this gift warrant two annual exclusions? No. Only one is allowed for the present interest transferred to *B*; the future interest given to C is disqualified. Thus, if the value of the property transferred to the trust is $15,000 and *B*'s life interest is properly valued at $6,000, and *C*'s remainder interest at $9,000, then the gift, after taking account of the exclusion, is $9,000 ($15,000 less $6,000, the excludible portion).

The disqualification of future interests for the annual exclusion has created some problems in the making of excludible gifts to minors; current statutory relief from such difficulties is considered in a later chapter.[26]

Also excluded from the clutches of the gift tax, regardless of whom the payments benefit, or the amount of the payments, are tuition payments and medical expense payments that are made directly to an educational organization or to a provider of medical care.[27]

[4] Gift-Splitting

If one spreads one's generosity among numerous donees and over a considerable number of years, one can indeed transmit a substantial amount of wealth tax-free. In addition, gift-splitting offers a further ameliorating provision that sometimes has the effect of doubling this advantage.

A married donor can, with the donor's spouse's consent, elect to treat the donor's gifts as if they were made one half by each spouse.[28] Thus, if *A* makes a $22,000 gift to *B* and the requisite election is made, then for computation purposes *A*'s gift becomes an $11,000 gift by *A* and an $11,000 gift by *A*'s spouse, all tax-free because the gifts are within the annual exclusions of the two taxpayers. *A* could make $22,000 gifts to each of five donees (or any other number) and, with the advantage of the "split-gift" provision, entirely escape gift tax on gifts amounting to $110,000 (or $22,000 times the number).

---

[26] See ¶¶ 9.04[4], 9.04[5].

[27] See ¶ 9.04[6].

[28] See ¶ 10.03.

This, too, could be done annually and indefinitely. The concept is a wholly artificial one; the gifts in fact may be made entirely by one spouse and still be "considered" as if made one half by each. The split-gift provision may have a minimizing effect on tax liability in two other respects, as will subsequently be mentioned.

[5] Taxable Gifts

Gift tax rates apply only to a net figure, "taxable gifts," analogous to the "taxable estate" or "taxable income," so it becomes necessary to consider gift tax deductions. The gift tax statute provides for only two deductions in the computation of taxable gifts, and each bears resemblance to some of the estate tax deductions previously noted.

[a] Charitable Deduction

Charitable gifts escape gift tax by way of a deduction unrestricted by any dollar or other limitation.[29] However, to be deductible, a charitable contribution must meet certain formal requirements and must be made to a qualified recipient. Philanthropy mixed with private objectives raises gift tax problems similar to those suggested earlier with regard to the estate tax deduction for testamentary philanthropy.

[b] Marital Deduction

Finally, there is a gift tax marital deduction.[30] In general, it removes from taxable gifts the value of property given by one spouse to the other. "Terminable interest" rules and a transfer to a spouse who is not a citizen of the United States sometimes disqualify a transfer for the deduction, just as in the case of the estate tax, but there are again multiple exceptions to the rules. Exceptions to the terminable interest rule are made if the property will return to the donor or will be taxable either in the spouse's estate or upon an inter vivos transfer by the spouse to a third party. A transfer to a qualified domestic trust creates an exception to the noncitizen spouse rule. The deduction, again, is traceable to a congressional decision to allow interspousal transfers to be made without immediate tax consequences.

---

[29] See ¶ 11.02.
[30] See ¶ 11.03.

[6] Computation of the Gift Tax

The accumulative nature of the gift tax approach to rates fostered a recondite legislative prescription for computation of the tax. Congress has always sought to tax taxable gifts for a particular period at escalated rates pushed upward by taxable gifts made in all previous periods. The gift tax now shares the multi-purpose rate table with the estate tax. Like the estate tax, the gift tax is arrived at by a dual computation:

1. Determination of a tax figure under the current rate table for all taxable gifts, aggregating current and past taxable gifts.
2. Determination of a tax figure under the current rate table for past taxable gifts only, excluding those made in the current period. The tax for the period emerges when the second figure is subtracted from the first.[31]

While it might seem that somehow past gifts are being taxed again, this is clearly not so; subtraction of the second figure nullifies any tax attributable to past gifts in the first figure, and the only effect of taking past gifts into account is to make higher rates potentially applicable to current gifts than would apply if the current gifts were considered in isolation.

On the other hand, the split-gift provision should once more be called to mind. Because the tax rates escalate, it is obvious that gifts by two taxpayers of $2 million each may attract less tax liability than a $4 million gift by one. Thus, in the case of a married donor, not only may the election of the gift-splitting provision reduce taxable gifts by way of invoking another's annual exclusion, but also, to the extent that taxable gifts emerge, they may be subjected to lower rates. In addition, two unified credits may offset any gift tax liability rather than one.

Under the statutory system, past taxable gifts must be taken into account even if the taxpayer failed to report them or otherwise did not pay tax on them.[32] In determining the amount of such prior gifts, the law in effect at the time of the gift controls. Furthermore, if the statute of limitations has run, the taxpayer's treatment of the amount of such gifts, both valuation and the law involved may determine the amount of such gifts.[33] However, even if the amount of the donor's prior gifts is altered in the computation, this does not violate the limitations statute, as the effect is not to collect any tax on such prior gifts but only to see that they play their proper role in determining currently applicable rates.

---

[31] See ¶ 9.03[3].
[32] See ¶ 9.05.
[33] See ¶ 9.04[2].

[7] The Gift Tax Credit

A credit applies to the gift tax as well as the estate tax.[34] Similar to its role under the estate tax, the credit generally offsets $345,800 of gift tax liability or $1 million of taxable gifts, although unlike the estate tax credit which increases over the years, the gift tax credit is capped at that $345,800 amount.

Are two free transmissions of that magnitude granted, one during life and the other at death? No. When the gift tax credit takes the place of gift tax payment, it reduces dollar for dollar the reduction for gift tax payable in step 5 of the estate tax computation. Consequently, although it may require some reflection to understand it, the credit is used effectively only once to offset transfer tax liability, albeit at the greater of the gift or estate tax credit amount.[35]

[8] Payment of the Gift Tax

As previously indicated, the gift tax is computed on an annual basis. Whether a return must be filed for any calendar year depends on whether a taxpayer has made gifts in that year that exceed the taxpayer's annual exclusions, that are not qualified transfers for tuition or medical care, and generally that do not qualify for the charitable deduction or the marital deduction. This is so even if no tax will be due because of gift-splitting, properly asserted deductions, or the unified credit. If a gift tax return is required to be filed for a year, it generally must be filed by April 15 of the following year, a date familiar to calendar-year income tax payers.

Perhaps only implicit in what has been said here, the gift tax is not imposed on an individual gift basis. It may be necessary, of course, to look at a particular gift and to identify the donee for the purpose of asserting the annual exclusion or the right to a deduction. However, the tax is computed on aggregate gifts by the donor during the taxable period, much as the estate tax is imposed, not on individual bequests or inheritances but on the decedent's transmission of the decedent's estate. Just as the tax is figured on the donor's gratuitous transmissions, so is the donor made primarily liable for payment of the tax.[36] However, every good donee should know that the donee may incur gift tax liability if the donor fails to pay the tax.[37] In fact, the donee's liability may be in an amount equal to the full value of the gift received, not merely the tax attributable to *the donee's* gift, as one of possibly many made by the donor in the same taxable period.

---

[34] See ¶¶ 3.02, 9.06.

[35] See ¶ 3.02.

[36] See ¶ 9.03[4].

[37] See ¶ 9.04[11].

¶ 1.04 THE TAX ON GENERATION-SKIPPING TRANSFERS

[1] Introduction

The estate tax and the gift tax apply to gratuitous transmissions of wealth by one who is its owner or by one to whom ownership may reasonably be imputed. Consequently, they generally do not apply to mere shifts in interests, such as occur upon distributions from an existing trust to a beneficiary or upon the termination of a trust or a trust beneficiary's interest, leaving others in possession of or with the enjoyment of trust property. For many years, therefore, estate planners had used the trust (and equivalent devices) to pass along a person's wealth, effectively cascading enjoyment among succeeding generations but skipping one or more of the generations as far as the federal taxes on gratuitous transfers were concerned.

Initially, Congress imposed a complex tax on generation-skipping transfers that encompassed certain terminations and distributions from trusts and similar devices. However, Congress repealed its initial effort and enacted another Chapter 13 because outright generation-skipping transfers to transferees well down the ancestral line avoided taxation at the intervening generations. The revised version of Chapter 13 is an attempt to provide greater uniformity in imposition of the tax and to simplify (generally at the taxpayer's cost) its computation.

[2] Terminology

The terminology of the generation-skipping transfer tax is unlike that of other taxes, even other transfer taxes. Thus, an elementary understanding of the key terms is crucial to understanding the taxation of generation-skipping transfers.

The terminology cycle begins with a "transferor," an individual who is generally either the decedent (if property has been subject to the estate tax) or the donor (if property has been subject to the gift tax).[1] In general, there is a new transferor any time property is subject to a tax imposed by Chapter 11 or Chapter 12. However, for purposes of Chapter 13, the qualified terminable interest property election may be disregarded, with the result that the original transferor spouse may continue as the transferor, even if the property is included in the transferee spouse's gross estate or is the subject matter of a gift by the transferee spouse.[2]

---

[1] See ¶ 17.02[1].

[2] See ¶ 17.02[1][c][i].

Assignment of a generation level is important under Chapter 13; an individual's generation level is determined with reference to the transferor.[3] If the individual is related to the transferor, the relationship to the transferor determines the individual's generation level.[4] Thus, the transferor's child, niece, or nephew is assigned a generation level one below that of the transferor; the transferor's grandchild, grandniece, or grandnephew is assigned a generation level two below that of the transferor. An appropriate special rule applies if a descendant (and sometimes other relatives) of the transferor is dead at the time of the transfer. The rule has the effect of elevating the surviving relative into a higher generation. Thus, if one's child is deceased at the time of the transfer, the transferor's grandchildren who are children of the predeceased child are treated as the transferor's children because, as a practical matter in such circumstances, the transferor is not "skipping" a generation.[5] An individual marrying a person related to the transferor is assigned to the same generation level as that individual's spouse. Adopted persons are treated as related persons.[6] The generation level assigned to a person unrelated to the transferor is determined by the number of years separating that person in age from the transferor.[7] Persons twelve and one-half to thirty-seven and one half years younger than the transferor are assigned to a generation level one below that of the transferor. Persons unrelated to the transferor and more than thirty-seven and one half years younger than the transferor are assigned a generation level at least two below that of the transferor.

The assignment of generation levels is significant in identifying "skip persons"[8] who are the key to determining whether a generation-skipping transfer has occurred. Skip persons can be natural persons, trusts, or trust equivalent arrangements.[9] A natural person is a skip-person if the generation level to which the individual is assigned is two or more levels below that of the transferor.[10] A transferor's grandchildren and great-grandchildren, as well as unrelated persons more than thirty-seven and one half years younger than the transferor, are usually classified as skip persons. Generally, a trust or a trust equivalent arrangement is a skip person if all persons having an immediate right to receive income or corpus from the trust and all permissible noncharitable recipients of income or corpus are skip persons.[11] A trust providing income

---

[3] See ¶ 17.01.

[4] See ¶ 17.01[2][a].

[5] See ¶ 17.01[2][a][ii].

[6] See ¶ 17.01[2][a].

[7] See ¶ 17.01[2][b].

[8] See ¶ 13.03.

[9] See ¶¶ 13.03[2], 13.03[3].

[10] See ¶ 13.03[2].

[11] See ¶ 13.03[3].

to a transferor's child for life and a remainder to a grandchild is not a skip person; however, a trust with income to a transferor's grandchild for life and a remainder to anyone in any generation is a skip person. Sensibly enough, any natural person or trust or trust equivalent arrangement that is not a skip person is treated as a non-skip person.[12]

[3] The Three Types of Generation-Skipping Transfers

Chapter 13 imposes a tax on three types of generation-skipping transfers: direct skips, taxable terminations, and taxable distributions. A single event may trigger more than one generation-skipping transfer, but only one generation-skipping transfer tax will be imposed. To determine which type of generation-skipping transfer occurs, a pecking order has been established.[13] Direct skips prevail. Next in line are taxable terminations. Taxable distributions come last, acting as a backstop when other transfers are not present. The three types of transfers are considered in that order.

[a] Direct Skips

A direct skip is the transfer of an interest in property that is subject to either estate tax or gift tax and is made to a skip person (either a natural person or a trust or trust equivalent arrangement).[14] An inter vivos or a testamentary transfer to one's grandchild is a direct skip, as is an inter vivos or a testamentary transfer to a trust with income to grandchildren and remainder to their heirs. Because such transfers skip estate and gift taxation at one generation level, the child's generation, Congress deems it appropriate to impose a generation-skipping transfer tax. In general, inter vivos direct skip transfers that would be included in the transferor's gross estate if the transferor died immediately after making the transfer are not treated as occurring until the possibility of estate tax inclusion is removed.[15] Congress is not concerned with how many generations are skipped in a direct skip; an outright gift or estate tax transfer to the transferor's great-grandchild or great-great-grandchild is treated as a single generation-skipping transfer.

When a direct skip occurs, a generation-skipping tax is imposed even though a gift tax or an estate tax is also imposed. If the direct skip is inter vivos, the generation-skipping transfer tax paid by the transferor is treated as

---

[12] See ¶ 13.03[5].
[13] See ¶ 13.02[1][b].
[14] See ¶ 13.02[4].
[15] See ¶¶ 13.02[4][d], 16.02[7].

an additional inter vivos gift, with the result that there are two gift transfers[16] as well as a generation-skipping transfer.

[b] Taxable Terminations

A taxable termination occurs only with respect to a trust or a trust equivalent arrangement. It occurs upon the termination of the entire interest of a beneficiary who has an immediate right to receive income or corpus from the trust or who is a permissible noncharitable current recipient of income or corpus from the trust and the property held in the trust is not subject to federal estate or gift tax at the time of the termination, when immediately thereafter there is either (1) no non-skip person having such an interest in the trust or (2) no one having any such interest in the trust but a subsequent distribution may be made to a skip person.[17] In simpler terms, this generally means that if the entire interest of a current actual or permissible interest holder terminates, the property held in the trust is not subject to federal estate or gift tax at the termination, and that interest is subsequently acquired by a beneficiary who is a skip person in relation to the transferor of the trust, there is a taxable termination.

The classic taxable termination occurs when transferor T creates a trust with income to child C for life, then income to grandchild GC (C's only child) for life and a remainder to GGCs, T's great-grandchildren. There is a taxable termination generation-skipping transfer at C's death (as C's interest terminates without imposition of any gift or estate tax) and another at GC's death (as GC's interest terminates without any imposition of gift or estate tax). Imposition of the tax is appropriate at each level as a generation is skipped. If C had held a general power of appointment over the corpus and the power lapsed at C's death, the property subject to the power would have been included in C's gross estate; and, as a result, C would have become the transferor of subsequent generation-skipping transfers from the trust. Because GC is a non-skip person with respect to C, no taxable termination would occur with respect to the trust until GC's death and the termination of GC's interest.

[c] Taxable Distributions

The catchall in the generation-skipping transfer tax structure is the taxable distribution.[18] If a distribution is made from a trust or equivalent arrangement to a skip person and the distribution is neither a direct skip nor a taxable termination, it constitutes a taxable distribution. For example, if a transferor es-

---

[16] See ¶ 10.05.
[17] See ¶¶ 13.02[2][a], 13.02[2][b], 13.02[2][c], 13.02[2][d].
[18] See ¶ 13.02[3].

tablishes an inter vivos or a testamentary trust with income to child for life and a remainder to adult grandchildren, but permits the third-party trustee to give income or corpus to any of the grandchildren, a taxable distribution occurs on a distribution of income or corpus to a grandchild if the distribution does not deplete the entire trust corpus (in which case a taxable termination would occur). Such a distribution skips the child's generation and imposition of a generation-skipping transfer tax is warranted; imposing a tax on taxable distributions effects a backstop to support other generation-skipping transfers in the same manner that the gift tax backstops the estate tax.

Payment out of trust funds of any portion of Chapter 13 tax imposed on a taxable distribution is treated as an additional taxable distribution.[19] A taxable distribution occurs because liability for payment of the generation-skipping transfer tax is imposed on the skip person transferee, and if the trust satisfies that obligation, in substance the trust is making another taxable distribution to the skip person.

The nature of the generation-skipping transfer tax is easily recognized once the three types of generation-skipping transfers are understood. Chapter 13 imposes a tax on wealth cascading down through generations where the intervening generations escape any imposition of either of the two other types of wealth transfer tax.

[4] Exclusions

A transfer that falls within any of the three classifications of generation-skipping transfers will not be treated as a generation-skipping transfer in two situations. First, a testamentary direct skip, a taxable termination, or a taxable distribution made directly to an educational institution for the tuition of a skip person or to a person providing medical care for the medical expenses of a skip person that, if made inter vivos by the transferor, would have qualified for the gift tax exclusion under Section 2503(e) is not treated as a generation-skipping transfer.[20] Second, as the basic concept of the generation-skipping transfer tax generally is to impose a transfer tax where property has not been subject to the estate tax or gift tax at one generation level, Congress imposes the Chapter 13 tax on such property only once at each generation level.[21]

---

[19] See ¶ 13.02[3][c].

[20] See ¶ 13.01[2][a].

[21] See ¶ 13.01[2][b].

[5] Computation of the Generation-Skipping Transfer Tax

The computation of the generation-skipping transfer tax, like that of most taxes, is determined by multiplying the tax base by the tax rate.[22] The tax base is the taxable amount of the generation-skipping transfer and the tax rate is statutorily defined as the applicable rate. The generation-skipping transfer tax is essentially a flat-rate tax imposed at the maximum federal estate tax rate. Its sting is partially alleviated by the allowance of a generous exemption to each individual transferor.[23]

[a] The Taxable Amount

The taxable amount borrows the concepts of valuation and deductions from both the estate tax and the gift tax structure. It makes the generation-skipping tax a tax-inclusive tax when there is a taxable termination and a taxable distribution, but generally only a tax-exclusive tax when there is a direct skip. The taxable amount is best understood by looking at each of the three types of generation-skipping transfers separately.

[i] **Direct skip.** The taxable amount of a direct skip transfer is the value of the property received by the transferee.[24] Deductions are disregarded because the amount is based on the amount actually received by the transferee. The tax imposed is tax-exclusive in that the tax is based on the amount received by the transferee after the payment of transfer taxes. In the case of an inter vivos direct skip, however, the amount of Chapter 13 tax imposed on the transferor is treated as a further Chapter 12 gift transfer by the transferor.[25] Valuation occurs at the time that the direct skip occurs, and it is generally the fair market value of the property at that time.[26] However, if the property that is the subject matter of the direct skip is included in the transferor's gross estate, the Chapter 11 valuation method employed by the estate (which includes Section 2032 and Section 2032A valuation) is generally used to determine the taxable amount of the direct skip.[27]

[ii] **Taxable termination.** The taxable amount of a taxable termination is the fair market value of all the property with respect to which the termination has occurred.[28] Deductions against the value of the property for claims and

---

[22] See ¶ 12.02.
[23] See ¶ 15.02.
[24] See ¶ 14.04.
[25] See ¶ 10.05.
[26] See ¶ 14.05[1].
[27] See ¶ 14.05[2][a].
[28] See ¶ 14.03[2].

charges against the property similar to those under Section 2053 of the estate tax are allowed.[29] The tax imposed is tax-inclusive. Valuation is generally accomplished at the time the interest terminates,[30] although, if the termination occurs as a result of the death of an individual, Section 2032 valuation may be used.[31]

[iii] Taxable distribution. The taxable amount of a taxable distribution is the amount received by the transferee in the distribution.[32] Expenses incurred with respect to the determination, collection, or refund of the Chapter 13 tax are deductible in computing the taxable amount.[33] The property is valued at its fair market value at the time of the taxable distribution.[34] The transferee is liable for the Chapter 13 tax imposed on taxable distributions, and as a result, the tax is tax-inclusive.[35] If payment of the tax is made by the trust, that payment is treated as a further taxable distribution.[36]

[b] The Applicable Rate

The applicable rate establishes the rate of tax imposed on a generation-skipping transfer. It is the product of the maximum federal estate tax rate and the inclusion ratio with respect to the transfer.[37]

[i] The maximum federal estate tax rate. Chapter 13 borrows the maximum federal estate tax rate from the multipurpose rate table.[38] The use of a flat rate is purportedly intended to simplify the computation.

[ii] The inclusion ratio. The "inclusion ratio" is the mechanism by which an individual's generation-skipping transfer exemption amount (GST exemption) is incorporated into the computation of the generation-skipping transfer tax. The amount of the GST exemption roughly parallels the amount of the estate tax unified credit.[39] The individual or the individual's executor may allocate the GST exemption among the individual's generation-skipping transfers.[40]

---

[29] See ¶ 14.03[3].

[30] See ¶ 14.05[1].

[31] See ¶ 14.05[2][b].

[32] See ¶ 14.02[2].

[33] See ¶ 14.02[3].

[34] See ¶ 14.05[1].

[35] See ¶ 12.03[1].

[36] See ¶¶ 13.02[3][c], 14.02[4].

[37] See ¶ 16.01.

[38] See ¶ 2.01[3].

[39] See ¶ 15.02.

[40] See ¶ 15.03.

In addition, the statute provides a variety of inter vivos and testamentary automatic allocation rules attempting to ensure that not only will a transferor's GST exemption not be wasted, but that it will be also allocated in what is likley the most effective manner. The GST exemption allows most small and moderate-sized estates to avoid the imposition of any generation-skipping tax.

The inclusion ratio is a decimal fraction composed of one minus another fraction, the "applicable fraction."[41] The numerator of the applicable fraction is equal to the GST exemption amount allocated to the generation-skipping transfer and the denominator is generally equal to the value of the property involved in the transfer.[42] For example, if a transferor makes a $3 million direct skip and allocates $1 million of GST exemption to it, the applicable fraction is 0.333 and the inclusion ratio is 0.667 (one minus 0.333). Assuming a maximum federal estate tax rate of 50 percent, the applicable rate of tax on the transfer is 33.350 percent. If an individual transfers $1 million to a trust with income to a child for life, then income to a grandchild for life, and a remainder to the grandchild's grandchildren, and immediately allocates $1 million GST exemption to the trust, the applicable fraction is one and the inclusion ratio is zero. As a result, no generation-skipping transfer tax will be imposed on the trust at the death of either the child or the grandchild.

The inclusion ratio is generally recomputed where the transferor allocates additional GST exemption to a trust after the initial transfer,[44] where more than one transfer is made to a generation-skipping trust,[43] and where a single trust to which a GST exemption allocation has been made is involved in more than one taxable termination with respect to the same transferor.[45]

[c] Credit for State Taxes

Again borrowing from the estate tax,[46] the Chapter 13 tax allows a maximum 5 percent credit for state generation-skipping transfer taxes until 2005.[47] The credit is allowed only where a taxable termination or taxable distribution occurs at the same time as and as a result of the death of an individual.

---

[41] See ¶ 16.02.

[42] See ¶ 16.02.

[44] See ¶ 16.02[5].

[43] See ¶ 16.02[5].

[45] See ¶ 17.03[2][a].

[46] See ¶ 3.03.

[47] See ¶ 12.04.

[6] Liability for the Generation-Skipping Transfer Tax and Return Filing Responsibility

The responsibility for seeing that the tax is paid is the transferor's in the case of direct skip not made from a trust, the trustee's where there is a taxable termination or a direct skip from a trust, and the transferee's where there is a taxable distribution.[48] The Service generally requires that the person responsible for seeing that the tax is paid also files the necessary tax returns.[49]

¶ 1.05 WEALTH TRANSFER TAXATION AFTER THE YEAR 2009

The opening words of this chapter urge one to "squander it!" as the best way to avoid federal wealth transfer taxes. After the enactment of the Economic Growth and Tax Relief Reconciliation Act of 2001, the words "or die after 2009 but before 2011" can be added. This is because that 2001 legislation opens a window of opportunity for only one year to die and avoid both the estate and generation-skipping transfer taxes.[1] The possibility both of abusive assignments of income and of donors making large inter vivos gifts in the one-year window of opportunity in 2010 prompted Congress to continue to levy the gift tax after the scheduled demise of the estate and generation-skipping transfer taxes.[2] The estate tax and generation-skipping transfer tax window of opportunity currently is not open for long, because if Congress fails to take further action, the "repeal" of the estate and generation-skipping transfer taxes is subject to a "sunset" provision at the end of 2010. Under the sunset provision, all of the estate, gift, and generation-skipping transfer tax laws that were in effect prior to the 2001 Act are resurrected as if the 2001 Act had never been enacted.[3] As one of our colleagues has suggested, "the 2001 Act was drafted in quicksand!"

---

[48] See ¶ 12.03.

[49] See ¶ 18.02[3].

[1] See ¶ 8.10[1].

[2] See ¶¶ 8.10[4], 9.01.

[3] See ¶ 8.10[5].

¶ 1.06 CONCLUSION

The foregoing panoramic picture was obviously taken at a very long range. Even the beauties of the Taj Mahal are not apparent from a distance of several miles. Although great beauty may not be discovered in the chapters that follow, their careful consideration is urged, and at least some surprises may be found. This overview is cross referenced in such a way that some of the surprises can be turned up quite quickly.

PART **II**

The Estate Tax

CHAPTER 2

Imposition of Estate Tax

¶ 2.01 SECTION 2001. IMPOSITION AND RATE OF TAX

The federal estate tax is imposed by Section 2001(a) of the Internal Revenue Code (the Code) on the transfer of the taxable estate of every decedent who is either a citizen or a resident of the United States.[1] "Taxable estate" is a term of art defined in Section 2051.[2] The term "transfer" has less statutory significance than might at first be supposed;[3] the statutory plan presumes the requisite transfer of a property interest if its value is required to be included in the gross estate of a decedent.[4]

The method of computing the tax is provided by Section 2001(b) and the rates to be used are presented in a multipurpose rate table provided in Section 2001(c).[5] Prior to 1977, computation of the estate tax involved only the application of rates in a graduated rate table to the taxable estate. However, with the enactment of Section 2001(b) in the Tax Reform Act of 1976, Congress took steps toward integration of the gift and estate taxes. The estate tax computation involves essentially figuring a tentative tax on all gratuitous transfers made inter vivos or at death after 1976 and then subtracting an amount for tax payable on lifetime gifts after 1976. The computation does not tax any gratuitous transfers twice; the taxable estate is still the only amount being taxed. However, the rates at which the taxable estate is taxed depend on the aggregate value of the taxable estate *and* "adjusted taxable gifts," a term discussed here.

The following is a basic, narrative analysis of congressional thinking on the present death tax:

- We shall tax the value of property owned by a decedent transmitted to others at death.[6] We shall also tax the value at death of property that, although not owned by the decedent at death, was the subject of some

---

[1] The questions of citizenship and residence are discussed ¶ 6.01[3] in connection with the tax imposed on estates of nonresidents who are not citizens. IRC §§ 2101–2108; see also IRC §§ 2208, 2209. Cf. ¶¶ 9.02[1], 18.03[2].

[2] See ¶ 5.02.

[3] However, it is of constitutional significance that the estate tax is imposed on wealth *transfers*, not on wealth itself. An indirect tax such as a tax on the transmission of wealth is constitutional as long as it is imposed uniformly throughout the United States. In contrast, a direct tax on wealth must be apportioned among the states in accordance with their respective populations. See Tribe, American Constitutional Law, 841 (3d ed. 2000).

[4] IRC §§ 2031–2046, discussed in Chapter 4.

[5] For years after 1976 through 2009 and after 2010 (see ¶ 8.10[5]), the Section 2001(c) rate schedule is multipurpose, because it is used in computing the estate tax, the gift tax, and, to a limited extent, the tax on generation-skipping transfers.

[6] IRC § 2033. See IRC § 2031(c) (allowing an exclusion from the gross estate), discussed ¶ 4.02[7].

lifetime ownership or control resulting in a testamentary-like transfer by the decedent.[7]

- We shall allow certain deductions from the gross estate, as determined previously.[8] This is to say, we shall impose a tax only on "the transfer of the taxable estate."[9]
- But, as the rates are progressive, shall we be content to have the applicable rates determined solely by the amount of the taxable estate? No. That is the beginning.[10]
- The rates should depend upon all the decedent's philanthropy, i.e., the value of what the decedent transmits at death (or earlier in a testamentary manner) and the value of all lifetime gratuitous transfers—

  — Not separately considered if they were testamentary in nature so as to form a part of the decedent's taxable estate and be subject to the tax in that manner[11] and
  — Not made before 1977,[12] the year in which the cumulative (life and death) approach to estate tax rates was first invoked.

Although some minor liberties are taken here, this presents the general picture of the computation of the federal estate tax, which may be of some help if kept in mind as background for the more detailed analyses that follow.

[1] Computation of the Tentative Tax

The first step in computing a decedent's estate tax liability is to compute a tentative tax[13] on the aggregate amount of the decedent's "taxable estate" and "adjusted taxable gifts." The tax is determined by applying the Section 2001(c) graduated rates to that aggregated amount.[14]

[a] Taxable Estate

The term "taxable estate" is discussed in detail in Chapters 4 and 5. It constitutes the decedent's gross estate reduced by allowable deductions.[15] Prop-

---

[7] See, e.g., IRC § 2036. See generally IRC §§ 2035–2044.

[8] See generally IRC §§ 2051–2058.

[9] IRC § 2001(a).

[10] IRC § 2001(b)(1)(A).

[11] IRC § 2001(b) (last clause).

[12] IRC § 2001(b) (penultimate clause).

[13] IRC § 2001(b)(1).

[14] See infra ¶ 2.01[3].

[15] See Chapters 4, 5.

erty included in a decedent's gross estate is valued under either the method provided by Section 2031 or Section 2032A at the date of the decedent's death under Section 2031 or on the alternate valuation date under Section 2032.[16]

[b] Adjusted Taxable Gifts

The term "adjusted taxable gifts," defined in Section 2001(b), is the total amount of taxable gifts (within the meaning of Section 2503)[17] made by the decedent after December 31, 1976, other than gifts that are taken into account in determining the gross estate.[18] The gross estate reduced by allowable deductions yields the taxable estate, which is the first component in the computation.[19] The exclusion of gifts included in the decedent's gross estate from adjusted taxable gifts prevents the value of the same gift from being included twice in the estate tax computation.[20]

The amount of adjusted taxable gifts is the fair market value of the property gifted at the time the gift tax transfer was completed. However, this does not necessarily mean that the decedent's lifetime determination of the amount of the property gifted controls its amount in the estate tax computation. The

---

[16] See ¶¶ 4.02, 4.03, 4.04.

[17] Taxable gifts are gifts after gift-splitting under Section 2513, exclusions under Sections 2503(b) and 2503(e), and deductions allowed by Sections 2522 and 2523 as limited by Section 2524. See Chapters 9–11.

[18] See Chapter 4.

[19] IRC § 2001(b)(1)(A).

[20] See HR Conf. Rep. No. 1380, 94th Cong., 2d Sess. 3, 13 (1976), reprinted in 1976-3 CB (Vol. 3) 735, 747. See also Rev. Rul. 84-25, 1984-1 CB 191, which appropriately holds that a legally binding note issued by the decedent during life and subject to the gift tax (see ¶ 10.01[3][h] note 124), but unpaid at death, is not included in adjusted taxable gifts, because the assets to satisfy the note are included in the gross estate.

Similarly, the amount of adjusted taxable gifts is reduced by the amount of gifts made by the decedent's spouse that are included in the decedent spouse's gross estate under Section 2035 where a Section 2513 election applied to the transfer. IRC § 2001(e). This reduction prevents a gift to a third person that is included in the donor's gross estate under Section 2035 from increasing the marginal rate of tax imposed on the estate of the donor's spouse (decedent here) who has been treated as making one half of the gift. See Priv. Ltr. Rul. 8747001 (Mar. 12, 1987). Congress should have applied the Section 2001(e)(2) rule to inclusions of property in the estate of the decedent's spouse under Sections 2036–2038, as well as Section 2035, especially in view of the limited scope of Section 2035(a). See ¶ 4.07[2][b].

rules governing the amount of adjusted taxable gifts depend upon the date that gift was made.

[i] Gifts made through August 5, 1997. The fair market value of property transferred by gift prior to August 6, 1997,[21] may be redetermined in the determination of the amount of adjusted taxable gifts at the time of filing the estate tax return, notwithstanding the expiration of the statute of limitations on the assessment of gift tax on such transfers.[22] In addition, legal issues involving the interpretation of gift tax law (such as deductions and qualification for the annual exclusion) may also be raised even though the gift tax statute of limitations has run.[23]

[ii] Gifts made after August 5, 1997. The amount of adjusted taxable gifts made after August 5, 1997,[24] is not subject to an adjustment in the estate tax computation if: (1) the gift was either reported on a return, or disclosed in a statement attached to a return, in a manner adequate to apprise the government of the nature of the gift;[25] (2) the transferred property's value is finally determined for gift tax purposes;[26] and (3) the statute of limitations with respect to the gift has expired.[27] Even though the statute refers merely to valuation, the nonadjustment rule applies to adjustments involving all issues relating to the *amount* of the gift, including valuation issues and legal issues involving

---

[21] Prior to August 6, 1997, there was no statute that required the value of a gift as determined for gift tax purposes be used in valuing adjusted taxable gifts in a decedent's estate tax computation. Cf. IRC § 2504(c).

[22] Reg. §§ 20.2001-1(a), 25.2504-2(c) Ex. 3; Evanson v. United States, 30 F3d 960 (8th Cir. 1994); Levin v. Comm'r, 986 F2d 91 (4th Cir. 1993), cert. denied, 510 US 816 (1993); Estate of Smith v. Comm'r, 94 TC 872 (1990). Contra Boatmen's First Nat'l Bank of Kans. City v. United States, 705 F. Supp. 1407 (WD Mo. 1988). See Morris, "Troubling Transfer Tax Tie-Ins," 1991 Utah L. Rev. 749; Schlenger, Madden & Hayes, "IRS Can Revalue Gifts for Estate Tax Purposes," 21 Est. Plan. 366 (1994).

[23] Reg. § 20.2001-1(a).

[24] The Taxpayer Relief Act of 1997, Pub. L. No. 105-34, § 506(a), 111 Stat. 788, 855 (1997), reprinted in 1997-4 CB (Vol. 1) 1, 386. The regulations provide that these rules apply only if the estate tax return is filed after the date the regulations became final, December 3, 1999. Reg. § 20.2001-1(f). Arguably, for gifts made after August 5, 1997, where the estate tax return is filed prior to December 4, 1999, prior Proposed Regulation §§ 20.2001-1(b) through 20.2001-1(g) should apply. Notice of Proposed Rulemaking and Notice of Public Hearing, 63 Fed. Reg. 70,701, 70,704 (1998), represented in 1999-1 CB 813, 816. But see ¶ 9.05[2][b] note 20.

[25] IRC § 2001(f)(2) (flush language); Reg. § 20.2001-1(c)(1). See IRC § 6501(c)(9).

[26] IRC § 2001(f)(2).

[27] IRC § 2001(f)(2)(A). See Reg. § 20.2001-1(b). The rule applies to Section 2701(d) transfers as well. IRC § 2001(f)(1)(B). See ¶ 19.02[5][a].

the interpretation of the gift tax law.[28] If these requirements are not all satisfied, then the amount of the adjusted taxable gifts may be redetermined in computing the decedent's estate tax.[29]

Adequate Disclosure. The rules of adequate disclosure apply for purposes of both the estate tax computation and the limitations period for the gift tax.[30] Adequate disclosure may be made either on the gift tax return reporting the transfer or on a statement attached to the gift tax return.[31] Adequate disclosure[32] essentially requires a description of the nature of the gift and the basis for determining the value of the reported gift.[33] The regulations provide a safe harbor to satisfy the adequate disclosure requirements that must include: (1) a description of the transferred property and any consideration received by the transferor;[34] (2) a listing of the identity of, and relationship between, the transferor and each transferee;[35] (3) if the property is transferred in trust, the trust's identification number and either a brief description of the terms of the trust *or* a copy of the trust instrument;[36] (4) *either* a detailed description of the method used in determining the fair market value of the property, including any relevant financial data (such as balance sheets), and a description of any discounts

---

[28] IRC § 2001(f); Reg. § 20.2001-1(b). See Reg. § 301.6501(c)-1(f)(7) Ex. 2. This is a liberalization of the U.S. Treasury's policy prior to the adoption of final regulations. See TD 8845, Supplementary Information, Finalty with Respect to Adequately Disclosed Gifts, 64 Fed. Reg. 67,767, 67,768 (1999), reprinted in 1999-2 CB 683, 685. The proposed regulations had applied the nonadjustment rules only to issues of valuation. See Prop. Reg. §§ 20.2001-1(b), 20.2001-1(d), 20.2001-1(f) Ex. 2. Notice of Proposed Rulemaking and Notice of Public Hearing, 63 Fed. Reg. 70,701, 70,704. (1998), reprinted in 1999-1 CB 813, 816. Seemingly, this change led the Treasury to use the term "amount" of adjusted taxable gifts in the final regulations rather than the term "value," which had been used in the proposed regulations.

[29] For example, even though the "adequate disclosure" regulations have been satisfied sufficiently to commence the running of the statute of limitations, the reported amount is not binding for purposes of computing adjusted taxable gifts unless the "final determination" requirement is also met.

[30] IRC §§ 2001(f), 6501(c)(9). See ¶ 9.05[2].

The adequate disclosure regulations also provide adequate disclosure rules with respect to nongift completed transfers and transactions (Reg. § 301.6501(c)-1(f)(4), see Reg. § 301.6501(c)-1(f)(7) Ex. 6), incomplete transfers (Reg. § 301.6501(c)-1(f)(5)), and split gifts (Reg. § 301.6501(c)-1(f)(6)). See ¶ 9.04[10][b] text accompanying notes 230–237.

[31] IRC §§ 2001(f)(2) (flush language), 6501(c)(9).

[32] See Reg. §§ 301.6501(c)-1(f)(2), 301.6501(c)-1(f)(3). The adequate disclosure safe-harbor rules apply to gifts made after December 31, 1996, but only if the gift tax return for the gift is filed after the date that the regulations became final, December 3, 1999. Reg. § 301.6501(c)-1(f)(8). See supra note 24; ¶ 9.04[10] note 220.

[33] Reg. §§ 301.6501(c)-1(f)(2), 301.6501(c)-1(f)(3).

[34] Reg. § 301.6501(c)-1(f)(2)(i).

[35] Reg. § 301.6501(c)-1(f)(2)(ii).

[36] Reg. § 301.6501(c)-1(f)(2)(iii).

claimed in valuing the property;[37] *or in the alternative*, an adequate appraisal of the property[38] by a qualified appraiser[39]; and (5) a statement describing any position taken that is contrary to any proposed, temporary, or final Treasury regulations or revenue rulings published at the time of the transfer.[40]

Final Determination. The nonadjustment rules for adjusted taxable gifts in the computation of the estate tax also require a final determination of the prior amount of the adjusted taxable gifts.[41] A final determination occurs if (1) the

---

[37] Reg. § 301.6501(c)-1(f)(2)(iv).

If the transfer is of an *actively traded entity* on an established exchange, it will be considered adequately disclosed if the description includes the CUSIP number of the security and the mean between the highest and lowest quoted selling prices on the applicable valuation date. Reg. §§ 301.6501(c)-1(f)(2)(iv), 301.6501(c)-1(f)(7) Ex. 1.

If the transfer is of a *nonactively traded entity*, there is a more detailed requirement. If the valuation is based on the net value of the assets, a statement must be provided as to the valuation of 100 percent of the entity (without discounts), the pro rata portion subject to the transfer, and the fair market value reported on the return. Reg. §§ 301.6501(c)-1(f)(2)(iv), 301.6501(c)-1(f)(7) Ex. 3. The final step takes into consideration any discounting of the value of the property transferred. Id. See ¶ 4.02[4]. If 100 percent of the value of the entity is not disclosed, the taxpayer bears the burden of demonstrating that the fair market value is properly determined by a method other than a method based on the net fair market value of the assets held by the entity. Reg. § 301.6501(c)-1(f)(2)(iv).

Furthermore, if the nonactively traded entity that is transferred owns an interest in another nonactively traded entity or entities, the same analysis must be employed for each such entity, if such information is relevant and material in determining the value of the transferred interest. Reg. §§ 301.6501(c)-1(f)(2)(iv), 301.6501(c)-1(f)(7) Ex. 4. If the appraisal alternative is employed (see infra text accompanying notes 38 and 39), this requirement will be a part of the appraisal. Reg. § 301.6501(c)-1(f)(7) Ex. 5.

[38] The appraisal must provide all of the following information in order to meet the safe-harbor requirements: (1) the appraiser's background and credentials that qualify the appraiser to perform the appraisal; (2) the dates of the transfer and the appraisal, and the purpose of the appraisal; (3) a description of the property; (4) a description of the appraisal process; (5) a description of the assumptions, hypothetical conditions, and any limiting conditions and restrictions on the transferred property that affect the valuation reported; (6) the information considered in determining the appraised value, including all financial data used in determining the value of an ownership interest of a business so that another person can replicate the process and arrive at the appraised value; (7) the appraisal procedures used and the reasoning that supports them; (8) the valuation method used, the rationale for its use, and the procedure used in arriving at the fair market value; and (9) the specific basis for the valuation, such as specific comparable sales or transactions, sales of similar interests, asset-based approaches, merger-acquisition transactions, etc. Reg. §§ 301.6501(c)-1(f)(3)(ii), 301.6501(c)-1(f)(7) Ex. 5.

[39] Reg. §§ 301.6501(c)-1(f)(2)(iv), 301.6501(c)-1(f)(3).

The appraiser must not be the donor or the donee of the property, must not be related to the transferor (as defined in Section 2032A(e)(2), see ¶ 4.04[3][b][vii]), and must be qualified to appraise the type of property transferred. Reg. § 301.6501(c)-1(f)(3)(i).

[40] Reg. § 301.6501(c)-1(f)(2)(v).

[41] Section 2001(f) was amended in 1998 legislation to add a definition of the term "final determination." Internal Revenue Service Restructuring and Reform Act of 1998,

amount of the taxable gift as shown by the taxpayer on a gift tax return (or on a statement attached to the return) is not contested by the Service before the period for assessing gift tax on the transfer expires;[42] (2) the Internal Revenue Service (the Service) establishes an amount that is not contested by the taxpayer within the limitations period;[43] (3) the courts establish the amount in a final determination that is no longer subject to appeal;[44] or (4) the amount is established through a settlement agreement between the taxpayer and the Service.[45]

[2] Reductions in the Tentative Tax

The tentative tax on the sum of the taxable estate and adjusted taxable gifts is then reduced by the amount of gift taxes that would have been payable on gifts made after 1976[46] had those gifts been taxed under the rate schedule[47] in effect at the decedent's death.[48] In computing the amount of gift taxes that would have been payable on gifts made after 1976,[49] the gift tax credit that would have been allowed at the time of the gift is taken into account in arriving at the gift tax that would have been payable.[50] This yields the total amount of estate tax, after which credits are allowed under Sections 2010 through 2016 to determine the net estate tax payable. Since gifts made after 1976 are

---

Pub. L. No. 105-206, § 6007(e)(2)(B), 112 Stat. 685, 810 (1998), reprinted in 1998-3 CB 145, 270.

[42] IRC § 2001(f)(2)(A).

[43] IRC § 2001(f)(2)(B).

[44] IRC § 2001(f)(2)(C). See Reg. § 20.2001-1(d).

[45] IRC § 2001(f)(2)(C). A settlement agreement includes a Section 7121 closing agreement, a Section 7122 compromise, or a settlement of a valuation issue binding on both parties. Reg. § 20.2001-1(d).

[46] As the Section 2001(b)(2) reduction relates only to post-1976 gifts, pre-1977 gifts that become a part of the decedent's taxable estate identified in Section 2001(b)(1)(A) are still permitted to qualify for the Section 2012 credit for the gift tax paid. The Section 2012 credit will eventually fade away as it is inapplicable to post-1976 gifts. See IRC §§ 2012(a), 2012(e); ¶ 3.04.

While Section 2001(b)(2) applies only to post-1976 gifts, the rate of tax paid on such gifts is affected by pre-1977 gifts (see ¶ 9.03[3]) that must be taken into account in making the Section 2001(b)(2) reduction. TAM 9642001 (Nov. 30, 1994).

[47] IRC § 2001(c), discussed infra ¶ 2.01[3].

[48] IRC § 2001(b)(2). Even though the reduction for gift taxes payable is not so labeled, it is essentially a credit because it is a direct reduction of tax liability, and not merely a reduction of the tax base.

[49] IRC § 2001(b)(2).

[50] Priv. Ltr. Rul. 9250004 (Aug. 24, 1992). See IRC § 2505; ¶ 9.06.

pulled into the estate tax computation,[51] a reduction is properly provided for gift taxes on those gifts. Those gifts are not taxed again, but they do affect the tax rate applied to the taxable estate.

The Code specifically requires a reduction for the amount of gift taxes that would have been payable on the post-1976 gifts had the rate schedule *in effect at death* applied at the time of the gifts. This recomputation is required to prevent changes in the rate schedule from retroactively affecting the amount of tax effectively paid on prior gifts.[52] In instances in which taxpayers have not made any pre-1977 taxable gifts and their adjusted taxable gifts do not exceed $2 million, the tentative tax will be reduced by the gift taxes that were payable on gifts made after 1976 without recomputation based on rates effective at death, because the tax rate schedules on those gifts and estates are identical.[53] However, as a result of the reduction in the maximum Section 2001(c) unified tax rates in the years from 2002 through 2009, the rule applying the rate schedule at the time of the decedent's death to the rate of taxation on post-1996 gifts takes on an increased importance.[54]

Even if there is no change in the rate schedule, if there is a difference between taxes *actually paid* and taxes *payable*, the reduction is based on the latter. Thus, subject to the rules of Section 2001(f),[55] an error in prior computation of the gift tax may be disregarded and the reduction is based on

---

[51] Post-1976 gifts are part of the amount identified in Section 2001(b)(1)(A) if they are brought within the gross estate. If such gifts are not brought within the gross estate, they appear in Section 2001(b)(1)(B).

[52] HR Conf. Rep. No. 201, 97th Cong., 1st Sess. 38, 156 (1981), reprinted in 1981-2 CB 352, 376. In the case of a rate reduction, this would result in a reduction of taxes.

Assume that Donor made $1 million of taxable post-1997 gifts that were subject to a Section 2001(c) 55 percent tax rate, that Donor died with a $1 million taxable estate when the maximum Section 2001(c) tax rate was 50 percent, and that those maximum rates applied to both the gifts and the estate. At Donor's death, the tax on the taxable estate and the adjusted taxable gifts would be $1 million (50 percent of $2 million). If the liability were reduced by the 55 percent tax paid on the gifts ($550,000), the estate tax would be only $450,000. Using the maximum Section 2001(c) tax rate at Donor's death (50 percent) in computing the tax on the gifts, the estate tax would be $500,000. The latter result taxing the taxable estate at a 50 percent rate is appropriate. The former result would reduce the estate tax by $50,000, effectively retroactively reducing the tax on the gifts by $50,000.

[53] See IRC §§ 2001(c)(1), 2001(c)(2).

[54] See infra ¶ 2.01[3], especially note 66. Thus, the rule becomes important in some situations where the decedent or the decedent's spouse made adjusted taxable gifts exceeding $2 million or made pre-1997 taxable gifts. Prior to the 2001 enactment of Section 2001(c)(2), the amount of adjusted taxable gifts resulting in such a potential recomputation was $3 million.

[55] See supra ¶ 2.01[1][b][ii].

the amount of tax that should have been paid.[56] In addition, if the Section 2505 unified credit under the gift tax, although allowable, was not actually used, the amount of gift tax payable is reduced by the amount of credit that was allowable; again, it is tax *payable* not tax *paid* that determines the amount to be subtracted.[57]

The reduction of an amount for gift tax payable may include not only an amount for gift tax payable by the decedent but also, in limited situations, an amount for gift tax payable by the decedent's spouse. If Section 2513 gift-splitting[58] was elected on a lifetime transfer actually made by the decedent and the value of the property transferred was subsequently pulled into the decedent's taxable estate, then an amount for gift tax payable by the decedent's spouse is also used to reduce the tentative tax.[59] The reduction is proper; as the value of all of the property is being pulled into the decedent's gross estate, the estate ought to be allowed a reduction in the estate tax computation for gift taxes on the value of the entire property. However, in codifying this rule, Congress expressly approved a complementary rule that in some circumstances is

---

[56] For open years there may be an assertion of a deficiency or a right to a refund if the gift tax liability was improperly determined at the time of the gift. See ¶ 9.04[10].

[57] See ¶ 9.06. This result is harsh and was probably not intended by Congress. See McCord, 1976 Estate and Gift Tax Reform—Analysis, Explanation and Commentary 23 (West 1977). The taxpayer is not given an opportunity to postpone use of the Section 2505 unified gift tax credit. If it is not used as allowed in post-1976 gifts, it cannot be used against subsequent gifts. Rev. Rul. 79-398, 1979-2 CB 338. The credit allowable in a year is the maximum credit reduced by the credit "allowable" in prior calendar periods. IRC § 2505(a)(2). See ¶ 9.06[2]. Under prior law, the somewhat related Section 2521 $30,000 lifetime exemption was not required to be used at the earliest possible time. Reg. § 25.2521-1(a). See Stephens, Maxfield & Lind, Federal Estate and Gift Taxation, ¶ 10-2 (Warren, Gorham & Lamont, 3d ed. 1974).

[58] See ¶ 10.03.

[59] IRC § 2001(d). This rule parallels pre-1977 law, which allowed a credit for gift tax under Section 2012 for payment by a donor spouse of gift tax on split gifts if the gift was also taxed in the donor's estate.

Under Section 2001(e), when the consenting spouse dies, the Section 2001(b)(2) reduction of an amount for the gift tax payable is reduced by the amount of the tax treated under Section 2001(d) as payable by the donor spouse if Section 2035 required inclusion of the gift in the donor spouse's estate. See supra ¶ 2.01[1][b] note 20. This adjustment, however, should not be greater than the Section 2001(d) amount that actually qualified as a Section 2001(b)(2) reduction in the donor spouse's estate. In this situation, the total amount of adjusted taxable gifts of the consenting spouse does not include the split portion of the donor decedent's gift included in the donor decedent's estate under Section 2035. See supra ¶ 2.01[1].

If the consenting spouse dies before the donor decedent and the gift is included in donor decedent's gross estate under Section 2035, the consenting spouse's federal estate tax return will likely have to be amended. See Rev. Rul. 81-85, 1981-1 CB 452.

If the donor spouse dies within three years and if the consenting spouse pays tax on one half of the gift and lives beyond the reach of Section 2035, it is possible to have payment of the federal estate tax with dollars that are never included in the gross estate.

Section 2001

disadvantageous to the decedent's spouse: any Section 2505 credit used ineffectively (as it now turns out) by a spouse on the "split" lifetime transfer of the decedent is not restored for further use by the spouse in case of subsequent lifetime transfers.[60]

As indicated earlier, in addition to a reduction for an amount for gift tax payable, the tentative tax is further reduced by tax credits,[61] the most important of which is the unified credit provided by Section 2010.[62] Other credits,[63] which are discussed in Chapter 3, also reduce the net amount of estate tax payable.[64]

[3] Tax Rates

The multipurpose rate table for estate and gift taxes[65] for the years 2002 through 2009 appears in Section 2001(c).[66] Over the years since the 1976 uni-

---

[60] Cf. Norair v. Comm'r, 65 TC 942 (1976), aff'd, 556 F2d 574 (4th Cir. 1977); Ingalls v. Comm'r, 336 F2d 874 (4th Cir. 1964); English v. United States, 284 F. Supp. 256 (ND Fla. 1968). The legislative history of Section 2001(d) expresses congressional approval of these results. HR Conf. Rep. No. 1380, 94th Cong., 2d Sess. 3, 13 (1976), reprinted in 1976-3 CB (Vol. 3) 735, 747.

[61] See Chapter 3.

[62] That credit replaced the Section 2052 $60,000 exemption, which operated as a deduction under pre-1977 law. The current credit is phased in over several years. See ¶ 3.02.

[63] See IRC §§ 2011–2016.

[64] Although Section 2001(b)(2) largely eliminates the use of the Section 2012 credit for gift taxes, that credit is still applicable with respect to pre-1977 gifts that find their way into the estate tax computation as part of the taxable estate, not as adjusted taxable gifts. See supra note 46.

[65] The maximum tax rate imposed by the table is also used in computing the rate of tax on generation-skipping transfers. IRC § 2641. See ¶ 16.01.

[66] The basic table as provided in Section 2001(c)(1) is modified in subsequent years according to the rules of Section 2001(c)(2). Under those modifications, the maximum rate under Section 2001(c) is as follows:

Calendar Years	Maximum Rate
1977–1981	70 percent
1982	65 percent
1983	60 percent
1984–2001	55 percent
2002	50 percent
2003	49 percent
2004	48 percent
2005	47 percent
2006	46 percent
2007–2009	45 percent

fication of the estate and gift taxes, the table has undergone a variety of changes, with the current rate schedule being the most favorable to taxpayers. In 1977, the top rate was 70 percent, which by 1984 was reduced to 55 percent.[67] Both rates also were subject to a 5 percent surtax on transfers in excess of $10 million.[68] The top marginal rate is 50 percent for the year 2002 and the

---

Under the "sunset" provision effective on January 1, 2011, the top rate of 55 percent is restored. In addition, the 5 percent surtax on transfers in excess of $10 million, which eliminates the graduated tax rates, is also restored. Economic Growth and Tax Relief Reconciliation Act of 2001, Pub. L. No. 107-16, § 901(a)(2), 115 Stat. 38, 150 (2001), reprinted in 2001-__ CB __, __. The "sunset" provision is discussed more fully at ¶ 8.10[5].

[67] See supra ¶ 2.01 note 6. In the Economic Recovery Tax Act of 1981, Pub. L. No. 97-34, § 402, 95 Stat. 172, 300 (1981), reprinted in 1981-2 CB 256, 324, Congress adopted legislation that would, over time, have reduced the maximum rate under the multipurpose rate table from 70 percent to 50 percent. The rate reduction, which ultimately would have affected only taxable estates in excess of $2.5 million, was intended to help prevent forced sales of "highly successful" closely held and family businesses, and to conform the maximum rate under Section 2001(c) to the then maximum income tax rate of 50 percent. The first motive was suspect because, in all likelihood, wealthy individuals who did not engage in closely held and family businesses would benefit the most from the reductions. The 20 percent maximum rate reduction was scheduled to occur over an eleven-year period, from 1982 through 1992. See the Tax Reform Act of 1984, Pub. L. No. 98-369, § 21(a), 98 Stat. 506 (1984), reprinted in 1984-3 CB (Vol. 1) 1, 14, and the Omnibus Budget Reconciliation Act of 1987, Pub. L. No. 100-203, § 10401(a), 101 Stat. 1330, 1430 (1987), reprinted in 1987-3 CB 1, 150. The rate reduction to a maximum federal estate tax rate of 50 percent from 55 percent originally scheduled to occur in 1985 in the Economic Recovery Tax Act of 1981, Pub. L. No. 97-34, § 402, 95 Stat. 172, 300 (1981), reprinted in 1981-2 CB 256, 324, was first postponed to 1988 by the Tax Reform Act of 1984, Pub. L. No. 98-369, § 21(a), 98 Stat. 506 (1984), reprinted in 1984-3 CB (Vol. 1) 1, 14, and later postponed to 1993 by the Omnibus Budget Reconciliation Act of 1987, Pub. L. No. 100-203, § 10401(a), 101 Stat. 1330, 1430 (1987), reprinted in 1987-3 CB 1, 150. Ultimately, the proposed maximum rate reduction from 55 to 50 percent was stricken by the Revenue Reconciliation Act of 1993, Pub. L. No. 103-66, § 13208(a), 107 Stat. 416, 469 (1993), reprinted in 1993-3 CB 1, 57.

The 1993 legislation was signed into law on August 10, 1993, and it retroactively increased the maximum tax rate (which had technically dropped to 50 percent on January 1, 1993) to 55 percent. The retroactive increase has withstood constitutional attack. Kane v. United States, 942 F. Supp. 233 (ED Pa. 1996), aff'd without published opinion, 118 F3d 1576 (3d Cir. 1997); Quarty v. United States, 170 F3d 961 (9th Cir. 1999); Nationsbank of Texas, N.A. v. United States, 269 F3d 1332 (Fed. Cir. 2001); US Bank, N.A. v. United States, 74 F. Supp. 2d 934 (D. Neb. 1999). Cf. Nat'l Taxpayers Union v. United States, 68 F3d 1428 (DC Cir. 1995).

[68] For years from January 1, 1988, through December 31, 1997, the 5 percent surtax could eliminate both the then $192,800 unified credit and the graduated tax rates. It applied to taxable transfers of up to $21.04 million (in effect, when fully applied, imposing a flat 55 percent tax on such transfers without the benefit of the unified credit). Thus, if in 1997 a decedent had taxable transfers of $21.04 million, the decedent would incur under Section 2001 a regular tax of $11,212,800 reduced by a Section 2010 credit of $192,800, or $11.02 million, plus a Section 2001(c)(2) surtax of 5 percent of $11.04 million, or

5 percent surtax does not apply to estates of decedents dying after 2001.[69] The top marginal rate is scheduled to be gradually reduced from 50 percent to 45 percent prior to 2010, the year of the termination of the estate tax.[70]

However, the rates can properly be analyzed only by examining them in conjunction with the Section 2010 credit.[71] As a result of both the applicable credit amount,[72] which offsets tax attributable to the lower rates, and the ceiling on maximum rates, the effective marginal rates of estate tax ranged from

---

$552,000, for a total of $11,572,000. That $11,572,000 amount is equal to a flat 55 percent of $21.04 million.

Section 2001(c)(2) was amended by the Taxpayer Relief Act of 1997, Pub. L. No. 105-34, § 501(a)(1)(D), 111 Stat. 788, 845 (1997), reprinted in 1997-4 CB (Vol. 1) 1, 59. For years beginning in 1998, the surtax wiped out only the graduated rates but not the unified credit, and, as a result, it was capped at $17,184,000. A flat 55 percent tax on $3 million (where the 55 percent rate kicked in under Section 2001(c)(1) as it applied in years from 1998 through 2001) is $1,650,000 which is $359,200 in excess of the $1,290,800 amount of tax in the tables. Since 5 percent of $7,184,000 equals $359,200, and the surtax applied only to taxable amounts over $10 million, the 5 percent surtax terminated at $17,184,000 ($10 million plus $7,184,000).

The surtax applied only to taxable transfers made after December 31, 1987. Gifts made prior to that date, however, were included in total transfers for the purpose of determining the tax on transfers after the effective date. Conf. Rep. No. 495, 100th Cong., 1st Sess. 993–994 (1987), reprinted in 1987-3 CB 193, 273–274. Thus, if a donor made taxable transfers of $25 million prior to 1988, any subsequent transfers the donor may have made were not subject to the surtax. If a donor made gifts of $8 million prior to 1988 and $5 million subsequent to that time, $3 million of the latter transfer was subject to the surtax.

The surtax did not affect the maximum federal estate tax rate for purposes of computing the generation-skipping transfer tax. Conf. Rep. No. 495, 100th Cong., 1st Sess. 993–994 (1987), reprinted in 1987-3 CB 193, 273–274. See ¶ 16.01 text accompanying note 9.

The Section 2001(c)(2) 5 percent surtax was repealed by the Economic Growth and Tax Relief Reconciliation Act of 2001 for years after 2001. Pub. L. No. 107-16, § 511(b), 115 Stat. 38, 70 (2001), reprinted in 2001-__ CB __, __. But see infra note 70.

[69] IRC § 2001(c)(1). See the Economic Growth and Tax Relief Reconciliation Act of 2001, Pub. L. No. 107-16 § 511(b), 115 Stat. 38, 70 (2001), reprinted in 2001-__ CB __, __. But see infra note 70.

[70] IRC § 2001(c)(2). See supra note 66.

Under the "sunset" provision effective on January 1, 2011, the top rate of 55 percent is restored as is the 5 percent surtax on transfers in excess of $10 million that eliminates the graduated tax rates. Economic Growth and Tax Relief Reconciliation Act of 2001, Pub. L. No. 107-16, § 901(a)(2), 115 Stat. 38, 150 (2001), reprinted in 2001-__ CB __, __. The "sunset" provision is discussed more fully at ¶ 8.10[5].

[71] The credit also determines estate tax filing requirements. See IRC § 6018, discussed at ¶ 3.02 text accompanying notes 22–30.

[72] See IRC § 2010(b), discussed ¶ 3.02. If a recomputation of the gift tax payable is required by Section 2001(b)(2), the gift tax history of the decedent's spouse (not of the decedent) is applied to the spouse's portion of the split gifts included in the decedent's gross estate. IRC § 2001(d). See supra ¶ 2.01[2] text accompanying note 59.

37 to 55 percent from 1984 through 2001, changing to 41 to 50 percent in the year 2002, 41 to 49 percent in the year 2003, 45 to 48 percent in the year 2004, and 45 to 47 percent in the year 2005, and they result in a flat 46 percent rate in the year 2006, and a flat 45 percent rate in years 2007 through 2009, prior to the termination of the estate tax in 2010.[73]

[4] Tax Planning

For decedents who die prior to the year 2010,[74] lifetime gifts made after 1976 are automatically pulled into the estate tax structure in computing the rate of tax on the taxable estate and are subject to the same multipurpose rate table. An initial reaction might be that inter vivos gifts made after 1976 will not result in any overall tax savings. Although the government, not the taxpayer, has use of any gift tax dollars paid during the donor's lifetime, there are offsetting factors. While lifetime gifts play a part in the computation of the estate tax, appreciation of the transferred property between the date the gift is made and the date of the donor's death is not included as a taxable amount. This is because adjusted taxable gifts are included in the transfer tax base at their value when the gift is complete. Second, income generated by the gift property between the time of the gift and the time of death is not included in a decedent's gross estate. In addition, assuming a post-gift survival period of more than three years,[75] the amount of any gift tax payable is not included in the transfer tax base. Therefore, federal gift taxes paid on lifetime transfers reduce the tax base in a way that the federal estate taxes do not. Finally, there are still tax savings available by use of the annual exclusion under Section 2503(b),[76] which may be doubled by the provision that permits married taxpayers to split gifts,[77] and by use of the exclusion under Section 2503(e) for qualified transfers for tuition and medical expenses.[78] Congress has consciously retained these tax advantages for lifetime gifts.

---

[73] See IRC § 2001(c). The table actually shows minimum rates of 18 percent, gradually rising to 41 percent, identified here as the lowest current effective estate and gift tax rates. Forty-one percent is the lowest current effective rate because all estate and gift taxes imposed at the lower rates are eliminated by the unified credit. As the text indicates, when the unified credit increases (see IRC § 2010(c)), the lowest effective rate also increases. The lower part of the table was needed when enacted to compute the tax previously imposed on generation-skipping transfers. The original tax on generation-skipping transfers was retroactively repealed in 1986. See ¶ 18.05.

[74] See IRC § 2210(a); ¶ 8.10[1].

[75] IRC § 2035(b). See ¶ 4.07[3].

[76] Section 2503(b) is discussed ¶¶ 9.04[1]–9.04[3]. See also ¶¶ 9.04[4], 9.04[5].

[77] IRC § 2513. See ¶ 10.03.

[78] Section 2503(e) is discussed ¶ 9.04[6].

Planning for estates is, of course, much more difficult because of the uncertainty after 2009. It appears that the best thing to do taxwise, but not necessarily otherwise, is to die during 2010![79] With respect to other planning, the gift tax exclusions of Sections 2503(b) and 2503(e) and the use of the Section 2505 $1 million applicable exclusion amount remain the only safe bets with respect to inter vivos estate planning.[80]

[5] Tax on Excess Retirement Distributions

For decedents dying after December 31, 1986, and prior to January 1, 1997, there was a provision imposing an estate tax that was hidden in Section 4980A(d) of the excise taxes and that imposed a 15 percent estate tax on a decedent's "excess retirement accumulation."[81] It was repealed in 1997.[82]

¶ 2.02 SECTION 2002. LIABILITY FOR PAYMENT

Section 2002 requires the executor to pay the estate tax.[1] According to the regulations, the executor's duty to pay the tax "applies to the entire tax, regardless of the fact that the gross estate consists in part of property which does not come within the possession of the executor. . . . "[2] Taken literally, the Code and the corresponding regulations state that once one assumes the position of executor, the individual is required to pay the entire estate tax, even though that individual must dig into personal funds to do so. That is, the executor might be looked upon as fully responsible to the government, even if the executor is entitled to reimbursement from others. Although there is some authority

---

[79] A "sunset" provision restores the estate tax in the year 2011. Economic Growth and Tax Relief Reconciliation Act of 2001, Pub. L. No. 107-16, § 901(a)(2), 115 Stat. 38, 150 (2001), reprinted in 2001-__ CB __, __. The "sunset" provision is discussed more fully at ¶ 8.10[5].

[80] See ¶¶ 9.04, 9.06 (especially ¶ 9.06[3]).

[81] The provision is discussed in detail at Stephens, Maxfield, Lind & Calfee, Federal Estate and Gift Taxation, ¶ 2.05 (Warren, Gorham & Lamont, 7th ed. 1997).

[82] Section 4980A(d) was repealed by the Taxpayer Relief Act of 1997, Pub. L. No. 105-34, § 1073, 111 Stat. 788, 948 (1997), reprinted in 1997-4 CB (Vol. 1) 1, 162, effective for decedents dying after December 31, 1996.

[1] The term "executor" has a broad meaning that is not confined to one appointed as executor of a will or even to one named as the administrator of an estate. The statutory definition of the term appears in Section 2203. See ¶ 8.02. Cf. IRC § 7701(a)(47).

[2] Reg. § 20.2002-1. For an example of such a possibility, see Section 2036, discussed at ¶ 4.08, in part concerning transfers with retained life estates.

for this view,[3] it seems unacceptable in the light of other statutory provisions that fasten personal liability onto the executor only in specified circumstances.[4] A better view is that the executor incurs personal liability only for a fiduciary impropriety[5] and that, except with regard to priorities, the executor's duty regarding the payment of estate taxes is not appreciably different from the executor's obligation under state law to other creditors of the estate.[6] The clear thrust of the statute is to centralize responsibility in the executor, and, in the usual case where estate assets available to the executor are sufficient to pay the tax, a simple and orderly method for payment is the result.

[1] Estate Tax Return

The estate tax return, Form 706, United States Estate (and Generation-Skipping Transfer) Tax Return (or Form 706-NA, United States Estate (and Generation-Skipping Transfer) Tax Return, in the case of a decedent who is neither a citizen nor a resident), generally must be filed within nine months after the decedent's death.[7] An extension can be obtained for filing the return. Section 6081 grants general authority to the Service to extend the time for filing tax returns required by the Code or by regulations, and it provides for a six-month limit on extensions, except for taxpayers who are abroad.[8] For estate tax returns filed on Form 706 the six-month extension is automatic if a timely appli-

---

[3] Baldwin v. Comm'r, 94 F2d 355 (9th Cir. 1938).

[4] See the comments on discharge of the executor from personal liability in the discussion of Section 2204, at ¶ 8.03.

[5] See Reg. § 20.2002-1; Schwartz v. Comm'r, 560 F2d 311 (8th Cir. 1977); Leigh v. Comm'r, 72 TC 1105 (1979). These cases are considered in Huchberg & Silbergleit, "Recent Cases Narrow Scope of Executor's Personal Liability for Taxes," 7 Est. Plan. 2 (1980). See also Bank of the West, Trustee v. Comm'r, 93 TC 462 (1989); Estate of Pittard v. Comm'r, 69 TC 391 (1977), in which executor was found liable for civil fraud penalty for errors in estate tax return. Cf. Occidental Life Ins. Co. of Cal. v. Comm'r, 50 TC 726 (1968).

[6] The problem is elaborately considered in 6 Mertens, Law of Federal Gift and Estate Taxation, §§ 43.02–43.12 (1960). See also Alexander, "Personal Liability of Executors and Trustees for Federal Income, Estate and Gift Taxes," 9 Tax L. Rev. 1 (1953).

[7] IRC § 6075(a). For estates of decedents who died before 1971, the statutory period was fifteen months. See Section 6075(a) prior to amendment by the Excise, Estate, and Gift Tax Adjustment Act of 1970. Pub. L. No. 91-614, § 101(b), 84 Stat. 1836 (1970), reprinted in 1971-1 CB 533. In both instances, the period expires on the later date numerically corresponding to the date of death or, if there is no such date, on the last date of the appropriate month. When the due date falls on a Saturday, Sunday, or legal holiday, the due date for filing the return is the next day that is not Saturday, Sunday, or a legal holiday. Reg. § 20.6075-1.

[8] IRC § 6081(a). See Form 4768, "Application for Extension of Time to File a Return and/or Pay U.S. Estate (and Generation-Skipping Transfer) Taxes" (Rev. Aug. 2001),

cation is made.⁹ However, it appears that for estate tax returns other than a Form 706, the regulations indicate that an application for extension will be granted only if "good and sufficient cause" is demonstrated.¹⁰ An extension of time for *filing* of the return under Section 6081 does not operate to extend the time for *payment* of the tax.¹¹

Section 6651(a)(1) imposes a penalty of 5 percent (with a maximum of 25 percent) of the amount of the tax for each month of delinquency in filing (determined with regard to any extension of the time for filing),¹² unless the delay is "due to reasonable cause and not due to willful neglect."¹³ Generally, the executor has a nondelegatable duty to file the return on time. That duty is not satisfied, that is, reasonable cause is not shown, by the executor's reliance on an attorney or an accountant who either fails to inform the executor of the correct filing deadline or fails to file the return within that deadline.¹⁴ However,

---

which must be filed in conjunction with any request for an extension. Reg. § 20.6081-1(a).

⁹ Reg. § 20.6081-1(b). The Form 4768 request for an automatic extension of time to file a Form 706 must be filed before the due date for filing the Form 706. See supra note 8.

¹⁰ Reg. § 20.6081-1(c). It appears that the automatic extension does not apply to filing Form 706A "United States Additional Estate Tax Return," Form 706D, "United States Additional Estate Tax Under Section 2057," Form 706NA, "United States Estate and Generation-Skipping Tax Return Estate of Nonresident not a Citizen of the United States" and Form 706QDT "United States Estate Tax Return for Qualified Domestic Trusts." See Notice of Proposed Rulemaking and Notice of Public Hearing, Supplementary Information, 65 Fed. Reg. 63,025, 63,026 (2000), reprinted in 2000-2 CB 465, 466.

A request for an extension of time to file beyond the six-month automatic extension where the executor is abroad should be filed early enough to permit the Service time to consider the matter before the due date of the return. Reg. § 20.6081-1(c). This same rule applies where an estate or person required to file forms other than Form 706 is seeking an extension of time to file. Id. An extension of time to file Form 706 may be granted to an estate that did not request an extension of time to file Form 706 prior to the due date at the discretion of the Service if good cause is shown; however, failure to request an extension of time before the due date may indicate negligence and constitute cause for denial of the extension of time to file. Id.

The Tax Court has jurisdiction to determine whether the Commissioner's denial of an extension of time to file the estate tax return is an abuse of discretion. Estate of Gardner v. Comm'r, 82 TC 989 (1984).

¹¹ Reg. § 20.6081-1(e). See infra ¶¶ 2.02[2], 2.02[3].

¹² But see Rev. Rul. 81-237, 1981-2 CB 245 (in computing failure to file penalty, no reduction in amount of tax due for payments made during extension period); Constantino v. United States, 85-2 USTC ¶ 13,629 (ND Cal. 1985) (payment of tax during extension period did not reduce amount of failure-to-file penalties).

Section 6651(a)(2) also imposes a penalty for late *payment* of tax.

¹³ IRC § 6651(a)(1).

¹⁴ United States v. Boyle, 469 US 241 (1985); United States v. Blumberg, 86-1 USTC ¶ 13,658 (CD Cal. 1985); Estate of Cox v. United States, 637 F. Supp. 1112 (SD Fla. 1986); Constantino v. United States, 85-2 USTC ¶ 13,629 (ND Cal. 1985); Estate of

reasonable cause is established and the penalty is inapplicable if the executor relies on substantive advice by a tax adviser that filing a return is not required.[15] The reasonable cause test is also met under some other extenuating conditions.[16]

In filing an estate tax return, the executor is treated as providing the requisite notice of qualification as executor.[17] However, anyone who acts in a fi-

---

Newton v. Comm'r, 59 TCM (CCH) 469 (1990); Maltaman v. Comm'r, 73 TCM (CCH) 2162 (1997); Estate of Hinz v. Comm'r, 79 TCM (CCH) 1289 (2000). In the *Boyle* case, the Supreme Court resolved a conflict among several circuits by drawing what it described as a "bright line" to conclude that reliance on a tax expert to file the return or inform the executor when the return was due was not "reasonable cause" under Section 6651(a)(1) because the executor could have easily filed the return himself or ascertained when the return was due. *Boyle* may draw a "bright line," but it leaves many "reasonable cause" questions unanswered. See Estate of Campbell v. Comm'r, 62 TCM (CCH) 1514 (1991) (neither the fact that the estate could not obtain appraisal information on its principal asset nor reliance on the attorney's advice not to file incomplete estate tax return constituted reasonable cause); Estate of Melville v. Comm'r, 66 TCM (CCH) 1076 (1993) (neither reliance on erroneous advice of an attorney that penalty for late filing of estate tax return would be waived nor lack of funds to pay tax constituted reasonable cause). See also Brookens, "Section 6651(a)(1) Penalty for Late Filed Returns: Reasonable Cause and Unreasoned Decisions," 35 Case W. Res. L. Rev. 183 (1985); Newmann, "Supreme Court Holds that Reliance on Attorney Was Not Reasonable Cause for Late Filing," 13 Tax'n for Law. 266 (1985); Trost, "Supreme Court Rules Reliance on Counsel Is Not Reasonable Cause to Abate Late Filing Penalty," 12 Est. Plan. 138 (1985).

[15] See United States v. Boyle, 469 US 241, 250 (1985); Estate of Paxton v. Comm'r, 86 TC 785 (1986) (executor relied on advice of counsel that certain trusts were not includable within the gross estate and consequently no return was required to be filed); Estate of Chagra v. Comm'r, 60 TCM (CCH) 104 (1990) (executrix reasonably relied on advice of attorney that a return was not required); Estate of Lennon v. Comm'r, 62 TCM (CCH) 326 (1991) (personal representative reasonably relied on the advice of attorney that the date-of-death value of the estate did not require the filing of a return). Cf. Estate of Buring v. Comm'r, 51 TCM (CCH) 115 (1985) (reliance on advice from accountant that certain gifts were loans, and no gift tax return was required to be filed).

[16] Brown v. United States, 630 F. Supp. 57 (MD Tenn. 1985) (in which an old, inexperienced executor in ill health was incapable of ordinary business care and prudence when an emergency arose with his attorney). The Service has compiled a list of extenuating circumstances that satisfy the reasonable cause test, such as unavoidable postal delays, timely filing of a return with the wrong IRS office, erroneous Service advice, destruction by casualty of a taxpayer's records, and death or serious illness of executor or a member of the executor's immediate family. Internal Revenue Manual (CCH) § 4350, (22)22.2(2) (June 1998) (Audit Technique Manual for Estate Tax Examiners).

[17] Until 1970, an executor had two tax forms to file before the estate tax return: namely, the preliminary notice, Form 704 (Form 705 for estates of nonresident aliens), and a notice of qualification as executor. IRC § 6036. Neither is required with respect to decedents dying after 1970. The preliminary notice was abandoned, apparently because of the shortened period for filing the estate tax return itself, which is discussed supra note 7.

duciary capacity for another, including an executor and an administrator, is required to give notice of the fiduciary relationship.[18]

Although the statute dealing with the location where a decedent's estate tax return is to be filed generally provides that the return of a resident decedent is filed with the Service center of the Service district in which the decedent was domiciled at death, the statute also permits the Service to designate other locations.[19] Under this authority, the Service has centralized filing locations. If a resident files using the U.S. Postal Service, the return is filed at the Service center in Cincinnati, Ohio.[20] If an authorized private delivery service is used, the return is filed at the Service center in Covington, Kentucky.[21] In the alternative, a resident may hand-deliver the return to the Service center in the Service district where the decedent was domiciled at death.[22]

Returns of decedents who were citizens or residents must always be accompanied by a certified copy of the will, if the decedent died testate.[23] Even though this requirement is clearly stated in the instructions for the return,[24] it is often not observed, which, as the instructions warn, delays the processing of the return. Other documentation may be required[25] or permitted and desirable.

---

[18] IRC § 6903; Reg. § 301.6903-1(a); Estate of McElroy v. Comm'r, 82 TC 509 (1984). Form 56, "Notice Concerning Fiduciary Relationship," is provided for this purpose and for notice of termination. Notice of termination must be given to relieve the fiduciary of any further duty or liability. Reg. § 301.6903-1(b).

[19] IRC § 6091(b)(3). Returns of decedents who were not domiciled in the United States, whether they were citizens or noncitizens, are filed with the Service center in Philadelphia, PA 19255. IRC § 6091(b)(4); Reg. § 20.6091-1(b); Instructions for Form 706 "United States Estate (and Generation-Skipping Transfers) Tax Return" (Rev. Nov. 2001) at 2, Instructions for Form 706-NA, "United States Estate (and Generation-Skipping Transfer) Tax Return" (Rev. Sept. 1999) at 1.

[20] Instructions for Form 706, "United States Estate (and Generation-Skipping Transfer) Tax Return (Rev. Nov. 2001) at 2. The address is Internal Revenue Service Center, Cincinnati, OH 45999. Id.

[21] Instructions for Form 706, "United States Estate (and Generation-Skipping Transfer) Tax Return" (Rev. Nov. 2001) at 2. The address is Internal Revenue Service Center, 201 W. Rivercenter Blvd., Covington, KY 41019. Id.

[22] IRC § 6091(b)(4); Reg. § 20.6091-1(a). Presumably, the hand-delivery rule is to enable executors to convieniently ensure timely filing without relying on the timely mailing rule of Section 7502.

[23] Reg. § 20.6018-4(a).

[24] See Instructions for Form 706, "United States Estate (and Generation-Skipping Transfer) Tax Return" (Rev. Nov. 2001), Supplemental Documents, at 2.

[25] Instructions for Form 706, "United States Estate (and Generation-Skipping Transfer) Tax Return" (Rev. Nov. 2001), Supplemental Documents, at 2. See Reg. § 20.6018-4.

[2] Payment of the Estate Tax

In general, Section 6151 requires that the estate tax be paid at the time and place fixed for the filing of the return.

[3] Extension of Time for Payment

The Code presents several provisions that permit deferral of payment of the estate tax. The principal sections are 6159, 6161, 6163,[26] and 6166. Each deserves some comment.[27]

[a] Section 6159

This is a general provision applicable to any tax (not just an estate tax) under which the Service is authorized to enter into a written agreement with a taxpayer to satisfy a tax liability by installment payments if the Service determines that such an arrangement will facilitate collection of the tax liability.[28] The agreement generally remains in effect for the term specified therein.[29] However, the Service may terminate the agreement if the taxpayer provides inaccurate or incomplete information,[30] or if the Service determines that collection of any tax to which an agreement relates is in jeopardy.[31] In addition, the Service may alter, modify, or terminate an agreement if the taxpayer fails to

---

[26] Section 6163, permitting extension for tax on remainders, is discussed ¶ 3.07.

[27] Potential estate tax savings derived from the use of the installment payment provisions of the Code are discussed in several articles that may be useful even if some are not entirely current. E.g., Kiziah, "Deferring Estate Tax Is Not Always a Beneficial Move," 20 Est. Plan. 12 (1993); Sheffield, "Liquidity Problems of Owners of Closely-Held Corporations: Relief Provided by Sections 303 and 6166," 38 Fla. L. Rev. 787 (1986); Was, "How to Defer Estate Tax on a Closely-held Business Interest and When It Is Advisable," 13 Tax'n for Law. 206 (1985); Hardee, "How to Solve the Liquidity Problems of an Illiquid Estate," 16 Prac. Acct. 59 (1983); Brown, "Possibilities for Deferring Estate Taxes Increase as a Result of Recent Developments," 22 Tax'n for Acct. 4 (1979); Byars, "Sections 6166 and 6166A Elections—Estate Planning Opportunities," 57 Taxes 265 (1979); Perkins, "Should You Mortgage Your Estate?" 57 Taxes 270 (1979). Opportunities discussed in these articles are related to fluctuations in the interest rate on underpayments of tax. See infra ¶¶ 2.02[3][b] note 39; 2.02[3][c][v].

[28] IRC § 6159(a). Interest would be due on any deferral. See IRC §§ 6601, 6621. Section 6159(a) applies to installment agreements entered into after November 10, 1988. Technical and Miscellaneous Revenue Act of 1988, Pub. L. No. 100-657, § 6234(c), 102 Stat. 3342, 3736 (1988), 1988-3 CB 1, 396. A user fee of $43 is imposed for entering into an installment agreement under Section 6159. TD 8589, 1995-1 CB 225.

[29] IRC § 6159(b)(1).

[30] IRC § 6159(b)(2)(A).

[31] IRC § 6159(b)(2)(B).

pay an installment when it is due,[32] fails to pay any other tax liability when it is due,[33] or fails to provide any updated financial information requested by the Service.[34] If the Service makes a determination that there is a significant change in the financial condition of the taxpayer, the Service may also alter, modify, or terminate the agreement.[35]

[b] Section 6161

[i] **Short extensions.** The general rule of this long-standing provision complements the Section 6081 extension of time for filing returns. Here, extension of the time for payment may be made by the Service for as much as twelve months.[36] To the statutory rule expressed in terms of discretion, the regulations add a requirement of "reasonable cause."[37] Routine requests for brief extensions of time for filing may encompass a companion request for deferred payment of up to six months or a year.[38] Of course, as there is no contrary

---

[32] IRC § 6159(b)(4)(A). A user fee of $24 is imposed for restructuring or reinstating an installment agreement entered into under Section 6159. TD 8589, 1995-1 CB 225.

[33] IRC § 6159(b)(4)(B).

[34] IRC § 6159(b)(4)(C). The legislative history adds that any such request must be reasonable. HR Conf. Rep. No. 1104, 100th Cong., 2d Sess. 219–220 (1988), reprinted in 1988-3 CB 473, 709–710.

[35] IRC § 6159(b)(3). This action may be taken only if the Service notifies the taxpayer of its determination at least thirty days prior to the date of the action and provides in the notification an explanation why it intends to take such action. These requirements do not apply if the Service believes that the collection of tax covered by the agreement is in jeopardy. IRC § 6159(b)(5).

[36] IRC § 6161(a)(1).

[37] Reg. § 20.6161-1(a)(1). See infra note 44 for a discussion of examples involving "reasonable cause."

[38] See Form 4768, "Application for Extension of Time to File a Return and/or Pay U.S. Estate (and Generation Skipping Transfer) Taxes" (Rev. Aug. 2001). See supra ¶ 2.02[1] note 8.

special rule, normal interest[39] will be payable from the date prescribed for payment without regard to the extension.[40]

[ii] **"Reasonable cause" extensions.** Section 6161(a)(2) permits a much longer extension of the time for payment, up to ten years.[41] In this instance, however, the statute itself requires a showing of "reasonable cause." The reasonable cause requirement in Section 6161(a)(2) replaced a required showing of "undue hardship."[42] Congress intended to provide estates with greater relief from liquidity problems,[43] and the term "reasonable cause" here should be interpreted in line with the meaning given it in the regulations applicable to Section 6161(a)(1).[44] If an extension of time for payment is granted under Section

---

[39] The interest rate fluctuates and approximates the prime rate. IRC § 6621(b). See, e.g., Rev. Rul. 2001-22, 2001-1 CB 556. Rev. Proc. 95-17, 1995-1 CB 556, contains uniform tables for computing interest using the daily compounding rule for all computations made after December 31, 1994. See also Rev. Proc. 83-7, 1983-1 CB 583, for procedures to be followed in computing interest and for examples of such procedures for interest computations made before January 1, 1995.

The interest is generally deductible by the estate under Section 2053(a)(2). Estate of Bahr v. Comm'r, 68 TC 74 (1977); Estate of Buchholtz v. Comm'r, 70 TC 814 (1978); Rev. Rul. 81-154, 1981-1 CB 470. Cf. Rev. Rul. 80-250, 1980-2 CB 278, allowing a Section 2053 deduction for interest only when it accrues on extensions to pay under Section 6161 and 6163. See ¶ 5.03[3][c] text accompanying notes 79–80. A Form 706 with the supplemental information must be filed to annually deduct interest and recompute the estate tax as authorized in Rev. Proc. 81-27, 1981-2 CB 548, where an estate has been granted an extension of time to pay estate tax under Section 6161. Priv. Ltr. Rul. 9241002 (July 23, 1992).

[40] IRC §§ 6601(a), 6601(b)(1).

[41] See comments on extensions and on installment payments under Section 6166 infra ¶ 2.02[3][c]. See also supra note 39.

[42] Tax Reform Act of 1976, Pub. L. No. 94-455, § 2004(c), 90 Stat. 1520, 1867–1868 (1976), reprinted in 1976-3 CB (Vol. 1) 343–344.

[43] HR Conf. Rep. No. 1380, 94th Cong., 2d Sess. 3, 31 (1976), reprinted in 1976-3 CB (Vol. 3) 735, 765.

[44] HR Conf. Rep. No. 1515, 94th Cong., 2d Sess. 399, 611 (1976), reprinted in 1976-3 CB (Vol. 3) 807, 961. *Compare* Regulations Section 20.6161-1(a)(1) Exs. 1–4 of reasonable cause, involving:

1. Difficulty in marshaling adequate liquid assets scattered in several jurisdictions;

2. Substantial portion of assets in the form of royalty or similar rights to future payment against which estate cannot borrow upon reasonable terms;

3. Substantial estate assets not collectible without litigation; and

4. Lack of funds or reasonable accessibility thereto to pay estate tax and to provide survivors' support during administration and to pay claims that are due;

with Regulations Section 20.6161-1(a)(2)(ii), now obsolete because of a change in Section 6161(a) by Technical Amendments of 1958, Pub. L. No. 85-866, § 206(c), 72 Stat. 1606

6161(a)(2) other than with regard to installment payments under Section 6166 discussed in the following section, interest is payable for the usual time at normal rates.[45]

[c] Section 6166

[i] **Introduction.** In effect, Congress has long held that it can identify some situations that are *res ipsa loquitur* payment deferral cases. Section 6166 is one of those situations, providing deferral of estate taxes attributable to certain interests in closely held businesses.[46] Estate tax within Section 6166 generally may remain entirely unpaid for five years, after which the tax generally may be paid over a maximum of ten installments, one each year with the first due at the end of year five, thus extending the time to pay the estate tax attributable to the value of the interest for up to fourteen years.[47] Interest is charged on the unpaid tax, but it is charged at preferential rates.[48] Section 6166 may

---

(1958), reprinted 1958-3 CB 254, 332, which said that "undue hardship" means more than inconvenience and that a sale of estate assets at fair market value is not undue hardship, and that illustrates "undue hardship" in Regulations Sections 20.6161-1(a)(2)(ii) Ex. 1 and 20.6161-1(a)(2)(ii)(2), comprehending:

1. A required sale of part of a closely held business to pay taxes where other relief is not available and
2. A forced sale of other assets at a sacrifice price to pay taxes.

See also HR Conf. Rep. No. 1380, 94th Cong., 2d Sess. 3, 28 (1976), reprinted in 1976-3 CB (Vol. 3) 735, 762; Estate of Doster v. Comm'r, 83 TCM (CCH) 1044 (2002) (no abuse of discretion in denying extension for lottery payments).

[45] IRC §§ 6601(a), 6621. See supra ¶ 2.02[3][b] note 39. There is no "reasonable cause" exception for the payment of interest. Church v. United States, 79-2 USTC ¶ 13,306 (EDNY 1979).

[46] Prior to the 1981 amendment of Section 6166 by Pub. L. No. 97-34, § 422, 95 Stat. 172, 314 (1981), reprinted in 1981-2 CB 256, 331, the Code contained two provisions, Sections 6166 and 6166A, providing similar, but somewhat different payment extensions. See Stephens, Maxfield & Lind, Federal Estate and *Gift Taxation* ¶¶ 2.02[3][b], 2.02[3][c] (Warren, Gorham & Lamont, 4th ed. 1978) and HR Conf. Rep. No. 201, 97th Cong., 1st Sess. 38, 180 (1981), reprinted in 1981-2 CB 352, 388. In essence, the two provisions were combined and liberalized under the 1981 Act. See Smith & Guyton, "New Law Makes it Easier to Qualify for Estate Tax Deferral and Sec. 303 Redemptions," 56 J. Tax'n 14 (1982).

The Section 6166 extension of time for payment is available for payment of the generation-skipping transfer tax attributable to an interest in a closely held business, where that business interest is the subject matter of a direct skip generation-skipping transfer occurring at the time of and as a result of an individual's death. IRC § 6166(i). See ¶ 18.01[2][a].

[47] IRC §§ 6166(a)(1), 6166(a)(3).

[48] See infra ¶ 2.02[3][c][v].

work in combination with other provisions providing estate tax assistance to closely held businesses such as Section 303,[49] Section 2032A,[50] and Section 2057.[51]

[ii] Qualification for extension. A variety of technical requirements must be satisfied to permit a decedent's estate to defer payment of part of a decedent's estate taxes under Section 6166. The decedent must have been a citizen or resident of the United States at the date of the decedent's death.[52] In addition, an election to employ Section 6166 must be made by the decedent's executor.[53] Finally, the section applies only when the value of certain closely held business interests constitute more than 35 percent of the decedent's adjusted gross estate.[54]

Election. An election[55] under Section 6166 is made with the decedent's return[56] at the time of filing the return.[57] Further, a timely but unsuccessful election made in good faith under Section 6166 is treated as a timely reasonable cause application for extension under Section 6161.[58] If the decedent's estate has a deficiency and the other requirements of Section 6166 are satisfied, the section allows an executor to pay the deficiency attributable to the qualify-

---

[49] See Bittker & Eustice, Federal Income Taxation of Corporations and Shareholders, ¶ 9.08 (Warren, Gorham & Lamont, 7th ed. 2000). Cf. infra text accompanying note 143.

[50] See ¶ 4.04, infra text accompanying note 103.

[51] See ¶ 5.08, especially ¶ 5.08[6].

[52] IRC § 6166(a)(1).

[53] IRC § 6166(a)(1).

[54] IRC § 6166(a)(1).

[55] See Rev. Proc. 79-55, 1979-2 CB 539, for IRS procedures in processing requests. "No news is good news!" If the executor's request is proper, it is likely no communication will be received. But see Rocovich v. United States, 1989-2 USTC ¶ 13,819 (Cl. Ct. 1989), aff'd, 933 F2d 991 (Fed. Cir. 1991) (Service not equitably estopped from disallowing taxpayer's Section 6166 election upon audit nearly three years after return was filed because of failure to deny the deferral earlier; silence was not a misrepresentation of fact).

[56] Reg. § 20.6166-1(b).

[57] IRC § 6166(d). See Priv. Ltr. Rul. 8512003 (Nov. 30, 1984) (election invalid because not attached to timely filed return where request for extension of time to file denied).

If an election was made with the return, deficiencies are also covered. IRC § 6166(e). Reg. § 20.6166-1(c)(2). See also IRC § 6166(f)(3) with regard to interest on the assessment of the deficiency.

A protective election may be made to defer payment of any portion of tax remaining unpaid at the time the values are finally determined and any deficiencies attributable to the closely held business interest. Reg. § 20.6166-1(d).

[58] Reg. § 20.6161-1(b). See the discussion of Section 6161, including its regulatory requirements, supra ¶ 2.02[3][b].

ing closely held business interests in installments, even if no election was made when the return was filed.[59]

Value of Interests in Closely Held Businesses Must Exceed 35 Percent of the Decedent's Adjusted Gross Estate. The value of the closely held active business assets must constitute a significant portion of the value of the decedent's gross estate in order to defer the payment of estate tax related to those assets. The determination whether this requirement is met is a three-step process: (1) the decedent must own an interest in a closely held business;[60] (2) the active business assets in the closely held business must be separated from the other business assets;[61] (3) the value of such active assets in the closely held business must exceed 35 percent of the decedent's adjusted gross estate.[62]

Closely Held Business. A decedent's interest in a sole proprietorship qualifies as a closely held business under Section 6166.[63] If the decedent was a partner in a business, the decedent's partnership interest in that business qualifies as a closely held business under Section 6166, if at least 20 percent of the total capital interests in the partnership are included in the decedent's gross estate or if the partnership has no more than forty-five (fifteen for years prior to 2002) partners.[64] The decedent's ownership in a corporation similarly qualifies if at least 20 percent of the voting stock is included in the decedent's gross estate or if the corporation has no more than forty-five (fifteen for years prior to 2002) shareholders.[65]

---

[59] IRC § 6166(h)(1); Reg. § 20.6166-1(c)(1). If an election was not made with the return and there is a deficiency, an election is timely if made within sixty days after notice and demand for payment. IRC § 6166(h)(2). The election will cause a proration of the amount of the deficiency among all past and future installment dates created by an existing election or those that would have been created had a timely election occurred with the return. All amounts allocated to installment dates that preceded the election will be due at the time of the deficiency election. IRC § 6166(h)(3).

[60] IRC § 6166(b)(1).

[61] IRC § 6166(b)(9).

[62] IRC § 6166(a)(1).

[63] IRC § 6166(b)(1)(A).

[64] IRC § 6166(b)(1)(B). Seemingly, a limited liability company (which is taxable as a partnership for federal income tax purposes) should be treated as a partnership for purposes of Section 6166.

The increase of the number of partners from fifteen to forty-five was made by the Economic and Tax Relief Reconciliation Act of 2001, Pub. L. No. 107-16, § 571(a), 115 Stat. 38, 92 (2001), reprinted in 2001-__ CB __, __ and is effective for the estates of decedents dying after December 31, 2001. Id. at § 571(b), 115 Stat. 38, 92 and 2001-__ CB __, __. Under the "sunset" provision effective January 1, 2011, the forty-five-member rule reverts back to fifteen members. Economic Growth and Tax Relief Reconciliation Act of 2001, Pub. L. No. 107-16, § 901(a)(2), 115 Stat. 38, 150 (2001), reprinted in 2001-__ CB __, __. The "sunset" provision is discussed more fully at ¶ 8.10[5].

[65] IRC § 6166(b)(1)(C). See supra note 64.

The 20 percent ownership and forty-five-member tests applicable to part-nership or corporate interests are determined immediately before the dece-dent's death.[66] Several special rules apply in measuring the ownership or membership tests. First, stock and partnership interests held by spouses as community property or in any form of joint ownership with or without survi-vorship rights are treated as if they are held by one shareholder or one partner for purposes of the forty-five-member limitation.[67] Second, ownership by an entity is attributed to the owners of the entity.[68] Third, stock or a partnership interest held by a member of the decedent's "family" (within the meaning of Section 267(c)(4))[69] is treated as if it were owned by the decedent.[70] The gov-ernment, seemingly inappropriately, contends that the foregoing second and third attribution rules apply only for measurement of the forty-five-member test and that the attribution rules apply in measuring the 20 percent tests only if a Section 6166(b)(7)(A) election is made.[71] Section 6166(b)(7)(A) treats the

---

[66] IRC § 6166(b)(2)(A).

[67] IRC § 6166(b)(2)(B). This rule is not limited to the decedent and the decedent's spouse but applies to all spousal owners. Thus, if a partnership has ninety partners, con-sisting of forty-five sets of spouses whose interests are held as community property, then decedent's ownership of one half of the community property will qualify for measurement in the 35 percent test because the statute treats the partnership as if it is owned by only forty-five partners.

[68] IRC § 6166(b)(2)(C). These rules attributing ownership from an entity to an owner can be helpful in qualifying the estate for the 20 percent ownership requirement, but they can also operate to disqualify the estate from the forty-five-member requirement. For ex-ample, if a decedent owned a 15 percent interest in a corporation and a 10 percent interest in a partnership owning a 50 percent interest in the same corporation, an additional 5 per-cent is attributed to the decedent under Section 6166(b)(2)(C), and the decedent's now 20 percent interest qualifies as a closely held business interest. However, if the corporation has only ten shareholders, including the partnership previously mentioned, and the dece-dent owned only a 5 percent interest in the partnership, which has 50 partners, the Section 6166(b)(2)(C) attribution rule will disqualify the decedent's otherwise qualifying share-holder interest from treatment as a closely held business. Without attribution, the decedent would be within the forty-five-member limitation; but with attribution, the corporation is treated as having more than forty-five shareholders, and the decedent is treated as owning only a 17.5 percent interest in the corporation.

[69] For these purposes, "family" means brothers and sisters (whether by the whole or the half blood), spouses, ancestors, and lineal descendants. IRC § 267(c)(4). In determin-ing whether any of these relationships exists, full effect is given to a legal adoption. Reg. § 1.267(c)-1(a)(4).

[70] IRC § 6166(b)(2)(D).

[71] Priv. Ltr. Rul. 8428088 (Apr. 12, 1984) (involving the Section 6166(b)(1)(D) fam-ily attribution rule); Priv. Ltr. Rul. 9644053 (Aug. 1, 1996) (involving the Section 6166(b)(1)(C) entity attribution rule). While Section 6166(b)(7) is more specific than Sec-tions 6166(b)(2)(C) and 6166(b)(2)(D) with respect to its interrelationship with Sections 6166(b)(1)(A)(i) and 6166(b)(2)(A)(i), they are not inconsistent and both can operate inde-pendently in different situations. As a result, the government's position based on a very weak legislative history comment (see HR Conf. Rep. No. 1380, 94th Cong., 2d Sess. 32

decedent's estate as owning the interests not only for the 20 percent tests of Sections 6166(b)(1)(B)(i) and 6166(b)(1)(C)(i) but also for purposes of Section 6166(c)[72] and it pulls such attributed property into the decedent's gross estate for purposes of the 35 percent test[73] if the decedent's executor so elects.[74] However, if the executor makes the Section 6166(b)(7) election, there is a relinquishment of two of the benefits normally provided under Section 6166, namely, the 2 percent interest rate on the tax on the qualifying interest[75] and the five-year deferral for the payments.[76]

The Active Business Requirement. The deferral provisions inherently require the closely held business[77] to be carrying on an active trade or business and not to be a mere holding company.[78] There is no requirement that the decedent materially participate or even actively participate in the closely held business for the estate to utilize the election.[79] However, even where an active trade or business is carried on, for purposes of measuring whether the closely held business meets the 35 percent test, the portion of the business attributable to passive assets is disregarded.[80] This rule precludes the decedent from "stuffing" an otherwise active business with passive assets in order to satisfy the 35 percent test. A "passive asset" is any asset other than an asset used in carrying on a trade or business.[81] Lines here can be difficult to draw, especially where the trade or business involves the holding of real estate.[82] However, in some

---

(1976), reprinted in 1976-3 (Vol. 3) CB 738, 766, which is quoted in Priv. Ltr. Rul. 9644053, supra) seems incorrect. The Sections 6166(b)(2)(C) and 6166(b)(2)(D) attribution rules should apply to Sections 6166(b)(1)(B)(i) and 6166(b)(1)(C)(i) both where a Section 6166(b)(7) election is not made and where one is made.

[72] IRC § 6166(c). See infra text accompanying notes 112–114.

[73] IRC § 6166(b)(7)(A)(i). See infra text accompanying notes 109–110.

[74] IRC § 6166(b)(7)(A)(i).

[75] IRC § 6166(b)(7)(A)(iii). See infra text accompanying notes 125–129.

[76] IRC § 6166(b)(7)(A)(ii). See infra text accompanying at notes 116–117.

[77] See IRC § 6166(b)(9)(A).

[78] See IRC §§ 6166(b)(1)(A), 6166(b)(1)(B), 6166(b)(1)(C) (each subparagraph refers to the "carrying on" requirement).

[79] Cf. IRC §§ 469(c)(1)(B), 469(h)(1), 469(i)(1), 1402(a)(1), 2032A(b)(1)(C)(ii), 2032A(c)(6)(B), 2032A(e)(6), 2057(b)(1)(D)(ii), 2057(f)(1)(A).

[80] IRC § 6166(b)(9)(A).

[81] IRC § 6166(b)(9)(B)(i).

[82] In Rev. Rul. 75-367, 1975-2 CB 472, some of the decedent's holdings qualified as active business interests, but others were merely managed investment assets. Decedent's "business" interests consisted of a corporation that engaged in home building on land owned and developed by decedent's sole proprietorship, together with a business office and warehouse, which the decedent and the corporation shared in the home-building and land development activities. On the other hand, the decedent's activities in maintaining eight owned and rented homes were held to constitute the mere management of investment assets. In Rev. Rul. 75-366, 1975-2 CB 472, operation of farm realty by the dece-

instances, Section 6166 expressly permits residential property (even if it is a passive asset) to be included in valuing a closely held farming business for purposes of the 35 percent test.[83]

Generally the stock of a mere holding company does not qualify for Section 6166 deferral. However, under a special rule, Section 6166 permits the decedent's executor to elect to have stock of a holding company pierced to determine the extent to which the holding company owns stock in a closely held active trade or business which stock may then qualify for deferral.[84] If all of the pierced stock is non–readily tradable stock, deferral is permitted to any pierced stock that qualifies for deferral.[85] However, in such circumstances, the benefits of both the 2 percent interest rule and the five-year deferral rule are automatically waived.[86] If some of the pierced stock is publicly traded, deferral is permitted to the non–publicly traded pierced stock that otherwise qualifies for deferral.[87] However, in such circumstances, in addition to automatic waiver

---

dent under agreements with tenant farmers who absorbed a percentage of the farm's expenses in return for a percentage of the crops was an active business of the decedent because the decedent was operating a farm for a gain based on its production rather than merely securing a return as fixed rental income. However, in Rev. Rul. 75-365, 1975-2 CB 471, rental property was held to be a "passive" investment asset. A host of private letter rulings deal with the issue whether real estate activities meet the active trade or business requirement. The following held that there was an active business: Priv. Ltr. Ruls. 8244003 (May 1, 1981); 8251015 (Sept. 27, 1982); 8601005 (Sept. 24, 1985); 9410011 (Dec. 2, 1993); 9422052 (Mar. 9, 1994); 9602017 (Oct. 11, 1995); 9801009 (Sept. 26, 1997); 200000634 (Nov. 12, 1999); 200114005 (Dec. 15, 2000). The following held that there was a mere passive investment: Priv. Ltr. Ruls. 7917006 (Jan. 11, 1979); 8451014 (Aug. 30, 1984); 8515010 (Jan. 8, 1985); 8625005 (Mar. 6, 1986); 9403004 (Oct. 8, 1993); 9621007 (Feb. 13, 1996). See Houghton & Solomon, "Installment Payment of Estate Taxes: IRS Interpretation of Legislative Intent Denies Election to Many Real Estate Owners," 13 J. Real Est. Tax'n 177 (1986).

[83] IRC § 6166(b)(3).

[84] IRC § 6166(b)(8). In measuring voting rights for purposes of the Section 6166(b)(1)(C)(i) 20 percent voting control test (see supra text accompanying note 65), the pierced stock is treated as voting stock to the extent that the voting stock in the holding company owns directly (or through voting stock of one or more other holding companies) voting stock in the business company. IRC § 6166(b)(8)(C).

[85] IRC § 6166(b)(8)(B)(i).

[86] IRC §§ 6166(b)(8)(A)(ii), 6166(b)(8)(A)(iii). See infra text accompanying at notes 116, 117, 125, 126, 127, 128.

[87] IRC § 6166(b)(8)(B)(ii). This provision applies to estates of decedents dying after December 31, 2001. Under the "sunset" provision effective January 1, 2011, this rule is terminated. Economic Growth and Tax Relief Reconciliation Act of 2001, Pub. L. No. 107-16, § 901(a)(2), 115 Stat. 38, 150 (2001), reprinted in 2001-__ CB __, __. The "sunset" provision is discussed more fully at ¶ 8.10[5].

of the 2 percent interest rule and the five-year deferral rules, the payment period is shortened from the normal ten years to five years.[88]

Similarly, if a business owns stock in another business, that stock will generally be treated as a passive asset for purposes of the preceding rules.[89] However, another special rule allows the subsidiary shell to be pierced and a corporate subsidiary to be treated as part of its parent corporation if (1) the parent owns 20 percent or more of the value of the subsidiary's voting stock or the parent is one of forty-five (fifteen for years prior to 2002) or fewer shareholders of the subsidiary;[90] (2) 80 percent or more of the value of each corporation's assets (excluding the value of the subsidiary's stock held by the parent) is used in carrying on that corporation's trade or business;[91] and (3) the decedent's executor makes an election under the holding company rule discussed earlier.[92]

A third special rule treats certain stock in a "qualifying lending and finance business" as an active trade or business[93] if the executor so elects.[94] A lending and finance business is a business that meets loans, purchases or discounts financial obligations, engages in the rental and leasing of property, and renders services or makes facilities available in the regular course of a lending and financial business and its own business.[95] The business is a "qualifying" business if it satisfies either a "facts and circumstances" test[96] or a mechanical

---

[88] IRC §§ 6166(b)(8)(A)(ii), 6166(b)(8)(A)(iii), 6166 (b)(8)(B)(ii). See infra text accompanying notes 115–117, 125–128.

[89] IRC § 6166(b)(9)(B)(ii).

[90] IRC § 6166(b)(9)(B)(iii)(I). See supra note 64.

[91] IRC § 6166(b)(9)(B)(iii)(II).

[92] IRC § 6166(b)(9)(B)(ii)(I). See supra text accompanying at notes 86–88, discussing the costs of such election.

[93] IRC § 6166(b)(10)(A). This rule applies to estates of decedents dying after December 31, 2001. Economic Growth and Tax Relief Reconciliation Act of 2001, Pub. L. No. 107-16, § 572(b), 115 Stat. 38, 93 (2001), reprinted in 2001-__ CB __, __.

[94] IRC § 6166(b)(10)(A). Under the "sunset" provision effective January 1, 2011, this rule is terminated. Economic Growth and Tax Relief Reconciliation Act of 2001, Pub. L. No. 107-16, § 901(a)(2), 115 Stat. 38, 150 (2001), reprinted in 2001-__ CB __, __. The "sunset" provision is discussed more fully at ¶ 8.10[5].

[95] IRC § 6166(b)(10)(B)(ii). The services and facilities made available in connection with its own business may be carried on by another corporation that is a member of the same affiliated group (as defined in Section 1504 without regard to Section 1504(b)(3)).

The definition of "qualifying lending and finance business" does not include an interest in an entity if the stock or debt of the entity (or a controlled group of which the entity was a member) was readily tradeable on an established securities market or secondary market at any time in the three years preceding the decedent's death. IRC § 6166(b)(10)(B)(iii).

[96] IRC § 6166(b)(10)(B)(i)(I). The test concerns whether, based on all the facts and circumstances, immediately before the decedent's death there was substantial activity with respect to the business. Id.

test,[97] both of which in essence require it to be an *active* trade or business. If the executor elects to use this special rule, there is no five-year deferral of payments[98] and the payments must be paid over a five- (rather than a ten-) year period.[99]

The 35 Percent Test. The value of the active business interests in a closely held business that meets the requirements described earlier must exceed 35 percent of the value of the decedent's adjusted gross estate.[100] The valuation used for testing purposes is expressly identified as the estate tax value.[101] This contemplates possible use of the alternate valuation under Section 2032,[102] as well as special real property valuation under Section 2032A.[103]

The term "adjusted gross estate" is defined as the gross estate less the allowable[104] Section 2053 and 2054 deductions.[105] Although the statute seemingly does not require it, the legislative history indicates that for purposes of measuring the numerator of the 35 percent test, the value of the active assets in the closely held business is reduced by allowable expenses, losses, and indebtedness related to those assets.[106]

---

[97] IRC § 6166(b)(10)(B)(i)(II). The test requires that, for at least three of the five taxable years preceding the decedent's death, the business had: (1) at least one full-time employee substantially all of whose services were the active management of such business; (2) ten full-time, nonowner employees substantially all of whose services were directly related to such business; and (3) $5 million in gross receipts from the lending or finance business. Id.

[98] IRC § 6166(b)(10)(A)(ii). See IRC §§ 6151(a), 6166(a)(3).

[99] IRC § 6166(b)(10)(A)(iii). See infra ¶ 2.02[3][c][iii].

[100] IRC § 6166(a)(1). Eligibility is not affected by subsequent redemptions required by a stock transfer agreement. ILM 200141015 (July 2, 2001).

The use of Section 2057, relating to qualified family-owned business interests, does not affect the value, since that provision provides a deduction, not a change in value. See ¶ 5.08[6][c]. The interrelationship of the Section 2031(c) qualified conservation easement exclusion and the 35 percent test is discussed ¶ 4.02[7][e][ii].

[101] IRC § 6166(b)(4).

[102] See ¶ 4.03.

[103] See ¶ 4.04.

[104] Even if Section 2053 or Section 2054 deductions are forgone under the estate tax and are instead deducted under the estate's income tax pursuant to Section 642(g), a reduction occurs in computing the adjusted gross estate because such amounts are "allowable" under Section 2053 or Section 2054.

[105] IRC § 6166(b)(6). As the amount of the adjusted gross estate is partially dependent upon post-death occurrences, a timing rule is supplied that is not very satisfactory and leaves much to the regulations. IRC § 6166(b)(6). See IRC § 6166(j).

[106] HR Conf. Rep. No. 201, 97th Cong., 1st Sess 38, 181 (1981), reprinted in 1981-2 CB 352, 388. A net business value is consistent with its comparison to the net figure, the adjusted gross estate; but the statute itself speaks only of "the value . . . included in . . . the gross estate." IRC § 6166(a)(1). Cf. Rev. Rul. 80-202, 1980-2 CB 363 (only the net value of a sole proprietorship (seemingly reduced by Section 2053 or Section 2054 deductions)

In measuring the adjusted gross estate, the gross estate computation[107] differs from the normal computation in several ways. First, the estate must satisfy the 35 percent test both by including and by not including in the decedent's gross estate all property gratuitously transferred within three years of the decedent's death that is included in the decedent's gross estate under Section 2035(a).[108] Second, if the family attribution election is made under Section 6166(b)(7) to qualify for the 20 percent closely held business requirement,[109] that election triggers the attribution of ownership of interests for purposes of the 35 percent test as well.[110] In measuring the amount of the decedent's gross estate, the attributed family-owned stock is also treated as owned by the decedent.[111]

Generally, each closely held business interest is treated separately under the 35 percent test.[112] However, interests in two or more closely held businesses may be aggregated and treated as interests in a single business under the 35 percent test, if the decedent's gross estate includes 20 percent or more of the total value of each separate business.[113] Solely for purposes of determining the 20 percent aggregate requirement, business interests held by a spouse

---

is used in measuring the test). See infra text accompanying note 113 where the net value test should be applied.

[107] Property included within the gross estate under Section 2044 is eligible for Section 6166 deferral. Reg. § 20.2044-1(b). Under the *Bonner* line of cases, Bonner Estate v. United States, 84 F3d 196 (5th Cir. 1996), the value of interests included in the gross estate under Section 2044 may be eligible for discounts that could affect the availability of Section 6166. See ¶¶ 4.02[4][b] text accompanying notes 157, 158, 4.16 text accompanying notes 19–23.

[108] IRC § 2035(c)(2). See ¶ 4.07[2][d].

[109] See supra text accompanying notes 71–76, especially notes 75, 76 discussing the relinquishment of benefits when making such an election.

[110] IRC § 6166(b)(7)(A)(i).

[111] IRC § 6166(b)(7)(A)(i). For example, assume decedent *D* owns a 10 percent interest that is worth $100,000 in a widely held partnership, that *D*'s sibling *S* also owns a $100,000, 10 percent interest in the partnership, and that *D*'s actual adjusted taxable estate is $300,000. Only the 10 percent interest *D* actually owns is used in measuring the Section 6166(b)(1)(B)(i) 20 percent test and the Section 6166(a)(1) 35 percent measurement and *D* is unable to elect Section 6166 because *D*'s $100,000 interest does not meet the 20 or 35 percent tests. Assume *D*'s executor elects to use Section 6166(b)(7). That subsection attributes *S*'s interest to *D*'s gross estate for purposes of the Section 6166(a)(1) 35 percent test as well as for the Section 6166(b)(1)(B)(i) 20 percent test. Now, *D* is treated as owning a $200,000, 20 percent interest in the partnership. The attributed interest meets the 20 percent test of Section 6166(b)(1)(B)(i) and it exceeds 35 percent of *D*'s now $400,000 adjusted gross estate. Thus, *D*'s actually owned $100,000 interest qualifies for Section 6166 deferral.

[112] IRC § 6166(a)(1).

[113] IRC § 6166(c).

as community property or in any form of joint ownership with or without sur-vivorship rights are treated as included in the decedent's gross estate.[114]

[iii] **Period of extension.** If an estate qualifies under Section 6166, the executor generally may elect to defer payment of all or a portion of the estate tax attributable to the qualifying interest for a period of up to five years, after which the unpaid tax may be paid in up to ten annual installments.[115] The first installment is due on or before the date selected by the executor, which may not be more than five years after the regular filing and payment date provided by Section 6151(a) (nine months after death), with subsequent installments due on the anniversaries of the first payment thus extending the time to pay the tax to up to fourteen years.[116] In limited circumstances, the estate may not use the five-year period and must immediately make payments for the maximum ten-year period.[117]

[iv] **Maximum amount of deferral.** Section 6166 does not necessarily permit installment payments of the entire estate tax. Generally, the section lim-its deferral to the tax attributable to the value of the active business assets of

---

[114] IRC § 6166(c) (last sentence). Except for these interspousal rules, attribution is in-applicable here. Thus, actual ownership is required for the 20 percent test. If a decedent owned 25 percent of *X* corporation and 22 percent of *Y* sole proprietorship, the values of both are combined for the 35 percent test of Section 6166(a)(1). If both of the interests mentioned previously are held in joint tenancy with decedent's spouse, then under the last sentence of Section 6166(c), the interests qualify for the 20 percent test of Section 6166(c). But attribution is limited to that test as the statute provides "for purposes of the 20 percent requirement of the preceding sentence." Thus, the decedent's Section 6166(b)(6) adjusted gross estate includes only the value of a 12.5 percent interest in *X* and 11 percent in *Y* for computation of the Section 6166(a)(1) 35 percent test.

[115] IRC §§ 6166(a)(1), 6166(a)(3). See IRC § 6503(d) extending the limitations pe-riod on collections when Section 6166 applies.

[116] IRC § 6166(a)(3). Section 6165 allows the Secretary to require security for a Sec-tion 6166 extension. Section 6324A provides a special lien for the payment of estate tax where the time for payment is extended under Section 6166. The maximum value of prop-erty subject to a lien, where the executor elects to be released from personal liability and the Section 2204 requirement of furnishing a bond, is the amount of the unpaid estate tax liability plus interest for the first four years of a deferral period. "If an election has been made under Section 6324A, the executor may not thereafter substitute a bond pursuant to Section 2204 in lieu of that lien. If a bond has been supplied under Section 2204, how-ever, the executor may, by filing a proper notice of election and agreement, substitute a lien under Section 6324A for any part or all of such bond." Reg. §§ 20.2204-3, 301.6324A-1(d). If the property in the probate estate is insufficient, the difference can be made up by furnishing a bond. IRC § 6324A(b)(3). Cf. infra note 133.

[117] See IRC §§ 6166(b)(7)(A)(ii), 6166(b)(8)(A)(ii), 6166(b)(9)(B)(ii)(I), 6166(b)(10)(B)(ii), and 6166(b)(10)(A)(iii) (under which the maximum ten-year period is reduced to five years) discussed supra text accompanying notes 76, 86, 88, 92, 98, and 99. Cf. infra text accompanying note 129.

the closely held business interest.[118] The balance of the tax is payable in a lump sum on the usual date. The formula for this limitation makes use of the adjusted gross estate figure as follows:

$$\text{Qualified amount of tax}^{119} \;=\; \frac{\text{closely held business amount}^{120}}{\text{adjusted gross estate}^{121}} \;\times\; \text{tax less credits}^{122}$$

[v] **Interest.** Although Section 6166 permits deferred payment of the estate tax, interest must be paid annually for the first five years, or any shorter period of outright deferral.[123] Subsequently, interest is paid along with and as a part of annual tax installments.[124] However, the interest imposed on a Section 6166 deficiency is substantially lower than the interest required on most tax deficiencies. Interest is generally imposed at a 2 percent interest rate on the "2 percent portion" of the deferral and at a rate of only 45 percent of the normal interest rate on any deferred amount in excess of the "2 percent portion."[125] The "2 percent portion" is the deferred tax due on the lesser of the entire amount of extended tax or the first $1 million (adjusted for inflation)[126] of es-

----

[118] Seemingly the business could be included in the gross estate and make up 50 percent of the adjusted gross estate and could also fully qualify either for a charitable deduction under Section 2055, a marital deduction under Section 2056, or a qualified family-owned business interest deduction under Section 2057 and thus generate no estate tax liability. Nevertheless the numerator of the Section 6166(a)(2) fraction uses the amount of the business included in the gross estate (reduced by Sections 2053 2054 deductions) and not the net amount included in the taxable estate.

[119] IRC § 6166(a)(2).

[120] IRC § 6166(b)(5). Cf. Rev. Rul. 80-202, 1980-2 CB 363.

[121] IRC § 6166(b)(6). See supra text accompanying notes 104–110.

[122] Although this formula determines the amount of tax that may be deferred for five years and then paid in ten annual installments, as previously explained, only a portion of the deferred tax may qualify for the favorable 2 percent interest rate. See infra text accompanying notes 125–129.

[123] IRC §§ 6166(f)(1), 6166(f)(4); see IRC § 6601(a).

[124] IRC § 6166(f)(2).

[125] IRC § 6601(j)(1).

[126] IRC § 6601(j)(3). The inflation adjustment applies to estates of decedents dying after 1998. Id. The adjustment uses the Consumer Price Index (CPI) for a base year of 1997. IRC § 6166(j)(3)(B). However, upward adjustments of the $1 million amount are made only in increments of $10,000, and are rounded down to the next lowest multiple of $10,000. IRC § 6166(j)(3) (flush language). An explanation of a similar adjustment is found at ¶ 9.04[1] text accompanying notes 6–9. The "2 percent portion" is $1.01 million, for the calendar year 1999 (Rev. Proc. 98-61, 1998-2 CB 811, 816), $1.03 million for the calendar year 2000 (Rev. Proc. 99-42, 1999-2 CB 568, 572), $1.06 million for the calendar year 2001 (Rev. Proc. 2001-13, 2001-1 CB __), and $1.1 million for the calendar year 2002 (Rev. Proc. 2001-59, 2001-2 CB __, __).

tate tax liability attributable to the qualifying closely held business interest.[127] If the deferred amount of tax bears interest at both the 2 percent and 45 percent of normal rates, any payments of the deferred tax reduce the 2 percent and the 45 percent interest portions ratably.[128] In limited circumstances, an estate may not be eligible for the 2 percent interest rate.[129]

The benefit of both of the low interest rates applicable to the tax on Section 6166 property comes at a cost. The interest paid under the special low interest rates is neither deductible under the estate tax as a Section 2053 administrative expense[130] nor deductible as interest under the income tax.[131] The interest rates were reduced and the interest made nondeductible to eliminate the necessity to file annual supplemental estate tax returns and to make complex mathematical computations to claim an estate tax deduction for the interest paid.[132]

[vi] **The "gotcha."** In several situations, an estate may lose its right to defer the payment of taxes with the result that the payment of the taxes will be

---

[127] IRC § 6601(j)(2). Thus, the 2 percent rate of interest applies to the amount of deferred estate tax attributable to the first $1 million (adjusted for inflation) in *taxable* value of the closely held business (i.e., the first $1 million in value in excess of the applicable exclusion amount under Section 2010(c)). Thus, disregarding any inflation, in 2007 when the Section 2010(c) applicable exclusion amount is $2 million, the amount of estate tax attributable to the value of the closely held business between $2 million and $3 million is eligible for the 2 percent rate (i.e., the first $1 million of Section 6166 value that actually increases out-of-pocket estate tax liability). This is a liberalization of prior law that applied the preferential (then 4 percent) interest rate to only $1 million less the applicable credit amount. See IRC §§ 6601(j)(1), 6601(j)(2) prior to amendment by the Taxpayer Relief Act of 1997, Pub. L. No. 105-34, § 503(a), 111 Stat. 788, 852 (1997), reprinted in 1997-4 CB (Vol. 1) 1, 66.

[128] IRC § 6601(j)(4).

[129] See IRC §§ 6166(b)(7)(A)(iii), 6166(b)(8)(A)(iii), 6166(b)(8)(B)(ii), 6166(b)(9)(B)(ii)(I), discussed supra text accompanying notes 75, 86, 88, and 92. Cf. supra text accompanying note 117.

[130] IRC § 2053(c)(1)(D).

[131] IRC § 163(k). See Priv. Ltr. Rul. 9903038 (Oct. 2, 1998) allowing a potentially appealing alternative to the use of Section 6166 in a situation where the entire amount of interest on a loan to pay estate taxes was deductible as an administrative expense under Section 2053(a)(2) where there was fixed interest on a seven-year loan with no possible prepayment of interest.

[132] See HR Conf. Rep. 148, 105th Cong., 1st Sess. 356 (1997), reprinted in 1997-4 CB (Vol. 1) 319, 356.

Section 6601(j)(2) is applicable to decedents dying after December 31, 1997. The Taxpayer Relief Act of 1997, Pub. L. No. 105-34, § 503(d)(1), 111 Stat. 788, 853 (1997), reprinted in 1997-4 CB (Vol. 1) 1, 67. For decedents dying prior to January 1, 1998, interest was imposed at a 4 percent rate on a "4 percent portion" that was an amount equal to the lesser of the tax due on $1 million reduced by the unified credit or the tax due. Thus, where it applied, the limitation under former Section 6601(j) effectively reduced the maximum amount of the Section 6166 deferral that was eligible for the 4 percent rate to

accelerated.[133] For example, in order to properly police the statute, Congress provides a first rule that penalizes tardy payment of any principal or interest installment. If any installment is not paid when due or within six months following the due date, the entire unpaid portion of the tax must be paid upon notice and demand.[134] If payment is made within six months of the due date, the unpaid portion of the tax is not subject to payment on demand;[135] however, the late payment is not eligible for the special reduced interest rates[136] and a penalty is assessable on the payment.[137]

Under a second rule, the time for the payment of deferred installments is accelerated and any unpaid tax becomes due if the reason for deferral ceases. Expressed in general terms, the reason may cease to exist if: (1) any portion of the qualified business interest is "distributed, sold, exchanged, or otherwise disposed of,"[138] or money or other property is withdrawn from the qualifying closely held business[139] and (2) the aggregate amount of distributions, sales, exchanges, or other dispositions and withdrawals of money or other property from the qualifying closely held business interest equals or exceeds 50 percent

---

the tax imposed on $400,000 ($1 million less the $600,000 exemption equivalent) or $153,000. Normal deficiency interest was imposed on the remainder of the deficiency. However, such interest was deductible for estate tax purposes under Section 2053 (see Rev. Rul. 80-250, 1980-2 CB 278) or, if elected, for income tax purposes under Section 163(h)(2)(E).

Estates of decedents dying before 1998 with deferred estate tax under Section 6166 were allowed to make a one-time irrevocable election before January 1, 1999, to use the lower interest rates provided for decedents dying after 1997. Under the election, the 2 percent interest rate is available only for the amount that qualified for the 4 percent interest rate under prior law. Where the amount of tax deferred by an estate making the election exceeds the 4 percent portion, a rate equal to 45 percent of the annual rate provided in Section 6601(a) is available. The price tag on the election is nondeductible for estate or income tax purposes of the interest paid. IRC §§ 163(k), 2053(c)(1)(D). The lower interest rates apply to any installments due after the effective date of the election. Taxpayer Relief Act of 1997, Pub. L. No. 103-34, § 503(d)(2), 111 Stat. 788, 853 (1997), reprinted in 1997-4 CB (Vol. 1) 1, 67. Procedures for making such an election are set forth in Rev. Proc. 98-15, 1998-1 CB 374.

[133] IRC § 6166(g). See IRC § 6324A(d)(5), which also triggers Section 6166(g). Section 6324A is discussed supra note 116.

[134] IRC § 6166(g)(3)(A). See Eichheim v. United States, 1988-1 USTC ¶ 13,764 (D. Colo. 1988).

[135] IRC § 6166(g)(3)(B)(i).

[136] IRC § 6166(g)(3)(B)(ii).

[137] IRC § 6166(g)(3)(B)(iii). The penalty is equal to 5 percent of the payment that was originally due times the number of months between the due date and the payment date. In making the computation, a fraction of a month is counted as a full month. Id.

[138] IRC § 6166(g)(1)(A)(i)(I).

[139] IRC § 6166(g)(1)(A)(i)(II). The notion here is that to require tax payment when there have been such significant withdrawals does not menace the business.

of the value of the qualifying interest.[140] In such circumstances, the entire un-paid portion of the tax must be paid upon notice and demand.[141]

A series of special rules apply in determining whether or to what extent a distribution, sale, exchange, disposition, or withdrawal of money or property accelerates the tax. A distribution to a legatee or to one entitled to the property under local laws of descent and distribution is placed outside the scope of the acceleration rules.[142] In general, a Section 303 redemption (and sometimes a Section 304 redemption) also is not a disqualifying distribution or withdrawal if the redemption proceeds are used to make Section 6166 payments.[143] Fur-ther, restructuring of a business does not trigger acceleration. Thus, stock re-ceived in a tax-free D, E, or F reorganization under Section 368(a)(1), in a Section 355 tax-free corporate division, or on a Section 351 or Section 721 transfer is not a disqualifying distribution.[144] However, if stock in a holding company is treated as business stock,[145] a disposition of the holding company stock or withdrawal of money or other property from the holding company[146] and any disposition by the holding company of its business company stock or withdrawal of money from the business company are dispositions or withdraw-als under Section 6166(g)(1)(A).[147]

Under a third rule, if the estate has undistributed net income[148] for any year in which an installment payment is due and fails to pay an amount equal

---

[140] IRC § 6166(g)(1)(A)(ii). The manner in which the 50 percent computation is made is discussed and illustrated in outdated Regulations Sections 20.6166A-3(d)(2) and 20.6166A-3(d)(3) Ex. 1, respectively.

[141] IRC § 6166(g)(1)(A).

[142] IRC § 6166(g)(1)(D). A similar rule applies to a subsequent transfer of the prop-erty by reason of death as long as the transferee is a Section 267(c)(4) family member. Id. See supra note 69. See Priv. Ltr. Rul. 200043031 (July 26, 2000) (also involving other transactions related to a limited liability company that were not Section 6166(g) disposi-tions).

[143] IRC § 6166(g)(1)(B). Compare Rev. Rul. 72-188, 1972-1 CB 383 (allowing a cu-mulative approach in measuring the scope of the exception), with Rev. Rul. 86-54, 1986-1 CB 356 (permitting the use of either a cumulative approach or a redemption-by-redemp-tion approach in the measurement). Excess Section 303 (and some Section 304) distribu-tions may trigger an acceleration of tax. Section 303 and Section 304 redemptions are discussed in Bittker & Eustice, Federal Income Taxation of Corporations and Sharehold-ers, ¶¶ 9.08, 9.09 (Warren, Gorham & Lamont, 7th ed. 2000).

[144] IRC § 6166(g)(1)(C); Reg. § 20.6166A-3(e)(2). See Priv. Ltr. Rul. 200129018 (transfer of assets of a closely held business to a limited liability company (in what would be a Section 721 transfer) was not within Section 6166(g)(1)(A)). The statutory rule does not apply to a Section 368(a)(1) "A," "B," or "C" reorganization.

[145] IRC § 6166(b)(8)(A). See supra text accompanying notes 84–88.

[146] IRC § 6166(g)(1)(E).

[147] IRC § 6166(g)(1)(F).

[148] IRC § 6166(g)(2)(B).

to such undistributed net income in liquidation of the unpaid portion of the tax, the unpaid portion of the tax generally becomes payable on demand.[149]

Since Congress enacted Section 6166 because it identified a possible liquidity problem, the second and third rules make sense. When the property is disposed of, or when the estate has undistributed net income, there is no longer a liquidity problem and, accordingly, the deferred tax is made due.

Under a similar rule, an elimination of the deferral of an installment of estate tax under Section 6166 may occur when there is an overpayment of estate tax. If an estate makes an overpayment of estate tax, the overpayment must first be applied toward unpaid Section 6166 installments.[150] Any refund of any estate tax paid by the taxpayer will only be made to the taxpayer under Section 6402 once the total amount of estate tax ultimately owed is eliminated.[151]

[vii] Declaratory judgments with respect to Section 6166. Prior to the enactment of Section 7479, an estate could not litigate either its qualification for use of Section 6166 or the termination of its qualification for an exclusion without first paying the entire estate tax due. Since this was not in keeping with the deferral policy of Section 6166, Section 7479(a) was enacted[152] to give the Tax Court authority to issue declaratory judgments in response to either of these questions. The provision allows estates to assert eligibility for Section 6166,[153] or to argue that such eligibility has not been lost,[154] without the burden of paying the entire tax due before being eligible for a judicial review of the issue.[155] A Section 7479 action may be brought by the executor of

---

[149] IRC §§ 6166(g)(2)(A), 6166(g)(3). In addition, if stock in a holding company is treated as stock in a business company (see IRC § 6166(b)(8)(A) and supra text accompanying notes 84–88), a dividend paid to the holding company is to be treated as if it were paid to the decedent's estate for purposes of the undistributed income rule. IRC § 6166(g)(2)(C).

[150] IRC § 6403.

[151] Estate of Bell v. Comm'r, 928 F2d 901 (9th Cir. 1991) (overpaid installment); ILM 200141013 (June 28, 2001) (overpayment of tax due prior to a Section 6166 election reduced amount qualifying for Section 6166 treatment).

[152] Taxpayer Relief Act of 1997, Pub. L. No. 105-34, § 505(a), 111 Stat. 788, 854 (1997), reprinted in 1997-4 CB (Vol. 1) 1, 68. Section 7479 is applicable to estates of decedents dying after August 5, 1997. For prior law, see Darmstadter & Jennings, "Can a Judicial Forum Be Obtained for Estate Tax Deferral Disputes?" 82 J. Tax'n 74 (1995).

[153] IRC § 7479(a)(1). See supra ¶ 2.02[3][c][ii]. The section also allows a declaratory judgment whether particular property in an estate qualifies for Section 6166 deferral. IRC § 7479(a)(1).

[154] IRC § 7479(a)(2). See supra ¶ 2.02[3][c][vi].

[155] No proceeding may be instituted under Section 7479 unless it is commenced within ninety days of the IRS mailing notice by certified or registered mail of its denial of eligibility or continued use of Section 6166. IRC § 7479(b)(3).

the estate or any person who has assumed the obligation to make Section 6166 payments.[156]

---

[156] IRC § 7479(b)(1). If more than one person has an obligation to make payments, all such persons must be joined in the action. IRC § 7479(b)(1)(B). The taxpayer must have exhausted its administrative remedies before it is entitled to declaratory judgment. IRC § 7479(b)(2).

CHAPTER 3

Credits Against Estate Tax

¶ 3.01 INTRODUCTION

This chapter deals with credits against the estate tax, which can be claimed after the basic computation of the tax to determine the net estate tax payable. All estates are entitled to one or more such credits.

These highly technical provisions cannot readily be understood without prior knowledge of the other estate and gift tax provisions of the Internal Revenue Code (the Code). Although discussion of credits appears early in the text in accordance with the place of the credit provisions in the Code, a reader who has little previous experience with federal estate and gift taxes would probably do well to skip most of this chapter initially and to return to it only after reading the other portions of the book dealing with the estate and gift taxes. The "unified credit" is the exception to this suggestion. It is straightforward, applies to all estates, and should be examined without deferral.

Congressional policy has been to provide for both credits and deductions.[1] Tax credits are direct reductions in tax otherwise payable, differing in this way from deductions, which are subtractions from the taxable amount. Every dollar of tax credit allowed results in a corresponding dollar reduction of tax to be paid. On the other hand, one dollar of deduction produces a reduction in tax payable that is equal to one dollar times the applicable rate of tax.[2] Credits can be viewed as more equitable because they reduce tax liability equally for taxpayers in all tax brackets (to the extent there is tax otherwise payable), while deductions confer greater tax savings on taxpayers in higher brackets.[3]

¶ 3.02 SECTION 2010. UNIFIED CREDIT AGAINST THE ESTATE TAX

Estates of decedents dying after 1976 are allowed a Section 2010 credit, which reduces and, in the case of most decedents, eliminates any estate tax liability.[1] If the amount of the credit available under Section 2010 exceeds tax liability, no refund is allowed.[2] As a result of the Section 2010 credit, if the decedent

---

[1] See IRC §§ 2010–2016, 2051–2058. See also text ¶¶ 3.01–3.08, 5.01–5.09.

[2] A dollar of deduction could produce a tax reduction equivalent to a dollar of credit only if the rate were 100 percent, a rate of tax not provided under the present rate structure. See IRC § 2001(c).

[3] See HR Conf. Rep. No. 1380, 94th Cong., 2d Sess. 15 (1976), reprinted in 1976-3 CB (Vol. 3) 738, 749.

[1] For example, in 1998 the estate tax was levied on less than 2 percent of decedents. The Congressional Budget Office, Budget Options Chapter 6 (Feb. 2001).

[2] Section 2010(c) limits the amount of the credit to the amount of estate tax imposed under Section 2001.

has no "adjusted taxable gifts" and the decedent's "taxable estate"[3] does not exceed the "applicable exclusion amount"[4] available in the year of the decedent's death, the estate will incur no estate tax liability.[5]

The unified credit was enacted with phased increases from 1977 until 1987, and then it remained flat until 1997.[6] The credit was again increased for

---

Prior to 1977, all estates were allowed a $60,000 specific exemption, which operated as a deduction in computing the taxable estate. IRC § 2052, repealed with respect to estates of decedents dying after 1976 by the Tax Reform Act of 1976, Pub. L. No. 94-455, § 2001(a)(4), 90 Stat. 1520, 1848 (1976), reprinted in 1976-3 CB (Vol. 1) 1, 324. In the Tax Reform Act of 1976, Congress eliminated the exemption, replacing it with a credit in the amount of $47,000, which was phased in from 1977 to 1981. Tax Reform Act of 1976, Pub. L. No. 94-455, § 2001(a)(2), 90 Stat. 1520, 1848 (1976), reprinted in 1976-3 CB (Vol. 1) 1, 324. In 1981, Congress substantially enlarged the credit to $62,800 in 1982 and, further phased in annual increases, to $192,800 in 1987. Economic Recovery Tax Act of 1981, Pub. L. No. 97-34, §§ 401(a)(1), 401(a)(2), 95 Stat. 172, 299 (1981), reprinted in 1981-2 CB 256, 323.

The credit of Section 2010 injects an element of progression into the estate tax separate from the progressive rates of Section 2001(c). If, for example, a decedent who died in 2002 had a taxable estate of $1.05 million and no adjusted taxable gifts, the decedent's estate would pay $20,500 of tax ($366,300 tax less a $345,800 credit), while the estate of a decedent who also died in 2002 with a taxable estate of $1.15 million and no adjusted taxable gifts (less than 10 percent larger) would pay $61,500 of tax ($407,300 tax less a $345,800 credit) or three times as much. One may question whether this kind of acceleration at lower levels is appropriate. There is an interesting analysis under pre-1977 law in Bittker, "Federal Estate Tax Reform: Exemptions and Rates," 57 ABA J. 236 (Foundation Press 1971), reprinted in Goldstein, Readings in Death and Gift Tax Reform 278 (1971).

[3] IRC §§ 2001(b)(1)(A), 2001(b)(1)(B), discussed ¶ 2.01[1].

[4] IRC § 2010(c). See infra text accompanying note 9.

[5] For example, the tax under Section 2001(c) on the first $1 million of taxable estate is $345,800, exactly the amount of tax offset by the Section 2010 credit for decedents dying between January 1, 2002, and December 31, 2003.

Even if the decedent had made "adjusted taxable gifts," the estate would incur no estate tax liability as long as the total amount of the adjusted taxable gifts and the "taxable estate" reduced by the amount of gift tax payable under Chapter 12 at rates in effect at the decedent's death do not exceed the "applicable exclusion amount" available in the year of the decedent's death.

[6] The amount of the credit from 1977 to 1997 was as follows:

Year of death	Credit	Maximum taxable estate without tax liability (assuming zero adjusted taxable gifts)
1977	$ 30,000	$120,667
1978	34,000	134,000
1979	38,000	147,333
1980	42,500	161,563
1981	47,000	175,625
1982	62,800	225,000
1983	79,300	275,000
1984	96,300	325,000

years after 1997[7] and is scheduled for further phase increases for years 2002 through 2009.[8]

The Section 2010 credit is statutorily expressed as the "applicable exclusion amount," which is converted to an "applicable credit amount."[9] For the years 2002 through 2009,[10] those amounts are as follows:[11]

1985	121,800	400,000
1986	155,800	500,000
1987-1997	192,800	600,000

See supra note 2. However, from 1988 through 1997, the Section 2010 credit and the progressive rates under Section 2001(c) were phased out for persons with large taxable transfers through the imposition of a 5 percent surtax on taxable transfers where the transferor's total taxable transfers exceeded $10 million. IRC § 2001(c)(2) prior to amendment by the Taxpayer Relief Act of 1997, Pub. L. No. 105-34, § 501(a)(1)(D), 111 Stat. 788, 845 (1997), reprinted in 1997-4 CB (Vol. 1) 1, 59. From 1998 through 2001, the 5 percent surtax eliminated the progressive rates under Section 2001(c), but it did not eliminate the benefit of the Section 2010 credit. See ¶ 2.01[3] text accompanying note 68.

[7] See The Taxpayer Relief Act of 1997, Pub. L. No. 105-34, § 501(a)(1), 111 Stat. 788, 845 (1997), reprinted in 1997-4 CB (Vol. 1) 1, 59, which increased the credit as follows:

Year of Death	Applicable Exclusion	Applicable Credit Amount
1998	$ 625,000	$202,050
1999	650,000	211,300
2000 and 2001	675,000	220,550
2002 and 2003	700,000	229,800
2004	850,000	287,300
2005	950,000	326,300
2006 and thereafter	1,000,000	345,800

The exclusion amount was not to be adjusted for inflation. HR Conf. Rep. No. 220, 105th Cong., 1st Sess. 394 (1997), reprinted in 1997-4 CB (Vol. 2) 1457, 1864.

Under the "sunset" provision effective January 1, 2011, the $1 million applicable exclusion amount for the year 2006 will apply to the estates of decedents dying after the year 2010. Economic Growth and Tax Relief Reconciliation Act of 2001, Pub. L. No. 107-16, § 901(a)(2), 115 Stat. 38, 150 (2001), reprinted in 2001-__ CB __, __. The "sunset" provision is discussed more fully at ¶ 8.10[5].

[8] The Economic Growth and Tax Relief Reconciliation Act of 2001, Pub. L. No. 107-16, § 521(a), 115 Stat. 38, 71 (2001), reprinted in 2001-__ CB __, __. See IRC §§ 2010(a), 2010(c).

[9] IRC §§ 2010(a), 2010(c).

[10] For years after 2009, see IRC § 2210 discussed, ¶¶ 8.10[1], 8.10[2]. But see also the sunset provision discussed ¶ 8.10[5].

[11] IRC § 2010(c).

Year of Death	Applicable Exclusion	Applicable Credit Amount
2002 and 2003	$ 1 million	$ 345,800
2004 and 2005	$1.5 million	$ 555,800
2006 and 2008	$ 2 million	$ 780,800
2009	$3.5 million	$1,455,800

The credit is sometimes subject to a very minor reduction in amount. If a decedent made inter vivos gifts between September 8, 1976, and January 1, 1977, and used all or any portion of the Section 2521[12] $30,000 specific lifetime exemption to reduce such gifts, Section 2010(b) requires a reduction in the amount of the Section 2010 credit by 20 percent of the amount of exemption so used.[13]

The credit generally effectively exempts from the federal transmission taxes otherwise taxable transfers not exceeding the applicable exclusion amount for the year of the decedent's death.[14] The Section 2010 estate tax credit is referred to as unified because it is also used to offset the federal transmission tax imposed on lifetime gifts.[15] For years prior to the year 2004, Section 2505, the gift tax unified credit, generally provides an identical amount of credit against gift tax liability for inter vivos transfers after 1977.[16] However, after the year 2003, the estate and gift tax unified credits are no longer equal in amount, and the gift tax applicable exclusion amount is capped at $1 million.[17]

---

[12] This section was repealed by the Tax Reform Act of 1976 for years after 1976. See Pub. L. No. 94-455, § 2001(b)(3), 90 Stat. 1520, 1849 (1976), reprinted in 1976-3 CB (Vol. 1) 1, 325.

[13] This results in a maximum Section 2010 credit reduction of $6,000 if the full $30,000 exemption was used during such period. Between the adoption of the Tax Reform Act of 1976 and December 31, 1976, there were substantial tax incentives for taxpayers with large estates to make inter vivos gifts at lower tax rates. Although Congress condoned a full use of the $30,000 exemption against gifts made before September 9, 1976, with no reduction in the Section 2010 credit, a credit reduction in the amount indicated was considered a proper cost for last-minute use of the exemption. A potential donor's prior gift history was an obvious factor in the decision whether to elect to use the Section 2521 exemption during that period. See Priv. Ltr. Rul. 7937010 (May 31, 1979) (a Section 2010(b) credit reduction was not restored even though the gift was subsequently included in decedent's estate under Section 2035).

The constitutionality of Section 2010(b) was upheld in United States v. Hemme, 476 US 558 (1986).

[14] See supra text accompanying notes 9–11.

[15] IRC § 2505, discussed ¶ 9.06.

[16] There was a difference in the amount of the two credits, in the first half of 1977, when only $6,000 of the unified credit could be used against liability for gift tax, as compared with the $30,000 available estate tax credit. See Tax Reform Act of 1976, Pub. L. No. 94-455, §§ 2001(a)(2), 2001(b)(2), 90 Stat. 1520, 1848, 1849 (1976), reprinted in 1976-3 (Vol. 1) 1, 324, 325.

[17] IRC § 2505(a)(1). Thus, the Section 2505 credit amount is $345,800. See ¶ 9.06.

Although the credit is spoken of as "unified," use of the Section 2505 gift tax credit does not reduce the amount of the Section 2010 estate tax credit. This appears to allow a decedent who made lifetime gifts the advantage of the use of two credits, but it does not.[18] Under the system, the unified credit is effectively used only once, although at an amount equal to the larger estate tax applicable credit amount after the year 2003. This is so because, before credits, the amount of the estate tax is the tentative tax on the sum of the taxable estate plus adjusted taxable gifts, reduced by gift taxes that would have been payable on the gifts made by the decedent after 1976 at rates in effect at the time of the decedent's death. Use of the gift tax credit reduces taxes payable on the gifts and correspondingly reduces the reduction in estate tax liability permitted for gift taxes that would have been payable.[19]

Use of the gift tax credit is mandatory.[20] Failure to use the gift tax credit, if available, may result in no credit effectively being allowed. Furthermore, if more than the necessary gift tax is paid, estate tax liability will still be reduced only by gift taxes "payable" at rates in effect at the decedent's death, and,

---

Even though the Section 2010 credit and the Section 2505 credit are not equal in amount after the year 2003, the credits are still "unified" because a single use of the credits is effectively allowed. See infra text accompanying notes 18–19.

[18] For years after 2003, the estate tax credit is determined by the larger estate tax applicable exclusion amount for the year involved. See supra text accompanying note 11 and infra note 19.

[19] Because the lifetime use of the credit merely neutralizes gifts that otherwise would have generated a gift tax, which in turn would have reduced the estate tax under Section 2001(b)(2), the credit has not been used in an estate tax sense when applied to lifetime gifts. In the end, the unified credit causes a single reduction for gift tax and estate tax purposes that does not exceed the larger estate tax unified credit.

For example, if in 2002, Decedent, who had previously not made any gifts, made inter vivos taxable gifts of $1 million and died in 2003 having a taxable estate of $1 million, the amount of gift tax liability on the $1 million inter vivos taxable gift would have been zero, $345,800 of tax less a $345,800 Section 2505 credit. At death, Decedent's taxable estate and adjusted taxable gifts would equal $2 million, generating a potential tax of $780,800 under Section 2001(b)(1). The Section 2001(b)(2) reduction for gift tax payable would be zero because use of the Section 2505 credit would eliminate any gift tax payable in computing the gift tax. If the Section 2010 credit of $345,800 were not allowed to Decedent's estate, Decedent effectively would not have been allowed any credit on the $2 million of total wealth transfers. If Decedent, in this example, had died in 2006 rather than in 2003, there again would have been no gift tax payable on the $1 million gift in 2002, $780,800 of potential tax under Section 2001(b)(1), and a zero reduction under Section 2001(b)(2). However, because the Section 2010 credit is $780,800 (see supra text accompanying note 11) for the year 2006, the unified credit would eliminate any estate tax liability.

[20] See Staff of Joint Comm. on Tax'n, 94th Cong., 2d Sess., General Explanation of the Tax Reform Act of 1976, at 531 (1976), reprinted in 1976-3 CB (Vol. 2) 1, 543 and Rev. Rul. 79-160, 1979-1 CB 313, illustrating the use of the Section 2505 credit.

overall, an overpayment of gift taxes could effectively wipe out the estate tax credit.[21]

The Section 2010 credit not only directly affects tax liability, but also indirectly affects the requirement for an estate to file an estate tax return. Section 6018(a) provides the rules for filing estate tax returns. The filing requirements are based on the amount of the gross estate.[22] The amount of gross estate for which no return is required to be filed is closely equivalent to the amount of taxable estate that, as a result of the Section 2010 credit, results in no tax liability.[23] If the decedent's gross estate exceeds the applicable exclusion amount for the year of the decedent's death set forth in Section 2010(c), a return must be filed.[24]

---

[21] See ¶ 2.01[2]. For example, if in the initial example, supra note 19, Decedent had not used Decedent's Section 2505 credit and had paid $345,800 of gift taxes on the 2002 gift, at Decedent's death, Decedent's gift tax payable on the 2002 gift would still have been zero (after the Section 2505 credit available in the year of the gift is applied) and $345,800 of estate taxes would still be due, resulting in $691,600 and effectively eliminating the unified credit.

[22] See Chapter 4.

[23] See supra text accompanying notes 3–13. This is similar to the pre-1977 filing requirement that was based on the $60,000 specific exemption. See Tax Reform Act of 1976, Pub. L. No. 94-455, § 2001(a)(1)(J), 90 Stat. 1520, 1848 (1976), reprinted in 1976-3 CB (Vol. 1) 1, 328 (amending Section 6018).

[24] Subject to the two reductions discussed infra text accompanying notes 25–28, the Section 6018(a) filing requirements are as follows:

Year of death	A return must be filed if the gross estate exceeds
1977	$ 120,000
1978	134,000
1979	147,000
1980	161,000
1981	175,000
1982	225,000
1983	275,000
1984	325,000
1985	400,000
1986	500,000
1987 through 1997	600,000
1998	625,000
1999	650,000
2000 and 2001	675,000
2002 and 2003	1,000,000
2004 and 2005	1,500,000
2006 through 2008	2,000,000
2009	3,500,000

Under the sunset provision effective January 1, 2011, the $1 million applicable exclusion amount for the year 2006 will apply to the estates of decedents dying after the year

Returns are sometimes required for smaller gross estates. The critical gross estate figures for years after 1976 must be reduced by adjusted taxable gifts.[25] The reason for this reduction is that adjusted taxable gifts may operate to increase the tax rate. For example, if in 2003 a decedent had a taxable estate of $1 million and had made no adjusted taxable gifts, the decedent's estate tax would be only $345,800, which would be offset by the unified credit. However, if the decedent had made adjusted taxable gifts, the tax on the $1 million taxable estate would be greater than the amount of the unified credit. Appropriately, a return must then be filed.

In addition, but less significantly, the critical gross estate figures must be reduced by the amount of the decedent's exempted lifetime transfers of property made between September 8, 1976, and January 1, 1977.[26] This is required because of the reduction in the amount of credit required in these circumstances.[27] This reduction of the critical gross estate figures cannot exceed $30,000, the amount of the prior specific lifetime exemption.[28]

Even though an estate tax return is not required to be filed, it may be wise to file one. The statute of limitations on assessment, the period specified in Section 6501 within which the government may assess tax in addition to that reported, does not commence until a return is filed. Filing a return with sufficient information starts the time clock.[29] An ancillary benefit of filing a return is that it provides a permanent source of information that may be used for determination of the income tax basis of assets acquired from the decedent.[30]

¶ 3.03 SECTION 2011. CREDIT FOR STATE DEATH TAXES

[1] Introduction

Section 2011 provides a limited credit against the federal estate tax to decedents dying prior to January 1, 2005, for death taxes actually paid to any state

---

2010. Economic Growth and Tax Relief Reconciliation Act of 2001, Pub. L. No. 107-16, § 901(a)(2), 115 Stat. 38, 150 (2001), reprinted in 2001-__ CB __, __. The sunset provision is discussed more fully at ¶ 8.10[5].

[25] IRC § 6018(a)(3)(A). See supra note 24.

[26] IRC § 6018(a)(3)(B).

[27] IRC § 2010(b). See supra text accompanying notes 12 and 13.

[28] See IRC § 2521 (prior to repeal in the Tax Reform Act of 1976, Pub. L. No. 94-455, § 2001(b)(3), 90 Stat. 1520, 1849 (1976), reprinted in 1976-3 CB (Vol. 3) 1, 325).

[29] Estate of Lohman v. Comm'r, 31 TCM (CCH) 96 (1972) ("tentative return" put the Service on notice for statute of limitations purposes in an estate tax case).

[30] See IRC § 1014. Cf. ¶ 8.10[3].

or the District of Columbia with respect to property included in the decedent's gross estate for federal estate tax purposes.[1] State taxes paid on property that escapes the federal estate tax do not qualify for the Section 2011 credit.[2]

The credit permitted is not dependent on the form in which the state death tax is imposed; it is available whether the state tax is an estate tax on the transmission of property at death, an inheritance tax on the succession to property at death, or some variation or combination of the two.[3] No doubt the statute contemplates a validly imposed state tax,[4] but "[i]t is the policy of the Internal Revenue Service generally not to question the application of state death tax statutes or to intervene in controversies regarding their application."[5] Therefore, when taxes are paid to two states with respect to the same property, both taxes potentially qualify for the credit.[6] Of course, state taxes paid in connection with the death of someone other than the decedent are not to be taken into account; property included in the decedent's gross estate may have been subjected to state death taxes in the estates of other decedents, but a parenthetical provision in Section 2011(a) expressly forecloses consideration of such other taxes.[7]

To the extent that the federal tax allows a credit,[8] a state tax places no additional tax burden upon a decedent's estate. The total tax burden is the same as if there were no state tax; some of the federal estate tax is simply diverted to the states rather than going to the federal government. Consequently, some

---

[1] IRC § 2011. See IRC § 2011(f) and infra text accompanying note 14.

Certain generation-skipping transfers (other than direct skips) taxed under state law may give rise to a credit against the generation-skipping transfer tax imposed under Section 2601 for generation-skipping transfers prior to January 1, 2005. IRC §§ 2604(a), 2604(c). See ¶ 12.04 note 2.

[2] See Reg. § 20.2011-1(a); Second Nat'l Bank of New Haven v. United States, 422 F2d 40 (2d Cir. 1970); Estate of Owen v. Comm'r, 104 TC 498 (1995). See also Turner, "The Gross Estate and the Death Tax Credit," 28 Wash. & Lee L. Rev. 254 (1971).

[3] A state tax imposed on a generation-skipping transfer for which a credit is allowed under Section 2604 for decedents dying prior to December 31, 2004, will not qualify for the Section 2011 credit against the federal estate tax because the credit against estate tax arises only out of state tax paid "in respect of . . . property included in the gross estate." Transfers "subject to" the federal estate tax (and, therefore, transfers where the value of the property is included in the gross estate) can only be subjected to the generation-skipping transfer tax as direct skips. IRC § 2612(c)(1). See IRC § 2612(b); Reg. § 26.2612-1(b)(1)(i); ¶¶ 13.02[2][d], 13.02[3][b][ii]. State tax imposed on a direct skip generation-skipping transfer does not qualify for the Section 2604 credit. IRC § 2604(a). See ¶ 12.04.

[4] See Mim. 3971, XI-2 CB 427 (1932). Death taxes paid to a municipality do not qualify for the credit. Cf. McFarland v. United States, 80 AFTR2d 97-8348 (ED La. 1997).

[5] Rev. Rul. 60-88, 1960-1 CB 365, 366.

[6] Rev. Rul. 60-88, 1960-1 CB 365; Rev. Rul. 70-272, 1970-1 CB 187.

[7] IRC § 2011(a) (parenthetical).

[8] See infra ¶¶ 3.03[3], 3.03[4].

states impose death taxes in a manner designed to assure them of their share of the death duties being imposed. Such taxes are commonly referred to as pick-up taxes, because the states merely "pick up" as much of the federal tax as they can without imposing any additional tax burden on the decedent's estate. Nothing, of course, prevents a state from imposing death taxes in excess of the amount of the credit available against the federal estate tax, and some states do have death taxes that exceed the Section 2011(b) credit limitation.[9] All the states have enacted some type of death tax.

Regrettably for the states, the federal government is substantially reducing and, in some instances, totally eliminating[10] this indirect subsidy to the states. As discussed later,[11] the federal government has substantially reduced the credit by allowing only a portion of the prior credit for decedents dying in years from 2002 to 2004[12] with the consequence that the federal government will pick up only a declining percentage of federal taxes during the period.[13] For estates of decedents dying after 2004, the credit is converted to a deduction under new Section 2058.[14] Even though the credit becomes a deduction, that deduction constitutes an indirect subsidy to the states to the extent that a decedent's federal tax is reduced by the deduction, which depends upon the decedent's top federal estate tax rates.[15] However, depending upon the nature

---

[9] See, e.g., Oklahoma Stat. tit. 68 § 803 (West 2002); Rhode Island § 44-22-1 (Lexis 2001). Compare Fla. Stat. § 198.02 (1969) with Fla. Stat. § 198.02 (2001).

The constitutionality of Section 2011 has been upheld. Florida v. Mellon, 273 US 12 (1927).

[10] To the extent that the Section 2010 credit is increased (see IRC § 2010(c)), some decedents' estates will no longer pay a federal estate tax with the result that no Section 2011 credit will be allowed. IRC § 2011(e).

[11] See infra ¶¶ 3.03[3][d], 3.03[4].

[12] IRC § 2011(b)(2).

[13] Thus, if a state has enacted a pick-up tax that fluctuates with the federal credit (see infra note 16) and the federal unified credit is increased and the federal credit for state death taxes is reduced, the amount of state revenues will decline. If states enact higher state death taxes (beyond the amount of the federal credit), there will be an increase in the tax burden of the estates of decedents subject to the state tax. See infra note 16. See Blattmachr & Detzel, "Estate Planning Changes in the 2001 Tax Act—More Than You Can Count," 95 J. Tax'n 74 (2001); Weiss, "Estate Planning Remains Crucial Despite Estate Tax Repeal," 67 Prac. Tax Strat. 68 (2001).

[14] See ¶ 5.09. The conversion also requires a revision of the Section 2053(d) rule. See ¶ 5.03[8] text accompanying note 168.

[15] For example, in 2007 the federal estate tax rate is 45 percent (see IRC § 2001(c)(2)(B)) after a $2 million applicable exclusion amount (see IRC § 2010(c)) with the result that estates of decedents will pay federal estate tax at a flat 45 percent rate. Thus, in 2007 to the extent that a decedent's estate pays federal estate taxes, the federal government will subsidize 45 percent of such taxes. For decedents who are subsidized to the extent of 45 percent, this results in an increase in the mere 25 percent subsidy that the federal government would have provided to such estates if the decedent had died in the

of the state pick-up tax beginning in the year 2002 or 2005 and thereafter, state pick-up taxes will no longer be taxes that result in no additional taxation to state residents, a phenomenon that will likely create some anxiety for state legislators and some friction between state residents and their legislators.[16]

[2] The "Actually Paid" Requirement

An estate becomes entitled to a credit for state taxes only insofar as such taxes are "actually paid."[17] This requirement has been interpreted strictly, although a discharge of the tax obligation either by a cash payment or a transfer of prop-

---

year 2004. See IRC § 2011(b)(2)(B). The relationship of credits and deductions, as well as policy considerations are discussed in Surrey, "Tax Incentives as a Device for Implementing Government Policy: A Comparison With Direct Government Expenditures," 83 Harv. L. Rev. 705 (1970). See also ¶ 3.01 text accompanying notes 2, 3.

[16] Whether the state death taxes result in an additional tax to state residents between the years 2002 and 2004 depends upon the nature of the state pick-up tax. If the state pick-up tax is flexible because it flucturates with the amount of the federal credit, then no additional *state* tax will be imposed, although state revenues will be reduced in the years 2002 through 2004 and eliminated in the year 2005. See Fla. Stat. § 198.02 (2001); Cal. Rev. & Tax Code § 13302 (West 2001). On the other hand, if the state pick-up tax is based on the amount of the federal credit on a specific date, for example, January 1, 2001, then the state tax remains constant even though the federal credit is reduced, generating the same amount of revenue to the state but increasing the decedent's estate's overall state and federal taxes. See, e.g., Code of Va. § 58.1-901 (2001) (Section 2011 as it existed on Jan. 1, 1978).

[17] Some states treat state gift tax as a prepayment of state death tax where the property subject to the state gift tax is included in the estate for state death tax purposes. This is so regardless of whether the state gift tax was paid prior to the decedent's death. At one time the Commissioner had agreed that this gift tax qualified as a "payment" of state death taxes under Section 2011. However, if the state gift tax that so qualified was paid prior to the decedent's death, the Commissioner contended that it should be included in the decedent's gross estate under Section 2033 (Rev. Rul. 75-63, 1975-1 CB 294); or if the state tax was not paid prior to the decedent's death, no deduction should be allowed under Section 2053 (Rev. Rul. 71-355, 1971-2 CB 334). The Commissioner was unsuccessful in the courts in both instances, losing on the Section 2033 issue in Estate of Gamble v. Comm'r, 69 TC 942 (1978), acq. 1981-2 CB 1, and Horton v. United States, 79-2 USTC ¶ 13,316 (MDNC 1979), see ¶ 4.05[2][a] note 8, and losing on the Section 2053 issue in Estate of Lang v. Comm'r, 613 F2d 770 (9th Cir. 1980), see ¶ 5.03[5][a] note 105. The Commissioner has revoked these rulings. Moreover, the Commissioner has appropriately taken the position that the state gift tax credit is in substance a gift tax and not a "payment" of estate tax within Section 2011. Rev. Rul. 81-302, 1981-2 CB 170. However, the Tenth Circuit adopted the Commissioner's prior position, allowing a Section 2011 credit but denying a Section 2053 deduction for a posthumously paid gift tax. First Nat'l Bank & Trust Co. of Tulsa v. United States, 787 F2d 1393 (10th Cir. 1986).

erty may qualify for the credit.[18] Proof of payment must be made,[19] and, if an estate takes advantage of a discount allowed by a state for prompt payment and pays less than the amount assessed, only the amount paid qualifies for the credit.[20] A deposit made as security for payment of state death taxes has been held not to meet the "actually paid" test in the statute.[21]

Seasonable payment is also required. Under Section 2011(c), the general rule is that the credit will be allowed for state taxes paid only when the credit is claimed within four years after the filing of the estate tax return.[22] Although a cutoff date is desirable, there are circumstances in which the four-year rule could work an improper hardship, so Section 2011(c) recognizes three exceptions to the general rule.

1. For reasons explained later on, some states base their death duties directly on the federal tax, thus, in such circumstances, the state tax cannot be determined until the amount of the federal tax is established. Controversy over the amount of the federal tax arising out of the government's assertion of a deficiency can be litigated in the Tax Court, subject to review in the courts of appeals and the U.S. Supreme Court. Such proceedings may take many years, with the possible result that the state tax cannot be accurately determined until after the expiration of the four-year limitation period that usually applies. To overcome such difficulties, Section 2011(c)(1) supplies an alternative limitation period: If the taxpayer files a timely petition in the Tax Court, the credit is allowed for state taxes that are paid and for which the credit is claimed within sixty days after the Tax Court decision becomes final, even if both the payment and the claim occur beyond the four-year period.[23]

2. If an extension of time is granted under Section 6161 or Section 6166 for payment of the federal estate tax, which may be granted for a pe-

---

[18] Rev. Rul. 86-117, 1986-2 CB 157.

[19] Reg. § 20.2011-1(c)(2); Bell v. Comm'r, 82 F2d 499 (3d Cir. 1936); Estate of Giacopuzzi v. Comm'r, 29 TCM (CCH) 1777 (1970); Schuneman v. United States, 783 F2d 694 (7th Cir. 1986) (taxpayers who, contrary to the direction in Regulation Section 20.2011-1(c)(2) that evidence of payment be submitted with the return or as soon as practicable, waited for no apparent reason to file proof of payment for almost three years, were allowed the credit but were required to pay interest on the state tax credit amount from the date the return was filed until the date proof of payment was submitted).

[20] Commonwealth Trust Co. of Pittsburgh v. Driscoll, 50 F. Supp. 949 (WD Pa.), aff'd per curiam, 137 F2d 653 (3d Cir. 1943), cert. denied, 321 US 764 (1944).

[21] Estate of Damon v. Comm'r, 49 TC 108 (1967), acq. 1968-2 CB 2; Aronauer v. United States, 37-1 USTC ¶ 9052 (SDNY 1937).

[22] Courts do not have the power to extend this period. Howard v. United States, 40 F. Supp. 697 (ED La. 1941), aff'd on other grounds, 125 F2d 986 (5th Cir. 1942).

[23] See Estate of Damon v. Comm'r, 49 TC 108 (1967), acq. 1968-2 CB 2.

riod of up to fourteen years with respect to the tax shown on the return[24] or up to four years or more with respect to amounts determined as a deficiency,[25] Section 2011(c)(2) extends the period within which the state death tax payment must be made and credit claimed to either the usual four-year period or the expiration date of any such extension, whichever is later. It should be noted that an extension of time for payment of the state tax is irrelevant;[26] here it is the extension of time for payment of the federal tax that operates to extend the usual limitation period.[27]

3. Section 2011(c)(3) permits the credit to be claimed if the state tax has been paid within sixty days after a federal estate tax refund claim has been denied or, even later, within sixty days after the final decision in a refund suit that is based on such a claim. In effect, this leaves the matter of timely payment open when final settlement of federal estate tax liability is postponed by a pending claim or suit for refund; however, it is clear that the exception can be invoked only if a timely[28] claim has been filed.

Section 2011(c) expressly provides that a timely claim for refund based on the credit for payment of state death taxes can be made within the limitation periods just discussed, notwithstanding Code provisions that usually require refund claims to be filed within three years from the time the return was filed or two years from the time the tax was paid, and despite other Code provisions that usually foreclose the payment of refunds when the taxpayer has filed a Tax Court petition. Nonetheless, such refunds are to be made without the usual payment of interest.[29] The limitation period provided here is in addi-

---

[24] IRC § 6166. See also IRC § 6161(a)(2). An extension of twelve months after the due date for the last installment is allowed in the case of extensions for reasonable cause under Section 6161(a)(2)(B).

[25] IRC § 6161(b)(2). In some circumstances, a deficiency payment may be extended for more than four years. See IRC § 6166(e).

[26] Rev. Rul. 86-38, 1986-1 CB 296. See also In re Harkavy's Estate, 34 NYS2d 910 (1942); Estate of Spillar v. Comm'r, 50 TCM (CCH) 1285 (1985).

[27] Rev. Rul. 86-38, 1986-1 CB 296.

[28] Cf. Empire Trust Co. v. United States, 214 F. Supp. 731 (D. Conn.), aff'd per curiam, 324 F2d 507 (2d Cir. 1963). See also HR Conf. Rep. No. 775, 85th Cong., 1st Sess. 36 (1957), reprinted in 1958-3 CB 811, 846.

[29] But see Edinburg v. United States, 617 F2d 206 (Ct. Cl. 1980); Rev. Rul. 61-58, 1961-1 CB 414 (concerning the allocation of interest on the portion of a refund based on Section 2011 and that portion based on some other ground). See also Rev. Rul. 79-219, 1979-2 CB 401 (holding that interest an estate paid on a prior deficiency is also not recoverable in a subsequent refund suit based on Section 2011).

tion to, not in lieu of, other limitation periods; a claim for refund can always be filed within two years after the estate tax was paid.[30]

[3] Limitations on Amount of Credit

[a] No Refund

The credit is not permitted, in conjunction with the unified credit,[31] to result in a tax refund. This is accomplished by limiting the credit to the amount of tax imposed by Section 2001, reduced by the unified credit.[32]

[b] The Section 2011 Ceiling

Section 2011(a) fixes the potential credit at the amount of state death taxes "actually paid." However, a further limitation is imposed on the amount of the credit by Section 2011(b)(1) that links the maximum credit permitted to the amount of the adjusted taxable estate. The "adjusted taxable estate" is the taxable estate reduced by $60,000.[33] To determine the Section 2011(b)(1) limitation, a rate table is provided that resembles the rate table in Section 2001, which is used to determine the federal estate tax.[34] The maximum credit for state death taxes becomes progressively larger as the adjusted taxable estate increases in size. No credit is allowed for the first $40,000 of the adjusted taxable estate. The credit allowed ranges from eight-tenths of 1 percent of the next

---

[30] IRC § 6511(a); Rev. Rul. 81-263, 1981-2 CB 169.

[31] IRC § 2010.

[32] IRC § 2011(e).

[33] IRC § 2011(b)(3). The invention of the adjusted taxable estate was a means of continuing the pre-1977 credit for state death taxes in the same amount, notwithstanding the elimination of the $60,000 exemption. IRC § 2052 (prior to repeal in the Tax Reform Act of 1976, Pub. L. No. 94-455, § 2001(a)(4), 90 Stat. 1520, 1848 (1976), reprinted in 1976-3 CB (Vol. 1) 1,324. Taxable estates took a $60,000 jump with this development, although the simultaneous enactment of the Section 2010 credit effects more than a corresponding reduction in federal tax. And if the state death tax credit in the first bracket, for example, were still limited to 0.8 percent of the amount by which the taxable estate exceeds $40,000, the credit would have been greatly enlarged. The status quo is maintained by working with an adjusted taxable estate, which is $60,000 less than the taxable estate would now be; and, of course, the same differential is reflected in each bracket of the limiting table. See infra ¶ 3.03[5] for the earlier development of this provision.

[34] The credit table has its roots in prior law under which there were a basic estate tax and an additional estate tax. A credit was allowed for state death taxes up to 80 percent of the basic tax. See infra ¶ 3.03[5]. The terms are obsolete under the 1954 and 1986 Codes, because there is now a single estate tax, and the credit is allowed directly against that tax.

$50,000 to 16 percent of the amount of the adjusted taxable estate in excess of $10.04 million.[35]

[c] Further Limitation if State Death Tax Deduction Allowed

In 1956, Congress amended Section 2053 by adding subsection (d), which in some cases allows a deduction for state death taxes imposed upon charitable transfers.[36] State death taxes that are allowed as a deduction from the gross estate should not also be allowed as a credit against the federal tax, and to prevent this double benefit, Congress adopted Section 2011(d) as a companion to Section 2053(d). The detailed rules of Section 2011(d), which foreclose this double advantage, are applicable only when the deduction is claimed.

The basic rule, Section 2011(d)(1), is that no Section 2011 credit is allowed for state death taxes that are allowed as deductions under Section 2053(d). Such deductible taxes are includible in determining the credit, however, if they are not actually claimed as deductions; Section 2053(d), which is discussed in Chapter 5, leaves it up to the executor to elect use of the credit or the deduction, subject to severe restrictions.[37]

Beyond this basic rule, Section 2011(d)(2) establishes a further limitation on the credit for state death taxes in situations in which they are allowed as deductions. The limitation is expressed in alternatives. First, the credit cannot exceed the maximum specified in the table in Section 2011(b), using as the adjusted taxable estate for the purpose of that subsection an amount that reflects the deduction for the state death taxes on the charitable transfer. As far as this first alternative is concerned, it would seem that the deduction should be taken even though it reduces the maximum credit. This is so because the tax rates in Section 2001 are always higher than the maximum credit rates in Section 2011, and the amount of the maximum credit will not be reduced as much as the deduction will reduce the tax. Of course, if the adjusted taxable estate is $40,000 or less, the deduction permitted will yield a tax advantage, because in that situation no credit for state taxes will be available. When a credit is available and the deduction is taken, the second alternative limitation on the amount of the credit must be considered because it may result in a lower maximum credit for state death taxes.

The second alternative limitation may be expressed in terms of the following formula: The maximum credit cannot exceed an amount that bears the same ratio to the maximum determined under the table in Section 2011(b) (us-

---

[35] IRC §§ 2011(b)(1), 2011(b)(3). See supra notes 33, 34.

[36] See IRC § 2053(d), discussed ¶ 5.03[8].

[37] See ¶ 5.03[8]. The conversion of the Section 2011 credit to a deduction in the year 2005 (see infra ¶¶ 3.03[3][d], 3.03[4]) requires a revision of the Section 2053(d) rule. See ¶ 5.03[8] text accompanying note 168.

ing an adjusted taxable estate not reduced by the tax claimed as a deduction) as the state death taxes reduced by the amount of such taxes claimed as a deduction bear to such state taxes without regard to the deduction. This may be expressed as follows:

$$\frac{\text{alternative no. 2 maximum}}{\substack{\text{maximum under Section 2011(b) ignoring} \\ \text{Section 2053 state death tax deduction}}} = \frac{\text{state taxes reduced by the deduction}}{\text{total state death taxes}}$$

or:

$$\text{alternative no. 2 maximum} = \frac{\text{state taxes reduced by the deduction}}{\text{total state death taxes}} \times \substack{\text{maximum under} \\ \text{Section 2011(b)} \\ \text{ignoring Section} \\ \text{2053 state death} \\ \text{tax deduction}}$$

The effect of this alternative is to limit the maximum credit for state death taxes usually allowed under Section 2011(b) to a portion of such maximum based on the relationship between state death taxes for which no deduction is claimed and total state death taxes paid. In some circumstances, after subtracting deductible state taxes from the entire amount of state taxes, the remaining amount might still exceed the maximum credit reflected in the rate schedule. But such maximum is not allowed when the deduction is taken. Instead, a percentage of the credit for state death taxes is eliminated by the required alternative computation. Sections 2011 and 2053 present alternatives, and as always when the Code presents opportunities for election, the only safe course is to compute the resulting tax liability both ways and then to choose the more advantageous alternative.

[d] Phase-out of the Credit

The amount of the credit, subject to all the limitations just discussed, is phased out with only 75 percent of the credit (a 25 percent reduction) allowed in 2002, 50 percent of the credit (a 50 percent reduction) allowed in 2003, and 25 percent of the credit (a 75 percent reduction) in 2004.[38] In years beginning

---

[38] IRC § 2011(b)(2). For example, if in the year 2004 Decedent had a taxable estate of $3.1 million and no adjusted taxable gifts, Decedent's Section 2011 credit would be equal to a maximum of $47,700 (25 percent of 190,800). See IRC §§ 2011(b)(1), 2011(b)(2), 2011(b)(3). If the state in which Decedent was a resident imposed a tax of $190,800, Decedent would owe $143,100 of taxes to the state in excess of the federal Section 2011 credit. If the state imposed a tax based on the maximum federal credit, the state would recover only $47,700 in taxes.

in 2005, the credit is terminated[39] and replaced by a deduction.[40] The phase-out of the credit and the conversion to a deduction both increases federal tax revenues and works to the detriment of the states, either reducing their revenues or increasing their taxes.[41]

[4] The Section 2058 Deduction

In 2005, a deduction rather than a credit for state death taxes is allowed in the computation of the decedent's taxable estate.[42] The deduction employs several rules that applied to the repealed credit. The provision allows a deduction for "the amount of *any* estate, inheritance, legacy, or succession taxes[43] *actually paid*[44] . . . in respect of any property included in the gross estate[45] (not including any such taxes paid with respect to the estate of a person other than the decedent)."[46] Section 2058 is discussed in detail later in the treatise.[47]

[5] Background of Section 2011

In 1924, in response to the argument that death taxes were a traditional source of state revenues that the federal estate tax was displacing, Congress allowed a credit of 25 percent of the federal estate tax for death taxes paid to the states. In 1926, in response to further pressure to relinquish this field of taxation en-

---

[39] IRC § 2011(f).

It is worth noting that the effect of the repeal of the credit actually increases the top *federal* estate tax rates. For example, under the law in effect prior to the 2001 Act, the top federal estate tax rate under Section 2001(c) was 55 percent; however, the top state tax credit rate under Section 2011(b) was 16 percent, resulting in a maximum *federal* tax rate of 39 percent. After the repeal of the credit in 2005, the top federal tax rate is 47 percent reduced to a top rate of 45 percent in 2007. Thus, the top *federal* tax rate actually increases from 39 percent to at least 45 percent as a result of the repeal of the credit.

[40] IRC § 2058. See infra ¶ 3.03[4]. See also ¶ 5.09.

Under the sunset provision effective on January 1, 2011, the Section 2011 credit is restored to its status prior to the year 2002 and the Section 2058 deduction is eliminated. Economic Growth and Tax Relief Reconciliation Act of 2001, Pub. L. No. 107-16, § 901(a)(2), 115 Stat. 38, 150 (2001), reprinted in 2001-__ CB __, __. The sunset provision is discussed more fully at ¶ 8.10[5]. See supra ¶ 3.03[1].

[41] See supra ¶ 3.03[1].

[42] See supra ¶ 3.03[1] text accompanying notes 13, 14.

[43] IRC § 2058(a) emphasis added. See supra ¶ 3.03[1] text accompanying notes 3–6.

[44] IRC § 2058(a) emphasis added. See supra ¶ 3.03[2].

[45] IRC § 2058(a). See supra ¶ 3.03[1] text accompanying note 1.

[46] IRC § 2058(a). See supra ¶ 3.03[1] text accompanying note 7.

[47] See ¶ 5.09.

tirely to the states, the credit was raised to 80 percent. When, in 1932, it was decided to effect a major increase in the federal estate tax rates, it was necessary to make some modification in the credit provisions to prevent the bulk of the increase from passing by way of the credit to the states. Accordingly, the 1926 tax was continued as the "basic tax," which served to determine the amount of the credit, and an additional tax was separately imposed, against which no credit for state death taxes was allowed. This accomplished the congressional purpose but unduly complicated computation of the federal tax; a dual computation was required, and computation of the basic tax served no purpose other than to fix the maximum credit for state death taxes. Nevertheless, this situation continued until the enactment of the 1954 Code. The rules adopted in that Code and presently continued represent a substantial simplification.

¶ 3.04 SECTION 2012. CREDIT FOR GIFT TAX

Upon enactment of the Tax Reform Act of 1976, which is applicable to transfers made after 1976, a substantial measure of integration of the federal gift tax and the federal estate tax was achieved.[1] The general plan imposes a tax on any significant gratuitous transfer of wealth, whether during life or at death, taking into account the aggregate amount of all prior gratuitous transfers.[2]

Integration has not been undertaken in a fully retrospective fashion, however. Persons who made gifts before 1977 did so under a system that separately taxed lifetime gifts and testamentary transfers. Prior to 1976, the gift tax rates were equal to 75 percent of the then-existing estate tax rates. If, after integration, gifts made before 1997 had been taken into account in determining (increasing) the rate of tax applicable to post-1976 testamentary transfers, it would have had the practical effect of increasing the tax on pre-1977 gifts from 75 percent to 100 percent of the current estate tax rates. To avoid this result, the definition of "adjusted taxable gifts," which was adopted as one element of the post-integration estate tax computation, prevents pre-1977 gifts from entering into the estate tax calculation[3] unless they are gifts that are pulled back into the transferor's gross estate under specific estate tax provisions.[4] Because pre-1977 gifts (other than those pulled back into the gross estate) are

---

[1] See IRC §§ 2001, 2502.

[2] See IRC § 2001(b), discussed ¶ 2.01[1]; IRC § 2502, discussed ¶ 9.03.

[3] See IRC § 2001(b), discussed ¶ 2.01[1].

[4] IRC § 2001(b)(1)(A), discussed ¶ 2.01[1]. Lifetime transfers can be pulled into estates of decedents who die even many years after the transfer. See, e.g., IRC §§ 2036, 2037, 2038.

not taken into account in determining post-1976 estate tax, the two-step estate tax computation does not subtract from the tentative estate tax an amount equal to the gift tax that would have been payable on the decedent's pre-1977 gifts that are not includible in the gross estate. On the other hand, Congress has never intended the estate tax and the gift tax to effect two exactions on the same gratuitous transfer;[5] and thus, an allowance must be made for gift tax paid on those pre-1977 lifetime transfers that are included in the gross estate. This is the limited continuing mission of Section 2012.

Section 2012 is on the endangered species list. It provides for no credit against the estate tax for gift tax payable on post-1976 gifts.[6] Why? Because there is a subtraction of an amount equal to that gift tax that is built into the unified estate tax computation.[7] And that subtraction is made without regard to whether a post-1976 gift is includible in the gross estate. The subtraction is simply an integral part of the computation of the estate tax.

The foregoing comments indicate that it is too soon to deliver Section 2012 the coup de grace. We continue to give it space. However, the following comments will eventually shade off toward ministrations to a dying friend.

When applicable, Section 2012 supplies a number of detailed rules for determining the amount of the gift tax that was paid that is to be credited against the estate tax. The general approach is to determine the gift tax attributable to the decedent's lifetime transfer of the property in question.[8] That becomes the potential credit. However, the credit actually allowed will be either that amount or the estate tax attributable to the inclusion of such property in the transferor's estate, whichever is less.[9]

---

[5] After early fumbling with the relationship of the two taxes, the U.S. Supreme Court cleared up the matter. Compare Estate of Sanford v. Comm'r, 308 US 39, 45 (1939), with Smith v. Shaughnessy, 318 US 176, 179, 180 (1943).

[6] IRC § 2012(e).

[7] IRC § 2001(b)(2), discussed ¶ 2.01[2].

[8] If the decedent and another own property as joint tenants with the right of survivorship and the decedent properly treats their transfer to a third person as decedent's gift, only one half of the tax paid qualifies for the credit, the tax on decedent's actual gift. Rev. Rul. 76-471, 1976-2 CB 260.

[9] The third edition of this treatise (Stephens, Maxfield & Lind, Federal Estate and Gift Taxation, Warren, Gorham & Lamont, 3d ed. (1974) Chapter 3, § 2012, note 3) spoke as follows:

> Question might be raised whether any IRC § 2012 credit would be allowed in the following circumstance. D transfers property to a trust, income to be paid to B for life, reversion to D if living but, if not, remainder to R or R's estate. B dies survived by D, and when D dies the reacquired property is part of his Section 2033 gross estate. D paid gift tax on the lifetime transfer of the life interest to B and the contingent remainder to R. Smith v. Shaughnessy, 318 US 176 (1943). But, while interests in the very property transferred to and received back from the trust were subjected to gift tax, no Section 2012 credit results. No amount "in respect of such gift[s]" is in-

[1] Computation of Potential Credit

In determining the gift tax attributable to the property, it must be remembered that gift tax liability is not determined with respect to individual gifts; instead, the tax is imposed annually on the aggregate of gifts made during the calendar year.[10] Further, the credit is allowed only for gift tax paid on gift property, the value of which is included in the gross estate.[11] If several gifts were made during the calendar year, it is necessary to determine what part of the transferor's gift tax liability for that year is attributable to the gift property that qualifies for the credit by reason of its inclusion in the decedent's gross estate.[12] Section 2012(d)(1) supplies the rule for applying the general provision of Section 2012(a) in these instances. The rule can be expressed in terms of the following formula: The potential credit is an amount that bears the same ratio to total gift tax liability for the year in which the gift was made as the amount of the gift in question bears to total taxable gifts for that year. The formula, stated here only in general terms, which are explained later in this section, may perhaps be better understood in the following form:

$$\frac{\text{credit (unknown)}}{\text{total gift tax}} = \frac{\text{amount of the gift}}{\text{total taxable gift}}$$

This, again, may be started as follows:

$$\text{credit} = \frac{\text{amount of the gift}}{\text{total taxable gifts}} \times \text{total gift tax}$$

In this fashion, a portion of the gift tax paid for the year is allocated to the gift in question and becomes the potential credit. There is no need to use a

---

cluded in D's gross estate within the meaning of Section 2012(a); the property is being taxed because D owned it at death, not for reason of any lifetime gifts.

Rev. Rul. 76-470, 1976-2 CB 259, properly echoes this view, denying any credit where the decedent reacquires the gift property.

[10] For years after 1970 and before 1982, gifts were generally reportable on a quarterly basis. If a computation here involves a year after 1970 and before 1977, the computations would be made on a quarterly rather than an annual basis. See ¶ 9.04[9] note 197.

[11] The gift tax credit may be claimed by the decedent's estate as long as the decedent was the one liable for the tax even if the tax was paid by one other than the decedent, such as a co-owner of the gift property (Rev. Rul. 76-471, 1976-2 CB 260), the grantor of a reciprocal trust (Rev. Rul. 74-533, 1974-2 CB 293), a spouse in the case of a split gift (Reg. § 20.2012-1(e), or even the donee (Rev. Rul. 74-363, 1974-2 CB 290).

[12] Returns for gifts made between January 1, 1971, and December 31, 1976, were generally required to be filed on a quarterly rather than an annual basis. For such gifts the same apportionment method was used, except that it was a ratio of the gift tax to total taxable gifts for that quarter.

formula if the gift giving rise to the credit was the only gift made during the year; in such a case, the gift tax paid for the year is the potential credit.

The precise meaning of the terms used in the formula must now be considered.

[a] Total Gift Tax

As used in the formula, total gift tax is the gift tax imposed on the decedent (who was the donor) for the year in which the gift was made.[13] However, if Decedent and Decedent's Spouse elected to treat the gift as if it were made half by Decedent and half by Spouse for gift tax purposes, as is allowed under Section 2513[14] and corresponding provisions of prior law, the amount of gift tax incurred by Spouse with respect to the gift is to be added to the gift tax imposed upon Decedent.[15] Spouse's gift tax liability attributable to the gift in question is also determined under the formula just given. The reason for this addition is that the split-gift provision in the gift tax laws is an artificial concept designed only to equalize gift tax treatment in community and noncommunity property states. But the equalization is not complete because the gift remains a gift by the one who supplied the thing given; the entire value of the gift may be included in Decedent's gross estate, and Decedent may even have paid the tax on the part of the gift artificially attributed to Spouse. The adjustment to total gift tax simply takes into account this reality.

[b] Amount of the Gift

Basically, the "amount of the gift" is the *included* amount of the gift for the year. Thus, the pre-1982, $3,000 annual exclusion, if allowed under Section 2503 for pre-1977 gifts (or similar exclusion of prior law),[16] is to be subtracted from the value of the gift. Section 2012(d)(2) requires this. Under this rule, if a transferor made a $3,000 pre-1977 gift to a minor child under the Uniform Gift to Minors Act,[17] making no other gifts to the child in the year,

---

[13] The credit is available even though the gift tax is paid after death by the decedent's executor. Reg. § 20.2012-1(a).

[14] Section 2513 is discussed ¶ 10.03.

[15] IRC § 2012(c).

[16] Section 2503 is discussed ¶ 9.04. The current annual exclusion of $10,000 adjusted for inflation after 1998 is not a factor in the determination of the Section 2012 credit. Section 2012 is not applicable to gifts made after December 31, 1976, and the current annual exclusion was effective only after December 31, 1981. See IRC § 2012(e); ¶ 9.04[1]. The pre-1977 annual exclusion that is employed in determining the Section 2012 credit was either $5,000, $4,000, or $3,000 depending on the year of the gift. See ¶ 9.04[1]. Subsequent comments in this paragraph will assume a $3,000 pre-1977 annual exclusion.

[17] See IRC § 2503(c); ¶ 9.04[5].

and the gift was subsequently included in the transferor's gross estate,[18] the transferor's estate would not get a gift tax credit for that gift, even though the transferor paid substantial gift tax for the year in which the gift was made.[19] Application of the exclusion would reduce the amount of the gift to zero and foreclose any credit. This is logical, because the excludible $3,000 gift did not cost the transferor anything in gift tax, and the estate tax is the only federal transfer tax effectively applied to this transfer. If a gift tax charitable or marital deduction was allowed with respect to a gift, under Section 2522 or Section 2523,[20] respectively, a further downward adjustment in amount of the gift equal to the permitted deduction is required by Section 2012(d)(2).[21]

[c] Total Taxable Gifts

In the preceding formula, the amount of total taxable gifts is to be determined without any reduction for the gift tax specific exemption previously provided by Section 2521,[22] taking into account the pre-1977 annual exclusion under Section 2503.[23] Section 2012(d)(1) requires this. Experimentation with this equation will show that to take the specific exemption into account in determining total taxable gifts might make it appear as if just one substantial gift among many was responsible for the entire tax for the year. The effect of not taking the specific exemption into account is merely to reduce the gift tax attributable to each taxable gift, including the gift in question.

The foregoing comments relate to a determination of gift tax attributable to a transfer of property, the value of which is required to be included in the transferor's gross estate. But the amount of such tax is only potentially the credit against the estate tax; a second limitation on the amount of the credit, based on the extent to which estate tax liability is attributable to the property in question, is now considered.

---

[18] See IRC §§ 2036(a), 2038; ¶¶ 4.08, 4.10.

[19] This possibility exists because, in the same year, the transferor might have made gifts to others that were not of such a nature as to be included in the transferor's gross estate, but did cause gift tax liability.

[20] These sections are discussed in Chapter 11.

[21] Cf. Rev. Rul. 80-185, 1980-2 CB 250.

[22] Section 2521 was repealed as to gifts made after 1976. Tax Reform Act of 1976, Pub. L. No. 94-455, § 2001(b)(3), 2001(d)(2), 90 Stat. 1520, 1849, 1854 (1976), reprinted in 1976-3 CB (Vol. 1) 1, 325, 330. However, the Section 2012 credit relates only to pre-1977 gifts to which the Section 2521 specific exemption applied.

[23] See supra ¶ 3.04[1][b] text accompanying note 16.

[2] Limitation on the Credit

Under Section 2012(a), the amount of the credit is limited by a formula that can be expressed as follows: The amount of the credit cannot exceed an amount that bears the same ratio to the federal estate tax as the value of the gift bears to the decedent's gross estate. This formula may perhaps be better understood in the following form:

$$\frac{\text{credit (unknown)}}{\text{federal estate tax}} = \frac{\text{value of the gift}}{\text{decedent's gross estate}}$$

This, again, may be started as follows:

$$\text{credit} = \frac{\text{value off the gift}}{\text{decedent's gross estate}} \times \text{federal estate tax}$$

The purpose of this limitation is to restrict the amount of the credit to the amount of the federal estate tax that is attributable to the inclusion in the gross estate of the value of the property that has previously been subjected to gift tax. The formula is stated only in general terms, and the following comments relate to some adjustments that must be made in various terms used.[24]

[a] Federal Estate Tax

In the formula, "federal estate tax" is the estate tax minus the unified credit allowed under Section 2010 and the credit for state death taxes actually paid and allowed under Section 2011. Taking account of these credits, of course, reduces the possible gift tax credit. Reduction with regard to the Section 2011 state death tax credit is arguably appropriate because the amount representing the state death tax credit does not go to the federal government

---

[24] A special circumstance arises if a decedent has made gifts that qualify for the credit in more than one year. For example, as to gift property included in the gross estate, a 1970 gift might have resulted in a $200 gift tax, and a 1972 gift in an $800 gift tax. The estate tax attributable to such gifts in the aggregate might be $1,200. If so, is the full $1,000 credit allowable after the application of the limitation provisions of Section 2012(a)? Maybe not. The regulations provide that "[w]hen more than one gift is included in the gross estate, a separate computation of the two limitations on the credit is to be made for each gift." Reg. § 20.2012-1(b). Even if $600 of the estate tax is attributable to the 1970 gift, that gift will still support only a $200 credit, no more than the gift tax on that gift. If $600 of the estate tax is attributable to the 1972 gift, that will support a credit of only $600, no more than the estate tax attributable to that gift. The separate computation required by the regulations would thus produce an allowable credit of only $800, whereas an aggregate computation would support a $1,000 credit. The point can hardly be regarded as settled, however. Compare Burns v. United States, 242 F. Supp. 947 (DNH 1965), with Estate of Budlong v. Comm'r, 8 TC 284 (1947), acq. 1947-1 CB 1 (withdrawn), nonacq. 1964-2 CB 8, and Estate of Chapman v. Comm'r, 32 TC 599 (1959).

and, therefore, to that extent, two federal taxes are not being imposed on the same transfer.[25] Similarly, to the extent that estate tax liability is reduced by the unified credit, a smaller amount of estate tax is actually attributable to the lifetime gift.

[b] Value of the Gift

Basically, the "value of the gift" is the value at the date of the gift or at the date of death, whichever is lower. The effect of this is to reduce the credit if the gift property shrinks in value between the date of the gift and the date of death, but not to allow an increase in the credit if appreciation occurs during such period. The following two examples, which for the moment disregard other special rules, are provided to aid in the understanding of this concept.

> **EXAMPLE 3-1:** If Transferor made a gift of property worth $10,000 to child, the gifted property is included in Transferor's gross estate, and the property has become worthless by the date of Transferor's death, then the value of the gift in the formula is zero.[26] Another glance at the formula will show that the potential credit is completely eliminated. This, of course, is entirely appropriate, because inclusion in the gross estate of property with a zero valuation does not produce any estate tax liability, so this transfer is in no sense being taxed twice. The same principle applies to diminution in value, even if the property has not become valueless by the time of death; only the smaller value at death is productive of estate tax liability, and only to that extent would there be, in effect, a double tax.

> **EXAMPLE 3-2:** On the other hand, if Transferor made a gift of property worth $10,000 to child, the gifted property is included in Transferor's gross estate, and the property has increased in value to $15,000 by the date of death, then the value of the gift in the formula is only $10,000. To be sure, the $15,000 may produce estate tax liability, but only $10,000 is effectively being subjected to both gift tax and estate tax; the $5,000 increase in value was not subjected to gift tax, and in determining estate tax liability traceable to property previously subject to gift tax, the additional $5,000 is accordingly disregarded.

---

[25] A counterargument can be made that to the extent of the Section 2011 pick-up tax credit (see ¶ 3.03[1]), the federal government has merely assigned part of its tax to the states; thus, the tax is a federal (not state) tax and the reduction is unfair. The issue becomes moot after the year 2004 when the Section 2011 credit is repealed. See ¶¶ 3.03[1], 3.03[3][d], 3.03[4].

[26] No gross-up problem is presented, because Section 2035(b) applies only to post-1976 gifts to which the Section 2012 credit is inapplicable.

The situation is complicated when a partial interest in property is subject to the credit. For example, if a decedent created a trust retaining the income from the trust for life, with the remainder to another, the lifetime gift of the remainder would be subject to the Section 2012 credit.[27] In computing the value of the gift in the decedent's gross estate, the Service has ruled that the value of the trust corpus at the date of the gift or at death, whichever is lower, times the actuarial factor determining the value of the remainder at the time of the gift is the value of the gift for purposes of the second limitation of Section 2012.[28] This seems an appropriate way to measure the extent of the double taxation that Section 2012 is intended to alleviate.

Beyond the determination of the basic value of the gift, certain adjustments are required.

1. *Annual Gift Tax Exclusion.* The value is to be reduced to reflect the annual gift tax exclusion[29] if such exclusion applied to the gift in question. Section 2012(b)(1) so specifies. Thus, if Transferor's only gift to a child in a pre-1977 year was $10,000, the gifted property qualified for the $3,000 annual exclusion available at the date of the gift, and the gift was included in Transferor's gross estate, the value of the gift in the formula becomes $7,000 and the credit is reduced accordingly. This is appropriate because inclusion of $3,000 of the $10,000 in the gross estate does not result in estate tax liability traceable to property previously subject to gift tax.[30]

2. *Marital Deduction.* Under Section 2012(b)(2), the estate tax marital deduction allowed under Section 2056[31] may affect the value of the gift in the formula.[32] If the marital deduction has the effect of taking out of the estate the entire value of property both included therein and subject to gift tax upon a lifetime transfer, no gift tax credit is or should be allowed, because estate tax liability is not traceable to property that was previously the subject of gift tax liability. For ex-

---

[27] This assumes a completed gift of the remainder and gross estate inclusion under Section 2036(a)(1). No Section 2702 problem is presented because Section 2702 applies only to transfers after October 8, 1990, to which the Section 2012 credit is inapplicable.

[28] Rev. Rul. 67-319, 1967-2 CB 319. The ruling is clarified and its principles applied to a charitable remainder unitrust in Revenue Ruling 74-491, 1974-2 CB 290.

[29] See supra ¶ 3.04[1][b] note 16.

[30] Only if the value of the property at the date of the gift is the lower figure is the full amount of the exclusion taken into consideration. If the value of the property at the date of death is lower, the value of the gift is reduced by only a portion of the annual exclusion. The reduction is an amount that bears the same ratio to the exclusion as the value of the property at the date of death bears to its value at the date of gift. See Reg. § 20.2012-1(d)(2)(i).

[31] Section 2056 is discussed ¶ 5.06.

[32] Cf. Rev. Rul. 80-185, 1980-2 CB 250.

ample, assume Transferor made a gift to Spouse of $50,000 that is later included in Transferor's gross estate and the gift, treated as passing to Spouse, qualified for the estate tax marital deduction.[33] In this situation, the value of the gift is reduced to zero by subtracting the amount of the estate tax marital deduction, and no gift tax credit is allowed, because the marital deduction effectively blocks the potential second federal transfer tax on the property.[34]

3. *Charitable Deduction.* Regarding the value of the gift, Section 2012(b)(3) may require an adjustment with respect to the estate tax charitable deduction. The principle here is the same as that with respect to lifetime marital deduction transfers that subsequently are included in the transferor's gross estate and qualify for the estate tax marital deduction; to the extent that property subjected to gift tax upon a decedent's lifetime transfer and included in the decedent's gross estate upon death is removed from the taxable estate by way of a charitable deduction, there is no need for a credit for gift tax because the property is not being subjected to a second federal transfer tax.[35]

4. *Gift-Splitting.* Regarding adjustments in the value of the gift, Section 2012(c)(2) deals with the situation in which the gift was made by Decedent but treated for gift tax purposes as if made half by Decedent and half by Spouse, as is permitted by Section 2513. If the full amount of the gifted property is included in Decedent's gross estate, each half of the gift is included in value of the gift, but each half must be reduced by the amount of the gift tax exclusion that was allowed. This, again, simply recognizes the reality that, regardless of special gift tax rules, the entire value of such a gift (not merely one half) may be included in Decedent's estate, and Decedent may have paid the tax on the entire gift, even though the amount of tax was determined by artificially attributing one half of the gift to Spouse.

---

[33] Prior to 1977, a gift tax marital deduction was allowed under Section 2523(a) only with respect to one half of the value of property given to one's spouse.

If the credit is to be determined for the estate of a decedent who died after 1976, amendments to Section 2056 by the 1976 and 1981 legislation will, of course, play a part. See ¶ 5.06[10].

[34] This feature of the computation became complex when property treated as passing to the surviving spouse exceeded the limitation on the amount of estate tax marital deduction prior to its repeal. See ¶ 5.06[10].

[35] Restrictions on the deduction of mixed private and charitable transfers, added to the statute, discussed ¶¶ 5.05[4]–5.05[8], make this adjustment somewhat less likely than it once was.

[c] Decedent's Gross Estate

Decedent's gross estate in the formula determining the estate tax attributable to the gift property is to be reduced by the amount of estate tax marital and charitable deductions allowed.[36] The formula generally calls for a determination of the relationship between the value of the gift and decedent's gross estate. Since the value of the gift is to be adjusted with respect to these deductions, however, it is necessary to make a similar reduction in decedent's gross estate.

[d] The Limitation

It is the fraction established by the ratio of the value of the gift to the decedent's gross estate, taking into account all the adjustments previously discussed, that is applied to the federal estate tax to determine the limitation on the potential gift tax credit. In effect, if the gift tax found to be attributable to the property included in the decedent's gross estate exceeds the estate tax attributable to the gift property, the amount of the estate tax becomes the amount of the gift tax credit that will be allowed.

The principles discussed here are illustrated and explained in somewhat different fashion in the regulations.[37]

¶ 3.05 SECTION 2013. CREDIT FOR TAX ON PRIOR TRANSFERS

Section 2013, like vanishing Section 2012, allows a credit against the estate tax based on the tax paid on another transfer. Here, however, the credit arises out of a tax (estate tax) paid by someone other than the decedent, unlike the gift tax credit in Section 2012, which involves a tax (gift tax) paid by the decedent on a lifetime transfer made by the decedent. Further, unlike Section 2012, Section 2013 is alive and well and enjoying a long life expectancy.[1]

---

[36] IRC § 2012(a).

[37] See generally Reg. § 20.2012-1.

[1] In fact, legislation in 1988 gave it a new responsibility. Technical and Miscellaneous Revenue Act of 1988, Pub. L. No. 100-647, § 5033(a)(1), 102 Stat. 3342, 3670 (1988), reprinted in 1988-3 CB 1, 330. The credit is allowed (without any restrictions related to time) for some inclusions within the gross estate of a surviving spouse if that spouse is not a citizen of the United States. IRC § 2056(d)(3), discussed ¶ 5.06[9] text accompanying notes 441–447.

The purpose of this credit is to alleviate a hardship that could otherwise result from the death in quick succession of two or more persons.[2] If *A* who owned a substantial amount of property, died leaving it all to *B*, and *B* died soon thereafter leaving it all to *C*, the imposition of two estate taxes, one on *A*'s and one on *B*'s estate, would have the practical effect of an imposition of extra high rates on a death transfer essentially the equivalent of a single transfer of *A*'s property from *A* to *C*. The remedial device under the Code is, in general, to credit against estate tax payable by *B*'s estate the tax paid by the estate of *A*. And, in general, if only a part of *A*'s estate was left to *B*, the credit for *B*'s estate will be a portion of the estate tax on *A*'s estate commensurate with the part of *A*'s estate that went to *B*. The section also allows *C*'s estate a credit if *C* dies soon after *B*. The credit allowed *C*'s estate is based on the tax on *B*'s estate, without taking into account the credit to which *B*'s estate was entitled under this section.[3]

[1] General Rule—Section 2013(a)

Under the general rule of Section 2013(a), an estate is entitled to a credit for all or a part of the estate tax paid with respect to a transfer of property to the decedent by another person who died not more than ten years before or two years after the decedent. The one who transferred the property to the decedent is designated the "transferor" in the statute, and that term is used in this discussion.[4] The section provides for the reduction of the credit as the span of time between the transferor's death and the decedent's death increases. The general rule of Section 2013(a) prompts several basic observations.

[a] Transfer to Decedent

It is the transfer of property to the decedent, not the decedent's possession of previously received property or converted property at the decedent's death, that is a condition to the allowance of the credit. Under the predecessor to

---

[2] Section 2013 replaced a deduction from the gross estate of the value of the property previously taxed, not a credit against tax, which was allowed under Section 812(c) of the 1939 Code. See Rudick, "The Estate Tax Credit for Tax on Prior Transfers," 13 Tax L. Rev. 3 (1957); Chirelstein & Shieber, "Property Previously Taxed Under the Revenue Act of 1954," 33 Taxes 773 (1955); Redd, "When and How to Take Maximum Advantage of the Credit for Prior Transfers," 12 Est. Plan. 162 (1985).

[3] See Rev. Rul. 59-73, 1959-1 CB 234. This phenomenon is explained infra ¶ 3.05[3][a].

[4] Although in some instances it may be advantageous to the transferee-estate to claim a credit for only one of two qualified transfers, the Treasury has interpreted the "shall" language of Section 2013 to indicate that the credit is mandatory. Rev. Rul. 73-47, 1973-1 CB 397. Cf. Rev. Rul. 59-123, 1959-1 CB 248; Rev. Rul. 79-398, 1979-2 CB 338.

Section 2013 in the 1939 Code, the property previously taxed had to be identified in the decedent's estate for the corresponding deduction (in lieu of the present credit) to be allowed. No such tracing is required under Section 2013. If a transferor dies leaving the decedent a life interest in property and the decedent dies shortly thereafter, even though the value of the life interest is not included in the decedent's gross estate because the interest expires with the decedent,[5] tax considered paid on the transfer of the life interest to the decedent qualifies for the credit.[6]

Nonetheless, there must be a transfer to the decedent. Suppose Transferor's entire estate is left to Friend, and nothing is left to Transferor's children by a prior marriage—a classic setting for a will contest. If a settlement upsets the terms of the will by permitting amounts to be paid to the children, do those amounts nevertheless constitute property passing to Friend from Transferor for purposes of a Section 2013 credit on Friend's death? The Second Circuit thought *Lyeth v. Hoey*[7] was persuasive authority against the credit in this situation.[8] If the will contest successfully removed the will as an obstacle to the children's heirship, what they received came to them as heirs from Transferor; it was not property that passed to Friend from Transferor and from Friend to them. It may be true that neither in this case nor in the life interest situation will the property transferred be included in Friend's gross estate; however, in the life interest situation, Friend's estate will at least have been enlarged in some measure by the interest received from Transferor, whereas in the will contest case, the interest in question completely bypasses Friend's estate. In our example, the death of any *child* within the statutory ten-year period would invoke the credit for the child's estate.[9]

The principal companion requirement is, of course, that the value of the property must have been included in the transferor's gross estate; no credit arises with respect to property not so included, even though the decedent may have received the property from the transferor. For example, a post-1981 inter vivos outright cash gift will give rise to no credit.[10]

[b] "Property"

The term "property" as used in Section 2013 encompasses any interest in property, but it also extends to some things that are not customarily accorded

---

[5] See ¶ 4.05[5][b].

[6] Reg. § 20.2013-1(a); Rev. Rul. 59-9, 1959-1 CB 232. See Rev. Rul. 66-271, 1966-2 CB 430; Rev. Rul. 70-292, 1970-1 CB 187; infra ¶ 3.05[3][b].

[7] Lyeth v. Hoey, 305 US 188 (1938).

[8] In re Estate of McGauley, 504 F2d 1030 (2d Cir. 1974).

[9] Cf. Lyeth v. Hoey, 305 US 188 (1938).

[10] See ¶ 4.07[2].

property-law recognition as property. Under Sections 2514 and 2041, Congress treats general powers of appointment as if they were ownership interests in the property subject to the power for gift and estate tax purposes. It is therefore appropriate that Section 2013(e) defines "property" as "any beneficial interest in property," expressly including a general power of appointment.[11]

[c] "Transfer" Used Broadly

Section 2013(a) provides that if the transferor fails to exercise a general power of appointment[12] with the result that the appointive property passes to the decedent, the failure to exercise the power constitutes a "transfer" of property from the transferor to the decedent. Moreover, the legislative history[13] of the section makes it clear that almost any shifting of an interest in property included in the transferor's gross estate[14] constitutes a transfer for the purpose of this credit provision.[15] Nevertheless, there are some limitations. An estate is not entitled to a credit under Section 2013 with respect to property that the decedent acquired as a creditor of the transferor. The Treasury has appropriately recognized the logical inconsistency in the allowance of a credit for tax on a prior transfer with respect to an item that was deductible in the transferor's estate.[16] The inconsistency is avoided by a slight narrowing of the meaning of the term "transfer.[17]" No Section 2013 credit is allowed if, as a condition to the receipt of property from the transferor, the transferee decedent must convey property of equal or greater value to another.[18] This may occur in the case of a community property widow's election to take under a spouse's will, relinquishing the surviving spouse's share of the community property for a life interest in all the community property.[19]

---

[11] Cf. Rev. Rul. 77-156, 1977-1 CB 269. But see Rev. Rul. 84-179, 1984-2 CB 195, which is discussed ¶ 4.14[4][e] text accompanying note 73.

[12] "General power" is defined in Section 2041, discussed ¶¶ 4.13[3], 4.13[4]. See Rev. Rul. 66-38, 1966-1 CB 212. See also Rev. Rul. 79-211, 1979-2 CB 319.

[13] S. Rep. No. 1622, 83d Cong., 2d Sess. 463 (1954).

[14] See IRC §§ 2035–2042, discussed ¶¶ 4.07–4.14.

[15] See Reg. § 20.2013-5(b).

[16] Rev. Rul. 60-247, 1960-2 CB 272, 274. See infra ¶ 3.05[3][b] text accompanying notes 47, 48.

[17] In some instances, it is difficult to say whether property is acquired from a transferor as a beneficiary of the transferor's estate or as a creditor. If the transferee decedent was a creditor of the transferor and waived the creditor's claim, the transferee decedent does not automatically convert anything received from the estate to a credit-producing inheritance, and especially not if the transferee decedent was both creditor and sole beneficiary. Rev. Rul. 60-247, 1960-2 CB 272, 274.

[18] Estate of Sparling v. Comm'r, 552 F2d 1340 (9th Cir. 1977).

[19] Estate of Sparling v. Comm'r, 552 F2d 1340 (9th Cir. 1977). See ¶ 4.08[7][c].

It may be important to identify accurately the transferor for Section 2013 purposes. A ruling[20] reveals this disappointing circumstance. In 1954, *A* transferred property to *B* but retained a life estate. Upon *B*'s death in 1956, *A* surviving, *B*'s remainder interest in the property was devised to *C*. The remainder was taxed in *B*'s estate under Section 2033. *A* died in 1967 and *C* died in 1970, having acquired full ownership of the property through *C*'s remainder interest. In a sense, the source of *C*'s property is *A*, and *A*'s estate was taxed on the property under Section 2036. Should *C*'s estate be credited under Section 2013? Not at all. *C*'s transferor was *B*, who devised the remainder to *C*, and *B*'s death occurred too long before *C*'s for *C*'s estate to be allowed any credit.

[d] Death Before That of Transferor

It may seem difficult to understand why the credit is allowed if the so-called transferor dies within two years after the decedent. In many situations, the value of property transferred during a transferor's life is included in the transferor's gross estate at death. A gift of a remainder interest after a life estate retained by the donor is a clear example.[21] If such a gift is made to the decedent before death and the transferor dies after the decedent's death but within two years, this credit provision comes into play. Thus, the decedent's estate may be entitled to a credit for estate tax paid by the transferor's estate, even though the transferor died after the decedent. The two-year period, a question of where one draws the line, is supported by considerations of administrative convenience. It seems obvious that the provision should not encompass all taxable lifetime transfers.

[2] Computation of Credit in General

The basic credit, which is subject to limitations, is the amount of estate tax paid[22] by the transferor's estate on property transferred to the decedent. This might not present a problem if the transferor's entire estate passed to the decedent; but if only a part passes to the decedent, it is essential to determine what portion of the tax paid by the transferor's estate is attributable to the property so transferred. To solve this problem, Section 2013(b) provides the rule for determining the basic credit: The credit is an amount that bears the same ratio to

---

[20] Rev. Rul. 71-480, 1971-2 CB 327.

[21] See IRC § 2036(a)(1), discussed ¶ 4.08.

[22] IRC § 2013(a). See Rev. Rul. 83-15, 1983-1 CB 224, showing the interrelationship of the Section 2013 credit to deferred tax payments under Sections 6161, 6163, and 6166. Cf. Priv. Ltr. Rul. 8714001 (Oct. 29, 1986) applying Revenue Ruling 83-15 in a situation with a marital deduction formula clause.

the estate tax on the transferor's estate as the value of the property transferred to the decedent bears to the transferor's taxable estate. This general statement of the rule, which is subject to further explanation, may be better understood in the following form:

$$\frac{\text{credit (unknown)}}{\text{transferor's estate tax}} = \frac{\text{value of the property transferred}}{\text{transferor's estate tax}}$$

This, again, can be stated differently as:

$$\text{credit} = \frac{\text{value of the property transferred}}{\text{transferor's taxable estate}} \times \text{transferor's estate tax}$$

[a] Transferor's estate tax

Accordingly, the rule yields a fraction to be applied to the transferor's estate tax to determine the amount of the basic credit. Having stated the rule in general terms, it is now necessary to explain the statutory adjustments to be made in each term. As suggested here, the whole purpose of this computation is to identify the part of the estate tax paid on the estate of the transferor that is attributable to the property transferred to the decedent.

[3] Adjustments

[a] Transferor's Estate Tax

In the preceding formula, "transferor's estate tax" means the estate tax paid by the transferor's estate subject to two adjustments required under Section 2013(b).

1. The estate tax paid is increased by the amount of any Section 2012 credits for gift tax[23] that the transferor's estate was allowed. This adjustment is made because the prior gift tax payments with respect to property included in the gross estate, while not paid at the transferor's death, are appropriately treated as mere advance payments of the estate tax. The formula contemplates these gift tax payments as a part of the estate tax cost of the transfer to the decedent even though they were made before the transferor's death. It is difficult to see why any gift tax attributable to the transferor's post-1976 transfer of a beneficial interest also included in the transferor's taxable estate should not

---

[23] See discussion of Section 2012 at ¶ 3.04.

likewise be added to the figure for the transferor's estate tax. Failure to provide for this in the estate tax computation has resulted in an unintended reduction in the Section 2013 credit.

2. The estate tax paid is increased by the amount of any credits allowed under Section 2013 for death taxes paid with respect to prior transfers to the transferor, if the transferor had acquired property from one who died within ten years before the present decedent's death. The general objective of this adjustment is to avoid the diminution of the credit when the transferor's estate has also benefited from this credit provision. Thus, Congress sought "to subject property to estate tax only once where two or more decedents all die within a ten-year period."[24] Usually this objective is achieved,[25] but it will not be if the immediately prior decedent's estate was not taxable even without regard to the credit.[26] In such a case, the estate tax "paid" increased by any credit "allowed" under this section is zero. And this is so even if the property was all taxed recently in another estate.[27]

[b] Value of Property Transferred

Section 2013(d) requires essentially that the property value used in the foregoing formula be the value at which the property was included in the transferor's gross estate.[28] Recognized valuation principles generally apply to determine that value. In most circumstances, the recognized valuation principles used in the valuation of interests, such as annuities and interests for life, as well as remainder and reversionary interests that depend on the life of a person are limited to the mortality and actuarial tables.[29] However, the actual life expectancy of an individual whose life measures the value of the interest is generally[30] taken into account if the individual was terminally ill at the time of

---

[24] S. Rep. No. 1622, 83d Cong., 2d Sess. 464 (1954).

[25] See Rev. Rul. 59-73, 1959-1 CB 234.

[26] United States v. Denison, 318 F2d 819 (5th Cir. 1963).

[27] Estate of La Sala v. Comm'r, 71 TC 752 (1979). See also discussion infra ¶ 3.05[4][b] of the percentage limitation that may result in another modification of the general congressional objective.

[28] It is immaterial that the recipient decedent may have disposed of the property for a higher or lower value before death.

[29] Reg. § 20.2013-4(a). See IRC § 7520; Reg. §§ 20.7520-1, 20.7520-2, 20.7520-3, 20.7520-4. See also ¶ 4.02[5]. Generally, the method of valuation and the time of valuation used in the transferor's estate are controlling. See IRC §§ 2031, 2032, 2032A. See also Rev. Rul. 81-118, 1981-1 CB 453.

[30] See infra text accompanying notes 34–36.

the decedent's death.[31] An individual is considered "terminally ill" if, at the transferor's death, the individual is known to have an incurable illness or other deteriorating physical condition and there is at least a 50 percent probability that the individual will die within one year.[32] However, if the individual survives the transferor for eighteen months or longer, the individual is presumed not to have been terminally ill at the date of the transferor's death, unless the contrary is established by clear and convincing evidence provided by either the government or the executor of the estate of the decedent qualifying for Section 2013.[33] The "terminally ill" exception to use of the valuation tables is inapplicable in valuing a life estate qualifying for a Section 2013 credit in a transferee's estate if the life estate was required to be valued in the transferor's gross estate and if a final determination[34] of estate tax liability has been made with respect to the transferor's estate.[35] The value assigned to the life estate in the transferor's gross estate is used in computing the transferee's Section 2013 credit.[36] Use of the actuarial tables is also inappropriate if the transferor and the individual who is the measuring life die as a result of a common accident or other occurrence.[37] Thus, if Transferor created a testamentary trust, leaving

---

[31] Reg. § 20.7520-3(b)(3)(i).

[32] Reg. § 20.7520-3(b)(3)(i).

[33] Reg. § 20.7520-3(b)(3)(i). See ¶ 4.02[5].

For the applicable law regarding this issue prior to December 14, 1995 (see Reg. § 20.7520-3(c)). See Continental Ill. Nat'l Bank & Trust Co. of Chicago v. United States, 504 F2d 586 (7th Cir. 1974); Merchants Nat'l Bank of Topeka v. United States, 369 F. Supp. 1080 (D. Kan. 1973); Rev. Rul. 66-307, 1966-2 CB 429; Rev. Rul. 80-80, 1980-1 CB 194. See also TAM 199917066 (Jan. 19, 1999) (date of transferor's death determines effective date).

[34] The regulations fail to define the term "final determination." Seemingly, it includes a final judicial decision or a closing agreement and should include the expiration of the statute of limitations of the transferor's return. Cf. IRC § 2001(f)(2).

[35] Reg. § 20.7520-3(b)(3)(ii). A life estate would be required to be valued in a transferor's gross estate, for example, where the life estate was for the life of another and was a separate asset included in the transferor's gross estate under Section 2033 or where property included in the gross estate was transferred in trust and a life estate was given to a third person and a remainder given to a surviving spouse and the value of each interest had to be determined for computing the amount of the Section 2056 deduction.

[36] Reg. § 20.7520-3(b)(3)(ii).

[37] Reg. § 20.7520-3(b)(3)(iii). This rule applies even if the terms of the will and applicable state law presume the transferor died first. Reg. §§ 20.7520-3(b)(3)(iii), 20.7520-3(b)(4) Ex. 2. See ¶ 4.02[5].

For the applicable law prior to December 14, 1995, see Reg. § 20.7520-3(c); Estate of Carter v. United States, 921 F2d 63 (5th Cir. 1991), cert. denied, 502 US 817 (1991); Estate of Marks v. Comm'r, 94 TC 720 (1990); Estate of Lion v. Comm'r, 52 TC 601 (1969), aff'd, 438 F2d 56 (4th Cir. 1971); Old Kent Bank & Trust Co. v. United States, 292 F. Supp. 48 (WD Mich. 1969), rev'd on other grounds, 430 F2d 392 (6th Cir. 1970); Estate of Harrison v. Comm'r, 115 TC 161 (2000). See Comment, Lee, "The Common Disaster: The Fifth Circuit's Error in Estate of Carter v. United States and the Glitch in

a life interest in property to Decedent with a remainder to others, but Transferor and Decedent died simultaneously, no credit is allowed to Decedent's estate because the value of the life interest received by Decedent is zero.

If the value of the decedent transferee's interest is not susceptible to valuation on the date of death of the transferor, no Section 2013 credit is allowed.[38] An income interest for life that is subject to discretionary powers of a trustee may be incapable of such valuation.[39] However, an income interest subject to termination upon remarriage is capable of valuation under Section 2013.[40]

The value of the property transferred as conventionally determined is subject to three expressly required adjustments.

1. It is reduced by the amount of any death tax—federal, state, or other-payable out of such property; if by reason of any state[41] or federal law[42] or a provision in the will, a part of the financial burden of death taxes falls on the property, the net value to the decedent of the property transferred is diminished accordingly, which is why this adjustment is made.

2. For the same reason, "value of property transferred" as used in the formula is reduced by the amount of any encumbrance on the property[43] and the amount of any obligation imposed on the decedent by the transferor with respect to the property, just as if the value of a gift to the decedent were being determined.[44]

3. If the decedent was the transferor's spouse at the time of the transferor's death, "value of property transferred" to the decedent is re-

---

the 'Tax on Prior Transfer' Credit in Valuing Life Estates Created in a Common Disaster," 40 Emory LJ 1269 (1991).

[38] Rev. Rul. 67-53, 1967-1 CB 265.

[39] Compare Estate of Lloyd v. United States, 650 F2d 1196 (Ct. Cl. 1981), and Rev. Rul. 70-292, 1970-1 CB 187, with Estate of Pollock v. Comm'r, 77 TC 1296 (1981), Holbrook v. United States, 575 F2d 1288 (9th Cir. 1978), and Rev. Rul. 67-53, 1967-1 CB 265. Cf. Rev. Rul. 75-550, 1975-2 CB 357 (regarding valuation of nonmarital deduction trusts).

[40] Rev. Rul. 85-111, 1985-2 CB 196.

[41] Many states have statutes that apportion the financial burden of the tax among those interested in the estate. See discussion of Section 2205 at ¶ 8.04.

[42] See IRC §§ 2206, 2207, 2207A, 2207B, discussed ¶¶ 8.05–8.08.

[43] Donaldson v. Comm'r, 49 TCM (CCH) 564 (1985). The value is reduced by the full amount of the encumbrance even if the property is qualified for a marital deduction (see infra note 45) because only the net value of the property would qualify for a marital deduction. Reed v. United States, 743 F2d 481 (7th Cir.), cert. denied, 471 US 1135 (1985). Cf. In re Estate of McGauley, 504 F2d 1030 (2d Cir. 1974).

[44] See the discussion of Section 2512 at ¶ 10.02[2][a]. See also Rev. Rul. 78-58, 1978-1 CB 279; Estate of Sparling v. Comm'r, 552 F2d 1340 (9th Cir. 1977).

duced, possibly to zero, by the amount of the marital deduction allowed to the transferor's estate.[45]

Regarding this third adjustment, to the extent that a marital deduction was allowed to the transferor's estate, property received by the surviving spouse was, in effect, not taxed in the transferor's estate. Thus, no credit should be allowed with respect to possible tax on the prior transfer. The general effect of the provision is to recognize a right to the credit in the estate of the surviving spouse to the extent that property received from the transferor did not qualify for the marital deduction and was therefore responsible for a part of the estate tax liability with respect to the transferor's estate.[46]

While the statute does not expressly say so, it is the position of the Treasury that the value of property transferred must also reflect any diminution caused by administration expenses in the prior estate, which are "estate trans-

---

[45] Reduction to take account of the marital deduction is required whether the deduction is allowed initially on the basis of the estate tax return or only later as a result of a refund suit. Shedd's Estate v. Comm'r, 320 F2d 638 (9th Cir. 1963).

[46] See Rev. Rul. 58-167, 1958-1 CB 340; TAM 9145004 (July 12, 1991). Conceivably, there could be an advantage in causing the property passing from the transferor's estate to fail to qualify for the marital deduction so as to increase the amount of the Section 2013 credit. This might create some tax liability in the transferor's estate, payment of which would reduce the estate tax of a decedent transferee who died soon thereafter, because a Section 2013 credit for the tax payment would be allowed in the transferee's estate. In the event of a disclaimer of, for example, a general power of appointment over the property by the transferee or the transferee's executor, an income interest in the property might still pass to the transferee spouse. See IRC § 2518(b)(4)(A); Reg. § 25.2518-3(a)(1)(iii). However, a waiver of the marital deduction is generally not permitted, as the marital deduction provision is expressed in mandatory terms. Estate of La Sala v. Comm'r, 71 TC 752 (1979); Rev. Rul. 59-123, 1959-1 CB 248. However, if the transferor creates a trust providing a Section 2056(b)(7) qualified terminable income interest for a spouse and if the transferor's executor opts not to make an election to treat the property as qualifying terminable interest property thereby forgoing the marital deduction (resulting in the property in the transferor's gross estate being taxed), the spouse's income interest qualifies for the Section 2013 credit. Cf. TAM 8512004 (Dec. 11, 1984); Estate of Howard v. Comm'r, 91 TC 329 (1988). See Mulligan, "When the Credit for Prior Transfers May Be More Valuable Than the Marital Deduction," 52 J. Tax'n 26 (1980); Fowler & Jones, "The Trade-Off Between the Marital Deduction and the Section 2013 Credit," 44 Tax Notes 207 (July 10, 1989). An extension of time to file the federal estate tax return increases by six months the time to determine whether to make the election to qualify the transfer for the marital deduction. See IRC § 6081. The extension is generally automatic. See Reg. § 20.6081-1(b); ¶ 2.02[1] text accompanying note 9. This post-mortem estate planning tool has lost some of its appeal as the result of amendments to Regulations Section 20.7520-3(b)(3)(i) that take into account the transferee spouse's *actual* life expectancy in valuing the income interest for purposes of the Section 2013 credit if the transferee spouse is "terminally ill" at the transferor spouse's date of death or if there is a simultaneous death. See supra text accompanying notes 30–37.

mission" expenses (as opposed to "estate management" expenses)[47] generally regardless of whether such expenses are claimed for estate or for income tax purposes.[48] The legislative history of Section 2013[49] strongly supports this diminution position, which has received judicial support.[50]

[c] Transferor's Taxable Estate

In the previously mentioned formula, the transferor's taxable estate is also subject to adjustment. The taxable estate, as defined in Section 2051,[51] is reduced by the amount of any death taxes—federal, state, or other—paid with respect thereto. The general effect of this, taken together with a like adjustment made in the value of property transferred, is to make the comparison of the two amounts called for by the formula a comparison of net amounts after charges against the property.[52]

With these adjustments in mind, the formula set out earlier (i.e., value of property transferred over transferor's taxable estate times transferor's estate tax) determines the basic credit for tax on prior transfers; but this basic credit is subject to two other limitations that are now considered.

[4] Limitations on Credit

To this point, this chapter has explored the statutory rules for determining estate tax caused to the transferor's estate by the transferred property. That will be the amount of the credit, unless one of two limitations discussed later in this section apply.

---

[47] Reg. § 20.2013-4(b)(3)(i). The regulation incorporates the principles of Regulations Section 20.2056(b)-(4)(d), which is discussed in detail at ¶ 5.06[5][b]. In general, "transmission" expenses are expenses incurred because of the prior decedent's death, while "management" expenses are expenses that would have been incurred in any event. Reg. §§ 20.2056(b)-4(d)(1)(i), 20.2056(b)-4(d)(1)(ii).

[48] But see Reg. §§ 20.2056(b)-4(d)(3), 20.2056(b)-4(d)(4), 20.2056(b)-4(d)(5) Ex. 3.

[49] S. Rep. No. 1622, 83d Cong., 2d Sess. 467 (1954).

[50] Estate of Gilruth v. Comm'r, 50 TC 850 (1968).

[51] For purposes of this computation, only deductions taken under Section 2053 are taken into consideration. Estate of Wood v. Comm'r, 54 TC 1180 (1970). Compare supra ¶ 3.05[3][b] text accompanying notes 43–46.

[52] In the case of estates of decedents who died before 1977, a transferor's taxable estate was increased by the amount of the $60,000 deduction (exemption) provided by Section 2052. This, of course, was an artificial deduction allowed in computing the taxable estate, but which was out of place in making a comparison between a net value of the property transferred and what amounts to a more realistic net estate. Cf. Rev. Rul. 79-317, 1979-2 CB 318.

[a] Tax Caused in Decedent's Estate

The first limitation takes into account the amount of the estate tax on the decedent's (not the transferor's) estate that is attributable to inclusion in the decedent's estate of an amount equal to the value of the property transferred to the decedent by the transferor. The credit actually allowed cannot exceed that amount.

The amount of tax on the decedent's estate attributable to the value of the property transferred is determined by computing estate tax liability in two ways: once on the entire taxable estate and again on a so-called reduced taxable estate, which is the taxable estate recomputed by excluding from the gross estate the value of the property transferred, taking into account in both instances the unified credit[53] and the state death tax, gift tax, and foreign tax credits,[54] but disregarding the credit for tax on prior transfers.[55] This limitation may be considered generous because it reflects an assumption that the highest graduated estate tax rates were applicable to the value of the transferred property. The value of the property transferred, as used in this limitation, is the same as it is for the purpose of determining the formula that is used to calculate the estate tax on the transferor's estate attributable to the property transferred.[56]

    1. *Charitable Deduction.* If a charitable deduction is allowable in the decedent's estate, one additional adjustment must be made. In computing estate tax on the decedent's estate without the value of the property transferred, the amount of the charitable deduction must be reduced in such a way as to attribute to that deduction a portion of the value of the property transferred. This reduces the difference in the results of the two computations and places a corresponding lower limit on the amount of the credit. The statute fixes the amount of the reduction by the following formula: The reduction in the charitable deduction shall be in an amount that bears the same ratio to the entire charitable deduction as the value of the transferred property bears to the decedent's gross estate, less deductions for expenses and claims

---

[53] See IRC § 2010.

[54] See IRC §§ 2011, 2012, 2014. (Section 2011 does not apply to the estates of decedents dying after December 31, 2004. IRC § 2011(f).) The diminishing role of the Section 2012 credit for gift tax paid is discussed at ¶ 3.04 text accompanying notes 1–7.

[55] Rev. Rul. 67-110, 1967-1 CB 262.

[56] See discussion supra ¶ 3.05[3][b] on the value of property transferred. Recall that this figure is the value of the property included in the transferor's gross estate, but that the value of the property may not actually be reflected at all in the decedent's gross estate. Rev. Rul. 59-9, 1959-1 CB 232.

under Section 2053 and losses under Section 2054.[57] What the statute does, in effect, is to presume conclusively that any charitable deduction or bequest that gives rise to a deduction in the decedent's estate is satisfied proportionately out of all the assets in the estate and, therefore, in part out of the value of the property transferred to the decedent by the transferor. To the extent that part of the value of the property transferred is treated as a charitable deduction, that part of the value is not taxed again, and the maximum credit is reduced accordingly.

2. *Property From Two or More Transferors.* One further necessary detail is covered by Section 2013(c)(2). A decedent may have received property from two or more transferors, and thus the decedent's estate may be entitled to the credit for tax on prior transfers with respect to tax paid by several transferor decedents. This does not create a problem with respect to the initial determination of the credit, for the amount is determined initially by establishing the amount of tax attributable to the transferred property in each of the transferor's estates. In determining the tax attributable to the value of the transferred property in the decedent's estate, the statute requires the values of the properties transferred to be aggregated to determine the overall limitation on the amount of the credit. This overall limitation is then apportioned to the several properties transferred in proportion to their relative values. Thus, the basic credit with respect to each transfer of property to the decedent is to be tested separately against its proper portion of the tax on the decedent's estate attributable to all the property transferred to the decedent.[58]

For example, *A* and *B* die in year one, each leaving property of equal value to the decedent, and the decedent dies in year two. *A*'s estate paid no estate tax, and *B*'s estate paid a large estate tax, $1,000 of which was attributable to the property that *B* transferred to the decedent. If the tax attributable to both properties together in the decedent's estate is $1,000, this amount is ap-

---

[57] IRC § 2013(c)(1) (flush language). The formula for the reduction algebraically stated is:

$$\begin{array}{l} \text{Reduction in} \\ \text{the charitable} \\ \text{deduction} \end{array} = \frac{\text{value of the transferred property}}{\begin{array}{c}\text{gross estate less Section 2053 and}\\\text{Section 2054 deductions}\end{array}} \times \begin{array}{l}\text{entire charitable}\\\text{deduction}\end{array}$$

Sections 2106(a)(1) and 2106(a)(2) apply instead of Sections 2053 and 2054 if the decedent was a nonresident noncitizen. See ¶ 6.06[1].

See also Rev. Rul. 90-2, 1990-1 CB 170; Rev. Rul. 61-208, 1961-2 CB 148.

[58] Estate of Meyer v. Comm'r, 83 TC 350 (1984), aff'd per curiam, 778 F2d 125 (2d Cir. 1985).

portioned between the properties equally (in accordance with their values); the amount attributed to the property received from *A* is canceled because *A*'s estate paid no tax. The basic credit under Section 2013(b), as limited by Section 2013(c), becomes $500, the amount of tax paid by *B*'s estate ($1,000) that is within the limitation based on the tax in the decedent's estate on the value of such property ($500).

[b] The Percentage Limitation

Section 2013(a) superimposes a further limitation on the amount allowed as a credit. A percentage table indicates the allowable portion of the potential credit determined after application of the transferor's and the decedent's limitations. The percentage applicable depends on when the transferor's death occurred in relation to the death of the decedent as illustrated in the following table:

Transferor's death in relation to decedent's death	Percentage applicable
2 years before or after	100
more than 2 years and up to 4 years before	80
more than 4 years and up to 6 years before	60
more than 6 years and up to 8 years before	40
more than 8 years and up to 10 years before	20
more than 10 years before or 2 years after	0

If more than one transferor is involved, the percentages are to be applied to the amounts determined separately, as indicated in the preceding paragraph, depending on the gap between the decedent's death and that of each transferor.[59]

This percentage approach, which was introduced in the 1954 Code, is a substantial improvement over prior law. The old property-previously-taxed deduction was allowed in full if the second death occurred within five years of the death of the prior decedent, but it was lost entirely if the second death occurred as much as one day beyond the five-year period. A diminishing credit certainly seems preferable to the former all-or-nothing approach.

The principles discussed here are illustrated and explained in a somewhat different fashion in the regulations.[60]

---

[59] Estate of Meyer v. Comm'r, 83 TC 350 (1984), aff'd per curiam, 778 F2d 125 (2d Cir. 1985).

[60] See generally Reg. §§ 20.2013-1–20.2013-6. See also Bevan, "The Estate Tax Credit for Property Previously Taxed," 23 NYU Inst. on Fed. Tax'n 1117 (1965).

[5] Treatment of Additional Tax Imposed Under Section 2032A

Section 2032A provides that certain real property included in the gross estate may be valued at an amount approximating actual use value rather than fair market value.[61] The federal estate tax savings from the valuation relief afforded by Section 2032A may be recaptured in whole or in part in certain instances. Recapture is accomplished by the imposition of an additional tax provided for in Section 2032A(c).[62] Imposition of an additional tax with respect to property valued pursuant to Section 2032A in the transferor's estate supports a recomputation of the Section 2013 credit for the transferee's estate if the recapture event occurs before the second anniversary of the transferee's death.[63] The additional tax imposed by Section 2032A(c) is treated as an estate tax imposed on the estate of the transferor[64] at the transferor's death, even though the "qualified heir" is made personally liable for it.[65] Clearly, the amount of the transferor's taxable estate is to be determined disregarding the Section 2032A valuation of the property with respect to which an additional tax is imposed.[66] Less certainly, but logically, the value of other property valued initially under the provisions of Section 2032A, but with respect to which no recapture event has occurred, remains the same in the computation of the taxable estate. The recapture property is to be valued for this purpose on the basis of its fair market value on the applicable valuation date for the transferor's estate.[67]

¶ 3.06 SECTION 2014. CREDIT FOR FOREIGN DEATH TAXES

Subject to some limitations discussed in the next paragraphs, the estate of a U.S. citizen may claim a credit against the federal estate tax for all or a part of the amount of death taxes[1] actually paid to any foreign country with respect to property included in the decedent's gross estate but situated in the foreign

---

[61] Section 2032A is discussed at ¶ 4.04.

[62] The additional tax imposed by Section 2032A(c) is discussed at ¶ 4.04[7].

[63] IRC § 2013(f). Cf. HR Conf. Rep. No. 1380, 94th Cong., 2d Sess. 27 (1976), reprinted in 1976-3 CB (Vol. 3) 735, 761.

[64] IRC § 2013(f)(1).

[65] See HR Conf. Rep. No. 1380, 94th Cong., 2d Sess. 27 (1976), reprinted in 1976-3 CB (Vol. 3) 735, 761.

[66] IRC § 2013(f)(2).

[67] Although not specifically provided for in the statute, seemingly, additional tax recaptured with respect to Section 2057 deduction should be similarly treated. See ¶ 5.08[5].

[1] No credit is available if the nature of the foreign tax is an income tax. Estate of Ballard v. Comm'r, 85 TC 300 (1985).

country. The question of where property is situated is determined in accordance with principles provided in the sections of the Code relating to estates of nonresident noncitizens,[2] Sections 2101 through 2108, which are discussed in Chapter 6. Tax conventions, which are discussed in Chapter 7, also play a role. Although these sections are used to determine whether property is situated in the United States, the same principles are applied to determine whether property is situated in a foreign country.[3] A parenthetical provision in Section 2014(a) makes it clear that only the foreign death taxes paid with respect to the decedent whose estate tax liability is being determined give rise to this credit; death taxes paid with respect to the same property in other estates are disregarded.

Estates of U.S. residents who are not citizens are entitled to the same credit as estates of U.S. citizens, subject to one qualification. The Foreign Investors Tax Act of 1966[4] authorized the President of the United States to deny the foreign tax credit to resident noncitizens if the President finds that

- The foreign country imposing the tax does not allow U.S. citizens residing in the foreign country a credit similar to the foreign tax credit allowed by the United States to citizens of that foreign country residing in the United States.
- The foreign country has denied or ignored a request to provide a similar credit to U.S. citizens residing in that foreign country.
- It is in the public interest to allow the tax credit to citizens of the foreign country who reside in the United States only if the foreign country allows a similar credit to U.S. citizens residing in the foreign country.

Of course, a presidential proclamation may prompt the foreign country to adopt a provision allowing a credit similar to that provided by Section 2014 to estates of U.S. citizens resident there at death. If the adoption occurs before death, the estate of a citizen of the adopting country who is resident in the

---

[2] Reg. § 20.2014-1(a)(3).

[3] Reg. § 20.2014-1(a)(3). Application of the principles is not without controversy. See Estate of Schwartz v. Comm'r, 83 TC 943 (1984), acq. 1986-1 CB 2 (concerning bank deposits in Spanish branches of Spanish banks situated in Spain); Riccio v. United States, 1971-2 USTC ¶ 12,801 (DPR 1971) (holding life insurance policies issued by U.S. companies and bank accounts in the United States are not situated in foreign countries). See also Borne v. United States, 577 F. Supp. 115 (ND Ind. 1983).

[4] Pub. L. No. 89-809, § 106(b)(3), 80 Stat. 1539, 1569 (1966), reprinted in 1966-2 CB 656, 685. Substantial changes in the estate and gift taxation of noncitizens, brought about by the Foreign Investors Tax Act of 1966 and the Tax Reform Act of 1969, were incorporated into the regulations by TD 7296, 38 Fed. Reg. 34,190 (Dec. 12, 1973), reprinted in 1974-1 CB 255. Eroded some by later developments, such as the Tax Reform Act of 1976, the document is of continuing interest to persons concerned with the affairs of noncitizens.

United States is allowed the credit notwithstanding the proclamation.[5] The regulations also make it clear that the President may revoke the proclamation.[6] In that case and, of course, in the absence of a presidential proclamation denying the credit, the credit is allowed to resident noncitizens.[7]

Estates of decedents who are neither citizens nor residents of the United States are not entitled to the benefits of this section at all, but this creates no hardship because of the manner in which the federal estate tax applies to such estates.[8]

At one time, prior to the enactment of Section 2014, the allowance of any credit for foreign death taxes depended solely on treaty agreements; now the taxpayer may elect the benefits of Section 2014 or the provisions of a treaty, if any, whichever provides the greater credit.[9] Death taxes of U.S. possessions, deemed to be foreign countries for this purpose,[10] and of possessions and political subdivisions of foreign countries[11] also qualify for the credit.

[1] Computation of Credit

No credit is allowed under this section unless the property in question is subject to both foreign and U.S. death taxes. The primary reason for the credit is to obviate the harsh effect of double taxation resulting from the imposition of a foreign tax on a transfer of property also taxed by the United States. Since 1962, this credit provision has taken on somewhat greater importance; only since that time has foreign realty been included in the gross estate of a U.S. citizen or resident.[12] When some credit is available, Section 2014(b) limits the credit allowed to the lesser of two amounts: either the amount of foreign death tax or the amount of federal estate tax attributable to the foreign property.

---

[5] IRC § 2014(h) (last clause).

[6] Reg. § 20.2014-1(c)(2)(iii).

[7] Rev. Rul. 72-6, 1972-1 CB 306.

[8] Reg. § 20.2102-1(a). See ¶ 6.02 text accompanying note 5.

[9] S. Rep. No. 781, 82d Cong., 1st Sess. (1951), reprinted in 1951-2 CB 458, 617; Reg. § 20.2014-4. The regulations (Reg. § 20.2014-4(a)(2)) caution that as regards the treaty and the statutory credit for foreign taxes, the most may not be the best because of the interrelation of the Sections 2013 and 2014 credits. Prudence may require dual computations.

[10] IRC § 2014(g).

[11] Reg. § 20.2014-1(a)(1).

[12] See Revenue Act of 1962, Pub. L. No. 87-834, § 18(a), 76 Stat. 960, 1050 (1962), reprinted in 1962-3 CB 111, 189–190 (amending IRC § 2031 and other sections defining the gross estate in this respect).

[2] The Foreign Death Tax Formula

The following formula is provided to determine the amount of foreign death tax attributable to the foreign property. The credit cannot exceed an amount that bears the same ratio to the foreign death tax as the value of the property situated in the foreign country and included in the decedent's gross estate bears to the value of all property subject to the foreign tax. This formula, which is stated in general terms only, may be better understood in the following form:

$$\frac{\text{credit (unknown)}}{\text{foreign death tax}} = \frac{\text{value of property}}{\text{all property subject to foriegn tax}}$$

This equation can also be started as

$$\text{credit} = \frac{\text{value of property}}{\text{all property subject to foreign tax}} \times \text{foreign death tax}$$

Accordingly, the formula yields a fraction that, when applied to the amount of the foreign death tax, gives the amount of foreign tax attributable to the property situated in the foreign country that is being subjected to both foreign and U.S. death taxes.

The statute and regulations spell out the meaning to be given to the terms in the previously stated formula. "Foreign death tax" is the entire death tax actually paid[13] to the foreign country.[14] "Property" means only property that is: (1) situated within the foreign country (the term does not include property not situated therein, even though taxed by the foreign country);[15] (2) subject to death tax in the foreign country;[16] and (3) included in the gross estate for federal estate tax purposes.[17] All three conditions must be met; thus, property situated in a foreign country, but exempt from tax there, will not enter into the computation. If the property meets the threefold test, then, for the purpose of computing foreign tax that may qualify for the credit, Section 2014(c) defines "value of property" as the value determined for the purpose of the foreign death tax.

The foregoing discussion presupposes a foreign estate tax. If the foreign country imposes an inheritance tax, which may involve several taxes on the succession to property by more than one beneficiary, separate computations us-

---

[13] IRC § 2014(a).

[14] The foreign death tax must be expressed in terms of dollars. This is accomplished by using the exchange rate in effect at the time of each foreign tax payment. Rev. Rul. 75-439, 1975-2 CB 359. Cf. Rev. Rul. 80-260, 1980-2 CB 277.

[15] Reg. § 20.2014-1(a)(3). See supra ¶ 3.06 note 3.

[16] Reg. § 20.2014-1(a)(1).

[17] Reg. § 20.2014-1(a)(1).

ing the previously mentioned formula may be necessary to determine the total of the qualifying death taxes on the interests passing to the several benefi-ciaries.[18]

[3] The Federal Estate Tax Formula

The other limitation, which is based on the amount of federal estate tax attrib-utable to the property in question, is to be determined in accordance with the following formula: The credit cannot exceed an amount that bears the same ra-tio to the federal estate tax as the value of the property bears to the gross es-tate. This formula, which again is stated in general terms only, may be better understood in the following form:

$$\frac{\text{credit (unknown)}}{\text{federal estate tax}} = \frac{\text{value of the property}}{\text{gross estate}}$$

This equation can also be started as

$$\text{credit} = \frac{\text{value of the property}}{\text{gross estate}} \times \text{federal estate tax}$$

Accordingly, the formula yields a fraction that, when applied to the fed-eral estate tax, gives the amount of that tax attributable to the property that is being subjected to both foreign and U.S. death taxes. The statute defines the terms used in this formula.

[a] Adjustments: Federal Estate Tax

The "federal estate tax" used in the formula is the tax imposed by Section 2001,[19] less the unified credit under Section 2010 and the credits for state death taxes and for gift taxes under Sections 2011 and 2012, respectively.[20] The apparent objective is to base this limitation on the amount of federal tax actually to be paid. It should be noted that Section 2014 was included in the 1954 Code from prior law without taking into account the change in treatment of estate taxes previously paid on property transferred to the decedent. For-merly, there was a deduction for property previously taxed in arriving at the net or taxable estate. Now, under Section 2013, a credit is allowed in these cir-cumstances that probably should be, but is not, taken into account in determin-

---

[18] This is well illustrated in the regulations. See Reg. § 20.2014-3(d).

[19] The 1976 change in the method of computation of estate tax effects no change here in computation of the foreign tax credit.

[20] IRC § 2014(b)(2). Section 2011 is repealed for estates of decedents dying after De-cember 31, 2004. IRC § 2011(f). See ¶¶ 3.03[1], 3.03[3][d], 3.03[4].

ing federal estate tax as used in the foregoing formula. This anomaly, observed in earlier editions of this book, persists.

[b] Value of the Property

As used in the federal estate tax formula, "value of the property" is the value determined for federal estate tax purposes, as Section 2014(c) specifies. However, such value is reduced to reflect charitable or marital deductions[21] that are allowed with respect to the property. The statute does not specify how such an adjustment is to be made, leaving the details to the Secretary of the Treasury. The regulations[22] provide for a reduction of the value of the property in accordance with rules that seek to attribute to the foreign property a proper portion of the marital and charitable deductions. The reason for this adjustment is to restrict the offset for foreign taxes to that part of the value of property effectively taxed in the United States.

[c] Gross Estate

The gross estate, as customarily determined, is reduced by the total amount of charitable and marital deductions allowed under Sections 2055 and 2056, respectively, to conform to the similar reduction in value of the property.[23]

[4] Payment

Section 2014(d) requires, as a condition to the allowance of the credit, that the taxpayer establish "to the satisfaction of the Secretary" the amount of taxes actually paid to the foreign country, the amount and date of each such payment, the description and value of the property with respect to which the taxes are imposed, and any other information needed to verify or compute the credit.[24]

Note that the credit for foreign death taxes, like the credit for state death taxes under Section 2011, is dependent on the taxes being "actually paid."[25] Again, this actually paid requirement, when considered together with limitation

---

[21] See IRC §§ 2055, 2056, discussed ¶¶ 5.05, 5.06. Value of the property is also reduced in the less likely event of a deduction claimed for foreign taxes under Section 2053(d). IRC § 2014(f).

[22] Reg. § 20.2014-3(b).

[23] IRC § 2014(b)(2). See also IRC § 2014(f), relating to a Section 2053(d) deduction.

[24] Reg. § 20.2014-5.

[25] See supra ¶ 3.03[2]. Section 2011 is repealed for estates of decedents dying after December 31, 2004. IRC § 2011(f). Cf. IRC § 2058(b), applicable after 2004. See ¶¶ 3.03[1], 3.03[3][d], 3.03[4], 5.09.

periods and related rules, could cause hardship in many circumstances. This potential hardship with respect to the credit for foreign death taxes is mitigated by Section 2014(e), which is similar to Section 2011(c), and serves the same purposes as Section 2011(c) serves regarding the credit for state death taxes. Seasonable payment is again required. Under Section 2014(e), the general rule is that the credit will be allowed only where the foreign death taxes are paid and the credit is claimed within four years after the filing of the estate tax return.[26] Although a cutoff date is desirable, there are circumstances in which the four-year rule could work an improper hardship, so Section 2014(e) recognizes two exceptions[27] to the general rule governing when the foreign tax must be paid and the credit claimed:

1. Under Section 2014(e)(1), if a taxpayer files a timely petition in the Tax Court, the credit is allowed for foreign death taxes paid within sixty days after the Tax Court decision becomes final if the credit is claimed within that same period, even if this occurs beyond the four-year period.[28]

2. If an extension of time is granted under Section 6161 for payment of the federal estate tax, which may be granted for a period of up to twelve months with respect to the tax shown on the return[29] or up to four years or more with respect to amounts determined as a deficiency,[30] Section 2014(e)(2) extends the period within which the state death tax payment must be made and credit claimed to either the usual four-year period or the expiration date of any such extension, whichever is later. It should be noted that an extension of time for payment of the foreign death tax is irrelevant;[31] here it is the extension of time for payment of the federal tax that operates to extend the usual limitation period.[32]

---

[26] See Reg. § 20.2014-6; Winer v. United States, 153 F. Supp. 941 (SDNY 1957). Courts do not have the power to extend this period. Cf. Howard v. United States, 40 F. Supp. 697 (ED La. 1941), aff'd on other grounds, 125 F2d 986 (5th Cir. 1942).

[27] Section 2014 does not provide for an extension of the usual limitations periods if an estate tax refund claim or suit is pending. Compare IRC § 2011(c)(3).

[28] Cf. Estate of Damon v. Comm'r, 49 TC 108 (1967), acq. 1968-2 CB 2.

[29] IRC § 6161(a)(2). An extension of twelve months after the due date for the last installment is allowed in the case of extensions for reasonable cause under Section 6161(a)(2)(B).

[30] IRC § 6161(b)(2). While Section 2011(c)(2) recognizes extensions under Section 6166, Section 2014(e)(2) does not recognize a Section 6166 extension.

[31] Cf. Rev. Rul. 86-38, 1986-1 CB 296; In re Harkavy's Estate, 34 NYS2d 910 (1942); Estate of Spillar v. Comm'r, 50 TCM (CCH) 1285 (1985).

[32] Cf. Rev. Rul. 86-38, 1986-1 CB 296.

Section 2014(e) expressly provides that a timely claim for refund based on the credit for payment of foreign death taxes can be made within the limitation periods just discussed, notwithstanding Code provisions that usually require refund claims to be filed within three years from the time the return was filed or two years from the time the tax was paid, and despite other Code provisions that usually foreclose the payment of refunds when the taxpayer has filed a Tax Court petition. Nonetheless, such refunds are to be made without the usual payment of interest.[33] The limitation period provided here is in addition to, not in lieu of, other limitation periods; a claim for refund can always be filed within two years after the estate tax was paid.[34]

¶ 3.07 SECTION 2015. CREDIT FOR DEATH TAXES ON REMAINDERS

There is a special rule with respect to the credit for state or foreign death taxes on reversionary or remainder interests in property. The rule applies generally to estates of citizens or residents and to estates of nonresident noncitizens as regards the credit for state death taxes. It reflects the requirement that a credit for state or foreign death taxes is available only if the state or foreign tax is actually paid; and it is, in effect, a further extension of the usual limitation periods that are extended in certain other respects under Sections 2011(c) and 2014(e), which were discussed earlier in this chapter.[1]

The value of a reversionary or remainder interest in property that generally is includible in a decedent's gross estate under Section 2033 and does not expire upon the owner's death may be taxable under state or foreign estate or inheritance tax statutes. On the other hand, these interests are not readily salable and in some instances may not be salable at all. Thus, the imposition of death taxes with respect to them, especially if they constitute a major portion of the inheritance, may make it difficult to raise the cash needed to pay the tax. In recognition and mitigation of this situation, some state and foreign death tax statutes permit postponement of the payment of the tax (and, in some instances, even postponement of the computation of the tax) with respect to

---

[33] But cf. Edinburg v. United States, 617 F2d 206 (Ct. Cl. 1980); Rev. Rul. 61-58, 1961-1 CB 414 (concerning the allocation of interest on the portion of a refund based on Section 2011 and that portion based on some other ground); Rev. Rul. 79-219, 1979-2 CB 401 (holding that interest an estate paid on a prior deficiency is also not recoverable in a subsequent refund suit based on Section 2011).

[34] IRC § 6511(a). Cf. Rev. Rul. 81-263, 1981-2 CB 169.

[1] See ¶¶ 3.03[2], 3.06[4]. Section 2011(c) is repealed for estates of decedents dying after December 31, 2004. IRC § 2011(f). Cf. IRC § 2058(b), applicable after 2004. See ¶¶ 3.03[1], 3.03[3][d], 3.03[4], 5.09.

these future interests until the preceding interest or interests have been terminated.

Section 6163(a) permits postponement of the payment of the part of the federal estate tax attributable to such interests[2] until at least six months after the interest takes effect in actual enjoyment.[3] The executor may elect postponement by way of a letter to the district director, which should be filed before the tax is due.[4] However, the postponement provision is limited "to cases in which the reversionary or remainder interest is included in the decedent's gross estate as such and [does] not extend to cases in which the decedent creates future interests by his own testamentary act."[5]

Section 2015 comes into play only if the estate elects under Section 6163(a) to postpone payment of the part of the federal estate tax attributable to a reversionary or remainder interest, not if it merely postpones payment of the state or foreign tax. Subject to all the limitations imposed with respect to the computations of the amount of the state and foreign death tax credits, such credits attributable to these future interests are allowed if the state or foreign death taxes are paid and credit is therefore claimed before the time for payment of the federal tax as postponed under Section 6163.[6] The result is that the state or foreign tax may be "actually paid" and the credit allowed many years after the death of the decedent, if the election is made to postpone payment of the part of the federal tax attributable to the future interests specified. This provision thus may extend the time for payment of the state or foreign taxes

---

[2] Reg. § 20.6163-1(c) prescribes a formula for computing tax attributable to the future interest.

[3] See Reg. § 20.6163-1. Section 6163(b) permits a further administrative extension of three years upon a showing of "reasonable cause." The "reasonable cause" standard replaced the "undue hardship" standard for discretionary extensions of time for payment of estate tax attributable to reversionary and remainder interests in the Tax Reform Act of 1976, Pub. L. No. 94-455, § 2004(c)(3), 90 Stat. 1520, 1868 (1976), reprinted in 1976-3 CB (Vol. 1) 1, 344. This was done to ease the liquidity problems experienced by decedent's estates by making discretionary extensions easier to obtain. HR Conf. Rep. No. 1380, 94th Cong., 2d Sess. 30, 31 (1976), reprinted in 1976-3 CB (Vol. 3) 735, 764, 765. "Reasonable cause" for this purpose is defined in Regulation Section 20.6161-1(a)(1). HR Conf. Rep. No. 1515, 94th Cong., 2d Sess. 611 (1976), reprinted in 1976-3 CB (Vol. 3) 807, 961. See ¶ 2.02[3][b].

If an extension of time within which to pay tax is granted, security to assure payment may be required. IRC § 6165.

[4] Reg. § 20.6163-1(b).

[5] Reg. § 20.6163-1(a)(1). See IRC § 2037, discussed ¶ 4.09.

[6] Payment within the periods established by Sections 2011(c) or 2014(e), if later, will also qualify the state or foreign tax for the credit. See Reg. § 20.2015-1(a)(1).

Section 2015

well beyond the extensions permitted under Sections 2011(c)(2)[7] and 2014(e)(2).

Section 2015 became less attractive in 1975 when the statute regarding interest on tax payments deferred under Section 6163 was changed. For many years, those payments incurred interest at a rate of only 4 percent, in lieu of the then-usual 6 percent figure.[8] Most postponed federal taxes, including those postponed under Section 6163 on reversionary and remainder interests, incur interest at a standard[9] but fluctuating rate established under Section 6621, which has been as high as 20 percent[10] and as low as 6 percent[11] since the statute was amended.[12]

¶ 3.08 SECTION 2016. RECOVERY OF TAXES CLAIMED AS CREDIT

Section 2016 is designed to protect the interests of the government when an amount paid as state or foreign death tax and claimed as a credit against federal estate tax is subsequently recovered[1] from the state[2] or foreign country involved. The statute imposes a duty on the executor or other person recovering the money to give notice to the government of the recovery, at a time and in a manner prescribed in the regulations.[3] Thereupon, a redetermination of estate tax liability, taking into account the recovery, is to be made, and the executor or other person making the recovery is required upon notice and demand to

---

[7] Section 2011(c)(2) is repealed for estates of decedents dying after December 31, 2004. IRC § 2011(f). Cf. IRC § 2058(b)(2)(B), applicable after 2004. See ¶¶ 3.03[1], 3.03[3][d], 3.03[4], 5.09.

[8] IRC § 6601(b) (prior to amendment by Pub. L. No. 93-625, § 7(b)(1), 88 Stat. 2109, 2117 (1975), reprinted in 1975-1 CB 510, 514, effective July 1, 1975).

[9] IRC § 6601(a).

[10] See Rev. Rul. 81-260, 1981-2 CB 244; ¶ 2.02[3][b] note 39.

[11] See Rev. Rul. 77-411, 1977-2 CB 480.

[12] The standard rate does not apply to the estate tax extended under Section 6166. See IRC § 6601(j) discussed ¶ 2.02[3][c][v].

[1] Whether an amount received from a foreign government is a proscribed tax recovery may be a question. Cf. Rev. Rul. 73-240, 1973-1 CB 399, raising a similar question under the United States-Canada Death Tax Convention of 1962.

[2] The Section 2011 credit is repealed for estates of decedents dying after December 31, 2004 (see IRC § 2011(f)), and Section 2016 is amended on such date to delete the reference to "section 2011." In the year 2005, the Section 2011 credit is replaced by a deduction under Section 2058 (see ¶¶ 3.03[4], 5.09). Seemingly, Section 2016 should be further amended to apply to a recovery under Section 2058.

[3] Such notification is to be made to the district director within thirty days of receipt. See Reg. § 20.2016-1.

pay the tax due, if any, as a result of such redetermination. Most important, the redetermination and demand may be made regardless of the usual limitation periods prescribed by Section 6501 for assessment of tax.[4] Section 2016 serves the double purpose of compelling the disclosure of refunds of state or foreign death taxes and removing limitation periods as obstacles to the appropriate readjustment of federal estate tax liability resulting from any such refund.

Normally, of course, interest must be paid on tax deficiencies. However, with respect to additional tax due as a result of a refund of foreign taxes, Section 2016 provides that no interest shall be assessed or collected for periods prior to the receipt of the refund, except to the extent that the foreign country paid interest on the amount refunded.[5] No such provision appears with respect to a refund of state death taxes, and the Treasury has ruled[6] that interest is payable at the regular rates on a deficiency arising out of a refund of such taxes. This difference in treatment between foreign and state taxes is probably due to the uncritical adoption by Congress of phraseology found in Section 905(c), which concerns a credit against the federal income tax for foreign income taxes.[7] There is no corresponding income tax credit for state income taxes, and, accordingly, no reference is made in Section 905(c) to the question of interest on a deficiency based on a refund of state income taxes. It seems that Congress may have failed to adjust the language of Section 905(c) to take into account the question of interest on an estate tax deficiency arising out of a refund of state death taxes. If an oversight, its correction seems overdue, but the difference persists.

---

[4] It seems clear that only the recovered tax, not other computational errors, may be the basis for additional liability in the extended-limitation period. Cf. Rev. Rul. 72-525, 1972-2 CB 443. See FSA 200051044 (Sept. 27, 2000) (state tax refund).

[5] IRC § 2016 (last sentence). In all likelihood, interest is charged with respect to accrued foreign taxes that have been adjusted. See Rev. Proc. 62-27, 1962-2 CB 495.

[6] Rev. Proc. 60-17, 1960-2 CB 942, 971.

[7] See S. Rep. No. 1622, 83d Cong., 2d Sess. 468 (1954); HR Conf. Rep. No. 1337, 83d Cong., 2d Sess. A313 (1954).

The Gross Estate

¶ 4.01 INTRODUCTION

This chapter discusses the determination of the decedent's gross estate for federal estate tax purposes. How this determination relates to the computation of the tax is indicated in broad terms in the Overview Chapter in Part 1. In general, the gross estate is arrived at by:

1. Identifying interests in property that must be taken into account;
2. Ascertaining the time at which the interests must be valued; and
3. Employing an accepted method of valuation to determine the fair market value of the identified assets at the specified time.

Thus, the elements discussed in this chapter are asset identification, time of valuation, and method of valuation.

As will soon be apparent, Section 2031 assigns the job of identifying includable interests to Sections 2033 through 2046. If an interest in property is identified as a part of the decedent's gross estate, regardless of the reason for its inclusion, the time for its evaluation is invariably the date of the decedent's death,[1] unless the alternate valuation date is elected.[2] Similarly, all of the valuation methods utilized, with one exception, have as their goal the determination of the fair market value of the many types of property interests included in the gross estate, regardless of the reason for their includability or the time at which they are to be valued. The one exception to market valuation is Section 2032A, which generally values property at its actual use rather than its highest and best use.[3]

It is useful, therefore, to present a general analysis of valuation methods in connection with the discussion of Section 2031, which follows in the next section. The methods of valuation discussed are applicable to most interests brought into the gross estate, even if the alternate valuation date is elected under Section 2032. These methods of valuation are essentially nonstatutory, resting as they do primarily on the meaning of the general term "value."[4]

---

[1] IRC § 2031(a); ¶ 4.02.

[2] IRC § 2032; ¶ 4.03.

[3] Section 2032A provides a limited elective, nonmarket valuation method for certain real property. Section 2032A is examined in detail later in ¶ 4.04. The ensuing discussion assumes that this provision is either inapplicable or not elected.

[4] For a more complete discussion of the significance and methods of valuation, see Bogdanski, Federal Tax Valuation (Warren, Gorham & Lamont 1996).

¶ 4.02 SECTION 2031. DEFINITION OF "GROSS ESTATE"

Section 2031 defines "gross estate" to include the value of all property, real[1] or personal, tangible or intangible, to the extent provided by Sections 2033 through 2046, although there is a limited exclusion with respect to land subject to a qualified conservation easement.[2] Thus, other than the specific exclusion, unless property is described in one of these sections, all of which are discussed in this chapter, it is not part of the gross estate. However, the definitional sections will be seen to be quite comprehensive.[3]

It is apparent that Section 2031 lacks much substance; on identification questions, it merely directs attention to other sections, for the gross estate is to be determined by including property "to the extent provided for" by other sections.[4] It does, however, focus attention on the matter of valuation. It is the "value" of property that must be taken into account in determining the "value" of the gross estate. Just as school children learn not to add apples and oranges, taxes must be computed in terms of dollars, not objects. Section 2031 also expresses the presumptive date-of-death rule for the time of valuation. The remainder of this discussion addresses the nonstatutory meaning of "value," along with the fundamental principles and methods of valuation for estate tax purposes.

---

[1] Eliminating a time-honored statutory exclusion, the Revenue Act of 1962, Pub. L. No. 87-834, § 18, 76 Stat. 960, 1052 (1962), reprinted in 1962-3 CB 189, 189-190, provided that foreign real estate is included in the gross estate if the decedent died on or after July 1, 1964. If the decedent died before October 17, 1962, the foreign realty was excluded. Transitional rules for death after October 16, 1962, and before July 1, 1964, are set forth in Reg. § 20.2031-1(c). See also Rev. Rul. 69-165, 1969-1 CB 220.

[2] IRC § 2031(c). See infra ¶ 4.02[7].

[3] Compare Section 61, which defines "gross income" to include "all income from whatever source derived," with Section 2033, which includes in the gross estate "all property to the extent of the interest therein of the decedent."

[4] The Service annually releases revisions of its procedures relating to (1) the issuance of rulings and determination letters; (2) closing agreements; (3) the issuance of technical advice to District Directors and Chiefs, Appeal Officers; and (4) taxpayers' rights. See Rev. Proc. 2002-1, 2002-1 CB __. See Rev. Proc. 2002-3, 2002-1 CB __, regarding areas in which the Service will generally not issue advance rulings on domestic matters, and Rev. Proc. 2002-7, 2002-1 CB __, regarding areas in which advance rulings will generally not be issued on international matters. The Service has issued checklist questionnaires that must accompany all ruling requests relating to estate, gift, and generation-skipping transfer tax issues effective March 13, 1991. Rev. Proc. 91-14, 1991-1 CB 482. Rev. Proc. 2002-1 § 9, 2002-1 CB __ and Rev. Proc. 2002-1 App. C, 2002-1 CB __ contain a general update of the Service's checklist procedures.

[1] Introduction

After determining what interests in property are to be included in the gross estate, the importance of valuation becomes obvious; actual tax liability is highly
sensitive to variation in valuation, just as it is to variation in the tax rates, inclusion in or exclusion from the gross estate, or allowance or disallowance of
deductions or credits. Viewed in this light, it is surprising that so little on valuation appears in the statute. In fact, Section 2031(a) provides only that the
"value" of property shall be included in the gross estate.[5] The method of valuation is left to the administrative regulations, rulings,[6] and judicial decisions.
The general lack of statutory rules and the infinite variety of property interests
that may form a part of the gross estate make it impossible to present adequately here even a survey of valuation problems. Instead, some general principles will be presented, and some concrete approaches will be illustrated.

[2] Fair Market Value

[a] Introduction

The "value" spoken of in Section 2031(a) is fair market value, which is
the main guidepost for estate tax valuation. A long-standing regulation defines
the fair market value of an asset as "the price at which the property would
change hands between a willing buyer and a willing seller, neither being under
any compulsion to buy or sell and both having reasonable knowledge of relevant facts."[7] The determination of fair market value is a question of fact.[8]

The factual nature of the valuation question has important overtones. An
executor may well hope to resolve valuation difficulties with the examining
agent. Undoubtedly, most such controversies are settled in the administrative
process,[9] although litigation involving valuation is certainly common. As may

---

[5] Section 2031(b) provides some limited guidance regarding the valuation method for
unlisted stocks and securities. See infra ¶ 4.02[3][f]. Section 2703 sometimes disregards
valuation established by an agreement. See infra ¶ 4.02[2][c].

[6] The Service ordinarily will not issue advance rulings on valuation issues because
they present questions of fact. Rev. Proc. 2002-3 § 4.02(1), 2002-1 CB ___.

[7] Reg. § 20.2031-1(b).

[8] Estate of Lauder v. Comm'r, 64 TCM (CCH) 1643, 1660 (1992); Messing v.
Comm'r, 48 TC 502, 512 (1967); McGuire v. Comm'r, 44 TC 801, 812 (1965). The Service ordinarily will not issue advance rulings on valuation issues because they present
questions of fact. Rev. Proc. 2002-3 § 4.02(1), 2002-1 CB ___.

[9] E.g., Estate of Colyear v. Comm'r, 6 TCM (CCH) 1157 (1947); Scott v. Henrick-
sen, 1941-2 USTC ¶ 10.098 (WD Wash. 1941); Taylor v. Rogan, 1942-2 USTC ¶ 10,192
(SD Cal. 1942), rev'd and remanded on other issues, 136 F2d 598 (9th Cir. 1943). See
Bosland, "Tax Valuation by Compromise," 19 Tax L. Rev. 77 (1963).

be expected, the final determination of value often represents a compromise between the figure asserted by the taxpayer and that asserted by the Commissioner.[10] However, if a controversy is not settled in the administrative process, the Commissioner's determination of value is prima facie correct, leaving the taxpayer with the accustomed burden of proof, whether the taxpayer litigates in a refund suit[11] or in the Tax Court.[12] Moreover, the taxpayer's chances of upsetting a valuation finding by the Tax Court, the claims court, or a district court, the possible courts of original jurisdiction, are limited.[13]

Cash on hand and checking and savings accounts carry their own indicia of value.[14] For liquid and other regularly traded assets, valuation is not an especially difficult issue. The fair market value of such assets can be determined by reference to comparable sales in the open market.[15]

Fair market value is a more problematic issue for assets that are not commonly sold in the open market.[16] In some cases, the asset to be valued is unique, irreplaceable in the market.[17] In other cases, the value of an asset is af-

---

[10] OE.g., Worthen v. United States, 192 F. Supp. 727 (D. Mass. 1961) (stock); Singer v. Shaughnessy, 198 F2d 178 (2d Cir 1952), aff'g 96 F. Supp. 506 (NDNY 1951) (partnership interest); Estate of Lowenstein v. Comm'r, 17 TC 60 (1951), acq. 1951-2 CB 3 (real property); Estate of Nelson v. Comm'r, 41 TCM (CCH) 400 (1980) (land); Estate of Iacono v. Comm'r, 41 TCM (CCH) 407 (1980) (real property).

[11] E.g., Hays v. Heiner, 15 AFTR 935 (WD Pa. 1933).

[12] E.g., Estate of Fox v. Comm'r, 69 TCM (CCH) 1719 (1995); Estate of Pridmore v. Comm'r, 20 TCM (CCH) 47 (1961).

[13] See First Nat'l Bank v. Comm'r, 125 F2d 157 (6th Cir. 1942). See also Estate of Berg v. Comm'r, 976 F2d 1163 (8th Cir. 1992) (Tax Court's adoption of Service's experts over estate's experts valuation was not clearly erroneous even though both calculations were valid). But see Estate of Mitchell v. Comm'r, 250 F3d 696 (9th Cir. 2001) (Circuit Court reversed the Tax Court requiring it to adequately explain any valuation conclusions reached).

[14] See Rev. Rul. 78-360, 1978-2 CB 228 (coins or paper currency with a fair market value in excess of face amount, such as in a collection, are valued at fair market value).
Cf. ¶ 4.05[3] note 28 for a discussion of whether outstanding checks are included in a decedent's gross estate.

[15] For example, the regulations state that the fair market value of an automobile is equal to the retail price for a used vehicle of the same make, model, and condition. Reg. § 20.2031-1(b).

[16] Valuation can also be difficult where the asset is traded only in the black market. For example, the Service advised that marijuana should be valued according to "the price an ultimate consumer would pay in the illicit marketplace," meaning its retail street value where the decedent, a drug smuggler, was in possession of the marijuana at the time of a fatal plane crash, and the property was included in the decedent's gross estate under Section 2033. FSA 1999-1132 (undated).

[17] See, e.g., Estate of Pascal v. Comm'r, 22 TCM (CCH) 1766 (1963) (valuation of rights to produce one play and two motion pictures); Goodall v. Comm'r, 391 F2d 775 (8th Cir. 1968) (valuation of oil and gas interests); Donehoo v. United States, 1968-1 USTC ¶ 12,519 (WD Pa. 1968) (valuation of rights to compensation); Estate of Lennon v.

fected by too many factors to make any one valuation method authoritative. In general, any factor that would reasonably be considered in determining at what price property would be purchased or sold is relevant in determining fair market value for estate tax purposes.[18] These factors include income yield, appraisals, sales prices of similar property near the date of death, bids made for the asset, and general economic conditions. Even the location of an asset may be a factor in determining its value; a snowmobile located in Miami, Florida is less valuable than the same snowmobile located in Bangor, Maine.[19]

Because the definition of "fair market value" sets forth an objective standard for computation, it requires consideration of both a hypothetical willing buyer and a hypothetical willing seller. Accordingly, if an appraisal considers only the perspective of the willing buyer, for example, a court may give the appraisal little weight.[20] Moreover, an appraisal should present the price that would be agreed to between hypothetical parties, not the price the actual parties to a transfer would agree upon.[21] Still, an appraisal should consider the identity of other owners. In one case, the court chastised the Service's expert for not taking into account the fact that a hypothetical buyer would be entering into a family corporation and thus, in effect, would have little influence over management.[22]

Assets included in the gross estate are generally valued (other than valuation under Section 2032) at the moment of the decedent's death. This rule is consistent with the fact that the federal estate tax is a tax imposed upon the transfer of wealth. The focus is not on the value of the asset in the decedent's hands, but instead on the value of the asset that is available for transfer. For

---

Comm'r, 62 TCM (CCH) 326 (1991) (valuation of interest in decedent's personal injury claim); Estate of Biagioni v. Comm'r, 42 TCM (CCH) 1663 (1981) (allowing a discount for attorney fees in valuing decedent's interest in litigation); Estate of Tompkins v. Comm'r, 13 TC 1054 (1949), acq. 1950-1 CB 5 (valuation of growing crops).

[18] See Estate of Smith v. Comm'r, 57 TC 650, 658 n.7 (1972), aff'd on other grounds, 510 F2d 479 (2d Cir. 1957).

[19] Estate of Swan v. Comm'r, 24 TC 829 (1955), acq. 1956-2 CB 8, rev'd on other issues, 247 F2d 144 (2d Cir. 1957) (valuation of securities held abroad and subject to wartime restrictions).

[20] See, e.g., Estate of Lehmann v. Comm'r, 74 TCM (CCH) 415 (1997).

[21] Estate of Bright v. United States, 658 F2d 999, 1005–1006 (5th Cir. 1981); Priv. Ltr. Rul. 9719001 (Nov. 19, 1996) (identities of donees of nine separate gifts of stock from the donor were irrelevant for purposes of determining the value of each gift). Cf. infra ¶ 4.02[2][c].

[22] Mandelbaum v. Comm'r, 69 TCM (CCH) 2852 (1995), aff'd 91 F3d 124 (3d Cir. 1996). This brings to mind words of caution from the Tax Court: while the willing buyer and willing seller are hypothetical persons and not the actual parties, "otherwise, the process of valuation considers actual conditions as they exist at the time of valuation." Estate of Dunn v. Comm'r, 79 TCM (CCH) 1337, 1341 n.3 (2000). See also Estate of Simplot v. Comm'r, 249 F3d 1191 (9th Cir. 2001) (reversing a Tax Court decision that constructed particular possible purchasers).

valuation purposes, the moment of death is a very brief, perhaps immeasurably small, instant.[23] Accordingly, any restrictions that apply solely to the decedent's own ability to transfer or enjoy any beneficial interest in an asset should be ignored, as such restrictions necessarily lapse at the decedent's death.[24] Likewise, any value added to an asset by the decedent's presence, like goodwill, should be disregarded in computing the value of the asset included in the gross estate.[25] Further, because the interests of the decedent's beneficiaries have not yet vested in the assets at the moment of death, valuation does not consider the ultimate disposition (or recipient) of the assets.[26]

Valuation should not be affected by events occurring after death unless such events were known or reasonably foreseeable at the moment of death.[27] This is not to say that after-death events may never be considered in establishing the original value of an interest. For example, the value of an illiquid asset can be determined with reference to the price at which the asset, or a similar

---

[23] United States v. Land, 303 F2d 170, 171 (5th Cir. 1962).

[24] Estate of McClatchy v. Comm'r, 106 TC 206 (1996) (restrictions on the decedent's stock ownership under Rule 144 of the Securities Act of 1933 ignored in valuing stock because restrictions did not carry over to decedent's estate) rev'd, 147 F3d 1089 (9th Cir. 1998) (the stock's value did not increase until stock was actually owned by the estate, which could not occur until the personal representatives had letters testamentary; therefore, the Rule 144 restrictions should have been considered in valuing stock at the moment of death). The guiding principal of the Tax Court decision—that restrictions applicable only to the decedent should be ignored—is still viable, even after the Ninth Circuit's reversal.

[25] However, any goodwill not attributable to the decedent should still be considered. Estate of Sharp v. United States, 97-1 USTC ¶ 60,268 (ED Tenn. 1997).

[26] Estate of McClatchy v. Comm'r, 147 F3d 1089 (9th Cir. 1998); Estate of Chenoweth v. Comm'r, 88 TC 1577, 1582 (1987); Estate of Curry v. United States, 706 F2d 1424 (7th Cir. 1983); Ahmanson Foundation v. United States, 674 F2d 761 (9th Cir. 1981). But see Estate of Nowell v. Comm'r, 77 TCM (CCH) 1239 (1999) (limited partnership interest which would under local law generally become less valuable assignee interests were treated as partnership interests under partnership agreement because they passed to a general partner).

[27] Necastro v. Comm'r, 68 TCM (CCH) 227 (1994); Estate of Bennett v. Comm'r, 65 TCM (CCH) 1816 (1993); Estate of Mueller v. Comm'r, 63 TCM (CCH) 3027 (1992); Estate of Pattison v. Comm'r, 60 TCM (CCH) 471 (1990); Estate of Spruill v. Comm'r, 88 TC 1197 (1987); Estate of Gilford v. Comm'r, 88 TC 38 (1987). See also Estate of Andrews v. United States, 94-2 USTC ¶ 60,170 (ED Va.).

asset, was sold after death.[28] However, the longer the period between death and sale, the less probative the sale is of the asset's value.[29]

When the Service and the taxpayer disagree as to the value of an asset, both parties typically obtain appraisals from qualified valuation experts. Technically, the taxpayer has the initial burden to prove that the Service's valuation in the deficiency notice is wrong, unless the Service's valuation is shown to be arbitrary and capricious[30] or the Service's own trial experts demonstrate that the value used in the deficiency notice is wrong.[31] But once the taxpayer submits a qualified appraisal, the burden is met[32] and the dispute often becomes a battle of the experts. While a court may be reluctant to determine the value, it will do so when necessary.[33] In many cases, a court will simply follow the better of the appraisals[34]; other times, the court will balance or even average the competing determinations.[35] Courts will carefully consider all appraisals sub-

---

[28] Morrissey v. Comm'r, 243 F3d 1145 (9th Cir. 2001) (sale of stock two months after death established value); Freeman v. Comm'r, 72 TCM (CCH) 373 (1996); Scanlan v. Comm'r, 72 TCM (CCH) 160 (1996); Estate of Jung v. Comm'r, 101 TC 412 (1993); Gettysburg National Bank v. United States, 92-2 USTC ¶ 60,108 (DC Pa. 1991); Estate of Andrews v. Comm'r, 79 TC 938 (1982).

[29] Estate of Spruill v. Comm'r, 88 TC 1197 (1987) (sale fourteen months after death did not establish fair market value); Morton v. Comm'r, 73 TCM (CCH) 2520 (1997) (prospectus two years after death not relevant, but valuation by accounting firm fifteen months after death held admissible); Estate of Sharp v. Comm'r, 97-1 USTC ¶ 60,268 (ED Tenn. 1997) (price paid for business sixteen months after death irrelevant, but value of goodwill based upon purchase offer five months after death held relevant).

[30] Tax Court Rules of Practice and Procedure, Rule 142(a), 109 TC 507, 617 (1997); Helvering v. Taylor, 293 US 507, 514–515 (1935). See infra ¶ 4.02[6][b].

[31] Estate of Mitchell v. Comm'r, 250 F3d 696 (9th Cir. 2001).

[32] Estate of Sharp, Jr., v. United States, 97-1 USTC ¶ 60,268 (ED Tenn. 1997).

[33] The U.S. Tax Court has signaled its hope to limit the number of valuation disputes, claiming "[w]e continue to believe that valuation disputes are better settled than litigated." Estate of Mueller v. Comm'r, 63 TCM (CCH) 3027, 3029 (1992). But see Estate of Scanlan v. Comm'r, 72 TCM (CCH) 160 (1996), aff'd, 116 F3d 1476 (5th Cir. 1998) (court derived a 30 percent discount on its own after both sides submitted inadequate expert testimony as to the value of the decedent's undivided community property share).

[34] Estate of Strangi v. Comm'r, 115 TC 478 (2000); Smith v. Comm'r, 78 TC 745 (1999); Estate of Furman v. Comm'r, 75 TCM (CCH) 2206 (1998); Estate of Newhouse v. Comm'r, 94 TC 193, 217 (1990), nonacq. 1991-1 CB 1; Estate of Dailey v. Comm'r, 82 TCM (CCH) 710 (2001).

[35] See, e.g., Estate of Fleming v. Comm'r, 74 TCM (CCH) 1049 (1997) (court held value of decedent's interest in closely held finance company was $875,000, not the $1,100,000 value presented by the Service or the $604,000 value advocated by the taxpayer); Estate of Wright v. Comm'r, 73 TCM (CCH) 1863 (1997) (court determined the value of decedent's stock at $45 per share, rejecting Service's appraisal at $50 per share and the petitioner's appraisal at $38 per share); Estate of Lauder v. Comm'r, 68 TCM (CCH) 985 (1994) (court set value of stock at $7,474 per share—nearly the average between the taxpayer's per share value of $4,300 and the Service's asserted value of

mitted by parties, and courts do not hesitate to critique inadequate or self-interested valuations; it is clear that the courts are requiring experts to have a sound basis to their appraisals and to explain them thoroughly.[36]

While appraisals should determine the value of the asset at or near the subject valuation date (date of death or alternate valuation date for the federal estate tax), the date on which the appraisal is actually performed does not matter. Thus, a court will not automatically suspect an appraisal performed after the Service issues a notice of audit; in determining value on the appropriate valuation date, the courts will look at appraisals of value at a date close to the subject valuation date.[37]

[b] General Valuation Methods

There is no set formula for valuing an asset included in the gross estate. Instead, one or more of several different valuation methods are employed to determine value. As a result, the choice of valuation method sets the paradigm. Where more than one valuation method is applicable to an asset, each applica-

---

$10,890 per share); Estate of Mueller v. Comm'r, 63 TCM (CCH) 3027 (1992) (court valued decedent's minority interest at $1,700 per share, not $2,000 as advocated by the Service nor $1,505, as claimed on the estate tax return).

A court will also disregard the appraisals from both sides where circumstances merit such action. Estate of Kaufman v. Comm'r, 77 TCM (CCH) 1779 (1999) (Service's appraisal not admitted into evidence and taxpayer's appraisal generally unpersuasive; consequently, because the taxpayer bears the burden of proof, Service's original determination of value accepted). See also Rabenhorst v. Comm'r, 71 TCM (CCH) 2271 (1996) (Service's expert appraisal disregarded when expert admitted unfamiliarity with minority interest discounts and taxpayer's evidence given little consideration where taxpayer's expert demonstrated poor analysis of comparables).

[36] See Estate of Hinz v. Comm'r, 79 TCM (CCH) 1289 (2000); Estate of Hagerman v. United States, 81 AFTR2d 98-2208 (CD Ill. 1998); Estate of Freeman v. Comm'r, 72 TCM (CCH) 373 (1996); Estate of Gloeckner v. Comm'r, 71 TCM (CCH) 2548 (1996), rev'd on other grounds, 152 F3d 208 (2d Cir. 1998); Estate of Ford v. Comm'r, 66 TCM (CCH) 1507 (1993), aff'd, 53 F3d 924 (8th Cir. 1995). See also Mandelbaum v. Comm'r, 69 TCM (CCH) 2852 (1995), aff'd without published opinion, 91 F3d 124 (3d Cir. 1996) (expert chastised for making conclusions that contradicted another opinion rendered by the same expert in a different case).

[37] Rabenhorst v. Comm'r, 71 TCM (CCH) 2271 (1996). But see Estate of Kaufman v. Comm'r, 77 TCM (CCH) 1779 (1999) (Service's expert appraisal as of December 8, 1993, not close enough to valuation date of April 14, 1994); Estate of Necastro v. Comm'r, 68 TCM (CCH) 227 (1994) (petitioner's environmental audits were rejected by the court because they tested on dates not sufficiently close to the applicable valuation date); Estate of Mitchell v. Comm'r, 74 TCM (CCH) 872 (1997) (court considered both an offer to purchase a business made several months before the decedent's death and an alleged offer following the decedent's death), rev'd, 250 F3d 696 (9th Cir. 2001) (Tax Court failed to adequately explain rationale for its valuation conclusion).

ble method should be considered, though the weight given to each method can (and should) vary.[38]

[i] **Income approach.** For rental property and other income-producing assets, value can be determined with reference to the present value of the expected future income and other benefits to be derived from the subject property. This "income approach" begins with a determination of the anticipated return from the subject property. The return is best measured by the asset's actual return in prior years, with greater weight given to more recent years.[39] A capitalization rate is then applied to the anticipated return to compute the final value. For many assets, a capitalization rate based on the yield of modern conservative investments, such as government bonds, is suitable where appropriately adjusted for risk. For closely held businesses, a capitalization rate can be derived by taking the inverse of the price-earnings ratios of comparable, publicly traded business entities and, appropriately, adjusting for the amount of risk.[40]

[ii] **Market approach.** In valuing an illiquid asset, reference can be made to comparable assets that are publicly traded. This "market approach" is most often used with closely held business interests and real property not held for rent. Once comparable publicly traded assets are found,[41] the market approach then requires some adjustment to reflect the illiquid nature of the subject property.[42]

Not surprisingly, the greatest disputes in the use of the market approach relate to the selection of comparable assets and the adjustment made to the comparable price. The Tax Court once criticized an expert retained by the Service to value a minority interest in a closely held corporation that operated

---

[38] Estate of Andrews v. Comm'r, 79 TC 938, 945 (1982). See infra ¶ 4.02[2][b][iv]. Notably, selection of the wrong valuation method can cause the appraisal to be wholly or partially disregarded. Estate of Furman v. Comm'r, 75 TCM (CCH) 2206 (1998); Estate of Hendrickson v. Comm'r, 78 TCM (CCH) 322 (1999); Estate of Klauss v. Comm'r, 79 TCM (CCH) 2177 (2000).

[39] See Rev. Rul. 59-60 § 4.02(d), 1959-1 CB 237, 240.

[40] See, generally, IRS Valuation Training for Appeals Officers (CCH 1998) 1-12, 1-13. See also Estate of True v. Comm'r, 82 TCM (CCH) 27 (2001).

[41] If there is no comparable publicly traded asset, the class of permissible comparables can expand. See Estate of Jann v. Comm'r, 60 TCM (CCH) 23 (1990) (no comparable publicly traded company in the same line of business as the subject corporation, so publicly traded companies in similar lines of businesses were taken into consideration); Estate of Heck v. Comm'r, 83 TCM (CCH) 1181 (2002) (since no adequate comparables for winery, income approach adopted). In *Heck*, the court stated "As similarity to the company to be valued decreases, the number of required comparables increases in order to minimize the risk that the results will be distorted by attributes unique to each of the guideline companies." Id. at __.

[42] See infra ¶ 4.02[4][d].

several grocery stores. Although the expert considered comparable grocery store chains in computing the value of the decedent's stock, the expert failed to take into account the local economies relevant to the subject corporation and the increased competition in those economies.[43]

[iii] **Asset-based (cost) approach.** The "asset-based approach" (sometimes called the "cost approach") is more suitable for holding companies and other non-income-producing assets that have no reliable comparables with known values.[44] The asset-based approach simply aggregates and nets the value of underlying assets and liabilities.[45] If the subject property represents an interest in several assets, the multiple valuation necessarily becomes more difficult, being based on multiple valuations of underlying assets.

[iv] **Combinations.** It is quite common for an appraisal to consider a variety of valuation approaches. The relative weight of each approach should vary according to the nature of the subject property. For example, in one case,[46] the gross estate included a 25.235 percent interest in a limited partnership that owned an apartment complex. The court used both the income approach and the net asset approach to value the apartment complex, but weighed the income approach more heavily (75 percent) than the net asset approach (25 percent).[47]

---

[43] Estate of Brookshire v. Comm'r, 76 TCM (CCH) 659 (1998).

[44] Estate of Ford v. Comm'r, 66 TCM (CCH) 1507 (1993), aff'd, 53 F3d 924 (8th Cir. 1995) (investment assets held by a corporation); Estate of Jameson v. Comm'r, 77 TCM (CCH) 1383 (1999) (net asset value of timber property held by a corporation), vacated and remanded on other grounds, 267 F3d 366 (5th Cir. 2001).

[45] The net asset value generally does not take into account liquidation costs and taxes. Estate of Dunn v. Comm'r, 79 TCM (CCH) 1337 (2000) (net asset value represents the aggregate, pre-liquidation asset values, not after-tax values). But see Estate of Jephson v. Comm'r, 87 TC 297 (1986) (government allowed reduction for liquidation costs where liquidation was imminent); infra ¶ 4.02[4][e][iii].

[46] Estate of Weinberg v. Comm'r, 79 TCM (CCH) 1507 (2000).

[47] From this computation, the court then applied the minority and marketability discounts discussed infra ¶¶ 4.02[4][c], 4.02[4][d]. The court also rejected the Service's argument that no weight should be given to the building's net asset value because the decedent's limited partnership interest restricted the decedent's ability to compel sale of the building. Estate of Weinberg v. Comm'r, 79 TCM (CCH) 1507, 1515 (2000).

See also Estate of Dunn v. Comm'r, 79 TCM (CCH) 1337 (2000) (stock in heavy equipment rental company properly valued by weighting income approach at 35 percent and net asset value appraoch at 65 percent); Estate of Smith v. Comm'r, 78 TCM (CCH) 745 (1999) (value of stock in corporation that owned and operated a farm based 70 percent on net asset value approach and 30 percent on income approach because the corporation served as both a holding company for valuable property and a going concern).

[c] Valuation Determined by Agreements

Closely held business owners often enter into agreements that spell out the consequences of an owner's retirement, withdrawal, expulsion, death, disability, or other event leading to the transfer of an ownership interest. These "buy-sell" agreements typically require the exiting owner to offer the ownership interest to be transferred to the other owners at a price determined under the agreement. In some cases, the agreement provides a fixed price for the ownership interest, but in most cases, the agreement contains a formula for valuing the ownership interest. Section 2703 generally provides that for estate, gift, and generation-skipping transfer tax valuation purposes, buy-sell agreements will not be considered in the valuation of property unless certain statutory tests are met.[48] Even where the buy-sell agreement survives Section 2703[49] and is taken into consideration, various factors may cause a court to discount or disregard the agreement's stated price.

Where Section 2703 is inapplicable and the buy-sell agreement is negotiated at arm's length between unrelated owners, courts have given considerable deference to the valuation method contained in the agreement because the parties are involved in a bona fide arm's length agreement.[50] The exiting owner will usually want the highest possible valuation, and the other owners will likely want the lowest possible valuation. In these cases, it is fair to assume that the agreed formula represents a compromise between the parties whose interests are economically adverse to one another.

Section 2703 is more likely to be applicable and courts are more apt to discount the formula price contained in a buy-sell agreement where the parties are related,[51] where there is evidence that the owners did not negotiate the formula at arm's length,[52] or where the formula is simply unreasonable given

---

[48] IRC § 2703(a). Section 2703 was enacted in 1990 as part of the Omnibus Budget Reconciliation Act of 1990, Pub. L. No. 101-508, § 11602(a), 104 Stat. 1388-1, 1388-498 (1990), reprinted in 1991-2 CB 481, 528. Section 2703 does not apply to buy-sell agreements applicable before enactment. For a discussion of such pre-1990 agreements, see Stephens, Maxfield, Lind & Calfee, Federal Estate and Gift Taxation, ¶¶ 4.08[9], 4.02[3][g] (Warren, Gorham & Lamont, 6th ed. 1991). See Estate of True v. Comm'r, 82 TCM (CCH) 27 (2001) (recent lengthy rejection of a pre-1990 buy-sell agreement).

[49] See ¶ 19.04[6].

[50] See, e.g., Gloeckner v. Comm'r, 152 F3d 208 (2d Cir. 1998); Cartwright v. United States, 457 F2d 567, 571 (2d Cir. 1972), aff'd, 411 US 546 (1973); Fiorito v. Comm'r, 33 TC 440 (1959).

[51] Bommer Revocable Trust v. Comm'r, 74 TCM (CCH) 346 (1997) (buy-sell agreement disregarded in valuing stock because agreement was held to be a device to transfer decedent's stock to beneficiaries for less than full consideration). Cf. Reg. § 25.2703-1(a)(3).

[52] Estate of Lauder v. Comm'r, 64 TCM (CCH) 1643 (1992) valuation fixed by buy-sell agreement disregarded in part because there was no evidence that owners negotiated the valuation formula to be used upon death or termination). Cf. IRC § 2703(b).

recent developments in the business. Furthermore, no respect is afforded to unilateral restrictions imposed by the decedent or transferor.[53] Section 2703 and agreements which pass muster under Section 2703 are considered in detail later in the treatise.[54]

[3] Basic Valuation Approaches to Property Interests

[a] Tangible Personal Property

Most decedents leave behind a number of miscellaneous personal effects—televisions, lamps, area rugs, and the like. Generally, each item should be valued separately,[55] although the nuisance of this rule is partially alleviated by the Treasury's willingness to accept a single value for a group of items (provided each is of relatively small value) or a single, unitemized figure given by an expert appraiser.[56] The value of personal property generally is determined with reference to the retail price at which the item would sell to the general public.[57] The detail required in preparing an inventory of household and personal effects, a headache for the casual personal representative, is a fairly routine matter for professional and other experienced personal representatives. Where an item's primary value lies in its utility to the owner (a bed's value typically is based on keeping the owner off a hard floor at night), the range of possible values is fairly limited and not subject to much controversy. But a work of art, by nature, often has a wide range of values, depending upon the beholder. Consequently, any such item with a value in excess of $3,000

---

[53] Citizens Bank & Trust Co. v. Comm'r, 839 F2d 1249 (7th Cir. 1988) (court rejected a 90 percent discount claimed because the subject property was held in an irrevocable trust with a ninety-seven-year term).

[54] See ¶ 19.04.

[55] Ownership of furniture and personal items may be uncertain. Some may be owned by a surviving spouse or may be merely on loan from relatives. Records should be kept regarding the ownership of items such as valuable antiques and paintings. Here, of course, includability in the decedent's gross estate is simply assumed.

[56] See Reg. § 20.2031-6(a). Appraisal usually entails relatively small cost, saves much time and effort, and may help avoid controversy. Although where the property value is relatively small and the property qualifies for the marital deduction, the likelihood of controversy is slight.

[57] Reg. § 20.2031-1(b). See also Goldberg, "Fair Market Value in the Tax Law: Replacement Value or Liquidation Value?" 60 Tex. L. Rev. 833 (1982).

must be listed separately and supported with an appraisal from a competent professional,[58] and valuation disputes over works of art are common.[59]

[b] Real Property

Generally, real property is valued according to "the highest and best use of the property" on the valuation date.[60] This rule causes the focus to shift away from the owner's actual use of the property and toward the objectively reasonable possible uses.[61] Thus, for example, if an orange grove worth $2,000 an acre as such could be sold for $5,000 an acre for use as a residential subdivision, its value would be $5,000 an acre for estate tax purposes.[62] While a parcel will be valued at its highest and best use, courts are hesitant to assume away any zoning changes that would be required to make the highest and best use of the subject property.[63] Indeed, courts will discount the value of real property by the costs that an owner would incur in converting the parcel to its highest and best use, including costs of rezoning the property.[64]

The assessed value of real property for local tax purposes is given little weight in computing fair market value[65] unless the assessed value bears a

---

[58] Reg. § 20.2031-6(b). The regulation lists the items most likely affected by this requirement as "jewelry, furs, silverware, paintings, etchings, engravings, antiques, books, statuary, vases, oriental rugs, [and] coin or stamp collections." Id.

[59] See Estate of O'Keeffe v. Comm'r, 63 TCM (CCH) 2669 (1992); Estate of Smith v. Comm'r, 57 TCM (CCH) 650 (1972), aff'd on other grounds, 510 F2d 479 (2d Cir. 1975) (estate initially valued decedent's metal sculptures at $714,000, but the Service ultimately contended that the value was over $5.2 million—the court fixed the value at $2.7 million); Estate of Scull v. Comm'r, 67 TCM (CCH) 2953 (1994) (different valuation methods used for different pieces of art in a collection). For a more comprehensive discussion, see Lerner, "Valuing Works of Art for Tax Purposes," 28 Real Prop. Prob. & Trust J. 593 (1993).

[60] Estate of Lloyd v. Comm'r, 71 TCM (CCH) 1903 (1996); Estate of Mitchell v. Comm'r, 27 TCM (CCH) 1568 (1968); Flanders v. United States, 347 F. Supp. 95 (ND Cal. 1972).

[61] Estate of Lloyd v. Comm'r, 71 TCM (CCH) 1903 (1996); Estate of Trenchard v. Comm'r, 69 TCM (CCH) 2164, 2169 (1995).

[62] However, if the personal representative can and does elect Section 2032A, the highest and best use of the property will, to some extent, give way to actual use value. See ¶ 4.04.

[63] Estate of Ratcliffe v. Comm'r, 63 TCM (CCH) 3068 (1992).

[64] Estate of Busch v. Comm'r, 79 TCM (CCH) 1276 (2000) (allowing discount for anticipated delays in developing subject property because of evidence that area residents would resist development plans contemplated at decedent's death); Estate of Spruill v. Comm'r, 88 TC 1197 (1987) (5 percent discount for rezoning costs and for negative effect of two homes on the subject property).

[65] Reg. 20.2031-1(b). See Estate of Sochalski v. Comm'r, 14 TCM (CCH) 72 (1955).

fixed, known relationship to the fair market value of the property.[66] Instead, an appraisal is necessary for all parcels and interests included in the gross estate. As seen before, courts will give greater weight to professional appraisals than mere guesses and will often choose between competing appraisers' values or select a mid-range value.[67] The appraisal should consider all of the following factors—and perhaps others, if relevant—in valuing the subject property:

1. Recent attempts to dispose of the property,[68] perhaps including offers made after death;[69]
2. Sales of similar property nearby;[70]
3. The condition of the property;[71]

---

[66] Estate of Cary v. Comm'r, 7 TCM (CCH) 731 (1948).

[67] See Estate of Dowlin v. Comm'r, 67 TCM (CCH) 2750 (1994) (court discounted value of personal residence based on the residence's condition, the fact that it had only a two-car garage and no swimming pool—unlike comparable parcels—and the fact that the personal representative obtained a $200,000 personal loan secured by the residence). See also Estate of Sharp v. Comm'r, 68 TCM (CCH) 1521 (1994) (court determined between appraisers' values); Estate of Dougherty v. Comm'r, 59 TCM (CCH) 772 (1990) (testimony of Service's appraiser—decedent's son—was more credible that of the appraiser testifying for the estate); Estate of Frieders v. Comm'r, 40 TCM (CCH) 403 (1980); Estate of Vinson v. Comm'r, 22 TCM (CCH) 280 (1963) (taxpayer's appraisal adopted).

[68] Estate of Wilson, 5 BTA 615 (1926), acq. VI-1 CB 6. Cf. Rev. Rul. 80-319, 1980-2 CB 252 (property was subject to a contract of sale, which was reduced by points the seller was required to absorb under the contract). But see Estate of Jennings v. Comm'r, 35 TCM (CCH) 688 (1976).

[69] Estate of Bond v. Comm'r, 25 TCM (CCH) 115 (1966); Estate of Mitchell v. Comm'r, 74 TCM (CCH) 872 (1997) (court considered both an offer to purchase a business made several months before the decedent's death and an alleged offer following decedent's death), rev'd, 250 F3d 696 (9th Cir. 2001) (Tax Court failed to adequately explain rationale for its valuation conclusion).

[70] Estate of Pattison v. Comm'r, 60 TCM (CCH) 471 (1990) (court rejected taxpayer's appraisal, which found the highest and best use of the subject property to be for agricultural pursuits, for failing to consider the parcel's location was across the street from a residential development; court accepted Service's appraisal using comparable sales of nearby parcels). See Crane v. Comm'r, 49 TC 85 (1967), acq., 1968-2 CB 2; Jones v. Comm'r, 25 TCM (CCH) 1066 (1996); Estate of Whitt v. Comm'r, 46 TCM (CCH) 118 (1983), aff'd on other grounds, 751 F2d 1548 (11th Cir. 1985); Morris v. Comm'r, 761 F2d 1195 (6th Cir. 1985). See Rev. Proc. 79-24, 1979-1 CB 565, for a detailed discussion of factors.

[71] Estate of Necastro v. Comm'r, 68 TCM (CCH) 227 (1994) (environmental damage reduced value of property); Estate of Lloyd v. Comm'r, 71 TCM (CCH) 1903 (1996) (reduced value due to topography and limited road access). See also Estate of Brown v. Comm'r, 28 TCM (CCH) 497 (1969), aff'd per curiam, 425 F2d 1406 (5th Cir. 1970). For more on the effects of environmental hazards on the value of real estate, see Lewandrowski, "Toxic Blackacre: Appraisal Techniques & Current Trends in Valuation," 5 Alb. Law J. Sci. & Tech. 55 (1994).

4. Assessed value for local tax purposes, assuming the relationship between assessed value and fair market value is ascertainable;[72]

5. The existence of an outstanding lease for a term of years that may either depress[73] or increase[74] the value of the decedent's interest in the property;

6. The amount of a nonrecourse mortgage loan secured by the property;[75]

7. A capitalization of current rentals;[76]

8. The prospect of proposed favorable or unfavorable zoning changes;[77]

9. The existence of easements on the property;[78]

10. The price of a post-death sale of the subject property,[79] absent evidence of changes in value after death;[80]

11. Any cloud on the property's title or other associated legal risks;[81]

12. The decedent's interest in the real property;[82] and

13. The highest and best use of the property, including any special uses for which the property may be realistically suited.[83]

Most certainly, these thirteen factors are not intended as an exhaustive list of considerations that might apply in valuing real property. As with any asset in-

[72] Estate of Cary v. Comm'r, 7 TCM (CCH) 731 (1948).

[73] Estate of Proctor v. Comm'r, 67 TCM (CCH) 2943 (1994); Estate of Barry v. Comm'r, 15 TCM (CCH) 502 (1956). Cf. Estate of Edwards v. Comm'r, 82 TCM (CCH) 471 (2001) (no depression in value because no proof leases existed).

[74] Van Dyke v. Kuhl, 78 F. Supp. 698 (ED Wis. 1945).

[75] Reg. § 20.2053-7. See ¶ 5.03[6].

[76] Van Dyke v. Kuhl, 78 F. Supp. 698 (ED Wis. 1945).

[77] Compare Estate of Wolfe v. Comm'r, 13 TCM (CCH) 22 (1954) with Knoell v. United States, 236 F. Supp. 299 (WD Pa. 1964).

[78] Estate of Vinson v. Comm'r, 22 TCM (CCH) 280 (1963).

[79] See First Nat'l Bank of Kenosha v. United States, 763 F2d 891 (7th Cir. 1985); Cobb v. Comm'r, 49 TCM (CCH) 1364 (1985); Estate of Keller v. Comm'r, 41 TCM (CCH) 147 (1980); Estate of Ballas v. Comm'r, 34 TCM (CCH) 506 (1975).

[80] See Estate of Keitel v. Comm'r, 60 TCM (CCH) 425 (1990); Estate of Hillebrandt v. Comm'r, 52 TCM (CCH) 1059 (1986); Estate of Ridgely v. United States, 1967-2 USTC ¶ 12,481 (Ct. Cl. 1967); Estate of Loewenstein v. Comm'r, 17 TC 60 (1951), acq., 1951-2 CB 3; Estate of Spruill v. Comm'r, 88 TC 1197 (1987).

[81] Estate of Sharp v. Comm'r, 68 TCM (CCH) 1521 (1994).

[82] For the applicability of minority interest and fractional interest discounts, see infra ¶¶ 4.02[4][c], 4.02[4][e][i].

[83] Again, however, attention should be given to the possibility of a Section 2032A election, if available. See ¶ 4.04.

cluded in the gross estate, the valuation is affected by all factors that would influence the hypothetical willing buyer and the hypothetical willing seller.[84]

[c] Publicly Traded Securities

While artwork and real estate frequently pose valuation problems, publicly traded securities—typically held in a brokerage account—usually pose few, if any, problems for the personal representative.[85] Because of the ready market for such securities, value is usually ascertainable with reference to accessible reports of actual market transactions.[86] Indeed, the regulations state that the fair market value of marketable securities is "the mean between the highest and the lowest quoted selling prices on the valuation date."[87] If no trades occurred on the valuation date, Treasury requires the personal representative to use a weighted average of the mean trade figures for dates before and after the valuation date.[88] If there are no actual trades close to the valuation

---

[84] See Estate of Lloyd v. Comm'r, 71 TCM (CCH) 1903 (1996) (court reduced the value of the subject property to take into account its difficult topography and limited road access available to make the highest and best use—in this case, commercial—of the property); Estate of Sirmans v. Comm'r, 73 TCM (CCH) 2846 (1997) (court considered several facts in computing the value of 56.5 acres of Florida land, including environmentally-sensitive wetlands on the property, a condemnation proceeding affecting five acres, and several appraisals on the property performed for different purposes).

[85] If the securities serve as collateral for a third-party loan, this fact will likely reduce the value of the securities. Estate of Hall v. Comm'r, 46 TCM (CCH) 479 (1983).

[86] Actual market transactions may reflect the value of some intangibles other than stocks or bonds, such as options, puts, calls, and commodity futures contracts; indeed, some fungible tangibles, such as eggs, soybeans, and pork bellies, can sometimes be valued with reference to quoted market prices.

[87] Reg. § 20.2031-2(b)(1). See Rev. Rul. 68-272, 1968-1 CB 394 (the mean price is used even though the security may sell only in fractional amounts). In most cases, the "valuation date" will be the date of death, although the alternate valuation date six months later may be elected. IRC §§ 2031(a), 2032. See ¶ 4.03.

Suppose that a U.S. citizen dies in Zurich, Switzerland, at 4:00 AM on April 1. In all time zones in the United States, it is technically March 31. The Treasury takes the position that the measurement date for purposes of this regulation is based on the time of the decedent's death at the decedent's domicile. Rev. Rul. 74-424, 1974-2 CB 294; Rev. Rul. 66-85, 1966-1 CB 213. Thus, if the decedent were domiciled in Zurich, the measurement date would be April 1. If the decedent were domiciled in the United States (on vacation in Zurich), the measuring date would be March 31. Similarly, if a California resident dies in San Francisco on April 1 at 10:00 PM, when it is April 2 for purposes of New York Stock Exchange quotations, the probable result is that the date of the decedent's death is the date of death in the decedent's domicile, California.

[88] The approach is described in Regulations Sections 20.2031-2(b)(2) and 20.2031-2(b)(3). See Rev. Proc. 84-17, 1984-1 CB 432, for similar methods used to value trust funds.

date, the personal representative can resort to taking the mean between the bid and asked prices for the securities on the valuation date.[89]

When the gross estate includes a large number of shares in one corporation's publicly traded stock, a blockage discount may come into play.[90] At this point, the mechanical formulas in the regulations give way to the expert appraisal.[91] Of course, other discounts may also apply.[92]

[d] Open- and Closed-End Funds

Investors frequently seek to diversify their investments through the purchase of shares in investment companies or mutual funds. The fund investor generally has no influence over the securities purchased and sold by a fund; those decisions are left to the fund's managers. But the expertise of the fund's managers is one of the attractions for these funds, along with owning a slice of the fund's investment portfolio. The estate tax valuation issues for these funds depend upon the nature of the investment company.

So-called closed-end funds have a fixed number of shares outstanding and are traded on stock exchanges. Closed-end funds tend to have specialized portfolios, limiting their investments to certain types of securities. Because the shares in closed-end funds are easily traded on an established market, the estate tax value is the mean between the highest and lowest selling prices on the valuation date, just as in the case of any other publicly traded security.[93]

An open-end fund, by contrast, constantly issues new shares to purchasers. Open-end funds also stand ready to redeem their outstanding shares at net asset value. Usually, shares in open-end funds are not traded on stock exchanges. There are two types of open-end funds: "no-load" funds, which impose no fee to purchase or redeem shares, and "load" funds, which impose fees upon purchase, redemption, or both.

---

[89] Reg. § 20.2031-2(c). See also Reg. §§ 20.2031-2(d), 20.2031-2(e), 20.2031-2(f) for even more indirect valuation methods.

[90] See infra ¶ 4.02[4][e][ii].

[91] See infra ¶ 4.02[4][e] note 207.

[92] See infra ¶ 4.02[4][e][iv] regarding possible application of securities laws discounts. Neither a minority discount or a marketability discount is an applicable discount for marketable securities. But where the decedent merely owns an interest in a nonmarketable entity that holds marketable securities, the marketability discount may also apply. See infra ¶¶ 4.02[4][c], 4.02[4][d].

[93] See supra ¶ 4.02[2][c]. In the market, closed-end funds tend to sell at a discount from their net asset value because of the perception that managers of closed-end funds are less responsive to considering other profitable investments, unlike the managers of open-ended funds. Barron's Downs and Goodman, Dictionary of Finance and Investment Terms (Barron's, 5th ed. 1998).

Estate tax valuation of no-load funds is not especially problematic. Because the shares are always purchased and redeemed at net asset value, the net asset value provides an easy mechanism for valuation. Load funds present more complex issues. In a "front-load" fund, for example, the investor pays a premium (usually between 3 and 9 percent of net asset value) to acquire shares. The shares are then redeemed at net asset value, as no additional charge is imposed. The Service originally argued that estate tax valuation of load funds should be based on replacement cost, which of course would include the premium required to purchase a number of shares equal to the number of shares included in the gross estate. But personal representatives argued that the redemption price (net asset value without any premium) was a more proper measure of the wealth transferred at death. In *Cartwright v. United States*,[94] the Supreme Court properly embraced the taxpayer view for reasons expressed at some length in an earlier edition of this book.[95] Load funds are thus valued at the redemption price.

[e] Bonds

Corporate bonds that are traded actively are valued in the same manner as stock.[96] The marketplace values such bonds with an eye to the financial position of the obligor, the interest rate paid, the date of maturity, and sometimes, the bonds' convertibility into stock. Except for convertibility, government bonds that are actively traded are accorded their marketplace value, which is determined in the same manner as other securities. One type of government bond, however, was valued differently. So-called "federal redeemable bonds" or "flower bonds" could be submitted at par value in payment of federal estate taxes and, for that reason, they were valued at par to the extent they could be so used.[97] However, such bonds are no longer issued and all have matured.[98]

---

[94] Cartwright v. United States, 411 US 546 (1973).

[95] See Stephens, Maxfield & Lind, Federal Estate and Gift Taxation, ¶¶ 4.10–4.12 (Warren, Gorham & Lamont, 3d ed. 1974).

[96] Reg. § 20.2031-2(b). See supra ¶ 4.02[3][c]. For a consideration of the valuation of untraded bonds in closely held businesses, see Reg. § 20.2031-2(f)(1) and infra ¶ 4.02[3][f] note 101.

[97] Such bonds are discussed in detail in Stephens, Maxfield, Lind & Calfee, Federal Estate and Gift Taxation, ¶ 4.02[3][e] text accompanying notes 68–71 (Warren, Gorham & Lamont 7th ed. 1996).

[98] Bonds that were issued after March 3, 1971 could not be used to pay federal estate taxes. See IRC § 6312, prior to repeal by an Act, Pub. L. No. 92-5, § 4(a)(2), 85 Stat. 5 (1971), reprinted in 1971-1 CB 553. All such bonds have now matured.

Some types of federal government bonds are nontransferable (and therefore are not traded on the market) and may merely be redeemed.[99] In general, their redemption value at the date of the decedent's death establishes their estate tax value. Series G and K U.S. Savings Bonds, if held by the owner for six months, may be redeemed at par and generally, therefore, their estate tax value is their par value.[100]

Series E U.S. Savings Bonds can be redeemed at gradually increasing prices prior to their maturity date; they are purchased at a discount and the increase reflects interest. If held beyond maturity, they pay interest at 6 percent semiannually and, after maturity, are redeemable at par. Whether held to maturity or not, their estate tax value is their redemption value at the date of decedent's death.

[f] Closely Held Corporations

Valuation is especially significant when the asset is an equity ownership interest[101] in a closely held business. In the absence of a public market, stock in a corporation is valued by reference to many factors. The regulations state only that the value of such stock is to be determined with reference to "the company's net worth, prospective earning power and dividend paying capacity, and other relevant factors."[102] Almost fifty years ago, the Service issued Reve-

---

[99] These include U.S. Savings Bonds. For a discussion of transferability of ownership of U.S. Savings Bonds, see discussion of Section 2040 at ¶ 4.12[2].

[100] Rev. Rul. 55-301, 1955-1 CB 242. If bonds are redeemable at par at death, but at a lower figure if notice of death is not given and redemption is delayed (which sometimes happens with Series G and K U.S. Savings Bonds), par value should be used for estate tax purposes. But compare Estate of Brown v. Comm'r, 21 TCM (CCH) 1321 (1962), and Estate of Haupfuhrer v. Comm'r, 9 TCM (CCH) 974 (1950), aff'd on another issue, 195 F2d 548 (3d Cir.), cert. denied, 344 US 825 (1952) (par value used) with Collins v. Comm'r, 216 F2d 519 (1st Cir. 1954) (employing a lower value). The *Collins* opinion seems to put misplaced reliance on the fact that the bonds were not *required* to be redeemed at death; but note that shares of stock need not be *sold* at death, either. See also United States v. Simmons, 346 F2d 213 (5th Cir. 1965).

[101] Where the decedent owned a debt obligation of a closely held business, the regulations generally indicate that the value of bonds in close corporations is to be arrived at by giving consideration to "the soundness of the security, the interest yield, the date of maturity, and other relevant factors." Reg. § 20.2031-2(f)(1). A question may arise whether such bonds are in substance stock to determine various income tax consequences. Gooding Amusement Co. v. Comm'r, 236 F2d 159 (6th Cir. 1956). Even though a purported bond may in substance be stock for income tax purposes, it should nevertheless still be considered a bond for estate tax valuation purposes. Under the vague criteria of the regulations, all the factors that caused it to be labeled as stock under the income tax will be considered in determining its estate tax value.

[102] Reg. § 20.2031-2(f)(2).

nue Ruling 55-60[103] to provide more comprehensive guidance in valuing closely held stock. This ruling continues to be the seminal authority for valuing closely held corporations that actively conduct a trade or business. In the ruling, the Service lists eight factors to consider in valuing the closely held business:

(a) The nature of the business and the history of the enterprise from its inception;[104]

(b) The economic outlook in general and the condition and outlook of the specific industry in particular;[105]

(c) The book value of the stock and the financial condition of the business;[106]

(d) The earning capacity of the company;[107]

(e) The dividend-paying capacity;[108]

---

[103] 1959-1 CB 237.

[104] This factor is discussed in more detail in Revenue Ruling 59-60, § 4.02(a), 1959-1 CB 237, 239. See also Estate of Lauder v. Comm'r, 68 TCM (CCH) 985, 987 (1994); Estate of Smith v. Comm'r, 9 TCM (CCH) 907 (1950); Holrick v. Kuhl, 62 F. Supp. 168 (ED Wis. 1945); Holmes v. Comm'r, 22 BTA 757, acq. X-1 CB 29 (1931). For guidelines applicable to the radio and television broadcasting business, see Rev. Proc. 75-39, 1975-2 CB 569.

[105] This factor is discussed in more detail in Revenue Ruling 59-60, § 4.02(b), 1959-1 CB 237, 239. See also Estate of Newhouse v. Comm'r, 94 TC 193 (1990), acq., 1991-1 CB 1; Estate of Titus v. Comm'r, 57 TCM (CCH) 1449 (1989); Zanuck v. Comm'r, 149 F2d 714 (9th Cir. 1945); Bishop Trust Co. v. United States, 1950-1 USTC ¶ 10,764 (D. Hawaii 1950).

[106] This factor is discussed in more detail in Revenue Ruling 59-60, § 4.02(c), 1959-1 CB 237, 240. See also Estate of Lauder v. Comm'r, 68 TCM (CCH) 985, 997 (1994); Estate of Hogan v. Comm'r, 3 TCM (CCH) 315 (1944); True v. United States, 51 F. Supp. 720 (1943); Brooks v. Willcuts, 78 F2d 270 (8th Cir. 1935). But see Estate of Maxcy v. Comm'r, 28 TCM (CCH) 783 (1969), rev'd on other grounds, 441 F2d 192 (5th Cir. 1971).

[107] This factor is discussed in more detail in Revenue Ruling 59-60, § 4.02(d), 1959-1 CB 237, 240. See also Estate of Dooly v. Comm'r, 31 TCM (CCH) 814 (1972); Harrison v. Comm'r, 17 TCM (CCH) 776 (1958); Wishon v. Anglim, 42 F. Supp. 359 (ND Cal. 1941); Laird v. Comm'r, 38 BTA 926 (1938), acq. and nonacq. 1939-1 CB 20, 53.

[108] This factor is discussed in more detail in Revenue Ruling 59-60, § 4.02(e), 1959-1 CB 237, 241. See also Poley Estate v. Comm'r, 6 TCM (CCH) 288 (1947), aff'd per curiam, 166 F2d 434 (3d Cir. 1948); Estate of Cook v. Comm'r, 9 TC 563 (1947), acq. 1947-2 CB 2; Northern Trust Co. v. Comm'r, 87 TC 349 (1986). But see Driver v. United States, 76-1 USTC ¶ 13,155 (WD Wis. 1976) (lack of dividends unimportant because compensation in close corporation is taken in other ways); Estate of Hogan v. Comm'r, 3 TCM (CCH) 315 (1944) (consideration of dividend payments improper for valuing stock in highly competitive business); Estate of Smith v. Comm'r, 78 TCM (CCH) 745 (1999) (dividend paying capacity not ignored in valuing corporation).

(f) Whether or not the enterprise has goodwill or other intangible value;[109]

(g) Sales of the stock and the size of the block of stock to be valued;[110]

(h) The market price of stocks of corporations engaged in the same or a similar line of business having their stocks actively traded in a free and open market, either on an exchange or over the counter.[111]

The ruling states that the weight of each factor varies according to each particular corporation,[112] and the Tax Court agrees, refusing to ascribe a fixed weight to any one factor.[113] Sometimes the courts have modified the factors as needed.[114]

Closely held partnerships and limited liability companies that conduct an active trade or business activity are valued in the same manner as active closely held corporations.[115] Where the rights and obligations of partners in a partnership or the members of a limited liability company differ from those of shareholders in a corporation, some variation in valuation is justified.[116]

---

[109] This factor is discussed in more detail in Revenue Ruling 59-60, § 4.02(f), 1959-1 CB 237, 241. See Rev. Rul. 65-193, 1965-2 CB 370, Rev. Rul. 68-609, 1968-2 CB 327 (both modifying § 4.02(f) of Revenue Ruling 59-60).

[110] This factor is discussed in more detail in Revenue Ruling 59-60, § 4.02(g), 1959-1 CB 237, 241. See First Nat'l Bank of Fort Smith v. United States, 85-2 USTC ¶ 13,627 (WD Ark. 1985) (sale of 2 percent of stock sixteen months before decedent's death). This factor may be subsequently adjusted for discounts and premiums. See infra ¶ 4.02[4].

[111] This factor is discussed in more detail in Revenue Ruling 59-60, § 4.02(h), 1959-1 CB 237, 242. This factor responds to the requirements of Section 2031(b) and Regulations Section 20.2031-2(f). See generally Estate of Hall v. Comm'r, 92 TC 312 (1989); Estate of Stoddard v. Comm'r, 34 TCM (CCH) 888 (1975); Estate of Ewing v. Comm'r, 9 TCM (CCH) 1096 (1950); Estate of Webb v. Comm'r, 3 TCM (CCH) 440 (1944).

Because publicly traded companies tend to be larger in size, one should not blindly apply the price-earnings ratios of comparable publicly traded companies to the closely held stock under examination. Estate of Smith v. Comm'r, 78 TCM (CCH) 745 (1999).

[112] Rev. Rul. 59-60, § 5, 1959-1 CB 237, 242.

[113] Estate of Andrews v. Comm'r, 79 TC 938 (1982); Messing v. Comm'r, 48 TC 502 (1967).

[114] Mandelbaum v. Comm'r, 69 TCM (CCH) 2852 (1995) (factors modified to determine discount for lack of marketability). See infra ¶ 4.02[4][d] note 186.

[115] See Moore v. Comm'r, 62 TCM (CCH) 1128 (1991).

[116] In Adams v. United States, 99-1 USTC (CCH) 60,340 (ND Tex. 1999), rev'd, 218 F3d 383 (5th Cir. 2000), the district court denied a minority interest discount in valuing the decedent's 25 percent partnership interest asserting that under state law the decedent's death caused the partnership to dissolve and entitled the estate as an assignee to have the right to obtain up to 25 percent of the partnership's assets. The court nonetheless found the strict fiduciary duties of the other partners to the hypothetical buyer prevented any discount. The Fifth Circuit reversed and remanded the case finding that it was not well established that a partner's assignee has a right to receive his proportionate share of the partnership's net asset value. On remand, the District Court applied substantial discounts

[g] Notes

Notes and similar contractual obligations representing amounts owed to the decedent are includable in the gross estate[117] and valued according to the hypothetical willing seller, willing buyer concept.[118] Interest rates and dates of maturity affect their valuation.[119] Accrued interest on such obligations is treated as separate property to be separately stated and valued on the estate tax return.[120] However, the regulations provide that notes owed to the decedent are included in the gross estate at their face amount, or in the amount of unpaid principal, unless the personal representative establishes that the value is lower or that the notes are worthless.[121] This provision in the regulations is intended to encompass all types of notes, including personal debts,[122] obligations under a mortgage,[123] installment sales notes,[124] and mere payments to be made under a contract.[125]

A personal representative, who has the burden of proof in such situations,[126] can establish that an obligation has a value lower than its face amount in several ways. For instance, if the debtor is insolvent, the obligation may be

---

for minority interest, portfolio, and marketability discounts. Adams v. United States, 88 AFTR2d 2001-6057 (ND Tex. 2001).

[117] When the obligation is formal, the estate will likely not succeed in arguing that the decedent intended a gift, meaning that the decedent owned no right to any amount at death. This is a Section 2033 issue. See Estate of Hamlin v. Comm'r, 9 TC 676 (1947); Estate of Hodge v. Comm'r, 2 TC 643 (1943), acq., 1943 CB 11.

[118] Recall that the fair market value "is not to be determined by a forced sales price." Reg. § 20.2031-1(b). See Estate of Frank v. Comm'r, 69 TCM (CCH) 2255 (1995); Eleanor Lansburgh v. Comm'r, 35 BTA 928 (1937), nonacq. 1937-2 CB 43, withdrawn and acq., 1943 CB 14.

[119] See Estate of Hamlin v. Comm'r, 9 TC 676 (1947) (Service and taxpayer agreed on a commuted value for an interest-free note).

[120] Reg. § 20.2031-4; Estate of Sharp v. Comm'r, 68 TCM (CCH) 1521 (1994).

[121] Reg. § 20.2031-4. See Smith v. United States, 923 F. Supp. 896 (SD Miss. 1996) (lower valuation upheld because note not easily tradeable and maker never formally acknowledged liability); Estate of Hoffman v. Comm'r, 81 TCM (CCH) 1588 (2001) (notes bore interest below normal market rate); Estate of M.R. Cross v. Comm'r, 5 BTA 621 (1926); Estate of C.W. Goodin v. Comm'r, 8 BTA 1277 (1927), acq. VII-2 CB 15; Rev. Rul. 76-112, 1976-1 CB 276.

[122] Estate of Hamlin v. Comm'r, 9 TC 676 (1947).

[123] Estate of Low v. Comm'r, 2 TC 1114 (1943), nonacq. 1944 CB 43, aff'd per curiam, 145 F2d 832 (2d Cir. 1945); Rev. Rul. 67-276, 1967-2 CB 321.

[124] Gump v. Comm'r, 124 F2d 540 (9th Cir. 1941), cert. denied, 316 US 697 (1942).

[125] Estate of H.F. Hammon v. Comm'r, 10 BTA 43 (1928), acq. VII-1 CB 13.

[126] Mulliken v. Magruder, 55 F. Supp. 895 (D. Md. 1944), aff'd on another issue, 149 F2d 593 (4th Cir. 1945).

worthless[127] or its value limited to the value of property held as security for the debt.[128] In one case, the insolvent debtor, a beneficiary of the estate, became solvent by way of bequests from the decedent. Nevertheless, the court concluded that in valuing the note, the debtor's affluence, by reason of the decedent's death, was not to be considered.[129] The court limited the value of the notes in the decedent's estate to the value of the assets held as security, plus the net worth of the debtor prior to any bequests from the decedent. However, in an income tax case,[130] the court held that in valuing notes for basis purposes under Section 1014, the debtor's intestate share of the decedent's estate was to be included in his net worth to determine his solvency. The notes were valued at their face amount. The prior approach is preferable because the emphasis of the federal estate tax is on the amount of wealth the decedent *could* pass on, a question that is unaffected by the fact that a debtor is also a beneficiary.[131] Likewise, if a statute of limitations bars procedures to collect the obligation, it may have no value[132] or it may be limited in value to the collateral securing the obligation.[133] A debtor's discharge in bankruptcy has about the same effect as the running of a statutory limitation period.[134] Controversy regarding liability to pay an asserted obligation is certainly relevant; in such cases, the likelihood of success in litigation is a factor in valuing the obligation.[135] However, value should be determined on the applicable date of valuation and should not be dependent on subsequent recoveries.[136]

---

[127] Estate of Lincoln v. Comm'r, 1 TCM (CCH) 326 (1942). But see Scher v. United States, 1976-2 USTC ¶ 13,163 (DNJ 1976).

[128] Estate of Harper v. Comm'r, 11 TC 717 (1948), acq. 1949-1 CB 2.

[129] Estate of Harper v. Comm'r, 11 TC 717 (1948), acq. 1949-1 CB 2. See also TAM 9240003 (June 17, 1992) (value of note owed to decedent by insolvent nephew was properly determined by nephew's ability to pay at date of death without regard to bequest to nephew in will or fact that note was canceled by will).

[130] Estate of Hodge v. Comm'r, 2 TC 643 (1943), acq. 1943 CB 11.

[131] But cf. Goodman v. Granger, 243 F2d 264 (3d Cir. 1957), cert. denied, 355 US 835 (1958).

[132] Philbrick v. Manning, 57 F. Supp. 245 (DNJ 1944). But see Estate of H.M. Springer v. Comm'r, 45 BTA 561 (1941), acq. 1942-1 CB 15 (statute of limitations tolled by debtor's absence from state).

[133] Estate of Walker v. Comm'r, 4 TC 390 (1944), acq. 1945 CB 7.

[134] Malloch v. Westover, 1951-1 USTC ¶ 10,816 (SD Cal. 1951).

[135] Mullikin v. Magruder, 55 F. Supp. 895 (D. Md. 1944), aff'd on another issue, 149 F2d 593 (4th Cir. 1945).

[136] Mullikin v. Magruder, 55 F. Supp. 895 (D. Md. 1944), aff'd on another issue, 149 F2d 593 (4th Cir. 1945). Cf. Estate of Smith v. Comm'r, 57 TC 650 n. 2 (1972). But see Rosskam v. United States, 64 Ct. Cl. 272 (1927), where it was impossible to value the notes at the decedent's death, so value was based on the amount received on sale five years later. The *Rosskam* approach has a certain appeal because of its "wait and see" approach. Cf. Comm'r v. Estate of Shively, 276 F2d 372 (2d Cir. 1960). But while this ap-

[h] Annuities and Life Insurance Policies

An annuity may be defined generally as a right to a stream of fixed payments over a specified term. Because the specified term is generally keyed to the life of the beneficiary, valuation can be a more complex issue. Fortunately, in the case of commercial annuities and endowment contracts, the issue is made fairly simple. The value of an annuity payable by a company regularly engaged in selling annuity contracts is the price at which comparable contracts are being sold by the company,[137] obviously an appropriate resort to marketplace valuation.[138]

Marketplace valuation may also be possible for an insurance policy[139] on the life of another owned by the decedent.[140] If the policy is paid up, its value is the amount that the company would charge for a single-premium policy on a person of the same age as the insured.[141] Policies on which premium payments remain to be paid are generally valued with respect to the company's interpolated terminal reserve (adjusted with respect to the most recent premium payment), which, in general, identifies the amount designated by the issuing company as needed at the valuation date to fund the death benefit that will ultimately become payable.[142]

For noncommercial annuity-type arrangements, there is no market to serve as a reference. In these cases, reference is made to mechanical rules under Section 7520, discussed in more detail later.[143]

---

proach works sometimes for income tax purposes (Burnet v. Logan, 283 US 404 (1931); Dorsey v. Comm'r, 49 TC 606 (1968)), awkward evaluations are not avoided for estate tax purposes. Cf. Smith v. Shaugnessy, 318 US 176, 180 (1943). The usual approach, therefore, is to take a still picture at the applicable valuation date. Ithaca Trust Co. v. United States, 279 US 151 (1929). See ¶ 5.03[5][b].

[137] Reg. § 20.2031-8(a)(3) Ex. 1.

[138] For a discussion of the valuation of an interest measured by the life or lives of terminally ill persons, see infra ¶ 4.02[5] text accompanying notes 253–255.

[139] There may be a question whether a combination life insurance and annuity contract should be valued as insurance or as an annuity. The regulations note the distinction. Reg. § 20.2031-8(a). Compare Helvering v. Estate of Le Gierse, 312 US 531 (1941) with Fidelity-Philadelphia Trust Co. v. Smith, 356 US 274 (1958).

[140] For policies on the life of the decedent, see Section 2042, discussed at ¶ 4.14.

[141] Reg. §§ 20.2031-8(a)(1), 20.2031-8(a)(3) Ex. 2. See also Rev. Rul. 78-137, 1978-1 CB 280. The correct mortality tables are now gender-neutral. Should the insurability of the insured be a factor?

[142] See Reg. §§ 20.2031-8(a)(2), 20.2031-8(a)(3) Ex. 3; Estate of DuPont v. Comm'r, 233 F2d 210, 212 (3d Cir.), cert. denied, 352 US 878 (1956). Cf. Estate of Pritchard v. Comm'r, 4 TC 204 (1944); Rev. Rul. 77-181, 1977-1 CB 272.

[143] See infra ¶ 4.02[5].

[i] Other Property Interests

The list of items previously mentioned for which valuation approaches are discussed is, of course, not exhaustive. Items that must be valued cover the whole range of property interests included under Section 2033 and all other provisions defining the gross estate. Although some of these miscellaneous items, because of their uniqueness, are quite difficult to value, the general principles previously recited are applicable: the "willing buyer, willing seller" test is still applied; difficulty of valuation should not preclude valuation; date of death is the normal valuation date; and, often determinative, the burden of proof is on the taxpayer.

[4] Adjustments for Premiums and Discounts

[a] Introduction

Once the value of an asset is determined, various increasing and decreasing adjustments may be made to such valuation to reflect the decedent's interest in the asset.[144] Upward adjustments are appropriate where the decedent's interest has special powers or leverage over the interests of others in the same asset.[145] Likewise, downward adjustments are required where the decedent's interest is comparatively weaker than other interests in the same asset or than other assets to which the subject property is compared.[146]

In most cases, the preadjustment base price is the "liquidation value" of the decedent's interest, generally expressed as the decedent's share of the underlying property to which the decedent's interest relates. For example, if the gross estate includes an 80 percent interest in a parcel of real property worth $100,000, the liquidation value of the decedent's 80 percent interest would be $80,000. However, $80,000 is probably not the price that a willing buyer would pay for the decedent's 80 percent interest.

Because of the importance of the various adjustments, which will be described, where the cost is justified, the personal representative might consider obtaining two separate appraisals—one that provides the unadjusted (or "liqui-

---

[144] See Estate of Newhouse v. Comm'r, 94 TC 193, 249 (1990). A more detailed discussion of premiums and discounts appears in Bogdanski, Federal Tax Valuation ¶¶ 4.01–4.04 (Warren, Gorham & Lamont 1996).

[145] See infra ¶ 4.02[4][b].

[146] See infra ¶¶ 4.02[4][c]–4.04[e]. Not all possible downward adjustments are considered, of course. See Estate of Jameson v. Comm'r, 77 TCM (CCH) 1383 (1999) (a 97 percent interest in a corporation was not discounted for a "nuisance discount" because local law allowed the 97 percent shareholder near-unfettered control over corporate actions), vacated and remanded on other grounds, 267 F3d 366 (5th Cir. 2001).

dation") value of the interest included in the gross estate, and a second appraisal that proves the proper adjustments to the liquidation value. This strategy has been successful,[147] although it is certainly not required. One appraisal can determine both the liquidation value and the fair market value.

[b] Premium for Control

[i] **Rationale.** When the subject property is a controlling interest in a business entity or some other asset, a willing buyer might indeed pay a premium in addition to the liquidation value of the interest.[148] Thus, for example, when the subject property is an 80 percent interest in a closely held business, a willing buyer might pay more than 80 percent of the total fair market value of the business.[149] The willing buyer will pay extra to guarantee unfettered control over the business. With an 80 percent interest, the willing buyer would control the election of officers, the timing and amount of distributions including liquidation, all votes of the owners, hiring and salary decisions, and all other aspects of the business.[150]

[ii] **Absence of attribution.** The fair market value of an interest included in the gross estate is determined without attribution to the decedent of interests owned by other individuals. Thus, when a decedent owns a 30 percent interest in a closely held business, no control premium is proper where the decedent's spouse, children, or other close family members own interests that, when combined with the decedent's interest, would create a controlling interest. This is true even when the decedent effectively enjoys close relationships with the other family owners and may effectively control the underlying asset because

---

[147] See Estate of Williams v. Comm'r, 75 TCM (CCH) 1758 (1998).

[148] See Reg. § 20.2031-2(e) (last sentence).

[149] This premium is frequently combined with a discount for a lack of marketability (see infra ¶ 4.02[4][d]) which can have the effect of partially or totally canceling out the premium. See infra ¶¶ 4.02[4][d] text accompanying notes 191–193, 4.02[4][f].

[150] See Estate of Murphy v. Comm'r, 60 TCM (CCH) 645, 658–659 (1990), which lists rights associated with control quoting Pratt, Valuing a Business: The Analysis and Appraisal of Closely Held Companies, 55–56 (Dow Jones–Irwin 1989). The listed rights are as follows: (1) elect directors and appoint management; (2) determine management compensation and perquisites; (3) set policy and change the course of business; (4) acquire or liquidate assets; (5) select people with whom to do business and award contracts; (6) make acquisitions; (7) liquidate, dissolve, sell out, or recapitalize the company; (8) sell or acquire treasury shares; (9) register the company's stock for a public offering; (10) declare and pay dividends; and (11) change the articles of incorporation or bylaws. See Pratt, Reilly, Schweihs, Valuing a Business: The Analysis and Appraisal of Closely Held Companies, 347–348 (McGraw-Hill, 4th ed. 2000).

of the close ties. The Service has conceded the issue[151] after several court defeats.[152]

Although the Service concedes the attribution issue,[153] it appropriately maintains that aggregation within the gross estate is proper. Thus, where a revocable trust created by the decedent for the decedent's sole benefit owns shares in a closely held corporation, any shares in the same corporation owned outright by the decedent will be added to the trust shares[154] in order to compute value.[155] Likewise, a minority interest transferred within three years of death in a manner that causes gross estate inclusion under Section 2035(a) will be added to whatever interest the decedent owned outright at the date of death.[156]

Where the decedent is a surviving spouse and beneficiary of a QTIP trust, shares owned by the surviving spouse outright or included in the surviving spouse's gross estate under other gross estate inclusion sections are not combined with the shares owned by the QTIP trust, even though Section 2044 requires inclusion of the QTIP trust shares in the surviving spouse's gross estate.[157] Although Section 2044 treats a surviving spouse as the owner of the shares held in the QTIP trust for purposes of computing the gross estate, such

---

[151] Rev. Rul. 93-12, 1993-1 CB 202. See also TAM 9432001 (Mar. 28, 1994) (decedent's 49 percent interest in corporate stock still given minority discount even though legatee, decedent's son, owned remaining 51 percent of stock). The rule against attribution is also recognized in the federal gift tax setting, where a transferor will fracture a controlling interest and give several smaller, noncontrolling interests. See ¶ 10.02[2][b] text accompanying notes 88–90. This technique is successful, as the Service conceded in Revenue Ruling 93-12, and TAM 9449001 (Mar. 11, 1994) (transfer of 9 percent interests to each of eleven children valued as eleven separate gifts, not one gift of controlling interest).

[152] See Estate of Bright v. United States, 658 F2d 999 (5th Cir. 1981), Estate of Andrews v. Comm'r, 79 TC 938 (1982), Propstra v. United States, 680 F2d 1248 (9th Cir. 1982); Estate of Lee v. Comm'r, 69 TC 860 (1978).

[153] Rev. Rul. 93-12, 1993-1 CB 202.

[154] For inclusion in the gross estate of stock owned by a decedent's revocable trust, see ¶ 4.10.

[155] See Rev. Rul. 79-7, 1979-1 CB 294; TAM 9403002 (Sept. 17, 1993).

[156] Rev. Rul. 79-7, 1979-1 CB 294. Cf. ¶ 4.16 text accompanying notes 19–23.

[157] See ¶ 4.16.

shares are not and have never been actually owned by the surviving spouse, so the courts consider such aggregation improper.[158]

[iii] **Amounts and cases.** There is no fixed adjustment to apply to controlling interests in property or a business.[159] The proper adjustment depends upon the degree of control possessed by the subject interest, and upon the nature of the underlying assets. For example, the control premium for a 60 percent interest in a business should be less than the control premium applicable to an 80 percent interest, because only the latter has the ability (under most state laws) to unilaterally compel liquidation, merger, or other extraordinary corporate action.

A control premium is not warranted when the interest lacks any voting control. Thus, if the decedent owns 90 percent of the equity in a closely held business but no portion of the business' voting power, no control premium should apply. Likewise, an interest should not be subject to a control premium simply because it is large enough to elect one member of a board of directors.[160]

In one case, the Tax Court held that a minority interest with significant voting power may warrant a control premium. In *Estate of Simplot v. Commissioner*, the court applied a premium equal to 3 percent of the total equity value to the 76.445 voting shares in the subject corporation, even though these shares represented only approximately $5/100$ of 1 percent (0.05 percent) of the total number of shares.[161] However, the case was reversed on appeal with the Ninth Circuit Court of Appeals finding several errors in the Tax Court's rationale.[162]

---

[158] Estate of Bonner v. Comm'r, 84 F3d 196 (5th Cir. 1996) (involving a parcel of real estate and a boat). The Tax Court followed *Estate of Bonner* in Estate of Mellinger v. Comm'r, 112 TC 26 (1999), acq., 1999-2 CB xvi; Estate of Nowell v. Comm'r, 77 TCM (CCH) 1239 (1999); Estate of Lopes v. Comm'r, 78 TCM (CCH) 46 (1999). Various aspects of the decisions are discussed in ¶ 4.16 text accompanying notes 19–23 and in Aucutt, "What Happens When Nothing Is Happening? *Mellinger* Acquiescence and Not Much Else," 26 Est. Plan. 496 (1999).

[159] Estate of Salsbury v. Comm'r, 34 TCM (CCH) 1441 (1975) (38 percent control premium where decedents owned 51.8 percent voting interest in a corporation); Estate of Trenchard v. Comm'r, 69 TCM (CCH) 2164 (1995) (40 percent control premium was applied to the decedent's 60 percent interest in a family corporation); Dooly v. Comm'r, 31 TCM (CCH) 814 (1972); Anderson v. Comm'r, 31 TCM (CCH) 502 (1972).

[160] Estate of Wright v. Comm'r, 73 TCM (CCH) 1863 (1997).

[161] Estate of Simplot v. Comm'r, 112 TC 130 (1999). The decedent owned eighteen of the voting shares (23.55 percent of the voting shares) and 3,942 nonvoting shares. Although no shareholder held a majority of the voting shares, the court determined that a willing buyer would pay a premium because ownership of any portion of the voting shares would give the willing buyer access to the corporation's "inner circle."

[162] Estate of Simplot v. Comm'r, 249 F3d 1191 (9th Cir. 2001). The Ninth Circuit was critical of the Tax Court finding imaginary scenarios as to potential purchasers, valu-

If the decedent owns a controlling block of stock in a closely held corporation immediately before death, the decedent might be tempted to transfer a fraction of the controlling interest to one or more beneficiaries and die holding a minority interest. For this reason, death-bed transfers of minority interests by a controlling shareholder are suspect, and a court has not only disallowed minority interest discounts (discussed later) but also applied a control premium to the decedent's interest.[163] The Service continues to be suspicious of any death-time "slicing and dicing" of a controlling interest.[164]

[iv] **Swing vote premium.** Suppose a decedent had owned 2 percent of the stock in a closely held corporation, and that the other two shareholders, who are unrelated to one another, each own 49 percent of the stock. A willing buyer might be willing to pay a premium for the decedent's shares above the price that would normally be paid for a minority interest[165] because the owner of the 2 percent interest will have the opportunity to have a significant say in corporate management and distributions, certainly much more so than most 2 percent shareholders. Further, if the owners of the 49 percent blocks are interested in gaining control of the corporation, the owner of the 2 percent interest will have a ready market unlike that available to many 2 percent shareholders of closely held businesses. This is the underlying theoretical construct that supports the concept of "swing vote premium." It was the justification for a decision to permit no minority interest discount in a situation in which the decedent owned a 10 percent block of voting stock in a corporation where another 40 percent was owned by members of the decedent's family and the

---

ing all the voting stock and assuming that each share held a proportionate share of such value, and adding a premium to value where no economics advantage was proved.

[163] Estate of Murphy v. Comm'r, 60 TCM (CCH) 645 (1990). The *Murphy* court stressed the fact that the decedent and her beneficiaries had an informal agreement among them to keep control of the corporation within the family. But see Estate of Frank v. Comm'r, 69 TCM (CCH) 2255 (1995), where a death-bed transfer from the decedent by decedent agent under a power of attorney to his spouse was respected and a 20 percent minority discount to the decedent's share of stock allowed. The *Frank* court did not cite the *Murphy* case, and found the decedent's motive was not solely tax avoidance. Id. at 2257–2259.

[164] See TAM 9719006 (Jan. 14, 1997) (the Service valued a partnership's assets as if owned outright by the decedent where the decedent's children created a family limited partnership while the decedent was on life support and sold partnership interests to the decedent's children under an installment note dated contemporaneously with the creation of the partnership). See also TAM 9723009 (Feb. 24, 1997), TAM 9725002 (Mar. 3, 1997) (both raising the same issues on similar facts). Outside the context of its own rulings on "death-bed partnerships," the Service's attempt to disregard the partnership and instead value its inside assets has been unsuccessful. See ¶ 19.04[2] text accompanying notes 20–26.

[165] See the discussion of discount for minority interests infra ¶ 4.02[4][c].

other 50 percent was owned by members of another family.[166] That decision was in turn relied upon by the Service to conclude that where three 30 percent blocks of stock were the subject of simultaneous gifts, all three blocks could be valued with a premium because of swing vote characteristics.[167] A review of the authorities suggests that such a premium seems most likely to be recognized where the ownership interest being valued can be combined with at least one (and possibly more) other ownership interests to gain control of the business, and where there are at least one or more of those ownership interests are held by persons who can reasonably be assumed (or proved) to want to gain control.[168] The Service has urged swing vote premium in a number of other cases with limited success.[169] The reasons for declining to apply the analysis in those cases have varied, and on the whole, the cases suggest that the theory is one that will affect value in some situations.[170]

---

[166] Estate of Winkler v. Comm'r, 57 TCM (CCH) 373 (1989) (stating, on the facts of that case, "we conclude that a 10 percent block of voting stock has 'swing vote characteristics' and that a minority discount would be inappropriate here"). Id. at 383. A somewhat similar result was reached in Estate of Hendrickson v. Comm'r, 78 TCM (CCH) 322 (1999) (holding that a large minority interest effectively controlled a business and thus was entitled to no minority interest discount, although allowing a marketability discount).

[167] Priv. Ltr. Rul. 9436005 (May 26, 1994). The ruling rejected an argument by the taxpayer that had the gifts been made seriatim, a different result would have been reached. The ruling also correctly notes that the swing vote analysis was examined in Estate of Bright v. Comm'r, 658 F2d 999 (5th Cir. 1981), a case better known for rejecting family ownership attribution for valuation purposes. It also included, however, a thoughtful discussion of swing vote concepts (id. at 1007, 1009), but concluded the point had not been timely raised by the government. Id. at 1008.

[168] This may explain why swing vote analysis was not raised in Revenue Ruling 93-12, 1993-1 CB 202 (where gifts of five 20 percent interests were made simultaneously to the donor's children and there was no mention of a swing vote analysis) and TAM 9449001 (March 11, 1994) (involving transfers of 11 nine percent interests). In neither situation could the owner of one of the interests combine with any other one owner to achieve control. The statement in the text is consistent with the result in Estate of Davis v. Comm'r, 110 TC 530 (1998), where the issue was the value of two 25.77 percent blocks of stock in a holding company given to the donor's two children. In valuing each gift of 25.77 percent, the court indicated that because the remaining shares were owned by the donor and the donor's other child, and those two owners were unlikely to seek to acquire control by obtaining the 25.77 percent held by the third shareholder, neither gifted block was likely to be able "to influence management and to be a swing block." Id. at 559.

[169] Estate of Simplot v. Comm'r, 112 TC 130 (1999), rev'd, 249 F3d 1191 (9th Cir. 2001); Estate of True v. Comm'r, 82 TCM (CCH) 27, 87 (2001); and Estate of Magnin v. Comm'r, 81 TCM (CCH) 1126 (2001) (where the Tax Court stated "we have recognized that a discount may not apply in situations where a minority block of stock has 'swing vote characteristics'"). Id. at 1138–1139.

[170] In Estate of Simplot v. Comm'r, 112 TC 130 (1999), the Tax Court referred to the eventual potential for swing vote power in determining the voting premium to attach to eighteen voting shares comprising a 23.55 percent voting block of a very valuable corporation. Id. at 179. Although the decision was reversed on appeal, Estate of Simplot v.

[c] Discount for Minority Interest

[i] **Rationale.** The minority interest discount reflects the inability both to compel liquidation of the underlying asset and to control its management. The rationale for allowing a minority interest discount is essentially the inverse of adding a control premium:[171] while a willing buyer is prepared to pay a premium for a controlling interest, a willing buyer will insist on paying less than the liquidation value for a noncontrolling interest.[172]

[ii] **Absence of attribution.** As with the control premium, there is no attribution of others' interests to the decedent.[173] In essence, the decedent's interest is valued in isolation, even though the decedent might have indirectly controlled the interests of others in the same asset or enterprise through the decedent's influence.[174]

[iii] **Amounts and cases.** Because valuation is a question of fact, there is no fixed minority discount amount.[175] As the following summary of important cases shows, the typical minority interest discount ranges from 10 to 30 percent.[176]

In *Estate of Berg v. Commissioner,*[177] the court sustained the Service's application of a 20 percent minority interest discount on the decedent's interest in a closely held corporation that managed unimproved real estate, completely

---

Comm'r, 249 F3d 1191 (9th Cir. 2001), the dissenting judge supported his dissent with an argument virtually identical to the argument that supports swing vote premium. In Estate of True v Comm'r, 82 TCM (CCH) 27, 87 (2000), the Tax Court rejected the application of the concept to a general partnership interest.

[171] See the factors listed supra ¶ 4.02[4][b] note 150.

[172] See Bogdanski, Federal Tax Valuation ¶ 4.03[6][c] (Warren, Gorham & Lamont 1996).

[173] See supra ¶ 4.02[4][b][ii].

[174] Although attribution will not prevent application of the minority interest discount, a court will not be blind to the identity of other owners in considering the proper discount figure. Moore v. Comm'r, 62 TCM (CCH) 1128 (1991) (court increased the minority interest discount for the decedent's partnership interest because a willing buyer would know that the surviving partners were related and thus the decedent's partnership interest would have much less influence than the parties' appraisals suggested).

[175] In some cases, a court may compute the minority discount with respect to the control premium applicable to a majority interest. For example, in Kosman v. Comm'r, 71 TCM (CCH) 2356 (1996) (4 percent minority discount after citing a study that controlling rights were worth a 2 to 4 percent premium); Rakow v. Comm'r, 77 TCM (CCH) 2066 (1999) (31 percent minority discount based on control premium).

[176] See also Estate of Barudin v. Comm'r, 72 TCM (CCH) 488 (1996) (19 percent minority interest discount for a 1/65 general partnership interest in partnership that owned depressed real estate in New York).

[177] 61 TCM (CCH) 2949 (1991).

rejecting the estate's expert claim for a higher discount. The Service includes *Berg* in its training guide for appeals officers,[178] apparently to proclaim its victory. Still, a 20 percent minority interest discount is quite significant. The *Berg* case should not be read for the proposition that the Service will concede a 20 percent minority interest discount in all cases, but one can use *Berg* to show that the Service will accept significant minority interest discounts for closely held businesses.[179]

In another case,[180] the Service asserted that the decedent's 50 percent interest in a closely held corporation should not receive a minority interest discount because the decedent's interest could block action by the other shareholders. But the court concluded that a 10 percent minority interest discount was proper because a 50 percent interest is not a controlling interest. Similar discounts should apply to a predeceasing spouse's 50 percent interest in property held as community property.[181]

Still another case sheds light on the minority discount applicable to nonvoting shares in a business enterprise. The subject property in the case was a corporation's Class B shares. The Class B shares were nonvoting with respect to most corporate matters, but consent of Class B shareholders was required for a corporate merger, liquidation, redemption, or other extraordinary corporate action. The Tax Court concluded that this veto power was significant enough to outweigh the general lack of voting rights; accordingly, it applied no minority discount in valuing the shares.[182] The Ninth Circuit Court of Appeals reversed, finding the veto powers alone insufficient to overcome the presumption that nonvoting shares receive a minority discount.[183]

Finally, it should be stressed that the minority discount is premised on the fact that the other, controlling interest or interests have actual control over the subject property. Thus, where the decedent owned an income interest in real property that was conveyed to a liquidating trust following a dispute between the decedent and the remainder beneficiaries, the decedent's minority income interest was not entitled to a minority interest discount because the remainder beneficiaries gave up control upon transfer to the liquidating trust.[184]

---

[178] IRS Valuation Training for Appeals Officers 9–5 (CCH 1998).

[179] Estate of Ford v. Comm'r, 66 TCM (CCH) 1507 (1993), aff'd, 53 F3d 924 (8th Cir. 1995) (the Service's use of a 20 percent minority interest discount approved for a minority interest in a real estate holding company).

[180] Wheeler v. United States, 96-1 USTC ¶ 60,226 (WD Tex. 1996), rev'd and rem'd on other grounds, 116 F3d 744 (5th Cir. 1997).

[181] Estate of Fleming, 74 TCM (CCH) 1049 (1997).

[182] Theophilos v. Comm'r, 67 TCM (CCH) 2106 (1994).

[183] Theophilos v. Comm'r, 85 F3d 440 (9th Cir. 1996).

[184] Estate of Casey v. Comm'r, 71 TCM (CCH) 2599 (1996). The estate, however, was entitled to a 15 percent marketability discount because of the anticipated delay in sale.

[d] Discount for Lack of Marketability

[i] **Rationale.** A readily marketable interest is easily sold by its owner. Where an interest cannot be readily sold because of a limited market of buyers, or because of restrictions on the owner's ability to transfer the interest, the value of the interest must be less than its liquidation value. The marketability discount reflects the fact that a willing buyer will consider the costs and delay involved in eventually reselling the subject property. The discount for lack of marketability applies to both controlling and minority interests in an asset or business.[185]

[ii] **Amounts and cases.** As with the minority interest discount, there is no fixed discount amount for a lack of marketability. Again, determining the appropriate amount of the discount is a fact-intensive inquiry.[186] Still, one can obtain a sense of the importance of the marketability discount through a review of some of the litigated cases. The following cases suggest that the typical range for a marketability discount will be from 15 to 40 percent, with the marketability discount generally falling nearer the high end of that range where the decedent's interest is a minority interest.

As suggested, many cases have permitted significant marketability discounts where the decedent also held a minority interest in the property. For example, in *Estate of Jung v. Commissioner*,[187] the court applied a 35 percent marketability discount in valuing the decedent's 20.74 interest in a closely held corporation. A 40 percent marketability discount was applied in *Estate of Lauder v. Commissioner*,[188] where the subject property was a minority interest in a successful, industry-leading corporation. A 40 percent marketability discount was also applied to the decedent's 9.8 percent interest in the stock of a closely held retail grocery store chain.[189] And a 26 percent marketability dis-

---

[185] See infra ¶¶ 4.02[4][d][ii], 4.02[4][f]. Attribution of ownership is again disregarded. See Estate of Andrews v. Comm'r, 79 TC 938, 953 (1982) (minority and marketability discount allowed where decedent and siblings owned 100 percent of a corporation).

[186] An in-depth analysis of factors which a court examines in determining the amount of a marketability discount appears in Mandelbaum v. Comm'r, 69 TCM (CCH) 2852 (1995), aff'd 91 F3d 124 (3d Cir. 1996). The Tax Court considered the following ten factors: (1) private versus public sales figures; (2) financial statement analysis; (3) corporate dividend policy; (4) corporation's economic outlook; (5) corporate management; (6) control exerted by subject shares; (7) restrictions on transfer; (8) holding periods; (9) corporate redemption policy; and (10) costs of making a public offering. See Estate of Marmaduke v. Comm'r, 78 TCM (CCH) 590 (1999) (sales of stock used to determine amount of marketability discount).

[187] 101 TC 412 (1993).

[188] 68 TCM (CCH) 985 (1994).

[189] Estate of Brookshire v. Comm'r, 76 TCM (CCH) 659 (1998). Beyond its relatively high percentage discount, *Brookshire* is interesting for two reasons. First, the corpo-

count was allowed for 1/95th general partnership interest in partnership that owned depressed real estate in New York.[190]

Significant marketability discounts have been allowed even where the decedent owned a controlling interest in property. In one case,[191] the court applied a 20 percent marketability discount to the decedent's 78 percent interest in an incorporated ranch. The court found the discount appropriate because of restrictions on the decedent's use of the land under the California Land Conservation Act. A controlling interest received a 15 percent marketability discount where the decedent owned an 82.49 percent interest in a family holding corporation.[192] A marketability discount of 30 percent was allowed for a minority interest in an entity that was treated as a controlling interest.[193]

Even where a decedent owns all of the interests in an asset or business entity, a marketability discount may be appropriate. The decedent was the sole beneficiary of a trust that owned 100 percent of the stock of a holding company where the court accepted the 25 percent marketability discount claimed by the petitioner's expert.[194] A 15 percent marketability discount was approved

---

ration's buy-sell agreement gave the estate the right to compel redemption of the decedent's shares at book value (or, if less, the total amount of life insurance the corporation held on the decedent's life). It is therefore curious that the court would approve such a high marketability discount, given the estate's ability to have the shares redeemed in short order. Second, the book value of the stock was higher than the estate tax value approved by the court. One would expect that the book value in this case would be the minimum value of the stock for estate tax purposes.

[190] Estate of Barudin v. Comm'r, 72 TCM (CCH) 488 (1996).

[191] Estate of Luton v. Comm'r, 68 TCM (CCH) 1044 (1994). But in the same case, the decedent's interest in a private trust holding an unsecured promissory note was given a marketability discount of only 10 percent because of the note's consistent payment history and the solid financial status of the note's maker.

[192] Gray v. Comm'r, 73 TCM (CCH) 1940 (1997). The court upheld a marketability discount despite the Service's assertion that a marketability discount was inappropriate for a controlling interest in an entity valued according to the net asset method. See Estate of Borgatello v. Comm'r, 80 TCM (CCH) 260 (2000) (82.76 percent interest allowed a 93 percent marketability discount).

[193] Estate of Hendrickson v. Comm'r, 78 TCM (CCH) 322 (1999) (30 percent marketability discount on 49.97 percent interest in closely held bank treated as a controlling interest). See supra ¶ 4.02[4][b] note 166.

For other marketability discount cases involving controlling interests see Estate of Ford v. Comm'r, 66 TCM (CCH) 1507 (1993), aff'd, 53 F3d 924 (8th Cir. 1995) (10 percent marketability discount given to decedent's 92.4 percent interest in a corporation); Estate of Newhouse v. Comm'r, 94 TC 193 (1990), acq. 1991-1 CB 1 (35 percent blended minority and marketability discount permitted even though decedent held largest outstanding ownership interest in the corporation). Trenchard v. Comm'r, 69 TCM (CCH) 2164 (1995) (40 percent marketability discount).

[194] Estate of Dougherty v. Comm'r, 59 TCM (CCH) 772 (1990).

in another case[195] that involved the valuation of a wholly owned holding company. Some cases have not allowed a marketability discount, but have reduced the value of a company by the estimated cost of liquidating the company.[196]

[e] Other Significant Discounts

[i] **Fractional interest discount.** Like a minority interest discount, a fractional interest discount recognizes the risks of co-ownership. While the minority interest discount applies to co-ownership of an *entity*, the fractional interest discount applies to co-ownership of an *asset*. Thus, assets held by the decedent and another as tenants in common or as community property eligible for a fractional interest discount.[197] The fractional interest discount reflects the fact that a willing buyer will not pay liquidation value for an undivided interest in an asset because of the costs to partition the property or sever the interest, not to mention the general headaches and compromises required of co-ownership. While these same risks may be present with respect to property held as joint tenants with rights of survivorship, Section 2040 provides specific rules for inclusion and valuation, and courts will not apply a fractional interest discount to the amount required for inclusion under Section 2040.[198]

A typical example of the fractional interest discount appears in a case[199] where the property was an undivided one-half interest in undeveloped Florida timberland. The Tax Court allowed a 30 percent discount because the decedent's interest lacked control, despite the Service's contention that a fractional interest discount beyond costs of partitioning the property should be disallowed in the absence of evidence of sales of fractional interests in comparable real property.[200] The Service's argument in the case apparently represented a

---

[195] Estate of Bennett v. Comm'r, 65 TCM (CCH) 1816 (1993). The discount would be reflected in the value of the asset or business entity under either the market approach or the asset-based approach described earlier.

[196] Estate of Jephson v. Comm'r, 87 TC 297 (1986) (decedent owned two investment companies holding only cash and marketable securities; the court found it sufficient to merely reduce the net asset value by the costs to liquidate the securities). A marketability discount was also denied in Estate of Cloutier v. Comm'r, 71 TCM (CCH) 2356 (1996), because none of the estate's appraisals followed an appropriate valuation method, not necessarily because the decedent owned a 100 percent interest in the subject corporation.

[197] Propstra v. United States, 680 F2d 1248 (9th Cir. 1982). See infra text accompanying notes 199–205. Cf. Estate of Bright v. Comm'r, 658 F2d 999 (5th Cir. 1981); Estate of Lee v. Comm'r, 69 TC 860 (1978).

[198] Estate of Young v. Comm'r, 110 TC 297 (1988); Estate of Fratini v. Comm'r, 76 TCM (CCH) 342 (1998).

[199] Estate of Williams v. Comm'r, 75 TCM (CCH) 1758 (1998).

[200] Estate of Williams v. Comm'r, 75 TCM (CCH) 1758, 1766 (1998). The very absence of such evidence supported the court's conclusion that there was no real market for

renewed attack against the fractional interest discount. In an earlier case involving real property, the Service unsuccessfully argued for a fractional interest discount of 5 percent plus the cost of partitioning the property.[201] At least in that case, the Service was receptive to a fractional interest discount that reflected more than simply the costs to partition the subject property. But as the former case suggests, the Service more recently will challenge the discount when it exceeds the partition costs.[202] To date, however, the Service generally continues to be unsuccessful.[203]

The fractional interest discount does create significant planning opportunities. The decedent's spouse in one case[204] created two inter vivos trusts for the benefit of the decedent. Fractional interests in real property were placed inside each trust. The assets of only one of the trusts were included in the decedent's gross estate, and the court upheld a 15 percent fractional interest discount in valuing the trust's share of the real property.[205]

[ii] **Blockage and market absorption discounts.** On some occasions, the size of the property included in the gross estate is so large that a discount is required for the effect of supply and demand on the market for such property. For example, if the decedent owned a significant share of the publicly traded

---

fractional interests in real property. Further, the court rejected the Service's argument that a fractional interest discount should be limited to the costs to partition the property. See Estate of Baird v. Comm'r, 82 TCM (CCH) 666 (2001) (60 percent discount for two undivided interests in Louisiana timberland, a ^{14}/₆₅ interest and a ^{17}/₆₅ interest); Estate of Forbes v. Comm'r, 81 TCM (CCH) 1399 (2001) (30 percent fractional discount for raw farmland).

[201] Estate of Cervin v. Comm'r, 68 TCM (CCH) 1115 (1994), rev'd and rem'd on other grounds, 111 F3d 1252 (5th Cir. 1997) (Tax Court granted a 20 percent fractional interest discount, noting the fact that a partition action would require agreement among all of the co-owners as to the relative values of each interest—a fact that apparently increases the fractional interest discount).

[202] See TAM 199943003 (June 7, 1999).

[203] See Estate of Brocato v. Comm'r, 78 TCM (CCH) 1243 (1999) (allowing the 20 percent fractional interest discount claimed by the taxpayer and rejecting the Service's attempt to limit the discount to costs of partition plus costs of anticipated delays). But see Estate of Busch v. Comm'r, 79 TCM (CCH) 1276 (2000) (the personal representative argued for a 40 percent fractional interest discount where the decedent owned an undivided 50 percent interest in real property, but the court allowed a 10 percent fractional interest discount, an amount based primarily on partition costs, because it was likely that the other co-owner would not resist any effort to sell the land). See Hoffman, "The Tax Court's Decisions on Undivided Interest Discounts," Valuation Strategies 19 (May/June 2001).

[204] Estate of Pillsbury v. Comm'r, 64 TCM (CCH) 284 (1992).

[205] The court distinguished Estate of McMullen v. Comm'r, 56 TCM (CCH) 507 (1998), where a fractional interest discount was disallowed because the real estate was owned by a trust whose governing instrument required any sale of the property to be in the form of a fee simple interest—the entire property. The trusts in Estate of Pillsbury v. Comm'r, 64 TCM (CCH) 284 (1992), did not contain this provision.

shares of one company and tried to sell the entire block at once, the decedent would not be able to sell each share for the same price. Because of the significant increase in the number of shares available for sale, the price per share will drop as the number of shares in the block increases. In the case of stock or other business interests, this is referred to as a "blockage discount." The Service acknowledges that a blockage discount can be proper,[206] but there has been litigation over the amount of the discount. The typical size of the blockage discount for business interests is smaller than the typical minority interest and marketability discounts; often the discount ranges from about 5 to 10 percent.[207] A discount at the higher end of the range is usually given to large ownership interests of thinly traded interests.[208]

For assets other than business interests, the corollary term often used is "market absorption discount."[209] The discount has been approved by courts in cases ranging from real property to art collections.[210] The market absorption

---

[206] Reg. § 20.2031-2(e). See also Rev. Rul. 83-30, 1983-1 CB 224 (underwriting fees on marketing a block of stock are not considered in blockage discount, but are allowed as a Section 2053 administrative expense).

[207] See, e.g., Estate of Branson v. Comm'r, 78 TCM (CCH) 78 (1999) (20 percent blockage discount applied to decedent's 62.5 percent stock interest in a small bank); Estate of Wright v. Comm'r, 73 TCM (CCH) 1863 (1997) (court considered the size of decedent's 23.8 percent block of stock in a holding corporation that owned all of the shares of a New York bank; court ultimately reduced Service's appraisal from $50 per share to $45 per share); Gillespie v. Comm'r, 23 F3d 36 (2d Cir. 1994) (4.8 percent blockage discount applied to decedent's 6.54 interest in a class of shares of the Washington Post Company).

[208] Estate of Wright v. Comm'r, 73 TCM (CCH) 1863 (1997) (court applied a blockage discount, highlighting the point that valuation considers both sides of a hypothetical sale transaction in responding to the Service's argument that a blockage discount was inappropriate because the subject property was thinly traded because of the lack of sellers, not any demonstrated lack of buyers).

[209] See Estate of Grootematt v. Comm'r, 38 TCM (CCH) 198 (1979).

[210] Real property market absorption discounts cases include Estate of Brocato v. Comm'r, 78 TCM (CCH) 1243 (1999) (11 percent market absorption discount applied to several rental properties located in San Francisco's Marina District); Estate of Rodgers v. Comm'r, 77 TCM (CCH) 1831 (1999) (permitting an unspecified market absorption discount in valuing real estate holdings of corporation in which decedent was a one-third shareholder, rejecting Service's position that entity-owned real estate should not be entitled to a market absorption discount; the real estate itself was valued in order to compute the value of the decedent's stock); Estate of Auker v. Comm'r, 75 TCM (CCH) 2321 (1998) (court approved a market absorption discount in excess of 6 percent for apartment complexes owned by decedent); Estate of Folks v. Comm'r, 43 TCM 427 (1982) (20 percent discount for five lumber yards).

Art collection market absorption discounts cases include Estate of O'Keeffe v. Comm'r, 63 TCM (CCH) 2699 (1992) (court awarded a 25 percent market absorption discount to paintings of decedent, a famous artist, that could be sold within a short time, and a 75 percent market absorption discount to those paintings that would take longer to sell); Estate of Smith v. Comm'r, 57 TC 650 (1972) (reduction in value for 425 sculptures).

discounts tend to be somewhat higher than the blockage discounts, perhaps because of the unique nature of the assets involved.[211]

[iii] **Capital gains discount.** Generally, expenses incurred to sell property are ignored in computing the fair market value.[212] At the decedent's death appreciated property included in the decedent's gross estate generally receives a Section 1014 "step-up" in basis so that the fair market value of the property is equal to its basis.[213] However, if the decedent's property is stock in a corporation and the corporation owns appreciated capital gain property, then as a result as the repeal of the *General Utilities* doctrine in 1986,[214] the corporation would have to pay tax on such gain on its liquidation reducing the net value of the corporation. Prior to the repeal of the *General Utilities* doctrine no tax would have been paid and no discount was allowed.[215] But with the repeal of the doctrine, the courts have recognized a discount related to the capital gains tax incurred.[216]

The first cases addressing the capital gains discount issue after the repeal of the *General Utilities* doctrine did not adjust the value of subject property by such lurking gains (often called a "capital gains discount") absent evidence that, at the moment of death, liquidation was planned in the near term.[217] More recently, however, courts have been willing to apply a capital gains discount, even when there is no evidence that a liquidation was contemplated at the valuation date. If the subject property is corporate stock, a capital gains discount

---

[211] Compare the results in the cases cited supra note 210 with those supra note 207.

[212] Estate of Wright v. Comm'r, 73 TCM (CCH) 1863 (1997). The court did acknowledge, however, that such expenses are generally deductible as administration expenses. See ¶ 5.03[3]. See also Estate of Luton v. Comm'r, 68 TCM (CCH) 1044, 1049 (1994); Estate of Andrews v. Comm'r, 79 TC 938, 942 (1982); Estate of Piper v. Comm'r, 72 TC 1062, 1087 (1979).

[213] This would not be the case with gifted property where as a result of Section 1015 the value of property may exceed its adjusted basis.

[214] General Utilities and Operating Co. v. Helvering, 296 US 200 (1935). See Bittker and Eustice, Federal Income Taxation of Corporations and Shareholders ¶¶ 8.20, 8.21 (Warren, Gorham & Lamont, 7th ed. 2000).

[215] Cf. Estate of Bennett v. Comm'r, 65 TCM (CCH) 1816 (1993); Estate of Andrews v. Comm'r, 79 TC 938, 942 (1982).

[216] Estate of Davis v. Comm'r, 110 TC 530 (1998) (the court increased the marketability discount on gifted stock by $9 million to account for the potential tax on built-in capital gains). See Estate of Jones v. Comm'r, 116 TC 121, 136 (2001) (no capital gains discount to a partnership interest because of the possibility of making a Section 754 election).

[217] Estate of Luton v. Comm'r, 68 TCM (CCH) 1044, 1050 (1994). See also Estate of Gray v. Comm'r, 73 TCM (CCH) 1940 (1997) (no capital gains discount for stock in corporation that held $2.265 million installment note because payment of the note depended upon sale of land by maker, making the risk of capital gain too speculative to be a factor in valuation).

is possible when a corporate liquidation cannot be accomplished without recognition of gain at the corporate level; plans to liquidate at the valuation date are not required.[218] The Service has acquiesced to some extent, conceding that a capital gains discount may be proper, but reserving the right to challenge the applicability and amount of the discount in each case.[219]

[iv] **Securities law discount.** Where the securities laws impose restrictions on the trading of the decedent's stock, a discount is appropriate, and sometimes courts will separately state the discount attributable to securities laws assuming the restrictions survive the decedent.[220] The Service has issued guidance for computing the effect of securities laws in valuing stock.[221]

[v] **Environmental hazards discount.** Where real property is contaminated or used for an activity that may present risks of environmental hazards, a willing buyer will not require an adjustment to the purchase price to reflect the extra costs the buyer may incur to clean up or restore the property. Where environmental hazards can be proved, courts are willing to discount the value of real property included in the gross estate.[222]

To claim a discount for environmental hazards, it is not enough simply to prove that an environmental hazard exists or is likely to occur on the property. Instead, one must show that a willing buyer would discover the hazard and, if so, that the willing buyer would demand an adjustment to the purchase price.[223]

[vi] **Key person discount.** If the decedent was instrumental to the value of a business, a discount to the value of the decedent's interest in the business

---

[218] Eisenberg v. Comm'r, 155 F3d 50 (2d Cir. 1998), acq. AOD 1999-001; Estate of Dunn v. Comm'r, 79 TCM (CCH) 1337 (2000); Estate of Jameson v. Comm'r, 267 F3d 366 (5th Cir. 2001); Estate of Davis v. Comm'r, 110 TC 530 (1998). The *Davis* court rejected the Service's argument that the tax could be avoided or substantially reduced through a subchapter S election, since the election would limit the universe of possible shareholders and would invoke potential double taxation under the ten-year rule in Section 1374. A discount for the full tax liability of liquidation was disallowed because there was no showing that the corporation planned to liquidate or sell substantially all its assets.

[219] AOD 1999-001 (Jan. 29, 1999).

[220] Estate of McClatchy v. Comm'r, 147 F3d 1089 (9th Cir. 1998). But see Estate of Davis v. Comm'r, 110 TC 530, 540–544 (1998) (disallowing a securities law discount for valuing shares of corporation that owned just over one percent of the stock of Winn-Dixie Stores' publicly traded stock).

Sometimes, the securities law restrictions are reflected in the marketability discount. See supra ¶ 4.02[4][d].

[221] Rev. Rul. 77-287, 1977-2 CB 319.

[222] Estate of Necastro v. Comm'r, 68 TCM (CCH) 227 (1994) (34 percent discount).

[223] Estate of Necastro v. Comm'r, 68 TCM (CCH) 227 (1994). See also Estate of Pillsbury v. Comm'r, 64 TCM (CCH) 284 (1992).

that reflects the decedent's death is often appropriate. Courts have recognized and applied a "key person discount," often in the range of about 10 percent.[224]

[vii] **Litigation discount.** Courts will also discount the value of an asset that is or will likely be subject to litigation.[225] The risk of litigation and the likelihood of loss greatly affect the size of the discount, making it impossible to describe a typical discount range. Thus, in one case, the Tax Court approved a litigation discount of only 2.5 percent in recognition of the fact that no lawsuit had been filed and that a willing buyer would, after some investigation, conclude that a lawsuit was unlikely.[226] But in another case, the court applied a 25 percent litigation discount because of evidence that the subject property was conveyed to the decedent through undue influence.[227]

[f] Combinations of Premiums and Discounts

It is common for several premiums and discounts to apply to the same interest. A common combination is a premium for control coupled with a discount for marketability.[228] A more common combination is discounts for a minority interest and a lack of marketability.[229] The adjustments for premiums and discounts are layered; they are not cumulative. For example, if a minority interest in a closely held business warrants a 20 percent minority interest discount and an additional 30 percent discount for lack of marketability, the total discount is 44 percent, not 50 percent. Suppose that the liquidation value of the minority interest is $100x. After application of the minority interest dis-

---

[224] Estate of Furman v. Comm'r, 75 TCM (CCH) 2206 (1998) (10 percent key person discount approved, along with combined discount for marketability and minority interest); Estate of Mitchell v. Comm'r, 74 TCM (CCH) 872 (1997) (10 percent key person discount, among other discounts, allowed), rev'd on appeal for failure to adequately explain overall valuation of stock, Estate of Mitchell v. Comm'r, 250 F3d 696 (9th Cir. 2001); Estate of Feldmar v. Comm'r, 56 TCM (CCH) 118 (1988) (25 percent discount).

[225] See Estate of Mitchell v. Comm'r, 74 TCM (CCH) 872 (1997) (court reduced value of decedent's stock by 10 percent to reflect contingent litigation regarding excessive deferred compensation paid to decedent's co-owner), rev'd on appeal for failure to adequately explain overall valuation of stock, Estate of Mitchell v. Comm'r, 250 F3d 696 (9th Cir. 2001).

[226] Estate of Mueller v. Comm'r, 63 TCM (CCH) 3027 (1992).

[227] Estate of Sharp v. Comm'r, 68 TCM (CCH) 1521 (1994). See Estate of Davis v. Comm'r, 65 TCM (CCH) 2365 (1993) (court applied a 5 percent discount for litigation risks in valuing a pending lawsuit alleging securities churning).

[228] See supra ¶ 4.02[4][d] text accompanying notes 191–193.

[229] See supra ¶ 4.02[4][d] text accompanying notes 187–190 and see the discussion of family limited partnerships and limited liability companies infra ¶ 4.02[4][g].

count, the value is $80x. The marketability discount is then subtracted from the reduced figure to obtain the fair market value, $56x in this case:[230]

$100x	Liquidation value of interest
($20x)	Less 20 percent minority interest discount
$ 80x	
($24x)	Less 30 percent marketability discount
$56x	Fair market value of interest

Because the parties are most concerned with the total discount, several re-ported cases only disclose the total discount, leaving the reader to guess the composition of the total discount.[231]

[g] Nonbusiness Assets Held in FLPS and FLLCs

Virtually all the examples and litigated cases involving the minority inter-est and marketability discounts concern the valuation of ownership interests in active businesses. In order to obtain an enhanced lack of marketability dis-count for other, *nonbusiness assets*,[232] many wealthy taxpayers have created

---

[230] See Estate of Frank v. Comm'r, 69 TCM (CCH) 2255 (1995); Estate of Andrews v. Comm'r, 79 TC 938 (1982). The order in which the discounts are applied does not matter; mathematically, layered discounts will produce the same aggregate discount re-gardless of order. Note that the results remain the same in the text example if the dis-counts are applied in reverse order: $100x less $30x marketability discount (30 percent) equals $70x; $70x less $14x minority interest discount (20 percent) equals $56x, the same result.

Similarly if there is a combination of a premium and a discount, the adjustments are layered as well. For example, if there is a 40 percent premium for control and a 20 per-cent discount for a minority interest, the fair market value of the interest is 112 percent of the estate's unadjusted value: either (1) 40 percent times 100 or 140 reduced by 20 per-cent of 140 or 28 to 112 or (2) 100 reduced by 20 percent of 80 which is increased by 40 percent or 32 to 112.

[231] See Knight v. Comm'r, 115 TC 506 (2000) (approved a 15 percent combined marketability and minority interest discount in valuing interests in a family partnership that owned a ranch); Furman v. Comm'r, 75 TCM (CCH) 2206 (1998) (awarded a 40 per-cent combined marketability and minority interest discount in valuing stock in a corpora-tion that owned and operated Burger King franchises); Dockery v. Comm'r, 75 TCM (CCH) 2032 (1998) (40 percent combined marketability and minority interest discount for an interest in a closely held Cayman Islands reinsurance program); Estate of Mitchell v. Comm'r, 74 TCM (CCH) 872 (1997) (allowed a 35 percent combined minority and mar-ketability discount in valuing decedent's 49.04 percent interest a closely held company), rev'd on appeal for failure to adequately explain overall valuation of stock. Estate of Mitchell v. Comm'r, 250 F3d 696 (9th Cir. 2001).

[232] This is not to say that valuation discounts do not apply to assets other than inter-ests in businesses, FLPs, or FLLCs. The fractional interest, minority interest, capital gains, environmental hazards, securities laws, and other discounts potentially apply to nonbusi-ness, nonentity interests. The estate tax advantage of the FLP or FLLC is to create or en-hance a marketability discount and make it easier to create minority interest discounts

family limited partnerships (FLPs) or family limited liability companies (FLLCs).[233] Suppose, for example, that a taxpayer owns $6 million in marketable securities, $3 million in investment real property, and another $1 million in artwork. The taxpayer might transfer these assets (or a portion of them) to an FLP or FLLC in exchange for all of the interests in the new entity. The taxpayer could then make lifetime transfers of entity interests to children, grandchildren, or other beneficiaries. To the extent the taxpayer transfers minority interests in the FLP or FLLC, the transfers will qualify for the minority interest discount. Further, because the transferred property is an interest in a holding company (and not undivided interests in the inside assets), the interest qualifies for a marketability discount. If, at the death of the decedent-transferor, the gross estate includes a noncontrolling interest in the FLP or FLLC, the estate in addition can claim a minority interest discount in valuing the included FLP or FLLC interest. In any event, any FLP or FLLC interests included in the decedent's gross estate can qualify for a marketability discount.

Although these FLPs or FLLCs do not actively conduct a trade or business, the eight factors provided in *Revenue Ruling 59-60* apply to the valuation of the FLP or FLLC interest, and the premiums and discounts typically applied to closely held corporations also apply in this context.[234] The Service has vigorously challenged the erosion to the transfer tax base occasioned by the discounts realized upon the transfer of interests in FLPs and FLLCs formed with passive assets. From its perspective, taxpayers create such FLPs and FLLCs solely to obtain higher valuation discounts and for no legitimate business or economic purpose.[235] While it is accepted that FLPs and FLLCs must be more closely scrutinized because of the familial nature of the entity,[236] the Service's attacks have fallen on deaf ears. In essence, the courts have said that

---

also, while nonetheless maintaining control in the senior generation of the family. These tax reasons are not the only reasons for creating an FLP or FLLC. See infra note 237.

[233] For estate tax valuation purposes, there need be little difference between an FLP and an FLLC. As a matter of applicable state law, of course, the FLP is a limited partnership and the FLLC is a limited liability company. Assuming the two entities are treated the same for state income tax purposes, the FLLC may be preferable because no member is personally liable for the debts and obligations (tort or contract) of the entity. In a limited partnership, the way to achieve limited liability for all owners is to name a corporate general partner, which invites unwanted complexity. See ¶ 4.05[7][c].

[234] See Estate of Weinberg v. Comm'r, 79 TCM (CCH) 1507 (2000); supra ¶¶ 4.02[4][a]–4.02[4][f].

[235] The Service typically cites Gregory v. Helvering, 293 US 465 (1935), for the proposition that transactions which lack economic substance other than tax avoidance should be disregarded. See FSA 200143004 (July 5, 2001) (restatement of government's economic substance argument in situation involving an S corporation).

[236] Frazee v. Comm'r, 98 TC 554, 561 (1992); Harwood v. Comm'r, 82 TC 239 (1984), aff'd without published opinion, 786 F2d 1174 (9th Cir. 1986); Estate of Kelly v. Comm'r, 63 TC 321 (1974); Kuney v. Frank, 308 F2d 719 (9th Cir. 1962).

if an entity is recognized under local law and it changes the relationship of the parties to the assets, it has economic substance for federal tax purposes.[237] The Service has similarly been unsuccessful in attacking FLPs and FLLCs on other grounds.[238]

In some cases, however, the Service is successful in looking through the partnership "device" and valuing the inside assets. If the FLP or FLLC owns only one asset or a few assets of the same type, there is authority for valuing the ownership interests as if they were partial interests in each of the entity's inside assets.[239] But where the entity itself alters the nature of the decedent's interest in the inside assets, it is not enough simply to aggregate the values of a fixed percentage of each asset. In most cases, of course, the FLP or FLLC arrangement does in fact substantively alter the nature of the owner's interest in the inside assets.[240]

It is also proper to disregard the FLP or FLLC entity when the owners have essentially disregarded the entity through their own actions. Thus, where

---

[237] See Estate of Strangi v. Comm'r, 115 TC 478 (2000); Kerr v. Comm'r, 113 TC 449 (1999); Knight v. Comm'r 115 TC 506 (2000); Estate of Dailey v. Comm'r, 82 TCM (CCH) 118 (2001). Cf. Estate of Murphy v. Comm'r, 60 TCM (CCH) 645 (1990). Several articles have stressed nontax business purposes for creating such activities. See Eastland, "Family Limited Partnerships: Non Transfer Tax Benefits," 7 Prob. & Prop. 10 (Mar./Apr. 1993).

[238] The Service has argued that Section 2703 requires disregard of the FLP or FLLC entity. The Service views the entire FLP or FLLC structure as a "restriction" on the inside assets of the FLP or FLLC that it asserts should not affect valuation under Section 2703. This argument misinterprets Section 2703 by reading the word "property" as a reference to the entity's inside assets. The Service has been similarly unsuccessful with its Section 2703 attack. Church v. United States, 2000-1 USTC (CCH) 60,369 (WD Tex. 2000), aff'd without opin., 2001-2 USTC (CCH) 60,415 (5th Cir. 2001); Estate of Strangi v. Comm'r, 115 TC 478 (2000). See ¶ 19.04[2] text accompanying notes 20–26. In the future, the Service may attack various provisions in the FLP or FLLC agreement or under state law as "restrictions" under Section 2703. See FSA 200143004 (July 5, 2001) (a full litany of the government's current arguments against FLPs or FLLCs in the context of an S corporation).

A further attack on such entities has occurred using Section 2704(b) to argue that the entities are subject to "applicable restrictions" that reduce the amount of the marketability discounts. Again, however, the Service has been unsuccessful in applying Section 2704(b). Kerr v. Comm'r, 113 TC 449 (1999); Knight v. Comm'r, 115 TC 506 (2000); Harper v. Comm'r, 79 TCM (CCH) 2232 (2000); Estate of Jones v. Comm'r, 116 TC 121 (2001). See ¶ 19.05[3][b] text accompanying note 59.

Finally, the Service has attempted to argue a "gift on formation" as a result of the reduced valuation resulting from discounts. But the courts, with some judges dissenting, have failed to buy into such an argument. Estate of Strangi v. Comm'r, 115 TC 478 (2000); Estate of Jones v. Comm'r, 116 TC 121 (2001). This argument is discussed at ¶ 10.01[2][b] text accompanying notes 23–25, and ¶ 10.02[2][c][v].

[239] See, e.g., Estate of Lehmann v. Comm'r, 74 TCM (CCH) 415 (1997) (limited partnership's asset was a leasehold interest in parcel of real estate).

[240] See Knight v. Comm'r, 115 TC 506 (2000).

a founding and controlling member of three FLPs continued to deposit entity funds into the member's own personal bank account, paid both personal and partnership expenses from the one account, and kept no separate books and records for the partnerships, the Service successfully disregarded the entities by pulling the assets into the funding member's gross estate under Section 2036(a)(1).[241]

[5] Temporal Property Interests

Athough valuing fractional interests in property involves application of minority and fractional interest discounts that vary from case to case,[242] the valuation of temporal property interests (like a term of years or a remainder) involves application of actuarial rules and tables. Furthermore, if the decedent's interest is measured with reference to the life of another person (such as a life estate pur autre vie), mortality tables will also come into play. Consider a relatively simple example: suppose that an irrevocable trust will pay income to A for A's life, with the remainder to be paid to B or B's estate. If B dies before A, the personal representative must determine the value of B's remainder interest which is included in B's gross estate under Section 2033. Stated differently, the amount included in B's gross estate is the present value of B's right to receive the trust assets outright upon A's death.[243]

For estates with valuation dates after April 30, 1989, Section 7520 and the regulations thereunder provide that the fair market value of annuities, interests for life or a term of years, and remainder or reversionary interests are calculated by means of a Section 7520 actuarial factor. This factor is derived by the using the applicable Section 7520 interest rate and, if the interest is measured with reference to a life, a mortality component.[244]

---

[241] Schauerhamer v. Comm'r, 73 TCM (CCH) 2855 (1997). See Estate of Reichardt v. Comm'r, 114 TC 144 (2000) (similarly applying Section 2036 because of an implied agreement that decedent had a right to income). Cf. Strangi v. Comm'r, 115 TC 478 (2000) (government's unsuccessful attempt to belatedly raise Section 2036 issue). See also ¶ 4.08[4][c] text accompanying note 49.

[242] See supra ¶¶ 4.02[4][c], 4.02[4][e][i].

[243] See IRC § 6163(a) (allowing an extension of time for payment of taxes on such interests) discussed at ¶ 3.07.

[244] IRC § 7520; Reg. §§ 20.7520-1(a)(1), 20.7520-1(b), 20.7520-1(c). See also Reg. § 20.2031-7(d)(1) for actuarial valuations after April 30, 1999. For estates with valuation dates after April 30, 1989, and before June 10, 1994, the personal representative may rely on tables published in Notice 89-24, 1989-1 CB 660, or Notice 89-60, 1989-1 CB 700 to value such interests. The present value of such interests for estates with valuation dates before May 1, 1999, is determined under regulations identified in Regulations Section 20.2031-7A.

The Section 7520 interest rate is equal to 120 percent of the applicable federal midterm rate in effect under Section 1274(d)(1) for the month in which the valuation date falls.[245] Gender-neutral tables for interest rates between 4.2 percent and 14.0 percent provide the actuarial factor to be used in calculating the present value of the property interest to be valued under Section 7520.[246] The regulations contain the tables to be used for estate tax purposes.[247] The precise method for using the tables to calculate the present value of ordinary remainder and reversionary interests, ordinary term-of-years and life interests, and annuities is also set out in the regulations.[248]

Where the Section 7520 tables produce an unrealistic valuation, it is unlikely that a court would consider other evidence of the value of a temporal interest in property. For example, there is disagreement with regard to the valuation of annuities in the form of lottery winnings where there are restrictions on the transferability of such winnings. See Estate of Gribauskas v. Comm'r, 116 TC 142 (2001) (no reduction under the Section 7520 tables); Estate of Cook v. Comm'r, 82 TCM (CCH) 154 (2001) (same). Compare Estate of Shackleford v. United States, 262 F3d 1068 (9th Cir 2001) (other evidence of and a reduction in value where the Section 7520 tables were not applied).

[245] IRC § 7520(a)(2). See Reg. § 20.7520-1(b)(1). The valuation date is the date of the transfer. Reg. § 20.7520-1(b)(1)(ii). The Section 7520 interest rate is determined and published monthly in the Internal Revenue Bulletin. Reg. § 20.7520-1(b)(1)(i). For estate tax purposes, this is the date of death or the Section 2032 alternate valuation date, if it is elected.

Special rules are provided for charitable transfers. See IRC § 7520(a) (flush language), Reg. § 20.7520-2, and ¶¶ 5.05[5][a] note 207, 5.05[5][b] note 265, 5.03[5][c] text accompanying note 290, 5.05[6][b] text accompanying notes 327, 328.

[246] Tables used for valuing Section 7520 property interests are scattered throughout the regulations, depending on the purpose of the valuation. The locations of the tables are identified in Regulations Section 20.7520-1(c)(1). The most recent actuarial tables relate to estates of decedent's dying after April 30, 1999. See supra note 244.

[247] Reg. § 20.2031-7(d)(6). The interest rate employed in the tables is rounded to the nearest ²⁄₁₀ of 1 percent (0.2 percent). IRC § 7520(a)(2) (parenthetical). The same tables are used for federal gift tax purposes. Reg. § 25.2512-5(a).

Many standard actuarial factors are not included in the tables under Regulations Section 20.2031-7(d)(6), but can be found in IRS Publication 1457, "Actuarial Values, Book Aleph," (7-1999). Reg. § 20.2031-7(d)(4). For example, Reg. § 20.2031-7(d)(6) does not contain tables with actuarial factors for life or term income interests, but those tables can be found in Publication 1457. Alternatively, Regulations Section 20.2031-7(d)(2)(iii) demonstrates how the factors can be determined mathematically using the tables in Regulations Section 20.2031-7(d)(6). If a special factor is required in order to value an interest, the Service will furnish the factor upon a request for a ruling. Reg. §§ 20.7520-1(c), 20.2031-7(d)(4).

[248] See Reg. §§ 20.2031-7(d)(2)(ii), 20.2031-7(d)(2)(iii), 20.2031-7(d)(2)(iv), respectively. For the present value of remainder interests in pooled income funds, charitable remainder annuity trusts, charitable remainder unitrusts, and the present value of life or term interests in charitable remainder unitrusts that are not calculated under the tables in Regulations Section 20.2031-7(d)(6), see ¶¶ 5.05[5][a][ii], 5.05[5][b][ii], 5.05[5][c][ii], 5.05[6][b]. The determination of the present value of an annuity or unitrust payable until the earlier of the lapse of a specific number of years or the death of an individual is made

Because Section 7520 values property interests by means of a projected rate of return and actuarial factors, there will be a discrepancy between the actual value of the interest and its value computed under Section 7520. The justification for the Section 7520 method of valuation is that it provides a system for uniform valuation. But in some circumstances the nature of the property interest is such that use of Section 7520 produces a value that is clearly distorted. Use of the Section 7520 method of valuation is inapplicable in some of these instances.[249] Section 7520 will not apply (nor will a special Section 7520 factor be required) if the property interest to be valued is subject to any contingency, power, or other restriction that is provided for in the governing instrument or caused by other circumstances and which changes the nature of the interest.[250] For example, Section 7520 will not apply for the purpose of valuing an income interest in unproductive property when the beneficiary does not have the legal right to compel investment in productive property.[251] The Section 7520 mortality component is also inapplicable if the decedent and the individual whose life is the measuring life, die as a result of a common accident or occurrence.[252]

When the value of an interest is measured by a life or lives, rather than by a fixed period, the physical condition of the measuring life will be taken into account in some cases. The Section 7520 mortality component is disregarded if the measuring life is "terminally ill" at the time of the decedent's death.[253] A person is considered to be terminally ill if: (1) the individual is "known to have an incurable illness or other deteriorating physical condition;" and (2) "there is at least a 50 percent probability" that the measuring life will die within one year of the decedent's death.[254] In those circumstances, the mea-

---

in accordance with Regulations Section 25.2512-5(d)(2)(iv). See Reg. § 20.2031-7(d)(2)(v).

[249] Reg. § 20.7520-3(a). See Reg. §§ 20.7520-3(a)(7), 20.7520-3(a)(8).

[250] Reg. §§ 20.7520-3(b)(1)(ii), 20.7520-3(b)(2). See Estate of Gribauskas v. Comm'r, 116 TC 142 (2001), for a discussion of such situations.

[251] Reg. § 20.7520-3(b)(2)(v) Ex. 1. Cf. Prop. Reg. § 1.643(b)-1.

[252] Reg. §§ 20.7520-3(b)(3)(iii), 20.7520-3(b)(4) Ex. 2.

[253] See Reg. §§ 20.7520-3(b)(3), 20.7520-3(b)(4) Ex. 1. Even before these regulations became effective for decedents dying after December 31, 1995, the courts and the Service had concluded that the actuarial tables were inappropriate where the death of the measuring life was imminent because of some incurable disease. In such cases, calculations were made with reference to the actual expected duration of the measuring life. See McLendon v. Comm'r, 66 TCM (CCH) 946 (1993); O'Reilly v. Comm'r, 973 F2d 1403 (8th Cir. 1992); Continental Ill. Nat'l Bank & Trust Co. v. United States, 504 F2d 586 (11th Cir. 1974); Jennings v. Comm'r, 10 TC 323 (1948); Rev. Rul. 80-80, 1980-1 CB 194; Priv. Ltr. Rul. 9504004 (Jan. 27, 1995). All of these precedents are now superseded by the regulations under Section 7520. See Rev. Rul. 96-3, 1996-1 CB 348.

[254] Reg. §§ 20.7520-3(b)(3)(i), 20.7520-3(b)(4) Ex. 1. But see ¶ 3.05[3][b] text accompanying notes 34, 35, explaining that the terminally ill valuation rules do not apply

suring life's actual physical condition is considered in valuing the relevant interest. But if the measuring life actually survives for at least eighteen months, the measuring life is presumed not to have been terminally ill at the time of the decedent's death, and the normal mortality tables will come into play, unless the contrary is established by "clear and convincing evidence."[255]

[6] Statutes Related to Valuation

[a] Understatement Penalty and Reasonable Cause: Sections 6662 and 6664

Apart from the proper computation of tax, valuation is also important from a more practical perspective. If an asset is undervalued on the federal estate tax return, an underpayment of estate tax will necessarily result. If the underpayment of estate tax is attributable to a "substantial estate or gift tax valuation understatement,"[256] the estate will owe, in addition to the underpayment amount, a penalty equal to 20 percent of the underpayment amount.[257] The penalty does not apply at all unless the underpayment attributable to a substantial estate or gift tax valuation understatement exceeds $5,000.[258] A substantial understatement occurs any time the value of property included in the gross estate (or the value of property transferred by gift for federal gift tax purposes) is 50 percent or less of the finally determined value.[259] Thus, if the personal representative states the value of an asset at $100,000 but the actual value of the asset is determined to be $200,000 or more, the substantial understatement penalty applies.

If the value of property included in the gross estate (or reported on the federal gift tax return) is 25 percent or less of the value finally determined, the penalty amount increases to 40 percent of the underpayment amount.[260] In the above example, the more drastic penalty would apply if the actual value of the asset is determined to be $400,000 or more.

---

for purposes of determining the value of a life interest received by a transferee that qualifies for a Section 2013 credit if there has been a final determination of the federal estate tax liability of the transferor estate requiring valuation of the life interest. See also Reg. § 20.7520-3(b)(3)(ii).

[255] Reg. § 20.7520-3(b)(3)(i).

[256] IRC § 6662(b)(5).

[257] IRC § 6662(a). If there is no tax due, for example because of the unlimited marital deductions or charitable deduction, no penalty is imposed because there is no underpayment.

[258] IRC § 6662(g)(2).

[259] IRC § 6662(g)(1).

[260] IRC §§ 6662(h)(1), 6662(h)(2)(C).

Section 6664(c) offers a safe harbor from the substantial understatement penalty. If the personal representative can prove that there was reasonable cause for the understatement and that the personal representative acted in good faith with respect to any portion of the valuation, the substantial understatement penalty will not apply to that portion.[261] Reliance on a professional appraisal will not, by itself, warrant relief from the penalty.[262] Consideration must also be given to the information supplied to the appraiser, the methodology used in the appraisal, the circumstances under which the appraisal was obtained, and the relationship, if any, of the appraiser to the parties in interest.[263] The Tax Court has held that a taxpayer who relied on the advice of a professional is not subject to the Section 6662 penalty if the following three-prong test is met: (1) the advisor was a competent professional who had sufficient expertise to justify reliance; (2) the taxpayer provided necessary and accurate information to the advisor; and (3) the taxpayer actually relied in good faith on the advisor's judgment.[264]

[b] Section 7491

In the context of valuation disputes, Section 7491 purports to shift the burden of proof to the Service if the taxpayer submits "credible evidence" in support of the taxpayer's valuation.[265] In reality, the burden shift is illusory. In most cases, the only "credible evidence" of valuation that will effectively shift the burden to the Service will be an expert appraisal.[266] In effect, the taxpayer must meet the traditional burden of proof to shift the burden to the Service.[267]

---

[261] IRC § 6664(c).

[262] Reg. § 1.6664-4(b)(1).

[263] Reg. § 1.6664-4(b)(1).

[264] DeCleene v. Comm'r, 115 TC 457 (2000) (an income tax case). See Reg. § 1.6664-4(c)(1); Shop Talk, "Will Tax Opinions of 'Interested' Professional Advisors Overcome Taxpayers' Penalties?" 94 J. Tax'n 189 (2001).

[265] IRC § 7491(a). The burden is shifted only if (1) the taxpayer kept records that meet the substantiation requirements of the Code; (2) the taxpayer cooperated with IRS requests for information and exhaust any available administrative remedies within the Service; and (3) the taxpayer is an individual or an estate, or, if the taxpayer is a trust, corporation or a partnership, its net worth does not exceed $7 million. IRC § 7491(b).

[266] The legislative history to Section 7491 defines "credible evidence" as "the quality of evidence which, after critical analysis, the court would find sufficient upon which to base a decision on the issue if no contrary evidence were submitted (without regard to the judicial presumption of IRS correctness)." S. Rep. No. 105-174, 105th Cong. 2d Sess. 1, 45 (1998), reprinted in 1998-3 CB 537, 581.

[267] See Jones, "The Burden of Proof Under the '98 Act—Not Much Substance Under All That Smoke" 90 J. Tax'n 133 (1999).

Additionally, the taxpayer must agree to several conditions for the burden shift to be effective.[268]

[c] Section 7517

Section 7517 is designed to reduce friction between taxpayers and the Service over estate, gift, or generation-skipping transfer tax valuation issues. If the Service challenges the value of an item stated on the estate tax return, the personal representative can require that within forty-five days of a request, the Service furnish the personal representative with a statement[269] that includes:[270] (1) the basis for the Service's conflicting valuation; (2) any computations used by the Service in arriving at the item's value; and (3) a copy of any expert appraisal performed for the Service.

This information is always helpful to a personal representative in deciding whether to contest the valuation issue, even though neither the value disclosed nor the valuation method used to determine the value disclosed is binding on the Service.[271]

[7] Exclusion of the Value of Land Subject to a Qualified Conservation Easement

[a] Introduction

Section 2031(c) allows an executor to elect to exclude a portion of the value of "land subject to a qualified conservation easement"[272] from a decedent's gross estate.[273] Section 2031(c) is unique in that it is the only provision that contains an exclusion from the gross estate. The exclusion is allowed where land included in the gross estate is subject to a qualified conservation easement. The exclusion is available even though an income tax deduction is allowed under Section 170 or an estate tax deduction is allowed under Section 2055 for the value of the qualified conservation easement.[274] However when

---

[268] IRC § 7491(a)(2).

[269] IRC § 7517(a). See Reg. § 301.7517-1.

[270] IRC § 7517(b). But see Estate of Abruzzo v. United States, 21 Cl. Ct. 351 (1990) (estate cannot delay discovery of its valuation reports until Service disclosed its report).

[271] IRC § 7517(c).

[272] IRC §§ 2031(c)(1), 2031(c)(8)(A). See infra ¶ 4.02[7][b].

[273] Section 2031(c) is discussed in Lindstrom & Small, "New Estate Tax Relief For Land Under Conservation Easement," 78 Tax Notes 1171 (Mar. 2, 1998).

[274] See infra ¶ 4.02[7][b] text accompanying notes 311–315.

either deduction is allowed, the amount of the exclusion may be reduced.[275] The qualified conservation easement may be granted by the decedent, a member of the decedent's family, the decedent's executor or a trustee if the land is held in trust.[276] Section 2031(c) may be elected to provide an exclusion to multiple estates as "land subject to the qualified conservation easement" is subsequently included in the gross estates of more than one family member.[277] The exclusion is subject to a ceiling limitation that increased over the years from $100,000 in 1998 to $500,000 in 2002 and thereafter.[278]

[b] Land Subject to a Qualified Conservation Easement

The exclusion applies only to "land subject to a qualified conservation easement."[279] As defined, that term imposes requirements related to the location[280] and the ownership[281] of the land. The qualified conservation easement[282] must be created by an applicable individual[283] either before, at, or after the death of the decedent.[284]

[i] Land to which the provision applies.

Location. The land whose value is to be partially excluded from the decedent's gross estate must be located in the United States or in a possession[285] of the United States.[286] As originally enacted and for the years 1998 through 2000, a more stringent location requirement applied.[287] The rule expanding the

---

[275] IRC § 2031(c)(1)(A). See infra ¶ 4.02[7][d][i], especially note 326.

[276] See infra ¶ 4.02[7][b] text accompanying notes 311–315.

[277] See infra ¶¶ 4.02[7][b], 4.02[7][c] text accompanying notes 319, 320.

[278] IRC § 2031(c)(3). See infra ¶ 4.02[7][d][iii]. The maximum estate tax savings resulting from an election of Section 2031(c) is $250,000 (50 percent (the maximum tax rate in 2002–2003) times of $500,000 (the maximum ceiling)). The maximum savings varies partially dependent upon the year involved. See IRC §§ 2011(c)(2), 2031(c)(3).

[279] IRC §§ 2031(c)(1), 2031(c)(8)(A).

[280] IRC § 2031(c)(8)(A)(i).

[281] IRC § 2031(c)(8)(A)(ii).

[282] IRC § 2031(c)(8)(A)(iii).

[283] IRC §§ 2031(c)(8)(A)(iii), 2031(c)(8)(C).

[284] IRC §§ 2031(c)(8)(A)(iii), 2031(c)(8)(C), 2031(c)(6). See infra ¶ 4.02[7][b] text accompanying notes 311–315.

[285] Cf. IRC §§ 2208, 2209; ¶ 8.09.

[286] IRC § 2031(c)(8)(i). The provision is effective for estates of decedents dying after December 31, 2000. Economic Growth and Tax Relief Reconciliation Act of 2001, Pub. L. No. 107-16, § 551(c), 115 Stat. 38, 86 (2001), reprinted in 2001-__ CB __, __.

[287] Under Section 2031(c)(8)(A)(i) prior to amendment in the Economic Growth and Tax Relief Reconciliation Act of 2001, the land had to meet one of three alternative location requirements on the date of the decedent's death. Economic Growth and Tax Relief Reconciliation Act of 2001, Pub. L. No. 107-16, § 551(a), 115 Stat. 38, 86 (2001), re-

scope of Section 2031(c) was enacted to allow more land to qualify in an effort to preserve environmentally significant land.[288]

Ownership. The land must have been owned by the decedent or a member of the decedent's family at all times during the three-year period ending on
the date of the decedent's death.[289] The term "member of the decedent's family" is broadly defined to include the decedent's ancestors, spouse, and lineal
descendants as well as the lineal descendants of the decedent's parents and
spouse and the spouses of all such lineal descendants.[290] If the land that is subject to a qualified conservation easement is held in a partnership, corporation
or trust, Section 2031(c) is applicable to the interest in the entity only if at
least 30 percent of the entity is owned directly or indirectly[291] by the decedent.[292]

[ii] Qualified conservation easement.

---

printed in 2001-__ CB __, __. It had to be located in or within (1) twenty-five miles of a
metropolitan area (see now-repealed IRC § 2031(c)(8)(A)(i)(I). The term metropolitan area
is defined by the Office of Management and Budget. See Office of Management and
Budget, Bulletin No. 96-08 (1996)); (2) twenty-five miles of a national park or wilderness
area that is part of the National Wilderness Preservation System (see now-repealed IRC
§ 2031(c)(8)(A)(i)(II). The National Wilderness Preservation System was established by
the Wilderness Act. Wilderness Act, Pub. L. No. 88-577, §2, 78 Stat. 890 (1964). Land
located within twenty-five miles of a national park or wilderness area, however, did not
qualify for the exclusion if the Secretary determined that the land was not under significant development pressure. IRC § 2031(c)(8)(A)(i)(II)); or (3) ten miles of an Urban National Forest (see now-repealed IRC § 2031(c)(8)(A)(i)(III). The Forest Service designates
what constitutes an Urban National Forest. Id.). However, under the "sunset" provision of
the 2001 legislation, these restrictions may return in 2011. See ¶ 8.10[5].

[288] H. Rep. No. 107-37, 107th Cong., 1st Sess. 33 (2001), reprinted in 2001-__ CB
__, __. In addition, the prior rules were technical and it was unclear how distances were
to be measured.

[289] IRC § 2031(c)(8)(A)(ii).

[290] IRC § 2031(c)(8)(D). See IRC § 2032A(e)(2); ¶ 4.04[3][b][vii]. A legally adopted
child of an individual is considered a child of the individual by blood. IRC § 2032A(e)(2).

[291] Section 2057(e)(3)(B) indirect ownership rules are employed to determine ownership for purposes of Section 2031(c)(10). IRC § 2031(c)(10). Ownership is determined
under Section 2057(e)(3)(A). IRC § 2031(c)(10). Thus, the 30 percent test should be applied to both combined voting power *and* total value with respect to a corporation (see
Section 2057(e)(3)(A)(i)) and 30 percent of the capital interests with respect to a partnership (see Section 2057(e)(3)(A)(ii)). See ¶ 5.08[2][c] text accompanying notes 62–64.

[292] IRC § 2031(c)(10). Land held in a trust should qualify for the exclusion where the
trust is included in the decedent's gross estate under Sections 2035, 2036, 2037, or 2038.
It is difficult to determine how the literal requirements of Section 2031(c)(8)(A)(iii)
can be satisfied if the land is owned by a corporation or partnership. If the easement was
created by an individual and transferred to the entity, the literal requirements could be
met. In the alternative, seemingly if the requirements of Section 2031(c)(10) are satisfied,
the corporate or partnership entity is pierced and the individual partner or shareholder is
treated as satisfying the Section 2031(c)(8)(A)(iii) requirements. In addition, the entity

Definition. The land qualifying for the Section 2031(c) exclusion must be subject to a "qualified conservation easement,"[293] which is defined as a restriction limiting the use of the land for "conservation purposes"[294] given in perpetuity[295] to a qualified organization.[296] The restriction on use must include a prohibition on use of a qualified real property interest[297] in the land for commercial recreational activity other than a use that is de minimis.[298] Conservation purposes include the preservation of land areas for outdoor recreation by, or for the education of, the general public;[299] the protection of a relatively natural habitat of fish, wildlife, plants or similar ecosystem;[300] and the preservation of open space (including farmland and forests) where the preservation is either for the scenic enjoyment of the public or pursuant to a clearly delineated governmental conservation policy and where the preservation will yield a significant public benefit.[301] However, no exclusion is allowed for an easement for the preservation of an historically important land area or a certified historic structure.[302]

---

would be pierced for purposes of satisfying the Section 2031(c)(8)(A)(ii) requirement. The legislative history provides no guidance; thus, regulatory guidance is needed.

[293] IRC §§ 2031(c)(1)(A), 2031(c)(8)(B).

[294] IRC §§ 170(h)(1)(C), 170(h)(4)(A)(i), 170(h)(4)(A)(ii), 170(h)(4)(A)(iii).

[295] IRC § 170(h)(2)(C).

[296] IRC § 2031(c)(8)(B). The term "qualified organization" is defined in Section 170(h)(3). See ¶ 5.05[7][c] note 346.

[297] A qualified real property interest may be the entire interest in the land (other than a qualified mineral interest), a remainder interest, or a restriction (granted in perpetuity) on the use which may be made of the real property. IRC § 170(h)(2).

[298] IRC § 2031(c)(8)(B). See HR Conf. Rep. No. 105-220, 105th Cong., 1st Sess. 403 (1997), reprinted in 1997-4 CB (Vol. 2) 1457, 1873. De minimis commercial recreational activity consistent with the conservation purpose, such as the granting of hunting or fishing licenses, will not prevent the land from qualifying for the Section 2031(c) exclusion. HR Conf. Rep. No. 105-220, 105th Cong., 1st Sess. 403 (1997), reprinted in 1997-4 CB (Vol. 2) 1457, 1873. The Secretary of the Treasury will provide guidance to indicate the scope of the de minimis exception. Id.

[299] IRC § 170(h)(4)(A)(i).

[300] IRC § 170(h)(4)(A)(ii).

[301] IRC § 170(h)(4)(A)(iii). See IRC §§ 170(h)(1)(C), 2031(c)(8)(B). The conservation policy may be that of the federal, state or local government.

[302] IRC §§ 2031(c)(8)(B), 170(h)(4)(A)(iv). The exclusion is not available for historic structures because the legislation was not intended to exclude structures, just land. The fact that the exclusion is not available for historically important land areas is in all likelihood merely a mistake. See Lindstrom & Small, "New Estate Tax Relief For Land Under Conservation Easement," 78 Tax Notes 1171, 1174 (Mar. 2, 1998).

Qualified Grantors. The qualified conservation easement must be conveyed by an individual[303] who is either the decedent,[304] a member of the decedent's family,[305] the executor of the decedent's estate,[306] or the trustee of a trust the corpus of which includes the land subject to the easement.[307] If land is subject to a qualified conservation easement that was created by anyone other than one of those applicable individuals is included in a decedent's gross estate, the land does not qualify for an exclusion under Section 2031(c).[308]

Timing. The qualified conservation easement must be placed on the land by the date of the election to use the Section 2031(c) exclusion.[309] Although the easement may have been placed on the land before the decedent's death or at the decedent's death, it may also be placed on the land after the decedent's death as long as it is placed on the land no later than the date of the Section 2031(c) election which is made on the decedent's federal estate tax return.[310]

Combining the qualified grantor and timing rules,[311] a "qualified conservation easement" that qualifies a portion of the value of land for the Section 2031(c) exclusion may be:

(1) created by a family member (or the family member's executor or trustee) prior to receipt of the property by the decedent (with a Section 170 or Section 2055(a) deduction to the family member but not to the decedent);[312]

---

[303] IRC § 2031(c)(8)(A)(iii). Cf. supra ¶ 4.02[7][b] note 292.

[304] IRC § 2031(c)(8)(C)(i).

[305] IRC § 2031(c)(8)(C)(ii). Members of the decedent's family means any member of the family as defined in Section 2032A(e)(2). IRC § 2031(c)(8)(D). See supra ¶ 4.02[7][b] text accompanying note 290.

[306] IRC § 2031(c)(8)(C)(iii). Although a qualified conservation easement is to be made by an "individual," a corporate fiduciary serving as executor of the decedent's estate should be a qualified grantor. See IRC §§ 2031(c)(8)(A)(iii), 2031(c)(8)(C).

[307] IRC § 2031(c)(8)(C)(iv). A corporate trustee, although not an individual, should be permitted to convey a qualified conservation easement. See supra note 306, ¶ 4.02[7][b] note 292.

[308] For example, if a decedent's land passes to a non–family member and that individual conveys a qualified conservation easement prior to the filing of the decedent's estate tax return, the decedent's gross estate does not qualify for a Section 2031(c) exclusion.

[309] IRC § 2031(c)(8)(A)(iii). The election is discussed infra ¶ 4.02[7][c].

[310] IRC §§ 2031(c)(8)(A)(iii), 2031(c)(9). See infra ¶ 4.02[7][c] text accompanying note 318.

[311] See supra text accompanying notes 303–310.

[312] This would result in an income or estate tax deduction to the family member and an inclusion in the decedent's gross estate of the value of the land reduced by the value of the easement and further reduced by the amount of the Section 2031(c) exclusion.

(2) created by the decedent or the trustee of the decedent's revocable trust during the decedent's lifetime (with a Section 170 deduction to the decedent during the decedent's lifetime);[313]

(3) created by the decedent's executor or trustee after the decedent's death and prior to the timely filing of the decedent's estate tax return (with a Section 2055(a) deduction to the decedent's estate);[314] or

(4) created by a family member after the land is distributed from the estate prior to the timely filing of the decedent's estate tax return (with a Section 170 deduction to the distributee).[315]

[c] The Election

Section 2031(c) applies only if an election is made by the decedent's executor[316] on the decedent's estate tax return.[317] The election must be made on or before the due date (including extensions) of the filing of the return, and once made, the election is irrevocable.[318]

More than one exclusion election may be made with respect to land subject to a qualified conservation easement. For example, if such land passes from the decedent to the decedent's surviving spouse[319] or some other family member, when that family member dies a Section 2031(c) exclusion may again be elected if the requirements of Section 2031(c) are otherwise met.[320]

---

[313] This would result in an income tax deduction for the decedent during the decedent's life, an inclusion in the decedent's gross estate of the value of the land reduced by the value of the easement and further reduced by the Section 2031(c) exclusion.

[314] This would result in both an exclusion under Section 2031(c) and an estate tax deduction under Section 2055(a) for the decedent's gross estate, but no Section 170 income tax deduction on the creation of the easement. See Priv. Ltr. Rul. 200143011 (July 25, 2001) (portion of property included in decedent's gross estate qualified for both Section 2031(c) and Section 2055 with no violation of Section 2031(c)(9), while portion not included in gross estate qualified for a Section 170 deduction).

[315] Cf. IRC § 2031(c)(9). This would result in a Section 2031(c) exclusion to the decedent's gross estate and a Section 170 deduction to the distributee, but no Section 2055(a) deduction to the decedent's estate. See infra ¶ 4.02[7][c] note 326.

[316] IRC § 2031(c)(1). See ¶ 8.02. The term would include the trustee of a living trust in the absence of any other executor of the estate. See ¶ 8.02 note 12.

[317] IRC § 2031(c)(6).

[318] IRC § 2031(c)(6).

[319] Cf. infra ¶ 4.02[7][e] text accompanying notes 375–379.

[320] The statute does not preclude multiple use of the exclusion with respect to a qualified conservation easement.

[d] The Amount of the Exclusion

The amount of the Section 2031(c) exclusion is determined by first adjusting the value of the land that is subject to the qualified conservation easement and then multiplying the adjusted land value by an applicable percentage.[321] However, the amount that may be excluded is also subject to a ceiling limitation.[322]

[i] **The value of the land.** In computing the amount of the exclusion, the determination of the value of the land begins with a determination of its value for federal estate tax purposes.[323] If the easement has been placed on the land prior to the date of the decedent's death, the value of the land is reduced for gross estate inclusion purposes by the value of the qualified conservation easement at the date of the decedent's death.[324] If the qualified conservation easement is placed on the land at or subsequent to the death of the decedent, then the value of the land included within the gross estate is not reduced by the value of the qualified conservation easement; instead, the date of death value of the land without regard to the easement is determined, and then that value is reduced by the amount of any Section 2055 deduction allowed to the estate for the qualified conservation easement.[325] Thus, the possibility of both a gross estate exclusion and an estate tax charitable deduction for the value of the qualified conservation easement is foreclosed.[326] For example, if a decedent

---

[321] IRC § 2031(c)(1)(A).

[322] IRC § 2031(c)(1)(B). See infra ¶ 4.02[7][d][iii].

[323] See IRC §§ 2031, 2032, 2032A. See infra ¶ 4.02[7][e][ii].

[324] See IRC §§ 2031, 2032, 2032A. Although the value of a qualified conservation easement is not included in the transfer tax base whether the transfer is inter vivos or testamentary, an inter vivos transfer has the added advantage of generating an income tax deduction. IRC § 170.

[325] IRC § 2031(c)(1)(A). See ¶ 5.05[7][c]. The Section 2055 deduction is limited to the fair market value of the qualified conservation easement. IRC §§ 2055(a), 2055(f).

Thus, the net value used in determining the amount of the Section 2031(c) exclusion is the same whether the qualified conservation easement is conveyed before the decedent's death or is conveyed by the estate after the decedent's death. Cf. infra note 326.

[326] If an income tax deduction is allowed to a family member for the creation of a qualified conservation easement by the family member after the decedent's death and prior to the timely filing of the decedent's federal estate tax return (see supra ¶ 4.02[7][b] text accompanying note 315), the value of the land should *not* be reduced by amount of the Section 170 deduction in computing the Section 2031(c)(1)(A) amount, because no Section 2055 deduction is allowed to the estate and hence no taxable estate reduction occurs for the value of the easement.

The statute does not preclude the possibility of both an income tax deduction and an estate tax exclusion for the full value of the property. Section 2031(c)(9) precludes an income tax deduction "*to the estate*" (emphasis added) if a Section 2055(f) deduction is allowed, but it seemingly does not preclude a Section 170 income tax deduction to a family member distributee of the estate prior to filing the decedent's estate tax return. This literal

owned land worth $100,000 subject to no acquisition indebtedness and no retained development rights, and the land was subject to a qualified conservation easement worth $30,000 for which the amount of the gross estate was reduced (if the easement was created prior to decedent's death) or for which a $30,000 Section 2055 deduction was taken by the estate, only the $70,000 net value would be multiplied by the applicable fraction in computing the exclusion.[327]

The value of the land used in the determination of the exclusion is subject to two further reductions that effectively prevent the allowance of an exclusion to the extent that the property is "debt-financed"[328] or to the extent that the qualified grantor has retained any "development rights"[329] in the property.[330]

Debt-Financed Property. The value of the land is reduced to the extent that the property is "debt-financed property."[331] Thus, generally only the decedent's equity interest in the property qualifies for an exclusion under Section 2031(c). This reduction makes sense because, to the extent the property is

---

reading of the statute is not necessarily inconsistent with the legislative history of Section 2031(c)(9) which states that "no income tax deduction is allowed to the estate or *the qualified heirs* with respect to such postmortem conservation easements [with respect to which a Section 2055(f) deduction is allowed]." (Emphasis added) S. Rep. No. 105-174, 105th Cong., 2d Sess. 161 (1998), reprinted in 1998-3 CB 537, 697.

[327] This interpretation of the Section 2031(c)(1)(A) computation eliminates the overlap of the deduction and the exclusion and is supported by the legislative history. HR Conf. Rep. No. 105-220, 105th Cong., 1st Sess. 402 (1997), reprinted in 1997-4 CB (Vol. 2) 1457, 1872. The legislative history provides that the "exclusion amount is calculated based on the value of the property after the conservation easement has been placed on the property." Id.

To apply the applicable percentage to the value of the land without accounting for the easement and then reduce the resulting figure by the amount of the Section 2055 deduction would result in a large disparity between the effect of an inter vivos and a testamentary transfer of a qualified conservation easement in the determination of the Section 2031(c) exclusion. For example, if Decedent conveyed just before death a qualified conservation easement worth $30,000 and the value of the land subject to the easement was $70,000 at Decedent's death, taking into account the easement, $28,000 could be excluded form Decedent's gross estate under Section 2031(c). Alternatively, assume that Decedent devised an easement worth $30,000 on land valued at $100,000 at death and a $30,000 Section 2055 deduction was allowed. If the 40 percent applicable percentage is applied to the value of the land, $100,000, and the result, $40,000, is then reduced by the Section 2055 deduction allowed, $30,000, only $10,000 of the value of the land would qualify for exclusion under Section 2031(c). However if the value of the land, $100,000, is reduced by the Section 2055 deduction, $30,000, before the 40 percent applicable percentage is applied, the Section 2031(c) exclusion amount is $28,000, an exclusion equaling the same amount excluded where the easement was conveyed before death. See also supra text accompanying note 326.

[328] IRC § 2031(c)(4).

[329] IRC § 2031(c)(5)(D).

[330] IRC § 2031(c)(5)(A).

[331] IRC § 2031(c)(4)(A).

debt-financed, the property is not included in the decedent's taxable estate even in the absence of Section 2031(c).[332] Debt-financed property is defined as property upon which there is acquisition indebtedness at the date of the decedent's death.[333] Acquisition indebtedness is defined to include indebtedness incurred in the acquisition of the property,[334] incurred prior to acquisition of the property that would not have been incurred but for such acquisition,[335] or incurred after the acquisition of the property if it would not have been incurred but for the acquisition and such indebtedness was reasonably foreseeable at the time of the acquisition.[336] The term also includes any extension, renewal, or refinancing of such acquisition indebtedness.[337]

Retained Development Rights. The value of the property is also reduced by the value of any development rights retained in the land by the qualified grantor in the conveyance of a qualified conservation easement.[338] A development right is a right to use the land for any commercial purpose which is not subordinate to *and* directly supportive of the use of the land as a farm for farming purposes.[339]

However, there is no reduction for the value of retained development rights to the extent that all persons who have an interest in the land (possessory or not) at the time of the agreement execute an agreement to extinguish permanently some or all of such development rights and such agreement is made prior to the date for filing the decedent's estate tax return.[340] Thus, if the parties agree to extinguish some or all of such rights, the exclusion *may*[341] be increased and the estate tax reduced. Any failure to implement the relinquish-

---

[332] See IRC § 2053(a)(4); ¶ 5.03[6].

[333] IRC § 2031(c)(4)(B)(i). One should question why this reduction is limited to acquisition indebtedness. It would seem that it should apply to any indebtedness on the property.

[334] IRC § 2031(c)(4)(B)(ii)(I).

[335] IRC § 2031(c)(4)(B)(ii)(II).

[336] IRC §§ 2031(c)(4)(B)(ii)(III). See also IRC § 514(b).

[337] IRC § 2031(c)(4)(B)(ii)(IV).

[338] IRC § 2031(c)(5)(A).

[339] IRC § 2031(c)(5)(D). The term "farming purposes" is defined in Section 2032A(e)(5). See ¶ 4.04[3][b][iii].

[340] IRC § 2031(c)(5)(B). Priv. Ltr. Rul. 200014013 (Dec. 22, 1999) (valid extinction of retained development rights).The agreement must be filed with the estate tax return. IRC § 2031(c)(5)(B). The Instructions for Form 706 list six items which must be included in the agreement and must be signed by all of the parties to the agreement. Instructions for Form 706, United States Estate (and Generation-Skipping Transfer) Tax Return, Schedule U Line 8 at page 24 (Revised July, 1999).Such extinguished development rights are also disregarded when determining the Section 2031(c)(2) applicable percentage. See infra text accompanying note 346.

[341] IRC § 2031(c)(5)(B). But see infra text accompanying note 353 demonstrating that the exclusion instead may be decreased.

ment agreement within two years of the date of the decedent's death (or on or before the date of sale of the land, if earlier) generally results in the imposition of additional estate tax taking such retained development rights into consideration in computing the amount of the exclusion.[342] The method to be employed to determine the amount of estate tax attributable to such retained development rights is to be specified by the Secretary.[343]

[ii] **The applicable percentage.** The applicable percentage is generally 40 percent.[344] However, the percentage is reduced (not below zero) by two percentage points for each percentage point (or fraction thereof) by which the value of the qualified conservation easement at the time of the contribution is less than 30 percent of the value of the land at such time.[345] The easement is disregarded in valuing the land for purposes of determining the denominator used in calculating the percentage reduction; however, in computing the denominator, the value of the land is reduced by the value of any development rights retained.[346] If the value of the qualified conservation easement is equal to 15 percent of the value of the land (both values determined at the time of the contribution and disregarding the qualified conservation easement) and if

---

[342] IRC § 2031(c)(5)(C). The additional tax will be due within six months of such triggering date. Id. But see infra text accompanying note 353. Even though the estate tax is terminated for decedents dying after December 31, 2009 (see IRC § 2210(a)), this recapture rule applies until December 31, 2011 for decedents dying prior to January 1, 2010. See ¶ 8.10[2][b][iii].

An agreement of this type may be used to defer payment of any additional estate tax related to the retained development rights until six months after the earlier of the date two years after the decedent's death or the date of the sale of the land.

[343] IRC § 2031(c)(7) last sentence. The Secretary is also directed to prescribe the forms to be used. Id.

[344] IRC § 2031(c)(2). The Instructions for Form 706 provide that if the easement was granted for consideration, the value of the easement is reduced by any consideration received. If the date of death value of the easement is different from the value at the time the consideration was received, the reduction is for the portion of the consideration received. The Instructions for Form 706, United States Estate (and Generation-Skipping Transfer) Tax Return, Schedule U Line 11 at 24 (Rev. July, 1999).

[345] IRC § 2031(c)(2). See IRC § 2031(c)(8)(B). Cf. supra ¶ 4.02[7][b] text accompanying notes 311–315.

[346] IRC § 2031(c)(2). See supra text accompanying notes 340–342.

This reduction in the denominator may work to a taxpayer's advantage, because a reduction in the denominator (of the value of the retained development rights) increases the percentage of the value of the qualified conservation easement to the adjusted value of the land and may increase the Section 2031(c)(2) applicable percentage. This result seems inappropriate and is probably based on the thinking that since such rights may not be excluded under Section 2031(c) (see supra text accompanying notes 338–342), they should result in a reduction of the amount used in computing the applicable percentage. However, this reduction may actually result in an increase of the exclusion. See infra text accompanying note 353.

there are no retained development rights, the applicable percentage is reduced to 10 percent.[347] If, at the time of the contribution, the value of the easement is equal to only 10 percent of the value of the land (disregarding the qualified conservation easement) and if there are no retained development rights, the applicable percentage is zero[348] and no exclusion is allowed under Section 2031(c).

[iii] **The exclusion limitation.** The value of land qualifying for the exclusion[349] is subject to an "exclusion limitation"[350] that imposes a ceiling on the maximum amount that can be excluded from the gross estate under Section 2031(c). The exclusion limitation was phased in between 1998 and 2002 and is currently $500,000.[351]

[iv] **Examples.** Some examples might be helpful in demonstrating the computation of the amount of the Section 2031(c) exclusion. If a decedent owned land worth $100,000, both at the date of the decedent's death and the time of the contribution, which was subject to no acquisition indebtedness and no retained development rights and the land was subject to a qualified conservation easement worth $30,000 (either created during decedent's life or by the decedent's executor), the amount of the Section 2031(c) exclusion would be $28,000. This amount of the exclusion is the product of the net value of the land at the decedent's death, $70,000, multiplied by a 40 percent applicable percentage. Because the ratio of the value of the easement to the value of the land (not reduced by the easement) at the time of the contribution is exactly 30 percent, no reduction of the applicable percentage occurs. In addition, regardless of the year involved, the exclusion limitation is inapplicable if the land were worth $100,000 at the time of the contribution, but $150,000 at the date of the decedent's death and the easement was worth $30,000 at both the date

---

[347] Because 15 percent is 15 percentage points below 30 percent, the 40 percent applicable percentage is reduced by 30 percentage points (two percentage points for each of those 15 percentage points) to 10 percent.

[348] Because 10 percent is 20 percentage points below 30 percent, the 40 percent applicable percentage is reduced by 40 percentage points to zero, 2 percentage points for each of those 20 percentage points.

[349] See IRC § 2031(c)(1)(A).

[350] IRC § 2031(c)(1)(B).

[351] IRC § 2031(c)(1). The phase-in schedule was as follows:

Year of Decedent's Death	Exclusion Limitation
1998	$100,000
1999	$200,000
2000	$300,000
2001	$400,000
2002 and thereafter	$500,000

of the creation of the easement and of the decedent's death, the amount of the exclusion would be $48,000, the net estate tax value of the property, $120,000, multiplied by the 40 percent applicable percentage. If the land was worth $1 million and the easement was worth $300,000, both at the date of the decedent's death and the time of the contribution, the potential exclusion would be $280,000, but the amount of the Section 2031(c) exclusion would depend on the year involved. If the decedent died prior to the year 2000, the exclusion would be limited, but if the decedent died after 1999, the full $280,000 exclusion would be allowed. If the easement on the $1 million property was valued at only $200,000, then the potential exclusion would be $160,000, the $800,000 net value of the land multiplied by a 20 percent applicable percentage.[352] If, however, the decedent had retained development rights worth $200,000 on the property, the amount of the potential exclusion would be increased to $180,000, $600,000 (the net value of the land reduced by the development rights) multiplied by a 30 percent applicable percentage.[353]

[e] The Interrelationship of Section 2031(c) and Other Estate Tax Sections and Other Taxes

[i] **Introduction.** The resolution of many of the issues that arise with respect to the interrelationship of Section 2031(c) with other estate tax sections and to other taxes depends upon the underlying nature of the Section 2031(c) exclusion. In all probability, the underlying nature of Section 2031(c) is an exclusion of *specific land* from the decedent's gross estate.[354] However, it can

---

[352] The percentage of the value of the easement to the land (not reduced by the easement) would be 20 percent ($200,000/$1 million), and the applicable percentage would be 20 percent, 40 percent reduced by 20 percent (two times 10 percent).

[353] The applicable percentage is 30 percent, because the $200,000 value of the easement over $800,000 (the $1 million value of the land not reduced by the easement but reduced by the $200,000 retained development rights) is 25 percent. As a result, the applicable percentage is 30 percent, 40 percent less 10 percent (2 times 5 percent). Thus, in some circumstances, a retention of development rights results in an *increase* in the amount of the exclusion. See supra note 346.

[354] As a result of the income tax basis rules of Section 1014(a)(4) (see infra text accompanying notes 393–404), it is likely that Section 2031(c)(1)(A) excludes a portion of the value of the land subject to the qualified conservation easement from the gross estate, and a specific asset is therefore excluded. Section 2031(c)(1)(B) can be interpreted as simply imposing a dollar ceiling on the amount of the exclusion of such assets.

When read in conjunction with Section 2033, Section 2031(c) also would seem to provide for such an asset exclusion. Section 2033 provides that "[t]he value of the gross estate shall include the value of all property to the extent of the interest therein of the decedent at the time of his death." IRC § 2033. Section 2031(c) then provides that " . . . there shall be excluded from the gross estate . . . the value of land subject to a qualified conservation easement. . . . " IRC § 2031(c)(1).

also be argued that Section 2031(c) provides an exclusion of *a dollar amount* (but not specific land) from the gross estate[355] or even a *combination* of the two alternatives, an exclusion of specific land if Section 2031(c)(1)(A) applies or of a dollar amount if Section 2031(c)(1)(B) applies.[356] In considering the three alternatives, the third alternative seems inappropriate in that different decedents' estates would be treated inconsistently with more stringent rules applied to a decedent with land with a smaller value.[357] The legislative history fails to deal with the issue of the nature of the exclusion[358] and, to date, the Treasury has not taken a position offering guidance with respect to the interrelationship of Section 2031(c) with other estate tax provisions and other taxes.

[ii] Interrelationships with other estate tax provisions.

The Interrelationship With Section 2032A. An election to use the Section 2031(c) exclusion does not preclude an election to value the property under Section 2032A.[359] Furthermore, if a qualified heir grants a qualified conservation easement over the property, the grant is not a disposition that triggers the recapture tax under Section 2032A(c).[360] However, beyond those conclusions, the interrelationship of Sections 2031(c) and 2032A is often unclear. Most of the interrelationship problems between the two sections involve the issue of the extent to which one section is taken into consideration in satisfying the qualification requirements under the other section. A chicken and egg type Section 2031(c)–Section 2032A interrelationship problem occurs when real

---

[355] It can be argued that Section 2031(c)(1)(B) excludes a dollar amount, $100,000 to $500,000 depending on the year of death and that Section 2031(c)(1)(A) limits the dollar amount to the value of the land included in the gross estate.

[356] It can be argued that when Section 2031(c)(1)(A) determines the exclusion, there is a specific exclusion of land and that when Section 2031(c)(1)(B) applies, it excludes a dollar amount but not specific land.

[357] In general, if the value of a decedent's land is small, then Section 2031(c)(1)(A) applies with more stringent rules limiting what would be an asset specific exclusion. If the land value is larger, Section 2031(c)(1)(B) applies a dollar amount exclusion with more lenient rules. It hardly seems that Congress would want to be more stringent on land with a smaller value than a larger one.

As a result, this alternative will be disregarded in the discussion below.

[358] See S. Rep. No. 105-33, 105th Cong., 1st Sess. 45 (1997), reprinted in 1997-4 CB (Vol. 2) 1067, 1125, HR Conf. Rep. No. 105-220, 105th Cong., 1st Sess. 403 (1997), reprinted in 1997-4 CB (Vol. 2) 1457, 1873.

[359] S. Rep. No. 105-33, 105th Cong., 1st Sess. 47 (1997), reprinted in 1997-4 CB (Vol. 2) 1067, 1127.

[360] IRC § 2032A(c)(8). See ¶ 4.04[7][b][i].

When additional estate tax is imposed under Section 2032A(c), the property initially valued under Section 2032A is effectively revalued at its fair market value. See ¶ 4.04[7][c][ii]. If this results in an alteration in the amount of the Section 2031(c) exclusion, it may change the amount of the additional estate tax imposed under Section 2032A(c). See ¶ 4.04[7][c][ii].

property that is potentially eligible for a Section 2032A reduction in value is also potentially eligible for a Section 2031(c) exclusion and an executor elects the application of both sections. It is unclear which section is applied first. The statutes do not explicitly state the impact of a Section 2032A reduction in value on the requirements to qualify for the Section 2031(c) exclusion.[361] Similarly, the impact of a Section 2031(c) exclusion on the qualification requirements for Section 2032A valuation is not specifically addressed.[362] The question is best resolved by assuming that the other section is applicable in determining qualification under each section, i.e., measuring the amount of the Section 2031(c) exclusion by using Section 2032A valuation and testing Section 2032A qualification by applying the Section 2031(c) exclusion.

The effect of a Section 2032A election on satisfying the requirements of Section 2031(c) is first considered. Recall that the value of the land is significant in determining the amount of the Section 2031(c) exclusion.[363] If the land subject to the qualified conservation easement is valued under Section 2032A,[364] any such special Section 2032A valuation should be used in measuring the amount of the Section 2031(c) exclusion.

The impact that an exclusion under Section 2031(c) has on the qualification for Section 2032A must be similarly analyzed. Section 2032A(b)(1) imposes two tests that an estate must satisfy in order for the estate to qualify for Section 2032A treatment. Under the first test, the adjusted value of the *real and personal property* being used on the decedent's date of death for a qualified use by the decedent or a member of the decedent's family which meets certain duration of ownership and material participation tests and that was acquired from or passed from the decedent to a qualified heir of the decedent must equal or exceed 50 percent of the adjusted value of the gross estate.[365] Under the second test, the adjusted value of only *real property* that meets similar requirements, must equal or exceed 25 percent of the adjusted gross estate.[366] Under both of the percentage tests, the denominator of the fraction is based on the value of the gross estate determined without regard to Section 2032A.[367] The numerator of both tests is based on the value of property included in the gross estate determined without regard to Section 2032A.[368] None of these definitions specifically provides for the exclusion under Section

---

[361] See IRC §§ 2031(c)(1)(A), 2031(c)(2). See supra ¶ 4.02[7][d].

[362] IRC §§ 2032A(b)(1)(A), 2032A(b)(1)(B).

[363] See supra ¶ 4.02[7][d] text accompanying note 323.

[364] The land may be valued at fair market value under Section 2031 or Section 2032 if the land is separate from the real property valued under Section 2032A.

[365] IRC § 2032A(b)(1)(A). See ¶ 4.04[3][b].

[366] IRC § 2032A(b)(1)(B). See ¶ 4.04[3][c].

[367] IRC § 2032A(b)(3)(A).

[368] IRC §§ 2032A(b)(1)(A), 2032A(b)(1)(B).

2031(c).[369] Because the denominator of both fractions is a function of the gross estate, the Section 2031(c) exclusion (regardless of its nature) should reduce the denominator of both fractions. The effect of Section 2031(c) on the numerator of both fractions depends upon a number of factors. If the land subject to the easement is not a part of the special valuation property, Section 2031(c) has no effect on the numerators. If the land is a part of the special valuation property, then the nature of the Section 2031(c) exclusion becomes relevant.[370] If, as is likely, the nature of the Section 2031(c) exclusion is effectively a reduction for estate tax purposes in the value of the specific land,[371] then the exclusion would reduce the numerators of both of the fractions.[372] In the alternative, if the nature of the Section 2031(c) exclusion is related to a dollar amount and not a specific asset,[373] then the numerators of neither fraction would be reduced by the Section 2031(c) exclusion.[374]

The Interrelationship With Section 2056. The question of the underlying nature of the Section 2031(c) exclusion is again significant in determining the interrelationship of Section 2031(c) with Section 2056. If, as is likely, the Section 2031(c) exclusion is an asset-specific exclusion,[375] then any excluded land passing to a surviving spouse would not qualify for the marital deduction because it would be a nondeductible interest.[376] Thus, although the Section 2031(c) exclusion might be applicable to the same land if it is included in both a decedent spouse's and a surviving spouse's gross estates,[377] the decedent spouse likely will not be allowed a marital deduction to the extent of the Section 2031(c) exclusion to the decedent spouse's gross estate. On the other hand, if the Section 2031(c) exclusion is a general exclusion of a specified dollar amount,[378] then the land subject to a qualified conservation easement passing to a surviving spouse would be a deductible interest for purposes of the marital deduction.[379]

---

[369] Note that Section 2032A was in existence before Section 2031(c) was conceived.

[370] See supra ¶ 4.02[7][e][i].

[371] See supra text accompanying note 354.

[372] This would make qualification for Section 2032A more difficult because subtracting the same amount from the numerator and the denominator of a fraction will always reduce the fraction to where the numerator is smaller than the denominator.

[373] See supra text accompanying note 355.

[374] This result would make it easier to satisfy the Section 2032A tests because a reduction in a denominator of a fraction without any reduction in its numerator will always increase the amount of the fraction.

[375] See supra text accompanying note 354.

[376] IRC § 2056(a) (last clause). Reg. § 20.2056(a)-2(b)(1).

[377] See supra ¶ 4.02[7][c] text accompanying notes 319 and 320.

[378] See supra text accompanying note 355.

[379] IRC § 2056(a) (last clause). Reg. § 20.2056(a)-2(b)(1).

Use of the Section 2031(c) exclusion is significant in estate planning. The exclusion effectively increases the amount that can bypass federal estate tax.[380]

The Interrelationship With Section 2057. The Section 2031(c) exclusion may be elected even if a deduction is allowed with respect to the property under Section 2057.[381] A problem similar to that arising under Section 2056 again arises. If, as is likely, the nature of the Section 2031(c) exclusion is asset specific (as opposed to a dollar amount), no Section 2057 deduction is allowed to the extent of any excluded value of the land.[382] If Section 2031(c) excludes a dollar amount, then no land per se is excluded and the full value of the land would qualify for a Section 2057 deduction.

The Interrelationship With Section 6166. Section 6166 was enacted after Congress identified potential liquidity problems for decedents owning closely held businesses.[383] The land subject to a qualified conservation easement may be a part of such a closely held business. To qualify for deferral of estate tax attributable to the closely held business interest, the closely held business interest[384] must be "included in determining the gross estate of a decedent,"[385] and it must exceed 35 percent of the adjusted gross estate[386] of the decedent.[387] There would be property other than the land involved in such a closely held business that would be in includible in the gross estate; therefore the exclusion of a portion of the value of land under Section 2031(c) should not preclude qualification for the Section 6166 deferral.[388] In addition, in computing the denominator of the 35 percent test under Section 6166,[389] regardless of the underlying nature of Section 2031(c), the Section 2031(c) exclusion should be taken into account in determining the "adjusted gross estate." If the portion of the land subject to the Section 2031(c) exclusion is not a part of the value of the closely held business, the end result would be no reduction in the numerator, but a reduction in the denominator, thereby making the 35 percent test easier

---

[380] The share bypassing federal estate taxation should be increased above the normal formula (based generally on the Section 2010 credit) by the Section 2031(c) exclusion amount.

[381] Cf. HR Conf. Rep. No. 105-220, 105th Cong., 1st Sess. 403 (1997), reprinted in 1997-4 CB (Vol. 2) 1457, 1873. See ¶ 5.08.

[382] IRC § 2057(b)(2)(A).

[383] See ¶ 2.02[3][c].

[384] IRC § 6166(b)(1).

[385] IRC § 6166(a)(1).

[386] IRC § 6166(b)(6).

[387] IRC § 6166(a)(1).

[388] Cf. S. Rep. No. 105-33, 105th Cong., 1st Sess. 40 (1997), reprinted in 1997-4 CB (Vol. 2) 1067, 1120, HR Conf. Rep. No. 105-220, 105th Cong., 1st Sess. 396 (1997), reprinted in 1997-4 CB (Vol. 2) 1457, 1866, allowing use of the now-repealed Section 2033A exclusion and Section 6166.

[389] IRC § 6166(b)(6).

to satisfy.[390] If the portion of the land subject to the Section 2031(c) exclusion is a part of the value of the closely held business interest for purpose of Section 6166, then the issue is whether or not the excluded portion reduces the numerator of the 35 percent test. If, as is likely, the nature of the Section 2031(c) exclusion is effectively a reduction for estate tax purposes in the value of the specific land,[391] then the excluded portion will reduce the numerator of the fraction (as well as the denominator) in applying the 35 percent test. In the alternative, if the nature of the Section 2031(c) exclusion is related to a dollar amount and not a specific asset,[392] then the excluded portion would not reduce the numerator of the 35 percent test.

[iii] Interrelationship to the income tax.

Income Tax Basis. Property excluded from the decedent's gross estate under Section 2031(c) takes a carryover basis from the decedent.[393] Recall that Section 2031(c) can apply in four situations.[394] In the first two situations, either the qualified conservation easement was created by a family member with the land subsequently held by the decedent at death or the easement was created inter vivos by the decedent, the income tax basis is the same amount. In both situations, if property worth $100,000 with a $50,000 basis is subject to a $30,000 easement, the $70,000 net value of the land potentially included in the gross estate would have a $35,000 adjusted basis prior to decedent's death[395] and would qualify for a $28,000 exclusion.[396] The included $42,000 portion of value would take a basis of $42,000[397] and the excluded portion would take a basis of $14,000 ($28,000/$70,000 times $35,000)[398] for a total basis of $56,000.

In the third situation, the easement is created at or subsequent to the decedent's death, and the issue is whether the total basis for the land is determined and a portion is then allocated to the charitable contribution or whether the charitable contribution is made and the retained portion absorbs all of the carryover basis. Assume a decedent had purchased land at a cost of $50,000 that appreciated to a fair market value of $100,000 at the date of the decedent's death, the easement is conveyed at or subsequent to the decedent's death, and

---

[390] A reduction in the denomination of a fraction without any reduction in its numerator will always increase the amount of the fraction.

[391] See supra text accompanying note 354.

[392] See supra text accompanying note 355.

[393] IRC § 1014(a)(4).

[394] See supra ¶ 4.02[7][b] text accompanying notes 311–315.

[395] Reg. §§ 1.170A-14(h)(3)(iii), 1.170A-14(h)(4) Ex. 9.

[396] See supra ¶ 4.02[7][d][iv].

[397] IRC § 1014(a)(1).

[398] IRC § 1014(a)(4).

the decedent's executor conveyed a qualified conservation easement worth $30,000 and properly elected to exclude $28,000 under Section 2031(c). If the total basis is determined and then allocated,[399] the total basis of the property would be $86,000, $72,000 for the land included in the decedent's gross estate ($100,000 less $28,000) plus $14,000 for the portion excluded under Section 2031(c) ($28,000/$100,000 of the Section 1012 basis of $50,000). The $86,000 basis would be apportioned between the qualified conservation easement and the land subject to the qualified conservation easement according to their relative fair market values with the land subject to the easement having a basis of $60,200 ($70,000/$100,000 times $86,000).[400] If the basis is allocated first and then the Section 1014(a)(4) reduction occurs, the retained value of the property would be $70,000 and that $42/70$ of the value of the property would receive a step-up to $42,000 and the remainder would receive a $14,000 carryover basis, resulting in a $56,000 total basis (identical to the basis where there was a pre-death contribution).[401]

Finally, if a family member made a post-distribution conveyance of the easement prior to the timely filing of the decedent's estate tax return and if the Section 2031(c) exclusion is $28,000,[402] the property would take a total $86,000 basis to the distributee ($72,000 plus $14,000). On the creation of the easement, that basis would be allocated between the retained and donated portions of the land.[403] The land subject to the easement would have a basis of $60,200 ($70,000/$100,000 times $86,000). If, however, the amount of the Section 2031(c) exclusion is $40,000,[404] the property would have a total basis of $80,000 ($60,000 plus $20,000) and on creation of the easement, 70 percent of that basis ($56,000) would be allocated to the retained property.

Section 303. Stock that qualifies for capital gain treatment under Section 303 must be included in the decedent's gross estate and all such corporate stock must, in general, exceed 35 percent of the decedent's gross estate.[405] Issues similar to those arising in determining the interrelationship of Section 2031(c) with Section 6166 and with Section 2032A arise with respect to the interrelationship of 2031(c) to Section 303.[406] Regardless of the nature of Sec-

---

[399] See supra ¶ 4.02[7][d][iv].

[400] See Reg. §§ 1.170A-14(h)(3)(iii), 1.170A-14(h)(4) Ex. 9.

[401] In this situation and in all three other situations one can concoct other possible results in determining the basis for the property. Therefore, regulatory guidance will be welcomed.

[402] But see supra ¶ 4.02[7][d] note 326.

[403] See Reg. §§ 1.170A-14(h)(3)(iii), 1.170A-14(h)(4) Ex. 9.

[404] No reduction of the value of the land should occur in computing the exclusion, with the result that the exclusion would be 40 percent of $100,000 or $40,000. See supra ¶ 4.02[7][d] note 326.

[405] IRC §§ 303(a), 303(b)(2)(A).

[406] See supra text accompanying notes 359–374, 383–391.

tion 2031(c), the measurement of the denominator of the fraction is based on "the value of the gross estate"[407] and the Section 2031(c) exclusion would reduce the denominator. If, as is likely, Section 2031(c) is an asset-specific exclusion, and if the land subject to the easement is in the corporation whose stock is being redeemed, then both the numerator and denominator of the fraction should be reduced and the 35 percent test would be more difficult to meet.[408] In the alternative, if Section 2031(c) is treated as excluding a dollar amount and not as an asset-specific exclusion,[409] or the land subject to the qualified conservation easement is not in the corporation whose stock is being tested, the stock is included in the gross estate and is also a part of the numerator of the 35 percent fraction. In these circumstances, a reduction of the denominator without any reduction of the numerator will make meeting the greater than 35 percent requirement easier to satisfy.[410]

[iv] Interrelationship to the generation-skipping transfer tax. Regardless of the underlying nature of Section 2031(c), the section should generally have no effect on consequences that occur under the generation-skipping transfer tax. Since Section 2031(c) is an estate tax provision, it is inapplicable to any inter vivos transfers made by a transferor. But even if a testamentary transfer is made by a transferor,[411] the fact that an exclusion has been allowed by Section 2031(c) does not preclude applicability of the generation-skipping transfer tax.[412] The definitions of a taxable termination[413] and a taxable distribution[414] are met even if the property was originally specifically excluded from a transferor's gross estate. One of the requirements for a direct skip is that there is "a transfer subject to a tax imposed by Chapter 11. . . . "[415] Even if the underlying nature of Section 2031(c) is that specific land is excluded from taxation under Chapter 11 by Section 2031(c),[416] such land is still "subject to"

---

[407] IRC § 303(b)(2)(A).

[408] See supra text accompanying notes 354, 371, 372.

[409] See supra text accompanying note 355.

[410] See supra text accompanying note 374.

[411] This testamentary transfer would include either direct transfers that could constitute direct skips or transfers to trusts that might potentially result in taxable terminations or taxable distributions.

[412] Since Section 2031(c) is not a valuation section, it has no effect on valuation of any property subject to a generation-skipping transfer. See IRC § 2624.

[413] IRC § 2612(a)(1).

[414] IRC § 2612(b).

[415] IRC § 2612(c)(1).

[416] If Section 2031(c) simply excludes a dollar amount (see supra text accompanying note 355), the "subject to" issue is not raised and Section 2031(c) has no generation-skipping transfer tax consequences.

Chapter 11 taxation.[417] The same "subject to tax imposed by Chapter 11" rationale applies to make the decedent the *transferor* of such property for purposes of the generation-skipping transfer tax.[418]

[f] Effective Date

Section 2031(c) applies to the estates of decedents dying after December 31, 1997.[419]

¶ 4.03 SECTION 2032. ALTERNATE VALUATION DATE

[1] Introduction

Section 2032 provides an optional date for valuing property required to be included in the gross estate. In general, the executor may elect the date six months after the decedent's death, instead of the date of death.[1] The election is made by proper notation on the estate tax return and cannot be withdrawn

---

[417] In effect the property was subject to such taxation but excluded by election from it. See the discussion of the relationship of Section 2503(e) (transfer not subject to taxation) and Section 2503(b) (transfer subject to but excluded from taxation) at ¶ 13.02[4][b] text accompanying notes 259–264.

It might be argued that the language of Regulations Section 26.2652-1(a)(2) ("a transfer is subject to Federal estate tax if the value of the property is includible in decedent's gross estate as determined under Section 2031....") provides that property excluded under Section 2031(c) is not "subject to" Chapter 11. However, this regulation was promulgated prior to the enactment of the Section 2031(c) exclusion, and it would be inconsistent with the treatment of exclusions under the gift tax, which are treated as "subject to" the gift tax, under the first sentence of Regulations Section 26.2652-1(a)(2).

[418] IRC § 2652(a)(1)(A). See ¶ 17.02[1][b] text accompanying note 21.

[419] Taxpayer Relief Act of 1997, Pub. L. No. 105-34, § 508(e)(1), 111 Stat. 788, 860 (1997), reprinted in 1997-4 CB (Vol. 1) 1, 74. The amendments made to Section 2031(c) in the Internal Revenue Service Restructuring and Reform Act of 1998 are effective as if included in the Taxpayer Relief Act of 1997. Internal Revenue Service Restructuring and Reform Act of 1998, Pub. L. No. 105-206, § 6024, 112 Stat. 685, 826 (1998), reprinted in 1998-3 CB 145, 286. In addition, the broadened location rules are applicable to estate of decedents dying after December 31, 2000. See supra ¶ 4.02[7][b] text accompanying notes 285–288.

[1] The six-month rule applies to estates of decedents dying in 1971 and later years. In the case of earlier death, the principal alternate date is one year after death. Where there is no date in the sixth month following the decedent's death that corresponds numerically to the date of death, the basic alternate valuation date is the last day of the sixth month. Rev. Rul. 74-260, 1974-1 CB 275.

once made.[2] For the election to be valid, the return must be filed within one year of the date of timely filing, including extensions.[3] Under Section 6075 of the Code, the basic statutory period for filing estate tax returns is "within 9 months after the date of the decedent's death." An extension, generally limited to six months, may be granted.[4] Therefore, except for the ever-present possibility of disagreement on valuation, the executor need not speculate whether the election of the alternate valuation date will be beneficial; the executor can make the decision with full knowledge concerning valuation on both permissible dates.

The provision permitting valuation of the estate as of a date after the date of death was enacted in 1935, which affords a clue to its purpose. At the time of the 1929 stock market crash and the attending general recession, which marked the beginning of the Depression, some persons died wealthy but, before administration of the estate could be completed, the value of their estates had shrunk to a figure less than the amount of estate tax based on the value of the estates at death. This extreme situation reflects the type of difficulty arising out of a strict date-of-death valuation rule; Section 2032 affords some tax relief from such difficulties.[5] The significance of the tax relief provided by this provision was reinforced by the bear stock market in 2000 and 2001.

---

[2] IRC § 2032(d)(1). See Form 706, "United States Estate (and Generation-Skipping Transfer) Tax Return" (Rev. November 2001) at 2. The election may not be revoked even if an attempt is made to revoke an election prior to the proper date for filing. See Joint Comm. on Taxation, General Explanation of the Revenue Provisions of the Deficit Reduction Act of 1984, at 1122 (1984). The Service has issued temporary regulations under Section 2032(d). Reg. § 301.9100-6T. See TD 8435, 57 Fed. Reg. 43,893 (1992), reprinted in 1992-2 CB 324. The temporary regulations provide that if a filed return does not indicate the election, such election may be made on a subsequent return, but *only* if the later return is filed by the due date, with extensions, of the original return.

A taxpayer may make a protective Section 2032 election conditioned upon a variety of factors. See, e.g., Estate of Mapes v. Comm'r, 99 TC 511, 527 (1992) (conditional upon failure to qualify for Section 2032A); TAM 9846002 (July 13, 1998) (conditional upon testamentary trust not qualifying for a marital deduction or surviving spouse's exercise of elective share rights); Priv. Ltr. Rul. 199942015 (July 22, 1999) (conditional upon date of death blockage discount).

[3] IRC § 2032(d)(2). Estate of Eddy v. Comm'r, 115 TC 135 (2000) (no timely election). But see supra note 2; Priv. Ltr. Rul. 200203031 (Oct. 27, 2001) (extension available under Regulations Section 301.9100-3).

[4] IRC § 6081. See Reg. § 20.6081-1(b), allowing an automatic six-month extension for filing a Form 706 if certain requirements are met; ¶ 2.02[1] text accompanying note 8.

[5] Since the time interval between a decedent's date of death and the basic alternate valuation date has been shortened from one year to six months, a necessary corollary to shortening the time for filing estate tax returns, there is less chance for sharp valuation changes. See S. Rep. No. 1444, 91st Cong., 2d Sess. 5 (1970), reprinted in 1971-1 CB 574, 576. See also IRC § 6075, discussed at ¶ 2.02[1] text accompanying note 7.

If the alternate valuation date is elected, the election applies to all the property included in the gross estate; the statute does not permit the alternate date to be used selectively with regard only to part of the estate.[6] Moreover, when any estate tax provision makes reference to the value of property at the time of the decedent's death, the provision must be read as value as of the alternate date if the benefits of Section 2032 are elected.[7] Section 2032(b) so specifies.

Election of the alternate valuation date affects not only the estate tax but also establishes the date-of-death value basis of property for the income tax.[8] Back in the good (bad?) old days when individual income tax rates were as high as 70 percent or 50 percent rather than the mid to upper 30 percent rates on ordinary income (and the generally 20 percent rate on net capital gain),[9] it was sometimes advantageous to elect Section 2032 when the value of property in the gross estate was higher on the alternate valuation date than on the date of death, if the tax rates on the estate were less than the potential income tax rates applicable to gain on a subsequent sale of the property.[10] With the current

---

[6] The high cost of confusion on this point is reflected in Rosenfield v. United States, 156 F. Supp. 780 (ED Pa. 1957), aff'd per curiam, 254 F2d 940 (3d Cir.), cert. denied, 358 US 833 (1958).

[7] See e.g., Estate of Luton v. Comm'r, 68 TCM (CCH) 1044 (1994). Cf. IRC § 1014(a)(2).

[8] IRC § 1014. See also Estate of Bary v. Comm'r, 368 F2d 844 (2d Cir. 1966). There are three other statutory exceptions to the date-of-death income tax basis rule. The first is that property valued at other than fair market value under Section 2032A is acquired with the Section 2032A value as its income tax basis. See ¶ 4.04. Second, Section 1014(c) denies a date-of-death basis to property that constitutes a right to receive an item of income in respect of a decedent. See IRC § 691; ¶ 4.05[4]. The final exception is contained in Section 1014(e). Under Section 1014(e), if "appreciated property" (see IRC § 1014(e)(2)(A)) is acquired by gift by the decedent within the one-year period ending on the decedent's death and if the property passes from the decedent to the donor of the property or the donor's spouse, the donor's basis or the spouse's basis in the property is the adjusted basis of the property in the hands of the decedent immediately *before* the decedent's death, i.e., its Section 1015 basis. IRC § 1014(e)(1). If the estate sells appreciated property that is covered by Section 1014(e) and the sale proceeds pass to the donor (or the donor's spouse), the same basis rule applies. IRC § 1014(e)(2)(B). Under the same circumstances the same rule also applies to a trust of which the decedent was the grantor. Id.

[9] IRC §§ 1(a), 1(b), 1(c), 1(d), 1(e), 1(h), 1(i)(2), 1222(11). Cf. IRC § 1(g).

[10] Prior to the enactment of Section 2032(c), if an estate was not required to pay any estate tax or was taxed at a lower estate tax rate, an executor would want to elect a higher alternate date valuation so as to increase the income tax basis of property. Prior to the enactment of Section 2032(c), the Treasury had conceded that the Code allowed the election of Section 2032 in a lower date-of-death value situation. Reg. § 20.2032-1(b)(1). See Rev. Rul. 55-333, 1955-1 CB 449. However, the Treasury refused to recognize such use of the alternate valuation date in a situation where the value of the gross estate was so small that no return was required to be filed. Reg. § 20.2032-1(b)(1). See Rev. Rul. 56-60, 1956-1 CB 443. Cf. IRC § 6018.

rate schedules, i.e., the effective estate tax rates ranging from 41 percent to 45 percent or more[11] and the individual income tax rates at a maximum of mid to upper 30 percent (or generally 20 percent rate on net capital gains),[12] there seems to be little incentive to elect a higher alternate valuation date.[13] Nevertheless, in a largely barn-door-locking gesture, Congress enacted Section 2032(c)[14] to ensure that Section 2032 is used only to provide estate tax relief and not to avoid income taxes. That subsection allows a Section 2032 election only where the election will result in both a decrease in the value of the decedent's gross estate and a decrease (after allowable credits) in the sum of the decedent's estate tax and the tax on generation-skipping transfers with respect to property included in the decedent's gross estate.[15]

[2] Identification of Gross Estate

As previously indicated, when the alternate provision is elected, the usual date for valuation of the estate is six months after death. It is very important to understand that this section does not require or permit a redetermination of what property is to be included in the gross estate; the identification of interests subject to tax is made as of the date of death and is generally unaffected by subsequent events,[16] regardless of whether the alternate date or the date of death is used for valuation purposes. The alternate date provision merely permits the election of a different time for valuation. The adoption of a time for valuation different from the time used for identification creates some problems that need discussion.

---

[11] See ¶ 2.01.

[12] IRC §§ 1(a), 1(b), 1(c), 1(d), 1(e), 1(h), 1222(11). Cf. IRC § 1(g).

[13] There is also little incentive to use a higher valuation date with respect to property taxed under the generation-skipping transfer tax which is imposed at the top estate tax rate. See IRC §§ 2641, 2642(b)(2)(A).

However, some incentive still existed with respect to estates paying a small amount of tax due to the unlimited marital deduction, the Section 2010 credit, or a combination of the two. See supra note 10.

[14] Section 2032(c) was originally enacted as part of the Deficit Reduction Act of 1984. Pub. L. No. 98-369, § 1023, 98 Stat. 495, 1030 (1984), reprinted in 1984-3 CB 1, 538. Section 2032(c)(2) was amended in 1986 to include the tax on generation-skipping transfers as well as the estate tax. Tax Reform Act of 1986, Pub. L. No. 99-514, § 1432(c)(1), 100 Stat. 2085, 2730 (1986), reprinted in 1986-3 CB (Vol. 1) 1, 647. See supra note 13; ¶ 14.05[2][a] text accompanying notes 15–17.

[15] IRC § 2032(c).

[16] A post-death agreement affecting only the use to which property may be put has been rejected as irrelevant. Flanders v. United States, 347 F. Supp. 95 (ND Cal. 1972). In TAM 9349003 (Sept. 3, 1993) (forged deeds recorded two days after the decedent's death did not affect value).

The gross estate may be thought of as consisting of two elements: the actual estate[17] and the artificial estate.[18] The provisions of Section 2032 apply alike to property interests owned by the decedent and to interests the ownership of which is merely imputed to the decedent. For purposes of simplicity, however, the impact of Section 2032 is discussed here largely with respect to property actually owned at death. It has probably always been clear that a disposition of estate assets after death would not remove the assets from the gross estate, even if Section 2032 is elected and the disposition occurs before the alternate date.[19]

Some related problems present greater difficulty. Should property that was not a part of the gross estate at death but that came into the estate during the six months after death be included in the valuation of the gross estate if the alternate provision is elected? For example, what about an ordinary cash dividend, payable to stockholders of record as of a date after death, received during the six-month period? Such a dividend is not a part of the gross estate because it cannot be identified at death as property owned by the decedent,[20] and its value is not to be included even if the alternate date is elected.[21]

[a] Bond Interest and Rent

The same principle generally applies to bond interest that accrues between the date of death and the alternative date, to an increase in the redemption price of a nontransferable government savings bond during that period,[22] and to rent on property owned by the decedent that accrues during the six-month pe-

---

[17] Section 2033 (and Section 2034) tax property to the extent of the decedent's actual interest in the property at death.

[18] Sections 2035 through 2042 and Section 2044 tax other property interests without regard to the decedent's date-of-death ownership, which are nevertheless considered properly within the reach of the death duty.

[19] See the comments infra ¶ 4.03[3] on exceptions to usual valuation date.

[20] Reg. § 20.2033-1(b). But see Reg. § 20.2031-2(i), properly indicating a different result if at death the stock is selling "ex-dividend" even though the record date has not been passed.

[21] Maass v. Higgins, 312 US 443 (1941); Reg. § 20.2032-1(d)(4). But see Estate of Fleming v. Comm'r, 33 TCM (CCH) 1414 (1974), improperly concluding that the value of stock included the amount of the dividend declared after the date of death and payable to shareholders of record after the alternate valuation date. In Bartram v. United States, 1975-1 USTC ¶ 13,041 (D. Conn. 1974), a capital gain dividend declared and paid after death was not included under the *Maass* rationale. The Service agrees, if the amount of such dividends is not substantial in relation to the value of the underlying stock. Rev. Rul. 76-234, 1976-1 CB 271.

[22] The increase is in substance an interest payment to be excluded from valuation. Reg. § 20.2032-1(d)(3).

riod.[23] Nevertheless, the Treasury maintains that an advance payment of bond interest or rent during the six-month period, which constitutes payment for a period subsequent to the alternate valuation date, may be identified as realistically a part of the gross estate at death and included in the alternate valuation along with the diminished value of the principal assets.[24] This principle is unassailable. Such prepaid interest or rent represents an immediate cash realization of a part of the value of the very property owned at death, and therefore must be viewed as "included" property, to use the term of the regulations.[25]

[b] Corporate Stock

Some transactions involving corporate stock raise much more difficult problems under the alternate valuation date provision. For example, a decedent might own shares of cumulative preferred stock on which there were substantial dividend arrearages at the time of the decedent's death. If such arrearages are discharged by dividends declared and paid during the alternate valuation period, are they "included" or "excluded" property? Passed preferred dividends are not analogous to accrued interest, since no debtor-creditor relationship arises between the shareholder and the corporation until the dividend is declared. On this ground, such dividends have been held to represent post-death income not includable when received during the alternate period if declared after death.[26] The decision seems too technical. In such circumstances, the right to the dividends when and if paid is an element in the value of the stock at the date of death and an absent element on the later date if the dividends have been paid in the meantime. Logically, the value of the hoped-for payment should be included, whichever date is selected; an all-or-nothing approach seems to tax either too much or too little. The difficulty well illustrates the problem arising out of the split identification and valuation dates.

Other corporate transactions can raise comparable difficulties, but not all do. During the boom stock market of the mid to late 1990s, many appreciated stocks split. On December 31, 1999, for example, wireless communication provider Qualcomm split its stock four for one. It is a safe assumption that some of its many shareholders died just before the split. If such a shareholder's personal representative elected the alternate valuation date, the personal representative held on the later date 4,000 shares of Qualcomm instead of the 1,000

---

[23] Reg. § 20.2032-1(d)(2). Interest and rent accrued at death are of course included. Estate of Sloane v. Comm'r, 3 TCM (CCH) 555 (1944). See ¶ 4.05[4].

[24] Reg. §§ 20.2032-1(d)(1), 20.2032-1(d)(2), 20.2032-1(d)(4).

[25] Reg. § 20.2032-1(d)(1). Within this provision, a payment of principal on a bond or note or mortgage is logically treated the same as an advance payment of interest and is included. Rev. Rul. 58-576, Situation 5, 1958-2 CB 625, 626.

[26] Peoples-Pittsburgh Trust Co. v. United States, 54 F. Supp. 742 (WD Pa. 1944).

shares owned at death by the decedent, and the personal representative was is-sued a new 3,000-share certificate at the time of the split. The old 1,000-share certificate may have been worth more at death compared to the value on the alternate date as a result of the split and market fluctuations. Could the dece-dent use the lower valuation figure, ignoring the new certificate? Clearly not. Both certificates simply represent the same interest in Qualcomm as the one certificate did prior to the split, and both are "included" property.

[c] Stock Dividends

Stock dividends (and, indeed, even extraordinary cash distributions), how-ever, are something else again. If the Sun Oil Corp. declares and distributes a 12½ percent stock dividend during the critical valuation period, which indeed had occurred in the case of *Estate of Schlosser v. Commissioner*[27] in 1953, is the dividend stock "included" property? The determinative question can easily be asked: Does it represent a part of the very property interest owned by the decedent at death or is it, in effect, new property first owned by the estate? The answer comes hard. The Third Circuit included the dividend shares in the gross estate, largely on the basis of an income tax case holding that a common stock dividend paid on common is not income within the meaning of the Six-teenth Amendment.[28] The result in *Schlosser* gets some support from the un-derlying fact that at the time of the decedent's death, the corporation's surplus was sufficient to cover both the stock dividend and cash dividends paid the same year.[29] Thus, even if the corporate veil were pierced, the dividend could be said to represent an interest in corporate assets that the decedent owned when he died. While the Third Circuit rejected this refinement, preferring to rest its decision on a broader ground, the source of a stock dividend may be

---

[27] Estate of Schlosser v. Commissioner, 277 F2d 268 (3d Cir.), cert. denied, 364 US 819 (1960).

[28] Eisner v. Macomber, 252 US 189 (1920).

[29] No assertion was made that the cash dividends should be included, and, even if this may be open to philosophical question, it seems settled that "ordinary dividends," whether paid in cash or stock, are not to be included. Maass v. Higgins, 312 US 443 (1941); Reg. § 20.2032-1(d)(4). Cf. Bartram v. United States, 1975-1 USTC ¶ 13,041 (D. Conn. 1974). However, the regulations would not include within the scope of "ordinary dividends" either (1) a cash dividend, distributed by a corporation in which decedent held a substantial interest, which consisted of "all" (or presumably a substantial part of) the earnings and profits accumulated at the date of decedent's death; or (2) a distribution in partial liquidation of the decedent's interest without a surrender of stock, except to the ex-tent paid out of earnings and profits earned after the decedent's death.

important. The Treasury[30] and other courts[31] have taken the position that post-death stock dividends escape tax if "they are out of earnings of the corporation after the date of the decedent's death." This basically acceptable principle is flawed, however, by the absence of any guide in the determination of what the dividend is paid "out of."[32] The need for legislative specification has long been recognized.[33]

[d] Other Types of Property

The income-versus-property problem under Section 2032 may arise with respect to other types of property. For instance, appreciation in the value of cattle during the alternate valuation period, even though it may represent new meat, is considered property included in the estate.[34] Oil and gas royalties collected during the alternate valuation period have been held includable in the gross estate when the alternate valuation date is elected.[35] Similar problems arise with respect to the valuation of life insurance. When the decedent owns a policy on the life of another, its increase in value during the six-month period

---

[30] Reg. § 20.2032-1(d)(4).

[31] Cf. Tuck v. United States, 282 F2d 405 (9th Cir. 1960); English v. United States, 270 F2d 876 (7th Cir. 1959); Estate of McGehee v. Comm'r, 260 F2d 818 (5th Cir. 1958); Rev. Rul. 80-142, 1980-1 CB 197.

[32] Compare Estate of McGehee v. Comm'r, 260 F2d 818 (5th Cir. 1958), where the corporate history answered the question in favor of post-death earnings, and in an analogous Section 2035(a) setting, the dividend stock was excluded, with Tuck v. United States, 282 F2d 405 (9th Cir. 1960), where the taxpayer failed to prove that a stock dividend was out of post-transfer earnings, yielding an adverse decision under Section 2040. Cf. Section 316(a), which is not applicable to the estate tax but for income tax purposes adopts a last-in, first-out (LIFO) approach to the distributions of corporate earnings.

[33] See Lowndes & Stephens, "Identification of Property Subject to the Federal Estate Tax," 65 Mich. L. Rev. 105, 113 (1966).

[34] Rev. Rul. 58-436, 1958-2 CB 366. In addition, the ruling holds that feed given to the cattle is included in the estate at its value on the date of its use, which is a disposition, but that its value is deductible under Section 2053 as an administration expense. Thus, the feed, which is converted into meat, is really not taxed twice.

[35] Estate of Holl v. Comm'r, 967 F2d 1437 (10th Cir. 1992); Johnston v. United States, 779 F2d 1123 (5th Cir.), cert. denied sub nom., Payne v. United States, 477 US 904 (1986). A discount is allowed to reflect properly only the value of the reserves in place. Rev. Rul. 71-317, 1971-2 CB 328. In Estate of Holl v. Comm'r, 54 F3d 648 (10th Cir. 1995), the Tenth Circuit reversed the Tax Court's valuation of reserves in place on the alternate valuation date and the decedent's date of death must be determined by apportioning services, pro rata, to quantities produced during the interim period and valuing the reserves as of the date of severance. See Selby, "Determining Estate Tax Value of Mineral Interests Under the Section 2032 Alternate Valuation Date; Estate of Holl v. Commissioner," 46 Tax Law. 865 (1993); Wacker, The In-Place Value of Oil and Gas Reserves Extracted During the Alternate Valuation Period of IRC 2032(a)(1)," 4 Oil & Gas Tax Q. 731 (1994).

is not included in the decedent's estate to the extent that it is attributable to premium payments or interest earned.[36] However, if the insured under the policy dies during the period, the proceeds are fully included in the decedent's gross estate, because an event has merely increased the value of the policy to face value.[37]

[3] Exceptions to Usual Alternate Date

The alternate valuation date is not invariably the date six months after death. In Section 2032(a), the applicable date is expressed in the form of three alternatives. It is more generally thought of, however, as the date six months after death, subject to two exceptions, one relating to property disposed of within the six months after death and the other to property whose value changes as a result of the mere passage of time.

[a] Property Disposed of

Section 2032(a)(1) requires that "property distributed, sold, exchanged, or otherwise disposed of" during the six-month period is to be valued as of the date of disposition. Thus, in the case of property sold by the estate within the six-month period, the alternate date is the date of sale, not the date six months after death. In the case of a "sale," the reason for this exception to the usual alternate date is easy to understand; conversion of an asset to cash forecloses any further concern about market fluctuations.[38] A distribution to beneficiaries has the same effect, as far as the estate is concerned, and at least enables the beneficiaries to convert the asset to cash if they choose to do so.[39] And an "ex-

---

[36] Rev. Rul. 55-379, 1955-1 CB 449.

[37] Rev. Rul. 63-52, 1963-1 CB 173.

[38] The sale price will not necessarily establish the property's alternate valuation if the sale is not at arm's length or if the decedent was not "locked into" the sales price. Estate of Critchfield v. Comm'r, 32 TC 844 (1959). See ¶ 4.02[2][c], ¶ 19.04.

[39] Reg. § 20.2032-1(c)(2) broadly defines what constitutes a distribution. However, actual distributions are not distributions within Section 2032 if the property may still be used by the executor to satisfy claims and expenses of the estate. Rev. Rul. 78-378, 1978-2 CB 229. The ruling is a reversal of an earlier position of the Commissioner, who successfully agreed to the contrary in Estate of Prell v. Comm'r, 48 TC 67 (1967). See also Hertsche v. United States, 244 F. Supp. 347 (1965), aff'd per curiam, 366 F2d 93 (9th Cir. 1966), holding that a final order directing distribution, which preceded actual distribution, constituted a Section 2032 distribution. Cf. Stoutz v. United States, 324 F Supp. 197 (ED La. 1970), aff'd per curiam, 439 F2d 1197 (5th Cir. 1971); Reardon v. United States, 429 F. Supp. 540 (WD La. 1977), aff'd per curiam, 565 F2d 381 (5th Cir. 1978); Land v. United States, 429 F. Supp. 545 (WD La. 1977), aff'd per curiam, 565 F2d 355 (5th Cir. 1978). Compare Rev. Rul. 73-97, 1973-1 CB 404, with Rev. Rul. 78-431, 1978-2 CB 230,

change"[40] would indicate at least that the executor had acquired the property so that the executor could deal with it to forestall losses. But it is important to understand that these words and the words "otherwise disposed of," according to the Treasury, comprehend "all possible ways by which property ceases to form a part of the gross estate."[41] Accordingly, as the regulations indicate, cash on hand at death, which is used to pay funeral or other expenses of, or charges against, the estate during the six-month period, is property "disposed of" within the meaning of the section.[42] This is entirely in keeping with the purpose of this relief provision. Of course, the estate may get a deduction for such expenses and charges, but their payment does not operate to reduce the *gross* estate, and it is appropriate to take the cash into account as it passes out of the probate estate.[43]

The disposition, which fixes the alternate valuation date, can be made by one other than the executor. For example, if a person owned a joint tenancy with right of survivorship interest in property fully funded by the decedent, the value of which is fully included in the decedent's gross estate because the property was funded by the decedent, and the surviving joint tenant disposes of the property by sale or otherwise during the six months after the decedent's death, the date of the disposition of the property becomes the alternate date.[44] There is an interesting hiatus here, however. If one who receives a lifetime transfer taxable under Section 2035(a) sells the property *before* the decedent's death, the very property transferred is still to be valued for estate tax purposes.[45] If the alternate valuation date is elected, is the property to be valued as of the date of disposition in this case as well? Apparently not. The date six months after death will control[46] because the property was not disposed of "*af-*

---

both dealing with the issue whether post-death divisions of included inter vivos trusts constitute Section 2032 distributions.

See Estate of Sawade v. Comm'r, 86-2 USTC ¶ 13,672 (8th Cir. 1986), holding that under state law a distribution of stock to beneficiaries occured only when the shares were transferred on the corporate books.

[40] See Estate of Smith v. Comm'r, 63 TC 722 (1975), holding that to the extent warrants (boot) were received for stock in a merger, there was an "exchange" of stock under Section 2032(a)(1). The Commissioner conceded that stock received for stock was not an exchange, but a mere change in the form of ownership. See also Estate of Aldrich v. Comm'r, 46 TCM (CCH) 1295 (1983) (amount received in settlement of a contingent fee case constituted an "exchange" to the decedent attorney's estate).

[41] Reg. § 20.2032-1(c)(1); Rev. Rul. 54-444, 1954-2 CB 300; Rev. Rul. 55-123, 1955-1 CB 443. Cf. Rev. Rul. 71-317, 1971-2 CB 328.

[42] Reg. § 20.2032-1(c)(1).

[43] A third exception can be said to apply to decedents who died prior to 1971 for whom the original one-year period remains applicable.

[44] Reg. § 20.2032-1(c)(3).

[45] Rev. Rul. 72-282, 1972-1 CB 306. See ¶ 4.07[2][c].

[46] IRC § 2032(a)(2).

ter the decedent's death" so as to invoke the exception to the usual rule.[47] Anomalous? It seems so. Indeed, if alternate valuation is elected, the value on the date of disposition seems just as relevant if disposition occurs the day before the decedent's death as it does when it occurs the day after.

[b] Value Affected by Time Lapse

Section 2032(a)(3) supplies a special rule for dealing with property whose value is affected by a mere lapse of time. A patent, which of course has a limited life span and may diminish in value as time passes for that reason alone, is one example of such property.[48] To use the date six months after death to value a patent would give effect to normal shrinkage in value unrelated to market conditions, which is not the aim of Section 2032. The statute requires such property to be valued as of the date of death (expressly ruling out the later date), but with adjustment for differences in value not attributable to a mere lapse of time. Suppose the patent is sold three months after death. Are both the "disposition" rule and the "lapse of time" rule applicable? They are, and the regulations illustrate the method of applying them.[49]

The Tax Court has properly held that a decrease in the value of an annuity occasioned by the death of the annuitant after the decedent's death does not reflect a difference in value due to mere lapse of time.[50] Such a property interest, if included in the gross estate,[51] must be valued as of the date of death be-

---

[47] IRC §§ 2032(a)(1), 2032(a)(2).

[48] Other examples include annuities, life insurance proceeds, or interests in a trust or other property whose value is dependent upon individuals' life expectancies. Estate of Welliver v. Comm'r, 8 TC 165 (1947); Reg. § 20.2032-1(f).

[49] Regulations Section 20.2032-1(f)(2), which involves the old one-year alternate valuation date, provides the following illustration: If a patent owned by the decedent had ten years to run at death and was sold by the estate six months after death, the patent's value under Section 2032 is its value at the time of *sale* divided by 0.95. This may appear at odds with the statute, but in fact it makes the adjustment for passage of time *and* all other factors by using the date of sale, and then restores shrinkage due to mere lapse of time by recognizing that the patent was worth only 95 percent of its date-of-death value at the time of sale because one twentieth, or 5 percent, of its remaining life had lapsed by that time. To update the regulation's example, assume the patent was sold only three months after the decedents' death. Under Section 2032, its value would be 97.5 percent of its value at the time of sale reflecting the expiration of one fortieth, or 2.5 percent, of its useful life.

[50] Estate of Hance v. Comm'r, 18 TC 499 (1952), acq. 1953-1 CB 4. See also Estate of Hull v. Comm'r, 38 TC 512 (1962), acq. 1964-2 CB 6, rev'd on another issue, 325 F2d 367 (3d Cir. 1964) (compromise of a claim held by the decedent that occurred during the alternate valuation period was relevant in valuing the claim because the compromise did not reflect a difference in value due to mere lapse of time).

[51] See IRC § 2039; ¶ 4.11.

cause its value is affected by mere lapse of time;[52] but the adjustment in value that the statute permits may take into account the annuitant's death within the six-month period. In the case referred to, the effect was to reduce the value of the annuity from approximately $120,000 to approximately $5,000.[53] Similarly, an increase in annuity payments due to a cost-of-living adjustment does not reflect a difference in value due to mere lapse of time and must be considered in valuing the annuity at the alternate date.[54]

[4] Effect of Election on Deductions

Section 2032(b) provides special rules that apply in determining estate tax deductions if the alternate valuation date is elected.

[a] General Impact on Deductions

Any deduction otherwise allowed in determining the taxable estate is disallowed if the item in question is in effect taken into account by the election of the alternate date. If an asset of the estate is destroyed by fire or other casualty during the six months following death, and the loss is not compensated for by insurance or in some other manner, Section 2054 allows a deduction for such loss in computing the taxable estate.[55] However, if the alternate date is used, the loss will be reflected in the value at which the asset is included in the gross estate. In these circumstances, the usual loss deduction under Section 2054 is sensibly disallowed. If, for example, by reason of the election of the alternate valuation date, an asset wholly destroyed shortly after death is included in the gross estate at a zero valuation, obviously no casualty loss de-

---

[52] Estate of Welliver v. Comm'r, 8 TC 165 (1947).

[53] This result should be compared with the alternate valuation date special rule concerning the marital deduction, which is discussed infra ¶ 4.03[4][b].

[54] Rev. Rul. 69-341, 1969-1 CB 218.

[55] See ¶ 5.04.

duction should be allowed with respect to the asset.[56] The same principle applies if the loss is something less than a total loss.[57]

[b] Relation to Charitable and Marital Deductions

The second special rule, expressed in Sections 2032(b)(1) and 2032(b)(2), is that if the alternate valuation date is elected, the valuation of property for the purpose of determining the charitable deduction and the marital deduction under Sections 2055 and 2056 respectively must be made on the basis of the value of the property at the date of death.[58] However, adjustment is made for any difference in value as of the alternate date that is not due to the mere lapse of time or to the occurrence or nonoccurrence of some contingency. As a practical matter, if shares of stock specifically bequeathed to charity are worth $10,000 at death, but only $8,000 as of the date six months after death, and if the alternate valuation date is elected, $8,000 is the amount includable in the gross estate and also the amount deductible in determining the taxable estate, provided, of course, the stock is not disposed of in the interim. The date-of-death value is used as the starting point, even though the alternate date is elected, but a full adjustment would be made in these circumstances to reflect the smaller value as of the later date.[59] If there is a disposition within the six months after death, such as an actual transfer to the charity, the date of disposition becomes the date to be used in determining the adjustment in the date-of-death value.

---

[56] Reg. § 20.2032-1(g). In addition, the estate would not be allowed a Section 165(c) income tax casualty loss deduction for the property because, by being valued as of the alternate valuation date, the Section 1014 basis for the property would be zero and Section 165(b) would disallow any income tax deduction. With regard to the income tax, Section 642(g) disallows any income tax deduction for the decedent's estate for casualty losses allowable in determining the taxable estate, unless the estate tax deduction is waived and not claimed. But Section 642(g) does not expressly foreclose the income tax deduction merely because a casualty loss is given estate tax effect by election of the alternate date. No such rule was seriously needed because Section 1014 date-of-death (or alternate date) basis provisions effectively restrict the potential income tax deduction.

[57] If the property were not totally destroyed, there would be an income tax basis for the property and arguably an income tax deduction for the loss. See Reg. § 1.165-7(b)(1), especially subsection (ii). An alternative argument is that the income tax basis already reflects the loss and no further loss is justified. This problem and the problem raised supra note 56 do not arise if the loss occurs after the alternate valuation date. Cf. IRC § 642(g).

[58] See IRC §§ 2106(a)(2), 2106(a)(3) as to estates of nonresident aliens, which are discussed at ¶¶ 6.06[2], 6.06[3].

[59] If the decedent provides that an amount equal to a percentage of the decedent's gross estate is to pass under Section 2055 or Section 2056, and if Section 2032 is elected, then the amount of the gross estate is determined as of the alternate valuation date. Cf. Rev. Rul. 70-527, 1970-2 CB 193.

No adjustment is to be made for changes in value that result from the mere lapse of time or the occurrence or nonoccurrence of a contingency. For example, if the decedent devised a residence worth $40,000 at the decedent's death to a child for the child's life, with a remainder to a qualified charity, the death of the child during the six months following the decedent's death would be the occurrence of a contingency that would affect the value of the interest passing to the charity. The present interest of the charity at the later date would be more valuable than the future interest dependent upon the child's death. However, the date-of-death value of the charity's interest would fix the amount of the charitable deduction without adjustment for the increase in the value of the charity's interest that resulted from the child's death. On the other hand, if the residence itself decreased in value during the six months, that decrease would require an adjustment in the valuation of the charitable remainder and a corresponding reduction in the charitable deduction if the alternate date is used.[60]

In this light, the special rule on valuation for purposes of the charitable deduction seems to yield a sound result. The decedent's philanthropy, which gives rise to the deduction, is measured by circumstances existing at the decedent's death, except for market fluctuations.[61]

The rule might appear to yield a less supportable result with regard to the marital deduction. In the *Hance* case,[62] the Tax Court properly took into account the death of a surviving annuitant, the decedent's wife, in determining the value to be included in the decedent's gross estate under the alternate valuation provisions, and included the annuity at a value of only $5,000, rather than $120,000. The decedent had died in 1947, and the estate tax marital deduction was not an issue. If the marital deduction applied,[63] should the property be valued for that purpose without regard to the wife's death? The statute specifically says that such a contingency shall be disregarded. On the facts in the *Hance* case, it might seem that property entering into the gross estate at only $5,000 would then support a $120,000 marital deduction. However, the seeming problem under Section 2032 is taken care of by Section 2056(a), in its last clause, which limits the marital deduction to the value at which the interest passing to the surviving spouse is included in the decedent's gross es-

---

[60] The remainder interest discussed here qualifies for a charitable deduction. But see IRC § 2055(e), discussed at ¶¶ 5.05[4]–5.05[8], which sometimes disallows deductions for such interests.

[61] The statute does not invariably follow this principle with regard to the charitable deduction. See IRC § 2055(a), discussed in Chapter 5, which in some circumstances permits a qualified disclaimer made after death to enlarge the deduction. See IRC §§ 2046, 2518 on qualified disclaimers.

[62] Estate of Hance v. Comm'r, 18 TC 499 (1952), acq. 1953-1 CB 4.

[63] See IRC §§ 2056(b)(1), 2056(b)(6), which are discussed at ¶¶ 5.06[7], 5.06[8][c]. An annuity does not necessarily run afoul of the "terminable interest" rule.

tate. Thus, in the *Hance* situation, the marital deduction with respect to the annuity would be limited to $5,000, and no distortion results from the different Section 2032 rules on inclusions and deductions.

¶ 4.04 SECTION 2032A. VALUATION OF CERTAIN FARM, ETC., REAL PROPERTY

[1] Introduction

The alternate *time* of valuation under Section 2032, just discussed, has long been a familiar estate tax phenomenon. This part of the chapter covers other *methods* of valuation designed, when available, to afford relief to estates in which a farm or other real property utilized in a closely held business forms a substantial part of a decedent's estate.

Section 2032A "provides optional methods of valuation"[1] based on actual use for a limited amount[2] of "qualified real property"[3] required to be included in the gross estate. This section represents an elective statutory exception to the general rule that the value of an item includable in the gross estate is its fair market value on the applicable valuation date;[4] for familiar fair market valuation, approximate actual-use value may be substituted. Fair market value, the price a willing buyer would pay a willing seller, takes account of the highest and best use to which the real property could be put, rather than the actual use of the property.[5] Section 2032A is the product of a congressional determination that potential use valuation is inappropriate for certain real property,

---

[1] IRC §§ 2032A(e)(7), 2032A(e)(8). See Goggans & Hartman, "Current Application of Special Use Valuation Under Section 2032A," 63 Taxes 511 (1985); Milner, "Scope of Special-Use Valuation Eligibility and Recapture Made Clearer by New Developments," 11 Est. Plan. 82 (1984); Uchtmann & Fischer, "Agricultural Estate Planning and the Economic Recovery Tax Act of 1981," 27 SD L. Rev. 422 (1982).

[2] IRC § 2032A(a)(2).

[3] IRC § 2032A(b).

[4] Reg. § 20.2031-1(b). Either the date of death or the alternate valuation date may be used in conjunction with a Section 2032A election. Rev. Rul. 83-31, 1983-1 CB 225. If alternate valuation is elected, it must also be used to determine if the Section 2032A requirements are met. Rev. Rul. 88-89, 1988-2 CB 333. A taxpayer may make a protective election to use Section 2032 in the absence of qualifying for Section 2032A. Estate of Mapes v. Comm'r, 99 TC 511, 527 (1992).

[5] HR Rep. No. 1380, 94th Cong., 2d Sess. 3, 21 (1976), reprinted in 1976-3 CB (Vol. 3) 735, 755; Estate of Hankins v. Comm'r, 42 TCM (CCH) 229 (1981).

particularly that used before and after death as a farm[6] for farming purposes[7] or in other closely held business[8] activities. This section is designed to encourage or facilitate continued use of real property for farming and other small business purposes and to curtail forced sales of this type of property to pay estate tax.[9] The valuation relief afforded by this section is not unlimited; the reduction in the value of the gross estate may not exceed $750,000,[10] adjusted for inflation for the estates of decedents dying in a year after 1998.[11] Nor is the tax benefit derived from use of this section unconditional; tax avoided may be recaptured in whole or in part if the qualifying real property is disposed of or converted to a nonqualifying use.[12] Gaining the benefits provided by Section 2032A requires an election by the executor,[13] accompanied by a specified agreement.[14]

Much of the momentum for legislative action to repeal the estate tax[15] was generated by the appealing argument that there was a "need for tax relief for all decedents' estates, decedents' heirs, and businesses, including small businesses, family-owned businesses, and farming businesses . . . [to] provide . . . relief . . . from the unduly burdensome . . . taxes."[16] This is not to say that such interests are not already provided special relief under the transfer tax structure. Section 6166 permits a deferral of payment of taxes on certain

---

[6] IRC § 2032A(e)(4).

[7] IRC § 2032A(e)(5).

[8] See Sections 2032A(g) and 6166(b)(1) for the determination of whether a business other than a sole proprietorship is closely held, discussed infra ¶ 4.04[3][b][v], ¶ 2.02[3][c] text accompanying notes 64–76.

[9] HR Rep. No. 1380, 94th Cong., 2d Sess. 3, 21, 22 (1976), reprinted in 1976-3 CB (Vol. 3) 735, 755, 756.

[10] IRC § 2032A(a)(2). See infra ¶ 4.04[5] note 171 involving the measurement of the ceiling when discounts are taken.
Section 2032A, in effect, provides a conditional exemption. Viewed in this manner, the section runs counter to stated policy reasons for the enactment of the unified credit (IRC §§ 2010, 2505) to replace the specific exemptions (IRC §§ 2052, 2521), now repealed, in that the section confers more tax savings on larger estates. See HR Rep. No. 1380, 94th Cong., 2d Sess. 3, 15 (1976), reprinted in 1976-3 CB (Vol. 3) 735, 749.

[11] The statutory figure of $750,000 is adjusted for increases in the cost of living, in $10,000 increments, based on the increase in the Consumer Price Index over the base year 1997. IRC § 2032A(a)(3). The limitation is $760,000 for the estate of a decedent dying in 1999 (Rev. Proc. 98-61, 1998-2 CB 811, 816) and $770,000 for the estate of a decedent dying in 2000. Rev. Proc. 99-42, 1999-2 CB 568, 572.

[12] IRC § 2032A(c). The recapture provisions of Section 2032A will cause a "lock-in" effect that tends to restrict the allocation of capital between those competing sources.

[13] IRC §§ 2032A(a)(1)(B), 2032A(d)(1).

[14] IRC §§ 2032A(a)(1)(B), 2032A(d)(2).

[15] IRC § 2210(a). See ¶ 8.10[1]. But see also ¶ 8.10[5].

[16] H. Rep. No. 107-37, 107th Cong., 1st Sess. 19 (2001), reprinted in 2001-__ CB __,

---

closely held businesses,[17] and for decedents dying prior to the year 2004, Section 2057 allows a deduction for qualified family-owned business interests.[18] This section, Section 2032A, is a third relief provision which provides a reduction in valuation generally to the extent that the actual use valuation of property used by small businesses or in farming is less than the highest and best use valuation of such property. Regrettably, there is no uniform set of requirements which apply to trigger the three relief provisions and, even worse, the three provisions are each very complicated with potentially complex and sometimes uncertain interrelationships.[19] Thus, Congress, while lamenting the impact of the estate tax on small business, has itself contributed to the problem for small businesses by enacting relief provisions that are exceedingly complex, not properly coordinated, and, in an attempt to be targeted at only specific situations, probably too restrictive.

The details of this very intricate piece of legislation will be analyzed in the following paragraphs.

[2] Qualification for Special-Use Valuation in General

Elective special-use valuation is available for a limited amount of real property if both the decedent's estate and the real property itself satisfy separate eligibility prerequisites.

A decedent's estate qualifies for use of Section 2032A if the following three conditions are satisfied: (1) The estate must be that of a citizen or resident of the United States;[20] (2) at least 50 percent of the adjusted value of the gross estate must consist of the adjusted value of real or personal property,[21] used for a qualified use by the decedent or the decedent's family on the date of the decedent's death,[22] which passes to a qualified heir;[23] and (3) a minimum of 25 percent of the adjusted value of the gross estate must consist of the adjusted value of real property that passes to a qualified heir and that, for periods aggregating at least five years in the eight-year period immediately preceding the decedent's death, was owned by the decedent or a member of the

---

[17] IRC §§ 2032A(g), 6616(b)(1); ¶ 2.02[3][c] text accompanying notes 64–76.

[18] IRC § 2057, especially IRC § 2057(j). See ¶ 5.08.

[19] See, e.g., ¶ 5.08[6][b] discussing the interrelationship of Section 2057 to Section 2032A.

[20] IRC § 2032A(a)(1)(A).

[21] IRC § 2032A(b)(1)(A). "Adjusted value" is discussed infra ¶ 4.04[3][b][i].

[22] IRC § 2032A(b)(1)(A)(i). See IRC § 2032A(e)(2).

[23] IRC § 2032A(b)(1)(A)(ii).

decedent's family and used for a qualified use generally involving material participation by the decedent or a member of the decedent's family.[24]

If the estate qualifies for Section 2032A valuation, the real property to be valued under that section must satisfy additional requirements in order to be denominated "qualified real property." It must (1) be located in the United States;[25] (2) have been acquired from or have passed from the decedent to a qualified heir of the decedent;[26] (3) have been used on the date of the decedent's death for a qualified use by the decedent or the decedent's family;[27] (4) have been owned by the decedent or a member of the decedent's family and used for a qualified use that required material participation by the decedent or a member of the decedent's family generally for periods aggregating at least five years in the eight-year period immediately preceding the decedent's death;[28] and (5) be designated in a written agreement signed by all persons having an interest in the property consenting to the potential imposition of a recapture tax.[29]

[3] Estate Qualification

[a] Citizens or Residents Only

The decedent must have been a citizen or resident of the United States at the time of death for the decedent's estate to take advantage of Section 2032A. The usual means of acquiring status as a citizen of the United States is, of course, birth within this country. In other instances, the Immigration and Naturalization Act determines whether an individual is a citizen. Generally, a person is classified as a resident if the person lives in the United States with no definite intention of leaving.[30]

---

[24] IRC § 2032A(b)(1)(B). See IRC §§ 2032A(b)(1)(A)(ii), 2032A(b)(1)(C). See also IRC § 2032A(b)(4).

[25] IRC § 2032A(b)(1).

[26] IRC § 2032A(b)(1).

[27] IRC § 2032A(b)(1).

[28] IRC § 2032A(b)(1)(C). See also IRC § 2032A(b)(4).

[29] IRC §§ 2032A(b)(1)(D), 2032A(d)(2).

[30] The questions of citizenship and residence are discussed in Chapter 6 in connection with the estate tax on nonresident noncitizens. IRC §§ 2101–2108. See ¶ 6.01[2]. See also IRC §§ 2208, 2209; ¶ 8.09.

[b] The 50 Percent Test

For the decedent's estate to qualify for special-use valuation, one half of the decedent's estate must consist of assets devoted to a trade or business that is retained by the decedent's family after the decedent's death. Specifically stated, at least one half of the adjusted value of the gross estate must consist of the adjusted value of real or personal property meeting two requirements.[31] The real or personal property must have been (1) used for a qualified use by the decedent or the decedent's family on the date of the decedent's death[32] and (2) acquired from or passed from the decedent to a qualified heir of the decedent.[33]

[i] Adjusted value. The numerator of the fraction posited by the 50 percent test is the adjusted value of certain real and personal property. The denominator is the adjusted value of the gross estate. "Value" here means value on the applicable valuation date,[34] determined without regard to Section 2032A, employing the usual valuation techniques to arrive at fair market value. "Adjusted value" is that value reduced by amounts allowable as deductions for unpaid mortgages and indebtedness under Section 2053(a)(4). The gross estate denominator is to be reduced by all amounts allowable under Section 2053(a)(4);[35] and the value of each item of real or personal property in the numerator is to be reduced by amounts allowable with respect to the particular item.[36]

These adjusted value determinations include any transfers within three years of death, even though the transferred property is excluded from the decedent's gross estate.[37] This prevents a decedent from qualifying the estate for Section 2032A valuation with near-death transfers of nonqualifying property.[38] Near-death outright transfers of property not devoted to a qualified use reduce the decedent's gross estate,[39] thereby reducing the adjusted value of the gross

---

[31] IRC § 2032A(b)(1)(A).

[32] IRC § 2032A(b)(1)(A)(i).

[33] IRC § 2032A(b)(1)(A)(ii).

[34] See Rev. Rul. 83-31, 1983-1 CB 225.

[35] IRC 2032A(b)(3)(A). Generally, Section 2053(a)(4) allows a deduction for indebtedness for which the decedent's estate is liable where payment of the indebtedness is secured by property included in the gross estate. The deduction allowable under Section 2053(a)(4), in addition to the principal sum due, includes any interest on the indebtedness accrued to the date of death. Reg. § 20.2053-7. For a discussion of IRC § 2053(a)(4), see ¶ 5.03[6].

[36] IRC § 2032A(b)(3)(B).

[37] IRC § 2035(c)(1)(B). See IRC § 2035(a)(2). See also Estate of Slater v. Comm'r, 93 TC 513 (1989); Estate of Holmes v. Comm'r, 62 TCM (CCH) 839 (1991).

[38] See ¶ 4.07[2][e].

[39] See IRC § 2035(a).

estate, the denominator of the fraction. Although possibly not contemplated by Congress, outright transfers within three years of death to qualified heirs of real or personal property devoted to a qualified use before and after the transfer will be included in both the numerator and the denominator of this fraction.[40]

[ii] **Qualified use.** Property is used for a qualified use if it is used as a farm for farming purposes[41] or in a trade or business other than that of farming.[42] There is no statutory prohibition against lumping farm and other trade or business property together for purposes of satisfying the 50 percent test.[43] But the dichotomy between farm and nonfarm business may affect the method of valuing the property under Section 2032A.[44]

The question of whether the leasing of a farm constitutes a qualified use of a farm has arisen in several contexts.[45] In general, if there is an element of risk to the owner, there is a qualified use. For example, if there is a percentage lease or a sharecropping arrangement, there is a qualified use;[46] however, generally a mere net cash rental is not a qualified use.[47] Since qualified use can be made by either the decedent or a family member,[48] a cash lease by the dece-

---

[40] A decedent's near-death transfer to a qualified heir of property devoted to a qualified use should be considered acquired from or passed from the decedent. Section 2032A(e)(9)(A) defines property as acquired from or passed from a decedent if the property is so considered under Section 1014(b). Near-death transfers of property required to be included in the decedent's gross estate by Section 2035 are considered acquired from the decedent under Section 1014(b)(9). See Reg. §§ 1.1014-2(b)(2), 1.1014-2(b)(3); Priv. Ltr. Rul. 8514032 (Jan. 8, 1985). Pretend inclusion under Section 2035(a) for purposes of Section 2032A results in pretend acquisition from the decedent under Section 1014(b).

[41] IRC § 2032A(b)(2)(A).

[42] IRC § 2032A(b)(2)(B).

[43] Rev. Rul. 85-168, 1985-2 CB 197. However, personal property related to an unqualified trade or business cannot be included. Estate of Geiger v. Comm'r, 80 TC 484 (1983).

[44] See discussion of IRC §§ 2032A(e)(7), 2032A(e)(8) infra ¶ 4.04[5].

[45] See infra ¶ 4.04[3][c] note 143, infra ¶ 4.04[7][b] text accompanying notes 283–288.

[46] Schuneman v. United States, 783 F2d 694 (7th Cir. 1986) (leasing a farm property for a percentage of the farm's production constituted a qualified use). See infra text accompanying note 68.

[47] Heffley v. Comm'r, 884 F2d 279 (7th Cir. 1989) (cash rental to an unrelated party did not constitute a qualified use); Brockmann v. Comm'r, 903 F2d 518 (7th Cir. 1990) (same); Estate of Abell v. Comm'r, 83 TC 696 (1984) (same); Bruch v. United States, 86-2 USTC ¶ 13,692 (ND Ind. 1986) (same).

[48] IRC §§ 2032A(b)(1)(A)(i), 2032A(b)(1)(C)(i).

dent to a family member who makes a qualified use of the property will qualify the property[49] for Section 2032A valuation.

[iii] Farm and farming. The term "farm" encompasses a very wide range of agricultural and horticultural pursuits. It is defined[50] to include plantations, ranches, nurseries, ranges, orchards, and woodlands. Greenhouses or other similar structures used primarily to raise agricultural or horticultural commodities are classified as farms.[51] Various types of farms specifically included within the definition are stock, dairy, poultry, fruit, and truck farms as well as fur-bearing-animal farms.[52]

The term "farming purposes" is broadly defined in the statute.[53] It encompasses cultivating the soil and raising or harvesting any agricultural or horticultural commodity (including the raising, shearing, feeding, training, care, and management of animals) on a farm.[54] Property used for farming purposes includes property used for "handling, drying, packing, grading, or storing on a farm any agricultural or horticultural commodity in its unmanufactured state,"[55] if the owner, operator, or tenant regularly produces more than half of the commodity so treated.[56] If more than one half of the commodity so treated is produced by others, the property will be considered to be used in a trade or business other than farming, a qualified use, and will still aid in satisfying the 50 percent test. Farming purposes additionally include the planting, cultivating, care, or cutting of trees,[57] or the preparation of trees for market, excluding milling.[58] However, property devoted to the milling of trees should constitute property used in a trade or business other than farming, a qualified use.[59]

[iv] Other business use. The term "trade or business" is not defined in Section 2032A or any other place in the Code. What amounts to trade or busi-

---

[49] See HR Rep. No. 795, 100 Cong., 2d Sess. 590 (1988).

[50] IRC § 2032A(e)(4).

[51] IRC § 2032A(e)(4).

[52] IRC § 2032A(e)(4).

[53] IRC § 2032(A)(e)(5). Participation in "Payment-in-Kind" and other related land diversion programs offered to farmers by the Department of Agriculture will not have an adverse effect on qualifying for or maintaining Section 2032A treatment for either the owner decedent or the qualified heir. IRS Announcement No. 83-43, 1983-10 IRB 29 (Mar. 7, 1983). Cf. TAM 9212001 (Mar. 20, 1992).

[54] IRC § 2032A(e)(5)(A).

[55] IRC § 2032A(e)(5)(B).

[56] IRC § 2032A(e)(5)(B).

[57] IRC § 2032A(e)(5)(C)(i). Estate of Holmes v. Comm'r, 62 TCM (CCH) 839 (1991) (test not met).

[58] IRC § 2032A(e)(5)(C)(ii).

[59] The only difference ultimately is the restriction on choice of methods of valuation of the real property contained in Sections 2032A(e)(7) and 2032A(e)(8).

ness use within the meaning of Section 2032A(b)(2)(B) is not determined by reference to a broad concept of "business," a case-law definition for purposes of deductions under Section 162[60] or Section 167, or provisions in the regulations under Section 513.[61] Past struggles with the trade or business concept may be of little guidance.

The term as used in this section applies only to active businesses, not passive investment activities.[62] Maintaining an office and regular hours for the management of income-producing property does not necessarily constitute a trade or business under Section 2032A.[63] Mere passive rental of land constitutes a passive investment and not an active trade or business.[64] An activity not engaged in for profit is not a trade or business.[65]

[v] Indirect ownership and use. The 50 percent test may be affected by property devoted to a business use in a partnership, trust, estate, or corporation. If the business is such that the decedent's relation to it constitutes an interest in a closely held business as defined in Section 6166(b)(1),[66] regulations are to indicate how Section 2032A is to be applied.[67] Property owned by a de-

---

[60] Reg. § 20.2032A-3(b).

[61] A definition of "trade or business" is contained in Regulations Section 1.513-1(b), regarding unrelated trade or business of certain exempt organizations.

[62] Reg. § 20.2032A-3(b).

[63] Reg. § 20.2032A-3(b).

[64] Estate of Trueman v. United States, 6 Cl. Ct. 380 (1984); Estate of Abell v. Comm'r, 83 TC 696 (1984); Sherrod Estate v. Comm'r, 774 F2d 1057 (11th Cir. 1985) (rental land was not qualified even though rental income from the land was used to pay taxes on contiguous active business land). But see Priv. Ltr. Rul. 8516012 (Dec. 28, 1984). Query whether rental to an unrelated third person for a percentage of profits constitutes a qualified use under Regulations Section 20.2032A-3(b).

[65] Reg. § 20.2032A-3(b). See IRC § 183; Priv. Ltr. Rul. 8820002 (Feb. 8, 1988).

[66] IRC § 2032A(g). A closely held business within the meaning of Section 6166(b) includes a partnership with forty-five (fifteen prior to 2002) or fewer partners or one in which 20 percent or more of the capital interest is included in determining the gross estate of the decedent or a corporation with forty-five (fifteen prior to 2002) or fewer shareholders or one in which at least 20 percent of the voting stock is included in the decedent's gross estate. See ¶ 2.02[3][c] text accompanying notes 64–76. No "trust interest" is defined as an interest in a closely held business by Section 6166(b)(1).

Beneficial ownership of trust property will be treated as constituting an interest in a closely held business as defined in Section 6166(b)(1) if the requirements of Section 6166(b)(1)(C) would be satisfied if the property were owned by a corporation and all beneficiaries having vested interests in the trust were shareholders in the corporation. See Reg. § 20.2032A-3(d). Beneficial ownership of estate property will be treated like trust property in the application of Section 2032A. Cf. Reg. § 20.2032A-3(f)(2). Beyond this, Section 6166 presents a parallel requirement that the closely held unit must be "carrying on a trade or business" to qualify under Section 6166. See supra note 61.

[67] The Secretary had indicated that the decedent's interest in a business "must, in addition to meeting the tests for qualification under section 2032A, qualify under the tests of

cedent that is leased to a partnership, corporation, or trust may qualify for valuation under Section 2032A and the numerator of the 50 percent test if, at death, the decedent's interest in the lessee qualifies as an interest in a closely held business as defined in Section 6166(b)(1).[68] Real property leased to a farming corporation owned and operated by the decedent and the decedent's child is eligible for the numerator of the 50 percent test.[69]

The statute states that the property must be used for a qualified use by the decedent or a member of the decedent's family on the date of the decedent's death.[70] The statute does not preclude including in the numerator the value of property located outside the United States but included in the decedent's gross estate that at death is used for a qualified use by the decedent or a member of the decedent's family, if the property passes to a qualified heir.[71] The question considered here is satisfaction of the 50 percent estate eligibility test, not ultimate valuation of a particular parcel of real property under Section 2032A. There is, generally speaking, no requirement that property, real or personal, entering into the numerator be held by the decedent or a member of the dece-

---

section 6166(b)(1) as an interest in a closely held business on the date of the decedent's death and for sufficient other time (combined with periods of direct ownership) to equal at least 5 years of the 8-year period preceding the death." Reg. § 20.2032A-3(b). This statement in the regulation raises an issue whether an interest in a closely held partnership, trust, or corporation must qualify under the tests of Section 6166(b)(1) combined with periods of direct ownership for at least five years of the eight-year period preceding death to be considered in the numerator of the 50 percent test. This issue should be answered in the negative to prevent unfair discrimination against indirectly owned business property. The five-out-of-eight-year test should be applied only where that test is generally applied in Section 2032A.

[68] Reg. § 20.2032A-3(b). This regulation provides that to be "qualified real property," the decedent's interest in the partnership, trust, or corporation must qualify as an interest in a closely held business under Section 6166(b)(1) on the date of the decedent's death and "for sufficient other time (combined with periods of direct ownership) to equal at least five years of the eight-year period preceding the death." Cf. Minter v. United States, 19 F3d 426 (8th Cir. 1994) (the Section 6166(b)(1) test was applied to post-death leasing). The 5-out-of-8-year test should not be a prerequisite for the inclusion of the decedent's interest in a closely held business in the numerator of the 50 percent test. The 50 percent test deals with the determination of an estate's qualification, not whether an interest in a closely held business is qualified real property.

[69] Reg. § 20.2032A-3(b). Unresolved and left for further consideration by the Secretary pursuant to Section 2032A(g) is the question of participation in a closely held business by a decedent and nonfamily members. It is idle to speculate on the requirements that will have to be met, under the broad grant of authority to promulgate regulations, for property devoted indirectly to a qualified use to qualify for consideration under Section 2032A.

[70] IRC § 2032A(b)(1)(A)(i).

[71] This is so even though only real property located in the United States may ultimately qualify for valuation under Section 2032A.

dent's family for any length of time.[72] The only requirement is that the property be used for a qualified use by the decedent or a member of the decedent's family on the date of the decedent's death.

[vi] **Nature of use.** Real property devoted to a qualified use includes roads, buildings, and other structures and improvements functionally related to the qualified use.[73] Elements of value that are not functionally related to the qualified use are not to be taken into account. For example, the legislative history identifies mineral rights as an element of value not to be taken into account in the valuation of qualified-use property.[74]

Residential buildings and related improvements are classified as real property used for a qualified use if the following three requirements are satisfied by such property:[75] (1) The residential building and related improvements must be located on or contiguous to[76] qualified real property;[77] (2) the real property on which the structures are located, for periods aggregating five years in the eight-year period immediately preceding the decedent's death, must have (a) been owned by the decedent or a member of the decedent's family, (b) been used for a qualified use by the decedent or a member of the decedent's family, and (c) generally involved material participation by the decedent or a member of the decedent's family;[78] and (3) the residential or other structures must have been occupied on a regular basis by the owner or lessee, or employee of either, for the purpose of operating or maintaining real property used for farming or in another trade or business.[79]

---

[72] The one exception to this rule is residential buildings and related improvements, which may be treated as used for a qualified use. See IRC § 2032A(e)(3), discussed infra ¶ 4.04[3][b][vi].

[73] IRC § 2032A(e)(3).

[74] HR Rep. No. 1380, 94th Cong., 2d Sess. 3, 24 (1976), reprinted in 1976-3 CB (Vol. 3) 735, 758. See also Sherrod Estate v. Comm'r, 774 F2d 1057 (11th Cir. 1985); TAM 9443003 (Oct. 28, 1994).

[75] Residential buildings qualify under either qualified use, use as a farm for farming purposes, or use in a trade or a business other than farming, if the qualifications specified are satisfied. Compare the language of Section 2032A(e)(3) with that of Section 6166(b)(3).

[76] The legislative history states that "residential buildings or related improvements shall be treated as being on the qualified real property if they are on real property which is contiguous with qualified real property or would be contiguous with such property except for the interposition of a road, street, railroad, stream, or similar property." HR Rep. No. 1380, 94th Cong., 2d Sess. 3, 24 (1976), reprinted in 1976-3 CB (Vol. 3) 735, 758.

[77] IRC § 2032A(e)(3).

[78] IRC § 2032A(e)(3). See IRC § 2032A(b)(1)(C). See also IRC §§ 2032A(b)(4), 2032A(b)(5).

[79] IRC § 2032A(e)(3). As a practitioner becomes submerged in the intricacies of Section 2032A, one may begin to wonder whether the game is worth the candle.

Tangible personal property devoted to a qualified use is included in the numerator of the 50 percent estate qualification test. Personal property as used in Section 2032A(b)(1)(A) may also include intangible personal property, such as goodwill, devoted to a qualified use. An important question is whether inventory held for sale or consumption in connection with a qualified use is to be treated as personal property devoted to a qualified use. Treatment of inventories as personal property devoted to a qualified use would simplify and aid estate qualification. Business capital invested in inventories represents capital committed to a qualified use. It should be noted that the personal property itself will not qualify for special-use valuation; it is merely a factor in the 50 percent estate qualification test. Similarly, working capital used in the activity is counted in the 50 percent measurement.[80]

The value of real property used as a farm for farming purposes includes the value of trees and vines on the property. An unanswered question is whether growing crops are to be considered as property used as a farm for farming purposes. Unharvested crops on land used in a trade or business are artificially defined as property used in a trade or business for income tax purposes if certain requirements are met under Section 1231(b)(4).[81] Exclusion of the value of growing crops from the numerator of the 50 percent estate qualification test would work to preclude estate qualification, rather than being merely a neutral factor. It seems reasonable to suggest that growing crops ought to be treated as property used for qualified use. A further question whether a growing crop on real property may ever be valued as real property devoted to a qualified use has been answered affirmatively in at least one instance. Trees growing on qualified woodland are not treated as a crop[82] and may be valued as real property devoted to a qualified use.[83] Generally, however, growing crops are not treated as qualified real property.[84]

[vii] **Member of the family.** Real and personal property entering the numerator of the 50 percent test must be used for a qualified use by the decedent or a member of the decedent's family.[85] The decedent's family includes only the decedent's ancestors,[86] spouse, and lineal descendants as well as the lineal

---

[80] Estate of Mapes v. Comm'r, 99 TC 511 (1992).

[81] But see Watson v. Comm'r, 345 US 544 (1953).

[82] IRC § 2032A(e)(13).

[83] See infra ¶ 4.04[3][c].

[84] HR Rep. No. 201, 97th Cong., 1st Sess. 38, 166 (1981), reprinted in 1981-2 CB 352, 380.

[85] IRC § 2032A(b)(1)(A)(i).

[86] While the legislative history indicates that the ancestral chain does not extend any further than the decedent's parents, Conf. Rep. No. 215, 97th Cong., 1st Sess. 253 (1981), reprinted in 1981-2 CB 481, 510, the statutory language employed is not so limited.

descendants of the decedent's parents and spouse and the spouses of all those lineal descendants.[87] Legally adopted children are treated as children by blood.

[viii] **Acquired from the decedent.** The 50 percent test speaks of property "acquired from or passed from the decedent," not a new phrase to those familiar with Section 1014(b) concerning income tax basis. Property is considered to be acquired from or passed from the decedent for purposes of Section 2032A if it would be so treated under Section 1014(b).[88] Property acquired by inheritance, bequest, devise, or as a result of a qualified disclaimer,[89] as well as property transferred inter vivos but included in the gross estate by reason of death, form of ownership, or through the exercise or nonexercise of a power of appointment, is considered property acquired from the decedent.[90] Property acquired from the decedent includes property acquired from the decedent's estate[91] as well as from a trust to the extent that the trust assets are included in the decedent's gross estate.[92] Property acquired from the decedent's estate includes property purchased from the estate, whether under an option granted by the decedent or upon a sale by the personal representative, as well as property acquired in satisfaction of a right to a pecuniary bequest.[93]

---

[87] IRC § 2032A(e)(2).

[88] IRC § 2032A(e)(9)(A).

[89] Rev. Rul. 82-140, 1982-2 CB 208. See ¶ 10.07.

[90] Whether real property is qualified is determined at the time of the decedent's death, and a transfer preceding death might disqualify the property.

An interesting question will arise if property transferred inter vivos to a qualified heir, but required to be included in the decedent's gross estate, is transferred by that qualified heir to a family member prior to the decedent's death. If gross estate property devoted to a qualified use upon the date of the decedent's death was, before death, transferred to another qualified heir by the decedent's donee (who was also a qualified heir), the question whether the property was acquired by the second qualified heir from the decedent arises. Strictly speaking, the second qualified heir did not acquire the property from the decedent. However, after death, a qualified heir may dispose of an interest in qualified real property to any member of the qualified heir's family who thereafter is treated as the qualified heir. IRC § 2032A(e)(1).

[91] IRC § 2032A(e)(9)(B).

[92] IRC § 2032A(e)(9)(C).

[93] HR Rep. No. 201, 97th Cong., 1st Sess. 38, 176 (1981), reprinted in 1981-2 CB 352, 385.

When a qualified heir purchases property from an estate or trust valued under Section 2032A, Section 1040(c) provides the qualified heir's basis *shall* be limited to the Section 2032A value of the property increased by the gain recognized to the estate or trust on the transaction. Gain is recognized to the estate or trust only to the extent that the fair market value of the property on the date of transfer exceeds the value of the property for estate tax purposes on the applicable valuation date disregarding Section 2032A. IRC §§ 1040(a), 1040(b). See Reg. § 1.661(a)-2(f)(3) (which at times may reach a result inconsistent with Section 1040(c) which overrides the regulation).

Section 2032A

Property may be acquired or passed from the decedent outright or in trust. The regulations provide that if qualified property passes in successive interests (e.g., life estates and remainder interests), an election under Section 2032A is available only with respect to property (or a portion of property) in which qualified heirs receive *all* such successive interests.[94] For example, the Service would contend that if a decedent established a trust income to a child for life, remainder to other family members, and the child also was granted a nongeneral power of appointment, the remainder interest would not be treated as passing to a qualified heir if the child could exercise the power in favor of a nonfamily member, thereby divesting the other family members of their interests.[95] The courts have not always agreed with the Service and have held the Treasury regulation invalid where a trust has a remote contingent charitable beneficiary[96] and where grandchildren holding life estates after life estates in their parents hold special powers to appoint to nonqualified heirs,[97] where a small portion of income could be paid to one not a qualified heir,[98] or in a combination of such situations.[99] The holdings are in keeping with the policy of Section 2032A, and the regulations should be amended to allow other than qualified heirs to hold remote contingent interests in such trusts.[100]

[ix] Qualified heirs. A qualified heir is a member of the decedent's family who acquired property from, or to whom property passed from, the dece-

---

[94] Reg. § 20.2032A-8(a)(2). The Service has generally interpreted the regulation literally. See Rev. Rul. 81-220, 1981-2 CB 175; Rev. Rul. 82-140, 1982-2 CB 208; Priv. Ltr. Rul. 8337015 (June 7, 1983), Priv. Ltr. Rul. 8346006 (July 29, 1983). Priv. Ltr. Rul. 8441006 (June 26, 1984). But see Priv. Ltr. Rul. 8643005 (July 18, 1986), Priv. Ltr. Rul. 8321007 (Feb. 2, 1983).

[95] See Reg. § 20.2032A-8(a)(2). The possibility of divestment in favor of a nonfamily member may be eliminated by a qualified disclaimer of the nongeneral power of appointment. Rev. Rul. 82-140, 1982-2 CB 208. See infra ¶ 4.04[7][a] note 263.

[96] Estate of Davis v. Comm'r, 86 TC 1156 (1986); Estate of Pliske, 51 TCM (CCH) 1543 (1986).

[97] Estate of Clinard v. Comm'r, 86 TC 1180 (1986); Estate of Smoot v. Comm'r, 892 F2d 597 (7th Cir. 1989).

[98] Estate of Thompson v. Comm'r, 864 F2d 1128 (4th Cir. 1989).

[99] Estate of Thompson v. Comm'r, 864 F2d 1128 (4th Cir. 1989).

[100] See Begleiter and Bellatti, "Draft Regulations on Successive Interests Under § 2032A," 27 Real Prop., Prob. & Tr. J. 185 (1992).

It once appeared that a qualified heir must also hold a present interest in the trust. See IRC § 2032A(g), last sentence. See also Priv. Ltr. Rul. 8532007 (Apr. 22, 1985), Priv. Ltr. Rul. 8244001 (Jan. 14, 1982). That requirement does not appear in the Code and has been eliminated in the regulations.

The *present* interest requirement for property to have passed from the decedent has had an interesting history. It first appeared in the Conference Committee Report accompanying the Tax Reform Act of 1976: "Trust property shall be deemed to have passed from the decedent to a qualified heir to the extent that the qualified heir has a *present interest*

dent.[101] For this purpose, the decedent's "family" includes only ancestors, spouse, and lineal descendants, as well as the lineal descendants of parents, spouse, and spouses of all lineal descendants.[102] Adopted children are treated as children by blood.[103]

[c] The 25 Percent Test

Seeking still to determine an estate's qualification for use of Section 2032A, the third hurdle is the 25 percent test. Twenty-five percent or more of the adjusted value of the gross estate must consist of the adjusted value of real property that was acquired from a decedent by a family member or passed

---

in that trust property." HR Rep. No. 1515, 94th Cong., 2d Sess. 610 (1976), reprinted in 1976-3 CB (Vol. 3) 807, 960 (emphasis added). The regulations initially promulgated for Section 2032A mentioned the present interest requirement. Reg. §§ 20.2032A-3(b), 20.2032A-8(a)(2).

The Report of the House Committee on Ways and Means, dated July 24, 1981, on the Economic Recovery Tax Act of 1981 acknowledges the present interest requirement in Regulations Section § 20.2032A-3(b), HR Rep. No. 201, 97th Cong., 1st Sess. 38, 166 n.8 (1981), reprinted in 1981-2 CB 352, 380, and discusses the purpose of a statutory amendment to the present interest rule that treats property passing to a discretionary trust as qualifying for Section 2032A valuation if all beneficiaries of the trust are qualified heirs even though no beneficiary has a present interest under Section 2053 because of the trustee's discretion. Id. at 176, 1981-2 CB at 385. The Conference Committee Report dated August 1, 1981, merely restates the position set forth in the House Report and acknowledges that the conference agreement follows the House bill. Conf. Rep. No. 215, 97th Cong., 1st Sess. 252-253 (1981), reprinted in 1981-2 CB 481, 510. The 1981 statutory amendment clearly anticipating the present interest rule was the addition of the last sentence in Section 2032A(g) that was signed into law August 13, 1981.

On August 26, 1981, TD 7786, final IRS regulations on Special Use Valuation of Farms and Closely Held Business Real Estate for Federal Estate Tax Purposes, was published. The regulations after this amendment were devoid of any direct reference to the present interest rule and Section 2053. Indirect reference was present in Regulations Section 20.2032A-8(d)(2), now repealed.

It appears that the present interest rule, now not directly referred to in the Code or regulations, no longer exists. If the present interest requirement for property passing as first espoused in the Conference Committee report on the Tax Reform Act of 1976 were to remain, it ought to be put in the statute or at the very least be clearly presented in the regulations so as not to present a trap for the unwary.

[101] IRC § 2032A(e)(1).

[102] A widow or widower of a lineal descendant of the decedent is a qualified heir. Rev. Rul. 81-236, 1981-2 CB 172; Priv. Ltr. Rul. 8412014 (Dec. 2, 1983). A grandniece of the decedent's spouse is not within the term "family" and thus is not a qualified heir. Estate of Cowser v. Comm'r, 736 F2d 1168 (7th Cir. 1984). Nor is a lineal descendant of decedent's spouse's parents. Estate of Cone v. Comm'r, 60 TCM (CCH) 137 (1990).

[103] See IRC § 2032A(e)(2). An acknowledged child under Illinois law does not qualify as an adopted child. Whalen v. United States, 86-1 USTC ¶ 13,661 (CD Ill. 1986); Rev. Rul. 81-179, 1981-2 CB 172.

from the decedent to a family member and that, generally for periods aggregating at least five years in the eight-year period ending with the decedent's death, was owned and used for a qualified use involving material participation by the decedent or a member of the decedent's family.[104] Only real property enters the numerator of the 25 percent test, but the adjusted value of personal property is a part of the adjusted value of the gross estate, the denominator, just as it is in the 50 percent test. There is no statutory prohibition against the use of foreign real property to satisfy the 25 percent estate qualification requirement.[105]

Growing crops are generally not treated as part of the real property and are thus not included in the numerator of the 25 percent test.[106] The executor may, however, irrevocably elect[107] to treat trees growing on qualified woodland[108] as real property and add their value to the numerator of the 25 percent test.

The term "adjusted value," whether modifying real property or the gross estate, has the same meaning here as in the 50 percent test.[109] Similarly, the requirement that real property entering into the computation of the numerator of the 25 percent test must have been acquired or passed from the decedent to a member of the decedent's family presents concepts previously considered.[110] In general, at least one fourth of the estate must consist of real property passing from the decedent to the decedent's family members.[111]

[i] **Ownership and use requirements.** Real property that enters into the numerator of the 25 percent test must have been owned and used as a farm for

---

[104] IRC § 2032A(b)(1)(B). See Miller v. United States, 88-1 USTC ¶ 13,757 (CD Ill. 1988), holding Regulations Section 20.2032A-8(a)(2) invalid in requiring the estate to elect special-use valuation with respect to 25 percent of the adjusted value of the gross estate. The statute merely requires that such property make up 25 percent of the adjusted value of the gross estate. And see IRC §§ 2032A(b)(1)(A)(ii), 2032A(b)(1)(C). See also IRC §§ 2032A(b)(4), 2032A(b)(5).

[105] See supra ¶ 4.04[3][b] text accompanying note 71.

[106] See supra ¶ 4.04[3][b] text accompanying note 84.

[107] IRC § 2032A(e)(13)(D). This election is made on the federal estate tax return.

[108] IRC § 2032A(e)(13)(B). Qualified woodland is an identifiable area of land for which records are maintained and that is used in timber operations. IRC §§ 2032A(e)(13)(B), 2032A(e)(13)(C).

[109] "Adjusted value" is discussed supra ¶ 4.04[3][b][i]. Allocation problems will undoubtedly arise in determining the adjusted value of real property when a single indebtedness is secured by a group of assets. The indebtedness should be apportioned to the various assets securing payment on a pro rata basis using the fair market value of each asset.

[110] See supra ¶¶ 4.04[3][b][vii], 4.04[3][b][viii].

[111] Real property used as a farm and real property in another trade or business may be combined to satisfy the 25 percent test. Rev. Rul. 85-168, 1985-2 CB 197.

farming purposes, or in a trade or business other than farming, by the decedent or a family member generally for periods aggregating at least five years in the eight-year period ending on the decedent's death.[112] The ownership and devotion to a qualified use need not have been continuous; ownership and devotion to qualified use by any combination of the decedent, members of the decedent's family, and qualified closely held businesses[113] must merely aggregate five years in the critical eight-year period. However, only periods during which both the required ownership and the required use coincide may be aggregated. Moreover, the real property need not have been used for a qualified use on the date of the decedent's death, as is required of property entering into the numerator of the 50 percent test. However, qualifying improvements must have been made at least five years prior to the date of the decedent's death to satisfy the five-year ownership requirement.[114]

Generally, periods of ownership and qualified use of real property acquired in a like-kind exchange under Section 1031 or after an involuntary conversion under Section 1033 may be tacked on to periods of ownership and qualified use of the real property exchanged or converted.[115] Tacking is available if the use of the replacement property[116] and the replaced property[117] is the

---

[112] The liberalization of the period during which material participation is required, Section 2032A(b)(1)(C)(ii), by a retired or disabled decedent, Section 2032A(b)(4)(A), does not apply to the time period required for ownership and use of the real property by the decedent or a member of the decedent's family, Section 2032A(b)(1)(C)(i), which is incorporated into the 25 percent test of Section 2032A(b)(1)(B).

[113] Property transferred to a corporation or partnership is considered continuously owned to the extent of the decedent's equity interest if the transfer met the requirements of Section 351 or Section 721 and if the decedent's interest in this business qualifies under Section 6166(b)(1) as an interest in a closely held business. See supra ¶ 4.04[3][b] note 66. Property transferred to a trust is considered continuously owned if, treating all the beneficiaries having vested interests in the trust as shareholders of a corporation, the requirements of Section 6166(b)(1)(C) would be met. Any period during which the decedent's interest in the corporation, partnership, or trust does not meet the requirements of Section 6166(b)(1) is not counted toward satisfying the five-out-of-eight-years ownership requirement. Reg. § 20.2032A-3(d).

[114] Possibly, real property devoted to a variety of qualified uses for periods no one of which aggregates five years will be considered in the composition of the numerator of the 25 percent test. For example, if a decedent owned a parcel of real property for the entire eight-year period preceding death, and for four years the land was devoted to use as a farm for farming purposes and for the four years thereafter the land was used as a golf course—a trade or business other than farming—it can be argued that the land, if otherwise qualifying, satisfies the five-year requirement. Neither the statute nor the legislative history indicates that the real property is required to have a single use for the required five-year period.

[115] IRC § 2032A(e)(14).

[116] IRC § 2032A(e)(14)(C)(i).

[117] IRC § 2032A(e)(14)(C)(ii).

same,[118] and then only to the extent that the fair market value of the replace-ment property, on the date of acquisition, does not exceed the fair market value of the replaced property on the date of disposition.[119]

[ii] **Material participation.** The real property entering into the computa-tion of the numerator must have been devoted for five years to a qualified use involving material participation by the decedent or a member of the decedent's family.[120] Contemporaneous material participation by the decedent and one or more family members during any year will not satisfy more than one year of the five-year requirement.[121] Brief absence from the farm or other business during periods requiring material participation will be disregarded in ascertain-ing the five aggregate years if preceded by and followed by substantial periods of uninterrupted material participation.[122] Generally, the periods of material participation aggregating five years must be in the eight-year period ending with the date of the decedent's death.[123] However, if this requirement cannot be met with respect to the decedent, the eight-year period ends on the earlier of the date of disability or the date that old-age Social Security benefits com-menced if the disability or benefits were continuous until the decedent's

---

[118] IRC § 2032A(e)(14)(C).

[119] IRC § 2032A(e)(14)(B).

[120] Activities of a member of the decedent's family are considered only if the requi-site relationship existed at the time the activities occurred. Reg. § 20.2032A-3(e)(1). The material participation requirement cannot be satisfied with a marriage after the fact. A marriage of convenience would have to last at least five years.

[121] Reg. § 20.2032A-3(c)(2).

[122] Reg. § 20.2032A-3(c)(2) suggests a brief period of absence as thirty days or less and a substantial period of material participation as 120 days or more.

[123] IRC § 2032A(b)(1)(C).

death.[124] A disability is a physical or mental impairment preventing material participation by the decedent.[125]

The decedent or a member of the decedent's family is not required to have carried on the business, just to have materially participated.[126] The required material participation is to be determined in a manner similar to that used in Section 1402(a)(1), relating to net earnings from self-employment.[127] Active management by a surviving spouse may be treated as material participation.[128]

Section 1402(a)(1) deals essentially with the determination of material participation in the production of agricultural or horticultural commodities. However, for purposes of Section 2032A, these same rules are to be applied to determine material participation by the decedent or a member of the decedent's family in a trade or business other than farming. Generally, under Section 1402(a)(1), which Congress uses by analogy, material participation results where there is actual participation in the production or the management of pro-

---

[124] IRC § 2032A(b)(4)(A). This provision was designed to alleviate inequities resulting from the requirement that the decedent or a member of the decedent's family must materially participate in the farm or other business for periods aggregating five years of the eight years immediately preceding the decedent's death. If the decedent was receiving Social Security benefits and materially participated in the farm, any income derived from the farm was treated as earned income for Social Security purposes, resulting in the potential for reduced Social Security benefits. The interaction of these two rules forced some people to choose between receiving Social Security benefits and obtaining special-use valuation for their estates.

While this provision itself would go far to rectify the inequity, Congress at the same time modified the qualified-use provision. In order to be "qualified real property," the real property must, on the date of the decedent's death, have been used for a qualified use by the decedent or a member of the decedent's family. IRC § 2032A(b)(1); Bruch v. United States, 86-2 USTC ¶ 13,692 (ND Ind. 1986). There is no exception to this requirement, even if the decedent is retired or disabled on the date of death. Therefore, the question becomes whether it is ever possible to have the requisite use at the date of death without having at the same time material participation.

[125] IRC § 2032A(b)(4)(B).

[126] HR Rep. No. 1380, 94th Cong., 2d Sess. 3, 23 (1976), reprinted in 1976-3 CB (Vol. 3) 735, 757.

[127] IRC § 2032A(e)(6). The material participation test is similar but not identical to the material participation test under income tax Section 469. See S. Rep. No. 99-313, 99th Cong., 2nd Sess. 732 (1986), reprinted in 1986-3 CB (Vol. 3) 1, 732. Cf. TAM 9428002 (July 15, 1994) (treatment of an activity as a passive activity under Section 469 is a significant factor in determining material participation under Section 2032A).

See Begleiter, "Material Participation Under Section 2032A: It Didn't Save the Family Farm but It Sure Got Me Tenure," 94 Dick. L.Rev. 561 (1990).

[128] IRC § 2032A(b)(5). This subsection is discussed at infra text accompanying note 144.

duction of agricultural or horticultural commodities,[129] or a combination of both, that is material with respect to either or both combined.[130]

"Production" refers to the physical work performed and the expenses incurred in producing an agricultural or horticultural commodity or goods or services in a trade or business other than farming.[131] Production of farm commodities includes such activities as the actual work of planting, cultivating, and harvesting of crops and the furnishing of machinery, implements, seed, and livestock. An individual is treated as materially participating in the production if the individual engages to a material degree in the physical work related to production of the commodity produced or the goods and services rendered. Furnishing machinery, equipment, and livestock or paying expenses is not in and of itself sufficient to constitute material participation, but such activities combined with some physical labor, even only to a nonmaterial degree, may constitute material participation when the undertaking to furnish capital is substantial in relation to the total amount of capital required for the production of the commodity or the goods and services in a business. Although no single factor is determinative, doing physical work and participating in management decisions are the principal factors to be considered.[132]

"Management of production" refers to deciding the what, how, when, and where of the productive output of a trade or business.[133] The services rendered must be engaged in to a material degree to result in material participation. To qualify, the activity generally must involve not only planning but continued activity throughout production, such as inspection of the production activities and ongoing, periodic consultation in the production process.[134]

Direct involvement in the operation of a directly owned farm or other business on substantially a full-time basis by the decedent or the decedent's family constitutes material participation.[135] Activities of agents or employees who are not family members do not count in the determination of whether there has been the requisite material participation. Direct participation that is less than full-time but sufficient to fully manage the farm or other business

---

[129] IRC § 1402(a)(1).

[130] Reg. § 1.1402(a)-4.

[131] Reg. § 1.1402(a)-4(b)(3)(ii).

[132] See Reg. § 20.2032A-3(e)(2). Compare Mangels v. United States, 828 F2d 1324 (8th Cir. 1987) (material participation); Estate of Sherrod, 82 TC 523 (1984), reversed on other grounds, 774 F2d 1057 (11th Cir. 1985), cert. denied, 479 US 814 (1986) (material participation); Estate of Heffly v. Comm'r, 884 F2d 279 (7th Cir. 1989) (no material participation); Brockman v. Comm'r, 903 F2d 518 (7th Cir. 1990) (no material participation).

[133] Reg. § 1.1402(a)-4(b)(3)(iii).

[134] See Reg. § 20.2032A-3(e)(2).

[135] Reg. § 20.2032A-3(e)(1) indicates that thirty-five hours or more a week will be considered substantially full time.

also constitutes material participation.[136] A person performing all functions necessary to the operation of a directly owned farm requiring only seasonal activity participates materially, even though there is little activity other than in the producing season.

If the decedent or a member of the decedent's family is self-employed, the material participation test is met if earnings generated by the farm or other business are earned income for self-employment tax purposes. If no self-employment taxes have been paid, material participation is presumed not to have occurred.[137] If it is established that material participation did occur but no self-employment tax was paid, the self-employment tax due plus penalties and interest must be paid in order to qualify for Section 2032A valuation.[138]

If the property is directly owned but used by a nonfamily member, trust, or other business entity, less than full-time involvement must be pursuant to an arrangement, oral or written, capable of proof, providing for material participation and specifying the services to be performed.[139] This requirement also applies to property indirectly owned, even if there is full-time involvement.[140] For example, if the property to be valued pursuant to Section 2032A is owned by a trust, the requisite arrangement providing for material participation may result from appointment as trustee, an employer-employee relationship, a management contract, or the trust instrument expressly granting management rights.[141]

[iii] **Active management.** Active management will satisfy the requirement of material participation in one particular instance. If a surviving spouse acquires from the decedent real property that would have been eligible for special-use valuation[142] and such real property is then included in the estate of the

---

[136] Reg. § 20.2032A-3(e)(1).

[137] Reg. § 20.2032A-3(e)(1). Payment of self-employment tax does not, however, establish material participation.

[138] Reg. § 20.2032A-3(e)(1). See Rev. Rul. 83-32, 1983-1 CB 226, so holding but also holding that there is an exception where assessment is barred by the statute of limitations.

[139] Reg. §§ 20.2032A-3(e)(1), 20.2032A-3(g) Ex. 1.

[140] Reg. §§ 20.2032A-3(f)(1), 20.2032A-3(g) Ex. 5.

[141] Reg. § 20.2032A-3(f)(1).

[142] Special-use valuation need not have been elected by the first decedent's estate, but the real property must have been eligible for special-use valuation had the election been made and the agreement filed. IRC § 2032A(b)(5)(B).

surviving spouse, active management of the farm or other business by the surviving spouse[143] is treated as material participation.[144]

Active management is the making of management decisions of a business other than the daily operating decisions.[145] Whether active management occurs is a factual determination, but it is not dependent upon the surviving spouse's payment of self-employment tax under Section 1401.[146] Farming activities that may constitute active management include "inspecting growing crops, reviewing and approving annual crop plans in advance of planting, making a substantial number of the management decisions of the business operation, and approving expenditures for other than nominal operating expenses in advance of the time the amounts are expended."[147] Management decisions include "what crops to plant or how many cattle to raise, what fields to leave fallow, where and when to market crops and other business products, how to finance business operations, and what capital expenditures the trade or business should make."[148]

---

[143] Whereas the material participation requirement may be satisfied by either the decedent or a member of the decedent's family, active management will be treated as material participation only if the surviving spouse personally undertakes the active management. That is, active management by a member of the surviving spouse's family will not be deemed material participation. See IRC §§ 2032A(b)(1)(C)(ii), 2032A(b)(5)(A).

A net cash lease by the surviving spouse or a lineal descendant of a decedent to a member of the spouse's or descendant's family will not result in a recapture of the decedent's Section 2032A tax saving. See IRC § 2032A(c)(7)(E); infra ¶ 4.04[7][b] text accompanying notes 287, 288. Seemingly in such a situation, the family member will satisfy both the qualified use and material participation tests to qualify the surviving spouse's or the lineal descendant's estate for a Section 2032A election. See IRC §§ 2032A(b)(1)(A)(i), 2032A(b)(1)(C)(i).

[144] IRC § 2032A(b)(5)(A). If the first decedent was retired or disabled on the date of the decedent's death, both Section 2032A(b)(4) and Section 2032A(b)(5) may be applied. This, in effect, tolls the time period during which the first decedent was receiving Social Security benefits. The surviving spouse is given the benefit of satisfying the five-out-of-eight-year required material participation rule by combining the spouse's years of active management after the first decedent's death with the first decedent's years of material participation before becoming retired or disabled. IRC § 2032A(b)(5)(C).

[145] IRC § 2032A(e)(12).

[146] HR Rep. No. 201, 97th Cong., 1st Sess. 38, 170 (1981), reprinted in 1981-2 CB 352, 382.

[147] HR Rep. No. 201, 97th Cong., 1st Sess. 38, 170-171 (1981), reprinted in 1981-2 CB 352, 382.

[148] HR Rep. No. 201, 97th Cong., 1st Sess. 38, 171 (1981), reprinted in 1981-2 CB 352, 383.

[d] Estates Involving Community Property

Estates of decedents owning qualified real property as community property are to be treated on a parity with those involving separate property.[149] Community property is to be taken into account under the provisions of Section 2032A in a manner that provides a result consistent with that obtained had the qualified real property not been held as community property.[150] The entire value of the community-qualified real property, not just the decedent's one-half interest, may be considered in determining whether the percentage qualification requirements imposed on the estate are satisfied. Without this rule, estates of decedents owning community-qualified real property would be at a disadvantage.[151]

[4] Real Property Qualification

If an estate qualifies, real property in the gross estate must satisfy six requirements to be classified as "qualified real property" subject to special valuation under Section 2032A. First, the property must be located in the United States.[152] Property located in a possession of the United States does not qualify.[153] Second, the property must be devoted to use as a farm[154] for farming purposes[155] or to use in a trade or business other than farming on the date of the decedent's death by the decedent or the decedent's family.[156] Third, the

---

[149] IRC § 2032A(e)(10).

[150] IRC § 2032A(e)(10). See Rev. Rul. 83-96, 1983-2 CB 156.

[151] Assume an estate with an adjusted value of $800,000 contains property devoted to a qualified use with an adjusted value of $400,000 and no community property. The 50 percent estate qualification test is met. Alternately, if the property devoted to the qualified use is community property, without the special rule the adjusted value of the gross estate would be only $600,000 and the adjusted value of property devoted to a qualified use would be only $200,000. The 50 percent test would not be satisfied, because the adjusted value of property devoted to a qualified use would represent only 33 percent of the adjusted value of the gross estate. Note that only the interest of the surviving spouse in community *qualified real property* is taken into account. An estate in which the nonqualifying property is community property and the qualifying real property is the separate property of the decedent has a greater likelihood of satisfying both the 25 percent and the 50 percent estate qualification tests because of a reduced denominator.

[152] IRC § 2032A(b)(1). This includes property in one of the states or in the District of Columbia. See IRC § 7701(a)(9).

[153] See IRC §§ 2032A(b)(1), 7701(a)(9).

[154] The term "farm" is discussed supra ¶ 4.04[3][b] text accompanying notes 50–52.

[155] The term "farming purposes" is discussed supra ¶ 4.04[3][b] text accompanying notes 53–59.

[156] IRC § 2032A(b)(1).

property must have been acquired from or passed from the decedent[157] to a qualified heir[158] of the decedent.[159] Fourth, the property[160] must have been owned directly or indirectly and used for a qualified use[161] by the decedent or a member[162] of the decedent's family for periods aggregating five years in the eight-year period immediately preceding the decedent's death.[163] Fifth, the decedent or a member of the decedent's family must have materially participated[164] in the operation of the farm or other business generally for periods aggregating five years in the eight-year period immediately preceding the date of the decedent's death.[165] Sixth, the property must be designated in the agreement required to be filed by the executor.[166] Only real property satisfying these six requirements is classified as "qualified real property."

[5] Valuation Methods

Two statutory methods are prescribed for valuing "qualified real property": a formula method and a multiple-factor method.[167] Both methods seek a value for qualified real property approximating its actual-use valuation. The formula method may be employed only in the valuation of qualified real property used as a farm for farming purposes,[168] not in the valuation of qualified real property devoted to use in a trade or business other than farming. The multiple-factor method is required in the latter instance. The multiple-factor method may, however, be employed to value real property used for farming, as an elective alternate[169] to formula method valuation. When applicable and appropriate, these methods of valuation may be used to value qualified real property required to be included in the decedent's gross estate by virtue of outright ownership or of the decedent's interest in a partnership, trust, or corporation as

---

[157] Property acquired or passed from a decedent is discussed supra ¶ 4.04[3][b][viii].

[158] The term "qualified heir" is discussed supra ¶ 4.04[3][b][ix].

[159] IRC § 2032A(b)(1).

[160] The property must be real property meeting the tests discussed here.

[161] The term "qualified use" is discussed supra ¶ 4.04[3][b][ii].

[162] The phrase "members of the decedent's family" is discussed supra ¶ 4.04[3][b] text accompanying notes 102, 103.

[163] IRC § 2032A(b)(1)(C)(i).

[164] "Material participation" is discussed supra ¶ 4.04[3][c][ii].

[165] IRC § 2032A(b)(1)(C)(ii). Section 2032A(b)(4) provides the exception to this general rule if the decedent was disabled or receiving old age Social Security benefits at death. It is discussed supra ¶ 4.04[3][c] text accompanying notes 124, 125.

[166] IRC § 2032A(b)(1)(D). This agreement is discussed infra ¶ 4.04[6].

[167] IRC §§ 2032A(e)(7), 2032A(e)(8).

[168] IRC § 2032A(e)(7).

[169] IRC § 2032A(e)(7)(C)(ii).

long as the decedent's interest is an interest in a closely held business.[170] The regulations are to prescribe how, under Section 2032A, to value qualified real property held in a partnership, trust, or corporation in which the decedent has an interest.[171]

If real property held by a corporation in which the decedent owned all outstanding shares is valued under Section 2032A, the value of the qualified real property so determined would be used in attempting to establish a value for the shares of stock required to be included in the decedent's gross estate.

Even though real property is valued at its actual-use value for gross estate inclusion purposes, any claims against the estate, including mortgages on such property, are deducted under Section 2053 at the full value of such claims.[172] However, because Section 2032A establishes the value of the property "for purposes of this chapter," the actual-use valuation should be used in determining the amount of the marital deduction[173] and the amount of the qualified family-owned business interest deduction.[174]

---

[170] An "interest in a closely held business," as that term is defined in Section 6166(b)(1), is discussed supra ¶ 4.04[3][b] note 66.

[171] IRC § 2032A(g). No minority discount (see ¶ 4.02[4][c]) is taken into account in valuing such interests. Estate of Maddox v. Comm'r, 93 TC 228 (1989). However, for purposes of imposing the maximum Section 2032A(a)(2) reduction in value under Section 2032A (see supra ¶ 4.04[1] text accompanying note 10), a minority discount is allowed in measuring the fair market value of an interest, as compared to its Section 2032A special valuation that is computed without any minority discount. Estate of Hoover v. Comm'r, 69 F3d 1044 (10th Cir. 1995), acq. 1998-2 CB xix.

[172] Rev. Rul. 83-81, 1983-1 CB 230. In the case of a nonrecourse liability on such property, only the Section 2032A value of the property reduced by the principal amount of the nonrecourse liability should be included within the gross estate. See Reg. § 20.2053-7; ¶ 5.03[6].

[173] Priv. Ltr. Rul. 8422011 (Feb. 8, 1984). Nevertheless, in private rulings the Service has ruled that where a formula clause establishes the maximum amount of the marital deduction (a pecuniary formula marital bequest) and provides that property shall be valued at its fair market value at the date of distribution to satisfy the formula, then such property may be valued at its fair market value to determine the amount of the marital deduction. Priv. Ltr. Ruls. 8314001 (Sept. 22, 1982), 8314005 (Dec. 14, 1982). If these letter rulings represent Service policy, this presents some estate tax-saving possibilities. See Kolb, "Special Use Valuation and the Marital Deduction," 6 J. of Agric. Tax. & Law 624 (1985). However, it also presents some income tax problems. Cf. Kenan v. Comm'r, 114 F2d 217 (2d Cir. 1940).

[174] See ¶¶ 5.08[3][c] text accompanying note 125, 5.08[6][b] text accompanying note 278.
    Note that such property will not qualify for a charitable deduction under Section 2055 because a charity is not a qualified heir. Section 2032A valuation should also be used in determining the amount of a Section 2054 loss.

[a] Formula Farm Valuation

The general rule for valuing qualified real property devoted to farming involves a capitalization of hypothetical earnings. The average annual gross cash rental of comparable land, less the average annual state and local real estate taxes for the comparable land,[175] is divided by the average annual effective interest rate for all new Federal Land Bank (now Farm Credit Bank) loans.[176] If there is no comparable land from which average annual gross cash rental can be derived, the same formula may be applied using the average annual net share rental of comparable land.[177] The annual figures in the five calendar years ending just prior to the year of death are to be used in the computation of each annual average.[178] Each annual average of the five required years need not be derived from the same tract of comparable farm land.[179] This formula may not be used if (1) there is no comparable farmland in the locality from which the average annual gross cash or net share rental may be determined,[180] or (2) the executor elects to use the multiple-factor method to determine the value of the farm for farming purposes.[181]

[i] **Gross cash rental.** The statutory formula requires an actual annual gross cash rental figure for comparable land when available.[182] Annual gross cash rental is the total amount of cash rents received in the calendar year, undiminished by any expenses.[183] Cash rental contingent upon production does

---

[175] IRC § 2032A(e)(7)(A)(i). Whether properties are comparable is a factual determination. Reg. § 20.2032A-4(d) lists some factors that are to be considered in determining comparability.

[176] IRC § 2032A(e)(7)(A)(ii). Rev. Rul. 2001-21, 2001-1 CB 1144, lists the average annual effective interest rates on new Farm Credit Bank loans for 2001 to be used under Section 2032A(e)(7)(A)(ii) by estates that value farmland under Section 2032A as of a date in 2000 and cites rulings applicable to earlier years. See infra note 201.

[177] IRC § 2032A(e)(7)(B)(i).

[178] IRC § 2032A(e)(7)(A) (last sentence).

[179] Reg. § 20.2032A-4(b)(2)(iv).

[180] IRC § 2032A(e)(7)(C)(i). TAM 9328004 (Mar. 31, 1995). There may be controversy over whether there is any rented comparable land used for farming in the locality of the qualified farm property.

[181] IRC § 2032A(e)(7)(C)(ii).

[182] Area averages of rentals compiled by the U.S. Department of Agriculture or other statements regarding rental value may not be used; actual cash rental is required. Reg. § 20.2032A-4(b)(2)(iii). See Estate of Thompson v. Comm'r, 76 TCM (CCH) 426 (1998) (requirement not met).

[183] Reg. § 20.2032A-4(b)(1). Estate of Klosterman v. Comm'r, 99 TC 313 (1992) (payment to irrigation district for water could not be deducted). Where comparable farmland is the subject matter of a net lease, the specified expenses of the landlord paid by the tenant constitute constructive cash rent and should be included in the gross cash rental. Improvements placed on the leasehold by the lessee may constitute additional rent for in-

not qualify for use in this formula.[184] The rent must be equivalent to that received in an arm's-length transaction between unrelated private individuals leasing for profit not involving actual or contemplated material participation by the lessor or the lessor's family.[185] If cash rentals received for the use of comparable real property include the use of farm equipment, a portion of the rent may be attributed to the use of personal property and thereby excluded from consideration in the valuation formula, but only if the lease specifies that a reasonable amount of total rent is attributable to the use of the personal property.[186]

[ii] **Net share rental.** It is not uncommon to rent farmland for a specified share of the crop rather than a specified amount of cash. If the personal representative cannot identify actual tracts of comparable farmland rented solely for cash in the same locality as the decedent's farmland, the dollar value of the average annual net share rental may be substituted for the average annual gross cash rental in the formula.[187] Net share rental is the value of the crop or other product received by the lessor, less the cash operating expenses of growing the produce, other than real property taxes paid by the lessor under the lease.[188]

---

come tax purposes. Reg. § 1.61-8(c). But see IRC § 109. If so, is this figure to be included in the gross cash rental in the formula as constructive cash rent? The alternative is that comparable rented land improved by the lessee, which improvements are additional rent for income tax purposes, is not comparable land from which the annual gross cash rental may be determined. Further regulations should deal with these problems and also with the treatment to be accorded advance rentals and lease-cancellation payments in the computation of the annual gross cash rental.

[184] Prior to the enactment of Section 2032A(e)(7)(B) providing for the use of net share rentals in formula valuation for estates of decedents dying after December 31, 1981, the Treasury vacillated on the question whether farmland rented on a crop-share basis qualified as comparable land from which the average annual gross cash rental could be determined. Proposed Regulations Section 20.2032A-4(b) initially permitted crop share rentals to be converted to a cash equivalent to be used in some cases as a substitute for cash rental in the formula but, by later amendment, prohibited it. The exclusion of crop share rentals from the definition of "cash rentals" is contained in final Regulations Section 20.2032A-4(b)(2)(iii).

[185] Reg. § 20.2032A-4(b). Federal, state, and local government leases for amounts less than those demanded by private lessors are not considered arm's-length transactions. Reg. § 20.2032A-4(b)(2)(ii).

[186] Reg. § 20.2032A-4(b)(2)(v).

[187] IRC § 2032A(e)(7)(B). The net share rental approach to formula valuation is available for estates of decedents dying after 1981. Economic Recovery Tax Act of 1981, Pub. L. No. 97-34 § 421(k)(1), 95 Stat. 172, 313 (1981), reprinted in 1981-2 CB 256, 330.

[188] IRC § 2032A(e)(7)(B)(ii). Both the House Report and the Senate Report indicate that real property taxes are not to be considered cash operating expenses. HR Rep. No. 201, 97th Cong., 1st Sess. 38, 172 (1981), reprinted in 1981-2 CB 352, 383; S. Rep. No. 144, 97th Cong., 1st Sess. 135 (1981), reprinted in 1981-2 CB 412, 464.

The produce may be received actually or constructively by the lessor. If the lessor receives a set share of the proceeds upon sale of the crop by the tenant rather than a share of the produce, the arrangement is to be treated the same as a net share rental.[189] If the crops and other products received by the lessor are sold in an arm's-length transaction within five months[190] of the date of receipt, actual or constructive, the gross amount received is the value of the produce in the determination of the net share rental. Alternatively, if the produce received by the lessor is not disposed of in the prescribed time and manner, the produce is to be valued using the weighted average price of the produce of the closest national or regional commodities market on the date of actual or constructive receipt.[191]

[iii] **Comparable land.** The comparable land must actually be rented for farming purposes; an offer to rent for a price is not sufficient.[192] Formula farm valuation requires a computation of the average annual gross cash or net share rental, less real estate taxes for the five calendar years ending before the calendar year of the decedent's death. The same tract of comparable land need not be rented throughout the full five-year period. All that is necessary is that an actual tract of farmland meeting the requirements of this section be identified for each year.[193]

The comparable real property must be situated in the same locality as the decedent's farmland.[194] There is no fixed rule to determine what constitutes the same locality, but neither mileage nor political divisions alone are the standards. "Same locality" is to be judged according to generally accepted real property valuation rules.[195]

A difficult question is the determination of comparability. Comparability of land is a factual question requiring consideration of a number of factors, no one of which is determinative.[196] The factors to be considered include the size, topography, condition, and soil capacity of the land, the similarity in the quan-

---

[189] HR Rep. No. 201, 97th Cong., 1st Sess. 38, 172 n.18 (1981), reprinted in 1981-2 CB 352, 383.

[190] This period actually is to be no longer than the period established by the U.S. Department of Agriculture for its price support program. HR Rep. No. 201, 97th Cong., 1st Sess. 38, 172 (1981), reprinted in 1981-2 CB 352, 383.

[191] HR Rep. No. 201, 97th Cong., 1st Sess. 38, 172 (1981), reprinted in 1981-2 CB 352, 383.

[192] Reg. § 20.2032A-4(b)(2)(iii).

[193] Reg. § 20.2032A-4(b)(2)(iv).

[194] Reg. § 20.2032A-4(d). Cf. Estate of Hughan v. Comm'r, 61 TCM (CCH) 2932 (1991).

[195] Reg. § 20.2032A-4(d). Cf. Estate of Hughan v. Comm'r, 61 TCM (CCH) 2932 (1991).

[196] Reg. § 20.2032A-4(d). See Rev. Rul. 86-99, 1986-2 CB 159.

tity and quality of the agricultural and horticultural commodities that are or may be produced, and the improvements made to the land.[197] Undoubtedly, this determination will be a source of controversy and litigation. Land producing agricultural and horticultural commodities similar in ·kind and quantity to that produced on the farm to be valued pursuant to the formula should be classified as comparable. When a farm to be specially valued under the formula method has a variety of improvements, uses, and land characteristics, the property must be segmented and comparable land identified for each different segment.[198] For example, when the executor elects under Section 2032A(e)(13) to treat trees growing on qualified woodlands as real property rather than as a crop, the trees may be valued under the formula method if there is comparable timber land from which the average annual cash or net share rental may be ascertained. Although the size of the particular parcel may dictate a different rental rate and render the land not comparable, in the situation where the size does not affect the rate per acre, the comparable land's gross rental will be converted to a per-acre rate in the application of the formula.

[iv] **Real estate taxes.** The average annual state and local real estate taxes to be subtracted from average annual gross cash or net share rental in formula valuation are the taxes that are assessed by a state or local government on the comparable real property and that are allowable as income tax deductions under Section 164.[199]

[v] **The divisor.** After determining an adjusted rental income figure (average rent, less taxes), that figure is divided by the average annual effective in-

---

Note that the formula may not be used to value a farm "where it is established that there is no comparable land. . . . " IRC § 2032A(e)(7)(C)(i). This "exception" places the burden to establish comparability on the taxpayer.

[197] Reg. § 20.2032A-4(d) lists ten factors that may be considered in determining comparability.

[198] Reg. § 20.2032A-4(d). The statute, Section 2032A(e)(7)(A)(i), states that the value of a "farm for farming purposes" is to be determined with the formula. The formula uses the gross cash or net share rental from comparable "land used for farming." Comparable land used for farming is not the same as a comparable farm. Qualified real property devoted to use as a farm for farming purposes may include residential buildings. IRC § 2032A(e)(3). Is comparable land without residential buildings to be treated as comparable to a farm with residential buildings that are classified as qualified real property? The improvements located on the farm could be a factor used to deny comparability. Alternately, both parcels may have residential structures, but the residential buildings on the farm to be valued may not qualify as qualified real property devoted to use as a farm for farming purposes. See IRC § 2032A(e)(3). The point is that in establishing comparability, the real property qualifying for special formula valuation must be actually comparable with the rented land. Segment-by-segment valuation will most likely be the rule rather than the exception. See Reg. § 20.2032A-4(d), Estate of Rogers v. Comm'r, 79 TCM (CCH) 1891 (2000) (timberland comparable, pastureland not comparable).

[199] Reg. § 20.2032A-4(c).

terest rate for the same period on all new Farm Credit Bank loans.[200] The average annual effective interest rate for new Farm Credit Bank loans is defined in the regulations as the average billing rate adjusted for the required purchase of land bank stock charged on new agricultural loans in the farm credit district in which the real property to be valued is located.[201] The statute requires use of the average annual effective interest rate for "*all* new Federal Land Bank loans." It is entirely unlikely that the average annual effective interest rate for new Farm Credit Bank loans in any one farm credit district, which varied in 2000 from 8.18 percent to 9.82 percent, will equal the rate for *all* new Farm Credit Bank loans. It would appear that the estate could properly use either the statutory or the administrative (regulations) figure.

Interest rate increases have a reverse effect on Section 2032A valuation. For example, if the rental figure to be used is $10,000, a 10 percent rate will yield a value of $100,000. Rates of 12 percent or 8 percent would reflect values of $83,333 and $125,000, respectively. The apparent and logical thesis is that farmland has a greater use value when it can be acquired and operated at a lower cost for borrowed money. This situation leads to the sliding rates at which income figures are to be capitalized.

[vi] Objectives of formula valuation. Formula valuation is designed to eliminate from consideration in the valuation of farmland nonfarm uses and speculative inflation of farm real estate values. The mechanical formula accomplishes this desired result. The legislative history indicates that formula method valuation of farmland will provide greater certainty in farm valuation, reducing subjectivity and controversy. Certainty of valuation results under the formula, however, only after some familiar subjective determinations regarding the value of farm real property have been completed. Conventional fair market value of the real property devoted to farm use must be determined to ascertain initial qualification for formula valuation.[202] That fair market value determination may be critical, possibly leading the executor reluctantly into controversy.[203]

---

[200] IRC § 2032A(e)(7)(A)(ii).

[201] Reg. § 20.2032A-4(e). Rev. Rul. 2001-21, 2001-1 CB 1144, lists the average annual effective interest rates on new Federal Credit Bank loans for each of the twelve farm credit districts for 2001. The ruling also lists the states within each Farm Credit Bank district and cites rulings with rates applicable to earlier years. Prior to 1988, the Farm Credit Banks were known as Federal Land Banks. Comparable rulings for prior years are cited in Rev. Rul. 88-59, 1988-2 CB 332.

[202] See discussion supra ¶¶ 4.04[2], 4.04[3][b], 4.04[3][c].

[203] The fair market value of the farm property is crucial for more than mere initial qualification. In the event the tax benefit provided by Section 2032A valuation is recaptured under Section 2032A(c), the fair market value of the real property that may be established at the time of filing the estate tax return controls in the computation of the imposition of additional tax. The recapture tax may equal the difference between the es-

[b] Multiple-Factor Valuation

The multiple-factor method of valuation[204] is the only special-use valuation method that may be employed for qualified real property used in a trade or business other than farming. It is also an elective alternative to formula valuation of qualified property devoted to farming.[205] The statute requires the consideration of several factors in the special-use valuation of any qualified real property not valued under formula valuation:

1. The capitalized value of reasonable anticipated earnings;[206]
2. The capitalized value of the fair rental value based on the farming or other actual use;[207]
3. Assessed land value in a state that has a differential or use value assessment law for qualifying property;[208]
4. Comparable sales of land in the geographical area, but in locations in which nonagricultural use is not a significant factor in the sales price;[209] and
5. Any other factor that tends to establish a value based on actual use of property.[210]

The statute does not require that each of these factors be applied with equal weight to determine the multiple-factor value of qualified real property. The regulations should recognize that at times one factor may be entitled to more weight than another, even though this may come close to an uncherished

---

tate tax imposed using Section 2032A and the estate tax liability that would have been imposed had the qualified property been included in the gross estate at fair market value. See infra ¶ 4.04[7][c].

[204] IRC § 2032A(e)(8).

[205] IRC § 2032A(e)(7)(C)(ii). If an executor elects use of Section 2032A, but does not satisfy the requirements of Section 2032A(e)(7), then Section 2032A(e)(8) applies. Reg. § 20.2056A-4(b)(2)(i). See Estate of Wineman v. Comm'r, 79 TCM (CCH) 2189 (2000).

[206] Precisely stated: "The capitalization of income which the property can be expected to yield for farming or closely held business purposes over a reasonable period of time under prudent management using traditional cropping patterns for the area, taking into account soil capacity, terrain configuration, and similar factors." IRC § 2032A(e)(8)(A). See FSA 9924019 (Mar. 17, 1999) (estimation of zero income because of Section 2032A(c) recapture rule was inappropriate).

[207] IRC § 2032A(e)(8)(B).

[208] IRC § 2032A(e)(8)(C).

[209] IRC § 2032A(e)(8)(D). Estate of Hughan v. Comm'r, 61 TCM (CCH) 2932 (1991).

[210] IRC § 2032A(e)(8)(E). However, all factors that are relevant to the particular valuation must be used. Rev. Rul. 89-30, 1989-1 CB 274.

"all the facts and circumstances" approach. The factors are not new.[211] They are frequently employed outside the tax area by appraisers ascertaining the fair market value of real property. The difference is that the statutory factors are to be applied in a manner that results in a valuation approximating a value based on the actual use of the qualified property, eliminating elements of value attributable to factors other than current actual use.

[6] Election and Agreement

In General. Section 2032A valuation of certain real property is an elective alternative to fair market valuation of all qualified real property required to be included in the gross estate. If any property is to be valued pursuant to Section 2032A, the executor must elect the application of the section and file the appropriate agreement.[212]

The election is made by attaching a notice of election[213] and the appropriate agreement to the decedent's federal estate tax return.[214] The election may be made on a late return if it is the first return filed.[215] Once made, the election is irrevocable.[216] The notice of election must contain the information necessary to indicate satisfaction of the separate eligibility prerequisites of the decedent's estate and the real property to be valued under Section 2032A.[217]

---

[211] See ¶ 4.02[3][b].

[212] IRC § 2032A(a)(1)(B). Rev. Proc. 81-14, 1981-1 CB 669, contains a sample form of the required agreement.

[213] Reg. § 20.2032A-8(a)(3).

[214] IRC § 2032A(d)(1). See Priv. Ltr. Rul. 200143014 (July 26, 2001) (time for making election may be extended under Regulations Section 301.9100-3). The election for estates of decedents dying prior to 1982 was required to be made not later than the time for filing the federal estate tax return, including extensions. IRC § 2032A(d)(1), prior to amendment by the Economic Recovery Tax Act of 1981, Pub. L. No. 97-34, § 421(j)(3), 95 Stat. 172, 313 (1981), reprinted in 1981-2 CB 256, 330. Reg. § 20.2032A-8(a)(3). This rule was changed because Congress felt that the benefits of Section 2032A valuation should not be forfeited when the estate tax return is not filed on time. HR Rep. No. 201, 97th Cong., 1st Sess. 38, 171 (1981), reprinted in 1981-2 CB 352, 383.

[215] IRC § 2032A(d)(1). Regulations Section 301.9200-2 provides rules for the extension of the time to make the election if it is not made on time. It allows an automatic twelve-month extension if the Service has not yet begun an examination of the return and if the top of the document states "FILED PURSUANT TO § 301.9100-2."

[216] IRC § 2032A(d)(1). Further, additional property may be added. Priv. Ltr. Rul. 8222018 (Feb. 11, 1982).

[217] Reg. § 20.2032A-8(a)(3). To facilitate some verification of estate qualification, this notice is to contain the decedent's name and Social Security number and the adjusted value of the gross estate as well as to identify items of real and personal property used for a qualified use passing from the decedent to qualified heirs. The adjusted value of these items must be shown. Disclosure is required in the notice of periods in the requisite pe-

If Section 2032A is not initially available to value real property included in a decedent's gross estate, a protective election may be made pending final valuation for estate tax purposes.[218] The protective election is made by filing a notice of election with the estate tax return.[219] If the property included in the decedent's gross estate ultimately qualifies for valuation under Section 2032A, an additional notice of election must be filed within sixty days after the determination is made.[220] The new notice of election accompanied by the requisite agreement is to be attached to an amended federal estate tax return.[221]

The written agreement required to be filed by the executor must designate the real property to be valued pursuant to Section 2032A[222] and signify the consent of the signatories to the imposition of an additional tax under Section 2032A(c).[223] The required signatories are all the persons in being who have an

---

riod preceding the decedent's death, generally eight years, in which the required ownership, qualified use, or material participation by the decedent or his family was absent. Regarding the real property to be specially valued, the notice is to indicate the schedule on the federal estate tax return on which it appears and its item number, legal description, qualified use, fair market value, copies of written appraisals of the fair market value, special-use value, and identification of the method used in determining the special-use value. Additionally, the notice is to contain a statement that the decedent or a family member has owned the real property to be specially valued for the requisite five-year period preceding the decedent's death, affidavits describing the activities comprising material participation, and the identity of the material participants, as well as the names, addresses, Social Security numbers, and relationships of the persons to whom the specially valued property passes and the fair market value and special-use value of the interests passing to each person. All of these rules are contained in a list of fourteen requirements found in Regulations Section 20.2032A-8(a)(3).

[218] Reg. § 20.2032A-8(b). This protective election does not extend the time for payment of estate tax. Letter rulings have allowed a protective election even where a regular election is available. Priv. Ltr. Rul. 8532003 (Apr. 11, 1985), Priv. Ltr. Rul. 8407005 (Nov. 8, 1983). A protective election does not provide an option to file a special-use valuation election at a later time. TAM 9013001 (Mar. 30, 1990). See Estate of Kokernot v. Comm'r, 112 F3d 1290 (5th Cir. 1997) (taxpayer actions constituted waiver of a protective election).

[219] Reg. § 20.2032A-8(b). The notice of election is to indicate that it is a protective election pending final valuation. It reveals the decedent's name and taxpayer identification number and identifies the real and personal property listed on the federal estate tax return that passes to qualified heirs and states the qualified relevant use. Id.

[220] Reg. § 20.2032A-8(b); Priv. Ltr. Rul. 8706006 (Oct. 10, 1986); TAM 9230002 (Apr. 9, 1992); TAM 9441003 (Oct. 14, 1994) and TAM 9508002 (Nov. 2, 1994) (involving sixty-day periods commencing with a closing letter).

[221] Reg. § 20.2032A-8(b). The new notice of election is to contain the fourteen requirements required by Regulations Section 20.2032A-8(a)(3). See supra note 217. The amended return is to be filed with the same office as the original return.

[222] IRC § 2032A(b)(1)(D).

[223] IRC § 2032A(d)(2). The imposition of additional tax under Section 2032A(c) is discussed infra ¶ 4.04[7]. Although the statute does not specify a time period in which the appropriate agreement must be filed, the agreement must be filed within the time specified

interest in the real property designated in the agreement, whether or not their particular interests are possessory.[224] Signatories include owners of remainder and executory interests, holders of general or nongeneral powers of appointment, takers in default of the exercise of powers, joint tenants of the decedent, directors of a corporation, and trustees of a trust holding an interest in the qualified real property.[225] However, the rule does not apply to owners of undivided interests in property where only the decedent's undivided interest is included in the decedent's gross estate and the other co-owners do not acquire the decedent's interest at the decedent's death.[226] Creditors of the estate are not required signatories solely by reason of their status as creditors.[227] Each person signing the agreement consents to the imposition of recapture tax with respect to real property valued pursuant to Section 2032A in which the person has an interest. Qualified heirs consent to personal liability;[228] persons other than qualified heirs consent to collection of the additional tax from the qualified real property.[229] In addition, the agreement must designate an agent for the signatories with whom the Service may deal on all matters involving continued qualification and the special lien under Section 6324B.[230]

In 1984, Congress relaxed these stringent requirements with the addition of Section 2032A(d)(3) to the Code.[231] Under that provision, if the election of special-use valuation or the written agreement submitted with the election evidenced "substantial compliance"[232] with the Section 2032A requirements, the

---

for the election by the executor. Reg. § 20.2032A-8(a)(3); Estate of Gunland v. Comm'r, 88 TC 1453 (1987).

[224] IRC § 2032A(d)(2). The interest may be present or future, vested or contingent. See Reg. § 20.2032A-8(c)(2); Estate of Smoot v. Comm'r, 892 F2d 597 (7th Cir. 1989). See TAM 9038002 (June 8, 1990) (signature of remote contingent qualified heir not required).

[225] IRC § 2032A(d)(2). See also Rev. Rul. 85-148, 1985-2 CB 199 (spouse's inchoate dower interest).

[226] Estate of Pullian v. Comm'r, 84 TC 789 (1985); Estate of Bettenhausen v. Comm'r, 51 TCM (CCH) 488 (1986); TAM 9027004 (Mar. 22, 1990) (all involving tenancies-in-common). But see Priv. Ltr. Rul. 8645004 (July 28, 1986) (one partner could not sign for the partnership).

[227] Priv. Ltr. Rul. 8536004 (May 20, 1985).

[228] See IRC § 2032A(c)(5); Priv. Ltr. Rul. 8422008 (Feb. 2, 1984). A qualified heir may request from the Secretary a statement of the maximum amount of any additional estate tax for which the qualified heir may be personally liable. If the qualified heir furnishes a bond in that amount, the qualified heir is discharged from personal liability. IRC §§ 2032A(e)(11), 2032A(c)(5).

[229] Reg. § 20.2032A-8(c)(1).

[230] Reg. §§ 20.2032A-8(c)(1), 20.2032A-8(c)(4).

[231] Deficit Reduction Act of 1984, Pub. L. No. 98-369, § 1025, 98 Stat. 494, 1030 (1984), reprinted in 1984-3 CB (Vol. 1) 1, 538.

[232] IRC § 2032A(d)(3)(B) (prior to amendment in 1997).

election or agreement was considered valid, but only if the technical defect or flaw was cured within ninety days from the time of the Service's notification to the executor that the defect or flaw existed.[233] In keeping with the legislative history,[234] the Service had interpreted the substantial compliance requirement narrowly.[235] The courts agreed, allowing slight technical defects to pass muster

---

[233] IRC § 2032A(d)(3). Prior to 1984, Form 706 did not indicate all the information required to be filed with a Section 2032A election. Consequently Congress provided that estates of individuals dying before 1986 that provided *"substantially all"* of the necessary information required under Form 706 were allowed a period of ninety days after being notified of their errors by the Treasury to perfect their defective elections. Tax Reform Act of 1986, Pub. L. No. 99-514, § 1421, 100 Stat. 2085, 2716 (1986), reprinted in 1986-3 CB (Vol. 1) 1, 633. The election could be made on a late-filed return as long as that return was the first return filed. Technical and Miscellaneous Revenue Act of 1988, Pub. L. No. 100-647, § 1014(f), 102 Stat. 3342, 3562 (1988), reprinted in 1988-3 CB 1, 222.

The "substantially all" test was more easily satisfied than the "substantial compliance" test. Prussner v. United States, 896 F2d 218 (7th Cir. 1991). The "substantially all" test was satisfied in Prussner v. United States, supra (failure to attach a recapture agreement satisfied the "substantially all" test, even though it did not satisfy the Section 2032A(d)(3) "substantial compliance" test); Estate of Doherty, 982 F2d 450 (10th Cir. 1992) (failure to provide written appraisal of fair market value); Parker v. United States, 90-2 USTC ¶ 60,038 (ED Ark 1990) (failure to state property's fair market value where required, reveal a family member's interest in property, and property not identified). The test was not met in Estate of Collins v. United States, 91-1 USTC ¶ 60,060 (WD Okla. 1991) (failure to submit notice of election and appraisals); Estate of Merwin v. Comm'r, 95 TC 168 (1990) (failure to attach notice of election or recapture agreement); Killion v. Comm'r, 55 TCM (CCH) 1004 (1988) (almost no information filed).

[234] The legislative history of the 1984 Act gives examples of such technical defects or flaws. See Staff of Joint Comm. on Taxation, General Explanation of the Revenue Provisions of the Deficit Reduction Act of 1984, at 1124.

[235] An election has been treated as satisfying the substantive compliance requirement in the following: Rev. Rul. 85-84, 1985-1 CB 326 (lack of a full legal description of the property where the property was nevertheless described with reasonable clarity); Priv. Ltr. Rul. 8617005 (Dec. 31, 1985) (no separate notice of the election although all appropriate information included with the return), Priv. Ltr. Rul. 8647002 (Aug. 6, 1986) (lack of a full legal description of the property where documents submitted provided reasonably clear description), Priv. Ltr. Rul. 8725002 (Mar. 18, 1987) (failure to include written appraisal of fair market value of property); TAM 9038002 (Sept. 21, 1990) (beneficiary with remote interest did not sign agreement); TAM 9225002 (Jan. 30, 1992) (choice of valuation method but insufficient substantiation); TAM 9228005 (Mar. 31, 1992) (signature on recapture agreement as qualified heir but not as trustee); TAM 9245002 (June 12, 1992) (signature as qualified heir but not as shareholders, partners, or trustees); TAM 9346003 (Aug. 9, 1993) (same).

The substantive compliance requirement was not met where there was an election in the following: Priv. Ltr. Rul. 8650002 (Sept. 5, 1986) (no separate notice of election with the return and no appropriate information with the return), Priv. Ltr. Rul. 8704002 (Sept. 25, 1986) (property not designated with reasonable clarity).

The agreement satisfied the substantial compliance test in the following: Rev. Rul. 85-148, 1985-2 CB 199 (failure of a qualified heir (spouse with a mere inchoate dower interest) to sign); Priv. Ltr. Rul. 8617007 (Jan. 10, 1986), Priv. Ltr. Rul. 8637001 (Apr. 21,

under the "substantial compliance" test,[236] but refusing to find such compliance in the case of more significant defects.[237]

In 1997, Congress further liberalized the Section 2032A election provisions by amending Section 2032A(d)(3) to permit signatures to be added to the recapture agreement after it is filed and required information to be supplied late, so long as the election was made and the agreement was submitted within the prescribed time.[238] The executor again has a reasonable period of time, not exceeding ninety days after being notified of the failure to provide the required information or signatures, to make the necessary corrections.[239]

1986), Priv. Ltr. Rul. 8632001 (Mar. 14, 1986), Priv. Ltr. Rul. 8646007 (July, 31 1986), and Priv. Ltr. Rul. 87130011 (Dec. 3, 1986) (signature of qualified heir not in appropriate capacity).

Substantial compliance with respect to the agreement was not satisfied in the following: Priv. Ltr. Rul. 8614006 (Dec. 30, 1985), Priv. Ltr. Rul. 8520006 (Feb. 1, 1985), Priv. Ltr. Rul. 8532010 (May 2, 1985), Priv. Ltr. Rul. 8527007 (Mar. 14, 1985), Priv. Ltr. Rul. 8711003 (Nov. 28, 1986) (failure of a qualified heir to sign), Priv. Ltr. Rul. 8528003 (Mar. 22, 1985) (failure of legal guardian of qualified heir to sign), Priv. Ltr. Rul. 8540003 (July 21, 1985), and Priv. Ltr. Rul. 8602007 (Sept. 7, 1985) (signature not in appropriate capacities as directors of corporation).

[236] McAlpine v. Comm'r 968 F2d 459 (5th Cir. 1992) (trustee signed the recapture agreement but beneficiaries who had little chance of acquiring the property within ten years didn't); Gettysburg Nat'l Bank v. United States, 92-2 USTC ¶ 60,108 (MD Penn. 1992) (owners of 62 percent of property signed recapture agreement).

[237] McDonald v. Comm'r, 853 F2d 1494 (8th Cir. 1988) (failure of children who received a partial interest in property to sign election and recapture agreement); Grimes v. Comm'r, 937 F2d 316 (7th Cir. 1991) (failure to attach a recapture agreement); Prussner v. United States, 896 F2d 218 (7th Cir. 1991) (same); Estate of Hudgins v. Comm'r, 57 F3d 1393 (5th Cir. 1995) (same); Estate of Lucas v. United States, 97 F3d 1401 (11th Cir. 1996) (same); Parker v. United States, 91-2 USTC ¶ 60,082 (ED Ark. 1991) (failure to include residuary taker as person with interest in the property); Estate of Strickland v. Comm'r, 92 TC 16 (1989) (failure to choose and substantiate method of special valuation); Estate of Collins v. United States, 91-1 USTC ¶ 60,060 (WD Okla. 1991) (failure to submit notice of election and appraisals); Estate of Merwin v. Comm'r, 95 TC 168 (1990) (failure to attach notice of election or recapture agreement); Killion v. Comm'r, 55 TCM (CCH) 1004 (1988) (almost no information filed); Estate of Doherty v. Comm'r, 982 F2d 450 (10th Cir. 1992) (failure to substantiate either fair market valuation or special-use valuation of property).

[238] The Taxpayer Relief Act of 1997, Pub. L. No. 105-34, § 1313(a), 111 Stat. 788, 1045 (1997), reprinted in 1997-4 CB 1471, 1736.

[239] IRC § 2032A(d)(3). The revised provision is effective for estates of decedents dying after August 5, 1997. The Taxpayer Relief Act of 1997, Pub. L. No. 105-34, § 1313(b), 111 Stat. 788, 1045 (1997), reprinted in 1997-4 CB 1471, 1737. The legislative history specifies that these corrections may be made without regard to Treasury Regulations Section 20.2032A-8. The legislative history also states that technically defective Section 2032A elections made prior to the date of enactment should be corrected under prior law in a manner consistent with the new provisions. H Conf. Rep. No. 105-220, 105th Cong., 1st Sess. 330, 720 (1997), reprinted in 1997-4 CB (Vol. 2) 1457, 2190. Cf. Estate

Effect of Election and Agreement. If the election is made and the appropriate agreement filed, all "qualified real property" included in the gross estate must be valued pursuant to Section 2032A.

However, this mandate is not so broad as it seems. Property is not qualified real property unless it is designated in the agreement that the executor is required to file.[240] Any real property capable of satisfying all the prerequisites for classification as "qualified real property" may possibly be excluded from mandatory Section 2032A valuation by excluding it from the agreement. Although the election need not include all real property eligible for valuation under Section 2032A, the regulations purport to require that sufficient property to satisfy the threshold requirements of Section 2032A(b)(1)(B) be valued under the election.[241] Real property with an adjusted value[242] equaling 25 percent of the adjusted value of the gross estate[243] must, according to the regulations, be valued under Section 2032A. This requirement is not in the statute. Its wisdom and perhaps its validity are questionable.[244]

At the time the election is filed, a special lien in the amount of the estate tax saved by special-use valuation is imposed on the real property valued under Section 2032A by Section 6324B.[245] Other security may be substituted for this lien.[246] The lien continues with respect to an interest in qualified real property as long as there is any potential liability for recapture tax with respect to the interest.[247] The contingent liability for recapture tax may be extinguished by satisfaction, lien unenforceability because of lapse of time, expiration of ten

---

v. Wineman, 79 TCM (CCH) 2189 (2000) (discussing congressional intent under current Section 2032A(d)(3)).

[240] IRC § 2032A(b)(1)(D).

[241] Reg. § 20.2032A-8(a)(2). IRC § 2032A(b)(1)(B) is discussed supra ¶ 4.04[3][c].

[242] IRC § 2032A(b)(3)(B). Adjusted value is discussed supra ¶ 4.04[3][b][i].

[243] IRC § 2032A(b)(3)(A). Adjusted value is discussed supra ¶ 4.04[3][b][i].

[244] How will this regulation be administered when the application of Section 2032A(e)(10) or Section 2035(c)(1)(B), either alone or in combination, results in satisfaction of the 25 percent estate qualification test but there is insufficient real property included in the gross estate to satisfy the regulation requirement? Is special valuation prohibited when the real property that must be specially valued under the regulation exceeds the Section 2032A(a)(2) limit? This requirement should be dropped.

[245] IRC § 6324B(a). Standing timber valued under Section 2032A will be subject to this lien to the same extent as the land on which it stands. HR Rep. No. 201, 97th Cong., 1st Sess. 38, 175 n.27 (1981), reprinted in 1981-2 CB 352, 385.

[246] IRC § 6324B(d). See Reg. § 20.6324B-1(c).

[247] IRC § 6324B(b). This lien will be transferred to qualified exchange property or qualified replacement property when the qualified real property is discharged from the lien. HR Rep. No. 201, 97th Cong., 1st Sess. 38, 174 ns. 24-25 (1981), reprinted in 1981-2 CB 352, 384.

years after the decedent's date of death, or death of the potentially liable qualified heir.[248]

[7] Recapture

What Congress gives, Congress may take away. Section 2032A was enacted to encourage the continued use of real property in family farms and other small business operations.[249] If this favored use is not continued for a reasonable time after the decedent's death, the estate tax saved by special-use valuation may be recaptured in whole or in part. Recapture is accomplished by the imposition of an additional tax.[250] The "gotcha"[251] has invaded the estate tax.

An additional estate tax is imposed,[252] generally within ten years after the decedent's death, if the qualified heir (1) disposes of an interest in property valued under Section 2032A to one other than a member of the qualified heir's family[253] or (2) ceases to use the qualified property or a portion thereof for the qualified use.[254] Death of the qualified heir usually terminates potential recapture liability.[255]

---

[248] This lien, which is in lieu of any lien under Section 6324, must be filed as provided in Section 6323(f) to have priority against any purchaser, holder of a security interest, mechanic's lien, or judgment lien creditor. See Section 6324B(c)(1), which makes reference to Section 6324A(d)(1). The priority this lien has, once filed, is specified in Sections 6324A(d)(1) and 6324A(d)(3). See IRC § 6324B(c)(1).

[249] HR Rep. No. 1380, 94th Cong., 2d Sess. 3, 22 (1976), reprinted in 1976-3 CB (Vol. 3) 735, 756.

[250] IRC § 2032A(c)(1).

[251] See IRC §§ 1245 and 1250 for examples of the income tax "gotcha." The "gotcha" has also been applied to the Section 2057 deduction. See ¶ 5.08[5].

[252] IRC § 2032A(c)(1).

[253] IRC § 2032A(c)(1)(A).

[254] IRC § 2032A(c)(1)(B). Form 706-A, "United States Additional Estate Tax Return," is used to report the additional tax due because of the application of Section 2032A(c). The form is filed and the tax paid within six months after the taxable disposition or cessation of qualified use. Instructions for Form 706-A, "United States Additional Estate Tax Return" (Rev. August 1999). See Le Fever v. Comm'r, 100 F3d 778 (10th Cir. 1996) (taxpayers estopped under the "duty of consistency" doctrine from avoiding recapture by contending that the property had not met the requirements of Section 2032A at the time of the election).

[255] IRC § 2032A(c)(1).

[a] The Ten-Year Period

Any potential liability for additional tax generally lapses at the end of the ten-year period immediately following the date of the decedent's death.[256] Generally, if property qualifying for special-use valuation is sold or converted to a nonqualified use more than ten years after the decedent's death, no additional tax is imposed.

The ten-year period begins on the date of the decedent's death or on the date the qualified heir commences qualified use if within two years of the date of the decedent's death. A qualified heir has a two-year period following the death of the decedent in which to commence qualified use of the real property without triggering recapture.[257] The ten-year period is justifiably extended by the period that elapses after death and before commencement of qualified use. The period of potential liability for the recapture tax may be further extended when property valued under Section 2032A is involuntarily converted and qualified replacement property acquired.[258] The period is extended by any period, beyond the two-year period referred to in Section 1033(a)(2)(B)(i), during which the qualified heir is allowed to replace the qualified real property.[259]

The statutory rule that the recapture event must precede the death of the qualified heir for an additional tax to be imposed with respect to the interest of that heir may be subject to one very important qualification if successive interests in qualified property are involved. If two or more qualified heirs acquire successive interests in property valued under Section 2032A, potential liability for the imposition of additional tax does not abate on the death of a qualified heir until the death of the last qualified heir.[260] The critical inquiry is whether the heir with the succeeding (future) interest is a qualified heir. Qualified heir status generally requires property to have passed to the individual from the de-

---

[256] IRC § 2032A(c)(1).

[257] IRC § 2032A(c)(7)(A).

[258] IRC § 2032A(h)(2)(A). See IRC § 2032A(h)(3)(B).

[259] IRC § 2032A(h)(2)(A). The Section 1033(a)(2)(B)(i) period is "2 years after the close of the first taxable year in which any part of the gain upon the conversion is realized." This two-year period may be extended upon a showing of reasonable cause for qualified heir's inability to replace the converted property within the specified period. Reg. § 1.1033(a)-2(c)(3). The ten-year recapture period is extended by any additional time granted. If the qualified heir replaces the converted qualified real property with qualified replacement property within two years after the close of the taxable year in which any gain on the conversion is realized, the recapture period is not extended. Additionally, if no gain is realized on the conversion, the ten-year recapture period is not extended because the two-year period referred to in Section 1033(a)(2)(B)(i) begins to run only after the close of the taxable year in which gain on the conversion is realized.

[260] HR Rep. No. 1380, 94th Cong., 2d Sess. 3, 26 (1976), reprinted in 1976-3 CB (Vol. 3) 735, 760. See Reg. § 20.2032A-3(c)(2).

cedent.[261] Generally, qualified property passing in trust is deemed to have passed to a qualified heir to the extent that the qualified heir has a present interest in the trust.[262] A future interest in trust property, under the general rule, is not considered to have passed, and, therefore, the remainderperson is not treated as a qualified heir. However, a remainder interest is treated as being received by a qualified heir if it is not contingent on surviving a nonfamily member and is not subject to divestment in favor of a nonfamily member.[263] If a decedent devises qualified real property in trust (e.g., income to the decedent's daughter for life, remainder to the decedent's grandchild), the death of the income beneficiary within ten years of the decedent's death should not affect the potential liability for the imposition of an additional tax.[264] Congress probably did not intend to abate the recapture liability in the event of the death of a qualified heir unless the decedent's interest in qualified property was required to be included in the qualified heir's gross estate. This would support the exception calling for no abatement of recapture tax liability until the death of those holding successive interests, but this also creates another problem. If one who holds a present interest also possesses a general power of appointment over the property, the death of the power holder *should* result in abatement of any potential liability for recapture tax with respect to the qualified real property subject to the general power of appointment. The successive interest rule should be applied only to successive holders if the property is not required to be included in the gross estate of the preceding holder.[265] The un-

---

[261] IRC § 2032A(e)(1).

[262] HR Rep. No. 1515, 94th Cong., 2d Sess. 610 (1976), reprinted in 1976-3 CB (Vol. 3) 807, 960. Property acquired or passed from a decedent is discussed supra ¶ 4.04[3][b][viii].

[263] Reg. § 20.2032A-8(a)(2). When the holder of the present interest possesses a power of appointment, the remainderperson may or may not be treated as a qualified heir. The remainderperson's status depends on whether any permissible appointee is a nonfamily member. Cf. Rev. Rul. 82-140, 1982-2 CB 208.

[264] Reg. § 20.2032A-3(c)(2).

[265] How should the successive interest rule be applied when otherwise qualified real property is placed in trust income to A for life, remainder to B, and C possesses a general power of appointment over the entire trust corpus? Is the general power of appointment to be treated as an interest in the property? (Section 2041 and Regulations Section 20.2032A-8(c)(2) treat a general power of appointment as if it were an interest in property.) Assuming the general power is to be treated as an interest in property for purposes of Section 2032A, then the question is whether the power "interest" overrides the present income interest and remainder interest. Should the override depend on whether the power is one that may be exercised by will or by deed? It seems if the property passing into trust is subject to a general power of appointment presently exercisable to the extent that the income and remainder interests are subject to divestment at the will of the power holder, the property ought to be treated as passing to the power holder and the successive interest rule should not be applied.

certainty and difficulty suggested here indicate a need for further Congressional refinement of the statute.

If a decedent's spouse and child acquire qualified property from the decedent as tenants in common, the death of either tenant within ten years frees that tenant's interest in the qualified property from potential liability for the recapture tax.[266] Under these facts, a sale of the deceased tenant's interest in the qualified property to an unrelated third party within ten years of the decedent's death is not an event giving rise to the imposition of an additional tax. Sale by the surviving tenant of that tenant's interest in the qualified property to an unrelated third party within ten years of the decedent's death is an event that results in the imposition of an additional tax.[267]

Death of a qualified heir after disposal of qualified real property to a member of the qualified heir's family does not affect any potential liability for recapture tax on the property transferred.[268]

[b] Recapture Events

[i] **Dispositions.** Not all dispositions of property valued under Section 2032A within the prescribed ten-year period invoke the additional estate tax. A disposition to a member of the qualified heir's family[269] does not result in the

---

[266] HR Rep. No. 1380, 94th Cong., 2d Sess. 3, 26 (1976), reprinted in 1976-3 CB (Vol. 3) 735, 760.

[267] The additional tax imposed will be one half of the amount that would have been imposed had both tenants survived and joined in the sale. Property acquired by two or more qualified heirs from the decedent as joint tenants with right of survivorship should be treated like a tenancy in common. Upon the death of the first to die, the value of that decedent's proportionate interest will be included in that decedent's gross estate. See IRC § 2040(a). That portion should not be subjected to recapture tax if the surviving joint tenant sells the property within a ten year period.

[268] For example, if A inherited qualified property from the decedent and sold it to B, a member of A's family, B thereafter is the qualified heir. IRC § 2032A(e)(1). The death of A after the sale to B would not affect the potential recapture liability with respect to the qualified property held by B at A's death.

[269] "Family" here includes only the qualified heir's ancestors, spouse, and lineal descendants, as well as the lineal descendants of the qualified heir's parents and spouse and the spouses of all those lineal descendants. See IRC § 2032A(e)(2); Rev. Rul. 85-66, 1985-1 CB 324. A member of the qualified heir's family need not be a member of the decedent's family, but, after the disposition, the member of the qualified heir's family is treated as the qualified heir of the decedent with respect to the transferred property or property interest. IRC § 2032A(e)(1). See also Rev. Rul. 89-22, 1989-1 CB 276 (recapture tax applied where the transferee was not a member of qualified heir's family, even though the transferee was a member of the decedent's family).

imposition of the recapture tax;[270] nor, in general, does a testamentary disposition by a qualified heir.[271] In addition, a contribution of a qualified conservation easement does not constitute a disposition.[272]

The additional tax is imposed if the qualified heir sells or exchanges any interest[273] in qualified property to a nonfamily member in a taxable transaction within the proscribed period. Nontaxable sales and exchanges under Section 1031 or Section 1033 will result in additional tax only to the extent that the transferor liquidates the property; there is no recapture tax when the qualified property involuntarily converted or exchanged for like-kind property is exchanged solely for real property or the proceeds of conversion are timely reinvested in real property to be used for the same qualified use as the qualified real property exchanged or converted.[274] A gift of qualified property to a nonfamily member within the proscribed period will also trigger the imposition of the additional tax. Measurement of the recapture tax in instances of transfers

---

[270] IRC § 2032A(c)(1)(A). Cf. TAM 9333002 (Apr 20, 1993) If the qualified heir makes a gift of an interest in qualified real property to a member of the qualified heir's family, valuation for gift tax purposes is not affected by the possible imposition of a recapture tax. Rev. Rul. 81-230, 1981-2 CB 186. Section 2032A is not applicable to Chapter 12, the gift tax, nor is there a comparable provision in Chapter 12. A cash lease of property to a qualified heir does not constitute a "disposition" to a qualified heir. Williamson v. Comm'r, 974 F2d 1525 (9th Cir. 1992). But see infra text accompanying notes 283–288.

[271] The death of the qualified heir before disposition generally eliminates any potential additional tax. IRC § 2032A(c)(1). For a discussion of the exception to this rule, see the discussion supra ¶ 4.04[7][a] text accompanying note 260.

[272] IRC § 2032A(c)(8) (applying to qualified conservation easements granted after 1997). See Estate of Gibbs v. United States, 161 F3d 242 (3d Cir. 1998) (a sale of such an easement is not a "contribution").

[273] Estate of Gibbs v. United States, 161 F3d 242 (3d Cir. 1998) (sale of development easement was a disposition even though the development easement was not a property interest under state law).

[274] IRC §§ 2032A(h), 2032A(i). If some "boot" gain is recognized, there is recapture tax. See infra ¶ 4.04[7][c] text accompanying notes 317–321. Priv. Ltr. Rul. 8526032 (Apr. 1, 1985); (IRC § 1031 like kind exchange); Priv. Ltr. Rul. 9604018 (Oct. 30, 1995) (same); Priv. Ltr. Rul. 9945046 (Aug. 12, 1999) (same); TAM 9333002 (Apr. 20, 1993) (foreclosure did not constitute an involuntary conversion). The provision relating to exchanges applies to exchanges after December 31, 1981, regardless of the decedent's date of death. Economic Recovery Tax Act of 1981, Pub. L. No. 97-34, § 421(k)(3), 95 Stat. 172, 313 (1981), reprinted in 1981-3 CB 256, 331.

If land is condemned, perhaps the proceeds may be used to improve the remaining land that originally qualified for special-use valuation. That might preclude nonrecognition of gain; the government has taken the position that the construction of improvements on land already owned by the taxpayer does not constitute replacement with property of a like kind within the meaning of Section 1033(g), because "land is not of the same nature or character as a building. . . . " Rev. Rul. 67-255, 1967-2 CB 270, 271. This position has been rejected by one court. Davis v. United States 411 F. Supp. 964 (D. Haw. 1976), aff'd on other grounds, 589 F2d 446 (9th Cir. 1979).

for less than full consideration is discussed later.[275] Severance of, or disposition of a right to sever, any standing timber treated as real property rather than as a crop under a Section 2032A(e)(13)(A) election is to be treated as a disposition.[276]

Mere changes in the form of business ownership are not intended to result in the imposition of the additional tax.[277] The transfer of qualified property by the qualified heir tax-free to a corporation under Section 351 or to a partnership under Section 721 does not constitute a disposition resulting in the imposition of the additional tax if three conditions are satisfied: (1) The qualified heir retains the same equitable[278] interest in the qualified property after the transfer; (2) the qualified heir's interest in the corporation or partnership after the transfer is an interest in a "closely held business," as that term is defined in Section 6166(b);[279] and (3) "the corporation or partnership consents to personal liability for the recapture tax if it disposes of the real property or ceases to use the property for qualified purposes during the period in which recapture may occur."[280]

The second requirement, that the heir's interest in the partnership or corporation be a closely held interest, should not apply if all shareholders or partners are members of the qualified heir's family. A qualified heir may give or sell separate interests in a parcel of qualified property to an infinite number of

---

[275] See infra ¶ 4.04[7][c].

[276] IRC § 2032A(c)(2)(E). Although the statute expressly treats "severance" as a "disposition," should severance followed by use on the farm be treated as a disposition resulting in the imposition of recapture tax? For example, if timber on qualified woodland is severed and used to fence the remaining woodland, should the recapture tax be imposed?

[277] HR Rep. No. 1380, 94th Cong., 2d Sess. 3, 25 n.3 (1976), reprinted in 1976-3 CB (Vol. 3) 735, 759; Priv. Ltr. Rul. 8416016 (Jan. 13, 1984). Similarly, a partition of property is not a recapture event even if the interests received are commensurate with those given up. TAM 9113028 (Mar. 29, 1991).

[278] The regulations should clarify the requirement that the qualified heir retain "the same equitable interest in the property" transferred to a corporation or a partnership. Except for a transfer to a wholly owned corporation, it would be impossible to retain the same equitable interest in the property. Seemingly, the legislative history means that the qualified heir not liquidate in whole or in part the heir's interest, i.e., that no Section 351(b), Section 731 or Section 707(a)(2)(B) boot be received in return for the transfer of the qualified property.

[279] A qualified heir's interest in a partnership is a closely held business interest if the heir owns at least 20 percent of the total capital interest in the partnership or if the partnership has 45 (15 prior to 2002) or fewer partners. IRC § 6166(b)(1)(B). If the qualified heir owns at least 20 percent of the value of the voting stock or is one of 45 (15 prior to 2002) or fewer shareholders, the interest in the corporation is classified as an interest in a closely held business. IRC § 6166(b)(1)(C). See supra ¶ 4.04[3][b] note 66.

[280] HR Rep. No. 1380, 94th Cong., 2d Sess. 3, 25 n.3 (1976), reprinted in 1976-3 CB (Vol. 3) 735, 759.

family members without triggering additional tax. The only limitation is proclivity for prolificacy.

If a qualified heir sells the interest in the partnership or a corporation to a nonfamily member, the qualified heir should incur liability for any recapture tax that is imposed. Sale by the qualified heir should not result in recapture tax liability at the corporate or partnership level. If the corporation or partnership owning qualified real property disposes of it to a person who is not a member of the qualified heir's family, the liability for recapture tax should also be discharged by the qualified heir or heirs who own the closely held business interests. Sale by the corporation or partnership to a member of the contributing qualified heir's family should not trigger imposition of the additional tax. Furthermore, if property held by a corporation or partnership is exchanged for like-kind property or is involuntarily converted, the recapture tax should be avoided to the extent that like-kind property is received in the exchange or the real property acquired with the proceeds is used for the same qualified use as the qualified real property exchanged or converted.[281]

[ii] **Cessation of qualified use.** The additional tax is imposed if within the recapture period the property valued pursuant to Section 2032A ceases to be devoted to the use originally qualifying the property for special-use valuation.[282]

As was the case with respect to qualification of property for Section 2032A treatment,[283] the question whether the leasing of a farm constitutes a qualified use raises some complicated issues.[284] Again, if the lease creates an element of risk to the qualified heir, there should be no cessation of qualified use.[285] Generally, a net cash lease of the property, even to a member of the qualified heir's family, constitutes a cessation of use and triggers the recapture

---

[281] See the discussion at supra text accompanying note 274.

[282] IRC § 2032A(c)(1)(B). Participation in "Payment-in-Kind" and other related land diversion programs offered to farmers by the Department of Agriculture will not have an adverse effect on qualifying for or maintaining Section 2032A treatment for either the owner decedent or the qualified heir. IRS Announcement No. 83-43, 1983-10 IRB 29 (Mar. 7, 1983). Cf. TAM 9212001 (Mar. 20, 1992).

[283] See supra ¶ 4.04[3][b] text accompanying notes 45–49.

[284] See Edwards, "Section 2032A: Cash Leases and Cessation of Qualified Use," 10 Va. Tax Rev. 731 (1991).

[285] Estate of Gavin v. United States, 113 F3d 802 (8th Cir. 1997). Cf. Schuneman v. United States, 783 F2d 694 (7th Cir. 1986).

tax.[286] However, if a surviving spouse[287] or a lineal descendant of a decedent who qualified for Section 2032A treatment leases a farm or business to a member of the family of such spouse or descendant for a net cash lease, there is no cessation of qualified use or triggering of the recapture tax.[288]

Either conversion to another use or mere disuse may constitute cessation of a qualified use. Conversion of qualified real property used as a farm for farming purposes at the decedent's death to use in a trade or business other than farming results in the imposition of the additional tax,[289] but the exact outer reaches of this rule are unclear. It is possible that if the actual use of qualified real property is varied at all in the recapture period, the additional tax will be imposed. For example, if land devoted to use as a fruit stand is con-

---

[286] Williamson v. Comm'r, 974 F2d 1525 (9th Cir. 1992) (cash lease to family member); Stovall v. Comm'r, 101 TC 140 (1993) (same); Fisher v. Comm'r, 65 TCM (CCH) 2284 (1993) (same); Shaw v. Comm'r 62 TCM (CCH) 396 (1991) (same); Martin v. Comm'r, 783 F2d 81 (7th Cir. 1986) (cash lease to nonfamily member); Hohenstein v. Comm'r, 73 TCM (CCH) 1886 (1997) (same after qualified heir physically incapacitated); Hight v. Comm'r, 58 TCM (CCH) 1457 (1990) (same). A cash rental to a family member constitutes a cessation of qualified use that triggers a recapture tax, even though a cash sale to a family member of a qualified heir would not trigger such tax. IRC § 2032A(c)(1)(A).

See also Minter v. United States, 19 F3d 426 (8th Cir. 1994) (cash lease to family-held corporation satisfying Reg. § 20.2032A-3(b)(1) pre-death requirements constituted post-death qualified use).

[287] See HR Rep. No. 795, 100 Cong. 2d Sess. 590 (1988) which explains the rationale for the spousal rule as follows:

> Under present law, property may qualify for special use valuation if the decedent leases the property to a member of his family. The recapture tax is imposed, however, if the property is not used in a qualified use by the qualified heir. Thus, if a decedent leases the qualified real property to a member of his family and the property passes to his spouse, a recapture tax will be imposed under present law unless the spouse begins to use the property in a qualified use.
>
> The committee believes that the surviving spouse should not be subject to more onerous rules than the decedent. . . .

[288] IRC § 2032A(c)(7)(E). Under the rule a legally adopted child of an individual is treated as a child by blood. Id. The rule applies to leases entered into after 1976. The Taxpayer Relief Act of 1997, Pub. L. No. 105-34, § 504(c), 111 Stat. 788, 854 (1997), reprinted in 1997-4 CB 1457, 1540. To provide relief where a tax has previously been triggered as a result of a cash lease, the Economic Growth and Tax Relief Reconciliation Act of 2001, Pub. L. No. 107-16, § 581, 115 Stat. 38, 93 (2001), reprinted in 2001-__ CB __, __, provides that a claim for refund or credit of any overpayment of tax resulting from the application of Section 2032A(c)(7)(E) is allowed if the claim is filed prior to June 7, 2002, a date one year after the date of the enactment of the 2001 Act.

The Service, relying on United States v. Zacks, 375 US 59 (1963), initially took the position that such retroactivity did not waive the general statute of limitations for refund claims (Section 6511(a)), thus substantially limiting any such refund claims. TAM 9843001 (July 8, 1998).

[289] IRC § 2032A(c)(6)(A).

verted to use as a processing plant, the additional tax may be imposed. But conversion from producing to processing would seem more significant. The normal rotation of crops on a farm should not trigger recapture; of less certain consequences would be the conversion to a vineyard of farmland that, until the decedent's death, had been used to raise various grains. Literally, the statute can and should be interpreted to interdict conversions only when they involve a shift from a Section 2032A(b)(2)(A) use to a Section 2032A(b)(2)(B) use.[290]

Generally, the qualified heir's mere failure to use property valued under Section 2032A for its qualified use during the recapture period results in imposition of a recapture tax.[291] There are exceptions to this rule. A qualified heir is allowed a grace period of two years immediately after the decedent's death in which to begin qualified use of the real property without triggering a recapture tax.[292] Failure to use the property for its qualified use after the grace period expires and before the end of the recapture period may result in the imposition of the recapture tax.[293] When an interest in qualified property is involuntarily converted,[294] cessation of qualified use during the replacement period specified in Section 1033(a)(2)(B) does not trigger a recapture tax.[295] Seasonal inactivity on property devoted to a qualified use by the qualified heir should not constitute cessation of qualified use. As a general rule, qualified use of property ceases and an additional tax is imposed if, in any eight-year period ending after the decedent's death within the recapture period, tacking on periods when the decedent or any qualified heir held the property, there have been periods aggregating more than three years in which either holder (decedent or qualified heir) or a member of their families did not materially participate[296] in the operation of the farm or other business.[297]

---

[290] IRC § 2032A(c)(6)(A).

[291] IRC § 2032A(c)(1)(B).

[292] IRC § 2032A(c)(7)(A)(i). See Priv. Ltr. Rul. 8240015 (June 29, 1982) (requiring the qualified heir to personally commence such use during the two-year period).

[293] HR Rep. No. 201, 97th Cong., 1st Sess. 38, 173 (1981), reprinted in 1981-2 CB 352, 384. The grace period terminates on the earlier of commencement of qualified use by the qualified heir or the date two years subsequent to the date of the decedent's death.

[294] Section § 2032A(h)(3)(A) defines involuntary conversion as a compulsory or involuntary conversion within the meaning of Section 1033.

[295] IRC § 2032A(h)(2)(C)(i). The replacement period specified in Section 1033(a)(2)(B) is the period beginning on the earlier of the date of disposition of the converted property or the earliest date of the threatened condemnation and ending on the later of two years after the close of the taxable year in which any gain on the conversion is realized or at any later date that the Secretary approves.

[296] Material participation is discussed supra ¶ 4.04[3][c][ii].

[297] IRC § 2032A(c)(6)(B). See Priv. Ltr. Rul. 8429058 (Apr. 18, 1984).

If an interest in qualified property is involuntarily converted, the period of time between the involuntary conversion[298] and acquisition of qualified replacement property[299] is disregarded in the determination of any eight-year period ending after the decedent's death or the more-than-three-year period.[300] Additionally, no recapture tax is to be imposed if the qualified heir commences use of the qualified property within two years of the decedent's death.[301] The Service should take the position that the grace period up to two years should be disregarded in determining any eight-year period and the more-than-three-year period also. The consecutive eight-year period may include seven years before the decedent's death and one year after death, or other combinations. Periods aggregating more than three years are all that is required; the periods need not be consecutive. Assume, for example, a decedent dies on January 1, 1997, holding qualified property that is valued pursuant to Section 2032A in the computation of the decedent's gross estate. Assume that neither the decedent (who has been dead a while) nor a member of the decedent's family materially participated in the qualified use for the last six months of 1992 and again for nineteen months in 1995 and 1996. If the qualified heir or a member of the qualified heir's family does not materially participate in the qualified use of the property for the last eleven and one half months of 1999, the recapture tax will be imposed, assuming, of course, that the qualified heir survives the critical date and that the property involved was not involuntarily converted during the requisite eight-year period.

When qualified property is held by a qualified heir, active management[302] by an eligible qualified heir, or in certain instances the eligible qualified heir's fiduciary,[303] will be treated as material participation.[304] A qualified heir is an eligible qualified heir if the qualified heir is the decedent's surviving spouse,[305]

---

[298] See IRC § 2032A(h)(3)(A).

[299] See IRC § 2032A(h)(3)(B).

[300] IRC § 2032A(h)(2)(C)(i).

[301] IRC § 2032A(c)(7)(A)(i).

[302] Active management is discussed supra ¶ 4.04[3][c][iii].

[303] If the qualified heir is an eligible qualified heir because the qualified is not yet age twenty-one or is disabled, active management by a fiduciary of the eligible qualified heir will be treated as material participation by the eligible qualified heir. In all other instances, the eligible qualified heir must personally engage in the active management of the farm or other business. IRC § 2032A(c)(7)(B). Active management by a member of the eligible qualified heir's family will not suffice.

[304] IRC § 2032A(c)(7)(B).

[305] IRC § 2032A(c)(7)(C)(i).

is under age twenty-one,[306] is disabled,[307] or is a student.[308] A qualified heir who is an eligible qualified heir by virtue of being under age twenty-one, disabled, or a student remains an eligible qualified heir only during the period such heir is under age twenty-one, disabled, or a student,[309] as the case may be.

[c] Measuring the Recapture Tax

[i] **Introduction.** The amount of the additional tax imposed on the occurrence of a recapture event[310] is essentially the estate tax that was saved by special-use valuation, that is, the amount of tax that was avoided when the qualified real property was included in the gross estate at its special-use value rather than at its fair market value. Thus, the additional tax, when added to the estate tax initially paid, will never exceed the federal estate tax that would have been imposed had all property in the gross estate been included at its fair market value.[311] Interest on the additional tax is payable only if the payment is not timely or if the qualified heir elects to increase the basis of the property.[312] Consequently, even if the entire tax saving under Section 2032A is recaptured and assuming no elected basis increase, the decedent's beneficiaries will have had, in effect, an interest-free loan from the government in the amount of the additional tax imposed for the period extending nine months after the decedent's death until as much as six months after the occurrence of the recapture event.

Disregarding a special rule for the disposition of certain timber,[313] and speaking now more explicitly, the amount of the additional tax imposed is the lesser of two amounts: (1) the "adjusted tax difference" attributable to the af-

---

[306] IRC § 2032A(c)(7)(C)(ii).

[307] IRC § 2032A(c)(7)(C)(iii). A qualified heir is disabled if the qualified heir has a mental or physical impairment that renders the qualified heir unable to participate materially in the operation of the farm or other business. IRC § 2032A(b)(4)(B).

[308] IRC § 2032A(c)(7)(C)(iv). A qualified heir is a student if the heir is a full-time student at an organization described in Section 170(b)(1)(A)(ii) during each of five calendar months during the calendar year. IRC §§ 2032A(c)(7)(D), 151(c)(4).

[309] IRC § 2032A(c)(7)(B).

[310] See supra ¶ 4.04[7][b].

[311] In a letter ruling, the Service has taken the position that, in computing the recapture tax, the actual value of the property at the date of death can be redetermined even if the statute of limitations has run on the decedent's return. However, the recapture may not exceed the Section 2032A(a)(2) limit. Priv. Ltr. Rul. 8403001 (Sept. 9, 1983).

[312] See IRC § 1016(c)(5)(B). The elective basis adjustment for additional tax imposed is discussed infra ¶ 4.04[7][h].

[313] The special rule is discussed infra ¶ 4.04[7][c][v].

fected interest[314] and (2) the excess of the amount realized in an arm's-length sale or exchange of the interest over the Section 2032A value of the interest sold or exchanged.[315] When qualified real property or any interest therein is transferred, triggering recapture other than in a sale or exchange at arm's length, or ceases to be used for a qualified use, fair market value at the date of the recapture event replaces the amount realized in the second of the two measures.[316]

When qualified real property is involuntarily converted and the cost of the qualified replacement property[317] is less than the amount realized on the conversion, or when qualified real property is exchanged not solely for qualified exchange property,[318] a recapture tax is imposed[319] However, the amount of the additional tax imposed is reduced if all or a part of the amount realized is reinvested in or exchanged for real property to be used for the same qualified use as the original qualified real property converted or exchanged. The reduction permitted is the amount that bears the same ratio to the additional tax as the cost of the qualified replacement property bears to the amount realized on the involuntary conversion[320] or as the fair market value of the qualified exchange property bears to the qualified real property exchanged.[321]

[ii] **The adjusted tax difference.** The amount of the adjusted tax difference attributable to an interest acquired by a qualified heir is essentially the additional federal estate tax that would have been imposed with respect to that interest had the interest been included in the gross estate at its fair market value rather than at its special-use value. Since the tax is actually imposed on the entire taxable estate, a formula is provided to determine tax attributable to any interest or portion. Thus, the adjusted tax difference attributable to an interest is defined as an amount that bears the same ratio to the adjusted tax difference with respect to the estate as the excess of the fair market value of the interest over the special-use value of the interest bears to a similar excess de-

---

[314] IRC § 2032A(c)(2)(A)(i).

[315] IRC § 2032A(c)(2)(A)(ii). The Section 2032A value of the interest actually sold or exchanged is determined on a pro rata basis. See IRC § 2032A(c)(2)(D)(i).

[316] IRC § 2032A(c)(2)(A)(ii).

[317] IRC § 2032A(h)(3)(B).

[318] IRC § 2032A(i)(3).

[319] No recapture tax is imposed by Section 2032A(c) if the amount realized in an involuntary conversion or like-kind exchange is all reinvested in or exchanged solely for qualified real property. See IRC §§ 2032A(h)(1)(A)(i), 2032A(i)(1)(A). These sections are discussed in greater detail supra ¶ 4.04[7][b][i].

[320] IRC § 2032A(h)(1)(B).

[321] IRC § 2032A(i)(1)(B). The fair market values are determined at the time of the exchange.

termined for all qualified real property.[322] The adjusted tax difference with respect to the estate is the excess of what would have been the estate tax liability, but for Section 2032A, over the estate tax liability.[323] The estate tax liability, as that term is used here, is the tax imposed by Section 2001 reduced by credits allowable against the tax.[324] The formula describing the adjusted tax difference attributable to an interest in the estate may be better understood in terms of the following equation:

$$\begin{array}{c}\text{adjusted tax}\\\text{difference}\\\text{attributable to}\\\text{the interest}\end{array} = \frac{\begin{array}{c}\text{excess of fair market value of the interest}\\\text{over § 2032A value of the interest}\end{array}}{\begin{array}{c}\text{excess of fair market value of all qualified}\\\text{real property over § 2032A}\\\text{value of all qualified real property}\end{array}} \times \begin{array}{c}\text{estate tax}\\\text{without}\\\text{§ 2032A minus}\\\text{estate tax}\\\text{liability with}\\\text{§ 2032A}\end{array}$$

Assume that a decedent who dies in 2002 not survived by a spouse had, utilizing Section 2032A, a taxable estate of $1,500,000 on which a tax of $161,700 was imposed. The estate included qualified real property with a fair market value of $500,000, which was taken into account in the gross estate at its special-use value of $300,000. The qualified real property was devised to two of the decedent's children in equal shares. Assume that one child sells the

---

[322] IRC § 2032A(c)(2)(B).

[323] IRC § 2032A(c)(2)(C).

[324] IRC § 2032A(c)(2)(C). If a state does not impose additional death tax in such circumstances, the Section 2011 credit used in the computation is the lesser of the maximum allowable credit under Section 2011(b) if there had been no Section 2032A election or the state death taxes actually paid. Cf. Rev. Rul. 82-35, 1982-1 CB 128 (computation of a Section 6324B lien). If a state does impose a recapture tax, the Service has taken the position that the Section 2011 credit used in the computation is the lesser of the maximum credit allowable under Section 2011(b) if there had been no Section 2032A election or the sum of the state death taxes actually paid and the potential state recapture tax. TAM 9940005 (June 2, 1999). Cf. Rev. Rul. 82-35, supra. The later position is at variance with the legislative history which does adjust the credit to take account of the state recapture tax because it does not treat such recapture tax as a state death tax. See HR Rep. No. 201, 97th Cong., 1st Sess. 38, 167 n.14 (1981), reprinted in 1981-2 CB 352, 381. Cf. IRC § 2011(f) repealing Section 2011 for estates of decedents dying after December 31, 2004; ¶ 3.03[3][d].

Additional problems may be encountered in recomputing the estate tax without Section 2032A where the Economic Recovery Tax Act of 1981, Pub. L. No. 97-34, § 403(e)(1), 95 Stat. 172, 305 (1981), reprinted in 1981-2 CB 256, 326, applies, negating the unlimited marital deduction otherwise available for decedents dying after 1981. For a discussion of these problems, which were more prevalent prior to the enactment of ERTA, see Stephens, Maxfield & Lind, Federal Estate and Gift Taxation, ¶ 4.04[9][c] (Warren, Gorham & Lamont, 4th ed. 1978).

child's share of the qualified real property to an unrelated third party for a price of $200,000 five years after the decedent's death. The additional tax imposed is the lesser of the adjusted tax difference and the amount realized less the special-use value of the interest. The first amount, the adjusted tax difference, is $39,900, computed using the preceding formula:

$$\frac{\text{adjusted tax difference}}{\text{attributable to the interest}} = \frac{\$250,000 - \$150,000}{\$500,000 - \$300,000} \times (\$241,500 - \$161,700)^{325}$$

$$= \frac{\$100,000}{\$200,000} \times \$79,800$$

$$= \$39,900$$

The second amount, the amount realized ($200,000), less the actual-use value of the interest sold ($150,000) equals $50,000. Therefore, the amount of additional tax imposed on the sale is $39,900, the adjusted tax difference of the selling child's interest, which is the lesser of the two amounts.[326]

[iii] **Recapture of portions of an interest.** The first recapture event involving a portion of an interest in qualified real property acquired from a decedent requires application of the general rule used to compute the amount of the additional tax imposed. When the qualified heir disposes of a portion of an interest in qualified real property acquired from the decedent or there is cessation of qualified use of only a portion of the interest acquired from the decedent, the amount of the additional tax imposed under the general rule may

---

[325] The federal estate tax imposed is computed as follows:

	With § 2032A	Without § 2032A
Taxable estate	$1,500,000	$1,700,000
§ 2001(b)(1) tentative tax	$ 555,800	$ 645,800
§ 2001(b)(2) amount	–0–	–0–
Tax imposed	$ 555,800	$ 645,800
§ 2010 credit	(345,800)	(345,800)
§ 2011 credit (75% of § 2011(b)(1) amount) (no state recapture tax)	(48,300)	(58,500)
Tax payable	$ 161,700	$ 241,500

See Priv. Ltr. Rul. 8350035 (Sept. 1983) for another illustration of this computation.

[326] If the child had sold the interest for $160,000, the first amount, the adjusted tax difference remains the same as in the example above, $39,900; but the second amount (the amount realized, $180,000, less the special-use value of the interest, $150,000) equals $30,000. Under these facts, the second amount is the lesser, so the amount of additional tax imposed is $30,000.

not exceed the amount realized with respect to the portion of the interest disposed of, or the fair market value of the portion of the interest where applicable, reduced by the Section 2032A value of the portion of the interest where applicable, reduced by the Section 2032A value of the portion of the interest involved in the recapture event. Thus, the general rule imposes additional tax in an amount equal to the lesser of (1) the adjusted tax difference and (2) the excess of the fair market value of or amount realized on the portion of the interest over the Section 2032A value of the portion of the interest. The Section 2032A value attributed to the portion of the interest involved in the recapture event is a pro rata share of the Section 2032A value of the entire interest acquired by the qualified heir from the decedent.[327] The recapture tax imposed on a portion of the interest is the same as the recapture tax imposed on the disposition of the entire interest, except where the amount realized or fair market value, as the case may be, of the interest reduced by the pro rata Section 2032A value attributed to the portion is less than the adjusted tax difference.[328]

In contrast, computation of the recapture tax involving the second or any subsequent portion of the same interest requires that the adjusted tax difference be reduced by the additional tax imposed on all prior transactions involving

---

[327] IRC § 2032A(c)(2)(D)(i).

[328] Thus, disposition or cessation of use of a portion of an interest may result in a recapture of the adjusted tax difference attributable to the entire interest in qualified property. HR Rep. No. 1380, 94th Cong., 2d Sess. 3, 26 (1976), reprinted in 1976-3 CB (Vol. 3) 735, 760.

For example, assume a decedent not survived by a spouse has a taxable estate in 2002 of $1,500,000 on which a tax of $161,700 is imposed. See supra note 325. The estate includes only one parcel of qualified real property with a fair market value of $500,000 included in the gross estate at its special-use value of $300,000. The parcel of qualified property is devised to the decedent's son. Assume that the son sells one third of the qualified real property to an unrelated third party for $200,000 five years after the decedent's death. The additional tax imposed is the lesser of (1) the adjusted tax difference attributable to the entire parcel acquired by the son from the decedent or (2) the amount realized, less the pro rata share of the special-use value of the interest attributed to the portion of the parcel sold. The first amount, the adjusted tax difference, is $79,800, computed as follows:

$$\frac{\$500,000 - \$300,000}{\$500,000 - \$300,000} \times (\$241,500 - \$161,700) = \$79,800$$

See supra note 325. The second amount, the amount realized, $200,000, less the pro rata share of the special-use value of the entire parcel attributed to the portion of the parcel sold, $100,000 ($300,000 × ⅓), equals $100,000. The amount of additional tax imposed on the sale of one third of the parcel to a third party is therefore $79,800, the lesser of the two amounts. See Priv. Ltr. Rul. 8434085 (May 23, 1984); Priv. Ltr. Rul. 8531004 (1985).

that interest.[329] Thus, the formula for the additional tax on subsequent dispositions of portions of the same interest is the lesser of (1) the adjusted tax difference less the additional tax imposed on prior transactions involving the interest
and (2) the excess of the fair market value of or amount realized on the portion of the interest over the Section 2032A value of the portion of the interest.

[iv] **Successive interests.** The statute does not specifically discuss the imposition of additional tax when two or more qualified heirs acquire successive
interests in qualified real property. Presumably, if all qualified heirs with interests in a particular parcel of qualified real property join in a sale of the qualified real property to an unrelated third party, the amount of additional tax
imposed should be divided on the basis of the amount realized by each qualified heir possessing an interest in that parcel of real property.[330] In the event
the qualified real property is held in trust, the tax should be paid out of the
proceeds of sale if the proceeds of sale are received by the trustee.[331]

When two or more qualified heirs acquire successive interests in qualified
real property and any one qualified heir disposes of the qualified heir's interest
or portion thereof, the additional tax is imposed. The amount of tax imposed
will generally be only the tax computed under the general rule attributable to
the interest in qualified real property of that heir;[332] but although there is no
authority, if one qualified heir has the power to extinguish the successive interests of other qualified heirs and does so in a transaction resulting in the imposition of an additional tax, the power holder should be responsible for any
additional tax that is imposed.

A successive interest holder may incur personal liability prior to the time
the holder's interest ripens into a possessory interest. For example, one qualified heir may acquire from the decedent a legal life estate in qualified real
property and, while in possession of the property, cease to use the entire parcel
for a qualified use. This event will trigger the imposition of additional tax with
respect to any successive interests in this parcel of qualified real property acquired from the decedent. Qualified heirs with successive interests may be required to discharge the liability prior to the time their respective interests ripen

---

[329] IRC § 2032A(c)(2)(D)(ii). A similar adjustment is made when the special rule for
disposition of timber applies. See infra ¶ 4.04[7][c][v].

[330] It is unclear whether an allocation would prorate the tax on the basis of the actuarial values of their respective interests computed at the date of the decedent's death or the
date of the sale.

[331] Discharge of the additional tax by the trustee with trust funds may result in a constructive distribution from the trust to the qualified heirs possessing the qualified interests
in the property with income tax consequences. See IRC §§ 661, 662.

[332] A disposition of an interest in qualified property resulting in the imposition of an
additional tax on one qualified heir, where other qualified heirs also have an interest in
the same parcel of real property, should trigger the tax attributable to the interest of that
qualified heir, not the interests of other qualified heirs in the same parcel of real property.

into possessory interests. It is entirely possible that an extension of time for payment of the additional tax will be allowed in this situation, similar to that provided by Section 6163 for remainder or reversionary interests required to be included in the gross estate prior to the termination of the preceding interest or interests in the property. If no extension is provided, the qualified heirs acquiring successive interests in qualified real property may experience difficulty in raising money to discharge the additional tax liability, a factor that may prevent their consenting to Section 2032A valuation of real property otherwise qualifying for special-use valuation.

[v] **Special rule for dispositions of timber.** Disposition, severance, or disposition of a right to sever any standing timber on qualified woodland[333] classified as qualified real property[334] is treated as a disposition of a portion of the qualified heir's interest in all qualified real property acquired from the decedent.[335] The amount of additional estate tax imposed on a first disposition or severance is the lesser of two amounts: (1) the amount realized[336] and (2) the amount of additional tax that would be imposed if the qualified heir disposed of the heir's entire interest in the qualified woodland.[337] This latter amount is the lesser of (1) the adjusted tax difference attributable to the qualified heir's entire interest in the qualified woodland and (2) the excess of the amount realized over the special-use value of the qualified heir's entire interest in the qualified woodland.[338] Computation of the recapture tax involving any subsequent disposition or severance of standing timber on qualified woodland requires that the amount of additional estate tax that would be imposed if the qualified heir disposed of the entire interest in the qualified woodland be reduced by the amount of additional estate tax imposed on all prior dispositions or severances of standing timber on qualified woodland.[339] In addition, if the qualified heir actually does dispose of the qualified woodland itself, the amount of additional estate tax imposed on the disposition is reduced by the

---

[333] IRC § 2032A(e)(13)(B). This section is discussed supra ¶ 4.04[3][c] text accompanying notes 107, 108.

[334] IRC § 2032A(e)(13)(A). See supra ¶ 4.04[4].

[335] IRC § 2032A(c)(2)(E); S. Rep. No. 144, 97th Cong., 1st Sess. 136 (1981), reprinted in 1981-2 CB 412, 465. Possibly all severances should not be treated as dispositions. See supra ¶ 4.04[7][b] note 276.

[336] IRC § 2032A(c)(2)(E)(ii)(I). In any case other than an arm's-length sale, the fair market value of the timber severed or disposed of is used.
    The effect of this special rule is to treat the sale or disposition to the extent of the amount realized as a sale of the entire property and not a portion of the property which is the general rule on recapture of a portion of an interest. Compare supra ¶ 4.04[7][c][iii] especially text accompanying notes 327, 328.

[337] IRC § 2032A(c)(2)(E)(ii)(II).

[338] IRC § 2032A(c)(2)(A).

[339] IRC § 2032A(c)(2)(E)(ii)(II).

amount of additional estate tax previously imposed on the disposition or severance of standing timber on that qualified woodland.[340]

[d] Imposition of Only One Additional Tax

Only one additional tax may be imposed on any portion of an interest in
qualified real property acquired from a decedent by a qualified heir.[341] If there
has been a recapture event described in Section 2032A(c)(1)(B), such as the
cessation of qualified use, that triggers the imposition of an additional tax with
respect to a portion of an interest, the sale thereafter to an unrelated third party
of the same portion of the interest, although a recapture event described in
Section 2032A(c)(1)(A), will not result in the imposition of any additional tax.
This rule may operate to the advantage of a qualified heir. Assume a qualified
heir acquires one parcel of qualified real property from a decedent. Subsequent
to the decedent's death, this parcel declines in value until its fair market value
equals its special-use value. At that point, the qualified heir ceases to use the
property for the qualified use, and the cessation of qualified use is a recapture
event. The additional tax imposed under Section 2032A(c)(1)(B) amounts to
zero, because the fair market value of the parcel on the date the additional tax
is imposed equals its special-use value.[342] The subsequent sale of the same parcel by the qualified heir within ten years of the decedent's death to a non-
family member for an amount in excess of the special-use value does not
result in the imposition of additional tax, because a second additional tax may
not be imposed upon the occurrence of the second recapture event involving
the same parcel of qualified real property.[343]

[e] Due Date for the Additional Tax

The additional tax imposed under Section 2032A(c) is due and payable
within six months after the recapture event.[344] The six-month period expires on
the date numerically corresponding to the date of the recapture event.[345] No interest is imposed in the event that the recapture tax is paid when due.

---

[340] IRC § 2032A(c)(2)(E).

[341] IRC § 2032A(c)(3).

[342] IRC § 2032A(c)(2)(A)(ii).

[343] IRC § 2032A(c)(3).

[344] IRC § 2032A(c)(4). Form 706-A, "United States Additional Estate Tax Return,"
(Rev. August 1999) is used to report the additional tax due because of the application of
Section 2032A(c).

[345] Presumably, if there is no date in the sixth month following the date of the recapture event corresponding to the date of the recapture event, the last day of the sixth month
is the due date.

Any additional tax imposed should, if there is reasonable cause, qualify for an extension of time for payment for a reasonable period under Section 6161(a)(2)(A) as a tax imposed by Chapter 11.[346] Although the estate of the decedent may qualify for deferral of payment under Section 6166 for the estate tax imposed by Section 2001, payment of the additional tax does not qualify for Section 6166 deferral. The additional tax is imposed by Section 2032A(c). Since it is neither a tax imposed by Section 2001 nor a deficiency in the tax imposed by Section 2001, Section 6166 is inapplicable.[347]

[f] Liability for the Additional Tax

The qualified heir is personally liable, generally for a ten-year period following the decedent's death, for any additional tax imposed with respect to the qualified heir's interest in qualified real property unless a bond is furnished in lieu of personal liability.[348] The qualified heir who incurs personal liability need not acquire the qualified property directly from the decedent. A qualified heir may dispose of an interest in qualified real property to a family member without the imposition of an additional tax.[349] Thereafter, the member of the qualified heir's family to whom the property is transferred becomes "the qualified heir" with respect to the interest transferred[350] and incurs personal liability for the recapture tax, even though the family member may have purchased the property for its full fair market value.[351]

A qualified heir may be discharged of personal liability for recapture tax by furnishing a bond. The bond must cover the requisite period of time and be in an amount equal to the maximum additional tax that may be imposed with respect to the interest in qualified real property.[352] Upon written request, the qualified heir must be provided a determination of the maximum amount of

---

[346] Under Section 6161(a)(2), an extension of time for payment of estate tax may be granted for a reasonable period, not in excess of ten years, for reasonable causes.

[347] See IRC §§ 6166(a)(1), 6166(h).

[348] IRC § 2032A(c)(5). See also IRC § 2032A(e)(11). The ten-year period begins on the date of the decedent's death or on the date the qualified heir commences qualified use if within two years of the date of the decedent's death. See IRC § 2032A(c)(7)(A), discussed supra ¶ 4.04[7][a]. Furthermore, the ten-year period may be extended where the qualified property is involuntarily converted. This extension is discussed more fully supra ¶ 4.04[7][a] text accompanying notes 258, 259.

[349] See IRC § 2032A(c)(1)(A).

[350] IRC § 2032A(e)(1).

[351] HR Rep. No. 1380, 94th Cong., 2d Sess. 3, 26, 27 (1976), reprinted in 1976-3 CB (Vol. 3) 735, 760, 761. The special estate tax lien for potential recapture tax remains on the property also. The lien is discussed supra ¶ 4.04[6] text accompanying notes 245–248.

[352] IRC § 2032A(e)(11).

additional tax that may be imposed with respect to the interest.[353] The Secretary is required to furnish the determination of the amount within one year of the request at the latest, but preferably as soon as possible.[354]

[g] Statute of Limitations

The additional tax imposed under Section 2032A(c) has its own statute of limitations, which takes precedence over any other law or rule of law.[355] The statutory period for assessment of an additional tax expires three years after the date the Service is notified of the recapture event.[356] If qualified real property is the subject of a Section 1031 like-kind exchange[357] or a Section 1033 involuntary conversion,[358] the limitations period expires three years after the Service is notified of the exchange, replacement, or intention not to replace the converted property.[359] Even if the occurrence of a recapture event[360] results in the imposition of an amount of additional tax equaling zero under Section 2032A(c)(2), prudence dictates notification be given to the Service to start the statute of limitations running.[361]

[h] Basis Adjustment for Additional Tax

If Section 2032A applies to value property, the basis of the qualified property in the hands of a qualified heir is its value determined under Section 2032A.[362] If the additional estate tax is imposed under Section 2032A(c)(1), the qualified heir, for a price, may elect to increase the basis in the qualified real property by an amount equal to the difference between the fair market value of the interest on the applicable valuation date[363] and the special-use

---

[353] IRC § 2032A(e)(11).

[354] IRC § 2032A(e)(11).

[355] IRC § 2032A(f)(2).

[356] IRC § 2032A(f)(1). Stovall v. Comm'r, 101 TC 140 (1993) (notification is not limited to a Form 706A; response to an IRS questionnaire will suffice).

[357] See IRC § 2032A(i).

[358] See IRC § 2032A(h).

[359] IRC § 2032A(f)(1).

[360] IRC § 2032A(c)(1).

[361] Such notification would also help avoid potential multiple recapture taxation. See supra ¶ 4.04[7][d].

[362] IRC § 1014(a)(3).

[363] That is, either the date of death, Section 2031, or the alternate valuation date, Section 2032.

value of the interest.[364] On a partial disposition of qualified real property, only a commensurate amount of increasing adjustment is made to the qualified heir's basis.[365] The adjustment is in an amount that bears the same ratio to the increase that would be allowed if the qualified heir disposed of the entire interest as the recapture tax actually imposed on the partial disposition bears to the total potential recapture tax.[366] If the additional estate tax is imposed with respect to qualified replacement property[367] or qualified exchange property[368] previously acquired in an involuntary conversion under Section 1033 or an exchange to which Section 1031 applied, the basis adjustment under Section 1016(c)(1) is made by reference to the property involuntarily converted or exchanged.[369]

Any increase in basis under Section 1016(c) is deemed to occur immediately prior to the event resulting in the imposition of the additional tax.[370] Therefore, if a disposition triggers recapture, the increased basis is used for purposes of determining gain or loss on that disposition. No retroactive changes in depreciation or other deductions or credits may be made to reflect the increased basis.[371]

There is a price, literally, for making the elective increase to basis: The qualified heir must pay interest on the additional estate tax from the time the estate tax return was required to be filed[372] until the date the additional tax is paid.[373]

---

[364] IRC § 1016(c)(1). Generally, this will increase the basis of the qualified real property to its fair market value on the date of the decedent's death or the alternate valuation date, whichever was employed. However, in some instances the qualified heir's basis in the qualified real property will be increased above the fair market value on the applicable valuation date. See IRC § 1040(c).

[365] IRC § 1016(c)(2)(A). A partial disposition is limited to the situations discussed supra ¶ 4.04[7][c][iii]. IRC § 1016(c)(2)(B).

[366] IRC § 1016(c)(2)(A). This ratio formula is illustrated as follows:

$$\text{amount of increase} = \frac{\text{recapture tax actually imposed on the partial disposition}}{\text{potential recapture tax if the entire property had been disposed of}} \times \frac{\text{fair market value on the applicable valuation date less the special-use valuation under § 2032A}}{}$$

[367] IRC § 2032A(h)(3).

[368] IRC § 2032A(i)(3).

[369] IRC § 1016(c)(4).

[370] IRC § 1016(c)(3).

[371] HR Rep. No. 201, 97th Cong., 1st Sess. 38, 174 (1981), reprinted in 1981-2 CB 352, 384.

[372] IRC § 6075.

[373] IRC § 1016(c)(5)(B).

¶ 4.05 SECTION 2033. PROPERTY IN WHICH THE DECEDENT HAD AN INTEREST

[1] Introduction

Section 2033 requires that there be included in the gross estate the value of all property to the extent of the decedent's interest therein. It would be simpler to refer to property owned by the decedent, and such a statement might well reflect the typical layman's notion of the gross estate for tax purposes. However, the provision is framed more precisely to avoid any possible inference that only the value of property owned outright by the decedent is to be included. It is the value of property to the extent of any interest therein of the decedent that is to be included.

If the value of property interests must be included in a decedent's estate under Section 2033, such interests must first be identified and then their value ascertained. In the discussion here, and in the discussion that follows of other Code sections defining "gross estate," only the identification question is emphasized. Applicable valuation principles are explored in an earlier part of this chapter in connection with Sections 2031, 2032, and 2032A.

This discussion concerns only property interests that are brought into a decedent's gross estate by Section 2033. Sometimes, under other sections that are part of the statutory definition of "gross estate," a decedent's retention until death of an interest in property that the decedent has transferred during life will cause something more than the value of the retained interest to be included.[1] Such a possibility will not be further anticipated in this section.

[2] Beneficial Interest

The interest of the decedent that gives rise to tax liability under Section 2033 is, of course, a beneficial interest.[2] If one held title to property only as a guardian or trustee or in some other fiduciary capacity, the person did not have an interest in property that is recognized by Section 2033.[3] If legal title to

---

[1] See IRC §§ 2036, 2037, 2039, 2040, 2042. Also, of course, if a decedent's attempted lifetime transfer was ineffective, the decedent's interest in the property will be included under Section 2033. See Estate of Fox v. Comm'r, 69 TCM (CCH) 1719 (1995); Broadhead Trust v. Comm'r, 31 TCM (CCH) 975 (1972).

[2] Reg. § 20.2033-1(a).

[3] Reed v. Comm'r, 36 F2d 867 (5th Cir. 1930). Cf. Estate of Rose v. Comm'r, 32 TCM (CCH) 461 (1973).

property was in the decedent, the estate must establish that the decedent had no beneficial interest, which may present a difficult problem of proof.[4]

[a] State Law

If the federal estate tax is imposed on property in which the decedent had an interest, what law determines whether the decedent had an interest and, if so, the extent of the interest? It is still essentially accurate to say, as the Supreme Court did fifty years ago, "State law creates legal interests and rights. The federal revenue acts designate what interests or rights, so created, shall be taxed."[5] Consequently, the estate tax, as is true of all federal taxes, is not to be dealt with in a federal vacuum. Instead, it is a federal exaction superimposed on locally determined rights and interests.[6] At one time, the Commissioner seized on this principle to attempt to include as property of the decedent under Section 2033 some state gift taxes paid by the decedent on transfers during life where state law deemed such payments prepayment of inheritance taxes.[7] The

---

[4] E.g., Sharp v. Comm'r, 91 F2d 802 (3d Cir. 1937), rev'd per curiam, 303 US 624 (1938); Estate of Bloise v. Comm'r, 25 TCM (CCH) 251 (1966); Estate of Rosenblatt v. Comm'r, 36 TCM (CCH) 63 (1977); Estate of Holmes v. Comm'r, 62 TCM (CCH) 839 (1991), aff'd per curiam, 978 F2d 1261 (7th Cir. 1992); Estate of H. Stimson, 63 TCM (CCH) 2855 (1992); Estate of Glass v. Comm'r, 41 TCM (CCH) 1303 (1981). But see Miglionico v. United States, 323 F. Supp. 197 (ND Ala. 1971); Levine v. Comm'r, 27 TCM (CCH) 284 (1968); Estate of Spruill v. Comm'r, 88 TC 1197 (1987) (where burden of proof was met).

[5] Morgan v. Comm'r, 309 US 78, 80 (1940). Federal law may also create legal rights and interests. First Victoria Nat'l Bank v. United States, 620 F2d 1096 (5th Cir. 1980). See, e.g., Longshoremen's and Harbor Workers' Compensation Act, 33 USC §§ 901 et seq. (1976); Death on the High Seas by Wrongful Act Act, 46 USC §§ 761 et seq. (1976). Cf. Asenap v. United States, 283 F. Supp. 566 (WD Okla. 1968); Rev. Rul. 69-164, 1969-1 CB 220. In addition, a defrauded decedent's right to recover from an insider under Section 10b-5 of the Securities Exchange Act of 1934 would clearly constitute an interest in property includable under Section 2033.

[6] Blair v. Comm'r, 300 US 5 (1937). See Estate of Quinn v. United States, 93-1 USTC ¶ 60,136 (DC Minn. 1993), aff'd, 23 F3d 1400 (8th Cir. 1994); Estate of Frazier v. Comm'r 77 TCM (CCH) 2197 (1999); Estate of Forrest, Jr. v. Comm'r, 60 TCM (CCH) 621 (1990); TAM 9018002 (Jan. 17, 1990); TAM 9005001 (July 7, 1989). Some citizens', such as indians, rights are determined by federal law. See Rev. Rul. 69-164, 1969-1 CB 220; Priv. Ltr. Rul. 200128021 (Apr. 12, 2001) (land excluded from gross estate); Priv. Ltr. Rul. 9646003 (July 29, 1996).

[7] Rev. Rul. 75-63, 1975-1 CB 294.

Commissioner was unsuccessful in the attempt[8] and reversed the position in Revenue Ruling 81-302.[9]

On the other hand, the meaning to be accorded the term "interest" in Section 2033 (and that term elsewhere or any other term in the estate tax statute) is a purely federal question; local nomenclature and characterization are not controlling.[10] Thus, if a state statute undertook to say that the rights of the remainderperson of a trust do not constitute an interest in property, this would by no means foreclose a court deciding a federal estate tax case from interpreting the term "interest" to encompass such rights. State law would govern the relationship of the remainderperson to the trust property; but whether the relationship fixed by local law amounted to an interest in the property would present a purely federal question.[11]

[b] State Decrees

If there is uncertainty regarding a decedent's relationship to property, a federal court in an estate tax case may have to decide that underlying issue, even though it is determined by local law, as a necessary part of settling any federal estate tax controversy. Thus, a federal court may decide whether the decedent had title to property only as a trustee or whether instead had a beneficial interest in the property. But it will apply state statutory and common-law principles in the decision of that underlying issue. Suppose, after a decedent's death, such an issue is litigated in the state probate courts and decided before adjudication of estate tax liability. Does that settle the matter, or can it be reopened in a subsequent estate tax case? The state court might have held, for example, that the decedent was only a trustee and that the property belonged to child A for whom the trustee held it, rather than that the decedent had full ownership of the property so that it would pass to child B, who was residuary legatee under the decedent's will. Strange as it must surely seem, even though the state court decision, if final, fixes the interests of A and B and does so on

---

[8] Estate of Gamble v. Comm'r, 69 TC 942 (1978); Horton v. United States, 79-2 USTC ¶ 13,316 (MDNC 1979).

[9] 1981-2 CB 170, revoking Rev. Rul. 75-63, 1975-1 CB 294. See ¶ 5.03[5][a] note 105. See also ¶ 3.03[2] note 17 (recognizing the Commissioner's proper contention that such payments do not qualify for Section 2011 credit).

[10] Allen v. Henggeler, 32 F2d 69 (8th Cir. 1929), cert. denied, 280 US 594 (1929). In Lyeth v. Hoey, 305 US 188, 193 (1938), the Court stated:

> The question as to the construction of a term in the federal statute is not determined by local law . . . the question whether what the heir has thus received has been "acquired by inheritance" within the meaning of the federal statute necessarily is a federal question. It is not determined by local characterization.

[11] Cf. Price v. United States, 470 F. Supp. 136 (ND Tex. 1979), aff'd per curiam, 610 F2d 383 (5th Cir. 1980).

the ground that the decedent had no beneficial interest, the beneficial interest question can probably be relitigated in the federal tax controversy. It cannot be reopened in any way that will affect the rights of A or B, which are res judicata and fixed under the local court's decision. But the court deciding the tax controversy can decide, contrary to the local decision, that the decedent had a beneficial interest in the property and that it is therefore subject to estate tax under Section 2033. In *Commissioner v. Estate of Bosch*,[12] the Supreme Court indicated it will not give finality in a tax controversy to a state court's decision on an underlying state law issue, unless the local decision is by the state's highest court.[13]

What has just been said may seem outrageous and, indeed, in this respect *Bosch* seems to rest on a false analogy to the philosophy supporting the doctrine of *Erie Railroad v. Tompkins*.[14] The doctrine permitting reexamination of local decisions in federal tax cases seems more supportable when the difficulty that engendered the rule is understood. Within a family group (children A and B in the prior example), it may be far less important whether A or B gets the property than whether some part of the property goes to the government in the form of federal estate tax. Therefore, it may be wondered whether state court litigation in which the rights of parties are seemingly asserted is really adversarial in nature, or worse, whether it is collusive, or whether it may not even edge up toward outright fraud; hence it also may be wondered whether the local decision handed down should be viewed at all as an adjudication of the in-

---

[12] Comm'r v. Estate of Bosch, 387 US 456 (1967).

[13] The *Bosch* principle does not apply, however, to a determination of rights and interests settled by local adjudication and res judicata at a time before events that raise a federal tax question occur. Rev. Rul. 73-142, 1973-1 CB 405. See Ufford, "Bosch and Beyond," 60 ABAJ 334 (1974), discussing procedures instituted by some states to broaden access to the highest court of the state in an effort to comply with *Bosch*. In addition, retroactive changes of legal effects of a transaction through judicial nullification of a transfer or a document do not have retroactive effect for federal tax purposes and thus do not alter results under Section 2033. Priv. Ltr. Rul. 9609018 (Nov. 27, 1995). Cf. Estate of Hill v. Comm'r, 64 TC 867 (1975) aff'd without opinion, 568 F2d 1365 (5th Cir. 1978); American Nurseryman Publishing Co. v. Comm'r, 75 TC 271, 276–277 (1980), aff'd without opin., 673 F2d 1333 (7th Cir. 1982).

[14] 304 US 64 (1938). *Erie* held that only the highest court of a state can make a final determination of what the state's common-law principles are. But any court whose decision becomes final, if it has not been defrauded or otherwise imposed upon by way of collusion, has settled the property interests at issue in the case, even if it has done so in a way later found to be at variance with the law of the state. Application of *Erie* to these federal tax questions has been criticized. E.g., Brown & Hinkle, "Tax Effects of Non-Tax Litigation: *Bosch* and Beyond," 27 NYU Inst. on Fed. Tax'n 1415, 1421-1423 (1969); Note, "*Bosch* and the Binding Effect of State Court Adjudication Upon Subsequent Federal Tax Litigation," 21 Vand. L. Rev. 825, 840-841 (1968); Note, "Taxation: The Role of State Trial Court Decisions in Federal Tax Litigation," 21 Okla. L. Rev. 227, 229-230 (1968); Note, "Binding Effect of State Court Judgment in Federal Tax Cases," 21 Sw. LJ 540, 544-545 (1967).

terests of the parties litigant. At best, the government, which is really an interested party to the extent that the local litigation may bear on estate tax liability (none in the prior example, if the decedent was a mere trustee for *A*), will not have been an actual party whose cause is heard by the local court. Before the Supreme Court undertook to lay down the broad principle now established, the lower courts labored to mark off identifiable circumstances in which the Tax Court was not bound by local adjudications; but the result was largely confusion.[15]

If the current answer seems draconian, at least the Supreme Court has not disturbed the settled principle that state law is determined by state statute and the decisions of the highest court of the state. In fact, it extends that principle to accord full recognition to state determinations of the rights of parties, if the determinations are made by a state's highest court.[16] However, in the absence of such decisions, only "proper regard," not finality, is to be given a prior local decision. The results reached by federal courts in giving proper regard to such decisions have varied.[17] While it might be hoped that the proper regard admonition would cause tax courts to accord recognition to prior local decisions except in fishy circumstances, there is only slight indication that this will be the case.[18] In fact, the lower courts labor under a confusion as to the meaning of the phrase "proper regard,"[19] which leaves them in somewhat the same uncertainty they were in before *Bosch.*

The three problems alluded to very briefly here—the importance of state law, the interpretation of a term in a federal statute, and the significance of a local decision—are all-pervasive in federal tax matters and surface again in many places throughout this book.[20]

---

[15] See Stephens & Freeland, "The Role of Local Law and Local Adjudications in Federal Tax Controversies," 46 Minn. L. Rev. 223 (1961).

[16] See Porter v. Comm'r, 49 TC 207 (1967); Estate of Sholes v. Comm'r, 42 TCM (CCH) 837 (1981).

[17] Compare Lake Shore Nat'l Bank v. Coyle, 296 F. Supp. 412 (ND Ill. 1968), rev'd on other grounds, 419 F2d 958 (7th Cir. 1970) and Underwood v. United States, 407 F2d 608 (6th Cir. 1969) (state court decision followed) with Krakoff v. United States, 313 F. Supp. 1089 (SD Ohio 1970), aff'd, 439 F2d 1023 (6th Cir. 1971) and Schmidt v. United States, 279 F. Supp. 811 (D. Kan. 1968) (opposite conclusion reached). "Proper regard" for a state court decision may turn out to be "no regard" if the decision was handed down in a nonadversary suit. Lakewood Plantation, Inc. v. United States, 272 F. Supp. 290 (DSC 1967). In this respect, the pre-*Bosch* melody lingers on.

[18] Estate of Nilson v. Comm'r, 31 TCM (CCH) 708 (1972).

[19] Lake Shore Nat'l Bank v. Coyle, 296 F. Supp. 412, 418 (ND Ill. 1968), rev'd on other grounds, 419 F2d 958 (7th Cir. 1970), refers to "proper regard, whatever that may mean."

[20] Estate of Cone v. Comm'r, 60 TCM (CCH) 137 (1990).

[3] Routine Inclusions

Drawing the perimeter of Section 2033 presents some difficult questions regarding the full reach of the section, which are dealt with subsequently in this discussion; but in many instances the applicability of the section is not questionable.

If the decedent is the sole owner of real property, its value is included in the decedent's gross estate. This is so even if the property is not subject to administration, because, under local law, title passes directly to the heirs or devisees.[21] Thus, while it is generally accurate to suggest that Section 2033 essentially describes the "probate" estate, the two concepts are not identical.[22] Moreover, "homestead" or similar state law exemptions that may shield property from some state taxes or creditors' claims do not keep the value of property out of the gross estate.[23] The regulations provide that a cemetery lot owned by a decedent is included in the decedent's gross estate, but only that part of the lot that is not designed for the interment of the decedent and members of the decedent's family.[24] The thought here may be that with respect to such a plot of ground, the decedent *can* take it with her.

Tangible personal property solely owned by the decedent is also clearly swept into the decedent's gross estate by Section 2033. As a pure question of law, there is no doubt that jewelry, automobiles, boats, furniture, and other personal and household effects owned by the decedent are includable in the decedent's gross estate under Section 2033.[25] However, the factual question of whether a particular item was owned by the decedent can be very troublesome. Indeed, some day a court may be asked to determine whether the decedent or the surviving spouse was the owner of the marital bed.[26]

---

[21] Reg. § 20.2033-1(a).

[22] Nor are estate tax gross estate concepts the same as "estate" concepts for income tax purposes. Compare Reg. § 1.661(a)-2(e) with Reg. § 20.2033-1.

[23] Reg. § 20.2033-1(b); Estate of Johnson v. Comm'r, 718 F2d 1303 (5th Cir. 1983), appropriately reversing a controversial contrary Tax Court holding at 77 TC 120 (1981); Estate of Hinds v. Comm'r, 11 TC 314 (1948), aff'd on another issue, 180 F2d 930 (5th Cir. 1950); Priv. Ltr. Rul. 8651001 (Aug. 8, 1986). This is clearly supported by the Supremacy Clause of Article VI of the U.S. Constitution. Cf. Carli v. Comm'r, 84 TC 649 (1985).

[24] Reg. § 20.2033-1(b).

[25] Cf. Estate of Fried v. Comm'r, 445 F2d 979 (2d Cir. 1971), cert. denied, 404 US 1016 (1972).

[26] Some estate planners, in drafting wills, suggest that the testator not make any disposition of household furniture, fearing that the Service agent will use the language of the will as authority to establish factually that the decedent was the owner of all the furniture and household effects. Inter vivos documentation of actual ownership should be maintained.

Many intangible property interests raise no questions. Thus, Section 2033 includes in the gross estate currency in the decedent's safe-deposit box, unless it can be shown that it was not the decedent's.[27] Likewise, the balance in one's personal checking and savings accounts and any credit balance in one's personal account with a brokerage firm are includable.[28] Note that a joint tenancy account, like other joint tenancy interests in property, would not be included under Section 2033, since the decedent's interest terminates at death, but would be tested for inclusion under Section 2040.[29] Investment-type intangibles, such as stocks and bonds[30] and certificates of deposit, if owned solely by the decedent,[31] are obvious Section 2033 inclusions, as are amounts

---

[27] Estate of Van Dever v. Comm'r, 11 TCM (CCH) 1179 (1952). Cf. Estate of Maxcy v. Comm'r, 441 F2d 192 (5th Cir. 1971), involving the question of ownership of stock in a closely held corporation located in the corporation's vault.

[28] Checks executed by a decedent while living but honored after death that are not incurred for adequate and full consideration or are not payable to charitable payees are included in a decedent's gross estate under Section 2033. Rosano v. United States, 245 F3d 212 (2d Cir. 2001); McCarthy v. United States, 806 F2d 129 (7th Cir. 1986); Estate of Dillingham v. Comm'r, 88 TC 1569 (1987); Estate of Gagliardi v. Comm'r, 89 TC 1207 (1987); Estate of Newman v. Comm'r, 111 TC 81 (1998), aff'd per curiam 99-2 USTC ¶ 60,358 (DC Cir. 1999). Cf. Metzger v. United States, 38 F3d 118 (4th Cir. 1994) (a gift tax case applying the relation back doctrine to the date checks were written but in circumstances where decedent was alive when checks honored); Rev. Rul. 96-56, 1996-2 CB 161; ¶ 10.01[3][h]. Such checks executed in discharge of bona fide legal obligations of the decedent incurred for adequate and full consideration reduce the gross estate. Reg. § 20.2031-5. Similar noninclusion occurs with respect to checks executed to charitable donees. Estate of Belcher v. Comm'r, 83 TC 227 (1984). Note that in the two noninclusion situations above, any inclusion would be coupled with a deduction resulting in a "wash" in the taxable estate. Cf. Estate of Devlin v. Comm'r, 78 TCM (CCH) 948 (1999) (cash gifts authorized by court but not made at death included in donor estate).

[29] See ¶ 4.12.

[30] This includes municipal and other bonds whose interest is exempt from federal income taxation. Reg. § 20.2033-1(a); Rev. Rul. 81-63, 1981-1 CB 455. See also Estate of Bograd v. Comm'r, 55 TCM (CCH) 11 (1988), where bearer bonds were included in the decedent's gross estate, even though such bonds could not be located.

A storm of controversy over whether public housing bonds under the Federal Housing Act of 1937 had to be included in a decedent's gross estate was quieted by The Deficit Reduction Act of 1984, which required inclusion. Deficit Reduction Act of 1984, Pub. L. No. 98-369, § 641, 98 Stat. 494, 939 (1984), reprinted in 1984-3 CB (Vol. 1) 1, 447. The Supreme Court resolved the dispute for cases arising prior to the 1984 Act holding that such bonds were not exempted from the estate tax. United States v. Wells Fargo Bank, 485 US 351 (1988).

Special rules attend the transfer of certain U.S. bonds, which raise the questions concerning their ownership. See the comments in the discussion of Section 2040 at ¶ 4.12[2].

[31] See Estate of Patterson, 46 TCM (CCH) 618 (1983), aff'd, 736 F2d 32 (2d Cir. 1984).

due to the decedent on notes, secured or not, arising out of the decedent's life-time loans or deferred-payment sales.[32]

[4] Income Items

For some purposes, the tax laws seek to differentiate property from the income from property as well as property from the value of a right to be paid for ser-vices.[33] One may wonder, therefore, whether income rights of the decedent at death must be treated as property in which the decedent had an interest within the scope of Section 2033. They must.

Salary due at death is a classic example of an item of "income in respect of a decedent" that, under Section 691, is taxed as income to the decedent's estate or other recipient when received.[34] But, as with other such items, this does not foreclose its treatment as a property interest for estate tax purposes.[35]

Bonuses payable to the decedent at the time of death are included in the decedent's gross estate,[36] and this is the case even though the right to the bo-

---

[32] Such notes and other claims are included even if they are canceled by the dece-dent's will. Reg. § 20.2033-1(b); Rev. Rul. 81-286, 1981-2 CB 177. See also Leopold v. United States, 1972-1 USTC ¶ 12,837 (CD Cal. 1972), aff'd on other grounds, 510 F2d 617 (9th Cir. 1975). In Estate of Musgrove v. Comm'r, 33 Fed. Cl. 657 (1992), the Court of Claims held that decedent's transfer of money to his son, in exchange for a promissory note that provided that it would be forgiven as of decedent's death if no prior demand for repayment had been made. Following Buckwalter v. Comm'r, 46 TC 805 (1966), the court held that the transaction was a loan made for less than adequate and full considera-tion, not an annuity, and should be included in the decedent's gross estate pursuant to Section 2033.

If, however, the obligation to pay the notes is extinguished at the decedent's death *and* this was a part of the bargained-for consideration of the sale, there is in substance an annuity and no Section 2033 or Section 2039 (see ¶ 4.11) inclusion. Estate of Moss v. Comm'r, 74 TC 1239 (1980), acq. 1981-1 CB 2. Cf. Estate of Costanza, 81 TCM (CCH) 1693 (2001) (inadequate consideration received resulted in a Section 2511 gift).

[33] See, e.g., IRC §§ 351, 721, concerning the transfer of "property" for corporate stock or a partnership interest; Reg. §§ 1.351-1(a)(1)(i), 1.721-1(b)(1). See also Hempt Bros. v. United States, 490 F2d 1172 (3d Cir.), cert. denied, 419 US 826 (1974); United States v. Frazell, 335 F2d 487 (5th Cir. 1964).

[34] See Johnson, Westphal, & Bolling, "Estate Tax Implications of IRD," 71 Taxes 35 (1993).

[35] Cf. IRC § 691(c), which reflects the assumption that estate tax may be paid on such "income" items; Findlay v. Comm'r, 332 F2d 620 (2d Cir. 1964). See Blanton III, "Who Gets a Dead Man's Gold? The Dilemma of Lottery Winnings Payable to a Dece-dent's Estate," 28 U. Rich. L. Rev. 443 (1994); Colgate, "Win, Lose or Draw: The Tax Ramifications of Winning a Major Lottery," 10 Cooley L. Rev. 275 (1993); "Uncashed Checks: Part of the Drawer's Gross Estate?" 5 Conn. Prob. LJ 340 (1991).

[36] Estate of King v. Comm'r, 20 TC 930 (1953); Estate of McKitterick v. Comm'r, 42 BTA 130 (1940).

nus is subject to contingencies until the time of the decedent's death.[37] However, bonuses in which a decedent has no interest at death but that are awarded only subsequent to death at the employer's discretion, are not included in the decedent's gross estate even if they are paid to the decedent's estate.[38]

Compensation due for services other than as an employee (such as fees due a lawyer, accountant, or physician) are treated the same as salary.[39] At first glance, it would seem that deferred compensation arrangements would be included in the decedent's gross estate, except that under most such arrangements the decedent's interest terminates at death and the proceeds of such payments (normally in the form of an annuity of a lump sum) are paid third parties, with the result that an instant after death, the decedent has no interest in the payments. This does not preclude gross estate inclusion.[40] If the dece-

---

[37] Cf. Goodman v. Granger, 243 F2d 264 (3d Cir.), cert. denied, 355 US 835 (1957). If such bonuses or other employee-type benefits are payable to persons other than the decedent or the decedent's estate, they may not be includable under Section 2033. Estate of Tully v. United States, 528 F2d 1401 (Ct. Cl. 1976). This would appear to be the case even if the decedent had the right until death to alter the beneficiary. Dimock v. Corwin, 19 F. Supp. 56 (EDNY 1937), aff'd on other grounds, 99 F2d 799 (2d Cir. 1938), aff'd, 306 US 363 (1939). However, the question is largely academic because, absent an express exemption such as appeared in now-repealed Section 2039(c), in such circumstances inclusion would probably result under other sections. See IRC §§ 2037, 2038, 2039, 2041; Estate of Bogley v. United States, 514 F2d 1027 (Ct. Cl. 1975); Rev. Rul. 76-304, 1976-2 CB 269; Rev. Rul. 78-15, 1978-2 CB 289; Comment, "Estate Taxation of Employer Death Benefits," 66 Yale LJ 1217 (1957).

[38] Estate of Barr v. Comm'r, 40 TC 227 (1963), acq. 1964-1 CB 4; Worthen v. United States, 192 F. Supp. 727 (D. Mass. 1961); Estate of Bogley v. United States, 514 F2d 1027 (Ct. Cl. 1975). See Rev. Rul. 65-217, 1965-2 CB 214, differentiating bonuses awarded to the decedent before death but paid to the decedent's estate after death (includable) from bonuses awarded and paid after death (not includable).

[39] See Reg. § 1.691(c)-1(d) Ex. 1. If the payment of a fee is contingent, there is no right to recovery in quantum meruit, and all rights the decedent might otherwise have to payment terminate at the time of death, and the decedent would have no Section 2033 property interest. Estate of Nemerov v. Comm'r, 15 TCM (CCH) 855 (1956). On the other hand, in the more usual case, the estate would be entitled to recover the reasonable value of services performed by the attorney before the decedent's death, and that right is a Section 2033 interest. Rev. Rul. 55-123, 1955-1 CB 443. A contractual right to payment for a portion of contingent attorney fees is included under Section 2033. Estate of Curry v. Comm'r, 74 TC 540 (1980). If all services under a contingent-fee agreement have been performed but, for instance, a favorable judgment not yet rendered at death is a condition to payment, a Section 2033 property interest in the decedent exists at death, even though its valuation may be difficult. Duffield v. United States, 136 F. Supp. 944 (ED Pa. 1955). Cf. Aldrich v. Comm'r, 46 TCM (CCH) 1295 (1983), where a Section 2032 election established valuation.

[40] See ¶ 4.11[6] discussing the inclusion of annuity arrangements within Section 2039. A lump sum amount with a third party designated beneficiary where the decedent had the power to alter the beneficiary until death is included in the decedent's gross estate under Section 2038. Cf. Rev. Rul. 76-304, 1976-2 CB 269.

dent's estate was the recipient of the proceeds or held a reversionary interest in such proceeds, Section 2033 would arguably include the proceeds and would definitely include the reversionary interest in the decedent's gross estate.[41]

Rent accrued at death on real or personal property owned by the decedent is a Section 2033 gross estate inclusion.[42]

Accrued interest, whether it be on savings in a bank account, on a bond, on a note arising out of an installment sale,[43] or on some less formal credit extension or loan made by the decedent during life, is a Section 2033 gross estate inclusion.[44]

Dividends on shares of stock that are payable to the decedent at the time of death are also a part of the decedent's gross estate. However, a decedent's right to a dividend does not accrue with the mere passage of time in the manner of interest on a bond. Instead, the decedent has no right to a dividend until the dividend is declared by the board of directors of the corporation and, even then, since the dividend is made payable on a future date only to stockholders of "record" on a date somewhere between the "declaration" and the "payment" date, the right does not arise until the record date.[45]

If the annuity or lump sum were paid to the decedent's surviving spouse, it would qualify for a marital deduction. See IRC § 2056, especially ¶ 5.06[7][c] note 193. Cf. IRC § 2056(b)(7)(C), ¶ 5.06[8][d] text accompanying notes 339–341.

[41] The reversionary interest would be included under Section 2033. As to the proceeds themselves, see infra ¶ 4.05[6] note 76 questioning whether inclusion occurs under Section 2033 or Section 2041.

[42] Reg. § 20.2033-1(b). But see Estate of Watson v. Comm'r, 94 TC 262 (1990).

[43] Cf. Wilson v. Comm'r, 56 TC 579 (1971), acq. 1972-1 CB 2; Estate of Swezey v. Comm'r, 35 TCM (CCH) 1637 (1976).

[44] The instruction for Schedule C of Form 706, "United States Estate (and Generation-Skipping Transfer) Tax Return" (Rev. November 2001), does not make clear that interest on a note, for example, is to be included. Nevertheless it is appropriate practice to state as separate items the principal amount of the note and interest accrued to the date of death. Cf. Reg. § 20.2032-1(d)(1).

[45] If a D dies owning stock on which a dividend has been declared, the dividend is separately included in D's gross estate, if not yet received by D, only if D's death followed the record date. Reg. § 20.2033-1(b). On the record date the dividend becomes separate property in which D had an "interest." This conforms to practice in the marketplace. Before the record date, the stock trades cum-dividend, and, to some extent at least, the forthcoming dividend is reflected in the price and value of the stock. After the record date — strictly speaking, five days before the record date with respect to listed securities to take account of major stock exchange settlement procedures — the stock trades ex-dividend; the dividend has become the property of the one who held the stock on the record date, and the owner is entitled to it even if the owner then sells the stock. If the owner relinquishes the stock by death after the record date, both the value of the dividend and of the stock (presumably now a lower value no longer reflecting the forthcoming dividend) are a part of the owner's gross estate. Reg. § 20.2031-2(i); Estate of McNary v. Comm'r, 47 TC 467 (1967). These comments relate only to Section 2033 and to date-of-death value under Section 2031. Some problems under other Code provisions are examined elsewhere.

[5] Partial Interests in Property

[a] Shared Interests in Property

A decedent may, at the time of death, share property with another. If the interest is one that the decedent can pass on to others, it is generally an interest within the scope of Section 2033.[46] Thus, if the decedent and another owned Blackacre as tenants in common, the interest will pass as the decedent directs by will or by laws of intestacy. A decedent's interest in community property is a similar inheritable or bequeathable interest and is not now differentiated from a tenancy in common for gross estate purposes.[47] The value of both types of interests is includable in the gross estate under Section 2033.

On the other hand, some interests in shared property are treated differently. During life, the co-owners' rights in property owned as joint tenants with right of survivorship or as tenants by the entirety are similar to the rights of tenants in common, except that a tenant by the entirety cannot make an independent disposition of the tenant's interest. But, in contrast to tenancies in common, other joint owners' rights cease on death and the property becomes that of the surviving tenant or tenants. These interests are not inheritable and, as they are not subject to the decedent's testamentary direction, are not interests covered by Section 2033.[48] To rule them out under Section 2033 is not to say, however, that they are without estate tax significance. Shared property interests that carry survivorship rights are the subject of specific estate tax provisions.[49]

For example, if the record date follows the decedent's death, the dividend is generally not treated as a property interest covered under Section 2033, even if the alternate valuation date is elected. Reg. § 20.2032-1(d)(4). But see Estate of Fleming v. Comm'r, 33 TCM (CCH) 1414 (1974).

[46] Estate of Mladinich v. Comm'r, 62 TCM (CCH) 1065 (1991).

[47] But see IRC § 811(e)(2) (1939); Fernandez v. Wiener, 326 US 340 (1945). During the period that Section 811(e)(2) was effective, just prior to the enactment of the marital deduction now found in Section 2056, community property was accorded estate treatment quite like that now accorded jointly held property under Section 2040. Much Section 2033 litigation arises over the question whether property is held as community property. E.g., Parson v. United States, 460 F2d 228 (5th Cir. 1972); Murrah v. Wiseman, 449 F2d 187 (10th Cir. 1971); Kern v. United States, 491 F2d 436 (9th Cir. 1974); Hundemer v. United States, 293 F. Supp. 1063 (ED La. 1968); Estate of Lepoutre v. Comm'r, 62 TC 84 (1974); Jackson v. United States, 88-1 USTC ¶ 13,750 (ND Tex. 1987); Wilmington Trust Co. v. United States, 4 Cl. Ct. 6 (1983), aff'd per curiam, 85-2 USTC ¶ 13,625 (Fed. Cir. 1985); Rev. Rul. 74-284, 1974-1 CB 276.

[48] Even if they were, their value would seem to be zero, if they are properly viewed as expiring rather than being transmitted at death.

[49] See IRC § 2040, discussed at ¶ 4.12.

[b] Successive Interests in Property

Tenants in common share all the rights in property concurrently; each owns a percentage of the entire property, but not a specific portion that can be identified. On the other hand, property can also be divided into interests that are successive in point of time rather than concurrent. Suppose A owns Blackacre outright but, for good consideration, A leases it to B for twenty years. Both A and B now have interests in Blackacre that, upon death, may be taxable under Section 2033. Thus, if B dies when the lease term has ten years still to run, B's estate includes the value of the leasehold. If A were to die at that time, A's estate would include the value of A's reversionary interest in the property, which is the value of the property reduced by the current outstanding interest in B.[50] Both are inheritable interests in property well within the scope of Section 2033.

In the foregoing example, B has a terminable interest in property that will end when the twenty-year lease has run its course. But a property interest may terminate upon the occurrence (or even nonoccurrence) of an event instead of upon the mere passage of time. Thus, B might have a life estate in Blackacre or, more commonly these days, B might be the life beneficiary of a trust. In these cases, B has no interest that B can transmit to others at B's death[51] and any such interest that terminates with B is not a Section 2033 interest in property.[52] But if the arrangement was that B's interest would terminate upon some other event, such as on the death of C who survived B, the value of B's interest at B's death, an estate *pur autre vie*, would be a Section 2033 inclusion,

---

[50] Any reversionary or remainder interest in property, if it is not a contingent interest that terminates upon the decedent's death, Rev. Rul. 55-438, 1955-2 CB 601, is within the scope of Section 2033. Estate of Hamilton v. Comm'r, 35 TCM (CCH) 1609 (1976). However, it may present a difficult valuation problem. Karlson v. Comm'r, 1974-2 USTC ¶ 13,014 (SDNY 1974). Cf. Estate of Jennings v. Comm'r, 10 TC 323 (1948).

[51] But see Priv. Ltr. Rul. 8820003 (Feb. 8, 1988) (under local law, the Rule in Shelley's Case converted a life estate to a fee simple includable in the decedent's gross estate).

In the past, B's death in these circumstances has been a neutral federal tax event because the estate and gift taxes have been exactions on the *transmission* of wealth. Numerous red flags must now be raised to caution against possible liability for the tax on generation-skipping transfers. See Chapters 12–18.

[52] Williams v. United States, 41 F2d 895 (Ct. Cl. 1930). See also Estate of Williams v. Comm'r, 62 TC 400 (1974); Estate of Dickinson v. Comm'r, 41 TCM (CCH) 787 (1981); Rev. Rul. 74-492, 1974-2 CB 298. On the other hand, a life tenant of a farm, for example, may own the crop on the land, even an unharvested crop; if so, the value of the crop is includable, for the life tenant's interest in it does not expire at death. Martin v. United States, 121 Ct. Cl. 829, 1952-1 USTC ¶ 10,844 (1952). Similarly accumulated income to which a decedent income beneficiary had a legal right even after death is included in the decedent's gross estate. Estate of Mitchell v. Comm'r, 41 TCM (CCH) 1290 (1981).

the value and duration of which now would have to be determined with reference to *C*'s life expectancy.

For purposes of Section 2033, a reversionary interest in property that the decedent has transferred is not distinguished from a remainder interest in property that has been transferred to the decedent by another. If *A* has a reversionary interest that will take effect upon the happening of an event (instead of simply upon the expiration of a period of time) this, too, is a property interest within Section 2033. A reversionary interest may, however, be contingent. If *A*'s reversion is contingent upon *A*'s surviving *B* and *B* in fact survives, *A* has no inheritable interest within Section 2033 because *A*'s reversionary interest expires when *A* dies. But if *A*'s reversion is dependent, for instance, upon *C*'s not surviving *B* and both are still living when *A* dies, the reversion does not expire on *A*'s death and is includable in *A*'s gross estate under Section 2033.

A person's death may prevent the acquisition of property that would otherwise have come to the person. Suppose *A* dies leaving all *A*'s property to *B* and *B* dies shortly thereafter while *A*'s estate is in probate. Clearly, *B*'s gross estate includes *B*'s interest in *A*'s estate.[53] However, *A*'s bequest to *B* may be conditional on *B* surviving *A* by six months. If *B* dies within the stated period, *B*'s inchoate rights in *A*'s estate are terminated by *B*'s death, and *B*'s interest in *A*'s estate is no more includable under Section 2033 than if it were a life interest or contingent remainder cut off by death.[54]

In contrast to the situation in which a decedent's death may terminate the decedent's interest in property, there are some situations in which the death may assure or enlarge the interest. Suppose *A* creates a trust, income payable to *B* for life, remainder to *C* or *C*'s estate, subject however to the contingency that if *D* predeceases both *B* and *C*, the remainder is to go to *E*. If *C* dies survived by *B* and *D*, what is included in *C*'s gross estate? The problem is that immediately before *C*'s death *C*'s remainder was contingent on *D*'s not predeceasing *C*. Upon *C*'s death, with *D* surviving, *C*'s remainder is assured. Is *C*'s includable interest the contingent remainder or the assured remainder? It seems settled now that the identification (and therefore the valuation) of *C*'s includable interest must take account of the fact that *C*'s death terminated the contin-

---

[53] Estate of Miller v. Comm'r, 58 TC 699 (1972); Estate of Hanch v. Comm'r, 19 TC 65 (1952), acq. 1953-1 CB 4.

[54] See Comm'r v. Rosser, 64 F2d 631 (3d Cir. 1933); Priv. Ltr. Rul. 8538007 (1985). Similarly, *A*'s will might provide that *B* would receive property only if *B* survived *A* and, in addition, that in the event of their simultaneous deaths, *A* would be presumed to have survived *B*. In such a case, if *A* and *B* died simultaneously, nothing would pass from *A* to *B*, and *A*'s property would not be included in *B*'s estate. The same result would follow, even if no such presumption was expressed in *A*'s will, if the administration of *A*'s estate was subject to the Uniform Simultaneous Death Act of 1940, 8 ULA 608, under which each person is presumed to be the survivor with respect to that person's property unless the person's will provides to the contrary. See Rev. Rul. 66-60, 1966-1 CB 221; Rev. Rul. 76-303, 1976-2 CB 266.

gency and assured the ultimate fruition of *C*'s interest.[55] Perhaps the most compelling argument in favor of this result is the fact that until death there is no decedent and no estate to be determined; therefore, it is necessary to look at Section 2033 property interests as of the moment after death.[56] In a sense this is the logical converse of the proposition that a contingent remainder extinguished by death is to be disregarded. Nevertheless, the question is difficult and the accepted rule comes close to an inheritance tax approach, looking to what is received by survivors rather than what is transmitted by the decedent. Certainly the decedent, *C*, never had the *assured* remainder interest.

Is a partial interest in property that can be extinguished at any time by the action of another person a Section 2033 property interest? For example, if *A* creates a trust, income payable to *B* for twenty years, remainder to *C* or *C*'s estate, both *B* and *C* have includable interests if either should die during the twenty-year period. Is the result altered by *A*'s retention of a power to revoke the trust? It is the Treasury's position that the interests of *B* and *C* are taxable interests.[57] The ruling may have a brittle technical underpinning but should be seriously questioned. As a practical matter and for estate tax and gift tax purposes, *A* remains the owner of the whole property. There is a logical inconsistency in saying that others have recognizable interests in it, if "the whole is equal only to the sum of its parts."[58]

[c] Cautions

The foregoing remarks require two areas of caution and some further elaboration.

---

[55] Goodman v. Granger, 243 F2d 264 (3d Cir.), cert. denied, 355 US 835 (1957); United States v. Harris Trust & Sav. Bank, 470 F2d 6 (7th Cir.), cert. denied, 409 US 1059 (1972).

[56] Christiernin v. Manning, 138 F. Supp. 923 (DNJ 1956).

[57] Rev. Rul. 67-370, 1967-2 CB 324. The ruling treats the power to revoke as immaterial for purposes of *identifying* taxable interests and, on the related *valuation* question, indicates that such subordinate interests are to be accorded more than nominal value. For valuation of irrevocable remainder interests, see Reg. §§ 20.2031-7(a), 20.2031-7(d), 20.2031-7A. On occasion, if an interest is very remote, it has been held that nothing is includable in the gross estate. Estate of Cardeza v. Comm'r, 5 TC 202 (1945), acq. and nonacq. 1946-1 CB 1, 5, aff'd, 173 F2d 19 (3d Cir. 1949). Although remoteness of the interests should bear only on the question of valuation, Estate of Hill v. Comm'r, 193 F2d 724 (2d Cir. 1952); Estate of Henry v. Comm'r, 4 TC 423 (1944), acq. and nonacq. 1945 CB 4, 8, aff'd on other grounds, 161 F2d 574 (3d Cir. 1947), the opposite pragmatic result seems supportable.

[58] A remote interest is one of those interests to be taken into account in identifying the entire ownership of property; whereas if one person owns "the whole thing," there is no room for other interests. Cf. IRC § 2037(b) (last sentence).

1. The only question that has been considered here is includability under Section 2033; a decedent's possession of terminable rights relating to income or enjoyment or of reversionary rights, even if in either case they expire at death, will sometimes be a reason for gross estate inclusion under other Code sections.[59]

2. A further word of caution relates to the nontaxability of beneficial interests in the decedent that terminate at the decedent's death. It is this concept that gives rise to what reformers have called "generation skipping." Thus, if, by will, a parent creates a trust with income payable to a child for life, remainder to a grandchild, the trust property may be taxed under the federal estate tax in the first and third generations but not the second. Failure to impose an estate tax at the death of one who may have enjoyed a life interest is quite in keeping with the general philosophy of the current etate tax, which, as other comments in this section suggest, looks to the transmission of property by the decedent.[60] There is a shifting of interests when a life tenant dies, but the shift cannot be said to constitute a transmission by the life tenant. Chapter 13 of the Code, which taxes that shift and some related generation-skipping transactions as well, is considered in Chapters 12 through 18 of this treatise. Although the tax imposed on generation-skipping transfers is a separate tax, nevertheless there are numerous statutory interrelationships with the estate and gift taxes.

3. An explanatory word should be addressed to the question whether several rights or interests in property, no one of which would be a sufficient reason for a Section 2033 inclusion, may together amount to an ownership interest. Income tax lawyers will think of *Helvering v. Clifford*,[61] in which tax ownership was attributed to a trust settler even though the settler lacked legal title and many other ownership attributes. There has been a growing common-law estate tax ownership concept,[62] but the estate tax has not experienced the same judge-made ownership development under Section 2033 as had occurred for income tax purposes under the predecessor of Section 61 before the enactment of the statutory grantor trust provisions.[63] A power of appointment, even a general power, is not recognized as an interest in

---

[59] See especially discussion of IRC §§ 2036, 2037 at ¶¶ 4.08, 4.09.

[60] See YMCA v. Davis, 264 US 47, 50 (1924).

[61] Helvering v. Clifford, 309 US 331 (1940).

[62] See Stephens, "The Clifford Shadow Over the Federal Estate Tax," 4 Ga. L. Rev. 233 (1970).

[63] IRC §§ 671-679. See Murray, "Income Taxation of Short-Term and Controlled Trusts," 7 USC Tax Inst. 497 (1955).

property under property law,[64] and it is accorded similar nonrecognition under Section 2033.[65] If one has a right to the current income
from property and a testamentary power to appoint it to anyone the
person chooses, does the person have enough of the bundle of rights
to be a Section 2033 owner? The Supreme Court has held not; neither
the terminating income interest nor the power alone is taxable under
Section 2033, and the Supreme Court has refused to give them Section 2033 status together.[66]

[6] Insurance Proceeds Under Section 2033

Proceeds of insurance on a decedent's life are the subject of a special estate
tax statutory rule.[67] However, the decedent may be the owner of a life insurance policy on the life of another person, such as the decedent's spouse or
business partner, who survives the decedent. The special provisions of Section
2042 do not apply to insurance on the lives of others; but an insurance policy
is property, and the value[68] of the decedent's interest in it will be included in
the decedent's gross estate under Section 2033.[69]

Inclusion results under Section 2033 even in a situation in which the insured and one who is both the owner of the policy and the primary beneficiary
die simultaneously if their affairs are governed by the Uniform Simultaneous

---

[64] 5 Casner, American Law of Property § 23.4, at 467 (1952).

[65] Estate of Noland v. Comm'r, 47 TCM (CCH) 1640 (1984). See special statutory
treatment of powers in the discussion of Section 2041 at ¶ 4.13.

[66] Helvering v. Safe Dep. & Trust Co., 316 US 56 (1942). See Ellis v. United States,
280 F. Supp. 786 (D. Md. 1968).

[67] See discussion of Section 2042 at ¶ 4.14. Among other things, Section 2042 includes insurance proceeds on the decedent's life that are "receivable by his executor,"
even though Section 2033 might include such proceeds without the aid of Section 2042.
See Mimnaugh v. United States, 66 Ct. Cl. 411, 1 USTC ¶ 339 (1928), cert. denied, 280
US 563 (1929), involving such inclusion under a statutory forerunner of Section 2033. But
see infra note 76.

[68] On the valuation of insurance policies, see Reg. § 20.2031-8 and the discussion at
¶ 10.02[2][e]. If the decedent owned a policy of insurance on the life of another, election
of the alternate valuation date can greatly increase the amount to be included in the gross
estate. If the insured dies within six months after the decedent's death, value under the alternate date election will include the added increment occasioned by the death of the insured. Rev. Rul. 63-52, 1963-1 CB 173. The amount to include is not increased, however,
with respect to added values arising from the payment of premiums or interest earned on
the policy after the decedent's death. Rev. Rul. 55-379, 1955-1 CB 449.

[69] Estate of DuPont v. Comm'r, 233 F2d 210 (3d Cir.), cert. denied, 352 US 878
(1956); Estate of Donaldson v. Comm'r, 31 TC 729 (1959).

Death Act or a similar statute.[70] If the owner of the policy is not the primary beneficiary of the proceeds, nothing is included in the owner's estate under Section 2033 when owner and insured die simultaneously.[71]

If the decedent owned a community property interest in a policy on the life of another person, one half of the value of the policy will be included in the decedent's gross estate.[72]

---

[70] Under the Uniform Simultaneous Death Act of 1940, the normal presumption is that the owner of property survives in the event of a simultaneous death. See supra ¶ 4.05[5][b] note 54. However, an overriding presumption assumes that the insured survives if the insured and the primary beneficiary die simultaneously. Thus, if the insured and one who is both an owner and primary beneficiary of a policy die simultaneously, the insured is deemed to have survived. Taxpayer-estates, originally ignoring this overriding presumption, argued that the decedent (owner-primary beneficiary) had no beneficial interest in the policy, because the secondary beneficiaries received the proceeds as a result of the simultaneous deaths. This argument, which would have resulted in the policy's being included in the estate of neither the insured nor the owner, has been uniformly rejected. Estate of Meltzer v. Comm'r, 439 F2d 798 (4th Cir. 1971); Estate of Wien v. Comm'r, 441 F2d 32 (5th Cir. 1971); Old Kent Bank & Trust Co. v. United States, 430 F2d 392 (6th Cir. 1970); Estate of Chown v. Comm'r, 428 F2d 1395 (9th Cir. 1970). Cf. Estate of Goldstone v. Comm'r, 78 TC 1143 (1982), where the Tax Court stated that it would no longer follow its prior decisions in *Chown* and *Wien*, which were reversed by the Ninth and Fifth Circuits, respectively.

Losing on the includability issue, taxpayer estates have contended that if there is a Section 2033 inclusion, it is not the proceeds of the policy that are included but its value as determined under Regulations Section 20.2031-8 (because of the presumption that the insured survives the decedent beneficiary). The government had argued that the *proceeds* of the policy should be included in decedent's estate because, in fact, the policy matures at the simultaneous death of the insured and the owner beneficiary. On this issue, it is the government that had sought to ignore the overriding presumption of the Uniform Simultaneous Death Act. The courts uniformly rejected the government's argument and have concluded that value should be determined pursuant to Regulations Section 20.2031-8. Estate of Meltzer v. Comm'r, supra; Estate of Wien v. Comm'r, supra; Old Kent Bank & Trust Co. v. United States, supra; Estate of Chown v. Comm'r, supra. The government has agreed with that position. Rev. Rul. 77-181, 1977-1 CB 272. See Note, "Simultaneous Death—The Ownership Interest in a Life Insurance Policy Should Be Valued on the Basis of the Interpolated Terminal Reserve," 49 Tex. L. Rev. 924 (1971); Ketchum & Johnson, "Traditional Simultaneous Death Planning Must Be Reviewed in Light of ERTA Social Changes," 10 Est. Plan. 90 (1983).

[71] Under the normal presumption of the Act, the owner is presumed to have survived the insured. Thus, at the instant of the insured's death, the right to the proceeds passes irrevocably to the beneficiary from the owner and it is a lifetime transfer subject to gift tax. Goodman v. Comm'r, 156 F2d 218 (2d Cir. 1946). But with respect to decedents dying after December 31, 1976, it is pulled back into the owner decedent's estate under Section 2035(a). See ¶ 4.07[2].

[72] This commonly occurs in a community property state when a husband and wife own a community property policy on the husband's life and the wife predeceases the husband. United States v. Stewart, 270 F2d 894 (9th Cir. 1959), cert. denied, 361 US 960 (1960); California Trust Co. v. Riddell, 136 F. Supp. 7 (SD Cal. 1955); Rev. Rul. 67-228, 1967-2 CB 331. Cf. Rev. Rul. 80-242, 1980-2 CB 276. But see United States v.

If, before death, the decedent has acquired an interest in the proceeds of an insurance policy on the life of another person who predeceased the decedent, the nature of the interest will determine whether anything is to be included in the decedent's gross estate with respect to such proceeds. For example, if all the decedent ever acquired was an annuity for life, nothing would be included in the decedent's gross estate[73] even if, after the decedent's death, benefits continue to be paid to others.[74] Similarly, if the decedent was entitled only to interest on the proceeds for life, and the proceeds were to be paid to a third party at the decedent's death, nothing would be included in the decedent's estate under Section 2033, as in both cases all the rights would expire at the decedent's death.[75]

An area of controversy has grown up around the situation in which the decedent is entitled only to interest on insurance proceeds for life and the proceeds are to be paid to *the decedent's* estate upon the decedent's death. Although it is tempting to equate these rights with outright ownership so as to include the entire value of the proceeds in the decedent's estate under Section 2033, close analysis reveals that the decedent's rights are only (1) temporary enjoyment of the interest income that ends at death, and (2) a right by will to say who shall have the proceeds, exercisable through the control of disposition of property that becomes a part of the probate estate. Neither is a Section 2033 property interest.[76]

Waechter, 195 F2d 963 (9th Cir. 1952), questionably relying on a state court decision, since overruled, that purported to interpret Washington law.

[73] Estate of Minotto v. Comm'r, 9 TCM (CCH) 556 (1950). However, if the decedent was given the option to receive the proceeds in a lump sum or in some other manner and the decedent elected an annuity with subsequent payments to a third party after the decedent's death or the decedent elected to receive only a life estate with a remainder to a third party, the courts will look at the substance of the transaction and treat decedent as if the decedent received the proceeds and subsequently transferred them, possibly causing inclusion in the decedent's gross estate under Section 2039 or Section 2036, respectively. Estate of Tuohy v. Comm'r, 14 TC 245 (1950); Estate of Morton v. Comm'r, 12 TC 380 (1949).

[74] Insurance and annuity arrangements may, however, be treated as a "trust" for generation-skipping transfer tax purposes. See ¶ 17.02[2].

[75] Cf. Second Nat'l Bank of Danville v. Dallman, 209 F2d 321 (7th Cir. 1954).

[76] This is not to say that the decedent's estate would not be taxed on the proceeds but only that it would not be taxed under Section 2033. In one early case, the court correctly refused inclusion under Section 2033 but erred with respect to the application of other Code provisions. Second Nat'l Bank of Danville v. Dallman, 209 F2d 321 (7th Cir. 1954). There, the decedent additionally had a lifetime power to designate a contingent beneficiary ultimately to receive the proceeds. This right was never exercised and, since it was a pre-1942 power of appointment, its nonexercise occasioned no estate tax. See discussion of IRC § 2041 at ¶ 4.13. However, the court refused to regard the decedent's power in effect to direct disposition of the proceeds by will as a testamentary power. It may be true, as the court said, that the decedent was powerless to divert the proceeds from the estate, ex-

[7] Business Interests

[a] Corporations and Proprietorships

If a decedent's business was incorporated, Section 2033 includes in the gross estate the value of the decedent's shares of stock, which may be viewed as investment assets.[77] This is so even if the decedent is the sole shareholder of the corporation. The value of a decedent's interest in an unincorporated business is, of course, a part of the decedent's gross estate as well. In the case of a sole proprietorship, no entity stands between a decedent and the business assets. The decedent's Section 2033 interest in property therefore encompasses the ownership of all the various assets of the business.[78]

Various business-type property interests lie between a sole proprietorship and a closely held corporation, and, generally, the value of each is included in a decedent's gross estate under Section 2033. For instance, several persons may own a piece of rental property as tenants in common, which may not make them partners for tax purposes[79] but which gives them essentially a business-type investment. The decedent's proportionate interest in such property, the same as in any tenancy in common, is an interest in property to be included in the decedent's estate.

---

cept by the exercise of the lifetime power that was not exercised. Upon payment of the proceeds to her estate, however, her will *did* direct the ultimate disposition of the proceeds, pretty clearly amounting to an exercise of a general testamentary power over the proceeds. This analysis of the problem was clear to the Fifth Circuit, which rejected the rationale of the Seventh Circuit in the *Second National Bank* case. Keeter v. United States, 461 F2d 714 (5th Cir. 1972), rev'g 323 F. Supp. 1093 (ND Fla. 1971). See Rev. Rul. 55-277, 1955-1 CB 456, rejecting the Seventh Circuit's analysis of the "powers" issue. See also Note, "Tax Evasion Through Settlement Options: Another Defeat for Substantial Ownership in Estate Taxation," 64 Yale LJ 137 (1954). There is some indication the government has not abandoned its Section 2033 argument on the facts here considered. See Keeter v. United States, supra, at 719 n.3. If the Fifth Circuit view on the "powers" issue prevails, the Section 2033 argument becomes relatively insignificant, especially since, different from the facts in the two cases cited, future controversy is more likely to evolve around post-1942 powers of appointment that need not be exercised to have estate tax significance. See discussion of IRC § 2041 at ¶ 4.13.

[77] If the decedent also owns bonds issued by the corporation, the value of the bonds is likewise included, whether treated as equity or debt securities, a distinction that is immaterial for estate tax purposes. See, e.g., Gooding Amusement Co. v. Comm'r, 236 F2d 159 (6th Cir. 1956), cert. denied, 352 US 1031 (1957). Valuation of such interests is discussed at ¶ 4.02[3][e].

[78] Cf. Williams v. McGowan, 152 F2d 570 (2d Cir. 1945). The difference in what we look to in a close corporation and in a proprietorship is largely formal; however, the important *valuation* question is approached in much the same way in either case. Reg. §§ 20.2031-2(f), 20.2031-3; Rev. Rul. 68-609, 1968-2 CB 327; Rev. Rul. 59-60, 1959-1 CB 237. See ¶ 4.02[3][f].

[79] IRC § 761(a); Reg. § 1.761-1(a).

[b] Partnership Interests

A decedent's interest in a partnership is likewise a business property interest included in the decedent's gross estate. The interest to be included in the estate may vary, however, depending on the decedent's rights in the partnership at death. For example, if the decedent owned a one-quarter interest in a partnership with no agreement as to what would occur if a partner died, state law would likely accord the decedent's estate a right to one quarter of the partnership's assets, essentially a tenancy in common interest. However, the decedent should not be viewed as owning any specific assets; instead, the decedent has a proportionate share of *each* asset, including partnership goodwill, which injects a "going concern" element into the identification of the Section 2033 interest.[80] Alternately, the partnership agreement might provide that a deceased partner's estate would receive a flat dollar amount for the interest. If so, the agreed amount may identify and measure the interest to be included in the decedent's gross estate.[81]

The rights of partners, living or dead, are about as varied as the ingenuities of the draftsmen who prepare their agreements. Thus, the agreement may provide that a deceased partner's estate is to receive a percentage of the partnership's profits over a period of time in lieu of other amounts to which it would otherwise be entitled. That right also constitutes an interest in property

---

[80] Uniform Partnership Act § 42, 6 ULA 521 (1969); Kihchel v. United States, 105 F. Supp. 523 (WD Pa. 1952). Income tax analysis may vary. See generally IRC §§ 736(b), 741, 751. An issue may arise as to what specific assets the partnership owns. Heath v. United States, 1968-1 USTC ¶ 12,508 (D. Colo. 1967). Similarly, an issue may arise whether a partnership exists; if it does not exist, the decedent's interest in the individual assets is included in the decedent's gross estate. Estate of Kjorvestad v. Comm'r, 81-1 USTC ¶ 13,401 (DND 1981).

Difficult problems of valuation occur with respect to the goodwill of the partnership and the effect of the decedent's death on its value. Estate of Goodall v. Comm'r, 391 F2d 775 (8th Cir. 1968); Estate of Leopold Kaffie v. Comm'r, 44 BTA 843 (1941), nonacq. 1942-1 CB 25; Blodget v. Comm'r, 18 BTA 1050 (1930), acq. IX-2 CB 6. Valuation problems also arise with respect to the fact the decedent owned a one-quarter interest which would qualify for discounts as a minority interest and for lack of marketability. See ¶¶ 4.02[4][c], 4.02[4][d].

[81] Estate of Weil v. Comm'r, 22 TC 1267 (1954), acq. 1955-2 CB 10. Note that in this situation, the concepts of identification and valuation for purposes of Section 2033 generally merge. See the comments on agreements in the discussion of IRC § 2031 at ¶ 4.02[2][c] and in the discussion of IRC § 2703 at ¶ 19.04. In Priv. Ltr. Rul. 9151045 (Sept. 26, 1991), the right of a withdrawing managing partner to future annual payments of $100,000 was characterized as a private annuity or a similar form of debt rather than as a retained interest in the entity that would be subject to the Chapter 14 special valuation rules. The Service concluded that this was so because the partnership agreement provided that a withdrawing partnership agreement would no longer hold any interest or right to participate in partnership profits or losses.

to be included in the decedent's estate under Section 2033.[82] And, of course, an agreement might provide that the decedent's estate would receive such a share of profits or a fixed dollar amount in addition to the value of the decedent's proportionate interest in the partnership's assets. In these circumstances, both amounts are included in the decedent's gross estate as interests in property.[83]

If a partnership does not terminate at the death of a partner and the estate becomes a partner in a continuing business, the value of the decedent's partnership interest is still to be included in the decedent's gross estate, and value then may be partially determined by the partnership's potential to earn future profits.[84] Under such an agreement, the decedent's right to future profits is not an interest in property to be separately included under Section 2033 because the decedent's estate is merely a continuing partner, which may not only share in profits but must also be liable for losses. A mere right to participate in a business is clearly distinguishable from a right to a portion of future earnings.[85]

[c] Limited Liability Companies

A decedent's interest in a limited liability company is similarly a business property interest included in the gross estate. A limited liability company has been described as "a cross between a close corporation and a limited partner-

---

[82] Estate of Riegelman v. Comm'r, 253 F2d 315 (2d Cir. 1958); McClennen v. Comm'r, 131 F2d 165 (1st Cir. 1942); Rev. Rul. 66-20, 1966-1 CB 214. Note the difficult practical problem of valuing such earnings. Winkle v. United States, 160 F. Supp. 348 (WD Pa. 1958). Cf. Estate of Davison v. United States, 292 F2d 937 (Ct. Cl.), cert. denied, 368 US 939 (1961), concerning related income tax questions. However, *interest* on such amounts, paid to the estate for a period during which distributions to the estate were delayed, has been held to be simply estate income and without estate tax significance. Mandel v. Sturr, 266 F2d 321 (2d Cir. 1959).

[83] See Estate of Lincoln v. Comm'r, 1 TCM (CCH) 326 (1942).

[84] Profit-making potential is a factor in valuing any continuing business interest. Reg. § 20.2031-3; Rev. Rul. 68-609, 1968-2 CB 327.

[85] Cf. Bull v. United States, 295 US 247 (1935). In general, *Bull* reached this conclusion. The rationale of the decision was that because the future profits would be taxed as estate income, their value could not also be subjected to the estate tax. Congressional rejection of such thinking is implicit in Section 691(c), which was enacted in 1942 *after* the *Bull* decision. *Bull* involved an interest in a services partnership that the Court concluded had no assets. Consequently, the Court held that the partnership interest had no value and nothing, other than the decedent's share of previously earned profits, was included in decedent's estate. Arguably, although the value of the future profits themselves should not have been separately included in the decedent's estate, the partnership interest itself would have some includable value because of its potential to earn future profits. See also Minskoff v. United States, 349 F. Supp. 1146 (SDNY 1972), aff'd per curiam, 490 F2d 1283 (2d Cir. 1974).

ship."[86] At present, every state and the District of Columbia has adopted legislation for the creation of such an entity.[87] In similar fashion to a corporation, the limited liability company protects its owners (called members) from the debts and liability of the entity. However, it also may have several traits of a partnership.[88] Overall, in many jurisdictions, limited liability companies may offer a variety of estate planning advantages over other business entities.[89]

[8] Compensation for Death

A decedent's death may be caused by the unlawful or wrongful conduct of another. At early common law, any cause of action the decedent had against the wrongdoer was ended by the decedent's death.[90] One statutory change that has been made in the common law takes the form of a "survival" statute[91] under which a decedent's rights against a tortfeasor can be enforced after death; the cause of action "survives." The English change in the early common law was effected by the enactment of Lord Campbell's Act.[92] Lord Campbell's Act and

---

[86] Willis, Pennell & Postlewaite, Partnership Taxation ¶ 2.06 (Warren, Gorham & Lamont, 5th Ed. 1995). See ¶ 4.02[4][g]. See also Bishop & Kleinberger, Limited Liability Companies: Tax and Business Law ¶ 8.04 (Warren, Gorham & Lamont 1994); Roche, Keatinge, & Spudis, "Limited Liability Companies Pass-Through Benefits Without S Corp. Restrictions," 74 J. Tax'n 248 (1991); Keatinge et al., "The Limited Liability Company: A Study of the Emerging Entity," 47 Bus. Law. 375 (1992); Gazur, "The Limited Liability Company Experiment: Unlimited Flexibility, Uncertain Role," 58 Law & Contemp. Probs. 135 (1995).

[87] See Scocca, "The 'Check-the-Box' Treasury Regulations: The Calm Before the Storm," 29 Rutgers L. J. 201, 204 n. 13 (1997).

[88] The Internal Revenue Service for many years was unclear whether a limited liability company should be treated as a partnership or a corporation for tax purposes. This issue was resolved, however, with the issuance of a revenue ruling, which held that a Wyoming limited liability company could be classified as a partnership. Rev. Rul. 88-76, 1988-2 CB 360. With the replacement of the formal classification tests by the "check-the-box" regulations, limited liability companies with more than one member are easily granted partnership status for federal tax purposes. See Reg. §§ 301.7701-1(a)(1), 301.7701-2(a), 301.7701-3(a), 301.7701-3(b)(1); Scocca, "The 'Check-the-Box' Treasury Regulations: The Calm Before the Storm," 29 Rutgers L. J. 201 (1997).

[89] See Caron, "Ten Estate Planning Advantages of Limited Liability Companies," 70 Tax Notes 998 (Feb. 19, 1996); Rothberg, "Estate Planning with Limited Liability Companies," 67 NY St. BJ 38 (1995); Hollingsworth, "The Optional Basis Adjustment Provides Another Tax Planning Advantage for LLC's," 2 J. Ltd. Liab. Cos. 114 (1995); Callison & Sullivan, Limited Liability Companies: A State-By-State Guide to Law and Practice, § 12.42 (West 1995).

[90] Prosser & Keeton, Law of Torts 940 (West 5th ed. 1984).

[91] Typical survival statutes are those of Connecticut and Iowa. See Conn. Gen. Stat. §§ 52-599, 52-555, 45(a)-448 (2000); Iowa Code §§ 611.20, 611.22, 633.336 (2000).

[92] Fatal Accidents Act of 1846, 9 & 10 Vict., ch. 93.

its later copies are called "wrongful death acts" and, in lieu of continuing the decedent's rights, they confer a fresh cause of action on survivors that may be enforced for their own benefit. It is well settled that rights to recover under such "wrongful death act" statutes do not represent any interest in property of the decedent under Section 2033, because it is rights of others, not the decedent, that may be enforced against the wrongdoer, even though such rights grew out of the decedent's death.[93]

Some early cases held that survival statute rights, since they were not terminated by death, constituted Section 2033 interests in property includable in the decedent's gross estate.[94] But more recent cases have refused to distinguish

---

[93] Maxwell Trust v. Comm'r, 58 TC 444 (1972), acq. 1973-2 CB 2; Rev. Rul. 54-19, 1954-1 CB 179. This includes survival benefits under no fault insurance. See Rev. Rul. 82-5, 1982-1 CB 131. Note, however, that a wrongful death claim then becomes an interest held by the survivor; if the survivor dies while the claim is outstanding, it is included in the survivor's estate at the value as of the date of the survivor's death. Estate of Houston v. Comm'r, 44 TCM (CCH) 284 (1982).

[94] This logical proposition was accepted in Connecticut Bank & Trust Co. v. United States, 330 F. Supp. 997 (D. Conn. 1971); the *Connecticut Bank* decision was reversed by the Second Circuit, 465 F2d 760 (2d Cir. 1972). The prior conflict between "survival" and "wrongful death act" statutes often resulted in interesting underlying conflict-of-laws questions that pointed up the importance of local law. In Maxwell Trust v. Comm'r, 58 TC 444 (1972), acq. 1973-2 CB 2, the decedent's death in a plane crash occurred in Japan due to the negligence of a Washington-based corporation. The decedent was an Iowa resident, but suit was brought in Illinois. The case was settled, but the Tax Court, in determining the decedent's estate tax consequence, concluded that if the Illinois court had rendered judgment, it would have applied Japanese law (wrongful death act) to allow recovery. According the same consequence to the settlement of the case, there was no inclusion under Section 2033. An application of Iowa law (survival act) would have involved enforcement of Section 2033 rights of the decedent with attending adverse tax consequences. In contrast, in *Connecticut Bank*, supra, the decedent was killed in Virginia as a result of the negligence of a New Jersey corporation; he was a resident of Connecticut, but suit, which was brought in New York, was settled without a trial. The district court, in determining the decedent's estate tax consequences, concluded that the New York court would have deferred to the state of domicile of the decedent and applied Connecticut law (survival act) to allow recovery. The settlement, therefore, represented a taxable Section 2033 interest of the decedent. The conflict-of-laws question was not an issue on appeal, but the Second Circuit reversed on the applicability of Section 2033. An interesting extension of the wrongful death exclusion was recognized in Revenue Ruling 68-88, 1968-1 CB 397, in which a recovery under the Virginia uninsured motorist act was excluded (after a determination that it was not life insurance under Section 2042) on the ground that it merely reflected rights to recover under the state's wrongful death statute.

There was a matter relating to survival-type statutes that had been given inadequate judicial and administrative consideration. Interests includable in a decedent's estate are to be identified at the date of death; they are likewise to be valued as of that time. See discussion of Section 2032 at ¶ 4.03 for alternate valuation dates. Therefore, if a decedent's death occurred under circumstances that gave rise to a right of recovery under a survival-type statute, the prior Section 2033 inclusion would be the somewhat speculative value at the time of the decedent's death of what *may* be recovered by suit or settlement in the

survival actions from wrongful death actions and have held that survival recoveries are not included in the decedent's gross estate under Section 2033.[95] The Commissioner has ruled that recoveries under survival statutes as well as wrongful death acts[96] are not includable in decedent's gross estate under Section 2033.[97] However, recoveries under survival statutes for a decedent's pain, suffering, or related expenses during the decedent's lifetime are not within the exclusion.[98]

The exclusion of wrongful death recoveries is supportable on the ground that the decedent never had an interest in the amounts recovered. It is likewise clear that, in general, the decedent could not control the disposition of the amounts recovered. These two factors are also characteristic of some death benefits payable outside the area of negligence or intentional torts, and they support a similar exclusion for post-death payments. Thus, a fairly early ruling excluded Social Security benefits payable to a decedent's widow and chil-

---

subsequent enforcement of the decedent's rights. This could well be much less (but possibly more) than what is ultimately recovered. However, there seems to be an uncritical assumption that the actual recovery fixes the amount to include. Connecticut Bank & Trust Co. v. United States, supra. See also Maxwell Trust v. Comm'r, supra, which expresses the same view of amounts recovered under a survival statute. Admittedly, to require a speculative valuation as of the date of death is awkward; but valuation difficulties are a generally accepted part of the administration of the federal transfer taxes. See Smith v. Shaughnessy, 318 US 176, 180 (1943), where valuation of a contingent remainder is discussed. But see Robinette v. Helvering, 318 US 184 (1942), in which an interest of uncertain value was ignored but only in a manner that worked against the taxpayer. The problem is discussed at ¶ 10.01[3][c]. For income tax purposes, purely speculative values are more likely to be ignored. See Burnet v. Logan, 283 US 404 (1931); Dorsey v. Comm'r, 49 TC 606 (1968). If the present statute presents a problem, legislative change might be considered; Congress could require a hindsight approach to require inclusion of what in fact was recovered. Cf. IRC § 2056, which permits a marital deduction for dower upon a post-death assertion of dower rights. Rev. Rul. 72-8, 1972-1 CB 309.

[95] Connecticut Bank & Trust Co. v. United States, 330 F. Supp. 997 (D. Conn. 1971); Lang v. United States, 356 F. Supp. 546 (SD Iowa 1973); Estate of Vanek v. United States, 1973-2 USTC ¶ 12,943 (SD Iowa 1973). The Second Circuit's theory in *Connecticut Bank & Trust Co.*, seemingly open to question, is that until death no rights arose that could represent property of the decedent under Section 2033 or property over which he had a Section 2041 power. It is arguable that *rights* arose at the time of the tort, although their *value* may have been affected by the decedent's death. See Goodman v. Granger, 243 F2d 264 (3d Cir.), cert. denied, 355 US 835 (1957); Keeter v. United States, 461 F2d 714 (5th Cir. 1972).

[96] Acq. in Maxwell Trust v. Comm'r, 58 TC 444 (1972), acq. 1973-2 CB 2. Cf. Rev. Rul. 54-19, 1954-1 CB 179.

[97] Rev. Rul. 75-126, 1975-1 CB 296; Rev. Rul. 75-127, 1975-1 CB 297. The rulings also state that there is no inclusion under Section 2041.

[98] Rev. Rul. 75-127, 1975-1 CB 296. Cf. Rev. Rul. 69-8, 1969-1 CB 219.

dren.[99] Similar results were later reached regarding payments under state workers' compensation acts,[100] the Federal Railroad Retirement Act,[101] and the Federal Coal Mine Health and Safety Act of 1969;[102] amounts paid under the Public Safety Officers' Benefit Act;[103] and allowances paid to survivors because of a decedent's death in the armed forces have likewise been excluded.[104] Seemingly a closer question, the same result has also been reached in instances in which a decedent employee has an agreement with an employer that if the employment relationship continued until the employee's death, the surviving spouse would be paid a fixed sum or an annuity. Although such payments have been held to be outside the reach of Section 2033,[105] the cases so holding deal only with circumstances in which the decedent had no interest in the payments, such as a contingent right to receive payments at a future time,[106] or any control over the determination of who was to receive the payments.[107]

As a matter of statutory interpretation, it is difficult to quarrel with the results reached regarding death benefits discussed here, whether they be based on tort, contract, or independent statutes such as workmen's compensation acts. Still, in some of these circumstances, perhaps especially those involving contractual employee death benefits but only less directly workers' compensation awards, the wealth enjoyed by survivors is traceable to the lifetime efforts of the decedent.[108] The question may be raised, therefore, whether Congress should differentiate death payments, taxing just those employee death benefits

---

[99] Rev. Rul. 67-277, 1967-2 CB 322. See Rev. Rul. 81-182, 1981-2 CB 179. See also Rev. Rul. 75-145, 1975-1 CB 298.

[100] Rev. Rul. 56-637, 1956-2 CB 600.

[101] Rev. Rul. 60-70, 1960-1 CB 372. Cf. Rev. Rul. 73-316, 1973-2 CB 318.

[102] Rev. Rul. 76-102, 1976-1 CB 272.

[103] Rev. Rul. 79-397, 1979-2 CB 322.

[104] Rev. Rul. 55-381, 1955-2 CB 381; Rev. Rul. 76-501, 1976-2 CB 267, involving death payments arising out of death while on active duty or from a service-connected disability.

[105] E.g., Hinze v. United States, 1972-1 USTC ¶ 12,842 (CD Cal. 1972); Harris v. United States, 1972-1 USTC ¶ 12,845 (CD Cal. 1972); Kramer v. United States, 406 F2d 1363 (Ct. Cl. 1959); Molter v. United States, 146 F. Supp. 497 (EDNY 1956). If the decedent had a right to receive payments during life, includability might turn on Section 2039, discussed infra ¶ 4.11. See Estate of Wadewitz, 339 F2d 980 (7th Cir. 1964); Estate of Bahen v. United States, 305 F2d 827 (Ct. Cl. 1962); Rev. Rul. 75-505, 1975-2 CB 364.

[106] In Goodman v. Granger, 243 F2d 264 (3d Cir.) cert. denied, 355 US 835 (1957), decedent had such an interest.

[107] See Harris v. United States, 1972-1 USTC ¶ 12,845 (CD Cal. 1972).

[108] See the judicial soul-searching in Estate of Porter v. Comm'r, 442 F2d 915 (1st Cir. 1971), properly decided for the government under Section 2035 but ranging over the other sections defining the gross estate as well. See also Note, "Employer-Financed Widow's Benefits—Definition of Transfer Extended," 1971 U. Ill. LF 343.

and similar awards traceable to the decedent's "good doing" and continuing to exclude wrongful death payments that emanate only from another's "wrong doing." The question is not rhetorical and, against initial impulse, the answer may well be no. Whether something should be subjected to estate tax raises more sophisticated questions than whether there is some rational basis for saying a decedent had an interest in it when the decedent died or that the decedent generated the wealth enjoyed by others after the decedent's death.

¶ 4.06 SECTION 2034. DOWER OR CURTESY INTERESTS

The important thing about Section 2034 is that it forecloses argument that a decedent's gross estate should be reduced by the value of a surviving spouse's dower or curtesy or similar interest in the decedent's property. Reaching fairly well back into estate tax antiquity,[1] Section 2034 is accorded the kind of unquestioned deference that used to be a right of old age, even though it has never received the expressed blessing of the Supreme Court. It has been sustained against constitutional attack by some lower courts,[2] and properly so, because whatever interest the survivor has by way of dower, curtesy, or some statutory equivalent, upon the decedent's death there is a ripening of the interest and a shifting of property rights from the decedent that is, and rather clearly can properly be, regarded as a suitable occasion for a federal excise, even one based essentially on the decedent's transmission of property at death.[3]

Most likely, the present language of Section 2033 would include the entire value of property owned by a decedent without reduction for a surviving spouse's dower or curtesy interest, which, at most, imposes conditional restrictions on disposition of property owned by the decedent; these restrictions, in turn, are not operative until the decedent dies and are never operative if the decedent's spouse predeceases. This reduces Section 2034 to a status of cautious redundancy.[4]

---

[1] The provision was first enacted in 1918. Revenue Act of 1918, Pub. L. No. 65-254, § 402(b), 40 Stat. 1051, 1097 (1918).

[2] E.g., Mayer v. Reinecke, 130 F2d 350 (7th Cir.), cert. denied, 317 US 684 (1942); United States v. Waite, 33 F2d 567 (8th Cir. 1929), cert. denied, 280 US 608 (1930); Allen v. Henggeler, 32 F2d 69 (8th Cir. 1929).

[3] E.g., Mayer v. Reinecke, 130 F2d 350 (7th Cir.), cert. denied, 317 US 684 (1942); United States v. Waite, 33 F2d 567 (8th Cir. 1929), cert. denied, 280 US 608 (1930); Allen v. Henggeler, 32 F2d 69 (8th Cir. 1929).

[4] This was not always so. Before there was an express provision on dower, the earliest forerunner of Section 2033 spoke in terms of the inclusion in the gross estate of property interests of the decedent that were "subject to the payment of charges against his

There may be a question of whether rights accorded to a surviving spouse are "dower or curtesy" or statutory rights in lieu thereof within the meaning of Section 2034.[5] The best general expression on this point seems to be: "It was the legislative intent by Section 2034 to tax only the inchoate interest of the surviving spouse which existed during the decedent's life, made consummate by the latter's death. . . . "[6] According to this view, "dower," as used in Section 2034, does not encompass a spouse's right to a child's share of the decedent's estate, considered not a substitute for dower for lack of any inchoate lifetime interest.[7] However, the current longer reach of Section 2033 renders such distinctions of little or no present importance. For the same reason, it is not now of much estate tax significance that some states have abolished dower and curtesy without providing any rights that are statutory estates in lieu thereof within the scope of Section 2034.[8]

This section, forbidding the exclusion of a surviving spouse's dower or curtesy or similar interest from the gross estate, does not necessarily mean that the interest will fully enter into the final determination of the estate's tax liability. When such an interest takes effect, it is treated as "passing" to the surviving spouse,[9] and so, subject to detailed considerations, it may be removed

---

estate and the expenses of its administration and . . . subject to distribution as part of his estate." Revenue Act of 1916, Pub. L. No. 64-271, § 202, 39 Stat. 756, 777 (1916). In any instance in which dower was protected against such expenses or charges or was not distributed as part of the estate, the surviving spouse's dower interest was thus excluded from the decedent's gross estate. Under such circumstances, estate tax liability was held to turn on whether the wife elected to take protected dower or received an unprotected interest under the will. Schuette v. Bowers, 40 F2d 208 (2d Cir. 1930). Moreover, after express provision for the inclusion of dower and curtesy was made in the Revenue Act of 1918, Pub. L. No. 65-254, § 402(b), 40 Stat. 1051, 1097 (1918), the restrictive language of the predecessor of Section 2033 continued until 1926. Revenue Act of 1926, Pub. L. No. 69-20, § 302(b), 44 Stat. 9, 70 (1926). Thus, the dower provision could still play an affirmative role. For example, if under state law a decedent's real property passed directly to his heirs or devisees, it was not "subject to distribution as part of his estate" and therefore escaped inclusion under the basic definition of the gross estate. However, under express language such as is now found in Section 2034, it is held that a surviving spouse's dower interest in such property is includable, even if it was not includable under the predecessor of Section 2033. Henderson v. United States, 18 F. Supp. 404 (Ct. Cl. 1937). And, under this language, it is immaterial whether she elected dower, took under the will, or asserted no rights whatever in the decedent's estate. Id.

[5] For a general discussion of dower, curtesy, and statutory rights in lieu thereof, see Atkinson, Law of Wills 105 n.6 (West 2d ed. 1953).

[6] Tait v. Safe Dep. & Trust Co., 3 F. Supp. 51, 58 (D. Md. 1933), aff'd, 70 F2d 79 (4th Cir. 1934).

[7] Tait v. Safe Dep. & Trust Co., 3 F. Supp. 51, 58 (D. Md. 1933), aff'd, 70 F2d 79 (4th Cir. 1934).

[8] See Atkinson, Law of Wills 108 (West 2d ed. 1953).

[9] IRC § 2056(c)(3).

from the taxable estate by way of the marital deduction allowed under Section 2056.[10]

Section 2034 must not be regarded as covering all property interests involving the marital relationship. For one thing, the rights of a surviving spouse with regard to jointly owned property are obviously outside the concept of dower or curtesy or any statutory equivalent and are unaffected by this section. Section 2033[11] and Section 2040[12] determine the extent to which joint property interests affect the gross estate. It is likewise clear that other interests created by the decedent, rather than by statute, are not covered by Section 2034, even though the interests are created in lieu of statutory rights.[13]

Furthermore, state community property laws are not statutory equivalents for common-law rules on dower or curtesy within the scope of this section. In many respects, the economic status of a spouse in a community property state is substantially similar to that of a spouse in a common-law state. But in the community property state each spouse does at least have an interest in the community property that can be disposed of by will regardless of which spouse dies first.[14] This has always been accepted as a differentiating factor, even though Congress has vacillated on the proper estate tax treatment of community property.[15]

The integrity of the statutory treatment of dower and curtesy interests under Section 2034 is protected by estate and gift tax rules regarding what may constitute consideration for a lifetime transfer or for an obligation incurred by the decedent for which the estate may claim a deduction.[16] -

---

[10] Rev. Rul. 72-7, 1972-1 CB 308; Rev. Rul. 72-8, 1972-1 CB 309. See ¶ 5.06.

[11] See ¶ 4.05[5][a].

[12] See ¶ 4.12, especially IRC § 2040(b) discussed at ¶ 4.12[10].

[13] Estate of Byram v. Comm'r, 9 TC 1 (1947), acq. 1947-2 CB 1. An inter vivos trust created by a decedent husband under an antenuptial agreement to satisfy his dower obligation to his wife was not included in the husband's estate.

[14] See Eisenstein, "Estate Taxes and the Higher Learning of the Supreme Court," 3 Tax L. Rev. 395, 536-561 (1948), for an illuminating discussion of community property in relation to estate tax.

[15] See Eisenstein, "Estate Taxes and the Higher Learning of the Supreme Court," 3 Tax L. Rev. 395, 536-561 (1948), for an illuminating discussion of community property in relation to estate tax. Compare IRC § 811(e)(2) (1939) with IRC §§ 2033, 2056 (1986), as discussed in this chapter and Chapter 5.

[16] See IRC §§ 2043(b), discussed ¶ 4.15[1]; 2053(c)(1)(A), discussed ¶ 5.03[5][e]; Merrill v. Fahs, 324 US 308 (1945).

¶ 4.07 SECTION 2035. ADJUSTMENTS FOR GIFTS MADE WITHIN THREE YEARS OF DECEDENT'S DEATH

[1] Introduction

For many years, the Section 2035 concepts of "contemplation of death" and "within three years of death" guarded the estate tax against nimble oldsters who sought to rid themselves of their wealth just in time so that when the estate tax collector came to exact what was due, the cupboard would be bare. The Commissioner had little success under the subjective "contemplation of death" test,[1] so Congress expanded the rule to an automatic three-year inclusion rule for all transfers in years after 1976.[2] In 1981, except for details that will be mentioned, Congress reversed course and retracted a significant portion of Section 2035.[3] However, this was not an act of congressional philanthropy.[4] When Congress largely merged the estate tax with the gift tax in 1976,[5] gifts entered the layering process that determines estate tax rates. The result is that if a transfer is subject to gift tax when made, it pushes increments of the estate into higher estate tax brackets, yielding a result much like an estate tax on at least the lifetime value of the gift, reduced by a credit for gift tax earlier paid. The most that can be said is "much like." This fiscal fornication puts two simple thoughts together to enlarge and complicate the transfer tax family. So there is much more to say here.

Current Section 2035[6] is essentially two disparate rules: (1) Subsection (a) is a limited class gross estate inclusion section subject to a series of exceptions and special rules found in Subsections (c) through (e);[7] and (2) Subsection (b) includes in the gross estate gift taxes paid on some lifetime transfers.[8]

---

[1] See Stephens, Maxfield & Lind, Federal Estate and Gift Taxation ¶ 4.07[7] (Warren, Gorham & Lamont, 4th ed. 1978), for a discussion of pre-1977 Section 2035. Prior to the substantial integration of the gift and the estate taxes in 1977, inclusion under Section 2035 carried more onerous consequences than under the integrated rules. Id. at ¶ 4.07[6].

[2] As amended, Section 2035(a), prior to 1982, generally included in a decedent's gross estate the date-of-death value of any property interest transferred by the decedent within three years of death. Tax Reform Act of 1976, Pub. L. No. 94-455, § 2001(e)(5), 90 Stat. 1525, 1848 (1976), reprinted in 1976-3 (Vol. 1) CB 1, 324.

[3] Economic Recovery Tax Act of 1981, Pub. L. No. 97-34, § 424(a), 95 Stat. 172, 317 (1981), reprinted in 1981-2 CB 256, 332.

[4] See infra ¶ 4.07[2][a] text accompanying notes 34–39.

[5] See ¶ 2.01[2].

[6] Current Section 2035 applies to decedents dying after 1981. Economic Recovery Tax Act of 1981, Pub. L. No. 97-34, § 424(a), 95 Stat. 172, 317 (1981), reprinted in 1981-2 CB 256, 332.

[7] See infra ¶ 4.07[2].

[8] See infra ¶ 4.07[3].

The first prong of Section 2035 is a product of piecemeal drafting. The rule is principally a composite of pre-1977 law,[9] amendments made by the Tax Reform Act of 1976,[10] further amendments made by the Economic Recovery Tax Act (ERTA) in 1981,[11] and a 1997 streamlining and clarification[12] of prior drafting. The end result is current Section 2035(a) and the exceptions and special rules related to it which are found in current Sections 2035(c) through (e). However, even after these congressional efforts, a firm grasp of Section 2035(a) can be achieved only by being familiar with the other Code sections that define the gross estate; accordingly, those sections should be examined prior to a detailed consideration of this section.[13]

The second prong of Section 2035 is Section 2035(b), which was originally enacted in 1976.[14] It performs the function of including in the decedent's gross estate gift taxes paid by the decedent or the decedent's estate on near-death transfers, regardless of whether the gifted property transferred is included in the decedent's gross estate.[15]

[2] The Section 2035(a) Rule (the First Prong)

[a] Section 2035(a) Inclusion

Section 2035(a) requires that property be pulled back into a decedent's gross estate if there is a transfer of an interest in property or the relinquishment of a power with respect to property inclusion and if the transfer or relinquishment is one that was made by the decedent within three years of death[16] for less than adequate and full consideration in money or money's worth.[17] But the section's scope is narrowed to apply only if the decedent transfers an interest or relinquishes a power over either (1) an insurance policy that, without the transfer or relinquishment, would have been included in the decedent's gross estate under Section 2042 or (2) an interest in property or power over property that, if not transferred or relinquished, would have required an amount to be

---

[9] IRC § 2035(d).

[10] IRC §§ 2035(a)(1), 2035(c)(3).

[11] IRC § 2035(a)(2).

[12] Taxpayer Relief Act of 1997, Pub. L. No. 105-34, § 1310(a), 111 Stat. 788, 1043 (1997), reprinted in 1997-4 CB 1457, 1735.

[13] See ¶¶ 4.05, 4.06, 4.08–4.14, 4.16.

[14] The Taxpayer Reform Act of 1976, Pub. L. No. 94-455, § 2001(a)(5), 90 Stat. 1520, 1848 (1976), reprinted in 1976-3 CB (Vol. 1) 324.

[15] See infra ¶ 4.07[3].

[16] IRC § 2035(a)(1).

[17] IRC § 2035(d).

included in the decedent's gross estate under Section 2036, Section 2037, or Section 2038.[18] Prior to the 1997 legislation, Section 2035(a) specifically referred only to transfers of property. The relinquishment of powers were treated as transfers of property under case law,[19] but they were not specifically referred to in the statutory language. The 1997 change clarifies Section 2035(a) to include such relinquishments.[20] However, in the discussion of the subsection when the text uses the term "*transfer*," the term encompasses both *transfers* of property and *relinquishments* of powers.

[i] **Section 2035(a)(1).** Transfers made more than three years before the decedent's death are explicitly outside the scope of Section 2035; however, no amnesty is provided for transfers that may be within other sections.[21] For Section 2035(a) to be applicable, the decedent must have made a transfer while alive and within three years of death. The courts look to local law to determine whether the decedent made a transfer. Once the transfer is established, the date the transfer was effective must be determined in order to establish whether the transfer was outside the three-year period. In general, the transfer occurs when the gift is complete for gift tax purposes.[22]

[ii] **Section 2035(a)(2).** Section 2035(a), prior to ERTA,[23] included in a decedent's gross estate the date-of-death value of *any* property interest transferred by the decedent within three years of the decedent's death.[24] Section 2035(a)(2), which applies to estates of decedents dying after 1981,[25] limits Section 2035(a) inclusions to transfers specifically listed in Section 2035(a)(2).

---

[18] IRC § 2035(a)(2).

[19] Cf. Rifkind v. United States, 5 Cl. Ct. 362 (1984). Since, for estate tax purposes, a decedent is deemed to own property over which certain powers are held (see IRC §§ 2036(a)(2), 2037(b)(2), 2038), a relinquishment of such powers is in essence a transfer of such property.

[20] IRC §§ 2035(a)(1), 2035(a)(2). Taxpayer Relief Act of 1997, Pub. L. No. 105-34, § 1310(a), 111 Stat. 788, 1043 (1997), reprinted in 1997-4 CB 1457, 1735.

[21] See, e.g., IRC § 2036, 2037, 2038. The three-year cut-off date under Section 2035 has been a part of the law since 1950.

[22] See discussion of Section 2511 at ¶ 10.01. See also infra ¶ 4.07[3][b].

[23] Economic Recovery Tax Act of 1981, Pub. L. No. 97-34, 95 Stat. 172 (1981), reprinted in 1981-2 CB 256.

[24] See supra ¶ 4.07[1] text accompanying note 2.

[25] Economic Recovery Tax Act of 1981, Pub. L. No. 97-34, § 424(a), 95 Stat. 172, 317 (1981), reprinted in 1981-2 CB 256, 332. A provision added by the Technical Corrections Act of 1982, Pub. L. No. 97-448, § 104(d)(3), 96 Stat. 2365, 2383 (1982), reprinted in 1983-1 CB 451, 460, applied to the estate of a decedent who died before August 13, 1984 having made gifts before August 13, 1981 that occurred within three years of the decedent's death and on which gift taxes were paid by August 16, 1982. The provision allowed the executor of the decedent's estate to elect to make the estate and gift tax amendments made by the Economic Recovery Tax Act of 1981 inapplicable to the dece-

Because of these limitations, very few transfers within three years of death are likely to be included in the decedent's gross estate under Section 2035(a) as it now applies, although when it does apply, the results are likely to be significant to the estate involved.

When Section 2035(a) applies, the overall effect on the determination of a decedent's gross estate is generally the same as including the appreciation on the transferred property which occurred between the date of transfer and the date of the transferor's death.[26] Congress concluded that inclusion of post-transfer appreciation on all gifts made within three years of death is generally unnecessary.[27] Outright transfers of property or cash that, if retained, would have been included in a decedent's gross estate under Section 2033 are unaffected by and not included under Section 2035(a). Nor do transfers of property that would otherwise be within the ambit of Section 2039, Section 2040, or Section 2041,[28] even if within three years of death, cause inclusion in a decedent's gross estate under Section 2035(a). Thus, Section 2035(a)(2) applies only if the interest transferred by the decedent was one that, had it been retained by the decedent, would have enlarged the decedent's gross estate under Section 2036, Section 2037, Section 2038, or Section 2042.

For example, if a donor gives a $100,000 face value insurance policy on the donor's life to a donee when it is worth $15,000, the fair market value of

---

dent. Regulations were to prescribe the manner in which the election was to be made. Once made, the election was irrevocable.

[26] Gift tax paid with respect to the transfer is also included in the gross estate under Section 2035(b). See infra ¶ 4.07[3].

[27] HR Rep. No. 201, 97th Cong., 1st Sess. 186–187 (1981), reprinted in 1981-2 CB 350, 390–391. Congressional leniency here may well have been motivated by the realization that Section 2035 inclusion would be coupled with a Section 1014 "stepped-up" basis in the property, while noninclusion would be coupled with a Section 1015 "carry-over" basis. See infra text accompanying notes 34–39.

[28] The 1981 enactment of Section 2035(a)(2) included Section 2041 general powers of appointment within the group of Code sections to which it applied. Section 2041 was appropriately deleted from Section 2035(a)(2) by the Technical Corrections Act of 1982, Pub. L. No. 97-448, § 104(d)(2)(B), 96 Stat. 2365, 2383 (1982), reprinted in 1983-1 CB 451, 460. The intent behind Section 2041 of the estate tax (and Section 2514 of the gift tax) is to equate general powers of appointment to outright ownership of property. If property were owned outright and transferred within three years of death, there would be no Section 2035 inclusion because Section 2033 is not listed within Section 2035(a)(2). Thus, the 1982 legislation, again equating general powers of appointment to outright ownership, appropriately deleted the reference to Section 2041 from Section 2035(a)(2).

But see IRC §§ 2041(a)(1)(B) and 2041(a)(2), which, under some circumstances, make Section 2035 applicable to general powers of appointment. For example, if a taxpayer held a general power of appointment and exercised it inter vivos retaining a life estate but transferring a remainder, and then, within three years of death, the taxpayer gave the retained life estate to the remainderperson, the property would be included in the taxpayer's gross estate. Inclusion would occur under Section 2041, however, and not under Section 2035.

the policy, $15,000, is subject to the gift tax. Had the donor retained the policy until death, the proceeds of $100,000 would have been included in the donor's gross estate under Section 2042. If the gift to the donee occurs within three years of the donor's death, Section 2035(a) operates to pull the life insurance policy back into the donor's gross estate at its fair market value on the date of the donor's death, the proceeds of $100,000. A transfer within three years of a decedent's death of property that, had it been retained until death, would have been included in the decedent's gross estate merely by reason of Section 2033 escapes inclusion under Section 2035(a). If, within three years of death, the donor merely gave $15,000 cash outright to the donee, that transfer would not be included in the donor's gross estate under Section 2035(a). This would be so even if the donee independently purchased an insurance policy on the donor's life. What if the donor purchased the policy in the donee's name, or gave the donee the money with the understanding that the donee would buy the policy, or the donee purchased the policy but the donor paid the $15,000 premium? Later in the text the interrelationship of Sections 2035 and 2042 is dealt with in more detail and the issues just raised are discussed.[29]

Section 2035(a)(2) speaks of "the value of . . . property (or an interest therein) [which] would have been included . . . under section 2036, 2037, 2038, or 2042 if such transferred interest . . . had been retained by the decedent on the date of his death." Sometimes the interest transferred within three years of death is identical to the property whose value is included in the decedent's gross estate. In the Section 2042 life insurance example stated earlier, the interest that is transferred, the life insurance policy, is the very property whose value would have been included had the transfer not occurred. This is also the case under Section 2038.[30]

With respect to other situations enumerated in Section 2035(a)(2), the interest that is transferred is not identical to the property included under Section 2035. For example, if a donor makes a transfer, retains a life estate, and holds the life estate until death, Section 2036(a)(1) pulls the entire trust corpus into the donor's gross estate.[31] If within three years of death the donor gratuitously transfers the life estate to the remainderperson or some other person, Congress intends Section 2035 to treat the transfer of the interest as not having been made and to include the entire trust corpus in the donor-decedent's gross estate under Section 2035(a).[32] The same type of analysis is applied where a rever-

---

[29] See ¶ 4.14[9][b]. Things become even more complicated if trusts or controlled corporations are used to carry out the listed transactions. Id. See also Estate of Kurihara v. Comm'r, 82 TC 51 (1984); Rev. Rul. 82-141, 1982-2 CB 209.

[30] See ¶ 4.10[8].

[31] See ¶ 4.08[8].

[32] See ¶ 4.08[8][b]. Although the question might be raised whether inclusion occurs under Section 2035 or Section 2036(a)(1), a proper interpretation of the statute requires inclusion under Section 2035. See also TAM 199935003 (May 19, 1999) (trustee's action

sionary interest that, but for the transfer, would have been included under Section 2037 is transferred by a decedent within three years of death. The amount of inclusion under Section 2035(a) is the same as the amount that would have resulted under Section 2037 had the transfer not been made.[33]

The benefits to be derived from elimination of most transfers from the scope of Section 2035(a) are largely illusory, and the statutory change may in some instances result in an overall estate-planning disadvantage. Under the current unified estate tax computation, noninclusion of a taxable gift in the decedent's gross estate generally means only that increases in value between the date of the gift and the date of death escape transfer taxation.[34] Since Section 2035 applies only to transfers within three years of death, even assuming appreciation of the property, it is only post-gift appreciation in value for a maximum period of three years that escapes taxation. In many situations this will not be of significant advantage to the estate. But enter the income tax! Because the property is not pulled into the gross estate, it retains its Section 1015 transferred basis, as opposed to a Section 1014 fair market value basis, for income tax purposes.[35] This can result in a significant income tax disadvantage if, at the time of the donor's death, the gift property had a value substantially higher than its income tax basis at the time of the gift.[36]

The difference in income tax bases may provide the rationale for the current scope of Section 2035(a). Section 2035(a)(2) includes property where there is a strong possibility of a substantial post-gift appreciation in value,

---

in commuting a trust constituted a transfer by decedent of a retained life estate triggering Section 2035(a)(2)).

[33] See ¶ 4.09[6].

[34] Under the current estate tax computation, any substantial lifetime gift may affect estate tax liability. Review the computation method prescribed by Section 2001(b). The questions are (1) whether the lifetime gift merely affects estate tax *rates* by reason of inclusion in the tax base at its date of *gift* value as a part of "adjusted taxable gifts" or (2) whether it affects estate tax by increasing the *gross estate*, and hence the "taxable estate," which relates to the death value of the property. A simplified answer is that most lifetime gifts after 1976 merely work to push the estate up the rate table. But if a gift is included in the gross estate, then post-gift fluctuations in value are taken into consideration in measuring not just the rates, but the amounts to which the rates apply.

[35] But see IRC § 1014(c), 1014(e).

[36] For example, assume a terminally ill donor has some highly appreciated property the donor wishes to give to the donor's children *right now*, but the donor wants them to take it with a Section 1014 basis. Rather than transferring the property outright to them, the donor might first retain a life estate in the property (see IRC § 2036) and subsequently relinquish the interest so as to trigger Section 2035 inclusion in the donor's gross estate. Of course, the substance of the transaction doctrine might be employed to telescope the transfers into a transfer not within Section 2035(a)(2).

Section 2035

such as under Section 2042[37] or Section 2038,[38] or where the property pulled into the gross estate differs from (i.e., is substantially greater than) the interest that was transferred, such as under Sections 2036 and 2037.[39] Congress continues to apply Section 2035 and allow a Section 1014 fair market value basis where there is a strong possibility of significantly increased estate tax inclusion, but has eliminated inclusion in return for a Section 1015 transferred basis where the likelihood of increased estate tax inclusion is less.

[b] Exceptions to Section 2035(a) Inclusion

[i] **Section 2035(d): bona fide sales.** Section 2035 is essentially aimed at gratuitous transfers. If, in connection with a transfer, the decedent receives full consideration in money or money's worth, then the transfer amounts only to a substitution or exchange of assets, the gross estate is not reduced, and no estate tax is avoided.[40] The Section 2001(b)(1)(A) element in the estate tax computation, the "taxable estate," is unaffected by such a transfer, since the potential taxable estate is the same immediately after as immediately before the transfer. Therefore, Section 2035(d) removes from the scope of Section 2035(a) a bona fide sale for an adequate and full consideration in money or money's worth. When there is a sale for partial consideration in money or money's worth, Section 2035(d) is inapplicable and Section 2043(a) provides some inclusion relief.[41]

---

[37] See the example supra text accompanying note 29.

[38] Under Section 2038, there is a possibility that an interest that was subject to the decedent's power of alteration might sizably increase as a result of the decedent's death. For example, assume a decedent grantor *G* created a trust with income to *A* for *G*'s life, then a remainder to *B* if *A* predeceased *G* and, if not, a remainder to *C*, but *G* could substitute another for *C*. If, within three years of death, *G* relinquished the power to alter *C*'s interest, *G* would make a taxable gift of the value of the remainder, which would have significantly less value than the value of the entire corpus. However, the value of the remainder subsequently pulled into *G*'s estate under Section 2035(a) would include the full value of the corpus.

A question may be raised as to why Section 2035(a)(2) includes Section 2038, since Section 2038 would include the remainder even without the application of Section 2035. See IRC §§ 2038(a)(1), 2038(a)(2), both referring to relinquishment of such powers within three years of death.

[39] See supra text accompanying notes 31–33.

[40] But see Estate of Musgrove v. United States, 33 Fed. Cl. 657 (1995) (a loan to a son within one month of lender's death in exchange for an unsecured demand note, that was canceled at death, was not treated as transferred). Cf. IRC § 691(a)(5).

[41] IRC § 2043(a); ¶ 4.15[2].

The statute does not specify what constitutes "adequate" consideration.[42] Moreover, the statute does not precisely say for what the decedent must receive full consideration. Where the interest transferred and the property included are the same, no problem is presented. For example, if a decedent transfers a $100,000 insurance policy on the decedent's life worth only $15,000 at the time of the transfer in return for a cash payment of $15,000, the Section 2035(d) exception is applicable. The same may not be said where the interest transferred and the property included are not identical.[43] What if the interest transferred is a Section 2036(a)(1) retained life estate worth $15,000 in a trust with a corpus of $100,000? Is a $15,000 cash payment adequate consideration? The estate tax answer should be no! When confronted with this problem, a court created an estate tax ownership concept requiring consideration equal in value to the potential estate tax inclusion.[44] Thus, the $15,000 received represents only partial consideration,[45] and the date-of-death value of the trust property (here, assume it is still $100,000)[46] less the consideration received ($15,000) is included.[47] In prior editions of this book, the authors applauded the result but suggested that Congress should tidy up the statute.[48] Congress amended the statute but failed to indicate either approval or disapproval of the prior judicial result. The courts should continue to observe this judicial gloss on the statutory language of Section 2035(d).

[ii] **Section 2035(e): certain transfers from revocable trusts.** For years, there was controversy whether inter vivos gifts from revocable trusts within three years of the grantor's death were to be included in the grantor's gross estate under Section 2035(a).[49] Section 2035(e) resolves this controversy by mak-

---

[42] See Mauck v. United States, 85-2 USTC ¶ 13,631 (D. Kan. 1985), where adequate consideration was not present under "old" Section 2035.

[43] See supra ¶ 4.07[2][a] text accompanying notes 31–33.

[44] United States v. Allen, 293 F2d 916 (10th Cir. 1961).

[45] Cf. IRC § 2043(a); ¶ 4.15[2].

[46] Measurement of adequate and full consideration ought to be based on the property potentially included in the gross estate valued at the time of the gift transfer. Under Section 2036, this is the corpus of the trust less any unrelated outstanding life estates; similarly, under Section 2037, this would include the trust corpus less any unrelated interests.

[47] IRC § 2043(a). See United States v. Allen, 293 F2d 916 (10th Cir. 1961).

[48] See Stephens, Maxfield & Lind, Federal Estate and Gift Taxation ¶ 4.08[8][b] (Warren, Gorham & Lamont, 4th ed. 1978). See also ¶ 4.08[8][b].

[49] If the trustees of the trust could invade trust corpus only for the grantor's benefit, then it was as though the transfer was made from the trust to the grantor and then by the grantor outright to the third party, with the result that the predecessor of Section 2035(a)(2) would not apply and there was no gross estate inclusion. Jalkut v. Comm'r, 96 TC 675 (1991), acq. 1991-2 CB 1; Estate of Collins v. United States 94-1 USTC ¶ 60, 162 (ED Mich. 1994); Estate of Frank v. Comm'r, 69 TCM (CCH) 2255 (1995) (invasion for grantor by son using power of attorney). The result was consistent with the govern-

ing Section 2035 (as well as Section 2038) inapplicable[50] to "any transfer from any portion of a trust during any period that such portion was treated under section 676 [the revocable grantor trust rule] as owned by the decedent by reason of a power in the grantor."[51] The rule treats all such transfers as being made directly by the decedent. Although Section 2035(e) speaks of "transfers" from a portion of a trust, it should also apply if a transferor relinquishes a power to revoke all or a part of the corpus of a trust.[52] This provision does not totally gut the interaction of Section 2035 with Section 2038; Section 2035 still interacts with Section 2038 where a Section 2038 power other than a power to revoke is relinquished within three years of a decedent's death.[53]

---

ment's position in a series of private letter rulings: TAM 9010005 (Nov. 17, 1989), TAM 9010004 (Nov. 17, 1989) and TAM 9017002 (Jan. 5, 1990) (all resulting in no inclusion). Whereas, if the trustees had the power to invade corpus for third parties as well as the grantor, then the transfer was deemed to be made directly from the trust and Section 2035(a)(2) applied to include the transfer in the grantor's gross estate. TAM 9015001 (Dec. 29, 1989), TAM 9016002 (Dec. 29, 1989) and TAM 9049002 (Aug. 29, 1940) TAM 9226007 (Feb. 28, 1992) (resulting in inclusion).

The latter result seemed to be avoided even though the trustee had broader powers if the property were removed from the trust, titled in grantor's name, and then gifted to the donee, or if the donor retained the power to designate in writing the persons who would receive such property. McNeely v. United States, 16 F3d 303 (8th Cir. 1994). Cf. Estate of Barton v. Comm'r, 66 TCM (CCH) 1547 (1993). See Klimczak, "Gift Giving and Revocable Trusts—The Right Way and the Wrong Way," 22 Tax Adv. 422 (1991).

[50] Section 2035(e) also makes Section 2038 inapplicable in such circumstances. See ¶ 4.10[8] text accompanying notes 87–91. Section 2035(e) applies to estates of decedents dying after August 5, 1997. The Taxpayer Relief Act of 1997, Pub. L. No. 105-34, § 1310(c), 111 Stat. 788, 1044 (1997), reprinted in 1997-4 CB 1457, 1736.

[51] The rule disregards Section 672(e), under which, for income tax purposes, the grantor is deemed to hold a power to revoke because the grantor's spouse holds such a power.

[52] See Estate of Kisling v. United States, 32 F3d 1222 (8th Cir. 1994), acq. 1995-2 CB 1, holding Section 2035 inapplicable where the grantor of a trust relinquished a power to revoke a portion of the trust within three years of grantor's death and HR Rep. No 105-220, 105th Cong. 1st Sess. 330, 717 (1997), reprinted in 1997-4 CB 1457, 2187, stating that Section 2035(e) is "not intended to modify the result reached in the Kisling case." If Section 2035(e) were interpreted to apply only to actual transfers from the trust, other transactions would be forced to revert to the pre-Section 2035(e) form-over-substance approach discussed supra note 49. Cf. ¶ 4.07[2][a] text accompanying notes 19, 20.

[53] For example, if grantor, G, created an irrevocable trust with income to A for G's life and a remainder to B or C whomever G selected and, within three years of death, G relinquished the power over B and C's interests by splitting the remainder equally between them, either Section 2035(a) acting in conjunction with Section 2038 or Section 2038(a) acting alone would include the entire corpus in G's gross estate at G's death. See ¶ 4.10[8] text accompanying notes 85–91.

[c] The Amount to Be Included Under Section 2035(a)

As is true of all the sections defining the gross estate, Section 2035 does not speak simply of transferred property, but looks instead to interests in property that the decedent may have transferred during life.[54] Property interests brought into the gross estate by way of Section 2035 do not enjoy any exception from the standard rules on the time of valuation. The interests are to be valued as of the date of death or the alternate valuation date.[55] Valuation presents difficulties. For example, when an individual makes a gift within the reach of Section 2035, one cannot know how it may affect the tax liability of one's estate; in addition to uncertainty whether the gift itself may be included under Section 2035, if it is so included, the value will not be determinable until death.[56] Furthermore, questions can arise as to specifically what property is included under Section 2035. For example, assume that a decedent transfers property to a trust within three years of death, that Section 2035 applies to the transfer, and that the trustee sells the property originally transferred and reinvests the proceeds prior to the decedent's death. The issue is whether the original property or that acquired upon reinvestment is to be valued. This issue is resolved by considering the purposes of Section 2035. Remember that, as modified by Section 2035(a)(2), Section 2035(a) operates to treat certain transfers within three years of death as if they had not occurred if, had they actually not occurred, there would have been inclusion of the property in the transferor's gross estate under Section 2036, Section 2037, Section 2038, or Section 2042.[57] Thus, Section 2035(a) should result in inclusion in the decedent's gross estate of an amount commensurate with that required to be included by Section 2036, Section 2037, Section 2038, or Section 2042 if the transfer that made them inoperable had not occurred.

For example, if a decedent, within three years of death, transfers an insurance policy on the decedent's life to a donee and the donee sells this policy and reinvests the proceeds, it is the value of the policy at the decedent's death, the proceeds payable on the policy, that should be included in the decedent's gross estate. Admittedly, there are three possible amounts of inclusion under these circumstances: (1) the value of the policy at the date of the decedent's death; (2) the sale price of the policy; or (3) the value of the subsequently acquired property at the date of the decedent's death.

---

[54] See supra ¶ 4.07[2][a] text accompanying notes 31–33.

[55] See IRC § 2031, 2032; ¶¶ 4.02, 4.03; Reg. § 20.2035-1(e). Cf. IRC § 2032A, discussed ¶ 4.04.

[56] This difficulty is minimized by the three-year rule and by state statutes apportioning the tax burden, to which reference is made in the discussion of Section 2205 at ¶ 8.04.

[57] See supra ¶ 4.07[2][a][ii].

In comparable circumstances involving an outright transfer of property, the Service has ruled that the first alternative is the proper result relying on the language of the statute.[58] The same result is reached with respect to inclusions under Section 2035(a) of Sections 2036-, 2037-, and 2038-type transfers. Again, the statute seems to justify the result, which is consistent with congressional policy. The congressional intent of Section 2035(a) is to apply Sections 2036 through 2038 as if no Section 2035 transfer had occurred, and it is in keeping with congressional policy simply to include that particular property over which the decedent had held the interest or power. Because no power or interest is held at death (it is relinquished within three years of death), the property included and valued should not be the property owned at death but rather the property over which the decedent held a power or interest.[59] Thus, the property held at the time of the Section 2035 transfer should be included at its date-of-death value.

The gross estate does not include income earned by the property after the gift is made, even if the income is added to the corpus of a trust that was created within the three-year period, provided the decedent had no interest whatsoever in or control over the income when the decedent died.[60] This may not quite accord with the idea expressed above that Section 2035 is intended to make the transferred property cause the same estate tax result as if the decedent had kept it until death; if the decedent had kept the property, the income might have enlarged the decedent's estate. Nevertheless, all the decedent could transfer was the decedent's interest in the property; and, if the decedent never

---

[58] Rev. Rul. 72-282, 1972-1 CB 306. Although the statutory language has been amended, the current language would reach the same result. See also Estate of Humphrey v. Comm'r, 162 F2d 1 (5th Cir.), cert. denied, 332 US 817 (1947). The ruling and *Humphrey* involve outright transfers of property under pre-1982 law, but there is no conceptual or other reason why a different result should apply to a transfer of a life insurance policy, and indeed the ruling hints at no such distinction.

[59] When a transfer is to a trust, it may be tempting to think that it is relatively easy to trace the property originally transferred into other assets that make up the fund at the critical date of death. This would support the application of alternative (3) in the text. Actually, as explained later, trust income would have to be excluded, and, if the trustee has made discretionary distributions out of corpus or has acquired new property with accumulated income, identification of assets becomes very difficult. Thus, practical reasons for a different rule for trusts in this setting are lacking, just as are conceptual reasons for the strict language of the statute. A different result is justified where Sections 2036 through 2038 operate independently from Section 2035. See ¶ 4.10[10].

[60] Burns v. Comm'r, 177 F2d 739 (5th Cir. 1949); Estate of Frizzell v. Comm'r, 9 TC 979 (1947), acq. 1966-1 CB 2. Compare the discussion of what constitutes income for purposes of Section 2032. See ¶ 4.03[2]. However, income earned after a transfer taxed under Section 2036 or Section 2038 may present a difficult problem. See United States v. O'Malley, 383 US 627 (1966). An aging article that deals with problems of this sort is Lowndes & Stephens, "Identification of Property Subject to the Estate Tax," 65 Mich. L. Rev. 105 (1966).

had an interest[61] in the income earned after the gift, it could not have been the subject of a taxable transfer by the decedent.

Any increase in value that results from improvements made by the donee after the gift need not be included in the decedent's gross estate.[62] Post-transfer stock dividends, even if payable before the transferor's death, at least if they represent a capitalization of post-transfer earnings, are not includable in the gross estate.[63] On the other hand, shares received in a post-transfer stock split are clearly includable. The in-between problems are not settled and are not precisely answerable under the present statute.[64]

As an illustration of the difficulties with Section 2035 in determining the amount includable, suppose a donor makes a transfer of an interest in property that results in inclusion in the donor's gross estate under Section 2035(a) of the corpus of a trust. Suppose the corpus is a valuable tract of timber and between the time of the transfer and the decedent's death the trustee sells the timber for $10,000 but retains the land. What is includable in the gross estate? To limit the amount to the date-of-death value of the denuded realty would open an obvious avenue for estate tax avoidance. To value the land as if the trees were still on it would be more supportable but would produce an irksome valuation question. As there is some authority for including the value of what was received by way of conversion of the original gift property,[65] perhaps the best result would be to include the value of the denuded realty plus the $10,000 cash received by the trustee.

Section 2035 may apply to shared property. For example, where the decedent owned property in joint tenancy or as community property and the property was transferred to a third person subject to a retained life estate in the decedent, and then within three years of the decedent's death the life estate was also transferred, only the value of the decedent's fractional interest in the property is included in the gross estate and not the value of the interest transferred by the co-owner.[66]

---

[61] This is not an appropriate place for application of an estate tax ownership concept. But see United States v. O'Malley, 383 US 627 (1966), ¶ 4.08[8][a].

[62] Estate of McGhee v. Comm'r, 260 F2d 818 (5th Cir. 1958). Cf. Reg. § 20.2032-1(d)(4). But see Estate of Schlosser v. Comm'r, 277 F2d 268 (3d Cir.), cert. denied, 364 US 819 (1960); Rev. Rul. 80-336, 1980-2 CB 271.

[63] See Lowndes & Stephens, "Identification of Property Subject to the Estate Tax," 65 Michigan L. Rev. 105 (1966).

[64] Reg. § 20.2035-1(e).

[65] See Estate of Dewitt v. Comm'r, 68 TCM (CCH) 1136 (1994). See also, Estate of Kroger v. Comm'r, 145 F2d 901 (6th Cir. 1944), cert. denied, 324 US 866 (1945).

[66] Estate of Sullivan v. Comm'r, 175 F2d 657 (9th Cir. 1949); Estate of Borner v. Comm'r, 25 TC 584 (1955), acq. 1969-2 CB xxiii (see also 1962-1 CB 4; 1957-2 CB 4); Estate of Brockway v. Comm'r, 18 TC 488 (1952), acq. 1969-2 CB xxiv (see also 1962-1 CB 4; 1955-2 CB 4), aff'd on other issues, 219 F2d 400 (9th Cir. 1954).

Transactions within three years of death relating to transfers with life interests retained, to transfers taking effect at death, to alterable transfers, and to transfers of life insurance are dealt with further in the discussions of Sections 2036, 2037, 2038, 2041,[67] and 2042, respectively.[68]

[d] Special Applications of the Section 2035(a) Rule

Although Section 2035(a)(2) limits inclusion in the gross estate under Section 2035(a), it does not limit inclusion in the gross estate under Section 2035(a) for all purposes. Section 2035(c)(1) sometimes makes Section 2035(a)(2) inoperative. It requires *all* transfers within three years of death (other than those made in a bona fide sale for adequate and full consideration)[69] to be included in the gross estate under Section 2035(a)[70] for purposes of applying Section 303(b) (relating to stock redemptions),[71] Sections 2032A (relating to special-use valuation),[72] and 6321 through 6326 (relating to liens for taxes).[73] However, any Section 2035(a) transfer (other than a transfer of a life insurance policy) is excepted from the Section 2035(c)(1) rules if the transfer is a de minimis transfer for which no gift tax return is required by Section 6019(1).[74]

Section 2035(c)(2) goes even further to impose a dual test (both using Section 2035(a) and making it inoperative) for purposes of meeting the 35 percent of the adjusted gross estate test of Section 6166(a)(1) (relating to extension of time for payment).

---

[67] See supra ¶ 4.07[2][a] note 28 for possible inclusion under Section 2041 as opposed to Section 2035, although Section 2041 may act in conjunction with Section 2035.

[68] See ¶¶ 4.08[8], 4.09[6], 4.10[9], 4.14[7].

[69] IRC § 2035(d). This is an appropriate result, although one which is difficult to read into the current statutory scheme. It was the result under the prior statute. See Stephens, Maxfield, Lind & Calfee, Federal Estate and Gift Taxation, ¶ 4.07[2][a] text accompanying notes 40, 41 (Warren, Gorham & Lamont, 7th ed. 1996).

[70] The constructive expansion of the gross estate applies only for purposes of the estate's qualification for benefits offered by these sections. See HR Rep. No. 97-201, 97th Cong., 1st Sess. 187 (1981), reprinted in 1981-2 CB 352, 390.

[71] IRC § 2035(c)(1)(A).

[72] IRC § 2035(c)(1)(B).

[73] IRC § 2035(c)(1)(C). See Armstrong v. Comm'r, 114 TC 94 (2000) (predecessor of Section 2035(c)(1)(C) applied to hold recipients of gifts within three years of donor's death liable for transferee liability).

[74] IRC § 2035(c)(3). Although a transfer under Section 6019(3) to a charity for which no gift tax return is required to be filed would also literally fall within the exception (which only excludes Section 6019(2) transfers), the failure to also exclude transfers covered by Section 6019(3) from the exception appears to be a legislative error unintended by Congress. A technical correction should be made.

[3] The Section 2035(b) Rule (the Second Prong)

[a] The Gift Tax Gross-Up Rule

Prior to the Tax Reform Act of 1976, even if lifetime taxable gifts were pulled into the donor's gross estate under Section 2035, an estate tax saving often occurred because the gross estate was reduced by the amount of any gift tax paid on the transfer. Not surprisingly, if a bit gruesome, these gifts were often "death bed transfers." The tax saving resulted because only the value of the gift was included in the decedent's gross estate, not the gift tax paid or payable on the gift.[75]

In the Tax Reform Act of 1976, Congress enacted current Section 2035(b) to close this loophole as to taxes paid on gifts after 1976 made within three years of death. The provision requires the federal gift tax paid by the decedent or the decedent's estate on *any* transfers made after 1976 by the decedent or the decedent's spouse within three years of the decedent's death to be included in the decedent's gross estate. The inclusion of the tax is a "gross-up" of the gift tax.[76] As the introduction suggests, Section 2035(b) may well be looked upon as an entirely separate section, because Section 2035(b) is operative regardless of whether the gift subject to the tax is included in the decedent's gross estate.

The Section 2035(b) gross-up is affected by the gift-splitting provision of Section 2513.[77] If a *decedent's spouse makes a transfer*, the spouses elect gift-splitting, and the decedent dies within three years, the tax the decedent paid will be pulled into the decedent's estate under Section 2035(b), even though there is, of course, no basis for including any part of the value of the property the spouse transferred in the decedent's estate.[78] Section 2035(b) is express on this, because, without this rule, a collateral death bed transfer could occur; a survivor's gift could effect an artificial reduction in the decedent's gross estate. Further, if the decedent pays all the tax on a split-gift transfer made by spouse, no gift to the decedent's spouse results,[79] but the full gift tax is included in the

---

[75] The savings, of course, rested in part on the Section 2012 credit against the estate tax for tax paid on the gift. For a more complete discussion of the "death bed transfer" device, see Stephens, Maxfield & Lind, Federal Estate and Gift Taxation, 4-73 (Warren, Gorham & Lamont, 3d ed. 1974).

[76] The fact that the gift tax is paid after the decedent's death by the decedent's estate does not preclude a "gross-up." Section 2035(b) expressly applies to federal gift taxes paid by the decedent or the decedent's estate.

[77] See ¶ 10.03.

[78] Rev. Rul. 82-198, 1982-2 CB 206.

[79] See Reg. §§ 25.2511-1(d), 25.2513-4.

decedent's estate.[80] If the *decedent makes a transfer* and gift splitting is elected and the decedent pays the full amount of the tax on the entire transfer, the full tax is again pulled into the decedent's estate. These literal results under the statute are essential to prevent artificial diminution of the decedent's estate. Under similar reasoning, the amount of gift tax paid by a decedent's spouse on transfers split under Section 2513 is not included in the decedent's gross estate because such payments do not reduce the decedent's gross estate.[81]

One method of making gifts has been to make net gifts, where, by agreement, the donee pays the donor's gift tax liability, effectively reducing the amount that the donor is treated as transferring to the donee as a gift.[82] In substance, the transaction involves in part a gift by the donor and in part a tax payment made indirectly by the donor arising out of a single transfer to the

---

[80] See TAM 9729005 (April 9, 1997) (where an individual made a gift to his spouse of the amount of the gift tax which the spouse then used to pay the gift tax due on a gift that had been split by the couple, the Service asserted substance over form and concluded that the gift tax was actually paid by the individual and was includable in the individual's gross estate under Section 2035(b)).

[81] If the decedent was the donor of a gift made after December 31, 1976, required to be included in the decedent's gross estate, one half of which was considered as made by the decedent's spouse, generally any tax paid by the spouse reduces the Section 2001(b)(1) tentative estate tax under Section 2001(b)(2). See IRC § 2001(d). This is so even though the amount of the gift tax paid by the surviving spouse is not included in the decedent's gross estate and occurs even when the spouse pays the entire tax on the split gift. If there is a problem here, it is with the potential gross estate of the survivor; the decedent's gross estate is not reduced by gift tax paid by the survivor. After the 1976 legislation was enacted, a problem appeared regarding correlation of the Section 2035(b) gross-up and the Section 2513 gift-splitting provision. If a spouse's gift was attributed one half to the other spouse under Section 2513, that portion would surface as a part of adjusted taxable gifts under Section 2001(b)(1)(b) upon death of the nondonor spouse. But the *entire* gift might already have formed a part of the donor spouse's taxable estate by reason of Section 2035. Obviously, this should not be; so Congress enacted Section 2001(e) to remove the attributed portion from the adjusted taxable gifts of the nondonor spouse in these circumstances. Logically, tax paid on that portion is also not to be a part of Section 2001(b)(2) gift tax payable in computing tax on the nondonor's estate, as the statute also expressly provides. Thus, even though the decedent paid the tax that is included in the decedent's estate under Section 2035(b), in this situation it is not deemed a tax paid by the decedent for purposes of Section 2001(b)(2). See Rev. Rul. 82-198, 1982-2 CB 206. As framed, the statute seems to create a problem if the nondonor spouse dies first; at that juncture, the questionable portion of the split gift will not be "includible in the gross estate of the decedent's spouse by reason of section 2035." The remedial provision is given full effect if the donor spouse dies before the estate tax return of the other is filed or by way of a refund in other cases. Rev. Rul. 81-85, 1981-1 CB 452. The critical question will always be resolved within the presumptive three-year limitation period for filing refund claims. IRC § 6511(a). See also ¶¶ 2.01[1][b] note 20, 2.01[2] note 59.

[82] See ¶ 10.02[6][d]. This may result in adverse income tax consequences to the donor. Diedrich v. Comm'r, 457 US 191 (1982). See Lefter, "Income Tax Consequences of Encumbered Gifts: The Advent of *Crane*," 28 U. Fla. L. Rev. 935 (1977).

donee. If the donor dies within three years of such a transfer, the gift tax should be pulled into the decedent's gross estate under Section 2035(b). It is fair to say the tax is paid "by the decedent" within Section 2035(b).[83] A similar issue also arises if gift tax paid by a surviving spouse is recovered under Section 2207A(b). This payment, too, should be treated as gift tax paid by the surviving spouse for purposes of Section 2035(b).[84] The person from whom the surviving spouse recovers the gift tax under Section 2207A(b) should not be treated as having paid gift tax for purposes of Section 2035(b).

[b] Gifts Made Within Three Years of Death

Questions can be raised as to the date a taxable gift was effective in order to determine whether the transfer was outside the Section 2035(b) three-year period. In general, the transfer occurs when the gift is complete for gift tax purposes.[85] For instance, the date of the execution of a deed to property has been held to be the date of transfer, even though the deed is not recorded until a later date.[86] In some situations, a transfer of land has been held to occur prior to transfer of actual legal title.[87] Delivery of stock certificates to the donee has been held to be a transfer of stock even though the stock is not transferred on the corporation's books until a later date.[88] However, execution of a power of attorney over a bank account is not a transfer of the funds in the account, and no transfer occurs until funds are actually disbursed from the account.[89] Similarly, no transfer of funds occurs in a joint bank account until there is a disbursement to the donee.[90]

---

[83] This result was reached in Estate of Sachs v. Comm'r, 88 TC 769 (1987).

[84] See ¶¶ 8.07[3], 8.07[4], ¶ 10.08[3].

[85] This can occur as a result of an actual transfer of an interest in property or a relinquishment of a power over property. See supra ¶ 4.07[2][a] text accompanying notes 19, 20; IRC § 2511, discussed at ¶ 10.01.

[86] Estate of Green v. Comm'r, 4 TCM (CCH) 286 (1945); Gerry v. Comm'r, 22 BTA 748 (1931), acq. X-2 CB 26. These cases involve situations in which state law did not require recording in order to transfer title. Cf. Estate of Raab v. Comm'r, 49 TCM (CCH) 662 (1985).

[87] Beeler v. Motter, 33 F2d 788 (D. Kan. 1928) (involving an oral gift of land under which donee took possession and made improvements prior to transfer of actual legal title). See also Mather v. McLaughlin, 57 F2d 223 (ED Pa. 1932).

[88] Cf. Grissom v. Sternberger, 10 F2d 764 (4th Cir. 1926); Estate of Connell v. Comm'r, 11 BTA 1254 (1928), acq. VII-2 CB 9; Stark Lavelle v. Comm'r, 8 BTA 1150 (1928), acq. VII-1 CB 30. But see Rev. Rul. 54-135, 1954-1 CB 205; Estate of Sawade v. Comm'r, 86-2 USTC ¶ 13,672 (8th Cir. 1986).

[89] Estate of Hite v. Comm'r, 49 TC 580 (1968).

[90] Estate of Zaiger v. Comm'r, 64 TC 927 (1975), acq. in result 1976-1 CB 1; Estate of Green v. Comm'r, 64 TC 1049 (1975), acq. in result 1976-2 CB 2; Haneke v. United States, 404 F. Supp. 98 (D. Md. 1975); Wilson v. Comm'r, 56 TC 579 (1971).

Stocks, bonds, and notes are not the only intangibles that can be the subject of a transfer taxed under the gift tax. Any contract right is property that may be the subject of such a transfer. There has never been any question that an insurance policy can be transferred in a manner resulting in the imposition of gift tax, and gift tax incurred on procurement of an insurance policy for another within three years of the purchaser's death results in the inclusion of the gift tax in the purchaser's gross estate at death.[91]

[4] Pre-1982 Section 2035 and Its Background

A provision pulling some completed inter vivos transfers into the gross estate has been in the estate tax statute since its inception in 1916.[92] The first provision and those that followed until 1926 contained a rebuttable presumption that gifts made within two years of death were made in contemplation of death, which was one of the criteria for inclusion.[93] A congressional effort in 1926 to strengthen the Commissioner's hand by making the presumption conclusive[94] was held unconstitutional by the Supreme Court in 1932[95] on the premise that to impose a tax on the basis of a factual assumption that the taxpayer is not permitted to rebut is so arbitrary as to offend the Fifth Amendment. Congress thereupon replaced the conclusive presumption with a rebuttable one.[96] In 1950, the rebuttable presumptive period was extended to three years, and a three-year cutoff date was added that precluded a finding of the requisite motive when that period had expired. The contemplation-of-death criterion and the three-year rebuttable presumption applied to transfers made through December 31, 1976.[97]

In 1976, Congress eliminated motive or intent as a criterion for inclusion under Section 2035; all tests for inclusion became objective for transfers after 1976.[98] Additionally, in 1976, Congress required inclusion in the gross estate

---

[91] Cf. Rev. Rul. 71-497, Situation 2, 1971-2 CB 329; Bel v. United States, 452 F2d 683 (5th Cir. 1971), cert. denied, 406 US 919 (1972). Cf. Porter v. Comm'r, 442 F2d 915 (1st Cir. 1971).

[92] Revenue Act of 1916, Pub. L. No. 64-271, § 202(b), 39 Stat. 756, 777 (1916).

[93] Revenue Act of 1916, Pub. L. No. 64-271, § 202(b), 39 Stat. 756, 777 (1916).

[94] Revenue Act of 1926, Pub. L. No. 69-20, § 302(c), 44 Stat. 9, 70 (1926).

[95] Heiner v. Donnan, 285 US 312 (1932).

[96] Revenue Act of 1932, Pub. L. No. 72-154, § 803(a), 47 Stat. 169, 279 (1932).

[97] For a discussion of the critical motive in the contemplation-of-death provisions, see Stephens, Maxfield & Lind, Federal Estate and Gift Taxation ¶ 4.07[7] (Warren, Gorham & Lamont, 4th ed. 1978).

[98] Tax Reform Act of 1976, Pub. L. No. 94-455, § 2001(a)(5), 90 Stat. 1520, 1848 (1976), reprinted in 1976-3 CB (Vol. 1), 324.

of gift taxes paid by the decedent or his estate on near-death transfers.[99] In 1981, Congress dramatically limited the scope of application of Section 2035(a).[100]

¶ 4.08 SECTION 2036. TRANSFERS WITH RETAINED LIFE ESTATE

Section 2036 is designed to prevent what would otherwise be a simple and effective device for the avoidance of estate tax. It has been explained previously that, if the decedent had a mere life estate or other life interest in property that expired at death, such an interest is not includable in the gross estate under Section 2033.[1] Thus, as far as that section is concerned, a person could gratuitously transfer property in trust, ridding the person of legal title, and yet retain the right to the income from the property for life without having one's estate suffer any estate tax liability with respect to the property upon death. This, of course, would be a real cake-and-eat-it scheme, but it is frustrated by Section 2036(a)(1). In general, this section includes in the gross estate the entire value of property so transferred by the decedent. Congress also looks disparagingly upon the similar situation where a decedent retains the mere power to determine who, other than oneself, will receive the income. In such a situation, Section 2036(a)(2) operates to pull the property over which the decedent held the power into the decedent's gross estate.

Section 2036 has been used more recently by Congress to avert other taxpayer cake-and-eat-it schemes. Section 2036(b) was added to the Code to treat transferors retaining voting rights in a corporation as retaining enjoyment of the corporation to include the stock of the corporation in decedent's gross estate under Section 2036(a)(1).[2]

---

[99] Tax Reform Act of 1976, Pub. L. No. 94-455, § 2001(a)(5), 90 Stat. 1520, 1848 (1976), reprinted in 1976-3 CB (Vol. 1), 324.

[100] See supra ¶¶ 4.07[2][a], 4.07[2][a][ii].

[1] See ¶ 4.05[5][b]. Beyond the estate tax frying pan, the IRC Chapter 13 fire threatens generation-skipping arrangements. See Chapters 12–18.

[2] See Stephens, Maxfield, Lind & Calfee, Federal Estate and Gift Taxation ¶ 4.08[9] (Warren, Gorham & Lamont, 6th ed. 1991) for a discussion of Section 2036(c) (prior to repeal in the Omnibus Budget Reconciliation Act of 1990, Pub. L. No. 101-508, § 11601(a), 104 Stat. 1388-1, 1388-490 (1990), reprinted in 1991-2 CB 481, 524) concerning estate freezes.

[1] Excluded Transfers

[a] Sales for Full Consideration

Section 2036 is inapplicable to a transfer which is "a bona fide sale for an adequate and full consideration in money or money's worth."[3] The value at the time of the transfer of the transferred interests that would be included in the gross estate if there were no consideration paid should be used as the measure to determine whether the consideration received is sufficient to negate Section 2036.[4] Thus, if A transfers property to R, retaining a life estate, a payment equal to the value of R's *remainder* interest should defeat the section. The rationale for stating that such a payment *should* defeat the section is that such a payment would not operate to deplete A's gross estate. This is due to the fact that if the proceeds paid for the remainder were invested at an interest rate equal to the rate assumed under the current tables at the time of the transfer,[5] and if A lived for a period of time equal to A's life expectancy, the value of the accumulated amount at A's death would equal the value of the corpus originally transferred. At death, A would hold the original value of the corpus and, in addition, would have received all the income from the corpus. Thus, there is no artificial diminution of A's estate such as Section 2036 seeks to proscribe.[6]

---

[3] IRC § 2036(a). The reason for this exclusion is the same as that discussed above concerning the similar exclusion from the provisions of Section 2035. IRC § 2035(d). See ¶ 4.07[2][b][i].

[4] At the time of the transfer, if A has retained a life interest, it diminishes the interest transferred to others and thus removed from A's estate. The retained interest is not consideration for the transfer and is also not a transferred interest.

[5] See Reg. §§ 20.2031-7(d)(7) Table S (for transfers after April 30, 1999); 20.2031-7A(e)(4) Table S (for transfers after April 30, 1989 and before May 1, 1999). See also IRS Notice 89-24, 1989-1 CB 660 (adopting actuarial tables for transfers after April 30, 1989); IRS Notice 89-60, 1989-1 CB 700; TD 8819, 1999-1 CB 1000 (adopting actuarial tables for transfers after Apr. 30, 1999).

[6] Some authors have agreed: See Moore, "The Use of Life Estates and Remainder Interests in Estate Planning," 19 U. Miami Est. Plan. Inst. Chapter 12 at ¶ 1201.2 (1985). See also the articles cited infra notes 7, 8.

This argument disregards any actual appreciation or depreciation which occurs in the transferred property whose value under this rationale is "frozen."

Recent cases[7] in the Court of Appeals in the Third,[8] the Fifth,[9] and the Ninth[10] Circuits have come to this conclusion and parsed Section 2036(a) to hold that the section is inapplicable where consideration is received in a bona fide sale

---

[7] Several prior community property widow's election cases have held that adequate and full consideration is received only if the amount paid as consideration equals or exceeds the entire value of the property (corpus) transferred. Estate of Gradow v. United States. 11 Cl. Ct. 808 (1987) (community property widow's election where transferor died within three years) aff'd, 897 F2d 516 (Fed. Cir. 1990); Estate of Gregory v. Comm'r, 39 TC 1012 (1963) (transfer in a community property widow's election where inadequate consideration was received under either test); United States v. Past, 347 F2d 7 (9th Cir. 1965) (transfer in a divorce settlement (not a community property widow's election) but which reached a comparable result). For a more detailed discussion of the community property widow's election, see infra ¶ 4.08[7][c]. One community property widow's election case appears to agree that full payment for the *remainder* interest satisfies the adequate consideration test. Estate of Christ v. Comm'r, 54 TC 493 (1970), aff'd, 480 F2d 171 (9th Cir. 1973). Cf. infra text accompanying notes 8–11. Several articles prior to the *D'Ambrosio* line of cases (see infra text accompanying notes 8–10) were critical of the *Gradow* result: see Jordan, "Sale of Remainder Interests: Reconciling Gradow v. United States and Section 2702," 14 Va. Tax Rev. 671 (1995); Horowitz, "Economic Reality in Estate Planning: The Case for Remainder Interest Sales" 73 Taxes 386 (1995); Pennell, "Cases Addressing Sale of Remainder Wrongly Decided," 22 Est. Plan. 305 (1995).

It can be argued that the community property widow's election cases are distinguishable from the cases infra notes 8–10, because there is *no bona fide sale* even though adequate and full consideration is received for the transferred interest. See infra ¶ 4.08[7][c] text accompanying notes 145, 146.

[8] Estate of D'Ambrosio v. Comm'r, 101 F3d 309 (3d Cir. 1996), cert. denied, 520 US 1230 (1997) (sale of a remainder interest to a closely held corporation for an annuity where the court (1) parsed the statute and interpreted the exception to apply to "property to the extent of any interest therein of which the decedent . . . has made a transfer" to refer only to the remainder interest that was transferred on the exchange and not the full fee simple interest and (2) used the time value of money approach used in the text to justify its statutory conclusion).

For articles discussing the *D'Ambrosio* line of cases, see Jensen, "Estate and Gift Tax Effects of Selling a Remainder: Have *D'Ambrosio, Wheeler* and *Magnin* Changed the Rules?" 4 Fla. Tax Rev. 537 (1999); Connolly, "Estate of D'Ambrosio v. Commissioner: Reinterpretation of Internal Revenue Code Section 2036(a) Nets Estate $330,000 in Tax Savings," 42 Vill. L. R. 1949 (1997).

[9] Wheeler v. United States, 116 F3d 749 (5th Cir. 1997) (sale of a remainder interest to transferor's sons in return for a note which was paid off prior to transferor's death where the court determined that the sale was a bona fide sale for adequate consideration using a time value of money approach).

[10] Estate of Magnin v. Comm'r, 184 F3d 1074 (9th Cir. 1999) (transfer of remainder to family members in consideration for a transfer from father where the court agreed with the *D'Ambrosio* and *Wheeler* results of parsing Section 2036(a)); on remand, it was determined that taxpayer had not received adequate and full consideration for the remainder interest thus triggering Sections 2036(a) and 2043. Estate of Magnin v. Comm'r, 81 TCM (CCH) 1126 (2001).

for the full value of the *remainder* interest.[11] Payment of full consideration for *R*'s remainder interest should likewise defeat application of Section 2036 if *A* creates an intermediate life estate in *B* preceding *A*'s retained interest, because only the remainder interest is potentially includable under Section 2036.[12]

[b] Pre–March 4, 1931 Transfers

Section 2036 is also inapplicable to transfers made before certain critical dates. Section 2036 *never* applies to a transfer made before March 4, 1931, and it may be inapplicable to transfers made between March 3, 1931, and June 7, 1932.[13]

[2] Period for Which Interest Is Retained

In order for Section 2036 to apply, the decedent must have retained an interest[14] in the property for a specified period. The period for which the interest must have been retained is discussed before the nature of the interest is considered. To determine whether the decedent has retained an interest in property

---

[11] If the exception is inapplicable, Section 2043(a) applies. See ¶ 4.15[2]. Elimination of the application of Section 2036 may not be as beneficial to the transferor as at first appears, because the inter vivos transfer creating the trust may trigger the application of gift tax Section 2702 providing a zero valuation for the transferor's retained income interest. See ¶ 19.03. Unless the remainder (along with any other transferred interest) is transferred to a nonfamily member (see IRC §§ 2702(e), 2704(c)(2) and ¶ 19.03[2][a][ii]) or one of the exceptions to Section 2702 applies (see IRC §§ 2702(a)(2)(B), 2702(a)(3)(A)(ii), 2702(b) and ¶¶ 19.03[3][b][i], 19.03[3][d]), there will be a gift for gift tax purposes of the value of the entire corpus less the consideration received for the transferred remainder. For example, if Transferor transfers $1 million to a trust with a retained life estate worth $800,000 and a remainder to Transferor's Child worth $200,000 and Child pays Transferor $200,000 for the remainder, Transferor makes an $800,000 gift as a result of Section 2702. See ¶ 19.03[2][a] text accompanying note 30.

[12] See infra ¶ 4.08[8].

[13] IRC § 2036(c). See IRC § 2045. TAM 9140003 (June 19, 1991) (consequences under Section 2036 of a trust created by the decedent before March 4, 1931). The reasons for this exclusionary rule and for the two critical dates are indicated briefly at the end of this discussion, infra ¶ 4.08[9]. There may be a question whether a transfer to a trust is "made" when property is turned over to the trustee, if the trust is revocable. It should not be so viewed. Comm'r v. Estate of Talbott, 403 F2d 851 (4th Cir. 1968), cert. denied, 393 US 1022 (1969). Cf. Wilson v. Comm'r, 56 TC 579 (1971), acq. 1972-1 CB 2. But see Comm'r v. Estate of Canfield, 306 F2d 1 (2d Cir. 1962); Comm'r v. Estate of Ridgeway, 291 F2d 257 (3d Cir. 1961). The question is to be differentiated from that of when a power of appointment is "created." See Reg. § 20.2041-1(e); United States v. Merchant's Nat'l Bank of Mobile, 261 F2d 570 (5th Cir. 1958).

[14] It is not technically accurate to speak of retention of an "interest." See discussion infra ¶ 4.08[3].

for the prescribed period, a threefold test is applied. Has the decedent retained an interest:

1. For the decedent's life?
2. For a period not ascertainable without reference to the decedent's death?
3. For a period that does not in fact end before the decedent's death?

The first of the three tests needs little explanation. It would obviously be met if the decedent transfers property in trust providing for income to be paid to the decedent "for his life" and, at death, the corpus to be distributed to others.

Regarding the second and third tests, the section is not limited to a straight life interest situation. Under the second, if the period for which the interest is retained is geared to the time of the decedent's death, the section applies. For example, assume that under the terms of a trust created by a decedent, the decedent is entitled to the income payable quarterly for life, but the trust agreement specifies that the decedent is to receive none of the trust income for the calendar quarter in which the decedent dies. In these circumstances, the decedent technically would not be entitled to the income "for his life," for the decedent would not get the full income from the trust up to the time of death.[15] Nevertheless, the period for which the decedent was entitled to the income would not be "ascertainable without reference to his death."[16] The section would therefore apply. In this fashion, the statute defeats avoidance schemes that might succeed if the statute used only the language "for his life." This language also catches a secondary life estate situation in which another interest intervenes before the decedent's interest takes effect in enjoyment. An example is a transfer by D to X for life, then to D for life, remainder to children. Even if D predeceases X, the value of the property, less the value of X's outstanding life estate, is included in D's gross estate, because the period for which D has retained an interest cannot be described without reference to D's death.[17]

---

[15] The technicality is not always accorded judicial recognition. Compare Bayliss v. United States, 326 F2d 458 (4th Cir. 1964) (applying Section 2036 on these precise facts on the ground that the decedent had retained an interest "for life"), with Comm'r v. Estate of Arents, 297 F2d 894 (2d Cir.), cert. denied, 369 US 848 (1962).

[16] Reg. § 20.2036-1(b)(1).

[17] Reg. § 20.2036-1(b)(1)(ii); Marks v. Higgins, 213 F2d 884 (2d Cir. 1954); Comm'r v. Estate of Nathan, 159 F2d 546 (7th Cir. 1947), cert. denied, 334 US 843 (1948). Cf. Kasishke v. United States, 426 F2d 429 (10th Cir. 1970). As these cases indicate, such provisions may be within the third as well as the second of the three timing tests.

The text comment reflects one sharp difference between Sections 2036 and 2038. Section 2036 may apply even if at death the decedent has no currently effective interest, right, or power. In contrast, Section 2038 applies only to interests that are "subject . . . to . . . change" when the decedent dies.

The third period specified makes the statute applicable to the retention of an interest for a period not stated in terms of the decedent's life or death if, in fact, the period does not end before death. Thus, a decedent at age forty might create a trust under which the decedent was entitled to the income for ten years, at the end of which period the trust was to terminate and the corpus was to be distributed to the decedent's child or the child's estate. If the decedent then died within the ten-year period, the decedent would have retained an interest for a period that did "not in fact end before his death," although the decedent had retained an interest not "for his life," and although the period for which the interest was retained was "ascertainable without reference to his death." The regulations under the 1939 Code provided that the retention of an interest for a stated period that happened not to end prior to death resulted in estate tax liability only if the period was such as to evidence the decedent's intention "that it should extend at least for the duration of his life. . . ."[18] As a matter of tax policy, the Treasury's former position seems supportable, and the legislative history is in accord with the old regulations.[19] However, no case has been decided in accordance with the quoted provision in the old regulations, and even when consideration has been given to the legislative history, the section has been applied where the retention of an interest merely does not in fact end before the decedent's death.[20] For many years now, the regulations have omitted any reference to this problem indicating a stricter Treasury policy in accord with the decisions. Perhaps the statute should be changed, but, until it is, the literal interpretation should prevail. Legislative history is not a substitute for unequivocal statutory language.

For a limited situation in which the secondary life estate rule would not be applied, see ¶ 11.03[4][c] text accompanying note 78.

[18] Reg. § 105, § 81.18. Cf. IRC § 673(a), a statutory adoption of this approach for income tax purposes.

[19] S. Rep. No. 665, 72d Cong., 1st Sess. (1932), reprinted in 1939-1 (pt. 2) CB 496, 532.

[20] Estate of Nicol v. Comm'r, 56 TC 179 (1971) (transfer of farm with retention of a five-year lease and death after three years); National Bank of Commerce in Memphis v. Henslee, 179 F. Supp. 346 (MD Tenn. 1959) (trust during minority of another who did not attain majority during decedent's life); Estate of Yawkey v. Comm'r, 12 TC 1164 (1949), acq. 1949-2 CB 3 (reservation of income rights until children, age fifteen and sixteen at time of transfer and twenty-three and twenty-four at death, attained the age of twenty-five); Estate of Fry v. Comm'r, 9 TC 503 (1947), acq. 1948-2 CB 2 (reservation of first $15,000 of dividends from transferred property having substantial value); Estate of Cooper v. Comm'r, 74 TC 1373 (1980) (retention of interest coupons for eight years after transfer of bonds with death occurring three years after transfer).

Section 2036

[3] Nature of the Interest Retained

Very broadly speaking, paragraphs (1) and (2) of Section 2036(a) make the section applicable if the decedent has transferred property but retained beneficial *interests* (first paragraph) or control over *others' interests* (second paragraph). Each of the alternative concepts requires some scrutiny.

[4] Beneficial Interests in the Decedent

The section is invoked if the decedent retains "the possession or enjoyment of" or "the right to the income from" the transferred property or property interest.[21] This, of course, requires a retention of an interest in the very thing transferred, and the decedent's right to other property, such as an annuity, in return for the transferred property does not trigger application of Section 2036[22] even if the amount of the annuity is closely equated to the anticipated income from the transferred property.[23]

[a] Possession or Enjoyment

Although the term "possession or enjoyment" is a quaint relic of earlier legislation, it is clear enough that if, for example, one makes a gift of a valuable painting but reserves the right to keep it for life,[24] or makes a gift of a residence but reserves the right to live in it for life, one has made a transfer comprehended by Section 2036. On the other hand, if the transferred property produces income to which the transferor remains entitled, the statutory language expressly treats this "right to the income" exactly the same as a retention of the "possession or enjoyment" of the property. The philosophy underlying these rules is not troublesome; if the transferor retains in the transferor essentially full lifetime benefits from transferred property, the ultimate shifting of enjoyment at the transferor's death is sufficiently akin to testamentary disposition of property to justify the imposition of estate tax at that time.

If a third person is entitled to all the income from income-producing property, no other person can realistically be said to have the enjoyment of the

---

[21] But see Estate of Goldstone v. Comm'r, 78 TC 1143 (1982), where a retained life estate was too ephemeral to invoke the provisions of Section 2036(a)(1).

[22] See Rev. Rul. 77-193, 1977-1 CB 273. Compare the situation where the decedent retained an annuity or unitrust interest in the transferred property itself and Section 2036(a)(1) applies. See infra ¶ 4.08[8] note 168

[23] Estate of Becklenberg v. Comm'r, 273 F2d 297 (7th Cir. 1959); Estate of Bergan v. Comm'r, 1 TC 543 (1943), acq. 1943 CB 2. See the discussion of private annuities at ¶ 4.11[5].

[24] Cf. IRC § 170(a)(3).

property even if the person is in a position to derive some benefit from it.[25] This essentially sound precept has defanged Section 2036 in some circumstances in which philosophically its bite seems needed.[26] Accordingly, Congress has added subsections enlarging the statutory concept of enjoyment with regard to interests in incorporated businesses.[27]

[b] Right to Income

The term "right to the income" in Section 2036(a)(1) encompasses a right to have the income used for the transferor's benefit;[28] this must be more than a mere expectancy,[29] but the transferor need not have a right to receive the income directly. For example, if the decedent transfers property in trust directing the trustee to use the income from the property for the support of the decedent's dependent, the property is includable in the decedent's gross estate.[30] The theory is that if the income is required to be used to discharge the decedent's obligation, it is the same as if the decedent actually received the income during life and then used it in that manner.[31] On the other hand, if trustees of

---

[25] See United States v. Byrum, 408 US 125, reh'g denied, 409 US 898 (1972).

[26] IRC § 2036(b).

[27] See infra ¶ 4.08[6][d]. See also former IRC § 2036(c) (prior to repeal in the Omnibus Budget Reconciliation Act of 1990, Pub. L. No. 101-508, § 11601(a), 104 Stat. 1388-1, 1388-490 (1990), reprinted in 1991-2 CB 481, 524) regarding frozen enterprises, which was subsequently repealed. Stephens, Maxfield, Lind & Calfee, Federal Estate and Gift Taxation ¶ 4.08[9] (Warren, Gorham & Lamont, 6th ed. 1991), for a discussion of Section 2036(c) (prior to repeal in the Omnibus Budget Reconciliation Act of 1990, Pub. L. No. 101-508, § 11601(a), 104 Stat. 1388-1, 1388-490 (1990), reprinted in 1991-2 CB 481, 524).

[28] There are various forms of income retention. See Estate of Cooper v. Comm'r, 74 TC 1373 (1980); Rev. Rul. 78-26, 1978-1 CB 286; infra ¶ 4.08[8] note 168.

[29] Estate of Wyly v. Comm'r, 610 F2d 1282 (5th Cir. 1980) (a "right" to income did not include an inchoate right created by operation of law and arising in very limited circumstances). The Service agrees. Rev. Rul. 81-221, 1981-2 CB 178. Cf. United States v. Byrum, 408 US 125, reh'g denied, 409 US 898 (1972); Estate of Uhl v. Comm'r, 241 F2d 867 (7th Cir. 1957).

[30] Reg. § 20.2036-1(b)(2); Richards v. Comm'r, 374 F2d 997 (10th Cir. 1967); Comm'r v. Estate of Dwight, 205 F2d 298 (2d Cir.), cert. denied, 346 US 871 (1953); Helvering v. Mercantile-Commerce Bank & Trust Co., 111 F2d 224 (8th Cir.), cert. denied, 310 US 654 (1940); Estate of Lee v. Comm'r, 33 TC 1064 (1960); Estate of Gokey v. Comm'r, 72 TC 721 (1979).

[31] Cf. Old Colony Trust Co. v. Comm'r, 279 US 716 (1929), applying like theory for income tax purposes. A ruling of questionable validity holds that a trust's requirement that the trustee use trust funds to pay any federal or state income tax liability incurred by its grantor due to the trust's status as a grantor trust will *not* cause the trust's corpus to be included in the grantor's estate, notwithstanding that the grantor trust rules make the grantor liable for the income tax payment and thus the trust would be satisfying a liability of the grantor. The ruling simply asserts that because the distributions on the taxpayer's be-

whom the decedent is not one are merely given discretion to use income for the support of the transferor decedent's dependent, Section 2036 does not apply. Interests or rights must be retained by the *decedent*, or at least by the decedent in conjunction with another, for Section 2036 to apply.[32] Midway between these circumstances (trustee required to use funds for support and trustee, other than decedent, having such discretion) is the situation in which the decedent, as trustee,[33] has discretion to use the income of a trust created by the decedent for support of the decedent's dependents. This is a taxable situation within Section 2036.[34] In such circumstances, it is irrelevant whether the trust income was actually used for support purposes;[35] under Section 2036 it is "the right to the income," which the decedent has if the decedent can direct that it be used for the decedent's benefit, that brings the section into play.[36] It is relevant, however, to consider the extent of the support obligation that may be discharged by income payments. Thus, if in the circumstances, $8,000 a year will discharge the obligation and the trust earns more than that, and the decedent has no direct or indirect interest in the excess income and no control over its disposition,[37] the decedent will be viewed as having reserved the right

---

half represent tax payments allocable to the trust's income, the distributions do not constitute the retention of a right to income as described in Section 2036(a). Priv. Ltr. Rul. 9922062 (Feb. 26, 1999). See Priv. Ltr. Rul. 200120021 (Feb. 13, 2001) (similar power with no Section 2036(a) inclusion but trustee's power was discretionary).

[32] Comm'r v. Estate of Douglass, 143 F2d 961 (3d Cir. 1944); Estate of Mitchell v. Comm'r, 55 TC 576 (1970), acq. 1971-1 CB 2; Estate of Chrysler v. Comm'r, 44 TC 55 (1965), acq. in result only 1970-2 CB xix, rev'd on another issue, 361 F2d 508 (2d Cir. 1966). The estate tax provisions do not include a "related or subordinate party" concept such as appears in the income tax provisions. See IRC § 672(c). However, see Rev. Rul. 95-58, 1995-2 CB 191, considered infra ¶ 4.08[5][a] text accompanying note 61, in which the Treasury attempts to "legislate" such a test into Sections 2036 and 2038.

[33] A question may arise whether decedent was the trustee at the time of death or relinquished such position within three years of death. See TAM 9043074 (July 12, 1990) (a settlor who actively controlled the affairs of a trust was the de facto trustee of the trust). Cf. Estate of Ware v. Comm'r, 480 F2d 444 (7th Cir. 1973); United States v. Allen, 293 F2d 916 (10th Cir. 1961), discussed infra ¶ 4.08[8][b]; IRC § 2035(a)(2).

[34] See IRC § 2036(a)(2), infra ¶ 4.08[5]; National Bank of Commerce in Memphis v. Henslee, 179 F. Supp. 346 (MD Tenn. 1959); Exchange Bank & Trust Co. of Fla. v. United States, 694 F2d 1261 (Fed. Cir. 1982); TAM 9122005 (Feb. 5, 1991). Cf. Rev. Rul. 59-357, 1959-2 CB 212. See also discussion at ¶ 4.10[4][f] on pitfalls in the use of gifts to minors legislation.

[35] The parallel grantor trust income tax provision is different. See IRC § 677(b).

[36] Estate of Pardee v. Comm'r, 49 TC 140, 148 (1967); Estate of McTighe v. Comm'r, 36 TCM (CCH) 1655 (1977).

[37] See infra ¶ 4.08[5].

to only a portion of the trust income, and a commensurate amount of the trust corpus will be included in the decedent's estate.[38]

If a decedent's estate is to be taxed under Section 2036 on the ground that the income of a trust is to be used until the decedent's death to discharge decedent's obligation, it is essential that the obligation to be discharged exist. Thus, if trust income may initially be used to support a minor child but the child reaches the age where the support obligation ceases before the decedent's death, the decedent will not have retained the prescribed right for a period that does not in fact end before the decedent's death.[39] The support obligation may also terminate in other ways. If property is transferred to a trust by a husband in exchange for an effective release of support obligations, such as his wife's support rights, or if local law would so permit those of his minor children, the obligations cease upon the transfer[40] and, even if the trust income is used thereafter to support the wife and children, it cannot properly be said to be used any longer to discharge obligations of the husband; his support obligations are discharged when the trust is created, and further payments merely discharge his contract. Upon his death, therefore, nothing should be included in his gross estate under Section 2036.[41]

[c] Enjoyment "Retained"

Section 2036 is framed in part in terms of actual possession or enjoyment or the right to income *retained* by a decedent transferor. However, the question

---

[38] See Estate of Pardee v. Comm'r, 49 TC 140, 150 (1967) (decedent, as co-trustee, had the power to use trust corpus to satisfy legal obligation to support his wife, but only after first considering his wife's needs and other sources of assistance; the portion of the trust corpus needed to satisfy his support obligation was included under Section 2036(a)(1)). Estate of Sullivan v. Comm'r, 66 TCM (CCH) 1329 (1993).

[39] Estate of Pardee v. Comm'r, 49 TC 140, 150 (1967). Even if the decedent dies within three years of the cessation of the support obligation, Section 2035(a) acting in conjunction with Section 2036(a) is inapplicable because there is no Section 2035(a) "transfer" or relinquishment of a power over the property at the time of the cessation of the obligation. IRC § 2035(a)(1).

[40] See, e.g., Sherman, Jr. v. United States, 462 F2d 577 (5th Cir. 1972).

[41] See, contra, Estate of McKeon v. Comm'r, 25 TC 697 (1956), acq. 1958-2 CB 6, including a part of the value of such a trust on the mistaken impression that includability turned on the question of whether the release of the support rights constituted consideration for the transfer to the trust and, further, mistakenly treating a wife's relinquishment of support rights as not consideration properly taken into account. On the latter point, see discussion of Section 2043(b) at ¶ 4.15[1][a]. If tax liability turns on something other than the use of trust income for discharge of a support obligation, such as the revocable nature of a trust, the question whether a release of support rights is recognizable consideration for the transfer may of course be relevant. See Chase Nat'l Bank v. Comm'r, 225 F2d 621 (8th Cir. 1955), decided under the revocable transfer provisions of Section 2038, discussed ¶ 4.15[1][a] text accompanying note 26.

whether there is a retention raises a pragmatic, not a legal, issue, and something may be "retained" in the absence of an enforceable right. It is enough that the decedent has arranged to keep the present use, economic benefit, or income from transferred property either directly or by implication.[42] Is there the necessary implied arrangement or understanding in the case of a residence if the transferor merely continues to live in the residence? The Commissioner has frequently taken the position that the mere fact of continued occupancy evidences an implied understanding.[43] If the transferee is a family member other than the spouse of the transferor,[44] there is mixed authority whether there was an implied understanding that the transferor would occupy the residence rent-free resulting in inclusion of the residence in the transferor's gross estate under Section 2036(a)(1). If the family member does not co-occupy the residence with the transferor, courts generally have concluded that the transferor has retained an interest in the residence under an implied agreement with the family member.[45] If a family member occupies the residence with the transferor, there is a split of authority whether Section 2036(a)(1) applies, with the courts gen-

---

[42] Estate of Whitt v. Comm'r, 751 F2d 1548 (11th Cir. 1985), cert. denied, 474 US 1005 (1985); Estate of McCabe v. United States, 475 F2d 1142 (Ct Cl. 1993); Tubbs v. United States, 348 F. Supp. 1404 (ND Tex. 1972), aff'd per curiam, 472 F2d 166 (5th Cir. 1973); Lee v. United States, 86-1 USTC ¶ 13,649 (WD Ky. 1985). See Rev. Rul. 79-109, 1979-1 CB 297 (retention for a portion of a year). This construction is clearly in accord with Congressional intent. See HR Rep. No. 708, 72d Cong., 1st Sess. (1932), reprinted in 1939-1 (Part 2) CB 457, in reference to the changes made by the 1932 Act to the Joint Resolution of March 2, 1931. But cf. Rev. Rul. 81-164, 1981-1 CB 458.

[43] See, e.g., Rev. Rul. 78-409, 1978-2 CB 234.

[44] If the transferee is the spouse of the transferor, the courts have consistently held that the transferor's continued occupancy of a residence is not a Section 2036(a)(1) retained interest. Union Planters National Bank v. United States, 361 F2d 662 (6th Cir. 1966) (stating that the transferor spouse continues to occupy the residence "as a natural incident to the marital relationship" and not as a result of an implied understanding with the transferee); Estate of Brinkley v. United States, 358 F2d 639 (3d Cir. 1966); Bridgforth v. United States, 73-1 USTC ¶ 12,916 (SD Miss. 1973); Estate of Gutchess v. Comm'r, 46 TC 554 (1966); Stephenson v. United States, 238 F. Supp. 883 (WD Va. 1965). Even the Commissioner generally agrees. Rev. Rul. 70-155, 1970-1 CB 189 (stating that "co-occupancy, where the donor and donee are husband and wife, does not of itself support an inference of an agreement or understanding as to retained possession or enjoyment by the donor."). With an unlimited marital deduction (see ¶ 5.06[1]), the issue is academic, because even if the transferor was deemed to have retained a Section 2036(a)(1) interest, the transferor would be entitled to a marital deduction equal in value to the residence included in the transferor's gross estate.

[45] Guyn v. United States, 437 F2d 1148 (4th Cir. 1971); Estate of Honigman v. Comm'r, 66 TC 1080 (1976); Estate of Kerdolff v. Comm'r, 57 TC 643 (1972); Estate of Linderme v. Comm'r, 52 TC 305 (1969); Estate of Rapelje v. Comm'r, 73 TC 82 (1979); Estate of Trotter v. Comm'r, 82 TCM (CCH) 633 (2001); Estate of Baggett v. Comm'r, 62 TCM (CCH) 333 (1991) (farm including farmhouse included in transferor's gross estate). See Rev. Rul. 70-155, 1970-1 CB 189.

erally looking to surrounding facts, especially whether the transferee assumed an ownership role by paying the property taxes and other expenses related to the property.[46] The same issue arises in a situation where a decedent has deeded a portion of a residence to a transferee, but has continued to reside in the residence until death.[47] In determining whether to apply Section 2036(a)(1) to the transferred portion of the residence, the courts should apply the same tests that they apply when an entire residence is transferred.[48]

An implied agreement to retain the income from property has also been found in situations where a transferor creates a family limited partnership and transfers interests in the partnership to other family members and, under the partnership agreement, the partnership or other family members have the rights to partnership income, but the transferor diverts all the partnership income for the transferor's personal use.[49] Where a decedent has actually been receiving

---

[46] Compare Diehl v. United States, 68-1 USTC ¶ 12,506, 21 AFTR2d 1607 (WD Tenn. 1967), Estate of Roemer v. Comm'r, 46 TCM (CCH) 1176 (1983) (no implied agreement where transferee paid property taxes) with Estate of Douglas v. Comm'r, 32 TCM (CCH) 5 (1973) (implied agreement where transferor paid property taxes). See also Estate of Spruill v. Comm'r, 88 TC 1197 (1987) (no implied agreement but not indication of who paid the property taxes); Rev. Rul. 78-409, 1978-2 CB 234 (stating that the Service would not follow *Diehl* and that "where the decedent's possession and enjoyment of the residence continue without limitation," the decedent has retained a Section 2036(a)(1) interest).

[47] A more common transfer of a partial interest occurs where a decedent has transferred the residence to a personal residence trust while retaining the use of the residence for a term of years. See IRC § 2702(a)(3)(A)(ii), ¶ 19.03[3][d]. In that situation, if the decedent dies during the term of years, Section 2036(a)(1) applies. See supra ¶ 4.08[2] text accompanying notes 18–20.

[48] See supra text accompanying notes 45, 46. Estate of Callahan v. Comm'r, 42 TCM (CCH) 362 (1981) (residence included under Section 2036(a)(1) where decedent gifted a 47/57 interest and lived with one child but paid all the property taxes); Estate of Wineman v. Comm'r, 79 TCM (CCH) 2189 (2000) (Section 2036(a)(1) inapplicable when decedent transferred a 24 percent minority interest in her homestead to her children, but did not have exclusive possession of the property and did not pay the property taxes).

If the residence is transferred to a family limited partnership with interests in the family limited partnership deeded to family members while the decedent continues to live in the residence, there is a likelihood that Section 2036(a)(1) will be applied. Cf. Estate of Schauerhamer v. Comm'r, 73 TCM (CCH) 2855 (1997); Estate of Reichardt v. Comm'r, 114 TC 144 (2000) (both cases in essence disregarding the partnership and holding Section 2036(a)(1) applicable to a family limited partnership where all the income was paid to the transferor of the partnership interests). See infra text accompanying note 49, supra text accompanying note 45.

[49] Estate of Schauerhamer v. Comm'r, 73 TCM (CCH) 2855 (1997) (implied agreement among the partners); Estate of Reichardt v. Comm'r 114 TC 144 (2000) (same). In these cases the partnership entity was in essence disregarded. If the parties each had made separate capital contributions to the partnership and one partner received all of the income from the partnership, Section 2036(a)(1) would not apply to pull the noncontributed capital into that transferor's gross estate because there would have been no Section 2036(a)(1)

the income from property, rather than, for instance, merely sharing a house that the decedent has transferred to a child, the fact of receipt of the income may create a stronger inference of the required retention by arrangement than does the mere continued use. This is because the decedent's receipt of the income necessarily constitutes a deprivation to the transferees who might otherwise receive it; in contrast, the decedent's continued use of a house (and possibly other property) may enhance rather than diminish the enjoyment of it by a sharing transferee.

A similar problem can arise if a decedent has transferred property to a trust with provision for the payment of income and ultimately corpus to others but has given the trustee, an individual other than the settlor decedent, complete discretion to make income payments to the decedent.[50] Section 2036(a)(1) requires that the decedent retain either "possession or enjoyment" or "the right to the income." If the decedent has no legal right to income, the "income" phrase would not support inclusion under Section 2036.[51] Perhaps it may be said the decedent has retained "enjoyment."[52] However, if some meaning is to be accorded the word "retained," some showing of an arrangement, more than the fact that income was paid to the decedent, should be required.[53]

---

transfer of that portion of the capital. Cf. Jones v. Comm'r, 116 TC 121 (2001) (holding no gift on pro rata creation of a family limited partnership); ¶ 10.01[2][b][ii].

[50] If the trustee were required under a standard such as support to make income payments to the transferor, then the corpus necessary to produce the support payments would be included in the decedent's estate. IRC § 2036(a)(1).

[51] Estate of Wyly v. Comm'r, 610 F2d 1282 (5th Cir. 1980); Priv. Ltr. Rul. 200120021 (Feb. 13, 2001) (no Section 2036 inclusion where independent trustee discretion to make payments for decedent's obligations from a defective grantor trust). Where the question is whether a decedent has retained a "right" to income (as opposed to whether the decedent has in fact retained enjoyment), the connotation may be a legal right. But see United States v. O'Malley, 383 US 627 (1966) (which speaks in terms of "power" rather than "right"); United States v. Byrum, 408 US 125, reh'g denied, 409 US 898 (1972); Estate of Gilman v. Comm'r, 65 TC 296 (1975) (speaking of a legally enforceable power). See also White, J., dissenting in United States v. Byrum, supra.

[52] There might be a basis for saying that the term "enjoyment" in Section 2036(a)(1) should have reference only to physical possession or use of non-income-producing property and that if an income interest is in question, mere retained "enjoyment" is not a substitute for the legal "right" to the income. However, precedent runs the other way. See, e.g., Estate of McNichol v. Comm'r, 265 F2d 667 (3d Cir.), cert. denied, 361 US 829 (1959); Estate of Skinner v. United States, 316 F2d 517 (3d Cir. 1963).

[53] Estate of Wells v. Comm'r, 42 TCM (CCH) 1305 (1981); Estate of Uhl v. Comm'r, 241 F2d 867 (7th Cir. 1957); Comm'r v. Irving Trust Co., 147 F2d 946 (2d Cir. 1945); Estate of McCabe v. United States, 475 F2d 1142 (Ct. Cl. 1993); Estate of German v. United States, 85-1 USTC ¶ 13,610 (Cl. Ct. 1985). Cf. Estate of Gutchess v. Comm'r, 46 TC 554 (1966). Since such transfers are treated as complete when made for gift tax purposes (see Rev. Rul. 77-378, 1977-2 CB 347, discussed ¶ 10.01[9]), there is even less reason for the imposition of estate tax liability under Section 2036.

[5] Control Over Others' Interests

The foregoing comments concern a transferor decedent's lifetime retention of beneficial interests in transferred property. The enjoyment of property or the right to income it produces are such substantial ownership attributes as clearly to support the inclusion in the gross estate required by Section 2036(a)(1). Paragraph (2) identifies far less significant ownership attributes that invoke the provisions of Section 2036. Most obviously, under Section 2036(a)(2), if a transferor retains the right for life (or for any similarly prescribed period) to say who may enjoy transferred property[54] or the income therefrom, even if the transferor has put it beyond the power to claim enjoyment or income for the transferor's own benefit, Section 2036 applies.[55] If this seems fair enough, what are some of the further reaches of the provision?

[a] Right to Designate Retained Indirectly

The right to designate may be indirectly retained.[56] If the decedent names a third party as trustee and gives the trustee the right to designate who shall enjoy the income, the decedent has not retained the proscribed control. But if, in such circumstances, the decedent has the right to discharge the trustee and name the decedent as trustee with the same right, the decedent has indirectly retained the condemned control even if the decedent never becomes the trus-

---

In these situations, one eye must be kept on local law. If under local law, the power of the trustee to give income and principal to the grantor gives the grantor's creditors the right to reach the trust assets, the transfer is revocable and Section 2036(a)(1) also applies. See ¶ 10.01[9] text accompanying note 205; Estate of Paxton v. Comm'r, 86 TC 785 (1986); TAM 199917001 (Jan. 15, 1999). The Section 2036(a)(1) result also applies if the trustees and creditors had such a right with respect to only the income, not the principal of the trust. Priv. Ltr. Rul. 9646021 (Aug. 16, 1996).

These problems, along with the corresponding gift tax consequences, are discussed in Lowndes, "Some Doubts About the Use of Trusts to Avoid Estate Taxes," 47 Minn. L. Rev. 31, 41-52 (1962); Covey, "Power to Distribute to Grantor," 98 Tr. & Est. 322 (1959).

[54] By statute, amounts held in a Qualified Tuition Plan or an Education Savings Account are generally not includable in the contributor's gross estate even though the contributor held the right to select new designated beneficiaries. IRC §§ 529(c)(4)(A), 530(d)(3). But see IRC §§ 529(c)(4)(B), 529(c)(4)(C); Prop. Reg. § 1.529-5(d)(2). See also ¶ 9.04[3][g] text accompanying notes 133, 134.

[55] If a trustee has discretion regarding the disposition of trust income, this will not invoke Section 2036 unless the decedent is the trustee. Especially where the decedent has been trustee and has sought to resign as such, a difficult evidentiary question may arise. E.g., Estate of Ware v. Comm'r, 480 F2d 444 (7th Cir. 1973). Similarly, a question may arise whether the decedent actually had the right to designate. Estate of Edmonds v. Comm'r, 72 TC 970 (1979); Estate of Bowgren v. Comm'r, 105 F3d 1156 (7th Cir. 1997) (power held under local law). Cf. Rev. Rul. 79-177, 1979-1 CB 298.

[56] Rifkind v. United States, 5 Cl. Ct. 362 (1984).

tee.[57] Further, even if the decedent has the right to become the trustee with the same right only in the case of the trustee's inability to serve, resignation, or removal by a proper court for cause, Section 2036(a)(2) still applies.[58] Again, the section may apply even if the retained right is not currently operative.[59]

The Service has reconsidered its long-held position that the reservation of the right to replace one trustee with another, even absent the right to name oneself as trustee, constitutes a retention of the trustee's powers for purposes of Section 2036(a)(2).[60] The Service now pretty much agrees that the grantor's reservation of the right or power to substitute one trustee for another will not result in an attribution of the trustee's powers to the grantor, but only if the potential appointees do not include a trustee who is related or subordinate to the grantor under Section 672(c).[61]

[b] Illusory "Control"

Seeming authority of the decedent to shift income or enjoyment may be quite illusory and still be within Section 2036(a)(2). If the decedent may direct income to others only with the consent of some other person, the decedent is still within the provision.[62] This is so even if the one who must join in the de-

---

[57] Reg. § 20.2036-1(b)(3).

[58] Estate of Farrell v. United States, 553 F2d 637 (Ct. Cl. 1977); Rev. Rul. 73-21, 1973-1 CB 405. This identification of indirect control is clearly within the present statutory language. Where complete discretion is lodged in a trustee who cannot be removed, however, it is still likely the trustee may comply with the settlor's wishes. See Estate of Goodwyn, 32 TCM (CCH) 740 (1973), holding, under the rationale of *Byrum*, that the decedent has no "right" to control in such situations, making Section 2036(a)(2) inapplicable. See infra text accompanying notes 60, 61.

[59] See supra ¶ 4.08[2] text accompanying note 17.

[60] Rev. Rul. 95-58, 1995-2 CB 191, revoking Rev. Rul. 79-353, 1979-2 CB 325 and Rev. Rul. 81-51, 1981 CB 458, and modifying Rev. Rul. 7-182, 1977-1 CB 273. The Service reconsidered its earlier position in light of the decisions in Estate of Wall v. Comm'r, 101 TC 300 (1993) and Estate of Vak v. Comm'r, 973 F2d 1409 (8th Cir. 1992), rev'g, 62 TCM (CCH) 942 (1991). In Estate of Wall, the Tax Court thoroughly analyzed Rev. Rul. 79-353 and concluded that the position taken by the Service was wrong, noting that the trustee had a duty of complete loyalty to the interests of the beneficiary. Notably, the Tax Court subsequently assessed attorney's fees against the Service. Estate of Wall v. Comm'r, 102 TC 391 (1994).

[61] Rev. Rul. 95-58, 1995-2 CB 191. This effort to "legislate" Section 672(c) into Section 2036(a)(2) is inappropriate. See supra ¶ 4.08[2][b] note 32.

[62] The decedent has the proscribed right to designate even if it is expressly lodged in another but made subject to the decedent's veto or consent. Cf. Estate of DuCharme v. Comm'r, 164 F2d 959 (6th Cir. 1947), on reh'g, 169 F2d 76 (6th Cir. 1948); Estate of Thorp v. Comm'r, 164 F2d 966 (3d Cir. 1947), cert. denied, 333 US 843 (1948); Rev. Rul. 70-513, 1970-2 CB 194. However, if the transfer was made before June 7, 1932, the power must be in the decedent alone. Reg. § 20.2036-1(a)(ii).

cedent's action has an interest adverse to the exercise of the power. Thus, if, under a trust created by *D*, *B* had the right to the income but with *B*'s consent *D* could designate *C* as income beneficiary, *D* has the prescribed "right" to designate.[63] Here and in some other places Congress recognizes that concepts of enlightened self-interest do not work in a typical family setting.

[c] Right to Designate Who Benefits

The right to designate need not be authority to decide at large who shall enjoy the property or receive its income. Authority to choose only between two named beneficiaries is enough.[64] Moreover, the *O'Malley* case[65] holds squarely that a mere right to direct the accumulation of trust income that would otherwise be payable to named beneficiaries is a proscribed power to designate within paragraph (2), if the accumulation will eventually pass to a third-person remainderperson or even if it will only possibly pass to a third-person remainderperson.

What if, under a power to accumulate, income not paid to the current income beneficiary may later be paid to the beneficiary or will at least ultimately be paid to the beneficiary's estate? Does this fall within the concept of a right to designate the persons who shall enjoy the income? Some courts have held that it does. In *Struthers v. Kelm*,[66] the trust created by the decedent grantor provided for the payment of the income to the decedent's daughter for the grantor's life, then remainder to the daughter. The decedent held a power to accumulate income. Under the local law, the beneficiary had the right to dispose of her remainder interest by will in the event she predeceased her mother;

---

[63] Reg. § 20.2036-1(b)(3). This may not be so, and should not be, if all persons with an interest in the property must join. Cf. Reg. § 20.2038-1(a)(2); Helvering v. Helmholtz, 296 US 93 (1935); ¶ 4.10[6]. See Old Colony Trust Co. v. United States, 423 F2d 601, 602 n.2 (1st Cir. 1970).

[64] Industrial Trust Co. v. Comm'r, 165 F2d 142 (1st Cir. 1947). See, however, the argument of Magruder, J., dissenting, that the right to designate under Section 2036 should be restricted to instances of broader control than under Section 2038, because the broader reach of Section 2036 argues for a narrower application of its principles.

Appropriately, the Service has taken the position that a Section 2036(a)(2) power does not include changes of beneficial interests as a result of after-born or after-adopted children of the transferor becoming beneficiaries of a trust. Rev. Rul. 80-255, 1980-2 CB 272. Cf. Estate of Tully v. United States, 528 F2d 1401 (Ct. Cl. 1976).

[65] United States v. O'Malley, 383 US 627 (1966). In *O'Malley*, the Supreme Court did not state the actual terms of the trust in which the decedent grantor held a power as trustee to accumulate income. The briefs of the case indicate that the income beneficiary had a right to income for a term of years with a remainder to the income beneficiary after those years if living but if not, a remainder to a third party. Thus, accumulation might have resulted in the income's eventually going to the third-party contingent remainderperson and that triggers IRC § 2036(a)(2).

[66] Struthers v. Kelm, 218 F2d 810 (8th Cir. 1955).

if she made no will, the property would have passed as hers under Minnesota laws on descent and distribution. Smitten by the then-recent decision in *Lober v. United States*,[67] a Section 2038 case,[68] the court held that the property was included in the decedent's gross estate under the predecessor of Section 2036(a)(2). The *Struthers* holding and the *O'Malley* dictum seem to suggest that under any circumstances, a retention of a power to accumulate income is the retention of the proscribed Section 2036 power to designate. But the authors believe that it is not, and that *Struthers* is wrong and *O'Malley* distinguishable, even though the Tax Court expressly disagrees, and its opinion has been affirmed by the Fourth Circuit.[69]

Granting that Sections 2036 and 2038 have much in common, their tests for applicability are different and the effects of their application are not the same. On the latter point, if the power to accumulate is a power to alter—at least a power to alter as to *time* of enjoyment—as it should invariably be viewed, the application of Section 2038 would include only the income interest subject to such alteration. In contrast, if the power to accumulate is a right to designate the *persons* who will enjoy the property, as it should only sometimes be, then the entire trust corpus may be swept into a grantor's gross estate. It is very well for the Treasury to say in its regulations that a mere power to alter the time of enjoyment is a Section 2038 power, "even though the identity of the beneficiary is not affected."[70] The Treasury wisely does not include any such "even though" clause in the Section 2036 regulations. After all, a power "to designate the persons who shall possess or enjoy" connotes some ability to choose between persons, however limited the circles of selection may be.[71] Authority over the timing of a single individual's enjoyment is simply not a power to designate under Section 2036(a)(2), and a rejection of the decisions to the contrary is urged.[72]

Thus, a power to accumulate given facts such as those in *Struthers* should invoke only Section 2038, menacing the income interest subject to the power.[73] A power to accumulate under the facts (known from the briefs) in *O'Malley*, in addition to being within Section 2038, though innocuous there because of the limited inclusion, is properly viewed as a power to designate under Section 2036, sweeping the trust corpus into the gross estate. This is because in

---

[67] Lober v. United States, 346 US 335 (1935).

[68] See ¶ 4.10[3] text accompanying note 17.

[69] Estate of Alexander v. Comm'r, 81 TC 757, 763 (1983), aff'd in unpub. op. (4th Cir. 1985).

[70] Reg. § 20.2038-1(a); Lober v. United States, 346 US 335 (1935).

[71] Cf. Industrial Trust Co. v. Comm'r, 165 F2d 142 (1st Cir. 1947).

[72] See supra notes 66, 69. The authors' thinking is reinforced by the Magruder dissent in Industrial Trust Co. v. Comm'r, 165 F2d 142 (1st Cir. 1947). See supra note 64.

[73] This would have involved a zero inclusion in *Struthers*, because the income interest terminated on the decedent's death; but that is appropriate.

O'Malley, unlike *Lober*, accumulated income might ultimately pass to third parties, not merely the named beneficiary or the beneficiary's estate. This ability to shift income to others is clearly a power to designate who shall enjoy the income.

[6] Indirect Interests or Controls

A pervasive problem in the estate tax area, which has an active counterpart in income tax and gift tax matters, is that circumstances, relationships, interests, rights, and obligations that bear importantly on questions of tax liability very often arise in something quite different from a marketplace setting. The cast of characters, seemingly distinct personal entities, often have subsurface personal, familial, fraternal, or business ties, which make them much more cronies than arm's-length bargainers. Naturally, too, they are likely to be in league against that outsider, the tax gatherer. And perhaps the problems are the greatest when one of the players is wearing several hats. For example, the settlor of a trust may play the role of principal owner of the stock of the corporation forming the trust res and the roles of employee and director of the corporation as well. The settlor may also be the trustee and, as such, have substantial managerial powers. To talk in formal terms of rights and interests in such settings approaches sophistry; but, since the statute does so, the game must be played.

[a] Settlor Trustee

If a trust settlor names oneself as trustee, it now seems settled, although subject to a statutory exception,[74] that the settlor may as such retain the typical managerial powers of a fiduciary without running afoul of Section 2036. It will be conceded that such powers can affect the enjoyment of the trust property, because, if the settlor may control investments, the settlor's decision to prefer high-yield bonds, for example, over growth stocks increases the rewards of income beneficiaries at the possible expense of remainderpersons, and vice versa. There is similar latitude regarding discretion as to the allocation of receipts or charges between principal and income. Nevertheless, both ancient[75] and modern[76] precedents reject such powers as a basis for applying Section 2036.

---

[74] See the anti-*Byrum* amendment to Section 2036(a)(1), discussed infra ¶ 4.08[6][d].

[75] Reinecke v. Northern Trust Co., 278 US 339 (1929).

[76] Old Colony Trust Co. v. United States 423 F2d 601 (1st Cir. 1970). Cf. United States v. Byrum, 408 US 125, reh'g denied, 409 US 898 (1972). Between *Reinecke*, 278 US 339 (1929), and *Old Colony*, the First Circuit held that broad administrative powers held by the grantor trustee were sufficient to result in a Section 2036(a)(2) inclusion. State St. Trust Co. v. United States, 263 F2d 635 (1st Cir. 1959). Several cases reached the op-

Again without incurring tax liability under Section 2036, somewhat more direct control over enjoyment may be retained by a settlor trustee if the settlor restricts the powers to compliance with an ascertainable standard. The trustee may, for example, have authority to distribute income otherwise to be accumulated (literally, "to designate" who "shall ... enjoy ... the income") if the trustee may do so only to ensure a beneficiary's accustomed manner of living, for the beneficiary's educational needs, or in case of sickness.[77] The notion here is that the trustee is not permitted to be an innovator; the trustee simply carries out directions found in the trust instrument, and, being limited by a standard, does not have a power to designate.[78] However, if the discretion is limited only by the trustee's appraisal of what will make the beneficiary "happy" or "comfortable," the trustee has gone too far; in the words of Judge Aldrich, the string the trustee has held on the property will produce "a rope burn."[79] Section 2036 applies.[80]

There may be a pernicious fallacy in all of this. After a certain amount of wealth is accumulated, all a trust settlor may wish to do is pass along to others at death as much as the settlor can, perhaps giving them some enjoyment of the trust property also while the settlor is living. A question, then, is whether the settlor can freeze the tax liability (to value at the time of gift) and yet work to enlarge the settlor's estate for life without estate tax attrition at death. A power to control investments (merely fiduciary) coupled with a restricted power over enjoyment (an adequate standard) may permit one to accomplish virtually all one's lifetime wishes with respect to property and still escape estate tax. This is hostile to the general philosophy underlying Section 2036 but

---

posite result on only slightly distinguishable facts. Estate of Ford v. Comm'r, 53 TC 114 (1969), aff'd per curiam, 450 F2d 878 (2d Cir. 1971), nonacq. 1978-2 CB 3; Estate of Budd v. Comm'r, 49 TC 468 (1968); Estate of Peters v. Comm'r, 23 TCM (CCH) 994 (1964); Estate of King v. Comm'r, 37 TC 973 (1962), nonacq. 1963-1 CB 5. The First Circuit subsequently overruled *State Street Trust* in the *Old Colony Trust* case. See Crump, "The State Street Trust Doctrine, 1959–1970: R.I.P.," 49 NC L. Rev. 811 (1971); Beausant, "Estate and Gift Tax Consequences of Administrative Powers," 115 Tr. & Est. 246 (1976).

Allocations by a trustee to adjust total return between principal and income under Section 104 of the Uniform Principal and Income Act (1997) should not cause gross estate inclusion under Section 2036 where the settlor is trustee. See, e.g., Calif. Prob. Code § 16336 (West 2001).

[77] Leopold v. United States, 510 F2d 617 (9th Cir. 1975); Estate of Wier v. Comm'r, 17 TC 409 (1951), acq. 1952-1 CB 4; Priv. Ltr. Rul. 199903025 (Oct. 27, 1998). Noninclusion here results only if the grantor is under no obligation of support that might require the grantor to meet such needs. See supra ¶ 4.08[4][b] text accompanying note 39.

[78] Compare the effect of a standard under Section 2036(a)(1), supra ¶ 4.08[4][c] note 50.

[79] Old Colony Trust Co. v. United States, 423 F2d 601, 605 (1st Cir. 1970).

[80] Estate of Cutter v. Comm'r, 62 TC 351 (1974). For examples of standards here and under Section 2038, see ¶ 4.10[5].

not to its language, as properly interpreted. Should anything be done about this? Can anything be done about it?[81]

[b] Enjoyment Retained in Commercial Transactions

The term "enjoyment" of property under Section 2036(a)(1) connotes "substantial present economic benefit" from the property.[82] Where a donor transfers land to another but they agree the donor will use the land rent-free for the donor's lifetime, there is a retention of enjoyment of the property.[83]

[c] Rent Paid by Transferor

An intriguing situation under the present statute is presented by a gratuitous transfer of real property coupled with a leaseback agreement under which the transferor pays rent for continued possession. Generally, when full market value is paid, the transfer is outside the estate tax under parenthetical exceptions to the lifetime transfer provisions, but those provisions relate to value *received* by the decedent for property interests transferred. A decedent's agreement to *pay* full rental value for continued possession of property that the decedent transfers will work a further diminution (beyond the transfer of the property) in the decedent's estate. Gratuitous transfers and leasebacks under which taxpayers have, often without success,[84] sought income tax advantage should not be equally vulnerable to the estate tax. A series of cases have held that Section 2036(a)(1) is inapplicable where the property is business property that is leased back for its fair rental value.[85] However, if enjoyment is exclu-

---

[81] Cf. ¶¶ 19.01–19.05.

[82] Cf. Comm'r v. Estate of Holmes, 326 US 480, 486 (1946). See Rev. Rul. 75-259, 1975-2 CB 361, holding that a "family estate" trust is includable in a grantor decedent's estate under Section 2036(a)(1) because there is a retention of a substantial present economic benefit in the property transferred. See also Rev. Rul. 75-257, 1975-2 CB 251; Rev. Rul. 75-258, 1975-2 CB 503, Rev. Rul. 75-260, 1975-2 CB 376, dealing with the income and gift tax consequences of "family estate" trusts.

[83] Estate of Baggett v. Comm'r, 62 TCM (CCH) 333 (1991). Cf. infra ¶ 4.08[5][c].

[84] E.g., Van Zandt v. Comm'r, 341 F2d 440 (5th Cir.), cert. denied, 382 US 814 (1965); Mathews v. Comm'r, 520 F2d 323 (5th Cir. 1975). But see Brooke v. United States, 468 F2d 1155 (9th Cir. 1972). See also current Section 673, eliminating the ten-year reversionary safe harbor allowed when these cases were litigated.

[85] Estate of Barlow v. Comm'r, 55 TC 666 (1971), acq. 1972-2 CB 1; Estate of Giselman v. Comm'r, 55 TCM (CCH) 1654 (1988). Cf. Estate of Stubblefield v. Comm'r, 42 TCM (CCH) 342 (1981).

sively retained and inadequate rent is paid[86] or there is *no* agreement to pay rent,[87] then Section 2036(a)(1) appropriately has been applied.

The government has asserted that if a residence is leased back at its fair market value, the business property rule should not be followed and Section 2036(a)(1) should apply.[88] The government's distinction between business and nonbusiness property is meaningless and the courts should not accept it.[89] However, a recent somewhat distinguishable case[90] involving a sale and lease-back gives cause for concern of the eventual outcome of the issue. In that case, two years before her death, the decedent "sold" her personal residence to her son and his wife for $270,000, with the applicable gift tax annual exclusion amounts of $20,000[91] forgiven simultaneously with the sale. A mortgage note was executed for the $250,000 balance. Following the "sale," the decedent leased the house from her son and daughter-in-law for an amount that closely approximated the annual mortgage interest owed by them to her. The decedent resided in the house until her death. In each of the years following the sale, decedent forgave the mortgage debt equal to the then annual exclusion amounts of $20,000; and, in her will, which was executed *two days after the sale*, the decedent forgave the balance of the debt. The Second Circuit agreed with the Tax Court that the "sale" did not constitute a sale but, instead, a transfer within Section 2036 because it was anticipated that there would be no payment of any portion of the purchase price. Even though the decedent dotted every "i" and crossed every "t," the court applied substance over form to apply Section 2036(a). The case casts a shadow over inclusions in the gross estate of inter vivos transfers well beyond the retained residential context in which it arose.

---

[86] In Estate of Du Pont v. Comm'r, 63 TC 746 (1975) the rent to be paid was not commensurate with the value of the property and the arrangement seemed to involve an elaborate tax-saving plan. The Tax Court viewed the arrangement as a kind of sham and simply treated the transfer as one with enjoyment retained within Section 2036(a)(1). "[W]e are firmly convinced," said the court (id. at 764) "that the series of legal steps . . . comprised a single device, wholly lacking in substance, by which decedent attempted to divest himself of title to the property without relinquishing his possession or enjoyment thereof." In these circumstances, the court said, "it is quite beside the point that decedent paid some, albeit inadequate 'rent'. . . . " Id. at 766.

[87] See supra ¶ 4.08[4][c] text accompanying notes 42–48.

[88] Priv. Ltr. Rul. 9146002 (July 31, 1991).

[89] A similar issue arises where a transferor of a personal residence trust leases the residence after the termination of the trust. See ¶ 19.03[3][d] note 177.

[90] Estate of Maxwell v. Comm'r, 3 F3d 591 (2d Cir. 1993), aff'g 98 TC 594 (1992).

[91] See ¶ 9.04[1].

[d] Section 2036(b) Transfer of Stock

Gifts of corporate stock create a unique problem under Section 2036. If one makes an outright transfer to an independent trustee and retains no interest in or control over the trust, Section 2036 seems inapplicable. Of course, if it is corporate stock that is transferred and the transferor retains control over the corporation, the trust and its beneficiaries may continue to feel the transferor's presence.

Generally, there is no overlap of the Section 2036(a)(1) statutory concepts of the "right to income" from property and the "possession and enjoyment" of property because the former applies to income-producing property and the latter to non-income-producing property. However, if during life a decedent had transferred voting stock of a "controlled" corporation to a trust irrevocably naming a third party as the income beneficiary, but the decedent had retained the right to vote such stock, Section 2036(a)(1) includes the voting stock within the decedent's gross estate. Even though the decedent did not retain the right to the income from the stock, Section 2036(b) provides nevertheless that there is a Section 2036(a)(1) retention of enjoyment of the stock. Under Section 2036(b),[92] referred to as the "anti-*Byrum*" provision,[93] the direct or indirect retention of voting rights in a "controlled corporation" is "considered" a retention of the "enjoyment" of transferred property so as to trigger application of Section 2036(a)(1).[94] The requirements for inclusion are essentially twofold: First, there must be a "controlled corporation;" and second, the decedent must have retained voting rights with respect to the corporation.

Section 2036(b)(2) defines "controlled corporation" as one in which the decedent owns, directly or by attribution under Section 318,[95] stock possessing at least 20 percent of the combined voting power of all classes of stock of the corporation. Even in the absence of stock ownership, actual or attributed, a corporation is controlled if the decedent has a right to vote (either alone or in

---

[92] See Revenue Act of 1978, Pub. L. No. 95-600, § 702(i), 92 Stat. 2763, 2931 (1978), reprinted in 1978-3 CB (Vol. 1) 1, 165. Section 2036(b) is effective for transfers made after June 22, 1976. See Plant & Wintress, "Planning for Shareholders Who Wish to Retain Control Without Invoking the Anti-*Byrum* Rules," 11 Est. Plan. 74 (1984).

[93] See United States v. Byrum, 408 US 125, reh'g denied, 409 US 898 (1972).

[94] IRC § 2036(b)(1). Although the *Byrum* case involved possible application of both Section 2036(a)(1) and Section 2036(a)(2), nevertheless the anti-*Byrum* provision relates only to retained enjoyment under Section 2036(a)(1). Congress clearly did not focus only on the effect voting rights might have on dividend payments and thus on the designation of who might enjoy the trust income.

[95] Section 318 provides a set of rules for attribution of stock ownership under which stock actually owned by other persons or entities is treated as owned by the taxpayer involved. For a discussion of the intricacies of Section 318, see Bittker & Eustice, Federal Income Taxation of Corporations and Shareholders, ¶ 9.02 (Warren, Gorham & Lamont, 7th ed. 2000).

conjunction with any other person)[96] at least 20 percent of the combined voting power.[97] The ownership of stock or voting rights must have been at a time after the decedent's transfer of the property to the trust and during the three-year period ending with the decedent's death.[98]

The second requirement, that a decedent have directly or indirectly[99] retained the voting rights of the stock in question,[100] is met if the decedent transferred stock to a trust naming decedent as trustee with the trustee having power to vote the stock. The requirement is also met if the decedent was a co-

---

[96] This power could be held by the decedent as a co-trustee or with an adverse party. See Prop. Reg. § 20.2036-2(c); supra ¶ 4.08[5][b]. However, if the transferor is a co-trustee and state law permits each trustee to vote a proportionate number of the shares held, the transferor should not be treated as having a right to vote the co-trustee's shares because those shares are not held in conjunction with the co-trustee.

[97] See Prop. Reg. § 20.2036-2(d)(2). Voting power is determined by the stock's power to elect directors. Stock that may vote only on extraordinary matters such as mergers and liquidations is disregarded. Treasury stock and stock that is authorized but unissued is also disregarded. The statute allows Section 318 attribution only to determine actual ownership of stock, not to attribute voting rights as well. IRC § 2036(b)(2). Prop. Reg. § 20.2036-2(c), fourth sentence, is consistent with the statute. However, Prop. Reg. § 20.2036-2(d)(1) is drafted too broadly in also permitting use of Section 318 attribution to determine the portion of voting rights. Prop. Reg. § 20.2036-2(d)(1) should be amended to permit attribution only to determine ownership, not to determine voting rights. Cf. Prop. Reg. § 20.2036-2(d)(2)(iii) Ex. which is vague as to the rationale for Section 318 attribution.

[98] See IRC § 2036(b)(3). Thus, if a decedent who had held 50 percent of the stock or voting rights of a corporation transferred 70 percent of the stock or rights (reducing the decedent's stock rights to 15 percent) to unrelated parties more than three years prior to the decedent's death, there would be no "controlled corporation" and the decedent's possession of voting rights over the retained 15 percent would not trigger the application of Section 2036(a)(1), although practically speaking, even with only 15 percent, the decedent might control the corporation. On the other hand, if the decedent transferred only 5 percent of the stock of a corporation to a trust and the decedent retained only voting rights (no right to income or power to designate) in the stock transferred to the trust, but the decedent was also an independent trustee of an unrelated trust with only third-party beneficiaries, and in that capacity held voting rights over another 16 percent of the stock, the 5 percent transferred to the first trust is included in the decedent's gross estate.

[99] Prop. Reg. § 20.2036-2(c); Rev. Rul. 80-346, 1980-2 CB 271.

[100] An inter vivos relinquishment of such voting rights might prevent their being held for one of the disqualifying periods required by Section 2036. See supra ¶ 4.08[2]. However, Section 2036(b)(3) provides that if such rights are relinquished or cease within three years of death, the relinquishment will be treated as a transfer of property for Section 2035 purposes. Thus, if a decedent who holds voting rights in a "controlled corporation" releases them within three years of death, the release will be treated as a transfer of the property that, if held until death, would have been included in the decedent's gross estate under Section 2036. Cf. IRC § 2035(a)(2); Prop. Reg. § 20.2036-2(b).

trustee,[101] or was not a trustee but had the power to name decedent as trustee, if the trustee has the required voting rights.[102] If the provision is to have its intended effect, the requirement will have to be considered met in a situation where the decedent transfers cash to a trust on the understanding that the trust will purchase stock and the decedent will have the right to vote the stock.[103] Stated more clearly, if a decedent transfers cash to the trust and several years later, as trustee, the decedent invests in stock of a controlled corporation over which the decedent holds the voting rights, this also falls within the concept of indirect retention of voting rights and results in inclusion in the decedent's estate.[104] Further, the subsection should also apply where the stock of one corporation is sold or exchanged for stock with voting rights of another controlled corporation.[105]

Thus, if a decedent "controls" a corporation and transfers its voting stock to a trust with decedent as trustee, providing the income is paid to A for A's life, remainder to B, the decedent's ability as trustee to vote the stock leaves the property in the decedent's estate under Section 2036(a)(1) if the decedent dies before or less than three years after the death of A.[106] What results in this situation if the corporation has both voting and nonvoting stock and the decedent transfers only nonvoting stock to the trust? An initial thought is that the nature of the decedent's control over the trust property is much the same as if the decedent had transferred the voting stock. However, under the *statute*, that may be a misleading thought. With regard to controlled corporations, Congress chose to attack retained "enjoyment" under paragraph (1) of Section 2036(a), not powers to "designate" enjoyment under paragraph (2). Consequently, solely as a matter of statutory interpretation (not as a matter of tax policy), it is not surprising to find a comment in the legislative history[107] placing a transfer of nonvoting stock outside the reach of Section 2036 in such an instance,

---

[101] Prop. Reg. § 20.2036-2(c). Cf. Gilman v. Comm'r, 547 F2d 32 (2d Cir. 1976); TAM 199938005 (June 7, 1999) (stock transferred to limited partnership, but decedent retained right to vote stock separately).

[102] See supra ¶ 4.08[5][a].

[103] See Prop. Reg. § 20.2036-2(e)(2). Cf. infra ¶ 4.08[8][a]; Prop. Reg. §§ 20.2036-2(e)(1) (second sentence), 20.2036-2(e)(4) Ex. 2.

[104] HR Rep. No. 700, 95th Cong., 1st Sess. 76–77 (1977). The proposed regulations incorporate these rules. See Prop. Reg. § 20.2036-2(e). Generally, the proposed regulations seem valid, although they may be unreasonable in some circumstances. See, for example, Prop. Reg. § 20.2036-2(e)(4) Ex. 3, where it would seem that some showing of a step transaction would be mandatory (see also Skifter v. Comm'r, 468 F2d 699 (2d Cir. 1972); Rev. Rul. 84-179, 1984-2 CB 195, both discussed at ¶ 4.14[4][e]); and Prop. Reg. § 20.2036-2(e)(4) Ex. 4 based on a questionable formula provided in Proposed Regulations Section 20.2036-2(e)(2).

[105] Prop. Reg. § 20.2036-2(e)(3). Cf. Prop. Reg. § 20.2036-2(b).

[106] See IRC §§ 2036(b)(3), 2035(a)(2); supra note 98.

[107] HR Rep. No. 700, 95th Cong., 1st Sess. 76-77 (1977).

even though the decedent has and keeps control of sorts by way of retained voting stock. The proposed regulations adopt the same interpretation.[108] This same line of reasoning supports an interpretation of the statute to make Section 2036 applicable only to the value of voting stock transferred, if a decedent transfers some voting and some nonvoting stock of a controlled corporation. The apparent sense of the statute is that the decedent has retained "enjoyment" only of the voting stock; again, control, if any, over the transferred nonvoting stock is irrelevant for purposes of Section 2036(b).

On a policy level, it may be questioned whether there is a kind of de facto power to designate enjoyment of the transferred interest when the decedent controls the valve freeing or restraining dividend payments.[109] An amendment could be framed to make that a relevant question under Section 2036. However, if that is done, Congress should at the same time address itself to other circumstances in which a decedent may have de facto control over enjoyment of others—the case of the friendly or at least nonadverse trustee, and so forth. Additionally, when Congress looks only to paragraph (1) enjoyment and disregards paragraph (2) control, it invites manipulation. Much of what could be done by transferring voting stock retaining voting rights can be accomplished by a transfer only of nonvoting stock, even if a recapitalization is required to create the nonvoting stock. It is difficult, therefore, to feel that Congress has responded significantly to the problems brought into sharper focus by the *Byrum* decision; however, with the repeal of the short-lived Section 2036(c) and the enactment of Chapter 14,[110] Section 2036(b) applies in very limited circumstances.[111]

[e] Other Legislative Possibilities

Without attempting detailed legislative proposals, the following ideas might be advanced. Congress could provide that if a trust settlor names settlor trustee and retains that position until death (or relinquishes it within three years of death), the settlor's gross estate will include the value of the property transferred to the trust. If this approach were taken, it would seem prudent to apply the same rule to a settlor who makes the settlor's spouse trustee and of course to one who reserved the right to substitute oneself for the named trus-

---

[108] Prop. Reg. § 20.2036-2(a); Rev. Rul. 81-15, 1981-1 CB 457; Priv. Ltr. Rul. 9710021 (Dec. 6, 1996) (nonvoting stock transferred to a business trust which was treated as a partnership). The proposed regulations cited also contain the Service's definition of voting stock for purposes of Section 2036(b) inclusion. Compare the definition of "voting power" for control purposes. See supra note 97.

[109] Note that in *Byrum*, question was raised whether the decedent had such control.

[110] Chapter 14 is discussed at ¶¶ 19.01–19.05.

[111] Perhaps that is why the Treasury, who promulgated proposed regulations under the subsection in 1983, has failed to finalize those regulations.

tee.[112] The problem, however, if it really is one, is nearly as great where others are named trustees because of the high probability that they will simply comply with the settlor's wishes. Congress could provide that if any "related or subordinate party"[113] other than the grantor or his spouse is named trustee, the same result would follow. If this were thought to go too far, as indeed it seems to, then the result might be made to turn on whether such a related or subordinate party was given more than mere fiduciary powers.

[7] Transfer by the Decedent

Section 2036 is applicable only with regard to an interest in property that has been transferred by the decedent.[114] Transfers by others, which create rights in the decedent, do not invoke the provisions of this section, except for others' transfers imputed to the decedent, such as by way of the reciprocal trust doctrine.[115] For example, a classic estate-planning tool has been the grandfather trust, which is simply a transfer by an individual providing for the payment of income to a child for life, remainder to a grandchild. The interest received by the child terminates on the child's death and nothing is includable in the child's estate under Section 2036, as the child was not the transferor.[116] Moreover, the question whether a decedent has made a transfer of an interest in property[117] generally depends on whether under local property law the decedent had an interest that the decedent could transfer.[118] There are some circumstances, however, in which the courts have invented an estate tax concept of

---

[112] Cf. IRC § 672(c)(1).

[113] See IRC § 672(c)(2). Such action, if taken, should be taken by Congress, not the Treasury. See supra ¶¶ 4.08[4][b] note 32, 4.08[5][a] note 61.

[114] This requires an actual or imputed transfer by decedent. Estate of Brown v. Comm'r, 73 TCM (CCH) 2655 (1997) (transaction was not a transfer by decedent); Priv. Ltr. Rul. 200203045 (Oct. 19, 2001) (trustee was not the transferor to a trust where transfer made by trustee pursuant to court order). A mere computational election to split gifts under Section 2513 effects no transfer recognized by Section 2036. Cf. Rev. Rul. 74-556, 1974-2 CB 300. For examples of an imputed transfer by a decedent see TAM 9043074 (July 12, 1990); TAM 9506004 (Nov. 1, 1994).

[115] See infra ¶ 4.08[7][d].

[116] The trust would be subject to the tax on generation-skipping transfers because there would be a taxable termination at child's death. See ¶ 13.02[2].

[117] A contingent interest in property can be the subject of a Section 2036 transfer. Rev. Rul. 72-611, 1972-2 CB 256.

[118] Heasty v. United States, 239 F. Supp. 345 (D. Kan. 1965), aff'd, 370 F2d 525 (10th Cir. 1966). See Estate of Anderson v. Comm'r, 32 TCM (CCH) 1164 (1973); American Nat'l Bank & Trust Co. v. Comm'r, 33 TCM (CCH) 1158 (1974), raising the issue whether there was ownership by a donee decedent of property held in trust or whether the donor made the transfer to the trust. See infra ¶ 4.08[8][a] text accompanying notes 175–179.

ownership to identify a property interest that has been the subject of a transfer, even though no interest in the transferor would be recognized under local law.[119] This problem raises a question whether the requisite transfer has taken place to render Section 2036 applicable, and it also may bear on the amount to be included in the gross estate if Section 2036 is found applicable.[120]

[a] Indirect Transfers

Under certain circumstances another's transfer of an interest in property is imputed to the decedent; the decedent may be treated as having made a transfer of property that the decedent, personally, never really transferred at all. In some instances, this is not difficult to understand; if the decedent pays another person $10,000 to transfer real estate of like value into a trust, it is not unrealistic to treat the decedent as the one who transferred such real estate to the trust, even though the decedent never owned it.[121] Section 2036 is silent on this point, but the reality is discernible to the tax administrators and the courts in the application of this section and others that concern transfers by the decedent.[122]

Indirect transfers have been found in other unusual circumstances. In the *Vease* case,[123] for example, after a decedent's death, all of the beneficiaries under his executed will agreed, as part of a family settlement, to substitute a distribution arrangement specified in an unexecuted will. The courts properly held that this agreement constituted a transfer by the beneficiaries under the executed will, just as if they had actually received their respective interests and had then made transfers of them. A similar result has been reached by treating as a transfer a beneficiary's agreement to extend a trust when the beneficiary had the right, instead, to receive the trust corpus.[124] When a husband, instead of repaying his wife for a loan she had made to him, transferred funds to a

---

[119] United States v. O'Malley, 383 US 627 (1966). See Estate of Thomson v. Comm'r, 495 F2d 246 (2d Cir. 1974).

[120] See infra ¶ 4.08[8][b].

[121] Estate of Shafer v. Comm'r, 749 F2d 1216 (6th Cir. 1984). But see Mahoney v. United States, 86-1 USTC ¶ 13,653 (SD Ohio 1985). See infra ¶ 4.08[8][b].

[122] See the quote from Lehman v. Comm'r, 109 F2d 99, 100 (2d Cir.), cert. denied, 310 US 637 (1940), infra ¶ 4.08[7][d] note 155.

[123] Comm'r v. Estate of Vease, 314 F2d 79 (9th Cir. 1963). See also Estate of Hoffman v. Comm'r, 78 TC 1069 (1982); National City Bank of Cleveland v. United States, 371 F2d 13 (6th Cir. 1966).

[124] Sexton v. United States, 300 F2d 490 (7th Cir.), cert. denied, 371 US 820 (1962). See Estate of Miller v. Comm'r, 58 TC 699 (1972) (a surviving wife's failure to assert her right to income from a portion of her husband's estate was treated upon her death as a Section 2036 transfer). But see Estate of Tull v. United States, 1974-2 USTC ¶ 13,010 (ED Mich. 1974).

trust in which she received a life interest, he was held to have acted as her agent in transferring corpus in the amount of the loan, and she was properly treated as the transferor.[125] A wife may be treated as transferring one half of the proceeds of a community property life insurance policy at the insured husband's death;[126] and where she holds Section 2036 powers over the proceeds, they are included in her estate at her death.[127]

[b] Transfers by Election

Transfers of an indirect nature may also arise out of some types of election situations. For example, if a beneficiary has a right to receive a fixed dollar amount of insurance proceeds upon another's death, but the beneficiary elects instead to have the insurance company hold the proceeds and pay interest on them for one's life with the proceeds passing at death to one's children, the election constitutes an indirect transfer, and upon one's death, the proceeds are included in one's gross estate under Section 2036(a)(1).[128]

[c] Spouse's Election

The recognized transfer may be less apparent in other election-type situations. For instance, if a husband bequeaths to his wife a life interest in a trust created by his will on the condition that she transfer outright to an unrelated person property equal in value to the life interest, she would be looked upon as having received consideration for her transfer to the unrelated person if she elects to make it, and thus would not have made a taxable lifetime gift.[129] However, at her death she should be viewed as a settlor of the husband's trust (as having made a transfer to it) to the extent that she procured an interest in it by way of her transfer to the unrelated person. Taking account of her "re-

---

[125] Estate of Marshall v. Comm'r, 51 TC 696 (1969), nonacq. 1969-2 CB xxvi. Cf. Rev. Rul. 81-166, 1981-1 CB 477.

[126] See ¶ 4.14[8] note 117.

[127] Estate of Bothun v. Comm'r, 35 TCM (CCH) 1008 (1976).

[128] Estate of Tuohy v. Comm'r, 14 TC 245 (1950); Estate of Morton v. Comm'r, 12 TC 380 (1949). Cf. Estate of Haggett v. Comm'r, 14 TC 325 (1950), acq. 1950-2 CB 2; Rev. Rul. 70-84, 1970-1 CB 188. Note that if the owner of the policy had simply provided in the policy that the decedent would receive the interest for life with a remainder to the decedent's children, nothing would be included within the decedent's estate, as the decedent would have made no transfer. But see IRC § 2612(a)(1); ¶ 13.02[2].

[129] IRC § 2512. If her transfer were to a family member, Section 2702 would apply. See ¶ 19.03.

tained" life interest, at her death Section 2036 would apply to the portion of the trust of which she is treated as the transferor.[130]

The transaction just described has a familiar counterpart which historically was employed in community property states and was commonly called a "*community property widow's*[131] *election.*"[132] Under the counterpart and assuming the husband predeceased the wife, the husband's will would provide that the widow would take none of the husband's community property unless she elected to transfer her interest in the community property to the decedent's testamentary trust, to which his community property was also transferred. If she did so, the corpus of the trust was made up of both spouses' community property, she received in return a life interest in the entire trust, and the remainder was left to third persons, generally their children. The decedent husband's property was fully included in his estate at his death,[133] and the wife, who made the election at the time of her husband's death, was deemed to have made a gift in an amount equal to the excess of the value of the property interest she gave to others (a remainder to the children in her community property) over the consideration she received (a life interest in the husband's community property).[134] The sought-after tax-saving aspect of the widow's election oc-

---

[130] Consideration received from her husband would reduce her gross estate inclusion. See IRC § 2043(a), infra text accompanying notes 136–143. Such consequences should also follow as a result of a widow's electing a life estate in some of a deceased husband's property in exchange for relinquishing her dower or statutory rights in lieu thereof. See Westfall, "Estate Planning and the Widow's Election," 71 Harv. L. Rev. 1269, 1284 (1968).

[131] The term "widow's" election is somewhat outdated. At the time the technique was initially employed, a widow generally survived her spouse. However, most plans also provide for an alternate widower's election if the wife predeceases.

[132] The historically employed community property widow's election is discussed in the following articles: Wilson, "The Widow's Election Viewed in the Light of the 1976 Tax Reform Act and the 1975 California Probate Code Revision," 28 Hastings LJ 1435 (1977); Kahn & Gallo, "The Widow's Election: A Return to Fundamentals," 24 Stan. L. Rev. 531 (1972); Lane, "The Widow's Election as a Private Annuity: Boon or Bane for Estate Planners?" 44 S. Cal. L. Rev. 74 (1971); Johanson, "Revocable Trusts, Widow's Election Wills, and Community Property: The Tax Problems," 47 Tex. L. Rev. 1247 (1969); Halbach, "The Community Property Widow's Election and Some of Its Counterparts," 107 Tr. & Est. 108 (1968).

[133] IRC § 2033.

[134] Comm'r v. Siegel, 250 F2d 339 (9th Cir. 1957). See ¶ 10.01[3][b].

One common variation was to give the widow a special power of appointment over the remainder to the children. See Johanson, "Revocable Trusts, Widow's Election Wills, and Community Property: The Tax Problems," 47 Tex. L. Rev. 1247, 1295 (1969). This would avoid any gift by the wife at the time of her election because her transfer would be incomplete for gift tax purposes. Estate of Sanford v. Comm'r, 308 US 39 (1939). See ¶ 10.01[6]. However, providing the wife a special power over the remainder could create other problems. The bargain or exchange aspect of the widow's election seems to disappear and the creation of the trust may involve only a straight bequest by the husband and

curred at the time of the widow's death.[135] Although the widow transferred her property and retained a Section 2036(a)(1) life interest in it, she received consideration equal to the value of her life interest in her husband's community property for her transfer and, consequently, only a portion, possibly none,[136] of her community property that she previously owned outright would be included in her gross estate under Section 2036(a)(1).[137]

Over the years, legislation[138] and case law have created obstacles which have dramatically altered the possibility of benefiting from using the commu-

---

a concurrent transfer by the wife to the trust for no consideration. Lack of consideration for her transfer would increase the amount included in her estate under Section 2036(a)(1). See Johanson, "Revocable Trusts, Widow's Election Wills, and Community Property: The Tax Problems," 47 Tex. L. Rev. 1247, 1309 (1969). In addition, with an eye to the income tax, if the wife never transferred anything of value in acquiring her life interest, it would not have been acquired by purchase and would not be amortizable (IRC § 273) and would have no cost basis on a separate sale (IRC § 1001(e)); but in addition there would seem to be no purchase or sale with possible adverse income tax consequences to the husband's estate. See infra note 151.

[135] Note, however, that income generated by all the trust property, including that transferred by the decedent husband, that was not consumed or given away by the widow, enlarged her wealth and would be included in her gross estate under Section 2033. It is this fact that supports the notion that the widow receives partial consideration for her transfer and, taken into account with gift tax that may be paid at the time of election, might substantially reduce the supposed tax savings.

[136] See the hypothetical infra note 137.

[137] Assume that husband (H) transferred his one half of the community property worth $1 million to a trust with income to his wife (W) for life with a remainder to their children at a time when W's life estate and the remainder each had a 50 percent actuarial value. The results under the historically employed widow's election were as follows:

H's community property subject to estate tax: § 2033 inclusion and no § 2056 deduction	$1 million
W's community property gift: $500,000 remainder transferred minus $500,000 life estate consideration received	0
W's community property subject to estate tax: no § 2036 inclusion because adequate and full consideration was received for the transferred remainder	0
Total of their $2 million of community property subject to transfer tax taxation	$1 million

This hypothetical disregards any consideration of use of a Section 2010 credit shelter trust. See ¶ 3.02 note 2; ¶ 5.06[6]. Use by both spouses of a shelter trust would not alter the end result: subjection of only one half of the community property in excess of any sheltered amount to transfer taxation.

[138] The QTIP exception to the marital deduction terminable interest rule provides a likely alternate way to use a community property widow's election. IRC § 2056(b)(7). See ¶ 5.06[8][d]. As a result of this provision, the husband's estate can qualify a portion of

nity property widow's election technique. However, as a result of recent case

---

the husband's transfer to the community property trust for a marital deduction. However, the husband's property qualifying for a marital deduction is generally then included in the widow's gross estate under Section 2044. See ¶ 4.16. This alternate does not impose an obstacle to use of the widow's election.

A hypothetical may be helpful to illustrate the consequences here. Assume, in facts similar to those supra note 137, that *H* (husband) has community property worth $1 million and that he creates a community property widow's election with a GRAT or GRUT for *W* (widow) which has an actuarial value equal to 50 percent of the corpus. The hypothetical assumes that a GRAT or GRUT is a "qualifying income interest" under Section 2056(b)(7)(B)(ii); however, that assumption may not be valid. See ¶ 5.06[8][d] notes 342–344. The consequences are as follows:

No QTIP election (supra note 137 hypothetical):

H's community property subject to estate tax:	$1 million
W's community property gift: $500,000 transferred remainder minus $500,000 consideration received	0
W's community property subject to estate tax—no § 2036 inclusion because adequate and full consideration was received for the remainder	0
Total	$1 million

QTIP election:

H's community property subject to estate tax: $1 million less § 2056 marital deduction, $500,000 (the amount of $1 million subject to the § 2056(b)(7) election less consideration *H* received, $500,000, see United States v. Stapf, 375 US 118 (1963), ¶ 5.06[5][b])	$ 500,000
W's community property gift: $500,000 transferred remainder minus $500,000 consideration received	0
W's gross estate: none of her community property included under § 2036(a), but § 2044 would include $500,000 (the portion of *H*'s property that qualified under § 2056(b)(7))	0
Total	$1 million

The hypothetical illustrates that where there is no appreciation in the value of the property subject to the QTIP election, the use of a QTIP election results in no difference in tax liability. However, as a practical matter, failure to make a QTIP election will result in a payment of estate tax dollars at the time of *H*'s death. This disadvantage in failing to make a QTIP election must be weighed against the potential QTIP disadvantage of including the appreciation in the portion of the property subject to the QTIP election in *W*'s gross estate under Section 2044.

Section 2036

law,[139] there may be an opportunity to revitalize its use. For many years, the first obstacle was *Estate of Gradow*,[140] which represented the prevailing view among both the courts and the Service of the manner in which Section 2036(a) applied to the widow's gross estate.[141] In *Gradow*, the Federal Circuit held that whether the Section 2036(a) exception for a bona fide sale for full and adequate consideration applied to a transfer of the widow's community property interest was dependent upon the entire value of the widow's community property transferred, not the value of the remainder interest she transferred.[142] More recently, however, several other Circuit Courts of Appeal have held (but not in the context of a community property widow's election) that if there is a bona fide sale of the remainder interest for its fair market value (with a retained life estate), Section 2036(a) is inapplicable, because the transferor has received full and adequate consideration for the transferred remainder.[143] This result is more sound than the result reached in *Gradow*.[144] However, it may be argued that *Gradow* is still the applicable law in a community property widow's election

---

[139] Estate of D'Ambrosio v. Comm'r, 101 F3d 309 (3rd Cir. 1996); Wheeler v. United States, 116 F3d 749 (5th Cir. 1997); Estate of Magnin v. Comm'r, 184 F3d 1074 (9th Cir. 1999). The cases are discussed in more detail at ¶ 4.08[1][a] notes 8–10.

[140] Estate of Gradow v. United States, 11 Cl. Ct. 808 (1987) aff'd, 897 F2d 516 (Fed. Cir. 1990).

[141] See Estate of Vardell v. Comm'r, 307 F2d 688 (5th Cir. 1962) (recognizing Section 2043(a) consideration but not considering what is adequate and full consideration); Estate of Gregory v. Comm'r, 39 TC 1012 (1963) (Section 2036(a) applied where inadequate consideration was received for the remainder or the corpus). See Brown, "The *Allen* Case and the Widow's Election," 36 S. Cal. L. Rev. 229 (1963); Bomash v. Comm'r, 432 F2d 308 (9th Cir. 1970) (variation on the standard community property widow's election); Estate of Sparling v. Comm'r, 552 F2d 1340 (9th Cir. 1977) (dealing with the Section 2013 credit in a community property widow's election situation).

[142] Thus, at the widow's death the full value of the widow's one half of the community property was included in her gross estate reduced only by the dollar value of the consideration she received from the husband. IRC §§ 2036(a)(1), 2043(a). Thus, under the *Gradow* case in the hypothetical, supra note 137, Section 2036(a)(1) would have applied with the result that the value of *W*'s one half of the community property at her death would be included in her gross estate reduced under Section 2043(a) by only the dollar amount ($500,000) of consideration she received.

[143] Estate of D'Ambrosio v. Comm'r, 101 F3d 309 (3d Cir. 1996); Wheeler v. United States, 116 F3d 749 (5th Cir. 1997); Estate of Magnin v. Comm'r, 184 F3d 1074 (9th Cir. 1999). The cases are discussed in more detail supra ¶ 4.08[1][a] text accompanying notes 8–10.

[144] In *Gradow*, the court likely inappropriately applied Section 2036(a). See supra ¶ 4.08[1][a]. See also Estate of Christ v. Comm'r, 54 TC 493 (1970), aff'd, 480 F2d 171 (9th Cir. 1973) (seemingly disagreeing with *Gradow*) and Parker v. United States, 75 AFTR2d 95-2509 (ND Ga. 1995) (where the court acknowledged that it had "some reservations about the correctness of *Gradow*").

context, because while full and adequate consideration may have been received,[145] the widow's transfer was not "*a bona fide sale.*"[146]

Another obstacle[147] to the historically employed community property widow's election is the enactment of Section 2702.[148] If the remainder transfer is to a family member, Section 2702 values the wife's retained interest at zero for gift tax purposes,[149] increasing the amount of the widow's gift transfer by the value of the retained income interest.[150] Uncertain income consequences have also created a potential obstacle to the use of the community property widow's election.[151] In summary, although the line of cases disagreeing with the *Gradow* result *may* remove an obstacle to the use of the community property widow's election, other obstacles continue to cast a shadow over employment of the community property widow's election technique.[152]

---

[145] See supra text accompanying note 143.

[146] Jordan, "Sales of Remainder Interests: Reconciling Gradow v. United States and Section 2702," 14 Va. Tax Rev. 671, 716-718 (1975); Jensen, "Estate and Gift Tax Effects of Selling a Remainder: Have *D'Ambrosio, Wheeler,* and *Magnin* Changed the Rules?" 4 Fla. Tax Rev. 537, 585-589 (1999). However, note that a bona fide sale is recognized in community property widow's election situations for income tax purposes. See infra text accompanying note 151.

[147] The Section 2702 obstacle is seemingly avoided if the widow retains a "qualified income interest" in the form of a GRAT or a GRUT or avoids the Section 2702 zero valuation rule in some other manner. See IRC §§ 2702(a)(2)(A), 2702(b)(1), 2702(b)(2); ¶¶ 19.03[3][b], 19.03[3][b][i]. See also Jordan, "Sales of Remainder Interests: Reconciling *Gradow v. United States* and Section 2702," 14 Va. Tax Rev. 671 (1995); Croman, "Remainder Interests May Again Be Viable," 23 Tax. for Law. 74 (1994).

Seemingly, a transfer of a remainder interest in a qualified personal residence trust would also result in an avoidance of the Section 2702 zero valuation rule. See IRC § 2702(a)(3)(A)(ii); ¶ 19.03[3][d].

[148] See ¶ 19.03.

[149] IRC §§ 2702(a)(1), 2702(a)(2)(A).

[150] Thus, in the hypothetical posed, supra note 137, *W* would make a gift at the time of her election equal to $1 million less $500,000 or $500,000. See ¶ 19.03[2][a] text accompanying note 30.

[151] Some cases have allowed the widow to amortize the cost of her income interest in the husband's property on the theory that she purchased the husband's income interest in a bona fide sale. Gist v. United States, 423 F2d 1118 (9th Cir. 1970); Estate of Christ v. Comm'r, 480 F2d 171 (9th Cir. 1973). However, if she purchased the husband's income interest, then the husband would have sold that interest with potentially disastrous income tax consequences under Section 1001(e)(1), unless the Section 1001(e)(3) exception is applicable. See Freeland, Lind, and Stephens, "What Are the Income Tax Effects of an Estate's Sale of a Life Interest?" 34 J. Tax'n 376 (1971); Wilson, "The Widow's Election Viewed in the Light of the 1976 Tax Reform Act and the 1975 California Probate Code Revision," 28 Hastings L. J. 1435 (1977).

[152] See supra text accompanying notes 147–151.

[d] Reciprocal Trusts

A transfer may be attributed to the decedent under a sophisticated judicial doctrine of "reciprocal" or "crossed" trusts.[153] For example, assume A sets up a trust for the benefit of B and at the same time B creates a trust of equal value for A, and under the provisions of A's trust, the income is to be paid to B for life with a remainder to B's children; and the trust B created provides for income to A for life, remainder to A's children. Literally, neither A nor B has made a transfer under which the transferor has retained a life interest; nevertheless, A and B are both in the same circumstances they would have been if they had done so. Consequently, the courts have developed the reciprocal trust doctrine, under which the grantors of the trusts are switched and each grantor is regarded as creating a trust under which the grantor retained a life interest, resulting in inclusion of the corpus in the grantor's gross estate.[154]

Although it is easy to state the theory underlying the reciprocal trust doctrine, it has been difficult to harness the theory so as to determine whether, on any particular facts, trusts will be treated as crossed. The Second Circuit, in first developing the doctrine, spoke in terms of one grantor paying a "quid pro quo" for the other grantor's transfer and of the trusts being established in consideration for one another.[155] For some time thereafter, the application of the reciprocal trust doctrine turned mainly on the crucial factor of consideration, which in turn depended in part on a determination of the subjective intent of the grantors.[156] However, in its first encounter with the reciprocal trust doctrine,[157] the Supreme Court in the *Grace* case[158] imposed a less stringent test to

---

[153] The doctrine applies not only under Section 2036 but also under other provisions, such as Section 2038, which depend on transfers by the decedent. See In re Lueder's Estate, 164 F2d 128 (3d Cir. 1947); Lehman v. Comm'r, 109 F2d 99 (2d Cir.), cert. denied, 310 US 637 (1940); Estate of Newberry, 6 TCM (CCH) 455 (1947), aff'd per curiam, 172 F2d 220 (3d Cir. 1948); Exchange Bank & Trust Co. of Fla. v. United States, 694 F2d 1261 (Fed. Cir. 1982); Estate of Bischoff v. Comm'r, 69 TC 32 (1977). But see Estate of Green v. United States, 68 F3d 151 (6th Cir. 1995) (refusing to apply the doctrine where the transferors did not personally have retained economic interests in the trusts, a decision that is too narrow an application of the reciprocal trust doctrine).

[154] United States v. Estate of Grace, 395 US 316 (1969); Lehman v. Comm'r, 109 F2d 99 (2d Cir.), cert. denied, 310 US 637 (1940).

[155] The court quoted Scott, Law of Trusts § 156.3, for the proposition that "a person who furnishes the consideration for the creation of a trust is the settlor, even though in form the trust is created by another." Lehman v. Comm'r, 109 F2d 99, 100 (2d Cir.), cert. denied, 310 US 637 (1940).

[156] McLain v. Jarecki, 232 F2d 211 (7th Cir. 1956); In re Lueder's Estate, 164 F2d 128 (3d. Cir. 1947); Estate of Newberry v. Comm'r, 201 F2d 874 (3d Cir. 1953).

[157] United States v. Estate of Grace, 395 US 316 (1969).

[158] It seems likely that given the broader *Grace* test, the courts deciding some earlier cases would not have rejected application of the reciprocal trust doctrine. See, e.g., McLain v. Jarecki, 232 F2d 211 (7th Cir. 1956); In re Lueder's Estate, 164 F2d 128 (3d Cir.

switch grantors, seemingly expanding the scope of the reciprocal trust doctrine. The Court said that application of the reciprocal trust doctrine is not dependent on questions of consideration, subjective intent, or a tax avoidance motive; instead, the Court said:[159] "Application of the reciprocal trust doctrine requires only that the trusts be interrelated, and that the arrangement, to the extent of mutual value, leaves the settlors in approximately the same economic position as they would have been in had they created trusts naming themselves as life beneficiaries."[160]

While the *Grace* decision unquestionably broadens the scope of the reciprocal trust doctrine, its still-value test leaves some doubt regarding to what extent the Commissioner may attempt to extend the doctrine. In *Grace*, the Court applied the doctrine in circumstances in which the terms of the trusts were identical, there was no time differential in the creation of the trusts, and the trusts were of equal value. These were all factors that the lower courts had previously looked to in determining the subjective intent question under the consideration test,[161] and it would appear that while the doctrine has been expanded, the *Grace* decision has mostly relieved the Commissioner of the bur-

---

1947), although in *Lueder* the lapse of fifteen months between the creation of the trusts might mitigate its reciprocal aspects. However, the trusts involved in some earlier cases would still likely not constitute reciprocal trusts, even under the *Grace* test. See, e.g., Estate of Ruxton v. Comm'r, 20 TC 487 (1953), acq. 1953-2 CB 6. But see Note, "*United States v. Estate of Grace*: The Reincarnation of the Reciprocal Trust Doctrine," 17 UCLA L. Rev. 436 (1969).

[159] United States v. Estate of Grace, 395 US 316, 324 (1969).

[160] In Estate of Bischoff v. Comm'r, 69 TC 32 (1977), the full Tax Court, in the first decision subsequent to United States v. Estate of Grace, 395 US 316, 324 (1969), was faced with applying the reciprocal trust doctrine. The majority apparently held that the mere similarity and the establishment of the trust produced the necessary interrelationship to apply the doctrine. Three judges concurred in the opinion, and four judges dissented. See also Exchange Bank & Trust Co. of Fla. v. United States, 694 F2d 1261 (Fed. Cir. 1982).

Presumably, the requirement that the trusts be "interrelated" would preclude, as it should if such a circumstance could ever be proved, an application of the doctrine in a case where two settlors quite unknowingly and coincidentally happened to create similar trusts for each other.

[161] The following factors figured prominently in the earlier cases: (1) identity of trust terms, Estate of Moreno v. Comm'r, 260 F2d 389 (8th Cir. 1958); Estate of Hanauer v. Comm'r, 149 F2d 857 (2d Cir.), cert. denied, 326 US 770 (1945); Lehman v. Comm'r, 109 F2d 99 (2d Cir.), cert. denied, 310 US 637 (1940); Estate of Newberry v. Comm'r, 201 F2d 874 (3d Cir. 1953); (2) simultaneous creation, Estate of Cole v. Comm'r, 140 F2d 636 (8th Cir. 1944); Estate of Eckhardt v. Comm'r, 5 TC 673 (1945); Estate of Fish v. Comm'r, 45 BTA 120 (1941), acq. 1942-1 CB 6. But see Priv. Ltr. Rul. 9735025 (May 30, 1997) and Priv. Ltr. Rul. 9804012 (Oct. 22, 1997) (no reciprocal trusts where reciprocal powers created 26 years after creation of the trusts); and (3) equivalency of value, Estate of Moreno v. Comm'r, supra; Lehman v. Comm'r, 109 F2d 99 (2d Cir.), cert. denied, 310 US 637 (1940).

den of proving subjective intent.[162] If the trust terms are not substantially identical, the doctrine is inapplicable.[163]

If trusts of unequal value are held to be reciprocal, the amount that can be included in either grantor's estate under Section 2036 is no more than the value of the smaller trust at the applicable estate valuation date. For example, in *Estate of Cole*,[164] a husband had transferred 700 shares of X Corporation stock in trust for his wife, the decedent, who at the same time transferred 300 shares of identical stock in trust for the husband. Each party was the income beneficiary for life under the trust set up by the other. The trusts were held to be reciprocal, and the gross estate of the decedent wife was held to include the value of 300 shares of the 700-share trust of which she was beneficiary; but the decedent was not treated as the transferor of the other 400 shares of the trust.[165]

This consideration of the reciprocal trust problems and earlier consideration of other indirect transfer phenomena should not be permitted to obscure the basic proposition that the decedent must have made a transfer of the property in question, either actual or imputed, for Section 2036 to bring the value of the property into the decedent's gross estate.

[8] Amount to Be Included

Under Section 2036, it is not the value of the interest retained by the decedent (such as a life interest) or controlled by the decedent (under a right to designate), but the date-of-death value of the property interest transferred in the proscribed manner, in general the trust corpus, that finds its way into the decedent's gross estate.[166] The idea here is that for tax purposes it is appropriate to treat the lifetime transfer as the equivalent of a testamentary disposition, if the decedent postponed the real effect of the transfer until death (or for a related period) by retention of the income or use or control over who else should have the property.

---

[162] See Turley, "Supreme Court's *Estate of Grace* Decision: What Does It Mean?" 31 J. Tax'n 130 (1969); Note, "New Standards for Application of the Reciprocal Trust Doctrine," 1970 Wis. L. Rev. 571; Wilson & Butler, "With Proper Planning, Even Reciprocal Trusts May Not Be Subject to Estate or Income Tax," 11 Est. Plan. 348 (1984); Note, "*United States v. Estate of Grace*: The Reincarnation of the Reciprocal Trust Doctrine," 17 UCLA L. Rev. 436 (1969).

[163] Estate of Levy v. Comm'r, 46 TCM (CCH) 910 (1983); Priv. Ltr. Rul. 9643013 (July 19, 1996).

[164] Estate of Cole v. Comm'r, 140 F2d 636 (8th Cir. 1944).

[165] Accord, Estate of Ruxton, 20 TC 487 (1953), acq. 1953-2 CB 6. Cf. Rev. Rul. 74-533, 1974-2 CB 293 (dealing with the Section 2012 credit in such circumstances).

[166] IRC § 2036(a). Cf. Fidelity-Philadelphia Trust Co. v. Rothensies, 324 US 108 (1945).

Section 2036 can apply in such a way as to include only a portion of property transferred by the decedent. For example, if *D* transferred a residence to *S* and retained for life the use of two out of eight rooms (assuming equal value for all rooms), one fourth of the date-of-death value of the residence would be included in *D*'s gross estate.[167] Similarly, if *D* transferred property in trust and retained for *D*'s life the right to one half of the income from the trust property, one half of the value of the trust corpus would be included in *D*'s gross estate at death.[168] Moreover, if, in making a transfer generally within the scope of Section 2036, an interest is created that is unaffected by the interest retained by *D*, the value of such an "outstanding interest" is excluded. This applies, for instance, to a secondary life estate in which *D*'s right to the income arises only upon the termination of a life interest in another person. In such circumstances, the amount to be included is the value of the property transferred, less the value of the outstanding life interest, as of the date of *D*'s death.[169] The reduction for outstanding interests was clearer, perhaps, under earlier statutory language. When the question was whether the interest was "intended to take effect in possession or enjoyment only at or after the decedent's death," interests not deferred as to possession or enjoyment were clearly not included. The result must be reached under the present statute by identifying

---

[167] See Rev. Rul. 79-109, 1979-1 CB 297, where the decedent retained the right to use a vacation home for a portion of each year.

[168] See Comm'r v. Estate of Dwight, 205 F2d 298 (2d Cir.), cert. denied, 346 US 871 (1953). If the decedent retained an income interest subject to a standard of support, then the amount of corpus necessary to produce the amount of income for support would be included in the decedent's estate.

See Rev. Rul. 76-273, 1976-2 CB 268 and Rev. Rul. 82-105, 1982-1 CB 133, for the Treasury's position on the amount of corpus inclusion where there is a retained income interest in a charitable remainder unitrust or annuity trust, respectively. It might be questioned whether there is a retention of "the income" generated by the corpus in such circumstances. See Estate of Becklenberg v. Comm'r, 273 F2d 297 (7th Cir. 1959); Estate of Bergan v. Comm'r, 1 TC 543 (1943), acq. 1943 CB 2. Because in the charitable remainder trust area, the transferred property generates the annuity or unitrust amount and a flat dollar amount is treated as income in establishing the value of the remainder, the Treasury's position seems proper.

The holding of the charitable remainder rulings, above, should also apply to grantor retained annuity trusts (GRATs) and grantor retained unitrusts (GRUTs). Priv. Ltr. Rul. 9412036 (Dec. 23, 1993) (GRUT); FSA 200036012 (May 25, 2000) (GRAT). See ¶ 19.03[3][b] note 120. The Service maintains that Section 2039 also applies to GRATs and GRATs potentially including the entire corpus of the GRAT or GRUT in a grantor's gross estate as compared to only the portion of the corpus which would be included under the charitable remainder rulings, above. See ¶ 4.11 note 3.

[169] Marks v. Higgins, 213 F2d 884 (2d Cir. 1954). See supra ¶ 4.08[2] text accompanying note 17. The regulations improperly, or at least questionably, restrict this exclusion to an outstanding interest "which is actually being enjoyed" at the date of death. Reg. § 20.2036-1(a). See Lowndes & Stephens, "Identification of Property Subject to the Federal Estate Tax," 65 Mich. L. Rev. 105, 126 (1966).

the several interests transferred and raising the question in each case whether the decedent has retained any interest or rights with respect to each transferred interest. As in the case of all the gross estate provisions concerning lifetime transfers, partial consideration received for the interest transferred reduces the amount to be included in the gross estate.[170]

As it is only the value of interests transferred by the decedent that is caught by Section 2036, the effect of its application to a trust may depend on whether persons other than the decedent have transferred property to the same trust. If A and B have both transferred property to a trust under which A has the right to the income for life and A dies, the amount includable in A's estate is only the portion of the trust property that can properly be identified as transferred by A.[171]

---

[170] IRC § 2043(a); ¶ 4.15[2]; Greene v. United States, 237 F2d 848 (7th Cir. 1956); Estate of Bianchi v. Comm'r, 44 TCM (CCH) 422 (1982); Pittman v. United States 878 F. Supp. 833 (EDNC 1994). See Rev. Rul. 79-94, 1979-1 CB 296, and the widow's election consequences, supra ¶ 4.08[7][c].

[171] Thus, if community property in which spouses have equal interests is transferred to a trust in which only one spouse has the right to the income for life, upon the death of the life beneficiary, one half the value of the trust corpus is includable in that spouse's gross estate. Katz v. United States, 382 F2d 723 (9th Cir. 1967). See Schwartz, "Revocable Trusts and California Marital Property," 20 USC Tax Inst. 363 (1968).

A problem arises if property is transferred to the same trust at different times and, for instance, the property transferred by A appreciates prior to B's transfer and then the combined corpus appreciates prior to A's death. For example, A transfers in trust X stock valued at 10, and the terms of the trust give A the right to all the trust income for A's life. The X stock then appreciates to 20. At this point, a transfer of Y stock valued at 10 is made to the trust by B. Both stocks are immediately sold, and all proceeds are invested in Z stock, which is valued at 40 when A dies. To arrive at a date-of-death valuation of the property transferred by A (and thus includable in A's gross estate), the appreciation must be allocated in some manner between the property transferred by A and that transferred by B. Although no case has dealt specifically with this problem under Section 2036, there has been an analogous treatment of this type of situation under now-repealed Section 2515 (Reg. § 25.2515-1(c)(2)). See Stephens, Maxfield & Lind, Federal Estate and Gift Taxation ¶ 10.06Y3][a] (Warren, Gorham & Lamont, 4th ed. 1978); IRC § 2040 (see Estate of Peters v. Comm'r, 386 F2d 404 (4th Cir. 1967), aff'g 46 TC 407, 415 n.4 (1966)). These authorities suggest a solution. It would seem that the proper method of allocation would be as follows: (1) If any of the appreciation is directly and identifiably traceable to any of the property actually transferred, it should be so allocated; and (2) if it is not directly traceable to any such property, then allocation should be made with reference to the relative values of the properties transferred at the times of transfers. Applying this method to the hypothetical facts above, first, the appreciation of the X stock from 10 to 20 is directly traceable to the property transferred by A. Therefore, that appreciation should be allocated to the value of that property. Second, it is clear that after the X and Y stock is sold and the proceeds commingled and reinvested, none of the 10 of remaining appreciation is directly traceable to either of the transfers, and it must therefore be allocated in a ratio of 20 (value of X stock at time of Y transfer) to 10 (value of Y stock at that time). On this basis, two thirds of the post-Y transfer appreciation of 10 (or 6⅔;) is allocated to A's trans-

[a] Accumulated Income

What about income accumulations added to corpus? If a decedent transferred property to a trust, retaining only the right to direct the accumulation of trust income, it is likely that Section 2036 applies to tax, as part of the decedent's estate, the property that the decedent actually transferred.[172] If income is in fact accumulated, is the accumulated income also to be included? It is now settled that it is.[173]

The result depends on a judge-made estate tax concept of ownership. The accumulated income may become a part of the corpus and subject to the same provisions as income from the original trust property. However, it is not possible to find any actual property interest in the decedent in the income that the decedent may direct to be accumulated. Consequently, in conventional property terms, the decedent cannot possibly be said to have made a transfer of such income. It is therefore a question whether the decedent's estate's liability for tax on accumulated income should not be controlled only by Section 2041,[174] which deals with property interest not transferred by the decedent but subject to the decedent's power. The Supreme Court has decided otherwise, perhaps questionably, treating income accumulations as if owned and transferred by the decedent for purposes of measuring tax liability under Section 2036.

The accumulation situation is not the only instance in which a judge-made estate tax ownership concept might seem a useful device; but it is not uniformly invoked. For example, assume that a decedent and a child had owned property jointly that the decedent originally funded and they subsequently transferred to another, retaining joint-and-survivor income interests. The child predeceased the decedent, and the decedent was in receipt of all the income at death. Only one half of the value of the property is included in the decedent's estate,[175] the portion actually transferred by the decedent, even though the entire value of the property would have been included under Sec-

---

fer, and a total of 26⅔ would be included in A's estate. See Priv. Ltr. Rul. 9206006 (Oct. 24, 1991) (involving a more complicated joint contribution factual scenario).

[172] See supra ¶ 4.08[4][c] text accompanying note 65. But see supra ¶ 4.08[4][c] text accompanying notes 66–73.

[173] United States v. O'Malley, 383 US 627 (1966). See also Horner v. United States, 485 F2d 596 (Ct. Cl. 1973). This principle does not apply to accumulated income that is transferred to a separate fund over which the decedent has no Section 2036 or Section 2038 controls. See Leopold v. United States, 510 F2d 617 (9th Cir. 1975), in which accumulated income did not become part of a Section 2036 trust corpus but was put into a separate account to be given to the income beneficiary at age 21.

[174] See ¶ 4.13.

[175] Cf. Heasty v. United States, 239 F. Supp. 345 (D. Kan. 1965), aff'd, 370 F2d 525 (10th Cir. 1966).

tion 2040(a)[176] if the lifetime transfer had not been made. An estate tax ownership concept, with collateral support from Section 2040, might have been
invoked to treat the decedent as the transferor of the entire property.[177] Despite
judicial rebuff,[178] the Commissioner should not give up on this issue short of
rejection by the Supreme Court.[179]

[b] Lifetime Relinquishment of Prescribed Interests

Literally, Section 2036 raises only the question whether the decedent has
made a lifetime gratuitous transfer of property retaining certain interests for a
specified period. Accordingly, it could be argued that a later lifetime relinquishment of the retained interest or right does not alter the fact that a prescribed transfer was made and that, however such relinquishment is made, the
value of the transferred property should be included in the transferor's estate.[180] Nonetheless, the lifetime relinquishment of the retained interest may

---

[176] See ¶ 4.12.

[177] See also Glaser v. United States, 306 F2d 57 (7th Cir. 1962). It is curious that the
Tenth Circuit, which decided Heasty v. United States, 239 F. Supp. 345 (D. Kan. 1965),
aff'd, 370 F2d 525 (10th Cir. 1966), and which had accepted an estate by ownership concept in United States v. Allen, 293 F2d 916 (10th Cir. 1961), before the Supreme Court
sanctioned such an approach in United States v. O'Malley, 383 US 627 (1966), rejected
the concept in *Heasty*, seemingly the most compelling circumstance for involving the concept. On the other hand, a rejection of an estate tax ownership concept may favor the government. The *Heasty* rationale supports a tax on one half of the value of joint tenancy
property transferred in a Section 2036 manner even in the estate of one who contributed
nothing to the acquisition of the jointly held property. Miller v. United States, 325 F.
Supp. 1287 (ED Pa. 1971). If full ownership were attributed to the potential Section 2040
estate tax owner, presumably the result would be otherwise, as the one who had contributed nothing would be seen as having no estate tax interest to transfer.

[178] Cf. Sullivan v. Comm'r, 175 F2d 657 (9th Cir. 1949).

[179] But see Rev. Rul. 69-577, 1969-2 CB 173, issued prior to the enactment of Section 2040(b), in which the Commissioner concedes the issue, saying in effect that the Service will follow Heasty v. United States, 239 F. Supp. 345 (D. Kan. 1965), aff'd, 370 F2d
525 (10th Cir. 1966). The ruling involved a tenancy by the entirety rather than a joint tenancy and concluded that one half of the value of the property was included in the decedent husband's estate. See also Priv. Ltr. Rul. 8331005 (Apr. 22, 1983). However, if the
husband's interest was worth less than one half of the value of the property, cf. Reg.
§ 25.2515-2(b)(2), only the value of his lesser proportionate interest should be included in
his estate, even though the income from the property was split equally, if actual legal interests are to control.

[180] Section 2036 states that the section applies if "at any time" the prescribed transfer
was made. See Breitenstein, J., concurring in United States v. Allen, 293 F2d 916, 918
(10th Cir. 1961).

This result has some theoretical justification. It is possible that a young person could
transfer property to a trust retaining a life estate and giving a remainder with a small actuarial value to a third person. At a later date, close to, but more than, three years prior to

Section 2036

render Section 2036 inapplicable, provided the relinquishment is not made within three years of death.[181] Such a two-step transaction should not be differentiated from a one-step transaction by which the decedent divests all interest in the property at the time of the initial transfer.

On the other hand, as a policy matter, few would argue that a "death bed" relinquishment of a life interest should be a recognized escape hatch from Section 2036. Section 2036 is deficient in this respect; it is silent on the issue. However, Section 2035(a) is applicable.[182] Section 2035 mandates inclusion where an interest that would have generated inclusion under Section 2036 if retained by the decedent until death is relinquished within three years of death. In effect, Section 2036 is exhumed by the application of Section 2035(a).

The problem is aggravated if the tainting life interest is *sold* for its full value. Retention of the interest until death might, for instance, make a $100,000 trust fully includable in the decedent's gross estate; but the value of the life interest (if the individual who has it is old) might be $1,000. Can the life interest be sold for its full value, $1,000, to defeat an inclusion of $100,000?[183] To avoid this absurdity, the convenient device of an estate tax ownership concept has been judicially applied here with seemingly good reason.[184] The transaction is seen to involve the value of the property that would have been included absent the transfer. Thus, the $1,000 received represents only partial consideration, and the date-of-death value of the trust property (maybe $100,000), less the consideration received ($1,000), is included.[185] Congress did not tighten up Section 2035 as we have urged, but, even so, the

---

the transferor's death (when the value of the income interest is small), the transferor could give the remaining income interest to a third person. The effect of such transfers, even if the income interest is transferred for adequate and full consideration, may be to remove most of the value of the corpus from transfer tax consequences (but see Section 2702 discussed ¶ 19.03), although such a result is theoretically inappropriate.

[181] Cf. IRC § 2035(a). Although perhaps theoretically inappropriate, it is the authors' opinion that United States v. Allen, 293 F2d 916 (10th Cir. 1961), in the context of Section 2036(a)(1) should be limited to its facts, i.e., a situation in which the transfer of a retained life estate occurs within three years of the transferor's death. If such transfers beyond three years of the decedent's death are to be pulled into the decedent's gross estate, Congress should provide for such a result. But see supra note 180.

The *Allen* case should be applied where there is a commutation of a trust within three years of the death of the transferor who held a retained life estate if the transferor was instrumental in the commutation action (cf. Priv. Ltr. Rul. 9815023 (Apr. 10, 1998)) (no ruling on *Allen* issue) or there was an implied agreement with the commuting trustee (cf. Priv. Ltr. Rul. 9935003 (May 18, 1999)) (ruling treated original transferor as commuting the trust implying an implied agreement).

[182] See ¶ 4.07[2][a].

[183] Generally, a transfer for full consideration is outside the special provisions on lifetime transfers. IRC §§ 2035, 2036, 2037, 2038.

[184] United States v. Allen, 293 F2d 916 (10th Cir. 1961).

[185] United States v. Allen, 293 F2d 916 (10th Cir. 1961).

courts should continue to interpret it in this manner to reach an appropriate re-sult.[186]

Further problems arise if a transferor retains a Section 2036(a)(2) power to designate the beneficiary, which is relinquished by the transferor within three years of death. For example, if a transferor provides an income interest to *A* or *B*, whomever the transferor selects, for the transferor's life and a re-mainder to *C*, and the transferor relinquishes the power within three years of death, the property would be included in its entirety in the transferor's gross estate; note that Section 2035(a), which triggers such inclusion under Section 2035(a), applies expressly to a transfer of an "interest in property," or a "relin-quished power."[187]

[9] Background of the Section

A limitation on the application of Section 2036 is set forth in Subsection (c), which is of diminishing importance because it relates only to transfers made a long time ago. The section is expressly made inapplicable to transfers made before March 4, 1931, and in some cases to transfers made before June 7, 1932.[188] The origin of this limitation provision is to be found in a strange bit of legislative and judicial history. In the Revenue Act of 1916, the first enact-ment of the federal estate tax, and in subsequent acts, the statute required that there be included in the gross estate the value of property "to the extent of any interest therein of which the decedent has at any time made a transfer . . . in-tended to take effect in possession or enjoyment at or after his death. . . . "[189] No language such as is now found in Section 2036 was included, but it might appear obvious that the original provision was meant to catch a lifetime gratui-tous transfer under which a decedent retained for life the enjoyment of the transferred property. Under such circumstances, certainly, enjoyment by the transferee is deliberately postponed until the decedent's death. Surprisingly, however, in 1930, the Supreme Court held that although a decedent had re-served a secondary life interest in the property transferred to a trust, no part of the value of the trust property was includable in the decedent's gross estate.[190] In 1931, the Court held that the presence of an intervening life interest in the earlier case was not the basis for that decision and that a reservation of an im-mediate life interest in the settlor with the remainder to named beneficiaries

---

[186] See ¶ 4.07[2][b][i]. In some situations the results may have been altered. See dis-cussion of Section 2702, ¶ 19.03[2].

[187] See ¶ 4.07[2][a].

[188] See also supra ¶ 4.08[6][d] note 92 for the effective dates of Section 2036(b).

[189] Revenue Act of 1916, Pub. L. No. 64-271, § 202(b), 39 Stat. 756, 777 (1916).

[190] May v. Heiner, 281 US 238 (1930).

did not result in the trust's inclusion in the gross estate.[191] These decisions apparently rested on the ground that the decedent retained no interest that passed to another at death; the retained life interest simply expired at that time.[192] Congress immediately enacted a joint resolution[193] overruling the Supreme Court decisions. The language now appearing in Section 2036(a) arrived there in part by way of the joint resolution[194] and in part by way of an amendment made June 6, 1932.[195]

In 1938, the Supreme Court ruled that the forerunner of Section 2036 did not apply retroactively to affect transfers effected prior to its enactment.[196] This decision reflects the law in its present form. There was an interim flurry, however, which is no longer of much importance. In 1949, the Supreme Court overruled *May v. Heiner* and held that a transfer with the right to enjoyment retained by the decedent until death was a transfer intended to take effect in enjoyment at death,[197] under the original "possession or enjoyment" clause of the statute, in effect nullifying its earlier decisions that the 1931 and 1932 amendments did not apply retroactively.[198] Congress was dissatisfied with this result,[199] and so, under Section 2036(c), the statute is expressly made inapplicable to transfers made before the critical dates in 1931 and, in some cases,

---

[191] Burnet v. Northern Trust Co., 283 US 782 (1931); Morsman v. Burnet, 283 US 783 (1931); McCormick v. Burnet, 283 US 784 (1931).

[192] Cf. Reinecke v. Northern Trust Co., 278 US 339 (1929).

[193] 46 Stat. 1516 (1931). This joint resolution was enacted the very next day following the decisions by the Court.

[194] 46 Stat. 1516 (1931). The two periods stated in the joint resolution were "for his life" and "for any period which does not in fact end before his death."

[195] Revenue Act of 1932, Pub. L. No. 72-154, § 803(a), 47 Stat. 169, 279 (1932), adding the third time period "for any period not ascertainable without reference to his death." Despite the abundance of legislative history, only one court of appeals has accepted the clearly sound proposition that transfers after March 3, 1931, and before June 7, 1932, are includable in the gross estate only if they are within the scope of the joint resolution. Estate of Hubbard v. Comm'r, 250 F2d 492 (5th Cir. 1957). Two courts of appeals have taken the position that a transfer includable only under the 1932 amendment (namely, a transfer where the period was merely not ascertainable without reference to the decedent's death) was nevertheless includable even though the transfer took place before June 7, 1932. Comm'r v. Estate of Arents, 297 F2d 894 (2d Cir.), cert. denied, 369 US 848 (1962); Bayliss v. United States, 326 F2d 458 (4th Cir. 1964), analyzed in Maxfield, "Federal Estate and Gift Taxation," 1964 Annual Survey of American Law 199-200.

[196] Hassett v. Welch, 303 US 303 (1938).

[197] Comm'r v. Estate of Church, 335 US 632 (1949). Despite its legislative interment, the *Church* doctrine may not be entirely dead. See White, J., dissenting, in United States v. Byrum, 408 US 125, 165, reh'g denied, 409 US 898 (1972).

[198] Hassett v. Welch, 303 US 303 (1938).

[199] See Technical Changes Act of 1949, Pub. L. No. 81-378, § 7(b), 63 Stat. 891, 895 (1949), reprinted in 1949-2 CB 275, 279.

1932.[200] Clearly, this is not a general estate tax amnesty with respect to early transfers; other sections of the Code must still be considered in determining whether the value of property transferred prior to 1931 or 1932 must be included in the gross estate.[201]

¶ 4.09 SECTION 2037. TRANSFERS TAKING EFFECT AT DEATH

[1] Introduction

From the inception of the estate tax Congress has been concerned that lifetime transfers essentially testamentary in nature might be used as a means to avoid the tax.[1] The earliest statutory obstacle to such avoidance was a provision that included in the gross estate the value of any property interest that was the subject of a lifetime transfer by the decedent "in contemplation of or intended to take effect in possession or enjoyment only at or after his death."[2] It does not take much imagination to see that the deferred possession or enjoyment aspect of this clause is the basic concept expressed in Section 2036. It is also expressive of the philosophy underlying Section 2038, and it is closely akin to Section 2037, here under discussion. Somewhat narrow judicial interpretation of the original possession or enjoyment language prompted Congress to proliferate the concept, creating three substantially more explicit provisions that convey, but in much more detail, essentially the same thought. Of course, the greater detail in the statute reduces judicial flexibility; however, it is not inappropriate to hark back to the original language and its fundamental concept as an aid to interpretation.

Section 2037 draws into the gross estate the value of some interests in property that the decedent has transferred conditionally during life. In its present form, the section applies only if:

---

[200] E.g., Florida Nat'l Bank v. United States, 336 F2d 598 (3d Cir. 1964), cert. denied, 380 US 911 (1965), followed in Estate of Cohn v. United States, 371 F2d 642 (2d Cir. 1967). Cf. Estate of Thomson v. Comm'r, 495 F2d 246 (2d Cir. 1974).

[201] See Estate of Thomson v. Comm'r, 495 F2d 246 (2d Cir. 1974), involving the interrelationship between *O'Malley*, 383 US 627 (1966), and the effective dates.

[1] See ¶¶ 4.07[1], 4.08[1].

[2] Sections 2035 through 2038 all have common parentage in this original statutory language. Revenue Act of 1916, Pub. L. No. 64-271, § 202(b), 39 Stat. 756, 777 (1916).

A third dimension to the estate and gift tax area should be mentioned: the tax on generation-skipping transfers. See Chapters 12–18.

1. The possession or enjoyment of the property is conditional upon surviving the decedent, *and*
2. The decedent has retained an interest in the property that may bring the property back to the decedent or to the decedent's estate or back into the decedent's power of disposition.

This double test is discussed later in this section, but two statutory exceptions should first be noted.

[2] Excluded Transfers

In common with Sections 2035, 2036, and 2038, all of which concern lifetime transfers by the decedent, Section 2037 is expressly made inapplicable to a bona fide sale for an adequate and full consideration in money or money's worth.[3] Second, but of ever-diminishing importance, this section does not apply to a transfer made on or before September 7, 1916, a rule that excludes transfers made before the first enactment of the federal estate tax. If the decedent has made a transfer[4] that is not covered by one of these exclusionary rules, the general applicability of Section 2037 depends on whether the tests of survivorship and of retention of an interest by the decedent are satisfied. Both tests must be met in order for the section to be applied.

[3] The Survivorship Requirement

A characteristic of any testamentary disposition of property is that the testator is dead before the possession or enjoyment of the property by the devisee or legatee begins. This characteristic is adopted as the primary test for attaching estate tax liability to a lifetime transfer under Section 2037. If the transferee of a property interest can get possession or enjoyment (through ownership of the interest transferred) while the decedent transferor is living, Section 2037 does not apply to the transfer. For example, assume that *D*, more than three years prior to death, transfers property to a trust under the following terms and conditions:

1. The income is to be paid to *A* for *A*'s life.

---

[3] See ¶¶ 4.07[2][b][i], 4.08[1][a], 4.10[2].

[4] As is true under other sections, a transfer not actually made by the decedent may be imputed to the decedent. Estate of Fried v. Comm'r, 445 F2d 979 (2d Cir. 1971), cert. denied, 404 US 1016 (1972); Estate of Bogley v. United States, 514 F2d 1027 (1975); Rev. Rul. 78-15, 1978-1 CB 289 (all involving contractual death benefits payable by a corporation to decedent employee's surviving widow or to employee's estate); Estate of Hill v. Comm'r, 229 F2d 237 (2d Cir. 1956). See ¶ 4.08[7][a].

2. Upon *A*'s death, the corpus is to be distributed to *B*, if living.
3. If *B* predeceases *A*, the corpus is to revert to *D*, if living.
4. If both *B* and *D* predecease *A*, remainder is to go to *R*.

Assume, further, that *D* dies, survived by *A* and *B*.[5] Is the property or some part of it includable in *D*'s gross estate under Section 2037?[6] The answer depends on an analysis of each interest transferred to others—the life interest in *A*, the contingent remainder in *B*, and the contingent remainder in *R*.

It is apparent that *A*'s life interest, which takes effect in enjoyment immediately, is outside the section; *A* enjoys that interest without regard to whether *D* is living or dead. Although slightly less apparent, the same is true of the interest transferred to *B*. *B* will get the property upon *A*'s death if *B* is then living; and *B* can get such possession even if *D* is living. As *B* need not survive *D* to get possession, *R*'s interest fails the primary test for inclusion under Section 2037. *R*'s interest is in a different posture. *R* (and anyone taking by virtue of *R*'s interest) cannot acquire the property until both *B* and *D* are dead. As *R*'s interest cannot take effect in possession until *D* dies, *R*'s interest meets the first test of Section 2037.[7]

Careful congressional use of the terms "interest" and "property" supports the above analysis. It is *interests* in property transferred by the decedent, under which possession or enjoyment of the *property* is deferred until the decedent's death, that are included in the decedent's gross estate under Section 2037. *R*'s interest is of that type but the other transferred interests are not; thus, the value of *R*'s contingent remainder at the time of *D*'s death is included in *D*'s gross estate, because the second test is obviously met too.[8]

It is almost frivolous to mention that *R*, in this example, *could* get immediate enjoyment of the property, with *D* still living, if *A* transferred *A*'s immediate income right to *R*. Is the analysis in error then? Not at all; Congress thought of this, too. Whether an interest escapes the clutches of Section 2037

---

[5] It is obvious that if *B* and then *A* should die before *D*, the property will return to *D* and simply be a part of *D*'s Section 2033 estate unless, before death, *D* makes some other disposition of it.

[6] Note that Section 2033 will include nothing, as *D*'s reversion is cut off by *D*'s death. Section 2036 is probably also inapplicable; however, an argument can be made that if *D* retained a reversionary interest in property, other than one that could only arise after *D*'s death, during *D*'s life the property might have reverted to *D* and *D* would have retained the right to the income from it under Section 2036(a)(1). Compare the secondary life estate situation under Section 2036(a)(1), discussed at ¶ 4.08[2] text accompanying note 17. Since the transfer was not revocable or otherwise alterable, Section 2038 will not apply; and, even if made within three years of *D*'s death, Section 2035 would not apply to the interests of *A* and *B*. IRC § 2035(a)(2).

[7] A further test for taxability is discussed infra ¶ 4.09[4].

[8] It would make no difference if *A* died survived by *B* the day after *D*'s death, cutting off *R*'s contingent remainder unless, for valuation purposes, Section 2032 was elected. See ¶ 4.03[3][b].

depends on whether the transferee of an interest can get possession or enjoyment of the property "through ownership of *such* interest" without surviving the decedent transferor. The fact that *R* may secure early possession or enjoyment in some other way is immaterial.[9]

There is one situation in which a transferred interest that cannot itself produce possession or enjoyment until the decedent transferor's death is placed outside Section 2037, even if the other statutory tests for inclusion are met. If possession or enjoyment could be obtained while the decedent was living by way of the exercise of a general power of appointment over the interest that was exercisable immediately before the decedent's death, all bets are off under Section 2037.[10] The one to whom an interest in question has been transferred need not have the power. In the preceding example, if *B* had the requisite general power, it would remove *R*'s contingent remainder from the reach of the section.[11] And it seems equally clear that the general power need not be held by one who has an interest in the transferred property; by adding a general power in *E* in the example, the section can be avoided.[12]

---

[9] It is likewise immaterial that the transfer under consideration will, except for the value of *D*'s retained contingent reversion, be fully subject to gift tax when made. Smith v. Shaughnessy, 318 US 176 (1943). See ¶ 10.01[3][d]. But the gift tax paid will be a Section 2001(b)(2) subtraction in the computation of the estate tax or, if the gift was made before 1977, a credit for gift tax paid may be allowed against the estate tax. Cf. IRC § 2012(e); ¶ 3.04.

[10] IRC § 2037(b) (last sentence).

[11] Cf. Reg. § 20.2037-1(e) Ex. 6.

[12] It should be noted, however, that the statutory exception raises the question whether "any beneficiary" could obtain possession by the exercise of a general power. The quoted phrase is puzzling, because neither the section nor the excepting sentence is limited to trusts, and the term "beneficiary" is not aptly used to indicate owners of successive or contingent legal interests. If the exception is intended to require that someone who has at least some interest in the property might be able to get possession through exercise of a power, not just any general power over the property will defeat the section. For example, if *E* in this illustration could appoint only to *E*'s estate, *E*'s power would be a general power (IRC § 2041(b)); but no one with an interest in the property (no "beneficiary"?) could obtain possession by way of an exercise of the power. This seems too narrow a view of the exception, and perhaps, the phrase "any beneficiary" should be ignored. See HR Rep. No. 1412, 81st Cong., 1st Sess. 9 (1949), reprinted in 1949-2 CB 295, 299, which omits the phrase. If Congress abhors estate tax ownership in the transferor here, where under Section 2041 another is simultaneously the estate tax owner of the entire property, why is this policy not more generally expressed in the statute?

It is quite possible that a decedent will have made a transfer generally within the scope of Section 2037 but will have given a third party a general power, not to appoint the entire property, but only to appoint the property after termination of another's interest, such as a power to appoint the remainder of a trust after termination of an interest for a term. This should be viewed as a power to appoint "the property," and, if it is exercisable immediately before the decedent's death and extends to the very interest otherwise included under Section 2037, it should render the section inapplicable. "Property" is some-

The first test of Section 2037 is precisely phrased to raise the question: Can possession be obtained without surviving the decedent? The question is clearly not whether possession was obtained before the decedent's death. Thus, a transfer to a trust with provision for accumulation of the income for ten years and then distribution of corpus and accumulated income to a beneficiary seems well outside the section; possession can be obtained (when ten years expire) before the decedent's death. The decedent's death within the ten-year period does not make the section applicable.[13]

The same may be said in general of alternative contingencies under which possession may be obtained. For example, if an accumulation trust[14] was to terminate after ten years or upon the settlor's death, whichever occurred first, the primary test of Section 2037 would again not be met. Possession could be obtained after ten years, even if the settlor is still living. Suppose, however, termination were to occur upon the death of the settlor A, or twenty years after the death of X (life expectancy forty years at the time of transfer), whichever came first. If A is ninety at the time of the transfer, the termination contingency that is an alternative to A's death could hardly be taken seriously. The Treasury expressly refuses to take it seriously, indicating in the regulations[15] that if an alternative contingency is "unreal" and if the decedent's death does precede it, the transfer will be considered one taking effect only at the death of the decedent.[16] With regard to this illustration, however, the regulations do not purport to deal with a situation in which possession or enjoyment is not geared at all to the decedent's death. Suppose, in the above example, the trust was simply to terminate twenty years after the death of X, whether A, the settlor, died earlier or not.[17] The transfer still should be considered within Section 2037; the case is not realistically distinguishable from the alternative contingency situation, although in that situation possession or enjoyment will be accelerated to the date of A's death.[18]

---

times used in the Code to mean *an interest* in property. Cf. IRC § 2503(c); Comm'r v. Herr, 303 F2d 780 (3d Cir. 1962).

[13] The concept of Section 2036, regarding a "period which does not in fact end before" the decedent's death, is not adopted in Section 2037.

[14] Since enactment of the Tax Reform Act of 1969, it may be less realistic to talk of accumulation trusts. See IRC §§ 665, 666, 667, 668, concerning income tax consequences of accumulation distributions. See also IRC § 2601, taxing generation-skipping transfers, discussed ¶¶ 12.02, 12.03, 12.04.

[15] Reg. § 20.2037-1(b).

[16] See also Reg. § 20.2037-1(e) Ex. 5.

[17] To meet the second test of the statute, it may be assumed that upon termination the corpus is to be distributed to Y, if living, and, if not, to A or A's estate.

[18] This is where the original language, "intended to take effect . . . at or after . . . death" should be remembered. Although "intended" has been interpreted to raise no question of *subjective* intent, Estate of Spiegel v. Comm'r, 335 US 701 (1949), the natural consequence of the transfer considered is to defer enjoyment until after A's death. If, until

Although it may seem contrary to the statutory language, Section 2037 can apply to a case in which the transferee gets both possession and enjoyment of the property at the time of the transfer. If *A* transfers property to *B* for life, reversion to *A*, but provides that if *A* predeceases *B*, *B* shall take the property in fee simple at *A*'s death, Section 2037(a)(1)is satisfied. Here it is necessary to recognize that *B* receives two interests, the life estate and a contingent remainder. The life estate does not depend on *A*'s death for enjoyment and is outside Section 2037. But possession and enjoyment of the property under the remainder interest cannot be obtained except "by surviving the decedent."[19]

The same result follows if *B* in the example is given a remainder subject to a condition subsequent (*B*'s death prior to that of *A*) that would defeat the remainder.[20] Under the present statute at least, these principles are sound, but they may be subject to misapplication. In *Estate of Thacher v. Commissioner*,[21] *D* created a trust with income payable to his wife for her life with remainder over to others. However, the trust instrument also provided that if his wife predeceased him, or in case of their legal separation or divorce, the corpus was to be returned to *D*. It also provided that upon the wife's remarriage after the death of *D*, her life interest would terminate and the corpus would be distributed to the remainderperson. It is clear, on these facts, that the transferred interests that followed the wife's life interest meet the test of Section 2037(a)(1), because as long as *D* was alive, the property would revert to him upon the wife's death. When *D* died survived by his wife, however, the litigated issue concerned includability of the wife's income interest. Contrary to the court's decision in *Thacher*, her enjoyment of that interest is no way dependent upon her surviving the decedent. Its full enjoyment can be secured by her not di-

---

death, *A* has retained the requisite reversionary interest (IRC § 2037(a)(2), discussed infra ¶ 4.09[4]), Section 2037 should apply. Possession or enjoyment is attainable only by surviving the decedent, and then some. Shukert v. Allen, 273 US 545 (1927), deciding against inclusion under the early "possession or enjoyment" clause where there was a similar postponement of enjoyment, is not contrary authority, as the decision seems to turn on the lack of any retained interest by the decedent transferor. Nor would it seem relevant under the present statute that the transfer is "unaffected by whether the grantor lives or dies." See Estate of Spiegel v. Comm'r, supra at 705, if it is clear that "possession or enjoyment . . . can . . . be obtained only by surviving the decedent."

[19] Klein v. United States, 283 US 231 (1931).

[20] Helvering v. Hallock, 309 US 106 (1940). For a time the law was otherwise, Helvering v. St. Louis Union Trust Co., 296 US 39 (1935); Becker v. St. Louis Union Trust Co., 296 US 48 (1935), seemingly on the theory that in such circumstances no interest passed from the decedent at death; the decedent's possibility of reversion simply expired. This was also the reasoning supporting the surprise decision in May v. Heiner, 281 US 238 (1930), subsequently overruled by statute. See Roberts, J., dissenting in Helvering v. Hallock, 309 US 106, 123 (1940); Reinecke v. Northern Trust Co., 278 US 339 (1929) (questioned in Estate of Spiegel v. Comm'r, 335 US 701 (1949)). See also supra ¶ 4.08[9].

[21] Estate of Thacher v. Comm'r, 20 TC 474 (1953), acq. 1954-1 CB 7.

vorcing the decedent while he is living and by not remarrying after his death. His death merely eliminates the divorce condition. If it is suggested that *he* might divorce *her* while living, it still must be said that she *can* fully enjoy the interest if he does not do so.[22] Thus, while it is true that one who has immediate enjoyment of property may also have an interest within the scope of Section 2037(a)(1), *Thacher* is not such a case. The decision is wrong.[23]

[4] Retention of Reversionary Interest

Even if the survivorship requirement is met, nothing will be included in the decedent's gross estate unless the decedent retained a reversionary interest in the property transferred as required by Paragraph (2) of Section 2037(a).[24] Questions of how the interest was retained and of what the value of the interest was, both of which may bear on the final decision whether the section applies, are discussed next. The first problem is determining what constitutes a "reversionary interest," as the term is used in the statute.

[a] Definition of "Reversionary Interest"

Under Section 2037(b), the term is defined to include the possibility that the property may return to the decedent transferor, as well as the possibility that it may return to the decedent's estate. It should be noted that this requirement is satisfied by the existence of the possibility; it is not necessary to show the property will return. Even if the possibility ends with the decedent's death, the decedent has retained the requisite interest long enough within the statutory

---

[22] In Estate of Thacher v. Comm'r, 20 TC 474 (1953), acq. 1954-1 CB 7, the wife's interest could be said to be enjoyable only by surviving the decedent if he could terminate it any time in his absolute discretion. He could, of course, have terminated it by obtaining a divorce. At the time of *Thacher*, however, no-fault divorce did not exist, and consequently, she would have had to provide him with grounds for obtaining a divorce. Hence, her full enjoyment would be assured by not giving him grounds for divorce. If *Thacher* had occurred today, under a no-fault divorce jurisdiction, the result should still be the same. As a practical matter, a life interest should not be considered conditional if a transferor would have to give up his wife to reacquire the property.

[23] In Estate of Thacher v. Comm'r, 20 TC 474 (1953), acq. 1954-1 CB 7, the Tax Court puts misplaced reliance on Helvering v. Hallock, 309 US 106 (1940). None of the three cases litigated nor the three others principally discussed there dealt with the *Thacher* problem. Instead, in each instance, the life interest transferred was assured, but whether the life beneficiary obtained a larger interest was conditional upon her surviving the decedent.

[24] The Tax Reform Act of 1986 Act imposed a similar 5 percent reversionary test for purposes of the *Clifford* trust income tax reversionary rule. IRC § 673(a). Tax Reform Act of 1986, Pub. L. No. 99-514, §1402(a), 100 Stat. 2085, 2711 (1986), reprinted in 1986-3 CB (Vol. 1) 1, 628.

concept. For example, if *D* transferred property to a trust providing that the income be paid to *B* for life and that upon *B*'s death the corpus be distributed to *D* if living and, if not, to *C* or *C*'s estate, *D* has the requisite reversion even though it is cut off by *D*'s death if *D* is survived by *B*. Moreover, the term is further defined to include the possibility that the property may become subject to a power of disposition by the decedent, even though the property could not return to the decedent or the decedent's estate as beneficial owner. The decedent has been held to have retained a reversionary interest if, after the decedent's death, the property might go into a trust set up under the decedent's will.[25] The Commissioner's contention that a contingent power that could not be exercised to benefit the decedent or the decedent's creditors constitutes a reversionary interest has been judicially approved.[26]

In any event, at the time the decedent made the transfer, the decedent must have *retained* the interest or right that may bring the property or power of disposition back. If a decedent provided in a lifetime trust instrument that upon termination of the trust, the property was to go to the decedent's spouse or the spouse's estate, should the decedent be held to have a reversionary interest in the property on the ground that the decedent might be entitled to

---

[25] Estate of Tarver v. Comm'r, 255 F2d 913 (4th Cir. 1958).

[26] Costin v. Cripe, 235 F2d 162 (7th Cir. 1956); Estate of Klauber v. Comm'r, 34 TC 968 (1960), nonacq. 1964-2 CB 8. These cases have the potential of vastly increasing the scope of Section 2037, although there is a broad overlap with the other grantor provisions. In Costin v. Cripe, the decedent created a trust under which he retained the right to the income for his life, after which provision was made for payment of the income to *A* and *B* for their joint lives, with a remainder to *C* or *C*'s estate. Because the transfer was made in 1923, Section 2036 did not apply. See IRC § 2036(c). The decedent also retained a special power of appointment over the remainder, exercisable if he survived *A* and *B*. The court included the value of *C*'s interest in the decedent's estate under Section 2037 when the decedent predeceased *A* and *B*. Note that Section 2038, as well as Section 2036, would be inapplicable as, *at the time* of his death, the decedent had no power to change interests. See ¶ 4.10[8] text accompanying note 79. However, Section 2036(a)(2), if applicable, would arguably include *C*'s remainder interest. If the trust provided income to *A* and *B* for their joint lives with a special power in the decedent at any time to appoint the remainder and, on failure of appointment, remainder to *C*, Sections 2037, 2038, and likely Section 2036(a)(2), would all apply to include the remainder interest. In *Klauber*, supra, the decedent created a trust with income to *A* and a remainder to *B*, with the decedent indirectly retaining the cumulative power to invade corpus up to $4,000 per year for *A*'s benefit. It was held that Section 2037 applied to the value of $4,000 multiplied by the number of years of the decedent's life expectancy immediately prior to his death. In contrast, in Estate of Valentine v. Comm'r, 54 TC 200 (1970), the trustees were required to pay the decedent settlor $150,000 annually from the corpus. In applying Section 2037, the court included the entire value of the trust in the decedent's gross estate, since the possession or enjoyment of the corpus could be obtained by the remainderperson only by surviving the decedent. *Klauber* was distinguished on the ground that the decedent's power of invasion in *Valentine* embraced the entire corpus, because the large amounts that were required to be paid out annually could have depleted the trust.

share in the spouse's estate? Viewed superficially, there is a possibility that the decedent will get the property or part of it at the spouse's death, which may seem to satisfy the statutory requirement. However, the possibility should not be regarded as "retained" by the decedent any more than one might be said to "retain" a reversionary interest in property transferred outright to any near relative on the ground that upon the transferee's death, the transferor might be entitled to or hope to share in the estate. In other words, the statutory requirements should not be regarded as being satisfied unless the condemned possibility arises directly out of action by the decedent. The Treasury has now accepted this line of reasoning.[27]

In contrast to the foregoing situation, a decedent might properly be regarded as having retained a reversionary interest, by operation of law, if the decedent provided for distribution of the trust corpus "to such person or persons who would be entitled thereto under the intestate laws of the State" as if the life beneficiary owned the trust property outright at death, if the decedent was among such persons.[28] Under such circumstances, however, if the decedent ever got the property, the decedent would receive it because of rights reserved by inference in the trust instrument; the decedent would receive it from the trustees, and it would not be subject to the debts of the deceased life beneficiary; nor could the decedent's rights be defeated by some other dispositive provision in the life beneficiary's will.

Subsection (b) of Section 2037 specifies that the term "reversionary interest" does not include a possibility merely that the income from property or the power to designate who shall have the income may return to the decedent. The consequences of retention of such possibilities must be considered under Section 2036.[29]

---

[27] Reg. § 20.2037-1(c)(2). See Bartlett v. United States, 146 F. Supp. 719 (Ct. Cl. 1956). The rationale for this established principle is well expressed by Looker, "Estate Taxation of Living Trusts: The *Church* and *Spiegel* Decisions," 49 Colum. L. Rev. 437 n.3 (1949):

> These interests [reversionary interests], whether expressed in the instrument or arising by operation of law, must be distinguished from expectancies. See *Restatement, Property* c. 24 (1936). Where the settlor is a blood relative of the remainderman, he may conceivably re-acquire the trust property as an heir of the remainderman. But the settlor will not take under the terms of the trust instrument; he will receive the trust property not from the trustees, but from the executor or administrator of the remainderman's estate, subject, for example, to prior payment of the remainderman's debts.

[28] See Comm'r v. Estate of Marshall, 203 F2d 534, 535 (3d Cir. 1953), decided in favor of the estate on other grounds.

[29] A complementary Section 2036 rule appears at Regulations Section 20.2036-1(b)(3).

[b] How the Interest Is Retained

Regarding the manner in which the reversionary interest arises, the statute differentiates transfers on or after October 8, 1949 from those made earlier. In the case of earlier transfers, only reversionary interests that arise "out of the express terms of the instrument of transfer" are to be taken into account. The effect and purpose of this parenthetical provision is to disregard any such interest that arises only by operation of law.[30]

Incomplete provision for distribution of the corpus of a trust, which fails to take into account all contingencies, might, by operation of local law, leave the decedent with a possibility of reverter.[31] With respect to pre-1949 transfers, this reversionary interest arising by operation of law does not satisfy the retained interest requirement. With regard to transfers made on or after October 8, 1949, however, the requisite reversionary interest need not be expressly retained; it is enough if it arises by operation of law. Accordingly, the "express" requirement is not a factor in present-day drafting.

[c] Negligible Reversionary Interests

The value of the reversionary interest is not the amount to be included in the gross estate. The statute requires valuation of that interest only to determine whether Section 2037 applies at all. If it does, the amount to be included has no connection with the value of the reversionary interest.

A reversionary interest retained by the decedent does not meet the requirement of Paragraph (2) of Section 2037(a) unless its value, immediately before the decedent's death, exceeds 5 percent of the value of the transferred property.[32] This is congressional acceptance of the de minimis principle rejected by the Supreme Court in a case that did much to shape the present statutory language;[33] if the reversionary interest retained is inconsequential, it is ignored.

---

[30] Section 811(c)(2) (1939) expressly excluded such interests arising "by operation of law."

[31] Cf. Reg. § 20.2037-1(e) Ex. 5.

[32] As explained earlier (see supra ¶ 4.09[3] text accompanying note 10), a general power over property otherwise taxable under Section 2037 may render the section inapplicable. It would seem that even an outstanding nongeneral power could have that effect if it bore on the possibility of the property's returning to the decedent or his estate in such a way as to reduce the value of that possibility to less than 5 percent of the value of the property. Cf. Rev. Rul. 67-370, 1967-2 CB 324.

[33] See Burton, J., dissenting in Estate of Spiegel v. Comm'r, 335 US 701, 727 (1949).

[d] Mortality Tables and Actuarial Principles

Section 2037(b) provides that in undertaking to value the decedent's reversionary interest for the purpose of determining the applicability of the section, the fact of the decedent's death is to be disregarded and usual valuation methods are to be employed, including the use of gender-neutral mortality tables and actuarial principles. Under these tables and principles, the state of a decedent's health immediately prior to death is disregarded.[34] Controversy has developed around the question whether mortality tables and actuarial principles may be used as the sole determinants of value or whether the decedent's physical condition before death should also be taken into account.

[e] Decedent's Physical Condition

The Tax Court and the Treasury have recognized that to take account of physical condition just before death, whether or not the physical condition involves a terminal illness, would largely nullify the statute.[35] Yet, one court[36] has allowed the decedent's physical condition immediately prior to death to be considered in valuing her reversion, on the basis that Section 2037(b), providing for valuation "by usual methods of valuation, including the use of gender-neutral tables of mortality and actuarial principles," does not require valuation to be determined in all cases solely by reference to mortality and actuarial tables.[37] The Tax Court and Treasury approach have such strong policy support that even though it stretches the statute, it should prevail.

---

[34] Reg. § 20.7520-3(b)(3)(ii) (last sentence).

[35] See Estate of Roy v. Comm'r, 54 TC 1317, 1322–1323 (1970), citing the second edition of this treatise, wherein the court stated: "A drastically foreshortened actual life expectancy would bring any retained reversion below the 5 percent level. Section 2037 would then be applicable only in cases of sudden death." Reg. § 20.7520-3(b)(3)(ii) (last sentence). See also Robinson v. United States, 632 F2d 822 (9th Cir. 1980); Estate of Jones, Jr. v. Comm'r, 36 TCM (CCH) 380 (1977); Rev. Rul. 80-80, 1980-1 CB 194, and Rev. Rul. 66-307, 1966-2 CB 429 (last paragraph), both rulings taking this position but declared obsolete for the estates of decedents dying after December 13, 1995, in Rev. Rul 96-3, 1996-1 CB 348, in view of the promulgation of Regulations Section 20.7520-3(b)(3)(ii) (last sentence).

[36] Hall v. United States, 353 F2d 500 (7th Cir. 1965). Arguably, the statutory provision authorizes the Treasury by regulation to specify *usual* methods of valuation, including mortality tables and actuarial principles, and, under the provision in question, it could be said to be unusual to take account of the decedent's condition just before death. Note the comma placement in Section 2037(b) (second sentence).

[37] Hall v. United States, 353 F2d 500, 503 (7th Cir. 1965).

[f] Application of the 5 Percent Test

If physical condition is ignored, in general, application of the 5 percent rule becomes primarily a determination of the decedent's mathematical chances, on the basis of age just prior to death, of surviving some contingency or contingencies. An extreme set of facts may illustrate the problem. Suppose the decedent transferred property in trust to pay the income to the decedent's children for the decedent's life and, in the case of death of any child prior to the decedent's death, to pay that share to the child's children or, if the child has none, to the decedent's other children, and with the further provision that, upon the decedent's death, the corpus be distributed in the same manner but that if no child or grandchild survived the decedent, the trust corpus be paid over to the decedent's estate. This is a transfer taking effect at death under which the decedent has retained a reversionary interest. However, if the decedent was survived by numerous children and grandchildren, the decedent's chances, as of the moment before death, of surviving all of them would be negligible. In substantially similar circumstances, the Supreme Court has recognized that a reversionary interest of the decedent in a $1 million trust might at death be worth as little as $70.[38] As $70 is only a small fraction of 1 percent of $1 million, the 5 percent test would not be met.

Complexities in a trust instrument that may make it very difficult to value a reversionary interest do not foreclose application of the section.[39] The legislative history of the 1954 Code indicates that a reversionary interest is not to be regarded necessarily as having no value because the value cannot be measured precisely.[40] However, there is a point at which a reversionary interest becomes so remote that it will simply be accorded a zero value.[41]

[g] Base for the 5 Percent Test

It is clear from the forerunner of Section 2037 that "in determining whether the value of the reversionary interest exceeds five percent, it is to be compared with the entire value of the transferred property, including interests that are not dependent upon survivorship of the decedent."[42] Accordingly, in the foregoing example, the value of the life estate is not subtracted from the

---

[38] Estate of Spiegel v. Comm'r, 335 US 701 (1949).

[39] If a special factor is required to ascertain the value of a reversionary interest, the personal representative of the decedent's estate may get it from the Internal Revenue Service. See Reg. §§ 20.2037-1(c)(3), 20.2031-7(d)(4).

[40] S. Rep. No. 1622, 83d Cong., 2d Sess. 469 (1954).

[41] Estate of Cardeza v. United States, 261 F2d 423 (3d Cir. 1958). Cf. Robinette v. Helvering, 318 US 184 (1943).

[42] HR Rep. No. 1412, 81st Cong., 1st Sess. 7 (1949), reprinted in 1949-2 CB 295, 297.

value of the corpus for the purpose of the 5 percent test, even though its value is ultimately excluded from the gross estate as a separate interest not subject to survivorship and not taxable.

If a decedent retains a reversionary interest in only one half of the trust corpus, the value of his reversionary interest will be compared with the value of one half of the trust corpus.[43]

Recall that the possibility the transferred property may become subject to a power of disposition by the decedent, even though such a disposition cannot operate to the decedent's financial benefit, is included within the definition of the term "reversionary interest." Valuation of such an interest is to be made just as if that possibility were in fact a possibility that the property may return to the decedent.[44]

[5] Pre-Death Termination of Reversion

A transfer made by the decedent during life, which would at the time of transfer meet the general tests for liability under this section, nevertheless will not result in tax includability unless the tests are also met at death. The requirement that the decedent's reversionary interest "immediately before death" exceed 5 percent of the value of the property suggests that if the decedent's reversionary interest was extinguished prior to death, nothing would be includable in the decedent's estate under Section 2037. This conclusion was reached under prior law, under less compelling circumstances, where the decedent's reversionary interest was cut off before the decedent's death by an event over which the decedent had no control.[45] However, if the transferor relinquished the transferor's prescribed reversionary interest within three years of death, Section 2035(a) will be invoked to cause inclusion in the gross estate.[46] The problem is similar to that discussed earlier in connection with Section 2036.[47] The discussion is not extended here, except to suggest that numerous such problems seem to call for congressional attention.

---

[43] Reg. § 20.2037-1(c)(4). It should be noted that the value of the reversionary interest and the corpus are determined an instant before the decedent's death. Therefore, the fact that the decedent's executor elects the alternate valuation date is of no significance in applying the 5 percent test. Reg. § 20.2037-1(c)(3).

[44] IRC § 2037(b) (third sentence). See Costin v. Cripe, 235 F2d 162 (7th Cir. 1956).

[45] Estate of Matthews v. Comm'r, 3 TC 525, 539 (1944), acq. 1944 CB 19.

[46] IRC § 2035(a). The relinquished reversionary interest would have to be reconstructed and artificially valued at death for purposes of applying the 5 percent test, which must be met immediately prior to death for Section 2035 to be applicable. Rev. Rul. 79-62, 1979-1 CB 295. Cf. United States v. Allen, 293 F2d 916 (10th Cir. 1961).

[47] See ¶ 4.08[8][b].

[6] Amount to Be Included

To recapitulate briefly, Section 2037 will apply if, after September 7, 1916, the decedent has made a transfer of property to take effect only at or after the decedent's death and has retained a reversionary interest in such property (perhaps expressly) that has a value just before the decedent's death in excess of 5 percent of the value of the property transferred. The remaining question is: What is to be included in the gross estate when Section 2037 is applicable? As previously explained, reference to the value of the decedent's reversionary interest can be wholly misleading; valuation of that interest is undertaken only to determine the applicability of the section and bears no relation to the value to be included in the gross estate if the section is applicable. It is not the value of the decedent's reversionary interest that is to be included in the gross estate under Section 2037.[48]

Somewhat obscured by detail, the rule of Section 2037 is that the gross estate shall include the value at the date of death (or as determined under the alternate valuation provisions of Section 2032) of any interest in property that has been transferred in such a way as to take effect in possession or enjoyment at or after the decedent's death, subject, of course, to all the qualifications discussed here. Thus, in order to ascertain the amount to include in the gross estate it is necessary to identify the taxable interests and then to value them. Two examples will illustrate this. Suppose the decedent, _D_, transferred property in trust providing that the income from the trust be paid to _D_'s spouse during _D_'s life and upon _D_'s death the corpus be paid over to _D_'s spouse, if living, and if not, to _D_'s estate. _D_'s spouse survives _D_. Assuming that _D_'s chance of surviving the spouse just before _D_'s death was such that the value of _D_'s reversionary interest exceeded 5 percent of the trust corpus, the amount to be included in _D_'s estate is the entire value of the trust property, for that is the value of the interest that has been transferred by _D_ that is to take effect in possession or enjoyment at _D_'s death.[49]

However, as just suggested, if one inter vivos transaction involves the transfer of more than one interest in the same property, each such interest must

---

[48] In Estate of Klauber v. Comm'r, 34 TC 968 (1960), nonacq. 1964-2 CB 8, the decedent settlor acting with another nonadverse party could only direct $4,000 annual payments of principal to those who were the income beneficiaries. The value of such prospective distributions exceeded 5 percent of the value of the trust corpus at the decedent's death. Only $31,280, the value of the portion of the trust deemed subject to the power, was included; the balance of the trust property was held not to have been transferred conditionally. Compare Estate of Valentine v. Comm'r, 54 TC 200 (1970), where a similar power to invade for the decedent was deemed substantial enough to encompass the entire corpus, and _Klauber_ was distinguished. Cf. Rev. Rul. 66-87, 1966-1 CB 217, construing Section 2041(b)(2)(B) (powers of appointment), discussed at ¶ 4.13[7][f] text accompanying note 111.

[49] Costin v. Cripe, 235 F2d 162 (7th Cir. 1956).

be viewed separately to determine the amount to include in the gross estate under Section 2037. Suppose *D* transferred property to a trust providing for the payment of the income from the trust to *D*'s spouse, *S*, for *S*'s life and upon *S*'s death for distribution of the corpus to *D*, if living, and if not, to child, *C*, or *C*'s estate. Assume *C* and *S* survive *D*. Here, it will be observed, the income interest passing to *S* is in no way dependent upon *D*'s death, for *S* gets immediate enjoyment to continue for *S*'s life, whether *D* lives or dies. The value of *S*'s interest, accordingly, is not included in *D*'s gross estate under Section 2037.[50] However, neither *C* nor the beneficiaries of *C*'s estate can get possession or enjoyment through ownership of the remainder interest except by surviving *D*. Therefore, the value of the remainder interest will have to be included in *D*'s gross estate upon *D*'s death. Stated differently, Section 2037 requires in this situation that the entire value of the trust corpus, less the value of *S*'s outstanding life estate, be included in *D*'s gross estate.

If, instead, the trust had provided for income to *S* for *S*'s life and, upon *S*'s death, distribution of one half of the corpus to *D* if living and, if not, to *C* or *C*'s estate and for the other half of the corpus to pass at *S*'s death to grandchild, *GC*, or *GC*'s estate, then only one half of the value of the corpus less one half of the value of *S*'s outstanding life estate would be included within *D*'s gross estate under Section 2037.[51]

The Supreme Court has expressed the rule now found in Section 2037 in this way: "The value of the property subject to the contingency, rather than the actuarial or theoretical value of the possibility of the occurrence of the contingency, is the measure of the tax."[52]

[7] Background of the Section

As indicated at the outset of this discussion, the first federal estate tax statute contained a provision that included in the gross estate the value of any interest in property that had been the subject of a gratuitous lifetime transfer by the decedent "intended to take effect in possession or enjoyment at or after his death." The administrative, judicial, and legislative proliferation of this language involves a story too long and complex to be presented here even in

---

[50] Reg. § 20.2037-1(e) Ex. 3; Dixon v. United States, 319 F. Supp. 719 (EDNY 1970). Cf. Comm'r v. Estate of Nathan, 159 F2d 546 (7th Cir. 1947), cert. denied, 334 US 843 (1948).

[51] Cf. Reg. § 20.2037-1(c)(4), and note that the 5 percent reversionary interest test is based on the value of the decedent's reversionary interest in relation to the value of one half of the corpus. See supra ¶ 4.09[4][g] text accompanying note 43.

[52] Fidelity-Philadelphia Trust Co. v. Rothensies, 324 US 108, 112 (1945).

broad outline,[53] but mention of a few high points may aid in understanding the present section.

The current survivorship requirement is discernible in the original language, in the preceding quote.[54] If "intended" was ever supposed to be important in the sense of actual motive, the Supreme Court obliterated that word in 1949 by holding that the subjective intent of the decedent was irrelevant.[55] So, in retrospect at least, the basic test for liability under the "possession or enjoyment" provision has always been approximately the same as the present explicit survivorship test. No other test appeared expressly in the statute until 1949, but in 1929 the Supreme Court had found that a second test was implicit: Did the decedent retain an interest in the property until death?[56]

From this it can be seen that the twofold test, explicit in Section 2037, developed out of the original language concerning transfers "intended to take effect in possession or enjoyment at or after . . . death." Recent developments have largely centered around the retained-interest requirement. In 1949, the Supreme Court indicated, though it did not squarely hold, the statute did not require that an interest be retained by the decedent, and thus suggested abandonment of a rule that had been accepted for twenty years.[57] The same year, Congress adopted that judicial pronouncement as the statutory rule for future transfers, keeping and embellishing the old retained-interest rule for transfers before October 8, 1949.[58] The present section reflects a full return to the retained-interest requirement and a "value" test, added at first only with respect to pre-1949 transfers in the 1949 legislation. With regard to the earlier transfers, a reversionary interest continues to be significant only if expressly retained.

To summarize, differentiation of transfers on or after October 8, 1949, from those made earlier on the basis of express reservation of a reversionary

---

[53] The early history is recounted in Eisenstein, "Estate Taxes and the Higher Learning of the Supreme Court," 3 Tax L. Rev. 395, 421-502 (1948). Some later developments are discussed in Bittker, "The *Church* and *Spiegel* Cases: Section 811(c) Gets a New Lease on Life," 58 Yale LJ 825 (1949); Bittker, "*Church* and *Spiegel*: The Legislative Sequel," 59 Yale LJ 395 (1950); Stephens, "Federal Estate Tax: Section 811(c) Revisited," 3 U. Fla. L. Rev. 33 (1950).

[54] Shukert v. Allen, 273 US 545 (1927).

[55] Estate of Spiegel v. Comm'r, 335 US 701 (1949).

[56] Reinecke v. Northern Trust Co., 278 US 339 (1929). The notion at that time was that the estate tax was not intended to apply to property unless some interest in it passed *from the decedent* to others at the time of his death. Cf. May v. Heiner, 281 US 238 (1930). See Roberts, J., dissenting, in Helvering v. Hallock, 309 US 106 (1940).

[57] Estate of Spiegel v. Comm'r, 335 US 701 (1949).

[58] See IRC §§ 811(c)(2), 811(c)(3) (1939), as amended by the Technical Changes Act of 1949, Pub. L. No. 81-378, § 7(a), 63 Stat. 891, 895 (1949), reprinted in 1949-2 CB 275, 278.

interest is traceable to the 1949 legislation, which first established the express reservation requirement regarding earlier transfers.[59]

¶ 4.10 SECTION 2038. REVOCABLE TRANSFERS

[1] Introduction

If, as Webster's tells us, to "revoke" means to "recall," Section 2038 is very badly named. It is by no means limited in its reach to a decedent's lifetime transfers that may be recalled, transfers that are "revocable." It might better be named "alterable transfers"; for a decedent's power to change the enjoyment of transferred interests may invoke the section, even though the power cannot be exercised for the decedent's own benefit. Here again, however, it may be misleading to speak in terms of a power in the decedent, because the section sometimes applies when, although there is a nominal power in the decedent to change transferred interests, as a practical matter the decedent has no power at all. It is hoped these mysteries are dispelled in the pages that follow, but a further introductory word about the section is in order.

As Sections 2035 through 2038 all have common parentage,[1] all share certain characteristics. Each applies only to interests in property that have been transferred by the decedent.[2] However, in each instance another's transfer may be imputed to the decedent. In fact, although the problem is included in the previous discussion of Section 2036, it was a revocable transfer case under the forerunner of Section 2038 that first introduced the concept of reciprocal or crossed trusts.[3] Moreover, the common parentage of the transfer sections causes them to overlap substantially, and this is especially true with respect to

---

[59] See IRC §§ 811(c)(2), 811(c)(3) (1939), as amended by the Technical Changes Act of 1949, Pub. L. No. 81-378, § 7(a), 63 Stat. 891, 895 (1949), reprinted in 1949-2 CB 275, 278.

[1] All are traceable to the original statutory language concerning transfers "in contemplation of or intended to take effect in possession or enjoyment at or after death." Revenue Act of 1916, Pub. L. No. 64-271, § 202(b), 39 Stat. 756, 777 (1916).

[2] E.g., Comm'r v. Estate of Hagar, 173 F2d 613 (3d Cir. 1949) (taxing one half the value of a trust to which decedent and wife had each made like contributions); Estate of Levin v. Comm'r, 90 TC 723 (1988) (transfer by decedent's controlled corporation was imputed to decedent). But see Rev. Rul. 74-556, 1974-2 CB 300 (holding that an elective transfer under Section 2513 does not constitute a transfer for purposes of Section 2038); Estate of Folks v. Comm'r, 43 TCM (CCH) 427 (1982) (holding Section 2038 inapplicable because the decedent did not make a transfer of the property over which he held custodial powers).

[3] Lehman v. Comm'r, 109 F2d 99 (2d Cir.), cert. denied, 310 US 637 (1940). See ¶ 4.08[7][d].

Sections 2036 and 2038. Indeed, a close analysis will show that it is difficult to find circumstances in which Section 2038 applies that are not also covered by Section 2036, sometimes with more onerous consequences. When two or more of the transfer sections are applicable, obviously the Commissioner quite properly will apply that section or combination of sections requiring the maximum inclusion in the decedent's gross estate. Although the transfer sections are discussed seriatim in this book, it is always necessary to keep an eye on the other sections that are not the subject of immediate consideration[4] as well as those on the generation-skipping transfer tax.[5]

[2] Excluded Transfers

All the transfer sections, including Section 2038, are made inapplicable to "a bona fide sale for an adequate and full consideration in money or money's worth." On the other hand, since Section 2038 involves transfers that are subject to change, it is unlikely in transactions within its scope that a transferee will have paid consideration for the transferred interest.

In effect, the last sentence of Section 2038(a)(2) excludes from the provisions of Section 2038(a)(1) transfers made before June 22, 1936. There are four differences between Paragraphs (1) and (2) that are traceable to amendments made in 1936 to the revocable transfer provision, but even so, the differences in the two paragraphs are more apparent than real. First of all, the pre-1936 language "alter, amend, or revoke" was changed to read "alter, amend, revoke, or *terminate*." This has been held to be merely declaratory of prior law and not a substantive change in the statute.[6] Similarly, the addition of the parenthetical phrase "in whatever capacity exercisable" has been deemed a mere clarifying amendment,[7] and therefore these two formal differences in the two paragraphs may be disregarded. However, to overcome the result of a Supreme Court decision,[8] Congress added the further parenthetical phrase, "without regard to when or from what source the decedent acquired such power." Congress also made a change regarding the consequences of the relin-

---

[4] See the comparison of the provisions infra ¶ 4.10[10].

[5] See Chapters 12–18.

[6] Lober v. United States, 346 US 335 (1953). See Comm'r v. Estate of Holmes, 326 US 480 (1946), which had left some doubt about this equivalence.

[7] Union Trust Co. of Pittsburgh v. Driscoll, 138 F2d 152 (3d Cir.), cert. denied, 321 US 764 (1943); Welch v. Terhune, 126 F2d 695 (1st Cir.), cert. denied, 317 US 644 (1942). See Reg. § 20.2038-1(a)(3).

[8] White v. Poor, 296 US 98 (1935), discussed in Van Beuren v. McLoughlin, 262 F2d 315, 320 (1st Cir. 1958), cert. denied, 359 US 991 (1959).

quishment of some proscribed powers.[9] These two substantive changes are taken into account in the discussion that follows, but it is unnecessary to present a full, separate discussion of the two paragraphs.

[3] Any Change in Enjoyment

A key to the section is the question whether the enjoyment of an interest in property transferred by the decedent during life is subject to "any change" at the decedent's death. A further question is whether the possible change may be brought about by the decedent through the decedent's exercise of "a power." First, a word about the kind of possible change that taints a lifetime transfer.

It is obvious that if the decedent could until death take back property that the decedent has transferred, the interests given to others would be dramatically subject to change, that is, to elimination. A similarly dramatic potential change can exist even if the decedent cannot take the property back. For example, if D transfers property in trust, income to A for life and remainder to B or B's estate, but reserves the right to invade corpus for the benefit of either A or B, invasion for the benefit of either tends to defeat the enjoyment of the interest of the other; and so both interests are subject to change within the meaning of the section.

In other circumstances, the question becomes more subtle. Suppose instead that D may invade corpus only for the benefit of A. B's interest is clearly threatened by such a power of invasion and may indeed be cut off. The question is whether A's interest is likewise subject to change. The Treasury's position is that if the "time or manner" of enjoyment of an interest may be altered, the interest is subject to change.[10] It might appear that A's interest is within that concept, but it is not. In all events, A has a present right to the income from the property that will continue for A's life. It may be said that if D turns the entire corpus over to A, the "manner" of A's enjoyment of A's interest will be changed (from life beneficiary to outright owner); but if the regulation was intended to suggest that this is a tainting potential change, it would be in error.

It is necessary to consider closely the nature of the interests involved. In effect, the entire ownership of the property is divided in a *time* sense between A and B. A has a present interest enjoyable from the outset; B has a future in-

---

[9] See Reg. § 20.2038-1(e)(2). Cf. IRC §§ 2035(a)(2), 2035(e); infra ¶ 4.10[8] text accompanying notes 87–91. Of course, the transfer in issue must occur prior to the relinquishment of the decedent's power (or decedent's death) otherwise the transfer will be outside the scope of Section 2038. Estate of Halpren v. Comm'r, 70 TCM (CCH) 229 (1995) (Sections 2038 and 2041 are mutually exclusive; Section 2038 relates to the powers of a grantor while Section 2041 relates to the powers of the grantee).

[10] Reg. § 20.2038-1(a).

terest. If D could shift the future interest of B only to C, no one would argue that A's interest was subject to change. The situation is no different with regard to A's lifetime income interest if the future interest can be shifted to A. A will still have the right to the income for life, albeit as outright owner rather than as life beneficiary.[11] Actually, this analysis is in accord with a judicial decision[12] and current administrative practice.[13] Indeed, the example in the regulations following the "time or manner" expression is not at variance with the conclusion suggested.[14]

On the other hand, a possibility of mere acceleration of enjoyment is a potential change that is within the section.[15] Thus, if a trust gave A the right to the income for ten years and the remainder at the end of that time, but the settlor could terminate the trust earlier and turn the corpus over to A or A's estate, it might seem that A was in effect the sole owner of the property, as A had all the interests in it. Still, except for A's ten-year income interest, the time and manner of enjoyment of A's other interest in the property remains within the settlor's control and thus remains subject to "change." It may be said that any change will merely benefit A, because at worst A will become the outright owner of the property sooner than expected. But there is nothing in Section 2038 stating that the threatened change in an interest must be adverse for the section to apply.[16] The thought is that if the decedent kept a hand on the property until death, even by a right to accelerate the enjoyment of an interest, the transfer is so much akin to testamentary disposition that the affected interest should be subjected to estate tax.[17] Some further facets of the question of potential change emerge in the next segment of this discussion, which considers whether the decedent has the prescribed *power* to effect a change.

---

[11] Cf. IRC § 2503(b)(1) (last sentence).

[12] Walter v. United States, 341 F2d 182 (6th Cir. 1965). See Estate of DuCharme v. Comm'r, 164 F2d 959, 963 (6th Cir. 1947), reh'g, 169 F2d 76 (6th Cir. 1948).

[13] Rev. Rul. 70-513, 1970-2 CB 194.

[14] See the example at Reg. § 20.2038-1(a), in which A's income interest is additionally subject to change because the grantor reserved the right to accumulate income.

[15] Section 2038 is compared with other sections infra ¶ 4.10[10]. It may be noted here that a mere power of acceleration is proscribed by Section 2038 but should not be by Section 2036. See ¶ 4.08[5][c]. Appropriate? Probably so. Section 2038 will tax only the interest subject to the minor change. If Section 2036 applied, it would tax the entire property in which the changeable interest existed.

[16] Thus, in the example, while the actuarial value of A's term of years would be excluded from the value of the trust included in the settlor's estate, the value of the remainder is includable.

[17] Lober v. United States, 346 US 335 (1953); Comm'r v. Estate of Holmes, 326 US 480 (1946).

[4] Power in the Decedent

The scope of this section can best be understood by a recognition of the fact that almost any authority in the transferor to tamper with the enjoyment of interests transferred during life constitutes a proscribed power to "alter, amend, revoke, or terminate." Because the statute is framed in terms of the disjunctive "or," any one of the enumerated powers will invoke the provisions of Section 2038. However, a power recognizable under Section 2038 must be demonstrable, real, apparent, and evident, not merely speculative.[18]

[a] Power to Revoke

The broadest type of power that a decedent might hold over an interest in property is a power to revoke (take back) that interest. A gratuitous lifetime transfer subject to revocation by the decedent has always been subject to the estate tax, even before there was an express provision on revocable transfers.[19] The more general language of the first estate tax statute that caught such transfers is not of much present importance, but logically, if the decedent retains the right to get the property back, it is appropriate to tax the property "given" as a part of the decedent's estate. Since 1924, the statue has specifically done so. If state law provides that a particular transfer is revocable if not specifically made irrevocable,[20] the resulting power of revocation, even though not expressly retained,[21] results in inclusion under Section 2038.[22] Whether inter vivos transfers are revocable by the decedent depends on the decedent's powers as determined under state law. For example, if a transferor makes an inter vivos transfer to a trust for the benefit of third parties, names a third-party trustee, and grants the trustee absolute discretion to invade corpus for the transferor, if under local law the creditors of the transferor can reach the trust corpus, the transferor has retained an indirect power to revoke the trust.[23]

---

[18] Estate of Tully v. United States, 528 F2d 1401 (Ct. Cl. 1976) (no power retained); Estate of Musgrove v. Comm'r, 33 Fed. Cl. 657 (1995) (power retained).

[19] Reinecke v. Northern Trust Co., 278 US 339 (1929).

[20] See Calif. Prob. Code § 15400 (West 2001).

[21] In contrast to Section 2036, there is no "retained" requirement at all under Section 2038 regarding post-1936 transfers. The question is simply whether the decedent had the power at death. But see White v. Poor, 296 US 98 (1935). See also infra ¶ 4.10[7].

[22] Vaccaro v. United States, 149 F2d 1014 (5th Cir. 1945); Howard v. United States, 125 F2d 986 (5th Cir. 1942); Estate of Casey v. Comm'r, 55 TC 737 (1971); Estate of Davis v. Comm'r, 51 TC 361 (1968); Priv. Ltr. Rul. 8623004 (Feb. 18, 1986).

[23] Rev. Rul. 76-103, 1976-1 CB 293. Cf. Paolozzi v. Comm'r, 23 TC 182 (1954), acq. 1962-1 CB 4; Outwin v. Comm'r, 76 TC 153 (1981); Rev. Rul. 77-378, 1977-2 CB 347 (all treating such transfers as revocable gifts under the gift tax).

Seemingly, any retained power to revoke a trust directly or indirectly which is held at death also triggers Section 2036(a)(1) because it is a retained right to income which does

Substantial litigation has occurred with respect to the issue whether a transfer made by a person holding a power of attorney over an individual's property or who is a conservator or guardian for an individual has made a completed gift which escapes the individual's gross estate[24] or has made an incomplete revocable transfer subsequently includable in the decedent's gross estate under Section 2038.[25] Where a transfer is made on a decedent's behalf pursuant to a power of attorney, or by a court-appointed fiduciary, its effectiveness is also determined by local law.[26]

Despite the fact that revocable transfers are pulled into a decedent's gross estate, the use of inter vivos revocable trusts has become increasingly popular. Revocable trusts are not used to save gift[27] or estate taxes. A variety of nontax

---

not terminate prior to the decedent's death. See Estate of Paxton v. Comm'r, 86 TC 785 (1986); ¶ 4.08[4][c] note 53.

[24] The following transfers were held to be *complete* and not included in the decedent's gross estate under Section 2038: Estate of Ridenour v. Comm'r, 36 F3d 332 (4th Cir. 1994) (complete gift made under power of attorney under Virginia law, distinguishing Casey v. Comm'r, 948 F2d 895 (4th Cir. 1991)); Neff v. Comm'r, 73 TCM (CCH) 2606 (1997) (complete gift made under power of attorney under Oklahoma law which was orally directed and ratified); Estate of Pruitt v. Comm'r 80 TCM (CCH) 790 (2000) (complete gifts under power of attorney under Oregon law); TAM 9708004 (Oct. 31, 1996) complete gift under broad power of attorney under New York law in conjunction with supplemental letter from decedent; Priv. Ltr. Rul. 9839018 (June 25, 1998) (conservator gifts complete under amended state law allowing consideration of estate planning issues); TAM 199944005 (July 19, 1999) (gifts under power of attorney which were not specifically authorized but were complete based on decedent's intent and gift-giving history).

[25] The following transfers were held to be *incomplete* and included in the decedent's gross estate under Section 2038: Estate of Casey v. Comm'r, 948 F2d 895 (4th Cir. 1991) (gift made under power of attorney under Virginia law beyond the attorney's power to make gifts); Estate of Swanson v. United States, 46 Fed. Cl. 388 (2000), aff'd 2001-1 USTC 60,408 (gifts made under power of attorney under California law beyond scope of authority even though decedent orally ratified gifts); Townsend v. United States, 889 F. Supp. 369 (D. Neb. 1995) (gifts made under power of attorney under Nebraska law beyond express authority); Estate of Goldman v. Comm'r, 71 TCM (CCH) 1896 (1996) (gifts made under power of attorney under New York law beyond scope of attorney's authority); Estate of Gaynor v. Comm'r, 82 TCM (CCH) 379 (2001) (gifts made under power of attorney under Conn. law beyond scope of authority); TAM 9601002 (Sept. 22, 1995) (gifts made under power of attorney under Oregon law beyond scope of authority); TAM 9731003 (Mar. 31, 1997) (gifts by guardian approved by Maryland court under substitution of judgment doctrine held invalid). Cf. Estate of Christensen v. Comm'r, 80 TCM (CCH) 790 (2000) (gifts from decedent by another joint tenant of a joint bank account funded by decedent were revocable by decedent under Washington law).

[26] Most of such transfers involve gifts of cash or near-death transfers. Under the unified transfer tax system, the issue whether or not they are revocable has little fiscal significance (see ¶ 2.01[4]) because most involve transfers which, if complete, qualify for a gift tax exclusion and totally escape the clutches of the unified transfer tax base. See IRC §§ 2503(b), 2503(c); ¶¶ 9.04[1], 9.04[6].

[27] See ¶ 10.01[5].

considerations have increased the incidence of establishment and use of revocable trusts.[28]

[b] Power to Alter or Amend

It has long been recognized that Section 2038 is not limited to powers
that can be exercised to benefit the decedent.[29] The power to "alter" or
"amend" under the section encompasses a power generally to name new beneficiaries of a trust;[30] and a mere power to change beneficial interests among a
limited group of persons, such as the power to shift proportionate interests
among persons already enjoying rights as beneficiaries, is also within the section.[31] In such circumstances, the decedent "has not divested himself of that
degree of control which [Section 2038] requires in order to avoid the tax."[32]
The power to alter the interests of beneficiaries is sufficient to bring the alterable interests into the decedent's gross estate, even though the decedent could
exercise the power only by will and had no right during life to make adjustments.[33]

---

[28] The principal reasons for use of revocable trusts are (1) avoiding the administrative
hassles of probate; (2) avoiding ancillary probate; (3) maintaining privacy; and (4) providing for simplified property management during the grantor's lifetime especially if the
grantor becomes incapacitated. Saving probate costs can be a factor, but at least in jurisdictions where probate fees may be charged on an hourly basis, such cost saving is usually not a significant factor. The reasons for using revocable trusts are discussed in more
detail at Henkel, Estate Planning and Wealth Preservation ¶¶ 7.02, 7.03 (Warren, Gorham
& Lamont 1997); Price, Price on Contemporary Estate Planning § 10.12 (Little, Brown, &
Co. 1992); Weinstock, Planning an Estate §§ 7.2–7.39 (Shepard's McGraw-Hill 1995).
See also "The Revocable Living Trust As an Estate Planning Tool," 7 Real Prop., Prob. &
Tr. J. 223 (1979); Covey, "The Advantages and Disadvantages of the Revocable Trust in
Estate Planning," 26 NYU Inst. on Fed. Tax'n 1379 (1968); Heffernan & Williams, "Rev-
ocable Trusts in Estate Planning," 44 Cornell LQ 524 (1959).

[29] Porter v. Comm'r, 288 US 436 (1933); Florida Nat'l Bank v. United States, 336
F2d 598 (3d Cir. 1964), cert. denied, 380 US 911 (1965).

[30] But see Rev. Rul. 80-255, 1980-2 CB 272 (decedent's ability to have more children and thereby add new beneficiaries to a trust created by him was not a power to
change beneficial interests).

[31] Porter v. Comm'r, 288 US 436 (1933); Florida Nat'l Bank v. United States, 336
F2d 598 (3d Cir. 1964), cert. denied, 380 US 911 (1965); Chickering v. Comm'r, 118 F2d
254 (1st Cir.), cert. denied, 314 US 636 (1941).

[32] Lober v. United States, 346 US 335, 337 (1953).

[33] Adriance v. Higgins, 113 F2d 1013 (2d Cir. 1940); Holderness v. Comm'r, 86 F2d
137 (4th Cir. 1936); Comm'r v. Chase Nat'l Bank of NY, 82 F2d 157 (2d Cir.), cert. denied, 299 US 552 (1936); Marshall v. United States, 338 F. Supp. 1321 (D. Md. 1971).

[c] Administrative Powers

It is probably now a settled principle that mere administrative or managerial powers over trust assets do not constitute powers to alter beneficial interests in the trust within Section 2038.[34] However, such a statement of principle invites the inquiry: What powers are merely administrative or managerial? For openers, if an individual has the power to allocate receipts and disbursements between principal and income, does one have merely administrative powers? It must be admitted that the exercise of such powers may very well affect the enjoyment of interests in a trust.[35] On the other hand, there is an obvious need for some flexibility in a trustee's performance of fiduciary duties.[36] For example, a trust settlor might very well wish to reject the rigidity of statutory rules such as those of the 1962 Revised Uniform Principal and Income Act, which allocates to principal dividends paid in the form of stock of the issuing corporation.[37] This might be so whether a trust settlor or a bank is trustee. The trustee's discretion to allocate stock dividends to principal or income should not be regarded as a Section 2038 power.[38] This is because the exercise of such a fiduciary power is required to be undertaken evenhandedly for the benefit of all interests in a trust and is subject to control in this respect by a court of equity.[39] Thus, principal and income allocation decisions by a trustee generally

---

[34] See Old Colony Trust Co. v. United States, 423 F2d 601 (1st Cir. 1970), overruling State St. Trust Co. v. United States, 263 F2d 635 (1st Cir. 1959), in which the court stated (perhaps too broadly): "No aggregation of purely administrative powers can meet the government's amorphous test of 'sufficient dominion and control' so as to be equated with ownership." Old Colony Trust Co. v. United States, 423 F2d 601, 603 (1st Cir. 1970). Cf. United States v. Byrum, 408 US 125, reh'g denied, 409 US 898 (1972).

[35] See Comm'r v. Estate of Hagar, 173 F2d 613 (3d Cir. 1949); Ritter v. United States, 297 F. Supp. 1259 (SD W. Va. 1968) (decided under IRC § 2036(a)(2)).

[36] See Estate of Pardee v. Comm'r, 49 TC 140, 147 (1967).

[37] See Fla. Stat. Chapter 738.06 (2001); Unif. Principal & Income Act, §§ 3(b)(4), 6(a) (Revised 1962). The governing instrument may vary the statutory rule. Id. at § 2(a)(1).

[38] See Old Colony Trust v. United States, 423 F2d 601 (1st Cir. 1970); Estate of Ford v. Comm'r, 53 TC 114 (1969), nonacq. 1978-2 CB 3, aff'd per curiam, 450 F2d 878 (2d Cir. 1971); Estate of Budd, 49 TC 468 (1968); Estate of Pardee v. Comm'r, 49 TC 140 (1967); Estate of Peters v. Comm'r, 23 TCM (CCH) 994 (1964); Estate of Wurts v. Comm'r, 19 TCM (CCH) 544 (1960); Estate of Fiske v. Comm'r, 5 TCM (CCH) 42 (1946).

[39] IIIA Scott, The Law of Trusts § 232 (Little, Brown & Co., 4th ed. 1987). The Uniform Principal and Income Act approved by the National Conference of Commissioners on Uniform State Laws in 1997 authorizes a trustee to adjust total returns between principal and income under Section 104 of the Act. Unif. Principal & Income Act, § 104 (Revised 1997). Section 2038 should not be applicable where the settlor as trustee is under Section 104 authorized to adjust total return between principal and income. Unif. Principal & Income Act, § 104 (Revised 1997). See, e.g., Calif. Prob. Code § 16336 (West 2001).

cannot be made for the purpose of changing beneficial interests, even if they have some such effect.

Discretionary authority to make those allocations clearly may go too far. For example, if a nontrustee grantor reserved complete allocation discretion and if such discretion was subject to no judicial restraint, the grantor should be viewed as holding a proscribed power. Consider in such circumstances the status of the income beneficiary if the grantor allocates all receipts to principal, or of the remainderperson if all receipts are allocated to income. However, the hypothetical may not be very realistic; in such circumstances, the grantor may be a kind of quasi-fiduciary, restrained in actions by equitable principles.[40] If the grantor is unbridled, however, and trust agreements can be drafted to meet the parties' wishes, the allocation power should be regarded as being within Section 2038.

Similarly, even if an individual has allocation powers as *trustee*, if they are validly expressed in such a way as to foreclose restraint by a court of equity,[41] they go beyond needed flexibility, involve affirmative authority to tamper with beneficial interests, and should be regarded as Section 2038 powers. Thus, if an individual has the unrestrained power to allocate capital gains either to principal or to income, the status of the remainderperson is rendered so tenuous as to be regarded as "subject to change." For if, in fairly active trading, the trustee allocated all gains to income and charged all losses to principal,[42] most of the trust property might soon be placed in the pockets of the income beneficiaries at the expense of the remainderperson even if, on the whole, the investment practices were quite successful.[43] It is clear, therefore, that the broad principle removing managerial and administrative powers from the scope of Section 2038 does little more than require attention to be focused on any power to determine whether, under its terms and applicable local law, it is properly considered a fiduciary power or whether it really amounts to a power to change beneficial interests.

---

[40] Cf. Estate of Chalmers v. Comm'r, 31 TCM (CCH) 792 (1972) (decedent grantor's powers could be exercised only with the trustees; consequently, although the court does not rest its decision on it, the fiduciary restraints on the trustees spilled over to the decedent); Estate of King v. Comm'r, 37 TC 973 (1962), nonacq. 1963-1 CB 5 (court found that a nontrustee grantor's investment powers were reserved in a fiduciary capacity).

[41] Ritter v. United States, 297 F. Supp. 1259 (SD W. Va. 1968); Comm'r v. Estate of Hagar, 173 F2d 613 (3d Cir. 1949).

[42] See Unif. Principal & Income Act, § 3(b) (Revised 1962); Unif. Principal & Income Act, § 401 (Revised 1997).

[43] See Comm'r v. Estate of Hagar, 173 F2d 613 (3d Cir. 1949).

[d] Powers of Investment

While the foregoing discussion is centered around a power of allocation, the same principles should apply to powers of investment. It is obvious that a trust's terms cannot anticipate and provide the answer for all investment decisions. Some fiduciary flexibility in investing is usually needed to protect the interests of the beneficial owners of the trust property. And investment discretion that is subject to judicial restraint should again be classified as a mere administrative or managerial power.[44] However, if an individual has uncontrolled power over trust investments, it is obvious that the remainderperson's interest is threatened if the power holder invests in speculative high-yield mortgages and that the income beneficiary's interest may be virtually eliminated if the power holder opts for non-dividend-paying growth stocks. Therefore, in these circumstances, the interests may be subject to change through the investment power.[45] The somewhat unhappy conclusion is that no final answers are reached by noting that a power goes only to principal and income allocation or only to investment; in each instance, the exact nature and scope of the power must be considered.[46]

[e] Power to Terminate

A power to terminate a trust is an expressly proscribed Section 2038 power.[47] If a grantor can terminate a trust, does this bring the entire corpus into the grantor's gross estate? Not necessarily; there is a risk of focusing so

---

[44] Old Colony Trust Co. v. United States, 423 F2d 601 (1st Cir. 1970); United States v. Powell, 307 F2d 821 (10th Cir. 1962); Estate of Jordahl v. Comm'r, 65 TC 92 (1975), acq. 1977-1 CB 1; Estate of Chalmers v. Comm'r, 31 TCM (CCH) 792 (1972); Estate of King v. Comm'r, 37 TC 973 (1962) nonacq. 1963-1 CB 5; Estate of Wilson v. Comm'r, 13 TC 869 (1949), acq. in part 1950-1 CB 5, nonacq. in part 1950-1 CB 8, aff'd per curiam, 187 F2d 145 (3d Cir. 1951). Some earlier cases seem to reach this conclusion uncritically without examining the actual extent of the decedent's control: Estate of Neal v. Comm'r, 8 TC 237 (1947), acq. 1947-1 CB 3; Estate of Hall v. Comm'r, 6 TC 933 (1946), acq. 1946-2 CB 3; Fifth Ave. Bank of NY v. Nunan, 59 F. Supp. 753 (EDNY 1945) (involving a grantor's power to amend trustee's investment powers under a trust); Estate of Downe v. Comm'r, 2 TC 967 (1943), nonacq. 1944 CB 37.

[45] Cf. Commonwealth Trust Co. of Pittsburgh v. Driscoll, 50 F. Supp. 949 (WD Pa.), aff'd per curiam, 137 F2d 653 (3d Cir. 1943), cert. denied, 321 US 764 (1944).

[46] The principles expressed here are equally applicable under Section 2036(a)(2). See ¶ 4.08[6][a]. For a discussion of this general area, see Gray & Covey, "State Street—A Case Study of Sections 2036(a)(2) and 2038," 15 Tax L. Rev. 75 (1959); Van Vechten, "The Grantor's Retention of Powers as Trustee or Otherwise; Income and Estate Tax Consequences," 25 NYU Inst. on Fed. Tax'n 943 (1967).

[47] Despite the omission of the term "terminate" from Section 2038(a)(2), the two paragraphs (IRC §§ 2038(a)(1), 2038(a)(2)) do not differ in this respect, because the United States Supreme Court has held that authority to terminate a trust is within the

hard on the phrase "power . . . to alter, amend, revoke or terminate" as to for-
get that the only interests taxed are those the enjoyment of which was subject
to "change" through the exercise of such powers. Nevertheless, the termination
of a trust generally will change beneficial interests. For example, if *D* creates a
trust under which the income is to be paid to *B* for life, remainder to *C* or *C*'s
estate, but reserves the right at any time to terminate the trust, effecting an immediate corpus distribution to *C*, the entire trust corpus is includable in *D*'s
gross estate. *B*'s interest is clearly subject to change, as it can be terminated.
C's interest is likewise subject to change, as it can be accelerated and that
change, even though favorable to *C*, is within the scope of the section.

The situation is different if *D* has only the power to direct a distribution
of the trust corpus to the life beneficiary, *B* in this example. In these circumstances, although the remainder interest is clearly subject to change within
Section 2038, the income beneficiary's right to the income for life merely continues, albeit as outright owner of the property. Consequently, *B*'s life interest
is excluded if *D* dies possessing the power.[48]

[f] Gifts to Minors

The fact that acceleration of enjoyment is a "change" within Section 2038
has implications outside the area of formal trusts. For example, under state
statutes such as the Uniform Gifts to Minors Act and the Model Gifts of Securities to Minors Act, the custodian may apply income or principal for the
minor's benefit in the custodian's sole discretion, if it seems advisable for the
support and maintenance of the minor. The Service has ruled that under these
statutes, property transferred by a decedent naming oneself as custodian is includable in the decedent's gross estate if the decedent dies before the minor attains majority.[49] The Service's position has been sustained in several judicial
decisions.[50] There is an easy escape from estate tax liability in this situation;
generally, the objectives of a gift tax exclusion[51] and the benefit to the minor

---

meaning of the term "alter," which appears in both paragraphs. Lober v. United States,
346 US 335 (1953); Comm'r v. Estate of Holmes, 326 US 480 (1946).

[48] Walter v. United States, 341 F2d 182 (6th Cir. 1965); Rev. Rul. 70-513, 1970-2
CB 194. See Estate of DuCharme v. Comm'r, 164 F2d 959 (6th Cir. 1947), reh'g, 169
F2d 76 (6th Cir. 1948). This question is analyzed more fully supra ¶ 4.10[3].

[49] Rev. Rul. 70-348, 1970-2 CB 193; Rev. Rul. 59-357, 1959-2 CB 212; Rev. Rul.
57-366, 1957-2 CB 618. Cf. Rev. Rul. 74-556, 1974-2 CB 300.

[50] Stuit v. Comm'r, 452 F2d 190 (7th Cir. 1971) (Illinois law); Estate of Eichstedt v.
Comm'r, 354 F. Supp. 484 (ND Cal. 1972) (California law); Estate of Prudowski v.
Comm'r, 55 TC 890 (1971), aff'd per curiam, 465 F2d 62 (7th Cir. 1972) (Wisconsin
law); Estate of Jacoby v. Comm'r, 29 TCM (CCH) 737 (1970) (Missouri law).

[51] See discussion of Section 2503(c) at ¶ 9.04[5].

can be achieved as well by naming someone other than the decedent as custodian.[52]

[g] Power in "Whatever Capacity"

Section 2038 applies to a power "in whatever capacity exercisable" by the decedent.[53] However, if the decedent has no connection with an outstanding power over property the decedent has transferred, the statute, of course, does not apply. For example, if the decedent has made a lifetime transfer creating a power in some third party (such as one's spouse) to alter or amend, Section 2038 does not require the value of the transferred property to be included in the decedent's gross estate.[54] However, if the decedent has the unrestricted power to remove or discharge a trustee at any time and to appoint the decedent as trustee, the decedent is considered to have all the powers of the trustee.[55] The decedent's reservation of the power to substitute a trustee with someone other than oneself will not, by itself, result in inclusion under Section 2038.[56] As a practical matter, the exemption from tax where only a third party has a power over property clearly leaves substantial room for tax-free control by the decedent through careful selection of the person or persons who alone will have the power.[57]

---

[52] Section 2038 will not apply if one other than the decedent has a power, and Section 2036 will not be invoked if only a third-party custodian has discretion to use income and principal for support of the transferor's dependent. See supra ¶ 4.08[4][b] note 32. But see Exchange Bank & Trust Co. of Fla. v. United States, 694 F2d 1261 (Fed. Cir. 1982), discussed ¶ 4.08[7][d] note 153. However, Section 677(b) may leave the transferor subject to income tax liability on income actually used for support.

[53] IRC § 2038(a)(1). Despite the 1936 addition in Paragraph (1) of the clause "in whatever capacity exercisable," it seems settled that the capacity in which the decedent can exercise a power has never made any difference. Reg. § 20.2038-1(a). See Estate of Levin v. Comm'r, 90 TC 723 (1988) (power held as controlling shareholder of corporation). On the other hand, if the power is held in a fiduciary capacity, a power that might otherwise invoke Section 2038 may, by reason of potential judicial restraint, be held not a power to change enjoyment. See discussion supra ¶ 4.10[3].

[54] Reg. § 20.2038-1(a)(3). See, e.g., Estate of Hofheimer v. Comm'r, 2 TC 773, 783 (1943), nonacq., 1944 CB 40, rev'd on other issues, 149 F2d 733 (2d Cir. 1945). For income tax purposes the rule is otherwise. IRC §§ 672(e), 674, 676, 677.

[55] Reg. § 20.2038-1(a)(3); Mathey v. United States, 491 F2d 481 (3d Cir. 1974); Estate of Edmonds v. Comm'r, 72 TC 970 (1979). Cf. Rev. Rul. 73-21, 1973-1 CB 405 (Section 2036(a)(2) case). Of course, if the trustee does not hold sufficient powers to require inclusion under Section 2038, a decedent's power to name himself trustee will not cause Section 2038 inclusion. Miller v. United States, 325 F. Supp. 1287 (ED Pa. 1971).

[56] Rev. Rul. 95-58, 1995-2 CB 1, discussed at ¶ 4.08[4][b] note 32; ¶ 4.08[5][a], text accompanying note 61.

[57] The results are impossible to justify. For example, if the decedent makes a tranfer retaining the power to accumulate income only if the life beneficiary agrees, Section 2038

[5] Powers Restricted by Standards

It has been suggested here that judicial restraint on the exercise of fiduciary powers may neutralize apparent control in a decedent for purposes of Section 2038.[58] The same neutralization may arise out of limitations expressed in the governing instrument itself. If the trust instrument directs the decedent as trustee in identifiable circumstances to shift interests between trust beneficiaries, a person entitled to the benefit of such a shift may have the rights enforced by a court of equity. In such circumstances, the decedent is merely a lieutenant, not a general, and a power to change enjoyment only in stated circumstances does not invoke Section 2038.[59] If the decedent's discretion whether and how to exercise a power is subject to independent review by a court of equity under an objective standard, the power is ignored because the decedent really holds no "power." The leading case establishing this principle is *Jennings v. Smith*.[60] In the *Jennings* case, the decedent's power as trustee to pay out income to the son or his children if necessary in order to enable the beneficiary to keep himself and his family in comfort, "in accordance with the station in life to which he belongs,"[61] was held not to be a Section 2038 power. On the other hand, if the decedent's power to invade is exercisable simply if "the circumstances so require," the property will be includable in the decedent's gross estate.[62] If the results of these two examples seem inconsistent, the differentiating factor is that in the first instance, the decedent is carrying out terms of the trust, although with some discretion, whereas in the second instance, the trust leaves it up to the decedent to make up the terms or conditions for invasions of the corpus.[63]

---

applies. On the other hand, if the decedent's spouse has the power to revoke the transfer, Section 2038 is inapplicable. Nevertheless, the construction placed on the section requires these questionable results.

[58] See supra ¶ 4.10[4][d].

[59] Note that Section 2036(a)(2) would also be inapplicable in such circumstances. See ¶ 4.08[6][a]. See also Note, "The Doctrine of External Standards Under Sections 2036(a)(2) and 2038," 52 Minn. L. Rev. 1071 (1968); Harris, "Ascertainable Standard Restrictions on Trust Powers Under the Estate, Gift and Income Tax," 50 Tax Law. 489 (1997).

[60] Jennings v. Smith, 161 F2d 74 (2d Cir. 1947).

[61] Jennings v. Smith, 161 F2d 74, 76 (2d Cir. 1947).

[62] Hurd v. Comm'r, 160 F2d 610 (1st Cir. 1947). See Rev. Rul. 73-143, 1973-1 CB 407. A power to "accelerate payments . . . in case of need for educational purposes or because of illness or for any other good reason" has been held subject to an ascertainable standard. Estate of Wilson v. Comm'r, 13 TC 869 (1949), acq. in part 1950-1 CB 5, nonacq. in part 1950-1 CB 8, aff'd per curiam, 187 F2d 145 (3d Cir. 1951).

[63] In the early New Deal period, the proliferation of federal administration agencies was attacked on the ground of improper delegation of legislative power. The maxim "Delegata potestas non potest delegari" was invoked to challenge legislative abdication of power in favor of administrators. A question, however, was whether the authority con-

The broad proposition here, as stated in the opinions, is that a power that is restricted by an objective standard is not a power within the meaning of Section 2038. The rationale is not always clearly stated, but such a power involves authority to *execute* rather than to *determine or to change* the terms of the transfer. Thus, if *D* creates a trust with the income payable to *A* and the remainder to *B*, but the trust terms require *D* to give *A* such corpus as is necessary for *A*'s support and maintenance, *D* must merely comply with a requirement of the trust, and *D* holds no independent power. However, if, in *D*'s discretion, *D* may distribute to *A* such amounts of corpus as *D* feels *A* should have, then *D* has a power to change the terms of the original transfer, and the value of the remainder interest is included in *D*'s estate. Whether and to what extent seeming discretion is restricted depends on the terms of the transfer instrument as interpreted under state law, which makes it impossible to frame a flat rule for neutral trust terms. Of course, whether any restriction found to exist defeats the application of Section 2038 is a purely federal question.[64]

---

ferred was to be carried out pursuant to an "adequate standard" or some "intelligible principle" legislatively prescribed. This now seems long ago; nevertheless, the problem as then viewed is analogous to that under discussion here. Some of the United States Supreme Court's higher learning on the subject will be found in Schecter Poultry Corp. v. United States, 295 US 495 (1935); Panama Ref. Co. v. Ryan, 293 US 388 (1935); Hampton & Co. v. United States, 276 US 394 (1928).

[64] The effect of state law is discussed broadly at ¶ 4.05[2][a]. Although interpretations of trust terms may vary widely from state to state, nevertheless here is a group of *cases in which neutralizing standards for powers have been found to exist*: United States v. Powell, 307 F2d 821 (10th Cir. 1962) ("maintenance, welfare, comfort, or happiness"); Leopold v. United States, 510 F2d 617 (9th Cir. 1975) ("support, education, maintenance and general welfare . . . solely in the uncontrolled discretion of the Trustees"); Estate of Klafter v. Comm'r, 32 TCM (CCH) 1088 (1973) ("support, maintenance, health, education and comfortable living"); Estate of Ford v. Comm'r, 53 TC 114 (1969), nonacq. 1978-2 CB 3, aff'd per curiam, 450 F2d 878 (2d Cir. 1971) ("need of funds . . . for the purpose of defraying expenses occasioned by illness, infirmity or disability . . . or for his support, maintenance, education, welfare and happiness"; court concluded that "need" limited "happiness"); Estate of Pardee v. Comm'r, 49 TC 140 (1967) ("education, maintenance, medical expenses, or other needs . . . occasioned by emergency"; case contains a collection of cases on what constitutes an ascertainable standard).

The following cases found no ascertainable standard: Stuit v. Comm'r, 452 F2d 190 (7th Cir. 1971) (for minor's "benefit" under the Illinois Uniform Gift to Minors Act); Estate of Nettleton v. Comm'r, 4 TC 987 (1945), acq., 1946-1 CB 3 (trustees' uncontrolled discretion "as they may consider suitable and necessary in the interest and for the welfare of such beneficiary"); Estate of Perrin v. Comm'r, 3 TCM (CCH) 225 (1944) ("may in his discretion deem necessary or proper for the comfort, support and/or happiness"); Estate of Bell v. Comm'r, 66 TC 729 (1976) ("funds for a home, business, or for any other purpose believed . . . to be for her benefit"). Many of these cases involved both Sections 2036(a)(2) and 2038, and what constitutes a standard for one also constitutes a standard for the other.

[6] Power Exercisable Only With Another

Even if a mere power that may be exercised only subject to an ascertainable standard is not a power for Section 2038 purposes, this does not mean that a decedent must have a cogent power to be caught by Section 2038. In general, a requirement that the decedent obtain the concurrence or consent of another person in the exercise of a power does not defeat the section; and, again in general, the status of the other person or person's interest in the property subject to the power is not a relevant consideration. The statute applies to a power exercisable by the decedent alone or by the decedent in conjunction with *any* other person.[65] Section 2038 applies even though the person with whom the power is held has an interest that would be adversely affected by the exercise of the power and would be unlikely to concur in its exercise. Thus, Section 2038 applies to the remainder interest of a trust in which the income is payable to *A*, remainder to *B*, but that gives the decedent a power to invade the corpus for *A*'s benefit with *B*'s approval. Even though the power is held conjunctively with *B*, whose remainder interest would be diminished by its exercise, and the decedent can be looked upon as powerless, Section 2038 nevertheless applies to include the remainder interest in the decedent's gross estate.[66]

Prior to the enactment of the forerunner of Section 2038 in 1924, the value of transferred property was not includable in the decedent's estate if the decedent's power over the property could be exercised only in conjunction with beneficiaries whose rights would be adversely affected by such exercise. And that rule has continuing vitality with respect to pre-1924 transfers otherwise within the scope of the section.[67] However, the present provision has been interpreted strictly in this regard and sustained against constitutional attack on the ground that, under any other rule, the decedent could easily avoid the tax by joining in the exercise of the power an interested party who is reasonably certain to comply with the decedent's wishes.[68]

---

[65] IRC §§ 2038(a)(1), 2038(a)(2); Reg. § 20.2038-1(a); Estate of Bowgren v. Comm'r, 105 F3d 1156 (7th Cir. 1997); Swain v. United States, 147 F3d 564 (7th Cir. 1998); Adolphson v. United States, 90-2 USTC ¶ 60,048 (CD Ill. 1990). Cf. Swain v. United States, 85 AFTR2d 2000-910 (7th Cir. 2000). See TAM 9502005 (Jan. 13, 1995).

[66] Cf. Helvering v. City Bank Farmer's Trust Co., 296 US 85 (1935).

[67] Reg. § 20.2038-1(d). But see New England Merchant's Nat'l Bank of Boston v. United States, 384 F2d 176 (1st Cir. 1967) (involving a pre-1924 transfer in which, however, the institutional trustee had no adverse interest, so Section 2038 was applicable); Rev. Rul. 78-16, 1978-2 CB 289 (a substantial adverse interest in a pre-1924 transfer was created in 1940; the ruling held that since the decedent was not subject to an adverse interest that existed in 1924, subsequent adverse interests were subject to the post-1924 rule, and, therefore, Regulations Section 20.2038-1(d) was not applicable).

[68] Helvering v. City Bank Farmer's Trust Co., 296 US 85 (1935).

The Treasury and the courts do not differentiate between a power in the decedent to act with the consent of another and a power in another to act only with the decedent's consent.[69] Each is treated as a power in the decedent, which may result in tax liability under Section 2038. Obviously, as an interpretation of the statute, this is a realistic approach; in either case, both must join in the exercise of the power, and verbalistic differences should be ignored.

One exceptional case in which a decedent transferor may hold a power with others will be disregarded under Section 2038. If the decedent holds a power that can be exercised only with the consent of all persons having an interest, vested or contingent, in the property subject to the power and if the power adds nothing to the rights of the parties under local law, the power is ignored.[70] This exception rests upon two factors: (1) the required consent of all interested persons and (2) a provision of local law that would allow such persons to alter the terms of the trust in any event. Neither factor standing alone is enough to defeat Section 2038. Apart from this exception, the term "any other person" in Section 2038 is held to mean literally *any* other person.[71]

[7] Source of the Power

As previously discussed, Section 2036 expressly raises the question whether, with respect to a lifetime transfer, the decedent has "retained" enjoyment or continuing rights. In contrast, the Section 2038 transfer provision has always raised only the question whether interests were subject to change by way of a power in the decedent at the time of death. Nevertheless, the 1935 Supreme Court decision in *White v. Poor*[72] gave the revocable transfer provision as it then existed a restrictive interpretation along the lines of the "retained" requirement of Section 2036. In that case, the decedent had created a trust naming herself and others as trustees and giving the trustees the power to revoke. Later she resigned, only to be appointed trustee by a vote of the then trustees upon the occurrence of another resignation. At death, as a trustee, she had the power with the others to revoke the trust. Her estate successfully argued that the estate tax provision concerning revocable transfers was inapplicable because the decedent had acquired the power by virtue of the action of the other trustees and not because she had *retained* any power to control the enjoyment of the property.

---

[69] Rev. Rul. 55-683, 1955-2 CB 603; Estate of DuCharme v. Comm'r, 164 F2d 959 (6th Cir. 1947), reh'g, 169 F2d 76 (6th Cir. 1948).

[70] Reg. § 20.2038-1(a)(2), echoing the result reached in Helvering v. Helmholz, 296 US 93 (1935).

[71] Helvering v. City Bank Farmer's Trust Co., 296 US 85 (1935).

[72] White v. Poor, 296 US 98 (1935), discussed in Van Beuren v. McLoughlin, 262 F2d 315, 320 (1st Cir. 1958), cert. denied, 359 US 991 (1959).

This argument is of no avail regarding transfers made after June 22, 1936.[73] When Congress enacted what is now Paragraph (1) of Section 2038(a), it expressly provided that it makes no difference "when or from what source" the decedent acquired the proscribed power. However, there should be some linkage between the required transfer by the decedent and the decedent's power. Section 2038 should be held inapplicable in situations where the decedent makes a complete, absolute transfer and, by a totally unrelated reconveyance, the decedent has some fiduciary power or control at death.[74]

A power arising by operation of law is very likely within both Section 2038(a)(1) and Section 2038(a)(2). For example, if a state statute gives a parent the right to revoke any lifetime transfer to a minor child, the parent may properly be regarded as having "retained" the power to revoke, even though the retention rests on the statutory provision rather than on language expressed in the transfer instrument.[75] The *White* case restricts the scope of Section 2038(a)(2) with regard to powers conferred on the decedent by some independent outside force. Revenue Ruling 70-348[76] reflects the difference between pre-1936 and later transfers. In that ruling, a decedent had transferred property to another as custodian for a minor. Under relevant local law, the custodian had powers over the property that, if held by the decedent, would invoke Section 2038. Later, the original custodian transferred the property to the decedent as custodian, and in that way the decedent acquired the tainted power over the property that the decedent had originally transferred. *White v. Poor* places this case outside Section 2038(a)(2) for lack of *retention* of a power by the decedent,[77] but the Treasury properly ruled that the property was includable in the decedent's estate under Section 2038(a)(1). It will be observed that in the case governed by the ruling, the decedent's transfer created the power that the decedent ultimately acquired.[78]

[8] When Power Must Exist

In general, of course, the power must exist at the date of the decedent's death.[79] However, Section 2038(b) lays down specific rules regarding the exis-

---

[73] See Fabian v. United States, 127 F. Supp. 726 (D. Conn. 1954).

[74] Reed Estate v. United States, 1975-1 USTC ¶ 13.073 (MD Fla. 1975). Cf. Estate of Skifter v. Comm'r, 468 F2d 699 (2d Cir. 1972); Rev. Rul. 84-179, 1984-2 CB 195, discussed ¶ 4.14[4][d].

[75] Cf. IRC § 2037(a)(2).

[76] 1970-2 CB 193.

[77] For the same reason, Section 2036 is inapplicable.

[78] See Reed Estate v. United States, 1975-1 USTC ¶ 13,073 (MD Fla. 1975).

[79] Reg. § 20.2038-1(b); Estate of Webster v. Comm'r, 65 TC 968 (1976). See Estate of Yawkey v. Comm'r, 12 TC 1164 (1949), acq. 1949-2 CB 3. Thus, property subject to a

tence of the power in order to prevent artful drafting from frustrating Section 2038. The statute provides that the power shall be treated as existing at the date of death, even though the exercise of the power is subject to a precedent giving of notice or even though the amendment, revocation, or termination takes effect only upon the expiration of a stated period after the exercise of the power. For example, if, under a trust instrument, the decedent could not exercise a power to revoke until thirty days after giving notice of revocation, enjoyment of the interest affected by the power would not be subject to change at date of death if no such notice had been given. Section 2038(b) provides that a power such as this, which requires a notice before exercise, shall be considered to be a power that the decedent possesses on the date of death, despite the necessity of giving notice. This principle has been applied to a related situation without the benefit of the precise statutory rule. In a case in which the trustee had a power to amend and the decedent had the right to discharge the trustee and appoint himself trustee, but only after giving notice, the decedent was held to have the prescribed power at death even though no such notice had been given.[80]

On the other hand, the inference can properly be drawn from Section 2038(b) that if there are other contingencies (other than giving notice or a deferred effective date for the decedent's action), Section 2038 does not apply.[81] The inference merely confirms the apparent general requirement that the power exist at death. For example, assume D transfers property in trust providing that the income is to be paid to A for life, then to B and C for their lives as D may direct, with remainder payable to E. If D dies while A is alive, Section 2038 is

---

power exercisable only upon circumstances beyond the decedent's control, which had not occurred by the time of the decedent's death, is not within the section. Jennings v. Smith, 161 F2d 74 (2d Cir. 1947). For example, if the settlor has a power to appoint the settlor as a successor trustee only if the existing trustee should resign and at the settlor's death such resignation has not occurred, the settlor will not be deemed to have the powers of the trustee at death. See also Round v. Comm'r, 332 F2d 590 (1st Cir. 1964).

[80] Estate of Loughridge v. Comm'r, 183 F2d 294 (10th Cir.), cert. denied, 340 US 830 (1950).

[81] But see Rev. Rul. 68-538, 1968-2 CB 406, which appears to be at odds with the above conclusion. In the ruling, the decedent had created a revocable trust and later executed amendments to the trust by which she waived her right of revocation for a period of several years. This restriction was in effect at the date of her death. The Service recognized that the decedent did not have the power to revoke at her death, but found that she did have at that time the power to revoke in the future, namely, when the duration of the waiver expired, and ruled that the existence of such a power was sufficient to bring the trust within Section 2038. The value of the trust, however, was discounted for the period from the date of the decedent's death until the date when the waiver would have lapsed. Note that inclusion would occur under Section 2036 even when subject to a contingency beyond the decedent's control, and the ruling, very questionable under Section 2038, would seem to be correct if Section 2036 had been applied. See Reg. § 20.2036-1(b)(3)(iii); ¶ 4.08[2].

inapplicable because *D* does not have the power to alter or amend the interests of *B* and *C* at the time of *D*'s death.[82]

The decedent, of course, can avoid Section 2038 by relinquishing the power prior to death. However, both Paragraphs (1) and (2) of Section 2038(a) deal adversely with relinquishments made within three years of death.[83] In general, and in contrast to the omission in Section 2036,[84] Congress has expressly provided that the relinquishment of a power within three years of death does not defeat the section.[85] Here again, however, there are substantive differences in Sections 2038(a)(1) and 2038(a)(2). The provision applicable to earlier transfers nails only relinquishments made by *the decedent* within three years of death. Under Section 2038(a)(2), if the decedent had a power exercisable only with *A* and *A* relinquished the power within three years of the decedent's death, which under local law nullified the decedent's power, Section 2038 will not apply. However, as to later tranfers subject to Section 2038(a)(1), the question is only whether the power was *relinquished* within three years of the decedent's death; under that provision, *A*'s relinquishment of *A*'s power within three years of the decedent's death would not defeat the section.[86] However, both provisions are partially overridden by Section 2035(e). Section 2035(e) provides that for purposes of Section 2035 and 2038, any transfer of any portion of a trust (while the trust was treated under Section 676 as owned by de-

---

[82] Of course, if the contingency is one over which *D* has control, then the power is deemed to exist at the time of *D*'s death. See supra note 79. Note, too, that if the text example reflects a post-1932 transfer, the estate escapes the left feint of Section 2038 only to be hit by the right cross of Section 2036.

[83] E.g., Estate of Hofheimer v. Comm'r, 2 TC 773 (1943), nonacq. 1944 CB 40, rev'd on other issues, 149 F2d 733 (2d Cir. 1945) (decided for the taxpayer on the factual issue of in contemplation of death); Estate of Sanford v. Comm'r, 308 US 39 (1939); Lehman v. Comm'r, 109 F2d 99 (2d Cir.), cert. denied, 310 US 637 (1940) (prompted Congress to make some very limited exceptions to the rule regarding relinquishment of powers). See IRC § 811(d)(4) (1939); Pub. L. No. 378, ch. 720, § 6(c), 63 Stat. 891, 894 (1949), reprinted in 1949-2 CB 275, 278; S. Rep. No. 1622, 83d Cong., 2d Sess. 469 (1954). Consider also IRC § 2038(c) prior to repeal in the Tax Reform Act of 1976, Pub. L. No. 94-455, § 1902(a)(3), 90 Stat. 1520, 1804 (1976), reprinted in, 1976-3 CB (Vol. 1) 1, 280; Reg. § 20.2038-1(f); Bank of NY v. United States, 314 F. Supp. 1167 (SDNY 1970), for an application of Section 2038(c) and its interrelationship with Section 2037. See also IRC §§ 2035(a), 2035(e) regarding transfers within three years of death.

[84] See ¶ 4.08[8][b].

[85] Subordinate concepts of Section 2035, such as the three-year cutoff and the exception of transfers for full consideration, are applied in this context. Reg. § 20.2038-1(e)(1). See also IRC § 2035(e) which specifically overrides Section 2038. See infra text accompanying notes 87–91.

[86] Reg. § 20.2038-1(e)(2).

cedent by reason of a power of revocation in the grantor)[87] will be treated as a transfer made directly by the decedent.[88] Thus, transfers from a revocable trust or the relinquishment of a power to revoke part or all of a revocable trust[89] within three years of a decedent's death are treated as outright gifts by the decedent and are no longer within the grasp of either Section 2038 or Section 2035. However, this does not make the three-year language of paragraphs (1) and (2) of Section 2038(a) a dead letter. The provisions continue to apply to powers other than a Section 676 power of revocation that are held under Section 2038[90] and are relinquished within three years of a decedent's death. For example, if a decedent created an irrevocable trust with lifetime income and remainder interests but retained the power to change the designated beneficiaries or to alter the timing of a beneficiary's enjoyment and the decedent relinquished the power within three years of death, the affected interests would be pulled into the decedent's gross estate under Section 2035 and Section 2038.[91]

[9] Amount to Be Included

In arriving at the proper figure for the gross estate, all the sections defining it require (1) an *identification* of included interests;[92] (2) a determination as to the *time* for valuing the interests;[93] and (3) the *valuation* of the included interests in accordance with an accepted method.[94] Regarding identification, Section 2038 includes in the gross estate the value of any interest in property transferred by the decedent if the enjoyment of such interest was subject at the date of the decedent's death to change through one of the proscribed powers.[95] The fact that the decedent had no beneficial rights in the property is irrelevant. The question is: What is the value of the interest in property, the enjoyment of

---

[87] Section 676 is the revocable grantor trust provision. Section 2035(e) disregards Section 672(e), under which, for income tax purposes, the grantor is deemed to hold a power to revoke because the grantor's spouse holds such a power.

[88] Section 2035(e) is discussed in more detail elsewhere in the treatise. See ¶ 4.07[2][b][ii]. The subsection applies to estates of decedents dying after August 5, 1997. The Taxpayer Relief Act of 1997, Pub. L. No. 105-34, § 1310(c), 111 Stat. 788, 1044 (1997), reprinted in 1997-4 CB 1457, 1736.

[89] See ¶ 4.07[2][b] text accompanying notes 50–52.

[90] See generally supra ¶¶ 4.10[4]–4.10[7].

[91] IRC §§ 2035(a), 2038(a). Cf. Estate of Kisling v. Comm'r, 32 F3d 1222 (8th Cir. 1994), acq. 1995-2 CB 1.

[92] See infra ¶ 4.10[10][f].

[93] This presents a date-of-death, Section 2031, or alternate date, Section 2032, option.

[94] See Reg. §§ 20.2031-1(b), 20.2031-2–20.2031-9; IRC §§ 2032A, 7520.

[95] Reg. § 20.2038-1(a) (first sentence).

which is subject to a power held by the decedent, either alone or with others? The answer to this question is the amount to be included in the gross estate.

Assume, for example, that the decedent, *D*, made a transfer of property in trust under which the beneficiary, *B*, was entitled to the income until *B* attained age thirty, at which time *B* was to receive one half of the corpus. Thereafter, *B* was entitled to receive the income from the balance of the trust until *B* attained age thirty-five, at which time *B* was to receive the balance of the corpus. *D*, having retained the power to terminate the trust at any time with the corpus to be distributed to *B*, died without exercising the power when *B* was twenty-seven years old. As *D* retained the right to terminate the trust, the corpus is includable in *D*'s gross estate, except for the value (determined actuarially at the time of *D*'s death) of *B*'s right to receive the income from the trust until age thirty and from half the trust from that time until age thirty-five.[96] In effect, in a case such as this, death terminates *D*'s control over the enjoyment of the trust property, identifying a kind of transmission reasonably subjected to tax, but not with regard to the assured income interests for which an exception is noted.

[a] Interests Subject to Change

Sometimes it is easy to identify the includable interests that are subject to change. If the power possessed by the decedent at the time of the decedent's death affects only certain interests, only those interests will be included in the decedent's gross estate. For example, if the decedent has power to change only an income interest, Section 2038 requires that there be included in the gross estate only the value of that income interest.[97] If the income interest of a particular beneficiary of a trust is not subject to change, only the value of the other interests that are subject to change is included in the decedent's gross estate. Thus, if a fixed amount of the income from a trust is to be paid to a named beneficiary and no power exists to change the amount, the value of the beneficiary's interest cannot be included in the decedent's gross estate under Section 2038, even though other income interests may be within the section.[98]

Similarly, if a power in the decedent could not effectively be exercised at death because of a requirement of giving notice, the power is recognized under Section 2038(b), but the amount to be included in the gross estate is subject to adjustment. The adjustment excludes the value of the interest that could not have been affected by an exercise of the power if the decedent had lived. For example, suppose that a trust could be revoked only one year after the dece-

---

[96] Walter v. United States, 341 F2d 182 (6th Cir. 1965); Rev. Rul. 70-513, 1970-2 CB 194. Contra Estate of Inman v. Comm'r, 203 F2d 679 (2d Cir. 1953).

[97] Industrial Trust Co. v. Comm'r, 165 F2d 142 (1st Cir. 1947).

[98] Industrial Trust Co. v. Comm'r, 165 F2d 142 (1st Cir. 1947).

dent had given notice. If the decedent had not given notice at death, a beneficiary who had an income interest in the property would, at the date of death, be assured of the continuance of that interest for one more year. In such circumstances, Section 2038(b) provides that the amount otherwise includable in the gross estate shall be reduced by the value of the assured interest. For this purpose, the statute says that the notice shall be considered given on the date of the decedent's death. A similar adjustment is to be made if the exercise of a power will take effect only after the expiration of a stated period.

[b] Sections 2036 and 2038 Compared

Although Sections 2036 and 2038 have a considerable overlap,[99] one of the principal differences between them is the amount to be included in a decedent's gross estate when one or the other of the sections applies. Here is a comparative illustration of the operation of the two sections. If the decedent retained a power to designate who should have the income from the property transferred for one of the prescribed periods, the value of the entire property is includable in the decedent's gross estate under Section 2036(a)(2). However, under Section 2038 such a transfer would be includable only to the extent of the value of the alterable income interest. On the other hand, in some situations the same result will be reached whichever section is applied. For example, if the decedent transferred property to A for life, remainder to B, and retained the power to revoke, clearly both sections would apply and the value of the entire property would be includable under either. Both sections also apply to tax the entire property, if the decedent creates a trust with income to A for life, remainder to B, and the decedent in the decedent's discretion retains the unlimited power to invade the corpus for the benefit of the remainderperson.[100] In other circumstances, of course, the Commissioner will assert that provision of the statute that results in the greatest inclusion in the gross estate.

[10] A Reprise of the Lifetime Transfer Sections

At the end of this discussion of Sections 2035 through 2038, all of which are addressed to the estate taxation of a decedent's lifetime transfers, some general comments may be advanced on two types of problems generated by these sections. One type, which will be seen to be largely academic, arises out of the substantial *overlap* of the several statutory rules. The other is that of *identifying* the taxed interest, regardless of what section may be applicable. As no new concepts are advanced here and the principles discussed are all presented else-

---

[99] See infra ¶ 4.10[10].

[100] IRC § 2036(a)(2); Lober v. United States, 346 US 335 (1953).

where with proper documentation, these comments are framed in general terms.

[a] Overlap: Sections 2036 and 2038 Applicable

Suppose that D transfers 1,000 shares of XYZ stock in trust with provision for payment of the income to A for life and then to D for life and with further provision for the payment of the remainder after the death of D and A to whomever D appoints by will but, in default of the exercise of D's power, remainder to B if living and, if not, to D's estate. In this situation, Sections 2036, 2037, and 2038 are applicable because D has made a transfer retaining an income interest in the property (Section 2036), but the transfer of the remainder interest is conditional upon D's death and D's testamentary power gives D a reversionary interest (Section 2037), and the remainder remains subject to a power to change at the time of D's death (Section 2038). If these three sections apply, is it necessary to examine the scope of each? It usually is, unless one section pulls in the entire corpus. If D is survived by A, each of the sections, whichever is applied, includes the value of the property reduced by the value of A's outstanding life interest. If D survives A, each of the sections includes the entire value of the trust property upon D's death; but of course the trust property will be taken into account only once in any event.

[b] Overlap: Only Section 2037 Applicable

In the case of a transfer whose only taint is that it is conditional and the decedent has retained no more than a reversionary interest and no recognized right to affect the interests of others, only Section 2037 can cause inclusion of the value of the transferred property in the decedent's gross estate. Although it is true, therefore, that any given transfer can invoke the inclusionary rules of Sections 2036, 2037, and 2038, in many instances only Section 2037 will apply. This is because that section supplies a unique test (relating to conditional reversions) that, even if met, will not invoke the application of the other transfer sections.

[c] Only Section 2036 Applicable

It is also true that Section 2036 can be the sole section applicable to a lifetime transfer. Examples are a decedent's transfer in trust in which the decedent simply retains the right to the income from the trust for life and a decedent's direct transfer retaining a legal life estate.

[d] Only Section 2038 Applicable

It is more difficult to present a situation in which only Section 2038 will apply. This is because tax liability under Section 2038 rests on control or imputed control over transferred property by the decedent; and Section 2036(a)(2) is also brought into play by a retention of control over income or enjoyment.[101] Of course, Section 2037 may also be brought into play by a retention of a conditional power to dispose of the transferred property. The questions then, admittedly largely academic, are: When does Section 2038 have a significant role to play? When is it something more than a second reason for including the value of a property interest in the gross estate? Phrased this way, the questions are largely academic because, when Section 2036 applies, its power to pull interests into the gross estate generally exceeds that of Section 2038.

Section 2036(a)(2) is couched in terms of powers "retained" by the decedent, while Section 2038 merely requires that the transferred interest be subject to the decedent's power at the time of death. Thus, Section 2038 may be applicable, but Section 2036(a)(2) will be inapplicable, if the decedent does not *retain* a power in connection with a lifetime transfer. For example, assume that D creates an inter vivos trust with income to A for life and a remainder to B or B's estate, giving an independent trustee the power to pay the income to C during A's life. Assume further that although D retains no power to name D trustee, the independent trustee resigns and the court appoints D as trustee. If D then dies during A's life, Section 2038 applies to pull the income interest

---

[101] Beyond the common requirement that, to be included, a property interest must be one that the decedent transferred during life, some of the similarities of Sections 2036(a)(2) and 2038 include the following:

1. Both are subject to the full and adequate consideration exception and to the Section 2043(b) partial consideration rule;
2. Neither section applies if the decedent's power is limited by an adequate external standard, and a standard adequate for one provision is also a standard adequate for the other;
3. Both sections treat the decedent as holding any powers the trustee holds if the decedent could appoint the decedent as trustee;
4. Both sections apply whether the decedent's power was held alone or in conjunction with any other person (seemingly the Helmholz exception, Helvering v. Helmholz, 296 US 93 (1935), extends to Section 2036(a)(2) as well as to Section 2038);
5. Neither section applies if powers are held only by a third, albeit friendly, party;
6. The *O'Malley* doctrine is applicable to both sections; and
7. Regarding relinquishments by the decedent, both sections invoke the principles of Section 2035 including Section 2035(e), even though only Section 2038 contains specific statutory language to that effect. See Reg. § 20.2035-1(b).

into D's estate. Section 2036(a)(2), which if applicable would tax the entire trust, does not apply because D's power at death is not a retained power.[102]

There is another situation in which Section 2038 may have a longer reach than Section 2036(a)(2). If the decedent's power, whether retained or otherwise, affects only the remainder and not the income interest, Section 2038 may be in exclusive control. Suppose, for example, that D creates an inter vivos trust with income to A for D's life remainder to B or B's estate, and D retains the power to give the remainder to C or C's estate. D dies survived by A. Section 2038 is clearly applicable to the remainder interest as it is subject to change through the exercise of a power by D. Although the literal wording of the statute would seem to require inclusion under Section 2036(a)(2) as well, as the power would seem to be a "right . . . to designate the persons who shall possess or enjoy the property or the income therefrom," the regulations treat Section 2036(a)(2) as inapplicable.[103] According to the regulations, Section 2036(a)(2) powers do "not include a power over the transferred property itself which does not affect the enjoyment of the income received or earned during the decedent's life."[104] On the other hand, a perceptive reader will see that this supposed transfer is taxable under Section 2037 in the same manner as under Section 2038 and that the value of the remainder interest at D's death is equal to the value of the corpus.

The scope of the foregoing regulation is uncertain. For example, it is questionable whether Section 2036(a)(2) applies in the hypothetical if A's income interest is for A's life rather than D's life and D dies survived by A. Given these facts, during D's life it was possible that A might have predeceased D, and if so, by naming the remainderperson D could have determined whether B or C received the income while D was still alive, and D would have had a power that could have affected the enjoyment of the income from the property during D's life. This problem is again largely academic because,

---

[102] Section 2037 similarly requires that D's reversionary interest be "retained." Although instances in which Section 2038 has exclusive significance are stressed here, a second subtle difference in the two provisions sometimes leaves the field to Section 2036. If D has retained a power, but it is subject to a contingency beyond D's control that has not occurred prior to D's death, Section 2038 will not apply because the enjoyment of the transferred property will not be "subject at the date of the decedent's death to any change." Section 2038(b), of course, contains a limited exception to this rule. In contrast, however, Section 2036(a)(2) simply requires that a power of designation be retained for a proscribed period, which can be a period to begin at a future time. Thus, Section 2036 can apply even if the power was not exercisable at D's death but was, instead, subject to a contingency beyond D's control.

[103] Reg. § 20.2036-1(b)(3).

[104] Reg. § 20.2036-1(b)(3). See also the discussion at ¶ 4.08[5][c] for another situation in which Section 2038 may be applicable and Section 2036(a)(2) inapplicable. But see Alexander v. Comm'r, 81 TC 757 (1983), aff'd unpub. op. (4th Cir. 1985).

except in very narrow circumstances,[105] even if Section 2036(a)(2) is applicable, the amount of the inclusion under that section is equal to the amount of the Section 2038 inclusion.[106]

[e] Only Section 2035 Applicable

Prior to the 1981 changes in the Code, Section 2035 had a substantially broader scope encompassing all transfers made within three years of death. It now encompasses only transfers within three years of death of interests that would have been included under Sections 2036, 2037, 2038, and 2042 if no subsequent transfer had been made. Generally, there is no longer any statutory overlap between Section 2035 and Sections 2036 through 2038[107] but, instead, statutory combination, with Section 2035 acting in conjunction with Sections 2036 through 2038 to require inclusion in the same manner as if they were directly applicable. With one exception, there is inclusion only under Section 2035.[108]

[f] Identification of Taxed Interest

The discussion of the various lifetime transfer sections in this chapter reflects a dual inquiry under each section. One question is whether the section is applicable at all. When the first question is answered affirmatively, the other is: What transferred interest is taxed? This second identification question is the subject of some general observations here.

---

[105] There is not a total overlap of the two sections here because if *D*'s power had been subject to a contingency beyond *D*'s control that had not occurred prior to *D*'s death, Section 2038 would be inapplicable, whereas Section 2036(a)(2) would apply. For example, assume *D* creates an inter vivos trust with income to *A* for *A*'s life and a remainder to *B* or *B*'s estate, but *D* retains a power to give the remainder to *C* if *B* becomes divorced. If *D* dies during *A*'s life at a time when *B* is still married, Section 2038 is inapplicable; but if the exception recognized in Reg. § 20.2036-1(b)(3) is narrowly interpreted, Section 2036(a)(2) will include the remainder in *D*'s estate.

[106] Section 2036(a)(2) would include the value of the corpus less the unaffected income interest (or an amount equal to the remainder interest), which would likewise be the amount included under Section 2038.

[107] One instance in which there would be such overlap is a situation where within three years of death an insured transfers a life insurance policy on the insured's life to a trust in which the insured retains a life estate. Both Section 2035(a) and Section 2036(a)(1) would be applicable on the insured's death.

[108] There is overlap between Sections 2035 and 2038 caused by the express provisions of the last clause of Section 2038(a)(1) and the three-year provision of Section 2038(a)(2). But see IRC § 2035(e) which narrows the overlap and is discussed supra ¶¶ 4.10[8] text accompanying notes 87–91, 4.07[2][b][ii].

All the transfer sections share a characteristic that is troublesome at best. Each requires an identification of an included property interest on the basis of an occurrence at one time, the time of the transfer, but the valuation of the included interest at another time, the applicable valuation date. Thus, the included interest must be again identified at the later valuation date. The same difficulty arises even with respect to property included under Section 2033 if the executor elects the alternate valuation date under Section 2032. That section has its own expressed rules for post-identification date dispositions of property prior to the usual valuation date, easing some but not all[109] of the problems otherwise inherent in the split dates.

With regard to transfers taxed because they were made within three years of death, it is fairly well established that the value of the very property involved at the time of the near-death transfer is the measure for the tax.[110] What about interests transferred during life but included in the gross estate other than by reason of the near-death three-year rule? Where the property originally transferred is sold and the proceeds are reinvested, is the appropriate result to pull in the interests in the property originally transferred or to include the other property (or money, if no investment is made)? All the other lifetime transfer sections rest on some actual or imputed relationship of the decedent to the property, loosely the decedent's retention of some enjoyment, a reversionary interest, or control. It seems sensible to say that the included property must be that to which the decedent bears the required relationship at death, and although the statute falls far short of saying so expressly, this seems a reasonable inference.

Suppose, for example, that A gives B A's residence but reserves a legal life estate. If A and B subsequently agree to a sale of that residence and a reinvestment of the proceeds in another in which their present and future interests are the same, it is sound to value the second residence for inclusion in A's estate.[111] Perhaps, a fortiori, the same rule should apply if A transfers securities to a trust retaining the right to the trust income for life, remainder to B. If, under common trust powers, the trustee changes the investments, the value of B's remainder interest, which is the value of the trust assets as altered by the time of A's death, is what should be included in A's estate.[112] In all probability, in these cases the settlor's wishes will largely govern the trustee's investment decisions. Thus, a better result may be reached than if an attempt was made to value the property that was actually transferred. Suppose, for ex-

---

[109] See discussion of IRC § 2032 at ¶ 4.03[3].

[110] See ¶ 4.07[2][c].

[111] A reinvestment of more or less than the proceeds would seem to be a manageable problem.

[112] In point of fact, United States v. O'Malley, 383 US 627 (1966), even extends this approach to income retained in the trust.

Section 2038

ample, *A* placed $100,000 cash in the trust initially. If this is invested in securities by the trustee (maybe at *A*'s suggestion) and the securities are worth $200,000 when *A* dies, the statutory plan seems better implemented by including the larger death value of the trust in *A*'s estate, and the same rationale supports a smaller inclusion if the trust investments prove to be unwise.

Although the foregoing thoughts are expressed in terms of Section 2036 examples, they seem equally applicable to the other transfer sections, except Section 2035. On the other hand, they leave open the question of identification and value in a situation in which *A* makes a taxable transfer to a trust and others, either simultaneously or at different times, make transfers to the same trust.[113]

¶ 4.11 SECTION 2039. ANNUITIES

It has been said that people are unique among the animals in the possession of the knowledge that they will die. This, coupled with a person's familial instinct and capacity for affection, which are not unique, causes one to devise numerous direct and indirect means for the transmission of wealth to others. A person's efforts in this respect often have a purely personal motivation quite detached from tax considerations. However, informed persons are aware that tax consequences have an impact on the accomplishment of their personal objectives. In any event, whether the means of conferring financial benefits on another are prompted purely by personal wishes or partly by tax thinking, Congress must examine the means to determine how a particular mode of wealth transmission fits into the federal taxing scheme. Section 2039, addressed to annuity arrangements, is another result of such examination and determination.[1]

Annuity contracts take a variety of forms. The simplest is a single-life annuity without any refund feature. Under this type of contract, an amount is paid to the annuitant for life, and at death, all rights under the contract terminate. If a decedent purchases such an annuity for life, it will have no effect on the decedent's gross estate at death; this is an instance of the decedent's consumption of wealth during life, and it results in no transmission of anything to others either during life or at death.[2] Logically, nothing in Section 2039 seeks to alter this conclusion.

---

[113] A suggested approach to this problem is advanced in the discussion of Section 2036 at ¶ 4.08[8].

[1] The gift tax consequences of annuity transactions are determined largely by the application of general principles. See Chapter 10.

[2] Of course, amounts received under the annuity prior to death may enlarge the decedent's actual estate subject to tax under Section 2033.

Other annuity contracts provide definitely or contingently for something to be paid to others upon the death of the primary annuitant. For example, a contract may contain provisions under which, if the amount paid the annuitant during life does not equal the cost of the contract (or sometimes, in the case of annuity contracts arising out of employment relationships, the contributions of the employee), the difference will be paid to either the primary annuitant's estate or to named persons upon the annuitant's death. Under other contracts, upon the death of one annuitant, the payment that the annuitant has been receiving may be paid to another for the other's life; this is a self-and-survivor annuity or a survivorship-or-longer-life annuity. Still another common type of annuity is a joint-and-survivor annuity, under which a specified sum may be payable to two annuitants jointly during their lives and the same or a reduced amount paid to the survivor for life. It is agreements of these types, all of which involve some survivorship feature, that may have estate tax consequences under either Section 2039 or other general provisions, and properly so to the extent that they achieve a transmission of some of a decedent's wealth to others.

Section 2039 covers many annuity contracts, but it is important to note that it does not purport to be exclusive. If the application of some other section would result in amounts being included in the gross estate beyond what would be included under Section 2039, the other section will be applied.[3]

[1] General Rule

Regarding annuity contracts with survivorship features, the general rule under Section 2039 is that the value of amounts receivable by beneficiaries by reason of their surviving the decedent is to be included in the decedent's gross estate. A modification is expressed in Section 2039(b). First, however, it should be noted that Section 2039(a), which states the general rule, makes two explicit exceptions and several important qualifications.

---

[3] S. Rep. No. 1622, 83d Cong., 2d Sess. 472 (1954); Reg. § 20.2039-1(a). An example would be a purchase for another of an annuity for a term of years extending beyond the decedent's life with the decedent retaining the power during life to alter the beneficiary between two persons other than the decedent, taxable under Section 2038. See Estate of Siegel v. Comm'r, 74 TC 613 (1980). The amounts of inclusion under both Section 2038 and Section 2039 would be equal. But if Section 2039 includes a greater amount than some other section, it will be applied. See FSA 200036012 (May 25, 2000) (full corpus of a GRAT included under Section 2039 because only a portion of the corpus was included under Section 2036(a)).

[2] Exceptions Expressed in Section 2039(a)

[a] Life Insurance Policies

Section 2039(a) is expressly inapplicable to "insurance under policies on the life of the decedent." Therefore, amounts receivable under such policies, although often payable in the form of annuities and even though received by reason of surviving the decedent, are unaffected by Section 2039(a) regardless of whether other requirements of the section are met. This exception makes it easy to place outside the scope of Section 2039 the ordinary straight-life, term, or limited payment insurance policies. It is clear that the proceeds of these policies are includable in the decedent's gross estate in accordance with the provisions of Section 2042, which is discussed later in this chapter.[4] It is equally clear that annuity contracts without insurance features, if includable in the gross estate, will be governed by Section 2039 or general provisions other than Section 2042. However, the common current practice of issuing combination policies having an insurance and an endowment aspect, such as retirement policies with death benefits, raises a question whether the estate tax consequences of such policies are determined under Section 2039 or Section 2042. According to the legislative history of Section 2039[5] and the regulations,[6] if a policy is properly classified as life insurance, Section 2042 controls. The remaining question, then, is: When is a combination policy insurance? This question is dealt with in the discussion of Section 2042 later in this chapter, but some brief comments should be made here.

Risk shifting and risk distribution are the principal characteristics of insurance.[7] Accordingly, if, under a combination policy, an insurance company assumes the risk of the insured's premature death by way of a commitment at any given time to pay death benefits in excess of the total premiums that have been paid at such time (plus interest, which would of course represent part of the return under an annuity policy),[8] a risk element is present that makes the policy one of insurance governed by Section 2042. However, it should be

---

[4] See ¶ 4.14.

[5] S. Rep. No. 1622, 83d Cong., 2d Sess. 472 (1954).

[6] Reg. § 20.2039-1(d).

[7] Compare Helvering v. Estate of Le Gierse, 312 US 531 (1941) with Fidelity-Philadelphia Trust Co. v. Smith, 356 US 274 (1958). In All v. McCobb, 321 F2d 633 (2d Cir. 1963), the Second Circuit held that an unfunded death benefit plan for certain survivors of employees represented a personal liability of the employer that did not constitute an insurance contract for purposes of the exception to Section 2039(a). Cf. Essenfeld v. Comm'r, 311 F2d 208 (2d Cir. 1962) (involving exclusions from gross income).

[8] See Estate of Keller v. Comm'r, 312 US 543 (1941); Estate of Montgomery v. Comm'r, 56 TC 489 (1971), aff'd per curiam, 458 F2d 616 (5th Cir.), cert. denied, 409 US 849 (1972) (rejecting as unimportant "investment" as opposed to "insurance" risk).

noted that a combination policy, properly classified as insurance at its inception, may change its character at a later date when the insurance risk evaporates. The regulations properly make the applicability of Section 2042 or Section 2039 depend on the nature of the contract at the time of the decedent's death; if a retirement income policy with death benefits has matured during the life of the decedent (i.e., payments to the decedent have commenced), there is no longer an insurance element at death and Section 2039 controls the amount to be included in the gross estate.[9] However, the insurance element can disappear before such a policy matures. Thus, the regulations provide that "if the decedent dies after the reserve value equals the death benefit, there is no longer an insurance element under the contract," and Section 2039 controls, even though the policy may not have matured before the decedent's death.[10] Similarly, the regulations also specify that "a contract under which the death benefit could never exceed the total premiums paid, plus interest, contains no insurance element."[11]

[b] Pre-1931 Contracts

Section 2039 is effective for estates of decedents dying after August 16, 1954.[12] But Section 2039(a) is, by its own language, limited to contracts and agreements entered into after March 3, 1931, which, it will be recalled, is one of the critical dates with respect to the application of Section 2036.[13]

[3] Qualifications

Under Section 2039, the gross estate will include the value of an annuity or other payment receivable by any beneficiary only if, under a contract or agreement, an annuity or other payment was payable to the decedent or the decedent possessed the right to receive such annuity or payment, either alone or in conjunction with another, for the decedent's life or some similar period.

---

[9] Reg. § 20.2039-1(d).

[10] Reg. § 20.2039-1(d).

[11] Reg. § 20.2039-1(d).

[12] IRC § 7851(a)(2)(A).

[13] The unstated assumption seems to be that annuities now taxed under Section 2039 first became taxable upon the enactment of the forerunner of Section 2036 in 1931 and have continued to be taxable since that time either under Section 2036 or Section 2039. Prior to that time, the decedent's expiring interest was not the occasion for a tax. Cf. May v. Heiner, 281 US 238 (1930). See ¶ 4.08[9] text accompanying note 190. The assumption may be shaky if Section 2036 cannot properly be applied. See infra ¶ 4.11[7]. Still, an attack on the application of Section 2039 to pre-1954 transfers should meet with no success. Cf. Comm'r v. Estate of Church, 335 US 632 (1949).

[a] Contract or Agreement

Section 2039 requires that there be a contract or agreement. According to the regulations, contracts and agreements include understandings, arrangements, or plans.[14] Rulings exclude benefit payments paid under public laws where the decedent has no voice in the designation of beneficiaries or payments to them, such as certain veteran's benefits to a surviving spouse[15] and other survivor's benefits.[16] Also, the required contract or agreement is lacking in a situation where either the decedent or the beneficiaries have only a mere expectancy. The problem of a mere expectancy is not likely to arise in the case of ordinary commercial annuities; in fact, most of the provisions of Section 2039 can be rather routinely applied to such contracts. Not so, however, with regard to employees' annuities; most of the interpretation problems under Section 2039 arise in the employment setting, which is why much of the discussion of this section centers around employees' annuities. For example, if an employer retains complete discretion to determine whether payments will be made to the decedent and the decedent's survivors, there is no contract subject to Section 2039.[17] A question arises as to whether related employment contracts, plans, or agreements can be combined to determine whether the various requirements of Section 2039 are satisfied. The regulations provide:[18] "All rights and benefits accruing to an employee and to others by reason of the employment . . . are considered together in determining whether or not Section 2039(a) and (b) applies." There has been some appropriate judicial acceptance of the conglomerate approach required by the regulations.[19] However, the

---

[14] Reg. § 20.2039-1(b)(1). See FSA 200036012 (May 25, 2000) (holding that a grantor retained annuity trust was a contract or agreement). See supra ¶ 4.11 note 3.

[15] Rev. Rul. 76-501, 1976-2 CB 267, and rulings cited therein.

[16] Rev. Rul. 60-70, 1960-1 CB 372 (Railroad Retirement Act); Rev. Rul. 76-102, 1976-1 CB 272 (Federal Coal Mine Health and Safety Act); Rev. Rul. 79-397, 1979-2 CB 322 (Public Safety Officers' Benefit Act); Rev. Rul. 81-182, 1981-2 CB 179 (Social Security benefits).

[17] Estate of Barr v. Comm'r, 40 TC 227 (1963), acq. 1964-1 (pt. 1) CB 4; Courtney v. United States, 84-2 USTC ¶ 13,580 (ND Ohio 1984). The result is essentially consistent with Reg. § 20.2039-1(b)(2) Ex. 4, although the regulations warn that where the decedent's employer consistently makes discretionary payments, such payments will be considered as made under a "contract or agreement." Cf. Rev. Rul. 75-505, 1975-2 CB 364, holding that a state employer's unilateral right to reduce benefits by a reduction in salaries of continuing employees was related to the valuation of payments rather than to the existence of a binding contract.

[18] Reg. § 20.2039-1(b)(2) Ex. 6.

[19] Estate of Bahen v. United States, 305 F2d 827 (Ct. Cl. 1962) (two separate but related plans, adopted by the same employer on different dates, were treated as a combination). See also Gray v. United States, 410 F2d 1094 (3d Cir. 1969); All v. McCobb, 321 F2d 633 (2d Cir. 1963); Eichstedt v. United States, 354 F. Supp. 484 (ND Cal. 1972); Looney v. United States, 569 F. Supp. 1569 (MD Ga. 1983). But see Estate of Schelberg

courts have balked when the Commissioner has attempted to carry the matter too far. For example, salary payments to which the decedent had a right at death do not constitute "an annuity or other payment" to which the decedent was entitled so as to bring within Section 2039 post-death payments to the decedent's surviving spouse, in which the decedent never had any interest whatever.[20] However, if a decedent employee had a right to retirement benefits, which did not simply represent compensation for continuing services, that right may be viewed along with the decedent's survivor's benefits as a part of an annuity contract within the scope of Section 2039.[21] To link survivorship benefits arising out of the decedent's employment with the decedent's regular salary benefits[22] seems supportable as a policy matter, if Congress really seeks to tax survivors' benefits that represent testamentary transfers; but there are obstacles under the present statute.

[b] Period for Which Interest Is Retained

The duration of the decedent's interest does not present fresh problems of statutory interpretation. In this respect, the statutory language of Section 2039 has been lifted directly from Section 2036. The question is whether the decedent had the specified right or interest (1) for his life, (2) for a period not ascertainable without reference to his death, or (3) for a period that did not in fact end before his death. The meaning of this trilogy is the same as the meaning of the identical language in Section 2036[23] and is covered in the discussion of that section earlier in this chapter.[24]

---

v. Comm'r, 612 F2d 25 (2d Cir. 1979) (refusing to combine plans where one plan was a disability benefits plan under which taxpayer's right to any lifetime payments was too contingent to constitute a right to receive payment); Young, "A Proposal to Limit the Application of Section 2039 in Light of the Schelburg Reversal," 61 Taxes 627 (1983).

[20] Kramer v. United States, 406 F2d 1363 (Ct. Cl. 1969); Estate of Fusz v. Comm'r, 46 TC 214 (1966), acq. 1967-2 CB 2. See Estate of Barr v. Comm'r, 40 TC 227 (1963), acq. 1964-1 (pt. 1) CB 4. A later revenue ruling followed the courts' rationale in receding from the conglomerate approach where one of two plans covering the decedent was a wage continuation paid to survivors. Rev. Rul. 77-183, 1977-1 CB 274.

[21] Gray v. United States, 410 F2d 1094 (3d Cir. 1969). See Silberman v. United States, 333 F. Supp. 1120 (WD Pa. 1971) which distinguishes Kramer v. United States, 406 F2d 1363 (Ct. Cl. 1969). See also Rev. Rul. 71-507, 1971-2 CB 331.

[22] Cf. Rev. Rul. 77-183, 1977-1 CB 274.

[23] S. Rep. No. 1622, 83d Cong., 2d Sess. 472 (1954). For an application of the Section 2036 rules in the context of Section 2039, see Estate of Wadewitz v. Comm'r, 39 TC 925, 939 (1963), aff'd, 339 F2d 980 (7th Cir. 1964).

[24] See ¶ 4.08[2].

[c] Nature of Decedent's Interest

A difficult portion of Section 2039(a) is the language requiring that "an annuity or other payment was payable to the decedent, or the decedent possessed the right to receive such annuity or payment." At the outset it should be emphasized that the section is not restricted to conventional annuity payments but rather includes "annuity or other" payments, which the regulations state "may be equal or unequal, conditional or unconditional, periodic or sporadic" and of which there may be "*one* or more payments extending over any period of time."[25]

It is clear that the two statutory clauses, "payable to the decedent" and "possessed the right to receive," have separate and distinct meanings. The former clause applies to a case where the decedent at death was actually receiving payments without regard to the question whether the decedent could require their continuation.[26] On the other hand, the "right to receive" clause is satisfied if "the decedent had an enforceable right to receive payments at some time in the future, whether or not, at the time of his death, he had a present right to receive payments."[27] The regulations so interpreting the statute find support in the legislative history, which refers to the rules applicable under Section 2036 for determining whether the decedent had the "right to the income."[28] Under Section 2036, it has been held that one has such right even if another interest intervenes or if the right is contingent.[29]

If the payments to the decedent have not commenced at the decedent's death, Section 2039 will not apply unless, at death, the decedent's rights to future payments are nonforfeitable.[30] However, this requirement will be satisfied if the decedent has control of the conditions that must be fulfilled to prevent forfeiture[31] or, at least, the conditions are beyond the control of a person other than the decedent.[32] Obviously, the nonforfeiture and contract or agreement requirements under Section 2039 overlap, since an extreme case of forfeiture

---

[25] Reg. § 20.2039-1(b)(1) (emphasis added). Even a "lump sum" payment qualifies. S. Rep. No. 1622, 83d Cong., 2d Sess. 470 (1954). See Estate of Montgomery v. Comm'r, 56 TC 489 (1971), aff'd per curiam, 458 F2d 616 (5th Cir.), cert. denied, 409 US 849 (1972).

[26] Reg. § 20.2039-1(b)(1).

[27] Reg. § 20.2039-1(b)(1); Estate of Wadewitz v. Comm'r, 339 F2d 980 (7th Cir. 1964); Estate of Bahen v. United States, 305 F2d 827 (Ct. Cl. 1962).

[28] S. Rep. No. 1622, 83d Cong., 2d Sess. 472 (1954).

[29] E.g., Marks v. Higgins, 213 F2d 884 (2d Cir. 1954). See ¶ 4.08[2].

[30] Estate of Wadewitz v. Comm'r, 339 F2d 980 (7th Cir. 1964); Estate of Bahen v. United States, 305 F2d 827 (Ct. Cl. 1962).

[31] Estate of Wadewitz v. Comm'r, 339 F2d 980 (7th Cir. 1964).

[32] Estate of Bahen v. United States, 305 F2d 827 (Ct. Cl. 1962) (decedent entitled to lifetime payments only if prior to retirement he becomes totally incapacitated to perform other duties).

would be complete discretion in the employer to determine whether payments will be made. However, considerable doubt exists as to whether a contract or plan that has a comprehensive formula for determining benefits should be beyond the reach of Section 2039 merely because the employer retains the typical unilateral power to revoke or modify. The probability that such plans will not be revoked or substantially modified, except under unusual circumstances and generally only with the concurrence of the employee or the employee's union, should not be ignored.[33]

[d] Nature of Beneficiary's Interest

Most of the problems just discussed in connection with the decedent's interest are not, of course, present in the case of the beneficiary's interest. To the extent that problems are common, the phrase "annuity or other payments" will have the same meaning for the decedent's and beneficiary's interests.[34] The regulations properly indicate that a forfeiture provision in connection with the beneficiary's interest will not defeat the application of Section 2039 but will be taken into consideration in the valuation of the interest.[35] It is interesting to note that an employer who has contributed to the cost of the decedent's and beneficiary's benefits will not be treated as a beneficiary for purposes of Section 2039, even though under the contract the employer is entitled to a refund of contributions after the decedent's death.[36] Clearly, in such circumstances the decedent should not be viewed as making the kind of testamentary transmission of wealth to the decedent's employer that Congress seeks to subject to estate tax.

[4] Amount to Be Included

The general rule expressed in Section 2039(a) indicates that the value of amounts receivable by beneficiaries "by reason of surviving the decedent" shall be included in the gross estate when Section 2039 applies, but Section 2039(b) restricts this broad statement in an important manner. Before considering the Section 2039(b) restrictions, two points should be made regarding the value of amounts receivable.

---

[33] See Note, "Estate Taxation of Survivor Annuities: Section 811(c) and the Proposed IRC of 1954," 6 Stan. L. Rev. 473 (1954).

[34] Reg. § 20.2039-1(b)(1). See FSA 200036012 (May 25, 2000) (lump sum payment to a remainderperson of a grantor retained annuity trust was a Section 2039 "payment"). See supra ¶ 4.11 note 3.

[35] Reg. § 20.2039-1(b)(2) Ex. 2.

[36] Estate of Allen v. Comm'r, 39 TC 817 (1963), acq. 1964-1 (pt. 1) CB 4.

[a] Valuation

Under Sections 2031 and 2032, the value of the survivor's interest is to be determined at the date of death or as of the alternate valuation date, and it is the fair market value of the interest that is to be considered.[37] Annuities under contracts issued by companies regularly engaged in their issuance are to be valued in accordance with principles set out in Regulations Section 20.2031-8, which provides for valuation, as a rule, in accordance with the cost of "comparable" contracts issued by the company. Usually, the test of value is what it would cost at the date of death to acquire a policy for the survivor with benefits such as exist under the contract in question.[38] It is the survivor's rights immediately after the decedent's death, not as of the moment just before death, that are to be valued in this fashion.[39]

If the annuity payments receivable by survivors are not to be paid by a company that regularly engages in such business, a replacement-cost approach to valuation cannot be used. Instead, the valuation of such annuities is to be determined in accordance with appropriate valuation tables.[40] An amount taxable under Section 2039 may be expressed in terms of a lump sum payable over a future period. In such cases, it is not the amount of the lump sum that must be included, but the lower commuted value that is the present value of the rights to future payments.[41]

---

[37] Reg. § 20.2031-1(b). For a discussion of the valuation of annuities on the alternate valuation date, see ¶ 4.03[3][b].

[38] Cf. Estate of Welliver v. Comm'r, 8 TC 165 (1947). So-called variable annuities are becoming increasingly common. As future payments under such annuities are dependent upon the investment experience of a fund, it might appear that a serious valuation question is presented. However, such annuities are issued by companies regularly engaged in the business, so the replacement-cost approach to valuation eliminates the problem.

[39] Christiernin v. Manning, 138 F. Supp. 923 (DNJ 1956).

[40] Reg. § 20.2031-7 (for annuities after April 30, 1999). See Reg. § 20.2031-7A (with regard to valuation of annuities for estates of decedents dying before May 1, 1999); Rev. Rul. 84-162, 1984-2 CB 200. However, the mortality component of the actuarial tables may not be used if the measuring life is "terminally ill." The term "terminally ill" is defined to be an individual who has an incurable illness or other deteriorating physical condition that contributes to at least a 50 percent probability that the individual will die within one year. Reg. § 20.7520-3(b)(3).

There is disagreement with respect to valuation of annuities in the form of lottery winnings. Compare Estate of Gribauskas v. Comm'r, 116 TC 142 (2001), Estate of Cook v. Comm'r, 82 TCM (CCH) 154 (2001), and TAM 199909001 (Oct. 19, 1998) (employing the actuarial tables with no reduction in value for lack of transferability) with Shackleford v. United States, 262 F3d 1028 (9th Cir. 2001) (reducing the values under the tables to reflect a lack of marketability because of restrictions on transferability).

[41] Estate of Beal v. Comm'r, 47 TC 269 (1966), acq. 1967-2 CB 1.

[b] Percentage Restriction

Section 2039(b) specifies that the amount actually includable in the decedent's gross estate under Section 2039 is to be determined by reference to the following two factors: (1) the value of what is payable to survivors, which has just been discussed, and (2) the portion of the purchase price of the annuity or other contract that was paid by the decedent. In a nontechnical way these factors can be seen to raise two questions: First, what value have the survivors received? And second, to what extent does that value represent a transmission of wealth by the decedent? If *A* buys and pays for a joint-and-survivor annuity under which *A* and *B* receive payments while both are living and the payments are continued to *A* after the death of *B*, the value of *A*'s continuing right is within Section 2039(a) and therefore potentially taxable in *B*'s estate. But, as all the wealth giving rise to *A*'s continuing annuity originated with *A*, there is no transmission of *B*'s wealth that Congress would wish to tax. On these facts, Section 2039(b) produces the expected result (no inclusion), because under that provision the amount to be included is only such part of the value of the annuity or other payment receivable by beneficiaries as is proportionate to the part of the purchase price contributed by the decedent (zero). In this respect, the section resembles Section 2040(a), relating to joint interests.[42] The Section 2039(b) restriction can be expressed as follows:

$$\frac{\text{amount included (unknown)}}{\text{value of annuity}} = \frac{\text{decedent's contribution}}{\text{purchase price}}$$

$$\text{amount included} = \frac{\text{decedent's contribution}}{\text{purchase price}} \times \text{value of annuity}$$

Thus, if, in the case of a joint-and-survivor annuity for husband and wife, the wife paid all the cost of the policy and the husband survives, the entire value of amounts payable to the husband is to be included. As suggested earlier, if in the same circumstances, it is the wife who survives, nothing will be included in the gross estate of the husband because he made no contribution.

The decedent's contribution, as used in the foregoing formula, has a broader meaning than amounts paid directly by the decedent. For one thing, Section 2039(b) specifies that any contribution toward the purchase price of the contract made by an employer or former employer of the decedent by reason of the decedent's employment shall be treated as a contribution by the de-

---

[42] See ¶ 4.12.

cedent.[43] The Senate Finance Committee Report[44] indicates that employer contributions may be treated as those of the employee decedent, even in the absence of any express statement to this effect in the contract of employment. So the words "by reason of his employment" may be given a broad interpretation. It is possible that an employee's annuity arrangement within the scope of Section 2039 is entirely unfunded so that there are no formal contributions by either employer or employee to the "purchase price" of a contract, the employer simply assuming the obligation to make future payments. In such circumstances, the statute should be interpreted to treat the purchase price as contributed 100 percent by the employer, which contribution is then, by Section 2039(b), attributed to the employee.[45] Despite some deficiencies in the statute, there is no reason why unfunded plans should be treated differently from those that are funded.

The statute does not deal expressly with indirect contributions, such as the payment of a part of the purchase price by a wife with funds supplied by the husband. Sections 2039 and 2040(a) are similar in general scope and purpose and, despite uncertainties under Section 2039, the phrase "contributed by the decedent" should be interpreted to square with the far more precise language in Section 2040(a).[46]

[5] Private Annuities

It is sometimes difficult to determine whether a noncommercial arrangement constitutes a gratuitous transfer with a reservation of income rights for life or a transfer for consideration in the form of an agreement by the transferee to pay an annuity. If a decedent has transferred property reserving the right to the income for life, Section 2036 places the value of the property in the decedent's gross estate. On the other hand, if a decedent has transferred property to another person who agrees to pay, periodically, amounts equal to the anticipated income from the property for the rest of the decedent's life, Section 2036 probably does not apply. The rationale is that such an arrangement does not constitute a reservation of the right to the income from the property; the dece-

---

[43] If the employer contributions were treated as community property under state law, then they should be treated as made one half by decedent and one half by decedent's spouse.

[44] S. Rep. No. 1622, 83d Cong., 2d Sess. 471 (1954).

[45] See Estate of Beal v. Comm'r, 47 TC 269 (1966), acq. 1967-2 CB 1, which involved an annuity program that was not funded by the employer until after the decedent's death.

[46] See ¶¶ 4.12[4]–4.12[8].

dent acquires a mere contractual right to a specified payment.[47] Thus, the transaction constitutes the purchase of an "annuity" rather than the retention of a life estate. The same result may follow even if the decedent retains a security interest in the property transferred to ensure payment of the contractual amounts.[48]

The noncommercial aspect of a transaction does not foreclose the application of Section 2039 to private annuities. For example, assume that the decedent D transferred property to X, an individual, in exchange for X's agreement to pay D a specified sum each year for D's life and, upon D's death, to make like payments to D's child for life. Section 2039 would bring the value of the child's interest into D's gross estate.[49]

Although a private annuity with no survivorship rights would appear to be a device that would avoid the gift and estate taxes, this is not necessarily the case. Because the annuity is not in an ordinary business context, if the value of the property transferred by the decedent exceeds the value of the annuity to be paid, the excess is a gift subject to tax.[50] Similarly, an annuity is an estate tax—

---

[47] Estate of Becklenberg v. Comm'r, 273 F2d 297 (7th Cir. 1959), which was distinguished in an income tax case, Samuel v. Comm'r, 306 F2d 682 (1st Cir. 1962); Cain v. Comm'r, 37 TC 185 (1961), acq. 1962-2 CB 4; Estate of Bergan v. Comm'r, 1 TC 543 (1943), acq. 1943 CB 2; Rev. Rul. 77-193, 1977-1 CB 273. Cf. Greene v. United States, 237 F2d 848 (7th Cir. 1956) (where decedent retained the right to the income from the property but not less than $1,500 per year, any deficit to be paid by the transferee, and Section 2036(a)(1) was held to apply); Lazarus v. Comm'r, 58 TC 854 (1972) (income and gift tax liability incurred).

These cases are distinguishable from Rev. Rul. 76-273, 1976-2 CB 268, and Rev. Rul. 82-105, 1982-1 CB 133, involving a charitable remainder unitrust and a charitable remainder annuity trust, respectively, where a unitrust or annuity trust interest retained by the transferor triggered Section 2036(a)(1) when the transferor predeceased the term of the retained interest. See ¶ 4.08[8] note 168. Cf. ¶ 19.03[3][b] note 120. Since with respect to a charitable remainder trust, a flat dollar amount is treated as income generated by the property in establishing the value of the remainder, the Treasury's position seems proper, but the cases cited above are distinguishable because the underlying property does not necessarily generate the income.

[48] Compare Lincoln v. United States, 65 Ct. Cl. 198 (1928) with Tips v. Bass, 21 F2d 460 (WD Tex. 1927).

Retention of a security interest has the adverse income tax consequence of accelerating the gain on the transferred property to the time of the transfer. Compare Comm'r v. Kahn's Estate, 174 F2d 357 (3d Cir. 1949) (unsecured promise with no immediate capital gain) and Estate of Bell v. Comm'r, 60 TC 469 (1973) (secured promise with immediate recognition of gain).

[49] IRC § 2039(a). However, a survivorship annuity for the decedent's surviving spouse would result in a "wash" for estate tax purposes, because the value of the surviving spouse's interest would qualify for a marital deduction in the decedent's gross estate. See ¶ 5.06[7][c] note 193.

[50] Rev. Rul. 69-74, 1969-1 CB 43. See Estate of Bell v. Comm'r, 60 TC 469 (1973). The creation of a private annuity will not trigger Section 2702. See ¶ 19.03[2][a] note 78.

defeating device only if the annuity payments received are spent or otherwise disposed of. Where the annual annuity payments plus the decedent's other income exceed the decedent's expenses, any accumulated excess will be included in the decedent's gross estate under Section 2033.[51] Thus, generally, the transfer of property for a private annuity for the transferor's life that is equal to the value of the property reaps a financial estate planning benefit if the transferor predeceases the transferor's life expectancy,[52] although the transferor may not think of death as being beneficial. However, if the transferor outlives the transferor's life expectancy, the transaction can increase the transferor's gross estate and be costly to the transferee. It is that type of gamble that has led some planners to pursue alternate methods of transferring property to family members for its full fair market value.[53]

The private annuity creates some interesting income tax consequences for both the decedent and the transferee; those consequences must also be taken into consideration in determining whether use of the private annuity device is advisable.[54]

---

[51] Lifetime gifts up to the amount of the Section 2503(b), $11,000 per donee, annual exclusion can be helpful in reducing such accumulation. See ¶¶ 9.04[1]–9.04[5].

[52] But see Reg. § 25.7520-3(b)(3), which applies if the annuitant is terminally ill.

[53] One alternate method which provides greater simplicity and certainty and which "freezes" the value of the transferor's gross estate is an installment sale of the property. The note is included in the transferor's gross estate under Section 2033. See ¶ 4.05[3] note 32. Collection of the note is an item of income in respect of a decedent. IRC § 691.

A second more glamorous alternate method is the use of a self-canceling installment note. The technique has the advantage of no inclusion of the extinguished note in the transferor's gross estate. Estate of Moss v. Comm'r, 74 TC 1239 (1980), acq., 1981-1 CB 2. See ¶ 4.05[3] note 32. However, this does not avoid the transferor's estate's recognition of income from the note. See Frane v. Comm'r, 998 F2d 567 (8th Cir. 1993) (holding that the gain inherent in the note is taxable to the transferor's estate under Section 691). See Roszak, "Installment Sales Terminating at Death Versus Private Annuities as Estate Planning Devices," 59 J. Tax'n 20 (1983); Banoff and Hartz, "New Tax Court Case Expands Opportunities for Self-Cancelling Installment Notes," 76 J. Tax'n 332 (1992).

[54] The income tax consequences to the transferor are summarized in Rev. Rul. 69-74, 1969-1 CB 43. However, the ruling predated the enactment of Sections 72(b)(2) and 72(b)(3) which must currently also be taken into consideration in determining the income tax consequences to the transferor of annuities purchased after July 1, 1986. See Midgley, "Federal Income Taxation of Private Annuitants," 40 Geo. Wash. L. Rev. 679 (1972). The income tax consequences to the transferee are discussed in Rev. Rul. 55-119, 1955-1 CB 352.

For a general discussion of private annuities, see Ellis, "Private Annuities," Tax Mgmt. Portfolio (BNA) No. 195 (1969); Vernava, "Tax Planning for the Not-So-Rich: Variable and Private Annuities," 11 Wm. & Mary L. Rev. 1 (1969); Fair, McKinster & Zisman, "The Private Annuity," 40 Colo. L. Rev. 338 (1968); Salomon, "The Private Intra-Family Annuity," 21 U. Miami L. Rev. 777 (1967); Wallace, "Taxation of Private Annuities," 40 BU L. Rev. 349 (1960). An excellent discussion of estate tax planning opportunities including private annuities is Cooper, "A Voluntary Tax? New Perspectives on Sophisticated Estate Tax Avoidance," 77 Colum. L. Rev. 161 (1977).

[6] Exempt Annuities

For a thirty-year period from 1954 to 1985, Congress to some extent excluded different types of income tax deferred compensation arrangements from the gross estate of an employee or self-employed decedent.[55] The exclusion provisions were exclusive; even though another gross estate provision such as Section 2036 seemed operative, the Section 2039 exclusion prevailed.[56] The rules that dealt with qualification for the exclusion involved the types of arrangements, the form of benefit payments, and the classification of the annuity recipients. These rules were complex.[57]

In 1982, Congress reduced what had been a blanket Section 2039 exclusion to a maximum $100,000 exclusion.[58] Both before and after the 1982 restriction, prior editions of this text stated with respect to the Section 2039 exclusions:

> There may be good reason for the *income* tax deferral. . . . The income tax deferral is of some benefit to most who qualify for it but, as many estates of employees are too small to incur any estate tax liability in any event, the . . . exemptions confer advantages only on estates of rather well-to-do decedents. There is reason to wonder whether Congress should not carefully reconsider the exclusions with a view to their complete elimination. . . .[59]

In enacting the Tax Reform Act of 1984, whether or not Congress did "carefully reconsider" the exclusions, it repealed them entirely for estates of decedents dying after 1984.[60] In addition, Section 2517, which accorded

---

[55] See IRC §§ 2039(c), 2039(d), 2039(e), 2039(f) (prior to repeal in the Deficit Reduction Act of 1984, Pub. L. No. 98-396, § 525(a), 98 Stat. 494, 873 (1984), reprinted in 1984-3 CB (Vol. 1) 1, 381), which were applicable to various types of employee benefits, self-employed (or HR 10) plans, and individual retirement arrangements.

[56] See IRC §§ 2039(c), 2039(e) (prior to repeal in the Deficit Reduction Act of 1984, Pub. L. No. 98-396, § 525(a), 98 Stat. 494, 873 (1984), reprinted in 1984-3 CB (Vol. 1) 1, 381).

[57] See IRC §§ 2039(c), 2039(f) (prior to repeal in the Deficit Reduction Act of 1984, Pub. L. No. 98-396, § 525(a), 98 Stat. 494, 873 (1984), reprinted in 1984-3 CB (Vol. 1) 1, 381); Stephens, Maxfield, Lind & Calfee, Federal Estate and Gift Taxation ¶ 4.11[5] (Warren, Gorham & Lamont, 5th ed. 1983).

[58] See IRC § 2039(g) (prior to repeal in the Deficit Reduction Act of 1984, Pub. L. No. 98-396, § 525(a), 98 Stat. 494, 873 (1984), reprinted in 1984-3 CB (Vol. 1) 1, 381).

[59] Stephens, Maxfield, Lind & Calfee, Federal Estate and Gift Taxation 4.11¶ 4.11[5][c] (Warren, Gorham & Lamont, 5th ed. 1983).

[60] Deficit Reduction Act of 1984, Pub. L. No. 98-369, § 525(a), 98 Stat. 494, 873 (1984), reprinted in 1984-3 CB (Vol. 1) 1, 381. At the same time, Congress enacted a new subsection 2039(c), which was repealed in the Tax Reform Act of 1986. Pub. L. No. 99-514, § 1852(e)(1)(A), 100 Stat. 2085, 2868 (1986), reprinted in 1986-3 CB (Vol. 1) 1, 785.

comparable gift tax treatment to retirement benefits qualifying for the estate tax exclusion, was belatedly repealed in the Tax Reform Act of 1986.[61]

[7] Background of the Section

With respect to ordinary commercial annuities purchased in whole or in part by a decedent under which survivors or the decedent's estate receive benefits upon the decedent's death, the enactment of Section 2039 in 1954 did not represent a significant change in the law. For example, it has generally been assumed that if a contract provides for a refund to the decedent's estate of a portion of the cost in the event of the decedent's premature death, the amount of such refund could be treated as any other property interest of the decedent, includable in the gross estate under Section 2033.[62] In the case of an ordinary commercial joint-and-survivor annuity or a self-and-survivor annuity, the estate tax consequences were very largely settled before the enactment of Section 2039 by the application of less explicit provisions to reach a result similar to that reached under the explicit section.[63] On the other hand, prior to the 1954 Code, employees' annuities were generally held not to be includable in the gross estate of the annuitant,[64] and it is in this area that Section 2039 has the greatest impact, particularly in light of the continued if not increased importance of employee benefit plans and the renewed interest in unfunded deferred-compensation arrangements.

Prior to 1954, in instances in which the employee's estate had no continuing rights after the employee's death so that Section 2033 would not bring anything into the employee's estate, the Treasury sought to impose estate tax on the value of the survivor's interests under principles expressed in Sections 2035 through 2038. Because these rules applied only if the decedent had made

---

The repealed subsections are still effective for estates of decedents either dying before 1985 or in "pay status" (with regard to the annuity) before 1985, if such decedents had irrevocably elected the form of the benefit before July 18, 1984. Deficit Reduction Act of 1984, Pub. L. No. 98-369, § 525(b), 98 Stat. 494, 874 (1984), reprinted in 1984-3 CB (Vol. 1) 1, 382. The effective date is the same for subsection (c). Tax Reform Act of 1986, Pub. L. No. 99-514, § 1852(e)(1)(b), 100 Stat. 2085, 2868 (1986), reprinted in 1986-3 CB (Vol. 1) 1, 785.

[61] Tax Reform Act of 1986, Pub. L. No. 99-514, § 1852(e)(2)(A), 100 Stat. 2085, 2868 (1986), reprinted in 1986-3 CB (Vol. 1) 1, 785.

[62] S. Rep. No. 1622, 83d Cong., 2d Sess. 471-472 (1954).

[63] E.g., Estate of Mearkle v. Comm'r, 129 F2d 386 (3d Cir. 1942); Comm'r v. Clise, 122 F2d 998 (9th Cir. 1941), cert. denied, 315 US 821 (1942); Comm'r v. Estate of Wilder, 118 F2d 281 (5th Cir.), cert. denied, 314 US 634 (1941).

[64] E.g., Estate of Howell v. Comm'r, 15 TC 224 (1950), acq. 1953-1 CB 4; Estate of Twogood vs. Comm'r, 15 TC 989 (1950), acq. 1953-1 CB 6, nonacq. 1951-2 CB 6 (withdrawn), aff'd, 194 F2d 627 (2d Cir. 1952).

a transfer of property, the Treasury had to establish, first, that there was a transfer and second, that the transfer satisfied the prerequisites for inclusion under Section 2035, Section 2036, Section 2037, or Section 2038.

Whether an identifiable transfer occurred in these circumstances was never fully settled. In some circumstances, the Tax Court held that an employee's arrangements with the employee's employer for the payment of benefits to survivors constituted a transfer of property that might provide a basis for estate tax liability.[65] In slightly different circumstances, the Tax Court held the other way.[66] In two Tax Court cases reaching opposite conclusions on the question whether there was a transfer, the Second and Third Circuits both held for the taxpayer on the ground that even if there was a transfer, the requisite interest was not retained by the decedent to bring into play the principles of Section 2036.[67] After the enactment of the Technical Changes Act of 1949,[68] the Treasury shifted its main line of attack on this problem from what is now Section 2036 to what is now Section 2037. It continued to argue that some such arrangements constituted transfers[69] and that such transfers might fit the requirements of the provision concerning transfers taking effect at death.[70] Restoration in 1954 of the requirement in Section 2037 that the decedent retain a reversionary interest in the property transferred would have made the Treasury's job more difficult. However, Section 2039 now affords a different basis for taxing employees' annuities that makes irrelevant the "transfer" question and makes more explicit the nature of the interest the decedent must have retained or possessed in order for tax liability to be imposed.

The 1954 legislation makes apparent the congressional acceptance of the proposition that employees' annuities "purchased" either by employee contributions or by the performance of services for the employer represent testamentary-like transfers that could just as properly be subject to estate tax as are transfers inherent in ordinary commercial annuities with survivorship features.[71] However, as seen previously,[72] from 1954 to 1985, the numerous exemptions written into the statute very substantially eroded this basically sound proposition.

---

[65] E.g., Estate of Leoni v. Comm'r, 7 TCM (CCH) 759 (1948).

[66] E.g., Estate of Twogood v. Comm'r, 15 TC 989 (1950), acq. 1953-1 CB 6, nonacq. 1951-2 CB 6 (withdrawn), aff'd 194 F2d 627 (2d Cir. 1952).

[67] E.g., Estate of Twogood v. Comm'r, 15 TC 989 (1950), acq. 1953-1 CB 6, nonacq. 1951-2 CB 6 (withdrawn), aff'd 194 F2d 627 (2d Cir. 1952); Estate of Higgs v. Comm'r, 184 F2d 427 (3d Cir. 1950).

[68] See IRC § 2037; ¶ 4.09[7].

[69] Rev. Rul. 53-158, 1953-2 CB 259.

[70] Rev. Rul. 53-260, 1953-2 CB 262.

[71] See Note, "Estate Taxation of Survivor Annuities: Section 811(c) and Proposed IRC of 1954," 6 Stan. L. Rev. 473 (1954).

[72] See supra ¶ 4.11[6].

¶ 4.12 SECTION 2040. JOINT INTERESTS

[1] Introduction

The lot of Congress, like that of a police officer, is often not a happy one. An initial decision is made to tax the transmission of wealth at death. Section 2033 is born, appropriately but unimaginatively measuring the tax by the value of property owned at death by a decedent and, at that time, passed on to others. Peripheral questions clamor for answers.[1] One such question is what to do about the decedent's co-ownership of property with another or others at the time of the decedent's death. Co-ownership does not necessarily present fresh problems. An ordinary interest as a tenant in common is something that a decedent can pass along to others in the same way as any interest in property owned solely by the decedent. No special provision is needed and none has been enacted for such an interest; it is taxed under Section 2033.[2] A parallel approach is taken, quite supportably, to a decedent's interest in community property.[3] What if the decedent's joint property interest is one that cannot be passed on by will? If it is one that merely expires at death, Section 2033 will not tax it.[4] Should it (a thorny question) be accorded estate tax significance? As determined by Congress, the answer is yes, but with qualifications.

The qualified statutory answers to the riddle of joint ownership with survivorship rights must take account of the special rule of Section 2040(b), which applies only to property owned jointly by the decedent and the dece-

---

[1] Are transfers near to (and prompted by thoughts of) death also taxed? Prior to 1976, transfers made within three years of and "in contemplation of death" were included in the decedent's gross estate. In 1976, this largely subjective test was replaced by a flat rule that transfers made within three years of death were to be included in the decedent's gross estate. After 1981, transfers, regardless of proximity to death, are not included in the decedent's gross estate for purposes of computing the estate tax, unless they would have resulted in inclusion in the decedent's gross estate under Section 2036, Section 2037, Section 2038, or Section 2042 if the interest had been retained by the decedent. Are transfers with income or enjoyment or some measure of control retained taxed? Yes, but according to some detailed rules. IRC § 2036. Are transfers that are not fully effective until the transferor's death taxed? Certainly, but with some afterthoughts at least as to what conditions should invoke the tax and as to whether the decedent must retain some interest in the property, suggesting a death-time transfer by the decedent, even if the tax is measured differently. IRC § 2037. How about a transfer made during life but revocable until death? No problem; but what lines should be drawn in identifying control or imputed control in the decedent? IRC § 2038. Annuities payable to others after death but generated by the decedent's wealth are taxed (IRC § 2039) and even property never owned by the decedent that at death the decedent effectively controlled is taxed (IRC § 2041).

[2] See ¶ 4.05[5][a]. See also Reg. § 20.2040-1(b).

[3] See ¶ 4.05[5][a].

[4] See ¶ 4.05[5][a]. But see First Kentucky Trust Co. v. United States, 737 F2d 557 (6th Cir. 1984).

Section 2040

dent's spouse. That problem is discussed later in this segment;[5] where the special rule does not apply, four answers are essentially possible:

1. If the decedent's interest and that of the other co-owners were acquired gratuitously from outsiders (as by gift or bequest from others), a co-owner's estate is taxed at death on the co-owner's ratable share of the property, even though the co-owner's interest simply expires with the co-owner.[6]

2. If the decedent's wealth created all the joint interests (the decedent bought the property and gave others their interests in it), the entire value of the property is taxed in the decedent's estate.[7]

3. If the decedent's interest was acquired entirely gratuitously from another co-owner (one to whom the purchaser gave an interest), the decedent's estate is not taxed at all at death.[8]

4. If wealth of the decedent and that of the other co-owner went into their acquisition of the property (each paid a part of the cost of acquisition), Congress attributes to the decedent, and taxes the decedent's estate on, a portion of the property commensurate with the decedent's share of the cost of acquisition.[9]

The foregoing introductory remarks seek to suggest what Section 2040 is all about. A more detailed analysis of the section is attempted in the following discussion.[10]

---

[5] See infra ¶ 4.12[10]; note the exception to the Section 2040(b) rule discussed infra ¶ 4.12[10] text accompanying notes 85–94.

[6] IRC § 2040(a) (last sentence). Why, one might ask (but like jesting Pilot not awaiting an answer), when the expiring interest of a life tenant similarly acquired is an estate tax cipher?

[7] IRC § 2040(a) (first clause), subject to the Section 2040(b) exception. Why, one might ask again, when others had present interests fully enjoyed at death (and on which gift tax may have been paid by the decedent), such as would prompt an exclusion under Section 2036? Does the philosophy behind Section 2037 supply a reason by analogy? Estate of Fox v. Comm'r, 69 TCM (CCH) 1719 (1995).

[8] IRC § 2040(a); the "except" clause provides a full exclusion unless Section 2040(b) is applicable. This result is appropriate on the theory there has never been any gratuitous transmission of anything to anyone by the decedent.

[9] IRC § 2040(a); the "except" clause, as interpreted, nails the decedent's estate for "such part" unless Section 2040(b) is applicable. Reg. § 20.2040-1(c)(2). Accepting the valuation-at-death concept (see discussion of IRC § 2031 at ¶ 4.02), does this not fairly reflect the value transmitted by the decedent to surviving co-owners?

[10] Section 2040 is also discussed in some somewhat outdated articles: Dean, "Federal Tax Consequences of Joint Ownership," 53 Geo. LJ 863 (1965); Riecker, "Joint Tenancy: The Estate Lawyer's Continuing Burden," 64 Mich. L. Rev. 801 (1966). See also Maxfield, "Some Reflections on the Taxation of Jointly Held Property," 35 Rec. AB City NY 156 (1980); Barton, "Jointly Owned Spousal Properties: Reassessment Under ERTA," 41 NYU Inst. on Fed. Tax'n 41-1 (1983); Terrazzano, "Joint Tenancy Is Simple Way of

[2] Forms of Ownership Covered

Section 2040 applies specifically to three types of property interests:

1. *Joint Tenancies.* Property held by the decedent and another or others as "joint tenants" with a right of survivorship[11] is within the section. Neither the name given a property interest by the parties themselves nor the characterization under state law is controlling. State law may be a critical factor in the determination of whether Section 2040 applies, but only as it bears on the respective rights of the parties and not as it relates to labels or terminology.[12]

2. *Tenancies by the Entirety.* Tenancies by the entirety are expressly within the section, although they will generally be subject to the rules contained in Section 2040(b).[13] In general, although there are some differences, a tenancy by the entirety is a joint tenancy with a right of survivorship in which the only tenants are husband and wife.[14]

3. *Joint Bank Accounts.* The statute specifically encompasses joint bank accounts where the deposit is payable to either co-owner or the survivor.[15]

Holding Property but May Not Produce the Best Tax Results," 30 Tax'n Acct. 348 (1983).

[11] Cf. Reg. § 20.2040-1(a).

[12] In some states, if property is transferred to two or more persons in joint tenancy they are mere tenants in common, unless the controlling document expressly provides for a right of survivorship. E.g., Fla. Stat. § 689.15 (2001). In other states, the term "joint tenancy" automatically carries the survivorship right. E.g., Mass. Ann. Laws ch. 184, § 7 (West Pub. Co. 2001); NY Est. Powers & Trusts Law § 6-2.2 (McKinney 2001).

See Rev. Rul. 87-98, 1987-2 CB 207 (joint tenancy property with a right of survivorship was treated as community property under state law and, therefore, both halves of the community property were accorded a fair market basis under Section 1014(a)(1) and Section 1014(b)(6)). The ruling is discussed (with some skepticism) in Andrews, "Community Property with Right of Survivorship: Uneasy Lies the Head That Wears a Crown of Surviving Spouse for Federal Income Tax Basis Purposes," 17 Virg. Tax Rev. 577 (1998).

[13] See infra ¶ 4.12[10].

[14] A joint tenancy is usually unilaterally severable by any of the joint owners, but in the case of a tenancy by the entirety, neither spouse acting alone can defeat the right of the survivor to take the entire property. Cf. Reg. § 25.2515-2(b)(2).

The nature of a tenancy by the entirety is examined in Powell & Regan, 7 Powell on Real Property, Chapter 52 (Lexis Pub. 2000). See, e.g., NY Est. Powers & Trusts Law § 6-2.2(b) (McKinney 2001).

[15] Again, local law may bear importantly on the coverage of the section, and, despite the layman's notion, it is often far from clear whether a joint bank account survivor succeeds to the deposit. See Stephens, Jr., "Survivorship Rights in Joint Accounts," 24 U. Fla. L. Rev. 476 (1972).

In addition to forms of co-ownership already referred to, Section 2040 includes "a bond or other instrument, in the name of the decedent and any other person and payable to either or the survivor."[16]

An issue sometimes arises as to whether at the decedent's death the property was jointly held.[17] Although this issue must be determined under controlling documents and local property law,[18] a local adjudication of the issue is not necessarily determinative.[19] Controversy arose in some cases over whether U.S. savings bonds purchased by the decedent and held initially by the decedent and another in joint ownership had been transferred outright to the survivor during the decedent's life. The Treasury Savings Bond Regulations[20] provide that no inter vivos gift by one co-owner to another is effective unless the bonds are reregistered or reissued by the government in the donee's name. The courts of appeals disagreed on whether mere delivery of such bonds without reregistration or reissuance was sufficient to convert them from joint ownership within the scope of Section 2040 to outright ownership in a transferee, foreclosing the imposition of estate tax under Section 2040.[21] The controversy was settled by the Supreme Court in the *Chandler* case,[22] in which the Court held that outright ownership cannot be established in a manner at variance with the bond regulations. Thus, in the case of U.S. savings bonds, registration

---

[16] Reg. § 20.2040-1(b). Under local property law, the registration of a bond in joint names may not effect any transfer of a present property interest to the noncontributing party, such as is a usual characteristic of joint tenancies. A transfer takes place when the latter properly cashes in the bonds for personal use or upon the death of one of the co-owners. Nevertheless, such an arrangement seems to be within the term "joint tenancy" as used in Section 2040. See Rev. Rul. 68-269, 1968-1 CB 399, Situation 5. The ruling attempts to classify some other co-ownership arrangements as well.

[17] E.g., Estate of Kincade v. Comm'r, 69 TC 247 (1977); Wilson v. Comm'r, 56 TC 579 (1971), acq., 1972-1 CB 2; Buckley v. Comm'r, 42 TCM (CCH) 1592 (1981); Estate of May v. Comm'r, 37 TCM (CCH) 137 (1978); Black v. Comm'r, 765 F2d 862 (9th Cir. 1985).

[18] Crosby v. United States, 298 F. Supp. 172 (ED Mo. 1969); Estate of Freedman v. Comm'r, 23 TCM (CCH) 1628 (1964); Estate of Tennant v. Comm'r, 8 TCM (CCH) 143 (1949). Cf. Rev. Rul. 80-241, 1980-2 CB 273.

[19] See Comm'r v. Estate of Bosch, 387 US 456 (1967); ¶ 4.05[2][b].

[20] 31 CFR § 315 (2001).

[21] The Third and Ninth Circuits held that mere delivery is sufficient to transfer ownership. Silverman v. McGinnes, 259 F2d 731 (3d Cir. 1958); Chandler v. United States, 312 F. Supp. 1263 (ND Cal. 1970), aff'd per curiam, 460 F2d 1281 (9th Cir. 1972). However, the Sixth Circuit and other lower courts relied on the bond regulations to support the application of Section 2040. Curry v. United States, 409 F2d 671 (6th Cir. 1969); Estate of Elliot v. Comm'r, 57 TC 152 (1971), aff'd per curiam after Chandler, 474 F2d 1008 (5th Cir. 1973); Chambless v. United States, 1970-1 USTC ¶ 12,655 (DSC 1970).

[22] United States v. Chandler, 410 US 257 (1973). See also Dumbrill v. United States, 354 F. Supp. 1107 (D. Wyo. 1973); Estate of Elliot v. Comm'r, 57 TC 152 (1971), aff'd per curiam, 474 F2d 1008 (5th Cir. 1973).

or reissuance is needed to convert joint ownership to outright ownership outside the reach of Section 2040.

[3] Some Section 2040 Misconceptions

The impact of Section 2040 is considered in the next segment of this discussion, but it is important here that some common misconceptions be set aside.

1. It is immaterial that jointly owned property is not part of a decedent's estate for purposes of probate or administration. As in the case of other estate tax provisions,[23] liability for the federal estate tax is not dependent upon the decedent's having a transferable property interest when the decedent died.

2. The value of the decedent's interest in the jointly held property prior to the decedent's death is by no means the measure of what is to be included in the decedent's gross estate. All, a part, or none of the value of the jointly held property may be included in the gross estate regardless of the value of the decedent's particular interest prior to the decedent's death.[24] Thus, the fact that a decedent held a one-half interest in a joint tenancy prior to death is not determinative of the amount included in the estate under Section 2040.

3. The estate tax treatment of property owned by the decedent and another as joint tenants is not affected by the fact that the creation of tenancy was treated as a gift for gift tax purposes, except with regard to the possible availability of a credit for gift tax paid.[25] Payment of the gift tax does not make the property any less subject to estate tax; that is, the rules discussed here still determine what is to be included in the gross estate, even though for gift tax purposes there has been a completed gift of an interest in the property.[26] The gift tax paid may

---

[23] See, e.g., IRC §§ 2035, 2036, 2037, 2038.

[24] Compare the philosophy of Section 2040(a), which bases the amount of inclusion on the source of the property, with that of Section 2033, under which the interest in the property at a decedent's death measures the amount included in the decedent's estate.

[25] See the discussion of vanishing Section 2012 at ¶ 3.04; Estate of Horner v. Comm'r, 130 F2d 649 (3d Cir. 1942). Cf. IRC § 2001(b)(2).

[26] Between 1954 and 1981, the creation of a joint tenancy between spouses was not treated as a gift unless the spouses elected to treat it as such. IRC § 2515 (prior to repeal in the Economic Recovery Tax Act of 1981, Pub. L. No. 97-34, § 403(c)(3)(B), 95 Stat. 172, 302 (1981), reprinted in 1981-2 CB 256, 325). With the enactment of the unlimited marital deduction (see ¶ 11.03), Section 2515 generally became unnecessary, and it was repealed. Economic Recovery Tax Act of 1981, Pub. L. No. 97-34, § 403(c)(3)(B), 95 Stat. 172, 302 (1981), reprinted in 1981-2 CB 256, 325). But see ¶ 10.01[3][f] note 112, where Sections 2515 and 2515A (each prior to repeal in the Economic Recovery Tax Act

reduce the actual amount of estate tax to be paid by way of the gift tax credit[27] or the subtraction for gift tax payable in the estate tax computation.[28]

[4] Amount to Be Included

As stated previously, the basic policy of Section 2040(a) is to include in the decedent's gross estate the value of jointly owned property, except to the extent that the surviving tenant or tenants contributed to the cost of the acquisition of the property. The general effect of this policy is to treat property owned jointly by the decedent and another as if it were owned outright by the one who was financially responsible for its acquisition. Thus, if A pays for Blackacre and has it conveyed to A and B as joint tenants, upon A's death, B surviving, the entire value of Blackacre is included in A's gross estate.[29] But if B is the first to die, no part of the value of Blackacre will be included in B's estate, for Section 2040 does not treat B as owner of the property to any extent where A paid the purchase price.[30]

Section 2040(a) goes well beyond the obvious examples just discussed. The section provides that the decedent's estate includes the entire value of the jointly held property, except such part as may be shown to have originally belonged to the survivor and never to have been received or acquired by the survivor from the decedent for less than an adequate and full consideration in money or money's worth. If the survivor made a contribution, that part of the value of the property that is commensurate with the consideration furnished by the survivor is excluded from the decedent's gross estate. Accordingly, the crucial question is: What part of the value of jointly held property, if any, can be

---

of 1981, Pub. L. No. 97-34, § 403(c)(3)(B), 95 Stat. 172, 302 (1981), reprinted in 1981-2 CB 256, 325) have been resurrected in very limited circumstances.

[27] The philosophy behind the estate tax is different from that behind the gift tax in this area. The gift tax (like Section 2033) looks to the property interest created, whereas Section 2040(a) looks to the origin or source of the funds.

[28] See discussion of Section 2001(b) at ¶ 2.01. Gift tax paid on transfers within three years of death is included in the decedent's gross estate. IRC § 2035(b), discussed ¶ 4.07[3].

[29] E.g., Third Nat'l Bank & Trust Co. v. White, 45 F2d 911 (D. Mass. 1930), aff'd per curiam, 58 F2d 1085 (1st Cir.), aff'd per curiam, 287 US 577 (1932).

[30] Estate of Koussevitsky v. Comm'r, 5 TC 650 (1945), acq. 1945 CB 4. If A and B (nonspouses) die simultaneously, then all of the property would be included in A's estate under Section 2040(a). Estate of Julian Peabody v. Comm'r, 41 BTA 1 (1940). If the Uniform Simultaneous Death Act applied, one half would be included in A's estate under Section 2040(a) and the other half under Section 2033; in addition, one half of the property would be included in B's estate under Section 2033. Cf. Rev. Rul. 76-303, 1976-2 CB 266. See also Rev. Rul. 66-60, 1966-1 CB 221.

excluded from the gross estate? Some exclusion depends on the estate establishing two facts: (1) that the surviving joint tenant did make a contribution to the acquisition of the property or did receive the property jointly with the decedent by gift, bequest, devise, or inheritance from a third party; and (2) that the contribution does not represent cash or property acquired from the decedent for less than an adequate and full consideration.

[5] Survivor's Contribution

Specifically, Section 2040(a) as modified by Section 2040(b) provides that if the decedent owned property jointly with another other than only the decedent's spouse, the amount to be excluded from the decedent's gross estate is that part of the value of the property that bears the same ratio to the entire value of the property as the consideration furnished by the survivor (which did not come from the decedent gratuitously) bears to the entire consideration paid for the property. This relationship can be stated as follows:

$$\frac{\text{amount excluded}}{\text{entire value of property}} = \frac{\text{survivor's consideration}}{\text{entire consideration paid}}$$

$$\text{amount excluded} = \frac{\text{survivor's consideration}}{\text{entire consideration paid}} \times \text{entire value of property}$$

It is important to note that the ratio obtained is applied to the value of the property at the date of death or the alternate valuation date. The value may of course be higher or lower than the amount of the purchase price. For example, if A contributed $7,500 and B contributed $2,500 to the acquisition of Blackacre for $10,000 as joint tenants, and if A dies survived by B at a time when the property is valued at $20,000, $15,000 will be included in A's gross estate. If, instead, the property is valued at $8,000, then $6,000 will be included in A's gross estate.

[6] Property Acquired by Gift From Others

The statute takes express notice that property owned by joint tenants with right of survivorship may have been acquired by the owners by gift, bequest, devise, or inheritance from another. In general, in such circumstances, upon the death of one of the owners, the property is treated for estate tax purposes just as if each owner had contributed an equal part of the purchase price. Inasmuch as there are always just two owners in the case of a tenancy by the entirety, it has long been specified in Section 2040(a) that if property so owned was acquired by gift, bequest, devise, or inheritance, then one half of the property is to be included in the estate of the first to die. It is interesting to note that even without that specification, this result would be reached under Section 2040(b).

On the other hand, property acquired gratuitously from others may be held by several persons as joint tenants with rights of survivorship. Subsection (b) generally does not apply here, and, if their interests are equal, the amount to be included in the estate of the first to die is determined by dividing the value of the property by the number of joint tenants. If there are only two joint tenants, then one half of the value of the property will still be included in the estate of the first to die. But if there are three, the part of the value to be included is one third, and so on. It should be reemphasized that the rule applies only if the jointly owned property was acquired from outsiders by gift, bequest, devise, or inheritance.

[7] Property Paid for by the Co-Owners

[a] The Tracing Requirement

Unfortunately, the exclusionary rules of Section 2040(a) inject into the statute an irksome tracing problem. Section 2040(a) specifically disregards any contribution toward the acquisition of jointly held property made by the surviving tenant out of property gratuitously acquired from the decedent.[31] By proper interpretation, the proceeds from a disposition of such property are likewise generally disregarded.[32] The main thrust of the statute is that only contributions from separate funds of the survivor are taken into account under the exclusionary rules. For example, if the decedent, D, gave A $10,000, which A later used to pay one half of the purchase price of the property held by A and D at death as joint tenants, the entire value of the property would be included in the D's gross estate. Similarly, if D originally gave the property itself to A, and A subsequently reconveyed it through a straw man to A and D as joint tenants, A is not treated as having contributed to the acquisition of the property, and its entire value is included in D's gross estate if D is the first to die.[33] No part of the value would be included in A's estate under Section 2040 in either instance, if A was the first to die.[34]

Clearly, the statute adopts a tracing rule by requiring a determination whether a contribution to the purchase price by the surviving tenant was from

---

[31] See Estate of Lyons v. Comm'r, 35 TCM (CCH) 605 (1976).

[32] Estate of Edward T. Kelley v. Comm'r, 22 BTA 421 (1931), acq. X-2 CB 37.

[33] Estate of Hornor v. Comm'r, 130 F2d 649 (3d Cir. 1942); Stuart v. Hassett, 41 F. Supp. 905 (D. Mass. 1941).

[34] There would also be no Section 2035 inclusion. See IRC § 2035(a)(2); ¶ 4.07[2].

the surviving tenant's own funds.[35] More precisely, Section 2040(a) says the consideration provided by the survivor must never have been "acquired . . . from the decedent for less than an adequate and full consideration in money or money's worth. . . . " It is well established that a contribution originating as income from property acquired gratuitously from the decedent constitutes a contribution from the survivor's separate funds, and the regulations so provide.[36] Thus, a surviving tenant's contribution to the purchase of jointly held property out of dividends from stock given to the survivor by the other tenant, the decedent, has been treated as made out of the survivor's own separate funds.[37]

What is "income" for these purposes? A troublesome question is whether a contribution made out of gain representing appreciation in the value of property received gratuitously from the decedent is attributable to the decedent or, instead, is to be treated as income from the property and thus separate funds of the surviving tenant. Proposed regulations under the 1954 Code, not finally adopted, took the flat position that such appreciation is not "income" from property within the rule that permits income from gift property to be treated as the surviving tenant's separate contribution.[38] A similar position in the current regulations is not expressed so comprehensively.[39] Two distinct situations should be recognized. In one circumstance, the surviving tenant who received property gratuitously from the decedent may have sold the property and thereafter contributed the proceeds, including the survivor's gain. In this situation, the gain, measured by the appreciation from the time of the receipt of the gift to the time of the sale,[40] has been treated as income and as part of the surviving tenant's contribution.[41] For example, assume the decedent, D, buys prop-

---

[35] Cf. Rev. Rul. 78-418, 1978-2 CB 326.

[36] Reg. § 20.2040-1(c)(5).

[37] Estate of Howard v. Comm'r, 9 TC 1192 (1947), acq. 1948-1 CB 2; Estate of Drazen v. Comm'r, 48 TC 1 (1967); Estate of Fratini v. Comm'r, 76 TCM (CCH) 342 (1998). An issue can arise over whether a stock dividend is "income" attributable to the surviving tenant or a division of capital attributable to the decedent. See Tuck v. United States, 282 F2d 405 (9th Cir. 1960); English v. United States, 270 F2d 876 (7th Cir. 1959); Rev. Rul. 80-142, 1980-1 CB 197. This question is not unique to Section 2040(a) and is discussed in an analogous setting at ¶ 4.03[2][c].

[38] Prop. Reg. § 20.2040-1(a)(2), Notice of Proposed Rulemaking, 21 Fed. Reg. 7850, 7879 (1956).

[39] Reg. § 20.2040-1(c)(4).

[40] Swartz v. United States, 182 F. Supp. 540 (D. Mass. 1960).

[41] Harvey v. United States, 185 F2d 463 (7th Cir. 1950); Estate of Goldsborough v. Comm'r, 70 TC 1077 (1978); Rev. Rul. 79-372, 1979-2 CB 330. This treatment of gain on property acquired by gift from the decedent as separate funds of the survivor pays no obeisance to income tax concepts, which seems appropriate because the estate tax and the income tax are not in pari materia. Farid-Es-Sultaneh v. Comm'r, 160 F2d 812 (2d Cir. 1947). Thus, the donee's gain that is treated as the donee's property is measured by appreciation that occurs while the donee holds the property, rather than with reference to the

erty for $1,000 and the property appreciates to $2,000, at which point D gives the property to A. A holds the property until its value reaches $5,000 and then sells it and uses the proceeds for A's contribution in the acquisition of jointly held property that is held by D and A at the time of D's death. The appreciation from the time of the gift to the time of the sale, $3,000, would be treated as income from the gift property, qualified as a contribution by surviving tenant A.[42]

In the second situation, the surviving tenant, A, receives property gratuitously from the decedent, D, it appreciates, and thereafter A uses the property itself as A's contribution to the acquisition of jointly held property. Here, at least according to the regulations, all of the property will be treated as having been paid for by D.[43] Does this realization concept have an appropriate place in the estate tax? Maybe so, as it is conceptually difficult to carve out any separate funds where the very thing received gratuitously from the decedent constitutes the survivor's contribution, but the conclusion seems less acceptable as a policy matter than as a matter of statutory interpretation. Obviously, the rules on survivor contributions create a unique tracing and allocation problem; under them, the proceeds of the sale of appreciated gift property are partly the separate funds of the donee and partly attributable to the donor decedent, but quite different consequences may attend the economically similar contribution of property freighted with unrealized gain. With the enactment of Section 2040(b), the statute has moved away from these difficulties with respect to husband-and-wife joint tenancies.

The first situation, involving a realized gain on property owned by the survivor,[44] may have to be differentiated from a situation in which the donee never owns the property outright. For example, what if the decedent, D, transfers property to D and the surviving tenant, A, as joint owners and the property appreciates in value, is sold by them while jointly owned, and the proceeds (including the realized gain) are reinvested in other jointly owned property? It has been held that the full value of the property is included in D's

---

donee's income tax basis under Section 1015. The income tax concept of realization (cf. Eisner v. Macomber, 252 US 189 (1920)) necessarily creeps in because, absent a disposition of the gift property, the contribution of the gift property itself would simply be property "acquired by the donee . . . from the decedent" gratuitously, which the statute expressly says cannot be considered. However, there is no estate tax requirement that realized gain be "recognized." Thus, a donee's contribution of property acquired in a tax-free exchange, even though the donee's gain went unrecognized under Section 1031, for example, should be treated as the donee's separate contribution, except for the value at the time of the gift of the property acquired by gift.

[42] A rejection of income tax basis rules (IRC § 1015) and gain-measuring devices (IRC § 1001) seems appropriate here.

[43] Reg. § 20.2040-1(c)(4).

[44] Harvey v. United States, 185 F2d 463 (7th Cir. 1950).

gross estate.[45] The court rejected the estate's argument that one half of the realized gain from the sale of the property should be treated as a separate contribution by A on the ground that A never held an outright, as opposed to a joint, interest in the property.[46] Although treating a part of such realized appreciation as the property of and a contribution by A would allow an easy partial avoidance of Section 2040(a) by means of a near-death sale and repurchase of property,[47] such a result would nevertheless be consistent with the "property ownership" (as opposed to "tax ownership") theory adopted in other Section 2040(a) situations that also permit an easy partial avoidance of the section.[48]

[b] Additions and Improvements

In addition to establishing the respective contributions to the initial cost of acquisition, it may be necessary to take account of amounts subsequently contributed. The regulations state that the total cost of acquisition includes the cost of "capital additions."[49] Curiously, the regulations and the cases as well are virtually silent on the exact significance of the cost of capital additions.[50] For example, assume that D and A each contribute $100 to the purchase of unimproved real estate, taking title in the name of D and A as joint tenants. Assume that the property greatly appreciates over time to a value of $1,100. If D then makes a capital improvement at a cost to him of $100 and thereafter dies, how much is includable in D's gross estate? Applying the regulations literally, D has contributed $200 and A contributed $100. Accordingly, if the property at the time of D's death is worth $2,400 ($1,100 fair market value at the time of improvement, plus $100 improvement, plus $1,200 appreciation from date of last improvement to death), two thirds of that amount, or $1,600, would be includable in D's estate on the theory that D contributed two thirds of the cost.

---

[45] Endicott Trust Co. v. United States, 305 F. Supp. 943 (NDNY 1969).

[46] The propriety of the result in *Endicott* is questionable. If income in the form of interest, dividends, or rent generated by jointly held property paid for one person is used to purchase other jointly held property, the property is deemed funded equally by both joint owners. Estate of Otte v. Comm'r, 31 TCM (CCH) 301 (1972); Rev. Rul. 56-519, 1956-2 CB 123. On the other hand, unrealized appreciation on jointly held property originally paid for by a decedent would result in no separate contribution by the co-owner if that property were exchanged for other property to be held jointly. *Endicott* falls somewhere between these two situations. A realization of the appreciation on jointly held property would establish a portion of that appreciation as the survivor's property under local law, seemingly bringing it within the ambit of Harvey v. United States, 185 F2d 463 (7th Cir. 1950).

[47] There is an income tax obstacle, Section 1001.

[48] See infra ¶ 4.12[9].

[49] Reg. § 20.2040-1(a)(2).

[50] The second and third sentences of Regulations Section 20.2040-1(a)(2) are vague, to say the least. Compare Reg. § 25.2515-1(c)(2).

Stated more in terms of the statutory language, because A, who survives, contributed one third of the cost, one third of the date-of-death value is excluded from D's estate. This first possible approach seems incorrect, because D's contribution to the final value is exaggerated. In addition, in contemplation of a decedent's death, a likely survivor could make a relatively minor capital improvement and effectively remove substantial value from a decedent's estate.[51]

A second and seemingly correct approach would be to allocate to each of the co-owners a part of the appreciation commensurate with the co-owners' contributions prior to the appreciation.[52] Thus, in applying the exclusionary rules of Section 2040(a), D should be treated as having contributed the following sums: $100 ($D$'s share of the original cost), $450 (one half of the appreciation from the time of acquisition until the time of improvement), and $100 ($D$'s capital improvement), for a total of $650. Using like reasoning, A's contributions would be $100 ($A$'s share of the original cost) and $450 (one half of the pre-improvement appreciation), for a total of $550. The total cost of acquisition should be treated as $1,200 (fair market value after the improvement) for purposes of the exclusionary rule. Thus, the amount to be excluded from D's estate would be 550 ÷ 1200 multiplied by $2,400, or $1,100 (the portion of date-of-death value commensurate with A's contribution to total cost), as a result of A's "contributions,"[53] and only $1,300 would be included. The estate may have severe practical problems in establishing the value at the time of the improvement.

A third possible approach should be rejected along with the first one suggested. It would be merely to reduce the value of the property included in D's gross estate by actual cash value of A's contribution; on the facts of this example, $2,300 would be included. This mechanical approach would completely ignore the appreciation attributable to A's contribution. Only one case has faced the issue,[54] and the court may have adopted either the second or the third solution. In the *Peters* case, the decedent inherited some property and placed it in a joint tenancy, and the co-owners made improvements on it. The surviving joint tenant subsequently made further improvements before the decedent co-owner's death. The Tax Court found in *Peters* that the property did not appreciate in value subsequent to any of the survivor's improvements, and it taxed

---

[51] Thus, in the text example, if D made no improvement but A made a $400 capital improvement immediately prior to D's death, then five sixths of the value of the property would not be included in the D's estate, and only $400 would be included.

[52] This would be in accord with the gift tax regulations under Section 2515 (prior to repeal in the Economic Recovery Tax Act of 1981, Pub. L. No. 97-34, § 403(c)(3)(B), 95 Stat. 172, 302 (1981), reprinted in 1981-2 CB 256, 325). Reg. § 25.2515-1(c)(2). It should be subject to the qualification of those regulations that the allocation would be made, unless appreciation is directly and identifiably traceable to a particular contribution.

[53] Postimprovement appreciation continues to be partly contributed to A.

[54] Estate of Peters v. Comm'r, 386 F2d 404 (4th Cir. 1967).

the decedent's estate on the value of the property less the cost of the survivor's improvements. Thus, under the *Peters* facts, the same result would have been reached under either the second or the third solution, as none of the appreciation could be ascribed to the survivor's contribution. However, the Tax Court indicated that if there had been appreciation after that contribution, a formula or ratio might have been needed to reach the proper result, which implies the court's acceptance of the second solution.[55] Although the Fourth Circuit in affirming did not expand the Tax Court's rationale, nevertheless the result reached was correct.[56]

[8] Burden of Proof

The burden of showing original ownership or contribution to the purchase price[57] by the survivor falls upon the estate. Section 2040(a) specifically requires inclusion of the entire value of jointly held property, "except such part thereof as may be shown" to have originated with the survivor. As the cases illustrate, this can be a difficult burden,[58] although where evidence indicates that the survivor did make a contribution, courts have held that the burden is met and been willing to estimate the amount.[59] Clearly, then, the lesson is simple: The decedent's estate may be called upon through records, memoranda, canceled checks, duplicate deposit slips, and other documentary evidence to establish the time at which the transactions took place and the respective contributions.[60] As in most areas of tax controversy, inadequacy of records usually works to the disadvantage of the taxpayer.

---

[55] Estate of Peters v. Comm'r, 46 TC 407, 415 n.4 (1966).

[56] The Fourth Circuit, in affirming, did state that Regulations Section 20.2040-1(a)(2) is limited to a purchase as opposed to an inheritance situation. Estate of Peters v. Comm'r, 386 F2d 404, 407 (4th Cir. 1967). Such a conclusion seems unwarranted. See a discussion of the *Peters* case in Speranza, "IRC § 2040: Allocation of Contribution Problems," 5 USF L. Rev. 166, 168 (1970).

[57] As discussed supra ¶ 4.12[7][b] in connection with the contribution by the surviving tenant, the purchase price includes not only the cost of acquisition but also any improvements made to the property.

[58] E.g., Estate of Heidt v. Comm'r, 8 TC 969 (1947), aff'd per curiam, 170 F2d 1021 (9th Cir. 1948); Estate of Balazs v. Comm'r, 42 TCM (CCH) 632 (1981).

[59] Courts have adopted the principle of Cohan v. Comm'r, 39 F2d 540 (2d Cir. 1930), in estimating the survivor's contribution. Estate of Carpousis v. Comm'r, 33 TCM (CCH) 1143 (1974); Estate of Fratini v. Comm'r, 76 TCM (CCH) 342 (1998); Estate of Selecman v. Comm'r, 9 TCM (CCH) 997 (1950). Cf. Estate of Van Tine, 76 TCM (CCH) 530 (1998) (no *Cohan* estimation because original costs of property not shown). See also infra text accompanying note 69.

[60] Estate of Giacopuzzi v. Comm'r, 29 TCM (CCH) 1777 (1970) (entire value of a home owned jointly by mother and daughter was included in the mother's estate because the daughter was unable to trace her earnings that she had given to her mother into pay-

In the case of bank accounts owned jointly at death, the burden of proof is even more difficult. Here, the decedent's estate must show not only that the survivor made a contribution but also that the survivor did not withdraw the contribution made.[61] As the nontax advantages of owning property jointly are limited, these requirements raise a question whether, other than in the case of husband and wife, joint ownership should not be largely avoided.[62]

If the surviving tenant has made a contribution to the acquisition of jointly owned property out of property acquired from the decedent, but acquired for full consideration, this constitutes a contribution out of the survivor's separate funds. Prior to the enactment of current Section 2040(b) in 1981,[63] many issues arose with respect to various types of interspousal contributions.[64] For joint interspousal interests created after 1981, those issues are

---

ments on the home); Estate of Harden v. Comm'r, 72 TCM (CCH) 1139 (1996) (mother's estate was unable to prove any deposits made to a joint bank account by son). Cf. Blood v. Comm'r, 22 BTA 1000 (1931) (entire value of property held as tenants by the entirety was included in the husband's estate for lack of evidence of contribution by the surviving wife); Hudson v. United States, 79-1 USTC ¶ 13,292 (WD Okla. 1979) (decedent's estate was unable to show bank account deposits made by surviving spouse).

A surviving joint tenant may find it advantageous that all or a part of the value of jointly held property was included in the predeceasing joint tenant's gross estate because the basis of the property included may be increased. IRC §§ 1014(a), 1014(b)(9). However, the survivor does not have an option, and, for income tax purposes, the survivor may later have the burden of proving that any portion of the property was required to be included in the predeceasing joint tenant's gross estate. Madden v. Comm'r, 52 TC 845 (1969), aff'd per curiam, 440 F2d 784 (7th Cir. 1971).

[61] Estate of Drazen v. Comm'r, 48 TC 1 (1967); Estate of Brandt v. Comm'r, 8 TCM (CCH) 820 (1949). In Tuck v. United States, 282 F2d 405 (9th Cir. 1960), and English v. United States, 270 F2d 876 (7th Cir. 1959), there was a failure of proof that the survivor contributed separate funds to the acquisition of jointly held property.

[62] If an estate planner encounters jointly owned property, the planner must make a careful study of the gift tax consequences of a possible severance of the property, as well as being alert to possible gift tax liability ignored at the time the joint ownership originated.

[63] See infra ¶ 4.12[10].

[64] For estate tax purposes, a relinquishment of dower, curtesy, or other marital rights in another's estate does not constitute consideration. IRC § 2043(b), discussed ¶ 4.15[1]. A wife's performance of ordinary domestic services did not constitute a contribution on her part, under Section 2040(a). Estate of Lyons v. Comm'r, 35 TCM (CCH) 605 (1976). However, it was difficult to say, beyond the situation of domestic services, whether a wife had furnished consideration by virtue of work performed for her husband in a business setting, or whether she received a mere gratuity when he had property transferred to them jointly. Compare Berkowitz v. Comm'r, 108 F2d 319 (3d Cir. 1939); Richardson v. Helvering, 80 F2d 548 (DC Cir. 1935); and Estate of Otte v. Comm'r, 31 TCM (CCH) 301 (1972) (representing joint business efforts by husband and wife) with Rogan v. Kammerdiner, 140 F2d 569 (9th Cir. 1944) (reaching a like result seemingly based on a mere agreement to share profits). Cf. Estate of Carpousis v. Comm'r, 33 TCM (CCH) 1143 (1974). But see Estate of Ensley v. Comm'r, 36 TCM (CCH) 1627 (1977), aff'd unpub.

generally moot, because Section 2040(b) simply includes only one half of interspousal survivorship property in the predeceasing spouse's gross estate.[65]

Under what circumstances in a non–Section 2040(b) situation will mortgage liability be treated as a contribution by the surviving tenant? At least one case has appropriately held that if the parties acquire property taking title as joint tenants and jointly assuming a mortgage, initially each joint tenant will be treated as making a contribution in the amount of one half of the mortgage liability assumed;[66] the Service accepts that position.[67] If the mortgage liability so assumed is discharged with income from the property, the respective proportionate contributions would remain unchanged if the income from the property legally belongs one half to each tenant.[68] Even though the mortgage liability is assumed jointly, if one of the two tenants discharges the liability out of separate funds, their respective contributions should be realigned and the amount paid treated entirely as a contribution by the tenant who paid off the mortgage; but here, as elsewhere,[69] evidentiary problems regarding payments are difficult. There is no authority dealing with the question whether an acquisition of property subject to a mortgage (not assumed) will be treated similarly. For income tax purposes, the treatment is the same,[70] and there are equally strong reasons for a similar estate tax result.

[9] Termination Prior to Death

Under the present case law, a pre-death disposition of property held jointly presents a planning technique for the reduction of the estate tax.[71] If a decedent

---

opinion (7th Cir. 1979); Estate of Ehret v. Comm'r, 35 TCM (CCH) 1432 (1976). See Whitesell, "Estate Taxation of Joint Tenancy Property Acquired by Spouses With Funds Generated From the Family Business — 'The Family Partnership' Exception to Section 2040," 21 Wm. & Mary L. Rev. 191 (1979); now repealed Section 2040(c). See infra text accompanying note 85. The wife's contribution was easier to show in a community property state where all earnings of either spouse are deemed earned one half by each.

[65] See infra ¶ 4.12[10]. But see infra ¶ 4.12[10] text accompanying notes 85–94.

[66] Bremer v. Luff, 7 F. Supp. 148 (NDNY 1933).

[67] Rev. Rul. 79-302, 1979-2 CB 328; Rev. Rul. 81-183, 1981-2 CB 180; Rev. Rul. 81-184, 1981-2 CB 181.

[68] Cf. Estate of Otte v. Comm'r, 31 TCM (CCH) 301 (1972).

[69] Estate of Awrey v. Comm'r, 5 TC 222 (1945), acq. 1945 CB 1.

[70] Crane v. Comm'r, 331 US 1 (1947); Parker v. Delaney, 186 F2d 455 (1st Cir. 1950), cert. denied, 341 US 926 (1951).

[71] The technique requires a valid termination of the joint tenancy. See Estate of Bettin v. Comm'r, 33 TCM (CCH) 499 (1974), aff'd per curiam, 543 F2d 1269 (9th Cir. 1976) (involving an invalid termination). See also Ellis, "Estate and Gift Tax Planning for the Termination of Joint Interests," 31 J. Tax'n 98 (1969), for a discussion of this area prior to the enactment of Section 2040(b). Pre-death disposition of jointly held property to

provided all of the consideration for property held by the decedent and someone other than the decedent's spouse as joint tenants and the decedent predeceases the other person, the entire value of the property is included in the
decedent's gross estate under Section 2040(a).[72] If, however, near the decedent's death they sever the joint tenancy and create a tenancy in common, then
only one half of the property is included in the decedent's gross estate.[73]

   If the decedent and the other joint tenant transfer the property outright to
a third party gratuitously, even within three years of the decedent's death, none
of the value of the property is includable in the decedent's gross estate.[74] The
result follows no matter what would have been includable under Section
2040(a) had the property been retained until death. If the decedent and the
other joint tenant transfer the property to a trust reserving a life estate for their
joint lives, only one half of the property is includable in the decedent's gross
estate under Section 2036.[75] The Commissioner has argued that the whole
property should be included in the decedent's estate, relying on the estate tax
ownership concept embraced in *United States v. Allen*,[76] discussed in connection with Section 2036.[77] This approach, however, has been rejected and a
straight property ownership concept has been applied. The rationale for this result is that at the time of the transfer, the decedent had only a one-half interest
in the property under local law, which was all the decedent could have trans-

---

avoid Section 2040(a) may not be advantageous in all circumstances. The unified credit
and the income tax basis of the property should also be considered.

   [72] E.g., Third Nat'l Bank & Trust Co. v. White, 45 F2d 911 (D. Mass. 1930), aff'd
per curiam, 58 F2d 1085 (1st Cir.), aff'd per curiam, 287 US 577 (1932).

   [73] IRC § 2033.

   [74] Neither Section 2040(a) nor Section 2035(a) is applicable. See IRC § 2035(a)(2);
¶ 4.07[2]. The transfer is, of course, subject to gift tax with the decedent and the joint
tenant each making a gift of one half of the value of the property. Under the unified transfer tax, the value of the gift is instrumental in determining the estate tax. See IRC
§ 2001(b)(1)(B); ¶¶ 2.01[1],¶ 2.01[2]. See also IRC § 2035(b); ¶ 4.07[3].

   The same result would be reached if the property had been held jointly as a tenancy
by the entirety, cf. Glaser v. United States, 306 F2d 57 (7th Cir. 1962), although it can be
argued that the interest transferred by the decedent represented something different from a
one-half interest in the property. Reg. § 25.2515-2(b)(2).

   [75] Heasty v. United States, 370 F2d 525 (10th Cir. 1966); Black v. Comm'r, 765 F2d
862 (9th Cir. 1985); Glaser v. United States, 306 F2d 57 (7th Cir. 1962) (involving a tenancy by the entirety); Estate of Borner v. Comm'r, 25 TC 584 (1955), acq., 1969-2 CB
xxiii (tenancy by the entirety); Rev. Rul. 69-577, 1969-2 CB 173. But see Estate of May
v. Comm'r, 37 TCM (CCH) 137 (1978), questionably holding that a joint tenancy still exists if the property is transferred to a revocable trust.

   [76] United States. v. Allen, 293 F2d 916 (10th Cir.), cert. denied, 368 US 944 (1961).
See United States v. O'Malley, 383 US 627 (1966).

   [77] See ¶ 4.08[8][b].

ferred.[78] The principle, which seems settled, is not invariably favorable to the estate. A possible adverse consequence could arise if the noncontributing tenant predeceased the other tenant because, in that situation, one half of the corpus would be included in the decedent's gross estate.[79] If no trust had been created, the noncontributor would still have enjoyed one half of the income from the jointly owned property for noncontributor's life, but nothing would have been included in noncontributor's gross estate.[80]

The results of the cases square with a literal reading of Sections 2035 and 2036 but patently undermine the policy of Section 2040. Caution is in order; such circumstances invite legislative, even judicial, change. Legislation would be appropriate.

[10] The Section 2040(b) Exception

Many spouses own property, both realty and personalty, in joint ownership with right of survivorship principally to avoid the formal probate process. However, the estate tax consequences have often been adverse or at least complex; difficulty often arose in determining relative contributions to the acquisition of the property.[81] In Section 2040(b), Congress created a major exception to the general rule of Section 2040(a) that alleviates the difficulty.

Section 2040(b)(1) provides a flat rule that one half of the value of property jointly owned is included in the estate of the predeceasing tenant in the case of a "qualified joint interest,"[82] a term defined in Section 2040(b)(2). An interest qualifies only if the only co-owners are husband and wife and there is a right of survivorship.[83] Thus, with respect to such interests, no matter who

---

[78] Heasty v. United States, 370 F2d 525 (10th Cir. 1966). See Stephens, "The Clifford Shadow Over the Federal Estate Tax," 4 Ga. L. Rev. 233 (1970).

[79] Miller v. United States, 1971-1 USTC ¶ 12,769 (ED Pa. 1971); Rev. Rul. 76-348, 1976-2 CB 267.

[80] Estate of Koussevitsky v. Comm'r, 5 TC 650 (1945), acq. 1945 CB 4.

[81] See supra ¶¶ 4.12[7][a], 4.12[8].

[82] A post-1980 "qualified joint interest" should not be confused with a pre-1981 "qualified joint interest." Section 2040(b), as it existed from 1977 through 1980, contained a similar rule that also resulted in inclusion of only one half of the value of the property in the predeceasing spouse's gross estate. However, the earlier Section 2040(b) had several further requirements that had to be met before it became applicable. Those further requirements, some very intricate rules in now-repealed Sections 2040(d) and 2040(e) for qualifying pre-1977 joint tenancies for post-1976 Section 2040(b) treatment, and a second interspousal exception enacted in 1978 under Section 2040(c) related to farm and other business property held jointly, are considered in Stephens, Maxfield, & Lind, Federal Estate and Gift Taxation ¶ 4.12[11] (Warren, Gorham & Lamont, 4th ed. 1978).

[83] IRC § 2040(b)(2)(B). Both requirements are always met in a tenancy by the entirety.

provided the consideration or in what relative proportion, one half of the value of the property is included in the predeceasing spouse's gross estate.[84]

There are two exceptions to the Section 2040(b) rules. First, the rule is inapplicable to qualified joint interests created prior to 1977.[85] Second, concerned about collecting tax revenues from a surviving spouse who is not a U.S. citizen,[86] Congress has generally made the Section 2040(b) rule inapplicable where the surviving spouse is not a U.S. citizen.[87] Thus, with respect to a joint tenancy held only by spouses or a tenancy by the entirety where the surviving spouse is a noncitizen, the normal Section 2040(a) tracing rules generally apply.[88] However, if prior to the filing of a decedent's estate tax return,

---

[84] Inclusion under Section 2040(b) will essentially result in a "wash" (no net increase situation) as the included value of such property will qualify for the Section 2056 marital deduction. See ¶ 5.06. Full inclusion of such property would also result in a wash. Id. However, if only one half of the property is included in the decedent's gross estate, only one half of the property will qualify for a Section 1014 basis. If property were funded with community property, it may be more advantageous to hold title to the property as community property. See IRC § 1014(b)(6) which steps up the basis of both halves of community property on the death of the predeceasing spouse. Cf. Rev. Rul. 87-98, 1987-2 CB 206 (property held by spouses as joint tenants with rights of survivorship classified as community property under state law.)

[85] Section 2040(b) as originally enacted applied only to joint interests created after 1976 (Tax Reform Act of 1976, Pub. L. No. 94-455, § 2002(d)(3), 90 Stat. 1520, 1856 (1976), reprinted in 1976-3 (Vol. 1) CB 1, 332 and the amendment of the section by the Economic Recovery Tax Act of 1981, Pub. L. No. 97-34, § 403(c)(1), 95 Stat. 172, 301 (1981), reprinted in 1981-2 CB 256, 325, did not explicitly or implicitly repeal the effective date. Gallenstein v. United States, 975 F2d 286 (6th Cir. 1992) (an income tax case where a husband provided the entire consideration for a farm in which he and his spouse took title as joint tenants prior to 1977, the full value of the farm was properly included in his estate. His surviving spouse was therefore entitled, under Section 1014, to a stepped-up basis in the property equal to the property's fair market value at the time of the husband's death). The same result was reached in Patten v. United States, 116 F3d 1029 (4th Cir. 1997); Hahn v. Comm'r, 110 TC 140 (1998), acq., 2001-2 CB __.

[86] Seemingly, the thinking of Congress in making Section 2040(b) inapplicable is that if the joint property was funded by the decedent, it should be included in the decedent's gross estate in the event that the Treasury might not be able to tax the property in the noncitizen spouse's estate.

[87] IRC § 2056(d)(1)(B). The provision could hardly be more hidden!

The Section 2040(a) rules also apply if the decedent spouse is not a U.S. citizen, but the property is subject to United States taxation under Section 2103. Reg. § 20.2056A-8(a)(1).

[88] See supra ¶¶ 4.12[4]–4.12[9]. See Reg. § 20.2056A-8(c) Ex. 3. If the spouses acquired the property by gift, bequest, devise, or inheritance, only one half is includable in the decedent's gross estate where the spouses are the only tenants. See supra ¶ 4.12[6].

In conjunction with the enactment of Section 2056(d)(1)(B), Congress generally restored the gift tax provisions of Section 2515 and 2515A related to the creation of such joint tenancy and tenancy-by-the-entirety interests as they existed prior to their repeal in 1982. Economic Recovery Tax Act of 1981, Pub. L. No. 97-34, § 403(c)(3)(B), 95 Stat. 172, 302 (1981), reprinted in 1981-2 CB 256, 325). See IRC § 2523(i)(3). See also

the surviving spouse becomes a U.S. citizen and the surviving spouse was a U.S. resident at all times after decedent spouse's death and prior to becoming a citizen, Section 2040(b) remains applicable.[89] If the noncitizen surviving spouse does not obtain citizenship, Section 2040(a) remains applicable,[90] but to the extent that such property is included in the decedent spouse's gross estate under Section 2040(a)[91] and the surviving spouse transfers it to a qualified domestic trust (QDOT)[92] it qualifies for a marital deduction and QDOT treatment resulting in a postponement of decedent spouse's estate tax.[93] To the extent that the property is included in the gross estate of both spouses, a Section 2013 credit is allowed regardless of the time span between their deaths.[94]

¶ 10.01[3][f] note 112 explaining the interrelationship of Section 2040(a) and Section 2523(i)(3). As a result, in applying Section 2040(a), pursuant to the rules above, if the donor spouse predeceases the donee spouse, a transfer by the donor spouse made in creating a joint tenancy or a tenancy by the entirety prior to July 14, 1988, that was treated for gift tax purposes as a gift by donor to donee is treated as consideration originally belonging to the donee spouse in determining the value of the tenancy included in the donor spouse's gross estate. Reg. § 20.2056A-8(a)(2). Omnibus Budget Reconciliation Act of 1989, Pub. L. No. 101-239, § 7815(d)(16), 103 Stat. 2106, 2419 (1989), reprinted in 1990-1 CB 210, 275. Accordingly, if the donee spouse survives, the amount of joint tenancy property included in the donor spouse's gross estate is reduced proportionately by the amount of the gift. HR Rep. No. 247, 101st Cong., 1st Sess. 1429 (1989). See Reg. §§ 20.2056A-8(a)(2), 20.2056A-8(c) Ex. 1. If the donee spouse predeceases the donor spouse, any consideration treated as a gift by the donor spouse to the donee spouse is disregarded in applying Section 2040(a) to the donee spouse's gross estate. Reg §§ 20.2056A-8(a)(2), 20.2056A-8(c) Ex. 2.

[89] IRC § 2056(d)(4). See Reg. § 20.2056A-8(b); ¶ 5.06[9] text accompanying notes 431–433.

[90] See supra text accompanying note 88.

[91] See supra note 88.

[92] See ¶ 5.07[2][b]. QDOTs are explained in detail at ¶ 5.07.

[93] Supplementary Information, I. § 20.2056A-8 Special rules for joint property, 1995-2 CB 192, 196. Reg. § 20.2056A-8(a)(3). See ¶¶ 5.06[9], 5.07.

Although this does not seem to be a literal interpretation of the Code (see Section 2056(d)(2)), the Service has taken this position in the regulations. Supplementary Information, I. § 20.2056A-8 Special rules for joint property, 1995-2 CB 192, 196. See Reg. §§ 20.2056A-8(a)(1), 20.2056A-8(a)(3).

[94] IRC § 2056(d)(3). See ¶ 5.06[9] text accompanying notes 441–447. A hypothetical example might help to demonstrate the alternate consequences here. Assume donor *D* purchased real property in a joint tenancy with spouse *S*, who was not a U.S. citizen. No gift would occur on the purchase of the joint tenancy. IRC § 2523(i)(3). See ¶ 10.01[3][f] note 112. At *D*'s death, predeceasing *S*, if the property were worth $100,000 and the property were not transferred by *S* to a QDOT, $100,000 would be included in *D*'s gross estate (IRC § 2040(a)) and taxable estate (IRC § 2056(d)(1)(A)). At *S*'s death, if *S* still held the property that was then worth $200,000, the property would be included in *S*'s gross estate under Section 2033 or Section 2103 and *S*'s estate would qualify for a Section 2013 credit based on the prior $100,000 of inclusion in *D*'s gross estate.

[11] Background of the Section

Section 2040 traces its origin to the original enactment of the federal estate tax in 1916.[95] Without such provisions, joint tenancies created by way of gifts by others to the joint tenants might have entirely escaped estate taxation on the death of the first such tenant even though tenancies created by purchase by the tenant first to die might have been fitted into the provisions, also in the tax laws since 1916, concerning transfers taking effect at death.[96] In any event, in the early years when there was no gift tax, there was good reason for taxing the estate of a person who created a joint tenancy. This reason became less compelling with the advent of the gift tax provisions in 1932. Temporarily, for a period between 1954 and 1981, it once more became cogent with the adoption of gift tax provisions of the 1954 Code under which, in some circumstances, no gift tax liability arose upon the creation of the tenancy.[97]

At an early date, the estate tax provisions on joint tenancies came in for their share of attack on constitutional grounds, but such attacks were uniformly unsuccessful. An early argument was that a joint tenancy created prior to the enactment of the estate tax was not subject to the special provisions on jointly held property, but the provisions were applied retrospectively.[98] Another principal decision sustaining the constitutionality of Section 2040 is *Tyler v. United States*,[99] and a brief history of other important constitutional decisions is recounted in *United States v. Jacobs*.[100]

Alternately, if *S* timely transferred the property to a Section 2056A QDOT at *D*'s death and *D*'s executor made an election on *D*'s estate tax return, Section 2040(a) would still apply, and only $100,000 would be included in *D*'s gross estate; in addition, D would be allowed a $100,000 marital deduction (see IRC § 2056(d)(2)(A)). However, the property would be subject to estate tax under Section 2056A at its value at S's death ($200,000), which tax would be imposed at *D*'s estate tax rates. Remember that the effect of a QDOT is merely to postpone payment of estate tax on property valuing that property at the time of the payment of the tax. See IRC §§ 2056A(b)(1)(B), 2056A(b)(2); ¶ 5.07[4][b]. Assuming, again, that *S* still held the property, the property also would be included in *S*'s gross estate under Section 2033 or Section 2103 at its $200,000 value. *S*'s gross estate would again qualify for a Section 2013 credit for *D*'s Section 2056A estate tax on *D*'s $200,000 of inclusion.

[95] Revenue Act of 1916, Pub. L. No. 64-271, § 202(c), 39 Stat. 756, 778 (1916).

[96] See discussion of IRC § 2037 at ¶ 4.09.

[97] See generally IRC § 2515 (prior to repeal in the Economic Recovery Tax Act of 1981, Pub. L. No. 97-34, § 403(c)(3)(B), 95 Stat. 172, 302 (1981), reprinted in 1981-2 CB 256, 325).

[98] Gwinn v. Comm'r, 287 US 224 (1932).

[99] Tyler v. United States, 281 US 497 (1930).

[100] United States v. Jacobs, 306 US 363 (1939).

¶ 4.13 SECTION 2041. POWERS OF APPOINTMENT

[1] Introduction

A person who has a power of appointment over property has the authority to determine who, possibly including that individual, will become the beneficial owner of the property.[1] This authority, which of course always goes along with outright ownership of property, is not, however, considered an interest in the property.[2] If *A* creates a trust with suitable provision for income distribution and ultimately for distribution of the remainder but gives *B* a power of appointment over the trust, *B* has no property interest by virtue of *B*'s power. If *B* exercises the power by directing the trustee to transfer the property to *C* (the appointee), the property is considered to pass from *A* (the donor of the power) to *C* rather than from *B* (the donee of the power) to *C*. General principles of tax law respect this property law analysis of the nature of the power of appointment. Consequently, an individual who has a power of appointment over property at the time the individual dies does not have an "interest" in the property taxable in the individual's estate under Section 2033. By the same token, if the individual has exercised the power during the individual's life, such as the foregoing supposed appointment to *C*, the power holder has made no transfer of an "interest" in property such as could be taxed under Sections 2035 through 2038 if the exercise was testamentary in nature.

Nevertheless, the right to determine who may become the beneficial owner of property is such an important attribute of outright ownership that the question may be raised whether, for transfer tax purposes, it should be considered the equivalent of an ownership interest. Section 2041 (and Section 2514 of the gift tax) reflect a policy determination by Congress that sometimes this equivalence should be recognized. There is, however, a difference between retained control over property once owned by and transferred by an individual to others and control over property never actually owned by the power holder but simply received from an outside source. With regard to powers retained by a decedent in connection with lifetime transfers, Congress is content to rest tax liability on a fairly slender thread.[3] In contrast, as is more fully developed in the discussion that follows, if all the decedent ever had was a power over the property, Congress requires that the power give the decedent a more significant kind of control to be equated with ownership for estate tax purposes.

---

[1] See Casner, 5 American Law of Property § 23.1 (Little, Brown 1952). Perthman, "A Look at the Principles and Uses of Powers of Appointment," 132 Tr. & Est. 38 (Aug. 1993).

[2] The point is developed more fully in the discussion of Section 2033 at ¶ 4.05[5][c].

[3] See discussion of Sections 2036, 2037, and 2038 at ¶¶ 4.08, 4.09, 4.10.

The intricacies of Section 2041, especially the statutory definition of "general power of appointment" in Section 2041(b), reflect the congressional struggle with the question of when a power over property is sufficiently broad in scope to justify treating it as the equivalent of ownership. If a power is equated with ownership, other portions of Section 2041 attempt to say whether possession of the power at death or some type of lifetime exercise of the power are appropriate reasons for imposing a tax on the power holder's estate with respect to the property subject to the power.

[2] Powers Within Section 2041

Generally, a power of appointment is a right that may be exercised either during life or by will, not necessarily both,[4] to direct who shall become the owner of the property subject to the power. The holder of the power also often has some interest in the property; for example, a person might be the income beneficiary of a trust and at the same time have the power to appoint the principal of the trust to whomever the power holder wished, either during life or at death; but a power holder can have a power of appointment over property with respect to which the power holder has no property interest whatsoever.

A power of appointment exists if an individual has a power to appoint to anyone in the world or merely to appoint to *A* or to *B*, as the power holder may choose. Although a trust instrument may expressly give someone a "power," nomenclature is of no importance in determining whether a particular right constitutes a power of appointment.[5] A right to consume the principal of a trust is a power of appointment for federal tax purposes, and so is an unrestricted right of a person to substitute oneself for the existing trustee of a trust, if the trustee has a power of appointment.[6] In the latter case, a person may appear to have only the power to name oneself trustee, but, realistically, if the effect of the designation is to give the person a power of appointment over the property in question, the person has a power within the scope of Section 2041.

---

[4] Snyder v. United States, 203 F. Supp. 195 (WD Ky. 1962); Jenkins v. United States, 428 F2d 538 (5th Cir. 1970) (Section 2041 applicable even though the decedent could exercise the power only during life).

[5] Maytag v. United States, 72-2 USTC ¶ 12,895 (D. Colo. 1972), aff'd, 493 F2d 995 (10th Cir. 1974).

[6] Reg. § 20.2041-1(b)(1). See Estate of Small v. Comm'r, 3 TCM (CCH) 2 (1944). See also ¶ 4.08[5][a]. But see Priv. Ltr. Rul. 9741009 (July 8, 1997) (no power to appoint oneself trustee even though trustee held a general power) and Priv. Ltr. Rul. 200024007 (Mar. 7, 2000) (power to appoint self trustee but as trustee no power to appoint property to oneself), both citing Rev. Rul. 95-58, 1995-2 CB 191.

[a] Relationship to Other Sections

A power of appointment exists if the decedent has the power to affect the beneficial enjoyment of trust property or its income by altering, amending, or revoking a trust instrument or terminating the trust.[7] Such authority in the decedent is sometimes the basis for the imposition of tax under Sections 2036 and 2038 and so a question arises about an apparent statutory overlap. The regulations attempt to say which section applies, appropriately emphasizing that Section 2041 never operates to exclude from a decedent's gross estate the value of property that is includable under other sections.[8]

If *D* created a trust for the benefit of *B* but reserved an unlimited right to amend the trust, *D* would have a power of disposition over the property that is in the nature of a power of appointment. However, it is not considered a power within the scope of Section 2041. The Treasury interprets the section not to apply to powers "*reserved* by the decedent to himself," which are within the scope of other sections, such as here Section 2038.[9] Thus, Section 2038, or maybe Section 2036 but not Section 2041, would determine what was includable in the decedent's gross estate on these facts. By the same line of reasoning, it is possible for a decedent to have both a Section 2038-type power and a Section 2041-type power over different portions of property in a single trust. If *D* created the trust reserving an unlimited right to amend its terms, *D*'s power would be within the scope of Section 2038. If another person later transferred property to the same trust and it came within reach of *D*'s power to amend, *D*'s power over the latter transferred property would not be a "reserved" power, and the includability of that portion of the trust would be determined under Section 2041.[10]

---

[7] Reg. § 20.2041-1(b)(1).

[8] Reg. § 20.2041-1(b)(2). See Estate of Halpern v. Comm'r, 70 TCM (CCH) 229, 234 (1995) ("The structure of subtitle B—Estate and Gift Taxes—requires the contrary interpretation that sections 2038 and 2041 are mutually exclusive").

[9] Reg. § 20.2041-1(b)(2). The "reserved" power exception in the regulations is not as explicit as it should be, and the weakness has generated other problems. The non–Section 2041 powers should be identified explicitly as powers over property interests that have been transferred by the decedent. Thus, if *D* transfers property in trust reserving a right to appoint the remainder to other than the one named in the trust instrument, *D*'s power is outside Section 2041 regarding the property transferred. What about the subsequent income accumulations? It can be argued on these facts that post-transfer income was never *D*'s (see United States v. O'Malley, 383 US 627 (1966), contra, discussed at ¶ 4.08[8][a]) and that the power over it is outside the scope of Sections 2036 and 2038. Thus, Section 2041 might properly be applied to determine whether the accumulated income was taxable in *D*'s estate. The discussion that follows will indicate that under Section 2041, *D* would have to have more significant control over the income for it to be taxed to *D*'s estate than would be the case under either Section 2036 or Section 2038. Is this not appropriate?

[10] Estate of Shaeffer v. Comm'r, 12 TC 1047 (1949); Buckley v. Comm'r, 42 TCM (CCH) 1592 (1981). The *Shaeffer* case also reflects the possibility that, depending on lo-

[b] Powers That Overlap Interests

If the decedent has an actual ownership interest in the property, Section 2033 brings the value of that interest into the decedent's gross estate even if the decedent also has a power of appointment over the interest that, under Section 2041, would require something less or perhaps nothing at all to be included. The regulations illustrate this principle as follows:[11]

> [I]f a trust created by S provides for payment of the income to A for life with power in A to appoint the remainder by will and, in default of such appointment for payment of the income to A's widow, W, for her life and for payment of the remainder to A's estate, the value of A's interest in the remainder is includible in his gross estate under section 2033 regardless of its includibility under section 2041.

However, if, in this case, a gift to A's estate does not create a Section 2033 property interest in A, Section 2041 seems to handle the problem adequately.[12]

A power of appointment recognized under Section 2041 may arise outside the area of express trusts. For example, a testamentary bequest to a beneficiary "with full power to sell or dispose of same" and further provision for disposition of property undisposed of upon the beneficiary's death has been held to create a Section 2041 power in the beneficiary.[13] The court determined under local law that even though the beneficiary could not dispose of the property by gift, she could, under the terms of the testamentary bequest, appoint the property received under the bequest to herself or her creditors during her lifetime.[14]

Another uniquely created power may be seen to rise out of the terms of an insurance policy that provides for the payment of the income from the pol-

---

cal law, "a power of appointment may be created by implication." Estate of Shaeffer v. Comm'r, 12 TC 1047, 1051 (1949). But see First Nat'l Bank of Middlesex County v. United States, 72-2 USTC ¶ 12,872 (DNJ 1972). On the other hand, a power of appointment seemingly expressly created may lose its estate tax significance if there is an agreement, binding under state law, that the power will not be exercised. Estate of Cook v. Comm'r, 29 TCM (CCH) 298 (1970).

[11] Reg. § 20.2041-1(b)(2).

[12] It is difficult to read this example as giving A anything more than a life interest plus a general testamentary power; the remainder comes into being upon A's death, and A's estate is hardly A. This is not the equivalent of a gift to A or A's estate that would simply give A outright ownership. However, Section 2041 would tax the entire value of the property in A's estate because, by forgoing the exercise of A's express power, A can direct the disposition of the property by A's will, giving A implicitly a general power of appointment. Cf. United States v. Keeter, 461 F2d 714 (5th Cir. 1972). It is unimportant, therefore, whether A's express power is general or nongeneral and whether A has a recognizable "interest" in the property at death.

[13] Condon Nat'l Bank of Coffeyville v. United States, 349 F. Supp. 755 (D. Kan. 1972).

[14] See also Rev. Rul. 69-342, 1969-1 CB 221; infra ¶ 4.13[3].

icy proceeds to a beneficiary for life and then a distribution of the proceeds to the beneficiary's executors or administrators. It is obvious that such a disposition confers no beneficial interest on the fiduciary and that the proceeds would go to the beneficiary's heirs in case of intestacy, but that provisions in the beneficiary's will could determine who receives the proceeds. The last possibility indicates the beneficiary has a general testamentary power over the proceeds, as one court has held,[15] even though it may take some ingenuity to find it.[16]

[3] Definition of "General Power"

While it is profitable to explore what is meant by the term "power of appointment," Section 2041 generally imposes estate tax liability only with respect to the value of property subject to a *general* power of appointment.[17] The way in which the section applies depends in part on when the power was created; and, in some instances, the question whether a power is "general" depends on the date of the creation of the power. The critical date is October 21, 1942. In the discussion that follows, a power created on or before October 21, 1942, will be referred to as a pre-1942 power; one created after October 21, 1942, will be referred to as a post-1942 power. In either case the statute deals only with general powers; it seems wise to depart from the order of Section 2041 and begin with paragraph (1) of Section 2041(b), which defines "general power."

The estate tax definition of "general power" is at variance with traditional property law concepts. The basic rule in Section 2041(b)(1) is that a power is general if it "is exercisable in favor of the decedent,[18] his estate, his creditors, or the creditors of his estate"—roughly speaking, one that can be exercised directly or indirectly for the decedent's own benefit. If the decedent can appoint

---

[15] United States v. Keeter, 461 F2d 714 (5th Cir. 1972). See also Pittsburgh Nat'l Bank v. United States, 319 F. Supp. 176 (WD Pa. 1970) (a decedent's power as co-trustee to sell the trust corpus, which under the governing instrument would cause a termination of the trust and distribution to the decedent and others, was held to constitute a Section 2041 power).

[16] Contra Second Nat'l Bank of Danville v. Dallman, 209 F2d 321 (7th Cir. 1954). See ¶ 4.05[6] note 76.

[17] IRC § 2041(a)(3), discussed infra ¶ 4.13[8][b], indicates one very minor exception. See Texas Commerce Bank v. United States, 807 F. Supp. 50 (SD Tex. 1992).

[18] See Rev. Rul. 79-159, 1979-1 CB 301; Priv. Ltr. Rul. 9936052 (June 16, 1999) (right to take larger distributions than provided in an IRA was a general power of appointment); TAM 9431004 (Aug. 5, 1994) (ability to mortgage real estate held in trust constituted a general power of appointment, rather than an administrative power); FSA 199930026 (Apr. 29, 1999) (fiduciary obligation as trustee precluded a power of appointment to oneself). Cf. Rev. Rul. 77-460, 1977-2 CB 323.

to any of these appointees,[19] the decedent has a general power, subject to important exceptions discussed later.

Whether one has the legal right to appoint to oneself or others is determined by the interpretation of the governing instrument under local law.[20] This issue sometimes arises in connection with the marital deduction.[21] The extent of the legal right to appoint depends on local statutes and local case law, but not necessarily on a local adjudication.[22] If, under state law, a trust provision purporting to give the decedent a right to invade the corpus of a trust is invalid, the decedent does not have a power of appointment under Section 2041, general or otherwise.[23] However, whether the rights the decedent enjoys under state law constitute a general power for estate tax purposes is a federal question as to which local characterization of one's right is not controlling.[24]

---

[19] Emphasizing the use of the disjunctive "or" in the phrase "the decedent, his estate, his creditors or the creditors of his estate," the Tax Court has held that a power to appoint only to the decedent's estate is a general power. Estate of Edelman v. Comm'r, 38 TC 972 (1962). Smith v. United States, 557 F. Supp. 723 (D. Conn. 1982), also so holds. Cf. supra ¶ 4.13[4] text accompanying note 4. However, relying on First Nat'l Bank of Omaha v. United States, 681 F2d 534 (8th Cir. 1982), cert. denied, 459 U.S. 1104 (1983), the Service has ruled that when the language in a trust conferring a power of appointment over property is precatory in nature, the person to whom the power is conferred is not considered to hold a general power of appointment. See Priv. Ltr. Rul. 9304020 (Nov. 2, 1992).

[20] Cf. Rev. Rul. 76-502, 1976-2 CB 273.

[21] See ¶¶ 5.06[8][b][iii], 5.06[8][b][iv].

[22] Estate of Bosch v. Comm'r, 387 US 456 (1967); Estate of Carson v. Comm'r, 33 TCM (CCH) 1434 (1974). State courts' interpretations of trusts determining a decedent's powers often are effective in determining whether a decedent holds a general power. See Pitt v. United States, 98-2 USTC ¶ 60,314 (E.D. Mich. 1998) (no general power); Powers v. United States, 37 Fed. Cl. 709 (Ct. Cl. 1997) (general power); Priv. Ltr. Rul. 200043036 (July 27, 2000) (no general power); Priv. Ltr. Rul. 200045004 (June 30, 2000) (same); Priv. Ltr. Rul. 9743033 (July 25, 1997) (ruling conditional on favorable state court ruling).

[23] Rev. Rul. 54-153, 1954-1 CB 185 (NY law); Priv. Ltr. Rul. 200014002 (Nov. 29, 1999) (Mo. law). See also Rev. Rul. 53-243, 1953-2 CB 267 (the power is a general power in the absence of such a statute).

[24] Morgan v. Comm'r, 309 US 78 (1940), opinion amended and reh'g denied, 309 US 626 (1940). Cf. Blair v. Comm'r, 300 US 5 (1937); Estate of Aldrich v. Comm'r, 425 F2d 1395 (5th Cir. 1970). See discussion of state and federal law question under Section 2033 at ¶ 4.05[2]. The Service has indicated that it will not recognize state legislation that retroactively changes an individual's property rights or powers after federal tax consequences have attached. Rev. Proc. 94-44, 1994-2 CB 683.

[4] Exceptions to General Definition

There are a number of exceptions to the basic rule on what constitutes a general power of appointment.

[a] Power Limited by a Standard

The first exception relates to a power exercisable in favor of the decedent. The decedent may be given a power to appoint to anyone in the world; this is clearly a general power of appointment. In other cases, the decedent may be given a power to consume, invade, or appropriate property for the decedent's own benefit; this is also within the basic definition of "general power," as it is a power to appoint to oneself. However, under Section 2041(b)(1)(A), if a power may be exercised only in accordance with an ascertainable standard relating to the decedent's health, education, support, or maintenance, it is not treated as a general power of appointment.[25] An otherwise ascertainable standard that does not relate to the decedent's health, education, support, or maintenance is inadequate. This is one of several provisions in Section 2041 that create substantial flexibility in the use of powers to accomplish legitimate family objectives without onerous estate tax consequences. Especially in the case of modest trusts, the maintenance of the beneficiary may sometimes require an encroachment on the principal. If the beneficiary has the right to get at principal only for that purpose, there seems to be little reason for imposing tax on the beneficiary's estate with respect to that right.[26]

A critical question is whether the decedent's power is in fact limited by an ascertainable standard.[27] The regulations provide that a power exercisable for "comfort, welfare, or happiness" of the power holder is not limited by an ascertainable standard.[28] They also treat the statute as raising the question whether the right to invade[29] is "reasonably measurable in terms of . . . needs for health, education or support (or any combination of them)" and treat "maintenance" as a useless appendage having the same meaning as "sup-

---

[25] IRC § 2041(b)(1)(A). See generally Randall & Schmidt, "The Comforts of the Ascertainable Standard Exception," 59 Taxes 242 (1981); Schneider & White, "Current Interpretations of Ascertainable Standard' Affect the Drafting of Powers," 11 Est. Plan. 16 (1984); Harris, "Ascertainable Standard Restrictions on Trust Powers Under the Estate, Gift and Income Tax," 50 Tax Law. 489 (1997) (in part comparing standards under Section 2041 with standards under Sections 2036 and 2038).

[26] See infra ¶ 4.13[8][a]. However, some features of the tax on generation-skipping transfers are antagonistic to this concept. See IRC § 2612(b); ¶ 13.02[3].

[27] Reg. § 20.2041-1(c)(2). Cf. Jennings v. Smith, 161 F2d 74 (2d Cir. 1947).

[28] Reg. § 20.2041-1(c)(2).

[29] See discussion of an ascertainable standard under Section 2038 at ¶ 4.10[5].

port."[30] With regard to "support," early proposed regulations in the same paragraph provided: "The meaning is not limited to the bare necessities of life *and includes other reasonable living expenses, but it does not necessarily extend to all expenditures that might be considered customary in the decedent's position in life.*" However, the adopted regulations reflect a somewhat less narrow view of the support concept by omitting the italicized portion of the preceding quotation.[31]

The draftsman can stay within the Treasury's view of the invasion exception by limiting the right to exercise for the holder's "support," "support in reasonable comfort," "support in his accustomed manner of living," "education, including college and professional education," "health," and "medical, dental, hospital and nursing expenses and expenses of invalidism."[32] Beyond these guidelines it is difficult to generalize. Seemingly inconsistent results are not uncommon. For example, "support, care and comfort" has been held not to constitute an ascertainable standard,[33] while "maintenance, comfort and happiness" has been upheld.[34] The reason for these inconsistencies is that the federal courts generally look to state law to determine whether a standard exists.[35] Although the federal courts are rarely bound by the local adjudication of a case, they do nevertheless give proper regard to state adjudications of cases employing similar standards.[36] This leads to the type of discrepancy illustrated earlier.[37]

---

[30] Reg. § 20.2041-1(c)(2); Priv. Ltr. Rul. 9713008 (Dec. 10, 1996) ("care" was also synonymous with support where the standard examined authorized invasion for "proper care, maintenance and support").

[31] Reg. § 20.2041-1(c)(2).

[32] Reg. § 20.2041-1(c)(2). The regulations provide that a power to invade for support can be within the exception regardless of "whether the beneficiary is required to exhaust his other income before the power can be exercised."

[33] Whelan v. United States, 81-1 USTC ¶ 13,393 (SD Cal. 1980) (California law).

[34] Brantingham v. United States, 631 F2d 542 (7th Cir. 1980) (Massachusetts law).

[35] Morgan v. Comm'r, 309 US 78 (1940), opinion amended and reh'g denied, 309 US 626 (1940). Retroactive state legislation may not be respected. See supra ¶ 4.13[3] note 24.

[36] Estate of Bosch v. Comm'r, 387 US 456 (1967); Rev. Rul. 69-285, 1969-1 CB 222; Estate of Lanigan v. Comm'r, 45 TC 247 (1965) (local adjudication not binding on federal court); ¶ 4.05[2][b]. Cf. Priv. Ltr. Rul. 8339004 (1983); Priv. Ltr. Rul. 8346008 (1984).

[37] See supra text accompanying notes 33, 34. Cases and rulings have held the following standards *adequate*: Vissering v. Comm'r, 990 F2d 578 (10th Cir. 1993) (Florida law) (decedent's power to invade trust corpus to the "extent required for his continued comfort" did not constitute a general power of appointment); invasion "if she the beneficiary desires," Finlay v. United States, 752 F2d 246 (6th Cir. 1985) (Tennessee law); "emergency or illness," Sowell v. Comm'r, 708 F2d 1564 (10th Cir. 1983) (New Mexico law); "any emergency," Hunter v. United States, 597 F. Supp. 1293 (WD Pa. 1984) (Pennsylvania law); "financial emergency . . . as a result of accident, illness, or other natural cir-

It is apparent that a trust can be set up for a beneficiary and a considerable amount of leeway provided for the beneficiary's use of the corpus without inviting estate tax liability upon the death of the beneficiary. Nevertheless, close cases decided for and against taxpayers suggest caution.[38]

[b] Certain Pre-1942 Powers

Under Section 2041(b)(1)(B), another power that is within the basic definition of "general power" is not to be treated as a general power. This exception concerns only pre-1942 powers. If a pre-1942 power can be exercised by the decedent only in conjunction with some other person, it is not a general power for estate tax purposes. It is immaterial who the person may be or what rights or interests the person may have or have had in the property. The reasons for the exception are more historical than logical.[39] This exception is clear cut, but it affords little or no opportunity for current estate planning, relating, as it does, only to powers that have been created at a much earlier date.

---

cumstances," Wahlfield v. United States, 47 AFTR2d 81-1565 (CD Ill. 1980) (Illinois law); invasion "as he the beneficiary may . . . request, being . . . the sole judge of his needs," Pittsfield Nat'l Bank v. United States, 181 F. Supp. 851 (D. Mass. 1960) (Massachusetts law); "the right to use all or any part of the principal as she the beneficiary may see fit," Barritt v. Tomlinson, 129 F. Supp. 642 (SD Fla. 1955) (Florida law); "reasonable support, care, maintenance and education" or "proper care, maintenance and support," Priv. Ltr. Rul. 9713008 (Dec. 10, 1996).

Following are cases and rulings finding an *inadequate* standard: "exercise for taxpayer's benefit," De Oliveira v. United States, 767 F2d 1344 (9th Cir. 1985) (California law); "for whatever purpose she the beneficiary desires," Independent Bank of Waukesha v. United States, 761 F2d 442 (7th Cir. 1985) (Wisconsin law); "comfort and care as she the beneficiary may see fit," First Va. Bank v. United States, 490 F2d 532 (4th Cir. 1974) (Virginia law); "use, benefit, comfort, support, and maintenance," Lehman v. United States, 448 F2d 1318 (5th Cir. 1971) (Texas law); invasion as spouse "may require; she to be the sole judge," "care and comfort," Estate of Strauss v. Comm'r, 69 TCM (CCH) 2825 (1995) (Illinois law); Estate of Little v. Comm'r, 87 TC 599 (1986) (California law); "for business purposes," Estate of Penner v. Comm'r, 67 TC 864 (1977) (New York law); "care, maintenance, health, welfare and well-being," Estate of Jones v. Comm'r, 56 TC 35 (1971) (New Jersey law); "necessary and desirable," Estate of Hyde v. Comm'r, 950 F. Supp. 418 (DNH 1996) (New Hampshire law); "proper comfort and welfare," Rev. Rul. 77-194, 1977-1 CB 283 (New Jersey law); "health, care, maintenance and enjoyment," Rev. Rul. 76-547, 1976-2 CB 302 (Washington law); "advisable for . . . happiness, health, support, and maintenance," United States v. Forsee, 76 F. Supp. 2d 1135 (D Ka. 2001) (Kansas law).

For a further listing of cases, see the table in Randall & Schmidt, "The Comforts of the Ascertainable Standard Exception," 59 Taxes 242, 247 (1981).

[38] See supra note 37.

[39] See IRC § 811(f)(3)(B) (1939), prior to amendment in the Powers of Appointment Act of 1951, Pub. L. No. 82-58, § 2(a), 65 Stat. 91, 92 (1951), reprinted in 1951-2 CB 343, 344.

[c] Post-1942 Powers With Another Person

A much more complicated set of exceptions to the basic definition of "general power" is found in Section 2041(b)(1)(C). As noted, Section 2041(b)(1)(B) places *pre*-1942 powers, exercisable by the decedent only in conjunction with another person, *any* other person, outside the category of general powers. Under Section 2041(b)(1)(C), three exceptions are provided relating to *post*-1942 powers that may be exercised by the decedent only in conjunction with another person. In the following discussion of these three rules, it is important to keep in mind that the question is only whether or to what extent the power is to be treated as a general power; if the power is found to be general, further considerations, subsequently discussed, then come into play to determine the effect of the power on the decedent's gross estate. But a determination that the power is *not* general usually means that the property subject to the power will not be included in the decedent's gross estate.

[i] **Power held with the creator of the power.** If the decedent can exercise a power only in conjunction with its creator, the decedent does not have a general power of appointment. Of course, in these circumstances, Sections 2036 and 2038 may bring the value of the property or some part of it into the estate of the creator of the power for federal estate tax purposes. Either estate or gift tax liability will result upon the death of the creator of the power or the creator's lifetime exercise or relinquishment of it, and perhaps both estate *and* gift tax liability in the case of such exercise or relinquishment. These reasons support the exception.[40]

[ii] **Power held with an adverse party.** If the decedent can exercise a power only in conjunction with someone who has a substantial interest in the appointive property, which interest will be adversely affected by an exercise of the power in favor of the decedent, the decedent does not have a general power of appointment. It has been held that *A* has an interest adverse to the exercise of a power in favor of *B* if *A* has "a present or future chance to obtain a personal benefit from the property" subject to *B*'s power.[41] But a mere co-trustee has no interest, adverse or otherwise.[42] Similarly, if *C* has a beneficial interest in a trust that would be adversely affected by an exercise of the power in favor of *D*, *D*'s power is not rendered nongeneral by a requirement that *C*'s spouse, *E*, join in the exercise of the power; *E* might suffer some ad-

---

[40] S. Rep. No. 382, 82d Cong., 1st Sess. 5 (1951).

[41] Estate of Towle v. Comm'r, 54 TC 368 (1970); Rev. Rul. 79-63, 1979-1 CB 302.

[42] Miller v. United States, 387 F2d 866 (3rd Cir. 1968). Cf. Picciano v. United States, 81-2 USTC ¶ 13,433 (WD Ohio 1981). See also Rev. Rul. 82-156, 1982-2 CB 216 (general power could be exercised either with an adverse party or with a trustee (who was not adverse) was held to be a Section 2041 power), Priv. Ltr. Rul. 8704005 (Oct. 9, 1986) (trustee was an adverse party, and, thus, no general power).

versity if C is deprived of C's interest, but E has no chance for direct personal benefit from the property.[43]

Other interpretations of the adverse interest exception, even if settled, seem more controversial. For example, if D has a power to appoint to D the corpus of a trust under which B is otherwise entitled to the income for life and R to the remainder, D has a general power of appointment. But such a power is rendered nongeneral under the exception if D can exercise the power only in conjunction with B, or only with R, for both have interests adverse to an exercise of the power in D's favor.[44] The statute seems to contemplate a "total" exemption of such powers,[45] even though realistically it would seem that if the power could be exercised only with B, D could buy off B for the value of B's life interest and thus gain the right to defeat R altogether. Should D then be regarded as having a general power to the extent of the value of the remainder interest?[46] The problem seems to be more muddled than clarified by the statement in the Senate Finance Committee Report on the Powers of Appointment Act of 1951 that "principles developed under the income and gift taxes will be applicable in determining whether an interest is substantial and the amount of property in which the adversity exists."[47]

Perhaps within permissible limits of interpretation better sense can be made of the statute if it is recognized that what may be referred to broadly as a general power may in fact authorize the holder to deal with the property in several different ways. If so, the holder should be viewed as having several powers, which can be tested separately to see if they are general.[48] Thus, in the preceding example, D's general power might enable D to appoint the remainder, after B's interest, to anyone. If so, should D not be viewed as having a general power over the remainder interest even if exercisable only with B? B's interest would not be adverse to an exercise of such a power.

The statute makes it unnecessary to speculate whether one who would have a right to appoint the property in question to oneself after the death of the decedent has an interest in the property and, if so, whether such an interest would be adversely affected by an exercise of the decedent's power. By ex-

---

[43] Cf. Pittsburgh Nat'l Bank v. United States, 319 F. Supp. 176 (WD Pa. 1970); Latta v. Comm'r, 212 F2d 164 (3d Cir.), cert. denied, 348 US 825 (1954). It is unlikely, also, that collateral agreements regarding the exercise of a power, even if enforceable, will bring into play the exceptions of Section 2041(b)(1)(C)(ii). See Witkowski v. United States, 451 F2d 1249 (5th Cir. 1971).

[44] Reg. §§ 20.2041-3(c)(2) Exs. 1, 2; Priv. Ltr. Rul. 199933020 (May 19, 1999).

[45] S. Rep. No. 382, 82d Cong., 1st Sess. 5 (1951).

[46] Cf. Camp v. Comm'r, 195 F2d 999, 1004 (1st Cir. 1952).

[47] S. Rep. No. 382, 82d Cong., 1st Sess. 5 (1951).

[48] See Rev. Rul. 79-63, 1979-1 CB 302; Priv. Ltr. Rul. 199933020 (May 19, 1999) (5 or 5 power in part was a general power of appointment but not a general power to the extent held with an adverse party).

press provision, such a future power is to be deemed an *interest* and the interest so recognized is deemed to be *adverse* to the exercise of the decedent's power. If this seems so logical as not to need statutory expression, it must be remembered that a power is not an "interest" in property. Consequently, without the statutory assist, the contingent power could not qualify as an interest, adverse or otherwise.

[iii] **Power held with an equally interested party.** After the application of the first and second rules, just discussed, the decedent may have a general power, even if the power was exercisable only in conjunction with another person, if the person was not the creator of the power and did not have a substantial interest in the property that would be adversely affected by an exercise in favor of the decedent. However, clause (iii) of Section 2041(b)(1)(C) makes a further limited exception applicable to a case in which the other person who must join is one in whose favor the power *may* be exercised. The rule appears to be based on a concept of self-interest. If the decedent's power to appoint to himself, his estate, his creditors, or the creditors of his estate can be exercised only in conjunction with one other person in whose favor the power may also be exercised, only one half of the value of the property will be treated as subject to a general power of appointment in the decedent. The apparent reasoning here is that upon an exercise of the power, the other person would, or at least could, insist that half of the property be appointed to that other person so that in practical effect the decedent should be treated as if the decedent owned only one half of the property.[49] This reasoning carries over to a situation in which more than one other person in whose favor the power may be exercised is required to join. Thus, if there are two other possible appointees with whom the decedent must join in order to exercise the power, only one third of the value of the property is treated as subject to a general power of appointment for the purpose of determining the decedent's gross estate.[50]

This rule creates an interesting situation from the point of view of a drafter of a will. By requiring that several persons who are possible appointees join in the exercise of a power, the drafter can reduce the value of a property interest that may be included in the estate of a particular decedent. But, of course, the estate of any of the others may include a portion of the value of the property. If the estate of one who must join is to be protected from possible estate tax liability, such person must be removed from the class of persons in whose favor the property can be appointed, which may defeat the drafter's purpose, or the power must be exercisable by the survivors alone after death.

---

[49] If the exceptions in Clauses (ii) and (iii) of Section 2041(b)(1)(C) appear similar, the difference is that (iii) will come into play where (ii) is not applicable because the co-holder's power does not survive the decedent's death.

[50] Reg. § 20.2041-3(c)(3); Rev. Rul. 77-158, 1977-1 CB 285; Rev. Rul. 76-503, 1976-2 CB 275.

In applying the second and third rules just discussed, which may operate to render a post-1942 power that is otherwise general, nongeneral in whole or in part because another who must join in its exercise is a permissive appointee, the statute expressly indicates that a power is to be treated as exercisable in favor of a person if it can be exercised to benefit the person directly, or in favor of the person's estate, creditors, or the creditors of the estate. This, of course, parallels the basic test of whether a person has a general power of appointment.

[d] Judicious Use of Powers

The major revision of the powers-of-appointment provisions in 1951, since which time there has been no substantial change,[51] was not designed to raise the greatest possible amount of revenue. On the contrary, a principal purpose was to make the law simple and definite enough to be understood and applied by the average lawyer. It may surely be questioned whether the "simple and definite" objective was achieved, but even so, one should recognize that Congress has left considerable room for the judicious use of powers of appointment in planning at substantial tax savings. To some extent, this is reflected in the previous discussion of the numerous exceptions to the basic definition of general powers. It will be further evident in the ensuing discussion of the actual tax treatment of such powers.[52] In making advantageous use of powers, the tax on generation-skipping transfers also must be considered.[53]

[5] Introduction to Treatment of General Powers

With the foregoing discussion of what constitutes a general power of appointment in mind, it is now necessary to consider the statutory estate tax treatment of powers. The need for a statutory provision dealing specifically with powers arises in part out of the fact that a power of appointment, even when it strongly resembles ownership, is not an interest in property within the scope of Section 2033. The Supreme Court has so held with respect to a trust created by another under which the decedent had the exclusive enjoyment of property during life, the right to absolute ownership upon attaining a specified age, *and* the sole and unrestricted right to designate who should have the trust property

---

[51] Cf. IRC §§ 2045, 2518.

[52] See infra ¶ 4.13[8][a]. See also Halbach, "The Use of Powers of Appointment in Estate Planning," 45 Iowa L. Rev. 691 (1960); "Use and Drafting of Powers of Appointment," 1 Real Prop., Prob. & Tr. J. 307 (1966). Both articles are concerned with the pre-1986 law under which there was no tax on generation-skipping transfers.

[53] See Chapters 12–18, especially ¶¶ 13.02[2][d], 17.02[3][b].

after the decedent's death.[54] The present effect of this decision is to foreclose the application of Section 2033 to property with respect to which the decedent had only a power of appointment, even though the combination of circumstances just suggested seems to identify realistic ownership of property. The decision has not been overruled. When the decedent has a power of appointment but no interest recognized as within Section 2033, and when other sections are likewise inapplicable, what, if anything, may be included in the decedent's gross estate must be determined under Section 2041.

As previously indicated, pre-1942 and post-1942 powers must be considered separately. In general, a pre-1942 power, as the term is used here, is one that was created on or before October 21, 1942; the date of its creation is the date the instrument creating it became effective. Thus, if the power was created by an inter vivos instrument, the date of creation was the date of delivery of the instrument, even if the instrument was revocable, because it would be effective until revoked.[55] A power created by will is created at the date of the creator testator's death, because a will is not effective until then.[56]

[6] Treatment of Pre-1942 Powers

A pre-1942 power of appointment held by the decedent gives rise to estate tax inclusion only if the power is a *general* power and the decedent *exercises* the power. It is perfectly clear that if the decedent had a general power and took appropriate action under local law to exercise that power by will, a renunciation by the appointees that may prevent the property from "passing" under the power will not save the decedent's estate from liability under Section 2041.[57] This once-settled principle is probably unaffected by the provisions on disclaimers[58] that retract the transfer but not necessarily the exercise of the power.[59] Moreover, it also appears to be settled that even if the decedent by will exercises a general power of appointment in favor of the takers in default of exercise so that the exercise is ineffective in the sense that the appointees

---

[54] Helvering v. Safe Dep. & Trust Co., 316 US 56 (1942).

[55] Reg. § 20.2041-1(e).

[56] Under Section 2041(b)(3), some powers not actually coming into existence until later are treated as pre-1942 powers. Specifically, a power created by a will executed on or before the critical date is to be considered a pre-1942 power even if the creator of the power does not die until later; but this special rule on the date of creation applies only if the creator has died before July 1, 1949, without republishing one's will, by codicil or otherwise, after the critical 1942 date.

[57] Reg. § 20.2041-1(d); S. Rep. No. 382, 82d Cong., 1st Sess. 5 (1951).

[58] IRC §§ 2045, 2518.

[59] See HR Rep. No. 1380, 94th Cong., 2d Sess. 1, 65–67 (1976), reprinted in 1976-3 CB (Vol. 3) 735, 799–801.

would have received the property anyway, the statute is satisfied.[60] However, an invalid attempt to exercise is not treated as an exercise of the power.[61]

[a] Exercise of Power

The risk in the present rule is one of an unwitting exercise of a pre-1942 power.[62] In *Keating v. Mayer*[63] the power was not expressly exercised but tax liability resulted, because, under a Pennsylvania statute, a general devise of real estate or a bequest of personal property described in a general way operated as an exercise of a power over such property unless a contrary intention appeared in the will. An exercise of a pre-1942 power in favor of the takers in default gives rise to tax that is entirely avoidable without any change in the disposition of the property, for nonexercise of a pre-1942 power is not taxable.

Although it is suggested in the court's opinion in the *Keating* case[64] that the exercise need not be "effective" to constitute an exercise within Section 2041, the use of the term may be misleading. The taxpayer's argument was that the Pennsylvania courts viewed the exercise to those who would take in default as a nullity because they would get the property anyway. That an exercise was "ineffective" in this sense will not save the estate from Section 2041. But the Treasury recognizes that there is no exercise unless the decedent takes the appropriate steps under local law to accomplish such exercise.[65] For example, in the *Keating* case there was an exercise only because Pennsylvania law said the general provisions in the will had that effect.[66] An express attempt to exercise a power by a provision in a will that was subsequently held invalid would not be within the statute. In this sense, at least, an ineffective exercise is not an exercise under Section 2041.

Of course, not every exercise of a general pre-1942 power will cause the value of the property subject to the power to be included in the decedent's gross estate; the power must be exercised either *by will or in some other man-*

---

[60] Keating v. Mayer, 236 F2d 478 (3d Cir. 1956); Reg. § 20.2041-1(d). See also United States v. Keeter, 461 F2d 714 (5th Cir. 1972).

[61] Estate of Minot v. Comm'r, 45 TC 578 (1966).

[62] Pennell & Stansfield, "Inadvertent Exercise of Powers of Appointment," Ests., Gifts & Tr. J., at 34 (Nov.-Dec. 1980). See Priv. Ltr. Rul. 199924014 (Mar. 16, 1999) (division of trust and designation of beneficiaries constituted an exercise).

[63] Keating v. Mayer, 236 F2d 478 (3d Cir. 1956). See also Stewart v. United States, 512 F2d 269 (5th Cir. 1975); United States v. Merchant's Nat'l Bank, 261 F2d 570 (5th Cir. 1958); Bartol v. McGinnes, 185 F. Supp. 659 (ED Pa. 1960).

[64] Keating v. Mayer, 236 F2d 478, 481 (3d Cir. 1956).

[65] Reg. § 20.2041-1(d). See also Rev. Rul. 55-486, 1955-2 CB 605; Estate of Minot v. Comm'r, 45 TC 578, 587 (1966).

[66] But see White v. United States, 81-1 USTC ¶ 13,404 (SD Ind. 1981) (New York and Illinois law).

ner akin to testamentary disposition in order to cause estate tax liability.[67] It is clear enough that if a person who has a general pre-1942 power exercises the power by will, the person's gross estate will include the value of the property subject to the power. If the power is exercised only in part, that is, if by will the decedent appoints only a part of the property subject to the power and permits the rest to pass by default, possibly only the value of the property actually appointed is included in the person's gross estate.[68] On the other hand, there is authority for including the whole property even though the exercise of the power related to only a part (a life estate) of the property.[69] Caution suggests a conscious hands-off policy with regard to pre-1942 powers, if non–estate tax considerations permit it.[70]

What other manner of exercise will also result in estate tax liability? Section 2041(a)(1)(B) provides that if a pre-1942 general power is exercised by a disposition of a type that would be caught by Sections 2035 through 2038 if an actual transfer of property were involved, estate tax liability results. Accordingly, an exercise with retained life interests (Section 2036), an exercise effective at the decedent's death (Section 2037), or a revocable exercise of the power (Section 2038) is an exercise of a power that is treated the same as an exercise by will at death.[71] For example, assume X created a trust before 1942 under which the income was payable to B for life, remainder to whomever D may appoint by deed during D's life and, in default of appointment, to R. D has a general power of appointment over the remainder. If D exercises the power by providing that upon the death of B, the income is to be paid to D for life with a remainder to R, D has made a lifetime exercise of a power within the purview of Section 2036, that is, an exercise with a reservation of the right to the income for life.[72] If D later dies while B is still living, Section 2041 brings into D's gross estate the value of the property over which D exercised

---

[67] The possibility of gift tax liability arising out of a lifetime exercise is dealt with in the discussion of Section 2514 at ¶ 10.04.

[68] Estate of Wooster v. Comm'r, 9 TC 742 (1947); Reg. § 20.2041-2(f).

[69] Estate of Gartland v. Comm'r, 293 F2d 575 (7th Cir. 1961), cert. denied, 368 US 954 (1962).

[70] However, income tax basis considerations combined with a large unified credit may lead to a different course of action.

The exercise of a pre-1942 power may result in a direct skip generation-skipping transfer. See ¶ 13.02[4][b] notes 265–268.

[71] Under current law, a pre-1942 power can interact with Section 2035 only in extremely limited circumstances. If a decedent had held a pre-1942 power that the decedent previously exercised retaining a Section 2036, 2037, or 2038 interest or power and the decedent then relinquished such interest or power within three years of death, Section 2041(a)(1)(B) would apply interacting with Section 2035.

[72] Reg. § 20.2041-2(c) Ex. 2. See the discussion of Section 2036 at ¶ 4.08. See Henderson v. Rogan, 159 F2d 855 (9th Cir. 1947), cert. denied, 331 US 843 (1947) (decided the same way under the forerunner of Section 2037).

the power, that is, the entire value of the trust property less the value of B's outstanding life interest. If D dies after B, the entire value of the trust property is included in D's estate because it is the date-of-death or alternate date value of the interest over which D exercised the power that is to be included in D's gross estate,[73] and B's outstanding interest will have been extinguished by B's death.

[b] Failure to Exercise

The statute is explicit that a failure to exercise shall not be deemed an exercise (not treated as a negative exercise) of a pre-1942 power. Although this seems superfluous, it is likely in many cases that inaction on the part of the decedent accomplishes the same thing that the decedent would undertake to accomplish by an exercise of the power; the one who takes in default may be the one to whom the decedent would appoint. Be that as it may, inaction with respect to a pre-1942 power does not result in estate tax liability.

[c] Complete Release

Moreover, the statute also specifies that a complete release of a general pre-1942 power is not to be deemed an exercise of the power. Again, this may be the rough equivalent of an exercise of the power, for by such release the decedent may have secured the rights of the taker in default, which may be just what the decedent would have otherwise done by an exercise of the decedent's power at death. In any event, such complete release will not cause estate tax liability because, with respect to pre-1942 powers, liability results only from an *exercise of a general* power, and the statute says expressly that a complete release shall not be deemed an exercise.[74] There is a problem, however, as to what constitutes a "complete" release; the regulations include a somewhat obscure example of a partial exercise of a power coupled with a subsequent complete release, which may be viewed as an exercise rather than a release.[75] In this light, unless non−estate tax reasons call for an exercise of a pre-1942 power, inaction rather than release seems the safest course, although income tax basis considerations combined with the unified credit may lead to a different course of action. In the case of inaction, all the decedent needs to worry about is inadvertent exercise, such as apparently occurred in the *Keating* case discussed earlier, if the decedent would escape estate tax liability.

---

[73] See discussion of Sections 2031 and 2032 at ¶¶ 4.02, 4.03.

[74] Estate of Mitchell v. Comm'r, 835 F2d 138 (6th Cir. 1987).

[75] Reg. § 20.2041-2(d).

[d] Partial Release of Pre-1942 Powers

The statute also deals expressly with the effect of partial release and subsequent exercise of pre-1942 general powers. The problem dealt with here is whether by a partial release of a general pre-1942 power it can be converted to a nongeneral power, the exercise of which will not result in estate tax liability. The general answer is that it cannot be converted; this is only implicit in the statute, but the regulations expressly and appropriately provide, subject to a minor exception,[76] that the exercise of a pre-1942 power that was a general power but that has been partially released so as to make it no longer a general power will constitute the exercise of a general power of appointment.[77] Such an interpretation seems warranted, as any other rule would obviously permit a frustration of the clear statutory purpose.

---

[76] In very limited circumstances, powers that were originally pre-1942 general powers may be effectively removed from the general power category. The statutory rule is that if a pre-1942 general power is partially released either (1) prior to November 1, 1951, or (2) not later than six months after the termination of a legal disability if the donee of the power was under such disability on October 21, 1942, whichever date is later, so that the power is no longer a general power of appointment, the exercise of the power shall not be deemed to be an exercise of a general power of appointment. IRC § 2041(a)(1) (last sentence). This, of course, does not present a major tax loophole; conversion of a general pre-1942 power to a nongeneral one can be accomplished to defeat the application of Section 2041 only if action was reasonably taken in 1951 or earlier, or if the donee was under a disability in 1942 and the action is taken shortly after the removal of the disability.

There is litigation on whether a pre-1942 general power has been effectively reduced to a nongeneral power before the critical dates. See, e.g., Estate of Drake v. Comm'r, 67 TC 844 (1977). In one case, the decedent had a general power created in 1931. Simons v. United States, 135 F. Supp. 461 (EDNY), aff'd per curiam, 227 F2d 168 (2d Cir. 1955), cert. denied, 350 US 949 (1956). In 1940, she executed her will, under which she appointed property to certain relatives. In 1941, illness caused her to become legally incapacitated, and she died in 1949 without ever regaining testamentary capacity. The estate's argument was that the execution of the will followed by the decedent's incapacity was the practical equivalent of a reduction of the general power to a nongeneral power to appoint only to those named in the will. But the court treated the will provision as a taxable exercise of a general power.

The Tax Court has held that a transaction, which in form was an exercise of a general pre-1942 power followed by a release prior to November 1, 1951, was in *substance* a reduction of the power followed by a release so that Section 2041 was inapplicable. Estate of Lombard v. Comm'r, 46 TC 310 (1966), acq. 1967-1 CB 2. The court stated that the Congressional purpose for this exemption from estate tax in the case of a pre-November 1, 1951 release was to protect from tax a donee of a power who disabled himself from exercising the power for the benefit of others than those in the exempted class. Other courts have also advanced this liberal interpretation of the provisions regarding release before November 1, 1951. Kynett v. United States, 201 F. Supp. 609 (ED Pa. 1962); Emery v. United States, 153 F. Supp. 248 (D. Mass. 1957).

[77] Reg. § 20.2041-2(e).

[7] Treatment of Post-1942 Powers

As previously stated, post-1942 powers are treated differently than pre-1942 powers. The principal differences are that the later created powers need not be exercised by the decedent in order to cause tax liability to the decedent's estate, and that estate tax liability may result even from the complete release of these powers. Here, a release is treated as a negative exercise of the power, but, again, the power must as a rule be a general power to be caught by the statute.

The rules on post-1942 powers appear in Section 2041(a)(2). Several tests determine whether the value of property subject to a post-1942 general power of appointment in the decedent must be included in the decedent's gross estate.

[a] Possession

First, did the decedent *have* a general power of appointment at the time of death? In other words, possession of a post-1942 general power of appointment is now treated as the equivalent of ownership of the property subject to the power for federal estate tax purposes.[78] The Treasury has ruled that a person can have a general power even though at all times after its creation the person is under a legal disability to exercise it,[79] and the courts agree.[80] It has also been held that mere possession of a post-1942 general power of appointment is sufficient to cause inclusion of the property in a decedent's gross estate even though the decedent is unaware of the power's existence.[81] Moreover,

---

[78] In Estate of Council v. Comm'r, 65 TC 594 (1975), acq. 1976-2 CB 1 (decedent had made an inter vivos exercise of a power so there was no possession of the power at her death).

[79] Rev. Rul. 75-351, 1975-2 CB 368, Rev. Rul. 55-518, 1955-2 CB 384. It is probably of no significance that while this principle was expressed in Prop. Reg. § 20.2041-3(b), Notice of Proposed Rule Making, 21 Fed. Reg. 7850, 7882 (1956), it does not appear in the current regulations.

[80] All circuits that have considered this issue agree that the incompetency of a holder of a power will not make the power unexercisable for estate tax purposes. Boeving v. United States, 650 F2d 493 (8th Cir. 1981); Estate of Gilchrist v. Comm'r, 630 F2d 340 (5th Cir. 1980); Estate of Rosenblatt v. Comm'r, 633 F2d 176 (10th Cir. 1980); Estate of Alperstein v. Comm'r, 613 F2d 1213 (2d Cir. 1979), cert. denied, 446 US 918 (1980); Pennsylvania Bank & Trust Co. v. United States, 597 F2d 382 (3d Cir.), cert. denied, 444 US 980 (1979); Fish v. United States, 432 F2d 1278 (9th Cir. 1970). The anomalous lower court cases have been overruled. See Stephens, Maxfield, & Lind, Federal Estate and Gift Taxation, ¶ 4.13[6][a] note 77 (Warren, Gorham & Lamont, 4th ed. 1978).

[81] Estate of Freeman v. Comm'r, 67 TC 202 (1976). In *Freeman*, the decedent was aware of the existence of the trust itself as he was receiving an income interest from the trust and was simply unaware of his power over the trust. It is possible to parade a "horrible" here: *D* confers on *A*, a mortal enemy, a lifetime general power of which *A* is unaware either because *D* hides its existence or *A* is in a coma and mortally ill. *D* does this

even if the decedent has only an inter vivos power that cannot be exercised by will, the decedent is treated as having the power at death.[82]

Does the decedent *have* a general power of appointment *at the time of death* if the decedent's exercise of the power is not to be effective until a stated period after exercise, or if the decedent cannot exercise the power except after giving notice for a stated period of the decedent's decision to do so, and if, in either event, prior to death the decedent has taken no such action? An express affirmative answer to this question is given by the statute, foreclosing the obvious controversy that might otherwise ensue but leaving open a related problem. It is clear that if the decedent's power is exercisable only upon the happening of some event, such as attaining age thirty, and the event has not occurred before the decedent's death, the decedent does not have a power at death.[83] However, if the event is within the decedent's control, such as dismissal of a trustee if one has such a right and the right to appoint oneself, and if one can thus acquire a power exercisable by the trustee, it seems equally clear that the decedent will be treated as possessing the power even though the decedent has taken no action toward obtaining the power, and notwithstanding the fact that the decedent might be required to give the trustee notice prior to dismissal.[84] The Commissioner successfully advanced this argument in a case arising under analogous language in Section 2038 concerning the existence of a power to alter, amend, revoke, or terminate,[85] even though the statute concerns notice prior to *exercise* or prior to effectiveness of an exercise rather than notice prior to actual *acquisition* of the power. If the power can be exercised only after giving notice, presumably the value of the property included in the gross estate would be discounted for the period required to elapse between the time of the decedent's death and the time the power could have been exer-

---

simply to charge *A*'s estate with a higher tax. Certainly, an enlightened judge would hold Section 2041 inapplicable under these facts.

There is less a lack-of-knowledge problem with respect to a pre-1942 power of appointment because mere possession of the power does not trigger adverse tax consequences.

[82] Snyder v. United States, 203 F. Supp. 195 (WD Ky. 1962); Jenkins v. United States, 428 F2d 538 (5th Cir. 1970) (Section 2041 applicable even though the decedent could exercise the power only during life).

[83] Reg. § 20.2041-3(b). See Priv. Ltr. Rul. 8516011 (Jan. 3, 1985).

[84] Reg. § 20.2041-3(b). See Estate of Kurz v. Comm'r, 101 TC 44 (1993), reconsideration denied 67 TCM (CCH) 2978 (1994) (holding that there was a general power but stating that to preclude the possession of a general power due to a contingency or condition, the condition must not be illusory, and must be accompanied by some significant nontax consequences independent of the power holder's ability to exercise the power).

[85] Estate of Loughridge v. Comm'r, 183 F2d 294 (10th Cir.), cert. denied, 340 US 830 (1950).

Section 2041

cised.[86] An acceptable way to view this is that the defined power is equivalent only to a future interest in the property subject to the power.

As is true, mutatis mutandis, with respect to all special statutory provisions defining the gross estate, it is not necessary that a decedent's power extend to an entire property or fund. For example, a decedent might have a power to invade the corpus of a $100,000 trust only to the extent of $5,000. This would constitute a power of appointment to the extent of $5,000 that, if in existence at the time of the decedent's death, would require $5,000 to be included in the decedent's gross estate even though the entire corpus of the trust greatly exceeded that amount.[87]

[b] Exercise

Second, a pre-death exercise of a post-1942 general power in a testamentary fashion requires inclusion of the value of the property subject to the power in the gross estate. It will be observed that the statute does not specify tax liability in the event of an exercise of a post-1942 general power *by will* as it does in the case of pre-1942 powers. This does not relieve an estate of liability, however, for if the power is exercised by will, the decedent "has" the power at death, and of course, as to post-1942 powers, this brings the value of the property into the estate without regard to the question of exercise.

The statutory rule on the effect of lifetime exercise (though not what constitutes exercise) is the same for both pre-1942 and post-1942 general powers. Again, the question is whether the exercise involves a disposition that would be covered by Sections 2035[88] through 2038 if the exercise were a conventional transfer of property. The significance of this is previously indicated more fully in connection with the discussion of pre-1942 powers. It is worth noting that if a decedent has exercised a power by appointing to the decedent, such a lifetime exercise of a power is not a testamentary exercise within the statute, because the decedent has made no transfer to *another* such as is contemplated by Sections 2035 through 2038. This is entirely appropriate, how-

---

[86] Cf. Reg. § 20.2038-1(b). Nevertheless, the discounted value might be included in the decedent's estate. For example, if the decedent had an income interest with a general power exercisable after six months' notice, there would be a Section 2041 "adjustment" in the amount of inclusion, but since the decedent would receive the income during that period, the value of the "adjustment" would be included in the decedent's estate under Section 2033.

[87] Cf. Reg. § 20.2038-1(b).

[88] A post-1942 power can interact with Section 2035 only in extremely limited circumstances. If a decedent had held a post-1942 power that the decedent previously exercised retaining a Section 2036, 2037, or 2038 interest or power *and* the decedent then relinquished such interest or power within three years of death, Section 2041(a)(2) would apply, interacting with Section 2035.

ever, because after invasion by the decedent, the property acquired in that fashion becomes property actually owned by the decedent. If retained until death, it will be a part of the decedent's actual estate covered by Section 2033. If given away before then, it may be subject to gift tax or remain a part of the decedent's gross estate under other sections, or both. But in any event, Section 2041 need not and will not apply.

[c] Release

The third basic rule with respect to post-1942 general powers is that a lifetime release of the power by the decedent is the equivalent of an exercise of the power. If the release is made in a testamentary fashion, the value of the property is in the decedent's gross estate for federal tax purposes. This should be contrasted with the express provision in Section 2041(a)(1) to the effect that a complete release of a *pre*-1942 power shall not be deemed an exercise of the power, exercise being necessary with respect to estate tax liability concerning such powers. Thus, it may be said, no estate tax liability will result from a complete lifetime release of a pre-1942 power, but if a post-1942 power is released during life, estate tax liability with respect to the property subject to the power depends on the manner of release. The same test applies here as applies with regard to lifetime exercise of pre-1942 powers, namely: Does the release involve a disposition that would be covered by Sections 2035 through 2038 if the release were a conventional transfer of property? If a general power is released and the power holder retains no interest in or power over the property, there are no estate tax consequences, even if that release occurs within three years of the power holder's death.[89] Other releases may result in estate tax consequences. For example, if the decedent is the income beneficiary of a trust and has a general power to appoint the entire property to anyone, the decedent's inter vivos release of the power is treated as a transfer under Section 2514(b)[90] and, upon the decedent's death, the property subject to the power will be included in the decedent's estate under Section 2041(a)(2) because, had the release been a transfer of property, the property would be includable in the decedent's gross estate under Section 2036.[91]

A release of a general power of appointment may be indirect. For example, if, during life, an individual holds a nongeneral power of appointment over the corpus of a trust created by another along with a general power to ap-

---

[89] The release is treated as a transfer of property for gift tax purposes. See IRC § 2514(b).

[90] Estate of Robinson v. Comm'r, 101 TC 499 (1993) (no taxable gift of the residuary trust because there was no transfer).

[91] See De Oliveira v. United States, 767 F2d 1344 (9th Cir. 1985). Cf. Rev. Rul. 86-39, 1986-1 CB 301.

point it by will, an inter vivos exercise of the nongeneral power also constitutes a release of the general power.[92]

[d] Disclaimer or Renunciation

Section 2518[93] provides a uniform rule for disclaimers under the estate,[94] gift,[95] and generation-skipping transfer taxes[96] that allows an individual who is given a post-1942 general power of appointment to avoid any tax consequences[97] with respect to the power.[98] The basic disclaimer problem cannot arise with regard to pre-1942 powers, for even if a supposed disclaimer or renunciation of such a power were treated as a release, the release in any event is without estate tax significance. Section 2518 is intended to clear up many of the disclaimer problems under Section 2041[99] and other Code sections.

Disclaimers can arise in some unexpected circumstances. For example, a revenue ruling[100] properly held that a widow's failure to exercise her statutory

---

[92] Cf. Reg. § 25.2514-1(b)(2).

[93] IRC § 2518 discussed ¶ 10.07.

[94] IRC § 2046; ¶ 4.18.

[95] For a discussion of the requirements of Section 2518, see ¶ 10.07[2].

[96] IRC § 2654(c) discussed at ¶ 17.04[3] regarding disclaimers in the case of generation-skipping transfers.

[97] Cf. IRC § 2514(b).

[98] See especially IRC § 2518(c)(2).

[99] Prior to the enactment of the Tax Reform Act of 1976, Pub. L. No. 94-455, 90 Stat. 1520 (1976), reprinted in 1976-3 CB (Vol. 1) 1, there were several problems created by Section 2041(a)(2), which expressly stated that "a disclaimer or renunciation of such a power of appointment shall not be deemed a release of such power." IRC § 2041(A)(2) prior to amendment in the Tax Reform Act of 1976, Pub. L. No. 94-455, § 2009(b)(4), 90 Stat. 1520, 1894 (1976), reprinted in 1976-3 CB (Vol. 1) 1, 370. A beneficiary's attempted renunciation of an intestate share in another's estate had been held to constitute an actual taxable transfer of the property interest involved subject to gift or estate tax, rather than a mere rejection, due to the court finding that the beneficiary's interest had vested. Hardenbergh v. Comm'r, 198 F2d 63 (8th Cir.), cert. denied, 344 US 836 (1952). Compare Brown v. Routzahn, 63 F2d 914 (6th Cir.), cert. denied, 290 US 641 (1933). The quoted provision clearly contemplated a right to renounce a power tax-free without regard to the question of vesting; and the regulations, at least by inference, indicated that a renunciation could be made within "a reasonable time" after one learned of the existence of the power. Reg. § 20.2041-3(d)(6). See also S. Rep. No. 382, 82d Cong., 1st Sess. 6 (1951). But this had nothing to do with the renunciation of a vested property interest. Furthermore, the Treasury appropriately took the position that (1) after acceptance, a power could not be renounced—attempted renunciation would then be treated as a release; and (2) a power could not be accepted in part and renounced in part—renunciation contemplated an "unqualified refusal to accept the rights to which one is entitled." Reg. § 20.2041-3(d)(6).

[100] Rev. Rul. 74-492, 1974-2 CB 298.

right to her forced share of her predeceasing spouse's estate prior to her death constituted a disclaimer of a general power of appointment. The ruling arose prior to the effective date of Section 2518;[101] after the enactment of that provision, the opposite result might be reached due to a failure to meet the statutory requirement that disclaimers be written.[102]

[e] Lapse

Section 2041(b)(2) defines "release of a post-1942 power" to include the lapse of a power during the donee's lifetime, subject to some important exceptions.[103] Thus, basically, both release and lapse are the equivalent of exercise.[104] For example, if one has a noncumulative power to invade a trust to the extent of $20,000 each calendar year, one's failure to exercise the power in any year involves a lapse of the power, which in turn has the same estate tax significance as an exercise of the power in favor of the person who will take in default.[105] However, it should be remembered that not every release (or lapse) causes estate tax liability. If, in the example as given, the one who has the power is also the life income beneficiary of the trust, the person will be regarded as having made a transfer of a portion of the corpus (which one could have appointed to oneself), while retaining a right to the income from such portion for life, making the lapse taxable within the principle of Section 2036[106] but subject to the "five-or-five" qualifications. If the one who has the power has no other right or interest in the trust property, the lapse may cause gift tax liability but will not cause estate tax liability.

[f] The Five-or-Five Rule

The exceptions to the general rule (lapse equals release) are generous. The statute expressly makes the general rule inapplicable if the power that lapsed was such that during any calendar year its exercise was limited to $5,000 or to 5 percent of the value of the property out of which the exercise

---

[101] Section 2518 is effective only after Dec. 31, 1976. Reg. § 25.2518-1(a). See ¶ 10.07[3].

[102] IRC § 2518(b)(1).

[103] See infra ¶ 4.13[7][f].

[104] The Service has indicated that state legislation preventing a trustee-beneficiary from exercising a power of appointment in favor of oneself will not be considered a lapse for purposes of Section 2041(b)(2). Rev. Proc. 94-44, 1994-2 CB 6 (Florida statute); Priv. Ltr. Rul. 9852031 (Sept. 29, 1998) (California statute).

[105] A lapse has been accorded a full significance even though the power holder was incompetent. Fish v. United States, 432 F2d 1278 (9th Cir. 1970).

[106] Reg. § 20.2041-3(d)(3).

of the power could have been satisfied, whichever is greater.[107] Moreover, if the lapsed power exceeds $5,000 or 5 percent, its lapse is to be treated as a release only to the extent of the excess.

Under these exceptions, if the decedent could invade a $200,000 trust fund to the extent of $5,000 each year, and the decedent never exercised the power and the value of the fund remained unchanged, the decedent's failure to exercise the right for any year prior to the year in which the decedent died (and the attending lapse of the power) would be without estate tax significance. Both the $5,000 rule and the 5 percent rule would shield the estate from liability on these facts. If the decedent withdrew amounts under the decedent's power, or if, for other reasons, the fund diminished in value even to less than $100,000, the decedent's estate would still escape all possibility of liability for a lapse in any year under the $5,000 rule. That is, if a decedent's power is restricted to a withdrawal of $5,000, the lapse can be ignored. If the 5 percent rule must be resorted to, however, it is 5 percent of the value *at the time of the lapse* from which the amount of the exception is determined, as will be explained.

It is very important to note that the lapse rule applies only to lapses *during life*. If the decedent had not exercised the power in the year the decedent died,[108] the decedent would have held the power at death, and the value of the property subject to the power at death would be included in the decedent's gross estate.[109]

What if the decedent had a noncumulative right to invade a $30,000 trust fund of which the decedent was the life beneficiary in an amount not to exceed $10,000 each year? From what has been said, it might seem that if the decedent let ten years go by and never exercised the right the decedent would

---

[107] Failure of a taxpayer to establish the value of the trust will result in use of the $5,000 amount as the floor. Estate of Noland v. Comm'r, 47 TCM (CCH) 1640 (1984). See Covey, "The Estate Planning Benefits Available Via a $5,000 and 5 Percent Withdrawal Power," 34 J. Tax'n 98 (1971).

[108] The same result would occur to the extent that the decedent had not exercised the power if the decedent had exercised only part of the power during life. Reg. § 20.2041-3(d)(3).

[109] Estate of Dietz v. Comm'r, 72 TCM (CCH) 1058 (1996); Rev. Rul. 79-373, 1979-2 CB 331; Priv. Ltr. Rul. 199933020 (May 19, 1999). A common method of avoiding inclusion of the five-or-five power in the power holder's gross estate at death is to limit its exercise to a limited period of time during the year (e.g., a particular month of the year or a particular day of each month) so that if the power holder dies on a day of the year when the power holder does not hold the power, the power holder does not have the general power at death. IRC § 2041(a)(2).

For example, assume G gives C a five-or-five power over corpus only in the month of January of each year. If G dies in the month of January, the property subject to the power would be included in G's gross estate under Section 2041(a)(2). If, instead, C dies in any month other than January, none of the corpus is included in C's gross estate under Section 2041(a)(2).

have made ten transfers of $5,000 (the excess over the annual $5,000 exemption) within the concept of Section 2036. The regulations appropriately provide, however, that the total amount included cannot exceed the date-of-death or alternate date value of the trust. The actual amount to be included raises some complexity. Broadly, the regulations require a determination annually of the percentages of the trust fund (valued at the date of the lapse of the power as stated above) that could have been appointed under the lapsed power in excess of the allowed $5,000 or 5 percent exemptions. The aggregate of these percentages is to be applied to the date-of-death or alternate date value of the trust to determine the amount to include, which cannot exceed 100 percent in light of the limitation mentioned above.[110]

The operation of the 5 percent rule can be illustrated by an example. Suppose X makes a transfer in trust to D for life, remainder to R. D is given a noncumulative power to invade corpus to the extent of $20,000 per year. At the end of the first year, assume that the corpus is worth $200,000 and, at relevant times in the second year, the corpus is worth $300,000. If D never exercises D's power to invade and dies in the second year after the transfer, $35,000 will be included in D's gross estate. As to year one, D had a power to invade to the extent of $20,000, and as the corpus at the end of the year was worth $200,000, the 5 percent rule would seem to mean only $10,000 would be subject to tax. However, it is not $10,000 that would be includable in the gross estate, but rather $15,000 (10,000/200,000 multiplied by $300,000, the date-of-death value of the trust corpus, $200,000, representing the value of the property out of which the exercise of the power could have been satisfied at the time it lapsed). Since D died in the second year possessing the power to invade to the extent of $20,000, the full $20,000 would be includable with respect to the second year, for a total of $35,000.

If the decedent's power is limited to only part of the property, only that part is used to measure the 5 percent exclusion.[111] For example, assume the decedent was a lifetime beneficiary of a trust and, as the beneficiary, has had the noncumulative right to withdraw income from the trust each year. Any income not so withdrawn was to be accumulated and added to the corpus. For purposes of determining the 5 percent limitation provided by Section 2041(b)(2)(B), only the trust income is "the assets out of which . . . the exercise of the lapsed power could have been satisfied." Thus, the 5 percent exclu-

---

[110] Reg. § 20.2041-3(d)(4); S. Rep. No. 382, 82d Cong., 1st Sess. 7 (1951). The mechanical percentage approach to lifetime lapses does not yield a sound result if any year after a lapse the power is exercised. Presumably, in such a case, it would be necessary to make a less arithmetic determination of the portion of date-of-death value that should be included in the gross estate.

[111] Rev. Rul. 66-87, 1966-1 CB 217.

sion is based on the value of the trust income rather than on the trust corpus from which the income was derived.[112]

[8] Nongeneral Powers

[a] The Use of Nongeneral Powers

As one begins to digest the message of the last few pages related to exceptions as to the post-1942 general power of appointment rules, a planning opportunity begins to emerge. The net effect of the exceptions to the general rule on the lifetime lapse of currently exercisable powers, taken together with certain exceptions to the definition of "general powers" and the parallel gift tax provisions, has afforded planners great flexibility through an informed use of powers of appointment.[113] A beneficiary can be given significant interests in and powers over property held in a trust, that are not treated as a general power of appointment and they do not result in the property subject to the power being included in the beneficiary's gross estate. The property subject to the power bypasses the beneficiary's gross estate. For example, if a transferor gives a life estate in trust to a beneficiary, the beneficiary's life estate in the trust is not included in the beneficiary's gross estate at death under Section 2033 or any other estate tax provision.[114] A power to invade the corpus of the trust for the beneficiary's "health, education, support, and maintenance" does not result in the property subject to the power being included in the beneficiary's gross estate.[115] And a lifetime lapse of a power to invade corpus for the beneficiary to the extent of the greater of $5,000 or 5 percent of the corpus will not increase the beneficiary's gross estate,[116] except to the extent that such

---

[112] See Fish v. United States, 432 F2d 1278 (9th Cir. 1970).

[113] See Larson, "Limited Power of Withdrawal Still Can Be Effective Estate Planning Tool," 33 Tax'n for Acct. 322 (1984). See also Covey, "The Estate Planning Benefits Available Via a $5,000 and 5 Percent Withdrawal Power," 34 J. Tax'n 98 (1971). But see ¶ 13.02[2][e][ii].

[114] See ¶ 4.05[5][b] text accompanying notes 51, 52. However, the termination of the beneficiary's interest may trigger the generation-skipping transfer tax. See ¶¶ 4.05[5][c], 13.02[2].

[115] IRC § 2041(b)(1)(A). See supra ¶ 4.13[4][a].

[116] IRC § 2041(b)(2). See supra ¶ 4.13[7][f]. Technically, this is not a nongeneral power, but is an exception to the general power of appointment rules, generally (but see infra text accompanying note 117), if unexercised, it has the same consequences as a nongeneral power. If the power is exercised and the amount is retained until death, the amount will be included in the beneficiary's gross estate under Section 2033.

a power is held at the beneficiary's death.[117] The beneficiary may hold a testamentary power to appoint the property to anyone in the world other than the beneficiary's estate or the creditors of the beneficiary's estate. Generally, a testamentary nongeneral power of appointment is not drafted so broadly, but no matter how broadly it is drafted, subject to the limitation in the prior sentence, the power does not rise to the level of a general power of appointment and does not result in inclusion of the property in the beneficiary powerholder's gross estate.[118] In combination, the interests and powers granted a beneficiary may come very close to the equivalent of outright ownership, but without gross estate inclusion where the beneficiary is named trustee of the trust.[119] Such a trust is commonly referred to as a "bypass" trust because the corpus of the trust is not included in the beneficiary's gross estate, it simply bypasses the beneficiary's gross estate.

[b] Nongeneral Powers That Are Treated As General Powers

Thus far in this discussion of possible estate tax liability concerning powers of appointment, it has been assumed that a power that is not a general power as defined in the statute cannot result in estate tax liability under Section 2041. But there is one provision in the section that may require the inclusion in the gross estate of the value of property subject to a post-1942 nongeneral power. The provision is of very limited interest because of restrictions of local property law. Section 2041(a)(3) requires that there be included in the gross estate the value of property with respect to which the decedent by will, or otherwise in a testamentary fashion as indicated by Sections 2035 through 2037,[120] has exercised a post-1942 power (note omission of the word "general") by creating another power (note again it does not say "general") but only if under local law the newly created power can be exercised to post-

---

[117] IRC § 2041(a)(2). See supra ¶ 4.13[7][f] text accompanying notes 108, 109, especially note 109 suggesting that such a power be held only during a limited period of each year.

[118] See IRC § 2041(b)(1); Reg. § 20.2041-1(c)(1); Priv. Ltr. Rul. 199904001 (Oct. 19, 1998). See also supra ¶ 4.13[3].

[119] There is minimal potential gross estate inclusion (see supra note 117) and potential generation-skipping transfer tax consequences (see supra note 114).

Bypass trusts are commonly used on the death of a predeceasing spouse to bypass the estate of a surviving spouse to the extent of the Section 2010 credit (see ¶ 5.06[6] and supra ¶ 4.13[4][d] note 52) and to skip generations to the extent permitted by the Section 2631 generation-skipping transfer tax exemption (see ¶¶ 15.02[1], 15.02[2]). But their use is not limited to such situations, and they are an important estate planning technique in other situations as well. See Hess, "Federal Taxation of Nongeneral Powers of Appointment," 52 Tenn. LR 395 (1985).

[120] It is unclear why Section 2038 is omitted from this list.

pone[121] the vesting of the estate or interest in property or suspend ownership for a period ascertainable without regard to the date of creation of the first power.[122]

Even though this provision on nongeneral powers will rarely be of significance, the purpose behind it may be of interest. If local law permitted an indefinite suspension of absolute ownership of property through a succession of exercises of nongeneral powers of appointment, a nongeneral power could be created and exercised by the creation of another nongeneral power that again could be exercised by the creation of a nongeneral power, and so on indefinitely. In this fashion, except for the tax on generation-skipping transfers, practical ownership of property could be passed on from generation to generation, always outside the reach of federal estate tax, except for the provision under discussion.[123] Such potential avoidance is foreclosed by Section 2041(a)(3).

[9] Amount to Be Included

In the foregoing discussion, it has been necessary to anticipate the question of the amount to be included in a decedent's estate when, for one reason or another, Section 2041 is brought into play. In summary, when a pre-1942 power is involved, Section 2041 includes in the gross estate the date-of-death or alternate value of the property with respect to which the power was taxably exercised. When a post-1942 power is involved, there must be included the date-of-death or alternate date value of the property subject to the power the decedent had at death or with respect to which the decedent had in a taxable manner exercised or released the power. The special rule on lapsed powers will be recalled. The general proposition is that the power itself need not be valued; it is the value of the property that the decedent could or did appoint that is brought into the decedent's gross estate.[124]

---

[121] The section should not apply in states which have abolished the Rule Against Perpetuities because no postponement of vesting or suspending occurs.

[122] Estate of Murphey v. Comm'r, 71 TC 671 (1979) (Section 2041(a)(3) inapplicable because date of creation of first power not altered).

[123] See Blattmach and Pennell, "Adventures in Generation-Skipping, or How We Learned to Love the Delaware Tax Trap," 24 Real Property, Probate & Tr. J. 75 (1989) (explaining that Section 2041(a)(3) may now provide a tax planning opportunity). See also Greer, "The Delaware Tax Trap and the Abolition of the Rule Against Perpetuities," 28 Est. Plan. 68 (2001).

[124] See Estate of Hartzell v. Comm'r, 68 TCM (CCH) 1243 (1994) (holding that because stock was properly distributed, stock was not subject to the decedent's power of appointment).

[10] Background of the Section

The first federal estate tax statute did not deal expressly with powers of appointment,[125] and the Supreme Court held that a power of appointment was not an interest in property subject to tax under the forerunner of Section 2033.[126] Perhaps anticipating this decision, Congress added a section on powers in 1919.[127] The new provision taxed the value of property *passing* under a *general* power of appointment *exercised* by the decedent by will. It also subjected to estate tax the passing of property under a lifetime exercise of a general power, if such exercise was in contemplation of or intended to take effect at or after death, in keeping with the principles applicable at the time to other lifetime transfers. This was the estate tax statutory law on powers until 1942.

From 1919 to 1942, many serious difficulties were encountered in the administration of the powers provision. The statute did not define "general" power, and borrowing from property law concepts, the courts tended to give the term a very restricted definition.[128] Some doubt existed as to what constituted the "exercise" of a power, which is still a question under the present statute as to pre-1942 powers.[129] A further problem was presented when a general power was exercised in favor of the takers in default and they disclaimed any right under the appointment but took the property in their capacity as remainderpersons; in such circumstances, the property was held not to "pass" under the exercise of the power, leaving an essential element of the statute unsatisfied.[130]

In 1942, Congress undertook a general revision of the powers-of-appointment section.[131] The general power concept was abandoned in favor of a statutory definition of "taxable power of appointment." Moreover, the requirement of exercise was abandoned so that tax was imposed if the decedent *had* the power at death, but the statute also taxed lifetime exercise or releases of a testamentary nature. On the other hand, the section was not given full retroactive effect and persons were given an opportunity to make a tax-free release of tax-

---

[125] Revenue Act of 1916, Pub. L. No. 64-271, 39 Stat. 756 (1916).

[126] United States v. Field, 255 US 257 (1921). Restrictive language in the Revenue Act of 1916, Pub. L. No. 64-271, 39 Stat. 756 (1916), limited inclusion, inter alia, to property subject to the payment of charges against the estate. But if for that reason *Field* left a question of whether a power was a property "interest," that doubt is dispelled by Helvering v. Safe Dep. & Trust Co., 316 US 56 (1942).

[127] Revenue Act of 1918, Pub. L. No. 65-254, § 402(e), 40 Stat. 1057, 1097 (1918). But see Estate of Murphey v. Comm'r, 71 TC 671 (1979).

[128] E.g., Clauson v. Vaughan, 147 F2d 84 (1st Cir. 1945); Christine Smith Kendrick v. Comm'r, 34 BTA 1040 (1936).

[129] E.g., Keating v. Mayer, 236 F2d 478 (3d Cir. 1956).

[130] Helvering v. Grinnel, 294 US 153 (1935). But see Estate of Rogers v. Comm'r, 320 US 410 (1943).

[131] Revenue Act of 1942, Pub. L. No. 77-753, § 403, 56 Stat. 798, 942 (1942).

able powers created before the change in the statute. The date October 21, 1942, which figures prominently in the new section, is the date of adoption of the 1942 Act.

The 1942 revision was not successful. Some of the difficulties encountered under it cannot appropriately be set out here[132] In 1951, Congress again undertook extended revision by enactment of the Powers of Appointment Act of 1951,[133] which, without substantial change, was carried over into Section 2041 of the 1954 and 1986 Codes.

¶ 4.14 SECTION 2042. PROCEEDS OF LIFE INSURANCE

[1] Introduction

Section 2042 presents two basic inclusionary rules. The proceeds of insurance policies on a decedent's life are to be included in the insured's gross estate if they are (1) receivable by the executor or (2) receivable by other beneficiaries and the decedent had any incidents of ownership in the policy at death. But these are only seemingly simple and workable directives. Outside their obvious areas of coverage, these provisions leave the tax administrator and the courts, not to mention taxpayers, in some confusion. Both tests present difficulties, and neither is invariably clear as to its scope nor always supportable in its philosophy. These frailties emerge in the examination that follows, but first some preliminary observations should be made.[1]

It is important to recognize that this section deals only with insurance policies on the *decedent's* life. If a decedent owns an insurance policy on the life of another person and predeceases that person, this section is inapplicable. This is not to say that the value of such an insurance policy will escape taxation in the decedent's estate. On the contrary, it is property owned by the decedent at death and includable under Section 2033.[2] And a decedent's lifetime gratuitous

---

[132] But see Guterman, "The Powers of Appointment Act." 29 Taxes 631 (1951).

[133] Powers of Appointment Act of 1951, Pub. L. No. 82-58, 65 Stat. 91 (1951), reprinted in 1951-2 CB 343.

[1] Life insurance may play a significant role in estate planning. See Henkel, Estate Planning and Wealth Preservation ch. 12 (Warren, Gorham & Lamont 1997); Weinstock, Planning an Estate § 10 (Shepard's/McGraw-Hill 4th ed. 1995); Price on Contemporary Estate Planning ch. 6 (Little Brown 1992); Schwartz, "Life Insurance Estate Planning," 35 S. Cal. L. Rev. 1 (1961); Wright, "Life Insurance and Its Use in Estate Planning," 23 Okla. L. Rev. 125 (1970).

[2] E.g., Estate of DuPont v. Comm'r, 18 TC 1134 (1952), aff'd, 233 F2d 210 (3d Cir.), cert. denied, 352 US 878 (1956). If the decedent's executor elects Section 2032 and the insured dies within the six-month period after the decedent's death, the amount paid

transfer of an insurance policy on another's life may bring into play other sections,[3] but again Section 2042 would not result in inclusion. It should also be observed at the outset that when insurance on the decedent's life is involved so that Section 2042 is applicable, its provisions are not necessarily exclusive, and another section may also apply to produce a result yielding more or less tax than would be obtained from the application of Section 2042 alone.[4]

[2] What Is Insurance?

The significance of Section 2042 can be grasped only through an understanding of the term "insurance" as used in the federal tax laws. Conventional policies of all kinds, which guard against the financial hazards of premature death, are clearly within the concept. But either the distribution or the shifting of the risk of premature death is an essential element of life insurance. Conventional endowment-type policies also calling for the payment of death benefits cease to be insurance when the terminal reserve value equals the death benefit,[5] because, by that time, the insurer has, in effect, salted enough away out of premiums to pay the proceeds without incurring a loss.

Insurance that provides for unconditional payments only in the case of accidental death is within the insurance concept;[6] and so is the double indemnity feature of conventional life contracts.[7] The title or description of the agreement is unimportant as long as life insurance elements are present.

However, suppose a common carrier or other commercial or industrial company maintains liability insurance that obligates an insurer to reimburse or pay directly any damages that the company may incur in connection with an accident but that further provides that the insurer may negotiate a settlement with the injured party or the party's estate or survivors conditioned upon a release of the company from liability. Payments to an estate or survivors under

---

by the insurance company is included in the decedent's gross estate. Rev. Rul. 63-52, 1963-1 CB 173. See also discussion of IRC § 2033 at ¶ 4.05[6].

[3] See IRC §§ 2035, 2036, 2037, 2038, discussed at ¶¶ 4.07, 4.08, 4.09, 4.10, respectively.

[4] The relationship of Section 2042 to other inclusion sections is dealt with more fully infra ¶ 4.14[9].

[5] Reg. § 20.2039-1(d). Moreover, an employer's unfunded death benefits plan does not involve a shifting or spreading of the risk of premature death. All v. McCobb, 321 F2d 633 (2d Cir. 1963). See "Exceptions Expressed in Section 2039(a): Life Insurance Policies" in the discussion of Section 2039 at ¶ 4.11[2][a].

[6] Comm'r v. Estate of Noel, 380 US 678 (1965), rejecting an asserted distinction based on the proposition that while death is inevitable, accidental death is "evitable." Rev. Rul. 83-44, 1983-1 CB 228, involving no-fault automobile insurance. See Estate of Melville E. Ackerman v. Comm'r, 15 BTA 635 (1929).

[7] Comm'r v. Estate of Noel, 380 US 678 (1965).

such arrangements do not constitute the proceeds of insurance on the decedent's life and are not includable in the decedent's gross estate under Section 2042[8] or, probably, under any other section either.[9] Death benefits payable under such a policy are conditioned upon either a determination of legal liability of the insured company or a compromise of a claim of its liability.[10] If, in contrast, the policy called for unconditional payment of a fixed sum merely on proof of accidental death, Section 2042 would apply.[11]

Insurance is not restricted to policies issued by companies regularly engaged in the insurance business. Death benefits paid by fraternal beneficial societies operating under the lodge system are insurance,[12] and even less formal arrangements have been similarly classified. For example, if one purchases a seat on the New York Stock Exchange, one acquires a right to have the so-called Gratuity Fund of the Exchange pay one's survivors a minimum of $20,000 upon one's death. Depending on length of tenure, the maximum moves up to $100,000. Even at a time when other resources had made the fund self-supporting, making member contributions unnecessary, a court found present the element of distribution of risk of death and held that the amounts payable by the fund constituted insurance for estate tax purposes.[13]

Other death benefit arrangements arising in connection with employment present some difficulties. Of course, group life insurance policies are just as clearly life insurance policies as conventional individual policies.[14] On the other hand, death benefits in the form of a mere refund of an employee's contributions to a retirement plan that are paid to survivors do not constitute insurance, because there is no element of risk shifting or risk distribution.[15]

Death benefits not classified as insurance may be taxed as annuities, as indicated in the discussion of Section 2039,[16] and if such amounts are payable

---

[8] Rev. Rul. 57-54, 1957-1 CB 298.

[9] Cf. Rev. Rul. 54-19, 1954-1 CB 179; ¶ 4.05[8], concerning the taxability of amounts recoverable under so-called survival statutes.

[10] See Rev. Rul. 68-88, 1968-1 CB 397.

[11] Rev. Rul. 57-54, 1957-1 CB 298. Cf. Rev. Rul. 83-44, 83-1 CB 228.

[12] Reg. § 20.2042-1(a)(1). See also Rev. Rul. 65-222, 1965-2 CB 374.

[13] Comm'r v. Treganowan, 183 F2d 288 (2d Cir.), cert. denied, 340 US 853 (1950). It is understood that the payments by the Fund are again made possible by contributions from each of some 1,300-odd Exchange members upon the death of any other member. There is, therefore, further reason, beyond the circumstances in *Treganowan*, for treating the death benefits as insurance.

[14] E.g., Estate of Louis E. Flye v. Comm'r, 39 BTA 871 (1939), acq. 1939-2 CB 13, nonacq. 1939-2 CB 50. See the discussion of "Assignment of Group Term Insurance" infra ¶ 4.14[6].

[15] Cf. Reg. § 20.2039-1(b)(2) Ex. 3.

[16] Estate of Montgomery v. Comm'r, 56 TC 489 (1971), aff'd per curiam, 458 F2d 616 (5th Cir.), cert. denied, 409 US 849 (1972). See ¶ 4.11[2][a].

to the estate of the decedent as of right, they will be included in the decedent's gross estate as property owned by the decedent.[17] On the other hand, if the payments to the estate of the decedent or the decedent's survivors represent a mere expectancy or gift rather than a payment required by a contractual obligation of the employer, such payments will not be includable under Section 2042 or Section 2033, or under any other Code section.[18]

A contract that would usually constitute life insurance for purposes of Section 2042 may lose its character as insurance if it is acquired as part of a broader arrangement with an insurance company. For example, if a conventional life insurance policy is purchased in a transaction in which, for a single premium, the insured also acquires a single-life, nonrefundable annuity policy, no life insurance may emerge for estate tax purposes.[19] Life insurance and life-measured annuities are opposites; from the company's standpoint, its gain depends on longevity in the case of one and transiency in the case of the other. In other words, these combination arrangements lack the critical element of the shifting or distributing of the risk of premature death, if the insurer's gain on the early termination of the annuity payment will offset the insurer's loss on the early payment of the insurance proceeds.[20] Although the foregoing is not an exhaustive consideration of what constitutes insurance for estate tax pur-

---

[17] Cf. Rev. Rul. 65-217, 1965-2 CB 214 (involving bonuses awarded by the employer but unpaid at date of death); Goodman v. Granger, 243 F2d 264 (3d Cir.), cert. denied, 355 US 835 (1957).

[18] Cf. Rev. Rul. 65-217, 1965-2 CB 214 (involving bonuses awarded by the employer but unpaid at date of death); Goodman v. Granger, 243 F2d 264 (3d Cir.), cert. denied, 355 US 835 (1957); ¶ 4.05[4]. See also Estate of Barr v. Comm'r, 40 TC 227 (1963), acq. 1964-1 CB 4; Rev. Rul. 55-581, 1955-2 CB 381 (excluding six months' gratuity pay to survivors of a member of the Armed Forces). But see Estate of Porter v. Comm'r, 442 F2d 915 (1st Cir. 1971).

[19] Helvering v. Le Gierse, 312 US 531 (1941), Estate of Montgomery v. Comm'r, 56 TC 489 (1971), aff'd per curiam, 458 F2d 616 (5th Cir.), cert. denied, 409 US 849 (1972). The Le Gierse decision was followed for income tax purposes in Kess v. United States, 451 F2d 1229 (6th Cir. 1971), and in Rev. Rul. 65-57, 1965-1 CB 56.

[20] This takes a combination arrangement out of the mainstream of the discussion here but leaves open the question of how such arrangements affect estate tax liability. There are several possibilities: (1) if the insured retains both the annuity and the insurance, the annuity, expiring at death, will be ignored, but the insured's ownership of the policy will cause its inclusion under Section 2033, in the amount of the full proceeds (cf. Goodman v. Granger, 243 F2d 264 (3d Cir.), cert. denied, 355 US 835 (1957)); (2) if the insured makes a complete gift of both not within three years of death, only gift tax but no estate tax would result; (3) if the insured assigns the annuity but keeps the insurance policy, the results are the same as in (1) above; and (4) if the insured transfers the insurance policy outright but retains the annuity, the amount of the insurance proceeds will be included in the insured's gross estate, not under Section 2042 as insurance, but as an "other payment" under Section 2039. This result could not easily be reached under the statute as it existed prior to 1954. See Fidelity-Philadelphia Trust Co. v. Smith, 356 US 274 (1958). But the addition of Section 2039 changed the picture sharply. See Estate of Montgomery v.

poses, the statutory treatment of amounts that are recognized as the proceeds of insurance on the decedent's life will now be considered.

[3] Amounts Receivable by or for the Estate

If the proceeds of insurance on the decedent's life are "receivable by the executor" of the decedent's estate, they are a part of the decedent's gross estate for tax purposes. Section 2042(1) so provides. This provision is not interpreted strictly to require one named in a will as "executor" to be entitled to the proceeds. Certainly, if no will is executed but insurance proceeds come into the hands of an administrator, the statutory requirement is satisfied. In fact, the Treasury has long given this provision an even broader meaning, and insurance proceeds are "receivable by the executor" if they are "receivable by or for the benefit of the estate."[21] The test under Section 2042(1), then, is whether the proceeds are either payable into the estate or legally committed to the discharge of obligations of the estate.[22] Thus, insurance proceeds nominally payable to other named beneficiaries may still be "receivable by the executor" within the meaning of the statute if, or to the extent that, such beneficiaries are legally bound to use the proceeds to discharge the estate's obligations, such as taxes, debts, or other charges.[23] And insurance payable to a creditor as security for a loan to the decedent is "receivable by the executor," presumably up to the amount of the loan, although the amount included may be offset by a deduction under Section 2053.[24]

[a] Meaning of "Executor"

There is a technical flaw in the statute but it does not actually affect this insurance provision. Section 2203 purports to define "executor" for all estate tax purposes as the executor or administrator or, if neither is appointed, "then any person in actual or constructive possession of any property of the dece-

---

Comm'r, 56 TC 489 (1971), aff'd per curiam, 458 F2d 616 (5th Cir.), cert. denied, 409 US 849 (1972).

[21] Reg. § 20.2042-1(b)(1). For unusual applications of Section 2042(1), see Draper Estate v. Comm'r, 536 F2d 944 (1st Cir. 1976); First Kentucky Trust Co. v. United States, 737 F2d 557 (6th Cir. 1984).

[22] See Fox, "Estate: A Word to Be Used Cautiously If at All," 81 Harv. L. Rev. 992 (1968).

[23] Reg. § 20.2042-1(b)(1). If insurance proceeds are payable to a named beneficiary but in fact are used, though not legally required to be used, for estate obligations, the named beneficiary has made a gift to the estate beneficiaries.

[24] Reg. § 20.2042-1(b)(1). Bintliff v. United States, 462 F2d 403 (5th Cir. 1972). See discussion of IRC § 2053 at ¶ 5.03.

dent." Categorical as this definition may seem, it cannot properly be, and is not, taken into account in the interpretation of the clause "receivable by the executor" in the insurance section. The definition of "executor" serves other purposes, such as indicating who must file estate tax returns and pay the tax.[25]

Just as in some circumstances insurance payable to named beneficiaries may be "receivable by the executor" within the meaning of the statute, there are circumstances in which proceeds payable to the executor, according to the terms of the policy, will not be so regarded for tax purposes. In some states, statutes have provided that the surviving spouse and children are entitled to the husband's or father's life insurance proceeds that are not otherwise committed by will or by the terms of the policy.[26] Under such statutes, insurance proceeds nominally payable to the estate or the executor inure to the benefit of such survivors and are treated as insurance payable to other beneficiaries and are not within Section 2042(1),[27] although they still may be subject to inclusion under Section 2042(2), as is indicated in the following discussion. As is often true with respect to other sections as well, the vagaries of state law directly affect the practical operation of the insurance section.

[b] Simultaneous Death

A comparable problem is presented by the simultaneous death of the insured and a primary beneficiary if the beneficiary is not the owner of the policy on the insured's life.[28] In such circumstances, the Uniform Simultaneous Death Act presumes the insured survived.[29] If the secondary beneficiary is the insured's estate, the proceeds will be included under Section 2042(1). If some third party is the secondary beneficiary, the result under Section 2042(2) is not altered by the simultaneous deaths, because the result under that provision, as explained below, is dependent upon the decedent's incidents of ownership in the policy, not upon who is the beneficiary of the policy.

---

[25] See discussion of IRC § 2203 at ¶ 8.02.

[26] E.g., now-repealed (1985) ND Cent. Code § 26-10-18 (1978).

[27] Webster v. Comm'r, 120 F2d 514 (5th Cir. 1941).

[28] For an example of a situation of simultaneous death in a community property state, see Estate of Marks v. Comm'r, 94 TC 720 (1990), in which a husband and wife took out an insurance policy on the life of the other. The Tax Court held that under state (Louisiana) law, each policy was the separate property of the noninsured spouse who purchase and owned it, not the property of the spouse whose life was insured. See ¶ 4.05[6] for a discussion of the Section 2033 problems that arise on the simultaneous death of the insured and one who owns a policy on the insured's life.

[29] E.g., Fla. Stat. § 732.601(4) (2001); NY Est. Powers & Trusts Law § 2-1.6 (McKinney 2001).

[c] Is Insured's Wealth Transmitted?

Section 2042(1) of the insurance section may well be regarded as a precautionary and perhaps unnecessary provision. In an early case, the proceeds of an insurance policy owned by a decedent until death were paid to the decedent's executor. The court held that they were includable in the decedent's gross estate, as property owned by the decedent and subject to debts and claims, under the forerunner of present Section 2033.[30] It seems certain the same result would be reached today in the absence of Section 2042. The discussion here only concerns something clearly owned by the decedent that happens to increase in value at the moment of the decedent's death.[31] It is not clear that the same result would follow if another, who was the outright owner of a policy on the decedent's life, directed the payment of the proceeds to the decedent's estate by way of beneficiary designation. Here, the decedent would never have any interest in the proceeds. However, speculation under Section 2033 is hardly profitable when Section 2042(1) clearly includes in the decedent's gross estate the proceeds of insurance on the decedent's life that are paid to the decedent's estate.[32]

The philosophy behind Section 2042(1) is open to challenge. If a person, D, acquires insurance on D's life and holds onto it so that the proceeds actually fatten D's estate upon D's death, it seems fair enough to subject the proceeds to estate tax; that is, the usual transmission of wealth by D can be identified. The policy of Section 2042(1) that prescribes the same result if another, A, acquires the policy and holds onto it until D's death but designates D's estate as beneficiary, may be more open to question on the ground that it is A's wealth that is transmitted. What if A arranged for the policy but D paid all the premiums, or vice versa? In Section 2042(1), Congress looks only very narrowly at whether something is paid to or for the benefit of the estate and really not at all at who did what and with what and to whom; and this is not in keeping with other sections defining the gross estate that, although sometimes too sophisticatedly, seek to identify wealth transmission of a testamentary nature by D as a basis for taxing D's estate. Nevertheless, D can direct the transmission of the wealth involved.[33]

---

[30] Mimnaugh v. United States, 7 AFTR 8940 (Ct. Cl. 1928), cert. denied, 280 US 563 (1929).

[31] Cf. Goodman v. Granger, 243 F2d 264 (3d Cir.), cert. denied, 355 US 835 (1957).

[32] Adverse comments in this and the next paragraph should be measured against the competing philosophies of the Fifth and Seventh Circuits, reflected in the discussion of Second Nat'l Bank of Danville v. Dallman and United States v. Keeter, at ¶ 4.13[2][b] text accompanying notes 15, 16. The long reach of Section 2042(1) may be supported by the Fifth Circuit's view that a decedent has a general power under Section 2041 over amounts coming into the decedent's estate.

[33] See supra note 32.

[4] Amounts Receivable by Other Beneficiaries

The law has vacillated on the treatment of insurance proceeds paid to beneficiaries other than the estate. However, Section 2042(2) now provides a single test for determining whether amounts receivable by beneficiaries other than the estate under insurance policies on the decedent's life are includable in the decedent's gross estate. If at death the decedent had any of the incidents of ownership in the policy, exercisable alone or in conjunction with any person, the proceeds form a part of the decedent's gross estate. If the decedent had no such incident, they do not.[34] After an initial exploration of Section 2042(2), it is necessary to consider ownership incidents a decedent may have, not merely in the decedent's personal capacity but, for example, as trustee or in some similar position.

[a] Incidents of Ownership

The "incidents" test is statutory recognition of the concept of ownership as a bundle of rights. Full ownership is not required by Section 2042(2); if the decedent had at death one or more of the rights that go to make up complete ownership,[35] Congress has decided that is enough to bring the proceeds of the policy into the decedent's estate. Except in one respect soon to be mentioned, the statute does not define "incidents of ownership." However, in the course of enactment of the Revenue Act of 1942 when this provision was added to the statute, the House Ways and Means Committee listed some such incidents, although the list was not presented as exhaustive.[36] They are "the right of the insured or his estate to the economic benefits of the insurance, the power to

---

[34] Under Section 811(g) (1939), an alternate test, now long abandoned, was whether the decedent had directly or indirectly paid the insurance premiums. Doubt that premium payments could constitutionally support an estate tax on insurance payable to other beneficiaries was removed in United States v. Manufacturers Nat'l Bank of Detroit, 363 US 194 (1960).

[35] Estate of Margrave v. Comm'r, 618 F2d 34 (8th Cir. 1980). The decedent's inter vivos revocable trust was named beneficiary of a life insurance policy on the decedent's life owned by his spouse, but his spouse retained the right to change beneficiaries. At the decedent's death, he held only the mere expectancy of receiving the proceeds in the trust, and the court held that the expectancy was not sufficient to cause Section 2042(2) inclusion. The Service agrees. Rev. Rul. 81-166, 1981-1 CB 477. Estate of O'Daniel v. United States, 6 F3d 321 (5th Cir. 1993) (no legal power to exercise incidents of ownership). See also Estate of Keitel v. Comm'r, 60 TCM (CCH) 425 (1990) (decedent held incidents).

[36] HR Rep. No. 2333, 77th Cong., 1st Sess. (1942), reprinted in 1942-2 CB 372, 491.

change the beneficiary,[37] the power to surrender or cancel the policy,[38] the power to assign it, the power to revoke an assignment, the power to pledge the policy for a loan,[39] or the power to obtain from the insurer a loan against the surrender value of the policy."[40] In general, the Treasury and the courts have accepted these illustrations of incidents of ownership when they involve an economic benefit to the decedent.[41]

Thus, the Supreme Court has held flight insurance proceeds includable in a decedent's gross estate on the ground that the decedent had the legal right to change the beneficiary of the policy, even though as a practical matter the decedent could not exercise the right while the plane was in flight.[42] The Tax Court has also held insurance proceeds payable to the decedent's children includable, even though the decedent's retained incident of ownership in the policy was only the right to borrow on the policy for the purpose of paying the premiums.[43] Less surprisingly, perhaps, the Fifth Circuit has held a policy assigned to a third party includable in the decedent's gross estate where the policy was collateral for a loan taken out by the decedent.[44] However, the Third Circuit has held that a decedent's power to veto the assignment of a policy on the decedent's life to a person lacking an insurable interest is not an incident of ownership.[45]

---

[37] This has been held to include a power to veto another person's change of beneficiary. Schwager v. Comm'r, 64 TC 781 (1975). Cf. Rev. Rul. 75-70, 1975-1 CB 301.

[38] Priv. Ltr. Rul. 9745019 (Aug. 8, 1997) (no power to surrender split dollar life insurance policy where power subject to owner's option to pay the cash surrender value).

[39] Estate of Krischer v. Comm'r, 32 TCM (CCH) 821 (1973).

[40] Rev. Rul. 79-129, 1979-1 CB 306.

[41] E.g., Reg. § 20.2042-1(c)(2); Comm'r v. Treganowan, 183 F2d 288 (2d Cir.), cert. denied, 340 US 853 (1950). The Treasury's victory in *Treganowan* may have been abandoned in Rev. Rul. 72-307, 1972-1 CB 307. See infra ¶ 4.14[6] text accompanying note 101. The Tax Court has taken the position that there must be some right to initiate or consent to action in order for any "incident" to exist. See Estate of Smith v. Comm'r, 73 TC 307 (1979), acq. in result 1981-1 CB 2. Cf. Rev. Rul. 79-46, 1979-1 CB 303, which is distinguished and criticized in *Smith*. See also Eliasburg, "IRC § 2042—The Estate Taxation of Life Insurance: What Is an Incident of Ownership?" 51 Taxes 91 (1973); Simmons, "Incidents of Ownership—Some Haunting Reminders," 57 ABAJ 815 (1971).

[42] Comm'r v. Estate of Noel, 380 US 678 (1965).

[43] Estate of McCoy v. Comm'r, 20 TCM (CCH) 224 (1961).

[44] Prichard v. United States, 397 F2d 60 (5th Cir. 1968), involving a community property situation. It is possible where a policy has been assigned as security for a loan that both paragraphs (1) and (2) of Section 2042 will apply. See the district court's opinion in Prichard v. United States, 255 F. Supp. 552 (ND Tex. 1966). Compare Estate of Glade v. Comm'r, 37 TCM (CCH) 1318 (1978) with Bintliff v. United States, 462 F2d 403 (5th Cir. 1972).

[45] Rockwell v. Comm'r, 779 F2d 931 (3d Cir. 1985).

[b] Reversionary Interest

By express provision in Section 2042(2), a reversionary interest is an incident of ownership only if the value of the reversionary interest exceeded 5 percent of the value of the policy immediately before the decedent's death. It is immaterial whether the reversionary interest arose by express provision in the insurance policy or any instrument of transfer or by operation of law. The statute, not fully defining "reversionary interest," nevertheless specifies that it includes "a possibility that the policy, or the proceeds of the policy, may return to the decedent or his estate, or may be subject to a power of disposition by him."[46] These concepts are so closely parallel to the provisions of Section 2037(b) that a separate extended discussion is not undertaken here.[47]

As in the case of Section 2037, a reversionary interest is disregarded if its value does not exceed 5 percent of the vaue of the policy immediately before death. In other words, a very remote reversionary interest is not treated as an incident of ownership. The regulations recognize that the question of the relative value of the reversionary interest here is to be determined in accordance with the same principles as are applied under Section 2037,[48] But they also recognize that controlling powers in others, which would affect the value of the decedent's reversionary interest, must be taken into account, as illustrated by the following example from the regulations:[49]

> [T]he decedent would not be considered to have a reversionary interest in the policy of a value in excess of 5 percent if the power to obtain the cash surrender value existed in some other person immediately before the decedent's death and was exercisable by such other person alone and in all events.

Two further brief observations may be made. First, in making an assignment of an insurance policy with a view to escaping estate tax liability, the provisions of the policy must be closely examined. If the policy itself confers ultimate, indefeasible rights on the decedent or the decedent's estate, such provisions may give rise to a damaging reversionary interest no matter how complete and outright the assignment may otherwise be. In this connection, it should be said that pre-1954 and perhaps more recent assignments of many existing policies should be carefully reviewed. Before the enactment of the 1954 Code, an individual knew the individual's estate would include insurance on the individual's life if the individual had paid the premiums on such insurance. There was no occasion to worry about ownership of, or incidents of ownership

---

[46] IRC § 2042(2). Cf. Rev. Rul. 76-421, 1976-2 CB 280.

[47] See ¶ 4.09[4]. Cf. Priv. Ltr. Rul. 8819001 (Jan. 6, 1988).

[48] Reg. § 20.2042-1(c)(3). See ¶ 4.09[4][f].

[49] Reg. § 20.2042-1(c)(3).

in, the policy in these circumstances; the proceeds would be includable without regard to such considerations. Now, of course, a complete assignment of all interest in the policy, if not within three years of death, will defeat the estate tax, even if the decedent pays or has paid all premiums; but any effort to take advantage of this principle must be carefully undertaken.

Second, the statute makes no reference to a remainder, as opposed to a reversionary interest. Two thoughts occur. One, is a remainder interest an incident of ownership? The statute contains no express indication to the contrary. Two, the 5 percent rule that expressly excludes from "incidents of ownership" a remote reversionary interest (perhaps raising a negative inference that a remainder is an incident of ownership) is not phrased so as to apply to a remainder interest. If that exclusionary rule does not apply, a virtually valueless contingent remainder in a policy never otherwise owned by the decedent might be held to be an "incident of ownership" that would require the inclusion of the proceeds in the decedent's gross estate.

Suppose, for example, a wife takes out an insurance policy on her husband's life making herself primary beneficiary and their many children and grandchildren the contingent beneficiaries. The husband may have no interest in the policy except that, by its terms, his estate is the ultimate beneficiary if all other beneficiaries predecease him. He would have a remainder interest quite possibly of little or no value at the time of his death. However, if this is an incident of ownership and not a "reversionary interest," is the effect to tax his estate on the full proceeds of the policy?[50] The result should be rejected even if it requires bold judicial action. Elsewhere in this discussion,[51] it is suggested that something may be a Section 2042(2) incident in one setting but not in another. Here, if all the decedent ever had is a remote (less than 5 percent) contingent interest in a policy that never reached fruition and that terminated at the decedent's death, the decedent's estate simply should not be taxed. A very remote contingent remainder might be viewed as an incident of ownership of no "economic benefit" to the decedent.[52]

[c] Effect of Policy Terms

Whether a decedent had any of the incidents of ownership in an insurance policy is generally determined by the terms of the policy itself. If the decedent's estate claims that for some reason, the policy is not determinative, the courts may look to the substance of the transaction to determine who held the

---

[50] The point seems not to have been argued in Estate of Karagheusian v. Comm'r, 233 F2d 197 (2d Cir. 1956).

[51] See infra ¶ 4.14[4][e].

[52] See infra ¶ 4.14[4][f].

incidents of ownership.[53] However, the express language of the policy obviously prevails over any contrary unenforceable intentions of the parties,[54] and the burden of proof to overcome any terms of the policy is upon the decedent's estate.[55] Although this result may seem inequitable in some situations, the alternative of permitting wholesale exceptions to the application of the express policy language seems far less attractive,[56] particularly when attention to this matter by the decedent and counsel prior to the decedent's death will eliminate the problem.

[d] Buy-and-Sell Agreements

Partners, members of limited liability companies, and corporate shareholders sometimes enter into buy-and-sell agreements that are funded with life insurance.[57] The terms of the agreements may conflict with the terms of the supporting policies.[58] If, for example, surviving shareholders are required to purchase the stock of a deceased shareholder with the proceeds of insurance on the shareholder's life, the proceeds must be available to them for that purpose at the shareholder's death. Under local law, an agreement of this type may therefore amount to a surrender of the right to change beneficiaries, seemingly conferred on the decedent by the insurance contract, and support a decision that the decedent had no incidents of ownership.[59] It seems less likely, absent ownership incidents in the decedent under express terms of the insurance pol-

---

[53] Estate of Morton v. United States, 457 F2d 750 (4th Cir. 1972); Estate of Beauregard v. Comm'r, 74 TC 603 (1980), acq. 1981-1 CB 1; Estate of Dawson v. Comm'r, 57 TC 837 (1972), aff'd in an unpublished opinion (3d Cir. 1973); National Metropolitan Bank of Washington v. United States, 87 F. Supp. 773 (Ct. Cl. 1950); Watson v. Comm'r, 36 TCM (CCH) 1084 (1977).

[54] Comm'r v. Estate of Noel, 380 US 678 (1965); United States v. Rhode Island Hosp. Trust Co., 355 F2d 7 (1st Cir. 1966); Estate of Collino v. Comm'r, 25 TC 1026 (1956), acq. 1956-2 CB 5; Cockrill v. O'Hara, 302 F. Supp. 1365 (MD Tenn. 1969); Kearns v. United States, 399 F2d 226 (Ct. Cl. 1968). But see Estate of Piggott v. Comm'r, 340 F2d 829 (6th Cir. 1965).

[55] Kearns v. United States, 399 F2d 226 (Ct. Cl. 1968). See Estate of Jordahl v. Comm'r, 65 TC 92 n.5 (1975) (burden met).

[56] See United States v. Rhode Island Hosp. Trust Co., 355 F2d 7 (1st Cir. 1966).

[57] See Adams, Herpe & Carey, "Buy-Sell Agreements After Chapter 14," 132 Tr. & Est. 22 (May 1993); August, "Buy-Sell Arrangements: Estate, Business and Tax Considerations," 51 NYU Inst. on Fed. Tax'n 4.1 (1993); Gamble, "Buy-Sell Agreements, Transfer Restrictions and Section 2703; Have Buy-Sells Gone Bye-Bye?" 50 Inst. on Fed. Tax'n 19.1 (1992). See also ¶ 19.04.

[58] See TAM 9349002 (Aug. 25, 1993) (decedent's power under buy-sell agreement to withhold consent to exercise of policy rights under life insurance policy purchased by corporate trustee pursuant to buy-sell agreement provided decedent incidents of ownership of policy).

[59] First Nat'l Bank of Birmingham v. United States, 358 F2d 625 (5th Cir. 1966).

icy, that a court will find such incidents arising out of collateral agreements.[60] A person could also become outright owner of a policy by way of transfer by its initial owner,[61] without such complete ownership incidents being reflected at all in the terms of the policy. In the buy-and-sell agreement situation, matters are sometimes complicated by a potential problem of double inclusion, with the decedent's stock, interest in a limited liability company, or partnership interest being taxed as the decedent's property under Section 2033, but with that interest possibly including at least part of the value of the insurance taxed to the decedent's gross estate under Section 2042. The avoidance of the problem is examined more fully later in this discussion.[62]

[e] "Incidents" in Context

A certain amount of sophistication is required to interpret a statutory phrase one way in one circumstance and a different way in another. Nevertheless, if Section 2042(2) is to fit gracefully into the overall scheme of federal estate taxation, the Treasury and the courts must be just that ambidextrous. It usually seems fair enough to accord the term "incidents of ownership" a very broad meaning. Thus, if a person takes out and pays for a policy on the person's life, later assigning it to others but retaining a mere right to substitute A for B as beneficiary, Section 2042(2) taxes the person's estate at death on the proceeds. The circumstances are analogous to those governed by the lifetime transfer sections, Sections 2036 through 2038 (indeed may actually be within them), where relatively little retained interest or control is seen as a sufficient reason for the imposition of tax.

Suppose, however, that all the wealth represented by the policy is that of someone other than the decedent whose life is insured. Outside the area of insurance, such wealth is generally taxed in a decedent's estate either not at all[63] or only to the extent that the decedent has some control over the property that may be used directly or indirectly for the decedent's benefit.[64] The required administrative and judicial ambidexterity under Section 2042(2) then, is this: (1) if the origin of the insurance is such that some form of wealth transfer by the decedent is evident, very slender Section 2036-, Section 2037-, and Section 2038-type rights should be regarded as incidents of ownership; but (2) if the policy is not generated at all by the decedent's wealth or is disassociated from

---

[60] E.g., Estate of Infante v. Comm'r, 29 TCM (CCH) 903 (1970).

[61] If the transfer is for valuable consideration (not a gift) receipt of the proceeds by a corporate shareholder (but not a partner or member of a limited liability company) will result in income tax consequences. IRC § 101(a)(2).

[62] See infra ¶ 4.14[5]; Reg. § 20.2042-1(c)(6).

[63] Cf. IRC §§ 2039, 2040. But see IRC § 2040(b).

[64] Cf. IRC § 2041.

the decedent by a prior outright gift, then only stronger Section 2041-type rights should be recognized as incidents of ownership.[65] Such a reading of Section 2042(2) is in keeping with the clear inference in the legislative history that when Congress amended the life insurance rules in 1954, an objective was to bring the treatment of life insurance more in line with the treatment accorded other forms of wealth.[66] No doubt the statute should be more explicit; in its present form it offers a judge little guidance as to what kinds of "incidents" to look for in a given case.

In *Estate of Skifter v. Commissioner*,[67] the decedent had been the owner of a policy of insurance on his life. More than three years before his death, he transferred the policy to his wife. Upon her death, which occurred before his, the policy fell into a trust of which the decedent was trustee. Through his powers as trustee, he had the right to change beneficiaries under the policy, but not in any way to benefit himself. A mechanical, syllogistic approach to the problem would be to say: The right to change beneficiaries is an incident of ownership; decedent had that right; Section 2042(2) taxes the policy in his estate. But both the Tax Court and the Second Circuit rejected this line of reasoning, which would result in treating life insurance differently from other forms of property.[68] Instead, the decedent's power to change the beneficiaries was not treated as an incident of ownership. The critical factor in *Skifter* is clearly not that the decedent's power could be exercised only as a trustee. If the decedent had created the trust, the proceeds should be included in the decedent's estate.[69] If the decedent's right to change the beneficiaries included a

---

[65] Cf. IRC § 2041(b).

[66] S. Rep. No. 1622, 83d Cong., 2d Sess. 124 (1954): "No other property is subject to estate tax where the decedent initially purchased it and then long before his death gave away all rights to the property and to discriminate against life insurance in this regard is not justified."

[67] Estate of Skifter v. Comm'r, 468 F2d 699 (2d Cir. 1972), aff'g 56 TC 1190 (1971).

[68] It might be argued that Section 2038 would apply to this situation on the theory that the policy was once transferred gratuitously by the decedent and he could at death change interests in it. See White v. Poor, 296 US 98 (1935), contra. But see, overruling *White v. Poor*, the phrase in Section 2038(a)(1), "without regard to when or from what source the decedent acquired such power." But this interpretation should be rejected when, as here, the decedent has made a no-strings transfer of the property. Reed Estate v. United States, 1975-1 USTC ¶ 13,073 (ND Fla. 1975). It is the transferee's transfer to the trust that made the insurance proceeds only conditionally payable, and Section 2038 should be held inapplicable. The possible application of Section 2038 was apparently not raised in *Skifter*.

[69] Similarly, if the decedent transferred the policy to another person or to a trust but the decedent retained any incidents of ownership in it, inclusion would occur. Prichard v. United States, 397 F2d 60 (5th Cir. 1968). Cf. Estate of Lumpkin v. Comm'r, 474 F2d 1092 (5th Cir. 1973); Estate of Connelly v. United States, 551 F2d 545 (3d Cir. 1977) (in which the court improperly distinguished the Lumpkin case). In *Connelly*, the court

power to appoint proceeds to the decedent,[70] the decedent's estate would clearly be taxable.[71] Therefore, the *Skifter* result should apply only where the decedent either previously made an outright gift of the policy, completely dis-associating the policy, or never had any connection with the policy, and at the decedent's death the only power held was one under which the decedent could not obtain the economic benefits of the policy. While the Fifth Circuit dis-agrees with the *Skifter* result,[72] the Service has accepted the *Skifter* interpreta-tion of Section 2042(2).[73]

[f] Economic Benefit

The Tax Court seems prepared to give a narrow meaning to "incidents of ownership" under all circumstances, restricting the term to incidents from which the decedent derives some economic benefit. In the *Jordahl* case,[74] on facts something less than compelling, the court found no "economic benefit" in a decedent who as trustee could borrow on policies of insurance on his life held in a trust created by him, but only in order to pay premiums. The Sixth Circuit has taken a similar view.[75] It is a question of whether this position is too generous.[76] In any event, in some courts there is still room to argue that the term "economic benefit" in the regulations[77] modifies and limits the scope of the examples of ownership incidents that follow it.[78]

---

should have included the portion of the proceeds over which the decedent in conjunction with others held a power to alter the time of the beneficiary's enjoyment. In Rev. Rul. 81-128, 1981-1 CB 469, the Service announced it will not follow *Connelly* except in the Third Circuit. See also Priv. Ltr. Rul. 9832039 (May 13, 1998) (transferor's power to re-move trustee for cause and reappoint another trustee other than the transferor was not an incident of ownership).

[70] Cf. IRC § 2041(b).

[71] Estate of Fruehauf v. Comm'r, 427 F2d 80 (6th Cir. 1970); Estate of Karagheusian v. Comm'r, 233 F2d 197 (2d Cir. 1956); Gesner v. United States, 600 F2d 1349 (Ct. Cl. 1979). But see Hunter v. United States, 624 F2d 833 (8th Cir. 1980); Priv. Ltr. Rul. 9602010 (Sept. 29, 1995) (no inclusion where no general power to appoint to oneself).

[72] Terriberry v. United States, 517 F2d 286 (5th Cir. 1975), cert. denied, 424 US 977 (1976); Rose v. United States, 511 F2d 259 (5th Cir. 1975).

[73] Rev. Rul. 84-179, 1984-2 CB 195. See Folk, "Fiduciary Powers and Life Insur-ance: Putting Rev. Rul. 84-179 Into Perspective," 63 Taxes 417 (1985).

[74] Estate of Jordahl v. Comm'r, 65 TC 92, 101 (1975).

[75] Estate of Fruehauf v. Comm'r, 427 F2d 80 (6th Cir. 1970).

[76] The Tax Court's position was bolstered by the fact that any power the decedent had was limited by his fiduciary duties. Cf. United States v. Byrum, 408 US 125, reh'g denied, 409 US 898 (1972).

[77] Reg. § 20.2042-1(c)(2).

[78] Query whether the Tax Court's view gets some collateral support from the 5 per-cent test for reversions under Section 2042(2) and the regulations (Reg. § 20.2042-1(c)(6))

[5] Incidents Incidentally Held

The foregoing discussion of the meaning of the phrase "incidents of owner-ship" encompasses the question of whether the decedent had "possessed" in a direct way any such incidents. Further consideration must now be given to the question whether some indirect relationships that a decedent has to a policy on the decedent's life are enough to confer on the decedent proscribed ownership incidents.

[a] Shareholder in a Corporation

For example, the decedent may be a substantial shareholder in a corpora-tion that owns a policy of insurance on the decedent's life. If the proceeds of a policy on the life of a controlling shareholder of a corporation are payable to the corporation, the corporation's incidents of ownership will not be attributed to the decedent and Section 2042(2) will not apply to include the proceeds in the decedent's gross estate.[79] The rationale behind this provision is that inclu-sion of both the proceeds of the policy under Section 2042(2) and the value of the decedent's stock interest, which under the regulations[80] would be enhanced by the proceeds, would result in an unfair double inclusion in the decedent's gross estate.[81] However, if the proceeds are not paid to or for the benefit of the corporation, the regulation provides that if the decedent has legal or equitable ownership of more than 50 percent of the combined voting power of the stock of the corporation,[82] the corporation's ownership incidents[83] will be attributed

---

sometimes allocating proceeds between an insured's estate and his corporation in accor-dance with provision for payment.

[79] Reg. §§ 20.2042-1(c)(2), 20.2042-1(c)(6). See supra ¶ 4.14[4][d]. The regulations make it clear that the same rule applies if the proceeds must be used to defray corporate indebtedness so as to increase the net worth of the corporation.

[80] Reg. § 20.2031-2(f). Regulations Section 20.2042-1(c)(6) provides that if a portion of the proceeds are paid to the corporation and a portion to a third party, that portion paid to the corporation will not be included in the decedent's estate under Section 2042(2).

[81] See First Nat'l Bank of Birmingham v. United States, 1964-2 USTC ¶ 12,252 (ND Ga. 1964), rev'd, 358 F2d 625 (5th Cir. 1966).

[82] The decedent is then a controlling shareholder. Regulations Section 20.2042-1(c)(6) provides that this includes stock whose legal title is held directly by the decedent, by the decedent and another person jointly (to the extent of the decedent's Section 2040(a) share), and by a trustee of a voting trust (to the extent of the decedent's beneficial inter-est) or any other trust with respect to which at death the decedent was treated as an owner under Sections 671-679. See Priv. Ltr. Rul. 9746004 (Aug. 8, 1997) (no 50 percent own-ership where decedent and spouse each held only 36 percent of corporate stock as com-munity property). The regulation applies only if the proceeds are paid to a third person for a nonbusiness purpose. Reg. § 20.2042-1(c)(6).

[83] Reg. § 20.2042-1(c)(2). See Rev. Rul. 76-274, 1976-2 CB 278; Rev. Rul. 82-145, 1982-2 CB 213 (determining portion of incidents of ownership held by corporation). If the

to the decedent for purpose of Section 2042(2).[84] Such attribution has both legislative[85] and judicial[86] support where the decedent is the sole shareholder of the corporation. There is limited legislative and judicial authority to the same effect where the decedent owns something less than all the stock.[87] It is questionable whether the regulation should gain full judicial acceptance.[88] The attribution of one's ownership to another is of course common in the tax laws, but more often on the basis of the statute[89] than judicially or administratively.[90]

---

corporation held no incidents of ownership, there is no Section 2042(2) inclusion. Priv. Ltr. Rul. 9651030 (Sept. 20, 1996); Priv. Ltr. Rul. 9651017 (Sept. 18, 1996).

[84] Reg. § 20.2042-1(c)(6). Cf. Rev. Rul. 82-141, 1982-2 CB 209, applying the regulation in a Section 2035 situation. See Simmons, "Final Regs on Corporate Owned Life Insurance: Improved but Still Questionable," 41 J. Tax'n 66 (Aug. 1974); Finestein, "Corporate Owned Life Insurance and the Estate Tax—The New Majority Stockholder' Rule," 1 J. Corp. Tax'n 261 (1974); Davis, "Excluding Defined Benefit Plan Insured Death Benefits From the Gross Estate—Sole and Majority Shareholder," 9 Est., Gifts & Tr. J. 45 (1984).

However, the regulations specifically provide that in the case of group term life insurance (as defined in Regulations Sections 1.79-0, 1.79-1), the power to surrender or cancel a policy held by a corporation shall not be attributed to a decedent through the decedent's stock ownership. Cf. Rev. Rul. 83-148, 1983-2 CB 157, applying the group-term rule in a partnership context.

[85] HR Rep. No. 2333, 77th Cong., 1st Sess. (1942), reprinted in 1942-2 CB 372, 491.

[86] Cockrill v. O'Hara, 302 F. Supp. 1365 (MD Tenn. 1969); Estate of Dimen v. Comm'r, 72 TC 198 (1979), aff'd without op. (2d Cir. 1980).

[87] Estate of Levy v. Comm'r, 70 TC 873 (1978) (regulation upheld in the case of an 80.4 percent shareholder). Cf. Rev. Rul. 82-141, 1982-2 CB 209. Revenue Ruling 90-21, 1990-1 CB 172, amplifies Revenue Ruling 82-141 regarding application of the attribution role of Regulations Section 20.2042-1(c)(6) in a Section 2035 context. Revenue Ruling 82-141 provided that life insurance proceeds were includable in a deceased stockholder's gross estate under Section 2035(a), if, within three years of death, the decedent's corporation had transferred the incidents of ownership of a policy on the decedent's life. Revenue Ruling 90-21 amplifies Revenue Ruling 82-141 to provide that the same analysis would still apply upon a subsequent disposition of the controlling interest. In addition, Revenue Ruling 90-21 provides that life insurance proceeds will be included in a deceased stockholders estate under Section 2035(a) if, within three years of death, the decedent transfers the controlling interest in a corporation that owns a life insurance policy on the deceased stockholder's life.

See also Howard, "Corporate Control as an Incident of Ownership Under Section 2042 of the Internal Revenue Code," 13 Ariz. L. Rev. 619 (1971).

[88] But cf. Estate of Horne v. Comm'r, 64 TC 1020 (1975), especially 1024 n.5.

[89] E.g., IRC §§ 267(c), 318. See also IRC § 707(b).

[90] E.g., Helvering v. Clifford, 309 US 331 (1940).

[b] Partnership's Insurance on Partner

Parallel results may arise in the case of life insurance owned by a partnership on the life of a partner.[91] The aggregate (as opposed to corporate entity) nature of partnerships makes it possible to say more readily in such circumstances that the supposed partnership's ownership incidents are really those of all the partners as individuals. Therefore, the insured partner has ownership incidents "in connection with" the other partners, which would seem to bring the insurance proceeds into the partner's estate under Section 2042(2), and no doubt that result will follow if the proceeds are payable to an individual such as the decedent's spouse or child, without regard to the decedent's partnership interest.[92] There is no reason why Section 2042(2) should not be given its literal meaning in such circumstances.

However, in other instances it may be inappropriate to apply Section 2042(2) literally to insurance on the lives of the partners. If the policy is an asset of the partnership, it may, depending on agreement among the partners, enter into the measure of the value of the deceased partner's interest includable in the partner's gross estate under Section 2033. If so, Section 2042(2) should apply no more in this setting than in the corporate setting. The problem, again, is one of potential double inclusion, and the answer would seem to be, again, to take some liberties with the literal terms of Section 2042(2) when Section 2033 is adequate to handle the job.[93]

Nevertheless, the rights of partners are almost entirely a matter of contract or agreement. It is possible that the amount to which the estate of a deceased partner is entitled will be determined without regard at all to the proceeds of insurance on the partner's life, even though the proceeds may be paid directly to the partnership. If this is the case, the best analysis would seem to be that the deceased partner has, within the concept of Section 2042(2), transmitted wealth to the surviving partners. And this would seem to be so even if, voluntarily or in accordance with an agreement, they use the insurance proceeds to purchase the deceased partner's interest from the partner's estate. The thought

---

[91] Since a limited liability company is treated as a partnership for federal tax purposes, similar consequences are applicable to a life insurance policy on the life of a member of a limited liability company. See ¶ 4.05[7][c].

[92] Rev. Rul. 83-147, 1983-2 CB 158. But see Priv. Ltr. Rul. 200017051 (Jan. 24, 2000) (no Section 2042(2) where partnership agreement precluded insured partner from exercising incidents of ownership).

[93] Estate of Knipp v. Comm'r, 25 TC 153 (1955), aff'd on another issue, 244 F2d 436 (4th Cir.), cert. denied, 355 US 827 (1957) (no Section 2042(2) for ten policies on decedent's life owned and paid to partnership; however, 11th policy not owned by partnership was included under Section 2042(2)); Priv. Ltr. Rul. 9623024 (Mar. 6, 1996) (no Section 2042(2) double inclusion); Priv. Ltr. Rul. 9843024 (July 24, 1998) (same); Priv. Ltr. Rul. 200111038 (Dec. 15, 2000) (same). See supra ¶ 4.14[5][a] text accompanying notes 79–81.

here is analogous to the one found in the regulations relating to life insurance in the corporation setting; that is, if the insurance proceeds do not operate to enlarge the decedent's gross estate through the enhancement of a business interest, Section 2042(2) should be applied literally because of the essentially nonentity nature of a partnership. In other circumstances, both as to partnerships and corporations, one given to reading the statutory language closely cannot help but feel uncomfortable.

In general, no special problem is presented by a partner's personal ownership of an insurance policy on the life of a partner. If, under the policy, the insured partner has an incident of ownership such as the right to change beneficiaries, the proceeds of the policy should be included in the decedent's gross estate. Sometimes, however, it is the intention of the partners that the insured partner have no such control even though the policy expressly gives the partner the right to change beneficiaries. Despite such "policy" facts, the courts have been appropriately willing to hold that the decedent had no ownership incidents where the insurance company had merely erred and the incidents conferred on the decedent were inconsistent with an agreement between the partners.[94]

It is interesting to speculate whether reciprocal life insurance arrangements between partners should be treated under Section 2042(2) in a manner analogous to the treatment of reciprocal or crossed trusts under the lifetime transfer sections.[95] An argument can be made that if partner A insures the life of partner B, A retaining all ownership incidents in the policy, in exchange for partner B insuring the life of partner A, and each names beneficiaries in accordance with the wishes of the insured, upon the death of either partner, that partner should be treated as having incidents of ownership in the policy held by the other on the partner's life. The Treasury refused to apply this reciprocal concept in Revenue Ruling 56-397.[96] Even so, it would seem that the insured could sometimes control the distribution of the proceeds of the insurance on the insured's life under such circumstances. That may have been unlikely in the buy-and-sell setting of the revenue ruling,[97] but in other circumstances, a threat to direct the proceeds of the partner's policy to, for instance, the Red Cross might well ensure compliance with the wishes of the insured concerning the beneficiaries of the policy on the insured's life.

---

[94] Estate of Fuchs v. Comm'r, 47 TC 199 (1966), acq. 1967-1 CB 2. See also Estate of Infante v. Comm'r, 29 TCM (CCH) 903 (1970).

[95] See ¶ 4.08[7][d].

[96] 1956-2 CB 599.

[97] The factual situation of this ruling is distinguishable in that the proceeds were paid to the owner of the policy and not to beneficiaries named in accordance with the insured's wishes.

[6] Assignment of Group Term Insurance

Life insurance takes many forms. With today's emphasis on collective bargaining and fringe benefits, a popular form of insurance is employer-funded group term life insurance. Although such insurance has attributes that make it more difficult to assign than regular policies, an employee may effectively transfer all incidents of ownership in a group policy so that upon the employee's death the proceeds will not be included in the employee's gross estate.[98] Even a nonconvertible policy may be effectively assigned.[99] The Commissioner had contended that such policies were not fully assignable, because the employee's power to terminate the policy by terminating employment was an incident of ownership,[100] but that contention has been abandoned.[101] Consequently, an employee may effectively assign a nonconvertible group policy if the employee assigns all of the employee's rights. Even if the employee has a conversion privilege that would convert the policy to an individual policy should the individual cease employment, that is not an incident of ownership and the policy will not be included in the employee's estate.[102] Of course, an effective assignment of the policy does not preclude the possibility that the assignment will leave the employee's estate taxable under Section 2035(a).[103]

[7] Amount to Be Included

[a] In General

If insurance proceeds are includable in a decedent's gross estate, the amount to be included is "the full amount receivable under the policy."[104] If

---

[98] Rev. Rul. 69-54, Situation 3, 1969-1 CB 221. See Landorf v. United States, 408 F2d 461 (Ct. Cl. 1969). See also supra ¶ 4.14[5][a] note 84.

[99] Estate of Lumpkin v. Comm'r, 56 TC 815 (1971), rev'd on other grounds, 474 F2d 1092 (5th Cir. 1973). See also Landorf v. United States, 408 F2d 461 (Ct. Cl. 1969).

[100] Rev. Rul. 69-54, Situation 1, 1969-1 CB 221. See also Comm'r v. Treganowan, 183 F2d 288 (2d Cir.), cert. denied, 340 US 853 (1950).

[101] Rev. Rul. 72-307, 1972-1 CB 307.

[102] Estate of Smead v. Comm'r, 78 TC 43 (1982), holding that such a conversion privilege was too contingent and remote to be an incident of ownership under Section 2042(2). The Service agrees. Rev. Rul. 84-130, 1984-2 CB 194.

[103] Cf. Landorf v. United States, 408 F2d 461 (Ct. Cl. 1969); Kahn v. United States, 1972-2 USTC ¶ 12,890 (ND Ga. 1972). Cf. Rev. Rul. 80-289, 1980-2 CB 270. See infra ¶ 4.14[9][b].

[104] Reg. § 20.2042-1(a)(3). Compare the amounts to be included if the decedent owned a policy on the life of another that was included in the decedent's estate under Section 2033. Reg. § 20.2031-8(a). See ¶¶ 4.02[3][h], 4.05[6]. Form 712, Life Insurance Statement, must be completed by every life insurance company that issued a policy on the

the estate or beneficiary can take a lump sum as proceeds of the policy, that is the full amount receivable. If payments are to be made periodically in the form of an annuity with no option to take a lump sum, the amount receivable is the "sum used by the insurance company in determining the amount of the annuity."[105] However, if the periodic payments are merely payments of interest on the proceeds and not an annuity,[106] the face amount of the policy is included.[107] The amount to be included as insurance "proceeds" may include sums beyond the face amount of the policy if the beneficiary also receives additional amounts such as accumulated dividend additions or interest. However, includable proceeds do not include a mere return of prepaid premiums to one other than the decedent who purchased the policy;[108] of course, if the decedent was entitled to the prepaid premiums and they are payable to the decedent's estate, they are included in the decedent's gross estate under Section 2033.

[b] Inclusion of Only a Portion of Proceeds

It is possible that only a portion of the proceeds of a policy will be included in the decedent's gross estate. For example, if the decedent owned a paid-up policy on the decedent's life in the face amount of $10,000 that was pledged as security for a $5,000 note on which the decedent was liable, and, subject to the decedent's creditor's rights, more than three years prior to death the decedent assigned all the rights in the policy to the beneficiary, only $5,000 of the proceeds should be included in the decedent's gross estate.[109] That amount of proceeds would be an amount "receivable by the executor" under Section 2042(1).[110] It may be, additionally, that the pledge relationship constitutes an incident of ownership.[111] This further thought suggests the possible inclusion of the entire proceeds, but a proportionate concept seems prefera-

---

life of the decedent, and filed by the estate's executor with Form 706, United States Estate (and Generation-Skipping Transfer) Tax Return. Form 712, Life Insurance Statement (Rev. May 2000).

[105] Reg. § 20.2042-1(a)(3); Estate of Chisholm v. Comm'r, 37 BTA 167 (1938), nonacq. 1938-2 CB 39.

[106] Cf. IRC §§ 101(c), 101(d).

[107] Estate of Willis v. Comm'r, 28 BTA 152 (1933).

[108] Estate of Collino v. Comm'r, 25 TC 1026 (1956), acq. 1956-2 CB 5.

[109] The estate would also likely be allowed a Section 2053 deduction of $5,000. See ¶ 5.03[5][a].

[110] Reg. § 20.2042-1(b)(1); Estate of Matthews v. Comm'r, 3 TC 525 (1944), acq. 1944 CB 19; Bintliff v. United States, 462 F2d 403 (5th Cir. 1972).

[111] Prichard v. United States, 397 F2d 60 (5th Cir. 1968).

ble.[112] As the incident of ownership extends at most to half the date-of-death value of the policy, no more than that should be included under 2042(2).[113]

[8] Policy Purchased With Community Property Funds

The community property laws of some states effect a sharp difference in the estate tax treatment of the proceeds of life insurance. For example, an insurance policy on a husband's life paid for out of community property funds[114] is a community asset even if the proceeds are payable to the husband's estate. As the surviving wife has a right to half such proceeds, only one half is includable in the husband's estate upon his death, despite the usual consequences of Section 2042(1).[115] And if the proceeds are payable to a third party but the decedent had an incident of ownership in the policy that would invoke Section 2042(2), again only one half of the proceeds is includable in the decedent's estate despite the usual full inclusion consequences of Section 2042(2)[116] The theory here is that the decedent has incidents of ownership in only one half of the policy. Regarding the other half, the decedent acts only as an agent for the

---

[112] Cf. Rev. Rul. 79-129, 1979-1 CB 306.

The Service seems to adopt this proportionate approach with respect to split-dollar life insurance in which the insured decedent held incidents of ownership but a portion of the policy was owned by employer. Schwager v. Comm'r, 64 TC 781 (1975); Estate of Tomerlin v. Comm'r, 51 TCM (CCH) 831 (1986). Arguably, the decedent holds incidents of ownership over the entire policy, all of whose proceeds would be included in the decedent's gross estate under Section 2042(2) reduced by employer's claim against the estate under Section 2053(a)(3).

[113] The Service seems to adopt this proportionate approach with respect to split-dollar life insurance in which the insured decedent held incidents of ownership but a portion of the policy was owned by employer. Schwager v. Comm'r, 64 TC 781 (1975); Estate of Tomerlin v. Comm'r, 51 TCM (CCH) 831 (1986). Arguably, the decedent holds incidents of ownership over the entire policy, all of whose proceeds would be included in the decedent's gross estate under Section 2042(2) reduced by employer's claim against the estate under Section 2053(a)(3). Cf. Reg. § 20.2042-1(c)(5) (providing a like approach to community property insurance); Reg. § 20.2036-1(a) (adopting a similar proportionate approach to certain lifetime transfers).

[114] Questions can arise over whether the policy was acquired with community property funds. Daly v. United States, 1975-1 USTC ¶ 13,070 (D. Idaho 1975). Cf. infra text accompanying note 121.

[115] Reg. § 20.2042-1(b)(2). But see supra ¶ 4.14[3][c] note 32. See also Estate of Street v. Comm'r, 152 F3d 482 (5th Cir. 1998) (full proceeds included with court implying policy was not community property).

[116] Reg. § 20.2042-1(c)(5). But cf. Estate of Wildenthal v. Comm'r, 29 TCM (CCH) 519 (1970); Rev. Rul. 80-242, 1980-2 CB 276 (both involving a separate property policy with premiums paid with community property where the only right of the surviving spouse may be to receive repayment of the amount of premiums paid from the surviving spouse's share of community property).

decedent's spouse.[117] Of course, if the decedent's spouse predeceases the decedent, half of the value of community property insurance on the decedent's life will be included in the spouse's estate under Section 2033.[118]

Even if a policy is purchased with community property funds, it is possible for one spouse to make a gift of that spouse's one-half of the policy to the other spouse at the time of the acquisition.[119] Whether there has been an effective transfer of all ownership in the policy to one spouse depends on the effectiveness of the intended gift under local law,[120] which varies somewhat from state to state with regard to the formalities required. In general, the signature of one spouse on the policy or policy application is an insufficient affirmative act to overcome the community property presumption.[121] However, a specific "control clause" in the policy declaring that one spouse has or owns all incidents of ownership in the policy is generally sufficient to establish ownership of the policy in one spouse.[122]

Suppose community property funds are used to purchase separate policies on the lives of each spouse but there is an attempt to make each spouse both sole owner and beneficiary of the policy on the life of the other. If the attempt to convert ownership of each policy from community property to separate property is ineffective, then when the first spouse dies, one half of the value of

---

[117] If a decedent's spouse fails to assert the right to one half of the proceeds and they are paid to the decedent's executor and ultimately to some third party, or if they are paid directly to a third party, then the spouse has made a gift of the spouse's one half of the proceeds. Reg. § 25.2511-1(h)(9). Cf. Goodman v. Comm'r, 156 F2d 218 (2d Cir. 1946); Rev. Rul. 79-303, 1979-2 CB 332, involving various ramifications in a simultaneous death situation.

[118] United States v. Stewart, 270 F2d 894 (9th Cir. 1959), cert. denied, 361 US 960 (1960); California Trust Co. v. Riddell, 136 F. Supp. 7 (SD Cal. 1956); Rev. Rul. 67-228, 1967-2 CB 331. The amount of inclusion is determined under Regulations Section 20.2031-8(a). See Rev. Rul. 75-100, 1975-1 CB 303.

[119] Such a gift would not result in a taxable gift as it would fall within the exclusion of Section 2503(b) or qualify for the marital deduction of Section 2523. See Reg. § 25.2503-3(a); IRC § 2524. Additionally, any further premiums paid with community property funds, also likely intended as gifts, would similarly escape gift tax. IRC §§ 2503(b), 2523, 2524; Reg. § 25.2503-3(c) Ex. 6.

[120] See Kern v. United States, 491 F2d 436 (9th Cir. 1974) (Washington); Kroloff v. United States, 487 F2d 334 (9th Cir. 1973) (Arizona); Estate of Meyer v. Comm'r, 66 TC 41 (1976) (Washington); Catalano v. United States, 429 F2d 1058 (5th Cir. 1969) (Louisiana); Estate of Saia v. Comm'r, 61 TC 515 (1974), nonacq., 1978-2 CB 4 (Louisiana); Estate of McKee v. Comm'r, 37 TCM (CCH) 486 (1978) (Texas); Estate of Madsen v. Comm'r, 38 TCM (CCH) 1124 (1979), aff'd per curiam, 690 F2d 164 (9th Cir. 1982) (Washington); Estate of Hudnick v. United States, 83-2 USTC ¶ 13,539 (SD Tex. 1983) (Texas); Rev. Rul. 94-69, 1994-2 CB 241 (Louisiana).

[121] Freedman v. United States, 382 F2d 742 (5th Cir. 1967); Lutich v. United States, 1972-1 USTC ¶ 12,852 (ND Cal. 1972).

[122] Bintliff v. United States, 462 F2d 403 (5th Cir. 1972); Parson v. United States, 460 F2d 228 (5th Cir. 1972); Kern v. United States, 491 F2d 436 (9th Cir. 1974).

the proceeds is included in that spouse's estate under Section 2042(2) and one half of the value of the policy on the survivor's life is included in the survivor's estate under Section 2033.[123] If however, there is an effective conversion to separate property, then upon the death of the first spouse, none of the proceeds of the policy on the spouse's life is included in the spouse's estate under Section 2042 and only the full lifetime value of the policy on the survivor's life is included under Section 2033.[124]

If a husband and wife own a community property policy on the husband's life and the wife predeceases the husband, leaving her interest in the policy to him at her death, and if he continues to pay premiums on the policy and to retain incidents of ownership in it until his death, then the full amount of the proceeds is included in his estate under Section 2042.[125] However, if the wife's interest in the policy is bequeathed to a third person and thereafter the decedent pays all the premiums out of his own funds and retains incidents of ownership in the policy, the decedent and the third person own the policy as tenants in common. The portion of the proceeds includable in the decedent's estate is determined with reference to his contribution to the cost of the policy. Included are the full proceeds less the amount that bears the same ratio to the total proceeds as the wife's premium payments bear to the total premium payments.[126] While it might seem that this rule improperly invokes the old payment-of-premium test,[127] it does not. Reference to premium payment is made only to determine the relative ownership interests of the tenants in common. If, after his wife's death, one half of each of the decedent's premium payments is an effective gift to the third-party joint owner, then only one half of the proceeds plus any premium gifts made within three years of the decedent's death should be included in his gross estate.[128]

---

[123] Rev. Rul. 67-228, 1967-2 CB 331.

[124] Estate of Wilmot v. Comm'r, 29 TCM (CCH) 1055 (1970).

[125] But see Estate of Cavenaugh v. Comm'r, 51 F3d 597 (5th Cir. 1995) (only one half of proceeds of term policy included in survivor's gross estate because under state law the predeceasing spouse's death converted policy to a tenancy in common); Estate of Burris v. Comm'r, 82 TCM (CCH) 400 (210) (2001) (including one half of proceeds in husband's gross estate because the policy had been community property without considering aspects of the other half where proceeds paid to children).

[126] Scott v. Comm'r, 374 F2d 154 (9th Cir. 1967). See also Liebmann v. Hassett, 148 F2d 247 (1st Cir. 1945) (similar proportionate inclusion in Section 2035 joint payment-of-premiums context); Estate of Cervin v. Comm'r, 111 F3d 1252 (5th Cir. 1997) (one half proportionate inclusion where some premiums paid by decedent deemed paid by third parties with decedent having a claim against third parties for premiums).

[127] IRC § 811(g) (1939).

[128] Form should not control, but the gift might be clearer if the decedent gives cash equal to one half of the premium to the third party and the third party directly pays the third party's one half of the premium. Cf. Estate of Cervin v. Comm'r, 111 F3d 1252 (5th Cir. 1997) (one half of each premium was an account receivable of decedent against third

[9] Relation of Section 2042 to Other Sections Defining "Gross Estate"

[a] The Transfer Sections Generally

As previously indicated, the provisions of Section 2042 are not exclusive. Of course, if the particular policy involved is held not to be an insurance policy, Section 2042 is not applicable at all and other sections necessarily take over the determination of what is included in the gross estate. Even if insurance is involved, other sections will be applied if they bring into the gross estate something more than what would come in under Section 2042.

Section 2037 might easily be applicable if the decedent had made a lifetime gratuitous transfer of a policy on the decedent's life, but it is doubtful that the government will ever resort to that section. It contains a threefold test (transfer-survivorship-reversionary interest), and as the requirements of Section 2042 are met by satisfaction of the reversionary-interest test alone, it is difficult to see how resort to Section 2037 could produce a more onerous tax result than would follow from the application of Section 2042. For a similar reason, Section 2036 is not likely to be resorted to. If "insurance"[129] is involved and the decedent has transferred the policy in such a way as to reserve an income interest in it,[130] the decedent would have an incident of ownership that would activate Section 2042(2) without regard to Section 2036.[131]

Likewise, a power to alter, amend, revoke, or terminate that would bring into play Section 2038 would also satisfy the incident-of-ownership test of Section 2042(2).[132] Section 2039 is expressly made inapplicable to insurance,

---

party joint owner). For a general discussion of community property life insurance, see Thurman, "Federal Estate and Gift Taxation of Community Property Life Insurance," 9 Stan. L. Rev. 239 (1957).

[129] Fidelity-Philadelphia Trust Co. v. Smith, 356 US 274 (1958).

[130] Compare Estate of Larsh v. Comm'r, 8 TCM (CCH) 799 (1949) with Estate of Crosley v. Comm'r, 47 TC 310 (1966), acq. 1967-2 CB 2.

[131] It is not unlikely that Section 2036 will bring the value of an insurance policy on another's life into a decedent's gross estate. Such a result would be obvious if a third-party owner transferred a policy to a trust retaining income interests. A sneakier application of Section 2036 may arise out of a surviving beneficiary's election of a settlement option of income from proceeds for life, then proceeds to others. Compare Estate of Pyle v. Comm'r, 313 F2d 328 (3d Cir. 1963) (Section 2036 applied even though the decedent elected option before insured's death) with National City Bank of Cleveland v. United States, 371 F2d 13 (6th Cir. 1966) (Section 2036 held not applicable for lack of transfer by decedent where, while owner, she merely passively accepted income from proceeds for life and suffered proceeds to be paid to others at her death).

[132] See supra text accompanying notes 129–131; compare Estate of Skifter v. Comm'r, 468 F2d 699 (2d Cir. 1972), with Terriberry v. United States, 517 F2d 286 (5th Cir. 1975), cert. denied, 424 US 977 (1976).

and Section 2040 applies only to property in which the decedent has an owner-ship interest with others at death. A power of appointment, such as might be taxed under Section 2041, is certainly an "incident of ownership," although it is usually not treated as an interest in property.

[b] Near-Death Transfers

If the foregoing is correct, Section 2035(a), concerning transfers within three years of death, is the principal provision to stretch beyond the reach of Section 2042 to include amounts in a decedent's gross estate with respect to insurance policies on the decedent's life. If a transfer of a life insurance policy is within Section 2035(a), a question arises regarding the amount includable in the decedent's gross estate. A partial answer is the uniform date-of-death (or alternate valuation date) rule,[133] which runs through all the sections defining "gross estate." In the case of life insurance, its value takes account of the fact of the decedent's death. Thus, if a paid-up insurance policy was transferred by the decedent within three years of death, the full proceeds will be included in the decedent's gross estate;[134] and the amount included is increased by the amount of gift tax paid.[135]

Section 2035(a) applies only where the decedent actually held and trans-ferred Section 2042 incidents of ownership.[136] Cases involving transfers after

---

[133] IRC §§ 2031(a), 2032(a).

[134] Rev. Rul. 71-497, Situation 2, 1971-2 CB 329. As in other circumstances, a full and adequate consideration for the transfer of the policy will of course defeat the applica-tion of Section 2035(a). But a transfer for an amount equal to the cash surrender value of the policy clearly will not invoke this exclusionary rule. Estate of Pritchard v. Comm'r, 4 TC 204 (1944). In limited circumstances, the state of the insured's health may bear on what consideration will be adequate. Cf. Estate of Jennings v. Comm'r, 10 TC 323 (1948). Partial consideration will of course effect a reduction in the amount included in the gross estate. See the discussion of Section 2043(a) at ¶ 4.15[2] and the discussion of Section 2035(a) at ¶ 4.07[2][b].

[135] IRC § 2035(b).

[136] Estate of Headrick v. Comm'r, 93 TC 171 (1989) aff'd, 918 F2d 1263 (6th Cir. 1990); Leder v. Comm'r, 893 F2d 237 (10th Cir. 1989); Estate of Perry v. Comm'r, 927 F2d 209 (5th Cir. 1991); Estate of Chapman v. Comm'r, 56 TCM (CCH) 1451 (1989). All the above cases found Section 2035(a) inapplicable. In a follow-up development, in Perry, the Fifth Circuit has held that the estate was entitled to recover attorney fees for the cost of the appeal. Estate of Perry v. Comm'r, 931 F2d 1044 (5th Cir. 1991). These cases, along with various other planning aspects of life insurance trusts, are discussed in a short but excellent planning article by Aucutt & Hughes, "Irrevocable Life Insurance Trusts Still Have Planning Possibilities After TAMRA," 71 J. Tax'n 258 (1989). See also Lien, "Exclusion of Life Insurance Proceeds From the Value of the Decedent's Gross Estate: Estate of Perry v. Commissioner," 46 Tax Law. 295 (1992).

See also Salyer v. United States, 82 AFTR2d 98-5967 (ED Ky. 1998), aff'd, 99-2 USTC ¶ 60,362 (6th Cir. 1999) (Section 2035 applicable where policy transferred on

the amendment of Section 2035 in 1981 have refused to impute indirect acquisition of a policy to a decedent where the decedent did not actually hold incidents over the policy,[137] casting doubt on some cases arising under Section 2035 prior to its amendment in 1981.[138]

Suppose a policy is incompletely transferred by D. D might transfer a policy to another but continue under its terms to have the power to have the proceeds paid to D's estate if all of the beneficiaries predecease D, or D might retain the power to change the beneficiaries. These, of course, are incidents of ownership that would cause the proceeds to be included in D's gross estate under Section 2042(2). But now assume that D finally relinquishes all such powers within three years of D's death. The only logical conclusion is that the proceeds should still be included, and that is the Treasury's position.[139] The statute has been tidied up to support the result,[140] as the incidents-of-ownership test of Section 2042 would be largely a mockery if it could be defeated by last-minute, death-motivated relinquishment of proscribed incidents.[141]

---

company's records within three years of death). But see TAM 9615004 (Dec. 20, 1996) (corporate minutes evidenced transfer of policy more than three years before death even though transferred on company records within three years).

[137] For example, in Headrick v. Comm'r, 918 F2d 1263 (6th Cir. 1990), a trustee under no requirement to do so purchased a life insurance policy on the decedent's life with funds provided by the decedent, and in Leder v. Comm'r, 893 F2d 237 (10th Cir. 1989), the decedent's spouse applied for a policy on the decedent's life, and the decedent's wholly owned corporation paid the premiums on the policy. Neither case included the proceeds in the decedent's gross estate under Section 2035(a). See also TAM 9323002 (Feb. 24, 1993); Priv. Ltr. Rul. 9651004 (Aug. 26, 1996) (proceeds of a life insurance policy were not includable in decedent's gross estate under Section 2035(a)).

[138] Earlier cases under Section 2035, prior to its 1981 amendment (see supra ¶ 4.07[1]), found a constructive Section 2035 transfer or an agency relationship to pull the proceeds into a decedent's gross estate under the Section 2035(a) transfer requirement. See Bel v. United States, 452 F2d 683 (5th Cir. 1971), cert. denied, 406 US 919 (1972) (decedent took out a policy naming children as beneficiaries and paying premiums); Detroit Bank & Trust Co. v. United States, 467 F2d 964 (6th Cir. 1972), cert. denied, 410 US 929 (1973) (policy was taken out by the trust but decedent paid the only premium); First Nat'l Bank of Or. v. United States, 488 F2d 575 (9th Cir. 1973) (decedent's wife purchased policy on his life but decedent paid the premiums). See also Rev. Rul. 71-497, 1971-2 CB 329, Situation 2. The more recent cases require Section 2042 ownership prior to applying current Section 2035(a). Although Bel may still be followed, because the decedent can be viewed as owning the policy, and Headrick is distinguishable from Detroit Trust because there was no requirement for the trust to purchase the policy, Leder is directly contrary to First National Bank of Oregon, leaving these three cases in varying degrees of authority under current Section 2035(a).

[139] Reg. § 20.2042-1(a)(2).

[140] See IRC § 2035(a)(2); ¶ 4.07[2][a][ii]

[141] Cf. United States v. Allen, 293 F2d 916 (10th Cir.), cert. denied, 368 US 944 (1961). But see, e.g., Estate of Sullivan v. Comm'r, 175 F2d 657 (9th Cir. 1949); ¶¶ 4.08[8][b], 4.12[9].

The foregoing lifetime transfer discussion deals with paid-up policies. More often, premiums remain payable after a transfer. The four principal possibilities are as follows:

1. The decedent transfers the policy more than three years before death and the beneficiary pays all the premiums that subsequently come due. Nothing is included in the decedent's estate.[142]

2. The decedent's transfer is within three years of death, but again the beneficiary pays all post-transfer premiums. A part of the proceeds is includable in the decedent's gross estate.[143] The includable part of the proceeds is determined by subtracting from the full proceeds a portion of that amount commensurate with the portion of the premiums paid by the beneficiary.[144]

3. The decedent's transfer is within three years of death, and the decedent pays all the premiums that subsequently come due. The entire proceeds are includable in the decedent's gross estate.[145]

4. The decedent's transfer is made more than three years before death, but the decedent continues to pay all post-transfer premiums. The proceeds and the premiums are entirely excluded from the decedent's gross estate.[146]

---

[142] The decedent has no Section 2042(2) incidents at death, the transfer of the policy is outside the three-year rule of Section 2035(a), and the premium payments cannot be attributed to the decedent.

[143] Full inclusion might be expected here, since the decedent transferred the policy, the proceeds of which are paid at death. However, there is authority, long accepted as controlling, for treating the beneficiary's premium payments as in the nature of an improvement or betterment in something acquired from another. Liebmann v. Hassett, 148 F2d 247 (1st Cir. 1945). Cf. Rev. Rul. 67-463, 1967-2 CB 327. This is appropriate; the policy has become the property of the beneficiary that the beneficiary must "improve" if it is to retain its economic potential.

[144] Liebmann v. Hassett, 148 F2d 247 (1st Cir. 1945).

[145] The settled view seems to be that there is no basis for any reduction such as is recognized in the second situation just discussed. It could, however, be argued that the transfer of the policy is a complete transfer of an incomplete thing. Thereafter, the decedent's premium payments are not a further transfer of parts of the policy. Thus, the decedent's premium payments might be viewed the same as cash gifts to the beneficiary and subsequent premium payments by the beneficiary. If this view were taken, the part of the proceeds includable would be determined the same as in the second situation above, but to that would be added the amount of the post-transfer premiums paid by the decedent.

[146] If the decedent's premium payments within three years of death "engendered the entire right, title, and interest which" beneficiaries had in the policy, the entire proceeds may be includable. See Bel v. United States, 452 F2d 683, 690 (5th Cir.), cert. denied, 406 US 919 (1972). But see supra note 138. Cf. Leder v. Comm'r, 893 F2d 237 (10th Cir. 1989). See also Goodnow v. United States, 302 F2d 516 (Ct. Cl. 1962) (the life beneficiary of a trust who paid premiums on policies owned by the trust was not for that reason

[10] Background of the Section

No attempt is made here to trace the full history of Section 2042, but some of the highlights may be mentioned. The first federal estate tax statute did not deal expressly with insurance.[147] Nevertheless, it was held that insurance proceeds paid to the decedent's estate could be taxed as property owned by the decedent.[148] In 1918, in adding an insurance provision, Congress specifically taxed insurance receivable by the executor and also went after a tax on the proceeds of insurance policies "taken out by the decedent on his own life," even if the proceeds were payable to other named beneficiaries.[149] Seemingly a simple rule, this triggered a confusing series of administrative attempts to give meaning to the quoted language, which terminated in 1941 with a determination that the statute raised the question whether or to what extent the decedent had paid the premiums on the policy.[150] If the decedent had paid half the premiums, then one half of the policy was "taken out" by the decedent and half the proceeds were in the decedent's estate, and so forth. But the rule was not given full retrospective effect. Premiums the decedent had paid on or before January 10, 1941, were to be disregarded in applying this test, if, on that date, the decedent had no incidents of ownership in the policy.

From 1918 to 1942, the rule on includability of insurance proceeds payable to others was mitigated by a $40,000 exemption for such proceeds, which specific insurance exemption was not dropped from the statute until Congress undertook a general revision of the section in 1942. It was this insurance exemption that prompted the estate to argue in *Helvering v. Le Gierse*[151] that an insurance policy should be recognized as such even though it was taken out in combination with an annuity policy.

In 1942, Congress incorporated the Treasury's payment-of-premium test into the statute, including the rule that premiums paid by the decedent on or before January 10, 1941 were to be disregarded if, after that date, the decedent had no incidents of ownership in the policy.[152] Thus, a complete and irrevocable assignment before 1941 of a policy fully paid before that date would place the insurance outside the estate as far as the payment-of-premium test was concerned. It was this rule that prompted the taxpayer estate to argue in

---

deemed to be a settlor of the trust so as to make applicable Section 2036 to include trust assets in the life beneficiary's estate at death).

[147] Revenue Act of 1916, Pub. L. No. 64-271, 39 Stat. 756, 777 (1916).

[148] E.g., Mimnaugh v. United States, 7 AFTR 8940 (Ct. Cl. 1928), cert. denied, 280 US 563 (1929).

[149] Revenue Act of 1918, Pub. L. No. 65-254, § 402(f), 40 Stat. 1057, 1098 (1918).

[150] TD 5032, 1941-1 CB 427.

[151] Helvering v. Le Gierse, 312 US 531 (1941).

[152] Revenue Act of 1942, Pub. L. No. 77-753, § 404(c), 56 Stat. 798, 944 (1942).

Bohnen v. Harrison[153] and some other cases that an insurance policy should be recognized as such even though taken out in combination with an annuity policy.

In the 1942 revision, Congress added an alternative incidents-of-ownership test. Thus, from 1942 to 1954, insurance payable to others was included in the gross estate if the decedent had paid the premiums or if the decedent had any incidents of ownership in the policy at death. It is the incidents-of-ownership test, with some modifications, that survives as the sole test in the 1986 (and 1954) Code. The present provision is discussed above without precise reference to how it differs from the incidents-of-ownership test in the 1939 Code, but of course the differences are of importance in the case of decedents dying prior to August 17, 1954, on which date in general the 1954 Code became effective.

The insurance section has survived a number of constitutional squalls. It was sustained by the Supreme Court against constitutional attack in 1929,[154] after having lost a round with regard to an attempted retroactive application in 1925.[155] A serious constitutional shadow that was later thrown over the old payment-of-premium test has been removed.[156] There are few grounds upon which the section in its present form is open to serious constitutional challenge.

¶ 4.15 SECTION 2043. TRANSFERS FOR INSUFFICIENT CONSIDERATION

Section 2043 is divided into two parts. The first, Section 2043(a), contains an affirmative rule specifying the estate tax effect of a receipt by the decedent of partial consideration in connection with an inter vivos transaction giving rise to estate tax liability under Sections 2035 through 2038 and Section 2041. In brief, the section provides that a transfer includable under one of those sections will be exempted to the extent of the consideration received by the decedent.

The second part, Section 2043(b), contains generally a negative rule specifying certain advantages that may accrue to a decedent that cannot be treated as consideration to any extent for estate tax purposes. It applies to both claims against the gross estate and inter vivos transfers included in the gross estate.

---

[153] 199 F2d 492 (7th Cir. 1952), aff'd per curiam (by an equally divided court), 345 US 946, reh'g denied, 345 US 978 (1953).

[154] Chase Nat'l Bank v. United States, 278 US 327 (1929).

[155] Lewellyn v. Frick, 268 US 238 (1925).

[156] United States v. Manufacturer's Nat'l Bank of Detroit, 363 US 194 (1960).

An understanding of this Section 2043(b) restriction is necessary before considering Section 2043(a), and accordingly, the discussion will begin with the negative rule.

[1] Marital Rights: The Negative Rule

Section 2043(b)(1) provides that relinquishment or promised relinquishment of dower or curtesy or their statutory equivalents is not consideration in money or money's worth for estate tax purposes.[1]

An initial objective of Section 2043(b)(1) was to eliminate a form of estate tax avoidance that did not involve a lifetime transfer, specifically the contractual conversion of the wife's dower rights into a deductible claim against the estate. For example, if a husband died leaving an estate of $3 million and under state law the surviving spouse was entitled to one third, $1 million, as dower, this would not reduce the gross estate.[2] But without Section 2043(b)(1) the husband's estate would be entitled to a deduction of $1 million[3] if the surviving spouse and the decedent had entered into a contract by which she was to receive that amount from his estate in consideration for a waiver of her dower rights.[4] Although it was probably not initially intended, the Supreme Court has read Section 2043(b)(1) into the gift tax where it plays a role in determining whether lifetime interspousal transfers are gifts.[5]

The rule of Section 2043(b)(1) is closely related to the estate tax and gift tax marital deductions.[6] Prior to the Economic Recovery Tax Act of 1981[7] when there was a ceiling on those deductions, Section 2043(b)(1) played a more active role.[8] Now, however, there is an unlimited marital deduction for

---

[1] The predecessor of present Section 2043(b) was enacted in 1926 and amended by the Revenue Act of 1932. Revenue Act of 1926, Pub. L. No. 69-20, § 302(i), 44 Stat. 9, 71 (1926); Revenue Act of 1932, Pub. L. No. 72-154, § 804, 47 Stat. 169, 280 (1932). From that time on, it has been quite clear that a lifetime transfer is not saved from estate tax merely because it was made in exchange for the relinquishment of dower or curtesy rights or any statutory rights that are similar in purpose and effect.

[2] IRC § 2034.

[3] IRC § 2053(a)(3). If Section 2043(b)(1) presented no obstacle, such a claim could pass muster under Section 2053(c)(1)(A). See ¶¶ 5.03[5][a], 5.03[5][e].

[4] See S. Rep. No. 665, 72d Cong., 1st Sess. 50 (1931), reprinted in 1939-1 (Part 2) 496, 532.

[5] Merrill v. Fahs, 324 US 308 (1945). See ¶ 10.02[5][d].

[6] See ¶¶ 5.06, 11.03.

[7] Economic Recovery Tax Act of 1981, Pub. L. No. 97-34, 95 Stat. 172 (1981), reprinted in 1981-2 CB 256.

[8] But for Section 2043(b)(1), the estate in the hypothetical could conceivably argue for a deduction under Section 2053 in addition to the maximum marital deduction. If the husband left all his property to his surviving spouse, the result would have been a $2 mil-

most interspousal transfers either at death[9] or during life.[10] Thus, in the preceding hypothetical, if the husband leaves all his property to his surviving spouse, the husband's estate can receive a full $3 million deduction. The deduction, however, is under *Section 2056*. Section 2043(b)(1) still precludes a deduction of the claim under Section 2053 because the claim is founded on a promise or agreement that is not supported by consideration.

In view of the unlimited marital deduction, is Section 2043(b)(1) to be relegated to the scrap heap? Almost, but not quite. In a few situations, in which interspousal transfers do not qualify for a Section 2056 deduction,[11] the Section 2043(b)(1) preclusion of consideration for the transfer remains important.[12] Section 2043(b)(1) also has an impact in the divorce area with respect to post-divorce payments. If, in a divorce agreement, a spouse relinquishes the types of marital rights within the scope of Section 2043(b)(1), there may not be consideration for the transfer.[13] Despite some overlap in the interspousal and divorce negative consideration rules, there are sufficient differences to treat the two sets of negative rules separately.[14]

[a] The Negative Rule in a Marital Situation

The marital rights that are disqualified as consideration for estate tax purposes are explicit. In part, Section 2043(b)(1) echoes the provisions of Section

---

lion marital deduction under Section 2056 and a $1 million deduction under Section 2053. Cf. IRC § 2056(b)(9).

[9] IRC § 2056, as amended by the Economic Recovery Tax Act of 1981, Pub. L. No. § 97-34, 403(a), 95 Stat. 172, 301 (1981), reprinted in 1981-2 CB 256, 324. See infra text accompanying note 11.

[10] IRC § 2523, as amended by the Economic Recovery Tax Act of 1981, Pub. L. No. 97-34, § 403(b), 95 Stat. 172, 301 (1981), reprinted in 1981-2 CB 256, 324.

[11] See the terminable interest rule and the exceptions to the rule. IRC § 2056(b), discussed ¶¶ 5.06[7], 5.06[8]. See especially ¶ 5.06[7][b] text accompanying notes 176–181. Cf. ¶ 5.06[3][b]. The transfers may be either inter vivos transfers included in the decedent's gross estate under Sections 2035, 2036, 2037, 2038, and 2041 or testamentary transfers.

[12] For example, if *H* gratuitously transfers property to his children, reserving a twenty-year leasehold in the property, and then contracts with *W* that he will leave her the twenty-year leasehold in his will in exchange for her promised relinquishment of dower, the value of *H*'s interest in the leasehold is included in his gross estate under Section 2036. Are there any deductions? In the absence of a QTIP election under Section 2056(b)(7), a marital deduction under Section 2056 is foreclosed by the Section 2056(b)(1) terminable interest rule. See supra note 11. And a deduction under Section 2053 is precluded by Section 2043(b)(1). If it were not for Section 2043(b)(1), *W*'s nondeductible dower interests would have been contractually converted into a deductible claim against the estate under Section 2053.

[13] See infra ¶ 4.15[1][b].

[14] See infra ¶¶ 4.15[1][a], 4.15[1][b].

2034 in its reference to dower or curtesy and their statutory substitutes. The meaning of these terms, indicated in the comments on Section 2034,[15] is not further developed here, but it is not mere coincidence that these expressions are parallel, and their relationship should be made clear.

Now it will be seen, however, that Section 2043(b)(1) not only excludes dower, curtesy, or statutory equivalents, but it also goes on to disqualify as consideration "other marital rights in the decedent's property or estate." The question is: What further disqualification arises from this additional phrase? The answers come more readily if it is borne in mind that the disqualification aims at preventing the same kind of distortion that would result if dower and similar rights were treated as consideration.

One spouse's transfer may be at least in part in exchange for a relinquishment of the other partner's right to a share of the first spouse's estate at death under the laws of intestate succession. This right of the other spouse is disqualified by Section 2043(b)(1) as an "other" marital right.[16] It is an inchoate right "in the decedent's property or estate" that, like dower, even if asserted at death in a case of intestacy, will have no impact on the decedent spouse's gross estate. Therefore, for the same reasons as apply to dower, the right cannot be accorded estate tax recognition as consideration without serious distortion of estate tax liability.[17]

Other types of marital rights are not disqualified. For example, the interest a spouse has in community property is not a dower or curtesy interest, a statutory substitute therefore, or an "other" marital right within Section 2043(b)(1).[18] In fact, one spouse's community property interest is that spouse's property, not an interest in the property of the other spouse. Thus, if a wife transfers some of her noncommunity property to her husband in exchange for his interest of like value in community property, the exchange is for full consideration and is unaffected by Section 2043(b)(1). No distortion results because the husband's community property acquired by the wife in the exchange

---

[15] See ¶ 4.06.

[16] Cf. Estate of Herrmann v. Comm'r, 69 TCM (CCH) 1995 (1995), aff'd 85 F3d 1032 (2d Cir. 1996) (a waiver of right of equitable distribution (under New York law) in a prenuptial agreement did not provide consideration which is adequate and full in money or money's worth); Sutton v. Comm'r, 535 F2d 254 (4th Cir.), cert. denied, 419 US 1021 (1974) (prenuptual agreement forgoing marital rights did not constitute consideration for claim against decedent's estate). Cf. United States v. Davis, 370 US 65, 66 (1962).

[17] There is general agreement that "inheritance rights" are disqualified as consideration (cf. McMurtry v. Comm'r, 203 F2d 659 (1st Cir. 1953) (decided under the gift tax)), and the conclusion saves estate tax concern about what the value of the rights might be. But cf. United States v. Davis, 370 US 65 (1962).

[18] See Estate of Waters v. Comm'r, 48 F3d 838 (4th Cir. 1995) (under North Carolina equitable distribution statute, common law marital rights were converted to community property rights on divorce).

would not, but for the exchange, have been a part of her gross estate.[19] It replaces the property transferred, and the transfer therefore causes no artificial tax-free diminution of her gross estate.[20]

In a similar vein, a spouse's relinquishment of the spouse's right to support can be consideration.[21] If tunnel vision focuses only on the phrase "other marital rights," there will be trouble because a spouse's right to support is rather clearly a marital right other than a right such as dower. But if the whole phrase "other marital rights in the decedent's property or estate" is read, it will come closer to the correct conclusion because support rights are not rights in a spouse's property. Support rights are measured by a spouse's income and manner of living rather than by one's wealth or estate.[22] This close but proper reading of Section 2043(b)(1) to exclude support rights from the proscription of that provision has not invariably been followed,[23] but it has long been accepted by the Treasury.[24] The exclusion of support rights from the Section 2043(b)(1) proscription finds other collateral support. If the ejusdem generis canon of construction is applied,[25] and if the phrase "other marital rights in the decedent's property or estate" is properly read in the context of all of Section 2043(b)(1), the phrase "other marital rights" must mean rights such as dower, curtesy, and their statutory substitutes. But, as indicated, support rights are not like dower and similar property rights. Moreover, it is relevant to ask whether distortion will result from treating a relinquishment of support rights as consideration. If there is no settlement of support rights by way of a lifetime transfer, one spouse's lifetime payments for support during life do effect a natural

---

[19] Cf. Carli v. Comm'r, 84 TC 649 (1985) (interest in property received in relinquishment of community property rights under an antenuptial agreement is supported by adequate and full consideration); ¶ 4.05[2][a], supra ¶ 4.15[1] text accompanying note 5.

[20] Cf. ¶ 4.08[7][c] discussing the community property widow's election.

[21] But see Bowes v. United States, 77-2 USTC ¶ 13,212 (ND Ill. 1977), aff'd, 593 F2d 272 (7th Cir. 1979) (a purported relinquishment of support rights in a state that holds any such agreement void as against public policy did not constitute consideration).

[22] Cf. Bernatschke v. United States, 364 F2d 400 (Ct. Cl. 1966) (differentiating a property settlement from an alimony arrangement for purposes of determining whether Section 71 or Section 72 determined the income tax consequences of annuity payments received by a divorced wife prior to the 1984 amendment of Section 71).

[23] Estate of Meyer v. Comm'r, 110 F2d 367 (2d Cir.), cert. denied, 310 US 651 (1940).

[24] Rev. Rul. 68-379, 1968-2 CB 414, superseding ET 19, 1946-2 CB 166, which expressed the same principle. But compare Sherman, Jr. v. United States, 462 F2d 577 (5th Cir. 1972) and Estate of Iversen v. Comm'r, 552 F2d 977 (3d Cir. 1977) lifetime support rights were consideration even if payments extended beyond husband's death) with Estate of Ellman v. Comm'r, 59 TC 367 (1972) (post-death support rights are "marital rights" proscribed by Section 2043(b)). See also Sherman v. United States, 492 F2d 1045 (5th Cir. 1974) (determining the amount of deduction in the Sherman case).

[25] See Estate of Glen v. Comm'r, 45 TC 323, 340 (1966).

shrinkage in that spouse's estate with an attending reduction of estate tax liability. Presumably, if the obligation is discharged all at once by a lifetime transfer, only a corresponding shrinkage and tax reduction occur, which is unlike the artificial diminution that would attend a transfer for a relinquishment of dower rights. Thus, technical and policy reasons exist to differentiate support rights from dower for purposes of Section 2043(b)(1).[26]

[i] **Claims.** Testamentary transfers which qualify for the marital deduction under the unlimited marital deduction are permitted a Section 2056 deduction regardless of the nature of the property being transferred. But other testamentary transfers to a surviving spouse that do not qualify for a Section 2056 deduction[27] are deductible only if they are Section 2053 claims, which must then be founded on consideration as defined in Section 2043(b)(1). Thus, a surviving spouse's claim for statutory marital property rights generally would not be deductible under Section 2053, while a claim for liquidated support rights or community property rights would be deductible.[28]

[ii] **Gross estate inclusion of lifetime transfers.** The negative rule can apply to married couples in another context. A lifetime transfer that was testamentary in nature can generate gross estate inclusion under Sections 2035 through 2038 and 2041.[29] The transfer may be saved (or partly saved) from adverse estate tax consequences by recognized consideration passing to the transferor at the time of the transfer. Whether it is so saved requires an accurate identification of each right relinquished by the transferee that is tested against the Section 2043(b)(1) restrictions.[30] Any relinquished rights that qualify as consideration then must be valued. In the gross estate, the inter vivos transfer is either fully taxable, fully excluded (under the parenthetical exception to the transfer provisions), or partially taxable under the rules of Section 2043(a).[31]

---

[26] A transfer in exchange for the relinquishment of a child's right to support runs into no difficulty under Section 2043(b). It is a "filial" right, not a "marital" right, and besides, the policy reasons that support the relinquishment of a wife's support rights as consideration apply alike to the support right of children. McDonald Trust v. Comm'r, 19 TC 672 (1953), aff'd sub nom. Chase Nat'l Bank v. Comm'r, 225 F2d 621 (8th Cir. 1955).

[27] See supra ¶ 4.15[1] text accompanying note 11.

[28] See supra text accompanying notes 18–26. Cf. IRC § 2057, discussed ¶ 5.08.

[29] Much of the gross estate inclusion will, because of the unlimited marital deduction, result in a wash. However, see supra, ¶ 4.15[1] text accompanying notes 11, 12.

[30] See, e.g., Estate of Waters, 48 F3d 838 (4th Cir. 1995) (no recognized consideration for Section 2035 transfer, but other consideration for Section 2053 claims). The identification carries its own share of difficulties. In Estate of Glen v. Comm'r, 45 TC 323, 341 (1966), the court limits "other marital rights" to "inheritance rights," differentiating rights that would arise "immediately upon divorce." The rejection of this approach by Tannenwald, J., dissenting, id. at 349, is persuasive.

[31] See Comm'r v. Estate of Nelson, 396 F2d 519 (2d Cir. 1968); Estate of Scholl v. Comm'r, 88 TC 1265 (1987); Rev. Rul. 71-67, 1971-1 CB 271. The consideration is to be

Thus, if a surviving spouse's dower and similar marital rights do not reduce the decedent's gross estate at death, their relinquishment during life should not, as consideration, save a lifetime transfer from gross estate inclusion under Sections 2035 through 2038 or Section 2041. For example, suppose D, about to die, transferred an insurance policy to S, D's spouse, in exchange for S's relinquishment of S's marital rights having a value equal to the value of the policy. If there were no such transfer, as a result of Section 2034, S's marital rights would have been part of D's gross estate. To treat the transfer of the policy as being made for consideration so as to defeat an inclusion of the transferred insurance policy under Section 2035(a) would result in an obvious distortion, for nothing taxable would have replaced the policy that was transferred. A similar result would occur if D transferred a remainder interest in a trust to S in return for S's relinquishment of marital rights with D retaining a life estate in the trust. Because D did not receive money or money's worth consideration for the transfer,[32] Section 2036(a)(1) would include the trust corpus in D's gross estate.[33] If D's transfer had been in return for S's community property or a relinquishment of S's support right equal in value to the value of the remainder interest, Section 2036(a)(1) would likely be inapplicable.[34] If money or money's worth consideration were transferred but its value was less than the value of the transferred remainder, Section 2036(a)(1) would apply, but the amount included in the gross estate would be reduced by the dollar amount of consideration received at the time of the transfer.[35]

[b] The Negative Rule in a Divorce Situation

The picture becomes a bit more clouded when at the time of the decedent's death the spouses are divorced. Divorce, of course, eliminates the possibility of a marital deduction.[36] In general, the Section 2043(b) rule continues to apply to deny consideration status to "dower or curtesy, or . . . other marital rights," terms which have the same meaning as in the marital situation previously discussed. However, in some circumstances rights that constituted mere marital rights in the decedent's property and are not treated as consideration

---

valued as of the time of the transfer. United States v. Righter, 400 F2d 344 (8th Cir. 1968).

[32] IRC § 2043(b)(1).

[33] Puchner v. United States, 274 F. Supp. 704 (ED Wis. 1967) (marital rights were not valid consideration, although other property transferred was valid consideration).

[34] See ¶ 4.08[1][a].

[35] IRC § 2043(a). See infra ¶ 4.15[2], especially text accompanying notes 67–70.

[36] IRC § 2056(a). However, no particular conceptual difficulties arise with regard to an interspousal transfer effected in connection with mere separation unaccompanied by judicial proceedings. The results parallel those in the other marital situations previously discussed. See supra ¶ 4.15[1][a].

under Section 2043(b) may be elevated by case law or by the statute to rights that are in essence founded on consideration. Confusion in this area has also developed out of a merging of issues that are only loosely related: the deductibility of claims under Section 2053 and the taxability of lifetime transfers under the provisions defining the gross estate.

[i] **Claims.** In the claims area, recall that consideration must be shown to support a deduction only if a claim is founded on a promise or agreement;[37] if the claim arises in another way, it is deductible without regard to consideration. Thus, a claim based on a divorce decree that does not merely enforce the agreement of the parties is deductible without reaching any question of consideration.[38] It is not suggested that a claim against the estate becomes deductible without regard to consideration just because a court has rendered a judgment for the creditor. If *A* has merely made an enforceable promise to pay *B*, *A*'s child, $11,000, the claim is not deductible without a showing of consideration for *A*'s promise, even if *B* gets a judgment enforcing *B*'s claim against *A*'s estate after *A*'s death. Such a judgment does not alter the fact that the claim is "founded on" *A*'s promise.[39]

In a divorce setting, however, a decree may do more than merely enforce a prior agreement of the parties. If the divorce court under local law or as a result of an agreement being conditioned upon court approval has the power to determine on its own a settlement of property rights and even to vary the terms of any prior settlement agreement made by the parties, any indebtedness arising out of the court decree, even if there was a prior agreement, is not considered to be founded upon a promise or agreement but, rather, *upon the court decree*, and it is therefore deductible without regard to consideration.[40] This is true regardless of whether the claim is by the decedent's spouse or some third

---

[37] IRC § 2053(c)(1)(A). If there is consideration, the claim is deductible. Compare Estate of Kosow v. Comm'r, 45 F3d 1524 (11th Cir. 1995) (deduction allowed because consideration in the form of former spouse's reduction of support payments) with TAM 200011008 (Nov. 30, 1999) (no deduction because no proof of reduction of former spouse's support payments).

[38] Cf. Harris v. Comm'r, 340 US 106 (1950).

[39] Cf. Estate of Bowers v. Comm'r, 23 TC 911 (1955), acq. 1955-2 CB 4.

[40] Rev. Rul. 60-160, 1960-1 CB 374, 375. Compare Comm'r v. Estate of Watson, 216 F2d 941 (2d Cir. 1954) and Natchez v. United States, 705 F2d 671 (2d Cir. 1983) (deductible where court approved agreement) with Gray v. United States, 541 F2d 228 (9th Cir. 1976); Estate of Barrett v. Comm'r, 56 TC 1312 (1971); Estate of Satz v. Comm'r, 78 TC 1172 (1982); Estate of Bowers v. Comm'r, 23 TC 911 (1955), acq. 1955-2 CB 4. Estate of Edwards v. Comm'r 74 TCM (CCH) 748 (1997) (Calif.); Rev. Rul. 75-395, 1975-2 CB 370 (nondeductible despite judicial approval because court lacked power to alter the agreement). See also McMurtry v. Comm'r, 203 F2d 659 (1st Cir. 1953) (gift tax case).

person, such as a child, who is a beneficiary under the agreement.[41] If, however, the spouse's rights are not reduced or relinquished in return for a transfer to such third person, then, even though the agreement including the transfer to the third person is approved by a court decree, no deduction for the third person's claims is allowed under Section 2053.[42]

On the other hand, if a Section 2053 claim arising out of a divorce is founded upon a property settlement agreement (i.e., on a promise), rather than the divorce decree itself, whether there was consideration becomes significant and generally depends upon avoiding Section 2043(b).[43] However, in 1954, Congress enacted Section 2516, a gift tax amnesty rule, which provides that some transfers pursuant to an agreement are invariably to be treated as made for adequate consideration for *gift tax* purposes.[44] That section provides that any transfer of property pursuant to a written separation agreement is deemed made for a full consideration for gift tax purposes if a divorce occurs within the three-year period beginning one year before the agreement is made.[45]

In 1954, Congress did not enact an estate tax section analogous to the special gift tax amnesty rule, and it was criticized for failing to do so.[46] In response, in 1984 legislation, Congress finally took some action by enacting Section 2043(b)(2).[47] It expressly adopts the Section 2516 rule for estate tax purposes but only to provide adequate and full consideration for Section 2053 claims, not for lifetime transfers.[48] Thus, after 1984, claims against the estate are deductible either if they are founded upon a consideration in money or

---

[41] Leopold v. United States, 510 F2d 617 (9th Cir. 1975). Of course, such an agreement could result in a gift by the spouse.

[42] Hartshorne v. Comm'r, 48 TC 882 (1967), aff'd, 402 F2d 592 (2d Cir. 1968). Cf. Wiedemann v. Comm'r, 26 TC 565 (1956) (gift tax case).

[43] IRC § 2053(c)(1)(A).

[44] See ¶ 10.06.

[45] IRC § 2516.

[46] See Stephens, Maxfield, Lind & Calfee, Federal Estate and Gift Taxation, ¶¶ 4.15[1][e], 4.15[1][f] (Warren, Gorham & Lamont, 5th ed. 1983). See also the pre-Section 2043(b)(2) holdings of Estate of Satz v. Comm'r, 78 TC 1172 (1982) (Section 2516 was not to be read into the estate tax) and Natchez v. United States, 705 F2d 671 (2d Cir. 1983) (reaching the opposite conclusion). Cf. Estate of Glen v. Comm'r, 45 TC 323, 338 (1966).

[47] Deficit Reduction Act of 1984, Pub. Law No. 98-369, § 425(a)(1), 98 Stat. 494, 803 (1984), reprinted in 1984-3 CB (Vol. 1) 1, 311. See also IRC § 2053(e).

[48] Where a decedent transfers property to a trust to satisfy marital and property rights retaining a life interest that satisfies the requirements of Section 2516, the transferred property is includible in decedent's gross estate under Section 2036 without any reduction for consideration in money or money's worth because Section 2043(b)(2) only applies for purposes of Section 2053, not Section 2036. However, a deduction has been allowed under these circumstances under Section 2053(a) for the full value of the property passing to the former spouse. TAM 9826002 (Mar. 23, 1998). Section 2043(b)(2) should have been made applicable to the lifetime transfer provisions, Sections 2035, 2036, 2037 and

money's worth, founded upon a divorce decree, or if they meet the Section 2516 requirements.

[ii] Gross estate inclusion of lifetime transfers. A fair reading of the lifetime transfer provisions of Sections 2035 through 2038 and 2041 is that, absent qualified consideration, they prescribe gross estate inclusion in various circumstances whether the transfer was based on a promise or agreement or arose in some other manner. Thus, even if a transfer is directed by a judicial decree that does not merely enforce an agreement of the parties, the statute on its face still requires a showing of recognized consideration in order to avoid gross estate inclusion.

A development under the gift tax has raised a question of whether the estate tax transfer provisions should be construed in this manner. In *Harris v. Commissioner*,[49] the Supreme Court held that a wife's lifetime transfer to her husband, found to rest on a divorce decree, was free from gift tax without any showing of consideration. The inference to be drawn from the opinion is that consideration must be shown to avoid gift tax only if a transfer involving a relinquishment of marital rights[50] is founded on a promise or agreement, although the court does not expressly say so.[51] Is gross estate inclusion under the estate tax lifetime transfer sections similarly limited so that they too become inoperative if the transfer was either for recognized consideration or made pursuant to a divorce decree (i.e., not founded on a promise or agreement)?[52] The Tax Court has seemed to say so.[53] But other courts have disagreed. In *United States v. Past*,[54] the court refused to assume full recognized consideration for a transfer pursuant to a divorce decree to negate the effect of Section 2036 or Section 2038.[55] As a matter of literal statutory interpretation, the *Past* rule seems preferable to that of the Tax Court. Despite *Harris*, nothing in either the

---

2038, as well as Section 2053. Hopefully, the position set forth in the Technical Advice Memorandum will receive judicial acceptance or be incorporated in a legislative change.

[49] Harris v. Commissioner, 340 US 106 (1950).

[50] Cf. Spruance v. Comm'r, 60 TC 141 (1973), aff'd unpub. op. (3d Cir. 1974).

[51] The opinion of Douglas, J., in Harris v. Comm'r, 340 US 106 (1950), very logical to a point, disintegrates in the penultimate paragraph.

[52] Cf. IRC § 2043(b)(2) seemingly applicable only to claims deductible by the estate under Section 2053 and inapplicable to lifetime transfers. But see infra text accompanying notes 59–61.

[53] See Estate of O'Nan v. Comm'r, 47 TC 648, 656 (1967), acq. 1967-2 CB 3. See also Estate of Keller v. Comm'r, 44 TC 851 (1965) (expressing the same view except as to transfers to one other than the divorced spouse); Estate of McCoy v. Comm'r, 20 TCM (CCH) 224 (1961) (in which business as well as marital rights were settled).

[54] United States v. Past, 347 F2d 7 (9th Cir. 1965).

[55] Cf. Pope v. United States, 296 F. Supp. 17 (SD Cal. 1968). As noted in *Pope*, both *Pope* and United States v. Past, 347 F2d 7 (9th Cir. 1965), can be differentiated from United States v. Davis, 370 US 65 (1962), presuming full consideration in an interspousal

estate tax or the gift tax sections purports ever to waive the requirement of consideration in the case of lifetime transfers.

In the meantime, however, if there is to be a waiver of the consideration test under the gift tax for some divorce transfers, it is anomalous not to recognize a similar waiver for estate tax purposes. Thus, as the estate tax and gift tax are in pari materia,[56] it is not illogical for the Tax Court to suggest an estate tax treatment of lifetime transfers consistent with the gift tax treatment directed by *Harris*. Even if the *Harris* decision is questionable, the Supreme Court has the right to be wrong,[57] and, once it has fixed the gift tax philosophy, the same approach should be taken to like questions under the estate tax. In effect, therefore, the "founded on a promise or agreement" concept should be read into the estate tax lifetime transfer sections, just as it has been read into the gift tax, and a transfer pursuant to the independent determination of a divorce court should be relieved of gross estate inclusion. As the Tax Court decisions indicate, this elimination of the estate tax/gift tax anomaly seems to be within the reach of the judiciary.[58]

In a similar vein, Congress chose not to write Section 2516 gift tax consideration into the estate tax other than for purposes of deduction of claims under Section 2053.[59] Section 2516 does not provide consideration for the lifetime transfer provisions under the estate tax,[60] a result that seems inappropriate.[61]

---

transfer, but decided under the income tax that is free from any proscription regarding marital rights as consideration.

[56] Merrill v. Fahs, 324 US 308 (1945); Estate of Sanford v. Comm'r, 308 US 39, 44 (1939).

[57] See Jackson, J., concurring in Brown v. Allen, 344 US 443, 540 (1953): "We are not final because we are infallible, but we are infallible only because we are final."

[58] But see Tannenwald, J., dissenting in Estate of Glen v. Comm'r, 45 TC 323, 352 (1966): I do not believe that . . . we should pull ourselves up by our own bootstraps by accepting the importance of one provision of the estate tax into the gift tax via *Harris* and then reimporting that provision back into the estate tax—indeed, into another provision of the estate tax.

[59] IRC § 2043(b)(2). If property is included in a decedent spouse's gross estate under Sections 2035, 2036, 2037 or 2038 and the surviving former spouse has marital and property rights to such property after the decedent's death which satisfied the requirements of Section 2516, the Service treats such rights as a claim against the estate deductible under Section 2053 because Section 2043(b)(2) applies. TAM 9826002 (Mar. 23, 1998) (since surviving former spouse had rights to full value of the property at decedent's spouse's death, the full value of the corpus was deductible under Section 2053).

[60] See IRC § 2043(b)(2).

[61] Congress should have made Section 2043(b)(2) applicable to the lifetime transfer provisions, Sections 2035, 2036, 2037 and 2038, as well as Section 2053. If it had done so, the value of the consideration would be measured at the time of the inter vivos transfer. If the Service's position in TAM 9826002 (Mar. 23, 1998) is followed, the issue frequently is mooted. For example, if Decedent retains a life estate with a remainder to

[2] Partial Consideration: The Affirmative Rule

The sections providing for estate tax liability with respect to certain inter vivos transfers uniformly provide an exception for "a bona fide sale for adequate and full consideration in money or money's worth."[62] Section 2043(a) deals with transactions where there is some consideration in money or money's worth, but there is not a bona fide sale for adequate and full consideration. Although the flat exception of the various sections is not applicable, the partial consideration is to be taken into account. The rule provided is that the value of the consideration received by the decedent can be subtracted from the applicable valuation date value of the property included in the gross estate.

The rule and its rationale are easy to understand, although the application of the rule may be difficult and complicated.[63] If the property interest transferred by the decedent was replaced by something of money value, to the extent of such value there has been no reduction of the decedent's estate, regardless of motive or the form in which the transaction was carried out. Thus, the estate should not be taxed in the same way as if the transfer had been wholly gratuitous. It is important to note that the statute takes into account only a consideration in money or money's worth. This absolute rejection of the concept of consideration as known to the law of contracts is consistent with the purpose of the statute. A promise to marry may be a consideration for contract or other purposes, but a transfer for such a promise could reduce the gross estate, because the promise has no monetary value and in no way replaces the value of the property transferred.[64] Accordingly, such a promise is not consideration for estate tax purposes. For the same reason, a monetary detriment to the transferee without corresponding monetary advantage to the de-

---

Surviving former Spouse (founded on Section 2516 consideration) the property is included in Decedent's gross estate under Section 2036(a) but is fully deductible as a claim under section 2053. However, if Decedent created a similar trust with a secondary life estate in former Spouse (which satisfied the requirements of Section 2516) and a remainder to Children, and former spouse predeceased Decedent, the full corpus would be included in Decedent's gross estate with no reduction for the value of the former spouse's interest at the time of the transfer.

[62] The present requirement of "adequate and full" consideration to bring into play the flat exception of the various sections is appropriately stricter than its predecessors. Its origin is the Revenue Act of 1926, Pub. L. No. 69-20, § 302(i), 44 Stat. 9, 71 (1926), by which Congress replaced the earlier requirement of a "fair" consideration. E.g., Revenue Act of 1918, Pub. L. No. 65-254, § 402(c), 40 Stat. 1057, 1097 (1918).

It is sometimes unclear what constitutes "a bona fide sale for adequate and full consideration in money or money's worth." See infra text accompanying note 66; ¶ 4.08[1][a].

[63] See Lowndes, "Consideration and the Federal Estate and Gift Taxes: Transfers for Partial Consideration, Relinquishment of Marital Rights, Family Annuities, the Widow's Election and Reciprocal Trusts," 35 Geo. Wash. L. Rev. 50 (1966).

[64] Cf. Comm'r v. Wemyss, 324 US 303 (1945).

cedent transferor is not taken into account.[65] However, consideration that is recognized under Section 2043(a) need not be in the form of money or physical property received by the decedent. A promise to pay money in the future generally is consideration "reducible to a money value."[66]

If the decedent received property or money in connection with a transfer otherwise fully subject to estate tax, the amount of money received or the value of the property *at the time of receipt* is the amount to be subtracted under Section 2043(a).[67] This is the settled approach despite the fact that if a sale was for half price, it might appear that only 50 percent of the date-of-death value of the property should be included in the gross estate.[68] Increases or decreases in the value of the property transferred by the decedent, after the date of the transfer, are fully, not just partially, reflected in the gross estate, whereas under the rule, the value of the consideration is determined at the time of the transfer.[69]

For example, assume parent makes a transfer in trust retaining a life interest in the trust and designating parent's children as remainderpersons. At the time of the transfer, the corpus is worth $200,000 and the remainder is worth $100,000. The children pay parent $50,000 for their remainder interest. If the value of the remainder is $200,000[70] at parent's death, $150,000 will be included in parent's gross estate. If the value of the remainder is $50,000 at the decedent's death, nothing will be included in the gross estate.

If the decedent has made a transfer in exchange for a release from recognized legal obligations that have an ascertainable monetary value, the transfer

---

[65] Cf. Comm'r v. Wemyss, 324 US 303 (1945); Frothingham v. Comm'r, 60 TC 211 (1973).

[66] Reg. § 20.2043-1(a). But see infra text accompanying note 75.

[67] Reg. § 20.2043-1(a); Estate of Magnin v. Comm'r, 184 F3d 1074 (9th Cir. 1999); Schoenheit v. Lucas, 44 F2d 476, 490 (4th Cir. 1930).

[68] Estate of Davis v. Comm'r, 51 TC 269 (1968), rev'd on other grounds, 440 F2d 896 (3d Cir. 1971). See Estate of Marshall v. Comm'r, 51 TC 696, 703 (1969).

[69] The propriety of this approach is challenged in Lowndes & Stephens, "Identification of Property Subject to the Federal Estate Tax," 65 Mich. L. Rev. 105, 130 (1966), and discussed in Note, "Section 2043(a) of the Internal Revenue Code and the Additional Taxation of Property Transferred for Less Than Full and Adequate Consideration," 38 U. Cinn. L. Rev. 322 (1969); Burke, "Valuation Freezes after the 1988 Act: The Impact of Section 2036(c) on Closely Held Businesses," 31 Wm & Mary L. Rev. 67, 144-145 (1989); Holdsworth, "Report on Transfer Tax Restructuring," 41 Tax Law. 395, 410-411 (1988). By way of analogy, compare Section 170(e)(2) with Reg. § 1.1015-4(a). Question can be raised over whether the decedent has transferred the whole property for 50 percent consideration or half the property for full consideration and the balance for nothing.

[70] Where reference is made to a remainder following a life estate and the life tenant is dead, the value of the remainder equals the value of the corpus of the trust. Thus, the Section 2043(a) rule still comes into play in those instances.

is for consideration to the extent of such value. In one case,[71] the decedent, upon separation from his wife, created a trust in part for the support of his children during their minority in connection with the execution of a separation agreement and subsequent divorce. Notwithstanding his retention of a power to alter the trust, exercisable in conjunction with his divorced wife,[72] less than the entire value of the trust was included in his estate. The court found the value of the support obligation at the time the trust was created to be $30,000. This amount was subtracted from the date-of-death value of the trust corpus as consideration in money's worth for the transfer.[73] A good way to appraise this is that, except for creation of the trust and viewed as of the date of transfer, the decedent's estate would in any event have been reduced by $30,000 by way of payments that he would have had to make for support of his children. Thus, only the excess in value of what he transferred tended to result in an artificial reduction of his estate.

The most difficult question in applying the rule of Section 2043(a) is how to measure the consideration for the transfer when it is something less than "adequate and full" and is received by the decedent, especially in the form of an interest in property that is something less than outright ownership.[74] The Commissioner frequently has been successful in contending that promissory notes given by a transferee were not bona fide obligations contracted for consideration.[75] Again, the consideration is to be valued at the time of the transfer,

---

[71] McDonald Trust v. Comm'r, 19 TC 672 (1953), aff'd sub nom. Chase Nat'l Bank v. Comm'r, 225 F2d 621 (8th Cir. 1955). See supra ¶ 4.15[1][a] text accompanying note 26.

[72] See IRC § 2038; ¶ 4.10.

[73] A provision in proposed regulations, Prop. Reg. § 20.2043-1(b) (Notice of Proposed Rules, 21 Fed. Reg. 7850, 7886 (1956)), that in such circumstances the amount to be subtracted from the date-of-death value of the property is the date-of-death value of a child's continuing right to support, was appropriately omitted from the final regulations. See also Comm'r v. Estate of Nelson, 396 F2d 519 (2d Cir. 1968).

[74] Greene v. United States, 237 F2d 848 (7th Cir. 1956) (agreement to make up income deficiencies might constitute a partial consideration where there was a transfer in consideration of a promise to pay over the net income from the property, but not less than $1,500 annually). Cf. ¶ 4.08[1][a].

[75] Estate of Maxwell v. Comm'r, 3 F3d 591 (2d Cir. 1993) (interest bearing note given by children which was annually reduced in the amount of the annual exclusion and relieved by will was not a bona fide sale under Section 2036); Estate of Musgrove v. Comm'r, 33 Fed. Cl. 657 (1995). The Maxwell case is discussed at ¶ 4.08[6][c] text accompanying notes 90–91. Cf. Estate of Flandreau v. Comm'r, 63 TCM (CCH) 2512 (1992), aff'd 994 F2d 91 (2d Cir. 1993) (non-interest-bearing notes given to children not due until death or decedent reached age ninety-five were not valid Section 2053 claims against the estate).

not at the time of death,[76] even though the property includable in the estate is to be valued at the time of the decedent's death.[77]

¶ 4.16 SECTION 2044. CERTAIN PROPERTY FOR WHICH A MARITAL DEDUCTION WAS PREVIOUSLY ALLOWED

Sometimes a section makes little or no sense without an understanding of other provisions related to it. Section 2044[1] is such a section. It must be examined with Sections 2056(b)(7), 2523(f),[2] 2519,[3] and 2207A[4] to comprehend its message.

Generally, interspousal transfers of property are not subjected to estate tax or gift tax. However, when property previously transferred between spouses without estate tax or gift tax consequences moves outside the marital unit, it is then subjected to tax. Under Sections 2523(f) and 2056(b)(7), Congress allows a marital deduction to a transferor spouse or transferor spouse's estate for the total value of a gift or bequest of property to a transferee spouse, even though the transferee receives only an estate ("a qualifying income interest")[5] for the transferee's life[6] and all other interests in the property (including the remainder) pass to third parties.[7] Under both of these sections, *all* interests in the property are treated as if they were transferred outright to the transferee spouse in the determination of the amount of the marital deduction allowed to the transferor spouse or transferor spouse's estate.

This is where Section 2044 enters the picture. If the transferee spouse makes no inter vivos disposition of any part of the qualifying income interest[8]

---

[76] United States v. Righter, 400 F2d 344 (8th Cir. 1958); Estate of Vardell v. Comm'r, 307 F2d 688, 693 (5th Cir. 1962).

[77] Estate of Gregory v. Comm'r, 39 TC 1012 (1963). These rules are applied in a community property widow's election context. See ¶ 4.08[7][c].

[1] IRC § 2044. This section was added by the Economic Recovery Tax Act of 1981, Pub. L. No. 91-34, § 403(d)(3)(A)(i), 95 Stat. 172, 304 (1981), reprinted in 1981-2 CB 256, 326.

[2] IRC §§ 2056(b)(7), 2523(f). Both of these Sections (known as the QTIP, qualifying terminable interest property, provisions) are exceptions to the terminable interest rules of the estate tax and gift tax marital deduction provisions. See ¶¶ 5.06[8][d], 11.03[4][c].

[3] See ¶ 10.08.

[4] See ¶ 8.07.

[5] IRC §§ 2056(b)(7)(B)(ii), 2523(f)(2)(B).

[6] A more specific discussion of these requirements appears at ¶ 5.06[8][d].

[7] The sections present exceptions to the terminable interest rules of the estate tax and gift tax marital deduction provisions. See ¶¶ 5.06[7], 11.03[3].

[8] See IRC §§ 2056(b)(7)(B)(ii), 2523(f)(2), 2523(f)(3).

during the transferee's life,[9] Section 2044(a) includes the full value of the property in which the transferee had the qualifying income interest in the transferee's gross estate.[10] Because the transferee spouse is deceased, the qualifying income interest has expired[11] and all interests subsequent to transferee's life estate are included in the transferee's gross estate,[12] but, of course, these interests constitute *all* interests in the property.

If the transferor spouse's executor elected to treat only a portion of the transferred property as qualified income property, only that portion of the property is included in the transferee spouse's gross estate under Section 2044.[13] The included share is further reduced if it is established that principal distributions to the transferee spouse have been made pursuant to the trust instrument from the qualified terminable interest share during the term of the qualified income interest.[14] On the other hand, if the transferee spouse makes a

---

[9] IRC § 2044(b)(2).

[10] See Reg. §§ 20.2044-1(a), 20.2044-1(d), 20.2044-1(e) Ex. 1. The full value of the property is included even if the transferor spouse's transfer qualified for a Section 2503(b) annual exclusion. Reg. § 20.2044-1(a). Where a trust has been severed to make an election as to part of the property, referred to as a partial QTIP election (see Reg. §§ 20.2056(b)-7(b)(2)(ii), 25.2523(f)-1(b)(3)(ii); ¶ 5.06[8][d] text accompanying notes 376–381), only the value of the property in the QTIP severed trust is included. Reg. § 20.2044-1(d)(4).

Cf. Rev. Rul. 98-8, 1998-1 CB 541, discussed at ¶ 10.08[2] text accompanying note 41 (involving transferee spouse's lifetime "purchase" of the remainder); Rev. Proc. 2001-38, 2001-2 CB __, discussed at ¶ 5.06[8][d] note 384.

[11] See ¶ 4.05[5][b]. It is presumed that a marital deduction was "allowed" for purposes of Section 2044 if a marital deduction was taken on the return reporting the transfer creating the qualifying income interest. Reg. § 20.2044-1(c). To avoid Section 2044 inclusion, the transferee's executor must establish that a marital deduction was not taken. This may be accomplished by producing the return on which no election was made, by establishing that no return was required to be filed by the transferor, or by indicating that the transfer occurred before the effective date of Section 2056(b)(7) or Section 2523(f). Id. Cf. Estate of Letts v. Comm'r, 109 TC 290 (1997) (duty of consistency required inclusion of property in surviving spouse's gross estate (not necessarily under Section 2044) where decedent's estate took a marital deduction for the terminable interest property but no QTIP election was made); Estate of Soberdash v. Comm'r, 74 TCM (CCH) 295 (1997) (mismanagement of trust funds did not justify noninclusion under Section 2044).

[12] Any undistributed income earned during the term of the qualifying income interest, "stub income," is included in the transferee spouse's gross estate under Section 2044 (if not included under another section), even though it is in fact paid to a third party. Reg. § 20.2044-1(d)(2). See ¶ 5.06[8][d] at notes 321–323.

[13] Reg. §§ 20.2044-1(d)(1), 20.2044-1(e) Exs. 2, 3; Estate of Soberdash v. Comm'r, 74 TCM (CCH) 295 (1997). See TAM 9446001 (Nov. 18, 1994) (election of a dollar amount equal to the value of surviving spouse's income interest treated as an election of a fraction of the entire property). Cf. Reg. § 20.2044-1(e) Ex. 7 (where the QTIP election involves an annuity and the transfer was made prior to October 24, 1992).

[14] Reg. § 20.2044-1(d)(3). The executor of the transferee spouse's estate must establish the fair market value of the trust assets at the time of each distribution as a prerequi-

lifetime disposition of any portion of the qualifying income interest in the property, Section 2044 is inapplicable.[15] Although Section 2044 is inapplicable, if the transferee spouse makes a disposition of only a portion of the qualifying income interest, the Treasury contends that Section 2036(a)(1) applies and requires inclusion in the transferee's gross estate of the portion of corpus producing the retained portion of the qualifying income interest.[16]

Property included in the gross estate under Section 2044 is treated as passing from the transferee spouse to the persons who receive the property on the spouse's death.[17] Thus, if the property passes to charity or if transferee spouse has remarried and the property passes to new spouse, the transferee spouse's estate qualifies for a Section 2055 or Section 2056 deduction. The tax imposed on the property included under Section 2044 may qualify for estate tax installment payment under Section 6166.[18]

In general, an interest in property included in a decedent's gross estate under one Code section is aggregated with an interest in the same property included in the gross estate under another Code section in ascertaining the value of the interests for federal estate tax purposes.[19] However, a series of cases have held that property includible in the transferee spouse's gross estate under Section 2044 is valued without aggregating that property with similar property includible in that spouse's gross estate under other gross estate inclusion provi-

---

site to the reduction in the amount of Section 2044 inclusion. Reg. § 20.2044-1(d)(3)(iii). See Reg. § 20.2044-1(e) Ex. 4.

[15] IRC § 2044(b)(2). Section 2519 of the gift tax statute treats all third-party interests in the property as being transferred inter vivos by the transferee spouse. See ¶ 10.08[1].

[16] Reg. § 25.2519-1(a). See Reg. §§ 20.2044-1(e) Ex. 5, 25.2519-1(g) Exs. 4, 5. See also ¶ 10.08[1][a] note 15 (questioning the propriety of the Treasury's contention).

[17] IRC § 2044(c). See Reg. §§ 20.2044-1(b), 20.2044-1(e) Ex. 6.

[18] Reg. § 20.2044-1(b). See ¶ 2.02[3][c].

[19] IRC §§ 2031, 2032, 2032A. Cf. Reg. § 20.2044-1(b); IRC § 1014, especially IRC § 1014(b)(10).

sions,[20] and the Service has acquiesced in one of those decisions.[21] While these decisions are favorable to the surviving spouse's estate, they generate additional questions,[22] and one must not turn a blind eye to the tax consequences of these decisions on the predeceasing spouse's estate.[23]

---

[20] Estate of Bonner v. United States, 84 F3d 196 (5th Cir. 1996) (undivided interests in assets (a boat and land) owned outright by a decedent and by a trust included in the decedent's gross under Section 2044 were not aggregated into 100 percent ownership in the decedent's gross estate, but were instead separately valued as fractional interests in property); Estate of Mellinger v. Comm'r, 112 TC 26 (1999), acq. 1999-2 CB xvi (stock of publicly but thinly traded Frederick's of Hollywood held in a trust included in transferee spouse's gross estate under Section 2044 was not aggregated with stock held in transferee spouse's revocable trust, even though the aggregated stock would have constituted a majority controlling ownership block); Estate of Nowell v. Comm'r, 77 TCM (CCH) 1239 (1999) (a partnership interest held in a trust included under Section 2044 and a partnership interest held in a revocable trust were not aggregated in the transferee spouse's gross estate for valuation purposes); Estate of Lopes v. Comm'r, 78 TCM (CCH) 46 (1999) (interest in real estate in a trust included under Section 2044 not aggregated with interest in real estate held in transferee spouse's revocable trust for valuation purposes). See ¶ 4.02[4][b] text accompanying notes 157, 158. See also Bogdanski, "The Outer Limits of Minority Discounts," 23 Est. Plan. 496 (1999); Elliot, "A New Bright Line: Fractional Interest Discount Permitted for Property Interests Held by QTIP Trust and Decedent Outright," 13 J. P'ship Tax'n 358 (1997).

[21] Estate of Mellinger v. Comm'r, 112 TC 26 (1999), acq. 1999-2 CB xvi.

[22] A principal rationale behind the court's lack of aggregation of the interests appears to be the fact that the surviving spouse had no control over the ultimate disposition of the assets in the qualified terminable interest trust. See Estate of Bonner v. Comm'r, 84 F3d 196, 199 (5th. Cir. 1996) ("the assets . . . in fact were controlled at every step by [the predeceasing spouse]"); Estate of Mellinger v. Comm'r, 112 TC 26, 36 (1999) acq. 1999-2 CB xvi ("at no time did the decedent [surviving spouse] possess, control, or have any power of disposition over the [corpus] in the QTIP trust"). If this is the basis of the decisions, then the results should not be expanded to avoid aggregation of property included under other gross estate inclusion sections such as Section 2036, Section 2038, or Section 2041. See FSA 200119013 (Feb. 6, 2001) (stock included in decedent's gross estate under Section 2041 as a result of a predeceasing spouse's Section 2056(b)(5) marital deduction aggregated with stock included under Section 2033). The rationale also raises an issue whether the *Bonner* line of cases would apply if the surviving spouse were given directly or indirectly a general power of appointment over the qualified terminable interest corpus or even a nongeneral power of appointment over such corpus. Cf ¶ 5.06[8][f].

[23] Courts have recognized that discounts and premiums may be taken into account in determining the amount of a deduction under the estate tax deduction sections. See Estate of Chenoweth v. Comm'r, 88 TC 1577 (1987) (control premium allowed for gift to surviving spouse); Ahmanson Foundation v. United States, 674 F2d 761 (9th Cir. 1981) (stock given by decedent to charity discounted from its value in decedent's gross estate); Estate of Di Santo v. Comm'r, 78 TCM (CCH) 1220 (1999) (surviving spouse's valid partial disclaimer of marital bequest converted the bequest to a minority interest with the result that the marital deduction was reduced by an amount greater than the disclaimed portion of the bequest). See ¶¶ 4.02[4], 5.06[5] text accompanying notes 91–94.

¶ 4.17 SECTION 2045. PRIOR INTERESTS

Section 2045 contains the general rule concerning the time at which a transaction must have occurred to result in estate tax liability under Sections 2034 through 2042. The rule states that it makes no difference when the transaction took place unless a critical date for applicability is specifically provided by law.

By its own terms, Section 2035 does not apply to transfers that occur more than three years prior to death.[1] Section 2037 is expressly inapplicable to transfers made on or before September 7, 1916; moreover, by its express terms it provides different rules for transfers made before October 8, 1949, and transfers made on or after that date.[2] Specific critical dates or periods of broad or narrow importance appear in or for all the Sections from 2035 through 2041 and 2044; Sections 2034 and 2042 contain no critical dates.

The provisions of Section 2045 should not be confused with the matter of the effective date of the 1986 Code and amendments to it. When considering the possible application of Sections 2034 through 2042, two questions of timing may arise: (1) When did the transaction take place? and (2) When did the decedent die? In general, the estate tax provisions of the 1986 Code are applicable to estates of decedents who died after August 16, 1954, the date of the enactment of the 1954 Code.[3] Even this rule is not entirely free from exception, however. For example, treaty obligations in effect when the 1954 Code was enacted are excepted from contrary provisions in the 1954 Code.[4] Section 2039, concerning annuities, which had no direct counterpart in prior law, is generally applicable to estates of decedents who died after December 31, 1953 and in other circumstances only to estates of decedents who died after December 31, 1957, 1962, 1965, 1970, 1972, 1976, 1981, 1984, 1986, or 1987. Recent Revenue Acts have added substantially to instances in which a provision is limited to estates of decedents dying after a critical date.[5] These comments are not extended here, as critical dates are noted in the discussion of the various sections defining "gross estate."

---

[1] IRC §§ 2035(a)(1), 2035(b).

[2] IRC § 2037(a).

[3] IRC § 7851(a)(2)(A).

[4] IRC § 7852(d)(2).

[5] The only change in Section 2045 made by the Tax Reform Act of 1976 was to substitute the introductory phrase "Except as otherwise specifically provided by law" for "Except as specifically provided therein." See Tax Reform Act of 1976, Pub. L. No. 94-455, § 2001(c)(1)(m), 90 Stat. 1520, 1853 (1976), reprinted in 1976-3 CB (Vol. 1), 329. Thus, critical times for transactions may be expressed in statutes not incorporated into the Code.

¶ 4.18 SECTION 2046. DISCLAIMERS

Section 2046 is simply a cross reference to the uniform disclaimer rule of Section 2518, which is applicable to the estate tax provisions. A detailed discussion of the disclaimer rule appears in Chapter 10.[1]

---

[1] See ¶ 10.07.

CHAPTER **5**

The Taxable Estate

¶ 5.01 INTRODUCTION

There are six principal steps in the determination of federal estate tax liability. First, the gross estate is determined under Sections 2031 through 2046 of the Internal Revenue Code (the Code).[1] Second, the taxable estate is determined by subtracting from the gross estate the deductions permitted under Sections 2051 through 2058.[2] Third, adjusted taxable gifts are determined and added to the taxable estate.[3] Fourth, the estate tax rates found in Section 2001(c) are applied to that sum to determine a tentative tax.[4] Fifth, from that tax figure, an amount for the gift tax on post-1976 gifts is subtracted to determine the gross estate tax.[5] Finally, credits against the tax allowed by Sections 2010 through 2016 are subtracted from the tax to determine the estate's actual liability, the net estate tax payable.[6] This chapter deals with the second principal step, i.e., the subtraction of deductions allowed against the gross estate to establish the taxable estate.[7]

¶ 5.02 SECTION 2051. DEFINITION OF "TAXABLE ESTATE"

Section 2051 in Part IV of Chapter 11 of the Code defines the taxable estate[1] as the gross estate less "the deductions provided for in this part." Part IV includes Sections 2051 through 2058.[2] Those deductions can be separated into

---

[1] See ¶¶ 4.01–4.18.

[2] See ¶¶ 5.02–5.09.

[3] IRC § 2001(b)(1).

[4] IRC § 2001 (b)(1). See ¶ 2.01.

[5] IRC § 2001(b)(2). See Reg. § 20.0-2(b)(4).

[6] See ¶¶ 3.01–3.08; Reg. § 20.0-2(b)(5).

[7] The discussion in this chapter does not take into account special rules applicable to the determination of the taxable estate of a nonresident noncitizen. See IRC § 2106, discussed ¶ 6.06.

[1] "Taxable estate" is a term first used in the 1954 Code, and it essentially replaces the term "net estate," which was used in the earlier estate tax statutes.

[2] Prior to the Tax Reform Act of 1976, Section 2052 provided a flat $60,000 deduction from the gross estate of any citizen or resident in arriving at the taxable estate. The exemption, which applied to both large and small estates, was replaced under the Tax Reform Act of 1976 by the Section 2010 unified credit, which also reduces tax paid by large and small estates. Pub. L. No. 94-455, § 2001(a)(4), 90 Stat. 1520, 1948 (1976), reprinted in 1976-3 CB (Vol. 1) 1, 324. See discussion of Section 2010 at ¶ 3.02. Under prior law, because there was no tax on a gross estate of $60,000 or less, Congress required that an estate tax return be filed for citizen or resident decedents' estates only if the gross estate, properly valued at death, exceeded $60,000. IRC § 6018(a)(1); Reg. § 20.6018-1(a). After repeal of the $60,000 exemption by the Tax Reform Act of 1976, Section 6018(a)(1) now

two classifications: deductions that contribute to a realistic measure of what the decedent transfers to others and deductions that are allowed for other policy reasons. The deductions allowed under Section 2053 are designed to take into account the realities of the decedent's financial situation when the decedent died, the Section 2054 casualty loss deduction is concerned with post-death events that reduce the decedent's estate passing to others, and the Section 2058 deduction is for state death taxes incurred. The charitable deduction (Section 2055), the marital deduction (Section 2056), and the family-owned-business deduction (Section 2057) are all pretty clearly matters of congressional largess or of convenience.

¶ 5.03 SECTION 2053. EXPENSES, INDEBTEDNESS, AND TAXES

[1] Introduction

Section 2053 contains most of the estate tax rules designed to assure an application of the tax rates to a realistic taxable estate, determined by subtracting from the gross estate certain of the decedent's obligations existing at death and other reasonable charges involved in winding up the decedent's affairs and passing the property on to beneficiaries.[1] The value of property owned by a decedent at death, or treated as if owned by a decedent under the various sections defining the gross estate,[2] is obviously not a fair measure of the decedent's wealth or of what a decedent can actually pass on to survivors. A decedent's estate will be diminished by unavoidable funeral and related costs. The collection and distribution of a decedent's property will necessitate many expenditures. Creditors, including various tax collectors, may have substantial claims against a decedent that will have to be discharged out of the assets of a decedent's estate. Some of the decedent's property may be mortgaged and, even if the decedent had no personal liability for the mortgage debt, the value of the property is reduced by all the charges against it. Subject to detailed rules, Section 2053 takes all these matters into account in allowing deductions toward the determination of the taxable estate.

---

appropriately gears the return requirements to the available applicable exclusion amount in effect under Section 2010(c) for the calendar year of death. See IRC § 2010; ¶ 3.02.

[1] Items described in Section 2053 sometimes reduce the taxed amount of generation-skipping transfers too. See IRC § 2622(b), discussed at ¶ 14.03[3].

[2] See ¶¶ 4.01–4.18.

Five classes of deductions are authorized by Section 2053: four classes fall under Section 2053(a), and one is under Section 2053(b).[3] All five allowances are subject to important limitations[4] that are sometimes subject to a minor exception.[5] The five allowances will serve as the basic outline of the ensuing discussion followed by the limitations,[6] which often apply to several or even all the deduction provisions. There is no way to reduce the limitations to an apothegm; each limitation will be discussed in its most likely context with appropriate cross-references in other circumstances where the limitation may also apply.

On the other hand this seems to be the place for a brief introduction to the proper approach to Section 2053(a), an excellent small segment of legislation woefully buffeted about and otherwise abused by judge and scholar alike. It is a great place to pause and consider for a moment the interpretation of federal statutes.

Four categories of potentially deductible items are listed in Section 2053(a). The meaning of the terms "funeral expenses," "administration expenses," and the like are answered primarily by resort to federal law. We have known this at least since 1938.[7] The meaning of a term in a federal statute raises a question of *federal* law not governed by local characterization.[8] If Ohio passes a statute authorizing an executor to purchase a round-the-world trip for a bereaved widow and designates it a funeral expense, the Ohio executor may be authorized to expend the money, but the trip is not a Section 2053(a)(1) funeral expense merely because of its local characterization as a funeral expense, as it is clearly not within the *congressional* meaning for that term. So in each of the four categories of Section 2053(a), an initial question is the meaning of the term, a question of *federal law.*[9]

---

[3] First, funeral expenses, Section 2053(a)(1); second, expenses of administering the probate estate, Section 2053(a)(2); third, expenses of administering nonprobate, gross estate assets, Section 2053(b); fourth, claims against the estate, Section 2053(a)(3); and fifth, mortgages and other indebtedness on estate property for which the decedent is personally liable, Section 2053(a)(4).

[4] In addition to the requirements specified in Sections 2053(a) and 2053(b), see Section 2053(c).

[5] See IRC § 2053(d), allowing a deduction for certain state and foreign death taxes, despite the general proscription of Section 2053(c)(1)(B).

[6] See Reg. § 20.2053-1.

[7] Lyeth v. Hoey, 305 US 188 (1938).

[8] Lyeth v. Hoey, 305 US 188, 193 (1938). See also United States v. White, 853 F2d 107 (2d Cir. 1988), cert. denied, 493 US 5 (1989), rev'g and remanding 650 F. Supp. 904 (WDNY 1987), reinforcing the notion of a "federal standard" for deductible administration expenses.

[9] Even here an element of local law enters in. The term "expense" connotes a paid obligation. The obligation to pay can arise only by way of local law. Consequently, the

The next question is whether the item sought to be deducted falls within the meaning given the statutory term, a matter for a federal court's *decision*. A federal court deciding a tax case decides whether an item falls within a term of a federal statute; and it does so even if this may involve in some part a determination of how local law applies, notwithstanding that a state court, other than the highest state court, has already decided the local issue.[10]

Beyond these basics, there looms in Section 2053 a question of *state law* expressly raised. All the listed items in Section 2053(a) pass final muster as estate tax deductions only if they are "allowable" under applicable local law. There is *no* federal law that purports to say whether they are allowable,[11] in the obvious sense of this requirement. The question is whether state law permits the amount to be paid by the executor out of estate assets. This is a classic example of *express* reference to local law for a principle to be applied in the implementation of a federal statute. If Nevada expressly authorizes executors to purchase solid silver caskets and the cost of a casket *is* a funeral expense (as Congress has used the term), the cost of a solid silver casket becomes a funeral expense (federal question) allowable by local law (state question) that a federal judge cannot properly hold nondeductible because of some feeling of parsimony that the judge may harbor. Obviously, Congress is not *required* to allow estate tax deductions for the cost of solid silver caskets. Congress might instead allow a deduction for "reasonable funeral expenses."[12] *Local law* would not then play the same role. But in Section 2053(a) the selected litmus paper is the local rule of law on allowability.

Who decides whether local law actually allows the solid silver casket? Generally the federal judge deciding the tax case. The *Bosch* opinion[13] itself confuses local law versus local decision issues,[14] but at least the decision makes it clear that a decision regarding what state law allows by a state judge below the state's highest court is not binding on the federal judge. If the judge in a tax case decides that a probate judge erred in holding the purchase of a solid silver casket allowable under local law, the judge may disallow a deduction on the basis of a contrary interpretation of the local law, giving only "proper regard" to the local decision.[15]

---

discussion here is about *state*-recognized obligations to make payments that are, for example, within the *federal* concept of funeral expenses. Cf. Reg. § 20.2053-6(f).

[10] Comm'r v. Estate of Bosch, 387 US 456 (1967).

[11] See Burnet v. Harmel, 287 US 103 (1932).

[12] Cf. IRC § 162(a)(1), regarding a "reasonable allowance" for salaries.

[13] Comm'r v. Estate of Bosch, 387 US 456 (1967).

[14] The *Erie* doctrine concerns the controlling effect of local law, not local adjudications. See discussion of Section 2033 at ¶ 4.05[2][b] note 14.

[15] Comm'r v. Estate of Bosch, 387 US 456, 465 (1967); Reg. § 20.2053-1(b)(2).

To carry this a step beyond where it may need to be carried, suppose the local law authorizes the purchase of a casket "fitting to the decedent's economic situation in life." Local law is much more likely to raise this equivocal kind of issue than the black or white (silver or bronze?) issue suggested above. Judge Local approves the silver casket. Judge Federal, passing on the Commissioner's disallowance of the deduction, may reject Judge Local's *interpretation* of local law, reverse the decision, and hold the expenditure for the silver casket not "allowable" under the law governing administration of the estate (i.e., under local law).

These basic postulates are assumed in the discussion that follows, but, even if they are sound, the authors do not assert they are uniformly followed.

[2] Funeral Expenses

[a] In General

Funeral expenses deductible under Section 2053(a)(1) are not limited to the bare cost of the funeral ceremony. Reasonably interpreting the federal statutory term, the regulations have consistently recognized as funeral expenses reasonable expenditures for "a tombstone, monument, or mausoleum, or for a burial lot, either for the decedent or his family."[16] It is equally clear that costs for embalming, cremation, casket, hearse, limousines, and other amounts paid to the undertaker and for floral and other decorations are included. The cost of transporting the body to the place of burial is a funeral expense and so is the cost of transportation of the person accompanying the body.[17] Expenditures for the future care of the burial lot or mausoleum may qualify as a deduction,[18] but expenditures for the care of a lot in which the decedent is not buried[19] and expenditures made by a testamentary trust after settlement of the estate are not deductible as funeral expenses.[20]

---

[16] Reg. § 20.2053-2.

[17] Reg. § 20.2053-2. Estate of Berkman v. Comm'r, 38 TCM (CCH) 183 (1979).

[18] Reg. § 20.2053-2.

[19] Estate of Gillespie v. Comm'r, 8 TC 838 (1947) (amounts that may be allowed by Pennsylvania do not enlarge the meaning of the federal term).

[20] Carter v. United States, 1 USTC ¶ 238 (ED Mo. 1927). But see Comm'r v. Estate of Cardeza, 173 F2d 19 (3d Cir. 1949) (allowing a deduction for a testamentary trust established to maintain a mausoleum).

[b] The "Allowable" Test

Conceivably, the statute could be read to permit the deduction of the amount of funeral expenses that local law would allow without regard to the amount actually expended.[21] However, this is not the law. The terms "expenses" and "allowable," both of which appear in Section 2053(a), impose limiting concepts. The regulations properly assert as a ceiling on the deduction of expenses the amount "actually expended."[22] There is no "expense" within the scope of this provision unless there is an actual expenditure. The actual expense must then pass three further tests: (1) the funeral expense must be a funeral expense within the meaning of the federal statute; (2) it must be allowable under local law in that it is of the kind that governing law permits to be charged against estate assets;[23] *and* (3) the amount must not exceed that which local law permits.[24]

The term "allowable" obviously raises more than a mere question whether an expense can be paid; the question is whether it can be paid out of the decedent's estate, i.e., "out of property subject to claims."[25] This has presented problems in community property states. If funeral expenses are chargeable half and half against the decedent's and the surviving spouse's community property, only one half of the expenses are deductible—only the half allowable as properly payable out of the decedent's estate.[26] Predictably, state community

---

[21] The term "allowable" sometimes carries such a connotation, e.g., Virginian Hotel Corp. v. Helvering, 319 US 523 (1943), and indeed that may be its meaning as it affects the deduction of claims against the estate. See infra ¶¶ 5.03[5][a], 5.03[5][b].

[22] Reg. § 20.2053-2. Nevertheless, funeral expenses accrued but not paid when the return is filed, a likely occurrence with the nine-month filing period, should be deducted on the return. If appropriate payment is not made later, the executor should report nonpayment and pay the resulting additional tax. Cf. Reg. § 20.2053-3(b)(1).

[23] Compare Ingleheart v. Comm'r, 77 F2d 704 (5th Cir. 1935) (perpetual care of cemetery lot not chargeable against the estate under Florida law) with Comm'r v. Estate of Cardeza, 173 F2d 19 (3d Cir. 1949) (perpetual care of mausoleum an allowable expense under Pennsylvania law).

[24] Reg. § 20.2053-1(b)(1). Quantitative limitations respected by local law are most likely to arise out of testamentary insistence on a modest burial. Cf. Blackburn v. United States, 1960-2 USTC ¶ 11,964 (SD Ind. 1960) (no deduction for funeral expenses where a will contained no direction for payment, and absent such direction, funeral expenses were not payable out of the decedent's estate).

[25] Reg. § 20.2053-1(a)(1).

[26] United States v. Collins, 399 F2d 90 (5th Cir. 1968) (pre-1967 Texas law); Estate of Lang v. Comm'r, 97 F2d 867 (9th Cir. 1938) (Washington law); Estate of Pinkerton v. Comm'r, 33 TCM (CCH) 342 (1974) (pre-1977 California law); Rev. Rul. 70-156, 1970-1 CB 190 (pre-1977 California law). Cf. Estate of Orcutt v. Comm'r, 36 TCM (CCH) 746 (1977).

property laws have been amended to effect more satisfactory estate tax results.[27]

A somewhat similar problem may arise in a common-law state in which
the surviving spouse's duty of support imposes on the surviving spouse primarily liability for a deceased spouse's funeral expense.[28] If there is no provision
in the decedent's will specifying payment out of the decedent's estate, the estate is allowed no deduction, since the expenses are simply those of the surviving spouse and, not being properly chargeable against the decedent's estate, are
not allowable under local law.[29]

To recapitulate, the "allowable" test under Section 2053(a) is a clear case
of deference to, indeed express reference to, state or other local legal principles, for it permits such principles to be a factor and sometimes a controlling
factor in the determination of federal tax liability.[30] The effect of a local adjudication of rights and obligations under local law is, of course, a separate
question. The Supreme Court has directed courts deciding federal tax controversies to give proper regard to a local adjudication of significant rights and
obligations; at the same time, it holds that such adjudications are not binding
in the federal tax case unless they are decisions by a state's highest court.[31]
Thus, the Commissioner may successfully challenge the deductibility of funeral expenses actually allowed in a state probate court proceeding and paid by
the estate;[32] but, unless the contention is that the charges are not funeral expenses as Congress has used that term, the attack should address the question
whether the expenses are allowable under principles of local law.

---

[27] See Rev. Rul. 69-193, 1969-1 CB 222, Rev. Rul. 71-168, 1971-1 CB 271, reflecting the predictable changes in Texas and California law, respectively, and, for the future,
reversing the results indicated in United States v. Collins, 399 F2d 90 (5th Cir. 1968); Estate of Pinkerton v. Comm'r, 33 TCM (CCH) 392 (1974); Rev. Rul. 70-156, 1970-1 CB
190. See also Nev. Rev. Stat. § 150.230(4) (2001) (Nevada law amended to reach this result); Estate of Lee v. Comm'r, 11 TC 141 (1948) (funeral expenses fully deductible
under Idaho law).

[28] See Bradley v. Comm'r, 2 TCM (CCH) 609 (1943).

[29] Rev. Rul. 76-369, 1976-2 CB 281 (analyzing controlling local law in several
states). However, if the estate is secondarily liable and the surviving spouse is insolvent, a
deduction should be allowed if the estate pays the expenses and the payment is properly
approved by the local court. Id. If in a case of intestacy the estate is at least secondarily
liable under local law and pays the funeral expenses with proper judicial sanction, again
the deduction should be allowed, if the surviving spouse's insolvency saddles the estate
with the obligation. Id.

[30] Cf. Burnet v. Harmel, 287 US 103, 110 (1932); Priv. Ltr. Rul. 8838009 (June 17,
1988).

[31] Second Nat'l Bank of New Haven v. United States, 387 US 456 (1967). The doctrine is analyzed in the discussion of Section 2033 at ¶ 4.05[2][b].

[32] Cf. First Nat'l Bank of Ft. Worth v. United States, 301 F. Supp. 667 (ND Tex.
1969).

Veterans Administration payments to cover burial and funeral expenses, excluded from the gross estate, constitute a reimbursement that reduces the amount otherwise deductible. The same result follows if lump-sum Social Security benefits, also excluded from the gross estate, are paid to one other than a surviving spouse.[33]

A final hurdle for the deductibility of funeral expenses is imposed by Section 2053(c)(2), which, with an exception, limits the aggregate Section 2053(a) deductions to the value of estate assets subject to claims. This restriction is discussed later in this treatise[34] after a consideration of other deductions that are more likely to invoke the limitation.

[3] Administration Expenses

Section 2053(a)(2) authorizes the deduction of administration expenses. The expenses that fall into this category are those "actually and necessarily incurred . . . in the collection of assets, payment of debts, and distribution of property to the persons entitled to it."[35] The regulations specifically recognize as administration expenses executor commissions and attorney fees,[36] as well as such miscellaneous expenses as court costs, surrogates' fees, accountants' fees, appraisers' fees, and clerical costs.[37]

As in the case of funeral expenses, the concern here is only with expenses "actually incurred." The "allowable" concept, equally applicable here, is again a matter of limitation, not authorization.[38] And the question whether an admin-

---

[33] These possibilities are considered in Rev. Rul. 66-234, 1966-2 CB 436.

[34] See infra ¶ 5.03[7].

[35] Reg. § 20.2053-3(a). Cf. Rev. Rul. 80-260, 1980-2 CB 277 (dealing with the effect of foreign exchange rate fluctuations on Section 2053).

[36] Reg. §§ 20.2053-3(b), 20.2053-3(c).

[37] Reg. § 20.2053-3(d).

[38] See supra ¶ 5.03[2][b]. The regulations take the position that mere allowance of a deduction under state law is insufficient to permit a Section 2053(a)(2) deduction, unless the expense is a reasonable and necessary administration expense within the meaning of federal law. Reg. § 20.2053-3(a). The Seventh Circuit has improperly refused to follow that regulation and treats deductibility as governed by state law alone. Jenner v. Comm'r, 577 F2d 1100 (7th Cir. 1978). Some authors agree. See Tow, "Estate of Love and § 2053(c)(2): Why State Law Should Control the Determination of Deductible Administrative Expenses," 12 Va. Tax Rev. 283 (1992). Considering the same issue, see also Nantell & Rogers, "Deductibility of Administration Expenses Is Not Always Black and White," 16 Hamline L. Rev. 105 (1992); Caron, "The Estate Tax Deduction for Administrative Expenses: Reformulating Complementary Rules for Federal and State Laws Under IRC § 2053(a)," 67 Cornell L. Rev. 981 (1982).

The better rule to the contrary is adopted by the Second, Fourth, Fifth, Sixth, and Ninth Circuits, requiring not only allowance by state law but also that deductible expenses be administrative expenses within the meaning of that term in the federal statute. The registration expense is allowable raises a local law issue[39] and a question as to the effect of a local decree[40] similar to those discussed previously.

[a] Executor and Attorney Fees

The term "expense" clearly connotes outgo; it is therefore appropriate for the Treasury to condition a deduction for reasonable administration expenses on ultimate payment.[41] However, it is quite common for executor and attorney fees to be paid long after the filing of the estate tax return. It is therefore equally reasonable for the Treasury to permit the return to be prepared and filed on the basis of estimates, with suitable provision for adjustment in the case of disallowance on audit or in the case of nonpayment.[42] In this respect, attorney fees sometimes present a special problem, as they may depend on services performed in connection with an audit or even litigation of tax liability

---

ulations are an appropriate interpretation. Estate of Smith v. Comm'r, 57 TC 650 (1972), aff'd without determining the validity of the regulations, 510 F2d 479 (2d Cir.), cert. denied, 423 US 827 (1975); Estate of Love v. Comm'r, 923 F2d 335 (4th Cir. 1991); Pitner v. United States, 388 F2d 651 (5th Cir. 1967); Estate of Millikin v. Comm'r, 125 F3d 339 (6th Cir. 1997) overruling Estate of Park v. Comm'r, 475 F2d 673 (6th Cir. 1973); Hibernia Bank v. United States, 581 F2d 741 (9th Cir. 1978). See also Posen v. Comm'r, 75 TC 355 (1980); Estate of Reilly v. Comm'r, 76 TC 369 (1981); Payne v. United States, 1975-1 USTC ¶ 13,059 (MD Fla. 1975); Hefner v. United States, 880 F. Supp. 770 (WD Okla. 1993). The Tax Court opinion in *Smith* clearly rejects its improper earlier view rather casually expressed in Estate of Sternberger v. Comm'r, 18 TC 836 (1952), acq. 1953-1 CB 6, nonacq. 1953-1 CB 7, aff'd per curiam, 207 F2d 600 (2d Cir. 1953), rev'd on another issue, 348 US 187 (1955). See Goffe, J., dissenting, in *Smith*, 57 TC at 665, indicating the decision in *Sternberger* is contra to *Smith*.

Cf. Priv. Ltr. Rul. 8826003 (Mar. 14, 1988), which provides a simple illustration of the issue. In the ruling, the Internal Revenue Service (the Service) refused to allow the costs of pet care as an administration expense, notwithstanding that the expenses had been approved by the local probate court. It is the Service's position that Section 2053 applies only to those expenses necessary to preserve the property of the estate. Id.

[39] Malone v. United States, 493 F. Supp. 527 (SD Tex. 1980) (attorney fees limited by state law); Estate of Grant v. Comm'r, 78 TCM (CCH) 900 (1999) (executor's fees limited by state law); Estate of Rabe v. Comm'r, 34 TCM (CCH) 117 (1975) (extraordinary executor fees disallowed in absence of state court approval); Estate of Dowlin v. Comm'r, 67 TCM (CCH) 2750 (1994) (residence expense and extraordinary executor's fees not deductible in absence of proof of state court approval). See supra ¶ 5.03[1].

[40] E.g., First Nat'l Bank of Ft. Worth v. United States, 301 F. Supp. 667 (ND Tex. 1969) (unreasonable attorney fees not deductible even though allowed by probate court); Estate of Agnew v. Comm'r, 34 TCM (CCH) 758 (1975). Cf. infra ¶ 5.03[3][c] note 63. See supra ¶ 5.03[1].

[41] Reg. §§ 20.2053-3(b), 20.2053-3(c). See, e.g., Estate of Meriano v. Comm'r, 71 TCM (CCH) 2060 (1996) rev'd on other issue, 142 F3d 651 (3d Cir. 1998) (some fees excessive); Estate of O'Neal v. United States, 258 F3d 1265 (11th Cir. 2001) (no substantion of legal fees).

[42] Reg. §§ 20.2053-3(b), 20.2053-3(c).

after the estate tax return is filed. In deficiency or refund litigation, it is prudent, and permitted by the regulations,[43] to assert early a right to refund based on anticipated attorney fees even though the amount cannot be established at the time. If nothing is done in this respect until the litigation has run its course, a refund based on the attorney fees will likely be barred by the statute of limitations,[44] although last-minute thoughts that result in amendment of a petition or complaint before judgment may get the attorney fees recognized, if a claim for refund on other grounds has been timely asserted.[45] Indeed, it is not becoming for the government to deny an estate the tax advantage of a deduction for costs incurred in its struggles over tax liability, especially if the estate is successful in its contentions,[46] and a liberal approach to limitation concepts is in order in these cases.[47]

Of course, not every payment made by an estate to an executor or administrator or to an attorney will qualify as an expense of administration. The reason for the payment and the capacity in which the payee receives the payment will be relevant in determining whether the expenditure is deductible.[48] Thus, for example, a bequest to the executor, not paid as a commission, does not entitle the estate to a deduction.[49] However, even if the estate loses an estate tax deduction in the case of a bequest that takes the place of commissions, the executor benefits by being permitted to exclude the amount received from gross income for income tax purposes.[50] Obviously, this inverse relationship between income and estate taxes has resulted in tax planning that broadly considers the consequences in the case of an estate where the executor is a friend or relative. Even if the decedent has provided in a will for both a bequest to the executor and payment of commissions, an executor who is willing to forgo the latter

---

[43] Reg. § 20.2053-3(c)(2).

[44] Moir v. United States, 149 F2d 455 (1st Cir. 1945); United States v. Wells Fargo Bank, 393 F2d 272 (9th Cir. 1963); Estate of Swietlik v. United States, 779 F2d 1306 (7th Cir. 1985). Cf. Rev. Rul. 78-323, 1978-2 CB 240.

[45] Bankers Trust Co. v. United States, 438 F2d 1046 (2d Cir. 1970).

[46] Cf. Lykes v. United States, 343 US 118 (1952); IRC § 212(3). See also Section 7430 in some situations allowing an estate to recover reasonable administrative and litigation costs from the government. To the extent of recovery of such costs under this section, the estate would be made "whole," and no Section 2053 deduction should be allowed. Cf. IRC § 7430(c)(4)(A)(iii); Estate of Woll v. Comm'r, 44 F3d 464 (7th Cir. 1994).

[47] Cf. Lykes v. United States, 343 US 118 (1952) . But see Rev. Rul. 78-323, 1978-2 CB 240.

[48] E.g., Estate of Agnew v. Comm'r, 34 TCM (CCH) 758 (1975); Craft v. Comm'r, 68 TC 249 (1977), aff'd per curiam, 608 F2d 240 (5th Cir. 1979).

[49] Reg. § 20.2053-3(b)(2).

[50] The value of property acquired by bequest is excluded from gross income under Section 102. See United States v. Merriam, 263 US 179 (1923), criticized in Bank of New York v. Helvering, 132 F2d 773 (2d Cir. 1943), and in Wolder v. Comm'r, 493 F2d 608 (2d Cir. 1974).

fees may be able to avoid income and gift taxation on the fees if a timely waiver is executed.[51] On the other hand, an executor who is a lawyer may be paid deductible fees (subject to income tax) in both capacities, if the lawyer performs extraordinary legal services.[52]

No deduction is allowed for attorney fees if the attorney is performing services primarily for the benefit of individual legatees or beneficiaries rather than for the estate.[53] In many cases, payment of such personal expenses by the estate will not be proper under state law, and thus the "allowable under local law" requirement of Section 2053(a) will not be fulfilled.[54] Even if this is not the case, the disallowance of such expenses may be proper on the ground that if they are not primarily or directly related to the administration of the decedent's estate, they are not "administration expenses" as that term is used in Section 2053(a).[55] In some cases it is unclear whether the expense was incurred for the benefit of a beneficiary or for the estate. One court has drawn the line between expenses incurred in an internecine conflict among beneficiaries over their respective shares (not deductible) and those incurred in a dispute between the true beneficiaries as a group and other spurious contenders (deductible).[56]

---

[51] See Rev. Rul. 66-167, 1966-1 CB 20, applicable both to the income and the gift tax. Relative tax rates under the two taxes are a key to making decisions here.

[52] Rev. Rul. 69-551, 1969-2 CB 177.

[53] Reg. §§ 20.2053-3(a), 20.2053-3(c)(3); Jacobs v. United States, 248 F. Supp. 695 (D. Tex. 1965); Estate of Hecksher v. Comm'r, 63 TC 485 (1975); Estate of Bartberger v. Comm'r, 54 TCM (CCH) 1550 (1988); Estate of Baird v. Comm'r, 73 TCM (CCH) 1883 (1997). But see Dulles v. Johnson, 155 F. Supp. 275, 282 (SDNY 1957); rev'd on other issues, 273 F2d 362 (2d Cir. 1959), cert. denied, 364 US 834 (1960) (a deduction allowed for fees paid to counsel for legatees in proceedings initiated by the executors); Peirce v. United States, 80-1 USTC ¶ 13,338 (WD Pa. 1980); Estate of Reilly v. Comm'r, 76 TC 369 (1980); Rev. Rul. 75-509, 1975-2 CB 302.

[54] Estate of Baldwin v. Comm'r, 59 TC 654 (1973); Estate of McCoy v. Comm'r, 20 TCM (CCH) 224 (1961).

[55] Cf. Reg. §§ 20.2053-3(b)(3), 20.2053-3(c)(3). See Estate of O'Neal v. United States, 258 F3d 1265 (11th Cir. 2001) (attorney fees not deductible because of lack of substantiation that fees were incurred for work of the estate). But see Whitt v. Comm'r, 46 TCM (CCH) 118, 138 (1983), aff'd, 751 F2d 1548 (11th Cir. 1985).

[56] Pitner v. United States, 388 F2d 651 (5th Cir. 1967). The opinion is noteworthy also for its analysis of the meaning of "allowable" and its recognition that there can be administrative expenses when there is no "administration" because it is foreclosed by state law (Texas) for lack of necessity. Another case that fits within this distinction, Porter v. Comm'r, 49 TC 207 (1967), allowed a deduction for expenses incurred by two children successfully asserting against their surviving parent their deceased parent's interest in property held as community property under New Mexico law at the time of the parents' divorce.

[b] Commissions Paid to a Trustee

Commissions paid to a trustee generally do not qualify as administration expenses.[57] For example, fees paid to a trustee for services to be performed in the management of a testamentary trust after its creation are "not in settlement of a dead man's affairs, but for the benefit of the beneficiaries of the trust."[58] In fact, amounts paid to an executor for services, nominally for the settlement of the estate but actually in the capacity of trustee for beneficiaries, have been properly disallowed as deductions. This result was reached in a case in which the decedent in a will directed the executor to retain the residuary estate for a long period and to manage it for the beneficiaries.[59] On the other hand, if a trustee performs services concerning property included within the probate estate, services that would normally be undertaken by the executor, fees for such services may be proper administration expenses.[60] An example would be amounts paid to a trustee in connection with the setting up (not mere management) of a testamentary trust. When assets of an inter vivos trust are included in decedent's gross estate, a trustee's commissions for termination of the trust are either excludible from the gross estate or deductible as a Section 2053 expense.[61]

[c] Other Deductible Administration Expenses

It is not possible here to suggest even generally what expenses, other than executor commissions, attorney fees, and some of the miscellaneous items listed in the regulations, may constitute deductible administration expenses, but a few further examples may help to illustrate the controlling legal principles. If assets must be sold to realize cash to pay debts, expenses, and taxes, to preserve the estate, or to discharge cash legacies, then related brokerage charges[62] and other selling expenses are clearly administration expenses.[63] Similarly, ex-

---

[57] Reg. § 20.2053-3(b)(3).

[58] Estate of Sharpe v. Comm'r, 148 F2d 179, 181 (3d Cir. 1945). See also Estate of Carson v. Comm'r, 35 TCM (CCH) 330 (1976).

[59] Estate of Mary Eagan v. Comm'r, 18 BTA 875 (1930), acq. IX-2 CB 17. See Peckham v. Comm'r, 19 BTA 1020 (1930).

[60] Reg. § 20.2053-3(b)(3).

[61] Haggart's Estate v. Comm'r, 182 F2d 514 (3d Cir. 1950); Estate of De Foucaucourt v. Comm'r, 62 TC 485 (1974). Cf. infra ¶ 5.03[4].

[62] See Estate of Jenner v. Comm'r, 577 F2d 1100 (7th Cir. 1978); Estate of Joslyn v. Comm'r, 566 F2d 677 (9th Cir. 1977); Gillespie v. United States, 23 F3d 36 (2d Cir. 1994); Rev. Rul. 83-30, 1983-1 CB 224 (decisions permitting Section 2053(a)(2) deductibility of underwriting fees incurred in marketing a large block of stock). But see infra ¶ 5.03[3][d] note 78. Cf. Priv. Ltr. Rul. 8826003 (Mar. 14, 1988).

[63] Estate of Dudley S. Blossom v. Comm'r, 45 BTA 691 (1941), nonacq. 1966-2 CB 7; Estate of Papson v. Comm'r, 73 TC 290 (1979); Marcus v. Dewitt, 704 F2d 1227 (11th

penses incurred for investment counseling pending administration of the estate have been held deductible.[64] On the grounds that operation of a farm during administration of its owner's estate was a proper matter of maintenance, losses incurred on such operation have been held deductible as administration expenses,[65] but an estate cannot successfully claim expenses incurred in the development of estate property (as opposed to its maintenance) as deductible administration expenses.[66] Expenses allocable to tax-exempt income, for which an estate is denied an income tax deduction under Section 265, may be deductible for estate tax purposes.[67] If, for a purpose beneficial to the estate,[68] the decedent's executor permits interest to accrue on the decedent's debts after the decedent's death, such interest is an administration expense deductible if allowable under the state law.[69] However, any such postdeath interest must be determinable with reasonable accuracy.[70] Interest paid on amounts borrowed to

---

Cir. 1983). The regulations deny a deduction for selling expenses for other purposes (Reg. § 20.2053-3(d)(2)), and they have been upheld. Estate of Posen v. Comm'r, 75 TC 355 (1980); Estate of Smith v. Comm'r, 57 TC 650 (1972), aff'd, 510 F2d 479 (2d Cir.), cert. denied 423 US 827 (1975); Estate of Vatter v. Comm'r, 65 TC 633 (1975), aff'd per curiam, 1977-1 USTC ¶ 13,169 (2d Cir. 1976); Estate of Streeter v. Comm'r, 491 F2d 375 (3d Cir. 1974); Pitner v. United States, 388 F2d 651 (5th Cir. 1967); Estate of Grant v. Comm'r, 78 TCM (CCH) 900 (1999). The expenditure must be an "administration expense," as Congress used the term before the "allowable" issue arises under local law. See supra ¶ 5.03[1].

[64] Estate of Harold M. Lehman v. Comm'r, 39 BTA 17 (1939), acq. 1939-1 CB 20, aff'd on other issues, 109 F2d 99 (2d Cir.), cert. denied, 310 US 637 (1940).

[65] Estate of Fannie R. Brewer v. Comm'r, 1941 BTA (P-H) ¶ 41,574.

[66] Estate of HF Hammon v. Comm'r, 10 BTA 43 (1928), acq. VII-1 CB 13.

[67] Rev. Rul. 59-32, 1959-1 CB 245, clarified in Rev. Rul. 63-27, 1963-1 CB 57.

[68] Estate of Wheless v. Comm'r, 72 TC 470 (1979); Hibernia Bank v. United States, 581 F2d 741 (9th Cir. 1978); Estate of Graegin v. Comm'r, 56 TCM (CCH) 387 (1988). See Reg. § 20.2053-3(a). Cf. Rev. Rul. 77-461, 1977-2 CB 324. But see Jenner v. Comm'r, 577 F2d 1100 (7th Cir. 1978) (deductibility solely a matter of state law).

[69] Rev. Rul. 69-402, 1969-2 CB 176, issued after the Commissioner had failed to sustain a contrary contention in cases such as Ballance v. United States, 347 F2d 419 (7th Cir. 1965), and Maehling v. United States, 1967-2 USTC ¶ 12,486 (SD Ind. 1967). See TAM 9604002 (Oct. 6, 1995) (interest imposed by state law on a pecuniary bequest after a stated period was not an administrative expense, but in essence income paid to the recipient).

[70] Reg. § 20.2053-1(b)(3). For cases involving fluctuating interest rates, see Bailly v. Comm'r, 81 TC 949 (1983); Estate of Bliss v. Comm'r, 50 TCM (CCH) 1285 (1985); Snyder v. United States, 582 F. Supp. 196 (D. Md. 1984); Hoover v. Comm'r, 49 TCM (CCH) 1239 (1985); Estate of Harrison v. Comm'r, 52 TCM (CCH) 1306 (1986). See also Rev. Rul. 84-75, 1984-1 CB 193 (involving the possibility of loan acceleration); Estate of Graegin, 56 TCM (CCH) 387 (1988); Priv. Ltr. Rul. 9952039 (Sept. 30, 1999) (full amount of interest currently deductible because no possibility of acceleration).

pay the federal estate tax also qualifies as an administration expense.[71] However, for decedents dying after 1997, interest paid on estate taxes deferred under Section 6166 is not deductible under Section 2053.[72] Of course, interest

---

[71] Estate of Todd v. Comm'r, 57 TC 288 (1971), acq. 1973-2 CB 4; Hipp v. United States, 1972-1 USTC ¶ 12,824 (DSC 1971); Estate of Webster v. Comm'r, 65 TC 968 (1976); Estate of Bahr v. Comm'r, 68 TC 74 (1977), acq. 1978-1 CB 1. However, the estate must prove that the interest was "actually and necessarily incurred." Reg. § 20.2053-3(a); Estate of Todd v. Comm'r, supra; Estate of McKee v. Comm'r, 72 TCM (CCH) 324 (1996); Estate of Street v. Comm'r, 68 TCM (CCH) 1213 (1994) (burden not met because estate could not show there was a liquidity problem necessitating a loan to pay the taxes). The Service agrees. Cf. Rev. Rul. 78-125, 1978-1 CB 292 (involving interest on a Section 6166 obligation which is now not deductible, see infra text accompanying note 72), revoking Rev. Rul. 75-239, 1975-1 CB 304. Cf. Axtell v. United States, 860 F. Supp. 795 (D. Wyo. 1994) (no deduction for interest claimed after Section 6511 statute of limitations had run, even though interest would have been deductible had a Section 6166 election been made); Estate of Lasarzig v. Comm'r, 78 TCM (CCH) 448 (1999) (no interest deduction for loan to pay estate tax on QTIP trust whose assets were distributed and estate no longer being administrated).

Interest incurred on an estate tax deficiency is also a deductible administration expense to the extent allowable by local law. Rev. Rul. 79-252, 1979-2 CB 333; Rev. Rul. 81-154, 1981-1 CB 470. See also Rev. Rul. 81-287, 1981-2 CB 183; Rev. Proc. 81-27, 1981-2 CB 548; TAM 9051002 (Sept. 18, 1990) (interest expense on late filing of returns, even though returns filed five years late). Similarly, interest incurred on the deferral of state death taxes or foreign death taxes is also deductible. Rev. Rul. 81-256, 1981-2 CB 183, Rev. Rul. 83-24, 1983-1 CB 229. However, interest related to the Section 2032A(c) recapture tax is not deductible. Rev. Rul. 90-8, 1990-1 CB 173. Interest that is refunded or reimbursed to the estate is not deductible. Estate of O'Daniel v. United States, 6 F3d 321 (5th Cir. 1993); TAM 9333004 (May 3, 1993).

However, the Service has taken the position that if the interest in situations above cannot be immediately determined with reasonable accuracy (see supra text accompanying note 70), the interest is deductible only when it accrues. Rev. Rul. 80-250, 1980-2 CB 278; Rev. Rul. 84-75, 1984-1 CB 193. See also Rev. Proc. 81-27, 1981-2 CB 548 (explaining the method of computation).

If such deferred interest is deducted as a Section 2053 administrative expense, the Service takes the position that post-death interest accruing on deferred federal estate tax payable from a testamentary transfer is an expense that may reduce the value of the transfer for purposes of Section 2013 (see ¶ 3.05[3][b] text accompanying notes 47–50), and does reduce the value of the transfer for the purposes of Sections 2055 (see infra ¶ 5.05[3][b] text accompanying note 117) and 2056 (see infra ¶ 5.06[5][b] text accompanying note 119). See also Reg. §§ 20.2013-4(b)(3)(i), 20.2055-3(b)(3), 20.2055-3(b)(6), 20.2056(b)-4(d)(2), 20.2056(b)-4(d)(3), 20.2056-4(d)(5) Ex. 4.

[72] IRC § 2053(c)(1)(D). The rationale for this deduction disallowance as well as other aspects of the subsection are discussed at ¶ 2.02[3][c][v]. For prior law, see Rev. Rul. 78-125, 1978-1 CB 292; Rev. Rul. 80-250, 1980-2 CB 278; Estate of Shapiro v. Comm'r, 111 F3d 1010 (2d Cir. 1997), cert. denied, 118 S. Ct. 686 (1998).

For decedents dying before 1998, interest paid on estate taxes deferred under Section 6166 was not deductible under Section 2053 if there was an election to have Section 6601(j) as amended apply to installments due after the effective date of the election. Taxpayer Relief Act of 1997, Pub. L. No. 105-34, § 503(d)(2), 111 Stat. 788, 853 (1997), reprinted in 1997-4 CB 1457, 1539.

accrued before death for which the decedent was personally liable is deductible either as a claim against the estate under Section 2053(a)(3) or as a part of a secured indebtedness under Section 2053(a)(4).[73]

[d] The Section 642(g) Election

It should be apparent from the prior discussion that many administration expenses deductible for estate tax purposes are also deductible for income tax purposes under, for example, Section 162 or Section 212. However, Section 642(g) expressly prevents some items from being deducted for purposes of both taxes.[74] Affected items are not allowed in computing the taxable income of the estate[75] of any other person, which under Section 7701(a)(1) includes a trust, unless a statement is filed indicating that the items have not been allowed as estate tax deductions under Section 2053 or Section 2054 and that the rights to such estate tax deductions are waived. A portion of a single deduction may be taken under the estate tax and the remaining portion under the income tax.[76]

The limitation of Section 642(g) applies not only to deductions but also to reductions.[77] Thus, an estate may deduct the cost of selling securities for estate tax purposes; but the cost, such as a brokerage commission, cannot also be taken into account in the computation of gain or loss for income tax purposes.[78]

---

[73] Reg. § 20.2053-7. Cf. Rev. Rul. 77-461, 1977-2 CB 324.

[74] See also IRC § 213(c)(2), regarding post-death payment of medical expenses.

[75] See Burrow Trust v. Comm'r, 39 TC 1080 (1963), acq. 1965-2 CB 4, aff'd, 333 F2d 66 (10th Cir. 1964), which held that Section 642(g) did not prevent both an estate tax and an income tax deduction for a revocable inter vivos trust includible in the settlor's gross estate. The government followed *Burrow* by stipulation in Estate of Cohn v. United States, 249 F. Supp. 763 (SDNY 1966), aff'd on other issues, 371 F2d 642 (2d Cir. 1967). Of course, this result is not possible today because of the amendment of Section 642(g) by Pub. L. No. 89-621, 80 Stat. 872 (1966), reprinted in 1966-2 CB 604, 605 extending the proscription beyond the estate to "any other person."

[76] Reg. § 1.642(g)-2. Stack v. United States, 23 F3d 1400 (8th Cir. 1994).

[77] This rule, added by the Tax Reform Act of 1976, Pub. L. No. 94-455, § 2009(d), 90 Stat. 1520, 1896 (1976), reprinted in 1976-3 CB (Vol. 1) 1, 372, applies to all income taxable years ending after October 4, 1976.

[78] Prior to the 1976 amendment to Section 642(g), see supra text accompanying note 77, there was substantial contrary authority. Estate of Bray v. Comm'r, 46 TC 577 (1966), acq. 1971-1 CB 1, aff'd, 396 F2d 452 (6th Cir. 1968); Rev. Rul. 71-173, 1971-1 CB 204 (now obsolete, see Rev. Rul. 89-75, 1989-1 CB 319). Conceivably, perhaps where a large block of stock is sold by an estate through underwriters in a "secondary offering" to the public, expenses of the sale may be taken into account in valuing the stock under Section 2031. See ¶ 4.02[4][e] especially note 206. If so, did the *Bray* principle apply to also permit a Section 2053 deduction for the same expenses? The Tax Court has appropriately held it did not, Estate of Joslyn v. Comm'r, 57 TC 722 (1972), but the Ninth Circuit (in

A claim of a deduction on the estate tax return does not foreclose the income tax deduction if the estate tax deduction is not finally allowed, although the election of an income tax deduction must be made before the expiration of the statutory period of limitation for the taxable year for which the income tax deduction is claimed.[79] A waiver of estate tax deduction made in the form of the statement required by the regulations[80] is irrevocable.[81] Obviously, which deduction is more appropriate depends on the facts and circumstances of each situation; in many cases a simple mathematical computation of the respective tax benefits will determine the matter. However, in making the election, an executor must recognize that the executor's obligation is to all of the beneficial parties and that their interests may possibly conflict. For example, election of an income tax deduction will usually favor the income beneficiary while increasing the estate tax burden on the remainderpersons.[82]

It will be recalled that Section 2053(c)(2) generally limits aggregate Section 2053(a) deductions to the value of the estate assets subject to claims. A discussion of this restriction is again deferred.[83]

Joslyn) and Seventh Circuit disagreed, 500 F2d 382 (9th Cir. 1974) and, on reh'g 566 F2d 677 (9th Cir. 1977); Estate of Jenner v. Comm'r, 36 TCM (CCH) 241 (1977), rev'd, 577 F2d 1100 (7th Cir. 1978). The Service disagrees (Rev. Rul. 83-30, 1983-1 CB 224), as does the Second Circuit (Gillespie v. United States, 23 F3d 36 (2d Cir. 1994)).

Section 642(g) exempts from the double-deduction limitation items that are deductible as deductions in respect of decedents under Section 691.

[79] Reg. § 1.642(g)-1.

[80] Reg. § 1.642(g)-1. The statement must be filed in duplicate. Id.

[81] Reg. § 1.642(g)-1; Estate of Darby v. Wiseman, 323 F2d 792 (10th Cir. 1963). See also Priv. Ltr. Rul. 8022006 (Feb. 15, 1980). This prompts the sensible practice of deferring the filing of the waiver until the time of audit of the estate tax return. See McDaniel, Repetti & Caron, Federal Wealth Transfer Taxation, 516 (Foundation Press 4th ed. 1999).

[82] The fiduciary's problem is examined in Blattmachr, "The Tax Effects of Equitable Adjustments: An Internal Revenue Code Odyssey," 18 Miami Inst. on Est. Plan., §§ 1400–1415 (1984); Dobris, "Equitable Adjustments in Postmortem Income Tax Planning: An Unremitting Diet of *Worms*," 65 Iowa L. Rev. 103 (1979); Wyatt, "Problems of the Fiduciary in Deducting Administration Expenses," 14 Miami Inst. on Est. Plan. § 1300 (1980); Walsh, "Postmortem Estate Planning," 37 NYU Inst. on Fed. Tax'n Chapter 44 (1979); Wallace, "Current Problems in Postmortem Tax Planning," 3 Notre Dame Est. Plan. Inst. 657, 705 (1979); Fairchild, "Section 642(g) of the Internal Revenue Code: The Executor's Quandary," 24 U. Fla. L. Rev. 106 (1971); Lewis, "Shifting of Deductions From Estate to Income Tax Returns," 97 Trusts & Est. 936 (1958); Fager, "Administrative Expenses Deductible by Estates and Beneficiaries," 25 NYU Inst. on Fed. Tax'n 1167 (1967). More extensive postmortem estate planning is considered in Halbach, "Postmortem Estate Planning," 1963 U. Ill. LF 212; Simmons, "Tax Planning of the Administration of an Estate," 15 Vand. L. Rev. 437 (1962); Gallo, "Tax Considerations During Probate," 15 UCLA L. Rev. 1260 (1968).

[83] See infra ¶ 5.03[7].

[4] Expenses of Administering Property Not Subject to Claims

A person's death may necessitate the expenditure of money in the transmission of property that is not a part of the decedent's probate estate and is not subject to claims[84] but that as a part of the decedent's gross estate figures in the determination of the federal estate tax. If we are thus required to pretend that some property not owned by a decedent was the decedent's, elementary fairness seems to require the companion pretense that the estate is diminished by administration expenses incurred with respect to these imaginary assets. However, such expenditures may not be administration expenses allowable under local law, the test imposed by the last clause of Section 2053(a), because they are not payable out of the estate that is subject to claims. This is, therefore, what Section 2053(b) is all about.

Suppose, for example, that the decedent had created a trust taxable under Section 2036 because of the decedent's retention of the right to the income for life and that the assets in such trust are not subject to claims under local law. If the property is to be distributed to a remainderperson at the decedent's death, the activities of the trustee in terminating the trust and effecting the appropriate distribution of trust assets are scarcely different from the services performed by the executor with regard to probate assets; and on the termination of inter vivos trusts, there may be a substantial charge by the trustee in the form of principal commissions, which, from an overall estate tax view, are not easily differentiated from executor commissions. In general, Section 2053(b) makes these and similar charges deductible.[85]

[a] Scope

It is possible that some expenses incurred with respect to nonprobate property might be deductible without the assistance of Section 2053(b). Before that subsection was enacted, a trustee's termination charge on artificial gross estate property was allowed under what is now Section 2053(a).[86] However, for reasons suggested earlier, the appellate court refused to treat the charge as an administration expense, holding instead that it was deductible (or perhaps more accurately, would support an exclusion) under what is now Section 2053(a)(4).[87] Section 2053(b) might seem now to carry the inference that Section 2053(a) deductions are restricted to charges that fall on property subject to

---

[84] Cf. Estate of Snyder v. United States, 84 AFTR2d 99-5963 (Ct. Fed. Cl. 1999) (defining the term "subject to claims" for purposes of Section 2053(c)(2)).

[85] Reg. § 20.2053-8; Rev. Rul. 76-498, 1976-2 CB 1999. Related attorney fees fall within the same rule. Reg. § 20.2053-8(d) Ex. 1.

[86] George P. Davis v. Comm'r, 45 BTA 52 (1941), nonacq. 1942-1 CB 21, aff'd, 132 F2d 644 (1st Cir. 1942).

[87] See infra ¶ 5.03[6].

claims, but earlier doctrine regarding charges against gross estate assets is continued in the regulations.[88] In this light, Section 2053(b) might perhaps be viewed as mostly a clarifying change. However, if, for example, a person's entire estate consisted of insurance on that person's life payable to another, includible under Section 2042, or jointly held property, includible under Section 2040, there may be no charges against such nonprobate assets at death and yet the recipients could incur expenses, for items such as the preparation of the federal estate tax return.[89] As previously held,[90] these are not deductible administration expenses, and they are clearly not indebtedness in respect of estate assets. Thus, these appropriate charges would not reduce estate tax liability except for Section 2053(b), and they are deductible under its provisions.[91]

[b] Restrictions

Congress imposes two restrictions on the deduction of administration expenses under Section 2053(b). First, the expenses must be of a type that would be deductible under Section 2053(a) if they related to property that was subject to claims. Thus, all the comments in the preceding segment of this discussion are equally applicable here. Moreover, to be deductible, Section 2053(b) expenses must be paid before the limitation period for assessment of estate tax expires. In general, payment of such expenses is required within three years after the estate tax return is filed,[92] and of course, the return is generally due nine months after the decedent's death.[93] In some instances, however, the assessment period is extended;[94] therefore, the time of payment restriction is also extended.[95]

---

[88] Reg. § 20.2053-7, discussed infra ¶ 5.03[6].

[89] See IRC §§ 2002, 2203, 6324(a)(1); Reg. § 20.2002-1. Similarly, expenses might be incurred after death in the determination whether nonprobate assets were includible in the gross estate or with regard to the valuation of nonprobate assets for estate tax purposes.

[90] George P. Davis v. Comm'r, 45 BTA 52 (1941), nonacq. 1942-1 CB 21, aff'd, 132 F2d 644 (1st Cir. 1942).

[91] S. Rep. No. 1622, 83d Cong., 2d Sess. 474 (1954); Reg. § 20.2053-8(d); Central Trust of Cincinnati v. Welch, 304 F2d 923 (6th Cir. 1962).

[92] IRC § 6501(a). See Gillum v. Comm'r, 49 TCM (CCH) 240 (1984).

[93] IRC § 6075(a).

[94] E.g., no return, assessment at any time, IRC § 6501(c)(3); false return, same, IRC § 6501(c)(1); substantial omission of items from gross estate, six years, IRC § 6501(e)(2).

[95] See also ¶¶ 2.02[3] and 3.07 discussing situations in which the time for payment is extended either automatically or subject to discretion.

[5] Claims Against the Estate

Although Section 2053(a) groups several types of estate tax deductions, there are sharp philosophical differences in the allowance of funeral and administration expenses deductible under Sections 2053(a)(1) and 2053(a)(2) and the allowance of claims under Section 2053(a)(3). The first two paragraphs condition deductions on postdeath expenditures that must actually be made, and of course properly made under local law, to support a reduction in the taxable estate. The deduction under the third paragraph depends on whether there were "personal obligations of the decedent existing at the time of death."[96]

[a] Personal Obligations of Decedent

The required personal obligation exists only if a debt has a substantial economic effect on the person required to pay it. Thus, as manager of community property, one spouse might be personally liable at death for the full amount of community debts. But if the deceased spouse's obligation is accompanied by a right of recovery for half the amount against the surviving spouse's share of the community property, the deceased spouse has the required personal obligation for only one half of the community obligation.[97] Of course, the Section 2053 deduction is not increased by a will direction that the entire obligation be paid out of the deceased spouse's estate, for then the additional amount is merely an indirect bequest to the surviving spouse and not an obligation.[98] Similarly, the debt must be viable at the time of the decedent's death.[99] A claim barred by the statute of limitations or the doctrine of laches is

---

[96] Reg. § 20.2053-4. See George P. Davis v. Comm'r, 45 BTA 52, nonacq. 1942-1 CB 21, aff'd, 132 F2d 644 (1st Cir. 1992); Rev. Rul. 76-498, 1976-2 CB 199; Estate of Lineweaver v. Comm'r, 71 TCM (CCH) 3058 (1996) (obligation terminated); Elkins v. United States, 457 F. Supp. 870 (SD Tex. 1978) (intrafamily loan). The obligation must be bona fide. Estate of Bath v. Comm'r, 34 TCM (CCH) 493 (1975); Rev. Rul. 83-54, 1983-1 CB 229. An accrued liability to pay an inter vivos administration expense is a claim against an estate. TAM 9121002 (Jan. 18, 1991).

[97] United States v. Stapf, 375 US 118 (1963). Cf. Deobald Estate v. United States, 444 F. Supp. 374 (ED La. 1977). But see Estate of Fulmer v. Comm'r, 83 TC 302 (1984).

[98] United States v. Stapf, 375 US 118 (1963).

[99] See Greenburg v. Comm'r, 76 TC 680 (1981); Bailey v. Comm'r, 741 F2d 801 (5th Cir. 1984).

not an "existing" claim that will support a deduction,[100] assuming that such a claim would not be allowable under local law.[101]

Section 2053(c)(1)(B) expressly precludes any deduction for income taxes on income received after the decedent's death, property taxes not accrued before the decedent's death, and any "estate, succession, legacy, or inheritance" taxes[102] (but note the limited deduction for state and foreign death taxes under Section 2053(d)).[103] This negative rule seems hardly necessary in the light of the personal obligation requirement of Section 2053(a)(3) and the parallel concept under Section 2053(a)(4) discussed later. On the other hand, income taxes on income earned before death and any other taxes, such as unpaid gift taxes on the decedent's lifetime transfers, which are obligations of the decedent at the time of death,[104] represent deductible claims against the estate.[105]

---

[100] Estate of Honickman v. Comm'r, 58 TC 132 (1972), aff'd in unpub. op. (3d Cir. 1973); Jones v. United States, 424 F. Supp. 236 (ED Ill. 1976). Cf. Estate of Horvath v. Comm'r, 59 TC 551 (1973) (where the decedent's acknowledgment of an obligation precluded its being barred); Elkins v. United States, 457 F. Supp. 870 (SD Tex. 1978) (intrafamily loan).

[101] Cf. Estate of Ehret v. Comm'r, 35 TCM (CCH) 1432 (1976), where deduction of a valid claim was barred because the claim was not filed in state probate proceedings. But see Estate of Thompson v. Comm'r, 730 F2d 1071 (7th Cir. 1983). See Palmquist, "The Estate Tax Deductibility of Unenforced Claims Against a Decedent's Estate," 11 Gonzaga L. Rev. 707 (1976).

The Service takes the position that a claim valid under state law is not deductible if allowance of the claim would violate sharply defined public policy. TAM 9207004 (Oct. 21, 1991) (confiscation of illegal drugs). See Turnier, "The Pink Panther Meets the Grim Reaper: Estate Taxation of the Fruits of Crime," 72 NC L. Rev. 163 (1993).

[102] This preclusion includes a municipal inheritance tax. McFarland v. United States, 80 AFTR2d 97-8348 (ED La. 1997).

[103] Prior to 1997, Section 2053(c)(1)(B) contained an exception allowing a deduction for the now-repealed Section 4980A(d) 15 percent estate tax imposed on excess accumulations in retirement plans. IRC § 2053(c)(1)(B) prior to amendment by Taxpayer Relief Act of 1997; Pub. L. No. 105-34, § 1073(b)(3), 111 Stat. 788, 948 (1997), reprinted in 1997-4 CB 1457, 1637.

[104] Estate of Proesel v. United States, 585 F2d 295 (7th Cir. 1978), aff'g 77-2 USTC ¶ 13,217 (ND Ill. 1977), cert. denied, 441 US 961 (1979). See Reg. § 20.2053-6(f); Johnson v. United States, 742 F2d 137 (4th Cir. 1984). Cf. Estate of O'Neal v. United States, 258 F3d 1265 (11th Cir. 2001) (donees' claim for reimbursement of gift tax paid as transferees was a deductible claim); Priv. Ltr. Rul. 8837004 (June 2, 1988) (amount of deduction reduced by a surviving spouse's payment of part of a decedent's gift tax obligation, after a post-mortem election to split gifts).

[105] Some states treat state gift tax as a prepayment of state death tax if the property subject to the state gift tax is included in the estate for state death tax purposes. The Commissioner at one time took the position that if the state tax is not paid prior to decedent's death, the tax is a state "estate, inheritance, legacy or succession" tax not qualifying for a Section 2053(a)(3) deduction. Rev. Rul. 71-355, 1971-2 CB 334. This inappropriate position, questioned in the fourth edition of this text, was repudiated in Lang v. Comm'r, 613 F2d 770 (9th Cir. 1980). Cf. Reg. § 20.2053-6(d); Estate of Gamble v. Comm'r, 69 TC

Property taxes are deductible if they have become obligations[106] of the decedent or liens on the decedent's property[107] at the time of the decedent's death; accrual in the usual accounting sense is not enough.[108] Despite the special problems that sometimes arise with respect to state taxes, an obligation need not have matured to the point of being presently payable to be deductible. It is enough if the decedent's obligation to make the payment at some future time has become fixed by the date of the decedent's death.[109] Again, it will be seen that the guiding thread that runs through the important provisions of Section 2053 seeks to appraise the decedent's actual net worth at death (taking account, too, of taxable lifetime transfers), to determine the value of what the decedent can actually transmit to survivors, after costs incurred in transmitting it.

Section 2053 allows no deduction for any claim by a remainderperson[110] for property included in a decedent's gross estate under Section 2044.[111] Such a deduction, if allowed, would eliminate the property from the tax base in both the decedent's estate and the estate of the decedent's spouse.[112]

In some instances there is substantial uncertainty whether at the time of the decedent's death the decedent had any personal obligation to another.[113] For example, suppose the decedent was killed in an automobile accident in which another was injured. If the other person presents a claim against the decedent's estate, the decedent's obligation may depend on whether the decedent's negligence caused the injury. In such circumstances, an arm's-length

---

942 (1978), which rejects a comparable position taken under Section 2033 in Rev. Rul. 75-63, 1975-1 CB 294, and is discussed at ¶ 4.05[2][a]. The Commissioner has reversed the position in both rulings in Rev. Rul. 81-302, 1981-2 CB 170. However, the Commissioner has appropriately taken the position that such state gift taxes do not qualify for a Section 2011 credit and seemingly will take the position that they will not qualify for a Section 2058 deduction after 2004. But see First Nat'l Bank & Trust Co. of Tulsa v. United States, 787 F2d 1393 (10th Cir. 1986), considered at ¶ 3.03[1] note 17; and see ¶¶ 3.03[4], 5.09.

[106] A tax may become a personal obligation and deductible before it becomes a lien on property. Estate of Pardee v. Comm'r, 49 TC 140 (1967) (involving Michigan law).

[107] Reg. § 20.2053-6(b).

[108] Reg. § 20.2053-6(b). See Rev. Ruls. 68-335, 1968-1 CB 406; 65-274, 1965-2 CB 377.

[109] Rev. Rul. 67-304, 1967-2 CB 224.

[110] The term "remainderperson" as used in this section should be interpreted broadly to include any person having an interest in the property occurring subsequent to the decedent's qualifying income interest (e.g., a secondary life estate).

[111] See ¶ 4.16.

[112] See infra ¶ 5.06[8][d].

[113] See, e.g., Estate of Gray v. Comm'r, 73 TCM (CCH) 1940 (1997) (no debt to controlled corporation); Estate of Holland v. Comm'r, 73 TCM (CCH) 3236 (1997) (no debt to trust).

settlement between the claimant and the estate or a judgment calling for payment of the claim should be determinative of the existence of the requisite personal obligation and its amount.[114] Similarly, the amount of a decedent's
personal obligation may be quite uncertain, even if it is clear there is some obligation, as where at death the decedent's income tax returns for several years
are being audited. A postdeath arm's-length settlement or actual adjudication
again should determine the amount of the Section 2053 deduction.[115] This is
not to say that postdeath events are permitted to affect the deduction, for the
events mentioned (settlement of adjudication) purport only to determine the
validity and the amount of the claim as of the date of death.[116]

A decedent's personal obligations at death may be contingent in various
respects. For example, the decedent may be secondarily liable as an accommodation endorser of another's note. In a sense, the decedent has an obligation to
pay the amount of the note, but in fact neither the decedent nor the decedent's
estate may ever be called upon to do so. The settled doctrine in this area is
that no deduction will be allowed if at death it appears the estate will not be
required to pay anything.[117] However, a deduction will be allowed in full for a
claim arising out of the decedent's capacity as a secondary obligor (e.g., as in-
dorser or guarantor) if the decedent's rights against the primary obligor are
valueless.[118]

[b] Claims Affected by Postdeath Events

The contingency just mentioned is similar but not identical to another
type of claim that clearly exists at death but that is entirely dependent as to

---

[114] See, e.g., Estate of Nilson v. Comm'r, 31 TCM (CCH) 708 (1972) (deduction allowed for claim based on malicious prosecution, settled pending administration of the estate).

[115] Broadhead Trust v. Comm'r, 31 TCM (CCH) 975 (1972); Law v. United States,
83-1 USTC ¶ 13,514 (ND Cal. 1983). Cf. Estate of McMorris v. Comm'r, 243 F3d 1254
(10th Cir. 2001).

[116] See Estate of Kyle v. Comm'r, 94 TC 829 (1990) (taxpayers failed to prove there
was a valid claim at death). But see Estate of Smith v. Comm'r, 198 F3d 515 (5th Cir.
1999) nonacq. 2000-01 CB xvi (disagreeing with this distinction, but concluding that a
claim existed at death, therefore valuing the claim at death, and also considering the benefit of an estate's potential Section 1341 income tax deduction as part of the claim's
value).

[117] E.g., Estate of May v. Comm'r, 8 TC 1099 (1947), acq. 1947-2 CB 3; Rev. Rul.
84-42, 1984-1 CB 194.

[118] Compare Comm'r v. Wragg, 141 F2d 638 (1st Cir. 1944) (which cites numerous
earlier cases in the same vein) and First Interstate Bank of Ariz. v. United States, 86-1
USTC ¶ 13,665 (D. Ariz. 1986) (which looked at post-death events to value the claim),
with DuVal's Estate v. Comm'r, 152 F2d 103 (9th Cir. 1945), cert. denied, 328 US 838
(1946), and First Nat'l Bank of Pa. v. United States, 398 F. Supp. 100 (WD Pa. 1975).

amount on future events. The problem has arisen in several cases in which a decedent's divorced spouse has a deductible claim against the estate for ongoing payment of a fixed monthly or annual amount but the payments are to cease upon the former spouse's death or remarriage. It has never been suggested that these types of contingencies foreclose a Section 2053 deduction. The debated issue is instead whether the occurrence of either terminating event shortly after the decedent's death is determinative of the amount of the deduction. A seductive line of reasoning is that the valuation of such claims is difficult at best,[119] and if, by the time the estate tax return is to be filed, one of the events has occurred so that the actual amount to be paid out by the estate is known, the deduction should not exceed the actual payment. Some cases have been decided on that basis with the rationale that the purpose behind Section 2053 is to assure that a tax is imposed on the net estate allowing a deduction only where payment is required.[120] Even if these decisions reflect a reasonable policy decision that might well be adopted by Congress, they are not a sound interpretation of the statute in its present form, as the Tax Court and Ninth Circuit have recognized.[121] They fly in the face of early precedent and are inconsistent with the obvious purpose of the estate tax to measure the taxable estate at death, except where Congress clearly elects to recognize the postdeath events.[122]

The Treasury pushes its contention that postdeath events can affect the deductibility of claims even beyond the contingency area. In Revenue Ruling 60-247, it is asserted that "no deduction will be allowed for claims against the

---

[119] Compare Comm'r v. Maresi, 156 F2d 929 (2d Cir. 1946), with Estate of Lester v. Comm'r, 57 TC 503 (1972). This type of difficulty is more readily accepted for estate tax than for income tax purposes. In Burnet v. Logan, 283 US 404 (1931), the company interest of Mrs. Logan's parent, which had no ascertainable value for income tax purposes, was valued for estate tax purposes at $277,000.

[120] Comm'r v. Estate of Shively, 276 F2d 372 (2d Cir. 1960); Estate of Taylor v. Comm'r, 39 TC 371 (1962), aff'd sub nom. Gowetz v. Comm'r, 320 F2d 874 (1st Cir. 1963); Estate of Hagmann v. Comm'r, 60 TC 465 (1973), aff'd per curiam, 492 F2d 796 (5th Cir. 1974); Estate of Courtney v. Comm'r, 62 TC 317 (1974); Estate of Chesterton v. United States, 551 F2d 278 (Ct. Cl. 1977), cert. denied, 434 US 835 (1977). Cf. Rev. Rul. 80-260, 1980-2 CB 277; First Interstate Bank of Ariz. v. United States, 86-1 USTC ¶ 13,665 (D. Ariz. 1986) (which looked at postdeath events to value the claim).

[121] Estate of Van Horne v. Comm'r, 78 TC 728 (1982), aff'd, 720 F2d 1114 (9th Cir. 1983), cert. denied, 466 US 980 (1984).

[122] Cf. Ithaca Trust Co. v. United States, 279 US 151 (1929) (the value of a charitable bequest of a remainder interest in a testamentary trust was unaffected by the death of the life beneficiary shortly after the testator's death).
Examples of congressional recognition of postdeath events appear in this discussion. IRC §§ 2053(a)(1), 2053(a)(2) (relating to funeral and administrative expenses). See also, e.g., IRC §§ 2032 (providing an alternate valuation date); 2055(a) (permitting post-death disclaimers to affect the charitable deduction, just as Section 2056(a) permits post-death disclaimers to affect the marital deduction).

estate which have not been paid or will not be paid because the creditor waives payment, fails to file his claim within the time limit and under the conditions prescribed by local law, or otherwise fails to enforce payment."[123] This ruling is simply not acceptable under Section 2053(a)(3), and it should be rejected.[124] The authors stubbornly adhere to this position, which was expressed

---

[123] Rev. Rul. 60-247, 1960-2 CB 272, 274. See also Rev. Rul. 75-24, 1975-1 CB 306, which is a minor liberalization of Rev. Rul. 60-247 in limited circumstances.

[124] The ruling does recognize that if a creditor is sole beneficiary of the estate, the creditor's claim may be allowed as a deduction, without requiring the useless act of the creditor's pressing the claim. See also Estate of Wildenthal v. Comm'r, 29 TCM (CCH) 519 (1970). Rev. Rul. 60-247, 1960-2 CB 272, is a grotesque distortion of the sound precedents on which it purports to rest. Space for analysis is limited here, but these points might briefly be made:

1. If one is required to elect to proceed as a creditor against an estate or to accept a bequest, and chooses the latter, there is no claim against the estate. Jacobs v. Comm'r, 34 F2d 233 (8th Cir. 1929), cert. denied, 280 US 603 (1929).
2. If a state statute imposing liability for state taxes itself provides a means for securing immunity, there is no claim for taxes against the estate if the immunity is attained. John Jacobs v. Comm'r, 34 BTA 594 (1936).
3. If the amount of state taxes is subject to question, no estate tax deduction need be allowed for the amount initially asserted after death if it exceeds the liability. Estate of Metcalf v. Comm'r, 7 TC 153 (1946), aff'd, 1947-2 USTC ¶ 10,566 (6th Cir. 1947).
4. If one who is liable on a note as maker has full rights for a reimbursement from a solvent comaker, the note effects no reduction in the maker's taxable estate. DuVal's Estate v. Comm'r, 152 F2d 103 (9th Cir. 1945), cert. denied, 328 US 838 (1946); the Tax Court opinion in this case, 4 TC 722 (1945), comes closer to supporting Rev. Rul. 60-247. See also Estate of Pittard v. Comm'r, 69 TC 391 (1977).

These four sound principles are the holdings in the cases that are cited as support for Rev. Rul. 60-247, but clearly, the cases are miscited. There is no doubt that Congress has allowed a deduction only for bona fide claims that at death reduce the value of wealth otherwise controlled by the decedent, but what happens to such claims after death is immaterial. Cf. Ithaca Trust Co. v. United States, 279 US 151 (1929). There is an enlightened repudiation of Rev. Rul. 60-247 by Hoffman, J., in Russell v. United States, 260 F. Supp. 493 (ND Ill. 1966). Cf. Estate of Lester v. Comm'r, 57 TC 503 (1972). The ruling seeks to impose something in the nature of an actually paid requirement on the claims deduction. No doubt Congress could do this. It is fair to say it has done this in other parts of Section 2053(a) where deductions depend on an estate's expenses. There are no expenses, allowable or otherwise, unless some are incurred; but claims can exist at death and be perfectly bona fide and allowable even though the creditor never presses for, or even if the creditor expressly waives his right to, payment. The creditor's waiver may well be viewed as a taxable gift by the creditor to estate beneficiaries. See the discussion of Section 2511 at ¶ 10.01. See also Palmquist, "The Estate Tax Deductibility of Unenforced Claims Against a Decedent's Estate," 11 Gonzaga L. Rev. 707 (1976); Jones, "Estate and Income Tax: Claims Against the Estate and Events Subsequent to Date of Death," 22 UCLA L. Rev. 654 (1975); Lewis, "Effect of Events Subsequent to the Decedent's Death on the

in earlier editions of this text, and there has been growing judicial acceptance of the position.[125]

The decedent might have made specific provision in a will to discharge a debt to a creditor with a bona fide claim based on good consideration. Indeed, the decedent might have contracted to do so.[126] Such an arrangement does not convert the creditor's deductible claim to a nondeductible bequest,[127] and how and whether the obligation is in fact discharged should be immaterial in regard to the Section 2053 deduction. But, of course, there can be no deduction for a claim unless at death there is an obligation to be discharged.[128]

[c] Section 642(g) and Claims

The proscription of double deductions by Section 642(g) is generally inapplicable to claims against the estate.[129] If a claim is in the nature of a deduction in respect of the decedent specified in Section 691(b),[130] it is a deduction

---

Valuation of Claims Against His Estate Under Section 2053 of the Federal Estate Tax," 1972. U. Ill. L. Rev. 770 (1972).

[125] Estate of O'Neal v. United States, 258 F3d 1265 (11th Cir. 2001); Estate of McMorris v. Comm'r, 243 F3d 1254 (10th Cir. 2001); Estate of Smith v. Comm'r, 198 F3d 515 (5th Cir. 1999) nonacq. 2000-01 CB xvi (but also rejecting a distinction between claims which are certain at death and mere contingent claims, see supra text accompanying notes 113–118); Propstra v. United States, 680 F2d 1248 (9th Cir. 1982); Estate of Van Horne v. Comm'r, 78 TC 728 (1982), aff'd, 720 F2d 1114 (9th Cir. 1983), cert. denied, 466 US 980 (1984); Estate of McDowell v. Comm'r, 51 TCM (CCH) 319 (1986); Wilder v. Comm'r, 581 F. Supp. 86 (ND Ohio 1983); Estate of Cafaro v. Comm'r, 57 TCM (CCH) 1002 (1989).

[126] See First Nat'l Bank of Amarillo v. United States, 422 F2d 1385 (10th Cir. 1970); Wolder v. Comm'r, 493 F2d 608 (2d Cir.), cert. denied, 419 US 828 (1974).

[127] First Nat'l Bank of Amarillo v. United States, 422 F2d 1385 (10th Cir. 1970); Wolder v. Comm'r, 493 F2d 608 (2d Cir.), cert. denied, 419 US 828 (1974). Cf. Rev. Rul. 67-375, 1967-2 CB 60 (properly subjecting to income tax a bequest that was compensation for services, despite the exclusion of "bequests" from gross income under Section 102).

[128] Lazar v. Comm'r, 58 TC 543 (1972); Pennsylvania Bank & Trust Co. v. United States, 451 F. Supp. 1296 (D. Pa. 1978), aff'd, 597 F2d 382 (3d Cir. 1979), cert. denied, 444 US 980 (1980); Williams v. United States, 78-2 USTC ¶ 13,264 (WD Tex. 1978); Estate of Moore v. Comm'r, 54 TCM (CCH) 1167 (1987) (will contest settlements not deductible as claims). Gray v. United States, 541 F2d 228 (9th Cir. 1976) (valid claim, but case remanded on a question of adequacy of consideration, see infra ¶ 5.03[5][e]). See also Estate of Robinson v. Comm'r, 63 TC 717 (1975); Estate of DeVos v. Comm'r, 34 TCM (CCH) 933 (1975) (allowing a deduction in similar circumstances under Section 2053(a)(4)).

[129] See supra ¶ 5.03[3][d].

[130] The relevant provisions are Sections 162, 163, 164, 212, 611.

to which the Section 642(g) proscription is expressly inapplicable.[131] Of course, some claims that are deductible for estate tax purposes simply fall within no parallel income tax provision.[132]

[d] The Section 213(c)(2) Election

A claim against a decedent's estate for the sometimes considerable medical expenses for the decedent's last illness would usually qualify as a Section 2053(a)(3) deduction. However, Congress has provided that if such expenses are paid by an estate within one year of a decedent's death, they may be claimed as income tax deductions of the decedent in the decedent's income tax returns for the periods in which the expenses were incurred. This income tax allowance is accompanied by its own special double-deduction rule, which permits the income tax deduction only upon the filing of a statement that the estate tax deduction has not been allowed and a waiver of that deduction.[133]

[e] The Consideration Requirement

A further limitation on the deduction for claims appears in Section 2053(c)(1). A claim against the estate that is "founded on a promise or agreement" is deductible only to the extent that it was contracted in good faith and for an adequate and full consideration in money or money's worth.[134] The need for such a rule can be easily understood.

Begin with the general proposition that an enforceable claim against the estate gives rise to a deduction. For example, assume that at some time prior to death, Decedent promises to pay Child $100,000 and puts Child in a posi-

---

[131] Reg. § 1.642(g)-2; Rev. Rul. 67-304, 1967-2 CB 224, allowing a Section 2053(a)(3) deduction for the commuted value of periodic payment due the decedent's divorced spouse, notwithstanding the estate's income tax deduction of periodic payment as distributions under Section 661. See Rev. Rul. 71-422, 1971-2 CB 255.

[132] Compare a decedent's obligation to repay the principal of a loan, deductible under Section 2053(a)(3) but not for income tax purposes, with the decedent's obligation to pay interest accrued at death on the loan, deductible under both Sections 2053(a)(3) and 163 by virtue of Section 691(b). See IRC § 642(g), Reg. § 1.642(g)-2.

[133] IRC § 213(c)(2); Reg. § 1.213-1(d)(2). Medical expenses incurred by the decedent that are paid within one year of death may be deducted on the decedent's estate tax return or on the final income tax return at the executor's option. Section 642(g) prohibits a deduction for the same item on both returns. In Rev. Rul. 77-357, 1977-2 CB 328, the Service, with weak support, states its position that the deduction for estate tax purposes is subject to the same percentage of adjusted gross income limitations as are applied if the executor chooses to take the deduction on the final income tax return.

[134] See Estate of Fenton v. Comm'r, 70 TC 263 (1978); Estate of Scholl v. Comm'r, 88 TC 1265 (1987); Estate of Wilson v. Comm'r, 76 TCM (CCH) 350 (1998) (all holding that valuation of the consideration is made at the time of the promise or agreement).

tion to enforce the claim by giving Child an instrument under seal. Perhaps Decedent does the same with other children or other intended beneficiaries. Upon Decedent's death, should such claims operate to reduce the amount of Decedent's estate subject to tax? If so, the estate tax would be subject to very easy avoidance. Therefore, the statute denies a deduction for claims founded on a promise or agreement unless something with a monetary value came into the estate in exchange for the obligation undertaken by the decedent.[135] Because of the tax avoidance possibilities, intrafamily debt may be scrutinized carefully to determine whether a bona fide debt exists and whether the consideration requirement is satisfied.[136] The consideration requirement, which relates only to claims founded on a promise or agreement, does not affect the deductibility of claims reflecting "liabilities imposed by law or arising out of torts," which do not involve the avoidance possibilities discussed here.[137]

The two most difficult problems with respect to this limitation are: When is a claim founded on a promise or agreement? What is an adequate and full consideration in money or money's worth?

When is a claim founded on a promise or agreement? If a decedent merely made a gratuitous but enforceable promise, any claim resting on it is obviously founded on a promise, and lack of any consideration precludes any deduction for the claim. It is perhaps equally obvious that if the decedent was liable under a judgment based on some tortious act by the decedent during life, a claim under the judgment is not founded on a promise or agreement; thus,

---

[135] A seal is not a substitute for consideration under Section 2053(c)(1). Estate of Davis v. Comm'r, 57 TC 833 (1972). See Latty v. Comm'r, 62 F2d 952 (6th Cir. 1933); Young v. United States, 559 F2d 695 (DC Cir. 1977). Cf. Leopold v. United States, 510 F2d 617 (9th Cir. 1975).

In Bank of New York v. United States, 526 F2d 1012 (3d Cir. 1975), settlement of a claim by a third-party beneficiary against the surviving spouse in a joint and mutual will estate was held nondeductible under Section 2053(a)(3) for lack of consideration. A similar conclusion was reached in Estate of Huntington v. Comm'r, 16 F3d 462 (1st Cir. 1994); Luce v. United States, 444 F. Supp. 347 (WD Mo. 1977). See Estate of Harden v. Comm'r, 72 TCM (CCH) 1139 (1996) (denial of deduction for lack of consideration for non–family member obligation). Compare a surviving spouse's situation under a community property widow's election. See ¶ 4.08[7][c].

[136] For example, in Flandrau v. Comm'r, 994 F2d 91 (Fed. Cir. 1993), a gift to a family member equal to the annual exclusion amount followed by a loan of the same amount back to donor was a mere promise to pay not founded on consideration when donor died. See also Estate of Labombarde v. Comm'r, 58 TC 745 (1972), aff'd per curiam, 1973-2 USTC ¶ 12,953 (1st Cir. 1973); Estate of Ribblesdale v. Comm'r, 23 TCM (CCH) 1041 (1964); Childress v. United States, 1977-1 USTC ¶ 13,181 (ND Ala. 1977). In Beecher v. United States, 280 F2d 202, 204 (3d Cir. 1960), the court allowed a deduction for a claim by the decedent's children based on the decedent's agreement to leave a portion of his estate to them. The consideration issue was skirted by an unexplained express stipulation that the agreement was for "an adequate and full consideration in money or money's worth." See also Levin v. Comm'r, 355 F2d 987 (5th Cir. 1966).

[137] Reg. § 20.2053-4.

the claim is deductible without regard to any question of consideration. The difficult cases arise between these extremes. In the first example, the situation would not be altered merely because the claim was reduced to judgment; the judgment would merely enforce the claim, which would remain founded on a promise.[138] However, some judgments, even though they relate to previously made agreements, do more than enforce the agreements. A claim arising out of a divorce, even if the parties have entered into a separation agreement, will probably not be held to be a claim founded on an agreement.[139] On the other hand, a claim arising out of a prenuptial agreement probably cannot meet the consideration test in order to be deductible.[140]

What is consideration in money or money's worth? A further problem arises out of the requirement that consideration be in money or money's worth. If the value of what came in was less than the value of the obligation incurred by the decedent, the deduction is not permitted to exceed the value of what came in. In one respect the statute attempts to be explicit. Section 2053(e) refers to Section 2043(b)(2), which makes the relinquishment or promised relinquishment of the right to dower or curtesy, or statutory substitutes for either, or of other marital rights in the decedent's property or estate, to a limited extent a consideration in money or money's worth. Those rights are distinguishable from support rights.[141] The problem here is anticipated and discussed in the analysis of Section 2043.[142]

If a decedent was the accommodation endorser of another's note, the consideration requirement is satisfied by the money or money's worth that was received by the borrower, rather than the decedent.[143] In this connection it should

---

[138] Estate of Markwell v. Comm'r, 112 F2d 253 (7th Cir. 1940).

[139] Rev. Rul. 60-160, 1960-1 CB 374, modifying ET 19, 1946-2 CB 166. For a detailed discussion of this issue, see ¶ 4.15[1][b][i]. See also Bowes v. United States, 77-2 USTC ¶ 13,212 (ND Ill. 1977), aff'd on another issue, 593 F2d 272 (7th Cir. 1979) and Estate of Waters v. Comm'r, 48 F3d 838 (4th Cir. 1995) (agreement not founded on decree but deductible because consideration was provided in the form of vested property rights, not mere marital rights, under Section 2043(b)).

[140] Sutton v. Comm'r, 535 F2d 254 (4th Cir.), cert. denied, 419 US 1021 (1974); Estate of Morse v. Comm'r, 625 F2d 133 (6th Cir. 1980); Estate of Graegin v. Comm'r, 56 TCM (CCH) 387 (1988); Estate of Herrmann v. Comm'r, 69 TCM (CCH) 1995 (1995), aff'd, 85 F3d 1023 (2d Cir. 1996). But see Carli v. Comm'r, 84 TC 649 (1985). This problem and the cases related to it are discussed in depth with the discussion of Section 2043(b) at ¶ 4.15[1].

[141] Rev. Rul. 68-379, 1968-2 CB 414, superseding ET 19, 1946-2 CB 166, which expressed the same principle. Cf. Estate of Kosow v. Comm'r, 45 F3d 1524 (11th Cir. 1995) (waiver of support rights constituted valid consideration).

[142] See ¶ 4.15[1].

[143] E.g., Comm'r v. Wragg, 141 F2d 638 (1st Cir. 1944), citing numerous cases in which the Commissioner unsuccessfully advanced the contention that nothing was received by the decedent that could satisfy the requirements of Section 2053(c)(1)(A). All these cases, however, were decided prior to the Supreme Court's decision in Comm'r v.

be recalled, however, that the claim against the decedent as an endorser or possibly as comaker is deductible only to the extent that the right against the borrower is valueless.[144]

Section 2053(c)(1) expressly provides an important exception to the rule requiring consideration to support a claim based on a promise or agreement. A gratuitous promise to make a gift to a qualified donee for charitable purposes (as defined and specified in Section 2055), if enforceable, is treated as it would be, if the promise were, instead, a bequest to charity.[145]

The overriding limitation of Section 2053(c)(2), generally restricting allowable Section 2053(a) deductions to an amount not in excess of the value of estate assets subject to claims, remains to be considered. The limitation is discussed immediately after the next section.

[6] Mortgages

Section 2053(a)(4) allows a deduction for unpaid mortgages or other charges against property, if the value of the decedent's interest in the property is included in the decedent's gross estate without reduction for any such mortgage or charge. If only a portion of the property is included in the decedent's estate, then only that portion of the mortgage qualifies for the Section 2053(a)(4) deduction.[146] Although this provision might appear to afford the estate an election

---

Wemyss, 324 US 303, 307 (1945), in which for gift tax purposes the Court said, "[M]oney consideration must benefit the donor to relieve a transfer by him from being a gift." The estate tax deduction cases regarding accommodation indorsers seem at variance with this concept. On the other hand, some seemingly anomalous results look better under the sharp light of careful analysis. Suppose brother B borrows $11,000 from sister S. Parent D desires to free B of the obligation without making immediate payment. D assumes B's obligation to S who releases B, effecting a novation. D dies and S files a claim. Deductible? Yes. But did D not get anything? Yes, D did. If D has simply borrowed $11,000 from S and made a gift to B, clearly the claim would have been supported by the $11,000 D received. The earlier hypothetical case is not different in principle; what D might do with what he borrowed is not controlling. See Estate of Woody v. Comm'r, 36 TC 900, 904 (1961), acq. 1966-1 CB 3.

[144] See discussion of contingent claims supra ¶ 5.03[5][b].

[145] This paragraph overcomes the decision of the Supreme Court in Taft v. Comm'r, 304 US 351 (1938). See Reg. § 20.2053-5; Priv. Ltr. Rul. 9718031 (Feb. 4, 1997) (pledge to university building fund deductible); but see Estate of Levin v. Comm'r, 69 TCM (CCH) 1951 (1995); Estate of Sochalski v. Comm'r, 14 TCM (CCH) 72 (1955) (no deduction because not enforceable under state law). Of course, the restrictive rules of Section 2055, such as Section 2055(e), must be observed. See ¶ 5.05, especially ¶¶ 5.05[4]–5.08[8].

[146] Estate of Fawcett v. Comm'r, 64 TC 889 (1975); Rev. Rul. 79-302, 1979-2 CB 328; TAM 200104008 (Oct. 17, 2000) (involving a Section 2040(b) inclusion and allowing deduction of one half of the mortgage on property).

to include the full value and claim the deduction or to include only the value of the equity and claim no deduction, no such election is in fact recognized.[147] It seems to be settled that if the decedent is personally liable for the charge, the inclusion and deduction procedure must be followed; if the decedent is not personally liable (that is, there is only nonrecourse liability), only the value of the property less the amount of the charge is to be included in the gross estate, and then of course no deduction can be claimed.[148] So viewed, Section 2053(a)(4) often operates more as an exclusion than a deduction provision.[149] This provision may not be significant as a rule, but it could determine the need for filing a return.[150] In some cases, it would be nice to include the low gross value of property and to deduct the charge of a much larger amount against it.[151] However, this would not be in keeping with the purpose of Section 2053 to work toward a realistic taxable estate, for the decedent was not poorer to the full extent of the obligation if the obligation must be satisfied out of property worth less than the obligation.[152]

Beyond these considerations, the deduction for charges against property is subject to the same qualifications and limitations as the deductions for claims against the estate.[153] For example, if there is a charge against property arising

---

[147] Reg. § 20.2053-7.

[148] Comm'r v. Davis, 132 F2d 644 (1st Cir. 1943); Estate of Fawcett v. Comm'r, 64 TC 889 (1975).

The responsive regulation, Regulations Section 20.2053-7, is actually vague. It indicates that if the decedent was not personally liable, only the value of the equity of redemption "*need*" be included in the gross estate. The word "may" should be substituted for the word "need"; then, as the value of the property "undiminished by the . . . mortgage" is *not* included, no *deduction* would be allowed under the regulations. In a "taxable estate" sense, one is not poorer to the extent that a charge against property exceeds its value unless the obligor has a personal obligation to the creditor to make up the difference. Cf. Estate of Crail v. Comm'r, 46 BTA 658 (1942), acq. 1946-2 CB 2, nonacq. 1942-2 CB 23, withdrawn.

[149] E.g., Estate of Wildenthal v. Comm'r, 29 TCM (CCH) 519 (1970).

[150] See IRC § 6018. See also Reg. § 20.2032-1(b)(1) on election of the alternate valuation date. Cf. ¶ 6.06[1] note 9 explaining a difference in result in the estate of a nonresident-noncitizen.

[151] Despite the regulations, can Section 2053(a)(4) be read to offer this choice? Cf. Rev. Rul. 83-81, 1983-1 CB 230 (allowing full deductibility of the amount of personal liability, even though Section 2032A special valuation was employed with respect to the underlying property and the mortgage exceeded the special use valuation of the property); Priv. Ltr. Rul. 8423007 (Feb. 22, 1984) (properly allowing deductibility of the full amount of liability even though there was a low rate of interest on the mortgage).

[152] In Estate of Crail, 46 BTA 658 (1942), acq. 1946-2 CB 2, nonacq. 1942-2 CB 23, withdrawn, the decedent and his wife "gave their three year 5% note" secured by the mortgage in question, which created a personal liability in the decedent supporting a deduction in excess of the value of his interest in the property.

[153] Estate of Feinberg v. Comm'r, 35 TCM (CCH) 1794 (1976); Rev. Rul. 80-81, 1980-2 CB 203.

out of the decedent's agreement to put up security for a loan to someone else, the deduction (or exclusion) allowable under Section 2053(a)(4) may be offset by the value of the estate's claim against such other person.[154] The First Circuit accepted this principle in one case, although it held the deduction allowable in full on the ground that the estate's rights against the primary obligor were valueless.[155]

[7] Limitation Based on the Value of Property Subject to Claims

Funeral expenses, administration expenses relating to probate property included in the gross estate, claims against the estate, and charges against estate property are all generally allowed as deductions only to the extent that they do not exceed the value of property subject to claims.[156] Section 2053(c)(2) defines "property subject to claims" as that part of the gross estate that under local law will bear the burden of such expenses, claims, and charges, reduced, however, by any casualty loss deduction allowed under Section 2054.[157] A person may have a large gross estate for tax purposes, having made lifetime transfers subject to estate tax, and yet the decedent's probate estate may be hopelessly insolvent. In such a situation, it is not unreasonable to deny a deduction for expenses and claims that cannot be paid by the insolvent estate. If insolvency results from a deductible postdeath casualty loss, it is obviously reasonable to reduce correspondingly the general Section 2053(c)(2) ceiling on Section 2053(a) deductions.

However, it is not uncommon for family and friends of an insolvent decedent to discharge a decedent's obligations even if they are not required by law to do so. Perhaps this is not likely to occur where survivors are in receipt of life insurance proceeds, jointly held property, property subject to the decedent's general power of appointment, or any other property interest acquired from the decedent and taxable as a part of the decedent's gross estate which assume, under local law, is beyond the reach of the decedent's creditors. By way of exception to the usual ceiling on Section 2053(a) deductions, Congress has taken account of the artificiality of the gross estate and allowed additional

---

[154] Cf. Estate of Theis v. Comm'r, 770 F2d 981 (11th Cir. 1985); Estate of Hendrickson v. Comm'r, 78 TCM (CCH) 655 (1999).

[155] Comm'r v. Wragg, 141 F2d 638 (1st Cir. 1944). Cf. DuVal's Estate v. Comm'r, 152 F2d 103 (9th Cir.), cert. denied, 328 US 838 (1946).

[156] IRC § 2053(c)(2). Logically, this limitation does not apply to expenses deductible under Section 2053(b) for administration of nonprobate gross estate assets. See supra ¶ 5.03[4].

[157] See Snyder v. United States, 84 AFTR2d 99-5963 (Ct. Fed. Cl. 1999) (discussing "property subject to claims" and holding that property in a revocable trust was property subject to environmental claims under local law).

deductions for expenses, claims, and charges otherwise deductible, if they are paid before the estate tax return is due.[158] It might appear from the statute that timely payment from any source, including estate assets, works an upward adjustment in the ceiling, as the exception speaks in terms only of when such amounts must be paid. But the regulations appropriately limit the increase over the basic ceiling to timely payments "out of property not subject to claims."[159] Even so, there is neither any statutory requirement that the payment be made by someone who has a beneficial interest in the estate nor any statutory requirement that the source of the payment be nonprobate property included in the gross estate. Thus, timely payments by a mere volunteer may increase the general ceiling on the Section 2053(a) deductions beyond the value of probate assets.[160]

[8] State and Foreign Death Taxes on Charitable Bequests

In general, state and foreign death taxes are permitted to affect the amount of estate tax payable to the federal government only by way of the limited credits against tax provided by Sections 2011 and 2014. Although Section 2053(c)(1)(B) expressly denies a deduction for such taxes, Section 2053(d) gives the estate an election to adhere to the usual credit provision or, instead, to deduct state, District of Columbia, and foreign (subject to special restrictions) death taxes, but only those imposed on charitable bequests.[161] If the deduction is elected, appropriate adjustments must be made in the credit otherwise allowed.[162]

Under Section 2053(d)(2), the provision is severely restricted. The deduction can be claimed only if the resulting decrease in tax will inure solely to the benefit of a qualified charity, as defined in Sections 2055 and 2106(a)(2). However, if the financial burden of the federal estate tax is to be apportioned among those interested in the estate, equitably and with reference to interests that qualify for exemptions, credits, or deductions,[163] benefit of the deduction inures "solely" to the charity if its share of the tax is appropriately reduced by reason of the deduction, even though the amount of tax actually to be borne by other beneficiaries is also reduced. If no apportionment provision applies, the

---

[158] IRC § 2053(c)(2). Generally, such payment must be made within nine months of the decedent's death (Section 6075), but such payment is regarded as timely within the exception if made within any extension of time granted for filing the return. Reg. § 20.2053-1(c)(2). See IRC § 6081.

[159] Reg. § 20.2053-1(c)(2).

[160] Reg. §§ 20.2053-1(c) Exs. 1, 2, fail to reflect these possibilities.

[161] See Bush v. United States, 618 F2d 741 (Ct. Cl. 1980).

[162] See ¶¶ 3.03[3][c], 3.06[3][b].

[163] See, e.g., "State Statutes" in the discussion of Section 2205 at ¶ 8.04[2].

entire decrease in tax must inure to the benefit of a qualified charity in order for the deduction to be allowed.[164] The regulations provide a formula for the determinations of the amount of the state death tax attributable to the charitable transfer.[165] The significance of this elective provision is more fully explored in Chapter 3.[166]

Since the Section 2011 credit is repealed and converted to a deduction for estates of decedents dying after December 31, 2004,[167] Section 2053(d) is amended effective after such date to remove all references to the Section 2011 credit.[168] Thus, beginning after December 31, 2004, Section 2053(d) will apply only with respect to foreign death taxes.

¶ 5.04 SECTION 2054. LOSSES

Section 2054 permits a deduction from the gross estate for losses incurred during the settlement of the estate. Under this provision, the taxable estate, one of the principal elements in the tax computation under Section 2001(b), is affected by events that occur after the decedent's death. This is in contrast to the deduction for claims, for example, which depends on the existence of obligations of the decedent at the time the decedent died. Nevertheless, as transmission at death is not instantaneous, some postdeath losses and funeral and administration expenses all play a part in determining what the decedent can effectively pass on to others.

Only losses that are caused by certain kinds of casualties or theft are deductible under Section 2054. Losses resulting from ordinary fluctuations in market values give rise to no deduction. For obvious reasons, if a loss is compensated for by insurance or in some other manner,[1] the deductible loss is limited to the amount of the loss that is not so covered.[2] Thus, if a building owned by the decedent is destroyed by fire but is fully covered by insurance, no deduction is allowed. Moreover, if the asset subject to the loss has been distributed to a beneficiary before the loss occurs, the loss is not treated as one

---

[164] Reg. § 20.2053-9(b)(1); Watson v. McGinnes, 240 F. Supp. 833 (ED Pa. 1965). But see Estate of Darlington v. Comm'r, 302 F2d 693 (3d Cir. 1962).

[165] Reg. § 20.2053-9(d).

[166] See ¶¶ 3.03[3][c], 3.06[3][b].

[167] IRC § 2011(f). See ¶¶ 3.03[1], 3.03[3][d], 3.03[4], 5.09.

[168] Economic Growth and Tax Relief Reconciliation Act of 2001, Pub. L. No. 107-16, § 532(c)(5), 115 Stat. 38, 74 (2001), reprinted in 2001-__ CB __, __.

[1] See Estate of Bryan v. Comm'r, 74 TC 725 (1980).

[2] IRC § 2054. See Reg. § 20.2054-1.

incurred "during the settlement" of the estate and is not deductible by the estate.[3]

[1] Determining Amount of Loss

Neither the statute nor the regulations provide a method for determining the amount of the loss. Presumably, the computation of the amount of the loss for estate tax purposes is similar to that for income tax purposes. Accordingly, as a rule, the amount of the loss is the difference in the fair market value of the affected asset immediately before and immediately after the casualty. However, the value of the property on the applicable valuation date should be recognized as a ceiling on the deduction; the taxable estate should not be reduced by an amount in excess of the amount by which the property increased the gross estate.[4]

Under Section 2032, discussed in Chapter 4, a loss deduction, otherwise allowable, is disallowed to the extent that it is taken into account by the election of the alternate valuation date. Thus, if there is a total loss of an asset by fire during the six months after the decedent's death and the later valuation date is elected, there will be no deduction under Section 2054 because the loss will be reflected in the lower (zero) valuation for the asset involved. However, if the alternate valuation date is elected and the loss occurs more than six months after death, it is deductible. The estate tax value as of the applicable valuation date fixes a ceiling on the casualty loss deduction.[5] If the property had decreased in value before the casualty and is valued at the alternate date, the deduction may be diminished accordingly. If the alternate date is elected, an increase in value as of that date will effect a corresponding increase in the deduction ceiling. These suggestions are in keeping with the purpose of the alternate date and casualty loss sections and in accordance with the income tax basis approach to the computation of the estate tax deduction, as suggested in the preceding paragraph.

---

[3] Reg. § 20.2054-1. The beneficiary may of course have an income tax deduction under Section 165.

[4] See Rinaldi v. United States, 80 AFTR2d 97-5324 (Fed. Cl. 1997) (ceiling applied to citrus grove damaged in freeze by grouping of trees, not on a per tree basis). Cf. Reg. § 1.165-7(b)(1), limiting income tax casualty loss deductions to the amount of the adjusted basis of the property.

[5] Reg. § 20.2032-1(g). See IRC § 2032A; ¶ 4.04.

[2] "Casualty"

The term "casualty" does not stand alone in the statute. The statutory language is "losses . . . arising from fires, storms, shipwrecks, or other casualties, or from theft." Fires, storms, and shipwrecks produce losses that are expressly made deductible. What then is the scope of the phrase "other casualties"? There has not been much litigation under this estate tax provision to serve as an aid to interpretation of this term.[6]

Lord Tenderden's rule, more familiar as the ejusdem generis canon of construction, is that "where particular words of description ["fires, storms, shipwrecks" in this section] are followed by general terms ["other casualties" here], the latter will be regarded as referring to things of a like class with those particularly described. . . . "[7] Applying this guide of construction to Section 2054, the only casualties that give rise to deductions are casualties like fires, storms, and shipwrecks. Losses in the value of securities resulting from Great Britain's going off the gold standard may possibly be casualty losses in a general or popular sense, but it has been held that a deduction for such losses under Section 2054 is properly denied on the ground that they are not casualty losses like losses from fires, storms, or shipwrecks and therefore not within the meaning of "other casualties" as that term is used in this section.[8]

Similarly, a loss in the value of securities resulting from enemy action against property owned by the issuing corporation has not been allowed as a deduction under the estate tax casualty loss provision.[9] The court indicated that "fires" and "storms" have reference to "destruction of or damage to physical property where the extent of the loss can be fully measured as of the time the loss is allowed."[10] Although rejecting the claim of a deduction for loss in value of the securities, the court recognized nevertheless that "destruction of physical property . . . as a result of war" would support a casualty loss deduction.[11]

There has been a great deal more litigation concerning the meaning of a parallel casualty loss provision in the Code's income tax sections.[12] Decisions under that provision may have a direct bearing on the meaning of "other casu-

---

[6] On the parallel income tax question, see infra text accompanying note 13.

[7] Lyman v. Comm'r, 83 F2d 811, 813 (1st Cir. 1936).

[8] Lyman v. Comm'r, 83 F2d 811 (1st Cir. 1936).

[9] Leewitz v. United States, 75 F. Supp. 312 (Ct. Cl.), cert. denied, 335 US 820 (1948).

[10] Leewitz v. United States, 75 F. Supp. 312, 317 (Ct. Cl.), cert. denied, 335 US 820 (1948).

[11] Leewitz v. United States, 75 F. Supp. 312, 317 (Ct. Cl.), cert. denied, 335 US 820 (1948). See May v. Henslee, 45 AFTR 52-1285 (MD Tenn. 1952) (not officially reported).

[12] IRC § 165(c)(3).

alties" in Section 2054.[13] If a general test as to what constitutes a loss from "other casualties" can be stated, it seems to be: Did the loss result from "some sudden, unexpected, or unusual cause"?[14] No such general test can supply a ready answer for the borderline cases.

[3] "Theft"

There is no doubt that estate assets stolen after the decedent's death support a Section 2054 deduction. For example, valuable art objects stolen from the decedent's residence will effect a reduction in the taxable estate to the extent of their value when stolen, if that value is not in excess of the value at which they are included in the decedent's gross estate. The determination of what constitutes a "theft" is dependent on relevant state law.[15] If the theft occurred before the decedent's death, there probably would be no Section 2054 deduction, regardless of when the loss was discovered. It is uncertain whether such a loss could be treated as "incurred" during the settlement of the estate.[16] In any event, Section 2054 quite properly does not contemplate estate tax deductions for property that is not included in the gross estate.[17]

An executor's embezzlement of estate assets will support a deduction.[18] If a survivor was in possession of a decedent's property at death, perhaps by way

---

[13] Compare, e.g., Rosenberg v. Comm'r, 198 F2d 46 (8th Cir. 1952) with Fay v. Helvering, 120 F2d 253 (2d Cir. 1941), on the deductibility for income tax purposes of loss because of termite damage. But see Rev. Rul. 63-232, 1963-2 CB 97.

[14] Matheson v. Comm'r, 54 F2d 537, 539 (2d Cir. 1931). In White v. Comm'r, 48 TC 439 (1967), acq. 1969-1 CB 21, the taxpayer accidentally slammed the car door on a spouse's hand after helping the spouse alight from the car; the diamond fell out of her ring and was lost. The Tax Court held that an accidental and irrevocable loss of property can be the basis of a casualty loss deduction. The Service has accepted the principle that an accidental loss of property qualifies as a casualty provided the loss is: (1) identifiable; (2) damaging to property; and (3) sudden, unexpected, and unusual in nature. Rev. Rul. 72-592, 1972-2 CB 101.

[15] Estate of Meriano v. Comm'r, 142 F3d 651 (3d Cir. 1998). Cf. Estate of Shlensky, 36 TCM (CCH) 628 (1977) (similar holding as to an embezzlement).

[16] The income tax uncertainty on a parallel issue (see S. Rep. No. 1622, 83d Cong., 2d Sess. 198 (1954)) was settled by the enactment of Section 165(e), adopting a date-of-discovery rule.

[17] The date-of-discovery rule for income tax purposes does not extend to allowance of an income tax deduction for the estate, even if the theft occurred before death. Reg. § 1.165-8(b). If this Treasury concession is not wholly illusory, the decedent's basis for the stolen property should be used as the ceiling for the deduction. It is difficult to see how the estate itself could have any basis for property stolen before death such as would support a deduction under the Regulations Section 1.165-7(b)(1) computation.

[18] Cf. Miller v. Comm'r, 19 TC 1046 (1953), acq. 1953-2 CB 5, holding embezzlement a "theft" for income tax purposes under Section 23(e)(3) (1939). But see Estate of

of a loan, the survivor's misappropriation of the property would probably also constitute a theft under Section 2054. Suppose, however, that property not owned by the decedent but includible in the decedent's gross estate is squandered by its rightful owner after the decedent's death. An example would be a beneficiary's receipt and dissipation of insurance proceeds under a policy on the decedent's life in which the decedent had incidents of ownership.[19] The beneficiary might be liable for a part of the estate tax,[20] but if the beneficiary cannot pay the beneficiary's share of estate tax liability, there is a clear loss to the estate in the sense that the tax burden will fall more heavily on other beneficiaries. This may be a calamity, but it is not a "casualty" under Section 2054. Neither is it a theft, because the insurance beneficiary squandered only what was the beneficiary's; the loss arises out of the beneficiary's inability to discharge an obligation, not the taking of property that belonged to others. Thus, the estate could claim no Section 2054 deduction.[21]

[4] Relation to Income Tax

A casualty loss to estate property during the period of administration gives rise not only to a deduction from the gross estate for estate tax purposes but also to a deduction from gross income in determining the taxable income of the estate.[22] However, the estate cannot claim the deduction for both purposes. Section 642(g) provides for the disallowance of the income tax casualty loss deduction unless the estate files a statement that the loss has not been claimed as an estate tax deduction and a waiver of the right to claim it for estate tax purposes. Thus, the executor has an election that can be exercised at least with knowledge of which tax will be reduced the most by utilization of the deduction.[23]

It might appear that where the loss occurs within six months after the decedent's death, the election of the alternate valuation date would provide an escape from the proscription against both estate tax and income tax deductions for a single casualty loss. The idea would be that the loss could be given full estate tax effect by including the asset at the lower (or zero) value at the alternate date without claiming an estate tax deduction, leaving the estate free to

---

Shlensky v. Comm'r, 36 TCM (CCH) 628 (1977), denying a deduction where a co-executor's actions did not amount to an embezzlement under applicable state law. See also Harden v. Comm'r, 72 TCM (CCH) 1139 (1996) (embezzlement by third party).

[19] See IRC § 2042, discussed at ¶ 4.14.

[20] See IRC § 2206, discussed at ¶ 8.05.

[21] See Rev. Rul. 69-411, 1969-2 CB 177, which on these facts, however, calls attention to a possible Section 166 income tax bad-debt deduction.

[22] IRC §§ 165(c)(3), 641(b).

[23] See supra ¶ 5.03[3][d].

claim the income tax deduction. This theoretical possibility is largely illusory. The reason is that the election of the alternate valuation date would fix a lower (or zero) adjusted basis for income tax purposes, which in turn limits the income tax deduction.[24]

¶ 5.05 SECTION 2055. TRANSFERS FOR PUBLIC, CHARITABLE, AND RELIGIOUS USES

Section 2055 is the estate tax counterpart[1] of the more familiar Section 170 income tax charitable deduction provision. Although referred to as "charitable" deduction sections, neither is restricted to contributions to "charities" in the usual sense of the term, as the heading of Section 2055 suggests.[2] The estate tax charitable deduction is limited to the value of the property transferred to charity, but it is unlimited in the sense that it is not subject to percentage restrictions such as are applicable to the income tax deduction for contributions to charity.[3] On the other hand, it is conditioned on the satisfaction of many detailed requirements to which Congress (by legislation) and the courts and the administration (by interpretation) have added from time to time.[4]

---

[24] Reg. § 1.165-7(b)(1). Conceivably a partial loss because of casualty, recognized by way of the Section 2032 election, would leave some adjusted basis to support the Section 165(c) income tax deduction.

[1] See Henkel, "Estate Planning and Wealth Preservation" Pt. VIII (Warren, Gorham & Lamont 1997); Price, "Price on Contemporary Estate Planning" Chapter 8 (Little Brown and Co. 1992); Weinstock, Planning an Estate § 14 (Shepard's McGraw-Hill, 4th ed. 1995). See also Melfe, "Effective Planning for Charitable Giving," 40 NYU Inst. on Fed. Tax'n Chapter 1 (1982); Mangum, "Charitable Transfers and Estate Planning," 38 NYU Inst. on Fed. Tax'n Chapter 40 (1980); Moore, "The Role of Charitable Dispositions in Estate Planning," 13 Miami Inst. on Est. Plan. 600 (1979); Burke, "Charitable Giving and Estate Planning," 28 Tax Law. 289 (1975).

[2] Special rules applicable to estates of nonresident-noncitizens are provided in Section 2106(a)(2), discussed at ¶ 6.06[2].

[3] IRC § 170(b). See also Locke, "The Estate Tax and Charitable Donations," 20 Wayne L. Rev. 1227 (1974). The income tax charitable deduction, which is generally measured by the fair market value of donated property, must sometimes be reduced by the amount of, or a part of, the gain that would have resulted from a sale of the property. IRC § 170(e). No such limitation applies to the estate tax charitable deduction. This may be in part because of the date-of-death value basis principle of Section 1014, but it is equally true as regards bequests of items of income in respect of a decedent, which are denied a new basis by Section 1014(c). See infra ¶ 5.05[2][a] note 63.

[4] Matters for which rulings may be requested and areas in which the Service will not rule are generally set forth in Rev. Proc. 2002-1, 2002-1 CB __, § 5.05, and Rev. Proc. 2002-3, 2002-1 CB __. See also Rev. Proc. 2002-7, 2002-1 CB __.

[1] Qualified Recipients

[a] In General

It might be a charitable act to leave money to a poor person, but the statute authorizes no deduction for such direct philanthropy, requiring instead that bequests be made to qualified recipient organizations.[5] Moreover, no deduction is assured merely because a portion of the decedent's wealth actually reaches a qualified organization;[6] it must get there by way of a bequest, legacy, devise, or transfer by the decedent. This has produced some harsh results. For example, in one instance a bequest was made to a member of a religious order for saying masses for the dead. In fact, the property reached the religious order itself because of a vow of poverty made by the member. The charitable deduction was denied on the ground that the property reached the order, not by bequest, but by reason of the contractual arrangement between the member and the order.[7] This is not an isolated ruling but instead one supported by substantial precedent,[8] and the principle may be regarded as settled.

An estate tax charitable deduction is imperiled when the decedent's will fails to identify a particular qualified recipient.[9] A will provision directing the executor to distribute assets to such charitable organizations as the executor may select may produce no deduction for one of two reasons. First, such a bequest may be invalid under state law;[10] second, the possible distributees recog-

---

[5] Compare Priv. Ltr. Rul. 9630008 (Apr. 22, 1996) (deductible bequest to fund college scholarships for graduates of one high school) with TAM 9631004 (Apr. 30, 1996) (nondeductible bequest to provide scholarships for students with a particular family name who attend one of two universities where only 603 U.S. families had such name).

[6] If an executor has discretion to give the property to a private person, no charitable deduction is allowed even though the property passes to charity. Estate of Marine v. Comm'r, 990 F2d 136 (4th Cir. 1993).

[7] Rev. Rul. 68-459, 1968-2 CB 411. See Rev. Rul. 78-366, 1978-2 CB 241 (allowing a deduction where the masses would have been said anyway and the funds by law went directly to the general funds of the church); Estate of Hubert v. Comm'r, 66 TCM (CCH) 1064 (1993) (contributions were to the charity); TAM 9145005 (July 16, 1991) (bequests for saying of masses deductible).

[8] See, e.g., Estate of Barry v. Comm'r, 311 F2d 681 (9th Cir. 1962); Estate of Lamson v. United States, 338 F2d 376 (Ct. Cl. 1964) (both involving nondeductible direct gifts to a private individual).

[9] See Delaney v. Gardner, 204 F2d 855 (1st Cir. 1953) (executor discretion to use for noncharitable purposes); First Trust Co. of St. Paul v. Reynolds, 137 F2d 518 (8th Cir. 1943) (surviving spouse had to approve charitable beneficiaries); Paris v. United States, 381 F. Supp. 597 (ND Ohio 1974) (bequest not limited to charitable functions); Rev. Rul. 55-335, 1955-1 CB 455. But see Orphanos v. Comm'r, 67 TC 780 (1977) (qualified recipient determined under state law).

[10] Compare Rev. Rul. 71-441, 1971-2 CB 335 (deduction denied on the strength of a state court decision strictly limiting the cy pres doctrine legislatively adopted in Alabama),

nized by local law may extend beyond those qualified under the federal statute.[11]

Four general classes of recipients to which deductible bequests can be made are set out in Section 2055(a). Before they are identified, some general observations may be made about these qualified recipients. A basic congressional assumption is that charitable organizations perform services that are useful to the nation, services that might otherwise have to be paid for out of tax revenues. Where contributions are made to governmental units themselves,[12] the tax revenue relief is of course indisputable. In other circumstances, the cost to the government of reduced tax revenues plus the cost of private fund raising[13] may raise a question to which can be added some constitutional uncertainty regarding the preferred treatment of religious organizations.[14]

In any event, charitable tax preferences generally take one or both of two forms: (1) exemption of the organization from tax[15] and (2) a deduction for taxpayer contributions to the organization.[16] Although the exemption can exist without any accompanying deduction,[17] the two generally go together. Section 2055(a) makes some direct references to the income tax exemption sections, and, as the general objective of both the exemption and the deduction is the

---

with Rev. Rul. 72-442, 1972-2 CB 527 (in which a more liberal state (not identified) cy pres doctrine sustained the deduction).

[11] Compare State St. Bank & Trust v. United States, 634 F2d 5 (1st Cir. 1980), and Rev. Rul. 69-285, 1969-1 CB 222 (deduction allowed because the "charitable" concept under applicable Massachusetts law is at least as restrictive as that of Section 2055), with Rev. Rul. 71-200, 1971-1 CB 272 (deduction denied where distribution could be made to organizations qualifying for tax-free gifts under state law, which might go beyond qualified recipients under Section 2055). In this respect the income tax charitable deduction of an estate is more restrictively stated in Section 642(c) and strictly interpreted. See Ferguson, Freeland & Ascher, Federal Income Taxation of Estates, Trusts, and Beneficiaries, Chapter 6 (Aspen, 3d ed. 1998).

[12] See IRC § 2055(a)(1).

[13] See Rabin, "Charitable Trusts and Charitable Deductions," 41 NYU L. Rev. 912, 924 (1966), reprinted in Sander & Westfall, Readings in Federal Taxation, 373, 385 (Foundation Press 1970).

[14] See Schwarz, "Limiting Religious Tax Exemptions: When Should the Church Render Unto Caesar?" 29 U. Fla. L. Rev. 50 (1976); Cohen, Comment, "Constitutionality of Tax Exemptions Accorded American Church Property," 30 Alb. L. Rev. 58 (1966).

[15] See, e.g., IRC §§ 501(a), 501(c).

[16] See, e.g., IRC §§ 170, 2055, 2522.

[17] See, e.g., IRC §§ 501(c)(6), 501(c)(7), 501(c)(8). See also Rabin, "Charitable Trusts and Charitable Deductions," 41 NYU L. Rev. 912, 914 (1966), reprinted in Sander & Westfall, Readings in Federal Taxation, 373, 375 (Foundation Press 1970), referring to this practice in Great Britain.

same, it is not surprising to find a substantial parallel in the exemption and deduction sections.[18]

[b] Section 2055(a) Organizations

1. The United States, the several states and their political subdivisions, and the District of Columbia form one class of qualified recipients.[19] Counties, cities, and towns are of course included. The gift may be made directly to "or for the use of" any of these recipients. Numerous statutes authorize certain federal officials to receive gifts or bequests "for the use of" the United States within the meaning of Section 2055.[20] Gifts to recipients in this category are deductible only if made "for exclusively public purposes."

2. Corporations "organized and operated exclusively for religious, charitable, scientific, literary, or educational purposes" form a second group of qualified recipients.[21] This class includes, among others, churches, relief organizations such as the Red Cross, and schools. Also included are organizations that operate to encourage the arts, to foster amateur sports competition, and to prevent cruelty to children and animals.[22] It may not be enough that a

---

[18] Two parallels may be noted. First, there is a substantial similarity between Sections 170(c)(1), 170(c)(2), 170(c)(3), and 170(c)(4) and Sections 2055(a)(2) and 2055(a)(3). Thus, organizations that the Treasury recognizes as qualified to receive income tax deductions under Section 170(c)(2) (cumulative list, revised and republished periodically, available from the Government Printing Office) generally also qualify under Sections 2055(a)(2) and 2055(a)(3). Second, the exemption provisions of Section 501(c)(3) are substantially similar to those of Section 170(c)(2) and Sections 2055(a)(2) and 2055(a)(3). Thus, as nearly all charitable bequests are made to Section 501(c)(3) organizations, the existence of tax-exempt status under that provision and deductibility under Section 170(c)(2) are practical assurance of qualification under either Section 2055(a)(2) or Section 2055(a)(3). Cf. Rev. Rul. 76-307, 1976-2 CB 56; Rev. Rul. 82-39, 1982-2 CB 759.

[19] IRC § 2055(a)(1).

[20] See IRC § 2055(g). See also, e.g., Act of March 31, 1944, Pub. L. No. 78-274, § 1, 58 Stat. 135 (1944) (Secretary of the Navy accepts gifts for the Naval Academy); Act of Oct. 30, 1972, Pub. L. No. 92-603, § 132(c), 86 Stat. 1329 (1972) (provides for deductible gifts to Social Security); Pub. L. No. 95-91, § 652, 91 Stat. 601 (1977) (provides for deductible gift to the Department of Energy); Act of Oct. 2, 1964, Pub. L. No. 88-611, § 2, 78 Stat. 991 (1964) (gifts to the Department of Commerce); Nat'l Found. on the Arts and Humanities Act of 1965, Pub. L. No. 89-209, § 10(a), 79 Stat. 845, 853 (1965) (gifts to the National Foundation on the Arts and Humanities).

[21] IRC § 2055(a)(2).

[22] IRC § 2055(a)(2), Reg. § 20.2055-1(a)(2). See Priv. Ltr. Rul. 200001010 (Sept. 30, 1999) (estate may rely on IRS Pub. No. 78 for purposes of a Section 2055 deduction).

Generally, only amateur sports organizations that foster national or international sports competition and that do not provide athletic facilities or equipment qualify for the exemption. However, under the Tax Equity and Fiscal Responsibility Act of 1982, Pub. L. No. 97-248, § 286(a), 96 Stat 324, 569 (1982), reprinted in 1982-2 CB 462, 545, if an or-

corporation is currently "operated" exclusively for charitable purposes if it was not "organized" for such purposes.[23] In keeping with the statutory definition of "corporation,"[24] the regulations[25] make it clear that an unincorporated association may be within this qualified class.

Corporations and associations that qualify for this classification must meet three further tests. First, they must be set up in such a way that no part of their net earnings can inure to any private stockholder or individual "other than as a legitimate object" of their charitable or other purpose.[26] Therefore, a corporation does not lose its qualified status merely by paying salaries to employees.

Second, the corporation may lose its qualified status if it engages in a substantial way in propaganda or lobbying activities. For example, a bequest to a corporation, essentially charitable and educational in nature, but substantially engaged in drafting civil liberties legislation and seeking to have such legislation enacted, failed to qualify for the deduction.[27] In this setting, claims for deductions for contributions to bar associations and medical societies have resulted in considerable litigation.[28]

Third, as regards transfers after December 31, 1969, organizations that participate or intervene in political campaigns on behalf of (or in opposition

---

ganization is a "qualified sports organization" as defined in Section 501(j)(2), it will qualify for the deduction even though it provides athletic facilities or equipment and is only a regional or local organization. See IRC § 2055(a) (last sentence).

[23] Cf. Universal Oil Prods. Co. v. Campbell, 181 F2d 451 (7th Cir.), cert. denied, 340 US 850 (1950).

[24] IRC § 7701(a)(3).

[25] Reg. § 20.2055-1(a)(2).

[26] IRC § 2055(a)(2); Reg. § 2055-1(a)(2).

[27] Marshall v. Comm'r, 147 F2d 75 (2d Cir.), cert. denied, 325 US 872, reh'g denied, 326 US 804 (1945). See League of Women Voters v. United States, 180 F. Supp. 379 (Ct. Cl.), cert. denied, 364 US 822 (1960), in which the majority of the court found that the main purpose of the league was to influence legislation. The dissenting opinion suggests a distinction between lobbying for the self-interest of members and for the general public.

[28] A deduction was allowed for contributions to bar associations in St. Louis Union Trust Co. v. United States, 374 F2d 427 (8th Cir. 1967); Dulles v. Johnson, 273 F2d 362 (2d Cir.), cert. denied, 364 US 834 (1960); Rhode Island Hosp. Trust Co. v. United States, 159 F. Supp. 204 (DRI 1958). But see Rev. Rul. 77-232, 1977-2 CB 71, rev'g Rev. Rul. 59-152, 1959-1 CB 54, and disallowing a deduction under Section 2055(a)(1) for a contribution to an integrated bar because the state bar was not an arm of the state; it was a separate entity with private as well as public purposes. See also GCM 4805, VII-2 CB 58, disallowing a deduction for a contribution to voluntary bar associations. Disallowance of deductions for gifts to local medical societies, which might appear to be inconsistent with *Dulles*, seem justified in light of the records in the cases. Krohn v. United States, 246 F. Supp. 341 (D. Colo. 1965); Hammerstein v. Kelley, 235 F. Supp. 60 (ED Mo. 1964), aff'd, 349 F2d 928 (8th Cir. 1965).

to) candidates for public office are disqualified.[29] Although the earlier cases suggest the restrictive philosophy, they are not precedent with respect to estates of decedents dying after 1976. Section 2055(a)(2) now incorporates the concepts of Section 501(c) to determine whether activity aimed at influencing legislation precludes the deduction.[30]

Some of the qualifying objectives for corporations (e.g., religious, scientific, literary, educational) may seem more precise than they really are.[31] For an organization whose objects are not in these categories, it may be even more difficult to say whether the organization is organized and operated for "charitable" purposes, the other principal qualifying objective. The Treasury has accepted a general definition of "charity" as meaning "[supplying] benefits which are for an indefinite number of persons and are for the relief of the poor, the advancement of religion, the advancement of education or erecting or maintaining public buildings or works or otherwise lessening the burdens of government."[32] In this light, the operation of a public swimming pool, playground, or recreational facility, even where small charges are made for use, is regarded as charitable,[33] except where assess is restricted to less than the entire community.[34] A nonprofit hospital may be a qualified recipient for similar rea-

---

[29] The restriction was added to Section 2055(a)(2) by Section 201(d)(4) of the Tax Reform Act of 1969, Pub. L. No. 91-172, 83 Stat. 487, 561 (1969), reprinted in 1969-3 CB 10, 52. Reg. § 20.2055-1(a)(2).

[30] Tax Reform Act of 1976, Pub. L. No. 94-455, § 1307(d)(1)(B), 90 Stat. 1520, 1727 (1976), reprinted in 1976-3 CB (Vol. 1) 1, 203.

[31] Cf. Riker v. Comm'r, 244 F2d 220 (9th Cir.), cert. denied, 355 US 839 (1957) ("Christ's Church of the Golden Rule" not an exempt "religious" organization under Section 101(6) (1939) because of predominantly temporal and business purposes). But cf. Reg. § 1.501(c)(3)-1(d)(5); IRC §§ 512(b)(7), 512(b)(8), 512(b)(9), seemingly according very broad meaning to "scientific" and to scientific "research" for income tax exemption and unrelated business income purposes, respectively.

[32] Rev. Rul. 59-310, 1959-2 CB 146, 148. Rev. Rul. 73-74, 1973-1 CB 220, suggests that even broader objectives may qualify.

[33] Rev. Rul. 59-310, 1959-2 CB 146, 148.

[34] Rev. Rul. 67-325, 1967-2 CB 113. By the same token, a segregated private school probably is not within the qualified class identified in Section 2055(a)(2). Cf. Bob Jones Univ. v. United States, 461 US 574 (1983); Green v. Connally, 330 F. Supp. 1150 (DDC), aff'd per curiam, 404 US 997 (1971); McGlotten v. Connally, 338 F. Supp. 448 (DDC 1972). But see McCoy v. Shultz, 1973-1 USTC ¶ 12,906 (DDC 1973), rejecting the argument that qualified status should be denied because of discrimination based on sex. See also Bittker & Kaufman, "Taxes and Civil Rights: Constitutionalizing the Internal Revenue Code," 82 Yale LJ 51 (1972); Hobbit, "Charitable Contributions—How Charitable Must They Be?" 11 Seton Hall L. Rev. 1 (1980).

sons.[35] But a nonprofit cemetery association not exclusively for charitable purposes will not qualify.[36]

3. Trusts and certain fraternal organizations form a third class of qualified recipients; but because such organizations can qualify without being "organized and operated exclusively for" charitable and related purposes, the statute makes bequests to them deductible only if the bequests are to be used solely for such purposes. The principal difference between the second and third categories can be illustrated by reference to a case decided in 1943. An unrestricted bequest to the Presbyterian Hospital of New York would qualify for the deduction under the second classification as a gift to an institution organized and operated exclusively for charitable purposes; but a gift to a fund to be utilized by the director of such hospital would qualify only if use of the bequest was restricted to charitable purposes.[37] In this case, a direction that the fund's income be used to provide nursing care for graduate nurses who were patients in the hospital was held to meet the statutory test.

There is no language in Section 2055(a)(3) concerning the use of net income for individuals, because a bequest can qualify for the deduction under this section only if the bequest can be used solely for charitable or related purposes, as explained earlier. However, this section, like Section 2055(a)(2), disqualifies trusts that engage in propaganda or lobbying activities[38] and trusts that participate in political campaigns.[39]

---

[35] Old Colony Trust Co. v. United States, 438 F2d 684 (1st Cir. 1971). But cf. Rev. Rul. 69-545, 1969-2 CB 117 (exempt status under Section 501(c)(3) denied to a hospital found to be operated for private benefit).

[36] Child v. United States, 540 F2d 579 (2d Cir.), cert. denied, 429 US 1092 (1977); First Nat'l Bank of Omaha v. United States, 681 F2d 534 (8th Cir. 1982); Mellon Bank NA v. United States, 762 F2d 283 (3d Cir. 1985); Estate of Amick v. Comm'r, 67 TC 924 (1977); Smith v. United States, 84-2 USTC ¶ 13,595 (WD Mo. 1984); Estate of Alward v. Comm'r, 78 TCM (CCH) 243 (1999); Rev. Rul. 67-170, 1967-1 CB 272; Rev. Rul. 77-385, 1977-2 CB 331. But see Rev. Rul. 79-159, 1979-1 CB 308, allowing a deduction for a nonprofit church or government cemetery under Section 2055(a)(1). See Whalen, Note, "A Grave Injustice: The Uncharitable Federal Tax Treatment of Bequests to Public Cemeteries," 58 Fordham L. Rev. 705 (1990) (arguing that public cemeteries are qualified recipients for estate tax charitable deduction purposes).

[37] Estate of Gray v. Comm'r, 2 TC 97 (1943), acq. 1944 CB 12, nonacq. 1943 CB 32, withdrawn. See Langfitt v. United States, 321 F. Supp. 360 (WD Pa. 1970) (no deduction for bequest to charitable foundation for noncharitable purpose); Starkey v. United States, 233 F3d 694 (7th Cir. 2000) (ambiguity interpreted to limit to charitable purposes).

[38] See Buder v. United States, 7 F3d 1382 (8th Cir. 1993). As regards estate of decedents dying after 1976, the criteria for disqualification are the same as for trusts. Cf. Marshall v. Comm'r, 147 F2d 75 (2d Cir.), cert. denied, 325 US 872, reh'g denied, 326 US 804 (1945).

[39] Again, this restriction was added to Section 2055(a)(3) by Section 201(d)(4)(A)(ii) of the Tax Reform Act of 1969, Pub. L. No. 91-172, § 201 (d)(4)(A)(ii), 83 Stat. 487, 561, reprinted in 1969-3 CB 10, 51. It applies to transfers after December 31, 1969 Id.

4. Veterans' organizations incorporated by act of Congress and their local chapters and posts are qualified recipients under a 1954 addition to the estate tax charitable deduction provisions. This class is subject to the same restriction as corporations qualifying under Section 2055(a)(2) concerning the possible use of net earnings for the benefit of private shareholders or individuals, but there is no restriction against participation by these organizations in propaganda or lobbying activities or in political campaigns. Congress has presumably chosen to give such organizations a boost by making contributions to them qualify as tax deductions[40] without regard to their lobbying and political activities.

In the case of a bequest by a citizen or resident of the United States, there is no requirement that the recipient corporation, trust, or other organization be organized in the United States or that the bequest be utilized here.[41]

5. Section 2055(a)(5) allows a fifth charitable recipient that is not discussed in the text because of its limited applicability.[42]

[c] Tainted Organizations

Congress has long been concerned that organizations exempt from federal taxes might abuse their privileges. The Congress's concern is that charitable organizations funded by way of family or other limited contributions and controlled by their contributors may lack the attributes of public responsibility and dedication that should accompany status as qualified recipients of charitable contributions. Congressional concern has been expressed over, among other

---

Section 201(g)(4)(E), 83 Stat. 565, Reprinted in 1969-3 CB 54. See supra text accompanying note 29; Reg. § 20.2055-1(a)(3).

[40] See also IRC §§ 170(c)(3) (income tax), 2522(a)(4) (gift tax).

[41] Kaplun v. United States, 436 F2d 799 (2d Cir. 1971); Old Colony Trust Co. v. United States, 438 F2d 684 (1st Cir. 1971); National Sav. Trust Co. v. United States, 436 F2d 458 (Ct. Cl. 1971); Priv. Ltr. Rul. 200024016 (Mar. 13, 2000). Cf. Estate of Orphanos v. Comm'r, 67 TC 780 (1977). The Treasury now acquiesces in the aforementioned decisions provided the contributions are limited to exclusively charitable purposes under Sections 2055(a)(2) and 2055(a)(3). Rev. Rul. 74-523, 1974-2 CB 304. But see Continental Ill. Nat'l Bank & Trust Co. v. United States, 403 F2d 721 (Ct. Cl. 1968); IRC § 2106(a)(2), concerning estates of nonresident-noncitizens, discussed in ¶ 6.06[2]. See also Fields, "What Bequests to Foreign Charities Are Deductible for Estate Tax Purposes?" 32 J. Tax'n 33 (1970).

[42] This classification of charitable recipient involves employee stock ownership plans (ESOPs) given to charity if the ESOP was in existence on August 1, 1996, and the decedent died before January 1, 1999. This is an example of private legislation. IRC §§ 2055(a)(5), 664(g)(1)(A), 664(g)(2)(A). The subsection is neither discussed here nor in conjunction with remainder interests. See infra ¶¶ 5.05[5][a] note 186, 5.05[5][b] note 241.

things, their gradual acquisition of undue economic and political powers[43] and on whether they should be able to retain indefinitely contributions they receive that give rise to deductions while expending only the income from the property held by the charity.[44]

In response to these concerns, Section 2055(e)(1) disqualifies transfers to certain private foundations, trusts, and foreign organizations described in Sections 508(d) and 4948(c)(4).[45] Private foundations[46] that otherwise enjoy exempt status are subjected to a limited tax on their net investment income.[47] Merely to have such income is not a disqualifying circumstance. However, private foundations are taxed additionally if they fail to appropriately distribute their income,[48] if they have excessive business holdings,[49] if they make investments that jeopardize their charitable purpose,[50] or if they make certain taxable expenditures;[51] and they are taxed indirectly if they engage in self-dealing.[52] For a private foundation to be a qualified recipient under Section 2055, its governing instrument must contain provisions against engaging in any of the transactions that invoke such additional taxes.[53]

The special taxing provisions just discussed apply to private foundations. However, to foreclose the possibility that restrictions on the abuse of private foundations could be avoided and essentially the same abuses accomplished by

---

[43] S. Rep. No. 552, 91st Cong., 1st Sess. 25 (1969), reprinted in 1969-3 CB 423, 440.

[44] S. Rep. No. 552, 91st Cong., 1st Sess. 26 (1969), reprinted in 1969-3 CB 423, 441.

[45] These rules apply to estates of decedents who die in 1970 or later. Tax Reform Act of 1969, Pub. L. No. 91-172, § 201(g)(4), 83 Stat. 487, 565 (1969), reprinted in 1969-3 CB 10, 54; see Reg. §§ 20.2055-4(d), 20.2055-5(b), 20.2055-5(c). The effective date rules are discussed in detail infra ¶ 5.05[4][b] note 134.

[46] "Private foundations" is defined in Section 509.

[47] IRC § 4940.

[48] IRC § 4942.

[49] IRC § 4943.

[50] IRC § 4944.

[51] IRC § 4945. See Section 6684, assessing penalties if these taxes are imposed more than once. If they are imposed frequently there is also a possibility of termination. IRC §§ 507(a)(2), 507(c).

[52] IRC § 4941.

[53] IRC § 2055(e)(1), invoking the principles of Sections 508(d)(2)(A) and 508(e). Presumably, an organization is disqualified also for engaging in such transactions in violation of the terms of the governing instrument. Local law may be interpreted to preclude a foundation from violating these provisions in order not to jeopardize its charitable status. Cf. In re Barkey, 1971-1 USTC ¶ 9350 (NY Surr. Ct. 1971).

Otherwise qualified private foundations are also disqualified if they incur liability for the tax on termination of private foundation status. IRC § 508(d)(1). See IRC §§ 507(a), 507(c). In general, disqualification takes place only upon notification by the foundation of its intention to terminate private foundation status or upon notice by the Commissioner that the foundation has incurred liability for the termination tax, but may occur earlier with regard to one who has been a substantial contributor. IRC § 507(d)(2).

the use of nonexempt trusts,[54] Congress has extended the further qualifications imposed on private foundations to nonexempt trusts.[55] Foreign organizations that may be qualified recipients are subjected to similar additional qualifying rules.[56]

[2] Transfers to Charity

A deduction is allowed under Section 2055(a) if the transfer takes the form of a bequest, legacy, or devise to a qualified charity.[57] This section examines further restrictions that relate to the nature of a seemingly qualified recipient or are based on conditions or contingencies in otherwise qualified bequests.

[a] Outright Transfers

If a decedent leaves cash or other property outright[58]—say, to a church[59] or to the American Cancer Society—the decedent can feel reasonably confident that the estate will get the expected deduction. If the deduction is not in cash, its amount usually matches the value at which the property was included in the decedent's gross estate; quite reasonably, Congress provides it can never exceed that value.[60] An enforceable inter vivos pledge to charity that is paid by

---

[54] S. Rep. No. 552, 91st Cong., 1st Sess. 94 (1969), reprinted in 1969-3 CB 423, 483.

[55] IRC § 2055(e)(1) (invoking the principles of Sections 508(d)(2), 508(e), 4947).

[56] IRC §§ 2055(e)(1), 4948(c)(4). With some exceptions, new organizations that may qualify for income tax exemption under Section 501(c)(3) are also disqualified unless they have taken prescribed steps to establish their exemptions. IRC §§ 508(c), 508(d)(2)(B), 508(a).

[57] IRC § 2055(a).

[58] Compare Churchhill v. United States, 68 F. Supp. 267 (Wis. 1946) (restrictions on use precluded charitable deduction) with Polster v. Comm'r, 274 F2d 358 (4th Cir. 1960) (restrictions on use but a charitable deduction allowed because charity received property in all events). See infra ¶ 5.05[4][a] text accompanying note 128. Cf. Longue Vue Found. v. Comm'r, 90 TC 150 (1988) (right of voidability by forced heirs disregarded where not exercised); Proctor v. Comm'r, 67 TCM (CCH) 2943 (1994) (bequest subject to employee's right to lease property for fair market value for life was deductible and did not constitute a charitable remainder trust. See infra ¶ 5.05[8]); Priv. Ltr. Ruls. 8812003 (Dec. 17, 1987) (valid transfer of property even though property subject to bona fide lease and option to purchase at fair market value), 200116007 (Dec. 19, 2000) (bequest of land treated as outright even though permits required to use for public use, but if such permits not acquired property passed to another charity). Cf. infra ¶ 5.05[7][d].

[59] On what may constitute a "religious" purpose, see Schwarz, "Limiting Religious Tax Exemptions: When Should the Church Render Unto Caesar?" 29 U. Fla. L. Rev. 50 (1976).

[60] IRC § 2055(d). However, it is possible that the values will be less if the property included in the gross estate is not subject to a discount, but the transfer to charity is sub-

an executor to the charity is allowed as a deductible claim against the estate under Section 2053 if the payment would have constituted an allowable deduction under Section 2055 if it had been a bequest.[61]

A common type of property bequeathed outright to charity is the proceeds of some type of qualified deferred compensation arrangement.[62] Generally these proceeds are classified as items of income in respect of a decedent[63] and as such do not receive a new basis under Section 1014(a)[64] with the result that the proceeds are included in the gross income of the recipient when received.[65] The receipt of items of income in respect of a decedent by an exempt charity normally are not subject to income taxation.[66] The law governing charitable transfers of the proceeds of deferred compensation plans is complicated, and testamentary charitable bequests of such proceeds must be handled with care.[67]

---

ject to a discount. See infra ¶¶ 5.05[3][a] text accompanying notes 96, 97, 5.06[5] at notes 91–94.

[61] Reg. § 20.2053-5. See supra ¶ 5.03[5] text accompanying note 145.

[62] See ¶ 4.05[4].

[63] IRC § 691. Items of income in respect of a decedent may well be the subject of a charitable bequest. See Ferguson, Freeland, and Ascher, Federal Income Taxation of Estates, Trusts, and Beneficiaries, § 3.07[B][3] (Aspen, 3d ed. 1998).

The transfer of such arrangements to charity qualifies for a Section 2055 charitable deduction, and if the transfer is an outright transfer to charity, it is not income in respect of a decedent to the estate. See, e.g., Priv. Ltr. Ruls. 9723038 (June 6, 1997), 9818009 (May 1, 1998), 199901023 (Jan. 8, 1999), 199939039 (Oct. 1, 1999), 200002011 (Sept. 30, 1999).

[64] Compare IRC § 1014(c) (no step-up of basis for income in respect of decedent property) with IRC § 1014(a) (stepped-up basis for non–income in respect of decedent property).

[65] IRC § 691(a).

[66] IRC §§ 501(a), 501(c)(3). In selecting property to give to a charity and that to be given to a noncharitable beneficiary, compare a gift of an item of income in respect of a decedent to a charity with a gift of appreciated property to a noncharitable beneficiary. A gift of appreciated property to a noncharitable beneficiary receives a step-up in basis that will allow the noncharitable beneficiary to liquidate the property without recognizing any predeath gains. See IRC § 1014(a).

[67] See Petrie, "Estate Planning for Retirement Plans and IRAs," in Price on Contemporary Estate Planning 309 (Panel Supp. 1998), which points out that such charitable giving must be weighed against the economic growth that one's family might enjoy over an extended distribution period if the deferred compensation arrangement were left to the family. Id. at § 13.15. See generally Freeman, "When to Give Retirement Plan Assets to Charity," 21 Est. Plan. 348 (1994).

[b] Indirect Transfers

If, as a result of a settlement of a will contest,[68] an assertion of an elective share,[69] or a reformation of a will,[70] property passes outright to a charity or passes in a manner that otherwise qualifies for a charitable deduction and if the transaction is condoned by the local courts, a charitable deduction is allowed.[71] However, if the transaction is merely a collusive action by the parties to qualify property for a charitable deduction, no charitable deduction is allowed to the estate.[72] For example, if there is a charitable transfer under a will that does not otherwise qualify for a charitable deduction and the parties agree to an outright transfer of the same value to charity, then there is mere collusive action and no deduction is allowed.[73] In the alternative, if a third party with a legitimate intestate claim contests the will and the action is settled with local court approval and, as a result, the charity receives an outright transfer, a

---

[68] Estate of Flanagan v. United States, 810 F2d 390 (10th Cir. 1987); Northern Trust Co. v. United States, 78-1 USTC ¶ 13,229 (ND W. 1977); Estate of Strock v. United States, 655 F. Supp. 1334 (WD Pa. 1987); Terre Haute First Nat'l Bank v. United States, 91-1 USTC ¶ 60,070 (SD Ind. 1991) (valid split interest converted to outright transfer); Estate of Warren v. Comm'r, 981 F2d 776 (5th Cir. 1993) (valid split interest before and after the settlement); Priv. Ltr. Rul. 200032010 (May 5, 2000) (compromise of trust dispute). If an invalid split interest is converted to an outright transfer in a bona fide dispute, the Service allows a charitable deduction. Rev. Rul. 89-31, 1989-1 CB 277; TAM 200128005 (Mar. 22, 2001) (same). Cf. Estate of Carpenter v. Comm'r, 52 F3d 1266 (4th Cir. 1995); Davies v. United States, 87 AFTR2d 2001-614 (D. Me. 2000) (both disallowing a marital deduction for an outright bona fide settlement transfer where the surviving spouse's interest prior to the transfer would not have qualified for a Section 2056 deduction. See ¶ 5.06[3][a] note 30.

[69] First Nat'l Bank of Fayetteville, Ark. v. United States, 727 F2d 741 (8th Cir. 1984) (invalid split interest converted to valid split interest); Rev. Rul. 78-152, 1978-1 CB 296 (invalid split interest converted to outright transfer).

[70] Oetting v. United States, 712 F2d 358 (8th Cir. 1983) (invalid split interest converted to outright transfer); Priv. Ltr. Rul. 200027015 (Apr. 4, 2000) (reformation of a trust).

[71] See supra notes 68–70. These situations should be distinguished from a reformation of a split interest bequest under Section 2055(e)(3). See infra ¶ 5.05[8]. Similar consequences occur with respect to the marital deduction. See ¶ 5.06[3][a], but see supra note 68.

[72] When the sole purpose of the reformation is to qualify the bequest for a charitable deduction, the courts have ignored the state court results. See Estate of Burdick v. Comm'r, 96 TC 168 (1991), aff'd, 979 F2d 1369 (9th Cir. 1992); Estate of Johnson v. United States, 742 F. Supp. 940 (SD Miss. 1990); Estate of La Meres v. Comm'r, 98 TC 294 (1992). When the state court dispute involved the conveyance of a deed rather than the will itself, a charitable deduction has been disallowed. See Estate of Burgess v. Comm'r, 38 TCM 335 (1979), aff'd, 622 F2d 700 (4th Cir. 1980).

[73] Estate of Burdick v. Comm'r, 96 TC 168 (1991) aff'd, 979 F2d 1369 (9th Cir. 1992).

charitable deduction has been allowed.[74] Drawing these lines can be difficult. If the charity ends up with an interest that is more valuable than its uncontested interest under the will, the actions of the parties would appear to be collusive, although cases have treated such transactions as valid.[75] However, in one case, the court limited the charitable deduction to the value that the charity would have originally received under the will.[76]

[c] Disclaimers

Contingencies or powers that threaten ultimate receipt by a charitable recipient have always raised a question whether a deduction should be allowed. If a property interest left to charity is subject to a private power to consume, invade, or appropriate, the power would obviously render the value of the charitable interest too uncertain to support any charitable deduction. However, the statute[77] has long made it clear that the termination for any reason of any such unexercised power cures the defect if it occurs before the time for filing the estate tax return. This concept is now directly related to the statutory rules on disclaimers.[78] A timely termination of an offending power is made a "qualified disclaimer." A qualified disclaimer effects an ab initio elimination of the interest or "power" disclaimed.[79]

Special rules subsequently discussed apply to other mixed bequests where, for example, an individual may receive a temporary interest in property, and a qualified charity the remainder. Before such rules evolved, the charitable remainder was generally deductible, and in *Ithaca Trust* the Supreme Court held that its value was not affected by termination of the private interest by death of a life tenant after the decedent's death but before the estate tax return had to be filed.[80] Rules on the deductibility of portions of mixed bequests were tightened in 1969, but the Tax Reform Act of 1976 eased this matter in one respect. Under the disclaimer rules, one receiving a life interest in property, remainder to charity, may be able to assure the charitable deduction by making a

---

[74] Northern Trust Co. v. United States, 78-1 USTC ¶ 13,229 (ND W. 1977).

[75] Terre Haute First Nat'l Bank v. United States, 91-1 USTC ¶ 60,070 (SD Ind. 1991); Estate of Warren v. Comm'r, 981 F2d 776 (5th Cir. 1993) (estate ended up with greater charitable deduction because administrative expenses paid from other estate source).

[76] Terre Haute First Nat'l Bank v. United States, 91-1 USTC ¶ 60,070 (SD Ind. 1991). Cf. IRC § 2055(e)(3)(E), considered infra ¶ 5.05[8][c] text accompanying note 380.

[77] IRC § 2055(a) (penultimate sentence).

[78] IRC §§ 2045, 2518.

[79] IRC §§ 2518(a), 2518(c)(2). See also Rev. Rul. 80-66, 1980-1 CB 204.

[80] Ithaca Trust Co. v. United States, 279 US 151 (1929).

qualified disclaimer[81] of an interest. This will be effective only if the effect of the disclaimer is to give the entire interest in the property to a charity. In light of the rule with respect to *powers* (treating death of a power holder as a qualified disclaimer), it is odd that Congress has not elected to treat the *death* of one who has a property *interest* as a disclaimer of the interest.[82] But in this respect *Ithaca Trust* lives on.[83]

Qualified disclaimers of private bequests may work in another way to enlarge charitable bequests. For example, if a decedent, after making certain specific bequests, left the residuary estate to the Red Cross, a disclaimer effective under Section 2518 of any specific bequest that operates to enlarge the residue going to charity qualifies the affected interest for the deduction. However, under Section 2518, one should be cautioned that neither an asserted disclaimer of a bequest for which a legatee receives consideration[84] nor one made after the legatee has accepted benefits will be treated as a disclaimer for these purposes.[85] It is probably obvious that a private beneficiary's direction that a share of the estate be paid to a charity, where the beneficiary's mere rejection of the share would not have that result, is not a qualified disclaimer[86] and generates no deduction for the estate.

[d] Property Over Which Decedent Had a Power

Property over which the decedent had a power of appointment may in some circumstances be treated as part of the decedent's gross estate for estate tax purposes, whether or not the decedent exercised the power.[87] Section 2055(b), taking into account the foregoing treatment of powers for gross estate purposes, permits the estate a deduction to the extent that property brought

---

[81] IRC §§ 2045, 2518. But see Detroit Bank & Trust Co. v. United States, 80-2 USTC ¶ 13,382 (ED Mich. 1980). See infra ¶¶ 5.05[4], 5.05[5]. See also Priv. Ltr. Rul. 9635011 (May 23, 1996) (disclaimer of power resulted in valid charitable remainder unitrust (CRUT)).

[82] Cf. IRC § 2055(e)(3)(F), considered infra ¶ 5.05[8][d] text accompanying note 382.

[83] Merchants Nat'l Bank v. United States, 583 F2d 19 (1st Cir. 1978); Wells Fargo Bank v. United States, 79-2 USTC ¶ 13,317 (ND Cal. 1979); Rev. Rul. 76-546, 1976-2 CB 290. Both an interest and a power were terminated in Shriners' Hosp. for Crippled Children v. United States, 602 F2d 302 (Ct. Cl. 1979).

[84] Reg. § 25.2518-2(d); Priv. Ltr. Rul. 7809043 (Nov. 30, 1977).

[85] Reg. § 20.2055-2(c). See IRC § 2518(b)(3); Reg. § 25.2518-2(d); ¶ 10.07[2][c]. See also Reg. § 20.2055-2(c) providing similiar limitations on disclaimers under pre-Section 2518 law. An attempted disclaimer after an acceptance of a legacy might constitute a deductible gift by the legatee under Section 2522, discussed in Chapter 11. See also IRC § 170, potentially providing an income tax deduction for the legatee.

[86] IRC § 2518(b)(4). Cf. IRC § 2518(c)(3)(B).

[87] See IRC § 2041, discussed ¶ 4.13.

into the gross estate by Section 2041 is "received" by a qualified organization. Such property is to be "considered a bequest" to charity by the decedent.[88] This is entirely appropriate, for in order for the property to be included in the decedent's gross estate under Section 2041, the decedent must have had such power over the property that the decedent could have disposed of it for the decedent's own benefit or for the benefit of the decedent's estate. If the decedent directs or permits it to go to charity, a deduction is in order.[89]

[e] Lifetime Transfers

This deduction provision speaks in terms of "bequest, legacies, devises, or transfers" to qualified organizations. The use of the word "transfers"[90] needs some explanation.

A lifetime transfer to charity that leaves the value of the transferred property in the decedent's gross estate can give rise to an estate tax charitable deduction.[91] For example, if the decedent made a lifetime transfer of a personal residence to the Red Cross, reserving the right to its use for life, the value of the property will be included in the decedent's gross estate under Section 2036, but Section 2055 will permit an offsetting deduction.

Section 2055(a) speaks generally of transfers, which might appear to make all lifetime transfers to charities deductible for estate tax purposes. However, it must be read in connection with Section 2055(d), which limits the de-

---

[88] The bequest occurs at the time of the decedent's exercise or failure to exercise the power; this may create problems with respect to mixed charitable and private bequests. See Estate of Flanigan v. Comm'r, 743 F2d 1526 (11th Cir. 1984); Estate of Sorenson v. Comm'r, 72 TC 1180 (1979); Rev. Rul. 76-504, 1976-2 CB 286. See infra ¶¶ 5.05[4]–5.05[8].

[89] A 1956 amendment, applicable to estates of decedents dying after August 16, 1954 (Pub. L. No. 1011, § 1, 70 Stat. 1075 (1956)), added Section 2055(b)(2), which was of very limited applicability and was repealed for decedents dying after October 4, 1976. Tax Reform Act of 1976, Pub. L. No. 94-455, §§ 1902(a)(4)(A), 1902(c)(1), 90 Stat. 1525, 1804, 1806 (1976), reprinted at 1976-3 CB 1, 280, 282. For a discussion of the provision, see Stephens, Maxfield & Lind, Federal Estate and Gift Taxation 5-51 (Warren, Gorham & Lamont, 3d ed. 1974).

[90] In Senft v. United States, 319 F2d 642 (3d Cir. 1963), no deduction was allowed for property that escheated to the state, on the basis of Regulations Section 20.2055-1(a), which restricts deductions under Section 2055 to property transferred by the decedent during the decedent's lifetime or by will. In such circumstances, the requisite lifetime or testamentary transfer by the decedent is considered missing because the receipt by charity was because of some external force. See also Estate of Pickard v. Comm'r, 60 TC 618 (1973) (and cases cited therein), aff'd per curiam, 503 F2d 1404 (6th Cir. 1974).

[91] See the discussion of Sections 2035, 2036, 2037, and 2038 at ¶¶ 4.07–4.10; Rifkind v. United States, 5 Cl. Ct. 362 (1984); Rev. Rul. 72-552, 1972-2 CB 525, both allowing a charitable deduction under Section 2055 for a lifetime transfer to a charitable corporation.

duction for any transfer to an amount not in excess of the value of the transferred property that is included in the gross estate. Although the statute is not very precise, the effect of Section 2055(d) is generally to fix the amount of the deduction at the date-of-death value of the transferred property.[92] The alternate valuation date provision requires the use of date-of-death value, even when the later valuation date is elected, but provides for adjustment in value as of the alternate date for any differences "not due to mere lapse of time or the occurrence or nonoccurrence of a contingency."[93]

If a transfer to charity is something other than a lifetime transfer of property or a pecuniary or specific bequest, valuation difficulties may be increased. For example, a residuary bequest to a qualified organization may be reduced by amounts paid out of the estate to others as a result of settlement or judgment in a will contest.[94]

[3] The Amount of the Deduction

[a] In General

Absent a Section 2032 election of the alternate valuation date, date-of-death value generally controls the amount of the charitable deduction which is based on the amount that *passes* to charity.[95] However, this is not always the case. With the increased awareness by taxpayers, the government, and the courts that partial interests in unmarketable securities and real estate are subject to discounts,[96] a transfer to charity of only a portion of the decedent's interest in such property a larger portion of which is included in the decedent's gross estate may result in a charitable deduction that is less than the interest's proportionate share of the value of the entire property included in the decedent's gross estate.[97]

---

[92] But see infra ¶ 5.05[3][a] text accompanying notes 96, 97.

[93] See the discussion of Section 2032 at ¶ 4.03[4][b].

[94] Estate of Sage v. Comm'r, 122 F2d 480 (3d Cir. 1941), cert. denied, 314 US 699 (1942). See also Estate of Toulmin v. United States, 462 F2d 978 (6th Cir. 1972); Irving Trust Co. v. United States, 221 F2d 303 (2d Cir.), cert. denied, 350 US 828 (1955).

[95] If the decedent owned a temporal interest in property that is transferred to charity, the Section 7520 interest rate for either of the two months prior to death may be used in valuing the partial interest. Reg. § 20.7520-2(a)(2). If Section 2032 is elected, see IRC § 2032(b) (second sentence).

[96] See ¶ 4.02[4].

[97] For example, if the decedent dies owning 100 percent of the equity interests in a closely held business, the interests in the business would be valued for gross estate purposes without a minority interest discount and, perhaps, a relatively small marketability discount. If the decedent's testamentary plan calls for 49 percent of the equity interests to

If the Section 2032 alternate valuation date is elected, the inclusion and deduction rules, still usually the same, may vary with regard to valuation changes that result from the "occurrence or nonoccurrence of a contingency."[98] The accepted philosophy here is that a decedent's philanthropy (and the estate's deduction) should be measured at the time of the decedent's death and should not be affected by valuation changes that result from either a mere lapse of time or postmortem contingencies. Of course, if the value of property is affected by a mere lapse of time and alternate valuation is elected, valuation changes caused by the lapse are disregarded for gross estate *and* deduction purposes.[99] If the value of property is affected by a contingency that has not occurred at death, the contingency is ignored for all purposes if alternate valuation is not elected.[100] It is ignored only for *deduction* purposes if alternate valuation is elected.

For example, the value of an insurance policy owned by the decedent on the life of another person would be subject to the contingency of the other's death. If the other person died after the decedent but before the alternate valuation date, the later-date election would bring the entire proceeds of the policy into the gross estate. But, if the decedent had bequeathed the policy to a church, the deduction would be measured by the smaller date-of-death value of the policy on the then-living insured. The increase in value is viewed as a windfall for the charity, to which the decedent was insufficiently related to warrant an increased deduction for the decedent's estate.

[b] Expenses of an Estate Affecting the Deduction

[i] **Death taxes.** If, after certain specific bequests, a decedent by will leaves the residuary estate to charity, what is the value of the charitable transfer that can be claimed as a deduction? The residuary estate is determined by subtracting from the value of the estate the amount of the specific bequests

---

be distributed to charity, the value of the interests that pass to charity and that are deductible may be reduced due to a minority interest discount and, potentially, an additional marketability discount. As a result, the charitable deduction allowable may be less than it would appear to be if simply measured as 49 percent of the value of the equity included in the gross estate. See Ahmanson Found. v. United States, 674 F2d 761 (9th Cir. 1981). Cf. Estate of Schwan v. Comm'r, 82 TCM (CCH) 168 (2001) (redemption agreement imposed on the charity might reduce value passing to charity). See also ¶ 5.06[5] text accompanying notes 91–94; supra ¶ 5.05[2][a] note 60; infra ¶¶ 5.05[5][a] note 205; 5.05[5][b] note 262; 5.05[5][c] note 288. Cf. Priv. Ltr. Rul. 200202032 (Oct. 26, 2001) (full value of property included in gross estate passed to one or more of several charities with the result that the amount of deduction equaled the amount of inclusion.

[98] IRC § 2032(b) (last sentence).

[99] IRC § 2032(b) (last sentence).

[100] IRC § 2032(b) (last sentence).

and all debts and expenses. Is the charitable bequest what is left, or are death taxes payable out of the residuary estate also to be deducted to determine the charitable deduction? In other words, is the deduction restricted to what the charity actually receives? Before the statute dealt expressly with this problem, the Supreme Court held that the amount of the charitable deduction was the value of the residuary estate before taking into account the federal estate taxes to be paid.[101] The Court based its decision on the ground that the tax is on a net estate that is to be determined before the tax is computed; thus, the charitable deduction must be allowed for the full residuary estate left to charity, although the estate tax will take a bite out of the residuary estate, reducing the amount actually received.

Whether the decision was sound or not, Congress has specifically provided a contrary rule, and the "algebraic formulae . . . not lightly to be imputed to legislators"[102] now sometimes have to be dealt with. That is, the value of "two mutually dependent indeterminates"[103] must be determined. The tax may depend on the amount of the deduction, which, in turn, depends on the tax and the extent to which it reduces the amount actually passing to charity.

The need for this determination arises under Section 2055(c), which provides that the amount of federal estate tax or other death taxes[104] payable out of charitable "bequests, legacies, or devises" otherwise deductible must be subtracted from such "bequests, legacies, or devises"[105] to determine the amount of the charitable deduction.[106]

Fortunately, Section 2055(c) will often not have to be reckoned with. In some states, state and federal taxes are payable out of the residuary estate.[107] In

---

[101] Edwards v. Slocum, 264 US 61 (1924).

[102] Edwards v. Slocum, 264 US 61, 63 (1924).

[103] Edwards v. Slocum, 264 US 61, 63 (1924).

[104] Bush v. United States, 618 F2d 741 (Ct. Cl. 1980). See Rev. Rul. 80-66, 1980-1 CB 204. This includes the now-repealed Section 4980A(d) tax, which was, however, deductible under Section 2053(c)(1)(B). The Taxpayer Relief Act of 1997, Pub. L. No. 105-34, § 1073(a), 111 Stat. 788, 948 (1997), reprinted in 1997-4 CB (Vol. 1) 1, 162; Priv. Ltr. Rul. 9723038 (Mar. 11, 1997).

[105] Payment of such taxes out of the estate's post-death income does not allow the executor to decrease the Section 2055(c) reduction. Bowes v. United States, 593 F2d 272 (7th Cir. 1979); Waldrop v. United States, 137 F. Supp. 753 (Ct. Cl. 1956); Buchanan v. United States, 377 F. Supp. 1011 (WD Pa. 1974), aff'd, 511 F2d 1392 (3d Cir. 1975). Cf. infra ¶ 5.05[3][b][ii].

[106] Note that Section 2055(c) differs from Section 2055(a) in omitting the word "transfers." A possible interpretation is that amounts going to charity are reduced by death taxes only if they go by will and that lifetime transfers are not to be reduced correspondingly, even if the charity's share is burdened with the tax. The Treasury recognizes no such distinction (Reg. § 20.2055-3(a)), speaking simply of property "the transfer of which would otherwise be allowable as a deduction under section 2055."

[107] See discussion of Section 2205 at ¶ 8.04.

such states, unless the testamentary documents provide otherwise, a specific or pecuniary bequest to charity bears no part of the tax burden when the residuary estate is of sufficient magnitude to discharge the taxes, which makes it unnecessary to worry about the provisions of Section 2055(c).

Other states again, absent a direction otherwise in the controlling documents, apportion the tax burden equitably among those beneficially interested in the estate.[108] However, a common provision of such state apportionment statutes frees from the financial burden of death taxes interests that qualify for deductions under the statutes imposing the tax.[109] Accordingly, under such statutes, no part of the death taxes is attributed to the amount passing to charity, and again Section 2055(c) will not come into play.

However, the problem squarely arises when, for example, there is a residuary bequest to charity in a jurisdiction where there is no provision for apportionment, or where under the local apportionment rules a charitable bequest must bear a part of the financial burden of death taxes, or where the will itself provides for payment of estate taxes out of the residual charitable bequest.[110] The mathematics of this problem involving interdependent variables, while difficult, are not impossible. In fact, a laborious effort by trial and error would eventually lead to the correct balance of tax and deduction. But the solution is much easier under existing formulae too detailed for discussion in this book.[111]

[ii] **Administrative expenses and claims.** When a charitable bequest[112] bears administrative expenses or claims as a result of the provisions of the de-

---

[108] See discussion of Section 2205 at ¶ 8.04.

[109] See, e.g., NY Est. Powers & Trusts Law § 2-1.8(c)(2) (McKinney 2002). See Estate of Trunk v. Comm'r, 550 F2d 81 (2d Cir. 1977); Rev. Rul. 76-358, 1976-2 CB 291; Rev. Rul. 76-359, 1976-2 CB 293, interpreting the New York statute; Fla. Stat. § 733.817(2)(c) (2001). See also First Nat'l Bank of Omaha v. United States, 490 F2d 1054 (8th Cir. 1974) (discussed under the Nebraska apportionment statute); Mosher v. United States, 390 F. Supp. 1041 (D. Conn. 1975) (decided under the Connecticut statute). Cf. Estate of MacKay v. Comm'r, 68 TCM (CCH) 279 (1994) (taxes paid out of charitable share where the decedent intended that California proration statute not apply); Estate of Fagan v. Comm'r, 77 TCM (CCH) 1427 (1999) (will override North Carolina statute).

[110] See, e.g., Estate of Baumberger v. Comm'r, 551 F2d 90 (5th Cir. 1977); Chastain v. Comm'r, 59 TC 461 (1972); Estate of Leach v. Comm'r, 82 TC 952 (1984); Estate of Kunkel v. United States, 84-2 USTC ¶ 13,583 (MD Pa. 1984). See also Rev. Rul. 78-445, 1978-2, CB 242.

[111] See Pub. No. 904 (rev. May 1985), which is reproduced at 3 IRS Publications (CCH) ¶¶ 56,061–56,086. Cf. Rev. Rul. 76-358, 1976-2 CB 291, Rev. Rul. 76-359, 1976-2 CB 293; Estate of Baumberger v. Comm'r, 34 TCM (CCH) 332 (1975), aff'd, 551 F2d 90 (5th Cir. 1977). For the method of computation required to determine the deduction allowable for a CRUT that was subject to a portion of the estate's tax liability, see TAM 9419006 (Jan. 31, 1994).

[112] This includes both outright charitable gifts and deductible gifts of partial interests to charity. See infra ¶¶ 5.05[4]–5.05[8]; Reg. § 20.2055-3(b)(1)(iii).

cedent's will or local law, then the amount of the charitable deduction generally is reduced. If a charitable bequest is subject to deductible claims as a
result of the provisions of the decedent's will or local law, then the amount of
the charitable deduction is reduced because the amount the charity receives is
reduced.[113] To allow both deductions in their entirety would result in double
deductions.[114] The rules governing the effect of administrative expenses on the
amount of a charitable deduction for decedents dying after December 3, 1999,
are found in regulations that were promulgated after substantial litigation.[115]
Under those regulations, the Section 2055 deduction[116] is reduced if the administrative expenses (regardless of their nature) have been deducted under Sec-

---

[113] Cf. Estate of Hohensee v. Comm'r, 25 TC 1258 (1956).

[114] IRC § 2056(b)(9). See infra note 117.

[115] Reg. § 20.2055-3(b). The regulations are effective for the estates of decedents dying after December 3, 1999. Reg. § 20.2055-3(b)(7).

The issue originally arose as a question whether the charitable deduction amount was
required to be reduced where a Section 642(g) election was made to waive an estate tax
deduction for Section 2053 items if such items were paid out of income generated by the
property interests passing to charity rather than from corpus. Some lower courts held that
the charitable deduction should not be reduced by expenses paid out of post-death income
attributable to the charitable share. Estate of Hubert v. Comm'r, 63 F3d 1083 (11th Cir.),
aff'd, 520 US 93 (1997), aff'g 101 TC 314 (1993); Estate of Warren v. Comm'r, 981 F2d
776 (5th Cir. 1993) (reaching the same result with respect to a charitable lead annuity
trust). Cf. Estate of Street v. Comm'r, 56 TCM (CCH) 774 (1988), aff'd in part and rev'd
in part, 974 F2d 723 (6th Cir. 1992) (reaching the same result with respect to the marital
deduction). Other decisions supported the position that charging expenses to income from
the charitable share required a reduction in the charitable deduction. Burke v. United
States, 994 F2d 1576 (Fed. Cir. 1993) (reduction of charitable deduction for administrative
expenses other than interest). Cf. Estate of Street v. Comm'r, 974 F2d 723 (6th Cir.
1992); Fisher v. United States, 28 Fed. Cl. 886 (1993) (both reaching this result with respect to the marital deduction).

The Supreme Court resolved the issue in Estate of Hubert v. Comm'r, 520 US 93
(1997). The Court held that no reduction was automatically required, but indicated that a
reduction would occur if the anticipated expenses met a materiality test. Cf. Reg.
§ 20.2056(b)-4(a) (amended by TD 8846, 1999-2 CB 679, 682) which reduced the marital
deduction if there was "any material limitation" on the right to the income. The Court's
decision concluded that the payment of such expenses from income from the charitable
share should not affect the amount of the charitable deduction unless anticipated expenses
were material in relation to anticipated charitable share income. Hubert v. Comm'r, 520
US 93 (1997).

The Treasury subsequently recognized that the materiality test would be "too complex" and "administratively burdensome" (see REG-114663-97, Supplementary Information, 1999-1 CB 443, 444). It considered three alternatives to the materiality test (see
Notice 97-63, 1997-2 CB 322) prior to the adoption of the current regulations. See infra
text accompanying notes 116–126.

[116] If the expenses are paid out of income, which under the governing instrument or
applicable local law, the charity is not entitled to, then the payment is not out of the charitable share. Reg. §§ 20.2055-3(b)(1)(iii), 20.2055-3(b)(6), 20.2055(b)-4(d)(5) Ex. 7.

tion 2053.[117] This reduction precludes double estate tax deductibility. The Section 2055 charitable deduction is also reduced by the amount of administrative expenses that are deducted under the income tax as a result of a Section 642(g) election[118] and are paid out of the charitable share if the expenses are related to non–charitable share property.[119]

To the extent that administrative expenses attributable to the charitable share are deducted under the income tax as a result of a Section 642(g) election, the issue whether the charitable deduction is reduced depends on whether the administrative expenses are "management" expenses or "transmission" expenses. Management expenses are expenses that might have been incurred even if the decedent had not died and that are incurred in connection with the investment of estate assets or with their preservation and maintenance during the period of administration.[120] Examples of such expenses include investment advisory fees, stock brokerage commissions, custodial fees, and interest.[121]

Transmission expenses are expenses incurred as a result of the decedent's death, such as expenses incurred in collecting the decedent's assets; paying debts, estate, and inheritance taxes; or distributing the estate's property.[122] Examples of such expenses include most executor commissions and attorney fees (other than those related to the investment, preservation, and maintenance of assets), probate, appraisal, and will contest fees.[123] Any administrative expenses that are not management expenses are treated as transmission expenses.[124]

Transmission expenses reduce the amount of the charitable deduction, even if they are deducted under the income tax as a result of a Section 642(g) election.[125] Management expenses (to the extent that they are deducted under the income tax as a result of a Section 642(g) election) do not reduce the amount of the charitable deduction.[126]

---

[117] Regulations Section 20.2055-3(b)(3) properly references Section 2056(b)(9). See Reg. §§ 20.2055-3(b)(6), 20.2056(b)-4(d)(5) Ex. 4. The provision precludes a charitable deduction for the amount of any claims deducted under Section 2053 against the charitable property.

[118] See infra ¶ 5.03[3][d].

[119] Reg. § 20.2055-3(b)(4). Cf. Reg. § 20.2056(b)-4(d)(5) Ex. 3.

[120] Reg. § 20.2055-3(b)(1)(i).

[121] Reg. § 20.2055-3(b)(1)(i).

[122] Reg. § 20.2055-3(b)(1)(ii).

[123] Reg. § 20.2055-3(b)(1)(ii).

[124] Reg. § 20.2055-3(b)(1)(ii).

[125] Reg. §§ 20.2055-3(b)(2), 20.2055-3(b)(5) Ex. 2. If the transmission expenses are deducted under Section 2053, they also reduce the charitable deduction. See supra text accompanying notes 116, 117.

[126] Reg. §§ 20.2055-3(b)(3), 20.2055-(b)(6), 20.2056(b)-4(d)(5) Ex. 2. If the management expenses are deducted under Section 2053, they reduce the charitable deduction. See supra text accompanying notes 116, 117.

[4] Split Interests: Mixed Private and Charitable Bequests

The charitable deduction may be allowed even if a bequest is not one that vests an immediate and outright interest in a qualified recipient. A bequest of private interests in property that is ultimately to go to charity does not necessarily defeat the deduction. Similarly, it is possible to obtain a charitable deduction by way of a bequest of an income interest in property to a charity with the remainder, after a term, left to a private individual. Nevertheless, when private objectives are mixed with philanthropy, there may be reason to draw into question the true extent to which charities are benefiting. No doubt Congress has always intended the estate tax deduction to be measured only by the actual charitable benefits, and the Treasury has sought to administer Section 2055 in accordance with that intent. Consistent with these approaches, the Tax Reform Act of 1969 and subsequent legislation have added and amended Section 2055(e)(2) to superimpose qualifications for the deductibility of charitable transfers that carry with them private benefits as well.

[a] Background

For many years, the most controversial problems under the charitable deduction revolved around the following scenarios: (1) a bequest to a charity of a future interest following a private present interest, or vice versa; (2) a bequest to a charity of a contingent or conditional interest that might not materialize or might be withdrawn upon some happening in favor of a private interest; and (3) a bequest to a charity accompanied by a power held by a private person to invade the fund or otherwise diminish the charitable interest.

Mere deferral of a charity's enjoyment, or time limitations on its current enjoyment, as in item 1, raised largely valuation questions, or at least so it seemed at an earlier time.[127] Therefore, if the art of the actuary was not too sorely tested, bequests of this type usually yielded a deduction. On the other hand, conditions, contingencies, and powers more directly threatened the charitable interest. The Treasury and the courts generally took a pretty narrow view in these circumstances, and not content to place a marketplace price on the charity's chances, disallowed any deduction, unless the chance that the charita-

---

See Gans, Blattmachr & McCaffrey, "The Anti-Hubert Regulations," 87 Tax Notes 969 (May 15, 2000) (discussing the regulations and appropriately concluding that "[i]n virtually all cases, it will be preferable to take an income tax deduction for such [management] expenses" and providing several drafting suggestions with respect to the regulations); Budin, "Final *Hubert* Regulations Will Require Review of Many Estate Plans," 92 J. Tax'n 225 (Apr. 2000).

[127] But see infra ¶ 5.05[4][b].

ble transfers would not become effective was so remote as to be negligible.[128] We forgo a reexploration of the details of their pre-1970 solutions, directing interested readers to an earlier edition of this treatise and the considerable literature discussed there.[129]

Things are not always what they seem. The foregoing discussion indicates that a charitable deduction has been allowed for bequests of partial interests in property measured by the value of the interest passing to a charity. The partial charitable interest could be a present interest (a temporal lead interest followed by a private remainder) or a future interest (a remainder following a private interest granted for a term of years or for the life or lives of individuals). However, under prior law, the estate tax valuation of a charitable interest at the controlling date (death or the alternate date) could prove highly inaccurate. The valuation assumed a rate of return on the property in which the charity received an interest that could vary sharply from the actual experience of the property. The 3.5 percent rate of return that was assumed for many years was long open to question and was subsequently changed to a 6 percent rate, then to a 10 percent rate, and, more recently, to a variable rate.[130]

In the case of a charitable remainder, if the property was invested in high-yield, high-risk securities, the increased risk that the charity would never receive its remainder interest would reduce the actual value of the remainder well below the amount that was allowed as a charitable deduction.[131] Similarly,

---

[128] Reg. § 20.2055-2(b)(1). This test is still employed with respect to outright bequests and, although rarely applicable, to bequests of partial interests to charity. Seemingly, with respect to bequests of partial interests, the test will generally apply only where a trust has a relatively high payment rate with either a small initial asset value or a relatively young life beneficiary. See Priv. Ltr. Rul. 9443004 (Jan. 7, 1994) (allowing the test on an outright bequest, but reducing its value by the present value of the remote contingency); Estate of Moor v. Comm'r, 43 TCM (CCH) 1530 (1982) (partial interest). Cf. Rev. Rul. 77-374, 1977-2 CB 329 (amendment of charitable remainder annuity trust (CRAT) to reduce chance that charitable transfer will not occur to one so remote as to be negligible is not a valid reformation under Section 2055(e)(3)).

See also Rev. Rul. 81-20, 1981-1 CB 471 (pecuniary bequest to individual with residue to charity where bequest could be satisfied with property at its value on distribution does not violate Regulations Section 20.2055-2(b)(1)), clarified by Rev. Rul. 90-3, 1990-1 CB 174.

[129] See Stephens, Maxfield & Lind, Federal Estate and Gift Taxation, 5-44–5-53 (Warren, Gorham & Lamont 3d ed. 1974).

[130] IRC § 7520(a)(2). See Reg. §§ 20.7520-1(b)(1), 20.7520-2(a)(1), 20.7520-3.

[131] The Senate Report stated:

. . . The rules of present law for determining the amount of a charitable contribution deduction in the case of gifts of remainder interests in trust do not necessarily have any relation to the value of the benefit which the charity receives. This is because the trust assets may be invested in a manner so as to maximize the income interest with the result that there is little relation between the interest assumptions used in calculating present values and the amount received by the charity. For example, the trust corpus can be invested in high-income, high-risk assets. This enhances the

in the case of a charitable lead interest, an investment policy stressing growth but not yield would reduce the value of the charity's present interest well below the amount of the charitable deduction. In both cases, the value of the charitable gift might be far less than the amount of the deduction allowed, which was based on average investment experience.[132] The recognized disparity between the assumed (and allowed) value of the charitable bequest and its actual value was the reason for dramatic legislative changes to Section 2055 in the Tax Reform Act of 1969.[133]

[b] Present Law

In general, in the case of estates of decedents who die in 1970 or later,[134] charitable deductions are disallowed for many charitable bequests of partial in-

---

value of the income interest but decreases the value of the charity's remainder interest. The committee agrees with the House that a taxpayer should not be allowed to obtain a charitable contribution deduction for a gift of a remainder interest in trust to a charity which is substantially in excess of the amount the charity may ultimately receive.

S. Rep. No. 552, 91st Cong., 1st Sess. 87 (1969), reprinted in 1969-3 CB 423, 479.

[132] The Senate Report stated:

The purpose of the requirement is to assure that the amount received by the charity, in fact, bears a reasonable correlation to the amount of the charitable contribution deduction allowed the taxpayer.

S. Rep. No. 552, 91st Cong., 1st Sess. 92 (1969), reprinted in 1969-3 CB 423, 483.

[133] Pub. L. No. 91-172, § 201(d)(1), 83 Stat. 487, 560–561 (1969), reprinted in 1969-3 CB 10, 51. See S. Rep. No. 552, 91st Cong., 1st Sess. 86–92 (1969), reprinted in 1969-3 CB 479–483.

The limitations adopted in the estate tax area for deductible gifts of split interests are mirrored in the income tax and the gift tax provisions. See IRC §§ 170(f), 2522(c); ¶ 11.02[2]. The concept has also been extended to the special rules for valuation of transferred temporal interests that generally do not involve charitable recipients under Section 2702. See ¶ 19.03[3][b]. See also ¶ 19.03[3][c] for regulatory exceptions to the application of Section 2702, which largely parallel the split-interest charitable rules.

[134] The restrictions discussed here apply to estates that are affected by the Tax Reform Act of 1969. In general, they apply to estates of decedents who die after 1969 leaving charitable bequests by will. Reg. § 20.2055-2(e)(3). However, the law is not applicable to the estate of a decedent who died before October 9, 1972, without amending any dispositive will provision after October 9, 1969. Reg. § 20.2055-2(e)(3)(i)(a). In addition, it is not applicable to the estate of a decedent no matter when the decedent died if (1) at all times after October 9, 1969, the decedent had no right to change the provisions of the will providing for bequests to Section 2055(a) charitable organizations, or (2) the decedent did not amend any dispositive provision of the decedent's will after October 9, 1969, and before October 9, 1972, and, on October 9, 1972, and at all times thereafter until the decedent's death, the decedent was unable by reason of mental disability to amend the will. Reg. § 20.2055-2(e)(3)(i).

The restrictions apply to transfers to inter vivos trusts except in limited circumstances. Reg. § 20.2055-2(e)(3). They do not apply to property transferred by a decedent

terests in property that would have been deductible under prior law. Current law presents a rigorous and more mechanical attack on the valuation problems. The attack has not been limited to methods of valuing such interests; probably in recognition of the impossibility of arriving at realistic values in many circumstances, Congress has flatly denied deductions in some instances.[135] To state the matter affirmatively, Congress allows charitable deductions for bequests of partial interests only in circumstances in which the valuation uncertainties arising out of the beneficiaries' income rights and the trustee's investment discretion are minimal or nonexistent.

Outside the excepted areas described in the following paragraphs, the rules governing the deductibility of the present value of the charitable portion of split interests apply if an interest in the property passes or has passed without consideration from the decedent to a private person,[136] to an unqualified organization, or to a qualified organization for a disqualified use.[137] The concepts of "property" and an "interest in property" and of an interest that "passes" or "has passed" from the decedent are by no means new.[138] Thus, it is relatively easy to determine whether a split gift occurs.[139] However, if at the time of the

---

on or before October 9, 1969, to any inter vivos trust, but only if: (1) the decedent died before October 9, 1972, without having amended any dispositive provision of the governing instrument after October 9, 1969, or (2) regardless of when the decedent died, either (a) the charitable transfer on or before October 9, 1969, was an irrevocable interest given to, or for the use of, a Section 2055(a) charitable organization, or (b) the instrument was not amended at any time between October 9, 1969, and October 9, 1972, and the decedent was mentally disabled from October 9, 1972, until death. Reg. § 20.2055-2(e)(3)(ii).

The Treasury has broadly interpreted the terms "republish" and "amend" under the will republication and trust amendment limitations. See Reg. § 20.2055-2(e)(4).

Even though current law may be generally applicable to a bequest in trust, curative amendments of the trust instrument are nevertheless permitted by statute. See IRC § 2055(e)(3); infra ¶ 5.05[8].

[135] IRC § 2055(e)(2).

[136] The private interest must be a beneficial interest. Priv. Ltr. Rul. 8106022 (Nov. 7, 1980).

[137] These rules are inapplicable if a decedent leaves the decedent's entire interest in property to charity even though that interest is a partial interest, unless the decedent had previously divided the property to create the partial interest. Rev. Rul. 79-295, 1979-2 CB 349. However, courts will not allow a single trust to be partitioned in order for a portion of it to qualify as a wholly charitable gift. Zabel v. United States, 98-2 USTC ¶ 60,328 (D. Neb. 1998).

[138] The principles of Section 2056 and its regulations apply to determine whether an interest passes or has passed from the decedent. Reg. § 20.2055-2(e)(1)(i). For persons unfamiliar with the marital deduction, see the discussion of Section 2056 at infra ¶ 5.06[3], which indicates that the concept of an interest passing is broad enough to encompass all of the interests included in determining the decedent's gross estate.

[139] Compare Reg. §§ 20.2055-2(e)(1)(i) Exs. 1, 3, 4–6 (all involving the concurrent or nonconcurrent creation of split interests), with Reg. § 20.2055-2(e)(1)(i) Ex. 2 (no split

decedent's death, the private transfer is dependent on the performance of an act or on the happening of a precedent event in order to become effective and the possibility of the occurrence of the act or event is so remote as to be negligible, no interest is deemed to pass to the private person.[140] Of course, a valid disclaimer of the private interest resulting in the interest passing to charity would avoid the split-interest rules,[141] and a noncollusive judicially approved resolution of a bona fide conflict that results in a charity taking an outright transfer is treated as a bequest of a non-split interest.[142] However, the death of a private beneficiary of a charitable remainder trust before the filing of the decedent's estate tax return still results in a split gift.[143] If a transferor has made a post-1969 lifetime transfer in trust retaining the right to the income for life, with remainder to a qualified charity, the transfer is a mixed gift disqualified for a lifetime deduction;[144] however, at the transferor decedent's death,[145] the deduction is expressly allowed, as clearly it should be, because the offending private interest is "extinguished upon the decedent's death" and there is no split interest.[146]

Many of the restrictions on the deduction of split-interest charitable bequests are efforts to avoid the serious question of whether something close to the assumed value of the interest left to charity will actually reach the charita-

---

interest). But see Rev. Rul. 83-45, 1983-1 CB 233 (property whose income was paid to private individual during estate administration was a split interest not qualifying for a charitable deduction); Priv. Ltr. Rul. 9347002 (July 29, 1993) (provision of the decedent's will directing executor to pay income from estate to surviving spouse during period of administration created split interest in property otherwise devised to charity in fee simple). See also Kasner, "If Correct, a New Private Letter Ruling May Jeopardize Deductions for Many Estates," 62 Tax Notes 213 (Jan. 10, 1994); Levy, "When Will Administration Period Distributions Turn Charitable Bequests into Split Interests?" 11 Est. Plan. 38 (1984).

[140] Reg. §§ 20.2055-2(e)(1)(i), 20.2055-2(e)(1)(i) Ex. 4.

Similarly, if at the date of a decedent's death, a transfer to charity is dependent on the performance of an act or happening of a condition, or if a charitable transfer can be defeated by some subsequent event, and the possibility that the condition will occur or the subsequent event will not occur is so remote as to be negligible, then no transfer to charity occurs. Reg. § 20.2055-2(b)(1). Cf. supra ¶ 5.05[4][a] text accompanying note 128.

[141] See supra ¶ 5.05[2][c] text accompanying notes 80–83.

[142] See supra ¶ 5.05[2][b].

[143] Rev. Rul. 76-546, 1976-2 CB 290. But see infra ¶ 5.05[8][d] note 382. See also supra ¶¶ 5.05[2][b]text accompanying note 77, 5.05[2][c]text accompanying notes 82, 83 (cases involving a death of a beneficiary that results in a Section 2055(a) disclaimer of a power, but not a disclaimer of an interest).

[144] See IRC § 2522(c)(2), denying a gift tax charitable deduction; see also IRC § 170(f)(2)(A), denying an income tax deduction.

[145] The transfer is includible in the decedent's gross estate under Section 2036(a).

[146] IRC § 2055(e)(2) (second parenthetical). See Reg. § 20.2055-2(e)(1) (first parenthetical). Thus, the entire value of the property in the decedent's gross estate that was subject to the retained interest qualifies for a charitable deduction. See supra ¶ 5.05[2][e].

ble recipient. Toward that end, Congress requires these bequests to be cast in a particular form if the deduction is to be successfully claimed.[147] A charitable remainder is deductible only if it is a remainder in a "charitable remainder annuity trust," a "charitable remainder unitrust," or a "pooled income fund."[148] A charitable lead interest is deductible only if there is a present charitable interest in the form of either a guaranteed annuity or a fixed percentage of the annually determined value of the property (a "unitrust").[149] Only within these narrowly defined limits may split-interest bequests still qualify for the Section 2055 deduction. A brief description of these arrangements will make it clear that much of the uncertainty regarding what the charity will actually get is removed in the case of such interests. Several statutory exceptions to the rules will be discussed after consideration of the rules themselves.[150]

[5] Qualified Remainder Interests

The present value of a remainder interest in a "charitable remainder annuity trust," a "charitable remainder unitrust," or a "pooled income fund" qualifies for an estate tax charitable deduction.[151] The applicable rules make it unlikely that the property transferred will be fully expended for the benefit of the noncharitable income beneficiary or beneficiaries.[152] All three types of charitable remainders, which will be discussed in detail here,[153] borrow their definitions

---

[147] IRC § 2055(e)(2). Section 2055(e)(2) was held constitutional in Estate of Gillespie v. Comm'r, 75 TC 374 (1980).

[148] IRC § 2055(e)(2)(A). See infra ¶ 5.05[5].

Even though a partial bequest to charity meets all the requirements and would normally be deductible, no charitable deduction is allowed if the full value of the transfer qualifies for a marital deduction under Section 2056(b)(7). IRC § 2056(b)(9); Reg. § 20.2055-6. An example of such a disallowance is provided in Reg. § 20.2056(b)-9. See ¶ 5.06[8][e] text accompanying note 414.

The double deductibility limitation is not applicable to a deduction allowed by Section 2056(b)(8) where the separate interests (to a surviving spouse and to charity) are each deductible, but no double deductibility occurs. See infra ¶ 5.06[8][e] text accompanying notes 408–413.

[149] IRC § 2055(e)(2)(B). See infra ¶ 5.05[6].

[150] IRC § 2055(e)(2). See infra ¶ 5.05[7].

[151] IRC §§ 2055(e)(2)(A), 664(d), 642(c)(5).

[152] See supra ¶ 5.05[4][b].

[153] For discussions of entities qualifying for mixed bequests, including drafting suggestions, see Brier & Knauer, "Charitable Remainder Trusts and Pooled Income Funds," 435-2 TMP A-1 (BNA 1992); Schmolka, "Income Taxation of Charitable Remainder Trusts and Decedents' Estates," 40 Tax L. Rev. 1 (1984); Collister, "Charitable Remainder Trusts: An Overview," 51 Tax Law. 549 (1998); Schlesinger, "Split Interest Charitable Trusts," 51 NYU Inst. on Fed. Tax'n, § 17.00 (1993); Teitell, "Charitable Lead and Remainder Trusts," 32 USC Tax Inst. ¶ 1500 (1980); Sneed, "Charitable Remainder Trusts,"

from the income tax provisions of the Code.[154] As will be seen, the first two types of charitable remainder trusts (the annuity trust and the unitrust) bear substantial similarity to one another, although to qualify for a remainder deduction, a bequest must meet all the specific requirements of one type and may not mix and match between the two types.[155] A pooled income fund is a different type of vehicle. One common rule applicable to all three types of charitable remainders is that any failure to meet the requirements disqualifies the remainder gift from meeting the required definition, with the consequence that no charitable deduction is allowed. However, in some circumstances, invalid charitable remainder bequests may be reformed into deductible bequests.[156]

[a] The Charitable Remainder Annuity Trust

A charitable remainder annuity trust (CRAT) is defined in Section 664(d)(1). Essentially, a CRAT is a trust that initially pays a fixed annuity of between 5 percent and 50 percent of the original value of the trust corpus to the noncharitable beneficiary or beneficiaries of the trust, with a remainder having a value of at least 10 percent of the original value of the trust corpus passing to the charity. Although it may appear strange that a fixed amount must be paid for a noncharitable use, this fixed payment cures an old difficulty. It removes the "incentive to favor the income beneficiary over the remainder beneficiary by means of manipulating the trust's investments."[157] Unlike an interest in all of the trust's income, fixed payments for private use cannot be increased by high-yield investments, and the value of the remainder interest is therefore more accurately ascertainable. The Internal Revenue Ser-

---

25 USC Tax Inst. 87 (1973); Wren, "Charitable Remainder Trusts: Some Considerations to Draftsmanship," 8 U. Rich. L. Rev. 25 (1973); Crockett, "Charitable Remainder Trusts—New Trust Vehicles for Tax Planning," 19 St. Louis ULJ 161 (1974); Temple, "Using Deferred Charitable Gifts to Achieve Maximum Transmission of Family Wealth Tax Free," 11 Tax'n for Law. 312 (1983). Institutions that may benefit from carefully planned mixed gifts and bequests often offer technical assistance to potential donors.

[154] See IRC §§ 2055(e)(2)(A), 664(d), 642(c)(5). The text comments on qualification of a charitable remainder trust are by no means exhaustive. In some instances, the Treasury's requirements for qualification seem to go beyond the statute. For example, under the regulations some flexibility in investment policy must be accorded the trustee. Cf. Reg. § 1.664-1(a)(3). It is also notable that these trusts are accorded unique income tax attributes. For example, they are themselves exempt from tax (Section 664(c)), which may permit tax-free accumulation of excess income for the charitable remainderpersons. Further, the income tax rules on distributions differ from the usual rules of Subchapter J. See IRC § 664(b).

[155] Reg. § 1.664-1(a)(2).

[156] See IRC § 2055(e)(3); infra ¶ 5.05[8].

[157] S. Rep. No. 552, 91st Cong., 1st Sess. 88 (1969), reprinted in 1969-3 CB 423, 480.

vice (the Service) provides important assistance[158] in the form of model language for drafting deductible CRATs.[159]

[i] Annuity trust requirements. A CRAT must function as an annuity trust from its creation.[160] The governing instrument of an annuity trust must provide that, after the initial contribution, no additional contributions may be made to the trust.[161] However, in applying this rule, all property passing to an annuity trust by reason of the death of the grantor shall be considered a single contribution.[162] The governing instrument must also satisfy four definitional requirements:[163]

The Annuity Payments. A fixed amount (not less than 5 percent nor more than 50 percent of the net fair market value of the property at the time it is transferred to the trust)[164] must be paid at least annually to recipients (at least one of which does not qualify as a charity under Section 170(c)) for not more

---

[158] Some of the assistance may be outdated owing to recent legislative and administrative changes. See, e.g., infra text accompanying notes 169, 171–174, 200–204. See also Notice 2000-37, 2000-2 CB 118, indicating that the Service intends to revise its guidance to reflect statutory and regulatory changes to CRATs.

[159] Rev. Rul. 72-395, 1972-2 CB 340, modified by Rev. Ruls. 80-123, 1980-1 CB 205; 82-128, 1982-2 CB 71; 88-81, 1988-2 CB 127; 92-57, 1992-2 CB 123, clarified by Rev. Rul. 82-165, 1982-2 CB 117.

CRAT forms are found in Rev. Proc. 89-21, 1989-1 CB 842, and Rev. Proc. 90-32, 1990-1 CB 546. The Service will not issue determination letters as to the qualification of charitable remainder trusts substantially similar to the forms set forth in these rulings. Rev. Proc. 90-33, 1990-1 CB 551.

However, the Service does continue to rule on related issues not covered in the revenue rulings and procedures cited. Cf. Priv. Ltr. Rul. 9634019 (May 24, 1996) (a unitrust funded by grantor's retirement plan qualifies for a Section 2055 deduction).

[160] Reg. § 1.664-1(a)(4). A testamentary CRAT is deemed created at the date of death of the decedent, even though the trust is not funded until a later date. Reg. § 1.664-1(a)(5)(i). The annuitant's right to payments must arise at the date of death, although if permitted by the governing instrument or by local law, actual payments may be deferred until the end of the taxable year in which the trust is completely funded. Reg. § 1.664-1(a)(5)(i). Interest compounded annually must be paid on such deficiencies. Reg. § 1.664-1(a)(5)(i). See Reg. § 1.664-1(a)(5) for further rules applicable to deferred payments.

An inter vivos CRAT with an annuity to the transferor for life and then to secondary beneficiaries after the transferor's death, which annuity was included in the transferor's gross estate where the trust had failed to pay the annuities during the transferor's life, was not a valid CRAT, and transferor's estate was not permitted a charitable remainder deduction. Estate of Atkinson v. Comm'r, 115 TC 26 (2000).

[161] Reg. § 1.664-2(b). Failure to so provide disqualifies the trust for a Section 2055 deduction.

[162] Reg. § 1.664-2(b).

[163] IRC §§ 664(d)(1)(A), 664(d)(1)(B), 664(d)(1)(C), 664(d)(1)(D). See Reg. §§ 1.664-2; 20.2055-2(e)(2)(vi).

[164] Obviously, this may require payments out of principal. Such a distribution is considered a sale of the distributed property by the trust. Reg. § 1.664-1(d)(5).

than twenty years or, alternatively, for not more than the life or lives of living individuals.[165]

The fixed annuity amount may be stated as a flat dollar amount[166] or as a fraction or percentage of the original net fair market value of the corpus of the trust.[167] However, the annuity amount must not be less than 5 percent[168] nor greater than 50 percent[169] of the initial net fair market value of the property placed in the trust.

---

[165] IRC § 664(d)(1)(A).

[166] Reg. § 1.664-2(a)(1)(ii). The flat dollar amount may continue for successive non-charitable beneficiaries or may be an amount paid to joint beneficiaries. If, at the termination of the interest of one of the joint beneficiaries, that beneficiary's interest passes to charity, special rules apply under which the other recipients may continue to receive at least the annuity amount they were previously receiving. See Reg. § 31.664-2(a)(1)(ii). The amount of the annuity in such circumstances may drop below 5 percent. See Reg. § 1.664-2(a)(2)(ii), infra note 168.

[167] Reg. § 1.664-2(a)(1)(iii). The fraction or percentage must be based on the net value of the corpus of the trust as finally determined for estate tax purposes. Id. The fraction or percentage amount effectively becomes a flat dollar amount and may be paid to beneficiaries as discussed supra note 166.

[168] IRC § 664(d)(1)(A). This requirement has nothing to do with the estate or gift tax, but is instead imposed for income tax purposes. The legislative history of the provision (S. Rep. No. 552, 91st Cong., 1st Sess. 90 (1969), reprinted in 1969-3 CB 423, 481) stated that the 5 percent payment requirement:

> will prevent a charitable remainder trust from being used to circumvent the current income distribution requirement imposed on private foundations. In the absence of these rules, a charitable remainder trust could be established which provided for a minimal payout to the noncharitable income beneficiary (substantially less than the amount of the trust income). Since the trust generally is exempt from income taxes this would allow it to accumulate trust income in excess of the payout requirement of the unitrust or annuity trust without tax for the future benefit of charity.

The initial stated amount may drop below 5 percent on the death of a beneficiary or a termination of a term of years in limited circumstances in which a distribution is made to charity and the total amount paid to the remaining noncharitable beneficiaries bears the same ratio to 5 percent of the initial fair market value of the corpus as the net fair market value of the trust assets immediately after the distribution bears to the net fair market value of the assets immediately prior to the distribution. See Reg. §§ 1.664-2(a)(2)(ii), 1.664-2(a)(5)(ii)(e).

[169] IRC § 664(d)(1)(A). The 50 percent ceiling was imposed because of Congress's concern with accelerated charitable remainder trusts where "the interplay of the rules governing the timing of income from distributions from charitable remainder trusts . . . and the rules governing the character of distributions . . . have created opportunity for abuse. . . ." S. Rep. No. 33, 105th Cong., 1st Sess. 1, 201 (1997), reprinted in 1997-4 CB (Vol. 2) 1067, 1281. See Notice 94-78, 1994-2 CB 555, in which the Service had previously announced that it would challenge accelerated charitable remainder trusts. The 50 percent ceiling applies to transfers after June 18, 1997. The Taxpayer Relief Act of 1997, Pub. Law. No. 105-34, § 1089(a)(2), 111 Stat. 788, 960 (1997), reprinted in 1997-4 CB (Vol. 1) 1, 174.

The annuity payments must be made at least annually, although they can be made more frequently, such as quarterly or monthly.[170] Generally for annuity trust years ending after April 18, 1997, the annuity amount must be paid within the trust's taxable year.[171] This change was intended to prevent the use of so-called accelerated payment charitable remainder trusts, which relied, in part, on being able to have payments made from gains realized in a later year treated as payments made in the preceding years when the trust had no income, thus permitting the private beneficiary to recover the payment with no income tax consequences.[172] However, the rule is subject to several broad exceptions in nonabusive situations, permitting payment within a reasonable time[173] after the close of the year.[174]

Annuity trusts may have multiple named noncharitable beneficiaries,[175] and generally,[176] all those beneficiaries who are individuals must be living at the creation of the trust.[177] Even if the trustee of a testamentary trust has a power to alter the interests of named noncharitable beneficiaries, the trust gen-

---

See Reg. § 1.664-2(a)(1)(iv) for special computations involving short taxable years and the last taxable year of a period.

[170] IRC § 664(d)(1)(A). The value of the charitable remainder is reduced if the payment period is more frequent than an annual payment. See Reg. §§ 1.664-2(c); 20.2031-7(d)(6), Table J; 20.2031-7(d)(6), Table K.

[171] See Reg. § 1.664-2(a)(1)(i)(a). For trust taxable years ending on or before April 18, 1997, the annuity payment must be made within a reasonable time after the close of the taxable year. See Reg. § 1.664-2(a)(1)(i) (in force Jan. 1, 1998).

[172] See REG-209823-96, Supplementary Information, 1997-1 CB 763, 766.

[173] See Reg. § 1.664-2(a)(1)(i)(c) (reasonable time generally extends no later than the due date of the trust tax return).

[174] Exceptions apply in three situations: (1) the character of the annuity amount is income in the recipient's hands under Section 664(b)(1), Section 664(b)(2), or Section 664(b)(3), Reg. § 1.664-2(a)(1)(i)(a); (2) there is a distribution of property owned by the trust at the close of the taxable year to satisfy the annuity amount, but only if the trustee elects to treat the gain to the trust as having accrued in the year to which the distribution relates, Reg. § 1.664-2(a)(1)(i)(a); and (3) the trust has an annuity amount not in excess of 15 percent of the initial fair market value of the trust property, and the annuity trust was created prior to Dec. 10, 1998, Reg. § 1.664-2(a)(1)(i)(b).

[175] The noncharitable beneficiaries must be "persons." IRC §§ 664(d)(1)(A), 7701(a)(1). A person may include an entity as well as a natural person. Priv. Ltr. Rul. 9419021 (Feb. 10, 1994). See Rev. Rul. 78-105, 1978-1 CB 295 (pet animal is not an individual). Generally, if the beneficiaries are individuals, the individuals must be named individuals, although they may be within a named class of individuals, such as children. Reg. § 1.664-2(a)(3)(i).

[176] If there is a named class of beneficiaries for a term of years (rather than for life), the individuals need not be alive at the creation of the trust. Reg. § 1.664-2(a)(3)(i) (third sentence).

[177] IRC § 664(d)(1)(A). A testamentary trust is deemed created at the date of the decedent's death. Reg. § 1.664-1(a)(5)(i).

erally is not disqualified as a CRAT.[178] However, each noncharitable benefici-ary's interest must not extend beyond that beneficiary's life[179] or a term of years not to exceed twenty years.[180] Thus, in the case of any specific annuitant, the period may not exceed the longer of either the life of the named individual *or* a term of years not to exceed twenty years.[181] For example, a trust may pro-vide an annuity to *A* for life and then to *B* for life or for a term of years (not to exceed twenty years), whichever is *shorter* (but not longer), and remainder to charity.[182] Or a trust may provide an annuity to *A* for twenty years and an annuity to *B* (who was alive at the creation of the trust) for life, with a re-mainder to charity.[183] However, a period measured by a term of years may not be tacked onto a period measured by a life; thus, a trust may not provide an annuity to *A* for life, then an annuity to *B* for twenty years, because it is pos-sible for the term to exceed either the recipients' lives or a term of twenty years.[184] The regulations provide some enlightening examples of situations in-volving satisfaction of the minimum 5 percent rules and the time period rules.[185]

No Other Noncharitable Beneficiaries. Subject to one exception,[186] no other amounts may be paid for uses or to organizations other than those quali-fied for the charitable deduction.[187] For example, the trustee must not have a power to invade corpus for the annuitant (unless the invasion is of an amount

---

[178] The power to allocate the annuity amount among members of a class must not cause any person to be treated as the owner of any part or all of the trust under the gran-tor trust rules of Sections 671–678. Reg. § 1.664-2(a)(3)(ii). This limitation has very lim-ited application to a testamentary trust because the grantor is deceased, and the grantor trust provisions would be applicable only if Section 678 (nongrantor treated as owner of the trust) applied. Cf. Rev. Rul. 77-73, 1977-1 CB 175.

[179] Thus, a beneficiary's interest may not be based on the life of another person. IRC § 664(d)(1)(A); Reg. § 1.664-2(a)(5)(i).

[180] IRC § 664(d)(1)(A); Reg. § 1.664-2(a)(5)(i). See Rev. Rul. 78-105, 1978-1 CB 295. Cf. Rev. Rul. 76-291, 1976-2 CB 284.

[181] Reg. §§ 1.664-2(a)(5)(i), 1.664-2(a)(5)(ii)(b).

[182] Reg. § 1.664-2(a)(5)(i).

[183] Reg. § 1.664-2(a)(5)(ii)(c).

[184] Reg. § 1.664-2(a)(5)(i).

[185] See Reg. § 1.664-2(a)(5)(ii).

[186] There is a minor private legislative exception allowing the remainder of a trust funded with ESOP stock to be paid to an ESOP and to have the remainder still qualify for a charitable deduction. See IRC § 664(d)(1)(C); supra ¶ 5.05[1][b] text accompanying note 42.

[187] IRC § 664(d)(1)(B); Reg. § 1.664-2(a)(4). Of course, this requirement disqualifies any trust that may be invaded for any private purposes, regardless of what standards for invasion may be provided, except for an invasion required to make the annuity payment. To meet this requirement, the trust instrument must authorize the trustee to substitute a charity qualified under Section 170(c) if, at the time a charitable distribution is required, the charity named in the trust instrument no longer so qualifies. Reg. § 1.664-2(a)(6)(iv).

necessary to pay the annuity),[188] and if it is possible that death taxes or administrative expenses may be paid from the assets of an otherwise valid CRAT, the trust is an invalid annuity trust.[189] Any amount paid for which adequate and full consideration is received is not subject to this rule.[190] The rules do permit the charitable remainder interest to be commuted or accelerated;[191] put in other terms, the rules permit the noncharitable interests to be terminated on the happening of a "qualified contingency."[192] However, even if the annuity trust provides for a qualified contingency, the charitable interest is valued by disregarding that contingency.[193]

The Charitable Remainder. When the required payments[194] terminate, the remainder must be paid in whole or in part to, or for the use of, qualifying organizations qualified at that time[195] for a charitable deduction[196] or retained by the trust for the use of qualifying organizations.[197] The trust may provide that the remainder passes to a single organization or to concurrent or successive organizations.[198] In addition, if a person is given discretion to alter only the interests of qualified charities that receive the remainder, the trust is not disqualified.[199]

Rev. Rul. 72-395, 1972-2 CB 340, 343, § 4.03, gives an example of a suitable provision to include in the trust instrument.

[188] Rev. Rul. 77-58, 1977-1 CB 175 (invalid charitable remainder trust where trustee was not prohibited from exercising power granted under state law to invade corpus).

[189] Estate of Atkinson v. Comm'r, 115 TC 26 (2000). Cf. Rev. Rul. 82-128, 1982-2 CB 71.

[190] Reg. § 1.664-2(a)(4).

[191] Cf. Priv. Ltr. Rul. 8948023 (Sept. 1, 1989).

[192] IRC § 664(f)(1). A "qualified contingency" provides for a premature termination of the trust on the happening of a contingency (such as divorce or remarriage) when the private payments will terminate at a time not later than they would normally terminate under the trust. IRC § 664(f)(3). Cf. Reg. § 1.664-2(a)(4) (providing that if the trust is an inter vivos trust, the grantor may retain a power exercisable only by will to revoke or terminate a private interest).

[193] IRC § 664(f)(2). Thus, if an otherwise valid annuity trust provides for an annuity to *A* for life, but that *A*'s interest terminates if *A* divorces *A*'s spouse, with a remainder to charity, there would be a valid annuity trust. However, the remainder to charity would be valued ignoring the divorce contingency.

[194] See supra text accompanying notes 164–185.

[195] Reg. §§ 1.664-2(a)(6)(i), 1.664-2(a)(6)(iv).

[196] IRC §§ 170(c), 2055(a). Seemingly, in this situation the charity must qualify under both Sections 170(c) and 2055(a), although qualification only under Section 2055(a) would seem more appropriate. Cf. supra text accompanying notes 186, 187.

[197] IRC § 664(d)(1)(C). See Reg. § 1.664-2(a)(6).

[198] Reg. §§ 1.664-2(a)(6)(i), 1.664-2(a)(6)(iii).

[199] Reg. §§ 1.664-2(a)(3)(ii), 1.664-2(a)(4); Rev. Ruls. 76-7, 1976-1 CB 179 (power held by income beneficiary), 76-371, 1976-2 CB 305 (power held by trustee). Cf. Rev. Rul. 76-8, 1976-1 CB 179 (inter vivos trust power held by grantor).

The 10 Percent Remainder Floor. Finally, on the creation of the trust,[200] the value of the remainder interest must be equal to at least 10 percent[201] of the initial net fair market value of the property placed in the trust.[202] Prior to the adoption of this requirement, a transferor could practically "zero out" a charitable remainder interest, but at the same time use Section 664(c), which exempts CRATs from income tax on the gains on corpus, to allow the corpus to grow tax-free, similar to deferred compensation arrangements. Since Congress considered zeroing out the remainder interest to be abusive, it added the 10 percent requirement.[203] Several special reformation rules are added to provide relief for a trust that does not satisfy the 10 percent rule.[204]

[ii] The amount of the deduction. The amount of the deduction for a transfer to a CRAT is the net fair market value of the corpus of the trust[205] less

---

[200] See Reg. § 1.664-1(a)(5)(i); supra note 160.

[201] Section 7520 rules are used to determine the value of the remainder interest. IRC § 664(d)(1)(D). See ¶ 4.02[5].

[202] IRC § 664(d)(1)(D). Seemingly, even in view of the addition of the 10 percent requirement, Regulations Section 20.2055-2(b) must still be satisfied. Cf. Rev. Ruls. 77-374, 1977-2 CB 329; 70-452, 1970-2 CB 199.

[203] See HR Conf. Rep. 220, 105th Cong., 1st Sess. 330, 606 (1997), reprinted in 1997-4 CB 1457, 2075. The conference report indicates that the Treasury continues to have the power to promulgate regulations to curtail comparable abuses. Id. at 608, 2078. Pursuant to that power, the Treasury has promulgated Prop. Reg. §§ 1.643(a)-8, 1.664-1(d)(1)(iii); 64 Fed. Reg. 56,718 (Oct. 21, 1999).

The 10 percent requirement generally applies only to transfers in trust after July 28, 1997. The Taxpayer Relief Act of 1997, Pub. L. No. 105-34, § 1089(b)(6)(A), 111 Stat. 788, 961 (1997), reprinted in 1997-4 CB (Vol. 1) 1, 175. A special transition rule also applies. The 10 percent rule does not apply to a charitable remainder trust created by a testamentary instrument (will or revocable trust) executed before July 29, 1997, if the instrument is not modified after that date and the settlor dies before January 1, 1999, or the settlor was under a mental disability on that date and all times thereafter. Taxpayer Relief Act of 1997, Pub. L. No. 105-34, § 1089(b)(6)(B), 111 Stat. 788, 961 (1997), reprinted in 1997-4 CB (Vol. 1) 1, 175.

[204] IRC § 2055(e)(3)(J). Proceedings to declare such nonqualifying trusts void or to reform such trusts are discussed infra ¶ 5.05[8][d] text accompanying notes 383–386.

[205] This value is the federal estate tax value under Section 2031 or Section 2032. Reg. §§ 20.2055-2(f)(2)(i), 1.664-2(c). If the gift is made up of unmarketable assets (e.g., real property, closely held stock) and the trustee is a private beneficiary of the trust or is a related or subordinate party under Section 672(c) to either the decedent, the decedent's spouse, or a private beneficiary, the trustee must use a current qualified appraisal (see Reg. § 1.170A-13(c)(3)) by a qualified appraiser (see Reg. § 1.170A-13(c)(5)). Reg. § 1.664-1(a)(7). In addition, if the corpus of the trust is made up of less than all of the decedent's interest in a single issuer's unmarketable securities or interest in real estate, such appraisal may be required to incorporate a discount from the value used in valuing the securities or real estate in the gross estate. See supra ¶¶ 5.05[3][a] text accompanying notes 96, 97; 5.06[5] text accompanying notes 91–94. Cf. Estate of Chenoweth v. Comm'r, 88 TC 1577 (1987).

the value of the noncharitable interests in the trust.[206] Actuarial valuation is employed in valuing the noncharitable interests,[207] although the actuarial tables are disregarded if an individual whose life measures the noncharitable interest is "terminally ill" at the time of the decedent's death[208] or if both an individual whose life measures the noncharitable interest and the decedent died as a result of a common accident or occurrence.[209]

[b] The Charitable Remainder Unitrust

A charitable remainder unitrust (CRUT) is defined in Section 664(d)(2). A unitrust is very similar in its requirements to an annuity trust, except that the income beneficiary, rather than receiving a flat dollar annuity, receives payments based on a fixed percentage of the fair market value of the assets determined annually.[210] This share-of-current-value approach provides the income beneficiary with a hedge against inflation and the charity a hedge against loss in the value of the trust assets. Because the payments are flexible, in that they increase or decrease as the value of the corpus increases or decreases, there is no prohibition against additional contributions to a unitrust.[211] Similar to the annuity trust rules, the CRUT rules work toward a neutralization of investment decisions that might otherwise favor the current interest over the remainder interest.[212] As in the case of an annuity trust, the Service provides important drafting assistance in the form of model language for drafting deductible

---

[206] Reg. §§ 1.664-2(c), 20.2055-2(f)(2)(i).

[207] See IRC § 7520; Reg. §§ 1.664-2(c), 20.2055-2(f)(2)(i), 20.7520-1(a)(3). See IRC § 7520(a) (flush language), Reg. § 20.7520-2(a)(2), allowing the executor to use the interest rate component for either of the two months before the applicable valuation date.

[208] Reg. § 20.7520-3(b)(3)(i). See ¶ 4.02[5] text accompanying notes 253–255.

[209] Reg. § 20.7520-3(b)(3)(iii).

[210] Compare IRC § 664(d)(2) with IRC § 664(d)(1).

[211] Reg. § 1.664-3(b). However, the regulations provide a series of requirements that must be satisfied when additional contributions are made. Id. Compare the restriction on multiple contributions to a CRAT, supra ¶ 5.05[5][a] text accompanying notes 161, 162. Although a decedent would not make multiple contributions at death, it is possible the decedent would have made inter vivos contributions and an additional contribution at death.

If such a contribution would result in the trust ceasing to be a valid unitrust because of the Section 664(d)(2)(D) 10 percent remainder requirement (see infra text accompanying notes 255–260), the contribution will be treated as a contribution to a separate trust. IRC § 664(d)(4).

[212] See supra ¶ 5.05[5][a] text accompanying note 157. If the private beneficiary were to receive the income of the trust, rather than a fixed percentage of the value of its assets, the trustee might be tempted to make investments favoring the income beneficiary to the detriment of the charity's remainder.

CRUTs,[213] although some of the assistance may be outdated as a result of recent legislative and administrative changes.[214]

[i] **Unitrust requirements.** A CRUT must function as a unitrust from its creation in order to qualify for a deduction,[215] and it must satisfy the following four requirements.[216]

Unitrust Payments. A fixed percentage[217] of the net fair market value of the trust assets determined annually must be paid at least annually to recipients (at least one of which does not qualify as a charity under Section 170(c)) for not more than twenty years or, alternatively, for not more than the life or lives of living individuals at the creation of the trust.[218] The amount of the unitrust payment generally must not be less than 5 percent[219] nor more than 50 per-

---

[213] Rev. Rul. 72-395, 1972-2 CB 340, modified by Rev. Ruls. 80-123, 1980-1 CB 205; 82-128, 1982-2 CB 71; 88-81, 1988-2 CB 127; 92-57, 1992-2 CB 123, *clarified by* Rev. Rul. 82-165, 1982-2 CB 117.

CRUT forms are found in Rev. Proc. 89-20, 1989-1 CB 841, Rev. Proc. 90-30, 1990-1 CB 534, and Rev. Proc. 90-31, 1990-1 CB 539. The Service will not issue determination letters as to the qualification of charitable remainder trusts substantially similar to those following the forms set forth in the preceding rulings. Rev. Proc. 90-33, 1990-1 CB 551.

The Service does, however, continue to rule on related issues not covered in the revenue rulings and procedures cited. See, e.g., Priv. Ltr. Rul. 9634019 (May 24, 1996) (distribution of assets of a qualified plan to a unitrust).

[214] See, e.g., infra text accompanying notes 220, 228, notes 230–233, notes 255–260. See also Notice 2000-37, 2000-2 CB 118, indicating that the Service intends to revise its guidelines to reflect statutory and regulatory changes to CRUTs.

[215] Reg. § 1.664-1(a)(4). A testamentary CRUT is deemed created at the date of death of the decedent, although the trust is not funded until a later date. Reg. § 1.664-1(a)(5)(i). The right to payments of the unitrust amount must arise at the date of death, although if permitted by the governing instrument or by local law, actual payments may be deferred until the end of the taxable year in which the trust is completely funded. Reg. § 1.664-1(a)(5)(i). Interest compounded annually must be paid on such deferred payments. Reg. § 1.664-1(a)(5)(i). See Reg. § 1.664-1(a)(5) for further rules applicable to deferred payments. Cf. Estate of Atkinson v. Comm'r, 115 TC 26 (2000).

[216] IRC §§ 664(d)(2)(A), 664(d)(2)(B), 664(d)(2)(C), 664(d)(2)(D). See Reg. §§ 1.664-3, 20.2055-2(e)(2)(vii).

[217] The percentage may also be expressed as a fraction. Reg. § 1.664-3(a)(1)(ii). See supra ¶ 5.05[5][a] text accompanying note 157 for the rationale underlying the fixed amount requirement.

[218] IRC § 664(d)(2)(A).

[219] IRC § 664(d)(2)(A). See Rev. Rul. 74-19, 1974-1 CB 155 (unitrust disqualified where a portion of the trustee's fees charged against the unitrust amount even though unitrust amount may not be less than 5 percent). The 5 percent requirement has nothing to do with the estate or gift tax, but it is instead imposed for income tax purposes. See supra ¶ 5.05[5][a] note 168.

cent[220] of the annually determined net fair market value[221] of the property in the trust.[222] However, to lend some flexibility to the use of unitrusts where the unitrust amount may vary substantially (especially in a year when the value of the corpus increases significantly), a special "income only" rule allows the governing instrument of a unitrust to provide that if the amount of the trust income[223] for a year is less than the fixed percentage of value, the trust may pay the income beneficiary only the amount of the trust income for the year.[224] Such trusts are commonly referred to as NICRUTS (net income charitable remainder unitrusts). Further, the governing instrument of a unitrust with an income-only provision may add a "makeup" provision under which if trust income in any year is in excess of the fixed percentage of value, the excess must be paid to the income beneficiary to make up any unrecovered unitrust deficits from prior years.[225] These trusts are commonly referred to as NIMCRUTS (net income makeup charitable remainder unitrusts). Even though the governing instrument provides for an income-only rule or an income-only and an income makeup rule, the value of the charitable remainder is determined by disregarding the special rules and assuming that the unitrust percentage amount will be paid to the income beneficiary.[226] These types of trusts do not invite manipulation and therefore are permitted.[227] In limited circumstances,

---

The fixed percentage may not drop below 5 percent under any circumstances, including the death of a beneficiary or the expiration of a term of years. Reg. § 1.664-3(a)(2)(ii). Compare the rule applicable to CRATs. See supra ¶ 5.05[5][a] note 168.

[220] IRC § 664(d)(2)(A). The rationale for the rule is discussed at supra ¶ 5.05[5][a] note 169.

[221] See Reg. § 1.664-3(a)(1)(iv) for rules used in computing such net fair market value. The governing instrument must provide for additional payments to or repayments by the income beneficiary if an initial incorrect valuation is later corrected. Reg. § 1.664-3(a)(1)(iii).

The amount could continue for successive noncharitable beneficiaries or could be paid as an amount to joint beneficiaries. If at the termination of the interest of one joint beneficiary, that beneficiary's interest passes to charity, special rules apply under which the other recipients may continue to receive the percentage they were previously receiving, provided that the aggregate unitrust percentage does not drop below 5 percent. See Reg. §§ 1.664-3(a)(2)(ii), 1.664-3(a)(5)(ii)(e); supra note 219.

[222] IRC § 664(d)(2)(A). See Reg. § 1.664-3(a)(1)(v) for special computations involving short taxable years and the last taxable year of a period.

[223] Trust income is determined under Section 643(b). Reg. § 1.664-3(a)(1)(i)(b)(3).

[224] IRC § 664(d)(3)(A). See Reg. § 1.664-3(a)(1)(i)(b)(1). In the absence of such a provision, payments of the unitrust amount would have to be made out of principal. Such a distribution is considered a sale of the distributed property by the trust. Reg. § 1.664-1(d)(5).

[225] IRC § 664(d)(3)(B). See Reg. § 1.664-3(a)(1)(i)(b)(2).

[226] See Reg. § 1.664-4(a)(3).

[227] Cf. Rev. Rul. 76-310, 1976-2 CB 197 (trust not qualified as a CRUT because of potential manipulation).

the Service allows a one-time conversion of a NICRUT or a NIMCRUT to a regular CRUT.[228]

The unitrust payments must be made at least annually, although they can be made more frequently, such as quarterly or monthly.[229] Generally, for unitrust years ending after April 18, 1997,[230] the unitrust amount must be paid within the trust's taxable year.[231] However, the rule is subject to several broad exceptions in nonabusive situations permitting payment within a reasonable time[232] after the close of the year.[233]

---

[228] A flip is permitted if the governing instrument of the CRUT provides that the flip is triggered on a specific date, such as a beneficiary reaching a certain age, or by an event whose occurrence is not discretionary, such as a sale of unmarketable assets as defined in Regulations Section 1.664-1(a)(7)(ii) (assets other than those which can be readily saleable for cash or cash equivalents, such as real estate or closely held stock) or a marriage, death, divorce, or birth. Reg. §§ 1.664-3(a)(1)(i)(c)(1), 1.664-3(a)(1)(i)(d). Any prior net income makeup amount deficiency is forfeited if a flip occurs. Reg. § 1.664-3(a)(1)(i)(c)(3). The flip rules generally apply to trusts created on or after December 10, 1998. Reg. § 1.664-3(a)(1)(i)(f)(1). However, several reformation rules apply. See Reg. §§ 1.664-3(a)(1)(i)(f)(2), 1.664-3(a)(1)(i)(f)(3); Notice 99-31, 1999-1 CB 1185. See also McCoy, "Charitable Remainder Trust Regs Present Planning Opportunities," 138 Tr. & Est. 16 (Mar. 1999); Teitell, "Charitable Remainder Trusts—Final Regulations," 138 Tr. & Est. 36 (Aug. 1999); Clayton & Mirabello, "Donors and Charitable Remainder Trust Final Regs.," 90 J. Tax'n 204 (1999).

[229] IRC § 664(d)(2)(A). The value of the charitable remainder is reduced as the payment period is accelerated. See Reg. § 1.664-4(e)(6)(F).

[230] Reg. § 1.664-3(a)(1)(i)(l). As to pre–April 19, 1997, years, unitrust payments could be made within a reasonable time after the close of the year. Reg. § 1.664-3(a)(1)(i)(a) (in force Jan. 1, 1998).

[231] See Reg. § 1.664-3(a)(1)(i)(g). The rationale for this rule is discussed supra ¶ 5.05[5][a] text accompanying note 172.

[232] See Reg. § 1.664-3(a)(1)(i)(k) (reasonable time generally extends no later than the due date of the trust tax return).

[233] Exceptions apply in several situations: (1) The character of the unitrust amount is income in the recipient's hands under Section 664(b)(1), Section 664(b)(2), or Section 664(b)(3), Reg. § 1.664-3(a)(1)(i)(g); (2) There is distribution of property owned by the trust at the close of the taxable year to satisfy the unitrust amount, but only if the trustee elects to treat the gain to the trusts as having accrued in the year in which the distribution relates, Reg. § 1.664-3(a)(1)(i)(g); (3) the unitrust has a unitrust amount not in excess of 15 percent of the initial fair market value of the trust property and the unitrust was created prior to December 10, 1998, Reg. § 1.664-3(a)(1)(i)(h); and (4) the payments are made under the NICRUT or NIMCRUT exception, Reg. § 1.664-3(a)(1)(i)(j).

A unitrust may have multiple named noncharitable beneficiaries,[234] and generally,[235] all those beneficiaries who are individuals must be living at the time of the creation of the unitrust.[236] Even if the trustee of the testamentary unitrust has a power to alter the interests of such named noncharitable beneficiaries, the trust is generally not disqualified as a CRUT.[237] Each noncharitable beneficiary's interest must not extend beyond that beneficiary's life[238] or a term of years not to exceed twenty years.[239] The rules on measuring these periods are identical to the rules applicable with respect to CRATs.[240]

No Other Noncharitable Beneficiaries. Subject to one exception,[241] no other amounts may be paid for uses or to organizations other than those qualified for the charitable deduction.[242] For example, the trustee must not have a

---

[234] The noncharitable beneficiaries must be "persons." IRC §§ 664(d)(2)(A), 7701(a)(1). A person may include an entity as well as a natural person. Priv. Ltr. Rul. 9419021 (Feb. 10, 1994). See Rev. Rul. 78-105, 1978-1 CB 295 (pet animal is not an individual). Generally, if the beneficiaries are individuals, the individuals must be named individuals, although they may be within a named class of individuals, such as children. Reg. § 1.664-3(a)(3)(i).

[235] If there is a named class of beneficiaries for a term of years (rather than for life), the individuals need not be alive on the creation of the trust. Reg. § 1.664-3(a)(3)(i) (third sentence).

[236] IRC § 664(d)(2)(A). A testamentary trust is deemed created at the date of the decedent's death. Reg. § 1.664-1(a)(5)(i).

[237] The power to allocate the unitrust amount among members of a class must not cause any person to be treated as the owner of any part or all of the trust under the grantor trust rules of Sections 671–678. Reg. § 1.664-3(a)(3)(ii). This limitation has very limited application to a testamentary trust because the grantor is deceased and the grantor trust provisions would be applicable only if Section 678 (nongrantor treated as owner of the trust) applied. Cf. Rev. Rul. 77-73, 1977-1 CB 175.

[238] Thus, a beneficiary's interest may not be based on the life of another person. IRC § 664(d)(2)(A); Reg. § 1.664-3(a)(5)(i).

[239] IRC § 664(d)(2)(A); Reg. § 1.664-3(a)(5)(i). See Rev. Rul. 76-291, 1976-2 CB 284. Cf. Rev. Rul. 78-105, 1978-1 CB 295.

[240] See supra ¶ 5.05[5][a] text accompanying notes 179–184. The unitrust regulations provide some enlightening examples of situations involving satisfaction of the period rules and the 5 percent minimum payment rules. Reg. § 1.664-3(a)(5)(ii).

[241] A minor private legislative exception allows the remainder of a trust funded with ESOP stock to be paid to an ESOP and to have the remainder still qualify for a charitable deduction. See IRC § 664(d)(2)(C); supra ¶ 5.05[1][b] text accompanying note 42.

[242] IRC § 664(d)(2)(B); Reg. § 1.664-3(a)(4). This requirement, of course, disqualifies any trust that may be invaded for private purposes, regardless of what standards for invasion may be provided, except to the extent necessary to pay the unitrust amount. To meet this requirement, the trust instrument must authorize the trustee to substitute a charity qualified under Section 170(c) if, at the time a charitable distribution is required, the charity named in the trust instrument no longer qualifies. Reg. § 1.664-3(a)(6)(iv). Rev. Rul. 72-395, 1972-2 CB 340, 347, § 6.03, provides an example of a suitable provision to include in the trust instrument.

power to invade corpus for the unitrust interest holder except as necessary to pay the unitrust amount,[243] and if it is possible that death taxes or administrative expenses may be paid from the assets of an otherwise valid CRUT, the trust is an invalid unitrust.[244] Any amount paid for which adequate and full consideration is received is not subject to this rule.[245] The rules do permit the charitable remainder interest to be commuted or accelerated;[246] stated in other terms, the rules permit the noncharitable interest to be terminated upon the happening of a "qualified contingency."[247] However, even if the unitrust provides for a qualified contingency, the charitable remainder interest is valued by disregarding the contingency.[248]

The Charitable Remainder. When the required unitrust payments terminate,[249] the remainder must be paid to or for the use of organizations qualified at that time[250] for a charitable deduction[251] or retained by the trust for the use of qualified organizations.[252] The trust may provide that the remainder passes to a single organization or to concurrent or successive organizations.[253] In addition, if a person is given discretion to alter only the interests of qualified charities that receive the remainder, the trust is not disqualified.[254]

---

[243] Rev. Rul. 77-58, 1977-1 CB 75 (invalid charitable remainder trust where trustee was not prohibited from exercising power granted under state law to invade corpus).

[244] Rev. Rul. 82-128, 1982-2 CB 71. Cf. Estate of Atkinson v. Comm'r, 115 TC 26 (2000).

[245] Reg. § 1.664-3(a)(4).

[246] Priv. Ltr. Rul. 8948023 (Sept. 1, 1989).

[247] IRC § 664(f)(1). A "qualified contingency" provides for a premature termination of the trust on the happening of a contingency (such as divorce or remarriage) when the private payments will terminate at a time not later than they would normally terminate under the trust. IRC § 664(f)(3). Cf. Reg. § 1.664-3(a)(4) (providing that if the trust is an inter vivos trust, the grantor may retain a power exercisable only by will to revoke or terminate a private interest).

[248] IRC § 664(f)(2). Thus, if an otherwise valid unitrust provides for a unitrust interest to *A* for life, but that *A*'s interest terminates if *A* divorces *A*'s spouse, with a remainder to charity, there would be a valid unitrust. However, the remainder to charity would be valued ignoring the divorce contingency.

[249] See supra text accompanying notes 217–240.

[250] Reg. §§ 1.664-3(a)(6)(i), 1.664-3(a)(6)(iv).

[251] IRC §§ 170(c), 2055(a). Seemingly in this situation the charity must qualify under both Sections 170(c) and 2055(a), although qualification only under Section 2055(a) would seem more appropriate. Cf. supra text accompanying notes 241, 242.

[252] IRC § 664(d)(2)(C); Reg. § 1.664-3(a)(6).

[253] Reg. § 1.664-3(a)(6)(iii).

[254] Reg. § 1.664-3(a)(4). Rev. Rul. 76-7, 1976-1 CB 179 (power held by income beneficiary).

The 10 Percent Remainder Floor. With respect to each contribution to a unitrust,[255] the value of the remainder interest contributed must be equal to at least 10 percent[256] of the net fair market value of the contributed property at the time of the contribution.[257] However, if an additional contribution is made to a trust that satisfied the unitrust requirements prior to such contribution[258] and the additional contribution disqualifies the trust because of the 10 percent requirement, the additional contribution is treated as a contribution to a separate trust (thereby not disqualifying the original trust).[259] In addition, several special reformation rules are added to provide relief for trusts that do not satisfy the 10 percent rule.[260]

[ii] The amount of the deduction. Valuation of the remainder in a CRUT is determined in a manner somewhat similar to valuations of other valid charitable remainder interests.[261] The value of the charitable remainder depends on the value of the transferred property[262] and the value of the intervening non-

---

[255] See Reg. § 1.664-1(a)(5) for rules related to contributions at death. It is possible that a decedent would have made both inter vivos and testamentary transfers to a single unitrust. See supra note 211.

[256] Section 7520 rules are used to determine the value of such remainder interest. IRC § 664(d)(2)(D). See ¶ 4.02[5].

[257] IRC § 664(d)(2)(D). The rationale for this rule is discussed supra ¶ 5.05[5][a] text accompanying note 203.

Seemingly, even in view of the 10 percent requirement, Regulations Section 20.2055-2(b) must still be satisfied. Cf. Rev. Ruls. 77-374, 1977-2 CB 329; 70-452, 1970-2 CB 199.

[258] The 10 percent requirement generally applies only to transfers in trust after July 28, 1997. The Taxpayer Relief Act of 1997, Pub. L. No. 105-34, § 1089(b)(6)(A); 111 Stat. 788, 961, reprinted in 1997-4 CB (Vol. 1) 1, 175. A special transition rule also applies. See supra ¶ 5.05[5][a] note 203.

[259] IRC § 664(d)(4). Regulations are to be issued to illustrate these rules. Id.

[260] IRC § 2055(e)(3)(J). Proceedings to declare such nonqualifying trusts void or to reform such trusts are discussed infra ¶ 5.05[8][d] text accompanying notes 383–386.

[261] See supra ¶ 5.05[5][a][ii]; infra ¶ 5.05[5][c][ii]. Any valuation of the charitable remainder interest must be accompanied by documentation attached to the return. Reg. § 1.664-4(c).

[262] This is generally be the property's value as determined under Sections 2031 and 2032. If the gift is made up of unmarketable assets (e.g., real property, closely held stock) and the trustee is a private beneficiary of the trust or is a related or subordinate party under Section 672(c) to either the decedent, the decedent's spouse, or a private beneficiary, the trustee must use a current qualified appraisal (see Reg. § 1.170A-13(c)(3)) from a qualified appraiser (see Reg. § 1.170A-13(c)(5)). Reg. § 1.664-1(a)(7). In addition, if the corpus of the trust is made up of less than the decedent's entire interest in a single issuer's unmarketable securities or interest in real estate, such appraisal may be required to incorporate a discount from the value used in valuing the securities in the gross estate. See supra ¶ 5.05[3][a] text accompanying notes 96, 97; infra ¶ 5.06[5] text accompanying notes 91–94. Cf. Estate of Chenoweth v. Comm'r, 88 TC 1577 (1987).

charitable interests.[263] Valuation of the noncharitable interests depends on a host of factors, including the term of the noncharitable interest (taking into account life expectancies if the interest is for life),[264] the going interest rate under Section 7520,[265] and an assumption that payouts are distributed as provided in the governing instrument.[266] Even if an income-only clause is used, the value of the private interest assumes payment of the larger unitrust amount.[267]

[c] The Pooled Income Fund

The third type of charitable remainder interest that qualifies for a deduction under the split-interest rules is a pooled income fund.[268] Although in some aspects it differs dramatically from its two counterparts, like them, it avoids the type of split-interest problems that warrant the disallowance of a charitable remainder deduction. In general, a pooled income fund is a fund, not necessarily in a trust, in which a donor's contributed property is commingled with the property of other donors. The property is invested in a diversified investment portfolio fund that is administered by the charity, but not by any of the donors. Each donor or donor's designee (or designees) receives their share of the fund income for life, with an irrevocable remainder to the charity of their share at the donor's or designee's death. In such circumstances,[269] Congress allows a charitable remainder deduction because a transfer to such a fund maintained by the charity is not subject to investment manipulation; therefore, it may be realistically valued.[270]

[i] **Pooled income fund requirements.** A combination of the requirements summarized here must be met to qualify a fund as a pooled income fund. In a pooled income fund arrangement, a donor (in our case, a decedent)

---

[263] Reg. § 1.664-4(d)(6). See Reg. §§ 1.664-4T(d), 1.664-4T(e). These rules apply for transfers after April 30, 1999. Reg. §§ 1.664-4T(d), 1.664-4T(e). For prior transfers, see Reg. § 1.664-4T(d).

[264] Reg. §§ 1.664-4(a)(1), 1.664-4T(e)(4), 1.664-4T(e)(5), 1.664-4T(e)(6), 1.664-4T(e)(7). See also Reg. § 20.7520-3(b)(3).

[265] Reg. § 1.664-4(a)(2). See IRC § 7520(a) (flush language); Reg. § 20.7520-2(a)(2), allowing the executor to use the interest rate component for either of the two months before the applicable valuation date.

[266] Reg. § 1.664-4(a)(3).

[267] See Reg. § 1.664-4(a)(3); see also supra text accompanying notes 223–228.

[268] The term "pooled income fund" is defined in Section 642(c)(5).

[269] IRC §§ 2055(e)(2)(A), 642(c)(5).

[270] See S. Rep. No. 552, 91st Cong., 1st Sess. 88 (1969), reprinted in 1969-3 CB 423, 480. See also McClure, "Everybody Into the Pool," 127 Tr. & Est. 28 (Oct. 1988); Peckham, "Taxpayer's Tax, Investment, and Charitable Goals Can Be Met by Pooled Income Funds," 6 Est. Plan. 104 (1979); Teitell, "Philanthropy and Estate Planning: Pooled Income Funds . . . Almost Everything You Want to Know," 117 Tr. & Est. 708 (1978).

transfers property to or for the use of a charity[271] with the charity receiving an irrevocable, noncontingent remainder interest in the property[272] and to one or more beneficiaries receiving a life estate.[273] Each beneficiary must be living at the time of the transfer to the trust, and generally the beneficiary must be specifically named, although a named class (such as children) is permitted.[274] If there is more than one income beneficiary, the beneficiaries' interests may be concurrent, consecutive, or both concurrent and consecutive.[275] The charity receiving the remainder may also be named as one of the income beneficiaries.[276]

The property transferred by the decedent is commingled with property of other donors whose transfers must also meet the pooled income fund requirements,[277] and the fund must be made up of only such transfers.[278] The fund may receive and invest in a broad range of investments,[279] but may not receive or invest in tax-exempt securities.[280]

At the heart of the requirements for a pooled income fund (and a major justification for allowing a charitable deduction) is a requirement that the fund

---

[271] The charity must be a public charity, meaning a charity as defined in Section 170(b)(1)(A), other than Section 170(b)(1)(A)(vii) or Section 170(b)(1)(A)(viii), which qualifies under Section 2055(a).

Under the statutory and regulatory language, only one charity may be named as the charitable beneficiary of the fund. IRC § 642(c)(5)(A); Reg. § 1.642(c)-5(b)(1).

[272] IRC § 642(c)(5)(A). A contingent remainder interest transferred to charity does not qualify. Reg. § 1.642(c)-5(b)(1).

[273] IRC § 642(c)(5)(A). The life estate must be based on the beneficiary's own life. Rev. Rul. 79-61, 1979-1 CB 220.

[274] Reg. § 1.642(c)-5(b)(2). If the fund was created inter vivos, the transferor may retain the power exercisable by will to revoke or terminate the interest of any designated private beneficiary. Id.

[275] Reg. § 1.642(c)-5(b)(2). The governing instrument must specifically designate each beneficiary's share of income. Id.

Regulations Section 1.642(c)-5(b)(8) provides rules for severance of the fund at the termination of a life beneficiary's interest.

[276] Reg. § 1.642(c)-5(b)(2).

[277] IRC § 642(c)(5)(B). A public charity may maintain more than one pooled income fund, although there are some restrictions aimed at avoiding manipulation. Reg. § 1.642(c)-5(b)(3).

[278] IRC § 642(c)(5)(D). The fund must not include property transferred under arrangements other than the pooled income fund, although a fund is not disqualified if a portion of its properties is invested or reinvested jointly with non–pooled income fund properties held by the charity, such as a general endowment fund. Reg. § 1.642(c)-5(b)(3).

[279] See, e.g., Rev. Rul. 79-387, 1979-2 CB 247 (real estate).

[280] IRC § 642(c)(5)(C). The governing instrument of the fund must contain specific prohibitions against accepting or investing in such securities. Reg. § 1.642(c)-5(b)(4).

be maintained by the donee charity[281] and that no donor[282] or beneficiary of an income interest (other than the public charity) be a trustee of the fund.[283]

Each of the beneficiaries of the fund is entitled to receive income in an amount determined by the rate of return earned by the fund for the year equal to the beneficiary's proportionate share of the fund.[284] Such income must be paid within sixty-five days after the end of the fund's taxable year.[285] The Treasury has issued sample provisions for inclusion in declarations of trust and instruments of transfer to aid taxpayers in making deductible contributions to pooled income funds.[286]

[ii] The amount of the deduction. The method of valuation for a charitable remainder interest in a pooled income fund is partially prescribed by statute.[287] The determination of the value of the remainder is a three-step process, similar to the charitable remainder valuation of an annuity trust or unitrust. First, the fair market value of the property transferred to the pooled income fund is determined. In a Section 2055 deduction situation, this is the fair market value of the property for federal estate tax purposes.[288] The second step is

---

[281] IRC § 642(c)(5)(E). See Rev. Rul. 96-38, 1996-2 CB 44 (guidance on the maintenance requirement). The charity must maintain direct or indirect control over the fund, but it is not required to be a trustee. Reg. § 1.642(c)-5(b)(5). See Rev. Rul. 74-247, 1974-1 CB 152 (bank as trustee). However, if there are other trustees, the charity ordinarily must have the power to remove trustees and designate new trustees. Reg. § 1.642(c)-5(b)(5); Rev. Rul. 74-132, 1974-1 CB 152; Rev. Rul. 75-116, 1975-1 CB 182.

[282] Since the donor in our case is the decedent, this requirement is easily satisfied as to that donor. Other donors, however, may still be living and must be prohibited from serving as trustee.

[283] IRC § 642(c)(5)(E). The governing instrument must prohibit the donor or beneficiary from being designated as a trustee or having responsibilities normally exercised by a trustee. Reg. § 1.642(c)-5(b)(6). However, the fact that such person is an officer, director, etc., of the public charity will not prevent the trust from satisfying this prohibition. Reg. § 1.642(c)-5(b)(6).

[284] IRC § 642(c)(5)(F). Regulations Section 1.642(c)-5(c) provides rules for determining a beneficiary's proportionate share of income.

[285] Reg. § 1.642(c)-5(b)(7).

[286] Rev. Ruls. 72-196, 1972-1 CB 194; 82-38, 1982-1 CB 96; 85-87, 1985-1 CB 182; 90-103, 1990-2 CB 159. Sample forms are found in Rev. Proc. 88-53, 1988-2 CB 712. The Service will not issue determination letters as to the qualification of pooled income funds that are substantially similar to the forms set forth above. Rev. Proc. 88-54, 1988-2 CB 715.

[287] IRC § 642(c)(5) (flush language). See Reg. §§ 1.642-6 (valuation of transfers after April 30, 1989), 1.642(c)-6A (valuation of transfers prior to May 1, 1989).

[288] See Reg. § 1.642(c)-6(a)(2). This includes valuation on the alternate valuation date if Section 2032 is elected. Id.

If the corpus of the trust is made up of less than all of the decedent's interest in a single issuer's unmarketable securities or interest in real estate, the value may be required to incorporate a discount from the value used in valuing the securities or real estate in the valuation of the income interests. The rate of return used in valuing such interests depends on the rate of return of the transferee pooled income fund. If the fund has been in existence for at least three years, the assumed rate of return is the highest rate of return for any of the three taxable years immediately preceding the transfer to the fund.[289] If the fund has a shorter life, the assumed rate of return is a rate (rounded to the nearest 0.2 percent) one percentage point less than the highest annual average of the monthly Section 7520 rates for the three calendar years immediately preceding the calendar year in which the transfer is made.[290] The value of the income interest is determined by the actuarial valuation of the income beneficiaries' life expectancies[291] and the rate of return.[292] The third step determines the value of the charitable remainder by subtracting the value of the income interests from the value of the entire interest contributed.[293]

[6] Charitable Lead Trusts

A charitable organization may benefit financially not only from a bequest of a future remainder interest, but also from the bequest of a present interest in property, in what is commonly referred to as a charitable lead trust. Again, however, when a decedent mixes private objectives with philanthropy, the accurate measurement of the charity's interest on the applicable valuation date may be uncertain, even if the benefits begin at once.[294] In the case of mixed bequests, a present interest left to charity is deductible after 1969 only if it takes one of two forms, either a "guaranteed annuity" or a unitrust requiring the annual distribution of a "fixed percentage" of the value of the property as

---

gross estate. Cf. Estate of Chenoweth v. Comm'r, 88 TC 1577 (1987); see supra ¶¶ 5.05[3][a] text accompanying notes 96, 97; 5.06[5] text accompanying notes 91–94.

[289] IRC § 642(c)(5) (flush language).

[290] IRC § 642(c)(5) (flush language); Reg. § 1.642(c)-6(e)(3). See Rev. Rul. 96-1, 1996-1 CB 119, establishing the rate for transfers to new funds after April 30, 1989 (prior to such date, a 9 percent rate was generally assumed). See Reg. § 1.642(c)-6(b)(2) (in force Jan. 1, 1989).

[291] Reg. § 1.642(c)-6(e)(1). Generally Table S in Regulations Section 1.642-6(e)(6) is used if there is only a single income beneficiary. Reg. § 1.642-6(e)(5). However, Regulations Section 20.7520-3(b)(3) applies if the income beneficiary is terminally ill. Reg. §§ 1.642-6(e)(1), 20.7520-1(a)(2), 20.7520-3(b)(2)(iv).

[292] See generally Reg. § 1.642(c)-6(e)(6), Table S.

[293] The present value of the remainder is determined by multiplying the value of the property by the appropriate remainder factor (generally found in Table S). See supra note 291. Reg. §§ 1.642(c)-6(e)(3), 1.642(c)-6(e)(4), 1.642-6(e)(5). For other situations, see Reg. § 1.642(c)-6(b).

[294] See supra ¶ 5.05[4][a] text accompanying notes 131, 132.

determined annually.[295] The restrictions imposed on the deductibility of the present interests created in charitable lead annuity interests and charitable lead unitrusts have the same objectives as those directed at remainder interests. If the charity is entitled to a fixed annual payment or an amount determined annually with regard to the value of the property, incentives are removed for the kind of investment manipulation that might render uncertain the actual value passing to charity.

[a] Requirements

With some important differences noted in the next subsection, the restrictions on a charitable lead annuity interest[296] and a charitable lead unitrust interest[297] essentially mirror CRATs and CRUTs with many similar, although not identical, requirements.[298] While the definitions of charitable *remainder* annuity interests and unitrusts are borrowed from the income tax provisions,[299] the definitions of charitable *lead* interests are found in the estate tax regulations;[300] however, the regulations are similar to the income tax definitional requirements.[301] As in the case of charitable remainder trusts,[302] any failure to satisfy the requirements disqualifies the charitable lead interest for a charitable deduction.[303] Surprisingly, the Service has not issued assistance in the form of model language for drafting charitable lead interests similar to the drafting assistance it has issued for charitable remainder trusts.[304] Because of the substantial overlap in the requirements for charitable lead annuity interests and unitrusts, the

---

[295] IRC § 2055(e)(2)(B). The tax-avoidance possibilities inherent in Section 2055 and the use of the charitable lead trust are explored in Cooper, "A Voluntary Tax? New Perspectives on Sophisticated Estate Tax Avoidance," 77 Colum. L. Rev. 161 (1977).

[296] IRC § 2055(e)(2)(B). See Reg. § 20.2055-2(e)(2)(vi).

[297] IRC § 2055(e)(2)(B). See Reg. § 20.2055-2(e)(2)(vii).

[298] See S. Rep. No. 552, 91st Cong., 1st Sess. 92 (1969), reprinted in 1969-3 CB 483.

[299] See IRC §§ 642(d)(1), 644(d)(2), 2055(e)(2)(A); supra ¶ 5.05[5] text accompanying note 154.

[300] Reg. §§ 20.2055-2(e)(2)(vi), 20.2055-2(e)(2)(vii).

[301] See Reg. §§ 20.2055-2(e)(2)(vi), 20.2055-2(e)(2)(vii).

[302] See supra ¶ 5.05[5] text accompanying note 156.

[303] In some circumstances, invalid mixed charitable bequests may be reformed. See IRC § 2055(e)(3), discussed infra ¶ 5.05[8].

[304] See supra ¶¶ 5.05[5][a] text accompanying note 158; 5.05[5][b] text accompanying note 213; 5.05[5][c] text accompanying note 286. However, private letter rulings are regularly issued on the validity of charitable lead interests. See, e.g., Priv. Ltr. Ruls. 9716023 (Jan. 21, 1997); 9718032 (Feb. 4, 1997); 9721006 (Feb. 7, 1997).

following discussion will first consider the differences in those requirements and then the common requirements.[305]

[i] Differences in requirements. The major difference in the regulatory requirements of the two types of charitable lead interests is primarily related to the difference in their underlying natures. A charitable lead annuity interest (the interest is generally in a trust commonly referred to as a CLAT) is a split-interest arrangement under which a "guaranteed annuity" (flat dollar amount) is presently paid to the charitable beneficiary, with other interests in the property (generally only future interests) passing to noncharitable parties.[306] The guaranteed annuity can be expressed as a dollar amount or as a fraction or percentage of the net fair market value as finally determined for estate tax purposes, or it can be dependent on some other outside factor such as a fraction of the cost of living index on the particular date;[307] however, the amount cannot be an amount that will vary over time.[308]

A charitable lead unitrust interest (the interest is generally in a trust commonly referred to as a CLUT) is a split-interest arrangement under which a charity receives a present interest in the form of a fixed percentage[309] of the net fair market value of the property determined annually,[310] with some other interests in the property (generally only future interests) passing to noncharitable parties.[311] Thus, the payment to the charity fluctuates in amount as the value of the corpus fluctuates. Seemingly, because of the difference in their underlying natures, additional contributions made to a unitrust may be deductible while additional contributions made to a guaranteed annuity interest are not deductible.[312]

[ii] Similarities in requirements. The similarities in the two types of charitable lead interests far outnumber their differences. Neither type of lead

---

[305] See infra ¶¶ 5.05[6][a][i], 5.05[6][a][ii].

[306] IRC § 2055(e)(2)(B); Reg. § 20.2055-2(e)(2)(vi)(a).

[307] Reg. § 20.2055-2(e)(2)(vi)(a).

[308] Reg. § 20.2055-2(e)(2)(vi)(a). Thus, it cannot be based on a fraction of a fluctuating amount such as the cost of living index each year. Id. See Priv. Ltr. Rul. 199952044 (Sept. 30, 1999) (amount ascertainable at the decedent's death).

[309] Seemingly, this could be a fixed fraction, as well as a fixed percentage.

[310] The valuation may be made on one date of the year or may be an average of a combination of dates, as long as the same valuation method is used each year. Reg. § 20.2055-2(e)(2)(vii)(a). If the unitrust interest is held in a trust and the trust instrument does not specify a particular method, the trustee may so specify on the trust's first income tax return on Form 1041. Id.

[311] IRC § 2055(e)(2)(B).

[312] See Reg. §§ 20.2055-2(e)(2)(vi)(a), 20.2055-2(e)(2)(vii)(a), supra ¶¶ 5.05[5][a] text accompanying notes 161, 162; 5.05[5][b] text accompanying note 211. Nevertheless,

interest requires the property to be held in a trust,[313] although the regulations seek to tighten the statutory requirements to provide that if the property is not held in trust, the lead interest must be paid by an insurance company or an organization regularly engaged in issuing such annuity or unitrust interests.[314]

Both types of payments must be made not less frequently than annually;[315] again, they may be made quarterly or monthly.[316] Unlike CRATs and CRUTs, which have specific limitations on the periods for noncharitable interests, payments to charitable lead trusts may be made for any period. Payments may be for a specified term (not limited to twenty years), a measuring life or lives (but only if the measuring life is the decedent's spouse or a lineal ancestor or a spouse of an ancestor of all of the noncharitable remainder beneficiaries[317] who are living and ascertained at the time of the creation of the trust), or a combi-

---

all contributions made at death should be treated as a single contribution. Cf. Reg. § 1.664-2(b).

Another difference between charitable lead annuity interests and charitable lead unitrusts occurs in determining the inclusion ratio under the generation-skipping transfer tax where there is a charitable lead annuity trust. See IRC § 2642(e); ¶ 16.02[6].

[313] Reg. §§ 20.2055-2(e)(2)(vi)(a), 20.2055-2(e)(2)(vii)(a).

[314] Reg. §§ 20.2055-2(e)(2)(vi)(c), 20.2055-2(e)(2)(vii)(c).

[315] Reg. §§ 20.2055-2(e)(2)(vi)(a), 20.2055-2(e)(2)(vii)(a).

[316] If the payments are made more frequently than annually, the charitable deduction is increased. Cf. Reg. §§ 1.664-4(e)(6)(F) (unitrust interest); 20.2031-7(d)(6), Table J, 20.2031-7(d)(6), Table K (annuity interest).

[317] Reg. §§ 20.2055-2(e)(2)(vi)(a), 20.2055-2(e)(2)(vii)(a), which were promulgated to prevent the use of "vulture" or "ghoul" trusts that had used seriously ill, but not terminally ill, measuring lives. If there is a less than 15 percent probability that individuals who are not lineal descendants will receive any trust corpus, those beneficiaries may be disregarded in determining whether the measuring life is an ancestor of *all* of the noncharitable remainder beneficiaries. The probability must be computed as of the date of the decedent's death, taking into account the interests of all primary and contingent remainder beneficiaries who are living at that time and must be calculated based on the current applicable Life Table contained in Regulations Section 20.2031-7. Reg. §§ 20.2055-2(e)(2)(vi)(a), 20.2055-2(e)(2)(vii)(a). This rule allows nonlineal descendants to be named as contingent remainderpersons. These rules are generally effective in the case of transfers pursuant to wills and revocable trusts where the decedent dies on or after April 4, 2000. There are exceptions to the effective date (1) for persons who die on or before July 3, 2001, without having republished a will (or amended a revocable trust) that was in effect on April 4, 2000; and (2) for a decedent who was on April 4, 2000, under a mental disability to change the disposition of the decedent's property, and either does not regain competence to dispose of such property before the date of death, or dies prior to the later of ninety days after the date on which the decedent regains competence or July 3, 2001, without having republished the will (or amended the trust). Reg. § 20.2055-2(e)(3)(ii).

nation of the two.[318] With one exception,[319] there are no percentage floors or ceilings on the payments (thus, no requirement that the payout be at least 5 percent and less than 50 percent) and no floor on the value of the remainder (i.e., no 10 percent requirement).[320] These differences between charitable lead and charitable remainder interests are not surprising given that the charity's interest is the present interest; thus, a term longer than twenty years or a small remainder will benefit the charity. If the annuity or unitrust amount is less than the actual income of the property, the excess income may be paid to the charitable beneficiary, although the possibility of such potential payments does not increase the amount of the charitable deduction.[321] On the other hand, if the income is less than the annuity or unitrust amount and the governing instrument permits the smaller of such amounts (the income) to be paid, the charitable lead interest is disqualified.[322] The Service takes the position that an otherwise qualified charitable lead interest does not qualify for the deduction if the trustee has the discretion to commute and prepay the charitable interest based on the discounted value of the interest prior to the expiration of its specified term;[323] thus, a specific prohibition against commutation should be provided in the governing instrument. However, an otherwise valid charitable lead interest

---

[318] Reg. §§ 20.2055-2(e)(2)(vi)(a), 20.2055-2(e)(2)(vii)(a). See Priv. Ltr. Rul. 9631021 (May 3, 1996) (formula to determine term of years). Compare the rules applicable to CRATs and CRUTs, supra ¶ 5.05[5][a] text accompanying notes 179–185 with supra ¶ 5.05[5][b] text accompanying notes 238–240.

[319] The regulations for a charitable lead annuity interest provide that if the property is held in trust and the value of the charitable lead interest exceeds 60 percent of the net value of the trust assets, the charitable interest will not be a guaranteed annuity interest, unless the governing instrument prohibits the acquisition and retention of assets that would give rise to a Section 4944 tax if the trustee acquired such assets. Reg. § 20.2055-2(e)(2)(vi)(e). See IRC §§ 4947(a)(2), 4947(b)(3). Cf. Priv. Ltr. Rul. 9604015 (Oct. 27, 1995). No comparable rule is applied to charitable lead unitrusts.

[320] Compare IRC § 2055(e)(2)(B) with IRC §§ 664(d)(1)(A), 664(d)(2)(A), 664(d)(1)(D), 664(d)(2)(D).

[321] Reg. §§ 20.2055-2(e)(2)(vi)(d), 20.2055-2(e)(2)(vii)(d). This provision does not have the effect of depriving the charity of value left to it. Cf. Rev. Rul. 88-82, 1988-2 CB 336.

[322] Reg. §§ 20.2055-2(e)(2)(vi)(b), 20.2055-2(e)(2)(vii)(b). Cf. Rev. Rul. 77-300, 1977-2 CB 352 (inter vivos unitrust interest disqualified on this basis). Such a term, if allowed in the governing instrument, would represent a return to the perceived pre-1969 evils that Section 2055(e)(2) was enacted to avoid.

[323] Rev. Rul. 88-27, 1988-1 CB 331. Although the ruling involved a guaranteed annuity, it would be equally applicable to a unitrust interest. See Priv. Ltr. Rul. 9734057 (May 28, 1997). See also Priv. Ltr. Rul. 8745002 (July 15, 1987), where the prepayment clause was eliminated if it disqualified the charitable deduction. The Service will not issue an advance ruling with respect to a guaranteed annuity if the interest may be prepaid. Rev. Proc. 88-3, 1988-1 CB 579, 580.

is not disqualified if someone has a power to select between one or more qualified charitable recipients.[324]

Although the regulations provide that no deduction is allowed to either type of charitable lead interest if a noncharitable interest precedes the charitable interest,[325] the Tax Court does not agree.[326]

[b] The Amount of the Deduction

The regulations provide different rules for determining the value of charitable lead annuity and unitrust interests. Similar to the valuation of remainder interests, the value of a charitable lead unitrust interest is determined by subtracting the present value of all interests other than the unitrust interest from the net fair market value of the property to arrive at the value of the unitrust interest.[327] However, the value of a charitable lead annuity interest is generally determined as a stand-alone annuity interest.[328]

[7] Exceptions to the Split-Interest Rules

The estate tax provisions generally borrow from the income tax rules to create a series of exceptions, considered next, where the split-interest requirements need not be satisfied to qualify the charitable interest for an estate tax deduction.[329]

---

[324] See Priv. Ltr. Ruls. 9631021 (May 3, 1996) (a single choice involving a guaranteed annuity interest); 9801013 (Sept. 29, 1997) (an ongoing choice involving a unitrust).

[325] Reg. §§ 20.2055-2(e)(2)(vi)(f), 20.2055-2(e)(2)(vii)(e), 20.2055-2(f)(2)(iv) Ex. 4. See also Rev. Rul. 76-225, 1976-1 CB 281 (same result).

[326] Estate of Boeshore v. Comm'r, 78 TC 523 (1982), acq. in result only, 1987-2 CB 1, AOD 1987-OO3 (June 15, 1987). GCM 39163 (Nov. 2 1983). In *Boeshore*, the Tax Court held Regulations Section 20.2055-2(e)(2)(vii)(e) invalid with respect to a charitable lead unitrust interest preceded by a private unitrust interest. However, if one or more noncharitable interests is concurrent with the charitable interest, there are substantial limitations imposed on the noncharitable interests. Reg. §§ 20.2055-2(e)(2)(vi)(f), 20.2055-2(e)(2)(vii)(e). For example, payments to the noncharitable interests must not be preferred to the charitable interests.

[327] Reg. § 20.2055-2(f)(2)(v). Cf. Reg. §§ 1.664-4T(e), 20.7520-2(a)(2).

[328] Reg. § 20.2055-2(f)(2)(iv). See Reg. §§ 20.2055-2(f)(2)(iv) Exs. 1, 2, 3; 20.7520-2(a)(2). Regulations Section 20.2031-7 generally applies to value such an interest, although Regulations Section 20.2031-7A applies for periods prior to May 1, 1999, and Regulations Section 20.2031-8 applies if the interest is issued by an annuity company. Reg. § 20.2055-2(f)(2)(iv).

[329] IRC §§ 170(f)(3)(B); 2055(e)(2). See IRC §§ 2055 (e)(2)(A), 2055(e)(2)(B); supra ¶¶ 5.05[5], 5.05[6].

[a] Remainders in Residences and Farms

The first exception to the split-interest rules is that a direct (*not in trust*)[330] charitable bequest of a remainder interest either in a personal residence[331] or in a farm[332] is deductible. The exception is based on the theory that there is no possibility of manipulative variance in the value of the charitable interest.[333] The Service allows a deduction for a nontrust charitable remainder interest in only a portion of such property,[334] but it takes the position that the remainder interest must not be a contingent remainder.[335] It also takes the position that the interest must be the property, not the proceeds from the sale of the property;[336] however, the Tax Court appropriately has reached the opposite conclusion where there is no danger of abuse of the purposes underlying the split-gift rules.[337]

---

[330] See Reg. §§ 20.2055-2(e)(2)(ii), 20.2055-2(e)(2)(iii), which were held valid in Ellis First Nat'l Bank of Bradenton v. United States, 550 F2d 9 (Ct. Cl. 1977). See also Estate of Burgess v. Comm'r, 622 F2d 700 (4th Cir. 1980); Estate of Cassidy v. Comm'r, 49 TCM (CCH) 580 (1985); Rev. Rul. 76-357, 1976-2 CB 285; Priv. Ltr. Rul. 8742001 (Jan. 30, 1987).

[331] Any number of residences used as a personal residence will qualify, since the dwelling need not be the decedent's principal residence. Reg. § 20.2055-2(e)(2)(ii). In addition, stock in a cooperative housing corporation may also qualify. Reg. § 20.2055-2(e)(2)(ii). But see Rev. Rul. 76-165, 1976-1 CB 279 (holding household furnishings that are not fixtures are not within the personal residence exception).

[332] A broad range of agricultural uses qualify property as a farm for this purpose. Any land used by the decedent or a tenant for the production of crops, fruit, other agricultural produce, or for the sustenance of livestock (which is also broadly defined) qualifies. See Reg. § 20.2055-2(e)(2)(iii). But see Estate of Brock v. Comm'r, 71 TC 901 (1979), aff'd per curiam, 630 F2d 368 (5th Cir. 1980) (salt mining royalty does not qualify).

[333] See S. Rep. No. 552, 91st Cong., 1st Sess. 87–89 (1969), reprinted in 1969-3 CB 423, 479–480. The exception is accomplished by the Section 2055(e)(2) reference to Section 170(f)(3)(B).

The valuation of the remainder interests is determined under Section 7520. See Reg. §§ 20.7520-1, 20.7520-2, 20.7520-3 (especially Reg. §§ 20.7520-2(a)(2), 20.7520-3(b)(3)).

[334] See Rev. Rul. 87-37, 1987-1 CB 295, rev'g Rev. Rul. 76-544, 1976-2 CB 288; Rev. Rul. 78-303, 1978-2 CB 122. The proportionate interest must not be in a trust. See infra ¶ 5.05[7][b] text accompanying note 338.

[335] See Rev. Rul. 85-23, 1985-1 CB 327 (allowing an exception if the contingency is so remote as to be negligible). Cf. Reg. § 20.2055-2(b).

[336] Rev. Rul. 77-169, 1977-1 CB 286. Cf. Rev. Rul. 76-543, 1976-2 CB 287.

[337] Estate of Blackford v. Comm'r, 77 TC 1246 (1981), acq. 1983-2 CB 1 (residence qualified for charitable deduction where the decedent's will directed executor to sell residence on termination of income interest and distribute proceeds to four charities). See also Rev. Ruls. 83-158, 1983-2 CB 159 (deduction allowed where charity could choose between property and proceeds of its sale); 84-97, 1984-2 CB 196 (deduction allowed where charity required to dispose of farm after ten years). Cf. Priv. Ltr. Rul. 8141037 (July 9, 1981).

[b] An Undivided Portion of the Property

The statute also qualifies bequests of split interests that are not temporal divisions, but represent an undivided portion (*not transferred in trust*)[338] of the decedent's entire interest in property (i.e., a tenancy in common).[339] Obviously, if the decedent bequeaths Blackacre to a child and the Red Cross in equal shares, the charitable bequest is deductible. However, the "undivided portion" exception also applies to a case in which the decedent is the vested remainderperson (following a noncharitable life estate) of a trust created by another person,[340] and the decedent bequeaths a portion of the remainder to charity and a portion to a private person; although an interest in the property passes from the decedent to a noncharitable beneficiary, the deduction is allowed.[341]

[c] A Qualified Conservation Contribution

Another exception is provided for a "qualified conservation contribution."[342] To qualify for this exception, the contribution must consist of an interest in real property.[343] Further, the contributed real property interest must be the decedent's entire interest in the property (other than a qualified mineral interest,[344] which may be retained by the decedent's estate), a remainder interest

---

[338] Rev. Rul. 77-97, 1977-1 CB 285. See Priv. Ltr. Rul. 7735002 (May 23, 1977).

[339] IRC §§ 170(f)(3)(B)(ii); 2055(e)(2). See Reg. § 20.2055-2(e)(2)(i); Rev. Rul. 75-414, 1975-2 CB 371; Rev. Rul. 73-339, 1973-2 CB 68 (allowing a deduction for an open space or scenic easement in perpetuity as an undivided portion of an interest in property).

In determining whether a portion of the decedent's entire interest in property is transferred, the proportionate interest must be a "substantial" interest or right in the property. Reg. § 1.170A-7(b)(1)(i). If the interest or right is insubstantial, it is disregarded. Priv. Ltr. Rul. 9729024 (Apr. 18, 1997). For example, if the decedent leaves an unsubstantial interest in property to a private person and the remaining interests to charity, the transfer is treated as an outright transfer to charity, although the amount of the charitable contribution may be reduced by the value transferred to the private person. Priv. Ltr. Rul. 9729024 (Apr. 18, 1997). See Reg. § 1.170A-1(h)(2)(i).

[340] Cf. Rev. Rul. 79-295, 1979-2 CB 349. If the decedent was settlor of the trust, the interest that has passed from settlor to another would ordinarily preclude the deduction. Reg. § 20.2055-2(e)(2)(i).

[341] Cf. Rev. Rul. 72-419, 1972-2 CB 104 (allowing an income tax deduction under Section 170).

[342] IRC §§ 170(f)(3)(B)(iii), 170(h), 2055(e)(2). See generally Reg. § 1.170A-14. Property with respect to which a qualified conservation contribution is or has been granted may also qualify for a gross estate exclusion under Section 2031(c). See ¶ 4.02[7].

[343] IRC §§ 170(h)(1)(A), 170(h)(2).

[344] IRC § 170(h)(2)(A). A qualified mineral interest involves subsurface minerals and the right to access such minerals. IRC § 170(h)(6). But see IRC § 170(h)(5)(B).

in the property, or a perpetual easement.[345] The contribution must be made to a qualified charitable organization.[346] Where the transfer is of the decedent's entire interest or a remainder interest in property, the contribution must be exclusively for a statutorily defined "conservation purpose."[347] However, where the transfer is of a perpetual easement, the transfer may be made for any valid conservation purpose.[348]

[d] Works of Art and Their Copyrights

Generally a work of art and the federal copyright for it are treated as a single piece of property subject to the limitations on mixed private and charitable bequests. However, in some circumstances, Section 2055(e)(4)[349] permits a split-gift exception and allows an estate tax charitable deduction for the fair market value of the gift of the work of art, regardless of what is done with the copyright. The exception imposes two requirements: the gift of the work of art

---

[345] IRC § 170(h)(2).

[346] IRC § 170(h)(1)(B). Section 170(h)(3) defines "qualified organization" to include governments and publicly supported charities, IRC §§ 170(h)(3)(A) and 170(h)(3)(B)(i), and organizations controlled by such groups, IRC § 170(h)(3)(B)(ii).

[347] IRC § 170(h)(1)(C). The term "conservation purpose" is defined by Section 170(h)(4) to be for the preservation of land areas for public outdoor recreation or education, the environmental protection of wildlife, fish, plants, and the like, the preservation of open space for scenic enjoyment or pursuant to a clearly delineated governmental conservation policy, and the preservation of historically important land areas or structures. A transfer will not be considered as made exclusively for conservation purposes, unless the conservation purpose is protected in perpetuity. IRC § 170(h)(5)(A).

[348] IRC § 2055(f) provides that contributions of perpetual easements need not satisfy the income tax conservation purposes of Section 170(h)(4)(A). Thus, a mere bequest of a perpetual easement to a qualified organization for some conservation purpose (not limited to the income tax conservation purposes) satisfies the exception requirement and qualifies for an estate tax charitable deduction. See Joint Comm. on Tax'n, General Explanation of the Tax Reform Act of 1986, at 1257 (1987).

Such easements are generally valued by comparing the fair market value of the property before and after the granting of the easement. Cf. Rev. Ruls. 73-339, 1973-2 CB 68; 76-376, 1976-2 CB 53. These valuations may be difficult. Hilborn v. Comm'r, 85 TC 677 (1985).

[349] Section 2055(e)(4) was added to the code by the Economic Recovery Tax Act of 1981, Pub. L. No. 97-34, § 423, 95 Stat. 172, 316 (1981), reprinted in 1981-2 CB 256, 332. See Reg. § 20.2055-2(e)(1)(ii); Lerner, "Final Sec. 2055(e)(4) Regs May Result in Loss of Charity Deduction for Artist's Estate," 62 J. Tax'n 300 (1985).

must be to a public charity,[350] and the use of the work of art by the charity must be related to its charitable purpose or function.[351]

[e] Charitable Gift Annuity

A charitable gift annuity, which is similar to a split gift, qualifies for a charitable deduction even though it is not subject to any statutory exception. A charitable gift annuity is created through a decedent's outright transfer of cash or property to a charity under an agreement that the charity will pay an annuity to an individual or individuals.[352] Section 2055(e)(2) is appropriately inapplicable to such a transfer because none of the devious possibilities raised above occurs. The amount of the decedent's charitable deduction is the difference between the amount of cash or the value of the property transferred and the value of the future annuity payments.[353]

[8] Curative Amendments Permitted

[a] In General

Although Congress enacted Section 2055(e)(2) in 1969, imposing significantly different requirements for the deductibility of split-interest gifts to charity,[354] it was not until 1984 that Congress enacted permanent rules permitting the reformation of nonconforming governing instruments of both charitable lead and charitable remainder split-interest trusts to meet the requirements of the 1969 rules.[355] The provision in question, Section 2055(e)(3), in a parsimo-

---

[350] Section 2055(e)(4)(D) defines "qualified organization" as "any organization described in section 501(c)(3) other than a private foundation (as defined in section 509)." A private operating foundation, as defined in Section 4942(j)(3), is not treated as a private foundation. IRC § 2055(e)(4)(D). See also IRC § 2055(e)(4)(A), which requires a "qualified contribution," which is defined in Section 2055(e)(4)(C) to require a transfer to a "qualified organization."

[351] IRC § 2055(e)(4)(C). Cf. IRC § 2055(e)(4)(A). The second requirement would generally limit the scope of the exception to bequests to museums and, in selected instances, to churches and educational institutions.

[352] Priv. Ltr. Rul. 8045010 (July 22, 1980). The transaction is similar to a pooled income fund, although here an annuity is paid as compared with a pooled income fund, which pays out the income generated by the property. See supra ¶ 5.05[5][c].

[353] See generally supra ¶ 5.05[3].

[354] For a discussion of the rationale for the 1969 changes, see supra ¶ 5.05[4]. The limitations adopted in the estate tax area for deductible gifts of split interests are mirrored in income tax and gift tax areas. See IRC §§ 170(f), 2522(c).

[355] Deficit Reduction Act of 1984, Pub. L. No. 98-369, § 1022(a), 98 Stat. 1026 (1984), reprinted in 1984-3 CB (Vol. 1) 1, 534, which is the current version of Section

nious and complex fashion to further gifts to charity, permits a deduction under Section 2055(a) for a "qualified reformation."[356] Reformation under Section 2055(e)(3) is unnecessary if there is an arm's-length settlement of a bona fide will contest and, as a result, the charity ends up with an outright interest in property.[357] Because a qualified reformation must begin with a "reformable interest"[358] and end with a "qualified interest,"[359] it will be useful to look first at what constitutes a reformable interest and what is meant by a qualified interest.

[b] Reformable and Qualified Interests

Congress deliberately limited the availability of deductible reformations by defining the phrase "reformable interest" to encompass only two types of reformable interests. The legislative history indicates that an interest is only reformable when (1) there is a minor defect in the good-faith effort of the settlor of the trust to comply with the 1969 Act or (2) there is a major defect in the charitable gift, and an effort to reform the governing instrument in a judicial proceeding is instituted before the Service has the opportunity to audit the matter.[360] Both types of reformable interests must satisfy an initial requirement; they must have been allowed a deduction under the rules applicable to split-interest transfers prior to the 1969 Act.[361] Thus, the reformation provisions of Section 2055(e)(3) can remedy only those defects in governing instruments

---

2055(e)(3). The prior curative amendment provisions of Section 2055(e)(3) are discussed in Stephens, Maxfield, Lind & Calfee, Federal Estate and Gift Taxation, ¶ 5.05[8][f] (Warren, Gorham & Lamont, 5th ed. 1983).

See Laurice, "How to Achieve Reformation of Defective Split-Interest Charitable Trusts," 14 Est. Plan. 80 (1987); Baetz, "Tax Planning for Sophisticated Charitable Transfers: The Divide Between Downright Doable and Dangerous," 62 Taxes 996, 1004 (1984).

[356] IRC § 2055(e)(3)(A). The income tax and gift tax rules parallel Section 2055(e)(3) by permitting qualified reformations for deduction purposes. See IRC §§ 170(f)(7), 2522(c)(4), which adopt the rules of Section 2055(e)(3) for the income tax and gift tax provisions respectively.

[357] See supra ¶ 5.05[2][b].

[358] IRC § 2055(e)(3)(C).

[359] IRC § 2055(e)(3)(D).

[360] S. Rep. No. 169, 98th Cong., 2d Sess. (Vol. I) 731 (1984); Joint Comm. on Tax'n, General Explanation of Deficit Reduction Act of 1984, Joint Comm. Rep. 1116 (1984).

[361] IRC § 2055(e)(3)(C)(i). In general, the prior rules required that the possibility the charity would not take was so remote as to be negligible as well as inclusion in the gross estate and a valid charity. See Rev. Rul. 77-374, 1977-2 CB 329; Stephens, Maxfield & Lind, Federal Estate and Gift Taxation, 5-44–5-53 (Warren, Gorham & Lamont 3d ed. 1974).

that relate to the splitting of interests between charitable and noncharitable beneficiaries.[362]

A minor defect in a good-faith effort to comply with the 1969 Act rules qualifies as a reformable interest if, prior to reformation, the interests of all nonremainder beneficiaries are expressed as either a fixed percentage of the fair market value of the trust assets or as a fixed dollar amount.[363] A power of invasion for a noncharitable beneficiary is not such a minor defect.[364] The minor defects that qualify as reformable interests include errors in determining the payout in special circumstances such as a short taxable year or in years of additional contributions.[365] Unlike the reformable interest discussed in the next paragraph, the "fixed interest" type of reformable interest need not be reformed in a judicial proceeding so long as the reformation is effective under local law.[366]

The second type of reformable interest is not required to meet the "fixed interest" requirements just discussed. Instead, its ability to engage in a qualified reformation depends on the timeliness of an effort to reform the interest into a qualified interest. A reformation is timely if a judicial proceeding to reform is commenced no later than ninety days after the due date of the estate tax return (including extensions) or, if no estate tax return is required, the due

---

[362] See Rev. Rul. 85-23, 1985-1 CB 327.

[363] IRC § 2055(e)(3)(C)(ii). See TAMs 9326003 (Mar. 23, 1993), 199941004 (May 27, 1999) (for trusts failing to meet this requirement). This subsection refers only to the interests of noncharitable beneficiaries. IRC § 2055(e)(3)(C)(ii). The legislative history does not limit the interests to noncharitable beneficiaries but refers to "*all* current payouts from the trust." S. Rep. No. 169, 98th Cong., 2d Sess. (Vol. 1) 733 (1984); Joint Comm. on Tax'n, General Explanation of Deficit Reduction Act of 1984, Joint Comm. Rep. 1118 (1984). If this subsection permitted reformation of only the income interests of noncharitable beneficiaries, it would be applicable only to charitable remainder trusts and not to charitable lead trusts. This was not the intent of Congress, however; and the regulations, when promulgated, should adopt this view. This "fixed interest" requirement applies only to wills executed or trusts created after December 31, 1978. IRC § 2055(e)(3)(C)(iv); Wells Fargo Bank v. United States, 1 F3d 830 (9th Cir. 1993) (post-1978 codicil did not cause a will to be executed after 1978). It would seem that all wills executed or trusts created prior to 1979 are reformable interests, regardless of their terms and regardless of the timing of any judicial proceeding. See IRC §§ 2055(e)(3)(C)(i), 2055(e)(3)(C)(ii), 2055(e)(3)(C)(iii), 2055(e)(3)(C)(iv).

[364] S. Rep. No. 169, 98th Cong., 2d Sess. (Vol. 1) 733 (1984); Joint Comm. on Tax'n, General Explanation of Deficit Reduction Act of 1984, Joint Comm. Rep. 1118 (1984); TAM 9327006 (Mar. 31, 1993).

[365] S. Rep. No. 169, 98th Cong., 2d Sess. (Vol. I) 733 (1984); Joint Comm. on Tax'n, General Explanation of Deficit Reduction Act of 1984, Joint Comm. Rep. 1118 (1984); TAM 9327006 (Mar. 31, 1993).

[366] IRC § 2055(e)(3)(B). Cf. IRC § 2055(e)(3)(C)(iii). See also S. Rep. No. 169, 98th Cong., 2d Sess. (Vol. 1) 734 (1984); Joint Comm. on Tax'n, General Explanation of Deficit Reduction Act of 1984, Joint Comm. Rep. 1118 (1984).

date of the trust's first income tax return.[367] Congress intended that the initiating pleading must describe the nature of the defect requiring reformation in a manner more specific than a mere "general protective pleading."[368] The "timely commencement" reformable interest is designed to allow correction of "major, obvious defects (such as where the income interest is not expressed as an annuity interest or a unitrust interest),"[369] but only if the trustee or executor acts quickly without prodding from the Service.

With respect to both types of reformable interests, a "qualified interest" is defined simply as "an interest for which a deduction is allowable under" Section 2055(a).[370] However, to be deductible under Section 2055(a), the charitable gift must meet the requirements of Section 2055(e)(2). Thus, the process of converting a reformable interest into a qualified interest requires the terms of the trust instrument to achieve compliance with the split-interest rules.[371]

[c] Qualified Reformation

Now we come to the heart of the matter, the meaning of that vague phrase "qualified reformation." A "reformation" can include a change in the trust instrument by "amendment, construction or otherwise" as well as by for-

---

[367] IRC § 2055(e)(3)(C)(iii). Estate of Hall v. Comm'r, 93 TC 745 (1989), aff'd without op., 6th Cir. (1991); Zabel v. United States, 82 AFTR2d 98-5333 (D. Neb. 1998). According to the legislative history, a judicial proceeding commenced in the wrong court will count for purposes of the timeliness test. S. Rep. No. 169, 98th Cong., 2d Sess. (Vol. 1) 733 n.4 (1984); Joint Comm. on Tax'n, General Explanation of Deficit Reduction Act of 1984, Joint Comm. Rep. 1117 n.18 (1984).

[368] S. Rep. No. 169, 98th Cong., 2d Sess. (Vol. 1) 733 (1984); Joint Comm. on Tax'n, General Explanation of Deficit Reduction Act of 1984, Joint Comm. Rep. 1117 (1984).

[369] S. Rep. No. 169, 98th Cong., 2d Sess. (Vol. 1) 732 (1984); Joint Comm. on Tax'n, General Explanation of Deficit Reduction Act of 1984, Joint Comm. Rep. 1116 (1984); see Priv. Ltr. Rul. 8703069 (Oct. 23, 1986).

[370] IRC § 2055(e)(3)(D).

[371] This discussion of the split-interest rules ultimately refers not only to Section 2055(e)(2) but, more important, to Sections 642(c)(5) and 664(d) also. The 1984 Act establishing the permanent rules for qualified reformations also added Section 664(f), which permits certain contingencies that might accelerate a charitable remainder. Deficit Reduction Act of 1984, Pub. L. No. 98-369, § 1022(d), 98 Stat. 1026 (1984), reprinted in 1984-3 CB (Vol. 1) 1, 534; see also S. Rep. No. 169, 98th Cong., 2d Sess. (Vol. 1) 735 (1984); Joint Comm. on Tax'n, General Explanation of Deficit Reduction Act of 1984, Joint Comm. Rep. 1119 (1984).

See IRC § 2055(e)(3)(E) limiting the amount of the deduction for the qualified interest to the amount of the deduction for the unreformed interest; infra ¶ 5.05[8][c] text accompanying note 380.

mal judicial reformation,[372] and it must be binding on all parties under local law.[373]

A reformation is "qualified" if a reformable interest is converted into a qualified interest *and if* three other requirements are met. First, the difference between the actuarial values of both the reformable interest and the qualified interest cannot exceed 5 percent of the actuarial value of the reformable interest.[374] Second, in the case of a charitable remainder trust, the noncharitable interest must terminate at the same time under the reformed instrument as under the original instrument;[375] in the case of a charitable lead trust, the reformable interest and the qualified interest must be for the same period.[376] Third, the reformation changes must be retroactive to the decedent's date of death.[377]

These stringent requirements were adopted because Congress, rather puritanically, believed the reformation proceedings "should not be an opportunity to significantly revise the substance of the split-interest transfer, especially where the change reduces the charity's share of the trust."[378] Congress was also concerned that the reformation proceedings might be used to increase the

---

[372] IRC § 2055(e)(3)(B).

[373] S. Rep. No. 169, 98th Cong., 2d Sess. (Vol. 1) 734 (1984); Joint Comm. on Tax'n, General Explanation of Deficit Reduction Act of 1984, Joint Comm. Rep. 1118 (1984). There is no express provision to that effect, but presumably, the intent evinced by the legislative history will be followed as reasonable.

[374] IRC § 2055(e)(3)(B)(i). All of the values are determined as of the decedent's date of death. Id. Note that this rule does not prohibit changes affecting the relative interests of the noncharitable beneficiaries, whereas the legislative history suggests that such changes may be treated as gifts between such beneficiaries. S. Rep. No. 169, 98th Cong., 2d Sess. (Vol. 1) 733 n.1 (1985); Joint Comm. on Tax'n, General Explanation of Deficit Reduction Act of 1984, Joint Comm. Rep. 1117 n.15 (1985).

The rule appears to allow both positive and negative fluctuations. Thus, if the interest prior to reformation was worth $100,000, the value of the qualified interest may range from $95,000 to $105,000. See infra text accompanying note 380. Cf. IRC § 2055(e)(3)(E) limiting the deduction to a maximum of $100,000.

[375] IRC § 2055(e)(3)(B)(ii)(I). A pre-reformation interest in excess of twenty years is treated as satisfying this requirement if, after reformation, it is for a term of twenty years. IRC § 2055(e)(3)(B) (flush language). Of course, a reduction in the term would require an increase in the annual distributions so as to meet the 5 percent of actuarial value requirement. See S. Rep. No. 169, 98th Cong., 2d Sess. (Vol. 1) 733 n.3 (1985); Joint Comm. on Tax'n, General Explanation of Deficit Reduction Act of 1984, Joint Comm. Rep. 1117 n.17 (1985).

[376] IRC § 2055(e)(3)(B)(ii)(II).

[377] IRC § 2055(e)(3)(B)(iii).

[378] S. Rep. No. 169, 98th Cong., 2d Sess. (Vol. 1) 732 (1984); Joint Comm. on Tax'n, General Explanation of Deficit Reduction Act of 1984, Joint Comm. Rep. 1116 (1984).

amount of the charitable deduction;[379] consequently, it has provided in the statute that the deduction for a qualified interest cannot exceed the deduction that would have been allowable for the reformable interest had it been deductible.[380]

[d] Additional Rules Related to Reformations

Congress enacted several other rules related to charitable reformations. If the noncharitable income beneficiary dies or if, for some other reason, the trust should become "wholly charitable"[381] before the due date for filing the estate tax return, the reformable interest becomes deductible as though the split-interest rules had been satisfied on the decedent's date of death.[382] In the case of a charitable remainder trust that fails to meet the 10 percent remainder test,[383] such trust may be declared null and void ab initio[384] or may be reformed by reducing the payout rate or the duration of the annuity or unitrust interest.[385] The proceeding to reform or void the trust must commence no later than ninety days after the due date of the estate tax return (including extensions) or, if no

---

[379] S. Rep. No. 169, 98th Cong., 2d Sess. (Vol. 1) 732 (1984); Joint Comm. on Tax'n, General Explanation of Deficit Reduction Act of 1984, Joint Comm. Rep. 1116 (1984).

[380] IRC § 2055(e)(3)(E). One may question whether this provision was necessary in light of the first requirement of nearly equivalent actuarial values for the reformable interest and the qualified interest. See supra ¶ 5.05[8][c] text accompanying note 374.

[381] A trust is wholly charitable if its unexpired interests are devoted to the exempt purposes of exempt organizations. IRC § 4947(a)(1). Cf. IRC § 2055(e)(3)(F).

[382] IRC § 2055(e)(3)(F). See Rev. Rul. 76-545, 1976-2 CB 289 (application of reformation); Shriners Hospital for Crippled Children v. United States, 862 F2d 1561 (Fed. Cir. 1988); Harbison v. United States, 2000-2 USTC ¶ 60,389 (ND Ga. 2000); Rev. Rul. 82-97, 1982-1 CB 138 (amount of deduction on reformation); Priv. Ltr. Rul. 9623019 (Mar. 6, 1996). This rule seemingly adopts the principle of the *Ithaca Trust* case. See supra ¶ 5.05[2][c] text accompanying note 80. The legislative history, however, states that "in such a case, the charitable deduction is the actuarial value of the remainder interest before the reformation, adjusted for any payments made before the death or deaths to income beneficiaries." Joint Comm. on Tax'n, General Explanation of Deficit Reduction Act of 1984, Joint Comm. Rep. 1118 (1984); see S. Rep. No. 169, 98th Cong., 2d Sess. (Vol. 1) 734 (1984).

[383] IRC §§ 664(d)(1)(D), 664(d)(2)(D). See supra ¶¶ 5.05[5][a] text accompanying notes 200–204; 5.05[5][b] text accompanying notes 255–260.

[384] IRC § 2055(e)(3)(J)(i). In such event, no deduction is allowed for any transfer to the trust, and any transactions entered into by the trust prior to being declared void are treated as entered into by the transferor. IRC § 2055(e)(3)(J) (flush language).

[385] IRC § 2055(e)(3)(J)(ii). See Priv. Ltr. Rul. 200022014 (Feb. 29, 2000). The reformation may be made in conjunction with a reformation to satisfy other statutory tests. In that event, the other reformation (including the payout and duration) must satisfy the Section 2055(e)(3)(B) requirements. See supra ¶ 5.05[8][c] text accompanying notes 374–377.

estate tax return is required, the due date of the trust's first income tax return.[386] However, the statute of limitations for assessing any deficiency resulting from a null and void trust or from a qualified reformation does not run until one full year after the Secretary is notified of the reformation.[387]

Finally, Congress gave the Secretary broad authority to promulgate regulations to implement Section 2055(e)(3), including regulations relating to income taxation of trusts and estates as well as regulations permitting qualified reformations for split-interest arrangements involving pooled income funds, personal residences, and farms.[388] To date, the Secretary has not exercised that authority.

¶ 5.06 SECTION 2056. TESTAMENTARY TRANSFERS TO SURVIVING SPOUSE

[1] Introduction

The marital deduction provision came on the scene in 1948 with the general purpose and effect of permitting a decedent spouse to pass on to a surviving spouse approximately one half of decedent's estate free of tax. The background of the marital deduction provisions is considered at the end of this chapter, but a brief introductory comment on its origin is necessary. Estates of decedents owning community property with their surviving spouses are required to include in the gross estate only one half of that property. This is because the surviving spouse is deemed to own one half of the community property. The initial purpose of the marital deduction provision, speaking most generally, was to accord equal estate tax treatment to estates made up of separate property with those that include community property. Companion provisions, also enacted in 1948, sought more equal income and gift tax treatment in community and noncommunity property states.[1]

In the Tax Reform Act of 1976, Congress, in what was a compromise between limitations on the marital deduction and totally tax-free interspousal transfers, liberalized the marital deduction provision to allow tax-free inter-

---

[386] IRC §§ 2055(e)(3)(J)(ii), 2055(e)(3)(C)(iii).

[387] IRC § 2055(e)(3)(G).

[388] IRC §§ 2055(e)(3)(H), 2055(e)(3)(I).

[1] See IRC §§ 1(a), 2, 6013 (split-income provisions), 2513 (split-gift provision), 2523 (gift tax marital deduction).

spousal transfers in modest estates.[2] In the Economic Recovery Tax Act of 1981, Congress took the major step of allowing tax-free interspousal transfers regardless of the size of the estate.[3] The policy reason for the marital deduction has changed from attempting to equate noncommunity property with community property to allowing interspousal transfers without the imposition of estate tax. For fear of not being able to collect transfer taxes from a noncitizen, Congress denies a marital deduction to the gross estate of a decedent whose surviving spouse is not a citizen of the United States, except where the interest passes to the noncitizen spouse by way of a qualified domestic trust (QDOT).[4] Unless stated to the contrary, the discussion in this section assumes that the surviving spouse is a citizen of the United States and is not subject to such disallowance.

Only a careful study of the detailed language of Section 2056 will result in proper conclusions. It is still true, as the Supreme Court observed years ago, that "the achievement of the purposes of the marital deduction [remains] . . . dependent to a great degree upon the careful drafting of wills."[5] Accordingly, no problem dealing with the marital deduction should be considered in the abstract. Only a careful reading of all pertinent authorities will assure certainty as to the desired result.

The marital deduction is generally mandatory, not elective. At first blush, it would seem unlikely that the executor of the decedent's estate would ever want to waive the marital deduction, but in certain situations such a waiver, if possible, would be advisable. For example, if two spouses die within a short period, can the executor of the first to die waive the marital deduction in order to reduce the estate of the survivor? The reduction would cause added tax to be paid in the first estate, but if permitted, this could produce an overall lower estate tax, after taking account in the second estate of the Section 2013 credit

---

[2] Pub. L. No. 94-455, § 2002(a), 90 Stat. 1520, 1854 (1976), reprinted in 1976-3 CB (Vol. 1) 330. In general, the 1976 changes allowed tax-free interspousal transfers of up to $250,000 regardless of the amount of separate or community property in the estate.

[3] Pub. L. No. 97-34, § 403(a), 95 Stat. 172, 301 (1981), reprinted in 1981-2 CB 324. A comparable change was made in the gift tax marital deduction. IRC § 2523. See ¶ 11.03; Kurtz, "Marital Deduction Estate Planning Under the Economic Recovery Tax Act of 1981: Opportunities Exist, but Watch the Pitfalls," 34 Rutgers L. Rev. 591 (1982). A summary of the marital deduction limitations for prior periods is found in Regulations Section 20.2056(a)-1(c).

[4] Technical and Miscellaneous Revenue Act of 1988, Pub. L. No. 100-647, § 5033(a)(1), 102 Stat. 3342, 3670 (1988), reprinted in 1988-3 CB 1, 330. The rule is effective for estates of decedents dying after November 10, 1988. Id. at § 5033(d)(1), 102 Stat. 3673, 1988-3 CB 333. See infra ¶ 5.06[9] for a discussion of Section 2056(d); see also IRC § 2056A, which is discussed at ¶ 5.07; Reg. § 20.2056A-1(a)(1). In 1988, Congress also provided that a nonresident noncitizen whose spouse is a U.S. citizen is allowed an estate tax marital deduction. IRC § 2106(a)(3); ¶ 6.06[3].

[5] Jackson v. United States, 376 US 503, 511 (1964).

for estate tax paid in the first.[6] A more common circumstance occurs when a decedent spouse leaves all of that spouse's property outright to a surviving spouse depriving the decedent's estate of effective use of the decedent's unified credit.[7] The Service has ruled, no doubt correctly, that the estate tax marital deduction may not be waived for any purpose,[8] for it is not an elective provision. However, a surviving spouse (or often the personal representative of a surviving spouse where the surviving spouse dies shortly after the decedent's death) has the ability to avoid receipt of the property by means of a valid disclaimer, which, generally, has the effect of denying decedent's estate a marital deduction.[9] In addition, an indirect rejection occurs on the failure to make a qualified terminal interest property election under Section 2056(b)(7) or, where the surviving spouse is not a U.S. citizen, by failing to create a qualified domestic trust.[10]

[2] General Description

There are two basic features to the marital deduction. First, in general, the estate is allowed a deduction under Section 2056(a) for the value of any interest in property that either passes at death or has passed during life from a decedent spouse to a surviving spouse. The term "passes" is a special tax concept explained below, but it should be emphasized that the deduction is available for property interests that do not pass by will or intestacy, namely, property not in the probate estate.[11] Second, the interest passing to the surviving spouse must also be a "deductible interest"[12] in property in order to qualify for the marital deduction. An interest passing to a spouse is deductible if

1. It is included in the decedent's gross estate.[13]
2. It is not otherwise deductible under some other estate tax deduction provision.[14]

---

[6] See, generally, ¶ 3.05[3][b], especially text accompanying note 40.

[7] See, generally, infra ¶¶ 5.06[3][h] text accompanying notes 76, 80, 81; 5.06[6].

[8] Rev. Rul. 59-123, 1959-1 CB 248.

[9] IRC §§ 2046, 2518, discussed at ¶¶ 4.18, 10.07. See infra ¶ 5.06[3][h] text accompanying notes 75–81.

[10] See infra ¶¶ 5.06[8][d][iii], 5.06[9], 5.07, respectively.

[11] See infra ¶ 5.06[3].

[12] Reg. § 20.2056(a)-2(a).

[13] IRC § 2056(a).

[14] IRC § 2056(b)(9). This restriction includes a double deduction limitation for items otherwise deductible under Sections 2053 through 2058. For deductions otherwise deductible under Section 2053, such as a claim against the estate or a surviving spouse's commissions as the personal representative, see Reg. § 20.2056(a)-2(b)(2); infra ¶ 5.06[5][b][ii]. For deductions otherwise allowable under Section 2054, see Reg.

3. It is not a terminable interest. Generally, this is an interest that, if disposed of by gift or at death, may subject the transfer to the imposition of either gift or estate tax.[15]

The two basic features—interests passing and the requirement that these interests be deductible property interests—are discussed in that order, even though that arrangement requires a departure from the order of the presentation in the statute. The reason is that all other provisions in the section, important and detailed as they may be, merely operate in some fashion to qualify the two basic features; and the qualifying provisions can be much more readily understood with the broad outline of the section in mind.

[3] Interests Passing to a Surviving Spouse

The status of "surviving spouse" is determined at the date of death[16] by the law of the decedent's domicile.[17] Thus, a bequest to a former spouse gives rise

---

§ 20.2056(a)-2(b)(3). For the interrelationship of deductions under Sections 2055 and 2056, see infra ¶ 5.06[8][e]. For the interrelationship of Sections 2056 and 2057, see ¶ 5.08[4][a][i].

[15] Reg. § 20.2056(a)-2(b)(4). See infra ¶ 5.06[7].

[16] S. Rep. No. 1013, 80th Cong., 2d Sess. 1163, 1228 (1948), reprinted in 1948-1 CB 285, 335; see Rev. Rul. 79-354, 1979-2 CB 334.

[17] Estate of Steffke v. Comm'r, 538 F2d 730 (7th Cir.), cert. denied, 429 US 1022 (1976); Estate of Goldwater v. Comm'r, 539 F2d 878 (2d Cir.), cert. denied, 429 US 1023 (1976). If, as in this case, the decedent was divorced in another jurisdiction and a court in the decedent's domicile held the divorce invalid, the decedent's second marriage would not be valid and a transfer to the decedent's "spouse" of the second marriage would not qualify for a Section 2056 deduction. Similarly, if the decedent's first spouse "remarried" in their domicile, property bequeathed to the spouse by the spouse's second "spouse" would not qualify for the marital deduction. Estate of Steffke v. Comm'r, 538 F2d 730 (7th Cir.), cert. denied, 429 US 1022 (1976). Cf. Lee v. Comm'r, 550 F2d 1201 (9th Cir. 1977) (imposing the same test for the joint return requirements under the income tax); Rev. Rul. 67-442, 1967-2 CB 65. The Second Circuit may be more lenient in income tax cases using a federal "rule of validity" test. See Borax Estate v. Comm'r, 349 F2d 666 (2d Cir. 1965), cert. denied, 383 US 935 (1966); Wondsel v. Comm'r, 350 F2d 339 (2d Cir. 1965) (although it seems to be retreating from that test and examining the law of the decedent's domicile); see also Estate of Goldwater v. Comm'r, 539 F2d 878 (2d Cir.), cert. denied, 429 US 1023 (1976), which distinguished Borax and Wondsel as income tax cases.

An invalidation of the decedent's divorce by a court in a jurisdiction other than that of the decedent's domicile is not binding on decedent's estate. Estate of Spalding v. Comm'r, 537 F2d 666 (2d Cir. 1976). In such instances, the federal courts must make their own evaluation of what the highest court in the decedent's domicile would have concluded. Cf. Comm'r v. Estate of Bosch & Second Nat'l Bank v. United States, 387 US 456 (1967).

to no marital deduction.[18] However, one may remain a "spouse" for the purpose of the provision even after an interlocutory decree of divorce, if the decree has not become final and local law recognizes the spousal relationship until the decree is final.[19] To qualify for the Section 2056 deduction, the decedent spouse need not have been either a citizen or resident of the United States at the time of death.[20] However, if the surviving spouse is not a citizen, the deduction is generally allowed only if the interest passing to the noncitizen spouse does so through a qualified domestic trust[21] (QDOT).[22]

In general, if a predeceasing spouse owned or was treated as owning property and somehow the surviving spouse became the owner of that property, the "passing requirement" of the marital deduction section will probably be satisfied. This is not to say that a marital deduction will be allowed, but only that one requirement may be met. The statutory definition of the term

---

See also Rev. Rul. 76-155, 1976-1 CB 286 (claimed common law spouse was not a "surviving spouse" for purposes of Section 2056); TAM 200132004 (Apr. 25, 2001) (same); Ellsworth, "Prescribing TUMS: An Alternative to the Marital Deduction for Unmarried Cohabitants," 11 Va. Tax Rev. 137 (1992).

Marital status is not the only test here. This is also the survivorship requirement. Again, local law is important. See Reg. § 20.2056(c)-2(e); Estate of Gordon v. Comm'r, 70 TC 404 (1978), acq. 1979-1 CB 1 (the decedent's will presumed the decedent predeceased spouse); Estate of Racca v. Comm'r, 76 TC 416 (1981), acq. 1982-1 CB 1; Estate of Acord v. Comm'r, 946 F2d 1493 (9th Cir. 1991) (the decedent's will superseded Arizona statute that presumed spouse predeceased); TAM 9815008 (Dec. 22, 1997) (state "slayer" law did not determine order of death for purposes of disposition of slayer's property).

[18] Generally, the Treasury considers a divorce decree effective. But see supra note 17.

[19] Cf. Eccles v. Comm'r, 19 TC 1049, 1054, aff'd, 208 F2d 795 (4th Cir. 1953); Rev. Rul. 55-178, 1955-1 CB 322, revoked by Rev. Rul. 57-368, 1957-2 CB 896.

[20] IRC § 2106(a)(3). Section 2106(a)(3) is effective for decedents dying after November 10, 1988. Technical and Miscellaneous Revenue Act of 1988, Pub. L. No. 100-647, § 5033(d)(1), 102 Stat. 3342, 3672 (1988), reprinted in 1988-3 CB 1, 332. See ¶ 6.06[3]. For estates of decedents dying prior to November 10, 1988, Section 2106(a) provides for no marital deduction. However, the statute denying the marital deduction might have been overridden by the provisions of a treaty. For coverage of tax treaties, see Chapter 7.

[21] IRC § 2056(d)(2). See ¶ 5.07 for a discussion of Section 2056A and the requirements of a QDOT. Although a marital deduction is allowed, the establishment of a QDOT generally results in a mere deferral of the decedent spouse's estate tax. See infra ¶ 5.07[4]. See also IRC § 2056(d)(4) allowing a marital deduction if a resident noncitizen surviving spouse becomes a citizen by the time the decedent spouse's estate tax return is filed. See infra ¶ 5.07[5].

[22] Thus, if property situated in the United States is transferred from a nonresident, noncitizen decedent to a QDOT for a noncitizen surviving spouse, it will qualify for the marital deduction. IRC §§ 2056(d)(2), 2103, 2104, 2105, 2106(a)(3). See supra text accompanying note 21.

"passing" in Section 2056(c) is very broad,[23] as indicated in the ensuing discussion.

[a] By Will or Inheritance

An interest the surviving spouse receives from the decedent by bequest or devise or by inheritance under the laws of descent and distribution is treated as passing from the decedent to the surviving spouse.[24] The term "inherited," as used in Section 2056(c)(2), is given a broad interpretation.[25]

An interest in property need not be bequeathed directly[26] or outright to the spouse to meet the test of passing. For example, a surviving spouse's interest in a testamentary trust passes from the decedent testator whether it is an immediate income interest or a future interest that follows immediate interests in others, as long as, in either case, it is a beneficial interest.[27]

Controversy in this area is most likely to arise in cases of will contests.[28] If the surviving spouse surrenders an interest otherwise passing under the will, or assigns a testamentary interest to another in settlement, the interest is to be treated as not passing to the surviving spouse. The Treasury has so held for some time, and the law must be regarded as settled on this point.[29] However, if

---

[23] See particularly Section 2056(c)(4), which defines the term "passing" to include an interest in property which "has been transferred to such [surviving spouse] by the decedent at any time." See Estate of Lauder v. Comm'r, 68 TCM (CCH) 985 (1994) (redemption of stock from the estate of the deceased spouse at less than its fair market value by corporation partially owned by surviving spouse constituted a "passing" to surviving spouse of the proportionate benefit). See generally Reg. §§ 20.2056(c)-1, 20.2056(c)-2.

[24] IRC §§ 2056(c)(1), 2056(c)(2); Risher v. United States, 465 F2d 1 (5th Cir. 1972) (property bequeathed by will must be reduced by any valid pretermitted heir claims to determine the amount passing); Ritter v. United States, 297 F. Supp. 1259 (SD W. Va. 1968). There may also be a question whether an interest passes to someone other than the spouse. E.g., IRC § 2056(b)(1)(A). The same rules answer this question, as discussed infra ¶ 5.06[7][c].

[25] Rev. Rul. 55-419, 1955-1 CB 458.

[26] In Rev. Rul. 79-383, 1979-2 CB 337, the Service properly ruled that a bequest to the decedent's spouse's creditor constitutes a passage to the spouse for marital deduction purposes.

[27] Reg. §§ 20.2056(c)-2(a), 20.2056(c)-2(b).

[28] Reg. § 20.2056(c)-2(d). Passage under other types of litigation, such as a deed contest, does not qualify for the marital deduction. Cf. Estate of Burgess v. Comm'r, 38 TCM (CCH) 335 (1975).

[29] Reg. §§ 105, 81.47(a), 81.47(g), 20.2056(c)-2(d)(1); Schroeder v. United States, 924 F2d 1547 (10th Cir. 1991); Citizens & S. Nat'l Bank v. United States, 451 F2d 221 (5th Cir. 1971); Estate of Tebb v. Comm'r, 27 TC 671 (1957), acq. 1957-2 CB 7; Estate of Sikler v. Comm'r, 42 TCM (CCH) 1389 (1981); Estate of Frost v. Comm'r, 65 TCM (CCH) 2101 (1993). Cf. Priv. Ltr. Rul. 200025032 (Mar. 23, 2000) (no valid settlement where the surviving spouse transferred survivorship rights in a joint tenancy to the dece-

in settlement of the controversy the surviving spouse acquires an interest in the estate in "bona fide recognition of enforceable rights"[30] in the decedent's estate, such interest passes to the spouse from the decedent.[31] Tax litigation in the past,[32] raising questions whether amounts received in settlement of will contests are excludible inheritances for income tax purposes,[33] is indicative of the uncertainties in this area.[34]

---

dent spouse's bypass trust). See Land, "Property Surrendered by Surviving Spouse 'Flunks' the 'Passing' Requirement: The Tenth Circuit Denies the Marital Deduction in Schroeder v. United States," 69 Denv. UL Rev. 747 (1992).

[30] Rev. Rul. 83-107, 1983-2 CB 160. Cf. Ahmanson Found. v. United States, 674 F2d 761 (9th Cir. 1981) (no valid settlement); Estate of Brandon v. Comm'r, 828 F2d 493 (8th Cir. 1987) (no valid settlement); Estate of Fung v. Comm'r, 117 TC 247 (2001) (no valid settlement); Estate of Wegman v. Comm'r, 36 TCM (CCH) 497 (1977) (no valid settlement); Estate of Allen v. Comm'r, 60 TCM (CCH) 904 (1990) (no valid settlement); Estate of Suzuki v. Comm'r, 62 TCM (CCH) 1550 (1991) (no valid settlement); De Paoli v. Comm'r, 66 TCM (CCH) 1493 (1993) (no valid settlement); Estate of Mergott v. United States, 86 AFTR2d 2000-6634 (DNJ 2000) (no valid settlement).

See Estate of Carpenter v. Comm'r, 52 F3d 1266 (4th Cir. 1995) (even the valid settlement, the court denied a marital deduction because prior to the settlement the surviving spouse was not to receive an interest that qualified for a marital deduction because it violated the terminable interest rule); Davies v. United States, 87 AFTR2d 2001-614 (D. Me. 2000) (same). But see infra ¶ 5.06[3][b] text accompanying notes 47, 48.

[31] Reg. § 20.2056(c)-2(d)(2). See, e.g., Bel v. United States, 1973-1 USTC ¶ 12,925 (WD La. 1972), on remand from Fifth Circuit, 452 F2d 683 (1971), cert. denied, 406 US 919 (1972); Farley v. United States, 581 F2d 821 (Ct. Cl. 1978); Priv. Ltr. Ruls. 9610018 (Dec. 7, 1995) (valid settlement), 9733017 (May 20, 1997) (valid settlement), 200127027 (Apr. 4, 2001) (valid settlement). See also Peirce v. United States, 80-1 USTC ¶ 13,338 (WD Pa. 1980).

The amount actually received by the surviving spouse is critical. Pastor v. United States, 386 F. Supp. 106 (EDNY 1974); Estate of Moss v. Comm'r, 43 TCM (CCH) 582 (1982) (both cases limiting the amount qualifying for the marital deduction to the amount received in settlement of an intestacy claim, not the spouse's intestate share). Compare Rev. Rul. 83-107, 1983-2 CB 160 (further limiting the amount qualifying for the marital deduction to the value of the surviving spouse's claimed interest prior to the settlement), with Estate of Hubert v. Comm'r, 101 TC 314 (1993) aff'd on other issue, 63 F3d 1083 (11th Cir. 1995), aff'd on other issue, 520 US 93 (1997) (settlement resulted in the surviving spouse receiving generally deductible amounts in excess of amounts the spouse would have received had family members not contested the will).

[32] E.g., Lyeth v. Hoey, 305 US 188 (1938).

[33] IRC § 102.

[34] Cf. White v. Thomas, 116 F2d 147 (5th Cir.), cert. denied, 313 US 581 (1941).

[b] Dower

A surviving spouse's dower or curtesy interest, or any statutory substitute commonly now referred to as an elective share or a forced share,[35] is an interest in property passing to the spouse from the decedent by virtue of Section 2056(c)(3).[36] The claim for dower or curtesy must be timely filed under state law to qualify for the marital deduction.[37] Of course, if a spouse elects to take under a will or other transfer instrument in lieu of enforcing the right to dower, no interest passes to the spouse by way of dower within the meaning of the statute,[38] but the interest acquired by will or other transfer passes to the spouse for purposes of the deduction. It is obvious that, where a surviving spouse has an election, the estate should not get a deduction for both the interest elected and the dower interest that is rejected. An opportunity to elect to take against the will opens up postdeath estate planning possibilities. For example, in one case the decedent's will provided nothing for the surviving spouse because the survivor had substantial property; all the decedent's property was left to one of the children. When the survivor, on advice of counsel, elected to take a statutory share and then gave the property outright to the children, the court allowed a marital deduction to the decedent's estate.[39]

If property in which a spouse has a dower interest is sold with the spouse's consent to discharge estate obligations, residual amounts received by the spouse after the sale representing the spouse's interest in the property are amounts received as dower meeting the passing requirement of the statute.[40]

The same result should be reached if, by agreement or court order, cash or specific property is transferred to the surviving spouse in proper recognition of the spouse's dower interest or a statutory substitute in each of the various

---

[35] Dower and curtesy are common law rights that have been replaced by various statutory rights that are generally elective rights. When the term "dower" is used in the text, it is intended to encompass all such rights.

[36] Section 2056(c)(3) seems inapplicable to an interest passing to a spouse pursuant to an antenuptial agreement in which dower or curtesy rights are waived but, even if so, such interests meet the passing requirement. Rev. Rul. 68-271, 1968-1 CB 409.

[37] Estate of Goldstein v. Comm'r, 479 F2d 813 (10th Cir. 1973); Estate of Ahlstrom v. Comm'r, 52 TC 220 (1969). Each of these cases involved a state court approval of dower, even though the surviving spouse's claim was untimely filed. However, under the *Bosch* doctrine (Comm'r v. Estate of Bosch, 387 US 456 (1967)), the Tax Court refused to recognize the untimely claims for Section 2056 purposes. In *Goldstein,* the Tax Court was reversed because the claim had been allowed by mitigating circumstances under local law and federal law also recognized it.

[38] Reg. § 20.2056(c)-2(c). See Estate of Parker v. Comm'r, 62 TC 192 (1974), acq. 1974-2 CB 4; Estate of Mergott v. United States, 86 AFTR2d 2000-6634 (DNJ 2000).

[39] Harter v. Comm'r, 39 TC 511 (1962), acq. 1963-2 CB 4.

[40] Crosby v. United States, 151 F. Supp. 497 (ND Fla. 1957), aff'd, 257 F2d 515 (5th Cir. 1958).

estate assets. As it is almost impossible to excise a portion of each piece of realty and personalty in which a surviving spouse has an interest and transfer the
specific portion to the surviving spouse,[41] the practice is to satisfy the right by
way of an allocation of whole assets in an appropriate amount.[42] The property
thus received clearly passes to the surviving spouse from the decedent for marital deduction purposes,[43] but the amount of the deduction is less certain. In the
usual case, it would seem appropriate to measure the spouse's right at death
and allow the marital deduction in an amount equal to the value of what the
surviving spouse receives (determined at the time of distribution) but not in
excess of the value of the right at death, as excess amounts can hardly be
viewed as paid "in bona fide recognition" of the spouse's enforceable rights.[44]
If the estate elects the alternate valuation date and the value of the surviving
spouse's interest at that date is greater than its date-of-death value, the later
value should fix the upper limit for the deduction. This is because the spouse's
dower interest is in the nature of a specific bequest; and, when specific property is left to a spouse, the amount of the marital deduction for the property
varies in accordance with its value at the alternate date when the later date is
elected.[45] But it is still the survivor's interest in all the assets that measures or
limits the deduction. The fact that there has been an increase in the value of
the assets actually transferred to the spouse, which might result in the spouse
receiving an amount in excess of the value of the spouse's interest in the estate
at the applicable valuation date, is not material in measuring the deduction.[46]

On the other hand, the character of the property actually received by the
surviving spouse may bear on the marital deduction in another respect; where
a spouse's dower rights to nondeductible terminable interests in property[47] can

---

[41] See, e.g., In re Ginsberg's Estate, 50 F2d 539 (Fla. 1951).

[42] E.g., Florida Bank at Lakeland v. United States, 443 F2d 467 (5th Cir. 1971). Cf.
Carrieres v. Comm'r, 64 TC 959 (1975), acq. in result 1976-2 CB 1, aff'd per curiam, 552
F2d 1350 (9th Cir. 1977).

[43] Cf. Reg. § 20.2056(c)-2(d)(2).

[44] Cf. Reg. § 20.2056(c)-2(d)(2).

[45] IRC § 2032(b)(2).

[46] Florida Bank at Lakeland v. United States, 443 F2d 467 (5th Cir. 1971). This case
stands essentially for the proposition expressed in the text in that the excess alternate date
value of assets transferred to the spouse was disallowed. However, on the alternate date,
which was elected, the estate assets overall had increased $650 in value, and the court
nevertheless limited the deduction to one third (the spouse's statutory share) of the value
of the estate assets at death. The error, which was trivial on the facts, is important in principle.

The problem here is outside the area of Rev. Proc. 64-19, 1964-1 (pt. 1) CB 682, discussed infra ¶ 5.06[6][a], as the marital deduction would never exceed the amount actually received by the surviving spouse, eliminating any possible distortion.

[47] See infra ¶ 5.06[7].

be and are satisfied by assignments of property to the spouse outright, that property received passes to the spouse as a *deductible* interest.[48]

[c] Transfers

If an interest in property has at any time been transferred by the decedent spouse to the surviving spouse, Section 2056(c)(4) provides that the interest "has passed" to the spouse within the requirement of the section. Accordingly, an inter vivos transfer may give rise to an estate tax marital deduction. The transferee need not have been the decedent's spouse at the time of the transfer for the deduction to be available; the question is whether the transferee was the spouse at the time of death. For example, if before marriage Decedent created a trust, reserving the right to the income for Decedent's life, with a remainder to Decedent's significant other, and if they later marry and are still married at Decedent's death when the remainder passes to Decedent's former significant other who is now Decedent's spouse, Decedent has made a transfer that meets the passing (and all other) requirements of the marital deduction provision.[49]

Several further observations should be made here. First, this part of the definition of "passing" obviously does not qualify all a decedent's lifetime gifts to a spouse for the estate tax marital deduction; recall the requirement, which will be discussed more fully, that the interest be included in the decedent's gross estate.

Second, the definition of "passing" in Section 2056(c) is not confined to interests passing to a spouse. This is because the definition section has to do double duty. It has to say when an interest passes or has passed to a spouse, because that is an essential element of the deduction; but it has to provide, as well, a basis for saying when an interest passes or has passed to someone other than a spouse. That question becomes important in determining whether the terminable interest rule, discussed later, forecloses a deduction for some interests admittedly passing to a spouse.

Third, it is also important to understand that interests are to be treated as passing to a surviving spouse only if they pass to the spouse as beneficial owner. No interest passes to a surviving spouse merely because a decedent has transferred property to a spouse as trustee for others or subject to an enforceable requirement that, without any personal benefit, the spouse dispose of the

---

[48] Stephens v. United States, 270 F. Supp. 968 (D. Mont. 1967); American Nat'l Bank & Trust Co. v. United States, 266 F. Supp. 1008 (ED Tenn. 1967). See also Rev. Ruls. 72-7, 1972-1 CB 308; 72-8, 1972-1 CB 309. We pass beyond the "passing" problem here to the terminable interest qualification, a matter discussed in detail infra ¶ 5.06[7][b]. See especially infra ¶ 5.06[7][b] text accompanying notes 176–181.

[49] S. Rep. No. 1013, 80th Cong. 2d Sess. 1163, 1228 (1948), reprinted in 1948-1 CB 285, 335; Rev. Rul. 79-354, 1979-2 CB 334.

property for the benefit of others. This principle, of course, is applicable to all the paragraphs of Section 2056(c)[50] defining "passing."

[d] Jointly Held Property

If the decedent and spouse held property jointly with others with rights of survivorship, the surviving spouse's interest in the property after the decedent's death is treated as though it "passes" to the spouse from decedent under Section 2056(c)(5). If the property was owned only by spouses as a tenancy either by the entirety or as joint tenants with rights of survivorship, the entire value of the property is treated as passing to the surviving spouse,[51] but the deduction will in any case be limited to the value that was included in the decedent's gross estate. Thus, if the property was jointly owned only by spouses, and one spouse predeceases, generally only 50 percent of the value of the property will be included in the decedent spouse's gross estate,[52] and therefore only 50 percent will qualify for the marital deduction.[53]

If a married couple own property by the entirety or as joint tenants and have executed *joint and mutual wills* that provide for the disposition of the property upon the death of the survivor, the courts have consistently allowed the marital deduction in the estate of the first to die, to the extent that Section 2040 includes the property in the decedent's gross estate.[54] Judicial opinions in

---

[50] Reg. § 20.2056(c)-2(a).

[51] E.g., Estate of Awtry v. Comm'r, 221 F2d 749 (8th Cir. 1955); Estate of Richman v. Comm'r, 68 TCM (CCH) 527 (1994).

[52] IRC § 2040(b). Section 2040(b) does not apply if the surviving tenant is not a citizen of the United States. IRC § 2056(d)(1)(B). See also Gallenstein v. United States, 975 F2d 286 (6th Cir. 1992), discussed ¶ 4.12[10] text accompanying note 85.

[53] Suppose spouses owning property either in a tenancy by the entirety or as joint tenants with rights of survivorship die together in a situation where there is no clear and convincing evidence to determine who dies first. How much is includible in the estate of each, and is the marital deduction allowable? The Uniform Simultaneous Death Act provides that, where there is no clear and convincing evidence of whether one spouse survived the other by 120 hours or more, the property will be distributed one-half as if one spouse has survived and one-half as if the other has survived. The Uniform Simultaneous Death Act is adopted in almost all states. Cf. Priv. Ltr. Rul. 8239004 (June 18, 1982) (involving a presumption of survival clause). The end result is that one half of the value of the jointly held property is included in each spouse's estate under Section 2033. Applying Section 2040(b) to that one-half results in the inclusion of one quarter of the value of the property in each spouse's gross estate. Cf. Rev. Rul. 76-303, 1976-2 CB 266. That one quarter passes to the other spouse under Section 2056(c)(5) and qualifies for the marital deduction, leaving only one half of the value of the property to be included in each spouse's estate under Section 2033. This result is appropriate because the full value of the property passing to others is included only once in the combined estates.

[54] E.g., Ford v. United States, 377 F2d 93 (8th Cir. 1967); McLean v. United States, 224 F. Supp. 726 (ED Mich. 1963), aff'd per curiam, 65-2 USTC ¶ 12,326 (6th Cir.

these cases, which of course range beyond the mere question whether an interest in property has passed to the surviving spouse, are reasonably consistent in basic philosophy. For example, in the *Awtry* case[55] the Eighth Circuit held that the jointly owned property qualified for the marital deduction because the property passed to the surviving spouse under the express language of what is now Section 2056(c)(5) and, further, that the contract between the spouses could not convert the survivor's interest to a terminable one. In the *McLean* case[56] the court, also recognizing that the requisite interest passed to the surviving spouse, held that the decedent's will could not transfer an interest in the jointly owned property to any other person and that the *terminable interest rule*[57] therefore was not an obstacle to the deduction. If the *McLean* rationale seems to overlook provisions in the regulations on terminable interests, which assert that it makes no difference whether an interest passing to a third party passes by will or otherwise,[58] it is still accurate if it can correctly be said that no interest in the property passed to others from the decedent, because it was the act of the survivor (contractual or testamentary or both) that generated the rights of those who ultimately received the property. Policy considerations are not at odds with allowing the deduction, if the property will be effectively taxed in the estate of the surviving spouse.[59] Outside the area of joint and mutual wills, the disposition of jointly owned property is entirely unaffected by provisions in a will.

Tenancies in common and community property do not "pass" at all under Section 2056(c)(5), which is confined to property interests held jointly with survivorship rights. A decedent can bequeath an interest in a tenancy in common or community property to a surviving spouse and satisfy the passing requirement of Section 2056(c)(1).[60]

[e] Property Subject to a Power

Under Section 2056(c)(6), an interest in property over which the decedent had a power passes to the one who takes by reason of a lifetime or testamentary exercise of the power by the decedent, or merely by default in the case of

---

1965), 15 AFTR2d 65-1355 (6th Cir. 1965); Estate of Awtry v. Comm'r, 221 F2d 749 (8th Cir. 1955); Rev. Rul. 71-51, 1971-1 CB 274. Cf. IRC § 2040(b).

[55] Estate of Awtry v. Comm'r, 221 F2d 749 (8th Cir. 1955).

[56] McLean v. United States, 224 F. Supp. 726 (ED Mich. 1963), aff'd per curium, 15 AFTR2d 65-1355 (6th Cir. 1965), 65-2 USTC ¶ 12,326 (6th Cir. 1965).

[57] See infra ¶ 5.06[7].

[58] Reg. § 20.2056(b)-1(e)(1).

[59] IRC § 2036(a)(1); see Rev. Rul. 71-51, 1971-1 CB 274. This matter will have to be accorded further thought if the ultimate beneficiary of the joint and mutual wills ever successfully asserts a deductible claim against the estate of the second spouse to die.

[60] Cf. Greer v. United States, 448 F2d 937 (4th Cir. 1971).

release or nonexercise of the power. This provision makes no reference to the date of creation of the power or to whether the power was a general power; and, with Section 2041 in mind, it might appear to go too far. However, recall again that the mere passing of an interest in property to a surviving spouse does not assure a deduction; an interest treated as passing is deductible only to the extent that its value is included in the decedent's gross estate.[61] Thus, this part of the passing definition seems quite appropriate when read in conjunction with Section 2041.

Note that this portion of the definition concerns only property over which the decedent had a power of appointment. If the decedent spouse gives the surviving spouse a power of appointment, this in itself does not constitute an interest in property passing to the spouse.[62] However, it is of great significance, as explained later, in determining whether an interest that does pass to the spouse, otherwise disqualified as a terminable interest, will be allowed as a deduction.[63]

[f] Insurance

The includibility of proceeds of insurance on a decedent's life in a decedent's gross estate is covered principally by Section 2042.[64] Section 2056(c)(7) requires interests in such insurance proceeds to be treated as passing from the decedent to those who receive them. For example, proceeds of insurance policies that had been assigned as security for loans to the decedent's corporation were held not to pass to the surviving spouse from the decedent when the company received the proceeds, even though a resolution provided that the surviving spouse be reimbursed for any of the proceeds applied against the corporation's debt.[65] Of course, even if the proceeds are held to pass from the decedent to a surviving spouse, the deduction still hinges on whether the proceeds are includible in the decedent's gross estate.

Whether insurance proceeds are payable in a lump sum, are payable periodically, or are left at interest, an interest in the proceeds may be treated as

---

[61] IRC § 2056(a) (last clause). See infra ¶ 5.06[4].

[62] S. Rep. No. 1013, 80th Cong., 2d Sess. 1163, 1225 (1948), reprinted in 1948-1 CB 285, 333.

[63] See IRC §§ 2056(b)(5), 2056(b)(6), discussed infra ¶¶ 5.06[8][b], 5.06[8][c].

[64] See ¶ 4.14. Cf. IRC § 2035(a); ¶ 4.07[3].

[65] Estate of Heinold v. Comm'r, 24 TCM (CCH) 26 (1965), aff'd, 363 F2d 329 (7th Cir. 1966) (holding that post-death corporate commitments to the surviving spouse did not establish that the surviving spouse was in effect the beneficiary); see also Estate of Maxcy v. Comm'r, 28 TCM (CCH) 783 (1969), rev'd on another issue, 441 F2d 192 (5th Cir. 1971) (where under similar circumstances only the net proceeds actually paid to the wife qualified for the marital deduction, because she had no right of reimbursement under state law to the amount of proceeds used to satisfy the loan obligation).

passing to the surviving spouse.[66] However, the terminable interest rule and the exceptions to that rule, discussed later, must be taken into account to determine whether and to what extent a deduction will be allowed.[67]

[g] Other "Passing" Problems

The legislative history of the marital deduction provision[68] indicates that "[t]he definition of an interest passing from the decedent is broad enough to cover all the interest included in determining the value of the decedent's gross estate under the various [sections defining the gross estate]. . . . "[69] In general, this is borne out by the preceding discussion. There was once a question whether a surviving spouse's allowance for support during the administration of the estate constitutes an interest passing to the spouse from the decedent, because it cannot easily be brought within the "passing" definition of Section 2056(c), which purports to be exclusive. Of course, if the interest is disqualified as a terminable interest, it is idle to speculate on the passing point, because no deduction will be allowed in any event.[70] What if, under local law, the amount is to be paid to the surviving spouse or, upon the spouse's death, the full amount is to be paid to the spouse's estate and thus escapes the terminable interest rule? The Treasury concedes that support payments meet the passing requirement;[71] and some judicial decisions, taking the same view, have allowed marital deductions for a surviving spouse's allowances where it is determined that the spouse's estate would receive payment if the spouse died prematurely.[72]

This result finds some support in the legislative history of a provision in the Revenue Act of 1950 eliminating the old deduction for support of dependents, indicating that, subject to conditions, amounts previously deductible

---

[66] Reg. § 20.2056(c)-2(b)(3).

[67] Reg. § 20.2056(c)-2(b)(3).

[68] S. Rep. No. 1013, 80th Cong., 2d Sess. 1163, 1223 (1948), reprinted in 1948-1 CB 285, 332.

[69] S. Rep. No. 1013, 80th Cong., 2d Sess. 1163, 1224 (1948), reprinted in 1948-1 CB 285, 333. Although Section 2056(c) does not specifically provide for Section 2039 annuities passing to a surviving spouse, nevertheless the regulations properly state that an annuity interest may qualify for the marital deduction. Reg. § 20.2056(c)-1(a)(6). See TAM 9008003 (Nov. 13, 1989) (annuity property under various retirement plans passed to the surviving spouse). See also IRC § 2056(b)(7)(C). Cf. Priv. Ltr. Rul. 9729015 (Apr. 16, 1997) (IRA (which could have been taken as an annuity) taken as a lump sum and allocated to an IRC § 2056(b)(7) trust).

[70] Jackson v. United States, 376 US 503 (1964).

[71] Rev. Rul. 53-83, 1953-1 CB 395; Reg. § 20.2056(c)-2(a).

[72] E.g., Dickson v. United States, 240 F. Supp. 583 (D. Md. 1965); King v. Wiseman, 147 F. Supp. 156 (WD Okla. 1956).

under the support provision "will be allowable as a marital deduction."[73] The
passing requirement is not affected by the question whether payments will be
made to the spouse's estate in the case of the spouse's premature death.[74] But,
if they will not, the terminable interest rule, discussed later,[75] presents an obstacle to a deduction.

[h] Disclaimers

If, under Section 2046, a surviving spouse disclaims an interest in property that would be treated as passing under the definitional provisions of Section 2056(c), and the interest is treated as passing to someone other than the
spouse, the marital deduction is foreclosed for the interest.[76] In a sense this
overrides the general proposition that the marital deduction is mandatory.[77] But
this loss of the deduction occurs, quite properly, only if others will acquire the
interest as a result of the disclaimer.[78] Accordingly, a surviving spouse's disclaimer of rights under a will in favor of a larger share of the estate under
dower or other statutory rights will not run afoul of this disclaimer provision.[79]
Similarly, if the surviving spouse is the residuary legatee, a disclaimer of a
specific bequest to the surviving spouse, which will only enlarge the spouse's
residuary estate, will not operate to reduce the amount treated as passing to the
spouse. However, a surviving spouse may make a qualified disclaimer with respect to property where the surviving spouse continues to own an interest in
the property.[80] Such a disclaimer is often used as a postmortem planning technique where the decedent has left property qualifying for a marital deduction
to a surviving spouse and, as a result of the qualified disclaimer, the property
passes to a bypass trust in which the surviving spouse holds only an income
interest.[81]

---

[73] S. Rep. No. 2319, 81st Cong., 2d Sess. (1950), reprinted in 1950-2 CB 380, 478.

[74] Estate of Rensenhouse v. Comm'r, 252 F2d 566, 567 (6th Cir. 1958). See Reg.
§ 20.2056(b)-1(g) Ex. 8.

[75] See infra ¶ 5.06[7]. See IRC § 2518; ¶ 10.07. See also infra ¶ 5.06[8].

[76] Reg. § 20.2056(d)-2(a). See IRC § 2518; ¶ 10.07. See also Mulligan, "Spouse's
Use of Disclaimer on Outright Bequest Maximizes Credit and Adds Flexibility," 11 Est.
Plan. 328 (1994); Erbacher, "Federal Estate Tax: Minimization by Renunciation of Be-
quest or Devise," 40 UMKC L. Rev. 170 (1971–1972). Cf. Estate of Swenson v.
Comm'r, 65 TC 243 (1975).

[77] See Rev. Rul. 59-123, 1959-1 CB 248.

[78] See IRC § 2518(b)(4)(B).

[79] Cf. In re Uihlein's Will, 59 NW2d 641 (Wis. 1953).

[80] See IRC § 2518(b)(4)(A).

[81] Such disclaimers are used in situations where a surviving spouse wishes to reduce
the amount of property qualifying for the marital deduction. See ¶ 10.07[2][d][i]. Care
must be used in drafting the bypass trust. See ¶ 10.07[2][d] notes 88–89.

There is a converse rule with respect to a disclaimer of an interest by someone other than the surviving spouse. An interest in property left to someone other than a spouse, but disclaimed by that person in circumstances that cause the interest to go to the surviving spouse, does "pass" to the spouse for marital deduction purposes. Again, the result depends on that third person's meeting the Section 2518 disclaimer requirements.[82] However, the statute does not go so far as to increase the marital deduction by way of postdeath, third-party gifts to the surviving spouse. It is obvious that the rules on disclaimers add a further dimension to postmortem estate planning in circumstances in which a surviving spouse's testamentary or statutory share of the estate is in an amount that does not minimize estate tax liability.

[4] The Gross Estate Requirement

As stated earlier, a determination that an interest in property passes or has passed to a surviving spouse does not alone assure a marital deduction. Under Section 2056(a), the value of the property interest can enter into the computation of the marital deduction "only to the extent that such interest is included in determining the value of the gross estate."[83] The reason for this rule is not difficult to understand. Property interests that are not includible at all in the decedent's gross estate do not contribute at all to estate tax liability.[84] If the interest is not productive of estate tax liability in any event, no deduction should be allowed merely because it is left to a surviving spouse. Two simple examples illustrate this principle. In the first, one spouse, perhaps with motives associated with death, gives property outright to the other spouse. Because the gift will not be included in the donor spouse's gross estate, no estate tax marital deduction will be allowed.[85] In the second, property owned jointly by the spouses with right of survivorship is included in the gross estate of the prede-

---

[82] Reg. § 20.2056(d)-2(b). See IRC §§ 2046, 2518(b); ¶ 10.07[2]. See, for example, TAM 9228004 (Mar. 31, 1992), TAM 9301005 (Sept. 30, 1992). Cf. Estate of Boyd v. Comm'r, 819 F2d 170 (7th Cir. 1987); TAM 9818005 (Jan. 6, 1998).

The relationship of disclaimers and the marital deduction is discussed in Henkel, Estate Planning and Wealth Preservation ¶ 47.03[1] (Warren, Gorham & Lamont, 1997); Price, Price on Contemporary Estate Planning § 5.16.2 (Little, Brown and Co. 1992); Weinstock, Planning an Estate § 15.43 (Shepard's McGraw-Hill, 4th ed. 1995).

[83] See, e.g., Estate of Agnello v. Comm'r, 103 TC 605 (1994).

[84] It is not clear whether Section 2031(c) excludes a property interest or a mere dollar amount. The nature of the Section 2031(c) exclusion determines whether this limitation is applicable. See ¶ 4.02[7][e] text accompanying notes 375–380.

[85] See IRC § 2035, discussed at ¶ 4.07. But see IRC § 2523, allowing a gift tax marital deduction.

ceasing spouse generally only to the extent of one half of its value.[86] As just discussed, the gross estate requirement appropriately limits the possible marital deduction for jointly held property to the value included in the gross estate with respect to the property, even though, under the definition of "passing" in Section 2056(c)(5), the entire interest in such property passes to the surviving spouse.

[5] Valuation of Interests Passing

The gross estate requirement also has a direct bearing on the basic valuations of interests passing to a surviving spouse. Valuation for marital deduction purposes must be undertaken in accordance with the method of valuation[87] and the valuation date adopted for valuing the gross estate. If the date of death is used, it must be used for both gross estate and for marital deduction valuation purposes. If the alternate valuation date is elected, Section 2032(b) lays down a special rule for valuation for marital deduction purposes.[88] If real property valued pursuant to Section 2032A is specifically bequeathed or passes by operation of law to a surviving spouse, that value is used in the determination of the amount of the marital deduction.[89] Similarly, if real property is valued under Section 2032A, that valuation must be used in computing the amount of any marital deduction determined under a formula clause if the formula is applied to a group of assets that includes the real property valued under Section 2032A.[90]

Where a transfer of property to a surviving spouse[91] consists of less than a decedent's entire interest in property, it is appropriate to value the interest in

---

[86] IRC § 2040(b). But see IRC § 2056(d)(1)(B); Gallenstein v. United States, 975 F2d 286 (6th Cir. 1992).

[87] Estate of Evers v. Comm'r, 57 TCM (CCH) 718 (1989). See IRC § 2032A, discussed at ¶ 4.04.

[88] The rule is explained in the discussion of Section 2032. See ¶ 4.03[4][b].

[89] IRC § 2032A(a)(1); Priv. Ltr. Rul. 8422011 (Feb. 8, 1984). Cf. Reg. § 20.2056(a)-2(b)(1). Generally, no Section 2032A election will be made for real property specifically bequeathed or passing by operation of law to a surviving spouse. Although the estate tax inclusion will be offset by a corresponding estate tax deduction, the basis of the property in the hands of the surviving spouse will be less if the Section 2032A election is made. IRC § 1014(a)(3).

[90] Priv. Ltr. Rul. 8422011 (Feb. 8, 1984). However, fair market value may be used to fund any such bequest if the executor either is required or has discretion to do so. Simpson v. United States, 92-2 USTC ¶ 60,118 (DNM 1992); Priv. Ltr. Rul. 8314005 (Dec. 14, 1982). Cf. Priv. Ltr. Rul. 8708001 (May 9, 1986) (the executor with discretion funded with Section 2032A value). See generally infra ¶ 5.06[6].

[91] The same principle should apply to a Section 2055 charitable deduction. See ¶ 5.05[3][a] note 97.

that property passing to the surviving spouse as a separate interest in property,[92] rather than as an undivided portion of the decedent's entire interest.[93] For example, if a decedent owned 100 percent of the stock of a corporation and only 49 percent of the stock is transferred to the decedent's surviving spouse in a transfer that qualifies for a marital deduction, the value of the property qualifying for a marital deduction is subject to a minority discount.[94]

---

[92] See the discussion of premiums and minority discounts in ¶ 4.02[4].

[93] TAM 9050004 (Aug. 30, 1990). Cf. Chenowith v. Comm'r, 88 TC 1577 (1987) (in which a premium was placed on the value of a majority interest transferred to a surviving spouse); Ahmanson Found. v. United States, 674 F2d 761 (9th Cir. 1981) (stock given by the decedent to charity discounted from its value in the decedent's gross estate). See ¶ 4.02[4].

[94] See, e.g., Estate of DiSanto v. Comm'r, 78 TCM (CCH) 1220 (1999) (the surviving spouse's valid partial disclaimer of marital bequest converted the bequest from a controlling corporate interest to a minority interest with the result that the marital deduction was reduced by an amount greater than the disclaimed portion of the bequest). See ¶ 4.02[4][c].

Property included in a decedent's gross estate may have one value for gross estate inclusion purposes and, because of a minority discount, another lower value for marital or charitable deduction purposes. Thus, assume that in the year 2003, the decedent's gross estate consisted solely of stock of a wholly owned corporation worth $3 million, with one third of the stock transferred outright to the charity, one third of the stock transferred outright to the surviving spouse, and one third of the stock transferred to a bypass trust. Each of the one-third interests was worth $1 million for gross estate inclusion purposes. However, as a result of the minority discounts applicable to the marital and charitable deductions, there would be a taxable estate in excess of $1 million (the gross estate value of the bypass trust) generating tax liability in excess of the amount of the Section 2010 credit.

On a similar note, if a dollar amount of marital deduction is deducted on a decedent's estate tax return as a result of a direct pecuniary bequest formula clause (see infra ¶ 5.06[6]), but because of discounts related to such property the value of the property actually transferred pursuant to the bequest is less than the amount claimed, the difference in amount may be treated as an indirect transfer by the surviving spouse to the recipients of other property in the predeceasing spouse's estate. See Rev. Rul. 84-105, 1984-2 CB 197. For example, assume in the year 2003, a decedent owning a 100 percent interest in a corporation worth $1.5 million makes a direct pecuniary formula bequest of $500,000 to the surviving spouse and the remainder passes to a bypass trust with income to the surviving spouse for life and a remainder to their children. If the executor transfers one third of the stock to the surviving spouse and if a 30 percent minority discount is warranted with respect to that transferred stock, the stock transferred to the surviving spouse is worth only $350,000 ($500,000 less 30 percent of $500,000, $150,000). The Service appropriately takes the position that the surviving spouse receives $500,000 and then transfers the $150,000 difference in value to the bypass trust. The transfer is a transfer to which Section 2702 applies, resulting in a zero value retained interest and a $150,000 gift by the surviving spouse to the children. Additionally, the surviving spouse retains a life estate in a portion of the bypass trust equal to the ratio of $150,000 to the value of the bypass trust on its creation, which will result in that portion of the trust being pulled into the surviving spouse's gross estate under Section 2036(a)(1). A similar result should apply if a fractional share bequest is funded with a minority interest, i.e., the surviving spouse should have received one third of the gross estate but would have received only $350,000 out of

Section 2056(b)(4) lays down two special rules on valuation, discussed in the following sections.

[a] Taxes on Surviving Spouse's Interest

Additional valuation principles are to be applied if property interests passing to a surviving spouse are subject to charges or indebtedness. Section 2056(b)(4)(A) provides that if interests passing to a surviving spouse share the economic burden of any death taxes, state or federal, the value of such interests must be diminished accordingly in computing the marital deduction.[95]

---

the $1.5 million estate. Furthermore, if a reverse pecuniary bequest were funded, leaving only a minority interest in the stock to the surviving spouse, a similar reduction should be made to the amount of the transfer to the surviving spouse. This would result in either a reduction of the Section 2056 marital deduction (creating tax liability to the predeceasing spouse's estate), or if there were no reduction of the marital deduction, there would be an indirect transfer by the surviving spouse with the same results as in the preceding example. Some of these issues, as well as others, are raised in Aucutt, "What Happens When Nothing is Happening? Mellinger Acquiescence and Not Much Else," 26 Est. Plan. 496 (1999).

If two different shares in the same property are transferred to a surviving spouse (one either outright or under Section 2056(b)(5) and the other under a Section 2056(b)(7) QTIP trust) or if a surviving spouse owns property outright or in a revocable trust and has an interest in a QTIP trust, the QTIP trust included in the surviving spouse's gross estate under Section 2044 is not merged with the surviving spouse's other interest. They are separately valued (possibly with minority discounts) in the same manner as in the first example here (involving a transfer to a charity and to a surviving spouse). See Bonner v. United States, 84 F3d 196 (5th Cir. 1996); Estate of Mellinger v. Comm'r, 112 TC 26 (1999), acq. 1999-2 CB xvi; Estate of Nowell v. Comm'r, TC Memo 1999-15 (1999); Estate of Lopes v. Comm'r, 78 TCM (CCH) 46 (1999); ¶¶ 4.02[4][b] text accompanying note 158, 4.16 text accompanying notes 20–23 and articles cited therein.

[95] In Estate of Wycoff v. Comm'r, 506 F2d 1144 (10th Cir.), cert. denied, 421 US 1000 (1975), the court required a reduction of the value of the surviving spouse's interest where taxes merely could be paid out of the surviving spouse's interest. Viewed in isolation, Section 2056(b)(4)(A) does not seem to require this result. Nevertheless, it can be supported on the ground that, if the possible payment of tax out of the spouse's interest is taken into account, to that extent the interest fails to qualify under the terminable interest rule. Unhappily, the court in *Wycoff* accepts this as only an alternative basis for the decision. See also Adec v. United States, 83-2 USTC ¶ 13,534 (D. Kan. 1983) (reaching the same result): Rev. Rul. 79-14, 1979-1 CB 309 (the Service takes the same position). The question of where the estate tax burden falls is considered in the discussion of Sections 2205, 2206, 2207, and 2207A in Chapter 8. See also Kahn, "The Federal Estate Tax Burden Borne by a Dissenting Widow," 64 Mich. L. Rev. 1499 (1966). Cf. Chiles v. United States, 843 F2d 367 (9th Cir. 1987) (holding that Section 2056(b)(4)(A) was unaffected by the 1981 legislation).

Schedule M of the Estate Tax Return[96] reflects this requirement essentially as follows:

1. Value of interests passing to spouse $ _____
2. Less:
    a. Federal estate tax payable out of such interests: $ _____
    b. Other death taxes payable out of such interests: $ _____
    c. Federal and state generation-skipping transfer
        taxes payable out of such interests: $ _____
    Total of a, b, and c: $ _____
3. Net value of such interests $ _____

If interests passing to the surviving spouse are unaffected by death and generation-skipping transfer taxes, the preceding item 2 will be zero, and the net value will equal the total in item 1. If death or generation-skipping transfer taxes will be paid in part out of property interests passing to the surviving spouse, the proper figures must be inserted in item 2. This cannot be done until the amount of the taxes and the surviving spouse's share thereof is known. And that amount and share cannot be known until the marital deduction is ascertained, which is accomplished partly by correctly filling out Schedule M.[97]

Where and to what extent any interest passing to a surviving spouse must bear a part of the federal or state death tax burden is often a question of local law.[98] The consequence of local law is frequently determined by the federal

---

[96] Form 706, U.S. Estate (and Generation-Skipping Transfer) Tax Return (rev. Nov. 2001), Schedule M lines 4-6.

[97] The problem here, of course, is that the marital deduction and the amount of the tax are interrelated, and neither can be determined until the other is known. The problem can be solved, however, on a straight trial-and-error approach, by assuming a figure for the marital deduction, computing the tax with that figure, then checking to see whether the marital deduction as reduced by the spouse's share of the tax corresponds to the figure assumed for the marital deduction. By repeated trials and gradual correction of the error, a balance can be struck that can be proved to be the correct computation.

However, an easier method is usually available. A pamphlet explaining a detailed algebraic approach to this problem can be obtained from the Service. Even if the problem cannot be solved by the use of a mathematical formula, which is sometimes the case if a state apportionment rule is applicable, one may gain some assistance in the trial-and-error approach from other suggested procedures. See, e.g., Fed. Est. & Gift Tax Rep. (CCH) ¶ 6745 (1999); Fed. Taxes Est. & Gift (P-H) ¶ 120,576 (1988); IRS Publication 904, "Interrelated Computations for Estate & Gift Tax" (Rev. May 1985). See also Rev. Rul. 77-345, 1977-2 CB 337.

[98] Riggs v. del Drago, 317 US 95 (1942); Estate of Dawson v. Comm'r, 62 TC 315 (1974); Jeschke v. United States, 814 F2d 568 (10th Cir. 1987); Estate of Reed, 90 TC 304 (1988); Estate of Phillips v. Comm'r, 90 TC 797 (1988); Estate of Fine v. Comm'r, 90 TC 1068 (1988); Rev. Rul. 88-12, 1988-1 CB 330. But see IRC §§ 2205, 2206, 2207, 2207A, discussed in Chapter 8.

court determining the federal tax controversy.[99] Where a state statute is specific, there may be no substantial interpretation problems in the application of local law.[100] However, whether or not a state statute controls, a state court's determination of the property's liability for estate taxes is generally not finally determinative of the Section 2056(b)(4)(A) adjustments, which may be made by the federal court deciding a tax controversy under the principle of the *Bosch* case.[101]

[b] Encumbrances on Surviving Spouse's Interest

The second special rule on valuation comes from Section 2056(b)(4)(B), which requires a similar adjustment if interests passing to the spouse are encumbered or if the spouse incurs an obligation with respect to the interests.

[i] **Mortgages.** The most obvious illustration is a devise to a surviving spouse of realty subject to a mortgage. If the decedent was personally liable for the charge against the property, the full value of the property will be included in the gross estate,[102] which might make it seem that the marital deduction could take into account the entire value. Section 2056(b)(4)(B) forecloses

---

[99] Reno v. Comm'r, 945 F2d 733 (4th Cir. 1991); Robinson v. United States, 518 F2d 1105 (9th Cir. 1975); Estate of Penney v. Comm'r, 504 F2d 37 (6th Cir. 1974); Folkerds v. United States, 494 F2d 749 (8th Cir. 1974); Cox v. United States, 421 F2d 576 (5th Cir. 1970); Patterson v. United States, 181 F3d 927 (8th Cir. 1999) (determination based on postmortem trustee action involving a QTIP trust); Estate of Short v. Comm'r, 68 TC 184 (1977); Estate of Haskell v. Comm'r, 58 TC 197 (1972); American Nat'l Bank v. United States, 1976-2 USTC ¶ 13,141 (DNJ 1976); First Trust Co. of St. Paul v. United States, 402 F. Supp. 778 (D. Minn. 1975); Northeastern Pa. Nat'l Bank & Trust Co. v. United States, 360 F. Supp. 116 (MD Pa. 1973); Reed v. United States, 316 F. Supp. 1228 (ED Mo. 1970); Estate of Leeds v. Comm'r, 54 TC 781 (1970); Estate of Woll v. United States, 809 F. Supp. 643 (DC Ind. 1992); Estate of Lewis v. Comm'r, 69 TCM (CCH) 2396 (1995).

[100] Rev. Rul. 72-612, 1972-2 CB 528, holding Md. Code Ann., Est. & Trusts art. 93, § 3-203 (1969), precludes the surviving spouse's elective share of the decedent's estate being liable for taxes.

[101] Greene v. United States, 476 F2d 116 (7th Cir. 1973); Merchants Nat'l Bank v. United States, 246 F2d 410 (7th Cir.), cert. denied, 355 US 881 (1957); Estate of Sawyer v. Comm'r, 73 TC 1 (1979), acq. 1980-2 CB 2; Estate of Pangas v. Comm'r, 52 TC 99 (1969); Thayn v. United States, 386 F. Supp. 245 (D. Utah 1974); Estate of Swallen v. Comm'r, 65 TCM (CCH) 2332 (1993), rev'd on another issue, 98 F3d 919 (6th Cir. 1996). Rev. Rul. 78-419, 1978-2 CB 244. See discussion of the *Bosch* case infra ¶ 5.06[8][b][iii] and at ¶ 4.05[2][b].

Even if a federal court determines that local law would follow a decedent's intent to pay taxes out of the nonmarital deduction share (see supra text accompanying note 99), the marital deduction is reduced if there are insufficient assets in the nonmarital share to satisfy the tax liability. Martin v. United States, 923 F2d 504 (7th Cir. 1991).

[102] See "Mortgages" in the discussion of Section 2053 at supra ¶ 5.03[6].

this possibility, and only the value of the spouse's equity will be taken into account;[103] otherwise a double deduction could result, because the marital deduction would duplicate a deduction also allowed under Section 2053.[104] This conclusion, sound as a matter of tax policy, is also entirely in accord with the legislative history of the marital deduction provision, because the Senate Finance Committee Report indicates unequivocally that a mortgage operates to reduce the value of the interest passing to a surviving spouse whether or not the decedent was personally liable.[105]

If, under applicable local law, the encumbrance on property bequeathed to a spouse must be discharged out of assets not passing directly to the spouse; if it is so discharged, a downward adjustment in value under Section 2056(b)(4)(B) will not actually operate to reduce the marital deduction. The

---

[103] Regulations Section 20.2056(b)-4(b) provides for a reduction by the amount of the mortgage. Seemingly, this is the principal amount of the mortgage as compared to fair market value of the mortgage. Cf. Reg. § 20.2053-7, which uses the principal amount under Section 2053. In a similar but distinguishable situation, in Priv. Ltr. Rul. 9113009 (Dec. 21, 1990), the Service took the position that the value of property qualifying for a marital deduction (in this case an estate trust) that was subject to an unsecured guarantee had to be reduced by the aggregate principal amount (not fair market value) of the guarantee. The ruling was criticized in August & Kalunas, "Guarantors Have Unexpected Gift Tax and Marital Deduction Consequences in IRS Ruling," 74 J. Tax'n 346 (1991). The ruling was reconsidered in TAM 9409018 (Dec. 1, 1993) which properly reduces the deduction by the fair market value of the guarantee obligation rather than its principal amount. See August, "IRS Reverses Prior Ruling on the Impact of Guarantees on the Marital Deduction," 80 J. Tax'n 324 (1994).

[104] See IRC § 2056(b)(9) and "Mortgages" in the discussion of Section 2053 at supra ¶ 5.03[6]. As in the case of taxes, the question of the extent of the liability for encumbrances is a question of local law frequently determined by the federal court determining the federal tax controversy. See supra text accompanying notes 98, 99; Estate of Preisser, 90 TC 767 (1988); Estate of Williams v. Comm'r, 103 TC 451 (1994); Estate of Tenenbaum v. Comm'r, 112 F3d 251 (6th Cir. 1997) (case held in abeyance until local law determination in similar case); TAM 200104008 (Oct. 17, 2000) (marital deduction reduced by one half of the amount of a liability in a Section 2040(b) inclusion situation).

[105] S. Rep. No. 1013, 80th Cong., 2d Sess., 1163, 1227–1228 (1948), reprinted in 1948-1 CB 285, 335; cf. Rev. Rul. 73-98, 1973-1 CB 407 (charitable deduction reduced), modified by Rev. Rul. 93-48, 1993-1 CB 270. A contrary argument can be made. The statute requires valuation of the spouse's interest as if the value of a gift to the spouse were being determined. In Estate of Gwinn v. Comm'r, 25 TC 31, 41 (1955), acq. 1956-1 CB 4, the Tax Court took a gift tax decision, Comm'r v. Procter, 142 F2d 824 (4th Cir.), cert. denied, 323 US 756 (1944), to mean that "where the debt for which the property was pledged could have been paid otherwise than out of the pledged property the value for gift tax purposes would be the value of such property unreduced by the debt." Such an approach should be rejected as not consistent with the purpose of Section 2056(b)(4)(B). See also the discussion of gifts of encumbered property at ¶ 10.02[2][a].

Treasury's position,[106] with which the legislative history[107] and the Tax Court[108] agree, is that even if such an adjustment is required, it is offset by treating the payments made as additional interests passing to the surviving spouse.

　　[ii] Administrative expenses. In general, if pursuant to a decedent's will or local law a marital bequest bears the cost of paying administrative expenses or claims, the amount of the marital deduction is reduced.[109] To allow both deductions in their entirety would result in a similar double deductibility.[110] However, recently a much disputed issue has arisen whether the amount of marital deduction should be reduced if administrative expense items were deducted under the income tax because of a Section 642(g) election and they were paid out of income generated by an interest passing to the surviving spouse.[111] The Supreme Court, relying on a prior long-standing regulation,[112] held in *Hubert v. Commissioner*[113] that no reduction in the amount of the marital deduction was automatically required, but a reduction would be made if the amount re-

---

　　[106] Reg. § 20.2056(b)-4(b). See also Wachovia Bank & Trust Co. v. United States, 163 F. Supp. 832 (Ct. Cl. 1958).

　　[107] S. Rep. No. 1013, 80th Cong., 2d Sess. 1163, 1228 (1948), reprinted in 1948-1 CB 285, 335.

　　[108] Estate of Gwinn v. Comm'r, 25 TC 31, 42 (1955), acq. 1956-1 CB 4.

　　[109] IRC § 2056(b)(4)(B). Reg. §§ 20.2056(b)-4(a) (amended by TD 8846, 64 Fed. Reg. 67,763–67,767, 26 CFR pt. 20, reprinted in 1999-2 CB 679, 682), 20.2056(b)-4(b) Ex. 2. Estate of Roney v. Comm'r, 33 TC 801 (1960), aff'd, 294 F2d 774 (5th Cir. 1961).

　　[110] See IRC § 2056(b)(9).

　　[111] Some courts held that the marital deduction should not be reduced by expenses paid out of post-death income attributable to the marital share, on the theory that such expenses do not come into existence until after death and thus do not reduce the amount that the surviving spouse receives. Estate of Hubert v. Comm'r, 63 F3d 1083 (11th Cir. 1995) aff'd, 520 US 93 (1997), aff'g 101 TC 314 (1993); Estate of Street v. Comm'r, 56 TCM (CCH) 774 (1988), aff'd in part and rev'd in part, 974 F2d 723 (6th Cir. 1992). Other courts had held that expenses charged to marital share income effectively reduce the value, as of the date of the decedent's death, of the property passing to the surviving spouse. Estate of Street v. Comm'r, 974 F2d 723 (6th Cir. 1992); Fisher v. United States, 28 Fed. Cl. 88 (1993). Cf. Burke v. United States, 994 F2d 1576 (Fed. Cir. 1993) (reduction of charitable deduction for administrative expenses) some of the courts that required a reduction in the amount of the marital deduction for expenses charged to marital share income had taken the view that discretionary post-death interest paid on deferred or delinquent taxes or other obligations and claimed as an administrative expense should not cause a reduction. Estate of Street v. Comm'r, 974 F2d 723 (6th Cir. 1992). The Service agreed with this latter position. Rev. Rul. 93-48, 1993-2 CB 270, clarifying, but in essence expanding Rev. Rul. 80-159, 1980-1 CB 206, and revoking a contrary position taken with respect to the charitable deduction in Rev. Rul. 82-6, 1982-1 CB 137. The issue is also discussed at ¶ 5.05[3][b][ii].

　　[112] See Reg. § 20.2056(b)-4(a) (amended by TD 8846, 64 Fed. Reg. 67,763–67,767, 26 CFR pt. 20, reprinted in 1999-2 CB 679, 682).

　　[113] Hubert v. Comm'r, 520 US 93 (1997).

sulted in a "material limitation" on the surviving spouse's right to income.[114] After *Hubert*, the Treasury concluded that applying the material limitation test would be "too complex" and "administratively difficult,"[115] and promulgated regulations that took a different position regarding such "double" deductibility[116] with respect to the marital share.[117]

Under those regulations, the marital deduction is reduced if the administrative expenses (regardless of their nature[118]) are deducted under Section 2053.[119] This reduction precludes double deductibility.[120] The marital deduction is also reduced by the amount of administrative expenses that are deducted under the income tax as a result of a Section 642(g) election[121] and are paid out of the marital share but are related to nonmarital share property.[122]

To the extent that the administrative expenses attributable to the marital share are deducted under the income tax as a result of a Section 642(g) election, the issue of whether the marital deduction is reduced depends on whether the administrative expenses are "management" expenses or "transmission" expenses. Management expenses are expenses that might have been incurred even if the decedent had not died and that are incurred in connection with the investment of estate assets and their preservation and maintenance during a reasonable period of administration.[123] Examples of such expenses include in-

---

[114] The Supreme Court's decision in *Hubert*, relying on Regulations Section 20.2056(b)-4(a) (prior to amendment by TD 8846, 64 Fed. Reg. 67,763–67,767, 26 CFR pt. 20, reprinted in 1999-2 CB 679, 682) held that expenses charged to marital share income effectively reduced the value, as of the date of the decedent's death, of the property passing to the surviving spouse, but concluded that under the regulation, the reduction would not affect the amount of the marital deduction unless anticipated expenses were material in relation to anticipated marital share income. See Dodge, "Lifting the Shroud Obscuring *Estate of Hubert*: The Logic of the Income and Estate Tax Treatment of Estate Administration Expenses," 3 Fla. Tax Rev. 647 (1998).

[115] Notice of Proposed Ruling Making and Notice of Public Hearing, REG-114663-97, Supplementory Information, 1999-1 CB 443, 444.

[116] See Reg. § 20.2056(b)-4(d), which is effective for estates of decedents dying after December 2, 1999. Reg. § 20.2056(b)-(4)(d)(6). Prior to such date, the "material limitation" test continues to apply. See FSA 199921004 (Feb. 2, 1999).

[117] Reg. § 20.2056(b)-4(d)(1)(iii). The marital share is property passing from a decedent that is deductible under Section 2056(a). If under the governing instrument or local law the marital share is not entitled to income produced by the property during the period of administration, no reduction of the marital deduction occurs if the administration expenses are paid from such income, regardless of the nature of the administrative expenses. See Reg. § 20.2056(b)-4(d)(5) Ex. 7. See also Reg. § 20.2056(b)-5(f)(9).

[118] See infra text accompanying notes 123–129.

[119] Reg. §§ 20.2056(b)-4(d)(2), 20.2056(b)-4(d)(3), 20.2056(b)-4(d)(5) Ex. 4.

[120] IRC § 2056(b)(9).

[121] See supra ¶ 5.03[3][d].

[122] Reg. §§ 20.2056(b)-4(d)(4), 20.2056(b)-4(d)(5) Ex. 3.

[123] Reg. § 20.2056(b)-4(d)(1)(i).

vestment advisory fees, stock brokerage commissions, custodial fees, and interest.[124]

Transmission expenses are expenses incurred as a result of the decedent's death, such as expenses incurred in collecting the decedent's assets; paying debts, estate, and inheritance taxes; or distributing the estate's property.[125] Examples of such expenses include most executor's commissions and attorney fees (other than fees related to the investment, preservation, and maintenance of assets), probate, appraisal, and will contest fees.[126] Any administrative expenses not falling into the management category are treated as transmission expenses.[127]

Transmission expenses reduce the amount of the marital deduction even though they are deducted under the income tax as a result of a Section 642(g) election.[128] However, managerial expenses (to the extent that they are deducted under the income tax as a result of a Section 642(g) election) do not reduce the value of the marital deduction.[129]

[iii] **Assumption of an obligation.** A bequest to a spouse conditioned on the spouse's assuming an obligation operates to reduce the value of the property passing to the spouse for purposes of the marital deduction. And this would seem to be true regardless of how the obligation is in fact discharged.[130]

In *United States v. Stapf*,[131] the decedent's will provided that if the surviving spouse permitted that spouse's interest in the community property to

---

[124] Reg. § 20.2056(b)-4(d)(1)(i).

[125] Reg. § 20.2056(b)-4(d)(1)(ii).

[126] Reg. § 20.2056(b)-4(d)(1)(ii).

[127] Reg. § 20.2056(b)-4(d)(1)(ii).

[128] Reg. §§ 20.2056(b)-4(d)(2), 20.2056(b)-4(d)(5) Ex. 1. If the transmission expenses are deducted under Section 2053, they also reduce the marital deduction. See supra text accompanying notes 118, 119.

The regulations contain two examples involving transmission expenses and formula clauses involving a nontaxable estate, one with a direct pecuniary bequest (Reg. § 20.2056(b)-4(d)(5) Ex. 5) and one with a reverse pecuniary bequest (Reg. § 20.2056(b)-4(d)(5) Ex. 6).

[129] Reg. §§ 20.2056(b)-4(d)(3), 20.2056(b)-4(d)(5) Ex. 2. If the management expenses are deducted under Section 2053, they reduce the amount of the marital deduction. See supra text accompanying note 119.

See Gans, Blattmachr & McCaffrey, "The Anti-Hubert Regulations," 87 Tax Notes 969 (May 15, 2000) (discussing the regulations and appropriately concluding that "[i]n virtually all cases, it will be preferable to take an income tax deduction for such [management] expenses" and providing several drafting suggestions with respect to the regulations); Budin, "Final *Hubert* Regulations Will Require Review of Many Estate Plans," 92 J. Tax'n 225 (Apr. 2000).

[130] Reg. § 20.2056(b)-4(b) Ex. 1. Cf. Reg. §§ 20.2056(b)-4(b) Exs. 2, 3, and the discussion of joint and mutual wills infra ¶ 5.06[8][d][iv].

[131] United States v. Stapf, 375 US 118 (1963).

pass to a trust for the benefit of the children, the surviving spouse would receive one third of the community property and of the decedent's separate property, and the estate would bear the community property debts and its
administration expenses. By electing to take under the will, the surviving
spouse surrendered (net) one sixth of the whole community property, to which
the spouse was otherwise entitled, and received by devise under the will about
$5,000 less than the value of the property interest relinquished.[132] The execu-
tors claimed a marital deduction for the value of the one-third interest in the
decedent's separate property passing to the surviving spouse. The Supreme
Court held that the marital deduction is permissible only insofar as the property devised to the surviving spouse exceeds in value the property the surviving spouse is required to relinquish in order to take under the will. The Court
took occasion to endorse the following example in the regulations:[133]

> A decedent bequeathed certain securities to his wife in lieu of her in-
> terest in property held by them as community property. . . . The wife
> elected to relinquish her community property interest and to take the be-
> quest. For purposes of the marital deduction, the value of the bequest is to
> be reduced by the value of the community property interest relinquished
> by the wife.

Payments by a surviving spouse or by persons other than the estate in discharge of obligations with respect to property passing to the spouse will never
prevent a downward adjustment in value otherwise required by Section
2056(b)(4)(B).[134] In this connection, a general thought expressed in the legislative history of the marital deduction provision is relevant:[135]

> The interest passing to the surviving spouse from the decedent is
> only such interest as the decedent can give. If the decedent by his will
> leaves the residue of his estate to the surviving spouse and she pays, or if
> the estate income is used to pay, claims against the estate so as to in-
> crease the residue, such increase in the residue is acquired by purchase
> and not by bequest. Accordingly, the value of any such additional part of
> the residue passing to the surviving spouse cannot be included in the
> amount of the marital deduction.

---

[132] The transaction can be accurately described in more than one way. See United
States v. Stapf, 375 US 118, 122 n.6 (1963).

[133] Reg. § 20.2056(b)-4(b) Ex. 3.

[134] Estate of Hohensee v. Comm'r, 25 TC 1258 (1956); Murray v. United States, 687
F2d 386 (Cl. Ct. 1982); TAM 200131001 (Feb. 26, 2001).

[135] S. Rep. No. 1013, 80th Cong., 2d Sess. 1163, 1228 (1948), reprinted in 1948-1
CB 285, 335. See also Estate of Horne v. Comm'r, 91 TC 100 (1988); Priv. Ltr. Rul.
8823001 (Feb. 19, 1988).

[6] Formula Clauses

The marital deduction has been dramatically altered from a maximum deduction of roughly one half of a decedent's estate, first, to an unlimited marital deduction for modest estates, and, currently, to an unlimited deduction for all estates.[136] Although the objectives of this book are not geared to estate planning, it must be noted that in most situations the predeceasing spouse may not wish to transfer all of his or her property to the surviving spouse, regardless of the fact that the transfer would fully qualify for the marital deduction. In many of those situations, the decedent's objective would be one of estate *tax* planning. No estate tax planning problem is present where the amounts included in the combined estates of both spouses are well below an amount of inclusion that would be sheltered from taxation by the Section 2010 credit and are expected to remain so.[137] Once the combined estates approach or exceed the shelter of the Section 2010 credit, efforts should be made to reduce the predeceasing spouse's deductible bequest to the surviving spouse at least by the amount of the applicable exclusion amount provided by the Section 2010 credit (or a sufficient amount of it so that the surviving spouse's estate will likely be less than the applicable exclusion amount available to the survivor)[138] so as to reduce the combined estate taxes on both estates. This is frequently accomplished by means of a trust in which the surviving spouse has a terminable interest that does not qualify for the marital deduction. This type of trust is commonly referred to as a bypass trust or a credit shelter trust. In smaller estates, the surviving spouse generally enjoys the full economic benefit of the property through a life estate combined with invasion powers subject to an ascertainable standard, but at death the trust bypasses the surviving spouse's gross estate because no amount is required to be included in the gross estate of the surviving spouse.[139]

---

[136] See supra ¶ 5.06[1].

[137] In 1987 and thereafter, if no inter vivos gifts have been made, the Section 2010 credit will shelter a taxable estate of up to the applicable exclusion amount from taxation. Thus, if after 1997 the combination of both spouses' estates is well below the applicable exclusion amount, no estate tax planning is necessary. See ¶ 3.02 for a discussion of the applicable exclusion amount and the exemption provided by the credit.

[138] See ¶ 3.02; supra ¶ 5.06[1]. From 1987 through 2009, the Section 2010 credit shelters taxable estates from $600,000 to $3.5 million from estate tax, assuming the decedent had made no taxable lifetime gifts.

[139] Of course, generally in large estates, a bypass (or credit shelter) trust may completely bypass a surviving spouse. Planning for bypass trusts is discussed at Henkel, Estate Planning and Wealth Preservation ¶¶ 4.03, 4.04, 49.02[2][b], 49.02[2][c] (Warren, Gorham & Lamont, 1997); Price, Price on Contemporary Estate Planning § 5.9 (Little Brown and Co. 1992); Weinstock, Planning an Estate § 5 (Shepard's McGraw-Hill, 4th ed. 1995).

There are many other estate planning aspects to the marital deduction,[140] which are beyond the scope of this book.[141] However, when the marital deduction is used, some type of will provision known as a formula clause will likely be used to achieve the decedent's objectives. Formula clauses usually take the form of a pecuniary or fractional share bequest. The following examples illustrate typical will provisions and formula clauses:[142]

1. Pecuniary bequest, e.g., a bequest of "$100,000 to my loving spouse." This requires a prediction of the desired amount.
2. A more sophisticated variation—a formula pecuniary bequest. An example is, "I hereby bequeath to my spouse an amount equal to the maximum marital deduction less interests passing to my spouse which are includible in my gross estate but not in my probate estate and less an amount which takes account of all available credits and deductions to the maximum extent without causing any federal estate tax."
3. Another variation is the nonformula fractional share bequest. An example is, "I hereby leave to my spouse an amount equal to [*some fraction of*] my residuary estate."
4. The most sophisticated type—a formula fractional share. This form varies from the straight fractional share approach only in that the fraction is fixed by a formula.[143] This formula, which establishes a fraction to be applied to the residuary estate, may have as its numerator the amount of the maximum marital deduction computed in the

---

[140] See, e.g., Henkel, Estate Planning and Wealth Preservation ¶¶ 4.01–4.07, 49.01–49.08 (Warren, Gorham & Lamont, 1997); Price, Price on Contemporary Estate Planning § 5 (Little Brown and Co. 1992); Weinstock, Planning an Estate § 4 (Shepard's McGraw-Hill, 4th ed. 1995); Gingiss, "Marital Deduction Planning Under ERTA '81," 60 Taxes 269 (1982); Smith, "Unlimited Marital Deduction Increases Planning Flexibility and Triggers Redrafting," 8 Est. Plan. 336 (1981); Keydel, "Estate and Gift Tax Changes Made by the Economic Recovery Tax Act of 1981," 17 Real Prop., Prob. & Tr. J. 18 (1982); Garlock, "Estate Tax Unlimited Marital Deduction Has Limited Advantages in Larger Estates," 56 J. Tax'n 236 (1982); Mulligan, "Drafting Marital Deduction Formula Clauses After ERTA," 29 St. Louis BJ 28 (1982); Llewellyn, "Computing the Optimum Marital Deduction: Is a Zero-Tax Formula Appropriate?" 24 Real Prop., Prob. & Tr. J. 331 (1989); Kasner, "The 'Optimum' Marital Deduction—Pay Now or Pay Later," 43 NYU Inst. on Fed. Tax'n 54.1 (1985).

[141] Arguably, pursuing a preoccupation with tax considerations may be unwarranted in many estates.

[142] These examples are intended only to illustrate a general pattern of bequests and are not "forms" or model bequests.

[143] See Henkel, Estate Planning and Wealth Preservation ¶ 49.02[2][a][vi] (Warren, Gorham & Lamont, 1997); Price, Price on Contemporary Estate Planning § 5.38 (Little Brown and Co. 1992); Weinstock, Planning an Estate § 4.32 (Shepard's McGraw-Hill, 4th ed. 1995); Casner, "How to Use Fractional Share Marital Deduction Gifts," 99 Tr. Est. 190 (1960). (This early article must be viewed with an eye on subsequent statutory changes.)

same manner as in the second example, over the residuary estate as the denominator.

[a] Special Problem With a Pecuniary Bequest to a Surviving Spouse

A pecuniary marital deduction bequest with the valuation of property distributed in kind to be made on the date of distribution shifts postdeath appreciation from the surviving spouse to the residuary legatees, who also are called on to absorb postdeath shrinkage in value.[144] One drawback to a pecuniary marital deduction bequest is that the estate will have a realized gain if appreciated property is paid to the surviving spouse in satisfaction of a pecuniary bequest; the discharge of the obligation produces realized gain to the extent of the difference between the basis of the property and the obligation discharged.[145] Alternatively, if the assets in the estate decline in value prior to distribution, the surviving spouse will receive a disproportionately large portion of the estate.[146]

Both problems could be eliminated if the executor were allowed to satisfy the bequest with assets valued at their federal estate tax value rather than their date of distribution value. However, the Service, in Revenue Procedure 64-19,[147] has established guidelines restricting the use of pecuniary bequests that are to be satisfied with estate tax values.[148] Revenue Procedure 64-19 will disallow the marital deduction if the executor is required to or has an opportunity to satisfy the bequest by a transfer of property in kind, using estate tax values,

---

[144] For example, assume an estate in 2003 of $1.5 million using estate tax values, and the pecuniary amount under the formula clause is $500,000. If the estate assets appreciate to $1.9 million at the date of distribution, the amount payable to the surviving spouse remains $500,000 and the residuary legatees receive $1.4 million; but if the property declines in value to $900,000, the surviving spouse still receives $500,000 with the residuary legatees receiving only $400,000.

Under a fractional share formula clause, the surviving spouse and the bypass trust would generally share proportionately in any post-death appreciation or depreciation in the value of the assets.

[145] Suisman v. Eaton, 15 F. Supp. 113 (D. Conn. 1935), aff'd, 83 F2d 1019 (2d Cir), cert. denied, 299 US 573 (1936); Kenan v. Comm'r, 114 F2d 217 (2d Cir. 1940); Rev. Rul. 60-87, 1960-1 CB 286. Cf. United States v. Davis, 370 US 65 (1965). See IRC § 1014(a).

[146] See supra note 144. An income tax deduction may be allowed for such losses. See, generally, IRC §§ 165(c), 267(b)(13), 1223(11).

[147] Rev. Proc. 64-19, 1964-1 (pt. 1) CB 682.

[148] The procedure only deals with the pecuniary bequest; it does not apply to transfers by will of specific assets or a fractional share of the estate, which proportionately reflects appreciation or depreciation on the dates of distribution.

Section 2056

unless applicable state law including a state statute,[149] common law,[150] or provisions of the will require that the fiduciary distribute to the surviving spouse either (1) assets having an aggregate fair market value, on the dates of distribution, not less than the amount of the pecuniary bequest as finally determined for federal estate tax purposes[151] or (2) assets fairly representative of appreciation or depreciation in the value of all property available for the distribution in satisfaction of the pecuniary bequest.[152] On the other hand, the revenue procedure will not disallow the deduction if the fiduciary must satisfy the pecuniary bequest solely in cash, or possesses no discretion in selecting the assets that may be distributed in kind, or must value the assets selected for distribution in kind at the values as of the dates of distribution.

The rationale of the ruling is clear. If the executor is permitted to distribute property to the surviving spouse in satisfaction of the bequest and the property will discharge the obligation at its estate tax value even though the property has greatly appreciated or depreciated in value since the federal estate tax valuation, the amount passing to the surviving spouse is not ascertainable at the moment of death. And the date of death is the time at which the bequest to the surviving spouse must be determinable.[153] To this technical reason for disallowance may be added the practical thought that the executor could possibly distribute to the surviving spouse property that had become valueless and distribute appreciated property to the other recipients of the estate;[154] even if the surviving spouse's property had substantial value at death, it would be

---

[149] E.g., NY Est. Powers & Trusts Law § 2-1.9 (McKinney 2002) and Special Ruling (Oct. 14, 1964); Cal. Prob. Code § 21120 (West 2001); Fla. Stat. § 733.810 (2001).

[150] Estate of Hamelsky v. Comm'r, 58 TC 741 (1972), nonacq. 1973-1 CB 2 (recognizing that New Jersey cases require the executor under his fiduciary obligation to distribute to the surviving spouse assets that are fairly representative of appreciation and depreciation in value).

[151] See Estate of de St. Aubin v. Comm'r, 76 TCM (CCH) 409 (1998) (the decedent died in 1967, but the trust was not funded until 1983 with huge appreciation escaping the Service's grasp).

[152] The disallowance is based on a violation of the terminable interest rule. See infra ¶ 5.06[7].

The importance of Rev. Proc. 64-19 1964-1 (pt. 1) CB 682, is considered at length in Covey, The Marital Deduction and the Use of Formula Provisions 99 (1978); see also Edwards, "Marital Deduction Formula, A Planner's Guide," 1967 Duke LJ 254 (1967); Polasky, "Marital Deduction Formula Clauses in Estate Planning—Estate and Income Tax Considerations," 63 Mich. L. Rev. 809 (1965). These early articles must be viewed with one eye on later statutory changes. See also Featherston, "The Funding of Formula Marital Deduction Gifts After the Economic Recovery Tax Act of 1981," 27 S. Tex. LJ 99 (1986).

[153] Jackson v. United States, 376 US 503 (1964).

[154] Compare Rev. Rul. 90-3, 1990-1 CB 174, where the Treasury sanctioned the use of a pecuniary bequest to a bypass trust with assets valued at the date of the distribution. Although there was a possibility at the decedent's death that the residual marital bequest

anomalous to allow a marital deduction for property that was worth nothing going to the spouse. Where the executor has, in effect, the power to fix the amount the surviving spouse will receive, the certainty requisite to the marital deduction is lacking.[155]

[b] Outdated Formula Clauses

The unlimited marital deduction is generally applicable to estates of decedents dying after December 31, 1981. However, under a transitional rule,[156] the unlimited marital deduction may not apply to estates of decedents dying after December 31, 1981, if the decedent's will or trust agreement contains a maximum formula marital deduction clause and was executed prior to September 12, 1981. The transitional rule, which rarely applies today, prevents unintended dispositions of a decedent's property due to congressional action to change the amount of the marital deduction.[157]

---

might be underfunded, there was no dual threat of overfunding the bypass trust as could have occurred in the situation disapproved of in Rev. Proc. 64-19, 1964-1 (Pt. 1) CB 682.

[155] Admittedly, such flexibility is allowed with respect to QTIP trusts through an executor's ability to elect or not to elect QTIP treatment (see infra ¶ 5.06[8][d][iii]) especially where the surviving spouse's right to receive all or part of an interest is contingent on the election. See Reg. § 20.2056(b)-7(d)(3)(i); infra ¶ 5.06[8][d] text accompanying notes 317–320. Such a distinction seems appropriate because QTIP is an exception to the terminable interest rule and not the terminable interest rule itself.

With respect to bequests under instruments executed prior to October 1, 1964, the revenue procedure provides transitional rules for possible allowance of deductions that would otherwise be denied.

[156] Under the transitional rule, the unlimited estate tax marital deduction provision does not apply to trusts and wills if five factors are present:

1. The decedent dies after December 31, 1981;
2. The property passes from the decedent pursuant to a will executed (or trust created) prior to thirty days after enactment of the Economic Recovery Tax Act of 1981 (i.e., prior to Sept. 12, 1981);
3. The will (or trust) contains a formula providing that the surviving spouse is to receive a maximum amount of property qualifying for the marital deduction;
4. The formula clause is not amended before the decedent's death in order to refer specifically to an unlimited marital deduction; and
5. The applicable state law does not construe the formula as referring to the unlimited marital deduction allowable by federal law as amended by the 1981 Act.

Economic Recovery Tax Act of 1981, Pub. L. No. 97-34, § 403(e)(3), 95 Stat. 172, 305 (1981), reprinted in 1981-2 CB 256, 325. See Bay, "The Transitional Rule for Marital Deduction Formula Clauses," 20 Real. Prop., Prob. and Tr. J. 965 (1985); DiCenso, "Handling the Unlimited Marital Deduction in Pre-ERTA Instruments," 8 Prac. Tax Law. 63 (1993).

[157] For example, without the transitional rule, a decedent who bequeaths to a surviving spouse an amount equal to the maximum allowable marital deduction would be trans-

If the unlimited marital deduction provision does not apply under the transitional rule, the Section 2056(c) limitation prior to its repeal by the Economic Recovery Tax Act of 1981[158] remains in effect.[159]

[7] The Terminable Interest Rule

Not every interest in property that passes from a decedent to a surviving spouse qualifies for the marital deduction. The disqualification of terminable interests is discussed here. The pattern is, first, to discuss the general denial of the marital deduction for terminal interests in property passing to a surviving spouse and exceptions of long standing, and then, to examine the phenomenon of, the now predominantly employed, qualified terminable interest property (QTIP). Comments made in this initial terminable interest discussion must be tested against the QTIP concept.

---

ferring the decedent's entire estate to the surviving spouse (as opposed to one half of the estate). In determining whether or not to allow an unlimited marital deduction, both the courts and the Treasury appear amenable to looking to the decedent's intent. See Estate of Neisen v. Comm'r, 89 TC 939 (1987) acq. 1990-1 CB 1 (unlimited marital deduction); Estate of Kendall v. Comm'r, 60 TCM (CCH) 1045 (1990) (unlimited marital deduction); Estate of Levitt v. Comm'r, 95 TC 289 (1990) (unlimited marital deduction); In re Estate of Khadad, 135 Misc. 2d 67 (NY Surr. Ct. 1987) (unlimited marital deduction); Estate of Bruning v. Comm'r, 54 TCM (CCH) 1469 (1988), aff'd in unpub. op. (5th Cir. 1989) (unlimited marital deduction); Estate of Lassister v. Comm'r, 80 TCM (CCH) 541 (2000); Estate of Christmas v. Comm'r, 91 TC 769 (1988) (no unlimited marital deduction); Erwin v. United States, 88-1 USTC ¶ 13,753 (WD Tex. 1988) (no unlimited marital deduction); Liberty Nat'l Bank & Trust Co. v. United States, 867 F2d 302 (6th Cir. 1989) (no unlimited marital deduction); Estate of Klein v. Comm'r, 60 TCM (CCH) 953 (1990) (no unlimited marital deduction); Estate of Amiel v. Comm'r, 74 TCM (CCH) 239 (1997) (no unlimited marital deduction).

There are also numerous letter rulings determining decedents' intent: compare, e.g., Priv. Ltr. Ruls. 8548007 (Sept. 4, 1985) (unlimited marital deduction) and 9731029 (May 5, 1997) (unlimited marital deduction with a disclaimer to use the unified credit bypass) with Priv. Ltr. Ruls. 8528007 (Apr. 3, 1985) (marital deduction limited to 50 percent of adjusted gross estate), 8832001 (Apr. 28, 1988), 8834005 (May 17, 1988), 8837002 (May 27, 1988), and 8826002 (Dec. 10, 1987) (marital deduction limited to greater of $250,000 or 50 percent of adjusted gross estate). Cf. Estate of Hall v. United States, 39 F3d 102 (6th Cir. 1994) (state court holding as to intent as a result of state statute resulted in an unlimited marital deduction).

[158] Economic Recovery Tax Act of 1981, Pub. L. No. 97-34, § 403(a)(1)(A), 95 Stat. 172, 301 (1981), reprinted in 1981-2 CB 256, 324.

[159] See Stephens, Maxfield & Lind, Federal Estate and Gift Taxation ¶ 5.06[5] (Warren, Gorham & Lamont, 4th ed. 1978). Need we add that any will or trust executed prior to September 12, 1981, should either be re-executed or amended to appropriately reflect the testator's or the grantor's intent as to the marital deduction.

[a] General Rule and Purpose

The terminable interest rule renders an interest in property passing to a surviving spouse nondeductible if (1) the interest is terminable; (2) the decedent has also given an interest in the property to another; and (3) on the termination or failure of the spouse's interest, the other person *may* come into possession or enjoyment of the property by way of that person's interest. The example most easily understood is that of a devise of a life estate in realty to the surviving spouse, remainder to the child or child's estate. Under the devise, a valuable property interest passes to the surviving spouse that meets all the general requirements of Section 2056. Nevertheless, subject to some exceptions discussed hereinafter, the threefold terminable interest rule found in Section 2056(b)(1) renders the interest nondeductible because the spouse's interest will terminate on the occurrence of an event, the spouse's death; an interest, the remainder, passes from the decedent to another, the child, gratuitously; and by reason of the interest the child, or the child's estate, will possess and enjoy the property on termination of the spouse's interest at the spouse's death.[160]

Before examining these principles in greater detail, a word as to their purpose. Although Congress sanctions interspousal transfers without the imposition of a transfer tax, it wants a transmission tax when the property is transferred to others. In general, the terminable interest rule seeks to assure that result by allowing the marital deduction only where the nature of the interest passing to the spouse is such that, if retained until death, it unquestionably will be taxed in the spouse's estate.

If a surviving spouse received from a predeceasing spouse only a life estate in property with a remainder going to others, none of the transferred property would be included in the surviving spouse's gross estate because the spouse's interest would expire at death.[161] The statute denies the decedent's estate a marital deduction for interests of this kind passing to a surviving spouse. In this light, a safe generalization is that if the interest acquired by the surviving spouse would not, if held until death, subject the spouse's estate to liability upon the spouse's death, then it will not automatically be a deductible interest. However, as will appear in the ensuing discussion, the converse of this gener-

---

[160] See Baker, "The Marital Deduction and the Terminable Interest Rule," 40 Tenn. L. Rev. 195 (1973); see also Estate of Baker v. Comm'r, 56 TCM (CCH) 417 (1988) (terminable interest).

[161] See "Partial Interests in Property" in the discussion of Section 2033 at ¶ 4.05[5].

Congress might have applied the terminable interest rule in a gentler manner by employing a mechanism similar to a QDOT (see infra ¶ 5.07) under which it would effectively postpone the disallowance of the marital deduction until the surviving spouse's terminable interest terminates. This would allow for marital deduction trusts to be eligible for the deduction until some event occurs (e.g., death or remarriage of the surviving spouse) that terminates the surviving spouse's interest under the trust terms. See infra ¶ 5.07[4][a].

alization will not invariably hold true; there are circumstances in which the interest will be nondeductible even though it will cause estate tax liability when the surviving spouse dies. Therefore, the suggested generalization cannot be substituted for a careful scrutiny of the precise statutory rules. In fact, the Supreme Court has stated, "[T]here is no provision in the Code for deducting all terminable interests which become nonterminable at a later date and therefore taxable in the estate of the surviving spouse."[162]

[b] Identifying Terminable Interests

As indicated previously, a legal life estate or life interest in a trust is terminable because it will terminate or fail upon, in the statutory language, "the occurrence of an event."[163] But under Section 2056(b)(1), an interest is likewise terminable if it will terminate or fail upon a "lapse of time" (e.g., the expiration of the stated period of years), the occurrence of a contingency (e.g., a surviving spouse's remarriage),[164] or on the failure of an event or contingency to occur (e.g., the decedent's daughter does not marry by the time she is thirty years old).[165]

Despite certain obvious illustrations of terminable interests, a number of questions have arisen and more will arise concerning the scope of the term. One type of interest that has been the subject of considerable litigation and has resulted in a decision by the Supreme Court is the "widow's allowance."[166] Many states grant an allowance to the surviving spouse, typically referred to as a widow's allowance, to provide funds for living expenses during the adminis-

---

[162] Jackson v. United States, 376 US 509 (1964).

[163] State law is relevant in determining whether an interest is terminable. See Estate of Boydstun v. Comm'r, 48 TCM (CCH) 311 (1984), aff'd in unpub. op. (9th Cir. 1985) (terminable interest); Estate of McCune v. Comm'r, 48 TCM (CCH) 1510 (1984) (mere precatory language did not make the interest terminable).

[164] Brown v. United States, 1972-2 USTC ¶ 12,887 (ND Ala. 1972). The question whether a property interest will so terminate depends on an interpretation of the will under local law, which interpretation may be made by the federal court deciding the tax case. Estate of Urge v. Comm'r, 31 TCM (CCH) 275 (1972); Estate of Fields v. Comm'r, 42 TCM (CCH) 1406 (1981); Jeschke v. United States, 814 F2d 568 (10th Cir. 1987); Rev. Rul. 77-98, 1977-1 CB 288. Cf. Stubbs v. United States, 76-2 USTC ¶ 13,162 (Ct. Cl. 1976).

[165] Estate of Edmonds v. Comm'r, 72 TC 970 (1979). Except for specific exceptions to the terminable interest rule discussed subsequently in the text, Section 2056(b)(1) was intended to be "all-encompassing with respect to various kinds of contingencies and conditions." S. Rep. No. 1013, 80th Cong., 2d Sess. 1163, 1229 (1948), reprinted in 1948-1 CB 285, 336.

[166] This term is now commonly called a family allowance, and it encompasses state statutes authorizing payments from an estate for support of a surviving spouse and children prior to the closing of an estate.

tration of the estate.[167] Does the terminable interest rule render such allowances nondeductible? In 1964, this question was resolved by the Supreme Court in the *Jackson* case.[168] The Court held that the issue of terminability and, accordingly, deductibility must be determined at the time of the decedent's death; subsequent events that may render an interest indefeasible do not cure a marital deduction defect. Under the local law applicable in the *Jackson* case, the surviving spouse's right to the allowance was contingent until the order of support was entered, and remarriage or death of the surviving spouse prior to the order of support prevented any award, and the spouse's remarriage or death, even after an award, cut off any future rights. Looking at the moment of death, it was possible that the interest would fail; accordingly, the marital deduction was not allowed.[169] Thus, the widow's allowance is nonterminable only if it vests immediately at death; that is, it must survive the spouse's death or remarriage.[170]

If a provision in the decedent's insurance contract stipulates that proceeds be paid to a beneficiary other than the surviving spouse if the spouse "be not living when the company receives due proof of death," the surviving spouse's interest in the insurance proceeds is a nondeductible terminable interest, even if the spouse does in fact survive and receives the proceeds.[171] The spouse's interest remains disqualified by the terminable interest rule even if the alternate

---

[167] E.g., Mo. Rev. Stat. § 474.260 (2001); Okla. Stat. Ann. tit. 58, § 314 (2002); Tenn. Code Ann. § 30-2-102 (2001).

[168] Jackson v. United States, 376 US 503 (1964). See Reg. § 20.2056(b)-1(g) Ex. 8.

[169] Although the terminable interest requirement was met, the other two requirements (interest passing to others, such interest taking effect on the spouse's death) must also be met in order to disallow the marital deduction; and if in *Jackson*, the surviving spouse had been the residuary legatee of the decedent's estate, the marital deduction would not have been denied on the widow's allowance to the extent that it did not exceed the amount that would otherwise have passed under the residuary clause. See Reg. § 20.2056(b)-1(g) Ex. 8.

[170] Hamilton Nat'l Bank v. United States, 353 F2d 930 (6th Cir.), cert. denied, 384 US 939 (1966) (Tennessee law rights do not qualify); Rev. Rul. 53-83, 1953-1 CB 395; Iowa-Des Moines Nat'l Bank v. United States, 306 F. Supp. 320 (SD Iowa 1969) (Iowa rights do not qualify); Rev. Rul. 72-153, 1972-1 CB 309 (Washington rights do not qualify); Estate of Abely v. Comm'r, 60 TC 120 (1973), aff'd, 489 F2d 1327 (1st Cir. 1974) (Massachusetts rights do not qualify); Estate of Snyder v. Comm'r, 84 TC 75 (1985) (Texas rights do not qualify); Estate of Green v. United States, 1970-1 USTC ¶ 12,650 (ED Mich. 1970), aff'd, 441 F2d 303 (6th Cir. 1971) (Michigan widow's allowance qualifies); Estate of Watson v. Comm'r, 94 TC 262 (1990) (Mississippi qualifies); Rev. Rul. 76-166, 1976-1 CB 287 (Arizona qualifies); Estate of Radel v. Comm'r, 88 TC 1143 (1987) (Minnesota qualifies); cf. Dickson v. United States, 240 F. Supp. 583 (D. Md. 1965). See supra note 169.

[171] Eggleston v. Dudley, 154 F. Supp. 178 (WD Pa. 1957), rev'd on state law issue, 257 F2d 398 (3d Cir. 1958).

valuation date is elected under Section 2032 and the contingency is satisfied by that date.[172]

If the decedent bequests property to a surviving spouse "if living at the time of the distribution of my estate," the interest taken by the spouse is a nondeductible terminable interest,[173] unless under applicable state law such a will provision can be given "the legal effect of vesting and making [i]ndefeasible in the [surviving spouse], as of the time of the testator's death, the property . . . bequeathed to [the spouse]."[174] A literal reading of such a bequest, unaffected by any special rule of local law, would certainly foreclose any marital deduction.[175]

In some states, a surviving spouse's dower interest is a terminable interest.[176] If, however, at decedent's death, the surviving spouse has a choice to receive either a terminable dower interest or a lump-sum amount in lieu of dower and elects the lump-sum amount, the courts have consistently, though questionably, held that receipt of the lump sum qualifies for the marital deduction.[177] Similarly, if the property in which the surviving spouse has a terminable interest is sold with the spouse's consent to discharge obligations of the estate, amounts received outright by the spouse in lieu of the spouse's dower

---

[172] Rev. Rul. 88-90, 1988-2 CB 335; Rev. Rul. 85-100, 1985-2 CB 200.

[173] Kaspar v. Kellar, 217 F2d 744 (8th Cir. 1954); Estate of Heim v. Comm'r, 914 F2d 1322 (9th Cir. 1990); Estate of Street v. Comm'r, 25 TC 673 (1955); Dunn v. United States, 80-1 USTC ¶ 13,347 (MD Fla. 1980); Estate of Harmon v. Comm'r, 84 TC 329 (1985).

[174] Kellar v. Kasper, on remand, 138 F. Supp. 738, 744 (DSD 1956). Similarly, the marital deduction was preserved by application of local law to overcome the apparent effect of a condition in the will in Estate of Tilyou v. Comm'r, 470 F2d 693 (2d Cir. 1972); Estate of Horton v. Comm'r, 338 F2d 51 (2d Cir. 1967); Estate of Doughty v. United States, 1970-1 USTC ¶ 12,651 (CD Cal. 1969); Berger v. United States, 285 F. Supp. 92 (ED Pa. 1968). Cf. Planters Nat'l Bank & Trust Co. v. United States, 1977-1 USTC ¶ 13,171 (EDNC 1977).

[175] Fried Estate v. Comm'r, 445 F2d 979 (2d Cir.), cert. denied, 404 US 1016 (1972); United States v. Mappes, 318 F2d 508 (10th Cir. 1963); Bookwalter v. Lamar, 323 F2d 664 (8th Cir.), cert. denied, 376 US 969 (1964); Werbe's Estate v. United States, 273 F2d 201 (7th Cir. 1959); Kidd v. United States, 334 F. Supp. 631 (SD Ohio 1971), aff'd, 451 F2d 1026 (6th Cir. 1972); Pirrie v. United States, 318 F. Supp. 274 (D. Mont. 1970); Nielsen v. United States, 1968-2 USTC ¶ 12,549 (CD Cal. 1968); Silvey v. United States, 265 F. Supp. 25 (ND Ala. 1966).

[176] E.g., Crosby v. United States, 151 F. Supp. 497 (ND Fla. 1957), aff'd, 257 F2d 515 (5th Cir. 1958) (involving dower under Alabama law).

[177] Estate of Kennedy v. United States, 320 F. Supp. 343 (DSC 1969); Bradham v. United States, 287 F. Supp. 10 (WD Ark. 1968); American Nat'l Bank & Trust Co. v. United States, 266 F. Supp. 1008 (ED Tenn. 1967); see Rev. Rul. 72-153, 1972-1 CB 309. If, however, the surviving spouse has no right of election and a state court misinterprets state law to award the spouse a nonterminable interest in lieu of a terminable dower interest, the spouse's award does not qualify for the marital deduction. Cox v. United States, 421 F2d 576 (5th Cir. 1970).

may qualify for the marital deduction;[178] and the Treasury has since abandoned its position that a "conversion" of a nondeductible dower interest cannot support the deduction.[179] It is equally clear that the marital deduction will be allowed if a surviving spouse renounces an interest left by will in favor of dower or similar statutory interests for which an election is made after the decedent's death.[180] In addition, if the surviving spouse elects a dower interest, which under state law is either terminable or not, but, because of a bona fide dispute about the spouse's right to take dower (perhaps based on an antenuptial agreement) a settlement is made, the payment qualifies for the marital deduction.[181]

There is a doctrinal weakness here if full effect is given to the *Jackson* case,[182] which stresses determinability at death. For example, especially if a surviving spouse's election of dower (or similar marital right) must be made personally, not by the spouse's personal representative after the spouse's death, the dower interest may well be viewed as terminable at the time of the predeceasing spouse's death. If the election is not made or is not timely made, the spouse's dower interest will fail. Still, Section 2056(c)(3), the express provision treating dower as "passing" from the decedent, would seem to have little point if the terminable interest rule generally disqualified dower for marital deduction purposes. Seemingly, the Treasury has decided not to probe the doctrinal weakness.[183]

Several courts further extended this doctrinal weakness to permit a marital deduction where a surviving spouse elects to receive a cash bequest in lieu of

---

[178] Crosby v. United States, 151 F. Supp. 497 (ND Fla. 1957), aff'd, 257 F2d 515 (5th Cir. 1958).

[179] Rev. Rul. 72-7, 1972-1 CB 308, revoking Rev. Rul. 53-279, 1953-2 CB 275; cf. Rev. Rul. 83-107, 1983-2 CB 159; Moore v. United States, 214 F. Supp. 603 (WD Ky. 1963) (allowing the conversion as a result of a bona fide settlement as well as a court proceeding). See supra ¶ 5.06[3][b] text accompanying note 48.

[180] Traders Nat'l Bank v. United States, 148 F. Supp. 278 (WD Mo. 1956), aff'd, 248 F2d 667 (8th Cir. 1957); Hawaiian Trust Co. v. United States, 412 F2d 1313 (Ct. Cl. 1969).

[181] Stephens v. United States, 270 F. Supp. 968 (D. Mont. 1967) (involving an election against a will in favor of dower and a subsequent settlement of a fee interest in lieu of a terminable dower interest); Waldrup v. United States, 499 F. Supp. 820 (ND Miss. 1980); Rev. Ruls. 66-139, 1966-1 CB 225, 76-199, 1976-1 CB 288 (where the settlement was conditioned on the Service's determination that the marital deduction would be allowed and the deduction was allowed). See Reg. § 20.2056(c)-2(d)(2). Cf. Rev. Rul. 76-155, 1976-1 CB 286, Rev. Rul. 83-107, 1983-2 CB 159.

[182] Jackson v. United States, 376 US 503 (1964).

[183] See Rev. Rul. 72-8, 1972-1 CB 309 (Florida dower deductible).

a life income interest within a reasonable time after the decedent's death.[184] The Treasury now agrees with these results.[185]

The interest of a surviving spouse in homestead property is a nondeductible interest if, under local law,[186] the spouse receives the property for life with the remainder to the decedent's lineal descendants. However, if residential property is converted before death into a tenancy by the entirety, making the homestead law inapplicable and the spouse's interest as surviving tenant not terminable, the interest may pass to the spouse as a deductible interest.[187] Similarly, if the surviving spouse has a right to a nonterminable award in lieu of a homestead right and elects the award, that award qualifies for the marital deduction,[188] just as a nonterminable award in lieu of dower qualifies.[189]

The marital deduction is not defeated by a bequest of a terminable interest to another prior to a vested interest in the surviving spouse. For example, if the decedent leaves property in trust, the income to be paid to parent for life, and upon the mother's death the remainder to be paid to decedent's surviving spouse or the spouse's estate, it is the parent's interest that is terminable. In this example, the surviving spouse's remainder interest is a deductible interest and the only complexity is its valuation.[190]

---

[184] Mackie v. Comm'r, 64 TC 308 (1975), aff'd per curiam, 545 F2d 883 (4th Cir. 1976); Newgass Estate v. Comm'r, 555 F2d 322 (2d Cir. 1977); Estate of Tompkins v. Comm'r, 68 TC 912 (1977). But see Estate of Edmonds v. Comm'r, 72 TC 970 (1979).

[185] Rev. Rul. 82-184, 1982-2 CB 215.

[186] E.g., Fla. Stat. § 732.401 (2000).

[187] Nelson v. Comm'r, 232 F2d 720 (5th Cir. 1956).

[188] Rev. Rul. 72-153, 1972-1 CB 1. Cf. Rev. Rul. 76-166, 1976-1 CB 287.

[189] See supra text accompanying note 177. The technical nature of the terminable interest rule is emphasized by the *Allen* case. Allen v. United States, 359 F2d 151 (2d Cir. 1966). Accord Ray v. Comm'r, 54 TC 1170 (1970). In *Allen*, the decedent had bequeathed property to a spouse on the condition the spouse execute an agreement that would provide the property to pass, upon the spouse's death, to a child of the decedent by a prior marriage, and which agreement was to be approved by the probate court; if the spouse failed to satisfy the condition, then the decedent bequeathed to the spouse a statutory share. The spouse met the condition and received the property. The court held that at the moment of the decedent's death the bequest to the spouse was terminable on the ground that either the spouse could fail to satisfy the condition imposed under the first part of the will or the probate court would not approve such agreement. The estate argued in the alternative that a marital deduction should be allowed at least for the statutory share that the spouse would have received under the second part of the will. But the court correctly held that as the spouse in fact received nothing under the alternative will provision, it would support no deduction.

[190] Reg. § 20.2056(b)-4(d). See IRC § 7520.

[c] Other Elements of the Terminable Interest Rule

It is worth emphasizing that the terminable nature of the spouse's interest does not by itself foreclose the marital deduction. Something more is required to invoke the limitation; even when the three elements of the terminable interest rule are satisfied, there are some exceptions, which are suggested in the following paragraphs. An easy illustration of the threefold nature of the requirement is a bequest of a patent to a surviving spouse. A patent has a limited life and is clearly within the terminable interest category.[191] But if a decedent owned a patent outright and left it outright to a surviving spouse, the interest is a deductible interest. The reason is that the two other elements of the terminable interest rule are missing: (1) no interest in the property has passed gratuitously to another[192] and (2) no other person will acquire the property on termination of the surviving spouse's interest by reason of any interest that person may have.[193]

A marital deduction is also allowed in the case of an "estate trust" where property is bequeathed in trust with income to the surviving spouse for life and the remainder to the spouse's estate. No nondeductible terminable interest is present because no interest passes to one other than the surviving spouse "or the estate of such spouse."[194] Even though the income from such an interest

---

[191] Reg. § 20.2056(b)-1(b).

[192] Rev. Rul. 76-404, 1976-2 CB 294. Cf. Priv. Ltr. Rul. 9606008 (Nov. 9, 1995) (the third person is required to pay fair market value on termination).

[193] Other examples of terminable interests that are deductible because these two requirements are missing are a survivorship annuity paid only to a surviving spouse (Rev. Rul. 77-404, 1977-2 CB 333, Rev. Rul. 79-420, 1979-2 CB 335); an installment sales payment (Rev. Rul. 79-224, 1979-2 CB 335); and a corporate recapitalization plan directed by the decedent's will (Provident Nat'l Bank v. United States, 581 F2d 1081 (3d Cir. 1978)).

[194] IRC § 2025(b)(1)(A). Cf. Reg. §§ 20.2056(c)-2(b)(1)(i), 20.2056(c)-2(b)(1)(ii). The parenthetical phrase in Section 2056(b)(1)(A), which treats property passing to "the estate" of a surviving spouse as not passing to any other person, seems to suggest a congressional assumption that a spouse and the spouse's estate are one, so that property that passes to the spouse's estate at death is the spouse's for purposes of Section 2033 and therefore includible in the spouse's gross estate. Unless the interest will be taxed in the spouse's estate, the deduction should not be allowed. See Rev. Rul. 77-170, 1977-1 CB 290. However, the application of Section 2033 in this situation is by no means clear. Compare Second Nat'l Bank of Danville v. United States, 209 F2d 321 (7th Cir. 1954), with Keeter v. United States, 323 F. Supp. 1093 (ND Fla. 1971), rev'd, 461 F2d 714 (5th Cir. 1972). See ¶ 4.05[6] note 76. If in this light the reason for the parenthetical phrase may once have been dubious, it seems adequately supported now by the Section 2041 treatment of general powers of appointment, because that section will assure inclusion in the spouse's estate even if Section 2033 does not. The provisions of Section 2056(b)(1), analyzed in this way and supported philosophically by reference to the power of appointment provisions of Section 2041, do not conflict with special exceptions to the terminable interest rule expressed in Section 2056(b)(5), discussed infra ¶ 5.06[8][b]. There, it is as-

could be accumulated and added to the corpus in the absolute discretion of a trustee, nevertheless, the fact that the corpus and accumulated income will be paid to the surviving spouse's estate leaves the bequest outside the terminable interest rule and justifies the allowance of a marital deduction for the entire corpus.[195]

Moreover, the surviving spouse may have a terminable interest followed by a remainder interest to another and the deduction will still be allowed in some circumstances. The first parenthetical phrase in Section 2056(b)(1)(A) makes this possible. To apply the terminable interest rule, the interest that passes or has passed to someone other than the spouse, under which such other person may possess the property on termination of the surviving spouse's interest, must have passed to such person from the decedent "for less than an adequate and full consideration in money or money's worth." Thus, if X sells Blackacre to Y for $10,000 but reserves possession for a term of twenty years, and if $10,000 is a full consideration for the interest purchased by Y, a bequest by X to a surviving spouse of what remains of X's twenty-year term qualifies for the marital deduction. This should be contrasted with a deed of gift of Blackacre by X to Y for no consideration, under which X retains a

---

sumed that the spouse's interests do pass to others (e.g., a contingent remainder to the children), thus defeating the deduction under Section 2056(b)(1) but for the special exceptions. The difference between an "estate trust" (deductible as a nonterminable interest) and a "power of appointment trust" (which, while involving a terminable interest, may be deductible under Section 2056(b)(5)) is well illustrated in Rev. Rul. 72-33, 1972-2 CB 530, allowing a full marital deduction for a trust that combined both elements.

Suppose you have essentially an "estate trust" for the surviving spouse, involving possible income accumulation during the spouse's life but providing for payment of accumulated income and corpus to the spouse's estate at death, and additionally the draftsman gives the spouse a post-1942 power. If the addition affords no means for avoidance of tax in the spouse's estate, the estate trust should still qualify for the deduction. In Rev. Rul. 75-128, 1975-1 CB 308, the Treasury says it will not because, as we would agree, we are not within Section 2056(b)(5) (inadequate current right to income, etc.) *and* as we do *not* agree, we are nailed by the terminable interest rule: "the possible appointees ... are ... persons other than the surviving spouse to whom an interest in the property [subject to the power] passes," etc. The quoted statement is nonsense. From an estate tax perspective, the permissible appointees have expectancies at best, not interests in property. So we are not faced at all with a terminable interest situation; no interest passes to anyone other than the surviving spouse or the spouse's estate. Is a deduction consistent with Section 2056 policy? Yes. It matters not whether the spouse's post-1942 power is inter vivos or testamentary, general or nongeneral. Its exercise will be either a gift-taxed exercise of a general power (the power itself) or a release of general power, the spouse's right to dispose of the property by will. IRC § 2514. See Keeter v. United States, 323 F. Supp. 1093 (ND Fla. 1971), rev'd, 461 F2d 714 (5th Cir. 1972). Its nonexercise will leave the property subject to the power as part of the spouse's gross estate. IRC § 2041. See *Keeter v. United States,* supra. The ruling is therefore at odds with both the language of the section and its underlying philosophy and should be repudiated.

[195] Rev. Rul. 68-554, 1968-2 CB 412; Priv. Ltr. Rul. 9634020 (May 24, 1996).

twenty-year term. Here, if X dies before the expiration of the term and bequeaths the retained interest to a surviving spouse, all elements of the terminal
interest rule are satisfied and the surviving spouse has received a nondeductible interest.

If a terminable interest passing to a spouse can be a deductible interest, it
is also true that an interest in property can pass to someone other than the
spouse without defeating the marital deduction for the interest in the same
property that passes to the spouse. For example, if the decedent left Blackacre
to a surviving spouse and child as tenants in common, the surviving spouse's
interest would qualify for the deduction. This emphasizes that the marital deduction is lost only if all three elements of the terminable interest rule are present.

[d] The Executor-Purchaser Provision

In one circumstance, a terminable interest passing to a surviving spouse is
disqualified even if no interest in the property passes or has passed to another.
The circumstance is that of a terminable interest that the decedent directs an
executor or a trustee to acquire for a surviving spouse. Section 2056(b)(1)(C)
prohibits any deduction with respect to such an interest. The regulations contain the following illustration:[196] "A decedent bequeathed $100,000 to his wife,
subject to a direction to his executor to use the bequest for the purchase of an
annuity for the wife. The bequest is a nondeductible interest." The reason for
this proscription is probably to be found in the similarity between a directed
executor purchase of a terminable interest and the more conventional bequest
of a life interest in a trust. For example, if a surviving spouse is seventy-six
years old at the predeceasing spouse's death and if the interest rate is 8 percent, a life interest in property left in trust for the surviving spouse would be
worth about one half the value of the trust property.[197] If the decedent left
$200,000 in trust for surviving spouse for life, the value of the spouse's inter-
est would at that time have been about $100,000 but would be a nondeductible
terminable interest. Decedent could have accomplished much the same thing,
economically speaking, by a direct bequest of $100,000 to the remainderper-
sons, the value of the interest they would have received in the trust,[198] and a
direction to an executor to use the remaining $100,000 to purchase an annuity
for the surviving spouse. Spouse's receipt of annuity payments would be much
the same as the receipt of trust income; and also similarly, the arrangement
would cause the spouse's estate no estate tax. This apparent possibility of circumvention of the usual terminable interest rule supports the executor-pur-

---

[196] Reg. § 20.2056(b)-1(g) Ex. 7.
[197] Reg. § 20.2031-7(d)(7), Table S. Cf. IRC § 7520.
[198] Reg. § 20.2031-7(d)(7), Table S. Cf. IRC § 7520.

chaser proscription. In addition, if a decedent directs an executor to purchase a Section 2056(b)(1)(C) terminable interest, the interest will not qualify for the marital deduction as QTIP under Section 2056(b)(7).[199] However, if money or other property is left outright to the surviving spouse, what a spouse does with it is of no consequence; that is, the spouse's voluntary purchase of a terminable interest such as an annuity does not defeat the marital deduction.

[e] The "Tainted Asset" Rule

An effort to take full advantage of the marital deduction by way of a general bequest to a surviving spouse may be upset by the so-called tainted asset rule. Section 2056(b)(2) has the practical effect of creating a conclusive presumption that, to the extent a bequest may be satisfied out of assets that would not qualify for the marital deduction, it is so satisfied. It is enough that the bequest could be satisfied out of the proceeds of such assets in order to run afoul of the rule. The actual statutory approach is to require a reduction in the value of the interests passing to the surviving spouse in the amount of the value of the tainted assets.

The application of the rule can be understood by way of the following example. Suppose a decedent made general bequests of approximately one half of decedent's estate to a child and left the residue to a surviving spouse. On its face, it might appear that the estate would get a marital deduction in an amount equal to one half of the value of the estate. Nevertheless, if the estate included a twenty-year leasehold that the decedent has reserved upon making a gratuitous transfer of the property earlier to the child, the value of the property interests passing to the surviving spouse would be reduced by the value of the leasehold. This is so simply because the leasehold, or the proceeds from its sale, might be used to satisfy the residuary bequest to the spouse; it is not necessary that in fact it be so used. Thus, something less than the expected marital deduction may be achieved, even though the property that actually goes to the surviving spouse would have supported a larger marital deduction. This problem can be avoided by a provision in the will that the surviving spouse's bequest cannot be satisfied with a nondeductible interest or the proceeds therefrom.[200] Similarly, if in this illustration the leasehold had been left by specific bequest to someone other than the spouse, it would not be an asset out of which the bequest to the spouse could be satisfied, and the tainted asset rule would not apply.

The disclaimer provisions[201] seem broad enough often to afford an opportunity for postmortem avoidance of the tainted asset rule. It is a draconian rule

---

[199] Reg. § 20.2056(b)-7(b)(1)(i). See infra ¶ 5.06[8][d] note 344 (last paragraph).

[200] Reg. § 20.2056(b)-2(d).

[201] IRC §§ 2046, 2518.

and this avoidance should be condoned when, as would usually seem to be the case, no tax distortion will result.

[8] Terminable Interests That Do Qualify

[a] Common Disaster and Related Provisions

A customary common disaster provision in a will could, from what has so far been said about the terminable interest rule, defeat the marital deduction. That is, a will provision diverting the surviving spouse's interest to others if the spouse should die after the decedent as a result of a common disaster could[202] render the spouse's interest terminable and otherwise meet the three-fold test of the terminable interest rule, even if the spouse did not die and actually received the interest in the estate. The same result would follow from a will provision defeating the surviving spouse's interest if the spouse should fail to survive the decedent for a stated period such as six months.

Section 2056(b)(3) marks out a limited exception to the terminable interest rule to permit the use of these familiar useful provisions without the loss of the marital deduction. The statutory provision is that an interest passing to a surviving spouse is not to be considered a terminable interest if it will fail only upon (1) the surviving spouse's death within six months after the decedent's death; (2) the surviving spouse's death as a result of common disaster, causing the death of the decedent as well;[203] or (3) the occurrence of either of such events if, in any event, such failure does not in fact occur. Thus, will provisions of the type here mentioned defeat the marital deduction, appropriately, only when they come into play in fact to defeat the interest that might otherwise pass to a surviving spouse.

However, this exception to the terminable interest rule has been strictly construed. For example, in one instance, an insurance policy provided that the interest of the surviving spouse who was the primary beneficiary would fail upon the spouse's death prior to the date the insurance company received proof of the death of the insured. Such proof would almost certainly be made within a six-month period following death. Nevertheless, the Treasury ruled the marital deduction was not allowable, because the policy did not precisely adopt the accepted six months' or common disaster principles. The case was

---

[202] "If no possibility exists at the moment of the decedent's death that his surviving spouse will die as a result of a common disaster, the mere fact that there is a clause in his will which would prevent the passing of an interest in property to her if she did so die does not make her interest terminable." S. Rep. No. 1013, 80th Cong., 2d Sess. 1163, 1238 (1948), reprinted in 1948-1 CB 285, 342.

[203] Rev. Rul. 66-60, 1966-1 CB 221 (dealing with other aspects of death in a common disaster).

not within the exception to the terminable interest rule because "submission of due proof of the insured's death may occur either within the 6-month period following the decedent's death or thereafter."[204] It is important to note that the question here is not when such proof was made; this exception to the terminable interest rule can be invoked only if contingent failure of the surviving spouse's interest is necessarily limited to the six months or common disaster situations.[205]

[b] Life Interests With Powers

Section 2056(b)(5) makes an exception to the terminable interest rule to permit the marital deduction with respect to life interests passing to a surviving spouse, even though contingent interests pass to others, if the spouse enjoys other controls over the property that in effect make the spouse the complete owner of the property.[206] The statutory requirements are far more explicit than this general statement would suggest, but an idea of the scope and purpose of the exception can be gained from the following statements in the legislative history:

> These provisions have the effect of allowing a marital deduction with respect to the value of property transferred in trust [or otherwise under present provisions] by or at the direction of the decedent where the surviving spouse, by reason of her right to the income [or use] and a power of appointment, is the virtual owner of the property. This provision is designed to allow the marital deduction for such cases where the value of the property over which the surviving spouse has a power of appointment will (if not consumed) be subject to either the estate tax or the gift tax in the case of such surviving spouse.[207]

---

[204] Rev. Rul. 54-121, 1954-1 CB 196, 197. See also Reg. § 20.2056(b)-3(b).

[205] Hansen v. Vinal, 286 F. Supp. 394 (D. Neb. 1968), aff'd, 413 F2d 882 (8th Cir. 1969); California Trust Co. v. Riddell, 136 F. Supp. 7 (SD Cal. 1955); Kasper v. Kellar, 217 F2d 744 (8th Cir. 1954), on remand 138 F. Supp. 738 (DSD 1956); Rev. Rul. 76-166, 1976-1 CB 287. See Priv. Ltr. Ruls. 8816001 (Dec. 30, 1987), 8809003 (Oct. 30, 1987), 8810002 (Nov. 19, 1987).

[206] Section 2056(b)(5) used to be a significant player in the exceptions to the terminable interest rule game. But with the 1981 advent of QTIP trusts (IRC § 2056(b)(7), see infra ¶ 5.06[8][d]) and the ability of such trusts to qualify as transfers by the decedent spouse for generation-skipping transfer tax purposes (IRC § 2652(a)(3), see ¶ 17.02[1][c][i]), Section 2056(b)(5) is no longer widely used, and it has largely taken a back seat to the QTIP exception. Nevertheless, there follows a detailed description of the Section 2056(b)(5) requirements, many of which are identical to the Section 2056(b)(7) requirements.

[207] S. Rep. No. 1013, 80th Cong., 2d Sess. 1163, 1238 (1948), reprinted in 1948-1 CB 285, 342.

The five statements that introduce the following five subsections are taken from the regulations,[208] and these requirements all must be met if the exception is to apply.

[i] **The surviving spouse must be entitled for life to all of the income from the entire interest or a specific portion of the entire interest, or to a specific portion of all the income from the entire interest.** The original marital deduction provisions of the 1939 Code did not provide an exception to the terminable interest rule for legal life estates coupled with powers[209] and required, moreover, in a trust situation that the surviving spouse be entitled to all the income from the trust, not merely a portion of the trust, in order for the exception to apply.[210] However, the Technical Amendments Acts of 1958 retroactively eliminated these differences.[211]

The income requirement is met if under the terms of a trust and applicable local law, the surviving spouse gets "substantially that degree of beneficial enjoyment of the trust property during . . . life which the principles of the law of trusts accord to a person who is unqualifiedly designated as the life beneficiary of a trust."[212] Within this concept, the exception to the terminable interest rule is not likely to be defeated by trust provisions (1) requiring stock dividends or the proceeds from the conversion of trust assets to be treated as corpus[213] or (2) prohibiting assignment or alienation of the spouse's right to the income.[214] The income requirement is satisfied if the spouse is entitled to income as defined under a state statute that provides for a reasonable apportionment between the income and remainder beneficiaries of the total return of the trust.[215] The exception is not lost merely because the survivor will not receive

---

[208] Reg. §§ 20.2056(b)-5(a)(1), 20.2056(b)-5(a)(2), 20.2056(b)-5(a)(3), 20.2056(b)-5(a)(4), 20.2056(b)-5(a)(5). The first two requirements are identical to the income requirements for a qualifying income interest under Section 2056(b)(7). IRC § 2056(b)(7)(B)(ii). See Reg. § 20.2056(b)-7(d)(2); infra ¶ 5.06[8][d][ii].

[209] IRC § 812(e)(1)(F) (1939).

[210] E.g., Estate of Shedd v. Comm'r, 23 TC 41 (1954), aff'd, 237 F2d 345 (9th Cir. 1956), cert. denied, 352 US 1024 (1957).

[211] Technical Amendments Act of 1958, Pub. L. No. 85-866, § 93(a), 72 Stat. 1606 (1958), reprinted in 1958-3 CB 254, 316.

[212] Reg. § 20.2056(b)-5(f)(1). See Rev. Rul. 69-56, 1969-1 CB 224; Rev. Rul. 85-35, 1985-1 CB 328 (income interest valid where trustee could expend income for the spouse who became disabled). Cf. Priv. Ltr. Ruls. 9739015 (June 26, 1997) (division of contingent payment allocated to income based on applicable federal rate as a discount rate), 9613016 (Dec. 27, 1995) (allocation of lottery proceeds between income and principal).

[213] Reg. § 20.2056(b)-5(f)(3).

[214] Reg. § 20.2056(b)-5(f)(7).

[215] Prop. Reg. § 20.2056(b)-5(f)(1). The provision must satisfy the requirements of Prop. Reg. § 1.643(b)-1(a). A reasonable apportionment may be accomplished through a 3 percent to 5 percent unitrust definition of income or by giving the trustee the power to

the income from the trust property for the period before distribution of the property by the personal representative, unless there is a will provision authorizing or directing unreasonable delay in such distribution.[216] Even if the trustees are given the discretionary power to retain cash without investment and to allocate receipts between income and principal, the marital deduction is allowed if local law imposes on the trustees a duty to use the degree of care a prudent person would use if the person owned the trust assets.[217] On the other hand, a general provision for accumulation of trust income or for income accumulation at the discretion of someone other than the surviving spouse leaves the spouse without the current income right that is a prerequisite to the exception.[218]

The subordinate principles just discussed seem responsive to the statutory mandate that the surviving spouse be entitled to all the income from the property interest in question, and are said to apply as well to legal life estates as to trusts.[219] However, the Treasury takes the further position that, if the trust includes property that is not likely to produce income during the spouse's life, the income requirement of the exception is not met unless applicable administrative rules require, or the spouse has the right to require, the trustee to make the property productive or to convert it to income-producing property or at least to make up the income deficiency out of other trust assets.[220] Application of the same principle may defeat the deduction in the case of a devise of a le-

---

make equitable adjustments between income or principal. Prop. Reg. §§ 1.643(a)-3(e) Exs. 1, 9, 1.643(b)-1.

[216] Reg. § 20.2056(b)-5(f)(9); Rev. Rul. 77-346, 1977-2 CB 340. Such a loss of income may affect valuation of the interest. See Reg. § 20.2056(b)-4(a).

[217] Reg. § 2056(b)-5(f)(4); Rev. Rul. 66-39, 1966-1 CB 223, Rev. Rul. 75-440, 1975-2 CB 372.

[218] Reg. § 20.2056(b)-5(f)(7). Wisely v. United States, 893 F2d 660 (4th Cir. 1990). But see Estate of Todd v. Comm'r, 57 TC 288 (1971), where the Tax Court concluded that although the trustees could distribute income to the surviving spouse as "in their conclusive discretion should be so expended to accomplish the purpose of [the] trust," nevertheless, the quoted language did not authorize the trustees to withhold income, since another part of the trust stated that its purpose was to qualify for the marital deduction. See also Estate of Mittelman v. Comm'r, 522 F2d 132 (DC Cir. 1975) (court looked at surrounding circumstances to determine the spouse had the right to all the income); Merchant's Nat'l Bank v. United States, 326 F. Supp. 384 (ND Iowa 1971) . But cf. Estate of Nicholson v. Comm'r, 94 TC 666 (1990) (distinguishing *Mittelman* and holding right to income for usual standard of living was not a right to all the income).

[219] Reg. § 20.2056(b)-5(e).

[220] Reg. §§ 20.2056(b)-5(f)(4), 20.2056(b)-5(f)(5); Rev. Rul. 66-39, 1966-1 CB 223, recognizes that if state law prohibits an unreasonable retention of uninvested cash, the marital deduction is not to be denied on the ground that cash accumulations deprive the surviving spouse of the requisite right to the income for life. See Estate of Smith v. Comm'r, 37 TCM (CCH) 745 (1978), holding the above-cited regulations inapplicable to its facts. Cf. Priv. Ltr. Ruls. 9242006 (July 15, 1992) (legal life estate in artwork provided

gal life estate in nonproductive property.[221] No unproductive property rule appears in the statute either expressly or by inference. Accordingly, these requirements are questionable as a matter of interpretation. They are also subject to challenge as a matter of policy. Consider this: *D*'s will creates a testamentary trust under which the income is to be accumulated for the life of spouse *S*; upon *S*'s death the corpus and accumulated income are to be paid to *S*'s estate. Whether the property is productive or not, *S* will have no current enjoyment of the property while alive. And yet upon *D*'s death survived by *S*, the marital deduction is allowed because, as no interest passed to one other than *S* or *S*'s estate, the basic thrusts of the terminable interest rule are not offended.[222] Moreover, if *D* wished to tie up the property, even though unproductive, in anticipation of appreciation in value, this can hardly be a matter of significance to the federal fisc. If *D* is right, the estate tax on *S*'s estate may be burdensome. Perhaps Congress would like a make-property-productive concept in the Section 2056(b)(5) exception (maybe even like the regulation provision); but, if so, they should provide some statutory underpinning for such a substantive requirement.

The phrase "specific portion" that appears in Section 2056(b)(5)[223] has been subject to substantial controversy. Although a surviving spouse's interest in a portion of a trust can qualify for the deduction, the portion must be identifiable;[224] and as to the portion, the current income test and all the other five tests under discussion here must be met. The Treasury initially took the position that a trust as to which a spouse has an income interest expressed in a fixed dollar amount or a general power of appointment over a fixed dollar amount will not qualify for the special exception to the terminable interest rule, because likely variations in trust income or corpus made it impossible to express the spouse's income interest or power in terms of a "fractional or percentile share."[225]

In *Northeastern Pennsylvania National Bank & Trust Co. v. United States*,[226] the Supreme Court rejected this narrow view of the regulations concerning the identification of a specific portion of an *income interest*. The case involved a decedent's creation of a trust requiring payment to the surviving

---

the surviving spouse with required beneficial enjoyment of property), 9604003 (Oct. 10, 1995) (life estate in a remainder interest did not satisfy regulation in a QTIP situation).

[221] Reg. § 20.2056(b)-5(e) (last sentence).

[222] See supra ¶ 5.06[7][c] text accompanying notes 194, 195.

[223] The term also appears in Sections 2056(b)(6) and 2056(b)(7). See infra ¶¶ 5.06[8][c], 5.06[8][d].

[224] Rev. Rul. 79-86, 1979-1 CB 311 (Section 2056(b)(5) held inapplicable because no income interest was assured).

[225] See Reg. § 20.2056(b)-5(c) (prior to its amendment Mar. 1, 1994, by TD 8522, 1994-1 CB 236).

[226] Northeastern Pa. Nat'l Bank & Trust Co. v. United States, 387 US 213 (1967).

spouse of $300 income per month, with excess income to be accumulated and a general power of appointment over the entire corpus by will. The government argued that the trust did not qualify for the marital deduction because the spouse's income interest was not expressed as a fractional or percentile share of the income from the trust corpus. A majority of the Court, three judges dissenting, allowed the deduction, because they found "no indication . . . that Congress . . . intended that the deduction . . . would be defeated merely because the specific portion or the undivided part was not expressed . . . in terms of a fractional or percentile share of the whole corpus";[227] and they rejected the conclusion in the regulations[228] that "if the annual income of the spouse is limited to a specific sum . . . the interest is not . . . deductible."[229] Relying on *Northeastern*, the Tax Court subsequently held that a *general power of appointment* over a specific dollar amount of trust corpus would also qualify for the Section 2056(b)(5) exception to the terminable interest rule.[230] The Tax Court result was philosophically wrong because the specific dollar amount would not reflect appreciation or depreciation in the value of the corpus.[231]

---

[227] Northeastern Pa. Nat'l Bank & Trust Co. v. United States, 387 US 213, 220–221 (1967).

[228] See Reg. § 20.2056(b)-5(c) (prior to its amendment Mar. 1, 1994, by TD 8522, 1994-1 CB 236).

[229] The Seventh Circuit had previously held the "specified portion" test of income under the regulations invalid. Citizens Nat'l Bank of Evansville v. United States, 359 F2d 817 (7th Cir.), cert. denied, 387 US 941 (1966); cf. Estate of Schildkraut v. Comm'r, 368 F2d 40 (2d Cir.), cert. denied, 386 US 959 (1966). The result in *Northeastern* was theoretically correct because, as the Court pointed out, its decision "will not result in any of the combined marital estate escaping taxation in either the decedent's or the surviving spouse's estate." Northeastern Pa. Nat'l Bank & Trust Co. v. United States, 387 US 213, 224 (1967). This includes the Supreme Court's conclusion as to the amount to be deducted. See Note, "Federal Taxation: Supreme Court Disapproves Treasury Regulation's Imposition of Fractional or Percentile Share Requirement on Section 2056(b)(5) Marital Deduction," 1967 Duke LJ 1261.

[230] Estate of Alexander v. Comm'r, 82 TC 34 (1984), aff'd without opinion (4th Cir. 1985). Several other courts had allowed a general power to appoint a pecuniary amount to satisfy the specific portion requirement. Gelb v. Comm'r, 298 F2d 544 (2d Cir. 1962) (where the spouse held a life estate with a general power of appointment over corpus, but trustee held a power to invade corpus to the extent of $5,000 per year for the child, deduction allowed to the extent of corpus less $5,000 times the spouse's and child's joint life expectancy); Allen v. United States, 250 F. Supp. 155 (ED Mo. 1965) ($5,000 deduction allowed where a widow was given income from a trust and a general power to appoint $5,000 from corpus per year); see Estate of Hollingshead v. Comm'r, 70 TC 578 (1978) (a widow was given income and a general power of appointment to appoint the greater of 5 percent of corpus and $5,000 per year, and the Commissioner conceded that the 5 percent amount qualified under Section 2056(b)(5)).

[231] See Stephens, Maxfield, Lind & Calfee, Federal Estate and Gift Taxation ¶ 5.06[8][b] notes 226–233 (Warren, Gorham & Lamont, 6th ed. 1990); see also Lake, "Qualification of a Specific Portion of a Trust for the Marital Deduction" 19 Stan. L. Rev.

In 1992, Congress added Section 2056(b)(10), which silenced the controversy and sided with the Service's original position providing that the term "specific portion" includes only a portion based on a fractional or percentage basis.[232] The provision is generally effective in the case of estates of decedents dying after October 24, 1992, and to gifts after that date.[233]

If the specific portions identified for income interest and general power of appointment purposes are in differing amounts, Section 2056(b)(5) is applicable only to the smaller of the portions.[234] Thus, it is clear that if the surviving spouse is entitled to only one half (or some other fraction) of the income, the deduction under Section 2056(b)(5) will be limited to the value of one half (or the relevant fraction) of the trust corpus, even if the surviving spouse has larger powers over the corpus.[235]

[ii] The income payable to the surviving spouse must be payable annually or at more frequent intervals. By and large, this requirement speaks

---

468 (1967); Boudett, "Dollar Amount Income as a Specific Portion for Marital Deduction," 2 USF L. Rev. 107 (1967). The Treasury agreed with this conclusion, and while it accepted the *Northeastern* result with respect to an income interest, it was unwilling to accept the *Alexander* result as to a general power of appointment interest. It took that position in Proposed Regulations Sections 20.2056(b)-5(c)(3), 1984-1 CB 598, 604; 20.2056(b)-5(c)(5) Ex. 1, 3, 1984-1 CB 598, 605. See TD 8522, 1994-1 CB 236, 237.

[232] IRC § 2056(b)(10). This section is applicable to Sections 2056(b)(6) and 2056(b)(7) as well as Section 2056(b)(5). See also IRC § 2523(f)(3) providing the same rule under the gift tax. Energy Policy Act of 1992, Pub. L. No. 102-486, § 1941, 106 Stat. 2776, 3036 (1992) reprinted in 1993-1 CB 246, 258.

[233] The legislative history of this subsection provided that no inference should be drawn regarding the law prior to its enactment. HR Conf. Rep. No. 1018, 102nd Cong., 2d Sess. 394, 433 (1992), reprinted in 1993-1 CB 268, 286. The Treasury adopted final regulations providing that for transfers prior to the effective date, it accepted the results of *both* the *Northeastern* and the *Alexander* cases. Reg. §§ 20.2056(b)-5(c)(3)(i), 20.2056(b)-5(c)(5) Exs. 1, 3. However, the results of the cases are not accepted with respect to estates of decedents dying after the effective date; thus, only a fraction or percentage amount will suffice for the subsequent decedents' estates. Reg. §§ 20.2056(b)-5(c)(2), 20.2056(b)-5(c)(5) Ex. 4.

The October 24, 1992, effective date is delayed three years to October 24, 1995, if the decedent had executed the will or revocable trust prior to October 24, 1992. The October 24, 1992, effective date is delayed to the date of the decedent's death if the decedent had a will or revocable trust executed prior to October 24, 1992, and was mentally disabled on such date and did not regain competence prior to death. Reg. § 20.2056(b)-5(c)(3)(iii). The extended date rules do not apply if the will or revocable trust is amended after October 24, 1992, in any respect that increases the marital deduction transfer or alters the terms by which the interest passes to the surviving spouse. Reg. § 20.2056(b)-5(c)(3)(iv).

[234] Reg. §§ 20.2056(b)-5(c)(2), 20.2056(b)-5(c)(5) Ex. 3. If the smaller specific portion relates to the general power of appointment, a Section 2056(b)(7) election may be available and preferable to use of Section 2056(b)(5). See infra ¶ 5.06[8][d].

[235] Reg. § 20.2056(b)-5(b).

for itself. The Treasury recognizes that the requirement need not be spelled out in the trust instrument if applicable local law compels such frequent distribution.[236] Of course, a contrary provision in the trust instrument or a contrary rule of local law, if applicable, would defeat the exception to the terminable interest rule. The Treasury takes the position that to satisfy this condition the income must be currently distributable to the surviving spouse;[237] and where there is a mandatory delay of one year before income may be paid out, such payment of income is not considered current.[238]

[iii] **The surviving spouse must have the power to appoint the entire interest or the specific portion to either surviving spouse or spouse's estate.** Although it is sometimes suggested that a power that is a general power under Section 2041 will meet this requirement of the terminable interest exception, the statutory provision echoed in the regulations is that the surviving spouse must be able to appoint to spouse or spouse's estate, one or the other; thus, a power only to appoint to spouse's creditors, which is a general power under Section 2041, will not meet the requirement of Section 2056(b)(5).[239] This illustrates the possibility alluded to earlier in this discussion that interests that will cause tax liability in a surviving spouse's estate do not necessarily qualify for the marital deduction; and it is curious that Congress did not simply adopt the general power definition of Section 2041(b).

If the spouse can appoint to spouse or if spouse can appoint to spouse's estate, the fact that spouse can also appoint to others does not defeat the exception to the terminable interest rule.[240] Of course, in line with the general principles of the marital deduction provision, it should be observed here that in such circumstances the property will be the subject of either gift or estate tax liability, and possibly both, depending on what action the spouse takes. Thus, no policy reason exists for a denial of the deduction.

Is a power to consume equivalent to a power of appointment? A problem that has given rise to considerable litigation is whether, when there is a bequest in trust with income to the surviving spouse for life, an attending power in the spouse to consume corpus is the equivalent of a power of appoint-

---

[236] Reg. § 20.2056(b)-5(e); Friedman v. United States, 364 F. Supp. 484 (SD Ga. 1973). But cf. Priv. Ltr. Rul. 8705002 (Oct. 8, 1986).

[237] Reg. § 20.2056(b)-5(f)(8). Priv. Ltr. Rul. 9936052 (June 16, 1999) (power to distribute income to the surviving spouse).

[238] Rev. Rul. 72-283, 1972-1 CB 311. Cf. Rev. Rul. 77-346, 1977-2 CB 340.

[239] Cf. Condon Nat'l Bank of Coffeyville v. United States, 349 F. Supp. 755 (D. Kan. 1972).

[240] Estate of Smith v. Comm'r, 37 TCM (CCH) 745 (1978); Rev. Rul. 72-154, 1972-1 CB 310. The surviving spouse's power may be held as an executor or trustee. Robertson v. United States, 310 F2d 199 (5th Cir. 1962).

ment.[241] If a court decides that the power to consume is the equivalent of an inter vivos power of appointment, the further issue is whether the power is exercisable by the surviving spouse "alone and in all events."[242] The leading case is *Estate of Pipe v. Commissioner*.[243] In that case, the court held that the surviving spouse's power to consume[244] was not broad enough to allow her to appoint the corpus to herself as the owner, a right that is required by Section 2056(b)(5),[245] even though there were no restraints whatever on her use of the property. Similarly, there is authority for denying the marital deduction for a bequest of a life estate unless the life tenant spouse has such power over the remainder that the spouse may dispose of it by gift.[246]

Application of these principles often raises close questions concerning the proper interpretation of a will provision[247] and the effect of state law on the scope of the power.[248] Even within the same state (Pennsylvania), a close reading of similar will provisions has thrown the marital deduction question in opposite directions.[249] In one case, a decedent gave a spouse the power to sell or otherwise dispose of property "as to her may seem best"; nevertheless, under local law the power was deemed merely administrative and not a power that

---

[241] IRC § 2056(b)(5).

[242] IRC § 2056(b)(5).

[243] Estate of Pipe v. Comm'r, 241 F2d 210 (2d Cir.), cert. denied, 355 US 814 (1957). Cf. United States v. First Nat'l Trust & Sav. Bank of San Diego, 335 F2d 107 (9th Cir. 1964).

[244] The bequest to the surviving spouse was of a life estate with full power to use corpus "for such purpose or in such manner, as she [the surviving spouse] in her uncontrolled discretion may choose."

[245] Accord Comm'r v. Ellis, 252 F2d 109 (3d Cir. 1958); Estate of Carpenter v. Comm'r, 52 F3d 1266 (4th Cir. 1995). See Reg. § 20.2056(b)-5(g)(3); Estate of Nelson v. Comm'r, 46 TCM (CCH) 377 (1983).

[246] Reg. § 20.2056(b)-5(g)(3); May v. Comm'r, 283 F2d 853 (2d Cir. 1960), cert. denied, 366 US 903 (1961); Condon Nat'l Bank of Coffeyville v. United States, 349 F. Supp. 755 (D. Kan. 1972); Burnett v. United States, 314 F. Supp. 492 (DSC 1970), aff'd per curiam, 436 F2d 975 (4th Cir. 1971); Lincoln Rochester Trust Co. v. United States, 188 F. Supp. 839 (WDNY 1960), rev'd, 297 F2d 891 (2d Cir.), cert. denied, 369 US 887 (1962); Estate of Adams v. Comm'r, 60 TCM (CCH) 1324 (1990). But see IRC § 2056(b)(7).

[247] E.g., McGehee v. Comm'r, 260 F2d 818 (5th Cir. 1958) (deduction allowed).

[248] Tyler v. United States, 468 F2d 959 (10th Cir. 1972); Guiney v. United States, 425 F2d 145 (4th Cir. 1970); Stewart v. Usry, 399 F2d 50 (5th Cir. 1968); May v. Comm'r, 283 F2d 853 (2d Cir. 1960), cert. denied, 366 US 903 (1961); Edwards v. Comm'r, 58 TC 348 (1972), nonacq. 1972-2 CB 3; Estate of Cline v. Comm'r, 43 TCM (CCH) 607 (1982).

[249] Compare Comm'r v. Ellis, 252 F2d 109 (3d Cir. 1958), with Hoffman v. McGinnes, 277 F2d 598 (3d Cir. 1960).

would qualify a terminable interest for the marital deduction.[250] The real problem is whether authority conferred on the surviving spouse by the decedent, not phrased or interpreted to accord with the exact terms of Section 2056(b)(5), creates a power of the kind required.[251] Prudence suggests that the draftsman follow closely the statutory language, even though variations in the principles of local law may still upset the applecart.

As in other areas, local law is interpreted to determine the parties' property interests. Until 1967, the question of what weight federal courts were required to accord local decisions was in doubt. However, in a case involving Section 2056(b)(5), the Supreme Court dealt with the problem.[252] In that case, the decedent had, during life, created a revocable trust for a spouse over which the spouse was given a general power of appointment. Later, the spouse purported to release the power, after which the decedent died. The issue before the court was whether the decedent's estate was allowed the marital deduction for the interest that had passed to the spouse, which was included in the decedent's gross estate. The court of appeals held that, although it was not "bound by" a decision of a state court with respect to local rights, in this case a state court had "authoritatively determined the rights under state law of a party to the federal action," and that decision was conclusive as to those rights for purposes of federal taxation. Accordingly, since the state court had held that the release was a nullity, the court of appeals recognized the existence of the power that supported the marital deduction. One judge dissented.[253] The Supreme Court reversed (with three judges dissenting).[254] In dicta the Court stated that the federal courts would accord finality to a state court's decision only if the local decision is made by the highest court of the state. However,

---

[250] Cass v. Tomlinson, 1957-1 USTC ¶ 11,692 (SD Fla. 1957); see also Estate of Flake v. Comm'r, 68 TCM (CCH) 1232 (1994) (power to revoke constituted a general power of appointment); McMillan v. Comm'r, 76 TC 170 (1981); Evans v. United States, 719 F2d 201 (6th Cir. 1983); Estate of Raisler v. Comm'r, 54 TCM (CCH) 1390 (1987); Estate of Stockdick v. Phinney, 65-2 USTC ¶ 12,351 (SD Tex. 1965); TAMs 9021002 (Feb. 9, 1990), 9023004 (Feb. 20, 1990).

[251] Piatt v. Gray, 321 F2d 79 (6th Cir. 1963); Estate of Holland v. Comm'r, 64 TC 499 (1975); Estate of Field v. Comm'r, 40 TC 808 (1963); Estate of Prox v. Comm'r, 35 TCM (CCH) 1003 (1976); Estate of Johnson v. Comm'r, 36 TCM (CCH) 1557 (1977); Estate of Smith v. Comm'r, 37 TCM (CCH) 745 (1978); Estate of Flake v. Comm'r, 68 TCM (CCH) 1232 (1994); Rev. Rul. 74-120, 1974-1 CB 282.

[252] Comm'r v. Estate of Bosch, 387 US 456 (1967). A discussion of the Supreme Court's holding and its implications under Section 2033 is found at ¶ 4.05[2][b]. See Gans, "Federal Transfer Taxation and the Role of State Law: Does the Marital Deduction Strike the Proper Balance?" 48 Emory LJ 871 (1999).

[253] Friendly, J.; see also Friendly, "In Praise of Erie And of the New Federal Common Law," 39 NYU L. Rev. 383 (1964).

[254] A companion case, Second Nat'l Bank v. United States, 351 F2d 489 (2d Cir. 1966), heard with the *Bosch* case, was affirmed.

in the absence of such a decision, only "proper regard," not finality, is to be accorded a prior local decision. The Supreme Court remanded the case; on remand, the Second Circuit concluded that the state's highest court would hold the release valid and that the marital deduction should have been denied.[255]

The meaning of the term "specific portion" again crops up with respect to a general power of appointment over a specific portion of the corpus. Against a controversial background, Congress has simply provided that a specific portion includes only a portion based on a fractional or percentage basis.[256]

[iv] The power in the surviving spouse must be exercisable by the spouse alone and (whether exercisable by will or during life) must be exercisable in all events. As the parenthetical phrase suggests, it is enough that the surviving spouse have either an inter vivos power or a testamentary power, or both.[257] Moreover, if the spouse has one or the other under which the spouse may appoint to the spouse or spouse's estate, the spouse may also have other lesser powers without defeating the exception. For example, if a surviving spouse was left a lifetime interest in a trust with a lifetime power to appoint the corpus only to the spouse's children and a power by will to appoint the corpus to the spouse's estate, this requirement of Section 2056(b)(5) would be met.[258] This may seem at odds with the general principles of the marital deduction provisions, but it is not. The reason is that although an exercise of a nongeneral power such as the lifetime power to appoint to the children would not ordinarily be a taxable transaction, in the circumstances here under discussion the exercise would constitute a release of the general testamentary power with attending gift or estate tax consequences.[259]

A requirement that someone join with the spouse in the exercise of the power will defeat the exception, because the power must be exercisable "alone."[260] This may go further than is necessary to assure a sensible result, because a post-1942 power can be a general power giving rise to estate or gift

---

[255] Comm'r v. Estate of Bosch, 382 F2d 295 (2d Cir. 1967).

[256] IRC § 2056(b)(10). The history of this area and the effective date rules are discussed supra ¶ 5.06[8][b] text accompanying notes 223–233.

[257] Estate of Prox v. Comm'r, 35 TCM (CCH) 1003 (1976); Rev. Rul. 77-30, 1977-1 CB 291.

[258] Reg. § 20.2056(b)-5(g)(5).

[259] ET 23, 1950-1 CB 133. Both the gift tax (Reg. § 25.2514-3(c)(4)) and the estate tax (Reg. § 20.2041-3(d)(1)) regulations make it clear that a release "need not be formal or express in character."

[260] IRC § 2056(b)(5) (last sentence). Draper v. Comm'r, 55 TCM (CCH) 797 (1988); Estate of Wilson v. Comm'r, 64 TCM (CCH) 576 (1992) (spouse power to act alone); Rev. Rul. 82-156, 1982-2 CB 216.

tax liability in some circumstances even if not exercisable by the decedent alone.[261]

The further requirement that the power be "exercisable in all events" is strictly construed against the taxpayer. If the spouse's power can be cut off during the spouse's life other than by the spouse's exercise or release of the power, as for example by the spouse's remarriage, or if the exercise of the power is otherwise restricted or conditional, it is not "exercisable in all events."[262] To meet the "all events" test the power must arise upon the death of the decedent and be exercisable, for example, before the estate makes distribution of the property subject to the power; but it is permissible that actual distribution to the appointee be delayed.

In one case, a decedent by will left property in trust for a spouse, giving the spouse also an unlimited right to invade the corpus, considered in the case a power to appoint to the spouse.[263] However, the will also provided that the spouse's power to invade should cease "in case of the spouse's legal incapacity from any cause or upon the appointment of a guardian, conservator, or other custodian of spouse's person or estate." The appeals court agreed with the Tax Court that the spouse's power was not "exercisable in all events."[264] A provision of local law that merely suspends powers of appointment in case of legal incapacity[265] does not defeat the exception to the terminable interest rule. If it did, the provisions of Section 2056(b)(5) could rarely be satisfied. In the case under discussion, the court pointed out that by the terms of the will, "the power of appointment ceases, finally and absolutely, upon the occurrence of the legal incapacity."[266] In another case in which under the terms of the will the spouse's power would cease on the appointment of a guardian, conservator,

---

[261] See discussions of Section 2041(b)(1)(C) at ¶ 4.13[4][c] and Section 2514(c)(3) at ¶ 10.04[2][b].

[262] Reg. §§ 20.2056(b)-5(g)(3), 20.2056(b)-5(g)(4); Estate of Foster v. Comm'r, 725 F2d 201 (2d Cir. 1984); Winkle v. United States, 381 F. Supp. 536 (SD Ohio 1974); Estate of Walsh v. Comm'r, 110 TC 29 (1998) (power terminated on incompetency); Rev. Rul. 76-446, 1976-2 CB 295; Priv. Ltr. Rul. 8924003 (Feb. 27, 1989). However, the deduction is not lost by qualifying the exercise of the power within the six months and by the common disaster principles of Section 2056(b)(3), discussed supra ¶ 5.06[8][a]. Reg. § 20.2056(b)-5(h).

[263] Starrett v. Comm'r, 223 F2d 163 (1st Cir. 1955); Reg. § 20.2056(b)-5(g)(1)(i). See Priv. Ltr. Rul. 9936052 (June 16, 1999) (power to accelerate IRA benefits was a general power of appointment).

[264] Starrett v. Comm'r, 223 F2d 163, 166 (1st Cir. 1955). See McCombs v. United States, 248 F. Supp. 568 (WD Ky. 1965).

[265] See Rev. Rul. 75-350, 1975-2 CB 367; TAM 9511002 (Dec. 2, 1994). Query as to a trust provision to the same effect?

[266] Starrett v. Comm'r, 223 F2d 163, 167 (1st Cir. 1955).

or other custodian, in circumstances short of legal incapacity, the deduction was denied.[267]

[v] The entire interest or the specific portion must not be subject to a power in any other person to appoint any part to any person other than the surviving spouse. A power in another to appoint only to the surviving spouse need not defeat the exception to the terminable interest rule, because if it is exercised the property subject to the power simply becomes property owned outright by the spouse subject to usual gift or estate tax consequences depending on the spouse's disposition of the property. Thus, as the statute indicates and the regulations provide, "a power in a trustee to distribute corpus to ... a surviving spouse will not disqualify the trust."[268] However, if another person had a special power to appoint to the decedent's children, which could be exercised so as to defeat a spouse's inter vivos or testamentary power, property might be released from the surviving spouse's estate free of tax, and such a power would disqualify the trust.[269] If the other person's power is exercisable only after the death of the surviving spouse, the Treasury properly agrees that the trust is not disqualified because such a power is not "in opposition to that of the surviving spouse."[270] Also, if the surviving spouse had a qualifying interest under Section 2056(b)(5), it is not disqualified by the fact that the spouse could invade the corpus for the benefit of third parties.[271] An example in the regulations dealing with this point is worth setting out in full to reflect also the rule of the 1986 Code, retroactively incorporated into the 1939 Code provisions, regarding the deduction of the value of specific portions of property left in trust:[272]

> Assume that the decedent created a trust, designating his surviving spouse as income beneficiary for life and as donee of a power to appoint by will the entire corpus. The decedent further provided that the trustee could distribute 30 percent of the corpus to the decedent's son when he reached the age of 35 years. Since the trustee has a power to appoint 30 percent of the entire interest for the benefit of a person other than the sur-

---

[267] Estate of Tingley v. Comm'r, 22 TC 402, 405 (1954). A power exercisable only for a period of one year is not exercisable "in all events." Rev. Rul. 66-38, 1966-1 CB 212.

[268] Reg. § 20.2056(b)-5(j); Estate of Smith v. Comm'r, 79 TC 974, acq. 1984-2 CB 2.

[269] Estate of McCabe v. United States, 475 F2d 1142 (Ct. Cl. 1973) (no marital deduction where wife's income and inter vivos general power were subject to the trustee's authority to invade corpus for a third person). See Rev. Rul. 69-56, 1969-1 CB 224; Priv. Ltr. Rul. 9147065 (July 12, 1991).

[270] Reg. § 20.2056(b)-5(j) (see particularly Reg. § 20.2056(b)-5(j) Ex. 1).

[271] Rev. Rul. 72-154, 1972-1 CB 310.

[272] Reg. § 20.2056(b)-5(j) Ex. 2.

viving spouse, only 70 percent of the interest placed in trust satisfied [the fifth requirement]. . . . If, in this case, the surviving spouse had a power, exercisable by her will, to appoint only one-half of the corpus as it was constituted at the time of her death, it should be noted that only 35 percent of the interest placed in the trust would satisfy [the third requirement].

If all five tests of Section 2056(b)(5) are met, the decedent's estate qualifies for the marital deduction.[273] The Treasury has recognized that even though a Section 2056(b)(5) marital trust is combined with an "estate trust,"[274] the property qualifies for the marital deduction.[275] The decedent involved in the ruling had created a trust income to a surviving spouse for life, and at the spouse's death, corpus necessary to meet the administration expenses of the spouse's estate was to be distributed to the spouse's executor, with the remaining corpus subject to a general power by the surviving spouse to appoint by will and designated beneficiaries to take in default of the spouse's appointment. The ruling concluded that although it was impossible to determine what portion of the property would be within the estate trust and what portion subject to Section 2056(b)(5), the entire trust property had to fall within one or the other of the two concepts; therefore, both portions qualified for the marital deduction. A marital deduction was allowed for the entire value of the property left in trust.

[c] Insurance With Powers

Insurance proceeds that pass outright and unconditionally to a surviving spouse constitute a "deductible interest" for marital deduction purposes.[276] Similarly, an insurance policy on the life of one other than the decedent can be transferred or bequeathed outright so as to qualify for the deduction. If the proceeds of a policy on the decedent's life or an existing policy on the life of another are left in trust for a surviving spouse and interests pass as well to other persons, availability of the marital deduction depends on the terminable interest rule exception discussed earlier under Section 2056(b)(5). However, if the proceeds of a life insurance, annuity, or endowment contract[277] are to be

---

[273] This is so even though the exact amount of property passing may not be determined until a later time because of a formula clause equalizing taxes in both spouse's estates. Estate of Smith v. Comm'r, 66 TC 415 (1976), aff'd, 565 F2d 455 (7th Cir. 1977), nonacq. 1978-1 CB 3. See also Laurin v. Comm'r, 645 F2d 8 (6th Cir. 1981).

[274] See supra ¶ 5.06[7][c] text accompanying notes 194, 195.

[275] Rev. Rul. 72-333, 1972-2 CB 530. But see Rev. Rul. 75-128, 1975-1 CB 308 (discussed at supra ¶ 5.06[7][c] note 194).

[276] Reg. §§ 20.2056(a)-2(b), 20.2056(c)-2(b)(3).

[277] The principles of Section 2056(b)(6) are expressly applicable to annuity and endowment contracts as well as to insurance on the decedent's life.

paid in installments or are to be held by the insurer under an agreement to pay interest, and an interest in such proceeds passes as well to someone other than the surviving spouse, then availability of the marital deduction depends on the insurance exception to the terminable interest rule in Section 2056(b)(6).[278]

The insurance exception follows closely the exception concerning life interests with powers; accordingly, discussion is abbreviated here. The fivefold statutory test for application of the insurance exception is expressed by the Treasury essentially as follows:[279]

1. The proceeds, or a specific portion of the proceeds, must be held by the insurer subject to an agreement either to pay the entire proceeds or a specific portion thereof in installments, or to pay the interest thereon; and all or a specific portion of the installments or interest payable during the life of the surviving spouse must be payable only to spouse.

2. The installments or interest payable to the surviving spouse must be payable annually, or more frequently, commencing not later than thirteen months after the decedent's death.[280]

3. The surviving spouse must have the power to appoint all or a specific portion of the amounts so held by the insurer to either the spouse or the spouse's estate.

4. The power in the surviving spouse must be exercisable by the spouse alone and (whether exercisable by a will or during life) must be exercisable in all events.[281]

5. The amounts or the specific portion of the amounts payable under such contract must not be subject to a power in any other person to appoint any part thereof to any person other than the surviving spouse.

Although these five requirements largely parallel the requirements of Section 2056(b)(5), some differences exist in application. For example, an interest in trust income expressed in terms of a fixed dollar amount is disqualified under Section 2056(b)(5) for failing to identify a fractional or percentile share,

---

[278] Reg. § 20.2056(b)-6(a). If, at the date of the decedent's death, the surviving spouse has several options, none of which violates the terminable interest rule exceptions, then the proceeds qualify for the marital deduction even though the option is not exercised until a later time. Estate of Fiedler v. Comm'r, 67 TC 239 (1976). In the alternative, Section 2056(b)(7) may be elected if its requirements are met. See infra ¶ 5.06[8][d].

[279] Reg. §§ 20.2056(b)-6(a)(1), 20.2056(b)-6(a)(2), 20.2056(b)-6(a)(3), 20.2056(b)-6(a)(4), 20.2056(b)-6(a)(5).

[280] As long as the payments can begin within thirteen months and the surviving spouse is the only person with any voice in the decision, this requirement is satisfied. Estate of Fiedler v. Comm'r, 67 TC 239 (1976).

[281] See Estate of Fiedler v. Comm'r, 67 TC 239 (1976).

as explained earlier.[282] In contrast, under Section 2056(b)(6), installment or interest payments to which a surviving spouse is entitled under an insurance policy may be so expressed if "it is shown that such sums [reflect an interest in] a definite or fixed percentage or fraction of the total proceeds."[283]

It is enough that a surviving spouse has a right that in effect is a power to appoint to the spouse or the spouse's estate; the term "power to appoint" need not be used in the contract.[284] Thus, a surviving spouse's right to "withdraw any proceeds" constitutes a power to appoint to the spouse;[285] again, state law is examined to determine the extent of the spouse's rights.[286] A right to direct an insurance company to pay the proceeds to the surviving spouse's "executors, administrators or assigns" has been recognized as a power to appoint to the estate of the surviving spouse.[287] The conclusion is supportable.[288]

Preoccupation with the terminable interest rule and its exceptions should not obscure the fact that a part of the proceeds of an insurance policy can sometimes qualify for the marital deduction entirely outside the terminable interest rule and without regard to its exceptions, even though an interest in the proceeds passes to someone other than the surviving spouse.[289] This would always be so if, say, one half of the proceeds were left outright to the spouse, but there are less obvious possibilities as well. In one case, the proceeds of insurance on the decedent's life were to be distributed to the surviving spouse in equal installments for ten years certain with like installments to the surviving spouse thereafter for the spouse's life; but if the surviving spouse should die within the ten-year period, the remaining certain installments were to be paid to the decedent's children. Reversing the Tax Court,[290] the appeals court held that although the portion of the proceeds covering the ten-year installments constituted a nondeductible terminable interest, the amount the insurance company designated as required for the payment of installments for life to the surviving spouse after the ten-year period was a deductible interest that did qualify for the marital deduction.[291] As regards that part of the proceeds, no in-

---

[282] IRC § 2056(b)(10); Reg. § 20.2056(b)-5(c)(2). See supra ¶ 5.06[8][b] text accompanying notes 223–233.

[283] Reg. § 20.2056(b)-6(c)(1).

[284] Reg. § 20.2056(b)-6(e)(4).

[285] Estate of Wynekoop v. Comm'r, 24 TC 167 (1955), acq. 1955-2 CB 10.

[286] Estate of Wynekoop v. Comm'r, 24 TC 167 (1955), acq. 1955-2 CB 10; Moore v. United States, 1970-2 USTC ¶ 12,715 (ND Ohio 1970).

[287] Rev. Rul. 55-277, 1955-1 CB 456.

[288] Compare Second Nat'l Bank v. United States, 209 F2d 321 (7th Cir. 1954), with Keeter v. United States, 323 F. Supp. 1093 (ND Fla. 1971), rev'd, 461 F2d 714 (5th Cir. 1972).

[289] Rev. Rul. 77-130, 1977-1 CB 289.

[290] Estate of Reilly v. Comm'r, 25 TC 366 (1955).

[291] Estate of Reilly v. Comm'r, 239 F2d 797 (3d Cir. 1957).

terest passed to any other person. The exact holding of the case has been upset by the Supreme Court's decision in *Meyer*.[292] On the facts presented, the Supreme Court held that the insurer's bookkeeping division of the proceeds of a policy into two parts was not enough to make such parts separate properties to be tested separately for marital deduction purposes. The Supreme Court did not, however, purport to decide whether a single life insurance policy could create several properties or funds.[293]

[d] Election With Respect to Life Estate for Surviving Spouse

Congress, perhaps after visiting Oz, Disney World, and even Lewis Carroll's Wonderland, apparently discovered how intriguing make-believe can be. We are authorized by Section 2056(b)(7) to pretend that one who is *not* the owner, really *is* the owner of property. Why? A decedent may wish the decedent's surviving spouse to have the enjoyment during spouse's life of the property that decedent leaves, but not unlimited control over its disposition either during spouse's life or upon spouse's death. The decedent's will may therefore provide that spouse receive the income from the property for life and also give spouse a limited lifetime right to invade the principal or give another person broad or limited authority to distribute principal to spouse.[294] What is left upon spouse's death, the remainder, is disposed of according to further provisions in decedent's will, not merely *spouse's* wishes. With the current high divorce rate, spouse is often a second (or at least not a first) spouse; and very likely it is children of an earlier marriage to whom decedent wishes to give the remainder. This disposition of the decedent's property passes to the surviving spouse only a terminable interest that, when coupled with the interests given to others, would not qualify for the marital deduction absent some authority permitting us to pretend that spouse is the owner of the property for transfer tax purposes.[295] Section 2056(b)(7) provides another, albeit quite different, exception to the general terminable interest rule; it permits the entire value of property disposed of in this manner (both the life estate and the remainder) to qualify for the marital deduction, and combined with Sections 2519 and 2044, is the authority for the required fantasy.[296]

---

[292] Meyer v. United States, 364 US 410 (1960).

[293] But see Rev. Rul. 77-130, 1977-1 CB 289.

[294] The invasion power may be limited by an ascertainable standard relating to health, education, support, or maintenance. Cf. IRC § 2041(b)(1)(A), ¶ 4.13[4][a].

[295] IRC § 2056(b)(1).

[296] Economic Recovery Tax Act of 1981, Pub. L. No. 97-34, § 403(d), 95 Stat. 172, 305 (1981), reprinted in 1981-2 CB 256, 325. The Section 2056(b)(7) QTIP provision is effective for the estates of decedents dying after December 31, 1981. Reg. § 20.2056(b)-(7)(a).

If the property in the disposition just discussed is "qualified terminable interest property," the terminable interest rule need not apply. The statute provides that, in the case of proper election, "no part of [the] property [is] treated as passing to anyone other than the surviving spouse," even though the surviving spouse has only a life interest and the remainder actually passes to others.[297] As the entire value of qualified terminable interest property is treated as passing to the surviving spouse, a marital deduction may be claimed for its full value.[298] The equalizer here[299] is that all interests in such property may be subjected to transfer taxes on the spouse's disposition of any part of the income interest during spouse's lifetime[300] or upon spouse's death.[301] Neither the surviving spouse nor spouse's estate need bear the actual burden of transfer taxes on property that has been treated as qualified terminable interest property. An apportionment rule provides that the transfer taxes imposed on interests, other than the spouse's income interest, in qualified terminable interest property may be borne by the property.[302]

Three requirements must be met for property to be classified as qualified terminable interest property: (1) the property must pass from the decedent;[303] (2) the surviving spouse must have a qualifying income interest for life in the property;[304] and (3) the decedent's executor must elect to apply Section 2056(b)(7).[305]

[i] The passing requirement. Although this requirement may appear repetitious, it is needed to assure that an interest qualifying for the marital deduction under the qualified terminable interest property rules "passes," as the term is used in Section 2056(a) and as defined in Section 2056(c),[306] from the decedent to whoever receives the interest. If an interest is to qualify for the marital

---

See Cornfeld, "A Tin Cup for QTIPs—The Tenth Anniversary of the Unlimited Marital Deduction and QTIPs," 26 Miami Inst. Est. Plan. Chapter 14 (1992); Jones, "Marital Deduction Planning With QTIPs After 1984 Tax Reform Act: The Flexibility and Some Problems Continue," 4 Boston UJ Tax Law 139 (1986); Landroche, "The Qualified Terminable Interest Rule: An Overview," 34 U. Fla. L. Rev. 737 (1982); McCaffrey & Kalik, "Qualified Terminable Interest Property (III)," 189 NYLJ 1 (1983); Schain, "Marital Trust v. QTIP: Advice for Estate Planners," 49 Mo. L. Rev. 741 (1984).

[297] IRC § 2056(b)(7)(A)(ii).

[298] IRC § 2056(b)(7)(A)(i).

[299] The proper cliché is "there is no such thing as a free lunch."

[300] IRC §§ 2511, 2519, 2702. Section 2519 is discussed at ¶ 10.08.

[301] IRC § 2044, discussed at ¶ 4.16. Cf. infra ¶ 5.06[8][e] text accompanying note 415.

[302] IRC § 2077A, discussed at ¶ 8.07.

[303] IRC § 2056(b)(7)(B)(i)(I).

[304] IRC § 2056(b)(7)(B)(i)(II).

[305] IRC § 2056(b)(7)(B)(i)(III).

[306] See supra ¶ 5.06[3].

deduction, it must be included in the decedent's gross estate and pass from the decedent.[307] If a decedent held an income interest for *spouse's life* in a trust that had been created by a third party and their child was the remainderperson of the trust, only the income interest would be included in the decedent's gross estate.[308] If the decedent bequeaths the income interest to surviving spouse, the full trust corpus did not pass from the decedent, and it should not be treated and is not treated as a qualified terminable interest property interest qualifying for the marital deduction.[309] The income interest, as opposed to the entire corpus, does qualify for the marital deduction, because it passes from the decedent and is not a disqualified terminable interest.[310]

[ii] **The qualifying income interest requirement.** The "qualifying income interest" requirement involves two components. The surviving spouse must have, first, a right to all the income from the property for spouse's life, payable annually or more frequently (or have a usufruct interest for life in the property);[311] and second, no one may have a power to appoint any part of the property during spouse's lifetime except for spouse's benefit.[312]

The income interest. The surviving spouse's income interest must generally commence at decedent spouse's death and extend for surviving spouse's entire life.[313] Income interests granted for a term of years or to terminate on the occurrence of a specified event, such as remarriage, are not qualifying income interests.[314] Even though the language of Section 2056(b)(7) is not identical to that of Section 2056(b)(5), the income interests required by these sections are generally identical.[315] When dealing with the income interest re-

---

[307] IRC § 2056(b)(7)(B)(i)(I).

[308] IRC § 2033.

[309] See IRC § 2056(b)(7)(B)(i)(I).

[310] The interest is not a disqualified terminable interest because the requirements of Section 2056(b)(1)(A) are not satisfied. Cf. Estate of Harper v. Comm'r, 93 TC 368 (1989).

[311] IRC § 2056(b)(7)(B)(ii)(I). Estate of Rapp v. Comm'r, 71 TCM (CCH) 1709 (1996), aff'd, 140 F3d 1211 (9th Cir. 1998) (requirement not met where federal court not bound by state court reformation of will); TAM 9818005 (Jan. 6, 1998) (disclaimer did not result in a qualifying income interest).

[312] IRC § 2056(b)(7)(B)(ii)(II). See Priv. Ltr. Rul. 200106008 (Oct. 20, 2000) (local court reformed a trust for a scrivener's error; the reformed trust then satisfied this requirement).

[313] HR Rep. No. 201, 97th Cong., 1st Sess. 161 (1981), reprinted in 1981-2 CB 352, 378. But see Reg. §§ 20.2056(b)-5(f)(9), 20.2056(b)-7(d)(2).

[314] HR Rep. No. 201, 97th Cong., 1st Sess. 161 (1981), reprinted in 1981-2 CB 352, 378. Reg. §§ 20.2056(b)-7(d)(3), 20.2056(b)-7(h) Ex. 5.

[315] Reg. § 20.2056(b)-7(d)(2). See Reg. § 20.2056(b)-5(f).

quired by Section 2056(b)(7), an examination of the discussion of income interests recognized under Section 2056(b)(5) is in order.[316]

The government originally took the position that if a surviving spouse's income interest was contingent on an executor's making a qualified terminable interest property election, the interest was not a qualifying income interest.[317] The rationale for that position was that the determination of whether property passing to a surviving spouse qualifies for the marital deduction is to be made at the instant of death.[318] The government claimed that the surviving spouse must have a qualifying income interest in the property from the moment of death, regardless of whether the executor ultimately made an election with respect to the property. The courts did not agree with the government, and allowed the qualified terminable interest property election and the marital deduction even though under the deceased spouse's testamentary document, the surviving spouse's income interest was contingent on the executor's election.[319] The government finally conceded and issued regulations providing that an income interest for life that is contingent on the executor's election to treat the trust as a qualified terminable interest property will not, on that basis, fail to be a qualifying income interest for life.[320]

At the opposite end of the spectrum, some of the judiciary and the Service agree that a trust provision allocating "stub income" to remainder benefi-

---

[316] See supra ¶¶ 5.06[8][b][i], 5.06[8][b][ii]. For example, compare Reg. § 20.2056(b)-7(h) Ex. 2 (the surviving spouse had power to force trustee to invest in productive property) with the discussion in Reg. §§ 20.2056(b)-5(f)(4), 20.2056(b)-5(f)(5); see also supra ¶ 5.06[8][b] text accompanying note 215 discussing the fact that the income required is satisfied if the spouse is entitled to income as defined under a state statute that provides for a reasonable apportionment between the income and remainder beneficiaries of the total return of the trust including a 3 percent to 5 percent unitrust. Prop. Reg. § 20.2056(b)-5(f)(1).

[317] Reg. §§ 20.2056(b)-7(d)(3), 20.2056(b)-7(h) Ex. 6, as finalized Feb. 28, 1994, in TD 8522, 1994-1 CB 236.

[318] Cf. Jackson v. United States, 376 US 503 (1964).

[319] Estate of Spencer v. Comm'r, 43 F3d 226 (6th Cir. 1995); Estate of Robertson v. Comm'r, 15 F3d 779 (8th Cir. 1994); Clayton v. Comm'r, 976 F2d 1486 (5th Cir. 1992); Estate of Clack v. Comm'r, 106 TC 131 (1996). Cf. Patterson v. United States, 181 F3d 927 (8th Cir. 1999) (similar rationale used for tax apportionment).

[320] Reg. § 20.2056(b)-7(d)(3)(i). The regulation applies to estates of decedents whose estate tax returns are due after February 18, 1997. Id. The estates of decedents whose returns were due prior to February 18, 1997, are granted an extension to make a QTIP election if (1) the period of limitations on filing a claim for credit or refund under Section 6511(a) has not expired with respect to the estate; (2) a claim for refund or credit is filed; and (3) the estate submits a statement providing that, pursuant to Section 2044, the surviving spouse's gross estate will include the value at the date of the surviving spouse's death of the property for which the QTIP election is made. The statement must be signed under penalties of perjury by the surviving spouse, the spouse's legal representative, or the surviving spouse's executor if the surviving spouse is deceased. Reg. § 20.2056(b)-7(d)(3)(ii).

ciaries does not disqualify an otherwise qualifying income interest.[321] Stub income is undistributed income that has accrued between the last payment date and the date of death of the surviving spouse.[322] Stub income generated by trust property in which the surviving spouse had a qualifying income interest is included in the surviving spouse's gross estate generally under Section 2044.[323]

---

[321] Estate of Howard v. Comm'r, 910 F2d 633 (9th Cir. 1990); Estate of Shelfer v. Comm'r, 86 F3d 1045 (11th Cir. 1996); Talman v. United States, 37 Fed. Cl. 741 (1997); Reg. § 20.2056(b)-7(d)(4), effective with respect to decedents dying after March 1, 1994. The Tax Court did not agree. See Estate of Shelfer v. Comm'r, 103 TC 10 (1994); Estate of Howard v. Comm'r, 91 TC 329 (1988). *Howard* is discussed in Odeku, "Section 2056(b)(7) Qualified Terminable Interest Property Marital Deduction in Estate of Rose D. Howard v. Commissioner," 44 Tax Law. 907 (1991).

[322] Reg. § 20.2056(b)-7(d)(4).

[323] Reg. § 20.2056(b)-7(d)(4). Unless otherwise included under some other section, inclusion occurs under Section 2044. Reg. § 20.2044-1(d)(2). Attempted codification of this essentially noncontroversial stub income rule has thus far not been enacted. See, e.g., HR Rep. No. 3419, 103d Cong., 1st Sess. §§ 603(a)(1), 603(e) (1994) (Tax Simplification and Technical Corrections Bill of 1993).

The surviving spouse must have a right to all[324] the income from the property[325] or a right to all the income from a "specific portion"[326] of the property. In the latter case, the specific portion is treated as the qualified terminable interest property.[327] The income interest must be payable to the surviving spouse at least annually.[328] Local law is taken into account in determining whether the annual distribution requirement is satisfied.[329] Section 2056(b)(7) imposes no restriction on the surviving spouse's disposition of a qualifying in-

---

[324] But see the text accompanying supra notes 321–323.

[325] IRC § 2056(b)(7)(B)(ii)(I). See Estate of Doherty v. Comm'r, 95 TC 446 (1990) (no QTIP election was permitted where the trustee could accumulate income and the surviving spouse trustee could be replaced during the spouse's lifetime); Estate of Novotny v. Comm'r, 93 TC 12 (1989) (limitations imposed on an income interest did not disqualify it, because the limitations were virtually identical to those imposed by state law); Estate of Nicholson v. Comm'r, 94 TC 666 (1990) (the spouse's income rights are subject to a standard, so no right to all income); Estate of Ellingson v. Comm'r, 964 F2d 959 (9th Cir. 1992) (the spouse had right to all income because power to accumulate income beyond the spouse's best interests would preclude clear intent to qualify for a QTIP election); *Ellingson* is discussed in Lazarus, "Limitations on the Qualified Terminable Interest Property Marital Deduction: Estate of Ellingson v. Commissioner," 46 Tax Law. 959 (1993)); Estate of Wells v. United States, 746 F. Supp. 1024 (D. Haw. 1990) (the spouse had no right to all income, because the income could be distributed to the children). Priv. Ltr. Rul. 9325002 (Feb. 26, 1993) (the income interest did not qualify because of a potential court power to modify income rights; this ruling is criticized in Kasner, "Ruling on Marital Deduction Is Dangerous and Unsupportable," 61 Tax Notes 91 (1993)); TAM 9237009 (May 21, 1992) (the unproductive art work qualified for QTIP treatment under Reg. §§ 20.2056(b)-5(f)(4), 20.2056(b)-5(f)(5)).

Even if a Section 2056(b)(7) election has been made, a spouse's subsequent Section 2518 disclaimer of the income interest nullifies any marital deduction. Rev. Rul. 83-26, 1983-1 CB 234. Cf. Priv. Ltr. Rul. 9320015 (Feb. 17, 1993) (the surviving spouse's Section 2518 disclaimer of an outright receipt of property resulted in funds going into trust that qualified for QTIP treatment).

On the other hand, valid Section 2518 disclaimers by third parties of income leaving a surviving spouse with all the income from a trust that otherwise satisfies the requirements of Section 2056(b)(7) qualify the trust for a marital deduction. Estate of Lassiter v. Comm'r, 80 TCM (CCH) 541 (2000); Priv. Ltr. Rul. 200030012 (Apr. 26, 2000).

[326] See IRC § 2056(b)(10); Reg. § 20.2056(b)-7(b)(1)(ii); supra ¶ 5.06[8][b] text accompanying notes 223–233.

[327] IRC § 2056(b)(7)(B)(iv).

[328] IRC § 2056(b)(7)(B)(ii)(I). In Rev. Rul. 2000-2, 2000-1 CB 305, it was held that an executor may elect to treat an IRA and a trust as a qualifying income interest where the surviving spouse has the authority to compel the trustee of the trust to withdraw all of the IRA's income from the trust at least annually and the trust's terms were consistent with QTIP treatment. Compare Priv. Ltr. Ruls. 9320015 (Feb. 17, 1993), 9932001 (Apr. 29, 1999), and 9704029 (Oct. 31, 1996) (same) with TAM 9220007 (Jan. 30, 1991) (not qualified).

[329] Reg. § 20.2056(b)-7(g); Estate of Cavenaugh v. Comm'r, 100 TC 407 (1993) (the trustee held some discretion over distributions, but local law required distributions to be paid at least annually).

come interest. However, disposition of the interest has transfer tax consequences.[330] If a spendthrift clause restricts the surviving spouse's right of disposition, the spouse's income interest nevertheless may be "qualified" under Section 2056(b)(7).[331]

Qualifying income interests are not limited to interests in property placed in a trust.[332] Property subject to a legal life estate may be qualified terminable interest property. A qualifying life estate or interest in nontrust property must accord the recipient surviving spouse with income rights of the same character as those required by Section 2056(b)(5).[333] A common example of a legal life estate constituting a qualified terminable interest is a legal life estate in a residence. Assuming the surviving spouse has a right to use the residence, or to rent it and receive all the rent, and must consent to any disposition of it, the surviving spouse's interest constitutes a qualifying income interest.[334] An income interest in a pooled income fund also qualifies as a qualifying income interest.[335]

Strictly speaking, an annuity is not a qualifying income interest, since it is not an arrangement calling merely for payments of income.[336] Nevertheless, there are two special qualified terminable interest property rules under which an annuity is treated as a qualifying income interest facilitating the treatment of the annuity as qualified terminable interest property.[337] Section

---

[330] See IRC §§ 2511 (tax consequences on transfer of the income interest), 2519 (tax consequences on transfer of the other interests). Section 2519 is discussed at ¶ 10.08. Cf. IRC §§ 2207A(b), 2702; ¶¶ 8.07, 19.03.

[331] See Reg. §§ 20.2056(b)-5(f)(7), 20.2056(b)-7(d)(2). Estate of Miller v. United States, 949 F. Supp. 544 (ND Ohio 1997).

[332] Reg. § 20.2056(b)-7(d)(2).

[333] Reg. §§ 20.2056(b)-7(d)(2), 20.2056(b)-5(f). See Priv. Ltr. Rul. 9242006 (July 15, 1992) (legal life estate in artwork qualified for the QTIP election).

[334] Reg. § 20.2056(b)-7(h) Ex. 1; Peacock v. United States, 914 F2d 230 (11th Cir. 1990). If the surviving spouse had a right to only one half of the income generated by the property if it were sold, then there is a qualifying income interest in only one half of the residence. TAM 9040001 (June 8, 1990). See Kyle v. Comm'r, 94 TC 829 (1990) (Texas homestead interest is not a qualifying interest because the spouse's interest terminates if the spouse abandons residence); TAMs 9033004 (May 2, 1990) (no qualifying interest if no right to rent), 9229004 (Mar. 31, 1992) (no qualifying interest where the surviving spouse's interest terminates if the spouse is not occupying residence). Cf. Priv. Ltr. Rul. 9126020 (Mar. 29, 1991) (vacation residence in trust qualified because even though third parties (children) had a right to use the residence, their rights were subordinate to that of the spouse).

[335] Reg. §§ 20.2056(b)-7(d)(5), 20.2056(b)-7(h) Ex. 13. For this reason, a pooled income fund does not qualify for the Section 2056(b)(8) terminable interest exception. See infra ¶ 5.06[8][e] note 409 and text accompanying notes 414, 415.

[336] IRC § 2056(b)(7)(B)(ii)(I); cf. Estate of Becklenberg v. Comm'r, 273 F2d 297 (7th Cir. 1959); Estate of Bergan v. Comm'r, 1 TC 543 (1943), acq. 1943 CB 2.

[337] IRC §§ 2056(b)(7)(C), 2056(b)(7)(B)(ii) (flush language last sentence).

2056(b)(7)(C) treats the value of an annuity as qualified terminable interest property if a surviving spouse is the only payee *during spouse's life* of an annuity that was either included in the decedent spouse's gross estate under Section 2039 or, as a community property interest, was included in the decedent spouse's gross estate under Section 2033.[338] The rule only applies to annuities which are classifed as terminable interests, where there are third-party annuitants or recipients under the annuity.[339] Under Section 2056(b)(7)(C), if the third party or parties have no rights to any payments before the death of the surviving spouse, the surviving spouse's interest is treated as a qualifying income interest for life.[340] When the rule applies, the decedent spouse's executor is deemed to have made an election to treat the survivorship annuity as qualified terminable interest property unless the executor makes an irrevocable contrary election on the estate tax return.[341]

The second annuity rule is similar to the first in that an annuity interest will be treated as a qualifying income interest. The second rule applies to annuity interests created at the decedent spouse's death, not annuities included in the decedent's gross estate under Section 2039. The second rule is to be pro-

---

[338] Section 2033 applies in a situation where a nonparticipant spouse predeceases a participant spouse and the spouses owned a retirement plan subject to community property laws. HR Conf. Rep. No. 220, 105th Cong., 1st Sess. 1718 (1997), reprinted in 1997-4 CB (Vol. 2) 1457, 2188. The provision is applicable only to the estates of decedents dying after August 5, 1997. The Taxpayer Relief Act of 1997, Pub. L. No. 105-34, § 1311(a), 111 Stat. 788, 1044 (1997), reprinted in 1997-4 CB (Vol. 1) 1, 258. The conference report indicates that the provision is not intended to modify the result of Boggs v. Boggs, 520 US 833 (1997) (holding that ERISA preempted Louisiana community property law and allowing a predeceasing participant spouse's testamentary transfer of the spouse's interest in retirement benefits). HR Conf. Rep. No. 220, 105th Cong., 1st Sess. 1, 717–718 (1997), reprinted in 1997-4 CB (Vol. 2) 1457, 2188.

[339] If all benefits are to be paid to the surviving spouse and no one else, then there is no terminable interest, and the Section 2056(b)(7)(C) rule does not apply.

[340] IRC § 2056(b)(7)(C)(i).

[341] IRC § 2056(b)(7)(C)(ii). Cf. IRC §§ 2523(f)(6)(A), 2523(f)(6)(B).

Section 2056(b)(7)(C) annuities include qualified annuities. IRC § 417(b). See HR Rep. No. 795, 100th Cong., 2d Sess. 522 (1988). Part of the reason for the enactment of this statutory rule is that the Retirement Equity Act generally requires a joint-and-survivor annuity as an automatic form of benefit under a qualified pension plan. See HR Rep. No. 795, 100th Cong., 2d Sess. 522 (1988). Cf. Reg. § 2056(b)-7(h) Ex. 10, which treats IRA payments within IRC § 2056(b)(7)(B)(ii) without regard to IRC § 2056(b)(7)(C); Rev. Rul. 2000-2, 2000-1 CB 305; Priv. Ltr. Rul. 9317025 (Jan. 29, 1993). Congress also enacted a comparable but more complex gift tax marital deduction rule under Section 2523(f)(6). See ¶ 11.03[4][c][ii].

The Treasury has reserved regulations on all joint-and-survivor annuities, including those under Section 2056(b)(7)(C). See Reg. § 2056(b)-7(f) and infra note 344. However, the Service will issue rulings on whether an annuity will qualify for Section 2056(b)(7)(C) treatment, subject to what the regulations may specify in the future. See, e.g., Priv. Ltr. Rul. 9822031 (Feb. 25, 1998).

vided for in regulations pursuant to statutory directive.[342] The regulations only provide a second annuity rule for decedent's dying before October 25, 1992, and certain individuals dying thereafter with wills or revocable trusts executed prior thereto.[343] The regulation rule for other decedents is yet to be promulgated.[344]

With respect to a decedent dying before October 25, 1992, under the second special rule, a surviving spouse's lifetime annuity interest payable from a

---

[342] IRC § 2056(b)(7)(B)(ii) (flush language, last sentence).

[343] Reg. § 20.2056(b)-7(e). This regulation applies to decedents dying after October 24, 1992, if the property passes under a will or revocable trust executed before October 25, 1992, and either the decedent was under a mental disability on October 25, 1992, that continued until death or the decedent dies prior to October 24, 1995. Reg. § 20.2056(b)-7(e)(5)(ii). The transitional rule is inapplicable if the will or revocable trust is amended in any respect after October 24, 1992, which increases the amount of the marital deduction or alters the terms of the interest passing to the surviving spouse. Reg. § 20.2056(b)-7(e)(5)(iii).

[344] Section 2056(b)(10), defining the term "specific portion" for purposes of the exceptions to the terminable interest rule in Sections 2056(b)(5), 2056(b)(6), and 2056(b)(7)(b)(iv), is effective generally in the case of decedents dying after October 24, 1992. See supra ¶ 5.06[8][b] text accompanying notes 223–233. Since the meaning of the term "specific portion" is more narrowly defined in Section 2056(b)(10) than under case law prior to its enactment, the Treasury has reserved regulations on annuities generally for estates of decedents dying after October 24, 1992, for the first special rule under Section 2056(b)(7)(C), as well as the second special rule. See Reg. §§ 20.2056(b)-7(e), 20.2056(b)7-(f).

There is substantial uncertainty regarding the regulatory rules that will eventually be promulgated under the second special rule. The government has been unclear whether an annuity interest bequeathed to a surviving spouse followed by other interests in third parties qualifies as a Section 2056(b)(7)(B)(ii) qualified income interest. In Rev. Ruls. 76-273, 1976-2 CB 268, and 82-105, 1982-1 CB 133, the Service ruled that the unitrust and annuity interests in a CRUT and a CRAT, respectively, were retained rights to the income from the property under Section 2036(a)(1), implying that such interests would constitute "the income from the property" under Section 2056(b)(7)(B)(ii)(I). Cf. ¶ 4.08[8] note 168. The Service has taken inconsistent positions in private letter rulings whether an annuity interest qualifies as a qualifying income interest involving Section 2056(b)(7). Compare Priv. Ltr. Ruls. 8730004 (Apr. 15, 1987) (no Section 2056(b)(7) election permitted for a CRAT with an annuity to a surviving spouse) and 9409005 (Oct. 29, 1993) (the surviving spouse's annuity interest from a trust did not qualify for a Section 2056(b)(7) election) with Priv. Ltr. Rul. 9021001 (Jan. 1, 1990) (the surviving spouse's annuity interest from a trust qualified for a Section 2056(b)(7) election). Cf. supra note 316

It seems clear that the regulations will not permit a deduction if the annuity violates the executor purchase rule. See supra ¶ 5.06[7][d]. Example 14 contained in prior Proposed Regulations Section 20.2056(b)-7(e) (LR-211-76, 1984-1 CB 598, 607) does not appear in the final regulations. The example permitted an executor-purchased annuity for a surviving spouse to qualify for a marital deduction as qualified terminable interest property even though it would not qualify for a marital deduction under the executor purchase rule of Section 2056(b)(1)(C). The current regulations state that "[t]erminable interests described in Section 2056(b)(1)(C) cannot qualify as qualified terminable interest property." Reg. § 20.2056(b)-7(b)(1)(i).

trust or other group of assets passing from the decedent is treated as a qualifying income interest for life.[345] However, an annuity interest will be treated as a qualifying income interest for life only if no other person may receive distributions from the property funding the annuity during the life of the surviving spouse.[346] If the other Section 2056(b)(7) requirements are also met,[347] the amount of the marital deduction generated by the annuity is the specific portion of the property that, using an appropriate interest rate,[348] would produce income equal to the minimum annuity amount paid annually to the surviving spouse.[349] If property from which the annuity is payable is insufficient to produce an amount of income equal to the minimum annuity amount, the entire value of the property qualifies for the deduction.[350] The amount of the marital deduction may not exceed the value of the property funding the annuity.[351]

Powers over Property During the Surviving Spouse's Life. An interest is a qualifying income interest only if no one, including the surviving spouse,[352] has a power to appoint the underlying property to anyone other than the surviving spouse during spouse's lifetime.[353] If there is a disqualifying power and

---

[345] Reg. § 20.2056(b)-7(e)(1).

[346] Reg. § 20.2056(b)-7(e)(3).

[347] See IRC §§ 2056(b)(7)(B)(i)(I), 2056(b)(7)(B)(i)(III).

[348] Reg. § 20.2056(b)-7(e)(4). The applicable interest rate for valuing annuities is determined using Sections 2031 and 7520 and the regulations promulgated for these sections. See Reg. §§ 20.2031-7, 20.2031-7A, 20.7520-1.

[349] Reg. § 20.2056(b)-7(e)(2). If the amount of the annuity may be increased, as where the annuity is subject to an upward adjustment for inflation, the increased amount is not taken into account in determining the amount of the marital deduction generated by the annuity. Id. See Reg. § 20.2056(b)-7(h) Ex. 11.

[350] Reg. § 20.2056(b)-7(e)(2). See Reg. § 20.2056(b)-7(h) Ex. 12.

[351] Reg. § 20.2056(b)-7(e)(2). See Reg. § 20.2056(b)-7(h) Ex. 12. Furthermore, if the annuity amount may increase, the increased amount is not taken into account involving the deductible interest. Reg. § 20.2056(b)-7(e)(2); Estate of Sansone v. United States, 87 AFTR2d 2001-2345 (CD Cal. 2001).

[352] Reg. § 20.2056(b)-7(d)(1).

[353] IRC § 2056(b)(7)(B)(ii)(II); see Reg. §§ 20.2056(b)-7(d)(6), 20.2056(b)-7(h) Ex. 4; Estate of Manscill v. Comm'r, 98 TC 413 (1992); Estate of Bowling v. Comm'r, 93 TC 286 (1989); Estate of Rinaldi v. United States, 80 AFTR2d 97-5324 (Fed. Cl. 1997); TAM 199903031 (Sept. 30, 1998). A very indirect spousal power was found in a field service advice (undated, but reported by 1999 TNT 100-87) involving conversion rights of a partnership interest.

A power under applicable state law that permits the trustee to adjust between income and principal to fulfill the trustee's duty of impartiality between the income and remainder beneficiaries that meets the requirements of Prop. Reg. § 1.643(b)-1 is not a power to appoint trust property to one other than the surviving spouse. Prop. Reg. § 20.2056(b)-7(d)(1).

In Priv. Ltr. Rul. 9113009 (Dec. 21, 1990), the Service took the position that if the property were transferred to a surviving spouse along with a guarantee of a nonrecourse obligation and if the spouse also received a separate otherwise valid QTIP trust interest,

it is validly disclaimed under Section 2518, it is disregarded and the interest may qualify.[354] There is no restriction on the surviving spouse, or anyone else for that matter, having a power to invade the corpus during the spouse's lifetime as long as the invasion is only for surviving spouse's benefit.[355] The invasion power is allowed regardless of whether it is subject to a standard.[356] The regulations concede the fact that the surviving spouse may circumvent this restriction by transferring the distributed property to a third person in a transfer that would be a gift transfer under Section 2511.[357] However, the regulations do provide that the third person invasion restriction is violated if surviving spouse is legally bound to transfer the distributed property to a third person without adequate and full consideration.[358]

The restriction against a power to appoint the property to someone other than the surviving spouse does not apply to a power exercisable only at or after the death of the surviving spouse.[359] If the surviving spouse or some third party is given a nongeneral power over the remainder, "exercisable only at or

---

the QTIP trust was totally disqualified for a marital deduction because the bequests violated Section 2056(b)(7)(B)(ii)(II). The ruling was criticized in August & Kalunas, "Guarantors Have Unexpected Gift Tax and Marital Deduction Consequences in IRS Ruling," 74 J. Tax'n 346 (1991). In Priv. Ltr. Rul. 9409018 (Dec. 1, 1993), the Service reconsidered the issue and held that the borrower does not possess an "interest in" or a "power to appoint the property" under Section 2056(b) and the mere presence of a loan guarantee does not cause the total disallowance of the Section 2056(b)(7) bequest. The prior ruling was withdrawn. See August, "IRS Reverses Prior Ruling on the Impact of Guarantees on the Marital Deduction," 80 J. Tax'n 324 (1994). See supra ¶ 5.06[5][b] note 103. See also FSA 200018020 (Jan. 20, 2000) (sale of property at a discount prior to funding of a QTIP trust did not violate Section 2056(b)(7)(B)(ii)(II)).

[354] See Reg. § 20.2056(b)-7(h) Ex. 4. See Priv. Ltr. Ruls. 8429085 (Apr. 19, 1984), 8443005 (July 12, 1984) (both applying Section 2056(b)(7) after valid Section 2518 disclaimers of third-party interests).

[355] Section 2056(b)(7)(B)(ii)(II) proscribes an invasion only for "any person other than the surviving spouse." See Reg. § 20.2056(b)-7(d)(6); Estate of Bowling v. Comm'r, 93 TC 286 (1989). But see Parasson v. United States, 87-1 USTC ¶ 13,708 (ND Ohio 1987). If, however, there is a power to invade for the minor children to satisfy the spouse's support obligation, any invasion is for the surviving spouse and the requirement is met. Cf. Reg. §§ 20.2056(b)-5(j), 20.2056(b)-7(h) Ex. 4. But see TAM 9005002 (Aug. 31, 1989) (the requirement not satisfied because there was no support obligation as the children were adults).

[356] It is possible that a trust will satisfy the requirements of both paragraphs (5) and (7) of Section 2056(b), if the surviving spouse can invade the corpus only for the spouse's own benefit and the invasion power is held by the spouse alone and is exercisable in all events. If the surviving spouse is given an invasion power for the spouse's benefit not limited by a standard of health, education, support, or maintenance, the spouse holds a general power over the property. See IRC §§ 2514, 2041, 2056(b)(5); infra ¶ 5.06[8][f].

[357] Reg. § 20.2056(b)-7(d)(6).

[358] Reg. § 20.2056(b)-7(d)(6).

[359] IRC § 2056(b)(7)(B)(ii) (flush language).

after" the spouse's death, the property may be qualified terminable interest property. If there appears to be a gap in the net here (and a hungry tax collector left hungry), do not lose sight of Section 2044.[360]

The statutory restrictions against powers in qualified terminable interest property arrangements are unnecessarily broad. The legislative history indicates that the purpose of these restrictions is to ensure that the value of the property not consumed by the spouse be a part of the measure of the estate tax on spouse's death or of the gift tax upon spouse's earlier disposition of the property.[361] The restriction on powers held by a surviving spouse over the qualified terminable interest property is not needed to accomplish this purpose. Regardless of the type of power held by a surviving spouse, the government would be assured of tax on the transfer of the property, whatever action the spouse takes or does not take.[362]

The rule that only powers exercisable at or after the death of the surviving spouse are innocuous is also overly restrictive. There should be no question when any person holding a power to dispose of only a remainder interest may act even if the power is exercisable during the surviving spouse's life. If there is a power, exercisable not merely at the surviving spouse's death but also during spouse's life, to dispose of only the remainder interest, it will not alter the surviving spouse's life income interest. The spouse would still be entitled to all the income from the property for life. The property would be included in the spouse's gross estate under Section 2044, and the government would get its tax bite. For example, assume Decedent left property in trust, income to Spouse for life, remainder to their Children, but added an inter vivos power in Spouse or some third party to alter Children's interests. An alteration of Children's interests does not affect the Spouse's income interest; it should still be a qualifying income interest. It is not the time of exercise but the time the exercise is effective that should be significant here. The Service may agree with this conclusion because they seem to provide that a power "the exercise

---

[360] See ¶ 4.16.

[361] HR Rep. No. 201, 97th Cong., 1st Sess. 161 (1981), reprinted in 1981-2 CB 352, 378.

[362] The surviving spouse might be given a general power over the corpus, a general power over the remainder, a nongeneral power over the corpus or a nongeneral power over the remainder, or some combination of these powers. Whatever combination of such powers was granted, if the spouse took no action during the spouse's lifetime, the property would be included in the spouse's gross estate under Section 2044 and possibly Section 2041. If the spouse's power were over only the remainder, the property would also be included under Section 2044 and possibly Section 2041. If the spouse exercised a general power over corpus during life in favor of a third party, the spouse would make a transfer of property under Sections 2514 and 2519. If the spouse exercised a nongeneral power over corpus, this would constitute a transfer of the income interest under Section 2511 (see ¶ 10.04[3][c]), which would trigger a transfer of the remainder interest under Section 2519. See ¶ 10.08.

of which takes effect only at or after [surviving spouse's] death" does not violate the qualified terminable interest property requirement.[363]

[iii] **The election.** Section 2056(b)(7) is an elective provision,[364] operative only if an election[365] is made by the executor[366] of the decedent's estate on the estate tax return to treat property as qualified terminable interest property.[367] An election can be made for all or a specific portion[368] of the property passing from the decedent in which the surviving spouse receives a qualifying income interest.[369] Sometimes only a portion of a piece of property is within the qualified terminable interest property provision. For example, if Decedent creates a trust, one half of the income payable to Spouse for Spouse's life and one half to Decedent's Sibling for Sibling's life, remainder to Decedent's Children, a Section 2056(b)(7) election can be made only with respect to one half of the corpus; and for purposes of both Decedent's and Spouse's estates, Spouse is treated under the exception to the terminable interest rule as receiving and owning one half of the corpus outright.[370] Even if Spouse is to receive *all* the income from the trust for Spouse's life, the executor may elect to qualify only

---

[363] See Reg. § 20.2056(b)-7(h) Ex. 4 (fourth sentence).

[364] IRC § 2056(b)(7)(B)(i)(III).

[365] A decedent spouse's executor also may want to make a "reverse QTIP election" with respect to QTIP. IRC § 2652(a)(3). The purpose of such an election is to continue to treat the decedent spouse as the "transferor" of the property for generation-skipping transfer tax purposes. Generally, this is done to maximize the decedent spouse's use of the GST exemption. Reverse QTIP elections are considered in detail at ¶ 17.02[1][c][i].

[366] Cf. IRC § 2203. An executor makes the election even though the executor is not in possession of the property. However, if there is no appointed executor, a person in actual or constructive possession of the property may make the election. Reg. § 20.2056(b)-7(b)(3). For example, the trustee of an inter vivos trust included in the decedent's gross estate could make an election in the absence of an appointed executor. Reg. § 20.2056(b)-7(b)(3).

[367] IRC § 2056(b)(7)(B)(v).

[368] IRC § 2056(b)(10). See supra ¶ 5.06[8][b] text accompanying notes 223–233.

[369] IRC § 2056(b)(7)(B)(iv). Reg. § 20.2056(b)-7(b)(2). See Priv. Ltr. Ruls. 8814002 (Oct. 29, 1987), 9915015 (Jan. 6, 1999) (the trustee allowed extension pursuant to Reg. § 301.9100-3 to convert full election to partial election).

[370] Reg. § 20.2056(b)-7(h) Ex. 3.

a specific portion of the trust as QTIP.[371] The election effectively treats a "specific portion" of property as "separate property."[372]

If the election is for only a specific portion of property in which the surviving spouse receives a qualifying income interest, the portion must be expressed as a percentage or fractional share of identifiable property passing from the decedent.[373] The percentage or fractional share requirement assures that the elective portion will reflect a proportionate share of the appreciation or depreciation of all property passing from the decedent in which the surviving spouse has a qualifying income interest.[374] The percentage or fraction may be expressed by a formula.[375]

A trust may be divided into separate trusts to reflect a partial election if authorized either under the governing instrument or local law.[376] The division must be made by the termination of the period of estate administration, and if not divided by the time of filing the estate tax return, an intent to divide must be unequivocally indicated on the estate tax return.[377] The severed trust must be divided on a fractional or percentage basis,[378] which may be determined by a formula.[379] The trust need not be funded with a proportionate share of each asset,[380] but the division must be required either by the governing instrument

---

[371] See IRC § 2056(b)(10); Reg. § 20.2056(b)-7(h) Ex. 3. If there is an election made with respect to only a specific portion of a trust corpus in which the spouse has only a proportionate qualifying income interest, only that specific portion of the proportionate interest qualifies for QTIP treatment, i.e., if there is a 40 percent election with respect to the trust in which the spouse has a 50 percent qualifying income interest (supra text accompanying note 368), only 20 percent of the corpus qualifies for QTIP treatment. Reg. § 20.2056(b)-7(h) Ex. 3.

[372] IRC § 2056(b)(7)(B)(iv). If the executor has an invasion power over the entire trust for the spouse's benefit, the decedent's will may require the portion that qualifies for Section 2056(b)(7) treatment to be exhausted by the invasion power prior to the remainder of the corpus in order to reduce overall inclusion in the spouse's gross estate. The unqualified portion of the corpus is merely a terminable interest that expires on the spouse's death and is not included in the spouse's gross estate. Reg. § 20.2056(b)-7(h) Ex. 9.

[373] IRC § 2056(b)(10). Reg. § 20.2056(b)-7(b)(2)(i). See supra ¶ 5.06[8][b] text accompanying notes 222–233.

[374] Reg. § 20.2056(b)-7(b)(2)(i).

[375] Reg. § 20.2056(b)-7(b)(2)(i). See Reg. §§ 20.2056(b)-7(h) Exs. 7, 8; Priv. Ltr. Rul. 9724016 (Mar. 17, 1997). Cf. TAM 9327005 (Mar. 31, 1993).

[376] Reg. § 20.2056(b)-7(b)(2)(ii)(A).

[377] Reg. § 20.2056(b)-7(b)(2)(ii)(A).

[378] Reg. § 20.2056(b)-7(b)(2)(ii)(B).

[379] Reg. § 20.2056(b)-7(b)(2)(i). See Reg. § 20.2056(b)-7(h) Ex. 9.

[380] Reg. § 20.2056(b)-7(b)(2)(ii)(B).

or local law to be based on the fair market value of the assets at the time of the division.[381]

The decedent's will can either direct the executor to make the QTIP election or leave it to the executor's discretion. Postmortem estate planning flexibility is enhanced when the choice is left to the executor.[382]

The election is to be made on the last estate tax return filed on or before the due date (including extensions), or if a timely return is not filed, on the first return filed after the due date.[383] An election once made on a return is irrevocable.[384] If an election is made prior to the due date, the election may be altered on a subsequent timely filed return.[385]

The courts have been consistently strict in requiring taxpayers to elect affirmatively to use the qualified terminable interest property provisions,[386] but the executor can make the qualified terminable interest property election sim-

---

[381] Reg. §§ 20.2056(b)-7(b)(2)(ii)(C), 20.2056(b)-7(h) Ex. 14. This requirement of valuing the assets at fair market value on the date of the division is a stricter requirement than the requirement for a discretionary division of a trust for generation-skipping transfer tax purposes that allows *either* fair market valuation of the assets at the date of the division where the governing instrument requires a division based on a pecuniary bequest *or* a division in a manner that fairly reflects the net appreciation or depreciation in the value of the assets measured from the date of valuation (usually death) to the date of funding. See Reg. § 26.2654-1(b)(1)(ii)(C). Cf. Rev. Proc. 64-19, 1964-1 (Pt. 1) CB 682.

[382] The executor has a window of opportunity to determine whether or to what extent a QTIP election should be made.

[383] Reg. § 20.2056(b)-7(b)(4)(i). Regulations Section 301.9001-1(a) permits the Service to grant a reasonable extension of time to make an election where (1) the time for making the election is not prescribed by the statute; (2) the request for an extension is made within a period that the Commissioner considers reasonable; and (3) the Commissioner is satisfied that the interests of the government will not be jeopardized. The Service has granted an extension in numerous rulings where a marital deduction was claimed for a trust that qualified under Section 2056(b)(7) even though the original return did not unequivocally manifest an intent to make a QTIP election or did not properly list the property. See, e.g., TAMs 9414019 (Jan. 4, 1994), 9307001 (Mar. 11, 1992); Priv. Ltr. Rul. 9702006 (Sept. 30, 1996); TAM 9411010 (Dec. 13, 1993) (a regulation is applied to make a Section 2652(a)(3) reverse QTIP election). Cf. Priv. Ltr. Rul. 9752022 (Sept. 23, 1997) (relying on Reg. § 301.9100-3T).

[384] IRC § 2056(b)(7)(B)(v). However, an election that is unnecessary because the estate tax liability of an estate is zero prior to the election is treated as null and void for purposes of Sections 2056(b)(7), 2044(a), 2519, and 2652(a). Rev. Proc. 2001-38, 2001-1 CB 1335. The Revenue Procedure is inapplicable where a partial QTIP election was necessary to reduce the liability to zero and the executor made the election to more property than needed, where there is a formula clause designed to reduce the estate tax to zero, or to a protective election. Id.

[385] Reg. § 20.2056(b)-7(b)(4)(ii). Priv. Ltr. Rul. 8523006 (Feb. 4, 1985); cf. Priv. Ltr. Ruls. 8746004 (Aug. 7, 1987), 8418005 (1983).

[386] Higgins v. Comm'r, 897 F2d 856 (9th Cir. 1990); Estate of McCants, 61 TCM (CCH) 2038 (1991); Estate of Spohn, 90-2 USTC ¶ 60,027 (ND Ind 1990); Robinson v. United States, 90-2 USTC ¶ 60,045 (SD Ga. 1990).

ply by listing the trust property and the value thereof as a deduction on Schedule M.[387]

A protective election is allowed if at the time the federal estate tax return is filed the executor reasonably believes that there is a bona fide issue whether an asset is required to be included in the gross estate or a bona fide issue as to the amount or nature of property a surviving spouse is entitled to receive.[388] Once made, the protective election is irrevocable and binding when the issue is resolved.[389]

[iv] **Joint and mutual wills.** A terminable interest problem, possibly affected by Sections 2056(b)(5) and 2056(b)(7), sometimes arises with respect to joint and mutual wills.[390] Generally, such wills encompass agreements for a disposition of the predeceasing spouse's property to the survivor with disposition of all their property at the survivor's death to mutually-agreed-on third parties. There are various views on the legal effect of joint and mutual wills. A terminable interest problem arises only if on some accepted theory the planned disposition of the property is binding on the survivor, not merely precatory.[391] Even if binding, local law varies on the time at which the parties become bound,[392] the freedom of disposal over the property that the surviving spouse has during life,[393] and the theory under which third parties may recover if the surviving spouse fails to dispose properly of the property by will.[394]

---

[387] See Form 706, U.S. Estate (and Generation-Skipping Transfer) Tax Return (Rev. Nov. 2001).

[388] Reg. § 20.2056(b)-7(c)(1). The protective election must identify either the specific asset, group of assets, or trust and the specific basis for the protective election. Id.

[389] Reg. § 20.2056(b)-7(c)(2). No comparable protective QTIP election is available for inter vivos transfers. TD 8522, Supplementary Information (to the final Section 2056 regulations) 1994-1 CB 236, 238.

[390] In general, a joint will is a single will entered into by persons jointly disposing of their property, while mutual wills are two separate wills drafted in consideration for one another, under a jointly-agreed-on testamentary scheme. See Atkinson, Law of Wills 222–227 (West Pub. Co., 2d ed. 1953).

[391] The mere presence of joint or mutual wills is not sufficient to raise a presumption that they were executed pursuant to a binding contract. Atkinson, Law of Wills 225 (West Pub. Co., 2d ed. 1953).

[392] Compare Brown v. Webster, 90 Neb. 591, 134 NW 185 (1912) (binding on execution) with Smith v. Thompson, 250 Mich. 302, 230 NW 156 (1930) (binding at time of the predeceasing spouse's death, the majority view) and Tooker v. Vreeland, 92 NJ Eq. 340, 112 A. 665 (1921) (binding on acceptance of benefits).

[393] Estate of Grimes, 937 F2d 316 (7th Cir. 1991) (under local law, the surviving spouse had no general power). See Cook, "The Contractual Will: Invitation to Litigation and Excess Taxation," 48 Tex. L. Rev. 909, 911 (1970).

[394] Compare In re Edwards Estate, 3 Ill. 2d 116, 120 NE2d 10 (1954) (specific performance under the original will) with Smith v. Thompson, 250 Mich. 302, 230 NW 156 (1930) (contractual claim against the decedent's estate, the majority view). For a discus-

Problems in this area are difficult enough if attention is focused only on the question whether the marital deduction is allowed in the estate of the spouse first to die. However, the analysis of any specific situation certainly prompts a look at the estate tax consequences to the survivor. There is no general principle that if, upon the death of one spouse, the other spouse receives an interest in property that will be included in the gross estate of the second spouse to die, the estate of the predeceasing spouse gets a marital deduction.[395] Nevertheless, that is the general philosophy on which Section 2056 is grounded, and uneasiness sets in when in this or other respects the deduction provision fails to mesh well with the provisions defining "gross estate."

It is academically exciting, but frustrating and unprofitable, to explore the details of state law regarding joint and mutual wills.[396] Questions can be raised, for example, as to whether ultimate recipients who take under the will are perhaps entitled to specific performance, or whether instead they acquire only rights as third-party beneficiaries under a contract. Recognition of the contract theory might suggest a deductible claim against the estate of the survivor[397] under Section 2053(a), which would be anathema to the marital deduction in the estate of the first to die, because the property would not be effectively taxed (or would be only partly taxed) in the estate of the second decedent. Although federal tax consequences in this and other areas often turn on rights and obligations under local law, the theories under which local law determines these rights and obligations are irrelevant in a federal tax controversy. It is necessary to accord recognition to rights and obligations acquired or incurred under joint and mutual wills, but not to the various theories on which such rights and obligations are based.[398]

---

sion of joint and mutual wills, see Atkinson, Law of Wills 222 (West Pub. Co., 2d ed. 1953); Cook, "The Contractual Will: Invitation to Litigation and Excess Taxation," 48 Tex. L. Rev. 909 (1970); Schapiro, "The Marital Deduction: Joint or Mutual Wills and the Survivorship Requirement," 24 NYU Inst. on Fed. Tax'n 359 (1966); Note, "Joint and Mutual Wills," 61 Harv. L. Rev. 675 (1948).

[395] See Jackson v. United States, 376 US 503 (1964); Estate of Pipe v. Comm'r, 241 F2d 210 (2d Cir.), cert. denied, 355 US 814 (1957).

[396] One who attempts this will shares the impatience of Drennen, J., dissenting in Estate of Opal v. Comm'r, 54 TC 154, 168 (1970), aff'd, 450 F2d 1085 (2d Cir. 1971), who rejected "the subtleties of New York law" in favor of a broader estate tax view of the economic consequences of a joint will. But cf. Brown v. Comm'r, 52 TC 50 (1969), acq. 1969-2 CB xxiv (analyzing Texas law on joint and mutual wills for gift tax purposes).

[397] This in turn presents problems of whether and, more important, to what extent there is consideration for the claim. IRC § 2053(c)(1).

[398] The approach to joint and mutual wills indicated in the text is in accordance with the long-recognized objective of Congress "to give a *uniform* application to a nationwide scheme of taxation." Burnet v. Harmel, 287 US 103, 110 (1932) (emphasis added). To this end, "State law may control only when the federal taxing act, by express language or necessary implication, makes its own operation dependent upon state law." Id. at 110. Cf. Lyeth v. Hoey, 305 US 188 (1938).

In general, the marital deduction consequences to the predeceasing spouse's estate depend on whether local law grants the surviving spouse that degree of ownership contemplated by the marital deduction provisions. If, under local law, there is insufficient intent to create joint and mutual wills or if the wills are interpreted merely to express a precatory desire, then a marital deduction is allowed because the property passes outright to the surviving spouse who has complete ownership of it.[399] This is comfortable enough because the deduction in the estate of the first spouse is purchased at the cost of a matching inclusion in that of the second.

Joint and mutual wills raise the following three estate tax questions:

1. Does the surviving spouse gain complete freedom to use and dispose of the property? If so, the property received from the first decedent qualifies for the marital deduction[400] and is in no way screened from inclusion in the gross estate of the second.[401]

2. Does the surviving spouse acquire no more than the right to use or receive the income from the property during life?[402] If so, a marital deduction is available only when the Section 2056(b)(7) exception to the terminable interest rule is satisfied.[403]

3. Does the surviving spouse acquire lifetime rights that include the right to the income from the property received together with some freedom of disposition of the property? If so, the marital deduction must be tested against the description of powers of appointment that qualify a terminable interest for marital deduction under Section 2056(b)(5).[404] In the alternative, if its requirements are met, Section 2056(b)(7) may be used to qualify the predeceasing spouse's estate for a marital deduction. Again, however, this test should be made with regard to the scope of the surviving spouse's economic control

---

[399] Estate of Aquilino v. Comm'r, 31 TCM (CCH) 906 (1972). Cf. Kellmann v. United States, 286 F. Supp. 632 (ED Mo. 1968); Poage v. Phillips, 202 F. Supp. 267 (SD Iowa 1961).

[400] IRC § 2056(b)(5); United States v. Spicer, 332 F2d 750 (10th Cir. 1964); Estate of Vermilyea v. Comm'r, 41 TC 226 (1963), acq. 1973-1 CB 2; Nettz v. Phillips, 202 F. Supp. 270 (SD Iowa 1962).

[401] Section 2041 includes a mere general power to appoint by deed unexercised at death. Snyder v. United States, 203 F. Supp. 195 (WD Ky. 1962).

[402] In this respect, it makes no difference whether the right is limited because the joint or mutual will must be specifically enforced or whether the limitation arises out of valid contractual claims by third-party beneficiaries.

[403] See supra ¶¶ 5.06[8][b][iii]–5.06[8][b][v]. There would be inclusion in the surviving spouse's gross estate regardless of the local law rationale for a claim against the spouse's control. See supra note 398.

[404] Estate of Siegel v. Comm'r, 67 TC 662 (1977); Estate of Opal v. Comm'r, 54 TC 154, 168 (1970), aff'd, 450 F2d 1085, 1089 (2d Cir. 1971).

Section 2056

over the property and without regard to theoretical local principles on which the control rests.

[e] Special Rules for Charitable Remainder Trusts

If a decedent bequeaths property outright to a qualified charity, a deduction is allowed for the full value of the property under Section 2055.[405] Similarly, if a decedent bequeaths property outright to a surviving spouse, a deduction is allowed for the full value of the property under Section 2056. Prior to 1982, a combination of the two in the form of a life estate to one's surviving spouse with a remainder to a qualified charity earned no deduction. A marital deduction for the life estate was foreclosed by the terminable interest rule,[406] and a charitable deduction for the remainder was precluded by the split-interest limitations.[407] The Economic Recovery Tax Act of 1981 changed this so that the bequest of a life estate in property to a surviving spouse with a remainder in the property to charity may result in a deduction in the decedent spouse's estate for the entire value of the property, under two alternative rules.

The first alternative emerges from Section 2056(b)(8),[408] which adds another exception to the terminable interest rule. The exception provides that the terminable interest rule does not apply to an interest in a CRAT or a CRUT[409] that passes or has passed to a surviving spouse from a decedent, if the surviving spouse is the only noncharitable beneficiary.[410] The surviving spouse's in-

---

[405] Section 2055 is discussed at ¶ 5.05.

[406] IRC § 2056(b)(1).

[407] IRC § 2055(e); see ¶¶ 5.05[4]–5.05[8].

[408] This section is effective for decedents dying after 1981. Economic Recovery Tax Act of 1981, Pub. L. No. 97-34, § 403(d)(1), 95 Stat. 172, 301 (1981), reprinted in 1981-2 CB 256, 325.

[409] See IRC § 664(d); ¶¶ 5.05[5][a], 5.05[5][b]. An income interest in a pooled income fund (see ¶ 5.05[5][c]) does not qualify for the Section 2056(b)(8) terminable interest exception, but statutory assistance for an income interest in a pooled income fund is unnecessary because such an interest can qualify for the QTIP exception. Reg. §§ 20.2056(b)-7(d)(5), 20.2056(b)-7(h) Ex. 13; see also S. Rep. No. 592, 97th Cong., 2d Sess. 20 (1982), reprinted in 1983-1 CB 475, 483. Cf. Roels v. United States, 928 F. Supp. 812 (ED Wis. 1996) (no deduction where income interest is not an annuity nor a unitrust interest).

[410] If there are noncharitable beneficiaries other than the spouse, Section 2056(b)(8) is inapplicable. IRC § 2056(b)(8)(A). A noncharitable beneficiary is a beneficiary other than an organization described in Section 170(c). IRC § 2056(b)(8)(B)(i). However, a valid disclaimer under Section 2518 by all such noncharitable beneficiaries will qualify as the spouse's interest for a Section 2056(b)(8) marital deduction. Priv. Ltr. Rul. 200204022 (Oct. 22, 2001).

With respect to decedents dying prior to October 24, 1992, a transfer of an annuity or unitrust interest to a surviving spouse where there is also an interest in another noncharita-

terest may be either for life or for a term of years not exceeding twenty years.[411] When the requirements of Section 2056(b)(8) are met, a decedent may claim a deduction for the full value of the property transferred, a marital deduction for the value of the income interest passing to the surviving spouse,[412] and a charitable deduction for the interest passing to the charity.[413]

The second alternative is a testamentary trust, income payable to the surviving spouse for life and remainder to charity, where the executor elects to qualify property held in the trust as qualified terminable interest property under Section 2056(b)(7).[414] This alternative also allows the decedent's estate a deduction for the full value of the trust property. If the value of the property is later included in the surviving spouse's gross estate under Section 2044,[415] the spouse's estate will be allowed a Section 2055 charitable deduction for the value of the property, resulting in a "wash."

Some substantial differences in the treatment of income interests and additional noncharitable interests may be provided under the two alternatives. If the surviving spouse is given a qualified income interest in a charitable remainder trust, the Section 2056(b)(8) interest is in the form of either an annuity or a fixed percentage of the annually valued trust property, as opposed to a Section 2056(b)(7) qualified terminable interest under which the surviving spouse simply has a right to all the income from the property for life. Additionally, the decedent may give a trustee (or the surviving spouse) the power to invade corpus for the benefit of the surviving spouse and could give the surviving spouse a limited testamentary power of appointment in the case of an

---

ble beneficiary may still qualify for a marital deduction under Section 2056(b)(7). Reg. § 20.2056(b)-8(b). This includes deaths after such date under the transitional rules of Reg. § 20.2056(b)-7(e)(5). After such date, the consequences are uncertain. See supra ¶ 5.06[8][d] text accompanying notes 342–344.

The 1997 amendment to Sections 2056(b)(8)(A) and 2056(b)(8)(B)(ii), addition allowing an ESOP to be an alternative beneficiary, is not discussed. See supra ¶ 5.05[2] text accompanying note 42.

[411] Reg. § 20.2056(b)-8(a)(2). Cf. ¶¶ 5.05[5][a] text accompanying notes 179–185, 5.05[5][b] text accompanying notes 239–240.

[412] A marital deduction is allowed even if the transfer is conditioned on the spouse's payment of state death taxes attributable to the charitable remainder trust. Reg. § 20.2056(b)-8(a)(3). But see Reg. § 20.2056(b)-4(c), which applies to the reduction of the marital deduction for such taxes.

[413] Reg. § 20.2056(b)-8(a)(1). See TAM 9244001 (Sept. 17, 1991) (alternative charitable remainder qualified). Thus, no election under Section 2056(b)(7) is required for the deduction.

[414] Even if the remainder qualifies for a deduction under Section 2055 (see ¶ 5.05[5], but see supra ¶ 5.06[8][d] note 344), a full deduction is allowed under Section 2056(b)(7) and no Section 2055 charitable deduction is allowed. IRC § 2056(b)(9). See Reg. §§ 20.2056(b)-9, 20. 2055-6.

[415] Section 2044 is discussed at ¶ 4.16.

interest that meets the tests of Section 2056(b)(7), but not in one that complies with the Section 2056(b)(8) requirements.

The opportunity to provide an invasion power makes the Section 2056(b)(7) alternative attractive; however, that alternative contains some potential problems for the surviving spouse. If the surviving spouse makes no transfers during life, the final result is a wash in the surviving spouse's estate.[416] If the spouse makes a lifetime transfer of the income interest to a noncharitable donee,[417] the spouse would make a gift not only of the income interest[418] but of the remainder as well, and the remainder gift would not qualify for the gift tax charitable deduction.[419] This problem could be avoided by the use of a spendthrift clause. An additional problem lurks in the decedent's possible provision of an interest, such as a secondary life estate to some third person. In such a situation the decedent will be allowed a full deduction, but the surviving spouse's estate will be allowed no deduction under Section 2055, unless the interests after the surviving spouse's death satisfy Section 2055(e). Care must be taken under either alternative to attain the desired deductions.

[f] Interrelationship of the Terminable Interest Exceptions

The several exceptions to the terminable interest rule are independent of one another, but there is some overlap. For example, a decedent's will may create a testamentary trust but make the spouse's interest subject to the Section 2056(b)(3) six-month survivorship or common disaster survivorship condition. Qualified terminable interest property is treated essentially the same as property that is the subject of an outright transfer to a surviving spouse; and since Section 2056(b)(3) applies to outright transfers, the two exceptions may be combined. If there is in fact no failure or termination of the survivor's interest, the surviving spouse has the "qualifying income interest for life" that supports a marital deduction.[420]

---

[416] If the value of the property is included in the spouse's gross estate, this could require the filing of an estate tax return where none otherwise was required. See IRC § 6018; the discussion at ¶ 2.02[1].

[417] Compare the result if Section 2056(b)(8) applies: the surviving spouse could give away a Section 2056(b)(8) income interest without a transfer of the remainder being attributed to the spouse; thus, the remainder would continue to meet the charitable deduction requirements. The transfer of the spouse's gift of the income interest would be subject to the imposition of gift tax. IRC § 2511.

[418] IRC § 2511.

[419] The Section 2519 transfer of the remainder, even though to charity, is not in the form of a unitrust, annuity trust, or pooled income fund. IRC § 2522(c)(2)(A).

[420] See IRC § 2056(b)(7)(B)(ii)(I). Cf. Reg. §§ 20.2056(b)-5(f)(8), 20.2056(b)-5(f)(9). This same analysis should apply to combine Section 2056(b)(3) with the Sections 2056(b)(5) and 2156(b)(6) exceptions.

There is some overlap, previously alluded to, between Sections 2056(b)(5) and 2056(b)(7). If the surviving spouse is given a qualifying income interest and a general power to appoint the remainder by *will*, both exceptions to the terminable interest rule are potentially applicable.[421] If the general power to appoint the remainder may be exercised by *deed*, both exceptions should still be applicable but are not.[422] Similarly, Sections 2056(b)(6) and 2056(b)(7) may overlap, if a surviving spouse is given a qualifying income interest and a general power of appointment with respect to life insurance or annuities. The determination of which exception is applicable in either of these combinations should depend on whether a Section 2056(b)(7) QTIP election is made.[423]

Regardless of any overlap, the statute appropriately forbids a double deduction for any single property interest in the decedent's estate.[424] This applies not only to double deductibility within Section 2056 but also to double deductibility under any two estate tax deduction provisions.[425]

[9] The Noncitizen Surviving Spouse

Section 2056(d) generally[426] disallows the marital deduction to the estate of any decedent if the decedent's surviving spouse is not a citizen of the United

---

[421] See supra ¶ 5.06[8][d] note 356. If both exceptions apply, the relationship of Section 2056(b)(7) to Sections 2519, 2044, and 2207A must be considered in deciding which exception to use. Primary in this consideration is the possibility of a small income gift triggering a Section 2519 gift of the entire remainder and the possibility, under Section 2207A, of shifting the tax burden to the remainder person. See ¶¶ 8.07, 10.08[1][a]. In addition, the overlap may raise valuation issues in the surviving spouse's gross estate. See ¶¶ 4.02[4][b] text accompanying notes 157, 158, 4.16 text accompanying notes 19–23.

[422] The existence of a lifetime power over the remainder that can be exercised only in favor of the spouse does not violate the Section 2056(b)(7) concept. However, the statute, quite improperly, provides that powers, even if held by the surviving spouse, in favor of any other person may only be exercisable at or after the spouse's death to qualify under Section 2056(b)(7). See the discussion supra ¶ 5.06[8][d] text accompanying notes 359–360. This flaw in the statute is ameliorated somewhat by the possible overlap of Section 2056(b)(5), discussed here.

[423] See supra ¶ 5.06[8][d][iii].

[424] IRC § 2056(b)(9). See Reg. §§ 20.2056(b)-9, 20.2055-6.

[425] See supra ¶ 5.06[5][b], especially text accompanying note 120; ¶ 5.05[3][b] text accompanying note 117.

[426] The Section 2056(d) marital deduction prohibition is generally inapplicable to the extent that it is inconsistent with a treaty provision under a treaty to which the United States is a party. An estate eligible to use such a treaty may choose either to use the marital deduction, exemption, or credit allowed under a treaty or to qualify for a marital deduction by using a QDOT under Section 2056A. See infra text accompanying notes 434–440. However, the estate cannot use a combination of both. Thus, an estate may not avail itself of marital deduction benefits under a treaty and then use a QDOT for the remainder of property that is not otherwise deductible under the treaty. Reg. § 20.2056A-1(c). See

States.[427] Section 2056(d) also generally makes Section 2040(b) inapplicable if the decedent's surviving spouse is not a citizen.[428] Section 2056(d) applies regardless of whether the surviving spouse is a U.S. resident.[429] Congress enacted Section 2056(d) out of concern for the subsequent collection of transfer tax from the estate of the noncitizen spouse in cases in which that spouse could avoid such tax by giving up U.S. residency.[430] Thus, neither of these Section 2056(d) prohibitions applies if the surviving spouse becomes a U.S. citizen before the decedent's estate tax return is made[431] and if such spouse was a U.S. resident[432] at all times after the decedent's death until becoming a U.S. citizen.[433]

---

also Omnibus Budget Reconciliation Act of 1989, Pub. L. No. 101-239, § 7815(d)(14) 103 Stat. 2106, 2418 (1989).

[427] IRC § 2056(d)(1)(A). Section 2056(d) is applicable to decedents dying after November 10, 1988. Technical and Miscellaneous Revenue Act of 1988, Pub. L. No. 100-647, § 5033(d)(1), 102 Stat. 3342, 3672 (1988), reprinted in 1988-3 CB 1, 332.

[428] IRC § 2056(d)(1)(B). See ¶ 4.12[10] text accompanying notes 86–93. Section 2040(b) generally includes in a decedent's gross estate only one half of the value of property held by the decedent and the decedent's spouse as tenants by the entirety or as joint tenants with a right of survivorship if the decedent and the spouse are the sole joint tenants. See ¶ 4.12[10].

In conjunction with the enactment of Section 2056(d)(1)(B), Congress generally restored the gift tax provisions of Sections 2515 and 2515A, which related to the creation of such joint tenancy and tenancy-by-the-entirety interests as they existed prior to their repeal in 1982 and the enactment of the unlimited marital deduction. IRC § 2523(i)(3). See ¶ 10.01[3][f] note 112 explaining the interrelationship of Sections 2040(a) and 2523(i)(3).

[429] Reg. § 20.2056A-1(a).

[430] In the legislative history, Congress pointed out that "[p]roperty passing to an alien surviving spouse is less likely to be includable in the spouse's estate, since to avoid taxation on the worldwide estate, the spouse must only give up United States residence." HR Rep. No. 795, 100th Cong., 2d Sess. 592 (1988).

[431] See IRC § 2056(d)(4)(A). The legislative history uses the term "filed," not "made." HR Rep. No. 247, 101st Cong., 1st Sess. 1430 (1989). There appears to be no intended difference in these two terms. The regulations clarify this timing rule by providing that for purposes of Section 2056(d)(4)(A), a return filed prior to the due date (including extensions) is considered filed on the last day the return is required to be filed (including extensions), and a late return filed after its due date is considered filed on the date it is actually filed. Reg. § 2056A-1(b).

[432] Residency is determined under the Reg. § 20.0-1(b)(1) definition. Section 7701(b) is not relevant to the determination except to the extent that the income tax residency of the spouse is pertinent in applying Regulations Section 20.0-1(b)(1). Reg. § 2056A-1(b). Thus, a resident must have "domicile" in the United States under the regulation. "A person acquires a domicile in a place by living there, for even a brief period of time, with no definite present intention of later removing therefrom. Residence without the requisite intention to remain indefinitely will not suffice to constitute domicile. . . . " Reg. § 20.0-1(b)(1).

[433] IRC § 2056(d)(4)(B). Cf. Reg. § 25.2501-1(b). See Priv. Ltr. Rul. 9021037 (Feb. 23, 1990) (application for citizenship at time of return was not acquisition of citizenship).

The marital deduction is allowed with respect to any of the decedent's property passing[434] to the noncitizen surviving spouse in a manner that would ordinarily qualify for a marital deduction if the property is transferred to a qualified domestic trust (QDOT), as defined in Section 2056A.[435] However, the QDOT arrangement merely allows a decedent's estate to postpone payment of the *decedent's* estate tax, generally until the surviving spouse's death.[436] The decedent's postponed estate tax is imposed on the QDOT property revalued at the time of taxation at the decedent's top marginal estate tax rate[437] and the property held in the QDOT is taxed as if it had been included in the decedent's gross estate.[438] Various QDOT requirements[439] assure the government an opportunity to collect the decedent spouse's postponed estate tax.[440]

If the property passing to a surviving noncitizen spouse will be subject to tax in the decedent spouse's gross estate, either because (1) a marital deduction is denied by Section 2056(d)(1)(A)[441] or (2) taxation of the property in the decedent's estate is postponed until a subsequent time as a result of its transfer to a QDOT,[442] *and* if the property is also subject to estate tax in the surviving spouse's gross estate,[443] then the surviving spouse's estate is allowed a Section 2013 credit for the estate tax paid by the decedent's estate.[444] The length of

---

See also ¶ 5.07[5] for additional situations in which a QDOT may be set aside if the surviving spouse becomes a citizen at a subsequent time.

[434] The passing requirement may be satisfied in several ways that are discussed at ¶ 5.07[2].

[435] IRC § 2056(d)(2)(A). QDOTs are discussed in detail at ¶ 5.07. Section 2040(b) remains inapplicable even if the property is transferred to a QDOT. See ¶ 4.12[10] text accompanying notes 90–93.

[436] IRC § 2056A(b)(1)(B). See ¶ 5.07[4][a]. The computation is based on the estate tax rates and the credit amounts in effect on the date of the decedent's death. See ¶ 5.07[4][b] text accompanying notes 159, 160.

[437] If the revaluation occurs upon the surviving spouse's death, there is a possibility of valuation under Section 2032 or Section 2032A. IRC § 2056A(b)(10). See ¶ 5.07[4][a] text accompanying notes 145, 146.

[438] IRC § 2056A(b)(2)(A). See ¶ 5.07[4][b].

[439] See IRC §§ 2056A(a), 2056A(b)(6).

[440] The requirements are discussed at ¶ 5.07[3].

[441] IRC § 2056(d)(3)(B). See Reg. § 20.2056A-7(b).

[442] IRC § 2056(d)(3), parenthetical, the flush language. See supra text accompanying note 436, explaining that taxation of property transferred to a QDOT is merely a deferral of the decedent spouse's estate tax.

[443] IRC § 2056(d)(3)(C). Cf. IRC §§ 2001, 2101, 2033, 2041(a)(2), 2044.

[444] IRC § 2056(d)(3). See Reg. § 20.2056A-7. Some special rules apply in computing the Section 2013 credit when the property is subject to a deferral of taxation in the decedent spouse's gross estate as a result of a QDOT election and is subject to subsequent taxation in the surviving spouse's gross estate. The amount treated as taxed in the decedent spouse's estate includes amounts taxed under both Sections 2056A(b)(1)(A) (distributions from the QDOT) and 2056A(b)(1)(B) (property in the QDOT at the noncitizen spouse's

time between the two spouses' deaths is not a factor in computing the amount of the Section 2013 credit; a 100 percent Section 2013 credit applies regardless of when the surviving spouse dies, even if the surviving spouse outlives the decedent spouse by more than ten years.[445]

As a result of these rules, property on which tax has been directly or indirectly[446] paid in both spouses' estates is taxed only once, thus carrying out the policy of Section 2056 to provide for tax-free interspousal transfers.[447]

[10] Background of the Section

The present Section 2056 has a curious history.[448] Before 1942, there was no specific statutory provision with respect to the estate tax imposed on community property. Generally, only one half of the community property was included in the gross estate of the decedent. Of course, this result depended on the nature of the interest the survivor had under state law. If the survivor's interest was a "mere expectancy" until the death of the decedent, the entire community property was includible in the decedent's estate.[449] Initially, to put the residents of common-law jurisdictions on a par with those of community property states, Section 811(e)(2) was added to the 1939 Code by the Revenue Act of 1942.[450] Under this provision, the community property was included in the estate of the first spouse to die, except to the extent that the executor could trace the property as being the separate property of or being attributable to the personal services of the surviving spouse.[451] Although this provision generally

---

death). Reg. § 20.2056A-7(a)(1). See IRC § 2013(b); Reg. § 20.2013-2; ¶ 5.07[4][a]. The amount treated as transferred to the surviving spouse is the value of the QDOT assets on the date of the surviving spouse's death not reduced by the Section 2056A estate tax imposed at the surviving spouse's death. Reg. § 20.2056A-7(a)(2). See IRC §§ 2013(c), 2013(d); Reg. §§ 20.2013-3, 20.2013-4; ¶ 5.07[4][a]. See also Reg. § 20.2056A-7(c) Ex., illustrating these rules and the computation of the Section 2013 credit.

[445] IRC § 2056(d)(3) (last clause). See Reg. §§ 20.2056A-7(a)(3), 20.2056A-7(b), 20.2056A-7(c), Ex.

[446] IRC § 2056(d)(3). Other special rules in applying Section 2013 are considered supra note 444.

[447] See supra ¶ 5.06[1] text following note 3. If the property is subject to a higher amount of tax in the decedent's estate than in the surviving spouse's estate, the amount of the Section 2013 credit is limited to the amount of tax on the property paid in the surviving spouse's estate. IRC § 2013(c)(1). See ¶ 3.05[4][a].

[448] See Lewis, The Marital Deduction (1984).

[449] Talcott v. United States, 23 F2d 897 (9th Cir.), cert. denied, 277 US 604 (1928).

[450] Revenue Act of 1942, 56 Stat. 802, 941 (1942).

[451] To exclude the property, the statute required a showing that it was received by the surviving spouse "as compensation for personal services . . . or derived originally from such compensation or from separate property of that spouse."

had the effect of putting the residents of common-law and community property jurisdictions on an estate tax par, the tracing requirement was so burdensome[452] that it led to the Revenue Act of 1948,[453] which repealed Section 811(e)(2) of the 1939 Code, and the estate tax treatment of community property reverted back to its pre-1942 status. In its place, the 1948 Act added the estate tax marital deduction, along with the related marital income tax and gift tax[454] provisions.

Reviewing the purpose of the marital deduction, Justice Goldberg once stated:

> The 1948 tax amendments were intended to equalize the effect of the estate taxes in community property and common-law jurisdictions. Under a community property system, such as that in Texas, the spouse receives outright ownership of one half of the community property and only the other one half is included in the decedent's estate. To equalize the incidence of progressively scaled estate taxes and to adhere to the patterns of the law, the marital deduction permits a deceased spouse, subject to certain requirements, to transfer free of taxes, one half of the non-community property to the surviving spouse. Although applicable to separately held property in a community property state, the primary thrust of this is to extend to taxpayers in common-law States the advantages of "estate splitting" otherwise available only in community property States.[455]

Under the 1948 Act, the marital deduction generally was limited to one half of the decedent's "adjusted gross estate," which was the gross estate reduced by decedent's community property and by the Section 2053- and Section 2054-type deductions attributable to decedent's separate property.[456] The Tax Reform Act of 1976 liberalized the deduction limit. The limitation on the deduction was expanded to the greater of $250,000 and one half of the decedent's adjusted gross estate to allow free interspousal transfers in small and moderate estates.[457] Congress, in the Economic Recovery Tax Act of 1981,

---

[452] Cf. IRC § 2040(a), discussed at ¶ 4.12[7][a].

[453] S. Rep. No. 1013, 80th Cong., 2d Sess. 1163, 1223 (1948), reprinted in 1948-1 CB 285, 304. A threatened stampede by the common-law states to gain the more significant income tax advantages of community property states was probably a greater stimulant to the 1948 legislation. Id. at 302.

[454] See ¶¶ 10.03, 11.03.

[455] United States v. Stapf, 375 US 118, 128 (1963).

[456] Pub. L. No. 80-471, § 361(a), 62 Stat. 110, 117 (1948), reprinted in 1948-1 CB 211, 218; see Reg. § 20.2056(a)-1(c)(1).

[457] Pub. L. No. 94-455, § 2002, 90 Stat. 1520, 1854 (1976), reprinted in 1976-3 CB (Vol. 1) 1, 330. See Reg. §§ 20.2056(a)-1(c)(2), 20.2056(a)-1(c)(3).

abolished the limit on the amount of the marital deduction entirely,[458] allowing unlimited interspousal transfers of deductible property interests including transfers of community property between spouses.[459] The original purpose for the marital deduction has been completely abandoned.

¶ 5.07 SECTION 2056A. QUALIFIED DOMESTIC TRUSTS

[1] Introduction

An estate tax marital deduction generally is not allowed for property that passes from a decedent to a surviving spouse who is not a citizen of the United States because of a congressional concern over the ability of the United States to subsequently collect tax from the noncitizen surviving spouse.[1] However, if the property *passes*[2] to the noncitizen surviving spouse in a qualified domestic trust[3] (QDOT),[4] a marital deduction is allowed.[5] However, unlike normal marital deduction transfers, which result in the transferred property being includible in the estate of the surviving spouse, the deduction merely results in the *postponement of* the imposition of estate tax on the QDOT

---

[458] Pub. L. No. 97-34, § 403, 95 Stat. 172, 301 (1981), reprinted in 1981-2 CB 256, 324. Exception is made for instruments falling under the transitional rules discussed supra ¶ 5.06[6][b].

[459] A summary of the marital deduction rules is found in Reg. § 20.2056(a)-1(c).

[1] IRC § 2056(d)(1)(A). In the legislative history, Congress pointed out that "[p]roperty passing to an alien surviving spouse is less likely to be includible in the spouse's estate, since to avoid taxation on the worldwide estate, the spouse need only give up U.S. residence." HR Rep. No. 795, 100th Cong., 2nd Sess. 592 (1988). But see IRC §§ 2056(d)(2), 2056(d)(3), 2056(d)(4), 2056(d)(5); ¶ 5.06[9]; infra ¶¶ 5.07[2][a], 5.07[5].

In addition, Section 2040(b) is inapplicable to a decedent whose surviving spouse is not a citizen of the United States. IRC § 2056(d)(1)(B). See ¶ 5.06[9] note 428; ¶ 4.12[10] text accompanying notes 86–93.

[2] See infra ¶ 5.07[2].

[3] IRC § 2056A(a). See infra ¶ 5.07[3].

[4] See Reg. § 20.2056A-1(a)(1)(i). QDOTs and the rules applicable to noncitizen surviving spouses are discussed in Plaine & Siegler, "The Federal Gift and Estate Tax Marital Deduction for Non-United States Citizen Recipient Spouses," 25 Real Prop. Prob. & Tr. J. 385 (1990); Adams, "The Limited Marital Deduction for Transfers to Noncitizen Spouses—Is It Fair?" 42 Fla. L. Rev. 749 (1990); Magaram & Abraham, "Transfers to Non-Citizen Spouses Significantly Affected by RRA '89," 72 J. Tax'n 266 (1990); Karr, "New Planning Required for Surviving Spouses Who Are Not U.S. Citizens," 70 J. Tax'n 140 (1989).

[5] IRC § 2056(d)(2)(A).

property as a part of the estate of the *transferor* spouse.[6] The QDOT property is revalued at the time of the postponed taxation, either during the surviving spouse's lifetime or at that spouse's death.[7] Thus, the QDOT rules are somewhat similar to the regular marital deduction rules, because they permit the postponement of the payment of tax from the death of the first spouse to die until the death of the surviving spouse.

[2] The Passing Requirement

Property must "pass" to the surviving spouse in a QDOT to qualify for postponement of taxation under Section 2056(d). Generally, the property will pass directly from the decedent's estate to the QDOT.[8] However, property may "pass" to the surviving spouse in a QDOT in three other ways.

[a] Reformation Into a QDOT

Property will be treated as passing to the surviving spouse in a QDOT even though it passes from the decedent to a trust which is not initially a QDOT if, after the decedent's death, the trust is re-formed to satisfy the QDOT requirements.[9] The trust can be reformed pursuant to the terms of the decedent's will, the terms of the trust itself, or a judicial proceeding.[10] If reformation occurs pursuant to the decedent's will or the trust, the QDOT quali-

---

[6] IRC § 2056A(b). The term "property" includes an interest in property. IRC § 2056A(c)(1). Cf. IRC § 2056(b)(1).

[7] IRC § 2056A(b). See infra ¶ 5.07[4][b]. Thus, if the property fluctuates in value between the decedent's death and the time the property held in the QDOT is taxed, there is a resulting increase or decrease in the amount of tax.

Section 2056A is applicable to estates of decedents dying after November 10, 1988. Technical and Miscellaneous Revenue Act of 1988, Pub. L. No. 100-647, § 5033(d)(1), 102 Stat. 3342, 3673 (1988), reprinted in 1988-3 CB 1, 333. Section 2056A(e) allows the Secretary to promulgate regulations necessary or appropriate to carry out the purposes of Section 2056A. Extensive regulations have been adopted. Reg. §§ 20.2056A-1–20.2056A-13. The regulations, other than Regulations Section 20.2056A-2(d), are effective with respect to estates of decedents dying after August 22, 1995. Reg. § 20.2056A-13. Regulations Section 20.2056A-2(d) is generally effective for estates of decedents dying after February 19, 1996. Reg. § 20.2056A-2(d)(6)(i). See also Reg. §§ 20.2056A-2(d)(6)(ii) (special rule in case of incompetency), 20.2056A-2(d)(6)(iii) (special rule for certain irrevocable trusts).

[8] IRC § 2056(d)(2)(A). See Reg. § 20.2056A-1(a)(1)(i). The requirements for a valid QDOT are discussed infra ¶ 5.07[3].

[9] IRC § 2056(d)(5)(A); Reg. § 20.2056A-1(a)(1)(ii). See infra ¶ 5.07[3]. Prior to its reformation, the trust must meet all of the other requirements for a marital deduction. Reg. § 20.2056A-4(a)(1). See ¶¶ 5.06[3], 5.06[4], 5.06[7].

[10] Reg. § 20.2056A-4(a)(1).

fication must be *completed* by the time prescribed (including extensions) for filing the decedent's federal estate tax return.[11] If there is a judicial reformation, the reformation must *commence* on or before the due date for decedent's return (including extensions actually granted).[12] If a reformation suit is filed, the statute of limitations for assessing any estate tax deficiency related to the issue of the QDOT's qualification remains open until one year after the Service is notified of the suit's resolution.[13]

[b] The Surviving Spouse's Transfer to a QDOT

If a decedent's property passes outright to a noncitizen surviving spouse—e.g., as a result of a bequest, devise, operation of law, or pursuant to an assignable annuity or similar arrangement[14]—a marital deduction is disallowed because the outright transfer is not held in a QDOT.[15] However, if the surviving spouse or the surviving spouse's representative[16] transfers or assigns the property to a QDOT, the property is treated as "passing" to the noncitizen spouse in a QDOT.[17] The transfer or assignment of property to the QDOT[18] must be in writing[19] and must occur before the decedent spouse's estate tax re-

---

[11] IRC § 2056(d)(5)(A)(i); Reg. § 20.2056A-4(a)(1). The statute uses the term "made." Cf. ¶ 5.06[9] note 431.

[12] IRC § 2056(d)(5)(A)(ii). The reformation must result in a trust that is effective under local law. Reg. § 20.2056A-4(a)(2). See Priv. Ltr. Rul. 9017015 (Jan. 25, 1990). The reformed trust may be revocable by the surviving spouse or subject to the surviving spouse's general power of appointment, provided no person (including the spouse) has a power to amend the trust so that it would no longer qualify as a QDOT. Reg. § 20.2056A-4(a)(2). Prior to the time that the judicial reformation is completed, the trust is treated as a QDOT, imposing various requirements on the trustee. Reg. § 20.2056A-4(a)(2). Failure to meet those requirements may violate the anti-abuse rule. See Reg. § 20.2056A-2(d)(1)(v); infra ¶ 5.07[3][c] text accompanying notes 114, 115.

[13] IRC § 2056(d)(5)(B).

[14] See Reg. § 20.2056A-4(b)(7) for rules applicable to assignable annuities.

[15] IRC § 2056(d)(1)(A).

[16] This includes a legal representative (if the surviving spouse is incompetent) and a personal representative (if the surviving spouse has died). Reg. § 20.2056A-4(b)(1).

[17] IRC § 2056(d)(2)(B); Reg. §§ 20.2056A-1(a)(1)(iii), 20.2056A-2(b)(2). See Priv. Ltr. Rul. 9623063 (Mar. 13, 1996) (rollover of IRAs into a QDOT).

[18] The QDOT must be a valid QDOT, except that since the surviving spouse already owns the property and is otherwise treated as transferring it (see infra text accompanying note 25), the terms of the QDOT are not required to satisfy Section 2056(b)(5), Section 2056(b)(7), Section 2056(b)(8), or the estate trust requirements. Reg. § 20.2056A-4(b)(1). See infra ¶ 5.07[3][e]. However, if other property is or has been transferred to the trust, all of the property in the trust must qualify for a marital deduction under Section 2056 in order to avoid complicated tracing problems. Reg. § 20.2056A-4(b)(1).

[19] Reg. § 20.2056A-4(b)(2).

turn is filed and during the period allowable for making a QDOT election.[20] If there is a timely valid assignment, the actual transfer of the assigned property to the QDOT must occur before the administration of the decedent's estate is completed.[21] Only assets that are included in decedent's gross estate and pass to the spouse at death (or the proceeds from the sale, exchange, or conversion of such assets) may be transferred or assigned to the QDOT.[22] Thus, the surviving spouse cannot fund the QDOT with property owned by such spouse before decedent's death in lieu of decedent's property. The transfer or assignment may be of a specific asset, group of assets, fractional share of assets, or pecuniary amount; if the transfer or assignment is of less than an entire asset or group of assets, it may be expressed as a formula amount.[23] A protective assignment or transfer of property to a QDOT is permitted if there is a bona fide controversy that concerns the residency or citizenship of the decedent, the citizenship of the surviving spouse, the inclusion of all or part of an asset in decedent's gross estate, or the specific property that the surviving spouse is entitled to receive.[24]

---

[20] IRC § 2056(d)(2)(B)(i). See Reg. §§ 20.2056A-1(a)(1)(iii), 20.2056A-2(b)(2), 20.2056A-4(b)(1). See also ¶ 5.06[9] text accompanying note 431 and infra ¶ 5.07[3][d] text accompanying note 118. If a decedent died prior to the December 19, 1989, date of enactment of this provision, the transfer or assignment could have been made at any time prior to December 19, 1990. Omnibus Budget Reconciliation Act of 1989, Pub. L. No. 101-239, § 2815(d)(4)(B), 103 Stat. 2106, 2415 (1989).

[21] IRC § 2056(d)(2)(B)(i); Reg. § 20.2056A-4(b)(6). If there is no estate administration, the deadline is one year after the due date (including extensions) for filing the decedent's estate tax return. Reg. § 20.2056A-4(b)(6). If the actual transfer is not timely made, the marital deduction is generally denied, although the Service can issue private letter rulings extending the time for completing the conveyance. Id. See, e.g., Priv. Ltr. Rul. 9816010 (Jan. 8, 1998). Cf. TAM 9228001 (Feb. 20, 1992).

[22] Reg. § 20.2056A-4(b)(3). See Priv. Ltr. Rul. 9918039 (Feb. 8, 1999) (assets transferred to corporation).

[23] Reg. § 20.2056A-4(b)(2). See Reg. §§ 20.2056A-4(d) Exs. 1 (group of assets), 2 (formula amount), 3 (fractional share).

If the transfer or assignment is in the form of a pecuniary amount, the assets actually transferred must meet one of two tests. They may have a value equal to the pecuniary amount on the transfer date. Reg. § 20.2056A-4(b)(4)(i). Alternatively, the amount can be satisfied on the basis of an estate tax valuation date if the assets are fairly representative of appreciation or depreciation in the value of all property available for transfer or assignment occurring between the estate tax valuation date and the date the assets are actually transferred to the QDOT. Reg. § 20.2056A-4(b)(4)(ii). Cf. Rev. Proc. 64-19, 1964-1 CB 682; ¶ 5.06[6][a].

[24] Reg. § 20.2056A-4(b)(8). A protective assignment must identify the specific assets and the reasons for the protective assignment. Id. It may be expressed by means of a formula. Id. A protective assignment is irrevocable once made. Id. The timing of the transfer related to a protective assignment must satisfy the timing requirements discussed supra text accompanying note 20.

Because the surviving spouse is the actual transferor of the property to the QDOT, the surviving spouse may have transfer tax consequences with respect to the transfer.[25] For example, the surviving spouse has gift tax consequences to the extent that there is a completed transfer to third persons[26] and may have eventual generation-skipping transfer tax consequences if the third persons are skip persons.[27]

[c] An Annuity or Other Arrangement Treated as Passing to a QDOT

An annuity or other arrangement[28] that is not assignable[29] or transferable to a QDOT under federal, state, or foreign law or under the terms of the plan or arrangement, and but for Section 2056(d)(1)(A) would otherwise qualify for a marital deduction to the decedent's estate, is treated as passing to a QDOT if the surviving spouse exercises one of two options.[30] Both options involve actions with respect to the "corpus portion"[31] of the annuity or other arrangement.[32] Under the first option, the surviving spouse must agree to pay the deferred QDOT tax annually on the corpus portion of each annuity or arrange-

---

[25] Reg. § 20.2056A-4(b)(5). There can be income, gift, estate, generation-skipping transfer, and excise tax consequences. Id. But see Reg. § 25.2702-1(c)(8) (exempting such transfers from the special valuation rules of Section 2702). See ¶ 19.03[3][c] note 154.

[26] Reg. §§ 20.2056A-4(b)(5), 25.2702-1(c)(8), 20.2056A-4(d) Ex. 5 (the surviving spouse transferred the property received outright to a trust retaining an income interest for life with a remainder to the grandchildren and, with Section 2702 inapplicable (see Reg. § 25.2702-1(c)(8)), the transfer resulted in a gift of the actuarial value of the remainder and potential inclusion in the surviving spouse's gross estate under Section 2036(a)(1) and a Section 2013 credit (see ¶ 5.06[9] text accompanying notes 441–447).

[27] Reg. §§ 20.2056A-4(b)(5), 20.2056A-4(d) Ex. 5. In such circumstances, because the surviving spouse transfers the property to the trust, and because the decedent spouse makes an outright transfer to the surviving spouse, the decedent's personal representative may not make a Section 2652(a)(3) reverse QTIP election with respect to the property in the trust. Reg. § 20.2056A-4(d) Ex. 5. See ¶ 17.02[1][c][i].

[28] The term "annuity or other arrangement" includes employee plan benefits, tax-sheltered annuities, and tax-deferred annuities. The annuity or other arrangement is not required to be part of a qualified retirement plan. Reg. § 20.2056A-4(c)(1).

[29] Even though assignable, an IRA under Section 408(a) is treated as not assignable and must satisfy the procedure set forth in Regulations Section 20.2056A-4(c). Reg. § 20.2056A-4(c)(1). See Reg. § 20.2056A-4(b)(7) with respect to requirements for assignable annuities.

[30] Reg. §§ 20.2056A-1(a)(1)(iv), 20.2056A-2(b)(3), 20.2056A-4(c).

[31] The corpus portion does not include the income portion of the annuity or arrangement that is not subject to the QDOT tax. Cf. infra ¶ 5.07[4][a] text accompanying note 131. Reg. § 20.2056A-4(c)(4) provides a formula used to compute the corpus portion that is illustrated in Reg. § 20.2056A-4(d) Ex. 4.

[32] Reg. §§ 20.2056A-4(c)(2), 20.2056A-4(c)(3).

ment payment that the surviving spouse receives.[33] Under the second option, the surviving spouse must agree to transfer or roll over the corpus portion of each payment to a QDOT within sixty days of the surviving spouse's receipt of the payment.[34] However, to the extent that all or a part of the corpus portion of the annuity or other arrangement would be eligible for a hardship exemption if paid from a QDOT,[35] a corresponding portion of the payment is exempt from the payment or rollover requirements.[36]

[3] Requirements of a QDOT

To qualify as a QDOT, the trust to which property passes must satisfy several statutory and regulatory requirements that principally ensure the government's ability to collect the federal estate tax on the decedent spouse's property passing to the QDOT.[37] The trust must be established by a document executed

---

[33] Reg. §§ 20.2056A-4(c)(2)(i), 20.2056A-4(c)(6). See infra ¶ 5.07[4].

In addition, pursuant to Regulations Sections 20.2056A-4(c)(2)(ii), 20.2056A-4(c)(2)(iii), 20.2056A-4(c)(2)(iv), the decedent's personal representative

1. Must file an Information Statement signed by the surviving spouse with the decedent's estate tax return, which must contain the items listed in Regulations Section 20.2056A-4(c)(5);
2. Must file an "Agreement To Pay Section 2056A Estate Tax" described in Regulations Section 20.2056A-4(c)(6) signed by the surviving spouse; and
3. Must make a timely QDOT election with respect to the nonassignable annuity or other payment. See infra ¶ 5.07[3][d].

[34] Reg. §§ 20.2056A-4(c)(3), 20.2056A-4(c)(7). The QDOT may be created by the decedent's will, decedent's executor, or the surviving spouse, and it must be established prior to the date the decedent's estate tax return is filed and during the time the QDOT election may be made. Reg. §§ 20.2056A-4(c)(3)(i), 20.2056A-4(c)(3)(ii). In addition, pursuant to Regulations Sections 20.2056A-4(c)(3)(iii), 20.2056A-4(c)(3)(iv), 20.2056A-4(c)(3)(v), the decedent's personal representative

1. Must file an Information Statement signed by the surviving spouse with the decedent's estate tax return which must contain the items listed in Regulations Section 20.2056A-4(c)(5);
2. Must file an "Agreement To Roll Over Annuity Payments" signed by the surviving spouse (see Reg. § 20.2056A-4(c)(7)); and
3. Must make a timely QDOT election with respect to the nonassignable annuity or other payment.

See infra ¶ 5.07[3][d]. See also Reg. § 20.2056A-5(c)(3)(iv) discussed infra ¶ 5.07[4][a] note 133; Priv. Ltr. Rul. 9729040 (Apr. 23, 1997) (illustrating the preceding rules).

[35] See infra ¶ 5.07[4][a] note 132.

[36] Reg. §§ 20.2056A-4(c)(2)(i), 20.2056A-4(c)(3)(i).

[37] IRC § 2056A(a); Reg. §§ 20.2056A-2(b), 20.2056A-2(d). See also infra ¶ 5.07[4].

under the laws of a state of the United States, the District of Columbia, or a foreign jurisdiction.[38] If executed under the laws of a foreign jurisdiction, the document must designate the laws of a particular state or the District of Columbia as governing the trust's administration, and such designation must be effective under the law of the designated jurisdiction.[39]

As provided by regulations, the term "trust" includes other equivalent arrangements that are not trusts but that have substantially the same effect as a trust.[40] This provision is designed to permit nonresident surviving spouses living in countries that prohibit the use of a trust to create some alternative structure that permits them to utilize the QDOT rules. These nontrust arrangements must allow the United States to retain jurisdiction and adequate security to assure collection of the deferred tax.[41] The legislative history suggests those conditions may be satisfied by a bilateral treaty that provides for tax collection from the noncitizen surviving spouse or by a closing agreement process under which a surviving spouse waives treaty benefits, allowing the United States to retain taxing jurisdiction and providing adequate security.[42]

[a] A United States Trustee

Except as provided in regulations,[43] the trust instrument must require that at least one trustee of the trust be a U.S. citizen or a domestic corporation that

---

[38] Reg. § 20.2056A-2(a).

[39] Reg. § 20.2056A-2(a). The trust must be maintained and administered under the laws of the designated jurisdiction. Id. The trust must also be an "ordinary trust" as defined in Regulations Section 301.7701-4(a). Reg. § 20.2056A-2(a). A trust will not fail to constitute an ordinary trust solely because of the nature of the assets transferred to it, regardless of its classification under Regulations Section 301.7701-2, Regulations Section 301.7701-3, or Regulations Section 301.7701-4. Reg. § 20.2056A-2(a).

[40] IRC § 2056A(c)(3). The provision is effective for estates of decedents dying after August 5, 1997. The Taxpayer Relief Act of 1997, Pub. L. No. 105-34, § 1312(b), 111 Stat. 788, 1044 (1997), reprinted in 1997-4 CB (Vol. 1) 1, 258.

[41] HR Conf. Rep. No. 220, 105th Cong., 1st Sess. 1, 721 (1997), reprinted in 1997-4 CB (Vol. 2) 1457, 2190.

[42] HR Conf. Rep. No. 220, 105th Cong., 1st Sess. 1, 721 (1997), reprinted in 1997-4 CB (Vol. 2) 1457, 2190.

[43] The relaxation of the United States Trustee requirement is intended to permit the establishment of a QDOT in circumstances where a foreign country prohibits a trust from having a U.S. Trustee. HR Conf. Rep. No. 220, 105th Cong., 1st Sess. 1, 721 (1997), reprinted in 1997-4 CB (Vol. 2) 1457, 2190. The legislative history indicates that the regulations should provide a waiver of the U.S. Trustee requirement where there is an alternative mechanism under which the United States would retain jurisdiction and adequate security with respect to the QDOT property. One suggested mechanism is a closing agreement process under which a surviving spouse waives treaty benefits, allowing the United States to retain taxing jurisdiction and providing adequate security. Id. The rule applies to decedents dying after August 5, 1997. The Taxpayer Relief Act of 1997, Pub. L.

is commonly referred to as a "United States Trustee."[44] All the trustees of the trust, whether United States Trustees or not, are personally liable for payment of the estate tax imposed on certain distributions from or property held in a QDOT.[45] The requirement of a United States Trustee provides the government with a taxpayer within the United States' jurisdiction who will be liable for the tax if trust assets are not available.

[b] The United States Trustee's Right to Withhold Tax

The QDOT instrument must provide that no corpus distribution can be made from the trust unless the United States Trustee has the right to withhold the amount of tax liability that will be imposed upon the distribution.[46] This right granted to the United States Trustee, together with the jurisdiction of the United States over the United States Trustee who is personally liable for the payment of the tax,[47] assures the United States of collection of the tax.

No. 105-34, § 1314(b), 111 Stat. 788, 1045 (1997), reprinted in 1997-4 CB (Vol. 1) 1, 259.

[44] IRC § 2056A(a)(1)(A); Reg. § 20.2056A-2(c). A domestic corporation is a corporation created or organized under the laws of the United States, any state, or the District of Columbia. Reg. § 20.2056A-2(c). See IRC § 7701(a)(4). Cf. infra ¶ 5.07[3][c] text accompanying notes 67–69.

If the United States Trustee is an individual U.S. citizen, the individual must have a tax home as defined in Section 911(d)(3) in the United States. Reg. § 20.2056A-2(d)(2). Thus, the person must be subject to the U.S. judicial process during the administration of the trust.

[45] IRC § 2056A(b)(6). See infra ¶ 5.07[4][c].

[46] IRC § 2056A(a)(1)(B). See IRC § 2056A(b)(1)(A). This power held by the United States Trustee does not disqualify the QDOT from meeting the terminable interest requirements under the exceptions of Section 2056(b)(5) or Section 2056(b)(7). IRC § 2056A(b)(14). See infra ¶ 5.07[3][e] text accompanying note 126.

The withholding requirement entered the statute in the Omnibus Budget Reconciliation Act of 1990, Pub. L. No. 101-508, § 11702(g)(2)(A), 104 Stat. 1388-1, 1388-515 (1990), reprinted in 1991-2 CB 481, 535. Prior to that time, under the 1988 legislation, all trustees (not just a single trustee) had to be U.S. citizens or domestic corporations. The Taxpayer Relief Act of 1997 added a transitional rule that provides that a QDOT created under an instrument executed prior to the enactment of the 1990 Act on October 8, 1990, is treated as satisfying the current withholding requirement if the instrument requires that all trustees of the trust be U.S. citizens or domestic corporations. The Taxpayer Relief Act of 1997, Pub. L. No. 105-34, § 1303(a), 111 Stat. 788, 1039 (1997), reprinted in 1997-4 CB (Vol. 1) 1, 253. The rule is treated as though it was included in the 1990 Act. The Taxpayer Relief Act of 1997, Pub. L. No. 105-34, § 1303(b), 111 Stat. 788, 1040 (1997), 1997-4 CB (Vol. 1) 1, 254.

[47] IRC § 2056A(b)(6). See infra ¶ 5.07[4][c].

[c] Regulatory Requirements to Ensure Collection of Deferred Tax

A QDOT must meet various additional requirements imposed by regulations[48] further designed to ensure the collection of the tax imposed on a QDOT.[49] The set of regulatory requirements that are applicable depend on the value of the assets that pass[50] to the QDOT. The primary determinant of which set of requirements applies is whether or not the value of the QDOT assets as finally determined for estate tax purposes exceeds $2 million.[51] In measuring the value of the QDOT assets for determining which set of regulatory requirements apply, the value employed is the fair market value as "finally determined"[52] for federal estate tax purposes at the date of the decedent spouse's death or the alternate valuation date (if applicable), determined without any re-

---

[48] These regulatory rules are applicable to decedents dying after February 19, 1996. Reg. § 20.2056A-2(d)(6)(i). There are grandfathering rules for incompetent decedents and for irrevocable trusts created by decedents on or before November 20, 1995, that are automatically deemed to satisfy the regulatory requirements. Reg. §§ 20.2056A-2(d)(6)(ii), 20.2056A-2(d)(6)(iii). The grandfathering rules are effective only if the U.S. Trustee provides a written statement with the estate tax return, binding on all successor trustees, that the trust is being administered in actual compliance with the regulatory requirement and will be so administered throughout its duration. Reg. §§ 20.2056A-2(d)(6)(ii), 20.2056A-2(d)(6)(iii).

The requirements to ensure collection may be incorporated into the trust document by reference. Reg. § 20.2056A-2(d)(1)(i). However, the Service has also issued sample language that can be used to incorporate the requirements in the trust document. Rev. Proc. 96-54, 1996-2 CB 386.

[49] IRC § 2056A(a)(2). See IRC § 2056A(b); Reg. § 20.2056A-2.

[50] See supra ¶ 5.07[2].

[51] See infra ¶¶ 5.07[3][c][i], 5.07[3][c][ii]. The Commissioner has reserved the right to alter the $2 million threshold amount. Reg. § 20.2056A-2(d)(5). See also infra text accompanying notes 55–63.

[52] The fair market value is finally determined at the earliest of (1) the entry of a final decision, judgment, decree, or other order by a court of competent jurisdiction; (2) the execution of a closing order under Section 7121; (3) any final disposition by the Service of a claim for refund; (4) the issuance of an estate tax closing letter if no claim for refund is filed; or (5) the expiration of the period of assessment. Reg. § 20.2056A-2(d)(1)(iii).

If the fair market value of the assets is originally reported to be $2 million or less but is finally determined to be more than $2 million, the United States Trustee has a reasonable period (not exceeding sixty days after the final determination) to meet the requirements applicable to QDOTs with assets in excess of $2 million. Reg. § 20.2056A-2(d)(1)(ii). See infra ¶ 5.07[3][c][i].

duction for indebtedness with respect to the assets.[53] If more than one QDOT is established, the value of the assets of the QDOTs is aggregated.[54]

In determining whether the $2 million threshold is exceeded, the executor of decedent's estate may elect[55] to exclude from the value of the QDOT up to $600,000[56] in value attributable to a personal residence wherever situated[57] (along with related furnishings)[58] that is owned directly by the QDOT and is used as the principal residence[59] or one other residence[60] of the surviving spouse.[61] If the residence ceases to be used as the surviving spouse's personal residence or is sold and the proceeds are not reinvested in another personal

---

[53] Reg. §§ 20.2056A-2(d)(1)(i), 20.2056A-2(d)(1)(ii). Generally, indebtedness is taken into consideration in taxing property under the estate tax (see IRC § 2053(a)(4); Reg. § 20.2053-7), and disregarding indebtedness in measuring the $2 million threshold seems inappropriate, although the Treasury disregards indebtedness in measuring the threshold because to take it into consideration would result in added "complexity" as to what indebtedness would and would not be considered. TD 8686, 1996-2 CB 152.

[54] Reg. § 20.2056A-2(d)(1)(ii)(A).

[55] The election is made by attaching a written statement to the decedent spouse's estate tax return on which the QDOT election is made. Reg. § 20.2056A-2(d)(1)(iv)(A). See infra ¶ 5.07[3][d].

[56] The Commissioner has reserved the right to alter the $600,000 exclusion amount. Reg. § 20.2056A-2(d)(5). See also supra note 51.

[57] The elective exclusion is not available in determining whether more than 35 percent of the QDOT assets consist of foreign real property. Reg. § 20.2056A-2(d)(1)(iv)(C). See infra ¶ 5.07[3][c][ii].

[58] Related furnishings include furniture, fixtures, appliances, decorative items, and china associated with normal household and decorative use. Reg. § 20.2056A-2(d)(1)(iv)(E). They do not include rare artwork, valuable antiques, or automobiles. Id.

[59] "Principal residence" is defined under Section 1034 (prior to its repeal by the Taxpayer Relief Act of 1997, Pub. L. No. 105-34, § 312(b), 111 Stat. 788, 839 (1997), reprinted in 1997-4 CB (Vol. 1) 1, 53) and the regulations promulgated for Section 1034. Reg. § 20.2056A-2(d)(1)(iv)(D). Cf. IRC § 121; Prop. Reg. § 1.121-1(b) (when this regulation is finalized, Regulations Section 20.2056A-2(d)(1)(iv)(D) should reference Section 121 rather than Section 1034).

[60] Reg. § 20.2056A-2(d)(1)(iv)(D).

[61] Reg. § 20.2056A-2(d)(1)(iv)(A). The residence may not be held in a corporation or partnership owned by the QDOT. Id. A personal residence may not be rented to a third party. Reg. § 20.2056A-2(d)(1)(iv)(D). A personal residence may include appurtenant structures and adjacent land reasonably appropriate for residential purposes. Id. Cf. ¶ 19.03[3][d][i].

This exception was made in recognition of the fact that it would be unfair to include a personal residence as part of the QDOT corpus if a significant portion of a QDOT consists of a personal residence that will generally produce no income, because of the potential cost of a bond, letter of credit, or bank trustee fees that must be incurred by QDOTs with more than $2 million in value. Cf. TD 8613, Supplementary Information, 1995-2 CB 216, 218.

residence within twelve months of the sale, the exclusion ceases to apply.[62] Should the executor elect to exclude a personal residence from the computation, the United States Trustee must file a report with respect to the exclusion in any year in which the residence is sold or ceases to be used as a personal residence.[63]

[i] **Requirements for QDOTS with assets that exceed $2 million in value.** If the value of the assets passing to the QDOT at the time of the decedent spouse's death finally valued in the manner described earlier[64] exceeds $2 million, then at all times during the term of the trust, the trust instrument must satisfy at least one of three requirements. The QDOT may alternate among the three requirements as long as, at any given time, one of them is satisfied.[65] The purpose of these requirements is to ensure collection of the Section 2056A estate tax.[66]

Bank Trustee. Under the first alternative requirement, the trust instrument must require either that at least one United States Trustee[67] be a domestic

---

[62] Reg. § 20.2056A-2(d)(1)(iv)(G). If the proceeds (technically, the adjusted sales price as defined in Section 1034(b)(1) (prior to its repeal by the Taxpayer Relief Act of 1997, Pub. L. No. 105-34, § 312(b), 111 Stat. 788, 839 (1997), reprinted in 1997-4 CB (Vol. 1) 1, 53)) are fully reinvested within the twelve-month period, the "cessation of use" rule is inapplicable. Where only a portion of the adjusted sales price is reinvested within the twelve-month period, the amount of the exclusion equals the amount reinvested in the new residence plus any amount previously allocated to any other residence that continues to qualify for the exclusion up to a total of $600,000. Reg. § 20.2056A-2(d)(1)(iv)(6). As a result of these rules, there may be a partial or total disallowance of the exclusion. If, after the disallowance, the value of the assets at the time of the initial valuation would have exceeded $2 million, the requirements applicable to QDOTs with assets in excess of $2 million (see infra ¶ 5.07[3][c][i]) must be satisfied no later than 120 days after the effective date of the disallowance for the QDOT to continue to be a valid QDOT. Reg. § 20.2056A-2(d)(1)(iv)(G).

[63] Reg. §§ 20.2056A-2(d)(1)(iv)(F), 20.2056A-2(d)(3)(i)(B). The reporting is discussed infra ¶ 5.07[3][c][iii].

A similar exclusion election, subject to the same rules and same reporting, may also be made by the executor to exclude a personal residence from the bond or letter of credit security requirements considered below. Reg. § 20.2056A-2(d)(1)(iv)(B). Because one may alternate between methods of security, this election may be made at any time during the term of the QDOT or may be canceled at any time by attaching a written statement to a Form 706-QDT, "U.S. Estate Tax Return for Qualified Domestic Trusts" (Rev. Apr. 2000). Id. See infra ¶ 5.07[3][c][i].

[64] See supra text accompanying notes 52–63.

[65] Reg. § 20.2056A-2(d)(1)(i).

[66] Reg. § 20.2056A-2(d)(1).

[67] See supra ¶ 5.07[3][a].

bank[68] or that a U.S. branch of a foreign bank is a co-trustee with a United States Trustee as another cotrustee.[69]

Bond. Under the second alternative, the trust instrument must require the United States Trustee to furnish a bond in favor of the Service in an amount equal to at least 65 percent of the fair market value of the trust corpus as finally determined for estate tax purposes.[70] The bond must generally remain in effect until the termination of the QDOT and the payment of any tax liability finally determined to be due under Section 2056A(b),[71] unless the QDOT notifies the Service that it will satisfy one of the two other requirements within thirty days of having notified the Service of failure to renew.[72] There are several additional requirements that the bond must satisfy.[73] In addition, the bond must be drafted as provided in the regulations,[74] and it is generally required to be filed by the executor with the decedent's federal estate tax return.[75]

---

[68] The regulations incorporate the Section 581 definition of "bank." Reg. § 20.2056A-2(d)(1)(i)(A). The term "bank" is defined in Section 581 in part as "a bank or trust company incorporated and doing business under the laws of the United States . . . , the District of Columbia . . . or any state."

[69] Reg. § 20.2056A-2(d)(1)(i)(A). This rule permits, for example, an individual to serve as a United States co-trustee with a U.S. branch of a foreign bank. See supra ¶ 5.07[3][a].

[70] Reg. § 20.2056A-2(d)(1)(i)(B). Fair market valuation is determined in the same manner as valuation of the QDOT assets in determining the $2 million threshold (see supra text accompanying notes 52–63); therefore, the personal residence exclusion may be elected (see supra text accompanying notes 55–63 and Reg. § 20.2056A-2(d)(1)(iv)(B)), and the value of the assets is not reduced by an indebtedness with respect to the assets (see supra text accompanying note 53). Reg. § 20.2056-2(d)(1)(i)(B).

Although the 65 percent test is higher than the top Section 2001(c) rate, the higher percentage is justified both to reflect inflation in the value of the assets and to preclude the need to revalue the assets on an annual basis.

[71] Reg. § 20.2056A-2(d)(1)(i)(B).

[72] Reg. § 20.2056A-2(d)(1)(i)(B)(1). If these requirements are not met, the Service will not draw on the bond for failure to renew if, within thirty days of the Service's receipt of failure to renew, the Service is notified that QDOT will satisfy one of the other two alternative collection requirements prior to or on expiration of the bond. Id. There are additional requirements with respect to draws on the bond. See Reg. § 20.2056A-2(d)(1)(i)(B)(3).

[73] See Reg. § 20.2056A-2(d)(1)(i)(B)(1). The bond must satisfy Section 7101 and Regulations Section 301.7101-1, must be subject to Service review, must be for a term of at least one year, and must be automatically annually renewable unless notice of failure to renew is provided to the Service and to the U.S. Trustee at least sixty days prior to the end of the term. Reg. § 20.2056A-2(d)(1)(i)(B)(1).

[74] Reg. § 20.2056A-2(d)(1)(i)(B)(2).

[75] Reg. § 20.2056A-2(d)(1)(i)(B)(4). Presumably, this requirement applies only if the bond is the security arrangement originally relied on by the QDOT, rather than a later adopted alternative method, although the regulations are not so phrased. An extension for filing the bond may be granted under Regulations Section 301.9100. Reg. § 20.2056A-

Letter of Credit. Under the third alternative, the trust instrument must require the United States Trustee to furnish security in the form of an irrevocable letter of credit[76] in an amount equal to at least 65 percent of the fair market value of the trust corpus as finally determined for estate tax purposes.[77] Unless another alternative is employed, the letter of credit must generally remain in effect until the termination of the QDOT and the payment of any tax liability finally determined to be due under Section 2056A(b),[78] unless the QDOT notifies the Service that it will satisfy one of the two other requirements within thirty days of having notified the Service of failure to renew or closure of the issuing U.S. branch of a foreign bank.[79] The other rules and additional requirements with respect to the letter of credit substantially parallel those applicable to the furnishing of a bond.[80] The letter of credit must be drafted as provided in the regulations,[81] and it is generally required to be filed by the executor with the decedent's federal estate tax return.[82]

2(d)(1)(i)(B)(4). See Priv. Ltr. Rul. 9803017 (Oct. 17, 1997). The U.S. Trustee must submit a written statement with the bond that includes a valuation of assets used to fund the QDOT and a statement whether the personal residence exclusion is elected (see supra text accompanying notes 55–63). Reg. § 20.2056A-2(d)(1)(i)(B)(4).

[76] The letter of credit must be issued by a domestic bank as defined in Section 581 (see supra note 68), a U.S. branch of a foreign bank, or a foreign bank and confirmed by a domestic bank. Reg. § 20.2056A-2(d)(1)(i)(C).

[77] Reg. § 20.2056A-2(d)(1)(i)(C). Fair market valuation is determined in the same manner as valuation of the QDOT assets in determining the $2 million threshold (see supra text accompanying notes 52–63); therefore, the personal residence exclusion may be elected (see supra text accompanying notes 55–63 and Reg. § 20.2056A-2(d)(1)(iv)(B)), and in valuing the assets, their value is not reduced by any indebtedness with respect to the assets (see supra text accompanying note 53). Reg. § 20.2056A-2(d)(1)(i)(C). See supra note 70 for a justification of the 65 percent of value requirement.

[78] Reg. § 20.2056A-2(d)(1)(i)(C).

[79] Reg. § 20.2056A-2(d)(1)(i)(C)(1). The Service will not draw on the letter if it is notified within thirty days of receipt of the notice of failure to renew or closure of the U.S. branch that the QDOT satisfies one of the other two alternatives collection requirements. Id.

[80] Reg. § 20.2056A-2(d)(1)(i)(C). Cf. Reg. § 20.2056A-2(d)(1)(i)(B). The letter of credit must provide for sight payment, and it must be for a term of at least one year and be automatically annually renewable unless notice of failure to renew is provided at least sixty days prior to the end of the term. Reg. § 20.2056A-2(d)(1)(i)(C)(1). If the letter of credit is issued by a U.S. branch of a foreign bank and such branch is closing, the branch or foreign bank must notify the Service at least sixty days prior to such closure. Reg. § 20.2056A-2(d)(1)(C)(1). There are additional requirements with respect to draws on the letter of credit. See Reg. § 20.2056A-2(d)(1)(i)(C)(4).

[81] Reg. § 20.2056A-2(d)(1)(i)(C)(2). The regulations also provide the appropriate form for the confirmation of a letter of credit issued by a foreign bank and confirmed by a domestic bank. Reg. § 20.2056A-2(d)(1)(i)(C)(3). See supra note 76.

[82] Reg. § 20.2056A-2(d)(1)(i)(C)(5). Presumably, this requirement applies only if the letter of credit is the security arrangement originally relied on by the QDOT, rather than a

Undervaluation. In some circumstances, where its assets exceed $2 million, a QDOT is disqualified and no marital deduction is allowed to decedent spouse's estate[83] if there has been substantial undervaluation of the assets in the QDOT. QDOT disqualification occurs if (1) the value of the QDOT assets as reported on decedent spouse's federal estate tax return are "substantially undervalued" and (2) either (a) a bond or letter of credit security arrangement alternative has been employed or (b) the property was initially valued at $2 million or less and was finally determined to have a value in excess of $2 million.[84] Substantial undervaluation occurs when the valuation of the QDOT property reported on the estate tax return is 50 percent or less than the amount finally determined as the value of the property.[85] The substantial undervaluation QDOT disqualification rule is inapplicable if there was reasonable cause for such undervaluation or if the fiduciary of the estate acted in good faith with respect to such undervaluation.[86]

[ii] Requirements for QDOTs with assets that do not exceed $2 million in value. If the finally determined value of the assets passing to the QDOT at decedent's death, valued in the preceding manner,[87] is not in excess of $2 million, the trust instrument may provide for the trust to satisfy any of the three preceding alternative requirements,[88] or it may require that no more than 35 percent of the fair market value of the trust assets determined annually[89] consist of real property located outside the United States.[90]

---

later adopted alternative method, although the regulations are not so phrased. An extension may be granted under Regulations Section 301.9100. Reg. § 20.2056A-2(d)(1)(i)(C)(5). The United States Trustee must submit a written statement with the letter of credit that includes a valuation of assets used to fund the QDOT and a statement whether the residence exclusion is elected (see supra text accompanying notes 55–63). Reg. § 20.2056A-2(d)(1)(i)(C)(5). If a confirmation is required by a domestic bank (see supra note 76), it must also be filed. Reg. § 20.2056A-2(d)(1)(i)(C)(5).

[83] See Reg. § 20.2056A-2(d)(1)(i)(D)(1).

[84] Reg. § 20.2056A-2(d)(1)(i)(D)(1). See supra note 52.

[85] Reg. § 20.2056A-2(d)(1)(i)(D)(1). Seemingly, the $600,000 residence exclusion is inapplicable in applying this test. Compare Reg. § 20.2056A-2(d)(1)(i)(D)(1) with Reg. § 20.2056A-2(d)(1)(iv)(A). See supra text accompanying notes 55–63.

[86] Reg. § 20.2056A-2(d)(1)(i)(D)(2). Regulations Section 1.6664-4(b) applies to the extent applicable in making this determination. Reg. § 20.2056A-2(d)(1)(i)(D)(2).

[87] See supra text accompanying notes 52–63.

[88] See supra ¶ 5.07[3][c][i].

[89] The determination is made on the last day of the taxable year of the trust or, if the trust does not have a taxable year, the last day of the calendar year. Reg. § 20.2056A-2(d)(1)(ii). Rules applicable to the annual reporting requirement are considered below. See infra ¶ 5.07[3][c][iii].

[90] Reg. § 20.2056A-2(d)(1)(ii).

If the 35 percent alternative is used, some special rules apply. First, the elective personal residence exclusion is not applicable.[91] Second, a special look-through rule applies if the QDOT owns directly or by family attribution[92] a significant interest in a corporation or partnership, either 20 percent or more of the voting stock or value in a corporation with fifteen or fewer shareholders or 20 percent or more of a capital interest in a partnership with fifteen or fewer partners.[93] The purpose of this look-through rule is to determine whether the QDOT owns real property located outside the United States through a corporation or partnership. Under the look-through rule, all assets owned by the corporation or partnership are deemed to be owned directly by the QDOT to the extent of the QDOT's pro rata share of *actual* ownership of the corporation or partnership.[94] In addition, interests owned by the QDOT in other entities (such as a trust) are subject to a similarly applied look-through rule.[95]

If the 35 percent foreign realty test is not met at the time of the annual reporting,[96] the QDOT is not disqualified[97] if one of the three other alternative requirements applicable to a QDOT with assets in excess of $2 million (a bank trustee, a bond, or a letter of credit)[98] is satisfied.[99] If the 35 percent test is not met because of distributions of QDOT principal during the year, fluctuations in the value of the currency in the jurisdiction where the real estate is located, or fluctuations of the relative values of assets in the QDOT, a special relief provi-

---

[91] Reg. § 20.2056A-2(d)(1)(iv)(C). See supra text accompanying notes 55–63. Thus, the personal residence is included as real estate in measuring the 35 percent test even though it may not have been included in measuring the $2 million test.

[92] Reg. § 20.2056A-2(d)(1)(ii)(B). In applying the 20 percent and fifteen member tests, stock or partnership interests owned by or for the benefit of the surviving spouse or members of the surviving spouse's family as defined in Section 267(c)(4) are treated as owned by the QDOT. Id. Section 267(c)(4) includes brothers and sisters (whether by whole or half blood), spouses, ancestors, and lineal descendants as members of one's family.

[93] Reg. § 20.2056A-2(d)(1)(ii)(B).

[94] Reg. § 20.2056A-2(d)(1)(ii)(B). In the case of a partnership, the pro rata share is determined by the greater of the QDOT's interest in capital or profits of the partnership. Id. The surviving spouse's and the spouse's family members' ownership is not used in determining the QDOT's pro rata share of the assets of the entity. Id.

For example, if the QDOT and the surviving spouse's brother each own 15 percent of a corporation with fourteen other unrelated shareholders, the look-through rule applies because under the family attribution rule there is more than 20 percent ownership and only fifteen shareholders. However, in making the 35 percent measurement, the QDOT is deemed to own only 15 percent of the corporation's assets, the percentage corresponding to its actual ownership.

[95] Reg. § 20.2056A-2(d)(1)(ii)(C).

[96] See supra note 89.

[97] See infra ¶ 5.07[4][a] text accompanying notes 152–154.

[98] See supra ¶ 5.07[3][c][i].

[99] Cf. Reg. § 20.2056A-2(d)(1)(i).

sion applies. If one of these circumstances occurs, the QDOT is not disqualified[100] if, by the end of the succeeding year, either the value of the foreign real property held by the QDOT does not exceed the 35 percent test or the QDOT meets one of the three alternative requirements applicable to a QDOT with assets in excess of $2 million.[101]

[iii] Rules applicable to both classifications of QDOTs. The United States Trustee of a QDOT is required to file an annual written report in several circumstances. If the QDOT uses the less than 35 percent foreign real estate alternative[102] and the QDOT owns any foreign real estate either directly or under the look-through rule[103] on the last day of its taxable year,[104] the United States Trustee is required to make an annual reporting.[105] The United States Trustee must also make a reporting if the personal residence exclusion applies to the QDOT and a sale of the residence occurs or the residence ceases to be used as a personal residence during the year.[106] As a result of the foreign realty annual reporting, it may be determined that the 35 percent rule has been violated, disqualifying the QDOT.[107] The personal residence annual report may disclose that either the QDOT exceeds the $2 million threshold or fails the 65 percent security test.[108]

In all the preceding situations in which a report is required, the report must include identification of the United States Trustee,[109] a current valuation of trust assets including those subject to the look-through rule,[110] and if applicable, information regarding any sale of a personal residence or cessation of use of a residence as a personal residence.[111] The report is generally required to be filed by April 15 of the year following any calendar year in which the

---

[100] See infra ¶ 5.07[4][a] text accompanying notes 152–154.

[101] Reg. § 20.2056A-2(d)(1)(ii)(D). See supra ¶ 5.07[3][c][i].

[102] See supra text accompanying notes 89–101. If the QDOT satisfies one of the requirements applicable for a trust whose assets exceed the $2 million value, Regulations Sections 20.2056A-2(d)(3)(i)(A) and 20.2056A-2(d)(3)(i)(C) are expressly inapplicable.

[103] See supra text accompanying notes 92–95.

[104] If the trust has no taxable year, the last date of the calendar year applies. Reg. §§ 20.2056A-2(d)(3)(i)(A), 20.2056A-2(d)(3)(i)(C).

[105] Reg. §§ 20.2056A-2(d)(3)(i)(A), 20.2056A-2(d)(3)(i)(C).

[106] Reg. § 20.2056A-2(d)(3)(i)(B). See supra text accompanying notes 55–63.

[107] But see supra text accompanying notes 96–101.

[108] See supra text accompanying notes 55–63, 70, 77. The personal residence exclusion is inapplicable to the 35 percent test (see supra text accompanying note 91); thus, the reporting requirement of the personal residence is unrelated to that test.

[109] Reg. § 20.2056A-2(d)(3)(iii)(A).

[110] Reg. § 20.2056A-2(d)(3)(iii)(B).

[111] Reg. §§ 20.2056A-2(d)(3)(iii)(C), 20.2056A-2(d)(3)(iii)(D).

report is required,[112] and failure to timely file may result in a disqualification of the QDOT.[113]

An anti-abuse rule also applies to disqualify either classification of QDOT if the QDOT utilizes any device or arrangement that has, as a principal purpose, the avoidance of liability for or prevention of the collection of the decedent spouse's deferred tax.[114] For example, the anti-abuse rule may apply if the United States Trustee is a domestic corporation established with insubstantial capitalization by the surviving spouse or members of the spouse's family.[115]

[iv] Alternative arrangements. Alternative plans or arrangements to the preceding regulatory requirements imposed to ensure collection of the deferred tax may be proposed to the Commissioner. They will be approved if the Commissioner is satisfied that such plans or arrangements ensure collection of the deferred estate tax.[116]

[d] A QDOT Election

The decedent spouse's executor must make an irrevocable QDOT election on the decedent's federal estate tax return.[117] The election must be made on the last federal estate tax return filed before the due date (including extensions that have been granted). If no timely return is filed, the election may be made on the first return filed after the due date, but only if such election is made within one year of the time (including granted extensions) such return is required to

---

[112] Reg. § 20.2056A-2(d)(3)(ii). It is to be accompanied by a Form 706-QDT, "U.S. Estate Tax Return for Qualified Domestic Trusts" (Rev. Apr. 2000). Id.

[113] Reg. § 20.2056A-2(d)(3)(ii). See Reg. § 20.2056A-2(d)(1)(v).

[114] Reg. § 20.2056A-2(d)(1)(v).

[115] Reg. § 20.2056A-2(d)(1)(v). Failure to file a required annual reporting may also be treated as a violation of the anti-abuse rule. Reg. § 20.2056A-2(d)(3)(ii) (last sentence). The anti-abuse rule may also apply to a judicial reformation of a trust that fails to file during the judicial reformation. Reg. § 20.2056A-4(a)(2).

[116] Reg. § 20.2056A-2(d)(4). If the Commissioner publishes guidance in the Internal Revenue Bulletin for such alternative plans or arrangements, and if such a plan or arrangement is adopted, the QDOT will be treated as meeting the additional regulatory requirements to ensure collection of deferred tax. Id. See Reg. § 20.2056A-2(d)(1). However, prior to such time, taxpayers should request private letter rulings for any alternative plans or arrangements. Reg. § 20.2056A-2(d)(4) (last sentence).

[117] IRC §§ 2056A(a)(3), 2056A(d). The election must meet any requirements imposed by the estate tax return or the instructions applicable to the return. Reg. § 20.2056A-3(d).

Pursuant to Regulations Section 301.9100-1(a), the Commissioner may allow a reasonable extension of time for the election. See Priv. Ltr. Rul. 9547005 (Aug. 9, 1995); Priv. Ltr. Rul. 9505007 (Nov. 3, 1994).

be filed.[118] An election is not allowed with respect to only a portion of the property in a trust,[119] but a separate QDOT election may be made for any severed QTIP trust if a trust is validly severed under Section 2056(b)(7).[120] The executor may file a protective QDOT election if there is a bona fide controversy as to "the residency or citizenship of the decedent, the citizenship of the surviving spouse, whether an asset is included in the decedent's gross estate, or the amount or nature of the property the surviving spouse [will] receive."[121]

[e] Marital Deduction Qualification

The property passing from a decedent directly to a QDOT must generally satisfy the requirements of Section 2056.[122] Thus, the property must be included in the decedent's gross estate,[123] must pass to the surviving spouse,[124] and must satisfy the terminable interest rule.[125] Since the property is held in a trust, the property may satisfy the terminable interest rule by complying with Section 2056(b)(5) (life estate with a general power of appointment), Section 2056(b)(7) (QTIP property, including joint and survivor annuities under Section 2056(b)(7)(C)), or Section 2056(b)(8) (surviving spouse is the only noncharitable beneficiary of a charitable remainder trust), or by constituting an estate trust.[126]

---

[118] IRC § 2056A(d). See Reg. § 20.2056A-3(a) (which does not specifically mention the one-year late filing limitation that nevertheless still applies). Cf. Reg. § 20.2056A-1(a)(1)(iii).

[119] Reg. § 20.2056A-3(b).

[120] Reg. § 20.2056A-3(b). See ¶ 5.06[8][d] text accompanying notes 376–381.

[121] Reg. § 20.2056A-3(c). The controversy must exist at the time the estate tax return is filed. Id. The protective election must list the specific reason for the election and the specific assets, although they may otherwise be defined by means of a formula. Id. Once made, the protective election is irrevocable with respect to the specific assets to which the election applies. Id.

[122] Reg. § 20.2056A-2(b)(1). This requirement does not appear on the face of the statute. See IRC § 2056A(a). It is contained in the legislative history (HR Rep. No. 101-247, 101st Cong., 1st Sess. 1431 (1989)), and it can be read into the statute as a result of Sections 2056(d)(2)(A) and 2056(a). However, if the property passes outright to a surviving spouse and has already qualified for a marital deduction, the surviving spouse's subsequent transfer need not be to a QDOT that satisfies the terminable interest rule. See supra ¶ 5.07[2][b] note 18.

[123] See supra ¶ 5.06[4].

[124] See supra ¶ 5.06[3].

[125] See supra ¶ 5.06[7]. But see supra note 122.

[126] Reg. § 20.2056A-2(b)(1). See ¶¶ 5.06[8][b], 5.06[8][d], 5.06[8][e], 5.06[7][c] at notes 194–195, respectively. See also IRC § 2056A(b)(14), discussed supra ¶ 5.07[3][b] note 46. An estate trust must meet the requirements of Regulations Sections 20.2056(c)-2(b)(1)(i), 20.2056(c)-2(b)(1)(ii), and 20.2056(c)-2(b)(1)(iii). Seemingly, property qualify-

[4] Taxation of QDOT Property

[a] Events Triggering the Tax

The imposition of estate tax on the property in the decedent spouse's estate that qualified as QDOT property is deferred by allowing the decedent's estate a marital deduction for the value of such property.[127] The decedent spouse's estate tax liability on the property is generally[128] deferred until corpus is distributed from the QDOT, the surviving spouse dies, or the QDOT ceases to qualify as a QDOT.[129]

[i] **Corpus distributions.** If there is a distribution of principal from the QDOT during the surviving spouse's lifetime, the distribution is generally subject to tax when made.[130] However, tax is not imposed if the distribution is a distribution of income,[131] a corpus distribution to the surviving spouse on ac-

---

ing for a Section 2056(b)(6) marital deduction does not qualify as a QDOT because it is not held in a trust.

[127] IRC § 2056(d)(1)(A).

[128] But see infra ¶ 5.07[5] for a series of rules disregarding the QDOT if the surviving spouse subsequently becomes a citizen.

[129] See IRC §§ 2056A(b)(1), 2056A(b)(4), 2056A(b)(9). Form 706-QDT, "U.S. Estate Tax Return for Qualified Domestic Trusts" (Rev. Apr. 2000) is required to be filed. Reg. § 20.2056A-11.

[130] IRC § 2056A(b)(1)(A). A distribution of principal includes the corpus portion of an annuity payment that is not rolled over. See supra ¶ 5.07[2][c] text accompanying note 33, infra ¶ 5.07[4][c] text accompanying notes 171, 172.

Section 6161(a)(1) may be used to defer the payment of such tax. Reg. § 20.2056A-11(c)(2). See ¶ 2.02[3][b]. Seemingly, Section 6166 should also be potentially applicable. Cf. infra text accompanying note 148.

In determining the basis of distributed property for income tax purposes under Section 1015, any distribution where estate tax is imposed is treated as a transfer by gift and any estate tax paid is treated as a gift tax paid. IRC § 2056A(b)(13). See IRC §§ 1015(d)(1), 1015(d)(6); Reg. § 20.2056A-12. Arguably, the property is being included in the decedent spouse's estate at its estate tax valuation at the time of the distribution (see infra ¶ 5.07[4][b] text accompanying note 157), and the property ought to receive a Section 1014 basis on the date of the distribution.

Even though the estate tax is generally terminated for estates of decedent's dying after the year 2009 (see IRC § 2210(a)) if a decedent spouse dies prior to that date establishing a QDOT for a surviving spouse, this section applies to any distributions made to the surviving spouse during surviving spouse's lifetime and prior to the year 2021. IRC § 2210(b)(1). See infra note 137; ¶ 8.10[2][a].

[131] IRC § 2056A(b)(3)(A). The term "income" means fiduciary accounting income as defined in Section 643(b), except that it does not include capital gains or other items that would be allocated to corpus under applicable local law (or, in the absence of local law, under general principles of law), although a trust provision specifically labels them as income. IRC § 2056A(c)(2); Reg. § 20.2056A-5(c)(2). See Prop. Reg. § 1.643(b)-1.

count of hardship,[132] a distribution to reimburse the surviving spouse for federal income tax paid by the spouse on an item of QDOT income that the surviving spouse is not entitled to receive under the terms of the trust,[133] or certain administrative distributions and for consideration dispositions.[134] Thus, many distributions to third persons,[135] or to the surviving spouse are taxed. The amount of a taxable distribution is grossed up to include any payment of Section 2056A tax by the QDOT on a taxable distribution made by the trust.[136]

[ii] **The surviving spouse's death.** The value of any property remaining in the QDOT on the date of the surviving spouse's death is also subject to estate tax in the decedent spouse's estate.[137] If QDOT property is subject to de-

---

[132] IRC § 2056(b)(3)(B). A distribution is for hardship if it is in response to "an immediate and substantial financial need relating to the spouse's health, maintenance, education, or support or the health, maintenance, education, or support of any person that the surviving spouse is legally obligated to support." Reg. § 20.2056A-5(c)(1). Cf. Reg. § 1.401(k)-1(d)(2)(i). If other resources, such as surviving spouse's publicly traded stock or certificates of deposit, are reasonably available to the surviving spouse, the hardship requirement is not satisfied. Reg. § 20.2056A-5(c)(1). A hardship distribution must be reported on Form 706-QDT, "U.S. Estate Tax Return for Qualified Domestic Trusts" (Rev. Apr. 2000) even though it is exempt from tax under Section 2056A. Id.

[133] IRC § 2056A(b)(15). For example, this would include capital gains on corpus that were taxed to surviving spouse but that were not distributed to surviving spouse. See also Reg. § 20.2056A-5(c)(3)(iv) (reimbursement for taxes paid on nonassignable annuity corpus payments that are subsequently transferred by a surviving spouse to a QDOT pursuant to Regulations Section 20.2056A-4(c)(3)). See supra ¶ 5.07[2][c] text accompanying note 34.

[134] Reg. §§ 20.2056A-5(c)(3)(i), 20.2056A-5(c)(3)(ii), 20.2056A-5(c)(3)(iii). The regulations include within this exclusion ordinary and necessary expenses of the QDOT, government taxes (other than the estate tax) on the QDOT, and dispositions of trust assets for full and adequate consideration. Reg. §§ 20.2056A-5(c)(3)(i), 20.2056A-5(c)(3)(ii), 20.2056A-5(c)(3)(iii).

[135] Because a QDOT must generally satisfy the requirements of Section 2056 in order to qualify as a QDOT (see supra ¶ 5.07[3][e]; but see supra ¶ 5.07[2][b] note 18), only limited distributions to third persons would be possible. However, distributions could occur on an exercise of a general power by surviving spouse in favor of a third party under a Section 2056(b)(5) marital deduction trust. If the property is subject to estate tax in the decedent spouse's gross estate on the transfer and if the surviving spouse's gift were subject to U.S. taxation (see ¶ 9.02[1]), the property would be subject to double transfer taxation because no Section 2013-type credit would apply. Compare the result if there were dual estate tax inclusion. See infra text accompanying notes 138, 139; ¶ 5.06[9] text accompanying notes 441–447.

[136] IRC § 2056A(b)(11). The amount of the distribution varies depending on whether the United States Trustee withholds estate tax from the amount of the distribution or pays the tax out of other assets of the QDOT. Reg. § 20.2056A-5(b)(1). Issues may arise here similar to the issues that arise under Section 2621(b). See ¶ 14.02[4].

[137] IRC § 2056A(b)(1)(B). See Reg. § 20.2056A-5(b)(2). Section 6161(a)(1) may be used to defer the payment of such tax. Reg. § 20.2056A-11(c)(2). Cf. supra ¶ 2.02[3][b]. See also infra text accompanying notes 147, 148. If the decedent spouse dies prior to the

ferred tax in the decedent spouse's gross estate on any of the taxable events under Section 2056A[138] and the property is also included in the surviving spouse's gross estate, the surviving spouse's estate is allowed a Section 2013 credit regardless of the length of time between the two spouses' deaths.[139]

If the property remaining in the QDOT at the surviving spouse's death is includible in the surviving spouse's gross estate (or would be includible if such spouse were a resident of the United States),[140] Section 2056A(b)(10)[141] provides that the property in the QDOT subject to tax may qualify for benefits

---

year 2010, this section does not apply to property remaining in the QDOT if the surviving spouse dies after the year 2009. IRC § 2210(b)(2). Cf. supra note 130; ¶ 8.10[2][a].

[138] IRC §§ 2056A(b)(1), 2056A(b)(4). See supra text accompanying notes 127–137.

[139] IRC §§ 2056(d)(3), 2056A(b)(7). The interrelationship of QDOTs and the Section 2013 credit is discussed in detail at ¶ 5.06[9] notes 441–447. See also supra note 135.

[140] This would encompass inclusion generally under Section 2033, Section 2041(a)(2), or Section 2044.

[141] Regulations Section 20.2056A-6(b)(1) provides that except as provided in Regulations Sections 20.2056A-6(b)(2), 20.2056A-6(b)(3), 20.2056A-6(b)(4), 20.2056A-6(b)(5), the rules of each of the credit deduction and deferral provisions listed must be complied with. However, in applying these provisions, the surviving spouse is presumed to be a resident of the United States for purposes of inclusion of the property in the surviving spouse's gross estate under Chapter 11 and for purposes of these credit, deduction, and deferral provisions. Reg. § 20.2056A-6(b)(2).

Section 2056A

provided by Sections 303,[142] 2011,[143] 2014,[144] 2032,[145] 2032A,[146] 2055, 2056,

---

[142] The estate of the surviving spouse may use the Section 2056A(b)(1)(B) tax payment as an estate tax payment for purposes of Section 303. IRC § 2056A(b)(10)(B). See IRC § 303(a)(1).

[143] Because the effect of a QDOT is merely to postpone the decedent spouse's federal estate taxes on the property included in the QDOT, the computation of the Section 2011 state death tax credit when there is a QDOT tax computation must reflect all prior taxable events with respect to the decedent's estate and all state death taxes paid with respect to the decedent's estate. Reg. § 20.2056A-6(b)(4). Thus, the Section 2011 credit for the QDOT must be based on the lesser of (1) the total state taxes paid by the decedent's estate at the decedent's death as well as those paid on the taxation of the QDOT property (which includes those paid on account of inclusion of the property in the surviving spouse's estate for such death tax purposes), and (2) the Section 2011(b) ceiling determined by the decedent's original taxable estate increased by any QDOT taxable amounts. Id. See Reg. §§ 20.2056A-6(d) Exs. 2(i), 2(ii). The computation with respect to increased QDOT amounts should reflect Section 2011(b)(2) for the year of the decedent spouse's death. Cf. IRC § 2056A(b)(2)(A)(i); infra ¶ 5.07[4][b] text accompanying note 159. See ¶ 3.03[3][d].

Section 2011 is repealed for estates of decedents dying after December 31, 2004. IRC § 2011(f). The credit is replaced by a deduction under Section 2058. See ¶¶ 3.03[1], 3.03[3][d], 3.03[4], 5.09. As a result, Section 2011 is replaced by Section 2058 in Section 2056A(b)(10) for years after 2004.

[144] Because the effect of a QDOT is merely to postpone the decedent spouse's federal estate taxes on property included in the QDOT, the computation of the Section 2014 foreign tax credit when there is a QDOT taxable event must reflect both (1) the decedent spouse's actual taxable estate increased by the QDOT's taxable amount, and (2) the foreign death taxes paid both at decedent's death and with respect to the QDOT property. Reg. § 20.2056A-6(b)(4). Cf. supra note 143.

[145] In computing the deferred estate tax, the Section 2032 election is made on the Form 706-QDT, "U.S. Estate Tax Return for Qualified Domestic Trusts" (Rev. Apr. 2000), that is filed with respect to the balance in the QDOT on the surviving spouse's death; in addition, and the separate requirements for Section 2032 must be met. See ¶ 4.03; Reg. § 20.2056A-6(b)(5)(i). Section 2032 alternate valuation is allowed only if the irrevocable election reduces both the value of the property remaining in the QDOT upon the death of the surviving spouse and the net amount of deferred estate tax due. Reg. § 2056A-6(b)(5)(ii). See IRC § 2032(c); Instructions for Form 706-QDT (Rev. Apr. 2000) at 3.

[146] In computing the deferred estate tax, the Section 2032A election is made on the Form 706-QDT, "U.S. Estate Tax Return for Qualified Domestic Trusts" (Rev. Apr. 2000), that is filed with respect to the balance in the QDOT on the surviving spouse's death. The separate requirements of Section 2032A must be met if Section 2032A is to be used. See ¶¶ 4.04[1]–4.04[4]. Reg. § 20.2056A-6(b)(5)(i). The total value of property valued under Section 2032A in the QDOT cannot be decreased from its fair market value by more than the maximum Section 2032A limitation. Reg. § 20.2056A-6(b)(5)(iii). See IRC § 2032A(a)(2); Instructions for Form 706-QDT (Rev. Apr. 2000) at 3.

2057, 6161(a)(2),[147] and 6166.[148] For example, if the surviving spouse holds a general power of appointment over property and if the surviving spouse exercises the power over the entire property in favor of surviving spouse's new spouse who is a U.S. citizen, the taxable amount would be reduced by a marital deduction and there would be no taxation of the corpus of the QDOT at the surviving spouse's death.[149] Similarly, if the decedent established a trust that qualified for the marital deduction by virtue of an election under Section 2056(b)(7), with income to surviving spouse for life and a remainder to charity, and if surviving spouse made no inter vivos disposition of the income interest, the full taxable amount would qualify for a charitable deduction resulting in a wash with respect to imposition of any tax on the corpus of the QDOT at the surviving spouse's death.[150] In addition, in the case of a QDOT in which the surviving spouse's interest qualifies for a marital deduction under Section 2056(b)(8), a charitable deduction is allowed at the surviving spouse's death in the computation of the tax, although the property held in the QDOT is not included in the surviving spouse's gross estate.[151]

[iii] **QDOT disqualification.** If the QDOT ceases to qualify as a QDOT, either because the United States Trustee requirements are no longer met[152] or other requirements aimed at assuring tax collection are not satisfied,[153] the property in the QDOT is subject to tax as if the surviving spouse had died on the cessation date.[154]

---

[147] See Reg. § 20.2056A-11(c)(1); ¶ 2.02[3][b]. In applying Section 6161(a)(2), the trustees of the QDOT replace the decedent's executor when the term "executor" is used in the Code. IRC § 2056A(b)(10)(C). A Section 6161(a)(1) extension may also be granted for QDOT taxes for either lifetime distributions or at the surviving spouse's death. Reg. § 20.2056A-11(c)(2). See ¶ 2.02[3][b]; supra notes 130, 137.

[148] See Reg. § 20.2056A-11(c)(1); ¶ 2.02[3][c]. Section 2057 should be added to this list of Code sections in the text. See ¶ 5.08. Cf. supra note 143.

[149] IRC § 2056A(b)(10)(A). See IRC §§ 2056(a), 2056(b)(5). Therefore, as a result of the use of a QDOT, the deferral of tax with respect to the decedent's estate can be permanent, both in the situation described here and the situation described infra text accompanying note 150.

[150] IRC § 2056A(b)(10)(A). See IRC §§ 2055, 2056(b)(7), 2044. If, in the alternative, there were an inter vivos distribution to charity by a trust qualifying under Section 2056(b)(5) (e.g., on the surviving spouse's exercise of an inter vivos Section 2056(b)(5) general power of appointment), there should be a charitable deduction allowed under Section 2056A(b)(1)(A), but no deduction is provided by Section 2056A. Cf. IRC §§ 2056A(b)(10)(A), 2522.

[151] Reg. § 20.2056A-6(b)(3).

[152] See supra ¶¶ 5.07[3][a], 5.07[3][b].

[153] See supra ¶ 5.07[3][c].

[154] IRC § 2056A(b)(4). Although the reference to the surviving spouse's death would seem to cause the cessation to constitute a Section 2056A(b)(1)(B) taxable event, it is unclear whether a taxable event occurring as a result of the trust's ceasing to qualify as a

[b] Computation of the Tax

On the occurrence of a Section 2056A taxable event,[155] a deferred estate tax is imposed on the decedent's estate.[156] The property is taxed as if it had originally been included in the decedent's taxable estate, but the property is valued on the date of the subsequent taxable event.[157] On the first imposition of tax on the QDOT property, the value of the property taxed[158] is added to the amount of the decedent's taxable estate and adjusted taxable gifts. A tax on that total amount is computed using the Section 2001(c) rates in effect on the date of the decedent's death.[159] That amount of tax is then reduced by the Section 2001(c) tax on the amount of decedent's original taxable estate and ad-

---

QDOT results in a taxable event under Section 2056A(b)(1)(A) (inter vivos distribution) or Section 2056A(b)(1)(B) (death of surviving spouse). Results under the two subsections differ with respect to the basis of the property for income tax purposes (see IRC §§ 2056A(b)(10)(A), 2056A(b)(13)), the time for payment of tax due under Section 2056A (see IRC §§ 2056A(b)(5)(A), 2056A(b)(5)(B); infra ¶ 5.07[4][c]), and the allowance of certain tax benefits (see IRC § 2056A(b)(10)).

In all likelihood, this is a Section 2056A(b)(1)(B) taxable event because Section 2056A(b)(4) provides that "the tax imposed by paragraph (1) shall apply *as if the surviving spouse died on the date of such cessation*" (emphasis added). Regrettably, the regulations do not specifically address this issue. See Reg. § 20.2056A-5(b)(3). They merely provide that the amount subject to tax is the value of the trust corpus on the date of disqualification. Id.

[155] See supra ¶ 5.07[4][a].

[156] IRC § 2056A(b)(1).

[157] For purposes of Section 2056(d), any Section 2056A tax shall be treated as a tax paid under Section 2001 with respect to the decedent's estate. IRC § 2056A(b)(7). See supra ¶¶ 5.07[4][a] text accompanying notes 137–139, 5.06[9] at notes 436–440.

[158] Property taxed under Section 2056A(b)(1)(A) on distribution is valued at its fair market value. Property taxed under Section 2056A(b)(1)(B) upon death may be valued at its fair market value, but Section 2032 or Section 2032A valuation rules may also apply. See IRC § 2056A(b)(10)(A); supra ¶ 5.07[4][a], notes 145, 146, 154.

[159] IRC § 2056A(b)(2)(A)(i); Reg. § 20.2056A-6(a). This computation includes any tax under the additional 5 percent rate of now-repealed Section 2001(c)(2). Reg. § 20.2056A-6(a). See ¶ 2.01[3] text accompanying note 68.

If there is more than one QDOT with respect to any decedent, the amount of tax will be determined by using the highest rate of tax imposed under Section 2001(c) as of the date of the decedent's death, rather than the rates determined under Section 2056A(b)(2)(A). IRC § 2056A(b)(2)(C). The rules relating to multiple QDOTs are inapplicable if the decedent's executor designates a "Designated Filer" (either a U.S. citizen with a tax home in the United States (see IRC § 911(d)(3)) or a domestic corporation) who is responsible for filing all returns with respect to all the QDOTs. IRC § 2056A(b)(2)(C); Reg. § 20.2056A-9. The United States Trustee of each of the QDOTs must provide the Designated Filer with all necessary information at least sixty days prior to filing the return, and the Designated Filer must allocate the deferred estate tax due from each QDOT on a pro rata basis (based on the ratio of the amount of each respective taxable events in each QDOT to the amount of all such taxable events), unless a different allocation is required in the governing instrument or under local law. Reg. § 20.2056A-9.

justed taxable gifts.[160] On any subsequent imposition of tax under Section 2056A, a similar computation is made by first computing a tax at the rates in effect at the date of decedent's death on the then value of the property involved in the taxable event,[161] the decedent's original taxable estate and adjusted taxable gifts, and the Section 2056A amounts previously taxed. That amount of tax is then reduced by the amount of tax that would be imposed at decedent's rates on the total amount of the property excluding the property involved in the current taxable event.[162]

On any Section 2056A imposition of tax, if the amount of Section 2001 tax with respect to a decedent's taxable estate has not been finally determined owing to the statute of limitations not having expired[163] or to some pending judicial determination,[164] a tentative Section 2056A tax is computed at the highest Section 2001(c) rate in effect at the date of the decedent's death.[165] If the amount of tax imposed at that rate exceeds the amount of tax due under Section 2056A when the decedent's estate tax is finally determined, the estate has a one-year period from the date of final determination to claim the excess amount as a credit or refund (with interest).[166]

---

[160] IRC § 2056A(b)(2)(A)(ii). In computing the taxes under each step, the credits under Sections 2010, 2011, 2013, and 2014 in effect on the date of the date of the decedent's death are taken into consideration unless the decedent is a nonresident noncitizen, in which case Section 2102 is applied. Reg. § 20.2056A-6(a). See ¶ 6.02. Thus, any of the decedent spouse's unused Section 2010 credit is allowed as a credit against the tax. Id. See Reg. § 20.2056A-6(d) Ex. 1. Cf. IRC § 2056A(b)(12)(C)(ii).

For example, if in the year 2002, the decedent spouse previously had a total taxable estate and adjusted taxable gifts of $1.5 million and if, in the year 2004, the taxable amount involved under Section 2056A is $500,000, the Section 2056A tax liability (considering only the Section 2010 credit) would be $225,000, which is the difference between the Section 2001(c) tax on $2 million ($435,000: $780,800 less $345,800 under Section 2010 at the date of the decedent's death) and the Section 2001(c) tax on $1.5 million ($210,000: $555,800 less $345,800 under Section 2010). See Reg. § 20.2056A-6(d) Ex. 1.

[161] See IRC § 2056A(b)(1); supra note 158.

[162] See IRC §§ 2056A(b)(2)(A)(i)(II), 2056A(b)(2)(A)(ii).

For example, if there were a subsequent $500,000 taxable amount under Section 2056A in 2005 in addition to the amounts determined in the example supra note 160, and applying the same assumptions, the tax on the $500,000 would be $245,000, the difference between the Section 2001(c) tax on $2.5 million ($680,000: $1,025,800 less $345,800 under Section 2010) and the Section 2001(c) tax on $2 million ($435,000: $780,800 less $345,800 under Section 2010).

[163] See IRC § 6501.

[164] See HR Rep. No. 1104, 100th Cong., 2nd Sess. 115 (1988), reprinted in 1988-3 CB 473, 605. A tax may be finally determined by a closing agreement. Id. See IRC § 7121.

[165] IRC § 2056A(b)(2)(B)(i). See IRC § 2001(c), ¶ 2.01[3].

[166] IRC § 2056A(b)(2)(B)(ii).

[c] Liability for and Payment of the Tax

The date for the payment of the tax depends on the taxable event[167] that triggers the tax.[168] If the tax is due as a result of the death of the surviving spouse,[169] the tax is to be paid nine months from the date of the death.[170] If the taxable event is a taxable distribution from the trust,[171] the tax is generally due on April 15 of the year following the calendar year in which the distribution occurs.[172] However, if the distribution occurs in the year of the surviving spouse's death, the tax is due on the earlier of April 15 of the succeeding year or nine months after the date of the surviving spouse's death.[173] If the tax is due as a result of the disqualification of the trust as a QDOT,[174] the death of the surviving spouse rules likely will apply.[175]

Each trustee of the QDOT (not just the United States Trustee) is personally liable for the payment of the tax.[176] In addition, the assets of any QDOT are subject to collection for any tax resulting from a taxable event with respect to any other QDOT established with respect to the same decedent.[177]

---

[167] IRC § 2056A(b)(9). See supra ¶ 5.07[4][a].

[168] IRC § 2056A(b)(5).

[169] IRC § 2056A(b)(1)(B).

[170] IRC § 2056A(b)(5)(B). See Reg. § 20.2056A-11(b), allowing an extension of time for filing a Form 706-QDT, "U.S. Estate Tax Return for Qualified Domestic Trusts" (Rev. Apr. 2000), of not more than six months if the Section 6081(a) conditions are met; and see supra ¶ 5.07[4][a] note 147 for extensions of time for tax payments under Sections 6161(a)(1) and 6161(a)(2). See also ¶¶ 2.02[1], 2.02[3][b].

[171] IRC § 2056A(b)(1)(A). See supra ¶ 5.07[4][a][i].

[172] IRC § 2056A(b)(5)(A). See Regulations Section 20.2056A-11(a), allowing an extension of time for filing a Form 706-QDT, "U.S. Estate Tax Return for Qualified Domestic Trusts" (Rev. Apr. 2000), of not more than six months if the Section 6081(a) conditions are met, Regulations Section 20.2056A-11(c)(2) allowing a six-month extension of time for payment under Section 6161(a)(1), and ¶¶ 2.02[1], 2.02[3][b]. See also Regulations Section 20.2056A-4(c)(6)(i) for filing with respect to corpus portions of annuity payments considered supra ¶ 5.07[2][c] text accompanying note 33.

[173] IRC § 2056A(b)(5)(A).

[174] IRC § 2056A(b)(4). See supra notes 170, 172, involving extensions for payment of tax and filing of returns.

[175] See supra ¶ 5.07[4][a] text accompanying note 154; supra text accompanying note 170.

[176] IRC § 2056A(b)(6). If there are multiple QDOTs with respect to the same decedent, all trustees of each trust (and not just the United States Trustee) are personally liable for the amount of tax imposed on any taxable event with respect to that trustee's QDOT, notwithstanding the appointment of a Designated Filer. Reg. § 20.2056A-11(d). See supra ¶ 5.07[4][b] note 159.

[177] Reg. § 20.2056A-11(d). There is a lien against the property giving rise to the tax until ten years from the date of the taxable event. IRC § 2056A(b)(8). Any tax imposed under Section 2056A shall be treated as an estate tax imposed with respect to a decedent

[5] Exceptions If Surviving Spouse Becomes a U.S. Citizen

Special rules apply if the surviving spouse becomes a U.S. citizen. If the surviving spouse becomes a U.S. citizen before decedent's estate tax return is filed[178] and if such spouse was a U.S. resident[179] at all times after the decedent's death until becoming a U.S. citizen, there is no need for a QDOT, and Section 2056(d) is inapplicable.[180]

If the surviving spouse becomes a U.S. citizen after the decedent's estate tax return is filed, a QDOT may be disregarded with respect to any subsequent distributions and at the surviving spouse's death, if there is no subsequent need for the QDOT.[181] A QDOT is disregarded if one of several alternative requirements are met. The requirements ensure that any prior taxable distributions from the QDOT do not escape the equivalent of taxation to the surviving spouse. A QDOT is disregarded after the surviving spouse becomes a citizen subsequent to decedent's estate tax return being filed if *either* (1) the surviving spouse was a resident of the United States at all times after the decedent's death prior to becoming a citizen[182] *or* (2) regardless of residency status, no QDOT tax was imposed under Section 2056A(b)(1)(A) on any distributions before the surviving spouse became a citizen[183] *and* under either of these alternatives, the United States Trustee notifies the Service and certifies in writing to the Service that the surviving spouse has become a U.S. citizen.[184] A separate alternative applies if the surviving spouse was not a resident at all times after the decedent's death prior to becoming a citizen and if there were prior

---

dying on the date of the taxable event, and the property involved shall be treated as included in the gross estate of such decedent. Id. See IRC § 6324.

[178] See Reg. § 20.2056A-1(b). See ¶ 5.06[9] text accompanying note 431.

[179] See ¶ 5.06[9] note 432.

[180] IRC § 2056(d)(4). See ¶ 5.06[9] text accompanying notes 430–433; Reg. § 20.2056A-1(b). Section 2040(b) also applies if surviving spouse becomes a citizen prior to such time. See ¶ 4.12[10] text accompanying note 89.

[181] IRC § 2056A(b)(12). Thus, there is no Section 2056A tax on a subsequent distribution or at surviving spouse's death. See IRC § 2056A(b)(1).

[182] IRC § 2056A(b)(12)(A). If the surviving spouse was a resident at all such times, any gift transfer made by the surviving spouse to a third party would be subject to a transfer tax as a result of the application of Section 2511, Section 2514, or Section 2519.

[183] IRC § 2056A(b)(12)(B). Even though there was a Section 2056A(b)(1)(A) distribution, no tax would be imposed if the tax liability was within the decedent's spouse's unused Section 2010 unified credit. Cf. IRC § 2056A(b)(12)(C). Arguably, no tax would be imposed if the distribution were to a charity. See supra ¶ 5.07[4][a] note 150.

[184] Reg. § 20.2056A-10(a)(2). Notice is made by filing a final Form 706-QDT, "U.S. Estate Tax Return for Qualified Domestic Trusts" (Rev. Apr. 2000). This filing must occur on or before April 15 of the year following the year in which the surviving spouse becomes a citizen, unless a Section 6081 extension on filing the Form 706-QDT is granted. Id. An extension of time in which to file the notice can be granted pursuant to Regulations Section 301.9100-3. Priv. Ltr. Rul. 200132013 (Apr. 19, 2001).

distributions upon which tax was imposed under Section 2056A(b)(1)(A).[185] In such circumstances, a QDOT is disregarded for periods after the surviving spouse becomes a citizen if the surviving spouse both (1) elects to treat the prior taxable QDOT distributions as taxable gifts made by the surviving spouse for purposes of determining the rate of tax imposed on gifts made by the surviving spouse in the current and subsequent years and on the computation of the surviving spouse's estate tax[186] and (2) elects to treat any of the *decedent spouse's* Section 2010 unified credit allowed against such distributions as though it was used by the surviving spouse, thus reducing the surviving spouse's own Section 2505 unified credit in determining the subsequent estate and gift tax liability of the surviving spouse.[187]

¶ 5.08 SECTION 2057. FAMILY-OWNED-BUSINESS DEDUCTION

[1] Introduction

Section 2057 provides an elective deduction for decedents dying before January 1, 2004,[1] subject to a ceiling amount,[2] from a decedent's gross estate for the "adjusted value"[3] of certain "qualified family-owned business interests."[4] Section 2057 was enacted to preserve family businesses by totally or partially

---

[185] IRC § 2056A(b)(12)(C).

[186] IRC § 2056A(b)(12)(C)(i). The effect of this requirement is to reflect any prior Section 2056A(b)(1)(A) distributions in the surviving spouse's subsequent transfer tax computations. Reg. § 20.2056A-10(b)(1).

[187] IRC § 2056A(b)(12)(C)(ii). See Reg. § 20.2056A-10(b)(2).

Both elections must be made by attaching notification of the election to a timely filed Form 706-QDT, "U.S. Estate Tax Return for Qualified Domestic Trusts" (Rev. Apr. 2000), on or before April 15 of the year following the year in which the surviving spouse becomes a citizen (unless a Section 6081 extension is granted). Reg. § 20.2056A-10(b)(3).

[1] IRC § 2057(j). Section 2057 does not apply to the estates of decedents dying after December 31, 2003. However, Title IX of the Economic Growth and Tax Relief Reconciliation Act of 2001 contains a "sunset" provision that would make Section 2057(j) inapplicable to estates of decedents dying after December 31, 2010. Economic Growth and Tax Relief Reconciliation Act of 2001, Pub. L. No. 107-16, § 901(a)(2), 115 Stat. 150 (2001), reprinted in 2001-__ CB __, __. See ¶ 8.10[5].

[2] Section 2057 allows a deduction of up to $675,000. IRC § 2057(a)(2). The deduction is interrelated with the Section 2010 applicable credit amount. IRC § 2057(a)(3). See infra ¶ 5.08[4][b].

[3] IRC § 2057(d). See infra ¶ 5.08[3][c][iii].

[4] IRC § 2057(a). See IRC § 2057(e), discussed infra ¶ 5.08[2].

eliminating federal transfer tax liability[5] with respect to family-owned farms and small businesses, thereby making their liquidation to pay federal estate taxes unnecessary.[6] Congress hoped that protecting family enterprises in this manner would "preserve jobs and strengthen the communities in which such enterprises are located."[7] The purpose of Section 2057 is similar to the purpose supporting Sections 2032A and 6166, and in some circumstances, all three sections may be applied in tandem.[8]

The predecessor of Section 2057 (Section 2033A) took the form of an exclusion from the gross estate.[9] The Internal Revenue Service Restructuring and Reform Act of 1998 converted the exclusion to a deduction.[10] The principal reason for the conversion was to avoid problems with the interrelationship between the exclusion and other tax provisions both within and beyond the estate tax.[11] The conversion largely achieves this result.[12]

Section 2057 is similar to Section 2032A. In fact, Section 2057 borrows many of its statutory provisions from Section 2032A.[13] However, the two sections differ in that Section 2032A provides special valuation for specific real

---

[5] A Sense of the Senate Resolution was passed by the Senate that "Congress should eliminate the Federal estate tax liability for family-owned businesses by the end of 2002 on a deficit-neutral basis." HR Conf. Rep. No. 220, 105th Cong., 1st Sess. 764 (1997), reprinted in 1997-4 CB (Vol. 2) 1457, 2234. The conference agreement did not include the Senate amendment. Id.

[6] See S. Rep. No. 33, 105th Cong., 1st Sess. 40 (1997), reprinted in 1997-4 CB (Vol. 2) 1067, 1120.

[7] S. Rep. No. 33, 105th Cong., 1st Sess. 40 (1997), reprinted in 1997-4 CB (Vol. 2) 1067, 1120.

[8] See ¶¶ 2.02[3][c], 4.04. See also infra ¶¶ 5.08[6][b], 5.08[6][c].

[9] Taxpayer Relief Act of 1997, Pub. L. No. 105-34, § 502(a), 111 Stat. 788, 847 (1997), reprinted in 1997-4 CB (Vol. 1) 1, 61.

[10] Internal Revenue Service Restructuring and Reform Act of 1998, Pub. L. No. 105-206, § 6007(b)(1)(B), 112 Stat. 685, 807 (1998), reprinted in 1998-3 CB 145, 267.

[11] The exclusion provision was unclear as to whether it excluded specific property or simply a dollar value from the gross estate. The legislative history of the Internal Revenue Service Restructuring and Reform Act of 1998 stated:

It [was] unclear whether the provision provide[d] an exclusion of value or an exclusion of property from the estate, and thus it is unclear how the . . . provision interact[ed] with other provisions in the Internal Revenue Code (e.g., secs. 1014, 2032A, 2056, 2612, and 6166).

S. Rep. No. 174, 105th Cong., 2nd Sess. 155 (1998), reprinted in 1998-3 CB 537, 691.

The conversion of the exclusion to a Section 2057 deduction resolves gross estate computation issues because the qualifying family-owned business interests are included in the gross estate.

[12] See infra ¶ 5.08[6].

[13] See IRC § 2057(i). Section 2057 has been criticized because of its complexity. Much of the complexity and difficulty in interpreting Section 2057 results from congressional borrowing from Section 2032A.

property, while Section 2057 provides a deduction when a decedent owns a specific type of property. This difference in the nature of the provisions creates difficulty in interpreting how the Section 2032A cross-references interact with Section 2057.

[2] Definition of "Qualified Family-Owned Business Interest"

[a] In General

A qualified family-owned business interest may be either an interest held as a proprietor in a trade or business[14] carried on as a sole proprietorship[15] or an interest held in an entity carrying on a trade or business if the decedent and members of the decedent's family directly or indirectly own a specified minimum interest in the entity.[16] A decedent is treated as engaged in a trade or business if any member of the decedent's family is engaged in that trade or business.[17] Thus, an individual's interest in property used in a trade or business by a member of the individual's family may be a qualified family-owned business interest.[18] For example, if a parent leases farmland to a child and the child uses the farmland in a trade or business as a proprietor, although the parent is not actually engaged in the trade or business, the parent is treated as engaged in the child's trade or business[19] and the parent has a qualified family-owned business interest that may qualify for the family-owned-business deduction.[20]

---

[14] See infra ¶ 5.08[2][b] text accompanying note 23.

[15] IRC § 2057(e)(1)(A).

[16] IRC § 2057(e)(1)(B). See infra ¶ 5.08[2][c][ii].

[17] IRC § 2057(e)(1).

[18] S. Rep. No. 174, 105th Cong., 2nd Sess. 157 (1998), reprinted in 1998-3 CB 537, 693.

[19] S. Rep. No. 174, 105th Cong., 2d Sess. 157 (1998), reprinted in 1998-3 CB 537, 693. "[I]f a brother and sister inherit farmland upon their father's death, and the sister cash-leases her portion to her brother, who is engaged in the trade or business of farming, the 'trade or business' requirement is satisfied with respect to both the brother and the sister." Id.

[20] The result should be the same if the child owns an interest in an entity carrying on a trade or business that leases the land from the parent. Technically, treating a decedent as engaged in any trade or business in which a member of the decedent's family is engaged does not by itself achieve this result. The mere fact that an entity engages in a trade or business probably does not cause the entity's owners to be engaged in that trade or business. Nevertheless, Section 2057(e)(3)(C) treats ownership interests in entities as proportionate ownership interests in the entity's property. Consequently, if a member of a decedent's family owns an interest in an entity that itself engages in a trade or business, Section 2057(e)(3)(C) treats that family member as engaged in the trade or business through the entity, and Section 2057(e)(1) treats the decedent as engaged in that same

trade or business through the family member. In addition, if a child owns an entity carrying on a trade or business that leases land from an entity owned by the parent, the parent should be treated as engaged in the child's trade or business and owning a qualified family-owned business interest that may qualify for the family-owned-business deduction.

For purposes of Section 2057, rules similar to those contained in Section 2032A(g) apply relating to the application of Section 2057 to interests in partnerships and corporations. IRC § 2057(i)(3)(L). Under Section 2032A(g) the Secretary is to "prescribe regulations setting forth the application of . . . [Section 2032A] . . . in the case of an interest in a partnership, corporation . . . which, with respect to the decedent, is an interest in a closely held business (within the meaning of paragraph (1) of section 6166(b))." IRC § 2032A(g). The regulations provide that

> [w]here the ownership is indirect . . . the decedent's interest in the business must, in addition to meeting the tests for qualification under section 2032A, qualify under the tests of section 6166(b)(1) as an interest in a closely-held business on the date of the decedent's death. . . . Directly owned real property that is leased by a decedent to a separate closely held business is considered to be qualified real property, but only if the separate business qualifies as a closely held business under section 6166(b)(1) with respect to the decedent on the date of . . . death.

Reg. § 20.2032A-3(b)(1). The incorporation into Section 2057 of Section 2032A(g) by reference raises an interesting issue. Must an entity that leases from a decedent property that is used by the entity in carrying on a business as a prerequisite to classification as a "qualified family-owned business interest" qualify as an interest in a closely-held business under Section 6166(b)(1) in addition to satisfying the other tests in Section 2057? If one entity owned by a decedent leases property to a second entity for use in carrying on a trade or business, do both entities have to qualify under Section 6166(b)(1) if the decedent is to be treated as having a qualified family-owned business interest? Regulations will in all likelihood never be promulgated for Section 2057 to address these issues. See infra ¶ 5.08[2][c][ii].

Section 2057

[b] Requirements and Limitations Applicable to Both Proprietorships and Entities

Several requirements must be satisfied by both a proprietorship and an entity in order to be classified as a qualified family-owned business,[21] and additional requirements are applicable only to entities.[22]

[i] **A trade or business.** To constitute a qualified family-owned business, the proprietorship or entity must engage in a trade or business, a term undefined by the Code.[23]

[ii] **Principal place of business in the United States.** The principal place of business of the trade or business must be located in the United States.[24]

[iii] **Ceiling on amount of personal holding company income.** The trade or business must generate most of its income from the active conduct of a trade or business rather than from mere passive income activities.[25] A trade or business is not a qualified family-owned business interest if, in the taxable year of the decedent's death, more than 35 percent of the adjusted ordinary

---

[21] See infra ¶¶ 5.08[2][b][i]–¶ 5.08[2][b][v].

[22] See infra ¶ 5.08[2][c].

[23] The phrase "trade or business" is frequently used in the Code, yet it is not defined in the Code or in Treasury Regulations; nor is there a prevailing clear definition of the term in the relevant case law. See Boyle, "What Is a Trade or Business?" 39 Tax Law. 737 (1986) (discussing the varied use of the term "trade or business" in the Code). See also Comm'r v. Groetzinger, 480 US 23 (1987) (discussing the phrase "trade or business" for purposes of Section 162); LDL Research & Development II, Ltd. v. Comm'r, 124 F3d 1338 (10th Cir. 1997) (noting "that the *Groetzinger* court was careful to observe that any effort to provide an all-purpose definition for 'trade or business' applicable to all Code contexts 'would be counterproductive, unhelpful, and even somewhat precarious for the overall integrity of the Code'"); Bittker & McMahon, Federal Income Taxation of Individuals ¶ 11.1[2] (Warren, Gorham & Lamont, 2d ed. 1995).

[24] IRC § 2057(e)(2)(A). The term "principal place of business" is an ambiguous phrase that is used in a number of instances in the Internal Revenue Code. Historically, for purposes of determining a corporation's principal place of business, courts have applied either the "nerve center" test, the "place of activities" test, or the "total activity" test. Levy, "Diversity Jurisdiction; Where Do Dead Corporations Live? Determining the Citizenship of Inactive Corporations for Diversity Jurisdiction Purposes," 62 Brook. L. Rev. 663, 673 (1996). Under the "nerve center" test, a corporation's principal place of business is "the site of executive and administrative functions." Id. Under the "place of activities" test, the corporation's center of production or center of service activities is its principal place of business. Id. Finally, under the "total activity" test, a court analyzes the corporation in light of the "nerve center" test and the "place of activities" test and determines the principal place of business by weighing all the relevant factors. Id.

[25] IRC § 2057(e)(2)(C).

gross income[26] is personal holding company income.[27] "Personal holding company income" consists of certain dividends, interest, royalties, annuities, rents, and a number of other similar items of income.[28] There are some exceptions to the 35 percent rule. The passive income limitation does not apply to banks,[29] domestic building and loan associations,[30] and trades or businesses whose principal source of income is as a dealer in property producing personal holding company income.[31] In addition, income from a net cash lease by a decedent to a member of the decedent's family is not treated as personal holding company income for this purpose if it would not be personal holding company income if the decedent used the property in the same manner as the lessee.[32]

[iv] **Certain assets excluded from value.** Even if a business is not denied qualified family-owned-business status owing to the personal holding company income rule, Congress will not allow a deduction for unneeded passive assets that are held by an active business. Thus, assets held in a trade or business activity that are mere passive assets and not directly related to the active conduct of the trade or business generally are not treated as a part of the trade or business, and they do not qualify for a Section 2057 deduction.[33] A qualified family-owned business interest does not include the portion of the value of a trade or business represented by cash and marketable securities in excess of reasonably expected day-to-day working capital needs.[34] Nor does a

---

[26] IRC § 543(b)(2).

[27] IRC § 2057(e)(2)(C).

[28] IRC § 543(a). In determining personal holding company income, the trade or business is treated as if it were a corporation and Section 543(a) is applied without regard to Section 543(a)(2)(B) (the dividend requirement for corporate entities). IRC § 2057(e)(2)(C).

[29] IRC § 581.

[30] IRC § 7701(a)(19).

[31] IRC § 2057(e)(2)(C). See IRC § 542(c)(2); S. Rep. No. 33, 105th Cong., 1st Sess. 42 (1997), reprinted in 1997-4 CB (Vol. 2) 1067, 1122.

[32] IRC § 2057(e)(2).

[33] IRC § 2057(e)(2)(D).

[34] IRC § 2057(e)(2)(D)(i). Working capital needs are to be determined by using an analysis similar to that set forth in Bardahl Mfg. Corp. v. Comm'r, 24 TCM 1030 (1965). S. Rep. No. 33, 105th Cong., 1st Sess. 42 (1997), reprinted in 1997-4 CB (Vol. 2) 1067, 1122. In *Bardahl*, the court applied a facts-and-circumstances test to determine the amount of the corporation's working capital needs. In calculating the amount of the corporation's available liquid assets, the court included the outstanding balance of all loans made by the corporation that were unrelated to its business activities, as well as the net investments of the corporation in unrelated real estate transactions. Working capital does not include amounts of capital held for capital acquisitions. S. Rep. No. 33, 105th Cong., 1st Sess. 42 (1997), reprinted in 1997-4 CB (Vol. 2) 1067, 1122. See Bittker & Eustice Federal Income Taxation of Corporations and Shareholders ¶ 7.03 (Warren, Gorham & Lamont, 7th ed. 2000).

qualified family-owned business interest generally include certain passive assets[35] such as assets that produce dividends, interest, rents, royalties, annuities, and certain other types of passive income;[36] an interest in a trust, partnership, or REMIC;[37] assets that produce no income;[38] assets that give rise to income from commodities transactions or foreign currency gains;[39] assets that produce income equivalent to interest;[40] or assets that produce income from notional principal contracts or payments in lieu of dividends.[41] However, these normally passive assets *are* included in the value of a qualified family-owned business interest in business such as banks,[42] domestic building and loan associations,[43] and dealers who use the assets in the active conduct of their business and in whose hands the assets are not passive.[44] Furthermore, property leased on a net cash basis by a decedent to a member of the decedent's family is included in the value of the qualified family-owned business interest and is not excluded as property held for the production of personal holding company income if the

---

[35] IRC § 2057(e)(2)(D)(ii). If a qualified family-owned business interest owns as an asset an interest in another business, the business interest held as an asset will not be a part of the qualified family-owned business interest under Section 2057(e)(2)(D)(ii), whether or not the business interest held as an asset is a qualified family-owned business interest. Nevertheless, the subsidiary business interest owned by the qualified family-owned business interest may itself be a qualified family-owned business interest. For example, where corporate stock is owned by a qualified family-owned business interest, that portion of the value of the qualified family-owned business interest attributable to the corporate stock would not be part of the qualified family-owned business interest as defined in Section 2057(e). IRC § 2057(e)(2)(D)(ii). The corporate stock owned by the qualified family-owned business interest may itself be a qualified family-owned business interest as defined in Section 2057(e). See infra ¶ 5.08[2][c] text accompanying notes 65–69.

[36] IRC § 543(a). In determining assets that produce personal holding company income, the trade or business is to be treated as if it were a corporation and Section 543(a) is applied without regard to Section 543(a)(2)(B) (the dividend requirement for corporate entities). IRC §§ 2057(e)(2)(D)(ii), 2057(e)(2)(C). Property leased on a net cash basis to a member of the decedent's family is not treated as an asset that produces personal holding company income if the activities of the lessee if carried on by the lessor directly would not generate personal holding company income. IRC § 2057(e)(2).

[37] IRC § 954(c)(1)(B)(ii).

[38] IRC § 954(c)(1)(B)(iii).

[39] IRC §§ 954(c)(1)(C), 954(c)(1)(D).

[40] IRC § 954(c)(1)(E).

[41] IRC §§ 954(c)(1)(F), 954(c)(1)(G).

[42] IRC § 581.

[43] IRC § 7701(a)(19).

[44] IRC § 2057(e)(2)(D)(ii); S. Rep. No. 33, 105th Cong., 1st Sess. 42 (1997), reprinted in 1997-4 CB (Vol. 2) 1067, 1122. See IRC § 542(c)(2).

property would have been included had the decedent directly engaged in the activities engaged in by the lessee.[45]

[v] **Interests passing to noncitizens.** Generally, a family-owned trade or business interest that passes to a qualified heir who is not a citizen[46] of the United States is not treated as a qualified family-owned business interest and does not qualify for a Section 2057 deduction.[47] However, if certain security requirements are met, the interest passing to a noncitizen qualified heir is treated as a qualified family-owned business interest.[48] The security requirement is satisfied if the interest passes to a "qualified trust."[49] A qualified trust is generally any trust organized under, and governed by, the laws of the United States or a state,[50] and whose governing instrument requires that at least one trustee of the trust be a citizen of the United States or a domestic corporation.[51] Alternatively, the security requirement is satisfied if the qualified heir furnishes a bond equal to the maximum amount of additional estate tax that could be imposed in the event additional estate tax actually is imposed.[52]

[c] Additional Requirements With Respect to Entities

An entity, including a corporation, partnership, or any entity treated as a partnership or corporation for federal tax purposes,[53] will be treated as a qualified family-owned business interest only if it also meets the following additional requirements.

[i] **Non–publicly traded equity and debt.** Equity or debt interests in the entity or in a controlled group[54] of which the entity was a member must not

---

[45] IRC § 2057(e)(2).

[46] See infra ¶ 5.08[3][a].

[47] IRC § 2057(g)(1).

[48] IRC § 2057(g)(1).

[49] IRC § 2057(g)(1).

[50] IRC § 2057(g)(2)(A). The Section 2057 qualified trust will, in all likelihood, bear a strong resemblance to a Section 2056A qualified domestic trust, which may be used to permit a marital deduction to a decedent's estate when there is a noncitizen surviving spouse. See IRC § 2056A; ¶ 5.07.

[51] IRC § 2057(g)(2)(B). This requirement may be altered by the regulations. Id. Cf. ¶ 5.07[3][a] note 43.

[52] IRC §§ 2057(g)(1), 2057(i)(3)(F), 2032A(c)(5). See infra ¶ 5.08[5][c].

[53] The term "entity" would include any limited liability company as well as any other entity treated as a partnership for federal tax purposes. See Reg. § 301.7701-3 (the "check-the-box" regulations). The entity may be owned directly or indirectly. See infra text accompanying notes 65–70.

[54] IRC § 267(f)(1).

have been readily tradable on an established securities market or secondary market at any time within three years of the decedent's date of death.[55]

[ii] **Ownership requirements.** The decedent and members of the decedent's family must directly or indirectly own one of several alternative specified interests in the entity:[56] (1) at least 50 percent of the entity[57] or (2) at least 30 percent of the entity if either (a) 70 percent of the entity is owned by members of two families[58] or (b) 90 percent of the entity is owned by members of three families.[59] The term "members of decedent's family" is broadly defined

---

[55] IRC § 2057(e)(2)(B). Although the statute provides "any time within three years of the date of decedent's death," the overall structure of the statute indicates that this period refers only to the three years immediately preceding the date of the decedent's death and should not indicate the three years immediately following the date of the decedent's death.

[56] IRC § 2057(e)(1)(B). For purposes of Section 2057, rules similar to those contained in Section 2032A(g) apply relating to the application of Section 2057 to interests in partnerships, corporations, and trusts. IRC § 2057(i)(3)(L). Under Section 2032A(g), the Secretary is to "prescribe regulations setting forth the application of . . . [Section 2032A] . . . in the case of an interest in a partnership, corporation, or trust which, with respect to the decedent, is an interest in a closely held business (within the meaning of paragraph (1) of section 6166(b))." IRC § 2032A(g). The regulations provide that "[w]here the ownership is indirect . . . the decedent's interest in the business must, in addition to meeting the tests for qualification under section 2032A, qualify under the tests of section 6166(b)(1) as an interest in a closely held business on the date of the decedent's death. . . . " Reg. § 20.2032A-3(b)(1). The incorporation into Section 2057 of Section 2032A(g) by reference raises the issue whether an entity, to be classified as a "qualified family-owned business interest," must qualify as an interest in a closely held business under Section 6166(b)(1) in addition to satisfying the other tests in Section 2057(e). If the answer is affirmative, then for a decedent's interest in a partnership to be a qualified family-owned business interest, at least 20 percent of the total capital interest in the partnership would have to be included in the decedent's gross estate or the partnership would have to have forty-five or fewer partners (fifteen for decedents dying prior to 2002). IRC § 6166(b)(1)(B). See ¶ 2.02[3][c] text accompanying note 64. If the decedent had an interest in a corporation, then at least 20 percent of the value of the voting stock of the corporation would have to be included in the decedent's gross estate or the corporation would have to have forty-five or fewer shareholders (fifteen for decedents dying prior to 2002). IRC § 6166(b)(1)(C). The limitation on the number of partners or shareholders could apply not only to the family member partners or shareholders but also could include the partners or shareholders of other families under the 70 and 90 percent tests. See IRC §§ 2057(e)(1)(B)(i)(II), 2057(e)(1)(B)(i)(III). The legislative history that accompanied the enactment of the deduction for qualified family-owned business interests is devoid of any reference to Section 6166(b)(1). Regulations to be promulgated for Section 2057 should address this issue.

[57] IRC § 2057(e)(1)(B)(i)(I).

[58] IRC §§ 2057(e)(1)(B)(i)(II), 2057(e)(1)(B)(ii).

[59] IRC §§ 2057(e)(1)(B)(i)(III), 2057(e)(1)(B)(ii). For example, assume that the corporation carrying on a trade or business is owned equally by three unrelated individual shareholders. Not one of the shareholders can satisfy the 50 percent test. IRC § 2057(e)(1)(B)(i)(I). Likewise, the 70 percent test is not satisfied because any two of the

to include the decedent's spouse, ancestors, and lineal descendants, as well as the lineal descendants of both the decedent's spouse and parents, and the

---

shareholders only own two thirds of the corporation. IRC §§ 2057(e)(1)(B)(i)(II), 2057(e)(1)(B)(ii). Nevertheless, each shareholder's stock may be a qualified family-owned business interest because the 90 percent test is satisfied. IRC §§ 2057(e)(1)(B)(i)(III), 2057(e)(1)(B)(ii).

The same result holds if the grandparent, a grandchild, and the grandchild's spouse owned one third of the corporation equally and two other shareholders each owned one third of the corporation. The grandparent, grandchild, and the grandchild's spouse are all members of a family. IRC §§ 2057(i)(2), 2032A(e)(2). Because 90 percent of the corporation is owned by three families and the grandparent and the grandparent's family members own at least 30 percent of the entity, the entity satisfies the general test for classification as a family-owned business interest. IRC §§ 2057(e)(1)(B)(i)(III), 2057(e)(1)(B)(ii). The decedent's interest in the corporation may have to qualify as an interest in a closely held business under Section 6166(b)(1) to be a qualified family-owned business interest as a result of the incorporation into Section 2057 of the rules contained in Section 2032A(g). IRC § 2057(i)(3)(L). See supra note 56. The decedent's interest in a corporation fits within the definition of an interest in a closely held business under Section 6166(b)(1) if at least 20 percent of the value of the corporation's voting stock is included in the decedent's gross estate or the corporation has forty-five or fewer shareholders (fifteen for decedents dying prior to 2002). IRC § 6166(b)(1)(C). In both of the examples presented here, the requirements of Section 6166(b)(1)(C) are satisfied in addition to the ownership requirements imposed by Section 2057(e)(1)(B). However, if there were fifty members in the second family holding the stock of the corporation in which the grandparent, grandchild, and grandchild's spouse own a one-third interest equally, then the grandparent's interest in the corporation would not be an interest in a closely held business under Section 6166(b)(1) because less than 20 percent of the value of the corporation's voting stock would be included in the grandparent's gross estate and there would be more than forty-five shareholders in the corporation. The attribution rule under Section 6166(b)(2)(D) generally applies only for the purpose of determining the number of partners and shareholders and is not used to determine whether 20 percent of the capital interest or value of voting stock is included in determining the gross estate of the decedent. HR Rep. No. 1286, 95th Cong., 2d Sess. 12–13 (1978). See Priv. Ltr. Rul. 8428088 (Apr. 12, 1984). However, there is a possibility that an executor can make an election under Section 6166(b)(7)(A) to have the attribution rule of Section 6166(b)(2)(D) apply for the purpose of determining whether 20 percent of the capital interest of the partnership or value of the voting stock of a corporation is included in the decedent's gross estate. IRC § 6166(b)(7)(A); HR Rep. No. 1286, 95th Cong., 2nd Sess. 13 (1978). See ¶ 2.02[3][c] text accompanying notes 72–76.

Section 2057

spouses, widows, or widowers of any such lineal descendants.[60] Legally adopted children are treated as children by blood.[61]

Special rules apply to determine what constitutes ownership and how such ownership is measured. If the entity is a corporate entity, ownership is measured by the percentage of the family's voting power *and* the total value of the

---

[60] IRC §§ 2057(i)(2), 2032A(e)(2). Death does not terminate a marital relationship, although a divorce does. Rev. Rul. 81-236, 1981-2 CB 172. When evaluating entity ownership by any family other than the decedent's family, any individual with an interest in the entity apparently can be used as the measure to satisfy the percentage tests. Assume that A, B, and C own stock in a corporation with other shareholders. A is B's mother-in-law, but no other family relationship exists between any shareholders. Assume C dies and it is necessary to determine if A and B are members of the same family to determine whether C's interest is a qualified family-owned business interest. B is A's daughter-in-law and, thus, a member of A's family as a spouse of a lineal descendant. IRC §§ 2057(i)(2), 2032A(e)(2)(C). A is not a member of B's family because ancestors of spouses are not family members. IRC §§ 2057(i)(2), 2032A(e)(2). Presumably, A could be used by C to satisfy the percentage tests.

Divorce eliminates spousal status. In the preceding example, if B and A's child are divorced, B is no longer a family member of A because B is no longer the spouse of a lineal descendant of A. If A's child died and was not divorced from B, B is still treated as the spouse of a lineal descendant, and although the statute and the regulations do not address the issue, the Instructions for Form 706, United States Estate (and Generation-Skipping Transfer) Tax Return, provide that the term member of the family includes the widow or widower of any lineal descendant of the individual, individual's spouse, or a parent of the individual. Instructions for Form 706, United States Estate (and Generation-Skipping Transfer) Tax Return (Rev. Nov. 2001), at 22. Thus, if A's child died, B is still a member of A's family. See Rev. Rul. 81-236, 1981-2 CB 172. The next question is if B remarries, is B still considered a widow or widower of a lineal descendant and a member of A's family? Possibly, it is like the scouts: "Once a scout, always a scout."

[61] IRC §§ 2057(i)(2), 2032A(e)(2). See Rev. Rul. 81-179, 1981-2 CB 172 (acknowledged child is not adopted child).

family's shares.[62] If the entity is a partnership, ownership is measured by the family's percentage ownership of capital interests[63] in the partnership.[64]

If a trade or business owns an interest in another trade or business, look-through rules apply.[65] Under the look-through rules, each trade or business in which the decedent and members of the decedent's family have a direct or indirect ownership interest is analyzed separately to determine whether it meets the requirements of a qualified family-owned business interest.[66] Thus, any interest that one trade or business owns in another trade or business is not included in the analysis of whether the first trade or business meets the requirements of a qualified family-owned business interest.[67] These rules should be applied sequentially to multitiered entities to look through each separate tier of the entity to determine if it meets the requirements of a family-

---

[62] IRC § 2057(e)(3)(A)(i). The legislative history explains this rule as follows:

For purposes of applying the ownership tests in the case of a corporation, the decedent and members of the decedent's family are required to own the requisite percentage of the total combined voting power of all classes of stock entitled to vote and the requisite percentage of the total value of all shares of all classes of stock of the corporation.

HR Conf. Rep. No. 220, 105th Cong., 1st Sess. 396 (1997), reprinted in 1997-4 CB (Vol. 2) 1457, 1866. For example, assume that the corporation carrying on a trade or business has two classes of stock outstanding: voting common stock worth $1 million and nonvoting preferred stock worth $2 million. The shareholder owns all the voting common stock and 20 percent of the preferred stock. Ten unrelated individuals own equal amounts of the balance of the preferred shares. Although the shareholder holds stock possessing the appropriate percentage of the total combined voting power of all classes of stock entitled to vote, the shareholder does not hold the appropriate percentage of the total value of shares of all classes of stock. The shareholder held 100 percent of the voting power, but only 46.67 percent of the total value of all classes of stock. The shareholder does not have a qualified family-owned business interest.

In determining the appropriate percentage of the total value of shares of all classes of stock, it is unclear whether discounts and premiums should be taken into account. For instance, in the example, should the interests of the unrelated preferred shareholders receive a minority discount or be discounted for lack of marketability either individually or collectively in the determination of whether the shareholder satisfies the 50 percent ownership test?

[63] The legislative history also requires the appropriate percentage of a profits interest. S. Rep. No. 33, 105th Cong., 1st Sess. 41 (1997), reprinted in 1997-4 CB (Vol. 2) 1067, 1121. Without a technical amendment or regulations, it appears that one should look only to the capital interest.

[64] IRC § 2057(e)(3)(A)(ii).

[65] IRC § 2057(e)(3)(B). See S. Rep. No. 33, 105th Cong., 1st Sess. 41 (1997), reprinted in 1997-4 CB (Vol. 2) 1067, 1121.

[66] IRC § 2057(e)(3)(B). The look-through rules also apply to qualified heirs and members of their families in determining ownership for purposes of the recapture rules. Id. See infra ¶ 5.08[5][b].

[67] IRC § 2057(e)(3)(B)(i).

owned business interest.[68] Finally, when one looks through an entity, a business interest owned by an entity is deemed to be proportionately owned "by or for the entity's shareholders, partners, or beneficiaries."[69] If a trust holds an interest in an entity carrying on a trade or business, a person must have a present interest in the trust to be considered as having any ownership interest under the look-through rules in some portion of the trade or business carried on by the entity held by the trust.[70]

---

[68] S. Rep. No. 33, 105th Cong., 1st Sess. 41 (1997), reprinted in 1997-4 CB (Vol. 2) 1067, 1121. Once each tier of a multitiered entity is analyzed to determine if it is a qualified family-owned business interest, the amount of deduction that may be allowed with respect to each tiered trade or business interest will require a reduction in the value of the qualified family-owned business interest by the amount of the value of any lower-tiered business interests. See supra ¶ 5.08[2][b] note 35.

[69] IRC § 2057(e)(3)(C); S. Rep. No. 33, 105th Cong., 1st Sess. 41 (1997), reprinted in 1997-4 CB (Vol. 2) 1067, 1121. The Senate Report provides the following example to explain how the look-through and the multitiered entity rules work together in the determination of the satisfaction of the percentage and other requirements of a qualified family-owned business interest:

> For example, if a holding company owns interests in two other companies, each of the three entities will be separately tested under the qualified family-owned business interest rules. In determining whether the holding company is a qualified family-owned business interest, its ownership interest in the other two companies is disregarded. Even if the holding company itself does not qualify as a family-owned business interest, the other two companies still may qualify if the direct and indirect interests held by the decedent and his or her family members satisfy the requisite ownership percentages and other requirements of a qualified family-owned business interest. If either (or both) of the lower-tier entities qualify, the value of the qualified family-owned business interests owned by the holding company are treated as proportionately owned by the holding company's shareholders.

S. Rep. No. 33, 105th Cong., 1st Sess. 41 (1997), reprinted in 1997-4 CB (Vol. 2) 1067, 1121.

[70] IRC § 2057(e)(3)(C). Rules similar to Section 2032A(g) apply for purposes of Section 2057. IRC § 2057(i)(3)(L). "[A]n interest in a discretionary trust all the beneficiaries of which are qualified heirs shall be treated as a present interest." IRC § 2032A(g). Just what is a discretionary trust? Presumably it is a trust where all, or any portion, of the income or corpus of a trust may be accumulated or distributed in the discretion of the trustee to one or more beneficiaries, none of whom has a present interest as defined in Section 2503(b). See HR Rep. No. 201, 97th Cong., 1st Sess., 38, 176 (1981), reprinted in 1981-2 CB 352, 385. Who are the beneficiaries of a discretionary trust? Presumably, any person who is a permissible distributee of income or corpus at any time during the existence of the trust is a beneficiary. This should include those who may receive income, as well as those entitled to the remainder upon the termination of the trust.

Section 2057(e)(3)(C) provides that "[f]or purposes of [Section 2057], an interest owned, directly or indirectly, by or for an entity described in paragraph (1)(B) shall be considered as being owned proportionately by or for the entity's shareholders, partners, or beneficiaries." IRC § 2057(e)(3)(C). Section 2057(e)(1)(B) deals with an interest in an entity carrying on a trade or business. IRC § 2057(e)(1)(B). Section 2057(e)(3)(A), which deals with ownership of entities for purposes of Section 2057(e)(1)(B), deals only with corporations and partnerships. IRC §§ 2057(e)(3)(A)(i), 2057(e)(3)(A)(ii). Where a trust

[3] Estate Qualifications

Once it is determined that the decedent owned a qualified family-owned business interest,[71] the decedent's estate must satisfy a variety of requirements to qualify for a Section 2057 deduction. The requirements are similar to, and have their roots in, the requirements that must be met by an estate to qualify for use of Section 2032A.[72]

A decedent's executor[73] may, on filing an appropriate agreement,[74] elect[75] to deduct from the decedent's gross estate value related to qualified family-owned business interests[76] owned and operated by the decedent or the decedent's family members[77] for at least five years in the eight years preceding the decedent's death if[78] (1) the decedent was a citizen or resident of the United States at the time of death;[79] (2) the adjusted value of the family-owned business interests[80] makes up a significant portion of the decedent's gross estate;[81] and (3) the property is acquired by or passes to a qualified heir.[82]

---

owns an interest in a partnership or corporation that carries on a trade or business, the entity is considered as owned proportionately by beneficiaries of the trust having a present interest in the trust. Presumably, any beneficiary who does not have a present interest in the trust, as defined in Section 2503(b), or who is not treated as having a present interest in the trust, as defined in Section 2032A(g), is not considered to own any proportion of the entity held by the trust.

If a trust holds a sole proprietorship business interest, even though the sole proprietorship is not an entity described in Section 2057(e)(1)(B), it ought to be treated as being owned proportionately by the beneficiaries possessing, or treated as possessing, a present interest in the trust.

[71] See supra ¶ 5.08[2].

[72] See ¶¶ 4.04[3], 4.04[6].

[73] IRC § 2203. See ¶ 8.02.

[74] IRC §§ 2057(b)(1)(B), 2057(h), 2057(i)(3)(H), 2032A(d)(1), 2032A(d)(3).

[75] IRC § 2057(b)(1)(B).

[76] IRC § 2057(a). See supra ¶ 5.08[2], infra ¶ 5.08[4].

[77] IRC § 2057(i)(2).

[78] IRC § 2057(b)(1)(D).

[79] IRC § 2057(b)(1)(A).

[80] IRC §§ 2057(b)(1)(C)(i), 2057(b)(2), 2057(d).

[81] IRC § 2057(b)(1)(C).

[82] See infra ¶ 5.08[3][f].

[a] Citizen or Resident Decedent

The decedent must have been a citizen[83] or resident[84] of the United States at the time of death to qualify for the deduction allowed under Section 2057.[85] Although classification as a citizen or a resident is critical to qualification for the family-owned business interest deduction, the estate tax provisions provide very little guidance in defining these terms.[86]

[b] Election and Agreement

Section 2057 applies only if the decedent's executor[87] affirmatively elects to use the section and files an appropriate agreement.[88] Rules similar to those relating to the election[89] and the agreement[90] under Section 2032A apply to the election and the agreement under Section 2057.[91]

[i] **The election.** The election to use Section 2057 is made by attaching a notice of election to the decedent's federal estate tax return.[92] The executor is deemed to have made the election to use Section 2057 by filing a completed Schedule T of the estate tax return[93] and by deducting any qualifying business

---

[83] See ¶ 6.01[3][a]; 8 USC §§ 1101–1537 (2001).

[84] See Reg. § 20.0-1(b)(1); ¶ 6.01[3][b].

[85] IRC § 2057(b)(1)(A).

[86] See IRC §§ 2208, 2209. Sections 2208 and 2209 provide whether a U.S. citizen who was a resident of a possession of the United States at death will be considered a citizen or a nonresident noncitizen for estate tax purposes. See ¶¶ 4.04[3][a], 6.01[3], 8.09.

[87] This term is defined broadly. See IRC § 2203, discussed ¶ 8.02.

[88] IRC §§ 2057(b)(1)(B), 2057(h). See infra ¶ 5.08[5].

[89] IRC §§ 2032A(d)(1), 2032A(d)(3). See ¶ 4.04[6].

[90] IRC § 2032A(d)(3). See ¶ 4.04[6].

[91] IRC § 2057(i)(3)(H).

[92] IRC §§ 2057(b)(1)(B), 2057(i)(3)(H), 2032A(d)(1); Reg. §§ 20.2032A-8(a)(1), 20.2032A-8(a)(3). When the election is made, a special lien in the amount of the deduction is imposed on the qualified family-owned business interest. See IRC §§ 2057(i)(3)(P), 6324B; ILM 200149033 (Nov. 1, 2001) (lien requirement, consequences, and operation). See also ¶ 4.04[6] text accompanying notes 245–248.

[93] Form 706, United States Estate (and Generation-Skipping Transfer) Tax Return (Rev. Nov. 2001) Schedule T, at 38–41.

interests from the gross estate.[94] Once made, the election is irrevocable.[95] If

---

[94] Form 706, United States Estate (and Generation-Skipping Transfer) Tax Return (Rev. Nov. 2001) Schedule T, Part 1— Election. See Instructions for Form 706, United States Estate (and Generation-Skipping Transfer) Tax Return (Rev. Nov. 2001) at 22.

The notice of election must contain the information necessary to indicate satisfaction of the eligibility requirements of Section 2057. IRC §§ 2057(i)(3)(H); 2032A(d)(1). See Reg. § 20.2032A-8(a)(3); Form 706, United States Estate (and Generation-Skipping Transfer) Tax Return (Rev. Nov. 2001), Instructions for Schedule A-1. Section 2032A Valuation at 6–7; ¶ 4.04[6].

The completion of Schedule T—Qualified Family-Owned Business Interest Deduction, Form 706, requires the attachment of a schedule identifying each qualified family-owned business interest for which the Section 2057 election is being made and the amount that is being deducted. Instructions for Form 706, United States Estate (and Generation-Skipping Transfer) Tax Return (Rev. Nov. 2001), at 23. Where a marital deduction is claimed for any part of the value of a qualified family-owned business passing to a surviving spouse for which a Section 2057 election is made, a schedule must be attached listing the amount of the qualified family-owned business interests for which the Section 2057 election is made for which the marital deduction is claimed. Instructions for Form 706, United States Estate (and Generation-Skipping Transfer) Tax Return (Rev. Nov. 2001), at 23. A schedule is required listing the amount of any federal estate or generation-skipping transfer taxes and any state inheritance tax paid out of any qualified family-owned business interest for which a Section 2057 deduction is claimed. Instructions for Form 706, "United States Estate (and Generation-Skipping Transfer) Tax Return" (Rev. Nov. 2001), at 23. A schedule is required listing any deductions, other than the marital deduction and the deductions taken for claims or mortgages deductible under Section 2053(a)(3) or Section 2053(a)(4), claimed with respect to each qualified family-owned business interest for which a Section 2057 deduction is claimed. Instructions for Form 706, United States Estate (and Generation-Skipping Transfer) Tax Return (Rev. Nov. 2001), at 23. This may result in an adjustment for deductions pursuant to Section 2053(a)(1), Section 2053(a)(2), Section 2054, or Section 2055. See infra ¶ 5.08[4][a].

[95] IRC §§ 2057(b)(1)(B), 2057(i)(3)(H), 2032A(d)(1).

Section 2057

Section 2057 is not initially available because of valuation uncertainties, a protective election may be made pending final valuation for estate tax purposes.[96]

[ii] **The agreement.** If the decedent's executor elects to use the Section 2057 deduction, the executor must file a written agreement,[97] which must designate the property that qualifies for a deduction under Section 2057 and which must be signed by each person having an interest in the property desig-

---

[96] IRC §§ 2057(b)(1)(B), 2057(i)(3)(H), 2032A(d)(1). See Reg. § 20.2032A-8(b). The protective election should be made by filing a notice of election with the estate tax return. Id.

An issue not directly addressed under Section 2057 is whether an election can be made with respect to a part of a qualified family-owned business interest. It is unclear what constitutes a business interest for purposes of Section 2057 and whether an election can be made for one line of business in a sole proprietorship if a qualified family-owned business has two distinct lines of business. Where the qualified family-owned business interest is an entity carrying on business as a corporation, it is also unclear whether the "business interest" is the whole of the decedent's ownership in the corporation or whether it is each separate share of stock owned by the decedent and whether an election can be made for some, but not all, of the decedent's stock? If the qualified family-owned business interest is an entity carrying on business as a partnership and the decedent owns both a general and limited partnership interest, it is unclear whether an election can be made for one type of partnership interest but not the other. If a family limited partnership with a corporate general partner operated a qualified family-owned business and the decedent, in addition to holding a limited partnership interest, was the sole shareholder of the corporate general partner, it is unclear whether an election can be made for just the value of the limited partnership interest. It is hoped that the regulations to be promulgated for this section will provide guidance to taxpayers resolving these issues.

[97] IRC §§ 2057(b)(1)(B), 2057(h).

nated in the agreement.⁹⁸ In the agreement, each signatory must consent to the potential imposition of additional estate tax with respect to the property.⁹⁹

[iii] Grace period. If the executor makes a timely election and submits an agreement, and either the election or agreement is deficient because of the failure to provide all the required information or because of a missing signature of a person required to enter into the agreement, the executor has a reasonable period of up to ninety days after notification of the deficiency to provide the missing signature or required information.¹⁰⁰

---

⁹⁸ IRC § 2057(h). Form 706, United States Estate (and Generation-Skipping Transfer) Tax Return (Rev. Nov. 2001) Schedule T, Part 5 is the "Agreement to Family-Owned Business Interest Deduction Under Section 2057." Form 706, Schedule T, Part 5 provides that "[t]here cannot be a valid election unless . . . [t]he agreement is executed by each and every one of the qualified heirs." Form 706, United States Estate (and Generation-Skipping Transfer) Tax Return (Rev. Nov. 2001) Schedule T, Part 5 at 40. The actual agreement provides:

We [*list all qualified heirs and other persons having an interest in the business required to sign this agreement*]—being all the qualified heirs and—being all other parties having interests in the business(es) which are deducted under section 2057 of the Code do hereby approve the election. . . .

Id.
Interested parties who are not qualified heirs are required to sign only if they have an interest in a business that is deducted under Section 2057. It is unclear whether only the qualified heirs who have an interest in the qualified family-owned business interest for which a deduction is taken under Section 2057 must sign the agreement, or whether all qualified heirs who have an interest in any qualified family-owned business must sign, even though they do not have an interest in the qualified family-owned business for which the Section 2057 deduction was taken.

⁹⁹ IRC §§ 2057(h), 2057(f). See infra ¶ 5.08[5]. The signatories must also consent to Section 6324B liens on their respective qualified family-owned business interest. IRC § 2057(i)(3)(P). See Form 706, United States Estate (and Generation-Skipping Transfer) Tax Return (Rev. November 2001) Schedule T, Part 5 at 40. In addition, the signatories must appoint a designated agent for all dealings with the Service. The designated agent has the authority to (1) receive confidential information concerning continued Section 2057 qualification and Section 6324B lien matters; (2) furnish any requested information about the interests to the Service; (3) notify the Service if any event triggering the imposition of additional estate tax under Section 2057 occurs; (4) receive Internal Revenue refund checks; (5) execute waivers of assessment or deficiency collection restrictions and notice of disallowance of a claim for refund or credit; and (6) execute Section 7121 closing agreements. Form 706, United States Estate (and Generation-Skipping Transfer) Tax Return (Rev. Nov. 2001) Schedule T, Part 5, at 40.

¹⁰⁰ IRC §§ 2057(b)(1)(B), 2057(i)(3)(H), 2032A(d)(3).

[c] The 50 Percent Test

[i] **In general.** The qualified family-owned business interest must constitute a significant portion of the decedent's wealth to qualify for a deduction. Stated technically, the adjusted value of the includible qualified family-owned business interests plus includible gifts of family-owned business interests must exceed 50 percent of the adjusted gross estate.[101]

A series of complicated steps, which will be discussed, must be followed in order to determine whether the 50 percent requirement is met. In taking those steps, community property qualified family-owned business interests are treated on a parity with such interests held as separate property.[102]

[ii] **Includible qualified family-owned business interests.** In computing the numerator of the 50 percent test fraction, the first step is to identify the includible family-owned business interests. An "includible qualified family-owned business interest"[103] is a business interest[104] whose value is included in

---

[101] IRC § 2057(b)(1)(C). When a decedent holds family-owned business interests in more than one trade or business, all of the qualifying business interests are aggregated in applying this test. HR Conf. Rep. No. 220, 105th Cong., 1st Sess. 398 (1997), reprinted in 1997-4 CB (Vol. 2) 1457, 1868.

[102] IRC §§ 2057(i)(3)(I), 2032A(e)(10). Thus, community property is to be taken into account under the provisions of Section 2057 in a manner that provides a result consistent with that obtained had the qualified family-owned business interests not been held as community property. IRC §§ 2057(i)(3)(I), 2032A(e)(10). See Rev. Rul. 83-96, 1983-2 CB 156. As a result of this rule, the entire value of the community property qualified family-owned business interests, not just the decedent's one-half interest, may be considered in determining whether the percentage qualification requirements imposed on the estate are satisfied. Without this rule, estates of decedents owning community property qualified family-owned business interests would be at a disadvantage. Assume a decedent's gross estate with an adjusted value of $1.6 million contains no community property and a qualified family-owned business interest with an adjusted value of $810,000. The 50 percent estate qualification test is met. Alternatively, if the qualified family-owned business interest is community property, without the special rule, the adjusted value of the gross estate would be only $1,195,000 and the adjusted value of property devoted to a qualified use would be only $405,000. The adjusted value of the qualified family-owned business interest would represent only 34 percent of the adjusted value of the gross estate, and the 50 percent test would not be satisfied. Note that *only the interest of the surviving spouse in community property qualified family-owned business interests* is taken into account under this rule.

[103] IRC §§ 2057(b)(2), 2057(e). See supra ¶ 5.08[2].

[104] For purposes of the 50 percent test, if the qualified family-owned business interest is a farm, then the interest also includes any interest in residential buildings and related improvements on the farm that are occupied on a regular basis by either the owner or lessee of the farm or by persons who are employed by such owner or lessee to operate or maintain the farm. IRC §§ 2057(i)(3)(N), 6166(b)(3).

the decedent's gross estate[105] and that is acquired by, or passed to, a qualified heir from the decedent.[106] There appears to be no statutory requirement that the includible family-owned business interest be owned, or that the decedent or members of the decedent's family must materially participate in the business, for any specified length of time to be considered in the satisfaction of the 50 percent test.[107]

Acquired or Passed from the Decedent. Includible qualified family-owned business interests are considered to be acquired or passed from the decedent for purposes of Section 2057 if they would be so treated under Section

---

[105] IRC § 2057(b)(2)(A). The value of a business interest that holds land that qualifies for an exclusion from the decedent's gross estate under Section 2031(c) is not an includible qualified family-owned business interest to the extent of the amount excluded. See infra note 121; ¶ 4.02[7][e][ii].

[106] IRC § 2057(b)(2)(B).

[107] See IRC § 2057(b)(1)(D). Section 2057(b)(1)(D) should be interpreted as imposing additional requirements that qualified family-owned business interests described in Section 2057(b)(2) and included in the numerator of the 50 percent test must satisfy for the estate to take a deduction for the qualified family-owned business interest under Section 2057. Section 2057(b)(1)(D) should not be interpreted as imposing additional requirements for a qualified family-owned business interest to satisfy to be included in the numerator of the 50 percent fraction. See also infra ¶¶ 5.08[3][d] note 150, 5.08[3][e] note 152.

Under this interpretation, a qualified family-owned business interest purchased from an unrelated individual within four years of a decedent's death would be included in the numerator of the 50 percent test but would not satisfy the five-year ownership test and therefore would not qualify for a deduction under Section 2057. It could be argued that this interpretation will allow a decedent to purchase new businesses near death to satisfy the 50 percent test. On the other hand, if recently acquired business interests are excluded from the numerator of the 50 percent test but included in the denominator of the 50 percent test, a decedent who is expanding by purchasing more business interests within five years of death would be penalized because it would be more difficult for that decedent's estate to satisfy the 50 percent test.

Thus, it appears that an individual could purchase business interests near death with cash and other liquid assets not qualifying for exclusion to facilitate the satisfaction of the 50 percent test and thereby qualify family-owned business interests that have been owned and operated by the decedent for at least five of the eight years immediately preceding the decedent's death. For example, assume an individual owns assets worth $4 million, $3 million in cash and marketable securities, and a sole proprietorship worth $1 million that the individual has owned and operated for many years. Assuming the values of the assets remain constant, the individual's estate would not qualify for the Section 2057 deduction because the 50 percent test would not be satisfied. If the individual used just over $1 million in cash and marketable securities to purchase a new business interest near death and the new business interest was worth just over $1 million at the individual's death, the 50 percent test would then be satisfied. If the original $1 million sole proprietorship satisfied the remaining statutory requirements, a portion of the value of the original sole proprietorship would qualify for a deduction under Section 2057, subject to the $675,000 ceiling.

1014(b), which presents the income tax basis rules.[108] The broad scope of Section 1014(b) includes property acquired by inheritance, bequest, devise, or as a result of a qualified disclaimer,[109] as well as property transferred inter vivos but included in the gross estate by reason of death, by form of ownership, or through the exercise or nonexercise of a power of appointment.[110] In addition, property acquired or passed from the decedent includes property acquired from the decedent's estate[111] as well as from a trust to the extent that the trust assets are included in the decedent's gross estate.[112]

Qualified Heirs. Members of the decedent's family constitute one group of qualified heirs under Section 2057.[113] "Member of the family" is broadly defined to include the decedent's spouse, ancestors, and lineal descendants (and the lineal descendants' spouses), as well as the lineal descendants of the decedent's parents, the decedent's spouse, and the spouses, widows, or widowers of these lineal descendants.[114] Legally adopted children are treated as children by blood.[115]

Section 2057 also includes another category of qualified heir unique to Section 2057.[116] For purposes of Section 2057, a qualified heir includes any active employee of the qualified family-owned business who has been employed by the business for at least ten years.[117]

[iii] Adjusted value of qualified family-owned business interests. The determination of the adjusted value of qualified family-owned business inter-

---

[108] See Section 2057(b)(2)(B), which directs one to Section 2032A(e)(9)(A), which redirects one to Section 1014(b).

[109] Rev. Rul. 82-140, 1982-2 CB 208. See ¶ 10.07.

[110] IRC §§ 2057(b)(2)(B), 2032A(e)(9)(A), 1014(b).

[111] IRC § 2032A(e)(9)(B). Property acquired from the decedent's estate may be purchased from the estate, for example under an option granted by the decedent, upon a sale by the personal representative, or acquired in satisfaction of a right to a pecuniary bequest. HR Rep. No. 201, 97th Cong., 1st Sess. 38, 176 (1981), reprinted in 1981-2 CB 352, 385.

[112] IRC § 2032A(e)(9)(C).

[113] IRC §§ 2057(i)(1)(A), 2032A(e)(1).

[114] IRC §§ 2057(i)(2), 2032A(e)(2); Rev. Rul. 81-236, 1981-2 CB 172 (death does not terminate a marital relationship); Instructions for Form 706, United States Estate (and Generation-Skipping Transfer) Tax Return (Rev. Nov. 2001), at 22. See supra ¶ 5.08[2][c] note 57; ¶ 4.04[3][b][vii].

[115] IRC §§ 2057(i)(2), 2032A(e)(2). See supra ¶ 5.08[2][c] note 61.

[116] IRC § 2057(i)(1)(B).

[117] IRC § 2057(i)(1)(B). Regulations to be promulgated for this section should define an "active employee" and consider both quantitative and qualitative elements and seasonal businesses.

ests is a two-step process.[118] First the qualified family-owned business interests are valued,[119] and then that value is adjusted.[120]

Valuation. The estate tax value of all qualified family-owned business interests is determined on the applicable valuation date using the applicable valuation method.[121] The business interests may be valued on either the date of the decedent's death[122] or the elective alternate valuation date[123] using either fair market valuation[124] or special use valuation, where applicable.[125]

Adjustments. The value of the includible qualified family-owned business interests is then adjusted. The value is reduced by all the amounts deductible under Sections 2053(a)(3) (claims against the estate)[126] and 2053(a)(4) (unpaid mortgages and indebtedness with respect to property),[127] other than any indebtedness on any qualified residence of the decedent the interest on which is deductible under Section 163(h)(3),[128] indebtedness incurred to pay educational or medical expenses of the decedent, the decedent's spouse, or the decedent's dependents (as defined in Section 152),[129] and any other individual item of indebtedness that does not exceed $10,000.[130]

[iv] Includible gifts of qualified family-owned business interests. Some inter vivos gifts of qualified family-owned business interests[131] that are not included in the decedent's gross estate are then added to the adjusted value of

---

[118] IRC § 2057(d).

[119] IRC § 2057(d).

[120] IRC §§ 2057(d)(1), 2057(d)(2).

[121] IRC § 2057(d). In determining such valuation, any Section 2031(c) exclusion is likely taken into consideration. See ¶ 4.02[7]. There is no restriction on a decedent's executor electing to use both Sections 2031(c) and 2057 to reduce a decedent's taxable estate. See ¶ 4.02[7][e] text accompanying notes 381, 382. However, if land subject to a qualified conservation easement is used in a trade or business and a portion of the value of the land is excluded under Section 2031(c), that value by definition is likely not an includible qualified family-owned business interest because it is not included in determining the value of the gross estate. IRC § 2057(b)(2)(A).

[122] IRC § 2031. See ¶ 4.02.

[123] IRC § 2032. See ¶ 4.03.

[124] IRC § 2031; Reg. § 20.2031-1(b). See ¶ 4.02[2]. If discounts are taken in the valuation of the qualified family-owned business interests under either Section 2031 or Section 2032A, those discounts must be taken into consideration in meeting the 50 percent test. See ¶¶ 4.02[4][c], 4.02[4][d], 4.02[4][e].

[125] IRC § 2032A. See ¶ 4.04; infra ¶ 5.08[6][b]; supra note 124.

[126] IRC §§ 2057(d)(1), 2053(a)(3). See ¶ 5.03[5].

[127] IRC §§ 2057(d)(1), 2053(a)(4). See ¶ 5.03[6].

[128] IRC § 2057(d)(2)(A).

[129] IRC § 2057(d)(2)(B).

[130] IRC § 2057(d)(2)(C).

[131] IRC §§ 2057(b)(1)(C)(ii), 2057(b)(3).

includible qualified family-owned business interests[132] at their gift tax value[133] in the computation of both the numerator and the denominator[134] of the fraction used to determine whether the 50 percent test is met.[135] Those includible gifts are the amount of gifts of qualified family-owned business interests from the decedent to members of the decedent's family,[136] other than the decedent's spouse,[137] which are included in adjusted taxable gifts under Section 2001(b)(1)(B)[138] or that qualified for the annual exclusion under Section 2503(b).[139] With respect to both types of gifts, the gifts must be continuously held by family members between the date of the gift and the date of the decedent's death.[140]

[v] **Adjusted gross estate.** The denominator of the fraction used in applying the 50 percent test is the adjusted gross estate, which is the gross estate

---

[132] IRC §§ 2057(b)(1)(C)(i), 2057(b)(2).

[133] S. Rep. No. 33, 105th Cong., 1st Sess. 43 (1997), reprinted in 1997-4 CB (Vol. 2) 1067, 1123. Includible gifts are not revalued at the date of the decedent's death in the determination of the numerator of the fraction. The statute refers to the "amount" of the gifts, not the value of the gifts. IRC §§ 2057(b)(1)(C)(ii), 2057(b)(3)(A), 2057(b)(3)(B).

[134] See infra note 145.

[135] IRC § 2057(b)(1)(C).

[136] IRC §§ 2057(i)(2), 2032A(e)(2).

[137] The parenthetical reference—"other than the decedent's spouse"—in the last clause of Section 2057(b)(3) gives rise to uncertainty in the interpretation of the statute. Although the statute could be read as requiring everyone other than the decedent's spouse to continuously hold the gifted qualified family-owned business interests until the decedent's death, it was intended to be read as eliminating any gifts to the decedent's spouse from includible gifts of qualified family-owned business interests. HR Conf. Rep. 220, 105th Cong., 1st Sess. 398 (1997), reprinted in 1997-4 CB (Vol. 2) 1457, 1868. Inter vivos gifts of qualified family-owned business interests to family members, other than inter vivos gifts of qualified family-owned business interests to the decedent's spouse, that are taken into account under Section 2001(b)(1)(B), as well as those excluded under Section 2503(b), that are continuously held from the date of the gift until the decedent's death are included in the numerator. Inter vivos gifts of qualified family-owned business interests to a spouse are to be excluded from the numerator of the 50 percent test.

[138] IRC § 2057(b)(3)(A). "Adjusted taxable gifts" is defined for purposes of Section 2001(b)(1)(B) as "the total amount of taxable gifts (within the meaning of section 2503) made by the decedent after December 31, 1976, other than gifts which are includible in the gross estate of the decedent." IRC § 2001(b). See ¶ 2.01[1][b].

Where pursuant to the provisions of Section 2513 a gift of a qualified family-owned business interest is treated as made one-half by a decedent and one-half by the decedent's spouse, one half of the value of the property transferred will be considered as an includible gift of a qualified family-owned business interest under Sections 2057(b)(3)(A) and 2057(b)(3)(B). See Priv. Ltr. Rul. 8515001 (Oct. 19, 1984) ("adjusted taxable gifts" includes one half of post-1976 gifts subject to Section 2513 treatment).

[139] IRC § 2057(b)(3)(B).

[140] IRC § 2057(b)(3) (last clause).

decreased by certain deductions and increased by several types of inter vivos transfers.[141] The term "adjusted gross estate" is defined as the value of the decedent's gross estate,[142] reduced by the amounts deductible under Section 2053(a)(3) for claims against the estate and under Section 2053(a)(4) for indebtedness and unpaid mortgages,[143] and increased by three classes of gifts and transfers valued at their gift or transfer valuation that are not otherwise included in the decedent's gross estate.[144] The three classes of gifts and transfers to be added are (1) the includible gifts of qualified family-owned business interests that are included in the numerator of the fraction;[145] (2) the amount of "other transfers" made within ten years of the decedent's death from the decedent to the decedent's spouse (other than such transfers that were de minimis at the time of the transfer);[146] and (3) the amount of the decedent's other gifts

---

[141] IRC § 2057(b)(1)(C).

[142] IRC § 2057(c). The value is the value of the gross estate determined on the applicable date using the applicable valuation method with regard to Section 2031(c). See supra text accompanying notes 121–125.

[143] IRC § 2057(c)(1). This reduction for claims and indebtedness is not adjusted by the items specified in Section 2057(d)(2) that are considered in the determination of the numerator of the 50 percent test. See supra text accompanying notes 126–130.

[144] IRC § 2057(c)(2).

[145] IRC § 2057(c)(2)(A)(i). See supra ¶ 5.08[3][c] text accompanying notes 131–139. The denominator of the 50 percent test includes any transfers of qualified family-owned business interests to family members, other than the spouse of the decedent, that have been continuously held by members of the decedent's family until the decedent's death. HR Conf. Rep. 220, 105th Cong., 1st Sess. 398 (1997), reprinted in 1997-4 CB (Vol. 2) 1457, 1868. Inter vivos gifts of qualified family-owned business interests to a spouse are not included in the amount of gifts determined under Section 2057(b)(3) and therefore are not included in the denominator of the 50 percent test under Section 2057(c)(2)(A)(i). See supra text accompanying note 137.

[146] IRC § 2057(c)(2)(A)(ii). Spousal status is determined at the time of the transfer. Section 2057(c)(2)(A)(ii) uses the term "other transfers." It is unclear whether this term includes or excludes transfers of qualified family-owned business interests. "Other transfers" might include any transfer not included in Section 2057(c)(2)(A)(i) that excludes any inter vivos transfers of qualified family-owned business interests to the decedent's spouse. Therefore, "other transfers" might include any transfer made to a spouse within ten years of the decedent's death. Transfers of qualified family-owned business interests and any other transfer to an individual who was the decedent's spouse at the time of the transfer, other than de minimis gifts, would be included in the denominator for the 50 percent test. See Instructions for Form 706, United States Estate (and Generation-Skipping Transfer) Tax Return (Rev. Nov. 2001), at 23.

On the other hand, "other transfers" might be interpreted as "any transfers of assets *other than qualified family-owned business interests* from the decedent to the decedent's spouse that were made within ten years of the date of the decedent's death." Staff of the Joint Comm. on Taxation, 105th Cong., General Explanation of Tax Legislation Enacted in 1997, at 68 (Comm. Print 1997) (JCS-23-97) (emphasis added).

It would seem that if transfers of qualified family-owned business interests to a spouse are excluded from the numerator for the 50 percent test, these transfers should also

made within three years of death, other than gifts to members of the decedent's family otherwise excluded by the annual exclusion under Section 2503(b).[147]

[d] Ownership Requirement

The qualified family-owned business interests that qualify for a deduction under Section 2057 must have been owned[148] by the decedent or a member of the decedent's family[149] for at least five of the eight years preceding the date of the decedent's death.[150] Ownership by any combination of the decedent and

---

be excluded from the denominator. It is hoped the regulations promulgated for Section 2057(c)(2)(A)(ii) will resolve the problem.

[147] IRC § 2057(c)(2)(A)(iii). If the Secretary so decides, de minimis gifts to persons other than members of the decedent's family may be excluded from the denominator. IRC § 2057(c) (flush language).

[148] The ownership requirements of Section 2057(e)(1) must be satisfied, which in the case of ownership of an entity includes the Section 2057(e)(1)(B) requirements. See supra ¶ 5.08[2][c] note 56.

[149] IRC § 2057(i)(2). "Member of the family" is defined for this purpose in Section 2032A(e)(2). See supra ¶ 5.08[3][c] text accompanying notes 114, 115; ¶ 4.04[3][b][vii].

[150] IRC § 2057(b)(1)(D)(i). "Such interests" are required to have been owned by the decedent or a member of the decedent's family for at least five years in the eight-year period ending with the decedent's death. "Such interests" should refer to those qualified family-owned business interests for which a deduction is sought under Section 2057 as defined in Section 2057(e). "Such interests" would encompass those qualified family-owned business interests described in Section 2057(b)(2) that are included in the numerator of the 50 percent test. Accordingly, Section 2057(b)(1)(D)(i) should be interpreted as an additional requirement that qualified family-owned business interests described in Section 2057(b)(2) and included in the numerator of the 50 percent test must satisfy for the estate to take a deduction for the qualified family-owned business interest under Section 2057. See supra ¶ 5.08[3][c] note 107.

A difficult distinction may have to be made between expanding an existing qualified family-owned business interest and creating a new qualified family-owned business interest. Every addition of a new asset to a trade or business should not start a new period running under the five-out-of-eight-years test. Whether the purchase of new assets is an expansion of an existing trade or business or is the creation of a new trade or business may be important to the deductibility of the value of those assets as a qualified family-owned business interest under Section 2057. It is hoped the regulations to be promulgated for Section 2057 will clarify and provide direction on the effect of expansions of existing businesses and a means for distinguishing a business expansion from the creation of a new trade or business interest.

Rules similar to those found in Section 2032A(e)(14) relating to treatment of replacement property acquired in Section 1031 or Section 1033 transactions apply for purposes of Section 2057. IRC § 2057(i)(3)(J). Section 2032A(e)(14) tacks periods of ownership by a decedent or any family member of replaced property onto replacement property if the replacement property was acquired in a Section 1031 or Section 1033 nonrecognition transaction and the use of the replacement and replaced property is the same, but only to the extent that the fair market value of the replacement property on the date of acquisition does not exceed the fair market value of the replaced property on the date of disposition. IRC § 2032A(e)(14). See ¶ 4.04[3][c] text accompanying notes 115–119. The question is how this rule "shall" be applied to Section 2057, specifically Section 2057(b)(1)(D)(i). Section 2057 provides a deduction for a "qualified family-owned business interest" which is an "interest . . . in a trade or business" as a proprietor or an "interest in . . . a trade or business" carried on by an entity. IRC § 2057(e)(1). Where the interest is owned by an entity, it is considered owned proportionately by its shareholders or partners. IRC § 2057(e)(3)(C). Section 2057 seems to refer to the decedent's interest in the trade or business, not the business's individual assets. Although the disposition of an individual asset may affect the composition of the property of a trade or business, it does not in all cases affect the ownership or existence of the business. Section 1031 or Section 1033 could apply to a disposition of an ownership interest in a trade or business (as opposed to the underlying property held by the business) only in the most unusual circumstances. Section 1031 does not apply to exchanges of interests in business entities. IRC §§ 1031(a)(2)(B), 1031(a)(2)(D). It is difficult to imagine a compulsory or involuntary conversion of corporate stock or a partnership that would trigger Section 1033. Theoretically, Section 1033 might apply to an entire proprietorship interest if all the trade or business assets were converted at once, or Section 1031 could apply to the disposition of an entire trade or business held as a proprietorship, but practically, it is very unlikely.

An alternative analysis may be that this provision was intended to apply to the disposition of property used by the trade or business and thereby not require the restarting of the five-out-of-eight-years-ownership clock each time any asset of the business is replaced in a transaction covered by Section 1031 or Section 1033. The problem with this analysis is the implication that the five-out-of-eight-years-ownership requirement applies to each individual asset of a trade or business. Certainly inventory sales, cash-financed equipment replacement, or business expansion should not reduce the likelihood that a trade or business interest would ultimately qualify for the Section 2057 deduction. Section 2057 was enacted to help businesses survive, and transactions involving property of a trade or business not qualifying for nonrecognition under Section 1031 or Section 1033 are the life-blood of a business and essential for survival. Regulatory guidance regarding the application of Section 2032A(e)(14) certainly would be helpful, if not essential.

Rules similar to those contained in Section 2032A(g) apply for purposes of Section 2057. IRC § 2057(i)(3)(L). See supra ¶ 5.08[2][c] text accompanying note 56; Reg. § 20.2032A-3(b)(1). See also ¶ 4.04[3][b][v]. It appears that satisfaction of the five-out-of-eight-years-ownership requirement contained in Section 2057(b)(1)(D)(i) requires the decedent's ownership of an interest in a partnership or a corporation carrying on a trade or business that is an interest in a closely-held business within the meaning of Section 6166(b)(1) for at least five years in the eight-year period immediately preceding the date of the decedent's death. Where a business interest is transferred from a proprietorship to a corporation or partnership that is a closely-held business within the meaning of Section 6166(b)(1) during the eight-year period ending on the date of the decedent's death, the time that the business interests were held as a sole proprietorship may be added to the periods the business interests are held by an entity, either a corporation or a partnership, to satisfy the five-year ownership requirement if the transfer meets the requirements of Section 351 or Section 721.

See Reg. § 20.2032A-3(d). Where a business interest is transferred to a trust, it is considered to be continuously owned if all the beneficiaries having vested interests in the trust are treated as shareholders of a corporation and that pretend corporation is a closely held corporation as defined in Section 6166(b)(1)(C). See Reg. § 20.2032A-3(d).

members of the decedent's family may aggregate the five years in the critical eight-year period. Any such ownership need not have been continuous.

[e] Material Participation Requirement

There must have been material participation[151] by the decedent or a member of the decedent's family for at least five of the eight years preceding the date of the decedent's death in the operation of the businesses that make up the qualified family-owned business interests.[152] Contemporaneous material participation by the decedent and one or more family members for a year does not satisfy more than one year of the five-year requirement.[153]

The existence of material participation is a factual determination. The types of activities and financial risks that will support a determination that material participation exists will vary, depending on the form of the ownership of the property and the nature of the business itself.[154] Although no single factor is determinative of the existence of material participation, physical work and participation in management decisions are the principal factors to be considered.[155] A brief absence from the operation of the businesses during periods of material participation will likely be disregarded in ascertaining the five aggregate years if preceded by and followed by substantial periods of uninterrupted

---

[151] Material participation has the meaning given to it by Section 2032A(e)(6). IRC § 2057(b)(1)(D)(ii). See ¶ 4.04[3][c][ii].

[152] IRC § 2057(b)(1)(D)(ii). See IRC §§ 2032A(e)(6), 2057(e)(1) (flush language), 2057(f)(3). Material participation is required in the operation of the business to which "such interests" relate. IRC § 2057(b)(1)(D)(ii). "Such interests" should refer to those qualified family-owned business interests for which a deduction is sought under Section 2057 as defined in Section 2057(e). "Such interests" would encompass those qualified family-owned business interests described in Section 2057(b)(2) that are included in the numerator of the 50 percent test. Accordingly, Section 2057(b)(1)(D)(ii) should be interpreted as an additional requirement that qualified family-owned business interests described in Section 2057(b)(2) and included in the numerator of the 50 percent test must satisfy for the estate to take a deduction for the qualified family-owned business interest under Section 2057. Section 2057(b)(1)(D)(ii) should not be interpreted as imposing an additional requirement for a qualified family-owned business interest to satisfy to be included in the numerator of the 50 percent fraction. See supra ¶¶ 5.08[3][c] note 107, 5.08[3][d] text accompanying note 150.

The Senate Report contains the following instructive example:

[I]f a father cash-leases farmland to his son, and the son materially participates in the trade or business of farming the land for at least five of the eight years preceding his father's death, the pre-death material participation and trade or business' requirements are satisfied with respect to the father's interest in the farm.

S. Rep. No. 174, 105th Cong., 2nd Sess. 157 (1998) reprinted in 1998-3 CB 693.

[153] Cf. Reg. § 20.2032A-3(c)(2).

[154] IRC §§ 2057(b)(1)(D)(ii), 2032A(e)(6); Reg. § 20.2032A-(3)(a).

[155] IRC §§ 2057(b)(1)(D)(ii), 2032A(e)(6); Reg. § 20.2032A-3(e)(2).

material participation.[156] Generally, the periods of material participation aggregating five years must be in the eight-year period ending with the date of the decedent's death.[157] However, if this requirement cannot be met with respect to the decedent because of retirement or disability,[158] the eight-year period ends

---

[156] Cf. Reg. § 20.2032A-3(c)(2) (suggesting that a brief period of absence is thirty days or less and a substantial period of material participation is more than 120 days).

Rules similar to those found in Section 2032A(e)(14) relating to treatment of replacement property acquired in Section 1031 or Section 1033 transactions apply for purposes of Section 2057. IRC § 2057(i)(3)(J). Section 2032A(e)(14) tacks periods of material participation by a decedent or any family member with respect to replaced property onto material participation by a decedent or any family member with respect to replacement property if the replacement property was acquired in a Section 1031 or Section 1033 nonrecognition transaction and the use of the replacement and replaced property is the same, but only to the extent that the fair market value of the replacement property on the date of acquisition does not exceed the fair market value of the replaced property on the date of disposition. IRC § 2032A(e)(14). The question is how this rule "shall" be applied to the Section 2057(b)(1)(D)(ii) requirement that there be material participation in the business to which the ownership interest relates. See supra ¶¶ 5.08 [3][c] note 107, 5.08[3][d] text accompanying note 150. Section 2057 provides a deduction for a "qualified family-owned business interest" which is an "interest . . . in a trade or business" as a proprietor or an "interest . . . in a trade or business" carried on by an entity. IRC § 2057(e)(1). Where the interest is owned by an entity, it is considered owned proportionately by its shareholders or partners. IRC § 2057(e)(3)(C). Seemingly, Section 2057 refers to the decedent's interest in the trade or business, not the business's individual assets. Although the disposition of an individual asset may affect the composition of the property of a trade or business, it does not in all cases affect the ownership or existence of the business. Section 1031 or Section 1033 could apply to a disposition of an ownership interest in a trade or business (as opposed to the underlying property held by the business) only in the most unusual circumstances. Section 1031 does not apply to exchanges of interests in business entities. IRC §§ 1031(a)(2)(B), 1031(a)(2)(D). It is difficult to imagine a compulsory or involuntary conversion of corporate stock or a partnership that would trigger Section 1033. Theoretically, Section 1033 might apply to an entire proprietorship interest if all the trade or business assets were converted at once, or Section 1031 could apply to the disposition of an entire trade or business held as a proprietorship, but practically it is very unlikely.

An alternative analysis may be that this provision was intended to apply to the disposition of property used by the trade or business and thereby not require the restarting of the five-out-of-eight-years material participation clock each time any asset of the business is replaced in a transaction covered by Section 1031 or Section 1033. The problem with this analysis is the implication that the five-out-of-eight-years material participation requirement applies to each individual asset of a trade or business. Certainly inventory sales, cash-financed equipment replacement, or business expansion should not reduce the likelihood that a trade or business interest would ultimately qualify for the Section 2057 deduction. Section 2057 was enacted to help businesses survive and transactions involving property of a trade or business not qualifying for nonrecognition under Section 1031 or Section 1033 are the lifeblood of a business and essential for survival. Regulatory guidance is needed.

[157] IRC § 2057(b)(1)(D)(ii).

[158] A disability is a physical or mental impairment preventing material participation by the decedent. IRC §§ 2057(i)(3)(A), 2032A(b)(4)(B).

on the earlier of the date of disability or the date that old-age Social Security benefits commenced[159] provided that the disability or benefits were continuous until the decedent's death, but the five-year requirement must still be met within the eight-year period determined under this special rule.[160]

Where a qualified family-owned business passes from a decedent to the decedent's surviving spouse, active management[161] by the surviving spouse will be treated as material participation in the determination of whether the business interest qualifies for the Section 2057 deduction in the surviving spouse's estate.[162]

[f] The Interest Must Pass to a Qualified Heir

The qualified family-owned business interest must pass to a qualified heir to qualify for a deduction under Section 2057.[163] Qualified family-owned business interests may pass outright to a qualified heir either as a sole proprietorship, corporation, or partnership interest. Qualified family-owned business interests may pass from an existing trust to a qualified heir,[164] and they may

---

[159] This provision is adopted from Section 2032A. It is designed to alleviate inequities resulting from the material participation requirement in cases where the decedent was receiving Social Security benefits and materially participated in the qualified family-owned business prior to commencement of those benefits. In such cases, any income derived from the qualified family-owned business would be treated as earned income for Social Security purposes, resulting in the potential for reduced Social Security benefits. The interaction of these two rules, in the absence of Section 2057(i)(3)(A), would force some people to choose between receiving Social Security benefits and obtaining the estate tax deduction for their qualified-family owned business interest.

[160] IRC §§ 2057(i)(3)(A), 2032A(b)(4). See ¶ 4.04[3][c] text accompanying notes 124, 125.

[161] Active management is the making of management decisions of a business other than daily operating decisions. IRC §§ 2057(i)(3)(B), 2032A(e)(12); ¶ 4.04[3][c][iii].

[162] IRC §§ 2057(i)(3)(B), 2032A(b)(5).

[163] IRC § 2057(b)(2)(B). The Senate Finance Committee Report on the Internal Revenue Service Restructuring and Reform Act of 1998 specifically states that "a qualified family-owned business interest must pass to a qualified heir in order to qualify for the deduction." S. Rep. No. 174, 105th Cong., 2d Sess. 158 (1998), reprinted in 1998-3 CB 537, 694. To qualify for the deduction, the qualified heirs (see supra ¶ 5.08[3][c] text accompanying notes 113–117) of the qualified family-owned business interest must consent to the potential application of the imposition of additional estate tax (see IRC §§ 2057(b)(1)(B), 2057(h)) in various circumstances related to the qualified heirs' holding of the property. IRC § 2057(f)(1). See infra ¶ 5.08[5][b].

[164] A qualified family-owned business interest that is an interest in an entity carrying on a trade or business held in an existing trust may qualify for a Section 2057 deduction as indicated by the reference in Section 2057(e)(3)(C) to "beneficiaries." Note that to be a "beneficiary," under Section 2057(e)(3)(C), the decedent or members of the decedent's family must hold a "present interest" in the trust. IRC § 2057(e)(3)(C) (last sentence). See supra ¶ 5.08[2][c] text accompanying note 70.

pass to a trust and be treated as passing to a qualified heir "if all beneficiaries of a trust are qualified heirs (and in such other circumstances as the Secretary of the Treasury may provide). . . . "[165]

[4] The Amount of the Deduction

Section 2057 allows a deduction for the adjusted value of qualified family-owned business interests. In computing the amount of the deduction, the adjusted value of the qualified family-owned business interests is to be reduced by any portion of the adjusted value that passes to a surviving spouse for which a marital deduction is claimed,[166] death taxes to be paid out of the deductible interests,[167] and certain other deductions.[168] In addition, a limitation is imposed on the maximum amount of the Section 2057 deduction.[169]

[a] Other Deductions and Expenses of Estates Affecting the Section 2057 Deduction

Although Section 2057 is silent on this issue, Form 706, "United States Estate (and Generation-Skipping Transfer) Tax Return,"[170] and the Instructions for Form 706[171] provide that if a marital deduction is claimed for the value of a qualified family-owned business interest passing to the surviving spouse, it may not be deducted under Section 2057.[172] Additionally, the return form and

---

[165] S. Rep. No. 174, 105th Cong., 2d Sess. 158 (1998), reprinted in 1998-3 CB 537, 694. Presumably, the term "beneficiaries" refers only to those beneficiaries who have a present interest in the trust as defined in Section 2503(b) or are treated as having a present interest in the trust under Section 2032A(g) (last sentence). IRC §§ 2057(e)(3)(C), 2057(i)(3)(L), 2032(A)(g). See HR Rep. No. 201, 97th Cong., 1st Sess. 38, 176 (1981), reprinted in 1981-2 CB 352, 385; supra ¶ 5.08[2][c] text accompanying note 70. See also ¶ 4.04[3][b][viii] text accompanying notes 95–100.

[166] See infra ¶ 5.08[4][a][i].

[167] See infra ¶ 5.08[4][a][ii].

[168] See infra ¶ 5.08[4][a][iii].

[169] IRC § 2057(a)(2). See infra ¶ 5.08[4][b].

[170] Form 706, United States Estate (and Generation-Skipping Transfer) Tax Return (Rev. Nov. 2001) Schedule T, Part 4, Line 15, at 39.

[171] Instructions for Form 706, United States Estate (and Generation-Skipping Transfer) Tax Return (Rev. Nov. 2001), at 23.

[172] A schedule is to be attached to the federal estate tax return that specifies the amount of the qualified family-owned business interests that is being deducted under Section 2056 for which the Section 2057 election is being made. Instructions for Form 706, United States Estate (and Generation-Skipping Transfer) Tax Return (Rev. Nov. 2001), at 23. Although the Instructions for Form 706, United States Estate (and Generation-Skipping Transfer) Tax Return (Rev. Nov. 2001), are not elevated to the same legal persua-

accompanying instructions require that in computing the amount to be deducted under Section 2057, the adjusted value of a qualified family-owned business interest must be reduced "by the amount of any Federal estate or . . . [generation-skipping transfer] tax and any state inheritance taxes paid out of, and any other deductions claimed with respect to, the interests"[173] to be deducted.

[i] **Marital deduction.** The prohibition of the Section 2057 deduction for the value of any qualified family-owned business interests passing to the surviving spouse for which a marital deduction is claimed under Section 2056 is not troublesome even though it is not found in the statutory language of Section 2057. If the Section 2057 deduction is claimed for the value of the qualified family-owned business interest passing to a surviving spouse, the marital deduction for this interest is denied.[174]

[ii] **Death taxes.** The adjusted value of the qualified family-owned business interest to be deducted under Section 2057 should be reduced by the amount of any federal estate or generation-skipping transfer tax and any state inheritance taxes paid out of the interest.[175] Although the statutory language of Section 2057 does not specifically provide for such a reduction, the omission is likely an oversight and the reduction should be made. Other deduction sec-

---

siveness as statutes, regulations, or judicial decisions, at least some courts are willing to grant them significant weight. Wilkes v. United States, 50 F. Supp. 2d 1281, 83 AFTR2d 99-1573 (MD Fla. 1999). But see Zimmerman v. Comm'r, 71 TC 367 (1978) (statutes, regulations, and judicial decisions are authoritative sources of federal tax law, not informal IRS publications).

[173] Instructions for Form 706, United States Estate (and Generation-Skipping Transfer) Tax Return (Rev. Nov 2001), at 23.

[174] IRC § 2056(b)(9). Section 2056(b)(9) provides that nothing in Section 2056 or any other provision of Chapter 11 (which includes Section 2057) shall allow the value of any interest in property to be deducted under this chapter more than once with respect to the same decedent. Possibly this provision is statutory authority for this Section 2057 reduction. Section 2056(b)(9) was enacted to insure that there was not a double deduction as a marital and charitable deduction for charitable remainder interests after the enactment of the unlimited marital deduction. Description of HR 6056 (Technical Corrections Act of 1982) Scheduled for a Hearing Before the Comm. on Ways and Means on April 27, 1982, at 11, JCS-12-82 (Joint Comm. Print Apr. 26, 1982).

[175] The Department of the Treasury takes this position. Instructions for Form 706, United States Estate (and Generation-Skipping Transfer) Tax Return (Rev. Nov. 2001), at 23. See Form 706, United States Estate (and Generation-Skipping Transfer) Tax Return (Rev. Nov. 2001) Schedule T, Part 4, Line 15, at 39.

A schedule is to be attached to the federal estate tax return that lists the amount of any taxes paid out of each qualified family-owned business interest. Instructions for Form 706, United States Estate (and Generation-Skipping Transfer) Tax Return (Rev. Nov. 2001), at 23.

tions provide for such a reduction.[176] An adjustment is provided for any estate, succession, legacy, or inheritance taxes payable out of property passing to a charity in determining the amount of the Section 2055 deduction.[177] Similarly, in determining the Section 2056 marital deduction, the value of any interest in property passing to the surviving spouse is reduced by death taxes that affect the net value of the property passing to the surviving spouse.[178] A similar death tax adjustment is appropriate in Section 2057. The adjustment keeps a parity between Sections 2056 and 2057 when the qualified family-owned business interests pass to a surviving spouse. The adjustment can be avoided by drafting the appropriate tax apportionment clause. It would just plain feel better to a New England conscience if the adjustment were provided for in the statute.

[iii] **Other deductions.** The Instructions for Form 706 provide that the adjusted value of the qualified family-owned business interests are to be reduced by "any other deductions claimed with respect to" the qualified family-owned business interests in determining the amount of Section 2057 deduction.[179] What are the "other deductions claimed"? Other deductions might include deductions under Section 2053(a)(1) for funeral expenses,[180] Section 2053(a)(2) for administration expenses,[181] Section 2054 for losses,[182] and Sec-

---

[176] It can be argued that it is the actual net adjusted value of the qualified family-owned business interest that *is acquired by or that passes to the qualified heir* that may be deducted under Section 2057, not just the adjusted value of the qualified family-owned business interest for which the election is made. IRC § 2057(b)(2)(B). See IRC §§ 2057(a)(1), 2057(b)(2). Congress certainly did not take this precise an approach in defining the adjusted value of the qualified family-owned business interest. IRC § 2057(d).

[177] IRC § 2055(c). It is worth noting that this statutory provision was added to the code after the Supreme Court held that the amount of the charitable deduction was the value of the residuary estate before taking into account the federal estate taxes to be paid out of the amount passing to the charity. Edwards v. Slocum, 264 US 61 (1924). See ¶ 5.05[3][b][i].

[178] IRC § 2056(b)(4)(A). See ¶ 5.06[5][a].

[179] Instructions for Form 706, United States Estate (and Generation-Skipping Transfer) Tax Return (Rev. Nov. 2001), at 23. See Form 706, United States Estate (and Generation-Skipping Transfer) Tax Return (Rev. Nov. 2001) Schedule T, Part 4, Line 15, at 39. A schedule is to be attached to the federal estate tax return that lists the type and amount of any other deductions claimed with respect to each qualified family-owned business interest to be deducted under Section 2057. Instructions for Form 706, United States Estate (and Generation-Skipping Transfer) Tax Return (Rev. Nov. 2001), at 23. Section 2056(b)(9) might be used as authority for this adjustment when it prohibits any provision in Chapter 11 allowing the deduction for any interest in property more than once with respect to the same decedent.

[180] IRC §§ 2053(a)(1), 2053(b). See ¶¶ 5.03[2], 5.03[4].

[181] IRC §§ 2053(a)(2), 2053(b). See ¶¶ 5.03[3], 5.03[4].

[182] IRC § 2054. See ¶ 5.04.

tion 2055 for charitable transfers.[183] Does it matter if the "other deductions" are subject to the Section 642(g) prohibition on double deductions and deducted for federal income tax purposes rather than for federal estate tax purposes?[184] Possibly the adjustment is only for those deductions claimed under Chapter 11 and not those deductions for which a waiver is filed because they are taken for federal income tax purposes. Even if the estate tax deduction is waived and the administration expenses are paid out of income generated by the qualified family-owned business interest that is deducted under Section 2057, a question arises as to whether a reduction in the value of the deduction for the qualified family-owned business interest is required. Regulations address this issue in the context of the Section 2055 charitable deduction and the Section 2056 marital deduction.[185] Although these regulations are not specifically applicable to the Section 2057 deduction, they should be applied to Section 2057 as well.[186] Applying these regulations, the value of the qualified family-owned business interest would be reduced by the amount of any "estate transmission expenses"[187] related to the business interest regardless of whether such transmission expenses were deducted in the computation of the estate tax or the income tax.[188] Also, the value of the qualified family-owned business interest would be reduced by the amount of any "estate management expenses"[189] if those expenses were deducted in the computation of the estate tax;[190] however, no reductions of the potential Section 2057 deduction would occur if the estate management expenses were deducted in the computation of the income tax.[191] If such management expenses are paid out of Section 2057 property, but they related to expenses on other property, there would be a reduction in the Section 2057 deduction.[192]

---

[183] IRC § 2055. See ¶ 5.05. Could "other deductions" include those deductions claimed under Section 2053(a)(3) or Section 2053(a)(4) that are added back in the determination of the adjusted value of the qualified family-owned business interests under Section 2057(d)(2)? These deductions listed in Section 2057(d)(2) are deductible under Section 2053 and may also be a charge against the value of the qualified family-owned business interests deducted under Section 2057.

[184] IRC § 642(g). See ¶ 5.03[3][d].

[185] Reg. §§ 20.2055-3(b), 20.2056(b)-4(d). These regulations were issued subsequent to Comm'r v. Hubert, 520 US 93 (1997).

[186] See ¶ 5.06[5][b] text accompanying notes 111–117.

[187] Reg. §§ 20.2055-3(b)(1)(ii), 20.2056(b)-4(d)(1)(ii).

[188] See IRC § 642(g). Cf. Reg. §§ 20.2055-3(b)(2), 20.2056(b)-4(d)(2); ¶ 5.06[5][b] text accompanying notes 119, note 128.

[189] Reg. §§ 20.2055-3(b)(1)(i), 20.2056(b)-4(d)(1)(i).

[190] Reg. §§ 20.2055-3(b)(3), 20.2056(b)-4(d)(3).

[191] Reg. §§ 20.2055-3(b)(3), 20.2056(b)-4(d)(3). See ¶ 5.06[5][b] text accompanying note 129.

[192] Reg. §§ 20.2055-3(b)(4), 20.2056(b)-4(d)(4). See ¶ 5.06[5][b] text accompanying note 122.

No language in Section 2057 expressly requires the adjustment for other deductions. Possibly Section 2056(b)(9) can be used as authority for this adjustment when it prohibits any provision in Chapter 11 allowing the deduction for any interest in property more than once with respect to the same decedent. Although generally no double deductions are allowed, Congress has provided for some items to be deducted twice. Congress provided a deduction for the adjusted value of the qualified family-owned business interest.[193] In determining the adjusted value of the qualified family-owned business interest, there is a reduction for any amounts deducted under Section 2053(a)(3) or Section 2053(a)(4).[194] This reduction is then further reduced by the indebtedness on any qualified residence of the decedent when the interest is deductible under Section 163(h)(3),[195] certain indebtedness incurred to pay educational and medical expenses,[196] and any indebtedness that does not exceed $10,000.[197] Each of these types of indebtedness, which are added back, increases the adjusted value of the qualified family-owned business interest and increases the amount of the Section 2057 deduction provided for statutorily by Congress. Congress expressly authorized a deduction under Section 2057 and one under Section 2053(a)(3) or Section 2053(a)(4) for these expenses. This authorization allows a double deduction for these types of indebtedness. If Section 2057 specifically allows double deduction of certain Section 2053(a)(3) and Section 2053(a)(4) deductions, should Section 2056(b)(9) be overridden, and if so, to what extent? Possibly, Section 2056(b)(9) is overridden only for the double deductions that are specifically provided for in Section 2057.[198]

[b] The Deduction Limitation

The amount of the Section 2057 deduction allowed for the adjusted values[199] of qualified family-owned business interests[200] may not exceed $675,000.[201] However, if the deduction is maximized at $675,000, the Section 2010(c) applicable exclusion amount, $1 million (for years 2002 and 2003), is limited to $625,000[202] with the result that the maximum total deduction-credit

---

[193] IRC § 2057(a)(1).

[194] IRC § 2057(d)(1). See supra ¶ 5.08[3][c][iii].

[195] IRC § 2057(d)(2)(A).

[196] IRC § 2057(d)(2)(B).

[197] IRC § 2057(d)(2)(C).

[198] See ¶ 5.06[8][f] text accompanying notes 424, 425.

[199] See supra ¶ 5.08[4][a].

[200] IRC § 2057(a)(1). The valuation of the business interests to be deducted reflects any discounts or premiums attributable to such property. See ¶ 4.02[4].

[201] IRC § 2057(a)(2).

[202] IRC § 2057(a)(3)(A).

relief equals $1.3 million.[203] However, if the amount of the Section 2057 deduction is less than the $675,000 ceiling, the special Section 2010 $625,000 applicable exclusion amount is increased by the excess of $675,000 over the amount of the Section 2057 deduction.[204] The increased Section 2010 applicable exclusion amount may not exceed the actual Section 2010(c) applicable exclusion amount for the year involved.[205] For example, if in 2002 Decedent died and qualified for only a $475,000 Section 2057 deduction, Decedent's Section 2010 applicable exclusion amount would be $825,000. The Section 2010 applicable exclusion amount is the total of $625,000 plus $200,000 ($675,000 less $475,000). However, if Decedent's Section 2057 deduction had been only $200,000, Decedent's potential $475,000 increase ($675,000 less $200,000) in the Section 2010 exclusion amount would be capped at $375,000 because the Section 2010(c) ceiling on the applicable exclusion amount is $1 million for 2002.[206]

All this statutory hocus pocus is aimed at providing taxpayers with some indirect relief. When originally enacted as an exclusion under the now-repealed Section 2033A,[207] the amount of the exclusion was reduced each year as the Section 2010 applicable exclusion amount increased, so that the total exclusion-credit relief was equal to $1.3 million.[208] The same $1.3 million of relief is available through the current deduction-credit mechanism. However, because the deduction comes "off the top" and provides a benefit at a decedent's highest estate tax brackets, while the credit comes "off the bottom" and provides relief at a decedent's lowest estate tax brackets, Congress opted to allow a full Section 2057 deduction "off the top" at a decedent's maximum estate tax brackets and to reduce the Section 2010 applicable exclusion amount, thereby providing taxpayers with indirect additional tax relief.[209]

---

[203] This was the total amount of the original exclusion-credit relief under now-repealed Section 2033A and Section 2010 in 1998. See Taxpayer Relief Act of 1997, Pub. L. No. 105-34, § 502(a), 111 Stat. 788, 847 (1997), reprinted in 1997-4 CB (Vol. 1) 1, 61. See infra text accompanying notes 210–212.

[204] IRC § 2057(a)(3)(B). Thus, generally a decedent's estate will be allowed $1.3 million of deduction-credit relief.

[205] IRC § 2057(a)(3)(B).

[206] Thus, the decedent's estate would be allowed total relief of $1.2 million ($200,000 plus $1 million).

[207] Internal Revenue Service Restructuring and Reform Act of 1998, Pub. L. No. 105-206, § 6007(b)(1)(B), 112 Stat. 685, 807 (1998), reprinted in 1998-3 CB 145, 267.

[208] See Taxpayer Relief Act of 1997, Pub. L. No. 105-34, § 502(a), 111 Stat. 788, 847 (1997), reprinted in 1997-4 CB (Vol. 1) 1, 61.

[209] S. Rep. No. 174, 105th Cong., 2d Sess. 155 (1998), reprinted in 1998-3 CB 537, 691.

The Section 2010(c) applicable exclusion amount increases to $1.5 million in 2004.[210] If a taxpayer elects to take the Section 2057 deduction, the amount of the deduction is limited to $675,000 and the applicable exclusion amount is fixed at $625,000, limiting the total benefit of an election to take the deduction under Section 2057 to $1.3 million.[211] When the applicable exclusion amount exceeds $1.3 million after 2003, no one would elect to take the Section 2057 deduction; therefore, Section 2057 no longer applies with respect to decedents dying after December 31, 2003.[212]

[5] The Recapture Rule

[a] Introduction

The Section 2057 deduction is designed to preserve family business enterprises by totally or partially eliminating the value of the business from the tax base, thereby possibly eliminating the forced disposition of family businesses to generate funds to pay federal estate taxes.[213] All or a portion of the estate tax saved by the deduction, however, may be recaptured through the imposition of an additional estate tax[214] on the occurrence of any one of four specified events. All four recapture events that trigger the additional estate tax occur in situations that are inconsistent with Congress's stated intention of keeping the business in the hands of the qualified heirs.[215] In imposing the additional estate tax, Section 2057 once again borrows significantly from Section 2032A.[216]

---

[210] IRC § 2001(c). Additional changes in the applicable exclusion amount are scheduled. Id. See ¶ 3.02.

[211] See supra text accompanying notes 201–203.

[212] IRC § 2057(j). Section 2057 was not repealed because there is still the possibility of recapture of the benefit provided by Section 2057 for decedents dying before January 1, 2004. HR Conf. Rep. No. 84, 107th Cong., 1st Sess. 186 (2001), reprinted in 2001-__ CB __, __. However, Title IX of the Economic Growth and Tax Relief Reconciliation Act of 2001 contains a "sunset" provision that would make Section 2057(j) inapplicable to estates of decedents dying after December 31, 2010. Economic Growth and Tax Relief Reconciliation Act of 2001, Pub. L. No. 107-16, § 901(a)(2), 115 Stat. 150 (2001), reprinted in 2001-__ CB __, __. See ¶ 8.10[5].

[213] See S. Rep. No. 33, 105th Cong., 1st Sess. 40 (1997), reprinted in 1997-4 CB (Vol. 2) 1067, 1120.

[214] IRC § 2057(f). See infra ¶¶ 5.08[5][c], 5.08[5][d].

[215] IRC § 2057(f). See also supra ¶ 5.08[1].

[216] IRC §§ 2057(f)(1)(A), 2057(i)(3). See IRC § 2032A(c); ¶ 4.04[7].

[b] Recapture Events

Generally, an additional estate tax is imposed, if at all, if a recapture event occurs within the recapture period, which is the shorter of the ten-year period after the date of the decedent's death or the period between the date of decedent's death and the date of death of the qualified heir.[217] Therefore, any potential liability for this additional estate tax generally lapses no later than ten years after the death of the decedent. However, the recapture period may be extended for up to two years because a qualified heir has up to two years following the death of the decedent in which to commence material participation.[218] The four recapture events are discussed next.

[i] Failure to meet material participation requirements. The material participation requirements for both the decedent or a member of the decedent's family[219] and the qualified heirs[220] are at the heart of the beneficial treatment accorded qualified family-owned business interests. Consequently, if the material participation requirement is not met for a significant length of time, a recapture event occurs. Rather than looking only at the qualified heir's failure to materially participate after the decedent's death, the rule looks at material participation during the decedent's lifetime as well. As a general rule, an additional estate tax is imposed if in any period there is an eight-year period that ends after the decedent's death and within the recapture period,[221] tacking on periods when the decedent[222] or any qualified heir held the property, there are periods aggregating more than three years in which either the holder (the dece-

---

[217] IRC § 2057(f)(1).

[218] IRC §§ 2057(i)(3)(G), 2032A(c)(7)(A). The recapture period is justifiably extended by the grace period that elapses after the decedent's death and before commencement of material participation. The period should also be extended for an involuntary conversion replacement period. IRC §§ 2057(i)(3)(M), 2032A(h). See ¶ 4.04[7][b] text accompanying notes 298–300.

[219] See supra ¶ 5.08[3][e].

[220] IRC § 2057(i)(1).

[221] IRC § 2057(f)(1)(A). The recapture period may be extended for up to two years because a qualified heir has up to two years following the death of the decedent to commence material participation. IRC §§ 2057(i)(3)(G), 2032A(c)(7)(A)(ii). See IRC § 2057(f)(2)(B). Prior to the expiration of this grace period, a failure of the qualified heir to materially participate with respect to the trade or business will not trigger an additional estate tax under Section 2057(f). IRC §§ 2057(i)(3)(G), 2032A(c)(7).

[222] If the decedent was disabled or receiving Social Security retirement benefits at death, then for purposes of material participation, the period ending on the date on which the disability or retirement began shall be treated as the period immediately before the decedent's death. IRC §§ 2057(i)(3)(A), 2032A(b)(4)(A), 2032A(b)(4)(C), 2032A(c)(6)(B)(i). Therefore, the period of the decedent's disability or retirement is disregarded for the material participation determination with respect to the period during which the decedent held the property.

dent or the qualified heir) or a member of the holder's family[223] did not materially participate[224] in the operation of the family business.[225]

Mere active management[226] by a qualified heir is treated as material participation[227] if the qualified heir is the decedent's surviving spouse,[228] is under the age of twenty-one,[229] is disabled,[230] or is a student.[231] In the case of a qualified heir other than the decedent's surviving spouse, active management suf-

---

[223] IRC §§ 2057(i)(2), 2032A(e)(2).

[224] Material participation is discussed supra ¶ 5.08[3][e] and in the context of Section 2032A at ¶¶ 4.04[3][c][ii], 4.04[7][b] text accompanying note 296.

[225] IRC §§ 2057(f)(1)(A), 2032A(c)(6)(B). See supra ¶ 5.08[3][e] note 156 for a consideration of the interrelationship of Sections 1031 and 1033 to the material participation requirement.

The consecutive eight-year period may include six years before the decedent's death and two years after death, or other combinations. Periods aggregating more than three years are all that is required; the periods counting toward the three years need not be consecutive. Assume, for example, that a decedent dies on January 1, 1998, holding a qualified family-owned business interest that qualified the estate for the Section 2057 deduction. Assume that neither the decedent, nor a member of the decedent's family, materially participated in the operation of the family-owned business interest for twelve months in 1993, ten months in 1995, and six months in 1997. Assuming no involuntary conversion takes place and that the qualified heir does not die before the end of the year 2000, if the qualified heir or members of the qualified heir's family fail to materially participate in the operation of the family-owned business for more than eight months before the end of the year 2000, an additional estate tax will be imposed.

It appears that if a family-owned business ceased operations owing to financial hardship during the period, the qualified heir could not, and therefore would not, satisfy the material participation requirement, and the additional estate tax would be imposed.

[226] See supra ¶ 5.08[3][e] text accompanying note 161. Active management is discussed at ¶ 4.04[3][c][iii]. See IRC §§ 2057(i)(3)(G), 2032A(c)(7)(B), 2032A(e)(12).

[227] IRC § 2057(i)(3)(G), 2032A(c)(7)(B).

[228] IRC § 2032A(c)(7)(C)(i). See also IRC §§ 2057(i)(3)(B), 2032A(b)(5).

[229] IRC § 2032A(c)(7)(C)(ii). Active management by the fiduciary of an individual qualified heir under the age of twenty-one will be treated as material participation by the heir. IRC § 2032A(c)(7)(B)(ii).

[230] IRC § 2032A(c)(7)(C)(iii). A qualified heir is disabled if he or she has a mental or physical impairment that renders the qualified heir unable to materially participate in the operation of the farm or other business. IRC § 2032A(b)(4)(B). Active management by the fiduciary of a qualified heir who is disabled will be treated as material participation by the disabled qualified heir. IRC § 2032A(c)(7)(B)(ii).

[231] IRC §§ 2032A(c)(7)(C)(iv), 2032A(c)(7)(D) (incorporating the Section 151(c)(4) definition of "student").

fices for material participation only during the period the qualified heir is under age twenty-one, disabled, or a student.[232]

[ii] **Dispositions.** Generally, a disposition of any portion[233] of an interest in a qualified family-owned business by a qualified heir during the recapture period[234] triggers the imposition of an additional estate tax.[235] However, there are several exceptions to the disposition rule where, in effect, no disposition outside the family occurs. Thus, a disposition to a member of the qualified heir's family[236] is not treated as a disposition, and various corporate transactions should not be treated as dispositions.[237] Finally, although outside the general scope of exceptions, a conveyance of a qualified conservation contribution as defined by Section 170(h)[238] does not constitute a disposition.[239] No disposition occurs to the extent that a disposition qualifies for nonrecognition under

---

[232] IRC § 2032A(c)(7)(B).

[233] IRC §§ 2057(i)(3)(C), 2032A(c)(2)(D).

[234] See supra ¶ 5.08[5][b] text accompanying notes 217, 218.

[235] IRC § 2057(f)(1)(B). "The conferees clarify that a sale or disposition, in the ordinary course of business, of assets such as inventory or a piece of equipment used in the business (e.g., the sale of crops or a tractor) would not result in recapture of the benefits of the qualified family-owned business exclusion." HR Conf. Rep. 220, 105th Cong., 1st Sess. 400 (1997), reprinted in 1997-4 CB (Vol. 2) 1457, 1870. See infra ¶ 5.08[5][c]; ILM 200149033 (Nov. 1, 2001) (transfer of Section 2057(i)(3)(P) lien property).

[236] IRC § 2057(f)(1)(B). It appears that a transfer by an unrelated qualified heir to a member of that unrelated qualified heir's family is not a disposition triggering the additional estate tax. Query whether Congress meant to also allow disposition by a related qualified heir to a ten-year employee qualified heir without imposition of estate tax.

If a qualified heir ceases to be engaged in a trade or business but a member of the family of the qualified heir is so engaged, there is no disposition of the qualified heir's interest. IRC § 2057(f)(3).

[237] IRC § 2057(f)(1)(B). It should be noted that there are other potential dispositions that would not trigger recapture if Section 2057(i)(3)(O) is read so as to apply Sections 6166(g)(1)(B), 6166(g)(1)(C), and 6166(g)(1)(D) to the recapture provisions. First, any stock redeemed under Section 303 (and sometimes under Section 304) will not be treated as a disposition for recapture purposes if tax is paid in an amount not less than the amount received on the redemption. IRC §§ 2057(i)(3)(O), 6166(g)(1)(B). Second, Section 2057(f) presumably will not apply to an exchange in either a tax-free "D," "E," or "F" reorganization under Section 368(a)(1) or in a Section 355 exchange (or so much of Section 356 as relates to Section 355). IRC §§ 2057(i)(3)(O), 6166(g)(1)(C). Finally, Section 2057(f) presumably will not apply to a distribution to a legatee or to one entitled to property under local laws of descent and distribution. IRC §§ 2057(i)(3)(O), 6166(g)(1)(D). See ¶ 2.02[3][c] text accompanying note 142.

[238] See ¶ 5.05[7][c].

[239] IRC § 2057(f)(1)(B).

income tax Sections 1031 and 1033 and the replacement property qualifies as Section 2057 property.[240]

[iii] **Loss of citizenship.** If a qualified heir loses U.S. citizenship "within the meaning of Section 877"[241] or an event described in subparagraph (A) or (B) of Section 877(e)(1) occurs with respect to the qualified heir[242] within the

---

[240] IRC §§ 2057(i)(3)(M), 2032A(h), 2032A(i). See ¶ 4.04[7][b] text accompanying note 274. To the extent that there is boot and the nonrecognition provisions are inapplicable, a recapture tax is imposed. See ¶ 4.04[7][c] text accompanying notes 317–321.

[241] This reference to Section 877 is problematic because Section 877 does not define loss of citizenship. It is unclear whether Congress intended for any loss of U.S. citizenship to trigger the possible imposition of the additional estate tax under Section 2057(f)(1)(C) or only where the loss of U.S. citizenship was to avoid the imposition of income, estate, gift or generation-skipping transfer taxes. The legislative history provides that the benefit of the Section 2057 deduction for qualified family-owned business interests is subject to recapture if "the qualified heir loses U.S. citizenship" without making any reference to Section 877. S. Rep. No. 33, 105th Cong., 1st Sess. 44 (1997); HR Conf. Rep. No., 220, 105th Cong., 1st Sess. 399 (1997), reprinted in 1997-4 CB (Vol. 2) 1457, 1869.

Section 877(a)(1) imposes an alternative tax on certain nonresident alien individuals who within the ten-year period immediately preceding the close of the taxable year have lost U.S. citizenship in order to avoid income or estate or generation-skipping transfer taxes. Under Section 877(a)(2), certain individuals are treated as having a tax avoidance purpose if certain income or net worth tests are met. IRC § 877(a)(2). However, Section 877(a)(2) does not apply and tax avoidance is not presumed in certain cases specified in Section 877(c). IRC §§ 877(a)(2), 877(c). It is possible for a qualified heir to lose U.S. citizenship and not lose U.S. citizenship within the meaning of Section 877. Seemingly if a qualified heir lost U.S. citizenship within ten years of the date of the decedent's death, the government would want the former U.S. citizen qualified heir to satisfy the security requirements for a noncitizen qualified heir regardless of whether the loss of citizenship was within the meaning of Section 877. See IRC § 2057(g). Possibly the statute should be amended to eliminate the parenthetical phrase "within the meaning of section 877."

[242] A qualified heir may trigger the imposition of an additional estate tax under Section 2057 if the heir ceases to be a lawful permanent resident of the United States or commences to be treated as a resident of a foreign country under a tax treaty without waiving the benefits of the treaty. IRC §§ 2057(f)(1)(C), 877(e)(1)(A), 877(e)(1)(B), 7701(b)(6).

Under Section 877(e)(1), a long-term resident of the United States who ceases to be a lawful permanent resident of the United States or commences to be treated as a resident of a foreign country under a treaty between the United States and the foreign country without waiving the benefits of the treaty applicable to residents of the foreign country is treated for purposes of Section 877 in the same manner as if the resident were a citizen of the United States who lost U.S. citizenship. A long-term resident is an individual "other than a citizen of the United States." IRC § 877(e)(2). If a qualified heir is a long-term resident and not a citizen of the United States, any interest passing to a noncitizen, long-term resident heir is treated as a qualified family-owned business interest only if the interest passes to a qualified trust. IRC § 2057(g). The occurrence of an event described in Section 877(e)(1)(A) or Section 877(e)(1)(B) should only infrequently, if ever, give rise to the imposition of an additional estate tax because of the required compliance with Section 2057(g) to have an interest held by the long-term resident treated as a qualified family-owned business interest. One possible application of this provision may be in the event

recapture period,[243] an additional estate tax may be imposed. The additional estate tax will not be triggered and the interest will continue to be treated as a qualified family-owned business interest[244] if the qualified heir complies with the security arrangements[245] that apply to qualify a family-owned business interest passing to a noncitizen qualified heir as a qualified family-owned business interest.[246]

[iv] Foreign principal place of business. Recapture also occurs if the principal place of business changes to a location outside the United States during the recapture period.[247]

[c] Measuring the Recapture Tax

[i] Introduction. The amount of the additional estate tax imposed on the occurrence of a recapture event is computed by multiplying the "adjusted tax difference"[248] by the "applicable percentage."[249] Essentially the "adjusted tax difference" is the estate tax savings afforded by the deduction for qualified family-owned business interests. The "applicable percentage" reduces the amount to be recaptured generally if the recapture event occurs more than six

---

that the qualified trust or bond terminated prior to the expiration of the recapture period. If it is possible to have the qualified trust or bond terminate prior to the end of the recapture period, a provision needs to be added to provide security for all noncitizens treated as receiving an interest in a qualified family-owned business interest under Section 2057(g).

[243] The recapture period is the ten-year period after the date of death of the decedent or, if shorter, the period between the date of death of the decedent and the date of death of the qualified heir. IRC § 2057(f)(1). However, the recapture period may be extended for up to two years. IRC §§ 2057(i)(3)(G), 2032A(c)(7)(A)(ii). See supra ¶ 5.08[5][b] text accompanying note 218.

[244] IRC § 2057(g)(1).

[245] IRC §§ 2057(f)(1)(C), 2057(g).

[246] See supra ¶ 5.08[2][b][v]. Thus, the qualified heir may place the qualified family-owned business interest in a qualified trust to avoid the imposition of the additional estate tax. IRC § 2057(g)(1). A qualified trust is any trust that is organized under, and governed by, the laws of the United States or a state, and that, subject to regulations, has a trust instrument requiring that at least one trustee of the trust be an individual citizen of the United States or a domestic corporation. IRC § 2057(g)(2). (The Section 2057 qualified trust will in all likelihood bear a strong resemblance to a Section 2056A qualified domestic trust that may be used to permit a marital deduction to a decedent's estate when there is a noncitizen surviving spouse. See IRC § 2056A; Reg. § 20.2056A; ¶ 5.07.) Alternatively, the qualified heir may furnish a bond for the maximum amount of additional estate tax that may be imposed for the remaining recapture period. IRC §§ 2057(i)(3)(F), 2032A(c)(5), 2032A(e)(11). See ¶ 4.04[6] text accompanying note 238.

[247] IRC § 2057(f)(1)(D). See supra ¶ 5.08[2][b][ii].

[248] IRC §§ 2057(f)(2)(A)(i), 2057(f)(2)(C).

[249] IRC §§ 2057(f)(2)(A)(i), 2057(f)(2)(B).

years after the decedent's death.[250] Interest is imposed from the due date of the estate tax to the due date of the additional estate tax.[251]

[ii] **Adjusted tax difference.** The starting point for the determination of the adjusted tax difference with respect to the disqualified family-owned business interest is the adjusted tax difference with respect to *all* qualifying family-owned business interests initially included in the gross estate. The adjusted tax difference with respect to the estate is determined on a "top incremental basis" because it is the excess of what the estate tax liability would have been if Section 2057 had not been elected less the estate tax liability given that Section 2057 was used.[252] The term "estate tax liability" means the tax imposed by Section 2001, reduced by credits allowable against the tax.[253]

The adjusted tax difference attributable to a disqualified family-owned business interest is then determined by multiplying the adjusted tax difference with respect to the estate by a fraction that represents the portion of the qualified family-owned business interest that is involved in the recapture event over the value of all qualified family-owned business interests described in Section 2057(b)(2).[254] Only a single additional tax may be imposed on any portion of a qualified family-owned business interest acquired from a decedent by a qualified heir.[255] Thus, multiple taxation cannot occur upon subsequent recapture events with respect to the same qualified family-owned business interest.

[iii] **Applicable percentage.** After determining the adjusted tax difference attributable to the qualified family-owned business interest involved in the recapture event, the applicable percentage[256] of that amount becomes the additional estate tax.[257] The applicable percentage depends on the year of material participation in which the recapture event takes place.[258] If the recapture event occurs within the first six years of material participation by the qualified heir or a member of the heir's family, the applicable percentage is 100 percent.[259] If

---

[250] IRC § 2057(f)(2)(B). The applicable percentage reduction actually occurs only after six years of material participation. See infra text accompanying notes 258–261.

[251] IRC § 2057(f)(2)(A).

[252] IRC § 2057(f)(2)(C)(ii).

[253] IRC § 2057(f)(2)(C)(ii).

[254] IRC § 2057(f)(2)(C)(i).

[255] IRC §§ 2057(i)(3)(D), 2032A(c)(3). See ¶ 4.04[7][d].

[256] IRC § 2057(f)(2)(B).

[257] IRC § 2057(f)(2)(A)(i).

[258] The year of material participation is used in determining the applicable percentage because the two-year grace period in the commencement of material participation may result in a two-year extension of the ten-year recapture period. See supra ¶ 5.08[5][b] text accompanying note 218.

[259] IRC § 2057(f)(2)(B).

the recapture event occurs in the seventh year of material participation by the qualified heir or a member of the heir's family, only 80 percent of the tax savings is recaptured.[260] This recapture percentage decreases in the eighth, ninth, and tenth years to 60 percent, 40 percent, and 20 percent, respectively.[261]

[d] Additional Aspects of the Recapture Tax

[i] **Due date.** Any recapture tax imposed is due and payable within six months after the recapture event.[262] Any additional tax imposed should, if there is reasonable cause, qualify for an extension of time for payment for a reasonable period under Section 6161(a)(2)(A).[263] Payment of the additional tax does not qualify for Section 6166 deferral because the additional tax is neither a tax imposed by Section 2001 nor a deficiency in the tax imposed by Section 2001.[264]

[ii] **Interest.** The additional estate tax includes interest on the additional estate tax liability computed at the underpayment rate[265] for the period beginning on the date the estate tax liability was initially due under Chapter 11 and ending on the date the additional estate tax is due.[266]

[iii] **Liability for the tax.** The qualified heir is personally liable for any additional tax imposed with respect to the qualified heir's qualified family-owned business interest during the recapture period, unless a bond is furnished in lieu of personal liability.[267] As seen earlier, when a qualified heir disposes of the qualified family-owned business interest to a family member, no recap-

---

[260] IRC § 2057(f)(2)(B).

[261] IRC § 2057(f)(2)(B). The period is extended in a Section 1033 situation. IRC §§ 2057(i)(3)(M), 2032A(h)(2)(A). See ¶ 4.04[7][a] text accompanying notes 258, 259.

[262] IRC §§ 2057(i)(3)(E), 2032A(c)(4). See ¶ 4.04[7][e]. The six-month period expires on the date numerically corresponding to the date of the recapture event.

[263] Under Section 6161(a)(2), an extension of time for payment of estate tax may be granted for a reasonable period, not in excess of ten years, for reasonable cause.

[264] IRC §§ 6166(a)(1), 6166(h).

[265] IRC § 6621.

[266] IRC § 2057(f)(2)(A)(ii). Legislation was proposed that would have eliminated the interest component of the additional estate tax. HR 1105, 106th Cong., 1st Sess. § 2 (1999).

[267] IRC §§ 2057(i)(3)(F), 2032A(c)(5), 2032A(e)(11). See ¶ 4.04[7][f]. It is unclear whether the term "qualified heir" means only those qualified heirs who have an interest in the qualified family-owned business interests deducted under Section 2057 or whether it includes all qualified heirs, even those who do not have an interest in the qualified family-owned business interest deducted under Section 2057.

ture event occurs;[268] however, the member of the qualified heir's family to whom the interest passes becomes the "qualified heir" with respect to the interest transferred.[269] If no bond is furnished in lieu of personal liability by the new qualified heir, that qualified heir incurs personal liability for any subsequent additional estate tax.[270] Additionally, all individuals who are not qualified heirs having an interest in any business that is deducted under Section 2057 must consent to the collection of any additional estate tax imposed under Section 2057(f) from the deducted interests.[271]

[iv] **Statute of limitations.** The statutory period for assessment of an additional tax imposed under this section[272] does not expire until three years after the date the Service is notified of the recapture event.[273] Even if the occurrence of the recapture event does not result in the imposition of additional estate tax,[274] prudence dictates that the Service be notified to start the running of the statute of limitations.

[6] Interrelationship of Section 2057 to Other Estate Relief Provisions

[a] The Interrelationship With Section 2031(c)

There is no restriction on a decedent's executor electing to use both Section 2057 and the qualified conservation easement exclusion under Section 2031(c).[275] However, if land subject to a qualified conservation easement is used in a trade or business, and as is likely, Section 2031(c)[276] excludes some portion of specific land from the gross estate (as opposed to excluding a dollar amount), that amount does not qualify for a Section 2057 deduction, as it is

---

[268] IRC § 2057(f)(1)(B). See supra ¶ 5.08[5][b] text accompanying note 236.

[269] IRC §§ 2057(i)(1)(A), 2032A(e)(1).

[270] See ¶ 4.04[7][f] for the rules as they have developed with regard to Section 2032A(c)(5). It is hoped that regulations promulgated for this section will address the issue of successor liability where a disposition of the property to a family member does not result in the imposition of additional estate tax. See also ¶ 4.04[7][c][iv].

[271] IRC § 2057(h); Form 706, United States Estate (and Generation-Skipping Transfer) Tax Return (Rev. Nov. 2001) Schedule T, Part 5, at 40.

[272] IRC § 2057(f).

[273] IRC §§ 2057(i)(3)(K), 2032A(f)(1). See supra ¶ 5.08[5][b]. See also ¶ 4.04[7][g].

[274] See IRC § 2057(f)(2).

[275] Cf. HR Conf. Rep. No. 220, 105th Cong., 1st Sess. 403 (1997), reprinted in 1997-4 CB (Vol. 2) 1457, 1873. See ¶ 4.02[7][e][ii].

[276] See ¶ 4.02[7][e][i].

not a "family-owned business interest," because it is not included "in deter-mining the value of the gross estate."[277]

[b] The Interrelationship With Section 2032A

Section 2057 may be used in tandem with Section 2032A.[278] If a family-owned farm or business is passed between family members, both sections could, when combined with the Section 2010 applicable exclusion amount, raise the effective total estate tax exclusion amount by $750,000,[279] from $1.3 million[280] to $2.05 million.[281] In addition, as seen earlier, Section 2057 is inter-related with Section 2032A because it often borrows provisions from Section 2032A.[282]

The interrelationship problems between the two sections relate to the ex-tent to which one section is considered in satisfying the qualification require-ments of the other section. The statutes do not explicitly state the effect of a Section 2032A reduction in value on the requirements to qualify for the Sec-tion 2057 deduction. Similarly, the effect of a Section 2057 deduction on the qualification requirements for Section 2032A valuation is not specifically ad-dressed.[283]

The effect of a Section 2032A election on satisfying the requirements of Section 2057 is the most complicated. Recall that, in general, to qualify for the Section 2057 deduction, "the adjusted value of the qualified family-owned bus-iness interests" must exceed "50 percent of the adjusted gross estate."[284] An es-

---

[277] IRC § 2057(b)(2)(A). It can be argued that Section 2031(c) merely excludes a dol-lar amount and not a portion of specific property. If so, both a Section 2031(c) exclusion and a Section 2057 deduction would be allowed for the full value of the land. See ¶ 4.02[7][e] text accompanying notes 381, 382; supra ¶¶ 5.08[3][b] note 105, 5.08[3][c] note 121.

[278] Even before Section 2057 was converted from an exclusion to a deduction, the legislative history of now-repealed Section 2033A implied that Congress intended that these two sections could be used in tandem. HR Conf. Rep. No. 220, 105th Cong., 1st Sess. 396 (1997), reprinted in 1997-4 CB (Vol. 2) 1457, 1866. See IRC §§ 2057(b)(1)(C), 2057(b)(2), 2057(c).

[279] This result disregards the fact that the Section 2032A(a)(2) limitation is subject to an inflation adjustment.

[280] See supra ¶ 5.08[4].

[281] The amount of the increase in the maximum effective exclusion amount under Section 2032A and Section 2057, disregarding any adjustments for inflation, is $1,425,000 ($750,000 plus $675,000). See supra ¶ 5.08[4][b] indicating that the maximum Section 2010 amount is reduced to $625,000 in the years 2002 and 2003 and that Section 2057 is teminated in the year 2004. See also infra ¶ 5.08[7].

[282] See ¶ 5.08[1] text accompanying note 13.

[283] IRC §§ 2032A(b)(1)(A), 2032A(b)(1)(B).

[284] IRC § 2057(b)(1)(C). See supra ¶ 5.08[3][c].

tate's ability to satisfy the test varies, depending on whether any property valued under Section 2032A is part of the includible qualified family-owned business interests. If the Section 2032A real property is *not* part of any includible qualified family-owned business interest, the Section 2032A special valuation does not affect the numerator, but does affect the denominator of the fraction required to determine satisfaction of the 50 percent test of Section 2057.[285] The denominator of the fraction is the "adjusted gross estate,"[286] which depends on the "value of the gross estate. . . . "[287] Any Section 2032A reduction in value is taken into account to reduce the value of the gross estate and, consequently, the value of the adjusted gross estate. The reduction of the denominator without any reduction in the numerator will make the greater-than-50-percent requirement easier to satisfy.[288]

On the other hand, if the real property valued under Section 2032A *is* a part of an includible qualified family-owned business interest, then the reduction in its value caused by Section 2032A is taken into account in both the numerator and denominator of the 50 percent test. The numerator for purposes of the 50 percent test is composed in part of includible qualified family-owned business interests.[289] Section 2057(b)(2)(A) provides that includible qualified family-owned business interests are "the interests which are included in determining the value of the gross estate. . . . " Thus, Section 2032A valuation is taken into account in determining the value of an includible qualified family-owned business interest.[290] Hence, if the estate tax value of real property that qualifies for Section 2032A treatment and is also part of an includible qualified family-owned business interest is reduced under Section 2032A, that reduction should be taken into account for purposes of determining the value of

---

[285] IRC § 2057(b)(1)(C). That test requires that the sum of the adjusted value of includible qualified family-owned business interests and the amount of certain gifts of qualified family-owned business interests exceeds 50 percent of the adjusted gross estate (as defined in Section 2057(c)).

[286] IRC § 2057(c). The "adjusted gross estate" is the gross estate reduced by amounts deductible under paragraphs (3) or (4) of Section 2053(a) and increased by a variety of gift transfers. Id.

[287] IRC § 2057(c). The value is the value of the gross estate determined on the applicable date using the applicable valuation method with regard to Section 2031(c). See supra ¶ 5.08[3][c] text accompanying notes 121–125.

[288] Subtracting a positive amount from the denominator of a fraction while subtracting nothing from its numerator will always increase the fraction. For example, if the original amounts are $400,000/$1 million, the 50 percent test is not met. However, if $300,000 is subtracted from the denominator, the fraction is $400,000/$700,000 and the 50 percent test is met.

[289] IRC § 2057(b)(1)(C). The other part of the numerator is composed of certain gifts of qualified family-owned business interests.

[290] The Section 2031(c) exclusion should also be taken into account. See ¶ 4.02[7]; supra ¶¶ 5.08[3][c] text accompanying note 121, 5.08[6][a].

the includible qualified family-owned business interest in the numerator of the fraction. Thus, as seen earlier,[291] the denominator of the fraction will also be reduced for the Section 2032A reduction in valuation. As a result, in most cases it would be harder for an estate to qualify for the Section 2057 deduction if the Section 2032A property is part of an includible qualified family-owned business interest.[292]

A Section 2057 deduction has no effect on qualification for Section 2032A. Recall that among the requirements to qualify for Section 2032A is that the adjusted value of real and personal property must exceed 50 percent of the adjusted value of the gross estate and the adjusted value of only the real property must exceed 25 percent of the adjusted gross estate.[293] Conversion of Section 2057 from an exclusion to a deduction avoids any qualification problems because the qualifying family-owned business interest property is included in the gross estate and the amounts of the adjusted value of such property and the amount of the gross estate are unaffected by the Section 2057 deduction.[294]

Another Section 2057–Section 2032A interrelationship problem occurs when real property that is eligible for a Section 2032A reduction in value is also part of an includible qualified family-owned business interest that is eligible for a deduction, and an executor elects the application of both sections. Although both operate to reduce the estate tax due, in a chicken-and-egg-type question, it is unclear which section comes first. The determination of which section applies first may control which set of recapture provisions applies in the event of a disposition more than six years after the decedent's death. If Section 2032A applies first, the entire amount of additional tax may be due.[295] If the interest is subject to Section 2057, then less than 100 percent of the additional tax may be due under Section 2057(f)(2)(B).[296]

---

[291] See supra text accompanying notes 284–288.

[292] That is because in virtually all cases, the Section 2032A reduction in value would be subtracted from something less than 100 percent of the adjusted gross estate in the numerator of the Section 2057(b)(1)(C) fraction and from 100 percent of the adjusted gross estate in the denominator, making the satisfaction of a more-than-50-percent test more difficult. For example, if $300,000 is subtracted from both the numerator and the denominator of the fraction $600,000/$1 million ($\frac{6}{10}$), the result is $300,000/$700,000 ($\frac{3}{7}$).

[293] IRC §§ 2032A(b)(1)(A), 2032A(b)(1)(B). See ¶¶ 4.04[3][b], 4.04[3][c].

[294] IRC § 2032A(b)(3). See supra ¶ 5.08[6][a].

[295] IRC § 2032A(c)(2). If the disposition is a partial one, the additional tax is prorated.

[296] IRC § 2057(f)(2). See supra ¶ 5.08[5][c].

[c] The Interrelationship With Section 6166

Section 6166, like Section 2057, was enacted after Congress identified potential liquidity problems for decedents owning closely-held businesses.[297] Therefore, it is not surprising to find that a qualified family-owned business interest should normally also qualify as a closely-held business interest under Section 6166.[298] To qualify for deferral of estate tax attributable to the closely-held business interest, the closely-held business interest[299] must also be "included in determining the gross estate of a decedent,"[300] and it must exceed 35 percent of the adjusted gross estate[301] of the decedent.[302] The conversion of the relief provided for qualified family-owned business interests from an exclusion to a deduction under Section 2057 avoids any interrelationship problem of a qualified family-owned business interest meeting the requirements under Section 6166 because all such Section 2057 property is included in the gross estate and is not deducted in computing the adjusted gross estate.[303] As a result, qualification for Section 6166 is unaffected by the Section 2057 deduction.

[7] Effective Date

Section 2057 applies to the estates of decedents dying after 1997[304] and before January 1, 2004.[305]

---

[297] See ¶ 2.02[3][c].

[298] IRC § 6166(b)(1). The legislative history accompanying now-repealed Section 2033A implied that even an exclusion under Section 2033A could act in conjunction with Section 6166. S. Rep. No. 33, 105th Cong., 1st Sess. 40 (1997), reprinted in 1997-4 CB (Vol. 2) 1067, 1120; HR Conf. Rep. No. 220, 105th Cong., 1st Sess. 396 (1997), reprinted in 1997-4 CB (Vol. 2) 1457, 1866.

[299] IRC § 6166(b)(1).

[300] IRC § 6166(a)(1).

[301] IRC § 6166(b)(6). The term "adjusted gross estate" is defined differently for purposes of Sections 6166 (see ¶ 2.02[3][c] text accompany notes 107–111) and 2057 (see supra ¶ 5.08[3][c][v]).

[302] IRC § 6166(a)(1).

[303] See IRC §§ 6166(a)(1), 6166(b)(6).

[304] Taxpayer Relief Act of 1997, Pub. L. No. 105-34, § 502(c), 111 Stat. 788, 852 (1997), reprinted in 1997-4 CB (Vol. 1) 1, 66. All the amendments to original Section 2033A were made retroactive to that date. Internal Revenue Service Restructuring and Reform Act of 1998, Pub. L. No. 105-206, § 6024, 112 Stat. 685, 826 (1998), reprinted in 1998-3 CB 145, 286.

[305] IRC § 2057(j). See supra ¶ 5.08[4][b] text accompanying notes 210–212. Section 2057 was not repealed because there is still the possibility of recapture of the benefit provided by Section 2057 for decedents dying before January 1, 2004. HR Conf. Rep. No. 84, 107th Cong., 1st Sess. 186 (2001), reprinted in 2001-__ CB __, __. However, Title IX of the Economic Growth and Tax Relief Reconciliation Act of 2001 contains a "sunset"

¶ 5.09 SECTION 2058. STATE DEATH TAXES

[1] Introduction

Section 2058 provides a deduction from the gross estate for death taxes actually paid to any state or the District of Columbia with respect to property included in the decedent's gross estate.[1] The deduction replaces the Section 2011 credit[2] and is effective for estates of decedents dying after December 31, 2004.[3] State taxes paid on property that escapes the gross estate do not qualify for the deduction.[4]

The deduction is not dependent on the form in which the state death tax is imposed; it is available whether the state tax is an estate tax on the transmission of property at death, an inheritance tax on the succession to property at death, or some variation or combination of the two.[5] No doubt the statute contemplates a validly imposed state tax,[6] but "[i]t is the policy of the Internal Revenue Service generally not to question the application of state death tax statutes or to intervene in controversies regarding their application."[7] Therefore, when taxes are paid to two states with respect to the same property, both taxes potentially qualify for the deduction.[8] Of course, state taxes paid in connection with the death of someone other than the decedent are not to be taken into account; property included in the decedent's gross estate may have been subjected to state death taxes in the estates of other decedents, but a parenthet-

provision that would make Section 2057(j) inapplicable to estates of decedents dying after December 31, 2010. Economic Growth and Tax Relief Reconciliation Act of 2001, Pub. L. No. 107-16, § 901(a)(2), 115 Stat. 150 (2001), reprinted in 2001-__ CB __, __. See ¶ 8.10[5].

[1] IRC § 2058(a). Section 2058 does not apply to estates of decedents dying after December 31, 2010, under the "sunset" provision. Economic Growth and Tax Relief Reconciliation Act of 2001, Pub. L. No. 107-16, § 901(a)(2), 115 Stat. 38, 150 (2001), reprinted in 2001-__ CB __, __. See ¶ 8.10[5].

[2] See ¶ 3.03. Since there is a substantial similarity between the two provisions, much of the authority under Section 2011 should be authority for Section 2058 as well.

[3] Economic Growth and Tax Relief Reconciliation Act of 2001, Pub. L. No. 107-16, § 532(d), 115 Stat. 38, 75 (2001), reprinted in 2001-__ CB __, __.

[4] Cf. Reg. § 20.2011-1(a); Second Nat'l Bank of New Haven v. United States, 422 F2d 40 (2d Cir. 1970); Estate of Owen v. Comm'r, 104 TC 498 (1995).

[5] Cf. Reg. § 20.2011-1(a), which provides that the Section 2011 credit applies for "estate, inheritance, legacy or succession taxes. . . ."

[6] Cf. Mim. 3971, XI-2 CB 427 (1932). Death taxes paid to a municipality do not qualify for the deduction. Cf. McFarland v. United States, 80 AFTR2d 97-8348 (ED La. 1997).

[7] Cf. Rev. Rul. 60-88, 1960-1 CB 365, 366.

[8] Cf. Rev. Rul. 60-88, 1960-1 CB 365; Rev. Rul. 70-272, 1970-1 CB 187.

ical provision in Section 2058(a) expressly forecloses consideration of such other taxes.[9]

[2] The "Actually Paid" Requirement

An estate becomes entitled to a credit for state taxes only insofar as such taxes are "actually paid."[10] This requirement has been interpreted strictly under Section 2011, the predecessor of Section 2058, although a discharge of the tax obligation either by a cash payment or a transfer of property may qualify for the deduction.[11] Proof of payment must be made,[12] and, if an estate takes advantage of a discount allowed by a state for prompt payment and pays less than the amount assessed, only the amount paid qualifies for the deduction.[13] A de-

---

[9] IRC § 2058(a) (parenthetical).

[10] IRC § 2058(a).

Some states treat state gift tax as a prepayment of state death tax where the property subject to the state gift tax is included in the estate for state death tax purposes. This is so regardless of whether the state gift tax was paid prior to the decedent's death. At one time the Commissioner had agreed that this gift tax qualified as a "payment" of state death taxes for purposes of Section 2011. However, if the state gift tax that so qualified was paid prior to the decedent's death, the Commissioner contended that it should be included in the decedent's gross estate under Section 2033 (Rev. Rul. 75-63, 1975-1 CB 294); or, if the state tax was not paid prior to the decedent's death, no deduction should be allowed under Section 2053. Rev. Rul. 71-355, 1971-2 CB 334. The Commissioner was unsuccessful in the courts in both instances, losing on the Section 2033 issue in Estate of Gamble v. Comm'r, 69 TC 942 (1978), acq. 1981-2 CB 1, and Horton v. United States, 79-2 USTC ¶ 13,316 (MDNC 1979), see ¶ 4.05[2][a] note 8 and losing on the Section 2053 issue in Estate of Lang v. Comm'r, 613 F2d 770 (9th Cir. 1980), see ¶ 5.03[5][a] note 105. The Commissioner has revoked these rulings. Moreover, the Commissioner has appropriately taken the position that the state gift tax credit is in substance a gift tax and not a "payment" of estate tax. Cf. Rev. Rul. 81-302, 1981-2 CB 170 (where this position was taken with respect to the Section 2011 credit). However, the Tenth Circuit adopted the Commissioner's prior position, allowing a Section 2011 credit but denying a Section 2053 deduction for a posthumously paid gift tax. First Nat'l Bank & Trust Co. of Tulsa v. United States, 787 F2d 1393 (10th Cir. 1986). Seemingly, the Tenth Circuit would allow a Section 2058 deduction for such a tax.

[11] Cf. Rev. Rul. 86-117, 1986-2 CB 157.

[12] Cf. Reg. § 20.2011-1(c)(2); Bell v. Comm'r, 82 F2d 499 (3d Cir. 1936); Estate of Giacopuzzi v. Comm'r, 29 TCM (CCH) 1777 (1970); Schuneman v. United States, 783 F2d 694 (7th Cir. 1986) (taxpayers who, contrary to the direction in Regulations Section 20.2011-1(c)(2) that evidence of payment be submitted with the return or as soon as practicable, waited for no apparent reason to file proof of payment for almost three years, were allowed the Section 2011 credit but were required to pay interest on the state tax credit amount from the date the return was filed until the date proof of payment was submitted).

[13] Cf. Commonwealth Trust Co. of Pittsburgh v. Driscoll, 50 F. Supp. 949 (WD Pa.), aff'd per curiam, 137 F2d 653 (3d Cir. 1943), cert. denied, 321 US 764 (1944).

posit made as security for payment of state death taxes does not meet the "actually paid" test in the statute.[14]

Seasonable payment is also required. Under Section 2058(b), the general rule is that the deduction will be allowed for state taxes paid only when the deduction is claimed within four years after the filing of the estate tax return.[15] Although a cutoff date is desirable, there are circumstances in which the four-year rule could work an improper hardship, so Section 2058(b) recognizes several exceptions to the general rule.

1. Some states base their death duties directly on the federal tax, thus, in such circumstances, the state tax cannot be determined until the amount of the federal tax is established. Controversy over the amount of the federal tax arising out of the government's assertion of a deficiency can be litigated in the Tax Court, subject to review in the courts of appeals and the United States Supreme Court. Such proceedings may take many years, with the possible result that the state tax cannot be accurately determined until after the expiration of the four-year limitation period that usually applies. To overcome such difficulties, an alternative limitation period is provided: If the taxpayer files a timely petition with the Tax Court,[16] the credit is allowed for state taxes that are paid and for which the credit is claimed within sixty days after the Tax Court decision becomes final, even if both the payment and the claim occur beyond the four-year period.[17]

2. If an extension of time is granted under Section 6161[18] or Section 6166[19] for payment of the federal estate tax, which may be granted for a period of up to fourteen years with respect to the tax shown on the return[20] or up to four years or more with respect to amounts determined as a deficiency,[21] the time period within which the state death tax payment must be made and credit claimed is extended to either the usual four-year period or the expiration date of any such exten-

---

[14] Cf. Estate of Damon v. Comm'r, 49 TC 108 (1967), acq. 1968-2 CB 2; Aronauer v. United States, 37-1 USTC ¶ 9052 (SDNY 1937).

[15] Courts do not have the power to extend this period. Cf. Howard v. United States, 40 F. Supp. 697 (ED La. 1941), aff'd on other grounds, 125 F2d 986 (5th Cir. 1942).

[16] IRC § 6213(a).

[17] IRC § 2058(b)(2)(A). Cf. Estate of Damon v. Comm'r, 49 TC 108 (1967), acq. 1968-2 CB 2.

[18] See ¶ 2.02[3][b].

[19] See ¶ 2.02[3][c].

[20] IRC § 6166. See also IRC § 6161(a)(2). An extension of twelve months after the due date for the last Section 6166 installment is allowed in the case of extensions for reasonable cause under Section 6161(a)(2)(B).

[21] IRC § 6161(b)(2). In some circumstances, a deficiency payment may be extended for more than four years. See IRC § 6166(e). See ¶ 2.03[3][c] note 57.

sion, whichever is later.[22] It should be noted that an extension of time for payment of the state tax is irrelevant;[23] here it is the extension of time for payment of the federal tax that operates to extend the usual limitation period.[24]

3. The deduction for state death taxes may be claimed on the latter of:[25] (a) sixty days after a federal estate tax refund claim has been denied;[26] (b) sixty days after the final decision in a refund suit that is based on such a claim;[27] or (c) two years after the date the executor files a Section 6532(a)(3) written waiver of the requirement that the executor be mailed a notice of disallowance of a refund claim.[28] In effect, this leaves the matter of timely payment open when final settlement of federal estate tax liability is postponed by a pending claim or suit for refund; however, it is clear that the exception can be invoked only if a timely[29] claim has been filed.

A timely claim for refund based on the deduction for payment of state death taxes can be made within the limitation periods just discussed, notwithstanding Code provisions that usually require refund claims to be filed within three years from the time the return was filed or two years from the time the tax was paid, and despite other Code provisions that usually foreclose the payment of refunds when the taxpayer has filed a Tax Court petition.[30] Nonetheless, such refunds are to be made without the usual payment of interest.[31] The limitation period provided here is in addition to, not in lieu of, other limitation periods; a claim for refund can always be filed within two years after the estate tax was paid.[32]

---

[22] IRC § 2058(b)(2)(B).

[23] Rev. Rul. 86-38, 1986-1 CB 296. See also In re Harkavy's Estate, 34 NYS2d 910 (1942); Estate of Spillar v. Comm'r, 50 TCM (CCH) 1285 (1985).

[24] Cf. Rev. Rul. 86-38, 1986-1 CB 296.

[25] IRC § 2058(b)(2)(C).

[26] IRC § 2058(b)(2)(C)(i).

[27] IRC § 2058(b)(2)(C)(ii).

[28] IRC § 2058(b)(2)(C)(iii).

[29] Cf. Empire Trust Co. v. United States, 214 F. Supp. 731 (D. Conn.), aff'd per curiam, 324 F2d 507 (2d Cir. 1963). Cf. also HR Rep. No. 775, 85th Cong., 1st Sess. 36 (1957), reprinted in 1958-3 CB 811, 846.

[30] IRC § 2058(b)(flush language).

[31] IRC § 2058(b)(last sentence). But cf. Edinburg v. United States, 617 F2d 206 (Ct. Cl. 1980); Rev. Rul. 61-58, 1961-1 CB 414 (concerning the allocation of interest on the portion of a refund based on Section 2011 and that portion based on some other ground). See also Rev. Rul. 79-219, 1979-2 CB 401 (holding that interest an estate paid on a prior deficiency is also not recoverable in a subsequent refund suit based on Section 2011).

[32] IRC § 6511(a). Cf. Rev. Rul. 81-263, 1981-2 CB 169.

[3] Consequences of the Conversion of the Section 2011 Credit to the Section 2058 Deduction

As the Introduction to this section points out, the Section 2058 deduction replaces the Section 2011 credit. The conversion to a deduction results in the federal government effectively paying a portion of the decedent's state death taxes equal to the maximum tax rates imposed on the decedent's estate.[33] However, this is a far cry from the consequences prior to the 2002 inception of the phase-out of the Section 2011 credit[34] when the federal government picked up 100 percent of the state death taxes up to the amount of the Section 2011 credit.[35] This change may create problems for states which impose a death tax based on the federal tax credit.[36]

An indirect consequence of the conversion is that the previous deduction for state death taxes imposed upon charitable transfers that was an alternative to the Section 2011 credit[37] is eliminated.[38] The effect of the elimination is to preclude any possible double deduction of the state taxes paid.[39]

---

[33] For example, if the deduction reduces a decedent's taxable estate which would otherwise be taxed at a 45 percent rate under Section 2001(c), the federal government is effectively paying up 45 percent of the decedent's state tax costs.

[34] For the years between 2002 and 2004, a portion of the prior Section 2011 credit is allowed. See ¶¶ 3.03[1] text accompanying note 13; ¶¶ 3.03[3][d].

[35] See ¶ 3.03[1] text accompanying notes 8–9.

[36] See ¶ 3.03[1] text accompanying note 16.

[37] See IRC § 2053(d) as amended by the Economic Growth and Tax Relief Reconciliation Act of 2001, Pub. L. No. 107-16, § 532(c)(5), 115 Stat. 38, 74 (2001), reprinted in 2001-__ CB __, __, applies to estates of decedents dying after December 31, 2004. Economic Growth and Tax Relief Reconciliation Act of 2001, Pub. L. No. 107-16, § 532(d), 115 Stat. 38, 75 (2001), reprinted in 2001-__ CB __, __.

[38] See ¶ 5.03[8], especially text accompanying note 168.

[39] But see IRC § 2056(b)(9) which could be applied to preclude any double deductibility under the estate tax. The section would thus preclude double deductibility of the taxes, even if this statutory change had not been made.

CHAPTER 8

Miscellaneous Estate Tax Provisions

¶ 8.01 SECTION 2201. COMBAT ZONE–RELATED DEATHS OF MEMBERS OF THE ARMED FORCES AND DEATHS OF VICTIMS OF CERTAIN TERRORIST ATTACKS

Section 2201 of the Internal Revenue Code (the Code) provides special reduced estate tax rates for estates of military personnel who are killed in a combat zone or who die as a result of wounds, disease, or injuries suffered while serving in a combat zone and for estates of specified terrorist victims.[1] The provision originated in 1949[2] as a measure affording retroactive relief to estates of decedents who were World War II casualties. It has subsequently been extended to cover later military conflicts and victims of terrorist attacks.[3] The section is elective, because the executor of the decedent's estate may elect out of the application of the provision.[4]

[1] Qualified Decedents

The Section 2201 special rates are available only to "qualified decedents,"[5] who are defined in Section 2201(b) and fall into one of two categories.[6]

[a] Certain Military Personnel

The first category of qualified decedents is military personnel who are in the "active service" of the armed forces and are killed in a combat zone or die as a result of wounds, disease, or injuries suffered while in a combat zone.[7]

---

[1] The Section 2201 reduction is claimed on page 1 of Form 706, United States Estate (and Generation-Skipping Transfer) Tax Return (Rev. Nov. 2001). See Instructions for Form 706, United States Estate (and Generation-Skipping Transfer) Tax Return (Rev. Nov. 2001), Instructions for Part 2. Tax Computation (Page 1 of Form 706), Lines 6–9 at 5.

[2] Technical Changes Act of 1949, Pub. L. No. 81-378, § 10(a), 63 Stat. 891, 896 (1949) (adding IRC § 939(a)).

[3] See the definition of "combat zone" infra ¶ 8.01[1][a][iii]. A similar estate tax military exemption applied to the World War I casualties. Revenue Act of 1918, Pub. L. No. 65-254, § 401, 40 Stat. 1057, 1097 (1919).

[4] IRC § 2201(a).

[5] IRC § 2201(a).

[6] IRC §§ 2201(b)(1), 2201(b)(2).

[7] IRC § 2201(b)(1).

This rule applies only to estates of citizens or residents;[8] estates of nonresident noncitizens do not qualify.

[i] **Active service.** A person in the inactive reserves or on retirement is not in active service.[9] But the person can be in active service without being in the field or in a theater of war, and one does not lose "active service" status merely because the person is "absent from duty on account of sickness, wounds, leave, internment by the enemy, or other lawful cause. . . ."[10]

[ii] **Member of the armed forces.** The armed forces of the United States include "all regular and reserve components of the uniformed services which are subject to the jurisdiction of" the Secretaries of Defense, the Army, the Navy, or the Air Force, and also the Coast Guard.[11] One is a member of the armed forces if one is an officer or enlisted person, but not if one is merely a civilian serving with the armed forces.[12] Members of the Merchant Marine are not members of the armed forces.[13]

[iii] **Death in a combat zone.** The estate of a decedent who meets the tests previously discussed is allowed the special rates if the decedent was killed in action while serving in a combat zone. A member in active service who became a prisoner of war or was missing in action while in a combat zone and who occupied that status until death, or occupied that status when the wounds, disease, or injury resulting in death were incurred, is treated as satisfying the requirement.[14]

Section 2201 adopts the Section 112(c)(2) definition of "combat zone,"[15] which in turn rests on presidential designation of an area as one in which our armed forces are engaged in combat, or have been so engaged after June 24,

---

[8] IRC § 2201(b)(1).

[9] Cf. Reg. § 20.2201-1(e). The Act of Jan. 2, 1975, Pub. L. No. 93-597, § 2(a)(2), 88 Stat. 1950, 1950 (1975), reprinted in 1975-1 CB 495, 495 eliminated a former requirement that there be an induction period in order for the estate of a serviceman to claim the tax exemption. This change became effective July 1, 1973—the day after the expiration of the Military Selective Service Act, which eliminated induction periods. Id. at § 2(c), 8 Stat. 1950, reprinted in 1975-1 CB 495.

[10] Reg. § 1.112-1(b)(1). See Reg. § 20.2201-1(e).

[11] IRC § 7701(a)(15).

[12] Estate of DuPont v. Comm'r, 18 TC 1134, 1141 (1952), aff'd, 233 F2d 210 (3d Cir.), cert. denied, 352 US 878 (1956) (estate of a decedent who was a civilian special assistant on the staff of the Commanding General of the United States Army Air Corps was denied the exemption, the court refusing to treat as members of the armed forces persons who were not "formally commissioned officers, warrant officers, or enlisted men.")

[13] Rev. Rul. 70-537, 1970-2 CB 17.

[14] Reg. § 20.2201-1(e).

[15] IRC § 2201(b)(1)(A).

1950.[16] In addition, Section 112(c)(3) indicates that one is serving in a combat zone only if one performs services thereafter the date designated by the President as the commencement of combat activities and before the date designated by the President as the termination of such activities.[17]

As previously stated, the provision was added initially to aid estates of decedents who were World War II casualties. Amendments in 1951[18] and 1953[19] liberalized the relief and extended it to the estates of persons who were casualties of the Korean conflict. June 25, 1950, is fixed by statute as the date of commencement of combat activities in the Korean conflict, for which President Truman designated a combat zone.[20] President Eisenhower designated January 31, 1955, as the date of termination of combat activities in the Korean conflict.[21] A subsequent act[22] provides that individuals detained during the seizure of the crew of the U.S.S. Pueblo by the government of North Korea in 1968 shall be treated as having served in a combat zone. A presidential proclamation[23] extended the military relief provision to estates of persons who were casualties of the fighting in Vietnam, with January 1, 1964, designated as the date of commencement of combat activities in Vietnam and adjacent waters[24] and June 30, 1996, designated as the date of termination of those combatant activities.[25] On January 17, 1991, President George H.W. Bush designated areas of the Persian Gulf as a combat zone.[26] Areas of former Yugoslavia were

---

[16] See Reg. § 20.2201-1(c)(1).

[17] See Reg. § 20.2201-1(c)(2).

[18] Revenue Act of 1951, Pub. L. No. 87–182, § 606, 65 Stat. 452, 567 (1951).

[19] Technical Changes Act of 1953, Pub. L. No. 83-287, § 106, 67 Stat. 615, 616 (1953), reprinted in 1953-2 CB 485, 487.

[20] Exec. Order No. 10,195, 15 Fed. Reg. 9177 (1950).

[21] Exec. Order No. 10,585, 20 Fed. Reg. 17 (1955).

[22] Act of Apr. 24, 1970, Pub. L. No. 91-235, § 1, 84 Stat. 200, 200 (1970), reprinted in 1970-1 CB 360, 360.

[23] Exec. Order No. 11,216, 30 Fed. Reg. 5817 (1965).

[24] Exec. Order No. 11,216, 30 Fed. Reg. 5817 (1965). See Reg. § 1.112-1(e), which includes, as within a combat zone, service in certain areas outside the zone that are in direct support of the zone. Compare Reg. § 1.112-1(e)(2) Ex. 5 (combat zone) with Reg. § 1.112-1(e)(2) Ex. 6 (no combat zone). See also Rev. Rul. 70-621, 1970-2 CB 17.

[25] Exec. Order No. 13,002, 61 Fed. Reg. 24,665 (1996).

[26] Exec. Order No. 12,744, 56 Fed. Reg. 2663 (1991). Notice 96-34, 1996-1 CB 379, states that under the Act of March 20, 1996 (Pub. L. No. 104-117, 110 Stat. 827 (1996), reprinted in 1996-3 CB 1), U.S. military and support personnel in the peacekeeping effort in Bosnia, Herzegovina, Croatia, and Macedonia are to be treated as if in a combat zone under Section 112 if they perform services in a qualified hazardous duty area. These countries were to be considered qualified hazardous duty areas if, as of the date of enactment of Pub. L. No. 104-117, U.S. Armed Forces members were entitled to special pay under 37 USC § 310, which they were. Accordingly, under Pub. L. No. 104-117, Section 2201 applies to members of the U.S. Armed Services serving in those countries.

designated by President Clinton as a combat zone with March 24, 1999, designated the date of commencement of combat activities.[27] On December 12, 2001, President George W. Bush designated Afghanistan, including the air space above it, as a combat zone with September 19, 2001, designated as the date of commencement of combat activities.[28]

[iv] **Service-connected death.** Even if one was not killed in action, a person's estate may benefit under the first classification if the person dies as a result of wounds, disease, or injury suffered while serving in a combat zone in the line of duty by reason of a hazard to which the service subjected the person.[29] The term "serving in a combat zone" has the same meaning here as indicated earlier.[30]

[b] Specified Terrorist Victims

The second classification of decedents to whom the Section 2201 special estate tax rates are available are "specified terrorist victims."[31] This group includes individuals who die from wounds or injury incurred as a result of the September 11, 2001, terrorist attacks,[32] the April 19, 1995, Oklahoma City terrorist attack,[33] or as a result of illness incurred due to an anthrax attack that occurred on or after September 11, 2001, and before January 1, 2002.[34] This classification is not limited to citizens or residents,[35] but it is inapplicable to any individual identified by the Attorney General to have been a participant or conspirator in any such terrorist attack or a representative of such individual.[36]

---

[27] Exec. Order No. 13,119; 64 Fed. Reg. 18,797 (1999). Tax Benefits for Serviceman in Bosnia and Herzegovina, Pub. L. No. 104-117, § 1(b), 110 Stat. 827, 827 (1996), reprinted in 1996-3 CB 1, 1. See Notice 96-34, 1996-1 CB 379.

[28] Exec. Order No. 13,239; 66 Fed. Reg. 64,904 (2001).

[29] IRC § 2201(b)(1)(B); Reg. § 20.2201-1(a)(2). See Reg. § 20.2201-1(d). If the Armed Forces official record states that the decedent was killed in action in a combat zone or died as a result of wounds, disease, or injury suffered in a combat zone, a presumption arises that the decedent qualifies for the exemption. Reg. § 20.2201-1(d).

[30] See Reg. § 1.112-1(f) Ex. 8; supra text accompanying notes 15–28.

[31] IRC § 2201(b)(2). Specified terrorist victims are defined in Section 692(d)(4).

[32] IRC § 692(d)(4)(A).

[33] IRC § 692(d)(4)(A).

[34] IRC § 692(d)(4)(B).

[35] See IRC § 692(d)(4).

[36] IRC § 692(d)(4) (flush language).

[2] Effects of the Relief Provision

[a] Rate Relief

Section 2201(c) provides a special rate schedule that is applicable to the qualified decedents described here.[37] The rate schedule is equal to 125 percent of the maximum state death tax credit amount allowed for years prior to 2002.[38] The Section 2201(c) rates are substituted for the Section 2001(c) rates in making the computations under Section 2001(b) in the case of a decedent who qualifies for the Section 2201 rates and who is a citizen or resident[39] and under Section 2101(b) in the case of a nonresident noncitizen[40] decedent who also qualifies under Section 2201. The Section 2201(c) rates are used in making the computations under both Sections 2001(b)(1) and 2001(b)(2) (for citizens or residents) and under both Sections 2101(b)(1) and 2101(b)(2) (for noncitizen nonresidents). As a result, a single graduated (albeit reduced) rate schedule applies to transfers made by a qualified decedent at death, based upon cumulative taxable transfers made both during life and at death.[41]

[b] Unified Credit Computation

While qualified decedents may use the Section 2201(c) reduced rates in the computation of their tax liability, they nevertheless are allowed a regular unified credit under either Section 2010[42] (for a citizen or resident) or Section 2102(c)[43] (for a noncitizen, nonresident).

---

[37] See supra ¶ 8.01[1].

[38] IRC § 2201(c). See IRC § 2011(b)(1); ¶ 3.03[3][b]. Section 2201(c) provides a separate rate schedule that is significantly different from the Section 2011(b)(1) schedule because the Section 2011(b)(1) schedule is based on the amount of the decedent's "adjusted taxable estate," which is the taxable estate reduced by $60,000. IRC § 2011(b)(3). See ¶ 3.03[3][b]. After the $60,000 adjustment is added back to the Section 2011(b) schedule and the amounts under that table are increased by 25 percent, the two schedules become identical.

[39] IRC § 2201(a). See ¶¶ 2.01[1], 2.01[2].

[40] IRC § 2201(a). See ¶ 6.01[2].

[41] See Joint Comm. on Tax'n, "Technical Explanation of the 'Victims of Terrorism Tax Relief Act of 2001' as Passed by the House and Senate on December 20, 2001" at 9 (2001).

[42] See ¶ 3.02. Under Section 2010(c) the credit amount is dependent on an applicable exclusion amount. Arguably, the Section 2201(c) rates could be used in computing the amount of the Section 2010 credit; however, Section 2201(d) provides that Section 2201(a) is not used in computing the Section 2010 credit with the result that the Section 2001(c) rates rather than the Section 2201(c) rates are used in computing the Section 2010 credit amount.

[43] See ¶ 6.02[4].

[3] Effective Dates

The provision generally applies to estates of decedents dying on or after September 11, 2001.[44] In the case of individuals dying as a result of the Oklahoma City terrorist attack, the provision applies to decedents dying after April 19, 1995.[45]

¶ 8.02 SECTION 2203. DEFINITION OF "EXECUTOR"

Section 2203 resolves a difficulty that might otherwise arise in the case of an estate for which a return should be filed or tax paid, but for which no executor was appointed. For example, Section 2002 requires "the executor" to pay the estate tax, and Section 6018 imposes upon "the executor" the duty of filing the estate tax return. With regard to these provisions, Section 2203 provides that the term "executor" includes the administrator of an estate, if one is appointed; if neither an executor nor an administrator is acting within the United States, the term "executor" also includes "any person in actual or constructive possession of any property of the decedent."[1]

The Treasury broadly construes the statutory language concerning persons in possession so as to include "among others, the decedent's agents and representatives; safe-deposit companies, warehouse companies, and other custodians of property in this country; brokers holding, as collateral, securities belonging to the decedent; and debtors of the decedent in this country."[2] However, if an executor is appointed, qualifies, and is acting, this definition, which may otherwise make persons in possession "statutory executors," is not applicable, and persons in possession cannot take advantage of the provisions concerning the

---

[44] Victims of Terrorism Tax Relief Act of 2001, Pub. L. No. 107-134, § 103(d)(1)(A), 115 Stat. 2427, 2431 (2001), reprinted in 2001-__ CB __, __. For prior law, see Stephens, Maxfield, Lind & Calfee, Federal Estate and Gift Taxation, ¶ 8.01 Warren, Gorham, & Lamont (7th ed. 1996) and see supra ¶ 8.01 text accompanying note 2.

[45] Victims of Terrorism Tax Relief Act of 2001, Pub. L. No. 107-134, § 103(d)(1)(B), 115 Stat 2427, 2431 (2001), reprinted in 2001-__ CB __, __. A special rule extends the period of limitations to permit the filing of a claim for refund resulting from this provision until one year after the date of enactment, if that period would otherwise have expired before that date. Id. at § 103(d)(2), 115 Stat. 2427, 2431 (2001), reprinted in 2001-__ CB __, __.

[1] De Niro v. United States, 561 F2d 653 (6th Cir. 1977); Estate of Guida v. Comm'r, 69 TC 811 (1978). See Hanna, "The Inadvertent Executor Under Section 2203 of the IRC," 137 Tr. & Est. 64 (Apr. 1998). Cf. IRC § 7701(a)(47).

[2] Reg. § 20.2203-1. Allen v. Comm'r, 78 TCM (CCH) 828 (1999) (son in fraudulent possession of the decedent father's assets).

discharge of the executor from personal liability under Section 2204, discussed later.[3]

The statutory definition can be important even when an executor has been appointed. Upon the discharge of the executor by the probate court, persons in actual or constructive possession of property of the decedent may become "statutory executors" to whom, among other things, a deficiency notice may properly be addressed.[4]

Section 2203 may cause a person to be recognized as the executor (albeit, a statutory one) in some circumstances in which the person would otherwise be a mere transferee of the decedent's property. In a proceeding involving the assertion of tax liability against an individual as a transferee of the taxpayer, the court does not have the jurisdiction to determine who may be entitled to a refund of an overpayment of tax made by the transferor.[5] However, in a transferee proceeding in which the transferee is also the "statutory executor," such a determination can be made.[6]

In the case of a missing person, an estate tax return must be filed by the "responsible person"[7] if the person determines from the existing facts that the absentee is dead. Facts indicating death depend on state law;[8] such facts are as follows:[9]

---

[3] Rev. Rul. 57-424, 1957-2 CB 623.

[4] See Estate of Brandt v. Comm'r, 7 TCM (CCH) 271 (1948). But see Detroit Trust Co. v. United States, 18 F. Supp. 776 (Ct. Cl. 1937) (discharged executor reappointed as administrator de bonis non, was proper party to bring suit for refund of estate tax), Estate of Sivyer v. Comm'r, 64 TC 581 (1975) (deficiency notice sent to the executor of an estate was valid, even though the executor had obtained a discharge of his personal liability, because a notice terminating the executor's fiduciary capacity had not been filed. Thus, the executor remained the proper person of record to receive deficiency notices on behalf of the estate). Cf. Estate of Guida v. Comm'r, 69 TC 811 (1978).

[5] Sniveley v. Comm'r, 20 TC 136 (1953), acq. 1955-1 CB 6. The significance of proper proceedings to assess transferee liability should not be minimized. The Seventh Circuit, in United States v. Cleavenger, 517 F2d 230 (1975), determined, where such proceedings had not been instituted, that the special ten-year lien for estate taxes was not extended by the mere commencement of litigation to foreclose under the special lien within the statutory period. Since the special lien expired before the foreclosure proceedings could be concluded, the Commissioner sought to rely on the general lien provisions to recover from the surviving joint tenant of the property that was the subject of the suit. These provisions were similarly unavailing to the Commissioner, since no deficiency had ever been assessed against the joint tenant. But see United States v. Saleh, 514 F. Supp. 8 (DNJ 1980).

[6] New York Trust Co. v. Comm'r, 26 TC 257 (1956), acq. 1956-2 CB 7; De Niro v. United States, 561 F2d 653 (6th Cir. 1977).

[7] Rev. Rul. 66-286, 1966-2 CB 485.

[8] Rev. Rul. 80-347, 1980-2 CB 342.

[9] Rev. Rul. 66-286, 1966-2 CB 485.

1. The absentee's property is administered pursuant to an adjudication by a court that the absentee is dead.
2. The absentee's property is transferred to or vested in a beneficiary under the state statute.
3. The absentee's property is taken by any person without a court order or statutory authority.
4. The absentee has been absent for seven years.[10]

In one respect, Section 2203 itself is deficient. It makes a statutory executor out of one who is "in actual or constructive possession of any property of the decedent," under the foregoing circumstances. This begs the question of whether the reference is only to property actually owned by the decedent or whether the phrase also encompasses property that the decedent did not own, but that is treated as a part of the decedent's gross estate. Although it strains the statutory language, the broader gross estate interpretation is accepted.[11] Thus, the term includes the trustee of a living trust in the absence of any other executor of the estate.[12]

A further problem is raised by the statutory executor concept: the laconic edict of Section 2002 is that "the tax imposed by this chapter shall be paid by the executor." However, exercising necessary restraint, the Treasury requires a statutory executor to pay the entire tax only "to the extent of the value of the property in his possession."[13] In some circumstances, one who is not a statutory executor and against whom proceedings are not properly brought as a transferee[14] may still be liable for estate tax under lien provisions designed to give still further assurance the estate tax can be collected.[15]

---

[10] But see Rev. Rul. 80-347, 1980-2 CB 342. See also Davie v. Briggs, 97 US 628 (1878).

[11] Estate of Wilson v. Comm'r, 2 TC 1059, 1083 (1943), acq. 1944-2 CB 30. Reg. § 20.6018-2 (which in this context makes specific reference to the "gross estate").

[12] See New York Trust Co. v. Comm'r, 26 TC 257 (1956), acq. 1956-2 CB 7 (trustees of inter vivos trusts created by decedent that were revocable, IRC § 2038, and involved retained enjoyment, IRC § 2036, were statutory executors).

[13] Reg. § 20.2002-1. It is also recognized that a statutory executor may be unable to make a complete return, in which case one is required to give whatever information one has on property interests not reported to enable the Service to require partial returns from others. Reg. § 20.6018-2.

[14] See IRC § 6901; ¶ 8.04 text accompanying note 4.

[15] IRC § 6324(a)(2). See United States v. Russell, 461 F2d 605 (10th Cir.), cert. denied, 409 US 1012 (1972), holding the transferee procedure provisions of Section 6901 "are not exclusive and mandatory, but are cumulative and alternative" to other recognized methods of tax collection.

¶ 8.03 SECTION 2204. DISCHARGE OF EXECUTOR FROM PERSONAL LIABILITY

Section 2204(a) enables an executor to secure a release from the personal liability imposed upon the executor for payment of estate taxes in general; of course, an executor is liable for estate taxes only in the executor's fiduciary capacity,[1] but every executor should know that improprieties in one's service as executor may result in personal liability for taxes imposed on the estate.

[1] Debts Due the United States

A general federal statute[2] provides that debts due the United States shall be satisfied first if the assets of the estate are insufficient to pay all debts. In these situations, a related statute[3] imposes personal liability on a fiduciary for estate debts to the United States whenever the fiduciary pays "any debts due by the . . . estate" to others before satisfying those due the United States.[4] Debts due the United States include all federal taxes, whether or not assessed.[5] The estate and gift tax regulations expressly state that an estate debt includes a beneficiary's distributive share of an estate.[6] Therefore, premature distributions to beneficiaries may create personal liability of the executor for federal taxes payable by the decedent or the estate. It is arguable that a distribution to a beneficiary, possibly excepting the payment of a pecuniary bequest,[7] should not constitute payment of a "debt" such as might invoke executor liability under the statute. However, the obvious purpose of the statute to keep the estate intact until federal tax liability has been discharged supports the broader interpretation of the regulations.[8]

It has been held that the United States does not have priority over prior specific and perfected liens[9] and certain other charges (e.g., funeral expenses,

---

[1] See IRC § 2002; ¶ 2.02.

[2] 1 USC § 3713(a) (2001).

[3] 1 USC § 3713(b) (2001).

[4] United States v. Estate of Kime, 950 F. Supp. 950 (D. Neb. 1996). Cf. Schwartz v. Comm'r, 560 F2d 311 (8th Cir. 1977).

[5] Price v. United States, 269 US 492, 499 (1926).

[6] Reg. §§ 20.2002-1, 25.2502-2. The estate tax regulations were upheld in Champlin v. Comm'r, 6 TC 280 (1946); United States v. First Huntington Nat'l Bank, 34 F. Supp. 578, 580 (SD W. Va. 1940). The gift tax regulations were upheld in Want v. Comm'r, 280 F2d 777 (2d Cir. 1960).

[7] Cf. Rev. Proc. 64-19, 1964-1 CB 682.

[8] The problem is analyzed in depth at 6 Mertens, Law of Federal Gift and Estate Taxation, § 43.06 (Lofit Publication 1960).

[9] Union Guardian Trust Co., 41 BTA 1306 (1940), acq. 1940-2 CB 7.

court costs, statutory allowances for widows, and administration costs) that are given priority by state law.[10] Consequently, there are some estate obligations that may be discharged by the executor without running the risk of personal liability.[11]

While the applicable statute does not expressly say so, a fiduciary is personally liable for federal taxes only if the fiduciary discharges obligations to creditors other than the United States with knowledge of tax liability to the United States.[12]

[2] Procedure to Gain Release From Personal Liability

Section 2204 provides a procedure under which the executor can be released from personal liability—which is important because the executor's discharge by the local probate court does not terminate the executor's liability for federal taxes.[13] Spreading the payment of estate taxes over a fourteen-year period under Section 6166 extends the period during which the executor will remain subject to personal liability. Thus, it is incumbent upon the executor to comply with Section 2204 and not just to obtain a discharge from the local probate court. The executor will remain subject to personal liability if the successor fails to pay any of the Section 6166 installments.[14] The executor may apply in writing to the IRS officer with whom the return is required to be filed[15] for a determination of the amount of the tax and a discharge from personal liabil-

---

[10] United States v. Weisburn, 48 F. Supp. 393 (ED Pa. 1943); IT 2518, IX-1 CB 158 (1930); SM 5032 V-1 CB 109 (1926); Jessie Smith v. Comm'r, 24 BTA 807 (1931), acq. 11-1 CB 6 (1932); Rev. Rul. 80-112, 1980-1 CB 306 (describing such items as charges against the property of decedent not debts of the decedent).

[11] See 6 Mertens, Law of Federal Gift and Estate Taxation, § 43.07 (Lofit Publication 1960).

[12] E.g., Irving Trust Co., 36 BTA 146, 148 (1937), acq. 1937-2 CB 15. See also 6 Mertens, Law of Federal Gift and Estate Taxation, § 43.10 (Lofit Publication 1960). The foregoing brief remarks are presented only to give point to the discussion of Section 2204. There is a comprehensive analysis of the executor's personal liability for federal taxes of a decedent and a decedent's estate in Ferguson, Freeland & Ascher, Federal Income Taxation of Estates, Trusts, and Beneficiaries, Ch. 13 (Aspen 3d ed. 1998). See also Miller, "The Fiduciary Personal Liability for Deficiencies in Federal Income, Estate and Gift Taxes of a Decedent or Decedent's Estate," 11 Gonz. L. Rev. 431 (1976).

[13] See United States v. First Huntington Nat'l Bank, 34 F. Supp. 578 (SD W. Va. 1940). Procedures under which a fiduciary may get prompt assessment of income and gift taxes are expressly inapplicable to the estate tax. IRC § 6501(d); Peterson v. Comm'r, 31 TCM (CCH) 269 (1972).

[14] Rev. Rul. 76-114, 1976-1 CB 290.

[15] Reg. § 20.2204-1. See IRC § 2002; ¶ 2.02.

ity.[16] Upon such application, Section 2204 requires that the executor be notified of the amount of the tax "as soon as possible," and the executor is discharged from personal liability upon payment of the amount determined or the posting of bond for payments that are deferred. Such notification must be given within nine months from the date the application is made or nine months after the return is filed if the application is made before the filing of the return.[17] Failure to give notification within nine months also releases the executor, but the nine-month period can probably be invoked only if the return filed is complete.[18] The notification need not be given after the expiration of the period within which the tax may be assessed under Section 6501.[19] If the Service is unable to complete the audit within the nine-month period and issue its report, it may ask the executor to withdraw the request. Presumably, a refusal by the executor to withdraw the request would result in an assertion of the largest possible deficiency, based on the agent's judgment of the particular facts, which would leave the executor vulnerable for premature distributions.

If the fiduciary pays the amount of tax specified in a notification made in response to the request, the fiduciary is discharged from personal liability for any deficiency subsequently determined and is entitled to a receipt reflecting such discharge.[20] The discharge of the executor from personal liability does not discharge the estate;[21] in fact, such a notice of deficiency sent to an executor after a discharge under Section 2204 has been held to confer jurisdiction on the Tax Court to adjudicate the liability of the estate notwithstanding the executor's release in a personal capacity.[22] Nor does the executor's release affect the lien for estate taxes on assets in the gross estate.[23]

Initially, the statute afforded no means for a fiduciary who was not an executor, as that term is defined in Section 2203, to seek assurance against personal liability. Consequently, the trustee of an inter vivos trust includible in

---

[16] An attorney for the estate has no authority as such to file the Section 2204 application, but may do so effectively if the attorney has a properly executed power of attorney to take any action the executor could take relative to estate tax liability. Rev. Rul. 65-186, 1965-2 CB 380.

[17] IRC § 2204(a).

[18] See United States v. Cruikshank, 48 F2d 352 (SDNY 1931), decided under Revenue Act of 1921, Pub. L. No. 67-98, § 407, 42 Stat. 227, 281 (1921), which specifically required the filing of a "complete return."

[19] That period is usually three years after the return was filed, but the fiduciary's liability may extend beyond this period. See, e.g., IRC § 6901(c)(3).

[20] Rev. Proc. 70-10, 1970-1 CB 437, states that the legal representative of an estate may use Form L-118, together with proof of payment, to establish that the representative's personal liability for the estate tax has been satisfied.

[21] E.g., Brainard v. Comm'r, 47 BTA 947 (1942).

[22] Estate of Tarver v. Comm'r, 255 F2d 913 (4th Cir. 1958).

[23] IRC § 6324(a)(3).

the decedent's gross estate might well hesitate to distribute trust assets for fear of incurring personal liability for estate taxes.[24] Section 2204(b) was added to give such fiduciaries an opportunity to secure release from personal liability in accordance with procedures generally similar to those applicable to executors under Section 2204(a).[25]

Section 2204(c) provides that an agreement that satisfies Section 6324A shall be treated as a furnishing of the bond[26] with respect to the tax for which the time for payment has been extended under Section 6166.

Section 2204(d)[27] provides that an executor may rely in good faith on gift tax returns filed by the decedent during life to determine the amount of adjusted taxable gifts made by the decedent. If the executor does rely on prior returns, the executor will not be personally liable for any estate tax deficiency attributable to gifts made after 1976 and more than three years before the decedent's death that are not shown on the returns. However, the executor continues to be personally liable for deficiencies attributable to post-1976 gifts made within three years of the decedent's death.

¶ 8.04 SECTION 2205. REIMBURSEMENT OUT OF ESTATE

Section 2205 is one of the five Code provisions[1] that bear on the question of where the ultimate financial burden of the tax will fall. This question must be differentiated from that of the means available to the government for collection of the tax. The statute imposes on the executor the primary obligation to pay the tax.[2] However, the tax is a lien on the gross estate property interests,[3] and

---

[24] See IRC § 6324(a)(2). Section 6324(a)(2) applies only if the trustee has property included in the decedent's gross estate under Sections 2034 through 2042. Seemingly, Section 6324(a)(2) should be extended to include Section 2044. Regardless, the trustee of a trust included under Section 2044 would still want to use Section 2204(b).

[25] Excise, Estate, and Gift Tax Adjustment Act of 1970, Pub. L. No. 91-614, § 101(d)(1), 84 Stat. 1835, 1836 (1970), reprinted in 1971-1 CB 533, 533. See S. Rep. No. 1444, 91st Cong., 2d Sess. 6 (1970), reprinted in 1971-1 CB 574, 577.

[26] The bond requirements are set out in Section 2204(a) or Section 2204(b). See Reg. § 301.6324A-1.

[27] Revenue Act of 1978, Pub. L. No. 95-600, § 702(p)(1), 92 Stat. 2763, 2937 (1978), reprinted in 1978-3 CB (Vol. 1) 1, 171.

[1] The others are Sections 2206, 2207, 2207A, and 2207B. For a discussion of all of these apportionment statutes, see Pennell, "Tax Payment Provisions and Equitable Apportionment," 22 U. Miami Inst. Est. Plan. Ch. 18 (1998).

[2] See IRC § 2002; ¶ 2.02.

[3] IRC §§ 6324(a)(1), 6324(a)(3).

transferees of estate assets may be held liable for all or part of the tax.[4] The problem dealt with in this Code section is, regardless of how or from whom the government collects the tax, whose interest in the estate must ultimately feel the pinch? Does one whose share of the estate has in fact been reduced by payment of the tax have a right to reimbursement or partial reimbursement from others? Section 2205 creates no rights in anyone prior to the final payment of the full amount of the estate tax due. This section is concerned only with the final impact of the estate tax, after the payment of the full amount due.[5]

Section 2205 has been aptly referred to as a challenging study in ambiguity.[6] No effort will be made here to explore fully its mysteries or those of the related Code provisions.[7] Still, some basic principles applicable in this troubled area can be identified.

The federal death duty is in the form of an estate tax and is thus a charge against the estate, as opposed to an inheritance tax that is a charge against the receipt of property by the several beneficiaries of an estate. Absent any special rule or principle to the contrary, the estate tax would be treated the same as any other obligation of the estate; that is, it would be paid out of the residuary estate or, if necessary, out of the particular bequests in accordance with the rules on abatement. This basic proposition seems to receive congressional recognition in the final clause of Section 2205, which expresses the intent that, if it is practicable and there is no contrary will provision, the tax shall be paid out of the estate before its distribution.[8] This obviously meshes well with Section 2002, making the executor liable for payment of the tax.

The section clearly does not fasten the burden of the tax inescapably upon the residuary legatees. If the tax is not paid by the executor in accordance with

---

[4] IRC § 6324(a)(2). Section 6324(a)(2) provides that the persons are liable to the extent of the value of such property at the decedent's death. See Armstrong v. Comm'r, 114 TC 94 (2000) (recipients of gifts within three years of the decedent's death were subject to estate tax liability for Section 2035(b) inclusion).

The circuit courts are split on the issue of whether interest accruing on the estate tax obligation may, when combined with the tax liability, exceed the value of the property. Compare Richard Baptiste v. Comm'r, 29 F3d 1533 (11th Cir. 1994) (imposing liability in excess of the value of the property because it treated the interest as a personal liability of the transferee) with Gabriel Baptiste v. Comm'r, 29 F3d 433 (8th Cir. 1994), cert. denied, 513 US 1190 (1995) (Richard's brother, whose liability was limited to tax and interest only equal to the value of the property). Cf. Poiner v. Comm'r, 858 F2d 917 (3d Cir. 1988), cert. denied, 490 US 1019 (1989) (gift tax liability limited to the value of the property).

[5] United States v. Melman, 530 F2d 790 (8th Cir. 1976).

[6] Paul, Federal Estate and Gift Taxation, § 13.54, at 775 (Little, Brown & Co. 1942).

[7] Detailed analysis appears in 6 Mertens, Law of Federal Gift and Estate Taxation, Ch. 44 (Lofit Publication 1960).

[8] IRC § 2205.

established fiduciary principles, beneficiaries whose interests have been diminished by the government's collection of tax, but who were not the ones upon whom the decedent imposed the tax burden, may be entitled to reimbursement from the estate or from other beneficiaries. While such possible rights to reimbursement are recognized in Section 2205, this section does not purport to *establish* the relative rights and obligations of the various beneficiaries,[9] which may arise from any one of several sources. The obligations of persons who have received insurance proceeds, power of appointment property, qualified terminable interest property (QTIP), or Section 2036 property are the subject of Sections 2206, 2207, 2207A,[10] and 2207B, which are discussed later in this chapter. When these sections are inapplicable, other possible sources of rights and obligations must be examined; these other sources are briefly reviewed in the following paragraphs.

[1] Will Provisions

Congress leaves it up to the decedent to say by will, if the decedent so wishes, what interests in the estate are ultimately to be diminished by the tax.[11] Thus, a decedent can specify that the entire tax is to be paid out of property otherwise specifically passing to a named beneficiary and, if the value of the beneficiary's interest is equal to or greater than the amount of the tax, no interest other than that of the named beneficiary will be reduced by payment of the tax. In fact, in the case of such a provision, if the tax were actually paid out of the residuary estate and the other property were distributed intact to the named beneficiary, Section 2205 recognizes that the residuary legatees would have a right to reimbursement from the named beneficiary. In contrast, of course, the will may require the residuary legatees to shoulder the entire tax burden.[12]

[2] State Statutes

Some states have enacted apportionment statutes that require proration of the estate tax among persons beneficially interested in the estate.[13] The premise be-

---

[9] Riggs v. Del Drago, 317 US 95 (1942).

[10] Section 2207A also applies in a gift tax context. See IRC § 2207A(b); ¶ 8.07[3].

[11] This is true even regarding interests otherwise subject to the special rules of Sections 2206 and 2207.

[12] See Chastain v. Comm'r, 59 TC 461 (1972), in which the residual charitable legatees had been so burdened.

[13] E.g., NY Est. Powers & Trusts Law, § 2-1.8 (McKinney 2001); Fla. Stat. Ch. 733.817 (2001). See Riggs, "Florida Estate Tax Apportionment," 25 U. Fla. L. Rev. 719 (1973). See also Fed. Est. & Gift Tax Rep. (CCH) ¶ 8675.16 (2000) for a listing of state

hind these statutes is that those who share financial benefit from the estate should also share the tax bite. Although a decedent can provide for this by will, the decedent may not be able to fasten tax liability on some who are in possession of assets subject to tax[14] but not subject to administration. These statutes extend the burden to such persons in accordance with a presumed testamentary intent in the absence of a contrary will provision, but of course, their effect is not limited to nonprobate property. These state apportionment statutes complement, rather than conflict with, Section 2205 and have been sustained against attack under the supremacy clause of the U.S. Constitution.[15] State apportionment statutes generally free deductible interests from any part of the tax burden. For example, if the entire interest passing from a decedent to a surviving spouse qualifies for the marital deduction, the spouse's interest, which in effect caused no tax liability to the estate, generally will bear no part of the burden of the tax. Such a rule can greatly simplify the computation of the marital deduction.[16]

Although a provision in a will can effectively allocate the tax burden in a manner different from a statutory apportionment rule, such a will provision must be drafted with great care to be assured of recognition.[17]

[3] State Common Law

Some states have recognized the apportionment principle without a specific statute.[18] A contrary will provision will also prevail over such a common-law

---

statutes. The National Conference of Commissioners on Uniform State Laws promulgated a Uniform Estate Tax Apportionment Act in 1964. See Unif. Estate Tax Apportionment Act, 8A ULA 331, 334 (2001).

[14] See discussion of Sections 2035–2042, 2044 at ¶¶ 4.07–4.14, 4.16, respectively.

[15] Riggs v. Del Drago, 317 US 95 (1942).

[16] See ¶ 5.06[5][a]. See also Estate of Ferrara v. United States, 94-2 USTC ¶ 60,181 (ND Ohio 1994) (residue passing to surviving spouse qualifying for marital deduction reduced by taxes on specific bequests); TAMs 9326002 (Mar. 18, 1993) (all liability fell on nonprobate property because all probate property constituted deductible interests), 9434004 (Aug. 26, 1994) (application of the Florida Estate Tax Apportionment Statute (Fla. Stat. Chapter 733.817 (2001)) on the funding of a credit shelter trust).

[17] See Second Nat'l Bank of New Haven v. United States, 387 US 456 (1967); In re Mill's Will, 70 NYS2d 746 (NY 1947), aff'd, 80 NE2d 535 (NY 1948). Compare Estate of Shannon v. Comm'r, 60 TCM (CCH) 1361 (1990) (will clause did not override state statute) with Estate of Ramsey v. United States, 765 F. Supp. 1388 (SD Ind. 1990) (will clause overrode state statute).

[18] E.g., McDougall v. Central Nat'l Bank, 104 NE2d 441 (Ohio 1952); Louisville Trust Co. v. Walter, 207 SW2d 328 (Ky. 1948).

rule,[19] but absent a will provision, such a common-law apportionment rule is as effective as a state statute to fix the ultimate tax burden.[20]

Depending on the circumstances, either a well-drawn will provision or a judicious silence can produce the desired results regarding the tax burden. Failure to consider the matter can, on the other hand, be catastrophic. The unexpected thrust of the tax burden on a particular interest in the estate can seriously upset an otherwise carefully constructed scheme for disposition of the estate.

It should be reemphasized that the apportionment rules under discussion here do not in any way restrict the governmental means of collecting the full estate tax due. As the regulations say of the Code's apportionment provisions:

> These provisions . . . are not designed to curtail the right of the district director to collect the tax from any person, or out of any property, liable for its payment. The district director cannot be required to apportion the tax among persons liable nor to enforce any right of reimbursement or contribution.[21]

¶ 8.05 SECTION 2206. LIABILITY OF LIFE INSURANCE BENEFICIARIES

Section 2206 provides that, in general, beneficiaries of insurance on a decedent's life are required to contribute to payment of the estate tax. However, the statute expressly permits the decedent to make a contrary direction by will.

Contribution is required only with respect to insurance proceeds that are a part of the decedent's gross estate, which is a realistic recognition of the proposition that if insurance proceeds do not in fact affect the amount of the tax, the recipient should not be called upon to bear any part of the tax burden. Moreover, the Treasury recognizes[1] that a superseding federal statutory exemption of the proceeds of National Service Life Insurance policies from the claims of creditors[2] relieves the beneficiaries of the policies from contribution

---

[19] McDougall v. Central Nat'l Bank, 104 NE2d 441 (Ohio 1952); Louisville Trust Co. v. Walter, 207 SW2d 328 (Ky. 1948); Cosby v. Shackelford, 408 F2d 1144 (10th Cir. 1969).

[20] Estate of Whipple v. United States, 419 F2d 494 (6th Cir. 1969).

[21] Reg. § 20.2205-1.

[1] Letter dated March 14, 1946, 1 United States Tax Reporter (RIA), ¶ 20,425.21(25) (2001).

[2] 38 USC § 5301 (2001). Cf. Estate of Hutson v. Comm'r, 49 TC 495, 498 (1968).

to the tax under this section, even though the proceeds of the policies can be included in the gross estate in determining the amount of tax.[3]

[1] Formula to Determine Amount of Contribution

If Section 2206 applies, subject to a qualification concerning proceeds passing to a surviving spouse, which is discussed next, a rigid formula determines the amount of contribution that the executor can exact from a beneficiary. The executor can collect an amount that bears the same relation to the total tax paid as the proceeds included in the gross estate[4] and received by the beneficiary bear to the taxable estate. This computation can be expressed as follows:

$$\text{beneficiary's share of tax} = \frac{\text{proceeds included in gross estate and received by the beneficiary}}{\text{taxable estate}} \times \text{total tax}^{[5]}$$

If there are several beneficiaries, the share of the tax burden for each is determined with reference to each beneficiary's share of the proceeds.

[2] Special Rule Concerning Marital Deduction

Insurance proceeds passing to a surviving spouse are the subject of a special rule that takes into account the marital deduction. Again, there is a statutory recognition of the proposition that if insurance proceeds do not in fact affect the amount of tax, the recipient should generally not be called upon to bear any part of the tax burden. The last sentence of Section 2206 clarifies that to the extent the insurance proceeds that pass to the surviving spouse qualify for the Section 2056 marital deduction, the spouse is not required to contribute to the payment of the tax on account of such insurance.

    A significant point here, however, is the manner used to determine whether the proceeds qualify fully. If a marital deduction for the proceeds is denied by the terminable interest rule,[6] the proceeds are taken into account in

---

[3] Similar rules should apply to Servicemen's Group Life Insurance. See 38 USC § 1970(g) (2001).

[4] Preferably, the value of the proceeds included in the gross estate should be adjusted to reflect expenses that are attributable to such proceeds and are deducted in arriving at the taxable estate. See ¶ 8.08[2] note 11.

[5] Seemingly, credits against the tax are taken into account in determining "total tax" for this purpose. But cf. United States Trust Co. of NY v. Sears, 29 F. Supp. 643 (D. Conn. 1939).

[6] IRC § 2056(b)(1). See Eggleston v. Dudley, 154 F. Supp. 178 (WD Pa. 1957), rev'd on state law issue, 257 F2d 398 (3d Cir. 1958).

determining the amount of the surviving spouse's contribution to the taxes due just as if they passed to someone other than the surviving spouse. If the proceeds qualify for a marital deduction, they generate no tax and the surviving spouse is not liable for any part of the tax with regard to those proceeds.[7]

[3] Contrary Will Provision

As indicated at the outset of the discussion of this section, a contrary provision in a will overrides this contribution section. Since 1942, the statute has expressly recognized that a contrary will provision is controlling.[8] Earlier, however, in holding a particular will provision insufficient to overcome the statutory prescription of contribution, one court at least indicated that an explicit will provision against payment of any part of the tax by the insurance beneficiary would prevail over the statute.[9] Even under the present statute, it may take a very explicit will provision to overcome the contribution rule.[10]

[4] State Law

Although Section 2206 does not authorize collection from insurance beneficiaries in the face of a contrary *will* provision, there remains the question whether it authorizes collection from insurance beneficiaries despite a contrary rule of local law. The statute makes no express exception for these cases. Although it has been long recognized that Section 2205 does not conflict with provisions of local law calling for apportionment, the Supreme Court once intimated that it might view differently the federal contribution rules on insurance and power of appointment property,[11] which do not pass through the hands of

---

[7] With the enactment of the *unlimited* marital deduction, Congress could have deleted the "except" clause of the last sentence of Section 2206. For interpretation of that provision under prior law, see Stephens, Maxfield & Lind, Federal Estate and Gift Taxation, ¶ 8.06[2] (Warren, Gorham & Lamont 4th ed. 1978).

[8] Revenue Act of 1942, Pub. L. No. 77-753, § 404(b), 56 Stat. 798, 945 (1942). This right may be disclaimed. See Estate of Boyd v. Comm'r, 819 F2d 170 (7th Cir. 1987) (disclaimer of contrary will provision).

[9] United States Trust Co. of NY v. Sears, 29 F. Supp. 643, 646 (D. Conn. 1939).

[10] In Priedeman v. Jamison, 202 SW2d 900 (Mo. 1947), contribution by insurance beneficiaries was enforced where a will provision generally exonerated each "legatee or devisee," but failed to make specific reference to insurance policies. See TAM 9915001 (Dec. 21, 1998) (sufficient provision to overcome Section 2206).

[11] See IRC § 2207; ¶ 8.06.

the executor.[12] Further, a 1986 case has held that the federal rule overrides conflicting local law.[13]

As indicated previously, Section 2206 excepts from its contribution requirements deductible interests passing to a surviving spouse. State apportionment statutes commonly afford a like exception to deductible interests passing to charity,[14] but Section 2206 does not.[15] This may be considered surprising, as deductible charitable interests do not generate estate tax liability any more than deductible marital interests do. In any event, the likely result is a clash between local and federal contribution rules; Section 2206 contains no express language suggesting that the federal rule should give way to that of the state. In light of the supremacy clause of the U.S. Constitution, it seems clear, therefore, that an explicit will provision, not merely the contrary rule of a state apportionment statute, is required to free charitable beneficiaries of includible insurance proceeds from contribution to the payment of the estate tax. However, there is no authority directly on point.[16]

The contribution rules of Section 2206, as in the case of Sections 2205, 2207, 2207A, and 2207B, do not operate to restrict governmental efforts to

---

[12] Riggs v. Del Drago, 317 US 95, 102 (1942).

[13] McAleer v. Jernigan, 804 F2d 1231 (11th Cir. 1986). Although the case recognizes the executor's ability to collect, it does not rule on the executor's duty to collect. One case has recognized such a duty. Pearcy v. Citizens Bank & Trust Co. of Bloomington, 96 NE2d 918 (Ind. Ct. App. 1951).

In one state under prior state law (see Rev. Rul. 72-612, 1972-2 CB 528), insurance proceeds passing to a surviving spouse and qualifying fully for the marital deduction had been subjected to a part of the tax burden in accordance with the state's apportionment statute. See Weinberg v. Safe Dep. & Trust Co. of Baltimore, 85 A2d 50 (Md. 1951). This might appear to have been a recognition of the proposition that a state apportionment statute is just as effective as a will to override the contribution principle of Section 2206, but the case was not a square holding on the point. The court said the state and federal statutes were not in conflict because the contribution rule of Section 2206 does not apply "to such proceeds except as to the amount thereof in excess of the aggregate amount of the marital deductions allowed." Id. at 57. Under this view, it might take a will provision to free a surviving spouse from contribution regarding insurance proceeds that do not qualify for the marital deduction, but a state would be free by statute to make its own contribution rules on insurance proceeds that do qualify.

[14] E.g., Fla. Stat. Ch. 733.817(1)(d) (2001), Fla. Stat. Ch. 733.817(3) (2001), Fla. Stat. Ch. 733.817(5) (2001).

[15] A rule similar to the marital deduction rule should be added where the proceeds qualify for a Section 2055 charitable deduction. Cf. ¶¶ 5.05 [3][b][i], 8.08[2] note 13.

[16] Cf. In re Will of King, 277 NYS2d 281 (Surr. Ct.), aff'd, 285 NYS2d 566 (App. Div. 1967), rev'd on other grounds, 239 NE2d 875 (NY 1968), cert. denied, 393 US 1086 (1969).

Section 2206

collect the tax.[17] When applicable, they simply establish rights and obligations among the persons interested in the estate.[18]

¶ 8.06 SECTION 2207. LIABILITY OF RECIPIENT OF PROPERTY OVER WHICH DECEDENT HAD POWER OF APPOINTMENT

Section 2207 provides, in general, that one who has or receives property subject to a power of appointment that is included in one's gross estate pursuant to Section 2041 must contribute to the payment of the estate tax. Again, a contrary provision in the will prevails; but it appears that a contrary rule under a state apportionment statute would not overcome the contribution requirement.[1] In the case of appointive property, a will provision may subject even a charitable recipient to greater liability for tax than would result from the application of the formula provided by Section 2207.[2]

One who acquired property by reason of the decedent's exercise, nonexercise, or release of a power of appointment may be called upon to contribute to payment of the tax only if the property was included in the decedent's gross estate.[3] The same basic formula is provided for determining the amount of contribution that may be enforced as is provided with respect to beneficiaries of insurance policies under Section 2206. In other words, the amount of the tax to be borne by one acquiring power of appointment property is determined as follows:

$$\frac{\text{value of such property in gross estate passing to the recipient}^4}{\text{taxable estate}} \times \text{total tax}^5 = \text{recipient's share of tax}$$

---

[17] Reg. § 20.2206-1.

[18] See Tannenbaum, "Insurance Proceeds and Estate Tax Apportionment: The Florida Dilemma," 29 U. Fla. L. Rev. 468 (1977).

[1] See IRC § 2206; ¶¶ 8.05[3], 8.05[4].

[2] In re King v. United Jewish Appeal, 239 NE2d 875 (NY 1968), cert. denied, 393 US 1086 (1969).

[3] See IRC § 2041; ¶ 4.13. Property subject to a nongeneral power of appointment is not subject to the contribution provision.

[4] Preferably, the value of such property in the gross estate should be adjusted to reflect deductible expenses that are attributable to such property and are deductible in arriving at the taxable estate. See ¶ 8.08[2] note 11.

[5] Seemingly, credits against the tax are taken into account in determining the "total tax" for this purpose. But cf. United States Trust Co. of NY v. Sears, 29 F. Supp. 643 (D. Conn. 1939).

If several persons acquire power of appointment property, each one bears a portion of the tax burden as determined by the foregoing formula with respect to the property received.[6]

As in the case of insurance proceeds,[7] this section also makes a special provision for property acquired by a surviving spouse; again, the effect of the marital deduction is recognized.[8] To the extent that property subject to a power of appointment and insurance proceeds includible in the gross estate and passing to the surviving spouse qualify for the Section 2056 marital deduction, such interests passing to the spouse bear no part of the estate tax burden. However, to the extent that such insurance proceeds and power of appointment property do not qualify for the marital deduction, the surviving spouse does bear a part of the tax burden on the proceeds and the appointment property.

This contribution provision, as is true of Sections 2205 and 2206, discussed earlier, and Sections 2207A and 2207B, discussed later, does not operate to restrict governmental efforts to collect the tax.[9] When applicable, it simply establishes rights and obligations among the persons interested in the estate.

There is one curious consequence of state and federal provisions that distribute the actual tax burden in accordance with the relative values of various property interests included in the gross estate. The executor's election of the alternate valuation date[10] may operate to shift the burden among the estate's beneficiaries. Assume, for example, that assets in the probate estate sharply declined in value during the six months after death, but that the gross estate included property subject to a general power that enjoyed an increase. Assume the amount of estate tax liability would be slightly less on the alternate date. The amount of tax liability borne by those interested in the probate estate and

---

[6] As applicable to estates of those who died on or before December 31, 1976, Section 2207 made reference to Sections 2502 and 2106(a), which provided specific exemption for citizens and residents and for nonresident noncitizens, respectively. These provisions were repealed in 1976. Tax Reform Act of 1976, Pub. L. No. 94-455, §§ 2001(a)(4), 2001(c)(1)(F), 2001(c)(1)(I), 90 Stat. 1520, 1848, 1852, 1854 (1976), reprinted in 1976-3 CB (Vol. 1) 1, 324, 328, 330.

[7] See IRC § 2206, discussed ¶ 8.05[2]. A provision similar to the marital deduction provision should be added when the property qualifies for a Section 2055 charitable deduction. Cf. ¶¶ 5.05[3][b][i], 8.08[2] note 13.

[8] The court in In re King v. United Jewish Appeal, 239 NE2d 875, 878 (NY 1968), cert. denied, 393 US 1086 (1969), noted that in light of the controlling provision of the will, it was unnecessary to decide whether, when Section 2207 was fully operative, Congress intended to exonerate charitable recipients from bearing their share of the tax burden. Surprisingly, as in the case of Section 2206, Section 2207 contains no such express exoneration. See ¶ 8.05[4] text accompanying note 15.

[9] Reg. § 20.2207-1.

[10] IRC § 2032. See IRC § 2032A, which may affect the value of interest in estate assets.

those in possession of the appointive property would be markedly affected by the choice of valuation date. It seems unlikely that legal principles regarding fiduciary obligations have developed to the point of answering the attending dilemma in cases such as this where a fiduciary's action affects not only interests in the probate assets, but somewhat related interests outside the probate estate.[11]

¶ 8.07 SECTION 2207A. RIGHT OF RECOVERY IN THE CASE OF CERTAIN MARITAL DEDUCTION PROPERTY

[1] Introduction

In 1981 Congress added the qualified terminable interest property (QTIP) exception to the terminable interest rule of both the federal estate tax[1] and gift tax[2] marital deductions.[3] Under the exception, a surviving or donee spouse is treated for marital deduction purposes as receiving all interests in qualifying terminable interest property, even though that spouse receives only an income interest for life.[4] The interests, other than the qualifying income interest, are either transferred for purposes of the gift and estate tax under Section 2519,[5] if the surviving or donee spouse makes an inter vivos disposition of any part of the qualifying income interest, or included in the spouse's gross estate under Section 2044,[6] if there is no inter vivos disposition. The recipient spouse or the spouse's estate is liable for the taxes resulting from the application of Section 2519 or Section 2044. This is so even though the spouse never actually owned or had the power to obtain the property interests taxed.

Section 2207A alleviates the seeming inequity of taxing the phantom transfers by permitting the spouse or the spouse's estate to call upon the persons who actually own the other interests in the property for reimbursement for the tax arising as a result of Section 2519 or Section 2044[7] attributable to their interests and for any concomitant interest and penalties.

---

[11] See Riggs, "Florida Estate Tax Apportionment," 25 U. Fla. L. Rev. 719 (1973).

[1] IRC § 2056(b)(7). See ¶ 5.06[8][d].

[2] IRC § 2523(f). See ¶ 11.03[4][c].

[3] Economic Recovery Tax Act of 1981, Pub. L. No. 97-34, § 403(d), 95 Stat. 172, 304 (1981), reprinted in 1981-2 CB 256, 325.

[4] IRC §§ 2056(b)(7)(B)(ii), 2523(f)(3).

[5] See ¶ 10.08.

[6] See ¶ 4.16.

[7] A right of recovery occurs only where there is a gift tax generated by a transfer under Section 2519 or estate tax generated by inclusion under Section 2044. IRC

[2] Estate Tax Recovery

If qualified terminable interest property is included in the spouse's gross estate under Section 2044[8] and if the spouse has not specifically provided to the contrary by will or in a revocable trust,[9] the spouse's estate[10] is entitled to recover the estate tax attributable to the inclusion from the persons receiving[11] the

---

§§ 2207A(a), 2207A(b). A disposition of all or part of a spouse's qualifying income interest is a transfer by the spouse for purposes of all three transfer taxes of all interests in the property other than the qualifying income interest. See Reg. § 25.2519-1(a); ¶ 10.08[1] text accompanying note 6. Furthermore, property transferred under Section 2519 escapes Section 2044 inclusion in the spouse's gross estate. IRC § 2044(b)(2). These rules can cause some surprising results. Assume a spouse has a qualifying income interest in a trust with a nongeneral power to appoint the remainder. If the spouse makes a gift of the qualifying income interest, there would be a Section 2511 transfer of the income interest, but the Section 2519 transfer of all other interests would not constitute a completed gift and there would be no tax generated by Section 2519 and no right of recovery. At the spouse's death, the property would be included in the spouse's gross estate under Section 2038, not Section 2044, and again there would be no right of recovery, although a creative judge might equitably apply Section 2207A(a) even though it is not literally applicable.

[8] See ¶ 4.16. The spouse's interest expires at the spouse's death, and the only interests in qualified terminable interest property included in the spouse's gross estate are the third-party interests, but of course they encompass the entire property. If the spouse made a Section 2519 transfer, nothing is included in the spouse's gross estate under Section 2044. IRC § 2044(b)(2). But see supra note 7.

[9] See IRC § 2207A(a)(2). The language in the decedent's will or revocable trust must specifically indicate the decedent's intent (e.g., by a reference to QTIP, the QTIP trust, Section 2044, or Section 2207A). HR Rep. No. 148, 105th Cong., 1st Sess. 1, 614 (1997), reprinted in 1997-4 CB (Vol. 1) 319, 936. A general provision specifying that all taxes be paid by the decedent's estate is not sufficient to waive the right of recovery. Id. If the executor waives recovery, no gift is made by the beneficiaries who would have benefitted from such recovery had it been made, since they cannot compel recovery. Reg. § 20.2207A-1(a)(3). Cf. Priv. Ltr. Rul. 200127007 (Mar. 30, 2001) (disclaimer of waived right of recovery resulted in charitable deduction).

[10] The right to claim recovery under Section 2207A is in the executor or administrator, but on their failure to exercise it, it passes to persons on whom the tax liability fell, generally the takers of the residuary estate. But see Reg. § 20.2207A-1(a)(3), discussed supra note 9.

[11] Immediate possession or enjoyment of the property may not occur. See infra ¶ 8.07[4]. If the property is in trust at the time of the spouse's death, the trustee is treated as the person receiving the property. Reg. § 20.2207A-1(d). If the property is distributed to any person prior to the expiration of the right of recovery, that person is treated as receiving the property. Id. These rules do not affect the right, if any, under local law of any person with an interest in property to reimbursement or contribution from another person with an interest in the property. Id.

property.[12] The amount of estate tax that may be recovered is determined by computing the federal estate tax liability (including interest and penalties)[13] of the spouse with and without the inclusion of the qualified terminable interest property in the spouse's gross estate. The difference is the amount the statute authorizes to be collected from the persons receiving the property.[14] Thus, the tax liability attributable to the Section 2044 inclusion is determined on a top incremental basis—"off the top"—rather than on a proportionate share basis.[15] For example, assume a spouse who has made no taxable gifts dies in 2002 with a taxable estate of $3 million, which includes $1 million of Section 2044 property. Considering the Section 2010 credit and assuming a state inheritance tax is imposed equal to Section 2011 credit, the tax on the spouse's estate with the Section 2044 inclusion is $793,500.[16] Without the Section 2044 inclusion and again applying Sections 2010 and 2011, the tax liability would be $360,300,[17] with the net result that $433,200 of tax liability is attributable to the Section 2044 inclusion and may be recovered from those persons receiving that property.

---

[12] IRC § 2207A(a)(1). The right of recovery arises when the federal estate tax with respect to the property includible under Section 2044 is paid by the estate. Reg. § 20.2207A-1(a)(1).

[13] IRC § 2207A(d); Reg. § 20.2207A-1(b).

[14] IRC § 2207A(a)(1). See Reg. §§ 20.2207A-1(b), 20.2207A-1(e) Ex. If more than one property interest is involved, the amount determined above is prorated among the property interests according to their relative amounts of inclusion in the gross estate after any deduction allowed with respect to each property. Reg. § 20.2207A-1(c). See infra ¶ 8.07[4] text accompanying notes 30, 31.

[15] Reg. § 20.2207A-1(b). As a result, there is no right of recovery from any person for the portion of property received by that person for which a deduction was allowed from the gross estate if no tax is attributable to that property, i.e., as a marital or charitable deduction. Reg. § 20.2207A-1(a)(1).

Although the regulations and statute do not specifically provide for considering Section 2053 deductions allowed to the decedent's estate in making this computation, they should be taken into account in some instances. If an expense for which a Section 2053 deduction is allowed in the computation of the estate tax is paid out of the qualified terminable interest property, it should be taken into consideration in the determination of the value of the Section 2044 property used in the apportionment formula. There should be no reduction in the value of the Section 2044 property used in the apportionment formula for expenses not paid out of the qualified terminable interest property or for those expenses for which a Section 2053 deduction is waived under Section 642(g) regardless of the source of payment. Cf. ¶ 8.08[2] note 11.

[16] The Section 2001 liability is $1,275,800 reduced by a $345,800 Section 2010 credit and a $136,500 Section 2011 credit ($182,000 under Section 2011(b)(1), reduced by $45,500 under Section 2011(b)(2)).

[17] The Section 2001 liability is $780,800 reduced by a $345,800 Section 2010 credit and a $74,700 Section 2011 credit ($99,600 under Section 2011(b)(1), reduced by $24,900 under Section 2011(b)(2)).

[3] Gift Tax Recovery

A similar rule applies to the recovery of gift tax generated by a Section 2519 inter vivos transfer.[18] The amount of the gift tax depends on the gift-giving history of the spouse.[19] Once again, the amount recoverable is determined on a top incremental basis, "off the top."[20] The amount of liability (including interest and penalties) the spouse would have had if the Section 2519 transfer had not occurred is subtracted from the spouse's gift tax liability for the year, including the Section 2519 transfer and interest and penalties.[21] The net result is the amount of tax that is apportioned to those receiving the property[22] and is therefore recoverable from them.[23] The Section 2519 transfer may use a part of the spouse's unified gift tax credit,[24] but there is no right of recovery for any amount of the unified credit consumed,[25] harsh as this rule may seem.

The spouse has the right to recover gift taxes paid on property treated as transferred under Section 2519 from the recipients of that property. If the spouse dies before exercising the right of recovery, the right to use the recovery provision does not die with the spouse. Recovery by the estate is permitted[26] if such recovery is claimed within a reasonable time after the tax is actually paid.[27]

---

[18] IRC § 2207A(b). The right of recovery arises at the time the gift tax is actually paid by the transferor. Reg. § 25.2207A-1(a).

[19] Cf. IRC § 2502.

[20] IRC § 2207A(b). See supra ¶ 8.07[2] text accompanying note 15.

[21] IRC §§ 2207A(b), 2207A(d); Reg. § 25.2207A-1(c).

[22] If the property is in trust at the time of the transfer, the trustee is treated as the person receiving the property. Reg. § 25.2207A-1(e). If the property, other than the qualifying income interest, is distributed to any person prior to the expiration of the right of recovery, that person is treated as receiving the property. Id. These rules do not affect the right, if any, under local law of any person with an interest in property to reimbursement or contribution from another person with an interest in the property. Id.

[23] IRC § 2207A(b). See Reg. §§ 25.2207A-1(c), 25.2207A-1(f) Ex. If more than one property interest is involved, the amount determined above is prorated among the property interests according to their relative amount of net taxable gifts made during the calendar year. Reg. § 25.2207A-1(d). See infra ¶ 8.07[4] text accompanying notes 30, 31.

[24] IRC § 2505.

[25] See HR Rep. No. 201, 97th Cong., 1st Sess. 1, 162 (1981), reprinted in 1981-2 CB 352, 379.

[26] Reg. § 25.2207A-1(a). Compare the interrelationship of Sections 2035(b) and 2207A. See ¶ 10.08[3].

[27] See Reg. § 25.2207A-1(a) (last sentence). If the spouse's will directs against recovery, the will provision should prevail. Cf. IRC § 2207A(a)(2).

[4] Whose Liability?

The Code provides that "if there is more than one person receiving the property, the right of recovery shall be against each such person."[28] Although neither the Code nor the legislative history suggests the extent to which the tax burden may be shifted to any one person receiving property,[29] the regulations provide that the recoverable tax is to be apportioned among the recipients of property interests according to the relative values of their interests at the time of the Section 2519 transfer or the Section 2044 inclusion, thus limiting the recovery from any one person receiving property.[30] The result is sensible, because the recovery is not the exaction of a tax but the enforcement of contribution to the payment of tax due. For example, if the remainder interest passes equally to two children, the recoverable tax is apportioned equally among the children.[31] If a recovery attributed to Section 2044 property occurs while the property is still held by the trustee prior to distribution to the beneficiaries, the tax is recovered from the trustee.[32]

The Section 2207A right of recovery may create a hardship in some situations.[33] A simple hypothetical example illustrates the difficulty. Suppose Donor makes an inter vivos transfer giving Donee Spouse a *legal life estate*, remainder to their children, and there is a valid QTIP election. At a time when Spouse's legal life estate is worth $100,000 and the remainder is worth $200,000, Spouse gives the legal life estate to a third party. As a result of the gift, Section 2519 applies and there is a transfer by Spouse that *should* be equal to the value of a net gift of the remainder worth $200,000 less the Section 2207A recoverable amount,[34] in addition to Spouse's routine Section 2511

---

[28] IRC § 2207A(c).

[29] Conceivably, under the statutory language the entire amount of the recoverable tax could be sought from one of multiple recipients of the property.

[30] See Reg. §§ 20.2207A-1(c), 25.2207A-1(d).

[31] If the childrens' interests were not equal in value, the recovery is made according to the relative values of the childrens' interests. Thus, if in the hypotheticals supra ¶ 8.07[2] text accompanying notes 16 and 17, Son received $400,000 and Daughter received $600,000 of the $1 million Section 2044 amount, the $433,200 amount of recovery would be allocated $173,280 to Son and $259,920 to Daughter. Reg. § 20.2207A-1(c).

[32] Reg. § 20.2207A-1(d). The fact that the trustee is treated as the person receiving the property alleviates any problem in the recovery of the tax under Section 2207A where the property continues in trust with a secondary life estate following the life estate of a spouse and where there are both contingent and vested remainderpersons. Reg. §§ 20.2207A-1(d), 20.2207A-1(e) Ex. Cf. ¶ 8.03[2] note 24

[33] Cf. IRC § 6163(a).

[34] Under proposed regulations, the Section 2519 transfer resulting in a taxable gift was treated as a "net gift." Prop. Reg. § 25.2519-1(a), 1984-1 CB 598, 612. The amount treated as transferred was reduced by "the amounts that the spouse is entitled to recover under Section 2207A (relating to the right to recover taxes attributable to the remainder interest)." Id. See ¶ 10.01[6][d]. The final regulations covering the effect of the gift tax

transfer of the legal life estate. The hardship is that the children may be called upon to pay the recoverable tax, even though they are not in possession of the property. Admittedly, they might be able to sell their future interest to generate the necessary tax dollars; but this seems so harsh that, if it is the result, Congress should provide at least for deferral of the payment of the tax.[35] If the transfer were *in trust*, and an equitable life estate rather than a legal life estate was established, the liability would fall on the trustee and the tax would be paid with assets comprising the corpus of the trust.[36] The Section 2519 transfer again *should* be the value of the remainder at the date of disposition less the amounts the spouse is entitled to recover under Section 2207A.[37] If so, determination of the amount of the Section 2519 transfer requires an interdependent variable computation.

The value of the income interest transferred under Section 2511 should be diminished if the gift tax imposed on the Section 2519 transfer is paid by the trustee out of trust corpus. If the spouse's qualifying income interest is gifted

---

recovered under Section 2207A on the amount of the transfer are reserved. Reg. § 25.2519-1(c)(4). But see Reg. § 25.2207A-1(f) Ex. (implying that there is no net gift where the amount of the remainder gift is not reduced to reflect any tax recovery).

Section 2207A(b) should be viewed as a statutory "net gift" agreement between the donor spouse and the person receiving the property, and the amount transferred as a result of Section 2519 should be reduced by any amount the spouse is entitled to recover under Section 2207A. As in the case of a net gift (where a donee agrees with the donor to discharge the donor's gift tax on a gift to the donee), the donor spouse is primarily liable for the tax. Although the statute allows a shifting of liability (see IRC § 2207A(b)), as in the case of a net gift, the shift is not a mandatory shift required by statute. Cf. Rev. Rul. 80-111, 1980-1 CB 208.

If there is a net gift, the value of the remainder interest transferred requires an interdependent variable computation because the amount of the tax affects the amount of the gift and the amount of the gift determines the amount of the tax.

If the donor waives the right of recovery that arises when the tax is actually paid (Reg. § 25.2207A-1(a) (last sentence)) there is an additional gift. In all likelihood, this gift will occur in the calendar year following the year in which the Section 2519 transfer occurs when the tax is paid on that transfer and the waiver is made. In the example in the text, the full value of the remainder, $200,000, would be subjected to the gift tax over two calendar years assuming the gift tax was paid when due and the waiver was made at that time.

[35] Cf. IRC § 6163(a). An alternative result that is not harsh and is consistent with the treatment of transfers in trust is to charge the tax to the assets producing the life estate, so that the burden is borne both by the recipient of the spouse's life estate and the children. The justification would be the language of Section 2207A(b) authorizing recovery from "the person receiving the property," in that both the life tenant and the children are receiving the property because the life estate and the remainder are inseparable unless the life estate is commuted.

[36] Reg. § 25.2207A-1(e). Cf. Reg. § 20.2207A-1(d).

[37] But see Reg. § 25.2519-1(c)(4) (reserving such a rule from the regulations); supra note 34. Cf. Reg. § 25.2207A-1(b). An appropriate result here might be to treat the life estate assets as a trust. See supra note 35.

and the gift tax attributed to the Section 2519 transfer is recovered from the trust corpus, the amount of the Section 2511 transfer of the income interest should be reduced to reflect the reduced value of the trust corpus.

A similar hardship could arise as a result of a Section 2044 inclusion. Generally, upon the spouse's death, the remainderpersons acquire possession of the property from which to pay the taxes. However, if the spouse's interest is followed by a secondary legal life interest, say, to the donor spouse's sibling, possession by the remainderpersons is delayed even though the tax recovery is due presently.[38]

[5] The Possibility of Indirect Gifts

When the spouse does not waive the right of recovery,[39] failure to assert rights of recovery of estate tax under Section 2207A(a) following a Section 2044 inclusion constitutes a transfer of property within Section 2511.[40] With regard to estate tax, the executor, or seemingly upon the executor's failure to act, those entitled to the residuary estate (or anyone whose hide bears the brunt of the tax) may seek recovery of the estate tax attributable to the inclusion of property under Section 2044 from the persons receiving the property.[41] Failure to seek recovery is an indirect gift by the persons whose interests are reduced by the tax (normally the residuary takers) to the persons from whom the tax was recoverable.[42] The amount of the gift is the value of the right of recovery. The Treasury has reserved regulations on whether an indirect gift may likewise occur upon a failure to recover gift tax arising out of a Section 2519 transfer.[43]

---

[38] Although it can be argued that Section 6163(a) might be used to postpone the estate's payment of tax, its application does not ensure a postponement of the estate's recovery under Section 2207A(a), even though regulations should provide for a postponement.

If the property is held in trust, the Section 2207A tax liability falls on the trustee. See Reg. § 20.2207A-1(d).

[39] Reg. § 20.2207A-1(a)(3).

[40] Reg. § 20.2207A-1(a)(2). The transfer is made when the right of recovery no longer exists under local law. Id. A delay in the exercise of the right of recovery may be an interest-free loan under Section 7872. Id. See ¶ 10.01[2][f]. Of course, there would have to be a recovery right to pose this problem. Recall that in some cases no right exists if the spouse's will or revocable trust directly precludes it. IRC § 2207A(a)(2). See supra ¶ 8.07[2] note 9.

[41] Reg. § 20.2207A-1(a)(1).

[42] Reg. § 20.2207A-1(a)(2).

[43] Reg. § 25.2207A-1(b). Cf. Reg. § 20.2207A-1(a)(2) (applicable only to Section 2044 recoveries.) See supra ¶ 8.07[4] notes 34, 37.

However, the spouse does make an indirect transfer to the persons from whom the spouse had a right of recovery, and the Treasury should treat it as such.[44]

[6] Effective Dates

Section 2207A is applicable to transfers after December 31, 1981.[45] The regulations are generally effective for decedents dying and dispositions made after March 1, 1994.[46] With respect to estates of decedents dying or gifts made on or before such date, any reasonable interpretation of the statutory provisions may be relied on.[47]

¶ 8.08 SECTION 2207B. RIGHT OF RECOVERY WHERE DECEDENT RETAINED INTEREST

[1] Introduction

With the enactment of Section 2207B, Congress has continued its trend of allowing a right of recovery for transfer taxes against recipients of property not passing through the probate estate[1] or in situations where one does not make

---

[44] Section 2207A should be viewed as a possible statutory "net gift" agreement between the spouse and the persons receiving the property in the Section 2519 transfer. The donor spouse remains primarily liable for the tax as is the case where the donee agrees with the donor to discharge the donor's gift tax on a gift to the donee. If a donor discharges gift tax that the donee had agreed to pay in a "net gift" agreement, the donor makes an additional gift to the donee. The same result should occur where the spouse disposing of all or a portion of a qualifying income interest elects not to seek reimbursement from the person receiving the property under Section 2207A or where the heirs of the donor spouse following a Section 2519 transfer that is a completed gift opt not to seek reimbursement from the recipient of the property under Section 2207A.

[45] Economic Recovery Tax Act of 1981, Pub. L. No. 97-34 § 403(e)(1), 95 Stat. 172, 305 (1981), reprinted in 1981-2 CB 256, 326.

[46] Reg. §§ 20.2207A-2, 25.2207A-2.

[47] Reg. §§ 20.2207A-2, 25.2207A-2. Regulations Sections 20.2207A-1 and 25.2207A-1 (as well as the proposed regulations appearing in LR-211-76, 1984-1 CB 598, 611–612) are considered to be a reasonable interpretation of the statute with respect to decedents dying or gifts made prior to March 1, 1994.

[1] A right of recovery presently exists against the beneficiaries of life insurance policies on a decedent's life under Section 2206; against the recipients of power of appointment property under Section 2207; and against persons receiving qualified terminable interest property upon termination of the interest of a surviving or donee spouse under Section 2207A(a). See ¶¶ 8.05–8.07.

an actual inter vivos transfer of property.[2] Section 2207B allows a right of recovery against a recipient of property included in a decedent transferor's gross
estate under Section 2036.[3] As with the previously allowed rights of recovery,
Section 2207B extends its right of recovery to include the amount of any penalties and interest attributable to the estate or gift tax liability involved.[4]

[2] Estate Tax Recovery

If property is included in a decedent's gross estate under Section 2036,[5] the estate is entitled to recover a pro rata share of the estate tax attributable to the
property from the recipient of the property.[6] By the very nature of Section
2036, property that is included in a decedent's gross estate is not part of the
decedent's probate estate. Thus, without some type of statutory assistance, probate property (generally the residuary estate) would potentially become liable
for the estate taxes on the nonprobate Section 2036 property.[7] To make the
rule inapplicable, a decedent must specifically direct in a provision of the decedent's will that the Section 2207B right of estate tax recovery is waived.[8] In

---

[2] Under Section 2519, a right of gift tax recovery exists where one does not actually
own a property interest but nevertheless is treated as transferring it. See IRC § 2207A(b);
¶ 8.07[3].

[3] IRC § 2207B(a). See IRC § 2036; ¶ 4.08.

[4] IRC § 2207B(c).

[5] Section 2036(a) is applicable where the decedent made a transfer and retained either
the right to the income or the possession or enjoyment of property or the right to determine who will receive such income or possession or enjoyment of the property for the decedent's life, for a period that cannot be ascertained without reference to the decedent's
death, or for any period that does not in fact end before the decedent's death. See ¶ 4.08.
In addition, Section 2036(b) treats certain retention of voting rights as a retention of the
enjoyment of property under Section 2036(a)(1). See ¶ 4.08[6][d].

[6] IRC § 2207B(a)(1). Section 2207B seems to apply when both Sections 2036 and
2038 are applicable to include the same property in a gross estate. For example, if a decedent sets up a revocable trust in which the decedent retains a life estate, both Sections
2036 and 2038 are applicable to pull the full amount of trust corpus into the decedent's
gross estate. Section 2207B should apply under such circumstances to provide for estate
tax recovery. One wonders why reimbursement provisions similar to Section 2207B have
not been added for other gross estate inclusion provisions such as Sections 2037, 2038,
2039, and 2040.

[7] But see the discussion of Section 2205 relating to will provisions or state law altering these consequences. See ¶¶ 8.04[1], 8.04[2]. Section 2207B(a)(1) (like Sections 2206,
2207, and 2207A) overrides these other rules unless Section 2207B(a)(3) applies.

[8] IRC § 2207B(a)(2). The directive must specifically state the decedent's intent, although a specific reference to Section 2207B is not required. For estates of decedents dying prior to August 6, 1997, specific reference to Section 2207B was required. See TAM
9915001 (Dec. 21, 1998). See also IRC § 2206; ¶ 8.05[3] text accompanying note 10;
IRC §§ 2207, 2207A(a)(2).

addition, Section 2207B permits a decedent to make such a direction by means of a revocable trust instrument.[9]

The amount that the estate is entitled to recover is computed on a proportional share basis. It is the amount that bears the same ratio to the total estate tax paid as the value[10] of the property included in the gross estate under Section 2036 bears to the total taxable estate.[11] This amount can be computed as follows:

$$\frac{\text{amount of Section 2036 property in gross estate}}{\text{taxable estate}} \times \text{total tax} = \text{recipient's share of tax}^{12}$$

If more than one person receives an interest in the property, the right of recovery extends to each such person.[13] The statutory language could conceiva-

---

[9] IRC § 2207B(a)(2). The legislative history states that this alternative applies only if the decedent dies without a will and so directs in a provision of a trust that serves as a substitute for a will. Joint Comm. on Tax'n, Explanation of Finance Committee Amendment to S. 2238 (Technical Corrections Act of 1988, as reported) (JCX-28–88) at 5 (Sept. 12, 1988).

[10] The property would be valued employing the same valuation date or valuation method used for the remainder of the gross estate. See IRC §§ 2031, 2032, 2032A.

[11] Preferably, the value of the property included under Section 2036 should be adjusted to reflect administrative and other expenses that are attributable to such property and are deducted in arriving at the taxable estate. See, e.g., IRC § 2053(a)(2). This would provide for a recovery of taxes more proportionate to the value of the property included in the taxable estate. The statute uses instead the gross value of the property for purposes of this ratio. In so doing, Congress is allowing recovery of more tax than the property might actually have generated. See also IRC §§ 2206, 2207, which are structured in the same manner. ¶¶ 8.05[1] text accompanying note 4, 8.06 text accompanying note 4. Cf. ¶ 8.07[2] note 15.

[12] IRC § 2207B(a)(1). Since the amount is based on tax "paid," credits against the estate tax should be allowed prior to this computation. But cf. United States Trust Co. of NY v. Sears, 29 F. Supp. 643 (D. Conn. 1939). See also IRC §§ 2206, 2207, discussed ¶¶ 8.05[1] note 5, 8.06 note 5.

[13] IRC § 2207B(c). However, there is no right of recovery against the charitable recipient of a charitable remainder trust, as described in Section 664. IRC § 2207B(d). Because the charitable remainder will qualify for a Section 2055 deduction and thus generate no estate tax, it would be inappropriate to allow a right of recovery from such property. Since this rule applies only to trusts described in Section 664 (charitable remainder annuity trusts and charitable remainder unitrusts), the rule is inapplicable to a pooled income fund under Section 642(c)(5). Cf. IRC § 2055(e)(2)(A).

Congress was too narrow in its exceptions to a right of recovery. It should provide an exception for any property included in the decedent's gross estate that qualifies for either a Section 2055 charitable deduction or a Section 2056 marital deduction from the gross estate. Because such property is not included within the taxable estate, it generates no estate tax liability and should not be responsible for any reimbursement. For example, if a decedent made an inter vivos transfer of property, either retaining a life estate with a re-

bly nail each person for the entire amount of the tax liability, but it more likely should be interpreted to apportion the liability among the recipients of the property interests according to the relative values of their interests at the time of the Section 2036 inclusion.[14]

The provision is effective for transfers after November 10, 1988, the date of the enactment of Section 2207B.[15]

¶ 8.09 SECTIONS 2208 AND 2209. CITIZENSHIP AND RESIDENCE OF CERTAIN RESIDENTS OF POSSESSIONS

These sections sometimes determine whether an estate is subject to tax under Section 2001, which applies to citizens and residents, or to tax under Section 2101, which applies to nonresident noncitizens. Section 2208 provides that a citizen of the United States who is a resident of a U.S. possession at death will be considered a U.S. citizen for estate tax purposes, unless the person acquired U.S. citizenship solely because the person was a citizen of such possession or because of birth or residence within such possession. This section, which is applicable to estates of decedents dying after September 2, 1958, overcomes a Tax Court decision that a native-born U.S. citizen who later became a resident and citizen of Puerto Rico without losing U.S. citizenship was a nonresident

---

mainder to charity or to a pooled income fund, the property would be included in the decedent's gross estate under Section 2036(a)(1); however, at the decedent's death it would fully qualify for a Section 2055 deduction as an outright transfer to charity and would generate no estate tax liability. Similar results apply with respect to property qualifying for the Section 2056 marital deduction. A technical correction is needed. Compare Sections 2206 and 2207, providing for the marital deduction, but note their omission of an exception for any charitable interests. See ¶¶ 8.05[2], 8.05[4] text accompanying note 15, 8.06 text accompanying notes 7, 8.

[14] This is the more sensible result, because the recovery is not the exaction of a tax but the enforcement of contribution to the payment of tax due. Regulations should endorse the apportionment concept. For example, if the remainder interest passes equally to three children, the recoverable tax should be apportioned equally among all three children. This liability should fall on any contingent as well as any vested remainderperson. Similarly, if the trust involves a secondary life interest (after the transferor's life interest) followed by a remainder, the secondary income beneficiaries, as well as the remainderpersons, should be liable for the recoverable tax. Cf. ¶ 8.07[4] text accompanying notes 30–32 applying these types of rules to rights of recovery under Section 2207A.

[15] Technical and Miscellaneous Revenue Act of 1988, Pub. L. No. 100-647, § 3031(h)(3), 102 Stat. 3342, 3639 (1988), reprinted in 1988-3 CB 1, 299; S. Rep. No. 445, 100th Cong., 2d Sess. 532 (1988).

noncitizen for estate tax purposes.[1] Section 2209, which was enacted in 1960 and is applicable to estates of decedents dying after September 14, 1960, confirms that residents and citizens of U.S. possessions who satisfy the "unless" clause of Section 2208 will be considered nonresident noncitizens.[2] A contrary result was reached under the 1939 Code.[3] Identical statutory definitions are provided for gift tax purposes in Sections 2501(b) and 2501(c).

¶ 8.10 SECTION 2210. TERMINATION

[1] Introduction

Section 2210[1] provides that decedents dying after December 31, 2009, are no longer subject to the Chapter 11 federal estate tax, effectively terminating the tax for such decedents.[2] Congressional thinking is that the estate tax is unduly burdensome to all taxpayers, especially those owning businesses, and more specifically small, family-owned, and farming businesses.[3] However, the estate tax is not repealed; it remains as a part of the Code. Thus, various provisions contained in the estate tax have continued viability after the year 2009 for decedents who died prior to January 1, 2010.[4] Although the estate tax terminates,

---

[1] Smallwood v. Comm'r, 11 TC 740 (1948), acq. 1949-1 CB 3. See also Fairchild v. Comm'r, 24 TC 408 (1955), which reached the same result in the case of a U.S. citizen who was a resident of the Virgin Islands at death. The cases were decided under the 1939 Code, which was applicable to estates of nonresident citizens who resided beyond the limits of the U.S. territories and possessions. IRC § 802, 53 Stat. 1, 119 (1939).

[2] Regulations Sections 20.2208-1 and 20.2209-1 contain illustrations of the rules. In Rev. Rul. 74-25, 1974-1 CB 284, the Service ruled that a decedent who acquired U.S. citizenship by birth in Puerto Rico and died in the Virgin Islands is considered a nonresident noncitizen under Section 2209. See IRC §§ 2501(b), 2501(c); ¶ 9.02[1] note 5; Priv. Ltr. Rul. 200105048 (Nov. 2, 2000) (Section 2209 applied to a gift transfer).

[3] Estate of Rivera v. Comm'r, 19 TC 271, aff'd, 214 F2d 60 (2d Cir. 1954).

[1] A prior version of Section 2210 provided for the transfer of liability for payment of the estate tax from an executor to an employee stock ownership plan (ESOP) or eligible worker-owned cooperative on the transfer of employer securities to the ESOP or EWOC. The section was repealed with respect to estates of decedents dying after July 12, 1989. Omnibus Budget Reconciliation Act of 1989, Pub. L. No. 101-239, § 7304(b), 103 Stat. 2106, 2353 (1989). The section is discussed in Stephens, Maxfield, Lind & Calfee, Federal Estate and Gift Taxation, ¶ 8.10, Warren, Gorham & Lamont (7th ed. 1997).

[2] IRC § 2210(a). Section 2664 provides for the termination of the generation-skipping transfer tax for generation-skipping transfers occurring after December 31, 2009. See ¶ 18.04.

[3] HR Rep. No. 37, 107th Cong., 1st Sess. 25 (2001), reprinted in 2001-__ CB __, __.

[4] See infra ¶ 8.10[2].

the gift tax continues to apply even after the year 2009,[5] and in general, transfers at death are subject to a modified carry-over basis system under the income tax.[6] However, the estate tax termination is currently scheduled to be terminated, with the result that the termination of the estate tax and the substitution of the modified carry-over basis are eliminated for years after the year 2010 under a "sunset" provision.[7]

[2] Nonterminating Provisions

Because Section 2210(a) makes Chapter 11 inapplicable only to the estates of decedents dying after December 31, 2009, several provisions of Chapter 11 have continued viability with respect to the estates of decedents who die prior to January 1, 2010. This is proper because the estates of those decedents have received tax benefits, and the commitments made under the estate tax in existence when they died should be kept, even though the estate tax is terminated for decedents who die after the year 2009.

[a] Qualified Domestic Trust Distributions

Because the qualified domestic trust (QDOT) provisions result in a mere deferral of tax on a decedent spouse's taxable estate,[8] if a decedent spouse died prior to the year 2010, the normal QDOT distribution rules[9] should continue to apply to the decedent spouse's estate, even though the distributions occur after the year 2009. In general, the distribution rules continue to apply; however, some generous rules apply that sometimes terminate the normal distribution rules.[10] The regular QDOT distribution rules are inapplicable to distributions from a QDOT upon the death of the surviving spouse in any year after

---

[5] Seemingly out of a concern for abusive assignments of income that could occur if the gift tax were repealed and the possibility that a donor would have a window of opportunity to make significant inter vivos gifts in the year 2010 (a year when the estate tax does not apply prior to the "sunset" provision taking effect in the year 2011, see infra ¶ 8.10[5]), the gift tax is not repealed in the year 2010 or thereafter. See ¶ 9.01. See Blattmachr & Gans, "Wealth Transfer Tax Repeal: Some Thoughts on Policy and Planning," 140 No. 2 Tr. & Est. 49 (Feb. 2001). The gift tax continues in its current form with the same $1 million applicable exclusion amount under the Section 2505 credit, the annual exclusion, and the exclusion of transfers for qualified education and medical expenses. See ¶¶ 9.04, 9.06. However, the gift tax is imposed at a flat 35 percent rate, equal to the maximum income tax rate imposed at that time. See ¶ 9.03[2].

[6] See infra ¶ 8.10[3].
[7] See infra ¶ 8.10[5].
[8] See ¶ 5.07[4][b].
[9] See ¶ 5.07[4].
[10] IRC § 2210(b).

the year 2009.[11] In addition, even if the surviving spouse is not dead, the distribution rules are terminated for any distributions made after December 31, 2020.[12]

[b] Other Nonterminating Estate Tax Provisions

Several other provisions also have continued vitality after the year 2009.

[i] Section 2032A. If the estate of a decedent who dies prior to the year 2010 elects to use the special valuation under Section 2032A, the recapture ("gotcha") provisions of Section 2032A[13] imposing an additional estate tax continue to apply if a disqualifying event occurs.[14] The additional estate tax possibly may be imposed until December 31, 2019.

[ii] Section 2057. Although Section 2057, the deduction for qualified family-owned business interests, does not apply to estates of decedents dying after December 31, 2003,[15] if the estate of a decedent who died prior to that date elected to use the deduction, the recapture provisions of Section 2057[16] potentially continue to apply until December 31, 2013.[17]

[iii] Section 2031(c). Failure to implement a plan to restrict redevelopment rights within two years of the decedent's death on property that has qualified for a conservation easement exclusion under Section 2031(c) in the estate of a decedent dying prior to the year 2010 may result in the imposition of ad-

---

[11] IRC § 2210(b)(2). See IRC § 2056A(b)(1)(B); ¶ 5.07[4]. Because the QDOT taxation provision is a tax on the decedent's estate (see ¶ 5.07[4][b]), without this special rule the QDOT distribution would have been taxed even where the surviving spouse died after the year 2009. Cf. infra ¶¶ 8.10[2][b], 8.10[5].

[12] IRC § 2210(b)(1). See IRC § 2056A(b)(1)(A); ¶ 5.07[4]. Without this special rule, since the QDOT taxation provision is a tax on the decedent's estate (see ¶ 5.07[4][b]), the QDOT distribution rules would have applied indefinitely. Cf. infra ¶¶ 8.10[2][b], 8.10[5].

[13] See IRC § 2032A(c); ¶ 4.04[7].

[14] HR Rep. No. 37, 107th Cong., 1st Sess. 186 (2001), reprinted in 2001-__ CB __,

__.

[15] IRC § 2057(j). See ¶¶ 5.08[1], 5.08[4][b].

[16] See IRC § 2057(f); ¶ 5.08[5].

[17] HR Rep. No. 37, 107th Cong., 1st Sess. 186 (2001), reprinted in 2001-__ CB __,

__.

ditional estate tax[18] under Section 2031(c)(5)(C). That subsection potentially applies until December 31, 2011.[19]

[iv] Section 6166. If the estate of a decedent who dies prior to the year 2010 is allowed to defer payments of the estate tax under Section 6166, the acceleration provisions contained in Section 6166 continue to apply if a disqualifying event occurs.[20] An acceleration of payment may occur until almost nine months after December 31, 2023.[21]

[3] Income Tax Consequences

[a] Introduction

The benefits of the termination of the estate tax are not granted without exacting potential income tax detriments to the recipients of the decedent's property.[22] Under current law, the income tax basis for most assets included in an individual's gross estate at the individual's death is automatically adjusted, *up or down*, according to the fair market value of the assets on the date of the individual's death.[23] This is commonly referred to as a step-up in basis for appreciated assets. With the termination of the estate tax for individuals dying after December 31, 2009,[24] Section 1014 is replaced by Section 1022 providing for a modified "carry-over" basis system. This carry-over basis regimen is similar in many respects to the basis determined under Section 1015 for lifetime gifts.[25] For some, this conjures up memories of the short-lived 1976 congressional experimentation with a carry-over basis at death under then Section

---

[18] See IRC § 2031(c)(5)(C); ¶ 4.02[7][d] note 342.

[19] See HR Rep. No. 37, 107th Cong., 1st Sess. 186 (2001), reprinted in 2001-__ CB __, __.

[20] See IRC § 6166(g); ¶ 2.02[3][c][vi].

[21] See IRC §§ 6166(a)(3), 6166(g); HR Rep. No. 37, 107th Cong., 1st Sess. 186–187 (2001), reprinted in 2001-__ CB __, __.

[22] Since the generation-skipping transfer tax is also terminated (see IRC § 2664, ¶ 18.04), no step-up in basis is allowed under Section 2654(a). See ¶ 17.04[1].

[23] IRC § 1014(a)(1). But see several exceptions to this rule under Sections 1014(a)(2), 1014(a)(3), 1014(c), and 1014(e). See also IRC § 2031(c).

[24] IRC § 2210(a); supra ¶ 8.10[1].

[25] However, because no estate tax is paid, there will be no increase in the basis of the transferred property that is directly related to transfer taxes paid as can occur with respect to gifts. See IRC §§ 1015(d)(1), 1015(d)(6).

1023.[26] After a public outcry, that provision was retroactively repealed in 1980, when Congress resurrected Section 1014.[27]

The modified carry-over basis regimen is applicable only to "property acquired from a decedent" after December 31, 2009.[28] The term "acquired from a decedent" is broadly defined to encompass any "*property*"[29] that would have been included in the decedent's gross estate under the current estate tax if it had not been terminated.[30] Thus, it includes property acquired by the decedent's estate from the decedent or property acquired from the decedent by bequest, devise, or inheritance.[31] It also includes property transferred inter vivos by the decedent to a qualified revocable trust[32] or to any trust with respect to which the decedent has reserved the right to make any change in enjoyment through the power to alter, amend, or terminate the trust.[33] Finally, the term broadly encompasses any other property passing from the decedent by reason of death, to the extent that such property passed without consideration.[34] This would include property held as joint tenants with a right of survivorship or as tenants by the entirety[35] or property held in an inter vivos trust created by a decedent where the decedent held an interest in the property in the trust, even

---

[26] Tax Reform Act of 1976, Pub. L. No. 94-455, § 2005(a)(2), 90 Stat. 1520, 1872 (1976), reprinted in 1976-3 CB (Vol. 1) 1, 348.

Section 1023 is distinguishable from the current Section 1022 legislation, because when Section 1023 was enacted, the estate tax continued in existence.

[27] Crude Oil Windfall Profit Tax Act of 1980, Pub. L. No. 96-223, § 401, 94 Stat. 229, 299 (1980), reprinted in 1980-3 CB 1, 71.

[28] IRC § 1022(a)(1). However, like the estate tax termination (see supra ¶ 8.10[1]), the carry-over basis regimen is currently slated to be sunsetted in the year 2011. See infra ¶ 8.10[5].

[29] The provision applies only to "property," so any cash received, especially the receipt of life insurance proceeds, would not be subject to these rules. Cf. IRC §§ 101(a), 2042. Similarly, cash payments included in a decedent's gross estate under Section 2035(b) (see ¶ 4.07[3]) would not be included. Cash would also include annuity payments in cash (cf. IRC § 2039); but see also IRC § 1022(f), which makes Section 1022 inapplicable to items of income in respect of a decedent. Cf. infra ¶ 8.10[3][b][iv].

[30] IRC § 1022(e). It also encompasses property that would have been subject to the Section 2031(c) exclusion. IRC § 1022(e)(3) infra text accompanying note 34. See ¶ 4.02[7].

Compare infra ¶ 8.10[3][b][iii] more narrowly defining "ownership," which is required in order to make any basis adjustments to such property. See infra ¶ 8.10[3][b].

[31] IRC § 1022(e)(1).

[32] IRC § 645(b)(1). Cf. IRC § 2038.

[33] IRC § 1022(e)(2). Cf. IRC § 2038; ¶ 4.08. Seemingly, in order to qualify for the adjustments considered infra ¶ 8.10[3][b], such property must be held in either type of such trusts at the date of the decedent's death. See infra ¶ 8.10[3][b] text accompanying note 75.

[34] IRC § 1022(e)(3).

[35] Cf. IRC § 2040; ¶ 4.12.

though the decedent held no powers over the trust.[36] It is unclear whether it in-cludes property subject to a general power of appointment created by another person and held by the decedent.[37] The rules are specifically inapplicable to any items of income in respect of a decedent.[38]

Although the carry-over basis rules apply to the broad range of property "acquired from a decedent," the advantageous rules allowing an upward adjust-ment to the carry-over basis apply only if the decedent "*owned*" such property, a term that is much more narrowly defined.[39]

Under the carry-over basis regimen, the income-tax basis of an asset pass-ing at death will generally be the lesser of the adjusted basis of the asset in the hands of the decedent or the fair market value of the asset on the date of the decedent's death.[40] Once the estate tax is eliminated, and the carry-over basis system applies to transfers of property at death, the decedent's estate or benefi-ciaries may incur an income tax upon sale of assets acquired from the dece-dent that had appreciated in value prior to the decedent's death. Property that has depreciated in value that is acquired from a decedent will have its basis adjusted downward to the property's fair market value on the date of the dece-dent's death, precluding the decedent's estate or beneficiaries from deducting the loss on sale of the property.[41]

---

[36] Cf. IRC §§ 2035, 2036, 2037; ¶¶ 4.07, 4.08, 4.09.

[37] IRC § 2041. Theoretically it would include such property, but statutorily such property might not be included. The question is academic because such property does not qualify for any basis adjustments (see infra ¶ 8.10[3][b] text accompanying notes 76–79), and such property will simply be allowed a carry-over basis in any event.

[38] IRC § 1022(f). See ¶ 4.05[4]. To the extent an item is an item of income in re-spect of a decedent, it is accorded a zero basis.

[39] IRC § 1022(d)(1)(A). See infra ¶ 8.10[3][b], especially ¶ 8.10[3][b][iii].

[40] IRC § 1022(a)(2). For decedents with taxable estates of $3.5 million or less who have done no taxable inter vivos giving or whose combined taxable estate and adjusted taxable gifts are less than $3.5 million, it may be beneficial to die in years prior to the year 2010, even though the estate tax is terminated in the year 2010. See ¶ 8.10[1]. The reason is that such persons will pay no estate tax because of the Section 2010 applicable exclusion amount (see ¶ 3.02), but their estates or heirs will still be able to take advantage of the Section 1014 step-up in basis. Of course, many such estates will also be stepped-up to fair market value as a result of the basis adjustments discussed infra ¶ 10.01[3][b]. The applicable exclusion amount is less than $3.5 million for years prior to 2009. See IRC § 2010(c); ¶ 3.02.

[41] However, such losses may be indirectly allowed. See IRC § 1022(b)(2)(C)(ii), infra ¶ 8.10[3][b] text accompanying note 53.

[b] Adjustments to the Carry-Over Basis

The executor[42] or administrator of the decedent's estate may "step up" the adjusted basis of a decedent's appreciated assets under two separate rules, in effect exempting an amount of unrealized gain from the income tax.[43] Under the first adjustment, the aggregate adjusted basis of the decedent's assets may generally be increased by an amount of $1.3 million, regardless of who is the recipient of the property.[44] In addition, the adjusted basis of assets transferred to a surviving spouse either outright or in certain other ways, may be increased by an additional $3 million.[45] The result is that, if the decedent is survived by the decedent's spouse, $4.3 million of basis increase is potentially available to assets acquired from the decedent. Adjustments are made on an asset-by-asset basis, for example, a block of stock or a single share of stock.[46] However, the adjusted basis of an asset may not be increased above its fair market value as of the date of the decedent's death (thus making it impossible to create artificial losses).[47] The basis adjustment rules are subject to some other limitations. They apply only to property "acquired from the decedent"[48] only if the property was "owned" by the decedent at death.[49] Furthermore, the adjustment rules are inapplicable to some types of property.[50]

[i] **Increase in basis regardless of the recipient.** Potentially an executor may increase the adjusted basis of the decedent's assets transferred to anyone generally by $1.3 million.[51] The $1.3 million amount is increased by the amount of the decedent's unused capital loss carryover at death under Section 1212(b) and the amount of any of the decedent's unused net operating loss carryover under Section 172, either of which would (but for the event of death) be carried from the decedent's last taxable year to a later taxable year.[52] The $1.3 million amount is also increased by the amount of any losses that

---

[42] IRC § 7701(a)(47). Cf. IRC § 2203; ¶ 8.02.

[43] IRC §§ 1022(b), 1022(c), 1022(d).

[44] IRC § 1022(b)(2). See infra ¶ 8.10[3][b][i].

[45] IRC § 1022(c). See infra ¶ 8.10[3][b][ii].

[46] See infra ¶ 8.10[3][b][v].

[47] IRC § 1022(d)(2).

[48] See supra ¶ 8.10[3][a] text accompanying notes 28–38.

[49] IRC § 1022(d)(1)(A). See infra ¶ 8.10[3][b][iii].

[50] See infra ¶ 8.10[3][b][iv].

[51] IRC § 1022(b)(2)(B). Nonresidents who are not U.S. citizens may increase the basis of their property by only up to $60,000. IRC § 1022(b)(3)(A). The Section 1022(b)(2)(C) adjustments discussed infra text accompanying notes 52 and 53 are inapplicable to the potential $60,000 adjustment available to a nonresident noncitizen. IRC § 1022(b)(3)(B).

[52] IRC § 1022(b)(2)(C)(i).

would have been deductible under Section 165 if the property acquired from the decedent had been sold at fair market value immediately before the decedent's death.[53] The $1.3 million amount is adjusted for inflation occurring after the year 2009.[54]

[ii] **Increase in basis for surviving spouses.** An executor may also increase the adjusted basis of property transferred to a surviving spouse[55] by a total of $3 million, if the property is "qualified spousal property," that is, property that passes "outright" to the spouse or passes as "qualified terminable interest property."[56] Outright bequests to a surviving spouse qualify only if they are not terminable interests under a test identical to the terminable interest rule applicable under the estate tax marital deduction provision.[57] The Section 2056(b)(3) condition on survival for a limited period exception to the terminable interest rule applies to such transfers.[58] However, property passing to a surviving spouse in a trust subject to a general power of appointment held by the spouse or a similar interest[59] is not treated as an outright transfer and does not qualify for the $3 million basis adjustment.[60] Qualified terminable interest

---

[53] IRC § 1022(b)(2)(C)(ii). The effect of this Section 165 rule is to allocate the amount of any "step-down" in the basis of assets, which have declined in value prior to the decedent's death and whose sale would result in a deduction under Section 165(c) because they are business or investment assets (see IRC §§ 165(c)(1), 165(c)(2)), to any other assets that have appreciated in value. The adjustment would not apply to any potential losses under Section 165(c)(3).

[54] IRC § 1022(d)(4)(A). A similar adjustment is made to the $60,000 amount applicable to nonresident noncitizens. Id. The inflation adjustments will be made in $100,000 and $5,000 increments, respectively. IRC § 1022(d)(4)(B).

[55] The $3 million adjustment does not apply to a nonresident, noncitizen surviving spouse. IRC § 1022(b)(3)(B).

[56] IRC § 1022(c).

[57] IRC § 1022(c)(4)(B). See IRC § 2056(b)(1); ¶ 5.06[7]. Although property transferred to a surviving spouse in a marital deduction estate trust is a transfer in trust, it does not violate the terminable interest rule (see ¶ 5.06[7][c] text accompanying notes 194, 195) and it should be treated as an "outright" transfer qualifying for the adjustment. For estate tax purposes, one's estate is essentially treated the same as oneself and consequently a transfer to a surviving spouse's estate should be treated as a transfer to the surviving spouse under Section 1022(c)(4)(A). Cf. IRC § 2056(b)(1)(A); ¶ 5.06[7][c] note 194.

[58] IRC § 1022(c)(4)(C). See IRC § 2056(b)(3); ¶ 5.06[8][a]. If there is such a clause and, as a result, the property does not pass to the surviving spouse, then there is no potential $3 million adjustment.

[59] IRC §§ 2056(b)(5), 2056(b)(6). See ¶¶ 5.06[8][b], 5.06[8][c]. See also supra ¶ 8.10[3][a] text accompanying note 37.

[60] IRC §§ 1022(c)(3), 1022(c)(4), 1022(c)(5). As a policy matter, it is questionable why such trusts do not qualify for the adjustment.

property[61] is similar to Section 2056(b)(7) property[62] in that it is property that passes from the decedent,[63] from which the spouse is entitled for life to all the income payable annually or at more frequent intervals,[64] and no portion of which may be appointed to anyone other than the surviving spouse during the surviving spouse's lifetime.[65] The $3 million amount is adjusted for inflation occurring after the year 2009;[66] however, unlike the $1.3 million adjustment, the amount is not adjusted for any income tax carryovers or potential losses.[67]

[iii] **Ownership.** To qualify for either type of increase in basis, the property must be "owned" or treated as owned by the decedent at the time of death.[68] "Ownership" is defined more narrowly than the current gross estate ownership inclusion provisions, and thus, it does not include all properties "acquired from the decedent" that are described earlier.[69] The statute provides some specific rules of ownership,[70] but it does not specifically define the term "owned" as that term is used under the statute. Congress needs to tighten up the statute by specifically defining the term "owned." It is arguable that any property "acquired from a decedent"[71] would be treated as "owned" by the decedent, unless the statute otherwise provides some special rule under the special rules that are discussed next:

Joint Tenancy with Spouse. In the case of property held as joint tenants or tenants by the entireties with the surviving spouse, the statute tracks Section

---

[61] IRC § 1022(c)(5).

[62] See ¶ 5.06[8][d]. However, no election is required. Cf. IRC § 2056(b)(7)(B)(i)(III).

[63] IRC § 1022(c)(5)(A)(i).

[64] IRC §§ 1022(c)(5)(A)(ii), 1022(c)(5)(B)(i). A usufruct interest in the property for life also qualifies. Id. To the extent provided in regulations, an annuity shall be treated similarly to an income interest in property (regardless of whether the property from which the annuity is payable can be separately identified). IRC § 1022(c)(5)(B) (flush language). See IRC § 2056(b)(7)(B)(ii) (flush language); ¶ 5.06[8][d][ii].

[65] IRC §§ 1022(c)(5)(A)(ii), 1022(c)(5)(B)(ii). See IRC § 2056(b)(7)(B)(ii)(II); ¶ 5.06[8][d][ii]. The definition of qualified terminable interest property also incorporates two other rules from Section 2056(b)(7). The term "property" includes an interest in property. IRC § 1022(c)(5)(C). See IRC § 2056(b)(7)(B)(iii). Furthermore, a specific portion of property is treated as separate property. IRC § 1022(c)(5)(D). See IRC § 2056(b)(7)(B)(iv); ¶ 5.06[8][d][ii].

[66] IRC § 1022(d)(4)(A). The inflation adjustments will be made in $250,000 increments. IRC § 1022(d)(4)(B)(iii).

[67] See supra text accompanying notes 52, 53. Any such adjustment would provide a double benefit of such attributes to the recipients of property.

[68] IRC § 1022(d)(1).

[69] See supra ¶ 8.10[3][a] text accompanying notes 28–38.

[70] IRC § 1022(d)(1)(B).

[71] See supra ¶ 8.10[3][a] text accompanying notes 28–38.

2040(b), and only one half of the property is treated as having been owned by the decedent and thus being eligible for the basis increase.[72]

Joint Tenancy with Others. In the case of property held as joint tenants with right of survivorship with a person other than the surviving spouse, the statute is patterned after Section 2040(a). The portion of the property attributable to the consideration furnished by the decedent is treated as having been owned by the decedent and is eligible for a basis increase.[73] If the property was acquired by the joint tenants by gift, bequest, devise, or inheritance, and their interests are not otherwise specified or fixed by law, the decedent shall be treated as the owner to the extent of the value of a fractional part, which is to be determined by dividing the value by the number of joint tenants.[74]

Revocable Trust. The decedent is treated as the owner of property if the property was transferred by the decedent during life to a qualified revocable trust (as defined in Section 645(b)(1)).[75] It makes sense that the property must be held in the trust at the time of the decedent's death to qualify for the adjustments under this provision, although the statute is not that specific.

Powers of Appointment. The decedent is not treated as owning any property solely by reason of holding a power of appointment with respect to such property (whether a special or general power of appointment).[76] Thus, such property is not provided any basis adjustments. Therefore, property held in a Section 2056(b)(5) general power marital deduction trust[77] does not qualify for the $3 million increase at the decedent spouse's death[78] nor a $1.3 million basis adjustment at the death of the surviving spouse. Presumably, if the surviving spouse held and exercised a general power in favor of the surviving spouse's estate, the property would be eligible for the basis adjustment.[79]

Community Property. The decedent is treated as owning the surviving spouse's one-half share of community property (which will be eligible for a basis increase) if at least one-half share of the whole of the community interest is treated as owned by, and acquired from, the decedent.[80] This rule applies to property that is not currently included in the decedent spouse's gross estate

---

[72] IRC § 1022(d)(1)(B)(i)(I). Cf. IRC § 2040(b); ¶ 4.12[10].

[73] IRC § 1022(d)(1)(B)(i)(II). Cf. IRC § 2040(a); ¶¶ 4.12[1]–4.12[8].

[74] IRC § 1022(d)(1)(B)(i)(III). Cf. IRC § 2040(a); ¶ 4.12[6].

[75] IRC § 1022(d)(1)(B)(ii). Cf. ¶ 4.10. Seemingly, a trust over which a decedent has a Section 2038 power under the current law (see ¶ 4.10[4]) other than a power to revoke the trust is not treated as "owned" by the decedent. Cf. supra text accompanying note 71.

[76] IRC § 1022(d)(1)(B)(iii). Cf. supra ¶ 8.10[3][a] text accompanying note 37.

[77] See ¶ 5.06[8][b].

[78] See supra text accompanying notes 59, 60.

[79] However, there may be nontax reasons, such as creditor issues, why making such an exercise would not be desirable.

[80] IRC § 1022(d)(1)(B)(iv). The surviving spouse's one-half share is also treated as acquired from the decedent. Id. Cf. IRC § 1014(b)(6).

and it is therefore distinguishable from the special rules, noted earlier. However, it is similar to the generally beneficial rule of Section 1014(b)(6), and it allows basis adjustments to the surviving spouse's one half of the community property, even though such property was not actually owned by the decedent.[81]

Qualified Terminal Interest Property. The statute does not provide any special rules with respect to a surviving spouse's ownership of qualified terminable interest property that is included in the surviving spouse's gross estate under Section 2044.[82] Without a special rule similar to Section 2044, it appears that property held in a QTIP trust at the death of the surviving spouse is ineligible for the *surviving spouse's* $1.3 million basis adjustment.[83]

[iv] Ineligible property. Certain types of property are made specifically ineligible for any of the adjustments to basis.[84]

Property Acquired Within Three Years of Death. Property that was acquired by the decedent by gift or by an inter vivos transfer for less than adequate and full consideration during the three-year period ending on the date of the decedent's death is ineligible for any adjustments.[85] There is an exception to this three-year rule for property acquired from the decedent's spouse, unless the decedent's spouse also acquired the property during such three-year period in whole or in part by gift or by inter vivos transfer for less than adequate and full consideration.[86]

---

[81] For example, if Decedent and Spouse own community property with an adjusted basis of $1.7 million that is worth $6 million (each owns $3 million of community property), the basis of both halves of the community property are stepped-up to $3 million at Decedent's death, even though only one-half is actually owned by Decedent.

[82] See ¶ 4.16. But see ¶ 4.16 text accompanying notes 20–23 not aggregating the interest with other property owned by the surviving spouse for valuation purposes.

[83] Seemingly, the result would be different if the trustee of the QTIP trust distributed the property out of the QTIP trust to the surviving spouse before the surviving spouse's death.

[84] Because property that constitutes a right to receive income in respect of a decedent is not within Section 1022 (IRC § 1022(f)), such property does not qualify for a basis adjustment.

[85] IRC § 1022(d)(1)(C)(i). This rule is similar to Section 1014(e) except that it involves a three-year (rather than one-year) time frame and it does not require a transfer of the property by the decedent back to the donor of the property. The purpose of the rule is to preclude near-death transfers of property taking advantage of the basis increases.

[86] IRC § 1022(d)(1)(C)(ii). This is consistent with the income tax policy of allowing tax-free interspousal transfers. See IRC § 1041. However, it precludes an interspousal transfer where the transferor spouse transfers property that violates the Section 1022(d)(1)(C)(i) rule. IRC § 1022(d)(1)(C)(ii). Thus, a surviving spouse may make a transfer to a decedent spouse (during that spouse's life) to take advantage of the $3 million adjustment (as the property is transferred back at decedent spouse's death to the surviving spouse) as long as the surviving spouse had not acquired the property by gift (in whole or in part) from a third person within three years of the decedent's death.

Foreign Personal Holding Company. Stock or securities of a foreign personal holding company are ineligible for any basis adjustments.[87]

Domestic International Sales Corporation. Stock of a domestic international sales corporation (or former domestic international sales corporation) is also ineligible.[88]

Foreign Investment Companies. Stocks of a foreign investment company and stock of a passive foreign investment company (except that for which a decedent shareholder had made a qualified electing fund election) are similarly ineligible.[89]

[v] Allocation of the basis adjustments. The executor of the decedent's estate[90] is permitted to allocate both the potential $1.3 million and the $3 million adjustments to any qualifying property;[91] however, the adjustments may not increase the basis of any asset above its fair market value.[92] The allocation is made on an asset-by-asset basis, with the result that generally an executor has a broad amount of discretion to decide which appreciated assets will receive a basis adjustment and the extent of the increase. The allocation is made on an informational return required after the year 2009 by Section 6018.[93] Once made, the allocation may be changed only as allowed by the Service.[94]

[c] Special Rules for Treatment of Gain

Several of the post-estate tax termination provisions deal with the treatment of gains under the income tax law.

[i] Character. The character of gain on the sale of property received from a decedent generally is treated the same as if the property had been acquired by gift.[95] Thus, the character of gain is normally determined by the character of the property in the donee's hands.[96] However, for example, real estate that has been depreciated and would be subject to ordinary income re-

---

[87] IRC § 1022(d)(1)(D)(i).

[88] IRC § 1022(d)(1)(D)(ii).

[89] IRC §§ 1022(d)(1)(D)(iii), 1022(d)(1)(D)(iv). See IRC § 1295.

[90] IRC § 7701(a)(47). Cf. IRC § 2203; ¶ 2.02.

[91] IRC § 1022(d)(3)(A). Although the federal law allows such discretion, state fiduciary law may impose important fairness restrictions with the respect to the allocation of such adjustments.

[92] IRC § 1022(d)(2).

[93] IRC § 1022(d)(3)(A). This is the return relating to large transfers at death. See infra ¶ 8.10[3][d][ii].

[94] IRC § 1022(d)(3)(B).

[95] IRC § 1022(a)(1).

[96] However, the tacking of holding periods would apply. IRC § 1223(2).

capture gain if sold by the decedent would be subject to recapture gain if sold by the recipient of the property.[97]

[ii] Pecuniary bequests. A nonrecognition rule provides that gain on the transfer of property by an executor in satisfaction of a pecuniary bequest is recognized only to the extent that the fair market value of the property at the time that the pecuniary bequest is satisfied exceeds the fair market value of the property on the date of the decedent's death (not the property's carry-over basis).[98] These same rules apply to trusts to the extent provided by regulations.[99] The adjusted basis of property acquired in an exchange to which the pecuniary bequest rule applies is the adjusted basis of the property held before the transfer appropriately increased by the amount of gain recognized on the transfer.[100]

[iii] Liability in excess of basis. Another nonrecognition rule provides that gain is not recognized at the time of death when an estate or beneficiary, other than a tax-exempt beneficiary,[101] acquires property from the decedent that is subject to a liability greater than the decedent's adjusted basis in that property.[102] Similarly, no gain is recognized by the estate on the distribution of such property to a beneficiary of the estate other than to a tax-exempt beneficiary.[103] Thus, except with respect to a tax-exempt beneficiary,[104] in determining whether gain is recognized and in determining the adjusted basis of such property, liabilities in excess of basis are disregarded.[105]

[iv] Sale of residence. The benefit of the decedent's income tax exclusion of up to $250,000 of gain on the sale of a principal residence[106] is extended to the decedent's estate, other recipients of the residence, or to a trust

---

[97] See IRC §§ 1250(b)(1), 1250(b)(3), 1250(d)(1).

[98] IRC § 1040(a). Prior to 2010, a similar rule applied to transfers of property to a qualified heir if the property was valued under Section 2032A. IRC § 1040(a).

[99] IRC § 1040(b). If regulations are not promulgated prior to the year 2010, a Section 645 election might be prudent with respect to a qualified revocable trust.

[100] IRC § 1040(c). The adjusted basis would include any Section 1022(b) or Section 1022(c) adjustments.

[101] Under Section 1022(g)(2), a tax-exempt beneficiary includes (1) the United States, any state or political subdivision thereof, any U.S. possessions, any Indian tribal government, or any agency or instrumentality of the above; (2) any organization exempt from tax (other than a Section 521 farmers' cooperative); or (3) any foreign person or entity (see IRC § 168(h)(2)).

[102] IRC § 1022(g)(1)(A).

[103] IRC § 1022(g)(1)(B).

[104] In the case of a transfer to a tax-exempt beneficiary, gain would be recognized to the extent of the excess of the liabilities over the adjusted basis of the property, because it represents the last opportunity for the government to capture such gain.

[105] IRC § 1022(g).

[106] IRC § 121.

that immediately before death was a qualified revocable trust established by the decedent.[107] If the decedent's estate or a person who acquired the residence from the decedent or a qualified revocable trust sells the decedent's principal residence, up to $250,000 of gain may be excluded provided that the decedent owned and used the property as a principal residence for two or more years during the five-year period prior to the sale.[108] In addition, if an heir or a beneficiary occupies the property as a principal residence, the decedent's period of ownership and use is tacked on to the recipient's subsequent ownership and use in determining whether the property was owned or used for two or more years as a principal residence during the five-year period prior to the sale.[109] As a result of this rule, an executor might not want to allocate a decedent's potential increase in basis adjustments to a principal residence.

[v] **Certain foreign transfers.** Gain is recognized on the transfer of an asset by a U.S. person to a foreign estate or trust or to a nonresident noncitizen.[110] The amount of gain is the difference between the fair market value of the property transferred and its adjusted basis.[111]

[d] Reporting Requirements

New reporting rules and penalties for failure to satisfy such rules are applicable after the year 2009.

[i] **Lifetime gifts.** A donor who is required to file a gift tax return under Section 6019(a)[112] is, in addition, required after the year 2009 to furnish certain information by written statement to each recipient of such property.[113] The statement must show the name, address, phone number of the donor,[114] and the information required on the gift tax return with respect to the property received by the person (e.g., a description of the property, the adjusted basis of the property, and the value of the property).[115] This information must be furnished

---

[107] IRC §§ 121(d)(9)(A), 121(d)(9)(B), 121(d)(9)(C). See also IRC §§ 645(b)(1), 1022(e).

[108] IRC §§ 121(a), 121(b)(1), 121(d)(9).

[109] IRC §§ 121(a), 121(b)(1), 121(d)(9) (flush language), 121(d)(9)(B). As a result of this rule, an executor may want to give close consideration to which heir or beneficiary to whom the residence is distributed.

[110] IRC § 684. Prior to 2010, Section 684 provided the same rule; however, it was inapplicable to a nonresident noncitizen.

[111] IRC § 684.

[112] See ¶ 9.04[9].

[113] IRC § 6019(b).

[114] IRC § 6019(b)(1).

[115] IRC § 6019(b)(2).

to the recipient of the property not later than thirty days after the date the gift tax return is filed.[116]

[ii] **Transfers at death.** Where transfers of property acquired from a decedent[117] of noncash assets exceeding $1.3 million[118] or transfers of appreciated property received by a decedent within three years of death that is ineligible for any basis adjustment[119] and which was required to be reported on a gift tax return,[120] the executor of the estate[121] is required to file an informational return.[122] The informational return must provide the following: (1) the name and taxpayer identification number of the recipient of the property; (2) an accurate description of the property; (3) the adjusted basis of the property in the hands of the decedent and its fair market value at the time of death; (4) the decedent's holding period for the property; (5) sufficient information to determine whether any gain on the sale of the property would be treated as ordinary income; (6) the amount of basis increase allocated to the property under Section 1022(b) or Section 1022(c);[123] and (7) any other information as the Treasury Secretary may prescribe.[124] If the executor is unable to make a complete return as to any property, the executor is to include in the return a description of the property and the name of every person holding a legal or beneficial interest therein.[125] Similar information (including the name, address, and phone number of the person filing the return) is required to be provided to each recipient of such property within thirty days after the date the return is filed.[126]

[iii] **Penalties for failure to file required information.** Any person required to report to beneficiaries and donees under Section 6018(e) or Section

---

[116] IRC § 6019(b) (flush language).

[117] IRC §§ 1022(e), 6018(d). See supra ¶ 8.10[3][a] text accompanying notes 28–38.

[118] IRC § 6018(b)(1). See IRC § 1022(b)(2)(B); supra ¶ 8.10[3][b][i]. The $1.3 million amount is adjusted for inflation after the year 2010. IRC § 1022(d)(4).

[119] See IRC § 1022(d)(1)(C).

[120] IRC § 6018(b)(2). See IRC § 1022(d)(1)(C), discussed supra ¶ 8.10[3][b] text accompanying notes 85, 86; IRC § 6019(a), discussed ¶ 9.04[9] text accompanying notes 197–205.

[121] IRC § 7701(a)(47). Thus, the term executor would include the trustee of a revocable trust. Id. Cf. IRC § 2203; ¶ 8.02.

[122] IRC § 6018(a). The provision also applies to a nonresident noncitizen decedent where tangible property situated in the United States and other property acquired from the decedent by a U.S. person has a value exceeding $60,000 (as adjusted for inflation). IRC §§ 1022(b)(3), 1022(d)(4), 6018(b)(3).

[123] See supra ¶ 8.10[3][b].

[124] IRC § 6018(c).

[125] IRC § 6018(b)(4). Upon notification from the Service, such persons shall file a similar return with respect to such property. Id.

[126] IRC § 6018(e).

6019(b)[127] will incur a penalty of $50 for each failure to report such informa-
tion to a beneficiary.[128] Any person required to furnish any information under
Section 6018 for transfers at death who fails to do so timely would be liable
for a penalty of $10,000 for the failure to report such information[129] (or $500
in the case of each failure to furnish information in accordance with Section
6018(b)(2) relating to gifts received by the decedent within three years of
death).[130] No penalty is imposed with respect to any failure that is due to reasonable cause.[131] If any failure to report to the Service or a beneficiary is due
to intentional disregard of the rules, then the penalty is 5 percent of the fair
market value of the property for which reporting was required, determined at
the date of the decedent's death (for property passing at death) or determined
at the time of gift (for a lifetime gift).[132]

[4] Section 2511(c)

After the year 2009, the gift tax survives the termination of both the estate and
the generation-skipping transfer taxes.[133] The rationale for the continuation of
the gift tax is to avert significant inter vivos gifts during the year 2010 window of opportunity and to avert assignments of income in any year.[134] In keeping with averting assignments of income, Congress enacted Section 2511(c)
seemingly to assure that if income from property placed in trust, either the income generated by the trust or the income on the corpus of the trust is assigned and it is not taxable to the grantor or the grantor's spouse under the
grantor trust rules,[135] the transfer of the property generating that income is a
transfer of property by gift.[136]

Section 2511(c) alters the normal rules of Section 2511 in very limited
circumstances. The provision does not appear to alter the well-established
transfer rules of Section 2511(a) with respect to completed gifts.[137] If a gift is

---

[127] See supra ¶¶ 8.10[3][d][i], 8.10[3][d][ii].

[128] IRC § 6716(b).

[129] IRC § 6716(a). See supra ¶ 8.10[3][d][ii].

[130] IRC § 6716(a) (parenthetical). See supra ¶ 8.10[3][d][ii].

[131] IRC § 6716(c). Cf. ¶ 2.02[1] text accompanying notes 14–16.

[132] IRC § 6716(d). The deficiency procedures of subchapter B of Chapter 63 do not
apply to the assessment or collection of any of the previously stated penalties. IRC
§ 6716(e).

[133] See supra ¶ 8.10[1] text accompanying note 5.

[134] See supra ¶ 8.10[1] note 5.

[135] IRC §§ 671–679. See Ferguson, Freeland & Asher, Federal Income Taxation of
Estates, Trusts, and Beneficiaries, Chapter 10 (Aspen 3d ed. 1998).

[136] IRC § 2511(c).

[137] See ¶¶ 10.04–10.09.

already treated as a completed gift under Section 2511(a), it remains a completed gift, even though the grantor or the grantor's spouse is treated as owning the property for income tax purposes.[138] A transfer that would not otherwise be a completed transfer under Section 2511(a), under which the income is shifted to the transferee in whole or in part, is subject to Section 2511(c). For example, if Donor creates an inter vivos trust with income to Donee for life, a reversion to Donor if living at Donee's death, and, if not, remainder to Donee's children and if the value of Donor's reversion on the creation of the trust is less than 5 percent of the value of the trust, the ordinary income from the trust would be taxed to Donee.[139] Even though Donor's reversion would normally not be treated as a completed gift,[140] Section 2511(c) converts the value of the reversionary interest to a completed gift.[141] Similarly, if Donor had a power to revoke a trust in which Donor was not a beneficiary, but held the power only after ascertainable events under which Donor's power was worth less than 5 percent of the value of the trust,[142] the value of Donor's power of revocation would be a completed gift.[143]

Section 2511(c) is not effective until the year 2010[144] and as a result of the "sunset" provision,[145] currently has only a one-year life expectancy.

---

[138] Thus, a "defective grantor trust," a transfer in trust that is complete for gift tax purposes, but is incomplete for income tax purposes (because either the grantor or the grantor's spouse is treated as owning the property for income tax purposes) is unaffected by Section 2511(c).

[139] IRC § 673(a). The corpus income would be taxed to Donor under Section 677(a)(2). Reg. § 1.671-3(b)(2).

[140] See ¶ 10.01[3][d]. But see IRC § 2702, ¶ 19.03.

[141] If either Donee or Donee's child were a member of Donor's family under Section 2704(c)(2), Section 2702 would have valued Donor's retained interest at zero and the entire value of the property would be a completed gift without the assistance of Section 2511(c). See ¶ 19.03.

[142] For income tax purposes, the ordinary income from the trust would be taxed to Donee, although the corpus income would be taxed to Donor. IRC § 676(b), Reg. § 1.671-3(b)(2).

[143] But see supra note 141.

[144] Economic Growth and Tax Relief Reconciliation Act of 2001, Pub. L. No. 107-16, § 511(f)(3), 115 Stat. 38, 71 (2001), reprinted in 2001-__ CB __, __.

[145] Economic Growth and Tax Relief Reconciliation Act of 2001, Pub. L. No. 107-16, § 901, 115 Stat. 38, 150 (2001), reprinted in 2001-__ CB __, __. See infra ¶ 8.10[5].

[5] The "Sunset" Provision

Each of the provisions of The Economic Growth and Tax Reconciliation Act of 2001 is currently scheduled to terminate after December 31, 2010.[146] This means the estate and the generation-skipping transfer taxes will be terminated for only one year and the concurrent income tax modified carry-over basis system will be in effect for only one year. The estate tax will not be imposed on the estates of decedents dying in the calendar year 2010, and generation-skipping transfers in the calendar year 2010 will not be subject to the generation-skipping transfer tax.[147]

Commencing in 2011, the estate and the generation-skipping transfer tax provisions in effect prior to the enactment of the Economic Growth and Tax Relief Reconciliation Act of 2001 will be resurrected and the gift tax provisions will be returned to their year 2001 status. The estate tax applicable exclusion amount will be $1 million,[148] and the maximum tax rate will be 55 percent (plus the 5 percent surtax, if applicable).[149] The GST exemption will be $1.1 million (adjusted for inflation since the year 2002) and the maximum generation-skipping transfer tax rate will be 55 percent.[150] Modified carry-over basis under Section 1022 for assets received from a decedent will no longer apply, and Section 1014 will return generally to provide a fair market value basis of property acquired from a decedent.[151] The gift tax Section 2505 applicable exclusion amount will continue to be $1 million,[152] but the maximum gift tax rates under the unified tax rates will rise to 55 percent with a possible 5 percent surtax.[153]

Other estate tax provisions will return to their 2001 status. The full Section 2011 credit for state death taxes will be restored, and Section 2058 will no longer apply.[154] The deduction for qualified family-owned business interests will be restored,[155] and the conservation easement exclusion qualification requirements return to their original form,[156] as do the rules under Section

---

[146] Economic Growth and Tax Relief Reconciliation Act of 2001, Pub. L. No. 107-16, § 901, 115 Stat. 38, 150 (2001), reprinted in 2001-__ CB __, __.

[147] See ¶¶ 8.10[1], 18.04.

[148] This is the applicable exclusion amount that under the pre-2001 law was to be phased-in to $1 million in the year 2006. See ¶ 3.02 note 7.

[149] See ¶ 2.01[3] text accompanying notes 67, 68.

[150] See ¶¶ 15.02, 16.01.

[151] See supra ¶ 8.10[3][a].

[152] See ¶ 9.06.

[153] See ¶ 9.03[2] text accompanying notes 6–7.

[154] See ¶¶ 3.03[3][d], 3.03[4], 5.09. Thus, the pick-up tax system enacted by many states again becomes effective. See ¶ 3.03[1].

[155] IRC § 2057. See ¶ 5.08.

[156] See ¶ 4.02[7][b] text accompanying note 287.

6166.[157] The estate tax will again be imposed on nonresident noncitizens.[158] Changes made by the legislation to the generation-skipping transfer tax are also sunsetted. The termination of the Section 2604 credit for state death taxes,[159] the Section 2632 special rules for allocation of the GST exemption,[160] and the Section 2642(a)(3) qualified severing of trusts rule[161] are all eliminated in the year 2011. The sunsetting of other less significant provisions will occur as well.[162]

The reasons for the "sunset" provision were apparently both procedural[163] and political. With multiple new Congresses, and at least one new President by the year 2009, and a constantly changing economic situation, it is futile to try to predict whether a future Congress and administration will either retain the transfer taxes in their 2009 form for 2010 and later years, retain the transfer taxes in some other form, make the rules that take effect in 2010 permanent, or allow the sunset provision to take effect in 2011. Total inaction will result in a sunsetting, although such inaction seems unlikely.

---

[157] See ¶ 2.02[3][c] text accompanying notes 64, 66, 87, 88, 93–99.

[158] See ¶ 6.01[1] text accompanying note 9. See also ¶¶ 6.01[2] text accompanying note 13, 6.02[1] text accompanying note 19, 6.06[4].

[159] See ¶ 12.04.

[160] See ¶¶ 15.03[4], 15.03[5].

[161] See ¶ 16.02[5][e].

[162] See, e.g., IRC § 2210(b), supra ¶ 8.10[2][a]; IRC § 2511(c), supra ¶ 8.10[4].

[163] The provisions were sunset to ensure compliance with the Byrd Rule. 2 USC § 644. The Byrd Rule imposes a ten-year limit on spending increases and (as here) revenue decreases enacted under procedural rules that preclude the possibility of a filibuster (i.e., may be broken only by a vote of sixty senators). 2 USC § 644. See Economic Growth and Tax Relief Reconciliation Act of 2001, Pub. L. No. 107-16, §§ 901(a)(2), 901(b), 115 Stat. 38, 150 (2001), reprinted in 2001-__ CB __, __.

PART III

The Gift Tax

CHAPTER 9

Gift Tax: Determination of Liability

¶ 9.01 INTRODUCTION

The gift tax should be viewed as a companion to the estate tax, although it bears a close relationship to the income tax as well. The gift tax reflects an attempt, not entirely successful, to backstop the other two taxes. With regard to the estate tax, the gift tax results in an exaction on lifetime transfers that take property, which might otherwise be subject to tax at death, out of the estate.[1]

---

[1] The efficacy of the gift tax in this respect must be appraised in the light of the gift tax progressive rate table that is the same as the estate tax rate table (IRC §§ 2001(c), 2502), the annual exclusion (IRC § 2503(b)), the exclusion for qualified transfers (IRC

With regard to the income tax, the fragmentation of large estates for the purpose of avoiding high surtax rates is somewhat discouraged or penalized by the imposition of a gift tax on lifetime gratuitous transfers. In some small measure at least, these policies may be conflicting because an objective of the estate tax is a broader distribution of wealth.[2]

On the other hand, the income, estate, gift, and generation-skipping transfer taxes are not a well-integrated body of law. As will appear in the ensuing discussion, a determination that a transfer constitutes a completed gift for gift tax purposes is no assurance that it will be regarded similarly when questions of income tax liability or determination of the taxable estate are at issue. Accordingly, the only safe course is to view the gift tax as a separate statutory phenomenon, except as it may be sensible and appropriate to urge a uniform administrative or judicial approach in unsettled areas of the law and to recommend harmonizing statutory changes, some of which have been recently forthcoming.

The United States has made only two excursions into the gift tax field. One was short-lived; our present gift tax is a continuation of the second. In 1924, Congress enacted the first federal gift tax.[3] The first effort was not successful and Congress abolished it in 1926.[4] A reason for abandoning the gift tax at that time was the simultaneous adoption of an estate tax provision under which gratuitous transfers made within two years of death were conclusively presumed to have been made in contemplation of death and, as such, were subject to the estate tax.[5] It is obvious that an effective device for frustrating that type of avoidance of estate tax would tend to reduce the need for a tax on lifetime transfers.

In 1932, the Supreme Court held the foregoing conclusive presumption unconstitutional,[6] having previously arrived at the same conclusion regarding a

---

§ 2503(e)), provisions for gift-splitting by married donors (IRC § 2513), and the gift tax credit (IRC § 2505), all discussed infra, as well as the fact that lifetime gifts are a factor in establishing the rate of estate tax (IRC § 2001(b)(1)(B)).

[2] It is difficult to appraise the incidental economic effect of estate and gift taxes. See Halbach, Death, Taxes, and Family Property (West 1977); Harriss, "Economic Effects of Estate and Gift Taxation," Joint Comm. on Economic Rep., Fed. Tax Policy for Economic Growth & Stability 855 (1955), reprinted in Goldstein, Readings in Death and Gift Tax Reform 41 (Foundation Press 1971); McCaffery, "The Uneasy Case for Wealth Transfer Taxation," 104 Yale LJ 283 (1994); "Colloquium on Wealth Transfer Taxation" 51 Tax L. Rev. 357 (1996).

[3] Revenue Act of 1924, Pub. L. No. 68-176, §§ 319–324, 43 Stat. 253, 313–316 (1924).

[4] Revenue Act of 1926, Pub. L. No. 69-20, § 1200, 44 Stat. 9, 125 (1926).

[5] Revenue Act of 1926, Pub. L. No. 69-20, § 302(c), 44 Stat. 9, 70 (1926).

[6] Heiner v. Donnan, 285 US 312 (1932). See ¶ 4.07[4] for the discussion of the constitutionality of Section 2035(a), which causes certain inter vivos transfers made within three years before death to be included in a decedent's gross estate.

similar state death tax provision.[7] The decision reestablished, or at least reem-phasized, the need for a tax on lifetime transfers, and Congress answered that need in the Revenue Act of 1932.[8] The 1932 date is of continuing significance, as is explained later in the discussion of Sections 2502 and 2504 of the Code.

After early judicial refusal to sanction a retroactive application of the gift tax[9] and congressional abandonment of any such efforts, the tax has had smooth sailing constitutionally. The most plausible argument against validity, and a weak one at best, failed when the Supreme Court sustained the tax as a valid excise not subject to the constitutional requirement that direct taxes be apportioned among the states in accordance with their respective populations.[10]

Ever since their inception, both the estate tax and the gift tax have under-gone frequent statutory change. Under the Tax Reform Act of 1976, a substan-tial unification of the two taxes—after having been suggested for more than a quarter of a century[11]—gained congressional acceptance.[12] Current gifts are taxed under Chapter 12 of the 1986 Code, which is effective for the calendar year 1987 and all subsequent calendar years.[13] An overview of the gift tax ap-pears in Chapter 1. This and the next two chapters present a more detailed analysis and explanation of the gift tax sections of the Code.

Although the estate tax and the generation-skipping transfer tax are termi-nated for decedents dying after and generation-skipping transfers occurring af-ter December 31, 2009,[14] the gift tax lingers on.[15] Seemingly, there are two reasons for the continuation of the gift tax. First, if there were no gift tax, it would open avenues for easy assignment of income to persons in lower brack-ets under the income tax. Second, if the gift tax were repealed, along with the estate tax, and both taxes were scheduled to be resurrected (sunsetted) in the year 2011,[16] there would be a strong incentive for individuals to make tax-free inter vivos transfers in the year 2010. For these reasons, the gift tax continues its existence.

---

[7] Schlesinger v. Wisconsin, 270 US 230 (1926).

[8] Revenue Act of 1932, Pub. L. No. 72-154, §§ 501–531, 47 Stat. 169, 245–259 (1932).

[9] Untermyer v. Anderson, 276 US 440 (1928).

[10] Bromley v. McCaughn, 280 US 124 (1929).

[11] See Goldstein, "Readings in Death and Gift Tax Reform," 77–111 (Foundation Press 1971).

[12] See the discussion of Section 2001 at ¶ 2.01.

[13] See IRC § 7851(a)(2)(B). Gifts for prior years were taxed under the same sections of the 1954 Code or under Sections 1000 through 1031 of the 1939 Code, or under other prior laws.

[14] IRC §§ 2210, 2664; ¶¶ 8.10[1], 18.04.

[15] This includes the special valuation rules of Chapter 14. See ¶¶ 19.01–19.05.

[16] See ¶ 8.10[5].

¶ 9.02 SECTION 2501. IMPOSITION OF TAX

Section 2501(a)(1) imposes a tax on "the transfer of property by gift."[1] However, under Section 2502, the Section 2001(c) tax rates (found in the multipurpose rate schedule discussed in Chapter 2) are applied to "taxable gifts" after recognition of the allowance of certain exclusions and deductions. Thus, there is a concept of gross or includible gifts and of net or taxable gifts, which somewhat parallels the gross estate and taxable estate concepts under the estate tax discussed in earlier chapters of this book. For estate tax purposes, Congress has provided an exclusive definition of "gross estate."[2] Some transfers subject to gift tax are expressly recognized in Sections 2511 through 2519, but Congress has not undertaken a parallel exclusive definition of what might be called "gross gifts." Therefore, the scope of the gift tax is somewhat less certain than that of the estate tax, although both present myriad interpretational problems.[3] Congress has expressly placed two types of gratuitous transfers beyond the reach of the gift tax.

[1] Transfers of Intangibles by Nonresident Noncitizens

In general, the gift tax statute does not tax the transfer of intangible property by one who is neither a citizen nor a resident of the United States.[4] The rules on citizenship and residence here parallel the rules previously discussed that bear upon the tax on estates of nonresidents who are not citizens.[5] As later indicated, as a general rule nonresident noncitizens are subject to gift tax only on transfers of property situated within the United States.[6] However, the provision under discussion here is an overriding exemption that says that gratuitous transfers of intangibles by nonresident noncitizens are not taxed, even if the

---

[1] The definition of the term "gift" and the determination of the date of a gift are considered in the discussion of Section 2511 and related sections. See Chapter 10.

[2] See IRC §§ 2031–2046, discussed in Chapter 4.

[3] See especially the discussion of Section 2033 at ¶ 4.05, under which vague statutory terms have led to broad inclusionary rules.

[4] IRC § 2501(a)(2). See Priv. Ltr. Rul. 8342106 (July 20, 1983) (gift of all shares of a domestic corporation to a U.S. resident by nonresident noncitizen not subject to the gift tax).

[5] See IRC § 2101; ¶ 6.01. See also IRC § 7701(a)(9); Reg. § 25.2501-1(b); United States v. Matheson, 400 F. Supp. 1241 (SDNY 1975), aff'd, 532 F2d 809 (2d Cir. 1976), cert. denied, 429 US 823 (1976). Sections 2501(b) and 2501(c), which bear on the citizenship of certain residents of U.S. possessions, are not discussed here, but they are considered in detail in Priv. Ltr. Rul. 9720029 (Feb. 13, 1997). Sections 2501(b) and 2501(c) are precisely parallel to Sections 2208 and 2209, which are discussed briefly at ¶ 8.09.

[6] IRC § 2511(a). Even property situated in the United States may not be subject to gift tax if a gift tax convention with a foreign country exempts it. Reg. § 25.0-1(a)(1).

properties are considered to be situated within the United States. Restrictive provisions designed to prevent abuse of this exemption apply to persons who within ten years of the date of the gift relinquished U.S. citizenship principally to avoid income, gift, estate, or generation-skipping transfer taxes.[7]

This exemption first appeared in the 1954 Code. Two factors seem to have motivated its adoption. First, under prior law, nonresident noncitizens may have been able to avoid the tax on transfers of intangibles, such as bonds, by moving the bonds outside the United States prior to making the gifts. If the tax was so easily avoided,[8] there was little reason for its imposition.[9] Second, efforts to avoid the tax tended to deny "United States financial institutions business as depositories for property" of nonresident noncitizens.[10] This business is encouraged by the present rule. Until 1966, the exception applied only if the nonresident noncitizen donor was not engaged in business in the United States. Elimination of this qualification is a further inducement to foreign investment in U.S. securities.

[2] Transfers to Political Organizations

The Service long took the position that gifts to political parties or candidates constituted taxable transfers within the scope of Section 2511(a).[11] With two

---

[7] IRC §§ 2501(a)(3), 2501(a)(4). The purpose of these restrictions is to thwart citizenship relinquishment as a deliberate gift tax avoidance device. See IRS Notice 97-19, 1997-1 CB 394. The rules with respect to a principal tax avoidance purpose (see IRC §§ 2501(a)(3)(A), 2501(a)(3)(B), 2501(a)(4)) are identical to the rules under Section 2107. See ¶ 6.07[1]. Cf. Rev. Rul. 92-109, 1992-2 CB 3, dealing with gift tax consequences of expatriates whose citizenship was retroactively restored.

A credit is allowed for any foreign gift tax actually paid with respect to a gift subject to tax solely by reason of Section 2501(a)(3). IRC § 2501(a)(3)(D).

[8] But see De Goldschmidt-Rothschild v. Comm'r, 168 F2d 975 (2d Cir. 1948) .

[9] S. Rep. No. 1622, 83d Cong., 2d Sess. 126 (1954).

[10] S. Rep. No. 1622, 83d Cong., 2d Sess. 126 (1954).

[11] Rev. Rul. 59-57, 1959-1 CB 626. Section 2511 is discussed at ¶ 10.01 (see especially ¶ 10.01[2][c]).

exceptions,[12] the Service was successful in its contention.[13] Controversy also developed over the extent to which political contributions qualified for the annual exclusion.[14]

In 1975, Congress added Section 2501(a)(5), which provides that the gift tax is inapplicable "to the transfer of money or other property to a political organization (within the meaning of Section 527(e)(1)) for the use of such organization."[15] No parallel exemption was added to the estate tax. Although in the congressional hearings the question was raised as to whether political contributions constituted gifts or "contributions to further the general political or good government objectives of the donor,"[16] the House Committee Report indicated that the Section 2501(a)(5) exemption was enacted "because the tax system should not be used to reduce or restrict political contributions."[17]

Under the exemption, the gift tax does not apply to a transfer made after May 7, 1974, to a "political organization."[18] Contributions to individuals are not excluded by the exemption.

---

[12] In Stern v. United States, 436 F2d 1327 (5th Cir. 1971), the taxpayer successfully argued that no taxable gift was made because the transfer was nontaxable under Regulation Sections 25.2512-8. See a discussion of the regulation at ¶ 10.02[4]. The Service declined to follow *Stern* except in the Fifth Circuit. Rev. Rul. 72-583, 1972-2 CB 534.

In Carson v. Comm'r, 71 TC 252 (1978), aff'd, 641 F2d 864 (10th Cir. 1981), nonacq. 1979-2 CB 2, the courts decided that the legislative history of the gift tax laws compelled the conclusion that such laws were never intended to apply to political campaigns, since the inevitable intent of the contributor is to further the contributor's own social and political interests, and not to benefit candidates personally.

[13] See Tax Analysts & Advocates v. Schultz, 376 F. Supp. 889 (DDC 1974), vacated sub nom. Tax Analysts & Advocates v. Simon, 1975-1 USTC ¶ 13,052 (DC Cir. 1975) (remand for dismissal of complaint as moot); du Pont v. United States, 97 F. Supp. 944 (D. Del. 1951).

[14] See Stephens, Maxfield & Lind, Federal Estate and Gift Taxation 8-15, 8-16 (Warren, Gorham & Lamont, 3d ed. 1974). See also Rev. Rul. 77-131, 1977-1 CB 295; Rev. Rul. 74-199, 1974-1 CB 285; Rev. Rul. 72-355, 1972-2 CB 532.

[15] Pub. L. No. 93-625, § 14(a), 88 Stat. 2108, 2121 (1975), reprinted in 1975-1 CB 510, 517. See Streng, "The Federal Tax Treatment of Political Contributions and Political Organizations," 29 Tax Law. 139 (1975).

[16] 120 Cong. Rec. 12,594 (Dec. 20, 1974) (statement of Congressman Ullman). See also S. Rep. No. 1357, 93d Cong., 2d Sess. 4 (1974), reprinted in 1975-1 CB 517, 519.

[17] HR Rep. No. 1502, 93d Cong., 2d Sess. 110 (1974).

[18] Reg. § 25.2501-1(a)(5). See Rev. Rul. 82-216, 1982-2 CB 220, which states that the Service will not seek to impose a gift tax on pre-1974 transfers to political organizations. However, contributions of appreciated property to "political organizations" result in income tax consequences to the donor. IRC § 84(a).

As defined in Section 527(e)(1), a political organization is a party, committee, association, fund, or other organization organized and operated primarily to accept contributions and make expenditures for the purpose of electing, appointing, selecting, or nominating public officials. See Reg. § 1.527-2, which discusses the definition in detail.

[3] Periodic Imposition

Under the current annual reporting system, a taxpayer who makes a reportable gift is required to file a gift tax return, Form 709, by April 15 of the year after the year in which the gift is made. If, however, the donor dies during the year of the gift, the gift tax return is due no later than the time for filing the estate tax return, including extensions.[19]

The gift tax is imposed on the *transfer* of property (not on the property itself), which is why it has been sustained as an excise.[20] In this respect, it parallels the estate tax, which also has been sustained as an excise on a transfer.[21] The tax is not imposed with respect to each separate gift; instead it is imposed with respect to aggregate gifts made during the calendar year.[22] In this respect, periodic imposition, it resembles the income tax. Although donees are secondarily liable, primary liability for the tax rests on the donor;[23] thus, in contrast with a tax on "income," it may aptly be viewed as a tax on "outgo." Actual computation of the gift tax differs fundamentally from computation of the income tax, and it bears a closer resemblance to the estate tax computation, as is explained in the ensuing discussion of Section 2502.

¶ 9.03 SECTION 2502. RATE OF TAX

Section 2502 specifies the method of computation to be used in the determination of gift tax liability. A two-step computation is required, as will be explained. However, it should be observed at the outset that the rates are always applied to "taxable gifts," a term that is akin to the "taxable estate" for estate

---

[19] See ¶ 9.04[9]. This is a sensible modification of the due date in the event of the donor's death because of the interplay in the calculation of the estate tax and the gift tax. See also ¶ 2.01.

[20] Bromley v. McCaughn, 280 US 124 (1929). Cf. See ¶ 2.01[3] text accompanying note 67 (upholding the validity of the *Bromley* result in estate tax cases).

[21] New York Trust Co. v. Eisner, 256 US 345 (1921).

[22] IRC § 2501(a)(1). From 1932 through 1970 and after 1981, gift taxes have been imposed on an annual basis, always using the calendar, not a fiscal year. There was quarterly reporting of gifts from 1971 through 1981. Excise, Estate, and Gift Tax Adjustment Act of 1970, Pub. L. No. 91-614, § 102, 84 Stat. 1836, 1838 (1970), reprinted in 1971-1 CB 533, 534. See Kahn, "A Guide to the Estate and Gift Tax Amendments of 1970," 17 Prac. Law. 13, 26 (1971); Price, "Recent Tax Legislation—The Excise, Estate and Gift Tax Adjustment Act of 1970," 47 Wash. L. Rev. 237, 241 (1972). The quarterly approach, employed from 1971 through 1981, caused a "paper blizzard," which is probably why Congress returned to an annual reporting method after 1981. Economic Recovery Tax Act of 1981, Pub. L. No. 97-34, § 442, 95 Stat. 320 (1981), reprinted in 1981-2 CB 334.

[23] IRC § 2502(c). See ¶ 9.03[4].

tax purposes and "taxable income" for income tax purposes. The term "taxable gifts," which is defined in Section 2503, represents a net figure to be arrived at by determining what gifts are generally within the scope of the tax, by possibly taking advantage of the Section 2503(b) exclusion,[1] and finally, by taking into account certain deductions allowed by the statute.

[1] Periodic Accounting for Gifts

Imposition of a gift tax based on taxable gifts for the year gives this tax a superficial resemblance to the federal income tax, which is based on taxable income for the year. One obvious difference is that gift tax liability is always determined with reference to the calendar year, whereas in determining income tax liability, the taxpayer may adopt a fiscal year.[2] There is another fundamental difference. Income tax rates are determined with reference only to the taxable income figure for the taxable period in question;[3] gift tax rates depend on the donor's aggregate sum of taxable gifts since June 6, 1932.[4] This cumulative method of applying progressive rates is the reason for the rather involved language of Section 2502(a).

[2] Rates

The Section 2001(c) rate schedule, which also applies to the estate tax, is the rate schedule for "taxable gifts."[5] Thus the rate brackets applicable to gifts are identical to the rate brackets applicable to estates. Prior to 2002, the maximum gift tax rate was 55 percent,[6] and it was increased by a 5 percent surtax on gifts over $10 million.[7] Beginning in the year 2002, the maximum rate de-

---

[1] See also IRC §§ 2503(e), 2503(f), 2503(g), which treat some transfers as nontransfers.

[2] See IRC §§ 441, 2501(a)(1).

[3] But see IRC § 1341.

[4] A decedent's taxable gifts made after December 31, 1976, not includible in the decedent's gross estate, also affect the estate tax rates applicable to the decedent's estate. IRC § 2001(b).

[5] IRC § 2502(a)(1).

[6] See IRC § 2001(c)(1), prior to its amendment by the Economic Growth and Tax Relief Reconciliation Act of 2001, Pub. L. No. 107-16, § 511(a), 115 Stat. 38, 70 (2001), reprinted in 2001-__ CB __, __. See ¶ 2.01[3] text accompanying note 67.

[7] See IRC § 2001(c)(2), prior to its repeal by the Economic Growth and Tax Relief Reconciliation Act of 2001, Pub. L. No. 107-16, § 511(b), 115 Stat. 38, 70 (2001), reprinted in 2001-__ CB __, __. The 5-percent surtax was imposed on gifts in excess of $10 million. IRC § 2001(c)(2), prior to its repeal by the Economic Growth and Tax Reconciliation Act of 2001, Pub. L. No. 107-16, § 511(b), 115 Stat. 38, 70 (2001), reprinted in

clines to 50 percent with no surtax,[8] with further declines in the maximum rate in the year 2003 to 49 percent, in the year 2004 to 48 percent, in the year 2005 to 47 percent, in the year 2006 to 46 percent, and to 45 percent in the years 2007 through 2009.[9] In 2010, gifts are effectively taxed at a flat rate of 35 percent, an amount equal to the maximum income tax rate.[10]

Prior to 1976, the gift tax rates were exactly 75 percent of the corresponding estate tax rates. As a justification for equalizing the rates, the House Committee Report states:

> The tax burden imposed on transfers of the same amount of wealth should be substantially the same whether the transfers are made both during life and at death or made only upon death. As a practical matter, the preferences for lifetime transfers are available only for wealthier individuals who are able to afford lifetime transfers. . . . [P]references for lifetime transfers principally benefit the wealthy and result in eroding the transfer tax base.[11]

The Committee Report recognizes that some advantages still exist with respect to inter vivos giving.[12] However, a strong objection can be made to the rate equalization.[13] When one makes a gift tax payment, the government imme-

---

2001-__ CB __, __. The surtax was phased out at $17,184,000, the point at which the rate of tax on all gifts was a flat 55 percent rate. Prior to 1998, the surtax also phased out the Section 2505 credit. See ¶¶ 2.01[3] text accompanying note 68, 9.06[1] note 10.

[8] IRC §§ 2001(c), 2502(a)(1). See ¶ 2.01[3] text accompanying note 68.

[9] IRC §§ 2001(c), 2502(a)(1). See ¶ 2.01[3].

[10] See IRC §§ 1, 2502(a)(2) as amended by the Economic Growth and Tax Relief Reconciliation Act of 2001, Pub. L. No. 107-16, § 511(d), 115 Stat. 38, 70 (2001), reprinted in 2001-__ CB __, __. Section 2502(a) effective for years after 2009 incorporates the current Section 2001(c) rates up to the 34 percent rate and then caps such rates on transfers in excess of $500,000 at 35 percent. Since Section 2505 provides a credit on the first $1 million of taxable gifts (see ¶ 9.05), the interrelationship of the Section 2505 credit and the Section 2502(a)(2) rates result in a flat 35-percent tax rate for taxes paid.

Under the sunset provision effective January 1, 2011, the top gift tax rate of 55 percent is restored, as is the 5-percent surtax on transfers in excess of $10 million, which eliminates the graduated tax rates. See Economic Growth and Tax Reconciliation Act of 2001, Pub. L. No. 107-16, § 901(a)(2), 115 Stat. 38, 150 (2001), reprinted in 2001-__ CB __, __. The sunset provision is discussed more fully at ¶ 8.10[5].

[11] HR Rep. No. 1380, 94th Cong., 2d Sess. 11 (1976), reprinted in 1976-3 CB (Vol. 3), 735, 745.

[12] HR Rep. No. 1380, 94th Cong., 2d Sess. 12 (1976), reprinted in 1976-3 CB (Vol. 3) 735, 746. See ¶ 2.01[4].

[13] In addition, while Congress provided for transfer tax rate equalization, it currently fails to provide for income tax basis equalization. Compare Section 1014, generally providing a fair market value basis at death for property taxed under the estate tax prior to its termination in 2010, with Section 1015, generally providing a carryover of the donor's basis for property taxed under the gift tax. In 1976, Congress enacted a modified carryover basis rule for property taxed under the estate tax, but the rule was retroactively repealed in

diately has the use of money that would otherwise be producing more wealth for the donor until the donor's death. That additional cost to the donor's overall wealth was seemingly overlooked by Congress in its rate "equalization." Avoidance of this additional cost was a justification for the previous rate discrepancy. Conceivably, a modest credit against the estate tax could be allowed, figured with regard to interest on what are in effect prepayments of estate tax with a view to the time elapsed between payment of the gift tax and the donor's death. Such a credit would encourage lifetime gifts, probably a desirable consequence of the abandoned rate differential.

After 1976, it is less likely than it was before 1977 that it is better to give than to bequeath,[14] but as indicated in the introduction to Chapter 2, prior to the year 2010 there are still significant advantages to inter vivos giving.[15]

[3] Method of Computation

To simplify the explanation of the gift tax computation, disregard for the moment the problem of determining taxable gifts and assume that the statute simply taxes all gifts. Section 2502 requires that (1) a tentative tax figure be determined by applying the current tax rates to all gifts made since June 6, 1932,[16] including gifts made in the current year for which tax liability is being determined and (2) a second tentative tax figure be determined by applying the current tax rates to all gifts made since June 6, 1932, but not including gifts made in the current year. The excess of the first tentative figure over the second is the tax on gifts for the current year.[17]

1980. See IRC § 1023 as enacted by the Tax Reform Act of 1976, Pub. L. No. 94-455 § 2005(a), 90 Stat. 1520, 1872 (1976), reprinted in 1976-3 CB (vol. 1) 1, 348, prior to repeal by the Windfall Profit Tax Act of 1980, Pub. L. No. 96-223 § 401, 94 Stat. 229, 299 (1980), reprinted in 1980-3 CB 1, 71. In the year 2010 when the estate tax is terminated (see IRC § 2210), Congress has reenacted a similar modified carryover basis provision. IRC § 1022. See ¶ 8.10[3].

[14] For an analysis of this issue under pre-1977 law, see Stephens, Maxfield & Lind, Federal Estate and Gift Taxation 8-8–8-10 (Warren, Gorham & Lamont, 3d ed. 1974).

[15] See ¶ 2.01[4].

[16] Section 2502(b) establishes the June 6, 1932, cut-off date.

[17] With the exception of Section 2505, there are no statutory credits against the gift tax, such as those against the estate tax discussed in Chapter 3; but in rare circumstances a treaty may provide a credit if the gift is subject to tax by the United States and a foreign country as well. See Form 709, "United States Gift (and Generation-Skipping Transfer) Tax Return" (2001), Part 2, Tax Computation, Line 13; Chapter 7. A few states impose gift taxes. This practice raises the question of whether there should be a federal credit or deduction for state gift taxes, as is provided for state death taxes against the federal estate tax by Section 2011 or Section 2058. See ¶¶ 3.03, 5.09.

Reference to the computation of a tax on gifts in preceding periods may make it appear that in some fashion the earlier gifts are again being subjected to tax. The statute has neither that purpose nor that effect; instead, the effect is only to fix the rates applicable to the current year's gifts by reference to the total of all gifts made since 1932. Similarly, while the post-1976 rates are being used in both computations, only the current year's gifts are actually being taxed at those rates. This may be more readily understood by a comparison with the computation of tax liability under the graduated income tax rates. With regard to that tax, the taxpayer may be viewed as beginning each year with an empty container marked off with the graduated rates. As income pours in, additional amounts become subject to higher tax rates,[18] but at the end of the year the container is emptied and the process starts all over again.

In the case of the gift tax, the container is never emptied.[19] Instead, any gift made since June 6, 1932, stays in the container and gifts made in later periods are poured in on top of earlier years' gifts to form a layer that is subject to higher rates than if the entire computation were begun afresh for each taxable period.

The effect of Section 2502 in this respect can best be illustrated by the use of round numbers that correspond to the multipurpose rate table brackets. Suppose an individual has made taxable gifts in the total amount of $1 million in prior years after the year 2001 and then makes taxable gifts of $200,000 in the current year prior to the year 2010. The computation would be as follows:

Tax on all gifts, including current year ($1.2 million)	$427,800
Less tax on gifts made in prior periods ($1 million)[20]	$345,800
Tax on current year's gifts	$ 82,000

The same result is reached if the 41 percent rate, applicable to gifts between $1 million and $1,250,000, is applied directly to the $200,000 amount of gifts for the current year. However, any such forthright approach to the problem would not be so easy if the amounts involved did not coincide exactly with the rate brackets. In any event, precisely the same result is accomplished by the statutory plan.

Section 2502(b) defines "preceding calendar period" to make it plain that gifts made on or before June 6, 1932, are to be disregarded in the computation of the tax. The critical date is the date of first enactment of the current gift tax law; by making the tax inapplicable to gifts made on or before that date, Con-

---

[18] IRC § 1.

[19] See, however, Section 2001(b), under which the container is emptied at the end of 1976 for purposes of computing *estate* tax liability under the unified rate table.

[20] Since the prior years' gifts were made after 2001, the gift tax liability on those gifts would have been eliminated by the Section 2505 credit discussed at ¶ 9.06.

gress escaped constitutional difficulties previously encountered under the earlier 1924 statute.[21] The definition also makes it clear that calendar quarters, used from 1971 to 1981 (inclusive) for purposes of gift tax administration, have been replaced by a return to the calendar year.[22]

[4] Liability for the Gift Tax

Section 2502(c) provides that the tax shall be paid by the donor. This fastens the primary liability for the tax on the donor; the donee's secondary liability for the tax is explained at the end of the discussion of Section 2503.[23] As between donor and donee, the ultimate financial burden may be shifted by an agreement that the donee will pay the tax.[24] Of course, such an agreement does not affect the right of the Commissioner to collect the tax from either donor or donee in accordance with established procedures.

¶ 9.04 SECTION 2503. TAXABLE GIFTS

The periodic imposition of the gift tax makes it necessary to determine a net gift figure for the calendar year. The net figure, termed "taxable gifts" (to correspond to "taxable income" and the "taxable estate"), is calculated by subtracting from "the total amount of gifts" for the period[1] the deductions authorized by Sections 2522 and 2523.[2] Section 2503(a), which defines "taxable gifts" in this manner, contemplates that the total amount of gifts for a period are to be matched with deductions for the same period to determine the net figure for the period.

The meaning of "gifts" in this context is left to Sections 2511 through 2519.[3] Section 2503(a) relies on other sections for delineation of inclusions in the total amount of gifts and still other sections for authorization of deductions; thus, it is not in itself much of a definition of "taxable gift." Section

---

[21] See ¶ 9.01.

[22] See ¶ 9.02 note 22.

[23] See ¶ 9.04[11].

[24] An incidental effect of these agreements is to reduce the amount of the gift and consequently the amount of the gift tax. See the discussion of Section 2512 at ¶ 10.02[6][d]. The income tax ramifications of such agreements are also discussed at ¶ 10.02[6][d] note 181.

[1] Prior to 1971 and after 1981, the period is the calendar year; from 1971–1981, the period is the calendar quarter. See ¶ 9.02 note 22.

[2] See Chapter 11.

[3] See Chapter 10.

2503(b), however, presents one specific rule that bears on what must be included in "the total amount of gifts" for a particular period.

[1] The Annual Exclusion

Under Section 2503(b), the taxpayer[4] may currently exclude from "the total amount of gifts" for a calendar year (the starting point in the computation of taxable gifts) the first $11,000 of gifts to *each* donee.[5] The annual exclusion amount is adjusted from an initial $10,000 amount for inflation in years after 1998.[6] The adjustment is based on the Consumer Price Index (CPI) for the calendar year 1997.[7] However, adjustments are made only in multiples of $1,000 and adjustments are rounded to the *lowest* multiple of $1,000.[8] Thus, the adjustment of the annual exclusion to $11,000 has been made because the post-1997 CPI inflation amount meets or exceeds 10 percent.[9]

With respect to any donee, the annual exclusion amount of $11,000 is reduced, until consumed, by the amount of previous gifts to the same donee in the same calendar year. Thus, the $11,000 figure is an annual allowance that may be used in a piecemeal fashion.[10] For example, unmarried taxpayer *A* may make a cash gift of $1,000 to cousin *B* in January and a further $7,000 cash gift to *B* in April, *A*'s only gifts in the year. The total amount of *A*'s gifts is reduced to zero by the exclusion. If *A* makes a third gift of $7,000 to *B* in the same year, only $3,000 of the annual exclusion remains, and the total amount

---

[4] A nonresident noncitizen who makes a gift subject to the gift tax qualifies for the annual exclusion. See ¶ 9.02[1].

[5] See Smith, "Should We Give Away the Annual Exclusion?" 1 Fla. Tax. Rev. 361 (1993); Steinkamp, "Common Sense and the Gift Tax Annual Exclusion," 72 Neb. L. Rev. 106 (1993).

[6] IRC § 2503(b)(2).

[7] IRC § 2503(b)(2)(B). A modified version of Section 1(f)(3) of the income tax applying the "calendar year 1997" rather than the "calendar year 1992" is used in making the adjustment. Id. See Rev. Proc. 98-61, 1998-2 CB 811; Rev. Proc. 2001-59, 2001-1 CB —, —.

[8] IRC § 2503(b)(2) (flush language).

[9] Subsequent adjustments will be dependent on comparable post-1997 CPI inflation. Thus, an adjustment to $12,000 will not be made until post-1997 CPI inflation amount meets or exceeds 20 percent of the 1997 price level.

[10] Where it is necessary to determine taxable gifts for a prior year in which annual computation was required, prior law relating to the exclusion continues in effect. See the discussion of Section 2504(b) at ¶ 9.05[3].

In the case of a gift to a spouse who is not a citizen of the United States, the amount of the annual exclusion is increased to $110,000. IRC § 2523(i)(2). An explanation of the rationale for this increase appears at ¶ 11.03[5].

of A's gifts for the year is $4,000. The statute is mandatory in this respect; A may not forgo the use of the exclusion.[11]

The annual exclusion can be claimed only in the case of transfers of present interests in property; the disqualification of future interests is discussed later. Aside from this restriction, every donor is entitled to an $11,000 exclusion for each person to whom the donor makes gifts, and this exclusion is renewed annually. The amount of the annual exclusion has varied over the years;[12] the significance of this fact in the computation of gift tax for current periods is indicated in the discussion of Section 2504.

The exclusion is as generous as it sounds. To illustrate, a donor could make $11,000 cash gifts to every person in the Manhattan telephone book during the current calendar year; the donor's $11,000 exclusion for each donee would leave the donor's "total amount of gifts" for the year at zero. Moreover, the donor could repeat the donations in the succeeding year and thereafter each year for life; in no year would the donor have any "total amount of gifts" after taking into account the annual exclusion.[13]

The exclusion operates not only to eliminate gifts of $11,000 or under from total gifts; as suggested in the preceding example, it also scales down larger gifts. Thus, if A makes a cash gift to B of $12,000 in a year, the gift tax treatment reflected in the return will be:

Gift to B	$12,000
Exclusion	11,000
Included amount	$ 1,000

The amount included in the total amount of gifts with respect to B will be included with all other gifts during the year that exceeds the exclusion.[14]

---

[11] See Section 2503(b), which provides that "the *first* $10,000 of such [present interest] gifts to such person shall not . . . be included in the total amount of gifts made during such year." [Emphasis added.] See also ¶ 16.02[2][b] note 63 for a situation in which A might want to forgo immediate use of the annual exclusion.

[12] The annual exclusion was $5,000 from 1932–1938, $4,000 from 1939–1942, and $3,000 from 1943–1981. It was $10,000 for years after 1981–2001 (see Reg. § 25.2503-2), and it is adjusted for inflation after 1997 (see supra text accompanying notes 6–9). There are frequent proposals in Congress to either alter the amount of the annual exclusion or to place a ceiling on the total amount of annual exclusions. See also infra ¶ 9.04[3][f] note 113.

[13] Compare Rev. Rul. 83-180, 1983-2 CB 169 (separate annual exclusion gifts each year), with Rev. Rul. 77-299, 1977-2 CB 343 (single gift in initial year).

[14] See supra text accompanying note 10.

[a] Purpose of Annual Exclusion

The congressional purpose for the annual exclusion is "to obviate the necessity of keeping an account of and reporting numerous small gifts . . . to fix the amount sufficiently large to cover in most cases wedding and Christmas gifts and occasional gifts of relatively small amounts."[15] This purpose is not at odds with the objective of making the gift tax support the income and estate taxes. Of course, the purpose could be achieved without permitting the exclusion to scale down a $100,000 gift to $89,000, which it does. However, to limit the exclusion to the elimination of small gifts (and not to the reduction of larger ones) would invite fragmentation of larger gifts to secure the tax benefit. If there are answers to that problem, Congress is not concerned with them, even though annual exclusions for several donees over the long life span of a generous donor may result in a very large tax-free transmission of property.

[b] Identification of Donees

Since a donor has an exclusion annually for each donee, it is of great importance to determine the meaning of the term "donee." Actually, the statute uses the expression "gifts . . . made to any person." No problem is encountered if, say, a parent makes outright gifts to children; each child is a person qualifying for the exclusion.[16] In other circumstances, it may be more difficult to determine the "person" in receipt of the gift.

[i] **Gifts in trust.** An early problem arose with respect to gifts in trust. Is the trustee the donee, the person to whom the gift is made? Or is a gift in trust a gift to the beneficiary or beneficiaries of the trust? The question is no longer open; transfers in trust constitute gifts to the beneficiaries.[17] Thus, a single transfer to a trust may qualify for several annual exclusions limited only by the number of beneficiaries and the future interest rule discussed in the next section.

If an exclusion is to be allowed at all in the case of transfers in trust, it is practically necessary to treat the beneficiaries as the donees. Otherwise, it might be possible to multiply the exclusion indefinitely to the advantage of a single beneficial donee by the simple expedient of using numerous trusts for

---

[15] S. Rep. No. 665, 72d Cong., 1st Sess. (1932), reprinted in 1939-1 (Pt. 2) CB 496, 525. See IRC § 2513, discussed ¶ 10.03, which since 1948 has had the practical effect of doubling the exclusion for gifts by some married taxpayers.

[16] But see Schultz v. United States, 493 F2d 1225 (4th Cir. 1974) (no annual exclusion for brothers' gifts to nieces and nephews where gifts were reciprocal transactions); Estate of Robinson v. Comm'r, 101 TC 499 (1993) (no annual exclusion for minor grandchildren who were not deeded an interest in transferred real estate).

[17] Helvering v. Hutchings, 312 US 393 (1941); Reg. § 25.2503-2.

the same donee.[18] Indeed, before the Supreme Court settled the uncertainty on this point, Congress deemed it necessary for a time to make gifts in trust ineligible for the exclusion;[19] but after the Supreme Court ruling, the ineligibility was removed in 1943.[20]

[ii] **Gifts to other entities.** Regarding gifts to entities other than trusts, the exclusion question may be somewhat more difficult. The Treasury's steady position has been that a transfer to a private corporation is a transfer to the corporation's shareholders.[21] This might seem to suggest an exclusion for each shareholder or, if the donor is also a shareholder, for each of the other shareholders.[22] The Tax Court, on the other hand, has held that for exclusion purposes a gift to a private corporation is to the corporation itself and thus to one "person," justifying at most a single exclusion.[23] The controversy is not significant because, in the same case on appeal, the U.S. Court of Appeals refused to pass on the point urged by the taxpayers—that the corporation's shareholders were the donees—on the ground that if it accepted the taxpayer's argument, the future interest rule, discussed next, would preclude any exclusions.[24] The Tax Court decision is at odds with the regulations and very difficult to square with the Supreme Court's treatment of the analogous problem concerning gifts in trust,[25] even if it has some support in other cases.[26] It has properly been repudiated.[27] But, although the effect is to multiply the donees, the result adversely affects taxpayers because the indirect gifts to the shareholders run afoul of the future interest rule.[28] Similarly, a gift to a partnership or to a lim-

---

[18] Helvering v. Hutchings, 312 US 393, 397 (1941).

[19] Revenue Act of 1938, Pub. L. No. 75-554, § 505, 52 Stat. 447, 565 (1938).

[20] Revenue Act of 1942, Pub. L. No. 77-753, § 454, 56 Stat. 798, 953 (1942).

[21] Reg. § 25.2511-1(h)(1).

[22] Reg. § 25.2511-1(h)(1).

[23] Heringer v. Comm'r, 21 TC 607 (1954).

[24] Heringer v. Comm'r, 235 F2d 149 (9th Cir.), cert. denied, 352 US 927 (1956).

[25] Helvering v. Hutchings, 312 US 393 (1941).

[26] E.g., Frank B. Thompson v. Comm'r, 42 BTA 121 (1940), settled while on appeal in Sixth Circuit.

[27] Chanin v. United States, 393 F2d 972 (Ct. Cl. 1968) (relied on in Rev. Rul. 71-443, 1971-2 CB 338, restating the position taken in the regulations).

[28] Heringer v. Comm'r, 235 F2d 149 (9th Cir.), cert. denied, 352 US 927 (1956); Stinson Estate v. United States, 214 F3d 846 (7th Cir. 2000); Chanin v. United States, 393 F2d 972 (Ct. Cl. 1968); Georgia Ketteman Trust v. Comm'r, 86 TC 91 (1986). See infra ¶ 9.04[3][e] text accompanying notes 89–91. Cf. Priv. Ltr. Rul. 9114023 (Jan. 7, 1991) (principal shareholder's transfer of stock to key employees was a future interest).

ited liability company is an indirect gift to the partners of the partnership or the members of the limited liability company.[29]

[iii] Gift by an entity. If a gift is made by an entity, the entity veil is again pierced; and the ratable portion of the gift ascribed to each owner of the entity may be offset by each entity owner's exclusion.[30] For example, if a corporation having four equal shareholders makes a $20,000 gift to shareholder *A*, there is a $5,000 gift from each of the other three shareholders to *A* and each of the three $5,000 gifts qualifies for the annual exclusion. The other $5,000 transfer is a nongift transfer from *A* to *A*.

[iv] Gifts to charitable organizations. Deductible gifts to charitable organizations qualify for the annual exclusion.[31] Of course, such organizations have no private beneficial owners who might be identified as the recipients of gifts to the organization in the way that the shareholders of private corporations are identified. In any event, to the extent that an exclusion might be denied, the result would be only to increase the gift tax charitable deduction.[32] A gift to a charitable organization that does not qualify for the charitable deduction is also treated as a single gift to the entity, eligible for one annual exclusion.[33]

[v] Straw person. It is clear that the number of a donor's exclusions cannot be increased by the use of a straw person. Two gifts to a single donee, one direct and one through a straw person, result in one exclusion only.[34] Thus, if a donor gives $11,000 to a child and $11,000 to a sibling's child and sibling gives $11,000 to a child and $11,000 to donor's child, the principle of the re-

---

[29] Gross v. Comm'r, 7 TC 837 (1946), acq. 1946-2 CB 2. Cf. Fischer v. Comm'r, 8 TC 732 (1947), acq. 1947-1 CB 2 (adequate consideration received for transfer). See infra ¶ 9.04[3][e] text accompanying note 92 and 93.

[30] See, e.g., Reg. § 25.2511-1(h)(1). If entity gifts were not ascribed to the entity's owners, they would escape gift tax entirely because the tax is imposed only on transfers by "individuals" (IRC § 2501(a)(1)), and it does not apply to "transfers by corporations or persons other than individuals" (Reg. § 25.0-1(b)).

[31] See Reg. § 25.2502-1(d) Ex. 3.

[32] See the discussion of Sections 2522, 2524 at ¶¶ 11.02, 11.04[1].

[33] Priv. Ltr. Rul. 9818042 (Jan. 28, 1998). See DuPont v. United States, 97 F. Supp. 944 (D. Del. 1951). See also Reg. § 25.2511-1(h)(1) (last sentence).

[34] Heyen v. United States, 945 F2d 359 (10th Cir. 1991); Estate of Cidulka v. Comm'r, 71 TCM (CCH) 2555 (1996); Estate of Bies v. Comm'r, 80 TCM (CCH) 628 (2000). Cf. Reg. § 25.2511-1(h)(2), appropriately stating that "the transfer of property to *B* if there is imposed upon *B* the obligation of paying a commensurate annuity to *C* is a gift to *C*."

ciprocal transaction doctrine[35] should be applied to make each transferor the donor of a $22,000 gift to his or her respective child.[36]

[vi] Joint donees. On the other hand, a single transfer of property to two persons as joint tenants or as tenants by the entirety is generally considered two gifts for the purpose of the exclusion.[37] This is consistent with the established principle that a gift is made to the one on whom the donor confers the benefit of the donation.[38] However, this principle also precludes the treatment of a tenancy by the entirety itself as a person for whom the donor can claim an exclusion. In a curious burst of optimism, a donor claimed three exclusions in one year for gifts (1) to his son; (2) to his daughter-in-law; and (3) to son and daughter-in-law as tenants by the entirety. This claim was not successful;[39] the transfer to the tenancy by the entirety was simply an additional gift to the two persons for whom he had already claimed his full exclusions.

Transfers into a tenancy by the entirety present a problem related to the valuation of the interests of the two tenants.[40] In the case of an ordinary joint tenancy with survivorship rights under which either party can act unilaterally to sever his or her interest, the interest of each tenant is of equal value.[41] Thus, a gift of property worth $22,000 to A and B as joint tenants is a gift of $11,000 to each and is fully offset by the annual exclusion if the exclusion has not been used by other gifts to the same persons earlier in the year. However, a tenancy by the entirety is not subject to unilateral severance; instead, the survivor is assured of ultimately becoming the full owner unless the parties act jointly to terminate the tenancy. In such circumstances, the tenant who has the

---

[35] Estate of Schuler v. Comm'r, 80 TCM (CCH) 934 (2000). See United States v. Estate of Grace, 395 US 316 (1969); ¶ 4.08[7][d].

[36] Schultz v. United States, 493 F2d 1225 (4th Cir. 1974); Sather v. Comm'r, 78 TCM (CCH) 456 (1999); Priv. Ltr. Rul. 8717003 (Jan. 17, 1987); Cf. Rev. Rul. 85-24, 1985-1 CB 329.

[37] Estate of Buder v. Comm'r, 25 TC 1012 (1956). But see Rev. Rul. 75-8, 1975-1 CB 309 (North Carolina law); Rev. Rul. 74-345, 1974-2 CB 323 (Tennessee law), holding that if under local law one spouse during the marriage has no enforceable rights to rents, profits, possession, or control of the property, that spouse has no present enjoyment of the property and only one annual exclusion is allowed. Rev. Rul. 74-345 has been revoked by Rev. Rul. 79-54, 1979-1 CB 313, because Tennessee law was changed, giving the spouse a "joint right to the use, possession, control and income of the property."

[38] Helvering v. Hutchings, 312 US 393 (1941).

[39] Estate of Buder v. Comm'r, 25 TC 1012 (1956).

[40] See ¶ 10.01[3][f].

[41] See Reg. § 25.2515-2(b)(1) (applicable to Section 2515 prior to repeal by the Economic Recovery Tax Act of 1981, Pub. L. No. 97-34, § 403(c)(3)(B), 95 Stat. 172, 302 (1981), reprinted in 1981-2 CB 256, 325).

longer life expectancy has the more valuable interest in the tenancy,[42] and the gift tax results will reflect that difference in valuation of interests. Thus, if *A* and *B* are of different ages, a gift by a third party to them as tenants by the entirety of property worth $22,000 may be a gift to *A* of $12,000 and to *B* of $10,000. In this circumstance, even if no part of the exclusion for *A* or *B* has been used in the year, the full exclusion will not be consumed, because this must be reflected on the return as:

Gift to *A*	$12,000
Exclusion	11,000
Included amount of gift	$ 1,000
Gift to *B*	$10,000
Exclusion	10,000
Included amount of gift	$ 0

The unused exclusion regarding the gift to *B* cannot be applied to offset a part of the gift to *A*. This is not always a problem, however; if the property were more valuable, the interest of each tenant could exceed the maximum exclusion anyway.

[2] Future Interests Disqualified for Exclusion

A parenthetical provision in Section 2503(b) forecloses any exclusion for gifts of future interests in property. There is some justification for this rule; remote or contingent future interests in property may be very difficult to value, and the ultimate donees may be difficult to identify. This was the congressional reason for adopting the future interest disqualification.[43] Nevertheless, the rule is applied mechanically, even in circumstances that bear little relationship to its supporting reasons, and sometimes with surprising results.

[3] Definition of "Future Interests"

A "future interest" is one that is "limited to commence in use, possession or enjoyment at some future date or time."[44] It is not enough that a donee re-

---

[42] See Reg. § 25.2515-2(b)(2) (applicable to Section 2515 prior to repeal by the Economic Recovery Tax Act of 1981, Pub. L. No. 97-34, § 403(c)(3)(B), 95 Stat. 172, 302 (1981), reprinted in 1981-2 CB 256, 325).

[43] S. Rep. No. 665, 72d Cong., 1st Sess. 41 (1932), reprinted in 1939-1 (Pt. 2) CB 496, 526.

[44] Reg. § 25.2503-3(a).

ceives a vested right to the property. Even if an interest can be sold,[45] the statutory test is the immediate right to use, possession, or enjoyment.[46] As the Supreme Court said in the *Fondren* case:

> [I]t is not enough to bring the exclusion into force that the donee has vested rights. In addition he must have the right presently to use, possess or enjoy the property. These terms are not words of art, like "fee" in the law of seizin . . . but connote the right to substantial present economic benefit. The question is of time, not when title vests, but when enjoyment begins.[47]

A remainder interest, thus, whether vested or contingent, is a future interest for which no exclusion is allowed. This should be related to the principle expressed earlier that recognizes the beneficiaries of a trust as the persons to whom a gift in trust is made. If a donor transfers property worth $22,000 in trust, the income to be paid to *A* for life and then the corpus to be distributed to *B*, can the donor claim two exclusions with respect to the gift? The answer is no. Although there are two donees, the gift to *B* is a gift of a future interest for which no exclusion is allowed. Moreover, the donor may not even get one full $11,000 exclusion. Although the present value of the gift to *A* admittedly qualifies for the exclusion, the excess amount of the $11,000 exclusion over the amount of the gift is simply lost unless the donor makes additional gifts to *A*. It cannot be applied to gifts to other donees.

[a] Separate Interests Tested

Whenever a single transfer constitutes a gift to several persons, it is necessary to identify each gift in deciding what exclusions may be claimed. Gifts that are of future interests in property are completely disqualified. A gift of a present interest supports an exclusion, but of course not in excess of the amount or value of that gift. Accordingly, in the trust situation suggested earlier, where the total value of the property placed in trust is $22,000, assume that *A*'s life interest is worth $7,000 and *B*'s remainder interest $15,000, taking into account current interest rates and *A*'s age.[48] On such facts, the donor's total amount of gifts would be $15,000 ($22,000 less an exclusion for the full value of the gift of the $7,000 present interest).

---

[45] Schuhmacher v. Comm'r, 8 TC 453 (1947), acq. 1947-1 CB 4; Howze v. Comm'r, 2 TC 1254 (1943).

[46] Braddock v. United States, 73-2 USTC ¶ 12,963 (ND Fla. 1973). See Rev. Rul. 76-360, 1976-2 CB 298; Wooley v. United States, 736 F. Supp. 1506 (SD Ind. 1990) (contribution to capital accounts of partners were present interests because of partner's immediate right of withdrawal).

[47] Fondren v. Comm'r, 324 US 18, 20 (1945) (emphasis added).

[48] See IRC § 7520; Reg. §§ 20.2031-7(d)(7) Table S, 25.2512-5(d)(2)(iii).

A gift in trust, of course, may not qualify at all for the annual exclusion. If one transfers property to a trust and provides for no current income distribution but for the income to be paid, only after a stated period, to A for life and the remainder ultimately to B, the donor has made a gift of a present interest to neither A nor B.[49] The entire value of the property transferred is a part of "the total amount of gifts" for the period in which the transfer is made.[50]

The future-interest rule often produces extreme results. If the transfer is one of $20,000 in trust for B, then twenty-one years old, the income to be paid to B until B is twenty-eight years old and then the corpus to be distributed to B, there are again gifts of present and future interests, this time both interests are gifts to the same person. Assuming a 10 percent rate under the applicable valuation tables, the present interest is worth $9,737 and the remainder is worth $10,263.[51] The exclusion for such a gift is limited to the smaller figure. Under these circumstances, the "taxable gift" is less if B's income interest is extended and B's right to the corpus is deferred until B reaches age 41.[52] B's income interest (the present interest for which the exclusion is allowed) is worth $17,027 and the remainder is worth $2,973.[53] As a matter of policy, this result seems wrong, since the taxable portion of the gift is smaller in the cir-

---

[49] Cf. Reg. § 25.2503-3(c) Ex. 2; Rev. Rul. 79-47, 1979-1 CB 312.

[50] United States v. Pelzer, 312 US 399 (1941). In one situation, a donor made a transfer of property in trust in December for the benefit of a then unborn child who was born in February of the following year. The trustee was directed to pay so much of the income to the child as necessary for support and to accumulate the balance of the income. When the child attained age 21, the trust was to terminate and the corpus with accumulated income was payable as the child might appoint or, in default, was payable to an identical trust created for his sister. The Service ruled that no present interest was created that would support an exclusion under Section 2503(b). While under Regulations Section 25.2503-3(b) an unrestricted right to the income from property is a present interest, an unborn child does not have such an unrestricted right. Moreover, Section 2503(c), discussed in the following paragraphs, was not satisfied because two conditions of the section would not be met if the child was stillborn. Rev. Rul. 67-384, 1967-2 CB 348.

Disqualification for the exclusion is not limited to gifts in trust. See Rev. Rul. 67-172, 1967-1 CB 276, involving donor's deed of realty with temporary reservation of surface right to crops and rents and to mineral rights.

One may wish to consider this question: Is it appropriate to deny an exclusion entirely if the only possible present interest is an income interest that begins one year after a trust is created when the value of the right to such future income would, in part, determine the value of the excludible income interest if income payments began immediately instead of being deferred for one year?

[51] See IRC § 7520; Reg. §§ 20.2031-7(d)(6) Table B, 25.2512-5(d)(2)(iii).

[52] Charles v. Hassett, 43 F. Supp. 432, 435 (D. Mass. 1942).

[53] See IRC § 7520; Reg. §§ 20.2031-7(d)(6) Table B, 25.2512-5(d)(2)(iii). Of course, the exclusion would be limited to $11,000 and $9,000 would go into the "total amount of gifts," unless a spouse's exclusion could also be invoked under Section 2513 to reduce the total amount of gifts to $2,973, as discussed at ¶ 10.03.

cumstance in which the donee's full rights in the property are no longer postponed.

An interesting issue is whether a life interest or a term of years should be treated as a present interest to the full extent of its present value. The Treasury has not always agreed that it should on the ground that a substantial part of the enjoyment is spread forward over the duration of the interest. However, the Treasury now recognizes the full value of such interests as present interests,[54] a point on which the courts also agree.[55]

A question can arise as to what constitutes separate interests in trust. If a donee receives an income interest for a term of years followed by a remainder interest, the income interest is treated as a separate interest and only its value qualifies for the annual exclusion. Suppose two donees each receive an income interest in the principal of a trust that is split equally for their joint lives, and upon the death of either, the principal is combined and all income is paid to the survivor for life. Has each received a single income interest that may be expanded, or has each received two income interests, a present right to one half the income for the beneficiaries' joint lives and a contingent future right to all the income if the donee survives? The Treasury takes the latter position and allows an annual exclusion for the value of each right to one half the income during the beneficiaries' joint lives but no exclusion for the contingent future rights to income.[56] This is probably sound under the present statute, but arguably, it is questionable as a matter of policy.

Where a donor gives a donee an income interest for a term of years but, prior to expiration of the first term of years, expands it to a longer term of years, two separate interests are created; indeed, two separate gifts are made. Since the second gift does not commence in enjoyment until the termination of the first, it is a future interest that does not qualify for an annual exclusion.[57] If, however, upon the second gift the donee becomes outright owner of the property, the second gift qualifies for the annual exclusion. In one case,[58] for example, the donor who had retained a reversionary interest in a trust gave the reversionary interest to the only beneficiary of the trust (the income beneficiary). Under local law the transfer resulted in complete ownership by the donee; thus, the gift of the reversion qualified for the annual exclusion. Similarly, a remainderperson's gift of the remainder interest to the only income benefici-

---

[54] Reg. § 25.2503-3(b).

[55] E.g., Sensenbrenner v. Comm'r, 134 F2d 883 (7th Cir. 1943); Fisher v. Comm'r, 132 F2d 383 (9th Cir. 1942); Mercantile-Safe Dep. & Trust Co. v. United States, 311 F. Supp. 670 (D. Md. 1970). See also Fondren v. Comm'r, 324 US 18 (1945).

[56] Rev. Rul. 75-506, 1975-2 CB 375. See also Herr v. Comm'r, 35 TC 732 (1961), nonacq. 1962-1 CB 5, nonacq. withdrawn, acq. substituted, 1968-2 CB 2, aff'd, 303 F2d 780 (3d Cir. 1962).

[57] Rev. Rul. 76-179, 1976-1 CB 290.

[58] Clark v. Comm'r, 65 TC 126 (1975), acq. 1977-1 CB 1.

ary of a trust is a gift of a present interest if there is a merger of the estates under local law.[59]

[b] Non-Income-Producing Property

A present interest in property qualifies for the exclusion only to the extent that it is susceptible to valuation at the time of the gift.[60] If, for example, one has the right to the income from a trust for a term of years or for life, it is possible to ascribe a value to the interest with regard to the duration (term) or probable duration (life) of the right and the value of the corpus. This is what the actuarial tables prescribed by the Secretary purport to do.[61] It is suggested below that if a term or life interest is alterable or otherwise subject to being defeated, it cannot be accorded a value for purposes of the exclusion. Here, however, we raise only the question of whether the nature of the property in which the interest exists may likewise prevent valuation and thus preclude any exclusion.

An argument can be made that an income interest in non-income-producing property either cannot be valued or has a zero value for annual exclusion purposes. The Commissioner has advanced this argument with some success[62] and adheres to it,[63] but it proves too much. Once it is conceded that temporary income interests can be excludible present interests, the actuarial approach is the only fair method to determine their value. The uncertainties are many; for example, consider the following:

1. If the interest is geared to life, expectations rest only on experience and averages.
2. Past productivity of property is no sure guide to what it will do in the future.
3. Inert property (raw land) may next week sprout oil wells.

---

[59] Rev. Rul. 78-168, 1978-1 CB 298. If there were a secondary income beneficiary, this ruling would not be applicable. If there were joint income beneficiaries, the ruling would be applicable only to the extent that a merger would occur under local law.

[60] Comm'r v. Disston, 325 US 442 (1945).

[61] Reg. §§ 20.2031-7(d)(7), 25.2512-5(d)(2)(iii). See also IRC § 7520.

[62] E.g., Berzon v. Comm'r, 63 TC 601 (1975), aff'd, 534 F2d 528 (2d Cir. 1976), acq. 1975-2 CB 1; Calder v. Comm'r, 85 TC 713 (1985); Stark v. United States, 345 F. Supp. 1263 (WD Mo. 1972), aff'd per curiam, 477 F2d 131 (8th Cir.), cert. denied, 414 US 975 (1973); Maryland Nat'l Bank v. United States, 609 F2d 1078 (4th Cir. 1979) (in which the Fourth Circuit distinguished its prior decision in *Rosen*); Rosen v. Comm'r, 48 TC 834 (1967), rev'd, 397 F2d 245 (4th Cir. 1968). But see Swetland v. Comm'r, 37 TCM (CCH) 249 (1978), and cf. O'Reilly v. Comm'r, 95 TC 646 (1990). See Baxter, "Application of Section 2503(b) of the Internal Revenue Code to Gifts in Trust of Nonincome-Producing Property," 102 Mil. L. Rev. 119 (1983).

[63] Rev. Rul. 69-344, 1969-1 CB 225.

4. Directors may reverse a prior policy of no dividend distributions.
5. A right to interest on insured savings in a large bank may be affected by changes in interest rates.
6. If trust assets are presently unproductive, the trustee may have discretion to convert them.
7. Absent a contrary provision in the governing instrument, state statutes on principal and income may generate some substantial economic benefit for the income beneficiary, even though the trust consists of non-income-producing property.

It appears to be improper to rule out present interests in property producing no income and allow an exclusion for an interest in assets (growth stocks?) presently producing very little income.[64] The matter poses no big threat to the fisc[65] nor any seriously proportioned matter of inequity among taxpayers. The Commissioner should abandon the practice of examining the nature of the underlying property and terminate this area of controversy and litigation. Yet the Commissioner continues to fight, often successfully.[66]

[c] Powers Affecting Present Interests

To revert to the original trust example in this section, if *A* receives a life interest in a trust and *B* the remainder, *A*'s interest will qualify for the exclusion. What if there is added a discretionary power in the trustee to distribute corpus to either *A* or *B*? This poses quite a different kind of valuation question. Such a power makes it impossible to determine the value of *A*'s present interest, for at any time the trustee may distribute the corpus to *B*, obliterating *A*'s income interest. Under these circumstances, the donor neither will nor

---

[64] Even if such a differentiation were made, would the latter interest be valued actuarially or on the basis of the actual income experience of a few years, something that is quite likely to change?

Cf. Prop. Reg. §§ 20.2056(b)-5(f)(1), 20.2056(b)-7(d)(1), 25.2523(e)-1(f)(1) all providing that a power under applicable state law that permits a trustee to adjust between income and principal to fulfill the trustee's duty of impartiality between the income and remainder beneficiaries of a trust where the power meets the requirements of Proposed Regulations Section 1.643(b)-1 is a valid income interest for marital deduction purposes. See, e.g., ¶ 5.06[8][b] text accompanying note 215.

[65] See Gelb v. Comm'r, 298 F2d 544, 552 (2d Cir. 1962), quoted in Rosen v. Comm'r, 397 F2d 245, 248 (4th Cir. 1968): "[T]he United States is in business with enough different taxpayers so that the law of averages has ample opportunity to work."

[66] Berzon v. Comm'r, 63 TC 601 (1975), aff'd, 534 F2d 528 (2d Cir. 1976), acq. 1975-2 CB 1; Maryland Nat'l Bank v. United States, 609 F2d 1078 (4th Cir. 1979). See Horvitz, "How the Nature of Trust Property Can Kill the Gift Tax Exclusion," 13 Tr. & Est. 490 (1974); Benya, "How to Qualify Gifts in Trust as Present Interests for the Gift Tax Exclusion," 7 Est. Plan. 194 (1980).

should get an exclusion for either interest.[67] If property is transferred in trust specifying named beneficiaries of present interests, but providing that after-born children share, the Service has sensibly ruled that exclusions are allowable for the named beneficiaries if a minimum value can be assigned to their interests.[68]

At one time, if the trustee held a discretionary power to invade the corpus only for the benefit of the one who had the immediate income interest, no exclusion was allowable. This was technically supportable because it is not possible on such facts to value the income interest.[69] However, in the enactment of the 1954 Code, Congress recognized the practical absurdity of this rule, which is the reason for the second sentence of Section 2503(b). Now if one has a present interest, such as *A* in this example, the possibility that *A*'s present interest may be diminished only by the exercise of a power in *A*'s favor is disregarded in valuing *A*'s income interest for the purpose of the annual exclusion. It is still true, however, that if the trustee held a discretionary power to invade for the benefit of either *A* or *B*, no exclusion is available.[70]

[d] Brief Postponement of Enjoyment

Any postponement of enjoyment defeats the exclusion. As indicated earlier, a transfer in trust with a provision for accumulation of the income cannot qualify. No beneficiary has a right to present use, possession, or enjoyment if the income is to be kept in the trust.[71] The same result follows even if the trustee is given authority to advance income to or for the beneficiaries, if a steady measurable flow of income to the beneficiaries is not assured.[72] Some special rules on gifts to minors, which may vary this general principle, are discussed in the following paragraphs.

The future interest disqualification has been applied with severity. In one case, on October 2, 1949, a donor gave each of her ten children a one-twentieth mineral royalty interest effective for production commencing January 1, 1950. It was of no avail to point out that the postponement of enjoyment was

---

[67] Prejean v. Comm'r, 354 F2d 995 (5th Cir. 1966); Riter v. Comm'r, 3 TC 301 (1944); Jacobson v. United States, 78-2 USTC ¶ 13,256 (D. Neb. 1975). Cf. Martinez v. Comm'r, 67 TC 60 (1976).

[68] Rev. Rul. 55-679, 1955-2 CB 390; Rev. Rul. 55-678, 1955-2 CB 389. On disqualification of the interests of unborn beneficiaries, see Rev. Rul. 67-384, 1967-2 CB 348.

[69] Evans v. Comm'r, 198 F2d 435 (3d Cir. 1952).

[70] Hockman v. United States, 327 F. Supp. 332 (D. Md. 1971) (income interest disqualified for exclusion, even though trust could be invaded only for the income beneficiary "or any member of his or her immediate family").

[71] United States v. Pelzer, 312 US 399 (1941).

[72] Comm'r v. Disston, 325 US 442 (1945); Fondren v. Comm'r, 324 US 18 (1945). Cf. Roderick v. Comm'r, 57 TC 108 (1971).

for less than three months, or that she could just as well have waited until January 1 and then made the gift one of an immediate interest, or that she could have permitted the children to share in the mineral royalty from October 2 on. The exclusion was denied.[73] This is not an isolated case.[74]

[e] Right to Enjoyment Suffices

On the other hand, one may be in receipt of a gift of a present interest in property without being in actual possession or enjoyment. It is the unrestricted right to such possession or enjoyment that is crucial.[75] This is forcefully illustrated by the treatment for exclusion purposes of gifts in the form of payment of insurance premiums. The regulations give this example:[76] "L pays premiums on a policy of insurance on his life. All the incidents of ownership in the policy (including the right to surrender the policy) are vested in M. The payment of premiums by L constitutes a gift of a present interest in property." This same principle supports the exclusion in the case of a gift in trust with a general provision for accumulation of income if the beneficiary has the right, nevertheless, to draw down the income or corpus as the beneficiary wishes.[77] Spendthrift provisions in a trust also do not defeat the exclusion for the value of the income interest.[78] Furthermore, the fact that the trustee is authorized to invest in non-income-producing property may not foreclose the exclusion.[79]

If a trustee's discretion stands between the beneficiary and the right to the income, no exclusion can be allowed for the income interest; the necessary

---

[73] Estate of Jardell v. Comm'r, 24 TC 652 (1955).

[74] See, e.g., Hessenbruch v. Comm'r, 178 F2d 785 (3d Cir. 1950) (income from a trust was to be accumulated for a similarly short time). See also Braddock v. United States, 73-2 USTC ¶ 12,963 (ND Fla. 1973); Estate of Kolker v. Comm'r, 80 TC 1082 (1983); Rev. Rul. 75-415, 1975-2 CB 374. But see Estate of Grossinger v. Comm'r, 44 TCM (CCH) 443 (1982). However, if the income is to be paid commencing with the creation of the income interest, the fact that it is paid periodically, not instantly as received, does not invalidate a present interest. A.D. Edwards, 46 BTA 815 (1942) (acq.), aff'd on another issue, 135 F2d 574 (7th Cir. 1943).

[75] Reg. § 25.2503-3(b). See Skouras v. Comm'r, 14 TC 523 (1950), aff'd, 188 F2d 831 (2d Cir. 1951).

[76] Reg. § 25.2503-3(c) Ex. 6. But see Reg. § 25.2503-3(c) Ex. 2.

[77] See Kieckhefer v. Comm'r, 189 F2d 118, 121 (7th Cir. 1951). But cf. Blasdel v. Comm'r, 58 TC 1014 (1972), aff'd per curiam, 478 F2d 226 (5th Cir. 1973).

[78] Rev. Rul. 54-344, 1954-2 CB 319.

[79] Gilmore v. Comm'r, 213 F2d 520 (6th Cir. 1954); Rosen v. Comm'r, 48 TC 834 (1967), rev'd, 397 F2d 245 (4th Cir. 1968). Contra Stark v. United States, 345 F. Supp. 1263 (WD Mo. 1972), aff'd per curiam, 477 F2d 131 (8th Cir.) cert. denied, 414 US 975 (1973); Rev. Rul. 69-344, 1969-1 CB 225.

right to enjoyment is lacking.[80] It is likewise possible that even if a beneficiary nominally has the right to the income from a trust, broad powers in the trustee to allocate receipts between principal and income may render the value of the interest too uncertain to support an exclusion.[81] However, one may have a present interest in a trust without being entitled to all or some stated percentage of the income. If a trustee is required under an identifiable standard to pay out income to or for the benefit of a beneficiary so that "a steady flow of some ascertainable portion" of the income is assured, an excludible present interest may be recognized,[82] but, if the standard is uncertain, the exclusion is lost.[83]

The Treasury concedes that the term "future interest" "has no reference to such contractual rights as exist in a bond, note (though bearing no interest until maturity), or in a policy of life insurance, the obligations of which are to be discharged by payments in the future"[84] but, at the same time cautioning that a future interest in such obligations may be created by limitations in an instrument of transfer.[85]

Generally, a gift of a partnership interest or corporate stock is a gift of a present interest because of a fiduciary duty on the general partners or board of directors to act for the benefit of the other partners or shareholders[86] and because such interests are transferable.[87] However, limitations on both a fiduciary duty to distribute income (other than for reasons related to the conduct of the entity), and on the ability to transfer the property may result in the gift being

---

[80] Hamilton v. United States, 553 F2d 1216 (9th Cir. 1977); King v. Comm'r, 28 TCM 614 (1969); McManus v. Comm'r, 40 TCM (CCH) 866 (1980); Reg. § 25.2503-3(c) Ex. 3.

[81] Van Den Weymelenberg v. United States, 397 F2d 443 (7th Cir.), cert. denied, 393 US 953 (1968); Rev. Rul. 77-358, 1977-2 CB 342, which properly disallows an annual exclusion for an income interest of a trust where the income has to be used to replenish trust corpus if there are losses incurred on the sale of trust assets. But see Quatman v. Comm'r, 54 TC 339 (1970) (exclusions for income interests were allowed despite substantial accounting discretion in the trustee and his authority to use income for maintenance of the trust res, which was a farm).

[82] See Comm'r v. Disston, 325 US 442, 449 (1945).

[83] E.g., Johnston v. Comm'r, 27 TCM (CCH) 1401 (1968).

[84] Reg. § 25.2503-3(a).

[85] Reg. § 25.2503-3(a). See Perkins v. Comm'r, 1 TC 982 (1943), nonacq. 1943 CB 38 (donee wife received only future interest in insurance policy).

[86] Priv. Ltr. Rul. 9415007 (Jan. 12, 1994) (general partner fiduciary duty to limited partner); Priv. Ltr. Rul. 9710021 (Dec. 6, 1996) (transfer of an interest in a business trust classified as a partnership interest was subject to a fiduciary duty of the transferor partner and constituted a present interest).

[87] TAM 9131006 (Apr. 30, 1991) (general partner fiduciary duty to limited partner and donees had a right to sell or assign their interests subject to a right of first refusal); Priv. Ltr. Rul. 199944003 (July 2, 1999) (same).

classified as a future interest.[88] Furthermore, a gift of capital to a corporation, although it is a gift to the shareholders of the corporation,[89] is not a gift of a present interest. Courts have held that each individual shareholder's inability to receive the individual's share of the capital without a corporate dividend or a liquidating distribution precludes any present enjoyment of the property.[90] The courts do not treat the shareholder's concurrent increase in the value of their stock or their ability to sell the stock as sufficient to constitute a present interest.[91] Seemingly, a gift of capital to a partnership, which is similarly a gift to each partner's capital account,[92] is a gift of a present interest to each partner if the partner has an unrestricted right to demand payment of the partner's capital account.[93]

[f] *Crummey* Powers

If a beneficiary or several beneficiaries of a trust receive future interests in the trust, which would not ordinarily qualify for annual exclusions under Section 2503(b), the interests may be accorded the status of excludible present interests if the beneficiaries are given what are commonly referred to as *Crum-*

---

[88] Hackl v. Comm'r, 118 TC 279 (2002) (an interest in a limited liability company was subject to restrictions which prevented its transfer from qualifying as a present interest); TAM 9751003 (Aug. 28, 1997) (limited partnership agreement restricted the limited partners' rights to assign their interests and from withdrawing their interests without the consent of others and authorized the general partner to distribute income to the partners in her "sole discretion" and to retain funds for partnership expenditures or for "any reason whatsoever"). The TAM ruling has received attention, see Kalinka, "Should the Gift of a Limited Partnership Interest Constitute a Future Interest?" 76 Taxes 12 (Apr. 1988); Lipshultz & Zysik, "Significant Recent Developments in Estate Planning (Part I)," 29 Tax Adviser 547 (1998).

[89] Reg. § 25.2511-1(h)(1).

[90] Stinson Estate v. Comm'r, 214 F3d 846 (7th Cir. 2000); Chanin v. United States, 393 F2d 972 (Ct. Cl. 1968); Heringer v. Comm'r, 235 F2d 149 (9th Cir.), cert. denied, 352 US 927 (1956); Georgia Ketteman Trust v. Comm'r, 86 TC 91 (1986); Rev. Rul. 71-443, 1971-2 CB 338.

[91] The courts dealing with the issue do not directly address this issue, merely comparing a corporate interest to a remainder interest in a trust. This may be a bit difficult to accept given the lenient treatment of bonds and life insurance as present interests. See supra text accompanying notes 84, 85. Nevertheless, the law seems well settled.

[92] Gross v. Comm'r, 7 TC 837 (1946), acq. 1946-2 CB 2. Cf. Fischer v. Comm'r, 8 TC 732 (1947), acq. 1947-1 CB 2 (adequate consideration received for the transfer).

[93] Cf. Wooley v. United States, 736 F. Supp. 1506 (SD Ind. 1990) (a transfer from one partner's capital account to other partners' capital accounts was a present interest because of the donee partners' rights to demand immediate payment of their capital accounts).

mey powers. Named after a Ninth Circuit case,[94] *Crummey* powers are powers given to beneficiaries to demand outright ownership of property held in trust.[95] The thinking is that a present right to possession is equal to possession. Such powers are commonly found in life insurance trusts, because the transfer of life insurance to the trust or the payment of premiums on the life insurance policies in the trust would normally not result in the creation of an excludible present interest,[96] but *Crummey* powers are not limited to such trusts. *Crummey* powers have traditionally been given to income beneficiaries of any trust in which a transfer to the trust does not qualify (either in whole or in part) for an annual exclusion.[97] They have also been given to trust beneficiaries who otherwise hold only remainder interests or secondary income interests, which also do not qualify for an annual exclusion.[98] Furthermore, *Crummey* powers are not limited to transfers made to trusts. They are also used with respect to transfers of partnership interests that may not otherwise qualify for an annual exclusion.[99]

The Service has employed a variety of attacks (thus far unsuccessfully) in an attempt to limit the use of *Crummey* powers. In its initial attack on *Crum-*

---

[94] Crummey v. Comm'r, 397 F2d 82 (9th Cir. 1968). The *Crummey* case involved an issue of the power of guardians of minor beneficiaries to demand an amount of up to $4,000 in cash or a pro rata amount of transfers to the trust, whichever was less. The court concluded that the demand rights were sufficient legal rights to qualify as present interests. The Commissioner did not challenge the qualification of the rights of the adult beneficiaries of the trust. The Service has subsequently agreed with the *Crummey* result, holding that it will not raise the *Crummey* issue where there is "no impediment under the trust or local law to the appointment of a guardian and the minor donee has a right to demand distribution." Rev. Rul. 73-405, 1973-2 CB 321.

[95] If the *Crummey* power is limited by trustee discretion, no exclusion is allowed. Priv. Ltr. Rul. 8213074 (Dec. 30, 1981). Cf. Hockman v. United States, 327 F. Supp. 332 (D. Md. 1971).

Furthermore, if a *Crummey* power is given to a skip person who has a present interest in a trust, the transfer will not automatically qualify for a zero inclusion ratio under the generation-skipping transfer tax unless the transfer also satisfies the requirements of Section 2642(c)(2). See ¶ 16.02[2][b][iii].

[96] See Reg. § 25.2503-3(c) Ex. 2. Cf. Reg. § 25.2503-3(c) Ex. 6. Several letter rulings have recognized the validity of *Crummey* powers in life insurance trusts funded only with life insurance. Priv. Ltr. Rul. 7826050 (Mar. 29, 1978) (term insurance); Priv. Ltr. Rul. 8006109 (Nov. 20, 1979) (group term insurance and $1,000 cash); Priv. Ltr. Rul. 8047131 (Aug. 29, 1980) (whole life insurance). The Service will not ordinarily issue a ruling regarding the Section 2503(b) consequences of a *Crummey* power in some life insurance situations. Rev. Proc. 95-3, 1995-1 CB 385, 396 § 5.21.

[97] See, e.g., supra ¶¶ 9.04[3][a] text accompanying note 49, 9.04[3][c] text accompanying note 67, 9.04[3][d] text accompanying note 71.

[98] See supra ¶ 9.04[3] text accompanying notes 44–47.

[99] See Priv. Ltr. Rul. 9710021 (Dec. 6, 1996) (donee granted withdrawal power with respect to a transfer to a business trust that was treated as a partnership for tax purposes). Cf. supra ¶ 9.04[3][e] text accompanying notes 87, 88.

mey powers in Revenue Ruling 81-7,[100] the Service held that if the power is "illusory" because of the beneficiary's lack of knowledge or because of an unreasonable time within which to exercise the power, the power does not qualify under Section 2503(b). The Service's position appears to be aimed at lack of knowledge,[101] with lack of time being less significant,[102] although lack of time was a factor in Revenue Ruling 81-7. The position seems invalid because the Service recognizes no comparable exception under other sections,[103] although prudence would suggest that compliance with the ruling would be advisable.

In a subsequent attempt to invalidate *Crummey* powers, the Service has held that in order to constitute a valid *Crummey* power, the holder of the power must have a "substantial economic interest" in the trust.[104] However, the essence of a *Crummey* power is that the recipient of the power has the right to extract the property subject to the power from the trust corpus. It would seem that there is no need for the *Crummey* power holder to have any beneficial interest in the trust to qualify for the annual exclusion. A step in this direction was taken by the Tax Court in the *Cristofani* case,[105] where the court upheld *Crummey* powers given to persons holding only contingent remainder interests in the trust.[106] Although the Service ultimately acquiesced in *Cristofani*,[107] it has since announced that it will continue to deny annual exclusions to persons with only contingent remainder interests or with no interests in a trust.[108] However, the Tax Court followed the *Cristofani* case in the *Kohlsaat* case[109] where *Crummey* powers were granted to sixteen contingent trust beneficiaries, all children, grandchildren, or spouses of the primary beneficiaries.

---

[100] Rev. Rul. 81-7, 1981-1 CB 474.

[101] Compare Rev. Rul. 81-7, 1981-1 CB 474, with Rev. Rul. 83-108, 1983-2 CB 167; Priv. Ltr. Ruls. 8004172 (Nov. 5, 1979), 8047131 (Aug. 29, 1980). But see Priv. Ltr. Rul. 7826050 (Mar. 29, 1978).

[102] See, e.g., Crummey v. Comm'r, 397 F2d 82 (9th Cir. 1968) (two weeks); Rev. Rul. 83-108, 1983-2 CB 167 (forty-five days); Priv. Ltr. Rul. 8022048 (Mar. 4, 1980) (three days).

[103] See, e.g., ¶ 10.07[2][b] note 62.

[104] See, e.g., TAMs 8727003 (Mar. 16, 1987) (no exclusion where *Crummey* power holders had only remote contingent interests or no interest in the trust), 9045002 (July 27, 1990) (no exclusion for remote contingent interests).

[105] Estate of Cristofani v. Comm'r, 97 TC 74 (1991).

[106] The case involved seven annual exclusions, two to the income beneficiaries of the trust and five to contingent remainderpersons. The transfer was held to qualify for seven annual exclusions.

[107] Acq. in result, 1992-1 CB 1; Action on Decision, 1992-09 (Mar. 23, 1992); Action on Decision, 1996-010 (Jul. 15, 1996).

[108] Cristofani, Action on Decision, 1992-09 (Mar. 23, 1992).

[109] Estate of Kohlsaat v. Comm'r, 73 TCM (CCH) 2732 (1997).

In its most recent attack on *Crummey* powers, the Service has argued that such powers should not be recognized when the facts and circumstances show that there is a prearranged understanding that the withdrawal power will not be exercised or that if they are not exercised, it will result in adverse economic consequences to its holder.[110] Thus far, the Service has been unsuccessful with such arguments.[111]

These attacks on *Crummey* powers indicate that their use continues to be of great concern to the Service. The Service can be expected to continue its attacks, especially in situations where a *Crummey* power is given to a nonbeneficiary of a trust[112] or where the Service finds an implied agreement not to exercise the *Crummey* power. The question of the extent to which a donor can create *Crummey* powers is one that has given rise to congressional proposals but, to date, no action.[113]

A problem may arise with respect to *Crummey* powers, relating to the amount of the property subject to withdrawal by exercise of the power. In general, the power is usually limited to the lesser of the amount transferred to the trust or the amount of the donor's annual exclusion.[114] However, with an an-

---

[110] Action on Decision, 1996-010 (Jul. 15, 1996); TAMs 9141008 (June 8, 1991) (prearranged understanding), 9628004 (Apr. 1, 1996) (prearranged understanding and adverse economic consequences because some power holders had no other economic interest in the trust except the withdrawal power), 9731004 (Apr. 21, 1997) (prearranged understanding).

[111] Estate of Kohlsaat v. Comm'r, 73 TCM (CCH) 2732 (1997); Estate of Holland v. Comm'r, 73 TCM (CCH) 3236 (1997). See Fogel, "The Emperor Does Not Need Clothes – The Expanding Use of 'Naked' *Crummey* Withdrawal Powers to Obtain Federal Gift Tax Annual Exclusions," 73 Tulane L. Rev. 555 (1998).

[112] See supra text accompanying notes 104, 105, 106, 110.

[113] There have been proposals to Congress to either deny an annual exclusion to *Crummey* powers or to set a maximum on the number of per donee annual exclusions a donor may be allowed. See, e.g., ALI Proposal, Federal Estate and Gift Tax Recommendations 19–21 (1969); Clinton administration proposal in 1998 to overrule the *Crummey* decision by making Section 2503(b) applicable only to outright transfers other than Section 2503(c). See Dept. of Treasury "General Explanations of the Administration's Revenue Proposals" 130 (Feb. 1998). The *Cristofani* case is discussed in Cavanaugh & Preston, "When Will *Crummey* Transfers to Contingent Beneficiaries Be Excludable Present Interests?" 76 J. Tax'n 68 (1992); Fiore & Ramsbacher, "*Crummey* Powers for Contingent Beneficiaries OK'D," 19 Est. Plan. 10 (1992).

[114] If there are several beneficiaries, the Service has appropriately concluded that each beneficiary's power to demand a pro rata share of the transferred amount qualifies that amount as an excludible present interest. Rev. Rul. 80-261, 1980-2 CB 279. But see Rev. Rul. 85-24, 1985-1 CB 329.

nual exclusion of $11,000[115] and, if gift-splitting is used,[116] a potential of $22,000 in annual exclusions for each donee, there is an important interrelationship between *Crummey* powers and the lapse exception to the general power of appointment rules.[117] Because of the potential for the interrelationship to cause unexpected gift, estate, and income tax consequences,[118] one would be prudent to limit the *Crummey* power holder's power to the least of (1) the

---

[115] IRC § 2503(b). In the Economic Recovery Tax Act of 1981, Pub. L. No. 97-34, § 441(c)(2), 95 Stat. 172, 319 (1981), reprinted in 1981-2 CB 256, 334, Congress provided a transitional rule that made the increase in the annual exclusion to $10,000 inapplicable with respect to *Crummey* power formula clauses created prior to thirty days after the Section 2503(b) increase. The transitional rule applies only if (1) the power is defined in terms of Section 2503(b); (2) there is no state law contrary; and (3) the instrument involved is not amended subsequently to the applicable date (thirty days after the Section 2503(b) amendment).

[116] See IRC § 2513, discussed ¶ 10.03.

[117] IRC § 2514(e); ¶ 10.04[4][c]. Cf. IRC § 2041(b)(2).

[118] The beneficiaries holding *Crummey* powers hold general powers of appointment. *Crummey* powers are, as a practical matter, rarely exercised and their lapse results in a potentially taxable transfer by the beneficiary to the extent that the lapse exceeds the greater of $5,000 or 5 percent of the aggregate value of assets out of which the lapsed powers can be exercised. See ¶ 10.04[4][c]. But see Rev. Rul. 85-24, 1985-1 CB 329. See also Rev. Rul. 85-88, 1985-2 CB 201, involving multiple *Crummey* powers given by a donor to a single donee. Regarding the excess, if the beneficiary of a *Crummey* power is the income beneficiary of the trust, the lapse may constitute a gift to the extent of the value of the remainder interest; and the beneficiary will have retained a life interest with adverse estate tax consequences. See Reg. § 20.2041-3(d)(3); IRC § 2702; Priv. Ltr. Rul. 8229097 (Apr. 22, 1982); ¶ 4.13[6][f]. See also Priv. Ltr. Rul. 7947066 (Aug. 23, 1979).

There may be unanticipated income tax consequences as well, because of the possibility that the trust becomes a grantor trust as to the beneficiary who lets the *Crummey* power lapse. The lapse of a *Crummey* power may result in the power holder being treated as the owner for income tax purposes of the property subject to the lapsed power if the power holder retains control over the property subject to the lapsed power that would subject a grantor of a trust to treatment as owner of the trust for income tax purposes under Section 671–677. IRC § 678(a)(2). The issue is to what extent there is a "release" of the general power of appointment under § 678(a)(2) when an $11,000 *Crummey* power lapses. There is no judicial authority on the issue. The Service takes the position that there is a release of the full $11,000 lapse and provides a method to compute the portion of the corpus whose income is taxed to the *Crummey* power holder. Priv. Ltr. Rul. 9034004 (May 17, 1990). Writers have taken different positions with respect to the result. Compare Westfall, "Lapsed Powers of Withdrawal and the Income Tax," 39 Tax L. Rev 63 (1983) ($11,000 is released) and Ferguson, et al., "Federal Income Taxation of Estates, Trusts, and Beneficiaries" § 10.16[8] (Aspen 3d ed. 1998) ($11,000 is released) with Peschel & Spurgeon, "Federal Taxation of Trusts Grantors and Beneficiaries" § 9.05B (Warren, Gorham & Lamont 1978) ($6,000 is released) and with Lawrence, "Structuring Irrevocable Trusts in Light of Tax Changes and Proposals," 44 NYU Tax Inst. § 55.03[1][c] (1985) and Early, "Income Taxation of Lapsed Withdrawal Powers Analyzing Their Current Status," 62 J. Tax'n 198 (1985) (nothing is released). See also Natboney, "The *Crummey* Trust and Five and Five Powers After ERTA," 60 Taxes 497 (1982).

power holder's pro rata share of the transferred amount; (2) the annual exclusion of the transferor or transferors; or (3) the lapse exception to the general power of appointment provision.[119] The potential adverse income, gift, estate, and generation-skipping transfer tax consequences of *Crummey* powers dictate that they be handled with care.[120]

[g] Qualified Tuition Programs and Education Savings Accounts

In the late 1990s, Congress became increasingly aware of the burdens of the costs of higher education upon taxpayers and enacted a series of income tax provisions to assist taxpayers (especially lower and middle range income taxpayers) in meeting those burdens.[121] Two of the provisions involve Quali-

---

[119] Such a provision would avoid the problems discussed supra note 118. The amount of the lapse exception may depend on whether the donee's power to appoint is merely out of the property transferred to the trust, as was the case in *Crummey*, or out of the entire trust corpus. See Rev. Rul. 66-87, 1966-1 CB 217; ¶ 4.13[7][f]. For example, if a donor transfers $11,000 to a trust that previously had a $209,000 corpus but gives the donee a power to withdraw only the property transferred, the five-or-five power protection would apply only to the extent of the greater of $5,000 or $550 (5 percent of $11,000). But if the power were to extract $11,000 from corpus, the five-or-five power protection would apply to the greater of $5,000 or $11,000 (5 percent of $220,000). Either type of provision should qualify as a valid *Crummey* power. See Priv. Ltr. Rul. 8006109 (Nov. 20, 1979). Cf. Rev. Rul. 81-7, 1981-1 CB 474.

An alternative planning device is a "hanging power" under which a donee continues to hold the *Crummey* power to the extent that it exceeds the $5,000 or 5 percent Section 2514(e) limitation. See Price on Contemporary Estate Planning §§ 7.37.4, 7.37.12 (Little Brown & Company 1992); Harrison, "Lapse of *Crummey* Power Need Not Result in Taxable Gift if Hanging Power Is Used," 17 Est. Plan. 141 (1990); Harris & Jacobson, "Maximizing the Effectiveness of the Annual Gift Exclusion," 70 Taxes 204 (1992).

[120] See ¶ 13.02[2][d][ii] for a discussion of the relationship of *Crummey* powers to the generation-skipping transfer tax.

A discussion of *Crummey* powers is found in the following articles: Lischer, "The 'Crummey' Trust," 79 Est., Gifts & Tr. J., July–Aug. 1979, at 17; Leimberg, "Section 2503(b)—Use of Trusts and the Gift Tax Exclusion," 39 NYU Inst. on Fed. Tax'n, Chapter 42 (1980); Szarwark, "Drafting *Crummey* Powers: The Current Rulings Scene," 5 Notre Dame Est. Plan. Inst. 483 (1980); Madden, "Restrictive Future Interest Gifts to Minors May Qualify for the Annual Exclusion," 49 J. Tax'n 348 (1978); Daniel, "*Crummey* Trusts for Minors," 24 Ariz. L. Rev. 905 (1982). Moore, "Tax Consequences and Uses of 'Crummey' Withdrawal Powers: An Update," 22 U. Miami Inst. Est. Plan. Chapter 11 (1988); Fried, "Various Aspects of *Crummey* Powers," 1 Cal. Tax. Law (3) 11 (1991); Harris & Jacobson, "Maximizing the Effectiveness of the Annual Gift Exclusion," 70 Taxes 204 (1992); Steinkamp, "Common Sense and the Gift Tax Annual Exclusion," 72 Neb. L. Rev. 106 (1993).

[121] See, e.g., IRC § 25A (The Hope Scholarship and Lifetime Learning Credits).

fied Tuition Programs[122] and Education Savings Accounts.[123] Currently,[124] both are subject to similar statutory estate and gift tax rules,[125] which differ from the normal estate and gift tax rules.

The principal gift tax event in connection with either a Qualified Tuition Program or an Education Savings Account occurs when a contributor makes a contribution of cash to such a plan on behalf of a beneficiary. Either type of contribution is treated as a completed gift of a Section 2503(b) present interest to the beneficiary,[126] and is not treated as a "qualified transfer" under Section 2503(e).[127] Because a contribution to an Education Savings Account is limited to $2,000 per year[128] per beneficiary, the qualification of such gifts for the annual exclusion will generally prevent taxpayers from making taxable gifts with

---

[122] IRC § 529. There are two types of such programs, prepaid tuition plans (which permit the purchase of higher education credit hours at the current price level at either public or private institutions) and college savings accounts (investment accounts that are subsequently used to pay education expenses at public institutions). IRC § 529(b)(1).

For income tax purposes, contributions to such programs are nondeductible, income earned by contributed funds is exempt from income taxation, distributions from such programs are excluded to the extent they are used to pay qualified higher education expenses, and excess distributions are taxed to the recipient beneficiaries using Section 72 annuity rules. See IRC §§ 529(a), 529(c)(3)(A), 529(c)(3)(B).

[123] IRC § 530. Technically, such savings accounts, which were previously labeled Education Individual Retirement Accounts, are named Coverdell Education Savings Accounts. Contributions to such accounts are nondeductible, income earned by contributed funds is exempt from the income tax and, generally, distributions from the accounts are excluded from gross income to the extent that the proceeds are used to pay qualified higher education expenses and qualified elementary and secondary education expenses. Excess distribution amounts are taxed using Section 72 annuity rules. See IRC §§ 530(a), 530(b)(2), 530(d)(2)(A).

[124] Contribution to Qualified Tuition Programs made after August 20, 1996, and before August 6, 1997, were subject to a different set of rules. Under those rules, a waiver of tuition by or payment of tuition to an educational institution was treated as qualified transfer under Section 2503(e) and, consequently, was not subject to the gift tax or to the generation-skipping transfer tax. IRC § 529(c)(2) prior to amendment in the Taxpayer Relief Act of 1997, Pub. L. No. 105-34, § 211(b)(3)(A)(i), 111 Stat. 788, 811 (1997), reprinted in 1997-4 CB 1457, 1495. IRC § 2642(c). See Prop. Reg. § 1.529-5(a). The value of any interest in such a Qualified Tuition Program at the date of the contributor's death attributable to contributions by the decedent was included in the contributor's gross estate. Prop. Reg. § 1.529-5(c).

[125] IRC §§ 529(c)(2), 529(c)(4), 529(c)(5), 530(d)(3).

[126] IRC §§ 529(c)(2)(A)(i), 530(d)(3). This is so even though the contributor retains a power to alter the beneficiary of the program, although such an alteration may result in a gift by the prior beneficiary. See infra text accompanying notes 136, 137.

The contributions are also treated as meeting the requirements of Section 2642(c)(2) if the beneficiary is a "skip person" under the generation-skipping transfer tax. Prop. Reg. § 1.529-5(b). See ¶ 16.02[2][b][ii].

[127] IRC §§ 529(c)(2)(A)(ii), 530(d)(3). See supra note 124; infra ¶ 9.04[6]

[128] IRC § 530(b)(1)(A)(iii).

respect to such transfers (unless transfers to the donee in the year plus transfers to the Savings Account exceed the annual exclusion amount). Contributions to a Qualified Tuition Program may exceed the annual exclusion amount.[129] Consequently, a special rule is provided that permits a donor to elect[130] for gift tax purposes to treat a transfer to a Qualified Tuition Program that is up to five times the annual exclusion amount[131] as if it was made ratably over a five-year period.[132] If the contributor dies during the five-year period, the portion of the contribution that has not yet been treated as a gift transfer is included in the contributor's gross estate.[133] Otherwise, generally, the contribution consumes the donor's annual exclusions over the five-year amortization period, and no amount is included in the contributor's gross estate; however, the value of any interest distributed on account of the death of a beneficiary to the beneficiary or the beneficiary's estate seemingly is included in the beneficiary's gross estate.[134]

Generally, since contributions to either a Qualified Tuition Program or an Education Savings Account are treated as transfers under the gift tax, distributions from such plans to a beneficiary are not treated as taxable gifts.[135] However, if, under either type of plan, there is a change in the designation of the beneficiary or a rollover from the account of one beneficiary to another benefi-

---

[129] Section 529 imposes no specific limit on the amount of such contributions, but it does provide that the Program must prevent contributions in excess of those necessary to provide for the qualified higher education expenses of the beneficiaries. IRC § 529(b)(6).

[130] See Prop. Reg. §§ 1.529-5(b)(2)(i), 1.529-5(b)(2)(ii), 1.529-5(b)(2)(iii). The election is made in the year of the transfer. See Prop. Reg. § 1.529-5(b)(2)(i). In appropriate circumstances, the transferor may also elect to use Section 2513 gift splitting. Prop. Reg. § 1.529-5(b)(2)(ii).

[131] If the annual exclusion amount is increased in any year for inflation pursuant to Section 2503(b)(2), the donor may make an additional nontaxable contribution in any year in an amount equal to the increase for the year. Prop. Reg. § 1.529-5(b)(2)(iv). See Prop. Reg. § 1.529-5(b)(2)(v) Ex.

[132] IRC § 529(c)(2)(B); Prop. Reg. § 1.529-5(b)(2)(i). Technically, this rule may apply to a transfer to an Education Savings Account as well. IRC § 530(d)(3).

[133] IRC § 529(c)(4)(C). Generally, other than this rule, on the death of the contributor, there is no gross estate inclusion of any amount under either a Qualified Tuition Program or an Education Savings Account in the contributor's gross estate. Prop. Reg. § 1.529-5(d)(1). See IRC §§ 529(c)(4)(A), 530(d)(3).

[134] IRC §§ 529(c)(4)(A), 529(c)(4)(B), 530(d)(3). "The gross estate of a designated beneficiary . . . includes the value of any *interest* in [the Qualified Tuition Program or Education Savings Account]." Prop. Reg. § 1.529-5(d)(3). Seemingly, to have an *interest* in such property and to trigger inclusion in the beneficiary's gross estate, the property must be distributed to the beneficiary or the beneficiary's estate.

[135] IRC §§ 529(c)(5)(A), 530(d)(3).

ciary and the new beneficiary is not a family member of the old beneficiary[136] or is assigned by the generation assignment rules of the generation-skipping transfer tax to a generation below the old beneficiary, there is a taxable transfer from the old beneficiary to the new beneficiary.[137]

[4] Gifts to Minors

Concern that even an outright gift to a minor must be treated as a gift of a future interest because of the minor's legal disability to deal fully with the property was long ago dispelled by the Treasury.[138] If a gift is outright, the exclusion is not lost merely because the donee is a minor. On the other hand, convenience in dealing with property beneficially owned by a minor may indicate a transfer to a custodian or trustee for the minor's benefit, rather than a direct gift. As indicated earlier,[139] a transfer in trust for the benefit of an adult, even though there are general provisions for accumulation of the income, does not preclude an exclusion if the adult donee is given an unrestricted right to deal with the property as the donee wishes. Does conferring on a guardian immediate rights to act for a minor convert what would otherwise be a future interest into a present one? Before the enactment of the 1954 Code, an interesting controversy raged over this question.[140] The Ninth Circuit, in the

---

[136] Prop. Reg. § 1.529-5(b)(3)(i). Seemingly, although this proposed regulation involves only Qualified Tuition Programs, it should also apply to an Education Savings Account. See IRC § 530(d)(3) incorporating the estate and gift tax rules of Section 529.

[137] IRC §§ 529(c)(5)(B), 530(d)(3); Prop. Reg. §§ 1.529-5(b)(3)(ii), 1.529-5(b)(3)(iii) Ex. See IRC § 2651. See ¶ 17.01. Such transfer may also constitute a generation-skipping transfer if the new beneficiary is a skip person in relation to the old beneficiary. Prop. Reg. § 1.529-5(b)(3)(ii).

The five-year spreading rule also applies to such transfers by beneficiaries. Prop. Reg. § 1.529-5(b)(3)(ii). See supra text accompanying notes 130–134.

[138] Rev. Rul. 54-400, 1954-2 CB 319.

[139] See supra ¶ 9.04[3][e] text accompanying note 77.

[140] The Sixth and Seventh Circuits took a view in favor of the taxpayer, holding that if the trustee had no discretion to withhold payment (Gilmore v. Comm'r, 213 F2d 520 (6th Cir. 1954)), or if, at least, the guardian could make effective demand on behalf of the minor (Kieckhefer v. Comm'r, 189 F2d 118 (7th Cir. 1951)), the gift would be treated as a gift of present interest. In this way, gifts to minors and to adults were placed on equal footing for exclusion purposes. On the other hand, the Second Circuit required that a guardian be appointed and authorized to act for the minor at the time of the gift in order to overcome the future interest obstacle. Stifel v. Comm'r, 197 F2d 107 (2d Cir. 1952). See also Rev. Rul. 54-91, 1954-1 CB 207, revoked by Rev. Rul. 73-405, 1973-2 CB 321. The Tax Court, in Crummey v. Comm'r, 25 TCM (CCH) 772 (1966) before being reversed by the Ninth Circuit accepted the view of the Second Circuit and refined it in a case in which a trust was established, providing that the beneficiaries could demand a fixed sum of money from the trustee each year. The court allowed the annual exclusion with respect to the adult beneficiary but, following the Second Circuit, disallowed the ex-

Crummey case[141] allowed an annual exclusion on the ground that under applicable California law, the minor beneficiaries could make effective demand for trust income even though no guardian had yet been appointed for them, because one could be appointed. The Service now agrees, and it allows a Section 2503(b) exclusion even though no guardian has been appointed, if there is no impediment under trust or local law to the appointment of a guardian and the minor donee has the right to demand distribution.[142]

In order to provide an area of certainty, Congress added Section 2503(c) in 1954.[143] Although, as will be seen in the subsequent discussion, Congress was not entirely successful in eliminating all controversy concerning the application of the annual exclusion to gifts to minors, Section 2503(c) does provide a way in which a gift to a minor (one that is not outright and does not require immediate expenditure for the minor's benefit) may qualify as a gift of a present interest. If the requirements of Section 2503(c) are satisfied, not just the income interest, but the entire corpus may qualify for the exclusion.

[5] Special Statutory Rule for Minor Donees

Section 2503(c) is phrased negatively. It states that no part of a gift to one under age twenty-one (establishing a federal rule that avoids conflicting provisions of local law on minority) shall be treated as a gift of a future interest if certain conditions are met. The conditions are as follows: (1) the property and the income therefrom may be expended by or for the donee before the donee reaches age twenty-one and (2) the property and income not so expended will pass to the donee when the donee attains age twenty-one, or to the donee's estate or pursuant to the donee's exercise of a general power of appointment if the donee dies before reaching that age.[144]

---

clusion for the young minor beneficiaries. An exclusion was allowed for one minor beneficiary who was eighteen years old on the ground that applicable local law gave an eighteen-year-old the legal capacity to enter into contracts involving real and personal property.

[141] Crummey v. Comm'r, 397 F2d 82 (9th Cir. 1968). See supra ¶ 9.04[3][f] note 94.

[142] Rev. Rul. 73-405, 1973-2 CB 321. See also Naumoff v. Comm'r, 46 TCM (CCH) 852 (1983).

[143] S. Rep. No. 1622, 83d Cong., 2d Sess. 127 (1954). See Polisher & Kapustin, "Gifts to Minors Qualifying for the Annual Gift Tax Exclusion Under the Internal Revenue Code," 81 Dick. L. Rev. 1 (1976); Madden, "Restrictive Future Interest Gifts to Minors May Qualify for the Annual Exclusion," 49 J. Tax'n 348 (1978).

[144] A gift that satisfies the requirements of Section 2503(c) and is within the annual exclusion amount generally will also have a zero inclusion ratio under the generation-skipping transfer tax where the donee of the gift is a skip person. See ¶ 16.02[2][b][iii], especially note 77.

[a] First Requirement

Substantial controversy has developed around the first requirement of Section 2503(c) concerning whether the transfer terms are such that the property and its income are properly expendable for the minor donee. There is of course no requirement that expenditure be mandatory; the statute clearly contemplates that a trustee or guardian may exercise discretion. However, the Treasury properly asserts broadly that there must be "no substantial restrictions" on the exercise of discretion.[145] The key to these problems is a recognition of the congressional intention of placing gifts to minors more on a par with gifts to adults for purposes of the annual exclusion.[146] Accordingly, if Section 2503(c) is to apply, someone should have much the same control over the property and income for the minor's benefit as an adult over the adult's own property. That control is lacking in the case of gifts for single or limited purposes. Therefore, if a grandparent wants to set up a trust for a grandchild, the income from which can be used only for educational purposes, the grandparent is perfectly free to do so, but the transfer will not be excludible by reason of Section 2503(c).[147]

---

[145] Reg. § 25.2503-4(b)(1).

[146] See HR Rep. No. 1337, 83d Cong., 2d Sess. 93 (1954).

[147] The profile of Section 2503(c)(1) emerges from a number of decided cases, even though some conflicts leave the edges a little blurred. Sufficiently expendable to support exclusion: Rev. Rul. 67-270, 1967-2 CB 349 (amounts may be spent for "support, care, education, comfort and welfare"); Ross v. United States, 348 F2d 577 (5th Cir. 1965) (trustee to deal with trust property "as if [he] were the guardian of the beneficiary's person and estate"); Upjohn v. United States, 72-2 USTC ¶ 12,888 (WD Mich. 1972) (may expend funds but not for "support or maintenance which the settlors [are] legally obligated to provide"); Craig v. Comm'r, 30 TCM (CCH) 1098 (1971) (may expend income for "proper care, support, maintenance and education" and principal for same purposes when income from all other sources is deemed insufficient); Heidrich v. Comm'r, 55 TC 746 (1971) (fiduciary may pay such income and principal "as may be necessary for . . . education, comfort and support . . . and shall accumulate . . . income not so needed"); Mueller v. United States, 69-1 USTC ¶ 12,592 (WD Mo. 1969) (trustee may spend as he "deems necessary for said child's support, health and education"); Williams v. United States, 378 F2d 693 (Ct. Cl. 1967) (may expend for "maintenance, education, medical care, support and general welfare . . . if the cost and expense incident thereto are not otherwise adequately provided for").

Subject to "substantial restrictions" that preclude exclusion: Faber v. United States, 439 F2d 1189 (6th Cir. 1971) (expend for "accident, illness or other emergency"); Pettus v. Comm'r, 54 TC 112 (1970) (expressly approving Regulations Section 25.2503-4(b)(1), may expend for child, if "in need of funds . . . because of illness, infirmity or disability"); Illinois Nat'l Bank of Springfield v. United States, 756 F. Supp. 1117 (CD Ill. 1991) (expend for education or disability); Rev. Rul. 69-345, 1969-1 CB 226 (expend for "care, support, education and welfare . . . [but] take into consideration other resources available to the beneficiary and other payments made to him or for his benefit").

[b] Second Requirement

The regulations[148] indicate that a trust instrument may provide for the extension of the trust at the election of the donee beneficiary upon the beneficiary's attaining age twenty-one without loss of the exclusion. In a reversal of its prior position,[149] the Service allows the interest to qualify even though the beneficiary must act affirmatively within a limited period to compel distribution of the interest.[150] The statute provides in Section 2503(c)(2)(B), that either of two alternative provisions is acceptable concerning the donee's death before age twenty-one. It is enough in such circumstances that the property will pass either to the donee's estate[151] or to whomever the donee may appoint under a general power of appointment. If the power of appointment alternative is relied on here, it is immaterial that "under the local law a minor is under a disability to exercise an inter vivos power or to execute a will,"[152] and either an inter vivos power or a testamentary power will suffice.[153] Further, a provision that the property and accumulated income will pass to others upon the donee's death before reaching age twenty-one, in default of the exercise of donee's power, does not defeat the exclusion.[154]

The following example illustrates a problem that, after substantial controversy, seems to have been settled in the taxpayer's favor. A donor makes a transfer of property in trust for minor beneficiaries to whom the trustee may distribute income and principal when the beneficiaries are minors. Upon the beneficiaries' attaining age twenty-one, the undistributed accumulated income, but not the corpus, is to be distributed to them. The corpus is to be distributed to the beneficiaries when they attain age thirty. The Commissioner initially disallowed any exclusion for such a transfer, relying on the statutory language, "no part of a gift . . . shall be considered a gift of a future interest . . . if the *property and income therefrom* . . . " meet the stated requirements [emphasis

---

[148] Reg. § 25.2503-4(b)(2).

[149] See Rev. Rul. 60-218, 1960-1 CB 378, superseding Rev. Rul. 59-144, 1959-1 CB 249.

[150] Rev. Rul. 74-43, 1974-1 CB 285; Priv. Ltr. Rul. 8434071 (May 23, 1984) (ninety days after reaching age 21 was a reasonable time). See also Buck v. Comm'r, 31 TCM (CCH) 1134 (1972) (no exclusion where interest would pass to others at donee's death regardless of whether donee could gain possession at age twenty-one under state law or only upon attaining age 25, as provided in the transfer instrument).

[151] Priv. Ltr. Rul. 8320007 (Feb. 1, 1983). See Ross v. Comm'r, 71 TC 897 (1979), aff'd, 652 F2d 1365 (9th Cir. 1981) (distinguishing "heirs at law" from "estate").

[152] Reg. § 25.2503-4(b). However, if restrictions on exercising the power under the instrument creating the interest are more restrictive than state law, no exclusion is allowed. Gall v. United States, 521 F2d 878 (5th Cir. 1975), cert. denied, 425 US 972 (1976).

[153] Reg. § 25.2503-4(b).

[154] Reg. § 25.2503-4(b)(3).

added]. The Commissioner's position was that "property" means the principal or corpus, and therefore gifts, of both principal and income must meet Section 2503(c) standards if either is to qualify for the exclusion. The Tax Court,[155] however, properly identified the income interest as "property" severable from the trust corpus. So viewed, the value of the income interest to age twenty-one qualifies for the exclusion, even though it is clear that the value of the corpus does not qualify.[156] After the Third and Fifth Circuits and the Claims Court accepted the Tax Court's approach,[157] the Commissioner capitulated.[158] Of course, it is useless to argue that the income interest should be viewed separately from the remainder interest for exclusion purposes under Section 2503(c), unless the income interest itself meets all the statutory tests.[159] In addition, if the trust itself is to extend beyond age 21, the right to the income interest from age 21 to age 30 is a separate interest,[160] which is a future interest not qualifying for an annual exclusion and that cannot be merged with the prior interest to qualify both for the exclusion.[161] Retrospective efforts to bring a faulty transfer within the scope of Section 2503(c) by amending the transfer instrument have not been successful.[162]

[c] State Statutes Simplifying Gifts

All fifty states have enacted laws simplifying the making of gifts, at least gifts of securities, to minors. The statutes are based on either the Uniform

---

[155] Herr v. Comm'r, 35 TC 732 (1961), nonacq. 1962-1 CB 5, nonacq. withdrawn, acq. substituted, 1968-2 CB 2, aff'd, 303 F2d 780 (3d Cir. 1962).

[156] Comm'r v. Thebaut, 361 F2d 428 (5th Cir. 1966).

[157] Herr v. Comm'r, 35 TC 732 (1961), nonacq. 1962-1 CB 5, nonacq. withdrawn, acq. substituted, 1968-2 CB 2, aff'd, 303 F2d 780 (3d Cir. 1962); Comm'r v. Thebaut, 361 F2d 428 (5th Cir. 1966); Rollman v. United States, 342 F2d 62 (Ct. Cl. 1965).

[158] Rev. Rul. 68-670, 1968-2 CB 413. See also Herr v. Comm'r, 35 TC 732 (1961), nonacq. 1962-1 CB 5, nonacq. withdrawn, acq. substituted, 1968-2 CB 2, aff'd, 303 F2d 780 (3d Cir. 1962).

[159] Compare Herzberg v. Comm'r, 30 TCM 1046 (1971) (no exclusion) with Konner v. Comm'r, 35 TC 727 (1961), acq. 1968-2 CB 2, and Weller v. Comm'r, 38 TC 790 (1962), acq. 1968-2 CB 3 (income interests qualified for exclusion).

[160] Rev. Rul. 76-179, 1976-1 CB 290.

[161] Estate of Levine v. Comm'r, 526 F2d 717 (2d Cir. 1975), rev'g 63 TC 136 (1974). The Service issued a nonacquiescence in the Tax Court decision, 1978-2 CB 3.

[162] E.g., Harris v. Comm'r, 461 F2d 554 (5th Cir. 1972); Van Den Weymelenberg v. United States, 397 F2d 443 (7th Cir.), cert. denied, 393 US 953 (1968); Davis v. Comm'r, 55 TC 416 (1970). See also Roderick v. Comm'r, 57 TC 108 (1971).

Transfers to Minors Act[163] or the Uniform Gifts to Minors Act.[164] Gifts under each type of act qualify for the annual exclusion.[165]

On the other hand, these statutes may contain hidden income and estate tax pitfalls. To the extent that the income from a gift to a minor under a custodian act is used to support the minor, the one who has a legal obligation to support the minor is subject to income tax on the income.[166] More clearly, if a donor serves as custodian (instead of transferring the property to another), the value of the property may be included in the donor's gross estate if the donor dies before the donee attains age twenty-one. The Treasury has expressly so ruled,[167] and this position seems sound under the estate tax provisions.[168] With knowledge these pitfalls can be avoided, and making the exclusion available in the case of gifts to minors seems desirable. However, nontax reasons may exist for not utilizing Section 2503(c).[169] For example, it may not be appropriate to provide for distribution of a trust corpus when the beneficiary attains age twenty-one.

Section 2503(c) is not exclusive; gifts that do not precisely meet its terms still qualify for the exclusion if they can successfully run the gauntlet without the special statutory assist. An example of a gift that does not meet the terms of Section 2503(c) but qualifies for the exclusion in part under Section 2503(b) is given in the regulations:

> [A] transfer of property in trust with income required to be paid annually to a minor beneficiary and corpus to be distributed to him upon his attaining the age of 25 is a gift of a present interest with respect to the

---

[163] E.g., Fla. Stat. § 710 (2001). See Peirsol, "Gifts to Minors: How Effectively Has the Uniform Act Functioned?" 25 NYU Inst. on Fed. Tax'n 1099 (1967).

[164] Alaska Stat. § 13.46 (2001).

[165] Rev. Rul. 59-357, 1959-2 CB 212. Such gifts qualify for an annual exclusion as a result of the application of Section 2503(c). See Rev. Rul. 56-86, 1956-1 CB 449. See also Rev. Rul. 73-287, 1973-2 CB 321, properly recognizing that the provisions of Section 2503(c) set forth the maximum restrictions on gifts to minors and that the amendment of states lowering the age of majority to eighteen and requiring distribution to a minor donee at that age do not breach the requirements of Section 2503(c)(2)(A).

[166] Rev. Rul. 59-357, 1959-2 CB 212. See also IRC § 677(b), which applies if the transferor has the support obligation.

[167] Rev. Rul. 59-357, 1959-2 CB 212. Cf. Rev. Rul. 74-556, 1974-2 CB 300.

[168] Estate of Prudowsky v. Comm'r, 465 F2d 62 (7th Cir. 1972); Eichstedt v. United States, 354 F. Supp. 484 (ND Cal. 1972). See discussion of Sections 2036, 2038 at ¶¶ 4.08, 4.10.

[169] See Newman, "Tax and Substantive Aspects of Gifts to Minors," 50 Cornell LQ 446 (1965). See also Weil & Heald, "Uniform Gifts to Minors Act—Some Second Thoughts on Its Usefulness as an Estate Planning Tool," 55 Taxes 271 (1977), and the sources cited supra ¶ 9.04[4] note 143.

right to income but is a gift of a future interest with respect to the right to corpus.[170]

This is consistent with a prior Treasury ruling.[171]

[6] Medical Expenses and Tuition

A person's payment of another's unreimbursed medical expenses or academic tuition to an educational organization, long recognized as indirect transfers possibly subject to gift tax, have always escaped the tax if they are made to discharge the payor's obligation under local law to provide medical care or education to the one for whom the expenses were paid. Section 2503(e)[172] expressly excludes *all* payments of this type from the gift tax and makes it immaterial whether the payor has any obligation to make the payments.[173] Transfers within the concepts of subsection (e) are designated "qualified transfers"[174] and are not treated as transfers of property by gift. These transfers fully escape the gift tax without consuming any part of the donor's annual exclusion for transfers of property by gift to the donee who benefits from the payment.[175]

Unreimbursed medical expenses that may qualify for the exclusion are defined in Section 213(d), which includes payments for medical insurance.[176] The expenses are not subject to any percentage limitation such as the one that appears in Section 213.[177] Only payment of medical expenses that are not reimbursed by insurance or otherwise are eligible for the exclusion. And payments must be made directly to the one who supplies the services[178] and not to reimburse the one who has paid for the services.[179]

---

[170] Reg. § 25.2503-4(c).

[171] Rev. Rul. 54-400, 1954-2 CB 319. See also Rev. Rul. 59-78, 1959-1 CB 690.

[172] IRC § 2503(e) was added by the Economic Recovery Tax Act of 1981, Pub. L. No. 97-34, § 441(b), 95 Stat. 319 (1981), reprinted in 1981-2 CB 333. The statute is cryptic in that it refers to Section 170(b)(1)(A)(ii) for a definition of "educational organization" as used here and Section 213(d) to define "medical care."

[173] Thus, the relationship between the donor and donee is irrelevant.

[174] IRC §§ 2503(e)(1), 2503(e)(2).

Such transfers, if they are for the benefit of "skip-persons," are also excluded from the generation-skipping transfer tax. See ¶¶ 13.01[2][a], 16.02[2][b] text accompanying notes 54–57.

[175] Reg. § 25.2503-6(a).

[176] Reg. § 25.2503-6(b)(3).

[177] See IRC § 213(a). A Section 213 income tax deduction may also be allowed for the payment.

[178] Reg. §§ 25.2503-6(b)(1)(ii), 25.2503-6(c) Ex. 3. Rev. Rul. 82-98, 1982-1 CB 141.

[179] Reg. § 25.2503-6(c) Ex. 4.

Educational expenses that may qualify are likewise unlimited in amount.[180] The exclusion applies to both full- and part-time students; but only "tuition" may be excluded.[181] Payments for books, supplies, housing, and related items are outside the statute and may constitute includible gifts.[182] Again, to be excludible, payment must be made directly to an educational organization.[183]

[7] Waiver of Survivorship Benefits

A waiver of survivorship benefits or a right to future benefits under a qualified joint-and-survivor annuity or a qualified preretirement survivorship annuity[184] by a nonparticipant spouse prior to the death of the participant is not treated as a transfer of property by gift.[185]

[8] Loans of Qualified Artwork

A loan of property without any charge is a transfer of an interest in the property for the period of the loan.[186] If such a loan is made to a charity, the trans-

---

[180] The Service has held that prepayments of tuition for future years for students who were attending a school qualified for the exclusion where the prepayments were not refundable. Priv. Ltr. Rul. 199941013 (July 9, 1999). Although the ruling related to a year prior to the enactment of Section 529 Qualified Tuition Programs (see supra ¶ 9.04[3][g]), the ruling involving nonrefundable payments should not be altered by the enactment of Section 529.

[181] IRC § 2503(e)(2)(A); Reg. § 25.2503-6(b)(2).

[182] Reg. § 25.2503-6(b)(2).

[183] Reg. §§ 25.2503-6(b)(1)(i), 25.2503-6(c) Ex. 2. The term includes payments to foreign institutions. Reg. § 25.2503-6(c) Ex. 1; Rev. Rul. 82-143, 1982-2 CB 220.

Payments made directly to an eligible educational organization are treated as being received by the student for purposes of the Section 25A income tax credit. Reg. §§ 1.25A-5(a)(1), 1.25A-5(a)(2) Ex.

For a limited period from August 20, 1996, through August 5, 1997, payments made to Qualified Tuition Programs were treated as qualified education expenses. See IRC § 529(c)(2) prior to amendment in the Taxpayer Relief Act of 1997, Pub. L. No. 105-34 § 211(b)(3)(A)(i), 111 Stat. 788, 811 (1997), reprinted in 1997-4 CB 1457, 1495. Such transfers are no longer so treated, but they do qualify for an annual exclusion. See supra ¶ 9.04[3][g] especially text accompanying note 126.

[184] See IRC §§ 401(a)(11), 417.

[185] IRC § 2503(f). The provision was added by the Tax Reform Act of 1986, Pub. L. No. 99-514, § 1898(h)(1)(B), 100 Stat. 2085, 2957 (1986), reprinted in 1986-3 CB (Vol. 1) 1, 874, effective for plans created after December 31, 1984. See infra ¶ 9.04[9] note 198, with respect to the requirement of filing a gift tax return.

[186] Cf. Crown v. Comm'r, 585 F2d 234 (7th Cir. 1979); IRC § 7872; ¶ 10.01[2][f].

fer would not qualify for a charitable deduction because of the special rules for gifts of partial interests in property to charity.[187] Section 2503(g) partially alleviates this problem by treating some charitable loans as though no transfer, and hence no gift, has occurred.[188]

The Section 2503(g) rule is applicable only to a loan of "a qualified work of art,"[189] which is defined as "any archaeological, historic, or creative tangible personal property."[190] To qualify for nontransfer treatment, the loan must be made either to a public charity or to a private operating foundation[191] and the artwork must be used by the charity for fulfilling its charitable purpose or function.[192]

If a loan of artwork is disregarded as a transfer for gift tax purposes under this subsection, it is disregarded for all transfer tax inclusion purposes.[193] Thus, if the person making the loan dies during the period of the loan, the full fair market value of the property is included in that person's gross estate.[194]

[9] Gift Tax Returns

The question of whether a gift tax return must be filed for any calendar year is related to the gift tax exclusions of Section 2503(b) and Section 2503(e),[195] the gift tax marital deduction under Section 2523, and the gift tax charitable deduction under Section 2522.[196] Returns are discussed here because of their relationship to the Section 2503 provisions.

Generally, Section 6019 requires any individual who makes a gift to file a gift tax return for the year in which the gift is made.[197] This rule has three ex-

---

[187] IRC § 2522(c)(2)(B). See ¶ 11.02[2].

[188] Section 2503(g) is effective for transfers after July 31, 1969. Technical & Miscellaneous Revenue Act of 1988, Pub. L. No. 100-647, § 1018(s)(2)(B), 102 Stat. 3342, 3587 (1998), reprinted in 1988-3 CB 1, 247.

[189] IRC § 2503(g)(1).

[190] IRC § 2503(g)(2)(A).

[191] IRC § 2503(g)(1)(A).

[192] IRC § 2503(g)(1)(B). Cf. IRC § 170(e)(1)(B)(i).

[193] Since no transfer occurs, no gift tax return is required to be filed. See IRC § 6019(a).

[194] S. Rep. No. 445, 100th Cong., 2d Sess. 473 (1988). Cf. IRC § 2033.

[195] See supra ¶¶ 9.04[1]–9.04[6].

[196] Sections 2522 and 2523 are discussed in detail at ¶¶ 11.02 and 11.03. See ¶ 2.02[1], relating to penalties and extensions for tax returns, applicable to both estate tax and gift tax returns.

[197] This was changed by the Economic Recovery Tax Act of 1981, Pub. L. No. 97-34, § 403(b)(3)(A), 95 Stat. 172, 301 (1981), reprinted in 1981-2 CB 256, 324. Prior law was explained in HR Rep. No. 201, 97th Cong., 1st Sess. 195, reprinted in 1981-2 CB 352, 394, as follows (footnotes omitted):

ceptions. First, an individual is not required to file a gift tax return if that individual's only transfers are not included in the "total amount of gifts" because they do not exceed the annual exclusion (Section 2503(b)), or they are "qualified transfers" (Section 2503(e)).[198] Second, a return is not required if the only transferred interest in excess of the annual exclusion[199] is allowed a marital deduction under Section 2523 other than a situation involving a Section 2523(f) QTIP election.[200] Finally, no gift tax return is required if the only interest transferred in excess of the annual exclusion[201] is a gift to charity deductible under Section 2522 of *either* (1) the donor's entire interest in property if no other interest in such property is or has been transferred (other than a transfer for adequate and full consideration in money or money's worth) to a nonchari-

---

Prior to 1971, gift tax returns were required to be filed, and any gift tax liability paid, on an annual basis. For gifts between 1971 and 1976, gift tax returns were required to be filed, and any gift tax liability paid, on a calendar quarter basis. For gifts made after December 31, 1976 [through 1981], a gift tax return is required to be filed, and any gift tax paid, on a quarterly basis if the sum of (1) the taxable gifts made during the calendar quarter plus (2) all other taxable gifts made during the calendar year (and for which a return has not yet been required to be filed) exceeds $25,000. If a gift tax return is required to be filed the gift tax return is due, and any gift tax payable, on or before the 15th day of the second month following the close of the calendar year.

If all transfers made in a calendar year that are subject to the gift tax filing requirements do not exceed $25,000 in taxable gifts, a return must be filed, and any gift tax paid, by the filing date for gifts made during the fourth calendar quarter of the calendar year. In 1979 . . . the due date for an annual return or a return for the fourth calendar quarter was conformed to due date for filing individual income tax returns, i.e., April 15 of the following year.

See also ¶ 9.02[3] note 22; Stephens, Maxfield & Lind, "Federal Estate and Gift Taxation" ¶ 9.04[6] (Warren, Gorham & Lamont, 4th ed. 1978).

[198] IRC § 6019(1). No return seems to be required for a Section 2503(f) waiver of survivorship benefits or a Section 2503(g) loan of qualified artwork. However, Section 2503(f) provides that waivers of survivorship benefits are not transfers by gift "for purposes of this chapter," i.e., Chapter 12. It can be argued that the waiver remains a transfer for purposes of other Code chapters, thus requiring an informational return with respect to a Section 2503(f) waiver under Section 6019. With regard to Section 2503(g), see supra note 193.

[199] See IRC § 2524; ¶ 11.04.

[200] IRC § 6019(2). If a donor is required to make an election under Section 2523(f) in order to qualify the gift transfer for a marital deduction, then a return is required to make the QTIP election. Reg. § 25.2523(f)-1(b)(4).

[201] See IRC § 2524; ¶ 11.04.

table donee[202] *or* (2) a qualified conservation easement.[203] Forms 709 (the regular gift tax return form) and 709-A (a short form used where there is gift-splitting and no tax is due)[204] are provided for reporting a donor's gift tax, and the regulations require the instructions on the form to be observed carefully.[205]

Returns required by Section 6019 for any calendar year generally are to be filed by April 15 of the following year.[206] The gift tax return filing date corresponds to the familiar income tax return filing date for calendar-year taxpayers.[207] General provision is made for extension of time for filing for as much as six months,[208] and there are special provisions for persons in or with the Armed Forces in a combat zone.[209] If a calendar-year taxpayer is granted an extension of time to file an income tax return, it is also deemed an extension of time to file a gift tax return required for the calendar year.[210] If a gift tax return is required for the calendar year in which the donor dies, the gift tax

---

[202] IRC § 6019(3)(A). Gifts involving transfers of only partial interests to charity must be reported. See IRC § 2522(c)(2); ¶ 11.02[1][e] note 43. The charitable transfer may be a Section 2522(a) transfer by a citizen or resident or a Section 2522(b) transfer by a noncitizen or nonresident. Even though the noncharitable portion of a split gift to charity qualifies for an annual exclusion or a marital deduction, a gift tax return is still required. IRC § 6019(3)(A)(ii).

[203] IRC § 6019(3)(B). See ¶¶ 5.05[7][c], 11.02[2][d] note 99. Section 6019(3) is applicable to transfers after August 5, 1997. Taxpayer Relief Act of 1997, Pub. L. No. 105-34, § 1301, 111 Stat. 788, 1039 (1997), reprinted in 1997-4 CB (Vol. 1) 1, 253.

[204] See ¶ 10.03[3][a].

[205] Reg. § 25.6019-3(a).

[206] IRC § 6075(b)(1). Failure to file a gift tax return when due will subject the donor to the penalty provisions of Section 6651 unless the failure is attributable to "reasonable cause." Compare Buckley v. Comm'r, 42 TCM (CCH) 1592 (1981) (no reasonable cause) with Lasater v. United States, 81-2 USTC ¶ 13,426 (ND Ill. 1981), and Autin v. Comm'r, 102 TC 760 (1994) (reasonable cause based on reliance on the advice of experts). See ¶ 2.02 note 14.

[207] IRC § 6072(a).

[208] IRC § 6081(a). No extension of time for filing a return may be granted unless the application is received by the Service before the time within which the return must otherwise be filed. Reg. § 25.6081-1.

[209] IRC § 7508. See ¶ 8.01[2].

[210] IRC § 6075(b)(2). Requests for an extension of time to file the income tax return are made by using Form 4868, "Application for Automatic Extension of Time to File U.S. Individual Income Tax Return" or Form 2350, "Application for Extension of Time to File U.S. Income Tax Return." Each form has a box to check for requesting an extension for filing Form 709, "United States Gift (and Generation-Skipping Transfer) Tax Return." An application for an additional extension of time to file an income or gift tax return is made by filing Form 2688, "Application for Additional Extension of Time to File U.S. Individual Income Tax Return." Form 2688 must be filed in sufficient time to receive a reply before the due date or extended due date where a previous extension of time to file was granted.

return is required to be filed not later than the due date of the federal estate tax return, including extensions.[211]

The statue provides flexibility as to *where* a gift tax return is to be filed and as a result, the Service generally requires a gift tax return to be filed with the Cincinnati, Ohio, Internal Revenue Service Center.[212]

In general, the tax is to be paid when the return is filed.[213] Only one copy of the return is required.[214] Donees are not required to file information returns. Special circumstances that may affect the requirement that a return be filed are discussed elsewhere.[215]

[10] Limitations on Assessment

[a] Commencement of Limitations Period

Generally,[216] for gifts made prior to 1997, the statute of limitations commences on the filing of a gift tax return.[217] However, with respect to gifts

---

[211] IRC § 6075(b)(3). If a donor dies prior to July 15 in any year and no extension of time to file the federal estate tax return is granted, the donor's gift tax return is due at the time of the donor's estate tax return within nine months of the donor-decedent's death. IRC §§ 6075(a), 6075(b)(3). If the donor dies after July 15 in any year, the donor's gift tax return barring any extensions is due on April 15 of the following year. IRC § 6075(b)(1).

[212] IRC § 6091(b), especially IRC § 6091(b)(1)(A)(ii). Generally, a donor must file a gift tax return in the internal revenue district in which is located the legal residence or principal place of business of the person making the return or as the secretary may designate. However, unless a return is hand-delivered the return must be filed in accordance with the Instructions for the return. Reg. § 25.6091-1(b). The Instructions for Form 709 direct that Form 709, United States Gift (and Generation-Skipping Transfer) Tax Return (2001) be sent by all donors, including nonresident donors to the Internal Revenue Service Center, Cincinnati, Ohio 45999. Instructions for Form 709, United States Gift (and Generation-Skipping Transfer) Tax Return (2001) at 4.

[213] IRC § 6151(a). An extension of time for filing a required return does not operate to extend the time for the payment of the corresponding tax, unless specified to the contrary in the extension. Reg. § 25.6081-1.

Payment of the gift tax may be made in installments as provided by Section 6159 (see ¶ 2.02[3][a]) or may be deferred under Section 6161(a) for a reasonable period not to exceed six months (see Reg. § 25.6161-1; ¶ 2.02[3][b]).

[214] Reg. § 25.6019-1(a).

[215] See, e.g., discussion of Section 2513 at ¶ 10.03, concerning splitting of gifts by married persons, and Section 2516 at ¶ 10.06, concerning certain property settlements.

[216] See infra note 218.

[217] See infra ¶ 9.04[10][b] text accompanying note 241.

made after December 31, 1996,[218] the statute of limitations does not commence running until an item is disclosed on a gift tax return, or on a statement attached to the return, in a manner adequate to apprise the Service of the nature of the item.[219] The regulations provide a broad general rule under which adequate disclosure requires a description of the nature of the gift and the basis for determining the reported value of the gift.[220] If adequate disclosure is provided, the statute of limitations runs with respect to all issues relating to the amount of the gift, including both valuation issues and legal issues involving the interpretation of the gift tax law.[221]

In addition to the broad general adequate disclosure rule, the regulations also provide safe-harbor adequate disclosure rules,[222] which require the following: (1) a description of the transferred property and any consideration received by the transferor;[223] (2) a listing of the identity of and relationship between the transferor and each transferee;[224] (3) if the property is transferred in trust, the trust's identification number and either a brief description of the terms of the trust or a copy of the trust instrument;[225] (4) *either* a detailed description of the method used in determining the fair market value of the property, including any relevant financial data (such as balance sheets), and a description of any discounts claimed in valuing the property,[226] *or*, in the alter-

---

[218] With respect to gifts arising as a result of the application of either Section 2701 or Section 2702, including an increase in taxable gifts required as a result of the application of Section 2701(d), the adequate disclosure rules applied to transfers made after October 8, 1990. Furthermore, with respect to such transfers, the regulations apply a separate set of requirements that must be met under the adequate disclosure test. Reg. § 301.6501(c)-1(e)(2). See ¶¶ 19.02[5][a], 19.02[5][d], 19.03[4][d].

[219] IRC § 6501(c)(9). The rules of adequate disclosure also apply in computing the amount of adjusted taxable gifts in the computation of a decedent's estate tax liability and in determining the amount of prior transfers to be used in determining current gift tax liability. IRC §§ 2001(f), 2504(c). See ¶¶ 2.01[1][b], 9.05[2][b].

[220] Reg. §§ 301.6501(c)-1(f)(2), 301.6501(c)-1(f)(3). The regulatory rules apply to gifts made after December 31, 1996, but only if the gift tax return for the gift is filed after the date the regulations became final, December 3, 1999. Reg. § 301.6501(c)-1(f)(8).

The regulations do not state the adequate disclosure requirements for post-1996 gifts reported in returns filed prior to December 4, 1999. Seemingly, any reasonable interpretation of the statutory provisions may be used, including the final regulations (Reg. §§ 301.6501(c)-1(f)(2)—301.6501(c)-1(f)(6)), the proposed regulations (Prop. Reg. §§ 301.6501(c)-1(f)(2)–301.6501(c)-1(f)(6) Notice of Proposed Rulemaking and Notice of Public Hearing, 63 Fed. Reg. 70,701, 70,707 (Dec. 22, 1988)), or possibly Reg. § 301.6501(c)-1(e)(2). Cf. Reg. § 301.6501(c)-1(e)(3).

[221] Reg. § 301.6501(c)-1(f)(7) Ex. 2.

[222] Reg. §§ 301.6501(c)-1(f)(2), 301.6501(c)-1(f)(3).

[223] Reg. § 301.6501(c)-1(f)(2)(i).

[224] Reg. § 301.6501(c)-1(f)(2)(ii).

[225] Reg. § 301.6501(c)-1(f)(2)(iii).

[226] Reg. § 301.6501(c)-1(f)(2)(iv).

native, an adequate appraisal of the property[227] by a qualified appraiser;[228] and (5) a statement describing any position taken that is contrary to any proposed, temporary, or final Treasury regulations or revenue rulings published at the time of the transfer.[229]

If the transfer is of an *actively traded entity* on an established exchange, the description must include the CUSIP number of the security and the mean between the highest and lowest quoted selling prices on the applicable valuation date. Id. See Reg. § 301.6501(c)-1(f)(7) Ex. 1.

If the transfer is of a *non–actively traded entity*, there is a more detailed requirement. If the valuation is based on the net value of the assets, a statement must be provided as to the valuation of 100 percent of the entity (without discounts), the pro rata portion subject to the transfer, and the fair market value reported on the return. Reg. §§ 301.6501(c)-1(f)(2)(iv), 301.6501(c)-1(f)(7) Ex. 3. The final step takes into consideration any discounting of the value of the property transferred. Reg. §§ 301.6501(c)-1(f)(2)(iv), 301.6501(c)-1(f)(7) Ex. 3. If 100 percent of the value of the entity is not disclosed, the taxpayer bears the burden of demonstrating that the fair market value is properly determined by a method other than a method based on the net fair market value of the assets held by the entity. Reg. § 301.6501(c)-1(f)(2)(iv).

Furthermore, if the non–actively traded entity that is transferred owns an interest in another non–actively traded entity or entities, the same analysis must be employed for each such entity, if such information is relevant and material in determining the value of the transferred interest. Reg. §§ 301.6501(c)-1(f)(2)(iv), 301.6501(c)-1(f)(7) Ex. 4. If the appraisal alternative is employed (see infra text accompanying notes 227 and 228), this requirement will be a part of the appraisal. Reg. § 301.6501(c)-1(f)(7) Ex. 5.

[227] The appraisal must provide all the following information in order to meet the safe-harbor requirements: (1) the appraiser's background and credentials that qualify the appraiser to perform the appraisal; (2) the date of the transfer and the appraisal, and the purpose of the appraisal; (3) a description of the property; (4) a description of the appraisal process; (5) a description of the assumptions, hypothetical conditions, and any limiting conditions and restrictions on the transferred property that affect the valuation reported; (6) the information considered in determining the appraised value, including all financial data used in determining the value of an ownership interest of a business so that another person can replicate the process and arrive at the appraised value; (7) the appraisal procedures used and the reasoning that supports them; (8) the valuation method used, the rationale for its use, and the procedure used in arriving at the fair market value; and (9) the specific basis for the valuation, such as specific comparable sales or transactions, sales of similar interests, asset-based approaches, and merger-acquisition transactions. Reg. §§ 301.6501(c)-1(f)(3)(i)(B), 301.6501(c)-1(f)(3)(ii).

[228] Reg. §§ 301.6501(c)-1(f)(2)(iv), 301.6501(c)-1(f)(3). A valid appraisal by a qualified appraiser is an alternative to the detailed description requirement. See Reg. § 301.6501(c)-1(f)(7) Ex. 5.

The appraiser must not be the donor or the donee of the property and not related to the transferor (as defined in Section 2032A(e)(2), see ¶ 4.04[3][b][vii]) and qualified to appraise the type of property transferred. Reg. § 301.6501(c)-1(f)(3)(i).

[229] Reg. § 301.6501(c)-1(f)(2)(v).

[b] Limitations Period

The regulations also provide adequate disclosure rules that relate to the commencement of the running of the limitations period in additional situations:

First, if the situation involves an asserted nongift completed transfer or transaction (such as a transaction in the ordinary course of business, including a bona fide sale between family members), the transfer or transaction is adequately disclosed if foregoing requirements (1), (2), (3), and (5) are met,[230] and there is also an explanation as to why the transfer is not a gift transfer.[231] In addition, completed transfers to members of one's family[232] that are made in operating a business are deemed to be adequately disclosed, even if not reported on a gift tax return, if the transfer is properly reported by all parties for income tax purposes.[233]

Second, if an incomplete transfer is adequately disclosed under the preceding rules and is reported as a completed transfer on a gift tax return, the gift tax statute of limitations begins to run when the return is filed, and once the period for assessment of the gift tax expires, the transfer will be subject to inclusion in the donor's gross estate for estate tax purposes only to the extent a completed gift would be so included.[234] On the other hand, if the transfer is reported as an incomplete transfer, whether or not adequately disclosed, the period for assessing a gift tax does not commence to run until the transfer is reported as a completed gift with adequate disclosure.[235]

Finally, if spouses elect to treat a gift as a split gift,[236] the adequate disclosure requirements are deemed satisfied with respect to the consenting spouse if the return filed by the donor spouse (who transferred the property) satisfies the adequate disclosure requirements.[237]

If a return is filed and *either* adequate disclosure is made with respect to gift transfers after December 31, 1996,[238] *or* the gift transfer was made prior to

---

[230] Reg. § 301.6501(c)-1(f)(4)(i). See supra ¶ 9.04[10][a] text accompanying notes 223, 224, 225, 229.

[231] Reg. § 301.6501(c)-1(f)(4)(ii).

[232] "Family" is defined by Section 2032A(e)(2). Reg. § 301.6501(c)-1(f)(4). See ¶ 4.04[3][b][vii].

[233] Reg. §§ 301.6501(c)-1(f)(4), 301.6501(c)-1(f)(7) Ex. 6.

[234] Reg. § 301.6501(c)-1(f)(5).

[235] Reg. § 301.6501(c)-1(f)(5). The estate tax consequences would also remain open in such circumstances.

[236] IRC § 2513. See ¶ 10.03.

[237] Reg. § 301.6501(c)-1(f)(6).

[238] If a post-1996 gift is not adequately disclosed on a return either because the adequate disclosure requirements are not met or a gift was not reported, Rev. Proc. 2000-34, 2000-2 CB 186, provides guidance for submitting information required to adequately disclose the gift. The statute will begin to run when the gift is adequately disclosed.

January 1, 1997,[239] the usual limitation period within which additional tax can be assessed is three years from the time the return was filed.[240] In applying this rule, the Service treats returns filed before the due date as if they were filed on such date.[241] If an includible gift of a value in excess of 25 percent of the total amount of gifts stated on the return is omitted from the return, the usual three-year limitation period is extended to six years.[242] Finally, if a fraudulent return is filed, the tax can be assessed at any time.[243]

[11] Donee and Fiduciary Liability

The recipient of a gift has a surprisingly important interest in being assured that the donor has paid the gift tax. The case of *Baur v. Commissioner*[244] should probably be required reading for all donees. It stands for the following propositions:

1. If the donor fails to pay the gift tax, the donee is personally liable for the tax to the extent of the value of the gift.[245]
2. The reason for the donor's failure to pay is immaterial; the donee can be held liable even if the donor could pay and even if the Commissioner made no effort to collect from the donor, if in fact the donor did not pay.[246]
3. Timely assessment against the donee can be made "within one year after the expiration of the period of limitation for assessment against the transferor."[247]

---

[239] Adequate disclosure rules also apply to some transfers made after October 8, 1990. See supra ¶ 9.04[10][a] note 218.

[240] IRC § 6501(a). See also IRC § 6511(a), which establishes the periods of limitations on refunds of claims.

[241] IRC § 6501(b)(1).

[242] IRC § 6501(e)(2). See Daniels v. Comm'r, 68 TCM (CCH) 1310 (1994) (Section 6501(e)(2) inapplicable where reorganization and gift of stock were treated as a single transaction).

A transfer is not treated as omitted from a return if it is adequately disclosed on a return. IRC § 6501(e)(2). Thus, as to transfers after December 31, 1996, which meet the adequate disclosure rules, the six-year rule would seem to be inapplicable.

[243] IRC §§ 6501(c)(1), 6501(c)(2), 6501(c)(3).

[244] Baur v. Comm'r, 145 F2d 338 (3d Cir. 1944).

[245] IRC § 6324(b). See Tilton v. Comm'r, 88 TC 590 (1987).

[246] O'Neal v. Comm'r, 102 TC 666 (1994). See IRC § 6901(a)(1)(A)(iii).

[247] IRC § 6901(c)(1). See O'Neal v. Comm'r, 102 TC 666 (1994) (in effect imposing a four-year statute of limitations on gift transfers); Ripley v. Comm'r, 103 F3d 333 (4th Cir. 1996) (one-year period ran from date of assessment agreement occurring prior to the running of the three-year statute of limitations).

4. With some exceptions for gifts of securities, the gift tax is a lien on the gift property for a period of ten years from the date of the gift.[248]

5. Most surprisingly of all, the recipient of a tax-free gift (in the *Baur* case, one that was entirely within the annual exclusion) can be held liable to the extent of the value of the gift for tax on all other gifts made by the donor in the same taxable period.

An executor of a donor's estate may also become personally liable for a donor-decedent's gift taxes in the same manner in which the executor may become personally liable for estate taxes imposed on the donor-decedent's estate.[249] Section 6905 provides a procedure, similar to the estate tax procedure under Section 2204, under which the executor may be released from personal liability for the decedent's gift taxes.[250]

¶ 9.05 SECTION 2504. TAXABLE GIFTS FOR PRECEDING CALENDAR PERIODS

Section 2504 answers a question raised by the two-step method for computing the gift tax provided by Section 2502 and described in a preceding section. Since the sum of taxable gifts for preceding calendar years (and, where relevant, calendar quarters) enters into the computation, what rules are to be applied in determining the sum of such gifts?

Under Section 2502(b), it is clear that only gifts made after June 6, 1932, are to be taken into account in determining taxable gifts for preceding periods. What gratuitous transfers made since that time can be disregarded? What statutory exclusions are to be recognized? What deductions from included gifts are to be allowed in arriving at taxable gifts? The statute could simply require the use of aggregate net or taxable gifts as shown on prior gift tax returns, but it does not. Fairer, if more complicated, rules are provided by Section 2504.

[1] Transfers Included for Prior Years

Any transfers made in preceding taxable periods (years or quarters as the case may be) are to be included in the sum of gifts made in those periods if the

---

[248] IRC § 6324(b). Upon expiration of the ten-year period, the lien is extinguished. The lien is durational and not limitational; thus enforcement must occur within the ten-year period. See New England Acceptance Corp. v. United States, 80 AFTR2d 97-6759 (DCNH 1997).

[249] See discussion of Section 2204 at ¶ 8.03.

[250] Reg. § 301.6905-1.

transfers were gifts under the applicable gift tax law when they were made.[1] This rule cuts both ways. A transfer that was not subject to gift tax when made need not be included, regardless of how it would now be treated. But a transfer that was subject to gift tax when made must now be included in the sum of gifts for preceding years even if it is a transfer that would not be subject to gift tax under present law.

To illustrate the second aspect of this rule, suppose that in 1945 Donor purchased Blackacre and had it conveyed to Spouse and Donor as tenants by the entirety. Until the enactment of the 1954 Code, such a transaction constituted a gift by Donor to Spouse. From 1954 to 1981, such a transaction constituted a gift only if Donor elected to have the creation of the tenancy treated as a transfer.[2] After 1981, such a transfer constitutes a gift without regard to any election, although it qualifies for a 100 percent deduction under Sections 2523 and 2524. Notwithstanding the present rule of law and regardless of whether the gift was reported in 1945, the 1945 transaction enters into the calculation of gifts for preceding calendar years.[3]

Note that prior gifts subject to tax when made must be included in gifts for preceding calendar periods, even if no gift tax return was filed when made and the expiration of limitation periods forecloses the imposition of tax with respect to such gifts.[4] Of course, this inclusion does not circumvent the statute of limitations so as now to tax such gifts, but only makes them play their proper role in the determination of rates applicable to gifts made in the current taxable period,[5] as is explained later in the discussion of the annual exclusion for gifts for preceding years.[6]

---

[1] IRC § 2504(a)(1).

[2] IRC § 2515. See Stephens, Maxfield & Lind, Federal Estate and Gift Taxation ¶ 10.06 (Warren, Gorham & Lamont, 4th ed. 1978) for a detailed discussion of this section.

[3] McMurtry v. Comm'r, 203 F2d 659 (1st Cir. 1953).

[4] S. Rep. No. 1622, 83d Cong., 2d Sess. 479 (1954).

[5] See, e.g., Clark v. Comm'r, 65 TC 126 (1975), acq. 1977-1 CB 1.

[6] The effect of a prior adjudication that a particular transfer did or did not constitute a gift may present a problem. Suppose many years ago when the gift tax concepts were not well developed, T transferred property to a trust, income to A for life with a reversion to T if living and, if not, to B or B's estate. The Commissioner asserted, it can be assumed, the value of the property transferred less only the value of the retained reversionary interest constituted a gift; but the taxpayer claimed the remainder, not just the reversion, was likewise excluded, because it would be subject to estate tax on T's death. Assume further that T litigated the matter and won a final judgment excluding the remainder interest. E.g., Smith v. Shaughnessy, 40 F. Supp. 19 (NDNY 1941). While in this actual case, the Court of Appeals reversed the district court, 128 F2d 742 (2d Cir. 1942), and the Supreme Court sustained the reversal, 318 US 176 (1943), as indicated at ¶ 10.01[3][d] note 102, assume for discussion purposes that the district court decision had not been appealed but that in a later case the Supreme Court had determined that the remainder was a part of the gift. Could T, forever after in determining gifts for prior years, exclude the value of the remainder interest transferred to B? Probably not. The earlier de-

[2] Valuation for Prior Years

Until 1954, the valuation of a gift made in earlier periods, not merely its includibility, could be reopened at any time for the purpose of determining the sum of taxable gifts for preceding calendar years.[7] This was consistent with the rules that permit the correction of improper omissions of gifts from earlier returns; and, as later explained,[8] similar principles may permit adjustments for exclusions and deductions improperly claimed. But it raised a problem, because in many instances it is very difficult to prove what the value of property was many years ago. In enacting the 1954 Code, Congress added Section 2504(c), which substantially alleviated the problem.[9] Under this provision, if certain conditions are met, an earlier *valuation* of a gift by the taxpayer or, in some circumstances, an earlier determination of *the amount of a gift*, becomes final[10] and no longer subject to reconsideration. Section 2504(c) was amended in 1997 with the result that one set of rules applies with respect to gifts made

---

cision is obviously not res judicata regarding gift tax liability for a later year and, if the prior decision has significance, it is only by reason of the doctrine of collateral estoppel or estoppel by judgment. There is some indication the earlier decision might aid *T* in such an assertion. Cf. Farish v. Comm'r, 2 TC 949 (1943), nonacq. 1944 CB 37 (settled while on appeal to the Fifth Circuit, perpetuating the effect of an annual exclusion judicially but erroneously allowed in a prior year). But see Comm'r v. Disston, 325 US 442 (1945) (rejecting a prior exclusion previously claimed (in a year against which the statute of limitations had run) where there had been no prior adjudication). However, *Farish* was decided before the Supreme Court educated the judiciary on the effect of collateral estoppel in tax cases. Comm'r v. Sunnen, 333 US 591 (1948) (an income tax case). Under the doctrine of the *Sunnen* case, a change in the interpretation of the law, such as occurred in Smith v. Shaughnessy, supra, in the Court of Appeals and the Supreme Court, would render collateral estoppel unavailable as a basis for perpetuating a prior erroneous judicial decision that a transfer did not constitute a gift. Of course, a change in the statute that makes a particular transfer a gift does not make gifts out of similar transfers made before the effective date of the change. However, the Treasury properly continues to assert (note the continued nonacquiescence in *Farish*) that erroneous "interpretations of the gift tax laws" (presumably whether judicial or administrative and whether ad hoc or in a case involving another taxpayer) may require adjustments to arrive at the proper figure for aggregate taxable gifts for preceding taxable years. Reg. § 25.2504-1(d). See also IRC § 6214(b) (jurisdiction (of the Tax Court) over other years and quarters). It may be a comfort to some to recognize that the principle expressed here works both ways; thus, collateral estoppel would not necessarily require the inclusion in prior years' gifts of amounts judicially but erroneously treated as gifts in earlier years.

[7] S. Rep. No. 1622, 83d Cong., 2d Sess. 479 (1954).

[8] See infra ¶¶ 9.05[3], 9.05[4].

[9] S. Rep. No. 1622, 83d Cong., 2d Sess. 127 (1954).

[10] See infra ¶¶ 9.05[2][a], 9.05[2][b]. In addition, while Section 2504(c) is applicable to the gift tax, it does not necessarily apply in computing "adjusted taxable gifts" under Section 2001(b)(1)(B). See ¶ 2.01[1][b].

through August 5, 1997[11] and another quite different set of rules applies to gifts made after that date.[12]

[a] Gifts Made Through August 5, 1997

With respect to gifts made through August 5, 1997, prior Section 2504(c) provides that *valuation* becomes final in the computation of gift tax due on additional gift tax transfers if[13] (1) a gift was made in a preceding calendar period; (2) a gift tax was assessed or paid for that taxable period;[14] and (3) the time for further assessment of tax for that taxable period has expired.[15]

If the appropriate conditions are met, the value of the prior gift, which must be included in the sum of the gifts for preceding calendar periods, is the value that was used in computing the tax for the last preceding taxable period for which a gift tax was assessed against or paid by the donor. This is not the same as saying that the gift is included at the value shown on the return for the year in which the gift was made. That value may be adjusted, even under the rule being considered, until such time as the year in which the gift was made becomes a closed year.[16] By adopting this somewhat complicated rule, Congress assures the use, in determining the tax on current gifts, of the last value that was determined for a gift made in a prior year before the running of the statute of limitations on the year in which such gift was made.

With respect to gifts before August 6, 1997, Section 2504(c) does not "prevent adjustment where issues other than valuation of property are involved;"[17] the section bears only on the question of *valuation*, not legal issues, such as whether a gift actually occurred or the propriety of exclusions or deductions that may have been claimed with respect to a gift.[18] Thus, even

---

[11] Reg. § 25.2504-2(a).

[12] Reg. § 25.2504-2(b).

[13] Reg. §§ 25.2504-1(d), 25.2504-2(a). Seemingly, this rule also applied to any Section 2701(d) gifts made after October 8, 1990, and prior to August 6, 1997, which were reported on the gift tax return or adequately disclosed under Section 6501(c)(9) as it existed between October 8, 1990, and August 5, 1997. See ¶ 19.02[5][a].

[14] Reg. §§ 25.2504-2(a), 25.2504-2(c) Exs. 1, 2, 3. Use of the gift tax credit under Section 2505 does not constitute a payment or assessment for purposes of Section 2504(c). Reg. § 25.2504-2(c) Ex. 1, Rev. Rul. 84-11, 1984-1 CB 201. Cf. Reilly v. United States, 88-1 USTC ¶ 13,752 (SD Ind. 1987).

[15] See the comments on limitation periods for gifts made before January 1, 1997, at ¶ 9.04[10][b] notes 239–243 and ¶ 9.04[10][a] note 218 for assessments on Section 2701(a), Section 2701(d), and Section 2702 transfers.

[16] See O'Neal v. Comm'r, 102 TC 666 (1994).

[17] S. Rep. No. 1622, 83d Cong., 2d Sess. 479 (1954).

[18] S. Rep. No. 1622, 83d Cong., 2d Sess. 479 (1954). Reg. §§ 25.2504-1(d), 25.2504-2(a). See Rev. Rul. 76-451, 1976-2 CB 304.

though a pre-August 6, 1997, gift was made, a gift tax was assessed, and the statute of limitations has run, the Service can alter the amount of the gift (not value) due, for example, to an improper annual exclusion or deduction.[19]

[b] Gifts Made After August 5, 1997

Under current Section 2504(c), with respect to gifts made after August 5, 1997,[20] if the statute of limitations has run on a gift because the gift was either reported on a return, or disclosed on a statement attached to a return, in a manner adequate to apprise the government of the nature of the gift,[21] the *amount*[22] of the gift as finally determined[23] for gift tax purposes may not be changed for purposes of determining the amount of tax on subsequent taxable gifts under the gift tax.[24] Current Section 2504(c) omits the second requirement of old Section 2504(c) that gift tax must be assessed or paid for the prior period,[25] and it extends protection to all issues relating to the gift, including valuation issues and legal issues involving the interpretation of gift tax law.[26] However, it also imposes a "final determination" requirement.[27] A final determination of the amount is made (1) by the taxpayer if the amount is shown on a gift tax return (or a statement attached to the return) and the Service does

---

[19] See Reg. §§ 25.2504-2(c) Exs. 2, 3.

[20] The rules apply only if the gift tax return for which the transfer is reported is filed after December 3, 1999. Reg. § 25.2504-2(d). This includes gifts made as a result of the application of Section 2701(d). IRC § 2504(c)(2). See ¶ 19.02[5][a].

Arguably, with respect to gifts made after August 5, 1997, where the gift tax return is filed before December 4, 1999, the prior proposed regulations that applied only to valuation, but not legal issues, apply (see Prop. Reg. § 25.2504-2(b) Notice of Proposed Rulemaking and Notice of Public Hearing, 63 Fed. Reg. 70,701, 70,705 (Dec. 22, 1998)), although allowing use of either the proposed regulations or the final regulations for such period would seem more appropriate.

[21] The reporting and disclosing language does not expressly appear in the statute, but it is incorporated via the Section 6501 time expiration requirement of Section 2504(c). See IRC § 6501(c)(9); Reg. § 25.2504-2(b) (last sentence). The adequate disclosure requirements applicable to gifts made after August 5, 1997, are discussed at ¶ 9.04[10][b].

[22] Seemingly, Regulations Section 25.2504-2(b) uses the term "amount" rather than "value" to incorporate legal as well as valuation issues.

[23] See IRC §§ 2001(f)(2), 2504(c); infra text accompanying notes 28–31.

[24] IRC § 2504(c). See Reg. §§ 25.2504-2(b), 25.2504-2(c) Exs. 1, 2.

[25] See supra ¶ 9.05[2][a] note 14. The difference in the pre– and post–Aug. 5, 1997 requirements is illustrated in the examples in Regulations Section 25.2504-2(c).

[26] Reg. §§ 25.2504-2(b), 25.2504-2(c) Ex. 1.

[27] Section 2504(c) incorporates the Section 2001(f)(2) definition of "final determination" that was added in 1998. Internal Revenue Service Restructuring and Reform Act of 1998, Pub. L. No. 105-206 § 6007(e)(2)(B), 112 Stat. 685, 810 (1998), reprinted in 1998-3 CB 145, 270.

not contest the amount before the period for assessing the gift tax expires;[28] (2) by the Service in a situation where the Service establishes an amount that is not contested by the taxpayer within the limitations period;[29] (3) by the courts in a final determination of the amount that is no longer subject to appeal;[30] or (4) by a settlement agreement between the taxpayer and the Service determining the amount.[31]

[3] Exclusions for Prior Years

The preceding general rule appears broad enough to cover the question of how the statutory annual exclusion enters into the determination of taxable gifts for preceding calendar periods. Any remaining doubt is dispelled by Section 2504(b), which deals with this question expressly. Whatever statutory exclusion was provided for the earlier period in which a gift was made continues to be recognized. This is important, because the annual exclusion was reduced from an original $5,000[32] to $4,000[33] and to $3,000[34] before being raised to $10,000[35] and adjusted for inflation to the present $11,000.[36] A gift made in a year when the annual exclusion was $5,000 and properly qualifying for the exclusion[37] is included in the gifts for preceding calendar years only to the extent it exceeded $5,000; and, of course, a like rule applies to gifts made during the period of the $4,000 and $3,000 exclusions. This is less of a congressional concession than a matter of necessity, because there would be no return reporting gifts that were entirely within the exclusion, and there may be no records at all.

If an exclusion was improperly claimed in a period for a transfer prior to August 6, 1997, or for a transfer subsequent to August 5, 1997, where there

---

[28] IRC § 2001(f)(2)(A).

[29] IRC § 2001(f)(2)(B).

[30] IRC § 2001(f)(2)(C). See Reg. § 20.2001-1(d).

[31] IRC § 2001(f)(2)(C). A settlement agreement includes a Section 7121 closing agreement, a Section 7122 compromise, or settlement of a valuation issue binding on both parties. See Reg. § 20.2001-1(d).

[32] Revenue Act of 1932, Pub. L. No. 72-154, § 504(b), 47 Stat. 169, 247 (1932), effective from 1932 to 1938.

[33] Revenue Act of 1938, Pub. L. No. 75-554, § 505, 52 Stat. 447, 565 (1938), effective from 1939 to 1942.

[34] Revenue Act of 1942, Pub. L. No. 77-753, § 454, 56 Stat. 798, 953 (1942), effective from 1943 to 1981. See also Reg. § 25.2504-1(a).

[35] Economic Recovery Tax Act of 1981, Pub. L. No. 97-34, § 441(a), 95 Stat. 172, 319 (1981), reprinted in 1981-2 CB 256, 333, effective for 1982 and later years.

[36] IRC § 2503(b)(2). See ¶ 9.04[1]; Rev. Proc. 2001-59, 2001-1 CB __, __.

[37] See Schuhmacher v. Comm'r, 8 TC 453, 464 (1947), acq. 1947-1 CB 4.

was no adequate disclosure,[38] the exclusion is not allowed in determining the sum of gifts for preceding calendar periods. An erroneous claim of an exclusion, even if, in the case of a pre-August 6, 1997, transfer, allowed and protected by the statute of limitations, does not establish the right to take such an erroneous exclusion into account in determining taxable gifts for prior periods.[39] Again, the statute of limitations is not circumvented and the amount that previously escaped tax is not subjected to tax after the limitation period. The effect, as in the case of includible gifts that were previously erroneously omitted from the gift tax returns, is only to increase the rates applicable to current gifts. This can be seen from the preceding discussion of Section 2502. Observe that the amount in question enters into both stages of the two-step computation. Any increase in the tentative tax computed on gifts for all periods including the current period is offset by a larger subtraction for the tax computed only on gifts for prior periods. In such situations, the statute prevents improper avoidance of tax in an earlier period from carrying the further advantage of reducing rates in later periods. However, if the transfer is subsequent to August 5, 1997, and the adequate disclosure requirement is met and the statute of limitations has run, an erroneous claim of an exclusion may be taken into account in determining the amount of gifts in prior periods.[40]

[4] Deductions and Exemptions for Prior Years

With just one important exception, which is discussed later, deductions allowed at the time the gift was made continue to be allowed in determining taxable gifts for preceding calendar periods. The term "taxable gifts" as used in the 1954 and 1986 Codes replaces the term "net gifts" that was used in the 1939 Code.[41] Section 2504(d) makes it clear that the two terms are to be treated as equivalents. Deductions allowed in computing "net gifts" under prior law continue to enter into the determination of "taxable gifts" for prior periods. Of course, only deductions that were provided by law in the year the gift was made are considered; obviously, no marital deduction can be claimed for gifts to a spouse made before the effective date of the marital deduction provision.[42]

---

[38] See supra ¶ 9.05[2].

[39] E.g., Comm'r v. Disston, 325 US 442 (1945), Berzon v. Comm'r, 63 TC 601 (1975), aff'd, 534 F2d 528 (2d Cir. 1976), acq. 1975-2 CB 1. But see Farish v. Comm'r, 2 TC 949 (1943), nonreq. 1944 CB 37 questioned supra ¶ 9.05[1] note 6.

[40] See supra ¶ 9.05[2][b], especially text accompanying note 26.

[41] See IRC § 1003(a) (1939).

[42] See discussion of Section 2523 at ¶ 11.03.

The important exception to the rule on deductions concerns the so-called specific exemption, which was allowed prior to 1977 by Section 2521.[43] Generally speaking, it was an arbitrary deduction of $30,000 that a taxpayer could use as a lump sum or piecemeal during life to offset gifts that would otherwise result in tax. It was scaled down from an original $50,000[44] to $40,000[45] to $30,000.[46] It was repealed by the Tax Reform Act of 1976,[47] and was, in effect, replaced by the Section 2505 credit.[48]

The $30,000 Section 2521 exemption, allowable[49] with respect to pre-1977 gifts, effects a reduction in taxable gifts in preceding calendar periods ending before January 1, 1977, without regard to whether the exemption was actually claimed. The excess exemption (beyond $30,000) of prior years is *not* allowed as a deduction in determining taxable gifts for preceding calendar periods for the purpose of computing liability for tax on current gifts. Upon repeal of the exemption, Congress could have provided that it be entirely disregarded in computing taxes on post-1976 transfers. Its continued allowance, in effect, allows current transfers to be taxed at lower rates.[50] Of course, none of this is of any consequence if the donor has made no pre-1977 transfers.

The different treatment of the exemption and the annual exclusion probably rests on considerations of convenience. Gifts made in early years that were entirely within the $5,000, $4,000, or $3,000 exclusion did not have to be disclosed on a return. To try in later years to pick up such gifts, to the extent they exceeded the exclusions in subsequent years, would present a hopeless task. In contrast, however, the exemption could be utilized only if a return was filed and a part or all of it claimed as a deduction in determining taxable or

---

[43] Section 2521 is discussed in detail in Stephens, Maxfield & Lind, "Federal Estate and Gift Taxation" ¶¶ 10.01–10.04 (Warren, Gorham & Lamont 3d ed. 1974).

[44] Revenue Act of 1932, Pub. L. No. 72-154, § 505(a)(1), 47 Stat. 169, 247 (1932), effective from 1932 to 1935.

[45] Revenue Act of 1935, Pub. L. No. 74-407, § 301(b), 49 Stat. 1014, 1025 (1935), effective from 1936 to 1942.

[46] Revenue Act of 1942, Pub. L. No. 77-53, § 455, 56 Stat. 798, 953 (1942), effective from 1943 to 1981. See also Reg. § 25.2504-1(b).

[47] Pub. L. No. 94-455, § 2001(b)(3), 90 Stat. 1520, 1849 (1976), reprinted in 1976-3 CB (Vol. 1) 1, 325.

[48] See ¶ 9.06.

[49] Compare the use of the word "allowable" in Section 2504(a), permitting a donor to reduce prior taxable transfers even though the specific exemption was not actually used by donor prior to its repeal, with "allowed" in Section 2505(c). See also Rev. Rul. 78-106, 1978-1 CB 300, involving revocability of the exemption.

[50] The prior reduction of the exemption from $50,000 and $40,000 down to the $30,000 post-1943 level had the opposite effect, increasing prior taxable transfers and pushing current taxable transfers into higher brackets.

net gifts. Thus, use of the exemption is a matter of record, and adjustment to accord with the $30,000 amount presents few difficulties.[51]

Section 2504(a)(3) expressly allows the pre-1977 exemption of $30,000, rather than the higher amounts permitted under prior law, to be applied in determining taxable gifts for prior years. The effect is that if one made included gifts of $100,000 in 1935 and correctly paid tax only with respect to net gifts of $50,000 after applying the specific exemption, such gifts now enter into taxable gifts for prior years in the amount of $70,000. The donor must add back the amount ($20,000) by which the exemption used in prior years exceeds the amount subsequently allowed. Again, of course, this $20,000 that previously lawfully escaped tax is not being taxed, because the $20,000 enters into both steps of the tax computation. The result is only to tax present gifts at higher rates than would be applicable if the full earlier exemption were allowed in the determination of taxable gifts from preceding calendar periods.[52]

¶ 9.06 SECTION 2505. UNIFIED CREDIT AGAINST THE GIFT TAX

Citizens and residents[1] of the United States are allowed a credit against the gift tax on transfers made after 1976.[2] Beginning in 2002, and at all times thereafter, the gift tax credit amount offsets the tax on $1 million of taxable transfers.[3] Congress sometimes seems inclined to state the obvious; Section 2505(c) makes it clear that no refund is allowed if the amount of the credit exceeds the gift tax liability imposed under Section 2501.[4] Prior to 1977, a $30,000 specific lifetime exemption was allowed,[5] but as part of the Tax Reform Act of

---

[51] See Lockard v. Comm'r, 166 F2d 409 (1st Cir. 1948).

[52] The question whether all or a part of the taxpayer's lifetime exemption was in fact used in a prior period is considered in the context of the Section 2505 credit in the discussion of Section 2513 at ¶ 10.03[2].

[1] Nonresident noncitizens are allowed no gift tax credit. HR Rep. No. 1380, 94th Cong., 2d Sess. 17 (1976), reprinted in 1976-3 CB (Vol. 3) 735, 751.

[2] IRC §§ 2505, 2010. See Phillips, "Planning for the Use of the Unified Credit," 41 NYU Inst. on Fed. Tax'n 47-1 (1983).

[3] IRC § 2505(a)(1). See infra ¶ 9.06[1].

[4] See IRC § 2010(c), providing an identical rule for the estate tax unified credit.

[5] Section 2521 was repealed by the Tax Reform Act of 1976, Pub. L. No. 94-455, § 2001(b)(3), 90 Stat. 1520, 1849 (1976), reprinted in 1976-3 CB (Vol. 1) 1, 325. Section 2521 is discussed in detail in Stephens, Maxfield & Lind, "Federal Estate and Gift Taxation" ¶¶ 10.01–10.04 (Warren, Gorham & Lamont 3d ed. 1974).

1976, Congress eliminated both the gift tax and estate tax exemptions[6] that were deductions and replaced them with credits.[7]

[1] Amount of Credit

There are similarities between the gift tax and estate tax credits. The amount of both credits is currently based upon an "applicable credit amount,"[8] which is a mechanism whereby the amount of dollars shielded from the gift tax by the "applicable exclusion amount" set forth in Section 2010(c) and cross-referenced in Section 2505 is converted to a credit amount. Like the estate tax credit, the gift tax credit was originally phased in from 1977 until 1987,[9] was a

---

[6] See ¶ 3.02.

[7] This is only one of several areas in which Congress has replaced deductions with credits. In such situations, congressional policy views credits as more equitable than deductions, because they reduce tax liability equally for taxpayers in all brackets, while deductions confer greater tax savings on taxpayers in higher brackets. See HR Rep. No. 1380, 94th Cong., 2d Sess. 15 (1976), reprinted in 1976-3 CB (Vol. 3) 735, 749. See also Surrey, "Tax Incentives as a Device for Implementing Governmental Policy: A Comparison with Direct Government Expenditures," 83 Harv. L. Rev. 705 (1970).

In other situations, credits have been replaced by deductions. See IRC §§ 2011, 2058; ¶¶ 3.03, 5.09. In such circumstances, congressional policy is reversed, although there may be additional motives, such as to raise additional federal revenue, for the policy reversal. See ¶ 3.03[3][d].

[8] IRC § 2505(a)(1). See IRC § 2010(c).

[9] Taxable gifts by donors prior to January 1, 1987, encountered the following phase-in schedule:

Year of gift	Credit	Maximum taxable gifts without tax liability
1977 (before July 1)	$ 6,000	$ 30,000
1977 (after June 30)	30,000	120,667
1978	34,000	134,000
1979	38,000	147,333
1980	42,500	161,563
1981	47,000	175,625
1982	62,800	225,000
1983	79,300	275,000
1984	96,300	325,000
1985	121,800	400,000
1986	155,800	500,000
1987	192,800	600,000

The maximum taxable gift amount (in column 3) assumes no prior gifts have been made in any year after 1932.

fixed amount from 1987 through 1997,[10] and was increased and again phased in from 1998 until 2002, when it reached $345,800, an amount that effectively excludes the first $1 million of taxable gifts from taxation.[11] The ceiling on the phase-in of the applicable exclusion amount continues to be $1 million for years after 2002,[12] with no increase in the amount for inflation.[13] In general, if

---

[10] The credit amount from 1987–1997 remained at $192,800 which effectively excluded the first $600,000 of taxable gifts.

From 1987–1997, the amount of the credit was phased out (along with the lower transfer tax rate brackets employed by Section 2001(c)(1)) for taxable gifts in excess of $10 million. The phase-out occurred as a result of a 5 percent surtax on taxable gifts in excess of $10 million up to taxable gifts of $21,040,000, with the result that on taxable gifts in excess of $21,040,000 there was a flat 55 percent tax rate and no Section 2505 credit. IRC § 2001(c)(2) prior to amendment by the Taxpayer Relief Act of 1997, Pub. L. No. 105-34, § 501(a)(1)(D), 111 Stat. 788, 845 (1997), reprinted in 1997-4 CB (Vol. 1) 1, 59. After 1997, the amount of the credit was not phased out. However, a 5 percent surtax which applied from 1998–2001 with respect to taxable gifts between $10 million and $17,184,000, had the effect of applying a flat 55 percent tax rate to all the taxpayer's taxable gifts. IRC § 2001(c)(2) (after 1997) was repealed by the Economic Growth and Tax Relief Reconciliation Act of 2001, Pub. L. No. 107-16, § 511(b), 115 Stat. 38, 70 (2001), reprinted in 2001-__ CB __, __.

[11] See IRC § 2505(a)(1) and the 1998–2002 phase-in schedule infra note 12. Since the credit was scheduled to increase to $1 million prior to the Economic Growth and Tax Relief Reconciliation Act of 2001, the sunset provision has no effect on the amount of the Section 2505 credit. See Economic Growth and Tax Relief Reconciliation Act of 2001, Pub. L. No. 107-16, § 901(a)(2), 115 Stat. 38, 150 (2001), reprinted in 2001-__ CB __, __. The sunset provision is discussed more fully at ¶ 8.10[5].

[12] For taxable gifts after 1997, the applicable exclusion amounts and credit amounts are as follows:

Year	Applicable Exclusion Amount	Applicable Credit Amount
1998	$ 625,000	$202,050
1999	650,000	211,300
2000 and 2001	675,000	220,550
2002 through 2009	1,000,000	$345,800
After 2009	1,000,000	330,800 to almost $345,800

The applicable credit amount depends upon the timing of the prior taxable gifts. If all the taxable gifts are made after 2009, the amount is $330,800. See IRC § 2502(a)(2) effective for years after 2009. If, however, some of the taxable gifts are made prior to such date, the applicable credit amount ranges from $330,800 to almost $345,800.

The applicable credit amounts for the gift tax and the estate tax are equal until the year 2003. Thereafter the gift tax applicable exclusion amount is $1 million, while the estate tax applicable exclusion amount increases in varying phases to $3.5 million in 2009. See ¶ 3.02 text accompanying notes 6–10.

[13] The Conference Report accompanying the Tax Relief Act of 1997 expressly provided that the effective exemption converted to the unified credit is not to be adjusted for inflation. HR Conf. Rep. No. 220, 105th Cong., 1st Sess. 394 (1997), reprinted in 1997-4 CB (Vol. 2) 1457, 1864.

a donor who has made no prior "taxable gifts" makes "taxable gifts" in a year after 2001 not exceeding $1 million, no gift tax liability is incurred.

The credit[14] is sometimes subject to a minor reduction in amount. If a decedent made inter vivos gifts between September 8, 1976, and January 1, 1977, and used the Section 2521 $30,000 specific lifetime exemption to reduce such gifts, Section 2505(b)[15] requires a reduction in the amount of the Section 2505 credit by 20 percent of the amount of exemption so used.[16]

Because of the phase-in rules,[17] a donor could be required to pay tax on a "taxable gift" in a year before the credit was fully phased in and yet be required to pay no tax on a transfer of a "taxable gift" in a subsequent year when the credit was larger. For example, if a donor having made no prior gifts made $750,000 of "taxable gifts" in 1999 and makes $200,000 of "taxable gifts" in 2004, the 1999 transfer would have generated gift tax liability of $248,300 that was reduced by $211,300 of Section 2505 credit resulting in $37,000 of gift tax payable.[18] The year 2004 transfer of $200,000 of "taxable gifts" results in no actual gift tax payable. The gift tax liability on that transfer is $78,000,[19] but that liability is eliminated by the remaining Section 2505 credit, which is $134,500 ($345,800 reduced by the $211,300 credit previously

---

[14] See supra text accompanying notes 9–12.

[15] See IRC § 2010(b), which requires an identical reduction in the estate tax credit.

[16] See supra text accompanying notes 5–7. This results in a maximum Section 2505 credit reduction of $6,000 if the full $30,000 specific exemption was used during such period. Between the adoption of the Tax Reform Act of 1976 and December 31, 1976, there were substantial tax incentives for taxpayers with large estates to make inter vivos gifts at lower tax rates. Although Congress condoned a full use of the $30,000 exemption against gifts made before September 8, 1976, with no reduction in the Section 2505 credit, a credit reduction in the amount indicated was considered a proper cost for last-minute use of the exemption. A potential donor's prior gift history was an obvious factor in the decision whether to elect to use the Section 2521 exemption during that period.

[17] See supra text accompanying notes 9–12.

[18] This would also constitute an amount of gift "tax payable" under Section 2001(b)(2). See ¶ 2.01[2].

[19] Under Section 2502, this amount is the difference between the tax on aggregate transfers of $950,000 equal to $326,300 of tax, less the tax on preceding transfers of $750,000 or $248,300 of tax.

allowable).[20] Thus, no tax is due. Of course, no refund of the prior $37,000 of taxes properly paid is allowed.[21]

[2] Required Use of the Credit

Use of the gift tax credit is mandatory;[22] failure to use the credit, when available, will result in denial of the credit to the extent it is not used.[23] Statutorily, the denial occurs because Section 2505(a)(2) provides that the amount of credit available for any subsequent gift must take account of a reduction for the credit "allowable" for preceding gifts.

However, use of the $30,000 lifetime exemption under pre-1977 law, with the one exception already discussed,[24] does not preclude use of the full Section 2505 credit. Thus, if a donor has made $300,000 of pre-1977 "taxable gifts" using the lifetime exemption,[25] the donor can still use the Section 2505 credit against post-1976 gifts. If in 2004 the donor made another $1 million of "taxable gifts," the Section 2505 credit would reduce, but not eliminate,[26] the donor's tax liability. Because the donor had made prior taxable gifts, the donor's tax computed under Section 2502 would be $382,000,[27] and the $345,800 credit would reduce tax liability to $36,200.

---

[20] IRC §§ 2505(a)(1), 2505(a)(2). The donor still has a remaining Section 2505 credit amount of $56,500 ($345,800 less $211,300 and $78,000). If the donor makes up to another $140,244 of taxable gifts after 2004 and before 2010, no gift tax is incurred. The amount is increased if the gifts are made in 2011 when the gift tax rates are reduced. See IRC § 2502(a)(2) as amended by the Economic Growth and Tax Relief Reconciliation Act of 2001, Pub. L. No. 107-16, § 511(d), 115 Stat. 38, 70 (2001), reprinted in 2001-__ CB __, __, which applies to gifts made after December 31, 2009. Economic Growth and Tax Relief Reconciliation Act of 2001, Pub. L. No. 107-16 § 511(f)(3), 115 Stat. 38, 71 (2001) reprinted in 2001-__ CB __, __. See supra note 12.

[21] Cf. IRC § 2505(c).

[22] Cf. IRC § 2521 (prior to repeal by the Tax Reform Act of 1976, Pub. L. No. 94-455, § 2001(b)(3), 90 Stat. 1520, 1849 (1976), reprinted in 1976-3 CB (Vol. 1) 1, 325), under which use of the $30,000 lifetime exemption was elective. The exemption could be used at any time in a taxpayer's gift-giving career.

[23] Rev. Rul. 79-398, 1979-2 CB 338; Rev. Rul. 79-160, 1979-1 CB 313. Failure to use the gift tax credit indirectly precludes use of the estate tax credit. See ¶ 3.02 text accompanying notes 20 and 21.

[24] See supra ¶ 9.06[1] text accompanying notes 14–16.

[25] This assumes no use of the exemption after September 8, 1976. Disregarding the exemption, the donor would have made $330,000 of "taxable gifts."

[26] See supra ¶ 9.06[1] note 15.

[27] The computation is as follows:

Section 2502(a)(1) tax on $1.3 million	$469,800
Less 2702(a)(2) tax on $300,000	87,800
Tax liability	$382,000

[3] Relation to the Section 2010 Credit

Section 2505 provides a credit against gift tax liability for inter vivos transfers after 1976 similar but not identical to the estate tax credit under Section 2010.[28] Although the credit is referred to as unified, use of the Section 2505 gift tax credit does not reduce the amount of the Section 2010 estate tax credit. At first glance, it may appear that a donor-decedent is allowed the double advantage of both credits; however, as previously explained, the donor-decedent is not provided a double benefit.[29] Under the system, the two credits are effectively used only once.[30] However, even if a decedent has used the $345,800 credit available for lifetime transfers, the decedent is allowed to use the larger estate tax Section 2010 credit at death.[31] For example, if decedent, who had never made any prior gifts, made $1.5 million of taxable gifts in 2004, decedent would have been required to pay gift tax for 2004 of $210,000 ($555,800 less a credit of $345,800). If decedent died in 2009 having a taxable estate of $2 million, decedent would pay no estate tax.[32]

---

[28] See supra ¶ 9.06[1] text accompanying notes 8–13; ¶ 3.02 text accompanying notes 15–17.

The estate tax return filing requirements are related to the applicable exclusion amount used to determine the amount of the estate tax Section 2010 credit. See IRC § 6018(a); ¶ 3.02. Gift tax return filing requirements are not related in any way to the amount of the Section 2505 credit. See IRC §§ 6019, 6075(b), which are discussed ¶ 9.04[9].

[29] See ¶ 3.02 text accompanying notes 18, 19.

[30] See ¶ 3.02 text accompanying notes 15–19. The amount of the estate tax, before credits, is the tentative tax on the sum of the taxable estate and adjusted taxable gifts, reduced by gift taxes payable on post-1976 gifts. Inter vivos use of the gift tax credit reduces taxes payable on the gifts and correspondingly reduces that reduction in estate tax liability. In effect, lifetime gifts are removed from the estate tax base (but not from the figure that determines estate tax rates) either by lifetime use of credit or that use plus estate tax reduction for gift tax after accounting for the gift tax credit. Because the lifetime use of the credit merely neutralizes gifts that otherwise would have caused gift tax, thereby reducing the estate tax under Section 2001(b)(2), the credit has not been used in an estate tax sense when applied to lifetime gifts. In the end, the Section 2505 and Section 2010 credits cause a single reduction for gift and estate tax purposes. Cf. supra note 28.

[31] See IRC §§ 2010(c), 2502(a)(1).

[32] Under Section 2001(b)(1) there would be a tentative tax on $3.5 million of $1,455,800 reduced by the gift taxes of $210,000 under Section 2001(b)(2) to $1,245,800 that would be well below the $1,455,800 estate tax Section 2010 credit amount. However, no recovery of the gift taxes previously paid is allowed. See IRC §§ 2010(c), 2502(a)(1); ¶¶ 2.01, 3.02.

CHAPTER 10

Gift Tax: Transfers Subject to Tax

¶ 10.01 SECTION 2511. TRANSFERS IN GENERAL

Congress has undertaken to make the gift tax comprehensive. Just as the income tax extends to the receipt of most any financial advantage, with only limited statutory and common-law exceptions,[1] and the "estate" tax applies to any interest in property owned by the decedent at death, with some expanding and a few limiting modifications,[2] so the gift tax is designed to apply to almost any actual gratuitous or partly gratuitous lifetime shifting of property and property rights. As a result of Chapter 14 of the Internal Revenue Code, a shifting of value of a property interest may occur for gift tax purposes even though no actual transfer of that property interest occurs.[3] Additionally, when shifts of property or of property interests occur with no actual transfer, the tax on generation-skipping transfers sometimes creates a transfer that is taxed.[4]

The scope of the gift tax is discernible in the broad language of Section 2511. Insofar as it relates to citizens and residents,[5] Section 2511(a) provides: "Subject to the limitations contained in this chapter, the tax imposed by section 2501 shall apply whether the transfer is in trust or otherwise, whether the gift is direct or indirect, and whether the property is real or personal, tangible or intangible. . . . " This brief provision and the cryptic imposition of tax "on the transfer of property by gift" under Section 2501 are all the statutory law there is on whether the vast majority of gratuitous transfers are subject to the gift tax.[6]

Transactions that receive specific statutory treatment in Sections 2513 through 2519 are taken up later in this chapter. The matter dealt with here is the general scope of the gift tax and the general meaning of "the transfer of property by gift" in circumstances that are not the subject of express statutory provisions. When the statute is as general and fragmentary as it is here, the judicial decisions, administrative rulings, and regulations take on an extraordinary importance to a general understanding of the law.[7]

---

[1] See Comm'r v. Glenshaw Glass Co., 348 US 426, reh'g denied, 349 US 925 (1955).

[2] See Chapter 4.

[3] See Chapter 19.

[4] See Chapters 12–18.

[5] The second clause of Sections 2511(a) and 2511(b), which deal with nonresident noncitizens, are considered infra ¶ 10.01[11].

[6] The effect of full or partial consideration received in connection with a transfer is treated in the discussion of Section 2512 at ¶ 10.02.

[7] Compare the general nature of Section 2033.

[1] Direct Gifts

Section 2511 indicates, at least, that "the transfer of property" by gift may occur "whether the transfer is in trust or otherwise" and "whether the gift is direct or indirect." Direct gifts are easily identified: *A* transfers some stock to *B*; *X* deeds some land to *Y*; *P* gives adult child *C* an expensive car. These gifts raise few tax difficulties, but there may be a question whether and when the transfer is fully effective so as to invoke gift tax liability.[8]

Even though there may be a direct gratuitous transfer of cash to a donee, the Commissioner will take a close look to determine whether the transfer is a gift if the proceeds are "loaned" back to the donor. The substance of such a transaction is that the donor does not really make a gift to the donee but merely promises to make a gift in the future on the repayment of the "loan."[9] Thus, the Commissioner may disallow an annual exclusion on the original transfer,[10] a deduction for interest payments on the "loan,"[11] or a deduction for a claim for the amount of the loan against the donor's estate if the donor dies prior to repayment.[12]

[2] Indirect Gifts

Indirect gifts, also encompassed by Section 2511, occur in a multitude of settings.[13] The discussion in Chapter 9 of Section 2503(b), which provides the annual exclusion, has anticipated some problems arising out of indirect transfers.

---

[8] See infra ¶ 10.01[4].

[9] Estate of Flandreau v. Comm'r, 63 TCM (CCH) 2512 (1992). See infra ¶ 10.01[3][h] text accompanying note 123.

On the other hand, a purported "loan" may in fact be a gift at the time of the loan. See Miller v. Comm'r, 71 TCM (CCH) 1674 (1996), aff'd in unpub. op., 113 F3d 1241 (9th Cir. 1997). Cf. Vinikoor v. Comm'r, 75 TCM (CCH) 2185 (1998).

[10] Talge v. United States, 229 F. Supp. 836 (WD Mo. 1964).

[11] Muserlian v. Comm'r, 932 F2d 109 (2d Cir. 1991).

[12] Estate of Flandreau v. Comm'r, 63 TCM (CCH) 2512 (1992).

[13] An indirect gift can occur in numerous situations within a family context. See, e.g., Doerr v. United States, 819 F2d 162 (7th Cir. 1987) (the donor payment of state gift tax liability of the donee); Snyder v. Comm'r, 93 TC 529 (1989) (failure to convert stock constituted a gift, but failure to put stock to the corporation did not constitute a gift); Estate of Maggos v. Comm'r, 79 TCM (CCH) 1861 (2000) (redemption of the mother's stock at less than fair market value was a gift to the sole shareholder son); Estate of Hendrickson v. Comm'r, 78 TCM (CCH) 655 (1999) (a gift where the income beneficiary of a trust permitted income to pass through a trust to the children); Estate of Bosca v. Comm'r, 76 TCM (CCH) 62 (1998) (the conversion of voting stock to nonvoting stock was a gift of value to the remaining voting shareholders); Cidulka v. Comm'r, 71 TCM (CCH) 2555 (1996) (gifts of stock to the donor's daughter-in-law and grandchildren were held to be gifts to the donor's son where, after a redemption of the donor's remaining

[a] Transfer in Trust

There was confusion for a time on the application of the annual exclusion to gifts in trust, but the fact that a gratuitous transfer is to a trust rather than to an individual has never been thought to preclude gift tax liability. The language "in trust or otherwise" has been in the statute since its inception.[14] A transfer in trust, then, is one example of an indirect gift; it is treated not as a gift to the trust, but as a gift of separate interests to the beneficiaries.[15] As subsequently explained, a transfer in trust may be a completed gift to some of the trust beneficiaries but not to others.

[b] Transfers to Entities

[i] Corporations. Transfers to corporations are analogous to transfers in trust. To be sure, a trust is essentially a conduit through which benefits flow to the beneficiaries, whereas a corporation is often viewed for tax and other purposes as an entity separate and distinct from its shareholders. The corporate entity concept has stood in the way of easy analogy of gifts to trusts to gifts to corporations. But for gift tax purposes, the corporate veil is disappearing.

An individual who makes a transfer to a trust exclusively for the individual's own benefit has made no gift; even if the individual has transferred property, it is only an indirect transfer to the same individual, and the relationship of the gift tax to the estate tax compels the conclusion that the gift tax applies

---

share and a subsequent liquidation of the corporation, the donor's son received all liquidating proceeds); Estate of Furman v. Comm'r, 75 TCM (CCH) 2206 (1998) (transfer of common stock for preferred stock resulted in a gift to other shareholders); du Pont v. Comm'r, 37 TCM (CCH) 115 (1978) (the husband made a gift when the wife transferred their life insurance policies to the children under a property settlement); Rev. Rul. 84-105, 1984-2 CB 197 (the spouse gift to residuary beneficiary on receipt of less than amount entitled to under marital deduction pecuniary bequest); TAM 200014004 (Dec. 10, 1999) (primary trust of the beneficiary's acquiescence to payment of excessive trustee fees to the beneficiary's children constituted a gift); TAM 9315005 (Dec. 31, 1992) (failure to enforce a stock redemption agreement held an indirect gift to another shareholder); Priv. Ltr. Rul. 8723007 (Feb. 18, 1987) (failure to pay noncumulative preferred dividends to the grandfather who owned the preferred stock and voting control of the corporation was a gift to the children's trust, which owned the common stock); Priv. Ltr. Rul. 8403010 (Sept. 30, 1983) (failure by the corporation to pay dividends (which were noncumulative) on the preferred stock constituted a taxable gift, because the preferred shareholder was legally entitled to be paid the dividends, and, since the preferred shareholder held voting control of the corporation, the failure to require a payment of the dividends constituted a transfer of property to the common shareholders). Cf. IRC § 2701; ¶ 19.02.

[14] Revenue Act of 1932, Pub. L. No. 72-154, Chapter 209, § 501(b), 47 Stat. 169, 245 (1932). Cf. Priv. Ltr. Rul. 199912027 (Dec. 23, 1998) (a trust extended by exercise of nongeneral power of appointment was a continuation of the same trust).

[15] Helvering v. Hutchings, 312 US 393 (1941).

only to transfers to others. What if an individual makes a transfer to a corporation wholly owned by the individual? Does the entity theory arise to suggest possible gift tax liability? Or is it again only an indirect transfer to the individual? Raised in this bald way, the question is settled; no gift tax liability will be asserted, although there may be some disagreement as to the reason.[16]

Notwithstanding the sensible result reached in the case of a transfer to a wholly owned corporation, the Tax Court in one case classified transfers to a corporation partly owned by the donors as fully subject to tax.[17] The entity theory was fully adopted, even to the point of the allowance of a single exclusion for the corporate donee. This is patent nonsense and, agreeing, the court of appeals on review pierced the corporate veil.[18] In this case, the donors owned 40 percent of the stock of the corporation and the court of appeals modified the Tax Court decision so as to treat the gift as only 60 percent of the value of the property transferred; there was no gift of "the 40 percent interest retained" by reason of the donors' ownership interest. Such a view rejects the entity concept, as it should be rejected in this setting, and brings the treatment of transfers to corporations into harmony with the treatment of transfers to trusts.

The appropriate gift tax view of a private corporation as a nonentity has other judicial and administrative support.[19] The regulations state flatly: "A transfer of property by B to a corporation generally represents gifts by B to the other individual shareholders of the corporation to the extent of their proportionate interests in the corporation."[20] On the subject of the annual exclusion, discussed in Chapter 9, this is not a taxpayer victory because the transfers to

---

[16] In one case involving such a transfer, the Board of Tax Appeals rejected the Commissioner's assertion of gift tax liability. Robert H. Scanlon v. Comm'r, 42 BTA 997 (1940), acq. 1941-1 CB 9. However, this eminently fair result was reached without judicial rejection of the concept of corporate entity in gift circumstances, to which the board had given full recognition earlier in the same year. Frank B. Thompson v. Comm'r, 42 BTA 121 (1940), settled while on appeal to the Sixth Circuit. Even if the transfer was to a separate entity, the board reasoned, the transferor received an adequate and full consideration for the property transferred in the form of a corresponding enhancement in the value of his shares. Robert H. Scanlon v. Comm'r, supra at 997, 999. Such full consideration precludes gift tax liability, as explained in the discussion of Section 2512 below. See infra ¶ 10.01[2][b] text accompanying notes 24, 25. The board also recognized the existence of an alternative that would have produced the identical economic result free of income tax and gift tax, namely, a transfer of property in exchange for stock, rather than a mere outright donation. See IRC § 351. See generally Bittker & Eustice, Federal Income Taxation of Corporations and Shareholders Chapter 3 (Warren, Gorham & Lamont, 7th ed. 2000).

[17] Heringer v. Comm'r, 21 TC 607 (1954).

[18] Heringer v. Comm'r, 235 F2d 149 (9th Cir.), cert. denied, 352 US 927 (1956).

[19] Chanin v. United States, 393 F2d 972 (Ct. Cl. 1968); Rev. Rul. 71-443, 1971-2 CB 337; Hollingsworth v. Comm'r, 86 TC 91 (1986); Kincaid v. United States, 682 F2d 1220 (5th Cir. 1982).

[20] Reg. § 25.2511-1(h)(1).

the corporation are regarded as gifts of future interests to the shareholders;[21] if the donor is a shareholder, however, the nonentity view works to reduce the amount of the gift.

[ii] **Partnerships or limited liability companies.** The general principles applicable to transfers of property to corporations apply as well to partnerships and limited liability companies. Thus, a transfer of property to a partnership in which the transferor owns only a portion of the partnership that is disproportionate to the investment made is a gift transfer of the remaining portion of the property to the remaining partners.[22] If, however, the partners form a partnership and receive interests in the partnership capital equal to their proportionate contributions, it is difficult to find any gift transfers. Nevertheless, in this era of discounting with respect to transfers of property to family limited partnerships (FLPs) and limited liability companies,[23] the Internal Revenue Service (IRS) has attempted to find a gift to the extent the value of the property contributed to the partnership or limited liability company exceeds the value of the entity interest received.[24] Courts have generally rejected the notion of a gift to the extent of the "disappearing value" holding there is no gift where each investor receives an interest in the entity proportionate to the investor's capital investment.[25]

[c] Gifts by Entities

The regulations have long pierced the corporate veil in the case of gifts by corporations.[26] The gift tax is imposed only on individuals,[27] and rigid application of the entity doctrine here would provide a wide avenue for tax

---

[21] Rev. Rul. 71-443, 1971-2 CB 337; Stinson Estate v. United States, 214 F3d 846 (2000); Georgia Ketteman Trust v. Comm'r, 86 TC 91 (1986); Chanin v. United States, 393 F2d 972 (Ct. Cl. 1968); Heringer v. Comm'r, 235 F2d 149 (9th Cir.), cert. denied, 352 US 927 (1956). See ¶¶ 9.04[1][b] text accompanying note 28, 9.04[3][e] text accompanying notes 89–91.

[22] See ¶ 9.04[1][b] text accompanying note 29.

[23] See ¶ 10.02[2][c].

[24] See FSA 199950014 (Sept. 15, 1999); TAM 9842003 (July 2, 1998); Estate of Strangi v. Comm'r, 115 TC 478 (2000).

[25] Jones v. Comm'r 116 TC 121 (2001); Church v. United States, 85 AFTR2d 2000-804 (WD Tex. 2000). See Estate of Strangi v. Comm'r, 115 TC 478 (2000) (minuscule proportion of disappearing value transferred). See ¶ 10.02[2][c][v].

[26] E.g., Reg. § 25.2511-1(h)(1).

[27] IRC § 2501(a); Reg. § 25.0-1(b).

avoidance by way of gifts by corporations.[28] Thus, the regulations continue to provide:

> A transfer of property by a corporation to B is a gift to B from the stockholders of the corporation. If B himself is a stockholder, the transfer is a gift to him from the other stockholders but only to the extent it exceeds B's own interest in such amount as a shareholder.[29]

Presumably, a similar analysis will apply to gratuitous transfers by partnerships and limited liability companies.

It is difficult to see why a corporation should be an entity donee and a nonentity donor. As just discussed, this artificial distinction seems to be on its way out in favor of uniform nonentity status for corporations and for partnerships and limited liability agencies as well.[30]

[d] Nature of the Transfer

An indirect transfer subject to gift tax can arise because of the way the transfer is made as well as because of the nature of the recipient. If one knows that one is entitled to an annual $11,000 exclusion for each donee, a person might believe that the person could make a $33,000 excluded gift to A by giving $11,000 each to A, B, and C, but requiring B and C to turn their portions over to A. Transfers to a straw person are not gifts to the straw person, and consequently, the transfers to B and C are obviously no more than indirect gifts to A.[31] The regulations deal with some slightly less patent illustrations of indirect gifts that take the form of transfers to individuals.[32]

---

[28] Consider also the possibility of numerous exclusions by the use of multiple corporations, if corporations were subject to the tax and if the corporation were treated as a donor. Cf. IRC § 1561.

[29] Reg. § 25.2511-1(h)(1).

[30] See supra ¶ 10.01[2][b]. Prior to May 8, 1974, political gifts raised somewhat similar questions, but with the enactment of Section 2501(a)(5), generally exempting gifts to political organizations, those questions are now moot. See also discussion of Section 2501(a)(5) and the law prior to the enactment of that subsection discussed at ¶ 9.02[2].

[31] Heyen v. United States, 945 F2d 359 (10th Cir. 1991). See Estate of Cidulka v. Comm'r, 71 TCM (CCH) 2555 (1996) (gifts of stock to the donor's in-laws and grandchildren held gifts to the donor's child where after redemption of the donor's share, the child received all proceeds upon liquidation).

Similarly, transfers by a straw person to the beneficial owner of a property are not subject to gift tax. Snyder v. Comm'r, 66 TC 785 (1976).

[32] Reg. §§ 25.2511-1(h)(2), 25.2511-1(h)(3). Cf. Rev. Rul. 77-732, 1977-2 CB 344.

[e] Discharge of Indebtedness

If, for no consideration, *A* discharges *B*'s legal obligation to *C*, *A* may have made a gift to *B*.[33] Similarly, a creditor's gratuitous discharge of a debtor's obligation may be a gift by the creditor.[34] On the matter of a gift arising out of the discharge of another's indebtedness, the Treasury recognizes a seeming exception in the case of payment of taxes by married persons. If a husband and wife file a joint income tax return[35] or if a husband and wife elect to have their gifts for a year treated as if made one-half by each,[36] the payment of all or more than half of the tax by either is not treated as a transfer that is subject to the gift tax.[37] Of course, in such circumstances, the spouses are both jointly and severally liable for the entire tax,[38] so this is not simply a case of one gratuitously discharging the liability of another. Each is discharging that spouse's own legal obligation even if one spouse pays the entire tax.

[f] Below-Market Interest Rate Loans

A gift may occur if a creditor forgives a debtor's obligation to pay interest that has accrued on a loan,[39] or if the creditor simply makes a below-market interest rate loan (which includes an interest-free loan) to the debtor. For many years, the treatment of below-market interest rate loans was a subject of controversy. The Service took the position that a loan for less than a normal rate of interest constituted a gift.[40] The Tax Court refused to follow the Service's position and held that interest-free intrafamily loans were not subject to gift tax.[41] Among the circuits, the Seventh Circuit agreed with the Tax Court and the Eleventh Circuit sided with the Commissioner.[42] The Supreme Court

---

[33] Payment by the taxpayer of an expense of a child constitutes a gift. See (Drybrough v. United States, 208 F. Supp. 279 (WD Ky. 1962); Edwards v. United States, 1970-1 USTC ¶ 12,654 (WD Pa. 1970)), unless the expense is one that the donor has a legal obligation to pay. See ¶ 10.02[5].

[34] Reg. § 25.2511-1(a); Estate of Kelley v. Comm'r, 63 TC 321 (1974); Rev. Rul. 81-264, 1981-2 CB 186. On an analogous income tax question, see IRC § 102. Compare Helvering v. American Dental Co., 318 US 322 (1943) with Comm'r v. Jacobson, 336 US 28 (1949).

[35] IRC § 6013.

[36] See ¶ 10.03.

[37] Reg. § 25.2511-1(d).

[38] IRC §§ 2513(d), 6013(d)(3).

[39] Cf. Reg. § 25.2511-1(a).

[40] Rev. Rul. 73-61, 1973-1 CB 408.

[41] Crown v. Comm'r, 67 TC 1060 (1977); Dickman v. Comm'r, 41 TCM (CCH) 620 (1980).

[42] Crown v. Comm'r, 585 F2d 234 (7th Cir. 1978); Dickman v. Comm'r, 690 F2d 812 (11th Cir. 1982).

settled the controversy in 1984 when it affirmed the Eleventh Circuit in *Dickman v. Commissioner*,[43] holding that an interest-free loan, even when evidenced by a demand note, represented a transfer of property rights constituting a transfer by gift.

In the year following the *Dickman* case, Congress enacted Section 7872, which appears to be the exclusive authority with respect to the tax consequences of below-market interest rate loans (including interest-free loans).[44] In general, such loans are recharacterized to impute the payment of interest by the borrower at the applicable federal rate.[45] For income tax purposes, this constructive payment may result in interest income to the lender and in an interest deduction for the borrower.[46] In addition, and of importance for gift tax purposes, the lender is treated as constructively providing the funds to the borrower for payment of the constructive interest. The characterization of this event depends on the nature of the loan. A gift occurs from the lender to the borrower if the lender's funding (forgoing) of the borrower's interest payments is characterized as a gift for gift tax purposes.[47]

---

[43] Dickman v. Comm'r, 465 US 330 (1984). For a summary of the judicial history of interest-free loans, see Webster, "Dickman v. Commissioner: The Supreme Court Applies the Gift Tax to Interest-Free Loans," 35 Ala. L. Rev. 553 (1984).

[44] See Prop. Reg. § 25.7872-1. The Section 7872 rules apply to term loans after June 6, 1984, and demand loans outstanding after June 6, 1984, that are not repaid before September 17, 1984. Deficit Reduction Act of 1984, Pub. L. No. 98-369, § 172(c)(2), 98 Stat. 494, 700 (1984), reprinted in 1984-3 CB (Vol. 1) 1, 208. See Prop. Reg. § 1.7872-1(b)(1). It is unclear whether Section 7872 applies to an interest-free loan by a trust to a beneficiary.

[45] The applicable federal rates are determined by the Secretary on a monthly basis. IRC § 1274(d)(1)(B). The rates in effect will reflect the average yields of outstanding marketable U.S. securities with comparable maturities. IRC § 1274(d)(1)(C).

Term of loan	Applicable rate
Not over 3 years	Federal short-term rate
Over 3 years but not over 9 years	Federal midterm rate
Over 9 years	Federal long-term rate

The applicable federal rate for a demand loan is the federal short-term rate for each day the loan is unpaid. IRC § 7872(f)(2)(B). See generally Prop. Reg. § 1.7872-3(b). Use of such rates for gift tax purposes has been judicially upheld as reasonable. Cohen v. Comm'r, 910 F2d 422 (7th Cir. 1990); Estate of Arbury, 93 TC 136 (1989).

[46] IRC §§ 61, 163. Through its recharacterization of the transaction, Section 7872 artificially turns what actually happened into what should have happened. Because the lender never actually received this deemed interest payment, choosing instead to forgo levying it upon the borrower, Section 7872 labels this amount as "forgone interest." IRC § 7872(e)(2).

[47] IRC § 7872(f)(3); Prop. Reg. § 1.7872-4(b). See ¶ 10.02[3]. Compare Comm'r v. Duberstein, 363 US 278 (1960). Other classifications of Section 7872 loans include com-

All Section 7872 loans, including gift loans, are classified into two categories: term loans and demand loans. A gift loan that is to be repaid on a specific date is classified as a "term loan."[48] The amount of the gift (i.e., the constructive interest) is the principal loaned less the present value of all principal and all actual interest payments to be made under the loan.[49] For example, assume that a parent makes a $100,000 interest-free gift loan to a child on January 1 in the current year and that the child is to repay the loan exactly four years later. Assume further that the applicable federal rate in effect in the current year when the loan is made is 12 percent. The present value of $100,000 for four years at 12 percent compounded semiannually is $62,742.24. The $37,258.76 difference is the constructive interest, and is the amount of the gift from the parent to the child. The gift is deemed to be made on the date the loan is made.[50] In addition, for income tax purposes, the child's possible interest deduction and the parent's corresponding interest income[51] are computed annually for each calendar year the loan is outstanding.[52]

A gift loan is classified as a "demand loan" if it carries no fixed date for repayment.[53] Again, a gift of the funds with which to pay the constructive interest is deemed to be made by the lender to the borrower.[54] However, no separate calculation of the amount of the gift need be made—the amount of the gift and the borrower's potential interest deduction, along with the lender's corresponding interest income, are simply determined by subtracting any actual interest payments due under the loan from the interest that would have accrued under the applicable federal rate (i.e., the forgone interest).[55] Because the loan

---

pensatory loans and dividends. See IRC § 7872(c); Prop. Reg. §§ 1.7872-4(c)–1.7872-4(g).

[48] See IRC § 7872(f)(6), which defines "term loan" as any loan that is not a demand loan; Prop. Reg. § 1.7872-10(a)(2). See Frazee v. Comm'r, 98 TC 554 (1992), applying Section 7872 to a term gift loan that took the form of a promissory note received on the transfer of the property.

[49] The total payments are discounted using the appropriate applicable federal rate. IRC § 7872(f)(1). See Prop. Reg. § 1.7872-7(a).

[50] IRC §§ 7872(b)(1), 7872(d)(2); Prop. Reg. § 1.7872-7(a)(1).

[51] See IRC §§ 61, 163 (especially IRC § 163(h)).

[52] IRC § 7872(a). The amount of interest that would have accrued for the year under the applicable federal rate is reduced by any actual interest payable that is properly allocable to the year, and the remainder is called forgone interest. IRC §§ 7872(a)(2), 7872(e)(2). In the hypothetical example above, since the parent's loan to the child called for no interest, the forgone interest for each year of the loan is simply 12 percent compounded semiannually on $100,000 or $12,360. The forgone interest is treated as having been paid on the last day of each calendar year during which the loan is outstanding. IRC § 7872(a)(2).

[53] IRC § 7872(f)(5). See Prop. Reg. §§ 1.7872-10(a)(1), 1.7872-10(a)(2).

[54] IRC § 7872(a)(1)(A).

[55] IRC §§ 7872(a), 7872(e)(2); Prop. Reg. § 1.7872-6(c).

has no fixed date for repayment, the lender is deemed to make a gift each year (or portion thereof) that the loan remains outstanding on the last day of each of the lender's taxable years.[56] Similarly, for income tax purposes, the lender recognizes interest income and the borrower earns a possible interest deduction, in the amount of the gift, during each year that the loan is outstanding.[57] For example, if the parent lends the child $100,000 interest-free on January 1, payable in full upon the parent's demand, and the loan remains outstanding throughout the entire calendar year, only one calculation is required. The determination of the interest on $100,000 at the assumed 12 percent rate compounded semiannually is $12,360. As no actual interest payments are called for, that amount is deemed to be a gift from parent to child on December 31.[58]

Section 7872 contains a de minimis exception for gift loans between individuals for any day on which the aggregate outstanding amount of loans between such individuals does not exceed $10,000.[59] There is no imputed interest and no gift in such a situation. This exception is not available, however, if the loan is directly attributable to the purchase or carrying of income-producing assets.[60]

[g] Gratuitous Services

In some respects, arguments supporting gift treatment for the permitted rent-free or interest-free use of property or money would support as well a gift tax on a person's gratuitous performance of services for another. However, the statute permits no such conclusion, as the tax is imposed only on "the transfer of property."[61] Property and services are differentiated for many tax purposes.[62] For example, the receipt of an interest in a corporation or partnership in exchange for services may be fully subject to income tax, whereas the receipt of an interest in exchange for property sometimes wholly escapes tax.[63] There-

---

[56] IRC § 7872(a); Prop. Reg. § 1.7872-6(b)(3).

[57] See supra text accompanying note 51.

[58] Similarly, the child is treated as paying that same amount back to the parent as interest, possibly earning the child a Section 163 deduction and creating Section 61 interest income for the parent.

[59] IRC § 7872(c)(2)(A). See generally Prop. Reg. § 1.7872-8.

[60] IRC § 7872(c)(2)(B). See Prop. Reg. § 1.7872-8(b)(3). Section 7872(d)(1) also contains an exception for income tax purposes with respect to the retransferred imputed interest where the amount of the outstanding loans does not exceed $100,000. But see IRC § 7872(d)(1)(B).

[61] IRC § 2501.

[62] Cf. Reg. § 1.170-1(a)(2), disallowing income tax charitable deductions for contributions of services.

[63] IRC §§ 351(a), 721; Frazell v. United States, 335 F2d 487 (5th Cir. 1964). But cf. Hempt Bros. v. United States, 490 F2d 1172 (3d Cir. 1974), involving accounts receivable

fore, if services are to give rise to gift tax liability, it must be by way of the would-be donor earning the right to compensation and then gratuitously shifting that right, a property right, to another. If an individual has earned a right to compensation for services but directs that it be paid to another, there is no question that the individual has made a gift to the ultimate recipient.[64] Both for income tax and gift tax purposes, a transaction of this sort is treated just as if the earner received the compensation and then made a gift of it.

What if a person merely rejects the compensation with the result that it passes to others? It certainly seems that an individual should be allowed to take the purely negative step of rejecting something to which that individual is entitled without suffering any tax consequences. Indeed, that may be the law for income tax purposes.[65] However, in the area of gift taxation (and estate tax and the tax on generation-skipping transfers are no different), a mere rejection of something often channels it to the very persons to whom the one rejecting it would otherwise make a gift. So there is a felt need to differentiate pure rejection from rejection that is much akin to a transfer. Left to their own devices, the administration and the courts were unable to deal smoothly with this problem. Congress opted for tax neutrality in the case of rejection by offering a person an opportunity to turn down a proffered interest in property[66] without tax consequences, if the refusal meets the requirements of Section 2518.[67] The provision is discussed later in this chapter.[68]

[h] Gift by an Incompetent

A gratuitous transfer by an incompetent is an extreme example of an indirect, indeed an unwitting, gift. A transfer by an incompetent's guardian pursu-

---

for services rendered to third parties. See also Bittker & Eustice, Federal Income Taxation of Corporations and Shareholders ¶ 3.03 (Warren, Gorham & Lamont, 7th ed. 2000); McKee, Nelson & Whitmire, Federal Taxation of Partnerships and Partners ¶ 4.02[2] n.66 (Warren, Gorham & Lamont, 3d ed. 1997).

[64] It is equally clear that the assignment of income will be disregarded for income tax purposes. Lucas v. Earl, 281 US 111 (1930). Cf. Estate of Di Marco v. Comm'r, 87 TC 653 (1986) (commencement of rendering services did not constitute a transfer of an interest in survivorship income benefits).

[65] See Comm'r v. Giannini, 129 F2d 638 (9th Cir. 1942) (seemingly requiring a rejection prior to rendering services); Rev. Rul. 66-167, 1966-1 CB 20 (seemingly reaching a more lenient result where there is a waiver of an executor's fees). See ¶ 5.03[3][a] text accompanying note 51.

[66] Including a power as an "interest." IRC § 2518(c)(2).

[67] IRC § 2518, applicable as well to Chapters 11 and 13, not just gift tax settings. See IRC §§ 2046, 2654(c).

[68] See ¶ 10.07.

ant to a judicial decree has been held to be a gift by the incompetent.[69] Presumably the gift tax treatment does not depend on whether court approval is required, although, generally, state law imposes such a condition.[70] The date of payment or transfer, rather than the date of court approval, is controlling for gift tax purposes, because prior to that time the court would have the power to amend or revoke the decree of approval.[71] An attempted transfer directly by one who has been adjudicated incompetent is not a gift if state law declares one of the elements of a valid gift to be competency of the donor to contract.[72]

[3] Property Interests Covered

The legislative history of the gift tax clearly indicates that "property" as used in the statute is to be given its broadest meaning to include "every species of right or interest protected by law and having an exchangeable value."[73] The same broad scope exists under Section 2033 of the estate tax provisions and, not surprisingly, items of property that would be included in a decedent's gross estate if owned at death are similarly subject to gift tax if transferred during life.

It is always necessary to identify accurately the donor's interest in property[74] and to determine what portion of the interest is the subject of the gift. In the absence of artificial statutory presumptions, an individual cannot make a transfer of any interest other than that in which the individual owns a beneficial interest.[75] For example, a transfer by a trustee holding only a legal interest

---

[69] Comm'r v. Greene, 119 F2d 383 (9th Cir.), cert. denied, 314 US 641 (1941); Rev. Rul. 73-612, 1973-2 CB 322; Rev. Rul. 67-280, 1967-2 CB 349. But see Priv. Ltr. Rul. 9639056 (June 24, 1996) (no gift because a transfer by the incompetent's guardian was incomplete); Priv. Ltr. Rul. 9831005 (Apr. 20, 1998) (same).

[70] See "Substitution of Judgment Doctrine and Making Gifts From an Incompetent's Estate," 7 Real Prop., Prob. & Tr. J. 479 (1972); Jorrie & Hofheinz, "Estate Planning for Those Without Testamentary Capacity," 46 Tex. BJ 579 (1983). See also Priv. Ltr. Rul. 9731003 (Mar. 31, 1997) (transfers not properly authorized by state law).

[71] Rev. Rul. 67-280, 1967-2 CB 349.

[72] Cf. Estate of Bettin v. Comm'r, 33 TCM (CCH) 499 (1974), aff'd per curiam, 543 F2d 1269 (9th Cir. 1976).

[73] S. Rep. No. 665, 72d Cong., 1st Sess. (1931), reprinted in 1939-1 CB (pt. 2) 496, 524. See Estate of Bosca v. Comm'r, 76 TCM (CCH) 62 (1998) (surrender of voting common stock for nonvoting common stock was a gift of property with a value equal to the difference between the voting and nonvoting stock).

[74] On the part played by the local law, see discussion of the *Bosch* principle at ¶ 4.05[2][b].

[75] See Estate of Davenport v. Comm'r, 184 F3d 1176 (10th Cir. 1999).

in property is not subject to gift tax.[76] If a lottery ticket holder transfers winnings to family members, there are gifts of the transfers; however, if the ticket is purchased on behalf of a pre-existing family partnership and the winnings are distributed in accordance with the partners' interests in the partnership, no gift occurs.[77] Thus, a transfer of property owned by a married couple as tenants by the entirety or as joint tenants usually represents gifts by two donors; in general, each is treated as making a gift of that spouse's interest in the property.[78] Similarly, a gift of community property owned by spouses is treated as a gift of one half of the property by each. Quite properly, the Treasury refuses to recognize any reduction in one spouse's gift with respect to the other spouse's marital elective share interest in the property, because it is an inchoate interest more in the nature of a mere expectancy.[79]

[a] Everyday Classes of Property

A house, a car, jewelry, furniture, books, cash, and intangibles such as stocks, bonds, patents, patent applications,[80] and real estate[81] are all property that may be the subject of a Section 2511 transfer.[82] But, of course, the scope of the term "property" under this section is much broader. Partial interests in property are also "property." Thus, an income interest in a trust,[83] a right to share in future rental payments,[84] a right to share in future mineral royalties,[85] and an option to purchase property including vested and exercisable stock op-

---

[76] Reg. § 25.2511-1(g)(1). See Saltzman v. Comm'r, 131 F3d 87 (2d Cir. 1997). However, if the trustee also owns a beneficial interest in the trust, there may be a gift. Reg. § 25.2511-1(g)(2).

[77] Estate of Winkler v. Comm'r, 73 TCM (CCH) 1657 (1997). Cf. TAM 9217004 (Apr. 24, 1992) (no gift on the distribution of winnings on a jointly owned winning lottery ticket that was required by state law to be held in one owner's name).

[78] Cf. Estate of Borner v. Comm'r, 25 TC 584 (1955), acq. 1969-2 CB xxiii, withdrawing nonacq. 1962-1 CB 4, acq. 1957-2 CB 4.

[79] Rev. Rul. 58-13, 1958-1 CB 342.

[80] Talge v. United States, 229 F. Supp. 836 (WD Mo. 1964).

[81] See O'Dell, "Intrafamily Transfers of Real Estate: Recent Law Changes Offer Planning Opportunities and Raise Problems," 9 J. Real Est. Tax'n 319 (1982).

[82] Recall that the Section 2503(b) annual exclusion may make many such gifts nontaxable. See ¶ 9.04.

[83] Rev. Rul. 79-327, 1979-2 CB 342.

[84] Galt v. Comm'r, 216 F2d 41 (7th Cir. 1954), cert. denied, 348 US 951 (1955); Rev. Rul. 57-315, 1957-2 CB 624.

[85] Estate of Jardell v. Comm'r, 24 TC 652 (1955). But see Estate of Hazelton v. Comm'r, 29 TC 637 (1958), acq. 1958-2 CB 5, intimating that a mere expectancy cannot be the subject of a gift.

tions[86] are all interests in property that can be the subject of a gift, notwithstanding possible difficulties of valuation. This is so even though for income tax purposes the donor continues to be treated as the owner of the property producing the income and must pay income tax on all the income.[87]

[b] Remainders

A remainder can be the subject of a gift,[88] even a contingent remainder. In one case, a court properly held the gratuitous transfer of a contingent remainder was subject to gift tax even though the remainderperson failed to survive the life tenant, so that the interest transferred never did ripen into a possessory interest.[89]

If a person transfers less than an entire interest in property, technically the person has made a gift only of the portion transferred.[90] The general principle applicable may be readily understood in terms of a donor who owns four acres of land and gives away only three; but interests in property are capable of division in ways other than geographically. If an individual makes a gift of real property but reserves a legal life estate, the individual has retained an interest susceptible to valuation and not subject to the gift tax, much like the donor who retained one acre of a four-acre tract. The individual has made a gift only of the remainder. If a donor transfers property in trust and reserves a right to a specified payment for life, again the donor's gift is reduced by the value of the retained interest.[91] Although these comments are "technically" correct, Con-

---

[86] Rev. Rul. 80-186, 1980-2 CB 280 (transfer of option to purchase real property); Priv. Ltr. Ruls. 199927002 (Mar. 19, 1999) (transfer of stock option), 199952012 (Sept. 22, 1999) (transfer of stock option), 9725032 (Mar. 24, 1997) (currently exercisable options that terminate if the employee's employment is terminated for causes constituted as transferable gifts). But see Heim v. Comm'r, 52 TCM (CCH) 1272 (1987) (option too indefinite to be enforced, thus transfer occurred when the option was exercised and the property was transferred). Rev. Rul. 98-21, 1998-1 CB 975 (transfer, for no consideration, of nonstatutory stock option is not exercisable until the employee performs additional services ("golden handcuffs" provision); not completed as gift until services are performed).

See Harrison, "Using Options to Allow Donees to Have the Donor's Cake and Eat It, Too," 72 Taxes 277 (Mar. 1999); Madden & Hayes, "New Ruling Turns Golden Handcuffs of Stock Options Into Estate Planning Ball and Chain," 25 Est. Plan. 310 (Aug.–Sept. 1998); Markstein & Pressgrave, "New Developments Create Opportunities Via Gifts of Stock Options," 24 Est. Plan. 403 (Nov. 1997).

[87] Galt v. Comm'r, 216 F2d 41 (7th Cir. 1954), cert. denied, 348 US 951 (1955).

[88] Lazarus v. Comm'r, 58 TC 854 (1972), aff'd, 513 F2d 824 (9th Cir. 1975); Estate of Kelley v. Comm'r, 63 TC 321 (1974).

[89] Goodwin v. McGowan, 47 F. Supp. 798 (WDNY 1942). See also Rev. Rul. 70-401, 1970-2 CB 197. Cf. Reg. § 25.7520-3(b)(3).

[90] Smith v. Shaughnessy, 318 US 176 (1943); Reg. § 25.2511-1(e).

[91] Bowden v. Comm'r, 234 F2d 937 (5th Cir.), cert. denied, 352 US 916 (1956).

gress has come up with some special rules under Section 2702 involving transfers made to a family member[92] where the donor or an "applicable family member" retains an interest in the property.[93] Under the rules, the retained interest or interests are valued at zero, thereby increasing the value of the transferred interest or interests.[94] In the discussion that follows, it is assumed the transfers are not to family members and, thus, Section 2702 is inapplicable.

[c] Uncertain Interests

If the interest retained by a donor is something less than a reversion, a legal life estate, an outright claim to the income, or a stated amount of income from the property, special problems are encountered. Suppose a donor creates a trust under which the trustee is required to utilize such part of the income or corpus as is necessary for the support of the donor during the donor's life and upon the donor's death to distribute the corpus and any accumulated income to others. Under established principles,[95] the donor has made a gift of the entire value of the property, unless the donor can show that the donor has retained an interest that is reasonably susceptible to valuation.[96] Where, as here, the standard supplied is one of support, valuation is possible and the value of the retained interest would be subtracted in computing the amount of the gift.[97] Perhaps the same result should be reached if the retained right is only the right to the income from non-income-producing property,[98] but there is authority to the contrary.[99] If a donor who initially retained an interest in property later relinquishes the interest, the donor makes a further gift of that interest at that time.[100]

---

[92] See IRC §§ 2702(a)(1), 2702(e), 2704(c)(2).

[93] IRC §§ 2701(e)(2), 2702(a)(1).

[94] IRC § 2702(a)(2)(A). Some exceptions apply. See IRC §§ 2702(a)(2)(B), 2702(a)(3). Section 2702 is discussed in detail at ¶ 19.03.

[95] Robinette v. Helvering, 318 US 184 (1943).

[96] TAM 9232002 (Aug. 7, 1992) (the donor could not prove value of retained income interest so there was a gift of all the property).

[97] Reg. § 25.2511-2(b). See also infra ¶ 10.01[9]; Priv. Ltr. Rul. 199908060 (Dec. 2, 1998) (the surviving spouse's transfer of right to receive payments from her deceased husband's pension plan for support, maintenance, care, and health, if her income was insufficient to provide for such, was a gift to be valued under the "willing buyer/willing seller" test, rather than as an annuity, because the likelihood of invasion was remote), Priv. Ltr. Rul. 199908022 (Nov. 25, 1998) (transfer by trust beneficiaries of income and remainder interests, contingent on surviving certain other persons, valued under Section 7520).

[98] See ¶ 9.04[3][b].

[99] Deal v. Comm'r, 29 TC 730 (1958), a decision that probably rested as much on the trustee's discretion.

[100] Rev. Rul. 79-421, 1979-2 CB 347.

[d] Reversionary Interests

The situation just presented involves the donor's retention of some type of income interest in the property. Naturally, the same principles are applicable if the donor retains a reversionary interest. Thus, if the donor creates a trust, income to A for fifteen years and reversion to the donor or the donor's estate, the amount of the gift is the value of the fifteen-year income interest or, stated differently, the value of the property less the value of the retained reversion.[101]

Suppose a donor transfers property in trust, income to A for life and, at death, remainder to A's child if living, and, if not, the corpus to return to the donor or the donor's estate. Three interests in the property are involved and must be considered separately for gift tax purposes. The value of A's life interest is clearly taxable as a gift. It is just as clear that the donor has not made a gift of the donor's reversionary interest. The Supreme Court has settled the question of the remainder. The value of the remainder, even though contingent, is an includible gift.[102] The donor has entirely relinquished control over the life interest and the remainder interest. Viewed another way, the donor has made a gift of the entire value of the property less the value of the contingent reversionary interest retained by the donor.

Whatever the proper view of transfers of interests that are difficult to value, the retained interest must be susceptible to valuation in order to support a reduction in the value of the gift. Therefore, the hypothetical situation discussed in the preceding paragraph must be differentiated from one in which the reversion is conditioned upon factors less predictable than survivorship. In a case in which the donor's reversionary interest would not take effect if A's child, who was unmarried at the time of the gift, married, had children, and the children lived to age 21, the Supreme Court said the reversionary interest could not be valued by recognized actuarial methods and refused to reduce the value of the gift by any amount with respect to the retained interest.[103]

[e] Transfers Conditional Upon Decision They Are Not Subject to Tax

In a case[104] in which the donor sought to make the transfer void to the extent that it was held to be taxable, the court treated the condition as void and

---

[101] Goulder v. United States, 1945-2 USTC ¶ 10,210 (ND Ohio 1945).

[102] Smith v. Shaughnessy, 318 US 176 (1943).

[103] Robinette v. Helvering, 318 US 184 (1943). See also Lockard v. Comm'r, 166 F2d 409 (1st Cir. 1948); Rev. Rul. 79-421, 1979-2 CB 347; Rev. Rul. 77-99, 1977-1 CB 295; Rev. Rul. 76-275, 1976-2 CB 299; Rev. Rul. 72-571, 1972-2 CB 533; Priv. Ltr. Rul. 8103130 (Oct. 27, 1980). For an extreme and questionable application of this principle, see McHugh v. United States, 142 F. Supp. 927 (Ct. Cl. 1956).

[104] Comm'r v. Procter, 142 F2d 824 (4th Cir.), cert. denied, 323 US 756 (1944).

upheld the Commissioner's assertion of a deficiency. Pointing out, among other things, that when the transfer was held taxable the condition would operate to set the decree aside, the court refused to condone "this sort of trifling with the judicial process."[105] The holding of the case has been extended to void an adjustment clause altering the amount of a gift transfer if, for federal tax purposes, it was finally determined that the value of the gift exceeded a stated amount.[106] Nevertheless, upon an intrafamily transfer of stock for an asserted adequate and full consideration in money or money's worth, subject to a price adjustment clause that is triggered if the Service determines the market value of the stock differs from the value set in the agreement, the price adjustment clause is not void as against public policy and no gift occurs.[107]

[f] The Creation of Joint Interests

A purchase of property by a person for oneself and another as tenants-in-common constitutes a gift of one half of the value of the property. Similarly, a conversion of separate property to community property is a gift of one half of the value of the property.[108] If there are several co-tenants, the purchaser makes gifts of the interests conferred on each of the others. If one person buys property and has it transferred to oneself and one or more joint tenants with rights of survivorship, there is a gift of a proportionate share of the value of the property.[109] Rights of equal value are created in the case of joint tenancies if, as usual, the survivorship rights of a party may be defeated by another party by severing one's interest. The acquisition with one spouse's funds of property transferred into a tenancy by the entirety also results in a gift of property.[110] Because there is no unilateral right in either spouse to sever the interests in

---

[105] Comm'r v. Procter, 142 F2d 824, 827 (4th Cir.), cert. denied, 323 US 756 (1944).

[106] Ward v. Comm'r, 87 TC 78 (1986). See also Rev. Rul. 86-41, 1986-1 CB 300; FSA 200122011 (Feb. 20. 2001) (formula clause allocating additional value to the charitable donee if gifted property revalued disregarded); TAMs 9309001 (Sept. 30, 1992) (adjustment of consideration if valuation contested disregarded); 9133001 (Jan. 31, 1990) (adjustment to consideration if valuation disregarded); Priv. Ltr. Rul. 8549005 (Aug. 30, 1985). Cf. Rev. Rul. 65-144, 1965-1 CB 442. But cf. Rev. Rul. 76-199, 1976-1 CB 288.

[107] King v. United States, 545 F2d 700 (10th Cir. 1976). But see Harwood v. Comm'r, 82 TC 239 (1984), aff'd in unpub. op., 786 F2d 1174 (9th Cir.), cert. denied, 479 US 1007 (1986) (gift occurred because no actual price adjustment was made). Cf. Dickinson v. Comm'r, 63 TC 771 (1975); Rev. Rul. 86-41, 1986-1 CB 300.

[108] Cf. Rev. Rul. 77-359, 1977-2 CB 24 (conversions of separate property owned by both spouses to community property). See also IRC § 2523; ¶ 11.03 (marital deduction for the gift).

[109] Reg. § 25.2511-1(h)(5). This would apply to down payments and any subsequent payments. Rev. Rul. 78-362, 1978-2 CB 248. See also Reg. § 25.2511-1(h)(4) and the subsequent discussion of revocable joint interests.

[110] But see IRC § 2523; ¶ 11.03.

such tenancies, the amount of the gift depends on the relative life expectancies of the tenants.[111] Special rules apply if the transfers are to a donee spouse who is not a citizen of the United States.[112]

[g] Insurance and Annuities

Many types of property interests may be the subject of a gift. An interest in a life insurance policy is property; and a purchase of a policy for the benefit of another, the transfer of an existing policy to another, or the payment of premiums on an existing policy owned by another, all may constitute gifts, if the one making the purchase, transfer, or payment retains no control over the policy.[113] An irrevocable designation of a new beneficiary or the relinquishment of a right to change existing beneficiaries has the same consequence if no

---

[111] See ¶ 9.04[1][b] text accompanying note 42.

[112] In the case of an inter vivos creation or termination of a joint tenancy or a tenancy by the entirety where there is a transfer by a donor spouse to a donee spouse who is not a U.S. citizen, the gift tax consequences depend on several factors. If the property is *personal property* there is generally a gift of one half of the value of the property. See Reg. § 25.2523(i)-2(c)(1). If severability of the tenancy may occur only by joint action of the parties, which is normally the case in a tenancy by the entirety, the amount of the gift is based on the parties' relative life expectancies. See Reg. § 25.2523(i)-2(c)(2). Subsequent gifts may occur on termination dependent on the manner in which the proceeds are split.

If the property is *real property*, there is generally no gift on creation of the joint tenancy or tenancy by the entirety, but on termination of either type of tenancy, the donor spouse is deemed to make a gift to the extent that the proportion of the total consideration furnished by the donor spouse multiplied by the value of the proceeds on termination (whether in cash or property) exceeds the value of the proceeds of termination received by the donor spouse. Reg. §§ 25.2523(i)-2(b)(1), 25.2523(i)-2(b)(2)(i), 25.2523(i)-2(b)(4) Ex. 1. However, if the real property joint tenancy or tenancy by the entirety interest was created after December 31, 1954, and before January 1, 1982, and an election was made under then Section 2515(c) or it was created after December 31, 1981, and before July 14, 1988, there was a gift on the creation of the interest. In that event, if the interest is terminated inter vivos, the preceding formula is applied, but the amount of the gift on the creation of the tenancy is treated as consideration originally belonging to and contributed by the noncitizen spouse. Reg. §§ 25.2523(i)-2(b)(2)(ii), 25.2523(i)-2(b)(4) Ex. 2. See Stephens, Maxfield & Lind, Federal Estate and Gift Taxation ¶¶ 10.06–10.07 (Warren, Gorham & Lamont, 4th ed. 1978). See also IRC §§ 2523(i)(1), 2523(i)(2), disallowing a marital deduction but allowing a $110,000 Section 2503(b) annual exclusion if there is a transfer to a noncitizen spouse, which would qualify for a marital deduction if the spouse were a U.S. citizen. See ¶ 11.03[5]. If there is no inter vivos termination of any of the preceding tenancies, Section 2040(a) generally applies. See IRC § 2056(d)(1)(B); ¶ 4.12[10] text accompanying notes 86–88. Cf. IRC § 2056(d)(2), discussed ¶ 4.12[10] text accompanying notes 83–93.

[113] Guggenheim v. Rasquin, 312 US 254 (1941); Halsted v. Comm'r, 28 TC 1069 (1957), acq. 1958-1 CB 5; Reg. § 25.2511-1(h)(8); Rev. Rul. 79-47, 1979-1 CB 312. Cf. Rev. Ruls. 76-200, 1976-1 CB 308; 78-420, 1978-2 CB 67; 76-490, 1976-2 CB 300

other control is retained over the policy.[114] If a third party is made the owner of a life insurance policy that was purchased with community property funds, generally it is treated as a gift made one-half by each spouse.[115] The purchase of an ordinary commercial annuity may constitute an indirect gift. No gift subject to tax could occur if an individual merely purchased a single-life, nonrefundable annuity for oneself; but the purchase of an annuity for another or the purchase of a joint or joint-and-survivor annuity for the purchaser and another can both constitute gifts.[116]

A private arrangement for the payment of an annuity does not differ in principle from the purchase of a commercial annuity[117] from the standpoint of whether there has been a gift. Thus, the regulations provide that[118] "[t]he transfer of property to B if there is imposed upon B the obligation of paying a commensurate annuity to C is a gift to C." If, in the example given, the annuity that *B* is to pay *C* is not commensurate with the value of the property transferred, there may be gifts to both *B* and *C*. And a transfer to a private person in exchange for such person's agreement to support the transferor for life constitutes a gift to the extent that the value of the property transferred exceeds the value of the support obligation assumed by the transferee.[119]

[h] Notes and Checks

If *A* who holds *B*'s promissory note gives it to *C*, *A* has made a gift to *C*.[120] The effect of one's issuance of one's own note or check is not necessarily the same, however. As previously indicated, in undertaking to say when a transfer becomes complete so as to be subject to the gift tax, it is necessary to differentiate transfers that are revocable or that otherwise remain subject to some control by the transferor from those that involve some future uncertainty because of conditions or contingencies not within the control of the trans-

---

(transfer of similar rights in a group-term policy not gift until premiums paid because policy at time of transfer had no ascertainable value).

[114] Reg. § 25.2511-1(h)(8).

[115] See infra ¶ 10.01[5][d] for further gift tax consequences of community property life insurance.

[116] E.g., Will of Ayer v. Comm'r, 29 BTA 945 (1934).

[117] Private annuities and commercial annuities are treated differently for valuation purposes. Reg. §§ 25.2512-5, 25.2512-6, 25.2512-9. See Dunigan v. United States, 434 F2d 892 (5th Cir. 1970). See also ¶¶ 10.02[2][b][ii], 10.02[2][b][iii].

[118] Reg. § 25.2511-1(h)(2). See also Estate of Bartman v. Comm'r, 10 TC 1073 (1948), acq. 1948-2 CB 1.

[119] Estate of Bergan v. Comm'r, 1 TC 543 (1943), acq. 1943 CB 2; Rev. Rul. 69-74, 1969-1 CB 43.

[120] See Prop. Reg. § 25.2512-4 with respect to valuation of the gift.

feror.[121] For example, if a parent hands a child a check as a gift, no taxable transfer occurs at that time because the parent could stop payment on the check and has consequently relinquished control over nothing.[122] Similarly, if a parent hands that parent's promissory note to a child as a gift, no transfer subject to tax takes place at that time because, in the absence of consideration, the child could not enforce payment of the note.[123] But if the parent's note is legally enforceable under state law, there is a completed gift because the child could enforce payment of the note.[124]

---

[121] Compare Sanford's Estate v. Comm'r, 308 US 39 (1939) with Smith v. Shaughnessy, 318 US 176 (1943).

[122] Dillingham v. Comm'r, 903 F2d 760 (10th Cir. 1990) (December 24, 1980, check not deposited until late January 1981; no gift until 1981, the transfer was revocable); Estate of Newman v. Comm'r, 111 TC 81 (1998) (checks were not completed gifts because they were not accepted or paid by the drawee bank until after the donor's death); Braum Family Partnership v. Comm'r, 66 TCM (CCH) 780 (1993) (December 31, 1983, checks not deposited until January 1984, and the court stated that the donor had not met the burden of proof that the donor had given up dominion and control). If the parent dies, such checks are included in the parent's gross estate under Section 2033. See ¶ 4.05[3] note 28.

Compare Estate of Metzger v. Comm'r, 38 F3d 118 (4th Cir. 1994) (where December 14, 1985, checks were deposited by donees on December 31, 1985, but the drawee bank did not pay the checks until January 2, 1986, and were appropriately held to be completed gifts (and qualify for the annual exclusion) on December 31, 1985, under the relation-back doctrine). The Service has agreed to follow the *Metzger* relation-back test. Rev. Rul. 96-56, 1996-2 CB 161. The ruling provides

that the delivery of a check to a noncharitable donee will be deemed to be a completed gift for federal gift and estate tax purposes on the *earlier* of (i) the date on which the donor has so parted with dominion and control under local law as to leave in the donor no power to change its disposition, *or* (ii) the date on which the donee deposits the check (or cashes the check against available funds of the donee) or presents the check for payment, if it is established that: (1) the check was paid by the drawee bank when first presented to the drawee bank for payment; (2) the donor was alive when the check was paid by the drawee bank; (3) the donor intended to make a gift; (4) delivery of the check by the donor was unconditional; and (5) the check was deposited, cashed, or presented in the calendar year for which completed gift treatment is sought and within a reasonable time of issuance.

Rev. Rul. 96-56, 1996-2 CB 162 (italics added).

Rev. Rul. 96-56, 1996-2 CB 161 modifies Rev. Rul. 67-396 (Situation 1), 1967-2 CB 351, although the result in Situation 1 would be the same under either ruling.

[123] Rev. Rul. 67-396 (Situation 2), 1967-2 CB 351. See also GCM 16460, XV-1 CB 369 (1936).

[124] Rev. Rul. 84-25, 1984-1 CB 191. See also ¶ 2.01[1][b] note 20.

In Priv. Ltr. Rul. 9113009 (Dec. 21, 1990), the Service took the position that an unsecured guarantee of an obligation constituted a gift at the time of the obligation. The ruling also stated that there would be gifts in the amount of any unreimbursed amounts on payment of any guarantee and also considered various marital deduction aspects of the guarantees (see ¶ 5.06[5][b] note 103). The ruling was criticized in August & Kulunas, "Guarantees Have Unexpected Gift Tax and Marital Deduction Consequences in IRS Rul-

[i] Enforceable Future Rights.

These established principles on checks and notes discussed earlier leave open the question whether a transfer subject to the gift tax may ever arise at the time an individual executes a contract under which the individual is required to transfer money or property at a future time. It is tempting to say, and essentially true, that an agreement to make a gift is not a gift either under basic property law or for federal tax purposes. As in the case of a gratuitous transfer of the maker's own note, the agreement would not be enforceable and consequently is accorded no significance. However, the agreement to make a future transfer is enforceable if it is supported by consideration. A likely thought here is that if there is consideration for the agreement, there will be no gift in any event; but this is simply not so. The reason is that consideration that may render an agreement enforceable may be entirely unrecognized for tax purposes or may be less than adequate and full consideration for the obligation assumed, and consideration that is unrecognized or inadequate by tax criteria does not foreclose the imposition of gift tax.[125]

Questions may still be raised, however, whether assumption of an enforceable obligation to do something in the future can ever be viewed as a gift, as it is "the transfer of property by gift" upon which the gift tax is imposed.[126] No Supreme Court decision deals squarely with this question, but respectable authority supports an affirmative answer.[127] Most cases take the form of transfers of identifiable property, such as an assignment of a deed of realty, physical transfer of personalty, or an effective assignment of all rights in intangibles such as securities. Nevertheless, an enforceable right acquired under a contract is itself a property right, and, if by contract an individual creates in another person an enforceable right to receive from the individual something of value, the individual has made a "transfer of property by gift" to the extent that the

---

ing," 74 J. Tax'n 346 (1991). The ruling was withdrawn by TAM 9409018 (Dec. 1, 1993), although that ruling discussed only the position with respect to the marital deduction consequences.

[125] See ¶ 10.02[5][d].

[126] Bradford v. Comm'r, 34 TC 1059 (1960). See IRC § 2501; ¶ 9.02.

[127] Rosenthal v. Comm'r, 205 F2d 505 (2d Cir. 1953); Comm'r v. Copley's Estate, 194 F2d 364 (7th Cir. 1952); Harris v. Comm'r, 178 F2d 861 (2d Cir.), rev'd on other grounds, 340 US 106 (1950); Rev. Ruls. 84-25, 1984-1 CB 191; 81-110, 1981-1 CB 479; 79-384, 1979-2 CB 344; 69-346, 1969-1 CB 227; 69-347, 1969-1 CB 227. See Alexander v. United States, 640 F2d 1250 (Ct. Cl. 1981) (where there was no gift because there was no legally binding commitment that donees could enforce). The Service's position on this issue has not been consistent. It has indicated that it was misled by the decision in Archbold v. Comm'r, 42 BTA 453 (1940), acq. 1969-1 CB 20, nonacq. 1965-2 CB 7, withdrawn, to believe the Tax Court would not hold that a gift could arise out of a mere enforceable promise. Ten years later, in Estate of Copley v. Comm'r, 15 TC 17 (1950), aff'd, 194 F2d 364 (7th Cir. 1952), the Tax Court recognized a gift by contract, and the Treasury acquiesced in Copley, 1965-2 CB 4.

transfer of the right was not supported by consideration recognized for gift tax purposes.[128]

Conceptually, the contractual creation of an enforceable property right in another gratuitously, or at least partly gratuitously, constitutes a gift even though there may be some uncertainty regarding what is to be paid or transferred in the future or even some uncertainty whether, because of conditions or contingencies, anything at all will ever have to be actually transferred. Uncertainties of these types that are not within the control of the putative donor usually concern only the value of the gift and not whether a gift has been made.[129] Settled principles in the gift tax area caution us to look to what the donor relinquishes, rather than to what the donee receives,[130] and tend to support the recognition of a gift arising out of an enforceable contract; the donor has created a claim against the donor's property. It might be relevant, however, to point out that the donee is in receipt of something at the time of the execution of the contract; the donee has acquired a property right that the donee could assign to another for valuable consideration. None of the foregoing observations seems to strain very hard established gift tax concepts and principles.[131]

[j] Qualified Tuition Programs and Education Savings Accounts

A contribution to either a qualified tuition program or an education savings account after August 5, 1997,[132] is treated as a completed gift of a present interest to the designated beneficiaries,[133] consequently, distribution from these plans to a beneficiary are not treated as taxable gifts.[134] However, if, under either type of plan, there is a change in the designation of the beneficiary or a rollover from the account of one beneficiary to another beneficiary and the new beneficiary is not a family member of the old beneficiary[135] or is assigned by the generation assignment rules of the generation-skipping transfer tax[136] to

---

[128] None of the authorities cited supra note 127 specifically treats the issue involved as a transfer of property issue.

[129] See Smith v. Shaughnessy, 318 US 176 (1943), treating the transfer of a contingent remainder interest in a trust as a gift even though subsequent events might destroy the interest with the result that the remainder person would take nothing from the trust.

[130] Burnet v. Guggenheim, 288 US 280 (1933).

[131] But see ¶ 10.02[1][b].

[132] Taxpayer Relief Act of 1997, Pub. L. No. 105-34, § 211(f)(5)(A), 111 Stat. 788, 811 (1977), reprinted in 1997-4 CB (Vol. 1) 1, 27.

[133] IRC §§ 529(c)(2)(A)(i), 530(d)(3). See ¶ 9.04[3][g].

[134] IRC §§ 529(c)(5)(A), 530(d)(3).

[135] Prop. Reg. § 1.529-5(b)(3)(i). Seemingly, although this proposed regulation involves only qualified tuition programs, it should also apply to an education savings account. See IRC § 530(d)(3) (incorporating the gift tax rules of Section 529).

[136] IRC § 2651. See ¶ 17.01.

a generation below the previous beneficiary, there is a taxable gift from the previous beneficiary to the new beneficiary.[137]

[4] When a Transfer Is Complete

A gift tax timing problem unavoidably intrudes on the discussion of gifts by contract. Broadly, the problem of when a gift is taxable raises the question: When did the donor relinquish dominion and control over the transferred property? The question may be more properly phrased: What degree of dominion and control retained by a donor defers completion for gift tax purposes? The statute is silent with respect to this problem but a well-developed pattern of law emerges from cases, rulings, and the regulations. However, this is a good place to abandon expressly any hope that the estate tax and gift tax rules on completeness are nicely parallel.[138]

A mere intention to make a gift is not a gift; objective action to effect a transfer to the donee is essential. Accordingly, in a case in which several donors who were determined to make gifts of securities to their spouses had their clerks make corresponding notations in their records, and took only initial steps to effect the transfer, the court held there were no completed gifts.[139] This principle is reflected in the regulations that recognize a gift as complete when properly endorsed stock certificates are delivered to a donee or the donee's agent but that provide that, if the certificates are delivered to the donor's bank or the donor's broker for transfer into the name of the donee, no gift occurs until the stock is transferred on the corporate books.[140] A transfer of real estate is complete when, under local law, it can no longer be transferred by the donor to a bona fide purchaser, generally when it is both deeded and recorded.[141]

Here, as elsewhere, the question is: When did the donor relinquish dominion and control? If the donor makes delivery to the donor's own agent, the do-

---

[137] IRC §§ 529(c)(5)(B), 530(d)(3); Prop. Reg. §§ 1.529-5(b)(3)(ii), 1.529-5(b)(3)(iii) Ex. The transfer may also constitute a generation-skipping transfer if the new beneficiary is a skip person in relation to the old beneficiary. Prop. Reg. § 1.529-5(b)(3)(ii).

[138] See infra ¶ 10.01[10].

[139] Richardson v. Comm'r, 126 F2d 562 (2d Cir. 1942); Cervi v. United States, 1974-2 USTC ¶ 13,027 (D. Colo. 1974). Compare Todd v. Comm'r, 51 TC 987 (1969) with Kraft v. Comm'r, 28 TCM (CCH) 1213 (1969). Cf. Davis v. United States, 378 F. Supp. 579 (ND Tex. 1974).

[140] Reg. § 25.2511-2(h). See Autin v. Comm'r, 109 F3d 231 (5th Cir. 1997) (special rule under Louisiana law); Estate of Davenport v. Comm'r, 184 F3d 1176 (1999) (constructive delivery under local law).

[141] Estate of Whitt v. Comm'r, 751 F2d 1548 (11th Cir. 1985); Warda v. Comm'r, 15 F3d 533 (6th Cir. 1994).

nor has not relinquished control and the gift is not complete.[142] Failure to collect a personal loan may constitute a completed gift on the running of the statute of limitations if affirmative action to effect a transfer does not occur at an earlier time.[143]

[5] Revocable Transfers

The greatest control a donor can retain over transferred property is a power to revoke the transfer and revest the beneficial title to the property in oneself. An early Supreme Court decision under the 1924 gift tax statute made it clear that a transfer subject to outright revocation by the donor is not a completed gift.[144] Although the creation of a trust by Settlor, income to A and remainder to B or B's estate, which Settlor retains a power to revoke, is not a completed gift at the time it is created, subsequent income distributions by the trust do constitute gifts.[145] As the gift tax law views Settlor as continuing owner of trust property, the income distributions are gifts by Settlor. Moreover, a complete relinquishment by Settlor of the initially retained dominion and control over the trust constitutes a completed gift of the trust corpus at that time.[146] If Settlor created the trust described here but expressly retained the power to revoke only the remainder interest, there would be a completed gift of the income interest to A even though the gift of the remainder to B or B's estate would be incomplete.[147] In the alternative, if there were a power to revoke only the income in-

---

[142] Cf. Carpenter v. United States, 4 Cl. Ct. 705 (1984); Estate of Cummins v. Comm'r, 66 TCM (CCH) 1232 (1993).

[143] Estate of Lang v. Comm'r, 613 F2d 770 (9th Cir. 1980). But see Miller v. Comm'r, 71 TCM (CCH) 1674 (1996), aff'd in unpub. op., 113 F3d 1241 (9th Cir. 1997) (parents purported loans to children were gifts when the loans were made); Vinikoor v. Comm'r, 75 TCM (CCH) 2185 (1998) (purported loans of stock gifts).

[144] Burnet v. Guggenheim, 288 US 280 (1933). See also Estate of Kelly v. Comm'r, 31 TC 493 (1958), rejecting a contention that transfers were void under local law, which, if true, would preclude gift tax liability.

[145] Reg. § 25.2511-2(f).

[146] Reg. § 25.2511-2(f); Latta v. Comm'r, 212 F2d 164 (3d Cir.), cert. denied, 348 US 825 (1954); Talge v. United States, 229 F. Supp. 836 (WD Mo. 1964); TAM 9127008 (Mar. 22, 1991) (complete gift when trust itself terminates). Cf. Estate of Vak v. Comm'r, 973 F2d 1409 (8th Cir. 1992) (complete gifts of portions of trust). If the power to revoke terminates because of the donor's death, no gift tax liability is incurred because the gift tax is imposed only on transfers by living donors. Reg. § 25.2511-2(f). However, such a situation would result in inclusion of the trust in the donor decedent's gross estate under Section 2038.

[147] Goldstein v. Comm'r, 37 TC 897 (1962), acq. 1964-2 CB 5. If the donor has a power to revoke that is subject to the donor's control, then these rules apply. Rev. Rul. 54-537, 1954-2 CB 316. If a power to revoke is beyond the donor's control, then there is a completed gift, although valuation may be difficult. Priv. Ltr. Rul. 8546001 (July 1985).

terest, there would be no completed gift of that interest, but the gift of the remainder would be complete.[148] That is to say, each property interest must be separately examined to determine whether the donor has relinquished dominion and control over it.

Transfers of property can be revocable for reasons other than the transferor's express reservation in the instrument of transfer of a power to revoke. For example, if a donor gives the trustee the power to revoke the trust and either names the donor as trustee or has the power to substitute the donor for the named trustee, the donor has retained a power to revoke the trust.[149] The test of revocability depends on whether the donor had a power to revoke under state law.[150] If under state law a transfer to a trust is deemed revocable unless expressly made irrevocable,[151] the power to revoke must be expressly renounced for a gift in trust to be complete.[152] And if under state law the corpus of the trust or an interest in it is subject to the claims of the donor's creditors, there is an incomplete transfer of the vulnerable portion that the donor indirectly retains a power to revoke.[153]

[a] Minor's Right to Revoke

If under local law a minor can rescind a gift, the minor's gifts are not recognized for gift tax purposes until the minor's power to rescind expires,

---

[148] Rev. Rul. 79-243, 1979-2 CB 343.

[149] Cf. Reg. § 20.2038-1(a)(3).

[150] Estate of Mandels v. Comm'r, 64 TC 61 (1975), acq. 1975-2 CB 2; Neal v. United States, 82 AFTR2d 98-5429 (WD Pa. 1998), aff'd in unpub. op., 187 F3d 626 (3d Cir. 1999) (state law equitable right of rescission permitted a taxpayer to be treated as continuing to hold contingent reversionary interests in a trust that had been released); Rev. Rul. 74-365, 1974-2 CB 324; TAM 9231003 (Apr. 9, 1992) (under state law holder of power of attorney had no power to make gifts; thus, transfers were revocable). But see Lange v. United States, 78 AFTR2d 96-6553 (ND Ind. 1996) (modification to disregard disclaimer did not affect tax consequences of disclaimer).

[151] See Cal. Prob. Code § 15400 (2001).

[152] Similarly, at a time when a Louisiana statute made gratuitous transfers by a husband to his wife revocable during the husband's lifetime, such transfers were not gifts for gift tax purposes. Cf. Vaccaro v. United States, 149 F2d 1014 (5th Cir. 1945).

[153] Paolozzi v. Comm'r, 23 TC 182 (1954), acq. 1962-1 CB 4; Hambleton v. Comm'r, 60 TC 558 (1973), acq. in result 1974-1 CB 1; Outwin v. Comm'r, 76 TC 153 (1981); Grynberg v. Comm'r, 79 TCM (CCH) 1355 (2000); Rev. Rul. 76-103, 1976-1 CB 293; Priv. Ltr. Rul. 9639056 (June 24, 1996). There is also an incomplete transfer if state law gives a donor an unqualified right to revest title in the donor as a result of a unilateral mistake on the donor's part. Touche v. Comm'r, 58 TC 565 (1972), acq. 1972-2 CB 3; Neal v. United States, 82 AFTR2d 98-5429 (WD Pa. 1998), aff'd in unpub. op., 187 F3d 626 (3d Cir. 1999).

which might be some time after the minor gains majority.[154] But in some states a minor's right to revoke a gratuitous transfer of realty may be postponed until the minor reaches majority.[155] If the minor does not have the right to revoke at any time but can revoke only upon attaining majority, the gift is complete at least to the extent of the assured interest, the term beginning with the date of transfer and ending with the date upon which the right to revoke arises.[156]

[b] Termination of Donor's Control

In instances in which the gift is treated as incomplete because of the donor's retention of control, a completed gift subject to gift tax occurs when the donor's control terminates either by operation of law, by some affirmative action by the donor, or upon the happening of an event other than the donor's death.[157] The situation of a minor, described previously, reflects the possibility of termination of a donor's control by operation of law. If a donor reserves a power only until the happening of a named event, such as a power in a donor to revoke until the death of a spouse, the happening of the event makes the gift complete and subject to tax at that time.[158]

Recall that if a donor hands a personal check to a donee, no taxable transfer occurs at that time because the donor may stop payment on the check. Thus, a check given by one family member to another at Christmas but not cashed, deposited, or negotiated until the next year is not treated as a gift until the year in which it is cashed.[159] Similarly, if for no consideration a donor gives a personal note to a donee, which is unenforceable under local law, the transfer is not a completed gift because the donee cannot enforce payment on the note.[160]

Agreements to make future transfers are merely revocable transfers, if they are transfers at all, unless or until they are supported by consideration recognized under local law.[161] To the extent that the value of enforceable rights under such agreements exceeds the consideration recognized for federal gift tax purposes,[162] there is a completed transfer taxable under the federal gift

---

[154] See Comm'r v. Allen, 108 F2d 961 (3d Cir. 1939), cert. denied, 309 US 680 (1940).

[155] CJS Infants § 132 (1978).

[156] Cf. Goldstein v. Comm'r, 37 TC 897 (1962), acq. 1964-2 CB 5.

[157] See supra ¶ 10.01[5] text accompanying note 146.

[158] Goodman v. Comm'r, 156 F2d 218 (2d Cir. 1946).

[159] See supra ¶ 10.01[3][h] note 122.

[160] See supra ¶ 10.01[3][h].

[161] See supra ¶ 10.01[3][i].

[162] See IRC § 2512(b), discussed ¶¶ 10.02[3]–10.02[6].

tax.[163] However, if the transfer itself is revocable, there is no gift, even though it is supported by binding consideration under local law.[164]

Contingent powers may cause difficulty, but if a power is exercisable upon a contingency that is within the donor's control, the contingency should be disregarded and the power recognized as an immediate one.[165] In other circumstances, restrictions on the time or conditions for exercise of a retained power may render a transfer only partly complete. An illustration may be helpful. D transfers property in trust with provision for payment of the income to B for life, remainder to R or R's estate, but D retains the right to revoke the trust after the death of R if B is still living. D has made a transfer subject to a power to revoke conditioned upon the death of R. What are the gift tax consequences? At least the value of B's assured right to the income until R's death is subject to gift tax, and so is the value of R's contingent remainder, as the contingency is not within D's control. That perhaps is the most that can be taxed at the time of the transfer.[166]

[c] Joint Accounts

Within the principle of revocable transfers, no gift occurs when one opens a joint bank account for oneself and another person on which either can draw without accounting to the other, because the depositor can defeat (revoke) the other's interest by withdrawal. But when the other draws an amount from the account, a completed transfer occurs, because the amount withdrawn then

---

[163] See supra ¶ 10.01[3] text accompanying note 125.

[164] Cf. Estate of Di Marco v. Comm'r, 87 TC 653 (1986), which was essentially a revocable transfer. See also Rev. Rul. 81-31, 1981-1 CB 475, which should have been decided on the rationale of a revocable transfer and that was revoked by Rev. Rul. 92-68, 1992-2 CB 257.

[165] Cf. Loughridge's Estate v. Comm'r, 183 F2d 294 (9th Cir.), cert. denied, 340 US 830 (1950).

[166] The value of income rights for B's life after R's death and of a remainder interest conditioned on B's surviving R are property interests over which the donor has not relinquished control. If, as seems likely, they can realistically be valued, their value is subtracted from the value of the trust property in determining the amount of the gift. But cf. Robinette v. Helvering, 318 US 184 (1943); Estate of Kolb v. Comm'r, 5 TC 588 (1945), acq. 1946-1 CB 3. Even though a part of the value of the transferred property may escape the gift tax, nevertheless that part and more may be subjected to estate tax upon D's death. If the contingency occurs prior to D's death, Section 2038 applies to include the entire value of the property. If D dies before the contingency occurs, the corpus (less a portion of B's income interest) is included in D's estate under Section 2036, but the excluded value of B's interest (considering R's advanced age) is less than the value that escaped gift tax at the time of the transfer. See the discussion of contingent Section 2036 interests and powers at ¶ 4.08[2] text accompanying note 17. Cf. IRC § 2012.

passes out of the depositor's control.[167] These same principles apply to purchase of U.S. savings bonds by the purchaser in the joint names of the purchaser and another person,[168] and to the creation of a joint brokerage account between the creator and a noncontributing third-party owner with securities registered in the name of a nominee of the firm.[169]

[d] Transfers of Community Property

If a revocable transfer of community property becomes complete upon the death of one spouse, the transfer of the survivor's interest may become a completed lifetime transfer at that time. The regulations contain an example of a possible gift arising out of transactions in life insurance in a community property state:

> Where property held by a husband and wife as community property is used to purchase insurance upon the husband's life and a third person is revocably designated as beneficiary and under the State law the husband's death is considered to make absolute the transfer by the wife, there is a gift by the wife at the time of the husband's death of half the amount of the proceeds of such insurance.[170]

The Treasury's position has been judicially accepted.[171] If, however, the surviving spouse receives some portion of the proceeds, the surviving spouse will be deemed not to have transferred those proceeds to another. Thus, if one half of the proceeds of a revocable community property life insurance policy on the decedent's life are paid to the surviving spouse, the surviving spouse has made no gift.[172]

---

[167] Reg. § 25.2511-1(h)(4). But see ¶ 10.02[5]. If the withdrawal is not treated as a valid transfer under state law, there is no completed gift. Estate of Bettin v. Comm'r, 33 TCM (CCH) 499 (1974), aff'd per curiam, 543 F2d 1269 (9th Cir. 1976). Cf. Estate of Sulavich v. Comm'r, 587 F2d 845 (6th Cir. 1978), involving the gift tax consequences of the creation of trustee savings accounts for third persons.

[168] Rev. Rul. 68-269, 1968-1 CB 399.

[169] Rev. Rul. 69-148, 1969-1 CB 226. But see First Wis. Trust Co. v. United States, 553 F. Supp. 26 (ED Wis. 1982), finding a completed gift where, under state law, the donor was obligated to account to the donee for one half of any proceeds removed from the account.

[170] Reg. § 25.2511-1(h)(9). Within this example, the husband's death could result in a taxable gift by his wife to the husband's mistress, if she were named the beneficiary of such a policy. Cf. Rev. Rul. 94-69, 1994-2 CB 241 (a gift of the entire proceeds, where policy funded with community property was owned by the surviving spouse at the insured's death).

[171] Cox v. United States, 286 F. Supp. 761 (WD La. 1968).

[172] Kaufman v. United States, 462 F2d 439 (5th Cir. 1972); Comm'r v. Chase Manhattan Bank, 259 F2d 231 (5th Cir. 1958), cert. denied, 359 US 913 (1959).

Similarly, in a community property widow's election situation,[173] no gift occurs until an affirmative election is made by the surviving spouse.[174] The spouse is deemed at that time to make a gift in an amount equal to the excess of the value of the property interests the spouse transfers to others (generally, a remainder to the children in the spouse's property that is valued applying Section 2702)[175] over the consideration the spouse receives (generally a life interest in the decedent's property).[176]

[e] Joint and Mutual Wills

Similar problems arise with respect to joint and mutual wills.[177] In general, any agreement entered into between spouses prior to the death of one spouse is revocable.[178] At the death of the predeceasing spouse, it can be argued that the surviving spouse makes a completed transfer of a remainder in the survivor's property less any consideration received from the deceased spouse, thus reaching a result comparable to the community property widow's election situation. However, the gift tax consequences to the surviving spouse depend on the spouse's rights in the spouse's property during the spouse's life.[179] If the spouse has complete freedom to use and dispose of the property after the predeceasing spouse's death, the spouse's transfer is essentially revocable and the spouse incurs no gift tax. If, however, the spouse is allowed only the income from the property during the spouse's life, a taxable transfer would occur, similar in consequence to a community property widow's election. Ob-

---

[173] See the discussion of this device at ¶ 4.08[7][c].

[174] Cf. Comm'r v. Siegel, 250 F2d 339, 344 n.10 (9th Cir. 1957); Brown v. Comm'r, 52 TC 50 (1969), acq. 1969-2 CB xxiv. The Commissioner takes the position that if an inter vivos contract to make the election is made when both spouses are alive and even if under state law the contract is binding from its inception, no completed gift is made by the survivor until the first spouse dies because the gift is not susceptible of valuation until that time. Rev. Rul. 69-346, 1969-1 CB 227. The ruling reaches the right result but for the wrong reasons. See ¶ 10.02[1][b] text accompanying note 16. See also Rev. Rul. 69-347, 1969-1 CB 227; supra ¶ 10.01[3] note 127.

[175] See ¶ 19.03. See also ¶ 4.08[7][c].

[176] Comm'r v. Siegel, 250 F2d 339 (9th Cir. 1957). See also IRC § 2512(b).

[177] See the discussion of joint and mutual wills at ¶ 5.06[8][d][iv].

[178] See ¶ 5.06[8][d][iv] text accompanying note 392; Rev. Rul. 69-346, 1969-1 CB 227, which confuses completion and valuation. There the Service inappropriately held that a transfer was complete but impossible to value. In fact, the agreement was revocable by both parties and not yet complete. See Macris, "Open Valuation and the Completed Transfer: A Problem Area in Federal Gift Taxation," 34 Tax L. Rev. 273 (1979); ¶ 10.02[1][b].

[179] Masterson v. Comm'r, 127 F2d 252 (5th Cir. 1942). A good summary of the cases in this area is found in Private Letter Ruling 7944009 (July 10, 1979). This is also the case in determining whether the decedent spouse's estate qualifies for a marital deduction. See ¶ 5.06[8][d][iv].

viously, if the spouse has some freedom of disposition over the property, local law must be examined to determine whether the degree of freedom reaches a power of revocation or other power that would make the transfer incomplete for gift tax purposes.[180]

[6] Power to Change Beneficiaries

A more limited type of dominion and control exists if a donor retains a power to change beneficial interests but not to revest the property in the donor. Uncertainty about the gift tax consequences of the donor's retention of this more limited power was dispelled by the Supreme Court in *Estate of Sanford v. Commissioner.*[181]

The *Sanford* case involved a refinement of the earlier pronounced *Guggenheim* principle.[182] In 1913, when there was no gift tax, the donor had set up a trust but had retained an unrestricted right to revoke the transfer. Later, in 1919, the donor relinquished all right to revoke or otherwise alter the trust for the donor's own benefit but reserved the right to modify the trust in other respects. Finally, in 1924, after the early gift tax statute was enacted, the donor relinquished donor's remaining powers over the trust. The question presented to the Court was when the transfer became complete for gift tax purposes. It could not be contended after *Guggenheim* that a fully revocable transfer constituted a gift, and it was not asserted that the 1913 transfer was complete. The taxpayer argued, however, that the gift was complete when, in 1919, the donor gave up any and all power to utilize the trust property for the donor's own benefit. If this argument had been accepted, the gift would have been complete before enactment of the gift tax statute and would therefore entirely have escaped gift tax. But the government contended that as long as the donor retained the right to change beneficial interests, even in a way not to benefit the donor, the gift was incomplete; thus, the gift should not be treated as complete until the relinquishment of the donor's remaining powers in 1924, which was

---

[180] Hambleton v. Comm'r, 60 TC 558 (1978), acq. in result 1974-1 CB 1; Brown v. Comm'r, 52 TC 50 (1969). Compare Pyle v. United States, 766 F2d 1141 (7th Cir. 1985) (gift completed because of limitations upon the survivor to dispose of the property under Illinois law) with Estate of Lidbury v. Comm'r, 800 F2d 649 (7th Cir. 1986) (no completed gift where no such restrictions upon the survivor under Illinois law). See infra ¶ 10.01[6].

[181] See supra ¶ 10.01[3][h] text accompanying note 121. Compare Sanford's Estate v. Comm'r, 308 US 39 (1939) with Smith v. Shaughnessy, 318 US 176 (1943).

[182] Burnet v. Guggenheim, 288 US 280 (1933).

of course after the enactment of the early gift tax. The government's contention was accepted by the Court.[183]

The *Sanford* opinion is not a model of clarity, but as subsequently explained by the Court[184] and indicated in the preceding discussion, the controlling factor in determining when a gift is complete for gift tax purposes is the donor's abandonment of control over the property. In more complicated circumstances, it is often difficult to identify the time at which the donor may be said to have given up control; some of the problems will be suggested here. First, however, it is interesting to note how the *Sanford* principle operates while a *Sanford*-type trust is in existence. If the donor can alter any beneficial interest in a trust set up by the donor, the creation of that interest does not constitute a gift by the donor, but amounts that the donor permits to be paid over to the beneficiary of the uncertain interest do constitute gifts; such amounts pass beyond the donor's control when paid out.[185] Thus, if a donor creates an irrevocable trust with income to be paid for twenty years to either *A* or *B*, as the donor may direct, and the remainder to *C* or *C*'s estate, there is a completed gift of the remainder interest, but no completed gift of the income interests. As income is actually paid to *A* or *B*, the amount paid constitutes a completed gift of a present interest, and if the donor later relinquishes the power to determine who receives the income or irrevocably accords *A* or *B* the entire right to future income, there is a completed gift of the remaining income interest at that time.

Briefly stated, the time of completion of a gift does not depend on when the donor relinquishes all power to take the property back (for a gift will still be incomplete if the donor has given up that power but retained a power to change others' interests) nor on when a donee becomes assured of an interest (for a gift that may be entirely defeated by the donor's reversionary interest

---

[183] See also du Pont v. Comm'r, 2 TC 246 (1943), nonacq. 1943 CB 30. It is late in the day to quarrel with the *Sanford* principle. Nevertheless, under the very general language of the gift tax statute, it could better be said that an individual has made a gift when the individual has gratuitously relinquished irrevocably to others all the individual's beneficial interest in property. Indeed, the result seems tidier. For estate tax purposes, Congress appropriately and expressly treats a transferor's retention of some nonbeneficial controls as a justification for imposition of death taxes. IRC §§ 2036, 2038. Even under the estate tax, however, the pervasive notion that transfers within those provisions are "incomplete" rather than merely taxable produces some questionable results. See United States v. O'Malley, 383 US 627 (1966), treating accumulated trust income as transferred by the decedent settlor who had no beneficial interest in it.

[184] Smith v. Shaughnessy, 318 US 176 (1943).

[185] Reg. § 25.2511-2(f); Comm'r v. Warner, 127 F2d 913 (9th Cir. 1942). Priv. Ltr. Rul. 200148028 (Aug. 27, 2001) (incomplete gift where the grantor retained a limited power to appoint trust property).

may still be complete), but it does depend on when the donor has fully relinquished dominion and control over the property.[186]

[7] Power to Alter Time or Manner

The degree of control a donor must retain to render a gift incomplete for gift tax purposes is greater in some respects than what the donor must retain to render a lifetime transfer taxable at death. Although reservation of a mere power to change the time or manner of enjoyment of a beneficiary's interest that cannot be shifted to another invokes estate tax liability,[187] it does not render the gift incomplete under the gift tax provisions. The regulations give this illustration:[188]

> [T]he creation of a trust the income of which is to be paid annually to the donee for a period of years, the corpus being distributable to him at the end of the period, and the power reserved by the donor being limited to a right to require that, instead of the income being so payable, it should be accumulated and distributed with the corpus to the donee at the termination of the period, constitutes a completed gift.[189]

Of course, a power to alter time or manner may be an indirect power to alter beneficial interests; if so, there is an incomplete gift of the interest involved. For example, if a donor transfers property to a trust, income payable to A and remainder to B or B's estate, and retains a power to accumulate the income, the power to accumulate is a power to shift income benefits from A to B, and only the transfer of the remainder interest is a completed gift.[190]

---

[186] Robinson v. Comm'r, 675 F2d 774 (5th Cir. 1982); Streck v. Comm'r, 44 TCM (CCH) 437 (1982). As in the case of a power to revoke, a power to alter beneficiaries may be indirectly retained by the donor. For example, if Donor creates a trust giving the trustee a power to distribute income to A or B and names Donor as trustee, Donor has not made a completed transfer of the income interest. If, however, Donor resigns as trustee and an independent trustee is named, and Donor does not have the power to reappoint Donor as trustee, at that time Donor has relinquished the indirect power to alter beneficial interests and there is a completed gift of the income interest. And this is so despite the continuing uncertainty of the interests of A and B. Cf. Rev. Rul. 72-571, 1972-2 CB 533; Priv. Ltr. Rul. 9821030 (Feb. 18, 1998). See infra ¶ 10.01[9].

[187] Reg. § 20.2038-1(a).

[188] Reg. § 25.2511-2(d).

[189] Such a transfer is at least partially subject to estate tax if the donor dies within the period stated. IRC § 2038; Lober v. United States, 346 US 335 (1953). See the discussion infra ¶ 10.01[10].

[190] Cf. Estate of Goelet v. Comm'r, 51 TC 352 (1968). Any actual distribution of income to A is a completed gift of a present interest. And if accumulated income becomes a part of corpus that cannot be distributed to A, income accumulations are completed gifts of future remainder interests to B when they are irretrievably committed to corpus.

[8] Donor's Power Exercisable Only With Third Persons

The general principles that emerge from the important gift tax cases are an inadequate substitute for explicit statutory rules on the gift tax treatment of incomplete transfers.[191] If a donor's lifetime transfer remains subject to changes, is it significant that the donor's powers can be exercised only with the consent of another person? Some answers are clear. If the one who must consent has no substantial economic interest in the transferred property adverse to the exercise of the power, the consent requirement is ignored; that is, the transfer is just as incomplete as if the donor alone had the power.[192] It is equally clear that if the donor's power can be exercised only with the consent of all persons having an interest in a trust, the so-called reserved power has no gift tax significance and does not render the gift incomplete.[193] Judge Magruder's opinion in *Camp v. Commissioner*[194] suggests an approach to the question of completed transfers where the donor retains a power that would normally make a transfer incomplete but that can be exercised only in conjunction with persons who have interests adverse to the exercise of the power:

1. If the trust instrument gives a designated beneficiary any interest in the corpus of the trust property or of the income therefrom, which is capable of monetary valuation, and the donor reserves no power to withdraw that interest, in whole or in part, except with the consent of such designated beneficiary, then the gift of that particular interest will be deemed to be complete, for the purposes of the gift tax. . . .

2. If the only power reserved by the donor is a power to revoke the entire trust instrument (not a power to modify the trust in any particular), and this power may be exercised only in conjunction with a designated beneficiary who is given a substantial adverse interest in the disposition of the trust property or the income therefrom, then the transfer in trust will be deemed to be a present gift of the entire corpus of the trust, for purposes of the gift tax. In such cases, the gift of the entire corpus will be deemed to have been "put beyond recall" by the donor himself.

3. If the trust instrument reserves to the donor a general power to alter, amend or revoke, in whole or in part, and this power is to be exercised only in conjunction with a designated beneficiary who has received an interest in the corpus or income capable of monetary valuation, then the transfer in trust will be deemed to be a completed

---

[191] Congress knows better how to deal with these problems. See IRC §§ 671–679 (income tax).

[192] Reg. § 25.2511-2(e).

[193] Camp v. Comm'r, 195 F2d 999 (1st Cir. 1952).

[194] Camp v. Comm'r, 195 F2d 999, 1004–1005 (1st Cir. 1952) (footnotes omitted).

gift, for purposes of the gift tax, only as to the interest of such designated beneficiary having a veto over the exercise of the power. As to the interests of the other beneficiaries, the gifts will be deemed to be incomplete, for as to such interests the donor reserves the power to take them away in conjunction with a person who has no interest in the trust adverse to such withdrawal. The gifts to the other beneficiaries have not been "put beyond recall" by the donor. . . .

Judge Magruder's first and third suggestions seem unassailable; however, the second may be questioned. Perhaps there the gift should be treated as complete only as to the interest of the beneficiary who must join in the exercise of the power. If the donor wished to revoke, could the donor not in all likelihood purchase that beneficiary's consent for the value of the beneficiary's interest? In this light, the other interests seem to remain within the donor's control. On the other hand, perhaps Judge Magruder's view can be justified on the assumption that the acquiring beneficiary would insist upon payment of more than the value of that beneficiary's interest. Because it is not clear how much more the beneficiary would insist upon, there is no basis for saying the extent to which the donor has retained an interest.[195]

It should be emphasized that the adverse interest possessed by one who must join in the donor's alteration of a trust to render the gift complete must be a financial interest, a "direct legal or equitable interest in the trust property."[196] A trustee, as such, is not one having an interest in a trust.[197] Moreover, if a donor sets up a trust for children and retains the right to revoke with donor's spouse's consent, donor's spouse having no other interest in the trust, the gift is incomplete. If donor and spouse have separated, the donor's spouse's desire to protect the interests of the children may very well be adverse to the donor's revocation, but an adverse interest of this type is not accorded tax recognition.[198]

The combination of powers held with adverse parties and the relinquishment or alteration of such powers can have strange and unsuspected gift tax consequences. For example, if a donor creates a trust with income to *A* and remainder to *B* or *B*'s estate and the donor retains a power to accumulate income or revoke the remainder with *A*'s approval, there is a completed gift of the income interest under the *Camp* doctrine. If *A* subsequently relinquishes the approval power, *A* will be seen to have made a gift of the income interest;

---

[195] Cf. Robinette v. Helvering, 318 US 184 (1943); Rev. Rul. 72-571, 1972-2 CB 533. See Macris, "Open Valuation and the Completed Transfer: A Problem Area in Federal Gift Taxation," 34 Tax L. Rev. 273 (1979).

[196] Comm'r v. Prouty, 115 F2d 331, 335 (1st Cir. 1940).

[197] Reg. § 25.2511-2(e).

[198] Latta v. Comm'r, 212 F2d 164 (3d Cir.), cert. denied, 348 US 825 (1954); Reg. § 25.2511-2(e).

A will have completely relinquished dominion and control over the income interest of which *A* was full owner by virtue of the power to negate income accumulations.[199] Moreover, if, after *A*'s relinquishment, the donor permits income to be distributed to *A*, the distributions will constitute further gifts from the donor to *A*.[200] Finally, if the donor subsequently releases the power both to accumulate the income and to revoke the remainder, donor has again made a gift of the income interest, along with a gift of the remainder interest, by relinquishing dominion and control over both interests.[201] Thus, by mere alterations of powers, the income interest of the trust has passed back and forth between donor and *A* like a ping-pong ball; each time it crosses the net, it subjects the parties to gift tax in a game where they both stand to lose.

[9] Powers Held Only by a Third Person

The test for completeness of a gift does not require that a donee be identifiable. Thus, if a donor creates a trust with income to *A* or *B*, whichever an independent trustee selects, remainder to *C*, and if the donor retains no power to appoint donor trustee, the donor has made a completed gift of the entire trust corpus.[202] The fact that the specific donee of the income interest is unknown is irrelevant.

Of course, a power held by a third party may be only an indirect means of retention of an interest by the donor. Assume a donor creates a trust with income to *A* for the donor's life, remainder to *B* or *B*'s estate, but requires the trustee to distribute to the donor such income as is necessary for donor's support and maintenance. Since the donor has limited the trustee's power by an ascertainable standard that is judicially enforceable, the donor has indirectly retained an interest in the trust property, and there is a gift only to the extent the value of the corpus exceeds the value of the donor's right to support and maintenance.[203] This situation must be differentiated, however, from one in which, under local law, the trustee's power is not required to be exercised, whether or

---

[199] Cerf v. Comm'r, 141 F2d 564 (3d Cir. 1944). Although *A* may continue to receive income, *A* has no control over whether *A* will, and under the principle of the *Robinette* case, *A* cannot prove the value of any retained interest that might reduce the amount of *A*'s gift. Robinette v. Helvering, 318 US 184 (1943).

[200] Cf. Reg. § 25.2511-2(f); Comm'r v. Warner, 127 F2d 913 (9th Cir. 1942). If there was some question about this result under general gift tax principles, the doubt is probably dispelled, subject to minor modification, by Sections 2514(b) and 2514(e), discussed ¶ 10.04[4][c] concerning the lapse of general powers of appointment.

[201] Cerf v. Comm'r, 141 F2d 564 (3d Cir. 1940).

[202] However, no measurable present interest exists that qualifies for an annual exclusion under Section 2503(b).

[203] Reg. § 25.2511-2(b).

not a standard under which the trustee may act is provided. Assume the donor creates a trust with income to A, remainder to B and, in addition, gives the trustee a power in the trustee's absolute discretion to invade the corpus for the benefit of the donor. Obviously, the entire property has passed from the control of the donor, and, as the donor has neither any control over it nor any interest in it, the donor has made a gift of the entire value of the property.[204] An opposite result may properly be reached if, under local law, the donor's creditors would have full access to the trust property under these circumstances, for then it is possible to assert the donor has indirectly retained control (in the form of a power to revoke) over all the property.[205]

A similar problem arises if the donor creates a trust with a right in donor to designate beneficiaries of income or corpus but, in addition, gives some third party a general power of appointment over the trust property. Under the *Sanford* principle, there is no gift to those to whom the donor may direct payments because, pro tempore, the donor has obviously retained control. If, under local law, the donor may still effect distributions to beneficiaries free and clear of the third party's power, the donor has made gifts to no one, for the donor still controls the entire trust property; but any distribution pursuant to the donor's designation constitutes a gift by the donor.[206] On the other hand, if, under local law, a donor can and does give another a general power of appointment over property that takes precedence over any interest in or control over the property by the donor, the donor has made a completed gift of the entire property. The only obstacle to this conclusion is the settled property law and tax law principle that a power is not an interest in property. How then can the do-

---

[204] Rev. Rul. 77-378, 1977-2 CB 347; Priv. Ltr. Ruls. 7833062 (May 18, 1978), 9332006 (Aug. 20, 1992), 9837007 (June 10, 1998). Cf. Estate of Wells v. Comm'r, 42 TCM (CCH) 1305 (1981).

[205] See Comm'r v. Vander Weele, 254 F2d 895 (6th Cir. 1958); Paolozzi v. Comm'r, 23 TC 182 (1954), acq. 1962-1 CB 4; Priv. Ltr. Rul. 9639056 (June 24, 1996) (the trustee's power limited by a standard but creditors could reach entire corpus). In Revenue Ruling 62-13, 1962-1 CB 181, the Commissioner sought to extend the acceptable doctrine of *Vander Weele* to a case in which broad discretionary powers in trustees to distribute income and corpus to the settlor merely create uncertainty that anything of value will ever go to the other named beneficiaries, without regard to any rights of creditors of the settlor to get at the trust assets. Cf. Estate of Gramm v. Comm'r, 17 TC 1063 (1951), nonacq. 1957-2 CB 8, withdrawn and acq. 1962-1 CB 4. The ruling is at variance with the doctrine of Robinette v. Helvering, 318 US 184 (1943), and has properly been limited. Rev. Rul. 77-378, 1977-2 CB 347. Cf. Rev. Rul. 77-99, 1977-1 CB 295; Rev. Rul. 76-275, 1976-2 CB 299. Some cases, such as Estate of Holtz v. Comm'r, 38 TC 37 (1962), acq. 1962-2 CB 4, seem mistakenly to analyze third-party power cases in terms of a retention of control in the donor, rather than in terms of a retention by the donor of an interest in the transferred property. Problems in this area are discussed in Lowndes, "Some Doubts About the Use of Trusts to Avoid Estate Taxes," 47 Minn. L. Rev. 31, 41–52 (1962), and Covey, "Power to Distribute to Grantor," 98 Tr. & Est. 322 (1959).

[206] Reg. § 25.2511-2(f).

nor be said to have transferred "property" by creation of the power? The answer is that the effect of the transaction is a complete shift of dominion and control over property actually owned by the donor to the one to whom the power is given, and it is immaterial that the shift in actual ownership is couched in terms of a gift of the power.[207]

[10] Relationship of the Gift Tax to the Income Tax and the Estate Tax

As a basic principle, it can be stated that a transfer treated as complete for gift tax purposes is not necessarily similarly treated for purposes of either the income tax or the estate tax. The proposition is not novel, is evident in numerous comments in preceding pages of this book, and is not developed here in detail. Some examples of awkward conceptual disparities among the taxes are presented here.

[a] Assignment of Income

The gift tax sometimes converts the well-known income tax "fruit" of Justice Holmes[208] into a "tree." A gratuitous assignment of rental income from property leaves the assignor taxable on the income.[209] Nevertheless, the assignment may constitute an immediate transfer subject to gift tax.[210] Perhaps this result follows even if the amount of rental is contingent upon such uncertain events that the gift cannot really be valued when made,[211] although the Commissioner continues to contend that a gift does not occur until such time as its value can be realistically determined.[212] Within the gift tax itself, there are therefore conceptual clashes on the questions whether (or when) a gift occurs and what amount is to be determined (or how). If the Commissioner succeeds in the above contention, gift tax principles will move somewhat closer to those

---

[207] See Cerf v. Comm'r, 141 F2d 564 (3d Cir. 1940). Cf. Reg. § 25.2514-1(b)(2), indicating correctly that if a life beneficiary of a trust, who has also a nongeneral power of appointment, exercises the power in favor of permissible appointees, the life beneficiary has made an actual transfer of the income interest, not dependent on tax rules regarding the exercise of powers. See ¶ 10.04[3][e].

[208] Lucas v. Earl, 281 US 111, 115 (1930).

[209] Galt v. Comm'r, 216 F2d 41 (7th Cir. 1954), cert. denied, 348 US 951 (1955). Cf. Helvering v. Horst, 311 US 112 (1940).

[210] Rev. Rul. 57-315, 1957-2 CB 624.

[211] Galt v. Comm'r, 216 F2d 41 (7th Cir. 1954), cert. denied, 348 US 951 (1955) (amount of rental measured by future volume of betting at racetrack).

[212] Rev. Ruls. 69-346, 1969-1 CB 227; 69-347, 1969-1 CB 227; 73-61, 1973-1 CB 408. See ¶ 10.02[1][b].

of the income tax,[213] although assignment of interest, conventional rental payment, or even measurable rights to patent royalties[214] may still be immediate gifts but merely assigned "fruit" for income tax purposes.

[b] Transfers Made Near to Death

Some gratuitous transfers made within three years of death are treated as testamentary in character and the value of the property is included in the transferor's gross estate.[215] But this does not mean that such transfers are incomplete for gift tax purposes. The courts have always recognized these transfers as possibly subject to both gift tax and estate tax.[216] This is an obvious circumstance in which the gift tax on a lifetime transfer is treated as a down payment on the estate tax liability.[217] Even if such a transfer occurs in the same year as the donor's death, the obligation falls on the executor to file a gift tax return and pay the gift tax, as well as to include the value of the property in the decedent's gross estate.[218]

One who receives property that has been taxed in the donor's gross estate under Section 2035(a) will likely be able to treat it as an excluded gift for income tax purposes. However, again, the tests for gift classification are disparate.[219]

[c] Transfers With Life Interests Retained

If one makes a lifetime gratuitous transfer of an interest in property, reserving to oneself the income for one's life, the entire value of the interest transferred is included in one's gross estate at death.[220] One might therefore assume that such a transfer would not incur gift tax liability. But, again, the two

---

[213] See Burnet v. Logan, 283 US 404 (1931); Dorsey v. Comm'r, 49 TC 606 (1968), both recognizing a departure from usual income tax realization principles where rights acquired cannot be valued.

[214] Talge v. United States, 229 F. Supp. 836 (WD Mo. 1964).

[215] See ¶ 4.07[2].

[216] E.g., Sanford's Estate v. Comm'r, 308 US 39 (1939).

[217] If the gift transfer occurred after 1976, the estate tax reduction is provided by Section 2001(b)(2). If the transfer occurred prior to 1977, Section 2012 allows a credit against the estate tax liability.

[218] In addition, Section 2035(b) requires the gift tax paid on all transfers within three years of the decedent's death to be included in the decedent's gross estate. IRC § 2035(b); ¶ 4.07[3].

[219] Compare IRC §§ 2035, 2043 with IRC §§ 2511, 2512 and with IRC § 102 as interpreted in Comm'r v. Duberstein, 363 US 278 (1960).

[220] See ¶ 4.08.

taxes are "not always mutually exclusive,"[221] and a transfer subject to gift tax has occurred. As the donor in this case has not transferred the donor's entire interest in the property, the value of the life interest retained by the donor is subtracted from the value of the property in determining the value of the gift subject to tax.[222] In this case, moreover, the gift tax and the income tax go hand in hand: Income received under the retained interest that escapes gift tax is taxed to the donor.[223]

[d] Conditional Transfers

If one makes a lifetime gratuitous transfer conditioned upon one's death, Section 2037 may bring a part or the entire value of the property transferred into the transferor's gross estate for estate tax purposes when the transferor dies.[224] But, again, this carries no assurance that the transfer, when made, will entirely escape the gift tax, as the key consideration for gift tax purposes is whether the transferor has relinquished dominion and control over the various transferred interests. In this area, the income tax and gift tax do not necessarily run parallel. In general, a grantor who transfers property in trust, relinquishing all rights and powers except an ultimate reversion, is subject to income tax on the income from the property unless the reversion has an insignificant value at the time of the creation of the trust.[225] Thus, while the gift (except for the reversion)[226] may be viewed as essentially complete for gift tax purposes, the donor and the donor's estate stand to be nailed for income tax during the donor's lifetime and for estate tax upon the donor's death.

[e] Powers Held by the Transferor

The degree of control that the donor must retain to render a gift incomplete for gift tax purposes is greater in some respects than what the donor must

---

[221] Sanford's Estate v. Comm'r, 308 US 39, 45 (1939).

[222] But see IRC § 2702, discussed ¶ 19.03. Under Section 2702 the value of the retained income interest will be valued at zero if the remainder is transferred to a family member.

[223] IRC §§ 652, 662. See also IRC §§ 674, 677, which may produce similarly parallel income and gift tax results. But see IRC § 2036, which subjects the estate to tax on the entire value of the property.

[224] See ¶ 4.09.

[225] As a result of a 1986 change in the legislation, the grantor of a trust generally will be taxed on the income from the trust if there is a retained reversion and if, at the inception of the trust, the value of the reversion exceeds 5 percent of the value of the trust. IRC § 673(a).

[226] But see IRC § 2702, discussed at ¶ 19.03, where the value of the retained version will be valued at zero if another interest in the property is transferred to a family member.

retain to render a transfer incomplete until death for estate tax purposes. A power to revoke or a power to change beneficiaries will render a gift incomplete under the gift tax,[227] but will also result in inclusion of the transferred property in the donor's gross estate.[228] To that extent, the two transfer taxes run parallel. However, reservation of a mere power to change the time or manner of enjoyment of a beneficiary's interest, provided the interest cannot be shifted to another, does not render a transfer incomplete under the gift tax provisions.[229] Nevertheless, such a retained power will subject the transferred property, or at least part of it, to estate tax; so again, both taxes may apply to the same transfer.[230]

Application of both gift and estate taxes to the same transfer is also possible in the case of a transfer in which the donor retains a power exercisable with someone having an adverse interest. The transfer is complete for gift tax purposes;[231] nevertheless, Sections 2036(a)(2) and 2038 generally overlook the fact that a power is jointly held for estate tax purposes. Therefore, the property subject to the gift tax will again be taxed at the donor's death.[232] Again, the income tax has its own set of rules regarding the effect of a taxpayer's powers over trust property.[233] Regrettably, no attempt has been made to provide a uniform gift-completion concept applicable to all the principal federal taxes.[234]

[11] Nonresident Noncitizens

Section 2511(b) has a message for nonresident noncitizen donors,[235] but really for only a very few persons who fall into that category. In general, one who is neither a citizen nor a resident of the United States is not taxed on transfers of

---

[227] Burnet v. Guggenheim, 288 US 280 (1933); Sanford's Estate v. Comm'r, 308 US 39 (1939).

[228] IRC §§ 2036(a)(2), 2038.

[229] Reg. § 25.2511-2(d).

[230] IRC §§ 2036(a)(2), 2038; Estate of Alexander v. Comm'r, 81 TC 757 (1983), aff'd in unpub. op. (4th Cir. 1985); Lober v. United States, 346 US 335 (1953). See ¶¶ 4.08[5][c] text accompanying note 58, 4.10[10][d] text accompanying notes 103, 104.

[231] See Camp v. Comm'r, 195 F2d 999 (1st Cir. 1952).

[232] Helvering v. City Bank Farmers Trust Co., 296 US 85 (1935). See also supra ¶ 10.01[5][b] text accompanying notes 165, 166 on contingent powers.

[233] See IRC §§ 671, 672, 674–678. See also S. Rep. No. 1622, 83d Cong., 2d Sess. 364–372 (1954).

[234] Lack of uniformity of the gift and estate tax rules with the income tax rules may work to a donor's wealth transfer advantage. See Mulligan, "Defective Grantor Trusts Offer Many Tax Advantages," 19 Est. Plan. 131 (1992); Parr, "Combining Defective Grantor Trusts With Other Types of Trusts," 21 Est. Plan. 82 (1994).

[235] Questions of citizenship and residence are considered in the discussion of Section 2101 at ¶ 6.01[3]. See also discussion of Section 2501 at ¶ 9.02[1].

intangible property.[236] However, the intangible property exemption is denied to some nonresident noncitizens.[237] As such persons are taxed only on transfers of property within the United States, Congress undertakes in Section 2511(b) to say what intangible property is to be treated as situated here.

Stock issued by U.S. corporations has long been treated as property situated in the United States and is expressly so classified now by Section 2511(b)(1). But at one time "bonds issued by United States persons, unlike other debt obligations, [were] considered to be situated where the instrument [was] located."[238] Section 2511(b)(2) alters that rule so that any debt obligation of a "United States person"[239] or of the United States, a state and its political subdivisions, and the District of Columbia, if owned by a nonresident noncitizen, is deemed to be situated in the United States.

Fitting this rule together with the rules of Section 2501(a) on the gift taxation of nonresident noncitizens, it will be seen that the situs of intangibles is rarely relevant. Citizens and residents are taxed on gifts of any property wherever situated; nonresident noncitizens are taxed on gifts of tangible property situated in the United States but generally escape tax on gifts of intangibles wherever situated. However, when the special provisions of Section 2501(a)(3) come into play, certain expatriates who are nonresident noncitizens become taxable on gifts, not only of tangible property within the United States, but also of intangibles if they are located here. It is then that the special situs rule of Section 2511(b)(2) on debt obligations may exact its toll.[240]

---

[236] See IRC § 2501(a)(2), discussed ¶ 9.02[1]. Nonresident noncitizens are generally subject to the gift tax on gifts of tangible property (IRC § 2501(a)(1)), but only if the property transferred is situated within the United States (IRC § 2511(a)).

[237] See IRC §§ 2501(a)(3), 2501(a)(4), briefly noted at ¶ 9.02[1] note 7.

[238] S. Rep. No. 1707, 89th Cong., 2d Sess. (1966), reprinted in 1966-2 CB 1059, 1099.

[239] Section 7701(a)(30) defines "United States person" as (1) a citizen or resident of the United States; (2) a domestic partnership; (3) a domestic corporation; and (4) any estate or trust other than a foreign estate or trust as defined in Section 7701(a)(31).

[240] The gift tax status of the nonresident noncitizen as indicated here reached its present stage by way of the Foreign Investors Tax Act of 1966, which amended the Code effective as regards transfers made in 1967 and thereafter. The principal differences from previous law are that earlier: (1) a nonresident noncitizen entirely escaped tax on the transfer of intangibles if the noncitizen was not engaged in business in the United States, and (2) where the noncitizen was engaged in business in the United States and liability turned on the question whether a transferred intangible was situated here, the statute expressly provided U.S. situs only for stock in domestic corporations. There is an excellent analysis of the change in the law in Ross, "United States Taxation of Aliens and Foreign Corporations: The Foreign Investors Tax Act of 1966 and Related Developments," 22 Tax L. Rev. 279 (1967). See also ¶ 6.07.

¶ 10.02 SECTION 2512. VALUATION OF GIFTS

Chapter 1 of the Code[1] gives promise of being an orderly statutory presentation. Subchapter A addresses itself primarily to matters of computation; Subchapter B, within which Section 2512 falls, identifies transfers subject to tax; and Subchapter C authorizes deductions that may be claimed in the determination of taxable gifts.[2] However, the internal arrangement of Subchapter B leaves much to be desired. Section 2511, which has just been considered, purports to be a general identification of taxable transfers, and Sections 2513 through 2519 accord specific treatment to transfers of various types.[3] In between, Section 2512, with which we are presently concerned, purports to present the gift tax rules on valuation; but it is disappointing. First, it affords much less than a full guide to the solution of gift tax valuation questions. Second, as interpreted, it often goes beyond the matter of valuation to determine the question whether a transfer is taxable at all. Third, many of the valuation rules established here are modified by a series of special valuation rules imposed by Chapter 14 of the Code.[4] Those special rules, when applicable, override the general rules found here.

In determining gift tax liability, the measurement of a gift under Section 2512 presents three principal problems: (1) At what point in time should the property be valued? (2) What method should be used to determine value? (3) What constitutes and what is the effect of consideration received for transferred property? Section 2512 does not completely answer any of these questions.

[1] Time of Valuation

Section 2512(a) is simple and seemingly forthright: "If the gift is made in property, the value thereof at the date of the gift shall be considered the amount of the gift." There is no alternate valuation date for gift tax purposes.[5] The requirement that a gift be valued at the time it is considered to be made is clear enough.

---

[1] IRC §§ 2501–2524.

[2] See Chapters 9 and 11, dealing with Subchapters A and C, respectively.

[3] Section 2518 provides rules on disclaimers. See ¶ 10.07.

[4] See ¶¶ 19.01–19.05.

[5] For estate tax purposes, Section 2032, discussed ¶ 4.03, provides an elective alternate valuation date.

[a] Valuation on Completion

Except with respect to outright transfers of cash or other property, there may be uncertainty regarding the time a gift becomes complete. The date of completion is "the date of the gift." For example, if a donor transfers property to a trust but retains the right to revoke the transfer, the initial transfer is not a gift. A gift subject to tax occurs when, during life, the donor relinquishes sufficient retained control over the transferred property.[6] Accordingly, the completion principles considered in the discussion of Section 2511 have a crucial bearing on the timing aspect of valuation under consideration here.[7]

It will be recalled that a transfer is not complete for gift tax purposes if the donor retains the power to alter the interests of others even though not for the donor's own financial benefit. This may create a situation in which a donor simply cannot afford to complete a lifetime gift. For example, if D transfers shares of Growth, Inc., to a trust, income to A and B for life, remainder to C or C's estate, but retains the power to vary the shares of income paid to A or to B and to encroach on corpus for the benefit of either, the gift is entirely incomplete. If, as sometimes happens, Growth, Inc., is worth ten times as much three years later, the gift tax cost of D's relinquishment of D's control then might be more than D's retained assets would bear.[8] The main point, however, is that tax liability is measured by value at the time of completion of the gift, not at the time of any earlier transfer.[9]

[b] Open Transactions Under the Gift Tax

A gift may occur when a donor enters into an enforceable agreement to make payments in the future[10] and when a donor transfers rights to receive future payments, such as rents and royalties, from a third party.[11] Conditions and contingencies surrounding such payments in these and other situations may create difficult valuation problems. The art of the actuary may be invoked to place an acceptable value on seemingly uncertain future rights. When this approach is possible, it is applied and rough approximations are accepted as a

---

[6] See Burnet v. Guggenheim, 288 US 280 (1933), discussed ¶ 10.01[5].

[7] See ¶¶ 10.01[4]–10.01[10].

[8] Of course, if the donor fails to relinquish control prior to death, such stock would then be included in the donor's gross estate for estate tax purposes. IRC §§ 2036, 2038. D may have nightmares about A or B dying, causing the gift of income to be complete and a portion of the gift tax due, and about A and B both dying and causing the gift to be entirely complete.

[9] A similar phenomenon occurs under the estate tax with respect to some lifetime transfers that are taxed at death. See discussion of Sections 2035–2038 at ¶¶ 4.07–4.10.

[10] See ¶ 10.01[3][i].

[11] See ¶ 10.01[3][a].

matter of course.[12] However, the art of the actuary has its limitations. If the occurrence of the condition or contingency upon which the future payment depends is not susceptible to conventional actuarial approximations, the circumstance presented is one in which a gift has occurred, but valuation of the gift may be extremely speculative.

The problem here is closely related to a similar problem encountered in income taxation. The income tax problem has been resolved by the open transaction doctrine.[13] Under the open transaction doctrine, an exchange that would ordinarily result in the determination of taxable gain or loss is not immediately taxable if the amount realized cannot be ascertained. In such cases, the transaction is considered open and, as amounts are received, they are applied against and reduce basis, resulting in taxable gain only after a full recovery of capital.

The open transaction doctrine is inapplicable to the estate tax.[14] The courts require valuation under the estate tax because there is only a single opportunity to exact a toll.[15]

Should the open transaction doctrine be applied to gift tax situations? The Service has taken the position that the taxation of a gift, arguably complete earlier according to conventional gift tax doctrine, will be deferred to the time at which the amount of the gift first becomes susceptible to valuation, if no realistic valuation can be made at an earlier date.[16] However, the Service has applied the open transaction doctrine unnecessarily to situations that involve incomplete gifts.[17]

---

[12] Smith v. Shaughnessy, 318 US 176 (1953); Rev. Rul. 79-421, 1979-2 CB 347. See also Rosenthal v. Comm'r, 205 F2d 505 (2d Cir. 1953).

[13] This doctrine originated in the case of Burnet v. Logan, 283 US 404 (1931). See Reg. § 15A.453-1(d)(2)(iii).

[14] Cf. Burnet v. Logan, 283 US 404 (1931), where the property was "impossible" to value for income tax purposes.

[15] Burnet v. Logan, 283 US 404 (1931), where the property was "impossible" to value for income tax purposes, but the same property was valued for estate tax purposes.

[16] Rev. Rul. 69-346, 1969-2 CB 227. The Service also applied the open gift tax transaction doctrine in Revenue Ruling 81-31, 1981-1 CB 475, concluding that the gift became complete at death. In DiMarco v. Comm'r, 87 TC 653 (1986), the court refused to follow Revenue Ruling 81-31 and held that there was no open transaction and no gift at death. The Service subsequently revoked Revenue Ruling 81-31. Rev. Rul. 92-68, 1992-2 CB 257. Cf. Reg. § 25.2511-2(f).

[17] The Service first applied the doctrine in Revenue Ruling 69-346, 1969-2 CB 227, where a couple signed an enforceable contract to make a community property widow's election. The Service left the transaction open, ruling that there was no completed gift until valuation was possible. The death of one of the spouses was the first time the gift was susceptible to valuation. Until the predeceasing spouse's death, the property that each was to transfer could be squandered, making their transfers revocable. See Macris, "Open Valuation and the Completed Transfer: A Problem Area in Federal Gift Taxation," 34 Tax L. Rev. 273, 293–294 (1979). This situation involved no relinquishment of dominion and no completed gift. A similar analysis can be made of a subsequent ruling purporting to apply

Application of the open transaction doctrine to the gift tax is analogous to its application to the income tax in that each tax is computed on an annual basis and each year presents a new opportunity to exact the tax toll. If a gift transfer is left open, however, it may escape taxation as a gift and taxation in the donor's estate as well. Suppose, for example, that a donor transfers a right to income from a third party and the valuation of the right is highly speculative. If the transaction is left open and the donor dies before receipt of all the income, the right to future income is not included in the donor's gross estate and it escapes both estate and gift taxes. If the donor instead had given the donee future income of highly speculative valuation from property the donor owned and the donor died prior to the donee's receipt of all the income, application of the open transaction doctrine would not preclude taxation under the estate tax.[18] In the first situation, the income right would have to be valued at the time of the gift in order for the government to be assured of recovering transfer tax liability. To maintain consistency under the gift tax, valuation should be required in both situations regardless of the obligor of the payment. To conclude otherwise creates a complex exception to the gift tax that would easily be misapplied. The open transaction doctrine should simply be inapplicable to the gift tax as well as to the estate tax.[19]

[2] Methods of Valuation

[a] Introduction

The method used to value property that is the subject of a taxable gift is of crucial importance in determining the gift tax consequence of the gift, and, because of the unification of the gift tax and estate taxes, ultimately is of im-

---

the open transaction doctrine. See Rev. Rul. 81-31, 1981-1 CB 475, which has been revoked by Rev. Rul. 92-68, 1992-2 CB 257.

[18] Suppose the donor dies, leaving behind an enforceable obligation of the donor under a contract that, while a completed gift, escaped tax during the donor's life because of valuation difficulty and application of the open transaction doctrine. No gift tax will have been paid on the transaction, yet there is less distortion than might at first appear. The donor's gross estate will include the value of assets that the donor still has and was only committed to transfer. If the payment relates to an enforceable agreement against the donor, see ¶ 10.01[3][i], the donee has a claim against the estate. But the claim is deductible only to the extent that recognized consideration was paid for the donor's promise to pay the royalty. IRC § 2053(c)(1)(A). Thus, with no estate tax deduction, the value of the property included in the donor's gross estate under Section 2033 will include the value of future royalties.

[19] See DiMarco v. Comm'r, 87 TC 653, 661 (1986); Macris, "Open Valuation and the Completed Transfer: A Problem Area in Federal Gift Taxation," 34 Tax L. Rev. 273, 297–306 (1979).

portance in determining the estate tax consequences of the transfer. To the extent the value of gifted property exceeds the consideration in money or money's worth paid by the transferee, the transferor is deemed to make a gift.[20] It is therefore surprising that the gift tax statutes are disappointingly silent with respect to valuation methods.[21]

On the other hand, basic valuation principles are well settled for both the gift tax and the related estate tax. The gift tax regulations, essentially parroting the corresponding estate tax regulations,[22] adopt the following general approach: "The value of the property is the price at which such property would change hands between a willing buyer and a willing seller, neither being under any compulsion to buy or to sell, and both having reasonable knowledge of relevant facts."[23] And, just as assets included in a decedent's gross estate are generally valued at the date of death,[24] a gift of property is valued as of the date of the gift.[25] The application of these principles is described in the discussion of Section 2031 in Chapter 4,[26] and for the most part, observations made there as to the methods of valuation[27] and the valuation of specific types of property are equally applicable here.[28] However, some issues unique (or more common) to gift tax valuation warrant special comment.[29]

---

[20] IRC § 2512.

[21] Similarly, the estate tax statutes are silent with respect to valuation methods for estate tax purposes. See discussion of valuation for estate tax purposes at ¶¶ 4.02[2]–4.02[6].

[22] Reg. § 20.2031-1(b).

[23] Reg. §§ 25.2512-1, 20.2031-1(b). An interesting difference between the contexts in which property is valued for the estate tax and the gift tax that is seemingly not considered in the regulations or the cases is the impact of potential gain. A buyer paying fair market value for property will have a basis equal to fair market value under Section 1012, as will the recipient of a bequest of appreciated property in many situations, thanks to Section 1014. A recipient of a gift of appreciated property will not receive a basis equal to the fair market value of the property under Section 1015. Would a willing buyer paying fair market value pay less if the purchased asset would not receive a basis equal to the fair market value price paid?

[24] IRC § 2031(a).

[25] IRC § 2512(a). See supra ¶ 10.02[1].

[26] See ¶ 4.02.

[27] See ¶ 4.02[2][b].

[28] See, e.g., valuation of tangible personal property (¶ 4.02[3][a]), real property (¶ 4.02[3][b]), publicly traded securities (¶ 4.02[3][c]), mutual funds (¶ 4.02[3][d]), bonds (¶ 4.02[3][e]), and closely held corporations (¶ 4.02[3][f]).

[29] For a more comprehensive discussion of valuation issues generally, see Bogdanski, Federal Tax Valuation (Warren, Gorham & Lamont, 1996).

[b] Special Approaches to Valuation

[i] **Encumbered property.** If property that is the subject matter of a gift has previously been pledged or assigned as security for a debt, is the amount of the gift the entire value of the property or only the value of the transferor's equity (the gross value less the amount of the indebtedness)?[30] In some circumstances the amount of the gift is the value of the property less the amount of the obligation. This was the square holding of the Board of Tax Appeals in an early case,[31] and there is no question that Congress intended this to be the usual result.[32] If the encumbrance is only a charge against the gifted property and the donor is not personally liable for the debt, this usual result is appropriate. Assuming the indebtedness would have reduced the amount included in the donor's gross estate if the property had been held until death,[33] no overall distortion results from treating the amount of the gift as the value of the donor's equity in the property. The gift reduces the potential gross estate only by the amount of the gift-taxed portion of the value of the property.

If the donor is personally liable for a debt secured by a mortgage on the gifted property, quite a different problem is presented. The donee may be in a position to enforce payment of the debt by the donor; and, if the creditor does collect the debt by proceeding against the pledged property, the donee may be surrogated to the creditor's rights against the debtor donor.[34] In these circumstances, the donor, both economically and for estate and gift tax purposes, has reduced wealth by the full value of the property to the corresponding financial

---

[30] For estate tax purposes, the statute quite logically deals with the effect of indebtedness on estate assets in the deduction sections (see IRC § 2053, discussed ¶ 5.03), but no parallel deduction rule, or indeed any rule, appears in the gift tax provisions.

[31] DS Jackman v. Comm'r, 44 BTA 704 (1941), acq. 1942-1 CB 9.

[32] Under Section 2056(b)(4)(B), bequests of encumbered property to a surviving spouse are to be valued "in the same manner as if the amount of a gift to such spouse . . . were being determined." At the time this language was adopted, the Senate Finance Committee Report indicated that "if the decedent by his will leaves his surviving spouse real estate subject to a mortgage . . . , the value of the interest passing to the surviving spouse does not . . . include the mortgage." S. Rep. No. 1013, 80th Cong., 2d Sess. (1948), reprinted in 1948-1 CB 285, 335.

[33] See IRC § 2053(c)(1)(A), limiting the reduction to instances in which there was monetary consideration for the indebtedness.

[34] Cf. Estate of Gwinn v. Comm'r, 25 TC 31, 43 (1955), acq. 1956-1 CB 4 (the donee of pledged life insurance policy "surrogated to the lender's right to enforce a claim against the [donor's] estate . . . "). This case is to be distinguished from the more common situation where an insurance policy owner takes out a policy loan and then makes a gift of the policy. In that instance, the loan is expected to be repaid from the policy—not the borrower.

advantage of the donee, which is the essence of a taxable gift.[35] A parallel estate tax problem arises with respect to a testamentary transfer of encumbered property to a surviving spouse. Usually, the marital deduction is measured by the value of the property reduced by the mortgage;[36] but if the executor is directed to pay off the debt, the payment constitutes an additional interest passing to the spouse so that, in effect, a deduction is allowed for the entire value of the property.[37]

If the debtor donor is personally liable for the indebtedness secured by a mortgage on the gift property but the donee has no right to be surrogated to the creditor's rights against the donor, then the amount of the gift should be the amount of the debtor's equity in the property.[38] The situation here falls between the two situations noted earlier; the subsequent action of the donor will determine who will actually pay off the liability. If after the transfer to the donee the donor pays off the liability, the donor increases the donee's equity in the property and, to that extent, makes subsequent gifts to the donee.[39] If, instead, the donee pays off the liability or the mortgagee forecloses, the donee's situation is identical to the donee who takes property subject to a mortgage on which the donor is not personally liable.[40] No statutory rule or common-law

---

[35] This thought may be subject to two refinements. First, a question may be raised regarding the solvency of the donor B whether the donor is good for paying the debt. There is some dictum to the effect that if the debt could be paid only from the gift property, then only the donor's equity in the gift is subject to the gift tax. Comm'r v. Procter, 142 F2d 824, 825 (4th Cir.), cert. denied, 323 US 756 (1944). But this should go only to ultimate valuation: What is the total value of the equity in the property plus the uncertain value of the donor's obligation to pay the debt? Second, a question may be raised how this conclusion relates to the estate tax. The value of the property will not be included in the decedent's gross estate; and yet an estate tax deduction should be allowed for the decedent's personal obligation if it persists until death. This does not seem to be foreclosed by the decedent's transfer of the encumbered property, because the deduction is allowed as a "claim" under Section 2053(a)(3). But see Reg. § 20.2053-7, disallowing deductions for mortgages on foreign realty when such property was excluded from the gross estate. There is nothing inappropriate, however, in this result. The decedent's taxable estate was potentially but properly reduced when for consideration the decedent incurred the debt; the decedent's gross estate is further reduced by the transfer of the property, but its full value is subject to the gift tax.

[36] IRC § 2056(b)(4)(B).

[37] Reg. § 20.2056(b)-4(b). See Estate of Gwinn v. Comm'r, 25 TC 31 (1955), acq. 1956-1 CB 4 (reaching the correct marital deduction result but, inappropriately, on the basis of the gift tax principles described in the text above).

[38] Alexander v. United States, 640 F2d 1250 (Ct. Cl. 1981).

[39] Alexander v. United States, 640 F2d 1250 (Ct. Cl. 1981).

[40] Although an argument could be made here that the donee incurred gift tax liability for the donee's discharge of the donor's personal obligation (cf. Old Colony Trust Co. v. Comm'r, 279 US 716 (1929)), the donee's payment is as much for the donee's own benefit as that of the debtor donor (cf. Crane v. Comm'r, 331 US 1 (1947)) and should not be viewed as a gift. See also Reg. § 25.2511-1(d) (no gift where a donor pays gift tax for

gift tax principle deals with the possibility that the donor may die prior to paying the mortgage and that the donor's estate may pay the obligation. Generally, the debt would be a deductible claim against the estate; but there would be no opportunity to exact a gift tax on the donor's estate upon its payment of the liability because the gift tax applies only to lifetime transfers. In this situation, if the estate tax and gift tax are to mesh properly, the deduction for the claim against the decedent donor's estate under Section 2053 should be disallowed.[41]

In the foregoing discussion, we assume of course that the initial transaction constituted a gift. In a business transaction, indebtedness with respect to transferred property, whether the transferee takes the property only subject to the indebtedness or assumes the indebtedness, constitutes a part of the amount realized by the transferor.[42] Whether a transfer under which the transferee takes the property only subject to an indebtedness constitutes a gift depends on whether the transaction falls within the "business" exception to the usual gift tax principles.[43] But even in a setting that might ordinarily result in a gift, the transferee's assumption of the transferor's indebtedness must be viewed as consideration for gift tax purposes.[44] The practical effect is that in the case of a gift of encumbered property where the donee assumes the encumbrance (rather than merely taking the property subject to it), the amount of the gift will be only the amount of the donor's equity in the property. This again appears appropriate when the gift tax is examined against the estate tax background. Even if no novation occurs and the donor remains liable to the creditor, and even if the donor's estate may be entitled to a deduction for the amount of the claim, the estate's right to reimbursement from the transferee who assumed the liability for the debt effects an offsetting inclusion in the donor's gross estate.[45] There is, therefore, no policy reason why gift tax should be imposed on an amount in excess of the donor's equity in the property. Of course, if the donor makes voluntary payments in discharge of the debt, in this setting, the donor

---

which the donor and spouse have used Section 2513 gift splitting and are jointly and severally liable).

[41] Section 2053 does not specifically provide for such disallowance; nevertheless, if property is not within the gross estate, there is some authority for treating claims that it secures as not deductible. See the limitation on deductions for mortgages on foreign realty when such property was excluded from the gross estate. Reg. § 20.2053-7.

[42] Crane v. Comm'r, 331 US 1 (1947); Comm'r v. Tufts, 461 US 300 (1983).

[43] See Reg. § 25.2512-8 and the discussion infra ¶ 10.02[4].

[44] A similar view will prevail for income tax purposes. See Citizens' Nat'l Bank of Waco v. United States, 417 F2d 675 (5th Cir. 1969).

[45] Cf. DuVal's Estate v. Comm'r, 152 F2d 103 (9th Cir. 1945), cert. denied, 328 US 838 (1946).

makes taxable gifts in the amount of the payments to the donee whose interest in the transferred property is enhanced by the reduction of the indebtedness.

[ii] **Insurance policies.** Gifts involving life insurance policies and annuity policies present some unique valuation problems. The classic case is *Guggenheim v. Rasquin,*[46] in which a donor purchased single-premium life insurance policies in the face amount of about $1 million for about $800,000 and immediately made a gift of the policies. No one would suggest the face amount of the policies measured the gift. The taxpayer's argument that the cash surrender value at the time of the gift, about $700,000, should be used was rejected by the Court, which held that the value of the gift was the cost of the policies, $800,000. If this result seems to be a departure from a fair market value approach (admittedly, the donee could realize only $700,000 on the policies immediately after the gift), it is nevertheless consistent with the basic pattern of federal estate and gift taxation. These federal taxes are imposed on the transmission of property rather than on its receipt by the donee.[47] Moreover, if the gift tax is properly to backstop the estate tax, the donor in the *Guggenheim* case must be taxed on the cost of the policies rather than the lower cash surrender value; otherwise there would be an artificial, tax-free $100,000 reduction in the donor's estate potentially subject to estate tax. The Court bolstered its opinion by pointing out as well that the donee had acquired more than the right to surrender the policies for cash; the donee had "the right to retain [them] for [their] investment virtues and to receive the face amount of the [policies] upon the insured's death."[48]

The principle expressed in the *Guggenheim* case answers a number of other insurance valuation questions. Thus, the payment of a premium on a life insurance policy over which the donor has relinquished all dominion and control is a gift having a value equal to the amount of the premium paid.[49] As regards a gift of an insurance policy upon which some or all of the premiums have been paid some time before the gift, either the replacement cost[50] or the interpolated terminal reserve at the time of the gift[51] may determine value.

---

[46] Guggenheim v. Rasquin, 312 US 254 (1941).

[47] Guggenheim v. Rasquin, 312 US 254 (1941).

[48] Guggenheim v. Rasquin, 312 US 254, 257 (1941).

[49] See Rev. Rul. 84-147, 1984-2 CB 201 (valuing an employee's gift of an assignment of an employer-funded group term policy). Cf. Gorman v. United States, 288 F. Supp. 225 (ED Mich. 1968); Rev. Rul. 71-497, 1971-2 CB 329.

[50] Reg. § 25.2512-6(a) Ex. 3.

[51] Reg. § 25.2512-6(a) Ex. 4.

If, in any of the circumstances described above, the transfer involves a gift of split dollar life insurance, the amount of the gift is determined under Regulations Section 25.2512-6(a) reduced by the value of the employer's interest in the policy. Rev. Rul. 81-198, 1981-2 CB 188.

Again, the *Guggenheim* principle supports a cost approach at variance with the measurement based on value to the donee.

[iii] **Temporal property interests.** Actuarial valuation is necessarily employed in valuing annuities; income, reversionary, and remainder interests in property; and other temporal property interests[52] under the gift tax. Other than determining the amount of annuity payments or the value of the corpus of a trust, such valuation generally[53] depends on two elements: a mortality factor dependent on life expectancies and an interest factor dependent on a projected relevant rate of return.[54] Over time, both elements have undergone substantial changes. Single unisex tables have replaced tables previously used in separately measuring male and female life expectancies.[55] Such tables are updated at least every ten years to reflect the most recent mortality experience available.[56] In addition, Section 7520[57] requires the Service to revise the applicable interest rate on a monthly basis.[58] The section prescribes an interest rate that is

---

[52] Section 7520 valuation is limited to the computation of the value of annuities, interests for life or term of years, or any remainder or reversionary interest. IRC § 7520(a). See Reg. § 25.7520-1(c). Revenue Procedure 78-21, 1978-2 CB 499, provides circumstances in which the Service will provide taxpayers with assistance in computing special actuarial factors and information the Service requires to be furnished in order to render such assistance.

Actuarial valuation may be used in combination with other valuation methods. See Priv. Ltr. Rul. 9802031 (Oct. 24, 1997) (beneficiary's rights to receive distributions for health, education, support, and maintenance for life).

[53] If a set term of years is involved, life expectancies are not a factor in valuation.

[54] See Reg. § 25.7520-1(b). Cf. Reg. §§ 25.2512-5, 25.2512-5A.

[55] See Reg. §§ 20.2031-7(d)(6), 25.2512-5. The prior gender-based mortality tables were held to be unconstitutional in Manufacturers Hanover Trust Co. v. United States, 775 F2d 459 (2d Cir. 1985), cert. denied, 475 US 1095 (1986).

[56] IRC § 7520(c)(3); Reg. §§ 25.2512-5(d), 25.7520-1(b)(2). See Life Table 90 LM, which is based on data compiled from the 1990 census. Transfers as of July 1, 1999, are subject to new, longer life expectancy tables. Taxpayers who made transfers after April 30, 1999, and before July 1, 1999, would use either the tables using the 1980 data or those using the 1990 data.

[57] Section 7520 applies not only to gift tax valuation but to income tax, estate tax, and generation-skipping transfer tax valuation as well. IRC § 7520(a). Cf. Notice 89-24, 1989-1 CB 660, which makes Section 7520 applicable to valuation under Sections 170, 642, 664, 2031, 2055, 2522, and 2624, as well as Section 2512. See also Reg. § 25.7520-1. Section 7520 is applicable to actuarial valuation after April 30, 1989. Reg. § 25.7520-1(a)(1).

[58] IRC § 7520(a)(2). In valuing charitable contributions, the interest rate for either of the two preceding months may be employed. IRC § 7520(a) (flush language); Reg. § 25.7520-2(a)(2).

See Estate of Cullison v. Comm'r, 75 TCM (CCH) 2489 (1998) (the taxpayer made a gift on sale of land from a private annuity where the taxpayer used state's going interest rate on sales of land rather than the Section 7520 rate).

equal to 120 percent of the federal midterm rate rounded off to the nearest two tenths of one percent.[59] The regulations provide tables to be used for gift tax valuation purposes.[60] The valuation of an interest may be altered where there are limitations or restrictions upon receipt of the interest.[61] In addition, the tables are disregarded if the interest is measured by the life of an individual and such individual is "terminally ill" at the time of the gift.[62]

[iv] **Excise taxes and other charges.** The effect of an excise tax on property that is the subject of a gift has prompted interesting controversies. The Second Circuit has held that if jewelry is purchased and soon thereafter is given to another, the gift tax value is the price paid including the excise tax paid at the time of purchase.[63] The same court has also held that if a substantial period of time elapses between the date of the purchase and the date of the gift, the same approach to valuation should be taken but adjustment should be made for changes in value during the period.[64] Essentially the same position is taken in the regulations.[65] When property is transferred in a completed gift upon creation of a trust, the amount of the gift is the value of the property transferred on the date of the transfer to the trust. The amount of the gift is not affected by the amount of trustee's commissions paid for receiving the prop-

---

[59] IRC § 7520(a)(2). The federal midterm rate is defined in Section 1274(d)(1). See Reg. § 25.7520-1(b)(1). Prior to 1971, interests actuarially valued were based on a 3.5 percent interest factor; the tables then used a 6 percent factor until 1983, when a 10 percent interest factor was adopted and used until April 30, 1989.

[60] Reg. §§ 20.2031-7(d)(6), 25.2512-5.

[61] See Reg. § 25.7520-3(b), especially Reg. § 25.7520-3(b)(2). These provisions are identical to Regulations Section 20.7520-3(b), which is discussed at ¶ 4.02[5] text accompanying notes 250–252.

[62] Reg. § 25.7520-3(b)(3). A person who is known to have an incurable illness or other deteriorating physical condition is considered terminally ill if there is at least a 50 percent probability that the person will die within one year. However, if the person survives for eighteen months or longer after the gift is completed, the person is presumed not to have been terminally ill at the date the gift was complete unless there is clear and convincing evidence to the contrary. Id. See Reg. § 25.7520-3(b)(4) Ex.

[63] Duke v. Comm'r, 200 F2d 82 (2d Cir. 1952), cert. denied, 345 US 906 (1953); accord, Estate of Gould v. Comm'r, 14 TC 414 (1950). These decisions find some support in Guggenheim v. Rasquin, 312 US 254 (1941).

[64] Publicker v. Comm'r, 206 F2d 250 (3d Cir. 1953), cert. denied, 346 US 924 (1954).

[65] Reg. § 25.2512-7. See also Rev. Rul. 55-71, 1955-1 CB 110.

erty; they are administrative expenses that neither increase nor reduce the amount of the gift.[66]

[v] **Stock options.** Generally, stock options are valued using the now-familiar willing seller–willing buyer test.[67] With the increasing use of non–publicly traded stock options providing the holder the right to acquire publicly traded stock as compensation,[68] the Treasury has issued a safe harbor procedure for valuing such options for purposes of all of the transfer taxes.[69] The procedure adopts the use of recognized option pricing models, but only if several factors are taken into consideration in making the valuation.[70]

[vi] **Restrictions on use.** Restrictions on the use or disposition of property may affect its value for gift tax purposes. The law in this area arising out of case law[71] and regulations[72] is substantially controlled by Sections 2703 and 2704(b), which are discussed in detail later in the book.[73]

[c] Premiums and Discounts for Interests in Property

It is common for donors to resist making lifetime transfers of fee simple interests in valuable assets to their beneficiaries because the donor does not want to lose control over (and income benefits from) the gifted property. As a result, donors instead commonly transfer undivided minority interests in assets. Such minority interest transfers permit the donor to deplete the donor's estate for federal transfer tax purposes while retaining control over the gifted property. Undivided interests are typically not subject to actuarial valuation rules because they are usually unaffected by the life expectancy of the donor or donee. Instead, undivided interests trigger various premiums and discounts that

---

[66] Rev. Rul. 67-230, 1967-2 CB 352.

[67] Reg. § 25.2512-1.

[68] Cf. ¶ 10.01[3][a] text accompanying note 86, for a discussion of such options.

[69] Rev. Proc. 98-34, 1998-1 CB 983. Thus, the procedure applies for purposes of the estate, gift, and generation-skipping transfer taxes. The procedure is discussed in Harrison, "Using Options to Allow Donees to Have the Donor's Cake and Eat It, Too," 77 Taxes 277 (Mar. 1999); Franz, Crawford & Campbell, "How to Value Gifts of Employee Stock Options," 29 Tax Adviser 848 (Dec. 1998).

[70] Rev. Proc. 98-34, 1998-1 CB 983, 984, § 4. Taxpayer employing the valuation method should indicate "FILED PURSUANT TO REV. PROC. 98-34" on the appropriate tax return.

[71] See, e.g., Spitzer v. Comm'r, 153 F2d 967 (8th Cir. 1946); Comm'r v. McCann, 146 F2d 385 (2d Cir. 1944); Berzon v. Comm'r, 63 TC 601 (1975), aff'd, 534 F2d 528 (2d Cir. 1976), acq. 1975-2 CB 1; Harwood v. Comm'r, 82 TC 239 (1984), aff'd in unpub. op., 786 F2d 1174 (9th Cir.), cert. denied, 479 US 1007 (1986).

[72] Cf. Reg. § 20.2031-2(h).

[73] See ¶¶ 19.04, 19.05[3].

are applied to the unadjusted fair market value of the underlying property to determine the value of the gift. The premiums and discounts discussed here are similar to the ones already described with respect to the federal estate tax.[74] Principles applicable to premiums and discounts in the estate tax context apply equally to the federal gift tax. Nonetheless, some cases and rulings applicable specifically to the federal gift tax are discussed here.

As with the estate tax, the premiums and discounts described next arise most frequently when valuing stock in closely held corporations and interests in other closely held business entities, such as limited partnerships and limited liability companies. Accordingly, much of the following discussion assumes the gifted property is an interest in a closely held business entity. Again, however, the premiums and discounts will apply to gifts of interests in any asset where relevant.[75]

[i] Control premium. A willing buyer will often pay a greater amount for a controlling interest in a business entity than its proportional value because it provides the buyer unfettered control over business affairs.[76] When a donor transfers a controlling interest in an asset or business entity to a donee, therefore, the interest is subject to a "control premium" for gift tax valuation purposes.

A control premium does not apply, however, where the donor transfers a minority interest that, when added to any other interests retained by the donor and those already owned by the donee or other family members, would constitute a controlling interest.[77] Similarly, when a donor fractures a controlling interest into several smaller, noncontrolling interests, and gives those interests simultaneously to separate beneficiaries, the donor makes gifts of several noncontrolling interests and not one comprehensive gift of a controlling interest.[78] The Service once ruled that where a donor transfers three blocks of 30 percent interests in an entity, the second block would be subject to a "swing vote pre-

---

[74] See ¶ 4.02[4]. Some of the discounts discussed in the estate tax valuation section are not discussed here. See ¶¶ 4.02[4][e][iv]–4.02[4][e][vii].

[75] Transfers of interests in real estate are a significant example. See Bringardner, "Discounting the Value of Undivided Interests in Realty," 72 J. Tax'n 12 (1990).

[76] See ¶ 4.02[4][b]. Depending on applicable laws and agreements, the buyer can acquire control by purchasing a simple majority interest or by purchasing a super-majority interest.

[77] Rev. Rul. 93-12, 1993-1 CB 202.

[78] Rev. Rul. 93-12, 1993-1 CB 202; TAM 9449001 (Mar. 11, 1994) (transfer of 9 percent interests to each of eleven children values as eleven gifts of noncontrolling interests, not one gift of interest subject to control premium). Compare this result to the result in connection with the valuation in the gross estate, where the decedent's testamentary division of the property into several noncontrolling "pieces" is not taken into account in determining the value included in the gross estate. See ¶ 4.02[4][b][ii]. Cf. ¶¶ 5.05[3][a] text accompanying notes 96, 97, 5.06[5] text accompanying notes 91–94.

mium" because it could join with one other shareholder to control entity affairs.[79] The Service gave no indication, however, of how this variation of the control premium was to be computed. In one case,[80] the court refused to apply a "swing vote" control premium to two gifts of 25.77 percent interests in a closely held business entity because the other shareholders, close family members of the donor, would be unlikely to join forces with a hypothetical willing buyer to compel key managerial decisions.

Because controlling interests are more likely to be passed at death rather than by inter vivos transfer for the reasons just described, the application of a control premium in a gift tax valuation matter is rare.

[ii] **Minority interest discount.** Just as a willing buyer is amenable to paying a premium for a controlling interest, a willing buyer is likely unwilling to pay proportionate value for a noncontrolling interest. This is the rationale for the minority interest discount.[81] Because the minority interest discount is the mirror image of the control premium, courts in some cases have simply computed the minority interest discount as the inverse of any applicable control premium.[82] Under this method, for example, if the premium applicable to a controlling interest in the subject property is 25 percent, the minority interest discount is 20 percent.[83]

More often, however, appraisers and courts determine minority interest discounts independently of the computation of control premiums. The proper discount is a function of state law, agreements pertaining to the business to be valued, and the rights of minority owners. As with estate tax valuation disputes, courts in gift tax valuation matters will consider the opinions of experts obtained by taxpayers and the Service. In some cases, a court will choose the better appraisal.[84] In other cases, the court will determine its own discount rate,

---

[79] TAM 9436005 (May 26, 1994).

[80] Estate of Davis v. Comm'r, 110 TC 530 (1998).

[81] See ¶ 4.02[4][c].

[82] Rakow v. Comm'r, 77 TCM (CCH) 2066 (1999) (inverse of 45 percent control premium produced 31 percent minority interest discount applied to the donor's gifts of stock to the grandchildren).

[83] One divided by 1.25 equals 0.80, and 0.80 is 20 percent less than 1.00.

[84] Dailey v. Comm'r, 82 TCM (CCH) 710 (2001) (the court applied the taxpayer's 40 percent combined minority and marketability discount to gifts of interests in an FLP, entirely rejecting the 15.72 percent combined discount advanced by the Service); Wall v. Comm'r, 81 TCM (CCH) 1425 (2001) (the court accepted the Service's 2 percent minority interest discount on gifts of nonvoting stock in the donor's previously wholly owned S corporation to twenty different trusts for benefit of the donor's children, rejecting the taxpayer's alleged 5 percent minority interest discount).

often a compromise between the discounts suggested by the competing experts.[85]

Because the minority interest discount is premised upon a lack of control over entity management, gifts of nonvoting stock or nonvoting interests in unincorporated business entities are eligible for the discount even where the amount transferred represents a majority equity interest in the business. In one case, the Tax Court determined the value of gifts of stock in a bank holding company by applying a 10 percent minority interest discount and an additional 4 percent discount to reflect the fact that the gifted shares lacked voting rights.[86] The court's distinction between the minority interest discount and a discount for nonvoting stock is unique.[87]

Although the federal gift tax is imposed on the property transferred by the donor, multiple gifts of fractional interests in the same property are not aggregated for valuation purposes. Thus, where a donor was deemed to have transferred a 50 percent voting interest in a closely held corporation in equal shares to each of the donor's two sons, the court valued the gifts as two gifts of 25 percent voting interests and not one gift of a single 50 percent interest.[88] This increases the applicability and amount of the minority interest discount. Likewise, where a donor gives minority interests in a business entity to family members and retains other interests, the Service will not aggregate the gifted interests and the donor's retained interests for purposes of denying a minority interest discount. The Service lost that argument in the cases where it raised it,[89] and has apparently abandoned the attribution strategy.[90]

[iii] Discount for lack of marketability. The marketability discount reflects the fact that a willing buyer would consider the lack of a ready market

---

[85] Janda v. Comm'r, 81 TCM (CCH) 1100 (2001) (the court applied 40 percent combined minority and marketability discount to gifts of stock in closely held corporation even though the taxpayer's expert applied a 65.77 percent combined discount and the Service's expert applied a combined discount of only 20 percent).

[86] Kosman v. Comm'r, 71 TCM (CCH) 2356 (1996).

[87] The experts hired by the taxpayer and the Service agreed that the proper minority interest discount was 10 percent, and both experts agreed that some additional adjustment was proper because the gifted shares lacked voting rights. This is perhaps why the court offered no analysis of the distinction. It also illustrates that the two separately stated discounts could have been combined into one overall discount for the nonvoting minority interest. The case should probably be read as approving an aggregate 14 percent minority interest discount, not two separate discounts of 10 percent and 4 percent.

[88] Estate of Bosca v. Comm'r, 76 TCM (CCH) 62 (1998).

[89] Mooneyham v. Comm'r, 61 TCM (CCH) 2445 (1991); Ward v. Comm'r, 87 TC 78 (1986); Carr v. Comm'r, 49 TCM (CCH) 507 (1985).

[90] Rev. Rul. 93-12, 1993-1 CB 202, revoking Rev. Rul. 81-253, 1981-2 CB 187.

of future buyers an impediment to acquiring the subject property.[91] If a buyer must wait several months or years to liquidate the buyer's interest, the buyer will offer less than full liquidation value to acquire it. Over the past forty years, the average marketability discount applied by the Tax Court is approximately 24 percent.[92] But this general conclusion is not helpful, for it ignores the fact that the determination of the proper discount in any case is highly dependent on several facts.[93] Generally speaking, the more impediments to liquidation, the higher the discount.

While the determination is highly factual, a look at some illustrative cases is helpful. Finding the taxpayers' expert testimony flawed and biased in many respects, one court[94] reduced the claimed 30 percent discount for lack of marketability on gifts of limited partnership interests to three trusts to a combined minority/marketability discount of 15 percent. This increased the taxpayers' gifts to each trust from $263,165 to $394,515, which was still less than the $450,086 value asserted by the Service. The court acknowledged that "some discount is proper" despite the flaws of the taxpayers' expert testimony, but it offered no basis for concluding that a combined 15 percent discount was appropriate.

In *Mandelbaum v. Commissioner*,[95] the court concluded that a 30 percent marketability discount was appropriate with respect to the taxpayer's several transfers of minority interests in a closely held corporation to family members over many years. The court concluded that the Service's expert failed to give sufficient weight to a shareholders' agreement that restricted transfers of the stock, but found that the taxpayer's expert similarly failed to give sufficient weight to the concept of a willing seller. In concluding that the taxpayer's proposed marketability discounts of 70 percent and 75 percent were too high, the court labeled "incredible the proposition that any . . . shareholder would be willing to sell his or her stock at such a large discount." The court then performed its own appraisal, considering ten separate factors affecting marketability, including the company's financial statements, its dividend policy, its management philosophy, its industry, its redemption policy, the shareholders'

---

[91] See ¶ 4.02[4][d]. One could argue that because the noncontrolling status of a minority interest reduces the market of potential buyers, the discount for minority status could be expressed as a function of marketability.

[92] Janda v. Comm'r, 81 TCM (CCH) 1100 (2001).

[93] For a detailed analysis of the factors a court will consider in determining the appropriate marketability discount, see Mandelbaum v. Comm'r, 69 TCM (CCH) 2852 (1995), aff'd, 91 F3d 124 (3d Cir. 1996).

[94] Knight v. Comm'r, 115 TC 506 (2000).

[95] Mandelbaum v. Comm'r, 69 TCM (CCH) 2852 (1995), aff'd, 91 F3d 124 (3d Cir. 1996).

agreement, and costs associated with taking the company public.[96] Ultimately, the court determined that the 30 percent discount used by the Service's expert was correct, even though it disagreed with that expert's approach in calculating the discount amount.

The size of the marketability discount can be affected by the size of the interest transferred, at least where the size of the interest affects the rights of the holder. In a revelant case,[97] the Tax Court determined the appropriate discounts for gift transfers involving two FLPs. In the first partnership, the donor transferred an 83.08 percent limited partnership interest to the donor's son. In the second partnership, the donor gave 16.915 percent limited partnership interests to each of the donor's four daughters. With respect to the first partnership, the taxpayer's expert applied a 55 percent "secondary market discount" and an additional marketability discount of 20 percent. The "secondary market discount" was a combined minority/marketability discount applicable to syndicated limited partnerships. The Service argued that no marketability discounts were appropriate, and with respect to the "secondary market discount," the court agreed. The court noted that the 83.08 percent interest transferred had unilateral power to remove the general partner of the partnership, so the restrictions assumed by the "secondary market discount" were not present. The court then reduced the 20 percent additional marketability discount to 8 percent. With respect to the second limited partnership, the court was more accepting of the 45 percent "secondary market discount" proffered by the taxpayer, concluding that a 40 percent discount was appropriate. This was because none of the interests transferred had the power to effect a dissolution of the partnership or even a distribution to the partners. As with the first partnership, the court also allowed an additional marketability discount of 8 percent.

Occasionally, taxpayers and the Service will agree on the proper discount, and when the stars are so aligned, courts are hesitant to disturb the agreement. In one such case,[98] the parties agreed to a 40 percent marketability discount for gifts of nonvoting common stock in an S corporation that manufactured and distributed office supplies. The parties fought principally over the minority interest discount amount: the taxpayer wanted a 5 percent discount and the Service insisted on a 2 percent discount.

---

[96] The Tax Court's willingness to criticize experts from both sides and engage in its own detailed analysis was also shown in Janda v. Comm'r, 81 TCM (CCH) 1100 (2001). There, the court found fault with an expert's reliance on the Quantitative Marketability Discount Model proposed by Z. Christopher Mercer in his book, Quantifying Marketability Discounts (Wiley, 1997). The court expressed "grave doubts about the reliability" of the model.

[97] Estate of Jones v. Comm'r, 116 TC 121 (2001).

[98] Wall v. Comm'r, 81 TCM (CCH) 1425 (2001).

Often a discount for lack of marketability is coupled with a discount for a minority interest.[99] Courts frequently will compute a single discount rate that encompasses both a minority interest discount and a discount for lack of marketability.[100] If the discounts are separately stated, they are layered, they are not cumulative.[101]

[iv] **Other discounts.** Although the minority interest and marketability discounts are the most common adjustments when valuing undivided interests, other discounts can apply in certain circumstances.

Fractional Interest Discount. Like the minority interest discount, the fractional interest discount recognizes the limitations of co-ownership. While the minority interest discount usually applies to co-ownership of an *entity*, the fractional interest discount typically applies to co-ownership of an *asset*.[102] The fractional interest discount applies to assets held as tenants-in-common, as well as property held as community property or tenants by the entirety.[103] It reflects the fact that a willing buyer will not pay liquidation value for an undivided interest in an asset because of the costs to partition the property or sever the interest if a dispute arises, not to mention the general headaches and compromises required by joint ownership.

Blockage Discount. Suppose a donor gives a large number of shares in a publicly traded corporation to a donee. If the donor sold all of the shares at once, the price per share would drop because of the significant increase in the

---

[99] See supra ¶ 10.02[2][c][ii].

[100] Dailey v. Comm'r, 82 TCM (CCH) 710 (2001); Janda v. Comm'r, 81 TCM (CCH) 1100 (2001); Barnes v. Comm'r, 76 TCM (CCH) 881 (1998) (combined 40 percent and 45 percent discounts on gifts of stock in two closely held telephone companies). See also Estate of Newhouse v. Comm'r, 94 TC 193 (1990); Estate of Andrews v. Comm'r, 79 TC 938 (1982).

[101] For example, if a minority interest in a closely held business warrants a 20 percent minority interest discount and an additional 30 percent discount for lack of marketability, the total discount is 44 percent not 50 percent. For this combination and a discussion of other combinations of premiums and discounts, see ¶ 4.02[4][f].

[102] Despite this basic distinction, the court in Shepherd v. Comm'r, 115 TC 376 (2000), applied a 15 percent "fractional interest discount" to the donor's gift of an interest in a partnership whose sole asset was a leasehold interest. The court said the discount was comprised as follows: (1) a 10 percent discount for the risk of disagreement between co-owners as to the terms and conditions of any sale of the partnership property; (2) a 3 percent discount for the lack of complete control over the management of the partnership property; and (3) a 2 percent discount for costs to partition the property, which was held unlikely in this case because the partnership's asset was a lease. To preserve the distinction between the minority interest discount and the fractional interest discount, the court should have called this a "minority interest discount." The court probably erred, technically, in calling it a "fractional interest discount," but this underscores the similarity between the two discounts. The analysis applicable to minority interest discounts should therefore also apply to fractional interest discounts.

[103] See ¶ 4.02[4][e][i].

Section 2512

number of shares available for purchase. To reflect the price depression that would accompany a hypothetical sale of the entire block of shares to one or more willing buyers, it is appropriate to apply a "blockage discount" to the liquidation value of the shares. The blockage discount is accepted by both the Treasury and the courts, although the amount of the discount tends to be much less than the typical minority interest and marketability discounts.[104] Of course, if a gift of a large block of shares is fractured into several smaller gifts, the applicable blockage discount will be less because the discount will be computed for each smaller gift.[105] In one recent case, the Tax Court held that no blockage discount applied to the donor's gift of stock in a holding company that owned a large block of publicly traded stock because the taxpayer failed to prove the amount of the discount.[106]

Capital Gains Discount. If the gifted property consists of stock in a corporation, the willing buyer might be reluctant to pay a price for the shares that equals the full value of the assets and business activity held by the corporation if the corporation would be taxable upon a substantial amount of built-in capital gain upon liquidation or a sale of its assets. Thus, courts have permitted application of a "capital gains discount" to gifts of corporate stock where a corporate liquidation cannot be achieved without recognition of gain at the corporate level.[107] The discount is apparently permissible even absent plans to liquidate the corporation in the near future and even though the corporation could, subject to a potentially lengthy delay, avoid much of the gain by electing to be taxed as an S corporation.[108] The discount is not allowed where the

---

[104] See ¶ 4.02[4][e][ii].

[105] TAM 9719001 (Nov. 19, 1996). This is because the donor is making several smaller gifts and not one large gift. See supra ¶ 10.02[2][c][i].

[106] Estate of Davis v. Comm'r, 110 TC 530 (1998). The court did observe that a blockage discount would be hard to prove because of the increasing value of the publicly traded (Winn Dixie Stores) shares at the time of the gift, but this was technically not the reason for denying the discount.

[107] See ¶ 4.02[4][e][iii].

[108] Estate of Davis v. Comm'r, 110 TC 530 (1998). The court noted that an S election was unlikely because it would limit the number of potential buyers in the future owing to the strict eligibility requirements to make and maintain an S election. Of possible significance here is that an S election will, as to an existing C corporation, involve a ten-year delay in avoiding the corporate level tax on built-in gains at the time of the election. IRC § 1374. See also Eisenberg v. Comm'r, 74 TCM (CCH) 1046 (1997), rev'd, 155 F3d 50 (2d Cir. 1998). The Second Circuit in *Eisenberg* cited *Estate of Davis* in vacating the Tax Court's decision rejecting a capital gains discount absent plans to liquidate the corporation or plans to sell or liquidate the corporation's sole asset. See also Estate of Jameson v. Comm'r, 267 F3d 366 (5th Cir. 2001); Estate of Dunn v. Comm'r, 79 TCM (CCH) 1337 (2001).

gifted property consists of interests in a partnership as long as the partnership could cure the entity-level gain by making a Section 754 election.[109]

Disallowed Discounts. In one case, the Tax Court rejected an asserted "small stock discount."[110] The taxpayer argued that the very small size of the gifted property (less than one percent of the corporation's stock) made the investment riskier for a hypothetical buyer.

The taxpayers' expert in another case argued for the application of a "portfolio discount."[111] The theory for this discount is that if a company owns two or more dissimilar assets or operations, the combination is not as attractive to a buyer who usually only wants one of the assets or operations.[112] Empirically, conglomerate corporations usually sell for about 10 to 15 percent less because the corporations have a portfolio of business operations.[113] The Tax Court disallowed the use of a portfolio discount in valuing interests in a partnership that owned real estate and marketable securities, finding no evidence that the mix of investments would be unattractive to a hypothetical buyer.[114]

[v] Discount resulting from a gift on formation. Suppose a donor forms a family limited partnership (FLP) or a family limited liability company (FLLC),[115] or a family corporation, by contributing investment assets worth $10 million to the entity in exchange for a 99 percent nonvoting interest in the entity. Then suppose the donor immediately gives the 99 percent interest to the donor's children. If the donor claims that the 99 percent interest is worth only $6.5 million because of applicable valuation discounts,[116] what happened to the remaining $3.5 million contributed to the entity? The Service has taken the position that the difference was a gift from the donor to the donees.[117] The argument has met with mixed results.

---

[109] Estate of Jones v. Comm'r, 116 TC 121 (2001).

[110] Barnes v. Comm'r, 76 TCM (CCH) 881 (1998).

[111] Knight v. Comm'r, 115 TC 506 (2000).

[112] See Pratt, Reilly & Schweihs, Valuing a Business: The Analysis and Appraisal of Closely-Held Companies 325 (Irwin Prof'l Publ'g, 3d ed. 1996). See also, Pratt, Reilly & Schweihs, Valuing a Business: The Analysis and Appraisal of Closely-Held Companies 325 (McGraw-Hill, 4th ed. 1996).

[113] See Pratt, Reilly & Schweihs, Valuing a Business: The Analysis and Appraisal of Closely-Held Companies 325 (Irwin Prof'l Publ'g, 3d ed. 1996).

[114] Knight v. Comm'r, 115 TC 506 (2000).

[115] For more on valuation issues with respect to FLPs and FLLCs, see ¶ 4.02[4][g].

[116] The interest would be subject to a marketability discount because a willing buyer would be unable to sell or transfer the limited partnership interest without restriction. It would also be subject to a minority interest discount because, as a limited partner, the interest holder would have no significant voting rights.

[117] FSA 199950014 (Sept. 15, 1999); TAM 9842003 (July 2, 1998).

In *Shepherd v. Commissioner*,[118] the Service prevailed because the relevant partnership agreement allocated all capital contributions pro rata to the partners' capital accounts. Thus, when the donor contributed property to the partnership and 50 percent of the value was immediately allocated to the capital accounts of the donor's two children (who themselves contributed nothing to the partnership), the court held that the donor had made a gift of half of the contributed assets to his children, as opposed to gifts of partnership interests. This is probably the right result when the donor-partner's capital contributions are immediately credited to the other partners; in this sense, it is the same as if the donor-partner conveyed assets to the other partners who then contributed the same to the partnership.[119] If the donor in *Shepherd* had first created a valid partnership, then had taken the partnership interests corresponding to the contributions and gifted half of the interests in equal shares to his two children, he would have avoided this trap.

Subsequent cases prove this to be true. In *Estate of Strangi v. Commissioner*,[120] the facts were very similar to the earlier hypothetical: the donor contributed various investment assets worth nearly $10 million to an FLP in exchange for a 99 percent interest in the partnership. The donor then conveyed the 99 percent interest to various donees and claimed to have made gifts totaling approximately $6.5 million. Armed with *Shepherd*, the Service argued that the donor made a gift of $3.5 million to the donees upon formation of the FLP. The court rejected the Service's argument, noting that the partnership agreement in this case credited only the donor's capital account for the property contribution. The reduction in the donor's wealth, said the court, was because of minority and marketability discounts, not because of any shift in equity for the benefit of the other partners.

The Service also lost the argument in another case.[121] There, the donor transferred investment assets worth approximately $17.6 million to an FLP in exchange for limited partnership interests that, after discounts, were worth only about $6.6 million. The Service argued that the donor made an $11 million gift at the time of the contribution transaction. The court held that no gift occurred because the donor's contribution was reflected only in the donor's capital account, and there was no resulting increase in the value of the interests of the other partners.

Thus, as long as certain formalities are followed with respect to contributions of property to an FLP or FLLC, the "gift on formation" argument should

---

[118] Shepherd v. Comm'r, 115 TC 376 (2000).

[119] See ¶ 9.04[1][b] text accompanying note 29, ¶ 10.01[1][b] text accompanying note 22.

[120] Estate of Strangi v. Comm'r, 115 TC 478 (2000).

[121] Estate of Jones v. Comm'r, 116 TC 121 (2001).

not apply.¹²² Specifically, donors should make sure that only their capital accounts are credited for their contributions to the entity.

[d] Statutes Applicable to Gift Tax Valuation

[i] Section 2504(c). Section 2504(c) generally provides that if the statute of limitations for assessment of federal gift tax has expired with respect to any prior calendar year, then the value of any property gifted during that closed year shall, for all gift tax purposes, be fixed at the value finally determined for gift tax purposes.¹²³ Taxpayers making use of valuation discounts have an incentive to file federal gift tax returns to take advantage of the possibility of closure under Section 2504(c). Even when a donor of discounted interests is not required to file a federal gift tax return, the donor might want to file a federal gift tax return so that the Service's opportunity to challenge the discount is limited.

[ii] Section 7517. As indicated in the estate tax discussion of Section 2031,¹²⁴ the Service is required to divulge certain information regarding its determination of value for computation of tax under Chapters 11, 12, and 13,¹²⁵ and to do so within forty-five days of a qualified request or of its valuation determination, whichever is later.¹²⁶ Now, therefore, a donor may request and will seasonably be furnished a written statement with regard to any item subject to tax that will:

1. Explain the basis on which the valuation was determined or proposed;
2. Set forth any computation used in arriving at such value; and
3. Contain a copy of any expert's appraisal made by or for the secretary.¹²⁷

[iii] Section 7477. Section 7477 provides that the donor of a gift who has exhausted the donor's administrative remedies may seek a declaratory judgment in the Tax Court as to the value of a gift where there is an actual controversy regarding the amount of a gift shown on a return or disclosed on a

---

¹²² See also Church v. United States, 85 AFTR2d (WD Tex. 2000).

¹²³ IRC § 2504(c), discussed ¶ 9.05[2].

¹²⁴ See ¶ 4.02[1].

¹²⁵ IRC § 7517(a). See Reg. § 301.7517-1.

¹²⁶ IRC § 7517(a). See Reg. § 301.7517-1.

¹²⁷ The provision is the subject of discussion in HR Rep. No. 1380, 94th Cong., 2d Sess. 60, reprinted in 1976-3 CB (Vol. 3) 735, 794.

statement attached to the return.[128] The donor's pleading must be filed within ninety days of the secretary's mailing of the notice of the determination of value with respect to the gift.[129] The court's determination has the same effect as a decision rendered by the Tax Court and is reviewable.[130]

[3] Consideration for a Transfer

The statutory rule of Section 2512(b) on consideration is brief: "Where property is transferred for less than an adequate and full consideration in money or money's worth, then the amount by which the value of the property exceeded the value of the consideration shall be deemed a gift. . . . " The phraseology used here has created an interesting situation. Because this language appears in a section purporting to deal with valuation, it might reasonably be assumed that the provision applied only in determining the value of property admittedly transferred by gift. However, the Supreme Court reads this provision instead as a part of the statutory definition of the term "gift." In holding common-law concepts of gifts and the question of donative intent irrelevant to a determination whether a transfer is subject to gift tax, the Court has said that Congress "formulated a much more workable external test, that where 'property is transferred for less than an adequate and full consideration in money or money's worth,' the excess in such money value 'shall, for the purpose of the tax imposed by this title, be deemed a gift. . . . '"[131] Thus, just as time of valuation and completeness are related concepts, method of valuation merges with the question of the meaning of the term "gift," and Section 2512 may affect the question whether a gift was made.[132]

---

[128] IRC §§ 7477(a), 7477(b)(2). Section 7477 is applicable to gifts made after August 5, 1997. Taxpayer Relief Act of 1997, Pub. L. No. 105-34, § 506(e)(1), 111 Stat. 788, 856 (1997), reprinted in 1997-4 CB (Vol. 1) 1, 70.

[129] IRC § 7477(b)(3). To revalue a gift adequately disclosed on a return or on a statement attached to a return, the Service must issue a final notice of redetermination of value within the statute of limitations applicable to the gift, even if the gift does not require any tax to be paid, such as where the Section 2505 credit is used. HR Conf. Rep. No. 220, 105th Cong., 1st Sess. 408 (1997), reprinted in 1997-4 CB (Vol. 2) 1457, 1878.

[130] IRC § 7477(a).

[131] Comm'r v. Wemyss, 324 US 303, 306 (1945). If accepted as a definition, there is no doubt that Section 2512(b) supplies a more "workable" test for a gift than that applied for income tax purposes. See Comm'r v. Duberstein, 363 US 278 (1960) (regarding the meaning of "gift" in Section 102). The *Wemyss* opinion adds that detriment to the donee fails to satisfy the adequate and full consideration requirement. *Comm'r v. Wemyss*, supra at 303, 307–308. Nonetheless, the existence of donative intent can help a court distinguish a gift from compensation. See Estate of Cavett v. Comm'r, 79 TCM (CCH) 1662 (2000); Estate of Powell v. United States, 88 AFTR2d 2001-5400 (WD Va. 2001).

[132] See, e.g., Fehrs v. United States, 620 F2d 255 (Cl. Ct. 1980) (value of property transferred exceeded value of a private annuity received). See also Krabbenhoft v.

[4] Transfers in the Ordinary Course of Business

A mechanical reading of Section 2512(b) in the manner just indicated would of course mean that every time an individual makes a bad bargain, that individual makes a gift within the scope of the gift tax. However, the Court hastens to add that the gift tax does not apply to "a sale, exchange, or other transfer of property made in the ordinary course of business (a transaction which is bona fide, at arm's length, and free from any donative intent)."[133] The regulations[134] echo this qualification. Such an exception is a recognition that Section 2512(b) is not really intended as a definition of the term "gift" and that it should be applied to determine value only if the transfer is otherwise recognizable as a gift. But it is much too late to argue the point seriously.

In any event, a grocer makes no gift subject to tax when the grocer runs a "loss leader" to entice customers into the grocer's store, and the Treasury is freed of the expense of hiring a staff of agents to determine which horse trader made the better deal. Peripheral questions like whether a transaction fits the business classification occasionally reach the litigation stage. In one case, the Supreme Court came very close to saying that negotiated interspousal transfers made in connection with a divorce were within the ordinary business exception.[135]

The Service has recognized that contributions of a group of citizens to a fund used to induce a company to locate an industrial plant in their area escape gift taxation under the business exception.[136] The Service's expression of its position is interesting for the light it sheds on the administrative interpretation of the language of the regulations, which was taken from the Supreme Court dictum quoted earlier. The parenthetical phrase "(a transaction which is bona fide, at arm's length, and free from any donative intent)" is seen as a description of a transaction "made in the ordinary course of business," not as a

---

Comm'r, 939 F2d 529 (8th Cir. 1991) (value of property transferred exceeded the present value of installment notes because the safe harbor of 6 percent interest found in income tax Section 483 did not apply for gift tax valuation purposes); Schusterman v. United States, 63 F3d 986 (10th Cir. 1995) (same). But see Ballard v. Comm'r, 854 F2d 185 (7th Cir. 1988) (contra).

[133] Comm'r v. Wemyss, 324 US 303 (1945).

[134] Reg. § 25.2512-8.

[135] Harris v. Comm'r, 340 US 106 (1950) (reaching a no-gift result but apparently on other grounds). The case is considered in the discussion of Section 2516 at ¶ 10.06.

In another case, gratuitous contributions to a citizens' group to establish a campaign fund for political aspirants were held to have been made bona fide, at arm's length, free from any donative intent, and, accordingly, made in the ordinary course of business and, therefore, not gifts. Stern v. United States, 304 F. Supp. 376 (ED La. 1969), aff'd, 436 F2d 1327 (5th Cir. 1971). The Service did not agree (Rev. Rul. 72-583, 1972-2 CB 534), but Congress did. See IRC § 2501(a)(5); ¶ 9.02[2].

[136] Rev. Rul. 68-558, 1968-2 CB 415.

further test.[137] So viewed, transactions that do not fit the income tax concept of the ordinary course of business[138] may nevertheless be well within the gift tax exception.[139] Sales of corporate stock by senior executives to unrelated junior executives, when the purpose was to assure continued, responsible owner-management of the business, have appropriately been placed outside the reach of the gift tax, even though the sales of the stock were obviously not a part of the transferor's ordinary business in the income tax sense.[140] In contrast, of course, a parent is likely to have difficulty establishing that a sale to children at less than market value fits the ordinary business exception.[141]

---

[137] "The phrase 'ordinary course of business' refers to a transaction that is bona fide, at arm's length, and free from any donative intent." Rev. Rul. 68-558, 1968-2 CB 415, 417. See Cobb v. Comm'r, 49 TCM (CCH) 1364 (1985).

[138] See, e.g., IRC §§ 165(c)(1), 167(a)(1), 1231(b). Compare Hazard v. Comm'r, 7 TC 372 (1946), acq. 1946-2 CB 3 with Grier v. United States, 218 F2d 603 (2d Cir. 1955).

[139] Cf. TAM 9217004 (Apr. 24, 1992) (no gift on distribution of winnings on jointly owned winning lottery ticket that was required by state law to be held in one owner's name).

[140] Estate of Anderson v. Comm'r, 8 TC 706 (1947), acq. 1947-2 CB 1. See Rev. Rul. 80-196, 1980-2 CB 32 (no gift on a transfer of stock by majority shareholders to corporate employees as a bonus for services). See also Chase Nat'l Bank v. Comm'r, 12 TCM (CCH) 455 (1953) (no gift upon transfer pursuant to a negotiated, judicially approved settlement of a controversy over the validity of a trust indenture).

[141] See Small v. Comm'r, 28 TCM (CCH) 1111 (1969). See also Estate of Campbell v. Comm'r, 59 TC 133 (1972) (a mother transferred an interest in property to her son under the belief that all she had to transfer was a life interest, accepting in return payment equal to the value of the life interest; upon the court's determination that she also held a general power of appointment and had effectively transferred the entire property, it was held that she had made a gift to the extent of the excess value); Estate of Slutsky v. Comm'r, 46 TCM (CCH) 1423 (1983) (a transfer of a hotel to a family member for inadequate consideration constituted a gift); Estate of Lenheim, 60 TCM (CCH) 356 (1990) (sale of stock to the son for inadequate consideration); Estate of Maggos v. Comm'r, 79 TCM (CCH) 1861 (2000) (redemption from the mother by the sole remaining shareholder). But see King v. United States, 545 F2d 700 (10th Cir. 1976) (upholding a price adjustment clause in an intrafamily stock sales contract, thereby precluding any gift tax consequences); Ellis Sarasota Bank & Trust Co. v. United States, 77-2 USTC ¶ 13,204 (MD Fla. 1977) (no gift in an intrafamily private annuity); Estate of Noland v. Comm'r, 47 TCM (CCH) 1640 (1984) (no gift in an intrafamily transfer of stock to resolve a valid legal dispute). In some instances, the determination of whether a transfer is in the ordinary course of business may play a role in determining the result of the developing controversy between the Service and taxpayers with respect to the transfer tax consequences of the creation of FLPs.

[5] Family Obligations

The gift tax has never been considered applicable to one's furnishing of food, clothing, or shelter for one's dependent spouse and children. This was given express recognition in proposed regulations released not long after the enactment of the 1954 Code, which provided "current expenditures by an individual on behalf of [a] spouse or minor child in satisfaction of [one's] legal obligation to provide for their support are not taxable gifts."[142] Although the current regulations do not include this statement, it is correct to treat the discharge of spouses' or parents' support obligations as consideration in money or money's worth, and the principle should continue to be recognized.[143] In addition, Section 2503(e) excludes payment of certain educational and medical expenses from gift tax liability even though there is no support obligation.[144]

On the other hand, in some circumstances, serious questions can arise both as to the existence of the obligation and as to the extent of the obligation,[145] and it seems evident that the existence of an obligation to support must be determined with reference to local law. *Commissioner v. Greene*[146] reflects a rejection of this proposition. Although California law imposed a duty to support adult children in specified circumstances, the court held that an incompetent's judicially sanctioned payments for such support were gifts, saying: "State law may control only when the federal taxing act, by express language or necessary implication, makes its own operation dependent upon state law."[147] This is a matter of misplaced reliance on a sound principle expressed by the Supreme Court in *United States v. Pelzer.*[148] There the question was only one of the proper interpretation of the term "future interest" as used in the federal statute, and the court properly dismissed local characterizations of future interests and made its own interpretation.[149] But there is no place to go other than to local law to determine the existence of support obligations, and the question cannot be confined to the interpretation of a term of the federal

---

[142] Prop. Reg. § 25.2511-1(f)(1), 22 Fed. Reg. 58 (1957).

[143] This is one of the many areas in which estate and gift tax problems are analogous and, even if the estate tax statute is more precise, like results should be reached under both taxes. Thus, under Section 2053, a decedent's obligations are deductible; but if found on a promise, they are not, unless incurred for full consideration in money or money's worth. Obligations imposed by law, however, are deductible without regard to consideration. By analogy, lifetime transfers that discharge obligations imposed by law are not subject to gift tax.

[144] See ¶ 9.04[6].

[145] Comm'r v. Greene, 119 F2d 383 (9th Cir.), cert. denied, 314 US 641 (1941).

[146] Comm'r v. Greene, 119 F2d 383 (9th Cir.), cert. denied, 314 US 641 (1941).

[147] Comm'r v. Greene, 119 F2d 383, 385 (9th Cir.), cert. denied, 314 US 641 (1941).

[148] United States v. Pelzer, 312 US 399 (1941).

[149] Cf. Roger's Estate v. Helvering, 320 US 410 (1943); Lyeth v. Hoey, 305 US 188 (1938).

statute. Instead, it is, in part, one of appraising private rights and obligations, which are necessarily locally determined under our system of dual sovereignties.[150]

Although the court in the *Greene* case[151] purports to deal with the matter as involving merely an interpretation of the term "consideration," the scope of the interpretation question would seem to extend only to whether a transfer to discharge an obligation to support is for consideration, and it is settled that it is. The remaining question whether the legal obligation to support exists must be settled by local law. It is significant that the portion of the proposed regulations quoted earlier used the term "legal obligation." At least since *Erie Railroad v. Tomkins*,[152] the federal courts are not at liberty to create general common-law rules concerning support.

[a] Extent and Value of Obligation

Once the existence of a legal obligation to support is recognized, an even thornier and less settled question arises: What is the extent or value of the obligation?[153] The Treasury once advanced the suggestion that "the extent of the donor's obligation to support his spouse or minor child must be ascertained from the facts and circumstances of the individual case."[154] In the absence of tax authority on this question, one court turned to principles developed in another area of the law concerning a person's liability for their spouse's purchases of items as necessaries.[155] Cases that rest upon the principle that the person may be acting as agent of the person are not relevant; but, if a person purchases items for the spouse for which the person would be liable as necessaries if the spouse had bought them, no gift tax liability is incurred. This criterion is not very clear, but it may at least be added that

> the term "necessaries" in its legal sense, as applied to a wife, is not confined to articles of food and clothing required to sustain life or preserve decency, but includes such articles of utility, or ornament, as are suitable to maintain the wife according to the estate and rank of her husband.[156]

---

[150] Cf. Hill v. Comm'r, 88 F2d 941 (8th Cir. 1937).

[151] Comm'r v. Greene, 119 F2d 383 (9th Cir.), cert. denied, 314 US 641 (1941).

[152] Erie RR v. Tomkins, 304 US 64 (1938).

[153] See Beck & Ekman, "Where Does Support End and Taxable Gift Begin?" 23 NYU Inst. on Fed. Tax'n 1181 (1965).

[154] Prop. Reg. § 25.2511-1(f)(1), 22 Fed. Reg. 58 (1957). The current regulations are silent on this point.

[155] Cf. Hill v. Comm'r, 88 F2d 941 (8th Cir. 1937).

[156] Hill v. Comm'r, 88 F2d 941, 944 (8th Cir. 1937), citing Bergh v. Warner, 50 NW 77, 78 (Minn. 1891). But see IRC § 2523.

This approach can produce surprising results. If a wealthy person purchases a $20,000 car for one's minor child, the person has probably just purchased a necessary. Would an artisan who used the artisan's life savings for the same purpose have made a gift on the ground that in the artisan's station in life the same car is not a necessary?[157]

There is bound to be a great deal of latitude in this area. As one writer suggests,[158] a technical gift can easily be found in the case of one who gives one's spouse a liberal allowance out of which to purchase needed items and run the home if the allowance exceeds the need and the spouse can save out of it amounts for the spouse's own separate use; yet there seems to be no likelihood that gift tax liability will be asserted here.[159] This same latitude has been identified in other settings. If a parent takes an adult child to dinner, having no obligation to support the child, should the cost of the dinner be treated as a gift of tax significance if other gifts to the child have exhausted the annual exclusion? Theory and practice are bound to diverge on such issues.

[b] Creation of a Trust

The discussion immediately above has been directed largely to a conventional discharge of support obligations. In some instances, however, a person may undertake an anticipatory discharge of a support obligation by the creation of a trust for that purpose. If the trustee is required to use the trust income for support purposes, has the settlor made a gift? Or is the transfer one for a recognized consideration to the extent of the value of the support rights? The Treasury's answer was once tentatively as follows:

> A transfer of property which, or the income from which, is to be used in the future to discharge a donor's obligation to support a dependent is not a transfer for a consideration in money or money's worth, unless under local law the transfer operates completely to discharge the donor's obligation.[160]

The regulations now make no reference to this principle. Nevertheless, it is supportable on the theory that if a trust that did not discharge the obligation

---

[157] Of course, the text question is made academic by the Section 2505 credit.

[158] Rudick, "Marriage, Divorce and Taxes," 2 Tax L. Rev. 123, 133 (1947). See also Thomas, Tax Consequences of Marriage, Separation and Divorce 96 (ALI-ABA 1986); Note, "Valuation of the Right to Support for Purposes of the Federal Tax System," 72 Colum. L. Rev. 132 (1972).

[159] This is especially so in view of Section 2523.

[160] Prop. Reg. § 25.2512-8, 22 Fed. Reg. 63 (1957). But cf. Helvering v. United States Trust Co., 111 F2d 576 (2d Cir.), cert. denied, 311 US 678 (1940); Estate of McKeon v. Comm'r, 25 TC 697 (1956), acq. 1958-2 CB 6 (differentiating discharge of child support and spouse support obligations).

became valueless and produced no income, the settlor would be in the same position regarding a support obligation as if the settlor had not set up the trust at all. Thus, no consideration is received. Similar reasoning brings such transfers into the gross estate on the theory that the transferor has retained an interest in the property (the income being used to discharge a continuing obligation) and has not received consideration for the transfer.[161]

[c] Divorce

Lump-sum arrangements in discharge of support obligations are most likely to arise in instances of divorce. Specific statutory rules concerning the gift tax significance of such arrangements are now provided in Section 2516, which is discussed later. But if Section 2516 is inapplicable, there is a gift to the extent that the value of the transfers for support exceed the value of the support rights.[162]

In a case in which an individual made a transfer to a prospective spouse in part to offset the prospective spouse's loss of income from a trust created by a former spouse in which the prospective spouse's rights would terminate upon remarriage, the court found no consideration for the transfer.[163] Such a view accords with the concept of the gift tax as a backstop for the estate tax, for otherwise there would have been a tax-free diminution of the transferor's estate.

[d] Elective Share Marital Rights

From what has been said so far, it might appear that a transfer in exchange for a relinquishment of dower, curtesy, and similar elective share marital rights would escape tax. Something of money's worth may flow to the transferor in such circumstances in the form of relief from a charge against the transferor's estate.[164] However, the gift tax law has developed the other way and logically so.[165] It will be recalled that for estate purposes, the statute speci-

---

[161] Comm'r v. Dwight's Estate, 205 F2d 298 (2d Cir.), cert. denied, 346 US 871 (1953). See the cases discussed in connection with Section 2036 in Chapter 4. See also Ellis v. Comm'r, 51 TC 182 (1968) (contractual agreement to release support rights cannot constitute consideration if the contract is void under state (Arizona) law).

[162] Rev. Rul. 77-314, 1977-2 CB 349. Cf. Rev. Rul. 80-82, 1980-1 CB 209.

[163] Comm'r v. Wemyss, 324 US 303 (1945). See Estate of Bartman v. Comm'r, 10 TC 1073 (1948), acq. 1948-2 CB 1 (the donor's gift to third parties is not reduced by the donor's spouse's release of the spouse's dower rights in the transferred property). But see IRC § 2513 on gift splitting by spouses.

[164] Cf. United States v. Davis, 370 US 65 (1962) (identifying realized gain for income tax purposes).

[165] See, e.g., Rev. Rul. 79-312, 1979-2 CB 29.

fies that a relinquishment or promised relinquishment of dower or curtesy or any statutory equivalent is not to be treated as consideration in money or money's worth.[166] Although no similar provision appears in the gift tax statute, the principle has been judicially incorporated into the gift tax.[167]

If the rule on relinquishment of dower, curtesy, or any statutory equivalent is open to debate as a matter of statutory interpretation, the interpretation adopted is at least abundantly supported by policy considerations. Again, the interrelation of the estate and gift taxes is the key. Since a surviving spouse's dower, curtesy, or similar interest is not excluded from a decedent's gross estate at death,[168] to treat relinquishment of such interests as consideration for gift tax purposes would result in a tax-free reduction of the value of the transferor's property otherwise subject to estate tax. Thus, this rule and the rule requiring that consideration be of financial benefit to the transferor have a common foundation in one of the principal purposes for the gift tax.[169]

[6] Other Receipts of Money's Worth

Of course, consideration need not be in money; money's worth will suffice, and many items that have money's worth are intangible in form. A transfer in discharge of a debt or a claim may be for consideration in money or money's worth,[170] and so is a transfer in exchange for a lifetime annuity,[171] or for a promise by the transferee to support the transferor for life.[172] In these instances, the value of the consideration must be weighed against the value of the property transferred, unless the payment of the debt was a business transaction, because under Section 2512(b), if the consideration is not "adequate and full," it operates only to reduce the amount of the gift.

---

[166] See discussion of Section 2043(b)(1) at ¶ 4.15[1]. Cf. IRC § 2043(b)(2).

[167] Merrill v. Fahs, 324 US 308, reh'g denied, 324 US 888 (1945). See ¶ 10.06[1].

[168] IRC § 2034.

[169] See Rev. Rul. 68-379, 1968-2 CB 414.

[170] Estate of Friedman v. Comm'r, 40 TC 714 (1963), acq. 1964-2 CB 5; Beveridge v. Comm'r, 10 TC 915 (1948), acq. 1949-1 CB 1. See also Rosenthal v. Comm'r, 205 F2d 505, 509 (2d Cir. 1953) (surrender of rights under earlier enforceable promise was consideration for later transfer). Cf. Abrams v. United States, 797 F2d 100 (2d Cir. 1986).

[171] Rev. Rul. 69-74, 1969-1 CB 43.

[172] Estate of Bergan v. Comm'r, 1 TC 543 (1943), acq. 1943 CB 2.

[a] Corporate Recipients

A transfer to a corporation partly owned by the transferor has been held to be supported by consideration to the extent of the transferor's proportionate ownership of the corporation.[173]

[b] Community Property Transactions

A conversion of community property into a tenancy in common has been held to result in no gift on the ground that the interest each party released in the community property constituted a full consideration for the interest acquired in the tenancy in common.[174] A similar result would occur if a joint tenancy were created on the conversion.[175]

The exercise of a community property election may constitute a transfer for consideration. In the typical situation, pursuant to an opportunity afforded by the decedent's will, a surviving spouse transfers that spouse's share of the community property to a trust that consists of both spouses' community property, and receives in return a lifetime income interest with a remainder to the children. In substance, the surviving spouse relinquishes a remainder interest in the spouse's share of the community property. Because the remainder is transferred to children who are family members under Section 2702,[176] the surviving spouse makes a transfer of that spouse's entire community property share,[177] but the amount of the spouse's taxable transfer is reduced by the consideration the spouse receives in the form of only the income interest in the decedent spouse's share of the community property.[178]

---

[173] Robert H. Scanlon v. Comm'r, 42 BTA 997 (1940), acq. 1942-1 CB 14. See Hollingsworth v. Comm'r, 86 TC 91 (1986); Kincaid v. United States, 682 F2d 1220 (5th Cir. 1982) (both cases involving a transfer for partial consideration to a partially owned corporation). See also Chanin v. United States, 393 F2d 972 (Ct. Cl. 1968) (involving contributions by more than one shareholder, in which an approach analogous to *Scanlon* is taken). The situation in *Scanlon* is more appropriately looked on as a gift by the transferor to the other shareholders to the extent of their proportionate interests. See Reg. § 25.2511-1(h)(1).

[174] Comm'r v. Mills, 183 F2d 32 (9th Cir. 1950).

[175] The creation of a tenancy by the entirety would result in a gift unless the spouses had equal life expectancies. The amount of the gift from the spouse with the shorter life expectancy would be the excess of the value of the interest in the property of the spouse with the greater life expectancy reduced by the value of one half of the property. See ¶ 10.01[3][f].

[176] IRC §§ 2702(e), 2704(c)(2).

[177] IRC § 2702(a)(2)(A).

[178] Cf. Comm'r v. Siegel, 250 F2d 339 (9th Cir. 1957). The surviving spouse's gift tax liability may be avoided if the spouse is given a power to alter the remainder interest in the trust because the spouse then holds the income interest in the spouse's community property share and a *Sanford* (Estate of Sanford v. Comm'r, 308 US 39 (1939)) power to

[c] Reciprocal Trusts

If two people create inter vivos reciprocal trusts,[179] one makes a gift to the other to the extent that the value of the property one transfers exceeds the value of the interest in the trust received. A similar result occurs if two joint owners of property transfer the property to a single trust in which they have equal income interests for their joint lives, and the survivor has the full income interest for life, with the remainder to go to another. Even if they held the transferred property as tenants-in-common or merely as joint tenants with right of survivorship (not as tenants by the entirety), so that at the time of transfer each had an equal interest in the property, the value of their retained interests in the newly created trust may be different because in contrast to the transferred property interests, the value of their interests in the trust is affected by their respective life expectancies. Consequently, although each has made a gift to the remainderperson of the same amount, one of the transferors may also have made a gift to the other.[180]

[d] Donee's Payment of Gift Tax

If by agreement a donor's gift tax liability on the transfer of property must be discharged by the donee, the value of the gift is reduced by the amount of the tax, either on the grounds that the donor has retained an interest in the property or that the donor has received consideration to the extent that the donor's tax obligation is to be discharged.[181] If the spouse is entitled to re-

---

alter the beneficiaries of the spouse's gift. A subsequent release of the power is a gift subject to no reduction for consideration because no consideration is received at the time of the release. Robinson v. Comm'r, 75 TC 346 (1980). Furthermore, if the surviving spouse is given a power to alter the remainder, it may jeopardize some of the income tax advantages of the community property election. See ¶ 4.08[7][c] note 134.

[179] See United States v. Grace, 395 US 316 (1969), discussed ¶ 4.08[7][d].

[180] See Rev. Rul. 69-505, 1969-2 CB 179, indicating the proper approach to this valuation problem, but likely obsolete in detail because the illustration is based on actuarial computations using assumed interest rates of 3.5 percent. Cf. IRC § 7520; supra ¶ 10.02[2][b][iii].

[181] Rev. Rul. 75-72, 1975-1 CB 310; Turner v. Comm'r, 49 TC 356 (1968), nonacq. 1971-2 CB, aff'd per curiam, 410 F2d 752 (6th Cir. 1969); Rev. Ruls. 80-111, 1980-1 CB 208; 81-223, 1981-2 CB 189. The formulas set forth in Revenue Ruling 75-72 deserve careful study. See also ¶ 8.07[4].

Income tax liability also lurks with respect to the donee's payment of the donor's gift tax if the amount of tax exceeds the donor's basis in the transferred property. Diedrich v. Comm'r, 457 US 191 (1982). There is an application of the part-gift, part-sale rules of Regulations Section 1.1015-4. Cf. Johnson v. Comm'r, 495 F2d 1079 (6th Cir.), cert. denied, 419 US 1040 (1974). See also Lefter, "Income Tax Consequences of Encumbered Gifts: The Advent of *Crane*," 28 U. Fla. L. Rev. 935 (1976); Ward, "Taxation of Gratuitous Transfers of Encumbered Property, Partial Sales and Section 677(a)," 63 Iowa L.

cover taxes under Section 2207A, the determination of the amount of taxes recoverable and thus also the determination of the value of the remainder interest treated as transferred under Section 2519 should be made by using the same interrelated computation applicable for other transfers in which the transferee assumes the gift tax liability (commonly referred to as net gifts).[182] This rule applies also if the transfer is to a trust pursuant to an agreement that the trustee will pay the tax.[183] A donee's payment of the donor's gift tax merely voluntarily, without any agreement express or implied, effects no reduction in the amount of the donor's gift,[184] and similarly, a donee's payment required under the donee's secondary liability does not reduce the amount of the gift.[185] If the amount of the donor's gift is reduced by the amount of the tax, a difficult computational problem arises, because the taxable value of the gift is dependent on the amount of the tax, which in turn is dependent on the value of the

Rev. 823, 857 (1978); Duhl & Cohen, "The Net Gift Technique: A Current Analysis of the Requirements for Its Successful Use," 42 J. Tax'n 158 (1975); Rief, "Donee-Paid Gift Tax: Some Considerations," 48 ABA J 1325 (1972).

[182] See ¶ 8.07[4] text accompanying note 34, ¶ 10.08[1][a] note 16.

[183] Lingo v. Comm'r, 13 TCM (CCH) 436 (1954); Harrison v. Comm'r, 17 TC 1350 (1952), acq. 1952-2 CB 2. However, if the gift tax is or may be payable out of the future trust income, the donor may incur income tax liability as payments are made. Compare Sheaffer's Estate v. Comm'r, 313 F2d 738 (8th Cir.), cert. denied, 375 US 818 (1963), and Krause v. Comm'r, 56 TC 1242 (1971) with Estate of Davis v. Comm'r, 30 TCM (CCH) 1363 (1971), aff'd per curiam, 469 F2d 694 (5th Cir. 1972). In *Krause*, the donors transferred income-producing securities to a trust with an agreement that the trustee would pay the gift taxes. The trustee borrowed money to pay the gift taxes. The Tax Court held that only dividends accruing up until the paying of the gift tax were taxable to the donor, relying on Section 671, and once the gift tax had been paid, the grantor was not taxed on any further income because the grantor had no further obligation to which the income could be applied. Cf. Davis v. United States, 378 F. Supp. 579 (ND Tex. 1974); "Tax Consequences of Gifts of Encumbered Property in Trust," 8 Real Prop., Prob. & Tr. J. 371 (1973). Moreover, if the donor has retained the right to have trust income applied to discharge the donor's tax obligation and the donor dies prior to the full payment of the gift tax, a part of the corpus of the trust may be included in the donor's gross estate under Section 2036. See IRC § 2035(b); Estate of Sachs v. Comm'r, 88 TC 769 (1987).

[184] Affelder v. Comm'r, 7 TC 1190 (1946).

[185] Moore v. Comm'r, 146 F2d 824 (2d Cir. 1945). The *Moore* case involved a solvent donor; it might be possible to find an implied agreement that the donee would pay the gift tax if the donor were insolvent. See Kopp, "Gifts Subject to Donee Payment of Tax: Timing, Risks, and Computations," 27 NYU Inst. on Fed. Tax'n 375, 378 (1969); Rief, "Donee-Paid Gift Tax: Some Considerations," 48 ABA J. 1325 (1972); Lowenstein, "Federal Tax Implications of Gifts Net of Gift Tax," 50 Taxes 525 (1972). See also Armstrong, Jr. Trust v. United States, 87 AFTR2d 2001-707 (2001) (the donee liability for gift tax contingent on value of property gifted to speculative to reduce value of gift).

gift and a cyclical problem occurs. However, the Service has advanced an algebraic formula for the solution of the problem.[186]

Although the foregoing discussion deals with a transferee's payment of the donor's gift tax, in point of fact the transferee's agreement to discharge any obligation of the transferor may reduce the amount of a gift,[187] subject to the question whether the assumed obligation is susceptible to valuation.

In all these circumstances in which consideration for a transfer is treated as reducing or eliminating a gift, the equilibrium of the estate that is potentially subject to estate tax is not disturbed. Either (1) an asset of money's worth has come in to replace what went out of the estate or (2) an obligation that would have been deductible in determining the taxable estate has been discharged. This twofold test can be applied as at least a general guide to the gift tax meaning of "consideration."[188]

¶ 10.03 SECTION 2513. GIFTS BY HUSBAND OR WIFE TO THIRD PARTY

[1] Introduction

The so-called split-gift provision came into the gift tax law in 1948 at the same time the estate and gift tax marital deduction provisions and the split-income provision were added to the Code.[1] This section was part of the 1948 congressional effort to equalize the tax treatment in community property and common-law states of transactions involving married persons.[2]

Under Section 2513(a), if a married person makes a gift to someone other than a spouse, the donor and the donor's spouse can elect to have the gift treated as if made one-half by each of them instead of as a gift made entirely

---

[186] Rev. Rul. 75-72, 1975-1 CB 310, 311. See also Rev. Ruls. 76-49, 1976-1 CB 294; 76-57, 1976-1 CB 297; Publication 904, Interrelated Computations for Estate and Gift Taxes (May 1985), Pt. III, Gift Tax. See also Publication 448, Federal Estate and Gift Taxes (Aug. 1992), Gifts in General, 31.

[187] See Harrison v. Comm'r, 17 TC 1350 (1952), acq. 1952-2 CB 2 (value of gift reduced by the trustee's obligation to pay the donor's income tax).

[188] Rev. Rul. 68-379, 1968-2 CB 414, includes a basic expression of the underlying philosophy in the context of relinquishment of support rights as consideration for a transfer.

[1] Revenue Act of 1948, Pub. L. No. 80-475, § 374, 62 Stat. 110, 127 (1948). It is effective as regards gifts made after April 2, 1948.

[2] Revenue Act of 1948, Pub. L. No. 80-475, § 374, 62 Stat. 110, 127 (1948). See ¶¶ 5.06, 11.03.

by the actual donor. Section 2513(b), discussed here, describes how the election is to be made.

The benefits of this provision are available only if both spouses are either citizens or residents of the United States; neither a nonresident noncitizen with a citizen spouse nor a citizen with a nonresident noncitizen spouse is permitted to make the election. The requisites of marital status and citizenship or residence are determined at the time of the gift.[3] A donor cannot split gifts made in the calendar year of but before the donor's marriage; nor can the donor split gifts made in any portion of a year in which the donor or the donor's spouse failed to meet the citizenship or residence requirement.[4] In the year of divorce or of the death of one spouse, gifts made before divorce or before death can be split, provided the surviving spouse does not remarry or, in the case of divorce, that neither spouse remarries in that calendar year.[5] Although gifts made after death cannot be split,[6] it is clear that gifts followed shortly by the death of a spouse can be split, subject to some questions with respect to consent that are discussed later.[7]

Community property gets no special mention anywhere in Section 2513, which at first may seem strange. An effect of the community property laws is to accomplish the gift splitting that is permitted by Section 2513 for taxpayers in the common-law states. Because the provision is aimed at equalizing the tax treatment of married taxpayers operating under the two different systems, it might seem that the section should be expressly made inapplicable to community property. But lack of reference to community property does not stem from inadvertence. As regards community property itself, an election under Section 2513 would not alter the tax result; if each spouse is treated as owning one half of the property that is the subject of a gift, an election under which each must treat one spouse's gift as made one-half by the other spouse will still leave each spouse making a gift of one half of the property. If the gift is of separate property, even though in a community property state, there is no reason to deny the benefit of the gift-splitting provision if the property in question did not emerge from a tax-free division or similar conversion of community

---

[3] Rev. Rul. 73-207, 1973-1 CB 409.

[4] Reg. § 25.2513-1(b)(2). Throughout Section 2513, with respect to gifts made after 1970 and prior to 1982, the applicable period is the calendar quarter rather than the calendar year.

[5] Reg. §§ 25.2513-1(a), 25.2513-1(b)(1).

[6] Rev. Ruls. 73-207, 1973-1 CB 409; 55-506, 1955-2 CB 609; Reg. § 25.2513-1(b)(1). A lifetime transfer by a married person may become a completed gift by the surviving spouse at the time of the death of the other spouse. As the decedent ceases to exist "at the time of the gift," the marital relationship ceases to exist at the death and, in addition, the decedent is probably not a "citizen or resident" at the crucial time, and such gifts do not qualify for splitting.

[7] Cf. Rev. Rul. 55-334, 1955-1 CB 449.

property.[8] As the split-gift provision makes no common-law, community property differentiation, the Treasury appropriately recognizes the application of the section to any separate property in a community property state.[9] The simplicity of the result may be applauded.[10]

Although the section is inapplicable unless a gift is made to someone other than a spouse, it will sometimes come into play in cases in which a single transfer includes a gift to the spouse and to third parties as well. For example, a gift in trust, the income to be paid to the donor's spouse for life, remainder to their children or the children's estates, is such a gift. The value of the interest transferred to the spouse cannot be split, but the value of the children's remainder can.[11] The only serious question in such circumstances is whether the value of the gift to the third party or parties is susceptible to valuation.[12] It clearly would be in the simple example given, because the value of the life and remainder interests can be fixed by the use of actuarial principles. And it may be even if the trust corpus can be invaded for the benefit of the life beneficiary spouse if such invasion may be undertaken only pursuant to a fixed standard, such as for the spouse's maintenance and support.[13] But if the value of the interest passing to third parties cannot be arrived at in some such accepted fashion, the split-gift provision cannot be applied because there is no way to fix the amount of the gift that is subject to the section.[14] The statute expressly denies gift splitting in one such circumstance: If in the preceding example, the donee spouse were given a general power of appointment over the trust corpus in addition to the life interest, Section 2513(a)(1) makes the section inapplicable. This provision seems almost unnecessary, because the existence of such a power in the donee spouse would make the value of the remainder merely conjectural.

---

[8] For all federal tax purposes, separate property owned by, and originating with, a community property spouse is the same as property owned outright by a spouse in a common-law state.

[9] E.g., Rev. Rul. 53-146, 1953-2 CB 292.

[10] If spouses effect a tax-free division of community property into the separate property of each and then one spouse gives that spouse's entire share to C, that spouse has parted with that spouse's entire interest in the property while the other spouse has retained the other share. This is quite different from a gift of one-half the community property itself to C, and yet the tax result to the spouses can be the same under Section 2513. However, the community property versus noncommunity property distinction is no longer relevant under Sections 2056 and 2523, and this hypothetical no longer creates even a philosophical problem. See ¶ 5.06[1].

[11] Robertson v. Comm'r, 26 TC 246 (1956), acq. 1956-2 CB 8.

[12] Reg. § 25.2513-1(b)(4); Falk v. Comm'r, 24 TCM (CCH) 86 (1965).

[13] Robertson v. Comm'r, 26 TC 246 (1956), acq. 1956-2 CB 8.

[14] Reg. § 25.2513-1(b)(4); Wang v. Comm'r, 31 TCM (CCH) 719 (1972); Kass v. Comm'r, 16 TCM (CCH) 1035 (1957); Rev. Rul. 56-439, 1956-2 CB 605.

Paragraph (2) of Section 2513(a) requires the consent of both spouses as a condition to the application of the section; this will be discussed further in connection with the method of giving consent under Section 2513(b). But Section 2513(a)(2) also specifies that the election, if made, applies to all gifts made during the calendar year[15] while the spouses are married to each other. It has previously been explained that the section is inoperative as regards gifts made while persons are not married; the significant point here is that the election cannot be made to apply only to specified gifts. It applies to all gifts that can come within the section made by either spouse in the year in question. An effective election to treat the donor's gifts as made one-half by the donor's spouse necessitates a similar treatment of the spouse's gifts for the same year.[16] However, the opportunity to elect arises afresh each year; an election one year does not bind the spouses to split-gift treatment for gifts made in others.[17]

Application of the section is not dependent on the consenting spouse having any interest whatever in the gift property. Thus, a prenuptial agreement under which each spouse waives all marital rights in the other's property does not preclude election of the split-gift provision.[18] It is unnecessary for the nondonor spouse to have any property at all; the election can still be made. The section must be viewed simply as permitting an artificial assumption quite contrary to fact as a part of the determination of gift tax liability. If both spouses have an interest in the gift property, but unequal interests, the election equalizes their interests solely for the purpose of the tax computation.

[2] Effect of Election

An important consequence of Section 2513 when its benefits are elected is to bring to bear on a gift made by one spouse, or partly by both spouses, the exclusions and credits of both spouses. A simple example will illustrate this result. After 2001, Donor, who has not previously made consequential gifts, could give Child $1,011,000 in cash in one calendar year without paying gift tax.[19] The first $11,000 would be excluded by Section 2503(b), discussed in

---

[15] As to gifts subsequent to December 31, 1970, and prior to January 1, 1982, the section applied to all gifts made during a calendar quarter. Reg. §§ 25.2502-1(c)(1), 25.2513-2(a)(1).

[16] Reg. § 25.2513-1(b)(5); Rev. Rul. 53-146, 1953-2 CB 292. See TAM 200147021 (July 31, 2001) (Section 2515 deemed gift is split between spouses under Section 2513 election).

[17] Reg. § 25.2513-1(b).

[18] Rev. Rul. 55-241, 1955-1 CB 470.

[19] The example assumes that the donor has not previously made any consequential gifts (i.e., taxable gifts). If the donor had made pre-1977 taxable gifts, those gifts would

Chapter 9. The remaining $1 million, potentially subject to tax, could be offset by the credit under Section 2505, also discussed in Chapter 9. If Donor's spouse has also never before made consequential gifts and each spouse has the Section 2505 credit intact, Donor could make a gift of $2,022,000 to Child in one year without tax by resort to the split-gift election. That is, the election will bring into play the spouse's exclusion and credit even though the gift is in fact solely that of the donor.

In some circumstances, the tax rate advantage will be greater than the other advantages just suggested. The graduated tax rates provided by Section 2001(c) and incorporated into the gift tax by Section 2502 are explained in Chapter 9. In general,[20] $1.5 million in taxable gifts would encounter higher rates than $1.5 million in gifts treated as taxable gifts in part by each of two donors. A comparison of some of the rates in the table in Section 2001(c) will indicate the amount of tax that can be saved by virtue of the split-gift provision. On the other hand, an election could backfire. If the donor spouse has never before made consequential gifts, but the nondonor spouse has made substantial gifts that will result in the donor's further gifts being subjected to very high rates, the election obviously should not be made.[21]

It should be emphasized that the split-gift provision is not simply an authorization to file joint gift tax returns. If a donor has fully utilized the donor's Section 2505 credit and the nondonor spouse still has the full credit intact, it might appear that a further gift by the donor could be offset by the nondonor spouse's credit. All the statute permits, however, is for such a gift to be treated as made one-half by each spouse. Thus, disregarding exclusions, one half of such a gift will be taxed to the donor and only the other half can be relieved of tax by the nondonor spouse's credit.[22]

When the benefits of Section 2513 are invoked, both spouses are jointly and severally liable for the entire gift tax of each spouse for the year. Section 2513(d) expressly so provides. Thus, no gift tax liability results from either spouse's full discharge of such liability.[23]

---

increase the rate of tax on post-1976 taxable gifts, reducing the scope of the exemption potential of the applicable credit amount for post-1976 gifts. See IRC § 2502(a), discussed ¶ 9.03[3]. The example also assumes that the Section 2503(b) annual exclusion has been adjusted for inflation. See IRC § 2503(b)(2); ¶ 9.04[1].

[20] See ¶ 9.03[2]. This comment is not correct if the transfers are made in the year 2010 when taxable gifts are subject to a flat 35 percent tax rate. See ¶ 9.03[2] text accompanying note 10.

[21] See Littenberg, "Gift Splitting as a Tax Planning Device: Advantages and Drawbacks," 27 NYU Inst. on Fed. Tax'n 355 (1969). See also Weiss & Etkin, "New Law Overhauls Estate and Gift Taxes, Triggering New Planning Strategies," 55 J. Tax'n 274 (1981).

[22] Cf. Rev. Rul. 54-30, 1954-1 CB 207.

[23] Reg. § 25.2511-1(d); TAM 9128009 (Mar. 29, 1991).

If the election is made to split gifts made after 1976 in the year of the donor's death and the executor pays the entire gift tax, the estate is entitled to deduct the entire amount of the tax paid as a tax accrued prior to death under Section 2053,[24] but is, of course, required to "gross up" (include the amount of the tax in the decedent donor's gross estate) under Section 2035(b),[25] creating a wash situation. The gross-up can be avoided by having the donor's spouse pay the tax.[26] This may seem again to be a mere wash situation as the donor decedent's estate would sacrifice the Section 2053 deduction to avoid the Section 2035(b) gross-up. However, if the gift is included in the decedent's gross estate,[27] tax paid by the nondonor spouse *would* reduce tax payable by the donor decedent's estate, as Section 2001(d) permits that payment to be treated as "tax payable" under Section 2001(b)(2) in the estate tax computation. The tax payment reduces the nondonor spouse's estate by the amount of the tax; it does not constitute a gift by the nondonor spouse; and, if the nondonor spouse lives three years, the tax paid will not be brought back into the nondonor spouse's estate by Section 2035(b). Consequently, the payment of the gift tax by the nondonor spouse has the advantage of reducing the donor's estate tax at the same time that it effects a transfer tax advantage for the family unit by way of a tax-free reduction of the survivor's estate.

Suppose it is the nondonor spouse who dies survived by the donor, and the nondonor spouse's estate consents to the split-gift provision and pays the entire tax. The consent "does not operate to create a liability retroactive to the date of [the nondonor spouse's] death."[28] In such circumstances, the nondonor spouse's estate is required to include the amount of the tax under Section 2035(b), but is entitled to no Section 2053 deduction for the gift tax.[29] Here, however, gross-up can be avoided if the executor makes the requisite split-gift election but the donor pays the gift tax. This gets back to the "wash" effect previously suggested, as the gross-up is avoided without gaining any estate tax deduction—or actual reduction by way of tax payment.

Suppose the donor spouse makes a gift and the nondonor spouse consents to the election of Section 2513 to have one half of the gift attributed to the nondonor, the nondonor using part or all of the nondonor's Section 2505 credit. Then the donor dies within three years of making the gift, and the do-

---

[24] Rev. Rul. 55-334, 1955-1 CB 449.

[25] The gross-up includes amounts paid by the decedent donor's "estate." See ¶ 4.07[3].

[26] See IRC § 2035(b); ¶ 4.07[3].

[27] See IRC § 2035 and especially IRC §§ 2035(a)(1), 2035(a)(2), discussed ¶¶ 4.07[2][a][i], 4.07[2][a][ii].

[28] Rev. Rul. 70-600, 1970-2 CB 194, 195.

[29] This results in double inclusion in the nondonor spouse's gross estate that can be avoided by the executor's not agreeing to pay either one-half or all of the gift tax liability arising from the Section 2513 election. Cf. Rev. Rul. 82-198, 1982-2 CB 206.

nor's gift is includible in the donor's gross estate.[30] In one such case, the nondonor argued that as the gift was includible in the donor's gross estate, the nondonor's credit[31] was "ineffectively utilized" and should be restored to the nondonor. The Fourth Circuit[32] properly held that the nondonor was not entitled to the restoration of the nondonor's credit.[33] The result has received congressional approval.[34] The fact that the gift was includible in the gross estate of the donor and subjected to estate tax did not mean that there was not also a transfer subject to gift tax against which the nondonor had used the nondonor's credit. This is a sad story, because the survivor's gift tax credit is wasted. The gift tax "saved" by its use might have fully reduced the estate tax liability of the decedent's estate[35] so that, overall, no more transmission tax would have been paid if the survivor's credit had been kept intact to offset future gifts.

There is a related problem. The survivor's unprofitable loss of credit against future gift tax is clear enough; will the profligate use of the credit have a corresponding adverse effect on estate tax payable on the *survivor's* estate? Not under the present scheme of things. No gift of the *survivor* escaped tax by use of the credit; and under Section 2001(e), no part of the gift will be included in the survivor's adjusted taxable gifts so as to increase the survivor's estate tax rate.[36] If the survivor's future gifts produce more gift tax "payable" because some of the credit was "wasted," that gift tax liability is nevertheless an offset against potential estate tax under Section 2001(b)(2). Thus, the "lost" credit will adversely affect only gift tax liability as regards the survivor.[37]

---

[30] See IRC § 2035 and especially IRC §§ 2035(a)(1), 2035(a)(2), discussed ¶ 4.07[2][a]. Cf. IRC § 2001(d)(2).

[31] Because the case involved a year prior to 1977, the issue involved the nondonor's use of the Section 2521 $30,000 specific exemption. Nevertheless, the same principles apply to use of the credit.

[32] Ingalls v. Comm'r, 336 F2d 874 (4th Cir. 1964). Accord, English v. United States, 284 F. Supp. 256 (ND Fla. 1968); Norair v. Comm'r, 65 TC 942 (1976).

[33] See supra note 31.

[34] HR Rep. No. 1380, 94th Cong., 2d Sess. 13 (1976), reprinted in 1976-3 CB (Vol. 3) 737.

[35] IRC § 2001(b)(2). For transfers prior to 1977, see IRC § 2012.

[36] See Rev. Rul. 81-85, 1981-1 CB 452. Cf. Rev. Rul. 82-198, 1982-2 CB 206.

[37] For a discussion of the interrelationship of Sections 2505 and 2513, see Schoenblum, "Working With the Unified Credit," 15 Miami Inst. on Est. Plan. Chapter 14, at 1404.5, 1404.6 (1981).

[3] Signifying Consent

[a] Manner

Section 2513(b) leaves the manner of signifying consent to have gifts by both spouses treated as made one-half by each to be spelled out in the regulations. Both spouses must consent and the gift tax return affords space in which to signify consent of the donor and "consent of spouse."[38] The regulations provide as follows:

> If both spouses file gift tax returns within the time for signifying consent, it is sufficient if (i) The consent of the husband is signified on the wife's return, and the consent of the wife is signified on the husband's return; (ii) The consent of each spouse is signified on his own return; or (iii) The consent of both spouses is signified on one of the returns.[39]

The Treasury has ruled that if each spouse executes the donor's consent on the donor's own return but each fails to execute his or her consent on the other's return, both spouses have signified their consent within the requirements of the statute and the split-gift provision applies.[40]

From the tax standpoint alone, it is clear that an executor can execute the consent of a decedent to bring the split-gift provision into play;[41] and the same is true of a guardian or committee of a legally incompetent spouse.[42] Such authority often exists as a rule under local law. It is possible that a recalcitrant

---

[38] Form 709, United States Gift (and Generation-Skipping Transfer) Tax Return (2001) at 1. See Nordstrom v. United States, 79 AFTR2d 97-612 (ND Iowa 1997) (no summary judgment denying gift splitting where applicable line on Form 709 was not answered "yes"). The Service allows an alternative Form 709A, United States Short Form Gift Tax Return (Rev. Nov. 2000) to be used generally if Section 2513 is applicable and all gifts, other than those qualifying for the marital deduction, do not exceed $22,000 per donee and are gifts of present interests in tangible personal property, cash, or listed stocks and bonds.

[39] Reg. § 25.2513-2(a)(1).

[40] Rev. Rul. 188, 1953-2 CB 292. Compare Rev. Rul. 54-6, 1954-1 CB 205 (regarding one spouse as the agent signifying consent of other), and Jones v. Comm'r, 327 F2d 98 (4th Cir. 1964) (where the wife failed to sign the husband's return signifying consent, but Section 2513 splitting was permitted because of intent of all parties to include the wife's consent) with Rev. Rul. 78-27, 1978-1 CB 387.

[41] Rev. Rul. 55-334, 1955-1 CB 449; Reg. § 25.2513-2(c). In limited circumstances where there is no executor or administrator of the estate, the decedent's spouse may make the election. Rev. Rul. 67-55, 1967-1 CB 278.

[42] Reg. § 25.2513-2(c).

executor can be compelled to signify consent to the election of the split-gift provision.[43]

[b] Time

In keeping with the requirement that gift tax returns be filed only after the end of the calendar year in which gifts were made, Section 2513(b)(2) requires the consent to be made after the close of the calendar year. After that time, the consent must be signified on or before April 15, except that, if neither spouse has filed a return by that time, the time for signifying consent is extended until either spouse files. It is important to recognize that the right to split gifts can be lost entirely if a return without consent is filed and the usual filing date passes with no election having been made or if, where neither spouse has filed on time, a late return is filed without the requisite consent.[44] To these hazards the statute expressly adds one other. The election cannot be made after a notice of deficiency has been sent to either spouse with respect to gift tax liability for the year in question.[45] The reference here is to the statutory deficiency notice;[46] there may be an opportunity to make the election after the receipt of a preliminary notice such as the "thirty-day letter."[47]

[c] Revocation

Section 2513(c) leaves it to the regulations to specify how a consent to split gifts can be revoked. The regulations specify that either spouse can revoke by filing with the District Director of Internal Revenue in duplicate a signed statement of revocation.[48] However, the statute indicates that an election under the section cannot be revoked after April 15 following the year in which the gifts were made[49] and that an election made after that date is irrevocable.[50]

---

[43] Cf. Floyd Estate (No. 2), 76 Pa. D&C 597 (1951), requiring the executor to file income tax return with the surviving spouse on ground that the refusal was unreasonable and arbitrary.

[44] Thorrez v. Comm'r, 31 TC 655 (1958), aff'd, 272 F2d 945 (6th Cir. 1959); Clark v. Comm'r, 65 TC 126 (1975); McLean v. United States, 79-1 USTC ¶ 13,293 (ND Cal. 1979); Rev. Rul. 80-224, 1980-2 CB 281. Cf. Rev. Rul. 78-27, 1978-1 CB 387.

[45] IRC § 2513(b)(2)(B).

[46] See IRC § 6212(a), authorizing the issuance of such notice. Cf. Rev. Proc. 98-54, 1998-2 CB 529, for rescission of such a notice.

[47] Cf. Estate of Gillespie v. Comm'r, 103 TC 395 (1994) (a thirty-day letter does not constitute a notice of deficiency for purposes of Section 7430 (awarding of costs and certain fees)).

[48] Reg. § 25.2513-3.

[49] IRC § 2513(c)(1).

[50] IRC § 2513(c)(2).

[4] Effect of Election on Return Requirement

Some comments on when a gift tax return must be filed were made in Chapter 9, because of the way in which the annual exclusion bears on that question.[51] Section 2513 may also be relevant. When elected, it is obviously taken into account to determine a taxpayer's "taxable gifts" for a year.[52]

¶ 10.04 SECTION 2514. POWERS OF APPOINTMENT

[1] Introduction

A power of appointment is a unique legal concept. One who has it does not, merely because of it, have an interest in the property under established property law and tax law principles.[1] The problem to which Section 2514 is addressed is whether a power holder may make a transfer subject to gift tax by some action or inaction that, because of his power, effects a shifting of interests in the property subject to the power. Because the power holder as such has no property interest, the holder's action or inaction cannot result in a conventional transfer of the holder's property; but, just as in the case of the estate tax, Congress has determined that in some circumstances for gift tax purposes the shifting of interests under the power should be treated as a transfer of property by the power holder.

The gift tax significance of the exercise, release, or lapse of a power of appointment is determined by Section 2514, which closely parallels Section 2041, the corresponding estate tax section on powers. The effect of a disclaimer of a power of appointment is determined by Section 2518. Both Sections 2041 and 2514, in approximately their present forms, originated in the Powers of Appointment Act of 1951.[2] Moreover, as in other areas, this gift tax provision backstops the estate tax, and lifetime efforts to escape the estate tax frying pan may put one in the gift tax fire. The extended discussion of the es-

---

[51] See ¶ 9.04[9].

[52] See supra ¶ 10.03[3][a] note 38.

[1] See discussion of Section 2033 at ¶ 4.05[5][c] text accompanying note 65 and the introduction to the discussion of Section 2041 at ¶ 4.13[1]. It is possible, however, that one who is the owner of property may make a gift tax transfer of the property by giving another a power over the property. See discussion of Section 2511 at ¶ 10.01[9]. But this is not because the new power holder has acquired a property interest; it is because the owner has effectively transferred an actual interest by relinquishing to another all dominion and control over the property, which is the essence of a gift for gift tax purposes.

[2] Powers of Appointment Act of 1951, Pub. L. No. 58, Chapter 165, 65 Stat. 91 (1951), reprinted in 1951-2 CB 343.

tate tax powers of appointment in Chapter 4 justifies abbreviating the treatment here of some parallel aspects of the gift tax provision.

With one minor exception,[3] Section 2514 is operative only with regard to transactions involving general powers of appointment. However, the applicability of the section may depend on when the power was created. The critical date, familiar from the estate tax provisions, is October 21, 1942. In the discussion that follows, a power created on or before that date is referred to as a pre-1942 power; powers created after that date are referred to as post-1942 powers. The later-created powers are treated differently in two respects: (1) different rules apply in determining whether the power is general and (2) different rules apply in determining the tax consequences of transactions involving powers properly classified as general.[4]

As the question whether a power is general is crucial to the applicability of Section 2514, Section 2514(c), defining "general powers," is considered first. It is essential to keep in mind that the exercise or termination of some powers accorded no significance for gift or estate tax purposes may result in a generation-skipping transfer subject to tax under Chapter 13.[5]

[2] General Power

[a] General Rule

The gift tax definition of a "general power" exactly parallels the estate tax definition.[6] One who has a power of appointment is referred to in the statute as the "possessor" of the power. The basic rule is that a general power is one that can be exercised in favor of the possessor of the power, the possessor's estate, the possessor's creditors, or the creditors of the possessor's estate. The power is general if it can be exercised in favor of any of such appointees; it is not

---

[3] IRC § 2514(d). See infra ¶ 10.04[5].

[4] Ordinarily a power is created on the date it becomes effective, but the statute in Section 2514(f) provides one special rule on the time of creation. If a power was created by a will executed on or before October 21, 1942, and if the testator died before July 1, 1949, without republishing the will by codicil or otherwise after October 21, 1942, the power is to be treated as a pre-1942 power, even though it became effective only at a later date upon the testator's death. A power created by an inter vivos instrument is considered as created on the date the instrument takes effect, even if the instrument is revocable. Reg. § 25.2514-1(e).

[5] See Chapters 12–18, especially ¶ 13.02[2][e][iii].

[6] A more extended discussion appears in the treatment of Section 2041 at ¶¶ 4.13[3], 4.13[4].

necessary that it be exercisable in favor of all of them.[7] But there are significant exceptions to the basic rule.

[b] Exceptions

Three numbered paragraphs under Section 2514(c) state the exceptions to the basic rule. The first paragraph applies to a power that can be exercised in favor of the possessor. Although such a power is generally within the basic rule, it is not treated as general if its exercise is restricted by an ascertainable standard relating to the possessor's health, education, support, or maintenance. This exception applies alike to both pre-1942 and post-1942 powers.[8]

The second paragraph applies only to pre-1942 powers. Such powers are not general if they can be exercised only in conjunction with another person. Thus, if the possessor of a pre-1942 power has no right to exercise it alone, the possessor does not have a general power regardless of who may be a permissible appointee.

The third paragraph applies only to post-1942 powers as the statute so specifies. In light of the exception just discussed, its application to pre-1942 powers would be meaningless anyway. It is divided into three subparagraphs. Under (A), a power is not general if it can be exercised only with the creator of the power. Under (B), a power is not general if it can be exercised only with one who has a substantial interest in the property subject to the power that would be adversely affected by an exercise of the power in favor of the possessor. Under (C), a power that is still a general power after applying the (A) and (B) exceptions is a general power as it pertains to only a portion of the property subject to the power, if others who must join in an exercise of the power are permissible appointees. These exceptions, which present their fair share of difficulties, are discussed in some detail in Chapter 4.[9]

[3] Treatment of Pre-1942 Powers

The special tax definition of a "general power," previously indicated, must, of course, be borne in mind in the discussion that follows. As previously indicated, pre-1942 and post-1942 powers must be considered separately. Section 2514(a), dealing with pre-1942 powers, is taken up first.

---

[7] For example, Regulations Section 25.2514-1(c)(1), treating a power as general if it can be exercised to meet the estate tax on the possessor's estate.

[8] Difficulties in the application of this exception are considered in the discussion of Section 2041 at ¶ 4.13[4][a]. With specific regard to the gift tax, compare Regulations Section 86.2(b)(3)(ii) with Regulations Section 25.2514-1(c)(2). See Rev. Rul. 76-547, 1976-2 CB 302.

[9] See ¶ 4.13[4].

[a] Exercise

The statute provides that the exercise of a pre-1942 general power shall be deemed a transfer of property.[10] In this manner, for gift tax purposes, Congress overrides the conventional concept of a power. When the statutory rule applies, we pretend (1) that the power holder has an interest in the property and (2) that the power holder transferred the interest.

It is important to recall, however, that not every transfer of property constitutes a gift subject to tax and that Section 2514, in isolation, does not contain all the law on the gift tax significance of an exercise of a pre-1942 general power. For example, B may be the life beneficiary of a trust created by another, with R as the remainderperson, and B may have as well a power to amend the trust in any way B wishes, even for B's own benefit.[11] If B during B's life appoints the remainder to C, B has exercised a general power of appointment and the statute makes this a transfer of property. But other gift tax principles must be applied to determine whether the transfer is a taxable gift. If B still retains the power to amend so that B could at any time defeat C's interest and name a different remainderperson, the transfer to C is incomplete,[12] for B has not relinquished dominion and control. In a like vein, if B altered the terms of the trust to give B a right to invade corpus during B's life and then appointed the trust corpus to B, this might constitute a "transfer" in that a general power had been exercised; but a transfer to the possessor of the power is not a gift by the possessor because one cannot make a gift to oneself. If B exercised B's power over the trust irrevocably in C's favor but received consideration from C, the amount of B's gift would be reduced by any consideration received.[13] Finally, if B could and did exercise B's power only at death by way of a provision in B's will, no transfer subject to gift tax would result; the gift tax applies only to transfers by living donors.[14] Enough has been said to indicate that Section 2514(a) undertakes to state only what transactions with respect to pre-1942 general powers constitute transfers; other principles must be considered to determine whether such transfers constitute gifts.

---

[10] As subsequently explained, a pre-1942 power is without gift tax significance unless it is exercised.

[11] While not termed a "power of appointment," B's power is treated as such (Reg. § 25.2514-1(b)(1)), and as long as B may exercise the power for B's own benefit, the power is a general power. IRC § 2514(c).

[12] Sanford's Estate v. Comm'r, 308 US 39 (1939).

[13] Cf. Estate of Campbell v. Comm'r, 59 TC 133 (1972) (involving a post-1942 power). In *Campbell*, the taxpayer sold what the taxpayer thought was a life estate realizing the fair market value for that interest; however, under local law, the taxpayer held a general power over the property and effectively transferred full ownership, and the excess value of the property over the consideration that the taxpayer received was held to be a taxable gift.

[14] Reg. § 25.2511-2(f).

[b] Release

Section 2514 also specifies that neither a failure to exercise nor the complete release of a pre-1942 power is to be treated as an exercise of the power. It is in this provision that the principal difference in the treatment of pre-1942 and post-1942 powers is found, as explained here. Section 2514(a) goes on to close what otherwise might be a loophole.

If a release of a power is not an exercise and only the exercise of a general power is a transfer, it might appear possible to convert a general power to a nongeneral power by way of a partial release and then to exercise the nongeneral power without adverse gift tax consequences. At least by implication, the statute indicates that such a step transaction will be telescoped and treated as the exercise of a general power, and the regulations state this rule affirmatively.[15]

There may be circumstances in which a nontaxable exercise of a general power followed by a complete release will constitute a taxable gift. The regulations contain the following example:

[A]ssume that A created a trust in 1940 providing for payment of the income to B for life with the power in B to amend the trust, and for payment of the remainder to such persons as B shall appoint or, upon default of appointment, to C. If B amended the trust in 1948 by providing that upon his death the remainder was to be paid to D, and if he further amended the trust in 1955 by deleting his power to amend the trust, such relinquishment will be considered an exercise and not a release of a general power of appointment.[16]

The principle is sound and the illustration appropriate. B's 1948 amendment would not be a taxable transfer for, as explained earlier, B would not have given up control. But on these facts, the subsequent release should be regarded as a taxable exercise of B's power.[17] The question, properly raised in general

---

[15] Reg. § 25.2514-2(d). The only exception, which is recognized by the statute, is that a pre-1942 general power can effectively be converted into a nongeneral power if the conversion is made before November 1, 1951, or within six months after the termination of a disability that on October 21, 1942, prevented such conversion. The exception is of diminishing importance. See IRC § 2041, discussed ¶ 4.13[6].

[16] Reg. § 25.2514-2(c).

[17] In proposed regulations first published after enactment of the 1954 Code, the statement of this illustration was erroneous because B's 1948 amendment simply purported to make C the remainder person. Although B then assured C's remainder interest by B's 1955 release, B could have accomplished precisely the same thing by an outright release without the 1948 amendment of the trust. However, if B amends in 1948 to replace C by D as remainder person and then releases the power, there is a shifting in beneficial interests that justifies treating the seeming release as an exercise of the power.

terms in the regulations, is whether "the relinquishment results in the reduction, enlargement, or shift in a beneficial interest in property."[18]

[c] Partial Exercise

The need to resort to gift tax principles not spelled out in Section 2514 itself is further illustrated by a partial exercise of a power. If *B* has a general lifetime power over a trust that *B* exercises by directing the trustee to distribute one-half the corpus to *C*, *B* has exercised the power and made a transfer subject to tax. But, of course, *B* is treated as having transferred only one-half the trust corpus and the value of that half is the amount of the gift.[19]

[d] Ineffective Exercise

If the statute makes the exercise of a general power a transfer, is the action of the appointee inconsequential? What if the appointee renounces or refuses to accept the property? The answer should be that there was only an attempt to make the transfer if, in fact, a renunciation leaves the possessor of the power precisely where the possessor was before. Nevertheless, history seems to be against this view; the Revenue Act of 1942 eliminated for estate tax purposes any requirement that property pass under an exercised power.[20] Furthermore, the estate tax decisions hold that a power is exercised at death and is subject to estate tax even if the appointee renounces[21] or if the exercise is essentially a nullity because it was made in favor of takers in default.[22] Should such estate tax history and decisions govern the gift tax approach? They should not.

The gift tax regulations adopt the view that there is a taxable transfer upon exercise of a pre-1942 power even if "the exercise is in favor of the taker in default . . . or . . . the appointee renounces any right to take under the appointment."[23] It is difficult to believe, however, that Congress undertook to tax "a mere gesture possessing no legal significance."[24] In the case of the estate tax, there is a cessation of the possessor's dominion over the property at the possessor's death that, whether appointees subsequently accept or reject the

---

[18] Reg. § 25.2514-2(c).

[19] Reg. § 25.2514-2(e).

[20] See ¶ 4.13[6].

[21] Wilson v. Kraemer, 97 F. Supp. 627 (D. Conn. 1950), aff'd, 190 F2d 341 (2d Cir.), cert. denied, 342 US 859 (1951).

[22] Keating v. Mayer, 236 F2d 478 (3d Cir. 1956).

[23] Reg. § 25.2514-1(d).

[24] Cf. Estate of Paul v. Comm'r, 16 TC 743, 749 (1951). See also Jorgensen v. United States, 152 F. Supp. 73, 76 (Ct. Cl.), cert. denied, 355 US 840 (1957).

property and regardless of to whom it goes, may justify imposition of the estate tax. But, if an appointee's renunciation in the case of a lifetime exercise simply leaves the parties where they were, no gift tax should be imposed. Such fruitless attempts at exercise should, for gift tax purposes, be equated with an attempt that is void as contrary to provisions of local law, such as the rule against perpetuities, which has been held not to constitute an exercise of a power even for estate tax purposes.[25] The argument made here finds at least oblique support in the legislative history of the Powers of Appointment Act of 1951, which indicates that it is an exercise of the power "which leaves in the holder no power to change the disposition of the property" that constitutes a taxable transfer.[26] The appointee's renunciation, if in compliance with Section 2518, should nullify the supposed transfer. Thus, not every attempted exercise of a power should be treated as a taxable transfer, and at least one frustrated by the appointee's renunciation should not be so treated.

[e] Interest Accompanying Power

If the possessor of a general power also has an interest in the property subject to the power, a transfer of the possessor's actual interest may be a gift without regard to Section 2514. Thus, if B is a life beneficiary of a trust and B assigns B's life interest to C gratuitously, B has made a gift even if B also has a testamentary power over the corpus that B has not exercised.[27] In one case, a life beneficiary of a trust, B, had a nongeneral lifetime power not exercisable for the benefit of B, B's creditors, B's estate, or the creditors of B's estate that B exercised by appointing the trust corpus to permitted appointees. Admitting that the exercise did not give rise to gift tax liability under the provisions on powers, the government argued, nevertheless, that the exercise of the power effected a taxable transfer of B's life interest. The court rejected this contention, regarding the life interest as merely terminated, not transferred, by the exercise of the power.[28] The government is still of the same opinion,[29] and it has received support from the Tax Court,[30] and properly so. The bare assignment of

---

[25] Estate of Paul v. Comm'r, 16 TC 743 (1951).

[26] S. Rep. No. 382, 82d Cong., 1st Sess. 4 (1951). Contrary to the regulations, a basis might exist for differentiating an exercise in favor of the taker in default (leaving "in the holder no power") from an exercise where the appointee renounces (leaving the holder where he was before the attempted exercise).

[27] Cf. Monroe v. United States, 301 F. Supp. 762 (ED Wash. 1969), aff'd per curiam, 454 F2d 1169 (9th Cir. 1972).

[28] Self v. United States, 142 F. Supp. 939 (Ct. Cl. 1956). See also Comm'r v. Walston, 168 F2d 211 (4th Cir. 1948).

[29] Reg. § 25.2514-1(b)(2); Rev. Rul. 79-327, 1979-2 CB 342.

[30] Regester v. Comm'r, 83 TC 1 (1984). The Treasury here has some support from the legislative history, which indicates that the power of appointment provisions "are not

the life interest would have constituted a gift and, realistically, that interest and all others in the property are assigned when the property is given outright to another person.

[f] Indirect Exercise

There may be an indirect as well as a direct exercise of a general power of appointment. If the holder of a presently exercisable general power of appointment and of a nongeneral power of appointment over the same property exercises the nongeneral power, the regulations appropriately take the position that the exercise of the nongeneral power constitutes an exercise of the general power to the extent that there is a decrease in the amount of property subject to the general power.[31] The regulations contain an important example of the interrelationship of a general five-or-five power and a nongeneral power over corpus as follows:

> [A]ssume A has a noncumulative annual power to withdraw the greater of $5,000 or 5 percent of the value of a trust having a value of $300,000 and a lifetime nongeneral power to appoint all or a portion of the trust corpus to A's child or grandchildren. If A exercises the nongeneral power by appointing $150,000 to A's child, the exercise of the nongeneral power is treated as the exercise of the general power to the extent of $7,500 (maximum exercise of general power before the exercise of the nongeneral power, 5 [percent] of $300,000 or $15,000, less maximum exercise of the general power after the exercise of the nongeneral power, 5 [percent] of $150,000 or $7,500).[32]

---

intended to limit the scope of other subdivisions of the Code . . . which apply to the transfer at death or during life of any interests possessed by the taxpayer." S. Rep. No. 382, 82d Cong., 1st Sess. 4, 6 (1951). See Note, "Special Powers of Appointment and the Gift Tax: The Impact of Self v. United States," 3 Val. UL Rev. 284 (1969); Taylor, "Gift Tax Results From Exercise of Special Powers of Appointment," 80 Tax Mgmt. Memo. No. 2, at 2 (1980).

[31] Reg. § 25.2514-1(d). The regulation applies to both pre-1942 and post-1942 general powers. It is arguable that this is merely a release of the general power. Nevertheless, the regulation is correct in concluding that this is, in substance, an exercise of the general power. Cf. supra ¶ 10.04[3][e] text accompanying notes 28–30.

[32] Reg. § 25.2514-1(d).

[4] Treatment of Post-1942 Powers

[a] In General

Under Section 2514(b) relating to post-1942 powers, not only the exercise but also the release of a general power of appointment is treated as a transfer of property.[33] Similar to the treatment of pre-1942 powers, the exercise (or release) of post-1942 powers may be indirect.[34] Again, however, other principles of gift taxation must be considered to determine whether the transfer deemed to have been made is such as to give rise to gift tax liability. For example, an exercise of the power in favor of the possessor of the power is no more a gift here than it is with respect to a pre-1942 power.

If a general power was created after October 21, 1942, but was converted to a nongeneral power by a partial release on or before May 31, 1951, it is not to be treated as a general power.[35] In any other circumstances, a partial release and subsequent exercise or release will be telescoped under the step transaction principle so that the ultimate action is treated as an exercise or release of a general power.[36] The principle here is similar to that noted in the discussion of pre-1942 powers.[37]

[b] Release or Disclaimer?

Although a release of a power is treated as a transfer, a "qualified disclaimer" of a power[38] under Section 2518 is not considered a release.[39] In order effectively to disclaim, the requirements of Section 2518(b) or Section 2518(c)(3)[40] must be met. Under Section 2518 it is important to note that a

---

[33] See Rev. Rul. 86-39, 1986-1 CB 301; Rev. Rul. 76-547, 1976-2 CB 302; Rev. Rul. 79-421, 1979-2 CB 347, involving releases of post-1942 general powers. See also Priv. Ltr. Ruls. 9725031 (Mar. 24, 1997) (no release of general power of appointment where the trust was ambiguous and a local court held power not general power based on extrinsic evidence); 200144018 (Aug. 3, 2001) (no release of general power of appointment where the local court reformed the trust instrument to correct the scrivener's error in manner consistent with state law as applied by the state's highest court).

[34] Reg. § 25.2514-1(d). See supra ¶ 10.04[3][f]; Priv. Ltr. Rul. 9741040 (July 15, 1997) (no indirect release of power of appointment where the power holder consented to reform trust giving the trustee greater discretion to make distributions to beneficiaries other than the power holder).

[35] Reg. § 25.2514-3(c)(2).

[36] Reg. § 25.2514-3(c)(3).

[37] See supra ¶ 10.04[3][b] text accompanying notes 16–18. See also Reg. § 25.2514-2(c).

[38] IRC §§ 2518(b), 2518(c)(2).

[39] IRC §§ 2518(a), 2518(c)(2).

[40] See ¶ 10.07; Reg. § 25.2514-3(c)(5).

power cannot be disclaimed or renounced after it has been accepted,[41] and a disclaimer in writing must, in general, be made not later than nine months after the general power is created.[42] The Section 2518 rule can create an inequitable situation where the taxpayer is not aware of the existence of the power within that period.[43]

A disclaimer or renunciation of a power will be recognized as such only if it is a complete and unqualified refusal to accept any rights under the power.[44] But it is not necessary for one also to renounce other interests in the property.[45] Thus, one who is given a life interest in a trust and a general power of appointment over the trust corpus can effectively disclaim the power while retaining a life interest. The disclaimer of the power as to one-half the trust corpus will also be treated as a valid disclaimer of one half of the corpus,[46] assuming the requirements of Section 2518(b) are met. Section 2518 governs disclaimers of powers created after 1976; the efficacy of earlier disclaimers is controlled by prior law.

[c] Lapse of Power

Under Section 2514(e), the lapse of a power is, in general, treated as a release. As the release of a post-1942 general power is deemed a transfer of property, gift tax liability can arise if the possessor merely permits the possessor's power to lapse. On the other hand, the Treasury concedes that the lapse of a power occasioned by the possessor's legal disability (in circumstances in which another cannot act on the possessor's behalf) is not to be treated as a lapse of the power.[47]

The general rule on lapse can be illustrated as follows. Assume one has a noncumulative right to invade a trust in the amount of $10,000 in each calendar year during one's life and that upon one's death the remainder is to go to

---

[41] IRC § 2518(b)(3).

[42] IRC §§ 2518(b)(1), 2518(b)(2).

[43] The regulations are more lenient for disclaimers of powers created before January 1, 1977, only requiring a disclaimer within a reasonable time after one has learned of the existence of the power. Reg. § 25.2514-3(c)(6). See Reg. § 25.2514-3(c)(5). See also ¶ 10.07[2][b] text accompanying notes 62–64, questioning whether Section 2518 is an exclusive rule.

[44] IRC § 2518(b).

[45] IRC § 2518(c)(2); Reg. § 25.2518-3(a)(1). See ¶ 10.07[2].

[46] Cf. IRC § 2518(c)(1).

[47] Reg. § 25.2514-3(c)(4). Cf. Rev. Proc. 94-44, 1994-2 CB 683 (state legislation preventing a trustee-beneficiary from exercising a power in favor of oneself does not constitute a lapse); Priv. Ltr. Rul. 9510065 (Dec. 14, 1994) (beneficiary, as co-trustee, held a general power of appointment, resigned as trustee, no lapse of the power occurred because of continued power to replace the trustee with another, including oneself).

others. If the person fails to exercise the right in any year, it lapses. Such a lapse constitutes a release and thus a transfer subject to gift tax, but with an important qualification, discussed next. The theory here is that by forgoing the exercise of the power, the possessor has, in effect, made a transfer to the remainderperson.

Before criticizing this rule, an important qualification should be noted. The statute limits the general rule by providing that a lapse constitutes a release only to the extent that the amount that could have been appointed exceeds $5,000 or 5 percent of the aggregate value of the assets subject to the power,[48] whichever is greater.[49] Consequently, we now proceed with this discussion with fingers partly crossed.

The purpose of the $5,000 or 5 percent exemption[50] is aptly expressed in the legislative history:

> Since the problem of the termination or lapse of powers of appointment during life arises primarily in the case of dispositions of moderately sized properties where the donor is afraid the income will be insufficient for the income beneficiary and therefore gives the income beneficiary a noncumulative invasion power, it is believed that the exemption . . . will be adequate to cover the usual cases without being subject to possible abuses.[51]

The following illustration of the lapse provision appears in the regulations:

> [I]f an individual has a noncumulative right to withdraw $10,000 a year from the principal of a trust fund, the failure to exercise this right of withdrawal in a particular year will not constitute a gift if the fund at the end of the year equals or exceeds $200,000. If, however, at the end of the particular year the fund should be worth only $100,000, the failure to exercise the power will be considered a gift to the extent of $5,000, the excess of $10,000 over 5 percent of a fund of $100,000.[52]

Here is an example of inaction resulting in a gift where an exercise of the power would not result in a gift, since a possessor's appointment to oneself does not constitute a gift. Nevertheless, this is consistent with general gift tax concepts, for if the possessor draws down the available property, the possessor

---

[48] Cf. Fish v. United States, 291 F. Supp. 59 (D. Or. 1968), aff'd, 432 F2d 1278 (9th Cir. 1970). See ¶ 4.13[7][f] for a discussion of the assets subject to the power.

[49] See Covey, "The Estate Planning Benefits Available Via a $5,000 and 5 Percent Withdrawal Power," 34 J. Tax'n 98 (1971). See also "Use and Drafting of Powers of Appointment," 1 Real Prop., Prob. & Tr. J. 307 (1966).

[50] IRC § 2514(e).

[51] S. Rep. No. 382, 83d Cong., 1st Sess. 4, 7 (1951).

[52] Reg. § 25.2514-3(c)(4).

is not in any way diminishing the possessor's estate;[53] and if the possessor fails to draw upon the property, it may pass to another.[54]

On the other hand, the illustration in the regulations is objectionable in certain respects and the Treasury's consideration of the consequences of lapse seems entirely inadequate. The statute itself makes a lapse the equivalent of release (subject to the $5,000 or 5 percent limitation) and also makes a release a transfer. But, as previously explained, it does not render every transfer subject to gift tax; nor does it lay down precise rules for valuation of the property interest transferred. The example in the regulations assumes a taxable transfer of $5,000. But has the possessor made a complete transfer of that amount when the possessor still has a right in future years to continue to draw down $10,000, possibly acquiring the entire trust during the possessor's lifetime? It is relevant to observe that such withdrawals will enlarge the possessor's estate subject to tax at the possessor's death. And if the possessor lives thirty years and never exercises the power, has the possessor made gifts of $150,000 (the $5,000 excess times thirty), notwithstanding the fact that the property subject to the power never exceeded $100,000 in value? Moreover, if we can detect a $5,000 transfer to the remainder person, it is a transfer of a future right to $5,000 that has a smaller present value.[55] The estate tax regulations deal with the corresponding estate tax problems somewhat more fully and intelligently.[56]

[5] Special Rule for Nongeneral Powers

The statute recognizes one circumstance in which the exercise of a post-1942 power of appointment that is not general can result in gift tax liability. The circumstance is one in which a nongeneral power is exercised by creating another power of appointment, if under applicable local law such new power can be validly exercised without regard to the date of creation of the first power. The reason for this special rule, which is of very limited applicability, is discussed in Chapter 4.[57]

---

[53] Cf. Comm'r v. Wemyss, 324 US 303 (1945).

[54] Consider the interrelationship of this provision with *Crummey* powers. See Crummey v. Comm'r, 526 F2d 717 (2d Cir. 1975); Rev. Rul. 85-88, 1985-2 CB 201; ¶ 9.04[3][f]. See also ¶ 13.02[2][e][ii].

[55] Cf. IRC § 2702, where if the remainder person is a member of the power holder's family, Section 2702 applies and there is a full $5,000 transfer to the remainder person. See ¶ 19.03.

[56] Reg. §§ 20.2041-3(d)(4), 20.2041-3(d)(5). See ¶ 4.13[7][f].

[57] See ¶ 4.13[8].

¶ 10.05 SECTION 2515. TREATMENT OF GENERATION-SKIPPING TRANSFER TAX

Some inter vivos gifts are potentially subject to not one, but two, transfer taxes: the gift tax and the generation-skipping transfer tax.[1] For example, if in the current year a donor makes a $30,000 inter vivos outright transfer to a grandchild whose parents are alive, we know that there is a gift tax transfer.[2] Regrettably, we are soon to discover that the transfer also constitutes an inter vivos direct skip potentially subject to the Chapter 13 generation-skipping transfer tax.[3] A single transfer subject to two transfer taxes! An inter vivos transfer to a trust may meet with the same treatment. For example, if, in the current year, a donor transferred $30,000 to an irrevocable trust with income to a grandchild for life and a remainder to great-grandchildren, the transfer is subject to both gift and generation-skipping transfer taxes.[4]

The liability for any generation-skipping transfer tax that is imposed[5] on an inter vivos direct skip (along with liability for the gift tax)[6] is placed on the donor.[7] As if the double tax were not painful enough, Section 2515 then treats the donor's Chapter 13 tax liability on an inter vivos direct skip as a further gift by the donor.[8] Suddenly, one actual transfer balloons into three transfers under the federal wealth transfer tax system.

Assume that the donor makes a $1 million gift transfer to the donor's grandchild[9] in a year when the ceiling on transfer taxes is 45 percent.[10] Assume also that the donor is in the 45 percent gift tax bracket, and disregard any exclusions[11] or exemptions.[12] There is a Section 2511 gift tax transfer of $1 million, generating $450,000 of Chapter 11 gift tax liability. Chapter 13

---

[1] See Chapter 13 of the 1986 Code, discussed in Chapters 12–18.

[2] IRC § 2511. The transfer may be subject to Section 2513 gift splitting and a Section 2503(b) annual exclusion.

[3] IRC § 2612(c)(1). See ¶ 13.02[4]. See also IRC § 2651(e); ¶ 17.01[2][a][ii].

[4] See ¶¶ 13.02[4][b][iii], 13.03[3].

[5] Generation-skipping transfers are subject to a GST exemption. See IRC § 2631, which is discussed at ¶ 15.02. Cf. IRC § 2632(b), discussed ¶ 15.03[3].

[6] IRC § 2502(c).

[7] IRC § 2603(a)(3).

[8] Section 2515 is effective generally for generation-skipping transfers occurring or treated as occurring after October 22, 1986. Tax Reform Act of 1986, Pub. L. No. 99-514, §§ 1433(a), 1433(b), 100 Stat. 2085, 2731 (1986), reprinted in 1986-3 CB (Vol. 1) 1, 648; Reg. §§ 26.2601-1(a)(1), 26.2601-1(a)(2).

[9] But see IRC § 2651(e), the deceased parent rule, which is discussed ¶ 17.01[2][a][ii].

[10] See IRC §§ 2001(c), 2502(a), 2602, 2641(a)(1).

[11] IRC § 2503(b).

[12] IRC § 2631. See supra note 5.

also imposes a $450,000 generation-skipping transfer tax[13] on the transfer, which is a direct skip.[14] Finally, there is a Section 2515 transfer of $450,000 (equal to the generation-skipping transfer tax liability), resulting in $202,500 of additional gift tax liability. Under these circumstances, the donor's gift of $1 million to the grandchild incurs $1,102,500 in transfer taxes.[15]

Although the gift tax survives the year 2010 termination of the estate tax and the generation-skipping transfer tax,[16] Section 2515 is effectively repealed in the year 2010 because the generation-skipping transfer tax is not imposed on inter vivos direct skips after December 31, 2009.[17]

¶ 10.06 SECTION 2516. CERTAIN PROPERTY SETTLEMENTS

[1] In General

Section 2516 represents a legislative effort to lay down precise statutory rules regarding the gift tax consequences of transfers between individuals in connection with divorce. Prior to the enactment of the 1954 Code, such matters were governed entirely by general gift tax principles.[1] In speaking about the purpose of Section 2516, the committee reports state: "Under present law property settlements between spouses are not regarded as taxable gifts if the property settlement is incorporated in the decree of divorce. However, the gift tax status under present law of settlements not incorporated in the decree of divorce is uncertain."[2] By enacting Section 2516, Congress attempted to carve out an area of certainty.

Nevertheless, it is well to observe that Section 2516 does not purport to be exclusive, and a divorce transfer that is not exempt under this section may still escape tax under general gift tax principles.[3]

---

[13] IRC §§ 2601, 2602, 2623, 2641.

[14] IRC § 2612(c)(1).

[15] The amount comprises $450,000 of Chapter 13 tax liability and $652,500 of Chapter 12 tax liability.

[16] See ¶ 9.01 text accompanying notes 14, 15. See also IRC §§ 2210(a), 2644; ¶¶ 8.10[1], 18.04.

[17] IRC § 2664. See ¶ 18.04. However the repeal may well be short-lived as the sunset provision resurrects the tax imposed on generation-skipping transfers on January 1, 2011. See ¶ 8.10[5].

[1] E.g., on the question of dower and similar marital rights and support rights as consideration, see ¶ 10.02[5]. See also IRC § 2043, discussed ¶ 4.15.

[2] S. Rep. No. 1622, 83d Cong., 2d Sess. 128 (1954).

[3] See Emmanuel, "Property Settlements: Ante-Nuptial, During Marriage, at Termination," 24 NYU Inst. on Fed. Tax'n 281 (1966).

In general, a transfer in exchange for a relinquishment of dower or curtesy or similar statutory rights, which is not within the protection of Section 2516, is not a transfer for consideration and will be subject to tax.[4] Such rights are to be distinguished from reasonable support rights of a spouse or minor children,[5] which are not in the nature of property rights; transfers in discharge of support rights have long been recognized as transfers for consideration to the extent they satisfy the transferor's support obligation.[6] Moreover, without regard to the question of consideration, a transfer in satisfaction of a spouse's dower, curtesy, or similar statutory right is not taxable if it is effected by a court decree and not merely founded on a promise or agreement between the spouses.[7] In the case of these support and judicially decreed transfers, no help is needed from Section 2516, even though in some situations it overlaps general gift tax principles.

In addition, no help is needed from Section 2516 for transfers made prior to a final divorce decree if those transfers qualify[8] (as outright transfers of property do) for the unlimited marital deduction.[9] Such qualifying transfers will result in no *taxable* gifts[10] and will not even require the filing of a gift tax return.[11]

What Section 2516 does, in broad outline, is make it unnecessary to show either consideration for a transfer, such as the discharge of a legal obligation, or that it was effected by a judicial decree; regardless of these factors, a transfer is exempt from the gift tax if the requirements of the section are met.[12]

-----

[4] Merrill v. Fahs, 324 US 308, reh'g denied, 324 US 888 (1945); Reg. § 25.2512-8.

[5] See Note, "Valuation of the Right to Support for Purposes of the Federal Tax System," 72 Colum. L. Rev. 132 (1972).

[6] Rev. Rul. 68-379, 1968-2 CB 414, superseding ET 19, 1946-2 CB 166, which expressed the same principle. S. Rep. No. 1622, 83d Cong., 2d Sess. 128 (1954). The scope of such rights for gift tax purposes is examined in the discussion of Section 2512 at ¶ 10.02[5]. See also Rosenthal v. Comm'r, 205 F2d 505 (2d Cir. 1953); Rev. Rul. 77-314, 1977-2 CB 349.

[7] Harris v. Comm'r, 340 US 106 (1950); McMurtry v. Comm'r, 203 F2d 659 (1st Cir. 1953). If, however, the transfer is responsive to an agreement between spouses that the court lacked judicial power to alter, there is a gift despite an enforcing decree, unless Section 2516 is applicable to the transfer. Cf. Spruance v. Comm'r, 60 TC 141 (1973), aff'd in unpub. op., 505 F2d 731 (3d Cir. 1974); Estate of Barrett v. Comm'r, 56 TC 1312 (1971). See also IRC § 2043(b), discussed ¶ 4.15[1].

[8] See IRC §§ 2523(b)–2523(f); ¶¶ 11.03[3], 11.03[4].

[9] See IRC § 2523(a); ¶ 11.03[1].

[10] See IRC § 2503(a).

[11] IRC § 6019(a)(2). See ¶ 9.04[9] text accompanying note 200.

[12] See Rev. Rul. 80-82, 1980-1 CB 209.

[2] Statutory Requirements

The statutory requirements for exemption under Section 2516 are, first, a written agreement relative to the marital and property rights of the spouses and, second, a final divorce within one year prior to, or two years after, execution of the agreement. If such requisites are met, then transfers pursuant to the agreement[13] are automatically treated as for a full and adequate consideration in money or money's worth if they are (1) either transfers to a spouse to settle marital or property rights or (2) transfers to provide reasonable support for the issue of the spouses during their minority. A transfer in trust for a spouse is a transfer "to" such spouse within the scope of this section.[14] The Section 2516 rules and their variance from the common-law principles can be illustrated by the following example.

Suppose a married couple decides to separate and one or the other begins divorce proceedings. They enter into a written agreement concerning their property rights and transfer property between them to settle their agreed interests. Under Section 2516, if divorce occurs one year prior to or within two years after the agreement is made, neither has made a taxable gift.[15] Of course, if the divorce occurs after the written agreement, there is uncertainty until the divorce decree becomes final, which may occur after the time at which a return would have to be filed if the transfer constituted a gift. The Treasury deals with this problem as follows:

> [T]he transfer must be disclosed by the transferor upon a gift tax return filed for the calendar year . . . in which the agreement becomes effective, and a copy of the agreement must be attached to the return. In addition, a certified copy of the final divorce decree must be furnished the internal revenue officer with whom the return was filed not later than 60 days after the divorce is granted. Pending receipt of evidence that the final decree of divorce has been granted (but in no event for a period of more than 2 years from the effective date of the agreement), the transfer will tentatively be treated as made for a full and adequate consideration in money or money's worth.[16]

Under Section 2516, it is not necessary to show that the agreement was adopted or approved by, or even submitted to, the court.[17] Nor is it necessary to allocate any part of the transfer to the discharge of support rights or to

---

[13] See Rev. Rul. 79-118, 1979-1 CB 315.

[14] Rev. Rul. 57-506, 1957-2 CB 65.

[15] See Reg. § 25.2702-1(c)(7), indicating that no gift is made for purposes of Section 2702 if a transfer to a spouse is within Section 2516 and all other interests in the trust are retained by the transferor spouse. See ¶ 19.03[2][a] text accompanying notes 53–59.

[16] Reg. § 25.6019-3(b).

[17] Reg. § 25.2516-1(a). See supra ¶ 10.06[1] text accompanying note 7.

dower or curtesy rights in an effort to prove actual consideration for at least part of the transfer;[18] the statute presumes adequate consideration.

The only type of decree that will make Section 2516 operative is a final decree of divorce;[19] a decree of separation, separate maintenance, or annulment apparently will not suffice. Of course, it should be remembered that a transfer that is founded on a separation decree will not result in gift tax.[20]

[a] Type of Transfer

To qualify under Section 2516, the transfer must be made in settlement of a spouse's marital or property rights[21] or for the support of issue. Uncertainty exists concerning the type of transfer that will be regarded as made in settlement of marital rights. The problem here is whether the statute shields from tax only transfers that are made in realistic recognition of the value of the marital rights of the transferee spouse. Some rulings indicate that the Treasury will attack a settlement, otherwise within the section, if the amount transferred is in excess of the value of the rights relinquished by a spouse;[22] and, as far as the statute is concerned, it can be argued that excessive transfers are entirely outside the statutory provisions or at least, as the ruling holds, that such transfers are not shielded from tax to the extent of the excess. Such an attack is contrary to congressional purpose to give certainty; but such a case is not likely to come up very often: A spouse normally does not transfer to a divorced spouse more than the divorced spouse rightfully demands.

[b] Amount for Child Support

Uncertainties exist as regards the amounts transferred to provide for the support of children. The Treasury interprets the term "issue of the marriage" to include legally adopted children,[23] which settles one problem; but the statute expressly raises the question what constitutes a reasonable allowance for support of children during their minority. Here it is clearly necessary to determine

---

[18] See Rev. Rul. 68-379, 1968-2 CB 414, superseding ET 19, 1946-2 CB 166; Reg. § 25.2516-2.

[19] Reg. § 25.2516-1(a). See also Reg. § 25.6019-3(b).

[20] See supra ¶ 10.06[1] text accompanying note 7.

[21] Burford v. Comm'r, 49 TCM (CCH) 755 (1985), aff'd in unpub. op., 786 F2d 1151 (4th Cir. 1986) (the transfer was not originally made pursuant to marital rights and was not converted to the same when the transfer was considered in reducing the transferor's alimony obligation).

[22] Rev. Rul. 75-73, 1975-1 CB 313. Cf. Spruance v. Comm'r, 60 TC 141 (1973), aff'd in unpub. op., 505 F2d 731 (3d Cir. 1974).

[23] Reg. § 25.2516-2.

the value of the children's support rights.[24] Any amounts transferred in excess of such value will not be shielded from tax by Section 2516. Thus, if a parent sets up a trust generally within Section 2516 to give the income to a child during minority with a remainder to the child upon reaching majority, and if the amount of anticipated income is a reasonable amount of support, the value of the remainder constitutes a taxable gift to the child. The apparent difference in the treatment of transfers in discharge of marital rights and transfers in discharge of children's support rights possibly reflects a congressional expectation of generosity in a person's dealings with children and of arm's-length bargaining in dealings between estranged spouses.[25]

[c] The Three-Year Rule

Section 2516 originally passed the House with a requirement that divorce occur within a reasonable time after execution of the agreement. The Senate can claim credit for reducing uncertainty in this respect by originally substituting a two-year rule for the reasonable time requirement.[26] The period was further extended in the Deficit Reduction Act of 1984 to include a period one year prior to the agreement.[27] Thus, the divorce must be final either one year prior to or two years after the written agreement. Yet this elimination of uncertainty may have been achieved at a cost to fairness. If the agreement is entered into prior to the divorce,[28] any delay in the divorce proceeding that carries the final decree beyond the two-year limitation may involve a heavy tax cost on any transfers that do not qualify for the marital deduction. The House and Senate concepts should be merged so that there would be certain exemption from tax if divorce occurred within two years, but also some flexibility as to possible exemption if divorce occurred more than two years but within a reasonable time after the execution of the agreement.[29] Although certainty can be achieved by judicious postponement of the execution of the agreement, the statute may unduly penalize ignorance and inadvertence.

A further statutory change would be appropriate. If death precludes divorce within two years of the agreement's execution, the result should be the

---

[24] See St. Joseph Bank & Trust Co. v. United States, 82-2 USTC ¶ 13,477 (ND Ind. 1982), aff'd, 716 F2d 1180 (7th Cir. 1983); Spruance v. Comm'r, 60 TC 141 (1973), aff'd in unpub. op., 505 F2d 731 (3d Cir. 1974). Cf. Helvering v. United States Trust Co., 111 F2d 576 (2d Cir. 1940); Estate of McKeon v. Comm'r, 25 TC 697 (1956), acq. 1958-2 CB 6.

[25] But see Rev. Rul. 75-73, 1975-1 CB 313.

[26] S. Rep. No. 1622, 83d Cong., 2d Sess. 128, 481 (1954).

[27] Deficit Reduction Act of 1984, Pub. L. No. 98-369, § 425, 98 Stat. 494, 803–804 (1984), reprinted in 1984-3 CB (Vol. 1) 1, 311–312.

[28] See supra ¶ 10.06[1] text accompanying notes 8–11.

[29] Cf. IRC §§ 1041(a)(2), 1041(c)(2); Reg. § 1.1041-1T(b), Q&A-7.

same as if divorce had occurred within the required period. Although the statute should expressly so provide, this principle is sufficiently in tune with the statute as presently written to justify its adoption by the Treasury under its Section 7805 authority to prescribe needful rules and regulations. Nevertheless, the Treasury does not seem inclined to take such action, and the Tax Court appears to be reluctant to extend the reaches of the statute.[30] With the enactment of the unlimited marital deduction, this issue becomes relevant only if the transfer violates the estate tax terminable interest rules.[31]

[3] Comparative Estate Tax Treatment

Prior to 1984, Section 2516 fostered a vexing disparity between gift tax and estate tax treatment of similar transactions. In the preceding paragraph, concern was expressed about the taxability of a lifetime transfer made under a separation agreement followed shortly by death of one of the parties. What about death after execution of the agreement and divorce but before the transfer was made? The agreement might result in a valid claim against the estate of the decedent, but the question is whether such a claim would be deductible. For many years Congress did not allow a deduction for such a claim.[32] In 1984, however, Congress permitted the gift tax provision to be read into the estate statute to support a deduction from the gross estate in these circumstances.[33]

[4] Income Tax Aspects

The income tax aspects of transfer incident to divorce or separation are beyond the scope of this book. The most common questions presented are whether amounts received by a spouse or former spouse constitute gross income and whether the paying spouse can claim a deduction for the amounts paid. The

---

[30] Estate of Hundley v. Comm'r, 52 TC 495 (1969), aff'd per curiam, 435 F2d 1311 (4th Cir. 1971). In *Hundley*, the Tax Court did not apply Section 2516 in a situation where the decedent, prior to his death, had taken no action to begin divorce proceedings; nevertheless, in dicta, the court indicated that even if the decedent had begun such action, it would not be "inclined" to apply Section 2516. Supra at 510.

[31] See ¶¶ 5.06[7], 5.06[8].

[32] See IRC § 2053(c)(1)(A). Of course if divorce had occurred and the court, with power to alter the agreement, had approved it, then the claim would be deductible because it would be founded on the decree. Rev. Rul. 60-160, 1960-1 CB 374. Cf. Harris v. Comm'r, 340 US 106 (1950).

[33] IRC §§ 2043(b)(2), 2053(e). Cf. Merrill v. Fahs, 324 US 308, reh'g denied, 324 US 888 (1945), incorporating an estate tax provision into the gift tax sections.

Code sections that deal with these questions are Sections 71, 215, and 682.[34] Prior to the Deficit Reduction Act of 1984, a possible income tax gain was required to be recognized on the transfer of appreciated property in satisfaction of a legal obligation arising out of an agreement or out of a judicial decree. Such a transfer resulted in realization of gain taxable to the transferor even if adverse gift tax consequences were successfully avoided.[35] Section 1041 now provides for nonrecognition of such gain and treats the transfer as a gift for income tax purposes.[36]

¶ 10.07 SECTION 2518. DISCLAIMERS

[1] Introduction

Section 2518[1] is an effort to provide uniform treatment for disclaimers under the estate tax,[2] the gift tax, and the tax on generation-skipping transfers.[3] Under prior law, there were different requirements for effective disclaimers under various federal transfer tax provisions.[4] In addition, because of differ-

---

[34] See Thomas, Tax Consequences of Marriage, Separation and Divorce (ALI-ABA 1986). See also 5 Mertens, Law of Federal Income Taxation §§ 31A.01–31A.06a (Callaghan, 1969); 6 Mertens, Law of Federal Income Taxation § 37.48 (Callaghan, 1968).

[35] United States v. Davis, 370 US 65 (1962). Compare Rev. Rul. 57-506, 1957-2 CB 65. See also Wren, "Tax Problems Incident to Divorce and Property Settlement," 49 Cal. L. Rev. 665 (1961).

[36] See IRC §§ 1041(a)–1041(c).

[1] Tax Reform Act of 1976, Pub. L. No. 94-455, §§ 2009(b)(1), 2009(e)(2), 90 Stat. 1520, 1893 (1896), reprinted in 1976-3 CB (Vol. 1) 1, 369, 372.

See Wenig, "Disclaimers," Tax Mgmt. Portfolio No. 848 (1992) (especially II dealing with both tax and nontax reasons for the use of a disclaimer); Pena, "Internal Revenue Code Section 2518 Disclaimers and the 1981 Economic Recovery Tax Act: Continued Unequal Treatment of Taxpayers," 22 Santa Clara L. Rev. 1179 (1982); Blazek & O'Donoghue, "Use of Disclaimers in Post Mortem Planning," 40 NYU Inst. on Fed. Tax'n Chapter 7 (1982); Frimmer, "The Federal Disclaimer Rules—E Pluribus Unum," 14 Miami Inst. on Est. Plan. 400 (1980); Frimmer, "A Decade Later: Final Disclaimer Regulations Issued Under Section 2518," 21 Miami Inst. on Est. Plan. Chapter 6 (1987); Saunders & Johnson, "Renunciation of Gifts and Bequests: New Law Clears Up Some but Not All of the Problems," 6 Est. Plan. 24 (1979); Evaul, "Federal Taxation: Section 2518 Disclaimers—Anything but Uniform," 31 U. Fla. L. Rev. 1988 (1978); Ellsworth, "On Disclaimers: Let's Renounce IRC Section 2518," 38 Vill. L. Rev. 693 (1993).

[2] See IRC § 2046, which makes Section 2518 applicable to the estate tax; ¶ 4.18.

[3] See IRC § 2654(c), which makes Section 2518 applicable to the generation-skipping transfer tax; ¶ 17.04[3].

[4] For example, a third party's disclaimer that would result in a marital deduction for a surviving spouse's receipt of property had to occur by the time for filing of the estate

ences in local law, a refusal to accept property in one state would be treated differently for federal tax purposes from an identical refusal in another.[5] This statute provides a uniform federal rule for disclaimers that is applicable to all three federal transfer tax laws.[6]

Under Section 2518, if a person (a transferor) makes a transfer of property or grants a power to another person who makes a "qualified disclaimer" thereof, federal tax law treats the situation as one in which the disclaimant (the would-be transferee) never received the property or power. It is a now-you-have-it, then-you-never-did situation. It is as if the property interest or power was never transferred to the disclaimant and the property or power passed directly from the transferor to some third person.[7] The disclaimer may alter the tax consequences not only of the disclaimant and the person receiving the property as a result of the disclaimer, but also the transferor of the property or

---

tax return. IRC § 2056(d)(2) (repealed by Tax Reform Act of 1976, Pub. L. No. 95-455, § 2009(b)(4)(D), 90 Stat. 1525, 1894 (1976), reprinted in 1976-3 CB (Vol. 1) 1, 370). However, in order to disclaim a general power of appointment over property, one had to disclaim within a reasonable time after learning of its existence. Reg. § 20.2041-3(d)(6)(ii). A case particularly disturbing to Congress was Keinath v. Comm'r, 480 F2d 57 (8th Cir. 1973), which arose during the period that lacked uniform rules. *Keinath* is tsk-tsked in the legislative history of Section 2518, HR Rep. No. 1380, 94th Cong., 2d Sess. 3, 66 (1976), reprinted in 1976-3 CB (Vol. 3) 735, 800, as follows: "In one case, a remainderman, who was aware of his interest, was considered to have made a disclaimer of his remainder interest within a 'reasonable' time for gift tax purposes when he disclaimed shortly after the expiration of a life tenancy which had continued for 19 years after the grantor's death." The *Keinath* result was also subsequently rejected by the Supreme Court in Jewett v. Comm'r, 455 US 305 (1982). See also United States v. Irvine, 511 US 224 (1994) (disclaimer occurring forty-seven years after creation was unreasonable even though it was disclaimed two months after it vested and was valid under state law).

A discussion of pre-1976 law is found in Stephens, Maxfield & Lind, Federal Estate and Gift Taxation 9-8 (Warren, Gorham & Lamont, 3d ed. 1974).

[5] In some states, local law deems that the property passing by intestacy vests in the intestate taker immediately upon the decedent's death with the result that a disclaimer of it may constitute a taxable transfer; in other states, however, a disclaimer in either a testate or an intestate situation may result in no transfer. Compare Hardenbergh v. Comm'r, 198 F2d 63 (8th Cir.), cert. denied, 344 US 836 (1952), with Brown v. Routzhan, 63 F2d 914 (6th Cir.), cert. denied, 290 US 641 (1933). Section 2518 would allow both to be effective disclaimers. See Martin, "Perspectives on Federal Disclaimer Legislation," 46 U. Chi. L. Rev. 316 (1979).

[6] Reg. § 25.2518-1(b). Disclaimers may occur with respect to property received from a decedent or donor. See ¶ 10.01[2][g]. In addition, disclaimers may be made with respect to property over which one has a general or nongeneral power of appointment. See ¶¶ 4.13[7][d], 10.04[4][b].

The fact that a disclaimer is voidable by creditors has no effect on whether it constitutes a qualified disclaimer. Reg. § 25.2518-1(c)(2). However, a disclaimer that is void or that is voided by creditors is not a qualified disclaimer. Id.

[7] Reg. § 25.2518-1(b). But see IRC § 2518(b)(4)(A), discussed infra ¶ 10.07[2][d][i].

the transferor's estate.[8] Although Section 2518 applies to a disclaimer of an *interest* in property, Section 2518(c)(2) makes a power with respect to property an interest in the property, facilitating the disclaimer of powers of appointment.[9] As a means of providing uniform treatment under state law, Section 2518 also accords disclaimer treatment to an actual transfer (as opposed to a mere disclaimer) of a disclaimant's entire interest in property to an individual who would have received the property if the transferor actually had made a disclaimer, if the transfer conforms generally with the timing and nonacceptance of benefits requirements of the disclaimer rules.[10]

[2] Definition of "Qualified Disclaimer"

A valid disclaimer occurs for purposes of each of the three taxes only if there is a "qualified disclaimer" as defined in Section 2518(b) or Section 2518(c)(3). Section 2518(a) provides that a "qualified disclaimer" may be made with respect to each separately created interest in property.[11] Separate interests in property include various different interests in a trust, including a power of appointment.[12] Thus, if a person receives both an income interest and a remainder in a trust or both an income interest and a general power to appoint a remainder under a trust, a disclaimer may be made with respect to the remainder or the power, without a disclaimer of the income interest.[13] However, where local law merges interests separately created by the transferor, a dis-

---

[8] Disclaimers may also affect the original transferor's gift or estate tax marital deduction (see ¶¶ 5.06[3][h], 11.03[2]) and gift or estate tax charitable deduction (see ¶¶ 5.05[2][c], 11.02).

[9] Cf. IRC § 2055(b). But see infra ¶ 10.07[2] text accompanying note 15.

[10] IRC § 2518(c)(3). See supra note 5, infra ¶ 10.07[2][d][ii].

[11] Reg. § 25.2518-3(a)(1)(i). See Estate of Boyd v. Comm'r, 819 F2d 170 (7th Cir. 1987); Priv. Ltr. Rul. 200127007 (Mar. 30, 2001).

[12] IRC § 2518(c)(2); Reg. §§ 25.2518-3(a)(1)(i), 25.2518-3(a)(1)(iii). See also Priv. Ltr. Ruls. 9203037 (Oct. 22, 1991) (the surviving spouse's valid disclaimer of power as co-trustee to invade trust corpus), 9329025 (Apr. 28, 1993) (the surviving spouse's valid disclaimer of power to remove trustee); TAM 9610005 (Nov. 9, 1995); Priv. Ltr. Ruls. 9633004 (May 6, 1996), 9852034 (Sept. 29, 1998) (involving disclaimers of rights to receive principal distributions from trusts, which resulted in valid charitable remainder trusts).

[13] See IRC § 2518(c)(2); Reg. §§ 25.2518-3(a)(1), 25.2518-3(d) Ex. 8 (a valid disclaimer of separate income and remainder interests in a trust), 25.2518-3(a)(1) Ex. 11 (a right as possible appointee of the corpus during life is a separate interest from a remainder interest); Estate of Lassiter v. Comm'r, 80 TCM (CCH) 541 (2000) (qualified disclaimers by descendants of the possibility of recovering income or corpus distributions prior to the death of the decedent's spouse while disclaimants retained remainder interest). Query whether one could disclaim an income interest but retain a general power to appoint corpus (rather than a remainder). See infra ¶ 10.07[2][d] note 80.

claimer of the merged interests or an undivided portion of the merged interests is required.[14] In addition, the regulations also take the position that a power of appointment over property can be validly disclaimed as a separate interest in property only if any retained interest in the same property (either a power or property interest) leaves the disclaimant without any future right to direct the property.[15] Thus, if the disclaimant has any further right to direct beneficial enjoyment of the property (as a result of a power or an ownership interest), there is a valid disclaimer only if the right is limited by an ascertainable standard.[16] If in such a situation the disclaimant continues to have the ability (not limited by an ascertainable standard) to determine who could receive the property, the interests are not treated as separate interests.[17]

A qualified disclaimer can be made with respect to severable property passing to the disclaimant such as items of jewelry, paintings, shares of corporate stock, and sufficiently identifiable acreage.[18] However, a disclaimer with respect to specific assets in a trust is ineffective, unless such assets are removed from the trust and pass to persons other than the disclaimant or to the decedent's spouse.[19]

---

[14] Reg. §§ 25.2518-3(a)(1)(i), 25.2518-3(d) Ex. 12 (merger of income and remainder interests precludes qualified disclaimer of either interest, but not a disclaimer of both interests). If a nominal interest was created as a device to prevent a merger, the nominal interest is disregarded and the interests will be regarded as merged. Reg. § 25.2518-3(a)(1)(i) (last sentence). A nominal interest is an interest in the property created by the transferor that (1) has an actuarial value of less than 5 percent of the total value of the property at the time of the transfer; (2) prevents a merger under local law; and (3) can be clearly shown to have been created primarily for the purpose of preventing the merger. Reg. § 25.2518-3(a)(1)(iv). Factors to be considered in determining whether the third test is met are listed in the regulations. Id. See Reg. §§ 25.2518-3(d) Ex. 13 (nominal interest disregarded), 25.2518-3(d) Ex. 14 (less than 5 percent of the interest is not disregarded because it was not created primarily for purpose of preventing the merger).

[15] See Reg. § 25.2518-3(a)(1)(iii).

[16] Reg. § 25.2518-3(a)(1)(iii). Seemingly, the rationale for this rule is found in the Section 2518(b)(4) qualified disclaimer requirement that an interest pass without direction on the part of the person making the disclaimer. See infra ¶ 10.07[2][d].

[17] See Reg. §§ 25.2518-3(d) Ex. 9 (general power (not limited by an ascertainable standard) to appoint corpus by deed and either a general or nongeneral power to appoint corpus by will not treated as separate interests), 25.2518-3(d) Ex. 10 (a disclaimer of a contingent remainder in corpus not treated as a separate interest from a nongeneral power to appoint by deed). Cf. Priv. Ltr. Rul. 9320015 (Feb. 17, 1993) (power limited by a standard).

[18] Reg. §§ 25.2518-3(a)(1)(ii), 25.2518-3(d) Exs. 1, 3.

[19] Reg. § 25.2518-3(a)(2). See Reg. §§ 25.2518-3(d) Ex. 5 (disclaimer not qualified because specific asset not removed), 25.2518-3(d) Ex. 6 (qualified disclaimer where specific asset removed as a result of disclaimer), 25.2518-3(d) Ex. 7 (disclaimer not qualified because specific asset not removed); Priv. Ltr. Ruls. 9725005 (Mar. 18, 1997) (qualified disclaimer where specific asset removed), 9845019 (Aug. 7, 1998) (qualified disclaimer where specific assets removed).

Section 2518(c)(1) further provides that a disclaimer of an undivided portion of an interest that meets the other requirements of Section 2518[20] is also a "qualified disclaimer" of such portion of the interest.[21] Thus, a disclaimer of an undivided portion of a separate interest, such as one half of an income interest or one quarter of a remainder interest qualifies as a qualified disclaimer.[22] However, a carved-out portion of an interest such as a disclaimer of a term of years by a person holding a life income interest or a disclaimer of a remainder interest in a fee simple will not qualify as an undivided portion.[23] A disclaimer of a specific pecuniary amount may qualify as an undivided portion if it is made out of either a pecuniary or nonpecuniary bequest or gift and if there is a segregation of the disclaimed amount from the gift or bequest.[24]

---

[20] See IRC §§ 2518(b)(1)–2518(b)(4), discussed infra ¶¶ 10.07[2][a]–10.07[2][d].

[21] See Reg. § 25.2518-3(d) Ex. 5 (a disclaimer of a portion of all interests in a trust). The portion may be determined by use of a formula; Reg. § 25.2518-3(d) Ex. 20 (fractional share formula); Priv. Ltr. Rul. 9203028 (Oct. 21, 1991) (specific pecuniary amount described by formula).

[22] Reg. §§ 25.2518-3(b), 25.2518-3(d) Ex. 4 (qualified disclaimer of a portion of income interest), 25.2518-3(d) Ex. 15 (qualified disclaimer of a portion of income interest where portion related to additional contribution to the trust), 25.2518-3(d) Ex. 20 (qualified disclaimer of a portion of remainder), 25.2518-3(d) Ex. 21 (qualified disclaimer of a portion of a power of appointment over the remainder).

[23] Reg. §§ 25.2518-3(b), 25.2518-3(d) Ex. 2 (invalid disclaimer of a carved-out income interest). See also supra text accompanying notes 15–17.

[24] Reg. §§ 25.2518-3(c), 25.2518-3(d) Ex. 16. See Priv. Ltr. Rul. 9822014 (Feb. 10, 1998) (valid disclaimer of pecuniary amount to facilitate use of the decedent's GST exemption).

The segregation must be made on the basis of the fair market value of the assets on the date of the disclaimer or on a basis that is fairly representative of valuation changes between the date of transfer and the date of disclaimer. Reg. § 25.2518-3(c). Cf. Rev. Proc. 64-19, 1964-1 CB (pt. 1) 682. See Reg. § 25.2518-3(d) Ex. 19.

However, an acceptance of a distribution of a gift or bequest prior to the disclaimer is considered an acceptance of a proportionate share of income by the disclaimant. See infra ¶ 10.07[2][c]. The proportionate amount of income considered to be accepted by the disclaimant is determined by the following formula:

$$\frac{\text{Amount of distribution received by disclaimant}}{\text{Total amount of income earned by the gift of bequest}} \times \begin{array}{c}\text{Total amount of gift or} \\ \text{bequest between the date} \\ \text{of transfer on the date of} \\ \text{the transfer and the date} \\ \text{of disclaimer}\end{array}$$

Reg. § 25.2518-3(c). See Reg. §§ 25.2518-3(d) Ex. 17 (portion of income accepted), 25.2518-3(d) Ex. 18 (all income accepted).

A "qualified disclaimer" requires an *"irrevocable*[25] *and unqualified refusal by a person*[26] *to accept an interest in property.'*[27] In addition, four other conditions generally must be met.

[a] Disclaimer Must Be Written

The refusal to accept the property must be in writing.[28] The purpose behind this requirement, generally not a requirement under prior law, appears to be evidentiary. Clearly, it is advisable to date, sign, and notarize a refusal with respect to an identified interest in property so as to establish not only the existence but also the timeliness of the disclaimer.[29]

[b] Disclaimer Must Be Timely

The written disclaimer of an interest must generally be received[30] by the transferor of the interest, the transferor's legal representative (such as the executor of an estate), or the holder of legal title to the property (the trustee in the

---

[25] See Priv. Ltr. Rul. 8239002 (June 2, 1982).

[26] As to the "person" making the disclaimer, see Estate of Goree v. Comm'r, 68 TCM (CCH) 123 (1994) (the parent's disclaimer on behalf of the minor children valid under state law valid for Section 2518); AOD 1996-001 (IRS's proposition that *Goree* court's use of appellate review of factual determination rather than making de novo factual determination was inappropriate under Comm'r v. Estate of Bosch, 387 US 456 (1967)); Nickel v. Estate of Estes, 122 F3d 294 (5th Cir. 1997) (the executor of beneficiary of pension plan had no power to disclaim). See also Fullerton, "When Can a Fiduciary Disclaim Property on Behalf of Another?" 17 Est. Plan. 272 (1990).

[27] IRC § 2518(b); Reg. § 25.2518-1(a)(1). See Priv. Ltr. Rul. 200127007 (Mar. 30, 2001) (benefit conferred by waiver of Section 2207A right of recovery is interest in property under Pennsylvania law that can be subject matter of qualified disclaimer). The Service takes the position that a disclaimer must adequately identify the property disclaimed. See also Reg. § 25.2518-2(b)(1); Estate of Chamberlain v. Comm'r, 77 TCM (CCH) 2080 (1999) (inadequate identification). Compare Priv. Ltr. Rul. 8240012 (June 28, 1982) (disclaimer of a pecuniary amount was an inadequate identification because the executor had a choice of assets) with Priv. Ltr. Rul. 8539004 (May 18, 1985) and Priv. Ltr. Rul. 8515005 (Dec. 20, 1984) (both holding that a disclaimer of pecuniary amount was an adequate identification because the amount constituted a portion of an identified class of property).

[28] IRC § 2518(b)(1). See Estate of Chamberlain v. Comm'r, 77 TCM (CCH) 2080 (1999) (inadequate written disclaimer).

[29] See IRC § 2518(b)(2); Reg. § 25.2518-2(b)(1).

[30] See Reg. § 25.2518-2(b)(2). A postmark of the U.S. Postal Service, a foreign postal service, or a designated private delivery service on a timely mailed, properly addressed written disclaimer generally is evidence of delivery. Reg. § 25.2518-2(c)(2). Cf. IRC § 7502. See Reg. §§ 301.7502-1(c)(1), 301.7502-1(c)(2), 301.7502-1(e), 301.7503-1(b). Designated private delivery services are set forth in Notice 2001-62, 2001-2 CB __, __. An electronic postmark meeting the requirements set forth in the regulations should also

case of a trust)[31] within nine months of the date of the transfer creating the interest.[32] The legislative history of the section is enlightening as to the date of the transfer creating the interest:[33]

> For purposes of this requirement, a transfer is considered to be made when it is treated as a completed transfer for gift tax purposes with respect to inter vivos transfers or upon the date of the decedent's death with respect to testamentary transfers.[34]

The test of timeliness of a disclaimer with respect to a testamentary transfer, being based on the date of death, is easily resolved;[35] however, the test of timeliness of a disclaimer of an inter vivos creation of an interest is more difficult because it is dependent on when a transfer becomes complete for gift tax purposes.[36] For example, if a settlor gives *A* an interest in a revocable trust, there is no completed transfer[37] for gift tax purposes, and a disclaimer with re-

---

be accepted as evidence of delivery. See Reg. § 301.7502-1(d)(3)(ii). A receipted copy of the disclaimer would be preferable.

[31] IRC § 2518(b)(2). In some situations, the disclaimant has a choice of persons to whom to transmit the disclaimer. For example, a disclaimer of an interest in an irrevocable inter vivos trust may be made to either the settlor or the trustee of the trust.

[32] IRC § 2518(b)(2)(A); Reg. §§ 25.2518-2(c)(1), 25.2518-2(c)(3)(i). See also IRC § 2518(b)(2)(B), discussed infra text after note 60.

[33] HR Rep. No. 1380, 94th Cong., 2d Sess. 3, 67 (1976), reprinted in 1976-3 CB (Vol. 3) 735, 801.

[34] HR Rep. No. 1380, 94th Cong., 2d Sess. 3, 67 (1976), reprinted in 1976-3 CB (Vol. 3) 735, 801. See Reg. § 25.2518-2(c)(3).
And when is the transfer made in the case of direct skips, distributions, or terminations taxable under Chapter 13? Presumably the event that triggers the nine-month period is the generation-skipping transfer. See HR Conf. Rep. No. 1515, 94th Cong., 2d Sess. 617 (1976), reprinted in 1976-3 CB (Vol. 3) 807, 967. But see Reg. § 25.2518-2(c)(5) Ex. 3 (implying that it is the date of the creation of the trust, not the date of the taxable termination). Cf. IRC § 2518(b)(2)(B).

[35] Reg. § 25.2518-2(c)(3)(i). See Reg. §§ 25.2518-2(c)(5) Ex. 5 (disclaimer not within nine months of death), 25.2518-2(c)(5) Ex. 11 (devise of one half of community property timely disclaimed); Estate of Fleming v. Comm'r, 974 F2d 894 (7th Cir. 1992) (time period is nine months after date of death, not admission of will to probate); Fitzgerald v. United States, 73 AFTR2d 93-2323 (WD La. 1993), aff'd without op., 35 F3d 562 (5th Cir. 1994) (nine-month period is not extended on receipt of an extension to file an estate tax return); Rev. Rul. 90-45, 1990-1 CB 175 (Situation 2; disclaimer of elected statutory share did not occur within nine months of death).
With the exception of the rule discussed infra text accompanying notes 58–60, the rules contained in Regulations Section 25.2518-2(c)(3)(i) are applicable for transfers creating the interest to be disclaimed made on or after December 31, 1997. Reg. § 25.2518-2(c)(3)(ii).

[36] Reg. § 25.2518-2(c)(3)(i). See Reg. § 25.2518-2(c)(5) Exs. 3, 4 (timely disclaimers). Gifts that qualify for the annual exclusion are completed transfers for this purpose. Reg. § 25.2518-2(c)(3)(i).

[37] See Burnet v. Guggenheim, 288 US 280 (1933); supra ¶ 10.01[5].

spect to A's interest[38] can be made at any time prior to nine months after the trust becomes irrevocable.[39] The trust may become irrevocable when the settlor relinquishes the power to revoke the trust or when the settlor dies. Even if the trust is irrevocable, if the settlor retains a power to distribute all the corpus either to A or to B, the transfer is not complete for gift tax purposes,[40] and A may validly disclaim A's interest in the trust until nine months after the settlor relinquishes the power by death or otherwise exercises it on A's behalf, whichever occurs first.[41] A gift is complete under this rule even though the property may subsequently be included in the transferor's gross estate.[42]

A person who receives an interest in property as a result of a qualified disclaimer of the interest must also disclaim the previously disclaimed interest no later than nine months after the date of the taxable transfer creating the interest in the preceding disclaimant to make a qualified disclaimer of the interest.[43] Thus, if property is left by will, a residuary beneficiary or an intestate taker must also disclaim any property that the person may subsequently receive as a result of a qualified disclaimer within nine months of decedent's death.[44]

In general, the date-of-creation rules with respect to tenancies with a right of survivorship are consistent with the above rules. If a donor creates a joint tenancy or a tenancy by the entirety, and the transfer to the tenancy is *revocable* by the donor (such as a transfer to a joint bank account or the purchase of a jointly held U.S. savings bond),[45] the donee need not disclaim until the earlier of nine months after the transfer is complete or nine months after the do-

---

[38] Any distributions to A from the trust would be completed gifts on the date of the distribution; for gift tax purposes, an effective disclaimer would have to be made within nine months of each distribution. Reg. § 25.2518-2(c)(5) Ex. 6.

[39] Reg. §§ 25.2518-2(c)(3)(i), 25.2518-2(c)(5) Ex. 6 (revocable trust), 25.2518-2(c)(5) Ex. 12 (revocable joint bank account). HR Conf. Rep. No. 1515, 94th Cong., 2d Sess. 617, 624 (1976), reprinted in 1976-3 CB (Vol. 3) 807, 974, appears vague and confused on this question; but the House Report comment is clear that this result should be reached. HR Rep. No. 1380, 94th Cong., 2d Sess. 3, 67 (1976), reprinted in 1976-3 CB (Vol. 3) 735, 801.

[40] See Estate of Sanford v. Comm'r, 308 US 39 (1939); supra ¶ 10.01[6].

[41] See Reg. § 25.2511-2(d); ¶¶ 10.01[4]–10.01[9] for other situations involving completion of inter vivos transfers. See also supra note 39.

[42] Reg. § 25.2518-2(c)(3)(i). For example, if the transferor creates an inter vivos trust with income to the transferor for a number of years or for life and a remainder to X, X must disclaim within nine months of the transfer because the gift of the remainder is complete even though the property may be included in the transferor's gross estate. See IRC § 2036(a).

[43] Reg. § 25.2518-2(c)(3)(i).

[44] Reg. § 25.2518-2(c)(3)(i); Priv. Ltr. Rul. 9625033 (Mar. 22, 1996) (multiple qualified disclaimers of the same property are all within nine months of the decedent's death).

[45] See Reg. § 25.2511-1(h)(4); ¶ 10.01[5][c].

nor's death.[46] If the donor creates a joint tenancy or tenancy by the entirety and the transfer is *irrevocable*, the donee of the completed gift interest[47] has nine months from the date of the creation of the joint interest to disclaim the portion of the transfer that is a completed gift.[48] On the death of one of the tenants in an irrevocable transfer, a surviving tenant has nine months to make a qualified disclaimer of the interest acquired by right of survivorship.[49] This survivorship rule applies regardless of whether there is a joint tenancy or a tenancy by the entirety, regardless of whether the survivorship interest can be unilaterally severed under local law,[50] regardless of the amount of considera-

---

[46] Reg. § 25.2518-2(c)(4)(iii). See Reg. §§ 25.2518-2(c)(5) Ex. 12 (a revocable joint bank account that the donee disclaims at the donor's death and therefore under state law are treated as the predeceasing donor; an account included in the donor's gross estate under Section 2033), 25.2518-2(c)(5) Ex. 13 (a revocable joint bank account that the donee of the predeceasing donor who may not disclaim because no completed transfer), 25.2518-2(c)(5) Ex. 14 (proportionate disclaimer by the donee of revocable joint account with disclaimed portion included in the donor's gross estate under Section 2033 and undisclaimed portion included under Section 2040).

Similarly, if there is a creation of a joint tenancy or tenancy by the entirety between spouses after July 14, 1988, and the donee surviving spouse is not a U.S. citizen and Section 2523(i)(3) applies (disallowing a marital deduction but currently providing a $110,000 annual exclusion (see ¶ 11.03[5])), the regulations treat the entire property as unilaterally severable and allow the noncitizen spouse to disclaim any portion of the interest that is included in the decedent's gross estate under Section 2040. Reg. §§ 25.2518-2(c)(4)(ii), 25.2518-2(c)(5) Ex. 9. For transfers prior to July 15, 1988 (the date of the enactment of Section 2523(i)(3)), a marital deduction was allowed and transfer treated as any other transfer to a joint tenant under the law in effect at that time.

[47] If the joint tenancy is created with two joint tenants, the completed gift is a gift of one half of the value of the property. The same principles apply to a smaller portion of a joint tenancy if there are more than two joint tenants, i.e., one-third if there are three joint tenants. If the creation is a nonunilaterally severable tenancy by the entirety the amount of the gift depends on the parties' relative life expectancies. See ¶ 10.01[3][c].

[48] Reg. § 25.2518-2(c)(4)(i).

[49] Reg. §§ 25.2518-2(c)(4)(i), 25.2518-2(c)(5) Exs. 7, 8. This rule is effective for disclaimers made on or after December 31, 1997. Reg. § 25.2518-2(c)(4)(iv). For a discussion of disclaimers by a surviving joint tenant prior to December 31, 1997, see Stephens, Maxfield, Lind & Calfee, Federal Estate and Gift Taxation ¶ 10.07[2][b] (Warren, Gorham & Lamont, 7th ed. 1997).

[50] The justification for treating tenancies by the entirety that are not unilaterally severable the same as severable joint tenancies and tenancies by the entirety is that persons purchasing such interests often are not aware that the decision to take title in that form would prevent the survivor from making a valid disclaimer of such survivorship interests within nine months of the death of the predeceasing spouse. TD 8744, Supplementary Information, 62 Fed. Reg. 68,183, 68,184 (1997).

tion furnished by the disclaimant,[51] and regardless of the portion of the property that is included in the decedent's gross estate under Section 2040.[52]

The date-of-creation rules are more complex with respect to powers of appointment. If the power is a nongeneral power, the holder, the permissible appointees, and takers in default all must disclaim within nine months of the creation of the nongeneral power.[53] The holder of a general power of appointment is treated as the owner of the property (to the exclusion of others with potential interests in the property) and the general power holder must disclaim within nine months of the transfer creating the power. A person to whom an interest in property passes upon the exercise, release, or lapse of a general power of appointment must disclaim within nine months after the exercise, release, or lapse regardless of whether the exercise, release or lapse is subject to estate or gift tax.[54] For example, if a decedent transfers property to a testamentary trust with income to A for life, also giving A a general power to appoint the remainder, and provides that B will receive the remainder in default of A's appointment, A must properly disclaim within nine months of the decedent's death to avoid any transfer tax consequences.[55] However, B's interest is contingent upon A's failure to exercise the power; it is an interest that is created upon the lapse of A's power. If A's power lapses, B's disclaimer need not be made until nine months after the lapse.[56] Similarly, if A exercises the power in favor of C, C's disclaimer need not be made until nine months after the creation of C's interest on A's exercise of the power. If C disclaims and, as a result, the property passes to B (as taker in default), B's disclaimer is effective only if made within nine months of the creation of C's interest (on A's exer-

---

[51] Thus, the original creator of the joint interest who made a completed transfer to the other joint owner may disclaim the survivorship interest that passes back to the original creator. Reg. §§ 25.2518-2(c)(4)(i), 25.2518-2(c)(5) Exs. 7, 8.

[52] Reg. § 25.2518-2(c)(4)(i). Compare Reg. § 25.2518-2(c)(5) Ex. 7 (if the parties are unmarried, zero Section 2040(a) inclusion) with Reg. § 25.2518-2(c)(5) Ex. 8 (one-half inclusion under Section 2040(b)).

[53] Reg. §§ 25.2518-2(c)(3)(i), 25.2518-2(c)(5) Ex. 1.

[54] Reg. §§ 25.2518-2(c)(3)(i), 25.2518-2(c)(5) Ex. 2.

[55] Reg. § 25.2518-2(c)(3)(i).

[56] Reg. §§ 25.2518-2(c)(3)(i), 25.2518-2(c)(5) Ex. 2; Priv. Ltr. Ruls. 9842060 (July 22, 1998), 9818053 (Feb. 2, 1998). If A makes a qualified disclaimer of the general power of appointment power rather than exercising it, releasing it, or allowing it to lapse the "person who receives an interest in property as the result of a qualified disclaimer of the interest must disclaim the previously disclaimed interest no later than nine months after the date of the transfer creating the interest in the preceding disclaimant." Reg. § 25.2518-2(c)(3)(i). In such circumstances, B would have to disclaim within nine months of the creation of A's interest on the decedent's death. When A makes a qualified disclaimer of the general power, A's interest in the property disappears and it is as though the power never existed. Once this occurs the property passes pursuant to the direction of the decedent. Since B has received the property from the decedent, B's time clock begins to run on the creation of B's interest.

cise of A's power) rather than within nine months of the date of C's disclaimer.[57]

In the case of qualified terminable interest property,[58] even though the transferee spouse is generally treated as the owner of the property for transfer tax purposes,[59] nevertheless, any third party who has an interest in the property must disclaim the interest within nine months of the transfer creating the interest.[60]

Section 2518(b)(2)(B) creates a special rule for an effective disclaimer by a recipient who is under age 21 at the time of the creation of an interest or power. Under the special rule, the recipient under age 21 need not file a written disclaimer within nine months of creation of the interest, but, instead, has until nine months after attaining age 21. This rule seems sensible when read in conjunction with the requirement that the interest disclaimed must pass to another person because generally under local law an attempted disclaimer by a minor would be ineffective, the property sought to be rejected would not pass to another person, and the federal requirements would not be met. The rule tolling the disclaimer deadline tends to harmonize federal and state law by creating a national standard that conforms to local law.[61]

The date-of-creation rule can create inequitable situations precluding disclaimers otherwise supported by Section 2518 if persons are unaware of the creation of an interest that could be disclaimed. For example, assume A creates an irrevocable inter vivos trust naming specific beneficiaries, but giving B a general power of appointment over the remainder. If B is not informed of the existence of the power until a year after its creation, B is unable to make a "qualified disclaimer" under Section 2518, even though B attempts to do so immediately upon learning of the existence of the power.[62] This situation raises

---

[57] See Reg. §§ 25.2518-2(c)(3)(i), 25.2518-2(c)(5) Ex. 2. Since B received B's interest in the property as a result of the exercise of A's general power of appointment, B effectively receives B's interest from A, and B's time within which to make a qualified disclaimer commences upon the exercise by A of the general power of appointment. Thus, B has nine months from the exercise of A's general power of appointment to make a qualified disclaimer. The result is different where A makes a qualified disclaimer of the general power of appointment and A's general power of appointment simply disappears. See supra note 56.

[58] IRC §§ 2056(b)(7), 2523(f). See ¶¶ 5.06[8][d], 11.03[4][c].

[59] IRC §§ 2044, 2519. Cf. IRC § 2652(a)(3). If a transferee spouse has any interests that would disqualify the qualified terminable interest property (commonly referred to as a QTIP election), those interests may be disclaimed by the transferee spouse within nine months of the transfer in order to qualify the property for qualified terminable interest property treatment.

[60] Reg. § 25.2518-2(c)(3)(i).

[61] See infra ¶ 10.07[2][d].

[62] Other horrors can be paraded here. For example, A creates a post-1942 trust essentially for A's children, but giving a general power of appointment over the trust to A's

the issue whether Section 2518 is the *exclusive* rule with respect to disclaimers under the federal tax laws. The intent of the section is to provide a uniform rule for disclaimers in the estate, gift, and generation-skipping areas, but the section need not be interpreted as exclusive.[63] Although Congress desired a uniform rule on disclaimers, it did not make the statute exclusive on its face,[64] and, in otherwise inequitable situations, even in the face of evidentiary difficulties, the courts should not treat the statute as the exclusive method of disclaimer under the three federal transfer taxes.

[c] Disclaimer May Not Follow an Acceptance

The third condition for a "qualified disclaimer" is that the person disclaiming an interest must not have accepted it or any of its benefits.[65] This condition generally echoes prior law. The regulations provide:

> Acceptance is manifested by an affirmative act which is consistent with ownership of the interest in property. Acts indicative of acceptance include using the property or the interest in property; accepting dividends, interest, or rents from the property; and directing others to act with respect to the property or interest in property. However, merely taking delivery of an instrument of title, without more, does not constitute acceptance. Moreover, a disclaimant is not considered to have accepted property merely because under applicable local law title to the property vests immediately in the disclaimant upon the death of a decedent.[66]

---

worst enemy, *B*. *A* does not inform *B* of the power during *B*'s lifetime. At *B*'s death, several years later but prior to *A*'s death, Section 2041 would include the property in *B*'s estate even though *B* was unaware of the power and consequently incapable of disclaiming it. This might be hazardous to *A*'s children, because depending on the language in the trust and state law, general language in *B*'s will might exercise the power. Compare Section 678(d) of the grantor trust provisions allowing a disclaimer within a "reasonable time" after the holder of a power becomes aware of its existence.

[63] Compare the interrelationship of Section 704(e) and Comm'r v. Culbertson, 337 US 733 (1949); IRC §§ 102, 1221, 1239. See also Rev. Rul. 62-102, 1962-2 CB 37.

[64] Note, however, HR Rep. No. 1380, 94th Cong., 2d Sess. 3, 66, 67 (1976), reprinted in 1976-3 CB (Vol. 3) 735, 800, 801, stating the congressional belief "that a uniform standard should be provided for determining the time within which a disclaimer must be made."

[65] IRC § 2518(b)(3).

[66] Reg. § 25.2518-2(d)(1). Compare Reg. §§ 25.2518-2(d)(4) Ex. 4 (recipient's request to the executor to sell property was acceptance of property), and 25.2518-2(d)(4) Ex. 5 (a pledge of property for a loan was an acceptance of property), with 25.2518-2(d)(4) Ex. 6 (the registration of stock in the recipient's name was not acceptance), and 25.2518-2(d)(4) Ex. 7 (mere execution of will exercising power of appointment was not acceptance of power of appointment), and Rev. Rul. 90-45, 1990-1 CB 175 (election of statutory share prior to disclaimer of a portion of such share is not an acceptance); Estate of Delaune v. United States, 143 F3d 995 (5th Cir. 1998), cert. denied, 525 US 1072

Generally, each interest in property is to be considered separately[67] and acceptance of an income interest in a trust in which the beneficiary has both an income and a remainder interest does not preclude a timely disclaimer of the remainder.[68] In addition, any action taken with regard to an interest in property by a beneficiary or custodian prior to the beneficiary's twenty-first birthday is not an acceptance of the interest, although any acceptance after that date disqualifies a Section 2518 disclaimer.[69] With respect to residential property held in joint tenancy or as community property, a resident's use of the property prior to a disclaimer is not an acceptance of the property.[70]

The regulations indicate that for purposes of this requirement, "[t]he exercise of a power of appointment to any extent by the donee of the power is an acceptance of its benefits."[71] This rule seems overly harsh especially in view of the Section 2518(c)(1) undivided portion rule. Under this rule of acceptance, if the recipient of a general power of appointment over the remainder of a trust appointed one half of it and subsequently disclaimed the power over the other one-half, there would be no "qualified disclaimer" of the second half. If, however, the timely disclaimer of one-half preceded the exercise of the power over

---

(1999) (payment of expenses by the surviving spouse out of community property account and not manifestation of affirmative act consistent with ownership of the deceased spouse's interest in the property); Priv. Ltr. Rul. 9036028 (June 12, 1990) (subsequent disclaimer of a portion of the income interest did not violate the acceptance rule, because the amount of income received prior to the disclaimer did not exceed income from a nondisclaimed portion). Cf. Reg. § 25.2518-2(c)(5) Ex. 6 (return of the check representing a trust income did not constitute acceptance of the income); Estate of Lute, II, v. United States, 19 F. Supp. 2d 1047 (D. Neb. 1998) (court refused to apply step transaction doctrine to find acceptance).

See Reg. § 25.2518-2(d)(2), which provides that the exercise of fiduciary powers to preserve or maintain the property by a fiduciary who is also a beneficiary does not constitute acceptance by the beneficiary; Priv. Ltr. Rul. 199932042 (May 19, 1999) (joint account transferred to the survivor's separate account then, after the survivor appointed the executor, the decedent's share retransferred to estate account not acceptance).

[67] See supra ¶ 10.07[2] text accompanying notes 11–24. Cf. Comm'r v. Herr, 303 F2d 780 (3d Cir. 1962).

[68] Reg. § 25.2518-2(d)(1). See Reg. § 25.2518-2(d)(4) Ex. 1.

[69] Reg. § 25.2518-2(d)(3). Compare Reg. §§ 25.2518-2(d)(4) Ex. 9 (valid disclaimer of interest even though income distributions prior to age 21), and 25.2518-2(d)(4) Ex. 11 (valid disclaimer even though dividends paid prior to age 21), with 25.2518-2(d)(4) Ex. 10 (invalid disclaimer if distribution of income after age 21 and prior to disclaimer).

[70] Reg. §§ 25.2518-2(d)(1), 25.2518-2(d)(4) Ex. 8 (occupancy of a community property residence). See Priv. Ltr. Rul. 9135043 (June 3, 1991) (postdisclaimer occupancy of a joint tenancy residence after a valid disclaimer of survivorship portion did not violate Section 2518(b)(3)). Cf. Reg. § 25.2518-2(d)(4) Ex. 3 (payment of property taxes out of personal funds did not constitute acceptance of property).

[71] Reg. § 25.2518-2(d)(1). This language is taken from the legislative history. See HR Rep. No. 1380, 94th Cong., 2d Sess. 3, 67 (1976), reprinted in 1976-3 CB (Vol. 3) 735, 801. See also Priv. Ltr. Rul. 8142008 (Dec. 31, 1980) (testamentary exercise of power of appointment is an acceptance that cannot be disclaimed by the executor).

Section 2518

the other one-half, there would be a "qualified disclaimer." The difference in results seems improper in view of the undivided portion rule.[72]

In addition, the regulations, following language from the legislative history, indicate that the acceptance of *any* consideration in return for making the disclaimer is to be treated as an acceptance of the benefits of the interest disclaimed.[73] The rationale behind the rule that acceptance of any consideration in return for making a disclaimer disqualifies the Section 2518 disclaimer is also suspect. If a disclaimant has a general power to appoint $100,000 and disclaims it for $50,000, the disclaimant has $50,000 of personal wealth and may have made a $50,000 gift, taking account of the consideration in the manner the regulations require. Yet if the disclaimant simply disclaims a power over one half of the property, and then sells the remaining interest to the taker in default for an adequate and full consideration in money or money's worth, $50,000, or merely appoints $50,000 to the disclaimant, the disclaimant's disclaimer would be valid and the disclaimant's personal wealth again would be $50,000, but there would be no gift tax.

[d] Persons to Whom the Interest Must Pass

The final condition of a "qualified disclaimer" relates to the persons to whom the property will pass.[74] As a result of the disclaimer, the interest generally[75] must pass to someone other than the person (or persons) disclaiming.[76] With one exception,[77] the interest must pass to the other person (or persons) as a result of the disclaimer and not as a result of any direction on the part of the disclaimant. Thus, the disclaimant generally must have no right to determine who will take the disclaimed property.[78] A disclaimant is treated as directing

---

[72] Query: What will result from a simultaneous exercise and disclaimer?

[73] Reg. § 25.2518-2(d)(1); HR Rep. No. 1388, 94th Cong., 2d Sess. 3, 67 (1976), reprinted in 1976-3 CB (Vol. 3) 735, 801. See Reg. § 25.2518-2(d)(4) Ex. 2 (disclaimer of property in return for possession of property for life). But see Estate of Monroe v. Comm'r, 124 F3d 699 (5th Cir. 1997) (unenforceable hope of future benefit, much of which was realized, did not constitute consideration).

[74] IRC § 2518(b)(4). This requirement assures the disclaimer must be valid under local law. Estate of Bennett v. Comm'r, 100 TC 42 (1993) (disclaimer invalid under Section 2518(b)(4) because no valid "passing of an interest" under state law).

[75] But see IRC § 2518(b)(4)(A) involving a disclaimant spouse discussed infra ¶ 10.07[2][d][i].

[76] IRC § 2518(b)(4)(B). See Priv. Ltr. Rul. 8326110 (Mar. 30, 1983) (a disclaimer by the daughter as a personal representative of the surviving spouse mother and was valid even though the property passed to the daughter).

[77] IRC § 2518(c)(3). See the discussion infra ¶ 10.07[2][d][ii].

[78] Reg. § 25.2518-2(e)(1)(i). Cleaveland v. United States, 88-1 USTC ¶ 13,766 (CD Ill. 1988). Compare Reg. §§ 25.2518-2(e)(5) Ex. 9 (ineffective disclaimer because disclaimant effectively determined which taker in default received the property), with 25.2518-

the transfer of a property interest if there is an express or implied agreement that the property is to pass to a person specified by the disclaimant.[79] A disclaimant is also treated as directing the transfer of property if the disclaimant disclaims a beneficial interest in property but continues to hold a fiduciary power that allows the disclaimant to distribute the interest to designated beneficiaries and the power is not subject to an ascertainable standard.[80] The no direction requirement assures that the disclaimer must be sufficient under state

---

2(e)(5) Ex. 10 (an effective disclaimer of specific property results in no direction on disclaimant's part). Precatory language used in naming the taker of disclaimed property is disregarded if applicable state law gives the language no legal effect. Reg. §§ 25.2518-2(e)(4), 25.2518-2(e)(5) Ex. 8; TAM 9509003 (Nov. 3, 1994).

A power of appointment may be disclaimed if there is no direction on the part of the disclaimant with respect to the transfer of the interest subject to the power or with respect to the transfer of the power. Reg. § 25.2518-2(e)(1).

[79] Reg. § 25.2518-2(e)(1); De Paoli v. Comm'r, 66 TCM (CCH) 1493 (1993).

[80] Reg. § 25.2518-2(e)(1). Compare Reg. §§ 25.2518-2(e)(5) Ex. 11 (invalid disclaimer where disclaimant continues to hold power to distribute corpus not limited by an ascertainable standard), with 25.2518-2(e)(5) Ex. 12 (valid disclaimer because retained power limited by an ascertainable standard), and Priv. Ltr. Ruls. 199929027 (Apr. 27, 1999) (qualified disclaimer where the property passed to a charitable foundation because disclaimant directors relinquished all power over the disclaimed property), 199903019 (Oct. 26, 1998) (valid disclaimer where the property passed to a charitable trust because the disclaimant also disclaimed potentially disqualifying powers over a charitable trust). See supra ¶ 10.07[2] text accompanying notes 15–17.

This raises an issue as to the result if the disclaimant continues to hold a nonfiduciary power. Suppose D dies, leaving property in trust, income to A, then income to B, remainder to C, also giving A a general power of appointment over the corpus of the trust. A disclaims the income interest. Is the disclaimer disqualified because, by virtue of A's power, A continues to have authority to redistribute interests in the trust? We think not. Probably, under the trust instrument or local law, B would gain the income interest upon A's disclaimer, certainly without direction by A. A's continuing power over the trust corpus does not violate the statutory requirement that "any interest" disclaimed (IRC § 2518(a)) must pass to "a person other than" the disclaimant (IRC § 2518(b)(4)) "without any direction on the part of" the disclaimant. Id. But see Reg. § 25.2518-2(e)(1)(i), which seemingly reaches the opposite conclusion. Our conclusion may seem more troublesome if A has only a nongeneral power and is not vulnerable to estate or gift tax, even if the trust may be exposed to Chapter 13 tax.

law to cause the property or a portion of the property[81] to pass to a third party.[82]

[i] **Disclaimer by a surviving spouse.** There is one exception to the requirement that the property pass to a third person.[83] If the spouse of a decedent disclaims and, as a result, the property, or some portion of the property, or an interest in the property, nevertheless passes to that spouse, the passing requirement is still met.[84] This exception was enacted to qualify a disclaimer by a decedent's spouse who seeks to disclaim an interest in property that qualifies for a marital deduction where, as a result of the disclaimer, the disclaimant spouse still has an interest in the property but that interest does not qualify for a marital deduction.[85] This provision may be helpful to a surviving spouse who disclaims a portion of the property received from a decedent spouse that exceeds the desired marital deduction in the decedent's estate.[86] For example, if the disclaimed property, which qualified for a marital deduction, passes to a residuary bypass trust in which the surviving spouse has only an income interest and that

---

[81] See Reg. § 25.2518-2(e)(3).

[82] See Reg. § 25.2518-2(e)(1)(ii). Thus, state law affecting disposition on a disclaimer is relevant in determining whether a third person takes the property. Compare Reg. §§ 25.2518-2(e)(5) Ex. 2 (valid disclaimer of all property because state law assumes disclaimant predeceases), with 25.2518-2(e)(5) Ex. 1 (valid disclaimer of only a portion of the property because under state law the other portion of the property passed to disclaimant by means of a residuary clause), and 25.2518-2(e)(5) Ex. 3 (valid disclaimer of only a portion of the property where the other portion of the property passed to the disclaimant as an heir at law). There would have been a valid total disclaimer in Regulations Section 25.2518-2(e)(5) Ex. 1, if the disclaimant had also disclaimed the interest in the residuary estate and in Regulations Section 25.2518-2(e)(5) Ex. 3, if the disclaimant had disclaimed any intestate share. See also Estate of Delaune v. United States, 143 F3d 995 (5th Cir. 1998), cert. denied, 525 US 1072 (1999) (disclaimer by heirs of a dead heir valid under state law).

Cf. Drye v. United States, 528 US 49 (1999) (regardless of differences in state law, a taxpayer whose property is subject to a federal tax lien under Section 6321 may not effectively disclaim inherited or bequeathed property because, under local law, the taxpayer has "property" or "rights to property" for federal tax purposes under Section 6321, which override any effective disclaimer under local law).

[83] IRC § 2518(b)(4)(A). This exception was added by the Revenue Act of 1978, Pub. L. No. 95-600, § 702(m)(1), 92 Stat. 2935 (1978), reprinted in 1978-3 CB 169.

[84] IRC § 2518(b)(4)(A). See Reg. § 25.2518-2(e)(2).

[85] See Reg. § 25.2518-2(e)(5) Exs. 4, 7 (disclaimed share of marital deduction trusts passed to nonmarital deduction trusts).

[86] See ¶ 5.06[6]. The rule can also be useful in making a qualified plan or individual retirement account eligible for a rollover. See Priv. Ltr. Ruls. 9752072 (Oct. 1, 1997), 9847026 (Aug. 25, 1998), 9609052 (Dec. 7, 1995). It may also be useful for other deferred compensation planning. See Priv. Ltr. Rul. 9723028 (Mar. 10, 1997).

does not qualify for a marital deduction, the disclaimer is still a qualified disclaimer.[87]

Suppose a spouse disclaims a trust interest and, as a result of the disclaimer, the spouse retains a power to direct the beneficial enjoyment of the property in a transfer that would *not* be subject to transfer tax. In that situation, unless the power is subject to an ascertainable standard, the spouse is treated as directing a transfer of the property and the spouse's disclaimer is invalid.[88] Such a power violates Section 2518(b)(4) because the property does not pass to the spouse (i.e., is not subject to a transfer tax on spouse's exercise of the power)[89] and yet the spouse holds a power (not limited to an ascertainable standard) to direct where it passes.[90] If the spouse holds no directive power, the spouse's disclaimer is not disqualified. Thus, if property otherwise validly disclaimed may be paid to the spouse pursuant to an independent trustee's power to distribute property to the spouse, there is a qualified disclaimer.[91]

[ii] Disclaimers ineffective under local law. While the federal rule is aimed at providing a uniform procedure for federal transfer tax purposes, nevertheless the efficacy of a disclaimer is often dependent on the property's pass-

---

[87] A decedent's spouse who seeks to disclaim an outright interest in the property where, as a result of the disclaimer, the property passes to a residuary trust in which the spouse has merely an income interest would fall within this rule. See Priv. Ltr. Rul. 9646010 (Aug. 12, 1996) (formula disclaimer by the surviving spouse to maximize use of the decedent's Section 2010 credit). Similarly, the rule is also useful to support the disclaimer of a portion of a general power or an excessive QTIP election if a marital deduction trust exceeds the predeceasing spouse's desired marital deduction and the surviving spouse has an interest in a residuary trust that does not qualify for a marital deduction.

[88] Reg. §§ 25.2518-2(e)(2), 25.2518-2(e)(5) Ex. 5 (invalid disclaimer where, as a result of the disclaimer, the surviving spouse held an inter vivos or testamentary nongeneral power of appointment over the remainder). The spouse could have avoided the result by also disclaiming the nongeneral power over the disclaimed portion of the property passing to the trust. Reg. § 25.2518-2(e)(5) Ex. 5. Compare Reg. §§ 25.2518-2(e)(5) Ex. 4 (valid disclaimer where the surviving spouse had only an income interest in the nonmarital trust), and 25.2518-2(e)(5) Ex. 6 (valid disclaimer where the spouse had an income interest, invasion power subject to a standard and third-party trustee could invade corpus of nonmarital trust for the spouse).

[89] For these purposes, a five-or-five power is treated as a transfer that would be subject to transfer tax even though for gift tax purposes it qualifies for a Section 2514(e) exclusion. Reg. § 25.2518-2(e)(5) Ex. 7 (five-or-five power over the disclaimed property did not invalidate the disclaimer); Priv. Ltr. Rul. 9818008 (Dec. 30, 1997) (five-or-five power over the disclaimed property did not invalidate the disclaimer).

[90] Cf. supra ¶ 10.07[2] text accompanying notes 15–17.

[91] Reg. § 25.2518-2(e)(5) Ex. 6; Priv. Ltr. Rul. 9320015 (Feb. 17, 1993) (qualified disclaimer by the surviving spouse despite the fact that the trustee may thereafter distribute principal to the disclaimant "as is necessary for maintenance in health and reasonable comfort").

ing to a third person, which in turn is dependent on the requirements of local law. Congress realized that it was overemphasizing local law[92] and subsequently added Section 2518(c)(3) to the statute, an exception allowing a valid disclaimer even though local disclaimer law was not satisfied.[93] Under this exception, certain transfers qualify as disclaimers for federal transfer tax purposes even if the disclaimer is not effective under local law. The following conditions must be met: there must be a written transfer of the transferor's entire interest in the property,[94] which is timely made,[95] to a person who would have received the property had the transferor made a qualified disclaimer,[96] and the transferor must not have accepted any of the interest or its benefits.[97]

[3] Effective Date

Section 2518 generally applies to a qualified disclaimer of a property interest created by a transfer made after December 31, 1976.[98] Section 2518(c)(3) is effective for disclaimers after 1981.[99]

---

[92] See Blazek & O'Donoghue, "Use of Disclaimers in Post Mortem Planning," 40 NYU Inst. on Fed. Tax'n ¶ 7.03[1] (1982); Evaul, "Federal Taxation: Section 2518 Disclaimers—Anything but Uniform," 31 Fla. L. Rev. 1988 (1978).

[93] For an example of a valid Section 2518(c)(3) disclaimer, see Priv. Ltr. Rul. 9135043 (June 3, 1991). The regulations applicable to Section 2518(c)(3) are reserved. Reg. § 25.2518-1(c)(1)(ii).

[94] IRC § 2518(c)(3).

[95] IRC §§ 2518(b)(2), 2518(c)(3)(A).

[96] IRC § 2518(c)(3)(B). See Rev. Rul. 90-110, 1990-2 CB 209 (disclaimer ineffective under state law).

[97] IRC §§ 2518(b)(3), 2518(c)(3)(A). Local law is still applicable in order to determine the identity of the transferee. An individual's direction of the transfer to the individual who would have taken under local law pursuant to an effective disclaimer will not be construed as an acceptance of the property. HR Rep. No. 201, 97th Cong., 1st Sess. 191 (1981), reprinted in 1981-2 CB 352, 391.

[98] See Reg. § 25.2518-1(a).

[99] It was added by the Economic Recovery Tax Act of 1981, Pub. L. No. 97-34, § 426(a), 95 Stat. 172, 318 (1981), reprinted in 1981-2 CB 256, 333. Cf. Reg. §§ 25.2518-1(c)(1)(i), 25.2518-1(c)(3).

¶ 10.08 SECTION 2519. DISPOSITION OF CERTAIN LIFE ESTATES

[1] The General Rule

Section 2519 is the gift tax counterpart to estate tax Section 2044.[1] It is an essential element of the statutory framework dealing with the qualified terminable interest property exception to the terminable interest rule of the gift tax and the estate tax marital deductions.[2] Congress allows a marital deduction to a transferor spouse or a transferor spouse's estate for the total value of a gift or a bequest of property for the life benefit of a transferee spouse, even though the transferee spouse receives only a qualifying income interest for life[3] and all other interests in the property pass to third parties. Under Sections 2056(b)(7) and 2523(f), *all* interests in the property are treated as if they were transferred outright to the transferee spouse in determining the amount of the marital deduction allowed. If the transferee spouse makes no inter vivos disposition of any part of the qualifying income interest during the transferee spouse's life, Section 2044 includes the full value of the property[4] in the transferee spouse's gross estate at the transferee spouse's death.[5]

On the other hand, if the transferee spouse makes an inter vivos disposition of *all or any part* of the transferee spouse's qualifying income interest in the trust property subject to a qualified terminable interest property election, Section 2519 treats the transferee spouse, for purposes of the gift and estate taxes, as making a transfer of all interests in the *entire property other than the*

---

[1] See ¶ 4.16. Section 2519 was added by the Economic Recovery Tax Act of 1981, Pub. L. No. 97-34, § 403(d)(3)(B)(i), 95 Stat. 172, 304 (1981), reprinted in 1981-2 CB 256, 326.

[2] IRC § 2056(b)(7), discussed ¶ 5.06[8][d]; IRC § 2523(f), discussed ¶ 11.03[4][c].

[3] IRC §§ 2056(b)(7)(B)(ii), 2523(f)(2)(B). If the transferee spouse receives a qualifying income interest for life in property, the regulations presume that a deduction was allowed under Section 2056 or Section 2523 by the application of Section 2056(b)(7) or Section 2523(f). Reg. § 25.2519-1(b). See ¶¶ 5.06[8][d], 11.03[4][c]. The regulations also indicate how the presumption may be rebutted, for example, by producing a copy of the return on which no election was made, by showing that because of the threshold amount under Section 6018, no estate tax return was made, or by proving that the transfer to the transferee spouse occurred prior to January 1, 1982, the effective date of Sections 2056(b)(7) and 2523(f). Reg. § 25.2519-1(b). See also Rev. Proc. 2001-38, 2001-1 CB 1335 (QTIP election disregarded for purposes of Section 2519(a) where proven not necessary to reduce estate taxes to zero).

[4] As the transferee spouse is deceased, the transferee spouse's life interest has expired and the transferee spouse's gross estate includes only interests subsequent to the transferee spouse's life interest. See ¶ 4.05[5][b].

[5] See IRC § 2044(b)(2); ¶ 4.16. See also infra ¶ 10.08[2] note 41.

qualifying income interest.[6] Since the qualifying income interest is a separate interest for transfer tax purposes and is directly owned by the transferee spouse, no assistance is needed from Section 2519 to accomplish the transfer of that interest, as it falls within the normal rules of Section 2511. But Section 2519 treats all other interests in the property as being transferred by the transferee spouse under the transfer taxes when the transferee spouse makes any inter vivos disposition of all or any part of the qualifying income interest.[7] Thus, to the extent that there are other interests subsequent to the transferee spouse's qualifying income interest (e.g., a secondary life interest and a remainder), the Section 2519 transfer includes the value of those other interests as well. These rules apply regardless of whether the qualifying income interest is in a trust or is simply a legal life estate followed by a remainder.[8]

A Section 2519 transfer can be avoided if the transferor spouse restricts the disposition of the transferee spouse's qualifying income interest by means of a spendthrift clause. In that event, the property subject to the qualified terminable interest property election will be included in the transferee spouse's gross estate under Section 2044.[9]

[a] Disposition of a Portion of the Transferee Spouse's Qualifying Income Interest

Arguably, a disposition of only a portion of the transferee spouse's qualifying income interest could be treated as a Section 2519 transfer of only a commensurate portion of the other interests in the property. This would be consistent with the underlying concept that treats the transferee spouse as the outright owner of the entire corpus and would produce a less harsh transfer tax

---

[6] IRC § 2519(a); Reg. § 25.2519-1(a). See infra ¶ 10.08[1][a].

Although Regulations Section 25.2519-1(a) specifically refers directly to a Section 2519 transfer as a transfer for gift and estate tax purposes, it should be treated as a transfer for generation-skipping transfer tax purposes as well unless a Section 2652(a)(3) reverse QTIP election has been made. See ¶ 17.02[1][c][i].

[7] IRC § 2519(a); Reg. § 25.2519-1(a). Section 2207A(b) authorizes the transferee spouse to recover from the donees the amount of gift tax paid on the Section 2519 transfer. See the discussion of Section 2207A(b) at ¶ 8.07[3]. If the transferee spouse utilizes Section 2207A(b), the donees are legally obligated to pay the gift taxes arising from such Section 2519 transfers without any recourse against the donor. This should be treated as a net gift, and the amount of any Section 2519 transfer should be reduced by the Section 2207A(b) recovery amount. That result has been reached in several private rulings. Priv. Ltr. Ruls. 200022031 (Mar. 3, 2000), 200027001 (Mar. 3, 2000), 199936036 (June 14, 1999); TAM 9736001 (May 21, 1997). Regrettably the Treasury has reserved issuing regulations on this issue. Reg. § 25.2519-1(c)(4). They should determine that it is a net gift. See ¶ 8.07[4] text accompanying note 34, ¶ 10.02[6][d].

[8] See ¶ 5.06[8][d].

[9] See supra text accompanying notes 4, 5.

result especially where the transferee spouse assigns only a small portion of the qualifying income interest.[10] However, the proportionate approach suggested was not adopted by the statute.[11] The statute provides that "any disposition of *all or part* of a qualifying income interest for life in any property . . . shall be treated as a transfer of *all interests in such property* other than the qualifying income interest."[12] If merely a portion of the transferee spouse's qualifying income interest is disposed of, *all* property subject to the qualifying income interest, other than the value of the qualifying income interest, is treated as transferred for both gift and estate tax purposes under Section 2519.[13] Thus, where only a portion of the qualifying income interest is transferred, a Section 2519 transfer can trigger Section 2702 (if another interest in the property is held by a member of the transferor's family)[14] and, the Treasury contends, can result in estate tax inclusion under Section 2036(a) (if the remaining portion of the qualifying income interest is retained until death).[15]

---

[10] See supra ¶ 10.08[1] text accompanying notes 3–5.

[11] IRC § 2519(a). As a result of this rule, if Section 2519 has previously applied, Section 2044 will include none of the property in the surviving spouse's gross estate. IRC § 2044(b)(2); Reg. § 20.2044-1(e) Ex. 5. See infra ¶¶ 10.08[1][b] note 27, 10.08[2] note 39. But see infra text accompanying note 15. Similarly, if Section 2519 applies when there is a transfer of a portion of a qualifying income interest, it does not apply to a subsequent inter vivos transfer of all or any part of a remaining portion of a qualifying income interest. Cf. IRC § 2044(b)(2).

The legislative history and the regulations are consistent with the statutory approach. HR Rep. No. 201, 97th Cong., 1st Sess. 161 (1981), reprinted in 1981-2 CB 352, 378. The legislative history was reinforced by the Technical Corrections Act of 1982, Pub. L. No. 97-448, § 104(a)(3)(A), 96 Stat. 2365, 2380 (1982), reprinted in 1983-1 CB 451, 459. Reg. §§ 20.2044-1(e) Ex. 5, 25.2519-1(a), 25.2519-1(g) Ex. 4.

[12] IRC § 2519(a) (emphasis added).

[13] Reg. § 25.2519-1(c)(1). In determining the value of the property subject to the qualifying income interest any accumulated income is included and no reduction is made even if some part of the property qualified for a Section 2503(b) annual exclusion on creation of the qualifying income interest. Id. The consequences of the transferee spouse's transfer of the portion of the qualifying income interest are determined under Section 2511. Id.

If the transferee spouse's qualifying income interest is in a trust consisting of only qualified income interest property as a result of a severed trust under Regulations Section 20.2056(b)-7(b)(2)(ii) or Regulations Section 25.2523(f)-1(b)(3)(ii), only the value of the property in the severed trust is subject to the Section 2519 rules. Reg. § 25.2519-1(c)(5).

[14] IRC § 2702(a)(1). Section 2702(e) relying on Section 2704(c)(2) defines the term "member of the family." See ¶ 19.03[2][a][ii]; Reg. §§ 25.2519-1(a), 25.2519-1(g) Ex. 4.

[15] See Reg. §§ 20.2044-1(e) Ex. 5, 25.2519-1(a), 25.2519-1(g) Ex. 4.

The Treasury's position should be challenged. When a QTIP election is made, the transferee spouse is not treated as the outright owner of the entire property. See supra text accompanying notes 10, 11. As a result, when the transferee spouse transfers a portion of the qualifying income interest triggering Section 2519, the transferee does not transfer the remaining income interest that was originally transferred by the transferor spouse and, consequently, under the statutory language of Section 2036(a) did not "transfer" or "[re-

To illustrate an application of this rule, assume there was a valid Section 2056(b)(7) or Section 2523(f) election with respect to a transfer of $1 million to a trust where Transferee Spouse's qualifying income interest is worth $400,000 and the remainder transferred to Children is worth $600,000. If Transferee Spouse makes an immediate gift of one quarter of the income interest worth $100,000, that gift of $100,000 is a completed transfer under Section 2511. There is also a deemed transfer for estate and gift tax purposes under Section 2519 of the *entire* remainder worth $600,000.[16] Since Transferee Spouse is deemed to transfer the remainder to Children who are family members, the remaining retained qualifying income interest (worth $300,000) is valued at zero under Section 2702[17] and the value of Transferee Spouse's Section 2519 transfer is increased by $300,000 to $900,000.[18] Finally, the Treasury contends that at Transferee Spouse's death, three quarters of the trust corpus is included in Transferee Spouse's gross estate under Section 2036(a).[19]

If there were a Section 2056 or Section 2523 deduction with respect to only a specific portion of the property subject to a qualified terminable interest property election under Section 2056(b)(7) or Section 2523(f),[20] only that portion of the property is subject to the Section 2519 rules.[21] For example, if there

---

tain] for . . . life . . . the right to the income from . . . the property." In applying Section 2036, Regulations Section 25.2519-1(a), as well as Regulations Sections 25.2519-1(g) Ex. 4, and 20.2044-1(e) Ex. 5, are unwarranted extensions of the QTIP provisions and inconsistent with the theory underlying those provisions.

[16] Theoretically, regarding the remainder, a $150,000 transfer seems a more appropriate result (one quarter of the qualifying income interest, so one quarter of the remainder); but, as seen above, that result is not consistent with either the statutory language, the legislative history, or the regulations. See supra note 11.

In addition, if the transferee spouse asserts the Section 2207A(b) right to recover the gift tax incurred on the Section 2519 transfer, a net gift transfer should occur, reducing the amount of the Section 2519 transfer. See supra ¶ 10.08[1] note 7; ¶ 8.07[4] text accompanying note 34, ¶ 10.02[6][d]. Further, payment of the tax from the corpus of the trust would reduce the value of the income interest and the amount of the Section 2511 transfer.

[17] IRC § 2702(a)(2)(A). See supra note 14.

[18] Cf. Reg. § 25.2519-1(g) Ex. 4. See also Reg. § 25.2519-1(g) Ex. 5. The Section 2702(d) exception is inapplicable because the transferee spouse transferred the entire remainder.

[19] Reg. §§ 25.2519-1(a), 25.2519-1(g) Ex. 4. See also Reg. §§ 20.2044-1(e) Ex. 5, 25.2519-1(g) Ex. 5. But see supra note 15. An adjustment is also made to the transferee spouse's adjusted taxable gifts under Section 2001(b)(1)(B). If the transferee spouse later disposes of all or part of the remaining qualifying income interest, there is a Section 2511 transfer of that interest and Regulations Section 25.2702-6 applies. See Reg. § 25.2519-1(g) Ex. 4; ¶ 19.03[4][c][i].

[20] See IRC §§ 2056(b)(10), 2523(f)(3).

[21] Reg. § 25.2519-1(c)(2). In determining the amount of the Section 2519 transfer, the same computation can be made as in supra text accompanying notes 16–18 (the value of the entire property subject to the qualifying income interest less the value of the qualify-

was a qualified terminable interest property election made with respect to only $200,000 of the trust (20 percent of the $1 million trust in the earlier example), the qualifying income interest would be worth $80,000 (20 percent of the $400,000 income interest). If the trust were not separated into qualified terminable interest property and non-qualified terminable interest property shares, and if Transferee Spouse made a gift of the entire $400,000 income interest in the trust, the amount of the Section 2519 transfer would be $120,000 (20 percent of the remainder of $600,000). Similarly, if only a part of the property in which Transferee Spouse has an income interest for life is subject to a qualified terminable interest property election and that portion is segregated, and if Transferee Spouse makes a disposition of any portion of the entire income interest or of the qualifying income interest, there is a Section 2519 transfer of the entire value of the portion of the property subject to qualified terminable interest property election.[22]

---

ing income interest increased by any Section 2702 amount), and that computation is then multiplied by the relevant fraction or percentage. Id. See Reg. § 25.2519-1(g) Ex. 3.

[22] Reg. § 25.2519-1(d). If the transferee spouse transfers only a portion of the entire income interest or a portion of the segregated qualified income interest, the amount of the Section 2511 transfer would differ, but the transferee spouse is deemed to have transferred the entire portion of the qualified terminable interest property. For example, under the facts of the hypothetical in the text, if the transferee spouse made a $100,000 Section 2511 transfer of one quarter of the entire $400,000 income interest (thereby making a $20,000 Section 2511 transfer of one quarter of the $80,000 qualifying income interest), there would be a Section 2519 transfer of the value of the QTIP portion of the remainder, or $120,000 (20 percent of $600,000), because the transferee spouse is deemed to transfer all interests in the QTIP property other than the qualifying income interest. In addition, that $120,000 transfer is further increased as a result of Section 2702 by $60,000 (the rest of the qualifying income interest) to $180,000. Under the formula of supra notes 20, 21, this is 20 percent of the $900,000 amount computed supra text accompanying note 18. Thus, the transferee spouse's total transfers are $280,000 ($100,000 under Section 2511 and $180,000 under Sections 2519 and 2702) if one quarter of the entire income interest is transferred. If the transferee spouse made a $20,000 Section 2511 transfer of the $80,000 qualifying income interest where the $200,000 QTIP portion had been segregated from the rest of the $1 million trust, the total gift would be $200,000 ($20,000 under Section 2511 and $180,000 under Sections 2519 and 2702). The amounts gifted in both of these situations should be adjusted if Section 2207A(b) is employed and its application is treated as a net gift. See supra note 16. Further, in either event the Service will contend that where there has been no appreciation in corpus at the transferee spouse's death, $150,000 of the corpus (three fourths of 20 percent of the value) would be included in the transferee spouse's gross estate under Section 2036(a)(1). See Reg. § 25.2519-1(g) Exs. 4, 5; supra note 15.

The Service has ruled that where a QTIP trust established under a decedent's will is validly severed under state law into two QTIP trusts that a disposition of the qualifying income interest in one QTIP trust does not result in the application of Section 2519 to the other QTIP trust. Priv. Ltr. Ruls. 200122025 (Feb. 27, 2001), 200116006 (Dec. 14, 2000), 200044034 (Aug. 8, 2000), 199926019 (Mar. 30, 1999).

When a qualified terminable interest property election is made with respect to only a portion of a trust, if inter vivos distributions of corpus are required to be made first from the qualified terminable interest property portion (so as to minimize inclusion in the transferee spouse's gross estate), if such distributions are made to the transferee spouse, and if the transferee spouse establishes the reduction in the qualified terminable interest property share based on the fair market value of the trust assets at the time of each distribution, then the proportionate amount under Section 2519 is appropriately reduced.[23]

[b] Section 2519 Transfer

Section 2519 artificially creates a "transfer," but that does not mean there is a completed gift for federal tax purposes.[24] For example, assume a transferor spouse creates a trust giving a transferee spouse a qualifying income interest for life with a testamentary power to appoint the remainder among their children and a valid election is made to treat the property as qualified terminable interest property. If the transferee spouse subsequently transfers the qualifying income interest to an unrelated third party,[25] Section 2519 treats the transferee spouse as having also made a transfer of the remainder interest. But the statute recognizes no completed gift of the remainder here, because the transferee spouse retains dominion and control in the form of a power to change the recipients of the remainder interest in the property.[26] When the transferee spouse dies, Section 2038 requires inclusion of the value of the property in the transferee spouse's gross estate.[27]

Although a Section 2519 transfer may be a completed transfer for federal gift tax purposes, it will generally not qualify for a Section 2503(b) annual exclusion. For example, assume a transferor spouse creates a trust with a qualifying income interest for life to a transferee spouse and a remainder to their children and a valid election is made to treat the property as qualified terminable interest property. If the transferee spouse gratuitously transfers the qualify-

---

[23] Reg. § 25.2519-1(c)(3). A numerical example of this rule appears at Regulations Section 25.2519-1(g) Ex. 5.

[24] See, e.g., supra ¶¶ 10.01[4], 10.04[3][a].

[25] This results in a Section 2511 transfer of the qualifying income interest.

[26] Sanford's Estate v. Comm'r, 308 US 39 (1939); Reg. § 25.2511-2.

[27] This is an example of the relationship of Section 2519 to the estate tax provisions. The *transfer* hypothecated by Section 2519, a gift tax section, carries over to bring into play Section 2038, an estate tax section. As a result, Section 2044 is inapplicable. IRC § 2044(b)(2). Cf. Reg. § 20.2044-1(e) Ex. 5. If there had been a transfer of only a portion of the qualifying income interest, the Treasury contends that the remaining portion of the property would also potentially be includible in the transferee spouse's gross estate under Section 2036(a). See supra ¶ 10.08[1][a] notes 15, 19. See also supra ¶ 10.08[1] note 7 involving Section 2207A.

ing income interest to a third party, the transferee spouse makes a completed transfer of the remainder to the children under Section 2519. The gift under Section 2519 does not qualify for any annual exclusions as it is a gift of future interests in the property.[28] If, however, the transferee spouse's gratuitous transfer of the qualifying income interest was to the children and there was a merger of the income and remainder interests of each child under local law, the gifts of each child's combined income and remainder interests would qualify for the annual exclusion.[29]

[2] Meaning of "Disposition"

The term "disposition" as used in Section 2519 is broadly interpreted,[30] but there are some reasonable limitations. If, for example, the transferee spouse has a qualifying income interest in a trust, a reinvestment of the trust corpus is not considered a disposition of the income interest; just a change of the income source.[31] Similarly, if there is a qualified terminable interest in property not in trust (i.e., a legal life estate) and the property is sold and fully reinvested in other property, there is no disposition of the qualifying income interest.[32] This is so even if the reinvested proceeds are transferred to a trust where the transferee spouse has a qualifying income interest.[33]

A Section 2519 disposition includes an outright transfer of the qualifying income interest by sale as well as by gift.[34] If, under the facts of the hypothetical case posed earlier (a qualifying income interest worth $400,000 to Trans-

---

[28] IRC § 2503(b). See ¶ 9.04[2].

[29] See ¶ 9.04[3][a] text accompanying note 59. There would, of course, be a single annual exclusion for each child. Cf. Reg. § 25.2519-1(c)(1) (parenthetical).

[30] See Priv. Ltr. Rul. 200022031 (Mar. 3, 2000) (nonqualified disclaimer of income interest constitutes a disposition). Cf. IRC § 453B. However, the exercise of a power of appointment by any person in favor of the transferee spouse is not treated as a disposition under Section 2519. Reg. § 25.2519-1(e). This is so even though the transferee spouse subsequently disposes of the property. Id. The transferee spouse's subsequent disposition is potentially a transfer under Section 2511.

[31] Reg. § 25.2519-1(f); Priv. Ltr. Rul. 9418013 (May 19, 1994) (QTIP corpus transferred in return for interest-bearing notes to be paid at the transferee spouse's death did not constitute a disposition); FSA 199920016 (Feb. 11, 1999) (transfer of QTIP trust assets for an FLP interest was not a disposition). Cf. Priv. Ltr. Rul. 199915052 (Jan. 20, 1999) (exchange of stock in a closely held company for stock of the publicly held company with the spouse receiving lump-sum distribution for delayed income was not a disposition).

[32] Reg. § 25.2519-1(f).

[33] Reg. § 25.2519-1(f).

[34] Reg. § 25.2519-1(g) Exs. 1, 2; HR Rep. No. 201, 97th Cong., 1st Sess. 161 (1981), reprinted in 1981-2 CB 352, 378.

feree Spouse and a remainder worth $600,000 to Children),[35] Transferee Spouse transfers the qualifying income interest for its $400,000 fair market value, there is no gift of the qualifying income interest because adequate consideration is received.[36] There is, however, a sale of the qualifying income interest that constitutes a disposition under Section 2519.[37] As a result, there is a $600,000 Section 2519 transfer of interests other than the qualifying income interest.[38] Similarly, under the preceding facts, a sale of one half of the income interest for $200,000 is treated (after the application of Section 2702) as an $800,000 Section 2519 transfer.[39]

If there is a sale of the property and the transferee spouse receives proceeds equal in value to the transferee spouse's qualifying income interest, there is a commutation of spouse's interest that constitutes a disposition triggering Section 2519.[40] One suggested method for potentially avoiding taxation of the qualified terminable interest property remainder in a surviving spouse's gross estate is for the surviving spouse to purchase the remainder for its fair market value during the spouse's lifetime, thereby merging the income and remainder interests in the spouse and getting the purchase price for the remainder, which would normally be included under Section 2033 in the surviving spouse's gross estate, out of the spouse's gross estate while delivering that value to the remainderpersons. The Service treats the purchase as a commutation of the trust's income interest and a Section 2519 transfer of the remainder.[41]

---

[35] See the discussion supra ¶ 10.08[1][a] text accompanying note 16.

[36] There is a Section 2511 "transfer," but full consideration shields the transfer from tax. See IRC § 2512, discussed at ¶ 10.02; Reg. § 25.2519-1(g) Ex. 2.

[37] Reg. § 25.2519-1(f).

[38] Reg. § 25.2519-1(g) Ex. 2.

[39] Since the retained income interest (worth $200,000) is valued at zero under Section 2702, the value of the gift of the remainder is increased from $600,000 to $800,000. See supra ¶ 10.08[1][a] text accompanying notes 17, 18.

In this situation, it is worth noting again that upon the transferee spouse's death, Section 2044 will not require any inclusion in the transferee spouse's gross estate, even if the transferee spouse retains one half of the income interest until death because, in the words of the statute, Section 2519 "did . . . apply" to the partial lifetime disposition. IRC § 2044(b)(2). However, see the discussion of the application of Section 2036(a)(1); supra ¶¶ 10.08[1][a] note 15, 10.08[1][a] text accompanying note 19, 10.08[1][b] note 27.

[40] Reg. § 25.2519-1(f). See Reg. § 25.2519-1(g) Ex. 2; Priv. Ltr. Rul. 200013015 (Dec. 22, 1999).

[41] Rev. Rul. 98-8, 1998-1 CB 541. The ruling also alternatively concluded that the transfer of the purchase price was a Section 2511 gift because the receipt of the remainder (potentially includible under Section 2033) did not increase the value of the surviving spouse's gross estate because the remainder would have been included under Section 2044 in any event. Cf. Priv. Ltr. Rul. 199908033 (Nov. 30, 1998) (gratuitous transfer of a remainder interest in a QTIP trust by the children to the surviving spouse was a gift by the children).

Beyond these examples, the meaning of the term "disposition" as used in Section 2519 becomes less certain. What if the transferee spouse transfers the qualifying income interest, but the transfer is incomplete for federal gift tax purposes? The application of Section 2519 should depend on whether the nature of the transfer is such that, for gift tax purposes,[42] the transferee spouse can be said to no longer own the income interest. For example, if the transferee spouse instructs the trustee of a trust in which the transferee spouse has a qualifying income interest for life to accumulate the income but retains the power to retrieve it, there is no disposition of the qualifying income interest because the transferee spouse still owns it. If, instead, the transferee spouse irrevocably instructs the trustee to accumulate the income for the benefit of the children but retains a power to allocate their portions of the accumulated income, the transferee spouse has seemingly made a disposition of the income interest that triggers a Section 2519 transfer of all subsequent interests, even though the disposition of the qualifying income interest is not a completed Section 2511 transfer for federal tax purposes.[43]

[3] Gift Tax Liability

Although the gift tax liability of the transferee spouse arising from a Section 2519 transfer can be recovered from the recipient of the property,[44] the transfer continues to be treated as a gift by the transferee spouse for other transfer tax purposes. For example, the gift tax liability resulting from a Section 2519 transfer is included for purposes of computing gift taxes on the transferee spouse's subsequent inter vivos transfers[45] and for purposes of computing the transferee spouse's estate tax liability.[46] As a result, the gift tax may consume the transferee spouse's Section 2505 credit, making it unavailable to offset subsequent taxable inter vivos transfers.[47] Gift tax paid by the transferee spouse or the transferee spouse's estate on a Section 2519 transfer within three

---

[42] See ¶¶ 10.01[5], 10.01[6].

[43] See ¶ 10.01[6].

[44] See IRC § 2207A(b), discussed ¶ 8.07[3]. Section 2207A(a) is applicable to estate tax liability under Section 2044. See ¶ 8.07[2].

[45] See IRC § 2502. In addition, if a recipient of a qualifying income interest has remarried, the gift will be treated as made one-half by the transferee spouse and one-half by the new spouse if they make a Section 2513 election for the year. See ¶ 10.03.

[46] See IRC §§ 2001(b)(1)(B), 2001(b)(2).

[47] This is so even though part of the gift tax liability is recovered from the recipient under Section 2207A(b). If the amount of a Section 2519 transfer is less than the amount of the transferee spouse's available applicable credit amount, there is no gift tax to recover from the recipient under Section 2207A(b). HR Rep. No. 201, 97th Cong., 1st Sess. 161, 162 (1981), reprinted in 1981-2 CB 352, 379.

years of death is included in the transferee spouse's gross estate under the gross-up concept of Section 2035(b).[48] Even if the transferee spouse or the transferee spouse's estate asserts the transferee spouse's Section 2207A(b) recovery rights, Section 2035(b) should apply to include the gift tax in the transferee spouse's gross estate.[49]

[4] Effective Dates

Section 2519 is applicable to transfers after December 31, 1981.[50] The regulations are generally effective after March 1, 1994.[51]

---

[48] See ¶ 4.07[3].

[49] Cf. Sachs v. Comm'r, 88 TC 769 (1987), discussed ¶ 4.07[3] text accompanying note 83. In the alternative, if Section 2035(b) is inapplicable, the recovered tax or the right to recover the tax is seemingly a property interest that would be included in the transferee spouse's gross estate under Section 2033.

[50] Economic Recovery Tax Act of 1981, Pub. L. No. 97-34, § 403(d)(3)(B)(i), 95 Stat. 172, 304 (1981), reprinted in 1981-2 CB 256, 326. A transitional rule and Section 2519 may be inapplicable if the transferor spouse died after December 31, 1981. See ¶ 5.06[6][b].

[51] Reg. § 25.2519-2. But see Reg. § 25.2519-1(g) Ex. 6, applicable only where the transferor spouse made a transfer of a spousal annuity payable from a trust subject to a QTIP election prior to October 24, 1992. With respect to Section 2519 transfers made prior to March 2, 1994, any reasonable interpretation of the statutory provisions may be relied on. Reg. § 25.2519-2.

CHAPTER **11**

Gift Tax Deductions

¶ 11.01 INTRODUCTION

Gift tax rates are applied to "taxable gifts," which are computed by applying three principal steps:

1. Identification of transfers subject to the gift tax,[1] which raises, among others, questions about whether a transfer is complete and whether it is for a recognized consideration;
2. Application of the annual exclusion to the extent that it is permitted to scale down such gifts;[2] and
3. Subtraction of the statutory deductions that may be taken into account in computing net or "taxable" gifts.[3]

This third step is the subject of this chapter.[4]

---

[1] See Chapter 10. Qualified transfers for educational and medical expenses are not treated as transfers subject to Chapter 12. See IRC § 2503(e) discussed ¶ 9.04[6].

[2] See ¶¶ 9.04[1]–9.04[5].

[3] A $30,000 lifetime exemption allowed as a deduction by Section 2521 was repealed by the Tax Reform Act of 1976, effective for gifts made after 1976. Tax Reform Act of 1976, Pub. L. No. 94-455, § 2001(b)(3), 90 Stat. 1520, 1849 (1976), reprinted in 1976-3 CB (Vol. 1) 1, 1325. The repealed exemption is discussed in Stephens, Maxfield & Lind, Federal Estate and Gift Taxation 10-1–10-4 (Warren, Gorham & Lamont, 3d ed. 1974). The Section 2505 credit, which replaces the Section 2521 exemption, is discussed at ¶ 9.06.

[4] Computation of the tax liability and the Section 2505 credit are discussed at ¶¶ 9.02, 9.03, 9.05, and 9.06.

¶ 11.02 SECTION 2522. CHARITABLE AND SIMILAR GIFTS

Lifetime philanthropy escapes the gift tax in much the same way that a charitable bequest generates no liability for estate tax, again by way of a deduction.[1] Similarities in Sections 2055 and 2522, the two deduction sections, justify a more abbreviated treatment here of Section 2522 on the assumption that the reader will closely coordinate a study of these materials with the discussion of Section 2055 in Chapter 5.

There is one major tax difference between inter vivos and testamentary charitable gifts. An inter vivos charitable gift is potentially deductible in the computation of taxable income[2] as well as in the computation of taxable gifts;[3] there is no double deduction proscription, such as the one that affects some estate tax deductions.[4] A testamentary charitable gift, on the other hand, is deductible under the transfer tax, but not under the income tax.[5] This difference provides an added incentive to make inter vivos rather than testamentary charitable transfers.[6]

[1] Charitable Transfers in General

[a] Qualified Recipients

Direct gratuities to poor or otherwise worthy individuals, no matter how much they may be inspired by charitable impulses, give rise to no gift tax charitable deduction.[7] To be deductible, gifts must be made to qualified recipient organizations.[8]

---

[1] IRC § 2055, discussed ¶ 5.05.

[2] IRC § 170. The income tax deduction rules are beyond the scope of this book, but they are complex and must be carefully studied when one is making an inter vivos charitable gift for which an income tax deduction is sought. See Henkel, Estate Planning and Wealth Preservation, ¶¶ 32.01–32.05 (Warren, Gorham & Lamont, 1997).

[3] IRC § 2522.

[4] See IRC § 642(g).

[5] See IRC §§ 170, 2055.

[6] See Henkel, Estate Planning and Wealth Preservation, ¶ 32.02[1] (Warren, Gorham & Lamont, 1997).

Although such inter vivos gifts are tempered by the lifetime loss of the use of the transferred funds, inter vivos giving to charities is increasing in this expanding economy in several forms such as gifts to community foundations and similar commercially run national programs, charitable split-dollar insurance, charitable lead and remainder trusts, and family limited partnership interests transferred to charity. A detailed discussion of most of these planning techniques is beyond the scope of this text.

[7] See ¶ 5.05[1].

[8] IRC § 2522(a).

Congress describes with some particularity the recipients that qualify for deductible contributions. With respect to gifts made by citizens or residents,[9] the qualified recipients described in Section 2522(a) are virtually the same as those described in Section 2055(a),[10] but it is surprising that these parallel sections are not identical.[11] Generally, the four categories of qualified recipients are as follows:

1. The United States, any state, territory, or political subdivision thereof, including the District of Columbia. Gifts to these governmental units are deductible, however, *only* if they must be used "for exclusively public purposes."[12]

2. Corporations, trusts, community chests, funds, or foundations organized and operated exclusively for religious, charitable, scientific, literary, or educational purposes, including the encouragement of art, the fostering of national or international amateur sports competitions,[13] and the prevention of cruelty to children or animals.[14] These organizations qualify, however, only if no part of their net earnings inures to the benefit of an individual; they carry on no lobbying or propaganda activities proscribed by Section 501(c)(3); and in the case of gifts af-

---

[9] See infra text accompanying notes 19–21 for gifts by nonresident noncitizens.

[10] See IRC § 2055, discussed ¶ 5.05[2]. Qualified recipients may include foreign charities. See ¶ 5.05[1][b] text accompanying note 41.

[11] Cf. infra ¶ 11.02[2][b] note 82.

[12] IRC § 2522(a)(1); Reg. § 25.2522(a)(1). Under numerous statutes not incorporated into the Code, gifts to various federal agencies and foundations are considered gifts to the United States and, as such, deductible: for example, Act of Oct. 2, 1964, Pub. L. No. 88-611, § 2, 78 Stat. 991 (1964) (gifts to Dep't of Commerce deductible); Nat'l Found. on the Arts and Humanities Act of 1965, Pub. L. No. 89-209, § 10(a), 79 Stat. 845, 853 (1965) (gifts to National Foundation on the Arts and Humanities deductible). See ¶ 5.05[1][b] note 20.

Gifts to a political party or to a candidate for public office are not gifts to the United States. Rev. Rul. 59-57, 1959-1 CB 626. But see IRC § 2501(a)(5), discussed ¶ 9.02[2], which excludes gifts to political organizations for the use of such organizations from the grasps of the gift tax.

[13] In general, no part of the activities may involve the provision of athletic facilities or equipment. However, if the organization is a "qualified amateur sports-organization" as defined in Section 501(j)(2), it will qualify for a deduction even though it provides athletic facilities and equipment and even though it is a regional or local organization. See IRC § 2522(a) (last sentence).

[14] IRC § 2522(a)(2). As deductibility is predicated on the recipient's being organized and operated exclusively for the enumerated purposes, the statute does not require that the donor specify a particular use for the gift. Specification of a particular use may, however, endanger the deduction. For example, it is clear that a gift to a college to be used for a scholarship for a named individual would not qualify. But see Rev. Rul. 60-367, 1960-2 CB 73, holding a gift to a college for fraternity housing, if made in accordance with certain terms, is deductible for income, estate, and gift tax purposes. See ¶ 5.05[1][a] note 7.

ter December 31, 1969, they do not participate in or intervene in any political campaign on behalf of (or in opposition to) any candidate for public office.[15]

3. A fraternal society, order, or association, operating under the lodge system. Here again, as with governmental entities, because of the varied activities of such organizations, the donor must restrict the use of the gift to religious, charitable scientific, literary, or educational purposes in order to achieve a deduction.[16] Under the statutory language of Section 2522, a fraternal society, order, or association, operating under the lodge system, is not a disqualified recipient by reason of its engaging in lobbying or political activities. Such activities, however, may disqualify these organizations under Section 2055.[17]

4. Posts or organizations of war veterans and auxiliary units or societies of any such posts or organizations.[18] The added requirements here are that such organizations must be organized in the United States or its possessions and that no part of their earnings may benefit a private individual.

With regard to gifts by a nonresident who is not a citizen of the United States, Section 2522(b) imposes two additional requirements for deductibility. First, gifts to an otherwise qualified corporation[19] are deductible only if the corporation is organized under the laws of the United States.[20] Second, a gift to a trust, community chest, fund, foundation, or fraternal order that meets all the previously described restrictions is deductible only if the gift is to be used within the United States.[21]

In addition to the criteria described previously, Congress has continually sought to prevent a dilution of the philanthropy for which it permits a deduction by way of indirect benefits returned to the donors out of their otherwise qualified gifts. The restrictions in Section 2522(c)(1)[22] sometimes cause private foundations, nonexempt trusts, and foreign organizations that are subject to

---

[15] These kinds of restrictions are considered in the parallel discussion of Section 2055, at ¶ 5.05[1][b] text accompanying notes 26–36.

[16] IRC § 2522(a)(3). See Rev. Rul. 56-329, 1956-2 CB 125. Such purposes specifically include the encouragement of art and the prevention of cruelty to animals and children, but not the fostering of national or international amateur sports competitions.

[17] Compare IRC § 2522(a)(3) with IRC § 2055(a)(3). But see Reg. § 25.2522(a)-1(a).

[18] IRC § 2522(a)(4). See Rev. Rul. 84-140, 1984-2 CB 56.

[19] IRC § 2522(b)(2).

[20] See Reg. § 25.2522(b)-1(a)(1).

[21] IRC §§ 2522(b)(3), 2522(b)(4).

[22] The restrictions are applicable to gifts made after Dec. 31, 1969. Tax Reform Act of 1969, Pub. L. No. 91-172, § 201(g)(4)(D), 83 Stat. 487, 565 (1969), reprinted in 1969-3 CB 10, 54.

special taxation to lose their status as qualified recipients of charitable contributions when they provide indirect benefits back to the donor.[23]

[b] The Amount of the Deduction

In general, the gift tax charitable deduction is measured by the amount of money given or, for gifts of property other than cash, by the fair market value of the property given.[24] If the donor owns only a temporal interest in property and the donor gives that entire interest to charity[25] or carves such an interest out of a fee simple,[26] the interest is valued under Section 7520.[27] The amount of any gift tax charitable contribution is reduced by the amount of any consideration received directly or indirectly by the donor.[28]

The same general approach also determines the amount to be included in the annual computation of taxable gifts, so that an included but deductible charitable gift is offset by a matching deduction and generates no tax liability.[29] No percentage or other limitation, such as those that restrict the amount of the income tax charitable deduction,[30] affects the gift tax deduction. However, a Section 2503(b) annual exclusion is allowed in the computation of taxable gifts and is applicable to charitable as well as private gifts.[31] Therefore, to assure that the charitable deduction removes only the amount of the charitable gift from the tax base and does not operate to reduce the donor's taxable gifts to others, Section 2524 limits the charitable deduction to the included amount of the charitable gifts.[32]

---

[23] See the discussion of Section 2055(e)(1), at ¶ 5.05[1][c] for a brief analysis of the restrictions. See also Reg. § 25.2522(c)-2.

[24] IRC §§ 2522(a), 2522(b). However, see infra text accompanying notes 31 and 32, discussing the interrelationship of Sections 2522 and 2524.

[25] See Rev. Rul. 86-60, 1986-1 CB 302.

[26] See infra ¶ 11.02[2].

[27] See Reg. §§ 25.7520-1, 25.7520-2 (especially § 25.7520-2(a)(2)), 25.7520-3. See also Reg. § 25.2522(c)-3(d) on valuation of deductible gifts of carved-out partial interests to charity.

[28] IRC § 2512. If a transfer is made to a qualified recipient for partial consideration, the consideration will reduce the amount of the gift (IRC § 2512), and will correspondingly reduce the amount of the deduction. Rev. Rul. 80-281, 1980-2 CB 282. Cf. IRC § 2524.

The transfer presents no serious part-gift, part-sale problem, such as the one that arises under the income tax (see IRC § 1011(b)), because the taxpayer's basis for property is not a factor in gift tax matters.

[29] See infra ¶ 11.02[1][e].

[30] IRC §§ 170(b), 170(e).

[31] See Reg. § 25.2502-1(d) Ex. 3.

[32] See IRC § 2524, discussed ¶ 11.04.

[c] Timing of the Deduction

The charitable deduction is allowed for the year in which a contribution is "made."[33] This is generally the year in which a gift is complete.[34] A transfer by check is generally deductible in the year in which it is delivered, provided that it is honored and paid and there are no restrictions on the time or manner of payment.[35] If one makes a charitable pledge, a deduction is allowed for the year in which the pledge becomes a binding obligation, rather than in the year in which payment of the pledge is made.[36]

[d] Property Passing From the Donor

A donor may make a charitable transfer in a direct or in some indirect manner. For example, if a donor exercises a general power of appointment[37] in favor of a charity resulting in a transfer that would be deductible if made in an outright transfer of the property, the donor qualifies for a charitable deduction.[38] Similarly, if as a result of a qualified disclaimer by the original donee[39] a donor's transfer passes to a charity, the transfer is treated as made directly by the donor to the charity, and the transfer qualifies for a charitable deduction. Various other types of indirect charitable transfers to charity may occur. For example, if a donor makes a transfer of property to X on the condition that X transfers a dollar amount to charity, the donor has made a gift to X of the value of the property less the dollar amount and a transfer of the dollar amount to charity.[40]

[e] Gift Tax Return

A Form 709 gift tax return[41] is not required to be filed for many transfers that, after consideration of Section 2524, fully qualify for a gift tax charitable

---

[33] IRC §§ 2522(a), 2522(b).

[34] See ¶¶ 10.01[4]–10.01[9].

[35] Rev. Rul. 54-465, 1954-2 CB 93. Cf. ¶ 10.01[3][h] text accompanying note 122.

[36] Rev. Rul. 81-110, 1981-1 CB 479.

[37] See IRC § 2514; ¶ 10.04.

[38] The transfer is effectively a wash for gift tax purposes. See supra ¶ 11.02[1][b] text accompanying notes 29–32.

[39] See IRC § 2518; ¶ 10.07.

[40] However, if a third party satisfies a binding charitable pledge of a pledgor, the third party makes a gift to the pledgor, not to the charity. Rev. Rul. 81-110, 1981-1 CB 479.

[41] Form 709, United States Gift (and Generation-Skipping Transfer) Tax Return (2001).

deduction under Section 2522.[42] No return is required for a transfer of the donor's entire interest in property[43] if no other interest in such property is or has been transferred (other than a transfer for adequate and full consideration in money or money's worth) from the donor to a person or for a use not described in Section 2522(a)[44] or Section 2522(b).[45] In addition, no return is required for a transfer of an easement in real property that qualifies for a deduction under Section 2522(d).[46]

[2] Mixed Private and Charitable Gifts

[a] Introduction

When a donor makes a charitable gift to a qualified recipient, but delays the recipient's enjoyment of the gift by reserving the present use or benefit of the gift for a private purpose or individual or, in the alternative, provides for a gift to charity in the form of a present use or benefit of property followed by other interests passing for private purposes, the deductible amount should equal only the present value of the interest the charitable recipient will receive. Although the concept is clear, determination of the present value of the charitable interest is difficult and has been a source of controversy and litigation. Further valuation complications arise if the ultimate enjoyment of the charitable interest is contingent upon the occurrence or nonoccurrence of some event, or if the interest may be diminished by a power of invasion. In 1969, Congress undertook to eliminate many of these problems by imposing formula requirements for deductible gifts that mix private and philanthropic objectives.[47]

---

[42] IRC § 6019(a)(3). This rule is applicable on transfers made after August 5, 1997. The Taxpayer Relief Act of 1997, Pub. L. No. 105-34, § 1301(a), 111 Stat. 788, 1039 (1997), reprinted in 1997-4 (Vol. 1) CB 1, 253. See ¶ 9.04[9] text accompanying notes 201–205; IRC § 2524, discussed ¶ 11.04.

[43] A gift tax return is required for mixed private and charitable gifts. See infra ¶ 11.02[2]. This is because such transfers will result in partial noncharitable gifts potentially subject to the gift tax. Even if such noncharitable gifts are fully within Section 6019(a)(1) (the annual exclusion) or Section 6019(a)(2) (the marital deduction), a return is nevertheless still required. IRC § 6019(a)(3)(A)(ii).

[44] Subsection 2522(a) involves transfers by citizens or residents. See supra ¶ 11.02[1][a] text accompanying notes 9–18.

[45] IRC § 6019(a)(3)(A). Subsection 2522(b) involves transfers by nonresidents and noncitizens. See supra ¶ 11.02[1][a] text accompanying notes 19–21.

[46] IRC § 6019(a)(3)(B). See infra ¶ 11.02[2][d] text accompanying note 100.

[47] IRC § 2522(c)(2). The rules are not retroactive; prior law applies to gifts made before August 1, 1969. Reg. § 25.2522(a)-2(c). See Reg. §§ 25.2522(a)-2(a), 25.2522(a)-2(b).

Section 2522(c)(2) provides generally that the charitable portion of certain mixed gifts made after July 31, 1969, is not deductible unless certain conditions are satisfied. When these conditions are satisfied, valuation problems are greatly simplified, and if the conditions are not satisfied, the deduction is completely precluded. However, the denial of a gift tax deduction for a charitable lifetime transfer does not necessarily preclude an estate tax deduction under Section 2055 with respect to the same transfer. If a decedent made a lifetime transfer in trust, retained the right to the income for life, and gave the remainder to charity, the rules may preclude a gift tax deduction for the remainder[48] but they do not affect the estate tax deduction, because the offending private interest is "extinguished upon the decedent's death."[49]

The rationale for and the substance of the rules for mixed private and charitable gifts under the gift tax substantially parallel the rules applicable to the estate tax split bequest charitable deduction rules.[50] Consequently, a briefer summary of the rules for charitable gifts of remainder interests, of the rules for gifts of charitable lead interests, of the exceptions to the rules, and of the reformation rules will be presented here highlighting differences between the gift and estate tax rules.[51]

[b] Qualified Remainder Interests

Restrictions are established for the deduction of charitable remainder gifts in an effort to assure that the assumed value of the interest left to charity will

---

Even under the prior law, if the conditions and circumstances surrounding the transfer indicated the charitable beneficiary might not receive the full benefit of its interest, only the minimum amount guaranteed to go to the charitable donee was allowed as a deduction. Reg. §§ 25.2522(c)-3(b)(1), 25.2522(c)-3(b)(2) Exs. 1, 2.

A part of the common law of both the estate tax and the gift tax requires that a transfer to charity should be assured to take effect in enjoyment and be reasonably ascertainable as to value in order to be deductible. This common law continues to be applicable to gifts whenever made, but regarding the mixed gifts discussed here, specific statutory restrictions usually deny a deduction without the need for considering the general principles discussed. Just as in the area of mixed charitable bequests, the controversies under prior gift tax law centered around three situations. See ¶ 5.05[4][a]. The controversies are attractive philosophically but are diminishing in importance with the passage of time. Consequently, we forgo here a reexploration of their pre-1970 solutions, directing readers interested in that area to an earlier edition of this treatise and its supplements, and to the considerable literature discussed there. See Stephens, Maxfield & Lind, Federal Estate and Gift Taxation, 5-44–5-53, 10-8–10-10 (Warren, Gorham & Lamont, 3d ed. 1974).

[48] Reg. § 25.2522(c)-3(c).

[49] Reg. § 20.2055-2(e)(1).

[50] See ¶ 5.05[4].

[51] A more detailed description of the remainder rules appears at ¶ 5.05[5], of the lead rules appears at ¶ 5.05[6], of the exceptions appears at ¶ 5.05[7], and of the reformation rules appears at ¶ 5.05[8].

actually reach the charitable recipient. Toward that end, Congress requires these gifts to be cast in a particular form if the deduction is to be successfully claimed.[52] The gift tax provisions borrow income tax sections of the Internal Revenue Code (the Code) to identify interests qualified under the rules.[53] A deductible gift of a remainder interest is valued in the same manner as gifts of bequests of deductible charitable remainder interests.[54] A charitable remainder is deductible only if it is a remainder in a "charitable remainder annuity trust," a "charitable remainder unitrust," or a "pooled income fund."[55] A brief description of these entities will make it clear that much of the uncertainty regarding what the charity will actually receive is removed in the case of such qualified remainders.

   [i] The charitable remainder annuity trust. A charitable remainder annuity trust (commonly referred to as a CRAT)[56] is defined in Section 664(d)(1).[57] Essentially, a CRAT is a trust that meets four tests:

   1. A fixed annuity amount (not less than 5 percent nor more than 50 percent of the original value of the property at the time it is transferred to the trust) must be paid at least annually to recipients (at least one of which does not qualify under Section 170(c) and who, if

---

[52] Cf. Estate of Gillespie v. Comm'r, 75 TC 374 (1980) upholding the constitutionality of the requirements; infra ¶ 11.02[2][d].

[53] IRC §§ 664(d)(1), 2522(c)(2)(A). See Reg. §§ 1.664-2, 25.2522(c)-3(c)(2)(v).

[54] See Reg. §§ 25.2522(c)-3(d)(2)(i), 25.2522(c)-3(d)(2)(ii), 25.2522(c)-3(d)(2)(iii); ¶¶ 5.05[5][a][ii], 5.05[5][b][ii], 5.05[5][c][ii].

[55] IRC § 2522(c)(2)(A); Reg. § 25.2522(c)-3(c)(2)(v).

See ¶ 11.03[4][d] for the interrelationship of the gift tax marital deduction and valid charitable remainder interests. In the case of a charitable remainder annuity trust or a charitable remainder unitrust, the income interest may also qualify for a marital deduction. IRC § 2523(g). Cf. ¶ 5.06[8][e].

[56] The Service provides useful, but potentially outdated, drafting assistance, including forms that may be used in creating the entities. Rev. Rul. 72-395, 1972-2 CB 340. Rev. Rul. 72-395 is modified by Rev. Ruls. 80-123, 1980-1 CB 205, 82-128, 1982-2 CB 71, 82-165, 1982-2 CB 117, 88-81, 1988-2 CB 127, 92-57, 1992-2 CB 123.

Charitable remainder annuity trust forms are found in Rev. Proc. 89-21, 1989-1 CB 842, and Rev. Proc. 90-32, 1990-1 CB 546. The Service will not issue determination letters as to the qualification of charitable remainder trusts substantially similar to those following the forms set forth in the rulings in this footnote. Rev. Proc. 90-33, 1990-1 CB 551.

The rulings and forms are essential reading for one creating such trusts, although both these rulings and the forms predate recent legislative changes in the statutory requirements. See Notice 2000-37, 2000-2 CB 118, indicating that the Service intends to revise its guidance to reflect statutory and regulatory changes to charitable remainder annuity trusts and unitrusts.

[57] Charitable remainder annuity trusts are discussed in more detail at ¶ 5.05[5][a].

an individual, is living) for not more than twenty years (or for not more than the life or lives of such living individuals).[58]

2. Generally, no other amounts can be paid for uses or to persons other than those organizations qualified for the income tax charitable deduction.[59]

3. When the payments described in test item 1 terminate, the remainder must be paid to or for the use of an organization qualified for the income tax charitable deduction, or retained by the trust for such a use.[60]

4. On the creation of the trust, the value of the remainder interest must be equal to at least 10 percent of the initial net fair market value of the property placed in the trust.[61]

Although it may appear strange that a fixed and even a substantial amount must be paid for the noncharitable use (the at-least-5-percent rule), this fixed payment cures an old difficulty.[62] It removes the "incentive to favor the income beneficiary over the remainder beneficiary by means of manipulating the trust's investments."[63] Payments for private use cannot be increased by high-yield investments, and the value of the remainder interest is therefore more accurately ascertainable. The 50 percent ceiling on annuity payments and the 10 percent floor on the remainder interest were also enacted to curb abuses in the operations of remainder trusts.[64]

In the case of a CRAT, the trust's governing instrument must prohibit additional contributions to the trust after the initial contribution.[65] Thus, an inter

---

[58] IRC § 664(d)(1)(A); Reg. § 1.664-2. See ¶ 5.05[5][a] text accompanying notes 164–185.

[59] IRC § 664(d)(1)(B); Reg. § 1.664-2(a)(4). See ¶ 5.05[5][a] text accompanying notes 186–193.

[60] IRC § 664(d)(1)(C); Reg. § 1.664-2(a)(6). See IRC § 170(c); ¶ 5.05[5][a] text accompanying notes 194–199.

[61] IRC § 664(d)(1)(D). See ¶ 5.05[5][a] text accompanying notes 200–204.

[62] Obviously, this may require payments out of principal.

[63] S. Rep. No. 552, 91st Cong., 1st Sess. 88 (1969), reprinted in 1969-3 CB 423, 480.

[64] See ¶ 5.05[5][a] note 169, text accompanying note 203. Other abuses are curbed by regulations. See, e.g., ¶ 5.05[5][a] text accompanying notes 171–174.

[65] Reg. § 1.664-2(b). The restriction is apparently founded on the premise that such additions would inject further complication into the valuation of the remainder interest. See also Rev. Rul. 72-395, § 4.05; 1972-2 CB 340, 343.

vivos CRAT should not be set up as the subject of a pour-over provision in a decedent's will.[66]

[ii] **The charitable remainder unitrust.** A charitable remainder unitrust (CRUT)[67] is a trust that meets four tests.[68] First, a fluctuating amount fixed in terms of a percentage of the annual value of the trust assets (and not less than 5 percent nor more than 50 percent of that value) must be paid at least annually to a nonqualified recipient (who, if an individual, is living) for not more than twenty years (or for not more than the life or lives[69] of such individuals).[70] The second, third, and fourth tests are the same as those for the CRAT;[71] and the second test again disqualifies any trust that can be invaded for private use.[72] This share-of-current-value approach also works toward a neutralization of investment decisions that might otherwise favor either the current or the remainder interest. Additional contributions may be made to the CRUTs (as opposed to CRATs), if certain provisions are included in the trust instrument.[73]

The unitrust statute injects a second element of flexibility into the unitrust (in a trust commonly referred to as a NICRUT) by permitting an "income only" rule under which, in lieu of payments fixed in terms of a percentage of

---

[66] However, testamentary trusts are not disqualified under the estate tax deduction section simply because all the property is not distributed to the trust simultaneously, since creation of the trust is considered a single distribution. Reg. § 1.664-2(b).

[67] The Service again provides important, but potentially outdated, drafting assistance and forms in creating such entities. See the revenue rulings cited supra ¶ 11.02[2][b] note 56.

Charitable remainder unitrust forms are found in Rev. Proc. 89-20, 1989-1 CB 841; Rev. Proc. 90-30, 1990-1 CB 534; Rev. Proc. 90-31, 1990-1 CB 539. The Service will not issue determination letters as to the qualification of charitable remainder trusts substantially similar to those following the forms set forth in the rulings stated in this paragraph. Rev. Proc. 90-33, 1990-1 CB 551.

The rulings and forms are essential reading for one creating such trusts, although both these rulings and the forms predate recent legislative changes in the statutory requirements. See Notice 2000-37, 2000-2 CB 118, indicating that the Service intends to revise its guidance to reflect statutory and regulatory changes to charitable remainder annuity trusts and unitrusts.

[68] IRC §§ 664(d)(2), 2522(c)(2)(A); Reg. §§ 1.664-3, 25.2522(c)-3(c)(2)(v). Charitable remainder unitrusts are discussed in more detail at ¶ 5.05[5][b].

[69] Cf. Rev. Rul. 76-291, 1976-2 CB 284; Rev. Rul. 74-149, 1974-1 CB 157.

[70] IRC § 664(d)(2)(A); Reg. § 1.664-3. See ¶ 5.05[5][b] text accompanying notes 217–240.

[71] IRC §§ 664(d)(2)(B), 664(d)(2)(C), 664(d)(2)(D); Reg. §§ 1.664-3(a)(4), 1.664-3(a)(6). See ¶ 5.05[5][b] text accompanying notes 241–260, supra ¶ 11.02[2][b]text accompanying notes 59–61.

[72] See supra ¶ 11.02[2][b] text accompanying note 59.

[73] Reg. § 1.664-3(b). See Rev. Rul. 80-83, 1980-1 CB 210.

annual value, payment to the noncharitable beneficiary is limited to the amount of the trust "income"[74] if that amount is less than the fixed percentage of value.[75] In addition, the unitrust instrument may provide a "make-up" clause (in a trust commonly referred to as a NIMCRUT) under which income in excess of the fixed percentage of value is to be paid to the current beneficiaries if, together with prior payments made when income was less than the fixed percentage, the total amount paid out does not exceed the amount that would have been paid out under the fixed percentage of value test.[76]

The settlor of a CRAT or CRUT may retain the power, exercisable only by will, to revoke or terminate the interest of a beneficiary that is not a charity without disqualifying a completed deductible gift of the remainder.[77] If the terms of a charitable remainder trust give the trustee the power to allocate the private benefits among members of a class of beneficiaries and the trustee is independent,[78] there is a complete gift of the entire corpus and a deductible gift of the remainder.[79] If the settlor retains, directly or indirectly, the power to change the charitable remainder beneficiary,[80] even though the power is limited to designating only charities that qualify under Section 2522(a), there is no completed gift of the remainder and consequently no charitable deduction.[81]

---

[74] See IRC § 643(b).

[75] IRC § 664(d)(3)(A).

[76] IRC § 664(d)(3)(B). Again, however, this does not invite manipulation. Cf. Rev. Rul. 76-310, 1976-2 CB 197. The amount of the charitable deduction of a charitable remainder unitrust disregards the income-only rule and a make-up clause in valuing the amount of the charitable remainder under Section 2522. See IRC § 664(e); Reg. § 1.664-4(a)(3).

In limited circumstances, the Service allows a one-time flip of a NICRUT or a NIMCRUT to convert to a regular charitable remainder unitrust. See ¶ 5.05[5][b] text accompanying note 228.

[77] Reg. §§ 1.664-2(a)(4), 1.664-3(a)(4), 25.2522(c)-3(c)(2)(v); Rev. Rul. 79-243, 1979-2 CB 343. See Rev. Rul. 72-395, § 5.07, 1972-2 CB 340, 346 for a sample provision.

[78] Reg. §§ 1.664-2(a)(3)(ii), 1.664-3(a)(3)(ii). See IRC §§ 672(c), 674(a), 674(c). If the power is subject to a standard and is held by a trustee other than the donor or the donor's spouse, there is also a complete gift and a deductible gift of the remainder. IRC § 674(d). Cf. IRC § 674(b).

[79] Reg. §§ 1.664-2(a)(3)(ii), 1.664-3(a)(3)(ii); ¶ 10.01[9].

[80] The settlor's power to revoke the interest of the charitable remainder beneficiary would foreclose any charitable deduction for that remainder interest. Of course, there would be no completed gift of the charitable remainder and thus no deduction would be warranted or needed.

[81] Priv. Ltr. Rul. 9517020 (Jan. 26, 1995). Cf. Estate of Sanford v. Comm'r, 308 US 39 (1939). If Section 2702 applied to the transfer because the lead interest was given to a family member, a zero value would be placed on the charitable remainder interest because it would be treated as an interest retained by the transferor. Reg. § 25.2702-2(a)(4).

However, if the settlor names a third-party trustee and provides the trustee with such a power, the gift is complete and the deduction is allowed.[82]

[iii] **The pooled income fund.** Congress qualifies the pooled income fund[83] as an organization in which a charitable remainder interest is deductible,[84] in large part because the charity entitled to the remainder controls the fund.[85] In addition, property transferred to such a fund is commingled with that of other donors,[86] no donor or beneficiary of an income interest of the fund may be a trustee,[87] and the private income beneficiary receives distributions that are determined by the rate of return on the entire fund.[88] Again, Congress clearly expected that charitable remainders in pooled income funds as defined would not be affected adversely by investment manipulation and could be valued realistically.[89]

However, the trust is a valid charitable remainder trust under Section 664 for income tax purposes. Rev. Rul. 76-8, 1976-1 CB 179.

[82] See Rev. Rul. 78-101, 1978-1 CB 301 (deduction allowed in a charitable lead unitrust where the recipients were all charities listed in Section 2522) and Rev. Rul. 76-371, 1976-2 CB 305 (deduction allowed where trustee was allowed only to select among Section 170(b)(1)(A) charities all of which were within Section 2522). However, a trustee's power to give to *any* Section 170 charity would include groups outside the scope of Section 2522(a) and would therefore preclude a deduction. If a trustee was given a power, the same principles apply whether the trust is a charitable lead trust or a charitable remainder trust. Cf. Rev. Rul. 76-307, 1976-2 CB 56.

[83] The Treasury has issued sample provisions for inclusion in declarations of trust and instruments of transfer to aid taxpayers in making deductible transfers to pooled income funds. Rev. Ruls. 72-196, 1972-1 CB 194; 82-38, 1982-1 CB 96; 85-87, 1985-1 CB 182; 90-103, 1990-2 CB 159. Sample forms are found in Rev. Proc. 88-53, 1988-2 CB 712. The Service will not issue determination letters as to the qualification of pooled income funds substantially similar to the forms set forth previously. Rev. Proc. 88-54, 1988-2 CB 715.

[84] IRC §§ 642(c)(5), 2522(c)(2)(A); Reg. §§ 1.642(c)-5, 25.2522(c)-3(c)(2)(v). For a more detailed discussion of pooled income fund requirements, see ¶ 5.05[5][c][i].

[85] IRC § 642(c)(5)(E).

[86] IRC § 642(c)(5)(B).

[87] IRC § 642(c)(5)(E).

[88] IRC § 642(c)(5)(F). Other parts of the Section 642(c)(5) definition require (1) that the charitable beneficiary be essentially a public charity (one described in Section 170(b)(1)(A) other than clauses (vii) or (viii) thereof, not merely one described in Sections 170(c)) (IRC § 642(c)(5)(A)); (2) that the private beneficiary be living at the time of the transfer (IRC § 642(c)(5)(A)); (3) that the trust not invest in tax-exempt securities (IRC § 642(c)(5)(C)); and (4) that the fund include only transfers sanctioned by Section 642(c)(5) (IRC § 642(c)(5)(D)).

[89] See S. Rep. No. 552, 91st Cong., 1st Sess. 88 (1969), reprinted in 1969-3 CB 423, 480.

[c] Temporary Interests Gifted to Charity: Charitable Lead Trusts

In addition to benefiting financially from gifts of future interests, a charitable organization may also benefit financially from the gift of a present interest in property through what is commonly referred to as a charitable lead trust.[90] Again, however, when the donor mixes private objectives with philanthropy, the measurement of the charity's interest on the applicable valuation date may be uncertain even if benefits begin at once.

In the case of mixed bequests, a present interest left to charity is deductible only if it takes the form of a "guaranteed annuity"[91] or requires the annual distribution of a "fixed percentage" of the value of the property as determined annually.[92] These restrictions adopt essentially the unitrust and annuity trust principles applicable to gifts of remainder interests.[93] However, in contrast to gifts of qualified remainder interests, generally gifts to charitable lead trusts may be made for any period and, generally, there are no percentage floors or ceilings on the amounts of the lead interest payments or on the value of the remainder.[94]

The restrictions imposed on the deductibility of present interests have the same objectives as those directed at remainder interests. If the charity is entitled to a fixed annual payment of an amount determined annually with regard to the value of the property, incentives are removed for investment manipulation such as might render uncertain the actual value of what has been left to

---

[90] The Service has not issued sample forms for charitable lead trusts even though it has issued such forms for charitable remainder trusts and pooled income funds. See supra ¶ 11.02[2][b] text accompanying notes 56, 67, 83.

[91] IRC § 2522(c)(2)(B); Reg. § 25.2522(c)-3(c)(2)(vi). See Rev. Rul. 77-327, 1977-2 CB 353; Rev. Rul. 85-49, 1985-1 CB 330 (valid guaranteed annuity lead interests).

[92] IRC § 2522(c)(2)(B); Reg. § 25.2522(c)-3(c)(2)(vii). But see Rev. Rul. 77-300, 1977-2 CB 352 (failure to satisfy Reg. § 25.2522(c)-3(c)(2)(vii)(b)).

[93] See supra ¶ 11.02[2][a]. For a more detailed discussion of charitable lead trust requirements, see ¶ 5.05[6][a]. See also S. Rep. No. 552, 91st Cong., 1st Sess. 91 (1969), reprinted in 1969-3 CB 423, 482.

[94] IRC § 2522(c)(2)(B). See ¶ 5.05[6][a] text accompanying notes 317–321 for a more detailed consideration of the rules. However, the Service takes the position that an otherwise qualified charitable lead trust (in this case a guaranteed annuity) does not qualify for the deduction if the trustee has the discretion to commute and prepay the charitable interest prior to the expiration of the specified term of the annuity. Rev. Rul. 88-27, 1988-1 CB 331. See also Priv. Ltr. Rul. 8745002 (July 15, 1987) (prepayment clause eliminated if it disqualified the charitable deduction). The Service will not issue an advance ruling with respect to a guaranteed annuity if the interest may be prepaid. Rev. Proc. 88-3, 1988-1 CB 579, 580.

the charity.[95] The valuation of inter vivos charitable lead trusts is similar to the valuation of testamentary charitable lead trusts.[96]

[d] Exceptions to the Split-Gift Rules

Congress provides a series of exceptions to the split-gift rules discussed here in situations in which a donor cannot engage in any hanky-panky that will deprive the charity of its interest. These exceptions, which for the most part grow out of analogous income tax exceptions, are identical to the estate tax exceptions. Thus, they are listed here with a cross reference to their estate tax deduction discussion:

1. A direct (not in trust) gift of a remainder interest in a personal residence or farm.[97]
2. A direct (not in trust) undivided portion of the donor's entire interest in property.[98]
3. A qualified conservation contribution of a real property interest.[99] This exception indirectly incorporates Section 2522(d), which allows a deduction of a perpetual easement given to charity.[100]
4. Although a work of art and the federal copyright for it are generally treated as a single piece of property, in some circumstances Section 2522(c)(3) permits a gift tax charitable deduction for the work of art regardless of what is done with the copyright.[101]

---

[95] The regulations seek to tighten the statutory restrictions with respect to deductible annuities by providing, among other things, that "[w]here a charitable interest in the form of a guaranteed annuity interest is not in trust, the interest will be considered a guaranteed annuity interest only if it is to be paid by an insurance company or by an organization regularly engaged in issuing annuity contracts." Reg. § 25.2522(c)-3(c)(2)(vi)(c). Similar restrictions are provided with respect to unitrust interests. Reg. § 25.2522(c)-3(c)(2)(vii)(c).

[96] Reg. §§ 25.2522(c)-3(d)(2)(iv), 25.2522(c)-3(d)(2)(v). See ¶ 5.05[6][b].

[97] IRC §§ 170(f)(3)(B)(i), 2522(c)(2). See Reg. §§ 25.2522(c)-3(c)(2)(ii), 25.2522(c)-3(c)(2)(iii); ¶ 5.05[7][a]. See also Rev. Rul. 76-473, 1976-2 CB 306, indicating that the value of a remainder interest in a personal residence for gift tax purposes is not reduced for depreciation during the noncharitable tenant's possession, allowing a higher gift tax deduction than income tax deduction (IRC § 170(f)(4)).

[98] IRC §§ 2522(c)(2), 170(f)(3)(B)(ii). See Reg. § 25.2522(c)-3(c)(2)(i); ¶ 5.05[7][b].

[99] IRC §§ 170(f)(3)(B)(iii), 2522(c)(2). See Reg. §§ 1.170A-14, 25.2522(c)-3(c)(2)(iv); ¶ 5.05[7][c]. Property subject to such a qualified conservation easement subsequently may also qualify a decedent's gross estate for a gross estate exclusion. See IRC § 2031(c) discussed ¶ 4.02[7].

[100] See ¶ 5.05[7][c] text accompanying note 348.

[101] IRC §§ 2055(e)(4), 2522(c)(3). See Reg. §§ 20.2055-2(e)(1)(ii), 25.2522(c)-3(c)(1)(ii); ¶ 5.05[7][d].

5. A charitable gift annuity where there is an outright transfer of property to charity under an agreement that the charity will pay an annuity to the donor or some third person.[102]

[e] Curative Amendments Permitted

Under Section 2522(c)(4), Congress allows split-gift curative amendments under the gift tax charitable deduction comparable to those allowed under the Section 2055(e)(3) estate tax charitable deduction.[103]

¶ 11.03 SECTION 2523. GIFTS TO SPOUSE

[1] Introduction

The gift tax counterpart of the estate tax marital deduction provision[1] is Section 2523, which has the general effect of allowing an unlimited deduction for interspousal gifts. When first enacted in 1948,[2] the predecessor of this section generally allowed a deduction for one half of the value of interspousal gifts.[3] The marital deduction was liberalized in 1976, essentially allowing modest interspousal gifts to be wholly tax-free.[4] The Economic Recovery Tax Act of

---

[102] Rev. Rul. 80-281, 1980-2 CB 282. See ¶ 5.05[7][e].

[103] Section 2055(e)(3) is discussed in detail at ¶ 5.05[8].

[1] IRC § 2056. See ¶ 5.06.

[2] Revenue Act of 1948, Pub. L. No. 80-471, § 372, 62 Stat. 110, 125 (1948).

[3] The gift tax marital deduction originated as an effort to equalize the gift tax consequences with respect to community and noncommunity property transfers. The prior inequality arose out of the fact that generally, under community property laws, each spouse acquires a one-half interest in property earned or acquired in certain ways by the other spouse. See De Funiak & Vaughn, Principles of Community Property § 66, at 140 (2d ed. 1971). The acquisition of the one-half interest in community property is not and was not treated as a transfer subject to gift tax. Some measure of equality was accomplished by allowing the earlier limited deduction for qualifying interspousal gifts of noncommunity property.

[4] Generally, under the amendments made by the Tax Reform Act of 1976, interspousal gifts up to the first $100,000 were tax-free. The second $100,000 of interspousal gifts qualified for no deduction. After $200,000 in gifts, one half of the value of subsequent gifts qualified for the marital deduction. Tax Reform Act of 1976, Pub. L. No. 94-455, § 2002(b), 90 Stat. 1520, 1855 (1976), reprinted in 1976-3 CB 1, 331. See HR Rep. No. 1380, 94th Cong., 2d Sess. 17 (1976), reprinted in 1976-3 CB (Vol. 3) 735, 751.

1981 removed the limitation on the deductibility of interspousal gifts.[5] Now, subject to certain qualifications, interspousal transfers are tax-free (fully deductible) regardless of the amount of the gift.[6] The changes in both the gift tax and the estate tax marital deduction provisions reflect a shift in congressional policy from that of seeking the tax equalization of noncommunity property and community property to a policy of allowing gratuitous interspousal transfers to be free from the imposition of estate and gift tax.[7]

A gift tax return is generally[8] not required for interspousal gifts that, except for Section 2524, fully qualify for a gift tax marital deduction under Section 2523.[9] The rationale behind this congressional action is that, as qualified interspousal transfers result in no gift tax liability, they should not invoke a requirement to file a gift tax return.[10]

[2] Basic Requirements

The gift tax marital deduction is available only if the donor and donee are married at the time of the gift. Thus, antenuptial transfers cannot qualify for the deduction, even if the donor and donee later marry in the same year in which the gift is made. Similarly, transfers that are made after divorce are denied the benefits of this provision.[11] Donors who are neither citizens nor residents of the United States but who make gifts subject to Chapter 12[12] are,

---

[5] Economic Recovery Tax Act of 1981, Pub. L. No. 97-34, § 403(b)(1), 95 Stat. 172, 301 (1981), reprinted in 1981-2 CB 256, 324. See ¶ 5.06[1].

[6] Economic Recovery Tax Act of 1981, Pub. L. No. 97-34, § 403(b)(1), 95 Stat. 172, 301 (1981), reprinted in 1981-2 CB 256, 324. See Reg. § 25.2523(a)-1(c) for a summary of the three rules previously mentioned and Reg. § 25.2523(a)-1(d) for some examples of the prior rules as well as the interrelationship of Sections 2523 and 2524. However, if the donee spouse is not a citizen of the United States, no gift tax marital deduction is allowed under Section 2523. IRC § 2523(i)(1). See infra ¶ 11.03[5].

[7] S. Rep. No. 144, 97th Cong., 1st Sess. 127 (1981), reprinted in 1981-2 CB 412, 461. See ¶ 5.06 text accompanying note 3.

[8] However, a QTIP election under Section 2523(f)(2)(C) (other than a deemed election for a joint and survivor annuity under Section 2523(f)(6)) must be made on a gift tax return for the calendar year in which the interest was transferred.

[9] IRC § 6019(a)(2); Reg. § 25.2523(f)-1(b)(4). See IRC § 2524, discussed ¶ 11.04.

[10] HR Conf. Rep. No. 201, 97th Cong., 1st Sess. 163 (1981), reprinted in 1981-2 CB 352, 379.

[11] S. Rep. No. 1013, 80th Cong., 2d Sess. 30 (1981), reprinted in 1948-1 CB 285, 352. See Rev. Rul. 67-442, 1967-2 CB 65. Cf. IRC § 2516; ¶¶ 4.15[1], 10.06.

[12] See IRC §§ 2501(a)(2), 2501(a)(3), 2511(b); ¶¶ 9.02[1], 10.01[11].

nevertheless, generally allowed a gift tax marital deduction.[13] However, if the donee is not a citizen of the United States at the time of the gift, no gift tax marital deduction is allowed.[14]

No marital deduction is allowed with respect to interests transferred to a spouse if the transfer is not treated as a gift. For example, if a transfer from one spouse to another prior to divorce is relieved of gift tax consequences by Section 2516, no marital deduction arises from the transfer.[15] A deduction is not needed because the transfer causes no gift tax liability, but the point is that no deduction is allowed because if it were allowed, it could operate to offset other includible gifts.

If the interest transferred to the spouse is only a partial interest in property rather than outright ownership, the marital deduction is limited by the value of the interest transferred. Thus, if the donor creates a trust, transferring the income to the donor's parent for life and providing for distribution of the corpus at the parent's death to spouse or spouse's estate, the gift tax marital deduction is dependent on the value of the spouse's remainder interest, not the value of the entire trust.[16] Similarly, an outright gift to a corporation in which the spouse is a shareholder qualifies for the marital deduction in an amount proportionate to the spouse's interest in the corporation.

Beyond the basic requirements that must be met for the marital deduction to be allowed, Section 2523 imposes some limitations relating to transfers of terminable interests between spouses and, as indicated in the preceding examples, Section 2524[17] imposes restrictions on the amount of the deduction in some instances. In addition, Section 2523(h) provides that the value of any interest in property that is deductible for gift tax purposes may be deducted only once with respect to each donor, although such interest may be deductible under one or more sections of the gift tax.[18]

---

[13] Reg. § 25.2523(a)-1(a). This rule parallels the estate tax marital deduction. See IRC § 2106(a)(3), ¶ 5.06[1]. Prior to July 14, 1988, no deduction was allowed. Reg. § 25.2523(a)-1(a).

[14] IRC § 2523(i)(1). See infra ¶ 11.03[5].

[15] Reg. § 25.2523(a)-1(b)(3)(ii). See ¶ 10.06 Cf. Reg. § 25.2523(a)-1(d) Ex. 8.

[16] Reg. § 25.2523(a)-1(e). If the donor spouse had retained the income interest (rather than transferring it to the parent), Section 2702 would apply to value the donor's interest at zero and increase the value of the remainder interest to the value of the corpus, with the result that the full value of the corpus would qualify for a marital deduction. See ¶ 19.03[2][c] text accompanying note 83.

[17] See ¶ 11.04[2].

[18] For example, if the donor makes a QTIP election with respect to a transfer to a trust, the remainder of which also qualifies for a charitable deduction, the entire value is deductible under Section 2523(f), but no Section 2522 deduction is allowed. Reg. § 25.2523(h)-1.

[3] The Terminable Interest Rule

This discussion of the terminable interest rule should seem familiar as a result of previous experience with parallel estate tax concepts.[19] Essentially, the rule precludes a marital deduction unless the transferee spouse receives an interest in property that will constitute a gift by that spouse if given away during the spouse's life or will be included in that spouse's gross estate if retained until the spouse's death, that is, unless the government will get its tax bite when the spouse gratuitously relinquishes the property.[20] Section 2523(b) sets forth the general rule denying a marital deduction if the spouse receives a disqualified terminable interest and Sections 2523(d), 2523(e), 2523(f), and 2523(g) provide four exceptions to the general rule.

[a] Section 2523(b)(1) Transfers

If the interest transferred to the spouse is a terminable interest,[21] then Section 2523(b)(1) may disallow a marital deduction in two situations.

1. *Donor Retains Interest.* The first situation, retention of an interest by the donor, is not present under the estate tax terminable interest rules because the donor is dead when the potentially deductible transfer to the spouse is deemed to occur. It is present, however, under the gift tax terminable interest rule, which takes account of situations in which a living donor retains an interest in the property. Under Section 2523(b)(1), if the interest transferred to the spouse is a terminable one, no marital deduction is generally allowed if the donor has retained an interest in the same property under which the donor may succeed to possession or enjoyment of the property upon termination of the spouse's interest.[22] An obvious illustration of this rule is as follows: A donor transfers property in trust, the income to be paid to spouse for life and the corpus to be returned to the donor or to the donor's estate upon the spouse's death. Even though the donor made a gift to the spouse in this situation, the gift does not qualify for the marital deduction because (1) the spouse's interest is terminable; (2) the donor has retained an interest in the property; and (3) by reason

---

[19] See ¶¶ 5.06[7], 5.06[8].

[20] The policy reasons that support this limitation, which are the same as those that support a like limitation on the estate tax marital deduction, are considered in the discussion of Section 2056 at ¶ 5.06[7][a].

[21] See IRC § 2056(b)(1). The estate tax and gift tax basic descriptions of terminable interests are identical. See ¶ 5.06[7]. Exceptions to the basic provisions are discussed infra ¶ 11.03[4].

[22] Some exceptions are indicated later. See infra ¶ 11.03[4].

of the donor's retained interest, the donor may enjoy the property upon termination of the spouse's interest.[23]

One may well ponder the rationale for this limitation. If the property will return to the donor or the donor's estate, either its full value (if the reversion takes effect before the donor's death) or at least the value of the remainder (if the donor predeceases the spouse)[24] may be taxed in the donor's estate at the donor's death. Consider, however, that shortly after the creation of the trust the donor might give the reversionary interest to a third party. In this fashion, in two steps the donor would have made a transfer clearly within the proscription of the terminable interest rule; and so, taking account of this possibility, Congress denies the deduction.

2. *Third Party Acquires Interest.* The second terminable interest situation under Section 2523(b)(1) is more easily identified with the estate tax terminable interest proscription. Under this rule, if the interest transferred to the spouse is a terminable interest[25] and the donor has gratuitously transferred to some third party an interest in the same property, under which that third person or that third person's heirs or assigns may succeed to possession or enjoyment of the property upon termination of the spouse's interest, no marital deduction is generally allowed.[26] This rule may be illustrated by the following example: A donor transfers property in trust, the income to be paid to spouse for the spouse's life and the corpus to be distributed to *A* or *A*'s estate upon the spouse's death.

Although the donor made a gift to the spouse, the donor cannot claim a marital deduction because (1) the spouse's interest is terminable; (2) the donor has transferred an interest in the property to *A*;[27] (3) the transfer to *A* was without consideration; and (4) by reason of

---

[23] Reg. § 25.2523(b)-1(c). No marital deduction is allowed even though Section 2702 values the retained interest at zero and as a result, the amount of the gift of the income interest is equal to the full value of the corpus. Although the property transferred may be included in the donor's gross estate, no double taxation occurs. See ¶ 19.03[4][c] text accompanying notes 327–331.

[24] See IRC § 2033, discussed ¶ 4.05[5][b].

[25] See supra note 21.

[26] Some exceptions are indicated later. See infra ¶¶ 11.03[4][b], 11.03[4][c], 11.03[4][d].

[27] A gift by donor to a corporation in which the spouse is a shareholder qualifies under Section 2523 and is not a disqualified terminable interest, because no part of the share of the property considered transferred to the spouse is transferred to any other person. Rev. Rul. 71-443, 1971-2 CB 337.

A's interest, *A* may enjoy the property upon termination of the spouse's interest.[28]

Disallowance of the marital deduction under the basic provision of the terminable interest rule requires the concurrence of all the elements enumerated in the preceding paragraph. The statute does not simply deny the marital deduction for transfers of terminable interests. These concepts have been explored more fully in the discussion of the estate tax marital deduction provision.[29]

The terminable interest rule precludes a deduction even if the proscribed interest that the donor transferred to another person was not transferred to such person at the same time the gift was made to the spouse. For example, if the donor transferred property in trust, reserving the right to the income for ten years and providing for the distribution of the corpus to *A* or *A*'s estate upon expiration of that period, the donor would have made a gift to *A* of the remainder interest at the time of the creation of the trust. A later gratuitous assignment of the retained income interest by the donor to the spouse would be a transfer of a nondeductible terminable interest described in Section 2523(b)(1) because the donor "has transferred" gratuitously an interest in the property to *A*, under which *A* will gain enjoyment of the property when the terminable interest transferred to the spouse expires.[30]

Moreover, the last sentence of Section 2523(b) resolves any uncertainty as to whether the donor has transferred an interest in the property to one other than the spouse. For example, the marital deduction is not allowed "[i]f a donor transferred property in trust, naming [the spouse] as the irrevocable income beneficiary for ten years, and providing that, upon the expiration of that term, the corpus should be distributed among [the spouse] and children in such proportions as the trustee should determine. . . . "[31] Because at the time of the gift it is uncertain who will receive the remainder interest, the last

---

[28] Reg. § 25.2523(b)-1(b). See Wang v. Comm'r, 31 TCM (CCH) 719 (1972) (no marital deduction where a spouse had a life estate with a third party remainder even though the trustee could invade the corpus for the spouse).

[29] See ¶ 5.06[7].

[30] Reg. §§ 25.2523(b)-1(b)(2), 25.2523(b)-1(b)(6)(v).

If *A* is a member of donor's family as defined in Section 2704(c)(2), there would have been a gift of the entire value of the corpus on the initial transfer as a result of Section 2702. Remedial relief is provided to prevent double taxation of the value of the retained income interest on the transfer to donee spouse. See ¶ 19.03[4][c][i]. Even though the amount of the subsequent transfer to the donee spouse is reduced, the transfer does not quality for a marital deduction.

[31] Reg. § 25.2523(b)-1(b)(3)(i).

sentence of Section 2523(b) requires that the gift be treated as "transferred to a person other than the donee spouse" and a marital deduction is disallowed.

3. *Caveat on Powers.* A donor's transfer of an interest in property to one other than a spouse will in some circumstances defeat the marital deduction even if the transfer is one that generally would not be recognized as a transfer for gift tax purposes. This possibility arises out of the penultimate sentence of Section 2523(b), which provides that a donor's exercise or release of a power over property is to be treated as a transfer of an interest for the purposes of the terminable interest rule even though it is not otherwise regarded as a transfer. Thus, although an exercise of a nongeneral power of appointment usually is not considered a transfer, it is considered as such for these purposes. Suppose that a third-party grantor establishes a trust under which a donee is entitled to the income for ten years and has a limited power to appoint the remainder during life. Upon expiration of the period, the trust corpus is to be distributed between the donee's spouse and child in accordance with the donee's appointment in any proportion that donee may determine, and, in default of appointment, the remainder passes to the spouse. The donee has a nongeneral power, the exercise or release of which is usually without gift tax consequences regardless of when the power was created.[32] Nevertheless, if the donee exercises the power in favor of the child and then assigns the income interest to the spouse, the donee is treated as having made a transfer of an interest in the property to the child which, under the terminable interest rule, bars the marital deduction for the gift to the spouse. If the donee first assigned the income interest to the spouse and then exercised the power by appointing the property to the child, Section 2523(b)(1) would not foreclose the deduction, but any such small shift in timing should not change the tax result and it will not, as explained in the next discussion.

[b] Section 2523(b)(2) Transfers

The marital deduction would not be saved, in this last example, by the postponement of the exercise of the nongeneral power because under Section 2523(b)(2) the donee would be viewed as having made a transfer with a "retained power." Under that provision, if (1) after a transfer of a terminable interest to the spouse (the assignment of the income interest in the previous example); (2) the donee has a power of appointment over the same property

---

[32] See IRC § 2514, discussed ¶ 10.04.

(our assumed retention); and (3) it can be exercised so that the appointee will possess or enjoy any part of the property after expiration of the spouse's interest (again our case), the marital deduction is denied.[33] Again, the power retained by the donee need not be a taxable power within the scope of Section 2514.[34] Moreover, it is immaterial whether the power is exercisable alone or only in conjunction with another person; statutory recognition of a power exercisable with any person probably should be interpreted literally, as it has been in the estate tax context.[35] But, again, each of the numbered elements identified here must exist in order for the deduction to be denied.

Section 2523(b)(2) can also foreclose a marital deduction for an interest transferred to the spouse if the donor had only a general power of appointment over the property in question and no interest in the property. For example:

> The donor, having [only] a power of appointment over certain property, appointed a life estate to . . . spouse. No marital deduction may be taken with respect to such transfer, since, if the retained power to appoint the remainder interest is exercised, the appointee thereunder may possess or enjoy the property after the termination or failure of the interest taken by the donee spouse.[36]

For purposes of Section 2523(b)(2), the fact that a donor's retained power is not immediately exercisable is immaterial. The statute specifies that the donor is to be treated as having retained the proscribed power, even though it cannot be exercised until after a certain amount of time has elapsed or until after the occurrence or nonoccurrence of some event or contingency. It is equally clear that a power immediately exercisable, but the exercise of which cannot take effect until some future time, will constitute a retained power for purposes of Section 2523(b)(2).

It should be reemphasized that the transfer of a terminable interest to the spouse is an essential element of the denial of a marital deduction under both Sections 2523(b)(1) and 2523(b)(2). Suppose, for example, that a donor created a trust under which the income was to be paid to the donor's sibling dur-

---

[33] Reg. § 25.2523(b)-1(d)(3). See infra text accompanying note 35. Furthermore, no Section 2523(f) QTIP election may be made where the spouse does not have a qualified income interest for life or where the donor spouse (the "donee" here) retains a Section 2523(b)(2) power to appoint an interest in qualified terminable interest property during the spouse's lifetime. IRC § 2523(f)(2)(B); Reg. § 25.2523(f)-1(a)(1). See infra ¶ 11.03[4][c] text accompanying notes 58, 62, 64.

[34] Reg. § 25.2523(b)-1(d)(2).

[35] Cf. Helvering v. City Bank Farmers Trust Co., 296 US 85 (1935). See also ¶ 4.10[6].

[36] Reg. § 25.2523(b)-1(d)(3) Ex. However, a marital deduction should be allowed if a QTIP election is made, even though the donor spouse has a power to alter the remainderperson after spouse's death. See infra ¶ 11.03[4][c] note 73.

ing the sibling's lifetime, and, upon the sibling's death, the corpus was to be distributed to the spouse or to the spouse's estate. Even if the donor retained a power to shift the sibling's income interest to others, the vested remainder transferred to the spouse would qualify for the marital deduction.[37]

Suppose a donor transfers property to a spouse for life, with a remainder to the spouse's estate. The terminable interest rule does not foreclose the deduction, for the only interest not passing directly to the spouse passes to the spouse's estate.[38] A marital deduction may be claimed, but should it be based on the value of the spouse's life estate or the entire value of the property transferred? The answer here depends on the answer to another question: Has the donor made a gift to the spouse of (1) the life estate or (2) the entire interest in the property? The deduction, subject of course to Section 2523(a)(2) limitations, is the value of the interest that the donor has given to the spouse.

Regarding a similar estate tax question, the regulations meet the problem head on: "If *H* devised property . . . [t]o *W* for life with remainder to her estate, the entire property is considered as having passed from *H* to *W*."[39] Thus, for estate tax purposes a bequest of this type gives rise to a marital deduction measured by the entire value of the property, not just the value of the spouse's life estate. No similar expression appears in the gift tax regulations, but it may reasonably be assumed that the Treasury will take a consistent position and treat the transaction in question as a transfer from the donor to the spouse of the entire value of the property for gift tax marital deduction purposes.[40]

[c] The "Tainted Asset" Rule

Section 2523(c), entitled "Interest in Unidentified Assets," supplies a rule to be applied when an interest transferred to a spouse can be satisfied either out of assets that qualify for the deduction or other assets that do not. The rule, which amounts to a flat presumption against the taxpayer, requires that for the purpose of determining the marital deduction, the value of the interest

---

[37] Cf. Rev. Rul. 54-470, 1954-2 CB 320; IRC § 2702. See ¶¶ 19.03[2][a][iv], 19.03[2][c] text accompanying note 83, indicating that as a result of Section 2702, the gift of the remainder would be equal to the value of the entire corpus and the entire value would qualify for a marital deduction.

[38] See the second parenthetical phrase in Section 2523(b)(1).

[39] Reg. § 20.2056(c)-2(b)(2)(ii). See also IRC § 2056(b)(1)(A) (second parenthetical).

[40] See Rev. Rul. 54-470, 1954-2 CB 320. Because the property will be included in the spouse's gross estate at death, a gift marital deduction should be allowed on the entire property. Cf. Keeter v. United States, 461 F2d 714 (5th Cir. 1972). But see Second Nat'l Bank of Danville v. Dallman, 209 F2d 321 (7th Cir. 1954). See also Rev. Rul. 55-277, 1955-1 CB 456, in which the Service announced that it will not follow *Second Nat'l Bank of Danville*. This issue is discussed with respect to Section 2033 at ¶ 4.05[6] note 76, and with respect to Section 2056 at ¶ 5.06[7][c] note 194.

transferred to the spouse must be reduced by the value of the tainted assets out of which or the proceeds of which the spouse's interest can be satisfied.

Thus, if a $20,000 interest in property transferred to the spouse could be satisfied out of $20,000 cash or out of an interest in property for a term of years worth $20,000 retained by the donor upon a gratuitous transfer of the property to the donor's child, the possible satisfaction of the gift to the spouse out of the nonqualifying term of years will reduce the interest transferred to the spouse to zero for the purpose of computing the marital deduction.

The gift tax "tainted asset" rule is virtually the same as its estate tax cousin, which is discussed in Chapter 5.[41] A better understanding of its gift tax application, and particularly of the method of computing the marital deduction when the rule applies, can be gained from a study of the following elaborate example from the regulations:

> H was absolute owner of a rental property and on July 1, 1950, transferred it to A by gift, reserving the income for a period of twenty years. On July 1, 1955, he created a trust to last for a period of ten years. H was to receive the income from the trust and at the termination of the trust the trustee is to turn over to H's wife, W, property having a value of $100,000. The trustee has absolute discretion in deciding which properties in the corpus he shall turn over to W in satisfaction of the gift to her. The trustee received two items of property from H. Item (1) consisted of shares of corporate stock. Item (2) consisted of the right to receive the income from the rental property during the unexpired portion of the twenty-year term. Assume that at the termination of the trust on July 1, 1965, the value of the right to the rental income for the then unexpired term of five years (item 2) will be $30,000. Since item (2) is a nondeductible interest and the trustee can turn it over to W in partial satisfaction of her gift, only $70,000 of the $100,000 receivable by her on July 1, 1965, will be considered as property with respect to which a marital deduction is allowable. The present value on July 1, 1955, of the right to receive $70,000 at the end of ten years is ... the value of the property qualifying for the marital deduction. ....[42]

[4] Exceptions to the Terminable Interest Rule

[a] Joint Interests

Section 2523(d) provides an exception to the terminable interest rule under which a gift arising out of the creation of a tenancy by the entirety or

---

[41] See ¶ 5.06[7][e].

[42] Reg. § 25.2523(c)-1(c) Ex.

joint tenancy with a spouse can qualify for the marital deduction. The interests of the co-owners are terminable, and upon creation of either tenancy the donor retains an interest under which the donor could gain sole possession of the property upon expiration of the spouse's interest at death. Nonetheless, the statute permits this retained interest to be disregarded for the purpose of the terminable interest rule.

The joint ownership exception to the terminable interest rule is appropriate. If the spouse survives, the entire property will become the spouse's outright and potentially subject to tax in the spouse's estate. If the donor survives, the full value of the property reverts to the donor and it will be a part of the donor's gross estate.[43] If the tenancy is terminated by severance, the property will have two separate owners, and all of it either will be subject to tax in their estates or if the spouses terminate the tenancy by giving the property away, such transfer will be subject to the imposition of the gift tax.[44] In general, joint tenancies solely between spouses do not present an opportunity for avoiding transfer taxes at the spouses' generation level, which the terminable interest rule is principally designed to guard against.

This exception to the terminable interest rule applies only to transfers between spouses and only to circumstances in which the spouses are the only tenants. This, of course, is invariably the situation in a tenancy by the entirety. In the case of a joint tenancy, the exception does not apply if there are other joint tenants.

The marital deduction allowed is based on the value of the interest transferred to the spouse. Thus, if a donor creates a joint tenancy in securities with the right of survivorship, and the donor supplies all the consideration for acquisition of the securities, the marital deduction is one half the value of the securities. One half of the value of the entire joint tenancy property is a gift to the spouse, and that is the amount of the deduction.[45] In the case of the creation of a tenancy by the entirety, although the valuation of the gift to the spouse presents more of a problem,[46] the same marital deduction principles apply, and the deduction is based on the value of the interest found to be transferred by gift to the spouse.[47]

---

[43] IRC § 2033. Cf. IRC § 2040(b), discussed at ¶ 4.12[10].

[44] If, in the case of a joint tenancy, a spouse makes a gift of that spouse's interest to a third party, the usual result is to convert the ownership to a tenancy in common between the donee and the continuing owner. Rasch, Real Property Law and Practice, § 624 at 3766 (1962). This, too, tends to support the exception.

[45] See Reg. § 25.2523(d)-1.

[46] See ¶ 10.01[3][f].

[47] See Reg. § 25.2523(d)-1.

[b] Life Interests With Powers

A second exception to the gift tax marital deduction terminable interest rule is a replica of an exception to the estate tax marital deduction terminable interest rule.[48] Matching Section 2056(b)(5) in the estate tax provisions, Section 2523(e) permits a marital deduction for certain otherwise unqualified life interests transferred to a spouse[49] if the spouse is also given a general power of appointment over the property or a "specific portion" of the property determined on a fractional or percentage basis.[50] This is only a general statement of the exception; certain specific statutory requirements must be met. However, the extended discussion in Chapter 5 of the parallel requirements under Section 2056 makes a detailed examination of this provision unnecessary.[51]

Section 2523(e) comes into play in the context of life insurance. In principle, the questions a gift of a policy of insurance on the life of the donor may raise under the terminable interest rule are no different from questions arising with respect to other kinds of property. If a donor owning a policy on the donor's life effectively transfers all rights and interests in the policy to the spouse and neither retains any interest nor transfers any interest to another, the gift is subject to the marital deduction. But, as in the case of other property, the assignment itself may create successive rights in others or, in contrast with most other property, the policy itself may name successive beneficiaries. In either of these circumstances, the deduction is threatened by the possibility that an interest transferred to the spouse is a nondeductible terminable interest, and this has generated litigation under Section 2523.

If the life insurance policy, as interpreted under applicable local law, gives others an interest in the policy after the death of the spouse, and if the spouse did not have complete power of disposition over the policy during the spouse's life, the gift of the policy to the spouse fails to qualify for the marital

---

[48] As in the case of the estate tax marital deduction, the life-estate-with-power exception to the terminable interest rule was first limited to property held in trust. Compare IRC § 1004(a)(3)(E) (1939), with IRC § 2523(e) (1954), as amended by the Technical Amendments Act of 1958, Pub. L. No. 866, 85th Cong., 2d Sess. § 893(a), 72 Stat. 1606 (1958) reprinted in 1958-3 CB 254, 316. In some instances, the effect of the addition of legal life estates (life interests in property not held in trust) is obvious; in others the results are less certain. See, e.g., Rev. Rul. 54-410, 1954-2 CB 321 (disallowing the gift tax marital deduction for a gift by the donor of Series E or G bonds in the name of the spouse with provision for payment to the donor if the spouse died before bonds were redeemed), which may be rendered obsolete by the 1958 change.

[49] See Rev. Rul. 69-56, 1969-1 CB 224.

[50] See IRC § 2523(e) (last sentence); ¶ 5.06[8][b] text accompanying notes 222–233; Reg. § 25.2523(e)-1(c), which parallels Reg. § 20.2056(b)-5(c).

[51] See ¶ 5.06[8][b]; Reg. § 25.2523(e)-1.

deduction.[52] But, if the spouse is "invested with the entire parcel of powers and rights with respect to" the policy, the transfer is brought within the exception to the terminable interest rule expressed in Section 2523(e), even though others may receive successive interests in the policy that would take effect in the case of inaction by the spouse.[53] The transfer of an insurance policy to a trust for the benefit of a spouse may more directly raise the question of whether the spouse has the right to the income from the transferred property. That right is an element in the gift tax marital deduction provision, just as it is in the estate tax area.[54]

[c] Qualified Terminable Interest Property

Under Section 2523(f),[55] a donor spouse may elect[56] to have gifts of certain life interests to a donee spouse treated as if they were not terminable interests if those interests meet the statutory definition of "qualified terminable interest property" (QTIP).[57] To meet the statutory definition of "qualified terminable interest property" (1) the property must pass from the donor; (2) the property must pass a qualifying income interest to the spouse for life; and (3) the donor must elect to use Section 2523(f).[58] To meet the qualifying income

---

[52] Berman v. Patterson, 171 F. Supp. 800 (ND Ala. 1959). But cf. Carlson v. Patterson, 190 F. Supp. 452 (ND Ala. 1961).

[53] Kidd v. Patterson, 230 F. Supp. 769, 772 (ND Ala. 1964).

[54] See Reg. § 25.2523(e)-1(f). See also Halsted v. Comm'r, 28 TC 1069 (1957), acq. 1958-1 CB 5; Estate of Smith v. Comm'r, 23 TC 367 (1954) (disallowing the marital deduction for premiums paid and amounts paid to a trust for premiums, respectively, on policies held in trust).

[55] Section 2523(f) is effective for gifts made after December 31, 1981. Reg. § 25.2523(f)-1(a)(1).

[56] The election is made on the return for the year in which the transfer is made (including extensions prescribed by Section 6075(b)) and once made is irrevocable. IRC § 2523(f)(4). See Reg. § 25.2523(f)-1(b)(4)(i). If the election is made for a calendar year in which the donor dies, the return must be filed no later than the time (including extensions) for filing the estate tax return. Reg. § 25.2523(f)-1(b)(4)(ii).

[57] IRC § 2523(f)(2).

[58] IRC § 2523(f)(2). Local law is taken into consideration in determining whether conditions (1) and (2) are satisfied. Reg. § 25.2523(f)-1(e). Cf. Prop. Reg. §§ 20.2056(b)-5(f)(1), 20.2056(b)-7(d)(1). No QTIP election may be made if a donor retains a power to appoint an interest in the qualifying terminable interest property. IRC § 2523(b)(2); Reg. § 2523(f)-1(a). Thus, any retained power in the donor to appoint the corpus during the spouse's life would disqualify a QTIP election. However, a retained power in the donor spouse to appoint the remainder after the donee spouse's death should not disqualify a QTIP election. See IRC §§ 2523(f)(2), 2523(f)(3), 2056(b)(7)(B)(ii) (flush language); Reg. § 25.2523(f)-1(a). See supra ¶ 11.03[3][b].

interest requirement[59] (1) the spouse must receive an immediate right to receive the income[60] from the entire property or a specific portion[61] thereof for
life;[62] (2) the income must be payable at least annually;[63] and (3) during the
donee spouse's life, neither the donee spouse nor anyone else may have the
power to appoint to any person other than the donee spouse any part of the
property from which the donee spouse is entitled to receive income.[64] These
requirements parallel the requirements contained in the corollary estate tax
provisions.[65]

[i] **Other QTIP consequences.** Recall that the objective of the terminable interest rule is to deny the marital deduction for property interests passing
from the donor to the spouse if the property passes in such a manner as to
avoid transfer taxes being imposed upon the spouse or the spouse's estate.[66]
The Section 2523(f) exception, standing alone, does not assure the government
its requisite tax bite, because qualified terminable interest property presents a
classic terminable interest situation. To the extent that qualified terminable interest property qualifies for a marital deduction to the donor, symmetry requires the government to impose at some subsequent time a tax on the
property as well as on the spouse's other wealth. Under Sections 2044 and
2519, which are discussed in more detail in other parts of this book,[67] qualifying property is treated as though it had been transferred outright to the spouse.

Essentially, Section 2519 provides that if the spouse disposes of any part
of the spouse's "qualifying income interest"[68] during the spouse's lifetime, all

---

[59] See Reg. §§ 25.2523(f)-1(c), 25.2523(f)-1(f) Exs. 1, 8. These examples essentially
parallel Reg. § 20.2056(b)-7(h) Exs. 1, 5, 11, 13. See also ¶ 5.06[8][d][ii].

[60] Reg. § 25.2523(f)-1(c)(2). When the donor retains a primary life estate and gives a
secondary life estate to the spouse, the spouse's interest does not qualify as a qualifying
income interest for life. Reg. § 25.2523(f)-1(f) Ex. 9.

[61] See IRC §§ 2056(b)(10), 2523(f)(3); Reg. § 25.2523(f)-1(b)(3)(i); supra
¶ 11.03[4][b] text accompanying note 50.

[62] IRC §§ 2056(b)(7)(B)(ii)(I), 2056(b)(7)(B)(iv), 2523(f)(3). A trust may be divided
into separate trusts to reflect a partial election. Reg. § 25.2523(f)-1(b)(3)(ii).

An annuity interest created by gift on or before Oct. 24, 1992, payable from a trust
or other assets passing from the donor is treated as a qualifying income interest. Reg.
§ 25.2523(f)-1(c)(3). See Reg. § 25.2523(f)-1(f) Exs. 6, 7. The Treasury has reserved regulations on annuities created after that date. See Reg. § 25.2523(f)-1(c)(4). The rationale
for the reservation is explained at ¶ 5.06[8][d] note 344. See also infra note 86.

[63] IRC §§ 2056(b)(7)(B)(ii)(I), 2523(f)(3).

[64] IRC §§ 2056(b)(7)(B)(ii)(II), 2523(f)(3). See supra ¶ 11.03[4][c] note 58.

[65] See ¶ 5.06[8][d]. Compare Reg. § 25.2523(f)-1 with Reg. § 20.2056(b)-7. Compare
also Reg. § 25.2523(f)-1(f) Exs. with Reg. § 20.2056(b)-7(h) Exs.

[66] See supra ¶ 11.03[3].

[67] See ¶¶ 4.16, 10.08.

[68] See IRC §§ 2056(b)(7)(B)(ii), 2523(f).

interests in the entire property that qualified for a marital deduction to the donor are transferred except, of course, the spouse's qualifying income interest, which is transferred in whole or in part under Section 2511.[69] The Section 2519 transfer is treated as if it were made by the spouse; if the transfer is a completed gift, tax rates are determined by the spouse's gift-giving history.[70] If the spouse makes no inter vivos disposition of the qualifying income interest, the property for which a marital deduction was allowed is included in the spouse's gross estate under Section 2044 and is valued at the spouse's death.[71] In addition, Section 2207A becomes applicable in conjunction with either Section 2519 or Section 2044, giving the spouse or the spouse's estate the right to recover the gift or estate taxes attributable to the transfer from the recipient of the property.[72]

Under the gift tax marital deduction terminable interest rule, a terminable interest exists where the donor retains an interest upon termination of the spouse's interest.[73] However, if all the qualified terminable interest property requirements are met, the full value of the property is treated as a gift to the spouse.[74] In essence, the qualified terminable interest property rules treat the property as owned by the spouse.[75] Thus, if the spouse makes a subsequent gift of all or part of the qualifying income interest, Section 2519 applies to all the spouse's other interests. When the spouse dies, all interests, including those of the donor, will be included in the spouse's gross estate by Section 2044.[76] Further, in keeping with the policy that the spouse owns the property, there are no gift tax consequences to the donor if the donor makes an inter vivos transfer of the donor's retained interest,[77] and the property is not included in the donor's gross estate under Section 2033, Section 2036, or Section 2037 if the donor re-

---

[69] IRC § 2519(a); Reg. § 25.2519-1. But see ¶ 10.08[2] text accompanying notes 42 and 43, which suggests that in some situations a disposition may not require a Section 2511 transfer.

[70] See IRC § 2502. The donee spouse's Section 2505 credit is used against such tax. There is no right of recovery of that credit from the recipients of the property; Section 2207A allows only a recovery of the tax that is paid.

[71] IRC §§ 2031, 2032, 2032A. In valuing the Section 2044 property, it is not aggregated with other interests in property owned outright by the surviving spouse or otherwise included in the surviving spouse's gross estate. See ¶ 4.02[4][b] text accompanying notes 157 and 158, ¶ 4.16 text accompanying notes 19–23.

[72] See ¶ 8.07.

[73] See supra ¶ 11.03[3][a] text accompanying notes 22, 23.

[74] IRC § 2523(f).

[75] IRC § 2523(f)(5)(A); Reg. § 25.2523(f)-1(a)(2). See generally Priv. Ltr. Rul. 9731009 (Apr. 30, 1997).

[76] IRC § 2523(f)(5)(A); Reg. § 25.2523(f)-1(a)(2).

[77] IRC § 2523(f)(5)(A)(ii).

tains a secondary life estate or a reversion until the donor's death.[78] However, after the spouse has made a Section 2519 transfer of the spouse's deemed interest or if that property interest has been included in the spouse's gross estate under Section 2044, the spouse is no longer treated as the owner of the property; in effect, the donor's interest is transferred back to the donor.[79]

Under the preceding rules, if the spouse is given a qualified terminable interest property interest in which the donor retains a reversion or contingent reversion, and the donor makes a Section 2523(f) election, a subsequent gift by the donor of the reversion is not deemed a Section 2511 transfer because the spouse "owns" the entire property for estate and gift tax purposes.[80] If the donor should predecease the spouse in these circumstances, there is no Section 2037 inclusion of the property in the donor's gross estate.[81] However, if the spouse makes a Section 2519 transfer or predeceases the donor and the property is included in the spouse's gross estate under Section 2044, the donor "owns" the donor's interest. The donor's subsequent gift of that interest is a Section 2511 transfer; at the donor's death, any noncontingent reversion is included in the donor's estate under Section 2033.[82]

[ii] Interspousal joint-and-survivor annuities. In 1988, Congress added Section 2523(f)(6) to the qualified terminable interest property rules.[83] Without this subsection, the creation of a joint-and-survivor annuity would violate the Section 2523(b)(1) terminable interest rule and might not qualify for qualified terminable interest property treatment because the spouse might not have a

---

[78] IRC § 2523(f)(5)(A)(i); Reg. § 25.2523(f)-1(d)(1). See Reg. § 25.2523(f)-1(f) Ex. 10.

[79] IRC § 2523(f)(5)(B); Reg. § 25.2523(f)-1(d)(2). However, the spouse is the transferor of such property and there is generally no inclusion in the donor's gross estate unless the fee interest is transferred back to the donor or a life estate is transferred back to the donor and the donee spouse's executor makes a QTIP election. See Reg. § 25.2523(f)-1(f) Ex. 11.

[80] Reg. § 25.2523(f)-1(d)(1). However, the spouse may not own the property for generation-skipping transfer tax purposes. IRC § 2652(a)(3). See ¶ 17.02[1][c][i].

[81] Reg. § 25.2523(f)-1(d)(1). Cf. Reg. § 25.2523(f)-1(f) Ex. 10.

[82] Reg. § 25.2523(f)-1(d)(2). There would be no Section 2037 inclusion of a contingent reversion because there would not be the necessary transfer of the property by the donor. Cf. Reg. § 25.2523(f)-1(f) Ex. 11.

[83] Technical and Miscellaneous Revenue Act of 1988, the provision is effective for decedents dying and transfers made after December 31, 1981. Pub. L. No. 100-647, § 6152(c)(1)(B), 102 Stat. 3342, 3725 (1988), reprinted in 1988-3 CB 1, 385. For joint-and-survivor annuities that were created before the enactment of this provision and were subject to the gift tax, Congress allowed a two-year grace period (from the date the section was enacted until Nov. 10, 1990) for the donor or donor's executor to seek a refund. See infra note 92.

qualifying income interest in the property.[84] Because annuities where only the spouses have the right to receive payments before the death of the survivor spouse can fit within the qualified terminable interest property scheme to be taxed to one of the spouses under the transfer tax mechanism, Congress has added Section 2523(f)(6) to the qualified terminable interest property rules, and such joint-and-survivor annuities now qualify for qualified terminable interest property treatment.[85]

The Section 2523(f)(6) rules contain several deviations from the normal qualified terminable interest property rules.[86] For example, under Section 2523(f)(6), if there is a transfer by the donor of an interest in a joint-and-survivor annuity,[87] where only the spouses have the right to receive any payments prior to the death of the survivor spouse,[88] the donee spouse's interest is treated as a qualifying income interest[89] and the donor is treated as having made the appropriate election unless the donor[90] elects out of qualified terminable interest property treatment.[91] This is a reversal of the normal requirement to make an affirmative qualified terminable interest property election.[92]

---

[84] IRC § 2523(f)(2)(B). See IRC § 2056(b)(7)(B)(ii). See also HR Conf. Rep. No. 795, 100th Cong., 2d Sess. 522 (1988); ¶ 5.06[8][d] note 336.

[85] Another reason for the enactment of this rule is that the Retirement Equity Act generally required a joint-and-survivor annuity as an automatic form of benefit under a qualified pension plan. See HR Conf. Rep. No. 795, 100th Cong., 2d Sess. 522 (1988).

[86] See IRC §§ 2044, 2519, 2523(f)(5). The Treasury has reserved the promulgation of regulations with respect to joint-and-survivor annuities. Reg. § 25.2523(f)-1(c)(4). Cf. Reg. §§ 25.2523(f)-1(c)(3), 25.2523(f)-1(f) Exs. 6, 7. See supra ¶ 11.03[4][c] note 62; ¶ 5.06[8][d] text accompanying notes 342, 344.

[87] Such annuities include qualified joint-and-survivor annuities. IRC § 417(b); see HR Conf. Rep. No. 795, 100th Cong., 2d Sess. 522 (1988).

[88] There may be third-party annuitants or benefit recipients, but they may have no right to any payments while either of the spouses is alive. The value of their interest (comparable to a remainder interest) also qualifies for the marital deduction.

[89] IRC § 2523(f)(6)(A).

[90] See IRC § 2523(f)(6)(D).

[91] IRC § 2523(f)(6)(B). The election is irrevocable. IRC § 2523(f)(6)(D). The creation of the survivorship annuity qualifies for a marital deduction even if the spouse is not a U.S. citizen. IRC § 2523(i) (last sentence). See Reg. §§ 25.2523(i)-(1)(b), 25.2523(i)-1(d) Ex. 2. Such annuities, if included in the donor's gross estate, automatically qualify for an estate tax marital deduction under a similar rule. IRC § 2056(b)(7)(C). See ¶ 5.06[8][d] text accompanying notes 337–341.

[92] IRC § 2523(f)(4)(A). A similar reversal applies under the estate tax. IRC § 2056(b)(7)(C)(ii). An election out of qualified terminable interest property treatment must be made by April 15 of the year following the creation of the annuity on a gift tax return reporting the gift, but the election need not have been made before Nov. 10, 1990. IRC § 2523(f)(6)(B); see IRC § 2523(f)(4)(A); HR Conf. Rep. No. 795, 100th Cong., 2d Sess. 522 (1988). Even if such an annuity had been created prior to the enactment of Section 2523(f)(6) on Nov. 10, 1988, the donor or the donor's executor had until Nov. 10,

Under the regular gift tax qualified terminable interest property rules, any interests in the qualified terminable interest property that are retained by the donor are for estate and gift tax purposes treated as owned by the donee.[93] Section 2523(f)(6), on the other hand, continues to treat the donor as owning the donor's interest in any joint-and-survivor annuities. Thus, if the donor makes an inter vivos gift of the donor's interest in the annuity, the transfer of that interest is subject to gift tax under Section 2511.[94] If the spouse transfers all or part of the spouse's annuity interest, Section 2519 does not treat the spouse as transferring any of the donor's interest, even though the spouse is treated as transferring third-party interests.[95] If the donor predeceases the spouse, the annuity is included in the donor's gross estate under Section 2039,[96] but the survivorship rights will qualify for qualified terminable interest property treatment unless the donor's executor elects out of such treatment.[97] Finally, if the spouse predeceases the donor, neither the donor's interest nor any third-party interests are included in the spouse's gross estate under Section 2044.[98] This final variation of the regular qualified terminable interest property rules goes even further than the foregoing variation in treating third-party interests as not owned by the spouse. The rule is no threat to the fisc, however, because all third-party interests will be subject to inclusion in the donor's gross estate.[99]

[d] Special Rule for Charitable Remainder Trusts

Section 2523(g) provides that if the donor and the spouse are the only noncharitable beneficiaries[100] of either a charitable remainder annuity trust or a charitable remainder unitrust,[101] the remainder qualifies for the charitable deduction, and the life interest in the spouse is not treated as a terminable inter-

---

1990, to seek a refund of any gift tax paid. HR Conf. Rep. No. 795, 100th Cong., 2d Sess. 522 (1988). See supra ¶ 11.03[4][c] note 83.

[93] IRC § 2523(f)(5)(A). See supra ¶ 11.03[4][c] text accompanying notes 73–82.

[94] IRC § 2523(f)(6)(C). Compare IRC § 2523(f)(5)(A)(ii).

[95] IRC § 2523(f)(6)(C).

[96] See ¶ 4.11.

[97] IRC § 2056(b)(7)(C). Any third-party interests would then be subject to Section 2519 or included in donee spouse's gross estate under Section 2044. See ¶ 5.06[8][d] text accompanying notes 336–351.

[98] IRC § 2523(f)(6)(D).

[99] IRC § 2039. See ¶ 4.11.

[100] If there are third-party noncharitable beneficiaries, a marital deduction is possible only under Section 2523(f). Reg. § 25.2523(g)-1(b). See also Reg. §§ 25.2523(f)-1(c)(3), 25.2523(f)-1(f) Exs. 6, 7.

[101] See Section 664(d) for the charitable remainder annuity trust and unitrust requirements. See also ¶¶ 5.05[5][a], 5.05[5][b].

est and hence qualifies for the marital deduction.[102] The parallel provision in the estate tax area is discussed in Chapter 5.[103]

[5] Noncitizen Donee Spouses

No gift tax marital deduction is allowed for any gift to a spouse who at the time the gift is made,[104] is not a U.S. citizen.[105] The denial of a gift tax marital deduction in this instance reflects congressional concern over the ability of the government to collect a transfer tax from a spouse who is not a citizen of the United States.[106] A $110,000 (rather than an $11,000) Section 2503(b) annual exclusion is allowed for these gifts.[107] To qualify for the exclusion, the present interest requirement under Section 2503(b) must be met;[108] the exclusion ap-

---

[102] See Reg. § 25.2523(g)-1(a).

[103] IRC § 2056(b)(8). See ¶ 5.06[8][e]. In addition, the decision of whether to use Section 2523(f) or Section 2523(g) is similar to the decision of whether to use Paragraph (7) or Paragraph (8) of Section 2056(b), which is discussed at ¶ 5.06[8][e]. See also Section 2523(h), which precludes any double deduction of the same interest. See supra ¶ 11.03[2] text accompanying note 18.

[104] Reg. § 25.2523(i)-1(a). See Reg. § 25.2523(i)-1(d) Ex. 5.

[105] IRC § 2523(i)(1). If the spouse is a U.S. citizen at the time of the gift, a transfer otherwise qualifying for a marital deduction is allowed a marital deduction regardless of whether the donor is a citizen or resident. Reg. § 25.2523(i)-1(a). Section 2523(i)(1) is effective with respect to gifts made on or after July 14, 1988. This disallowance may be altered by a treaty. Reg. § 25.2523(a)-1(a). Congress generally also disallows an estate tax marital deduction for a transfer to a surviving spouse who is not a U.S. citizen. IRC § 2056(d)(1)(A). But see IRC §§ 2056(d)(2), 2056(d)(3), 2056A. See ¶¶ 5.06[9], 5.07.

This rule is inapplicable to a transfer resulting from the acquisition of rights in a Section 2523(f)(6) joint-and-survivor annuity. IRC § 2523(i). See supra ¶ 11.03[4][c] note 91.

[106] For a more detailed explanation of that policy, see ¶¶ 5.06[9], 5.07 note 1. In addition to disallowing the marital deduction for transfers to noncitizen spouses, Congress has also altered the estate and gift tax rules for most joint-tenancy and tenancy-by-the-entirety property involving noncitizen spouses. See IRC § 2056(d)(1)(B); ¶¶ 4.12[10] notes 86–93, 5.06[9] note 428 for a discussion of the estate tax rules that generally make Section 2040(b) inapplicable and thus generally apply Section 2040(a) in such circumstances. Under the gift tax rules, Congress has generally reinstated Sections 2515 and 2515A as they existed prior to 1982. IRC § 2523(i)(3). See ¶ 10.01[3][f].

[107] IRC § 2523(i)(2). The amount was originally $100,000. Id. However, the amount is adjusted for inflation. Id. IRC §§ 2503(b)(1), 2503(b)(2). See ¶ 9.04[1] text accompanying notes 6–9.

The exclusion is available regardless of the citizenship or residency of the donor spouse. Reg. § 25.2523(i)-1(c)(2).

[108] See ¶¶ 9.04[1], 9.04[2], 9.04[3].

plies only to the extent of the value of the present interest;[109] and the transfer must be one that would qualify for a Section 2523 marital deduction if the donee spouse were a U.S. citizen.[110] The Service takes the position that a transfer to a noncitizen donee spouse that would qualify for a marital deduction if a qualified terminable interest property election were made fails the final requirement.[111]

¶ 11.04 SECTION 2524. EXTENT OF DEDUCTIONS

Section 2524 imposes a limitation on the amount of the charitable deduction and the marital deduction to prevent such deductions from offsetting gifts that are not themselves within the scope of the charitable and marital deduction provisions. The need for this restricting provision arises out of the annual exclusion[1] as explained in the next paragraphs.

[1] Charitable Deduction

If a donor who made a $15,000 gift to charity was allowed a full $15,000 deduction in determining taxable gifts for the year but the donor's gift to charity was reduced to $4,000 by the annual exclusion, $11,000 of the charitable deduction could apply improperly to offset otherwise taxable gifts to private individuals. Section 2524 limits the charitable deduction to $5,000 on these facts.

[2] Marital Deduction

Under Section 2523, the marital deduction, the same overuse possibility arises. But for the application of Section 2524, a donor who gives a spouse $15,000 outright during the year would be allowed both a $15,000 marital deduction

---

[109] Thus where there is a transfer qualifying for a gift tax marital deduction under Section 2523(e), only the value of the donee spouse's income interest qualifies for the exclusion. See Reg. § 25.2523(i)-1(d) Ex. 3.

[110] IRC § 2523(i)(2). See Reg. §§ 25.2523(i)-1(d) Ex. 1, 3. See TAM 9533001 (Jan. 23, 1995) (transfer neither qualified for annual exclusion nor marital deduction). This requirement applies only to transfers made after June 29, 1989. Reg. § 25.2523(i)-1(c)(1).

[111] Reg. § 25.2523(i)-1(d) Ex. 4. Because the spouse is not a citizen, a donor may not make a Section 2523(f)(4) QTIP election and thus the transfer does not satisfy the marital deduction qualification requirement.

[1] See IRC § 2503, discussed ¶ 9.04.

and an $11,000 annual exclusion. Section 2524 again limits the marital deduction to $4,000 on these facts.[2]

---

[2] See Reg. §§ 25.2523(a)-1(b)(3)(ii), 25.2523(a)-1(d) Ex. 8.

PART IV

Generation-Skipping
Transfer Tax

CHAPTER 12

Imposition of the Generation-Skipping Transfer Tax

¶ 12.01 SECTION 2601. TAX IMPOSED

[1] Reasons for the Tax

Since 1916, apart from some early, different exactions of a federal death duty,[1] the transmission of property at death has been subject to the federal estate tax. Efforts at avoidance invariably accompany the imposition of taxes; thus, even from the outset, Congress felt it necessary to subject to the estate tax lifetime transfers that were "in contemplation of or intended to take effect in possession or enjoyment at or after . . . death."[2] These concepts, and related devices designed to deter obvious tax avoidance schemes, have proliferated over the years as Congress has attempted to keep pace with the inventive genius of taxpayers and their counsel.[3] At times, Congress has had substantial administrative and judicial support.[4]

If the only gratuitous transfers taxed were those occurring or deemed to occur at death, large transmissions of wealth free of tax attrition by way of lifetime transfers, not so tainted as to fall prey to federal estate taxation, would be the order of the day. This simple truth so impressed itself on Congress, after abortive experimentation with taxes on lifetime gratuitous transfers from 1924 through 1926,[5] that there has been a federal tax on lifetime gifts since 1932.[6] The gift tax may properly be viewed as backstopping the estate tax because, although the two taxes were separate and distinct phenomena until 1977, the exaction on inter vivos transfers was designed to catch in the gift tax sieve wealth transmission that would escape estate tax upon the transferor's death. This was the thrust of the overall statutory plan, even though on close inspection one often found an overlapping of the two taxes[7] and ameliorating

---

[1] War Revenue Act of 1898, Ch. 448, §§ 29, 30, 30 Stat. 464–466 (1898). See Knowlton v. Moore, 178 US 41 (1900).

[2] Revenue Act of 1916, Pub. L. No. 64-271, Chapter 463, § 202(b), 39 Stat. 777–778 (1916). See ¶ 4.07[4].

[3] E.g., IRC §§ 2035, 2041, 2702, 2703, 2704.

[4] E.g., Lehman v. Comm'r, 109 F2d 99 (2d Cir.), cert. denied, 310 US 637 (1940); United States v. Estate of Grace, 395 US 316 (1969). In both cases, the Commissioner persuaded the courts that a person who is not in fact the grantor of a trust should be treated as the grantor of a trust created for that person by another, resulting in estate tax liability.

[5] Pub. L. No. 68-176, Ch. 234, 43 Stat. 253 (1924) (repealed Jan. 1, 1926).

[6] Pub. L. No. 72-154, Ch. 209, 47 Stat. 169, 245 (1932). See ¶ 9.01.

[7] See Smith v. Shaughnessy, 318 US 176 (1943).

credits or offsets where, in effect, a single transfer was subjected initially to gift tax and later to estate tax.[8]

It might appear that the arrangements described and examined closely in the preceding chapters of this book completely covered the federal taxation of wealth transmission, whether the congressional purpose was revenue raising or accumulation discouragement: The transmission of wealth was subjected to estate tax at the transferor's death; some lifetime transfers were treated as occurring at death, with the same resulting imposition of estate tax; and gratuitous lifetime transmissions of wealth were likewise subjected to a transfer tax. Nevertheless, a gap in this arrangement permitted tax-free "generation-skipping transfers." The gap arose out of the transmission nature of both the estate tax and the gift tax.

Prior to 1976, if a tax was to be imposed on a donor or on the estate of a decedent, it had to be because of the donor's or the decedent's transmission of wealth or the transmission of wealth realistically attributable to the donor or decedent. Thus, the mere termination of a person's interest in property, if that person never had an interest other than the one that terminated, was invariably viewed as a tax nullity, even though the termination was accompanied by the shift of a present interest to another person.[9] For example, if grantor G set up a trust with the income to child C for life, then income to grandchild GC for life, and a remainder to great-grandchild GGC, a federal transfer tax might have been imposed at the creation of the trust, but none would be imposed at C's death or at GC's death. The interests of C and GC would simply terminate, and GGC's possession of the property would not be effected by way of any transmission of wealth by C or GC. No transmission tax would be imposed because, in general, the distributions would be considered a mere fulfillment of the interests created by G.[10] If a third party had been made trustee with a power to distribute corpus, it would not have altered the lack of tax consequences at C's death or GC's death. Unless the trustee had a power that was the virtual equivalent of ownership,[11] the trustee would not be regarded as transmitting property at death.[12] If the trustee, who had no other connection with the trust, was given a power to appoint trust property only to another, another's estate, another's creditors, or the creditors of another's estate, the trus-

---

[8] Compare Section 2012, allowing a credit for gift tax paid on pre-1977 gifts, with the concept of "adjusted taxable gifts" and the estate tax computation under Section 2001(b).

[9] But see IRC § 2514(e).

[10] If the owner of a temporary present interest made a gift of it or otherwise released or relinquished the interest gratuitously (as opposed to merely letting it expire), the transfer would be subject to gift tax. Cerf v. Comm'r, 141 F2d 564 (3d Cir. 1944).

[11] IRC § 2041. Corpus distributions might also escape income taxation. IRC §§ 102, 652, 662, 663(a).

[12] Helvering v. Safe Deposit & Trust Co., 316 US 56 (1942).

tee's appointment of the property to *GGC* (or to anyone else for that matter) likewise would be without estate or gift tax significance.

This is a broad description of some arrangements under which property, prior to 1976, might have been enjoyed by way of its use, control of its use, or receipt of its income for several generations without the imposition of any federal transmission tax, as older beneficiaries dropped out of sight or amounts were distributed to persons well down the ancestral line.

There is nothing unconstitutional about the arrangements described. Indeed, cogent nontax reasons often support arrangements that suspend outright ownership of property. In 1976, however, Congress decided that the federal transmission taxes should generally take a bite out of accumulations of wealth once in each generation, at least where, between the persons who have outright ownership of property, there are others in intervening generations who have some interest in, or power over, it.[13]

Direct transfers of property that skipped over generations where, between the persons who had outright ownership of the property, there were others in intervening generations who had no interest in, or power over, the property, were free of tax prior to 1986. Although anyone could make a transfer of property that skipped a generation, generally only individuals of very substantial means could take advantage of the tax-planning opportunity to have their wealth skip one or more generation levels entirely. Thus, the imposition of the federal transfer taxes varied, depending on whether the property was passed directly to the immediately succeeding generation or was transferred in a way so as to skip an entire generation. Congress decided in 1986 that the federal transmission taxes should be imposed more uniformly and should take a bite out of direct skip transfers that skipped an entire generation level.[14]

[2] Imposition of the Chapter 13 Tax

When the statute taxing generation-skipping transfers is examined under the microscope, things that appear static to the naked eye remarkably begin to move about. The language of Section 2601 is characteristically crisp: "A tax is hereby imposed on every generation-skipping transfer (within the meaning of subchapter B)."[15] Viewed alone, this language is meaningless; it takes on meaning only after an examination of Chapter 13 in its entirety.

---

[13] See former IRC §§ 2613(a), 2613(b) (repealed by Tax Reform Act of 1986, Pub. L. No. 99-514, § 1431(a), 100 Stat. 2085, 2720 (1986), reprinted in 1986-3 CB (Vol. 1) 1, 637). Cf. IRC §§ 2612(a), 2612(b).

[14] IRC § 2612(c).

[15] IRC § 2601. The generation-skipping transfer tax is only imposed on generation-skipping transfers occurring prior to January 1, 2010. IRC § 2664. But see infra ¶ 12.01[3].

Chapter 13 imposes a federal excise that sometimes creates potential tax liability in two instances: (1) upon the transfer of property that skips a generation on its way to a younger generation and (2) upon a shifting of interests in property, even when the person who has a temporary interest in, or power over, the property does not actually transfer it to another person either during life or at death. In the latter instance, there is an event that can properly be seized upon as an occasion for the imposition of a federal tax.

A generation-skipping transfer must occur before the need arises to determine the generation-skipping transfer tax.[16] Generation-skipping transfers come in three varieties: taxable terminations, taxable distributions, and direct skips.[17] However, only certain taxable terminations, taxable distributions, and direct skips are treated as generation-skipping transfers.[18]

The generation-skipping transfer tax, like many other taxes, is determined by multiplying the tax base by the tax rate.[19] The tax base is the taxable amount of the generation-skipping transfer,[20] and it varies with the type of generation-skipping transfer being taxed.[21] The tax rate is the product of the maximum federal estate tax rate and the inclusion ratio.[22] The maximum federal estate tax rate is found in the multipurpose rate table of Section 2001(c).[23]

---

[16] IRC §§ 2601, 2611(a). See ¶¶ 13.01[1], 13.02[1][a].

[17] IRC § 2611(a). See IRC §§ 2612(a), 2612(b), 2612(c); ¶ 13.02.

[18] IRC § 2611(b). See ¶ 13.01[2].

[19] IRC § 2602. See ¶ 12.02.

[20] IRC §§ 2602(1), 2621, 2622, 2623, 2624. See ¶¶ 14.01–14.05.

[21] See generally ¶ 12.02 text accompanying notes 3–8. See also ¶¶ 13.01–13.02, for a discussion of the different types of generation-skipping transfers.

[22] IRC § 2641. See ¶ 16.01.

[23] IRC §§ 2641(b), 2001(c)(1). From 2002 to 2009 the maximum federal estate tax rate under Section 2010(c) ranges from 50 percent to 45 percent.

Calendar Year	Maximum Rate
2002	50%
2003	49%
2004	48%
2005	47%
2006	46%
2007	45%
2008	45%
2009	45%

See ¶¶ 2.01[3], 16.01.

Every transferor has a GST exemption.[24] The inclusion ratio is the mechanism that integrates the transferor's GST exemption into the tax rate structure.[25]

The approach taken here is to discuss separately each of the seven subchapters of Chapter 13. Some challenges to congressional policy and drafting are inescapable along the way. The first subchapter, Subchapter A, deals with the computation of the Chapter 13 tax under Section 2602, the liability for the payment of the tax and the credit for certain state taxes.[26] Subchapter B examines the definition of what is taxed and the three types of generation-skipping transfers.[27] Subchapter C explores the tax base of the generation-skipping transfer tax, the taxable amount.[28] Subchapter D discusses the GST exemption and its allocation among various generation-skipping transfers.[29] Subchapter E deals with the rate of tax imposed on generation-skipping transfers.[30] Subchapter F examines the definitions and special rules laid down by Congress that give more meaning to the critical statutory terms.[31] Finally, subchapter G considers the statutory expression of special administrative rules applicable to the reporting, payment, and enforcement of the generation-skipping transfer tax.[32]

---

[24] IRC § 2631. The GST exemption is $1 million adjusted upward for inflation until December 31, 2003. On January 1, 2004, the GST exemption amount equals the applicable exclusion amount under Section 2010(c). From 2004 to 2009, the GST exemption ranges from $1.5 million to $3.5 million.

Calendar Year	GST Exemption
2004	$1.5 million
2005	$1.5 million
2006	$2 million
2007	$2 million
2008	$2 million
2009	$3.5 million

IRC § 2010(c). As amended by Economic Growth and Tax Relief Reconciliation Act of 2001, Pub. L. No. 107-16, §§ 521(c), 521(e)(3), 115 Stat. 39, 72 (2001) reprinted in 2001- ___ CB ___, ___. See ¶¶ 15.02, 3.02.

[25] IRC § 2642. See ¶ 16.02.

[26] See ¶¶ 12.02, 12.03, 12.04.

[27] See ¶¶ 13.01, 13.02, 13.03.

[28] See ¶¶ 14.01–14.05.

[29] See ¶¶ 15.01, 15.02, 15.03.

[30] See ¶¶ 16.01–16.02.

[31] See ¶¶ 17.01–17.04.

[32] See ¶¶ 18.01–18.06.

[3] Termination

The generation-skipping transfer tax does not apply to generation-skipping transfers after December 31, 2009.[33] However, under a "sunset" provision the generation-skipping transfer tax will be reimposed and subject generation-skipping transfers after January 1, 2011, to tax.[34]

¶ 12.02 SECTION 2602. AMOUNT OF TAX

Section 2602 provides that the amount of tax imposed by Section 2601 is the product of the taxable amount[1] and the applicable rate.[2] The formula is relatively brief; however, that brevity does not equate with simplicity.

The taxable amount of a generation-skipping transfer[3] depends on whether the generation-skipping transfer is a taxable distribution, a taxable termination, or a direct skip.[4] The taxable amount of a taxable distribution is the amount actually or constructively[5] received by the transferee less expenses incurred in the determination, collection, or refund of the Chapter 13 tax imposed.[6] The taxable amount of a taxable termination is the value of the property with respect to which the termination has occurred, less deductions similar to those allowed by Section 2053.[7] The taxable amount of a direct skip is the amount received by the transferee.[8]

Section 2641(a) defines "applicable rate of tax" as the product of the maximum federal estate tax rate and the inclusion ratio with respect to the

---

[33] IRC § 2664. See ¶ 18.04. The estate tax does not apply to the estates of decedents dying after December 31, 2009. IRC § 2210(a). See ¶ 8.10[1].

[34] Economic Growth and Tax Relief Reconciliation Act of 2001, Pub. L. No. 107-16 § 901(a)(2), 115 Stat. 38, 150 (2001), reprinted in 2001-__ CB __, __. See ¶ 8.10[5] for a discussion of the "sunset" provision.

[1] IRC §§ 2621, 2622, 2623.

[2] IRC § 2641.

[3] See IRC §§ 2621, 2622, 2623, discussed at ¶¶ 14.02, 14.03, 14.04.

[4] See IRC §§ 2611, 2612, discussed at ¶¶ 13.01, 13.02. The interrelationship of the three types of generation-skipping transfers becomes significant when two types of generation-skipping transfers overlap. When there is overlap, a direct skip takes priority, followed by a taxable termination, and then a taxable distribution. See ¶ 13.02[1][b]; IRC § 2612(b) (parenthetical); Reg. § 26.2612-1(b)(1)(i) (preventing a direct skip from also satisfying the requirements of a taxable termination); Reg. § 26.2612-1(f) Ex. 5. See also Rev. Rul. 92-26, 1992-1 CB 314, 315.

[5] See IRC § 2621(b), discussed at ¶ 14.02[4].

[6] IRC § 2621. See ¶ 14.02.

[7] IRC § 2622. See ¶¶ 14.03, 5.03.

[8] IRC § 2623. See ¶ 14.04.

transfer.[9] The maximum federal estate tax rate is found in the multipurpose rate table of Section 2001(c).[10] It was the intent of Congress to simplify the computation of the generation-skipping transfer tax by using a flat tax rate.[11] This type of tax simplification may not be warmly greeted by taxpayers.[12] The inclusion ratio that integrates the transferor's GST exemption[13] into the tax rate structure[14] is a decimal fraction equal to one minus the applicable fraction.[15] The numerator of the applicable fraction is generally that portion of the transferor's GST exemption allocated[16] to the transfer,[17] and the denominator is generally the value of the property transferred.[18] As a result, generation-skipping transfers of up to the GST exemption attributed to any individual transferor[19] may be effectively exempted from the generation-skipping transfer tax.

The source of the funds with which to pay the Chapter 13 tax varies with the type of generation-skipping transfer. In the case of a taxable distribution or a taxable termination, the Chapter 13 tax is charged to the property being transferred.[20] In the case of an inter vivos direct skip, the transferor generally pays the Chapter 13 tax with assets other than the property transferred.[21] If the direct skip is from a trust, or with respect to property that continues to be held in trust, the trustee pays the tax out of trust assets.[22] The executor of the dece-

---

[9] See ¶ 16.01.

[10] IRC §§ 2641(b), 2001(c)(1); Reg § 26.2641-1. See ¶¶ 12.01[2] note 23, 16.01. See also HR Conf. Rep. No. 426, 99th Cong., 1st Sess. 827 (1986), reprinted in 1986-3 CB (Vol. 2) 1, 827.

[11] Staff of Joint Comm. on Tax'n, 100th Cong., 1st Sess., General Explanation of the Tax Reform Act of 1986 at 1259, 1263 (Comm. Print 1987). Under prior law, the amount of tax imposed on a generation-skipping transfer was computed using the Section 2001(c) graduated rate table and the rate progression dependent on the transferor's prior gift, estate, and generation-skipping transfer transactions. See former IRC § 2602(a)(1) (repealed by Tax Reform Act of 1986, Pub. L. No. 99-514, § 1431(a), 100 Stat. 2085, 2718 (1986), reprinted in 1986-3 CB (Vol. 1) 1, 635). Congress "simplified" the above computation by imposing a "flat rate" at the maximum Section 2001(c) rate. IRC §§ 2641(a)(1), 2641(b).

[12] See ¶ 16.01 note 10.

[13] IRC § 2631. See ¶¶ 12.01[2] note 24, 15.02.

[14] IRC §§ 2641, 2642. See ¶¶ 16.01, 16.02.

[15] IRC § 2642(a)(1).

[16] IRC § 2632. See ¶ 15.03.

[17] IRC § 2642(a)(2)(A). See ¶¶ 16.02[1]–16.02[3].

[18] IRC § 2642(a)(2)(B). See ¶¶ 16.02[1]–16.02[3].

[19] See IRC § 2652(a)(1).

[20] IRC §§ 2603(a)(1), 2603(a)(2), 2603(b). See ¶ 12.03; Reg. §§ 26.2662-1(c)(1)(i), 26.2662-1(c)(1)(ii).

[21] IRC § 2603(a)(3). See ¶ 12.03; Reg. § 26.2662-1(c)(1)(iii).

[22] See Reg. § 26.2662-1(c)(1)(iv).

dent's estate uses estate assets to liquidate the tax imposed on testamentary direct skips not involving trusts.[23]

Taxable distributions and taxable terminations are "tax-inclusive" transfers, whereas direct skips are generally[24] "tax-exclusive" transfers. In a tax-inclusive transfer, the tax is calculated on an amount which includes the assets used to pay the tax. The tax liability is extracted from the transferred property before the property reaches the recipient.[25] Disregarding any use of the GST exemption[26] and using a 50 percent generation-skipping transfer tax rate, the Chapter 13 tax imposed on a $2 million taxable distribution or taxable termination would be $1 million, leaving a net amount of only $1 million to pass to the transferee. Thus, disregarding any Chapter 11 or Chapter 12 taxes incurred at the creation of the trust,[27] it costs the transferor $2 million to transfer $1 million to a transferee in a tax-inclusive taxable distribution or taxable termination.

The tax liability in a tax-exclusive transfer, which occurs with respect to a testamentary direct skip,[28] is computed solely on the amount received by the transferee.[29] Again disregarding any use of the GST exemption and using the 50 percent generation-skipping transfer tax rate, the Chapter 13 tax imposed on the transferor's estate for making an outright $1 million testamentary direct

---

[23] See Reg. § 26.2662-1(c)(1)(v).

[24] As a result of Section 2515, which treats the Chapter 13 tax paid as an additional gift for gift tax purposes, an inter vivos direct skip might best be described as a hybrid tax-inclusive/tax-exclusive payment. See infra text accompanying notes 31–33; ¶ 10.05.

[25] The estate tax and the income tax are also tax-inclusive taxes, as the tax liability comes out of the property included in the gross estate or in gross income.

[26] IRC § 2631. See ¶ 15.02.

[27] On creation of the trust from which the taxable distribution or taxable termination was made, a Chapter 11 or Chapter 12 tax would have been imposed.

[28] See infra text accompanying notes 31–33 for a discussion of inter vivos direct skips.

[29] Even where the generation-skipping transfer tax imposed on a direct skip is to be paid out of the property constituting the transfer, the generation-skipping transfer tax is removed from the generation-skipping transfer tax base. In this situation, an interdependent variable computation is necessary to determine the generation-skipping transfer tax because the amount of the transfer subject to the tax is dependent on the amount of the tax. Form 706 solves this algebraic problem neatly by computing the tax imposed on the direct skip transfer by reducing the amount of the direct skip by the GST exemption allocated to it and then dividing the result by 2.818182. Form 706, United States Estate (and Generation-Skipping Transfer) Tax Return (Rev. Nov. 2001), Schedule R, Part 2, Line 8, at 34.

The gift tax is a tax-exclusive tax because the donor bears primary liability for the tax payment and is not required to include any gift tax paid as an additional gift subject to the gift tax. If a "net gift" is made, the transfer is still a tax-exclusive transfer and a cyclical computation must be made to determine the amount of net gift. See ¶ 10.02[6][d]. The tax-exclusive nature of the gift tax provides an estate tax planning opportunity if gifts are made more than three years prior to the donor's death. See IRC § 2035(b); ¶ 4.07[3].

skip to a transferee would be $500,000, where the tax is paid out of assets other than the $1 million transferred. Again disregarding any Chapter 11 tax imposed on the transfer,[30] the cost to the transferor of transferring $1 million in a tax-exclusive testamentary direct skip is $1.5 million.

Unlike a testamentary direct skip, an inter vivos direct skip is a hybrid tax-inclusive/tax-exclusive transfer; this is because Section 2515[31] of the Code treats the transferor's payment of the Chapter 13 tax imposed on an inter vivos direct skip as an additional transfer subject to the Chapter 12 gift tax. Thus, disregarding the Chapter 12 tax initially imposed on the $1 million transfer[32] and any use of the GST exemption, and assuming a 50 percent transfer tax rate, it costs the transferor $1,750,000 to transmit $1 million in an inter vivos direct skip to a transferee.[33]

¶ 12.03 SECTION 2603. LIABILITY FOR TAX

[1] General Rules

Section 2603 specifies who must pay the generation-skipping transfer tax.[1] Who pays the tax is determined in part by the type of generation-skipping

---

[30] Because this is a testamentary direct skip, estate tax would be imposed on the property transferred prior to the Chapter 13 transfer. Assuming a 50 percent estate tax rate, it could cost the decedent up to $3 million to transfer $1 million in a testamentary direct skip. If included in the transferor's gross estate, the $3 million is subject to a maximum 50 percent estate tax, leaving $1.5 million. As $1 million is distributed to the transferee, an additional $500,000 of Chapter 13 tax is imposed.

[31] See ¶ 10.05.

[32] This assumption parallels a disregard of the initial transfer tax in the examples mentioned previously. See supra text accompanying notes 27, 30.

[33] Because this is an inter vivos direct skip, a gift tax would be imposed on the property transferred prior to the Chapter 13 transfer. Assuming a 50 percent gift tax rate, the donor of a $1 million inter vivos transfer would have to pay $500,000 in gift tax. Using a 50 percent Chapter 13 tax rate, the donor would have to pay another $500,000 in Chapter 13 tax. Section 2515 would result in an additional $250,000 gift tax on the donor's payment of the Chapter 13 tax. As a result, it would cost the donor $2,250,000 to transfer $1 million to the transferee in an inter vivos direct skip.

[1] In general, the rules in Section 2603 are also used to identify the person who is required to file the generation-skipping transfer tax return. IRC § 2662(a)(1). See ¶ 18.02[3].

Section 164(a)(4) allows an income tax deduction for federal generation-skipping transfer tax imposed by Section 2601 and state generation-skipping transfer tax described in Section 2604 (tax on taxable terminations or taxable distributions) imposed on transfers included in the gross income of the distributee to which Section 666 does not apply. IRC §§ 164(a)(4), 164(b)(4).

transfer[2] that generates the tax liability.[3] Even though a person who is not the transferor may incur personal liability for the payment of the tax, the property involved in the transfer will be used to satisfy the tax liability unless the governing instrument directs otherwise by specific reference to the generation-skipping transfer tax.[4]

Section 2603 provides that the transferee is to pay the tax arising from a taxable distribution.[5] Although the term "transferee" for purposes of the Chapter 13 tax is not specifically defined in the Code, the transferee should be the person who receives the property or for whose benefit it is applied. If any amount of the generation-skipping transfer tax resulting from a taxable distribution is paid by the trustee, that amount is treated as an additional taxable distribution, and the liability for the tax on the imputed distribution again falls on the transferee.[6]

The tax imposed on any inter vivos direct skip that is not from a trust is to be paid by the transferor.[7] If the transferor fails to pay the tax, the transferee will be liable for the tax to the extent of the value of property received.[8] If the transferor dies before paying the tax imposed, the executor[9] of the transferor's estate may become personally liable for the tax in the same manner in which

---

[2] IRC § 2611(a). See IRC §§ 2612(a), 2612(b), 2612(c).

[3] IRC § 2603(a); Reg. § 26.2662-1(c)(1). The interrelationship of the three types of generation-skipping transfers becomes significant when the types of generation-skipping transfers overlap. When there is overlap, a direct skip takes priority, followed by a taxable termination, with a taxable distribution coming last. See ¶ 13.02[1][b]; IRC § 2612(b) (parenthetical); Reg. § 26.2612-1(b)(1)(i) (preventing a direct skip from also satisfying the requirements of a taxable termination); Reg. § 26.2612-1(f) Ex. 5. See also Rev. Rul. 92-26, 1992-1 CB 314, 315.

[4] IRC § 2603(b). See Priv. Ltr. Rul. 9731030 (May 5, 1997) (tax payment clause did not make specific reference to generation-skipping transfer tax). Section 2603(b) is an apportionment statute and, as such, may conflict with other federal or state apportionment statutes.

[5] IRC § 2603(a)(1). See Reg. § 26.2662-1(c)(1)(i).

[6] IRC § 2621(b). See ¶ 13.02[3][c].

[7] IRC § 2603(a)(3). See Reg. § 26.2662-1(c)(1)(iii).

[8] IRC §§ 2661(1), 6324(b). Timely assessment against the transferee can be made "within 1 year after the expiration of the period of limitation for assessment against the transferor." IRC § 6901(c)(1). Generally, the generation-skipping transfer tax constitutes a lien on the property transferred for a period of ten years from the date of the transfer. IRC §§ 6324(b), 6324(c); Reg. § 26.2662-1(f). See ¶ 9.04[11].

[9] IRC § 2203. See ¶ 8.02; Reg. § 26.2652-1(d).

the executor may become liable for the deceased transferor's gift taxes[10] and estate taxes.[11]

The executor of the transferor's estate is required to pay the generation-skipping transfer tax imposed on any direct skip transfer that is subject to the Chapter 11 estate tax, other than a direct skip from a trust.[12] In general, the executor will incur personal liability for the tax only where there is fiduciary impropriety.[13] Where estate assets are available to the executor to pay the generation-skipping transfer tax, they generally will be used for this purpose, thus eliminating the executor's liability.[14]

With all other types of generation-skipping transfers, such as taxable terminations of a trust or a trust equivalent arrangement and direct skips from a trust or from a trust equivalent arrangement occurring either during the transferor's life or at the transferor's death, the tax imposed is paid by the trustee,[15] except for a limited instance in which the executor is required to pay the tax.[16] Where the trust is an explicit trust,[17] the trustee is easily identified, and the trust corpus is used to satisfy the tax liability.[18]

---

[10] See IRC § 6905 (relating to the discharge from such liability). See also ¶¶ 8.03[1], 9.04[11].

[11] See IRC §§ 2002, 2204, discussed at ¶¶ 2.02, 8.03. The executor will incur personal liability for the tax only when there is fiduciary impropriety. Reg. § 20.2002-1. See ¶ 2.02 text accompanying note 5.

[12] Reg. § 26.2662-1(c)(1)(v). In addition, the executor of the transferor's estate is required to pay the generation-skipping transfer taxes imposed on direct skips from a trust equivalent arrangement occurring at the transferor's death (see IRC §§ 2652(b)(1), 2652(b)(3)) when the total value of direct skips with respect to the trustee of the trust arrangement is less than $250,000 for decedents dying after June 23, 1996, and $100,000 for decedents dying before June 24, 1996. Reg. §§ 26.2662-1(c)(2)(iii), 26.2662-1(c)(2)(iv). See infra ¶ 12.03[2] text accompanying notes 27, 28.

[13] See ¶¶ 2.02, 8.03.

[14] See ¶¶ 2.02, 8.03; IRC §§ 2661(2), 6905(a).

[15] IRC § 2603(a)(2); Reg. §§ 26.2662-1(c)(1)(ii), 26.2662-1(c)(1)(iv).

[16] See infra ¶ 12.03[2] text accompanying note 27.

[17] See Reg. § 26.2662-1(c)(2)(ii). An "explicit trust" is any trust that qualifies under the definition of "trust" found in Regulations Section 301.7701-4(a). The regulation defines "trust" as an arrangement "created either by a will or by an inter vivos declaration whereby trustees take title to property for the purpose of protecting or conserving it for the beneficiaries under the ordinary rules applied in chancery or probate courts."

[18] IRC § 2603(b). A trustee is not always as easily identified in a trust equivalent arrangement. See infra ¶ 12.03[2].

[2] Trust Equivalent Arrangements

Section 2652(b)(1) defines the term "trust" to include any trust equivalent arrangement having substantially the same effect as a trust.[19] The statute specifically lists life estates and remainders, estates for years, and insurance and annuity contracts as examples of trust equivalent arrangements and specifically excludes estates from such classification.[20] The person who is the "trustee" under a trust equivalent arrangement is generally the person liable for payment of the Chapter 13 tax.[21] Because the trustee of a trust equivalent arrangement is defined as the person in actual or constructive possession of the property subject to the arrangement,[22] the identity of the person who is treated as trustee for purposes of the Chapter 13 tax will depend on the type of trust equivalent arrangement involved. Sometimes that person may be difficult to identify.

In a life estate and remainder situation, for example, the person in actual or constructive possession of the property presumably is the life tenant. Therefore, the life tenant normally is the trustee for purposes of Section 2652(b)(2). However, if the life tenant is dead when a taxable termination occurs, the tenant obviously will not be able to pay the tax. The executor of the life tenant's estate could become liable for the payment of the tax, but such an arrangement seems unnecessarily complicated; the remainderperson would be in a better position to pay the tax and, in such instances, should be treated as the trustee.

In the case of an estate for years, the holder of the estate for years presumably is the "trustee" for purposes of Section 2652(b)(2). If the holder of the estate for years survives the term of years, the holder will be available to pay the tax with estate assets. If the holder of the estate for years dies before the term of years expires, the interest in the estate for years will pass to someone else, and the person receiving the interest in the remaining estate for years will be treated as trustee and will be liable for payment of the generation-skipping transfer tax.

Where the trust equivalent arrangement is a private annuity, the person paying the annuity presumably should be treated as "trustee" for purposes of Chapter 13. With commercial insurance and annuity contracts, the trustee is the company issuing the insurance or annuity contract.[23] The company issuing the contract is a good choice as the person to be liable for the tax because an insurance company can generally be relied on to be aware of the requirement

---

[19] See ¶ 17.02[2]. See also Reg. § 26.2662-1(c)(2)(ii).

[20] IRC §§ 2652(b)(1), 2652(b)(3). The list is not exclusive. See ¶ 17.02[2].

[21] An exception is provided for certain direct skips occurring at death with respect to property held in a trust equivalent arrangement. Reg. § 26.2662-1(c)(2). See Reg. §§ 26.2662-1(c)(2)(iii), 26.2662-1(c)(2)(iv); infra note 27. The Section 2652(b) trustee rules are considered at ¶ 17.02[2].

[22] IRC § 2652(b)(2). See ¶ 17.02[2].

[23] See Reg. § 26.2662-1(c)(2)(vi) Ex. 3.

to pay the tax and, in all likelihood, will possess the information needed to compute the generation-skipping transfer tax.[24] Problems regarding the funding of the tax can arise in the case of an insurance contract or a private or commercial annuity. An insurance or annuity contract will provide that the company or person issuing the contract should make certain payments to the beneficiary of the contract. Section 2603(b) provides that the generation-skipping transfer tax is paid out of the property being transferred unless the governing instrument directs otherwise by specific reference to the tax. Thus, unless an insurance or annuity contract specifically provides for payment of the generation-skipping transfer tax, the company or person issuing the contract may not be permitted to reduce the payments to the beneficiaries and may, therefore, be unable to pay the tax out of the property transferred. The statute should, but does not, provide for the tax liability to shift to the beneficiaries; nor does it allow the trustee to recover the amount of tax paid from the beneficiaries. Section 2663(3), however, authorizes the Secretary to prescribe regulations modifying the generation-skipping transfer tax rules for trust equivalents,[25] and the legislative history suggests that the Secretary may make the beneficiary of an insurance or annuity contract pay any generation-skipping transfer tax.[26]

---

[24] See PS-32-90, Supplementary Information, 1993-1 CB 907, 909. "An insurance company will generally be able to determine whether the proceeds are includible in the decedent's gross estate because it will have access to information regarding whether the proceeds are being paid to the decedent's estate or whether the decedent owned the policy or incidents of ownership in the policy." Id. at 909. The insurance company will generally possess the information necessary to determine whether or not the person receiving the benefits is a skip person or will be able to acquire the information from the executor of the decedent's estate if the proceeds are payable to the estate.

[25] See ¶ 18.03[3]; Reg. § 26.2662-1(c)(2)(ii).

[26] S. Rep. No. 445, 100th Cong., 2d Sess. 373 (1988); Staff of Joint Comm. on Tax'n, Description of the Technical Corrections Act of 1988 (HR 4333 and S. 2238) (JCS-10-88) 365 (Mar. 31, 1988). Note that Reg. §§ 26.2662-1(c)(2)(vi) Ex. 2 and 26.2662-1(c)(2)(vi) Ex. 3 make the insurance company, not the recipient of the proceeds of the policy, liable for the Chapter 13 tax. Although the Committee Report indicated that where the generation-skipping arrangement is in the form of an insurance or annuity contract, the regulation could provide that the beneficiary must pay the tax, "[i]t was determined, however, that it would be more appropriate if the primary burden for paying the tax remained on the trustee of the trust arrangement (or, in certain cases, upon the decedent's executor) because they are more likely to possess the information needed to compute the tax and file the return." PS-32-90, Supplementary Information, 1993-1 CB 907, 908. See ¶ 18.03[3] note 67.

However, see Reg. § 26.2662-1(c)(2)(v). Where a direct skip from a trust equivalent arrangement occurs and the value of the property with respect to the trustee of that trust equivalent arrangement is less than $250,000, the regulation permits the executor of a decedent's estate to recover the generation-skipping transfer tax attributable to the direct skip transfer from the recipient of the property.

There is only one situation in which the trustee of the trust equivalent arrangement is not liable for the payment of the generation-skipping transfer tax. If a direct skip transfer from such an arrangement occurs at the death of the transferor and the total value of the property involved in direct skips with respect to the trustee of that arrangement does not exceed $250,000, the executor of the transferor's estate (rather than the trustee of the trust equivalent arrangement) is liable for payment of the generation-skipping transfer tax.[27] However, the regulations treat the property involved in such a direct skip as any other nonprobate asset of the estate and allow the executor to recover the Chapter 13 tax from the property involved in the direct skip.[28] Thus, the search for a pseudo-trustee in a trust equivalent arrangement is sometimes unnecessary where a legal life estate was retained in the transferor, or where the transferor either owned a life insurance policy[29] or retained an annuity for the transferor's life and its value was less than $250,000. In such instances, the executor becomes responsible for payment of the tax.[30]

---

[27] Reg. §§ 26.2662-1(c)(2)(i), 26.2662-1(c)(2)(iii). In the case of transfers of decedents dying prior to June 24, 1996, if the transfer is less than $100,000, rather than $250,000, the executor of the transferor's estate is liable for payment. Reg. § 26.2662-1(c)(2)(iv).

This exception applies only if the aggregate value of policies issued by a particular company on an insured individual involved in direct skips with respect to the trustee of that trust arrangement is less than $250,000. See Reg. § 26.2662-1(c)(2)(vi) Ex. 2.

This exception facilitates the prompt payment of policy proceeds and the smooth administration of the imposition of the generation-skipping transfer tax. The proceeds can be paid once the insurance company determines that the policy proceeds are includible in the insured transferor's gross estate and that the aggregate value of the policies it has issued insuring the transferor is less than $250,000. The insurance company will generally possess enough information to determine if the insurance proceeds are includible in the insured's gross estate because it will know if the insured possessed incidents of ownership in the policy or if the proceeds are payable to the insured's executor. See IRC § 2042; Reg. § 26.2662-1(c)(2)(vi) Ex. 5; PS-32-90, Supplementary Information, 1993-1 CB 907, 909. The executor of the decedent's estate is in the best position to gather the information needed to determine the generation-skipping transfer tax liability of the deceased transferor.

[28] Reg. § 26.2662-1(c)(2)(v). For example, if Transferor in 2001 purchased an annuity for life with a refund feature to be paid to Grandchild, and if Transferor died in the current year, with Grandchild's parents surviving (see ¶¶ 13.02[4][c][i], 13.02[4][c][ii]), there would be a direct skip to Grandchild. If the value of the refund was less than $250,000, Transferor's executor would be liable for the tax but would be entitled to recover the amount of the liability from Grandchild. If the property is transferred to a trust or remains in a trust equivalent arrangement, the tax is recovered from the trustee. If the property passes outright, recovery is from the beneficiary. See Reg. §§ 26.2662-1(c)(2)(iii), 26.2662-1(c)(2)(iv).

[29] Reg. §§ 26.2662-1(c)(2)(vi) Ex. 1–4.

[30] The $250,000 limit applies to decedents dying after June 23, 1996. Reg. § 26.2662-1(c)(2)(iii). The limit for decedents dying on that date or before is $100,000. Reg. § 26.2662-1(c)(2)(iv). See supra note 27.

[3] Limitation of a Trustee's Liability

In two situations in which a trustee otherwise would be personally liable for the payment of the Chapter 13 tax, Section 2654(d) limits such liability.[31] A trustee is not personally liable for any increase in the generation-skipping transfer tax that is attributable to the fact that (1) Section 2642(c) does not apply to a transfer made to the trust during the life of the transferor for which a gift tax return was not filed[32] or (2) the inclusion ratio for the trust is greater than the inclusion ratio computed on the basis of the return on which an allocation of the transferor's GST exemption to property transferred to the trust was made.[33] However, the trustee's liability is not limited if the trustee could have reasonably concluded that a gift tax return was required or that the inclusion ratio was erroneous.[34]

If the trustee is not liable for payment of the increase in the generation-skipping transfer tax in the two situations described, then who is liable? Congress made no express provision for personal liability in this situation. In a taxable termination where property held in a trust is transferred to a transferee, it is logical that the transferee should become liable for the tax.[35] The transferee has the property and the means with which to pay the tax. But if a taxable termination occurs and the property transferred continues to be held in the trust, so that the transferee receives no property out of which the tax can be paid, the generation-skipping transfer tax should be paid by the trustee out of the trust property transferred,[36] even though the trustee has no personal liability.[37]

---

[31] See ¶ 17.04[4].

[32] IRC § 2654(d)(1). See Reg. § 26.2662-1(c)(3)(i). Section 2642(c) assigns a zero inclusion ratio to certain direct skip transfers to trusts that are not taxable gifts after application of the Section 2503(b) annual exclusion. IRC § 2642(c)(2). See ¶ 16.02[2][b].

[33] IRC § 2654(d)(2). See Reg. § 26.2662-1(c)(3)(ii). See also IRC § 2642(a); ¶¶ 16.02[1]–16.02[3].

[34] IRC § 2654(d) (last sentence). A trustee will be deemed to have knowledge of facts known to the trustee's agent, employee, partner, or co-trustee. Reg. § 26.2662-1(c)(3)(iii). For a more detailed discussion of Section 2654(d), see ¶ 17.04[4].

[35] See IRC §§ 2661, 6324.

[36] IRC § 2603(b).

[37] Congress may have intended that there be no personal liability for any party beyond the property involved in the event that the amount of the generation-skipping transfer tax is increased because no gift tax return was filed, or in the event that the inclusion ratio is erroneous. Congressional intent regarding this issue of personal liability is not clear. The issue should be clarified in regulations.

¶ 12.04 SECTION 2604. CREDIT FOR STATE TAX

The amount of federal estate tax liability has long been reduced by a credit for state death taxes paid.[1] Under Section 2604,[2] the federal tax imposed on a generation-skipping transfer may similarly be reduced by a credit for state taxes paid with respect to a taxable distribution or a taxable termination occurring at the same time as, and as a result of, the death of an individual.[3] However, Section 2604 does not allow a credit for state tax paid with respect to direct skip generation-skipping transfers.[4]

The basic measure of the credit is the amount of the generation-skipping transfer tax actually paid to a state with respect to the property transferred.[5] However, the amount allowed as a credit is limited to 5 percent of the amount of the federal tax imposed on the transfer by Chapter 13.[6]

It is common for states to enact death "pick-up" taxes, setting the amount of such taxes at the maximum credit allowable against the federal estate tax by Section 2011(b). The effect of a death pick-up tax is simply to divert to the states tax money that would otherwise find its way to the federal fisc.[7] The

---

[1] IRC § 2011. See ¶ 3.03. But see infra text accompanying notes 9–12.

[2] Section 2604 does not apply to generation-skipping transfers after December 31, 2004. IRC § 2604(c).

[3] IRC § 2604(a).

[4] IRC § 2604(a). Although the statute specifically excludes direct skips, the legislative history neither indicates that direct skips are excluded from the state tax credit nor why. The House Ways and Means Committee Report speaks of "[a] credit not exceeding five percent of the amended Federal tax ... " HR Conf. Rep. No. 426, 99th Cong., 1st Sess. 827 (1985), reprinted in 1986-3 CB (Vol. 2) 1, 827. The Conference Report indicates no modification with respect to the state tax credit. HR Conf. Rep. No. 841, 99th Cong., 2d Sess., Vol. II, 775 (1986), reprinted in 1986-3 CB (Vol. 4) 1, 775. The Staff of the Joint Committee Report alludes to "a credit not exceeding five percent of the amended Federal generation-skipping transfer tax." Staff of the Joint Comm. on Tax'n, 100th Cong., 1st Sess., General Explanation of the Tax Reform Act of 1986, 1266 (Comm. Print 1987).

[5] IRC § 2604(a). Section 2604 refers only to generation-skipping transfer taxes paid to states and does not mention taxes paid to the District of Columbia. Now-repealed Section 2602 specifically allowed a credit for taxes paid to the District of Columbia as well. IRC § 2602 (c)(5)(B) (repealed by Tax Reform Act of 1986, Pub. L. No. 99-514, § 1431(a), 100 Stat. 2085, 2718 (1986), reprinted in 1986-3 CB (Vol. 1) 1, 635). The legislative history of Section 2604 does not indicate any intention to exclude the District of Columbia. HR Conf. Rep. No. 426, 99th Cong., 1st Sess. 827 (1986), reprinted in 1986-3 CB (Vol 2) 1, 827; HR Conf. Rep. No. 841, 99th Cong., 2d Sess., Vol. II, 775 (1986), reprinted in 1986-3 CB (Vol. 4) 1, 775. See Staff of the Joint Comm. on Tax'n, 100th Cong., 1st Sess., General Explanation of the Tax Reform Act of 1986, 1266 (Comm. Print 1987). As a result of Section 7701(a)(10), Section 2604 should be interpreted to include the District of Columbia.

[6] IRC § 2604(b).

[7] See ¶ 3.03[2].

credit provided by Section 2604 also permits a state to impose a generation-skipping transfer pick-up tax at no additional tax cost to its residents. Many states have enacted statutes to take advantage of the credit provided by Section 2604.[8]

Section 2604 does not apply to generation-skipping transfers after December 31, 2004.[9] The termination of the provision is similar to the termination of Section 2011 under the estate tax,[10] although the estate tax credit is replaced with a deduction for state death taxes paid,[11] while no comparable generation-skipping transfer tax deduction is enacted to replace Section 2604. The effect of the termination of Section 2604 is to pull the rug out from under state generation-skipping transfer pick-up taxes similar to the rug pulling that has occurred under the estate tax with the termination of Section 2011.[12]

---

[8] See, e.g., Fla. Stat. Chapter 198.021, 198.031 (2001); Cal. Rev. and Tax Code § 16710 (West 2001). But see infra text accompanying notes 9–12. Any state that enacted such legislation before the existing version of the federal generation-skipping transfer tax was enacted in 1986 and tied the amount of pick-up tax to the now-repealed Section 2602 may want to adapt their statutes so that their residents may credit any state-imposed generation-skipping transfer tax against the federal tax before Section 2604 credit is eliminated in 2005. For example of a state that enacted a state generation-skipping transfer tax under the 1976 version of Chapter 13, but has yet to modify their laws to take into account the 1986 changes and the current federal credit offered, see W. Va. Code §§ 11-11-2, 11-11-4 (2001) (referring to repeated Section 2602 as amended or renumbered but imposing a tax only on generation-skipping transfers with respect to decedent's "taxable estate," a term that has no relevance under the current credit scheme of Section 2604).

[9] IRC § 2604. However, under the "sunset" provision, Section 2604 is resurrected in the year 2011. Economic Growth and Tax Relief Reconciliation Act of 2001, Pub. L. No. 107-16 § 901(a)(2), 115 Stat. 38, 150 (2001), reprinted in 2001-__ CB __, __. See ¶ 8.10[5].

[10] Section 2011, the estate tax credit for state death taxes paid is phased-out in years 2002 through 2004 and does not apply to the estates of decedents dying after December 31, 2004. IRC §§ 2011(b)(2), 2011(f). See ¶ 3.03[3][d]. There is no comparable phase-out of the Section 2604 credit.

[11] IRC § 2058. Section 2058 is applicable to the estates of decedents dying after December 31, 2004. Economic Growth and Tax Relief Reconciliation Act of 2001, Pub. L. No. 107-16 § 532(d), 115 Stat. 38, 75 (2001), reprinted in 2001-__ CB __, __. See ¶¶ 3.03[4], 5.09.

[12] See ¶ 3.03[1].

CHAPTER **13**

Generation-Skipping Transfers

¶ 13.01 SECTION 2611. "GENERATION-SKIPPING TRANSFER" DEFINED

[1] In General

The statute defines a "generation-skipping transfer" as a "taxable distribution,"[1] a "taxable termination,"[2] and a "direct skip."[3] Probe the labyrinth of the statute a little further and definitions of these three terms are to be found.[4] Those definitions, however, employ more unfamiliar terms that are the subjects of further definitions, and those further definitions are still further defined.[5] These definitions must be mastered and utilized simultaneously to identify generation-skipping transfers and to wrestle with their varying tax implications. This chapter analyzes the definitions of the three key terms and related statutory provisions in an effort to develop a working knowledge of the taxing rules of Chapter 13. Initially, dealing with all the definitions can easily lead to a case of vertigo. Patience is required; Latin was not learned in a day. Be optimistic; an interesting mosaic will emerge as the reader carefully puts the pieces in place one at a time.

[2] Transfers Excluded by Section 2611(b)

Some transactions or events that otherwise satisfy the definition of either a "taxable termination," a "taxable distribution," or a "direct skip" are not treated as generation-skipping transfers. Excluded are certain transfers for med-

---

[1] IRC § 2611(a)(1).

[2] IRC § 2611(a)(2).

[3] IRC § 2611(a)(3).

[4] IRC § 2612.

[5] For example, a taxable termination requires, in part, the termination of "an interest in property held in trust," unless there is a transfer of the property held in the trust subject to federal estate or gift taxation at the time of termination, or unless a "non-skip person" has an interest in the property immediately after the termination. IRC § 2612(a); Reg. §26.2612-1(b)(1)(i). What is an "interest in property?" See IRC § 2652(c). What is a "trust?" See IRC §§ 2652(b)(1), 2652(b)(3). When is a transfer "subject to" federal estate or gift taxation? See Reg. § 26.2652-1(a)(2). What is a "non-skip person?" See IRC § 2613(b).

Section 2613(b) of the Code defines "non-skip person" as "any person who is not a skip person." "Skip person" is defined in Section 2613(a), which, in part, essentially states that a natural person is a skip person if assigned to a generation two or more generations below that to which the transferor is assigned. IRC § 2613(a)(1). Generation assignment is determined by the rules of Section 2651, and a transferor is defined in Section 2652(a).

ical and educational expenses[6] and some transfers that have been previously subjected to the Chapter 13 tax.[7]

[a] Transfers for Educational and Medical Expenses

Section 2611(b)(1) of the Internal Revenue Code (the Code) excludes from treatment as a generation-skipping transfer "any transfer which, if made inter vivos by an individual, would not be treated as a taxable gift by reason of section 2503(e)."[8] Recall that Section 2503(e) provides an exclusion from the Chapter 12 gift tax for transfers of property that are made directly to an educational institution or a provider of medical care for educational or medical expenses of a donee.[9]

An individual's inter vivos transfer, which would be a direct skip but for its qualification for the Section 2503(e) exclusion,[10] is not a direct skip[11] and therefore not a generation-skipping transfer,[12] and it needs no assistance from Section 2611(b)(1). For example, assume that Grandparent makes an inter vivos transfer of $20,000 to a university to pay Grandchild's college tuition.

---

[6] IRC § 2611(b)(1).

[7] IRC § 2611(b)(2).

[8] IRC § 2611(b)(1).

[9] See ¶ 9.04[6]. The direct payment requirement is also applicable to the Section 2611(b)(1) exclusion. Section 2503(e) transfers are a means to indirectly transmit wealth inter vivos without incurring any federal gift or generation-skipping transfer taxes.

[10] Since Section 2611(b)(1) contains the clause "any transfer which, *if made inter vivos by an individual*" (emphasis added), the section itself indicates that an actual inter vivos direct skip transfer by an individual is not within the Section 2611(b)(1) rule.

[11] There is no Section 2612(c) direct skip when an inter vivos Section 2503(e) transfer is made. Chapter 12 generally imposes a tax on the "transfer of property by gift" (see IRC § 2501(a)), but Section 2503(e) removes transfers for educational and medical expenses from the gift tax base. They are not transfers of property by gift and, thus, not transfers subject to the tax imposed by Chapter 12. Accordingly, the Section 2612(c)(1) definitional requirement of a direct skip is not met because the transfer is "*not subject to a tax imposed by ... Chapter 12.*" See ¶ 13.02[4][b] text accompanying notes 259 and 260; Instructions for Form 709, "United States Gift (and Generation-Skipping Transfer) Tax Return" (2001) Transfers Not Subject to the Gift Tax, at 1–2.

Section 2642(c) (used in computing the generation-skipping transfer tax) provides for an inclusion ratio of zero in the case of a direct skip that is a nontaxable gift. Under Section 2642(c)(3)(B), a nontaxable gift for purposes of Section 2642(c) includes a Section 2503(e) transfer. The foregoing conclusion that there is no direct skip when an inter vivos Section 2503(e) transfer is made makes Section 2642(c)(3)(B) superfluous. See ¶ 16.02[2][b] text accompanying note 55.

Even if the conclusion that there is no direct skip when an inter vivos Section 2503(e) transfer is made is incorrect, there would still be no taxable generation-skipping transfer. If there were a direct skip, Section 2642(c) would assign it a zero inclusion ratio, with the result that there would be no tax liability for the transfer. See ¶ 16.02[2][b].

[12] IRC § 2611(a)(3).

There is an inter vivos Section 2503(e) transfer. Assuming that under state law Grandchild is liable for the tuition, there would appear to be a direct skip to Grandchild to satisfy the tuition obligation. However, because Section 2503(e) applies, there is no transfer of property by gift and, therefore, no direct skip requiring Section 2611(b)(1) assistance to avoid the imposition of a Chapter 13 tax.[13]

The Section 2611(b)(1) exclusion is applicable and is needed for other generation-skipping transfers that do not qualify for the Section 2503(e) exclusion, but would have qualified for the Section 2503(e) exclusion if made by a living donor (i.e., testamentary direct skip transfers, taxable distributions, and taxable terminations). The following examples illustrate how the exclusion operates.

If, by will, transferor G makes a $20,000 transfer to a university for grandchild GC's tuition, the transfer is a testamentary direct skip that needs the assistance of Section 2611(b)(1) to be excluded from generation-skipping transfer status.[14] If G established an irrevocable inter vivos trust or a testamentary trust, income to child C for life and a remainder to adult grandchild GC, and gave an independent trustee T the power to invade corpus for GC's tuition, T's invasion of corpus to make a payment directly to the university for GC's tuition would be a taxable distribution,[15] but it would not be a generation-skipping transfer because the taxable distribution would be excluded by Section 2611(b)(1).[16] If T's invasion of corpus for the payment to the univer-

---

[13] See supra note 11. If in the example given Parent of Grandchild were legally obligated to pay the tuition, there would be no transfer to a skip person and thus no generation-skipping transfer.

[14] This transfer does not qualify for the Section 2503(e) exclusion because it is a testamentary, not an inter vivos, transfer. It is assumed that GC's parents are alive (see IRC § 2651(e), discussed ¶ 17.01[2][a][ii]), that G's death occurs after 1989 (see the grandchild exclusion, discussed ¶ 13.02[4][c][ii]), and that GC's parents are not obligated by state law to pay GC's tuition. Section 2611(b)(1) provides an exclusion because there would have been a Section 2503(e) exclusion if the transfer had been an inter vivos transfer.

[15] IRC § 2612(b).

[16] See Priv. Ltr. Rul. 9109032 (Nov. 30, 1990) (payment of beneficiary's tuition not generation-skipping transfer). If the trust was an inter vivos trust and if G had been named trustee and had discretion to invade the corpus for either of two adult grandchildren's benefit, the transfer to the trust would not be a completed gift for Chapter 12 purposes. If G invades the corpus and makes a tuition payment directly to the university for the benefit of an adult grandchild, there is a completed gift (see Reg. § 25.2511-2(c)), and at that time, the gift qualifies for a Section 2503(e) exclusion. Accordingly, the distribution would not be subject to Chapter 12 and would not be a direct skip (see supra text accompanying note 11). Arguably, it would still satisfy the definition of a "taxable distribution" (see IRC § 2612(b)), and the taxable distribution would still require Section 2611(b)(1) assistance to avoid generation-skipping transfer status. Cf. IRC §§ 2642(c)(1), 2642(c)(3)(B). Where a single transfer satisfies the requirements of both a taxable distri-

sity depleted the entire trust corpus, the invasion would constitute a taxable termination,[17] but the taxable termination would be similarly excluded from generation-skipping transfer status by Section 2611(b)(1).

The Section 2611(b)(1) exclusion is inapplicable to an inter vivos or testamentary direct skip transfer[18] *to a trust*, even where the income or corpus of the trust is to be used exclusively for the payment of educational or medical expenses of skip persons. This is because Section 2503(e) requires that such payments be made directly *to* an educational institution or *to* any person providing medical care.[19] A transfer to a trust (even though the transfer qualifies as a direct skip) fails to satisfy the Section 2503(e) requirements because it is not a direct transfer *to* an educational organization as required by Section 2503(e)(2)(A).[20] For example, if a grandparent makes an inter vivos transfer of property to a trust, the entire corpus and income of which are to be used for the tuition of grandchildren or other skip persons, the transfer is a completed gift for purposes of the Chapter 12 gift tax, the transfer satisfies the requirements of a direct skip,[21] and therefore, it is a generation-skipping transfer.[22]

[b] Transfers Previously Subjected to Chapter 13 Tax

[i] General rule. Congress intended to restrict the imposition of Chapter 13 tax to transfers that may fairly be described as "generation-skipping." However, where the Chapter 13 tax has already taken its bite from a transfer of wealth to a particular generation, there remains the possibility of a second imposition of generation-skipping transfer tax. To prevent the double imposition

---

bution and a direct skip, the transfer is treated as a direct skip. IRC § 2612(b). If a transfer is not a direct skip, because, under Section 2503(e), it is not a transfer of property by gift, that should end the possibility of the imposition of a generation-skipping transfer tax with respect to that transfer. Furthermore, if a testamentary direct skip is not treated as a generation-skipping transfer by virtue of the application of Section 2611(b)(1), then that same transfer also should not be classified as a taxable distribution.

[17] IRC § 2612(a)(1)(A). If, at *C*'s death (with the remainder of the corpus passing to *GC* outright), the independent trustee also held a power to invade the corpus to make a direct payment to a clinic for *GC*'s medical expenses, the amount of any payment to the clinic would be a Section 2612(a)(1) taxable termination, but Section 2611(b)(1) would again exclude it as a generation-skipping transfer.

[18] IRC § 2612(c)(1).

[19] IRC § 2503(e)(2). See ¶ 9.04[6].

[20] See Reg. § 25.2503-6(c) Ex. 2. See also Priv. Ltr. Rul. 9823006 (June 5, 1998) (direct skip transfer to a trust did not qualify for exclusion under Section 2611(b)(1), where the purpose of the trust was to pay tuition).

[21] IRC § 2612(c)(1).

[22] IRC § 2611(a)(3).

of Chapter 13 tax in a single generation, Congress enacted Section 2611(b)(2), a brief but complex provision involving an exclusion based on prior transfers.

A transfer is excluded from the status of generation-skipping transfer and, therefore, is not subject to the Chapter 13 tax if three conditions are met. First, the property transferred was previously subject to Chapter 13 tax.[23] Second, the transferee in the previous transfer was assigned to the same or a younger generation than that to which the present transferee is assigned.[24] Third, the transfers as a whole do not have the effect of avoiding the Chapter 13 tax.[25]

An example illustrates this exclusion. Assume that a grantor *G* transfers property outright to grandchild *GC-1* in the current year. The transfer is subject in its entirety to the Chapter 11 estate tax or Chapter 12 gift tax.[26] Assuming the parents of *GC-1* are alive at the time,[27] the transfer is also a direct skip subject to the Chapter 13 generation-skipping transfer tax.[28] If, thereafter, *GC-1*, either inter vivos or by will, gratuitously transfers the property to *G*'s spouse *S* (*GC-1*'s grandparent), another transfer tax would be imposed under Chapter 11 tax or Chapter 12.[29] Assuming *S* subsequently transfers the property outright to another grandchild *GC-2*, there would be yet another imposition of tax under Chapter 11 or Chapter 12. In addition, assuming the parents of *GC-2* are alive at the time,[30] this transfer to *GC-2* satisfies the criteria for a direct skip. This second direct skip is excluded in whole or in part from generation-skipping transfer status by the Section 2611(b)(2) exclusion because the three requirements for the prior transfer exclusion are met. The property was subjected to the Chapter 13 tax at the time of *G*'s initial transfer to *GC-1*. *GC-1*, the transferee in the prior generation-skipping transfer, is in the same generation as *GC-2*, the transferee in the second direct skip. These two transfers do not appear to have the effect of improperly avoiding the Chapter 13 transfer tax.[31] Consequently, the direct skip transfer of the property from *S* to *GC-2* is

---

[23] IRC § 2611(b)(2)(A). A transfer is subject to Chapter 13, even if no generation-skipping transfer tax is imposed on the transfer, because the applicable rate of tax is zero owing to the amount of GST exemption allocated to the transfer. See ¶ 17.02[1][b] for a discussion of when property is "subject to" the estate or gift tax. See also Reg. § 26.2652-1(a)(2).

[24] IRC § 2611(b)(2)(B).

[25] IRC § 2611(b)(2)(C). See infra ¶ 13.01[2][b][ii].

[26] See IRC §§ 2001(a), 2501(a); Reg. § 26.2652-1(a)(2); ¶ 17.02[1][b].

[27] See IRC § 2651(e); ¶ 17.01[2][a][ii].

[28] IRC § 2612(c)(1).

[29] If *GC-1* received the property in a testamentary transfer and an estate tax was imposed on *GC-1*'s transfer under Chapter 11, there is always the possibility of a credit for tax on prior transfers. IRC § 2013. No credit for tax on prior transfers is generated by the imposition of a tax under Chapter 13. See IRC § 2013.

[30] See IRC § 2651(e); ¶ 17.01[2][a][ii].

[31] IRC § 2611(b)(2).

not treated as a generation-skipping transfer. Assuming no appreciation in the value of the property from the time it was transferred by *G* to *GC-1* to the time it was transferred by *S* to *GC-2*,[32] the entire value of the property qualifies for the exclusion.

There is no requirement that the property qualifying for this exclusion be in a trust or a trust equivalent arrangement[33] at the time of either transfer. The prior transfer exclusion is potentially applicable to situations in which there are (1) two or more outright transfers; (2) a transfer in trust followed by an outright transfer; (3) an outright transfer followed by a transfer in trust; (4) a transfer in one trust followed by a second transfer into another trust; and (5) two transfers within a single trust. However, where there are two or more possible generation-skipping transfers in a single trust, Section 2653(a) intervenes, repositioning the transferor to the generation just above the oldest person with an interest in the trust immediately after the generation-skipping transfer.[34] Thus, it is difficult (likely impossible) to conceive of a situation in which the prior transfer exclusion rule could apply to two transfers within a single trust.[35]

   [ii] The Section 2611(b)(2)(C) avoidance limitation. The legislative history and regulations are devoid of guidance or examples as to when the Section 2611(b)(2)(C) avoidance limitation is violated so as to make the prior transfer exclusion inapplicable. One situation in which the avoidance limitation ought to apply is when a transfer skips multiple generations, and thereafter, two or more of the intervening generations enjoy the property without the im-

---

   [32] IRC § 2611(b)(2). Any appreciation in the value of the property that was the subject matter of the direct skip transfers is a generation-skipping transfer and does not qualify for exclusion under Section 2611(b)(2). See infra ¶ 13.01[2][b][iii].

   [33] See ¶ 17.02[2].

   [34] See ¶ 17.03[1].

   [35] For example, assume that the terms of a trust provide for income to the transferor's child *C* for life, followed by income to the transferor's grandchild *GC* for life, a remainder to the transferor's great-grandchild *GGC*, if living, and, if there is no great-grandchild, then income to *GC*'s cousin (same generation as *GC*), with a remainder to the cousin's children. At *C*'s death, there is a taxable termination that is a generation-skipping transfer. IRC § 2612(a)(1). If *GC* dies and *GGC* is not surviving, the property passes to *GC*'s cousin. Since immediately following the generation-skipping transfer of the property at *C*'s death the property continues to be held in trust, under Section 2653(a), the transferor is assigned to *C*'s generation, so the transfer to *GC*'s cousin will not result in a generation-skipping transfer. See IRC § 2612(a)(1). The Section 2611(b)(2) exclusion would also have applied under these circumstances, but its application is moot because there is no generation-skipping transfer to exclude.

   The Section 2611(b)(2) prior transfer exclusion also may not be necessary when two trusts are involved and when Section 2653(a) precludes the possibility of either a taxable termination or a taxable distribution by eliminating the skip person in the dual trust situation.

position of Chapter 11 or Chapter 12 tax. The limitation ought to apply whether or not the person making the original transfer intended the avoidance.

For example, assume grantor *G* makes a direct skip to great-grandchild *GGC* who (whether with or without *G*'s urging) then transfers the property back to *G*'s spouse *S*. *S* subsequently transfers the property in trust to child *C* for life, then to grandchild *GC* for life, with a remainder to great-grandchild *GGC* (the original donee). The initial transfer to *GGC* skipped two generations, the generation of *C* and that of *GC*, but only one generation-skipping transfer tax was imposed. Under the facts of this example, the two generations that were previously skipped subsequently enjoyed *G*'s wealth. Had *G* simply initially transferred the property in trust, with income to *C* for life, then to *GC* for life, and the remainder to *GGC*, Chapter 13 would have imposed a tax at each intervening generation level as the property passed from the first generation, *G*'s, to the fourth, *GGC*'s.[36] Returning to the original example, if the GST tax imposed on the initial direct skip shields both the taxable termination of *C*'s interest and *GC*'s interest, only one Chapter 13 tax will have been imposed while two intervening generations will have enjoyed the property between outright owners. Therefore, where the Chapter 13 tax has been imposed on a multi-generation-skipping transfer, and, thereafter, two of the skipped generations have an interest in the property and enjoy the property without the imposition of a Chapter 11 or Chapter 12 tax, an additional Chapter 13 tax ought to be imposed.[37] In the absence of specific legislation or regulations as to which taxable termination should be taxed, the second taxable termination should be treated as a generation-skipping transfer and taxed accordingly under Chapter 13, because the second taxable termination has the effect of avoiding tax under Chapter 13.[38]

[iii] Scope of the Section 2611(b)(2) exclusion. Section 2611(b)(2) excludes any transfer "to the extent" of the amount subject to tax in the prior transfer. If the property initially subjected to Chapter 13 tax appreciates in value, the exclusion should be limited to only the value of the property previously subjected to the tax. Under prior law, the prior transfer exclusion was limited to the amount subject to tax in the prior transfer.[39] The same result is appropriate under the 1986 legislation; the amount of appreciation should be

---

[36] See IRC § 2612(a).

[37] If more than two generation levels are skipped in the original multigenerational direct skip, then a Chapter 13 tax should possibly be imposed for each intervening generation level. See ¶ 13.02[4][a] text accompanying note 244.

[38] IRC § 2611(b)(2)(C).

[39] IRC § 2613(b)(7)(B) (1954), repealed by the Tax Reform Act of 1986, Pub. L. No. 99-514, § 1431(a), 100 Stat. 2085, 2717 (1986), reprinted in 1986-3 CB (Vol. 1) 1, 634. See S. Rep. No. 1236, 94th Cong., 2d Sess. 620 (1976), reprinted in 1976-3 CB (Vol. 3) 807, 970.

subject to a generation-skipping tax. Thus, returning to an earlier example[40] where grantor *G* transferred property to grandchild *GC-1* and *GC-1* retransferred the property to *G*'s spouse, *S*, who then transferred the property to another grandchild *GC-2*, the Section 2611(b)(2) exclusion would apply. If the property was worth $200,000 at the time *G* transferred it to *GC-1*, and if the same property was worth $300,000 when *S* transferred it to *GC-2*, only $200,000 is not treated as a generation-skipping transfer; the remaining $100,000 is a generation-skipping transfer. The limitation on the *amount* of the exclusion provides an appropriate safeguard against shortchanging the fisc under the Section 2611(b)(2) exclusion.[41]

Where property involved in the original generation-skipping transfer is sold and the proceeds are reinvested, or the property is exchanged for other property prior to the second generation-skipping transfer, tracing should be used to identify the property that qualifies for the exclusion. If the transaction involves an exchange of property not held in a trust (as in the preceding example), then tracing the original property into the property received is appropriate.[42] If the transaction involves an exchange of property held in a trust, no tracing of the original property is required because the trust corpus itself traced.[43]

---

[40] See supra text accompanying notes 26–32.

[41] See also IRC § 2611(b)(2)(C), discussed supra ¶ 13.01[2][b][ii].

[42] For example, assume in the prior example that *G* transferred land worth $200,000 to *GS*. *GS* sold the land and used the proceeds to purchase a building that *GS* transfers to *S*. If *S* transfers the building to *GD* when it is worth $300,000, Section 2611(b)(2) would exclude $200,000, leaving $100,000 to be taxed as a generation-skipping transfer. The result would be the same if *GS* transferred the land to *S*, who sold it, purchased the building with the proceeds, and transferred the building to *GD*. The prior transfer rule is more restrictive than the Section 2013 credit for estate tax paid on a prior transfer, which does not require tracing. See ¶ 3.05[1][a]. But see ¶ 4.07[2][c] text accompanying notes 57–59.

[43] Cf. ¶ 4.10[10][f].

¶ 13.02 SECTION 2612. TAXABLE TERMINATIONS, TAXABLE DISTRIBUTIONS, AND DIRECT SKIPS

[1] Introduction

[a] In General

The three statutorily described events on which Chapter 13 imposes a tax[1] are a taxable termination, a taxable distribution, and a direct skip.[2] The occurrence of any one event will result in a generation-skipping transfer, unless the transfer is excluded by Section 2611(b).[3] Once an event is classified as a generation-skipping transfer, the amount of tax liability applicable to the transfer is then computed.[4]

[b] Interrelationship of the Three Types of Generation-Skipping Transfers

The termination of an individual's Chapter 13 interest[5] in a trust[6] or in a trust equivalent arrangement[7] may simultaneously satisfy the definitions of a "taxable termination"[8] and a "taxable distribution,"[9] but not a "direct skip."[10] A distribution from a trust that does not result in the termination of the trust may simultaneously satisfy the requirements of both a taxable distribution and a direct skip.[11] When there is overlap, the statute specifically provides that either a direct skip or a taxable termination takes precedence over a taxable distribution.[12]

---

[1] IRC § 2601.

[2] IRC § 2611(a). In determining whether an event is subject to the generation-skipping transfer tax, reference is made to the most recent transfer subject to the federal estate or gift tax. Reg. § 26.2611-1. See ¶ 17.02[1][b].

[3] See ¶ 13.01[2].

[4] See IRC §§ 2602, 2621–2642.

[5] IRC § 2652(c); Reg. § 26.2612-1(e). See ¶ 17.02[3].

[6] IRC § 2652(b)(1). See ¶ 13.03[3] text accompanying notes 25–28.

[7] IRC §§ 2652(b)(1), 2652(b)(3). As used throughout the remainder of this section, the term "trust" includes a trust equivalent arrangement.

[8] IRC § 2612(a).

[9] IRC § 2612(b).

[10] IRC § 2612(c); Reg. § 26.2612-1(b)(1)(i). Appropriate administrative action precludes the overlap of a taxable termination and a direct skip. See infra text accompanying note 14; ¶ 13.02[2][d].

[11] IRC §§ 2612(b), 2612(c).

[12] IRC § 2612(b) (parenthetical).

When the statutory criteria for both a direct skip and a taxable termination are satisfied, there is no specific statutory guidance as to which takes precedence,[13] but a transfer that satisfies the statutory requirements of both a direct skip and a taxable termination is treated as a direct skip as a result of appropriate administrative action.[14] For example, assume that a transfer in trust provides for income to be paid to the grantor *G* for life, with remainder to grandchild *GC*.[15] Statutorily, there is a taxable termination upon *G*'s death, because there is a termination of a Chapter 13 interest in trust property, and immediately thereafter, a skip person, *GC*, has such an interest in the property.[16] However, the property transferred to *GC* also constitutes a direct skip[17] because it is subject to the tax imposed by Chapter 11, since it is included in *G*'s gross estate under Section 2036 and it passes to a skip person. As a result of appropriate administrative action, this generation-skipping transfer is treated as a direct skip, not a taxable termination.[18]

Depending on the classification of a generation-skipping transfer as a direct skip, a taxable termination, or a taxable distribution, there can be a difference in the amount of the taxable transfer and the resulting tax liability.[19]

---

[13] At one point, Congress proposed to add a subsection under which a direct skip would take precedence over a taxable termination. The Technical Corrections Act of 1987 (HR 2636 and S. 1350 § 114(f)(3) (1987)) would have added Section 2612(a)(3) to the Code to provide that "the term 'taxable termination' shall not include any transfer which is a direct skip." However, the provision was deleted from the legislation without comment.

[14] The regulations supplement the statutory requirements of a taxable termination with one additional requirement that prevents any single transfer from satisfying the requirements of both a direct skip and taxable termination. Reg. § 26.2612-1(b)(1)(i). See infra ¶ 13.02[2][d]. The regulations add that a taxable termination is a termination of an interest in a trust, unless "[a] transfer subject to Federal estate or gift tax occurs with respect to the property held in the trust at the time of the termination." Reg. § 26.2612-1(b)(1)(i). The quoted language prevents any overlap because any direct skip generation-skipping transfer cannot satisfy this requirement of a taxable termination. See PS-32-90, Supplementary Information, 1993-1 CB 907, 908. See also Rev. Rul. 92-26, 1992-1 CB 314, 315, discussed infra ¶ 13.02[2][d] note 78.

[15] It is assumed that the grandchild's parents are alive and the transferor died after 1989. See IRC § 2651(e); ¶ 17.01[2][a][ii]; Tax Reform Act of 1986, Pub. L. No. 99-514, § 1433(b)(3), 100 Stat. 2085, 2731 (1986), reprinted in 1986-3 CB (Vol. 1) 1, 648, as amended by the Technical and Miscellaneous Revenue Act of 1988, Pub. L. No. 100-647, § 1014(h)(3)(A), 102 Stat. 3342, 3567–3568 (1988), reprinted in 1988-3 CB 1, 227–228, which is discussed infra ¶ 13.02[4][c][ii].

[16] IRC § 2612(a)(1)(A).

[17] IRC § 2612(c)(1). See infra ¶ 13.02[4].

[18] See supra note 14. See also Reg. § 26.2612-1(b)(1)(i).

[19] See IRC §§ 2621, 2622, 2623; ¶¶ 14.01–14.04.

There also may be a difference in the identity of the person who is liable for the Chapter 13 tax[20] and is required to file the tax return.[21]

[2] Taxable Terminations

[a] Introduction

The first of the three statutorily described events treated as a generation-skipping transfer is the taxable termination, which is generally thought of as the "classic" generation-skipping transfer. Assume that grantor *G* transfers property to an irrevocable trust, with income to child *C* for life, then income to grandchild *GC* for life, followed by income to great-grandchild *GGC* for life (and so on until the trust terminates to avoid violating any applicable Rule Against Perpetuities),[22] with a remainder to great-great-grandchildren *GGGC*. An estate or gift tax is imposed on *G* when property is transferred to the trust. Assuming that none of the beneficiaries make a gift of their interests, the property is not again subject to estate or gift taxation until each *GGGC* dies. The three skipped generations thus avoid estate or gift tax consequences. However, as the corpus of the trust cascades from each generation to the next, Chapter 13 imposes a wealth transfer tax on taxable terminations that occur on each of three events: *C*'s death, then *GC*'s death, and finally *GGC*'s death.[23]

For a transfer to be a taxable termination,[24] three requirements must be met: (1) There must be a "termination" of a Chapter 13 "interest[25] in property held in a trust;"[26] (2) immediately after the termination, no "non-skip person"[27] may have a Chapter 13 "interest" in such property,[28] *or*, if no one then has a Chapter 13 interest in such property, there must be a possibility that a subsequent distribution may be made to a "skip person;"[29] and (3) there must be no transfer subject to the federal estate or gift tax occurring with respect to such

---

[20] See IRC § 2603(a); ¶ 12.03.

[21] See IRC § 2662(a)(1); ¶ 18.02[3]; Reg. §§ 26.2662-1(c)(1), 26.2662-1(c)(2).

[22] See Gray, *The Rule Against Perpetuities* § 201 (Little, Brown & Company 4th ed. 1942). Cf. ¶ 15.02[2] note 44.

[23] IRC § 2612(a)(1).

[24] IRC § 2612(a)(1).

[25] IRC § 2652(c).

[26] IRC § 2612(a)(1). See IRC §§ 2652(b)(1), 2652(b)(3). See also ¶ 13.02[1][b] supra note 7.

[27] IRC § 2613(b).

[28] IRC § 2612(a)(1)(A).

[29] IRC § 2612(a)(1)(B). See IRC § 2613(a); Reg. § 26.2612-1(d).

property at the time of termination of the Chapter 13 interest.[30] These requirements contain numerous terms that have special meanings that will be explored in the sections that follow.

[b] First Requirement: Termination of an Interest

[i] **Interest.** The interest that must terminate to trigger a taxable termination is a "Chapter 13 interest," a form of beneficial relationship to a trust.[31] The statute recognizes three types of beneficial relationships as Chapter 13 interests in property held in trust.[32] The first type of beneficial relationship is a *present right* to receive income or corpus from the trust,[33] i.e., the conventional relationship of an income beneficiary to a trust or an annuitant to a trust equivalent. The second is that of a *permissible current noncharitable recipient* of income or corpus of the trust.[34] The third is that of a Section 2055 charitable organization[35] holding an interest in a charitable remainder annuity trust, a charitable remainder unitrust, or a pooled income fund.[36] However, Section 2652(c) refuses to recognize as a Chapter 13 interest any interest created "primarily to postpone or avoid any" generation-skipping transfer tax.[37] Only the first two types of Chapter 13 interests are discussed here because a termination of any interest in a trust having a charitable remainder interest will not result in a taxable termination.[38]

---

[30] Reg. § 26.2612-1(b)(1)(i).

[31] IRC §§ 2612(a)(1), 2652(c); Reg. §§ 26.2652-1(e), 26.2612-1(e). The regulations for Section 2652(c), Regulations Section 26.2652-1(e) "Interest in trust," simply cross-references Regulations Section 26.2612-1(e), which does little more than restate the Section 2652(c) statutory language.

[32] IRC § 2652(c)(1); Reg. § 26.2612-1(e)(1). See ¶¶ 13.03[3][a], 17.02[3].

[33] IRC § 2652(c)(1)(A); Reg. § 26.2612-1(e)(1)(i).

[34] IRC § 2652(c)(1)(B); Reg. § 26.2612-1(e)(1)(ii). A person who has a current ability to receive benefits under a sprinkling trust has such an interest in the trust.

[35] IRC § 2055(a). See ¶ 5.05[1][b].

[36] IRC § 2652(c)(1)(C); Reg. § 26.2612-1(e)(1)(iii). See IRC §§ 664(d)(1), 664(d)(2), 642(c)(5); ¶ 5.05[5].

[37] IRC § 2652(c)(2); Reg. § 26.2612-1(e)(2)(ii). Such noninterests are discussed at ¶ 17.02[3][d].

[38] A Section 2055(a) charity is deemed to be in the same generation as the transferor. IRC § 2651(f)(3). Any charity within Section 2651(f)(3) is also within Section 2055(a). Thus, charitable organizations holding remainder interests in any of the three types of charitable remainder trusts or funds mentioned are classified as non-skip persons. A termination of a Chapter 13 interest in such a trust (or trust equivalent) cannot result in a taxable termination because a non-skip person has a Chapter 13 interest in the trust or trust equivalent. IRC § 2612(a)(1)(A); see IRC § 2652(c)(1)(C).

For example, assume a transferor establishes a charitable remainder annuity trust with an annuity to child for life, then to grandchild for life, with a remainder to charity. There

A Present Right to Income or Corpus. A person[39] who has a right currently to receive income or corpus from the trust has an interest in property held in trust.[40] In general, a future right to trust income or corpus (a sigh from Simes) does not constitute a Chapter 13 interest in property held in trust.[41] If the right of enjoyment is deferred to some future time or conditioned upon a future event, the right is a future right.[42] A conventional or unavoidable delay in receipt should be disregarded. If a trust instrument requires income to be paid annually to the income beneficiary, the beneficiary has a present right, even if, as a practical matter, the income is to be paid periodically, not instantly as received.[43]

Assume grantor *G* transfers property to a trust that provides for income to child *C* for life, then income to grandchild *GC* for life, with a remainder to great-grandchild *GGC*. *C* has a Chapter 13 interest in the property held in trust, but *GC* and *GGC* do not. Admittedly, *GC* and *GGC* have beneficial interests in the property, a secondary life estate and a remainder, but those interests are not presently Chapter 13 interests in property held in trust because there is no right to receive income or corpus currently. Thus, *GC*'s death, with *C* surviving, does not constitute a taxable termination because a taxable termination can occur only as a result of a termination of a Chapter 13 interest.[44]

A person generally has a Chapter 13 interest in property held in trust if the trust instrument provides that trust assets may be used to discharge that person's legal obligations.[45] For example, if a trust instrument requires that trust assets be used to discharge a parental obligation to support a minor, the parent whose obligation it is to support the minor has a Chapter 13 interest in the property held in trust.[46]

---

is no taxable termination at the child's death because the charity, a non-skip person, has a Chapter 13 interest in the trust. IRC § 2612(a)(1)(A). However, the annuity distributions made to the grandchild constitute taxable distributions. IRC § 2612(b).

[39] The term "person" may apply to an individual, a trust, an estate, a partnership, or a corporation. IRC § 7701(a)(1). Section 2651(f)(2) provides that each individual having a beneficial interest in an entity shall be treated as having an interest in the property.

[40] IRC § 2652(c)(1)(A); Reg. § 26.2612-1(e)(1)(i). See ¶ 17.02[3][b]; Reg. § 26.2612-1(f) Ex. 14.

[41] IRC § 2652(c)(1)(A) (parenthetical). See Reg. § 26.2612-1(f) Ex. 14. A future charitable interest described in Section 2652(c)(1)(C) is the exception. See ¶ 17.02[3][c].

[42] Cf. Reg. § 25.2503-3(a).

[43] Cf. AD Edwards v. Comm'r, 46 BTA 815 (1942), acq. in part 1942-2 CB 6, aff'd on other grounds, 135 F2d 574 (7th Cir. 1943).

[44] IRC §§ 2612(a), 2652(c). A taxable termination cannot occur as a result of a termination of a future interest.

[45] IRC § 2652(c)(1)(A). See Reg. § 26.2612-1(e)(2)(i). See also infra note 46 for a discussion of the exception to the general rule.

[46] In general, a person is treated as holding an interest in property held in trust if discretionary amounts may be paid currently to discharge the person's legal obligation. IRC

A person who holds a presently exercisable general power of appointment over trust income or corpus has "a right to receive" income or corpus of the trust.[47] However, a person who holds only a nongeneral power of appointment does not have such a right to receive (i.e., has no right to appoint to oneself) trust income or corpus.[48]

A Permissible Noncharitable Current Recipient of Income or Corpus. A permissible noncharitable current recipient of income or corpus who has no absolute right to trust income or corpus is also treated as having a Chapter 13 interest in property held in trust.[49] The term "permissible current recipient" is not defined in the statute, and the concept of a permissible current recipient as a person with an interest in property held in trust is unique. The receipt of trust property by the person hinges only on another's authorized ("permissible") unimpeded action. It is not deferred until some future time or conditioned upon some future event.

Reflection will show that in identifying Chapter 13 interests, the termination of which may result in the imposition of the Chapter 13 tax, Congress seeks out persons who either are, or could be, munching on property or its fruit. The exercise of a presently exercisable power held by a trustee or another power holder will start the munching. For example, if a trustee is granted a "sprinkle" power to distribute current income to a person who does not have a legal right to trust income, Congress intends for the person to be treated as a permissible current recipient having a Chapter 13 interest in the property held in trust.[50] Likewise, if a trustee's or power holder's exercise of a presently exercisable power of appointment, whether general or nongeneral, may result in a noncharitable appointee's current receipt of trust income or corpus, the congressional plan is that the noncharitable appointee is treated as having a Chapter 13 interest in the appointive property.[51]

---

§ 2652(c)(1)(B). However, Section 2652(c)(3) provides that, for purposes of determining whether a person has a Chapter 13 interest in a trust, the fact that trust income or corpus may be used to satisfy an obligation of support arising under state law in either a discretionary manner or under a state law substantially equivalent to the Uniform Gifts to Minors Act shall be disregarded. Reg. § 26.2612-1(e)(2)(i). See Reg. § 26.2612-1(f) Ex. 15. The implications of Section 2652(c)(3) are discussed at ¶ 17.02[3][b] text accompanying notes 140–143. Cf. Old Colony Trust Co. v. Comm'r, 279 US 716 (1929).

The generation-skipping transfer consequences upon termination of a support obligation are discussed infra note 55.

[47] IRC §§ 2041(b)(1), 2514(c). This rule applies to both pre- and post-1942 general powers of appointment. See ¶ 18.05[2][b] text accompanying notes 37–39.

[48] The interrelationship of powers of appointment and the taxable termination rules is considered infra ¶ 13.02[2][e].

[49] IRC § 2652(c)(1)(B); Reg. § 26.2612-1(e)(1)(ii).

[50] IRC § 2652(c)(1)(B); Reg. § 26.2612-1(e)(1)(ii).

[51] See IRC § 2652(c)(1)(B); Reg. § 26.2612-1(e)(1)(ii); infra ¶ 13.02[2][e].

Although the event that will cause a future right to income or corpus to become a possessory interest may have a greater probability of occurring than the exercise of a discretionary power held by a third party to give financial benefit to a permissible current recipient, the recipient of a future right is not treated as having a Chapter 13 interest in property held in trust,[52] whereas the discretionary recipient is treated as having such an interest in the property.[53] If we discard conventional notions of property interests, we may find here a sufficient nexus between person and property to say, reasonably, that "a person has an interest in property."[54]

[ii] Termination of an interest. A taxable termination requires the termination of a Chapter 13 interest. The termination may occur in virtually any manner, "by death, lapse of time, release of power, or otherwise."[55] Although a taxable termination results in a transfer, the transfer does not always involve a physical element, a distribution of property. At times, the "transfer" is no more than an abstract shifting of opportunity to benefit.[56] If grantor *G* establishes a trust with income to child *C* for life and a remainder to grandchild *GC*, the death of *C* terminates *C*'s Chapter 13 interest in the property held in trust.[57]

---

[52] IRC § 2652(c)(1)(A) (parenthetical).

[53] IRC § 2652(c)(1)(B). In addition, if a trust agreement provides that one individual has a presently exercisable general power of appointment over the entire trust corpus and another individual is entitled to the income generated by the corpus of the trust, the power takes precedence over the right to income. In this situation, the power holder of a presently exercisable general power of appointment has an interest in the property held in trust by possession of the present right to income or corpus. See supra text accompanying note 47. The income beneficiary does not have a present right to trust income or corpus because that right is subordinate to the power holder's rights. Nevertheless, the income beneficiary in this situation should be treated as having an interest in the property held in trust because, until the power is exercised, the income beneficiary is a permissible current recipient of income. IRC § 2652(c)(1)(B). Thus, the power holder and the income beneficiary simultaneously have an interest in the trust property, one for the "right . . . to receive," and the other as a "permissible current recipient." IRC §§ 2652(c)(1)(A), 2652(c)(1)(B).

[54] IRC § 2652(c)(1).

[55] IRC § 2612(a)(1) (parenthetical). The termination of a support obligation upon a child attaining the age of majority, where the trust assets are required to be used to discharge the parent's legal obligation of support, may terminate a parent's Chapter 13 interest in the property and may result in a taxable termination. See supra text accompanying notes 45, 46; infra ¶ 13.02[2][c]. The transferor of the trust must be identified and the terms of the trust must be examined to determine whether there is a taxable termination upon the termination of the support obligation. If the parent established the trust that terminated with a remainder to child or provided for income from the trust to be paid to the child upon the child's reaching majority, there would be no taxable termination because the child is a non-skip person. IRC §§ 2612(a)(1)(A), 2613(b). See infra ¶ 13.02[2][c].

[56] See Reg. § 26.2612-1(f) Ex. 8.

[57] See Reg. § 26.2612-1(f) Ex. 4.

Similarly, if C's income interest were for a term of years, there would be a termination at the end of the term of years. Additionally, if C's interest were merely as a permissible recipient of a possible invasion of corpus by a nongeneral power holder, upon the relinquishment of the power, there would also be a termination of C's interest. There may be a taxable termination in each instance depending on what happens to the trust corpus, who has it or an interest in it, after such terminations;[58] but belay that, lest Hamlet be killed in the first act.[59]

A qualified disclaimer[60] of an interest does not constitute a termination of an interest in property held in trust. As under the estate and gift taxes, a qualified disclaimer effectively negates the initial transfer of the interest.[61]

A taxable termination requires a termination of the entire Chapter 13 interest in the property held in trust. Mere reduction in a person's interest in the trust is not a termination,[62] unless the person's interest is extinguished by the reduction.[63] The termination of an entire Chapter 13 interest, even if such interest does not extend to all the property held in the trust, is a termination of that interest. An individual who is given the right to one half of the income generated by property held in the trust has a Chapter 13 interest only in that portion of the property. Termination of the right to the one half of the income is the termination of an entire Chapter 13 interest in the property held in trust and may, pending satisfaction of the other two requirements, generate a taxable termination.[64]

[c] Second Requirement: No Non-Skip Interests or Possible Distributions to Skip Persons

Chapter 13 is meant to impose a tax on wealth that has avoided the traditional transfer taxes imposed by Chapter 11 and Chapter 12 as it passes to younger generations. Hence, there is the requirement that, immediately after the termination of an interest in property held in trust, no Section 2613(b) non-skip person (either an individual occupying a generation level that is not at

---

[58] IRC § 2612(a)(1).

[59] See infra ¶ 13.02[2][c].

[60] IRC §§ 2518, 2654(c). See ¶ 17.04[3].

[61] IRC § 2518(a); Reg. § 26.2612-1(e)(3). See ¶ 10.07.

[62] See Reg. § 26.2612-1(f) Ex. 12.

[63] IRC § 2612(a)(1). See Reg. § 26.2612-1(f) Ex. 9. The result is not altered if the trustee retains sufficient funds to pay winding-up expenses and any generation-skipping transfer tax imposed by reason of the taxable termination. Reg. § 26.2612-1(f) Ex. 9.

[64] IRC § 2652(c)(1)(A). See infra ¶¶ 13.02[2][c], 13.02[2][d]; See also infra ¶ 13.02[2][f].

least two levels below the transferor, or a non-skip person trust),[65] may have a Chapter 13 interest in the property.[66] If a non-skip person has such an interest in the property immediately after the termination, there is no generation skip, and, hence, no taxable termination.[67]

To illustrate the second requirement, suppose that grantor *G* establishes a lifetime trust, the income to be paid to *G*'s sibling *S* for life, then to *G*'s child *C* for life, with the remainder to *G*'s grandchild *GC*. At *S*'s death, with *C* surviving, the enjoyment of the trust property shifts to *C*, who is assigned to the generation level immediately below *G*'s and is, therefore, a non-skip person.[68] Under the facts of this example, there is no generation skip, and the termination of *S*'s interest in the trust property is not a taxable termination.[69] At *C*'s death, with *GC* surviving, *C*'s Chapter 13 interest in the trust property terminates, and, immediately thereafter, *GC*, who is a skip person (an individual at least two generation levels below *G*'s generation level),[70] has the only interest in the property. The interest in the property held in trust shifts to *GC* without being subject to the imposition of either Chapter 11 or Chapter 12 transfer tax, thereby skipping those taxes at *C*'s generation level. However, this shift constitutes a taxable termination "subject to" the tax imposed by Chapter 13 because there is the required termination of a Chapter 13 interest in the property held in trust (*C*'s life estate), immediately thereafter no non-skip person has an interest in the property, and no transfer subject to the federal estate or gift tax occurs with respect to the property at the time of *C*'s death. Assuming that *G* made great-grandchild *GGC* (rather than *GC*) the remainderperson of the trust, the result would be the same. There would be a single taxable termination even though two generation levels were skipped.[71]

A taxable termination also occurs on the termination of a Chapter 13 interest where the property is not subject to federal estate or gift tax at the time of the termination, unless, immediately after the termination, no person has a Chapter 13 interest in the property that continues to be held in trust and no subsequent distribution can ever be made to a skip person, even upon termina-

---

[65] A trust may be a skip person. IRC § 2613(a)(2). A trust that is not a skip person is a non-skip person trust. See ¶¶ 13.03[3], 13.03[5].

[66] IRC § 2612(a)(1)(A).

[67] IRC § 2612(a)(1)(A). But see IRC § 2612(a)(2), which is discussed infra ¶ 13.02[2][f].

[68] IRC §§ 2613(b), 2651(b).

[69] If *C* predeceases *S* and the corpus passes to *GC* at *S*'s death, there is no taxable termination at *C*'s death (see supra ¶ 13.02[2][b] text accompanying note 44), but there is a taxable termination at *S*'s death.

[70] IRC § 2613(a)(1). See IRC § 2651(b).

[71] Cf. Reg. § 26.2612-1(f) Ex. 10. See infra ¶ 13.02[2][g] text accompanying note 206.

tion of the trust.[72] For example, assume that a grantor establishes a trust, income to child *C* for life, then income to be accumulated until grandchild *GC* attains the age of majority and then distributed to *GC* for life, with the remainder at *GC*'s death to great-grandchild *GGC* or *GGC*'s estate.[73] If *C* dies before *GC* attains the age of majority, the income is to be accumulated and no person, skip person or non-skip person, has a Chapter 13 interest in the property until *GC* attains the age of majority or dies before attaining the age of majority. *C*'s death before *GC* reaches the age of majority results in a taxable termination because subsequent distributions may be made to skip persons, *GC* and *GGC*.[74]

Alternatively, if distributions can be made only to non-skip persons after a termination, no skip of a generation is possible and the termination is not a taxable one. Assume that Transferor has two children, *A* and *B*, and Transferor establishes a trust that provides for income to be paid to *A* for life, with a remainder to *B*, but if *A* dies prior to *B*'s attaining age 21, the income is to be accumulated and the distribution of the remainder delayed until *B* attains age 21. The termination of *A*'s life interest prior to *B*'s attaining age 21 may result in a taxable termination; the outcome depends on what happens to the trust income and corpus if *B* dies prior to attaining age 21. If the trust instrument provides that upon *B*'s death, prior to attaining age 21, the property passes to a Section 511(a)(2) charitable organization, there is no possibility that the property will be distributed to a skip person (neither *B* nor the charitable organization is a skip person[75]). Thus, there is no taxable termination at *A*'s death. However, if the trust instrument provides that upon *B*'s death, prior to attaining age 21, the property passes to the surviving children of *A* or *B*, it cannot be said at the time of *A*'s death that at no time after the termination of *A*'s interest can a distribution be made from the trust to a skip person. Under these circumstances, the termination of *A*'s interest is a taxable termination.

---

[72] IRC § 2612(a)(1)(B). A remote possibility, so remote as to be negligible, that a distribution may be made to a skip person is disregarded. A possibility is disregarded if it can be ascertained by actuarial standards that there is less than a 5 percent probability that the distribution will occur. Reg. § 26.2612-1(b)(1)(iii). See ¶ 13.03[3] note 24.

[73] While *GGC* is alive, *GGC* and *GGC*'s estate are treated as the same person. See ¶ 13.03[4][a] note 83.

[74] If *C* dies after *GC* has reached the age of majority, there, again, is a Section 2612(a)(1)(A) taxable termination at *C*'s death.

[75] See IRC § 2651(f)(3). Similarly, if the trust provides that upon *B*'s death prior to attaining age 21, the property passes to *B*'s estate, no generation-skipping transfer occurs with the parent as transferor because the property is included in *B*'s gross estate and "subject to" the tax imposed by Chapter 11. *B* replaces the parent as transferor of the trust. IRC § 2652(a)(1)(A).

[d] Third Requirement: Transfer Not Subject to Federal Estate or Gift Tax

If the property held in a trust is subject to federal estate or gift tax upon termination of a Chapter 13 interest, generally[76] there is no taxable termination.[77] This requirement precludes the possibility of the termination of an interest simultaneously satisfying the requirements of both a taxable termination and a direct skip generation-skipping transfer.[78] Upon the termination of an interest that, but for this requirement, would be both a taxable termination and a direct skip, the transfer may be subjected only to the Chapter 13 tax as a direct skip. This requirement, imposed by the regulations, appropriately fills a statutory gap by eliminating a statutory overlap.[79]

Assume that grantor G establishes a trust, with income to G for life and the remainder to grandchild GC or GC's estate. G dies, survived by GC whose parents are alive. At G's death, the statutory requirements of both a taxable termination and a direct skip are satisfied. Section 2036 requires the property held in the trust to be included in G's gross estate upon termination of G's retained life interest.[80] The termination of G's Chapter 13 interest in the property held in the trust at death is not a taxable termination, although the property is held thereafter by a skip person, because, at the time of the termination, the property is subject to the federal estate tax. The imposition of the third requirement for a taxable termination eliminates the possibility of overlapping taxable terminations and direct skips and fills the statutory gap.

Applying the regulatory requirement in another context, assume grantor G established a trust under which the income from the property is to be paid to spouse S for life, with the remainder to grandchild GC or GC's estate. If the transfer to the trust does not qualify for the marital deduction,[81] upon termination of S's interest at death the property will not be subject to the federal estate tax. Assuming the property is distributed at S's death to GC, a taxable

---

[76] The general rule is inapplicable if a reverse QTIP election has been made under Section 2652(a)(3). Reg. § 26.2652-2(d) Ex. 1. See infra text accompanying notes 83–87; ¶ 17.02[1][c][i].

[77] Reg. § 26.2612-1(b)(1)(i).

[78] The Treasury initially resolved the conflict by ruling that, where there was an overlap of a taxable termination and a direct skip, the direct skip took precedence over the taxable termination. Rev. Rul. 92-26, 1992-1 CB 314, 315.

[79] Although the language contained in the statute specifically provides that both a taxable termination and a direct skip override a taxable distribution, there is no statutory guidance on the result when there is an overlap of a taxable termination and a direct skip. IRC § 2612(b) (parenthetical). See supra note 78, ¶ 13.02[1][b].

[80] Section 2036 is discussed at ¶ 4.08.

[81] The transfer to the trust for the benefit of spouse S is a terminable interest which does not qualify for the marital deduction, unless a special election is made under Section 2523(f) or Section 2056(b)(7). See ¶¶ 5.06[7], 5.06[8][d], 11.03[3], 11.03[4][c].

termination results.[82] Alternatively, if *G*'s transfer qualifies for the marital deduction as a result of a QTIP election under either Section 2056(b)(7) or Section 2523(f) and *S* dies without disposing of the qualifying life interest, there
may or may not be a taxable termination at *S*'s death, depending on whether a
Section 2652(a)(3) election has been made. If no Section 2652(a)(3), "reverse
QTIP," election[83] has been made, the property is subject to the federal estate
tax upon the termination of *S*'s qualifying income interest in the property at
death[84] and there is no taxable termination,[85] but there is a direct skip generation-skipping transfer.[86] If a Section 2652(a)(3), reverse QTIP, election is
made, there will be a taxable termination at *S*'s death, even though the property held in the trust is subject to federal estate tax upon the termination of the
trust.[87]

[e] Relationship of Powers of Appointment to Taxable Terminations

[i] **Introduction.** A person who holds a presently exercisable general
power of appointment over trust income or corpus has a Chapter 13 interest in
property, while a person holding only a nongeneral power has no such inter-

---

[82] IRC § 2612(a)(1). *G* is the transferor of the generation-skipping transfer. IRC
§ 2652(a). The distribution of property to the grandchild, a skip person, is not treated as a
taxable distribution, because a taxable distribution is a distribution from a trust to a skip
person other than a taxable termination. IRC § 2612(b) (parenthetical).

[83] The estate of a decedent or donor spouse may elect for purposes of Chapter 13 to
ignore an election to treat property held in trust as qualified terminable interest property.
IRC § 2652(a)(3). The election is referred to popularly as a reverse QTIP election. See infra note 87.

[84] Section 2044 requires that the property held in the trust be included in *S*'s gross
estate at death.

[85] Reg. § 26.2612-1(b)(1)(i). See Reg. § 26.2612-1(f) Ex. 4.

[86] Reg. § 26.2612-1(f) Ex. 5. It is assumed that Section 2651(e), the predeceased parent rule, does not apply.

[87] Reg. § 26.2652-2(d) Ex. 1. Normally, when a QTIP election is made, the surviving
spouse becomes the Chapter 13 transferor of the property under Section 2652(a)(1) when
the property is subject to estate or gift taxation. When a Section 2652(a)(3), reverse QTIP,
election is made, the QTIP election is disregarded for purposes of the generation-skipping
transfer tax and the initial decedent or donor continues as the Chapter 13 transferor of the
property and is not supplanted by the surviving spouse when the property is subsequently
subject to the tax imposed by Chapter 11 or Chapter 12 and the surviving spouse is the
decedent or donor for purposes of those chapters. A Section 2652(a)(3), reverse QTIP,
election determines not only who is the Chapter 13 transferor, but also (since there is a
disregard of the property being subject to federal estate or gift tax with the surviving
spouse as the decedent or donor) the type of generation-skipping transfer that has occurred, namely a taxable termination, rather than a direct skip.

est.[88] Potential noncharitable appointees of either type of power who may currently receive trust income or corpus also have a Chapter 13 interest in the appointive property.[89] When a power is exercised, is released, or lapses,[90] one or more Chapter 13 interests may terminate and the termination may satisfy the requirements of a taxable termination.

[ii] **General powers of appointment.** The policy underlying the estate and gift taxation of property subject to any general power of appointment is that the power holder is generally treated as owning the property subject to the power.[91] A release or exercise of an inter vivos general power of appointment or the release of a testamentary general power of appointment during the power holder's life may constitute a Section 2514 transfer of property by the power holder,[92] and property subject to a testamentary general power at the power holder's death may be included in the power holder's gross estate.[93] To the extent that there is a Section 2514 transfer[94] or inclusion of property subject to a testamentary power in the power holder's gross estate under Section 2041,[95] the property subject to the power is *deemed* to be distributed to the power holder under Chapter 13.[96] If the property deemed distributed to the

---

[88] IRC § 2652(c)(1)(A). See IRC §§ 2041(b)(1), 2514(c). The interrelationship of powers of appointment and Chapter 13 interests is also considered supra ¶ 13.02[2][b][i] and ¶ 17.02[3][b].

[89] IRC § 2652(c)(1)(B). See supra ¶ 13.02[2][b] text accompanying note 51.

[90] The exercise, release, or lapse must be of the entire power to qualify as a taxable termination. See supra ¶ 13.02[2][b] text accompanying notes 62–64. See also infra note 100.

[91] See ¶¶ 4.13[1], 10.04[1].

[92] IRC §§ 2514(a), 2514(b). See IRC § 2514(e).

[93] IRC §§ 2041(a)(1), 2041(a)(2). Under Chapter 11, an inter vivos general power of appointment held until death is treated as a testamentary power of appointment. See ¶ 4.13[2] note 4.

[94] See IRC §§ 2514(a), 2514(b), 2514(e).

[95] See supra note 93. An inter vivos exercise or release of a power that was treated as an inter vivos transfer (see supra text accompanying note 92), but is subsequently included in the power holder's gross estate under Section 2041(a)(1) or Section 2041(a)(2), is not treated under Chapter 13 as a deemed distribution to and a deemed transfer by the power holder at death, since it was already deemed distributed and transferred inter vivos. See infra text accompanying note 96.

[96] Reg. § 26.2612-1(c)(1) (next to last sentence). The power holder then transfers the property to the appointee if there is an exercise of the general power, or the power holder is deemed to transfer the property to the taker-in-default if there is a release or lapse of the power. Cf. IRC § 2652(a)(1). Any transfer by the general power holder will occur on the date of the event described supra text accompanying notes 92–93.

The mere creation of the general power is not a taxable event under Chapter 13. The creation of a trust with a power holder having a general power over corpus is not treated as a transfer outright to the general power holder. See ¶ 13.03[3][b] note 71. See also Reg. §§ 26.2652-1(a)(5) Ex. 5, 26.2612-1(f) Ex. 3.

power holder under Chapter 13 passes to a third person, the power holder is deemed to have made a subsequent transfer to the third person. In determining the Chapter 13 consequences to a trust on the exercise, release, or lapse of a general power of appointment, both the Chapter 13 interests that terminate and the transferees of the property (both actual and deemed)[97] must be identified to determine whether a taxable termination or possibly some other type of generation-skipping transfer has occurred.[98]

For example, assume that in the current year grantor G transfers property to a trust, providing income to child C for life and a remainder to granddaughter GD. In addition, G gives grandson GS a general power to appoint trust corpus during C's life. If, during C's lifetime, GS appoints all the property to himself, all of the trust assets will be distributed to GS. The distribution to GS is a taxable termination of C's interest, GS's trust interest, and the interests of GS's potential appointees.[99] If GS exercised only part of the power and appointed part of the corpus to himself, there would be no taxable termination, but the distribution of trust property to GS would be a Chapter 13 taxable distribution.[100] If, instead, GS exercised his power to appoint the entire corpus to C or GD, under Chapter 13 there is a deemed distribution of the trust property to GS that would still result in a taxable termination of the trust.[101] If GS ap-

---

To the extent that the release or lapse of a general power is not treated as an inter vivos transfer of property subject to the power (e.g., the inter vivos lapse or release of a pre-1942 general power or the inter vivos lapse of a post-1942 power that is not treated as a release under the five-or-five rule. See infra text accompanying notes 113–160) and to the extent that property subject to a testamentary general power is not included in the power holder's gross estate (property subject to an unexercised pre-1942 general power of appointment), there is no deemed distribution to or transfer by the power holder. The property passes, under the original terms of the trust, and the original transferor of the trust remains as transferor. In the situations described here, except possibly in the case of the lapse of a post-1942 general power of appointment (see infra text accompanying notes 113–160), even though a taxable termination or taxable distribution may occur, there are no Chapter 13 consequences because the transfer to the trust would have occurred prior to the effective dates of Chapter 13. See ¶ 18.05.

[97] See supra note 96.

[98] IRC § 2612(a)(1).

[99] There is a termination of C's interest (C's life estate, which is a Section 2652(c)(1)(B) interest; see supra ¶ 13.02[2][b] note 53), GS's interest (his general power of appointment, which is a Section 2652(c)(1)(A) interest), and GS's potential appointees' Section 2652(c)(1)(B) interests. Upon termination of the interests, the property passes to GS, a skip person in relation to G. IRC § 2612(a)(1). Even though three different types of interests terminate, there is only a single taxable termination of the trust. See Reg. § 26.2612-1(f) Ex. 10.

[100] There is a distribution to a skip person, GS. IRC §§ 2612(b), 2613(a)(1). See infra ¶ 13.02[3]. There is no terminating distribution because neither C's, GS's, nor GS's potential appointees' interests completely terminate. See supra note 90.

[101] IRC § 2612(a)(1), Reg. § 26.2612-1(c)(1) (next to last sentence). See supra note 99. Thereafter, there would also be a Chapter 12 gift by GS to C or GD. IRC § 2514(b).

pointed all the property held in the trust to *GGGS* (*GS*'s grandson), under Chapter 13 there would be both a taxable termination of the trust[102] and a subsequent direct skip.[103] If *GS* exercised the general power and appointed the entire trust corpus to a second trust in a transfer that was not a complete gift or was a partially complete gift,[104] there would still be a deemed distribution of all the trust property to *GS* and a taxable termination of the first trust,[105] but there would likely be no immediate Chapter 13 consequences on the transfer by *GS* to the second trust.[106]

If *GS* predeceases *C* and holds a testamentary general power of appointment over property that is included in his gross estate under Chapter 11,[107] there is a deemed distribution of the trust property subject to the power to *GS* and a taxable termination.[108] In addition, if *GS* exercised his power, there is a

---

If, instead, *G*'s great-grandson *GGS* had held the general power and exercised it in favor of *C*, there would be a deemed distribution of the property held in the trust to *GGS* (Reg. § 26.2612-1(c)(1) (next to last sentence)), a taxable termination (see supra note 99), and a subsequent gift by *GGS* to *C*. IRC § 2514(b). If *C* then gave the property to her granddaughter *GGD*, there would likely be no subsequent direct skip. IRC § 2611(b)(2). But see IRC § 2611(b)(2)(C); supra ¶ 13.02[2][b], especially ¶ 13.02[2][b][ii].

[102] IRC § 2612(a)(1). See supra note 99.

[103] IRC § 2612(c)(1). There would be Chapter 12 gifts by GS to *GGGS* under both Sections 2514(b) and 2515. The transfer from *GS* to *GGGS* would constitute a direct skip. Id. See supra ¶ 13.02[1][b] note 15.

[104] See ¶ 10.01.

[105] IRC § 2612(a)(1). See supra note 99. Even though the property may subsequently be included in *GS*'s gross estate under Section 2041(a)(2), the taxable termination of the first trust still occurs on *GS*'s exercise of the power (not on its inclusion in his gross estate). See supra text accompanying notes 94–96.

[106] The transfer by *GS* will likely not result in any immediate direct skip (see IRC § 2642(f)(1) (last sentence)) by *GS*, and although *GS* may allocate GST exemption to the trust, the effect of the allocation will be delayed. IRC § 2642(f), discussed ¶ 16.02[7]. See ¶ 16.02[7] text accompanying notes 450–454. See also Reg. § 26.2632-1(c)(1).

[107] IRC §§ 2041(a)(1), 2041(a)(2). See supra note 93.

[108] IRC § 2612(a)(1). See supra note 99; Reg. § 26.2612-1(c)(1). See also supra notes 95 and 96. Cf. § 26.2612-1(b)(1)(i). The deemed distribution to *GS* and resulting taxable termination should be treated as occurring before inclusion in *GS*'s gross estate for this purpose. Regulations Section 26.2612-1(b)(1)(i) was promulgated to prevent overlap between a direct skip and a taxable termination, not overlap between a taxable termination and a taxable distribution.

If *C* predeceases *GS*, at *C*'s death, there will be an inter vivos lapse of *GS*'s general power. To the extent this lapse is treated as a release, *GS* will be treated as making a transfer of property by gift to *GD*, the remainderperson of the trust. The transfer is taxed under Chapter 12. IRC §§ 2511, 2514(b). There will be a termination of *C*'s, *GS*'s and *GS*'s potential appointees' interests. See supra note 99. To the extent that the lapse is treated as a release and taxed under Chapter 12 (see IRC §§ 2514(b), 2514(e)), the property is deemed transferred to *GS*. To the extent there is a nontaxable lapse under Section 2514(e), the property passes to *GD*. In either event, a skip person in relation to *G* holds

transfer to his appointees,[109] and, alternatively, if the power lapsed or was released, there would be a deemed transfer of the trust property by GS[110] to the takers-in-default of the power.[111] For example, if GS exercised his testamentary general power in favor of $GGGS$, in addition to the taxable termination, there would be a testamentary direct skip of the property by GS to $GGGS$.[112]

Lapse of a General Power. Generally, under the estate and gift taxes, the lifetime lapse of a post-1942 general power of appointment is treated as a release of the power that in turn is treated as a transfer of the property by the power holder,[113] and a lapse of such a power at death results in inclusion of the property within the power holder's gross estate.[114] Under Section 2514(e), however, the inter vivos lapse of a post-1942 general power, to the extent that it does not exceed the greater of $5,000 or 5 percent of the property from which it may be appointed, is not treated as a release.[115]

A *lifetime* lapse of an inter vivos post-1942 general power that is not treated as a release[116] results in a termination of the Chapter 13 interest of the power holder and of the potential appointees,[117] but under Chapter 13, a lapse that is not treated as a release should not result in a deemed transfer of the property from the trust to the power holder, nor a deemed transfer of the property by the power holder.[118] To the extent that the inter vivos lapse of a post-1942 general power of appointment *is* treated as a release, or the property is included in the power holder's gross estate as a result of a testamentary lapse, there is a termination of the power holder's power, a termination of potential appointees' interests, a deemed distribution by the trust to the power holder, and a deemed retransfer by the power holder to the trust under Chapter 13.[119] When an inter vivos lapse of a general power results in a gift, or there is only partial inclusion of the trust corpus in the power holder's gross estate, both the

---

the property after the termination, and a taxable termination of the entire corpus occurs. See generally infra text accompanying notes 113–160.

[109] See supra note 96.

[110] See supra note 96.

[111] In this case, it would pass to a trust providing income to C for life and the remainder to GD. This transfer would not be a generation-skipping transfer by GS. See IRC § 2612(c)(1). If the taker-in-default were a skip person in relation to GS, then GS would have made a direct skip transfer. IRC §§ 2612(c)(1), 2652(a)(1)(A).

[112] IRC §§ 2612(c)(1), 2613(a)(1). See supra text accompanying notes 102 and 103. Cf. IRC § 2651(e), which it is assumed is inapplicable.

[113] IRC §§ 2514(b), 2514(e).

[114] IRC § 2041(a)(2).

[115] See ¶ 10.04[4][c].

[116] IRC § 2514(e).

[117] IRC §§ 2652(c)(1)(A), 2652(c)(1)(B).

[118] See supra text accompanying notes 94–96.

[119] See supra text accompanying notes 91–98.

original transferor and the power holder become Chapter 13 transferors to the trust,[120] and the trust is treated as two trusts for Chapter 13 purposes.[121]

Two examples illustrate the operation of the lapse rules. Assume grantor *G* creates a trust with income to grandchild *GC* for life and a remainder to great-grandchild *GGC*. In addition, *G* gives child *C* a five-or-five noncumulative annual power to withdraw the greater of $5,000 or 5 percent of the corpus of the trust which *C* fails to exercise in any year of the trust.[122] *C*, a non-skip person, holds a Chapter 13 interest in the trust.[123] As a result, the trust is not a

---

[120] IRC § 2652(a)(1). See Reg. §§ 26.2652-1(a)(5) Ex. 5, 26.2652-1(a)(1); ¶ 17.02[1][d].

[121] IRC § 2654(b)(1); Reg. § 26.2654-1(a)(2)(i). See ¶ 17.04[2][a]. This analysis differs from the effective date ramifications. See ¶ 18.05[2][b] text accompanying note 38.

[122] A beneficiary is frequently granted a noncumulative annual general power to appoint the greater of $5,000 or 5 percent of the property from which the appointment may be made. This power is designed to conform to the exception for lapses and is commonly referred to as a "five-or-five power." There are two frequently employed types of five-or-five powers. The first type, present in this example, is an ongoing noncumulative right in each year to withdraw the corpus of a trust up to a maximum of the greater of $5,000 or 5 percent. The second type, present in the example in infra text accompanying note 143, is commonly known as a *Crummey* power (see Crummey v. Comm'r, 397 F2d 82 (9th Cir. 1968); ¶ 9.04[3][f]). A *Crummey* power is generally conditioned on contributions to a trust and allows the power holder to withdraw such contributions in order to qualify them for an annual exclusion under Section 2503(b). In order to maximize the use of the Section 2503(b) annual exclusion amount, a *Crummey* power may be granted which exceeds the $5,000 or 5 percent limitation of Section 2514(e). When the *Crummey* power exceeds the $5,000 limitation and the power of withdrawal may be satisfied from corpus, not merely the contribution to the corpus, the *Crummey* power might not exceed the 5 percent limitation.

A five-or-five power is typically given to the income beneficiary of the trust. If this example was a typical situation in which *G*'s trust provided income to *C* for life and a remainder to *GC*, and if *G* gave *C* a five-or-five power over corpus which was exercisable at any time during a calendar year (see infra note 142), there would be no Chapter 13 generation-skipping transfer until *C*'s death (see infra note 129), at which time the power terminates and *C*'s income interest terminates. As to the portion included in *C*'s gross estate under Section 2041(a)(2) (the greater of $5,000 or 5 percent of the corpus), there is no taxable termination to *C* because the property is included in *C*'s gross estate and, in addition, *C* is not a skip person in relation to *G*. Also there is no direct skip from *C* to *GC* of the portion included in *C*'s gross estate because GC is not a skip person in relation to the deemed transferor *C*. IRC §§ 2612(a)(1), 2612(c)(1), 2613(a)(1), 2652(a)(1)(A). As to the remaining portion not included in *C*'s gross estate, there is a taxable termination because *GC* is a skip person in relation to *G* and that portion of the property is not subject to the federal estate tax at the termination of *C*'s interest. IRC §§ 2612(a)(1), 2613(a)(1); Reg. § 26.2612-1(b)(1)(i). The less typical example in the text is used to better illustrate the lapse rules under Chapter 13.

[123] IRC §§ 2613(a)(1), 2613(b), 2652(c)(1)(A). *GC* also has a Chapter 13 interest in the trust property. IRC § 2652(c)(1)(A). See supra ¶ 13.02[2][b] note 53. It is assumed that *C*'s interest is not disregarded. See IRC § 2652(c)(2); Reg. § 26.2612-1(e)(2)(ii).

skip person[124] and there are no direct skips on *G*'s transfers to the trust.[125] In each year as *C*'s power lapses, there is no taxable event under Chapter 12[126] and no deemed distribution by the trust to *C* or recontribution to the trust by *C*.[127] There is a termination of *C*'s Chapter 13 interest in each year;[128] however, the termination is likely not a taxable termination because the property remains in a trust that is a non-skip person.[129] At *C*'s death, assuming the

---

[124] IRC § 2613(a)(2).

[125] IRC § 2612(c)(1). If *C* held no five-or-five power there would be direct skips on *G*'s transfers to the trust because *GC*, a skip person, would hold the only Chapter 13 interest in the trust. Id. See IRC § 2652(c)(1)(A).

[126] IRC § 2514(e). If *C* had been given an annual noncumulative general power over trust corpus that exceeded the greater of $5,000 or 5 percent of the value of the corpus, several different consequences would occur. To the extent of the five-or-five amount, the results would be the same as in the example in the text. See supra text accompanying notes 122–126; infra text accompanying notes 127–142. As to any excess, in each year of a lapse, there would be a Section 2514(b) transfer of property by *C* to the trust. That transfer of property results in a deemed distribution to *C* and a retransfer by *C* to the trust under Chapter 13. See supra text accompanying notes 94–96. The distribution to *C* would not be a taxable termination because *C* is a non-skip person in relation to *G* (see IRC §§ 2612(a)(1)(A), 2613(a)(1), 2613(b)), and *C*'s transfer would not be a direct skip because the trust is not a skip person in relation to *C* (*C* and *GC* both have Chapter 13 interests, and both are non-skip persons; thus, the trust is a non-skip person). See IRC §§ 2612(c)(1), 2613, 2652(c)(1); infra note 129. Both *G* and *C* would be transferors to the trust, and the trust would be treated as two trusts under Chapter 13. See supra text accompanying notes 120, 121; Priv. Ltr. Rul. 9801025 (Jan. 5, 1998) (no taxable event upon lifetime lapse where primary beneficiary of irrevocable trust granted power, exercisable for thirty days, to withdraw entire amount contributed to the trust).

[127] See supra text accompanying notes 116–118.

[128] IRC § 2612(a)(1). As income is distributed to *GC* from the trust, the distributions are Section 2612(b) taxable distributions. See infra ¶ 13.02[3].

[129] IRC § 2612(a)(1)(A). See supra text accompanying notes 123–124. It is likely not a taxable termination of *C*'s Chapter 13 interest and the trust likely retains its classification as a non-skip person. It is assumed that *C*'s Chapter 13 interest is continuous and does not terminate. When the right to withdraw lapses at precisely the last moment of the calendar year, it isimmediately replaced with a new right to withdraw which gives a fictional continuity to *C*'s Chapter 13 interest. Compare this situation with where *C* exercises the power during the year or the power to withdraw may be exercised only in one calendar month ofthe year and lapses during the year. From the point in time when the power lapses or is exercised until the power may be exercised again, *C* has no Chapter 13 interest. The lapse or exercise is a termination of *C*'s Chapter 13 interest that could be considered to result in a taxable termination of the entire trust corpus. Should *C*'s Chapter 13 interest be treated as not terminating each year? Should the definition of a Chapter 13 interest be fudged a little to include a Chapter 13 interest that is scheduled to appear each calendar year or regularly upon the mere passage of time? See infra note 142. These situations should be contrasted with a situation where an individual has the right to presently withdraw, a Chapter 13 interest, when a grantor contributes property to a trust, a *Crummey* power. See infra text accompanying notes 143–150.

power lapses[130] and *GC* survives,[131] two separate events occur. First, the greater of $5,000 or 5 percent of corpus is included in *C*'s gross estate and is subject to the tax imposed by Chapter 11.[132] As a result, the trust is deemed to make a distribution to *C* of that portion of the corpus.[133] Although *C*'s Chapter 13 interest terminates, there is no taxable termination of that portion because the property is deemed distributed to *C*, who is not a skip person in relation to *G*.[134] *C* is also deemed to transfer that portion back to the trust,[135] and *C* becomes the Chapter 13 transferor to that extent.[136] Second, with respect to the balance of the trust corpus that is not included in *C*'s gross estate, there is *likely* a taxable termination[137] because: (1) there is a termination of *C*'s interest as a power holder over the balance of the corpus and as a potential appointee;[138] (2) a transfer subject to the federal estate tax does not occur at the time of the termination of these Chapter 13 interests;[139] and (3) immediately after the termination *GC* (a skip person in relation to *G*) holds the only Chap-

---

[130] If, at *C*'s death, *C* exercises the power as to the five-or-five amount, the results are the same as if the five-or-five power lapsed (see infra text accompanying notes 132–136), except that if *C* exercises the power in favor of a skip person, *C* would also make a Section 2612(c)(1) direct skip of the five-or-five amount.

[131] If *GC* predeceased *C*, there would be a distribution of corpus to *GGC* and two simultaneous taxable terminations of the entire corpus that would result from a termination of *C*'s interest over the corpus and a termination of *GC*'s income interest. IRC § 2612(a)(1). See infra text accompanying notes 169, 179.

[132] IRC § 2041(a)(2).

[133] See supra text accompanying notes 94–96.

[134] IRC §§ 2612(a)(1)(A), 2613(a)(1), 2613(b). The distribution is also not a Section 2612(b) taxable distribution, again because *C* is a non-skip person in relation to *G*.

[135] See supra text accompanying note 96.

[136] IRC § 2652(a)(1)(A). The transfer by *C* is not a Section 2612(c)(1) direct skip to the trust because *C* makes a transfer to a trust that is not a skip person, because *GC* (a non-skip person in relation to *C*) holds all Chapter 13 interests in the trust. IRC § 2613(a)(2)(A).

[137] IRC § 2612(a)(1). See supra note 129.

[138] Although it might appear that *C*'s interest extended to only $5,000 or 5 percent of the corpus, the power holder's five-or-five power over many years potentially could have been exercised over the entire corpus of the trust. More important, if *C* had not held the five-or-five power, *G* would have made a direct skip generation-skipping transfer of the entire corpus to *GC* that would have been subjected to the tax imposed by Chapter 13 on creation of the trust. See supra note 125. *G*'s granting of a five-or-five power to *C* postponed the imposition of tax under Chapter 13. See supra text accompanying notes 123–125. At *C*'s death, the postponed Chapter 13 transfer occurs in the form of a taxable termination to the extent that the corpus is not included in *C*'s gross estate. But see supra note 129. Cf. infra text accompanying notes 157 and 158.

[139] Reg. § 26.2612-1(b)(1)(i).

ter 13 interest in the trust.[140] *G* remains the Chapter 13 transferor of that portion of the trust corpus not included in *C*'s gross estate, and the trust now has two transferors,[141] *G* and *C*, and it is treated as two separate trusts for purposes of Chapter 13.[142]

Similar, but not identical, results occur if *G* establishes the same trust (income to *GC* for life and a remainder to *GGC*), but *G* gives *C* only a *Crummey* power to withdraw *transfers to the trust* to the extent of the greater of $5,000 or 5 percent of such transfers.[143] *C* has a Chapter 13 interest in the trust when

---

[140] IRC §§ 2613(a)(1), 2652(c)(1)(A). See also Section 2653(a), which drops *G* down to *C*'s generation level for purposes of determining whether subsequent distributions from the portion of the trust of which *G* is still treated as transferor are generation-skipping transfers. See ¶ 17.03[1].

[141] See supra text accompanying note 96; Reg. § 26.2652-1(a)(5) Ex. 5.

[142] IRC § 2654(b)(1). See supra text accompanying notes 120 and 121.

A common method of avoiding inclusion of the five-or-five power in the power holder's gross estate at death is to limit its exercise to a limited period during the year (e.g., a particular month of the year or a particular day of each month) so that if the power holder dies on a day of the year when the power holder does not hold the power, the power holder does not have the general power at death. IRC § 2041(a)(2).

Using the example in supra text accompanying notes 122–142, assume *G* gives *C* a five-or-five power over corpus only in the month of January of each year. If *C* dies in the month of January, the results could be the same as in that example. The results will be the same as in the previous example if *C*'s Chapter 13 interest is not treated as terminating annually. See supra note 129. After the lapse of *C*'s Chapter 13 interest at the end of January, *C* no longer has a Chapter 13 interest in the trust. For eleven months, *C* merely has a future interest, and then beginning with the month of January, *C* has a Chapter 13 interest once again. If *C*'s Chapter 13 interest is treated as continuous, there will generally be no taxable termination until *C*'s death. Alternatively, if the lapse of *C*'s power at the end of January is treated as a termination of *C*'s Chapter 13 interest, the entire trust corpus will be the subject matter of a generation-skipping transfer at that point in time. This would move *G* into *C*'s generation under Section 2653(a). Subsequent distributions of income to *GC* would not be taxable distributions. If, instead, *C* dies in any month other than January, none of the corpus is included in *C*'s gross estate under Section 2041(a)(2), and there is no deemed distribution to or a transfer by *C*. *G* remains as the transferor of the entire corpus, and there is a taxable termination of the entire corpus of the trust at *C*'s death, assuming the termination of *C*'s power annually did not result in a taxable termination of the entire trust corpus. See supra note 129 and text accompanying notes 137–142.

[143] See supra note 122. The *Crummey* power might be given to *C*, for example, because the trust is funded with life insurance and there is no present interest in *GC* to qualify the trust for an annual exclusion. See Reg. § 25.2503-3(c) Ex. 2. Generally, a *Crummey* power is given to the income beneficiary of the trust. *C*, a third party, is given the *Crummey* power in this example so as to better illustrate the operation of the Chapter 13 rules. Cf. supra note 122. As a practical matter, the validity of a *Crummey* power held by a third party who is not a beneficiary will be questioned. See ¶ 9.04[3][f] text accompanying notes 104–106.

To maximize the annual exclusion, *G* could give *C* a *Crummey* power to withdraw up to $11,000 of contributions made to the trust in any calendar year. However, assuming *G*'s contributions in any year did not exceed $220,000 (5 percent of $220,000 equals

there is a contribution to the trust,[144] and, as *C* is a non-skip person, a contribution to the trust does not constitute a direct skip to the trust.[145]

Assuming that contributions in any one year to the trust do not exceed $5,000 and *C*'s power over any contributions to the trust lapses, there is no transfer of property by *C* taxable under Chapter 12.[146] As a result, there is no deemed distribution by the trust to *C* and the contributed property subject to the power that lapsed remains in the trust with *G* as transferor.[147] After any such lapse, there is a termination of *C*'s Chapter 13 interest in the trust and *C* has no Chapter 13 interest in the trust until another contribution is made to the trust.[148] The termination of *C*'s interest should be treated as a taxable termination because a transfer subject to federal gift tax does not occur at the termination of *C*'s Chapter 13 interest,[149] and, after *C*'s interest in the trust terminates, *GC* holds the only Chapter 13 interest in the trust, with the result that the trust is a skip person.[150] Similar treatment would be accorded to all future contributions to the trust; thus, all of *G*'s contributions to the trust will result in Chapter 13 taxable terminations as the property passes from *G* to *GC*, with *C* lapsing out of the scene.

However, if a contribution by *G* exceeds $5,000 and *C*'s $5,000 power lapses, then there should be a taxable termination only to the extent that the

---

$11,000) and *C*'s power lapsed, there would be a Section 2514(b) transfer by C to the extent the power was released. See IRC §§ 2514(b), 2514(e). To the extent of the release, there would be a termination of *C*'s interest and a deemed transfer from *G* to *C* (see supra text accompanying notes 94–96) that would not be a taxable termination because *C* is not a skip person in relation to *G*. See IRC §§ 2612(a)(1), 2613(a)(1). *C*'s deemed retransfer to the trust would not be a direct skip to the trust because *GC* (a non-skip person in relation to *C*) has the only Chapter 13 interest in the trust after *C*'s transfer. See IRC §§ 2612(c)(1), 2613(a)(1), 2652(c)(1)(A).

[144] Because *C* has a power to withdraw part of any contribution of corpus to the trust, *C* has a Chapter 13 interest in the trust. IRC § 2652(c)(1)(A). It is assumed that *C*'s interest is not disregarded. See IRC § 2652(c)(2); Reg. § 26.2612-1(e)(2)(ii).

[145] IRC § 2612(c)(1). *C* is not a skip person in relation to *G*; thus, a non-skip person has a Chapter 13 interest in the trust, and the trust is not a skip person. IRC §§ 2613(a)(1), 2613(a)(2), 2613(b). Even though non-skip person *C* may have an interest in only a portion of the trust, the contributions, that interest precludes the entire trust from being a skip person. IRC § 2613(a)(2)(A).

[146] IRC § 2514(e).

[147] Cf. supra text accompanying notes 94–98; IRC § 2652(a)(1).

[148] *C* has no presently exercisable interest and, hence, no Chapter 13 interest. See IRC § 2652(c)(1)(A); supra notes 129, 142. *C* will not have another Chapter 13 interest in the trust unless *G* makes another contribution to the trust.

[149] Reg. § 26.2612-1(b)(1)(i).

[150] IRC §§ 2612(a)(1), 2613(a)(2). The fact that *C* may never have another Chapter 13 interest in the trust mitigates against delaying the termination until *C*'s death.

lapse does not equal a release.[151] Because *C* held no Chapter 13 interest in the excess amount, there is no taxable termination of the excess.[152] Thus, if *G* made a $20,000 contribution to the trust and *C* had a power over $5,000 that lapsed, there should be a taxable termination of one fourth of the contribution but no taxable termination of the remaining three-fourths. At *C*'s death, *C* would hold no Chapter 13 interest in the corpus, and there would be no taxable termination of the trust,[153] except possibly with respect to a portion of a contribution made by *G* to the trust in the year of *C*'s death.[154] The result reached is inappropriate under Chapter 13. To the extent of *C*'s five-or-five power, there is a generation-skipping transfer on *G*'s contribution of property to the trust as it passes to *GC*'s generation. With respect to any contribution of property to the trust in excess of the five-or-five power, however, there is no generation-skipping transfer as the property passes from *G* to *GC*'s generation. There is no direct skip at the time of *G*'s transfers to the trust, because *C* holds a Chapter 13 interest in the trust that precludes the trust from being a skip person.[155] There is no taxable termination of the property in excess of the five-or-five power when *C*'s power lapses and the property passes to *GC*'s generation, because *C* had no Chapter 13 interest in the excess that could terminate. And at *C*'s death, *C* again has no Chapter 13 interest over the excess corpus. Hence, there is no taxable termination of the excess of the corpus as it passes to *GC*'s generation.[156]

The regulations must resolve this possibly significant escape hatch from the Chapter 13 tax. It is possible that the regulations could use the Section 2654(b)(2) separate share rule to divide the lapsed and non-lapsed portions of any contribution to the trust into separate trusts where a *Crummey* power is used. As a result, the portion over which there was no *Crummey* power (three

---

[151] IRC §§ 2514(b), 2514(e). Again, the transfer of any contributions to the trust are not direct skips to the trust because *C* has a Chapter 13 interest in the trust. See supra note 145.

[152] Because *C* held a power over only a portion of the contribution, there would be a taxable termination of only such a portion of the property. See supra ¶ 13.02[2][b] text accompanying note 64.

[153] IRC § 2612(a)(1). *C* had no presently exercisable power over the corpus of the trust and, thus, no Chapter 13 interest in the corpus of the trust. IRC § 2652(c)(1)(A).

[154] It is possible, although unlikely, that *C* would hold a Chapter 13 interest *over a contribution* made to the trust in the year of *C*'s death. For this to occur, *G* must make a contribution to the trust in that year and *C*'s power must not yet have lapsed as to that contribution at the time of *C*'s death. Even if this occurred, *C* would hold no power over the remaining corpus of the trust.

[155] See supra text accompanying note 145.

[156] Income distributions from the excess trust corpus to *GC* during *C*'s life result in a Section 2612(b) taxable distribution; however, the excess corpus is not subject to Chapter 13 tax until *GC*'s death.

fourths in this example) would be a transfer to a separate trust.[157] That trust would be a skip person and the transfer would be a direct skip.[158] As a result, all contributions to the trust would be taxed as they move from G to GC's generation level. A possible alternative would be to treat the five-or-five *Crummey* power as a Chapter 13 tax avoidance mechanism and disregard it under Section 2652(c)(2).[159] All contributions to the trust would then be direct skips[160] at the time of the contribution.

[iii] Nongeneral powers. Holding a nongeneral power over property does not constitute a Chapter 13 interest in property, but potential appointees who may presently receive income or corpus under the nongeneral power do hold Chapter 13 interests.[161] When a nongeneral power completely terminates[162] as the result of an exercise, release, or lapse, the appointees' interests also terminate. Whether the complete exercise, release, or lapse of a nongeneral power results in a taxable termination of a trust[163] depends on whether property passes to a skip person in relation to the transferor of the trust[164] and whether or not the property is subject to the federal estate or gift tax.[165] If property passes to a skip person and is not subject to federal estate or gift tax, there is a taxable termination.[166]

For example, assume transferor G creates a trust with income to child C for life and a remainder to one of C's children, GC. In addition, G gives C a nongeneral power to appoint the trust corpus either inter vivos or at death outright to any of G's descendants other than C. If C dies without exercising the power, or if C exercises the power at death in GC's sibling's favor, all appointees' interests (as well as C's income interest) terminate, and as the property

---

[157] See ¶ 17.04[2].

[158] IRC §§ 2612(c)(1), 2613(a)(2).

[159] See ¶ 17.02[3][d].

[160] It is possible that some combination of the two alternatives could be used. If the five-or-five power were small in relation to the contribution, the Section 2652(c)(2) rule could be applied; if it were large in relation to the contribution, the Section 2654(b)(2) rule could be applied.

[161] IRC § 2652(c)(1)(B). See supra text accompanying notes 88 and 89.

[162] A partial exercise, release, or lapse of the nongeneral power will not result in a Section 2612(a)(1) termination of the appointees' interests. See supra ¶ 13.02[2][b] text accompanying notes 62–64. It might generate a taxable distribution. IRC § 2612(b).

[163] IRC § 2612(a)(1).

[164] IRC §§ 2613(a), 2652(a)(1).

[165] Reg. § 26.2612-1(b)(1)(i). If the exercise of a nongeneral power of appointment is considered a transfer subject to the federal estate or gift tax by the holder of the power and the property passes to a skip person, there is a direct skip and no taxable termination. Cf. example infra text accompanying note 169.

[166] IRC § 2612(a)(1); Reg. § 26.2612-1(b)(1).

passes to *GC*'s sibling, there is a taxable termination of the trust.[167] If *C* appoints the property at death to *C*'s sibling *S*, there is no taxable termination because *S* is not a skip person in relation to *G*.[168] If *C* appoints the entire corpus at death to *GGC*, *C*'s grandchild, although both *C* and *GC*, who are at different generation levels, have Chapter 13 interests that terminate, according to the Treasury there is only one taxable termination because both Chapter 13 interests terminate at the same time as a result of one event.[169] If *C* appoints the property at death to a second trust, there is a taxable termination if the second trust is a skip person in relation to *G*.[170]

---

[167] See supra text accompanying notes 163–166. If *C* exercises the nongeneral power during lifetime, appointing all the property held in the trust to *GC*, *C*'s Chapter 13 interest in the trust terminates. *C* makes a transfer of property by gift of the value of the income interest to *GC*. IRC § 2511(a); Reg. § 25.2514-1(b)(2); Regester v. Comm'r, 83 TC 1 (1984). But see Self v. United States, 142 F. Supp. 939 (Ct. Cl. 1956) (inappropriately reaching an opposite result). See ¶ 10.04[3][e]. *C* is the Chapter 13 transferor of the value of the income interest given to *GC*, preventing a taxable termination of that portion of the transfer for want of a skip person, as well as the fact that a transfer subject to the gift tax occurs with respect to the property held in the trust at the time of the termination. The balance of the value of the trust property (the value of the remainder) satisfies the requirements of a taxable termination because *G* is the transferor of that portion of the trust property to *GC*, who is a skip person in relation to *G*, and at the time of termination of *C*'s interest, the property held in the trust is not subject to the federal estate or gift tax. All of the property held in the trust is appropriately subjected to transfer tax as the property passes from *C* to *GC*, with part of the property (the income interest) being taxed under Chapter 12 and the balance (the remainder interest) being taxed under Chapter 13.

   If *C* appoints only a portion of the trust corpus inter vivos to *GC*, there is a Section 2511 gift by *C* of the portion of the transfer attributable to the income interest transferred to *GC* from the trust and there is no taxable termination (see supra ¶ 13.02[2][b] text accompanying notes 62–64), but there is a Section 2612(b) taxable distribution of the transferred portion of the remainder interest to *GC* from the trust with *G* as the transferor. See infra ¶ 13.02[3].

[168] IRC §§ 2612(a)(1), 2613(a)(1).

[169] Reg. § 26.2612-1(f) Ex. 10. See infra ¶ 13.02[2][g]. There is a termination of *C*'s income interest under the trust. There is also a termination of *GC*'s interest and the interest of other potential appointees of *C* in both generation levels. The property passes without being subject to the federal estate or gift tax to *GGC*, who is a skip person. Should the two terminations result in two taxable events at descending generational levels? See infra ¶ 13.02[2][g] note 206. Cf. IRC § 2653(a).

   If the exercise of the nongeneral power in favor of *GGC* is an inter vivos exercise, there is an inter vivos gift by *C* of *C*'s remaining income interest (see supra note 167) which also constitutes a direct skip by *C* of the value of the income interest if *C*'s child, *GC*, is alive with *C* as transferor. In addition, there is a single taxable termination of the value of the remainder interest in the trust with *G* as the transferor. See supra note 167.

[170] See IRC §§ 2612(a)(1), 2613(a)(2). If the exercise is inter vivos, there is also an inter vivos gift transfer by *C* of the value of *C*'s remaining income interest that would constitute a direct skip with *C* as the Chapter 13 transferor and a taxable termination of the value of the remainder interest with *G* as the Chapter 13 transferor. See supra note 167.

A nongeneral power of appointment generally has neither Chapter 11 nor Chapter 12 consequences for the power holder,[171] and it is frequently used with an eye to avoiding those taxes. The use of a nongeneral power, however, may have significant Chapter 13 consequences. For example, assume that grantor *G* creates a trust with income to grandchild *GC* for life and a remainder to great-grandchild *GGC*. The transfer of property to the trust results in a direct skip,[172] and there will be a taxable termination at *GC*'s death.[173] However, if *G* also gave *GC* a nongeneral power to appoint the corpus to *GC*'s parent, *C* (*G*'s child) during *C*'s life, *C* will have a Chapter 13 interest in the trust.[174] Because *C*, a non-skip person, has an interest in the trust, the transfer of property to the trust is not a direct skip.[175] Any income distributions made to *GC* are taxable distributions.[176] If *C* predeceases *GC*, *C*'s interest terminates at death, and there is a taxable termination of the full value of the corpus.[177] There is another taxable termination at *GC*'s death.[178] If *GC* predeceases *C*, the corpus is distributed to *GGC* and both *C* and *GC*'s Chapter 13 interests terminate simultaneously upon the happening of a single event, and, according to the Treasury, only one taxable termination occurs.[179] Thus, by giving *GC*, a skip person, a nongeneral power of appointment to appoint trust property to *C*, a

---

[171] But see supra note 167 and the discussion at ¶ 10.04[3][e]. See also IRC §§ 2041(a)(3), 2514(d).

[172] IRC § 2612(c)(1). See supra ¶ 13.02[1][b] note 15.

[173] IRC § 2612(a)(1). Any income distributions to *GC* are not Section 2612(b) taxable distributions because *GC* is no longer a skip person by reason of Section 2653(a). See ¶ 17.03[1]; supra note 140.

[174] IRC § 2652(c)(1)(B).

[175] As a result of *C*'s interest, not all the Chapter 13 interests in the trust are held by skip persons. IRC § 2613(a)(2)(A). It is presumed that *C*'s interest is not disregarded under Section 2652(c)(2). Cf. supra text accompanying note 159. See IRC § 2613(a)(2)(B), which is also inapplicable because several persons hold Chapter 13 interests in the trust.

[176] IRC § 2612(b). See infra ¶ 13.02[3]. This will require the filing of a generation-skipping tax return in each year.

[177] IRC § 2612(a)(1). *C*'s Chapter 13 interest terminates, and, immediately thereafter, the only Chapter 13 interest in the trust property is held by *GC*, a skip person. This termination is a taxable termination of the full value of the corpus. Subsequent distributions of income to *GC* are not Section 2612(b) taxable distributions because *GC* is no longer a skip person by reason of Section 2653(a).

[178] IRC § 2612(a)(1).

[179] Reg. § 26.2612-1(f) Ex. 10. *C*'s Chapter 13 interest in the property terminates because *C* has a permissible right to receive corpus under *GC*'s exercise of a nongeneral power of appointment. IRC § 2652(c)(1)(B). *GC*'s right to income from the property also terminates. IRC § 2652(c)(1)(A). The property passes without being subject to federal estate or gift tax to GGC, who is a skip person, and a taxable termination results. IRC § 2612(a)(1)(A). Should the two terminations result in two taxable events at descending generational levels? See infra ¶ 13.02[2][g] note 206.

non-skip person, *G* defers the imposition of generation-skipping transfer tax, but may not decrease the number of Chapter 13 tax impositions on the corpus of the trust.[180]

[f] Terminations Followed by Multigenerational Interest Holders

The termination of a Chapter 13 interest[181] in property held in trust that does not result in a transfer subject to federal estate or gift tax[182] results in a taxable termination unless immediately thereafter a non-skip person[183] has a Chapter 13 interest in "*such property*,"[184] or if no one has such an interest immediately after the termination, no future distributions may be made to a skip person.[185] The termination of an interest in property held in trust followed by a distribution of all the trust property to both a skip person and a non-skip person will generally[186] prevent a distribution to a skip person[187] from being treated as a taxable termination.[188]

---

[180] Although the use of nongeneral powers may result in an effective deferral of Chapter 13 tax, the same number (but not the same taxable amounts) of Chapter 13 tax impositions may occur with respect to the corpus of a trust with or without the nongeneral power, assuming *GC* does not exercise the nongeneral power of appointment over the corpus in favor of *C*. There would have been a direct skip on the initial transfer if there was no nongeneral power because no non-skip person would have had an interest in the trust. See supra text accompanying note 172. At *GC*'s death there would be a taxable termination when the trust property passed to *GGC*. With the nongeneral power, there may be one or two taxable terminations of corpus: (1) if *C* predeceases *GC*, there is one at the death of *C*, a permissible appointee, and a second at the death of *GC*, the income beneficiary; and (2) if *GC* predeceases *C*, one event triggers the simultaneous termination of *GC*'s and *C*'s Chapter 13 interests (see supra note 179), and according to the Treasury this results in only one taxable termination. Reg. § 26.2612-1(f) Ex. 10. See supra note 169; infra ¶ 13.02[2][g] note 206. However, there are also numerous potential taxable distributions of income requiring numerous generation-skipping tax returns, although not necessarily significant amounts of generation-skipping transfers. See supra note 176.

[181] IRC §§ 2652(c)(1)(A), 2652(c)(1)(B).

[182] Reg. § 26.2612-1(b)(1)(i). See supra ¶ 13.02[2][d].

[183] IRC § 2613(b).

[184] IRC § 2612(a)(1)(A) (emphasis added).

[185] IRC § 2612(a)(1)(B). See IRC § 2613(a). Skip persons are discussed at ¶¶ 13.03[1]–13.03[4].

[186] But see infra text accompanying notes 189 and 190.

[187] The distribution to the skip person may result in a Section 2612(b) taxable distribution. See infra ¶ 13.02[3]. If the distribution resulted in a federal estate or gift taxable event to the transferor, it would constitute a direct skip rather than a taxable distribution. See IRC §§ 2612(b) (parenthetical), 2612(c)(1); infra ¶ 13.02[4]. The distribution to a non-skip person is not a generation-skipping transfer.

[188] A taxable termination does not occur if a non-skip person has an interest in "such property" immediately after the termination of a Chapter 13 interest in the property held in trust. IRC § 2612(a)(1)(A). "[S]uch property" refers to the trust property subject to the

Certain distributions that, strictly speaking,[189] are not taxable terminations are, with some statutory assistance, treated as taxable terminations. Section 2612(a)(2) provides: "If, upon the termination of an interest in property held in trust by reason of the death of a lineal descendant of the transferor, a specified portion of the trust's assets are distributed to one or more skip persons (or one or more trusts for the exclusive benefit of such persons), such termination shall constitute a taxable termination with respect to such portion of the trust property."[190] To illustrate the operation of Section 2612(a)(2), assume that transferor T establishes a trust, the income to be paid to son S for life. The remainder is to be divided equally between daughter D and granddaughter GD. When death terminates the interest of S, one half of the trust property is held outright by a non-skip person, D, and one-half is held by a skip person, GD. The distribution is not a taxable termination under Section 2612(a)(1) because D, a non-skip person, has an interest (outright ownership) in the property for-

---

Chapter 13 interest that terminated. Section 2612(a)(1)(A) should not be read to permit a taxable termination where a portion of the property subject to the interest that terminated passes to a skip person and a portion to a non-skip person. For example, assume that Transferor T establishes a trust, the income to be paid to T's nephew for life, with remainder to be divided equally between T's niece and the nephew's children. When death terminates the interest of the nephew, one half of the trust property is distributed to a non-skip person (the niece) and one-half to skip persons (the nephew's children). At that time, there is no Section 2612(a)(1) taxable termination of the interest, even to the extent the property passes to the nephew's children, because part of "such property" passed to the niece, a non-skip person. However, the distribution to the nephew's children does constitute a Section 2612(b) taxable distribution. If the property continues to be held in the trust for the niece and for the nephew's children, rather than distributed outright to the beneficiaries, there is no taxable termination at the nephew's death. Even if the Section 2654(b)(2) separate share rule applied at the nephew's death (see ¶ 17.04[2]), there would be no taxable termination. See infra text accompanying notes 197–200.

If the term "such property" in Section 2612(a)(1)(A) were interpreted to result in a taxable termination where a portion of the property subject to the interest that terminated passes to a skip person and a portion passes to a non-skip person, there would be no need for Section 2612(a)(2). That section would become excess verbiage. It might be administratively convenient for the Service to treat such terminations as taxable terminations rather than taxable distributions so that the reporting and tax-paying responsibility would lie with the trustee of the trust rather than the distributees. See IRC §§ 2603(a), 2662(a). However, such an administratively convenient interpretation would both thwart the statutory language and render Section 2612(a)(2) superfluous and, as such, would be an inappropriate exercise of administrative power by the Service without a statutory amendment by Congress.

[189] See infra text accompanying notes 191–193.

[190] See Reg. §§ 26.2612-1(b)(2), 26.2612-1(f) Ex. 11. It is assumed that a transfer subject to federal estate or gift tax does not occur with respect to the property held in the trust at the time of the termination. Reg. § 26.2612-1(b)(1)(i). See supra ¶ 13.02[2][d]. If the property held in the trust is subject to federal estate or gift tax at the time of termination, there is a direct skip and no taxable termination occurs.

merly held in the now-terminated trust.[191] However, because there is a termination of an interest upon the death of a lineal descendant of the transferor, *S*, and a portion of the trust assets is distributed to a non-skip person, *D*, the distribution to *GD* satisfies the Section 2612(a)(2) requirements of a taxable termination and is treated as such.[192] There is no taxable termination of the interest to the extent of the portion of the property that passes to *D*, because immediately after the termination of *S*'s Chapter 13 interest, a non-skip person, *D*, owns the property.[193]

The Section 2612(a)(2) rule applies where the property is distributed to a trust,[194] or where part of the property is distributed outright and a part remains in the trust.[195] When a person's Chapter 13 interest in property held in trust terminates and such interest continues to be held in trust but shifts to both skip persons and non-skip persons and no actual distribution of trust property occurs, a taxable termination generally is prevented by the non-skip person's possession of a Chapter 13 interest in the trust property.[196] Because no actual distribution of trust property occurs, the Section 2612(a)(2) rule is also inapplicable. However, the separate share rule of Section 2654(b)(2) may apply. Under the separate share rule, if skip persons and non-skip persons have substantially separate and independent shares in a trust and those shares existed from the creation of the trust, the shares are treated as separate trusts.[197] If the separate share rule applies,[198] the separate share of trust property held for the

---

[191] IRC § 2612(a)(1)(A). See supra note 187. The distribution to *GD* does satisfy the requirements of a taxable distribution. IRC § 2612(b). See infra ¶ 13.02[3].

[192] IRC § 2612(a)(2). Cf. IRC § 2612(b) (parenthetical). If Transferor *T* had established a trust with income to be paid to *T*'s nephew for life, remainder to be divided equally between *T*'s niece and *T*'s nephew's children, on the nephew's death, Section 2612(a)(2) would not apply because the nephew is not a lineal descendant of the transferor. The distribution to the nephew's children would constitute a taxable distribution. See supra text accompanying notes 186–188.

[193] IRC § 2612(a)(1)(A). Later, when the daughter dies or transfers the property by gift, that portion of the property will be taxed under Chapter 11 or Chapter 12.

[194] If the corpus of the original trust in the hypothetical in the text had been distributed to two separate trusts, one for *D* for life with a remainder to her children, and the second to *GD* for life with a remainder to her children, *GD*'s trust would be a Section 2613(a)(2)(A) skip person, and Section 2612(a)(2) would treat the transfer to *GD*'s trust as a taxable termination.

[195] Reg. § 26.2612-1(f) Ex. 11.

[196] See IRC § 2612(a)(1)(A).

[197] IRC § 2654(b)(2). See Reg. § 26.2654-1(a)(1)(i); ¶ 17.04[2]. If the trust has an inclusion ratio of between zero and one, it is possible, even likely, that the trust would have been severed in a Section 2642(a)(3) "qualified severance." See ¶ 16.02[5][e]. The qualifed severance rule will have the effect of narrowing the application of the Section 2612(a)(2) rule.

[198] See infra note 199.

skip person after the termination of the prior interest would be a Section 2612(a)(1)(A) taxable termination.

For example, assume grantor G establishes a trust, the income to be paid to son S for life, then the income to be split equally between daughter D and granddaughter GD and, at the death of either, the distribution of one half of the trust corpus to that beneficiary's children. At S's death, it appears that there is no taxable termination under Section 2612(a)(1)(A) because D, a non-skip person, has an interest in the trust, and Section 2612(a)(2) does not create a taxable termination because no actual distribution of trust property occurs. However, the separate share rule should apply[199] to divide the single trust into two separate trusts, one for D and one for GD, and upon S's death, there would be a Section 2612(a)(1) taxable termination of GD's separate share trust.[200] If the separate share rule does not apply and the trust is not separated, there is no taxable termination at S's death, but there are taxable distributions to GD as one half of the income of the trust is paid to GD.

[g] Simultaneous Terminations

When one individual possesses multiple Chapter 13 interests in the property held in a trust and the occurrence of a single event results in the simultaneous termination of each Chapter 13 interest, only one taxable termination of that individual's interests occurs.[201] For example, assume parent P established an irrevocable trust with the income payable to child C for life, remainder to grandchild GC, and the trustee was granted the power to invade the corpus of the trust for the benefit of C. C has two Chapter 13 interests, the right to receive the income from the trust[202] and the possible receipt of trust corpus under the trustee's currently exercisable power to invade corpus for C.[203] Upon the death of C, both of these Chapter 13 interests terminate, resulting in a single taxable termination generation-skipping transfer.

If the occurrence of a single event causes the simultaneous termination of the Chapter 13 interests of multiple beneficiaries assigned to the same generation level, there is only one taxable termination generation-skipping transfer. For example, assume that a parent established a trust with the income payable

---

[199] IRC § 2654(b)(2). It may be argued that the separate share rule does not apply here because separate shares did not exist from the creation of the trust as is required by the regulations, but that they existed only after S's death. Reg. § 26.2654-1(a)(1)(i). If S's interest can be bifurcated at the creation of the trust, the regulatory requirement is met. This would seem to be the appropriate result. Cf. supra note 197

[200] If the separate share rule applies at the creation of the trust, GST exemption may be allocated to either separate share trust. See ¶ 15.02.

[201] Reg. § 26.2612-1(b)(3).

[202] IRC § 2652(c)(1)(A).

[203] IRC § 2652(c)(1)(B).

in the discretion of the trustee to either of two children for parent's life with the remainder to a grandchild. A single event, the death of the parent, triggers the termination of the Chapter 13 interest of both children. Although the Chapter 13 interests of two individual beneficiaries terminate, there is a single taxable termination generation-skipping transfer when the trust terminates and the property is distributed to the grandchild.[204]

Even when a single event results in the simultaneous termination of the Chapter 13 interests of multiple beneficiaries assigned to different generation levels, the Treasury has taken the position that there is a single taxable termination generation-skipping transfer.[205] For example, assume that parent P established a trust providing that all income for P's life be distributed to child C, grandchild GC, or great-grandchild GGC in such amounts as the trustee discretionarily determines, with the remainder to GGC. The death of P, whose life measures the term of the trust, simultaneously terminates the Chapter 13 interests as permissible current noncharitable recipients of trust income of C, GC, and GGC. The Treasury's position is that P's death results in a single taxable termination generation-skipping transfer as the property passes outright to GGC.[206]

---

[204] Reg. § 26.2612-1(b)(3). The generation-skipping transfer tax was designed to bite only once at each generation level. See IRC § 2611(b)(2); ¶ 13.01[2][b]. See also IRC § 2653(a); ¶ 17.03[1].

[205] Reg. § 26.2612-1(f) Ex. 10.

[206] Reg. § 26.2612-1(f) Ex. 10. See Reg. § 26.2612-1(b)(3). This one example, which is quite significant from a Chapter 13 policy perspective, appears in the regulations without any other comment in the body of the regulations or the supplementary information accompanying the regulations. In the prior edition of this book, the authors took the position that when a single event resulted in the simultaneous termination of the Chapter 13 interests of individuals assigned different generation levels below the grantor, multiple taxable terminations occurred. See, Stephens, Maxfield, Lind & Calfee, Federal Estate and Gift Taxation ¶ 13.02[d], text accompanying notes 150, 160 (Warren, Gorham & Lamont, 6th ed. 1991). Admittedly, when any type of generation-skipping transfer (taxable distribution, taxable termination, or direct skip) results in the property skipping multiple generations, there is but one generation-skipping transfer. See supra ¶ 13.02[2][c] text accompanying note 71, infra ¶ 13.02[3][b] text following note 217, infra ¶ 13.02[4][a] text accompanying note 244. Even this approach may be questioned as a policy matter when an objective to be achieved with the imposition of the generation-skipping transfer tax is to achieve greater uniformity in the imposition of wealth transfer taxes. See infra ¶ 13.02[4][a] text accompanying note 244. To provide that there is only one taxable termination when a single event results in the simultaneous termination of the interests of beneficiaries assigned to different generation levels below the grantor is another matter.

From a policy perspective, this regulatory exemption of certain taxable terminations is inconsistent with the purposes behind and the construction of Chapter 13. The initial version of the generation-skipping transfer tax enacted in 1976 took a bite out of wealth accumulation in each generation where, between the persons who had outright ownership of property, there were others in intervening generations who had some interest in or power over the property. A person had an interest as a permissible recipient of income or

[3] Taxable Distributions

[a] Introduction

The tax on generation-skipping transfers is generally thought of as substantially equivalent to the estate and gift taxes that would have been imposed had the property actually been transferred outright down through each succes-

---

corpus. Direct transfers of property that skipped over generations where, between the persons who had outright ownership of the property, there were others in intervening generations who had no interest in or power over the property were initially free of tax. In the second version of the generation-skipping transfer tax enacted in 1986, the tax base was broadened to include the imposition of the Chapter 13 tax on direct skip transfers, where the intervening generations were not permissible recipients of income or corpus, to create a greater uniformity in the imposition of the federal wealth transmission taxes. The 1986 version retained the taxation of wealth transmission where the intervening generations had an interest in or power over the property. The fact that a particular generation level has an interest in or power over the property results in the entire property being subjected to the tax imposed by Chapter 13 regardless of whether the generation level actually receives any tangible pecuniary rewards. The mere possibility of current benefit is sufficient to incur a Chapter 13 tax. For example, if parent P establishes a trust in which an independent trustee may distribute or accumulate income to child C for C's life with a remainder to grandchild GC, and all of the income is accumulated, there is a taxable termination generation-skipping transfer at C's death even though C received no tangible pecuniary reward. The regulation example only taxes family wealth transmission to the extent of actual benefit and the fact that multiple generation levels may benefit is treated as only one level benefiting, as long as a single event terminates the Chapter 13 interests of those assigned to different generation levels. This is inconsistent with the theory to impose the Chapter 13 tax where generations have had a Chapter 13 interest in the property that terminates without the imposition of the federal estate or gift tax, as well as to tax where a generation has been skipped and enjoys no Chapter 13 interest. It is possible to structure wealth transmission to have different generations of a family enjoy the wealth and then avoid transmission taxes as the wealth moves on to a younger generation. For example, assume parent P establishes a trust in which the income may be distributed in the trustee's discretion to child C, grandchild GC, or great-grandchild GGC until the death of C, GC, or GGC, when the property passes to GGC or GGC's estate. If any generation level needs funds, they are available (although any distribution of funds to GC or GGC is a taxable distribution), and any funds not needed may be passed to GGC with the imposition of only one generation-skipping transfer tax although two other generation levels have had a Chapter 13 interest in the property. The bottom line is that a generation possessing a Chapter 13 interest in the property has been skipped for generation-skipping transfer tax purposes, a skipped generation-skipping transfer.

When those individuals classified as skip persons receive distributions prior to the termination of their interests, those distributions are classified as taxable distributions and are subject to the tax imposed by Chapter 13. It seems inconsistent to treat an individual who is a mere noncharitable permissible recipient of income or corpus as having a Chapter 13 interest in a trust, which upon termination results in the property being subject to the tax imposed by Chapter 13, and then treat someone who actually is benefiting from the trust, or is merely a permissible recipient, as having his or her interest terminated and not being subjected to federal estate, gift, or generation-skipping transfer tax.

Section 2612

sive descending generation, without the hiatuses afforded by trusts, forward gifts, and similar devices. Had the tax on generation-skipping transfers been imposed only upon the termination of an interest, when the benefits of a fund passed to a skip person or on direct skips, it would have been quite simple to avoid the tax entirely. The tax could have been avoided by merely shifting the benefits in the fund by a distribution to the desired skip person prior to any tainting termination and without incurring any estate or gift tax required in a direct skip. The imposition of a tax on taxable distributions effects a stopgap to support the transfer tax that may be imposed on terminations of an interest and on direct skips in a manner similar to that in which the gift tax backstops the estate tax.

A taxable distribution[207] is any distribution from a trust[208] to a skip person[209] that is not a direct skip[210] or a taxable termination.[211] The distribution may be from current or accumulated income or from corpus. Additionally, when Chapter 13 tax is incurred on a taxable distribution and the tax is paid using trust assets, the tax payment is also treated as a taxable distribution.[212]

[b] Basic Taxable Distributions

Any distribution from a trust is classified as a taxable distribution if it satisfies two requirements: (1) The distribution must be to a skip person,[213] and (2) the distribution must be neither a taxable termination nor a direct skip.[214]

[i] **First requirement: distribution to a skip person.** The first requirement is satisfied by any required or discretionary distribution of income or

---

[207] Certain transfers that are taxable distributions are excluded by Section 2611(b) and are not generation-skipping transfers. Transfers for educational and medical expenses are excluded by Section 2611(b)(1). See ¶ 13.01[2][a]. For example, assume grantor *G* creates a trust with income to child for life, but *G* gives the trustee the power to use income to pay grandchild's tuition directly to the university. Any tuition paid is a taxable distribution, but it is subject to the Section 2611(b)(1) exclusion, and it is not a generation-skipping transfer. In addition, some transfers previously subjected to the tax on generation-skipping transfers are excluded by Section 2611(b)(2). See ¶ 13.01[2][b].

[208] Again, the term "trust" includes any trust equivalent arrangement. IRC §§ 2652(b)(1), 2652(b)(3). See ¶ 17.02[2].

[209] IRC § 2613(a). See ¶ 13.03.

[210] IRC § 2612(c). See IRC § 2612(b) (parenthetical); infra ¶ 13.02[4].

[211] IRC § 2612(a). See IRC § 2612(b) (parenthetical); supra ¶ 13.02[2].

[212] IRC § 2621(b). See infra ¶ 13.02[3][c].

[213] IRC §§ 2612(b), 2613(a).

[214] IRC § 2612(b) (parenthetical).

corpus to a skip person. The skip person may be an individual[215] or a trust.[216] A taxable distribution that benefits a skip person who is more than two generations below the level of the transferor results in only a single taxable distribution. Thus, if transferor *T* creates an irrevocable trust with income to child *C* for life and the remainder to grandchild *GC*, and *T* gives an independent trustee the power to invade corpus for the benefit of *C* or *GC*, the trustee's invasion for *GC* is a taxable distribution.[217] If, instead, the trustee is given invasion power for the benefit of *T*'s great-grandchild *GGC*, a skip person who is more than two generations below *T*'s generation, and the trustee exercises the power for the benefit of *GGC*, such invasion is treated as a single taxable distribution even though two generations are skipped.

In determining whether a taxable distribution is made to a skip person, the multiple skip rule of Section 2653(a),[218] which relocates a transferor's generation level after a prior generation-skipping transfer if the property is held in trust, plays an important role. If transferor *T* creates an irrevocable trust with income to *GC* (whose parents are alive) for life and a remainder to *GGC*, the creation of the trust is a direct skip.[219] If an independent trustee also holds a power to invade corpus for *GC*, neither income distributions nor corpus invasions by the independent trustee for the benefit of *GC* constitute taxable distributions, because *T* will be treated as assigned to *C*'s generation as a result of Section 2653(a) and *GC* will no longer be a Section 2613(a)(1) skip person.

Although the statute is silent regarding the possibility of a constructive distribution from trusts or equivalent arrangements, the use of trust assets to secure a loan to a skip person beneficiary or a trustee's loan to a skip person beneficiary, especially if the loan is unsecured and bears little or no interest,

---

[215] IRC § 2613(a)(1). An individual is a skip person if assigned to a generation level two or more generation levels below the transferor. See ¶ 13.03[2].

[216] IRC § 2613(a)(2). A trust is classified as a skip person if all persons with Chapter 13 interests in the trust are skip persons. IRC § 2613(a)(2)(A). See ¶ 13.03[3][a]. If no person has such an interest in the trust, the trust is classified as a skip person only if no distribution from the trust may be made to a non-skip person. IRC § 2613(a)(2)(B). See ¶ 13.03[3][b]. The possibility of a distribution to a non-skip person that is so remote as to be negligible is disregarded. Reg. § 26.2612-1(d)(2)(ii). See ¶ 13.03[3] note 24.

The look-through rules apply in the classification of a trust as a skip person or non-skip person. They do not apply to treat a transfer to a trust as a transfer to the individual beneficiaries of the trust for any purposes other than classification of the trust. Reg. § 26.2612-1(c)(2). See infra ¶¶ 13.02[4][b][iii], 13.03[3][a].

[217] If the trustee invades the corpus to satisfy *C*'s obligation to support *GC*, the distribution would be treated as a distribution to *C*, a non-skip person, and it would not be a taxable distribution. See supra ¶ 13.02[2][b] note 55.

[218] See ¶ 17.03[1].

[219] IRC § 2612(c)(1). Cf. IRC § 2651(e).

may be treated as a taxable distribution.[220] Similarly, a distribution to a non-skip person with the understanding that the non-skip person will retransfer it to a skip person should also be treated as a constructive taxable distribution.

[ii] **Second requirement: not a taxable termination or a direct skip.** Any distribution to a skip person that simultaneously satisfies the requirements of a direct skip or a taxable termination is not a taxable distribution.[221] A distribution to a skip person that is subject to a tax imposed by either Chapter 11 or Chapter 12 is treated as a direct skip,[222] not a taxable distribution.[223] For example, if a transferor creates an inter vivos revocable trust, there would be no direct skip upon the transfer of property to the trust, because the property transferred would not have been subjected to the imposition of tax under Chapter 12 because of the revocable nature of the transfer. Section 2653(a) would also be inapplicable under these circumstances. All income or corpus distributions from the trust to skip persons will be subject to imposition of Chapter 12 tax and will result in Section 2612(c)(1) direct skips, thereby rendering the taxable distribution provision inapplicable.[224]

A taxable termination also overrides a taxable distribution, but differentiating a taxable termination from a taxable distribution is not always an easy task.[225] When an individual's interest in a trust terminates and all the trust property is distributed outright to a named individual who is a skip person, there is both a taxable termination and a taxable distribution, and the termina-

---

[220] Regulations proposed for the now-repealed 1976 version of the generation-skipping transfer tax, as well as the legislative history accompanying the 1976 version of Chapter 13, discussed this possibility. See (now repealed) Prop. Reg. § 26.2613-1(f)(1), 1981-1 CB 713, 718; HR Rep. No. 1380, 94th Cong., 2d Sess. 52 (1976), reprinted in 1976-3 CB (Vol. 3) 735, 786. The regulations would have applied if the loan were not a bona fide loan or if trust assets were used as security under an invalid security arrangement. Id. Cf. IRC § 7872(a); Dickman v. Comm'r, 465 US 330 (1984).

[221] IRC § 2612(b) (parenthetical). See supra ¶ 13.02[2][f]; infra ¶ 13.02[4][a] text accompanying notes 246, 247.

[222] If a transfer was not treated as a direct skip by reason of the $2 million exclusion afforded direct skips to grandchildren (see infra ¶ 13.02[4][c][ii]), it was not treated as a taxable distribution. See infra ¶ 13.02[4][c] text accompanying notes 325–328. If a transfer was not treated as a direct skip by reason of Section 2612(c)(2), prior to its replacement by Section 2651(e), which previously precluded direct skips to certain grandchildren whose parents were deceased at the time of the transfer, it was not treated as a taxable distribution. See Taxpayer Relief Act of 1997, Pub. L. No. 105-34, § 511(b)(1), 111 Stat. 788, 861 (1997), reprinted in 1997-4 CB (Vol. 1) 1, 75.

[223] IRC § 2612(c)(1). See infra ¶ 13.02[4][b].

[224] See IRC § 2612(b) (parenthetical). See ¶ 15.03[3][b].

[225] See supra ¶ 13.02[1][b].

tion overrides the distribution.[226] The taxable distribution classification prevails if there is a distribution without the termination of an interest, assuming the distribution is not subject to the tax imposed by Chapter 11 or Chapter 12.[227] Assuming the separate share rule is inapplicable[228] when an interest in property held in a trust terminates, and, thereafter, both skip persons and non-skip persons have an interest in that property,[229] any distributions to skip persons will generally be treated as taxable distributions.[230] However, when a termination of an interest is attributable to the death of a lineal descendant of the transferor, and thereafter a specified portion of the property held in the trust is distributed to one or more skip persons (or to trusts for their exclusive benefit), the distribution is treated as a taxable termination, not a taxable distribution.[231]

[c] Tax-Payment Taxable Distributions

When a taxable distribution occurs, the liability for payment of the generation-skipping transfer tax tax is imposed on the skip person transferee.[232] If

---

[226] IRC § 2612(b) (parenthetical). If the distribution met the statutory requirements of a taxable distribution, a taxable termination, and a direct skip, it is treated as a direct skip. See supra ¶ 13.02[1][b] notes 11–14.

If the trust were a charitable remainder unitrust, a charitable remainder annuity trust, or pooled income fund with the income interest to the grantor's child for life, then to grandchildren for life, and remainder to charity, the charity is a non-skip person. At the child's death, there would be no taxable termination (see IRC § 2612(a)(1)(A)), and, as a result, when the income is distributed to the grandchildren, there would be taxable distributions.

[227] See Reg. §§ 26.2612-1(f) Exs. 12–13.

[228] IRC § 2654(b). See ¶ 17.04[2]; infra note 231.

[229] This is so regardless of whether the trust itself terminates.

[230] See supra ¶ 13.02[2][f] text accompanying notes 181–188.

[231] IRC § 2612(a)(2). The application of the Section 2612(a)(2) rule is narrowed by the application of the Section 2642(a)(3) "qualified severance" rule and the application of the Section 2654(b) separate share rule. For example, if transferor T created an irrevocable trust with income equally to T's two children for life, but on the death of the predeceasing child, one half of the corpus would be distributed to that child's children (T's grandchildren), the trust would be separated and treated as two trusts, one of which would terminate under a Section 2612(a) taxable termination, precluding any consideration of a taxable distribution. Assume instead that, at one child's death, one quarter of the corpus was distributed to that child's children, but three quarters of the corpus remains in the trust with all income to the surviving child for life, and the remainder to be split one-third to the predeceasing child's children, and two-thirds to the surviving child's children. Here, the Section 2654(b) separate share rule seemingly is inapplicable, but the Section 2612(a)(2) rule applies to treat the distribution of one quarter of the corpus to the grandchildren as a taxable termination. See supra ¶ 13.02[2][f].

[232] IRC § 2603(a)(1). Cf. IRC § 164(a)(4), discussed ¶ 14.02[4] note 21.

any portion of the transferee's obligation is paid out of trust funds, however, the trust is indirectly making another taxable distribution to the skip person.[233]

Section 2621(b) treats the payment out of trust funds of any portion of the Chapter 13 tax on a taxable distribution as an additional Section 2612(b) taxable distribution. Although payment out of trust assets of the tax on the taxable distribution may be made after the close of the taxable year in which the distribution occurs, the tax-generated taxable distribution is treated as occurring in the same year as the taxable distribution that caused the imposition of tax.[234] The additional Section 2612(b) taxable distribution under Section 2621(b) is treated as having been made on the last day of the calendar year in which the original taxable distribution is made.[235] Increasing the tax base of the original taxable distribution by the Chapter 13 tax paid out of trust funds in a succeeding year transgresses the taxable year concepts employed in the determination of a taxable distribution.[236] Nevertheless, it is possible to determine the tax, even if it is not paid until a later year, employing a gross-up approach to determine the total amount of the taxable distributions. An interdependent variable computation will yield the amount of the Chapter 13 tax on the basic taxable distribution and on the tax-generated taxable distribution.[237] Although application of the gross-up approach accelerates the time for payment of the Chapter 13 tax imposed, it simplifies administration, thereby reducing the time and administrative costs incurred in the determination of any Chapter 13 tax and in return preparation.[238]

---

[233] IRC § 2621(b). See ¶ 14.02[4].

[234] Reg. § 26.2612-1(c)(1). Tax imposed by Chapter 13 on a taxable distribution is payable on the due date of the return, on or before the fifteenth day of the fourth month after the close of the calendar year in which the taxable distribution occurs. IRC § 2662(a)(2)(B). See Reg. § 26.2662-1(d)(1)(ii).

[235] Reg. § 26.2612-1(c)(1).

[236] IRC § 2662(a)(2)(B).

[237] The amount of the Chapter 13 tax imposed on any generation-skipping transfer is dependent upon the amount of the transfer, and the amount of the generation-skipping transfer is dependent on the amount of the tax imposed by Chapter 13 that is paid out of trust funds. For example, assume that there is a $1 million taxable distribution, no use of the Section 2631 GST exemption, and a 50 percent generation-skipping tax rate. If the Chapter 13 tax imposed on the $1 million taxable distribution is paid out of the trust, an additional taxable distribution under Section 2621(b) of $1 million is treated as being made on the last day of the taxable year in which the original $1 million taxable distribution is made.

[238] Assume that there is a $1 million taxable distribution in year 1, no use of the Section 2631 GST exemption, and a 50 percent generation-skipping transfer tax rate. Assume that any generation-skipping transfer tax imposed will be paid by the distributee and that additional trust distributions will be made to the distributee to pay the Chapter 13 tax imposed on any taxable distribution. In year 2, $500,000 is *distributed to the distributee* to facilitate the payment of the Chapter 13 tax imposed on the $1 million taxable distribution in year 1. The year 2 taxable distribution of $500,000 necessitates a distribution in year 3

[4] Direct Skips

[a] Introduction

The third type of generation-skipping transfer is the direct skip,[239] which is defined as a transfer of an interest in property to a skip person[240] that is subject to either estate tax or gift tax.[241] Generation-skipping transfers that are classified as direct skips result in the simultaneous imposition of two taxes: (1) the gift tax or estate tax (whichever is applicable) and (2) the generation-skipping transfer tax.

Prior to 1986, under the now-repealed generation-skipping transfer tax, an outright transfer of an interest in property to a person assigned to a generation level two or more levels below the transferor's level, although subject to the imposition of an estate tax or gift tax, was not subject to the tax imposed on generation-skipping transfers. This lack of uniformity in the imposition of the generation-skipping transfer tax under the old regime favored very wealthy individuals who could reduce the impact of the federal wealth transfer taxes by employing direct skips to transfer their wealth to subsequent generations.[242]

Congressional concern about the lack of uniformity in the imposition of wealth transfer taxes led in 1986 to the expansion of the generation-skipping

---

of $250,000 to the distributee to pay the Chapter 13 tax imposed on the year 2 taxable distribution. The year 3 taxable distribution will yield another taxable distribution in year 4, and so on ad infinitum. Ultimately, $1 million of generation-skipping transfer tax will be paid, the same amount of generation-skipping transfer tax incurred where the Chapter 13 tax on the initial $1 million taxable distribution in year 1 is paid from the trust assets and the amount of the initial distribution grossed up for the Section 2621(b) tax payment taxable distribution. Where Section 2621(b) is not triggered, the liability for the Chapter 13 tax on the initial $1 million taxable distribution may be structured and spread out ad infinitum. Spreading the tax to be paid over multiple years may result in substantial time value of money savings.

[239] IRC § 2611(a)(3).

[240] IRC § 2612(c)(1). "Skip person" is defined in Section 2613(a). See ¶¶ 13.03[1]–13.03[4].

[241] IRC § 2612(c)(1). The estate and gift taxes are imposed by Chapters 11 and 12, respectively, of the Code of 1986. See Reg. § 26.2652-1(a)(2).

[242] Consider, for example, the three generations of a family represented by a grandparent, a child, and a grandchild. If the family's wealth was sufficient to satisfy the child's needs without requiring the grandparent to transfer wealth to the child either outright or in trust, the grandparent could have transferred all the wealth to the grandchild and been liable for only one wealth transfer tax, the estate tax or gift tax. If it was necessary for the grandparent to provide for the child, the grandparent could have transferred the wealth into trust, with the income payable to the child for life and a remainder to the grandchild, thereby incurring two wealth transfer taxes: the estate tax or gift tax at the time the property was transferred into trust and a generation-skipping transfer tax at the child's death, when there would be a Section 2612(a)(1) taxable termination.

transfer tax base generally to include direct skips.[243] In its effort to close this apparent gap in the statutory framework, Congress made a major policy change from prior law. Under the prior generation-skipping transfer tax, the members of a generation on which no wealth transfer tax was imposed enjoyed some benefits of the property during their lives. If a grandparent established a trust with income to a child for life and a remainder to a grandchild, there would be a taxable termination generation-skipping transfer at the child's death, but the child would have enjoyed the benefits of the income generated by the property that skipped transfer taxation.

Under the 1986 version of Chapter 13, a tax is imposed on generation skips even where the skipped generation does not enjoy the property. While Congress imposes a tax on a completely skipped generation, Congress does not necessarily impose a tax on each skipped generation. For example, an individual's transfer of property to a great-grandchild skips two generations, the transferor's children and grandchildren, yet there is only one direct skip, and only one generation-skipping transfer tax is imposed. Overall, the property will pass through four generations with the imposition of only three transfer taxes. One transfer tax will be imposed at the transferor's generation level, another on the direct skip, and the third will be imposed upon the great-grandchild's disposition of the property. If that same property were to pass down to and through each generation level, a wealth transfer tax would be imposed four times, once at each generation level. Consequently, the reduction of wealth transfer taxes by the direct skip method is more readily available to families of very substantial means whose wealth is sufficient to satisfy the needs of family members without making outright or trust transfers benefiting family members at each generation level.

Perhaps from the prospective of policy purity, Congress should have gone a step further and imposed a generation-skipping transfer tax at each generation level that is skipped to achieve greater uniformity in the imposition of wealth transfer taxes. However, it should be recognized that the imposition of only one generation-skipping transfer tax on a multigenerational direct skip is balanced by the imposition of only one generation-skipping transfer tax on a multigenerational taxable distribution or taxable termination.[244]

---

[243] HR Rep. No. 426, 99th Cong., 2d Sess. 824 (1986), reprinted in 1986-3 CB (Vol. 2) 1, 824.

[244] See Reg. § 26.2612-1(f) Ex. 2; supra ¶ 13.02[2][c] text accompanying note 71, supra ¶ 13.02[2][g] text accompanying notes 205–206, supra ¶ 13.02[3][b] text following note 217. If Congress decides to impose a generation-skipping transfer tax at each generation level in a multigenerational direct skip, it must apply the same treatment to a multigenerational taxable distribution and a multigenerational taxable termination.

A direct skip may occur upon the direct or indirect transfer of property to an individual or to or from a trust.[245] If a particular transfer simultaneously satisfies the statutory criteria of a direct skip and a taxable distribution,[246] the transfer is treated as a direct skip.[247] A transfer cannot simultaneously satisfy the criteria of a direct skip and a taxable termination.[248]

The liability for any generation-skipping tax that results from a direct skip is generally imposed on the transferor or trustee.[249] If the direct skip is an inter vivos transfer, payment of the Chapter 13 tax imposed on the transferor is treated by Section 2515 (a gift tax provision) as an additional gift, thereby increasing the amount of the Chapter 12 gift by the amount of the Chapter 13 tax.[250]

As with most tax rules, the direct skip rule has been subject to exceptions,[251] some more equitable than others. For example, certain transfers to grandchildren before January 1, 1990, that, in the aggregate, did not exceed $2 million were not treated as direct skips.[252] In addition, some transfers that are direct skips are excluded from generation-skipping transfer status by Section 2611(b).[253]

---

[245] See Sections 2613(a)(1) and 2613(a)(2) for the definition of a "skip person" to whom a direct skip must be made.

[246] IRC § 2612(b).

[247] IRC § 2612(b) (parenthetical).

[248] Reg. § 26.2612-1(b)(1)(i). See supra ¶ 13.02[2][d].

[249] IRC §§ 2603(a)(2), 2603(a)(3). See ¶ 12.03[1].

[250] See ¶ 10.05. For example, assuming a 50 percent tax rate and no exclusions or exemptions, the Chapter 13 tax on a $1 million inter vivos gift made after 1989 to a grandchild whose parent is still alive would be $500,000. Section 2511 would treat the $1 million as a completed gift subject to Chapter 12 tax and Section 2515 would treat the $500,000 payment of Chapter 13 tax as an additional gift, resulting in total taxable gifts of $1.5 million ($1 million under Section 2511 and $500,000 under Section 2515) and $750,000 of gift tax liability. The total federal transfer tax on the $1 million transfer would be $1.25 million ($500,000 under Chapter 13 and $750,000 under Chapter 12). See generally ¶ 12.02 notes 31–33.

[251] See infra ¶ 13.02[4][c].

[252] Tax Reform Act of 1986, Pub. L. No. 99-514, §§ 1433(b)(3), 1433(d), 100 Stat. 2085, 2731 (1986), reprinted in 1986-3 CB (Vol. 1) 1, 648, as amended by the Technical & Miscellaneous Revenue Act of 1988, Pub. L. No. 100-647, § 1014(h)(3)(A), 102 Stat. 3342, 3567–3568 (1988), reprinted in 1988-3 CB 1, 227. See infra ¶ 13.02[4][c][ii].

[253] Excluded are certain testamentary transfers for educational and medical expenses (Section 2611(b)(1)) and certain transfers to the extent previously subjected to the Chapter 13 tax (Section 2611(b)(2)). IRC § 2611(b), discussed at ¶ 13.01[2].

[b] General Rule

A transfer is generally a direct skip if it satisfies two requirements: (1) The transfer must be subject to a tax imposed by Chapter 11 or Chapter 12, and (2) it must be a transfer of an interest in property to a skip person.[254]

[i] First requirement: transfer subject to estate or gift tax.

The statute specifies that only transfers "subject to a tax imposed by Chapter 11 or Chapter 12" qualify as direct skips. A precise meaning must be accorded the phrase "subject to a tax imposed by Chapter 11 or 12." Chapter 11 imposes a tax on "the taxable estate of every decedent who is a citizen or resident of the United States."[255] Chapter 11 also imposes a tax on the taxable estate[256] of any decedent who is a "nonresident not a citizen of the United States."[257] Chapter 12 imposes a tax on the transfer of property by gift "by any individual, resident or non-resident."[258]

Where an inter vivos transfer of property is excluded from treatment "as a transfer of property by gift" under Section 2503(e)(1),[259] the transfer is not "subject to" a tax imposed by Chapter 12 and, therefore, cannot result in a direct skip.[260]

---

[254] IRC § 2612(c)(1). See IRC § 2613(a).

[255] IRC § 2001(a).

[256] IRC § 2106. See ¶ 6.06. Property must be situated in the U.S. to be subject to estate tax. See ¶¶ 6.03[2], 6.04, 6.05.

[257] IRC § 2101(a). See also IRC § 2663(2); Reg. § 26.2652-1(a)(2).

[258] IRC § 2501(a)(1). Generally, no gift tax is imposed on the transfer of intangible property by a nonresident who is not a citizen of the United States. IRC §§ 2501(a)(2), 2501(a)(3). See ¶ 9.02[1] text accompanying notes 4, 7.

[259] See ¶ 9.04[6].

[260] IRC § 2612(c). The statutory pattern of Chapter 13 implies that an inter vivos transfer that satisfies the Section 2503(e) requirements may be a direct skip. Section 2642(c) provides a zero inclusion ratio in the case of a direct skip that is a "nontaxable gift," and Section 2642(c)(3)(B) includes a Section 2503(e) transfer within the scope of a "nontaxable gift." The implication is that such Section 2503(e) transfers are "subject to" the Chapter 12 gift tax. However, Section 2642(c)(3)(B) is superfluous and should be repealed. See ¶ 13.01[2][a] note 11. The Treasury seems to agree. The Instructions for Form 709 provide that transfers which qualify for the educational or medical exclusion are not subject to the gift tax. Instructions for Form 709, United States Gift (and Generation-Skipping Transfer) Tax Return (2001) at 1. The Instructions for Form 709 do not treat Section 2503(e) transfers as direct skips. The Instructions provide that "[a]n *inter vivos direct skip* is a transfer . . . that is: (a) subject to the gift tax. . . . A transfer is *subject to the gift tax* if it is required to be reported on Schedule A of Form 709 under the rules contained in the gift tax portions of these instructions. . . . Therefore . . . transfers that qualify for the medical or educational exclusions . . . are not subject to the GST tax." Instructions for Form 709, United States Gift (and Generation-Skipping Transfer) Tax Return (2001) at 2. The Instructions also state that Schedule A does not require the listing of "any gift or part of a gift that qualifies for the . . . educational, or medical exclusions." Instructions for Form

Similarly, the Treasury does not treat as a direct skip an inter vivos outright direct skip that fully qualifies for but does not exceed the Section 2503(b) annual exclusion.[261] This conclusion is theoretically justified under the structure of Chapter 13,[262] but it is difficult to justify statutorily. Inter vivos transfers of property that fully qualify for the Section 2503(b) annual exclusion ought to be considered "subject to" a tax imposed by Chapter 12 because Section 2501(a) imposes a tax on the transfer of property by gift[263] and Section 2503(b) merely excludes the first $11,000 of certain gifts from the "total amount of gifts," a figure in gift tax computation. As a result, the excluded amount, representing property transferred by gift, is "subject to" a tax imposed by Chapter 12 and is simply excluded in the computation of "total amount of gifts."[264]

Property over which a decedent has at death (or had during life) a general power of appointment and that is required to be included in the decedent's

---

709, United States Gift (and Generation-Skipping Transfer) Tax Return (2001) at 5. The effect of these Instructions is to make the Section 2503(e) inter vivos direct skip issue academic.

[261] See ¶ 9.04[1]. See Instructions for Form 709, United States Gift (and Generation-Skipping Transfer) Tax Return (2001) at 6. Page 6 of the Instructions for Form 709 also states that Schedule A does not require the listing of gifts "[i]f the total is $10,000 or less . . . (except gifts of future interests) . . . made to [a] donee," i.e., gifts fully excluded by Section 2503(b). For the calendar year 2002, the first $11,000 of gifts to any person (other than gifts of a future interest in property) qualify for the Section 2503(b) annual exclusion. See Rev. Proc. 2001-59, 2001-2 CB __, __. However, this rule is modified when the transfer is to a trust, unless the requirements of Section 2642(c)(2) are met. See Instructions for Form 709, United States Gift (and Generation-Skipping Transfer) Tax Return (2001) at 6; ¶ 16.02[2][b][iii].

Where the inter vivos outright direct skip qualifies and exceeds the Section 2503(b) annual exclusion, the transfer is treated as "subject to" the federal gift tax and must be listed on Schedule A of Form 709. See Instructions for Form 709, United States Gift (and Generation-Skipping Transfer) Tax Return (2001) at 6.

[262] Even if the transfer were treated as a direct skip, no generation-skipping transfer tax would be imposed as an indirect result of Section 2642(c). See IRC § 2642(c)(3)(A). However, Section 2642(c)(3) is not superfluous even with respect to an outright direct skip. Section 2642(c)(3)(A) includes as a nontaxable gift, which is assigned a zero inclusion ratio, a transfer that *in part* is excluded by Section 2503(b). As a result of the Treasury's position, Section 2642(c) is superfluous with respect to outright transfers that are fully excluded by Section 2503(b), but not with respect to transfers that are only partially excluded by Section 2503(b). See also ¶ 18.02[2][b] text accompanying notes 18–24.

[263] IRC § 2501(a)(1). See Reg. §§ 26.2612-1(a)(1), 26.2652-1(a)(2). See also Reg. § 26.2642-1(d) Ex. 2.

[264] With respect to outright transfers, this Section 2503(b) issue, like the Section 2503(e) issue, is academic. See supra note 260. Congress should have drafted the generation-skipping statute more carefully to reach this result.

gross estate[265] is "subject to" a tax imposed by Chapter 11. Similarly, property transferred by the inter vivos exercise of a pre-1942 general power of appointment[266] or by the release or exercise of a post-1942 general power during the life of the power holder[267] is "subject to" a tax imposed by Chapter 12 if that transfer constitutes a completed gift.[268] Property subject to an inter vivos general power of appointment that is allowed to lapse and is not treated as released[269] is not considered "subject to" a tax imposed by Chapter 12.[270]

In general, property subject to a nongeneral power of appointment is not required to be included in the power holder's gross estate,[271] and a transfer effected by the exercise or release of the power is not treated as a transfer of property for gift tax purposes.[272] Such a transfer is not "subject to" a tax imposed by Chapter 11 or Chapter 12.

Generally, when property is included in a decedent's gross estate under Section 2044, or when a Section 2519 transfer of property is a completed gift, the property is subject to the federal estate or gift tax. However, if a reverse QTIP election has been made under Section 2652(a)(3) to treat the property as if it were not qualified terminable interest property, neither Section 2044 gross

---

[265] IRC §§ 2041(a)(1), 2041(a)(2). Such powers would include a pre-1942 general power that was exercised at death or inter vivos in a manner that, if the decedent owned and transferred the property, the property would be included in the decedent's gross estate under Sections 2035 through 2038 (see IRC § 2041(a)(1)), and a post-1942 general power either held at death or exercised or released inter vivos in a manner that, if the decedent owned and transferred the property, the property would be included in the decedent's gross estate under Sections 2035 through 2038. See IRC §§ 2041(a)(2), 2041(b)(2); ¶¶ 4.13[6][a], 4.13[7][a], 4.13[7][b]. For Chapter 13 to be applicable, the Chapter 11 taxable event must occur after the effective date of Chapter 13. See ¶ 18.05.

[266] IRC § 2514(a).

[267] IRC § 2514(b). The term "release" includes a release of a general power as a result of a lapse of the power in excess of the five-or-five power exception. IRC § 2514(e). Cf. IRC § 2041(b)(2). The exercise of a pre-1942 power or the release or exercise of a post-1942 power must occur after the effective date of Chapter 13. See ¶ 18.05.

[268] IRC §§ 2501(a)(1), 2511. See Reg. §§ 26.2612-1(a)(1), 26.2652-1(a)(2).

[269] IRC § 2514(e). See ¶ 10.04[4][c]. Cf. IRC § 2041(b)(2).

[270] If the power lapses during the lifetime of the power holder and is not treated as a release, there is no transfer of property (see IRC §§ 2514(b), 2514(e)), no transfer of property by gift (see IRC § 2501(a)), no tax imposed by Chapter 12 on any property, and no direct skip. See Reg. § 26.2652-1(a)(5) Ex. 5.

[271] See IRC §§ 2041(a), 2041(b)(1).

[272] IRC § 2514. In some instances, however, the inter vivos exercise of a nongeneral power of appointment may trigger a Section 2511 transfer. See ¶ 10.04[3][e] notes 27–30. In addition, property that is controlled by way of a nongeneral power of appointment may be "subject to" the estate tax or the gift tax in two very limited instances. IRC §§ 2041(a)(3), 2514(d), discussed ¶¶ 4.13[8], 10.04[5]. If the application of one of these special rules results in the inclusion of the property in a decedent's gross estate or in a donor's total amount of gifts, the property is "subject to" the tax imposed by Chapter 11 or Chapter 12.

estate inclusion of the property nor a Section 2519 transfer of the property that is a completed gift result in the property being subject to the federal estate or gift tax for purposes of Chapter 13.[273]

[ii] Second requirement: transfer of an interest to a skip person. A direct skip must involve the transfer of an "interest in property" to a "skip person."[274] A direct outright transfer of property to a person[275] is a transfer of an interest in property to that person. In general, local property law determines whether there has been a transfer of an interest in property.[276] However, any transfer of an interest in property for estate or gift tax purposes will be recognized in determining whether a direct skip has occurred.[277]

If a transfer of an interest in property held in a trust is involved, only the transfer of a Chapter 13 interest will constitute a direct skip.[278] Thus, a direct skip occurs if the current income beneficiary of a trust gratuitously transfers the income interest to a skip person, whereas no direct skip occurs if the remainderperson of the trust gratuitously transfers the remainder to a skip person. Even though the remainderperson's transfer of the beneficial interest constitutes a gift under Chapter 12, there is no direct skip because that interest is not a Chapter 13 interest in property.[279]

---

[273] Reg. §§ 26.2612-1(a)(1), 26.2652-1(a)(3). See Reg. § 26.2652-1(a)(5) Ex. 5; supra ¶ 13.02[2][d] text accompanying notes 83–87.

If a reverse QTIP election has been made with respect to the qualified terminable interest property, and if the individual with the qualifying income interest or that individual's estate does not exercise a right of recovery under Section 2207A, the failure to exercise the right of recovery, even if it results in a transfer of property by gift, is not treated as a transfer of property to the trust for purposes of Chapter 13. Reg. § 26.2652-1(a)(5) Ex. 7. See ¶ 8.07[5]. Where a reverse QTIP election is made and the will of the individual possessing the qualified income interest provides that all death taxes are to be paid from the residuary estate, there is no constructive addition to the trust by virtue of the tax clause by the individual possessing the qualified income interest. Reg. § 26.2652-1(a)(5) Ex. 8.

[274] IRC § 2612(c)(1); Reg. § 26.2612-1(d).

[275] Section 7701(a)(1) defines "person" as an individual, an estate, a trust, a partnership, a corporation, a company, or an association. See infra ¶ 13.02[4][b][iii].

[276] The term "interest in property" as used here is substantially broader than the term "interest in property held in trust" as defined in Section 2652(c). See ¶¶ 4.05 (especially 4.05[2]), 10.01[3], discussing Sections 2033 and 2511, respectively. But see infra text accompanying notes 278 and 279.

[277] The exercise, release, or lapse of a general power of appointment over property may be treated as a transfer of property. See supra ¶ 13.02[4][b] text accompanying notes 265–272. Cf. United States v. O'Malley, 383 US 627 (1966).

[278] See IRC §§ 2612(c)(1), 2652(c); ¶ 17.02[3][e][i].

[279] See IRC §§ 2612(c)(1), 2652(c); ¶ 17.02[3][e][i]. The new remainderperson replaces the old remainderperson as the recipient of the property in determining whether a generation-skipping transfer occurs when the income interest terminates. For example, assume A establishes a trust, with income to brother B for life and a remainder to niece N.

A skip person may be either an individual or a trust.[280] An individual is classified as a skip person[281] if assigned to a generation level which is at least two generations below that assigned to the transferor.[282] Trusts are classified as skip persons if all Chapter 13 interests in the trust are held by skip persons,[283] or, if no person has such an interest, all permissible future distributions can be made only to skip persons.[284]

An outright inter vivos or testamentary transfer to one's grandchild or great-grandchild is generally a direct skip.[285] The exercise inter vivos or at death of a general power of appointment over a trust in favor of one's grandchild or great-grandchild is generally a direct skip,[286] as is a transfer to an inter vivos or testamentary trust created exclusively for one's grandchildren and great-grandchildren.[287] A transfer to a trust with a retained life estate in the grantor followed by a remainder to the grantor's grandchildren is generally a direct skip when the grantor dies.[288] A transfer to a trust that is treated as qualified terminable interest property under Section 2056(b)(7) or Section 2523(f) with a remainder to a grandchild generally[289] results in a direct skip of all or a

---

If, during B's life, N transfers her remainder interest to her grandchild, N makes a Chapter 12 gift, but the transfer is not a direct skip because it is not the transfer of a Chapter 13 interest. See ¶ 17.02[3][e][i]; Reg. § 26.2612-1(f) Ex. 14. See also supra ¶ 13.02[2][b][i]. At B's death, there is a taxable termination of the trust to N's grandchild, who is a skip person in relation to A. IRC § 2612(a)(1)(A). See ¶ 17.02[3][e][ii].

[280] IRC § 2613(a). Skip persons are discussed at ¶¶ 13.03[1]–13.03[4].

[281] IRC § 2613(a)(1).

[282] IRC § 2651. See ¶ 13.03[2].

[283] IRC § 2613(a)(2)(A).

[284] IRC § 2613(a)(2)(B). See ¶ 13.03[3]. Potential distributions to non-skip persons which are so remote as to be negligible are disregarded. Reg. § 26.2612-1(d)(2)(ii).

[285] IRC § 2612(c)(1). See Reg. §§ 26.2612-1(f) Exs. 1, 2; TAM 9534001 (May 1, 1995) (transfers made by the decedent's estate to the decedent's grandnephew and grand-niece to settle a will contest were not taxable distributions by testamentary trusts, but were testamentary direct skips by the decedent). But see infra ¶ 13.02[4][c]; IRC § 2651(e); ¶ 17.01[2][a][ii].

[286] IRC § 2612(c)(1). But see infra ¶ 13.02[4][c]; IRC § 2651(e); ¶ 17.01[2][a][ii].

[287] IRC §§ 2612(c)(1), 2613(a)(2). But see infra ¶ 13.02[4][c]; IRC § 2651(e); ¶ 17.01[2][a][ii].

[288] IRC §§ 2612(c)(1), 2642(f)(1). See infra ¶ 13.02[4][d]. But see infra ¶ 13.02[4][c]; IRC § 2651(e); ¶ 17.01[2][a][ii].

[289] It is assumed that there is no reverse QTIP election under Section 2652(a)(3). See supra ¶ 13.02[2][d] text accompanying notes 83–87; supra ¶ 13.02[4][b] text accompanying note 273. Additionally, it is assumed that, at the death of the holder of the qualified income interest, the parents of the grandchild are alive, precluding the application of Section 2651(e). See ¶ 17.01[2][a][ii].

portion of the property when the holder of the qualified income interest trans-fers all or a portion of the income interest or dies.[290]

[iii] **No trust look-through.** In determining whether a transfer of an in-terest in property to an entity is a direct skip, the look-through rules of Section 2651(f)(2)[291] generally provide that each individual who has a beneficial inter-est in the entity is treated as having an interest in the property. Thus, a transfer of property by gift to a corporation or partnership generally constitutes a direct skip to the extent that a skip person owns an interest in the entity.[292] However, Section 2612(c)(2) provides that "[s]olely for purposes of determining whether any transfer to a trust is a direct skip, the rules of section 2651(f)(2) shall not apply."[293] Initially this requirement seems peculiar because, when determining whether a trust is a skip person, it is necessary to look through the trust to as-certain whether the persons with an interest in the property in the trust[294] are skip persons or non-skip persons.[295] Section 2612(c)(2), however, is designed to ensure that the determination of whether a transfer to a trust is a direct skip is made solely on the basis of whether the trust, as the transferee in the trans-fer, is a skip person.[296] It ensures that the look-through rules are not to be ap-plied to create a direct skip to a beneficiary of the trust when the trust itself is the transferee.[297]

For example, suppose A makes a completed gift to a trust. Both A's child C and A's grandchild GC are potential recipients of the income from the trust during C's life, the distributions to be made at the discretion of the trustee, with GC as the remainderperson. There is a transfer of an interest in property that is subject to tax under Chapter 12. The only remaining requirement for a direct skip is that the transfer be made to a skip person.[298] The trust itself is not a skip person, because a Chapter 13 interest in the trust is held by C, a

---

[290] Reg. § 26.2612-1(f) Ex. 5. See IRC §§ 2044, 2519.

[291] See ¶ 17.01[2][c].

[292] IRC §§ 2612(c)(1), 2651(f)(2).

[293] IRC § 2612(c)(2). The legislative history of Section 2612(c)(2) states that, in the case of a direct skip, "the determination of whether a trust is a 'skip person' . . . is to be determined without regard to the entity look-through rules as they apply to trusts." Staff of the Joint Comm. on Tax., Description of the Technical Corrections Act of 1988 (HR 4333 and S. 2238) (JCS-10-88), 363 (Comm. Print Mar. 31, 1988). The "no trust look-through" rule also applies to taxable distributions to a trust. Reg. § 26.2612-1(c)(2).

[294] IRC § 2652(c).

[295] See IRC §§ 2613(a), 2613(b). Cf. Reg. § 26.2612-1(e)(3).

[296] IRC § 2613(a)(2). See Reg. § 26.2612-1(f) Ex. 3.

[297] See Reg. § 26.2652-1(a)(5) Ex. 5. See also Reg. § 26.2612-1(c)(2).

[298] See IRC § 2612(c)(1).

non-skip person.[299] Section 2651(f)(2), on its own, would treat the transfer to the trust as a transfer to the individuals having an interest in the trust, and, because a skip person, *GC*, has an interest in the trust, treat part of the transfer as a direct skip.[300] However, Section 2612(c)(2) intervenes to ensure the proper interpretation of Section 2613(a). As the trust itself is not a skip person, the transfer to the trust is not a direct skip generation-skipping transfer.

This result is consistent with the purpose of Chapter 13, namely, to impose a tax on transfers of wealth that skip a generation with respect to the estate or gift tax at the time the generation is skipped, or if the skipped generation has had the use of or the income from that property, at the time that generation's use of or enjoyment of income from that property ceases. In the preceding example, *A* is liable for Chapter 12 tax upon the transfer of property to the trust, but, because the trust is not a skip person and there is no direct skip, no Chapter 13 tax is imposed. Chapter 13 does impose a tax on any income distributions to *GC* during *C*'s lifetime, since these are taxable distributions,[301] and, as the property held in the trust is not taxed at *C*'s death under either Chapter 11 or Chapter 12, Chapter 13 imposes a tax on the taxable termination that occurs at *C*'s death.[302]

Given that Section 2612(c)(2) is designed to prevent the look-through rules from creating a generation-skipping transfer whenever there is a transfer to a trust, why is its statutory application limited to direct skips? With respect to taxable terminations, there is no need to prevent the application of the look-through rules to prevent the transfer from being a generation-skipping trans-

---

[299] IRC §§ 2613(a)(2)(A), 2613(a)(2)(B). See IRC §§ 2613(a)(1), 2613(b). See also Reg. § 26.2612-1(f) Exs. 3, 5.

[300] IRC §§ 2612(c)(1), 2613(a)(1).

[301] IRC § 2612(b). See supra ¶¶ 13.02[3][a], 13.02[3][b].

[302] IRC § 2612(a). See supra ¶¶ 13.02[2][a]–13.02[2][d].

fer.[303] A rule limiting the application of the look-through rules with respect to certain taxable distributions is provided in the regulations.[304]

---

[303] In determining whether there is a need for a prohibition on the application of the look-through rules (as they pertain to trusts) when there is a termination of a Chapter 13 interest in property held in trust, the trust in question has to be a beneficiary of the trust in which there is a termination. This is because the tests for a taxable termination require a termination of a Chapter 13 interest in a trust and focus on the classification of the persons with such an interest in the trust in which the termination occurred. On the other hand, the test for a direct skip is based on the classification of the person to whom the transfer is made and does not require that the transfer be made from a trust.

The first situation in which a taxable termination can occur is when there is a termination of a Chapter 13 interest in property held in trust and, immediately after the termination, only skip persons have an interest in the property. IRC § 2612(a)(1)(A). Assume that a donor makes a completed gift to trust one, in which several individuals and trust two have Chapter 13 interests, and also assume that both skip persons and non-skip persons have Chapter 13 interests in trust two. Upon termination of the interests of any of the individual beneficiaries of trust one, there will not be a taxable termination because a non-skip person has an interest in the property held in trust one. See IRC § 2612(a)(1)(A). Trust two is a non-skip person (see IRC §§ 2613(a)(2)(B), 2613(b)), and, if an argument is made to apply the look-through rules of Section 2651(f)(2), a non-skip person will still have a Chapter 13 interest in the property held in trust one. In this situation, therefore, there is no need to require expressly that the look-through rules are not to be considered in determining whether there is a taxable termination. Again, this is appropriate because the Chapter 13 tax will be imposed only when all of the non-skip persons no longer have the right to the income from the property held in trust.

A taxable termination also occurs when a Chapter 13 interest in a trust terminates, no one has such an interest in the trust immediately after the termination, and only skip persons remain as the trust beneficiaries. IRC § 2612(a)(1)(B). Whether or not the look-through rules are applied in these situations again will not cause any differences in result. This is because when a skip person trust is the only remaining beneficiary, or is one of several remaining skip person beneficiaries, even if the trust is pierced, there will still be only skip persons as beneficiaries. IRC § 2613(a)(2). Therefore, with respect to taxable terminations, there is no need to have an express prohibition against applying the look-through rules in testing for the occurrence of a taxable termination.

[304] Reg. § 26.2612-1(c)(2); supra ¶ 13.02[3][b] note 216. A taxable distribution is a distribution from a trust to a skip person. IRC § 2612(b). Since the test to determine whether a taxable distribution occurs parallels the direct skip test (i.e., whether the transfer is to a skip person) the need to preclude the look-through rules applies here as well.

In demonstrating the need for an express prohibition against the application of the look-through rules (as they pertain to trusts) when testing whether or not a taxable distribution has occurred, consider the arrangement where one trust is the beneficiary of another trust. To have a taxable distribution, there must be a distribution from a trust, and, in determining whether there needs to be an express prohibition against the application of Section 2651(f)(2) (with respect to trusts) in a taxable distribution, another trust must receive the distribution.

The beneficiary trust will be either a skip person or a non-skip person, depending on the persons who have a Chapter 13 interest in it. If the trust is a skip person, then the distribution to the beneficiary trust will be a taxable distribution, even if the look-through rules apply, because the distribution will always be to a skip person. However, if the beneficiary trust is a non-skip person, with both skip persons and non-skip persons having a

[c] Exceptions to the General Rule

[i] The deceased-parent exception for transfers made before January 1, 1998. Section 2612(c)(2), prior to its repeal by the Taxpayer Relief Act of 1997,[305] provided that if the parent of the transferor's grandchild was the lineal descendant of the transferor and was deceased at the time of the transfer,[306] the

---

Chapter 13 interest in the beneficiary trust, there should not be a taxable distribution at that time since the beneficiary trust is not a skip person. The look-through rules should not be applied in this situation to determine if there has been a taxable distribution with respect to the skip persons who have Chapter 13 interests in the beneficiary trust. This is because non-skip persons still have such an interest in the property that composed the taxable distribution, and the appropriate time to impose any Chapter 13 tax is when non-skip persons no longer have such an interest in the property in the beneficiary trust. This occurs when there is a taxable termination or a taxable distribution to a skip person from the beneficiary trust. The regulations expressly prohibit the application of the look-through rules of Section 2651(f)(2) in determining if a distribution from one trust to another trust is a taxable distribution. Reg.§ 26.2612-1(c)(2).

The legislative history of Section 2612(c)(2) can be used to support the regulatory prohibition of applying the look-through rules when a trust is involved in a transfer with possible Chapter 13 tax consequences. This legislative history does not limit the application of Section 2612(c)(2) to determinations involving direct skips. See Staff of the Joint Comm. on Tax., Description of the Technical Corrections Act of 1988 (HR 4333 and S2238), 363 (Mar. 31, 1988). Although the legislative history does not accurately reflect the manner in which Section 2612(c)(2) operates, it is apparent from the broad language used in the legislative history that this provision was intended to result in the uniform application of Chapter 13. The extension of the Section 2612(c)(2) rule in the regulations to certain taxable distributions results in a correct application of the rules governing the classification of trusts as skip persons or non-skip persons.

[305] Section 2612(c)(2) applied with respect to transfers made before January 1, 1998. Taxpayer Relief Act of 1997, Pub. L. No. 105-34, § 511(c), 111 Stat. 788, 861 (1997), reprinted in 1997-4 CB (Vol. 1) 1, 75. The "deceased-parent exception," embodied in Section 2612(c)(2) and applicable only to direct skips, was eliminated by the Taxpayer Relief Act of 1997 with respect to transfers after December 31, 1997. Taxpayer Relief Act of 1997, Pub. L. No. 105-34, § 511(b)(1), 111 Stat. 788, 861 (1997), reprinted in 1997-4 CB (Vol. 1) 1, 75. It was replaced with Section 2651(e), a special generation assignment rule for predeceased parents. IRC § 2651(e). Section 2651(e) is generally broader with respect to both the transferees covered and the types of generation-skipping transfers covered. However, as a practical matter, with respect to potential direct skips, the Section 2651(e) rule generally reaches the same end result as the provision it replaced. See ¶ 17.01[2][a][ii].

[306] A descendant of the transferor who died within ninety days after the transfer was treated as predeceasing the transferor to the extent so provided by the governing instrument or applicable local law. Reg. § 26.2612-1(a)(2)(i). A descendant who survived the transfer by ninety days was not treated as predeceasing the transferor for purposes of Section 2612(c)(2) (prior to repeal by the Taxpayer Relief Act of 1997, Pub. L. No. 105-34, § 511(b)(1), 111 Stat. 788, 861 (1997), reprinted in 1997-4 CB (Vol. 1) 1, 75) where a disclaimer was executed and the descendant was treated as predeceasing the transferor of the disclaimed property solely by reason of applicable state law. Id.

grandchild was treated as the child of the transferor for purposes of determining whether a transfer was a direct skip.[307] The rule also applied to transfers made to the grandchild of the transferor's spouse or former spouse if the grandchild's parent was a lineal descendant of the transferor's spouse or former spouse and was deceased at the time of the transfer.[308]

If a grandchild was treated as the transferor's child, an outright transfer to the grandchild was not a direct skip because the grandchild was no longer a skip person.[309] Rather than being assigned to a generation level that was at least two levels below that assigned to the transferor,[310] the grandchild was reassigned to the generation level one below that assigned to the transferor. Similarly, if the transfer was made to a trust in which a grandchild had a Chapter 13 interest, the trust was not a skip person,[311] and there was no direct skip.[312]

Once a transferor's grandchild was treated as the transferor's child, the lineal descendants below the grandchild's generation level were also reassigned.[313] The grandchild's children, the transferor's great-grandchildren, thus moved up one generation level and were treated as the transferor's grandchildren.[314] Under this rule, a transfer to a great-grandchild whose parent and

---

[307] IRC § 2612(c)(2) (prior to repeal by the Taxpayer Relief Act of 1997, Pub. L. No. 105-34, § 511(b)(1), 111 Stat. 788, 861 (1997), reprinted in 1997-4 CB (Vol. 1) 1, 75); Reg. § 26.2612-1(a)(2). The special rule for transfers to grandchildren was extended beyond transfers to grandchildren to transfers to any lineal descendant, disregarding any predeceased individual who was both an ancestor of the descendant and a lineal descendent of the transferor. Reg. § 26.2612-1(a)(2)(i). See Priv. Ltr. Rul. 9709015 (Nov. 26, 1996) (ruling that transfers from a taxpayer to the taxpayer's grandchildren who had been born to the taxpayer's deceased daughter would qualify for the predeceased child exception, even though the deceased daughter had been adopted away from the taxpayer).

[308] IRC § 2612(c)(2) (prior to repeal by the Taxpayer Relief Act of 1997, Pub. L. No. 105-34, § 511(b)(1), 111 Stat. 788, 861 (1997), reprinted in 1997-4 CB (Vol. 1) 1, 75); Reg. § 26.2612-1(a)(2). See supra note 307. Thus, if a transferor's spouse had a child by a former marriage who was deceased, and that child had children, those children (spouse's grandchildren) were treated as children of the transferor in determining if there had been a direct skip by the transferor. The same applied to children of the transferor's former spouse.

[309] IRC §§ 2612(c)(1), 2613(a)(1).

[310] IRC § 2651(b)(1).

[311] IRC §§ 2613(a)(2), 2612(c)(2) (prior to repeal by the Taxpayer Relief Act of 1997, Pub. L. No. 105-34, § 511(b)(1), 111 Stat. 788, 861 (1997), reprinted in 1997-4 CB (Vol. 1) 1, 75). See ¶ 13.03[3].

[312] See Reg. § 26.2612-1(f) Ex. 6. Cf. Reg. § 26.2612-1(f) Ex. 7.

[313] IRC § 2612(c)(2) (second sentence) (prior to repeal by the Taxpayer Relief Act of 1997, Pub. L. No. 105-34, § 511(b)(1), 111 Stat. 788, 861 (1997), reprinted in 1997-4 CB (Vol. 1) 1, 75).

[314] IRC § 2612(c)(2) (flush language, first sentence) (prior to repeal by the Taxpayer Relief Act of 1997, Pub. L. No. 105-34, § 511(b)(1), 111 Stat. 788, 861 (1997), reprinted in 1997-4 CB (Vol. 1) 1, 75). Great-grandchildren who were reassigned and treated as

grandparent were lineal descendants of the transferor and were deceased at the time of the transfer was treated as a transfer to the transferor's child. To illustrate, assume that a transferor had an only child, *C*, who had an only child, *GC*, and *GC* had an only child, *GGC*. Assume that the transferor had made an outright gift to *GC* in 1996. If *C* had been alive at the time of the transfer, the transfer would have been a direct skip. If *C* had been deceased, the transfer would not have been treated as a transfer of property to a skip person and, therefore, would not have been a direct skip.[315] If the gift had been made to *GGC* at a time when both *C* and *GC* were deceased, *GGC* would have been reassigned to the generation level of *C*, and again the transfer would not have been classified as a direct skip.[316]

Generational assignment under the Section 2612(c)(2) deceased-parent rule prior to its repeal applied not only to transfers in trust, but also to subsequent transfers of the trust corpus and of the income it generated.[317] If a transfer of property to a grandchild made in trust was not treated as a direct skip because of the Section 2612(c)(2) deceased-parent rule, subsequent distributions of income or corpus to the grandchild were not treated as taxable distributions or taxable terminations.[318] For example, assume a transferor, *T*, established a trust, with income to grandchild *GC* for life and a remainder to great-grandchild *GGC*. If *GC*'s parent, the lineal descendant of *T*, were dead at the time of the transfer, the transfer to the trust would not have been treated as a direct skip by reason of the Section 2612(c)(2) deceased-parent rule, and income distributions to *GC* would not have been treated as taxable distributions.[319]

Generational reassignment under Section 2612(c)(2) prior to its repeal applied only to the transfers from the portion of the property that qualified for

---

grandchildren under this rule did not qualify for the grandchild exclusion. See Temp. Reg. § 26.2601-1(d)(1), 1988-1 CB 332, 340.

[315] IRC §§ 2612(c)(1), 2612(c)(2) (prior to repeal by the Taxpayer Relief Act of 1997, Pub. L. No. 105-34, § 511(b)(1), 111 Stat. 788, 861 (1997), reprinted in 1997-4 CB (Vol. 1) 1, 75).

[316] Reg. § 26.2612-1(a)(2)(i).

[317] IRC § 2612(c)(2) (last sentence) (prior to repeal by the Taxpayer Relief Act of 1997, Pub. L. No. 105-34, § 511(b)(1), 111 Stat. 788, 861 (1997), reprinted in 1997-4 CB (Vol. 1) 1, 75); Reg. § 26.2612-1(a)(2).

[318] IRC § 2612(c)(2) (last sentence) (prior to repeal by the Taxpayer Relief Act of 1997, Pub. L. No. 105-34, § 511(b)(1), 111 Stat. 788, 861 (1997), reprinted in 1997-4 CB (Vol. 1) 1, 75); Reg. § 26.2612-1(a)(2).

[319] IRC § 2612(c)(2) (prior to repeal by the Taxpayer Relief Act of 1997, Pub. L. No. 105-34, § 511(b)(1), 111 Stat. 788, 861 (1997), reprinted in 1997-4 CB (Vol. 1) 1, 75); Reg. § 26.2612-1(a)(2)(i). See S. Rep. No. 445, 100th Cong., 2d Sess. 368 (1988); supra ¶ 13.02[3][b] text accompanying note 222. Similarly, if the trustee had a power to invade corpus for *GC* and appointed the entire corpus of the trust to *GC*, there would be no taxable termination of the trust.

the deceased-parent exception at the time of transfer to the trust.[320] If a transferor made an addition to an existing trust after the death of an individual who was an ancestor of the descendant and a lineal descendant of the transferor, the addition was treated as being held in a separate trust for Chapter 13 purposes.[321] For example, assume that transferor *T* created and funded a trust, with income to child *C* for life, then income to grandchild *GC* for life, and a remainder to great-grandchild *GGC*. After *C*'s death, with *T* surviving,[322] when the corpus was worth $1 million, assume the transferor made a second transfer, adding $1 million to the trust. Under the Section 2612(c)(2) deceased-parent exception, *GC* was assigned to *C*'s generation and was no longer a skip person. The second transfer was treated as being held in a separate trust for Chapter 13 purposes. The second transfer, which was treated as being made to a separate trust, was not a direct skip, and subsequent distributions of income to *GC* generated by the second transfer which were treated as being held in a separate trust were not taxable distributions.[323] Income distributions from the original trust also were not taxable distributions to a skip person because Section 2653(a) reassigned the transferor to *C*'s generation level.[324] However, there was a taxable termination of both trusts at *GC*'s death because *GGC* was a skip person with respect to both trusts.

[ii] **The grandchild exclusion.** Also excluded from the definition of a direct skip and from the imposition of the generation-skipping transfer tax was a transfer not exceeding $2 million made prior to January 1, 1990, to any

---

[320] IRC § 2612(c)(2) (last sentence) (prior to repeal by the Taxpayer Relief Act of 1997, Pub. L. No. 105-34, § 511(b)(1), 111 Stat. 788, 861 (1997), reprinted in 1997-4 CB (Vol. 1) 1, 75).

[321] Reg. § 26.2612-1(a)(2)(ii). The trust was treated in the same manner as a single trust with multiple transferors. Id. See ¶ 17.04[2][a]. Subsequent additions were also treated as being made to the separate trust. Reg. § 26.2612-1(a)(2)(ii).

[322] A Section 2612(a)(1) taxable termination occurred at *C*'s death, and, as a result of Section 2653(a), the transferor was shifted to *C*'s generation level. See ¶ 17.03[1].

[323] IRC § 2612(c)(2) (last sentence) (prior to repeal by the Taxpayer Relief Act of 1997, Pub. L. No. 105-34, § 511(b)(1), 111 Stat. 788, 861 (1997), reprinted in 1997-4 CB (Vol. 1) 1, 75). See supra text accompanying notes 318 and 319. Subsequent additions to the trust after the death of *C* were treated as made to the second transfer trust. Reg. § 26.2612-1(a)(2)(ii).

[324] See IRC § 2653(a); supra note 322.

grandchild of the transferor.[325] This major exception to the direct skip rules,[326] commonly referred to as "the grandchild exclusion,"[327] was the inequitable product of special-interest legislation,[328] and, until 1990, it severely undercut the rationale for taxing direct skips. Direct skips are now taxable because, in part, not taxing them would discriminate in favor of the super-wealthy taxpayer who, as a general proposition, is in a position to transmit a larger portion of wealth to future generations by bypassing the children's generation.[329] The grandchild exclusion, until it expired, reintroduced this discriminatory effect. Property that evaded the imposition of Chapter 13 tax by way of the grandchild exclusion will not, in most cases, reenter the transfer tax stream until the death of the grandchild, so it will be some time before this property is again subjected to any transfer tax.[330]

---

[325] The grandchild exclusion applied only to certain transfers made between September 26, 1985, and December 31, 1989. Transfers prior to such dates are safely outside the scope of Chapter 13. See the Tax Reform Act of 1986, Pub. L. No. 99-514, §§ 1433(b)(3), 1433(b)(4), 100 Stat. 2085, 2731 (1986), reprinted in 1986-3 CB (Vol. 1) 1, 648, as amended by the Technical & Miscellaneous Revenue Act of 1988, Pub. L. No. 100-647, § 1014(h)(3)(A), 102 Stat. 3342, 3567–3568 (1988), reprinted in 1988-3 CB 1, 227-228.

Although these transfers were not taxed as generation-skipping transfers, returns were still required to be filed for the transfers. See ¶ 18.02[2][b] note 27.

[326] There are other exceptions to the direct skip rules. See IRC § 2611(b), discussed ¶ 13.01[2].

[327] This exclusion should not be confused with the previous exclusion from direct skips for transfers to a grandchild whose parent, the lineal descendant of the transferor, is dead. See IRC §§ 2612(c)(2) (prior to repeal by the Taxpayer Relief Act of 1997, Pub. L. No. 105-34, § 511(b)(1), 111 Stat. 788, 861 (1997), reprinted in 1997-4 CB (Vol. 1) 1, 75); 2651(e). See supra ¶ 13.02[4][c][i]; ¶ 17.01[2][a][ii].

[328] Sheppard, "The Generation-Skipping Tax Loophole," 29 Tax Notes 882, 883 (Dec. 2, 1985). The exclusion has been dubbed the "Gallo Amendment" in reference to the suggestion that the lobbying efforts of California wine producers Ernest and Julio Gallo were responsible for the appearance of this exclusion in the proposed legislation on generation-skipping transfers considered in the House Ways and Means Committee. The amendment reportedly allowed the Gallo brothers and their wives to transfer $80 million to their twenty grandchildren without incurring a generation-skipping transfer tax. See Lassila, "Income Shifting and Generation-Skipping Under the House Tax Bill: Simplification and Cop-Out," 30 Tax Notes 1147, 1152 (Mar. 17, 1986). Cf. IRC § 2513.

[329] See supra ¶ 13.02[4][a] notes 242–244.

[330] This provision is explained in detail in prior editions of this treatise. See Stephens, Maxfield, Lind & Calfee, Federal Estate and Gift Taxation ¶ 13.02[4][c][ii] (Warren, Gorham & Lamont, 7th ed. 1997).

[d] Delayed Direct Skips

In some situations, even though the direct skip requirements are met,[331] the timing of the skip is postponed. Section 2642(f)(1) provides that when property that is the subject of an inter vivos direct skip would be included in the transferor's or the transferor's spouse's gross estate (other than by reason of Section 2035) if the transferor or the transferor's spouse had died immediately after making the transfer,[332] the direct skip is postponed[333] until the termination of the "estate tax inclusion period."[334] The "estate tax inclusion period" ends on the earliest of (1) the date that the property involved in the transfer is no longer potentially includable in the gross estate of the transferor[335] under Chapter 11 (other than by reason of Section 2035), (2) the date of any subsequent generation-skipping transfer with respect to the property, or (3) the date of the transferor's[336] death.[337]

The delayed direct skip rule of Section 2642(f)(1) has broad application.[338] It applies when an individual makes an inter vivos completed gift for purposes of Chapter 12 tax, either outright or in trust to a skip person, but retains an interest in the property or a power over its disposition that would render the property potentially includable in the individual's gross estate under Sections 2036 through 2038.[339] Section 2642(f)(1) also applies when a trans-

---

[331] IRC § 2612(c)(1).

[332] IRC § 2642(f)(4). See ¶¶ 16.02[7][a], 16.02[7][b][ii].

[333] IRC § 2642(f)(1) (especially the last sentence). The Section 2642(f) rule is discussed in detail at ¶ 16.02[7].

[334] IRC § 2642(f)(3).

[335] The reference to the transferor includes a reference to the transferor's spouse. IRC § 2642(f)(4).

[336] The reference to the transferor includes a reference to the transferor's spouse. IRC § 2642(f)(4).

[337] IRC § 2642(f)(3); Reg. § 26.2632-1(c)(3). See ¶ 16.02[7][c].

[338] However, under Section 2642(f), direct skips are not delayed if the possibility of inclusion is so remote as to be negligible. Reg. § 26.2632-1(c)(2)(ii)(A). See ¶ 16.02[7][a] text accompanying note 441. Additionally, a direct skip possibly should not be delayed until the close of the estate tax inclusion period if only a small portion of the value of the property transferred is required to be included in the transferor's gross estate.

[339] Some examples will illustrate the application of Section 2642(f) to a Section 2036 or a Section 2038 situation. If a transferor transfers a residence to a personal residence trust retaining use of the property for a term of years with a remainder in the trust to a grandchild whose parents are living (see ¶¶ 4.08, 17.01[2][a][ii], 19.03[5]), there is no direct skip transfer until the term of years expires, until the term interest is transferred, or until a generation-skipping transfer occurs, whichever occurs first. Similarly, if the transferor creates a trust with a transfer that is complete under the gift tax (see Reg. § 25.2511-2(d)) with income to a grandchild, whose parents are living, for twenty years and a remainder to either the grandchild or the grandchild's estate and transferor is named as trustee with an unlimited power to accumulate income or to invade corpus for the benefit of

feror funds a joint-and-survivorship annuity between the transferor and a skip person, which makes Section 2039 potentially applicable, and postpones the direct skip. Other situations in which Section 2642(f)(1) applies arise when a transferor's purchase of property held jointly by the transferor and a skip person potentially triggers Section 2040,[340] and when a transferor exercises (or, in the case of a post-1942 power, releases) a general power of appointment over property in a manner that would constitute a completed gift, but such property, had the transferor owned it at the time of death, would be included in the transferor's gross estate under Sections 2036 through 2038.[341]

An example will illustrate the rule. Assume that a grantor purchases property and has the title conveyed to grantor and grandchild as joint tenants with a right of survivorship. The transfer creating the grandchild's interest in one half of the property is a direct skip, but because the requirements of Section 2642(f)(1) are met, the occurrence of the direct skip is delayed until the end of the estate tax inclusion period. Assuming the tenancy is not partitioned or conveyed and the grantor predeceases grandchild, there is a direct skip of the entire property at its estate tax value to the grandchild at the end of the estate tax inclusion period at grantor's death.[342] If the grandchild predeceases the grantor, the property simply reverts to the grantor and there is no direct skip or any other generation-skipping transfer tax consequence.[343] If the joint tenancy is severed while both the joint tenants are alive and the property is split equally between them, there is a direct skip of one half of the value of the property at the time of the severance.[344] If, instead, the grantor and the grandchild jointly convey the property outright to the grantor's other grandchild, there is a direct skip of the entire value of the property at that time.[345] But if the property was jointly conveyed to the grantor's child (the grandchild's parent), there would be a direct skip of only one half of the property to the grandchild.[346]

---

the grandchild, no direct skip to the trust occurs until the termination of the estate tax inclusion period. See ¶ 4.10[4].

[340] See ¶ 4.12.

[341] IRC § 2642(f)(1). See supra note 339.

[342] Section 2642(f) also defers the effect of any allocation of the transferor's GST exemption and the valuation of the property until the date of death, when estate tax valuation is generally used. See IRC §§ 2642(f)(2)(A), 2642(f)(3)(B); ¶ 16.02[7][e]. A similar discussion of the interrelationship of joint tenancies and the Section 2642(f) direct skip rule is found at ¶ 16.02[7][d] text accompanying notes 494–505.

[343] But see infra note 346.

[344] See IRC § 2642(f)(3).

[345] IRC § 2612(c)(1). In effect, the grantor transfers one half of the property to the joint tenant grandchild and one-half to the other grandchild, both of whom are skip persons. See infra note 346; IRC §§ 2642(f)(1) (last sentence), 2642(f)(3)(A). A portion of each transfer may qualify as a nontaxable gift. See IRC §§ 2642(c)(1), 2642(c)(3)(A).

[346] The last sentence of Section 2642(f)(1) states that if a direct skip is postponed under the Section 2642(f) rule, "such skip shall be treated as occurring at the close of the

¶ 13.03 SECTION 2613. SKIP PERSONS AND NON-SKIP PERSONS

[1] Introduction

The definitions of "skip person"[1] and "non-skip person"[2] are essential to the determination of whether a generation-skipping transfer has occurred and whether a tax may then be imposed by Chapter 13.[3] A key component of the definition of each of the three generation-skipping transfers (a taxable termination, a taxable distribution, and a direct skip)[4] is either a skip person or a non-skip person.[5] Chapter 13 imposes a tax on transfers of property that have skipped the imposition of estate tax or gift tax at one or more generation levels. It is the definition of "skip person" that assures that the Chapter 13 tax is imposed only on transfers that skip the imposition of estate tax or gift tax at a particular generation level.

A skip person, the transferee of a generation-skipping transfer, can only be an individual (a "natural person")[6] or a trust[7] (the term "trust," as used throughout this section, includes a trust equivalent arrangement).[8] When a transfer is made to an entity that is not a trust, the entity is disregarded and the individuals or trusts having a beneficial interest in the entity are treated as the transferees and individually classified as skip or non-skip persons.[9]

---

estate tax inclusion period." The clause implies that one half of the property will pass to the grandchild in a direct skip transfer at the close of the estate tax inclusion period, and that one half of the property will be transferred from the grandchild to parent, the grantor's child.

[1] IRC § 2613(a).

[2] IRC § 2613(b).

[3] IRC § 2601.

[4] IRC § 2611(a).

[5] See IRC § 2612. A taxable distribution requires a distribution from the trust to a skip person. IRC § 2612(b). A taxable termination occurs whenever there is a termination of an interest in property held in trust which does not result in a transfer subject to federal estate or gift tax, unless a non-skip person has an interest in the property immediately after the termination or, if no person has a Chapter 13 interest, at no time after the termination can a distribution be made to a skip person. IRC § 2612(a); Reg. § 26.2612-1(b)(1)(i). A direct skip requires a transfer subject to estate or gift tax of an interest in property to a skip person. IRC § 2612(c). See ¶ 13.02[4].

[6] IRC § 2613(a)(1). Cf. IRC § 2651(f)(2).

[7] IRC § 2613(a)(2).

[8] IRC §§ 2652(b)(1), 2652(b)(3). See infra ¶ 13.03[3][c]; ¶ 17.02[2].

[9] IRC § 2651(f)(2). See infra ¶ 13.03[4].

A person who is not a skip person is a non-skip person.[10] Once skip persons are identified, non-skip persons are easily determined. The identification of skip persons and non-skip persons is made by reference to the transferor[11] and requires some familiarity with the generational assignment rules[12] and with the meaning of the term "interest" as it is used in Chapter 13.[13]

[2] Individuals as Skip Persons

A natural person,[14] or individual, is classified as a skip person if assigned to a generation level[15] that is at least two generations below that assigned to the transferor[16] of the property.[17] Thus, a transferor's grandchildren and great-grandchildren and the spouses of those grandchildren and great-grandchildren, as well as persons unrelated to the transferor who are more than thirty-seven and one-half years younger than the transferor, are skip persons.[18] On the other hand, a transferor's spouse, as well as the transferor's children, nieces, and nephews, and the parents and spouses of the transferor's nieces and nephews, are not skip persons.[19] Persons who are unrelated to the transferor and who are not more than thirty-seven and one-half years the transferor's junior are also not skip persons.[20]

[3] Trusts as Skip Persons

When the transferee of property is a trust,[21] the trust is a skip person if all Chapter 13 interests (as defined in Section 2652(c))[22] in the trust are held by

---

[10] IRC § 2613(b). See infra ¶ 13.03[5].

[11] See IRC § 2652(a).

[12] IRC § 2651. See ¶ 17.01.

[13] IRC § 2652(c). See ¶ 17.02[3].

[14] A natural person is classified as a skip person either as the transferee in an outright generation-skipping transfer or the beneficiary of a transferee trust. IRC § 2613(a). See IRC § 2651(d).

[15] IRC § 2651.

[16] IRC § 2652(a).

[17] IRC § 2613(a)(1); Reg. § 26.2612-1(d)(1).

[18] See IRC §§ 2651(b), 2651(c), 2651(d). See also ¶ 17.01. This assumes no application of the predeceased parent rule of Section 2651(e).

[19] See IRC §§ 2651(b), 2651(c).

[20] See IRC § 2651(d).

[21] The rules of Section 2613(a)(1) (natural persons as skip persons) do not apply.

[22] See ¶ 17.02[3].

skip persons,[23] or, if no person has a Chapter 13 interest in the trust, all future distributions, other than a distribution the probability of which is so remote as to be negligible, can be made only to skip persons.[24]

The term "trust" is not defined in Chapter 13[25] or, for that matter, under any part of the Code.[26] It is defined in part by the regulations,[27] which provide that "[i]n general, the term 'trust' as used in the Internal Revenue Code refers to an arrangement created either by a will or by an inter vivos declaration whereby trustees take title to property for the purpose of protecting or conserving it for the beneficiaries under the ordinary rules applied in chancery or probate courts."[28] The term "trust" also refers to any trust equivalent arrangements (other than an estate) that have substantially the same effect as a trust.[29] Trust equivalent arrangements include life estates and remainders, estates for years, and insurance and annuity contracts.[30]

To determine whether a trust is a skip person, one must first pierce the trust entity to ascertain whether any person holds a Chapter 13 interest[31] in the trust[32] and whether that person is a skip person or a non-skip person.[33] If no person holds a Chapter 13 interest in the trust, then all persons[34] owning *any*

---

[23] IRC § 2613(a)(2)(A); Reg. § 26.2612-1(d)(2)(i).

[24] IRC § 2613(a)(2)(B); Reg. § 26.2612-1(d)(2)(ii). If the chances of a distribution, including a distribution at the termination of the trust, are determined by actuarial standards to be less than 5 percent (one in twenty), the distribution possibility is classified as so remote as to be negligible and disregarded. Reg. § 26.2612-1(d)(2)(ii).

[25] See IRC § 2652(b)(1).

[26] See, e.g., IRC § 7701.

[27] Reg. § 301.7701-4.

[28] Reg. § 301.7701-4(a). The regulations not only provide a definition of an ordinary trust, but also discuss four specific types of trusts: the "business" trust, the "investment" trust, the "liquidating" trust and the "environmental remediation" trust. Reg. §§ 301.7701-4(b), 301.7701-4(c), 301.7701-4(d), 301.7701-4(e). Each of these types of trusts may be treated as a trust for generation-skipping transfer tax purposes.

[29] IRC § 2652(b)(1). See ¶ 17.02[2].

[30] IRC § 2652(b)(3). See infra ¶ 13.03[3][c].

[31] IRC § 2652(c).

[32] See IRC §§ 2613(a)(2)(A), 2613(a)(2)(B).

[33] As skip persons can only be individuals or trusts (see IRC §§ 2613(a)(1), 2613(a)(2)), any other entity holding a Chapter 13 trust interest must be pierced to determine whether each individual or trust with a beneficial interest in the entity is a skip or non-skip person. See IRC § 2651(f)(2); infra ¶ 13.03[4]. If one trust has a Chapter 13 interest in a second trust, the determination as to whether the first trust is a skip person will determine whether the second trust is a skip person. See infra ¶ 13.03[3][a] note 60.

[34] IRC § 7701(a)(1) defines "person" to include "an individual, a trust, estate, partnership, association, company or corporation." But see IRC § 2651(f)(2).

beneficial interests in the trust (not just Chapter 13 interests) are identified[35] to determine the possibility of a subsequent distribution to non-skip persons.[36]

[a] All Chapter 13 Trust Interests Held by Skip Persons

Where all Chapter 13 interests in the property held in trust are held by skip persons, the trust is treated as a skip person.[37] One generally thinks of "interests" as constituting all the beneficial interests in a trust; not so here. The term "interest" as used in Section 2613(a)(2) is given a special meaning by Section 2652(c), which provides a special definition to be used with respect to interests in trusts for generation-skipping transfer purposes.[38]

Under Chapter 13, a person has an interest in property held in trust if that person has a present right to receive income or corpus[39] or is a permissible current noncharitable recipient of income or corpus.[40] A charitable organization that is described in Section 2055(a) also has a Chapter 13 interest in a trust[41] if the trust is a qualifying charitable remainder annuity trust,[42] a charitable remainder unitrust,[43] or a pooled income fund.[44] However, if any interest in a trust was created primarily to postpone or avoid the imposition of Chapter 13 tax, it is not regarded as a Chapter 13 interest.[45]

Once the Chapter 13 interests in the trust have been identified, it must be determined whether these interests are held by skip persons or non-skip per-

---

[35] IRC § 2613(a)(2)(B)(ii) speaks of potential distributions, whereas the term "(trust) interest or interests" is used elsewhere in Section 2613(a)(2). See infra ¶ 13.03[3][b] note 62.

[36] IRC § 2613(a)(2)(B)(ii). See Reg. § 26.2612-1(d)(2)(ii).

[37] IRC § 2613(a)(2)(A). See Reg. § 26.2612-1(d)(2)(i).

[38] IRC § 2613(a)(2). Section 2652(c) is discussed in detail at ¶ 17.02[3] and is also considered at ¶ 13.02[2][b][i].

[39] IRC § 2652(c)(1)(A).

[40] IRC § 2652(c)(1)(B).

[41] IRC § 2652(c)(1)(C). See Priv. Ltr. Rul. 9532006 (May 4, 1995) (classification as charitable remainder trust under Section 2652(c) denied where no charitable deduction allowable under Section 2055 because of an excessive payout to noncharitable beneficiaries that made charitable remainder so remote as to be negligible).

[42] IRC § 664(d)(1).

[43] IRC § 664(d)(2).

[44] IRC § 642(c)(5). Any Section 2055(a) charitable organization is within Section 2651(f)(3) and is assigned to the transferor's generation level. Thus, if a Section 2055(a) charity has a remainder interest in a charitable remainder trust or a pooled income fund (trust equivalent), the transferee trust or fund will not be a skip person. See IRC § 2613(a)(2). However, distributions from such a trust or fund to a skip person prior to the termination distribution to the remainder interest will be Section 2612(b) taxable distributions. See ¶¶ 13.02[3], 13.02[2][b] note 38.

[45] IRC § 2652(c)(2). See ¶ 17.02[3][d].

sons.[46] If all Chapter 13 interests are held by skip persons, the trust is a skip person;[47] if any such interest is held by a non-skip person, the trust is not a skip person.[48] Assume that grantor *G* establishes a trust with income to adult grandchild *GC* for life and a remainder to great-grandchild *GGC* at a time when *G*'s child (the parent of *GC*) *C* is alive.[49] The trust is a skip person.[50] The only Chapter 13 interest in the trust[51] is held by a skip person, *GC*, who is assigned to a generation level that is two generations below that assigned to *G*.[52] The remainder interest of *GGC* is disregarded because it is a future right to income or corpus,[53] and *GGC* is not a current permissible recipient of income or corpus.[54] If the facts of this example were altered such that *G*'s child *C* was named the remainderperson, the trust would still be classified as a skip person, because *GC*, a skip person, still holds the only Chapter 13 interest in the trust.[55] *C*'s future interest is not a Chapter 13 interest[56] and is disregarded. If *G* had appointed a trustee, *T*, and given *T* a current discretionary power to invade corpus for *C*, a non-skip person, *C* would hold a Chapter 13 interest in the trust,[57] and the trust would not be classified as a skip person, because not all interests in the trust would be held by skip persons.

If a Chapter 13 interest in a trust is held by an estate, partnership, corporation, or other nontrust entity, the entity is pierced and each individual who has any beneficial interest in the entity is treated as having an interest in the property held in the trust.[58] Each individual with a beneficial interest in the entity must then be assigned a generation level to determine whether that individ-

---

[46] See generally IRC § 2613.

[47] IRC § 2613(a)(2)(A).

[48] IRC § 2613(a)(2)(A).

[49] If there was a potential direct skip transfer to a trust, and if the parent of the *GC* was deceased at the time of the transfer, Section 2651(e) would move *GC* up one generation and cause *GC* to become a non-skip person. A transfer to the trust would not be a direct skip. See ¶ 17.01[2][a][ii].

[50] IRC § 2613(a)(2)(A).

[51] IRC § 2652(c)(1)(A).

[52] IRC § 2651(b)(1).

[53] IRC § 2652(c)(1)(A) (parenthetical).

[54] IRC § 2652(c)(1)(B).

[55] IRC § 2652(c).

[56] IRC § 2652(c)(1)(A) (parenthetical).

[57] IRC § 2652(c)(1)(B). It is assumed that *C*'s interest is not used primarily to postpone or avoid the imposition of the generation-skipping transfer tax. Reg. § 26.2612-1(e)(2)(ii). However, as income is distributed to *GC*, the distributions would be taxable distributions under Section 2612(b). See ¶ 13.02[3].

[58] IRC § 2651(f)(2). In determining whether any transfer to a trust is a direct skip or a taxable distribution, the Section 2651(f)(2) look-through rules do not apply. IRC § 2612(c)(2); Reg. § 26.2612-1(c)(2). The rationale for this rule is discussed in detail at ¶ 13.02[4][b][iii].

ual is a skip person, so that it can be determined whether the trust is a skip person.[59] If one trust holds a Chapter 13 interest in a second trust, the determination as to whether the first trust is a skip person must be made in the process of determining whether the second trust is a skip person.[60]

[b] No Person Holds a Chapter 13 Interest but All Distributions Must Be to Skip Persons

Where no person holds a Chapter 13 interest in the trust,[61] but future distributions from the trust (including a terminating distribution) can be made only to skip persons, the trust is treated as a skip person.[62] Again, if the only beneficiaries of the trust are natural persons, the required determination is whether all possible beneficiaries are skip persons.[63] If a trust is a beneficiary, it must be determined whether that trust is a skip person.[64] If an entity other than a trust is a beneficiary of a trust, all beneficial interests in the entity must be owned by skip persons for the trust to be classified as a skip person.[65] The possibility of a distribution to a non-skip person, the probability of which is so

---

[59] For example, if a trust provides for income to a corporation for ten years with a remainder to the shareholders of the corporation at the end of ten years and if the corporation is owned by skip persons and non-skip persons, the trust is not a skip person. IRC §§ 2613(a)(2)(A), 2651(f)(2). However, if the corporation is owned only by skip persons, the trust is a skip person. IRC §§ 2613(a)(2)(A), 2651(f)(2). See infra ¶ 13.03[4][b] text accompanying notes 84–85.

[60] Assume that the terms of the first trust provide for income to the transferor's child for life and a remainder to the transferor's grandchild, and the terms of the second trust provide for income to the first trust for ten years, then a remainder to the transferor's grandchild. Under Section 2613(a)(2), the first trust is not a skip person because the child, who has the only Chapter 13 interest in the first trust, is not a skip person, and, therefore, the second trust is also not a skip person. IRC § 2613(a)(2)(A).

[61] IRC § 2613(a)(2)(B)(i). For purposes of Section 2613(a)(2)(B)(i), only beneficiaries holding Chapter 13 interests as determined under Section 2652(c) are considered. See supra ¶ 13.03[3][a] text accompanying notes 38–45. Any interest that is used primarily to postpone or avoid a Chapter 13 tax is disregarded. IRC § 2652(c)(2).

[62] IRC § 2613(a)(2)(B)(ii). See infra text accompanying note 66. However, Section 2613(a)(2)(B)(ii) does not use the term "interest"; therefore, one must look beyond "Chapter 13 interests." See supra note 61. In determining potential distributees, the Section 2652(c)(2) rule disregarding certain interests is inapplicable. All beneficial interests are considered in determining whether a distribution may be made to a non-skip person.

[63] IRC § 2613(a)(1).

[64] IRC § 2613(a)(2). See supra ¶ 13.03[3][a] note 60.

[65] IRC § 2651(f)(2). See IRC § 2612(c)(2); supra ¶ 13.03[3][a] text accompanying notes 58, 59. If a trust owns an interest in the entity, Section 2613(a)(2) tests again must be used to determine whether that trust is a skip person. See supra ¶ 13.03[3][a] note 60.

remote as to be negligible, is disregarded in determining whether or not the trust is a skip person.[66]

The following examples illustrate this second type of skip person trust. First, assume that a grantor G transfers property to a trust, income to be accumulated for ten years and then distributed to G's grandchild GC (whose parents are alive)[67] for life, with the remainder to G's great-grandchild GGC or GGC's estate. At the time of the transfer to the trust, no person has a Chapter 13 interest in the trust.[68] Nevertheless, the trust is classified as a skip person because no distribution may be made to a non-skip person at any time after the transfer; only distributions to skip persons are possible.[69] If the facts of this example are altered slightly and a testamentary nongeneral power over the remainder interest is given to GC (or, in default, to GC's heirs), the trust is no longer a skip person if the remainder interest may be appointed to a non-skip person. Although no person holds a Chapter 13 interest in the trust, distributions eventually may be made to non-skip persons.[70] Either GC may appoint the property to persons who are non-skip persons or GC's heirs may include non-skip persons.[71]

---

[66] Reg. § 26.2612-1(d)(2)(ii). If the actuarial probability that a distribution to a non-skip person will occur is less than 5 percent, the distribution possibility is classified as so remote as to be negligible. Id.

[67] See supra ¶ 13.03[3][a] note 49.

[68] IRC § 2613(a)(2)(B)(i). No person has other than a future right to income or corpus of the trust (see IRC § 2652(c)(1)(A)), and no person is a permissible current recipient of income or corpus. IRC § 2652(c)(1)(B). The Section 2652(c)(1)(C) definition of "interest" is also inapplicable here. See supra ¶ 13.03[3][a] note 44.

[69] IRC § 2613(a)(2)(B)(ii). Possible distribution to the estate of GGC is to be treated simply as a transfer to GGC. Cf. Walton v. Comm'r 115 TC 589 (2000). To interpret the term "estate" as other than to GGC would effectively erase Section 2613(a)(2)(B) from the Code. See infra ¶ 13.03[4][a] note 83.

[70] IRC § 2613(b). See IRC § 2613(a)(2)(B)(ii). But see Reg. § 26.2612-1(d)(2)(ii); supra text accompanying note 66.

[71] Alternatively, if GC held a general testamentary power of appointment over the remainder and in default to GC's heirs, the same result would be reached. Because GC could appoint to both skip and non-skip persons, or GC's heirs might include such persons, the Section 2613(a)(2)(B)(ii) requirement is not satisfied, the trust is not a skip person, and there would be no direct skip on a transfer to the trust. The result would be identical if the trust provided for a remainder to the estate of GC because, in essence, a remainder to the estate of GC is the same as giving GC a testamentary general power to appoint the remainder. See infra ¶ 13.03[4][a] text accompanying note 82.

It is tempting to treat a transfer to a trust in which GC has a testamentary general power to appoint as a transfer of the remainder to GC. But that treatment is inappropriate here. See Reg. §§ 26.2652-1(a)(5) Ex. 5; 26.2612-1(f) Ex. 3. At the point in time that Chapter 11 or Chapter 12 treats GC as transferring the property subject to the power (see ¶ 13.02[2][e] notes 95, 96), the property is treated as distributed by the trust to GC and transferred by GC, who becomes the Section 2652(a)(1) transferor of the property. See also Reg. § 26.2612-1(c)(1). But until that time, GC is not treated as the recipient of the

[c] Trust Equivalent Arrangements

If the transferee entity is a trust equivalent arrangement,[72] the entity is treated just like a trust for purposes of determining whether or not it is classified as a skip person.[73] The regulations provide the following example:

> On August 1, 1997, *T*, the insured under an insurance policy, dies. The policy provides that the insurance company shall make monthly payments of $750 to *GC*, *T*'s grandchild, for life with the remainder payable to *T*'s great grandchild, *GGC*. The face value of the policy is $300,000. Since the proceeds will continue to be held by the insurance company (the trustee), the proceeds are treated as if they were transferred to a trust for purposes of Chapter 13. The trust is a skip person (as defined in section 2613(a)(2)). . . .[74]

[4] Nontrust Entities

[a] Estates

An estate is a "person" for tax purposes,[75] but it is not a natural person and, thus, cannot be classified as a skip person.[76] Nor can an estate acquire skip person status as a trust equivalent arrangement, because estates are ex-

---

property. As a practical matter, this means that the generation-skipping transfer is postponed because *GC* has a general power of appointment. A transfer to the trust in which *GC* has the general power of appointment is not a transfer to a skip person, and there is no immediate direct skip to the trust. See also Reg. §§ 26.2652-1(a)(5) Ex. 5, 26.2612-1(f) Ex. 3. Income distributions to *GC* during life would constitute taxable distributions under Section 2612(b). At *GC*'s death, *GC*'s interests as income beneficiary, power holder, and potential appointee all terminate, and the property is deemed to be distributed to *GC* (see ¶ 13.02[2][e] text accompanying notes 107, 108) in a Section 2612(a)(1) taxable termination. The deemed distribution upon termination to *GC*, a skip person, is not a "transfer subject to the Federal estate or gift tax with respect to the property held in trust." Reg. § 26.2612-1(b)(1)(i). If *GC* exercised the power and appointed the property to a third party, there would be a deemed transfer subject to the federal estate or gift tax to the appointee. The deemed distribution would satisfy the requirements of a taxable distribution but for the parenthetical language contained in Section 2612(b). See also Reg. § 26.2612-1(c)(1). Thus, the generation-skipping transfer of the corpus of the trust is postponed until *GC*'s death.

[72] IRC §§ 2652(b)(1), 2652(b)(3).

[73] See supra ¶¶ 13.03[3][a], 13.03[3][b].

[74] Reg. § 26.2662-1(c)(2)(vi) Ex. 3.

[75] IRC § 7701(a)(1).

[76] IRC § 2613(a)(1).

pressly excluded from the definition of trust-like arrangements.[77] As an entity, a transferee estate is never a skip person. Instead, the estate loses its entity identity and each person having a beneficial interest in the estate is treated as having an interest in the property held by the estate.[78] Each beneficial interest held by an individual or a trust in a transferee estate will be classified separately as a skip person or a non-skip person.[79]

When a decedent dies and bequeaths property, the generation-skipping transfer consequences of the testamentary transfer are determined by disregarding the estate as an entity. For example, if the decedent's will provides a bequest to decedent's child and a bequest to decedent's grandchild, only the latter bequest, which is to a skip person, would constitute a direct skip.[80] If a transferor makes a transfer to the estate of an individual who has predeceased the transfer, the transferee estate is pierced and the individuals, trusts, or other entities with beneficial interests in the estate are ascertained and classified as either skip persons or non-skip persons.[81] A transfer to the estate of individual X who is still living essentially confers on X a general power to appoint the property by will,[82] whereas a transfer to an individual or an individual's estate should simply be treated as a transfer to the individual.[83]

---

[77] IRC § 2652(b)(1) (parenthetical).

[78] IRC § 2651(f)(2).

[79] IRC § 2613.

[80] IRC § 2612(c)(1).

[81] Assume that A makes an inter vivos or testamentary transfer to the estate of sibling B after B's death. Assume also that one third of B's estate passes to B's child C, one-third is transferred to a trust with income to B's grandchild GC for life and a remainder to B's great-grandchild GGC, and one-third is transferred to a corporation owned equally by C and GC. The first third is a transfer to a non-skip person and is not a Section 2612(c) direct skip. The second third is a transfer to a skip person trust (all Chapter 13 interests in the trust are held by GC, who is a skip person) and constitutes a Section 2612(c) direct skip. The final third is a transfer to a nontrust entity in which a skip person and a non-skip person each hold one half of the beneficial interest, with the result that there is a Section 2612(c) direct skip of one half of the final third transfer to the corporation. See infra ¶ 13.03[4][b] text accompanying note 84.

[82] The transfer to the estate of an individual will result in the property's being included in the individual's gross estate under Section 2041(a)(2). Cf. Keeter v. United States, 461 F2d 714 (5th Cir. 1972); ¶ 4.05[6] text accompanying note 76.

While the transfer is to an estate, it is essentially transferred to be held in some type of custodial arrangement until the power holder's death. As such, it is a Section 2652(b)(1) trust equivalent arrangement with income to be accumulated until X's death and a remainder to X's appointees. The trust equivalent is not a skip person because under Section 2613(a)(2)(B)(ii) the property may eventually pass to a non-skip person. As such, the transfer is not a Section 2612(c)(1) direct skip. However, a taxable termination to X occurs at X's death. See supra ¶ 13.03[3][b] note 71.

[83] If the transfer is to an individual or an individual's estate, the individual's estate is not an existing entity while the individual is alive, and the transfer should be treated as simply to the individual. A failure to reach this conclusion would effectively erase Section

[b] Other Nontrust Entities

When the transferee is not an individual, a trust, a trust equivalent arrangement, or an estate, the entity is disregarded and each individual or trust that has a beneficial interest in the entity is treated as having an interest in the property transferred to the entity. For example, a transfer of property to a corporation is a gift to each shareholder to the extent of the shareholder's proportionate interest in the corporation.[84] Each shareholder, rather than the corporation, is treated as the transferee and may qualify as the skip person.[85] Consequently, some portions of the gift may be generation-skipping transfers, while other portions may not. If, for example, the transferor's niece and the niece's two children each own one third of the corporation, two thirds of the property transferred to the corporation is essentially transferred to skip persons[86] and would constitute a Section 2612(c)(1) direct skip. If another corporation is a shareholder, it too is pierced to determine the extent to which the shareholders are skip persons. If a trust is one of the shareholders, the trust is a transferee and the trust will be either a skip person or a non-skip person, depending on the status of its beneficiaries.[87]

[5] Non-Skip Person

The definition of "non-skip person" may very well be the simplest in the Code. A non-skip person, sensibly enough, is any natural person or trust that is not a skip person.[88] Once the definition of "skip person" is mastered, the definition of "non-skip person" is child's play. Each individual or trust not classified as a skip person is a non-skip person.[89]

2613(a)(2)(B) from the Code because under Section 2613(a)(2)(B)(ii), one's estate would always potentially include a non-skip person.

[84] Reg. § 25.2511-1(h)(1). See ¶ 9.04[1][b].

[85] See IRC § 2613(a)(1).

[86] See IRC § 2613(a)(1).

[87] See supra ¶ 13.03[3]. If the corporation (in the text supra accompanying note 86) were owned one-third by the transferor's niece and two-thirds by a trust in which the niece's two children held an income interest for life, with a remainder to their children, the trust would be a Section 2613(a)(2)(A) skip person, and two thirds of the amount transferred to the corporation would be a Section 2613(c)(1) direct skip. Note that there was no look-through for determining whether there was a direct skip to the trust beneficiaries. IRC § 2612(c)(2). See supra ¶ 13.03[3][a] note 58.

[88] IRC § 2613(b). Entities other than trusts are pierced, and those individuals and trusts having beneficial interests in the entities are classified as skip persons or non-skip persons.

[89] See supra note 88; supra ¶ 13.03[2] text accompanying notes 19, 20.

A transferor's spouse as well as a transferor's children, nieces and nephews, and parents or spouses of such persons and unrelated individuals not more than thirty-seven and one-half years younger than the transferor are non-skip persons. A trust with income to a grantor's child for life and a remainder to grantor's grandchild is also a non-skip person.[90]

---

[90] Similarly, assume a decedent devises in a will a legal life estate in a personal residence to a child, with a remainder to a grandchild. This transfer is considered made to a trust because the legal life estate is a trust equivalent arrangement. IRC § 2652(b)(3). The trust is a non-skip person because a Chapter 13 interest in the trust is held by a non-skip person, the child, who is assigned a generation level just one level below the level assigned the decedent.

CHAPTER 14

Taxable Amount

¶ 14.01 INTRODUCTION

The amount of tax imposed on any generation-skipping transfer is determined by multiplying the "taxable amount" by the "applicable rate."[1] This chapter discusses the taxable amount, the tax base of the generation-skipping transfer tax. The applicable rate[2] is the product of the inclusion ratio[3] (a decimal fraction determined by the amount of GST exemption allocated to the property[4] and certain deductions)[5] and the maximum federal estate tax rate.[6] These concepts are discussed in Chapters 15 and 16.

The Internal Revenue Code (the Code) provides separate definitions of the taxable amount for each of the three types of generation-skipping transfers: taxable distributions,[7] taxable terminations,[8] and direct skips.[9] It also prescribes the time and method of valuation of the taxable amount.[10] The taxable amount of a generation-skipping transfer (both what is included and the method and time of valuation) is intended to be "closely analogous" to the taxable amount of estate and gift tax transfers.[11]

¶ 14.02 SECTION 2621. TAXABLE AMOUNT IN CASE OF TAXABLE DISTRIBUTIONS

[1] In General

The taxable amount of a taxable distribution[1] is the value of the property received by the transferee,[2] reduced by any consideration provided by the transferee[3] and any expenses incurred by the transferee in connection with the

---

[1] IRC § 2602.

[2] IRC § 2641(a). See ¶ 16.01.

[3] IRC § 2641(a)(2). See ¶ 16.02.

[4] IRC § 2631. See ¶ 15.02.

[5] IRC § 2642(a)(2)(B)(ii). See ¶ 16.02.

[6] IRC §§ 2641(a)(1), 2641(b). See ¶ 16.01.

[7] IRC § 2621. See ¶ 14.02.

[8] IRC § 2622. See ¶ 14.03.

[9] IRC § 2623. See ¶ 14.04.

[10] IRC § 2624. See ¶ 14.05.

[11] HR Conf. Rep. No. 426, 99th Cong., 1st Sess. 827 (1985), reprinted in 1986-3 CB (Vol. 2) 1, 827.

[1] IRC § 2612(b). See ¶ 13.02[3].

[2] IRC § 2621(a)(1).

[3] IRC § 2624(d). See ¶ 14.05[3].

determination, collection, or refund of the tax imposed by Chapter 13 with respect to the taxable distribution.[4] If the generation-skipping transfer tax imposed on a taxable distribution is paid by the trust, that payment constitutes another taxable distribution.[5]

[2] Valuation of Property Received by the Transferee

The first step in determining the taxable amount of a taxable distribution is to determine the value of the property received by the transferee.[6] The "value" to which the statute refers is the fair market value[7] of the property received by the transferee in the taxable distribution. Fair market valuation is the only method of valuation available in determining the taxable amount of a taxable distribution.[8]

The property received by the transferee in a taxable distribution is valued at the time of the generation-skipping transfer.[9] The statute allows no alternate date for valuing such property.[10]

[3] Reductions

The value of the property received by the transferee is reduced by any consideration provided by the transferee[11] and by any expenses incurred by the transferee in connection with the determination, collection, or refund of the tax imposed by Chapter 13 with respect to the taxable distribution.[12] The expenses that may be offset against the value of the property parallel those expenses for which a deduction is authorized by Section 212(3) of the Code in the determination of the federal income tax:[13] fees paid to attorneys, accountants, or ap-

---

[4] IRC § 2621(a)(2). See infra ¶ 14.02[3].

[5] IRC § 2621(b). See infra ¶ 14.02[4].

[6] IRC § 2621(a)(1).

[7] See Reg. § 20.2031-1(b).

[8] See IRC § 2624, discussed at ¶ 14.05. The valuation method provided by Section 2032A for the determination of the federal estate tax is inapplicable to the valuation of property for the determination of the taxable amount of a taxable distribution. Cf. IRC § 2624(b).

[9] IRC § 2624(a). See ¶ 14.05[1].

[10] IRC § 2642(a). See ¶ 14.05[1]. Cf. IRC §§ 2624(b), 2624(c). An alternate valuation date, like that provided for in Section 2032 for estate tax purposes, is not available. See IRC § 2032; ¶ 4.03.

[11] IRC § 2624(d). See ¶ 14.05[3].

[12] IRC § 2621(a)(2).

[13] See Reg. § 1.212-1(*l*).

praisers for tax advice, return preparation, and valuation[14] as well as expenses incurred in an administrative or judicial dispute with respect to the tax liability.[15]

To qualify for the reduction, the expenses must be incurred.[16] Expenses incurred but not paid, regardless of the transferee's method of accounting, qualify for the deduction. Such expenses must sometimes be estimated in determining the taxable amount in the same manner that expenses incurred in the administration of a decedent's estate are frequently estimated and deducted in the computation of the decedent's federal estate tax liability.[17] Once such expenses are ascertained, it may be necessary to amend the return filed with respect to the taxable distribution.

The Code provisions for the estate tax and the income tax both allow a deduction for certain administrative expenses and theft and casualty losses,[18] but Section 642(g) generally disallows deduction of the same amount under both taxes.[19] Although Section 2621(a)(2) allows a reduction of the taxable amount in a taxable distribution by the amount of Section 212(3) expenses, Section 642(g) generally disallows deduction of the same expenses under both Section 212(3) in the computation of the transferee's taxable income and Section 2621(a) in the computation of the amount of a taxable distribution.[20]

[4] Tax Payment as a Taxable Distribution

The Chapter 13 tax imposed on a taxable distribution is the liability of the transferee.[21] If any portion of that tax is paid by the trust from which the dis-

---

[14] See Bittker & Lokken, Federal Taxation of Income, Estates and Gifts, ¶ 20.5.4 (Warren, Gorham & Lamont 1999).

[15] Reg. § 1.212-1(*l*).

[16] IRC § 2621(a)(2).

[17] See Reg. §§ 20.2053-1(b)(3), 20.2053-3(b). See also ¶ 5.03[3][a], text accompanying notes 41–47. It is likely that the regulations will provide that where the amount of the expense is estimated, the reduction will be allowed only to the extent that the amount claimed will be paid.

[18] See IRC §§ 165, 212(2), 2053, 2054.

[19] In general, Section 642(g) (but see its last sentence) disallows an income tax deduction for the same amounts allowed under Section 2053 or Section 2054 as a deduction in computing the taxable estate of a decedent. The deduction allowable under Section 2053 or Section 2054 may be waived and the deduction allowed as an income tax deduction under Section 212(2) or Section 165. A portion of the deduction may be taken under each tax. Reg. § 1.642(g)-2. The role of Section 642(g) is discussed in depth at ¶ 5.03[3][d].

[20] IRC § 642(g) (second sentence). But see IRC § 642(g) (last sentence).

[21] IRC § 2603(a)(1). See ¶ 12.03[1] text accompanying note 5. Section 164(a)(4) allows the transferee an income tax deduction for generation-skipping transfer tax imposed

tribution is made, the Code appropriately treats an amount equal to the amount of tax paid as an additional taxable distribution.[22] This result would likely be reached, even without statutory assistance, under the income tax principle of the *Old Colony Trust* case.[23] Because the trust's payment of the tax is discharging a personal liability of the transferee,[24] it has (aside from possible timing differences[25]) the same substantive effect as an additional taxable distribution to the transferee, followed by the transferee's subsequent payment of the tax.

The tax-payment taxable distribution is treated as occurring on the last day of the calendar year in which the original taxable distribution is made.[26] The initial taxable distribution is grossed up by the amount of the additional tax-payment distribution. This is so even though the actual tax payment is made in the calendar year following the year of the initial taxable distribution.[27] The determination of the amount of the tax-payment taxable distribution requires an interdependent variable computation because the amount of the taxable distribution affects the tax to be paid, and the tax to be paid affects the taxable distribution.[28] For example, assume that a $1 million taxable distribu-

---

by Section 2601 and state tax described in Section 2604 imposed on transfers included in the gross income of the distributee to which Section 666 (accumulation distributions allocated to preceding years, commonly referred to as throwback distributions) does not apply. IRC §§ 164(a)(4), 164(b)(4).

[22] IRC § 2621(b). Payment of the Chapter 13 tax imposed on a taxable distribution by the trust should also be treated as a trust distribution to the transferee for income tax purposes under subchapter J. IRC §§ 651, 652, 661, 662, 663.

[23] Old Colony Trust Co. v. Comm'r, 279 US 716 (1929). See infra text accompanying note 32.

[24] IRC § 2603(a)(1). See ¶ 12.03[1].

[25] See infra text accompanying notes 26–29.

[26] Reg. § 26.2612-1(c). See ¶ 13.02[3][c].

[27] If the Chapter 13 tax is paid out of trust assets, the tax payment will generally occur in the calendar year following the initial taxable distribution because the tax imposed by Chapter 13 on a taxable distribution is due at the time the return reporting the taxable distribution is filed. IRC §§ 2661, 6151. The return is to be filed by April 15 of the year following the year in which the taxable distribution occurs. IRC §§ 664(a), 2662(a)(2)(B). If the generation-skipping transfer tax imposed on all taxable distributions is paid by the trust when the return is due and the tax-payment taxable distributions are treated as made in the year the tax payment is made, rather than grossed up and treated as paid in the year of the initial taxable distribution, transfers ad infinitum could result. Payment of the tax on the initial taxable distribution occurring in year one by the trust in year two would yield a tax-payment taxable distribution in year two. If the trust discharges the tax on the year two tax-payment taxable distribution when the return is due in year three, another tax-payment taxable distribution results in year three, and so it could go on ad infinitum. The regulations negate the possibility of transfers ad infinitum where the generation-skipping transfer tax on a taxable distribution is paid by the trust. Reg. § 26.2612-1(c).

[28] Although the gross-up approach makes the determination of the amount of the taxable distribution slightly more complex and accelerates the time of payment of the Chap-

tion is made from a trust and that the applicable rate of tax is 50 percent. If the Chapter 13 tax imposed on this $1 million taxable distribution is paid out of the trust, there is an additional tax-payment taxable distribution on the last day of the calendar year in which the $1 million distribution was made in the amount of $1 million, resulting in a total taxable distribution of $2 million for that calendar year.[29]

Expenses incurred in the determination of the Chapter 13 tax imposed on a taxable distribution should be paid by the transferee, who is personally responsible for paying the tax.[30] Payment of such expenses out of trust assets, if not reimbursed by the transferee, should also be treated as a taxable distribution[31] under the principle of the *Old Colony Trust* case.[32] These expenses may be deducted in computing the taxable amount of the taxable distribution to which the expenses are related,[33] regardless of the timing of the taxable distribution generated by their payment. Since the expense deduction will ultimately be matched by an amount equal to the expense-payment taxable distribution, it would be simpler to treat the expense deduction and expense-payment taxable distribution as a wash and not allow the deduction for these expenses for income or generation-skipping transfer tax purposes nor require an expense-payment taxable distribution in the first instance.

---

ter 13 tax, it simplifies the administration of Chapter 13 by reducing the number of returns required to be filed. The trustee can opt out of the tax-payment taxable distribution gross-up by merely making a distribution in the next calendar year to the distributee to cover the tax incurred on the prior year's distribution, rather than paying it directly from the trust. Ultimately, the same amount of tax will be paid, but payment of the tax will be delayed because it will be paid ad infinitum. See ¶ 13.02[3][c] text accompanying notes 235–238.

[29] The $1 million received by the transferee represents 50 percent of the sum of the $1 million distributed to the transferee and the $1 million tax payment distribution.

If there is a change in plans and the trustee does not pay all the taxes imposed on the taxable distribution, an adjustment to the grossed-up amount is required.

[30] IRC § 2603(a)(1).

[31] The trust's payment of the transferee's expenses in connection with the determination, collection, or refund of the Chapter 13 tax imposed on the distribution should also be treated as a constructive trust distribution to the transferee for income tax purposes under subchapter J. IRC §§ 651, 652, 661, 662, 663.

[32] Old Colony Trust Co. v. Comm'r, 279 US 716 (1929).

[33] IRC § 2621(a)(2). The expenses may be used to reduce the taxable amount of the taxable distribution or deducted for income tax purposes, but not both. IRC § 642(g). See supra ¶ 14.02[3] text accompanying notes 18–20.

¶ 14.03 SECTION 2622. TAXABLE AMOUNT IN CASE OF TAXABLE TERMINATIONS

[1] In General

The taxable amount of a taxable termination[1] is the value of all property involved in the taxable termination,[2] reduced by the amount of any deductions of the type allowed by Section 2053[3] and by the value of any consideration furnished by the transferee.[4] In general, the property involved is valued at its fair market value on the date of the taxable termination.[5] However, if the termination occurs as a result of the death of an individual, the property may be valued under the alternate valuation date rules.[6] The taxable amount of a taxable termination is essentially the net value of the wealth transferred to the transferee, but with no reduction for the Chapter 13 tax imposed on the property transferred.

[2] Valuation of Property Involved in a Taxable Termination

The determination of the taxable amount, or tax base, of a taxable termination requires the identification and valuation of all property with respect to which the taxable termination has occurred.[7] Identification of the property transferred in a taxable distribution or a direct skip is not difficult. By contrast, both the transfer and the property transferred in a taxable termination may be less obvious where the termination does not involve the complete termination of the

---

[1] IRC § 2612(a)(1). See ¶ 13.02[2].

[2] IRC § 2622(a)(1).

[3] IRC §§ 2622(a)(2), 2622(b). See ¶ 5.03.

[4] IRC § 2624(d). See ¶ 14.05[3].

[5] IRC § 2624(a). See ¶ 14.05[1].

[6] IRC § 2624(c). See ¶ 14.05[2][b]. See also IRC § 2032, discussed at ¶ 4.03.

[7] IRC § 2622(a)(1).

trust. This is because a termination may involve only a shift in interests in some[8] or all of the property held in trust with no actual transfer of property.[9]

Property that is the subject matter of a taxable termination must be valued at its fair market value in the determination of the taxable amount. No other method of valuation is allowed.[10] Valuation generally occurs at the time of the taxable termination, which is the time of the terminating event.[11] However, if the taxable termination occurs at the same time as, and as a result of, the death of an individual, an election may be made to have the property valued on an alternate date in accordance with the principles of Section 2032.[12] The election to value property according to the principles of Section 2032 for the purposes of Chapter 13 tax is not conditioned upon a Section 2032 election for the purposes of the estate tax.[13]

[3] Reductions

In determining the taxable amount of a taxable termination, the value of all property with respect to which the termination occurred is reduced by any consideration provided by the transferee,[14] as well as by Section 2053–type expenses attributable to that property.[15] Section 2053–type expenses encompass

---

[8] Generally, the entire value of the property held in the trust will not be taxed when a taxable termination of a Chapter 13 interest in the property held in the trust occurs if (1) substantially separate and independent shares of different beneficiaries in the trust are treated as separate trusts (see IRC § 2654(b)(2), discussed at ¶ 17.04[2]); (2) the portions of the trust attributable to different transferors are treated as separate trusts (see IRC § 2654(b)(1), discussed at ¶ 17.04[2]); or (3) a specified portion of trust assets is distributed to a skip person and the distribution is treated as a taxable termination under Section 2612(a)(2) (which is discussed at ¶ 13.02[2][f]).

[9] For example, assume grantor *G* establishes a trust providing for income to child *C* for life and a remainder to grandchild *GC*. At *C*'s death, there is a taxable termination of the trust itself. The fair market value of all the trust assets on the applicable valuation date is the value of the property involved in the taxable termination. If, instead, the trust provided for income to *C* for life, then income to *GC* for life, and a remainder to *G*'s greatgrandchild *GGC*, the trust itself would not terminate at the death of *C*, but there would be a taxable termination of *C*'s Chapter 13 interest in the property held in trust and a shift in the other beneficiaries' relationships to the property. The method of valuation of the property involved, however, would be the same.

[10] Thus, valuation under Section 2032A is not permitted.

[11] IRC § 2624(a). See ¶ 14.05[1].

[12] IRC § 2624(c). See ¶ 14.05[2][b].

[13] IRC § 2624(c). See ¶ 14.05[2][b] text accompanying note 28.

[14] IRC § 2624(d). See ¶ 14.05[3].

[15] IRC §§ 2622(a)(2), 2622(b). Although reduction of the taxable amount by Section 212(3) expenses is expressly authorized by Section 2621(a)(2) only for taxable distributions, reduction for such expenses is also allowed with respect to taxable terminations.

administration expenses, including trust termination fees,[16] unpaid mortgages and indebtedness with respect to the property,[17] claims against the property, and accrued expenses at termination.[18] These expenses are all allowed as deductions in determining the taxable amount of the taxable termination. Some expenses may have to be estimated.[19] Section 642(g) prohibits a deduction for certain Section 2053–type expenses both in the determination of the taxable amount of a taxable termination and in the computation of the taxable income of the trust.[20]

The 1976 generation-skipping transfer tax statute contained a provision allowing a deduction for theft and casualty losses similar to those allowed under Section 2054.[21] There is no similar provision in the current statute imposing the generation-skipping transfer tax. In failing to reenact the provision, Congress may have concluded that with the termination of one interest immediately activating another interest, there was no period analogous to the settlement period during which such losses might occur. The elimination of this loss deduction provision is mitigated to some extent by the availability, in some instances, of the election for alternate date valuation of the property subjected to tax[22] and, where alternate date valuation is not used, by the availability of an income tax deduction for such losses.[23]

Section 2053 clearly contemplates the deduction of the items described in Section 212(3). See Reg. §§ 20.2053-3(c), 20.2053-3(d), which describe the administrative expenses deductible under Section 2053; among them are expenses paralleling those described in Reg. § 1.212-1(l). Section 2053 is discussed in detail at ¶ 5.03.

[16] See IRC § 2053(a)(2), discussed at ¶ 5.03[3].

[17] See IRC § 2053(a)(4), discussed at ¶ 5.03[6].

[18] See IRC § 2053(a)(3), discussed at ¶ 5.03[5].

[19] See Reg. § 20.2053-1(b)(3) regarding estimated amounts. It is likely that the regulation promulgated under Section 2053 will be applied where expenses are estimated here. See also Reg. § 20.2053-3; ¶ 5.03[3][a] text accompanying notes 41–47, ¶ 14.02[3] text accompanying note 17.

[20] IRC § 642(g) (second and third sentences). See ¶¶ 5.03[3][d], 5.03[5][c]. See also ¶ 14.02[3] text accompanying notes 18–20.

[21] This was provided for in Section 2602(c)(5)(A) prior to its repeal by the Tax Reform Act of 1986, Pub. L. No. 99-514, § 1431(a), 100 Stat. 2085, 2717–2718 (1986), reprinted in 1986-3 CB (Vol. 1) 1, 634–635.

[22] See supra ¶ 14.03[2] text accompanying notes 12, 13.

[23] IRC § 165.

¶ 14.04 SECTION 2623. TAXABLE AMOUNT IN CASE OF DIRECT SKIPS

[1] In General

The taxable amount in the case of a direct skip[1] is the value of the property received by the transferee,[2] reduced by any consideration provided by the transferee.[3]

[2] Valuation of Property Received by the Transferee

The property is generally valued at the time of the direct skip transfer.[4] Where property is involved in a direct skip, the transfer may take place at the time the gift is complete for gift tax purposes,[5] at the close of the estate tax inclusion period,[6] or at the date of the transferor's death.

If property included in the transferor's gross estate is the subject matter of a direct skip, the transfer is treated as occurring on the transferor's date of death. The transfer may actually occur at death or it may be a delayed inter vivos direct skip that is treated as occurring at death under Section 2642(f).[7] When the property is included in the transferor's gross estate, the Chapter 11 value of the property is used in determining the taxable amount of the direct skip.[8] If the property is valued pursuant to Section 2032 or Section 2032A for purposes of the estate tax, the same time and method of valuation must be used for determining the taxable amount of the direct skip generation-skipping transfer.[9]

If the property that is the subject matter of the direct skip is not included in the transferor's gross estate, the direct skip is treated as occurring either at the time the gift is complete for gift tax purposes or at the close of the estate

---

[1] IRC § 2612(c). See ¶ 13.02[4].

[2] IRC § 2623. See TAM 9822001 (Sept. 18, 1997) (taxable amount of direct skip does not include generation-skipping transfer tax paid by estate or donor).

[3] IRC § 2624(d). See ¶ 14.05[3].

[4] IRC § 2624(a). See ¶ 14.05[1].

[5] Reg. § 25.2511-2.

[6] IRC § 2642(f)(1). See ¶ 16.02[7][a].

[7] IRC §§ 2642(f)(1) (last sentence), 2642(f)(3). See ¶ 16.02[7][a].

[8] IRC § 2624(b). See infra note 9.

[9] IRC § 2624(b). But see ¶ 14.05[2][a] note 21 and ¶ 18.03[1] text accompanying notes 10 and 11 considering whether fair market valuation may be used for generation-skipping transfer tax purposes even though Section 2032A valuation is used for estate tax purposes.

tax inclusion period.[10] In either event, the property can be valued only at its fair market value[11] on the applicable date.[12]

[3] Reductions

The value of the property received by the transferee in a direct skip is reduced by the amount of any consideration provided by the transferee.[13] In the case of an inter vivos direct skip, the transfer will be considered a sale to the extent of the consideration provided by the transferee, and to that extent, it will not be subject to the tax imposed by Chapter 12 and, thus, will not constitute a direct skip. The regular Section 2624(d) rules governing reductions for consideration apply to a testamentary direct skip.[14]

Because the transferor or trustee is liable for the generation-skipping transfer tax imposed on a direct skip, the transferor or trustee is responsible for the payment of any expenses related to the computation of the tax.[15] These expenses do not reduce the value of the property received by the transferee. As only the net value of the property actually received by the transferee is subject to tax, the statute appropriately does not authorize any reductions in value for Section 212(3) expenses or Section 2053-type expenses incurred with respect to the transfer.[16]

---

[10] See supra text accompanying notes 5, 6.

[11] Reg. § 20.2031-1(b).

[12] See supra text accompanying notes 4–6. No alternate date and no alternative method of valuation is permitted for these transfers.

[13] IRC § 2624(d). See ¶ 14.05[3].

[14] IRC § 2624(d). See ¶ 14.05[3].

[15] IRC §§ 2603(a)(2), 2603(a)(3). Where a direct skip occurs at death with respect to property held in a trust equivalent arrangement, the executor of the transferor's estate must pay the generation-skipping transfer tax if the total value of the property involved in direct skips with respect to the pseudo-trustee of that trust equivalent arrangement is less than $250,000. Reg. § 26.2662-1(c)(2)(iii). The executor is entitled to recover the generation-skipping transfer taxes attributable to the property from the pseudo-trustee, if the property remains in a trust equivalent arrangement, or the recipient, in the case of a transfer from a trust equivalent arrangement. Reg. § 26.2662-1(c)(2)(v). See ¶ 12.03[2] text accompanying note 28.

[16] See TAM 9822001 (Sept. 8, 1997) (interest payable on estate and generation-skipping transfer tax does not reduce amount of direct skip).

¶ 14.05 SECTION 2624. VALUATION

[1] The General Rule

Section 2624(a) provides the rules to be used for valuation of the property in-cluded in the taxable amount of taxable distributions, taxable terminations, and direct skips.[1] The general rule is that the property must be valued at the time of the generation-skipping transfer,[2] employing the now-familiar fair market value test.[3] Although the general rule as to time and method of valuation is used to determine the taxable amounts of all three types of generation-skipping transfers, the rule for identifying the property transferred is different for each type.[4] Thus, for purposes of valuing the taxable amount, it is necessary to properly identify the type of generation-skipping transfer that has occurred.[5]

In all three types of generation-skipping transfers, where property is sub-ject to a nonrecourse liability only, the equity of redemption (the value of the property less the nonrecourse liability) is included in the taxable amount.[6] If the property is subject to a recourse liability, the assumption of the recourse li-ability is treated as consideration provided by the transferee, reducing the value of the property transferred under Section 2624(d).[7]

In a taxable distribution, the taxable amount is measured by the value of the property received by the transferee.[8] The same general valuation procedure applies with respect to direct skips,[9] which also requires valuation of only the property received by the transferee.[10] In a taxable termination, valuation must

---

[1] See IRC §§ 2621, 2622, 2623.

[2] IRC § 2624(a).

[3] Reg. § 20.2031-1(b).

[4] Compare IRC §§ 2621(a)(1), 2622(a)(1), 2623.

[5] The interrelationship of the three types of generation-skipping transfers becomes significant here. When there is overlap of two types of generation-skipping transfers, a di-rect skip and a taxable termination take priority over a taxable distribution. See ¶ 13.02[1][b]. A direct skip and taxable termination never overlap. See ¶ 13.02[2][d].

[6] Cf. Reg. § 20.2053-7.

[7] See infra ¶ 14.05[3]. Thus, assuming properties with equal value and subject to lia-bilities of the same amount, the net taxable amount will be the same whether the liability is with or without recourse.

[8] IRC § 2621(a)(1). See ¶ 14.02. Because the distributee is liable for any generation-skipping transfer tax imposed under Section 2603(a)(1), the statute allows the value of the property received to be reduced by any Section 212(3)–type expenses incurred by the transferee with respect to the distribution in arriving at the taxable amount of the taxable distribution. See ¶ 14.02[3].

[9] But cf. IRC § 2624(b), discussed infra ¶ 14.05[2][a].

[10] IRC § 2623. See ¶ 14.04. Because the tax imposed on the direct skip transfer is the liability of the transferor or the transferor's estate under Section 2603(a)(3) or the trus-

be made of "all property with respect to which the taxable termination has occurred."[11] Section 2053–type expenses assumed by the transferee should be treated as consideration furnished by the transferee and reduce the value of the property transferred in the taxable termination under Section 2624(d). In no event should Section 2053–type expenses assumed by the transferee be subtracted once as Section 2053 expenses under Section 2622(a)(2) and also as consideration furnished by the transferee under Section 2624(d) in the determination of the taxable amount of the taxable termination.

[2] Exceptions to Fair Market Valuation on the Date of Transfer Rule

The fair market valuation on the date of transfer rule is subject to two exceptions. The first exception applies to any direct skip involving property that is included in the transferor's gross estate. The second applies to a taxable termination occurring at the same time as, and as a result of, the death of an individual.

[a] Direct Skip Property Included in Transferor's Gross Estate

If a direct skip involves property that is included in the transferor's gross estate, Section 2624(b) requires that both the time and method of valuation used for estate tax purposes under Chapter 11 be used to value the property in the computation of the tax imposed under Chapter 13.[12] It makes no difference whether the direct skip is a transfer to an individual or to a trust.[13] Use of the same valuation for Chapter 13 and Chapter 11 facilitates the administration of both taxes.

Chapter 11 valuation generally involves use of the standard fair market value on the date of death.[14] For property included in a decedent's gross estate,

---

tee under 2603(a)(2), the transferee is allowed no deductions for Section 212(3)–type expenses. See ¶ 14.04[3]. Cf. IRC § 2621(a)(2).

[11] IRC § 2622(a)(1). See ¶ 14.03[2]. Section 2053–type expenses are permitted to be deducted from the valuation of the property with respect to which the taxable termination has occurred in arriving at the net taxable amount of the taxable termination. IRC §§ 2622(a)(2), 2622(b). See ¶ 14.03[3].

[12] IRC § 2624(b). But see infra note 21.

[13] The gross estate may also include trust property that is not the subject matter of a direct skip at the decedent's death but may eventually be subject to the generation-skipping transfer tax. Such property may have to be valued under Section 2642 in order to allocate the transferor's GST exemption and compute the inclusion ratio. See ¶¶ 15.03[7], 16.02[4].

[14] IRC § 2031. See ¶ 4.02.

however, an election may be made under Section 2032 to use an alternate valuation date,[15] which is generally six months after death rather than the date of death.[16] The Section 2032 election is permitted in the determination of both the estate and generation-skipping transfer taxes, but only if use of the alternate date results in a reduction of both the value of the gross estate under Chapter 11 and the total amount of Chapter 11 and Chapter 13 taxes imposed after reduction for allowable credits.[17]

Chapter 11 also permits the election of special-use valuation under Section 2032A[18] if the transferor's estate satisfies certain requirements.[19] Section 2032A valuation may also be used to calculate the generation-skipping transfer tax imposed on a testamentary direct skip[20] involving property valued under Section 2032A for estate tax purposes.[21]

---

[15] IRC § 2032. See ¶ 4.03. If a Section 2032 election is made, all the property included in the decedent's gross estate must be valued under Section 2032. IRC § 2032(a).

[16] IRC § 2032(a)(2). But see IRC §§ 2032(a)(1), 2032(a)(3).

[17] IRC § 2032(c). It is possible that an election would reduce the value of the gross estate, but not the total amount of Chapter 11 and Chapter 13 taxes. For example, assume a single individual, T, makes a $1,011,000 inter vivos direct skip in 2002, using the Section 2505 credit and allocating $1 million of the Section 2631 GST exemption to the direct skip. At T's death, in 2007, T makes a $2 million testamentary direct skip. The $4 million residue of T's estate is bequeathed to a child. Assume that six months after T's death, the testamentary direct skip property appreciates in value to $2.8 million, while the residue of T's estate declines in value to $3 million. On the alternate valuation date, the value of the gross estate would be smaller ($5.8 million compared with $6 million) but the total amount of Chapter 11 and Chapter 13 taxes would be larger: $2,970,000 (estate tax of $2,160,000 plus a generation-skipping transfer tax of $810,000) as compared with $2.7 million (estate tax of $2,250,000 plus a generation-skipping transfer tax of $450,000). Under the facts of this example, an election of the alternate valuation date is precluded by Section 2032(c)(2).

[18] See ¶ 4.04.

[19] These requirements are discussed at ¶¶ 4.04[2]–4.04[4].

[20] Cf. ¶ 18.03[1] text accompanying notes 10, 11, 12 involving the amount of the testamentary direct skip if an additional estate tax is imposed under Section 2032A(c).

[21] IRC § 2624(b). The agreement to use special-use valuation required under Section 2032A(d)(2), which is contained in Form 706, indicates that the qualified heirs agree and consent to personal liability under subsection (c) of Section 2032A for additional estate and generation-skipping transfer taxes imposed by that subsection upon subsequent dispositions of the property or early cessation of qualified use. Form 706, United States Estate (and Generation-Skipping Transfer) Tax Return (Rev. Nov. 2001), Schedule A-1, Part 3. Agreement to Special Valuation Under Section 2032A at 10.

Although Section 2624(b) provides that property valued under Section 2032A for federal estate tax purposes that is the subject matter of a testamentary direct skip *shall* be valued under Section 2032A in determining the taxable amount of that direct skip, regulations to be promulgated for this section may provide for a valuation option. Possibly the regulations will provide that in determining the taxable amount of a testamentary direct skip, real property valued under Section 2032A for federal estate tax purposes may be valued at fair market value for Chapter 13 purposes. This option, in determining the taxable

[b] Taxable Terminations at Death

The second exception to the general valuation rule allows an election to be made to use the alternative valuation date if the taxable termination occurs at the same time as, and as a result of, the death of an individual.[22] Section 2624(c) provides that the use of the alternate valuation date should be made "in accordance" with Section 2032.[23] The election to use the alternate valuation date[24] must be made by the trustee[25] on the generation-skipping transfer tax return.[26] Section 2624(c) incorporates the valuation rules of Section 2032.[27] The Section 2624(c) election should be made, and is allowed, only if the amount of the taxable termination and the corresponding net Chapter 13 tax liability after allowable credits are both reduced.[28]

---

amount, would be similar to the one afforded in the determination of the inclusion ratio and would offer the qualified heirs the opportunity to eliminate the risk of the imposition of additional generation-skipping transfer tax upon a later disposition or cessation of qualified use. See ¶¶ 16.02[4][d][i], 18.03[1] notes 10, 11; Reg. § 26.2642-2(b)(1). See also Reg. § 26.2642-4(a)(4).

[22] IRC § 2624(c).

[23] IRC § 2624(c).

[24] See IRC § 2032(a); ¶¶ 4.03[1], 4.03[2], 4.03[3].

[25] IRC § 2603(a)(2).

[26] IRC § 2662(a)(2). The alternate valuation election is made by checking the box on Form 706-GS(T), Generation-Skipping Transfer Tax Return for Terminations (Rev. July 1999), Schedule A, Line 3, at 2. Once made, the election, like the Section 2032 election, should be irrevocable. If the alternate valuation date falls after the initial due date of the return, the return filing date must be extended. Instructions for Form 706-GS(T), "Generation-Skipping Transfer Tax Return for Terminations" (Rev. July 1999) at 4. The election may be made on a late filed return, provided it is not filed later than one year after the due date (including extensions). Id. See IRC § 2032(d)(2).

[27] See ¶¶ 4.03[1], 4.03[2], 4.03[3]. The "in accordance" language of Section 2624(c) would seem to be able to incorporate the deduction rules of Section 2032(b) as well. But incorporation of Section 2032(b) would be of no practical consequence because Section 2032(b) is inapplicable to any Section 2053 deduction. As the Section 2622 rules for computing the taxable amount do not provide a deduction for Section 2054 losses, any such losses should not be limited and should be reflected in the alternate valuation. See ¶ 4.03[4][a]. If the transfer is to charity or qualifies for a marital deduction, it would not generate a taxable termination and no valuation would be necessary. See IRC §§ 2612(a), 2651(c)(1), 2651(f)(3). Cf. ¶ 4.03[4][b].

[28] Instructions for Form 706-GS(T), "Generation-Skipping Transfer Tax Return for Terminations" (Rev. July 1999) at 4. Cf. 2032(c)(2). There is no reason to elect the alternate valuation date except to reduce Chapter 13 taxes. Even though the alternate valuation date would affect the amount of the basis adjustment for income tax purposes (see ¶ 17.04[1][d]), the discrepancy between the relative rates (the maximum rate for the income tax compared with the maximum rate for the generation-skipping transfer tax) would preclude an election of alternative date valuation when the value of the property was higher. Even if a transfer is fully shielded from Chapter 13 liability by the use of the

The election is available to each separate trust. If a single trust generates more than one taxable termination upon the death of an individual, and the election to use the alternate valuation date is made, all the property involved in the terminations must be valued using the alternate date.[29] But where a single trust is required to be treated as more than one trust for purposes of Chapter 13,[30] a separate election should be available for each portion of the single trust treated as a separate trust. If only one such separate trust satisfies the requirements for alternate valuation, it should be permitted to use the alternate valuation date.

In promulgating Section 2624(c), Congress apparently thought that a taxable termination resulting from the death of an individual is sufficiently similar to the inclusion of property in an individual's gross estate to warrant the use of estate tax alternate valuation date provisions. If Congress was so thinking, it also should have provided for the use of the Section 2032A valuation method for taxable terminations that qualify for such valuation.[31]

Section 2624(c) possibly should have been more restrictive in its application. As it stands, the exception permitting alternate date valuation applies not only when a taxable termination occurs at the death of the income beneficiary of the trust involved in the taxable termination, but also when a taxable termination occurs at the same time as, and as a result of, the death of any individual whose life is the measuring life, whether or not that person has an interest in the trust. Thus, if grantor G established a trust providing income to child C for the life of C's mother-in-law with a remainder to grandchild GC, Section 2624(c) would apply to allow Section 2032 valuation of the taxable termination of C's interest in C's mother-in-law's death.

[3] Reduction for Consideration

The taxable amount of any generation-skipping transfer is the value of the property transferred reduced by the amount of any consideration provided by the transferee.[32] Consideration comprises transferring money, assuming any

---

GST exemption, a higher valuation would not help because no basis adjustment would occur. See ¶ 17.04[1][d] text accompanying notes 45, 46.

[29] See Instructions for Form 706-GS(T), "Generation-Skipping Transfer Tax Return for Terminations" (Rev. July 1999) at 4.

[30] IRC § 2654(b). See ¶ 17.04[2].

[31] Compare IRC § 2624(b). That Congress did not so provide may be due to the complexity involved in any attempt to integrate the Section 2032A rules into taxable terminations. However, creating complexity in other parts of Chapter 13 has not precluded congressional action.

[32] IRC § 2624(d).

personal liability,[33] *or* taking the property subject to any liability or claim.[34] If there is a transfer of property subject to a nonrecourse liability, there is no reduction for consideration because only the net value of the property, the fair market value of the property less the liability, is treated as transferred.[35]

The consideration reduction rule is easy to apply if the transferee provides consideration at the time of the generation-skipping transfer, but it is not as easily applied if the transferee provided consideration sometime before the generation-skipping transfer. For example, assume grantor *G* makes an inter vivos transfer of $500,000 to a trust providing for income to child *C* for life and a remainder to grandchild *GC*. Assume further that *GC*'s remainder interest is worth 10 percent of the corpus at the time the trust is created[36] and that *GC* uses $50,000 of personal funds to purchase the remainder from *G* for its fair market value. The payment constitutes adequate and full consideration. Unlike the transfer provisions of the estate tax and gift tax,[37] the generation-skipping transfer tax statute contains no express exception for adequate and full consideration in money or money's worth. However, the Chapter 13 transferor is defined with reference to the transfer of property subject to the tax imposed by Chapter 11 or Chapter 12. Seemingly, the remainder interest was transferred for an adequate consideration in money or money's worth and is not subject to the tax imposed by Chapter 12. Thus, there is no Section 2652(a) transferor of the property and no generation-skipping transfer.[39] If *GC* has provided less than adequate and full consideration in money or money's worth, the value of the property at the time of the taxable termination, less the actual dollar amount of consideration received, would likely constitute a generation-skipping transfer. This treatment of the receipt of partial consideration under Chapter 13 parallels the treatment of the receipt of partial consideration under Chapter 11.[40]

---

[33] See supra ¶ 14.05[1] text accompanying note 7.

[34] See supra ¶ 14.05[1]. Cf. Reg. § 20.2053-4.

[35] This is consistent with the treatment of nonrecourse liabilities under the federal estate and gift tax provisions. See Reg. § 20.2053-7; ¶¶ 5.03[6], 10.02[2][a]. See also supra ¶ 14.05[1] text accompanying note 6.

[36] See IRC § 7520.

[37] IRC §§ 2035(d), 2036(a), 2037(a), 2038(a).

[39] This is appropriate because if the consideration received at the time the trust is created produces a rate of return commensurate with the actuarial tables, there is no depletion of *G*'s property. When the remainder passes to *GC*, there should not be a generation-skipping transfer.

[40] See IRC § 2043(a); ¶ 4.15[1].

CHAPTER 15

The Generation-Skipping
Transfer Exemption

¶ 15.01   INTRODUCTION

This chapter covers Sections 2631 and 2632 of the Internal Revenue Code (the Code). Section 2631 allows every individual essentially to exempt from the generation-skipping transfer tax imposed by Chapter 13 generation-skipping transfers of property equal in value to the amount of the GST exemption, statutorily referred to as the GST exemption. Section 2632 provides rules for allocating the GST exemption to gratuitous transfers of property, whether made during life or at death. Chapter 16 deals with Sections 2641 and 2642, which provide for the integration of an individual's GST exemption with the rate of tax to be imposed on generation-skipping transfers.

¶ 15.02 SECTION 2631. THE GST EXEMPTION

Every individual is allowed a GST exemption in the amount of $1 million[1] adjusted upward for inflation until December 31, 2003.[2] On and after January 1, 2004, the GST exemption amount equals the estate tax applicable exclusion amount under Section 2010(c).[3]

The $1 million GST exemption was adjusted for inflation for the calendar year 1999 to $1,010,000,[4] to $1,030,000 for the year 2000,[5] to $1,060,000 for the year 2001,[6] and to $1,100,000 for the year 2002.[7] An inflationary increase in the amount of the GST exemption for a calendar year before 2004 applies only to generation-skipping transfers made during or after that calendar year.[8] Thus, a deceased transferor may not use an inflationary increase in the GST exemption for a calendar year after the calendar year of the transferor's death.[9] Once an inflationary increase is made to the amount of the GST exemption,

---

[1] IRC § 2631(a).

[2] IRC § 2631(c)(1). The $1 million GST exemption is subject to inflationary increases after 1998 and before 2004. The amount of the inflationary adjustment is determined by multiplying the cost-of-living adjustment determined under a modified version of Section 1(f)(3) for the calendar year by $1 million. IRC § 2631(c)(1). The Section 1(f)(3) cost-of-living adjustment is modified by subtracting the Consumer Price Index for the calendar year of 1997 from the Consumer Price Index for the preceding calendar year. IRC § 2631(c)(1)(B). Inflationary adjustments to the GST exemption will be made only in multiples of $10,000, rounded to the next lowest multiple of $10,000. IRC § 2631(c)(1).

[3] IRC § 2631(c) (as amended by Economic Growth and Tax Relief Reconciliation Act of 2001, Pub. L. No. 107-16, § 521(c)(2), 115 Stat. 38, 72, reprinted in 2001-__ CB __, __). This section, as amended, is applicable to estates of decedents dying, and generation-skipping transfers, after December 31, 2003. Economic Growth and Tax Relief Reconciliation Act of 2001, Pub. L. No. 107-16, § 521(e)(3), 115 Stat. 38, 72 (2001), reprinted in 2001-__ CB __, __).

[4] Rev. Proc. 98-61, 1998-2 CB 811, 816.

[5] Rev. Proc. 99-42, 1999-2 CB 568, 572.

[6] Rev. Proc. 2001-13, 2001-1 CB 337, 341.

[7] Rev. Proc. 2001-59, 2001-2 CB __, __.

[8] IRC § 2631(c)(2) (prior to amendment by Economic Growth and Tax Relief Reconciliation Act of 2001, Pub. L. No. 107-16, § 521(c)(2), 115 Stat. 38, 72, reprinted in 2001-__ CB __, __). The increase is based on the statutorily granted $1 million exemption, not the $1 million exemption less amounts previously allocated by the taxpayer. An individual who allocates the entire GST exemption in a year is eligible to utilize post allocation increases that occur due to the inflation adjustment as they see fit.

[9] IRC § 2631(c)(2) (prior to amendment by Economic Growth and Tax Relief Reconciliation Act of 2001, Pub. L. No. 107-16, § 521(c)(2), 115 Stat. 38, 72, reprinted in 2001-__ CB __, __).

even if there is a deflationary period, there is no decrease in the amount of the GST exemption.[10]

The applicable exclusion amount of Section 2010(c) and therefore the GST exemption amount is scheduled to increase from $1.5 million in 2004, to $2 million in 2006, and to $3.5 million in 2009.[11] These scheduled step increases are not adjusted for inflation.[12] In what might be described as the ultimate unlimited GST exemption, generation-skipping transfers after December 31, 2009, are not subjected to the generation-skipping transfer tax imposed by Chapter 13.[13]

The GST exemption provided by Section 2631 is an important factor in the determination of the applicable rate of tax to be imposed on any generation-skipping transfer. The applicable rate of tax[14] is the product of the maximum Section 2001(c) federal estate tax rate[15] and the inclusion ratio.[16] The amount of the inclusion ratio is dependent on the amount of the transferor's GST exemption allocated to the transfer. The inclusion ratio is equal to one minus the applicable fraction.[17] The GST exemption allocated[18] to a transfer is the numerator of the applicable fraction,[19] and the value of the property trans-

---

[10] IRC § 2631(c)(1) (prior to amendment by Economic Growth and Tax Relief Reconciliation Act of 2001, Pub. L. No. 107-16, § 521(c)(2), 115 Stat. 38, 72, reprinted in 2001-__ CB __, __).

[11] IRC § 2010(c). See ¶ 3.02.

[12] IRC § 2631(c) (as amended by Economic Growth and Tax Relief Reconciliation Act of 2001, Pub. L. No. 107-16, § 521(c)(2), 115 Stat. 38, 72 (2001), reprinted in 2001-__ CB __, __). This section, as amended, is applicable to estates of decedents dying, and generation-skipping transfers, after December 31, 2003. Economic Growth and Tax Relief Reconciliation Act of 2001 § 521(e)(3), 115 Stat. 38, 72 (2001), reprinted in 2001-__ CB __, __.

[13] IRC § 2664. See ¶ 18.04. The tax imposed on generation-skipping transfers is scheduled to reappear on January 1, 2011, under a "sunset" provision contained in Economic Growth and Tax Relief Reconciliation Act of 2001. Economic Growth and Tax Relief Reconciliation Act of 2001, Pub. L. No. 107-16, § 901(a)(2), 115 Stat. 38, 150 (2001), reprinted in 2001-__ CB __, __. The "sunset" provision is discussed more fully at ¶ 8.10[5]. Once the "sunset" provision applies only the pre-existing inflationary adjusted GST exemption will apply. This leads to interesting speculation whether allocations of the GST exemption prior to January 1, 2010, in excess of the inflationary adjusted GST exemption will also disappear. Allocations of GST exemption in excess of the inflationary adjusted GST exemption should not be reduced in the post-sunset period.

[14] IRC § 2641(a). See ¶ 16.01.

[15] IRC § 2641(b).

[16] IRC § 2642(a)(1). See ¶ 16.02.

[17] IRC § 2642(a)(2). See ¶ 16.02.

[18] See IRC § 2632; infra ¶ 15.03.

[19] IRC § 2642(a)(2)(A). But see IRC § 2642(e)(2); ¶ 16.02[6].

ferred is generally the denominator of the fraction.[20] In general, if the amount of exemption allocated to a transfer is equal to the value of the property involved in the transfer, the applicable fraction is one, both the inclusion ratio and the applicable rate of tax are zero, and no generation-skipping transfer tax will be imposed on the property until there is a new transferor.[21]

[1] Individual Allocation

An individual may allocate GST exemption generally to any property transferred with respect to which the individual is the transferor.[22] The allocation of the exemption, if not made by the individual before death, may be made by the executor of the individual's estate[23] until the date for filing the individual's federal estate tax return.[24] As the GST exemption is cumulative over life and may be allocated to transfers made at death, the individual or the individual's executor may choose to allocate all, a part, or none of the available GST exemption to a particular transfer. An allocation, once made, becomes irrevoca-

---

[20] IRC § 2642(a)(2)(B)(i). However, Section 2642(a)(2)(B)(ii) provides for potential reductions in the denominator, and Section 2642(c) provides for an exclusion of nontaxable gifts from the denominator. See ¶¶ 16.02[2][b], 16.02[3][b][ii].

[21] But see supra notes 19, 20. In the alternative, if no GST exemption is allocated to a generation-skipping transfer, the applicable fraction is zero, the inclusion ratio is one, and the transfer is taxed at the maximum federal transfer tax rate.

[22] IRC §§ 2631(a), 2652(a). But see IRC § 2642(f); infra ¶ 15.03[3][b], ¶ 16.02[7]. Use of the exemption allows a major planning opportunity under the generation-skipping transfer tax. See Slade, "Lifetime Planning Under the GSTT Rules," 137 Tr. & Est. 46 (Dec. 1998); Gallo, "Estate Planning and the Generation-Skipping Transfer Tax," 33 Real Prop. Prob. & Tr. J. 457 (Fall 1998); Pennell & Williamson, "The Economics of Prepaying Wealth Transfer Tax," 136 Tr. & Est. 52 (Aug. 1997); Kalik & Schneider, "Generation-Skipping Transfer Taxes Under the Tax Reform Act of 1986," 21 U. Miami Inst. Est. Plan. 9-1, at ¶ 907 (1987); US Trust and Practical Drafting, "Generation-Skipping Transfers," 1149, 1255 (1987). See also Lang, "Allocating the GST Exemption Under the Generation-Skipping Transfer Tax," 41 Me. L. Rev. 43 (1989).

[23] See IRC § 2203; ¶ 8.02.

[24] IRC § 2632(a)(1), discussed infra ¶ 15.03. This date applies regardless of whether a federal estate tax return is required to be filed. Reg. § 26.2632-1(a). Regardless of whether a federal estate tax return is ultimately required to be filed, the deadline includes extensions actually granted. Reg. § 26.2632-1(a). See IRC § 6018(a); infra ¶ 15.03[6][a] text accompanying note 231. But see IRC § 2642(g); ¶ 16.02[9].

ble.[25] The allocation of GST exemption may be made by means of a formula.[26] If the allocation of GST exemption is made to property held in trust, the allocation is made to the entire trust rather than specific trust assets or a fractional share of the trust.[27] Generally,[28] an allocation of GST exemption is void to the extent the amount allocated exceeds the amount necessary to yield an inclusion

---

[25] IRC § 2631(b). A timely allocation of GST exemption becomes irrevocable after the due date of the return. Reg. § 26.2632-1(b)(2)(i). Thus, the allocation of GST exemption to property transferred inter vivos by the transferor may be modified by a subsequent allocation on an amended return filed on or before the date the Form 709 reporting the transfer is due, or would be due if no return is required to be filed. Reg. § 26.2632-1(b)(2)(ii)(A)(1). The later allocation must clearly identify the transfer and the nature and extent of the modification. Id. See Reg. §§ 26.2632-1(b)(2)(iii) Exs. 1, 2. Sections 2632(b) and 2632(c) automatically allocate GST exemption to inter vivos direct and indirect skips. IRC §§ 2632(b), 2632(c). The transferor may elect to prevent the automatic allocation of GST exemption to direct or indirect skips. IRC §§ 2632(b)(3), 2632(c)(5)(A). An election to prevent the automatic allocation of GST exemption to an inter vivos direct or indirect skip should also be subject to modification on an amended return filed on or before the due date of the Form 709 reporting the transfer. See Reg. § 26.2632-1(b)(1)(ii); infra ¶ 15.03[3][c] text accompanying notes 76, 77. See also IRC § 2642(g); ¶ 16.02[9]. Likewise, any timely allocation of GST exemption on Form 706 should be subject to modification by filing an amended Form 706 on or before the date prescribed for filing the return, including extensions actually granted. See Reg. § 26.2632-1(d)(1). A late allocation of GST exemption is irrevocable when made. Reg. § 26.2632-1(b)(2)(ii)(A)(2).

[26] Reg. §§ 26.2632-1(b)(2)(i), 26.2632-1(d)(1). The allocation may be expressed as the amount necessary to yield an inclusion ratio of zero for the trust after the transfer. Reg. § 26.2632-1(b)(2)(i). See also IRC § 2642(g)(2); ¶ 16.02[9][b].

When a transferor desires to prevent the automatic allocation of GST exemption to an inter vivos direct or indirect skip, a formula should be effective in describing the extent to which the automatic allocation is not to apply. See Reg. § 26.2632-1(b)(1)(i). However, a formula allocation of GST exemption with respect to a charitable lead annuity trust is invalid except to the extent the formula allocation is dependent on values as finally determined for federal estate or gift tax purposes. Reg. § 26.2632-1(b)(2)(i). See infra ¶ 15.03[6] text accompanying note 227. See also ¶ 16.02[6].

[27] Reg. § 26.2632-1(a). Even where the transfer is a direct skip to a trust, any of the transferor's GST exemption allocated to the transferred property is an allocation to the trust that is used in the computation of the applicable rate of generation-skipping transfer tax imposed on subsequent generation-skipping transfers from the trust attributed to that transferor, rather than an allocation of GST exemption to specific assets transferred in the direct skip. Id. If the GST exemption allocated is less than the total value of the assets in the trust, the result is that the trust has an inclusion ratio greater than zero, but less than one, as opposed to a fraction of the trust having an inclusion ratio of zero and the remaining portion of the trust having an inclusion ratio of one. Cf. IRC § 2642(a)(3), discussed ¶ 16.02[5][e] text accompanying notes 372–380.

[28] An exception is provided for allocation of GST exemption to charitable lead annuity trusts. Reg. § 26.2632-1(b)(2)(i). See Reg. § 26.2642-3(c) Ex. See also infra ¶ 15.03[6][a] note 237.

ratio of zero for the trust.[29] An allocation of GST exemption to a trust is also void if, at the time of the allocation, the trust has no potential to yield generation-skipping transfers attributed to the transferor whose GST exemption is allocated to the trust.[30] Any portion of an individual's GST exemption not allocated by the individual or the individual's executor is deemed allocated in a manner prescribed by Section 2632.[31]

Allocation of the GST exemption is needed only for potentially taxable generation-skipping transfers. It is not needed, for example, to protect transfers of property to grandchildren who are treated under the statutory scheme as the transferor's children,[32] transfers to grandchildren before 1990 that did not exceed $2 million,[33] transfers excluded by Section 2611(b),[34] transfers of certain nontaxable gifts under Section 2642(c),[35] or transfers that are grandfathered under the transitional rules.[36]

[2] Use of the Exemption

In general, an individual may allocate the GST exemption to any completed inter vivos transfer[37] or any testamentary transfer of property,[38] even though no

---

[29] Reg. § 26.2632-1(b)(2)(i). See Reg. § 26.2642-4(b) Ex. 3. This provision voiding excessive GST exemption allocations is intended to prevent a transferor from wasting GST exemption. TD 8644, Supplementary Information, 60 Fed. Reg. 66,898, 66,900 (1995).

[30] Reg. § 26.2632-1(b)(2)(i). This provision is intended to prevent a transferor from wasting GST exemption with respect to a testamentary or inter vivos transfer. TD 8644, Supplementary Information, 60 Fed. Reg. 66,898, 66,900 (1995). Priv. Ltr. Rul. 199929040 (Apr. 15, 1999) (allocation by settlor to qualified terminable interest property (QTIP) trust where no reverse QTIP election void). A trust is considered to have the potential to yield generation-skipping transfers with respect to the transferor whose GST exemption is allocated to the trust, even if the possibility of a generation-skipping transfer is so remote as to be negligible. Reg. § 26.2632-1(b)(2)(i).

[31] See IRC §§ 2632(b), 2632(c), 2632(e). Sections 2632(b) and 2632(c) require the GST exemption to be allocated to inter vivos direct and indirect skips unless the transferor elects to the contrary, and Section 2632(e) provides a rule allocating the GST exemption if the transferor and the transferor's executor do not totally deplete the transferor's GST exemption. These sections are discussed more fully infra ¶¶ 15.03[3], 15.03[4], 15.03[7].

[32] See IRC § 2651(e); ¶ 17.01[2][a][ii].

[33] See ¶ 13.02[4][c][ii].

[34] See ¶ 13.01[2].

[35] See ¶ 16.02[2][b].

[36] See ¶ 18.05[2].

[37] See IRC § 2652(a)(1)(B). But see IRC § 2642(f), discussed infra ¶ 15.03[3][b], ¶ 16.02[7].

[38] See IRC § 2652(a)(1)(A).

immediate generation-skipping transfer occurs.[39] However, if an inter vivos transfer is potentially includible in the gross estate of the transferor or the transferor's spouse, other than by reason of Section 2035, if such individual were to die immediately after the transfer, the allocation generally is not effective until the termination of the "estate tax inclusion period" (ETIP).[40]

Once the GST exemption allocated to property held in a trust is effective,[41] the applicable fraction structure effectively permits it to appreciate and depreciate with fluctuations in the value of the corpus of the trust to which it is allocated.[42] For example, assume A transfers property worth $1 million to an irrevocable inter vivos trust[43] and immediately allocates $1 million GST exemption to the property. The trust provides for income to A's child for life, then income to A's grandchildren for life, with a remainder to A's great-grandchildren. Assuming no application of the Rule Against Perpetuities[44] and no addition to the trust corpus, the property held in the trust is shielded from

---

[39] Instructions for Form 709, United States Gift (and Generation-Skipping Transfer) Tax Return (2001) Schedule C, Part 2, Line 5, at 11; Instructions for Form 706, United States Estate (and Generation-Skipping Transfer) Tax Return (Rev. Nov. 2001) How to Complete Schedule R, Part 1, Line 9, at 21. See IRC § 2632(c); infra ¶ 15.03[4].

[40] IRC §§ 2642(f)(1), 2642(f)(3), 2642(f)(4). The estate tax inclusion period is generally the period after the inter vivos transfer during which, should death occur, the property transferred would be included in the transferor's or the transferor's spouse's gross estate, other than by reason of Section 2035. Reg. § 26.2632-1(c)(2)(i). There are three exceptions to the general rule: (1) possible inclusion in the transferor's spouse's gross estate is disregarded if a Section 2652(a)(3), reverse QTIP, election is made (Reg. § 26.2632-1(c)(2)(ii)(C)); (2) possible inclusion is so remote as to be negligible (Reg. § 26.2632-1(c)(2)(ii)(A)); or (3) where the spouse holds a five-or-five power that expires within sixty days of the transfer (Reg. § 26.2632-1(c)(2)(ii)(B)). See ¶ 16.02[7][b][ii]. This period will not extend beyond the earlier of the generation-skipping transfer, the time at which no portion of the property is potentially includible in the gross estate of the transferor or the transferor's spouse, other than under Section 2035, or the death of the transferor or the transferor's spouse. IRC § 2642(f)(3); Reg. § 26.2632-1(c)(3). The estate tax inclusion period and other Section 2642(f) rules are more fully discussed infra ¶ 15.03[3][b] and at ¶ 16.02[7].

[41] This includes any trust equivalent. See IRC §§ 2652(b)(1), 2652(b)(3); ¶ 17.02[2].

[42] HR Rep. No. 426, 99th Cong., 1st Sess. 1, 826 (1986), reprinted in 1986-3 CB (vol. 2) 1, 826.

[43] The same principles would apply if the trust were a testamentary trust.

[44] The remainder interest under this trust would violate the Rule Against Perpetuities. If the trust had provided instead for income to be paid to A's child, then income to specifically named children of A's child who were living at the time the trust was created, with a remainder to those of A's great-grandchildren who are children of the grandchildren who are the income beneficiaries of the trust, there would be no violation of the Rule Against Perpetuities. We chose to use the looser provisions of the trust in our example, but technicians who prefer a common-law perpetuities-proper trust should substitute the above provisions for those in the text. See generally Gray, The Rule Against Perpetuities § 201 (Little Brown & Co., 4th ed. 1942).

the Chapter 13 tax throughout the duration and termination of the trust.[45] No Chapter 13 tax will be imposed on the taxable terminations occurring at the deaths of A's child and grandchildren, even if the trust corpus appreciates in value to tens of millions of dollars by the time the generation-skipping transfers occur because regardless of the value of the trust corpus, generation-skipping transfers are taxed at an applicable rate of zero.[46]

Alternatively, if A allocates \$500,000 of GST exemption to the \$1 million worth of property transferred to the trust, the trust's inclusion ratio will be 0.500.[47] Assuming that the trust is not severed in a qualified severance[48] and that there are no corpus additions or additional GST exemption allocations to the property held in trust, a generation-skipping transfer from this trust will be taxed at one-half the maximum federal estate tax rate; in effect, one half of the property transferred to the trust will be taxed and one-half will not, regardless of whether the property appreciates or depreciates in value.[49]

A number of states have modified the Rule Against Perpetuities. See Bloom, "The Generation-Skipping Transfer Tax Tail Is Killing the Rule Against Perpetuities," 87 Tax Notes 569 ns. 22, 23 (2000).

[45] HR Rep. No. 426, 99th Cong., 1st Sess. 1, 826 (1986), reprinted in 1986-3 CB (vol. 2) 1, 826.

[46] The Section 2642 inclusion ratio and the Section 2641 applicable rate of tax are both zero in this example: one minus (\$1 million/\$1 million is 1) one = zero.

As an alternative to the example in the text, consider the following example that results in both a generation-skipping transfer (a direct skip) at the creation of the trust and another generation-skipping transfer (a taxable termination or a taxable distribution) at a later time. Assuming an adequate allocation of the GST exemption, both generation-skipping transfers to and from the trust are shielded from the Chapter 13 tax.

For example, assume A transfers \$1 million to an irrevocable trust. The trust agreement provides that the income is to be paid to A's grandchild for life with a remainder to the grandchild's children (A's great-grandchildren) and permits the nongrantor trustee to invade corpus for the great-grandchildren. A's child, the parent of the grandchild, is alive at the time of the transfer to the trust. See IRC § 2651(e). If A allocates \$1 million of GST exemption to the property transferred, the trust's inclusion ratio and the applicable tax rate are zero. The transfer to the trust, as well as any generation-skipping transfers from the trust, assuming no corpus additions are made, will not generate any tax under Chapter 13 notwithstanding any increases or decreases in the value of the trust assets.

[47] The applicable fraction is 0.500 (IRC § 2642(a)(2)), and one minus 0.500 results in an inclusion ratio of 0.500. IRC § 2642(a)(1). See ¶ 16.02[1] note 6.

[48] A "qualified severance" of the trust would result in one trust with an inclusion ratio of one and another with an inclusion ratio of zero. See IRC § 2642(a)(3); ¶ 16.02[5][e].

[49] Assuming a maximum federal tax rate of 50 percent, a generation-skipping transfer from the trust would be taxed at a rate of 25 percent. This is the same as taxing one half of any generation-skipping transfer at a tax rate of 50 percent and the other one-half at a tax rate of zero.

The inclusion ratio for the trust must be recomputed after the initial generation-skipping transfer at the child's death to take into account the generation-skipping transfer tax borne by the trust. IRC § 2653(b)(1). See infra note 50. Under Section 2653(b)(1), assuming the \$1 million corpus has not appreciated in value at the child's death, the generation-

Should *A* subsequently allocate an additional amount of GST exemption to the property held in the trust, the applicable fraction must be recomputed,[50] resulting in the recomputation of the inclusion ratio and the rate of tax imposed on any subsequent generation-skipping transfer.[51]

[3] The Transferor Requirement

An individual's GST exemption may be allocated only to property with respect to which the individual is the transferor.[52] When there are multiple transferors and a single trust, each transferor's transfers must be segregated and each transferor treated as creating a separate trust for purposes of both allocation of the GST exemption and computation of the generation-skipping transfer tax.[53]

An individual may not assign GST exemption to property when another person is the transferor and may not apply the exemption of another person to property for which the individual is the transferor. However, when a transferor and the transferor's spouse elect under Section 2513 to split gifts for gift tax purposes,[54] that election also applies to transfers of property for generation-skipping transfer tax purposes.[55] Under these rules, each spouse is treated as a transferor to a single trust and each spouse is able to allocate GST exemption to the trust, thus effectively permitting an interspousal assignment of the GST exemption to the extent that the spouse is treated as a transferor.[56]

---

skipping transfer tax of $250,000 would be paid out of the trust corpus, leaving a $750,000 corpus, an applicable fraction of $500,000/$750,000 or 0.667, and an inclusion ratio of 0.333. Under Section 2653(b)(1), the generation-skipping transfer tax is treated as paid from the nonexempt portion of the trust. See ¶ 17.03[2][a].

[50] IRC § 2642(d)(4). The recomputation process is prescribed by Section 2642(d)(2). See ¶¶ 16.02[5][b][i], 16.02[5][b][iii]. The applicable fraction is also recomputed when additional property is transferred to the trust (see IRC § 2642(d)(1); ¶¶ 16.02[5][b][ii], 16.02[5][b][iii]), and when only a portion of the trust is shielded from tax and the trust is involved in a taxable termination without any substitution of transferor. See IRC § 2653(b)(1); supra note 49; ¶¶ 16.02[5][d], 17.03[2][a]. The applicable fraction also may be recomputed where separate trusts are consolidated. See Reg. § 26.2642-4(a)(2); ¶ 16.02[5][c]. Additionally, a recomputation of the applicable fraction may be necessary if additional estate tax is imposed under Section 2032A. See Reg. § 26.2642-4(a)(4)(i); ¶ 16.02[5][f].

[51] IRC §§ 2641(a), 2642(a); see ¶ 16.02[5].

[52] IRC § 2631(a). See also IRC § 2652(a).

[53] IRC § 2654(b)(1). See ¶ 17.04[2].

[54] See ¶ 10.03.

[55] IRC § 2652(a)(2). See ¶ 17.02[1][c][ii]. See also Reg. § 26.2632-1(b)(2)(iii) Ex. 5.

[56] The election also requires the trust to be treated as two trusts for computational purposes. See supra text accompanying note 53. For example, assume Transferor transfers $2 million to a trust with income to Child for life and a remainder to Grandchild. Transferor and Transferor's Spouse, both of whom have exhausted any available annual exclu-

[4] Duration of the Exemption

Once the amount of GST exemption allocated to a transfer of property equals the value of the property transferred, the GST exemption effectively protects that property from the imposition of the generation-skipping transfer tax whether it appreciates or depreciates in value.[57] However, the allocation effectively protects the property from Chapter 13 tax only as long as the individual who transferred the property and allocated GST exemption to it continues as the Chapter 13 transferor of the property.[58] When property held in trust is subject to taxation under the Chapter 11 estate tax or the Chapter 12 gift tax and the decedent or the donor is someone other than the original transferor, that the decedent or the donor generally[59] becomes the transferor of the property for purposes of Chapter 13.[60] That new transferor must allocate GST exemption to the property to shield it from the imposition of tax under Chapter 13.

When property that qualifies for the marital deduction as qualified terminable interest property (QTIP) is transferred in a generation-skipping transfer, the donee spouse usually replaces the donor spouse as the transferor of the property.[61] However, Section 2652(a)(3) permits the donor spouse or the donor spouse's executor to make an election, referred to as a reverse QTIP election, that retains the donor spouse as the Chapter 13 transferor and prevents the donee spouse from becoming the Chapter 13 transferor of the property.[62] Use of this reverse QTIP election permits the donor spouse to allocate GST exemption to a transfer that otherwise eventually would be attributable to the donee spouse and would require use of the donee spouse's GST exemption.

---

sion for gifts to Child in the year the trust is established, elect to use Section 2513 gift splitting, and each allocates $1 million of GST exemption to the transfer. As a result, the trust is treated as two separate trusts for computational purposes, with each trust having a zero inclusion ratio. In effect, Transferor's Spouse's GST exemption has been allocated to Transferor's transfer.

[57] See supra ¶ 15.02[2] text accompanying notes 41–46.

[58] Cf. IRC § 2652(a)(1). See ¶ 17.02[1].

[59] See infra text accompanying note 62.

[60] IRC § 2652(a)(1). See, e.g., IRC §§ 2041, 2514. For example, assume transferor T creates a trust that provides income to child C for life with a remainder to grandchild GC, but gives C a general power of appointment over the corpus. Even if C fails to appoint the corpus, it is included in C's gross estate under Section 2041(a)(2), and C becomes the Section 2652(a)(1) transferor of the property. See infra text accompanying notes 63–70.

[61] Under Section 2652(a)(1), the donee spouse would be the transferor of any property once that property is included in the donee spouse's gross estate under Section 2044, or once the donee spouse makes a gift of the qualifying income interest and under Section 2511 and Section 2519 the property held in trust is subject to the gift tax. See IRC §§ 2044, 2511, 2519. See also ¶¶ 4.16, 10.08.

[62] See ¶¶ 16.02[7][b] text accompanying notes 472–475, 17.02[1][c][i]. The election creates several tax-planning opportunities. See ¶ 17.02[1][c] text accompanying notes 56–60.

An allocation of an individual's GST exemption to a transfer that will not eventually be the subject matter of a generation-skipping transfer while the individual is the transferor of the trust is void.[63] For example, assume that grantor *G* transfers $1 million to a trust with income to child *C* for life, then income to grandchild *GC*, who is living at the creation of the trust, for life, and a remainder to grandchild's child *GGC*.[64] *G* allocates $1 million of GST exemption to the property held in the trust, shielding it from any Chapter 13 tax.[65] *G* also gives *C* a general power to appoint the entire corpus by will. At *C*'s death, the property held in the trust is included in *C*'s gross estate.[66] *C* becomes the transferor of the property held in trust,[67] and there is no generation-skipping transfer attributed to *G*.[68] Even if *C* fails to exercise the general power of appointment and, by default, the property remains in the trust created by *G*, *C* still becomes the Chapter 13 transferor of the trust and there is no generation-skipping transfer.[69] *G*'s GST exemption allocation is void because it was made with respect to a trust that had no generation-skipping transfer tax potential for the grantor at the time of the allocation of GST exemption by *G*.[70] Assuming *GC* survives *C*, *C*'s GST exemption must be allocated to the property held in trust to prevent the imposition of the generation-skipping transfer tax on any generation-skipping transfer with respect to the property held in the trust.

Assume the facts change and that instead *C* is granted only a noncumulative annual general power of appointment over 5 percent of the corpus. If, in any year, *C* exercises the general power and appoints the property to *GGC*, whose parents are still alive,[71] *C* (not *G*) is the Chapter 13 transferor of the direct skip generation-skipping transfer to *GGC*.[72] For this direct skip generation-

---

[63] Reg. §§ 26.2632-1(b)(2)(i), 26.2632-1(d)(1), 26.2632-1(d)(2).

[64] See generally supra ¶ 15.02[2] note 44.

[65] See supra ¶ 15.02[2] text accompanying notes 41–46.

[66] IRC § 2041(a)(2).

[67] See IRC § 2652(a)(1)(A); ¶¶ 13.02[2][e][ii], 17.02[1].

[68] Although *C*'s interest terminates, the property is deemed to pass to *C* (see ¶ 13.02[2][e] text accompanying notes 95, 96; see also Reg. § 26.2612-1(b)(1)), and as a result, there is no taxable termination, both because *C* is not a skip person in relation to *G* and there is a transfer subject to federal estate tax that occurs with respect to the property held in the trust at the time of the termination. See ¶ 13.02[2][d].

[69] See supra text accompanying note 67. Because *GC* is a non–skip person in relation to *C*, there is no direct skip on *C*'s deemed transfer of the property back to the trust.

[70] Reg. § 26.2632-1(b)(2)(i). See also Reg. § 26.2632-1(d)(1). Similarly, automatic allocation of GST exemption after death under Section 2632(e) does not occur if the entire trust will have a new transferor prior to the occurrence of any generation-skipping transfer. Reg. § 26.2632-1(d)(2). See infra ¶ 15.03[7].

[71] See IRC § 2612(c)(2).

[72] IRC §§ 2612(c)(1), 2652(a)(1)(B). See IRC § 2514(b). See also ¶ 13.02[2][e][ii]. However, to the extent that the exercise of the power results in outright transfers excluded

skipping transfer to escape tax, *C* must allocate GST exemption to the transfer.[73] If, instead, *C* allows the power to lapse each year, the entire amount of the lapse would come within the Section 2514(e) exception, and there would be no new transferor during *C*'s life.[74] At *C*'s death, however, 5 percent of the value of the property held in the trust would be included in *C*'s gross estate,[75] and that 5 percent of the corpus would thereafter be considered *C*'s transfer to the trust.[76] An allocation of *C*'s GST exemption would be needed to protect the 5 percent portion of the trust property that was included in *C*'s gross estate from the imposition of the generation-skipping transfer tax on the taxable termination that occurs at *GC*'s death.[77] Alternatively, if the trust instrument had not granted the general power of appointment to *C*, the property ultimately would have passed to *GGC* without imposition of any generation-skipping transfer tax by virtue of *G*'s GST exemption having been allocated to the property held in the trust.[78]

---

under Section 2503(b)(1) of the gift tax, the transfers are also exempted from Chapter 13 taxation. See IRC §§ 2642(c)(1), 2642(c)(3), discussed ¶ 16.02[2][b]. See also ¶ 13.02[4][b] text accompanying notes 261–264.

[73] See supra note 72. See also Section 2632(b)(1) (which would make a deemed allocation here in the absence of an election out of such deemed allocation under Section 2632(b)(3)); infra ¶ 15.03[3].

[74] IRC § 2514(e). In addition, each year's lapse of the power would not constitute a taxable termination. See ¶ 13.02[2][e] text accompanying notes 118, 129.

[75] IRC § 2041(a)(2). Inclusion of 5 percent of the value of the property held in the trust in *C*'s gross estate could possibly be avoided by limiting the time during the year when *C* holds and could exercise the 5 percent power. See ¶ 13.02[2][e] note 142.

[76] IRC § 2652(a)(1)(A). There is no immediate Section 2612(c) direct skip of that 5 percent of the corpus to the trust because the trust is not a skip person, due to the fact *GC* is not a skip person in relation to *C*. IRC § 2613. Cf. ¶ 13.02[2][e][ii]. Because there are now two transferors, the trust must be separated into two trusts. IRC § 2654(b)(1); see supra ¶ 15.02[3] text accompanying note 53. The first trust contains 5 percent of the original corpus and *C* is its transferor. A taxable termination of that trust occurs at *GC*'s death. IRC § 2612(a)(1). The second trust contains the remaining 95 percent of the original corpus with *G* as its transferor. There will be taxable terminations with respect to the second trust at *C*'s death and again at *GC*'s death. IRC § 2612(a)(1). Cf. IRC § 2653(b)(1).

[77] See supra note 76.

[78] See supra ¶ 15.02[2] text accompanying notes 41–46. This would also occur if *C* made a qualified disclaimer under Section 2518 of the general power of appointment. See ¶ 10.07.

¶ 15.03 SECTION 2632. SPECIAL RULES FOR ALLOCATION OF THE GST EXEMPTION

[1] In General

Section 2632 provides generally for the time and manner of allocating the transferor's GST exemption.[1] The transferor and the transferor's executor have the flexibility to allocate GST exemption to any property transferred by the transferor from the time of the transfer until the due date of the transferor's federal estate tax return.[2] The GST exemption is automatically allocated to certain lifetime direct and indirect skips of property.[3] Any residual GST exemption not allocated by the transferor or the transferor's executor within the time prescribed or not automatically allocated to inter vivos transfers is allocated automatically to property involved in at-death and postdeath generation-skipping transfers attributed to the deceased transferor.[4]

[2] Actual Allocation to Inter Vivos Transfers

A transferor may allocate unused GST exemption to any completed inter vivos gift[5] that has the potential to generate future generation-skipping transfers.[6] If the transferor dies before making any allocation of GST exemption to the inter vivos transfer, the transferor's executor may make the allocation.[7] If an inter vivos transfer is not a direct or indirect skip and has no potential to generate future generation-skipping transfers, any allocation of GST exemption to the transfer by the transferor is void.[8]

---

[1] IRC § 2631. See ¶ 15.02. Cf. IRC § 2642(f); ¶ 16.02[7].

[2] IRC §§ 2632(a)(1), 2632(d). See infra ¶¶ 15.03[2][a] note 10, 15.03[5]. To make the most effective use of the GST exemption, the transferor should have some plan in mind prior to making any taxable, or potentially taxable, generation-skipping transfers and should provide some testamentary guidance to the executor with respect to postdeath allocation of any then-unused GST exemption.

[3] IRC §§ 2632(b), 2632(c). See infra ¶¶ 15.03[3], 15.03[4]; IRC §§ 2641, 2642.

[4] IRC § 2632(e). See infra ¶ 15.03[7].

[5] Where the transfer is an inter vivos direct or indirect skip, the allocation of GST exemption is automatic. IRC §§ 2632(b)(1), 2632(c)(1). See infra ¶¶ 15.03[3][a], 15.03[4]. However, the transferor may opt out of any such automatic allocation. IRC §§ 2632(b)(3), 2632(c)(5)(A)(i). See infra ¶¶ 15.03[3][c], 15.03[4][e][i].

[6] IRC § 2632(a)(1).

[7] IRC § 2632(a)(1). See infra ¶ 15.03[6][c].

[8] Reg. § 26.2632-1(b)(2)(i). See ¶ 15.02[4] text accompanying notes 63–70. See also ¶ 15.02[1] text accompanying notes 32–36.

[a] Time of Allocation

An allocation of GST exemption to an inter vivos transfer generally may be made at any time after the transfer has become a completed gift[9] and on or before the date prescribed for filing the transferor's federal estate tax return.[10] However, generally if the transfer is an inter vivos transfer of property that would be includible in the transferor's or the transferor's spouse's gross estate (other than by reason of Section 2035) if death occurred immediately after the transfer, any allocation of the GST exemption is not effective before the close of the estate tax inclusion period.[11]

The timing of the allocation of an individual's GST exemption is important because the valuation of the transferred property for purposes of computing the inclusion ratio is made at the time the GST exemption allocation becomes effective.[12] Early allocation of the GST exemption that is effective with respect to appreciating assets beneficially leverages the GST exemption, as such allocation will result in the GST exemption effectively appreciating along with the assets to which it is allocated.[13]

[b] Manner of Allocation

The secretary is empowered to provide by regulations or forms the manner in which the GST exemption is to be allocated.[14] An individual or, if the individual is deceased, the individual's executor may allocate any available amount of GST exemption to property transferred to a trust, even though the transfer does not result in an immediate generation-skipping transfer. The allocation may be made by claiming the exemption on the transferor's federal gift tax return.[15] If the federal gift tax return reporting the transfer to which GST

---

[9] See Reg. § 25.2511-2(b); ¶ 10.01.

[10] IRC § 2632(a)(1). This deadline is determined with regard to extensions actually granted, but without regard to whether an estate tax return is required to be filed. Reg. § 26.2632-1(a).

[11] IRC §§ 2642(f)(1), 2642(f)(4); Reg. § 26.2632-1(c)(1). See infra ¶ 15.03[3][b]; Reg. § 26.2632-1(c)(2). The estate tax inclusion period is generally the period after the transfer during which, should death occur, the property transferred would be included in the transferor's or the transferor's spouse's gross estate, other than by reason of Section 2035. IRC § 2642(f)(3). See Reg. § 26.2632-1(c)(3); ¶ 15.02[2] note 40. The estate tax inclusion period and the other Section 2642(f) rules are more fully discussed at ¶ 16.02[7].

[12] See IRC § 2642(b), discussed at ¶ 16.02[4].

[13] See ¶ 15.02[2] text accompanying notes 41–46.

[14] IRC § 2632(a)(2).

[15] Reg. § 26.2632-1(b)(2)(i). Form 709, United States Gift (and Generation-Skipping Transfer) Tax Return, is used to report both inter vivos gifts and generation-skipping transfers. It contains a column titled "Generation-Skipping Transfer Exemption Allocated." Form 709, United States Gift (and Generation-Skipping Transfer) Tax Return (2001)

exemption is allocated is timely filed,[16] the allocation is generally effective as of the date the gift is complete.[17] If the GST exemption allocation is made on a federal gift tax return filed after the due date for reporting the transfer, the late allocation is effective on the day the return is filed.[18] A late allocation of

---

Schedule C, Part 3, Column C, at 4. An entry in this column will result in an allocation of the transferor's GST exemption to a generation-skipping transfer reported on Schedule C, Part 1 of Form 709. See Instructions for Form 709, United States Gift (and Generation-Skipping Transfer) Tax Return (2001) Schedule C, Part 3, Column C, at 11–12. A "Notice of Allocation" must be attached to Form 709 to allocate any GST exemption to generation-skipping transfers not listed on Schedule C, Parts 1 and 3 of Form 709. Instructions for Form 709, United States Gift (and Generation-Skipping Transfer) Tax Return (2001) Schedule C, Part 2, Line 5, at 11. The allocation must clearly identify the trust, the amount of GST exemption allocated, and if the allocation is late or if an inclusion ratio of greater than zero is claimed, the value of the trust assets at the effective date of the allocation. Reg. § 26.2632-1(b)(2)(i). The allocation should also state the postallocation inclusion ratio. See Reg. § 26.2632-1(b)(2)(i); Instructions for Form 709, United States Gift (and Generation-Skipping Transfer) Tax Return (2001) Schedule C, Part 2, Line 5, at 11. Failure to file a Notice of Allocation and literally comply with the procedural directions for making an allocation of GST exemption contained in the Instructions for Form 709 does not preclude an effective allocation of GST exemption where there is substantial compliance with the requirements for making an allocation. Priv. Ltr. Ruls. 200017013 (Jan. 20, 2000), 199919027 (Feb. 16, 1999), 199909034 (Dec. 4, 1998), 9721009 (Feb. 13, 1997).

[16] A federal gift tax return is "timely filed" if it is filed on or before April 15th following the close of the calendar year in which the reportable transfer is made, the due date of the transferor's federal estate tax return, if earlier, or the date that would be the date for reporting the transfer if it were a taxable gift where no return is required. Each of these time periods includes any extensions of time to file actually granted. IRC § 6075(b); Reg. § 26.2632-1(b)(1)(ii).

[17] IRC § 2642(b)(1)(B); Reg. § 26.2632-1(b)(2)(ii)(A)(1). The property will also be valued on such date. IRC § 2642(b)(1)(A). The allocation is not effective when the gift is complete if the property is subject to an estate tax inclusion period. See supra ¶ 15.03[2][a] note 11.

If more than one timely GST exemption allocation is made, a later allocation that clearly identifies the transfer and the extent of the modification will modify the earlier allocation. See Reg. §§ 26.2632-1(b)(2)(ii)(A)(1), 26.2632-1(b)(2)(iii) Exs. 1, 2; ¶ 15.02[1] note 25.

An extension of time may be granted to made an allocation of GST exemption under Section 2642(b)(1). See IRC § 2642(g)(1); ¶ 16.02[9][a].

[18] IRC § 2642(b)(3)(B); Reg. §§ 26.2632-1(b)(2)(ii)(A)(1), 26.2632-1(b)(2)(iii) Exs. 3, 4. The federal gift tax return is deemed filed on the date it is postmarked to the IRS Center. Reg. § 26.2632-1(b)(2)(ii)(A)(1). When an authorized private delivery service is used, the private delivery service can tell you how to get written proof of the mailing date. Instructions for Form 709, United States Gift (and Generation-Skipping Transfer) Tax Return (2001) General Instructions, D; When to File at 2. Note that if GST exemption is allocated to a trust on the same day as a generation-skipping transfer with respect to the trust, the GST exemption allocation is deemed to precede the generation-skipping transfer. Id. Reg. § 26.2632-1(b)(2)(iii) Ex. 4. The property will also be valued on such filing date. IRC § 2642(b)(3)(A). A late allocation may also be made on a federal gift tax

GST exemption after the transferor's death to an inter vivos transfer that is not included in the transferor's gross estate is made by the transferor's executor on the federal estate tax return, or a federal gift tax return filed on or before the due date of the transferor's federal estate tax return.[19] The executor's late allocation of GST exemption to such a transfer is effective as of the date the allocation is filed.[20] Once made, any allocation of GST exemption becomes irrevocable.[21]

For example, if grantor *G* transfers property to a trust and the terms of the trust provide for income to be paid to the grantor's child *C* for life, with a remainder to *G*'s grandchild *GC*, the transfer to the trust is a completed gift,

---

return that is timely filed with respect to another transfer. Reg. § 26.2632-1(b)(2)(ii)(A)(2).

There is no statutory requirement that the notice of allocation that is not made on a timely filed federal gift tax return must be made on or filed with a Form 709. IRC § 2642(b)(3)(B). However, the regulations and the instructions contemplate that the allocation will be made on or with a statement attached to a Form 709, a United States Gift (and Generation-Skipping Transfer) Tax Return. See Reg. §§ 26.2632-1(b)(2)(i), 26.2632-1(b)(2)(ii)(A)(1); Instructions for Form 709, United States Gift (and Generation-Skipping Transfer) Tax Return (2001) Schedule C, Part 2, Line 5, at 11. See also Reg. § 26.2632-1(b)(2)(ii)(A)(2).

If the decision to allocate GST exemption to the property held in trust is made after the federal gift tax return reporting the transfer to trust is filed, notice of the allocation filed with the secretary with a Form 709 used as a transmittal form should result in a valid GST exemption allocation. A late allocation made in this manner during the transferor's lifetime should become effective on the date notice of such allocation with the Form 709 used as a transmittal form is filed with the secretary. IRC § 2642(b)(3)(B); Reg. § 26.2632-1(b)(2)(ii)(A)(1). See Priv. Ltr. Rul. 200027009 (Mar. 31, 2000) (substantial compliance where donor mistakenly used Schedule C to allocate exemption to transfer other than direct skip and protective late allocation to produce zero inclusion ratio recognized), Priv. Ltr. Rul. 9721009 (Feb. 13, 1997) (substantial compliance with late allocation requirements without procedurally required Notice of Allocation). See also Priv. Ltr. Rul 199905009 (Oct. 29, 1999) (extension until end of 1998 to allocate GST exemption to trust effective November 19, 1985, under Regulations Section 301.9100-1(c)).

[19] Reg. § 26.2632-1(d)(1). See infra ¶ 15.03[6][c]. Postmortem allocation of GST exemption to inter vivos transfers that are included in the transferor's gross estate are discussed infra ¶ 15.03[6][b].

[20] Reg. § 26.2632-1(d)(1). See ¶ 16.02[4][c]. The opportunity for an executor to allocate GST exemption terminates after the date prescribed for filing the transferor's estate tax return, including extensions actually granted. IRC § 2632(a)(1). See Reg. § 26.2632-1(d)(2). At the termination of the power to make postdeath allocations, any unused GST exemption is automatically allocated. IRC § 2632(e). See infra ¶ 15.03[7].

[21] IRC § 2631(b). A late lifetime allocation is irrevocable when made. Reg. § 26.2632-1(b)(2)(ii)(A)(2). A late postmortem allocation of GST exemption to an inter vivos transfer not included in the transferor's gross estate should also be irrevocable when made. While timely allocations and automatic allocations of GST exemption generally become irrevocable after the due date of the return reporting the transfer (Reg. §§ 26.2632-1(b)(2)(i), 26.2632-1(b)(1)(ii). See also Reg. § 26.2632-1(b)(2)(iii)), a GST (see Reg. §§ 26.2632-1(b)(2)(ii)(A)(1), 26.2632-1(b)(2)(iii) Ex. 1; supra ¶ 15.02[1] note 25).

but not an immediate direct skip generation-skipping transfer.[22] At *C*'s death, however, the property held in the trust will be the subject matter of a taxable termination generation-skipping transfer[23] potentially subject to the tax imposed by Chapter 13. *G* or, if *G* is deceased, *G*'s executor may allocate any portion of *G*'s GST exemption to the property transferred to the trust by making an allocation on a federal gift tax return.[24] If the allocation is made on a timely filed gift tax return reporting the transfer, the allocation is effective as of the date of the gift transfer.[25] If the notice of allocation is made on a gift tax return that is filed after the due date for reporting the transfer, the allocation generally does not become effective until the date the return is filed.[26]

A timely allocation of GST exemption may be made for a transfer to a trust occurring in one year where another transfer of property to the trust is made in the succeeding year, prior to the due date of the federal gift tax return reporting the first transfer in the succeeding year.[27] This later transfer is referred to as an undisclosed transfer at the time the federal gift tax return is to be filed reporting the first transfer.[28] A timely allocation of GST exemption when there is an undisclosed transfer may result in an allocation of GST exemption to the undisclosed transfer, which is an early, albeit timely, alloca-

---

[22] The transfer to the trust is not a Section 2612(c) direct skip because the trust is not a skip person. A Section 2613(b) non−skip person, *C*, has a Section 2652(c) interest in the property held in the trust, precluding the trust from having skip person status. See ¶ 13.03.

[23] IRC § 2612(a).

[24] Reg. § 26.2632-1(b)(2)(i); Instructions for Form 709, United States Gift (and Generation-Skipping Transfer) Tax Return (2001) Schedule C, Part 2, Line 5, at 11. See supra note 15. However, if the allocation of GST exemption is a late allocation after the grantor's death to property transferred inter vivos that is not included in the grantor's gross estate, the allocation may be made on a federal estate tax return, Form 706, or a federal gift tax return, Form 709, filed on or before the due date of the grantor's federal estate tax return. Reg. § 26.2632-1(d)(1). See infra ¶ 15.03[6][c].

[25] IRC § 2642(b)(1)(B); Reg. § 26.2632-1(b)(2)(ii)(A)(1). See IRC § 2642(b)(1)(A); supra notes 16, 17. Technically, the allocation of GST exemption is made not "on," but rather "with," a timely filed gift tax return.

[26] IRC § 2642(b)(3)(B); Reg. § 26.2632-1(b)(2)(ii)(A)(1). See IRC § 2642(b)(3)(A); supra notes 18, 24. A late allocation by an executor after the grantor's death on Form 706 or Form 709 is effective as of the date the allocation is filed. Reg. § 26.2632-1(d)(1). See infra ¶ 15.03[6][c]. Relief from the late allocation may be granted under Section 2642(g)(1). See ¶ 16.02[9][a].

[27] For example, assume a transferor initially funded a trust in December and then, in the following January, added to the corpus of the trust. The timely filed federal gift tax return for the December transfer is due the following April 15. The January transfer is to be reported on a federal gift tax return required to be filed one year later than the federal gift tax return for the initial transfer.

[28] See Reg. §§ 26.2632-1(b)(2)(ii)(A)(1)(iii), 26.2642-4(b) Ex. 4. See ¶ 16.02[5][b][iii] for a detailed example of an allocation of GST exemption to an "undisclosed transfer."

tion.[29] A lifetime allocation of GST exemption combined with multiple transfers of property to a trust may result in an allocation of GST exemption to the property held in the trust that is timely, late, and early, as well as void. When it is unclear whether an allocation of GST exemption on a timely filed federal gift tax return is timely, late, or early, the allocation is effective as a timely allocation to any transfer disclosed on a timely filed federal gift tax return,[30] next as a late allocation to assets held in the trust,[31] then as an early, albeit timely, allocation to undisclosed transfers.[32] Once the allocation of GST exemption exceeds the amount necessary to exempt all the transferred property, it is void to the extent of the excess.[33]

[3] Deemed Allocation to Inter Vivos Direct Skips

[a] The Deemed Allocation

If an individual makes an inter vivos direct skip transfer, any unused portion of the individual's GST exemption is deemed allocated to the property transferred to the extent that it is available to reduce the inclusion ratio for such property, potentially to zero.[34] This automatic allocation of GST exemption is effective as of the date of the direct skip transfer.[35] Any portion of an individual's GST exemption that has not been previously allocated by the individual or deemed allocated to a prior direct or indirect skip[36] is automatically allocated to an inter vivos direct skip.[37] Outright direct skip transfers to individuals or trusts,[38] as well as direct skip transfers from a trust, are subject to

---

[29] See Reg. § 26.2642-4(b) Ex. 4(iii).

[30] Reg. § 26.2632-1(b)(2)(ii)(A)(1)(i). If the amount of GST exemption allocated exceeds the value of the transfers reported on the Form 709, the initial allocation is in the amount of the value of the transfers as reported on that return, even where there is a subsequent adjustment in value of the transfers reported on the return. Reg. § 26.2632-1(b)(2)(ii)(B).

[31] Reg. § 26.2632-1(b)(2)(ii)(A)(1)(ii). See Reg. § 26.2632-1(b)(2)(ii)(B).

[32] Reg. § 26.2632-1(b)(2)(ii)(A)(1)(iii). See Reg. § 26.2632-1(b)(2)(ii)(B).

[33] Reg. § 26.2632-1(b)(2)(i). See ¶ 16.02[5][b] note 356.

[34] IRC § 2632(b)(1).

[35] Reg. § 26.2632-1(b)(1)(ii).

[36] See IRC §§ 2632(a), 2632(b)(1), 2632(c)(1); Reg. § 26.2632-1(b)(1)(i); infra ¶ 15.03[4][c].

[37] IRC § 2632(b)(2).

[38] Allocation of GST exemption to a direct skip transfer to a trust is treated as an allocation of GST exemption to the trust by the transferor. Reg. § 26.2632-1(a). If a direct skip is made to a pre-existing trust with an inclusion ratio greater than zero, the inclusion ratio for the trust, not the value of the property transferred, should control the amount of

this deemed allocation rule.[39] Where the amount of the inter vivos direct skip exceeds the unused portion of an individual's GST exemption, the entire unused GST exemption is automatically allocated to the property transferred.[40] However, an individual may block the automatic allocation of GST exemption to any direct skip by making the appropriate election[41] or by paying the generation-skipping transfer tax.[42]

The purpose of the Section 2632(b) deemed allocation rule is to prevent individuals from inadvertently incurring generation-skipping transfer tax on inter vivos direct skips. The deemed allocation is made regardless of whether the required gift tax return is filed.[43] However, no GST exemption will ever be automatically allocated to a direct skip assigned an inclusion ratio of zero[44] because there is no need to allocate any portion of the individual's GST exemption in the computation of the applicable fraction.

[b] Delayed Direct Skips

When an individual makes an inter vivos direct skip transfer of property[45] and the value of that property would be includible in the individual's or the indi-

---

the unused GST exemption automatically allocated to the trust under Section 2632(b). This same issue arises where an indirect skip results in an automatic allocation of unused GST exemption under Section 2632(c). See infra ¶ 15.03[4][d] text accompanying notes 163–167.

[39] If grantor G creates a revocable trust with income to grandchild GC for life at a time when GC's parents are living, the income distributed to GC (even though through a trust) is a Section 2511 completed gift and is an inter vivos direct skip that is subject to Section 2632(b)(1). The language of Section 2632(b)(1), "[i]f any individual makes a direct skip," should be interpreted broadly to make all direct skips subject to the deemed allocation rule. The regulations provide for automatic allocation of GST exemption to any direct skip that "occurs during the transferor's lifetime." Reg. § 26.2632-1(b)(1)(i). When property is transferred to a skip person trust that is subject to an estate tax inclusion period, the direct skip is treated as occurring on the termination of the estate tax inclusion period. Reg. § 26.2632-1(c)(4).

[40] IRC § 2632(b)(1). If there are several simultaneous direct skips and their total value exceeds the unused portion of GST exemption, the exemption should be apportioned to the skips in proportion to their relative fair market values, after reduction for any nontaxable gift. See IRC § 2642(c); infra ¶ 15.03[7][c]. Cf. IRC § 2632(e)(2)(A).

[41] IRC § 2632(b)(3). See infra ¶ 15.03[3][c].

[42] Reg. § 26.2632-1(b)(1)(i). See infra ¶ 15.03[3][c].

[43] Reg. § 26.2632-1(b)(1)(ii).

[44] IRC § 2642(c). See ¶ 16.02[2][b]. Section 2503(e) transfers do not need the assistance of Section 2642(c)(1) because they are not direct skips. See IRC § 2611(b)(1); ¶ 13.01[2][a].

[45] IRC § 2642(f)(1)(A).

vidual's spouse's gross estate, other than by reason of Section 2035,[46] if death occurred immediately after the transfer,[47] the direct skip is delayed[48] and treated as occurring at the close of the estate tax inclusion period.[49] The deemed allocation of GST exemption to delayed inter vivos direct skips *should* take place when the delayed direct skip is treated as occurring, at the close of the estate

---

[46] Any reference in Section 2642(f) to the transferor generally includes a reference to the transferor's spouse. IRC § 2642(f)(4). But see ¶ 16.02[7][b] text accompanying notes 472–475.

[47] IRC § 2642(f)(1)(B).

[48] IRC § 2642(f)(1). See ¶ 16.02[7].

[49] IRC §§ 2642(f)(1), 2642(f)(3). See Reg. § 26.2632-1(c)(4). The estate tax inclusion period rules are discussed in detail at ¶ 16.02[7].

tax inclusion period,[50] and then only if the individual transferor is alive.[51]

---

[50] Section 2642(f)(1) provides "any allocation of GST exemption to such property shall not be made before the close of the estate tax inclusion period." However, the introductory language of Section 2642(f) starts off with the caution "[e]xcept as provided in regulations." The regulations, contrary to the statute, provide for the "allocation" of GST exemption to property during the estate tax inclusion period with merely a delayed effect until the end of the estate tax inclusion period. Regulations Section 26.2632-1(c)(1) provides "[a]n allocation of GST exemption (including an automatic allocation) to property subject to an estate tax inclusion period (ETIP) that is made prior to termination of the ETIP cannot be revoked, but becomes effective no earlier than the date of any termination of the estate tax inclusion period with respect to the trust." See Reg. §§ 26.2632-1(c)(5) Exs. 1, 2; 26.2642-4(b) Ex. 5. See also Reg. § 26.2642-1(b)(2); Priv. Ltr. Rul. 199922045 (Mar. 5, 1999) (allocation of GST exemption to property in trust during estate tax inclusion period prior to December 27, 1995, publication of Regulations Section 26.2632-1(c)(1) (providing that an allocation made during an estate tax inclusion period, although not effective until the close of the estate tax inclusion period, may not be revoked) was void). But see Instructions for Form 709, United States Gift (and Generation-Skipping Transfer) Tax Return (2001) Schedule C, Part 2, Note, at 11.

The regulations delay the effective date of automatic allocations of the GST exemption under Section 2632(b) as well as actual allocations of the GST exemption. Permitting, but delaying the effect of, actual allocations of GST exemption in these circumstances is sensible and appropriate. The regulations' treatment of automatic allocations is not. The automatic allocation of GST exemption to transfers of property under Section 2632(b) prior to the end of the estate tax inclusion period occurs if there is a direct skip generation-skipping transfer. Section 2642(f) provides that if a transfer during the estate tax inclusion period is a direct skip, "such skip shall be treated as occurring as of the close of the estate tax inclusion period." See Reg. § 26.2632-1(c)(4). Section 2632(b) provides "[i]f any individual makes a direct skip during his lifetime, any unused portion of such individual's GST exemption shall be allocated to the property transferred to the extent necessary to make the inclusion ratio for such property zero." Under Section 2632(b), an automatic allocation of GST exemption does not occur, if at all, until the direct skip is treated as occurring—which is as of the close of the estate tax inclusion period. However, under the regulations, an automatic allocation of GST exemption could be made prior to the time the direct skip is treated as occurring, with the effect of the automatic allocation of GST exemption merely being delayed until the end of the estate tax inclusion period.

The automatic allocation of GST exemption to a delayed direct skip should occur only at the close of the estate tax inclusion period when the direct skip is treated as occurring and then only if the estate tax inclusion period closes while the transferor is living. The automatic allocation rule was designed to protect an unsophisticated taxpayer from inadvertently incurring a generation-skipping transfer tax on a direct skip. The automatic allocation of GST exemption occurs to the extent of available exemption until a zero inclusion ratio and the resulting zero applicable rate of tax on the inter vivos direct skip transfer are achieved. The automatic allocation rule need not engage until there is, in fact, a direct skip at the termination of the estate tax inclusion period. Although a transferor may actually allocate GST exemption to a delayed direct skip transfer, which will take effect at the close of the estate tax inclusion period, the automatic allocation should not occur until the direct skip is treated as occurring during the transferor's life.

[51] IRC § 2642(f)(3). See supra ¶ 15.03[2][a] note 11. If the estate tax inclusion period closes on the date of the transferor's death, the deemed allocation rule of Section 2632(b)(1), is inapplicable. The deceased transferor's unused GST exemption can be allo-

Under the deemed allocation rule, unused GST exemption in an amount sufficient to produce a zero inclusion ratio is deemed allocated to the transfer. The amount deemed allocated is an amount equal in value to the amount of the delayed direct skip treated as occurring, less the amount of any GST exemption actually allocated previously to the delayed direct skip that takes effect upon the occurrence of the direct skip.

For example, assume grantor *G* establishes a trust with income to be paid to grandchild *GC* for ten years, with the remainder to *GC*, and *G* allocates no GST exemption to the trust. *G* retains the power to accumulate the income or invade the corpus for *GC* during the term of the trust. *G*'s child, *GC*'s parent, is alive.[52] The transfer to the trust, which is a skip person,[53] is a completed gift subject to the tax imposed under Chapter 12.[54] However, if *G* died immediately after the transfer, Section 2038 would require inclusion of the fair market value of the trust corpus in *G*'s gross estate.[55] Since there is an inter vivos transfer of property that would be included in *G*'s gross estate under Section 2038 if *G* died immediately after making the transfer, the direct skip generation-skipping transfer to the trust is treated as occurring at the close of the estate tax inclusion period.[56] If all the income is accumulated, no corpus distributions are made, and *G* is still alive, the estate tax inclusion period closes at the end of the ten-year term because at that time, there is no longer any potential inclusion in *G*'s gross estate. At the end of such term, the direct skip occurs, and there should[57] be a deemed allocation of available GST exemption to produce a zero inclusion ratio for the direct skip that was delayed, unless *G* elects otherwise. If during *G*'s life prior to the expiration of the initial ten-year term, *G* relinquishes the power to accumulate income and to invade corpus, the estate tax inclusion period should close,[58] a direct skip should occur, and the corresponding deemed allocation of available GST exemption should occur at that time.

If *G* does not exercise or relinquish the power to accumulate income and at the end of each year the income generated during the year is paid to *GC*, the estate tax inclusion period terminates as to the amount paid to *GC*.[59] A

---

cated to the then-completed direct skip by the executor under Section 2632(a)(1), or allocated under the residual allocation rule of Section 2632(e). See infra ¶¶ 15.03[6][a], 15.03[7].

[52] This negates the applicability of Section 2651(e). See ¶¶ 13.02[4][c][i], 17.01[2][a][ii].

[53] See ¶ 13.03[3]. The only Section 2652(c) interest in the trust is held by *GC*, who is a skip person.

[54] Reg. § 25.2511-2(d). See ¶ 10.01[7].

[55] IRC § 2038. See ¶ 4.10.

[56] IRC § 2642(f)(1). See ¶ 16.02[7][c].

[57] See supra note 50; IRC § 2632(b).

[58] See ¶ 16.02[7][c] text accompanying notes 485, 486.

[59] Reg. § 26.2632-1(c)(3)(iii). See Reg. § 26.2632-1(c)(5) Ex. 2.

portion of the delayed direct skip to the trust equal to the amount of the income paid should be treated as occurring on the termination of the estate tax inclusion period.[60] The trust now contains direct skip property and delayed direct skip property. The delayed direct skip portion has G assigned to two generation levels above GC. The direct skip portion of the trust has G assigned to the generation level one above GC, C's level, pursuant to the operation of Section 2653(a).[61] Since the trust now has a single grantor who is assigned to two different generation levels, one level with respect to the delayed direct skip property portion and another level with respect to the direct skip property portion, each portion should be treated as a separate trust for purposes of Chapter 13, just as if there were two separate grantors.[62] Since a direct skip has occurred during G's life, unused GST exemption is automatically allocated to the transferred property absent G's election otherwise.[63] Where the transfer is a direct skip to a trust, the allocation of GST exemption to transferred property is treated as an allocation of GST exemption to the trust.[64] Assuming sufficient unallocated GST exemption, the amount of GST exemption deemed allocated to the trust should equal the amount of the direct skip that is treated as occurring, the amount actually distributed to GC. The automatic allocation of GST exemption should be deemed allocated to the direct skip trust. Assuming sufficient unused GST exemption, the amount of GST exemption deemed allocated will equal the amount of the direct skip that is treated as occurring, and the direct skip trust will have an inclusion ratio of zero. The income paid should be treated as paid from the direct skip portion of the trust. If the income is considered paid from the direct skip portion of the trust, the payment of income to GC is not a generation-skipping transfer from the trust because G is assigned under Section 2653(a) to the first generation level above GC. After the payment of income, the direct skip portion of the trust should be eliminated and only the delayed direct skip portion of the trust should remain.[65]

---

[60] See Reg. § 26.2632-1(c)(4).

[61] See ¶ 17.03[1].

[62] See IRC § 2654(b)(1).

[63] Reg. § 26.2632-1(b)(1)(i).

[64] Reg. § 26.2632-1(a).

[65] A similar example will further illustrate the treatment suggested. Assume grandparent GP purchases property and has title conveyed to GP and grandchild GC as joint tenants with right of survivorship. The transfer creating the joint tenancy with right of survivorship is a lurking direct skip, which is treated as occurring as of the close of the estate tax inclusion period. One half of the value of the property is a gift to GC subject to tax under Chapter 12. GC is a skip person. The direct skip generation-skipping transfer is delayed because the transfer is an inter vivos transfer, and if GP dies immediately after the transfer, Section 2040 would require the property transferred to be included in GP's gross estate. IRC § 2642(f)(1). GP's subsequent transfer of the retained joint interest could close the estate tax inclusion period and result in the direct skip occurring. If and when that happens, the automatic allocation of available GST exemption should take place. If

[c] Opting Out of the Deemed Allocation

The transferor may prevent the automatic allocation of GST exemption to an inter vivos direct skip in whole or in part in two ways. The transferor may prevent it by making an appropriate election[66] or by payment of the generation-skipping transfer tax imposed on the direct skip.[67]

An election not to have the deemed allocation rule of Section 2632(b) apply in whole or in part to an inter vivos direct skip[68] generally must be made by the due date, including extensions actually granted, of the transferor's federal gift tax return[69] for the taxable year for which the election is to be effective.[70] The election is made by describing the transfer and the extent to which the automatic allocation is not to apply on the transferor's timely filed federal gift tax return for the taxable year in which the inter vivos direct skip occurs.[71] If a return is not required for the year of the inter vivos direct skip, a federal

---

GC predeceased GP, and the one-half interest in the property, the subject matter of the delayed direct skip, returns by operation of law to GP, the delayed generation-skipping transfer never occurs. If the jointly held property produces income, the annual income realized from the property by GC will result in a direct skip, which is not delayed and that will trigger the automatic allocation of available GST exemption until the zero inclusion ratio is achieved for the amount of income realized by GC.

[66] IRC § 2632(b)(3); Reg. § 26.2632-1(b)(1)(i).

[67] Reg. § 26.2632-1(b)(1)(i).

[68] IRC § 2632(b)(3). See Reg. § 26.2632-1(b)(1)(i). An individual who elects out of the deemed allocation rule may waste some GST exemption. For example, if an individual making an inter vivos direct skip does not allocate GST exemption to the transfer and elects to opt out of the deemed allocation rule, the direct skip will generate a tax under Chapter 13. If the individual dies without making any more inter vivos transfers or any testamentary direct skips or transfers to trusts that may generate generation-skipping transfers, the unused GST exemption will go unallocated. This results in the payment of a Chapter 13 tax when such tax could have been avoided or minimized.

[69] Reg. §§ 26.2632-1(b)(1)(i), 26.2632-1(b)(1)(ii). The time to make this election may be extended under Section 2642(g)(1). See IRC § 2642(g)(1)(A)(i), discussed at ¶ 16.02[9][a].

[70] Reg. § 26.2632-1(b)(1). When the transferor makes a direct skip and dies before the due date of the federal gift tax return, the transferor's executor may make the election. See infra ¶ 15.03[6][d].

[71] Reg. § 26.2632-1(b)(1). The automatic allocation should be prevented when a statement is attached to the return that (1) contains the name, address, and taxpayer identification number of the electing taxpayer; (2) states that it is an election not to allocate GST exemption to a direct skip under Section 2632(b); (3) states that the election is made pursuant to Section 2632(b)(3); (4) specifies the property or other items to which the election is to apply; and (5) provides any information required by the relevant statutory provisions and any information necessary to show that the taxpayer is entitled to make the election. Cf. Temp. Reg. § 301.9100-7T(a)(3)(i). Substantial compliance may be sufficient. See IRC § 2642(g)(2); ¶ 16.02[9][b]. The time to make the election under Section 2632(b)(3) may be extended under Section 2642(g)(1). See IRC § 2642(g)(1)(A)(i); ¶ 16.02[9][a].

gift tax return containing the election must be filed before the date for reporting the transfer as if it were a taxable gift, including any extensions of time to file actually granted.[72]

As an alternative, the automatic allocation of unused GST exemption to an inter vivos direct skip may be prevented, in whole or in part, even if no election is specifically made, by filing a timely federal gift tax return[73] accompanied by the payment of the generation-skipping transfer tax imposed on the inter vivos direct skip.[74] However, if the election is not made, or if the generation-skipping transfer tax is not paid, by the due date of the transferor's federal gift tax return, including extensions, an irrevocable deemed allocation automatically occurs.[75]

The election or the tax payment out of the deemed allocation rule is revocable until the time period to timely file the federal gift tax return expires.[76] After that time, a generation-skipping transfer tax is due on the direct skip and the election becomes irrevocable.[77]

Even if an irrevocable election out of the deemed allocation rule is made with respect to a direct skip transfer to a trust, the transferor or the transferor's executor may still subsequently allocate some GST exemption to the property held in the trust to shield subsequent generation-skipping transfers from Chapter 13 tax.[78] Assume *G* transfers property in trust, income to *GC* for life, and a remainder to great-grandchild *GGC*.[79] Even if *G* elects out of a deemed allocation and, as a result, pays a Chapter 13 tax on the direct skip transfer to the trust, *G* or *G*'s executor is allowed subsequently to allocate GST exemption to

---

[72] Reg. § 26.2632-1(b)(1)(ii).

[73] Reg. § 26.2632-1(b)(1)(ii).

[74] Reg. § 26.2632-1(b)(1)(i). This alternative merely alleviates the necessity of making an election. If the election is made, there is a direct skip unprotected from taxation by the GST exemption, requiring the payment of tax in any event.

[75] IRC § 2632(b). See Reg. § 26.2632-1(b)(1)(ii). The time to make the election to prevent the automatic allocation of GST exemption under Section 2632(b)(3) may be extended under Section 2642(g)(1). See IRC § 2642(g)(1)(A)(i); ¶ 16.02[9][a].

[76] Reg. § 26.2632-1(b)(1)(ii). See ¶ 15.02[1] note 25.

[77] Reg. § 26.2632-1(b)(1)(ii). To allow a revocation beyond that time limit would permit a transferor to postpone the election to revoke until the transferor determines the extent to which the property has appreciated or depreciated in value.

Any election to prevent an automatic allocation of GST exemption filed before January 26, 1996, became irrevocable on July 24, 1996. Reg. § 26.2632-1(b)(1)(iii).

[78] See infra ¶ 15.03[6][c] note 243.

[79] It is assumed that *GC*'s parents are living and that the transfer occurs after 1989 so that neither Section 2651(e) nor the grandchild exclusion would apply. See ¶¶ 13.02[4][c][ii], 17.01[2][a][ii].

the trust property to shield the taxable termination that occurs at *GC*'s death from the imposition of generation-skipping transfer tax.[80]

If an individual allocates a portion of unused GST exemption to a direct skip[81] and the amount allocated is less than the amount necessary to produce a zero inclusion ratio, the statute, consistent with the purpose behind the automatic allocation rule, will still allocate additional GST exemption to the direct skip in an amount sufficient to bring the inclusion ratio to zero, unless the automatic allocation is prevented.[82] It may be prevented by a timely filed federal gift tax return accompanied by the payment of the generation-skipping transfer tax imposed on the direct skip or by the making of the appropriate election.[83]

[4] Deemed Allocation to Inter Vivos Indirect Skips

Congress has expanded the instances in which the GST exemption is automatically allocated to transfers.[84] In addition to the deemed allocation of GST exemption to lifetime direct skips[85] and the automatic allocation of residual GST exemption after the death of the transferor,[86] Section 2632(c) provides for the deemed allocation of GST exemption to inter vivos nondirect skip transfers to trusts.[87] The provision is intended to be taxpayer friendly, covering situations where taxpayers desired to allocate GST exemption to inter vivos transfers that were not direct skips, but missed making the allocation by failing to make the

---

[80] For purposes of computing the applicable fraction, the property would be valued at the time of the allocation. IRC § 2642(b)(3)(A). If *G* had not elected out of the Section 2632(b)(1) deemed allocation, both generation-skipping transfers would have been shielded from tax if *G* had unused GST exemption equal to the value of the property transferred to the trust.

[81] The allocation would be made pursuant to Section 2632(a).

[82] IRC § 2632(b)(1). See supra ¶ 15.03[3][a] text accompanying note 44. A trust with an inclusion ratio of greater than zero, but less than one, may be severed in a "qualified severance" and thereafter recognized as two trusts under Chapter 13, one trust with an inclusion ratio of one and the other trust with an inclusion ratio of zero. See IRC § 2642(a)(3)(B)(ii); ¶ 16.02[5][e].

[83] IRC § 2632(b)(3); Reg. § 26.2632-1(b)(1)(i). The time to make the election to prevent the automatic allocation of GST exemption under Section 2632(b)(3) may be extended under Section 2642(g)(1). See IRC § 2642(g)(1)(A)(i); ¶ 16.02[9][a].

[84] IRC § 2632(c).

[85] IRC § 2632(b). See supra ¶ 15.03[3].

[86] IRC § 2632(e). See infra ¶ 15.03[7].

[87] IRC § 2632(c). Under the "sunset" provision this deemed allocation rule is repealed effective January 1, 2011. Economic Growth and Tax Relief Reconciliation Act of 2001, Pub. L. No. 107-16, § 901(a)(2), 115 Stat. 38, 150, reprinted in 2001-__ CB __, __. The "sunset" provision is discussed more fully at ¶ 8.10[5].

election on a timely filed gift tax return or by submitting a defective election.[88] Although the motives behind the enactment of the additional deemed alloca- tion of GST exemption are well intentioned, Section 2632(c) unfortunately adds additional complexity and uncertainty to the generation-skipping transfer tax provisions.[89] In many instances it may be very difficult for a donor, who the provision was designed to benefit, to determine whether the automatic allo- cation has taken place. This may make it difficult to determine how much of a donor's GST exemption remains unallocated in later years.

[a] In General

If an individual makes an "indirect skip" transfer[90] after December 31, 2000,[91] any unused portion of the individual's GST exemption[92] is deemed al- located to the property transferred to the extent necessary to reduce the inclu- sion ratio for such property to zero.[93] An individual can elect to forgo automatic allocation to an indirect skip[94] or to any or all transfers made to a particular trust.[95]

[b] Indirect Skip

The event that triggers the automatic allocation of unused GST exemption is an indirect skip.[96] An indirect skip is any lifetime *transfer of property sub-*

---

[88] See HR Rep. No. 37, 107th Cong., 1st Sess. 35 (2001), reprinted in 2001-__ CB __, __.

[89] This may be an example of the road to hell being paved with good intentions.

[90] IRC § 2632(c)(3)(A). See infra ¶ 15.03[4][b].

[91] Economic Growth and Tax Relief Reconciliation Act of 2001, Pub. L. No. 107-16, § 561(c)(1), 115 Stat. 38, 89, reprinted in 2001-__ CB __, __. The automatic allocation of unused GST exemption to indirect skips applies to inter vivos indirect skips occurring at the end of an estate tax inclusion period during the life of the transferor if the estate tax inclusion period ends after December 31, 2000. Id.

[92] IRC § 2632(c)(2). See infra ¶ 15.03[4][c].

[93] IRC § 2632(c)(1). See infra ¶ 15.03[4][d].

[94] IRC § 2632(c)(5)(A)(i)(I). See infra ¶ 15.03[4][e][i].

[95] IRC § 2632(c)(5)(A)(i)(II). See infra ¶ 15.03[4][e][i].

[96] IRC § 2632(c)(1).

ject to the gift tax imposed by Chapter 12 that is *not a direct skip* generation-skipping transfer and that *is a transfer to a GST trust.*[97]

[i] **Transfers of property subject to gift tax.** A transfer of property by completed gift by any individual is "subject to" the gift tax imposed by Chapter 12.[98] A transfer of property is "subject to" the gift tax imposed by Chapter 12 even though the transfer qualifies for an annual exclusion,[99] a marital deduction,[100] a charitable deduction,[101] or generates no gift tax liability[102] due to application of the Section 2505 credit.[103]

[ii] **Other than a direct skip.** An indirect skip does not include any direct skip generation-skipping transfer.[104] Because the Section 2632(b) automatic allocation of GST exemption rule for inter vivos direct skips applies to direct skips to trusts,[105] the application of the Section 2632(c) automatic allocation of GST exemption rule to direct skip transfers is unnecessary.[106]

[iii] **A GST trust.** An indirect skip requires a transfer of property to a "GST trust." A GST trust is a trust that could have a generation-skipping transfer with respect to the transferor[107] in the future.[108] Certain statutorily enumerated trusts are not treated as GST trusts,[109] and therefore no automatic allo-

---

[97] IRC § 2632(c)(3)(A). Section 2632(b) provides for the deemed allocation of unused GST exemption to direct skip generation-skipping transfers. IRC § 2632(b). See supra ¶ 15.03[3].

[98] IRC § 2501(a). See Reg. § 26.2652-1(a)(2). See also ¶ 17.02[1][b] text accompanying notes 18–38, ¶ 13.02[4][b][i].

[99] IRC § 2503(b). See ¶ 9.04.

[100] IRC § 2523. See ¶ 11.03.

[101] IRC § 2522. See ¶ 11.02.

[102] Reg. § 26.2652-1(a)(2). See ¶¶ 17.02[1][b] text accompanying notes 18–38, 13.02[4][b][i].

[103] IRC § 2505. See ¶ 9.06.

[104] IRC § 2632(c)(3)(A) (parenthetical clause). This rule includes direct skips that occur at the close of the estate tax inclusion period as a result of the application of Section 2642(f). Cf. IRC § 2632(c)(4). See ¶ 16.02[7].

[105] See supra ¶ 15.03[3][a] text accompanying notes 38, 39.

[106] In addition, Section 2632(b) overrides Section 2632(c) in allocating unused GST exemption. See infra ¶ 15.03[4][c].

[107] IRC § 2652(a). See ¶ 17.02[1].

[108] Although the term "GST trust" is broadly defined, as a practical matter, since an "indirect skip" does not include direct skips to or from such trusts (see supra ¶ 15.03[4][b][ii]), Section 2632(c) will apply only to a trust that is not classified as a skip person (see IRC § 2613(a)(2); ¶ 13.03[3]) and that can have taxable terminations or taxable distributions (see IRC §§ 2612(a), 2612(b); ¶¶ 13.02[2], 13.02[3]) with respect to the transferor in the future.

[109] IRC § 2632(c)(3)(B).

cation of unused GST exemption is made to, transfers of property to these trusts. The exceptions are designed to prevent the automatic allocation of GST exemption to a trust if a substantial portion of the trust corpus is not likely to be subject to the generation-skipping transfer tax because the trust terms make it likely the corpus will either be distributed to a non–skip person or included in a non–skip person's gross estate. However, a transferor may elect to treat a trust that is not a GST trust as a GST trust with respect to any indirect skip transfer or all indirect skip transfers to that trust and, as a result, an automatic allocation will be made.[110]

Although the statute lists six types of exceptions to the general definition of "GST trust,"[111] the exceptions can be broken down into two categories: (1) distributions to non–skip persons and (2) inclusions in non–skip persons' estates.

Distributions to Non–Skip Persons. A trust will not be treated as a GST trust if the trust instrument provides that more than 25 percent of the trust corpus[112] must be distributed to or may be withdrawn by one or more individual non–skip persons either before attaining age 46[113] or upon surviving another person identified in the trust instrument who is more than ten years older than the non–skip person.[114] Thus, for example, if Transferor creates a trust with income to Child for life and a remainder to Grandchildren, but also directs the trustee to distribute 30 percent of the trust corpus to Child at age 40, the trust is not classified as a GST trust.[115] Similarly, if Child held a power to

---

[110] IRC § 2632(c)(5)(A)(ii). See IRC § 2632(c)(5)(B)(ii); infra ¶ 15.03[4][e][ii].

[111] IRC §§ 2632(c)(3)(B)(i)–2632(c)(3)(B)(vi). In general, it is the uncertainty that arises from the application of these exceptions that makes application of the statute problematic.

[112] If the required distribution is to come from trust income, rather than trust corpus, it is not considered in determining whether the trust is a GST trust. IRC §§ 2632(c)(3)(B)(i), 2632(c)(3)(B)(ii). Discretionary distributions by trustees, or permissive withdrawals by beneficiaries, of income are also disregarded in classifying a trust as a GST trust. Where the trustee is required to pay an annuity to a non–skip person out of either income or corpus it maybe very difficult to determine whether there will be a required distribution out of corpus. In this situation, to provide certainty, an election should be made to opt out of automatic allocation of the individual's unused GST exemption. IRC § 2632(c)(5)(A)(i). See infra ¶ 15.03[4][e][i]. See also IRC § 2642(g)(1)(A)(ii); ¶ 16.02[9][a].

[113] IRC § 2632(c)(3)(B)(i). The trust instrument may provide that corpus distributions or withdrawals occur before the individual non–skip person attains age 46 (IRC § 2632(c)(3)(B)(i)(I)), on certain dates that will occur before the non–skip person is 46 years old (IRC § 2632(c)(3)(B)(i)(II)), or upon the occurrence of an event that is expected to occur before the individual non–skip person turns forty-six (IRC § 2632(c)(3)(B)(i)(III)). Regulations are to be promulgated to assist in the determination of when an event will reasonably be expected to occur. IRC § 2632(c)(3)(B)(i)(III).

[114] IRC § 2632(c)(3)(B)(ii). The decedent must be identified by name or by class. Id.

[115] IRC § 2632(c)(3)(B)(i).

withdraw up to 30 percent of the trust corpus after attaining age 40, the trust would not be treated as a GST trust.[116]

In making either of the 25 percent determinations noted here, mandatory distributions of corpus to non–skip persons are combined with permissive withdrawal powers held by one or more non–skip persons.[117] This same combination is made in the determination of whether the trust instrument provides that more than 25 percent of the trust corpus must be distributed to or may be withdrawn by one or more non–skip persons upon surviving another person identified in the trust instrument who is more than ten years older than the non–skip distributees or power holders.

In making the more than 25 percent determinations, the statute also provides two special rules related to the right of withdrawal held by a non–skip person. Under the first rule, "the value of transferred property shall not be considered to be . . . subject to a right of withdrawal by reason of such person holding a right to withdraw so much of such property as does not exceed the amount referred to in Section 2503(b) with respect to any transferor."[118] This special rule is aimed at what are commonly referred to as *Crummey* powers.[119] Thus, if an individual non–skip person is granted a power to withdraw an amount that does not exceed the annual exclusion provided by Section 2503(b) upon contribution of property to a trust by a transferor who has not made any

---

[116] IRC § 2632(c)(3)(B)(i).

[117] IRC §§ 2632(c)(3)(B)(i), 2632(c)(3)(B)(ii). If a trust instrument provides for both current distributions to or withdrawals by non–skip persons and future distributions to or withdrawals by non–skip persons upon surviving another individual identified in the trust instrument who is more than ten years older than the non–skip distributees or power holders, the statutory language does not provide for the current and future distributions to be considered together in determining whether the trust instrument provides that more than 25 percent must be distributed or may be withdrawn by one or more non–skip persons. Perhaps the statute should be amended to allow this combination or regulations should provide for this combination. Cf. IRC § 2632(c)(3)(B)(iii) where the combination is possible.

[118] IRC § 2632(c)(3)(B) (last sentence).

[119] Crummey v. Comm'r, 397 F2d 82 (9th Cir. 1968). See ¶ 9.04[3][f]. This simplifies application of the statute where a *Crummey* power is included in the trust instrument merely to qualify the transfer for the Section 2503(b) annual exclusion. *Crummey* powers may be granted to multiple non–skip persons. See Cristofani v. Comm'r, 97 TC 74 (1991).

A *Crummey* power holder may become a Chapter 13 transferor to the trust upon the lapse of the withdrawal power. If a power created after October 22, 1942, to withdraw lapses during the life of the power holder, the power holder may be treated as making a transfer to the trust that is subject to the tax imposed by Chapter 12, the gift tax. IRC §§ 2514(e), 2514(b). Where this transfer is a transfer of property by gift, the power holder becomes a Chapter 13 transferor to the trust. IRC § 2652(a)(1)(B); Reg. § 26.2652-1(a)(5) Ex. 5. See ¶ 17.02[1][b] text accompanying notes 34–38. This transfer by the power holder may also trigger an automatic allocation of the power holder's GST exemption under Section 2632(c).

prior gifts to the non–skip person in the calendar year, the withdrawal power is disregarded in the determination of whether an individual non–skip person may withdraw 25 percent of the trust corpus.[120] For example, if Transferor creates a trust with income to an individual who is more than ten years older than Child for life, then income to Child for life and a remainder to Grandchildren, and gives Child a *Crummey* power[121] to withdraw the annual exclusion amount on the creation of the trust, that withdrawal power is disregarded in making the 25 percent determination.[122]

If a transferor provides in a trust that a non–skip person has an annual noncumulative power to withdraw $5,000 of corpus each year or a noncumulative power to withdraw the greater of $5,000 or 5 percent of the corpus each year,[123] a broad reading of the special rule would disregard the withdrawal right to the extent of the annual exclusion amount each year.[124] However, this is the type of discretionary power that the exceptions to the classification as a GST trust should take into account. It would seem more appropriate to interpret the special rule narrowly to apply merely to powers to withdraw an amount not exceeding the Section 2503(b) amount only upon the contribution of property to a trust and not to annual noncumulative powers.

The second special rule provides that "it shall be assumed that powers of appointment held by non–skip persons will not be exercised."[125] This rule does not disregard the fact that any non–skip person holds a discretionary invasion power,[126] but simply assumes such powers are not exercised for purposes of measuring both the value of the corpus and the total amount of withdrawal powers under the 25 percent test. This direction is apparently designed to eliminate questions regarding calculation of the amount subject to withdrawal where, for example, multiple non–skip persons have a power, exercisable at different times, to withdraw specified percentages of the corpus. Without this second part of the special rule, the determination of the total amount of corpus

---

[120] IRC § 2632(c)(3)(B) (last sentence).

[121] See supra text accompanying notes 119, 120.

[122] If the *Crummey* power was given in the form of a "hanging power" (see ¶ 9.04[3][f] note 119), the power should still be disregarded in making the 25 percent determination.

[123] See IRC § 2514(e); ¶¶ 4.13[8][a], 10.04[4][c].

[124] The last sentence of Section 2632(c) could be read (emphasis added) "[T]he value of transferred property shall not be considered to be . . . subject to a right of withdrawal by reason of such [non–skip] person holding a right to withdraw so much of such property as does not exceed the amount referred to in Section 2503(b) *with respect to any transferor.* . . . " If one emphasizes the fact that the transferor can make an $11,000 annual exclusion gift to the non–skip person each year, this interpretation of the language is possible.

[125] IRC § 2632(c)(3)(B) (last sentence). This language is troublesome, since any discretionary power of withdrawal held by a non–skip person is a power of appointment.

[126] IRC §§ 2632(c)(3)(B)(i), 2632(c)(3)(B)(ii).

subject to withdrawal would be affected by assumptions regarding the exercise or nonexercise of the power by each power holder.

Charitable organizations are generally non−skip persons[127] and therefore property passing to a charitable organization does not require the protection of an allocation of GST exemption to avoid the imposition of the generation-skipping transfer tax. Thus, a charitable lead annuity trust,[128] a charitable remainder annuity trust,[129] and a charitable remainder unitrust[130] are not classified as GST trusts.[131] If a trust is a charitable lead unitrust (where a fixed percentage of the net fair market value of the property is distributed to the trust annually), which qualified for a gift tax charitable deduction,[132] it is not a GST trust if it is required to pay principal to a non−skip person if such person is alive on termination of the charitable lead interest.[133]

Inclusion in Non−Skip Persons' Estates. If a trust instrument provides that if a non−skip person dies before age 46[134] or before the death of another person more than ten years senior[135] that more than 25 percent of the trust corpus must be distributed to the estate or estates of one or more of such non−skip persons or is subject to a general power of appointment exercisable by one or more of such non−skip persons, the trust will not be treated as a GST trust.[136] For example, if Transferor creates a trust with income to Child for life, then a remainder to Grandchildren, but also provides that if Child dies prior to reaching age 45, one third of the corpus would be paid to Child's estate or would be subject to a general power of appointment by Child, the trust would not be a GST trust.[137]

---

[127] See IRC §§ 2651(f)(3), 2613(b), 2613(a).

[128] IRC § 2642(e)(3). See ¶ 5.05[6]. Cf. ¶ 16.02[6].

[129] IRC § 664(d)(1). See ¶ 5.05[5][a].

[130] IRC § 664(d)(2). See ¶ 5.05[5][b].

[131] IRC § 2632(c)(3)(B)(v).

[132] IRC § 2522. See ¶ 11.02[2][c].

[133] IRC § 2632(c)(3)(B)(vi).

[134] This includes not only a provision that specifically refers to the non−skip person's death before attaining age 46 but also on or before a date that will occur before the non−skip person is forty-six years old, or upon the occurrence of an event that is expected to occur before the individual non−skip person turns forty-six. IRC §§ 2632(c)(3)(B)(i), 2632(c)(3)(B)(iii). Regulations are to be promulgated to assist in the determination of when an event will reasonably by expected to occur. IRC § 2632(c)(3)(B)(i)(III).

[135] The older person may be identified in the instrument either by name or by class. IRC §§ 2632(c)(3)(B)(ii), 2632(c)(3)(B)(iii).

[136] IRC § 2632(c)(3)(B)(iii).

[137] IRC §§ 2632(c)(3)(B)(i), 2632(c)(3)(B)(iii). More than one non−skip person may be involved in this determination. For example, assume a trust instrument provides that 10 percent of the trust corpus will be distributed to a non−skip person's estate and that another non−skip person has a testamentary general power to appoint 20 percent of the trust corpus. If under the trust terms both non−skip persons are or were reasonably expected to

A trust also will not be treated as a GST trust if *any* portion of the trust would be included in the gross estate of a non–skip person, other than the transferor, if the non–skip person died immediately after the transfer.[138] For example, if Transferor creates a trust with a corpus of $500,000 with income to Child for life and a remainder to Grandchildren, but also provides that Child may at any time withdraw 10 percent of the trust corpus, the trust is not a GST trust.[139]

In applying both sets of inclusion in non–skip persons' estates rules, the first special rule discussed previously[140] applies. Thus, the value of transferred property shall not be considered to be includible in the gross estate of a non–skip person by reason of a right to withdraw so much of the transferred property as does not exceed the amount referred to in Section 2503(b) with respect to any transferor.[141] For example, assume that Transferor creates an inter vivos trust with income to Spouse for life,[142] then income to Child for life and remainder to Grandchildren, and that Transferor gives Child a *Crummey* power to withdraw the annual exclusion amount.[143] Since the power to withdraw is a general power of appointment,[144] if Child, who holds the power of withdrawal, dies at the moment the trust is established, prior to exercise or lapse of the power, Section 2041(a)(2) would require a portion of the value of the property transferred to be included in Child's gross estate, seemingly disqualifying the trust from GST trust status.[145] However, the transferred property is not considered to be includible in the gross estate of the Child, a non–skip person, by reason of the *Crummey* withdrawal power because the power is limited to the amount referred to in Section 2503(b) with respect to any transferor,[146] and that power will not prevent the trust from being classified as a GST trust.[147]

---

be under age 46 at the time of the trust invasion and no special election is made, the 10 and 20 percent corpus provisions will be aggregated. Therefore, the trust will not be classified as a GST trust and there will be no automatic allocation of GST exemption under Section 2632(c). IRC § 2632(c)(3)(B)(iii). See IRC § 2632(c)(5)(A)(ii); infra ¶ 15.03[4][e][ii].

[138] IRC § 2632(c)(3)(B)(iv).

[139] IRC § 2632(c)(3)(B)(iv).

[140] IRC § 2632(c)(3)(B) (last sentence). See supra text accompanying notes 118–124.

[141] IRC § 2632(c)(3)(B) (last sentence).

[142] This example assumes no Section 2523(f) QTIP election is made with respect to the trust. See infra text accompanying notes 148–150.

[143] See supra note 120. If the *Crummey* power was given in the form of a "hanging power" (see ¶ 9.04[3][f] note 119), it should be disregarded as well. See supra note 122.

[144] IRC § 2041(b).

[145] IRC § 2632(c)(3)(B)(iv).

[146] IRC § 2632(c)(3)(B) (last sentence).

[147] IRC § 2632(c)(3)(B) (last sentence). If a portion of the property held in the trust is included in the non–skip person power holder's gross estate for estate tax purposes, even though the inclusion is ignored under Section 2632(c)(3)(B), the power holder will become the

Under this exception, whenever a transferor establishes an inter vivos trust and makes an election under Section 2523(f) to treat the property transferred as QTIP,[148] the trust will not be treated as a GST trust. The automatic allocation rule will not apply because the trust would be included in the estate of the spouse, a non–skip person,[149] if the spouse's death occurred immediately after the transfer.[150] This application of the exception to the automatic allocation rule is appropriate. However, if the transferor also makes a reverse QTIP election under Section 2652(a)(3)[151] with respect to the trust, the trust should not be disqualified as a GST trust and the Section 2632(c) automatic allocation of GST exemption should apply if the trust is not otherwise disqualifed. If the Section 2652(a)(3) election is made, the property held in the trust is treated as if the Section 2523(f) election had not been made and as if there were no inclusion in the non–skip person spouse's gross estate; the trust also should be treated as if it is not included in the gross estate of the non–skip person spouse in the determination of whether the trust is a GST trust.

[c] Unused Portion of GST Exemption

The unused portion of an individual's GST exemption is determined by reducing the allowable amount of GST exemption[152] by the GST exemption allocated by the individual in the current and prior calendar years,[153] by the

---

Chapter 13 transferor of that portion of the trust. The power holder's GST exemption, not the GST exemption of the initial Chapter 13 transferor that was automatically allocated to the trust under Section 2632(c), must be allocated to the portion of the trust that the non–skip person power holder is the Chapter 13 transferor of if generation-skipping transfers may be made from the power holder's portion of the trust. Certainly, it is possible that a portion of the automatic allocation of the initial transferor's GST exemption automatically allocated to the GST trust may be wasted in such circumstances.

Alternatively, if Child has a power to withdraw an amount that exceeds the amount referred to in Section 2503(b) or holds a power to withdraw $5,000 or 5 percent of the corpus of the trust at the inception of the trust (see supra text accompanying notes 123, 124), the trust will not be treated as a GST trust and automatic allocation of the GST exemption under Section 2632(c) will not occur. That is because the power of withdrawal will not be ignored as it exceeds the amount referred to in Section 2503(b) and a portion of the trust would be included in the non–skip person power holder's gross estate for estate tax purposes if the power holder died immediately after the transfer. IRC § 2632(c)(3)(B)(iv).

[148] IRC § 2523(f). See ¶ 11.03[4][c].

[149] IRC §§ 2651(c)(1), 2613(b).

[150] IRC § 2044.

[151] IRC § 2652(a)(3)(B).

[152] IRC § 2631(a). See ¶ 15.02.

[153] IRC § 2632(c)(2)(A). See IRC § 2632(a); supra ¶ 15.03[2].

amount of GST exemption automatically allocated to inter vivos direct skips[154] in the current and prior calendar years,[155] and by the amount of GST exemption previously deemed allocated to the individual's indirect skips in prior years.[156] The determination of the unused portion of an individual's GST exemption cannot be made until after the end of the calendar year in which the indirect skip is made or treated as made[157] because GST exemption allocated by the individual during the year, as well as the amount of the individual's GST exemption automatically allocated to directs skips occurring anytime during the calendar year, must be considered in the computation of the unused portion of GST exemption available for automatic allocation to indirect skip transfers occurring during the calendar year. The unused portion is then allocated to indirect skips made during the year in chronological order.[158]

[d] The Amount Deemed Allocated

If an individual makes an indirect skip transfer, any unused portion of the individual's GST exemption[159] is deemed allocated to the property transferred to the extent necessary to reduce the inclusion ratio for the transferred property to zero.[160] The language of the statute for the automatic allocation of GST exemption to indirect skips mirrors that used in the automatic allocation of GST exemption to direct skips.[161]

If the indirect skip transfer occurs on the creation of a trust, the transferred amount makes up the entire corpus of the trust and the amount of the deemed allocation is clear. Unused GST exemption equal to the fair market value of the property transferred will be automatically allocated to the property transferred to the extent necessary to make the inclusion ratio for the transferred property and the trust zero.[162] If the indirect skip transfer occurs with respect to a pre-existing trust, which has an inclusion ratio of zero, the amount of the deemed allocation is again clear. The amount of unused GST exemption

---

[154] IRC § 2632(b). See supra ¶ 15.03[3].

[155] IRC § 2632(c)(2)(B).

[156] IRC § 2632(c)(2)(C).

[157] IRC § 2632(c)(4).

[158] IRC § 2632(c)(2)(C).

[159] In all the situations discussed here (see infra text accompanying notes 162–171), if the amount of the deemed allocation is greater than the individual's remaining GST exemption, the trust will not be totally exempted from the generation-skipping transfer tax because the inclusion ratio for the trust will be greater than zero.

[160] IRC 2632(c)(1).

[161] See IRC § 2632(b)(1). See supra ¶ 15.03[3][a].

[162] See IRC § 2632(c)(1).

automatically allocated under Section 2632(c) will equal the value of the property involved in the indirect skip transfer.

If an indirect skip transfer occurs with respect to a pre-existing trust, which has an inclusion ratio greater than zero, the amount of the deemed allocation is not as clear. It is arguable that the statute should be interpreted as allocating GST exemption equal to the value of the property transferred in the indirect skip. However, under the provisions dealing generally with GST exemption allocation, when an allocation of GST exemption is made for property held in a trust, the inclusion ratio for the trust is determined, not an inclusion ratio for the property transferred.[163] Thus, it is more appropriate to read the statute to provide that the inclusion ratio of the trust, not the value of the property transferred, controls the amount of the unused GST exemption to be allocated upon an indirect skip transfer to the trust in order to give the property transferred to the trust an inclusion ratio of zero.[164] Under that rationale, if a trust has an inclusion ratio of one prior to an indirect skip, the maximum amount of unused GST exemption deemed allocated to the transfer of property should equal the full value of the corpus of the trust. For example, if a trust with a corpus of $900,000 and an inclusion ratio of one prior to the addition by the grantor of an additional $100,000 of property in an indirect skip transfer that triggers the automatic allocation of GST exemption, an allocation of $1 million[165] of GST exemption is required.[166] Applying the same rationale, if prior to the indirect skip the trust had an inclusion ratio greater than zero and less than one, the maximum amount of unused GST exemption automatically allocated should be greater than the transferred amount but less than the value of the corpus of the trust.[167]

---

[163] IRC § 2642(a)(1)(A); Reg. § 26.2642-1(b).

[164] The legislative history does not provide an answer to this issue. It provides that "any unused portion of such individual's generation-skipping transfer tax exemption is allocated to the property transferred to the extent necessary to produce the lowest possible inclusion ratio for such property." HR Conf. Rep. No. 84, 107th Cong., 1st Sess. 198 (2001), reprinted in 2001-__ CB __, __. Possibly a trust may be severed or treated as severed to get an inclusion ratio of zero for the value of the property transferred with an allocation of GST exemption equal in value to the property transferred. See IRC §§ 2642(a)(3), 2654(b).

[165] If only $100,000 of GST exemption were automatically allocated, the inclusion ratio for the trust would be 0.900 (one minus 0.100 (100,000 ÷ 1,000,000)).

[166] Under this rationale, Section 2632(c), could automatically allocate unused GST exemption to transfers that were made to trusts prior to December 31, 2000, the effective date of Section 2632(c). See Economic Growth and Tax Relief Reconciliation Act of 2001, Pub. L. No. 107-16, § 561(c)(1), 115 Stat. 38, 89, reprinted in 2001-__ CB __, __.

[167] For example, if Transferor previously created a trust with $200,000 of corpus and allocated $100,000 of GST exemption to the trust and the corpus value increased to $400,000 when Transferor made an indirect skip transfer of $200,000 to the trust, a $400,000 deemed allocation of unused GST exemption would be required to reduce the trust's inclusion ratio to zero. Cf. ¶ 16.02[5][b].

To make the deemed allocation of unused GST exemption to the trust as a whole, the value of both the property transferred and the property in the trust must be determined.[168] This raises issues of when must the transferred property or trust corpus be valued and when is the allocation effective. It would seem that the property, which is the subject matter of an indirect skip, should be valued for this purpose when the inter vivos gift is complete for Chapter 12 purposes. However, when an indirect skip transfer is subject to the estate tax inclusion period rules contained in Section 2642(f),[169] the indirect skip transfer is deemed to be made at the close of the estate tax inclusion period.[170] The fair market value of an indirect skip transfer subject to the estate tax inclusion period rules is the "fair market value of the trust property at the close of the estate tax inclusion period."[171] Even though the amount to be allocated cannot be determined until the end of the year,[172] it appears that the allocation is also to take place at the time the gift is complete for gift tax purposes or if the estate tax inclusion period rules apply, at the close of the estate tax inclusion period.

[e] Elections

[i] **Preventing automatic allocation.** An individual may elect to prevent the automatic allocation of unused GST exemption to an indirect skip.[173] The election is to be made on a timely filed gift tax return for the calendar year in which the indirect skip transfer is made.[174] If the transfer is an indirect skip, which under Section 2642(f) is treated as made at the end of the estate tax inclusion period, the election is to be made on a timely filed gift tax return for the calendar year in which the estate tax inclusion period ends.[175] The secretary is authorized to and may prescribe later dates for an individual to make a valid election preventing the automatic allocation of unused GST exemption to an indirect skip.[176]

---

[168] IRC §§ 2632(c), 2642(b).

[169] IRC § 2642(f).

[170] IRC § 2632(c)(4).

[171] IRC § 2632(c)(4).

[172] See supra ¶ 15.03[4][c].

[173] IRC § 2632(c)(5)(A)(i)(I).

[174] IRC § 2632(c)(5)(B)(i). An election to prevent the automatic allocation of GST exemption to an indirect skip should be subject to modification on an amended return filed on or before the due date of the Form 709 reporting the transfer. See ¶ 15.02[1] note 25.

[175] IRC § 2632(c)(5)(B)(i).

[176] IRC § 2632(c)(5)(B)(i).

An individual may also elect to prevent the automatic allocation of un-used GST exemption to any or all transfers made to a particular trust.[177] This election can alleviate the burden of having to make numerous elections with respect to numerous transfers to a particular trust. The election generally is to be made on a timely filed gift tax return for the calendar year it is to become effective.[178]

[ii] Elective GST trusts. Even though a trust is not treated as a GST trust owing to the statutory exceptions,[179] an individual may elect to treat the trust as a GST trust for purposes of Section 2632(c).[180] The election may be made for any particular transfer or all transfers to the trust made by the indi-vidual during the year.[181] The election to treat a trust as a GST trust is gener-ally to be made on a timely filed gift tax return for the calendar year in which the election is to become effective.[182]

[5] Retroactive Allocations

When the transferor[183] of a trust anticipates that the trust is likely to benefit only non-skip persons,[184] and therefore is unlikely to result in any generation-skipping transfers, the transferor is unlikely to allocate GST exemption[185] to the trust.[186] The premature death of a non-skip person beneficiary after a transfer or transfers to the trust may upset the apple cart and result in an immediate or subsequent generation-skipping transfer with the imposition of generation-

---

[177] IRC § 2632(c)(5)(A)(i)(II).

[178] IRC § 2632(c)(5)(B)(ii). The time to make this election may be extended under Section 2642(g)(1). See IRC § 2642(g)(1)(A)(ii); ¶ 16.02[9][a].

[179] IRC § 2632(c)(3)(B). See supra ¶ 15.03[4][b][iii].

[180] IRC § 2632(c)(5)(A)(ii).

[181] IRC § 2632(c)(5)(A)(ii). This includes any Section 2642(f) transfers.

[182] IRC § 2632(c)(5)(B)(ii). The time to make this election may be extended under Section 2642(g)(1). See IRC § 2642(g)(1)(A)(ii); ¶ 16.02[9][a].

[183] IRC § 2652(a). See ¶ 17.02[1].

[184] IRC § 2613(b). See ¶ 13.03[5].

[185] IRC § 2631(a). See ¶ 15.02.

[186] See IRC §§ 2631(a), 2632(a)(1); supra ¶ 15.03[2]. The automatic allocation rules most likely would not apply here. Since non-skip persons enjoy the benefits of the trust, there would be no direct skip to the trust and no Section 2632(b) automatic allocation. See supra ¶ 15.03[3]. Similarly, since non-skip persons hold most of the interests in the trust, the trust would in all likelihood not be a GST trust under Section 2632(c). IRC § 2632(c)(3)(B). See supra ¶ 15.03[4][b][iii]. Even if it were a GST trust, if the transferor did not expect the trust to have a generation-skipping transfer, the transferor would likely elect out of Section 2632(c). IRC § 2632(c)(5)(A). See supra ¶ 15.03[4][e][i].

skipping transfer tax. When there is an unnatural order of death[187] and the transferor is still living and has unused GST exemption,[188] Section 2632(d)[189] permits the transferor retroactively to allocate unused GST exemption to the trust.[190]

[a] Requirements for a Retroactive Allocation

Several requirements must be satisfied before a transferor may make a retroactive allocation.

[i] Unnatural order of death of a non–skip person. A non–skip person[191] must have a Section 2652(c) interest[192] or a future interest[193] in the trust to which transfers have been made. The non–skip person must be a lineal descendant of a grandparent of the transferor or the transferor's spouse or former spouse,[194] must be assigned to a generation below the generation level of the transferor,[195] and must predecease the transferor.[196] For example, assume Transferor creates a trust that provides income to Transferor's Child until age 45 with a remainder to Child at age 45, but with a remainder to Grandchildren if

---

[187] See infra ¶ 15.03[5][a][i].

[188] See infra ¶ 15.03[5][a][ii].

[189] Section 2632(d) applies where the death of the non–skip person occurs after December 31, 2000, and it may therefore apply to transfers of property made to a trust prior to such date. Economic Growth and Tax Relief Reconciliation Act of 2001, Pub. L. No. 107-16, § __, 115 Stat. 38, __, reprinted in 2001-__ CB __, __. Section 2632(d) is eliminated from the Code after the year 2010 under the "sunset" provision. Economic Growth and Tax Relief Reconciliation Act of 2001 § 901(a)(2), 115 Stat. 150, 2001-__ CB __. See ¶ 8.10[5].

[190] IRC § 2632(d). See infra ¶ 15.03[5][b].

[191] IRC § 2613(b). See ¶ 13.03[5].

[192] See ¶ 17.02[3].

[193] IRC § 2632(d)(1)(A). A non–skip person has a future interest in a trust if trust income or trust corpus may be distributed to the non–skip person at some future date. IRC § 2632(d)(3).

[194] IRC § 2632(d)(1)(B)(i). Such non–skip persons would include a child, niece, nephew, or a child of a first cousin of the transferor or the transferor's spouse or former spouse. It would also include a descendant of a child, niece, or nephew who was assigned to the generation level of a non–skip person as a result of the application of Section 2651(e). See ¶ 17.01[2][a][ii].

[195] IRC § 2632(d)(1)(B)(ii). Thus, the death of a sibling or first cousin of the transferor would not trigger application of the section.

[196] IRC § 2632(d)(1)(C).

Child dies prior to age 45. An unnatural order of death would occur if Child subsequently predeceased Transferor prior to reaching age 45.

[ii] Unused GST exemption. A retroactive allocation is allowed only if the transferor has unused GST exemption. The amount of unused GST exemption available and allowable for retroactive allocation is determined immediately before the premature death of the non–skip person,[197] not at the time the transfer of property occurred.[198] The amount of the transferor's available unused GST exemption is determined by reducing the amount of GST exemption allowable at the time of the death of the non–skip person by the GST exemption allocated by the transferor[199] or deemed allocated by the transferor[200] prior to the death of the non–skip person.[201]

[iii] Transferor's allocation. The retroactive allocation is effective only if it is made on a timely filed gift tax return, including extensions,[202] for the calendar year of the non–skip person's death.[203]

---

[197] IRC § 2632(d)(2)(C).

[198] For example, assume a transferor established a trust in 1995 when the allowable GST exemption was $1 million. Assume further that a non–skip person beneficiary who qualified the transferor for retroactive allocation of the GST exemption died in 2002 when the allowable GST exemption was $1.1 million. The allowable amount of GST exemption used in the computation of the unused amount available for retroactive allocation is $1.1 million.

[199] IRC § 2632(a)(1). See supra ¶ 15.03[2].

[200] IRC §§ 2632(b), 2632(c). See supra ¶¶ 15.03[3], 15.03[4].

[201] IRC § 2632(d)(2)(C). Thus, in the example above (see supra note 198) even though the amount of the transferor's GST exemption is increased to $1.5 million in 2004, the transferor would not be able to allocate the 2004 increase retroactively to the trust notwithstanding the untimely death of the non–skip person in 2002 because the GST exemption amount allowable is determined immediately before the non–skip person's death.

[202] IRC §§ 6075(b), 6081. See ¶¶ 9.04[10], 16.02[4][a].

[203] IRC § 2632(d)(2). A return is required to make the retroactive allocation even if no gift tax return is otherwise required to be filed for the year.

[b] Consequences of a Retroactive Allocation

If a transferor satisfies the requirements for a retroactive allocation, Section 2632(d) is a pro-taxpayer rule, which maximizes the potential benefits to the transferor.

[i] Time of allocation. The retroactive allocation of unused GST exemption is generally[204] effective immediately before the death of the non–skip person.[205]

[ii] Inclusion ratio valuation. When a retroactive allocation of unused GST exemption is made to previous transfers of property, in determining the inclusion ratio,[206] the property transferred is generally[207] valued at its fair market value at the time that the transfer to the trust was complete for gift tax purposes.[208]

[iii] Chronological allocations to a trust. If there has been more than one transfer by the transferor to a trust, retroactive allocations of unused GST exemption to the prior transfers to the trust[209] are made on a chronological basis.[210]

[iv] Example. Assume Transferor created a trust with income to Transferor's Child until age 45 with a remainder to Child at age 45 but if Child died prior to age 45 remainder to Grandchild. Assume further that Child died in 2002, prior to reaching age 45, survived by Transferor. If Transferor had originally contributed $1 million to the trust in 1990 and when Child died the trust

---

[204] But see infra ¶ 15.03[5][c][i].

[205] IRC § 2632(d)(2)(B). For example, assume Transferor created a trust with income to Child until age 45 with a remainder to Child at age 45, but if Child dies prior to reaching age 45, the trust corpus passes to Grandchild. If Child dies prior to attaining age 45 there is a Section 2612(a) taxable termination. If Transferor survives Child and a Section 2632(d) retroactive allocation is made, the allocation of Transferor's unused GST exemption, determined immediately before the death of Child, is effective immediately prior to Child's death. The retroactive allocation is used in the determination of the inclusion ratio and applicable rate of tax imposed on the taxable termination generation-skipping transfer occurring upon the termination of Child's interest in the trust.

[206] See ¶ 16.02.

[207] But see infra ¶ 15.03[5][c][i].

[208] IRC § 2632(d)(2)(A). If the trust property has substantially appreciated since the original transfer, this valuation approach is potentially very advantageous.

[209] If a transferor has made transfers to multiple trusts that qualify for retroactive allocation, a Section 2632(d) allocation may be made with respect to any or all of such trusts, potentially adding further complexity and planning possibilities to the allocation of the transferor's GST exemption.

[210] IRC § 2632(d)(1). Retroactive allocation has an inclusion made on a chronological basis even though some GST exemption has been previously allocated to the trust.

corpus was worth $2 million and Transferor, in 2002, had an unused GST exemption of $1.1 million, Transferor could make a Section 2632(d) retroactive allocation of $1 million on a timely filed gift tax return for the year 2002. As a result of the allocation, the trust would have a zero inclusion ratio and Transferor still would have $100,000 of remaining unused GST exemption. If, instead, Child died in 2004 when Transferor had $1.5 million of unused GST exemption and Transferor had transferred another $1 million to the trust in the year 2000 and the first $1 million worth of property transferred to the trust was worth $3 million at Child's death and the second $1 million worth of property transferred to the trust was worth $2 million at Child's death, the chronological order rule would apply. The $3 million property (the first $1 million transfer) would be fully shielded from the generation-skipping transfer tax (a zero inclusion ratio) and one half of the $2 million property ($500,000 of Transferor's remaining unused GST exemption/$1 million transferred) would also be shielded with the result that $4 million of the $5 million corpus would be shielded from the generation-skipping transfer tax and the trust would have an inclusion ratio of 0.200.[211]

[c] Relationship to Other Provisions

The interrelationship of Section 2632(d) and most of the other generation-skipping transfer tax provisions is relatively straightforward. However, the interaction of the retroactive allocation rules of Section 2632(d) with the Section 2642(f) estate tax inclusion period rules and the Section 2642(a)(3) qualified severance rules are thought-provoking.

[i] The Section 2642(f) estate tax inclusion period rules. When a trust is subject to the estate tax inclusion period rules,[212] at the death of the non–skip person whose death triggers the possibility of a retroactive allocation, the estate tax inclusion period rules should override the retroactive allocation rules, both as to the effective date of the GST exemption allocation[213] and the time of valuation of the property in the determination of the inclusion ratio.[214] The

---

[211] See ¶ 16.02.

[212] IRC § 2642(f); ¶ 16.02[7].

[213] A retroactive allocation of GST exemption is generally effective immediately before the death of the non–skip person whose death prior to the transferor is a prerequisite to a retroactive allocation. IRC § 2632(d)(2)(B). See supra ¶ 15.03[5][b][i]. When the estate tax inclusion period rules of Section 2642(f) apply, the effect of the allocation of GST exemption in determining the inclusion ratio is delayed until the close of the estate tax inclusion period. Reg. § 26.2632-1(c)(1). See ¶ 16.02[7][a] text accompanying note 430.

[214] When a retroactive allocation is made to an inter vivos transfer, the transfer is valued at the time the gift is complete for federal gift tax purposes in determining the inclusion ratio. IRC § 2632(d)(2)(A). See supra ¶ 15.03[5][b][ii]. When the effect of an

effect of the retroactive allocation of GST exemption should be delayed until the close of the estate tax inclusion period[215] and the estate tax inclusion period valuation rules should be used in the determination of the inclusion ratio,[216] just as would have been the case if the transferor had allocated GST exemption to the trust during the estate tax inclusion period prior to the non–skip person's out of order death.[217]

Assume Transferor created a trust that initially provided for an annuity interest (a fixed dollar annual payment) to Transferor for fifteen years[218] followed by an income interest to Child until age 45 and a remainder to Child at age 45 and provided that if Child died before attaining age 45 remainder to Grandchild. Assume Child predeceases Transferor ten years after the creation of the trust. Upon the death of Child the prerequisites for a retroactive allocation of Transferor's GST exemption are satisfied, and the estate tax inclusion period rules apply to the trust. The estate tax inclusion period rules should take precedence. Any allocation of Transferor's unused GST exemption should not take effect until the close of the estate tax inclusion period, and the property should be valued at that time in the determination of the inclusion ratio for the trust.

[ii] **The Section 2642(a)(3) severance rule.** In some situations, the retroactive allocation rule may act in conjunction with the Section 2642(a)(3) severance rule.[219] For example, assume Transferor in a prior year transferred $3 million to a trust that provides income to each of Transferor's two Children (or their estates) equally until the youngest child reaches, or would have reached, age 45, with equal remainders to the Children at that time. In the event that either Child dies prior to reaching age 45, one half of the remainder of the trust passes to that Child's Children when the youngest Child reaches, or would have reached, age 45. Transferor, assuming that no generation-skipping transfers would occur, allocated no GST exemption to the trust. Assume one Child dies prior to reaching age 45 in 2004 when Transferor is still living and has $1.5 million of unallocated GST exemption[220] and the corpus of the trust is worth $6 million. Transferor may elect to retroactively allocate $1.5 million of

---

allocation of GST exemption is delayed due to the application of the Section 2642(f) estate tax inclusion period rules, the transfer is valued at the close of the estate tax inclusion period in determining the inclusion ratio for the trust. IRC § 2642(f)(2). See ¶ 16.02[7][e].

[215] IRC §§ 2642(b)(1)(B), 2642(f)(1). See ¶ 16.02[7][e].

[216] IRC §§ 2642(b)(1)(A), 2642(f)(2). See ¶ 16.02[7][e].

[217] See ¶ 16.02[7], especially ¶ 16.02[7][a] text accompanying note 430. IRC § 2642(f)(1); Reg. § 26.2632-1(c)(1).

[218] This is a grantor retained annuity trust (GRAT).

[219] See ¶ 16.02[5][e].

[220] See IRC §§ 2010(c), 2631(c).

GST exemption to the trust, giving the trust a 0.500 inclusion ratio[221] and then make a qualified severance of the trust under Section 2642(a)(3) and allocate the GST exemption to the trust benefiting the grandchildren. That trust would then have a zero inclusion ratio,[222] and the surviving Child's trust would have an inclusion ratio of one.[223] In the alternative, Transferor could make a Section 2642(a)(3) severance of the original trust[224] and then timely retroactively allocate $1.5 million of GST exemption to the trust benefiting the grandchildren, which again would have a zero inclusion ratio.[225]

[6] Allocations Made at or After Death

The executor of the transferor's estate has the opportunity at the transferor's death to allocate any unused GST exemption to four classifications of property transfers: direct skips occurring at death, property held in trusts included in the transferor's gross estate, property held in inter vivos trusts not included in the transferor's gross estate, and inter vivos direct or indirect skips occurring near death.[226] The allocation of the decedent's GST exemption may be made by use of a formula.[227] An allocation by the transferor's executor may be used to avoid, in whole or in part, the application of the automatic allocation of the residual GST exemption.[228]

---

[221] The allocation is effective as of the original $3 million transfer (IRC § 2632(d)(2)(A)) giving the trust an applicable fraction of 0.500 and an inclusion ratio of 0.500. IRC §§ 2642(a)(1), 2642(a)(2).

[222] See IRC § 2642(a)(3)(B)(ii).

[223] See IRC § 2642(a)(3)(B)(ii).

[224] If the trust were severed, each trust would still have an inclusion ratio of one because no GST exemption was allocated to the trust.

Arguably, the trust would have already been severed for purposes of Chapter 13 (although not actually severed) under Section 2654(b)(2). Because no GST exemption had previously been allocated to the trust, the trusts treated as severed would each still have an inclusion ratio of one. See ¶ 17.04[2]. See also ¶ 16.02[5][e].

[225] The $1.5 million GST exemption allocation would, as a result of Section 2632(d)(2)(A), provide the trust an applicable fraction of one and a zero inclusion ratio. IRC §§ 2642(a)(1), 2642(a)(2).

[226] IRC §§ 2631(a), 2632(a).

[227] Reg. § 26.2632-1(d)(1). See supra ¶ 15.02[1] note 26. A formula allocation of GST exemption with respect to a charitable lead annuity trust is invalid except to the extent the formula allocation is dependent on values as finally determined for federal estate or gift tax purposes. Reg. § 26.2632-1(b)(2)(i).

[228] IRC § 2632(e). See infra ¶ 15.03[7]. Seemingly, the transferor can direct the action to be taken by an executor in the postmortem allocation of the transferor's GST exemption.

[a] Direct Skips Occurring at Death

The deceased transferor's unused GST exemption may be allocated to direct skips of property occurring at death whether the transfers are outright, to a trust, or from a trust.[229] The executor may allocate the decedent's unused GST exemption at any time before the date prescribed for filing the decedent's federal estate tax return,[230] including extensions actually granted.[231] Failure to make a timely allocation of the exemption will result in any unused exemption being automatically allocated to the nonexempt value of the direct skip occurring, or treated as occurring, at death under the residual allocation rules.[232]

The allocation is made by the executor on the federal estate tax return.[233] The allocation is effective as of the date of the transferor's death.[234] The property involved in the direct skip occurring at death is generally valued at its federal estate tax value in the computation of the inclusion ratio.[235] When the property involved in a direct skip occurring at death is valued under Section 2032A for estate and generation-skipping transfer tax purposes,[236] the executor may allocate more GST exemption than the amount of the direct skip to re-

---

[229] This includes direct skips treated as occurring at death as a result of Section 2642(f). See ¶ 16.02[7]; supra ¶ 15.03[3][b]. A GST exemption may be allocated to a delayed direct skip with the effect of the allocation being delayed until the close of the estate tax inclusion period. See supra ¶ 15.03[3][b] note 50.

[230] Form 706, United States Estate (and Generation-Skipping Transfer) Tax Return (Rev. Nov. 2001).

[231] IRC § 2632(a)(1); Reg. § 26.2632-1(d)(1). Even if no federal estate tax return is required to be filed, the postdeath allocation of GST exemption is allowed to be made before the due date of the federal estate tax return, including any extensions of time to file the return that are actually granted. Reg. § 26.2632-1(a). However, if no return is required to be filed because of the size of the gross estate after considering prior inter vivos gifts (see IRC § 6018(a)), Section 2632(e) will automatically allocate GST exemption to the transferor's property without the need for any affirmative allocation. See infra ¶ 15.03[7].

[232] IRC § 2632(e). See infra ¶ 15.03[7]. See supra note 229.

[233] IRC § 2632(a)(2). Form 706, United States Estate (and Generation-Skipping Transfer) Tax Return (Rev. Nov. 2001) Schedules R and R-1 are used by a deceased transferor's executor to allocate the decedent's GST exemption to testamentary direct skips.

[234] IRC § 2642(b)(2)(B); Reg. § 26.2632-1(d)(1).

[235] IRC § 2642(b)(2)(A); Reg. § 26.2642-2(b). The federal estate tax value includes alternate valuation under Section 2032 and special use valuation under Section 2032A. See Reg. § 26.2642-2(b)(1). It also incorporates a special rule where requirements respecting postdeath changes in value are not met. See the last clause of Section 2642(b)(2)(A); Reg. §§ 26.2642-2(b)(2), 26.2642-2(b)(3); ¶¶ 16.02[4][d][ii], 16.02[4][d][iii].

[236] See ¶ 18.03[1][a] notes 10, 11.

duce the additional generation-skipping transfer tax that will be imposed in the event of the property's premature disposition or cessation of qualified use.[237]

[b] Trusts Included in the Gross Estate

The executor may allocate unused GST exemption to property held in a testamentary trust or an inter vivos trust that is includible in the decedent's gross estate.[238] The rules regarding the time and manner of allocation of the GST exemption by the executor to such trusts are similar to the rules for the allocation of the GST exemption to testamentary direct skips.[239] Thus, the allocation of the GST exemption to property held in trust included in the transferor's gross estate must be made by the due date of the federal estate tax return, including extensions actually granted;[240] the allocation is effective as of

---

[237] Form 706 may be used as a "Notice of Allocation" to allocate additional GST exemption to property valued pursuant to Section 2032A passing to individual skip persons. See Instructions for Form 706, United States Estate (and Generation-Skipping Transfer) Tax Return (Rev. Nov. 2001) Instructions for Schedules R and R-1, Generation-Skipping Transfer Tax, How to Complete Schedule R, Part 1—GST exemption reconciliation, Line 10, at 21. See also IRC § 2032A(c), which is discussed at ¶ 4.04[7]. If the executor fails to allocate additional GST exemption to the property valued pursuant to Section 2032A for generation-skipping transfer tax purposes, any unused GST exemption at the time of disposition or cessation of use will automatically be allocated to the earliest disposition or cessation of use of property valued under Section 2032A for generation-skipping transfer tax purposes. See infra ¶ 15.03[7][b][iii]. Although the Instructions for Form 706 do not specifically so state, it seems that a similar allocation may be made to property held in a trust that is a skip person, is includible in the transferor's gross estate, and is valued under Section 2032A. Id. See Reg. § 26.2642-2(b)(1); infra ¶ 15.03[6][b] note 242.

[238] The inter vivos trusts would be subject to the rules of Section 2642(f). See ¶ 16.02[7]. See Priv. Ltr. Rul. 199937026 (June 17, 1999) (no Schedule R filed but substantial compliance with allocation requirements due to information in trust agreement attached to return).

[239] See supra ¶ 15.03[6][a] text accompanying notes 230, 231. The statute provides, "If property is transferred as a result of the death of the transferor, the value of such property for purposes of subsection (a) shall be its value for purposes of Chapter 11. . . . " IRC § 2642(b)(2)(A). The transfer referred to in the statute should include a transfer subjected to the federal estate tax, which is not a generation-skipping transfer at the time of the transferor's death. Revaluation of the property at some later date after the transferor's death, before the filing of the federal estate tax return, generally would unduly complicate allocation of the unused GST exemption to property included in the decedent's gross estate, which was not the subject matter of a generation-skipping transfer at death. But see Reg. §§ 26.2642-2(b)(2), 26.2642-2(b)(3); ¶ 16.02[4][d].

[240] IRC § 2632(a)(1). See supra ¶ 15.03[6][a] note 231. Form 706 may be used to allocate the GST exemption to trusts for which the decedent is the Chapter 13 transferor and that may be the source of postdeath generation-skipping transfers of property. See Instructions for Form 706, United States Estate (and Generation-Skipping Transfer) Tax Return (Rev. Nov. 2001) Instructions for Schedules R and R-1. Generation-Skipping Transfer Tax, How to Complete Schedule R, Part 1—GST exemption reconciliation, Line 9, at 21.

the date of the transferor's death,[241] and the property is generally valued at its federal estate tax value in the computation of the inclusion ratio.[242]

[c] Inter Vivos Trusts Not Included in the Gross Estate

A transferor's executor may allocate any unused GST exemption to property held in an inter vivos trust that is not includible in the transferor's gross estate but that may be the subject matter of generation-skipping transfers attributable to the decedent transferor after the transferor's death.[243] Whether the allocation is an initial allocation or an additional allocation of the transferor's GST exemption to such a trust,[244] it is an allocation of GST exemption to an inter vivos transfer made by the transferor. If the transfer to the inter vivos trust occurs shortly before the transferor's death, and if the allocation is made on a timely filed federal gift tax return,[245] the allocation is effective on the date of the transfer to the trust,[246] and the property is valued on the date of the

---

Failure literally to comply with the instructions on Form 706 for making an allocation of GST exemption does not preclude an effective allocation where there is substantial compliance with the requirements for making an allocation. Priv. Ltr. Rul. 9534001 (May 1, 1995).

[241] IRC § 2642(b)(2)(B); Reg. § 26.2632-1(d)(1).

[242] IRC § 2642(b)(2)(A). See supra ¶ 15.03[6][a] note 235. Additional GST exemption may be allocated to trusts whose corpus is valued under Section 2032A to reduce the trust's inclusion ratio to zero and eliminate generation-skipping transfer tax imposed on taxable distributions or taxable terminations from the trust. The additional allocation of GST exemption is necessary to reduce the inclusion ratio to zero if, in determining the denominator of the applicable fraction, the value of the property included in the decedent's gross estate is valued at fair market value, not the Section 2032A value. Reg. § 26.2642-2(b)(1). See ¶ 16.02[4][d][i]. Allocation of GST exemption equal to the fair market value of the property, rather than the Section 2032A value of the property, will also reduce the amount of additional generation-skipping transfer tax that would be imposed in the event of a premature disposition or cessation of qualified use, which may trigger additional generation-skipping transfer tax. See Reg. § 26.2642-4(a)(4)(iii); supra ¶ 15.03[6][a] note 237; infra ¶ 15.03[7][b] text accompanying note 263; infra ¶ 15.03[7][b][iii].

[243] For example, this could include an inter vivos direct skip trust or GST trust with respect to which the transferor opted not to make an allocation of GST exemption under Section 2632(b)(3) or Section 2632(c)(5)(A)(i), respectively, but to which the transferor now wants to allocate GST exemption in order to shield future taxable distributions or taxable terminations. See the example supra ¶ 15.03[3][c] text accompanying notes 79, 80; supra ¶ 15.03[4]. See also supra ¶ 15.03[6] note 228. This may include a trust established when the transferor had no unused GST exemption, but where subsequent to the transfer the GST exemption amount increased. See IRC § 2631(c); ¶ 15.02.

[244] Cf. IRC §§ 2642(d)(2)–2642(d)(4). See ¶ 16.02[5][b].

[245] Reg. § 26.2632-1(d)(1).

[246] IRC § 2642(b)(1)(B); Reg. § 26.2632-1(b)(2)(ii)(A)(1). See infra ¶ 15.03[6][d] note 250.

transfer to the trust in the computation of the inclusion ratio.[247] If the allocation is not made on a timely filed federal gift tax return (a late allocation), the allocation is to be made on the federal estate tax return or a federal gift tax return filed on or before the due date of the transferor's federal estate tax return, it is effective on the date the allocation is filed,[248] and the valuation of the property for purposes of the inclusion ratio occurs on the date the allocation is filed.[249]

[d] Inter Vivos Direct and Indirect Skips Occurring Near Death

A transferor's executor may allocate GST exemption if the transferor has made an inter vivos direct or indirect skip[250] but dies before an allocation is made with respect to the transfer and before the time for filing the gift tax return.[251] In this situation, the executor should be able to take any action that the decedent could have taken with respect to the inter vivos direct or indirect skip. Thus, the executor may opt out of the deemed allocation rules for inter vivos direct or indirect skips,[252] make a partial or full allocation of the dece-

---

[247] IRC § 2642(b)(1)(A); Reg. § 26.2642-2(a)(1).

[248] Reg. § 26.2632-1(d)(1). A late allocation by an executor is effective as of the date of filing. Id.

[249] Reg. § 26.2642-2(a)(2). This is consistent with the Section 2642(b)(3)(A) statutory result. See infra ¶ 15.03[7][b] text accompanying note 282. But see Instructions for Form 706, United States Estate (and Generation-Skipping Transfer) Tax Return (Rev. Nov. 2001) Instructions for Schedules R and R-1. Generation-Skipping Transfer Tax, How to Complete Schedule R, Part 1—GST exemption reconciliation, Line 9, Column D, at 21, allowing an administrative variation under which a timely postdeath notice of allocation filed by the executor could be effective on the date of transferor's death, and the property could be valued on the date of the transferor's death in the computation of the inclusion ratio. It is possible that the administrative variation from the statute and regulations that is contained in the Instructions will be allowed with respect to any allocation to inter vivos trusts not included in the gross estate. These Instructions present a position consistent with the rule of valuation contained in proposed regulations not included in the final regulations. See Prop. Reg. § 26.2632-1(d)(1), 1993-1 CB 867, 876; Prop. Reg. § 26.2642-2(a)(2), 1993-1 CB 867, 877.

[250] IRC §§ 2632(b), 2632(c); supra ¶¶ 15.03[3], 15.03[4].

[251] If the transferor dies prior to July 15 of any year, the transferor's gift tax return generally is due at the time of the transferor's estate tax return. IRC § 6075(b)(3). If the transferor dies after July 15, the transferor's gift tax return generally is due on April 15 of the succeeding year. IRC § 6075(b)(1). See supra ¶ 15.03[6] note 228.

[252] IRC §§ 2632(b)(3), 2632(c)(5)(A)(i). See supra ¶¶ 15.03[3][c], 15.03[4][e][i].

dent's unused GST exemption to the transfer,[253] or do nothing, allowing the applicable deemed allocation rules to apply.[254]

[7] Allocation of Residual Exemption

[a] In General

Any portion of an individual's GST exemption not deemed allocated to inter vivos direct or indirect skips or not allocated by the individual transferor or the individual's executor by the date prescribed for filing the individual's federal estate tax return, including extensions actually granted,[255] is automatically and irrevocably allocated to generation-skipping transfers occurring at or after death.[256] The purpose of the automatic allocation of residual GST exemption after the death of a transferor is to make full use of the transferor's GST exemption, which effectively exempts property from the generation-skipping transfer tax base. If a transferor has unused GST exemption, it would be unreasonable not to allocate the unused GST exemption to reduce or eliminate generation-skipping transfer tax.

The residual portion of an individual's GST exemption is first allocated to the nonexempt value of property that is the subject matter of direct skips occurring, or treated as occurring, at the individual's death.[257] Any residual GST

---

[253] IRC § 2632(a). See supra ¶ 15.03[2]. But see also supra ¶ 15.03[3][c] text accompanying notes 81–83.

[254] IRC §§ 2632(b)(1), 2632(b)(2), 2632(c)(1), 2632(c)(2). See supra ¶¶ 15.03[3][a], 15.03[4][a].

[255] The automatic allocation of residual GST exemption occurs upon the expiration of the time the transferor or the transferor's executor is allowed to make allocations of the transferor's GST exemption. See Reg. § 26.2632-1(d)(2). The allocation of residual GST exemption occurs when extensions of time to file actually granted expire, regardless of whether an estate tax return is ultimately required to be filed. Id. See supra ¶ 15.03[6][a] note 231. The allocation of residual GST exemption may be affected, both as to timing and amount, by a Section 2642(g)(1)(A) extension to make an allocation of GST exemption described in Section 2642(b)(2). IRC § 2642(g)(1)(A)(i). See ¶ 16.02[9][a]. Section 2642(b)(2) deals with property transferred as a result of the death of the transferor, its valuation, and the effective date of GST exemption allocated to it. IRC § 2642(b)(2).

[256] IRC § 2632(e)(1). The automatic allocation is irrevocable, and any attempt to allocate GST exemption after the automatic allocation occurs is ineffective. Reg. § 26.2632-1(d)(2). See Priv. Ltr. Rul. 199937026 (June 17, 1999) (automatic allocation where no Schedule R filed and trust agreement filed with return silent regarding allocation between trusts).

[257] IRC § 2632(e)(1)(A); Reg. § 26.2632-1(d)(2). An inter vivos direct skip transfer subject to an estate tax inclusion period that terminates at the transferor's death is treated as occurring at the transferor's death. See IRC § 2642(f); Reg. § 26.2632-1(c)(4). See supra ¶ 15.03[6][a] note 229.

exemption not fully consumed by direct skips occurring, or treated as occurring, at death is then allocated to the nonexempt value of property held in trust with respect to which the individual is the transferor, and from which a taxable distribution or a taxable termination might occur at or after the individual's death.[258] Finally, any remaining unused GST exemption[259] will be deemed allocated to the nonexempt value of property upon the premature disposition or cessation of qualified use of property valued under Section 2032A for generation-skipping transfer tax purposes.[260] The three interclass allocation rules are considered in detail in the next section, along with consideration of allocations within a class.

[b] Allocation Between Categories

[i] **Direct skips.** Unused GST exemption is allocated first to direct skips occurring, or treated as occurring, at the transferor's death either outright or in trust to the nonexempt portion of the value of the transferred property generally as finally determined for purposes of Chapter 11.[261]

The first step in allocating residual GST exemption to direct skips occurring at the transferor's death is generally to determine the Chapter 11 value of the property involved in such direct skips. The Chapter 11 value, the value for federal estate tax purposes, is the fair market value[262] or the Section 2032A

---

[258] IRC § 2632(e)(1)(B). Cf. IRC § 2632(e)(2)(B). No GST exemption will automatically be allocated to a trust that will have a new transferor with respect to the entire trust prior to the occurrence of any generation-skipping transfer with respect to the trust. Reg. § 26.2632-1(d)(2). A GST exemption will not be automatically allocated to a trust if in the nine-month period following the transferor's death, no generation-skipping transfers occurred and, examining the trust at the end of the nine-month period, no future generation-skipping transfers can occur with respect to the trust. Id.

[259] See IRC §§ 2632(e)(1)(A), 2632(e)(1)(B); Reg. § 26.2632-1(d)(2).

[260] Reg. § 26.2642-4(a)(4)(i). The Section 2032A valuation may be used in the determination of the taxable amount of a testamentary direct skip or in the determination of the denominator of the applicable fraction. See ¶ 18.03[1]. See also Instructions for Form 706, United States Estate (and Generation-Skipping Transfer) Tax Return (Rev. Nov. 2001) Instructions for Schedules R and R-1. Generation-Skipping Transfer Tax, How to Complete Schedule R, Part 1—GST exemption reconciliation, Line 10, at 21. The instructions provide that "[i]f you do not allocate the GST exemption, it will be automatically allocated under the deemed allocation at death rules. To the extent any amount is not so allocated it will be automatically allocated (under regulations to be published) to the earliest disposition or cessation that is subject to the generation-skipping transfer tax."

[261] IRC § 2632(e)(1)(A); Reg. §§ 26.2632-1(d)(2), 26.2642-2(b).

[262] IRC § 2031. See ¶ 4.02[2].

value[263] of the property determined on the date of the transferor's death[264] or on the alternate valuation date.[265] When the date-of-distribution value or an adjusted Chapter 11 value overrides the Chapter 11 value in the determination of the denominator of the applicable fraction for testamentary direct skips[266] that occur before the due date for the filing of the decedent's federal estate tax return, that value should be used in the determination of the allocation of the residual GST exemption to testamentary direct skips.[267]

---

[263] IRC § 2032A. See ¶ 4.04. If the property that is the subject matter of a testamentary direct skip is valued under Section 2032A for estate tax purposes, that value is used in the determination of the taxable amount. IRC § 2624(b). However, in the determination of the applicable fraction, qualified real property valued under Section 2032A for federal estate tax purposes may be valued at fair market value in the determination of the denominator of the applicable fraction. Reg. § 26.2642-2(b)(1). See ¶ 18.03[1][a] note 11. If qualified real property is valued under Section 2032A in the determination of the taxable amount and at fair market value in the determination in the denominator of the applicable fraction, the fair market value of the property should be substituted for the Section 2032A Chapter 11 value in the determination of the allocation of residual GST exemption to testamentary direct skips. Id.

[264] IRC § 2031. See ¶ 4.02.

[265] IRC § 2032. See ¶ 4.03.

[266] IRC § 2642(b)(2)(A); Reg. §§ 26.2642-2(b)(2), 26.2642-2(b)(3). See ¶ 16.02[4][d].

[267] The purpose behind the automatic allocation of residual GST exemption after death of the transferor is to make full use of the transferor's GST exemption. If a transferor makes a testamentary direct skip that is required to be valued on the date of distribution in the determination of the applicable fraction (see ¶¶ 16.02[4][d][ii], 16.02[4][d][iii]) and has unused GST exemption, it would be unreasonable not to automatically allocate the unused GST exemption to the transfer and thereby reduce the inclusion ratio to zero and eliminate the imposition of any generation-skipping transfer tax. The substitution of the date-of-distribution value or the adjusted Chapter 11 value for the Chapter 11 value where that value is used in the determination of the denominator of the applicable fraction will assure that the direct skips occurring at death make full use of the deceased transferor's unused GST exemption. The value substituted for the Chapter 11 value should also be used in lieu of the estate tax value in determining the amount of the testamentary direct skip.

One potential problem occurs where the distribution is made after the time for filing the deceased transferor's federal estate tax return. It is not uncommon for pecuniary payments to occur subsequent to the time for filing the decedent's federal estate tax return. Seemingly, the residual allocation rules need another category to provide for the allocation of unused GST exemption remaining after the application of Section 2632(e) to testamentary direct skips if a substituted value, that is determined after the federal estate tax return is filed, is used in determining the amount of the testamentary direct skip. A problem with this approach is that it presupposes that the generation-skipping transfer tax on the testamentary direct skip pecuniary payment will be determined at some time after the federal estate tax return is required to be filed. How is it possible to have a testamentary direct skip pecuniary payment subject to the date-of-distribution valuation rules in the determination of the applicable fraction, which is reported on the transferor's federal estate tax return, and the generation-skipping transfer tax paid when the pecuniary payment is not

The second step is to determine the "nonexempt portion" of a direct skip. The nonexempt portion of a direct skip treated as occurring at death is determined by multiplying the Chapter 11 value of the direct skip by the inclusion ratio. Once the nonexempt portion is determined, the automatic allocation of unused GST exemption occurs on the date the federal estate (and generation-skipping transfer) tax return is due with respect to direct skips occurring, or treated as occurring, at the transferor's death.[268]

[ii] Trusts with generation-skipping transfer potential. Once the direct skips occurring at death have been neutralized for generation-skipping transfer tax purposes with unused GST exemption, any remaining GST exemption is then applied to trusts established by the decedent that may be the source of future generation-skipping transfers.[269] This category includes property transferred at death to a trust and inter vivos trusts included in the decedent's gross estate, and may include inter vivos trusts established by the decedent that are not required to be included in the decedent's gross estate that may be the source of future generation-skipping transfers.[270]

In two situations no automatic allocation of residual GST exemption is made to a trust. When the entire trust will have a new transferor[271] prior to the occurrence of any generation-skipping transfer with respect to the trust, there

---

made until after the federal estate tax return is to be filed? The regulations dealing with the special rules for pecuniary payments should deal with this situation.

[268] Reg. § 26.2632-1(d)(2). Working through the Section 2632(e) deemed allocation to direct skips occurring at the transferor's death is similar to a trip to Wonderland with Alice. A direct skip that occurs at death is required to be reported on a federal estate and generation-skipping transfer tax return. Generally, the generation-skipping transfer tax, if one is imposed, is paid by the estate from the property that is the subject matter of the direct skip. If an allocation of GST exemption is not made and the deemed allocation rules are relied on, is the executor required to pay the generation-skipping transfer tax imposed on the direct skip and then once the deemed allocation of GST exemption is triggered get a refund? The deemed allocation to testamentary direct skips is useful to protect an unknowing taxpayer who fails to file the required return and is salvaged from penalties due to the automatic application of GST exemption, but it is highly unlikely that anyone who reports the direct skip occurring at death on the appropriate return will ever knowingly rely on the deemed allocation of unused GST exemption.

[269] IRC § 2632(e)(1)(B); Reg. § 26.2632-1(d)(2).

[270] Section 2632(c) automatically allocates unused GST exemption to inter vivos transfers to trusts that would likely have generation-skipping transfers with respect to the transferor later. See IRC § 2632(c)(3)(B); supra ¶ 15.03[4]. A GST exemption may be allocated to the property transferred under Section 2632(e)(1)(B) to the extent the transferor elected out of the application of Section 2032(c) pursuant to Section 2632(c)(5), to the extent a trust received no allocation because it would unlikely be involved in a generation-skipping transfer, or where the unused GST exemption was less than the property transferred to the trust and the amount of the GST exemption subsequently increases. See IRC § 2631; ¶ 15.02.

[271] IRC § 2652(a). See ¶ 17.02[1].

is no automatic allocation of residual GST exemption to the trust.[272] Addition-ally, if during the nine-month period ending after the transferor's death no generation-skipping transfer has occurred with respect to the trust, and at the end of this period it can be determined that none can occur thereafter, no un-used GST exemption is deemed allocated to the trust.[273]

The unused GST exemption is allocated to the decedent's trusts with lurk-ing generation-skipping transfers generally on the basis of the Chapter 11 value of the nonexempt portion of the property included in the gross estate and the date-of-death value of the nonexempt portion of trusts not included in the gross estate.[274] The Chapter 11 value of the property held in a trust that is in-cluded in the deceased transferor's gross estate is the fair market value of property[275] or the Section 2032A value of qualified real property[276] determined on the applicable valuation date.[277] Property valued under Section 2032A for Chapter 11 purposes will be valued at fair market value on the applicable valu-ation date in the postdeath automatic allocation of residual GST exemption if the recapture agreement described in Section 2032A(d)(2) does not specifically provide for the "signatories' consent to the imposition of, and personal liability for, additional . . . [generation-skipping transfer] tax in the event additional es-tate tax is imposed under section 2032A(c)."[278] Additionally, when, instead of the Chapter 11 value, the date-of-distribution value or an adjusted Chapter 11 value is used in the determination of the denominator of the applicable fraction for trust property on or before the date the decedent's federal estate tax return is due (the point in time for the computation of deemed allocation of unused GST exemption), that date-of-distribution value or adjusted Chapter 11 value should be substituted for the Chapter 11 value in the application of Section 2632(e).[279] Use of the substitute Chapter 11 value in the automatic allocation of residual GST exemption will facilitate full use of the deceased transferor's unused GST exemption. Finally, property that is held in an inter vivos trust es-tablished by the transferor that is not included in the transferor's gross estate is valued at fair market value at the date of death for purposes of the allocation of the residual GST exemption to trusts with generation-skipping transfer tax

---

[272] Reg. § 26.2632-1(d)(2). See ¶ 15.02[4].

[273] Reg. § 26.2632-1(d)(2).

[274] Reg. §§ 26.2632-1(d)(2), 26.2642-2(b). This may require the decedent's estate or the trust that is not included in the decedent's gross estate, to incur eventually a valuation expense it would not otherwise incur with respect to a trust not included in the trans-feror's gross estate.

[275] IRC § 2031. See ¶ 4.02[2].

[276] IRC § 2032A. See ¶ 4.04; ¶ 16.02[4][d] text accompanying note 255; supra ¶ 15.03[6][b]. See also ¶ 18.03[1][b].

[277] IRC §§ 2031, 2032. See ¶¶ 4.02, 4.03.

[278] See Reg. § 26.2642-2(b)(1).

[279] See supra note 267.

potential.[280] Although the unused GST exemption is allocated on the due date of the federal estate tax return,[281] any allocation of GST exemption to property transferred as a result of the death of the transferor is effective as of the date of the transferor's death.[282] The allocation of residual unused GST exemption to property that is not transferred as a result of the death of the transferor should also be effective as of the date of the transferor's death.

[iii] Property valued under Section 2032A. If the transferor's unused GST exemption is not totally consumed by the allocations to direct skips treated as occurring at death and to properties held in the transferor's trusts that have generation-skipping transfer tax potential, it is then available for allocation to properties valued under Section 2032A for generation-skipping transfer tax purposes.[283] Residual allocation of unused GST exemption to property valued under Section 2032A for generation-skipping transfer tax purposes should be made only when a premature disposition or cessation of the qualified use of such property occurs.[284] This delayed allocation of unused GST exemption for property valued under Section 2032A for generation-skipping transfer purposes is available for property involved in a testamentary direct skip at the transferor's death. It is also available for allocation to trusts that are not skip persons at the transferor's death, but may be the source of generation-skipping transfers attributed to the transferor, and, nonetheless, hold property valued pursuant to Section 2032A in the computation of the denominator of the applicable fraction, which may require additional allocation of GST ex-

---

[280] Reg. § 26.2632-1(d)(2). This property is not specifically covered by a statutory valuation rule governing the computation of the inclusion ratio. See IRC § 2642(b). It is not property transferred as a result of the transferor's death under Section 2642(b)(2) nor is it property for which a notice of allocation needs to be filed with the secretary under Section 2642(b)(3), because the allocation is automatic. There is no statutory provision dictating when this property is to be valued for purposes of interclass allocation. Cf. infra ¶ 15.03[7][c] text accompanying note 294. The intraclass allocation rule does not apply to interclass allocations. IRC § 2632(e)(2). See infra ¶ 15.03[7][c][i].

[281] Reg. § 26.2632-1(d)(2).

[282] IRC § 2642(b)(2)(B).

[283] Reg. § 26.2642-4(a)(4)(i).

[284] Because it is unclear which property valued under Section 2032A for generation-skipping transfer tax purposes can take advantage of this administrative allocation of the GST exemption, the allocation is made at the time the additional generation-skipping transfer tax is imposed. Reg. § 26.2642-4(a)(4)(i). See infra ¶ 15.03[7][c][ii]; Instructions for Form 706, United States Estate (and Generation-Skipping Transfer) Tax Return (Rev. Nov. 2001) Instructions for Schedules R and R-1. Generation-Skipping Transfer Tax, How to Complete Schedule R, Part 1—GST exemption reconciliation, Line 10, at 21. The instructions provide that "[i]f you do not allocate the GST exemption, it will be automatically allocated under the deemed allocation at death rules. To the extent any amount is not so allocated it will be automatically allocated (under regulations to be published) to the earliest disposition or cessation that is subject to the generation-skipping transfer tax."

emption upon a premature disposition or cessation of qualified use of the property valued under Section 2032A.[285]

[c] Apportionment Within Categories

[i] Direct skips and trusts with generation-skipping transfer potential. Apportionment of the exemption within categories is required when there are multiple direct skips occurring at the transferor's death, or when there are multiple trusts and the residual GST exemption does not exceed the nonexempt value of the property involved in the direct skips or held in the trusts.[286] The exemption is apportioned among the properties or trusts as the case may be "in proportion to the respective amounts (at the time of allocation) of the nonexempt portions of such properties or trusts."[287] The nonexempt portion is the value of the property involved in the direct skip or held in a trust, multiplied by the inclusion ratio with respect to such property or trust.[288] If the properties or trusts have not previously had any GST exemption allocated to them, then their full value qualifies for the automatic pro rata allocation of the residual GST exemption. However, where some portion of the GST exemption has previously been allocated, the residual GST exemption is apportioned only among the nonexempt portions of the trusts or properties.

When apportionment of the residual GST exemption allocated to either direct skips or trusts is required, the property is to be valued at the time of allocation.[289] Is the time of allocation the date of the transferor's death, the date the property is distributed, or the due date for filing the transferor's federal estate tax return? The time of allocation is to be determined in conjunction with the allocation to the two statutory categories and the inclusion ratio valuation rules.[290] Not to do so would result in unnecessary revaluation of properties within each category. Therefore, when the apportionment is between direct skips occurring at the transferor's death, the rules for valuing transfers at death for purposes of computing the inclusion ratio apply.[291] Under these rules, the property value would generally be its Chapter 11 value.[292] In general, property

---

[285] Reg. § 26.2642-2(b)(1). See Reg. § 26.2642-4(a)(4). See ¶ 16.02[5][f].

[286] IRC § 2632(e)(2)(A). See Priv. Ltr. Rul. 199937026 (June 17, 1999) (automatic allocation of GST exemption apportioned between shares).

[287] IRC § 2632(e)(2)(A). See Reg. § 26.2632-1(d)(2).

[288] IRC § 2632(e)(2)(B). Residual GST exemption is disregarded in determining the nonexempt portion of the property involved in the direct skips or held in trusts.

[289] IRC § 2632(e)(2)(A).

[290] See supra ¶ 15.03[7][b]; IRC § 2642(b); Reg. §§ 26.2632-1(d)(2), 26.2642-2(b).

[291] IRC § 2642(b)(2)(A); Reg. §§ 26.2632-1(d)(2), 26.2642-2(b).

[292] Section 2642(b)(2)(A) provides in pertinent part that "the value of such property for purposes of subsection (a) shall be its value as finally determined for purposes of

held in trust that is included in the transferor's gross estate is also to be valued at its Chapter 11 value for apportionment purposes.[293] Property held in inter vivos trusts not included in the transferor's gross estate should be valued at its fair market value on the date of the transferor's death for purposes of intraclass apportionment, paralleling its valuation for purposes of interclass allocation and computation of the inclusion ratio.[294]

[ii] Property valued under Section 2032A. Apportionment of the residual GST exemption is required only when there are two or more simultaneous dispositions or cessations of use of properties valued under Section 2032A for generation-skipping transfer tax purposes. The residual GST exemption should be apportioned proportionately among the properties where Section 2032A is used for generation-skipping transfer tax purposes on which additional estate tax is imposed,[295] using the difference between the Section 2032A value of the properties and the fair market value of such properties at the transferor's date of death.[296]

Chapter 11. . . . " The Chapter 11 value generally will be the property's fair market value or its Section 2032A value on the applicable valuation date, the date of death, or the Section 2032 alternate valuation date. An exception to the general rule should apply where the requirements respecting postdeath changes in value are not met, and the property is valued at the date of distribution or an adjusted Chapter 11 value is used in the determination of the denominator of the applicable fraction. See supra ¶ 15.03[7][b] text accompanying notes 262–267; IRC § 2642(b)(2)(A) (last clause); ¶ 16.02[4][d][ii].

[293] IRC § 2642(b)(2)(A); Reg. § 26.2632-1(d)(2). See supra ¶ 15.03[7][b] text accompanying notes 275–279.

[294] Reg. § 26.2632-1(d)(2). See supra ¶ 15.03[7][b] text accompanying note 280.

[295] IRC § 2032A(c)(1).

[296] However, where the property valued under Section 2032A has depreciated in value, the amount realized or the fair market value of the property (in any case other than an arm's-length sale or exchange) at the time of the disposition or cessation of qualified use should be substituted for the fair market value of the property at the transferor's date of death. Cf. IRC § 2032A(c)(2)(A)(ii).

CHAPTER **16**

Applicable Rate and Inclusion Ratio

¶ 16.01 SECTION 2641. THE APPLICABLE RATE

The Internal Revenue Code sections discussed in this chapter provide the formula to determine the rate of tax on any generation-skipping transfer.[1] The rate, statutorily titled the "applicable rate,"[2] is the product of the "maximum Federal estate tax rate"[3] and the "inclusion ratio"[4] with respect to the transfer.[5]

   Unlike some other taxes, such as the income and estate taxes, the generation-skipping transfer tax does not have its own independent rate schedule.[6] Instead, it relies on the maximum rate of the federal estate tax schedule.[7] That maximum rate is determined at the time of the generation-skipping transfer.[8] The maximum federal estate tax rate[9] is scheduled to decrease in phases from 50 percent in 2002 to 45 percent in 2007.[10]

---

[1] Under Section 2602, the amount of generation-skipping transfer tax imposed on a generation-skipping transfer is the "taxable amount" (see IRC §§ 2621, 2622, 2623, and 2624, which are discussed in Chapter 14) multiplied by the "applicable rate" (see IRC § 2641(a)).

[2] IRC § 2641(a).

[3] IRC § 2641(b). This is also the maximum federal gift tax rate through the year 2009, as the gift and estate taxes are derived from the use of a unified rate table. See IRC §§ 2001(c), 2502.

[4] IRC § 2641(a)(2). This term is defined in Section 2642, which is discussed at ¶ 16.02. The inclusion ratio is one minus the applicable fraction. See IRC § 2642(a)(1).

[5] The inclusion ratio is stated in a decimal fraction rounded to the nearest one-thousandth, because it is derived by subtracting the applicable fraction, which is required to be rounded to the nearest one-thousandth, from one. See Reg. § 26.2642-1; ¶ 16.02[1] text accompanying note 6. The regulations do not provide for any rounding of the applicable rate of tax, which is the maximum federal estate tax rate times the inclusion ratio. The product of the inclusion ratio, expressed as a decimal fraction to the nearest one-thousandth, and the maximum federal estate tax rate, expressed as a decimal fraction in one-hundredths, results in a decimal fraction to the nearest one hundred-thousandth.

[6] See, e.g., IRC §§ 1 (income tax rates for noncorporate taxpayers), 11 (corporate income tax rates), 2001(c) (estate tax rates). But see IRC § 2502, which adopts the estate tax rates for computation of the gift tax through December 31, 2009.

[7] IRC § 2641(a)(1).

[8] IRC § 2641(b).

[9] IRC § 2001(c)(1).

[10] IRC § 2001(c)(2). From 2002 to 2009 the maximum federal estate tax rate under Section 2010(c) is:

Calendar Year	Maximum Rate
2002	50%
2003	49%
2004	48%
2005	47%
2006	46%
2007	45%
2008	45%
2009	45%

Prior to the Tax Reform Act of 1986, the generation-skipping transfer tax employed graduated rates.[11] In repealing and reenacting Chapter 13, Congress opted for a flat rate of tax seemingly for the purpose of tax simplification and ease of administration.[12]

The second factor in computing the applicable rate is the inclusion ratio, which is defined in Section 2642(a). The role of the inclusion ratio is to integrate the amount of the GST exemption[13] allocated to a transfer with the maximum federal estate tax rate to arrive at the applicable rate. The inclusion ratio is considered in detail in the next section.[14] Suffice it to say that if no GST exemption is allocated to a transfer, the inclusion ratio generally[15] is 100 percent

---

The generation-skipping transfer tax does not apply to generation-skipping transfers after December 31, 2009. IRC § 2664. See ¶ 18.04. On December 31, 2010, the "sunset" provision may restore the 55 percent maximum federal estate tax rate and the generation-skipping transfer tax if Congress does not act. Economic Growth and Tax Relief Reconciliation Act of 2001, Pub. L. No. 107-16, § 901(a)(2), 115 Stat. 38, 150 (2001), reprinted in 2001-__ CB __, __. See ¶ 8.10[5].

[11] Prior to its repeal, old Section 2602(a) used the rate schedule of Section 2001(c) to determine the tax imposed on a generation-skipping transfer. See IRC § 2602(a) prior to its repeal by Tax Reform Act of 1986, Pub. L. No. 99-514, § 1431(a), 100 Stat. 2085, 2718 (1986), reprinted in 1986-3 CB (Vol. 1) 1, 635. The tax imposed on the transfer was computed in a manner similar to the computation employed under the current gift tax by taxing the transfer at the deemed transferor's top rate based on the deemed transferor's prior wealth transfers. Under the prior generation-skipping transfer tax, a tentative tax was computed on an amount that included all current and prior generation-skipping transfers and gifts and, if the transferor was deceased, the transferor's taxable estate. IRC § 2602(a)(1) prior to its repeal by Tax Reform Act of 1986, Pub. L. No. 99-514, § 1431(a), 100 Stat. 2085, 2718 (1986), reprinted in 1986-3 CB (Vol. 1) 1, 635. A second tentative tax was then computed on an amount that included all prior generation-skipping transfers and gifts and, if applicable, the transferor's taxable estate. IRC § 2602(a)(2) prior to its repeal by Tax Reform Act of 1986, Pub. L. No. 99-514, § 1431(a), 100 Stat. 2085, 2718 (1986), reprinted in 1986-3 CB (Vol. 1) 1, 635. The amount of the tax on the current generation-skipping transfer was the difference between the two tentative tax computations. IRC § 2602(a) prior to repeal by Tax Reform Act of 1986, Pub. L. No. 99-514, § 1431(a), 100 Stat. 2085, 2718 (1986), reprinted in 1986-3 CB (Vol. 1) 1, 635. Under this system, the tax rate imposed under the now-repealed tax on generation-skipping transfers ranged from a low of 18 percent to a high of 65 percent.

[12] HR Rep. No. 99-426, 99th Cong., 2d Sess. 1, 824 (1985), reprinted in 1986-3 CB (Vol. 2) 1, 824. Using the maximum Section 2001 rate schedule eliminates any need to maintain an independent Chapter 13 rate schedule and provides a readily identifiable rate that can be used without regard to prior transfers made by the transferor. Future amendments of the Section 2001 rate schedule also effectively amend the rate of tax imposed under Chapter 13.

[13] IRC § 2631(a).

[14] See ¶ 16.02.

[15] Certain nontaxable gifts are assigned a zero inclusion ratio, thereby negating the necessity of allocating any GST exemption to the transfer to reduce the tax rate to zero. See IRC § 2642(c), discussed at ¶ 16.02[2][b].

and the transfer is taxed at the maximum federal estate tax rate. If the amount of the GST exemption allocated to a transfer is equal to the amount of the transfer, the inclusion ratio is zero and no generation-skipping transfer tax is imposed on the transfer.[16] If only part of a transfer is exempted, the inclusion ratio will be a fraction greater than zero and less than one.[17] The fraction when multiplied by the maximum federal estate tax rate yields the applicable rate of tax to be imposed on the generation-skipping transfer.[18]

¶ 16.02 SECTION 2642. THE INCLUSION RATIO

[1] In General

The Section 2642 inclusion ratio is a key factor in determining the rate of tax imposed on all generation-skipping transfers.[1] The inclusion ratio integrates the

---

[16] Again, to the extent that the transfer is a nontaxable gift, no allocation of GST exemption is required to reduce the inclusion ratio to zero. See IRC § 2642(c), discussed at ¶ 16.02[2][b].

[17] When the transfer is to a trust and the trust has an inclusion ratio greater than zero but less than one, it may be possible to sever the trust into multiple trusts with inclusion ratios of zero and one. See IRC § 2642(a)(3); ¶ 16.02[5][e].

[18] If property transferred will eventually be subject to generation-skipping transfer tax and will not be shielded from tax by the Section 2631 GST exemption (see supra text accompanying notes 15, 16), it may be beneficial not to skip a generation but, instead, to have the estate tax apply at the level of the generation immediately below the transferor. For example, assume grantor G who has $1 million of unused GST exemption transfers $3 million to a trust with a life estate to child C and a remainder to grandchildren or the grandchildren's estates. Unless C has a very substantial estate, G, if tax-motivated, most likely will prefer to transfer $1 million (using the unused GST exemption) to the trust and $2 million either outright to C, or to a second trust providing a life estate to C and giving C a testamentary general power of appointment with the grandchildren or their estates as takers in default of appointment. The $2 million transfer will ensure inclusion of that property in C's gross estate under Section 2033 or Section 2041(a)(2) and avoid a taxable termination under Section 2612(a)(1). In this fashion, any of C's unused applicable credit amount under Section 2010 and any of C's unfilled rate brackets lower than the top rate bracket can be used to reduce the transfer tax burden on the $2 million.

[1] The amount of tax imposed on a generation-skipping transfer is determined by multiplying the taxable amount of the generation-skipping transfer as provided in Sections 2621 through 2623 by the Section 2641 applicable rate. IRC § 2602. The applicable rate of the generation-skipping transfer is the product of the Section 2001(c) maximum federal estate tax rate and the Section 2642 inclusion ratio. IRC § 2641(a). See ¶ 16.01.

GST exemption[2] and reductions for certain taxes[3] and charitable transfers[4] into the calculation of the rate of tax to be imposed on any generation-skipping transfer.

The inclusion ratio is generally[5] one minus the applicable fraction.[6] The numerator of the applicable fraction is generally the amount of the transferor's GST exemption allocated to the property transferred.[7] The denominator of that fraction is generally the value of the property transferred,[8] reduced by the sum of any federal estate tax or state death tax attributable to the transferred property actually recovered from the trust and any charitable deduction allowed under either Section 2055, Section 2106, or Section 2522 with respect to the transferred property.[9]

The relationship between the GST exemption and the inclusion ratio is straightforward.[10] If none of a transferor's GST exemption is allocated to the

---

[2] IRC §§ 2631, 2642(a)(2)(A). See ¶ 15.02.

[3] IRC § 2642(a)(2)(B)(ii)(I).

[4] IRC § 2642(a)(2)(B)(ii)(II).

[5] See IRC § 2642(c)(1), discussed infra ¶ 16.02[2][b], which assigns a zero inclusion ratio to certain nontaxable gifts.

[6] IRC § 2642(a)(1). The applicable fraction is converted by the regulations to a decimal fraction. See, e.g., Reg. § 26.2642-2(c) Exs. 1, 2. In determining the inclusion ratio, the applicable fraction, converted to a decimal fraction, is rounded to the nearest one-thousandth. Rounding up to the highest one-thousandth occurs when the result falls midway between two one-thousandths. Reg. § 26.2642-1(a). Because the applicable fraction converted to a decimal fraction rounded to the nearest one-thousandth is subtracted from one in the determination of the inclusion ratio, the resulting inclusion ratio is also stated as a decimal fraction to the nearest one-thousandth. The regulation is effective with respect to generation-skipping transfers made after December 26, 1995. Reg. § 26.2601-1(c). However, taxpayers may rely on this regulation in the case of generation-skipping transfers made, and trusts that became irrevocable, after December 23, 1992. Id.

[7] IRC § 2642(a)(2)(A). But see IRC §§ 2642(e)(1)(A), discussed infra ¶ 16.02[6]; 2642(d)(2)(A), discussed infra ¶ 16.02[5]; 2642(f)(5); Reg. § 26.2642-1(b)(2), discussed infra ¶ 16.02[7].

[8] IRC § 2642(a)(2)(B)(i). See IRC § 2642(b), discussed infra ¶ 16.02[4]. The value of the portion of any transfer that is a nontaxable gift is not included. See IRC § 2642(c)(1), discussed infra ¶ 16.02[2][b].

[9] IRC § 2642(a)(2)(B)(ii); Reg. § 26.2642-1(c)(1)(ii).

[10] The rules for allocation of the GST exemption are not reconsidered here. See ¶ 15.03. However, two important points should be recalled. First, on the creation of a trust, the GST exemption can generally be allocated at any time prior to the occurrence of any generation-skipping transfer. For example, upon the creation of a trust, the transferor or the transferor's executor may allocate GST exemption to the trust or unused GST exemption may be automatically allocated to the property transferred to the trust even though no generation-skipping transfer may occur until a subsequent point in time. Second, the decision of when and how to use the GST exemption is one of the most important planning aspects related to the generation-skipping transfer tax. See ¶¶ 15.02[1], 15.03[3], 15.03[4].

property involved in the generation-skipping transfer, then the applicable fraction is zero, the inclusion ratio is one, and the generation-skipping transfer is taxed at the top marginal rate of the estate tax.[11] Alternatively, if there is an allocation of the transferor's GST exemption in an amount equal to the full value[12] of the property transferred, then the applicable fraction is one, the inclusion ratio is zero, and the generation-skipping transfer tax is imposed at an applicable rate of zero, negating the imposition of any generation-skipping transfer tax under Chapter 13.[13] Where some GST exemption amount (less than the value of the property transferred) is allocated to the property resulting in an applicable fraction greater than zero but less than one, the inclusion ratio will be a fraction that is one minus the applicable fraction.[14] The value of the property involved in the generation-skipping transfer[15] will be taxed at a rate equal to the inclusion ratio multiplied by the top marginal estate tax rate.[16]

The Code breaks the computation of the inclusion ratio into two separate classifications. One is the computation for direct skips, either inter vivos or testamentary, whether outright or in trust,[17] where the timing of the generation-skipping transfer and the determination of the inclusion ratio will coincide.[18] To the extent that the GST exemption is allocated to an outright direct skip, the GST exemption amount allocated is simply used and gone. If, instead, the direct skip is made to a trust from which subsequent generation-skipping transfers may occur, the inclusion ratio initially computed for the direct skip generally, under Section 2653(b)(1), continues to apply to any subsequent generation-skipping transfers from the trust.

The other classification of computation is one involving a transfer that is not a direct skip.[19] In this case, the computation of the inclusion ratio is generally made prior to any actual generation-skipping transfer. As in the case of a direct skip to a trust, the inclusion ratio initially computed generally continues to apply to any subsequent generation-skipping transfers from the trust.[20]

---

[11] IRC §§ 2001(c), 2641, 2642. But see IRC § 2642(c).

[12] IRC §§ 2642(b), 2642(e), 2642(f). But see IRC § 2642(c).

[13] See IRC §§ 2641, 2642.

[14] IRC § 2642(a)(1). When the transfer is to a trust and the trust has an inclusion ratio greater than zero but less than one, it may be possible to sever the trust into multiple trusts with inclusion ratios of zero and one. See IRC § 2642(a)(3); infra ¶ 16.02[5][e].

[15] IRC §§ 2621–2624.

[16] IRC §§ 2602, 2641.

[17] IRC § 2642(a)(1)(B). Cf. IRC §§ 2652(b)(1), 2652(b)(3). As used throughout the remainder of this section, the term "trust" includes a trust equivalent arrangement. See ¶ 17.02[2].

[18] But see IRC § 2642(f)(1) (last sentence), discussed infra ¶ 16.02[7][a].

[19] IRC § 2642(a)(1)(A).

[20] See IRC § 2653(b)(1), discussed at ¶ 17.03[2].

In the case of either a direct skip to a trust or an allocation of the GST exemption to a trust prior to any generation-skipping transfer, as long as the transferor of the trust does not change,[21] the inclusion ratio generally is not changed.[22] However, the inclusion ratio is changed if additional GST exemption is allocated to property held in trust,[23] additional property is transferred to the trust,[24] or separate trusts are consolidated.[25] In addition, the inclusion ratio may change if generation-skipping transfer tax is imposed on a generation-skipping transfer from the trust,[26] if a single trust is severed in a qualified severance[27] or if additional estate tax is imposed under Section 2032A.[28]

[2] Calculation of the Inclusion Ratio for Direct Skips

[a] In General

The statute singles out direct skip generation-skipping transfers, either outright or in trust, for separate treatment in computing the inclusion ratio.[29] In computing the inclusion ratio for a direct skip, the standard formula of one minus the applicable fraction generally applies.[30] The applicable fraction generally has a numerator equal to the amount of the transferor's GST exemption

---

[21] See IRC § 2652(a)(1). If there is a new transferor of a trust, that transferor's GST exemption is used to determine the applicable fraction and the inclusion ratio for subsequent Chapter 13 transfers from the trust.

If another person makes a transfer to a trust created by the original transferor, for Chapter 13 purposes, the additional transfer is treated as if made to a separate trust. IRC § 2654(b)(1). See ¶ 17.02[1][d]. As a result, the trust created by the original transferor maintains its separate identity and its inclusion ratio is not altered. Subsequent distributions from the combined trusts must be allocated between the separate trusts to determine the inclusion ratio and the Chapter 13 tax attributed to each transferor's trust.

[22] See IRC § 2653(b)(1), discussed at ¶ 17.03[2].

[23] IRC § 2642(d)(4); Reg. § 26.2642-4(a). See infra ¶¶ 16.02[5][b][i], 16.02[5][b][iii]. See also Reg. § 26.2642-4(a)(3); infra ¶ 16.02[7].

[24] IRC § 2642(d)(1); Reg. § 26.2642-4(a)(1). See infra ¶¶ 16.02[5][b][ii], 16.02[5][b][iii].

[25] Reg. § 26.2642-4(a)(2). See infra ¶ 16.02[5][c].

[26] IRC § 2653(b)(1). See infra ¶ 16.02[5][d]. See also ¶ 17.03[2][a].

[27] IRC § 2642(a)(3). See infra ¶ 16.02[5][e]. The severance of a single trust with an inclusion ratio of one or zero will not require a redetermination of the inclusion ratio because the resulting trusts created upon the severance will have the same inclusion ratio as the trust that was severed.

[28] Reg. § 26.2642-4(a)(4). See infra ¶ 16.02[5][f]. See also ¶ 18.03[1].

[29] IRC § 2642(a)(1)(B).

[30] IRC § 2642(a)(1).

allocated to the property transferred in the direct skip[31] and a denominator equal to the value of that property.[32] However, certain direct skips that are nontaxable gifts are automatically assigned a zero inclusion ratio,[33] negating both the need to compute the applicable fraction and the need to allocate any GST exemption to the transfer.

[b] Nontaxable Gifts

[i] **In general.** An inter vivos direct skip,[34] either outright or in trust, that is a nontaxable gift[35] is generally assigned a zero inclusion ratio.[36] An exception to this rule is provided for certain transfers in trust.[37] A nontaxable gift is an inter vivos transfer that is not taxed under the gift tax because it qualifies for either the annual exclusion[38] or the exclusion afforded certain transfers to medical providers or educational institutions.[39] The portion of a direct skip that is a nontaxable gift and assigned a zero inclusion ratio is essentially treated as a separate transfer, and it never generates any gift or generation-skipping transfer tax.[40] Any portion of a direct skip in excess of the portion assigned a zero inclusion ratio is treated as a separate direct skip transfer for which an applicable fraction and resulting inclusion ratio and applicable rate of tax must be computed.[41]

[ii] **Transfers not in trust.** An outright (not in trust) inter vivos direct skip to an individual is assigned an inclusion ratio of zero to the extent that the transfer qualifies for the gift tax annual exclusion.[42] To that extent, the

---

[31] IRC § 2642(a)(2)(A). See also IRC § 2642(f)(1).

[32] IRC §§ 2642(a)(2)(B), 2642(b), 2642(f).

[33] IRC § 2642(c). See infra ¶ 16.02[2][b].

[34] IRC § 2612(c).

[35] IRC § 2642(c)(3).

[36] IRC § 2642(c)(1).

[37] A direct skip to a trust that is a nontaxable gift is assigned a zero inclusion ratio only if certain other requirements are met. IRC § 2642(c)(2). See infra ¶ 16.02[2][b][iii].

[38] IRC §§ 2503(b), 2642(c)(3)(A). IRC § 2503(b) is discussed at ¶¶ 9.04[1], 9.04[2], 9.04[3]. See IRC § 2503(c), discussed at ¶¶ 9.04[4], 9.04[5].

[39] IRC §§ 2503(e), 2642(c)(3)(B). Section 2503(e) is discussed at ¶ 9.04[6]. Section 2642(c) provides an excellent inter vivos tax planning opportunity for grandparents and other transferors to make inter vivos transfers to skip persons without incurring any gift or generation-skipping transfer tax.

[40] Because the inclusion ratio is zero, the applicable rate of tax is zero and the amount of Chapter 13 tax imposed is zero. IRC §§ 2602, 2641(a).

[41] See Reg. § 26.2642-1(d) Exs. 3, 4.

[42] IRC §§ 2642(c)(1), 2642(c)(3)(A). See IRC § 2503(b), discussed at ¶¶ 9.04[1]–9.04[3].

transfer is removed from Chapter 13 taxation,[43] just as the annual exclusion removes these gifts or portions thereof from taxation under Chapter 12.[44] But for this rule, a grandparent's birthday gift to a grandchild could be taxed under Chapter 13. Thus, if transferor *T* gives grandchild *GC*[45] a birthday gift worth $11,000, *T* will be able to disregard the generation-skipping transfer tax if the transfer qualifies in its entirety for the gift tax annual exclusion because it is within the first $11,000 of gifts of a present interest made by *T* to *GC* within the year.[46]

If the amount of an outright inter vivos direct skip exceeds the available annual exclusion, only the amount of the transfer qualifying for the annual exclusion is assigned a zero inclusion ratio. The transfer in excess of the annual exclusion may generate Chapter 13 tax. For example, if grandparent *G* makes an outright gift of $25,000 to grandchild *GC*, and if $11,000 of the gift qualifies for the annual exclusion, the $11,000 amount is assigned a zero inclusion ratio in the generation-skipping transfer tax computation. The remaining $14,000 does not have a zero inclusion ratio unless $14,000 of *G*'s GST exemption is allocated to the transfer.[47] If *G* is married and *G* and *G*'s spouse elect under Section 2513[48] to split gifts for gift tax purposes, the $25,000 gift is also split for generation-skipping transfer tax purposes.[49] Thus, *G* and *G*'s spouse each are deemed to have made a gift of $12,500 and, assuming neither made any prior transfers to *GC* during the year, each transfer would be allowed an $11,000 annual exclusion and, to that extent, would be assigned a zero inclusion ratio. The remaining $1,500 of transfer made by each spouse would have an inclusion ratio of zero only if $1,500 of *each* transferor's GST exemption is allocated to the transfer.[50]

Although de minimis outright direct skips that qualify for the annual exclusion will not generate any generation-skipping transfer tax, there is no statu-

---

[43] See supra text accompanying notes 40, 41.

[44] IRC § 2503(b).

[45] Unless stated to the contrary, in all of the transfers to grandchildren in the examples in this chapter, it is assumed that the grandchildren's parents are alive, so Section 2651(e) does not apply. See ¶ 17.01[2][a][ii]. It is also assumed that the transfers occur after 1989, so as to avoid consideration of the grandchild exclusion. See ¶ 13.02[4][c][ii].

[46] Reg. § 25.2503-2(a).

[47] See IRC §§ 2632(a), 2632(b); ¶¶ 15.03[2], 15.03[3]. See also Reg. § 26.2642-1(d) Ex. 3.

[48] See ¶ 10.03.

[49] IRC § 2652(a)(2).

[50] See IRC §§ 2632(a), 2632(b); ¶¶ 15.03[2], 15.03[3]. See also Reg. § 26.2642-1(d) Ex. 3. If the transfer had been only $22,000, and gift splitting was employed under the same assumptions, both gifts (note the parenthetical language in Section 2642(c)(3)(A)) would be nontaxable gifts and no generation-skipping transfer tax would be imposed. There would be no need to allocate any GST exemption to the transfer in order to avoid Chapter 13 tax.

tory provision that exempts these generation-skipping transfers from disclosure on a generation-skipping transfer tax return. If an outright direct skip to an individual is totally excluded from gift taxation by Section 2503(b)[51] without the assistance of Section 2513, no generation-skipping transfer tax return ought to be required with respect to the transfer. While the statute does not specifically provide that no return is required,[52] Section 2662(a) allows the secretary to issue regulations with respect to the filing of returns. Those regulations can eventually be expected to incorporate the Internal Revenue Service's (IRS's) apparent position in the Instructions for the United States Gift (and Generation-Skipping Transfer) Tax Return that no return is required in such circumstances.[53]

A zero inclusion ratio is also assigned to any outright inter vivos direct skip if the transfer is to a medical care provider or an educational institution and is not treated as a transfer of property by gift by reason of Section 2503(e).[54] This zero inclusion ratio provision removes transfers that are excluded from Chapter 12 taxation by Section 2503(e) from taxation under Chapter 13. However, the Chapter 13 provision appears to be superfluous.[55] If a transferor makes an outright inter vivos transfer to a medical care provider or to an educational institution for the benefit of a skip person that qualifies for the Section 2503(e) exclusion, there is no transfer of property subject to tax

---

[51] No gift tax return would be required on such a transfer. See IRC § 6019(a)(1), discussed at ¶ 9.04[9]. Any Section 2503(e) transfer fully within that exclusion does not constitute a direct skip and, thus, requires no return. See supra text accompanying notes 54– 57.

[52] Cf. IRC § 6019(a)(1).

[53] Section 2662(a) mandates that the secretary prescribe regulations with respect to who is required to make a generation-skipping transfer tax return. Reg. § 26.2662-1(b)(3)(i) states that "Form 709 must be filed in accordance with its instructions for any direct skip . . . that is subject to [C]hapter 12 and occurs during the life of the transferor." The Instructions for Form 709, U.S. Gift (and Generation-Skipping Transfer) Tax Return (2001) Transfers Subject to the Generation-Skipping Transfer Tax, at 2, provide that a gift is subject to the Chapter 12 tax if it is required to be listed on Schedule A of the form. Note that this rule is modified where the transfer is to a trust, unless the requirements of Section 2642(c)(2) are met. See Instructions for Form 709, U.S. Gift (and Generation-Skipping Transfer) Tax Return (2001) Gifts Subject to Both Gift and Generation-Skipping Transfer Taxes, Direct Skip, at 6. Gifts that qualify entirely for the annual exclusion need not be listed on Schedule A. Additionally, the Instructions for Form 709, U.S. Gift (and Generation-Skipping Transfer) Tax Return (2001) Transfers Subject to the Generation-Skipping Transfer Tax, at 2, provide that "transfers that are fully excluded under the annual exclusion . . . are not subject to the generation-skipping transfer tax." Thus, although no statutory provision or regulation states that a return need not be filed if the entire amount of an outright direct skip qualifies for the annual exclusion, it seems that the Instructions for Form 709 do not contemplate a return being filed under such circumstances. See ¶ 18.02[2][b] text accompanying notes 19–24.

[54] IRC §§ 2642(c)(1), 2642(c)(3)(B). Section § 2503(e) is discussed at ¶ 9.04[6].

[55] See ¶ 13.01[2][a] text accompanying note 11.

imposed by Chapter 12, and as a result, there is no direct skip generation-skipping transfer.[56] Absent a generation-skipping transfer, there is no need to be concerned with the inclusion ratio of such a transfer.[57]

[iii] Transfers to trusts after March 31, 1988. The computation of the generation-skipping transfer tax on a direct skip to a trust is the same as the computation for an outright direct skip to an individual.[58] The amount of the transfer assigned a zero inclusion ratio is exempted from the imposition of any generation-skipping transfer tax,[59] and only the excess may generate such a tax.[60]

However, an inter vivos direct skip to a trust that is for the benefit of an individual and that qualifies for the gift tax annual exclusion will be assigned a zero inclusion ratio only if two additional requirements are satisfied. The first of these is that income or corpus of the trust may be distributed during the life of the individual only to, or for the benefit of, that individual.[61] The second is that if the trust does not terminate before the individual dies, the assets held in the trust will be included in the individual's gross estate.[62] In effect, even

---

[56] See IRC § 2612(c)(1); ¶ 13.02[4][b] text accompanying notes 259, 260. But see Reg. § 26.2652-1(a)(2).

[57] Section 2642(c)(3)(B) ought to be removed from the Code. The provision also has no effect if the Section 2503(e) transfer is made by a trust. See infra text accompanying notes 78–81.

[58] See supra text accompanying notes 42–50. See also supra ¶ 16.02[1] note 17.

[59] See supra note 40.

[60] See Reg. § 26.2642-1(d) Exs. 3, 4.

[61] IRC § 2642(c)(2)(A). The determination of whether the distribution is made for the benefit of a person other than the beneficiary of the gift is determined by applying the rules of Section 2652(c)(3). IRC § 2642(c)(2) (flush language). Use of trust property to satisfy any obligation of support that any person has to the named individual trust beneficiary arising by reason of state law is to be disregarded in determining whether a portion may be distributed to, or for the benefit of, a person other than the beneficiary of the gift if such use is discretionary or pursuant to any state law substantially equivalent to the Uniform Gift to Minors Act. IRC § 2652(c)(3), discussed at ¶ 17.02[3][b] text accompanying notes 140–143.

[62] IRC § 2642(c)(2)(B). Since the transfer to the trust will be included in the beneficiary's gross estate, the beneficiary will become the Section 2652(a) transferor of any subsequent transfer, and the former transferor and the former transferor's inclusion ratio are erased from the scene. See ¶ 17.02[1]. Initially, Section 2642(c)(2)(B) provided that if the individual died before the trust terminated, the assets held in trust must be included in the individual's gross estate. The statute was amended in 1990 to clarify that the assets of a trust that terminates on the beneficiary's death must be includible in the beneficiary's gross estate to qualify for a zero inclusion ratio. Revenue Reconciliation Act of 1990, Pub. L. No. 101-508, § 11703(c)(1), 104 Stat. 1388-400, 1388-517 (1990), reprinted in 1991-2 CB 481, 536. The 1990 change applies to transfers after March 31, 1988. Revenue Reconciliation Act of 1990, Pub. L. No. 101-508, § 11703(c)(4), 104 Stat. 1388-400, 1388-517(1990), reprinted in 1991-2 CB 481, 536.

when the property is transferred to a trust, the individual beneficiary of the trust must have the tax equivalent of outright ownership of the property.[63] As a result of the Section 2642(c)(2) requirements, a gift to a skip person of a present interest in trust does not necessarily qualify for a zero inclusion ratio under the generation-skipping transfer tax, although it qualifies for an annual exclusion under the gift tax. The additional requirements imposed on transfers in trust are aimed at preventing subsequent generation-skipping transfers *from* the trust from benefiting from the zero inclusion ratio,[64] as well as preventing the annual exclusion from shielding appreciation in trust assets from transfer taxes that would have been generated had the property been transferred outright rather than in trust.[65]

---

[63] This is similar to the marital deduction in Sections 2056(b)(5) and 2523(e), where the donee spouse must have the tax equivalent of outright ownership. See ¶¶ 5.06[8][b], 11.03[4][b].

Since a nontaxable gift under Section 2642(c) depends on that gift also qualifying for a gift tax annual exclusion under Section 2503(b), if there is more than one transfer to a skip person during a year, the order of transfers becomes significant. If transferor *T* intends to make both a $11,000 outright transfer to grandchild *GC* and a transfer of an income interest worth $11,000 in a trust to *GC* (with no additional trust interest to *GC*), the outright transfer must precede the trust transfer in order to be excluded under both the gift tax and the generation-skipping transfer tax. If the trust transfer precedes the outright transfer, although the trust transfer qualifies for a gift tax exclusion and is a nontaxable gift, it fails to satisfy the additional Section 2642(c)(2) requirements for transfers in trust and it is not assigned a zero inclusion ratio.

[64] See S. Rep. No. 445, 100th Cong., 2d Sess. 367, 376 (1988). For example, assume that grantor *G*, whose children are all alive, establishes an inter vivos trust with income to grandchild *GC* for life and a remainder to great-grandchild *GGC*. The transfer in trust is a direct skip. IRC § 2612(c)(1). Although the transfer to *GC* qualifies for the annual exclusion, no portion of the gift is assigned a zero inclusion ratio under Section 2642(c) because the interest held by *GC* is not includible in *GC*'s gross estate upon death. IRC § 2642(c)(2)(B). Assume instead that, to the extent that the transfer qualified for the annual exclusion (i.e., to the extent that the present value of the life income interest is within the Section 2503(b) annual exclusion limits), it was assigned a zero inclusion ratio. The zero inclusion ratio, to the extent of the annual exclusion, would have reduced the rate of tax imposed on the direct skip to the trust as well as the tax imposed on subsequent generation-skipping transfers from the trust and reduced the amount of GST exemption required to attain a zero inclusion ratio. The taxable termination occurring upon the death of *GC* would have been taxed at a rate established for the trust that included the zero rate for the nontaxable portion of the direct skip gift. Cf. infra ¶ 16.02[2][b][iv] for the computation of the inclusion ratio on nontaxable direct skip transfers to trusts prior to April 1, 1988.

[65] See S. Rep. No. 445, 100th Cong., 2d Sess. 367, 376 (1988). For example, if grantor *G* gives property valued at $100,000 to grandchild *GC* outright and the gift qualifies for an $11,000 Section 2503(b) annual exclusion, there is an $89,000 taxable gift. The transfer is also a direct skip, $11,000 of which is a nontaxable gift with an inclusion ratio of zero. The remaining $89,000 direct skip will generate a Chapter 13 tax unless $89,000 of GST exemption is allocated to the transfer. If the property doubles in value to $200,000 and *GC* transfers the property by gift outright to *GC*'s child, *GGC*, assuming *GC* made no

To illustrate these requirements, assume grantor *G* creates a trust with income to grandchild *GC* for life and a remainder to *G*'s great-grandchildren.[66] Even if the gift of the life interest to *GC* qualifies for the Section 2503(b) gift tax annual exclusion, no part of the transfer will be assigned a zero inclusion ratio under the generation-skipping transfer tax. This is because the transfer to the trust fails to satisfy the gross estate inclusion requirement,[67] because when *GC* dies, the assets held in the trust will not be included in *GC*'s gross estate. However, if *GC* had been granted a general power of appointment over the trust corpus with the great-grandchildren as takers-in-default of appointment, the corpus would be included in *GC*'s gross estate[68] and the transfer would have been assigned a zero inclusion ratio to the extent that the annual exclusion was allowed for gift tax purposes. Similarly, if *G* created the trust with income to *GC* for ten years and then a remainder to *GC* or *GC*'s estate, a zero inclusion ratio would be allowed to the extent of the annual exclusion amount because no portion of the trust income or corpus may be distributed to anyone other than *GC*. and if *GC* dies, the trust assets will be included in *GC*'s gross estate.[69] Under the last two examples, any portion of the transfer that qualifies for a gift tax annual exclusion is assigned a zero inclusion ratio and separated from the remainder of the transfer in computing the Chapter 13 tax.[70]

---

prior gifts to *GGC* in the year, Section 2503(b) again allows a $11,000 annual exclusion. The remaining $189,000 is a taxable gift. When there is an outright transfer, the appreciation in value of the portion of the property covered by the annual exclusion in a transfer is subject to a transfer tax.

Assume that instead of making an outright transfer of the property to *GC*, *G* had established a trust with income to *GC* for life and a remainder to *GGC*, and the $100,000 initial transfer qualified for an $11,000 gift tax annual exclusion. The transfer in trust is a Section 2612(c) direct skip, and, but for the Section 2642(c)(2) requirements, $11,000 of this transfer would be assigned a zero inclusion ratio. In order to appropriately compute the applicable fraction and the inclusion ratio, a dual transfer approach must be continued. Thus, 11 percent of the trust has a zero inclusion ratio and 89 percent of the trust has the same inclusion ratio as applied upon its creation. A taxable termination occurs at *GC*'s death. In comparison, if the property again appreciates in value to $200,000, the zero inclusion ratio assigned to the nontaxable gift would effectively appreciate to shield $22,000 of trust property from the generation-skipping transfer tax. The additional requirements of Section 2642(c)(2) prevent the appreciation in the value of trust assets qualifying for the annual exclusion from escaping the generation-skipping transfer tax. Thus, while the $100,000 transfer to the trust would still qualify for a gift tax annual exclusion, the transfer will not be assigned a zero inclusion ratio because the trust assets will not be included in *GC*'s gross estate upon death.

[66] See supra note 45.

[67] IRC § 2642(c)(2)(B).

[68] IRC § 2041(a)(2). See Priv. Ltr. Rul. 200114026 (Jan. 5, 2001) (after reformation of scrivener's error transfer qualifies as nontaxable gift). See also ¶ 16.01 note 18.

[69] IRC §§ 2033, 2041(a)(2). See ¶ 4.05[6] note 76. See also ¶ 16.01 note 18.

[70] For example, if $100,000 had been transferred to the trust and $11,000 of that amount qualified for an annual exclusion, the transaction would be separated into two

If a transferor makes a transfer to a trust and grants a beneficiary a *Crummey* power (a presently exercisable noncumulative general power of appointment over property transferred to the trust), it may be thought that, in substance, there is an outright transfer to the individual power holder to the extent of the property subject to the noncumulative general power. Such an analysis, however, is inappropriate. Instead, the entire transfer is treated as a transfer to a trust, and in order to qualify for a zero inclusion ratio, the requirements of Section 2642(c)(2) must be satisfied.[71] If this were not the rule, the zero inclusion ratio assigned to a nontaxable gift to a trust could be used, at least in part, to determine the applicable rate of tax imposed on subsequent transfers from the trust to younger generations.[72] In addition, the nontaxable

---

transfers. The first $11,000 transfer would not be subject to Chapter 13 tax. See supra text accompanying note 40. The remaining $89,000 would be subject to Chapter 13 tax, except to the extent that the grantor's GST exemption is allocated to the transfer. See supra ¶ 16.02[1] text accompanying notes 12–16; Reg. § 26.2642-1(d) Exs. 3, 4.

[71] See IRC §§ 2642(c)(2)(A), 2642(c)(2)(B); Reg. §§ 26.2642-1(d) Ex. 2, 26.2652-1(a)(5) Ex. 5. A transfer to a trust subject to a beneficiary's right of withdrawal is treated as a transfer to the trust rather than a transfer to the beneficiary. Reg. §§ 26.2612-1(f) Ex. 3, 26.2652-1(a)(5) Ex. 5.

[72] To the extent that there is an inter vivos lapse of the *Crummey* power that results in no Chapter 12 gift tax consequences to the holder of the power (see IRC § 2514(e)), the transferor of the trust continues to be the Chapter 13 transferor with respect to the trust property. Allowance of the zero inclusion ratio to that extent would permit subsequent tax-free generation-skipping transfers to younger generations from that transferor of the trust. Cf. supra note 64.

For example, assume that grantor *G* establishes a trust with income to grandchild *GC* for life and a remainder to great-grandchild *GGC*. The trust instrument provides *GC* with a *Crummey* power over trust additions. With respect to each addition of property to trust corpus, *GC* may demand at any time, up to and including December 31 of the year in which the addition is made, the lesser of $5,000 or the amount of the trust addition. *G* transfers $5,000 in trust and *GC* has a general power of appointment over $5,000; this amount qualifies for the gift tax annual exclusion. See ¶ 9.04[3][f]. For purposes of Chapter 13, the transfer is a direct skip to a trust and *G* is its transferor. Since the trust addition will not be included in the gross estate of *GC*, no portion of the transfer to *GC* should be assigned a zero inclusion ratio. IRC § 2642(c)(2)(B).

Assume that the original $5,000 transfer to the trust is treated as a separate outright transfer to the power holder and not as a transfer in trust. The additional Section 2642(c)(2) requirements for a direct skip to a trust to be assigned a zero inclusion ratio would not need to be satisfied. The transfer would be a nontaxable gift assigned a zero inclusion ratio without allocation of any of *G*'s GST exemption. If *GC* let the power lapse, the lapse would not constitute a release, *G* would still be the Chapter 13 transferor (cf. ¶ 13.02[2][e] text accompanying notes 113–121), and it would be necessary to look to the original transfer in trust to determine the inclusion ratio for that portion of the property transferred to the trust. The transfer of $5,000 to the trust would statutorily be assigned a zero inclusion ratio, and all subsequent generation-skipping transfers from the trust attributable to the $5,000 transfer would be taxed at an applicable rate of zero. For this reason, *G*'s transfer to the trust is treated as a transfer in trust and not as an outright transfer. See Reg. § 26.2652-1(a)(5) Ex. 5. See also Reg. § 26.2612-1(f) Ex. 3.

gift and zero inclusion ratio would appreciate with the property held in the trust.[73]

Direct skip generation-skipping transfers under the Uniform Gifts to Minors Act or the Uniform Transfers to Minors Act are assigned a zero inclusion ratio to the extent the transfer is not treated as a taxable gift owing to the annual exclusion.[74] Under these acts, the custodian is typically empowered to make payments only to, or for the benefit of, the minor.[75] If the minor dies, the custodial property must be transferred to the minor's estate.[76] These custodianship arrangements satisfy the two additional Section 2642(c)(2) requirements for a transfer to qualify for a zero inclusion ratio to the extent that the transfer is treated as a nontaxable gift.[77]

A transfer to an irrevocable trust providing for payment of an individual's medical care or educational expenses generally will not qualify for a zero inclusion ratio because it is not a direct transfer from the individual donor to a medical care provider or an educational institution, and therefore, it will not qualify for the Section 2503(e) exclusion.[78] If the transfer is to a revocable trust that made the transfer to the provider or institution, the trust should be disregarded and the transfer should be treated as having been made directly from the grantor of the trust to the provider or institution.[79] However, because

---

An alternative, albeit more complicated, solution to the *Crummey* power situation would be to have the zero inclusion ratio consequences depend on whether there actually is a lapse of the *Crummey* power. To the extent there is a nontaxable lapse under the gift or estate tax, the transfer would be treated as a transfer to the trust and would have to satisfy the Section 2642(c) requirements. To the extent that there is a release, exercise, or estate tax inclusion, the transfer would be treated as an outright transfer to the power holder qualifying as a nontaxable gift.

[73] Cf. supra note 65.

[74] Section 2652(b)(1) provides that the term "trust" includes any arrangement other than an estate that, although not a trust, has substantially the same effect as a trust. Custodianships established under these acts have substantially the same effect as trusts, so they are considered trusts for purposes of the generation-skipping transfer tax. Reg. § 26.2652-1(b)(2) Ex. 1. Thus, transfers under these acts are subject to the nontaxable gift to trust requirements of Section 2642(c)(2). See supra text accompanying notes 61–65.

[75] See, e.g., Fla. Stat. Chapter 710.116 (2001).

[76] See, e.g., Fla. Stat. Chapter 710.123 (2001).

[77] Under Section 2503(c), no part of such a transfer would be considered a future interest in property. See ¶¶ 9.04[4], 9.04[5]. Such transfers are therefore eligible for the Section 2503(b) annual exclusion.

[78] See ¶ 9.04[6]. The transfer to the trust will qualify for a zero inclusion ratio to the extent that it qualifies for a Section 2503(b) exclusion, if it satisfies the requirements of Section 2642(c)(2).

[79] Cf. ¶ 10.01[5][b] text accompanying note 157; IRC § 2035(e); ¶ 4.07[2][b][ii]; Priv. Ltr. Rul. 9333028 (May 21, 1993). Similarly, a transfer from a revocable trust to a skip person would be treated as a transfer by the grantor of the trust, potentially qualifying for an annual exclusion and zero inclusion ratio.

such a transfer is not a transfer of property subject to tax imposed by Chapter 12, it does not constitute a direct skip generation-skipping transfer.[80] Absent such a direct skip transfer, there is no need to be concerned with the inclusion ratio of the transfer.[81]

[iv] Nontaxable gift transfers to trusts prior to April 1, 1988. Section 2642(c), as amended by the Technical and Miscellaneous Revenue Act of 1988, only applies to transfers after March 31, 1988.[82] Generation-skipping transfers to trusts prior to April 1, 1988,[83] are governed by Section 2642(c) before it was amended.[84] The only significant change in the section as a result of the amendment was in the treatment afforded nontaxable gifts to trusts.[85]

---

[80] See supra text accompanying note 56.

[81] See supra text accompanying notes 54–57. Section 2642(c)(3)(B) is superfluous for trust transfers as well as outright transfers.

[82] Technical and Miscellaneous Revenue Act of 1988, Pub. L. No. 100-647, § 1014(g)(17)(C), 102 Stat. 3342, 3567 (1988), reprinted in 1988-3 CB 1, 227.

[83] The generation-skipping transfer tax generally applies to testamentary transfers made after October 22, 1986, and to inter vivos transfers made after September 25, 1985. The effective dates of the generation-skipping transfer tax are discussed at ¶ 18.05.

[84] Prior to amendment by Technical and Miscellaneous Revenue Act of 1988, Pub. L. No. 100-647, § 1014(g)(17)(A), 102 Stat. 3342, 3566, reprinted in 1988-3 CB 1, 226, Section 2642(c) read as follows:

(c) TREATMENT OF CERTAIN NONTAXABLE GIFTS.—

    (1) DIRECT SKIPS.—In the case of any direct skip which is a nontaxable gift, the inclusion ratio shall be zero.

    (2) TREATMENT OF NONTAXABLE GIFTS MADE TO TRUSTS.—

        (A) IN GENERAL.—Except as provided in subparagraph (B), any nontaxable gift which is not a direct skip and which is made to a trust shall not be taken into account under subsection (a)(2)(B).

        (B) DETERMINATION OF 1ST TRANSFER TO TRUST.—In the case of any nontaxable gift referred to in subparagraph (A) which is the 1st transfer to the trust, the inclusion ratio for such trust shall be zero.

    (3) NONTAXABLE GIFT.—For purposes of this section, the term "nontaxable gift" means any transfer of property to the extent such transfer is not treated as a taxable gift by reason of—

        (A) section 2503(b) (taking into account the application of section 2513), or

        (B) section 2503(e).

Note that, as a practical matter, Section 2642(c)(3) was not amended by Technical and Miscellaneous Revenue Act of 1988.

[85] After the amendments made by Technical and Miscellaneous Revenue Act of 1988, only nontaxable direct skip gifts to a trust that meet the requirements of amended Section 2642(c)(2) are assigned a zero inclusion ratio. See S. Rep. No. 445, 100th Cong., 2d Sess. 367, 376–377 (1988).

Nontaxable gifts[86] in trust made prior to April 1, 1988, were either assigned a zero inclusion ratio or excluded from the denominator of the applicable fraction.[87] A zero inclusion ratio was assigned to a nontaxable gift direct skip transfer to a trust and was also assigned to the *first* nontaxable gift *nondirect skip* transfer to a trust.[88] Subsequent nontaxable gift nondirect skip transfers to trusts were excluded from the denominator in the computation of the applicable fraction for the trust.[89]

Nontaxable Direct Skip Gift to a Trust. A nontaxable direct skip gift to a trust prior to April 1, 1988, was assigned a zero inclusion ratio.[90] When a direct skip to a trust prior to April 1, 1988, partly consisted of a nontaxable gift, the trust essentially had two inclusion ratios. The nontaxable portion of the direct skip was assigned a zero inclusion ratio.[91] The amount of the direct skip that was not a nontaxable gift had an applicable fraction, the numerator of which was the amount of the GST exemption allocated to the transfer[92] and the denominator of which was the amount of the direct skip that was not a nontaxable gift.[93] Such a trust may be the source of subsequent generation-skipping transfers attributed to a single transferor, and it should have a single inclusion ratio.[94] The appropriate method of computing a single inclusion ratio was to treat the transfer as two separate transfers to a single trust. The amount of the nontaxable gift was treated as one transfer, and the remaining amount of the

---

[86] Such gifts are essentially limited to transfers to a trust that qualify for a Section 2503(b) annual exclusion. IRC § 2642(c)(3)(A). Section 2642(c)(3)(B) is superfluous. See supra text accompanying notes 54–57, 78–81.

[87] See supra note 81. Nontaxable gifts made prior to April 1, 1988, were not required to satisfy the two requirements found in Section 2642(c)(2).

[88] IRC §§ 2642(c)(1), 2642(c)(2)(B) prior to amendment by Technical and Miscellaneous Revenue Act of 1988, Pub. L. No. 100-647, § 1014(g)(17)(A), 102 Stat. 3342, 3566 (1988), reprinted in 1988-3 CB 1, 226. See supra note 84.

[89] IRC § 2642(c)(2)(A) prior to amendment by Technical and Miscellaneous Revenue Act of 1988, Pub. L. No. 100-647, § 1014(g)(17)(A), 102 Stat. 3342, 3566 (1988), reprinted in 1988-3 CB 1, 226. See supra note 84.

[90] See supra note 84.

[91] See supra note 84.

[92] IRC § 2642(a)(2)(A). If the transferor made no allocation of unused GST exemption to the transfer, there would have been a deemed allocation under Section 2632(b)(1), unless the transferor elected under Section 2632(b)(3) to prevent the deemed allocation. See ¶ 15.03[3][c].

[93] IRC § 2642(a)(2)(B).

[94] The need for a single inclusion ratio seems clear, even though Congress stated that the effect of a nontaxable gift that is a direct skip to a trust upon the trust's inclusion ratio was unclear. See S. Rep. No. 445, 100th Cong., 2d Sess. 367, 376–377 (1988).

No such single inclusion ratio is required for a post–March 31, 1988, trust because the beneficiary of such a trust will become the transferor of the trust with respect to any subsequent transfers from the trust and the original inclusion ratio is erased from the picture. See supra note 62.

direct skip was treated as a second transfer. Section 2642(d), which provides a set of rules to use in computing the applicable fraction for a trust where multiple transfers of property are made to the trust, should be applied here to compute a single applicable fraction and a single inclusion ratio for the trust.[95]

To illustrate the computation of a single inclusion ratio, assume that on March 15, 1988, transferor T transferred $40,000 to a trust providing income to grandchild GC for life, with a remainder to great-grandchild GGC. Assume also that $10,000 of the transfer qualified as a nontaxable gift[96] and no part of T's GST exemption was allocated to the transfer. A single inclusion ratio is obtained by treating this transfer to the trust as two separate transfers. The $10,000 nontaxable gift transfer is treated as the initial transfer to the trust, and the $30,000 transfer is treated as a subsequent transfer. Section 2642(d) then can be used to compute a single applicable fraction. Using Section 2642(d), the numerator of the recomputed applicable fraction is the sum of the GST exemption allocated to the subsequent transfer—zero in this example— and the "nontax portion of the trust" immediately before the transfer.[97] The nontax portion of the trust immediately before the second transfer is the product of the value of all the property in the trust—the initial transfer of $10,000—and the applicable fraction for such trust—in effect, one.[98] The numerator of the recomputed applicable fraction is $10,000 (zero + $10,000). The denominator of the recomputed applicable fraction is $40,000, the sum of the property subsequently transferred ($30,000) and the value of all property in the trust immediately before the transfer ($10,000).[99] The recomputed applicable fraction is 0.250 ($10,000 ÷ $40,000), and the inclusion ratio for the entire trust is 0.750.[100]

Nontaxable Nondirect Skip Transfers to a Trust. The *first* nondirect skip transfer to a trust prior to April 1, 1988, was assigned a zero inclusion ratio to

---

[95] See infra ¶ 16.02[5][b]. As a result of such a single inclusion ratio, appreciation in the excluded property's value is generally not taxed on subsequent generation-skipping transfers.

[96] IRC § 2642(c)(3). See supra note 45.

[97] IRC § 2642(d)(2)(A).

[98] IRC § 2642(d)(3). Although no statutory provision specifies that the applicable fraction for a nontaxable gift is one, it is logical to assume this because Section 2642(c)(1) assigns an inclusion ratio of zero to a nontaxable gift and Section 2642(a)(1) defines the inclusion ratio as one minus the applicable fraction.

[99] IRC § 2642(d)(2)(B).

[100] See supra ¶ 16.02[1] note 6. If T allocates $15,000 of GST exemption to the remaining $30,000 of the transfer, the applicable fraction of the transfer that is not a nontaxable gift will be 0.500 ($15,000 ÷ $30,000). IRC § 2642(a)(2). When this is combined with the nontaxable gift, the numerator of the applicable fraction is $25,000 ($10,000 + $15,000); the denominator is $40,000 ($10,000 + $30,000); the applicable fraction is, therefore, $25,000 ÷ $40,000, or 0.625, and the inclusion ratio is 0.375.

the extent that it was a nontaxable gift.[101] Again, a single inclusion ratio should be ascertained to compute the tax on subsequent generation-skipping transfers from such a trust. The computation is identical to the computation for a non-taxable direct skip gift to a trust using Section 2642(d).[102]

Although subsequent nondirect skip transfers to a trust were not assigned a zero inclusion ratio, they were excluded from the denominator in the computation of the applicable fraction to the extent of the nontaxable gift.[103] If the full amount of a subsequent transfer prior to April 1, 1988, qualified as a nontaxable gift, recomputation of the applicable fraction was not required. However, subsequent transfers, to the extent that they were not classified as nontaxable gifts, required a recomputation of the inclusion ratio.

For example, assume that on March 15, 1987, grantor G, who had no remaining unused GST exemption, established a trust with income to child C for life and remainder to grandchild GC, with an initial transfer of $40,000 to the trust, of which $10,000 was a nontaxable gift. The initial $10,000 nontaxable gift was assigned a zero inclusion ratio.[104] The applicable fraction of the taxable portion of the gift was zero,[105] and the inclusion ratio was one. Combining the two gifts, taxable and nontaxable, resulted in a single applicable fraction of 0.250[106] and a recomputed inclusion ratio of 0.750.[107] If G then transferred $5,000 to the trust prior to April 1, 1988, which as a result of a *Crummey* power provision[108] was a nontaxable gift of $5,000, the applicable fraction re-

---

[101] IRC § 2642(c)(2)(B) prior to its amendment by Technical and Miscellaneous Revenue Act of 1988, Pub. L. No. 100-647, § 1014(g)(17)(A), 102 Stat. 3342, 3566 (1988), reprinted in 1988-3 CB 1, 226. See supra note 84.

[102] See supra text accompanying notes 96–100.

[103] IRC § 2642(c)(2)(A) prior to amendment by Technical and Miscellaneous Revenue Act of 1988, Pub. L. No. 100-647, § 1014(g)(17)(A), 102 Stat. 3342, 3566 (1988), reprinted in 1988-3 CB 1, 226. See supra note 84.

[104] IRC § 2642(c)(2)(B) prior to amendment by Technical and Miscellaneous Revenue Act of 1988, Pub. L. No. 100-647, § 1014(g)(17)(A), 102 Stat. 3342, 3566 (1988), reprinted in 1988-3 CB 1, 226. See supra note 84.

[105] IRC § 2642(a)(2). The numerator of the applicable fraction is zero because G has no unallocated GST exemption, which results in an applicable fraction of zero regardless of the value of the denominator.

[106] IRC § 2642(a)(2). The applicable fraction determined using the Section 2642(d) rules had a numerator of $10,000 and a denominator of $40,000.

[107] IRC § 2642(a)(1). See the computations supra text accompanying notes 96–100.

[108] Crummey v. Comm'r, 397 F2d 82 (9th Cir. 1968). Without the use of a *Crummey* power, only a portion of the $5,000 transfer, the actuarial value of C's life estate, would qualify for the annual exclusion. Use of a *Crummey* power with respect to a pre–April 1, 1988, transfer to a trust can create some interesting issues with respect to any lapse of the *Crummey* power. In such a situation, the power holder may become a transferor of a portion of the property held in the trust. See infra notes 114, 118; Reg. § 26.2652-1(a)(5) Ex. 5. See also ¶ 13.02[2][e] text accompanying notes 113–121. As a transferor, the power holder must compute his or her own applicable fraction and inclusion ratio, and lapses of

mained 0.250 because there was no GST exemption allocation, so the subsequent transfer had a numerator of zero, and the nontaxable gift was not a part of the denominator, so the denominator was zero.[109] The inclusion ratio remained at 0.750. If, however, when the trust corpus was worth $40,000, G instead transferred an additional $40,000 to the trust prior to April 1, 1988, $10,000 of which qualified for the annual exclusion, the $10,000 would have been disregarded in the determination of the denominator of the applicable fraction, which would have become 0.143 (($10,000 + 0)/($40,000 + $30,000)), and the inclusion ratio of the trust would have become 0.857.[110]

[v] **Ongoing nontaxable gift transfers to trusts.** Trusts containing *Crummey* powers[111] created after the effective date of the generation-skipping transfer tax provisions and prior to April 1, 1988, may be subject to both the pre– and post–March 31, 1988, rules. For example, assume that on November 30, 1987, transferor T established a trust with income to child C for life, with the remainder to grandchild GC, giving both C and GC a *Crummey* power over trust additions. With respect to each addition of property to the trust corpus, C and GC may each demand the lesser of the amount of the annual exclusion or one half of the amount of each addition at any time up to, and including, December 31 of the year in which the addition is made. Assume that on November 30, 1987, T funded the trust with a $20,000 transfer. C and GC each has a power over $10,000, and this amount qualifies for the annual exclusion.[112] Each $10,000 amount is a nontaxable gift.[113] The inclusion ratio for generation-skipping transfers from the trust attributed to the original transferor T is zero.[114]

---

powers may constitute both pre– and post–March 31, 1988, transfers. See supra notes 114, 118.

[109] Thus, the numerator is $10,000 plus zero plus zero, or $10,000, and the denominator is $10,000 plus $30,000 plus zero, or $40,000.

[110] If the property originally transferred to the trust appreciated in value prior to the subsequent transfer, the inclusion ratio in this example would decrease. If the value of the original property appreciated to $120,000, at which time G transferred the additional $40,000 to the trust, the applicable fraction would be 0.200, the numerator being $30,000 (0.250 × $120,000 + 0), and the denominator being $150,000 ($30,000 + $120,000). See supra ¶ 16.02[1] note 6.

[111] See Crummey v. Comm'r, 397 F2d 82 (9th Cir. 1968). See also supra note 108.

[112] IRC § 2503(b).

[113] IRC § 2642(c)(3)(A). However, the transfer is treated as a transfer to trust and not as an outright transfer. See supra text accompanying notes 71–73. See also Reg. § 26.2642-1(d) Ex. 2.

[114] IRC § 2642(c)(2)(B) prior to amendment by Technical and Miscellaneous Revenue Act of 1988, Pub. L. No. 100-647, § 1014(g)(17)(A), 102 Stat. 3342, 3566 (1988), reprinted in 1988-3 CB 1, 226. See supra note 84. If GC and C each allow their power to lapse, the lapse will be treated as a release to the extent that the property that could have been appointed by the exercise of the lapsed power exceeds the greater of $5,000 or 5

To continue the example, assume that on March 1, 1988, another $20,000 transfer that qualifies for the annual exclusion is made to the trust by *T.* Because this transfer occurs before April 1, 1988, the entire $20,000 will qualify as a nontaxable gift[115] that is not taken into account in the denominator of the applicable fraction.[116] Because the transfer is a nontaxable gift occurring on or before March 31, 1988, the applicable fraction need not be recomputed,[117] and the inclusion ratio remains at zero.[118]

Assume that in 1989, a third $20,000 transfer, which qualifies in its entirety for the annual exclusion, is made to the trust by *T.* This transfer is a nontaxable gift, but it will not be assigned a zero inclusion ratio. Because it does not satisfy the additional conditions imposed on transfers to trusts after March 31, 1988, for assignment of a zero inclusion ratio,[119] a recomputation of the inclusion ratio will be required.[120]

---

percent of the assets that could have been used to satisfy the exercise of the power. IRC § 2514(e). In this case, the lapse is treated as a release to the extent of $5,000. The release of a general power of appointment is treated as a transfer of property. IRC § 2514(b). The transfer of property will be a transfer of property by gift in an amount determined according to the relative values of the income interest and the remainder interest. On *C*'s $5,000 transfer, *C* will make a gift of a remainder interest to *GC*. On *GC*'s transfer, *GC* will make a gift of an income interest to *C*. To the extent that the property is subject to the gift tax (IRC § 2501), *GC* and *C* will each become the Chapter 13 transferors of property held in the trust. IRC § 2652(a)(1)(B); Reg. § 26.2652-1(a)(5) Ex. 5. Any portion of a trust that is attributable to a different transferor is treated as separate trust. IRC § 2654(b)(1). See Reg. § 26.2654-1(a)(2)(i). Now there are three transferors involved with this single trust, which is treated as three trusts. As a result, each distribution from the trust must be trifurcated. Reg. § 26.2654-1(a)(2)(i). See also ¶ 13.02[2][e] text accompanying notes 113–121. However, neither *C* nor *GC* makes a potential generation-skipping transfer because neither makes a transfer to a skip person.

[115] IRC § 2642(c)(3).

[116] IRC § 2642(c)(2)(A) prior to amendment by Technical and Miscellaneous Revenue Act of 1988, Pub. L. No. 100-647, § 1014(g)(17)(A), 102 Stat. 3342, 3566 (1988), reprinted in 1988-3 CB 1, 226. See supra note 84.

[117] See IRC § 2642(d)(1); supra text accompanying notes 108, 109.

[118] If *GC* and *C* both allow their powers to lapse, they will again be treated as each transferring $5,000 to the trust. See Reg. § 26.2652-1(a)(5) Ex. 5. For additional consequences, see supra note 114.

[119] IRC § 2642(c)(2). See supra ¶ 16.02[2][b][iii].

[120] IRC § 2642(d). See infra ¶ 16.02[5]; Reg. § 26.2642-4. If the prior transfers had not appreciated in value, the applicable fraction would have a numerator of $40,000 ($20,000 + $20,000 + 0) and a denominator of $60,000 ($20,000 + $20,000 + $20,000), or 0.667, and the inclusion ratio would be one minus 0.667, or 0.333. See infra ¶ 16.02[2][c].

[c] Direct Skips of Other Than Nontaxable Gifts

Where there is a direct skip, once any nontaxable gift that qualifies for a zero inclusion ratio is removed from the transfer and is treated as a separate transfer, computation of the inclusion ratio for the remaining portion of the transfer can generally[121] be accomplished with relative ease. Since the inclusion ratio is equal to one minus the applicable fraction,[122] the applicable fraction of the direct skip must be computed to determine the inclusion ratio.

[i] **Applicable fraction.** The numerator of the applicable fraction is the amount of the transferor's GST exemption allocated to the property transferred in the potentially taxable portion of the direct skip.[123] Generally, the transferor, or the transferor's executor, may allocate all, or any portion, of the transferor's GST exemption to any property that is the subject matter of a direct skip[124] and thereby determine the numerator of its applicable fraction.[125] In the event that no allocation is made to an inter vivos direct skip, the transferor's remaining GST exemption[126] is automatically allocated to the property transferred,[127] unless the transferor affirmatively elects to the contrary or pays the tax imposed on the direct skip.[128] If neither the transferor nor the transferor's executor makes an allocation of GST exemption to testamentary direct skips, any unused GST exemption is automatically allocated among them.[129] If none of the transferor's GST exemption is allocated to property transferred in a direct skip, the property, other than that qualifying for a zero inclusion ratio, will be taxed at the top marginal rate of tax.[130]

---

[121] But see the special rules for pre–April 1, 1988, transfers to trusts discussed supra ¶ 16.02[2][b][iv]. See Reg. § 26.2642-1(c)(1)(iii).

[122] IRC § 2642(a)(1).

[123] IRC § 2642(a)(2)(A); Reg. § 26.2642-1(b).

[124] IRC § 2632(a)(1). Allocation of the GST exemption is discussed at ¶ 15.03. An allocation of GST exemption to property transferred to a trust in a direct skip is, subsequent to the direct skip, treated as an allocation of GST exemption to the entire trust, rather than to the specific asset transferred, and is used in the determination of the inclusion ratio for future generation-skipping transfers attributed to the same transferor from the trust. Reg. § 26.2632-1(a). An individual's GST exemption can be allocated only to trusts with respect to which the individual is the transferor. IRC § 2631(a).

[125] IRC § 2642(a)(2)(A).

[126] IRC § 2632(b)(2).

[127] IRC § 2632(b)(1). See ¶ 15.03[3][a].

[128] IRC § 2632(b)(3); Reg. § 26.2632-1(b)(1)(i). See ¶ 15.03[3][c].

[129] IRC § 2632(e)(1)(A). See ¶ 15.03[6][a]. This automatic allocation occurs on the due date for filing the transferor's federal estate tax return, regardless of whether a return is required to be filed. Reg. § 26.2632-1(d)(2).

[130] IRC § 2641(b).

Section 2642

The denominator of the applicable fraction is the value of the property[131] involved in the potentially taxable portion of the direct skip.[132] Generally, in determining the denominator of the applicable fraction, there are two potential reductions from the value of the property: a reduction for any federal estate tax or state death tax recovered from the property,[133] and a reduction for any charitable deduction allowed under Section 2055, Section 2106, or Section 2522.[134] Neither reduction should occur in the computation of the denominator of the applicable fraction for a direct skip. First, the amount of property involved in the direct skip is the value of the property received by the transferee.[135] The amount of property received by the transferee is net of federal estate taxes and state death taxes, so there is no need for a reduction for these taxes. Second, it is impossible to have a direct skip to a charity or to a trust for which a deduction is provided by Section 2055, Section 2106, or Section 2522. Charitable institutions qualifying as recipients of deductible transfers have a Section 2652(c) interest in any trust transfer and are assigned to the transferor's generation, precluding the charity or the trust's classification as a skip person[136] and thereby precluding a direct skip.[137]

The following example illustrates the computation of the inclusion ratio for direct skips (including nontaxable gifts) and its relationship to the ultimate determination of the generation-skipping transfer tax. Assume that grantor *G*, who has never made any previous gifts, gives $1,011,000 in cash outright to grandchild *GC*.[138] The cash transfer is a $1 million taxable gift[139] and is a direct skip.[140] The $1,011,000 value of the property received by *GC* will constitute the taxable amount of the generation-skipping transfer.[141] To the extent that the transfer to *GC* qualifies for the $11,000 Section 2503(b) annual exclu-

---

[131] IRC § 2642(a)(2)(B)(i). See Reg. § 26.2642-1(c). The time and method of valuation are discussed infra ¶ 16.02[4].

[132] See supra ¶ 16.02[2][b][i]. The denominator of the fraction excludes the portion of the transfer that is a nontaxable gift. See Reg. § 26.2642-1(c)(1)(iii). However, special rules apply with respect to transfers to trusts prior to April 1, 1988. See supra ¶ 16.02[2][b][iv].

[133] IRC § 2642(a)(2)(B)(ii)(I). See Reg. § 26.2642-1(c)(1)(i).

[134] IRC § 2642(a)(2)(B)(ii)(II). See Reg. § 26.2642-1(c)(1)(ii).

[135] IRC § 2623.

[136] IRC §§ 2651(f)(3), 2652(c)(1)(C).

[137] IRC § 2612(c). See IRC §§ 2613(a)(2), 2652(c)(1)(C); Priv. Ltr. Rul. 9532006 (May 4, 1995) (classification as charitable remainder annuity trust under Section 2652(c) denied where no charitable deduction allowable under Section 2055 owing to an excessive payout to noncharitable beneficiaries).

[138] See supra ¶ 16.02[2][b] note 45.

[139] See IRC § 2503(b).

[140] IRC § 2612(c).

[141] IRC § 2623.

sion, it is a nontaxable gift[142] and it is assigned a zero inclusion ratio and not taxed.[143] An inclusion ratio for the remaining $1 million direct skip is computed by subtracting the applicable fraction from one.[144] Assume that $1 million of GST exemption is allocated to the transfer either by *G* or by an automatic allocation.[145] The numerator of the applicable fraction is $1 million, the amount of the GST exemption allocated to the property transferred.[146] The denominator is the value of the cash transferred ($1,011,000) less the nontaxable gift ($11,000), or $1 million.[147] The applicable fraction is one ($1 million/ $1 million), and the inclusion ratio and the applicable rate of tax will both be zero. No generation-skipping transfer tax will be imposed on this transfer,[148] and *G* will have used $1 million of GST exemption.

Assume instead that *G* had previously allocated $800,000 of the GST exemption to prior transfers.[149] *G* would have unused GST exemption remaining to allocate to the $1,011,000 cash transfer to *GC*. Again, under these assumptions, $11,000 of the cash transferred is a nontaxable gift and is assigned a zero inclusion ratio. If *G* allocates $200,000 of unused GST exemption to the transfer, *the balance of the gift*, $1 million, will have an applicable fraction with a numerator of $200,000 and a denominator equal to the value of the balance of the property that is not a nontaxable gift, or $1 million. The applicable fraction is 0.200,[150] the inclusion ratio is 0.800,[151] and the applicable rate, assuming a maximum tax rate of 50 percent, is 40 percent.[152]

[ii] Continuation of the inclusion ratio for subsequent generation-skipping transfers. After a direct skip to a trust, there may be a subsequent taxable termination or taxable distribution from the trust. In that event, the inclusion ratio for the determination of tax on the subsequent generation-skip-

---

[142] IRC § 2642(c)(3)(A).

[143] IRC § 2642(c)(1).

[144] IRC § 2642(a)(1).

[145] See IRC §§ 2632(a), 2632(b).

[146] IRC § 2642(a)(2)(A).

[147] IRC § 2642(a)(2)(B). See Reg. § 26.2642-1(c)(1)(iii).

[148] See supra ¶ 16.02[1] note 1.

[149] See IRC § 2632.

[150] The applicable fraction is converted to a decimal fraction rounded to the nearest one-thousandth. Reg. § 26.2642-1(a). See supra ¶ 16.02[1] note 6.

[151] Because the applicable fraction converted to a decimal fraction rounded to the nearest one-thousandth is subtracted from one in the determination of the inclusion ratio, the resulting inclusion ratio is a decimal fraction to the nearest one-thousandth also. See Reg. § 26.2642-1(a); supra ¶ 16.02[1] note 6.

[152] The applicable rate, 40 percent, is the product of the inclusion ratio, 0.800, and the assumed maximum federal estate tax rate, 0.50. Cf. Reg. § 26.2642-1(a). The 40 percent applicable rate applied against the taxable amount of $1 million results in a Chapter 13 tax liability of $400,000.

ping transfer is generally the same as the inclusion ratio computed on the prior direct skip to the trust.[153] For example, assume grantor *G*, having previously used some GST exemption, transfers $1 million[154] to a trust with income to grandchild *GC* for life and a remainder to *GC*'s children,[155] and allocates $700,000 of GST exemption, *G*'s entire unused GST exemption, to the trust transfer. There is a direct skip on the creation of the trust. The trust has an applicable fraction of 0.700[156] and an inclusion ratio of 0.300.[157] Assuming that the maximum federal estate tax rate is 50 percent,[158] the trust has an applicable rate of 15 percent and the Chapter 13 tax liability for the direct skip is $150,000.[159] Assume the trust corpus appreciates in value to $2 million at *GC*'s death when there is a taxable termination. Assuming that no additional GST exemption is allocated to the trust, the trust would continue to have an inclusion ratio of 0.300, with an applicable rate of 15 percent, assuming no change in the 50 percent maximum federal estate tax rate.[160] A generation-skipping transfer tax liability of $300,000 would be incurred on the taxable termination.[161]

---

[153] IRC § 2653(b)(1). See Reg. § 26.2632-1(a) (last sentence). The inclusion ratio will change if an additional amount of GST exemption is allocated to the trust, if additional property is added to the trust, or, in some circumstances, if there has been a prior taxable termination of the trust with no substitution of the transferor of the trust. The inclusion ratio may change when two trusts are consolidated or if a single trust is severed and will be redetermined where additional estate tax is imposed under Section 2032A. See supra ¶ 16.02[1] text accompanying notes 21–28; infra ¶ 16.02[5]; ¶ 17.03[2][a].

[154] See IRC § 2642(c)(2); supra ¶ 16.02[2][b][iii].

[155] See supra ¶ 16.02[2][b] note 45.

[156] The applicable fraction is $700,000 ÷ $1 million, or stated as a decimal fraction, 0.700. IRC § 2642(a)(2). See supra ¶¶ 16.02[1] note 6, 16.02(2)(c) note 150.

[157] IRC § 2642(a)(1). See supra ¶¶ 16.02[1] note 6, 16.02[2][c] note 151.

[158] See supra ¶ 16.02[2][c] note 152. If the maximum federal estate tax rate is 45 percent at the time of *GC*'s death, the applicable rate would be 13.5 percent.

[159] IRC §§ 2602, 2623, 2641. The applicable rate assuming a 50 percent maximum federal estate tax rate is 15 percent at *GC*'s death, which when multiplied by $1 million, equals $150,000. If the maximum federal estate tax rate is 45 percent at *GC*'s death, the applicable rate of tax would be 13.5 percent, which when multiplied by $1 million, equals $135,000.

[160] See supra ¶ 16.02[2][c] note 152. If the maximum federal estate tax rate is 45 percent at the time of *GC*'s death, the applicable rate would be 13.5 percent.

[161] This is the product of $2 million multiplied by the applicable rate of tax, 15 percent. If the maximum federal estate tax rate is 45 percent at *GC*'s death, the applicable rate of tax would be 13.5 percent, which when multiplied by $2 million, equals $270,000.

[3] Calculation of the Inclusion Ratio for Taxable Terminations and Taxable Distributions

[a] In General

Where a transfer to a trust[162] does not constitute a direct skip, but where GST exemption is allocated[163] to the trust transfer because a taxable termination or taxable distribution may subsequently occur, the applicable fraction[164] and resulting inclusion ratio[165] for the trust[166] must be determined once the exemption allocated to the transfer is effective.[167] The computations of the applicable fraction and the inclusion ratio in this case bear substantial similarity to the computations in the case of a direct skip to a trust.[168]

[b] Applicable Fraction

[i] **The numerator.** The numerator of the applicable fraction generally is the amount of the transferor's GST exemption allocated to the trust.[169] The ex-

---

[162] See supra ¶ 16.02[1] note 17.

[163] If the transferor has no unused GST exemption available or no allocation of GST exemption occurs because the transferor chooses not to have any GST exemption allocated, the applicable fraction will be zero, the inclusion ratio will be one, and the generation-skipping transfer will be taxed at the maximum federal estate tax rate. See IRC §§ 2602, 2641, 2642.

[164] IRC § 2642(a)(2).

[165] IRC § 2642(a)(1).

[166] When GST exemption is allocated to property transferred to a trust, the exemption allocation is to the entire trust rather than to specific trust assets. Reg. § 26.2632-1(a). However, when the inclusion ratio of a trust is greater than zero and less than one, in some circumstances, a qualified severance may be made splitting the single trust into two separate trusts, one with an inclusion ratio of zero and the other an inclusion ratio of one. IRC § 2642(a)(3). See infra ¶ 16.02[5][e].

[167] Section 2632 provides generally for the time and manner of allocation of the GST exemption. See ¶ 15.03 for a discussion of Section 2632. An allocation of GST exemption to property subject to an estate tax inclusion period (ETIP) is generally effective no earlier than the termination of the estate tax inclusion period, and the determination of the inclusion ratio and applicable fraction are delayed until the allocation of GST exemption is effective. See IRC § 2642(f), discussed infra ¶ 16.02[7].

[168] See supra ¶ 16.02[2][c]. If the transfer creating the trust is not a direct skip, either at the time of the transfer or at the close of the estate tax inclusion period, and if the transfer did not occur prior to April 1, 1988, there is no nontaxable gift to the trust. As a result, the computation is similar to the computation for most direct skips to trusts after March 31, 1988, that do not qualify for nontaxable gift status. Id. See Reg. § 26.2642-1(d) Ex. 1.

[169] IRC § 2642(a)(2)(A); Reg. § 26.2642-1(b)(1). Special rules are provided for the determination of the numerator of the applicable fraction: (1) where there is a charitable

emption can be allocated only to trusts with respect to which the individual making the allocation is the transferor.[170] All, or any portion, of the transferor's unused GST exemption may be allocated to a trust by the transferor or the transferor's executor at any time before the due date of the transferor's federal estate tax return.[171] At times, Chapter 13 requires an automatic allocation of a transferor's unused GST exemption to an inter vivos or testamentary transfer.[172] The rules governing the allocation of a transferor's GST exemption are discussed in detail in Chapter 15.[173]

[ii] The denominator.

In General. The denominator of the applicable fraction is the value of the property transferred to the trust,[174] less any federal estate and state death taxes recovered from the trust and the amount of any charitable deductions allowed for federal estate or gift tax purposes with respect to the property transferred.[175] The denominator reductions have the effect of reducing the amount of the GST exemption required to increase the applicable fraction, thereby reducing the inclusion ratio.[176]

Tax Reduction. The denominator of the applicable fraction is reduced by any federal estate or state death taxes actually recovered from the trust attribu-

---

lead annuity trust (see IRC § 2642(e) and Reg. § 26.2642-3, discussed infra ¶ 16.02[6]); (2) where the applicable fraction must be redetermined (see IRC § 2642(d) and Reg. § 26.2642-4, discussed infra ¶ 16.02[5]); and (3) where a generation-skipping transfer occurs during an estate tax inclusion period (see Reg. § 26.2642-1(b)(2), discussed infra ¶ 16.02[7]).

[170] IRC § 2631(a). Cf. IRC § 2652(a)(2).

[171] See IRC § 2632(a)(1). The due date is determined considering extensions of time to file actually granted, regardless of whether a return is required to be filed. Reg. § 26.2632-1(a).

[172] IRC §§ 2632(b), 2632(c), 2632(e).

[173] See ¶ 15.03.

[174] IRC § 2642(a)(2)(B)(i); Reg. § 26.2642-1(c). See IRC §§ 2642(b), 2642(f), discussed infra ¶¶ 16.02[4], 16.02[7]. In determining the denominator of the applicable fraction in the case of a charitable lead annuity trust, the property is valued immediately after the termination of the lead annuity trust. See IRC § 2642(e)(1)(B); Reg. § 26.2642-3(a)(2), discussed infra ¶ 16.02[6]. Special rules are provided for the determination of the denominator of the applicable fraction where a redetermination of the applicable fraction is required. Reg. § 26.2642-1(c)(1). Redetermination is required when additional GST exemption is allocated to the trust, additional property is added to the trust, trusts are consolidated, there is a qualified severance of a trust with an inclusion ratio greater than zero and less than one, or additional estate tax is imposed under Section 2032A. See IRC § 2642(d)(2); Reg. § 26.2642-4, discussed infra ¶ 16.02[5]. Redetermination is also required when the Chapter 13 tax imposed on a taxable termination is borne by the trust and the trust does not terminate. IRC § 2653(b)(1), discussed at ¶ 17.03[2][a].

[175] IRC § 2642(a)(2)(B)(ii).

[176] See infra text accompanying notes 178–182.

table to the property transferred to the trust.[177] This is proper because if the property had passed outright from one generation to the next, the value of the property received by each successive generation level would have been reduced by any federal estate and state death taxes imposed at the preceding generation level.

To demonstrate the operation of the reduction, assume grantor G establishes an inter vivos trust retaining the income from the property for life. The trust instrument provides that upon the death of G, the income is to be paid to G's child for life, with a remainder to G's grandchildren. When G dies,[178] the trust assets are valued at $100,000 and are included in G's gross estate.[179] Assume that the total federal estate and state death taxes apportioned to the trust under a state apportionment statute and paid by the trust are $32,000.[180] The denominator of the applicable fraction for the trust will be reduced by $32,000 to $68,000. For the trust to have an applicable fraction of one[181] and an inclusion ratio[182] of zero, $68,000 of G's GST exemption must be allocated to the trust.

Charitable Reduction Reduction. The reduction of the denominator of the applicable fraction for a trust by the amount of any federal estate or gift tax charitable deduction[183] exempts the charitable portion of the transfer from taxation under Chapter 13. The denominator reduction for charitable transfers is applicable only when the transfer to a trust is a gift, whether inter vivos or testamentary, that benefits both charitable and noncharitable beneficiaries.[184]

For example, assume transferor T, a single individual who has not previously made a gift or generation-skipping transfer, transfers $100,000 in cash inter vivos to a charitable remainder unitrust on January 1 of the current year,[185] which provides for an 8 percent annuity to T's GC and qualifies for a

---

[177] IRC § 2642(a)(2)(B)(ii)(I). This reduction does not apply to a direct skip. See supra ¶ 16.02[2][c] text accompanying notes 133–137.

[178] See IRC § 2642(f)(1), which requires postponement of any GST exemption allocation and valuation for purposes of computation of the inclusion ratio until G's death. See infra ¶ 16.02[7].

[179] IRC § 2036.

[180] See ¶ 8.04[2].

[181] See IRC § 2642(a)(2).

[182] See IRC § 2642(a)(1).

[183] IRC § 2642(a)(2)(B)(ii)(II). This includes a deduction allowed under Section 2055, Section 2106, or Section 2522. Reg. § 26.2642-1(c)(1)(ii). This reduction is inapplicable to a direct skip. See supra ¶ 16.02[2][c] text accompanying notes 133–137.

[184] See IRC §§ 2055(e)(2), 2522(c)(2). This is true regardless of whether the charitable interest is a lead interest or remainder interest. However, a special rule is provided for the computation of the inclusion ratio for a charitable lead annuity trust. See IRC § 2642(e), discussed infra ¶ 16.02[6].

[185] See IRC §§ 2522(c)(2)(A), 664(d)(2), discussed at ¶¶ 11.02[2][b][ii], 5.05[5][b], respectively.

charitable deduction of, $38,950.30.[186] Although the transfer to the trustee is a transfer of property by gift that results in a taxable gift,[187] the transfer is not a direct skip.[188] The distributions to *GC* are taxable distributions that are taxable under Chapter 13.[189] The denominator of the applicable fraction, $61,049.70, is the value of the property transferred to the trust, $100,000,[190] reduced by the charitable deduction allowed under Section 2522, $38,950.30. If $61,049.70 of *T*'s unused GST exemption is allocated to the trust,[191] it will result in an applicable fraction of one and an inclusion ratio and applicable rate of tax of zero,[192] and no generation-skipping transfer tax will be imposed on the taxable distributions to *GC*.

A similar reduction occurs in the computation of the denominator of the applicable fraction in the case of a trust where the charity has a qualified income interest rather than a remainder interest (a charitable lead trust).[193] If the transfer is inter vivos and a Section 2522 deduction is allowed for the income interest, the amount of the denominator reduction should not reflect the Section 2524 reduction of the Section 2522 deduction by any Section 2503(b) annual exclusion allowed for the interest.[194]

---

[186] See IRC § 2522(c)(2)(A); Reg. § 1.664-4(e)(4) Ex. This valuation assumes the trust instrument provides that quarterly on March 31, June 30, September 30, and December 31 for a period of twelve years, 8 percent of the fair market value of the trust assets on January 1 is to be paid to *T*'s grandchild, *GC*. It assumes that the Section 7520 rate for January 1 of the current year is 9.6 percent and that the remainder interest is held by a charitable organization described in Section 501(c)(3).

[187] The transfer results in a taxable gift of $50,049.70, which is equal to the total value of the property transferred by gift, $100,000, less the annual exclusion, $11,000 in this example, less the charitable deduction, $38,950.30. See Reg. § 1.664-4(e)(4), Ex.

[188] The trust is not a skip person because a Section 2652(c)(1)(C) interest in the property held in trust is held by a non–skip person, the charitable beneficiary that is assigned to the transferor's generation. IRC §§ 2612(c)(1), 2613, 2651(f)(3).

[189] IRC § 2612(b). See IRC §§ 2601, 2611(a)(1).

[190] Although the transfer to the trust qualifies for the annual exclusion ($11,000 under these facts), that portion does not qualify for an inclusion ratio of zero. See IRC § 2642(c)(2), discussed supra ¶ 16.02[2][b][iii].

[191] The allocation may be made on a timely filed gift tax return. See IRC § 2632(a)(1), discussed at ¶ 15.03[2][a]. The charitable remainder unitrust is not a GST trust. IRC § 2632(c)(3)(B)(v). However, *T* may elect to treat the trust as a GST trust resulting in an automatic allocation of unused GST exemption under Section 2632(c). IRC § 2632(c)(5)(A)(ii). See ¶ 15.03[4][e][ii].

[192] IRC §§ 2641, 2642(a).

[193] IRC §§ 2055(e)(2)(B), 2522(c)(2)(B). See Priv. Ltr. Ruls. 9840036 (July 6, 1998) (unitrust rate fixed but term of trust determined by formula to consume the transferor's available GST exemption), 9840008 (June 25, 1998) (term of trust fixed with formula payout percentage to consume transferor's remaining GST exemption).

[194] Section 2642(a)(2)(B)(ii)(II) provides for a reduction for any charitable deduction "allowed under . . . section 2522" with respect to such property. Technically the deduction

For example, assume grantor G transfers $100,000 to an inter vivos charitable lead unitrust under which 10 percent of the fair market value of the corpus determined annually is to be paid for five years to a charitable organization described in Section 501(c)(3), with a remainder to G's grandchildren. If the value of the charitable interest is $40,000, the Section 2522 reduction in the denominator of the applicable fraction should also be $40,000, reducing the denominator to $60,000. An allocation of $60,000 of GST exemption to the trust would then result in a zero inclusion ratio.[195] If the charitable lead trust is an annuity trust rather than a unitrust, Congress requires a special computation of the applicable fraction under the rules of Section 2642(e).[196]

[iii] Ongoing inclusion ratio. Once the inclusion ratio is established for a trust, it remains fixed for purposes of any future taxable terminations or taxable distributions, regardless of whether the property held in the trust appreciates or depreciates in value.[197] However, the inclusion ratio must be recomputed if additional property is added to the trust,[198] if additional GST exemption is allocated to the trust property at a later date,[199] if separate trusts created by the same transferor are consolidated,[200] if there is a qualified severance of a trust having an inclusion ratio greater than zero and less than one,[201] if an additional estate tax is imposed under Section 2032A,[202] or if an adjustment is required for Chapter 13 tax borne by the trust.[203]

For example, assume transferor T transfers $500,000 in trust. The trust instrument provides that the income is to be distributed at the trustee's discretion to T's three adult children for their joint lives, with a remainder to T's grandchildren. If $500,000 of T's unused GST exemption is allocated to the

---

"allowed" under Section 2522 is modified by the Section 2524 limitation on Section 2522. Since the income interest would qualify for a Section 2503(b) annual exclusion, the Section 2522 deduction "allowed" might be required to be reduced by the annual exclusion allowed. A more appropriate result would be to interpret the Section 2642(a)(2)(B)(ii)(II) amount to be the amount of deduction allowed by Section 2522 without modification by Section 2524. Such an interpretation can be read into the statute and produces an appropriate result. See IRC § 2524; ¶ 11.04[1].

[195] See supra note 194. If Section 2642(a)(2)(B)(ii)(II) is interpreted as the amount of the deduction allowed under Section 2522 as modified by Section 2524, the denominator of the applicable fraction would be $70,000 ($100,000 less $30,000), and an allocation of $70,000 of GST exemption would be required to reduce the inclusion ratio to zero.

[196] See infra ¶ 16.02[6].

[197] See ¶ 15.02[2].

[198] IRC § 2642(d)(1), discussed infra ¶ 16.02[5][b].

[199] IRC § 2642(d)(4), discussed infra ¶ 16.02[5][b].

[200] Reg. § 26.2642-4(a)(2), discussed infra ¶ 16.02[5][c].

[201] IRC § 2642(a)(3), discussed infra ¶ 16.02[5][e].

[202] Reg. § 26.2642-4(a)(4), discussed infra ¶ 16.02[5][f].

[203] IRC § 2653(b)(1), discussed at ¶ 17.03[2][a].

trust, no generation-skipping transfer tax will be imposed on the termination of the children's interest[204] because the applicable fraction is one ($500,000 ÷ $500,000) and the inclusion ratio for the trust is zero, which results in an applicable rate of tax of zero. This is true even if the trust property dramatically appreciates or depreciates in value after the transfer to the trust. If T instead had established the trust with income to children for their joint lives, then income to grandchildren living on creation of the trust for their joint lives, with a remainder to T's great-grandchildren who are alive at the death of the last of those grandchildren, the applicable rate of tax would still be zero at the taxable termination of the grandchildren's interest. Because the initial inclusion ratio for generation-skipping transfers from the trust attributed to T was zero, no generation-skipping transfer tax will ever be imposed on generation-skipping transfers from the trust, assuming no further transfers are made to the trust and the trust is not consolidated with another trust.

Alternatively, if only $125,000 of T's unused GST exemption was allocated to the $500,000 trust for children and grandchildren, the applicable fraction would have been 0.250 and the inclusion ratio would have been 0.750.[205] Assuming a 50 percent maximum federal estate tax rate, the applicable rate of tax imposed on future generation-skipping transfers from the trust would be 37.5 percent.[206] As a result, essentially 75 percent of the property held in trust would be taxed at the top marginal rate of tax, and 25 percent would be exempt from taxation.[207]

---

[204] A taxable termination occurs upon the termination of the children's interest. IRC § 2612(a).

[205] The 0.750 inclusion ratio is one minus the applicable fraction of 0.250, which is computed by dividing the GST exemption allocated to the trust ($125,000) by the value of the property transferred to the trust ($500,000). See supra ¶ 16.02[1] note 6.

[206] IRC § 2641(a). Upon the termination of the children's interest, the entire value of the property held in the trust would be taxed at a rate of 37.5 percent. This assumes that additional GST exemption is not allocated to the trust and that the maximum federal tax rate does not change. If the maximum federal estate tax rate is less than 50 percent at the time of the generation-skipping transfer, the property held in the trust would be taxed at a lower rate. For example, if the maximum federal tax rate is 45 percent at the time of the generation-skipping transfer, the property held in the trust would be taxed at a rate of 33.75 percent. Additionally, if the generation-skipping transfer occurred after December 31, 2009, and before December 31, 2010, no generation-skipping transfer tax would be incurred. IRC § 2664; Economic Growth and Tax Relief Reconciliation Act of 2001, Pub. L. No. 107-16, § 901(a)(2), 115 Stat. 38, 150 (2001), reprinted in 2001-__ CB __, __. But see ¶¶ 8.10[5], 18.04.

[207] If more than one generation-skipping transfer occurs from the trust (e.g., if the trust provides income to the children for their joint lives, then income to the grandchildren living on creation of the trust for their joint lives, with a remainder to the great-grandchildren who are alive at the death of the last of those grandchildren), an adjustment that will reduce the inclusion ratio must be made to the applicable fraction after the payment of Chapter 13 tax upon the children's death. See IRC § 2653(b)(1), discussed at

[4] Valuation Rules

Generally, when GST exemption allocated or deemed allocated to a transfer[208] is effective, the property transferred must be valued for purposes of determining the applicable fraction[209] and the inclusion ratio.[210] Sections 2642(b), 2642(e),[211] and 2642(f)[212] set forth the rules of valuation for the specific purpose of calculating the applicable fraction and the inclusion ratio.

Section 2642(b) provides the general rules for valuation of property in computing the applicable fraction and the inclusion ratio.[213] Generally, for purposes of computing the inclusion ratio, the GST exemption is effective and the property is valued at a time when it must otherwise be valued for either federal estate or gift tax purposes.[214] However, under Section 2642(b) both property that is transferred by the transferor inter vivos or is included in the transferor's gross estate may be valued for these purposes at a date subsequent to its valuation date for gift or estate tax purposes.[215] Sections 2642(e)[216] and 2642(f)[217] provide exceptions to the rules of Section 2642(b).

¶ 17.03[2][a]. Such an adjustment occurs only when the inclusion ratio is greater than zero and less than one.

[208] Section 2632 provides the allocation rules, which are discussed at ¶ 15.03. The GST exemption may be allocated by the transferor or the transferor's executor any time before the due date of the transferor's federal estate tax return, including extensions actually granted, regardless of whether a return is required to be filed. IRC § 2632(a). If the transferor does not allocate any GST exemption to an inter vivos direct or indirect skip, any unused GST exemption is deemed allocated under Section 2632(b)(1) or Section 2632(c)(1), unless the transferor makes an election under Section 2632(b)(3) or Section 2632(c)(5)(A)(i) negating the deemed allocation or negates the deemed allocation by paying the generation-skipping transfer tax on the direct skip with a timely filed return. Once the time period for allocation of the GST exemption expires, any unused GST exemption is deemed allocated under Section 2632(e).

[209] IRC § 2642(a)(2).

[210] IRC § 2642(a)(1).

[211] See infra ¶ 16.02[6] for a discussion of Section 2642(e).

[212] See infra ¶¶ 16.02[4][b], 16.02[7] for a discussion of Section 2642(f).

[213] See infra ¶¶ 16.02[4][a], 16.02[4][c], 16.02[4][d], 16.02[4][e] for a discussion of the Section 2642(b) rules.

[214] IRC §§ 2642(b)(1), 2642(b)(2), 2642(b)(4). See infra ¶¶ 16.02[4][a], 16.02[4][d], 16.02[4][e].

[215] IRC §§ 2642(b)(2)(A), 2642(b)(3). See infra ¶¶ 16.02[4][c], 16.02[4][d][ii], 16.02[4][d][iii].

[216] See infra ¶¶ 16.02[4][f], 16.02[6].

[217] See infra ¶¶ 16.02[4][b], 16.02[7].

[a] Timely Gift Tax Return Allocations

In several circumstances a transferor makes an inter vivos transfer and the transferor's GST exemption allocation is treated as effective on the date of the transfer.[218] In those circumstances the valuation as finally determined for purposes of Chapter 12,[219] the fair market value[220] of the property on the date the gift is complete for federal gift tax purposes,[221] is also used to compute the applicable fraction and the inclusion ratio.[222]

The rule valuing property on the date of the inter vivos transfer applies if the transferor actually allocates GST exemption to the property[223] on a gift tax return that is timely filed[224] or where an extension of time has been granted to allocate GST exemption.[225] The rule also applies where a retroactive allocation occurs as a result of the untimely death of a non–skip person,[226] where GST exemption is deemed allocated to a direct skip,[227] and where GST exemption is deemed allocated to an indirect skip.[228]

As a practical matter, a transferor has a maximum period of twenty-one and one-half months to determine whether and when to allocate any GST exemption to an inter vivos transfer without consideration of either the granting of an extension to allocate GST exemption under Section 2642(g)(1)[229] or the possibility of a retroactive allocation of GST exemption under Section 2632(d).[230] While the federal gift tax return for a transfer is generally required

---

[218] IRC § 2642(b)(1)(B). The allocation is effective on the date the gift is complete, whether or not the required gift tax return is filed for the transfer.

[219] IRC § 2642(b)(1). It is the valuation as finally determined for federal gift tax purposes within the meaning of Section 2001(f)(2). Id. See ¶ 9.05[2][b].

[220] See Reg. § 25.2512-1; ¶ 10.02.

[221] See Reg. § 25.2511-2; ¶¶ 10.01[4]–10.01[9].

[222] IRC § 2642(b)(1)(A).

[223] See IRC § 2632(a)(1), discussed at ¶ 15.03[2]. But see infra ¶ 16.02[4][b].

[224] IRC § 6075(b). The GST exemption allocation may be made on a timely filed gift tax return even though no return is required to be filed under Section 6019.

[225] IRC § 2642(g)(1)(A). If an extension of time is granted to make the GST exemption allocation under Section 2642(g)(1)(A), the value of the transfer, as finally determined for gift tax purposes, is used in the determination of the applicable fraction. Notice 2001-50, 2001-2 CB __; HR Conf. Rep. No. 84, 107th Cong., 1st Sess. 1, 202 (2001), reprinted in 2001-__ CB __, __. See infra ¶ 16.02[9].

[226] IRC § 2632(d)(2)(A). When a retroactive allocation is made to an inter vivos transfer (or transfers) under Section 2632(d)(1), in the determination of the inclusion ratio the property transferred is valued as if the allocation had been made on a timely filed gift tax return for the calendar year in which each transfer was made. See ¶ 15.03[5][b][ii].

[227] IRC § 2632(b)(1). See ¶ 15.03[3][a].

[228] IRC § 2632(c)(1). See ¶ 15.03[4].

[229] IRC § 2642(g)(1). See supra text accompanying note 225.

[230] IRC § 2632(d). See ¶ 15.03[5]; supra text accompanying note 226.

to be filed on or before April 15 of the year following the calendar year in which the gift is complete,[231] a six-month extension of time for filing is generally available.[232] With respect to a gift made on January 1 of year 1, the transferor may have until October 15 of year 2 to decide on the extent to which GST exemption should be allocated.[233] Thus, up to twenty-one and one-half months of valuation changes may be viewed retrospectively when deciding whether and how to allocate GST exemption to a particular inter vivos gift transfer. For example, assume transferor T makes two different generation-skipping transfers to two different non–skip person trusts, each holding securities worth $500,000 on January 1 of year 1. T can defer making the allocation of GST exemption until October 15 of year 2. Assume that the securities given to one donee trust appreciate in value to $2 million and the securities given to the other donee trust decline in value to $200,000 by that date. The allocation of $500,000 of T's unused GST exemption to the gift that appreciated in value will fully shield it from Chapter 13 tax.[234] As to the property that declined in value during the period, automatic allocation of the GST exemption should be prevented[235] and any allocation of GST exemption postponed beyond the maximum period of twenty-one and one-half months to take advantage of the reduced property value and consume only $200,000 of GST exemption to fully shield the property from Chapter 13 tax.[236] T should file the gift tax return without allocating any GST exemption to the declining value transfer. After the time for filing the gift tax return has expired, T should allocate $200,000 of GST exemption to the declining value transfer. Since there was no allocation on the timely filed gift tax return, the value of the property is generally determined when the allocation is filed with the secretary.[237]

---

[231] IRC § 6075(b)(1). The return due date is accelerated if the donor dies during the year in which the gift is made and the federal estate tax return is due before the normal April 15 gift tax due date. IRC § 6075(b)(3).

[232] IRC § 6081. See IRC § 6075(b)(2).

[233] See supra text accompanying notes 231, 232.

[234] This allocation may occur automatically under Section 2632(c)(1). IRC § 2632(c)(1). See ¶ 15.03[4]. If these automatic allocation rules do not apply, the allocation may be made by T under Section 2632(a)(1) on a gift tax return that is timely filed or deemed timely filed. IRC §§ 2642(b)(1), 2642(g)(1).

[235] IRC § 2632(c)(5)(A)(i). See ¶ 15.03[4][e][i]. The time to make the election to prevent the automatic allocation under Section 2632(c) may be extended. IRC § 2642(g)(1)(A)(ii).

[236] See infra ¶ 16.02[4][c]. Under Section 2642(b)(1), if the allocation of the GST exemption is made on a timely filed gift tax return, the value of the property is its value as finally determined for purposes of the gift tax within the meaning of Section 2001(f)(2), in this case, $500,000. Thus, T would have to allocate $500,000 of GST exemption on the gift tax return to have an applicable fraction of one and an inclusion ratio of zero.

[237] IRC § 2642(b)(3)(A); Reg. § 26.2642-2(a)(2). See infra ¶ 16.02[4][c] text accompanying notes 245–247. The property in this example is worth $200,000 when the alloca-

In addition, if either property is potentially subject to more than one generation-skipping transfer at the time of the gift, this twenty-one-and-one-half-month window also allows the transferor the opportunity to determine whether such multiple-skipping possibilities still exist at that later time. Assume *T* establishes trust one with $1 million on January 1 of year 1. The trust is to pay income to son *S* for life, then income to grandson *GS* for life, with the remainder to great-grandson *GGS*. On the same day, *T* establishes trust two with $1 million. Trust two is to pay income to *T*'s daughter *D* for life, then income to granddaughter *GD* for life, with the remainder to great-granddaughter *GGD*. *T* receives an extension for filing the gift tax return and the return is due on October 15 of year 2. *T* intends to allocate $500,000 of GST exemption to each trust. If *GS* dies on August 29 of year 2, *T* may wish to allocate $1 million of the GST exemption to trust two because only one taxable termination will occur with respect to trust one and two taxable terminations may occur with respect to trust two.[238]

[b] Certain Inter Vivos Transfers Possibly Includible in the Transferor's or the Transferor's Spouse's Gross Estate

When an individual makes an inter vivos transfer of property (whether it is complete or incomplete for gift tax purposes) and the property transferred would be included in the individual's or the individual's spouse's gross estate, other than by reason of Section 2035, if the individual or the individual's spouse died immediately after the transfer, the effective date of any allocation of the GST exemption is postponed under Section 2642(f)(1).[239] The delay lasts until the end of the "estate tax inclusion period" (ETIP), which is the time when the property is no longer potentially includible in the individual's gross estate, is subject to a subsequent generation-skipping transfer, or is in-

---

tion is filed with the secretary at a time that is more than the maximum of twenty-one and one-half months after the transfer. If $200,000 of GST exemption is allocated to the transfer, the applicable fraction is one ($200,000 ÷ $200,000) and the inclusion ratio is zero. *T* has established the same inclusion ratio and has saved $300,000 of GST exemption by allocating the GST exemption to the transfer at the later date after filing the gift tax return.

If the transfer was initially made to a skip person trust rather than a non–skip person trust and the facts were otherwise the same, there would be a direct skip and an automatic allocation of GST exemption. *T* would be required to elect out of the deemed allocation of GST exemption under Section 2632(b)(3) (see ¶ 15.03[3][c]) and would incur generation-skipping transfer tax. The generation-skipping transfer tax incurred is a factor that must be considered in making the decision to elect out of a deemed allocation and delay any allocation of GST exemption.

[238] See IRC § 2612(a)(1).

[239] If the transfer is a direct skip, the direct skip is also delayed. IRC § 2642(f)(1) (last sentence). Section 2642(f) is discussed infra ¶ 16.02[7].

cluded in the individual's gross estate, whichever occurs first.[240] In the case of an estate tax inclusion period arising by reason of an interest held by the transferor's spouse, the delay ends upon the death of the spouse or when no portion of the property would be includible in the gross estate of the spouse other than by reason of Section 2035, whichever occurs first.[241] When the effect of any GST exemption allocation is postponed under Section 2642(f)(1), there are special rules for valuing property in the computation of the inclusion ratio.[242]

[c] Allocation to Other Inter Vivos Transfers

The transferor may make a complete inter vivos transfer that is not subject to the Section 2642(f)(1) rule, but decide against an immediate affirmative allocation or deemed allocation[243] of any GST exemption to the property transferred. The transferor subsequently may have a change of mind and decide to allocate GST exemption to the transfer. The transferor can do this, but the allocation of GST exemption to the property transferred is effective only when the GST exemption is filed,[244] and the property is generally valued at its fair market value on that date.[245] However, when a late allocation is made during any month, the transferor may elect to value the trust assets on the first day of that month.[246] The first-of-the-month election is not effective with respect to a

---

[240] IRC § 2642(f)(3).

[241] Reg. § 26.2632-1(c)(3)(iv), discussed infra ¶ 16.02[7][c][iii].

[242] IRC §§ 2642(b)(1)(A), 2642(f)(2). See infra ¶ 16.02[7][e]. See also IRC § 2632(c)(4); ¶ 15.03[5][c][i].

[243] IRC §§ 2632(a)(1), 2632(b), 2632(c).

[244] IRC § 2642(b)(3)(B); Reg. § 26.2632-1(b)(2)(ii)(A).

[245] IRC § 2642(b)(3)(A); Reg. § 26.2632-1(b)(2)(i). The only method of valuation available is fair market value. To permit use of the earlier valuation date would provide a major escape hatch for appreciated property.

[246] Reg. § 26.2642-2(a)(2). The election is made by the transferor stating on Form 709, United States Gift (and Generation-Skipping Transfer) Tax Return, on which the late allocation of GST exemption is made, that the election is being made, the applicable valuation date, and the fair market value of the trust assets on that date. Id. An allocation of GST exemption subject to this election is not effective until filed. Id. The allocation of GST exemption is treated as effective on the first day of the month in which it is filed with the Service solely for the purpose of valuation of trust assets in the determination of the inclusion ratio. Id. See Reg. § 26.2642-2(c) Ex. 3.

Although this special valuation election is titled, "Special rule for late allocations during life," it should be available to the transferor's executor who makes a late allocation of GST exemption to property transferred inter vivos that is not required to be included in the transferor's gross estate, other than under Section 2035, for the transferor who could have made an effective late allocation of GST exemption. See Reg. § 26.2632-1(d)(1). The appropriate election could be made by stating the required information on Form 706 or a Form 709 filed on or before the due date of the transferor's federal estate tax return. Reg. § 26.2642-2(a)(2) (last sentence).

life insurance policy or a trust holding a life insurance policy if the insured has died.[247] The same valuation rules should apply if a transferor decides to allocate additional GST exemption to a prior transfer.[248]

As with all GST exemption allocations, a postponed allocation for a trust that is effective on the filing date of the allocation locks in the applicable fraction and inclusion ratio used in computing the tax imposed on subsequent generation-skipping transfers from the trust. The delay of allocation of GST exemption to an inter vivos transfer can either be costly or result in a more effective use of the GST exemption.[249]

---

[247] Reg. § 26.2642-2(a)(2). If the election were effective for life insurance or a trust containing life insurance after the death of the insured, it would be possible to allocate GST exemption to the trust containing the policy after the death of the insured and then elect to have the insurance policy valued for purposes of the inclusion ratio at its predeath value.

Since the election is unavailable for a late allocation of GST exemption to a trust containing life insurance if the insured individual has died, the life insurance and other trust assets are to be valued on the date the election is filed with the Service, not on the first day of the month in which the election is filed, unless the election is, in fact, filed on the first day of the month. Id.

[248] See IRC § 2642(d)(4), discussed infra ¶ 16.02[5].

[249] See supra ¶ 16.02[4][a] text accompanying notes 234–237. For example, assume transferor T establishes a trust, income to child for life and a remainder to grandchild. If T originally transferred $1 million to the trust and $1 million of GST exemption was initially allocated to the property held in trust, the entire corpus of the trust would be shielded from the generation-skipping transfer tax. Once the GST exemption allocated equals the fair market value of the property held in trust at the time of the allocation, all subsequent generation-skipping transfers attributed to T from the trust will not generate any Chapter 13 tax because the Section 2641(a) applicable rate of tax will be zero. If T postponed the allocation beyond the gift tax return filing date until a date when the corpus was worth $2 million, and T's unused GST exemption at that time is $1 million, only one half of the corpus would essentially be shielded from the generation-skipping transfer tax, with the other one-half effectively subject to the tax upon the child's death. Assuming, for ease in computation, a maximum 50 percent federal estate tax rate, although the entire value of the trust property is subject to tax, the applicable rate of tax is 25 percent. This is the same as taxing one half of the property at 50 percent and one half at zero percent. See ¶ 15.02[2]. However, if at that subsequent date the corpus had declined in value to $800,000 and T then allocated $800,000 of unused GST exemption to the property held in the trust, T would not only shield the entire trust from the generation-skipping tax, but would have more unused GST exemption remaining to apply to other transfers.

[d] Testamentary Transfers

[i] **The general rule.** Property transferred as a result of the transferor's death is generally[250] valued at its final federal estate tax value[251] in determining the denominator of the applicable fraction.[252] The federal estate tax value is generally the fair market value of the property at the date of the decedent's death.[253] When property is valued on the alternate valuation date for estate tax purposes, that value is used in computing the applicable fraction.[254] However, when real property is valued under Section 2032A for estate tax purposes, the Section 2032A value may be used in the computation of the applicable fraction only if the recapture agreement specifically provides for the imposition of, and liability for, additional generation-skipping transfer tax in the event additional estate tax is imposed.[255] If the recapture agreement does not contain this specific provision, the fair market value of the property is used in computing the applicable fraction.[256]

---

[250] Property used to satisfy a pecuniary payment in kind or a residual transfer of property after satisfaction of a pecuniary payment in kind is to be valued at the time of distribution if certain requirements with respect to postdeath appreciation are not satisfied. IRC § 2642(b)(2)(A) (last clause); Reg. §§ 26.2642-2(b)(2), 26.2642-2(b)(3), discussed infra ¶¶ 16.02[4][d][ii], 16.02[4][d][iii].

Use of the fair market value of real property valued pursuant to Section 2032A for federal estate tax purposes is required in some circumstances. Reg. § 26.2642-2(b)(1). See ¶ 18.03[1][a]; supra text accompanying note 255.

[251] IRC § 2642(b)(2)(A). See ¶ 2.01[1][b][ii].

[252] IRC § 2642(b)(2)(A). See Reg. § 26.2642-2(b)(1).

[253] IRC § 2031; Reg. § 20.2031-1(b).

[254] See IRC §§ 2032, 2642(b)(2)(A); infra ¶ 16.02[4][d][ii].

[255] Reg. § 26.2642-2(b)(1). See ¶ 18.03[1]. If additional estate tax is imposed under Section 2032A(c) and if the Section 2032A election was effective for generation-skipping transfer tax purposes, the applicable fraction and resulting inclusion ratio are generally redetermined as of the date of the transferor's death. Reg. § 26.2642-4(a)(4)(i). See ¶ 15.03[6][a] note 237. The denominator of the applicable fraction is the fair market value of the real property as of the date of the transferor's death reduced by any federal estate tax, state death tax, and additional estate and generation-skipping transfer tax chargeable to, and actually recovered from, the trust. It is further reduced by the amount of any charitable deduction allowed with respect to the transfer. Reg. § 26.2642-4(a)(4)(i). See infra ¶ 16.02[5][f]. See also Reg. § 26.2642-1(c).

The generation-skipping transfer tax imposed on any generation-skipping transfer from a trust holding the property valued under Section 2032A for Chapter 13 purposes occurring prior to the recapture event is recomputed using the redetermined applicable fraction and resulting inclusion ratio. Reg. § 26.2642-4(a)(4)(ii). Any such recomputed generation-skipping transfer tax is due six months after the event causing the imposition of additional estate tax under Section 2032A(c). Id. The redetermined applicable fraction and inclusion ratio are used in the determination of the tax imposed on generation-skipping transfers occurring subsequent to the recapture event. Reg. § 26.2642-4(a)(4)(iii).

[256] Reg. § 26.2642-2(b)(1).

The phrase "property . . . transferred as a result of the death of the transferor," as used in Section 2642(b)(2), encompasses more than just probate property, but it does not encompass all property included within the transferor's gross estate for federal estate tax purposes. Some items included in the gross estate are valued under the rules of Section 2642(f)[257] and some are valued under the inter vivos transfer rules.[258] Property included in the transferor's probate estate and taxed under Section 2033 is property transferred as a result of the death of the transferor. Insurance proceeds included in a decedent's gross estate under Section 2042 may also be within the term.[259] Property that is subject to a general power of appointment[260] and included in a decedent's gross estate under Section 2041 is treated as property transferred as a result of the decedent's death to the extent that the decedent holds the general power of appointment at death. This would include both a pre–October 22, 1942, general power of appointment exercised by will and a post–October 21, 1942, general power of appointment merely held at death.[261]

[ii] **Pecuniary amounts.** When a testamentary transfer involves a pecuniary amount and cash is used to satisfy the pecuniary amount, the denominator

---

[257] See infra ¶ 16.02[7] for a discussion of Section 2642(f). A list of property specifically included within Section 2642(f)(1) is found infra ¶ 16.02[7][b] text accompanying notes 445–449. As a practical matter, some property valued under Section 2642(f) may be valued in the same manner as property transferred at death. Compare IRC § 2642(b)(2)(A) with IRC § 2642(f)(2)(A). However, the valuation occurs under Section 2642(f), not under Section 2642(b)(2).

[258] Inter vivos transfers of property included in a decedent's gross estate under Section 2035 will not be treated as property transferred as a result of the death of the transferor. They will be governed by Section 2642(b)(1) or Section 2642(b)(3), not by Section 2642(b)(2). For example, an inter vivos outright transfer of a life insurance policy on a decedent's life that is pulled into the decedent's gross estate under Section 2035(a) is treated as an inter vivos transfer under Section 2642(b)(1) or Section 2642(b)(3).

[259] A life insurance policy included in a decedent's gross estate under Section 2042(1) is property transferred as a result of the decedent's death and is subject to Section 2642(b)(2). A life insurance policy on a transferor's life transferred inter vivos in an incomplete gift tax transfer, where the transferor retains incidents of ownership, is pulled into the transferor's gross estate under Section 2042(2) and is subject to Section 2642(f). See infra ¶ 16.02[7][b] note 449.

[260] IRC §§ 2041(b)(1), 2514(c). Although a power over property generally has not been treated as an interest in property under state property law, it is treated as an interest in property for federal estate and gift tax purposes. IRC §§ 2041, 2514.

[261] IRC §§ 2041(a)(1)(A), 2041(a)(2) (first clause). If property is required to be included in a decedent's gross estate under Section 2041 due to a power that was exercised or released in a manner such that, had the property been owned by the decedent and then so transferred, it would have resulted in inclusion in the decedent's gross estate under Section 2035; it also will be governed by Section 2642(b)(2), not Section 2642(f). Section 2642(f) applies only to inter vivos transfers that would have been included in a decedent's gross estate other than by reason of Section 2035.

of the applicable fraction is the pecuniary amount.[262] When property other than cash is used to satisfy the pecuniary amount, the denominator of the applicable fraction again is the pecuniary amount,[263] but only if the property used to satisfy the amount must be valued on the date of distribution.[264] If under the governing instrument the property used to satisfy the pecuniary amount is valued on another date, the denominator of the applicable fraction is the pecuniary amount only if the assets used to satisfy the pecuniary amount must fairly represent the net appreciation and depreciation in the value of all property available to satisfy the amount between the valuation date and the date of distribution.[265] When a pecuniary amount is satisfied with a distribution of property that does not satisfy those requirements, the denominator of the applicable fraction is the date-of-distribution value of the property used to satisfy the amount.[266] Thus, date-of-distribution valuation will be required when a pecuniary bequest or transfer in trust of a pecuniary amount is satisfied in kind with assets valued at their estate tax value, and the value of those assets does not fairly represent the appreciation and depreciation in the value of all property available for distribution.[267]

An example will demonstrate the rationale for these rules. Assume decedent *D* has an estate of $2 million and bequeaths $1 million to a trust for the benefit of grandchild[268] and the residue of the estate to child. *D*'s will provides that the executor may satisfy the trust bequest in kind with estate assets valued

---

Exercised or released general powers of appointment that result in inclusion in the decedent's gross estate under Section 2041 as if there had been an actual transfer of property that would have resulted in inclusion in the decedent's gross estate under Section 2036, Section 2037, or Section 2038 are governed by Section 2642(f), not Section 2642(b)(2). See IRC §§ 2041(a)(1), 2041(a)(2); infra ¶ 16.02[7][b] note 448.

If a decedent has a noncumulative general power of appointment resulting in inclusion under both the first and second clauses of Section 2041(a)(2) and also resulting in a generation-skipping transfer, only the inclusion under the first clause of Section 2041(a)(2) (decedent has a general power at the time of death) will be valued under Section 2642(b)(2). The part included under the second clause (decedent has, at any time, exercised or released a general power of appointment) will be valued under Section 2642(f), except where the property with respect to which the decedent exercised or released the power would have been includible under Section 2035.

[262] Reg. § 26.2642-2(b)(2)(i).

[263] Reg. § 26.2642-2(b)(2)(i).

[264] Reg. § 26.2642-2(b)(2)(i)(A).

[265] Reg. § 26.2642-2(b)(2)(i)(B). The last clause of Section 2642(b)(2)(A) legislatively allocates the same authority to the secretary as the secretary has administratively asserted previously in the estate tax marital deduction area. See Rev. Proc. 64-19, 1964-1 CB (pt. 1) 682, discussed at ¶ 5.06[6][a].

[266] Reg. § 26.2642-2(b)(2)(ii).

[267] Staff of Joint Comm. on Tax'n, 100th Cong., 2d Sess., Description of the Technical Corrections Act of 1988, at 362 (Comm. Print 1988).

[268] See supra ¶ 16.02[2][b] note 45.

at their federal estate tax value and that the executor has complete discretion in the selection of assets to be used to satisfy the bequest. On the date of distribution, one half of the estate's assets have doubled in value, from $1 million to $2 million, and the other half has declined in value, from $1 million to $500,000. If the assets that have appreciated in value are distributed in satisfaction of the specific bequest, but for the exception requiring date-of-distribution valuation, the executor would need to allocate only $1 million of D's GST exemption to transfer $2 million of D's appreciated assets. If the executor distributes the appreciated assets in satisfaction of the bequest, the assets are to be valued at their $2 million date-of-distribution value in the computation of the applicable fraction. However, if the executor must satisfy the pecuniary trust bequest in kind using date-of-death values on a basis that fairly reflects net appreciation and depreciation occurring between the date of valuation and distribution in all of the assets from which the pecuniary amount could have been satisfied, the date-of-death values may be used in computing the applicable fraction.[269] Thus, the executor could distribute assets worth $1.25 million in satisfaction of the pecuniary bequest, and those assets would be valued at their $1 million date-of-death value in the computation of the applicable fraction.

When valuation is required at the date of distribution, the property will generally be valued at its fair market value on that date. However, if the property being distributed was valued under Section 2032A for inclusion in the decedent's gross estate and qualified for Section 2032A valuation for generation-skipping transfer tax purposes,[270] this valuation method should be employed in the valuation on the date of distribution.[271]

[iii] **Residual transfer after a pecuniary payment.** A separate set of rules is used for valuing the denominator of the applicable fraction with respect to a residual transfer of property that occurs after the satisfaction of a pecuniary bequest.[272] Valuation of the residual property depends on whether the

---

[269] Reg. § 26.2642-2(b)(2)(i)(B).

[270] Section 2032A valuation of qualified real property is permitted for generation-skipping transfer tax purposes if the recapture agreement filed pursuant to Section 2032A(d)(2) specifically provides for the signatories' consent to the imposition of, and personal liability for, additional generation-skipping transfer tax in the event of the imposition of additional estate tax under Section 2032A(c). Reg. § 26.2642-2(b)(1). See ¶ 18.03[1].

[271] In making a distribution that is fairly representative of the net appreciation or depreciation in the value of available property on the date of distribution, the question is whether the executor must also make a distribution that is fairly representative of assets valued at their fair market value on the decedent's death as well as assets available for distribution valued under Section 2032A. The regulations are silent on this issue but ultimately may require distribution of a mix of assets valued under Sections 2032A and 2031.

[272] Reg. § 26.2642-2(b)(3).

pecuniary amount is satisfied with cash or in kind.[273] If the pecuniary amount is satisfied with cash that either carries appropriate interest[274] or is deemed to carry appropriate interest,[275] the denominator of the applicable fraction with respect to a residual transfer is the estate tax value of the assets available to satisfy the pecuniary payment reduced by the pecuniary amount.[276] If the pecuniary cash payment does not carry appropriate interest and is not deemed to carry it, time value of money concepts come into play. The estate tax value of the assets available to satisfy the pecuniary amount is reduced by the present value of the pecuniary payment at the transferor's death in the determination of the denominator of the applicable fraction, thereby increasing the valuation of the residual transfer.[277] This present value reduction with respect

---

[273] See Reg. §§ 26.2642-2(b)(3)(i), 26.2642-2(b)(3)(ii).

[274] Reg. § 26.2642-2(b)(4)(i). Appropriate interest has two components, time and rate. The time element requires payment of interest for the period commencing with either the transferor's date of death or the date specified under applicable state law requiring the payment of interest on pecuniary bequests, and ending with the date of payment. Id. The appropriate rate of interest must fall within a limited range. The rate must at least equal the statutory rate of interest applicable to pecuniary bequests under the law of the state governing the administration. Reg. § 26.2642-2(b)(4)(i)(A)(1). If there is no applicable state rate, the lowest rate is 80 percent of the Section 7520 rate in effect at the death of the transferor. Reg. § 26.2642-2(b)(4)(i)(A)(2). The rate may not exceed the greater of the statutory rate applicable to pecuniary bequests under the law of the state governing the administration or 120 percent of the applicable Section 7520 rate in effect at the date of the transferor's death. Reg. § 26.2642-2(b)(4)(i)(B).

[275] Reg. § 26.2642-2(b)(4)(ii). A pecuniary payment not carrying appropriate interest is deemed to carry appropriate interest to the extent that (1) within fifteen months after the transferor's death, the entire payment is made or property is irrevocably set aside to satisfy the pecuniary payment (Reg. § 26.2642-2(b)(4)(ii)(A)) or (2) the governing instrument or applicable local law specifically requires allocation to the pecuniary payment of a pro rata share of the income earned by the estate or trust between the date of the transferor's death and date of payment (Reg. § 26.2642-2(b)(4)(ii)(B)). A payment is treated as "set aside" if the amount is segregated and held in a separate account pending distribution. Id.

[276] Reg. § 26.2642-2(b)(3)(i).

[277] Reg. § 26.2642-2(b)(3)(i). The present value of the pecuniary payment at the transferor's death is determined by discounting the pecuniary payment by the applicable Section 7520 rate at the date of the transferor's death for the period of time elapsing between the date of the transferor's death and the date of the pecuniary payment. Id.

For example, assume a transferor's will provided a specific bequest of $100,000 to a sibling that was paid exactly three years after the transferor's death and neither the will nor state law provided for this bequest to bear interest or receive a pro rata share of estate income. Assume further that the transferor died when the applicable Section 7520 rate was 8.4 percent. The Section 7520 interest rate is "compounded annually, for purposes of section 1274(d)(1)" (Reg. § 20.7520-1(b)(1)) and, seemingly, should be compounded annually for purposes of this computation in the absence of directions to compound other than annually. Assuming annual compounding, this bequest would have a present value at the transferor's death of $78,507.68. The $21,492.32 difference would be treated as value

to a cash pecuniary payment may be easily avoided by making the entire pecuniary payment, or irrevocably setting aside the property with which to make the entire payment, within fifteen months after the transferor's death.[278]

If the pecuniary amount is satisfied with assets other than cash, the property involved in the residual transfer may be valued at its estate tax value for purposes of determining the denominator of the applicable fraction[279] only if (1) the property used to satisfy the preceding pecuniary amount must be valued on its date of distribution[280] or (2) the pecuniary amount must be satisfied with assets valued at a date other than the date of distribution that fairly reflect the net appreciation and depreciation between the valuation and distribution dates of all assets available to satisfy the pecuniary payment.[281] If the property used to satisfy the pecuniary payment in kind is not valued in one of these two ways, and there is a residual transfer of assets following the pecuniary payment in kind, the residual transfer of assets is valued on the date of distribution in the determination of the denominator of the applicable fraction.[282]

[e] Qualified Terminable Interest Property

Qualified terminable interest property (QTIP) not consumed by the recipient spouse either will have been disposed of in an inter vivos disposition by the recipient spouse and subjected to the gift tax[283] or will be included in the recipient spouse's gross estate.[284] When qualified terminable interest property is subjected to tax under Chapter 11 or Chapter 12, the recipient spouse generally becomes the Chapter 13 transferor of the property, supplanting the donor or decedent spouse.[285] However, a Section 2652(a)(3) "reverse QTIP" election may be made by the donor spouse or the donor spouse's estate to prevent the recipient spouse from becoming the Chapter 13 transferor of property by virtue of Section 2044, Section 2519, or Section 2207A subjecting the property to the

---

added to the residue of the estate and to the denominator of the applicable fraction of the residual transfer.

[278] This results in the pecuniary payment being deemed to carry appropriate interest. Reg. § 26.2642-2(b)(4)(ii)(A). In some states, if the will is silent on the matter, a pecuniary bequest in trust is entitled to a proportionate share of estate income, whereas a pecuniary bequest not in trust does not share proportionately in estate income. See, e.g., Fla. Stat. Chapter 738.05(2)(b) (2001).

[279] Reg. § 26.2642-2(b)(3)(ii). Cf. Reg. § 26.2642-2(b)(3)(i).

[280] Reg. § 26.2642-2(b)(3)(ii)(A).

[281] Reg. § 26.2642-2(b)(3)(ii)(B).

[282] Reg. § 26.2642-2(b)(3)(ii).

[283] IRC §§ 2519, 2511. See ¶ 10.08.

[284] IRC § 2044, discussed at ¶ 4.16. See also IRC § 2036(a)(1); Reg. §§ 25.2519-1(a), 25.2519-1(g) Ex. 4.

[285] IRC § 2652(a)(1). See Reg. § 26.2652-2(d) Ex. 3.

tax imposed by Chapter 11 or Chapter 12.[286] If the election is made, the transferor spouse generally continues as the Chapter 13 transferor of the property.[287]

If no Section 2652(a)(3) election is made and if the recipient spouse makes an inter vivos transfer of all or a portion of the qualifying income interest, under Section 2519, the recipient spouse is treated as making a transfer of all the interests in the property other than the qualifying income interest.[288] If the transfer of property is a transfer of property by gift, the recipient spouse is treated as the transferor of both interests for Chapter 13 purposes.[289] The valuation rules generally applicable to inter vivos transfers will apply in determining any inclusion ratio.[290]

If no Section 2652(a)(3) election is made and no Section 2519 transfer is made, the qualified terminable interest property is included in the recipient spouse's gross estate under Section 2044. The recipient spouse again becomes the Chapter 13 transferor of the property.[291] The estate tax valuation of the

---

[286] See ¶ 17.02[1][c][i]; Reg. §§ 26.2652-1(a)(3), 26.2652-2(a), 26.2652-2(d) Ex. 1.

[287] Reg. § 26.2652-2(d) Ex. 1. The election does not prevent the surviving spouse from becoming the Chapter 13 transferor of the qualifying income interest for life. See supra text following note 294. See also ¶ 17.02[1][c] note 48.

[288] For gift tax purposes, if the recipient spouse makes a gift transfer of only a portion of the income interest and the remainder in the property passes to a family member, Section 2702 applies and increases the amount of the Section 2519 transfer. Reg. § 25.2519-1(a). See Reg. § 25.2519-1(g) Ex. 4; ¶ 10.08 text accompanying note 14. As a result, for gift tax purposes, the full value of the corpus is transferred by the recipient spouse, consisting of a Section 2511 transfer of the portion of the income interest actually transferred and a Section 2519 transfer of the remaining income and the entire remainder. With respect to the portion of the income that the recipient spouse actually transfers under Section 2511, there is a transfer of that portion of the corpus and the spouse may allocate GST exemption to that portion of the corpus. As to the remaining portion, although there is a Section 2519 gift transfer of the remaining value of the corpus, there is no direct skip because the remainder interest is not a Section 2652(c) interest in property held in trust. See ¶ 19.03[4][e] text accompanying notes 373–376. With respect to the portion of the qualified remainder interest property in which the recipient spouse retains an income interest, the Treasury contends that portion of the property is potentially includible in the recipient spouse's gross estate under Section 2036. Reg. §§ 25.2519-1(a), 25.2519-1(g) Ex. 4. See ¶ 10.08 text accompanying note 15. If this contention is correct, the effect of any allocation of GST exemption to that portion of the transfer by the recipient spouse is postponed until the end of the estate tax inclusion period. IRC § 2642(f). See supra ¶ 16.02[7], ¶ 17.02[1][c] note 48. If Section 2036 is inapplicable, there has been a Section 2519 transfer of that portion of the corpus, the recipient spouse could allocate GST exemption, and the only issue is whether the interest valued under Section 2702 at zero increases the value of the corpus transferred with respect to which the recipient spouse may allocate GST exemption. See ¶ 19.03[4][e][iii].

[289] IRC § 2652(a)(1)(B). The recipient spouse is the donor of property subject to tax under Chapter 12.

[290] IRC §§ 2642(b)(1), 2642(b)(3), discussed supra ¶ 16.02[4][a]; IRC § 2642(f), discussed supra ¶ 16.02[4][b], infra ¶ 16.02[7].

[291] IRC § 2652(a)(1)(A). See Reg. § 26.2652-2(d) Ex. 3.

property in the recipient spouse's gross estate is used in the computation of that spouse's inclusion ratio for the property.[292] Any allocation of the recipient spouse's GST exemption to the property is effective upon the death of the recipient spouse.[293]

If, instead, a Section 2652(a)(3) election is made to treat the property as if it were not qualified terminable interest property for purposes of Chapter 13, the recipient spouse generally will not become the Chapter 13 transferor of the property. The transferor spouse generally remains as the Chapter 13 transferor of the property, and the inter vivos or testamentary valuation rules generally applicable to the transferor apply.[294] However, even if a Section 2652(a)(3) election is made, the recipient spouse actually owns the qualifying income interest. If the recipient spouse makes a gift of all or a part of the qualifying income interest, the recipient spouse is treated as transferring that interest in property and will become the Chapter 13 transferor of that property interest or the portion thereof.[295] The time of valuation and the effective date of the GST exemption allocation in the computation of the applicable fraction will be de-

---

[292] IRC § 2642(b)(4). Although the language "as finally determined" added to Section 2642(b)(2)(A) was not added to Section 2642(b)(4), that language should be added by a technical amendment or by regulations. See supra ¶ 16.02[4][d] text accompanying note 251.

The time of valuation may be the date of death under Section 2031 or the alternate valuation date under Section 2032. The method of valuation used will be either fair market value under Section 2031 or special-use valuation under Section 2032A in the case of qualified real property. Section 2642(b)(4) clearly mandates that the value of the property for purposes of Section 2642(a) that is included in a decedent's estate under Section 2044 "shall be its value for purposes of [C]hapter 11 in the estate of such spouse." The regulations governing valuation of property transferred at death for purposes of determining the inclusion ratio generally restrict the use of Section 2032A valuation of property for generation-skipping transfer tax purposes to those instances where the recapture agreement described in Section 2032A(d)(2) specifically provides for the signatories' consent to the imposition of, and liability for, additional generation-skipping transfer tax in the event that additional estate tax is imposed under Section 2032A(c). Reg. § 26.2642-2(b)(1). See supra ¶ 16.02[4][d] text accompanying note 255; ¶ 18.03[1]. Section 2642(b)(2)(A) provides that the value of property as finally determined for purposes of Chapter 11 is to be used in determining the inclusion ratio, except that if certain requirements regarding postdeath changes in value are not met, the property is to be valued at the date of distribution. Section 2642(b)(4) is devoid of any reference to the possibility of date-of-distribution valuation of property included in a decedent's gross estate under Section 2044, but it should incorporate the rules of Section 2642(b)(2)(A).

Valuation of property at the date of distribution in the determination of the inclusion ratio is discussed supra ¶¶ 16.02[4][d][ii], 16.02[4][d][iii].

[293] See IRC § 2642(b)(2)(B).

[294] IRC § 2652(a)(1). The applicable valuation rules depend on the transferor's use of GST exemption. See supra ¶¶ 16.02[4][a]–16.02[4][d].

[295] A transfer of the qualifying income interest to a grandchild would constitute a direct skip of such property with the recipient spouse as the Chapter 13 transferor. IRC § 2612(c)(1). See supra ¶ 16.02[2][b] note 45; ¶ 17.02[1][c] note 48.

termined for an inter vivos transfer of the recipient spouse's qualifying income interest under the rules generally applicable to inter vivos transfers.[296]

[f] Charitable Lead Annuity Trust Rule

A special valuation rule applies to charitable lead annuity trusts.[297] Under the rule, valuation of the property for purposes of determining the inclusion ratio is postponed until the termination of the charitable lead interest.[298] In addition, the amount of the GST exemption allocated to the transfer is adjusted.[299]

[5] Redetermination of the Applicable Fraction

[a] In General

After an initial determination of the applicable fraction,[300] subsequent events may occur that require a redetermination of the fraction.[301] A redetermination of the applicable fraction is required if additional GST exemption is allocated to property held in trust,[302] additional property is transferred to the trust,[303] or separate trusts are consolidated.[304] A redetermination may be necessary if generation-skipping transfer tax is imposed on a generation-skipping transfer from the trust,[305] if a single trust is severed,[306] or if additional estate tax is imposed under Section 2032A.[307] The redetermined applicable fraction is used to determine the rate of tax on subsequent generation-skipping transfers from the trust and may be used to redetermine the tax imposed on prior gener-

---

[296] See IRC §§ 2642(b)(1), discussed supra ¶ 16.02[4][a]; 2642(b)(3), discussed supra ¶ 16.02[4][c]; 2642(f), discussed supra ¶ 16.02[4][b], infra ¶ 16.02[7].

[297] IRC § 2642(e). The rule is discussed infra ¶ 16.02[6].

[298] IRC § 2642(e)(1)(B).

[299] IRC § 2642(e)(1)(A).

[300] IRC § 2642(a)(2).

[301] IRC §§ 2642(d), 2642(e)(4), 2642(f)(5); Reg. § 26.2642-4.

[302] IRC § 2642(d)(4); Reg. § 26.2642-4(a). See infra ¶¶ 16.02[5][b][i], 16.02[5][b][iii]. See also Reg. § 26.2642-4(a)(3); infra ¶ 16.02[7].

[303] IRC § 2642(d)(1); Reg. § 26.2642-4(a)(1). See infra ¶¶ 16.02[5][b][ii], 16.02[5][b][iii].

[304] Reg. § 26.2642-4(a)(2). See infra ¶ 16.02[5][c].

[305] IRC § 2653(b)(1). See infra ¶ 16.02[5][d]. See also ¶ 17.03[2][a].

[306] IRC § 2642(a)(3). See infra ¶ 16.02[5][e]. The severance of a single trust with an inclusion ratio of one or zero will not require a redetermination of the applicable fraction because the resulting trusts created upon the severance will have the same applicable fraction and inclusion ratio as the trust that was severed.

[307] Reg. § 26.2642-4(a)(4). See infra ¶ 16.02[5][f]. See also ¶ 18.03[1].

ation-skipping transfers.[308] The mechanics of the recomputation vary depending on the event necessitating the recomputation.

[b] Additional Exemption Allocations and Transfers to a Trust

Whenever an additional GST exemption allocated to a trust becomes effective or additional property is transferred to a trust, a recomputation of the applicable fraction is required.[309] The recomputed applicable fraction is used to determine the inclusion ratio,[310] which, in turn, is used to establish the applicable rate[311] of tax imposed on subsequent generation-skipping transfers from the trust.

[i] **Additional exemption allocations.** The applicable fraction and resulting inclusion ratio must be recomputed whenever an additional GST exemption allocated to the property held in trust becomes effective.[312] The numerator and denominator of the recomputed applicable fraction must reflect both the value of the property in the trust immediately before the subsequent allocation is effective and the extent to which the property held in trust is already covered by a previous effective GST exemption allocation.

The numerator of the recomputed applicable fraction is the sum of the amount of additional GST exemption allocated to the trust[313] and the "nontax portion" of the trust immediately before the additional allocation of GST exemption is effective.[314] The "nontax portion" is the product of the applicable fraction in effect for the trust immediately before the allocation of additional GST exemption[315] and the fair market value of trust assets immediately prior to the time the additional allocation of GST exemption is effective, adjusted for any charitable deduction allowed under Section 2055, Section 2106, or Section 2522 with respect to any transfer to the trust and for any unpaid federal estate and state death taxes incurred.[316] The nontax portion fluctuates in amount with

---

[308] See infra ¶ 16.02[5][f] text accompanying note 394 for a situation in which the tax imposed on prior generation-skipping transfers is redetermined.

[309] IRC §§ 2642(d)(1), 2642(d)(4).

[310] IRC § 2642(a). The inclusion ratio is one minus the applicable fraction. IRC § 2642(a)(1).

[311] IRC § 2641(a).

[312] IRC § 2642(d)(4); Reg. § 26.2632-1.

[313] IRC § 2642(d)(2)(A)(i).

[314] IRC § 2642(d)(2)(A)(ii).

[315] IRC § 2642(d)(3)(B).

[316] IRC § 2642(d)(3)(A). Section 2642(d)(3) provides that the nontax portion is the product of the applicable fraction and "the value of all of the property in the trust." The regulations simply provide that in determining the nontax portion, the applicable fraction is to be multiplied by the "value of the trust assets." Reg. § 26.2642-4(a). However, the

value of the property in the trust, the trust assets, must reflect the amount of any charitable deduction allowed under Section 2055, Section 2106, or Section 2522 with respect to any transfer to the trust. This conclusion is based on the fact that, in the initial determination of the denominator of the applicable fraction, the value of the property transferred to the trust is reduced by any charitable deduction allowed under Section 2055, Section 2106, or Section 2522. IRC § 2642(a)(2)(B)(ii)(II). See Reg. § 26.2642-1(c)(1)(ii).

An example will demonstrate the need for this adjustment in the determination of the nontax portion. Assume that Transferor establishes a charitable remainder trust with a transfer of $100,000. The trust instrument provides an annuity to grandchild for life, remainder to charity. The remainder qualifies for a charitable deduction. IRC § 2522(c)(2). Cf. IRC §§ 2055(e)(2), 2106(a)(2)(E). If the annuity interest and the charitable remainder are valued at $80,000 and $20,000, respectively, and $40,000 of GST exemption is allocated in a timely manner to the trust, the initial applicable fraction would be 0.500. The numerator of the fraction would be $40,000, the GST exemption allocated to the trust. The denominator would be $80,000, the value of the property held in the trust, $100,000, reduced by the charitable deduction allowed, $20,000. IRC § 2642(a)(2)(B)(ii)(II); Reg. § 26.2642-1(c)(1)(ii). Assume that the Transferor allocates an additional $40,000 of GST exemption to the trust within six months of the initial transfer, when the value of the property held in the trust has not changed. If the nontax portion of the numerator of the redetermined applicable fraction is determined by multiplying the applicable fraction, 0.500, by the value of all the assets in the trust, $100,000, the nontax portion is $50,000. The nontax portion, $50,000, when added to the additional GST exemption allocated to the trust, $40,000, yields a numerator of $90,000 for the redetermined applicable fraction. If the denominator is the "value of all of the property in the trust," $100,000, the redetermined applicable fraction would be 0.900. See IRC § 2642(d)(2)(B)(ii). *This is clearly wrong.* If the value of the property held in the trust has not changed, it seems that approximately $80,000 of GST exemption should produce an applicable fraction of one. Even if the denominator of the applicable fraction is reduced by the amount of the charitable deduction, an appropriate result is not reached. If the denominator is reduced by $20,000, the charitable deduction, the redetermined applicable fraction becomes one with an allocation of only an additional $30,000 of GST exemption to the trust. The problem is that if the regulation is followed literally, the nontax portion of the recomputed numerator and the denominator would both be overstated because of the charitable deduction.

The nontax portion must be determined with an adjustment for the charitable deduction allowed for any transfers to the trust. The question then is how to make this adjustment. One solution, possibly the best, is to multiply the fair market value of the property held in the trust at the time the additional allocation of GST exemption is effective by a fraction. The numerator of the fraction is the value of all the property held in the trust at the time the transfer qualifying for a charitable deduction is made to the trust, less the charitable deduction allowed at that time. The denominator of the fraction is the value of all the property held in the trust at the time of the transfer to the trust qualifying for the charitable deduction. If this adjustment is applied to the facts stated above to compensate for the charitable deduction allowed, the nontax portion of the trust would be $40,000, the product of the applicable fraction, 0.500, and the adjusted value of the property, $80,000. The adjusted value of the property is determined by multiplying the fair market value of the property held in the trust at the time of the additional allocation of GST exemption, $100,000, by a fraction, having a numerator of $80,000 ($100,000 − $20,000) and a denominator of $100,000. If the property held in the trust doubled in value to $200,000 between the initial transfer to the trust and the additional GST exemption allocation, the nontax portion would be $80,000. This is the product of the initial applicable fraction,

appreciation or depreciation in the value of the property held in the trust. The denominator of the recomputed applicable fraction is the fair market value of the property at the time the additional allocation is effective,[317] adjusted for any transfers to the trust for which a charitable deduction was allowed and for any unpaid federal estate and state death taxes incurred.[318]

0.500, and the adjusted value of the property held in the trust, $160,000. The adjusted value is determined by multiplying the value of the property held in the trust, $200,000, by the fraction of $80,000 ÷ $100,000.

One problem with this adjustment may be that it does not take into account that the proportionate values of the charitable portion and the noncharitable portion of the trust change over time. Another method of computing the nontax portion in this situation would be to revalue the charitable remainder at the time the additional GST exemption allocation is made, taking into account changes in the value of the trust assets, changes in the annuitant's life expectancy, and any changes in the discount rate. This redetermined value of the charitable remainder could then be subtracted from the current value of the trust assets, which would result in the current value of the annuity. The current value of the annuity could then be multiplied by the original applicable fraction, producing the current nontax portion of the trust.

The initial suggested adjustment is certainly much simpler than recomputing the amount of trust property passing to charity at the point in time when additional GST exemption is allocated to the trust and the applicable fraction redetermined. Regulations that address this issue hopefully will be promulgated soon.

In the foregoing example, it is assumed that any state death or federal estate taxes attributed to the property transferred to the trust have been discharged, thereby eliminating the necessity for a downward adjustment in the value of trust assets in the determination of the nontax portion. Admittedly, such an adjustment is possible; it is just not very likely. However, if the value of the property held in the trust was reduced for federal estate tax or state death taxes in the determination of the initial applicable fraction and those taxes are yet to be paid at the time of the determination of the nontax portion, the value of the property held in the trust must be reduced by the unpaid death and estate taxes to be paid in the determination of the nontax portion.

[317] Generally, when additional GST exemption is allocated by a transferor to an inter vivos transfer of property held in trust, it is considered a late allocation and is effective on the date the gift tax return containing the additional GST exemption allocation is filed. See ¶ 15.03[2]. When there is a retroactive allocation of GST exemption under Section 2632(d) it is generally effective immediately before the death of the non−skip person and the property is generally valued at the time the transfer to the trust was complete. See ¶ 15.03[5]. However, if a lifetime allocation of GST exemption is made during the estate tax inclusion period, the allocation is not effective until the close of the estate tax inclusion period. See infra ¶ 16.02[7]. If a late allocation to an inter vivos transfer is made after the death of the transferor by the transferor's executor to property that is not included in the transferor's gross estate, the allocation is effective as of the date it is filed. Reg. § 26.2632-1(d)(1). See ¶ 15.03[6][c].

[318] IRC § 2642(d)(2)(B)(i). See supra note 316 for the reasoning supporting the adjustment for the charitable transfers to the trust and suggested methods of computation of the adjustment. It is assumed that no additional property is transferred to the trust at the time of the allocation of additional GST exemption. For a discussion of the situation where additional property is transferred to the trust and GST exemption is allocated, see infra ¶ 16.02[5][b][iii].

For example, assume transferor T transfers $500,000 of property to a trust[319] and allocates $200,000 of GST exemption to the property in the trust on a timely filed gift tax return. The trust at that time has an applicable fraction of 0.400 ($200,000 ÷ $500,000).[320] When the corpus appreciates in value to $1 million, T allocates $500,000 of additional GST exemption to the trust. A recomputation of the applicable fraction is required to establish the rate of tax to be imposed on future generation-skipping transfers from the trust. The numerator of the recomputed applicable fraction is $900,000, the sum of T's fresh allocation of GST exemption to the trust ($500,000) and the $400,000 nontax portion of the trust immediately before the additional allocation of GST exemption is effective. The nontax portion of $400,000 is the product of the original applicable fraction of 0.400 and the $1 million value of the original corpus of the trust at the time the additional allocation is effective. The denominator of the applicable fraction is $1 million, the value of the trust corpus at the time the additional allocation of GST exemption is effective. Thus, the recomputed applicable fraction for the trust is 0.900 ($900,000 ÷ $1,000,000).

[ii] Additional transfers. After a transfer of property to a trust and once an allocation of a transferor's GST exemption is effective and the applicable fraction established, the transferor might transfer additional property to the trust.[321] When additional property is transferred, a recomputation of the trust's applicable fraction is required[322] on the date the additional transfer is complete.

The numerator of the recomputed applicable fraction is the "nontax portion" of the trust immediately before the transfer.[323] The nontax portion is the product of the fair market value of trust assets immediately prior to the transfer, adjusted for the value of any transfers to the trust for which a charitable deduction was allowed and for any unpaid federal estate and state death taxes incurred,[324] and the applicable fraction in effect for the trust immediately before the additional transfer to the trust.[325] The denominator of the recomputed applicable fraction is the value of the property held in the trust immediately after the transfer, reduced by the federal estate taxes and state death taxes

---

[319] Assume that no part of the transfer to the trust qualifies for a zero inclusion ratio under Section 2642(c) or for a charitable deduction under Section 2055, Section 2106, or Section 2522.

[320] See supra ¶ 16.02[1] note 6.

[321] It is assumed that no additional GST exemption is allocated to the trust at the time the additional property is transferred. For a discussion of the situation where additional property is transferred to the trust and additional GST exemption is allocated, see infra ¶ 16.02[5][b][iii].

[322] IRC § 2642(d)(1).

[323] IRC § 2642(d)(2)(A)(ii).

[324] See supra note 316.

[325] IRC § 2642(d)(3).

attributable to transfers to the trust to be paid from trust assets and the amount of any charitable deductions allowed for transfers to the trust.[326]

For example, assume transferor T initially transferred $500,000 of property to a trust[327] and allocated $200,000 of GST exemption to the property in the trust. The trust at that time has an applicable fraction of 0.400 ($200,000 ÷ $500,000). When the original corpus appreciates in value to $1 million, T transfers additional property valued at $1 million to the trust.[328] A recomputation of the applicable fraction is required[329] to establish the rate of tax to be imposed on future generation-skipping transfers from the trust. The numerator of the recomputed applicable fraction is the nontax portion of the trust, $400,000 (0.400 × $1 million). The numerator remains $400,000 because there was no additional GST exemption allocation. The denominator of the recomputed applicable fraction is $2 million, the current value of the initial transfer, $1 million, plus the $1 million corpus addition. The recomputed applicable fraction is 0.200 ($400,000 ÷ $2 million).

[iii] **Additional transfers and exemption allocations.** The applicable fraction is redetermined on the date additional GST exemption allocated to the property held in trust is effective,[330] or on the date a transfer of additional property to the trust is complete.[331] Generally, the effective date of a lifetime allocation by the transferor of GST exemption to the property held in trust is the date the property transferred to the trust is complete if the allocation is made on a timely filed federal gift tax return.[332] If the lifetime allocation by the transferor is not made on a timely filed federal gift tax return, it is considered a late allocation and it is effective on the date it is filed.[333] Thus, the property held in the trust may be valued on either of two dates in the redetermination of the applicable fraction, depending on whether the allocation is timely or late. A timely allocation of GST exemption may be made in year 2 for a transfer to a trust that occurred in year 1 after another transfer of prop-

---

[326] IRC § 2642(d)(2)(B). See supra note 316.

[327] It is assumed that no part of this transfer qualified for a charitable deduction under Section 2055, Section 2106, or Section 2522.

[328] It is assumed that no part of the additional transfer to the trust qualified for a charitable deduction under Section 2055, Section 2106, or Section 2522, or that any federal estate or any state death tax is chargeable to the trust by reason of the transfer that necessitates an adjustment to the denominator of the redetermined applicable fraction. IRC § 2642(d)(2)(B).

[329] IRC § 2642(d)(1).

[330] IRC § 2642(d)(4).

[331] IRC § 2642(d)(1).

[332] Reg. § 26.2632-1(b)(2)(ii)(A)(1). However, if the allocation of GST exemption is made during the estate tax inclusion period, the allocation is not effective until the close of the estate tax inclusion period. See infra ¶ 16.02[7].

[333] Reg. § 26.2632-1(b)(2)(ii)(A)(1).

erty has already been made to the trust in year 2, which is to be reported on a gift tax return in year 3.[334] The transfer to be reported in year 3 is referred to as an undisclosed transfer.[335] A timely allocation of GST exemption when there is an undisclosed transfer may result in an early allocation of GST exemption. Generally,[336] an allocation of GST exemption is void to the extent that on the effective date of the allocation the GST exemption allocated, when combined with the nontax amount, if any, exceeds the value of the property held in the trust.[337] A lifetime allocation of GST exemption combined with multiple transfers of property to a trust may result in an allocation of GST exemption to the property held in trust that is early, timely, late, and excessive.

When it is unclear whether an allocation of GST exemption on a timely filed federal gift tax return is early, timely, or late, the allocation is effective first as a timely allocation to any transfer disclosed on a timely filed return, next as a late allocation to assets held in the trust, then to undisclosed transfers to which the return filed would be timely.[338] Once the applicable fraction reaches one, any excess allocation of GST exemption is void.[339]

For an example involving an additional transfer to a trust and the allocation of additional GST exemption to the trust on the gift tax return reporting the transfer, assume transferor T established a trust with income to child for life and the remainder to grandchild. T originally funded the trust with $500,000 and initially allocated $200,000 of GST exemption to the trust on a timely filed gift tax return. The trust at that time has an applicable fraction of 0.400 ($200,000 ÷ $500,000). Further assume that the trust corpus appreciates in value to $1 million when T transfers an additional $1 million to the trust and that T allocates an additional $500,000 of GST exemption to the trust on a timely filed gift tax return. The numerator of the recomputed applicable fraction is the nontax portion of the trust, $400,000 (0.400 × $1 million), plus $500,000, the additional GST exemption allocated, or $900,000. The denominator of the applicable fraction is the fair market value of the corpus after the addition, $2 million. Thus, the recomputed applicable fraction is 0.450 ($900,000 ÷ $2 million).

To illustrate the allocation rule when it is unclear whether the GST exemption allocation is early, timely, or late, assume that transferor T establishes

---

[334] See Reg. § 26.2632-1(b)(2)(ii)(A)(1)(iii).

[335] See Reg. § 26.2642-4(b) Ex. 4.

[336] The exception to this general rule relates to charitable lead trusts. See Reg. § 26.2642-3, which is discussed infra ¶ 16.02[6].

[337] Reg. § 26.2632-1(b)(2)(i).

[338] Reg. § 26.2632-1(b)(2)(ii)(A)(1) (last sentence).

[339] Reg. § 26.2632-1(b)(2)(i).

an irrevocable trust in year 1 for the benefit of a child and grandchild.[340] The trust is funded with assets valued at $50,000. *T* allocates no GST exemption to the trust on the gift tax return reporting the initial transfer to the trust. On July 1 of year 2, *T* makes a second transfer in the amount of $40,000 to the trust. Immediately after the second transfer, the trust corpus has a fair market value of $100,000.[341] On February 1 of year 3, *T* adds an additional $50,000 to the trust,[342] the third transfer to the trust. Immediately after this third addition to the trust, the trust corpus has a fair market value of $200,000.[343] On April 15 of year 3, *T* files a timely federal gift tax return reporting the $40,000 transfer made on July 1 of year 2 and allocating $150,000 of GST exemption, *T*'s first allocation of GST exemption, to the property held in the trust.[344] On April 15 of year 3, the property held in the trust has a fair market value of $220,000.

The GST exemption allocation is effective first to the July 1 of year 2 transfer disclosed on the timely gift tax return filed on April 15 of year 3.[345] The GST exemption allocation was timely and effective to the extent of $40,000 on July 1 of year 2, the date that transfer was completed. On July 1 of year 2, the effective date, the property held in the trust immediately after the addition had a fair market value of $100,000 and an applicable fraction of 0.400.[346]

The GST exemption allocation made on the gift tax return filed on April 15 of year 3 is effective next as a late allocation to the property held in the trust on April 15 of year 3.[347] The value of the trust assets on that date, ex-

---

[340] The example that follows is borrowed from the regulations. See Reg. § 26.2642-4(b) Exs. 3, 4.

[341] The initial transfer of $50,000 has appreciated to $60,000, and once the additional transfer is complete, the corpus has a value of $100,000.

[342] It is assumed throughout this example that no transfer to the trust results in any federal estate tax or state death tax recovery from the trust.

[343] The trust corpus has appreciated from a value of $100,000 on July 1 of year 2 to $150,000 on February 1 of year 3 when, with the addition of $50,000, the trust corpus has a fair market value on February 1 of year 3 of $200,000.

[344] Whenever GST exemption is allocated to property held in a trust, the exemption applies to the trust, not to specific property transferred to or held in the trust. Reg. § 26.2632-1(a).

[345] Reg. § 26.2632-1(b)(2)(ii)(A)(1)(i).

[346] The numerator of the applicable fraction is $40,000, the amount of the portion of the GST exemption timely allocated, over the fair market value of the property held in the trust immediately after the addition on July 1 of year 2, $100,000, which yields an applicable fraction of 0.400 ($40,000 ÷ $100,000). See Reg. § 26.2642-4(b) Ex. 3(ii).

[347] Reg. § 26.2632-1(b)(2)(ii)(A)(1)(ii). A late allocation is effective on the date the gift tax return containing the GST exemption allocation is filed. Reg. § 26.2632-1(b)(2)(ii)(A)(1).

cluding the February 1 of year 3 transfer of $50,000,[348] must be determined to ascertain the amount of the late allocation of GST exemption and redetermine the applicable fraction. The value of the property held in trust on April 15 of year 3, excluding the February 1 of year 3 transfer, is $165,000.[349] The applicable fraction must be redetermined, treating the portion of the GST exemption allocated to the trust on the federal gift tax return filed on April 15 of year 3, which is considered a late allocation, as a second allocation of GST exemption to the property held in the trust. The numerator of the redetermined applicable fraction is the amount of the late allocation of GST exemption plus the "nontax portion" of the property held in trust on April 15 of year 3. The nontax portion is $66,000, which is determined by multiplying the applicable fraction immediately before the additional allocation, 0.400, by the value of the property held in the trust excluding the undisclosed transfer, $165,000. The nontax portion combined with $99,000 of late allocation of GST exemption yields a numerator of $165,000. The denominator of the redetermined applicable fraction is $165,000, the fair market value of the property held in trust on April 15 of year 3, excluding the undisclosed transfer of $50,000. The redetermined applicable fraction after the late allocation of GST exemption on April 15 of year 3 is one.[350]

T allocated $150,000 of GST exemption to the property held in trust on the gift tax return filed April 15 of year 3. Of this amount, $40,000 was considered a timely allocation and $99,000 was considered a late allocation, which leaves $11,000 remaining. This $11,000 is effective to the $50,000 undisclosed transfer to the trust, a transfer not disclosed on the April 15 of year 3 federal gift tax return.[351] Since the allocation is considered timely, it is effective on the date the $50,000 undisclosed transfer is complete, February 1 of year 3,[352] and

---

[348] The transfer on February 1 of year 3 must be excluded because that transfer is an "undisclosed transfer" that is to be reported on a gift tax return due April 15 of year 4. If a timely return is filed by April 15 of year 4, an allocation of GST exemption made with that return is timely and is effective February 1 of year 3, the date of the $50,000 transfer. If the undisclosed transfer were not excluded, the GST exemption allocation in excess of $40,000 would violate the ordering rule contained in the last sentence of Regulations Section 26.2632-1(b)(2)(ii)(A)(1).

[349] This amount, $165,000, is determined by multiplying the fair market value of the property held in trust on April 15 of year 3, $220,000, by a fraction that has as its numerator the fair market value of the trust assets on February 1 of year 3 immediately before the addition, $150,000, and as its denominator the fair market value of the trust assets on February 1 of year 3 immediately after the addition, $200,000 ($150,000 ÷ $200,000 × $220,000 = $165,000).

[350] If the applicable fraction is one, the inclusion ratio and rate of tax imposed on generation-skipping transfers from the trust are both zero. See Reg. § 26.2642-4(b) Ex. 4(ii).

[351] Reg. § 26.2632-1(b)(ii)(A)(1)(iii).

[352] Reg. § 26.2642-4(b) Exs. 4(i), 4(iii).

the applicable fraction must be redetermined on that date. On February 1 of year 3, the property held in the trust had a fair market value of $150,000 before the third addition in the amount of $50,000, the undisclosed transfer. The nontax portion of the trust prior to the third addition is the applicable fraction of 0.400 times the fair market value of the property held in trust immediately before the third addition, $150,000, or $60,000. This amount plus the remaining GST exemption, $11,000, yields the numerator of the redetermined applicable fraction on February 1 of year 3, $71,000. The denominator of the redetermined applicable fraction is the fair market value of the property held in the trust immediately after the third addition, $200,000. The redetermined applicable fraction on February 1 of year 3 is 0.355 ($71,000 ÷ $200,000).[353]

The redetermined applicable fraction of the property held in trust on April 15 of year 3 has as its numerator the nontax portion of $78,100 (0.355 × $220,000) and the $99,000 late allocation, which total $177,100. The denominator of the redetermined applicable fraction is $220,000, the fair market value of the property held in the trust on April 15 of year 3. The redetermined applicable fraction on April 15 of year 3 is 0.805 ($177,100 ÷ $220,000).[354]

Assuming alternatively that T allocates $200,000 of GST exemption to the trust on the federal gift tax return filed on April 15 of year 3, $40,000 is considered a timely allocation on July 1 of year 2, $99,000 is considered a late allocation on April 15 of year 3, $50,000 a timely allocation to an undisclosed transfer[355] on February 1 of year 3, and the remaining $11,000 a void excessive allocation of GST exemption.[356]

---

[353] Reg. § 26.2642-4(b) Ex. 4(iii).

[354] See Reg. § 26.2642-4(b) Ex. 4(iv).

[355] A GST exemption of $61,000 ($200,000 less $40,000 and $99,000) is available for any undisclosed transfers to the trust on the date the federal gift tax return is filed. Since the allocation of GST exemption to the undisclosed transfer is a timely allocation, it is effective on the date the undisclosed transfer is made, February 1 of year 3, and results in the allocation of an additional $50,000 of GST exemption to the property held in the trust.

The redetermined applicable fraction on February 1 of year 3 is 0.550. The numerator of this redetermined applicable fraction is $110,000. This is the total of the nontax portion of the property held in the trust, $60,000 (0.400 × $150,000), determined immediately before the $50,000 addition on February 1 of year 3, the undisclosed transfer, plus the additional GST exemption timely allocated on the April 15 of year 3 gift tax return to the undisclosed transfer, $50,000. The denominator of the applicable fraction is the fair market value of the property held in the trust immediately after the February 1 of year 3 addition, $200,000.

[356] Reg. § 26.2632-1(b)(2)(i). The allocation of GST exemption to this trust is void to the extent the amount allocated exceeds the amount necessary to obtain an inclusion ratio of zero with respect to the trust. Thus, once the applicable fraction of this trust is one (the numerator equals the denominator of the applicable fraction), any additional allocation of GST exemption is void.

[c] Consolidation of Separate Trusts

If a transferor creates separate trusts that are consolidated, a single applicable fraction must be determined for the consolidated trust.[357] The numerator of the applicable fraction of the consolidated trust is the sum of the nontax portions of each of the trusts immediately prior to consolidation. The nontax portion of each trust is determined by multiplying the applicable fraction of the

---

The redetermined applicable fraction on April 15 of year 3 is one, which results in an inclusion ratio of zero and a void allocation of $11,000. The numerator of the redetermined applicable fraction on April 15 of year 3 is the nontax portion on that date, $121,000 (0.550 × $220,000) plus the late allocation of GST exemption, $99,000, for a total of $220,000. The denominator of the redetermined applicable fraction is $220,000, the fair market value of the property held in trust on April 15 of year 3.

In summary, T allocated $200,000 of GST exemption to the property held in the trust on the federal gift tax return filed April 15 of year 3. Of this amount, $40,000 was considered effective July 1 of year 2, $50,000 was considered effective February 1 of year 3, $99,000 was considered effective April 15 of year 3, and $11,000 was a void allocation of GST exemption.

[357] Reg. § 26.2642-4(a)(2). See Priv. Ltr. Rul. 9801026 (Sept. 30, 1997) (distribution from one trust to another, both with zero inclusion ratios, created by the same transferor to facilitate payment of life insurance premiums viewed as consolidation of separate trusts with zero inclusion ratios).

trust by the fair market value[358] of the trust corpus[359] immediately prior to the

---

[358] Even if the trust contains real property that was valued under Section 2032A for generation-skipping transfer tax purposes and that value was used in the denominator of the initial applicable fraction, in the determination of the nontax portion in the redetermination of the applicable fraction, the fair market value of the property held in the trust should be used. Compare Reg. § 26.2642-4(a)(1) with Reg. § 26.2642-2(b)(1).

If the real property is subsequently subjected to additional estate tax under Section 2032A(c) after the trust consolidation, the applicable fraction of the trust containing the real property valued under Section 2032A must be recomputed as of the date of the transferor's death and the consolidated redetermined applicable fraction recalculated. See Reg. § 26.2642-4(a)(4); supra ¶ 16.02[4][d] note 255; infra ¶ 16.02[5][f].

For example, assume that Trust A and Trust B are to be consolidated. Trust A was funded with property worth $300,000 and valued at $200,000 under Section 2032A for generation-skipping transfer tax purposes. Trust A was allocated $200,000 of GST exemption and has an applicable fraction of one and a zero inclusion ratio. Trust B was funded with $100,000 of property not valued under Section 2032A for estate tax purposes, and $50,000 of GST exemption was allocated to Trust B, resulting in an applicable fraction of 0.500. The assets held in Trust A and Trust B have appreciated to $600,000 and $400,000, respectively. The nontax portion of Trust A at the time of consolidation is computed using the fair market value of the property at that time (see Reg. § 26.2642-2(b)(1)), which is $600,000 (the applicable fraction of 1 × $600,000). The nontax portion of Trust B is $200,000 (the applicable fraction of 0.500 × $400,000). The redetermined applicable fraction is then 0.800 ($600,000 + $200,000 ÷ $1 million). The $200,000 of value that is not covered by a GST exemption is the initial $50,000 of property in Trust B, which has appreciated to $200,000. If additional estate tax is imposed under Section 2032A with respect to the property held in Trust A, the applicable fraction for Trust A must be recomputed as of the date of the transferor's death, which would also require a recomputation of the determination of the consolidated trust's applicable fraction using Trust A's recomputed applicable fraction. See Reg. § 26.2642-4(a)(4); infra ¶ 16.02[5][f].

[359] The trust corpus must be adjusted for the amount of any charitable deduction allowed under Section 2055, Section 2106, or Section 2522 on the transfer to the trust that resulted in a reduction of the denominator used in the computation of the applicable fraction of the trust prior to consolidation. The reason for this adjustment is discussed supra ¶ 16.02[5][b] note 316.

For example, assume transferor T transferred $60,000 to Trust A and $80,000 to Trust B, and assume both are charitable remainder unitrusts. The lead beneficiary of each trust is T's grandchild, GC. Assume that the value of the charitable remainder for which a deduction is allowed under Section 2522 is $20,000 for Trust A and $40,000 for Trust B. The value of GC's lead interest is $40,000 in each of the trusts. T allocates $40,000 of GST exemption to Trust A and $20,000 of GST exemption to Trust B. The applicable fraction is 1.000 for Trust A and 0.500 for Trust B. The numerator of the applicable fraction for Trust A is $40,000, and the denominator is $60,000 minus $20,000, or $40,000. The numerator of the applicable fraction for Trust B is $20,000, and the denominator is $40,000 ($80,000 − $40,000). Assume further that these two trusts are consolidated after the property held in each has doubled in value. If the nontax portion is determined by merely multiplying the applicable fraction times the value of the trust principal, the nontax portion would be $120,000 for Trust A and $80,000 for Trust B. This would produce a redetermined applicable fraction for the consolidated trust of 0.714 ($200,000 ÷ $280,000).

If the two trusts had been consolidated upon formation and the same amount of GST exemption had been allocated, the applicable fraction would have been 0.750, $60,000

consolidation. The denominator of the redetermined applicable fraction of the consolidated trust generally is the fair market value of the property held in the consolidated trust.[360]

[d] Tax Imposed on Generation-Skipping Transfer

Unless a trust has an inclusion ratio of zero or one, a recomputation of the applicable fraction and the resulting inclusion ratio must also be made when there is a taxable termination of property in a trust, the generation-skipping transfer tax on the taxable termination is borne by the trust, *and* the trust continues with its original transferor.[361] Upon the taxable termination, the trust

---

($40,000 + $20,000) ÷ $80,000 ($60,000 − $20,000 + $80,000 − $40,000). If an adjustment is made to the value of the property held in the trusts in the determination of the nontax portion for the value of the charitable deduction allowed in the determination of the initial applicable fraction, the resulting redetermined applicable fraction is the same as if the trusts had been consolidated at inception. In determining the nontax portion of the value of the property held in each trust, the value of the property should be reduced by an amount that bears the same proportion to the value of the trust property at the time of the determination of the nontax portion as the charitable deduction allowed bore to the value of the property held in trust at the time the applicable fraction was computed. If this adjustment is made to the value of the property held in each trust for the charitable deduction allowed in the transfer of property to the trust, in determining the nontax portion of each trust, the nontax portion will be $120,000 (1.000 × [$120,000 − $40,000] + 0.500 × [$160,000 − $80,000]). If the values of trust assets used in the determination of the nontax portion are also used as the denominator of the applicable fraction, the consolidated trust will have a redetermined applicable fraction of 0.750.

Additionally, in the determination of the denominator of the applicable fraction, if a reduction was made for federal estate or state death taxes and those taxes have not been paid at the time of the consolidation, the principal of the trust must be reduced by the accrued but unpaid taxes in the determination of the nontax portion.

[360] The value of the trust property used as the denominator in the recomputed applicable fraction for the consolidated trust must be adjusted if a charitable deduction was allowed under Section 2055, Section 2106, or Section 2522 on the transfer to the trust. Any charitable deduction that was allowed would have resulted in a reduction of the denominator used in the computation of the applicable fraction of the trust prior to consolidation. The adjustment made in the denominator should be the same as that made to the value of the property held in the trust in the determination of the nontax portion. See supra note 359.

If a reduction was made in the determination of the denominator of the applicable fraction for federal estate and state death taxes that have not been paid at the time of the consolidation, the value of the consolidated trust property must be reduced in determining the denominator of the redetermined applicable fraction for the consolidated trust. The denominator of the redetermined applicable fraction of the consolidated trust is the fair market value of the property held in the consolidated trust, even if property was valued under Section 2032A in the determination of the applicable fraction of the trusts to be consolidated. See supra note 358.

[361] IRC § 2653(b)(1). The computation is discussed in detail at ¶ 17.03[2][a].

will have to pay some Chapter 13 generation-skipping transfer taxes that are treated as charged to the nonexempt portion of the trust for purposes of determining the ongoing applicable fraction. As a result, the applicable fraction must be recomputed (increased, with a resulting inclusion ratio decrease) prior to any subsequent imposition of generation-skipping transfer tax with respect to the trust.[362]

[e] Trust Severance

Severance of a single trust into two or more trusts has long been recognized for generation-skipping transfer tax purposes in limited circumstances.[363] Section 2642(a)(3) is an additional severance rule designed to make severance of a single trust into multiple trusts for generation-skipping transfer tax purposes less burdensome and less complex.[364] This provision not only provides additional opportunities for severing trusts, but in addition, it provides planning opportunities for more effective use of a transferor's GST exemption.[365]

Under Section 2642(a)(3), a trust may be severed with the resulting trusts recognized as separate trusts for purposes of Chapter 13 only if there is a "qualified severance" of the trust.[366] A "qualified severance" is the division of a single trust and the creation of *two or more* trusts if several requirements are met.[367] Either the governing instrument of the trust or a provision of local law must permit the severance of the trust.[368] The trust must be divided on a frac-

---

[362] IRC § 2653(b)(1). See ¶ 17.03[2][a].

[363] Reg. §§ 26.2654-1(a)(3), 26.2654-1(b). A single trust treated as a separate trust under Section 2654(b)(1) (multiple transferors) or Section 2654(b)(2) (separate and independent shares) may be divided into separate trusts where the new trusts are severed on a fractional basis and satisfy the funding requirements specified in the regulations. Reg. §§ 26.2654-1(a)(3), 26.2654-1(b)(1)(ii)(C). Additionally, a trust included in the transferor's gross estate or created under the transferor's will may be divided into two or more trusts that are recognized under Chapter 13 if certain requirements are satisfied. Reg. § 26.2654-1(b). See ¶ 17.04[2][b].

[364] See HR Rep. No. 107-37, 107th Cong., 1st Sess. 38 (2001). Section 2642(a)(3) also makes the application of the generation-skipping transfer tax less complex by allowing the severance of an existing trust with an inclusion ratio greater than zero and less than one into two separate trusts with inclusion ratios of zero and one. Id. See infra text accompanying notes 372–377.

[365] For example, see the combination of a qualified severance and a retroactive allocation discussed at ¶ 15.03[5][c][ii]. See also Harrington, McCaffrey, Plaine & Schneider, "Generation-Skipping Transfer Tax Planning After the 2001 Act: Mostly Good News," 95 J. Tax'n 143, 150–156 (2001).

[366] IRC § 2642(a)(3)(A).

[367] IRC § 2642(a)(3)(B).

[368] IRC § 2642(a)(3)(B)(i). The statute specifies the severance may be made by any means available under the governing instrument or local law, suggesting that a severance will be permissible even if the severance is accomplished under a broad power to dis-

tional basis.[369] The terms of the new trusts, in the aggregate, must provide for the same succession of interests of beneficiaries as are provided in the original trust.[370] For example, a trust that provides income to Child, C, for life with the remainder split 75 percent to a skip person and 25 percent to a non–skip person could be the subject of a qualified severance. This trust could be severed into two trusts both providing income to the child for life, but one with a remainder to the skip person and the other with a remainder to the non–skip person.[371]

Although trusts with inclusion ratios of zero and one may be severed under Section 2642(a)(3),[372] a principal purpose of the enactment was to eliminate complexity when an existing trust with an inclusion ratio of between zero and one was severed.[373] However, in that circumstance, an additional requirement must be satisfied to have a "qualified severance."[374] A single trust with an inclusion ratio greater than zero but less than one must be divided into two trusts with one trust receiving a fractional share of the total value of all trust assets equal to the applicable fraction of the single trust immediately before the severance.[375] The trust receiving the fractional share of assets based on the applicable fraction will have an inclusion ratio of zero.[376] The other trust will receive the balance of the trust's assets and have an inclusion ratio of one.[377]

---

tribute in further trust held by the trustee or even by a beneficiary holding an inter vivos limited power of appointment, rather than under a power expressly referencing severance for generation-skipping transfer tax purposes.

[369] IRC § 2642(a)(3)(B)(i)(I). A fractional basis requirement is also imposed where a single trust is actually severed into two or more trusts under Regulations Section 26.2654-1(a)(3) or Regulations Section 26.2654-1(b). Reg. § 26.2654-1(b)(1)(ii)(C)(1). The fractional basis requirement under Section 2642(a)(3)(B)(i)(I) will undoubtedly parallel the fractional basis requirement in Regulations Section 26.2654-1(b)(1)(ii)(C)(1). See ¶ 17.04[2][b] text accompanying note 66.

[370] IRC § 2642(a)(3)(B)(i)(II). This language parallels the language in Reg. § 26.2654-1(b)(1)(ii)(A). See ¶ 17.04[2][b] text accompanying note 70.

[371] Cf. Reg. § 26.2654-1(a)(5) Exs. 1, 2.

[372] IRC §§ 2642(a)(3)(A), 2642(a)(3)(B).

[373] See supra text accompanying note 363. Under the regulations, a single existing trust treated as multiple trusts after the application of Section 2654(b)(1) (multiple transferors) or Section 2654(b)(2) (separate and independent shares) may be divided into separate trusts where the new trusts are severed on a fractional basis and satisfy the funding requirements specified in the regulations. Reg. §§ 26.2654-1(a)(3), 26.2654-1(b)(1)(ii)(C). However, under Regulations Section 26.2654-1(a)(3) "a trustee cannot establish inclusion ratios of zero and one by severing a trust that is subject to the generation-skipping transfer tax after the trust has been created." HR Conf. Rep. No. 84, 107th Cong., 1st Sess. 200 (2001), reprinted in 2001-___ CB ___, ___.

[374] IRC § 2642(a)(3)(B)(ii).

[375] IRC § 2642(a)(3)(B)(ii).

[376] IRC § 2642(a)(3)(B)(ii).

[377] IRC § 2642(a)(3)(B)(ii).

For example, under the preceding example, assume that the trust with income to Child *C* for life and remainder 75 percent to a skip person and 25 percent to a non–skip person had an inclusion ratio of 0.250.[378] If this trust is severed in a qualified severance, one trust with 75 percent of the trust corpus would have an inclusion ratio of zero and the other trust with 25 percent of the corpus would have an inclusion ratio of one.[379] The allocation works nicely where the inclusion ratio and the corpus divisions are equal; however, even if they are not equal, a qualified severance may still be made.[380]

The regulations may provide for additional instances where a severance of the trust will be classified as a "qualified severance" and the resulting trusts recognized for purposes of Chapter 13.[381]

A qualified severance of a single trust may be made at any time[382] after December 31, 2000.[383]

---

[378] The trust would have an applicable fraction of 0.750.

[379] This, of course, is advantageous to the recipients of the property constituting the trust remainder. Had there been no qualified severance of the trust, there would have been generation-skipping transfer tax imposed on the taxable termination occurring at the death of the non–skip person for the value of the remainder passing to the skip person. However, because the trust severed with the remainder passing to the skip person has a zero inclusion ratio no generation-skipping transfer tax is imposed.

[380] For example, if the original trust had provided that 80 percent of the remainder go to a skip person and 20 percent to a non–skip person and the inclusion ratio was 0.250, the trust would still be severed with one trust having 75 percent of the corpus and an inclusion ratio of zero providing income to Child C and a remainder to the skip person. The second trust would provide income to Child C and 20 percent of the remainder of the second trust to the skip person and 80 percent of the remainder of the second trust to the non–skip person. The second trust would have an inclusion ratio of one. A qualified severance in this instance would still result in a 75 percent reduction of the generation-skipping transfer tax imposed on the taxable termination occurring upon the death of Child C with the income interest.

[381] IRC § 2642(a)(3)(B)(iii).

[382] IRC § 2642(a)(3)(C). The secretary is to provide by forms or regulations the manner in which the qualified severance is to be reported. Id.

[383] Economic Growth and Tax Relief Reconciliation Act of 2001, Pub. L. No. 107-16, § 562(b), 115 Stat. 38, 90 (2001), reprinted in 2001-__ CB __, __. Section 2642(a)(3) is subject to a "sunset" provision contained in Economic Growth and Tax Relief Reconciliation Act of 2001. Economic Growth and Tax Relief Reconciliation Act of 2001, Pub. L. No. 107-16, § 901(a)(2), 115 Stat. 38, 150 (2001), reprinted in 2001-__ CB __, __. See ¶ 18.04. See also ¶ 8.10[5].

[f] Recapture Tax Imposed Under Section 2032A

If additional estate tax is imposed under Section 2032A,[384] redetermination of the applicable fraction and the resulting inclusion ratio may be required.

[i] **Section 2032A value used in the denominator of the applicable fraction.** The applicable fraction is redetermined if property is valued under Section 2032A[385] in the determination of the denominator of the applicable fraction[386] and additional estate tax is subsequently imposed under Section 2032A(c).[387] The applicable fraction is redetermined *as of the date of the transferor's death.*[388] Any available GST exemption not allocated at the death of the transferor is automatically allocated to the property in the determination of the numerator of the redetermined applicable fraction.[389] The denominator of the redetermined applicable fraction is the fair market value of the property on the applicable Chapter 11 valuation date, the date of the transferor's death or the alternate valuation date,[390] reduced by any federal estate and state death tax,[391] including additional federal estate and state death tax[392] and additional generation-skipping transfer tax[393] chargeable to, and recovered from, the trust. The redetermined applicable fraction is then applied to any subsequent generation-skipping transfers from the trust that held the qualified real property valued initially pursuant to Section 2032A in the determination of the denominator of the applicable fraction.

Additionally, if additional estate tax is imposed under Section 2032A(c) on property valued under Section 2032A in the determination of the denomina-

---

[384] IRC § 2032A(c). See ¶ 4.04[7].

[385] IRC § 2032A. See ¶ 4.04.

[386] Reg. § 26.2642-2(b)(1). The fair market value of real property, valued for estate tax purposes under Section 2032A, is used in the determination of the denominator of the applicable fraction unless the recapture agreement "specifically provides for the signatories' consent to the imposition of, and personal liability for, additional . . . [generation-skipping transfer] tax in the event an additional estate tax is imposed under section 2032A(c)." Id. See ¶ 14.05[2].

[387] Reg. § 26.2642-4(a)(4)(i). The imposition of additional estate tax under Section 2032A(c) where property is valued pursuant to Section 2032A is discussed at ¶ 4.04[7].

[388] Reg. § 26.2642-4(a)(4)(i).

[389] Reg. § 26.2642-4(a)(4)(i).

[390] Cf. Reg. § 26.2642-4(a)(4)(i). The regulations overlook the possibility of the property being valued on the alternate valuation date in the determination of both the federal estate and generation-skipping transfer tax. See IRC §§ 2624(b), 2642(b)(2)(A). See also ¶ 4.04[1] note 4.

[391] Reg. § 26.2642-4(a)(4)(i); IRC § 2642(a)(2)(B)(ii)(I); Reg. § 26.2642-1(c)(1)(i).

[392] Reg. § 26.2642-1(c)(1)(i).

[393] Reg. § 26.2642-4(a)(4)(i).

tor of the applicable fraction of the trust, the generation-skipping transfer tax imposed on any transfers occurring between the date of death and the event triggering the additional estate tax must be recomputed and the additional generation-skipping transfer tax paid.[394]

[ii] Section 2032A property valued at fair market value in the denominator of the applicable fraction. Real property may be valued under Section 2032A for estate tax purposes and at its fair market value in the denominator of the applicable fraction.[395]

When additional estate tax is imposed on the disposition or cessation of the qualified use of qualified real property not held in a trust, as well as where the qualified real property is held in a trust, but not valued under Section 2032A in the determination of the denominator of the applicable fraction, and the additional estate tax is chargeable to, and recovered from, the trust, the applicable fraction for the trust must be recomputed. The denominator of the recomputed applicable fraction is reduced by any additional federal estate or state death tax imposed that is borne by the trust.[396] The difficult question is just how to recompute the applicable fraction in this instance. Clearly, the denominator of the recomputed applicable fraction should be reduced by the additional estate tax imposed that is charged to the trust assets. Are the assets held in the trust to be valued for purposes of the denominator of the recomputed applicable fraction at the date of the transferor's death, the alternate valuation date, the date the event that triggers the imposition of additional estate tax occurs, or the date the additional estate tax is paid by the trust? If generation-skipping transfers have occurred involving the trust property before the imposition of the additional estate tax, should the generation-skipping transfer tax previously incurred be recomputed using the recomputed applicable fraction? If the applicable fraction was one prior to the recomputation, the imposition of additional estate tax charged to, and paid from, the trust would reduce

---

[394] Reg. § 26.2642-4(a)(4)(ii). Any recomputed generation-skipping transfer tax on intervening generation-skipping transfers is due on the date that is six months after the recapture event. Id. See Reg. § 26.2642-2(b)(1).

[395] Reg. § 26.2642-2(b)(1). See Reg. § 26.2642-4(a)(4)(i). The fair market value is determined on the applicable valuation date, either the date of death or the alternate valuation date. See IRC § 2642(b)(2)(A); ¶ 18.03[1][a] note 11.

[396] Where the qualified property is held in the trust and not valued pursuant to Section 2032A for generation-skipping transfer tax purposes, the denominator is reduced for the additional estate tax just as it is for any federal estate tax and state death taxes incurred by reason of the transfer that is chargeable to, and recovered from, the trust. See IRC § 2642(a)(2)(B)(ii)(I); Reg. § 26.2642-1(c)(1)(i). Where the qualified property is not held in the trust and the additional estate tax is chargeable to, and recovered from, the trust, the recomputation of the denominator is necessary due to an adjustment in arriving at the fair market value of the property held in the trust rather than a deduction from the fair market value for taxes.

the denominator of the applicable fraction and would result in an excessive allocation of GST exemption to the property held in trust, which should be treated as void to the extent the allocation was excessive.[397] Hopefully, future regulations or rulings will provide guidance on these issues.

[6] Special Rules for Charitable Lead Annuity Trusts

When property is transferred to a trust under which a charitable organization receives an income interest and, upon termination of that income interest, the remainder passes to a noncharitable beneficiary, the trust is known as a charitable lead trust. The transfer of the income interest to a charitable beneficiary[398] qualifies for an estate or gift tax charitable deduction[399] only if the lead income interest is in the form of either a guaranteed annuity or a fixed percentage of the fair market value of the property determined and distributed yearly.[400] Such trusts are commonly referred to as charitable lead annuity trusts and charitable lead unitrusts, respectively.

The inclusion ratio for a charitable lead *annuity* trust[401] is determined under the special rule of Section 2642(e),[402] not under the general rule of Section 2642(a).[403] Congress enacted this special rule out of concern that the application of the general rule governing the computation of the applicable fraction would permit a "leveraging" of the GST exemption.[404] Generally, in

---

[397] Cf. Reg. § 26.2632-1(b)(2)(i).

[398] See IRC §§ 2055(a), 2522(a).

[399] IRC §§ 2055, 2522. If Section 2522 applies, see supra ¶ 16.02[3][b] note 191.

[400] IRC §§ 2055(e)(2)(B), 2522(c)(2)(B). See ¶¶ 5.05[6], 11.02[2][c].

[401] A charitable lead annuity trust is any trust in which there is a charitable lead annuity. IRC § 2642(e)(3)(A). A charitable lead annuity is any interest in the form of a guaranteed annuity with respect to which a deduction is allowed under the estate or gift tax provisions. IRC § 2642(e)(3)(B).

[402] See Reg. § 26.2642-3. This special rule applies with respect to property transferred after October 13, 1987.

[403] The special rule of Section 2642(e) applies only in determining the inclusion ratio for charitable lead annuity trusts and does not apply to charitable lead unitrusts. S. Rep. No. 445, 100th Cong., 2d Sess. 367, 368–369 (1988). See infra note 404 (explaining why the rule is inapplicable to unitrusts).

[404] S. Rep. No. 445, 100th Cong., 2d Sess. 367, 368–369 (1988). Leveraging the exemption occurs when more than one dollar of transfer is exempted from the generation-skipping transfer tax for each dollar of GST exemption used. If a transferor transfers property to a trust and allocates GST exemption to the trust, the corpus of which appreciates in value at the time of a subsequent generation-skipping transfer, leveraging of the GST exemption occurs. For example, if grantor *G* creates a trust with a corpus of $500,000 and allocates $300,000 of GST exemption to the trust, and the corpus of the trust appreciates in value to $1 million at the time of the generation-skipping transfer, *G* has used only $300,000 of GST exemption to effectively shield $600,000 from the generation-skipping

computing the denominator of the applicable fraction, the value of the property transferred to the trust is reduced by any estate or gift tax charitable deduction allowed on the transfer.[405] The effect of this reduction of the denominator is to increase the applicable fraction, thereby reducing the inclusion ratio and the applicable rate of Chapter 13 tax imposed on generation-skipping transfers from the trust and exempting the charitable portion of the transfer from taxation under Chapter 13.[406] The amount of the charitable deduction is based on the present value of the income interest received by the charitable organization using valuation tables that necessarily include a built-in assumed rate of return. If the assets in the trust earn a greater return than that assumed in computing the present value of the income interest under the tables, the amount passing to

---

transfer tax. Such leveraging is common for all allocations of GST exemption to appreciating property.

A transferor formerly could, however, substantially leverage the amount of GST exemption allocated to a charitable lead annuity trust. When the investment yield on trust assets exceeded the rate used in the tables to determine the amount of the charitable deduction, leveraging occurred because the amount of GST exemption required to be allocated to the transfer to achieve a zero (or other) inclusion ratio was effectively reduced by the amount of the charitable deduction, as it is subtracted from the denominator of the applicable fraction. While the charitable beneficiary would receive its flat dollar annuity, the value of which is computed under the tables, all trust earnings in excess of the projected rate used to compute the amount of the charitable deduction would pass to the noncharitable beneficiary at no additional generation-skipping tax cost. Thus, a transferor could achieve additional generation-skipping without using any additional GST exemption or paying any additional generation-skipping transfer tax. Congress enacted Section 2642(e) to prevent leveraging of the GST exemption in this manner. See infra text accompanying notes 408–412.

The special rule of Section 2642(e) is not applicable to a charitable lead unitrust. See supra note 403. The concern Congress had about the potential for leveraging is not present with a charitable lead unitrust, since the charitable beneficiary receives a fixed percentage of the total investment performance of the trust annually, regardless of how well the trust performs. Whenever a unitrust is the charitable lead interest, and the investment yield of the trust exceeds the rate used in the tables to compute the amount of the charitable deduction, the appreciation is shared between the charitable and noncharitable beneficiaries in accordance with their respective interests established at the inception of the trust. Although some leveraging can occur under such trusts, the amount of leveraging is not as great as in annuity trusts because the charity effectively shares in the proceeds of the amount of appreciation.

While charitable lead unitrusts may not be useful for leveraging, as would be charitable lead annuity trusts, unitrusts are still drawing some attention from planners. See Priv. Ltr. Ruls. 9840036 (July 6, 1998), 9840008 (June 25, 1998); supra ¶ 16.02[3][b] note 193. See also Priv. Ltr. Rul. 199917068 (Jan. 7, 1999).

[405] IRC § 2642(a)(2)(B)(ii)(II). See supra ¶ 16.02[3][b] text accompanying notes 183–196.

[406] See IRC § 2641, discussed supra ¶ 16.01. See also supra ¶ 16.02[3][b] text accompanying notes 175, 176.

noncharitable beneficiaries could exceed the amount that they would have received had there been no charitable lead interest in the trust.[407]

For example, assume that grantor *G* transfers $74,869 to a trust with the requirement that a designated charity be paid a guaranteed annuity of $10,000 a year, payable at the end of each year for three years, with the remainder to be paid to *G*'s grandchild *GC*.[408] Assume that the present value of the $10,000 annuity for three years is $24,869.[409] The present value of the remainder interest is the difference between the two amounts, or $50,000. Under the general applicable fraction rule, if *G* allocates $50,000 of GST exemption to the property transferred to the trust, the applicable fraction will be one and the inclusion ratio will be zero. If the trust earns a 10 percent rate of return each year, upon termination of the charitable lead annuity, $66,550[410] remains for distribution to *GC*. Using a 10 percent interest rate for three years, the $50,000 of GST exemption initially allocated to the trust by *G* would have increased in value to $66,550.[411] Thus, a zero inclusion ratio is justified if the trust earns the same rate of return that was used to determine the present value of the charitable lead annuity interest. If, however, the trust earns a rate of return slightly in excess of 15 percent, $80,000 would remain after the termination of the charitable lead annuity. The present value of an $80,000 remainder would have been $60,105.20 when the trust was established.[412] If the applicable fraction is not adjusted under Section 2642(e), a zero inclusion ratio results, even

---

[407] S. Rep. No. 445, 100th Cong., 2d Sess. 367, 368–369 (1988).

[408] See supra ¶ 16.02[2][b] note 45.

[409] Under Section 7520, the value of any annuity, any interest for life or term of years, or any remainder or reversionary interest is determined under tables prescribed by the secretary using an interest rate rounded to the nearest two tenths of 1 percent equal to 120 percent of the federal midterm rate, compounded annually, for purposes of Section 1274(d)(1), for the month in which the valuation date falls. Reg. § 20.2031-7(d)(6) provides valuation tables for term certain annuities with a valuation date after April 30, 1989. See Reg. §§ 20.7520-1(a)(1), 25.2512-5(a). These tables, applicable after April 30, 1989, are used when the Section 7520 interest rate is between 4.2 and 14 percent. Reg. § 20.2031-7(d)(6). See also Reg. §§ 20.2031-7(d)(4), 25.2512-5(d)(4).

Assume a federal midterm rate that, when multiplied by 120 percent, produces an interest rate of 10 percent, Reg. § 20.2031-7(d)(6) (Table B) provides a remainder factor of 0.751315 for a three-year annuity. The resulting valuation factor for the income interest is 0.248685, and the annuity factor is 2.48685. The present value of the annuity for three years is $24,869 ($10,000 × 2.48685). See Notice 89-24, 1989-1 CB 660, 661–662 Exs. 1–3; Reg. § 25.2512-5(d)(2)(iv).

[410] Using a 10 percent interest rate per year and subtracting a $10,000 annuity each year, $74,869 becomes $66,550 after three years.

[411] At 10 percent simple interest per year, $50,000 becomes $66,550 after three years.

[412] Table B of Reg. § 20.2031-7(d)(6) prescribes a factor of 0.751315 to determine the present value at 10 percent of a remainder interest postponed for three years. See supra ¶ 16.02[5][e] note 378.

Section 2642

though only $50,000 of the GST exemption is allocated to an interest that is actually worth $60,105.20.

In determining the inclusion ratio for a charitable lead annuity trust, Section 2642(e) provides a special computation that avoids leveraging and provides an equitable result, even if the property transferred to the trust declines in value.[413] In computing the applicable fraction, the numerator of the fraction is the "*adjusted* GST exemption."[414] The adjusted GST exemption is the amount of the GST exemption allocated to the trust, increased by an amount equal to the interest that would be earned on the GST exemption amount over the actual term of such annuity using the interest rate employed to determine the amount of the charitable deduction for the charitable lead annuity.[415] The denominator of the applicable fraction is the value of the property remaining in the trust immediately after the termination of the charitable lead annuity.[416]

To illustrate the special computation of the inclusion ratio under Section 2642(e), assume, as in the prior example, that grantor G transfers $74,869 in trust with the requirement that a designated charity be paid a guaranteed annuity of $10,000 a year, payable at the end of each year for a period of three years, and that the remainder be paid to G's grandchild GC. If the present value of an annuity of $10,000 a year for three years is $24,869,[417] G will receive a charitable deduction in that amount.[418] In addition, assume that G allocates only $50,000 of GST exemption to the transfer and, immediately after the termination of the charitable lead annuity, the value of the property held in trust is $80,000.[419] Under Section 2642(e), the numerator of the applicable fraction is the "adjusted GST exemption."[420] Where $50,000 of G's GST exemption was allocated to the trust, the adjusted GST exemption is the amount of GST exemption allocated to the trust, increased by the amount of interest

---

[413] See also infra note 425.

[414] IRC § 2642(e)(1)(A) (emphasis added).

[415] IRC § 2642(e)(2). See supra ¶ 16.02[5][f] text accompanying notes 390, 391. In determining the amount to be added for interest to the initial GST exemption amount, interest is to be compounded annually at the applicable rate. If a late allocation of GST exemption is made, the amount added for interest is computed from the date of the late allocation over the balance of the actual period of the charitable lead annuity. Reg. § 26.2642-3(b).

[416] IRC § 2642(e)(1)(B).

[417] See supra note 409.

[418] IRC § 2522(c)(2)(B). See supra ¶ 16.02[3][b] note 194.

[419] The trust would contain $80,000 at the expiration of the charitable lead annuity if the trust achieved a rate of return of slightly over 15 percent per year. Remember that, but for Section 2642(e), upon the taxable termination that occurs at the expiration of the charitable lead annuity, use of $50,000 of GST exemption would result in an inclusion ratio of zero, an applicable rate of zero, and no Chapter 13 tax. See supra text accompanying notes 410–412.

[420] IRC § 2642(e)(1)(A).

on the exemption amount generated by the 10 percent rate of return[421] used in computing the amount of the charitable deduction for the charitable lead annuity over its three-year term. This results in an adjusted GST exemption of $66,550.[422] The denominator of the Section 2642(e) applicable fraction is the value of all property in the trust immediately after the termination of the charitable lead annuity,[423] in this case, $80,000. Thus, the Section 2642(e) applicable fraction is 0.832 ($66,550 ÷ $80,000), resulting in an inclusion ratio of 0.168, one minus the applicable fraction.[424] This recomputation of the applicable fraction avoids the leveraging that would occur if no special rule were applied.[425]

---

[421] See supra notes 409, 412.

[422] IRC § 2642(e)(2). See supra note 412.

[423] IRC § 2642(e)(1)(B).

[424] IRC § 2642(a)(1). The amount of tax imposed on the taxable termination is the Section 2641 applicable rate (an inclusion ratio of 0.168 multiplied by the maximum federal estate tax rate in effect at the time of the termination) multiplied by the Section 2622 taxable amount of $80,000. IRC § 2602. The imposition of Chapter 13 tax may be prevented by the allocation of an additional $13,450 of GST exemption to the property held in the charitable lead annuity trust at the time of the termination of the charity's lead interest. See IRC §§ 2631(a), 2632(e).

[425] It should be noted that Section 2642(e) does not reduce the amount of GST exemption allocated to the transfer if the trust attains a rate of return that is lower than the rate used to compute the charitable deduction. The adjusted GST exemption is always the GST exemption allocated to the trust, increased by the assumed interest rate used to determine the charitable deduction. This may produce varying results.

Assume that the facts of the example in the text are the same except that, immediately after the termination of the charitable lead annuity trust, the value of the property held in trust is $55,000. The adjusted GST exemption and numerator of the applicable fraction are both still $66,550. The denominator of the applicable fraction is $55,000. The applicable fraction is $66,550 divided by $55,000. Section 2642(a)(1) states that the inclusion ratio is the excess, *if any*, of one minus the applicable fraction. In this case, there is no excess and the inclusion ratio is zero. Thus, due to the performance of the trust, *G* allocated more GST exemption than was necessary to attain an inclusion ratio of zero. The amount of the GST exemption allocated to the trust is not reduced and restored to the transferor even though a lesser amount would have resulted in a zero inclusion ratio. Reg. §§ 26.2642-3(b), 26.2642-3(c) Ex. This may be viewed as inequitable. However, had the trust performed better, more of the GST exemption would have been used to avoid the generation-skipping transfer tax.

Under different circumstances, the adjusted GST exemption will produce a clearly equitable result. Assume that the facts are the same as in the previous example except that *G* originally allocated $40,000 of GST exemption to the trust. Without Section 2642(e), the applicable fraction would have a numerator of $40,000 and a denominator of $50,000 ($74,869 transferred, less a charitable deduction of $24,869). The applicable fraction would have been 0.800 ($40,000 ÷ $50,000). The inclusion ratio would have been 0.200 (1 − 0.800). Using Section 2642(e), the numerator of the applicable fraction is the adjusted GST exemption of $53,240 ($40,000 increased at 10 percent per year for three years). The denominator of the applicable fraction is the value of the trust property immediately after the termination of the charitable lead annuity trust, in this case, $55,000. The

[7] Deferral of the Effect of Generation-Skipping Transfer Exemption Allocation and Direct and Indirect Skips on Certain Inter Vivos Transfers

[a] Introduction

If an inter vivos transfer of property is potentially includible in the gross estate[426] of the transferor, or the transferor's spouse,[427] if death occurred immediately after the transfer, any GST exemption allocated to the inter vivos transfer is irrevocable[428] but is generally[429] not effective[430] until the end of the "estate tax inclusion period."[431] The purpose of the Section 2642(f) deferral rule is to postpone the Chapter 13 consequences of an inter vivos transfer until it is complete for both gift and estate tax purposes.[432] The rationale for defer-

---

applicable fraction is 0.968 ($53,240 ÷ $55,000), and the inclusion ratio is 0.032 (1 − 0.968). The inclusion ratio is smaller than it would have been without Section 2642(e). This result is equitable, since the noncharitable beneficiary of the trust receives less than would have been received had there been no charitable lead annuity trust. See Priv. Ltr. Rul. 200107015 (Nov. 14, 2000) (effort to avoid Section 2642(e) by assignment of remainder).

[426] Inclusion under Section 2035 is disregarded. IRC § 2642(f)(1).

[427] Section 2642(f)(4) provides that, except as provided in regulations, any reference in Section 2642(f) to an individual (or transferor) shall be treated as including a reference to the spouse of such individual (or transferor). See infra ¶ 16.02[7][b][ii].

[428] Reg. § 26.2632-1(c)(1). But see Reg. § 26.2632-1(b)(2)(ii)(A)(1); ¶ 15.02[1] note 25; Priv. Ltr. Rul. 199922045 (Mar. 5, 1999) (allocation of GST exemption to property subject to estate tax inclusion period prior to issuance of final regulation treated as void rather than irrevocable).

[429] This rule is inapplicable to property with respect to which a Section 2652(a)(3), reverse QTIP, election has been made. See infra ¶ 16.02[7][b][ii].

[430] Section 2642(f)(1) provides "any allocation of GST exemption to such property shall not be made before the close of the estate tax inclusion period. . . . " However, pursuant to the authority granted in the introductory clauses of Section 2642(f), Reg. § 26.2632-1(c)(1) provides "[a]n allocation of GST exemption (including an automatic allocation) to property subject to an estate tax inclusion period (ETIP) . . . becomes effective no earlier than the date of any termination of the ETIP with respect to the trust." This language permits an allocation of GST exemption to property during the estate tax inclusion period and merely delays the effective date of the allocation. See Reg. §§ 26.2632-1(c)(5) Exs. 1, 2, 26.2642-4(b) Ex. 5; infra ¶¶ 16.02[7][e][i], 16.02[7][e][iii]. See also ¶ 15.03[5][c][i]. But see infra text accompanying notes 436, 437.

[431] IRC § 2642(f)(3). See infra ¶ 16.02[7][b].

[432] Section 2642(f) postponement may avoid a Section 2642(d) recomputation. Thus, if a transfer to a trust is within Section 2642(f) and a subsequent transfer is made by the same transferor to the trust, no allocation of the GST exemption is effective with respect to either transfer until the end of the estate tax inclusion period, thus avoiding the need for a Section 2642(d) recomputation. If Section 2642(f) applied to a transfer but an allocation of the GST exemption is made after the estate tax inclusion period ends, the applica-

ring the effective date of the allocation of any GST exemption is sensible. If a transferor makes a transfer that is sufficiently testamentary to require gross estate inclusion, then the transfer is essentially testamentary for Chapter 13 purposes as well and Chapter 13 consequences should be postponed until the potential for gross estate inclusion terminates. An irrevocable allocation of GST exemption may be made during the period,[433] but the effective date of the allocation is generally deferred until the close of the estate tax inclusion period.[434]

In addition, there is a second rule with a similar purpose under the estate tax inclusion period rules. Under the second rule, if the transfer during the estate tax inclusion period otherwise constitutes an inter vivos direct skip, the direct skip is also postponed until the end of the estate tax inclusion period.[435] When there is a direct skip that is delayed under Section 2642(f), automatic allocation of GST exemption[436] should not occur until the direct skip is treated as occurring, at the close of the estate tax inclusion period, and then only if the transferor is alive.[437]

The estate tax inclusion period rules of Section 2642(f) may affect both the amount of tax imposed on a generation-skipping transfer[438] and the timing of a direct skip generation-skipping transfer.[439]

---

ble fraction determined at that time is used in any subsequent Section 2642(d) computations. IRC § 2642(f)(5). See supra ¶ 16.02[5].

[433] Reg. § 26.2632-1(c)(1). See Reg. §§ 26.2632-1(c)(5) Exs. 1, 2; 26.2642-4(b) Ex. 5. The allocation of GST exemption during the estate tax inclusion period may be a retroactive allocation of GST exemption under Section 2632(d). IRC § 2632(d). See ¶¶ 15.03[5], 15.03[5][c][i].

[434] The computation of the applicable fraction, the resulting inclusion ratio, and the applicable rate of tax with respect to a generation-skipping transfer are also generally deferred until the close of the estate tax inclusion period. See supra note 430; infra ¶ 16.02[7][e]; ¶ 15.03[5][c][i]. But see infra ¶ 16.02[7][e][iii].

[435] IRC § 2642(f)(1) (last sentence). See infra ¶ 16.02[7][c]; ¶ 13.02[4][d].

[436] See ¶ 15.03[3]. When an indirect skip, which triggers the automatic allocation of GST exemption under Section 2632(c), is subject to the estate tax inclusion period rules, it is deemed to have been made at the close of the estate tax inclusion period. IRC § 2632(c)(4). The automatic allocation of unused GST exemption to the indirect skip occurs at the end of the estate tax inclusion period when the indirect skip is deemed to occur. See ¶ 15.03[4][d] text accompanying notes 169–172.

[437] See ¶ 15.03[3][b] text accompanying notes 45–51. A transferor may, however, allocate GST exemption to the delayed direct skip transfer, but the GST exemption allocation is not effective until the close of the estate tax inclusion period when the direct skip occurs. See supra note 430; infra ¶ 16.02[7][e].

[438] See infra ¶ 16.02[7][e].

[439] See an example of these rules infra ¶ 16.02[7][d].

Section 2642

[b] General Rules of Deferral

When a transferor makes a transfer, the estate tax inclusion period deferral rules may apply to defer the effect of an allocation of GST exemption or to defer a direct skip in two situations: (1) where the property is potentially includible in the transferor's gross estate and (2) where the property is potentially includible in the transferor's spouse's gross estate.[440] However, property is not to be considered potentially includible in the transferor's or the spouse's gross estate if the possibility that the property will be included is so remote as to be negligible.[441]

[i] Inclusion in the transferor's gross estate. The Section 2642(f) rule applies to any inter vivos transfer of property that would be includible in the gross estate of the transferor, other than pursuant to Section 2035,[442] and other than where the possibility of inclusion is so remote as to be negligible,[443] if the transferor were to die immediately after the transfer.[444] If an individual makes an inter vivos transfer but retains a life estate, a reversion conditioned upon survivorship, a power to revoke, a power to alter beneficiaries, or a power merely to alter the time of enjoyment, regardless of whether there is a completed inter vivos gift tax transfer, Sections 2036 through 2038 may, to some extent, require the property transferred to be included in the individual's gross estate with the result that the Section 2642(f)(1) postponement rules will likely apply.[445] If a transferor funds a joint-and-survivor annuity between the transferor and a skip person, Section 2039 potentially requires the property transferred to be included in the transferor's gross estate, triggering application of Section 2642(f).[446] Similarly, a transferor's purchase of property held jointly by the transferor and a skip person potentially results in inclusion under Section

---

[440] IRC §§ 2642(f)(1), 2642(f)(3); Reg. § 26.2632-1(c)(2)(i). This would include a transfer to a trustlike arrangement. See ¶ 17.02[2].

[441] Reg. § 26.2632-1(c)(2)(ii)(A). "A possibility is so remote as to be negligible if it can be ascertained by actuarial standards that there is less than a 5 percent probability that the property will be included in the gross estate." Id. This standard may be very difficult to apply. The Treasury might opt for a standard where an interest will be disregarded if, at the time of the transfer, the value of the interest in property to be included in the gross estate is less than a fixed percentage (say 5 percent) of the value of the transferred property at the time of the initial transfer.

[442] This Section 2035 limitation applies only to a transfer of a life insurance policy insuring the transferor's life that is potentially includible in the transferor's gross estate under Section 2035(a). See infra note 449.

[443] Reg. § 26.2632-1(c)(2)(ii)(A). See supra note 441.

[444] IRC § 2642(f)(1); Reg. § 26.2632-1(c)(2)(i).

[445] If any part of a trust is potentially includible in the gross estate of the transferor or the transferor's spouse, generally the entire trust is subject to the estate tax inclusion period rules. See Reg. § 26.2632-1(c)(1); infra text accompanying notes 450–454.

[446] IRC § 2642(f)(1).

2040 in the transferor's gross estate, and thus, the Section 2642(f) rules would apply with the result that the direct skip that would otherwise occur upon creation of the joint tenancy is deferred until termination of the estate tax inclusion period.[447] If a transferor exercises (or, in the case of a post-1942 power, releases) a general power of appointment in such a manner that, had the transferor owned the property, it would have been included in the transferor's gross estate under Sections 2036 through 2038, there is potential Section 2041 inclusion and the Section 2642(f) rules apply.[448] If a transferor transfers a life insurance policy insuring the transferor's life to a skip person, but retains an incident of ownership potentially triggering Section 2042(2), this section also applies.[449]

The term "property" under Section 2642(f)(1)(A) includes a mere property interest (as it does in most parts of the Code);[450] thus, the entire property transferred need not be subject to potential gross estate inclusion.[451] To illustrate, assume that grantor *G* establishes a trust with income to child *C* for life, a reversion to *G* if living at *C*'s death, and, if not, a remainder to *GC*. Further assume that *G*'s reversionary interest is, at all times prior to *G*'s death, worth greater than 5 percent of the corpus. Although on a transfer of corpus to the trust *G* makes a gift equal in value to the entire transferred corpus,[452] only a portion of the corpus (*GC*'s remainder) will be included in *G*'s gross estate under Section 2037 if *G* predeceases *C*.[453] Even though only a portion of the

---

[447] IRC § 2642(f)(1). See infra ¶ 16.02[7][d] text accompanying notes 494–505.

[448] IRC § 2642(f)(1). If a transferor exercises (or, in the case of a post-1942 power, releases) a general power of appointment in a manner such that, had the transferor owned the property, it would have been included in the transferor's gross estate under Section 2035, Section 2642(f) likely is inapplicable. See supra ¶ 16.02[4][d] note 261; infra ¶ 16.02[7][c] text accompanying note 486.

[449] IRC § 2642(f)(1). Since an incident of ownership is retained, there would be no completed gift of the policy. An outright transfer of a life insurance policy does not trigger these rules, even though the policy might be included in the transferor's gross estate under Section 2035, because the estate tax inclusion period disregards Section 2035 inclusion. Id. See IRC § 2035(a)(2).

[450] See, e.g., IRC §§ 2036(a), 2503(c); Comm'r v. Herr, 303 F2d 780 (3d Cir. 1962).

[451] Reg. § 26.2632-1(c)(1). The statutory language is clarified by this regulation. The term "property" as used in Section 2642(f)(1)(B) could mean the entire property or a mere property interest.

[452] See IRC §§ 2511, 2702.

[453] See ¶ 4.09.

corpus is potentially included in *G*'s gross estate, the entire trust is subject to the estate tax inclusion period rules.[454]

[ii] Inclusion in transferor's spouse's gross estate. Deferral of the effect of an allocation of GST exemption or of a direct skip also occurs where the value of the transferred property is potentially includible in the transferor's spouse's gross estate.[455] Again, a possibility that the transferred property will be included that is so remote as to be negligible is to be disregarded in determining potential gross estate inclusion.[456] In addition, if the transferee spouse holds a five-or-five power[457] to withdraw no more than the greater of $5,000 or 5 percent of the trust corpus that expires no later than sixty days after a transfer to the trust, although that property would be included within the spouse's gross estate if the spouse died during the period,[458] the power is disregarded in determining potential gross estate inclusion.[459]

These spousal deferral rules potentially apply to split gifts and to transfers qualifying for the marital deduction. The deferral rules may operate to the spouse's benefit by preventing ineffective allocations of GST exemption.

Split Gifts. If a donor makes an inter vivos transfer that is split under Section 2513 with a spouse for gift tax purposes,[460] the spouse becomes the transferor of one half of the property transferred for generation-skipping transfer tax purposes.[461] Even if no part of the property transferred would be includible in the spouse's gross estate immediately after the transfer, any allocation of GST exemption to the property by the spouse is not effective[462] until the end of the estate tax inclusion period if the property would be included in the donor's gross estate immediately after the transfer.[463] For example, assume Donor transfers property to a trust retaining an income interest for a term of years, with a remainder to Grandchild, and Donor and Spouse elect under Section 2513 to split the gift to Grandchild. Any allocation of GST exemption by Donor or Spouse does not take effect until the end of the estate tax inclusion period.[464] Deferral of the effect of GST exemption allocation avoids a waste of Spouse's GST exemption. If Donor dies during the term of years, the entire

---

[454] Reg. § 26.2632-1(c)(1). The same issue could arise with respect to inclusion of only a portion of the trust corpus under any of the gross estate inclusion provisions.

[455] IRC § 2642(f)(4); Reg. § 26.2632-1(c)(2)(i)(B).

[456] Reg. § 26.2632-1(c)(2)(ii)(A). See supra note 441.

[457] See IRC §§ 2041(b)(2), 2514(e).

[458] IRC § 2041(a)(2).

[459] Reg. § 26.2632-1(c)(2)(ii)(B).

[460] See ¶ 10.03.

[461] IRC § 2652(a)(2). See ¶ 17.02[1][c][ii].

[462] See infra ¶ 16.02[7][e].

[463] Reg. § 26.2632-1(c)(2)(i)(B).

[464] IRC §§ 2642(f)(1), 2642(f)(4). See Reg. § 2632-1(c)(5) Ex. 3.

property transferred is included in Donor's gross estate under Section 2036, and any GST exemption allocation by Spouse would be wasted because Donor becomes the sole transferor of the property for generation-skipping transfer tax purposes.[465] Any GST exemption allocated by Spouse that is ineffective should be treated as void and restored to Spouse.[466]

Marital Deduction Transfers. When an inter vivos interspousal transfer qualifies for a marital deduction,[467] Section 2642(f) prevents the allocation of GST exemption by either the donor or donee spouse from taking effect generally until the close of the estate tax inclusion period.[468] In most situations[469] no allocation of GST exemption should be made by the donor, because the donee will become the Chapter 13 transferor of the property prior to any generation-skipping transfer.[470] The deferral rule again generally prevents a waste of the donor's GST exemption.[471]

If the interspousal transfer qualifies for the marital deduction because an election is made to treat the property as qualified terminable interest property for gift tax purposes and a Section 2652(a)(3) "reverse QTIP" election has been made by the donor,[472] Section 2642(f) does not apply.[473] For example, if Donor establishes an inter vivos trust under which the income is to be paid to Spouse for life and the remainder to Grandchild and a Section 2523(f) qualified terminable interest property election is made, the Section 2642(f)(1) deferral rules generally apply.[474] However, if Donor makes a reverse QTIP election under Section 2652(a)(3) to disregard the qualified terminable interest property election for generation-skipping transfer tax purposes, the deferral rules do not apply.[475] This Section 2652(a)(3) exception is appropriate because the donor is

---

[465] IRC § 2652(a)(1)(A).

[466] See infra ¶ 16.02[7][e] note 511.

[467] IRC §§ 2523(d)–2523(g). See Rev. Rul. 68-554, 1968-2 CB 412.

[468] Reg. § 26.2632-1(c)(2)(i)(B).

[469] But see infra text accompanying notes 472–475.

[470] IRC § 2652(a)(1). This would be so regardless of whether the donee spouse made an inter vivos transfer of the property that resulted in a gift transfer, or whether the property was included in the donee spouse's gross estate.

[471] Any ineffective allocation of GST exemption by the donor should be treated as void. See infra ¶ 16.02[7][e] note 511.

[472] Section 2652(a)(3) allows the donor spouse, rather than the donee spouse who possesses a qualified income interest in qualified terminable interest property, to be treated as the transferor for generation-skipping transfer tax purposes if the appropriate election is made, even though the property will be included in the donee spouse's gross estate for federal estate tax purposes or treated as a transfer by the donee spouse of property subject to the federal gift tax. See ¶ 17.02[1][c][i]. See also IRC §§ 2044, 2519, 2652(a)(1).

[473] Reg. § 26.2632-1(c)(2)(ii)(C).

[474] Reg. § 26.2632-1(c)(2)(i)(B).

[475] Reg. § 26.2632-1(c)(2)(ii)(C).

treated as the transferor for generation-skipping transfer tax purposes to the exclusion of the donee spouse, and, therefore, there is no potential waste of the donor's GST exemption and no reason to delay the effect of the allocation of the donor's GST exemption.

[c] Termination of the Estate Tax Inclusion Period

[i] Potential inclusion in the transferor's gross estate. The estate tax inclusion period ends for property potentially includible in the transferor's gross estate on the *earliest* of (1) the date that the property involved in the transfer is no longer potentially includible in the gross estate of the transferor under Chapter 11 (other than by reason of Section 2035);[476] (2) the date of any subsequent generation-skipping transfer with respect to the property;[477] or (3) the date of the transferor's death.[478]

Although Section 2642(f)(3) defines the estate tax inclusion period to encompass inclusion in the gross estate as a result of Section 2035, the regulations define the termination of the estate tax inclusion period as occurring when no portion of the property is includible in the transferor's gross estate other than by reason of Section 2035.[479] This definitional difference is relevant in determining the end of the estate tax inclusion period if a transferor relinquishes an interest in, or power over, property that was the subject of a prior inter vivos transfer that was potentially includible under Section 2036, Section 2037, or Section 2038, or releases a previously retained Section 2042(2) incident of ownership. Under the statutory language of Section 2642(f)(3), the estate tax inclusion period does not end until three years after the date of the relinquishment of the interest or power, unless the transfer results in a generation-skipping transfer or the transferor's death intercedes. Under the regulatory rule that alters the Section 2642(f)(3) statutory language, the estate tax inclusion period ends upon the relinquishment of the interest or power.[480]

Section 2642(f)(1) prevents an allocation of GST exemption from taking effect while the transferor is treated as the owner of property transferred for

---

[476] Reg. § 26.2632-1(c)(3)(ii). See infra text accompanying notes 479–486.

[477] IRC § 2642(f)(3)(A). See Reg. § 26.2632-1(c)(3)(iii). If there is a generation-skipping transfer from a trust during the estate tax inclusion period, the estate tax inclusion period merely terminates with respect to the property involved in the generation-skipping transfer. See Reg. § 26.2632-1(c)(5) Ex. 2; infra ¶ 16.02[7][e][iii].

[478] IRC § 2642(f)(3)(B); Reg. § 26.2632-1(c)(3)(i).

[479] Reg. § 26.2632-1(c)(3)(ii). In defining the estate tax inclusion period, Section 2642(f)(3) makes no reference to Section 2035 even though Section 2642(f)(1) creates an exception for Section 2035 inclusion under the rule that makes Section 2642(f) applicable.

[480] Reg. § 26.2632-1(c)(3)(ii).

estate tax purposes.[481] Terminating the estate tax inclusion period before the expiration of the three-year period of exposure under Section 2035 is inconsistent with the purpose of delaying the effective date of the allocation of GST exemption under Section 2642(f)(1).[482] However, this appropriate regulatory shortening of the termination of the estate tax inclusion period likely can be justified on the basis of practicality. The property to which the GST exemption has been allocated must be valued when the estate tax inclusion period ends in order to compute the applicable fraction.[483] Ending the estate tax inclusion period when a retained interest is transferred will generally result in termination of the period when the property is also being valued for gift tax purposes. Waiting until the end of three years after a power or a retained interest is relinquished or transferred to terminate the estate tax inclusion period generally would require an additional valuation of the property solely for purposes of determining the applicable fraction at the end of the three-year period.[484]

Since Section 2035 inclusion is disregarded in determining the end of the estate tax inclusion period, Section 2038 inclusion resulting from relinquishment of a power within three years of death without any assistance from Section 2035[485] and instances where the exercise or release of a general power of appointment within three years of death results in Section 2041 inclusion by a disposition which, if it were a transfer of property, would be included in decedent's gross estate under Section 2035 should also be disregarded.[486]

[ii] **Terminations involving split gifts.** When a split gift is subject to the Section 2642(f)(1) deferral rules,[487] the estate tax inclusion period ends for the individual who is a transferor *solely by reason of the Section 2513 election* on

---

[481] This rule prevents the GST exemption allocated to property transferred from appreciating and depreciating with the property transferred while the transferor is still the owner of the property for estate tax purposes. Ending the estate tax inclusion period when the retained interest is transferred, rather than when estate tax inclusion is no longer possible at the end of the three-year period specified in Section 2035, results in the GST exemption appreciating or depreciating with the property for a maximum of an additional three years.

[482] See supra ¶ 16.02[7][a] text accompanying note 431.

[483] See infra ¶ 16.02[7][e].

[484] See infra ¶ 16.02[7][e]. However, if death intervenes during the three-year period, a valuation of the property will be required at that time for estate tax purposes in any event, not necessitating an additional valuation simply for generation-skipping transfer tax purposes. Additionally, if the relinquishment results in a generation-skipping transfer, the estate tax inclusion period ends and the property must be valued. The termination of the estate tax inclusion period when the retained interest is transferred will require a recomputation of the applicable fraction if the transferor dies within the three-year period and estate tax is paid out of the property held in trust. See supra ¶ 16.02[3][b][ii].

[485] IRC § 2038(a)(1). See ¶ 4.10[8]. See also IRC § 2035(e); ¶ 4.07[2][b][ii].

[486] See IRC §§ 2041(a)(1)(B), 2041(a)(2), 2041(a)(3)(B); ¶¶ 4.13[6][a], 4.13[7][b].

[487] See supra ¶ 16.02[7][b] text accompanying notes 460–466.

the earlier of the time at which no portion of the property would be includible in the gross estate of that individual's spouse (other than by reason of Section 2035), the death of that individual's spouse, or the time of a generation-skipping transfer with respect to the property subject to the generation-skipping transfer.[488]

[iii] Transferor's spouse's interest. The estate tax inclusion period following an inter vivos nontaxable interspousal transfer terminates at the first to occur of: (1) the death of the transferee spouse or (2) the time at which no portion of the property would be includible in the transferee spouse's gross estate (other than by reason of Section 2035).[489]

[d] Illustrations of the Deferral Rules

To illustrate the Section 2642(f) rules, assume grantor *G* transfers property to a trust with income to child *C* for life and a remainder to grandchild *GC* (*C*'s child), but *G* retains a power to revoke the trust. Since the property is potentially includible in *G*'s gross estate under Section 2038, no GST exemption allocated to the trust is effective until the termination of *G*'s estate tax inclusion period.[490] If *C* or *G* dies, or *G* relinquishes the power to revoke the trust, the estate tax inclusion period should end.[491] Alternatively, if the revocable trust provides income to *GC* for life with a remainder to *GGC*, *G*'s great-grandchild, there is no direct skip on *G*'s transfer of property to the revocable trust, but when *G* relinquishes the power to revoke, or when *G* or *GC* dies, the estate tax inclusion period should terminate[492] with a resulting direct skip transfer to the trust.[493]

To illustrate the Section 2642(f) rules that defer a direct skip transfer until the end of the estate tax inclusion period,[494] as well as the effect of an allocation of the GST exemption, assume that grandparent *G* purchases property and

---

[488] Reg. §§ 26.2632-1(c)(3)(i)–26.2632-1(c)(3)(iii). See especially Regulations Section 26.2632-1(c)(3)(ii), which indicates by implication that this set of alternatives applies.

[489] Regulations Section 26.2632-1(c)(3)(iv) applies when Regulations Section 26.2632-1(c)(2)(i)(B) triggers the estate tax inclusion period.

[490] IRC §§ 2642(f)(1), 2642(f)(3).

[491] If *G* dies within the estate tax inclusion period, the period ends at *G*'s death. IRC § 2642(f)(3)(B). If *G* relinquishes the revocation power, the period should also end. See supra text accompanying note 485. If *C* dies within the estate tax inclusion period, the period ends and the property passes to *GC* with a resulting transfer from *G* to *GC*, but the transfer is not a direct skip generation-skipping transfer because of the predeceased parent rule. IRC § 2651(e), discussed at ¶ 17.01[2][a][ii]. Cf. infra ¶ 16.02[7][e] note 511.

[492] IRC § 2642(f)(3)(A). See supra ¶ 16.02[7][c] text accompanying note 485.

[493] IRC §§ 2642(f)(1) (last sentence), 2642(f)(3). See Reg. § 26.2632-1(c)(3); supra ¶ 16.02[2][b] note 45. See also ¶ 15.03[3][b].

[494] IRC § 2642(f)(1) (last sentence).

title is conveyed to *G* and grandchild *GC* as joint tenants with a right of survivorship. The transfer creating the interests is a direct skip of one half of the value of the property from *G* to *GC*, but this direct skip is not treated as occurring until the end of the estate tax inclusion period, which has not occurred because the property transferred would be includible in *G*'s gross estate under Section 2040 if *G* died immediately after the transfer.[495] Assuming the property is non–income producing,[496] the tenancy is not partitioned or conveyed, and *G* predeceases *GC*, the estate tax inclusion period will end upon *G*'s death.[497] The effect of any allocation of the GST exemption is deferred by Section 2642(f) until the end of the estate tax inclusion period, the date of *G*'s death.[498] If *GC* predeceased *G* prior to any partition or conveyance, the property simply returns to *G*, and there is no direct skip or any other generation-skipping transfer.[499] Any GST exemption that has been allocated to the interest transferred to *GC* that has not taken effect should be treated as void and restored to *G*.[500] If, during the lives of the joint tenants, there is a severance of the joint tenancy with the property split equally between them, the estate tax inclusion period closes on the date the property is severed. The one half of the value of the property transferred to *GC* is no longer includible in the gross estate of *G*, and there is a direct skip generation-skipping transfer to *GC* of that one half of the value of the property. Any GST exemption allocated to the joint tenancy during the estate tax inclusion period is effective at the severance. The deemed allocation of GST exemption to the direct skip also occurs at severance.[501] If both joint tenants gratuitously convey the property to another of *G*'s grandchildren (the sibling of *GC*), the estate tax inclusion period terminates on the date of the conveyance, and there is a direct skip of the entire value of the property.[502] Again, as when the tenancy is severed, any GST exemption allocated to the property during the estate tax inclusion period is effective at that time, and

---

[495] IRC § 2642(f)(1). See supra ¶ 16.02[2][b] note 45.

[496] The estate tax inclusion period terminates with respect to one half of any income received by *GC*, which is a direct skip transfer from *G*. See IRC § 2642(f)(3)(A); ¶ 15.03[3][b] text accompanying notes 59–65; infra ¶ 16.02[7][e][iii].

[497] If *G* predeceases *GC*, at *G*'s death, there is a direct skip of the estate tax value of the entire value of property to *GC*, not merely one half of the value. See supra ¶ 16.02[2][b] note 45.

[498] See supra ¶ 16.02[7][b], infra ¶ 16.02[7][e].

[499] In this circumstance, the estate tax inclusion period never terminates prior to *GC*'s death. See IRC § 2642(f)(3).

[500] See infra ¶ 16.02[7][e] note 511.

[501] IRC § 2632(b)(1). See ¶ 15.03[3][b] note 65.

[502] IRC §§ 2642(f)(1), 2642(f)(3). In effect, *G* transfers one-half of the property in a direct skip to *GC*, who then transfers that one-half by gift to the sibling. Additionally, *G* transfers the other one half of the property by gift directly to the sibling of *GC*.

the deemed allocation of GST exemption to the direct skip occurs.[503] If the conveyance is to G's child (GC's parent), the delayed direct skip to GC of one half of the value of the property occurs as of the close of the estate tax inclusion period, and any GST exemption allocated or deemed allocated[504] to the property will be effective at that time.[505]

Section 2642(f)(1) deferral occurs also when Transferor makes a transfer in trust, providing that the income is to be paid to Spouse for life and giving Spouse a general power to appoint the remainder by will and in default of appointment, the remainder passes to grandchild GC. Assuming the transfer qualifies for the marital deduction under Section 2523(e),[506] if either spouse made an allocation of GST exemption to the trust,[507] the effect of the allocation is delayed until Spouse's death when Spouse becomes the Chapter 13 transferor. Any allocation of Transferor's GST exemption to the trust should be treated as void.[508] Alternatively, if Transferor makes a transfer in trust with income to GC for a term of years, remainder to Spouse, the estate tax inclusion period rules again apply, deferring the direct skip to the trust until the termination of the estate tax inclusion period.[509]

[e] Computation of the Applicable Fraction During the Estate Tax Inclusion Period

[i] **Introduction.** When the estate tax inclusion period deferral rules apply, special rules are used both with respect to the timing of the allocation of GST exemption in the determination of the numerator of the applicable fraction and the valuation of the trust property in the determination of the denominator of the applicable fraction.

Any allocation of GST exemption by the transferor prior to the termination of the estate tax inclusion period remains in limbo, and its effectiveness is delayed until the termination of the period[510] when it enters into the computation of the numerator of the applicable fraction.[511] At that time, the denomina-

---

[503] IRC § 2632(b)(1). See ¶ 15.03[3][b] note 65.

[504] IRC § 2632(b)(1). See ¶ 15.03[3][b] note 65.

[505] In effect, G transfers one-half of the property in a direct skip to GC, who then transfers that one-half by gift to parent C. G's transfer of one-half to child C (GC's parent) is not a generation-skipping transfer.

[506] See ¶ 11.03[4][c].

[507] See supra ¶ 16.02[7][b] text accompanying notes 467–471.

[508] See supra ¶ 16.02[7][b] text accompanying note 471.

[509] Reg. § 26.2632-1(c)(2)(i)(B). Cf. ¶ 15.03[3][b] text accompanying notes 52–65.

[510] Reg. § 26.2632-1(c)(1). Any such allocation is irrevocable. Id.

[511] See Reg. §§ 26.2632-1(c)(5) Exs. 1, 2, 26.2642-4(b) Ex. 5. If GST exemption is allocated during the estate tax inclusion period, but it never becomes effective because the

tor of the applicable fraction is determined under valuation rules that depend on the manner in which the estate tax inclusion period has terminated. The valuation rules, along with the recomputation rules for allocation of the GST exemption, are considered next.[512]

[ii] **Termination of the ETIP at death.** When death terminates the estate tax inclusion period,[513] the property is generally valued at its estate tax value in the computation of the denominator of the applicable fraction if the property is includible in the gross estate of the transferor or the transferor's spouse.[514] For example, assume that grantor G transfers $100,000 worth of property to a revocable trust with income to child C for life, followed by a remainder to grandchild GC (C's child), and that G immediately allocates $100,000 of GST exemption to the transfer. Because the trust is revocable, Section 2642(f) applies[515] to delay the effect of the allocation of GST exemption to the trust. Assuming G takes no inter vivos action, G's death, prior to C's death,[516] marks the close of the estate tax inclusion period.[517] If the corpus of the trust is valued at $150,000 in G's gross estate and no additional GST exemption is allocated to the trust, the numerator of the applicable fraction is $100,000, the GST exemption previously allocated that becomes effective at G's death on the termination of the estate tax inclusion period.[518] The denominator of the appli-

---

property returns to the transferor, the transferor of the transfer changes, or some other event occurs that results in the allocation disappearing prior to, or at the end of, the estate tax inclusion period, the allocation should be treated as void and the amount of the transferor's remaining GST exemption should be increased. See supra ¶¶ 16.02[7][b] text accompanying notes 466, 471, 16.02[7][d] text accompanying note 500.

[512] See infra ¶¶ 16.02[7][e][ii], 16.02[7][e][iii].

[513] Reg. §§ 26.2632-1(c)(3)(i), 26.2632-1(c)(3)(iv)(A).

[514] IRC § 2642(f)(2)(A). Estate tax valuation encompasses valuation under Section 2031, Section 2032, or Section 2032A, whichever is used for federal estate tax purposes. Although Section 2642(f)(2)(A) contains no qualifications on the method of valuation of property included in the gross estate of the transferor, the regulations provide that the estate tax value of qualified real property valued under Section 2032A is the fair market value of the qualified real property, rather than its value under Section 2032A, unless the recapture agreement specifically provides the signatories' consent to the imposition of, and personal liability for, additional generation-skipping transfer tax in the event additional estate tax is imposed under Section 2032A(c). Reg. § 26.2642-2(b)(1). See supra ¶ 16.02[4][d] note 255.

Where estate tax inclusion occurs under Section 2035, the lifetime termination of the estate tax inclusion period rules will apply. See infra ¶ 16.02[7][e][iii]. In disregarding Section 2035, Section 2035–type inclusions under Sections 2038 and 2041 should also be disregarded. See supra ¶ 16.02[7][c] text accompanying notes 485, 486.

[515] See supra ¶ 16.02[7][d] text accompanying notes 490, 491.

[516] See supra ¶ 16.02[7][d] text accompanying note 491.

[517] IRC § 2642(f)(3)(B).

[518] Reg. §§ 26.2632-1(c)(1), 26.2632-1(c)(3)(i).

cable fraction is the value of the corpus for estate tax purposes, $150,000.[519] The resulting applicable fraction is 0.667 ($100,000 ÷ $150,000).

[iii] **Lifetime termination of the ETIP.** Lifetime termination of the estate tax inclusion period occurs when trust property is no longer potentially includible in the transferor's or the transferor's spouse's gross estate, ignoring Section 2035 inclusion, or when there is a generation-skipping transfer of the property during the estate tax inclusion period.

Termination of Potential Estate Inclusion. When property subject to the Section 2642(f) deferral rules is no longer potentially includible in the gross estate of the transferor or the transferor's spouse, disregarding Section 2035,[520] the estate tax inclusion period ends.[521] If GST exemption has been allocated with its effect delayed during the estate tax inclusion period, or if GST exemption is allocated or deemed allocated on a timely filed gift tax return for the calendar year in which the possibility of gross estate inclusion other than under Section 2035 terminates, the numerator of the applicable fraction is the GST exemption allocated during the estate tax inclusion period plus any GST exemption allocated or deemed allocated on the timely filed return.[522] In these circumstances, the value used in determining the denominator of the applicable fraction is the fair market value of the property at the close of the estate tax inclusion period.[523]

---

[519] IRC § 2642(f)(2)(A). See supra text accompanying note 514.

[520] Reg. §§ 26.2632-1(c)(3)(ii), 26.2632-1(c)(3)(iv)(B). See supra ¶ 16.02[7][c] text accompanying notes 485, 486.

[521] Reg. §§ 26.2632-1(c)(3)(ii), 26.2632-1(c)(3)(iv)(B).

[522] Reg. § 26.2632-1(c)(1).

[523] IRC §§ 2642(b)(1)(A), 2642(f)(2)(B). Thus, the property is to be valued at its fair market value on the date of relinquishment or transfer in the determination of the denominator of the applicable fraction if the allocation of GST exemption is made, or treated as made, on a timely filed federal gift tax return for the calendar year in which such period ends. The normal due date of the federal gift tax return, April 15 following the close of the calendar year in which the gift is made, may be accelerated for gifts made in the year of death of the transferor to the due date for filing the federal estate tax return. IRC § 6075. However, if no allocation of GST exemption is, or has been, made at the close of the estate tax inclusion period other than at the transferor's death, generally the property is to be valued only when the allocation is filed. IRC § 2642(f)(2)(B) (parenthetical). However, an election may be made to value the property on the first day of the month in which the allocation is filed, except for the valuation of life insurance policies where the insured has died. Reg. § 26.2642-2(a)(2). See supra ¶ 16.02[3][c] text accompanying notes 246, 247. The allocation with respect to transfers for which no timely gift tax return is filed can be made by an executor on a timely filed estate tax return or a gift tax return filed on or before the due date of the estate tax return, and if that occurs, the date of valuation is the date the allocation is filed. Reg. § 26.2632-1(d)(1). This would include both untimely allocations to inter vivos transfers not included in the transferor's gross estate and allocations to property included in the transferor's gross estate under Section 2035(a).

For example, assume that grantor *G* transfers $100,000 worth of property to a revocable trust with income to child *C* for life, followed by a remainder to grandchild *GC* (*C*'s child), and that *G* immediately allocates $100,000 of GST exemption to the transfer. If *G* simply relinquishes the power to revoke the trust, the close of the estate tax inclusion period should occur at the time of the relinquishment of the power of revocation,[524] and the allocation of the GST exemption made to the property held in the trust should be effective at that time.[525] The GST exemption allocated to the trust during the estate tax inclusion period is treated as allocated[526] on a timely filed gift tax return for the year in which the estate tax inclusion period ends. The fair market value at the close of the estate tax inclusion period is used in the determination of the denominator of the applicable fraction.[527] If the corpus of the trust had a fair market value of $125,000 when the power to revoke was relinquished, the numerator is the $100,000 of previously allocated GST exemption, the denominator is $125,000, the fair market value of the trust corpus when the power was relinquished, and the resulting applicable fraction is 0.800 ($100,000 ÷ $125,000).[528]

Generation-Skipping Transfer Termination. The estate tax inclusion period terminates at the time of a generation-skipping transfer, but only with respect to the property involved in the generation-skipping transfer.[529] When this occurs, it is necessary to determine the applicable fraction and the resulting inclusion ratio for the property involved in the generation-skipping transfer in order to determine the tax liability for the transfer.[530] The regulations, in permitting an allocation of GST exemption during the estate tax inclusion period and merely delaying the effect of the allocation until the termination of the estate tax inclusion period, provide a workable solution to deal with generation-skipping transfers from a trust during the estate tax inclusion period.[531] If prop-

---

[524] IRC § 2642(f)(3). See Reg. §§ 26.2632-1(c)(3)(ii), 26.2632-1(c)(3)(iv)(B); supra ¶ 16.02[7][c] text accompanying note 486.

[525] IRC § 2642(f)(1). Valuation used for Chapter 12 gift tax valuation would also be applied here.

[526] See supra text accompanying notes 522, 523.

[527] IRC § 2642(f)(2)(B).

[528] If there is an allocation of GST exemption on a gift tax return that is not timely filed for the calendar year in which the estate tax inclusion period ends, the property is generally valued at its fair market value when an allocation is filed with the secretary. IRC § 2642(f)(2)(B) (parenthetical). However, an election may be made to value the property on the first day of the month in which the allocation is filed, except for life insurance policies where the insured has died. Reg. § 26.2642-2(a)(2). This valuation election is discussed supra ¶ 16.02[4][c] text accompanying notes 246, 247.

[529] Reg. § 26.2632-1(c)(3)(iii).

[530] See Reg. § 26.2642-1(b)(2).

[531] See Reg. §§ 26.2632-1(c), 26.2642-1(b)(2); ¶ 15.03[3][b] note 50.

erty is held in a trust, any allocation of GST exemption is made to the entire trust, not to specific assets held in the trust or to distributions from the trust.[532] The computations are straightforward if there is a generation-skipping transfer of the entire corpus of the trust, but they are more complex if the generation-skipping transfer involves only a portion of the trust.

For example, assume transferor T creates a trust that provides that trust income is to be paid to T for fifteen years, or until T's death if earlier, with a remainder to T's grandchild GC on the termination of T's interest, and that an independent trustee has the power to invade trust principal on behalf of GC at any time.[533] The trust is funded by T with $100,000 of cash, and T allocates $100,000 of GST exemption to the property held in the trust. Because the trust property would be includible in T's gross estate under Section 2036(a) if death occurred immediately after the transfer, the allocation of GST exemption is not effective until termination of the estate tax inclusion period.[534] On creation of the trust, the allocation of $100,000 of GST exemption remains in limbo.[535] If, during the fifteen-year period, the trustee invades the entire corpus of the trust for GC when the corpus is still valued at $100,000, the invasion constitutes a taxable termination, and there is no generation-skipping transfer tax because the applicable fraction is one and the inclusion ratio is zero. If the corpus has appreciated in value to $300,000, the applicable fraction would be 0.333 ($100,000 ÷ $300,000), and the inclusion ratio would be 0.667.

The determination of the applicable fraction and the inclusion ratio become more complicated when the generation-skipping transfer involves less than all of the property held in a trust. Subsequent generation-skipping transfers of portions of the property held in the trust during the estate tax inclusion period require redeterminations of the applicable fraction.[536] A redetermination of the applicable fraction is also required at the end of the estate tax inclusion period for any subsequent generation-skipping transfers with respect to the bal-

---

[532] Reg. § 26.2632-1(a).

[533] This basic factual pattern is similar to Regulations Sections 26.2632-1(c)(5) Exs. 1, 2, and 26.2642-4(b) Exs. 5(i), 5(ii). See supra ¶ 16.02[2][b] note 45.

[534] IRC § 2642(f)(1); Reg. § 26.2632-1(c).

[535] If T lives for fifteen years, when the value of the corpus appreciates to $500,000, and the trustee does not invade corpus for GC during that period, the applicable fraction is computed at the end of the fifteen-year period on the termination of the estate tax inclusion period. Reg. § 26.2632-1(c)(3)(ii). The numerator of the applicable fraction is the GST exemption amount initially allocated to the trust, $100,000 (Reg. § 26.2642-1(b)(1)), and the denominator is the value of the corpus at that time, $500,000 (Reg. §§ 26.2632-1(c)(1), 26.2642-1(c)(1)), resulting in an applicable fraction of 0.200 ($100,000 ÷ $500,000). See supra ¶ 16.02[7][e][iii]. If T dies within the fifteen-year period without any corpus invasions by the trustee for GC and the corpus is valued at $400,000 in T's gross estate, the applicable fraction is 0.250 ($100,000 ÷ $400,000). See supra ¶ 16.02[7][e][ii].

[536] See infra text accompanying notes 549, 550.

Section 2642

ance of the property held in the trust.[537] However, in any recomputation of the applicable fraction, since a portion of the trust property was previously distributed that carried a portion of the GST exemption allocated to the trust with it, the GST exemption allocated to the trust property that is not effective, the numerator of the applicable fraction, must be reduced by the nontax amount of the prior generation-skipping transfers with respect to the trust.[538] This reduction prevents multiple use of the GST exemption allocation. The nontax amount of a prior generation-skipping transfer with respect to a trust is the amount of the generation-skipping transfer multiplied by the applicable fraction attributable to the trust at the time of the prior generation-skipping transfer.[539]

Returning to the preceding example, if the trustee invades only a portion of the corpus for *GC* during the fifteen-year period, the invasion constitutes a taxable distribution generation-skipping transfer.[540] The estate tax inclusion period terminates at the time of invasion, but only with respect to the property involved in the generation-skipping transfer.[541] The applicable fraction and inclusion ratio for the trust must be computed in order to determine the generation-skipping transfer tax imposed on the taxable distribution.[542] Again, if *T* has allocated $100,000 of GST exemption to the trust and if the trustee distributes $25,000 of the corpus to *GC* when the entire trust corpus is valued at $100,000, $25,000 of the GST exemption is consumed by the disposition.[543] Computation of the applicable fraction for subsequent generation-skipping transfers from the trust requires a reduction of the GST exemption allocated to the trust, $100,000, by the nontax amount of any prior generation-skipping

---

[537] See infra text accompanying notes 551–555.

[538] Reg. § 26.2642-1(b)(2)(i)(A). If additional GST exemption is allocated to the trust after the termination of the estate tax inclusion period, it is added to the recomputed numerator of the applicable fraction. Reg. § 26.2642-1(b)(2)(i)(B).

[539] Reg. § 26.2642-1(b)(2)(ii)(A).

[540] IRC § 2612(b). See Reg. §§ 26.2632-1(c)(5) Ex. 2, 26.2642-4(b) Ex. 5(i).

[541] Reg. § 26.2632-1(c)(3)(iii).

[542] See IRC §§ 2602, 2641, 2642.

[543] The trust's applicable fraction is one. The numerator of the applicable fraction is $100,000, the value of the GST exemption allocated to the trust with delayed effect. The denominator is the fair market value of the trust corpus just prior to the distribution, $100,000. The inclusion ratio is zero, one minus the applicable fraction, and the applicable rate of tax is zero. The $25,000 distribution occurs without the imposition of any generation-skipping transfer tax because it is insulated from taxation by the GST exemption, and $25,000 of the GST exemption allocated to the trust has been consumed by the distribution.

transfers with respect to the trust.[544] The $25,000 taxable distribution to *GC* requires a reduction of $25,000 of the GST exemption allocated to the trust.[545]

Assume, instead, that the property held in the trust appreciates in value to $200,000 when the trustee distributes $25,000 to *GC*. The distribution to *GC* is a taxable distribution, the estate tax inclusion period terminates with respect to the $25,000 involved in the generation-skipping transfer,[546] and the applicable fraction must be determined to compute the generation-skipping transfer tax. The numerator of the applicable fraction is the GST exemption previously allocated to the trust, $100,000.[547] The denominator of the applicable fraction is the fair market value of the property held in the trust immediately prior to the distribution, $200,000. The resulting applicable fraction is 0.500 ($100,000 ÷ $200,000).[548]

If the remaining trust corpus appreciates to $275,000 in the next year when the trustee makes a second $25,000 taxable distribution to *GC*, the applicable fraction must again be redetermined. The numerator of the applicable fraction must be adjusted to reflect the portion of GST exemption consumed in the prior distribution. The GST exemption previously allocated to the trust, $100,000, is reduced by the nontax amount of the prior generation-skipping transfer with respect to the trust, $12,500,[549] and the numerator of the applica-

---

[544] Reg. § 26.2642-1(b)(2)(i)(A). The nontax amount of a prior generation-skipping transfer with respect to a trust is the amount of the generation-skipping transfer multiplied by the applicable fraction attributable to the trust at the time of the prior generation-skipping transfer, or here, $25,000 multiplied by 1, or $25,000. Reg. § 26.2642-1(b)(2)(ii)(A).

[545] See supra text accompanying note 544. The applicable fraction, inclusion ratio, and applicable rate of tax for another distribution would remain at one ($75,000 ÷ $75,000), zero, and zero, respectively, if the value of the underlying corpus remains at $75,000. If the remaining $75,000 of corpus appreciates in value to $375,000 on termination of the nine-year income interest and no further GST exemption is allocated to the trust, the applicable fraction is 0.200 ($75,000 ÷ $375,000) and the inclusion ratio is 0.800.

[546] Reg. § 26.2632-1(c)(3)(iii).

[547] Reg. § 26.2642-1(b)(2)(i). This regulation provides rules for the determination of the inclusion ratio (which involves the applicable fraction) with respect to taxable terminations and taxable distributions occurring during the estate tax inclusion period. Reg. § 26.2642-1(b)(2). These rules should also be applied where there is any subsequent generation-skipping transfer from the trust, including a direct skip.

[548] This results in an inclusion ratio of 0.500, an applicable rate of tax, assuming a maximum federal estate tax rate of 50 percent, of 25 percent (0.500 × 50 percent), and a tax of $6,250 ($25,000 × 25 percent). This is just as if $12,500 of the distribution is taxed at the maximum federal estate tax rate, an assumed rate of 50 percent in the example, and the remaining $12,500 is exempt from taxation owing to the allocation of GST exemption.

[549] Reg. § 26.2642-1(b)(2)(i)(A). The nontax amount of the prior generation-skipping transfer, $12,500, is the amount of the generation-skipping transfer, $25,000, multiplied by the applicable fraction attributable to the trust at the time of the prior transfer, 0.500. Reg. § 26.2642-1(b)(2)(ii). See supra text accompanying notes 538, 539.

ble fraction becomes $87,500. The denominator of the applicable fraction is $275,000, the fair market value of the trust property immediately prior to the second distribution. The applicable fraction is 0.318 ($87,500 ÷ $275,000).[550]

Assume that in the next year, when the remaining trust corpus has appreciated to $450,000, T transfers the retained income interest to child C, GC's parent. The estate tax inclusion period terminates with the transfer.[551] The lurking unused GST exemption allocated to the property is effective upon termination of the estate tax inclusion period. The applicable fraction must once again be redetermined. The numerator of the applicable fraction is $79,550. This is the amount of GST exemption initially allocated to the property held in the trust, $100,000, reduced by the nontax amount of both of the generation-skipping transfers occurring during the estate tax inclusion period, $20,450 ($12,500 + $7,950).[552] The denominator of the applicable fraction is the fair market value of the trust property at the time the income interest is transferred, $450,000. The applicable fraction is 0.177 ($79,500 ÷ $450,000).[553] After the final termination of the estate tax inclusion period, the applicable fraction used in the determination of the generation-skipping transfer tax remains 0.177 for any subsequent generation-skipping transfer from the trust,[554] unless a redetermination of the applicable fraction is required by a subsequent event, such as

---

[550] This results in an inclusion ratio of 0.682, the rate of tax assuming a 50 percent maximum federal estate tax rate is 34.100 percent (0.682 × 50 percent), and the generation-skipping transfer tax imposed is $8,525.00 ($25,000 × 34.100 percent).

If the trustee in the example had a discretionary power to pay income to GC during the fifteen-year period and exercised the power, distributions of income to GC would be treated in the same manner as the corpus distributions.

[551] Reg. § 26.2632-1(c)(3)(ii). No portion of the corpus is potentially includible in T's gross estate other than under Section 2035.

[552] Reg. § 26.2642-1(b)(2)(i)(A). The nontax amount of the first generation-skipping transfer during the estate tax inclusion period was $12,500. See supra note 517. The nontax amount of the second generation-skipping transfer during the estate tax inclusion period was $7,950 (0.318 × $25,000).

Although the termination of the estate tax inclusion period is not a generation-skipping transfer occurring during an estate tax inclusion period (see Reg. § 26.2642-1(b)(2)), the computation of the applicable fraction should be computed in the same manner as provided in the regulations. A reduction in the amount of exemption allocated for the nontax amount of any generation-skipping transfers occurring with respect to the trust during the estate tax inclusion period is necessary to properly compute the applicable fraction. See supra text accompanying notes 536–539.

[553] The inclusion ratio is 0.823 and the rate of tax assuming a 50 percent maximum federal estate tax rate is 41.150 percent (0.823 × 50 percent).

[554] Thus, at the end of the fifteen-year period, there is a taxable termination when C's income interest terminates and the corpus passes to GC, and the applicable fraction is 0.177.

the allocation of additional GST exemption or the addition of property to the trust.[555]

[8] Finality of Inclusion Ratio

[a] Direct Skips

The inclusion ratio applicable to a direct skip becomes final upon the expiration of the statute of limitations for assessment of the generation-skipping transfer tax.[556] This period includes the period during which additional generation-skipping transfer tax may be assessed as the result of the imposition of additional estate tax under Section 2032A(c).[557] This period will often coincide with the assessment period for the applicable estate or gift tax.[558]

[b] Taxable Terminations and Taxable Distributions

In the case of a taxable termination or a taxable distribution, the inclusion ratio for a trust generally becomes final upon the later of (1) the expiration of the period for assessment with respect to the first generation-skipping transfer tax return filed using that inclusion ratio[559] or (2) the expiration of the period for assessment of federal estate tax with respect to the transferor's estate.[560] The justification for this "later of" rule with respect to taxable terminations and taxable distributions is that the basis for challenging a claimed inclusion ratio will not exist until a deficiency in tax can be asserted.[561]

---

[555] See supra ¶ 16.02[5][b].

[556] Reg. § 26.2642-5(a).

[557] Reg. § 26.2642-5(a).

[558] Cf. IRC §§ 2661, 6501. See ¶ 18.01[1].

[559] This period for assessment is extended where Section 2032A valuation of real property is used for generation-skipping transfer tax purposes until the expiration of the period of assessment of any generation-skipping transfer tax due as the result of imposition of additional estate tax under Section 2032A(c). Reg. § 26.2642-5(b)(1).

[560] See Reg. § 26.2642-5(b). When the transferor dies after the first taxable distribution or termination from the trust has occurred, the inclusion ratio will become final three years and nine months from the transferor's death. IRC §§ 6075, 6501. This assumes the correct and timely filing of all returns. If no estate tax return is required to be filed, the period for assessments is determined as if a timely return was filed. Reg. § 26.2642-5(b)(2).

[561] See PS-73-80, Supplementary Information, 1993-1 CB 867, 869.

[9] Statutory Relief Provisions

An inadvertent failure to make a timely election with respect to the allocation of GST exemption may be excused.[562] In addition, substantial compliance with the requirements for an allocation of GST exemption will result in an allocation of GST exemption.[563]

[a] Election Relief

Section 2642(g)(1) provides relief in two situations: an inadvertent failure to allocate GST exemption on a timely filed return or an inadvertent failure to prevent automatic allocation of GST exemption on a timely filed return.[564] An extension of time may be granted under Section 2642(g)(1) to allocate GST exemption after an inadvertent failure to make an allocation of GST exemption to an *inter vivos transfer* on a timely filed gift tax return under Section 2642(b)(1).[565] A Section 2642(g)(1) extension will permit the taxpayer to value the property transferred at its value as finally determined under Chapter 12 on the date the transfer is complete in the determination of the applicable fraction[566] rather than on the date the generation-skipping transfer allocation is filed.[567]

An extension of time in which to allocate GST exemption to a testamentary transfer under Section 2642(b)(2) is also permitted.[568] When an extension is granted for the allocation of unused GST exemption to a testamentary transfer, the estate tax value as finally determined is generally used in the determination of the applicable fraction.[569] An extension to allocate GST exemption to a testamentary transfer allows the personal representative to alter the Section 2632(e) automatic allocation of residual GST exemption.[570]

---

[562] IRC § 2642(g)(1). See infra ¶ 16.02[9][a].

[563] IRC § 2642(g)(2). See infra ¶ 16.02[9][b].

[564] IRC § 2642(g)(1). See HR Rep. No. 37, 107th Cong., 1st Sess. 39 (2001).

[565] IRC § 2642(g)(1)(A)(i). An extension may be granted when a gift tax return is timely filed and seemingly may also be granted when a gift tax return is not timely filed.

[566] IRC § 2642(b)(1). See supra ¶ 16.02[4][a] text accompanying note 225.

[567] IRC § 2642(b)(3). See supra ¶ 16.02[4][c].

[568] IRC § 2642(g)(1)(A)(ii).

[569] IRC § 2642(b)(2)(A). The property may be valued at the time of distribution in some circumstances. IRC § 2642(b)(2)(A) (last sentence). See supra ¶¶ 16.02[4][d][ii], 16.02[4][d][iii]. An extension of the time to allocate GST exemption under Section 2642(b)(2) to a testamentary transfer generally does not change the effective date of the allocation of GST exemption or alter the date or method of valuation of the testamentary transfer. An extension of time to allocate GST exemption under Section 2642(b)(1) to an inter vivos transfer changes the effective date of the allocation of GST exemption and the date of valuation of the property transferred.

[570] IRC § 2632(e). See ¶ 15.03[7].

The time to prevent the Section 2632(b) automatic allocation of GST exemption to a direct skip under Section 2632(b)(3) may also be extended where there is an inadvertent failure to make a timely election preventing the allocation.[571] The time to prevent the Section 2632(c) automatic allocation of unused GST exemption to an indirect skip under Section 2632(c)(5)(A) may also be extended under Section 2642(g)(1).[572]

Regulations are to prescribe the circumstances and procedures under which extensions will be granted under Section 2642(g)(1).[573] In determining whether to grant relief under Section 2642(g)(1), the time prescribed by statute for making the allocation or election is to be disregarded and determined as if the statute did not provide any time for making the election or allocation.[574] The Procedure and Administration Regulations provide the standards used to determine whether to grant an extension of time to make an election whose date is prescribed by a regulation and not expressly provided by a statute.[575] Therefore an extension of time under Section 2642(g)(1) to make an allocation under Section 2642(b)(1) or Section 2642(b)(2) or an election described in Section 2632(b)(3) or Section 2632(c)(5) is to be determined under the Procedure and Administration Regulations.[576] Relief will be granted under those regulations if it is established that the taxpayer acted reasonably and in good faith and that the grant of an extension under Section 2642(g)(1) will not prejudice the interests of the government.[577] The basis of the determination is to include evidence of intent to make an allocation at an earlier time (e.g., the time of transfer) contained in the trust instrument or instruments of transfer and such other factors as the Treasury Secretary deems relevant. The requests for an extension under Section 2642(g)(1) are to follow the same procedures as a request for a private letter ruling.[578] Section 2642(g)(1) applies to requests pending on, or filed after, December 31, 2000;[579] however, it is noteworthy that comparable relief is to be allowed with respect to transfers made even before the date of enactment of Section 2642(g).[580]

---

[571] IRC § 2642(g)(1)(A)(ii). See ¶ 15.03[3][c] text accompanying note 71.

[572] IRC § 2642(g)(1)(A)(ii). See ¶ 15.03[4][e][i].

[573] IRC § 2642(g)(1)(A).

[574] IRC § 2642(g)(1)(B).

[575] Notice 2001-50, 2001-2 CB __, __.

[576] Reg. § 301.9100.

[577] Reg. § 301.9100-3.

[578] See Rev. Proc. 2002-1, 2002-1 CB __, __, § 5.02.

[579] Economic Growth and Tax Relief Reconciliation Act of 2001, Pub. L. No. 107-16, § 564(b)(1), 115 Stat. 38, 91 (2001), reprinted in 2001-__ CB __, __.

[580] IRC § 2642(g)(1)(A) (last sentence).

[b] Substantial Compliance

Under Section 2642(g)(2) a demonstration of substantial compliance with the statutory and regulatory requirements in the allocation of GST exemption will suffice to establish that the exemption was allocated to a particular transfer or trust.[581] Congress enacted this provision out of a concern that the complexity of the rules governing the allocation of GST exemption made it difficult for taxpayers to comply with the technical requirements for making a proper election.[582]

The substantial compliance rule has two different applications. First, where an allocation of GST exemption has not been successfully made, if there is substantial compliance in an attempted allocation, the allocation will be treated as successfully made.[583] Second, a taxpayer who, in allocating GST exemption under Section 2632, demonstrates an intent to have the lowest possible inclusion ratio with respect to a particular transfer or trust is deemed to have allocated so much of the taxpayer's unused GST exemption as will produce the lowest possible inclusion ratio.[584]

Substantial compliance will be determined by considering all relevant circumstances, including evidence of intent contained in the trust instrument or instrument of transfer and such other factors as the Treasury Secretary deems appropriate.[585] This provision applies to transfers subject to estate tax or gift tax made after December 31, 2000.[586]

---

[581] Close counts in dancing and now allocation of GST exemption as well.

[582] See HR Rep. No. 37, 107th Cong., 1st Sess. 40 (2001).

[583] HR Conf. Rep. No. 84, 107th Cong., 1st Sess. 1, 203 (2001), reprinted in 2001-__ CB __, __. This statutory rule is consistent with prior determinations by the Service. See TAM 9534001 (May 1, 1995) (allocation by executor deemed valid where only substantial compliance with procedural return instructions).

[584] IRC § 2642(g)(2).

[585] IRC § 2642(g)(2).

[586] Economic Growth and Tax Relief Reconciliation Act of 2001, Pub. L. No. 107-16, § 564(b)(2), 115 Stat. 38, 91 (2001), reprinted in 2001-__ CB __, __. No inference is intended with respect to the availability of a rule of substantial compliance prior to the effective date of this provision. Id. See HR Conf. Rep. No. 84, 107th Cong., 1st Sess. 1, 203 (2001), reprinted in 2001-__ CB __, __.

CHAPTER 17

Other Definitions and Special Rules

¶ 17.01 SECTION 2651. GENERATION ASSIGNMENT

[1] Introduction

To have a generation-skipping transfer, a generation must be skipped.[1] What does Congress mean by the term "generation"? "Generation" is easy to define when the skip involves only lineal descendants of the transferor; but of what generation are cousins or nieces and nephews or unrelated friends? To determine whether a generation has been skipped, Congress has come up with the terms "skip person"[2] and "non-skip person."[3] Classification of a person as a skip person or a non-skip person depends on the person's generation assign-

---

[1] Each of the three Section 2611(a) generation-skipping transfers (a Section 2612(a) taxable termination, a Section 2612(b) taxable distribution, and a Section 2612(c) direct skip) raises, inter alia, the question whether a Section 2613(a) skip person or a Section 2613(b) non-skip person has a Chapter 13 interest in property.

[2] IRC § 2613(a). See ¶¶ 13.03[1]–13.03[4].

[3] IRC § 2613(b). See ¶ 13.03[5].

ment, which is an essential element in the implementation of Chapter 13.[4] There are essentially three sets of rules for determining a person's generation assignment, depending on whether the person is related to the transferor, is an unrelated person, or is a beneficiary who is not an individual. Each is examined in the next section.

[2] Classes of Beneficiaries

[a] Related Beneficiaries

[i] **Ancestral chain.** A lineal descendant of a grandparent of a transferor[5] is assigned a generation by comparing the number of generations between the descendant and the grandparent with the number of generations between the transferor and the grandparent.[6] The latter figure is always one; only the generation of the transferor's parents stands between the transferor and the transferor's grandparents. A lineal descendant of a grandparent of the transferor's spouse[7] and of a grandparent of the transferor's former spouse[8] are "generated" in the same way, i.e., as if *they* were lineal descendants of a grandparent of the transferor.[9]

Generally, any individual who is a lineal descendant of a grandparent of the transferor (or of a grandparent of the transferor's spouse or former spouse) is classified as a skip person if there are three or more generations between that individual and the grandparent.[10] The grandchild of a transferor is assigned to the second generation below[11] (younger than) the transferor. Because the grandchild is a lineal descendant of the grandparent of the transferor, the grandchild's generation is statutorily determined by comparing the number of

---

[4] See supra note 1.

[5] IRC § 2652(a). See infra ¶ 17.02[1]. Section 2652(a) defines "transferor" except as provided in Section 2653(a). However, the Section 2653(a) definition does not apply for purposes of generation assignment under Section 2651. IRC § 2653(a) (parenthetical). See ¶¶ 17.02[1][a] text accompanying note 8, 17.03[1].

[6] IRC § 2651(b)(1).

[7] IRC § 2651(b)(2).

[8] IRC § 2651(b)(2).

[9] For example, if a transferor made a transfer to an unrelated individual who is the child of a spouse or former spouse, there would be one generation between the spouse or former spouse and the spouse's grandparents, and two generations between the child and those grandparents.

[10] IRC §§ 2613(a)(1), 2651(b)(1). See ¶ 13.03[2]. But see IRC § 2651(e) discussed infra ¶ 17.01[2][a][ii].

[11] See IRC § 2613(a)(1).

generations *between* the grandchild (fifth generation) and the transferor's grandparent (first generation), which is three, with the number of generations between the grandparent (first generation) and the transferor (third generation), which is one. A comparison of three with one yields two; therefore, under the statute, the grandchild is assigned to the second generation below the transferor.

Although it may seem complicated, this method of determining generation is a useful tool for assigning individuals to a generation in order to implement the tax on generation-skipping transfers. If blood is indeed thicker than water, most trusts are created for persons related to the transferor. It may seem strange to classify generations with reference to a grandparent of the transferor or the transferor's spouse or former spouse, but that is the statute's initial approach, and a little thought yields a good reason for it. The lineal descendants of a *grandparent* of the transferor or the transferor's spouse or former spouse, as opposed to the narrower chain directly descending from the *transferor* or the transferor's spouse or former spouse, fan out to include most of the likely trust beneficiaries. This is graphically reflected in the following chart, which schematically presents six generations, five of which represent lineal descendants of four persons. The four persons selected are the four grandparents of the transferor.

Most of the terminology used here is conventional (grandparent, father and mother, aunt and uncle, sister and brother, first cousin, child, niece and nephew, grandchild, grandniece and grandnephew, great-grandchild, and great-grandniece and great-grandnephew). Individuals designated second, third, and fourth cousins are not necessarily known that way to anthropologists, who use somewhat more precise terminology. Nevertheless, these designations serve to identify individuals classified according to the following generation chart:

Generation

First		Grandparents Δ=O		Δ=O Grandparents	
Second		Δ=O Aunt	Father Δ=O Mother	Uncle Δ=O	
Third	1st Cousin Δ=O	O=TRANSFEROR	Sister O=Δ	Δ=O 1st Cousin	
Fourth	2nd Cousin O=Δ	O=Δ Child	Niece O=Δ	Δ=O 2nd Cousin	
Fifth	3rd Cousin O=Δ	O=Δ Grandchild	Grandniece O=Δ	Δ=O 3rd Cousin	
Sixth	4th Cousin O	Δ Great-Grandchild	Great-Grandniece O	Δ 4th Cousin	

This chart covers quite a large group, since there will generally be ever-increasing numbers of lineal descendants of the transferor's (or the transferor's spouse's or former spouse's) grandparents in each succeeding generation.[12]

---

[12] There would be four more grandparents for the transferor's spouse and for any former spouse of the transferor.

Although an anthropologist would not consider a spouse or former spouse a lineal descendant, the statute provides that an individual who has been married at any time to the transferor will be assigned to the transferor's generation.[13] Further, the spouse of any person who is a lineal descendant of a grandparent of the transferor, the transferor's spouse, or the transferor's former spouse is placed in the same generation as the lineal descendant.[14] Neither death nor divorce changes these classifications.[15]

The statute expressly treats an adopted child as issue of the adopting parent, making it possible to establish the generation of an adopted child by the lineal descendant rules.[16] In addition, the statute provides that "[a] relationship by the half-blood shall be treated as a relationship of the whole-blood."[17]

[ii] Predeceased parent rule. A special generation assignment rule may apply in the determination of the generation level of an individual whose par-

---

[13] IRC § 2651(c)(1).

[14] IRC § 2651(c)(2). Thus, generally a transferor's grandchild's spouse is a skip person to the transferor, but the transferor's nephew's spouse is a non-skip person. But see IRC § 2651(f)(1).

[15] IRC §§ 2651(c)(1), 2651(c)(2).

[16] IRC § 2651(b)(3)(A).

[17] IRC § 2651(b)(3)(B). This relationship may be important for some purposes, but it is difficult to give the provision significance in Chapter 13. It may be questioned whether this provision is necessary, since lineal descendants of the grandparents of the transferor's spouse or former spouse are assigned a generation under the rules provided for lineal descendants. Is the half-blood rule half-baked and unnecessary excess statutory baggage? No. Under the lineal descendant generation assignment rules, most individuals with half-blood relationships to lineal descendants of the transferor are treated as lineal descendants of the grandparents of the transferor's spouse or former spouse. This generation assignment occurs even without assistance from the rule treating relationships by the half blood as relationships of the whole blood. However, treating half blood relationships as whole-blood relationships does expand the class of individuals assigned a generation under the lineal descendant rules. Moving to the outer fringe of the class of individuals assigned a generation under the lineal descendant rules, there is the possibility of adding half-blood relatives of lineal descendants of the transferor's spouse to the class of individuals who are under the lineal descendant umbrella for generation assignment. For example, assume that transferor *T* has a wife *W* who has a daughter *SD* by a prior marriage. *SD* has a half-blood brother *HB* who is the child of *W*'s former husband and his prior wife. Under the general rule, *SD* is assigned a generation as a lineal descendant, because she is a lineal descendant of the transferor's spouse, *W*. *HB* is not a lineal descendant of *W* and thus is not treated as a lineal descendant under the general rules. However, under the half-blood rules, *HB* is treated as a blood relative and the full-blood brother of *SD*. The question is whether *HB*, the half-blood brother of *W*'s daughter, is treated as a lineal descendant of *W*, the transferor's spouse. If the provision is to have any meaning, he *is* treated as a lineal descendant of *W*; his generation assignment is determined under the lineal descendant rules instead of the rules provided for unrelated beneficiaries. See infra ¶ 17.01[2][b]. See also TAM 200150003 (Aug. 22, 2001) (transferor's stepbrother's children not treated as lineal descendants of grandparent of transferor).

ent is deceased.[18] If the special rule applies, a grandchild may be assigned to the generation level of a child, the grandchild's parent's generation level. A grandniece or grandnephew may be assigned to the generation level of a deceased niece or nephew parent. When death has eliminated heirs at a generation level, and as a result, the transfer of family wealth skips a generation, Congress has decided that the transfer should not be treated as a generation-skipping transfer because a normal devolution of the property from one generation to the next available generation occurs and there is no motive to avoid transfer taxes.[19]

When the special generation assignment rule applies, the individual whose parent is deceased is assigned to the first generation below the transferor's generation or, if lower, the generation of the youngest living ancestor of the individual who is also a descendant of a parent of the transferor, a parent of the transferor's spouse or former spouse.[20] The generation assignment of the descendants of the individual assigned a generation under the predeceased parent rule are adjusted accordingly.[21]

If, under the predeceased parent rule, a grandchild is assigned to the generation level one below the transferor, the generation level of the transferor's children, an outright transfer to the grandchild is not a generation-skipping transfer, because the grandchild is not a skip person.[22] Rather than being assigned to a generation level that is at least two levels below that assigned to the transferor,[23] the grandchild is reassigned to the generation level one below that assigned to the transferor, the generation level of the transferor's children,

---

[18] IRC § 2651(e). This special rule may apply only to generation-skipping transfers occurring after December 31, 1997. Taxpayer Relief Act of 1997, Pub. L. No. 105-34, § 511(c), 111 Stat. 788, 861 (1997), reprinted in 1997-4 CB (Vol. 1) 1, 75.

The predeceased parent exception was formerly applicable only to direct skips. It was a part of the definition of a direct skip rather than a generation assignment rule. See IRC § 2612(c)(2) prior to its repeal with respect to direct skips occurring after December 31, 1997, in the Taxpayer Relief Act of 1997, Pub. L. No. 105-34, § 511(b)(1), 111 Stat. 788, 861 (1997), reprinted in 1997-4 CB (Vol. 1) 1, 75; Stephens, Maxfield, Lind & Calfee, Federal Estate and Gift Taxation ¶ 13.02[4][c][i] (Warren, Gorham & Lamont, 7th ed. 1997). The predeceased parent exception contained in the generation assignment rules may apply in the determination of all three types of generation-skipping transfers — taxable terminations, taxable distributions, and direct skips. In addition, the predeceased parent rule also applies in the generation assignment of collateral heirs (lineal descendants of the transferor's parents who are not lineal descendants of the transferor). See S. Rep. No. 33, 105th Cong., 1st Sess. 50 (1997), reprinted in 1997-4 CB (Vol. 2) 1067, 1130.

[19] See S. Rep. No. 33, 105th Cong., 1st Sess. 50 (1997), reprinted in 1997-4 CB (Vol. 2) 1067, 1130.

[20] IRC § 2651(e)(1).

[21] IRC § 2651(e)(1).

[22] IRC § §2613(a)(1), 2612(c)(1).

[23] IRC § 2651(b)(1).

and is classified as a non-skip person.[24] Similarly, if the transfer is made to a trust in which a grandchild has a Chapter 13 interest, the trust is not a skip person,[25] and there is no direct skip generation-skipping transfer.[26] Furthermore, distributions of either income or principal from the trust to the grandchild are treated as distributions to a non-skip person and are not classified as generation-skipping transfers.

Generally, the special predeceased parent rule applies if three conditions are satisfied. First, the individual whose generation assignment is being determined must be a descendant of a parent of the transferor, a parent of the transferor's spouse, or a parent of the transferor's former spouse.[27] Second, that individual's father or mother who was also a lineal descendant of such parent must be dead at the time the transfer establishing the individual's interest is first subject to the gift tax or the estate tax.[28] Third, the individual must be a lineal descendant of the transferor, the transferor's spouse, or the transferor's former spouse if the transferor has living descendants.[29] However, this third requirement does not apply if the transferor has no living lineal descendants at the time of the transfer.[30]

The second requirement under the predeceased parent rule is the trickiest of the requirements.[31] It essentially contains two timing requirements. The individual's father or mother who was also a lineal descendant of such parent must be dead at the *time of the transfer* establishing the individual's interest and must be dead at the time the transfer is *first subject to gift or estate taxation*. This combination of requirements is illustrated in the following examples.

Assume that Grantor creates an irrevocable trust that pays income to Grantor for life with a remainder to Grandchild. On the creation of the trust, there is a completed gift of the entire value of the corpus to the Grandchild.[32] However, there is no generation-skipping transfer at the time of the gift,[33] and

---

[24] IRC § 2613(b).

[25] IRC § 2613(a)(2). See ¶ 13.03[3].

[26] IRC § 2612(c)(1). See ¶ 13.02[4][b][ii].

[27] IRC § 2651(e)(1)(A).

[28] IRC § 2651(e)(1)(B).

[29] IRC § 2651(e)(2).

[30] IRC § 2651(e)(2). For example, the special predeceased parent rule would apply in assigning grandnieces and grandnephews a generation level if a transferor who had no living descendants transfers property to a grandniece or grandnephew when the transferor's nephew or niece who is the parent of the grandniece or grandnephew is deceased at the time of the transfer. See S. Rep. No. 33, 105th Cong., 1st Sess. 50 (1997), reprinted in 1997-4 CB (Vol. 2) 1067, 1130; Priv. Ltr. Rul. 200027002 (Mar. 3, 2000).

[31] IRC § 2651(e)(1)(B).

[32] IRC §§ 2511, 2702.

[33] This is not a direct skip to the trust because the trust is not a skip person because a non-skip person, the grantor, has a Section 2652(c) interest in the trust. IRC § 2613(a)(2).

assuming Grantor makes no gifts of the income interest, there may be a direct skip at Grantor's death.[34] The issue of whether there is a direct skip at Grantor's death depends on whether the predeceased parent rule applies. If, on the creation of the trust, Grandchild's Parent, who is the child of Grantor is deceased, the predeceased parent rule applies and there is no direct skip.[35] On the other hand, if Parent dies after the creation of the trust but prior to the potential direct skip, there is a direct skip because Parent was not dead at the time the transfer creating Grandchild's interest was *first* subject to gift or estate tax (here, the gift tax) at the time of the creation of the trust.[36]

If a transferor establishes a trust for the benefit of a grandchild prior to the death of the parent of the grandchild who is the child of the transferor and later, after the death of the child, makes an addition to the existing trust, the addition should be treated as being held in a separate trust for Chapter 13 purposes so that the grandchild could be treated as assigned to the higher generation just below the transferor.[37] Similar issues with the second requirement arise in a more practical context in conjunction with interspousal transfers.

The interaction of the predeceased parent rule and the estate tax marital deduction can create some interesting variations. For example, assume Grantor establishes a testamentary trust under which the income from the property is to be paid to Grantor's Spouse for life, with the remainder to Grantor's Grandchild, who is the child of Grantor and Spouse's only child. If Grantor and Spouse's child is dead at the time the trust is established, Grandchild will be assigned to the generation level one below that of Grantor and Spouse. Grandchild will be a non-skip person, and, upon the death of the Spouse, there will be no taxable termination regardless of whether the interest transferred to Spouse qualified for the marital deduction.

If the child in this example is alive at the time the trust is established but predeceases Spouse, the question whether the predeceased parent exception applies depends on whether the transfer to the trust qualifies for the marital deduction and whether both a qualified terminable interest property (QTIP) and Section 2652(a)(3) (reverse QTIP) elections have been made. When the child

---

[34] IRC §§ 2612(e)(1), 2651(e)(1).

[35] Section 2651 (e)(1) applies to convert the grandchild to a non-skip person with the result that there is no Section 2612(c)(1) direct skip.

[36] Section 2651(c)(1) is inapplicable, the grandchild is a skip person, and there is a Section 2612(c)(1) direct skip.

[37] The provisions of Section 2654(b)(1) and Regulations Section 26.2654-1(a)(2) should apply as if the portions of the single trust had separate transferors. See Reg. § 26.2612-1(a)(2)(ii), dealing with the similar situation under the predeceased parent exception applicable to direct skips occurring prior to January 1, 1998, under Section 2612(c)(2) prior to its repeal with respect to direct skips occurring after December 31, 1997, in the Taxpayer Relief Act of 1997, Pub. L. No. 105-34, § 511(b)(1), 111 Stat. 788, 861 (1997), reprinted in 1997-4 CB (Vol. 1) 1, 75.

is alive at the time the trust is established but predeceases Spouse and the transfer to the trust does not qualify for the marital deduction, the predeceased parent exception does not apply because the child was alive at the time of the transfer creating Grandchild's interest, and Grandchild is classified as a skip person. If a QTIP election is made qualifying Spouse's terminable interest for the marital deduction and a Section 2652(a)(3) (reverse QTIP) election is made, the predeceased parent exception will not apply in the determination of the generation level of Grandchild, again because the child was alive at the time of the transfer creating Grandchild's interest. However, if a QTIP election is made, qualifying Spouse's terminable interest for the marital deduction, and no Section 2652(a)(3) (reverse QTIP) election is made and Spouse dies without disposing of the qualifying life interest, the property is included in Spouse's gross estate under Section 2044. Spouse becomes the Chapter 13 transferor when the trust property is subject to tax under Chapter 11 after the child's death. The predeceased parent rule applies and assigns Grandchild to the generation level one generation below the transferor Spouse.[38] The termination of the Spouse's interest will not result in any generation-skipping transfer because Grandchild is not classified as a skip person.[39]

[iii] **Overlapping related beneficiaries.** As carefully as the generation placement rules of related parties may be stated, an overlap may occur. A beneficiary may be placed in two generations by the related beneficiary rules of

---

[38] "[A]t the time the transfer . . . is subject to a tax imposed by Chapter 11 . . . upon the *transferor*," the child is deceased, so Grandchild is assigned a generation under the predeceased parent rule. IRC § 2651(e)(1)(B) (emphasis added).

The legislative history provides a basis for arguing that the predeceased parent rule should not apply in this particular situation. The Senate Finance Committee Report provides "that transfers to trusts should be permitted to qualify for the predeceased parent exclusion where the parent of the beneficiary is dead at the time that the transfer is first subject to estate or gift tax." S. Rep. No. 33, 105th Cong., 1st Sess. 50 (1997), reprinted in 1997-4 CB (Vol. 2) 1067, 1130. However, the same report provides further that the predeceased parent exception is extended to "taxable terminations and taxable distributions, provided that the parent of the relevant beneficiary was dead at the earliest time that the transfer (from which the beneficiary's interest in the property was established) was subject to estate or gift tax." S. Rep. No. 33, 105th Cong., 1st Sess. 51 (1997), reprinted in 1997-4 CB (Vol. 2) 1067, 1131. Upon Spouse's death, the relevant generation-skipping transfer is a direct skip, not a taxable termination or a taxable distribution.

[39] Alternatively, if the grantor, rather than the spouse, was the income beneficiary of the trust, and the parent of the grandchild, the child of the grantor, died after the establishment of the trust but predeceased the grantor, the predeceased parent rule would not apply in assigning a generation to the grandchild. Although the parent of the grandchild is dead at the time the trust property is subject to tax under Chapter 11 in the Chapter 13 transferor's (the grantor's) gross estate, the predeceased parent rule does not apply because at the time the trust was established and the Chapter 13 transferor (the grantor) was subjected to a tax imposed under Chapter 12, Child, parent of the grandchild, was alive. Where a transfer is subject to a tax imposed by Chapter 11 or Chapter 12 on the trans-

Sections 2651(b) and 2651(c). What an awkward position! For example, looking back at the generation chart, assume that *A* is the transferor's fourth cousin on *A*'s mother's side and is therefore a lineal descendant in the sixth generation.[40] In a nonincestuous marriage,[41] *A* marries *B*, the transferor's third cousin on *A*'s father's side, who is assigned to the fifth generation. Since *A* is now *B*'s spouse and *B* is in the fifth generation, it would seem that *A* would also be classified in the fifth generation.[42] This dilemma of being placed in more than one generation is solved by Section 2651(f)(1), which generally[43] assigns individuals in such circumstances to the youngest of the two or more possible generations. In this case, *A* remains in the sixth generation. *A*'s marriage does not age *A*, at least for purposes of Chapter 13. *B*, however, may feel a flush of youth as *B* moves to the sixth generation because of marriage to fourth cousin *A*.[44]

The rule assigning an individual to the youngest of possible multiple generations prevents that individual from avoiding the sting of Chapter 13 by way of adoption or marriage. A transferor cannot avoid the imposition of the tax on a generation-skipping transfer by adopting a great-grandchild, thereby moving the great-grandchild to the first generation below the transferor.

Application of the rule of youngest-generation priority is predicated on there being no contrary rule expressed in the regulations.[45] Possible administrative exceptions to the basic rule of Section 2651(f)(1) to be provided for in regulations are currently a matter of speculation. In all probability, the rule will not be applied where there is an adoption or a marriage involving an individual assigned to different generations under the rules contained in Sections 2651(b) and 2651(c). The group of individuals who are assigned a generation under the rules contained in Sections 2651(b) and 2651(c) is very broad. The marriage of a remote lineal descendant of a grandparent of a transferor's spouse to a remote lineal descendant of the grandparent of a transferor should be excepted from the general rule where there is no tax avoidance motive.

---

feror more than once, the parent must be dead the first time the transfer is subject to tax under Chapter 11 or Chapter 12. IRC § 2651(e)(1)(B) (third parenthetical clause).

[40] IRC § 2651(b)(1). See supra ¶ 17.01[2][a][i] for the generation chart.

[41] A marriage invalid under state law presumably would not be recognized for generation-skipping transfer purposes.

[42] IRC § 2651(c)(2).

[43] Regulations may override the statutory rule. See IRC § 2651(f)(1) (introductory clause); infra text accompanying note 45.

[44] IRC § 2651(f)(1).

[45] IRC § 2651(f)(1).

[b] Unrelated Beneficiaries

Despite the broad group of possible beneficiaries within the ancestral chain,[46] some transfers may be made, at least in part, for persons unrelated to the transferor or the transferor's spouse or former spouse, e.g., for a friend or faithful employee. Such unrelated beneficiaries must also be classified as to generation, and Section 2651(d) points the way. Any individual who is not assigned a generation under Section 2651(b) or Section 2651(c) is assigned a generation under Section 2651(d), measured by comparing the date of birth of the individual with that of the transferor. Individuals not more than twelve and one-half years younger than the transferor are treated as members of the transferor's generation.[47] Individuals more than twelve and one-half but not more than thirty-seven and one-half years younger than the transferor are assigned to the first generation younger than the transferor, the generation of the transferor's children.[48] Similar rules are provided for the establishment of a new generation every twenty-five years thereafter.[49] For example, an unrelated individual born more than thirty-seven and one-half, but not more than sixty-two and one-half, years after the transferor is assigned to the same generation as the transferor's grandchildren.

Assume eighty-year-old transferor T established a trust providing for the income generated by the trust to be paid to a sixty-year-old friend for life, with a remainder to the friend's thirty-year-old child or the child's estate. T's friend, who was born more than twelve and one-half, but not more than thirty-seven and one-half, years after T's birth, is assigned to the first generation younger than T. The child of T's friend is assigned to the second generation younger than T, having been born more than thirty-seven and one-half, but not more than sixty-two and one-half, years after T's birth.

The youngest-generation assignment rule of Section 2651(f)(1) does not come into play if an individual seems to be assigned to one generation under Section 2651(d) and another under either Section 2651(b) or Section 2651(c), because Section 2651(d) injects itself into the fray only if an individual is *not* assigned to a generation under either Section 2651(b) or Section 2651(c).[50] Thus, the rule generally will not apply to the adoption of an unrelated individual by the transferor, the transferor's spouse, or the transferor's former spouse. Similarly, the rule generally will not apply to the marriage of an unrelated individual and the transferor, the transferor's spouse, or the transferor's former spouse.

---

[46] IRC §§ 2651(b), 2651(c). See supra ¶ 17.01[2][a][i] for the generation chart.

[47] IRC § 2651(d)(1).

[48] IRC § 2651(d)(2).

[49] IRC § 2651(d)(3).

[50] IRC § 2651(d) (introductory clause).

[c] Beneficiaries Who Are Not Individuals

A corporation, a partnership, a trust, the estate of a deceased person, or some other entity may be the transferee of an interest in property in a potential direct skip, may be the distributee of property in a taxable distribution or taxable termination, or may have an interest in property held in a trust after a transfer to a trust or the termination of an interest in a trust. Generally, when this occurs, the entity is pierced and each individual with a beneficial interest in the entity is treated as having an interest in the property and is assigned a generation level.[51] As previously discussed, generations are assigned to designate individuals as skip or non-skip persons in order to determine whether a generation-skipping transfer has occurred.[52] Since only individuals or trusts may be skip persons,[53] when there is a transfer to an entity or when an entity holds an interest in property held in a trust, the entity must be pierced to determine if, or to what extent, the property is held by skip persons and non-skip persons (either individuals or trusts).

[i] **Transfers to nontrust entities.** If an outright transfer or a trust distribution is made to a nontrust entity, such as a corporation, a partnership, or an estate, the entity veil is lifted[54] and each individual with a "beneficial interest" in the nontrust entity is treated as having an interest in the property transferred to the entity and is assigned to a generation level.[55] Section 2651(f)(2) not only facilitates the determination of whether there has been a generation-skipping transfer, but also facilitates the determination of the amount of the generation-skipping transfer. For example, assume that grantor G transfers property to a corporation owned equally by G's only child C and grandchild GC. After piercing the corporate veil, a familiar tax approach under the income and gift tax provisions,[56] the transfer is treated as being made one half to C and one half to GC.[57] C and GC are each assigned a generation level under the rule dealing with lineal descendants[58] to facilitate the determination of whether a generation-skipping transfer has occurred. In this example, there is a direct

---

[51] IRC § 2651(f)(2). The entity-piercing rule does not apply if the entity is a charitable organization described in Sections 511(a)(2) and 511(b)(2) or a governmental entity. IRC §§ 2651(f)(2) (introductory clause), 2651(f)(3). Such entities are assigned to the transferor's generation. IRC § 2651(f)(3).

[52] See supra ¶ 17.01[1].

[53] IRC § 2613(a). See ¶¶ 13.03[1]–13.03[4].

[54] IRC § 2651(f)(2).

[55] IRC § 2651(f)(2).

[56] See, e.g., IRC §§ 318(a)(2), 707(a), 707(b); Reg. § 25.2511-1(h)(1); ¶¶ 10.01[2][b], 10.01[2][c]Helvering v. Hutchings, 312 US 393 (1941).

[57] See ¶ 13.03[4][b], especially text accompanying note 86. Similar rules apply to all entities other than trusts.

[58] IRC § 2651(b).

skip transfer[59] of one half of the value of the property transferred, the portion of the property treated as transferred by *G* to *GC*.

[ii] Transfers to trust entities. In the case of a transfer or trust distribution to a trust entity, those individuals who have a "beneficial interest" in the trust must be identified in order to classify the trust as a skip person or non-skip person. A transfer to a trust is not considered to be made to individuals for Chapter 13 purposes; it is considered to be made to the individuals merely to facilitate the determination of whether the trust itself is to be classified as a skip person or non-skip person. When applying the piercing rule to a trust, those individuals with beneficial interests in the trust are treated as having an interest in the property held in the trust only if the beneficial interest held by the individual is an interest in property held in trust as defined in Section 2652(c).[60]

Similarly, if an estate, trust, partnership, or other entity has an interest in property held in a trust, then the interest in property must also be defined in Section 2652(c) before the piercing rule applies. For example, assume that a noncharitable entity is the beneficiary of another trust. If the beneficiary entity has the present right to receive income from the trust, the beneficiary has the required Section 2652(c) interest in property to apply the piercing rule. Alternatively, if the beneficiary entity is merely a remainderperson of the trust with only a future right to the corpus of the other trust, the beneficiary entity would not have an interest in the property of the other trust and the piercing rule would not apply.[61] Once it is determined that an entity has a Section 2652(c) interest in the property held in trust, each individual having a "beneficial interest" in the entity must be identified. Each individual having a "beneficial interest" is treated as having an interest in the property in which the entity has an interest, and each is assigned a generation under Section 2651.

The statutory language contained in Section 2651(f)(2) appears to provide a rule to determine whether an individual has an "interest in property" for all Chapter 13 purposes. The term "beneficial interest," which is used in Section 2651(f)(2), is not defined by the statute. When an entity holds an interest in property held in a trust, as defined in Section 2652(c), the term "interest" as used in the phrase "beneficial interest" should be defined in a manner consistent with the definition of an interest in property in Section 2652(c).

To illustrate this rule, assume that grantor *G* sets up two trusts. Trust Two is the current income beneficiary of Trust One, which has a noncharitable

---

[59] IRC § 2612(c)(1). See ¶ 13.02[4].

[60] See IRC § 2651(f)(2); ¶ 17.02[3].

[61] See IRC § 2651(f)(2); ¶ 17.02[3].

remainderperson.[62] *G*'s grandchild *GC*, a skip person, has the present right to the income of Trust Two, the beneficiary trust, and *G*'s niece *N*, a non-skip person, has the remainder interest in that trust. Does a transfer of property to Trust One constitute a direct skip?[63] *GC*, who has a right to income of beneficiary Trust Two, is an individual with a "beneficial interest" in Trust Two under the language of Section 2651(f)(2). *GC*'s interest is also an interest in property, as defined in Section 2652(c). What status is to be accorded *N*, the remainderperson of beneficiary to Trust Two? The remainderperson, who has no more than a future interest in the property held in Trust Two, should not be treated as having a Section 2651(f)(2) "beneficial interest" in the trust. The transfer to Trust One should constitute a direct skip.[64]

The same issue can also arise in the context of a taxable distribution or a taxable termination. For example, assume that Trust One provides income to grantor *G*'s child *C* for life and a remainder to Trust Two, which provides income to *G*'s grandchild *GC* for life and the remainder to *G*'s niece *N*. At *C*'s death, in piercing Trust Two to determine if there is a taxable termination of Trust One, only the beneficial Section 2652(c) interests in Trust Two should be considered in determining whether a taxable termination has occurred under Section 2612(a)(1)(A).[65]

A similar issue would arise in the case of an outright transfer to a corporation in which Trust Two is the sole shareholder. After piercing the corporate veil under Section 2651(f)(2) and turning up the trust shareholder, to what extent can the trust be pierced? Again, only Section 2652(c) beneficial interests

---

[62] Because the noncharitable remainder person does not hold a Section 2652(c) interest, it is irrelevant whether the remainder person is a skip person or a non-skip person in determining whether the trust is a skip person or a non-skip person.

[63] IRC § 2612(c)(1). A direct skip requires a transfer to a skip person. Id. Therefore, Trust Two must be a skip person in order for there to be a direct skip to Trust One. See ¶ 13.02[4].

[64] See also IRC § 2612(c)(2), which supports the result reached here and is discussed at ¶ 13.02[4][b][iii].

If *N*'s interest is not treated as a beneficial interest, she has no interest in the property held in the trust, and the transfer to the original trust constitutes a direct skip. If *N*'s interest is treated as a "beneficial interest," giving her an interest in the property in Trust Two, the transfer is not a direct skip. This is because *N* is not a Section 2613(a)(1) skip person.

[65] In fact, Section 2612(a)(1)(A) may itself reach the same result here. Seemingly, in determining whether a taxable termination occurs, only *GC*'s Chapter 13 interest after the termination is considered. To take the example a step further in order to raise the Section 2651(f)(2) "beneficial interest" issue, assume that Trust One terminates and pours over to another trust under which Trust Two is the income beneficiary. Seemingly, Section 2612(a)(1)(A) still calls for multiple piercing only to the extent of Chapter 13 interests.

in the trust should be considered. Since the trust is then a skip person, there is a direct skip of all transfers to the corporation.[66]

The veil-piercing provisions of Section 2651(f)(2) do not apply to organizations described in Section 511(a)(2), charitable trusts described in Section 511(b)(2), and governmental entities.[67] Each of these entities is assigned to the transferor's generation.[68]

¶ 17.02 SECTION 2652. OTHER DEFINITIONS

[1] Transferor

[a] Introduction

Anyone who lived through the first congressional frolic with a tax on generation-skipping transfers may recall with a certain weird fondness the "Deemed Transferor," who was supposed to play a very large role in that non-statute, which retroactively self-destructed when Congress enacted the current generation-skipping tax in the Tax Reform Act of 1986. The Deemed Transferor, always ephemeral, was nevertheless tenacious. Although the Deemed Transferor is still not always real, his ghost stalks the paragraphs of the current statute. Playing a different role, the Deemed Transferor is still often *deemed*, but with a lowercase "d." How is the deemed transferor identified? Section 2652(a) undertakes this task.

For every generation-skipping transfer, a transferor must be identified. A transferor is needed to ascertain the generation assignment of most individuals possessing interests in property subject to the tax,[1] to classify individuals as

---

[66] Compare IRC § 2612(c)(2), which arguably reaches the same result. See ¶ 13.02[4][b][iii]. Seemingly, Section 2612(c)(2) is applicable to a trust that holds an interest in a pierced (in this case, corporate) entity, and the same result arrived at here is reached using Section 2612(c)(2). The alternative of looking at both *GC*'s income interest and *N*'s remainder interest would mean that only part of the transfer to the corporation (the actuarial percentage of *GC*'s interest in the trust) would constitute a direct skip. Cf. Instructions for Form 706, United States Estate (and Generation-Skipping Transfer) Tax Return (Rev. Nov. 2001) Instructions for Schedules R and R-1. Generation-Skipping Transfer Tax, Determining Which Transfers Are Direct Skips, Example 4, at 20.

[67] IRC § 2651(f)(3).

[68] IRC § 2651(f)(3).

[1] IRC § 2651.

skip persons[2] or non-skip persons,[3] and to ascertain whether special generation assignment rules may apply to individuals whose parent is deceased.[4]

The term "transferor" includes a decedent who transfers any property in a manner that is subject to the estate tax[5] and a donor who transfers any property in a manner that is subject to the gift tax.[6] The determination of the transferor of property is fleeting, not permanent. Generally, anytime the property is again subjected to either the gift tax or the estate tax, a new transferor is recognized. There is only one exception to the general rule involving a special election for QTIP.[7] The initial phrase of Section 2652(a)(1) is deceptive, indicating that Section 2653(a) provides an exception to the general definition of "transferor." Actually, Section 2653(a) does no more than affect the generation level of the transferor in certain situations.[8] The transferor is not changed by Section 2653(a).

[b] General Rules

Section 2652(a)(1) provides that if any property subject to the tax imposed by Chapter 11 or Chapter 12 is in effect transferred, the decedent or the donor is the transferor of such property for purposes of Chapter 13. Even if there is no actual transfer of property for state law purposes, a new transferor emerges if the property is subject to the tax imposed by Chapter 11 or Chapter 12. For Chapter 13 purposes, "[a]n individual shall be treated as transferring any property with respect to which such individual is the transferor."[9]

Assume that in the current year parent P establishes a trust with income to be paid to child C for life and the remainder to anyone C appoints by will. In default, the trust corpus is to pass to C's children. Assume further that C dies without exercising the testamentary general power of appointment,[10] and the property passes to C's children, the takers in default. There is no actual transfer of property by C, but by virtue of the inclusion of the value of the trust corpus *in C's* gross estate,[11] C becomes the transferor under Chapter 13,

---

[2] IRC § 2613(a). See ¶¶ 13.03[1]–13.03[4]. Reg. § 26.2612-1(d).

[3] IRC § 2613(b). See ¶ 13.03[5].

[4] IRC § 2651(e); discussed ¶ 17.01[2][a][ii].

[5] IRC § 2652(a)(1)(A).

[6] IRC § 2652(a)(1)(B).

[7] IRC § 2652(a)(3), discussed infra ¶ 17.02[1][c][i].

[8] IRC § 2653(a), discussed ¶ 17.03[1].

[9] IRC § 2652(a)(1).

[10] IRC § 2041(b)(1). See ¶ 4.13[3].

[11] IRC § 2041(a)(2). See ¶ 4.13[7]. Where a general power of appointment results in the inclusion of the property subject to the power in the power-holder's gross estate, it is

replacing *P*, the original transferor, even though *C* had the only speaking part, so to speak.

The most troublesome and key statutory phrase of Section 2652(a)(1) is the term "subject to the tax." If there is a transfer of the type that is *subject to the tax* imposed by Chapter 11 or Chapter 12,[12] there is generally a new transferor. Thus, a precise meaning is to be accorded to the term "subject to."[13]

Chapter 11, the estate tax, is imposed on the taxable estate of every decedent who is a citizen or resident of the United States.[14] Chapter 11 also imposes a tax on certain U.S. situs property[15] of any decedent nonresident who is not a citizen of the United States.[16] A transfer is "subject to" the tax imposed by Chapter 11 if the value of the property is includible in the decedent's gross estate as determined under Section 2031 or Section 2103.[17] Chapter 12, the gift tax, is imposed on the transfer of property by gift by any individual, resident, or nonresident.[18] Property transferred in a way that qualifies for a deduction in the computation of the estate tax[19] or the gift tax,[20] escaping actual tax payment, is considered to be "subject to" the tax to the extent of the full value of the transferred amount.

Inter vivos transfers of property that qualify for the annual exclusion accorded by Section 2503(b) are also considered "subject to" the tax imposed by Chapter 12.[21] Section 2501(a) imposes a tax on the transfer of property by gift.

---

as though the property subject to the power was distributed outright to the power-holder who then transferred it. See ¶ 13.02[2][e][ii].

If *C* had no general power of appointment, there would have been no inclusion in *C*'s gross estate. However, there would have been a Section 2612(a) taxable termination with *P* as the transferor assuming at *C*'s death the remainder passed to *C*'s children.

[12] IRC §§ 2652(a)(1)(A), 2652(a)(1)(B), respectively. See Reg. § 26.2652-1(a).

[13] See Reg. § 26.2652-1(a)(2) and the discussion of "subject to" in the Section 2612(c)(1) discussion dealing with direct skips at ¶ 13.02[4][b][i].

[14] IRC § 2001(a). Cf. IRC § 2663(2).

[15] IRC §§ 2103, 2104. See also IRC § 2106.

[16] IRC § 2101(a). See also IRC § 2663(2).

[17] Reg. § 26.2652-1(a)(2).

[18] IRC § 2501(a)(1). In the case of a transfer by a nonresident who is not a citizen of the United States, the gift tax is not imposed on the transfer of property not situated within the United States. IRC § 2511(a). Furthermore, a transfer of intangible property by a nonresident noncitizen of the United States generally is not subject to the gift tax. IRC §§ 2501(a)(2), 2501(a)(3). Transfers of property by gift to political organizations, as defined in Section 527(e)(1), are not subject to the tax imposed by Chapter 12. IRC § 2501(a)(5). Cf. IRC § 2663(2).

[19] IRC §§ 2053, 2054, 2055, 2056, 2057, 2058. See ¶¶ 5.03–5.09.

[20] IRC §§ 2522, 2523. See ¶¶ 11.02, 11.03; Reg. § 26.2652-1(a)(2).

[21] IRC § 2501(a)(1). See Reg. §§ 26.2652-1(a)(2), 26.2652-1(a)(5) Ex. 1; PS-73-88, Supplementary Information, Transferor, 1993-1 CB 867, 867. Cf. ¶ 13.02[4][b] text accompanying notes 261–264.

Although Section 2503(b) excludes the first $11,000 of certain gifts each year from the "total amount of gifts," a figure used in the gift tax computation, nevertheless, the excluded Section 2503(b) amount is only excluded in the computation of "total amount of gifts," and it remains property transferred by gift, which is "subject to" the Chapter 12 tax.

An amount excluded under Section 2503(e)[22] is not "subject to" the Chapter 12 tax. The gift tax is imposed "on the transfer of property by gift,"[23] but an amount excluded under Section 2503(e) is, in the words of the statute, "not ... treated as a transfer of property by gift."[24] Thus, transfers excluded under Section 2503(e) are not "subject to" the tax.[25]

Property that is (or was) subject to a general power of appointment and is required to be included in the power-holder's gross estate is "subject to" the tax imposed by Chapter 11.[26] For purposes of Chapter 13, the power-holder is the transferor of the property subject to the power to the extent that the prop-

---

[22] Section 2503(e) excludes certain gratuitous inter vivos transfers for educational or medical expenses. See ¶ 9.04[6].

[23] IRC § 2501(a)(1).

[24] IRC § 2503(e)(1).

[25] See also Instructions for Form 709, United States Gift (and Generation-Skipping Transfer) Tax Return (2001) Purpose of Form, Transfers Subject to the Generation-Skipping Transfer Tax, at 2, which provide that the only generation-skipping transfer tax to be reported on Form 709 is the tax imposed on inter vivos direct skips. An inter vivos direct skip is a gift that is subject to the gift tax. The Instructions, at 2, provide that "[a] transfer is *subject to the gift tax* if it is required to be reported on Schedule A of Form 709." Id. The Instructions, Schedule A—Computation of Taxable Gifts, at 5, further provide that filers are not to enter on Schedule A "any gift or part of a gift that qualifies for the political organization, educational, or medical exclusions." Id. Gifts qualifying for the annual exclusion under Section 2503(b) are listed on Schedule A of Form 709, if a gift tax return is required to be filed. IRC § 6019. But see Reg. § 26.2652-1(a)(2).

However, Section 2642(c) implies that transfers qualifying for the Section 2503(e) exclusion are considered subject to the tax imposed by Chapter 12 for purposes of identification of a transferor under Chapter 13. Section 2642(c) deals with direct skips of nontaxable gifts. Section 2642(c)(3)(B) defines "nontaxable gift" to include a gift that is not a taxable gift because of Section 2503(e). A Section 2612(c)(1) direct skip occurs only when there is a transfer of property subject to a tax imposed by Chapter 11 or Chapter 12. If a nontaxable gift can be the subject matter of a direct skip, it must, by definition, be subject to a tax imposed by Chapter 12. But see Instructions for Form 709, United States Gift (and Generation-Skipping Transfer) Tax Return (2001). As stated before, the authors find Section 2642(c)(3)(B) to be superfluous. See ¶¶ 13.02[4][b] text accompanying notes 259, 260, 16.02[2][b] text accompanying notes 54–57.

[26] IRC §§ 2041(a)(1), 2041(a)(2). This would include both testamentary powers and inter vivos powers exercised or (in the case of a post-1942 power) released in a testamentary fashion (in a manner such that, had the power-holder actually owned the property, it would have been included in the power-holder's gross estate under Sections 2035 through 2038). See ¶ 4.13[7].

Section 2652

erty is included in the power-holder's gross estate.[27] Similarly, a general power of appointment created prior to October 22, 1942, that is exercised during the life of the power-holder, or a general power of appointment created after October 21, 1942, that is exercised or released during the life of the power-holder, effects a deemed transfer of the appointed property by the individual power-holder.[28] The property that is deemed transferred is "subject to" the tax imposed by Chapter 12 to the extent that the transfer constitutes a completed gift,[29] and to that extent, the power-holder is treated as a transferor for purposes of Chapter 13.[30] Property over which someone has a nongeneral power of appointment *generally* is not required to be included in the power-holder's gross estate;[31] nor is the exercise or release of the power treated as a transfer of property for gift tax or estate tax purposes by the power-holder.[32] The property therefore is not "subject to" tax imposed by Chapter 11 or Chapter 12, and with respect to the nongeneral power, no new Chapter 13 transferor is created.[33]

The same principles apply[34] when determining whether property is "subject to" the tax imposed by Chapter 11 or Chapter 12, when there is a lifetime lapse of a general power of appointment created after October 22, 1942. A lifetime lapse of a post-1942 general power *in excess of* the greater of $5,000 or 5 percent of the value of the property constitutes a release of the power, which is treated as a transfer of the property.[35] If the power-holder makes a

---

[27] IRC § 2652(a)(1)(A).

[28] IRC §§ 2514(a), 2514(b). This assumes that the deemed transfer occurs after the effective date of the generation-skipping transfer tax. See ¶¶ 10.04[3], 10.04[4]. Cf. ¶ 18.05[2][b] text accompanying notes 37–39.

[29] IRC § 2501(a)(1). See Reg. § 25.2511-2(b). See also Reg. § 26.2652-1(a)(2).

[30] IRC § 2652(a)(1)(B). Even though the gift is complete, the transfer and the effect of the GST exemption allocated may be postponed. IRC § 2642(f), discussed ¶ 16.02[7].

[31] See IRC § 2041. See ¶ 4.13. But see IRC § 2041(a)(3); infra note 33.

[32] IRC §§ 2514(b), 2514(c).

[33] Property that someone controls by way of a nongeneral power of appointment may, however, be subject to the estate tax or the gift tax in a very limited instance. IRC §§ 2041(a)(3), 2514(d), discussed ¶¶ 4.13[8], 10.04[5]. If the application of one of these special rules results in the inclusion of the property in a decedent's gross estate or in a donor's total amount of gifts, the property is subject to the tax imposed by Chapter 11 or Chapter 12, and the decedent or donor, as the case may be, is treated as a transferor for purposes of Chapter 13.

[34] See supra text accompanying notes 26–33. See also the discussion of the five-or-five powers at ¶ 13.02[2][e][ii].

[35] A congressional struggle with the question of when a power over property should be treated as ownership of the property resulted in a bit of congressional largess. The general rule, equating a lapse of a power of appointment created after October 21, 1942, with a release, applies only to the extent that the value of the property that could have been appointed by exercise of the lapsed power exceeds the greater of $5,000 or 5 percent of the value of the assets out of which an exercise of the power could be satisfied. IRC

completed gift on the release, there is a transfer of property by gift "subject to" the tax imposed by Chapter 12, and the power-holder of the lapsed general power of appointment becomes the transferor of the property.[36] However, property subject to a general power of appointment that lapses and is not considered released, or is considered released but is not a completed gift, is not "subject to" the tax imposed by Chapter 12,[37] and the original transferor remains as the Chapter 13 transferor of the property. If there is a transfer of property by gift upon the lifetime lapse of a post-1942 general power of appointment over property held in a trust, there will be two transferors, the power-holder (the donee of the power) and the donor of the power.[38]

Similarly, when the power-holder of an annual noncumulative five-or-five general power to appoint dies with the power,[39] there should be two transferors, the power-holder and the donor of the power. The power-holder is treated as the transferor of property to the extent that the property is required to be included in the power-holder's gross estate. The donor of the power is treated as the transferor of the balance of the property, which is the portion that is not required to be included in the power-holder's gross estate.[40]

---

§ 2514(e). See ¶ 10.04[4][c]. When a lifetime lapse is equated with a release, i.e., when the five-or-five limits are exceeded, the release is treated as a transfer of property. IRC § 2514(b).

[36] IRC § 2652(a)(1)(B); Reg. § 26.2652-1(a)(5) Ex. 5. If the transfer results in an incomplete gift, the power-holder becomes the Chapter 13 transferor when the gift of the property is complete under Chapter 12 or when it is included in the power-holder's gross estate under Chapter 11. IRC § 2652(a)(1). Even though the gift is complete, the transfer or the effect of the GST exemption allocated may be postponed. IRC § 2642(f), discussed ¶ 16.02[7].

[37] A lifetime lapse of a general power of appointment that is not considered released is not a transfer of property. IRC §§ 2514(b), 2514(e). Without a transfer of property, there is no "transfer of property by gift," subject to the tax imposed by Chapter 12. IRC § 2501(a)(1). The power-holder is not treated as the transferor of the portion of the value of property subject to a general power of appointment that lapses during the life of the power-holder and is not considered released, i.e., the five-or-five amount. Reg. § 26.2652-1(a)(5) Ex. 5.

[38] Cf. infra ¶ 17.02[1][d]. See also ¶ 13.02[2][e][ii].

[39] See IRC §§ 2041(a)(2), 2041(b)(2).

[40] See infra ¶ 17.02[1][d]. See also ¶ 13.02[2][e][ii]; Reg. §§ 26.2601-1(b)(1)(v)(A), 26.2601-1(b)(1)(v)(D) Ex. 1. For example, assume that parent P establishes a trust fund with a constant value of $100,000 for the benefit of child C and grandchild GC. The trust instrument provides that the trust income is to be paid to C for life, with the remainder to GC. The trust instrument also grants C a noncumulative power to withdraw $15,000 from the trust each year. If C lets the power lapse each year during life, the lapse equals a release to the extent of $10,000 each year. IRC § 2514(e). This release is treated as a transfer of property and, to the extent that the transfer of property is gifted to another (the remainder interest), it is "subject to" the tax imposed by Chapter 12. A valuation problem may arise here. See ¶ 10.04[4][c]. Cf. IRC § 2702; ¶ 19.03[4][e].

[c] Special Rules

[i] **Qualified terminable interest property.** There is one important exception to the general rule that any time property is "subject to" either the gift tax or the estate tax, a new transferor is recognized.[41] With respect to either the gift tax or the estate tax marital deduction,[42] a donor or decedent may give a spouse a "qualified terminable interest" in property in a trust and also name the remainderperson of the trust, in what is commonly referred to as a QTIP trust. Even though the spouse's interest is a terminable interest, the property will still qualify for a marital deduction if an election is made.[43] The price paid for allowance of a marital deduction to the donor or decedent is that the property is subject to transfer taxation through the application of Sections 2511 and 2519, if the spouse makes an inter vivos transfer of part or all of the qualifying income interest in the property,[44] or under Section 2044, if the spouse dies and there has been no inter vivos transfer.[45]

Under the general rule, the spouse becomes the transferor of the property when the property is included in the spouse's gross estate under Section 2044 or is treated as transferred by the spouse as a completed gift under Sections 2511 and 2519.[46] However, the estate of the decedent or the donor spouse (the original transferor) may elect under Section 2652(a)(3) to treat qualified terminable interest property as if it were not such property for purposes of Chapter 13.[47] The effect of this election is that the decedent or donor remains as transferor of the qualified terminable interest property, and the transferee spouse does not later become the Chapter 13 transferor of the property even though Sections 2044, 2207A, and 2519 apply.[48]

When *C*, who holds the power, dies, *C* should be treated as the transferor of the portion of the property required to be included in *C*'s gross estate under Section 2041; this would include any property subject to the power held at death (i.e., the power to appoint $15,000), as well as any prior releases under which there was a Section 2036 retained life estate. IRC § 2652(a)(1)(A). See IRC § 2041(a)(2); ¶ 4.13[7][f]. The donor of the power would be the transferor of the balance of the property held in trust not included in the power-holder's gross estate.

[41] IRC § 2652(a)(1).

[42] IRC §§ 2523, 2056. See Rev. Proc. 2001-38, 2001-1 CB __. (QTIP election disregarded for purposes of Section 2652(a) where proved that election not necessary to reduce estate taxes to zero).

[43] IRC §§ 2056(b)(7), 2523(f). See ¶¶ 5.06[8][d], 11.03[4][c].

[44] See ¶ 10.08. See also IRC § 2207A(b), discussed at ¶ 8.07[3].

[45] See ¶ 4.16. See also IRC § 2207A(a), discussed at ¶ 8.07[2].

[46] Reg. § 26.2652-1(a)(5) Ex. 3.

[47] IRC § 2652(a)(3). See Reg. § 26.2652-1(a)(3).

[48] See Reg. §§ 26.2652-1(a)(3), 26.2652-1(a)(5) Ex. 6, 26.2652-2(d) Ex. 1. If a reverse QTIP election is made under Section 2652(a)(3), the identity of the transferor is de-

If the Section 2652(a)(3) election is made, it must be made with respect to all qualified terminable interest property held in a trust.[49] For example, if an executor or donor makes a QTIP election[50] with respect to $1.3 million of a $2 million trust, the estate of the decedent or the donor may make the reverse QTIP election to disregard the QTIP election for Chapter 13 purposes with respect to the entire $1.3 million qualified terminable interest property portion of the trust.[51] If there are two trusts established by one spouse and both contain qualified terminable interest property, the election to disregard the QTIP election for purposes of Chapter 13 is available on a trust-by-trust basis. The election is available for "any trust" as long as the election treats "all of the property in such trust" as if the QTIP election had not been made for Chapter 13 purposes.[52]

---

termined without regard to the application of Section 2207A. Reg. § 26.2652-1(a)(3). See ¶ 16.02[4][e] text accompanying note 286. For example, if property is subject to a reverse QTIP election and the beneficiaries of the residue of the estate of a surviving spouse do not compel their right of recovery under Section 2207A, the beneficiaries of the residuary estate are not treated as making a constructive transfer to the trust, and are not treated as Chapter 13 transferors, because for purposes of Chapter 13 no right of recovery exists. Reg. § 26.2652-1(a)(5) Ex. 7. See Reg. § 26.2652-1(a)(5) Ex. 8; infra ¶ 17.02[1][d] text accompanying note 73; ¶ 18.05[2][b] text accompanying notes 45, 46.

When there is a gift of a portion of the qualifying income interest triggering Section 2519, there may be inclusion under Section 2036 of a portion of the corpus in the transferee spouse's gross estate. See Reg. §§ 25.2519-1(g) Ex. 4, 20.2044-1(e) Ex. 5; ¶ 10.08 text accompanying note 15. Arguably, even though a reverse QTIP election is made, the reverse QTIP election is terminated, and the transferee spouse becomes the Chapter 13 transferor of the portion included in the transferee spouse's gross estate under Section 2036 because the "identity of the transferor of the property is determined [only] without regard to the application of sections 2044, 2207A and 2519" and not Section 2036. See Reg. § 26.2652-1(a)(3). On the other hand, it can be argued that if the application of Section 2519 is disregarded for Chapter 13 purposes, as it is when a reverse QTIP election is made, there is no Section 2519 "transfer" of the property. Without a Section 2519 transfer, there is no satisfaction of the "transfer" requirement of Section 2036 and thus no Section 2036 inclusion to make the transferee spouse the Chapter 13 transferor of the property. This later result is consistent with the policy of Section 2652(a)(3).

[49] IRC § 2652(a)(3) (flush language); Reg. § 26.2652-2(a). See IRC § 2642(a)(3), discussed ¶ 16.02[5][e], which provides rules for severing a trust and could be used to sever a trust prior to making a QTIP election. See also Reg. § 26.2654-1(b), regarding severability of testamentary trusts considered at ¶ 17.04[2][b].

[50] IRC §§ 2056(b)(7)(B)(i)(III), 2523(f)(2)(C).

[51] IRC § 2652(a)(3) (flush language); Reg. § 26.2652-2(a); S. Rep. No. 76, 100th Cong., 1st Sess. 560 (1987); HR Rep. No. 391 (II), 100th Cong., 1st Sess. 1476 (1987).

[52] IRC § 2652(a)(3) (flush language); Reg. § 26.2652-2(a); S. Rep. No. 76, 100th Cong., 1st Sess. 560 (1987); HR Rep. No. 391 (II), 100th Cong., 1st Sess. 1476 (1987). See also Instructions for Form 706, United States Estate (and Generation-Skipping Transfer) Tax Return (Rev. Nov. 2001) Instructions for Schedules R and R-1. Generation-Skipping Transfer Tax, How To Complete Schedule R, Part 1-GST exemption reconciliation, Special QTIP election, at 21; Instructions for Form 709, United States Gift (and Genera-

The election is made on the tax return on which the QTIP election is made.[53] Thus, the election must be made on the last return filed before the due date, including extensions actually granted, or if a timely estate tax return is

---

tion-Skipping Transfer) Tax Return (2001) Schedule C-Computation of Generation-Skipping Transfer Tax, Part 2-GST Exemption Reconciliation, Special QTIP election, at 11. Thus, in the example at supra text accompanying note 50, the decedent or donor spouse might want to transfer the value of the qualified terminable interest property that exceeds the amount of the decedent's or donor's unallocated GST exemption to a separate trust. This would leave an amount equal to the decedent's or donor's remaining amount of GST exemption in the original qualified terminable interest property trust to which the decedent or donor would make a Section 2652(a)(3) election and allocate the remaining amount of GST exemption. See ¶ 16.02[7][a] note 429. As to the second trust, although a QTIP election would be made, no Section 2652(a)(3) election would be made, leaving the spouse as the eventual transferor of the trust and allowing the spouse to allocate GST exemption to the second trust. See ¶ 16.02[7][b][ii] text accompanying notes 472–475. See also Priv. Ltr. Rul. 9337006 (June 14, 1993).

If a reverse QTIP election was made with respect to a trust prior to December 27, 1995, to which GST exemption was allocated, the transferor (or the transferor's personal representative) was authorized to elect to treat the trust as two separate trusts, one with a zero inclusion ratio and one with an inclusion ratio of one, with the reverse QTIP election being treated as applicable only to the trust with the zero inclusion ratio. Reg. § 26.2652-2(c). That election was to have been made by June 24, 1996. Id. An extension of time for making this election may be granted pursuant to Regulations Sections 301.9100-1 and 301.9100-3 where a trust was administered as two separate trusts before the June 24, 1996, deadline and continues to be administered in that way. See Priv. Ltr. Rul. 199913022 (Dec. 30, 1998) (extension granted until Aug. 31, 1998).

[53] Reg. § 26.2652-2(b). If a protective QTIP election is made, no Section 2652(a)(3) election is effective unless a protective reverse QTIP election is also made. Id. If the QTIP election is made on the transferor's federal estate tax return, the reverse QTIP election under Section 2652(a)(3) is accomplished by merely listing the qualifying property in Part 1, Line 9 on Schedule R of Form 706. Form 706, United States Estate (and Generation-Skipping Transfer) Tax Return (Rev. Nov. 2001) Schedule R, Part 1, at 33. One no longer needs to check a box to make the reverse QTIP election for a testamentary transfer. If the QTIP election is made on the transferor's federal gift tax return, the reverse QTIP election under Section 2652(a)(3) is accomplished by checking a box on Schedule C of Form 709. Form 709, United States Gift (and Generation-Skipping Transfer) Tax Return (2001) Schedule C, Part 2, at 4.

not filed, the first return filed after the due date on which the QTIP election is made.[54] Once made, the election is irrevocable.[55]

There are various practical ramifications of using the reverse QTIP election.[56] Among other things, use of the election can facilitate full use of the GST exemption by each of the spouses.[57] It can also result in the conversion of a direct skip to a taxable termination with attendant consequences[58] and affect

---

[54] Reg. § 26.2652-2(b). See Priv. Ltr. Rul. 200028021 (Apr. 14, 2000); Priv. Ltr. Rul. 200018036 (Feb. 4, 2000) (both involving effective QTIP and reverse QTIP elections on first return filed where estate tax return not filed timely).

An extension of time to file a reverse QTIP election may be granted under Regulations Section 301.9100 generally for a period not to exceed six months (unless the taxpayer is abroad), where the taxpayer acts reasonably and in good faith and the extension will not prejudice government interests. See Reg. §§ 301.9100-1, 301.9100-3. See Priv. Ltr. Rul. 9611011 (Dec. 8, 1995) (extension of time to make reverse QTIP election). An extension of time to file a reverse QTIP election does not extend the time for allocating any remaining GST exemption. Priv. Ltr. Rul. 199908024 (Nov. 27, 1998).

[55] Reg. § 26.2652-2(a).

[56] See Kalik & Schneider, "Generation-Skipping Transfer Taxes Under the Tax Reform Act of 1986," 21 U. Miami Inst. Est. Plan. 9-1, at ¶ 902.1 (1987), in which these and other practical ramifications of Section 2652(a)(3) are discussed.

[57] IRC § 2631(a). Before 2003, the amount of the Section 2010 applicable exclusion amount was less than the GST exemption amount with the result that a Section 2652(a)(3) election was frequently made. After 2003 and before 2010, where a decedent has made an inter vivos transfer to a non-skip person using the Section 2505 credit, but not the GST exemption, the GST exemption amount will exceed the Section 2010 applicable credit amount and a Section 2652(a)(3) election may be beneficial.

Failure to establish separate QTIP trusts, with one using the Section 2652(a)(3) election and the other not using it, might deprive one of the spouses of use of their GST exemption. See supra note 52; ¶ 16.02[4][e]. See also ¶ 17.04[2].

[58] If the trust remainderperson is a skip person, the transfer at the death of the beneficiary spouse may satisfy the requirements of a direct skip if the Section 2652(a)(3) election is *not* made, but the transfer will satisfy the requirements of a taxable termination if the election *is* made. See Reg. §§ 26.2612-1(f) Ex. 5 (QTIP election direct skip), 26.2652-2(d) Ex. 1 (reverse QTIP election taxable termination). See generally IRC §§ 2612(a)(1), 2612(c)(1). See also IRC §§ 2642(a), 2642(f)(1), 2642(f)(4); Tax Reform Act of 1986, Pub. L. No. 99-514, § 1433(b)(3), 100 Stat. 2085, 2731 (1986), reprinted in 1986-3 CB (Vol. 1) 1, 648, as amended by Technical and Miscellaneous Revenue Act of 1988, Pub. L. No. 100-647, § 1014(h)(3)(A), 102 Stat. 3342, 3567 (1988), reprinted in 1988-3 CB 1, 227.

the generation assignment of beneficiaries[59] and the timing and method of valuation of assets.[60]

[ii] Gift-splitting by married couples. If the donor and a spouse make an election under Section 2513 to treat a gift as if it were made one half by each for gift tax purposes, the gift is also treated as split for purposes of Chapter 13.[61] Therefore, the donor and the spouse each become the transferor of one half of the gifted property.[62] The gift-splitting will have no effect on whether or not the transfer is a generation-skipping transfer because the spouse will be assigned to the same generation as the donor;[63] however, the gift-splitting will allow a married couple to use both of their GST exemptions[64] in determining the Chapter 13 tax on the transfer.

[d] Multiple Transferors

There are several situations in which more than one person may make actual or imputed transfers to a single trust. In such situations, there may be more than one transferor for a single trust, in which case a single trust will be split into separate trusts, one for each transferor, in determining the generation-skipping transfer tax to be imposed.[65]

---

[59] See ¶ 17.01[2][a][ii] text accompanying notes 37–39. Assume a trust established by a transferor provided income for life to a younger spouse and a remainder to very young unrelated friend who is forty years younger than the transferor and thirty years younger than the spouse. If the election is made, the unrelated friend is a skip person vis-à-vis the original transferor. If the election is not made, the unrelated friend is not classified as a skip person vis-à-vis the spouse.

[60] Compare IRC § 2624(b) with IRC § 2624(c). If a reverse QTIP election is made under Section 2652(a)(3), the estate tax inclusion period rules do not apply to delay the effect of GST exemption allocated to the property. Reg. § 26.2632-1(c)(2)(ii)(C). See ¶ 16.02[7][b] notes 473–475.

[61] IRC § 2652(a)(2); Reg. § 26.2652-1(a)(4). See also TAM 200147021 (July 31, 2001) (Section 2513 splits Section 2515 deemed gifts).

[62] IRC § 2652(a)(2); Reg. §§ 26.2652-1(a)(4), 26.2652-1(a)(5) Ex. 2. See Reg. § 26.2632-1(c)(5) Ex. 3 .

[63] IRC § 2651(c)(1). Cf. IRC § 2642(f)(4). See ¶ 17.01[2][a] text accompanying note 13.

[64] IRC § 2631. See ¶ 15.02. For example, if the donor makes a $2,022,000 outright inter vivos transfer to a skip person to whom neither spouse has made a prior gift during the year, and if they elect Section 2513 gift-splitting and both allocate $1 million of GST exemption to the transfer, there is no Chapter 13 tax on the transfer. See IRC §§ 2631, 2632, 2642(c)(1), 2642(c)(3)(A). Gift splitting is especially helpful where one spouse has a significant amount of wealth and the other a minimal amount. See also TAM 200201002 (Sept. 27, 2001) (automatic allocation of GST exemption to transfers attributed to spouse under Section 2513).

[65] IRC § 2654(b)(1). See infra ¶ 17.04[2][a]; Reg. § 26.2654-1(a)(2).

If spouses elect under Section 2513 to split their gifts, or if they transfer community property or they simultaneously transfer equally owned separate property to a trust, each spouse is treated as being the transferor of one half of the gifted property. A similar result should occur if two unrelated persons make equal contributions simultaneously to a trust.[66] If the contributions are unequal but are made simultaneously, the transferors are treated as transferors in proportion to their relative transfers.[67] For example, if one transferor transfers $2 million to a trust and a second transferor simultaneously transfers $4 million to the same trust, the two are transferors as to one third and two thirds of the trust, respectively.[68]

Application of the rule becomes more complicated when the contributions are not made simultaneously. In those situations, the relative contributions are determined by revaluing earlier contributions at the time when the subsequent contribution is made.[69] For example, if the $2 million contribution preceded the $4 million contribution and the trust corpus was valued at $4 million immediately before the $4 million contribution was made, then both transferors are treated as equal contributors to the trust.[70] This proposition parallels the determination of relative ownership of joint tenancy property under Section 2040, and the principles used there provide a guide to the determination of results here.[71]

Further complications arise as transfers become less direct and more frequent. The lapse of a noncumulative annual general power of appointment in excess of a five-or-five power may cause both the creator and the donee of the

---

[66] When separate contributions are made to a trust and the trust is treated as two separate trusts, the actual property contributed by each contributor generally is not traced and valued separately each time it is necessary to determine the Chapter 13 transferor. See Reg. § 26.2654-1(a)(2)(ii). For example, if both A and B contribute a parcel of land valued at $1 million to a trust, and A's parcel appreciates in value to $2 million and B's parcel depreciates in value to $500,000, A is generally treated as the transferor of the same portion of a generation-skipping transfer from the trust as B. Id. Additions are allocated pro rata unless otherwise provided expressly in the governing instrument. Reg. § 26.2654-1(a)(2)(i) (last sentence). The trust is a single trust, not two trusts, for the filing of returns and payment of tax. Reg. § 26.2654-1(a)(2)(i).

[67] IRC § 2654(b)(1); Reg. § 26.2654-1(a)(2)(i).

[68] See Reg. § 26.2654-1(a)(5) Ex. 5.

[69] The fractional portion of the entire trust attributed to each transferor is the fair market value of each transferor's separate contribution immediately after the most recent addition over the fair market value of the property held in the entire trust immediately after the transfer. Each transferor's separate contribution is the fair market value of that transferor's individual share of the trust determined immediately before the most recent addition plus the recent addition, if made by that transferor. Reg. § 26.2654-1(a)(2)(ii).

[70] See Reg. §§ 26.2654-1(a)(5) Exs. 6, 7.

[71] See ¶ 4.12[7].

general power of appointment to become transferors of a single trust.[72] The contribution of each may have to be determined annually. There can be multiple transferors to a trust in another, albeit obscure, situation. The surviving spouse ultimately becomes the Chapter 13 transferor of a trust containing qualified terminable interest property for which no reverse QTIP election is made under Section 2652(a)(3). If the beneficiary whose share bears the estate tax imposed on the value of the qualified terminable interest property included in the surviving spouse's estate fails to assert a Section 2207A right of recovery, that beneficiary becomes a transferor to the trust to the extent of the amount of the forgone Section 2207A right of recovery.[73] Thus, both the surviving spouse and the residuary beneficiary are transferors of the trust.

[2] Trusts and Trustees

The Section 2652(b) caption "Trust and Trustee" may be misleading, since the provision deals not with trusts and trustees, but rather with nontrust arrangements that are treated as trusts and nontrustees that are treated as trustees for purposes of Chapter 13.

Congress has looked under the bed, like the proverbial old maid, with a somewhat uncertain expectation and attitude. Are trustlike things lurking that could make a mockery of the generation-skipping transfer tax? If so, they should be brought into the open by calling them trusts. Basically, trust equivalents are trusts.[74] Congress rarely writes into the statute examples of items within terms that are not precisely defined.[75] The statute lists as possible trusts "life estates and remainders, estates for years, and insurance and annuity contracts."[76] The list is not exhaustive and certainly does not exclude other trust equivalent arrangements that are not specifically included. For example, custodianship under the Uniform Gifts to Minors Act or a similar state statute is treated as a trust for purposes of Chapter 13.[77] Generally, a transfer where the identity of the transferee is contingent on the occurrence of an event is

---

[72] See supra ¶ 17.02[1][b] notes 34–40; Reg. § 26.2652-1(a)(5), Ex. 5.

[73] See Reg. §§ 26.2652-1(a)(3), 26.2652-1(a)(5) Ex. 7 (where there is a QTIP trust but a Section 2652(a)(3) reverse QTIP election is made, the trust property is not treated as includible in the surviving spouse's estate, there is no Section 2207A right of recovery, and there are no multiple transferors to the trust). See supra ¶ 17.02[1][c][i] text accompanying note 48.

[74] IRC § 2652(b)(1).

[75] But see the use of "fire, storm, shipwreck, or other casualty" in Section 165(c)(3).

[76] IRC § 2652(b)(3).

[77] Reg. § 26.2652-1(b)(2) Ex. 1.

considered a transfer in trust.[78] This rule does not apply to a testamentary transfer where the identity of the transferee is contingent on an event that must occur within six months of the transferor's death.[79] If an arrangement is similar to a trust, whether or not it is in the form of one of the statutory examples, any reference in the statute to a trust is considered to refer to the similar arrangement as well. Chapter 13 specifically omits trust treatment for an estate.[80]

As an example of an arrangement that definitely falls within Section 2652(b), assume that a donor makes a gift of a residence to child A for life, with a remainder to B. There is neither a trust nor a fiduciary, and A has a legal life estate; yet there is some question about what there *is*. Section 2652(b)(3) makes it clear that this arrangement has substantially the same effect as a trust and is to be treated as a trust. However, this does not necessarily mean that a generation skip occurs upon A's death. On a kind of pari passu basis, the rules of Chapter 13 now take over. If this were a trust, A would have an interest.[81] A's death effects a termination of A's interest.[82] No transfer subject to federal estate tax occurs with respect to the property upon the termination of A's interest.[83] If B, the transferee of the property, is a skip person vis-à-vis the donor,[84] the termination of A's interest is a taxable termination,[85] which is a generation-skipping transfer,[86] the object of the tax imposed by Chapter 13.

Similarly, a donor might purchase a commercial annuity under which child A would have the right to payments for life and B would then be entitled to payments for life, with no refund feature to take account of the untimely death of both. This type of annuity will eventually burn out, which makes it

---

[78] Reg. § 26.2652-1(b)(1). For example, assume that parent makes a pecuniary bequest to a child provided the child survives parent by twenty-four months; if the child does not survive the parent by twenty-four months, the bequest is to be paid to grandchild. The bequest is a transfer in trust under Chapter 13. See Reg. § 26.2652-1(b)(2) Ex. 3.

[79] Reg. § 26.2652-1(b)(1). See Reg. § 26.2652-1(b)(2) Ex. 2.

[80] IRC § 2652(b)(1) (parenthetical). If estate administration is unduly prolonged, however, an estate is sometimes considered terminated and treated as a trust for income tax purposes. Reg. § 1.641(b)-3(a); Old Va. Brick Co. v. Comm'r, 44 TC 724 (1965). In terms of reality and substantive economic effect, this seems appropriate, and perhaps an estate in these circumstances should be treated as a trust under Chapter 13 as well. Indeed, there seems to be room for contrary administrative and judicial treatment in extreme cases. In view of the current Section 1(e) income tax rates, it is less likely that an estate will be unduly prolonged.

[81] IRC § 2652(c)(1). See infra ¶ 17.02[3].

[82] IRC § 2612(a)(1). See ¶ 13.02[2][b].

[83] Reg. § 26.2612-1(b)(1)(i). See ¶ 13.02[2][d].

[84] IRC § 2613(a). See ¶ 13.03[2].

[85] IRC § 2612(a)(1). Note that neither Section 2611(b)(1) nor Section 2611(b)(2) applies. See ¶ 13.01[2].

[86] IRC § 2611(a)(1). See ¶ 13.01[1].

different from most trusts, although trusts too may call for periodic or other payments out of corpus. In any event, an annuity arrangement with more than one annuitant is a device that may permit wealth to be passed along and enjoyed by successive generations. This is an arrangement having "substantially the same effect as a trust."[87] It would seem, therefore, that when *A* dies, there is a transfer to *B* of the then value of the annuity that does not result in a federal estate consequence to *A*.[88] *A*'s death is a Chapter 13 taxable termination[89] if *B* is a skip person in relation to the transferor, the purchaser of the annuity.[90]

These answers seem to come very easily, but a problem surfaces. The trustee in these cases may need to be identified, so that personal liability may be imposed for the tax if it is not paid when due.[91] The statute lifts the blanket of obscurity on this issue by identifying the trustee in a pseudo-trust arrangement as the person in actual or constructive possession of the property that is the subject of the arrangement.[92]

When one person holds a legal life estate (not an equitable interest in a trust) and another holds the remainder, who is the deemed trustee when the present interest, the legal life estate, terminates? The trustee is defined as the person in "actual or constructive possession of the property subject to such arrangement."[93] Is the trustee the one in possession immediately before the termination (in this case, the life tenant) or the one in possession immediately after (the remainderperson)? Generally, shifts in beneficial interests in real trusts have no effect on the trustee and leave the one in possession immediately before the termination still in possession after it. Had this legal life estate been an equitable life interest, the trustee would most likely have been the responsible party. The legal life tenant is the person in possession of the property immediately prior to death and should be treated as trustee until death. However, to treat the legal life tenant as the trustee after the transfer generally does not work, since the legal life tenant, in most cases, is the one upon whose death the transfer is effected. After the transfer, the remainderperson (or some other person who has a terminable interest) will be in possession of the property. In the legal life estate situation, the successor in interest, whether it is the one with the next terminable interest or the remainderperson, should be treated

---

[87] IRC § 2652(b)(1).

[88] Reg. § 26.2612-1(b)(1)(i). See ¶ 13.02[2][d].

[89] IRC § 2612(a)(1).

[90] IRC §§ 2652(a)(1), 2613(a)(1).

[91] IRC § 2603(a)(2). See ¶ 12.03.

[92] IRC § 2652(b)(2). See Reg. § 26.2652-1(c).

[93] IRC § 2652(b)(2).

as "trustee" and required to file the return and pay the tax.[94] Everything considered, regulations should provide for this procedure.[95]

In the case of an estate for years, the holder of the estate for years should be the trustee. If the holder of the estate for years dies before the term expires, the interest will pass to another who can assume the position of trustee.

If a private annuity is involved, the person paying the annuity should be treated as trustee under Chapter 13. In the case of ordinary commercial annuities, where an insurance company, in a sense, holds a fund as a fiduciary, the insurance company should be treated as the trustee[96] under an annuity that is treated as a trust under Chapter 13.[97] The Chapter 13 tax imposed on a testamentary direct skip should generally be computed and paid by the insurance company as pseudo-trustee out of funds that are the equivalent of the trust res.[98] An exception occurs when the annuity is the subject matter of a direct skip occurring at the transferor's death and the total value of the property involved is less than $250,000 with respect to the commercial annuity provider.[99] In this instance, the executor of the decedent's estate is liable for filing the required returns and paying the Chapter 13 tax.[100] If the property continues to be held by the annuity provider, the executor is entitled to recover the generation-skipping transfer tax attributable to the transfer from the annuity provider.[101] In the event the annuity provider has distributed the funds, the executor is entitled to seek recovery of the generation-skipping transfer tax attributable to the annuity from the recipient.[102]

---

[94] IRC § 2603(a)(2).

[95] See Section 2663(3), which provides for legislative regulations to fill in Section 2652(b) gaps such as this one. See ¶ 18.03[3].

[96] IRC § 2652(b)(2); Reg. § 26.2652-1(c).

[97] IRC § 2652(b)(3); Reg. § 26.2652-1(b)(1).

[98] Cf. Reg. §§ 26.2662-1(c)(2)(vi) Exs. 2, 3.

[99] Regulations Section 26.2662-1(c)(2)(iii) so provides for decedents dying on or after June 24, 1996. In the case of decedents dying prior to June 24, 1996, the executor is liable only if the property involved in the direct skip with respect to an annuity provider is less than $100,000, rather than $250,000. Reg. § 26.2662-1(c)(2)(iv). Cf. Reg. §§ 26.2662-1(c)(2)(vi) Exs. 1, 4.

[100] Reg. §§ 26.2662-1(c)(2)(i), 26.2662-1(c)(2)(iii).

[101] Reg. § 26.2662-1(c)(2)(v).

[102] Reg. § 26.2662-1(c)(2)(v). If the annuity provider determines that the amounts payable under all contracts it issued that are included in the decedent's gross estate are, in the aggregate, less than $250,000, it will be able to make a lump sum payment of the annuity proceeds without regard to the generation-skipping transfer tax. PS-32-90, Supplementary Information, 1993-1 CB 907, 908–909. See Reg. § 26.2662-1(c)(2)(vi) Ex. 5. This will not be the case where the annuity contract provider continues to hold a "fund" that is treated as a "trust." In this event, the executor of the decedent's estate may seek recovery for the generation-skipping transfer tax attributable to the annuity from the pseudo-trustee, the annuity provider. See Reg. § 26.2662-1(c)(2)(v). Where one provider has is-

Alternatively, if an annuity terminates with a final disbursement in the nature of a premium refund that is classified as a taxable termination, is the distributee, who is in possession of the property after the termination, treated as the trustee and required to compute and pay any tax imposed by Chapter 13? A commercial annuity presents a different situation from that of a legal life estate or a private annuity, which would be comparable to the legal life estate when the search for a trustee commences, since a commercial annuity involves a third-party stakeholder separate and apart from the beneficiaries. The distributee is not the one who is in possession immediately after the termination because the insurance company holds the "property" both before and immediately after the "transfer." A distributee under a commercial annuity policy or an insurance policy should not be treated as trustee upon a taxable termination.[103] The insurance company issuing the annuity or insurance policy treated as a trust under Chapter 13 should be treated as the trustee. If the trustee is to compute and pay the Chapter 13 tax, the insurance company, as pseudo-trustee, should be required to compute the tax and pay it out of funds that are the equivalent of the trust res unless the governing instrument provides otherwise.[104]

---

sued multiple contracts and there are both lump sum and annuity payouts and the total contracts issued by the provider do not, in the aggregate, exceed the $250,000 limit, the executor's recovery for the generation-skipping transfer tax incurred should be from both the annuity provider and the recipient. The executor should be able to recover only from the annuity provider or the recipient the generation-skipping transfer tax generated by the contract value each held or received.

[103] The possibility remains that the distributee under a commercial annuity or insurance policy could, although should not, be treated as trustee and incur the commensurate responsibilities and liabilities where the generation-skipping transfer is a taxable termination.

[104] See IRC § 2603(b). The insurance company would undoubtedly like to make a commensurate reduction in the continuing payments to a successor annuitant or beneficiary to take account of the tax it pays on the termination and the administrative costs incurred in the computation of the tax. The question is whether or not such a reduction can be made. Certainly state law or the contract may authorize withholding, but what if they are silent? The federal statute seems to authorize apportionment of the tax to the fund by providing that the tax imposed by Chapter 13 is to be charged against the property constituting the transfer. However, what if the contract provides certain benefits and these benefits cannot be paid as called for under the contract because of a reduction in the fund for payment of taxes? This is similar to the situation in which insurance proceeds are reduced for tax by application of the federal apportionment statute, Section 2206. Regulations to be promulgated under Section 2663(3) should offer guidance in this area.

Perhaps, if required to pay, an insurance company would have a right to seek reimbursement for tax that it paid from the fund from the transferee. Cf. Reg. § 26.2662-1(c)(2)(v). The simpler process is to pay the tax before the proceeds are distributed to the beneficiary. Insurance companies should insert clauses in contracts to allow for a reduction in benefits where a tax is imposed by Chapter 13. Additionally, a clause ought to be

The establishment of a joint tenancy with right of survivorship with multigeneration level joint tenants will never be treated as a trust. Although the establishment of such a joint tenancy may generate generation-skipping transfers,[105] and the termination of a joint tenant's interest may generate further generation-skipping transfers, the generation-skipping transfers will always take the form of direct skips and never taxable terminations.[106]

[3] Interest

[a] Introduction

One of the threshold questions in the discussion of most Chapter 13 problems is the meaning of the term "interest."[107] Chapter 13 defines the term "interest" only with respect to "an interest in property held in trust."[108] But there are other interests that are recognized for purposes of Chapter 13,[109] such as interests that are transferred directly to transferees outside a trust or a trust equivalent arrangement.[110] A fee simple interest may also be an interest in property for purposes of Chapter 13. With respect to such nontrust interests, Chapter 13 provides no special definition; therefore, a simple property interest should suffice.[111]

Section 2652(c) defines the term "interest" only for an interest in property held in a trust or a trust equivalent arrangement (other than an estate) that "has substantially the same effect as a trust."[112] A person has "an interest in prop-

---

inserted to recover costs incurred in determining the tax. See ¶ 12.03[2] text accompanying note 26.

[105] IRC § 2612(c). The transfer will not constitute an immediate direct skip if the transferor is a joint tenant. See IRC § 2642(f); ¶ 16.02[7][d] text accompanying note 495.

[106] A taxable termination requires the termination of an interest in property held in a trust or trust equivalent arrangement. If there is no trust or trust equivalent arrangement, there can be no taxable termination. The last sentence of Section 2040(a) would tax a portion of the transferred amount in the decedent joint tenant's gross estate. See ¶ 4.12[1] note 6.

[107] IRC § 2652(c).

[108] IRC § 2652(c)(1). See Reg. § 26.2652-1(e), referencing Reg. § 26.2612-1(e) for the definition of "interest in trust." The latter regulations section adds little to flesh out the bare bones of the statute.

[109] See IRC § 2612(c).

[110] IRC §§ 2652(b)(1), 2652(b)(3).

[111] See ¶¶ 4.05, 13.02[4][b][ii]. See also IRC § 2651(f)(2), discussed ¶ 17.01[2][c].

[112] IRC § 2652(b)(1).

erty held in trust"[113] (or in a trust equivalent arrangement)[114] if such person has a *present legal right* to receive trust income or corpus[115] or is a *permissible current noncharitable recipient* of income or corpus of a trust,[116] whatever the person's legal rights may be. The fact that a person's obligations may be discharged with trust income or corpus is not a Chapter 13 interest in the property held in a trust under some restricted circumstances.[117] In addition, charitable beneficiaries described in Section 2055(a) have an interest in property held in trust if the trust is a qualifying charitable remainder annuity trust, a charitable remainder unitrust, or a pooled income fund.[118] An interest in property held in trust that is used primarily to postpone or avoid the Chapter 13 tax is to be disregarded.[119] An interest does not exist to the extent it is the subject matter of a qualified disclaimer.[120]

It is necessary to ascertain if a person has an interest in property held in trust to determine whether there has been a taxable termination of the trust[121] and to determine whether a transfer to a trust is a direct skip.[122]

[b] Present Right to or Permissible Noncharitable Current Recipient of Income or Corpus

A person has a Chapter 13 interest in a trust if the person has a present right to receive income or corpus from the trust.[123] A future interest, even a clear-cut legal right to receive income or corpus from the trust at some time in the future, is not an interest in property held in trust under Chapter 13.[124] If enjoyment is deferred until a future time or if it is conditioned on the occurrence of a future event, the right is a future right. For example, assume that a trust

---

[113] IRC § 2652(c)(1).

[114] IRC §§ 2652(b)(1), 2652(b)(3). See supra ¶ 17.02[2]. As used throughout the remainder of this discussion, the term "trust" shall include a trust equivalent arrangement.

[115] IRC § 2652(c)(1)(A). See infra ¶ 17.02[3][b].

[116] IRC § 2652(c)(1)(B). See infra ¶ 17.02[3][b].

[117] IRC § 2652(c)(3). See infra ¶ 17.02[3][b] text accompanying note 140.

[118] IRC § 2652(c)(1)(C). See infra ¶ 17.02[3][c].

[119] IRC § 2652(c)(2). See infra ¶ 17.02[3][d].

[120] Reg. § 26.2612-1(e)(3). See IRC §§ 2518, 2654(c); ¶ 17.04[3].

[121] IRC § 2612(a)(1). See ¶ 13.02[2][b] for a detailed and similar discussion of the term "Chapter 13 interest" as it relates to taxable terminations.

[122] IRC § 2612(c)(1). See ¶ 13.02[4][b][ii] for a discussion of the definition of "interest" where there is a direct skip.

[123] IRC § 2652(c)(1)(A). Reg. § 26.2612-1(e)(1)(i). Such a right may be indirectly received, such as when the income from a trust is required to be used to satisfy a beneficiary's legal obligation, for example, an obligation of support. See infra text accompanying notes 140–143.

[124] IRC § 2652(c)(1)(A) (parenthetical). See Reg. § 26.2612-1(f) Ex. 14.

provides that the income is to be distributed to *A* for life, with the remainder to *B*. *A* has a Chapter 13 interest in the property held in trust,[125] but *B* does not. Although commonly termed a "future interest," *B* has only a *future* right to receive the property held in trust because *B* has to wait until *A*'s death to receive the corpus of the trust. Such a future interest is not a Chapter 13 interest.[126] Similarly, if the terms of the trust are expanded to provide *A*'s sibling *C* with a secondary life estate at *A*'s death and then a remainder to *B*, during *A*'s life, *C*'s secondary life estate is not a Chapter 13 interest in property. However, if the determination whether *C* has an interest is made at the time of *A*'s death, *C* has a present right to the income and therefore has a Chapter 13 interest in the trust property. Upon the death of both *A* and *C*, *B* has an interest in the property recognized by Chapter 13, that is, outright ownership of the property.

A person also has a Chapter 13 interest in property held in trust if the person is a permissible noncharitable current recipient of trust income or corpus.[127] A common example of a person having such an interest is a person who has the current ability to receive distributions from a sprinkling trust. A person may have an interest even if that person's receipt of income or corpus depends on the discretionary exercise of a power by a trustee, a beneficiary, or some other individual. To be a permissible current recipient of income or corpus under a power held by another, the power-holder must be able to exercise the power currently to give the recipient income or corpus either outright or through providing the recipient a present interest in a trust. A fortiori, a person does not have an interest for purposes of Chapter 13 if the person is merely a permissible recipient of property by way of a presently held power that can be exercised only at some future time or by way of a power that is presently exercisable over a future interest. For example, assume that a trust is established with the income to be paid to *A* for life, and the remainder to *B*. The trustee is given a power, exercisable before the death of *A*, to appoint the remainder to *C*. Under property law, *C* in this case has a mere expectancy and not a property interest. *C* cannot have a Chapter 13 interest in the property held in trust until the death of *A*. It is only upon the death of *A* that *C* may have a Chapter 13 interest, and then only if the trustee has exercised the power appointing the remainder to *C*. However, if the trustee holds a power to invade the trust corpus immediately (even during *A*'s life) to any extent for *C*'s benefit, then *C* has a Chapter 13 interest in the trust.

---

[125] A conventional or unavoidable delay in receipt should be disregarded. If a trust instrument requires income to be paid annually to the income beneficiary, the beneficiary has a present right, not a future right, to trust income even if, as a practical matter, the income is to be paid periodically and not instantly as received. Cf. Edwards v. Comm'r, 46 BTA 815 (1942) (acq. in part), aff'd on another issue, 135 F2d 574 (7th Cir. 1943).

[126] See Reg. § 26.2612-1(f) Ex. 14.

[127] IRC § 2652(c)(1)(B); Reg. § 26.2612-1(e)(1)(ii).

The holder of a general power of appointment[128] over trust property is classified as having a Chapter 13 interest in the property held in trust if the holder can presently exercise the power to take income or corpus by deed. The power-holder has a present "right . . . to receive income or corpus"[129] and is a permissible current recipient of income or corpus.[130] A general power of appointment presently exercisable, but only so as to affect the future enjoyment of trust property, is a future right (not a present right), and such a power-holder does not have a Chapter 13 interest in the property subject to the power. A general power exercisable only at a future time or upon the occurrence of a future event also does not give the power-holder a Chapter 13 interest in the property subject to the power. Thus, if a general power can be exercised only by will (a testamentary general power of appointment), the power-holder should not be treated as having an interest by virtue of the power. The holder of a noncumulative annual general power of appointment that is presently exercisable should be treated as having a Chapter 13 interest,[131] even if the terms of the instrument restrict the exercise of the power to a limited period, such as a single month in the year.[132]

A nongeneral power of appointment over property[133] generally is one that is not exercisable for the financial benefit of the power-holder.[134] This power does not give the power-holder a Chapter 13 interest in the trust property. The power itself gives the power-holder no right to trust income or corpus, nor is the power-holder a permissible current recipient of anything from the trust as a result of the power.[135]

A permissible noncharitable appointee of a currently exercisable general or nongeneral power of appointment has an interest in the property held in trust and is classified as having an interest for purposes of Chapter 13[136] if the appointee can currently receive income or corpus by way of an exercise of a general or nongeneral power.[137] Noncharitable permissible current appointees

---

[128] IRC §§ 2041(b), 2514(c). A person who merely holds a nongeneral power of appointment does not thereby have an interest, because there is no right to appoint income or corpus to oneself.

[129] IRC § 2652(c)(1)(A). See ¶¶ 13.02[2][e][ii], 10.04, 4.13.

[130] IRC § 2652(c)(1)(B). See ¶ 13.02[2][e][ii] for a discussion of Chapter 13 interest concerning a five-or-five power of appointment.

[131] IRC §§ 2652(c)(1)(A), 2652(c)(1)(B).

[132] See ¶ 13.02[2][e] note 142.

[133] A nongeneral power over property is a power that is not a general power of appointment. A general power of appointment is defined in Sections 2041(b) and 2514(c).

[134] See ¶¶ 4.13[3], 4.13[4], 10.04[2].

[135] IRC §§ 2652(c)(1)(A), 2652(c)(1)(B).

[136] IRC § 2652(c)(1)(B).

[137] The event that will cause a future right to become a possessory interest may have a greater probability of occurring than the exercise of a discretionary power held by a

of a presently exercisable noncumulative annual power, whether the power is general or nongeneral, also should be treated as having a Chapter 13 interest,[138] again regardless of whether the terms of the instrument restrict the exercise of the power to a limited period, such as a single month in the year.[139]

If a grantor establishes a trust whose income is required to be used exclusively for the support of a minor grandchild until the grandchild attains majority or is emancipated, the *parent* of the grandchild has a Chapter 13 interest in the property held in the trust. In addition, the parent is treated as having an interest in the property held in trust if the trust instrument mandates that the trust assets be used to satisfy a support obligation arising under state law.[140]

However, the parent will not be treated as having an interest in the property held in trust merely because "income or corpus of the trust may be used to satisfy an obligation of support arising under State law . . . if . . . such use is

---

third party needed to give financial benefit to a permissible current recipient. Nevertheless, although the former is characterized as a future right not treated as a Chapter 13 interest in property held in trust (see IRC § 2652(c)(1)(A) (parenthetical)), the latter discretionary recipient is treated as having such an interest in the property. IRC § 2652(c)(1)(B).

In addition, if a trust agreement provides that one individual is to have a general or nongeneral power of appointment over the entire trust corpus, and another individual is entitled to the income generated by the corpus of the trust, the power takes precedence over the right to income. In this situation, the power-holder of a presently exercisable general power of appointment has an interest in the property held in trust by possession of a present right to income or corpus. IRC § 2652(c)(1)(A). The income beneficiary does not have a present right to trust income or corpus, because the income beneficiary's right is subordinate to the power-holder's rights. Nevertheless, the income beneficiary in this situation should be treated as having an interest in the property held in trust because, until the power is exercised, the income beneficiary is a permissible current recipient of income. IRC § 2652(c)(1)(B). Thus, it is entirely possible that the power-holder and the income beneficiary may simultaneously have an interest in the trust property, one for the "right . . . to receive" and the other as a "permissible current recipient."

[138] IRC § 2652(c)(1)(B).

[139] For example, assume that grandparent *G* establishes a trust with income to child *C* for life, with a remainder to grandchild *GC*. *GC* also has a noncumulative annual power to withdraw the greater of 5 percent of the trust assets or $5,000, exercisable only during the month of January each year. *GC* should be treated as having a Chapter 13 interest in the trust. If, during the month of January, *GC* could exercise the power only to appoint property to great-grandchild *GGC* (*GC*'s child), *GC* would hold a nongeneral power and would have no Chapter 13 interest. However, *GGC* should be treated as having a Chapter 13 interest in the trust as a noncharitable permissible current recipient of trust income or corpus.

More detailed discussions of the interrelationship of powers of appointment with specific types of generation-skipping transfers are found elsewhere in the text. See ¶¶ 13.02[2][e], 13.02[4][b] notes 265–272.

[140] Reg. §§ 26.2612-1(e)(2)(i), 26.2612-1(f) Ex. 15. See Staff of Joint Comm. on Tax'n, 100th Cong., 2d Sess., Description of the Technical Corrections Act of 1988, Title I at 363 (Comm. Print. 1988). Cf. IRC § 2652(c)(1)(A).

discretionary, or . . . such use is pursuant to the provisions of any State law substantially equivalent to the Uniform Gifts to Minors Act."[141] The idea behind this provision is that parents should not be treated as having an interest in property given to their children merely because a gift to minors act (such as the Uniform Gifts to Minors Act) empowers the custodian to expend custodial property for the minor's support and maintenance. Support and maintenance, which is the legal obligation of the parent, may be satisfied with this property, and since the funds may be used to discharge the parent's legal obligations, it can be argued that the parent is an indirect permissible current recipient of income or corpus of the fund. This would be so whether or not the parent whose obligation may be discharged is, in fact, the custodian. The statute affords sensible relief by providing otherwise, namely, that even if income or corpus may discretionarily be used to discharge the support obligation arising under state law, that possibility is to be disregarded. This statutory relief is not limited to property held for a minor child under a Uniform Gifts to Minors Act. The relief provision applies to any arrangement whereby property may be expended to discharge a support obligation arising under state law, unless the trust instrument or its equivalent expressly provides that the property must be used to discharge the legal obligation.[142]

This relief provision may have the effect of accelerating the time of the payment of the generation-skipping transfer tax. A transfer by a grandparent to a custodian under a Uniform Gifts to Minors Act would constitute a direct skip to the grandchild. If the parent of the child is considered as having an interest in the fund, there would be no direct skip upon establishment of the custodianship because of the interest of the parent, a non-skip person. A generation-skipping transfer would occur upon the termination of the parent's legal obligation of support.

If, under the custodian's discretion, the income or corpus of property transferred under a Uniform Gifts to Minors Act is used for the support of a minor, thereby satisfying the parent's legal obligation, the parent still should not be treated as having a Chapter 13 interest in the property held in the trust. The transfer should be taxed under Chapter 13 at the time of the initial transfer to the custodian. Even if the subsequent event of discretionary use could be treated as giving the parents a Chapter 13 interest in a trust established by a grandparent for a grandchild, the termination of the parent's interest in the fund would generally not be treated as a generation-skipping transfer because of Section 2653(a) or application of the exclusion afforded by Section 2611(b)(2) for property previously subject to the generation-skipping transfer tax.[143]

---

[141] IRC § 2652(c)(3); Reg. § 26.2612-1(e)(2)(i). See Reg. § 26.2612-1(f) Ex. 15.

[142] IRC § 2652(c)(3); Reg. § 26.2612-1(e)(2)(i). See Reg. § 26.2612-1(f) Ex. 15.

[143] See ¶ 13.01[2][b]; infra ¶ 17.03[1]. See also IRC § 677(b).

[c] Special Rule for Charitable Remainders

A charitable beneficiary described in Section 2055(a) is treated as having an interest in property held in trust if the trust[144] is a charitable remainder annuity trust,[145] a charitable remainder unitrust,[146] or a pooled income fund, even though the charitable beneficiary has neither a present right to income or corpus nor is a permissible current recipient thereof.[147] These charitable beneficiaries are assigned to the transferor's generation under the generation assignment rules;[148] as a result, they are non-skip persons.[149] The consequences of these combinations of rules are primarily to preclude a transfer to such a trust from constituting a direct skip, even if the income beneficiary is a skip person.[150] However, if income distributions are made to a skip person income beneficiary, such distributions are taxable distributions.[151] Similarly, on the termination of any income interest (whether it is a primary or a secondary income interest), a Chapter 13 interest in the trust is held by a non-skip person (the charity) and no taxable termination may occur.[152] Again, if the primary or

---

[144] IRC § 2652(c)(1)(C); Reg. § 26.2612-1(e)(1)(iii).

[145] IRC § 664(d)(1). See ¶ 5.05[5][a]. A "charitable remainder trust" is a trust with respect to which a deduction is allowable under Section 170, Section 2055, Section 2106, or Section 2522. Reg. § 1.664-1(a)(1)(iii).

[146] IRC § 664(d)(2). See ¶ 5.05[5][b]. A "charitable remainder trust" is a trust with respect to which a deduction is allowable under Section 170, Section 2055, Section 2106, or Section 2522. Reg. § 1.664-1(a)(1)(iii).

[147] IRC § 642(c)(5). See ¶ 5.05[5][c]. A charitable contribution deduction for the value of the remainder interest may be allowed under Section 170, Section 2055, Section 2106, or Section 2522 where there is a transfer to a pooled income fund. Reg. § 1.642(c)-5(a)(4).

[148] IRC §§ 2651(f)(3)(A), 2651(f)(3)(B). If no charitable deduction is allowable for the trust, it is not a charitable remainder trust and the charity is not treated as having a Chapter 13 interest in property held in the trust. See IRC § 2652(c)(1)(C). If the charity does not have a Chapter 13 interest in the property held in trust, a non-skip person is not treated as having an interest in the trust and the trust may be a skip person. See Priv. Ltr. Rul. 9532006 (May 4, 1995) (trust was a skip person because a charitable deduction was denied for the unitrust remainder and the charity did not have a Chapter 13 interest in the trust).

[149] IRC § 2613(b).

[150] The non-skip person charity holds a Section 2652(c) interest in the trust so that all trust interests are not held by skip persons. The transferee trust is not a skip person; therefore, the transfer fails as a direct skip. IRC §§ 2612(c)(1), 2613(a)(2)(A).

[151] IRC § 2612(b). For example, assume that a grantor establishes a charitable remainder annuity trust with an income interest to a skip person and the remainder to charity. There is no direct skip on a transfer of property to the trust, but as annuity payments are made to the skip person, they are taxable distributions.

[152] IRC § 2612(a)(1)(A).

secondary income interest is held by a skip person, any income distributions to that beneficiary are taxable distributions.[153]

[d] Interests That Postpone or Avoid the Generation-Skipping Transfer Tax

Any interest in property held in trust (not just nominal trust interests) used primarily to postpone or avoid any tax imposed by Chapter 13 is required to be disregarded.[154] If transferor T transfers property worth $200,000 to a trust with one percent of the income to pass to a non-skip person and 99 percent to a skip person for a term of years, with a remainder to the skip person at the end of the term of years, the non-skip person's one percent will likely be disregarded and the transfer of the property will be treated as a Section 2612(c)(1) direct skip.[155] Similarly, if T creates a trust with income to child C for life and then income to grandchild GC, granting GC a limited nongeneral power to appoint to a non-skip person for GC's life, with a remainder at GC's death to GC's children, the non-skip person's Chapter 13 interest as a permissible recipient under GC's power may be disregarded. If so, a Section 2612(a)(1) taxable termination occurs at C's death.[156]

What is sauce for the goose is also sauce for the gander, and nominal interests, which cannot be used to postpone or avoid any tax, should not be used to cause an imposition of tax. For example, assume transferor T placed property in trust that will pay income to great-grandchild GGC for a relatively short period, after which it will pay income to child C for life and then to grandchild GC for life, with remainder going back to GGC. Recognition of GGC's initial interest would result in both the imposition of avoidance of multiple impositions of the generation-skipping transfer tax.[157] The income interest

---

[153] IRC § 2612(b). For example, assume that a grantor transfers property to a charitable remainder unitrust with income payments to child for life, then to grandchild for life, and a remainder to charity. On creation of the trust, there is no direct skip, and, at the child's death, there is no taxable termination. IRC §§ 2612(a)(1)(A), 2612(c)(1). But since income distributions are made to the grandchild, such distributions are taxable distributions. IRC § 2612(b).

[154] IRC § 2652(c)(2). An interest is considered as used primarily to postpone or avoid the tax imposed by Chapter 13 if a significant purpose for the creation of the interest is to postpone or avoid the tax. Reg. § 26.2612-1(e)(2)(ii).

[155] This would be an attempted postponement of a Chapter 13 transfer of corpus until the end of the term of years, even though there would be a Section 2612(b) taxable distribution as income was distributed to the skip person in each year of the term of years.

[156] Failure to disregard the non-skip person's interests would result in a postponement of the taxable termination at C's death until GC's death, when two taxable terminations would occur, although income distributions to GC during life would constitute Section 2612(b) taxable distributions.

[157] See IRC § 2653(a).

of *GGC* should be disregarded so that there would be a generation-skipping transfer tax at the deaths of both *C* and *GC*.[158]

[e] Assignment of a Trust Interest

If a beneficiary of a trust assigns an interest in a trust, there are potential generation-skipping transfer consequences to both the assignor and the trust. The assignor may make a generation-skipping transfer of the interest. In addition, there may be generation-skipping transfers from the trust either immediately after the assignment or at some subsequent time.

[i] **Consequences to the beneficiary assignor.** A beneficiary's assignment of an interest in a trust may involve the assignment of a Section 2652(c) Chapter 13 interest[159] or some other interest. When a beneficiary of a trust assigns a Chapter 13 interest in a trust, it is a transfer of property whose Chapter 13 consequences should be treated in the same manner as any other transfer of property. If a beneficiary of a Chapter 13 interest in a trust assigns an interest to a skip person, there should be a direct skip transfer of the interest.[160] For example, assume grantor *G* creates a trust, with income to nephew *N* for twenty years and a remainder to *G*'s grandchild, *GC*. *N*'s interest is a Chapter 13 interest in the trust.[161] A gratuitous outright transfer by *N* of his interest in the remaining twenty-year income interest results in a transfer subject to the Chapter 12 tax.[162] If *N* assigns his interest to a skip person, his grandchild *NGC*, for instance, there should be a direct skip,[163] whereas if *N* assigns the interest to

---

[158] *GGC*'s income interest would be disregarded, with the result that the transfer to the trust would not be a direct skip; however, income distributions to *GGC* would be taxable distributions. See Staff of Joint Comm. on Tax'n, 100 Cong., 2d Sess., Description of the Technical Corrections Act of 1988, Title I, at 364 (Comm. Print. 1988); infra ¶ 17.03[1] text accompanying notes 15–18.

[159] IRC § 2652(c)(1). See supra ¶¶ 17.02[3][a], 17.02[3][b].

[160] See IRC § 2612(c)(1). See ¶ 13.02[4].

[161] IRC § 2652(c)(1)(A).

[162] IRC §§ 2501, 2511. See Reg. § 26.2652-1(a)(5) Ex. 4.

[163] IRC § 2612(c)(1). Since the transfer of the Chapter 13 interest to *NGC* should be treated as a direct skip, the distribution of trust income to *NGC*, the assignee of the Chapter 13 interest, should not be classified as a generation-skipping transfer from a trust equivalent created by *N*. Section 2653(a) will move transferor *N* to the generation level just above *NGC*, preventing subsequent distributions to *NGC* from being treated as transfers to a skip person. See infra text accompanying notes 176, 177.

NGC becomes the owner of the income interest, which continues to be a Chapter 13 interest. If *NGC* were to assign this interest, it would be treated in the same manner as any other transfer of property.

his child *NC*, there is no direct skip.[164] If *N* assigns the interest to *NC* for life with a remainder to *NGC* and *NC* dies before the expiration of the twenty-year period, there should be a trust equivalent arrangement[165] with *N* as transferor that should result in a taxable termination at *NC*'s death.[166]

When there is an assignment of an interest in a trust that is not a Chapter 13 interest,[167] no Chapter 13 consequences should occur. Thus, the assignment of a remainder interest in a trust, even when the assignment is to a skip person in relation to the transferor, should not be a direct skip because the transfer does not involve the transfer of an "interest in property" under Section 2652(c).[168]

Returning to the prior example, if grantor's grandchild *GC* assigns the remainder interest in the trust to *GC*'s grandchild (*G*'s great-great-grandchild) *GGGC*, *GC*'s interest is not a Chapter 13 interest,[169] and even though *GC* makes a Chapter 12 transfer[170] and the transfer is to a skip person, *GGGC*,[171] there should be no direct skip.[172]

[ii] Consequences to the trust. Chapter 13 and its legislative history are both silent regarding the consequences to the trust of an assignment of an interest in a trust. Absent any future legislation, regulations will have to handle issues involving assignments.[173] When a beneficiary assigns an interest in a

---

[164] *NC* is not a skip person in relation to *N*; thus, the transfer is not to a skip person. See IRC §§ 2612(c)(1), 2613(a).

[165] See IRC §§ 2652(b)(1), 2652(b)(3). See supra ¶ 17.02[2].

[166] IRC §§ 2612(a)(1)(A), 2652(a)(1)(B). The amount of the taxable termination would be limited to the remaining value of the income interest.

At the end of the twenty-year period after any of the foregoing assignments by *N*, the income interest in the original trust will terminate and the entire corpus of the original trust will be the subject of a taxable termination. IRC § 2612(a)(1). Should this taxable termination not be treated as a generation-skipping transfer, if the property was previously subjected to Chapter 13 taxation on *N*'s assignment where the transferee in the prior transfer (*NGC*) was assigned to the same generation as, or a lower generation than, *GC*? See IRC § 2611(b)(2). Resolution of this issue depends on whether the same property is involved in two generation-skipping transfers. The previously assigned income interest that has now expired is not the same property held in the trust that passes to *GC* at the end of the twenty-year period. See Reg. § 26.2652-1(a)(5) Ex. 4; ¶ 13.01[2][b][iii].

[167] See IRC § 2652(c)(1).

[168] See IRC § 2652(c)(1); ¶ 13.02[4][b] text accompanying notes 278, 279. But see Priv. Ltr. Rul. 200107015 (Nov. 14, 2000) (assignor of remainder interest treated as Chapter 13 transferor of trust for value of remainder interest).

[169] See IRC § 2652(c)(1).

[170] IRC § 2511(a).

[171] IRC § 2613(a)(1).

[172] When the twenty-year income interest terminates, there is a taxable termination of the original trust to *GGGC*. See infra text accompanying notes 179, 180.

[173] See, e.g., Reg. § 26.2652-1(a)(5) Ex. 4.

trust and the assignee replaces the assignor as the holder of the interest, the regulations should provide that the consequences to the trust will depend on whether a Section 2652(c) interest or some other interest was assigned. The regulations should provide that if the assignment involved a Section 2652(c) interest in the trust, the assignment is disregarded and distributions from the trust in relation to the assigned interest should be treated as though they were made to the assignor of the interest (and then transferred by the assignor to the assignee). The regulations should further provide that if there is an assignment of an interest in a trust that is not a Section 2652(c) interest, the assignee replaces the assignor under the terms of the original trust as distributions are made to the assignee by the trust.

For example, again assume grantor G creates a trust with income to nephew N for twenty years and a remainder to grantor's grandchild GC. If N assigns his Section 2652(c) interest to his grandchild NGC, there is an assignment of a Chapter 13 interest,[174] but the assignment should not result in any generation-skipping transfer consequences to the original trust. At the time of the assignment, there is no termination of the twenty-year income interest in the trust and no taxable termination from the trust.[175] As income is paid to NGC, there is no taxable distribution from the original trust.[176] Each income distribution should be treated as though it was transferred under the original terms of the trust to N and then transferred from N to NGC.[177] In addition, if G's grandchild GC assigns the remainder interest to great-great-grandchild GGGC, that transfer is not a transfer of a Chapter 13 interest in the trust.[178] As a result, GGGC should replace GC under the original terms of the trust because GC's interest is not a Chapter 13 interest.[179] At the end of the twenty-year period, there is a taxable termination of the trust to GGGC.[180]

---

[174] See supra text accompanying notes 161–163.

[175] IRC § 2612(a)(1).

[176] IRC § 2612(b).

[177] N is a non-skip person; hence, there is no taxable distribution to N. IRC §§ 2612(b), 2613(a). The transfers from N to NGC initially would not be treated as direct skips because they have already been taxed as direct skips. See IRC § 2611(b)(2), discussed ¶ 13.01[2][b]; supra text accompanying notes 161, 162, 163. Once the transfers exceed the amounts initially taxed as direct skips, they will be taxed as direct skips. See ¶ 13.01[2][b][iii].

[178] See supra text accompanying note 168.

[179] See IRC § 2652(c)(1). But see Priv. Ltr. Rul. 200107015 (Nov. 14, 2000) (assignor treated as Chapter 13 transferor).

[180] IRC § 2612(a)(1)(A). Although it would appear that this escapes generation-skipping transfer tax, note that GC had no real possession or enjoyment of the trust property and that GC's transfer to GGGC was subject to a gift tax under Chapter 12.

The result here differs from the result that would have occurred if GC had received the remainder property and transferred it outright to GGGC. In that event, there again would have been a taxable termination on the distribution to GC, and a Chapter 12 trans-

If *N* instead assigns the income interest to the remainderperson *GC,* and if, under local law, that results in a merger of the interests and a termination of the trust,[181] there is a taxable termination of the original trust.[182] However, if there is no merger under local law, the income distributions during the remaining twenty-year period would be treated as if they were distributed by the trust to *N* and then by *N* to *GC,* and no taxable termination would occur until the termination of the twenty-year period.[183]

¶ 17.03 SECTION 2653. TAXATION OF MULTIPLE SKIPS

[1] Generation Level of Transferors of Multiple Skips

If there is a generation-skipping transfer of property and immediately after the transfer the property is held in trust, Section 2653(a) provides that the transferor of the property (when it is *subsequently* transferred) is assigned to the first generation level above the highest generation level of all persons who have a Chapter 13 interest[1] in the property held in the trust immediately after the prior generation-skipping transfer.[2] This rule prevents the imposition of a generation-skipping transfer tax on property transferred by a transferor more

---

fer by *GC* to *GGGC,* but there would have also been a direct skip by *GC* to *GGGC.* Admittedly, a tax has been avoided by *GC's* assignment of the remainder. Consider, however, how the Chapter 13 transfer by *GC* to *GGGC* would be taxed if *GC* predeceased *N.* There would be no mechanism for Chapter 13 taxation of the transfer of the remainder interest from *GC* to *GGGC.* There would be no taxable termination or direct skip because *GC* would not possess a Chapter 13 interest in the property held in the trust.

[181] Dukeminier & Krier, Property 296 (Little, Brown & Company, 3d ed. 1993).

[182] IRC § 2612(a)(1). *N's* interest would terminate and the corpus would pass to *GC,* a skip person.

[183] IRC § 2612(a)(1).

[1] IRC § 2652(c).

[2] See Reg. § 26.2653-1. A question may be raised about the meaning of the term "transfer" as last used in Section 2653(a), that is, whether "transfer" in this case refers to the initial generation-skipping transfer or to a subsequent transfer. It is the authors' opinion that the statute refers to the prior generation-skipping transfer so as to prevent certain generation-skipping transfers that should be taxed from escaping the grasp of Chapter 13. If the word "transfer" is interpreted to mean the subsequent transfer, no transfer to any lower generation beneficiary would give rise to a generation-skipping transfer, because the transfer would *never* be to a skip person. In each instance, the transferor's generation assignment would be just one above the new transferee, precluding the required two-generation split for a generation skip. IRC § 2613(a)(1). If "transfer" in the statute means the prior generation-skipping transfer, subsequent generation-skipping transfers are possible. See infra text accompanying notes 9, 10; Reg. §§ 26.2653-1(b) Exs. 1, 2.

than once at any generation level[3] by relocating the generation level of the transferor after a generation-skipping transfer.[4]

For example, assume transferor *T* creates a trust with income to *T*'s child *C* for life, then *T*'s granddaughter *GD* for life, and then *T*'s grandson *GS* for life, with a remainder to *T*'s great-grandchildren. At *C*'s death, there is a taxable termination of the property held in the trust because there is a termination of *C*'s interest, no transfer subject to the federal estate tax occurs at the termination, and immediately thereafter, a skip person (*GD*) holds a Chapter 13 interest in the property.[5] Without assistance from Section 2653(a), there would be a taxable distribution any time income is distributed to *GD* during her life because there would be distributions from the trust to a skip person in relation to *T*'s original generation level.[6] Again, without assistance from Section 2653(a), there would also be a taxable termination upon the death of *GD* when *GS* takes possession of the property because there would be a termination when *GD* dies and *GS* would be a skip person in relation to *T*'s original generation level, and *GS* would have a Chapter 13 interest in the property.[7] Congress rightly thinks it inappropriate to impose a second generation-skipping tax at the same generation level when a tax has already been imposed on a generation skip of the same property to that generation (or to a lower-level generation). Section 2653(a) solves the problem by reassigning the transferor to the first generation older than the oldest generation of any person who has a Chapter 13 interest in the trust immediately after the previous generation-skipping transfer. In this example, the only person having a Chapter 13 interest in the trust after the previous generation-skipping transfer is *GD*. As a result of Section 2653(a), *T* is shifted to *C*'s generation level at *C*'s death. When income is distributed to *GD* and, at *GD*'s death, when the property passes to *GS*, *GD* and *GS* are no longer skip persons with respect to *T*,[8] and there is no taxable distribution or taxable termination. However, when *GS* dies and the trust

---

[3] Cf. IRC § 2611(b)(2), discussed ¶ 13.01[2][b], which has a similar purpose.

[4] See Reg. § 26.2653-1(a). The rule neither changes the identity of the transferor nor fixes the tax rates. It simply relocates the transferor in a lower generation. It does not relocate the Section 2651 generation level of persons in their relationship to the transferor. See IRC § 2653(a) (parenthetical). See Reg. §§ 26.2653-1(b) Exs. 1, 2.

[5] IRC § 2612(a)(1); Reg. § 26.2612-1(b)(1). See IRC §§ 2613(a)(1), 2652(c).

[6] IRC § 2612(b). See IRC § 2613(a)(1). But see IRC § 2611(b)(2), which would negate the generation-skipping transfer.

[7] IRC § 2612(a)(1). See IRC §§ 2613(a)(1), 2652(c). But see IRC § 2611(b)(2), which would negate the generation-skipping transfer.

[8] Although *T*'s generation level is relocated, *GS*'s is not. See IRC § 2653(a) (parenthetical).

corpus passes to the great-grandchildren, they are skip persons in relation to the relocated *T*,[9] and there is another taxable termination.[10]

Section 2653(a) also operates in a situation in which multiple generations are skipped. Assume that a very elderly grantor, *G*, establishes a trust with income to child *C* for life, then to grandchild *GC* for life, and then to great-grandchild *GGC* for life, with a remainder to great-great-grandchild *GGGC*. If *GC* predeceases *C*, there is no taxable termination at that time,[11] but there is a taxable termination at *C*'s death.[12] When income is paid to *GGC*, there is no taxable distribution because Section 2653(a) reassigns *G* to *GC*'s generation at *C*'s death; as a result, income distributions to *GGC* during life are not taxable distributions because *GGC* is not a skip person.[13] At *GGC*'s death, there is another taxable termination because, although *G* has been reassigned to *GC*'s generation by Section 2653(a), the property passes to a skip person, *GGGC*.[14]

Does the Section 2653(a) rule permit possible abuse of the system? For example, could a transferor make a direct skip to a trust to provide for income to a great-grandchild for one year[15] (thereby shifting the transferor to the grandchild's generation under Section 2653(a))[16] and thereafter provide income to child for life, income to grandchild for life, with a remainder to great-grandchildren, thus avoiding taxable terminations at both child's and grandchild's deaths?[17] The answer is no. Section 2652(c)(2) would disregard the income interest of the great-grandchild in determining the subsequent potential generation-skipping transfers.[18]

However, if one or more great-grandchildren were given a prior legitimate interest in the trust, the Section 2653(a) rule would apply. For example, assume transferor *T* has an ill adult great-grandson, *GGS*, for whom *T* estab-

---

[9] Relocated *T* is in *C*'s generation, and the great-grandchildren are two generations below that generation. IRC § 2651.

[10] IRC § 2612(a)(1).

[11] Because *GC* held no Section 2652(c) interest at the time of death, there is no taxable termination. IRC § 2612(a)(1)(A).

[12] IRC § 2612(a)(1).

[13] IRC §§ 2612(b), 2613(a)(1). But see Priv. Ltr. Rul. 9823006 (Feb. 25, 1998) (taxable distributions after Section 2653(a) relocation of transferor).

[14] IRC §§ 2612(a)(1), 2613(a)(1). See Reg. §§ 26.2653-1(a), 26.2653-1(b) Ex. 1.

[15] IRC § 2612(c)(1). The trust would be a skip person because the only Section 2652(c) Chapter 13 interest in the trust (the great-grandchild's income interest) would be held by a skip person. See IRC § 2613(a)(2)(A).

[16] Since the Chapter 13 interest in the trust is held by the great-grandchild, Section 2653(a) would relocate the transferor to one generation above that level, to the grandchild's generation.

[17] As the transferor would be relocated to the grandchild's generation, neither the child nor the grandchild would be Section 2613(a)(1) skip persons, and there would be no taxable terminations at their deaths. IRC § 2612(a)(1)(A).

[18] See supra ¶ 17.02[3][d].

lishes an inter vivos irrevocable trust with trust income to be paid to *GGS* for life, then to *T*'s child *C* for life, and then to *T*'s grandchild *GC* for life, with a remainder to *T*'s great-granddaughter *GGD*. Assume further that *GGS*'s death is followed by the death of *C*, *GC*, and *GGD*, in that order. There is a direct skip on funding of the trust,[19] and under Section 2653(a), *T* is assigned to *GC*'s generation level.[20] Upon the death of *GGS*, no federal estate, gift, or generation-skipping transfer tax is imposed.[21] When *C* dies, survived by *GC*, there is no taxable termination or taxable distribution.[22] Upon the death of *GC*, the interest in the trust terminates and the property passes to *GGD*. Again, there is no taxable termination because *T* continues to be assigned to *GC*'s generation and *GGD* is not a skip person.[23] This example demonstrates that multiple skips can give rise to the imposition of only a single generation-skipping transfer tax if the initial interest in a trust is several generations lower than the transferor's generation and the interest is not used primarily to postpone or avoid Chapter 13 tax.[24]

[2] The Effect of Multiple Skips on the Inclusion Ratio

As a general rule, multiple generation-skipping transfers from a trust will not affect the inclusion ratio of the trust, regardless of their form.[25] Thus, if a trust has an inclusion ratio of 0.333 as a result of an allocation of the transferor's

---

[19] The transfer, which is subject to a tax imposed by Chapter 12, is to a skip person, the trust. See supra note 15.

[20] *GGS* holds a Chapter 13 interest in the trust. *T* is treated as assigned to the first generation older than the oldest generation of any person who has a Chapter 13 interest in the trust immediately after the previous generation-skipping transfer. The first generation above *GGS*'s generation, *GC*'s level, is the level to which *T* is assigned.

[21] Because *T* is assigned to the generation level of *GC* (see supra note 20), *C* is not a skip person.

[22] Upon *C*'s death, *C*'s interest in the property held in trust terminates, and *GC* acquires a Chapter 13 interest in the trust. But *GC* is not a skip person because *T* is assigned to *GC*'s generation. See supra note 20.

[23] IRC §§ 2612(a)(1)(A), 2613(a)(1). *GGD* is only one generation lower than the grandchildren's generation, where *T* is now located. See supra note 20.

[24] IRC § 2652(c)(2). Compare the results if the initial transfer to *GGS* had been an outright transfer and *GGS* had established a trust with income to *C*, then to *GC*, and a remainder to *GGD*. Section 2653(a) would have been inapplicable, and although Section 2611(b)(2) might come to the aid of the beneficiaries, a tax should be imposed at the intervening levels as a result of Section 2611(b)(2)(C). See ¶ 13.01[2][b][ii]. Perhaps Congress should enact a limitation similar to Section 2611(b)(2)(C) under Section 2653(a).

[25] IRC § 2653(b)(1). The inclusion ratio of a trust is altered when additional transfers of property or additional allocations of GST exemption are made to the trust. This is accomplished by means of a recomputation of the applicable fraction of the trust. IRC § 2642(d). See ¶ 16.02[5].

GST exemption and taxable distributions are made from the trust, on any subsequent generation-skipping transfer, such as a taxable termination, the inclusion ratio of the trust continues to be 0.333.[26] This general rule is subject to an exception. The inclusion ratio is altered when the ratio is less than 100 percent, there is a taxable termination, and the tax imposed is paid out of the trust corpus, but the property subject to the termination continues to be held in the same trust with the same transferor.[27] A special rule is also provided to determine the inclusion ratio when a generation-skipping transfer from one trust results in a pour-over transfer to a second trust.[28]

[a] Multiple Taxable Terminations With the Same Trust Transferor

The first exception to the general rule that the inclusion ratio of a trust is unaffected by multiple generation-skipping transfers is to be provided by regulations.[29] "Proper adjustment" is to be made to the inclusion ratio with respect to a trust where there has been an allocation of the transferor's GST exemption taxable termination has occurred with respect to the trust,[30] there is a continua-

---

[26] Generally, if the corpus of a trust is fully shielded from the generation-skipping transfer tax by the allocation of the transferor's GST exemption equal to the value of the corpus and no subsequent additions are made to the corpus of the trust, there will never be any tax imposed on generation-skipping transfers attributed to that transferor from the trust. See ¶ 15.02[2] text accompanying notes 41–46. Alternatively, if no GST exemption is allocated to a trust, the inclusion ratio will always be 100 percent. IRC § 2642(a)(1).

[27] IRC § 2653(b)(1). Section 2653(a) would also apply in such a situation. See supra ¶ 17.03[1].

[28] IRC § 2653(b)(2). Section 2653(a) would also apply in such a situation. See supra ¶ 17.03[1].

[29] IRC § 2653(b)(1).

[30] The rule provided by the regulations should not apply to either a direct skip or a taxable distribution. Although the rule of Section 2653(a) may apply to a direct skip transfer directly to a trust, allocation of the transferor's GST exemption is not effective until the direct skip occurs, and no inclusion ratio is established until that time. See ¶ 15.03[3][b]. Even if the transferor makes a transfer to a trust from which there is a subsequent direct skip with the property continuing to be held in the trust, Section 2642(f) delays the effect of any allocation of the GST exemption until the gift or estate taxable event occurs, and that event would coincide with the direct skip. See ¶ 16.02[4][b]. Thus, in the case of a direct skip, no inclusion ratio is determined until the taxable event occurs, and there is no need for an adjustment to the inclusion ratio for the generation-skipping transfer tax imposed. For example, assume T transfers $150,000 to an irrevocable trust. The trust instrument provides that trust income is to be paid to T for nine years or until T's prior death. Then the income is to be paid to T's grandchild GC for life, with the remainder to great grandchild GGC. T's children all survive T. The trust is subject to the estate tax inclusion period (ETIP) while T holds the retained income interest. T files a timely Form 709 reporting the transfer and allocates $50,000 of GST exemption to the trust. The allocation of the GST exemption is not effective until the close of the estate tax inclusion period. Because the trust property is subject to an estate tax inclusion period, the

tion of property (other than the property used to pay the generation-skipping tax) in the same trust,[31] and the original transferor of the trust continues as the transferor of remaining corpus of the trust.[32] The proper adjustment preserves the amount of GST exemption allocated to the property held in trust. The tax imposed is attributable to the portion of the property held in the trust to which no GST exemption is allocated, which is the portion of the property that essentially generates the tax.[33] The Chapter 13 tax payment reduces the nonexempt portion of the property held in trust, necessitating an adjustment in the inclusion ratio to preserve the GST exemption allocated to the property held in the trust. Because the nonexempt portion of the trust generates the Chapter 13 tax, that tax should be paid from the nonexempt portion, and the exempt portion of the trust should remain status quo. The proper adjustment will result in a downward adjustment of the transferor's inclusion ratio with respect to the trust.

For example, assume that transferor *T* funds a testamentary trust with a $3 million corpus and allocates $1 million of the GST exemption to the trust. The terms of the trust provide income to *T*'s child *C* for life, then income to *T*'s grandchild *GC* for life, with a remainder to *T*'s great-grandchildren. Upon

---

inclusion ratio for the trust is not determined until immediately prior to the occurrence of the generation-skipping transfer. See Reg. §§ 26.2632-1(c)(5) Exs. 1, 2. Assume the fair market value of the trust is $150,000 at *T*'s untimely death four years after establishment of the trust, that $150,000 is included in *T*'s gross estate under Section 2036, that no estate tax is paid or collected out of the trust corpus, that no additional GST exemption is allocated to the trust and that the maximum federal estate tax rate is 50 percent in the year of *T*'s death. A testamentary direct skip generation-skipping transfer occurs at *T*'s death in the amount of $116,686.11, the fair market value of the trust assets, $150,000, less the generation-skipping transfer tax, $33,313.89. An algebraic formula is needed to determine the amount of the generation-skipping transfer and the tax imposed because the tax is charged to the property and not included in the tax base. The generation-skipping transfer and the amount of tax imposed are interdependent variables. The trust's applicable fraction is $50,000/$116,686.11, or 0.429, and the resulting inclusion ratio is 0.571 (1 minus 0.429). Upon the death of *GC*, a taxable termination occurs and the 0.571 inclusion ratio established for the direct skip that occurred at *T*'s death is used in the determination of the generation-skipping transfer tax to be imposed on that taxable termination.

The regulatory rule also should not apply to a taxable distribution because the taxable distribution property will be distributed from the original trust. If it is transferred into another skip person trust, Section 2653(b)(2) applies and no "proper adjustment" is necessary. See infra ¶ 17.03[2][b], especially text accompanying notes 43–45.

[31] If there is a taxable termination generation-skipping transfer from one trust to another, the pour-over rule of Section 2653(b)(2) applies. See infra ¶ 17.03[2][b], especially text accompanying note 46.

[32] If there is a new transferor of the entire trust as a result of estate or gift taxation of the corpus to the new transferor (see IRC § 2652(a)(1)), any GST exemption of the original transferor allocated to the trust disappears.

[33] See ¶ 15.02[2] text accompanying note 49.

creation of the trust, the trust has a 0.667 inclusion ratio.[34] The corpus of the trust is still worth $3 million at *C*'s death. There is a Section 2612(a)(1) taxable termination, and, assuming a maximum federal estate tax rate of 50 percent, $1,000,500 of generation-skipping transfer taxes[35] are paid from the trust corpus, which, after payment of the tax, shrinks to $1,999,500. If the inclusion ratio of the trust were to remain constant at 0.667, *T* would effectively be deprived of part of the GST exemption allocation because the applicable fraction of 0.333 multiplied by the $1,999,500 corpus would in effect constitute only $665,833.50 (not $1 million) of GST exemption allocation. As a result, the regulations should provide that the applicable fraction and, concurrently, the inclusion ratio are to be properly adjusted to reflect the corpus that was paid out in generation-skipping transfer taxes. Since $1 million of GST exemption was allocated to a trust that now has a corpus of only $1,999,500, the applicable fraction should be increased to 0.500 (the ratio of $1 million to $1,999,500), and the inclusion ratio should therefore be lowered from 0.667 to 0.500.[36] The result is that the tax is paid out of the nonexempt portion of the corpus of the trust. The 0.500 inclusion ratio is to be employed on subsequent generation-skipping transfers, such as the taxable termination of the trust that occurs upon the death of *GC*.[37]

[b] Pour-Over Trusts

When a transferor makes a GST exemption allocation to one trust and that trust makes a generation-skipping transfer[38] to a second, or pour-over,

---

[34] The applicable fraction is 0.333, or the ratio of $1 million to $3 million. IRC § 2642(a)(2). See Reg. § 26.2642-1(a). The inclusion ratio is 0.667, or 1 minus 0.333. IRC § 2642(a)(1).

[35] The tax amount is computed by multiplying the taxable amount of $3 million by an applicable rate of 33.350 percent. The applicable rate is the 0.667 inclusion ratio multiplied by an assumed 50 percent maximum federal estate tax rate. IRC § 2641. See ¶ 16.01 note 5.

[36] If the corpus had appreciated in value *during C*'s life, the adjustment should still be made. For example, if the corpus had appreciated to $6 million at *C*'s death, then the generation-skipping transfer tax liability would be $2,001,000 ($6 million multiplied by the 33.350 percent applicable rate determined supra note 35). This would leave $3,999,000 of trust corpus, and the applicable fraction should again be increased to 0.500 to reflect the $2 million of GST exemption under the appreciated value of the trust corpus. The inclusion ratio would again be reduced to 0.500.

[37] If the remaining corpus of the trust had increased in value from $1,999,500 to $8 million at *GC*'s death, the generation-skipping transfer tax on that taxable termination assuming a 50 percent maximum federal estate tax rate would be $2 million, which is the product of $8 million multiplied by the 25 percent applicable rate (the assumed 50 percent maximum federal estate tax rate multiplied by the 0.500 inclusion ratio).

[38] If property pours over from one trust to another and the transfer is not a generation-skipping transfer, the applicable fraction of the first trust multiplied by the amount

trust, GST exemption is deemed allocated to property held in the pour-over trust in the determination of the inclusion ratio of the pour-over trust.[39] The "nontax portion" of the distribution is treated as if it were GST exemption allocated to the property held in the pour-over trust.[40] The nontax portion of a distribution is the pre-generation-skipping transfer tax amount of the distribution multiplied by the applicable fraction that applies to such distribution.[41] Section 2653(b)(2) applies regardless of whether the transferor of the first trust has previously been a transferor to the pour-over trust. If the transferor has previously been a transferor to the pour-over trust, then after the Section 2653(b)(2) GST exemption allocation amount is determined, the applicable fraction of the pour-over trust must be recomputed under the rules of Section 2642(d).[42]

For example, assume grantor *G* establishes Trust One, providing income to child *C* for life, then income to grandson *GS* for life, with a remainder to *GS*'s children. *G* gives the independent trustee of Trust One discretion to invade corpus of Trust One for the benefit of Trust Two. Trust Two, also created by *G*, provides income to *G*'s adult granddaughter *GD*[43] for life, with a remainder to *GD*'s children. Assume that *G* transfers $2 million to Trust One and that $500,000 of GST exemption is allocated to Trust One, and transfers $1 million to Trust Two and that no GST exemption is allocated to Trust Two. In the current year, the trustee distributes $1 million of corpus from Trust One to Trust Two in a Section 2612(b) taxable distribution. As a result, $375,000 of generation-skipping transfer tax is imposed on Trust Two on the taxable distribution from Trust One,[44] and only $625,000 is actually added to the corpus of Trust Two. Under Section 2653(b)(2), the nontax portion of the distribution is $250,000 (the 0.25 applicable fraction of Trust One multiplied by the distribution of $1 million). Section 2653(b)(2) treats *G* as making a $250,000 GST exemption allocation to Trust Two. If the corpus of Trust Two is still $1 million at the time of the pour-over, there is a $250,000 GST exemption allocation to Trust Two whose corpus after the pour-over is a total of

---

poured over should be treated as GST exemption allocated to the transfer to the pour-over trust in the determination of the inclusion ratio of the pour-over trust. If the transferor had previously made transfers to the pour-over trust, a recomputation of the applicable fraction of the pour-over trust is required. See IRC § 2642(d), discussed ¶ 16.02[5][b].

[39] IRC § 2653(b)(2).

[40] IRC § 2653(b)(2)(A).

[41] IRC § 2653(b)(2)(B).

[42] See ¶ 16.02[5][b].

[43] Assume that *GD*'s parents are alive. See IRC § 2651(e).

[44] IRC § 2603(a)(1). The tax is computed as follows: $1 million taxable amount is multiplied by a 37.5 percent applicable rate. The Section 2641(a) applicable rate, assuming a 50 percent maximum federal estate tax rate, is 50 percent multiplied by the 0.750 inclusion ratio (1 minus the 0.250 ($500,000/$2,000,000) applicable fraction).

$1,625,000. The resulting applicable fraction of the pour-over trust is 0.154 ($250,000/$1,625,000).[45]

Assume instead that Trust One provided for no invasion power by the trustee, but it provided that at *C*'s death, one half of the corpus was to be distributed to Trust Two, and one half of the corpus was to remain in Trust One. Further, at *C*'s death, the corpus of Trust One is still $2 million and the corpus of Trust Two is still $1 million. The pour-over of one half of the corpus of Trust One to Trust Two is a taxable termination, and the amount of GST exemption allocation for the pour-over trust is identical to the amount after the taxable distribution in the prior example, with the pour-over trust having an applicable fraction of 0.154 even though the generation-skipping transfer tax is paid by Trust One rather than Trust Two.[46]

---

[45] See Reg. § 26.2642-1(a). If, instead, *G* had also allocated $500,000 of GST exemption to Trust Two, which was worth $1 million at the time of the allocation and has a $2 million value at the time of the pour-over, then the applicable fraction after the pour-over is 0.476 ($1,250,000/$2,625,000). Under Section 2642(d)(2), the numerator of the applicable fraction is $1,250,000: (1) $250,000 (as a result of Section 2653(b)(2), there is $250,000 of allocation to the $625,000 of pour-over corpus from Trust One) plus (2) $1 million (there is $1 million of the nontax portion of GST exemption allocation to the current $2 million value of corpus of the pour-over trust immediately prior to the pour-over under Section 2642(d)(3)). The denominator of the applicable fraction is the value distributed from the first trust, $1 million, plus the value of the pour-over trust, $2 million, less the tax imposed on the taxable distribution, $375,000. IRC § 2642(d)(2)(B).

[46] At *C*'s death, the entire corpus worth $2 million is the subject matter of a taxable termination. IRC § 2612(a). Assuming the taxable amount of the taxable termination is $2 million, the generation-skipping transfer tax imposed is $750,000 (the assumed 50 percent maximum rate of tax multiplied by the inclusion ratio of 0.750, multiplied by the $2 million taxable amount). This tax is paid out of Trust One. IRC § 2603(a)(2). Of the $2 million, $1,250,000 remains after Chapter 13 tax on the taxable termination, to be divided between Trust One and pour-over Trust Two. Thus, $625,000 is poured over into Trust Two. The special rule of Section 2653(b)(1) (see supra ¶ 17.03[2][a]) applies in computing the inclusion ratio of Trust One. The applicable fraction of Trust One would initially be 0.250 ($500,000/$2 million), and the inclusion ratio would be 0.750. After application of Section 2653(b)(1), the Trust One applicable fraction should be $500,000/$1,250,000, or 0.400. The Section 2653(b)(2)(B) nontax portion from trust one would be 0.400 multiplied by $625,000, or $250,000. Trust Two would then have an applicable fraction computed under Section 2653(b)(2)(A) of $250,000 (GST exemption allocation)/$1,625,000 (the value of the corpus), or 0.154.

¶ 17.04 SECTION 2654. SPECIAL RULES

[1] Basis Adjustment

[a] Introduction

The unadjusted basis of property depends on how the property was acquired. If purchased, property has a cost basis.[1] The basis of property acquired
gratuitously depends on whether it was acquired from a transferor during life
or at death. An inter vivos gratuitous transfer of property to an individual or
into a trust generally takes a transferred basis from the transferor under Section
1015 in an amount equal to the transferor's basis for determining gain, and either that or the fair market value at the time of the transfer, if it is lower, for
determining loss.[2] Under Section 1015(d), the transferred basis is adjusted upward, though not in an amount in excess of fair market value at the time of
the transfer, by the amount of the gift tax attributable to unrealized appreciation in the gift property.[3] The gift tax adjustment is essentially treated as an
added cost of the gifted property. Under Section 1014(a), property, other than
land qualifying for the Section 2031(c) exclusion[4] acquired from a decedent
has a basis[5] equal to its valuation for estate tax purposes.[6]

A transferee's basis for property is significant for numerous tax consequences, primarily because it will be a determinant of gain or loss on a transferee's sales and exchanges[7] and will, in part, determine and limit the
transferee's depreciation deductions on depreciable property.[8]

All these basis principles have their fair share of intricacies, which are not
explored here. The issue to be discussed is the effect of Chapter 13 on the ba-

---

[1] IRC § 1012.

[2] IRC § 1015(a). Cf. IRC § 1041(b)(2).

[3] IRC § 1015(d)(6). See Reg. § 1.1015-5(c). See also Reg. § 1.1015-4 for basis of
property acquired in a part-gift and part-sale transfer.

[4] IRC § 1014(a)(4). The basis of property acquired from a decedent to the extent of
the applicability of the Section 2031(c) exclusion is the basis of the property in the hands
of the decedent. See IRC § 2031(c); ¶ 4.02[7][e][iii].

[5] IRC §§ 1014(a)(1), 1014(a)(2), 1014(a)(3).

[6] This would include the fair market value at date of death (IRC § 1014(a)(1)) or on
the alternate valuation date (IRC § 1014(a)(2); see IRC § 2032), or a value determined
under Section 2032A if elected (IRC § 1014(a)(3)). If the additional estate tax is imposed
under Section 2032A(c)(1), the qualified heir, for a price, may elect to increase the basis
in the qualified real property. See IRC §§ 1016(c)(1), 1016(c)(5)(B); ¶ 4.04[7][h].

[7] IRC § 1001.

[8] IRC §§ 167(a), 167(c), 168. See Section 167(d) and corresponding regulations for
allocation of depreciation deductions among life tenants and beneficiaries of trusts and estates. Cf. IRC § 167(e).

sis of property. A Chapter 13 transfer is accorded much the same effect on the basis of property as a lifetime or a testamentary transfer. Generally, when a generation-skipping transfer tax is imposed, a Section 1015(d)(6) type of adjustment is made to the property that is the subject of the transfer.[9] However, in the case of a testamentary direct skip, a Section 1014(a) adjustment is made and no adjustment should be necessary unless the direct skip involves appreciated land qualifying for the Section 2031(c) exclusion.[10] Furthermore, in the case of a taxable termination upon the death of an individual, a Section 1014(a) type of adjustment is made.[11]

[b] General Rule

It seems fair to say that, in general, the Chapter 13 tax is accorded the same significance as gift tax with respect to actual gifts. Basis is increased, but not above fair market value, by the amount of the Chapter 13 tax that is attributable to the excess of the fair market value of the property over the adjusted basis of the property immediately before the transfer, that is, the tax attributable to net appreciation.[12] If no Chapter 13 tax is imposed, no adjustment is made. For purposes of this basis adjustment, the Chapter 13 tax is computed without regard to Section 2604, the credit for state taxes.[13] The Chapter 13 adjustment is applied after any adjustment to the basis of the property under Section 1015 with respect to the transfer.[14] The two adjustments combined may not increase the basis of the property above its fair market value. The Chapter 13 tax adjustment to basis, like the gift tax adjustment, is treated as an added cost of the transferred property.

Application of this general rule requires a determination of the fair market value[15] of the property transferred in the generation-skipping transfer. The general rule uses the fair market value of the property in the computation of the basis adjustment available and as an overall limitation on the basis adjustment that may be made to the property. Generally, the determination of fair market

---

[9] IRC § 2654(a)(1).

[10] See infra ¶ 17.04[1][c], especially text accompanying notes 38–40.

[11] IRC § 2654(a)(2). See infra ¶ 17.04[1][d].

[12] IRC § 2654(a)(1).

[13] IRC § 2654(a)(1). See ¶ 12.04.

[14] IRC § 2654(a)(1) (last sentence). When a taxable gift that is a direct skip is made, the amount of the gift is increased by the Chapter 13 tax. IRC § 2515. See ¶¶ 10.05, 13.02[4][a]. The total gift taxes (including those generated by the Section 2515 portion of the gift) are taken into consideration in the adjustment to the basis of the property under Section 1015(d), as limited by Section 1015(d)(6). See infra text accompanying notes 23, 24.

[15] Reg. § 20.2031-1(b).

value will be made at the time of the generation-skipping transfer.[16] For example, if property with an adjusted basis of $50,000 is distributed from a trust in a taxable distribution[17] at a time when its fair market value is $75,000, and a $30,000 generation-skipping transfer tax is imposed, the property would have a $10,000 increase in basis, to $60,000.[18]

Property that is the subject matter of a generation-skipping transfer that generates a generation-skipping transfer tax sometimes qualifies simultaneously for more than one adjustment to basis. A single event may result in property qualifying for a basis adjustment under Section 2654(a)(1) as well as under Section 1014 or Section 1015.[19] When Section 1014(a)(1), Section 1014(a)(2), or Section 1014(a)(3) applies, no additional basis adjustment should occur under Section 2654(a)(1).[20] When Section 1014(a)(4) applies, a basis adjustment under Section 2654(a)(1) may occur.[21] Section 2654(a)(1) adjustments to basis are to be made after the application of the Section 1015 adjustments to basis.[22]

For example, if property with a $40,000 basis and a $100,000 fair market value had been the subject of a lifetime direct skip, and both a $43,500 gift

---

[16] IRC § 2624(a). See ¶ 14.05.

[17] IRC § 2612(b). See ¶ 13.02[3]. It is assumed that no Section 643(e)(3) election is made upon the distribution of the property. IRC § 643(e)(3). It is also assumed that the distribution is not treated as a taxable exchange upon the distribution in satisfaction of a pecuniary amount. See Kenan v. Comm'r, 114 F2d 217 (2d Cir. 1940).

[18] IRC § 2654(a)(1). The amount is computed by multiplying the fraction of the net appreciation, $25,000, over the fair market value, $75,000, or one-third, by the Chapter 13 tax, $30,000, to arrive at a $10,000 adjustment, which is then added to the $50,000 adjusted basis. If the property had an adjusted basis of $75,000 immediately prior to the transfer, no basis adjustment would be made. No basis adjustment would be made if a Section 643(e)(3) election was in effect for the year of the distribution. IRC § 643(e)(3).

If, after a term of years, there is a taxable termination of an income interest involving property with a basis of $40,000 and a fair market value of $100,000, and the property is subject to a $40,000 generation-skipping transfer tax, there would be a $24,000 increase in the basis of the property under Section 2654(a)(1); the property would then have a $64,000 adjusted basis. The adjustment is determined by the ratio of the appreciation ($60,000) to the fair market value of the property ($100,000) multiplied by the $40,000 tax (60 percent of $40,000 equals $24,000).

[19] An adjustment to basis is also available under Section 643(e). Section 643(e) involves the basis of property distributed in kind to a trust or estate beneficiary. When a Section 643(e)(3) election is made the property takes a fair market value basis, and no further Section 2654(a)(1) basis adjustment is necessary. See infra ¶¶ 17.04[1][c], 17.04[1][d].

[20] See infra ¶ 17.04[1][c]. See also infra ¶ 17.04[1][d].

[21] IRC § 1014(a)(4). Section 1014(a)(4) provides carryover basis for land subject to a qualified conservation easement acquired from a decedent to the extent of the applicability of the Section 2031(c) exclusion. See infra ¶ 17.04[1][c] text accompanying notes 38–40.

[22] IRC § 2654(a)(1) (last sentence). See infra note 24.

tax[23] and a $45,000 generation-skipping transfer tax were imposed on the transfer, then there should be an $18,000 Section 1015(d), as limited by Section 1015(d)(6), adjustment to basis, and there could be a $27,000 Section 2654(a)(1) adjustment to the basis with a resulting $85,000 adjusted basis for the property.[24]

---

[23] Under Section 2515, when there is an inter vivos direct skip, the amount of the taxable gift is increased by the amount of the Chapter 13 tax imposed on the transferor. Thus, the total gifts (disregarding any Section 2503(b) exclusion) would be $145,000. See supra note 14. The facts in the text assume a 30 percent gift tax rate. The $45,000 increase in the amount of the taxable gift is not an increase in the generation-skipping transfer.

[24] The $18,000 Section 1015(d) adjustment, as limited by Section 1015(d)(6), is the product of the net appreciation in the value of the gift over the amount of the gift, multiplied by the gift tax ($60,000/($100,000+$45,000) × $43,500).

The Section 2654(a)(1) adjustment to the basis of property subjected to a generation-skipping transfer tax is equal to the generation-skipping transfer tax attributable to the fair market value of the property, $100,000, over its adjusted basis immediately before the transfer. The last sentence of Section 2654(a)(1) provides that this basis adjustment "shall be applied after any basis adjustment under section 1015 with respect to the transfer." IRC § 2654(a)(1) (last sentence).

When a single transfer results in the imposition of both a gift tax and a generation-skipping transfer tax and qualifies simultaneously for more than one adjustment to basis, once the Section 1015(d) adjustment to basis for gift tax, as limited by Section 1015(d)(6), is calculated, a question arises whether this adjustment is to be added to the adjusted basis of the property transferred immediately before the gift in the determination of the Section 2654(a)(1) adjustment to basis for the generation-skipping transfer tax imposed. In the example, property with an adjusted basis of $40,000 and a fair market value of $100,000 is gifted to a skip person, and the Section 1015(d) adjustment to basis is $18,000. Is the "adjusted basis immediately before the transfer" to be used in the determination of the Section 2654(a)(1) adjustment, $40,000 (the adjusted basis of the property before the gift), or $58,000 (the adjusted basis, $40,000, increased by the Section 1015(d) adjustment, as limited by Section 1015(d)(6), of $18,000)?

As originally enacted in 1986, Section 2654(a)(1) contained only the first sentence of the present statutory language. Tax Reform Act of 1986, Pub. L. No. 99-514, § 1431(a), 100 Stat. 2085, 2727 (1986), reprinted in 1986-3 CB (Vol. 1) 1, 644. The second sentence was added in the Omnibus Budget Reconciliation Act of 1989. Omnibus Budget Reconciliation Act of 1989, Pub. L. No. 101-239, § 7811(j)(2), 103 Stat. 2106, 2411 (1989), reprinted in 1990-1 CB 210, 271. Initially, it was possible to make a gift tax basis adjustment that, when added to the pretransfer adjusted basis, did not exceed the fair market value of the property and a separate generation-skipping transfer tax adjustment to basis that, when added to the pretransfer adjusted basis, did not exceed the fair market value of the property. It was possible to make two separate adjustments to the basis of the property transferred, neither of which when added to the adjusted basis of the property before the transfer resulted in a basis that exceeded the fair market value of the property before the transfer, but in combination, the two basis adjustments could result in a basis that exceeded the fair market value of the property at the time of the transfer. To remedy this situation, the second sentence of Section 2654(a)(1) providing that "the preceding [the first sentence] shall be applied after any basis adjustment under section 1015 with respect to transfer" (IRC § 2654(a)(1)) was added to confirm "that the two adjustments combined

Property within the prior transfer exclusion of Section 2611(b)(2) does not generate a Chapter 13 tax. This precludes any Section 2654(a)(1) basis adjustment. If a single transfer is partly within and partly without the prior transfer exclusion, the unrealized appreciation should be allocated between the included and excluded amounts in accordance with their respective values, and the adjustment should be made with regard to tax on net appreciation in the included amount as so determined. Although Chapter 13 tax is not attributable to an excluded amount,[25] the statute does not clearly identify and exclude unrealized appreciation on the excluded amount from this basis computation.

[c] Testamentary Direct Skips

When property involved in a testamentary direct skip has a basis equal to its fair market value at the date of death,[26] no basis adjustment is made under Section 2654(a)(1). Section 2654(a)(1) provides that the basis of the property is to be increased, but not above fair market value, by an amount equal to the Chapter 13 tax attributable to the excess of fair market value over the adjusted basis immediately before the transfer. Therefore, when the basis of the prop-

---

cannot increase the basis in the property above its fair market value." HR Rep. No. 247, 101st Cong., 1st Sess. 1, 1436 (1989), reprinted in 1989 USCCAN 1906, 2906.

It is possible to interpret the second sentence as merely ensuring that the generation-skipping transfer tax basis adjustment and the gift tax basis adjustment when added to the adjusted basis of the property before the transfer does not exceed fair market value of the property without affecting the determination of the unrealized appreciation in the property used in the determination of the Section 2654(a)(1) basis adjustment. Under this interpretation, the adjusted basis used in the determination of the Section 2654(a)(1) adjustment would be $40,000. The Section 2654(a)(1) adjustment would be $27,000 ($60,000/ $100,000 × $45,000).

On the other hand, it may be argued that under the statute, as amended, the gift tax basis adjustment is added to the pretransfer adjusted basis of the property in the determination of the generation-skipping transfer tax basis adjustment. If this is done, it certainly "confirms that the two adjustments combined cannot increase the basis in the property above its fair market value" because it would be mathematically impossible. Under this interpretation, the adjusted basis used in the determination of the Section 2654(a)(1) adjustment would be $58,000. The Section 2654(a)(1) adjustment would be $18,900 ($42,000/100,000 × $45,000).

Taxpayers would favor the gift tax adjustment limiting only the amount of the generations-skipping transfer tax addition and not having the gift tax adjustment under Section 1015(d) being added to the pretransfer basis in the mechanics of calculation of the generation-skipping transfer tax basis adjustment. An example in the regulations addressing this issue would certainly be helpful.

[25] Nevertheless, any amount of basis adjustment should be allocated to adjust the basis of both the property subject to the exclusion and the property subject to tax.

[26] IRC § 1014(a)(1). See Reg. § 20.2031-1(b).

erty before application of Section 2654(a)(1) is equal to its fair market value, no further basis adjustment may occur for the Chapter 13 tax.[27]

The determination of fair market value is generally made at the time of the generation-skipping transfer.[28] However, if the property to be valued is transferred in a testamentary direct skip, the value for Chapter 13 purposes may, in some instances, be determined on the alternate valuation date.[29] If the property transferred is valued for Chapter 13 purposes on the alternative date, then, in all likelihood, that date will be the date of valuation for purposes of determining the basis adjustment under Section 2654(a). As a result of the operation of Section 1014(a)(2), no further Section 2654(a) basis adjustment shall be made.

Testamentary direct skips of property are mandatorily valued under Section 2032A for Chapter 13 purposes if the property is valued under Section 2032A for estate tax imposition purposes.[30] Although Section 2654(a) uses the term "fair market value," Section 2624(b), whenever applicable, should result in a Section 2032A valuation substitution for fair market value in the determination of the basis adjustment and application of the overall limitation in Section 2654.[31] Again, no further basis adjustment should occur under Section 2654(a)(1). Thus, if property involved in a testamentary direct skip has Section 1014(a)(2) or Section 1014(a)(3) basis, including valuation established under either Section 2032A[32] or Section 2032,[33] there should be no need for a basis adjustment under Section 2654(a)(1).[34]

---

[27] Assume that the basis to the transferor was $50,000, the date-of-death fair market value was $100,000, the property was not an item of income in respect of a decedent or excluded under Section 2031(c) from the transferor's gross estate, and the total Chapter 13 tax was $20,000. Assuming there is no Section 2032 or Section 2032A election, Section 1014(a)(1) provides that the basis of property acquired from a decedent is its fair market value at the date of the decedent's death, and the basis will be increased to $100,000. Section 2654(a)(1) will not increase the basis of the property taxed under Chapter 13 above its fair market value, so the basis of the property remains $100,000, unaffected by Section 2654(a)(1). See infra text accompanying notes 28–37, discussing the consequences when property is valued under Section 2032 or Section 2032A.

[28] IRC § 2624(a). See ¶ 14.05.

[29] IRC § 2624(b). See IRC § 2032. See ¶ 14.05[2][a].

[30] IRC § 2624(b). See ¶ 14.05[2][a] text accompanying notes 20, 21.

[31] This should be clarified in the regulations.

[32] IRC § 1014(a)(3).

[33] IRC § 1014(a)(2).

[34] For example, assume that property with an adjusted basis of $50,000 is worth $100,000 at the time of the testamentary direct skip, but a Section 2032 or a Section 2032A election is made, and the property is valued for estate tax purposes at $80,000. Assume that $20,000 of Chapter 13 tax is paid. In this situation, there is a potential Section 2654(a)(1) basis adjustment. But the federal estate tax value of $80,000 determined under either Section 2032 or Section 2032A should also be used as fair market value in the Sec-

If additional estate tax is imposed under Section 2032A(c),[35] additional generation-skipping transfer tax may also be imposed.[36] The imposition of an additional generation-skipping transfer tax should generate an additional basis adjustment on conditions similar to those required for a basis adjustment for the additional estate tax imposed.[37] However, if the imposition of additional estate tax results in a Section 1016(c) adjustment to basis, there should be no need for any basis adjustment under Section 2654(a)(1).

A portion of the value of land subject to a qualified conservation easement may be excluded from a decedent's gross estate under Section 2031(c).[38] Land subject to a qualified conservation easement that is acquired from a decedent receives a carryover basis under Section 1014(a)(4) to the extent that the exclusion under Section 2031 (c) is applicable.[39] A testamentary direct skip of property excluded from a decedent's gross estate for estate tax purposes is valued at its fair market value for generation-skipping transfer tax purposes.[40] The carryover basis of the property excluded from the decedent's gross estate may be greater than, equal to, or less than the fair market value of the property. If the excluded property has appreciated in value a Section 2654(a)(1) basis increase is made for the generation-skipping transfer tax attributable to the difference between the Section 1014(a)(4) carryover basis and the fair market value of the property qualified for the exclusion.

If the subject matter of a testamentary direct skip taxed under Chapter 13 is a right to receive an item of income in respect of a decedent,[41] a literal reading of Section 2654(a)(1) allows a basis adjustment. Section 2654(a)(1) contains no provision comparable to Section 1014(c). However, the regulations should prohibit a Section 2654(a)(1) basis adjustment for a testamentary transfer of a right to receive an item of income in respect of a decedent.

[d] Taxable Terminations at Death

If a taxable termination occurs at the same time as, and as a result of, the death of an individual, a step-up or step-down in basis occurs that is similar to

---

tion 2654(a)(1) computation to preclude any further Section 2654(a)(1) basis adjustment for the generation-skipping transfer tax.

[35] See ¶ 4.04[7].

[36] See ¶ 18.03[1][a] text accompanying notes 13, 14. The Secretary was charged by Congress specifically to promulgate regulations necessary to coordinate the provisions of Chapter 13 with the recapture tax imposed under Section 2032A. IRC § 2663(1). See Reg. §§ 26.2663-1, 26.2642-2(b)(1), 26.2642-4(a)(4).

[37] See IRC § 1016(c), especially IRC § 1016(c)(5)(B).

[38] IRC § 2031(c). See ¶ 4.02[7].

[39] IRC § 1014(a)(4).

[40] IRC § 2624(a).

[41] See IRC §§ 691, 1014(c).

the adjustment to basis provided under Section 1014(a).[42] If alternative valuation is not elected under Section 2624(c), the basis will generally be adjusted to the date-of-death fair market value.[43] If alternative valuation is elected under Section 2624(c),[44] the basis of the property will be adjusted to the Section 2032 value. Under Section 2624(b), Section 2032A valuation is permitted only for testamentary direct skips of property valued under Section 2032A for estate tax purposes; thus, Section 2032A valuation of property that is the subject matter of a taxable termination is not permitted.

If the Section 2642(a) inclusion ratio for property involved in a taxable termination at death is less than one, any increase or decrease in the adjustment to basis is limited to the amount derived by multiplying the adjustment by the inclusion ratio.[45] Where the inclusion ratio is less than 1, some of the property is essentially exempted from Chapter 13 tax by use of the transferor's GST exemption; to that extent, no increase in the property's adjusted basis is warranted.

For example, assume A has a life interest in property held in trust. The basis of the property is $100,000. When A dies, the fair market value of the property is $200,000. If, upon A's death, there is a taxable termination, as defined in Section 2612(a), and no GST exemption is allocated, resulting in an inclusion ratio of 1, the basis of the property will be adjusted by $100,000, to $200,000. If, instead, the inclusion ratio is 0.75, one quarter of the property is essentially exempted from Chapter 13 tax,[46] and the amount of the adjustment is only $75,000. Nevertheless, the $75,000 adjustment is made to the basis of all the property (both the included and excluded portions), and the entire property has an adjusted basis of $175,000.

[2] Single Trust Treated as or Divided Into Multiple Trusts

[a] Single Trust Treated as Multiple Trusts

The Chapter 13 consequences of a transfer of property may depend on whether assets are transferred in one trust or in more than one trust. In general,

---

[42] IRC § 2654(a)(2).

[43] An exception to this general rule may occur when the property that is the subject matter of the taxable termination is property that is excluded under Section 2031(c) from the gross estate of the individual whose death triggers the taxable termination; in this case, the basis of the property is determined under Section 1014(a)(4).

[44] See ¶ 14.05[2][b].

[45] IRC § 2654(a)(2).

[46] See ¶ 15.02[2] text accompanying note 49.

a single trust cannot be treated as multiple trusts.[47] However, in at least three circumstances, a single trust may be treated as if it were two or more trusts for Chapter 13 purposes.[48] Portions of a trust that are attributable to actual or imputed transfers from different transferors are treated as separate trusts.[49] Substantially separate and independent shares[50] of different beneficiaries are treated as separate trusts.[51] A pecuniary amount payable upon the death of the transferor from an inter vivos trust included in the transferor's gross estate, or from a testamentary trust, is treated as a separate trust in some circumstances.[52]

---

[47] IRC § 2654(b). Section 2642(a)(3) provides for a "qualified severance" of a single trust into multiple trusts. See ¶ 16.02[5][e]. When Section 2642(a)(3) applies, a single trust is severed into more than one actual trust. The single trust is not merely "treated" as multiple trusts after a Section 2642(a)(3) qualified severance.

[48] Section 2654(b) provides for this treatment in two instances. IRC §§ 2654(b)(1), 2654(b)(2). The regulations provide for it in one more instance. Reg. § 26.2654-1(a)(1)(ii). There may be another instance in which a single trust should be treated as two trusts, namely, where the grantor of a trust is assigned to two separate generation levels. See ¶ 15.03[3][b], especially text accompanying notes 61, 62.

This separation of a single trust into multiple trusts makes administrative sense, easing the Internal Revenue Service's burden with respect to determining the inclusion ratio for the trust and determining whether a generation-skipping transfer has occurred with respect to the trust.

However, Section 2654(b) does not apply during the period a trust is treated as part of an estate pursuant to Section 645. IRC § 2654(b) (last sentence). A Section 645 election to treat a trust as part of an estate has no other effect for generation-skipping transfer tax purposes. S. Rep. No. 174, 105th Cong., 2d Sess. 194 (1998), reprinted in 1998-3 CB 537, 730.

[49] IRC § 2654(b)(1); Reg. § 26.2654-1(a)(2). See ¶ 17.02[1][d], which involves the principal discussion of this concept; Reg. §§ 26.2654-1(a)(5) Exs. 5, 6, 7. See also IRC § 2652(a)(2); supra ¶ 17.02[1][c][ii]; ¶ 13.02[2][e][ii], dealing with multiple transferors where there are lapses of post-1942 general powers of appointment.

[50] The phrase "substantially separate and independent shares" is defined for this Chapter 13 purpose generally in Regulations Section 1.663(c)-3. Reg. § 26.2654-1(a)(1)(i). See Priv. Ltr. Rul. 200040010 (June 28, 2000) (Reg. § 1.663(c)-3 applied to conclude separate share with multiple beneficiaries).

[51] IRC § 2654(b)(2). See Reg. §§ 26.2654-1(a)(5) Exs. 1, 2. A portion of a trust that is a separate and independent share must exist at the creation of the trust and at all times thereafter. Reg. § 26.2654-1(a)(1)(i). See Reg. § 26.2654-1(a)(5) Ex. 8. A trust for this purpose is treated as created at the date of the transferor's death if the entire trust is included in the transferor's gross estate as defined in Section 2031. Reg. § 26.2654-1(a)(1)(i).

[52] Reg. § 26.2654-1(a)(1)(ii). The pecuniary amount is treated as a separate and independent share and therefore as a separate trust for purposes of Chapter 13 only if its payment is mandatory (nondiscretionary and noncontingent) and the trustee satisfies the amount within fifteen months of the transferor's death, or the trustee is required to allocate a pro rata share of the income earned by the fund from which the pecuniary payment is to be made between the date of death of the transferor and payment, or is required to pay appropriate interest on the amount. Reg. § 26.2654-1(a)(1)(ii)(A). See Reg. § 26.2642-2(b)(4). In addition, if the amount is payable in kind with assets valued at other

Even though a single trust is treated as more than one trust for purposes of Chapter 13, it is not treated as more than one trust for any other purposes, such as filing returns and payment of tax or the computation of any other tax imposed by the Internal Revenue Code.[53]

Additions to[54] and distributions from a single trust that is treated as multiple trusts are allocated on a pro rata basis among the separate trusts unless the governing instrument expressly provides otherwise.[55]

A GST exemption may be allocated to any of the separate shares treated as separate trusts for purposes of Chapter 13.[56] An inter vivos direct skip transfer[57] to a single trust treated as multiple trusts results in an automatic pro rata allocation of available GST exemption among the multiple trusts[58] unless prevented by the transferor.[59] The transferor may prevent the automatic allocation of GST exemption to each resulting multiple trust.[60]

Treatment of a single trust as multiple trusts can alter whether a generation-skipping transfer has occurred, the type of generation-skipping transfer that has occurred, and the applicable rate of tax to be applied to generation-

---

than the date of distribution, the trustee must be required to liquidate the amount in a manner that fairly reflects the net appreciation or depreciation that occurs in the fund that may be used to discharge the pecuniary amount between the date of valuation and the date of distribution. Reg. § 26.2654-1(a)(1)(ii)(B). See Reg. §§ 26.2654-1(a)(5) Exs. 3, 4. These concepts are discussed in more detail at ¶¶ 16.02[4][d][ii], 16.02[4][d][iii].

[53] Reg. § 26.2654-1(a)(1)(i). However, if the separate and independent share rule applies to a single trust, under Section 663(c) the shares of different beneficiaries are treated as separate trusts in the determination of distributable net income allocable to the respective beneficiaries under Sections 661 and 662 for income tax purposes. See Reg. § 1.663(c)-1(a).

[54] Additions to a trust with a single transferor treated as separate and independent shares are generally allocated pro rata among the separate trusts. Reg. § 26.2654-1(a)(1)(i). An addition to a trust created by a transferor but made by another grantor would be treated as a separate trust or an addition to an existing separate trust and would not be allocated pro rata. See Reg. § 26.2654-1(a)(2)(ii). Appreciation in assets held in a single trust with multiple grantors treated as multiple trusts is generally allocated between the multiple trusts on a pro rata basis. See Reg. § 26.2654-1(a)(2); ¶ 17.02[1][d] text accompanying notes 66–68.

[55] Reg. § 26.2654-1(a).

[56] Reg. § 26.2654-1(a)(4)(i). This is the rule regardless of whether the single trust has substantially separate and independent shares or multiple grantors. See Reg. § 26.2632-1; ¶ 15.03.

[57] IRC § 2612(c); ¶ 13.02[4].

[58] Reg. § 26.2654-1(a)(4)(ii). See IRC § 2632(b); ¶ 15.03[3].

[59] Reg. § 26.2654-1(a)(4)(ii). See Reg. § 26.2632-1(b)(1)(i); ¶ 15.03[3][c].

[60] Reg. § 26.2654-1(a)(4)(ii). The automatic allocation of GST exemption to a separate share of a single trust is prevented by describing on a timely filed United States Gift (and Generation-Skipping Transfer) Tax Return the transfer and the extent to which the automatic allocation rule is not to apply to a particular share. Id.

skipping transfers from the separate trusts. For example, assume that grantor *G* establishes a trust with one half of the income to be paid to grandchild *GC* (whose parents are living) and one half to be paid to child *C* for life, with a remainder to *GC*'s children. If the trust is separated, a transfer to the trust with income to be paid to *GC* constitutes a direct skip. There would not be a direct skip if there were a combined trust.[61] Similarly, assume that grantor *G* establishes a trust with income to child *C* for life; at *C*'s death, one half of the income goes to grandson *GS* for life, with one half of the remainder to *GS*'s children at *GS*'s death, and the other half of the income goes to granddaughter *GD* for life, with the other half of the remainder to *GD*'s children at *GD*'s death. If the trusts are appropriately separated, upon the death of *GD* or *GS*, a taxable termination, rather than a taxable distribution, occurs.[62]

[b] Division of a Single Trust Into Multiple Trusts

Treating a single trust as multiple trusts for purposes of Chapter 13 does not result in an actual severance of the single trust into more than one actual trust.[63] However, a single trust that is treated as separate trusts for Chapter 13 purposes[64] may be divided at any time.[65] If the trust is an inter vivos trust that is not included in the transferor's gross estate, the separate trusts must be divided and funded on a fractional basis[66] or, if required by the terms of the governing instrument, on the basis of a pecuniary amount.[67] If the trust is an inter

---

[61] IRC § 2612(c)(1). See ¶ 13.03[3][a]. See also supra text accompanying notes 57–59; ¶ 15.02[2].

[62] IRC § 2612(a)(2). See ¶ 13.02[2][f] at notes 194–200.

[63] See supra ¶ 17.04[2][a].

[64] See supra ¶ 17.04[2][a].

[65] Reg. § 26.2654-1(a)(3). In addition, a single trust may be severed in a qualified severance into multiple trusts. See IRC § 2642(a)(3), discussed at ¶ 16.02[5][e].

[66] Reg. § 26.2654-1(b)(1)(ii)(C)(1). If the new trusts are funded on a fractional basis, there is no requirement that a pro rata portion of each asset held by the trust to be divided be used to fund the new trusts. Id. However, if the trust is not funded on a pro rata basis, the new trusts must be funded using the fair market value of the assets on the date of funding or in a manner that fairly reflects the net appreciation or depreciation in the value of the assets between the dates of valuation and funding. Id.

[67] Reg. §§ 26.2654-1(b)(1)(ii)(C)(2), 26.2654-1(a)(3). If the trusts are divided on the basis of a pecuniary amount, the trust must pay appropriate interest on the pecuniary amount. Reg. §§ 26.2654-1(b)(1)(ii)(C)(2), 26.2654-1(a)(1)(ii)(A), 26.2642-2(b)(4). In addition, if the pecuniary amount is payable in kind with assets valued at a date other than the date of distribution, the assets distributed must fairly reflect net appreciation or depreciation in the value of assets available to fund the pecuniary amount between the dates of valuation and funding. Reg. § 26.2654-1(a)(1)(ii)(B). Cf. Rev. Proc. 64-19, 1964-1 (Pt. 1) CB 682.

If a single trust is divided and that division is not recognized for purposes of Chapter 13, generation-skipping transfers presumably will be treated as from each of the trusts on

vivos trust that is included in the transferor's gross estate or a testamentary trust created under the transferor's will that is treated as separate trusts under Chapter 13, it may be divided into separate trusts only if the governing instrument requires that the trust is to be divided upon the transferor's death,[68] or the trust is divided pursuant to discretionary authority granted by the instrument or local law and if three additional requirements are satisfied.[69] First, the terms of the new trusts must provide in the aggregate the same succession of interests and beneficiaries as the original trust.[70] Second, the severance must occur[71] prior to the due date for filing the transferor's federal estate tax return.[72] Third, the new trusts generally must be severed on a fractional basis,[73] or, if required

---

a pro rata basis. The allocation of GST exemption and the determination of the applicable fraction, inclusion ratio, and applicable rate of tax will be accomplished as though there were no severance.

[68] Reg. § 26.2654-1(b)(1)(i).

[69] Reg. § 26.2654-1(b)(1)(ii). See Reg. § 26.2654-1(b)(4) Ex. 1. See, e.g., Fla. Stat. Ann. § 737.403(1)(a)2 (2001); Ill. Comp. Stat. Ann. ¶ 5/4.25 (Smith-Hurd 2001), which specifically provide for severance to reduce potential generation-skipping transfer tax liability. Such a division would commonly occur to separate a trust for purposes of making a Section 2652(a)(3) reverse QTIP election. See ¶ 17.02[1][c][i]; Priv. Ltr. Rul. 9337006 (June 14, 1993); Priv. Ltr. Rul. 9126025 (Mar. 29, 1991); Priv. Ltr. Rul. 9126020 (Mar. 29, 1991); Priv. Ltr. Rul. 9707026 (Nov. 19, 1996) (trust, which followed QTIP trust after QTIP beneficiary's death, severed under state law before due date of QTIP beneficiary's federal estate tax return).

If the division of a single trust is not recognized for purposes of Chapter 13, generation-skipping transfers will presumably be treated as from each of the trusts on a pro rata basis. The allocation of GST exemption and the determination of the applicable fraction, inclusion ratio, and applicable rate of tax will be accomplished as though there was no severance.

[70] Reg. § 26.2654-1(b)(1)(ii)(A).

[71] If a reformation proceeding is required for severance, it is sufficient that it has commenced within the prescribed period. If a court order severing the trust has not been issued at the time the federal estate tax return is filed, a statement that indicates that the severance proceeding has commenced and contains a description of the proposed manner of severance must be attached to the return. A copy of the petition or other instrument commencing the proceeding must also be attached to the return. If the severance of the trust is to be accomplished pursuant to the governing instrument and the severance has not been completed prior to the filing of the federal estate tax return, this requirement is satisfied by the executor indicating on the federal estate tax return that separate trusts will be created and the manner of separation and funding. Reg. § 26.2654-1(b)(2).

[72] Reg. § 26.2654-1(b)(1)(ii)(B). The period in which the severance must occur is extended for the period that is actually granted to file the transferor's federal estate tax return. The time for severance should include the period to file a return, including extensions of time to file actually granted, even if no federal estate tax return is ultimately required to be filed.

[73] Reg. § 26.2654-1(b)(1)(ii)(C)(1). The trusts need not be funded with a pro rata portion of each asset held by the undivided trust. However, if the new trusts are not funded on a pro rata basis, the funding must be on the basis of either fair market value of the as-

by the terms of the governing instrument, on the basis of a pecuniary amount.[74]

[3] Disclaimers

The Chapter 13 rule on disclaimers is an express adoption of the gift tax disclaimer provision, Section 2518.[75] The virtue of Section 2518 is that it undertakes to create basically objective tests, resting as little as possible on principles of local law, to determine whether one has successfully rejected the receipt of an interest in, or a power over, property free from any involvement with federal taxes.[76]

Assume that grantor *G* transfers property in trust, income to be paid to grandchild *GC* for life,[77] then to great-grandchild *GGC* for life, with a remainder to *GGC*'s children. *G* then has a change of heart. According to *G*, *GC* does not really need the trust income; *GGC* is in only fair shape financially, is in poor health, and has five young children. *G* wonders why the trust was set

---

sets on the date of funding, or in a manner that fairly reflects the net appreciation or depreciation in the value of the assets from the date of valuation to the date of funding. Id. Cf. Reg. §§ 20.2056(b)-7(b)(2)(ii)(B), 20.2056(b)-7(b)(2)(ii)(C), which provide that when there is a division of a trust on a fractional or percentage basis to reflect a partial QTIP election, the separate trusts do not have to be funded with a pro rata portion of each asset held by the trust being divided, but require the funding to be on a basis of the fair market value of the assets at the time of the division.

[74] If a severance is made on the basis of a pecuniary amount, the trustee must pay appropriate interest on the pecuniary amount. Reg. §§ 26.2654-1(b)(1)(ii)(C)(2), 26.2654-1(a)(1)(ii)(A). Appropriate interest is as defined in Regulations Section 26.2642-2(b)(4). See ¶ 16.02[4][d][iii]. Additionally, if the pecuniary amount is payable in kind, the assets must be valued on the date of distribution or, if valued on a date other than the date of distribution, the assets distributed must fairly reflect net appreciation or depreciation, from the date of valuation until payment, in the value of the assets available to satisfy the pecuniary amount to satisfy the third requirement. Reg. §§ 26.2654-1(b)(1)(ii)(C)(2), 26.2654-1(a)(1)(ii)(B). See ¶ 16.02[4][d][ii].

[75] IRC § 2654(c). See ¶ 10.07. This multipurpose provision serves the estate tax as well. IRC § 2046.

[76] No matter what frailties the provision may have, a brief look backward suggests that it presents improvements over prior law. See, e.g., pre-1976 IRC § 2056(d). Compare Brown v. Routzahn, 63 F2d 914 (6th Cir.), cert. denied, 290 US 641 (1933) (the beneficiary may disclaim an interest by indicating an intent to reject the gift by deliberate and unequivocal acts prior to the time the beneficiary controls the property as beneficiary) with Hardenbergh v. Comm'r, 198 F2d 63 (8th Cir.), cert. denied, 344 US 836 (1952) (if title to an interest vests immediately upon an intestate's death, any renunciation of that interest is equivalent to a transfer by the beneficiary).

[77] Assume that Section 2651(e) does not apply. See ¶ 17.01[2][a][ii].

up as it was and what can be done about it. The first question to ask is, when did the transfer occur? The trust instrument should then be examined.[78]

Generally, the disclaimer must be made in writing within nine months of the transfer creating the property interest or power[79] for the disclaimer to be effective for tax purposes.[80] Assume that under the trust instrument the timely disclaimer of the interest of GC will accelerate GGC's interest. GC's disclaimer within the critical nine-month period would have the effect of converting G's original transfer into a trust with income to GGC for life, with the remainder to GGC's children, and of avoiding a taxable termination at GC's death, a seemingly desirable effect on these facts.[81]

Finally, it is important to emphasize another aspect of timeliness here. The efforts of GC to disclaim will fail if GC has accepted any of the benefits of the life interest.[82]

It is possible that Section 2518, adopted for Chapter 13 by Section 2654(c), will not be (and indeed should not be) interpreted as an exclusive rule on disclaimers. To return to the example, suppose that GGC was not informed of the secondary life interest until one year after G created the trust, or not until after GC dies or disclaims. GGC could not disclaim under Section 2654(c) because the nine-month period allowed would have expired. However, Section 2518, which Section 2654(c) adopts, states only what will be accorded ab initio rejection. It carries no clear negative inference. When Section 2518 is inapplicable or unavailable, the common law of taxation should be turned to for an answer. If there is no obstacle under local law, a disclaimer "within a reasonable time of learning" of the existence of the interest or power should be given the same force and effect as a qualified disclaimer under Section 2518.[83] In the final analysis, it seems that the Section 2518 disclaimer rules may work as well with respect to the tax on generation-skipping transfers as they do in the area of estate and gift taxes.

---

[78] Assume that the governing instrument in this example specifies the economic effect of possible disclaimers. Absent such specification, rules of local law vary.

[79] But see ¶ 10.07[2][b] text accompanying note 34, which considers the timeliness of a disclaimer for purposes of Chapter 13. A "power" is an "interest" for purposes of Section 2518(a). IRC § 2518(c)(2).

[80] IRC §§ 2518(b)(1), 2518(b)(2)(A). An individual who is under age 21 when an interest is created has nine months after attaining age 21 within which to act. IRC § 2518(b)(2)(B). For Chapter 13 purposes, the requisite written disclaimer should be delivered to the trustee who has "legal title to the property." IRC § 2518(b)(2).

[81] If GC is unable to make a qualified disclaimer, the attempt to disclaim will not cause a taxable termination on these facts. Instead, GC will make a Chapter 12 gift of the property and become the Section 2652(a)(1)(B) transferor of the trust, with the result that GGC will be a non-skip person. See IRC § 2612(a)(1)(A); ¶ 17.02[3][e][ii].

[82] IRC § 2518(b)(3). See Reg. § 25.2518-2(d)(4) Ex. 1.

[83] See ¶ 10.07[2][b] text accompanying notes 62–64.

[4] Limitation on Personal Liability of Trustees

Section 2654(d) limits personal liability of trustees in two situations. The first situation involves Section 2642(c),[84] which generally provides a zero inclusion ratio for property transferred in a direct skip that qualifies under the gift tax for a Section 2503(b) or Section 2503(e) exclusion. If the Chapter 13 tax is increased because Section 2642(c) does not apply to a transfer to the trust made during the life of the transferor, and if no gift tax return was filed for the transfer, the trustee will not be personally liable[85] unless the trustee should have known that a gift tax return was required to be filed.[86] Seemingly, the chances of this limitation being applicable are reduced by the enactment in the 1988 legislation of Section 2642(c)(2), which specifically limits the situations in which a direct skip transfer to a trust that qualifies for the annual exclusion is assigned a zero inclusion ratio.[87] In addition, a trustee should be aware that a direct skip to a trust will not qualify for the Section 2503(e) exclusion.[88]

The second situation in which the personal liability of a trustee is limited occurs when there is an increase in Chapter 13 tax because the inclusion ratio for the trust is greater than the inclusion ratio computed on the basis of the return on which an allocation of the GST exemption was made to property transferred to the trust. The trustee is not personally liable[89] unless the trustee should have known that the inclusion ratio was incorrect.[90]

---

[84] See ¶ 16.02[2][b].

[85] IRC § 2654(d)(1).

[86] IRC § 2654(d) (last sentence).

[87] See IRC § 2642(c)(2), added by the Technical and Miscellaneous Revenue Act of 1988, Pub. L. No. 100-647, § 1014(g)(17)(A), 102 Stat. 3342, 3567 (1988), reprinted in 1988-3 CB 1, 226.

[88] See ¶ 13.01[2][a] text accompanying notes 18–22.

[89] IRC § 2654(d)(2).

[90] IRC § 2654(d) (last sentence).

CHAPTER 18

Administrative and Miscellaneous Matters

¶ 18.01 SECTION 2661. ADMINISTRATION

[1] In General

The generation-skipping transfer tax is generally calculated independently of either the estate tax or the gift tax, but the methods by which it is assessed and collected are primarily adopted from the procedures for the assessment and collection of the estate and gift taxes. Section 2661 of the Internal Revenue Code (Code) incorporates into Chapter 13 all the administrative and procedural rules found in subtitle F of the Code in respect of the estate and gift taxes "[i]nsofar as applicable and not inconsistent with the provisions of [Chapter 13]."[1] Specifically, if the generation-skipping transfer at issue occurs "at the same time as and as a result of the death of an individual," then the provisions of subtitle F applicable to the estate tax, Chapter 11, or Section 2001 are made applicable to the generation-skipping transfer tax, Chapter 13, or Section

---

[1] IRC § 2661.

2601.² If the generation-skipping transfer occurs in other circumstances, the provisions of subtitle F applicable to the gift tax, Chapter 12, or Section 2501, are made applicable to the generation-skipping transfer tax, Chapter 13, or Section 2601.³

Subtitle F of the Code extends from Section 6001 through Section 7873, encompassing over 400 pages of statute. A detailed discussion of the application of each procedural and administrative rule of subtitle F to the Chapter 13 tax is beyond the scope of this book.⁴ A brief overview of some of the procedural matters covered in subtitle F is nonetheless provided. Section 2661 incorporates into Chapter 13 detailed rules prescribing for the proper assessment⁵ and collection of tax,⁶ including rules related to liens on property.⁷ It adopts and makes applicable to the generation-skipping transfer tax the deficiency and refund procedures,⁸ the interest⁹ and penalty provisions,¹⁰ and the limitation periods on assessment, collection, and refunds that generally govern the estate and gift taxes.¹¹

[2] Deferral of Payment

Payment of the generation-skipping transfer tax is usually required to be made at the time and place fixed for filing the generation-skipping transfer tax return.¹² However, Section 6161(a)(1) authorizes the Secretary to extend the time

---

² IRC § 2661(2). While reference "to the estate tax, to Chapter 11, or to Section 2001" in Section 2661(2) may appear repetitious, each of those terms is used in different sections in subtitle F. See, e.g., IRC §§ 6161(a)(1), 6163(a), 6166(a)(1).

³ IRC § 2661(1). As to possible repetition within the subsection, see supra note 2.

⁴ For a detailed discussion of subtitle F, see Saltzman, *IRS Practice and Procedure* (Warren, Gorham & Lamont, 1991).

⁵ IRC §§ 6201–6255.

⁶ IRC §§ 6301–6344.

⁷ See IRC §§ 6321, 6324, 6324A, 6324B; Reg. § 26.2662-1(f).

⁸ IRC §§ 6211–6216, 6401–6408.

⁹ IRC §§ 6601–6631.

¹⁰ IRC §§ 6651–6751. For example, Section 6651 imposes a penalty for the failure to file a tax return or to pay a tax when it is due.

¹¹ IRC §§ 6501–6515. For example, if a return "adequately discloses" all post-1996 gifts, and is made without fraud, then Section 6501(a) (by virtue of Section 2661) applies a three-year limitations period, commencing on the later of the due date or the filing date of the return, for the assessment of additional tax. Adequate disclosure of gifts is discussed at ¶ 9.04[10].

¹² IRC §§ 6151(a), 6151(c).

for payment of the tax,[13] and Section 6159 authorizes the Secretary to allow payment of the tax in installments.[14]

[a] Transfers at Death

If a generation-skipping transfer occurs at the same time as, and as a result of, the death of an individual, the time for payment of the tax may be extended for twelve months[15] and for up to ten years upon the showing of "reasonable cause."[16] Where the value of a reversionary or remainder interest in property is taxed under Chapter 13, an election is available to postpone the payment of the tax attributable to the reversionary or remainder interest until six months after the termination of the precedent interests in the property.[17] At the expiration of the six-month period, the Secretary may extend the time of payment for three additional years for reasonable cause.[18] For the privilege of deferral, interest is charged at a variable rate that is established quarterly.[19]

Section 6166 provides for deferral of payment of the *estate* tax attributable to an interest in a closely held business if certain qualifications are met.[20] Deferral generally may be permitted for as long as five years,[21] after which the tax may be paid in ten installments over the next nine years.[22] The amount of

---

[13] See also IRC § 6161(b).

[14] See ¶ 2.02[3][a].

[15] IRC § 6161(a)(1). The regulations add the requirement of showing reasonable cause. Reg. § 20.6161-1(a)(1). See infra note 16; ¶ 2.02[3][b].

[16] IRC § 6161(a)(2). The term "reasonable cause" is illustrated in Regulations Section 20.6161-1(a)(1) and is discussed at ¶ 2.02[3][b] note 44.

[17] IRC § 6163(a). See ¶ 3.07. Although a direct skip cannot occur as a result of a transfer of a reversionary or remainder interest in property in a trust or a trust equivalent (see ¶ 13.02[4][b] text accompanying notes 278, 279), nonetheless there could be a taxable distribution from a trust of a reversionary or a remainder interest in another trust.

[18] IRC § 6163(b).

[19] IRC §§ 6601(a), 6621(a)(2), 6621(b)(1).

[20] See ¶ 2.02[3][c].

[21] IRC § 6166(a)(3). The five-year deferral is not permitted if the executor makes an election qualifying non–readily tradable stock in a holding company or a lending and finance business as a closely held business. IRC §§ 6166(b)(8)(B)(ii), 6166(b)(10)(A)(ii). See ¶ 2.02[3][c] text accompanying notes 86, 98.

[22] IRC §§ 6166(a)(1), 6166(a)(3). If a personal representative elects to use a five-year deferral period and ten installment payments, the first installment is due five years after the date prescribed by Section 6151(a) for payment of the tax. Each of the subsequent nine annual installments would be due one year after the due date of the preceding installment. The tenth installment, the final installment, would be due nine years after the first installment payment. However, if a Section 6166(b)(8) election is made where some of the pierced stock is publicly traded or a Section 6166(b)(10) election is made, the tax deferred under the election may only be paid in five installments over four years. IRC

estate tax attributable to the first $1 million, adjusted upward for inflation, in taxable value of the closely held business may qualify for deferral at a 2 percent annual interest rate[23] with the balance of the tax deferred at 45 percent of a variable interest rate that is established quarterly.[24]

The Section 6166 extension of time for payment is made expressly available by statute for payment of the generation-skipping transfer tax attributable to an interest in a closely held business where that business interest is the subject matter of a *direct skip* occurring at the same time as, and as a result of, an individual's death.[25] However, the transferor's estate must qualify for an extension of time to pay the estate tax under Section 6166[26] before Section 6166 relief is available for the generation-skipping transfer tax liability.[27]

There is no similar specific statutory provision for deferral and installment payment of the generation-skipping transfer tax imposed on an interest in a closely held business where that interest is the subject matter of a taxable termination or a taxable distribution occurring at the time of, and as a result of, an individual's death.[28] Under the normal rules of statutory construction, the direct skip rule would be exclusive; however, Section 2661(2) invokes all the provisions of subtitle F, including Section 6166. Section 6166 justifies the deferral of estate tax payment on the grounds that lack of liquidity may make payment of the tax a hardship. Since Section 6166 relief is justifiable for the estate tax and for the generation-skipping transfer tax imposed on certain direct

---

§§ 6166(b)(8)(A)(ii), 6166(b)(10)(A)(iii). See ¶ 2.02[3][c] text accompanying notes 88, 99.

[23] IRC § 6601(j). See especially IRC §§ 2001(c), 6601(j)(1)(A), 6601(j)(2). See also ¶ 2.02[3][c][v]. The portion of the estate tax that is to bear interest at 2 percent is the entire extended amount, or, if less, the tentative estate tax on the sum of $1 million, adjusted for inflation, and the applicable exclusion amount in effect under Section 2010(c) determined under the Section 2001(c) rate table, reduced by the applicable credit amount in effect under Section 2010(c). IRC § 6601(j)(2). See IRC § 6601(j)(3); Rev. Proc. 98-61, 1998-2 CB 811, 816.

[24] IRC §§ 6601(a), 6621(a)(2), 6621(b)(1).

[25] IRC § 6166(i).

[26] See ¶ 2.02[3][c].

[27] It is questionable whether the 2 percent interest is available for the tax imposed on the first $1 million, adjusted upward for inflation, in taxable value of a closely held business interest under each tax, or whether a single 2 percent interest limitation applies to both taxes. The latter alternative would result in this benefit being split between the Chapter 11 tax and the Chapter 13 tax. If the latter alternative is adopted, a complicated apportionment could be avoided if the regulations were to allocate this benefit first to the deferred estate tax, with the balance of tax imposed on the $1 million, adjusted for inflation, taxable amount limitation allocated to the generation-skipping transfer tax.

[28] The 1976 version of Chapter 13 contained an explicit provision negating the applicability of the deferral payment provision of Section 6166 to Chapter 13 tax. See IRC § 2621(b) prior to repeal by the Tax Reform Act of 1976, Pub. L. No. 99-514, § 1431(a), 100 Stat. 2085, 2720 (1976), reprinted in 1986-3 CB (Vol. 1) 1, 637.

skips, it is difficult to justify the denial of such relief for the generation-skipping transfer tax incurred in a taxable termination or taxable distribution, where lack of liquidity may similarly pose a problem.[29] If Section 6166 is applicable to a taxable termination or taxable distribution, other issues may arise.[30]

[b] Transfers Other Than at Death

When a generation-skipping transfer occurs at any time other than at the same time as, and as a result of, the death of an individual, the time for payment of the tax imposed may be extended by six months.[31] To facilitate the collection of the tax, the Secretary may also allow the tax to be paid in installments.[32]

¶ 18.02 SECTION 2662. RETURN REQUIREMENTS

[1] In General

Chapter 13 does not specify what generation-skipping transfer tax returns are required to be filed, nor when or by whom. Section 2662 simply delegates to the Secretary the authority to require generation-skipping transfer tax returns, including information returns,[1] and the authority to prescribe who is responsible for the preparation of the returns and when the returns should be filed.[2] The statute offers some guidance, however. Section 2662 directs that "[t]o the

---

[29] In a previous edition of this treatise, it was observed that from a policy perspective, such a denial was inappropriate. Stephens, Maxfield, Lind & Calfee, Federal Estate and Gift Taxation ¶ 14.02[2] (Warren, Gorham & Lamont, 5th ed. 1983). But see Priv. Ltr. Rul. 9314050 (Jan. 13, 1993) (Section 6166 cannot be elected for a taxable termination).

[30] For example, only the trust itself (and not the combination of the decedent's gross estate and trust) should have to satisfy the closely held business qualifications. See ¶ 2.02[3][c]. If so, the closely held business assets of the trust must be involved in the taxable distribution or taxable termination. In addition, the issue of single or multiple application of the 2 percent interest rate also arises here. See supra note 27.

[31] IRC § 6161(a)(1). See also IRC § 6161(b); Priv. Ltr. Rul. 9314050 (Jan. 13, 1993) (Section 6161(a)(2) applied to the generation-skipping transfer tax).

[32] IRC § 6159. See ¶ 2.02[3][a].

[1] IRC § 2662(b).

[2] IRC § 2662(a).

extent practicable," the person liable for the tax[3] is required to file the return,[4] that the return reporting a direct skip (other than from a trust) is to be filed on or before the date on which the estate or gift tax return for the same transfer is due,[5] and that all other generation-skipping transfer tax returns for a transfer occurring within a calendar year are to be filed on or before the fifteenth day of the fourth month after the close of the taxable year of the person who is required to file the return.[6] The regulations promulgated pursuant to Section 2662 have slightly modified these statutory directives and provide specific guidance as to the who, what, and when of filing generation-skipping tax returns.[7]

[2] Returns Required

[a] Taxable Distributions and Taxable Terminations

Generally, a return is to be filed for each taxable distribution[8] and taxable termination[9] that is a generation-skipping transfer.[10] A return is generally re-

---

[3] See IRC § 2603(a).

[4] IRC § 2662(a)(1).

[5] IRC § 2662(a)(2)(A). But see infra ¶ 18.02[4][a] text following note 41.

[6] IRC § 2662(a)(2)(B). But see infra ¶ 18.02[4][a] text accompanying notes 47–53.

[7] Reg. § 26.2662-1.

[8] Reg. § 26.2662-1(b)(1).

[9] Reg. § 26.2662-1(b)(2).

[10] See IRC § 2611(b). Although Regulations Sections 26.2662-1(b)(1) and 26.2662-1(b)(2) require that a return be filed for any taxable termination as defined in Section 2612(a) and any taxable distribution as defined in Section 2612(b), the instructions for the returns are more lenient. Neither Form 706-GS(D-1) nor Form 706-GS(D) is required to be filed for a Section 2612(b) taxable distribution if the taxable distribution is not a generation-skipping transfer as a result of the application of Section 2611(b)(1) or Section 2611(b)(2). See Instructions for Form 706-GS(D-1), Notification of Distribution From a Generation-Skipping Trust (Rev. June 1999) at 1 (Distributions Subject to generation-skipping transfer Tax); Instructions for Form 706-GS(D), Generation-Skipping Transfer Tax Return for Distributions (Rev. June 1999) at 1 (Purpose of Form). See also ¶ 13.01[2] for a discussion of Section 2611(b). Form 706-GS(T) is not required to be filed for a Section 2612(a) taxable termination if the taxable termination is not a generation-skipping transfer as a result of the application of Section 2611(b)(1). See Instructions for Form 706-GS(T), Generation-Skipping Transfer Tax Return for Terminations (Rev. July 1999) at 2 (medical and educational exclusion). Seemingly, there is a requirement to file a Form 706-GS(T), even though the taxable termination is not a generation-skipping transfer by virtue of the application of Section 2611(b)(2). However, note that Form 706-GS(T) asks for a description of any terminations not reported because of the exception in Section 2611(b)(2) relating to prior payment of generation-skipping transfer tax. Form 706-GS(T), Generation-Skipping Transfer Tax Return for Terminations (Rev. July 1999) Part II, line 5, at 1.

quired to be filed whether or not any generation-skipping transfer tax is actually imposed.[11] A taxable distribution is reported on Form 706-GS(D),[12] and the trustee of the trust involved in the taxable distribution must file an informational Form 706-GS(D-1) with the Internal Revenue Service (the Service) for each distributee, as well as provide a copy of this form to each distributee.[13] A taxable termination is reported on Form 706-GS(T).[14]

---

[11] Appropriately, there are no exceptions to filing either a Form 706-GS(T) for a taxable termination or a Form 706-GS(D-1) for a taxable distribution that generates no generation-skipping transfer tax by reason of the transferor's GST exemption. The obligation to file such returns under Chapter 13, even where no tax is ultimately due, is consistent with the obligation to file a gift tax return under Chapter 12, even though no gift tax is due owing to the applicable credit amount of Section 2505. Without such returns, the Service would find it difficult, if not impossible, to monitor the taxpayer's use of credits and exemptions. There is an exception for filing Form 706-GS(D) when there are one or more taxable distributions and no tax is due on any such distribution by reason of the transferor's GST exemption. See Instructions for Form 706-GS(D), Generation-Skipping Transfer Tax Return for Distributions (Rev. June 1999) at 1 (Who Must File). Because the necessary information is gathered from the required filing of one or more Forms 706-GS(D-1), no duplication of such information is required by the filing of a Form 706-GS(D). A return is not required for a generation-skipping transfer that is not subject to the provisions of Chapter 13. For a discussion of generation-skipping transfers not subject to Chapter 13, see ¶ 18.05[2].

[12] Reg. § 26.2662-1(b)(1); Form 706-GS(D), Generation-Skipping Transfer Tax Return for Distributions (Rev. June 1999).

[13] Reg. § 26.2662-1(b)(1); Form 706-GS(D-1), Notification of Distribution From a Generation-Skipping Trust (Rev. June 1999). See Instructions for Form 706-GS(D-1), Notification of Distribution From a Generation-Skipping Trust (Rev. June 1999) at 1. See infra ¶ 18.02[6] text accompanying note 66. The trustee of a trust includes the pseudo-trustee of a trust equivalent arrangement.

[14] Reg. § 26.2662-1(b)(2); Form 706-GS(T), Generation-Skipping Transfer Tax Return for Terminations (Rev. July 1999).

[b] Direct Skips

Generally, a return must be filed for any inter vivos or testamentary direct skip.[15] An inter vivos direct skip is reported on Form 709,[16] whereas a testamentary direct skip is reported on Form 706.[17]

Direct skips that generate no generation-skipping transfer tax because of the transferor's GST exemption are not exempt from the filing requirements.[18] However, no generation-skipping transfer tax return is required to be filed for an inter vivos direct skip assigned a zero inclusion ratio under Section 2642(c)[19] if no federal gift tax return is required[20] for the transfer.[21]

---

[15] Reg. § 26.2662-1(b)(3). An inter vivos direct skip may be treated as a testamentary direct skip, with the result that the testamentary direct skip filing rules become applicable. See IRC § 2642(f), discussed at ¶¶ 16.02[4][b], 16.02[7]. Seemingly, no Form 706, United States Estate (and Generation-Skipping Transfer) Tax Return should be required to be filed to report testamentary direct skips from an estate that is otherwise not required to file a federal estate tax return under Section 6018. See Instructions for Form 706, United States Estate (and Generation-Skipping Transfer) Tax Return (Rev. Nov. 2001) at 1 (Which Estates Must File), 19 (Instructions for Schedules R and R-1. Generation-Skipping Transfer Tax). For example, if a decedent who is a U.S. citizen and who has never made a taxable gift dies in the current year and bequeaths an entire estate valued at $300,000 to a skip person, no Form 706, United States Estate (and Generation-Skipping Transfer) Tax Return, should be required to be filed to report the decedent's testamentary direct skip.

[16] Form 709, United States Gift (and Generation-Skipping Transfer) Tax Return (2001); Reg. § 26.2662-1(b)(3)(i).

[17] Form 706, United States Estate (and Generation-Skipping Transfer) Tax Return (Rev. Nov. 2001); Reg. § 26.2662-1(b)(3)(ii)(A). In general, testamentary direct skips from trusts or trust equivalent arrangements (see IRC § 2652(b)(3); Reg. § 26.2662-1(c)(2)(ii)) are required to be reported on Schedule R-1 of Form 706. Reg. § 26.2662-1(b)(3)(ii)(B). There are two exceptions to this rule when Schedule R is used: (1) where the executor is liable for making the return for direct skips of less than $250,000 from a trust equivalent arrangement and (2) where the executor is also the trustee of a trust. Instructions for Form 706, United States Estate (and Generation-Skipping Transfer) Tax Return (Rev. Nov. 2001) at 20. See Reg. § 26.2662-1(c)(2)(iii).

[18] The obligation to file a return under Chapter 13 where no tax is ultimately due is consistent with the obligation to file a gift tax return under Chapter 12 even though no gift tax is due because of the Section 2505 credit. Without such returns, the Service would find it difficult, if not impossible, to monitor the taxpayer's use of credits and exemptions. See supra ¶ 18.02[2][a] note 11.

[19] See ¶ 16.02[2][b].

[20] See IRC § 6019; ¶ 9.04[9].

[21] Regulations promulgated for this area provide that "Form 709 must be filed in accordance with its instructions for any direct skip (as defined in Section 2612(c)) that is subject to Chapter 12 and occurs during the life of the transferor." Reg. § 26.2662-1(b)(3)(i). According to the Instructions for Form 709, transfers fully excluded under the annual exclusion are not subject to the generation-skipping transfer tax. Instructions for Form 709, United States Gift (and Generation-Skipping Transfer) Tax Return (2001) at 2. Taxpayers are required to report the tax imposed on inter vivos direct skips on Form 709. "An 'inter vivos direct skip' is a gift that . . . is subject to the gift tax. . . . A gift is 'sub-

For example, a grandparent who makes a gift of a $200 wedding present to a grandchild (grandparent's only gift to the grandchild for the taxable year) is not required to file a gift tax return[22] or to pay a gift tax on the transfer because the transfer qualifies for, and is fully within, the annual exclusion provided by Section 2503(b). Although this transfer satisfies the requirement of a direct skip,[23] it is assigned a zero inclusion ratio under Section 2642(c) without an allocation of any of the grandparent's GST exemption, it generates no Chapter 13 tax,[24] and there is no reason to require that a return be filed. To require a return for every inter vivos direct skip assigned a zero inclusion ratio under Section 2642(c) would impose an onerous reporting obligation upon transferors.

In general, if a transfer does not constitute a direct skip, no generation-skipping transfer tax return is required to be filed.[25] Thus, where the Section

---

ject to the gift tax' if you are required to list it on Schedule A for Form 709." Instructions for Form 709, United States Gift (and Generation-Skipping Transfer) Tax Return (2001) at 6. If the total gifts to any donee are "$10,000 or less, you need not enter on Schedule A any gifts (except gifts of future interests) that you made to that donee." Id. However note that for the calendar year 2002, the first $11,000 of gifts to any person (other than gifts of a future interest in property) qualify for the Section 2503(b) annual exclusion and that amount will replace the "$10,000" amount in the preceding quote for calendar year 2002 returns. See Rev. Proc. 2001-59, 2001-2 CB __, __. See also ¶ 16.02[2][b] note 53. However, this rule is modified where the transfer is to a trust, unless the requirements of Section 2642(c)(2) are met. See Instructions for Form 709, United States Gift (and Generation-Skipping Transfer) Tax Return (2001) at 6; ¶ 16.02[2][b][iii]. There is one technical problem with the regulations and the instructions. A transfer fully excluded under the annual exclusion is nevertheless *subject to* the tax imposed by Chapter 12. See ¶ 13.02[4][b] text accompanying notes 261–264. However, if the transfer is a direct skip transfer that is assigned a zero inclusion ratio under Section 2642(c), it will never generate any generation-skipping transfer tax. Because no tax will ever be due, no return should be required.

[22] IRC § 6019(1).

[23] IRC § 2612(c). One additional fact is necessary to assure direct skip status for this transfer: the donor's child, the parent of the grandchild, must be alive. See IRC § 2651(e); ¶ 17.01[2][a][ii].

[24] Technically, this occurs because Section 2642(c)(1) provides that the "inclusion ratio shall be zero" for any outright direct skip that is a nontaxable gift. In turn, the phrase "nontaxable gift" is designed to include transfers that are not treated as a taxable gift because of the operation of the annual exclusion. Under Section 2641, the applicable generation-skipping transfer tax rate is a product of the maximum federal estate tax rate and the inclusion ratio for the transfer. The effect of these provisions is to ensure that no Chapter 13 tax will be imposed on an outright direct skip if the amount of the generation-skipping transfer is not in excess of the annual gift tax exclusion and the gift qualifies for the annual exclusion. See ¶ 16.02[2][b][ii].

[25] Inter vivos gifts to certain political organizations and inter vivos transfers to medical or educational institutions are not treated as transfers of property by gift under Chapter 12. IRC §§ 2501(a)(5), 2503(e). Because they are not subject to the tax imposed by Chapter 12, no federal tax return is required to be filed. See ¶¶ 9.02[2], 9.04[9]. Since such

2651(e) predeceased parent rule[26] precludes a direct skip, no generation-skipping transfer tax return is required.[27]

[3] Who Must File

Section 2662(a) authorizes the Secretary to prescribe who must file a return for the tax imposed by Chapter 13. To assist and guide the Secretary in the exercise of this discretion, the statute directs that "[t]o the extent practicable,"[28] the regulations shall provide that the person responsible for the filing of the return shall be the person liable for the payment of the tax under Section 2603(a).[29] With minor exceptions, the regulations merely implement the statutory directive.[30] These regulations prescribe general rules along with special rules for particular situations.

[a] General Rules

In a taxable distribution, the trustee is obligated to file the informational return and the transferee is obligated to file the tax return.[31] Where a taxable

---

transfers are not subject to the tax imposed by Chapter 12, they do not constitute inter vivos direct skips. Thus, no generation-skipping transfer tax return is required.

[26] See ¶ 17.01[2][a][ii].

[27] In addition, the term "direct skip" did not include any transfer before January 1, 1990, from a transferor to the transferor's grandchild to the extent that the transferor's transfers in the aggregate to any one grandchild did not exceed $2 million. Tax Reform Act of 1986, Pub. L. No. 99-514, § 1433(b)(3), 1002 Stat. 2085, 2731 (1986), reprinted in 1986-3 CB (Vol. 1) 1, 648, as amended by Technical and Miscellaneous Revenue Act of 1988, Pub. L. No. 100-647, § 1014(h)(3)(A), 102 Stat. 3342, 3567–3568 (1988), reprinted in 1988-3 CB 1, 227–228. See ¶ 13.02[4][c][ii]. Although there was no direct skip in this instance, the transfer was nonetheless required to be reported on an information return. Section 2662(b) confers broad discretion upon the Secretary to require the filing of information returns. Such transfers were to be reported on Forms 706 and 709, even though they were offset by the $2 million exclusion. See infra ¶ 18.02[6] note 69.

[28] IRC § 2662(a).

[29] IRC § 2662(a)(1). See ¶ 12.03.

[30] Reg. § 26.2662-1(c). When an individual is legally or mentally incapable of filing a return, the individuals's guardian is authorized to file the return. Reg. § 26.2662-1(c)(4)(i). If no guardian has been appointed, the return may be filed by a person charged with the care of the individual's person or property. Id. In addition, Regulations Section 26.2662-1(c)(4)(ii) adopts the provisions of Section 6012(b) concerning the filing of returns of decedents, persons under a disability, estates and trusts, and the filing of returns by joint fiduciaries.

[31] Reg. § 26.2662-1(c)(1)(i). See supra ¶ 18.02[2][a] text accompanying notes 12, 13; IRC § 2612(b). A transferee in a taxable distribution is required to file a tax return unless the inclusion ratio for all distributions reported to the transferee is zero. Instructions for

termination occurs, the trustee is obligated to file the tax return.[32] In the case of an inter vivos direct skip other than from a trust, the transferor is obligated to file the required tax return.[33] When an inter vivos or testamentary direct skip is made from a trust or when the property remains in the trust, it is the duty of the trustee to file the required tax return.[34] When an outright testamentary direct skip is not from a trust, the executor is required to file the required tax return.[35]

[b] Special Rule

In addition to the rules of general application, the regulations prescribe special filing obligations applicable to direct skips that occur at death with respect to property that is held in a "trust arrangement."[36] If a direct skip involving property held in a trust arrangement occurs at death and the total value of the property involved in direct skips with respect to the trustee of that trust arrangement is less than $250,000, the obligation to file a return is placed upon

---

Form 706-GS(D), Generation-Skipping Transfer Tax Return for Distributions (Rev. June 1999) at 1. See supra ¶ 18.02[2][a] note 11.

[32] Reg. § 26.2662-1(c)(1)(ii). See IRC § 2612(a)(1).

[33] Reg. § 26.2662-1(c)(1)(iii). See IRC §§ 2652(a)(1)(B), 2612(c)(1).

[34] Reg. § 26.2662-1(c)(1)(iv). See IRC § 2612(c)(1). Requiring the trustee to file the return for a direct skip from a trust is consistent with Section 2603(a)(2), which imposes the generation-skipping transfer tax liability on the trustee. However, Section 2603 is silent as to who is liable for the payment of tax when the property continues to be held in trust, e.g., when the person holding a general power of appointment over a trust with a skip person beneficiary releases the general power of appointment.

[35] Reg. § 26.2662-1(c)(1)(v). See IRC § 2612(c)(1). Section 2603(a)(3) seemingly calls for this result, as it places the burden on the transferor or, in this case, on the transferor's agent, the executor.

[36] Reg. § 26.2662-1(c)(2). Here, the term "trust arrangement" is defined to include "any arrangement (other than an estate) which, although not an explicit trust, has the same effect as an explicit trust." Reg. § 26.2662-1(c)(2)(ii). An "explicit trust" is any trust that qualifies as a trust under the definition found in Regulations Section 301.7701-4(a): namely, "an arrangement created either by a will or by an inter vivos declaration whereby trustees take title to property for the purpose of protecting or conserving it for the beneficiaries under the ordinary rules applied in chancery or probate courts."

The examples found in the regulations offer meager assistance in understanding what constitutes a "trust arrangement." Regulations Section 26.2662-1(c)(2)(vi) provides five separate examples, but they all deal with the payment of insurance proceeds. In Section 2652(b)(1), however, the term "trust" is defined for purposes of Chapter 13 to include "any arrangement (other than an estate) which, although not a trust, has substantially the same effect as a trust." Section 2652(b)(3) indicates that such trust arrangements would include "life estates and remainders, estates for years, and insurance and annuity contracts." See ¶ 17.02[2]. Each of the arrangements should also qualify as a trust arrangement for purposes of Regulations Section 26.2662-1(c)(2).

the executor of the decedent's estate.[37] Where the value of the property involved is at least $250,000, the obligation to file a return is placed upon the person serving as "trustee" of the trust arrangement.[38]

[4] When to File

[a] Timely Filing

Section 2662(a) directs the Secretary to issue regulations prescribing the due date of returns required to be filed under Chapter 13.[39] In the case of a direct skip other than from a trust, the Secretary's discretion is limited by the statutory directive that, to the extent practicable, the due date for such return is the same date on which the transferor's estate tax or gift tax return with respect to the transfer is required to be filed.[40] The regulations promulgated pursuant to the statute provide that the return for a direct skip is to be filed "on or before the date on which an estate or gift tax return is required to be filed with respect to the transfer."[41] The regulations do not exclude a direct skip from a trust from this filing rule. Thus, the return for a testamentary direct skip must be filed within nine months after the transferor's death,[42] unless an extension of time for filing is granted.[43] Returns reporting inter vivos direct skips generally must be filed on or before April 15 following the close of the calendar

---

[37] Reg. § 26.2662-1(c)(2)(iii). In the case of transfers of decedents dying prior to June 24, 1996, if the total value of the property involved in direct skips with respect to the trustee of that trust arrangement is less than $100,000, rather than $250,000, the executor of the transferor's estate is liable for payment. Reg. § 26.2662-1(c)(2)(iv). See ¶ 12.03[2] note 27. Compare Reg. § 26.2662-1(c)(2)(vi) Exs. 1, 4, with Reg. § 26.2662-1(c)(2)(vi) Exs. 2, 3. Although the executor is obligated to file a return, the executor has the right to recover from the trustee or the recipient of the property any generation-skipping transfer tax attributable to the transfer. Reg. § 26.2662-1(c)(2)(v).

[38] Section 2652(b)(2) defines "trustee" of a trust arrangement as "the person in actual or constructive possession of the property subject to such arrangement." Where an insurance policy is involved, such person would normally be the issuing insurance company. Reg. § 26.2662-1(c)(2)(vi) Exs. 2, 3. See ¶ 17.02[2] text accompanying notes 91–104. Cf. IRC § 2663(3); ¶ 18.03[3] note 67. See supra note 37.

[39] IRC § 2662(a).

[40] IRC § 2662(a)(2)(A).

[41] Reg. § 26.2662-1(d)(1)(i).

[42] IRC § 6075(a); Reg. § 26.2662-1(d)(1)(i). No returns for testamentary direct skips were due before June 13, 1988. Temp. Reg. § 26.2662-1(d)(2)(iii) (TD 8187, 1988-1 CB 332, 342).

[43] IRC §§ 2661(2), 6081. See infra ¶ 18.02[4][b].

year in which the transfer occurs,[44] unless the time for filing is extended.[45] This general rule is modified where the donor's death occurs in the same calendar year as the inter vivos direct skip; in that situation, the return is due on the earlier of April 15 of the following year or, if an estate tax return is required, on the date the donor's federal estate tax return (including extensions) is due.[46]

For any generation-skipping transfer other than a direct skip, the statute directs, again subject to the caveat of practicality, that the return required under Chapter 13 must be filed "on or before the 15th day of the 4th month after the close of the taxable year of the person required to make such return in which such transfer occurs."[47] The regulations provide that unless an extension of time to file is granted,[48] the return must be filed "on or before the 15th day of the 4th month after the close of the calendar year in which such transfer occurs,"[49] rather than the close of the taxable year of the person required to make the return.[50] Thus, the returns for taxable terminations and taxable distributions occurring in any year, regardless of whether they occurred at the same time as, and as a result of, the death of an individual, generally[51] are to be

---

[44] IRC § 6075(b)(1); Reg. § 26.2662-1(d)(1)(i). The return reporting an inter vivos direct skip made between September 25, 1985 and October 22, 1986, had to be filed on or before June 13, 1988. Temp. Reg. § 26.2662-1(d)(2)(i) (TD 8187, 1988-1 CB 332, 342).

[45] IRC §§ 2661(1), 6081. See infra ¶ 18.02[4][b].

[46] IRC § 6075(b)(3); Reg. § 26.2662-1(d)(1)(i). If a donor dies prior to July 15 in any year, the donor's gift tax return is generally due at the time of the donor's estate tax return. IRC § 6075(b)(3). If the donor dies after July 15 in any year, the donor's gift tax return is generally due on April 15 of the following year. IRC § 6075(b)(1).

For example, if a donor made a direct skip transfer in January and died on February 1, the return reporting the direct skip is required to be filed no later than the date by which the donor's federal estate tax return is required to be filed (generally within nine months after the date of the donor's death), November 1, unless the time for filing the federal estate tax return is extended. IRC §§ 6075(a), 6081. See Reg. § 20.6075-1. If the donor died on December 1 of the calendar year in which the inter vivos direct skip occurred, the generation-skipping transfer tax return would be due on April 15 of the following calendar year. The time may be extended, but not beyond the time for filing the decedent's federal estate tax return. Reg. § 25.6075-1(b)(2). If no federal estate tax return is required to be filed, the generation-skipping transfer tax return must be filed by the fifteenth day of April following the close of the calendar year unless an extension of time is granted. Id.

[47] IRC § 2662(a)(2)(B).

[48] IRC § 6081. See infra ¶ 18.02[4][b].

[49] Reg. § 26.2662-1(d)(1)(ii).

[50] IRC § 2662(a)(2)(B). Cf. IRC § 644(a). Again, the Secretary is within bounds because the filing date suggested by the statute was predicated upon practicality.

[51] An exception was provided for returns reporting taxable distributions and taxable terminations occurring after September 25, 1985, and before January 1, 1990. Such returns were to be filed on or before August 15, 1990. Ann. 90-54, 1990-16 IRB 21 (Apr. 16, 1990). See Temp. Reg. § 26.2662-1(d)(2)(ii) (TD 8187, 1988-1 CB 332, 342).

filed on April 15 of the following year.[52] However, in the case of a taxable termination with respect to which an election is made under Section 2624(c) to value property in accordance with Section 2032, the return may be filed on or before the tenth month following the month in which the death that resulted in the taxable termination occurred, if later.[53]

[b] Extensions of Time to File

The Secretary has broad authority to grant reasonable extensions of time, not to exceed six months, for the filing of any required tax return.[54] An extension of time for filing a required return does not operate to extend the time for the payment of the corresponding tax unless specified to the contrary in the extension.[55] Under the regulations,[56] a taxpayer's request for an extension of time to file a required return generally must be made before the due date of

---

[52] Reg. § 26.2662-1(d)(1)(ii). Section 2661(2) generally provides that all the subtitle F provisions applicable to the estate tax will apply "in the case of a generation-skipping transfer occurring at the same time as and as a result of the death of an individual. . . ." However, because the rules contained in Section 2662(a) are inconsistent with the subtitle F rules, they override these rules.

In a similar vein, Section 2661(1) provides that all the subtitle F provisions applicable to the gift tax, insofar as they are not inconsistent with the provisions contained in Chapter 13, will apply to taxable terminations and taxable distributions that do not occur at the same time as, and as a result of, the death of an individual. Should Section 6075(b)(3), which is in subtitle F and applicable to the gift tax, alter the general rule specifying that where the transferor dies in the calendar year in which the transfer occurs, the generation-skipping transfer tax return must be filed by April 15 of the following year? No. Section 2662(a)(2)(B) in Chapter 13 provides a specific rule that is inconsistent with the subtitle F provisions applicable to the gift tax. Section 2662(a)(2)(A) permits the application of Section 6075(b)(3) to inter vivos direct skips. See supra note 46.

[53] Reg. § 26.2662-1(d)(2). The supplementary information to the regulations clarifies that it is the *fifteenth* day of the tenth month on which the return may be due. 60 Fed. Reg. 66,898, 66,902 (1995).

[54] IRC § 6081. See IRC § 2661.

[55] Reg. §§ 20.6081-1(e), 25.6081-1.

[56] Reg. §§ 20.6081-1, 25.6081-1.

the return[57] at the IRS office where the return is required to be filed.[58] The application must be in writing and, where the extension is not automatic,[59] must give a full recital of the reasons for requesting an extension.[60]

---

[57] Reg. §§ 20.6081-1(b), 25.6081-1. The extension of time to file a return by a donor must be filed before the due date of the return. Reg. § 25.6081-1. The request for an automatic extension of time to file a Form 706, "United States Estate (and Generation-Skipping Transfer) Tax Return," must be filed before the due date for filing the Form 706. Reg. § 20.6081-1(b). A request for an extension of time to file beyond the six-month automatic extension where the executor is abroad should be filed early enough to permit the Service time to consider the matter before the due date of the return. Reg. § 20.6081-1(c). This same rule applies when an estate or person required to file forms other than Form 706 is seeking an extension of time to file. Reg. § 20.6081-(1)(c). An extension of time to file Form 706 may be granted to an estate that did not request an extension of time to file Form 706 prior to the due date at the discretion of the Service if good cause is shown; however, failure to request an extension of time before the due date may indicate negligence and constitute cause for denial of the extension of time to file. Reg. § 20.6081-1(c).

[58] Reg. §§ 20.6081-1(a), 25.6081-1. See also infra ¶ 18.02[5].

[59] If Form 4768, "Application for Extension of Time to File a Return and/or Pay United States Estate (and Generation-Skipping Transfer) Taxes" is filed in accordance with the procedures in the regulations on or before the due date for filing the Form 706, an estate will be allowed an automatic six-month extension of time to file. Reg. § 20.6081-1(b). The automatic extension is available for estate tax returns due after July 25, 2001. Reg. § 20.6081-1(e).

[60] See Reg. §§ 20.6081-1(b), 20.6081-1(c), 25.6081-1. If a donor is granted an extension for filing the donor's income tax return, the donor is also given an extension for filing the donor's gift tax return. IRC § 6075(b)(2). However, if the donor dies before filing the gift tax return, the extension for filing the gift tax return will not run beyond the time for filing the estate tax return (including extensions). IRC § 6075(b)(3). The extension of time would also be available for filing the generation-skipping transfer tax return for any transfer other than one occurring at the same time as, and as a result of, the death of an individual. IRC § 2661(1).

Requests for an extension of time to file the income tax return are made by using Form 4868, Application for Automatic Extension of Time to File United States Individual Income Tax Return, and Form 2350, Application for Extension of Time to File United States Income Tax Return. Each form has a box to check for requesting an extension for filing Form 709, United States Gift (and Generation-Skipping Transfer) Tax Return. An application for an additional extension of time to file an income or gift tax return is made by filing Form 2688, Application for Additional Extension of Time to File United States Individual Income Tax Return. Form 2688 must be filed in sufficient time to receive a reply before the due date or extended due date when a previous extension of time to file was granted. Form 4768, Application for Extension of Time to File a Return and/or Pay United States Estate (and Generation-Skipping Transfer) Taxes, is used to request an extension of time to file Form 706, United States Estate (and Generation-Skipping Transfer) Tax Return. When a discretionary extension is requested, Form 4768 needs to be filed early enough to permit a reply before the estate tax due date. Requests for an extension of the time to file Form 706-GS(D) and Form 706-GS(T) are made by filing Form 2758, Application for Extension of Time to File Certain Excise, Income, Information, and Other Returns. Form 2758 does not provide an automatic extension, so it must be filed in adequate time to permit the Service to consider it and reply before the return's due date.

[5] Where to File

Generation-skipping transfer tax return forms are to be filed at the Internal Revenue Service Center designated in the instruction accompanying the form to be filed. When Form 709 is used to report an inter vivos direct skip, it is generally to be filed with the Internal Revenue Service Center in Cincinnati, Ohio.[61] When Form 706 is used to report testamentary direct skips, generally it is also to be filed with the Internal Revenue Service Center, Cincinnati, Ohio.[62] When Form 706-GS(T) is used to report a taxable termination, when Form 706-GS(D) is used to report a taxable distribution, or when Form 706-GS(D-1)

---

[61] See Instructions for Form 709, United States Gift (and Generation-Skipping Transfer) Tax Return (2001), at 4. The place for filing returns required by Chapter 13 is to be determined under Section 6091. Reg. § 26.2662-1(e). Generally, a transferor must file a gift tax return in the IRS district in which is located the legal residence or principal place of business of the person making the return, or at a service center serving that internal revenue district. IRC § 6091(b)(1)(A). However, unless a return is filed by hand, whenever instructions provide that the return be filed with a service center, the return must be filed in accordance with the instructions. Reg. § 25.6091-1(b). Nonresident donors, who do not have a principal place of business located in an IRS district, file with the Internal Revenue Service Center, Philadelphia, Pennsylvania, or the Director of International Operations, Washington, D.C., depending on the place designated on, or the instructions for, the return form. Reg. § 25.6091-1(c). The Instructions for Form 709 direct that Form 709, United States Gift (and Generation-Skipping Transfer) Tax Return (2001) be sent by all donors, including nonresident donors, to the Internal Revenue Service Center, Cincinnati, Ohio 45999. Instructions for Form 709, United States Gift (and Generation-Skipping Transfer) Tax Return (2001), at 4.

[62] See Instructions for Form 706, United States Estate (and Generation-Skipping Transfer) Tax Return (Rev. Nov. 2001), at 2. The place for filing returns required by Chapter 13 is to be determined under Section 6091. Reg. § 26.2662-1(e). Generally, estate tax returns must be filed in the internal revenue district in which the decedent was domiciled at the time of death or at a service center designated as serving that IRS district. IRC § 6091(b)(3). However, whenever instructions provide that the return be filed with a service center, the return must be filed in accordance with the instructions. Reg. § 20.6091-1(a)(1). The Instructions for Form 706 direct that when Form 706, United States Estate (and Generation-Skipping Transfer) Tax Return (Rev. Nov. 2001) is filed using the United States Postal Service it is to be mailed to the Internal Revenue Service Center in Cincinnati, Ohio 45999.

This rule is subject to two exceptions. Where a private delivery service is used, the Form 706 is to be addressed to the Internal Revenue Service Center, 201 W. Rivercenter Blvd., Covington, KY 41019. Instructions for Form 706, United States Estate (and Generation-Skipping Transfer) Tax Return (Rev. Nov. 2001), at 2. Returns for nonresident citizens and noncitizens are to be filed with the Internal Revenue Service Center in Philadelphia, Pennsylvania, or with the Director of International Operations, Washington, D.C., depending on the place designated on, or the instructions for, the return form. Reg. § 20.6091-1(b). The instructions provide that the Form 706 filed for the estate of a nonresident United States citizen is to be filed with the Internal Revenue Service Center, Philadelphia, Pennsylvania 19255. Instructions for Form 706, United States Estate (and Generation-Skipping Transfer) Tax Return (Rev. Nov. 2001), at 2.

is used to provide notification of a taxable distribution, the form is filed with the Internal Revenue Service Center where the estate or gift tax return of the settlor must be filed to report the most recent transfer to the trust.[63]

[6] Information Returns

The Secretary is given broad authority to require the filing of information re-turns to assist in the proper administration and collection of the Chapter 13 tax.[64] When a taxable distribution occurs, the transferee is liable for the pay-ment of the Chapter 13 tax and the filing of the tax return, if required.[65] In ad-dition, the trust involved in the taxable distribution is required to file an information return, Form 706-GS(D-1), and provide each distributee with a copy.[66] When a direct skip is made from a trust included in the transferor's gross estate and the trustee is required to pay the tax,[67] the executor is required to file an information return, Schedule R-1 (Form 706),[68] with the trustee, noti-fying the trustee of the amount of the generation-skipping transfer tax due. In administering the Chapter 13 tax, the Secretary will, in all likelihood, impose additional information return requirements.[69]

---

[63] Instructions for Form 706-GS(T), Generation-Skipping Transfer Tax Return for Terminations (Rev. July 1999) at 1; Instructions for Form 706-GS(D), Generation-Skip-ping Transfer Tax Return for Distributions (Rev. June 1999) at 1; Instructions for Form 706-GS(D-1), Notification of Distribution From a Generation-Skipping Trust (Rev. June 1999) at 1. Where the settlor is, or was at death, a nonresident citizen or noncitizen, each of these forms is to be filed with the Internal Revenue Service Center in Philadelphia, Pennsylvania. See infra ¶ 18.02[6], especially note 66.

[64] IRC § 2662(b).

[65] Reg. § 26.2662-1(c)(1)(i). See supra ¶ 18.02[2][a] note 11.

[66] Reg. § 26.2662-1(b)(1). Form 706-GS(D-1) is required to be filed with the Internal Revenue Service Center where the estate or gift tax return of the settlor must be filed to report the most recent transfer to the trust. Instructions for Form 706-GS(D-1), Notifica-tion of Distribution From a Generation-Skipping Trust (Rev. June 1999) at 1.

[67] But see supra ¶ 18.02[3][b] text accompanying note 37.

[68] See Instructions for Form 706, United States Estate (and Generation-Skipping Transfer) Tax Return (Rev. Nov. 2001), at 19.

[69] For example, transfers that did not qualify as direct skips solely by reason of the $2 million grandchild exclusion, though not required to be reported on regular returns, were required to be reported on Forms 706 and 709 for informational purposes. See Tax Reform Act of 1986, Pub. L. No. 99-514, § 1433(b)(3), 1002 Stat. 2085, 2731 (1986), re-printed in 1986-3 CB (Vol. 1) 1, 648, as amended by Technical and Miscellaneous Reve-nue Act of 1988, Pub. L. No. 100-647, § 1014(h)(3)(A), 102 Stat. 3342, 3567–3568 (1988), reprinted in 1988-3 CB 1, 227–228.

¶ 18.03 SECTION 2663. REGULATIONS

Section 2663 directs the Secretary to issue such regulations "as may be necessary or appropriate" to implement the purposes of Chapter 13. This directive gives the Treasury the authority to promulgate legislative regulations that are given more weight by a court than the mere interpretative regulations promulgated solely by the authority of Section 7805, which merely directs the Secretary to "prescribe all needful rules and regulations."[1] In addition, Section 2663 specifically directs the Secretary to promulgate legislative regulations in three areas.

[1] Recapture Tax Under Section 2032A

Section 2663(1) requires the Secretary to issue regulations "necessary to coordinate the provisions of this chapter with the recapture tax imposed under section 2032A(c)."[2] Recall that for estate tax purposes, Section 2032A permits a special method of valuation for certain farm and other real property that passes to a qualified heir.[3] If the qualified heir[4] disposes of the qualified property[5] within ten years[6] of the decedent's death or ceases to make qualified use[7] of such property within the same period, generally there is an additional estate tax imposed,[8] for which the qualified heir is personally liable.[9]

[a] Testamentary Direct Skips

If the property passes to the qualified heir by way of a testamentary direct skip and the value of that property is determined under Section 2032A for purposes of Chapter 11, then the Section 2032A valuation is also statutorily assigned to the property in the determination of the taxable amount of the

---

[1] See Bittker & Lokken, Federal Taxation of Income, Estates and Gifts ¶ 110.4.2 (Warren, Gorham & Lamont, 1992). Cf. Rowan Cos. v. United States, 452 US 247, 253 (1981).

[2] IRC § 2663(1). See Reg. § 26.2663-1.

[3] See ¶ 4.04.

[4] IRC § 2032A(e)(1).

[5] IRC § 2032A(b).

[6] IRC § 2032A(c)(1).

[7] IRC § 2032A(b)(2).

[8] IRC § 2032A(c)(1)(B). If such disposition or cessation occurs within ten years, but only after the qualified heir's death, no additional estate tax is imposed. IRC § 2032A(c)(1).

[9] IRC § 2032A(c)(5). The amount of the additional estate tax is generally the amount of the estate tax that was saved owing to the special valuation. IRC § 2032A(c)(2).

testamentary direct skip under Section 2624(b)[10] and in the determination of the applicable fraction under Section 2642(b).[11] When Section 2032A is used to determine the taxable amount of a testamentary direct skip and additional

---

[10] Section 2624(b) mandates that, in the determination of the taxable amount of any testamentary direct skip, the value of such property for purposes of Chapter 13 "*shall* be the same as its value for purposes of Chapter 11 (determined with regard to sections 2032 and 2032A) (emphasis added)." IRC § 2624(b). However, it is possible that regulations to be promulgated for Section 2624(b) will disregard the statutory mandate and, as an option, allow testamentary direct skip property valued under Section 2032A for Chapter 11 purposes to be valued at fair market value in the determination of the Section 2624(b) taxable amount. See infra note 11.

[11] Section 2642(b) provides that, in the determination of the applicable fraction, the value of property, which is the subject matter of a testamentary direct skip, "shall be its value as finally determined for purposes of chapter 11." IRC § 2642(b)(2)(A); Reg. § 26.2642-2(b)(1). The regulations modify the dictate of the statute by providing that

> [i]n the case of qualified real property with respect to which the election under section 2032A is made, the value of the property is the value determined under section 2032A provided the recapture agreement described in section 2032A(d)(2) filed with the Internal Revenue Service specifically provides for the signatories' consent to the imposition of, and personal liability for, additional GST tax in the event an additional estate tax is imposed under section 2032A(c). . . . If the recapture agreement does not contain these provisions, the value of qualified real property as to which the election under section 2032A is made is the fair market value of the property determined without regard to the provisions of section 2032A.

Reg. § 26.2642-2(b)(1). It appears that real property can be valued under Section 2032A for purposes of the *estate tax* and in the determination of the *taxable amount* of the generation-skipping transfer, but valued at fair market value in the determination of the denominator of the *applicable fraction*.

However, the optional valuation afforded Section 2032A property in the determination of the inclusion ratio may be unavailable where real property is valued under Section 2032A in the determination of the taxable amount of a testamentary direct skip. The optional fair market valuation in the determination of the applicable fraction may be limited to use only where the real property is not the subject matter of a testamentary direct skip. When real property is valued under Section 2032A in the determination of the taxable amount, the Treasury should require a recapture agreement described in Section 2032A to be filed with the Internal Revenue Service specifically providing for the signatories' consent to the imposition of, and personal liability for, additional generation-skipping transfer tax imposed on the testamentary direct skip valued under Section 2032A in the event additional estate tax is imposed under Section 2032A(c). See infra note 12. If this agreement is a prerequisite to the use of the Section 2032A value of real property in the determination of the taxable amount of a testamentary direct skip, then that same agreement should preclude the use of fair market valuation of the same real property in the determination of the inclusion ratio.

Since real property may be valued pursuant to Section 2032A for Chapter 11 purposes and at fair market value in the determination of the applicable fraction, the Treasury needs to consider whether regulations promulgated for Section 2624(b) should modify the statutory dictate of Section 2624(b) in a similar fashion and provide taxpayers with an option to use Section 2032A for estate tax purposes, but use fair market value in the determination of the taxable amount and the inclusion ratio. See supra note 10, ¶¶ 14.05[2][a], 16.02[4][d][i].

estate tax is imposed under Section 2032A(c), a recomputation of the Chapter 13 tax imposed on the testamentary direct skip should also be required.[12] Additional generation-skipping transfer tax will be imposed on the testamentary direct skip unless one of two circumstances exist: (1) a sufficient amount of the transferor's GST exemption has been allocated[13] to the property to cover the Section 2032A value of the property and the difference between the Section 2032A value and the fair market value of the property or (2) sufficient unused residual GST exemption is available and automatically allocated to result in a zero inclusion ratio.[14]

The Treasury should specifically require testamentary direct skip property valued under Section 2032A for Chapter 11 purposes to be similarly valued for Chapter 13 purposes, both in the determination of the taxable amount and inclusion ratio. Furthermore, the Treasury should consider eliminating the fair market valuation option entirely with respect to property valued under Section 2032A for estate tax purposes by requiring the same valuation of property under Chapter 11 and Chapter 13. This could be accomplished by amending the regulations to provide that Section 2032A valuation for estate tax purposes is conditioned on a consent to the imposition of additional generation-skipping transfer tax and that if the recapture agreement does not contain these provisions, the value of real property is the fair market value of the property determined without regard to the provisions of Section 2032A for both estate and generation-skipping transfer purposes.

[12] If property passing to a skip person is valued under Section 2032A, a computation of the generation-skipping transfer tax saving attributable to direct skips for each skip person holding an interest in the property must be attached as part of the notice of election. Form 706, United States Estate (and Generation-Skipping Transfer) Tax Return (Rev. Nov. 2001) Schedule A-1, Part 2, Line 10, at 9. This is required to facilitate the computation of the additional generation-skipping transfer tax due upon the occurrence of a recapture event, the disposition or cessation of qualified use. Form 706, United States Estate (and Generation-Skipping Transfer) Tax Return (Rev. Nov. 2001), Instructions for Schedule A-1. Section 2032A Valuation, Part 2. Notice of Election, GST Tax Savings, at 6. Whenever additional estate tax is imposed under Section 2032A(c) and additional generation-skipping transfer tax is imposed, the qualified heir will likely be personally liable for the additional generation-skipping transfer tax imposed. However, the generation-skipping transfer tax imposed under Chapter 13 will not exceed the Chapter 13 tax previously saved by the special valuation.

Neither the statute nor the regulations specifically require revaluation of the taxable amount of the testamentary direct skip valued under Section 2032A or specifically impose an additional generation-skipping transfer tax on the increased taxable amount if additional estate tax is subsequently imposed under Section 2032A(c). See Reg. §§ 26.2663-1, 26.2642-4(a)(4). See also Reg. § 26.2642-2(b)(1). The regulations specially provide for the redetermination of the applicable fraction as of the date of the transferor's death. Reg. § 26.2642-4(a)(4)(i). The denominator of the redetermined applicable fraction is the fair market value of the property at the transferor's date of death, with any appropriate reductions. Id.

[13] IRC § 2632(a). See ¶ 15.03[6][a] note 237.

[14] IRC § 2632(e); Reg. § 26.2642-4(a)(4)(i). See ¶¶ 15.03[7][a], 15.03[7][b][iii], 15.03[7][c][ii].

[b] Other Testamentary Transfers

Property that is the subject matter of a testamentary transfer which is not a direct skip may also be valued under Section 2032A in the determination of the inclusion ratio.[15] If additional estate tax is imposed under Section 2032A(c) with respect to property valued under Section 2032A for generation-skipping transfer tax purposes, a recomputation of the applicable fraction[16] as of the date of the transferor's death is required.[17] Any unused GST exemption is automatically allocated to the property in the redetermination of the applicable fraction.[18] The denominator of the applicable fraction is the fair market value of the property on the date of the transferor's death, reduced by federal estate and state death taxes and any additional generation-skipping transfer tax charged to the trust.[19]

If property is valued under Section 2032A in the determination of the inclusion ratio and one or more post-death generation-skipping transfers occur prior to the cessation of qualified use and the imposition of additional estate tax, a recomputation of the generation-skipping transfer tax imposed on those intervening generation-skipping transfers is required.[20] Any additional generation-skipping transfer tax is due six months after the event causing the imposition of additional estate tax under Section 2032A(c).[21] Whether any additional generation-skipping transfer tax will be imposed depends on the amount of GST exemption allocated to the property. No additional generation-skipping transfer tax may be imposed if the executor of the estate allocated additional GST exemption to the property in an amount sufficient to cover the revalua-

---

[15] IRC § 2642(b)(2)(A); Reg. § 26.2642-2(b)(1). See ¶ 16.02[4][d] note 255. See also ¶ 15.03[6][b] note 242.

[16] Reg. §§ 26.2663-1, 26.2642-4(a)(4). See Reg. § 26.2642-2(b)(1). Recomputation of the applicable fraction is required if property is valued under Section 2032A in the determination of the taxable amount under Section 2624(b) and the applicable fraction, or only in the computation of the applicable fraction where the Section 2032A property is not the subject matter of a testamentary direct skip. See ¶ 16.02[5][f].

[17] Reg. § 26.2642-4(a)(4)(i).

[18] Reg. § 26.2642-4(a)(4)(i).

[19] Reg. § 26.2642-4(a)(4)(i) (last sentence). The federal estate and state death taxes charged to the trust may be incurred at death or upon the imposition of additional estate tax under Section 2032A(c) or a similar state statute. The denominator is to be reduced as provided in Reg. § 26.2642-1(c). See ¶ 16.02[3][b][ii].

[20] Reg. § 26.2642-4(a)(4)(ii).

[21] Reg. § 26.2642-4(a)(4)(ii). The additional generation-skipping transfer tax is to be remitted with Form 706-A (United States Additional Estate Tax Return). A statement disclosing the computation of the additional generation-skipping transfer tax is to be attached to Form 706-A. Id.

tion amount.[22] If the executor made no affirmative allocation of GST exemption, any available unused residual GST exemption will be automatically allocated until a zero inclusion ratio is achieved.[23]

If property, not the subject matter of a testamentary direct skip and valued under Section 2032A for federal estate tax purposes but at fair market value in the determination of the inclusion ratio,[24] is disposed of and additional estate tax is imposed under Section 2032A(c) prior to any post-death generation-skipping transfer, the regulations should require a recomputation of the inclusion ratio where the additional estate tax imposed is recovered from the trust.[25] This recomputation may void a portion of the GST exemption previously allocated to the property if the inclusion ratio prior to the imposition of additional estate tax under Section 2032A(c) was zero.[26]

[2] Nonresident Noncitizen Transferor

[a] In General

The regulations prescribe the manner in which the Chapter 13 tax is to be imposed when the transferor is a nonresident noncitizen of the United States.[27] Any transfer made after the effective dates for the generation-skipping transfer tax[28] by a nonresident noncitizen that is subject to the federal estate or gift tax is subject to the generation-skipping transfer tax in the same manner as a transfer by a resident or citizen of the United States.[29] Generally, property transferred by a nonresident noncitizen is subject to the federal gift or estate

---

[22] IRC § 2632(a). See ¶ 15.03[6][b] note 242. The regulations should permit the transferor's executor to allocate GST exemption to shield the property valued under Section 2032A from the imposition of additional Chapter 13 tax.

[23] Reg. § 26.2642-4(a)(4)(i). See ¶¶ 15.03[7][a] text accompanying notes 259–260, 15.03[7][b][iii], 15.03[7][c][ii].

[24] See Reg. § 26.2642-2(b)(1) (last sentence); supra ¶ 18.03[1][a] note 11; ¶ 15.03[6][b] note 242.

[25] See Reg. § 26.2642-1(c)(1)(i). See also Reg. § 26.2642-4(a)(4)(i).

[26] Reg. § 26.2632-1(b)(2)(i). See ¶ 15.02[1]. See also ¶¶ 15.03[7][b][ii], 15.03[7][b][iii].

[27] Reg. § 26.2663-2. Section 2663(2) directs the Secretary to prescribe the manner in which the Chapter 13 tax, consistent with Chapter 11 and 12, is imposed on nonresidents noncitizens of the United States. See Estate of Neumann v. Comm'r, 106 TC 216 (1996) (generation-skipping transfer tax was applied to the transfer of U.S. situs property by a nonresident alien decedent to her grandchildren, notwithstanding that at the time of the transfer, the regulations under Section 2663(2) had not yet been issued).

[28] Reg. § 26.2601-1(a)(1). See ¶ 18.05.

[29] See ¶ 6.01[3]. The rules of Chapter 11 and 12, the federal estate and gift tax provisions, are to be used in determining if an individual is a resident or a citizen for purposes of Chapter 13. Reg. § 26.2663-2(a).

tax if the property transferred is situated in the United States at the time it is transferred.[30] The application of Chapter 13 to a transfer by a nonresident noncitizen is mitigated to some extent by the GST exemption that is allowed every nonresident noncitizen transferor.[31] The regulations are not intended to override the provisions of any treaty limiting the jurisdiction of the United States to impose the generation-skipping transfer tax.[32]

[b] Transfer of Property Situated in the United States

Any transfer by a nonresident noncitizen that is subject to federal estate[33] or gift[34] taxation is subject to the generation-skipping transfer tax imposed by Chapter 13, generally[35] in the same manner as if the transfer were made by a resident or citizen of the United States.

Testamentary transfers of property situated in the United States by a decedent who is a nonresident noncitizen are subject to the provisions of Chapter 13.[36] Property that is situated in the United States for purposes of Chapter 11[37] is treated as similarly situated for purposes of Chapter 13.[38] The determination of the situs of the property for this purpose is to be made at the time of the initial transfer of the property to a skip person or to a trust that is not a skip person.[39] For example, assume Transferor, a nonresident noncitizen, devises real property situated in the United States for Chapter 11 purposes to a trust with income to Child for life and a remainder to Grandchild. Both Child and Grandchild are nonresidents and not citizens. The trustee sells the real property

---

[30] See infra ¶ 18.03[2][b].

[31] Reg. § 26.2663-2(a). The regulations provide that every nonresident noncitizen is allowed a GST exemption of $1 million. Id. Presumably the GST exemption afforded every nonresident noncitizen will be adjusted upward for inflation in the same manner and amount as the GST exemption afforded citizens under Section 2631 and after December 31, 2003, equal the applicable exclusion amount under Section 2010(c) afforded citizens. See IRC § 2631(c); ¶ 15.02.

[32] See Reg. § 25.0-1(a)(1); ¶ 7.06 text accompanying note 10. In the Supplementary Information to the proposed regulations, the Service stated that it believed that treaties negotiated prior to 1986 that covered the initial generation-skipping transfer tax, which was repealed retroactively in 1986, continue to apply to the present version of Chapter 13. PS-73-88, Supplementary Information, 1993-1 CB 867, 870. The Supplementary Information accompanying the final regulations make no mention of this policy. 60 Fed. Reg. 66,898, 66,902–66,903.

[33] See ¶¶ 6.01–6.07.

[34] See ¶ 9.02.

[35] See supra ¶ 18.03[2][a] note 31.

[36] Reg. § 26.2663-2(b). See ¶¶ 6.03[2], 6.04, 6.05.

[37] See ¶¶ 6.03[2], 6.04, 6.05.

[38] Reg. § 26.2663-2(b).

[39] See Reg. § 26.2663-2(b).

situated in the United States and reinvests in foreign real property. There is a taxable termination generation-skipping transfer subject to the tax imposed by Chapter 13 at Child's death regardless of the situs of the real property.[40]

Similarly, when a nonresident who is not a citizen makes an *inter vivos* transfer of property that is situated in the United States for purposes of Chapter 12 at the time of the transfer[41] and the transfer is subject to tax under Section 2501,[42] the transfer is also subject to the provisions of Chapter 13, even if the transfer is to a nonresident noncitizen.[43] The determination whether the property is subject to the federal gift tax is made at the time of the initial transfer to the skip person or trust that is not a skip person.[44] Assume that Transferor, a nonresident noncitizen, transfers only real property situated in the United States to a trust providing that the income from the property is to be paid to Child for life and the remainder to Grandchild and assume that neither Child nor Grandchild is a resident or citizen of the United States. Chapter 13 applies to the transfer to the trust because the real property transferred was situated in the United States for purposes of Chapter 12 at the time of the initial transfer to the trust and the transfer is subject to the federal gift tax under Section 2501(a).[45] At the death of Child, there is a taxable termination generation-skipping transfer.[46]

[c] Trusts Partially Subject to Chapter 13

A single trust created by a nonresident noncitizen may be funded with property subject to Chapter 13, as well as property that is not subject to Chapter 13. Property situated in the United States and property that either is not situated in the United States or is intangible property situated in the United States that is not subject to the federal gift tax, may be contributed to a single

---

[40] Reg. § 26.2663-2(b)(2). See also ¶ 6.03[2][a]. Alternatively, had Transferor funded the trust with a bequest of tangible personal property situated in the United States for Chapter 11 purposes, there would still be a taxable termination generation-skipping transfer subject to the tax imposed by Chapter 13 at Child's death, regardless of the situs of the tangible personal property.

[41] Reg. § 26.2663-2(b). See ¶ 9.02[1] text accompanying note 6.

[42] Reg. § 26.2663-2(b). See ¶ 9.02[1]. Generally, the transfer of intangible property situated in the United States by a nonresident noncitizen is not subject to taxation under Section 2501(a). IRC § 2501(a)(2). See Reg. § 25.2501-1(a)(3); ¶ 9.02[1]. But see IRC §§ 2501(a)(3), 2511(b); ¶¶ 9.02[1] note 7, 10.01[11].

[43] Reg. § 26.2663-2(d) Ex. 1.

[44] See Reg. § 26.2663-2(b).

[45] Reg. § 26.2663-2(b)(2). See also Reg. § 26.2663-2(d) Ex. 1.

[46] A termination of Child's interest in the trust is subject to Chapter 13 because the initial transfer to the trust was of property situated in the United States and that transfer was subject to tax under Section 2501(a). Reg. § 26.2663-2(b)(2).

trust. A trust, which has both types of property, is subject to Chapter 13 only to the extent that it is funded with property subject to taxation under Chapter 11 or Chapter 12 upon creation.[47] Generally, the applicable fraction for the trust is determined at the time of the transfer to the trust.[48] An exception to this rule occurs where an inter vivos transfer by a nonresident noncitizen is subsequently included in the gross estate of the transferor. Under this exception, the applicable fraction is redetermined at the date of the transferor's death.[49]

In computing the applicable fraction for a trust partially subject to Chapter 13, the numerator of the applicable fraction is the portion of the nonresident noncitizen transferor's GST exemption allocated[50] to the transfer, plus the value of the property held in the trust that is not subject to Chapter 13, the "nontax portion of the trust."[51] The nontax portion is expressed as a fraction, which, when multiplied by the fair market value of the entire trust, will yield the dollar value of the nontax portion to be used in the numerator of the applicable fraction.[52] The numerator of the nontax portion is the value of the property not subject to Chapter 13 as of the date of initial transfer, and the denominator is the fair market value of the entire trust on that date.[53] For example, assume a nonresident noncitizen transfers property worth $1 million to a trust. Assume that $200,000 of the property is situated in the United States and subject to the provisions of Chapter 13, and $800,000 of the property is not situated in the United States and is not subject to Chapter 13. The nontax portion of the trust is 0.8.[54] That decimal fraction times the fair market value of the trust would be added to the amount of GST exemption allocated to the transfer by the nonresident noncitizen transferor in arriving at the numerator of the applicable fraction.[55] The nontax portion of the trust is ascertained any time the applicable fraction for the trust is either determined[56] or redetermined.[57] The applicable fraction may need to be redetermined at a later date when prop-

---

[47] Reg. § 26.2663-2(b)(2). See Reg. § 26.2663-2(d) Exs. 2, 3, 4.

[48] Reg. § 26.2663-2(c)(1). See Reg. § 26.2663-2(d) Exs. 2, 3, 4.

[49] Reg. § 26.2663-2(c)(3). See Reg. § 26.2663-2(d) Exs. 6, 7; infra ¶ 18.03[2][d].

[50] The nonresident noncitizen's GST exemption is allocated to the property in the same manner as that of a citizen or resident. Reg. § 26.2663-2(a). See also Reg. § 26.2632-1; ¶ 15.03.

[51] Reg. § 26.2663-2(c)(1)(i). See Reg. § 26.2663-2(c)(2).

[52] See Reg. § 26.2663-2(c)(2).

[53] Reg. § 26.2663-2(c)(2).

[54] Reg. § 26.2663-2(c)(2). See Reg. § 26.2663-2(d) Exs. 3, 4.

[55] Reg. § 26.2663-2(c)(1)(i).

[56] See ¶ 16.02[3][b].

[57] See ¶ 16.02[5]; Reg. § 26.2663-2(d) Ex. 4.

erty is added to the trust, additional GST exemption is allocated to the trust, or other events occur that require a redetermination of the applicable fraction.[58]

The denominator of the applicable fraction is the fair market value of the trust corpus at the relevant time with three possible reductions.[59] The denominator of the applicable fraction is reduced by any federal estate and state death taxes imposed on the transfer and paid by the trust, the amount of any charitable deduction allowed for the transfer, and any portion of the transfer that qualified as a nontaxable gift for purposes of Chapter 13 by reason of the annual exclusion.[60]

[d] Nonresident Noncitizens and the Estate Tax Inclusion Period Rules

The estate tax inclusion period rules apply to nonresident noncitizen transferors only if the property transferred by the nonresident noncitizen is, in fact, subsequently included in the nonresident noncitizen's gross estate.[61] The estate tax inclusion period rules apply to citizens and residents when, should death occur immediately after the transfer, the value of the transferred property would be includible (other than by reason of Section 2035) in the transferor's or the transferor's spouse's gross estate.[62] The *possibility* of inclusion in the gross estate, not actual inclusion, results in the application of the estate tax inclusion period rules to transfers of citizens and residents. The generation-skipping transfer tax is applied to the transfer by a nonresident noncitizen of property subject to Chapter 13 during the life of the nonresident noncitizen, disregarding the estate tax inclusion period rules. However, if the property is, in fact, subsequently included in the gross estate of the transferor, the applicable fraction is redetermined at the date of the nonresident noncitizen's death.[63] This redetermined applicable fraction is then used in the computation of tax

---

[58] See Reg. § 26.2642-4; ¶ 16.02[5]; supra text accompanying note 49.

[59] Reg. § 26.2663-2(c)(1)(ii).

[60] Reg. § 26.2642-1(c)(1). See ¶ 16.02[3][b][ii].

[61] See Reg. § 26.2663-2(c)(3). Although this regulation is under subsection c titled, "Trusts funded in part with property subject to chapter 13 and in part with property not subject to chapter 13," the first sentence of this regulation says "[f]or purposes of this *section*, the provisions of § 26.2632-1(c) . . . apply . . . " (emphasis added). Id. The special rule with respect to the estate tax inclusion period for nonresident noncitizens is not limited in its application to trusts funded in part with property subject to Chapter 13 and in part with property not subject to Chapter 13. Regulations Section 26.2663-2(c)(3) should be redesignated Section 26.2663-2(d) to clarify the application of this special rule.

[62] IRC § 2642(f). See ¶ 16.02[7].

[63] See Reg. § 26.2663-2(c)(3).

imposed on generation-skipping transfers at death and thereafter from the trust.[64]

[3] Trust Equivalent Arrangements

Section 2663(3) directs the Secretary to issue such regulations as may be necessary to apply the provisions of Chapter 13 to "any arrangement which, although not a trust, is treated as a trust under section 2652(b)."[65] For the purposes of Chapter 13, the term "trust" is defined to include "any arrangement (other than an estate) which, although not a trust, has substantially the same effect as a trust."[66] Where the generation-skipping transfer tax rules applicable to trusts are not appropriate for dealing with trust equivalent arrangements, Section 2663(3) grants the Treasury authority to modify the rules generally applicable to trusts.[67]

¶ 18.04 SECTION 2664. TERMINATION OF THE GENERATION-SKIPPING TRANSFER TAX

Congress has determined the generation-skipping transfer tax to be unduly burdensome to all taxpayers, especially businesses, and more specifically small, family-owned, and farming businesses,[1] and it has scheduled the termination of

---

[64] The regulations do not consider whether in the event that the applicable fraction is redetermined at the death of a nonresident noncitizen owing to application of the estate tax inclusion period rules, the recomputed applicable fraction is used to recompute the tax imposed on all prior generation-skipping transfers occurring between establishment and the death of the transferor. Hopefully, the Treasury will address this issue in future regulations.

[65] IRC § 2663(3). See ¶ 17.02[2].

[66] IRC § 2652(b). See ¶ 17.02[2]; Reg. § 26.2662-1(c)(2)(ii).

[67] S. Rep. No. 445, 100th Cong., 2d Sess. 373 (1988). The legislative history provides an illustration of such a modification of rules. An insurance or annuity contract is a trust equivalent arrangement, and the insurance company is the trustee. IRC § 2652(b). Normally, the liability for payment of the Chapter 13 tax would fall on the trustee insurance company. IRC § 2603(a)(2). The legislative history suggests that regulations promulgated under Section 2663(3) require instead that the beneficiary pay the Chapter 13 tax. S. Rep. No. 445, 100th Cong., 2d Sess. 373 (1988). See Reg. §§ 26.2662-1(c)(2)(iii), 26.2662-1(c)(2)(v); ¶ 12.03[2] note 26. Compare Reg. § 26.2662-1(c)(2)(vi) Exs. 2, 3 with Reg. § 26.2662-1(c)(2)(vi) Exs. 1, 4.

[1] HR Rep. No. 37, 107th Cong., 1st Sess. 25 (2001), reprinted in 2001-__ CB __, __.

Chapter 13, the tax imposed on generation-skipping transfers.[2] The generation-skipping transfer tax will not apply to generation-skipping transfers that occur after December 31, 2009.[3] Several years must pass before Chapter 13, like the hero or heroine in a Zane Grey wild west novel, rides off into the sunset. Over those years there will be multiple new Congresses and at least one new president, possibly more. It is impossible to predict what, and even whether, alternative legislative action will be taken in the meantime. If no legislative changes are made, the scheduled termination will be short-lived and Chapter 13, like the sun, will rise again to tax generation-skipping transfers occurring on or after January 1, 2011, because of the "sunset" provision.[4] The sunset provision[5] not only eliminates Section 2664, but it restores Chapter 13 in its entirety to its state prior to the enactment of the Economic Growth and Tax Reconciliation Act of 2001.[6]

¶ 18.05 EFFECTIVE DATES

[1] General Rule

The generation-skipping transfer tax is generally applicable to any generation-skipping transfer occurring after October 22, 1986, and on or before December

---

[2] Economic Growth and Tax Relief Reconciliation Act of 2001, Pub. L. No. 107-16, §§ 501(b), 115 Stat. 38, 69 (2001), reprinted in 2001-__ CB __, __.

[3] IRC § 2664. In addition, the estate tax is terminated for the estates of decedents dying after December 31, 2009. IRC § 2210. See ¶ 8.10[1]. But see ¶ 8.10[2].

[4] Title IX of the Economic Growth and Tax Relief Reconciliation Act of 2001 contains a "sunset" provision that provides that Section 2664, which repeals the tax imposed on generation-skipping transfers occurring after December 31, 2009, magically disappears, like Cinderella's carriage and horses, at midnight on December 31, 2010. Economic Growth and Tax Relief Reconciliation Act of 2001, Pub. L. No. 107-16, § 901(a)(2), 115 Stat. 38, 150 (2001), reprinted in 2001-__ CB __, __. See ¶ 8.10[5].

[5] Economic Growth and Tax Relief Reconciliation Act of 2001, Pub. L. No. 107-16, § 901, 115 Stat. 38, 150 (2001), reprinted in 2001-__ CB __, __.

[6] Economic Growth and Tax Relief Reconciliation Act of 2001, Pub. L. No. 107-16, 115 Stat. 38 (2001), reprinted in 2001-__ CB __. If Chapter 13 is restored under the sunset provision, the amount of the GST exemption under Section 2631 will be $1.1 million (as adjusted for inflation occurring since 2002), the maximum tax rate under Section 2001(c) for purposes of Section 2641 will be 55 percent and the Section 2604 credit for state generation-generation skipping transfer taxes will be restored. The Section 2632(c) automatic allocation of GST exemption to indirect skips, the Section 2632(d) retroactive allocation of GST exemption, the Section 2642(a)(3) severance rules, the clarification of the Section 2642(b) valuation rules, and the relief provisions of Section 2642(g) will disappear.

31, 2009, as well as on or after January 1, 2011.[1] To render this rule equitable to both taxpayers and the government with respect to its inception, Congress has provided a number of transitional rules.[2]

[2] Transitional Rules

[a] Inter Vivos Transfers After September 25, 1985

On September 26, 1985, the House of Representatives first considered the package of measures that led to the Tax Reform Act of 1986, which included the current generation-skipping transfer tax. Congress presumably did not want to leave a window that would allow transfers made on or after that date, but prior to final passage of the legislation, to escape the imposition of the Chapter 13 tax. Thus, any inter vivos transfers subject to the Chapter 12 tax[3] that were made on or after September 25, 1985, and on or before October 22, 1986, are treated as if they were made on October 23, 1986,[4] the first day after the enactment of Chapter 13. If an inter vivos transfer made to a trust between those dates gave rise to distributions or terminations of an interest in the trust also occurring between those dates, it is treated as having been made on October 23, 1986.[5] Where more than one such transfer was made to and from a trust between those dates, all the transfers are treated as having occurred on October 23, 1986, in the order of their actual occurrence.[6] Although such transfers are treated as having been made on October 23, 1986, for the purposes of the imposition of Chapter 13 tax and the timing of filing returns, valuation of the property involved should occur on the actual date of the transfer.[7]

---

[1] Tax Reform Act of 1986, Pub. L. No. 99-514, § 1433(a), 100 Stat. 2085, 2731 (1986), reprinted in 1986-3 CB (Vol. 1) 1, 648. See Reg. § 26.2601-1(a)(1); IRC § 2664; Economic Growth and Tax Relief Reconciliation Act of 2001, Pub. L. No. 107-16, § 901(a)(2), 115 Stat. 38, 150 (2001), reprinted in 2001-__ CB __, __. See ¶¶ 8.10[5], 18.04.

[2] See infra ¶¶ 18.05[2][a], 18.05[2][b], 18.05[2][c], 18.05[2][d].

[3] A transfer after September 25, 1985, to a revocable trust that became irrevocable by reason of the transferor's death before October 23, 1986, is not treated as occurring on October 23, 1986, because the transfer is in the nature of a testamentary transfer that occurred prior to October 23, 1986. Reg. § 26.2601-1(a)(4).

[4] Reg. § 26.2601-1(a)(2).

[5] Reg. § 26.2601-1(a)(3). Thus, an inter vivos direct skip, taxable termination, or taxable distribution actually occurring before October 23, 1986, could be treated as occurring on such date.

[6] Reg. § 26.2601-1(a)(3). See Reg. § 26.2601-1(b)(1)(iv), which contains an allocation formula for additions to grandfathered trusts after September 25, 1985.

[7] Reg. § 26.2601-1(a)(2)(ii). See Reg. § 26.2601-1(a)(3) (last sentence).

[b] Trusts Irrevocable on September 25, 1985

In general, generation-skipping transfers from a trust or a trust equivalent arrangement[8] that was irrevocable on September 25, 1985, are not subject to the Chapter 13 tax.[9] There is probably no constitutional need to provide this amnesty.[10] Congress, however, intends to protect the trust fund, not some abstraction called a trust. Generation-skipping transfers by irrevocable trusts established prior to September 25, 1985, are not subjected to the Chapter 13 tax to the extent that they are made out of corpus added to the trust no later than September 25, 1985,[11] or out of income attributable to corpus added to the trust no later than September 25, 1985.[12]

[i] **The test of irrevocability.** A trust is not treated as irrevocable to the extent it would have been included in the transferor's gross estate for federal estate tax purposes by reason of Section 2038[13] if the transferor had died on September 25, 1985.[14] Basically, Section 2038 requires the inclusion of trust property in the transferor's gross estate where, at death, the transferor possesses a power to alter, amend, revoke, or terminate the enjoyment of the transferred property.[15] If a transferor creates an inter vivos trust and retains the

---

[8] IRC §§ 2652(b)(1), 2652(b)(3); Reg. § 26.2662-1(c)(2)(ii). See ¶ 17.02[2]. For purposes of this provision, Section 2652(b)(1) defines the term "trust" to include "any arrangement (other than an estate) which, although not a trust, has substantially the same effect as a trust." As used in the remainder of this section, the term "trust" includes any such trust equivalent arrangement. See Reg. § 26.2652-1(b).

[9] Tax Reform Act of 1986, Pub. L. No. 99-514, § 1433(b)(2)(A), 100 Stat. 2085, 2731 (1986), reprinted in 1986-3 CB (Vol. 1) 1, 648. See Reg. § 26.2601-1(b)(1)(i). See also infra text accompanying notes 38, 39.

[10] If the transitional rules were eliminated, simplicity might be served, but at the cost of the equitable purposes underlying the provisions. Cf., Kane v. United States, 942 F. Supp. 233 (DCPA 1996), aff'd, 118 F3d 1576 (3d Cir. 1997); Quarty v. United States, 170 F3d 961 (9th Cir. 1999).

[11] Tax Reform Act of 1986, Pub. L. No. 99-514, § 1433(b)(2)(A), 100 Stat. 2085, 2731 (1986), reprinted in 1986-3 CB (Vol. 1) 1, 648. See Reg. § 26.2601-1(b)(1)(iv).

[12] Tax Reform Act of 1986, Pub. L. No. 99-514 § 1433(b)(2)(A), 100 Stat. 2085, 2731 (1986), reprinted in 1986-3 CB (Vol. 1) 1, 648, as amended by Technical and Miscellaneous Revenue Act of 1988, Pub. L. No. 100-647, § 1014(h)(2)(B), 102 Stat. 3342, 3567 (1988), reprinted in 1988-3 CB 1, 227.

Where an addition is made after September 25, 1985, to an irrevocable trust established prior to that date, that portion of each distribution that is exempt from tax must be separated from that portion that is subject to tax. Reg. § 26.2601-1(b)(1)(iv).

[13] Section 2038 powers relinquished within the three years prior to September 25, 1985, are disregarded. Reg. § 26.2601-1(b)(1)(ii)(B). Cf. IRC §§ 2035(a)(2), 2038(a)(1) (last sentence).

[14] Reg. §§ 26.2601-1(b)(1)(ii)(B), 26.2601-1(b)(1)(ii)(D) Ex. 1. See infra ¶ 18.05[2][b][iii].

[15] IRC § 2038. See Reg. § 26.2601-1(b)(1)(ii)(D) Ex. 1. A trust is considered subject to a power, even though the exercise of such power is subject to the precedent giving of

right to amend the trust, the trust property is potentially includible in the transferor's gross estate by reason of Section 2038. If the transferor held the power on or after September 25, 1985, the trust will be considered revocable for purposes of the effective date rules and will generally be subject to the generation-skipping transfer tax.[16] On the other hand, if the transferor did not hold the power to alter, amend, revoke, or terminate enjoyment of the transferred property on or after September 25, 1985, the trust property is not potentially includible in the transferor's gross estate by reason of Section 2038 and the trust will be considered irrevocable for purposes of the effective date rules. The Treasury gets an "A" for tidiness in adopting Section 2038 concepts to test revocability.[17]

---

notice (or may be exercisable only within a stated period). But a trust is not considered to be subject to a power if, by its terms, the power is exercisable only on the occurrence of an event or contingency beyond the transferor's control that has not taken place. Reg. §§ 26.2601-1(b)(1)(ii)(B), 26.2601-1(b)(1)(ii)(D) Ex. 3. See Priv. Ltr. Rul. 9737026 (June 17, 1997) (settlor's power to make discretionary distributions of income to child between ages 21 and 30, where child had not attained age 21 on September 25, 1985, did not cause trust to be treated as revocable). Compare Priv. Ltr. Rul. 9738006 (June 17, 1997) (settlor's power to make discretionary distributions of income to child between ages 21 and 30, where the child was between ages 21 and 30 on September 25, 1985, caused a portion of the trust to be treated as revocable).

When someone other than the transferor holds a power of appointment over property held in a trust that was otherwise irrevocable on September 25, 1985, the trust generally will be considered irrevocable because the transferor did not hold the tainted power. Reg. § 26.2601-1(b)(1)(ii)(D) Ex. 2. The trust will be treated as irrevocable only until the power over the property held in the trust is exercised, released, or lapses in a manner that is treated as a taxable transfer of the property subject to the power under Chapter 11 or Chapter 12. See Reg. § 26.2601-1(b)(1)(i). See infra text accompanying note 38. However, if the transferor and some other person jointly hold a power, or if the transferor may at the transferor's own volition attain a third party's power, the transferor is treated as holding the power. These concepts along with other aspects of Section 2038 are considered at ¶ 4.10.

[16] But see the exception for revocable trusts discussed infra ¶ 18.05[2][c]; Reg. § 26.2601-1(b)(2)(ii).

[17] This does not mean that the standard, although tidy, is always precise. For example, under the authority of Rev. Rul. 79-353, 1979-2 CB 325, applied only prospectively pursuant to Rev. Rul. 81-51, 1981-1 CB 458, a grantor's power to remove and replace the corporate trustee of an irrevocable trust possessing Section 2038–type powers with another independent corporate trustee resulted in Section 2038 inclusion in the grantor's gross estate and in the trust being subject to the generation-skipping transfer tax provisions under the "tidy" rule. Thereafter, Estate of Wall v. Comm'r, 101 TC 300 (1993), followed by Rev. Rul. 95-58, 1995-2 CB 191, held that a grantor's power to remove and replace an independent corporate trustee with another corporate trustee, independent from the grantor, with Section 2038–type powers did not result in inclusion under Section 2038 in the grantor's gross estate, thereby possibly moving the trust in question, and other trusts similarly situated, to grandfathered status some eight years after the effective date of Chapter 13.

If a Section 2038 power is exercisable over a portion of the trust, only the remaining portion of the trust will be treated as irrevocable.[18] For example, if a transferor had a power to revoke one half of the corpus of a trust on September 25, 1985, the other half of the corpus would be considered irrevocable and only that half would escape the Chapter 13 tax.

Under the broad definition of "trust,"[19] a life insurance policy is treated as an irrevocable trust (for purposes of this transitional rule) if on September 25, 1985, the insured possessed no "incidents of ownership"[20] that would have caused the proceeds of the policy to be included in the insured's gross estate under Section 2042 if the insured had died on that date.[21] However, if on September 25, 1985, the insured possessed any incident of ownership, the insurance policy is treated as a revocable trust.[22] For example, if an individual purchased a life insurance policy, naming child and grandchild as beneficiaries, and had the right, on September 25, 1985, to obtain a loan from the insurer against the cash surrender value of the policy, this incident of ownership would result in the "trust" not being considered irrevocable for purposes of the transition rule.[23]

Under a special rule, an irrevocable trust existing on September 25, 1985, that holds qualified terminable interest property (QTIP)[24] will be treated for generation-skipping transfer tax purposes as if the election to treat the property as qualified terminable interest property had not been made.[25] The transferor will be deemed to have created the trust on its actual date of creation, and the donee spouse or the surviving spouse will not be treated as the transferor[26] of

---

[18] Reg. § 26.2601-1(b)(1)(ii)(D) Ex. 5. See Priv. Ltr. Rul. 9738006 (June 17, 1997) (portion of trust treated as other than irrevocable).

[19] IRC §§ 2652(b)(1), 2652(b)(3). See supra note 8.

[20] "Incidents of ownership" are defined in the same manner as in Reg. § 20.2042-1(c). See ¶¶ 4.14[4], 4.14[5].

[21] Reg. § 26.2601-1(b)(1)(ii)(C).

[22] Reg. § 26.2601-1(b)(1)(ii)(C).

[23] Reg. § 26.2601-1(b)(1)(ii)(D) Ex. 4.

[24] IRC §§ 2056(b)(7), 2523(f).

[25] Reg. § 26.2601-1(b)(1)(iii)(A). This has the same effect as a Section 2652(a)(3), reverse QTIP, election. IRC § 2652(a)(3). See ¶ 17.02[1][c][i]; Priv. Ltr. Rul. 9725014 (Mar. 19, 1997) (Section 2652(a)(3), reverse QTIP, election treated as made for qualified terminable interest property held in trust not subject to Chapter 13 due to an individual's mental disability continuously from October 22, 1986, until death), Priv. Ltr. Rul. 9735029 (June 2, 1997) (Section 2652(a)(3), reverse QTIP, election treated as made for qualified terminable interest property held in a trust created in June 1986 and amended in August 1986 not subject to Chapter 13 due to an individual's mental disability continuously from October 22, 1986, until death, although not in existence on September 25, 1985); infra ¶ 18.05[2][d] text accompanying notes 68–71.

[26] Cf. IRC § 2652(a)(3).

the property under Chapter 13. Generation-skipping transfers from such a trust will not be taxed under Chapter 13.[27]

All the preceding situations involving trusts or trust equivalent arrangements that are exempt from the Chapter 13 tax assume that no tainting additions or constructive additions were made to the trust or the trust equivalent arrangement.[28]

[ii] **Additions to corpus.** Some kinds of increases to corpus should not be viewed as tainted additions. Appreciation in the value of grandfathered corpus is not an addition to the corpus; it is merely a growth of the corpus.[29] Income generated by grandfathered corpus that is accumulated is not a corpus addition.[30] A "pour-over" to a grandfathered trust under a grandfathered instrument is not considered an addition to the corpus.[31] An inter vivos transfer to a trust will not be treated as a tainted corpus addition[32] if the transferred property would have been added to the trust in any event, pursuant to an instrument that satisfies a grandfather provision under the transitional rules.[33] On the

---

[27] Reg. § 26.2601-1(b)(1)(iii)(A). See Reg. § 26.2601-1(b)(1)(iii)(B) Exs. 1, 2.

[28] See infra ¶¶ 18.05[2][b][ii], 18.05[2][b][iii].

[29] Reg. § 26.2601-1(b)(1)(vi).

[30] Reg. § 26.2601-1(b)(1)(vi).

[31] Reg. § 26.2601-1(b)(5)(i). The instrument may be grandfathered as a result of transitional rules that apply to certain wills or revocable trusts (see infra ¶ 18.05[2][c]) or persons with a mental disability. See infra ¶ 18.05[2][d]. All of the examples in Regulations Section 26.2601-1(b)(5) involve the former type of pour-over. See, e.g., Reg. § 26.2601-1(b)(5)(ii) Exs. 1, 5.

This rule would also apply to some pour-overs from one trust to another. For example, assume that T and S are settlors of separate revocable trusts. Both trusts were established to benefit skip persons. S dies on December 1, 1985, and under the provisions of S's trust, the principal pours over into T's trust. If T dies before January 1, 1987, the entire corpus of the combined trust is excluded from the operation of Chapter 13. However, if T dies after December 31, 1986, the entire corpus of the combined trust will be subject to Chapter 13 taxation. See Reg. § 26.2601-1(b)(5)(ii) Ex. 3.

As another illustration, assume the same facts as in the preceding example, except that upon S's death, S's trust continues as an irrevocable trust and upon T's death, the corpus of T's trust is to be paid over to S's trust. If T dies before January 1, 1987, all of S's trust is excluded from the operation of Chapter 13. However, if T dies after December 31, 1986, the pour-over is considered an addition to the trust. Therefore, S's trust is not an excluded trust under the transitional rule contained in Regulations Section 26.2601-1(b)(2). Reg. § 26.2601-1(b)(5)(ii) Ex. 4. See Priv. Ltr. Rul. 9705011 (Oct. 31, 1996) (distribution of qualified terminable interest property held in trust not subject to Chapter 13 and the subject matter of deemed Section 2652(a)(3), reverse QTIP, election was not a tainted addition to two other trusts established by transferor and thus also not subject to Chapter 13).

[32] Reg. §§ 26.2601-1(b)(5)(i), 26.2601-1(b)(5)(ii) Ex. 2.

[33] Reg. §§ 26.2601-1(b)(2), 26.2601-1(b)(3). See infra ¶¶ 18.05[2][c], 18.05[2][d].

other hand, if the property would not have been added to the trust pursuant to a grandfathered instrument, it will be treated as a tainted corpus addition.[34]

Under the transitional rule,[35] various types of constructive additions are treated as tainted additions to corpus of an irrevocable trust.[36] Property remaining in a trust as a result of the exercise, release, or lapse of a power of appointment *may* constitute a constructive addition.[37] The exercise, release, or lapse of a general power of appointment over any portion of a pre-September 25, 1985 trust that is treated to any extent as a taxable transfer under Chapter 11 or Chapter 12 results in the value of the entire portion of the trust subject to the general power as withdrawn and immediately retransferred.[38] For exam-

---

[34] See Reg. § 26.2601-1(b)(5)(ii) Ex. 2. The effect of a corpus addition to an irrevocable trust is discussed infra ¶ 18.05[2][b][iii]. See also Priv. Ltr. Rul. 9644057 (Aug. 2, 1996) (beneficiaries' nonqualified disclaimers of interests in property held in trust established in 1970 and not subject to Chapter 13 were constructive additions to a trust and were subject to Chapter 13).

[35] See Reg. § 26.2601-1(b)(1).

[36] Reg. § 26.2601-1(b)(1)(v). See Reg. § 26.2601-1(b)(1)(i); Peterson Marital Trust v. Comm'r, 102 TC 79 (1994), aff'd, 78 F3d 795 (2d Cir. 1996). But see Simpson v. United States, 183 F3d 812 (8th Cir. 1999). See also infra note 38; Reg. § 26.2601-1(b)(1)(v)(D) Ex. 2 (illustrating *actual* additions, as opposed to *constructive* additions).

Numerous private letter rulings and technical advice memoranda address the question of whether a judicial amendment of a trust, an amendment by trustees pursuant to a power to amend included in the trust instrument, or a distribution in further trust constitutes a constructive addition. In response to the overwhelming number of ruling requests received, regulations have been issued to provide guidance with respect to the type of modifications that will not result in a constructive addition. See Reg. § 26.2601-1(b)(4); infra ¶ 18.05[2][e].

A modification may have the effect of changing the rights of the beneficiaries sufficiently to justify considering the trust as a new one created by the modification or as adding property to the trust after September 25, 1985.

[37] Reg. §§ 26.2601-1(b)(1)(v)(A), 26.2601-1(b)(1)(v)(B), 26.2601-1(b)(1)(v)(D).

[38] Reg. §§ 26.2601-1(b)(1)(v)(A), 26.2601-1(b)(1)(v)(D) Ex. 1, 26.2601-1(b)(1)(v)(D) Ex. 3. See Reg. § 26.2601-1(b)(1)(i). This transfer of property is treated as occurring when the exercise, release, or lapse of the power becomes effective in determining whether the transfer is a constructive addition to the trust that is subject to the tax imposed by Chapter 13. Reg. § 26.2601-1(b)(1)(v)(A). If any portion of the lapse is treated as a taxable transfer under Chapter 12, the rule applies even to the extent that the lapse is not treated as a release under Section 2041(b)(2) or Section 2514(e), referred to as the five-or-five exception. See Reg. § 26.2601-1(b)(1)(v)(D) Ex. 3. The treatment of general powers under the transitional rules differs from the treatment of powers suggested in ¶ 13.02[2][e][ii] with respect to the Chapter 13 taxation of such powers. See ¶ 13.02[2][e] text accompanying note 118.

To the extent that the property subject to the power is a taxable transfer under Chapters 11 and 12 (see Sections 2041 and 2514), it is as though the property were transferred to the power holder, who then retransferred it (as a constructive addition) to the trust. In this instance, the general power holder will be treated as the transferor. To the extent that there is no Chapter 13 or Chapter 12 taxable transfer, the creator of the power is treated as the transferor. See IRC § 2652(a); Reg. § 26.2601-1(b)(1)(v)(A). Cf. IRC § 2654(b)(1).

ple, assume *A* had a testamentary general power of appointment over the assets of an irrevocable trust created in 1980. The trust provides that on default of *A*'s exercise of the power, the property will continue to be held in the trust. On default of *A*'s exercise of the power at *A*'s death in 1988, the value of the entire trust is treated as if it were transferred to *A*, then retransferred to the trust as a tainted addition to corpus with *A* being the transferor.[39]

In general, property remaining in a grandfathered irrevocable trust after the release or lapse of a nongeneral power of appointment[40] over such property will not be treated as a tainted addition to corpus under the transitional rule.[41]

See also Priv. Ltr. Ruls. 9842060 (July 22, 1998) (failure to exercise pre-October 21, 1942, general power of appointment not constructive addition to grandfathered trust), 199923028 (Apr. 15, 1999) (proposed partial release of pre-October 22, 1942, general power of appointment where power holder retained testamentary general power not exercise or creation of power and not addition or distribution subjecting grandfathered trust to Chapter 13). The transfer of property for federal transfer tax purposes pursuant to the exercise, release, or lapse of a general power of appointment created in a pre-September 25, 1985, trust should not be treated as a transfer "under the exempt trust," but rather a transfer by the power holder occurring when the exercise, release, or lapse of the power becomes effective for purposes of determining whether or not the transfer is subject to the tax imposed by Chapter 13. See Reg. § 26.2601-1(b)(1)(i). This regulation was issued in response to, and takes a position contrary to, the decision in Simpson v. United States, 183 F3d 812 (8th Cir. 1999), where a generation-skipping transfer made pursuant to the exercise of a testamentary general power of appointment effective in 1993 under the terms of a trust that was irrevocable on September 25, 1985 (an "exempt" trust), was not subject to the generation-skipping transfer tax because it was a "generation-skipping transfer under a trust which was irrevocable on September 25, 1985." The regulations take a position consistent with the decision in Peterson Marital Trust v. Comm'r, 78 F3d 795 (2d Cir. 1996), where an inter vivos general power lapsed and the property subject to the general power was treated as an addition to the trust. See Supplementary Information, 64 Fed. Reg. 62,997, 62,998. See also, Bachler v. United States, 126 F. Supp. 2d 1279 (ND Cal. 2000) (following Peterson Marital Trust rejecting Simpson).

[39] Reg. §§ 26.2601-1(b)(1)(v)(A), 26.2601-1(b)(1)(v)(D) Ex. 1, 26.2601-1(b)(1)(v)(D) Ex. 3; Peterson Marital Trust v. Comm'r, 102 TC 79 (1994), aff'd, 78 F3d 795 (2d Cir. 1996). Depending on the date of *A*'s death, the outcome of this example may change if, instead, *A* executed a will on October 21, 1986. If *A* died before January 1, 1987, without exercising the power of appointment either in the will or before death, transfers pursuant to the will or under the trust will not be subject to Chapter 13 tax because the will qualifies as a grandfathered instrument and the trust is irrevocable. See Reg. § 26.2601-1(b)(5)(ii) Ex. 5. The outcome would be the same as in the example in the text if *A* died intestate before January 1, 1987. See Reg. § 26.2601-1(b)(5)(ii) Ex. 6. But see, Simpson v. United States, 183 F3d 812 (8th Cir. 1999) (exercise of a testamentary general power of appointment in 1993 over assets held in a trust which was irrevocable on September 25, 1985, appointing property to skip persons was a transfer under a trust which was irrevocable on September 25, 1985, and, therefore, was not subject to the tax imposed on generation-skipping transfers); supra text accompanying note 38.

[40] See Reg. § 26.2601-1(b)(1)(v)(B).

[41] Reg. § 26.2601-1(b)(1)(v)(B), especially Reg. § 26.2601-1(b)(1)(v)(B)(1). See Priv. Ltr. Rul. 199911008 (Dec. 4, 1998) (complete release of testamentary nongeneral power

However, property remaining in the trust as a result of the exercise of a nongeneral power in a manner that violates the common law Rule Against Perpetuities or the Uniform Statutory Rule Against Perpetuities will be considered a constructive tainted addition to the corpus.[42] A nongeneral power of appointment that is not exercised to postpone vesting beyond the prohibited period will not cause a constructive addition to the corpus of a grandfathered trust when the power is exercised.[43]

---

of appointment), Priv. Ltr. Rul. 199906003 (Oct. 19, 1998) (partial release of testamentary nongeneral power of appointment), Priv. Ltr. Rul. 199904001 (Oct. 19, 1998) (partial release of testamentary nongeneral power of appointment).

[42] Reg. § 26.2601-1(b)(1)(v)(B), especially Reg. § 26.2601-1(b)(1)(v)(B)(2). The prohibited period is the perpetuities period of lives in being at the creation of the trust plus twenty-one years plus, if necessary, a reasonable period of gestation. An exercise of a power of appointment will not be considered to violate the rule against perpetuities if it validly suspends ownership of an interest in property for a term of years not exceeding ninety years from the creation of the trust. If a power is exercised by creating another power, it is deemed to be exercised to whatever extent the second power may be exercised. Reg. § 26.2601-1(b)(1)(v)(B)(2). See Reg. §§ 26.2601-1(b)(1)(v)(D) Ex. 4, 26.2601-1(b)(1)(v)(D) Ex. 5, 26.2601-1(b)(1)(v)(D) Ex. 6, 26.2601-1(b)(1)(v)(D) Ex. 7. See also Gray, *The Rule Against Perpetuities* § 201 (4th ed. 1942).

For example, assume *B* has a nongeneral power of appointment over the assets of a trust created in 1982. If, in 1995, *B* exercises the power in favor of *C*'s children for their lives with a remainder to *C*'s grandchildren, assuming *C* is alive, the exercise of the power will cause a constructive addition to the corpus of the trust. *C* may have children born after the date of the creation of the trust whose lives would not be lives in being at the creation of the trust. The interest in *C*'s grandchildren does not vest until the last of *C*'s children dies. *C*'s last remaining child could have been a life not in being at the creation of the trust, and could survive *C*'s other children by more than twenty-one years. Therefore, vesting in *C*'s grandchildren would be postponed beyond the prohibited period. Because of this possibility, the portion of the trust subject to the power of appointment will be considered a tainted addition to the corpus of the trust by the creator of the trust. See also Reg. §§ 26.2601-1(b)(1)(v)(D) Ex. 4, 26.2601-1(b)(1)(v)(D) Ex. 5.

Another example may be helpful. Assume that prior to the effective date of Chapter 13 a grantor established an irrevocable trust giving the income to child, *C*, for life, and a testamentary power to *C* to appoint the remainder in further trust for the benefit of *C*'s children, and, in default, the property passes to charity. *C* dies in 1996 survived by a child, *GC*, who was alive when the trust was established and exercises the power to extend the trust. If the trust is extended for the life of *GC* plus twenty-one years, there is no constructive addition. Reg. § 26.2601-1(b)(1)(v)(D) Ex. 6. If it is extended for eighty years from creation, there is no constructive addition. Reg. § 26.2601(b)(1)(v)(D) Ex. 6. If it is extended until the first to occur of eighty years from creation or twenty-one years after the death of *GC*, there is no constructive addition. Reg. §§ 26.2601-1(b)(1)(v)(D) Ex. 6, 26.2601-1(b)(1)(v)(D) Ex. 7. If it is extended for the later of eighty years from creation or twenty-one years after the death of *GC*, there is a constructive addition. Reg. § 26.2601-1(b)(1)(v)(D) Ex. 6.

[43] Reg. § 26.2601-1(b)(1)(v)(B). See Priv. Ltr. Ruls. 9848018 (Aug. 27, 1998) (exercise of nongeneral power over trust exempt from generation-skipping transfer tax appointing trust property to new trust established under power holder's will not a constructive addition where perpetuities period measured from date of transfer creating

A constructive tainted addition may occur when a grandfathered irrevocable trust is relieved of any liability properly payable out of trust assets.[44] Thus, payment of a trust liability by the grantor is a constructive transfer to the trust on the date of payment. Similarly, if an estate fails to exercise a Section 2207A right of recovery with respect to a Section 2044 gross estate inclusion, the beneficiaries of the estate who bear the burden of the estate tax which could have been recovered under Section 2207A are considered to have made a transfer to the trust at the time the right of recovery lapses.[45] However, if a transferor makes a Section 2652(a)(3) election to treat the property as not qualified terminable interest property for Chapter 13 purposes, a reverse QTIP election, the beneficiaries of the estate who bear the burden of the estate tax are not treated as having made an addition to the trust by reason of the failure to exercise their right of recovery.[46]

[iii] Consequences when tainted corpus is added. A proportionate amount of every transfer out of an irrevocable trust in existence on September 25, 1985, to which a tainted corpus addition had been made, is subjected to the tax imposed by Chapter 13.[47] The amount is determined by multiplying every transfer from the trust by a fraction.[48] The numerator of the fraction is, in general, the fair market value of the addition to the trust on the date made; the denominator is, in general, the "total value of the entire trust"[49] immediately after the last addition.[50] If the addition to the corpus was a taxable generation-skipping transfer, both the numerator and denominator would be reduced

---

nongeneral power), 9839003 (June 19, 1998) (exercise of a nongeneral power of appointment to continue a trust exempt from generation-skipping transfer tax not a constructive addition).

[44] Reg. § 26.2601-1(b)(1)(v)(C).

[45] Reg. § 26.2601-1(b)(1)(v)(C). See also IRC § 2207B.

[46] Reg. § 26.2652-1(a)(5) Ex. 7. When the Section 2652(a)(3), reverse QTIP, election is made, the transferor of the property held in the trust is determined without regard to Section 2207A. Reg. § 26.2652-1(a)(3). The same rules should apply where the reverse QTIP election is deemed to have been made under Regulations Section 26.2601-1(b)(1)(iii)(A). See Priv. Ltr. Rul. 9627020 (Apr. 18, 1996).

[47] Reg. § 26.2601-1(b)(1)(iv)(A). See Reg. § 26.2601-1(b)(1)(iv). See supra ¶ 18.05[2][b][ii].

[48] Reg. § 26.2601-1(b)(1)(iv)(C). The fraction is required to be stated as a decimal fraction and rounded to five decimal places. Reg. § 26.2601-1(b)(1)(iv)(C)(1) (last sentence).

[49] The "total value of the entire trust" is generally the fair market value of the trust assets, reduced by any amount that would be similar to an amount allowed as a deduction under Section 2053. Reg. § 26.2601-1(b)(1)(iv)(C)(1).

[50] Reg. § 26.2601-1(b)(1)(iv)(C)(1). The computation is illustrated in Reg. §§ 26.2601-1(b)(1)(iv)(C)(2) Ex. 1, 26.2601-1(b)(1)(iv)(c)(2) Ex. 2. See also Reg. § 26.2601-1(b)(2)(v).

by the amount of any Chapter 13 tax imposed on the transfer and paid by the trust.[51]

Where multiple additions have been made to a grandfathered irrevocable trust, the fraction is revised after each addition.[52] The fair market value of the portion of the trust subject to Chapter 13 immediately before the latest addition is determined and added to the fair market value of the most recent addition to arrive at the numerator of the revised fraction.[53] The denominator of the revised fraction is the total value of the entire trust immediately after the addition.[54]

[c] Certain Wills and Revocable Trusts

Another transitional rule provides that Chapter 13 does not apply to generation-skipping transfers if: (1) they are made under a will executed prior to October 22, 1986, or from a revocable trust established prior to that date which was not amended after October 21, 1986 in a way that created or increased the amount of a generation-skipping transfer; (2) no impermissible additions were made to the trust; and (3) the decedent or grantor died before January 1, 1987.[55] Congressional thinking behind this amnesty is that such persons probably did not have sufficient notice of the revised generation-skipping tax laws to be able to amend their will or trust documents prior to death. In keeping with this line of thinking, Congress permitted such documents[56] to be amended[57] after October 21, 1986, if the amendments did not operate to create

---

[51] Reg. § 26.2601-1(b)(1)(iv)(C)(1).

[52] Reg. § 26.2601-1(b)(1)(iv)(C)(1).

[53] Reg. § 26.2601-1(b)(1)(iv)(C)(1).

[54] Reg. § 26.2601-1(b)(1)(iv)(C)(1). This computation is illustrated in Reg. §§ 26.2601-1(b)(1)(iv)(C)(2) Ex. 3, 26.2601-1(b)(1)(iv)(C)(2) Ex. 4. Both the numerator and denominator are reduced by the amount of any federal or state estate or gift tax imposed and subsequently paid by the recipient trust with respect to the most recent addition. Reg. § 26.2601-1(b)(1)(iv)(C)(1).

[55] Reg. § 26.2601-1(b)(2)(i). With respect to a qualified terminable interest property, rules comparable to those in supra ¶ 18.05[2][b] text accompanying notes 24–27 are to be applied. Reg. § 26.2601-1(b)(2)(iii).

[56] For purposes of the transitional rules, a revocable trust is any trust or trust equivalent arrangement except to the extent that (1) it was an irrevocable trust on October 22, 1986, or (2) it would have been an irrevocable trust on October 22, 1986, had it not been created or become irrevocable between September 25, 1985, and October 22, 1986. Reg. § 26.2601-1(b)(2)(ii).

[57] The amendment must become effective before it disqualifies the will or trust for this exception. If, for example, a codicil that would violate the requirements of this exception is executed but is subsequently revoked by a second codicil, then the first amendment will not disqualify the will. Compare Reg. § 26.2601-1(b)(2)(vii)(A) Ex. 4 with Reg. § 26.2601-1(b)(2)(vii)(A) Ex. 5).

or to increase the amount of any generation-skipping transfer[58] and, after that date, no additions were made to the revocable trust that created or increased the amount of any generation-skipping transfer.[59]

In two instances, an amendment to a will or revocable trust existing on October 21, 1986 will not be considered tainting even if it results in the creation or an increase in the amount of a generation-skipping transfer.[60] First, if the amendment was basically administrative, it was acceptable even though it incidentally increased the amount transferred.[61] For example, a codicil executed after October 21, 1986 to a will executed before that date removing one co-executor, thereby lowering the administrative costs and incidentally increasing the amount that can be transferred, would not cause a generation-skipping transfer under the will to be subject to the Chapter 13 tax.[62] Second, if the amendment was made to ensure that an existing bequest or transfer qualifies for the marital or charitable deduction, it would not taint a will or revocable trust otherwise protected by the transitional rule if the amount of a generation-skipping transfer under such will or from such trust is only incidentally increased.[63]

In some situations, it may not be immediately apparent whether an amendment has created or increased a generation-skipping transfer. For example, assume that an amendment made after October 21, 1986 to a revocable trust instrument adds a non-skip person to the class of remainder beneficiaries and provides that in the event the new beneficiary dies before the distribution, the new beneficiary's issue (who are skip persons) may take instead. In this situation, the amendment is presumed to create or increase the amount of a generation-skipping transfer, thereby disqualifying the trust for the exception, until a determination can be made.[64] Should events prove the amendment did

---

[58] Reg. § 26.2601-1(b)(2)(i)(A). Compare Reg. § 26.2601-1(b)(2)(vii)(B) Ex. 6 (no increase) with Reg. § 26.2601-1-1(b)(2)(vii)(b) Ex. 7 (creation of a generation-skipping transfer). The amendment must actually increase the amount that would have been received had the amendment not been made. For example, if, after October 21, 1986, a will, which was in existence on October 21, 1986, was amended to extinguish a specific bequest to a non–skip person, thus causing the bequest to fall into the estate residue (which contains generation-skipping provisions), then the transfers under the will are subject to Chapter 13. But if the potential beneficiary of the specific bequest predeceases the testator, and if local law would have caused the bequest to fall into the residue, then the amendment will not be considered to have increased a generation-skipping transfer. Reg. § 26.2601-1(b)(2)(vii)(A) Ex. 2.

[59] Reg. § 26.2601-1(b)(2)(i)(B). See also infra ¶ 18.05[2][e].

[60] Reg. § 26.2601-1(b)(2)(iv).

[61] Reg. § 26.2601-1(b)(2)(iv)(A).

[62] Reg. § 26.2601-1(b)(2)(vii)(A) Ex. 1.

[63] Reg. § 26.2601-1(b)(2)(iv)(B). But see Reg. § 26.2601-1(b)(2)(vii)(A) Ex. 3.

[64] Reg. § 26.2601-1(b)(2)(v).

neither, the Chapter 13 tax paid on any transfers from the trust can be recovered.[65]

In general, *any* addition to a revocable trust after October 21, 1986 will result in *all* subsequent generation-skipping transfers from the trust being subject to tax under Chapter 13.[66] However, additions after the death of the settlor to a grandfathered now irrevocable trust are afforded the same treatment as additions to an exempt irrevocable trust.[67]

[d] Mental Disability

Chapter 13 does not apply to any generation-skipping transfer made by an individual who was under a mental disability[68] on October 22, 1986 and thereafter until death,[69] provided the transfer is made under a trust[70] included in the individual's gross estate[71] or made by way of a testamentary direct skip.[72] Where the incompetent's property is held in a trust, this exception applies even if the person charged with the care of the incompetent's person or property has the power to revoke or modify the trust provisions as long as the person does not exercise that power after October 22, 1986 in a manner that increases the amount of generation-skipping transfers.[73] This rule does not apply to generation-skipping transfers made from a trust that is included in the incompetent's gross estate and which represents property transferred after October 22, 1986 by or for the incompetent individual during life.[74] This transitional rule protects individuals under a continuous mental disability, but it cannot be used by

---

[65] Reg. § 26.2601-1(b)(2)(vii)(B), Ex. 8. See also Reg. § 26.2601-1(b)(2)(vii)(A), Ex. 3.

[66] Reg. § 26.2601-1(b)(2)(vi).

[67] Reg. § 26.2601-1(b)(2)(vi). See Reg. § 26.2601-1(b)(1)(vi); supra ¶ 18.05[2][b][iii].

[68] Reg. § 26.2601-1(b)(3)(ii).

[69] Reg. § 26.2601-1(b)(3)(i).

[70] IRC §§ 2652(b)(1), 2652(b)(3). See Reg. § 26.2601-1(b)(3)(i)(A).

[71] Reg. § 26.2601-1(b)(3)(i)(A). See Priv. Ltr. Ruls. 9725014 (Mar. 19, 1997) (Section 2652(a)(3), reverse QTIP, election treated as made for a qualified terminable interest property held in trust not subject to Chapter 13 due to an individual's mental disability continuously from October 22, 1986, until death), 9735029 (June 2, 1997) (Section 2652(a)(3), reverse QTIP, election treated as made for a qualified terminable interest property held in trust created in June 1986 and amended in August 1986 not subject to Chapter 13 due to an individual's mental disability continuously from October 22, 1986, until death, although not in existence on September 25, 1985); supra ¶ 18.05[2][b] text accompanying notes 24–27.

[72] Reg. § 26.2601-1(b)(3)(i)(B).

[73] Reg. § 26.2601-1(b)(3)(v). See Reg. § 26.2601-1(b)(3)(vi) Ex.

[74] Reg. § 26.2601-1(b)(3)(i)(A) (parenthetical).

them or on their behalf to avoid the imposition of the generation-skipping transfer tax imposed on inter vivos transfers after October 22, 1986.

Mental disability, for purposes of this rule, means incompetence to execute an instrument governing the disposition of property.[75] This rule applies even if the mentally disabled individual has not been adjudicated mentally incompetent and no guardian of person or property has been appointed.[76] The rule applies only if the individual is continuously incompetent from October 22, 1986 until death.[77] If the individual has been adjudicated mentally incompetent on or before October 22, 1986 a copy of the judgment or decree and any modification thereof must be filed with Form 706.[78] If the individual has not been adjudicated mentally incompetent, the executor must demonstrate that the individual was mentally incompetent on October 22, 1986 and continuously thereafter until death.[79] This is accomplished by filing with Form 706 either a certification from a qualified physician,[80] other sufficient evidence of incompetency (provided a statement is filed explaining why no certification is available from a physician),[81] or any judgment or decree relating to the decedent's incompetency that was made after October 22, 1986.[82]

[e] Permissible Modifications to Exempt Trusts

Certain types of trust modifications will not affect a trust's exemption from the application of Chapter 13 under any one of the transitional rules.[83] A permissible modification may result from the exercise by a trustee of a discre-

---

[75] Reg. § 26.2601-1(b)(3)(ii).

[76] Reg. § 26.2601-1(b)(3)(ii).

[77] Reg. § 26.2601-1(b)(3)(i).

[78] Reg. § 26.2601-1(b)(3)(iv).

[79] Reg. § 26.2601-1(b)(3)(iii)(A).

[80] Reg. § 26.2601-1(b)(3)(iii)(A)(1).

[81] Reg. § 26.2601-1(b)(3)(iii)(A)(2).

[82] Reg. § 26.2601-1(b)(3)(iii)(A)(3). Any of these three items will be considered relevant, but not determinative, in establishing mental incompetency. Reg. § 26.2601-1(b)(3)(iii)(B).

A trust will not be disqualified from eligibility for the mental incompetency exemption solely as a result of failure to file the necessary documentation relating to the decedent's mental condition with the Form 706. See Priv. Ltr. Ruls. 9444016 (Aug. 2, 1994), 9437037 (June 21, 1994), 9335004 (May 18, 1993).

[83] See supra ¶¶ 18.05[2][b], 18.05[2][c], 18.05[2][d]. See also Harrington, McCaffrey, Plaine, Schneider, "Trust Modification Prop. Regs. and Other Significant GST Tax Developments," 92 J. Tax'n 212 (2000).

tionary power,[84] a court-approved settlement,[85] a judicial construction,[86] *or* a judicial or nonjudicial re-formation.[87] Although a modification may be neutral for Chapter 13 purposes, it may result in a taxable transfer for gift or income tax purposes or cause the trust to be included in the gross estate of a beneficiary.[88]

[i] **Trustee's discretionary powers.** A trustee may make a distribution of principal from one trust that is not subject to the provisions of Chapter 13 under any one of the transitional rules[89] to establish another new trust that will also be not subject to the provisions of Chapter 13 or retain trust principal in a continuing trust that will not cause the continuing trust to be subject to the provisions of Chapter 13, if two conditions are met.[90] First, the distribution or retention must be solely within the discretion of the trustee under the terms of the trust agreement[91] or authorized by state law at the time the exempt trust became irrevocable.[92] The first condition is not met if a beneficiary or court is required to consent to the distribution to the new trust or to the retention of trust principal in the continuing trust.[93] Second, the vesting of any beneficial interest in the trust pursuant to the governing instrument of the new or continuing trust must not be postponed beyond a perpetuities period[94] measured from the date the original trust became irrevocable.[95]

---

[84] Reg. § 26.2601-1(b)(4)(i)(A).

[85] Reg. § 26.2601-1(b)(4)(i)(B).

[86] Reg. § 26.2601-1(b)(4)(i)(C).

[87] Reg. § 26.2601-1(b)(4)(i)(D). The resolutions governing trust modifications are intended to diminish the need for private letter rulings regarding the effect of proposed modifications and constructions on an exempt trust. See Supplementary Information, 64 Fed. Reg. 62,997, 62,998.

[88] Reg. § 26.2601-1(b)(4)(i). See also Cottage Sav. Assoc. v. Comm'r, 499 US 554 (1991); Reg. § 1.1001-3.

[89] See supra ¶¶ 18.05[2][b], 18.05[2][c], 18.05[2][d].

[90] Reg. § 26.2601-1(b)(4)(i)(A). If the trustee uses a power of distribution to establish a new trust that is not a permissible modification of an exempt trust under the trustee's discretionary powers rule, it is possible that it may be treated as a permitted re-formation. See Reg. §§ 26.2601-1(b)(4)(i)(D), 26.2601-1(b)(4)(i)(E) Ex. 2; infra ¶ 18.05[2][e][iv].

[91] Reg. § 26.2601-1(b)(4)(i)(A)(1)(i).

[92] Reg. § 26.2601-1(b)(4)(i)(A)(1)(ii).

[93] Reg. § 26.2601-1(b)(4)(i)(A)(1).

[94] Reg. § 26.2601-1(b)(4)(i)(A)(2). The perpetuities period extends twenty-one years beyond any life in being at the date the original trust became irrevocable, plus if necessary, a reasonable period of gestation. Id. A distributive power that suspends vesting of property for a term of years that will not exceed ninety years measured from the date the original trust became irrevocable will not be considered beyond the perpetuities period. Id. If a trustee's distributive power is exercised by creating another power, it is deemed to be exercised to whatever the second power may be exercised. Id.

[95] Reg. § 26.2601-1(b)(4)(i)(A)(2).

For example, assume that Grantor established an irrevocable trust for the benefit of a child *C*, *C*'s spouse, and *C*'s issue that is exempt from the provisions of Chapter 13 under the transitional rules. The trust is to terminate upon the death of *C* and the principal is to be distributed to *C*'s issue, per stirpes. A corporate trustee has the power to distribute income or principal to any of the beneficiaries. Under the terms of the trust, the corporate trustee also has the discretion to distribute trust principal to one or more new trusts for the benefit of *C* or *C*'s issue under terms specified by the trustee. Any trust established by the trustee must terminate twenty-one years after the death of the last of *C*'s issue who was alive at the time of the establishment of the trust by Grantor. Assume that in the current year, without the need for approval of any beneficiary or court, the trustee distributes principal to establish a new trust for the benefit of *C*'s issue which will terminate upon the death of the last of *C*'s issue who was alive at the time Grantor established the trust. The terms of the new trust do not extend the time for vesting. Neither the trust established by Grantor nor the new trust established by the discretionary distribution of principal from Grantor's trust by the trustee is subject to the provisions of Chapter 13.[96]

[ii] Settlement. A reasonable[97] court-approved settlement[98] of a bona fide issue relating to the administration or the construction of terms of a trust will not affect the trust's exemption from the provisions of Chapter 13 under any of the transitional rules.[99]

[iii] Judicial construction. A court order in a proceeding that resolves an ambiguity in the terms of a trust agreement or corrects a scrivener's error will not cause a trust exempted from the provisions of Chapter 13 under any of the transitional rules to lose its exemption.[100] The proceeding must involve a bona fide issue,[101] and the construction must be consistent with the law that would

---

[96] This example is borrowed from the regulations. Reg. § 26.2601-1(b)(4)(i)(E) Ex. 1.

[97] The settlement must be "within the range of reasonable outcomes under the governing instrument and applicable state law addressing the issues resolved by the settlement." Reg. § 26.2601-1(b)(4)(i)(B)(2). For example, assume *A* and *B*, who are the sole remainder beneficiaries of a trust, disagree as to the portion each is to receive upon termination of the trust. A settlement dividing the corpus equally among *A*, *B*, and *C*, who is not a potential remainderperson under any construction of the trust agreement, would not be considered within the range of reasonable outcomes. Supplementary Information, 64 Fed. Reg. 62,997, 62,998.

[98] The settlement must be the product of arm's-length negotiations. Reg. § 26.2601-1(b)(4)(i)(B)(1).

[99] Reg. § 26.2601-1(b)(4)(i)(B).

[100] Reg. § 26.2601-1(b)(4)(i)(C). See Priv. Ltr. Rul. 200201020 (Oct. 2, 2001) (exempt status not affected by judicial reformation of scrivener's error).

[101] Reg. § 26.2601-1(b)(4)(i)(C)(1).

be applied by the state's highest court.[102] A court order construing the instrument does not alter or modify the terms of the instrument because it merely determines the settlor's intent at the time the instrument became effective.[103]

[iv] Other changes. A trust may be modified in a judicial or nonjudicial re-formation and retain its exemption from the provisions of Chapter 13 under any one of the transitional rules[104] as long as the modification does not shift a beneficial interest in the trust to a lower- or younger-generation-level beneficiary[105] nor extend the time for vesting of any beneficial interest in the trust beyond that initially specified in the trust agreement.[106] A change in trust situs,[107] a division of a trust,[108] a merger of two trusts,[109] a court-approved shift of income between beneficiaries,[110] conversion of an income interest into a unitrust interest,[111] allocation of capital gain to income,[112] or administrative changes to the trust terms[113] are all changes that may not subject the trust to the provisions of Chapter 13. A valid court-approved settlement, judicial construction or trustee's discretionary distribution that would subject a trust, initially qualifying for exemption from the provisions of Chapter 13 under any one of the transitional rules, to the provisions of Chapter 13 may not result in a loss of

---

[102] Reg. § 26.2601-1(b)(4)(i)(C)(2). See Reg. § 26.2601-1(b)(4)(i)(E) Ex. 3.

[103] See Supplementary Information, 64 Fed. Reg. 62,997, 62,998.

[104] Reg. § 26.2601-1(b)(4)(i)(D)(1). See ¶¶ 18.05[2][b], 18.05[2][c], 18.05[2][d].

[105] Reg. § 26.2601-1(b)(4)(i)(D)(1). A modification of a grandfathered trust will be treated as shifting a beneficial interest in the trust to a beneficiary in a lower generation if it results in either an increase in the amount of a generation-skipping transfer or the creation of a new generation-skipping transfer. Reg. § 26.2601-1(b)(4)(i)(D)(2). See Prop. Reg. § 26.2601-1(b)(4)(i)(D)(2). To make that determination, the effect of the instrument on the date of the modification is measured against the effect of the instrument in existence immediately before the modification. Reg. § 26.2601-1(b)(4)(i)(D)(2). If the effect of the modification cannot be determined, it will be deemed to have shifted a beneficial interest to a lower generation. Reg. § 26.2601-1(b)(4)(i)(D)(2).

[106] Reg. § 26.2601-1(b)(4)(i)(D)(1).

[107] See Reg. § 26.2601-1(b)(4)(i)(E) Ex. 4.

[108] See Reg. § 26.2601-1(b)(4)(i)(E) Ex. 5.

[109] See Reg. § 26.2601-1(b)(4)(i)(E) Ex. 6.

[110] See Reg. § 26.2601-1(b)(4)(i)(E) Ex. 7. The same result should be reached if the trustee had the power to legally shift the income between beneficiaries under the terms of the trust.

[111] See Reg. § 26.2601-1(b)(4)(i)(E) Ex. 8; Prop. Reg. § 26.2601-1(b)(4)(i)(E) Ex. 11. See also Priv. Ltr. Ruls. 200150016 (Sept. 12, 2001) (reformation of method of distribution no loss of exempt status), 200148034 (Aug. 29, 2001) (reformation of method of distribution no loss of exempt status).

[112] See Reg. § 26.2601-1(b)(4)(i)(E) Ex. 9; Prop. Reg. § 26.2601-1(b)(4)(i)(E) Ex. 12.

[113] See Reg. § 26.2601-1(b)(4)(i)(E) Ex. 10.

Chapter 13 exempt status if a beneficial interest is not shifted to a younger-generation beneficiary and the time for vesting is not extended.[114]

For example, assume that Grantor established an irrevocable trust for the benefit of a child C, C's spouse, and C's issue that is exempt from the provisions of Chapter 13 under the transitional rules. The corporate trustee has the power to distribute income or principal to any of the beneficiaries. The trust is to terminate upon the death of C and the principal is to be distributed to C's issue, per stirpes. Under state law, the corporate trustee had the power, with the consent of all beneficiaries, to distribute trust principal to a new trust as long as the exercise of discretion did not reduce the fixed income interest of any income beneficiary and was in favor of beneficiaries of the trust. In the current year, the trustee distributed one half of the trust's principal to a new trust that provides for the payment of trust income to C for life and the distribution of the remainder in equal shares to C's two children, or their issue, per stirpes. Because the modification does not shift any beneficial interest in the original trust to any younger-generation beneficiaries and the time for vesting of any beneficial interest is not extended beyond the period provided in the original trust, neither the trust nor the original trust will be subject to Chapter 13.[115]

¶ 18.06 REPEAL OF THE 1976 VERSION OF CHAPTER 13

Congress first attempted to impose a tax on generation-skipping transfers when it enacted Chapter 13 of the Code as part of the Tax Reform Act of 1976.[1] Owing to its complexity and its failure to tax generation-skipping transfers uniformly,[2] the 1976 version of Chapter 13 was retroactively repealed by the

---

[114] Reg. § 26.2601-1(b)(4)(i)(D).

[115] This example is borrowed from the regulations. See Reg. § 26.2601-1(b)(4)(i)(E) Ex. 2. The result in this example would not change if the corporate trustee had the power with the consent of the court upon notice to all of the parties to distribute trust principle. Id.

[1] Tax Reform Act of 1976, Pub. L. No. 94-455, § 2006, 90 Stat. 1520, 1879 (1976), reprinted in 1976-3 CB (Vol. 1) 1, 355. Chapter 13 was enacted on October 4, 1976, to operate retroactively to tax generation-skipping transfers made after June 11, 1976. Tax Reform Act of 1976, Pub L. No. 94-455, § 2006(c)(1), 90 Stat. 1520, 1889 (1976), reprinted in 1976-3 CB (Vol. 1) 1, 365, as amended by the Revenue Act of 1978, Pub. L. No. 95-600, § 702(n)(1), 92 Stat. 2767, 2935 (1978), reprinted in 1978-3 CB (Vol. 1) 1, 169.

[2] HR Rep. No. 426, 99th Cong., 1st Sess. 824 (1986), reprinted in 1986-3 CB (Vol. 2) 1, 824.

Tax Reform Act of 1986,[3] and it was replaced with another set of generation-skipping transfer tax provisions.[4] The 1986 Act provided that any assessments of tax that had been made under the first version of Chapter 13 were to be abated,[5] and any tax collected was to be credited or refunded with interest as an overpayment of tax.[6]

---

[3] Tax Reform Act of 1986, Pub. L. No. 99-514, § 1433(c)(1), 100 Stat. 2085, 2731 (1986), reprinted in 1986-3 CB (Vol. 1) 1, 648.

[4] Tax Reform Act of 1986, Pub. L. No. 99-514, §§ 1431–1433, 100 Stat. 2085, 2717–2732 (1986), reprinted in 1986-3 CB (Vol. 1) 1, 634–649.

[5] Tax Reform Act of 1986, Pub. L. No. 99-514, § 1433(c)(1), 100 Stat. 2085, 2731 (1986), reprinted in 1986-3 CB (Vol. 1) 1, 648.

[6] In general, the claim for a credit or refund had to be made before the expiration of the period for filing a claim as prescribed by Section 6511. However, if a refund or credit of any tax paid under the repealed version of Chapter 13 was barred by a statute of limitations on October 22, 1986, the statute of limitations was waived if the claim for refund or credit was filed before October 22, 1987. Tax Reform Act of 1986, Pub. L. No. 99-514, § 1433(c)(2), 100 Stat. 2085, 2731–2732 (1986), 1986-3 CB (Vol. 1) 1, 648–649.

PART V

Special Valuation Rules

CHAPTER 19

Special Valuation Rules

¶ 19.01 INTRODUCTION

[1] Estate Freeze Abuses

In general, estate freezes refer to actions taken by taxpayers with appreciating assets to stop or slow the growth in the estate tax value of certain of their assets while simultaneously transferring the future growth in value on those assets or value derived from them to younger generations at little or no transfer tax cost. The concept of estate freezes has long troubled the administrators of the transfer tax system. A major congressional action to curb a variety of types of estate freezes was the 1987 enactment of Section 2036(c),[1] which was substantially revised only one year later.[2] Section 2036(c) attempted to integrate a "cure" for numerous estate freeze schemes within the framework of the Code as it existed at the time by pulling the value of the entire entity as to which the freeze had been effected into the transferor's gross estate as a Section

---

[1] See ¶ 19.02[1]. Omnibus Budget Reconciliation Act of 1987, Pub. L. No. 100-203, § 10402(a), 100 Stat. 1330, 1431 (1987), reprinted in 1987-1 CB 1, 151.

[2] Technical and Miscellaneous Revenue Act of 1988, Pub. L. No. 100-647, § 3031, 102 Stat. 3342, 3634–3640 (1988), reprinted in 1988-3 CB 1, 294–300. See Blattmachr & Gans, "An Analysis of the Technical and Miscellaneous Revenue Act of 1988 Changes to the Valuation Freeze Rules," 70 J. Tax'n 14, 74 (1989).

2036(a)(1) retention of "enjoyment" of the property[3] and by finding an additional gift transfer on the relinquishment of a frozen interest or the transfer of a retained income interest.[4] Outcries that this mechanism, while meshing with existing Code provisions, nevertheless was vague, overly broad, unworkable, potentially unfair, and an inappropriate mechanism to deal with freezes resulted in its retroactive repeal in 1990.[5] Section 2036(c) was replaced by the special valuation rules of Chapter 14 of the Code.[6]

Chapter 14 consists of an independent set of special valuation rules also designed to combat abuses in certain estate freeze techniques.[7] These rules may be analyzed from two perspectives: by the conceptual approach taken to effect their purpose and by the mechanical workings of the provisions. Both perspectives must be understood to fully appreciate the workings of Chapter 14.[8]

Some estate freeze techniques manipulated the value of transfers with retained interests through recapitalizations that removed future appreciation in the recapitalized entity from the transferor's estate and through the exploitation of differences between actuarial values and real values. The congressional response of Chapter 14 is directed at particular abuses accomplished by a specific group of estate freeze transactions, which may occur in considerable variety. Therefore, much of the complexity of Chapter 14 is best understood in terms of the context against which it is directed.

Chapter 14 contains unique methods of valuation that differ from normal valuation mechanisms and from former approaches taken in response to estate freeze techniques. It consists of four Code sections, each of which operates in-

---

[3] IRC § 2036(c)(1) (repealed by the Omnibus Budget Reconciliation Act of 1990, Pub. L. No. 101-508, § 11601(a), 104 Stat. 1388-1, 1388-490 (1990), reprinted in 1991-2 CB 481, 524). See Stephens, Maxfield, Lind & Calfee, Federal Estate and Gift Taxation ¶ 4.08[9] (Warren, Gorham & Lamont, 6th ed. 1991). See also ¶ 19.02[1].

[4] IRC § 2036(c)(4) (repealed by the Omnibus Budget Reconciliation Act of 1990, Pub. L. No. 101-508, § 11602, 104 Stat. 1388-1, 1388-490 (1990), reprinted in 1991-2 CB 481, 524.). See ¶ 19.03. See also Stephens, Maxfield, Lind & Calfee, Federal Estate and Gift Taxation ¶ 4.08[9][d][ii] (Warren, Gorham & Lamont, 6th ed. 1991).

[5] Omnibus Budget Reconciliation Act of 1990, Pub. L. No. 101-508, § 11601, 104 Stat. 1388-1, 1388-490 (1990), reprinted in 1991-2 CB 481, 524.

[6] IRC §§ 2701–2704. Omnibus Budget Reconciliation Act of 1990, Pub. L. No. 101-508, § 11602, 104 Stat. 1388-1, 1388-490 (1990), reprinted in 1991-2 CB 481, 524. Chapter 14 is generally applicable to transfers made after October 8, 1990. Id. at § 602(e)(1).

[7] See, e.g., IRC §§ 2701(a)(3), 2702(a)(2), 2703(a), 2704(a).

[8] See Zaritsky & Aucutt, Structuring Estate Freezes Under Chapter 14 (Warren, Gorham & Lamont 1993) for a comprehensive discussion of Chapter 14 together with numerous forms, and Bogdanski, Federal Tax Valuation, Chapters 4–6 (Warren, Gorham & Lamont 1996). See also Harrison, "The Real Implications of the New Transfer Tax Valuation Rules—Success or Failure?" 47 Tax Law. (1994).

dependently, although there can be some overlap.[9] Section 2701 is aimed at curbing classic recapitalization estate freezes in which a frozen interest that does not have a fixed value in a corporate or partnership entity is retained and a growth interest is transferred to a family member.[10] Section 2702 attacks grantor retained income trusts (GRITs) and joint purchases of property where a transferor attempts to remove a remainder interest from the grantor's gross estate at little or no transfer tax cost.[11] Section 2703 applies to freezes in the form of various buy-sell agreements that are in the nature of a substitute for a testamentary disposition.[12] Finally, Section 2704 provides special rules for determining the effect of certain rights and restrictions that either exist or lapse at the time of valuation of an interest in a corporation or partnership.[13]

[2] Definitions

Two fundamental types of rules prevail throughout each of the four sections of Chapter 14. The first is a series of definitions that determine the overall scope and application of each provision. While attempting to avoid the overbreadth of Section 2036(c), the definitions under Chapter 14 provide flexibility to cover many variations in estate freeze techniques. Unfortunately, this means the definitions still result in considerable complexity and often counter-intuitive tax consequences. Chapter 14 thus represents its own self-contained mechanism in the sense that it comes complete with its own terms of art and approach. It represents the interests of a "transfer" tax, since the concept of a transfer is carefully defined and central to its operation and application. For example, as a result of the definitional approach to what constitutes an intrafamily transfer, the range of potentially subject transactions extends to some that would not otherwise be classified as transfers if they occurred between unrelated parties and to some that may not otherwise even be characterized as gifts.[14]

---

[9] See, e.g., ¶ 19.02[4][d][iv]; Reg. § 25.2704-1(c)(2)(ii).

[10] See ¶ 19.02. The term "partnership" as used in Sections 2701 and 2704 (see ¶ 19.05) should include a limited liability company that is a partnership for federal income tax purposes. See Priv. Ltr. Rul. 9947034 (Aug. 26, 1999) (Section 2701 potentially applicable to a limited liability company).

[11] See ¶ 19.03.

[12] See ¶ 19.04.

[13] See ¶ 19.05.

[14] See ¶ 19.02[2][a][i].

[3] Valuation

The second category of rules consists of the Chapter 14 valuation methodology and its concomitant assumptions. Once grasped, the application of the methodology is relatively straightforward, but may result in stark tax consequences. The pervasive theme in Chapter 14's approach can be roughly conceptualized as "estate maintenance." Wherever a transfer is deemed to occur through which the transferor is separated from a noncontemporaneous interest in and/or the appreciation from the transferred property, Chapter 14 will either (1) require valuation that imposes tax currently[15] or (2) force the transferor to accept the flow of an income stream that approximates the income and appreciation given up through the transfer.[16]

Unlike the approach of repealed Section 2036(c), Chapter 14 generally results in current recognition of a gift transfer and imposition of tax thereon, instead of future gross estate inclusion. Elections, however, are sometimes provided for those affected to opt in or out of certain provisions,[17] but a knowledgeable advisor is needed to point out and avail the taxpayer of such opportunities in a timely manner.

[4] Exceptions

Most important from a planning perspective are the exceptions created within the definitional framework of Chapter 14. Both the application and the tax consequences of the special valuation rules flow directly from compliance or noncompliance with strict definitional requirements. The framework generally provides for assumptions that adversely affect the taxpayer, unless a transaction fits within a specific exception. Where exceptions and exclusions exist, one of two themes is usually present. First, safe harbors exist where market safeguards or commercial reality operate to reasonably ensure arm's-length valuation.[18] Second, exceptions to unfavorable valuation are available when a retained interest is in a form that will pour sufficient income back into the transferor's estate as a surrogate for forgone income and appreciation.[19]

Estate planners will spend most of their efforts under Chapter 14 in structuring transactions to fit within the exceptions. However, a word of caution: Much of the effect of Chapter 14 is to create transfers where historically they have never before occurred. One must keep the principles of Chapter 14 firmly

---

[15] See, e.g., IRC §§ 2701(a)(3), 2702(a)(2)(A), 2703(a).

[16] See, e.g., IRC §§ 2701(d), 2702(a)(2)(B), 2702(b).

[17] See, e.g., IRC § 2701(c)(3)(C).

[18] See, e.g., ¶¶ 19.04[3], 19.04[4], 19.05[2][c].

[19] See, e.g., ¶¶ 19.02[3], 19.03[3].

in mind with respect to most estate plans, because the sections can appear on the scene when one least expects them.

¶ 19.02 SECTION 2701. SPECIAL VALUATION RULES

[1] Introduction

Section 2701 represents the latest congressional effort to curb certain types of estate freezes. Regrettably, simply reading the language contained in the statute sheds little light on either the problem that Congress is attempting to address or on the statutory solution to the problem.

[a] The Nature of an Estate Freeze

An understanding of the nature of an estate freeze is necessary in order to understand Section 2701. An estate freeze is a technique that has the effect of limiting the estate tax value of a property interest held by a member of an older generation at the time it is frozen and passing any subsequent appreciation in the value of the interest to a member of a younger generation without the imposition of any transfer tax on that appreciation.

One type of estate freeze involves the bifurcation of an entity into two interests, a frozen interest and a growth interest.[1] At the time of the bifurcation, the frozen interest[2] has a value that usually approximates the total value of the entity, while the growth interest[3] has little or no value. However, the growth interest has characteristics that permit it to absorb all future appreciation in the value of the entity. It is common for the frozen interest to retain income from and control over the entity. Although this type of estate freeze may take many forms,[4] it is most commonly the result of a tax-free recapitalization of a corporate or partnership entity and the creation of both frozen and growth equity interests with a retention of the frozen interest in an older generation and a transfer of the growth interest to a younger generation.

---

[1] Numerous articles discuss estate freezes prior to the enactment of Section 2701. See Elias, "Preferred Stock Recapitalizations: Income, Estate, and Gift Tax Issues," 13 J. Corp. Tax'n 332 (1987); Elias, "The Partnership Capital Freeze: A Path Through the Maze," 40 Tax Law. 45 (1986); Abbin, "The Value-Capping Cafeteria—Selecting the Appropriate Freeze Technique," 15 U. Miami Inst. Est. Plan. ch. 20 (1981).

[2] The frozen interest is a senior equity interest. See infra ¶ 19.02[2] note 25.

[3] The growth interest is a subordinate equity interest. See infra ¶ 19.02[2] note 24.

[4] Twelve freeze methods are described in Abbin, "The Value-Capping Cafeteria—Selecting the Appropriate Freeze Technique," 15 U. Miami Inst. Est. Plan. at 2014 (1981).

To illustrate, assume that an individual *A* owns all the stock of a corporation that owns *A*'s business.[5] *A* intends to leave the business to child *C* at death, but until *A*'s death, *A* wishes to retain control of the corporation and an income flow roughly equal to the current income generated by the business. At the same time, *A* wants to minimize the estate tax consequences of holding the business until death and to encourage *C*'s active involvement in the business by giving *C* a present stake in the future appreciation in the corporation. An estate freeze potentially accomplishes all of *A*'s objectives. First, in a nontaxable corporate reorganization,[6] *A*'s common stock is exchanged for two new classes of stock. One class is voting preferred stock with a liquidation preference placing a cap on its value equal to the present value of the business and with a dividend preference equal to the present income stream of the business. The other class is common stock (with either no or minority voting rights) having little or no current value but, because of the capped or frozen value of the preferred stock, the ability to absorb all future increases in the value of the business. *A* completes the freeze by giving or selling (for its nominal fair market value) the common stock to *C*.

The preferred stock in this example is "frozen" because its maximum value is established by its rights on liquidation. The common stock is not frozen, because any appreciation in the company's value will be reflected in an increase in the value of the common stock. Without special legislation, the transfer of the common stock is made with minimal gift tax consequences. To minimize those consequences there is a strong incentive to appear to attach as much value as possible to the frozen interest and indirectly reduce the value of the growth interest. This is commonly done by adding transferor-controlled discretionary rights (commonly referred to as bells and whistles) to the frozen interest. The discretionary rights arguably inflate the value of the frozen interest and concurrently reduce the value of the gifted growth interest. Additionally, the discretionary rights can be designed so that their value evaporates from nonpayment or nonexercise; as that occurs, the value is indirectly absorbed by the growth interest. Upon *A*'s death, only the frozen preferred stock is includible in *A*'s gross estate,[7] since *A* retains no testamentary interest in or power over the common stock.[8]

---

[5] Although the example assumes that the entity holds *A*'s business, the entity could hold any type of property, such as personal or business real estate, investments, stocks and bonds, or any combination of properties.

[6] See IRC § 368(a)(1)(E). A similar nontaxable restructure could occur if the entity were a partnership. See IRC §§ 721–723, 731–733.

[7] The preferred stock is included under Section 2033. Cf. IRC § 2704, discussed ¶ 19.05.

[8] See IRC §§ 2035–2038. Section 2036(b) is not applicable because *A* does not have the right to vote the common stock. See ¶ 4.08[6][d].

There are numerous variations on the basic estate freeze.[9] A freeze may also carried out in a similar manner through a partnership entity, creating frozen and growth equity interests in the partnership with results comparable to the corporate freeze technique.

[b] Prior Attacks on Freezes

Initially, the Service attempted both administrative and judicial attacks on freezes in an attempt to prevent the reduction of the transfer tax base. The Service first attempted to place greater value on the growth interest under the gift tax[10] and later attempted to have the growth interest pulled into decedent's gross estate as a retained enjoyment of property under Section 2036(a).[11] Neither of the Service's initial efforts was particularly successful.

Having been essentially unsuccessful on both the administrative and judicial fronts, the Treasury subsequently turned to Congress for assistance in curbing the estate freeze. Congress responded first by enacting Section 2036(c).[12] If the requirements of Section 2036(c) were met,[13] there was a Section 2036(a)(1) retention of the "enjoyment" of the transferred growth interest

---

[9] Freezes may take other forms. See ¶ 19.03 (dealing with grantor retained interest trusts (GRITs) and joint purchases), supra note 4.

[10] In Revenue Ruling 83-120, 1983-2 CB 170, the Service attacked the valuation of the inter vivos transfer of common stock by looking at significant factors in deriving the value of both types of stock in a freeze situation, such as their voting, dividend, and liquidation rights, as well as the common stock's exclusive rights to future appreciation. See also Rev. Rul. 83-119, 1983-2 CB 57 (treating a redemption premium to be paid on preferred stock in excess of its issue price as a Section 305(b)(4) stock distribution constructively received over the holder's life expectancy).

[11] Estate of Boykin v. Comm'r, 53 TCM (CCH) 345 (1987). See Estate of Harrison v. Comm'r, 52 TCM (CCH) 1306 (1987). See also Abbin & Kukin, "Have They Nuked the Freeze? Evaluating the Impact of Recent Decisions, Regulations, and Rulings," 19 U. Miami Inst. Est. Plan. ch. 5 (1985).

[12] See ¶ 19.01[1] text accompanying notes 1–4. Section 2036(c) also dealt with other estate freezing techniques, such as GRITs. See ¶ 19.03; IRC § 2036(c)(4) (repealed by the Omnibus Budget Reconciliation Act of 1990, Pub. L. No. 101-508, § 11601, 104 Stat. 1388-1, 1388-490 (1990), reprinted in 1991-2 CB 481, 524).

[13] Section 2036(c) required a transfer of a growth interest in an "enterprise" in which the decedent owned a "substantial interest" where the transferor retained "an interest in the income of, or rights in" the enterprise and the property transferred bore a "disproportionately large share of the potential appreciation" in the enterprise. IRC § 2036(c) (repealed retroactively), supra note 12.

Section 2036(c) is discussed in more detail in Stephens, Maxfield, Lind & Calfee, Federal Estate and Gift Taxation ¶ 4.08[9] (Warren, Gorham & Lamont, 6th ed. 1991); Averitt, "Entity Freezes—Corporations, Partnerships, and Trusts: A Practitioner's View of What's Left After Section 2036(c)," 14 Notre Dame Tax & Est. Plan. at 4-1 (Oct. 1988); Eastland, "Saving the Closely-Held Business After Congress Made Enterprise a Dirty Word," 47 NYU Inst. on Fed. Tax. ch. 20-1 (1989).

and the appreciated growth interest was pulled into the transferor's gross estate[14] along with the frozen interest.[15] Although the goal of Section 2036(c) was to eliminate the estate tax benefits of valuation freezes, the scope of the statutory language exceeded that goal and the section had the potential to achieve some far-reaching and uncertain results.[16] In 1990, the outcry against Section 2036(c) led Congress to retroactively repeal the Section and to enact Sections 2701 through 2704 (Chapter 14) to deal with several types of estate freezes.[17]

[c] Section 2701

Section 2701 is a gift tax provision that attacks the basic estate freeze transaction by establishing rules that tend to place minimal valuation on a retained frozen interest, thereby increasing both the value of the growth interest and the amount of the gift upon its transfer.[18] The special valuation rules of Section 2701 potentially apply when a transferor transfers a growth interest in a corporation or partnership, generally to a younger-generation family member, while a frozen interest, statutorily labelled an "applicable retained interest," generally with various discretionary rights (the bells and whistles), is retained by the transferor or by an ancestor of the transferor. Under Section 2701, the retained discretionary rights[19] are conclusively presumed to be worthless and are assigned a zero valuation on the basis of an underlying premise that they will never be exercised by a senior-generation member motivated to remove value from such member's gross estate. The value of the transferred growth interest is then determined by subtracting the Section 2701 value of the retained frozen interest from the value of the entire entity. This process transfers the

---

[14] Section 2036(c) reached property interests distinctly different from those historically encompassed by Section 2036(a). Property included in a decedent's gross estate under Section 2036 as a result of Section 2036(c) was generally a freestanding present interest in property rather than a mere future interest in property, such as a remainder. Cf. IRC § 2036(b).

[15] IRC § 2033. See supra ¶ 19.02[1][a] note 7.

[16] See Stephens, Maxfield, Lind & Calfee, Federal Estate and Gift Taxation ¶ 4.08[9][c] (Warren, Gorham & Lamont, 6th ed. 1991).

[17] See supra note 12; ¶ 19.01. See Begleiter, "Estate Planning in the Nineties: Friday the Thirteenth, Chapter 14: Jason Goes to Washington—Part I," 81 Kent. LJ 535 (1992–1993).

[18] Additionally, Section 2701 requires such value as is placed on the retained frozen interest to the supported by actual distributions to the owner of the interest, which will normally tend to increase the gross estate of the owner.

[19] The discretionary rights may be either noncumulative distribution rights (which may never be paid by the entity) or extraordinary payments rights (liquidation rights, puts, calls, conversion rights, or other similar rights that may never be exercised by their holder). See infra ¶ 19.02[2][b][ii].

value of the discretionary rights from the frozen interest to the growth interest, increasing the amount of the gift transfer.[20] If Section 2701 applies, the retained frozen interest may be valued at zero at the time the growth interest is transferred, resulting in a gift transfer of the full value of the entity or it may be valued at some higher amount dependent upon its terms. Whenever Section 2701 applies to a transfer, a minimum value is placed on every transferred growth interest to reflect its potential appreciation in value.[21] As a result of these valuation rules, when Section 2701 applies, to some extent it accelerates the transfer tax on the transferor's interest in the entity.[22] The transfer tax treatment of a basic estate freeze has shifted from taxation of only the transferor's frozen interest in the entity at transferor's death, to inclusion of the appreciated value of the entity in the transferor's gross estate, under Section 2036(c) and now to an increase in the amount of the gift transfer by an acceleration of the transfer tax on the frozen interest.[23]

Section 2701 is subject to several exceptions and special rules that are examined after consideration of its general statutory requirements.

---

[20] See infra ¶ 19.02[4][d].

[21] IRC § 2701(a)(4). See infra ¶ 19.02[4][f].

[22] Section 2701 may be inapplicable to the generation-skipping transfer tax; if so, the freeze device would still be effective for generation-skipping transfer tax purposes. See infra ¶ 19.02[5][f][iii]. Compare repealed Section 2036(c), which would have resulted in a direct skip of the appreciated value of the entity to a skip person at transferor's death. See IRC § 2642(f)(1) (last sentence); ¶ 16.02[7].

[23] While Section 2701 requires the transferor to prepay as gift tax some portion of the estate tax that would otherwise be imposed on the frozen interest at death and to pay gift tax on the value of the discretionary rights that would not otherwise be subject to transfer tax, transactions subject to Section 2701 may still offer some transfer tax advantages. First, post-gift appreciation in the value of the entity continues to avoid inclusion in the transferor's transfer tax base even though the transferor may continue to enjoy income generated by the asset "transferred" under Section 2701. Second, while some portion of the gift tax payment is a prepayment of estate tax and the transferor is deprived of the use of the money required to pay that gift tax, if the transferor survives the transfer by more than three years, the transferor's overall tax base is reduced by the amount of the gift tax incurred. See IRC § 2035(b), discussed at ¶ 4.07[3]. This results in a prepayment of estate tax with dollars that are not included in the transfer tax base. See IRC § 2001(b)(2). Disregarding any discretionary rights that would otherwise totally avoid inclusion in the transfer tax base, in some situations the exclusion of the gift tax from the transfer tax base may work to the transferor's overall transfer tax advantage. This would occur where the exclusion of the taxes from the transfer tax base saves more tax dollars than the income that could have been generated if the gift tax dollars had been retained. For example, assuming a flat 40 percent transfer tax rate, if Section 2701 resulted in a $1 million gift that required Taxpayer to pay $400,000 of gift tax and Taxpayer lived for more than three years after the gift, Taxpayer would remove the $400,000 from the transfer tax base and save $160,000 (40 percent of $400,000) in transfer taxes. One must weigh that savings against the net income that could be earned on the $400,000 and the increased transfer tax on that net income to determine whether a transaction subject to Section 2701 hurt or helped the taxpayer.

[2] The Requirements of Section 2701

The special valuation rules of Section 2701 essentially apply only if two basic requirements are met:

1. There must be a transfer of a growth interest referred to as a subordinate equity interest[24] in a partnership or a corporation to (or for the benefit of) a younger generation member of the transferor's family; and
2. A frozen "senior equity interest"[25] with certain rights statutorily labeled an "applicable retained interest" must be held by the transferor or an older generation applicable family member immediately after the transfer.

[a] The First Requirement

The first statutory requirement of Section 2701 is that there must be *a transfer of an interest in a corporation or partnership to (or for the benefit of) a member of the transferor's family.*[26]

[i] Definition of a transfer. The term "transfer" is interpreted broadly under Section 2701 and includes both indirect as well as direct transfers.[27] However, there is a Section 2701 transfer only if the transferor relinquishes sufficient dominion and control over the subordinate equity interest to constitute a completed transfer for gift tax purposes.[28] If there is no completed transfer of the subordinate equity interest under the gift tax rules, Section 2701 does not apply to increase the value of that interest until the transfer is com-

---

[24] A subordinate equity interest is an equity interest in an entity that has rights that are subordinate to a senior equity interest. Cf. Reg. § 25.2701-3(a)(2)(iii). Technically, Section 2701 applies only if the senior equity interest is an "applicable retained interest" in an entity. See IRC § 2701(b); infra ¶ 19.02[2][b][ii]). Thus under Section 2701, a subordinate equity interest is an interest in an entity as to which an applicable retained interest is a senior equity interest. Reg. § 25.2701-3(a)(2)(iii).

[25] A senior equity interest is an equity interest in an entity that has rights to distributions of income or capital that have preference over the rights of other "subordinate" equity interests. Cf. Reg. § 25.2701-3(a)(2)(ii).

[26] IRC § 2701(a)(1).

[27] See IRC § 2701(e)(5). For example, an indirect Section 2701 transfer occurs if Transferor owns an applicable retained interest and a subordinate equity interest in an entity and Family Member also owns a subordinate equity interest in the entity and Transferor transfers some or all of the subordinate equity interest to the entity for no consideration. See Reg. § 25.2511-1(h)(1). The transfer is not within the scope of a contribution to capital or a capital structure transaction (see infra text accompanying notes 30–45), but it is nevertheless an indirect Section 2701 transfer.

[28] See Reg. § 25.2701-1(b)(1); ¶¶ 10.01[4], 10.01[9].

plete. However, in determining whether a direct or indirect transfer occurs, the completed transfer need not constitute a "taxable" gift under Chapter 12 of the Code. If Section 2701 is otherwise applicable, it applies even if adequate and full consideration in money or money's worth is received for the interest transferred.[29] If a completed transfer of the subordinate equity interest is made in return for adequate and full consideration, the statute could be circumvented easily if the transfer is not treated as a Section 2701 transfer. Because the value of the subordinate equity interest is usually minimal, the receipt of a small amount of consideration could be used to avoid Section 2701 and the performance of its function of curtailing freeze transactions.

Contributions to Capital. A direct or indirect contribution to capital of a new or an existing entity is an indirect transfer,[30] which triggers Section 2701 if freeze consequences occur as a result of the contribution.[31] The regulations do not specifically define the term "contribution to capital." The term likely includes a transfer of money or property (other than an equity interest in the entity)[32] to a newly formed or existing entity in return for an interest in the entity or for no consideration. For example, if Parent and Child form a partnership or corporation with each contributing cash or property equal in value to the equity interests they receive in the new entity, and Parent receives a senior equity interest while Child receives a subordinate equity interest, there is a contribution to capital that is treated as an indirect transfer for purposes of Section 2701.[33] Similarly, if Parent, who owns a senior equity interest in an entity in which Child owns a subordinate equity interest, transfers cash or

---

[29] Reg. § 25.2701-1(b)(1). See Reg. §§ 25.2701-3(d) Exs. 4, 5; IRC §§ 2512(b), 2702(a)(3)(B), 2702(c)(2) (imposing similar rules for purposes of Section 2702). See also ¶¶ 19.03[2][a][i], 19.03[4][a].

[30] IRC § 2701(e)(5). Reg. § 25.2701-1(b)(2)(i)(A). See Reg. § 25.2701-1(b)(2)(i)(C); infra text accompanying note 48 (involving indirect contributions to capital).

[31] Compare IRC § 2701(e)(5) (requiring that freeze consequences result from a contribution to capital in order for the contribution to be a transfer) and Priv. Ltr. Rul. 9427023 (July 8, 1994) (applying Reg. § 25.2701-1(b)(3)(i) and holding that a contribution to capital was not a transfer where no freeze consequences occurred because family members held the same interests prior to and after the transaction) with Reg. § 25.2701-1(b)(2)(i)(A) (imposing no such requirement). The introductory clause to Section 2701(e)(5) allows the regulations to provide exceptions to the statute. The issue whether a contribution to capital where freeze consequences do not occur constitutes a Section 2701 "transfer" is academic, because if freeze consequences are not present, even though a "transfer" occurs, the other Section 2701 requirements will not be satisfied and Section 2701 will not apply.

[32] A "capital structure transaction," which is distinguished from a "contribution to capital" (see Reg. §§ 25.2701-1(b)(2)(i)(A), 25.2701-1(b)(2)(i)(B)), involves a transfer of an equity interest in an existing entity to the entity for consideration. See text infra accompanying notes 35–45.

[33] IRC § 2701(e)(5)(A).

property to the entity and receives no consideration, there is a transfer by Parent for purposes of Section 2701.[34]

Capital Structure Transactions. A redemption, recapitalization, or other change in the capital structure of an existing entity, referred to as a capital structure transaction,[35] is also treated as a transfer for purposes of Section 2701 if freeze consequences occur as a result of the transaction.[36] Generally, there are three situations in which a capital structure transaction will constitute a transfer for purposes of Section 2701. First, if a transferor or an applicable family member[37] receives an applicable retained interest[38] in a capital structure transaction, a transfer is deemed to occur.[39] For example, if Parent and Child both hold common stock in a corporation and Parent exchanges the common stock for preferred stock, the redemption constitutes an indirect transfer subject to Section 2701.[40] Similarly, if there is a recapitalization of the corporation and Parent receives preferred stock and Child receives common stock, a transfer subject to Section 2701 also occurs.

The second and third forms of capital structure transactions require a comparison of the equity interests in the entity both before and after the transaction. In the second situation, if the transferor or an applicable family member holding an applicable retained interest before a capital structure transaction surrenders a subordinate equity interest and receives property other than an applicable retained interest,[41] there is a capital structure transaction and an indirect transfer.[42] For example, if Parent owns both preferred stock and common stock and Child owns common stock in a corporation and if Parent's common stock is redeemed for cash, there is a capital structure transaction that is treated as a transfer under Section 2701. Child's common stock ownership percentage has increased just as if Parent had transferred the common stock directly to Child.

---

[34] IRC § 2701(e)(5)(B); Reg. § 25.2701-1(b)(2)(i)(A).

[35] Reg. § 25.2701-1(b)(2)(i)(B).

[36] IRC § 2701(e)(5); Reg. § 25.2701-1(b)(2)(i)(B). See supra note 31 considering whether freeze consequences are required to find a "transfer" on a contribution to capital.

[37] An "applicable family member" (essentially a senior generation family member of transferor's family) is defined in Section 2701(e)(2), which is discussed infra ¶ 19.02[2][b][i].

[38] An "applicable retained interest" (essentially a frozen interest) is defined in Section 2701(b), which is discussed infra ¶ 19.02[2][b][ii].

[39] Reg. § 25.2701-1(b)(2)(i)(B)(1).

[40] Reg. §§ 25.2701-3(d) Exs. 4, 5. In such a situation, if the preferred stock has a Section 2701 zero valuation, Parent is treated as making a gift transfer of the value of Parent's common stock to Child. Id.

[41] If an applicable retained interest is received, the first type of capital structure transaction occurs. See supra text accompanying notes 37–40.

[42] Reg. § 25.2701-1(b)(2)(i)(B)(2).

In the third situation, if a transferor or an applicable family member holds an applicable retained interest and surrenders an equity interest (other than a subordinate equity interest) and, as a result, the fair market value of the applicable retained interest is increased, there is a capital structure transaction and an indirect transfer subject to Section 2701.[43] For example, if Parent holds two types of preferred stock and Child holds common stock in a corporation and Parent transfers one class of preferred stock to the corporation and the transfer has the effect of increasing the value of the other preferred stock, there is an indirect transfer subject to Section 2701.

A capital structure transaction is not treated as a transfer under Section 2701 if the transferor, each applicable family member, and each member of the transferor's family hold substantially identical interests[44] both before and after the transaction, because freeze consequences do not occur as a result of the transaction.[45]

Indirect Transfers under the Attribution Rules. Section 2701 contains a series of comprehensive attribution of entity ownership rules that apply in the determination of whether and when a Section 2701 transfer occurs.[46] An indirect transfer can occur where a transferor owns an applicable retained interest in one entity and also owns an interest in another entity that owns a subordinate equity interest in the first entity. If the transferor transfers an interest in the second entity to a family member or if the second entity transfers the subordinate equity interest to a family member, an indirect transfer occurs.[47] For example, assume Parent owns preferred stock in Corporation *X* and also

---

[43] Reg. § 25.2701-1(b)(2)(i)(B)(3).

[44] In applying this rule, common stock with nonlapsing voting rights and nonvoting common stock are interests that are substantially the same. Reg. § 25.2701-1(b)(3)(i).

[45] IRC § 2701(e)(5) (flush language); Reg. § 25.2701-1(b)(3)(i). See Priv. Ltr. Ruls. 9511028 (Dec. 16, 1994), 9241014 (July 8, 1992), 9309018 (Dec. 3, 1992), 9947034 (Aug. 26, 1999) (each finding no transfer under Section 2701(e)(5)). See also Priv. Ltr. Rul. 9427023 (July 8, 1994), discussed supra note 31.

See Kasner, "How Recapitalization of Family Business Interests Affects Interests Held in Trust," 60 Tax Notes 1740 (Sept. 27, 1993), discussing the possibility of a "post-mortem" freeze in light of Private Letter Ruling 9321046 (Feb. 25, 1993). In that private ruling, the taxpayer proposed a pro rata recapitalization and the Service applied Regulations Section 25.2701-1(b)(3)(i) only to those shares issued outright to the transferor and not to the shares owned by a trust of which the transferor was an income beneficiary, but which trust was not included in the transferor's gross estate because no Section 2056(b)(7) QTIP election had been made.

The need for the substantially identical interests exception may be questioned in view of the statutory exception under Section 2701(a)(2)(C), which would otherwise seem to except the transfer from Section 2701. See infra ¶ 19.02[3][c].

[46] Reg. § 25.2701-6. The attribution of entity ownership rules and the situations in which they are applicable are considered in detail infra ¶ 19.02[2][d].

[47] Transferor owns an interest in the entity holding the subordinate equity interest. Reg. §§ 25.2701-6(a)(2), 25.2701-6(a)(3), 25.2701-6(a)(4). Transferor's indirect ownership

owns all the stock in Corporation Y, which holds common stock in Corporation X further assume that Parent transfers the Corporation Y stock to Child or Corporation Y transfers the common stock in Corporation X to Child. Parent has made an indirect transfer of the Corporation X subordinate equity interest to Child. The indirect transfer rules also apply where there is a contribution of capital by an entity to the extent that it is owned directly or indirectly by the transferor.[48]

Under the attribution rules, the transferor is generally attributed ownership of any subordinate equity interest held in the corpus of a grantor trust where the transferor is treated as the owner of the trust for income tax purposes.[49] An indirect transfer may occur when the transferor relinquishes the rights retained with respect to the property held in the grantor trust that caused it to be a grantor trust.[50] Since no Section 2701 transfer occurs until there is a transfer that is complete for gift tax purposes,[51] the timing of a Section 2701 transfer is often the same under both the completed gift transfer rule and the relinquishment of the rights causing the trust to be a grantor trust attribution rules. For example, if Grantor holds an applicable retained interest and transfers a subordinate equity interest to a revocable trust for the benefit of Child, there is a transfer subject to Section 2701 of the corpus of the trust under both rules when the power of revocation is relinquished.[52]

However, a transfer subject to Section 2701 may occur on the funding of a trust even though the grantor trust rules apply to the trust. When a subordinate equity interest is transferred to a trust in a transfer that is complete

---

of the subordinate equity interest is terminated upon a completed transfer of that entity interest.

[48] Reg. § 25.2701-1(b)(2)(i)(C). For example, if Transferor owns an applicable retained interest in Corporation X and Child owns a subordinate equity interest in Corporation X and Transferor also owns Corporation Y and Corporation Y makes a contribution to capital of Corporation X, Transferor makes an indirect transfer to Child subject to Section 2701. See Reg. § 25.2701-1(b)(2)(i)(C)(2).

[49] Reg. § 25.2701-6(a)(4)(ii)(C).
A person other than the grantor may also be treated as the owner of the corpus of a trust under Section 678 for income tax purposes, for example, where the person other than the grantor holds a general power of appointment over the trust corpus. If the corpus of the trust holds a subordinate equity interest, a completed gift exercise of the general power in favor of a family member would result in a Section 2701 transfer. Reg. § 25.2701-1(b)(2)(i)(C)(1). See infra note 62.

[50] Reg. § 25.2701-1(b)(2)(i)(C)(1).

[51] See supra text accompanying note 28; ¶¶ 10.01[4]–10.01[9].

[52] See IRC § 676; Reg. § 25.2511-2(c). Similarly if the donor retains a power to alter the income beneficiaries (see IRC § 674; Reg. § 25.2511-2(b)) and the donor relinquishes the power to alter the beneficiaries, there is a Section 2701 transfer when the power is relinquished at a time when there is both a Section 2511 transfer and a relinquishment of the Section 674 grantor trust power. Cf. Rev. Rul. 83-51, 1983-1 CB 48 (treating the grantor as owning the property for all income tax purposes).

for gift tax purposes, there may be several owners of the corpus of the trust under the entity attribution rules. Thus, both the transferor and the beneficiaries of a trust may be attributed ownership of the corpus of the trust.[53] When multiple ownership occurs with respect to a subordinate equity interest, the transferee beneficiaries are treated as owning the interest under ordering rules.[54] Even though the transferor is treated as the owner of the corpus under the grantor trust rules, the transferee is deemed to own the corpus for Section 2701 purposes and a Section 2701 transfer may occur.[55]

For example, if Transferor owns an applicable retained interest and transfers a subordinate equity interest to a trust with income to Transferor for a number of years and remainder to Child, or to a trust with income to Child and a reversion to Transferor, there is a Section 2511 transfer subject to Section 2701,[56] even though the transfer is to a trust where, under the grantor trust rules, Transferor is treated as owner of the trust for income tax purposes.[57]

An indirect transfer subject to Section 2701 also generally occurs when there is the termination of an indirect holding in an entity that would have

---

[53] Reg. §§ 25.2701-6(a)(4)(i), 25.2701-6(c)(4)(ii)(C). See infra ¶ 19.02[2][d] note 152.

[54] Reg. § 25.2701-6(c)(5)(ii). See infra ¶ 19.02[2][d] text accompanying note 167.

[55] See TAM 9321046 (Feb. 25, 1993). Although this result may initially appear to constitute regulatory overreaching, it appears consistent with the interrelationship of Sections 2701 and 2702. For example, if there is a complete transfer under Section 2511 to which Section 2702 applies, the interest retained by the transferor under the grantor trust rules is normally valued at zero and the transfer is viewed as a transfer of the entire property to the beneficiary. Thus, the treatment of the beneficiary as owning the interest outright under the attribution rules is consistent with the valuation of the beneficiary's interest under Section 2702. The interrelationship of Sections 2701 and 2702 is discussed infra ¶ 19.02[4][d] text accompanying notes 264–274.

[56] Section 2702 would also apply to the transfer with the result that either the income interest or the reversionary interest in Transferor would be valued at zero for gift tax purposes. See ¶ 19.03. The interrelationship of Sections 2701 and 2702 is considered infra ¶ 19.02[4][d] text accompanying notes 264–274.

[57] See IRC §§ 677, 673, respectively. Similarly, a transfer by Transferor of the subordinate equity interest to a defective grantor trust (where the transfer is complete for transferor tax purposes, but the grantor trust provisions apply for income tax purposes) would nevertheless constitute a Section 2701 transfer. For example, if Transferor creates a defective grantor trust by retaining a Section 675(4)(C) power to substitute assets and transfers a subordinate equity interest to the trust in which Child is a beneficiary, there is a transfer subject to Section 2701, even though the trust property is treated as owned by the grantor for income tax purposes. Regulations Section 25.2701-1(b)(2)(i)(C) would be inapplicable because Transferor would not hold an indirect interest in the entity. See supra text accompanying notes 54, 55. To read the regulations and statutes in any other manner would allow a transferor to avoid a Section 2701 transfer by establishing a defective grantor trust.

been included in the transferor's gross estate for federal estate tax purposes.[58] For example, an indirect Section 2701 transfer occurs on the termination of an interest in an entity where the remainderperson of a trust whose corpus holds a subordinate equity interest transfers the remainder interest in the trust to a family member while retaining an applicable retained interest in the entity.

The entity attribution rules and the indirect transfer rules are both broad. When they are combined, it is possible that more than one person, treated as the indirect holder of the property, may have an interest terminated resulting in indirect transfers by several persons.[59] If that occurs, an ordering rule provides which indirect holder is treated as making the indirect transfer.[60]

Limitations on the Transfer Rules. An indirect transfer also may occur on the inter vivos exercise of a pre-1942 general power or on the inter vivos exercise or release[61] of a post-1942 general power, all of which are transfers under the gift tax.[62] However, there are limitations on the scope of the indirect transfer rules. A transfer does not occur as a result of the exercise, release, or lapse of a power of appointment that would not be treated as a transfer under Section 2514.[63] Thus, the exercise, release, or lapse of any nongeneral power, the release or lapse of a pre-1942 general power, and the lapse of a post-1942

---

[58] Reg. § 25.2701-1(b)(2)(i)(C)(2). This rule applies only where the termination is not treated as the termination of an indirect holding of an interest under the grantor trust rules under Regulations Section 25.2701-1(b)(2)(i)(C)(1). Id.

[59] See, e.g., infra ¶ 19.02[2][d] text accompanying notes 151–158.

[60] Reg. § 25.2701-1(b)(2)(ii). The indirect transfer is attributed in the following order to indirect holders who: (1) transferred the interest to the entity (without regard to Section 2513); (2) possess a presently exercisable power to designate the person who shall possess or enjoy the property; (3) presently are entitled to receive the income from the interest; (4) are specifically entitled to receive the interest at a future date; and finally (5) to any other indirect holders proportionately. Id.

[61] A lifetime lapse is treated as a release to the extent that the property that could have been appointed by exercise of the lapsed power exceeds the greater of $5,000 or 5 percent of the aggregate value of assets out of which the lapsed power could have been satisfied. See IRC § 2514(e); ¶ 10.04[4][c].

[62] For example, an indirect transfer can occur where a person other than the grantor of a trust holds a general power of appointment over the trust corpus that contains a subordinate equity interest in an entity and also holds an applicable retained interest in the same entity. The power holder is treated as owning the property for income tax purposes under Section 678(a)(1). An indirect transfer occurs if the power holder exercises the power in a family member's favor. Reg. § 25.2701-1(b)(2)(i)(C)(1). Of course, the need for an indirect transfer here is minimal because Section 2514(a) or Section 2514(b) would also treat this as a transfer for gift tax purposes. An indirect transfer also occurs if this power holder exercised the power in a manner retaining powers that resulted in the transfer being incomplete for gift tax purposes and subsequently relinquishes those powers. See IRC § 678(a)(2). See supra text accompanying notes 49, 50.

[63] Reg. § 25.2701-1(b)(3)(iii).

general power that is within the exception of Section 2514(e) are not transfers for purposes of Section 2701.[64]

A shifting of rights as a result of a Section 2518 disclaimer does not constitute a transfer by the disclaimant for purposes of Section 2701.[65] Thus, assume Parent owns the senior equity interest in an entity and there is a gift of the subordinate equity interest to Parent but it is disclaimed in a manner that satisfies the requirements of Section 2518 and, as a result, the interest passes to Child. Parent has made no transfer for purposes of Section 2701 of the subordinate equity interest to Child. However, if Grandparent (Parent's parent) had made the original gift transfer that Parent disclaimed, there would be a transfer subject to Section 2701 from Grandparent to Child, assuming Grandparent (or some applicable family member with respect to Grandparent) holds a senior equity interest.

[ii] **An interest in a corporation or partnership.** There must be a transfer[66] of "an interest in a corporation or partnership"[67] to trigger Section 2701.[68] The interest must be in the nature of a growth interest, referred to as a subordinate equity interest, which is stock of a corporation or an interest in a partnership[69] that has rights as to income or capital that are subordinate to another more senior equity interest that is an applicable retained interest.[70]

[iii] **To (or for the benefit of) a member of the transferor's family.** Under Section 2701(e)(1), a member of the transferor's family includes only the transferor's spouse, lineal descendants of the transferor or the transferor's spouse, and the spouses of any such lineal descendants. Any relationship by legal adoption is treated as a relationship by blood.[71] Family members include only persons in the transferor's generation or in a generation younger than the transferor's generation. Neither the transfer of a subordinate equity interest to a relative in a higher generation nor a transfer to a brother or a sister or a niece or nephew is subject to the valuation rules of Section 2701.[72]

---

[64] See Section 2514; ¶¶ 10.04[3], 10.04[4].

[65] Reg. § 25.2701-1(b)(3)(ii). See ¶ 10.07.

[66] See supra ¶ 19.02[2][a][i].

[67] Cf. IRC §§ 7701(a)(2), 7701(a)(3); Reg. §§ 301.7701-2, 301.7701-3.

[68] IRC § 2701(a)(1). See IRC § 2701(a)(2)(B), discussed infra ¶ 19.02[3][b], making Section 2701 inapplicable if the transfer is of an interest of the same class as the retained interest.

[69] Cf. IRC § 2701(a)(4)(B)(ii); Priv. Ltr. Rul. 199952012 (Sept. 22, 1999) (option to acquire stock did not constitute equity interest).

[70] Reg. § 25.2701-3(a)(2)(iii). See supra ¶ 19.02[2] note 24.

[71] IRC § 2701(e)(4); Reg. § 25.2701-1(d)(3).

[72] However, if Grantor retains an applicable retained interest in an entity and transfers a subordinate equity interest to Grantor's Niece or Nephew (Grantor's Sibling's child) and Sibling retains an applicable retained interest in the entity and transfers a subordinate eq-

Section 2701 applies regardless of whether the transfer is an outright transfer "to" a family member or merely an indirect transfer "for the benefit of" a family member.[73] The attribution of entity rules apply to determine whether these tests are met.[74] For example, assume Transferor retains an applicable retained interest and transfers a subordinate equity interest either to a trust with income to Child and a remainder to an unrelated person or to a trust with income to unrelated person and remainder to Child. In either case, Child is deemed to own the trust property[75] and Section 2701 applies to the transfer.[76] Even if Transferor also retains an beneficial interest in the trust, there is a transfer "for the benefit of a family member" and Section 2701 may apply.[77]

[b] The Second Requirement

The second requirement of Section 2701 is that the transferor or *an applicable family member* must hold *an applicable retained interest* immediately after the transfer.[78]

[i] An applicable family member.

The term "applicable family member" is limited to the transferor's spouse, ancestors of the transferor or the trans-

---

uity interest to Sibling's Niece or Nephew (Grantor's child), the Service should apply the reciprocal trust doctrine and subject both transfers to the application of Section 2701. See United States v. Estate of Grace, 395 US 316 (1969); ¶ 4.08[7][d].

[73] IRC § 2701(a)(1).

[74] Reg. § 25.2701-6. See infra ¶ 19.02[2][d].

[75] Reg. §§ 25.2701-6(a)(4)(i), 25.2701-6(b) Exs. 4, 5. Cf. Reg. § 25.2701-6(a)(5)(ii).

[76] The amount of Transferor's gift reflects the Section 2701 value of the applicable retained interest. See infra ¶ 19.02[4]. Nevertheless, where a portion of the gift is to an unrelated party, the increase in the amount of the transfer as a result of the application of Section 2701 should not be allocated solely to the value of the family member's (here Child's) interest in the trust. Instead, the amount of the increase in the value of the property transferred to the family member should be based on the family member's actuarial interest in the trust. This issue can become relevant with respect to determining the amount of the Section 2503(b) annual exclusion or the amount of a charitable deduction. See generally infra ¶ 19.02[5][e] and compare infra ¶ 19.02[4][d] text accompanying notes 264–269 where there is no unrelated party transfer. Cf. ¶ 19.03[2][c] note 93.

[77] See supra ¶ 19.02[2][a][i] and supra text accompanying notes 49–55.

[78] IRC § 2701(a)(1)(B).

feror's spouse, and the spouses of any such ancestors.[79] Any relationship by legal adoption is treated as a relationship by blood.[80]

[ii] **An applicable retained interest.** The term "applicable retained interest" is the focal point of the Section 2701 requirements. It is defined as any equity interest[81] in a corporation or partnership with respect to which there is either (1) a "distribution right," but only if the transferor and a broad range of family members "control" the entity immediately before the transfer or (2) an "extraordinary payment right," which includes a put, call, or conversion right, a right to compel liquidation, or any similar right.[82] The rights composing an applicable retained interest are the discretionary rights that must be held by the transferor or applicable family member[83] as a prerequisite to the application of Section 2701 to a transfer.[84]

Distribution Rights. Distribution rights are rights to distributions from a corporation with respect to its stock or from a partnership with respect to a

---

[79] IRC § 2701(e)(2). Thus, an applicable family member includes only limited relatives in the transferor's generation or in a generation older than the transferor's generation. Note that a transferor's spouse is both a Section 2701(e)(1) "member of the family" and an "applicable family member."

The term "applicable family member" has a broader definition, including lineal descendants of the parents of the transferor or transferor's spouse for purposes of measuring control under Section 2701(b). See IRC § 2701(b)(2)(C); infra text accompanying notes 100–102.

[80] IRC § 2701(e)(4).

[81] The characterization of debt versus equity should be considered. See Bittker & Eustice, Federal Income Taxation of Corporations and Shareholders ¶¶ 4.01, 4.02 (Warren, Gorham & Lamont, 7th ed. 2000). Section 2701 is inapplicable to debt instruments that are not treated as equity interests. See Priv. Ltr. Rul. 9436006 (Sept. 9, 1994).

[82] IRC § 2701(b)(1). See Reg. §§ 25.2701-2(b)(1), 25.2701-2(b)(2), 25.2701-2(b)(3).

[83] If a transferor simultaneously transfers a subordinate equity interest to a family member and an applicable retained interest to an applicable family member, there would not only be an increased Section 2701 valuation of the transferred subordinate equity interest, but also a Section 2511 transfer of the applicable retained interest (valued without any application of Section 2701). A simultaneous transfer of 100 percent of the value of an interest in an entity may result in more than 100 percent of the value of the interest treated as transferred by gift. In this situation, relief from double taxation is provided. See IRC § 2701(e)(6); Reg. § 25.2701-5, infra ¶ 19.02[5][c] text accompanying note 438.

Compare Section 2702, which under Section 2702(a)(1) requires a "retained" interest (defined in Regulations Section 25.2702-2(a)(3) as an interest held both before and after the transfer) in order to apply with Section 2701(a)(1)(B), which requires that an applicable retained interest be "held" by an applicable family member only "after the transfer."

[84] As used here, the term discretionary rights are rights that may or may not be exercised by the taxpayer or in the case of an entity are not required to be paid. The discretionary rights are generally assigned a zero valuation by Section 2701. IRC § 2701(a)(3)(A). See infra ¶ 19.02[4].

partner's interest in the partnership,[85] but only if the corporation or partnership is a controlled entity.[86] In determining whether Section 2701 applies, it does not matter whether the distribution rights are cumulative or noncumulative,[87] although this distinction may become relevant in valuing such rights under Section 2701.[88] A distribution right does not include:

1. A right to dividends or distributions from an equity interest that is the same class as or subordinate to the transferred interest.[89] Thus, applicable retained interests include only distribution rights with respect to senior equity interests.

2. An extraordinary payment right (i.e., a put, call, liquidation, conversion right, or any similar right).[90] Extraordinary payment rights may make a senior equity interest an applicable retained interest, but the terms "distribution rights" and "extraordinary payment rights" are mutually exclusive.[91]

3. Any right to receive a guaranteed payment described in Section 707(c)[92] of a fixed amount with respect to a partnership equity interest.[93]

---

[85] IRC §§ 2701(c)(1)(A)(i), 2701(c)(1)(A)(ii). See Reg. § 25.2701-2(b)(3).

[86] IRC § 2701(b)(1)(A). See infra text accompanying note 94.

[87] See IRC § 2701(b)(1)(A).

[88] See IRC §§ 2701(a)(3)(A), 2701(a)(3)(B), 2701(c)(3); infra ¶ 19.02[4][c] (discussion of qualified payments).

[89] IRC § 2701(c)(1)(B)(i); Reg. § 25.2701-2(b)(3)(i); Priv. Ltr. Rul. 9415007 (Apr. 15, 1994) (distribution rights of the same class). See IRC § 2701(a)(4)(B)(i).

[90] IRC § 2701(c)(1)(B)(ii); Reg. § 25.2701-2(b)(3)(ii). See infra text accompanying notes 103–130.

[91] There is, for purposes of Section 2701, an important distinction between the two rights. A distribution right may be a qualified payment right and, in that event, it is valued at its fair market value (see infra ¶¶ 19.02[4][c][i], 19.02[4][c][ii]); whereas, an extraordinary payment right is valued at zero unless it is held in conjunction with a qualified payment right. See IRC § 2701(a)(3); infra note 104; ¶¶ 19.02[4][b] note 191, 19.02[4][c][ii].

Mandatory payment rights, non-lapsing conversion rights, and liquidation participation rights do not constitute distribution rights. Reg. §§ 25.2701-2(b)(3)(iii), 25.2701-2(b)(4). See infra text accompanying notes 110–122, 127–130.

[92] Section 707(c) applies to payments to a partner for services or for the use of capital that are determined without regard to the partnership's income. The amounts are ordinary income to the partner in the year in which the partnership deducts the payments as paid or accrued under its method of accounting. Reg. § 1.707-1(c). See generally McKee, Nelson & Whitmire, Federal Taxation of Partners and Partnerships ¶ 13.03 (Warren, Gorham & Lamont, 3d ed. 1997).

[93] IRC § 2701(c)(1)(B)(iii); Reg. §§ 25.2701-2(b)(3)(iii), 25.2701-2(b)(4)(iii). Guaranteed payment rights are neither distribution rights nor mandatory payment rights. See infra text accompanying notes 123–126. A guaranteed payment right is similar to a qualified payment interest, although since it is not a Section 2701 distribution right, it is not subject to the Section 2701(d) rules. See infra ¶ 19.02[5][a]. Since the rights to guaranteed pay-

Equity interests with distribution rights are applicable retained interests only if the transferor and a broad range of family members *control* the corporate or partnership entity immediately prior to the transfer of the subordinate equity interest.[94] If the transferor and the transferor's family do not have discretionary control over distributions, it is inappropriate both to assume that distributions on the applicable retained interests will not be made and to value the distribution rights at zero. Absent such control, any distribution rights are not discretionary rights. A corporation is controlled if the relevant family members hold 50 percent or more (by either voting rights or valuation) of the stock of a corporation.[95] A partnership is controlled if the relevant family members hold: (1) 50 percent or more of the capital or profits interests in a partnership[96] or (2) in the case of a limited partnership, hold any interest as a general partner.[97]

In determining whether the control requirement is met, entity attribution of ownership rules apply.[98] Any interest in a corporation or partnership that is held by an individual indirectly through a corporation, partnership, trust, estate, or other entity is treated as held by the individual directly in proportion to the individual's ownership of the entity.[99] Applicable family members are specially defined for purposes of control to include any lineal descendants of the parents of the transferor or the transferor's spouse and any direct or indirect (including

---

ments are so similar to the rights of a qualified payment interest, it might seem that Congress should have subjected guaranteed payments to the Section 2701(d) rules; however, if the partnership is on the accrual method of accounting, such payments will be taxed to the partner when deducted by the partnership, even though they are not actually received. See supra note 92.

See Priv. Ltr. Rul. 9808010 (Nov. 13, 1997), which may have treated a Section 707(c) guaranteed payment as an applicable retained interest. The ruling is discussed in Kasner, "Special Valuation Rules Applied to a Family Partnership," 79 Tax Notes 222 (Apr. 13, 1998) and Dees, "Valuation Rules and Partnerships Don't Mesh Well," 79 Tax Notes 1070 (May 25, 1998).

[94] IRC § 2701(b)(1)(A).

[95] IRC § 2701(b)(2)(A); Reg. § 25.2701-2(b)(5)(ii). Voting rights do not include rights to vote only on such matters as a liquidation, merger, or similar event, which rights are often given by corporate codes even to nonvoting stock. Reg. § 25.2701-2(b)(5)(ii)(B). Voting rights, however, will be counted whether they can be exercised alone or with others and where an individual can direct their exercise, but not if they are subject to a contingency that has not occurred and that is beyond the individual's control. Id. If voting rights are held in a fiduciary capacity, the rights are attributed to the beneficial owners of the entity, not to the fiduciary. Id.

[96] IRC § 2701(b)(2)(B)(i). Any guaranteed payment rights under Section 707(c) are disregarded in making this determination. Reg. § 25.2701-2(b)(5)(iii). See Reg. § 25.2701-2(b)(4)(iii).

[97] IRC § 2701(b)(2)(B)(ii).

[98] IRC § 2701(b)(1)(A).

[99] IRC § 2701(e)(3). See Reg. § 25.2701-6; infra ¶ 19.02[2][d].

entity attribution) holdings are taken into account in measuring control.[100] Thus, ownership interests held by siblings, nieces and nephews, and their descendants along with those of other applicable family members are considered in measuring control.[101] Relationships by legal adoption are again treated as relationships by blood in applying the family ownership rules.[102]

Extraordinary Payment Rights. An extraordinary payment right is a put, call, or conversion right, a right to compel liquidation, or any similar right, but only if the exercise or nonexercise of such right affects the value of the transferred interest.[103] Section 2701 generally values these discretionary extraordinary payment rights at a zero value, conclusively presuming that the owner of such rights will not exercise them.[104]

If payment rights are not discretionary, they are not treated as extraordinary payment rights and are not valued at zero under Section 2701. Extraordinary payment rights do not include[105] mandatory payment rights,[106] non-lapsing conversion rights,[107] rights to guaranteed payments of fixed amounts under Section 707(c),[108] and liquidation participation rights.[109]

Mandatory Payment Right. A mandatory payment right is a right that must be exercised at a specific time and in a specific amount and, therefore, it is not discretionary.[110] A mandatory redemption right in preferred stock requir-

---

[100] IRC § 2701(b)(2)(C). See IRC § 2701(b)(1)(A); Reg. § 25.2701-2(b)(5)(i).

[101] IRC § 2701(b)(2)(C). See IRC § 2701(b)(1)(A); Reg. § 25.2701-2(b)(5)(i). See supra ¶ 19.02[2][b][i]. Holdings of spouses of any members of the family of the transferor (other than applicable family members) and spouses of brothers and sisters and spouses of the descendants of brothers and sisters are not included in measuring control.

[102] IRC § 2701(e)(4).

[103] IRC § 2701(c)(2)(A); Reg. § 25.2701-2(b)(2). A call right includes any warrant, option, or other right to acquire one or more equity interests. Reg. § 25.2701-2(b)(2). See TAM 9447004 (Nov. 25, 1994) (lapsing conversion right constituted an extraordinary payment right). Priv. Ltr. Rul. 9848006 ruled that drag-along rights (entitling institutional investors to force other shareholders to sell), tag-along rights (requiring a selling shareholder to permit other shareholders to participate in a sale), and rights of first refusal, all granted in a shareholders' agreement, were *not* extraordinary payment rights for purposes of Section 2701(c)(1)(B)(ii) and Regulations Section 25.2701-2(b)(2).

[104] But see the Section 2701(a)(3)(B) "lower of" rule under which, in valuing a qualified payment right, value may be attributed to an extraordinary payment right. See the example infra ¶ 19.02[4][c] text accompanying note 210.

[105] Reg. § 25.2701-2(b)(4). In addition, these nondiscretionary payment rights are not treated as distribution rights. Id. See supra text accompanying notes 90, 91.

[106] IRC § 2701(c)(2)(B)(i); Reg. § 25.2701-2(b)(4)(i).

[107] IRC § 2701(c)(2)(C); Reg. § 25.2701-2(b)(4)(iv).

[108] Reg. § 25.2701-2(b)(4)(iii).

[109] Reg. § 25.2701-2(b)(4)(ii).

[110] IRC § 2701(c)(2)(B)(i); Reg. § 25.2701-2(b)(4)(i). If a right is assumed to be exercised in a particular manner under the Section 2701(a)(3)(B) "lower of" valuation rule

ing redemption on a specific date for a specific amount is a mandatory payment right.[111] The right to receive a specific amount on the death of the holder
of the right (for example, a mandatory buy-out of a partnership interest at
death) is also a mandatory payment right.[112]

Non-lapsing Conversion Right. A non-lapsing conversion right is a non-
lapsing right to convert a retained equity interest in a corporation or a partnership into a nondiluted interest that is the same as an interest in the entity that
has been transferred.[113] If the entity is a corporation,[114] the non-lapsing conversion right[115] must entitle the retained equity interest to be converted into a
fixed number or fixed percentage of shares of the same class as the transferred
interest.[116] The conversion right must be subject to proportionate adjustments
for any changes in the transferred equity ownership[117] and for accumulated but
unpaid distributions with respect to the retained interest.[118] Thus, if retained
preferred stock has a non-lapsing, nondiluted conversion right into common
stock, the value of the preferred stock reflects any increases in value of the
common stock and no freeze may occur with respect to the conversion right,
and it is not treated as an extraordinary payment right. If the entity is a partnership,[119] the conversion must be into a specified interest (other than an interest represented by a fixed dollar amount) of the same class as the transferred
interest[120] and must be subject to proportionate adjustments for changes in the

---

(see infra ¶ 19.02[4][c][ii]), that assumption is used in determining whether it is a
mandatory payment right. IRC § 2701(c)(2)(B)(ii).

[111] IRC § 2701(c)(2)(B)(i); Reg. § 25.2701-2(b)(4)(i).

[112] IRC § 2701(c)(2)(B)(i); Reg. § 25.2701-2(b)(4)(i). Cf. IRC § 2703.

[113] IRC § 2701(c)(2)(C).

[114] Reg. § 25.2701-2(b)(4)(iv)(A).

[115] IRC § 2701(c)(2)(C)(ii).

[116] IRC § 2701(c)(2)(C)(i). A conversion into an interest that would be of the same
class but for non-lapsing differences in voting power is treated as a conversion into the
same class. Id. Reg. § 25.2701-2(b)(4)(iv)(A).

[117] IRC § 2701(c)(2)(C)(iii). This would include adjustments for splits, combinations,
reclassifications, or similar changes in capital stock. Reg. § 25.2701-2(b)(4)(iv)(C).

[118] IRC § 2701(c)(2)(C)(iv); Reg. § 25.2701-2(b)(4)(iv)(D). The adjustment must provide for cumulative payments, compounding of any unpaid payments, and adjustments of
the number or percentage of shares of the interest into which it is convertible to take account of accumulated but unpaid payments on the retained interest. Reg. § 25.2701-
2(b)(4)(iv)(D). The computations are similar to the adjustments under Section 2701(d).
See infra ¶ 19.02[5][a][iv].

[119] See IRC § 2701(c)(2) (last sentence).

[120] This includes conversion into an interest that would be of the same class except
for non-lapsing differences in management rights or limitations on liability. Reg.
§ 25.2701-2(b)(4)(iv)(B).

equity ownership of the partnership[121] and for unpaid distributions with respect to the interest.[122]

Guaranteed Payment Rights. A right to guaranteed payments of a fixed amount under Section 707(c) is a guaranteed payment from a partnership entity[123] that is determined at a fixed rate.[124] It must not be contingent as to the time or the amount of the payment.[125] There is no discretionary element with respect to such guaranteed payment rights.[126]

Liquidation Participation Rights. When the transferor, members of the transferor's family, and applicable family members in the aggregate do *not* have the discretionary ability to *compel* the liquidation of the entity, they have a mere right to participate in a liquidation that is not an extraordinary payment right.[127] In determining whether the parties have the ability to compel a liquidation, the entity attribution rules apply.[128] The underlying rationale for this exception is similar to the rationale for requiring family control before a distribution right is subject to Section 2701. If this group of persons does not directly or indirectly have the power to liquidate the entity, the discretionary element present in other extraordinary payment rights is missing and no special reduced value should be assigned to the right to receive a distribution upon liquidation.[129] If those persons *do* have control of the entity, they have the discretionary ability to compel liquidation and their liquidation right is classified as an extraordinary payment right.[130]

---

[121] The convertible equity interest must be protected from dilution resulting from changes in the partnership structure. Reg. § 25.2701-2(b)(4)(iv)(C).

[122] Reg. § 25.2701-2(b)(4)(iv)(D). The computations are similar to the adjustments under Section 2701(d). See infra ¶ 19.02[5][a][iv]. The adjustment must provide for the items listed supra note 118.

[123] A Section 707(c) guaranteed payment is a payment of a fixed amount that is determined without regard to partnership income. Guaranteed payments are defined in more detail, supra note 92.

[124] Reg. § 25.2701-2(b)(4)(iii). This includes a rate that bears a fixed relationship to a specified market interest rate. Id.

[125] Reg. § 25.2701-2(b)(4)(iii).

[126] Neither the exception for guaranteed payment rights, nor the exception for liquidation participation rights is found in the statute, although both are appropriate because of their nondiscretionary nature.

[127] Reg. § 25.2701-2(b)(4)(ii). See Reg. § 25.2701-2(d) Ex. 4; IRC §§ 2701(e)(1), 2701(e)(2). Seemingly, the broader Section 2701(b)(2)(C) "applicable family member" definition is employed here. See supra text accompanying notes 100–102.

[128] See Reg. § 25.2701-6; infra ¶ 19.02[2][d].

[129] Reg. § 25.2701-2(b)(4)(ii). If the "lower of" rule of Section 2701(a)(3)(B) applies (see infra ¶ 19.02[4][c][ii]), the liquidation participation right is valued as though the ability to compel liquidation were exercised in a manner that is consistent with that rule. Id.

[130] The statute conclusively presumes that the right will not be asserted. The interest is valued at a zero value, as if the liquidation would never occur. IRC § 2701(a)(3)(A).

[c] Examples

Some examples will facilitate understanding of Section 2701 and its application. Assume Transferor recapitalizes a solely owned corporation and receives voting preferred stock, with a noncumulative preferred dividend right, and nonvoting common stock in return for all of the corporation's original common stock. Transferor then transfers the nonvoting common stock to Child. Because Transferor transfers an interest in the corporation to a family member and holds an applicable retained interest, Section 2701 applies.[131] Section 2701 applies in determining whether there is a gift and the valuation of the gift, even if the transfer is made to Child for consideration.[132] Furthermore, if a new corporation is formed by Transferor as a part of the transaction[133] (rather than recapitalizing an existing corporation), Section 2701 still applies. This is so even if Transferor and Child both make contributions to the corporation equal in value to the interests in the corporation they receive (Transferor's preferred interest and Child's common interest). Section 2701 would also apply if the interests created and transferred were interests in a partnership. If Transferor made any of the above-mentioned transfers, and simultaneously transferred the applicable retained interest to an applicable family member, Section 2701 would still apply.[134]

[d] Entity Attribution Rules Under Section 2701

Section 2701 contains an elaborate set of entity attribution rules.[135] Any equity interest, whether senior or subordinate in a corporation or partnership held by another corporation, partnership, estate, trust, or other entity is generally attributed to an individual who has an interest in the entity owning the equity interest in proportion to the individual's interest in that owning entity.[136] The rules further provide for multiple entity attribution.[137] Where one entity A, owns an interest in another entity B, which owns an equity interest in entity C, the equity interest in C is attributed through both the owning entities B and A

---

[131] IRC § 2701(a)(1). Cf. Reg. §§ 25.2701-1(a)(3), 25.2701-1(e) Ex.

Although a single interest will satisfy the statutory requirement of an applicable retained interest, in this example Transferor has two types of interests. Transferor has retained a senior equity interest with distribution rights in a controlled corporation and a liquidation right in the form of a liquidation power within the family.

[132] See Reg. § 25.2701-3(d) Exs. 4, 5. Cf. Reg. § 25.2701-1(b)(2)(i)(B).

[133] See IRC § 351. Cf. IRC § 721.

[134] See supra ¶ 19.02[2][b] note 83.

[135] IRC § 2701(e)(3).

[136] Reg. § 25.2701-6. But see infra ¶ 19.02[2][d][iv].

[137] Reg. § 25.2701-6(a)(1).

to the individuals who own entity A.[138] If an equity interest is treated as held by a particular individual in more than one capacity, the interest is treated as held by the individual in the manner that results in attribution of the largest total ownership of the equity interest to that individual.[139]

The entity attribution rules come into play in several circumstances under Section 2701:

1. They are applied both to determine whether and when there is a transfer and to determine whether it is to (or for the benefit of) a family member;[140]

2. They are used to determine whether there is an applicable retained interest by assessing (i) whether the control requirement is satisfied in connection with distribution rights[141] and (ii) whether liquidation participation rights constitute extraordinary payment rights;[142]

3. They are applied to measure the amount of the transfer under the subtraction method of valuation;[143] and

4. They are used in determining whether an exception to Section 2701 applies.[144]

   [i] Corporate attribution. Under the attribution rules, if a corporation[145] owns an equity interest, the corporation's ownership is attributed to any shareholder to the extent of the proportionate fair market value of that shareholder's stock in the corporation to the fair market value of all of the stock in the corporation.[146] A subsidiary corporation's ownership of an equity interest is attributed through its parent corporation to the shareholders of the parent

---

[138] Reg. § 25.2701-6(a)(1).

[139] Reg. § 25.2701-6(a)(1).

[140] A corporate or partnership equity interest deemed owned directly for ownership purposes by the attribution rules may be the subject of a direct or indirect transfer when an individual transfers an interest in the entity or the entity transfers the equity interest it holds. An indirect transfer may also be made to (or for the benefit of) a family member through a transfer of an interest in an entity to a corporation or a partnership in which the family member owns an interest or to an estate or trust in which the family member has an interest. See supra ¶¶ 19.02[2][a][i], 19.02[2][a][iii].

[141] See supra ¶ 19.02[2][b] text accompanying notes 98–102.

[142] See supra ¶ 19.02[2][b] text accompanying notes 127–128.

[143] See infra ¶ 19.02[4][d].

[144] See infra ¶ 19.02[3].

[145] This rule applies to any entity classified as a corporation for federal income tax purposes. Reg. § 25.2701-6(a)(2). See Reg. § 301.7701-2.

[146] Reg. § 25.2701-6(a)(2). The determination is made as if each class of stock were held separately by one individual. Id. See Reg. §§ 25.2701-6(b) Exs. 1, 2. In Example 2, a portion of its stock held by the entity to satisfy a deferred obligation is treated as held by an individual shareholder.

corporation. For example, if Parent Corporation owns 60 percent of Subsidiary Corporation, Parent owns 60 percent of Subsidiary's equity interest, and the interest attributed to Parent is then reattributed to Parent's shareholders to the extent of their proportionate interests in Parent.[147]

[ii] **Partnership attribution.** If an individual partner owns a capital or profits interest in a partnership that holds an equity interest,[148] the partnership's equity ownership is attributed to the individual partner in the proportion that the larger of the fair market value of the individual's capital or profits interest bears to the fair market value of the corresponding capital or profits interest in the partnership.[149] In a tiered partnership arrangement, an upper-tier partnership is treated as owning an equity interest owned by a lower-tier partnership in proportion to the greater of the upper-tier's capital or profits ownership share in the lower-tier partnership. For example, assume a lower-tier partnership A owns 50 percent of the common stock of a corporation, partnership B owns a 60 percent capital and 50 percent profits interest in partnership A and an individual partner owns a 20 percent capital interest and 30 percent profits interest in partnership B. Under the attribution rules, the individual partner is treated as owning 9 percent of corporation's common stock.[150]

[iii] **Estate, trust, and other entity attribution.** The attribution rules with respect to an estate, a trust, or other entities[151] are more complicated than those involving corporations or partnerships.[152] If a trust or an estate directly or indirectly holds[153] an equity interest, the equity interest is attributed to those individuals who have a beneficial interest in the trust or estate. A person is treated as holding a beneficial interest in a trust or an estate as long as the per-

---

[147] Reg. § 25.2701-6(a)(1).

[148] A partnership includes any entity classified as a partnership for federal income tax purposes. Reg. § 25.2701-6(a)(3). See Reg. § 301.7701-3.

[149] Reg. § 25.2701-6(a)(3). The determination is made as if each class of interest were held by one individual. Id.

[150] Reg. § 25.2701-6(a)(1). That is, the individual's 30 percent profits interest in B times B's 60 percent capital interest in A times A's 50 percent ownership of the corporate common stock.

[151] These rules apply to any entity that is not classified as a corporation (including an association) or a partnership for federal income tax purposes. Reg. § 25.2701-6(a)(4)(i). See Reg. §§ 301.7701-2, 301.7701-3, 301.7701-4.

[152] These attribution rules maximize an individual's attribution of any equity interest. Reg. § 25.2701-6(a)(4)(i).

The indirect transfer rules are closely related to the attribution of ownership rules. Compare Reg. § 25.2701-1(b)(2)(i)(C) (see supra ¶ 19.02[2][a][i]) with Reg. § 25.2701-6. It is important to recognize that without a "transfer," Section 2701 does not apply no matter who is deemed to "own" the trust or estate property.

[153] Property is held by an estate if the property is subject to claims against the estate and to expenses of administration. Reg. § 25.2701-6(a)(4)(ii)(A).

son *may* receive income or corpus distributions from the trust or estate, other than payments for full and adequate consideration.[154] A person is considered to hold an equity interest to the extent that the person's beneficial interest *may* be satisfied by the equity interest held in the estate or the trust, or the income or proceeds thereof.[155] Any person who may receive distributions from a trust is considered to hold an equity interest held by the trust to the extent that distributions can be made from current or accumulated income generated by that interest, or from proceeds on disposition of the equity interest, even though the interest could not be distributed to the person.[156] An individual owning a one-half interest in the income of a trust or a future right to one half of a trust's income is treated as holding one half of the equity interests held by the trust.[157] If a beneficiary has a right to receive all of a trust's income in the trustee's discretion or a future discretionary right to all of such income, the individual is deemed to hold all of the equity interests held by the trust.[158]

In applying these attribution rules, it is assumed that the executor or trustee uses the maximum exercise of discretion in favor of the person.[159] However, where a beneficiary of an estate or trust cannot receive any distribution with respect to an equity interest held by an estate or trust (including income generated thereby or proceeds on sale), none of the equity interest is attributed to the person.[160] Thus, where stock and its income is specifically bequeathed to one beneficiary of an estate, it cannot be attributed to any other beneficiaries of the estate.[161]

A person who is taxed as the owner of trust property under the grantor trust rules is treated as owning an equity interest owned by the trust.[162] This may include a third person who is not the grantor of the trust.[163] An individual treated as owning only a fractional share of a grantor trust because there are multiple grantors is treated as holding each equity interest owned by the trust up to the fair market value of the individual's fractional share of the trust.[164]

[iv] **Multiple attribution.** The attribution rules may attribute an equity interest to more than one individual. When this occurs, two different sets of

---

[154] Reg. § 25.2701-6(a)(4)(ii)(B).

[155] Reg. § 25.2701-6(a)(4)(i).

[156] Reg. § 25.2701-6(a)(4)(i).

[157] See Reg. § 25.2701-6(b) Ex. 3.

[158] See Reg. §§ 25.2701-6(b) Exs. 4, 5.

[159] Reg. § 25.2701-6(a)(4)(i).

[160] Reg. § 25.2701-6(a)(4)(i).

[161] Reg. § 25.2701-6(a)(4)(i).

[162] Reg. § 25.2701-6(a)(4)(ii)(C); IRC §§ 671–679.

[163] IRC § 678. See supra ¶ 19.02[2][a] notes 49, 62.

[164] Reg. § 25.2701-6(a)(4)(ii)(C). For example, if Grantor is treated as owner of one third of a trust for income tax purposes under the grantor trust rules, Grantor is treated as

ordering rules establish ownership of the equity interest for purposes of applying Section 2701. The first set of rules applies to allocation of ownership of an
applicable retained interest among the transferor and one or more applicable
family members.[165] Ownership is first attributed to the individual treated as the
owner of the trust for income tax purposes under the grantor trust rules, then
to the transferor of the subordinate equity interest, then to the transferor's
spouse, and finally pro rata among the applicable family members.[166]

The second set of ordering rules apply when ownership of a *subordinate
equity interest* is attributed to more than one individual in a class consisting of
the transferor, applicable family members, and members of the transferor's
family.[167] The subordinate equity interest is allocated in the following order to:
the transferee of the subordinate equity interest; each member of the transferor's family on a pro rata basis; the individual treated as the owner under the
grantor trust rules; the transferor; the transferor's spouse; and finally, each applicable family member on a pro rata basis.[168]

[3] Exceptions

The Section 2701 valuation rules do not apply in several situations.

[a] Market Quotations Available

If, on the date of the transfer, either the transferred interest[169] *or* the applicable retained interest[170] is an interest for which market quotations are readily
available on an established securities market, the Section 2701 rules do not apply.[171] In both instances, the interest is properly valued by the securities market
and Section 2701 special valuation is not needed to provide an accurate valuation of the equity interests involved.

---

holding each equity interest held by the trust to the extent that the value of the equity interest does not exceed the fair market value of Grantor's interest in the trust.

[165] Reg. § 25.2701-6(a)(5)(i). See Reg. § 25.2701-6(b) Ex. 4; Priv. Ltr. Rul. 9321046
(Feb. 25, 1993) (where the multiple attribution rules attributed an applicable retained interest to a transferor and a subordinate equity interest to a transferee where both interests
were held by the same trust).

[166] Reg. §§ 25.2701-6(a)(5)(i)(A)–25.2701-6(a)(5)(i)(D).

[167] Reg. § 25.2701-6(a)(5)(ii). See Reg. § 25.2701-6(b) Ex. 4; Priv. Ltr. Rul. 9321046
(Feb. 25, 1993); supra ¶ 19.02[2][a] text accompanying notes 54, 55.

[168] Reg. §§ 25.2701-6(a)(5)(ii)(A)–25.2701-6(a)(5)(ii)(F). Seemingly, the ordering
rules are designed to maximize the application of Section 2701.

[169] See Reg. § 25.2701-1(c)(1).

[170] See Reg. § 25.2701-1(c)(2); Priv. Ltr. Rul. 9725032 (Mar. 24, 1997).

[171] IRC §§ 2701(a)(1) (last sentence), 2701(a)(2)(A).

[b] Interests of the Same Class and Interests Proportionate to the Class

If the retained interest is the same class of equity as the transferred interest, the transfer has no potential for both freezing the retained interest and creating a growth interest out of the transferred interest.[172] As a result, Section 2701 is inapplicable.[173] The determination whether equity interests are of the same class is made without regard to non-lapsing differences in voting rights, or in the case of a partnership, non-lapsing differences with respect to management and limitations on liability.[174] For example, when voting common stock is retained and nonvoting common stock is transferred, the voting stock is treated as the same class of stock as the nonvoting stock and Section 2701 is inapplicable. When a general partnership interest is retained and a limited partnership interest is transferred, the interests are treated as the same class if the only differences in the interests are non-lapsing differences in management rights and limitations on liability. A right that lapses by reason of federal or state law is generally treated as a non-lapsing right.[175] This exception is inapplicable to a partnership interest that is transferred if the transferor or an applicable family member, acting individually or in concert, may alter the liability of the transferee of the transferred property.[176] The Section 2701(e)(7) separate interests rule[177] may be used in applying this exception to negate the applicability of Section 2701.[178]

If the retained interest is not the same class as, but shares proportionally the same rights as the transferred interest (using all of the same non-lapsing

---

[172] A transfer of stock in an S corporation is not subject to Section 2701 because an S corporation can issue only a single class of stock. IRC § 1361(b)(1)(D).

[173] IRC § 2701(a)(2)(B). See Priv. Ltr. Ruls. 9722022 (Feb. 27, 1997) (stock and options to acquire such stock treated as interests of same class), 9802004 (Sept. 30, 1997) (impossible to determine whether interests of same class until vote taken by owners).

[174] Reg. § 25.2701-1(c)(3). See Priv. Ltr. Rul. 9710021 (Dec. 6, 1996) (both non-lapsing voting rights and management control retained; voting rights appropriately treated as non-lapsing under Section 2701 but lapsing under Section 2704). In determining whether interests are of the same class, the statutory rules of Section 2701(a)(2)(C) (see infra ¶ 19.02[3][c]) are applied to Section 2701(a)(2)(B).

Non-lapsing provisions necessary to comply with Section 704(b) partnership allocations are non-lapsing differences with respect to limitations on liability. Reg. § 25.2701-1(c)(3). But see TAM 9933002 (Apr. 12, 1999) (where special allocation to make up for contributed capital by limited partners were not treated as within the exception).

[175] Reg. § 25.2701-1(c)(3); see IRC § 2701(a)(2) (flush language). The Treasury may determine by regulations or by a published revenue ruling when it is necessary to treat these rights as lapsing to accomplish the purposes of Section 2701. Reg. § 25.2701-1(c)(3).

[176] Reg. § 25.2701-1(c)(3). See IRC § 2701(a)(2) (flush language).

[177] See infra ¶ 19.02[5][b].

[178] See the example infra ¶ 19.02[5][b].

tests applicable to the same class exception),[179] Section 2701 does not apply. For example, if an entity has two classes of interests and one interest is transferred and the other retained, but both share income or dividends and liquidating distributions based on a fixed ratio, the two classes are proportionately the same interests, and Section 2701 is inapplicable. The potential for freezing an interest does not exist with respect to the transfer.

[c] Proportionate Transfers

A transfer that results in a proportionate reduction of each class of equity interest held by the transferor *and* all applicable family members in the aggregate immediately before the transfer is not subject to Section 2701.[180] The transferor need not transfer a proportionate interest in each class held, as long as the transfers are proportionate when the holdings of the transferor and all applicable family members are taken into consideration.[181] For example, assume an entity is owned:

	Applicable Retained Interest	Subordinate Equity Interest
Transferor	30%	50%
Applicable family member	30%	30%
Unrelated third parties	40%	20%

If Transferor transfers 15 percent of the total applicable retained interests and 20 percent of the total subordinate equity interests to Transferor's Child, Transferor has not made a proportionate transfer of Transferor's directly owned shares. However, in the aggregate, considering shares held by Transferor and Applicable Family Members, a proportionate one-quarter share of each class of equity interest is transferred (15 percent out of 60 percent and 20

---

[179] See IRC §§ 2701(a)(2) (flush language), 2701(a)(2)(C); Reg. § 25.2701-1(c)(3); supra text accompanying notes 174–178. See also Priv. Ltr. Ruls. 9451050 (Dec. 31, 1994) (real estate partnership transfer satisfied Regulations Section 25.2701-1(c)(3) exception); 9451051 (Sept. 23, 1994) (convertible preferred stock substantially the same interest as transferred common stock); 9933002 (Apr. 12, 1999) (general and limited partnership interests did not satisfy the exception).

[180] Reg. § 25.2701-1(c)(4); Priv. Ltr. Rul. 9248026 (Sept. 1, 1992) (a valid vertical slice exception to Section 2701).

Although this exception is not expressly provided by Section 2701, it is an appropriate administrative extension of Section 2701(a)(2)(C) to a situation where, in substance, there is a transfer of a vertical slice of the entity; again, no potential for freezing exists.

[181] Reg. § 25.2701-1(c)(4). In making this determination, attributed interests are taken into consideration. See Reg. § 25.2701-6; supra ¶ 19.02[2][d].

percent out of 80 percent), and Section 2701 is inapplicable.[182] Alternatively, assume Transferor transfers the 15 percent of the total applicable retained interests and only 10 percent of the total subordinate equity interests, but Transferor's Parent, an applicable family member, also simultaneously transfers 10 percent of the total subordinate equity interests to Child. The exception should apply to the combined transfers.

The proportionate transfer exception applies "to the extent that" a transfer results in a proportionate reduction of each class of equity interest.[183] For example, if the sole owner of an entity transfers 20 percent of the applicable retained interest and 30 percent of the subordinate equity interest in the entity to a member of transferor's family, the exception applies to the extent of the 20 percent proportionate interest, but not to the other 10 percent.[184] The 80 percent applicable retained interest and the 70 percent retained subordinate equity interest retain only 70 percent of the value of the potential appreciation with respect to the entity. The excess 10 percent subordinate equity interest is subject to Section 2701 because it effectively absorbs the discretionary rights of the excess 10 percent applicable retained interest.[185]

[4] Section 2701 Valuation Rules

[a] Introduction

The heart of Section 2701 is found in its valuation rules. If Section 2701 applies, the distribution and extraordinary payment rights attached to the appli-

---

[182] Reg. § 25.2701-1(c)(4). If Transferor transfers 15 percent of the total applicable retained interests and 25 percent of the total subordinate equity interests, there is proportionate (one-half) reduction of Transferor's interest but not a proportionate reduction of both Transferor and Applicable Family Member's interests. Transferor transfers 25 percent of the total applicable retained interests and 31.25 percent of the total subordinate equity interests, and Transferor's transfer is partially excepted from Section 2701. See infra note 184.

[183] Reg. § 25.2701-1(c)(4).

[184] Reg. § 25.2701-1(c)(4). In the example, supra note 182, 25 percent of the total transfer would be excepted under the "to the extent" rule. Only the 6.25 percent excess of the applicable retained interest of the Transferor and Applicable Family Member's total applicable retained interest, 3.75 percent of the total applicable retained interest of the entity (6.25 percent of 60 percent) would be valued under Section 2701.

[185] Only 10 percent of the value of the entity is subject to Section 2701 as a result of Step 3 of the subtraction method of valuation that allocates the special valuation between the transferred and other retained subordinate equity interests. See infra ¶ 19.02[4][d][iii]. Arguably, the sole owner's 80 percent retained interest could be treated as two separate interests under Section 2701(e)(7). See infra ¶ 19.02[5][b]; Reg. § 25.2701-7. However, this treatment is unnecessary in view of the Step 3 allocation process.

cable retained interest are valued under the Section 2701 valuation rules.[186] That valuation in turn is reflected in the corresponding valuation of the transferred subordinate equity interest. A subtraction method is used to determine the amount of the gift transfer.[187] If Section 2701 applies to a transfer, a minimum 10 percent valuation floor is placed on the value of the junior equity interests.[188] Before examining the subtraction method and the 10 percent rule, the special valuation rules for the distribution and extraordinary payment rights attached to the applicable retained interest must be explained.

[b] Extraordinary Payment Rights

Extraordinary payment rights[189] are rights attached to the retained interest that may affect the value of the transferred interest and the exercise of which is within the discretion of the owner of the retained interest.[190] The statute presumes that these rights will not be exercised and generally values them at zero unless the "lower of" rule applies.[191] By assigning extraordinary payment rights attached to the retained interest a zero value at the time of the transfer and using a subtraction method of valuation, the statute shifts any value attributable to the discretionary rights to the value of the transferred subordinate equity interest.

[c] Distribution Rights

Distribution rights in a controlled entity[192] generally[193] are also valued at zero.[194] Because of the family control requirement, the transferor and family members as a group have the discretion whether to make any distributions. The statute presumes that those persons will act in concert and the discretion will not be exercised and no distributions made. By so presuming and by use of the subtraction method of valuation, the statute shifts the value of the dis-

---

[186] IRC § 2701(a)(3).

[187] See infra ¶ 19.02[4][d].

[188] IRC § 2701(a)(4)(A). See infra ¶ 19.02[4][f], especially text accompanying note 301.

[189] Extraordinary payment rights that include a put, call, conversion right, a right to compel liquidation, or any similar right are defined in more detail supra ¶ 19.02[2][b] text accompanying notes 103–130.

[190] IRC § 2701(c)(2)(A); Reg. § 25.2701-2(b)(2).

[191] IRC § 2701(a)(3)(A). See Reg. §§ 25.2701-1(e) Exs. 1, 2, 25.2701-2(a)(5) Ex. But see IRC § 2701(c)(3)(B); supra ¶ 19.02[2][b] notes 91, 104, infra ¶ 19.02[4][c][ii], involving the "lower of" rule.

[192] IRC § 2701(c)(1). See supra ¶ 19.02[2][b] text accompanying notes 85–102.

[193] See infra ¶¶ 19.02[4][c][i], 19.02[4][c][ii].

[194] IRC § 2701(a)(3)(A).

cretionary distribution rights from the retained interest to the transferred subordinate equity interest.[195]

[i] Qualified payment rights. If a distribution right is a "qualified payment right," it is not assigned a zero valuation.[196] When an applicable retained interest has only a qualified payment right that is not held in conjunction with an extraordinary payment right,[197] the applicable retained interest is valued at its fair market value for purposes of Section 2701.[198]

A qualified payment right is the right to a *cumulative* dividend (or similar *cumulative* distribution right with respect to a partnership) payable on a periodic basis, at least annually, at a fixed rate[199] with respect to a senior equity interest.[200] A nondiscretionary distribution right in a family-controlled entity that is cumulative is a qualified payment right. For example, an annual cumulative dividend payable at a fixed rate on preferred stock[201] and a cumulative right to a fixed payment at least annually from a senior partnership interest are both qualified payment rights.[202]

An election may be made to treat a qualified payment right as though it is not qualified[203] or, in the alternative, to treat a distribution right that is not qualified as though it is qualified.[204] The election may be made to treat only a

---

[195] See Reg. §§ 25.2701-1(e) Ex. 2 (noncumulative preferred dividend rights and liquidation rights both valued at zero, shifting the entire value of the corporation to the transferred subordinate equity interest, the common stock); 25.2701-2(d) Ex. 2 (a zero value assigned to a noncumulative dividend right).

[196] See IRC § 2701(a)(3)(A); Reg. § 25.2701-2(a)(4).

[197] If an applicable retained interest has a qualified payment right held in conjunction with an extraordinary payment right. See infra ¶ 19.02[4][c][ii].

[198] IRC § 2701(a)(3)(C). See Reg. §§ 25.2701-1(e) Ex. 1, 25.2701-2(a)(4).

[199] A fixed rate includes a rate that bears a fixed relationship to a specified market interest rate. IRC § 2701(c)(3)(B); Reg. § 25.2701-2(b)(6)(ii).

[200] IRC § 2701(c)(3)(A).

[201] Reg. § 25.2701-2(b)(6)(i)(A). See Reg. § 25.2701-2(d) Ex. 1.

[202] Reg. § 25.2701-2(b)(6)(i)(B). See Priv. Ltr. Rul. 200114004 (Nov. 30, 2000) (a limited liability company's prepayments of annual distributions to its members would be qualified payments under Section 2701(c)(3)(A)).

[203] IRC § 2701(c)(3)(C)(i). See Reg. § 25.2701-2(c)(1).

[204] IRC § 2701(c)(3)(C)(ii). See Reg. §§ 25.2701-2(b)(6)(i)(C), 25.2701-2(c)(2). If the distribution payments are to be made to an applicable family member of the transferor, an election *must* be made to treat the payment right as a qualified payment right, even if the payment right meets the qualified payment right requirements. IRC § 2701(c)(3)(C)(i). See Reg. § 25.2701-2(c)(4); infra ¶ 19.02[5][a] text accompanying note 321.
A distribution right that is treated as a qualified payment right, either because it is a qualified payment right and there is no election out of such treatment or because it is a nonqualified right that is electively treated as a qualified payment right, is known as a qualified payment interest. Reg. § 25.2701-4(a). The decision whether to make an election

portion of each payment right as qualified or nonqualified.[205] To the extent that an otherwise qualified payment right is treated as not qualified, the payment right is valued at zero under Section 2701.[206] To the extent that a payment right that is not otherwise qualified is treated as a qualified payment right, the qualified payment right is valued at its fair market value.[207]

[ii] Qualified payment rights combined with extraordinary payment rights. If an applicable retained interest includes a distribution right that is treated as a qualified payment right[208] and also includes one or more extraordinary payment rights, then the value of all the rights is determined as if each extraordinary payment right were exercised in a manner that results in the *lowest* value for all the rights.[209] This rule is commonly referred to as the lower of rule. For example, assume Transferor retains cumulative preferred stock (with qualified payment rights) and gives nonvoting common stock to Child. Assume the cumulative dividend is $100 per year, and, under an extraordinary payment right, the stock may be redeemed for $1,000 at any time after two years. Applying the "lower of" rule, the value of the cumulative preferred stock is the lesser of: (1) the present value of two years of $100 dividends plus the present value of the $1,000 redemption right or (2) the present value of $100 paid every year into perpetuity.[210]

[d] The Subtraction Method of Valuation

Once an applicable retained interest is valued under Section 2701, the determination of the amount of the gift transfer is generally calculated using a

---

either into or out of qualified payment right status is dependent largely upon the potential application of Section 2701(d). See infra ¶ 19.02[5][a].

[205] IRC § 2701(c)(3)(C)(ii). See Reg. §§ 25.2701-2(c)(1), 25.2701-2(c)(2), 25.2701-2(c)(4).

[206] IRC § 2701(a)(3)(A). See supra text accompanying note 196.

[207] IRC § 2701(a)(3)(A); Reg. § 25.2701-2(a)(4). However, if the election is made, subsequent transfer taxes may be imposed on any cumulative unpaid distributions. IRC § 2701(d). See infra ¶ 19.02[5][a].

[208] This includes a payment right that is qualified as a result of an election. IRC § 2701(c)(3)(C)(ii).

[209] IRC § 2701(a)(3)(B). In determining the lowest total value, a consistent set of assumptions must be used with due regard to the entity's net worth, prospective earning power, and other relevant factors. Reg. § 25.2701-2(a)(3).

[210] HR Conf. Rep. No. 964, 101st Cong., 2d Sess. 1134 Ex. 1 (1990) reprinted in 1991-2 CB 560, 605; Reg. §§ 25.2701-2(a)(5) Ex., 25.2701-2(d) Ex. 3, 25.2701-3(d) Exs. 1, 2, 3 provide illustrations of the "lower of" valuation rule. See also Priv. Ltr. Rul. 200138028 (June 21, 2000) (application of the "lower of" valuation rule).

subtraction method of valuation.[211] Discretionary payment rights attached to an applicable retained interest are generally assigned a zero value.[212] In some situations[213] nondiscretionary payment rights may have more value,[214] including even fair market value.[215] Under the subtraction method, any reduction in the value of the applicable retained interest caused by Section 2701 valuation of the discretionary payment rights is transferred to the subordinate equity interests, which increases the amount of the gift transfer.[216] The subtraction method[217] generally involves a four-step procedure to determine the value of the transferred subordinate equity interests:[218]

Step 1: Determine the aggregate fair market value of all family-held interests[219] in the entity immediately after the transfer to which Section 2701 applies, computed as if all the interests were held by one person and without regard to Section 2701.[220]

Step 2: Generally subtract the following amounts from the amount determined in Step 1:[221]

---

[211] Reg. §§ 25.2701-3(a), 25.2701-3(b), 25.2701-3(d). See King, "Final Estate Freeze Rules Simplify Subtraction Method," 70 Taxes 460 (1992). An exception to the rule of determining the amount of a gift using the subtraction method occurs when the Section 2701(a)(4) minimum valuation rule applies. See infra ¶ 19.02[4][f].

[212] IRC § 2701(a)(3)(A); Reg. §§ 25.2701-1(a)(2)(i), 25.2701-1(a)(2)(ii). Distribution rights other than qualified payment rights and extraordinary payments rights fall into this category.

[213] See supra ¶ 19.02[4][c].

[214] Qualified payment rights combined with extraordinary payment rights generally fall into this category.

[215] IRC § 2701(c)(3)(A). See Reg. §§ 25.2701-2(a)(4), 25.2701-1(e) Ex. 1; supra ¶ 19.02[4][c] text accompanying note 198.

[216] A valuation analysis similar to the subtraction method is used where a donor retains an interest in transferred property. The value of the entire interest transferred is reduced by the value of retained interests to determine the value of the transferred interests. See Reg. § 25.2512-9(a)(1)(i). If there is a transfer to a family member with a retained temporal interest, Section 2702 provides a valuation methodology even more similar to that employed by Section 2701, because under Section 2702, the retained interests are generally valued at zero. See ¶ 19.03[1].

[217] An overview of the operation of Section 2701, with a simplified illustration of the subtraction method of valuation, is presented in the regulations. Reg. § 25.2701-1(a)(3) Ex. See TAM 9447004 (Nov. 25, 1994) (for a more detailed illustration of the subtraction method).

[218] Reg. § 25.2701-3(b).

[219] See infra text accompanying notes 235-237.

[220] Reg. § 25.2701-3(b)(1)(i).

[221] Reg. § 25.2701-3(b)(2)(i).

a. The sum of the fair market value of all family-held senior equity interests[222] other than applicable retained interests held by
   the transferor or applicable family members;[223]
b. The fair market value of any family-held equity interests of
   the same class as, or subordinate to, the transferred interests
   other than such interests that are held by the transferor, members of the transferor's family, and applicable family members
   of the transferor; and[224]
c. The *Section 2701 value* of the applicable retained interests
   held by the transferor and applicable family members.[225]

The effect of Step 2 is to isolate and place a value on all
subordinate equity interests[226] held by the transferor, members of
the transferor's family, and applicable family members of the
transferor.

Step 3: The Step 2 amount is allocated between the subordinate equity
interests that are the subject of the transfer and all other remaining subordinate equity interests (held by transferor, members of
the transferor's family, and applicable family members of the
transferor).[227] This step tentatively values the subordinate equity
interests that are transferred to members of the transferor's family.

Step 4: The amount allocated to the transferred subordinate equity interests in Step 3 is adjusted to take account of any minority or similar discount,[228] qualified interest under Section 2702,[229] and
consideration received.[230]

Prior to delving into the four-step subtraction method in greater detail,
two special valuation rules should be mentioned. A simplified subtraction
method of valuation applies if the nature of the transfer is a contribution to

---

[222] A senior equity interest is an equity interest in an entity that has a right to distributions of income and capital that is preferred as to the rights of the transferred interest.
Reg. § 25.2701-3(a)(2)(ii). See supra ¶ 19.02[2] note 25.

[223] Reg. § 25.2701-3(b)(2)(ii)(A). An adjustment may be required here. See infra text
accompanying notes 244–247.

[224] Reg. § 25.2701-3(b)(2)(i)(A).

[225] Reg. § 25.2701-3(b)(2)(i)(B).

[226] Subordinate equity interests are equity interests in the entity as to which an applicable retained interest is a senior equity interest. Reg. § 25.2701-3(a)(2)(iii). See supra
¶ 19.02[2] note 24.

[227] Reg. § 25.2701-3(b)(3).

[228] Reg. § 25.2701-3(b)(4)(ii).

[229] Reg. § 25.2701-3(b)(4)(iii). See ¶ 19.03.

[230] Reg. § 25.2701-3(b)(4)(iv).

capital.[231] In addition, whenever Section 2701 applies, it imposes a floor on the value of the transferred interest under which a minimum value is assigned to the class of subordinate equity interest from which the transfer is made that is based on an assumption that all subordinate equity interests in the entity have a total value equal to at least 10 percent of the value of the entity.[232]

[i] Step 1: Valuation of all family-held interests. Under the regular four-step subtraction method, the first step is to determine the fair market value[233] of all family-held equity interests in the entity immediately *after* the transfer without regard to Section 2701.[234] Family-held interests are all interests owned directly or by entity attribution[235] by the transferor, any applicable family members, and any lineal descendants of the parents of the transferor or the transferor's spouse.[236] Thus, the group includes brothers and sisters of the transferor or the transferor's spouse and their lineal descendants.[237] The fair market value is determined by assuming that the interests are all held by one individual.[238] This permits the valuation to reflect any control premium.[239]

[ii] Step 2: Reduction for the value of senior equity interests and some subordinate equity interests. The Step 1 amount is essentially reduced by three amounts: (1) the fair market value of all family-held senior equity interests other than applicable retained interests held by the transferor and applicable family members; (2) the Section 2701 value of the applicable retained

---

[231] See infra ¶ 19.02[4][e].

[232] IRC § 2701(a)(4). If the 10 percent amount exceeds the amount determined under the regular Section 2701 computation, the 10 percent based value applies. See infra ¶ 19.02[4][f].

[233] See Reg. § 25.2512-1.

[234] Reg. § 25.2701-3(b)(1)(i).

[235] See supra ¶ 19.02[2][d].

[236] Reg. §§ 25.2701-2(b)(5)(i), 25.2701-3(a)(2)(i). These are the same interests that are included in determining whether the transferor controls the entity when determining whether there are distribution rights under Section 2701. See supra ¶ 19.02[2][b] text accompanying notes 100–102.

[237] See supra ¶ 19.02[2][b] text accompanying note 101; infra text accompanying note 249.

[238] Reg. § 25.2701-3(b)(1)(i). The value is determined by applying Section 2704(b), thereby potentially disregarding a reduction in the value of any applicable restriction on the senior equity interest. See Reg. §§ 25.2704-2(c), 25.2704-2(d) Ex. 5; ¶ 19.05[3].

[239] See ¶¶ 4.02[3][f], 10.02[2][c]. This assumption, in effect, permits any minority discount with respect to a transferred interest to be taken into account at the last step in the four-step process. See Reg. § 25.2701-3(b)(4)(ii); infra text accompanying notes 262, 263.

This valuation should also reflect any marketability discount. See ¶¶ 4.02[4][d], 10.02[2][c]. See also Kordestani, "Section 2701 Valuation Issues in a Transfer of Family Business Interests," 73 Taxes 403 (1995).

interests held by the transferor or applicable family members; and (3) the fair market value of subordinate equity interests held by family members *other than* the transferor, members of the transferor's family, and applicable family members of the transferor.[240] Once the Step 2 computation is complete, the remaining value is the value of the subordinate equity interests held by the transferor, members of the transferor's family, and applicable family members of the transferor.

The Step 2 reduction involves interests valued at their fair market value[241] and interests valued by Section 2701. Three groups of interests are valued at their fair market value under the Step 2 reduction. First, all family-held senior equity interests, other than applicable retained interests[242] held by the transferor or applicable family members, are valued at their fair market value.[243] Second, under a special percentage rule some applicable retained interests are treated as not being held by the transferor or an applicable family member and are valued at their fair market value.[244] The special percentage rule applies if the percentage held by the transferor and applicable family members of any equity class that constitutes applicable retained interests (including any applicable retained interest received as consideration) exceeds *either* the highest family-held[245] percentage ownership (determined on the basis of relative fair market values) of any class of subordinate equity interests *or* all subordinate equity interests, valued in the aggregate.[246] The excess percentage of the applicable retained interests is treated as held by someone other than the transferor or an applicable family member and is valued at its fair market value.[247] Third, subordinate equity interests held by family members other than the transferor, members of the transferor's family, and applicable family members of the

---

[240] Reg. §§ 25.2701-3(b)(2), 25.2701-3(b)(5). But see infra text accompanying notes 244–247.

[241] For this purpose, the fair market value of an interest is its pro rata share of the fair market value of all family-held equity interests of the same class determined as if all such family-held equity interests were held by one individual. Reg. § 25.2701-3(b)(2)(i). By treating all family interests as if they were held by one individual, any control premium is allocated pro rata among family-held interests. Id.

[242] IRC § 2701(b). See supra ¶ 19.02[2][b][ii].

[243] Reg. § 25.2701-3(b)(2)(i)(A); IRC § 2701(e)(2). See supra ¶ 19.02[2][b][i]. Thus, an applicable retained interest held by the transferor's child would be a senior equity interest valued at is fair market value.

[244] Reg. § 25.2701-3(b)(5).

[245] Reg. § 25.2701-3(a)(2)(i).

[246] Reg. § 25.2701-3(b)(5)(ii).

[247] Reg. §§ 25.2701-3(b)(2)(i)(B), 25.2701-3(b)(5)(i). See Reg. § 25.2701-3(d) Ex. 2 (under Step 2, 10 percent of the transferor's applicable retained interests are valued at fair market value, not their Section 2701 value, because the transferor and applicable family members owned 60 percent of the entity's senior equity interests and only 50 percent of the subordinate equity interests are family-held interests).

transferor are also valued at their fair market value.[248] Recall that Step 1 includes the value of all family-held equity interests, which include those held by any lineal descendants of the parents of the transferor or the transferor's spouse. This chain of relations is broader than the Step 2 group that includes only transferor, members of the transferor's family, and applicable family members. The subordinate equity interests of those in the first group who are not in the second group (for example, brothers and sisters and their descendants) are eliminated here and those persons' subordinate equity interests are valued at their fair market value.[249]

The second type of interests that are deducted in Step 2 are interests that are valued under Section 2701.[250] These interests include all applicable retained interests held by the transferor or applicable family members other than an applicable retained interest received as consideration for the transfer and other than the excess percentage of such interests that falls into the fair market valuation category.[251] The Section 2701 valuation of these interests encompasses the zero valuation rules,[252] the "lower of" rule,[253] and a fair market value rule.[254] This special Section 2701 reduction in valuation of these interests effectively increases the value of the transferred interest under the subtraction method.

[iii] Step 3: Allocation between the transferred interests and other family-held subordinate equity interests. The value remaining after Step 2 is that attributed to subordinate equity interests held by the transferor, members of the transferor's family, and applicable family members of the transferor. The role of Step 3 is to value the subordinate equity interests transferred to members of the transferor's family, since only those transferred interests are being valued for gift tax purposes.[255] If the nature of a Section 2701 transfer is a capital structure transaction, such as a redemption of a subordinate equity in-

---

[248] Reg. § 25.2701-3(b)(2)(i)(A).

[249] The regulations seem to have made one error here. Under Section 2701(e)(1), members of the transferor's family include spouses of any descendants of the transferor or transferor's spouse. Such spouses are not encompassed within the "family-held" definition. This is possibly an unintended omission by the regulations.

[250] Reg. § 25.2701-3(b)(2)(i)(B) (referring to Reg. § 25.2701-2). See supra ¶¶ 19.04[4][a]–19.04[4][c].

[251] Reg. § 25.2701-3(b)(2)(i)(B). See supra text accompanying notes 244–247.

[252] IRC § 2701(a)(3)(A); Reg. §§ 25.2701-2(a)(1), 25.2701-2(a)(2). See Reg. § 25.2701-3(d) Exs. 4, 5.

[253] IRC § 2701(a)(3)(B). See Reg. §§ 25.2701-2(a)(3), 25.2701-3(d) Exs. 1, 2.

[254] See Reg. §§ 25.2701-1(e) Ex. 1, 25.2701-2(a)(4); supra ¶ 19.02[4][c] text accompanying note 198.

[255] Reg. § 25.2701-3(b)(3). See infra text accompanying notes 287, 292 for examples of the Step 3 process.

terest for a senior equity interest having a Section 2701 value,[256] the Step 3 process involves two phases. First, a determination of the amount of the Section 2701 transfer deemed to be made by the person whose interest was deemed transferred to members of that person's family, and then an allocation between the retained and transferred shares.[257]

In making the Step 3 allocation, if there is only one class of family-held subordinate equity interest, the allocation is made pro rata among the stock or interests.[258] If there is more than one class of family-held subordinate equity interests, the value remaining after Step 2 is first allocated to the most senior class of subordinate equity interests in a manner most fairly approximating their value if all rights valued under Section 2701 at zero did not exist.[259] If there is no clearly appropriate method of allocating value under the previously mentioned rules, the remaining value after Step 2 is allocated to the interests in proportion to their fair market values determined without regard to Section 2701.[260]

[iv] **Step 4: Adjustments to the value of the transferred interests.** Several final adjustments may be made to the value of the subordinate equity interests transferred to family members of the transferor as determined under Step 3.[261] A reduction is permitted for any minority or similar discount.[262] If the transferred interest would otherwise qualify for a minority or similar discount if Section 2701 were inapplicable, then the amount of the gift determined in Step 3 qualifies for a reduction. The amount of the reduction is the amount of any excess of the pro rata portion of the fair market value of the family-held interests of the same class (determined as if all voting rights conferred by family-held equity interests were held by one person who had no interest in the entity other than the family-held interests of the same class and otherwise without regard to Section 2701) over the fair market value of the transferred interest (also determined as if the holder had no other interest in the entity, thus taking a minority or similar discount into consideration, and determined without regard to Section 2701).[263]

---

[256] See supra ¶ 19.02[2][a] text accompanying notes 35–45.

[257] See Reg. §§ 25.2701-3(d) Exs. 4, 5 both of which provide applications of the rules in Step 3.

[258] See Reg. § 25.2701-3(d) Ex. 4 Step 3.

[259] Reg. § 25.2701-3(b)(3). Applicable retained interests not assigned a zero value are valued consistent with their valuation under Regulations Section 25.2701-2(a)(4). Id.

[260] Reg. § 25.2701-3(b)(3).

[261] Reg. § 25.2701-3(b)(4)(i).

[262] Reg. § 25.2701-3(b)(4)(ii). See ¶¶ 4.02[4], 10.02[2][c], infra ¶ 19.02[4][f] note 302.

[263] Reg. § 25.2701-3(b)(4)(ii). See Reg. § 25.2701-3(d) Ex. 3 (illustrating the minority discount computation where Transferor transfers 10 percent of a 75 percent ownership

A second adjustment involves the interrelationship of Section 2702[264] and Section 2701. In general, as a result of the trust attribution rules (including the ordering rules) of Section 2701,[265] Section 2701 operates independently of Section 2702, although it sometimes achieves the same results that would occur if both sections were applied.[266] For example, if Transferor retains an applicable retained interest and transfers a subordinate equity interest in an entity to a trust with income retained in Transferor for a term of years and remainder to Child, both sections would treat Child as owning all of the value of the subordinate equity interest. The Section 2701 attribution rules would treat the Child as owning all of the subordinate equity interest[267] and the Section 2702

---

of subordinate interests in an entity); TAM 9447004 (July 29, 1994) (also illustrating the computation of a minority discount). Cf. Reg. § 25.2701-3(d) Exs. 1, 2. The minority discount computation allows a reduction in value for the minority aspects of the transferred subordinate equity interest, but it disregards any minority aspects of the transferred value of the applicable retained interest.

Assume Transferor owns a majority of the stock of a corporation, no family member owns any other interest in the corporation, and the Transferor's stock is allocated a 20 percent control premium. Transferor transfers one quarter of Transferor's subordinate equity interest to Child retaining an applicable retained interest valued at zero under Section 2701. Assume Transferor's one-quarter minority interest qualifies for a 20 percent minority discount. Disregarding premiums and discounts, the subordinate equity interest has a $10,000 value and the applicable retained interest has a $40,000 value. The values are increased to $12,000 and $48,000, respectively, when combined with Transferor's other shares, with each appropriately assigned a 20 percent control premium, but the values are decreased to $8,000 and $32,000 respectively when transferred and a 20 percent discount is accorded to each interest. Under the first three steps of the subtraction method, Transferor's Section 2701 transfer would be $60,000 taking into account the zero value retained interest, the control premium, and the fact that one quarter of Transferor's subordinate equity interest is transferred. Under the Step 4 minority discount adjustment, there would be a $4,000 reduction, the pro rata share of Transferor's subordinate equity interests ($10,000) increased by the ($2,000) control premium, or $12,000, reduced by $8,000, the fair market value of the transferred interest determined without regard to Section 2701 and accorded a minority discount ($10,000 less 20 percent of $10,000). Thus, Transferor's Section 2701 transfer would be $56,000 ($60,000 less $4,000).

In this hypothetical case, it is arguable that since the zero value accorded the applicable retained interest under Section 2701 increases the value of the gift to $60,000 when the control premium is added, the minority discount should reflect a minority discount on the entire amount of the transfer or a discount of $20,000 (taking into account the 20 percent premium on the transfer and another $10,000, a 20 percent discount on the $50,000 Section 2701 amount of the transfer disregarding premiums and discounts) to result in a gift of $40,000 ($60,000 less $20,000).

The regulations apply to similar discounts, such as discounts for a lack of marketability. See ¶¶ 4.02[4][d], 10.02[2][c], infra ¶ 19.02[4][f] note 302. Similar rules should apply to such discounts.

[264] See ¶ 19.03.

[265] See supra ¶ 19.02[2][d][iii].

[266] See supra ¶ 19.02[2][a] note 55.

[267] Reg. § 25.2701-6(a)(5)(ii)(A). See supra ¶ 19.02[2][a] text accompanying note 55.

valuation rules would value Transferor's interest at zero,[268] effectively transferring all of the value of the subordinate equity interest to Child.[269] However, if
the amount of a Section 2702 transfer that would normally occur is reduced
because the transfer involves a "qualified interest" under which a fixed amount
or fixed percentage of the value of property must be paid to the income beneficiary annually,[270] the nature of the trust interest is similar, although not identical, to a qualified payment interest.[271] Seemingly because of the similarity, if
there is a Section 2701 transfer involving a trust with a Section 2702 qualified
interest, the amount of the Section 2701 transfer is reduced under Step 4 to reflect the value of the qualified interest.[272] For example, if Transferor retaining
an applicable retained interest transfers a subordinate equity interest to a grantor retained qualified interest trust[273] with a remainder to Child and Transferor's retained interest in the trust has a value of 60 percent of the corpus,
only 40 percent of the corpus is treated as transferred under Section 2702 and
only 40 percent of the amount otherwise determined under the subtraction
method is treated as a transfer under Section 2701.[274]

The final Step 4 reduction is for the amount of any consideration in
money or money's worth received by the transferor.[275] The amount of the reduction cannot exceed the amount of the gift determined without regard to
Section 2701.[276] If the consideration received is an applicable retained interest
in the entity, the value of the consideration is generally determined under Sec-

---

[268] IRC § 2702(a)(2)(A).

[269] If the Transferor had transferred the subordinate equity interest outright to Child
and transferred the applicable retained interest to a grantor retained income trust for a
term of years with a remainder to Child, although Section 2702 would transfer all of the
value of the applicable retained interest to Child, the Section 2701 attribution rules would
treat Transferor as owning all of the applicable retained interest. Reg. § 25.2701-6(a)(5)(i).
As a result, Section 2701 would apply to the transfer of the subordinate equity interest.

[270] IRC §§ 2702(a)(2)(B), 2702(b). See Reg. § 25.2702-2(d) Ex. 2.

[271] IRC § 2701(c)(3)(A). See supra ¶ 19.02[4][c][i]. When an interest is placed in a
trust requiring annuity-type payments to the interest holder, there is no statutory enforcement mechanism similar to Section 2701(d) for nonpayment or underpayment of the qualified interest payment rights valued under Section 2702(a)(2)(B).

[272] Reg. § 25.2701-3(b)(4)(iii).

[273] IRC §§ 2702(b)(1), 2702(b)(2).

[274] If Transferor transferred a subordinate equity interest outright to Child and an applicable retained interest to a trust with a qualified interest to Transferor and a remainder
to Child, Regulations Section 25.2701-3(b)(4)(iii) should apply. However, assuming the
qualified interest is worth 60 percent of the corpus, seemingly the reduction under the regulations should be only 60 percent of the difference between the fair market value and
Section 2701 value of the applicable retained interest.

[275] Reg. § 25.2701-3(b)(4)(iv). See IRC § 2512(b).

[276] Reg. § 25.2701-3(b)(4)(iv).

tion 2701.[277] For example, if a subordinate equity interest is transferred to an entity in a capital structure transaction[278] in exchange for an applicable retained interest, the value of the applicable retained interest received is determined under Section 2701.[279] In a contribution to capital,[280] any applicable retained interest received is always assigned a zero value.[281]

[v] **Examples.** Assume that all family-held interests in an entity have a fair market value of $1 million. Disregarding discounts, Transferor owns a senior equity interest worth $400,000 and a subordinate equity interest worth $100,000; Transferor's Parent owns a senior equity interest worth $200,000 and a subordinate equity interest worth $50,000; and Transferor's Sibling owns a senior equity interest worth $200,000 and a subordinate equity interest worth $50,000. Transferor transfers the $100,000 subordinate equity interest to Child in a Section 2701 transfer. Assume that when the interests are treated as owned by one individual under Step 1,[282] they are controlling interests in the entity, and they have a $1 million value that reflects the control factor. Transferor's and Parent's senior equity interests have a Section 2701(a)(3)(A) zero valuation. Under Step 2, the Step 1 amount is reduced by the values of all of the senior equity interests (Sibling's interest is valued at its $200,000 fair market value and Parent's and Transferor's applicable retained interests are valued at their Section 2701 zero value) and by Sibling's subordinate equity interest (valued at its $50,000 fair market value). Thus, the $1 million Step 1 amount is reduced under Step 2 by $250,000 to $750,000. Under Step 3, the $750,000 is allocated between the transferred interest and Parent's subordinate equity interest according to their relative fair market values ($100,000 and $50,000, respectively) with the result that two thirds of the $750,000 amount or $500,000 is allocated to Transferor's gift to Child of the subordinate equity interest. Assume there are no Step 4 adjustments.[283] As a result of Section 2701, Transferor makes a gift valued at $500,000 to Child. In the alternative, if Parent's senior equity interest was worth $300,000 and Sibling's was worth $100,000, the Step 1 result would be the same. The Step 2 amount would be $850,000 and under Step 3 Transferor would make a gift transfer to Child of two thirds of $850,000, or $566,667. If, instead, Parent's senior equity interest were

---

[277] Reg. § 25.2701-3(b)(4)(iv).

[278] See supra ¶ 19.02[2][a] text accompanying notes 35–45.

[279] Reg. § 25.2701-2(d) Exs. 4, 5 illustrate the application of this Step 4 rule in a capital structure transaction. See infra text accompanying note 288.

[280] See supra ¶ 19.02[2][a] text accompanying note 32.

[281] Reg. § 25.2701-3(b)(4)(iv).

[282] Reg. § 25.2701-3(b)(1).

[283] As a practical matter, the value of Child's interest should reflect a minority discount. See Reg. § 25.2701-3(b)(4)(ii); supra text accompanying notes 262, 263, ¶¶ 4.02[4][c], 10.02[2][c].

worth $100,000 and Sibling's were worth $300,000, the Step 1 amount would again be $1 million. The Step 2 amount would be $650,000 and, under Step 3, Transferor would make a gift transfer of two thirds of $650,000, or $433,333.

Assume instead Transferor and Child each own one half of the value of an entity that has one class of ownership and the entity is worth $1 million.[284] In a capital structure transaction one half of Transferor's equity interest is redeemed (one fourth of the entire interests) for a senior equity interest with a fair market value of $250,000. Assume Transferor's senior equity interest is an applicable retained interest that has a zero valuation under Section 2701.[285] Transferor is deemed to make an indirect transfer triggering Section 2701.[286] The Step 1 amount is $1 million, and it is reduced under Step 2 by the zero value of Transferor's applicable retained interest, leaving $1 million of value. Under Step 3, $250,000 of the $1 million value is allocated to the transferred (redeemed) stock that represents one fourth of the entire subordinate equity interest. Thus, the transferred stock is treated as a transfer of $250,000 to the corporation for no consideration. Since, after the transfer, Transferor owns one third of the subordinate equity interest and Child owns two thirds of such interest, two thirds of the transfer or $166,667 is deemed to be a gift transfer to Child.[287] Although Transferor received consideration for the transfer, under Step 4, the consideration was an applicable retained interest that is valued at zero, and as a result, there is no reduction for such consideration.[288] If, when the entity is still worth $1 million, Transferor subsequently redeems the remaining subordinate equity interest for a senior equity interest (again having a zero valuation under Section 2701), the first two steps would be the same. Under Step 3, $333,333 of the $1 million of value is allocated to the transfer to the corporation, the ratio of the transferred stock to the total outstanding stock (one third times the Step 2 amount of $1 million). Since after the transfer Transferor owns no subordinate equity interest, all of the transfer is deemed to be made to Child. Again, the Step 4 consideration adjustment is zero because the applicable retained interest received by Parent is valued at zero under Section 2701.[289] Thus, Parent's Section 2701 transfer is $333,333.[290]

Assume Transferor and Child are the sole owners of an entity and each owns 50 percent of the applicable retained interests that are worth $200,000

---

[284] This example is based on Reg. §§ 25.2701-3(d) Exs. 4, 5.

[285] IRC § 2701(a)(3)(A).

[286] Reg. § 25.2701-1(b)(2).

[287] Reg. § 25.2701-3(b)(3). See Reg. § 25.2701-3(d) Ex. 4 Step 3.

[288] Reg. § 25.2701-3(b)(4)(iv). See supra text accompanying note 279.

[289] See Reg. § 25.2701-3(d) Ex. 5.

[290] Note that in these examples where the Section 2701 value of the applicable retained interests received is zero, the total transfers equal the value of Transferor's total original interests of $500,000. See Reg. § 25.2701-3(d) Exs. 4, 5 (the value of the original interest totaled $750,000).

and 50 percent of the subordinate equity interests that are worth $200,000 with the entity having a total fair market value of $400,000. If Transferor exchanges Transferor's subordinate equity interests with Child in return for Child's applicable retained interests, Section 2701 applies to the transfer. Assume that under Section 2701(a)(3)(A), the applicable retained interests have a zero value. Under Step 1, the value of all family-held interests is $400,000. Under Step 2, there is a reduction of zero (the Section 2701 value of the applicable retained interest held by Transferor other than the interest received as consideration).[291] Under Step 3, the $400,000 Step 2 amount is allocated between the transferred and other subordinate equity interests or one half to each — $200,000.[292] Under Step 4, the amount is reduced for the amount of consideration received, except that where an applicable retained interest is received, it is assigned its Section 2701 value (here, zero),[293] and Transferor makes a gift transfer valued at $200,000 under Section 2701.

[e] Special Rule for Contributions to Capital

If the nature of the Section 2701 transfer is a contribution to capital,[294] a simplified subtraction computation is used to determine the amount of the Section 2701 transfer. Under Step 1, the fair market value of the transferor's contribution to capital is determined.[295] Under Step 2, that amount is reduced by the Section 2701 valuation[296] of any applicable retained interest received in exchange for the contribution to capital.[297] Step 3 is eliminated. The Step 4 adjustments remain in place; however, the reduction for consideration in the form of an applicable retained interest received is always zero.[298] Assume Parent and Child form a partnership and Parent receives only a senior equity interest that is an applicable retained interest valued at zero under Section 2701. The for-

---

[291] See Reg. § 25.2701-3(b)(2)(i)(B). See supra text accompanying note 251.

[292] Reg. § 25.2701-3(b)(3). See supra text accompanying note 255.

[293] Reg. § 25.2701-3(b)(4)(iv). See supra text accompanying notes 277–279.

[294] A contribution to the capital likely includes a transfer of money or property (other than an equity interest in the entity) to a newly formed or existing entity in return for an equity interest in the entity or for no consideration. See supra ¶ 19.02[2][a] text accompanying note 32. A contribution to capital constitutes a Section 2701 transfer. Reg. § 25.2701-1(b)(2)(i)(A). The regulations distinguish a contribution to capital from a "capital structure transaction" (a redemption, recapitalization, etc.) of an existing entity. See Reg. §§ 25.2701-1(b)(2)(i)(A), 25.2701-1(b)(2)(i)(B); supra ¶ 19.02[2][a] text accompanying notes 30–34.

[295] Reg. § 25.2701-3(b)(1)(ii). This is the fair market value of property transferred to the entity regardless of whether any consideration is received for the transfer.

[296] See Reg. § 25.2701-2; supra ¶¶ 19.02[4][b], 19.02[4][c].

[297] Reg. § 25.2701-3(b)(2)(ii).

[298] Reg. § 25.2701-3(b)(4)(iv).

mation is treated as a contribution to capital[299] and, under the simplified subtraction method, the value of Parent's contribution to capital of the partnership is reduced by zero, the Section 2701 value of the applicable retained interest that Parent received. Thus, the full value of Parent's contribution is a Section 2701 transfer to Child.

[f] Minimum Valuation of the Junior Equity Interest

If Section 2701 applies to a transfer, a special minimum valuation rule applies that establishes a minimum value for the transferred junior equity interest.[300] The amount of the Section 2701 transfer is the *greater* of the amount of the transfer determined under the subtraction method or the minimum value rule.[301] The value of the junior equity interest transferred may not be less than its pro rata portion of the value that would be determined if the total value of all junior equity interests in the entity were equal to 10 percent of the sum of the total value of all equity interests in such entity. Under the minimum value rule, the total amount of indebtedness of such entity owed to the transferor and to applicable family members is treated as an equity interest in the entity.[302] As a result, indebtedness may not be used to avoid or reduce the minimum value. In applying the rule, indebtedness does not include: short-term indebtedness incurred with respect to the current trade or business of the entity (such as accounts payable for current expenses);[303] indebtedness owed to a third party

---

[299] See Reg. § 25.2701-1(b)(2)(i)(A); supra ¶ 19.02[2][a] text accompanying note 33.

[300] The term "junior equity interest" refers to common stock or any partnership interest under which the rights to income and capital (or, to the extent provided in the regulations, the rights to either income or capital) are junior to the rights of all other classes of equity interests. IRC § 2701(a)(4)(B)(i). See Reg. § 25.2701-3(c)(2). A junior equity interest is a "subordinate equity interest," a term used elsewhere in the regulations. See Reg. § 25.2701-3(a)(2)(iii); supra ¶ 19.02[2] note 24.

[301] This minimum valuation rule has limited application. If Section 2701 applies, generally any applicable retained interest is valued at zero (IRC § 2701(a)(3)(A); see supra ¶¶ 19.02[4][b], 19.02[4][c] text accompanying notes 191, 194) usually resulting in a significant increase in the amount of a transfer under the subtraction method of Section 2701. However, the minimum value rule may result in a larger Section 2701 transfer than the amount of a transfer under the subtraction method where the "lower of" rule applies (see infra text accompanying note 307), where an entity has substantial indebtedness owed to the transferor and to applicable family members (see infra text accompanying note 302), which is generally disregarded under the zero valuation rules, or where Section 2701 applies, but the transferor and family members do not control the entity but transferor has an extraordinary payment right valued at zero and also has both noncumulative dividend rights and liquidation participation rights that have significant values.

[302] IRC § 2701(a)(4)(A). See Reg. § 25.2701-3(c)(1). No minority or similar discount is permitted for the transferred interest whose value is determined under the minimum value rule. See Reg. § 25.2701-3(b)(4)(ii).

[303] Reg. § 25.2701-3(c)(3)(i)(A).

solely because it is guaranteed by the transferor or an applicable family member;[304] amounts unavailable for use by the entity that are permanently set aside in a deferred compensation arrangement;[305] or obligations with respect to a lease requiring the payment of adequate and full consideration for use of the property.[306]

For example, if Transferor owns all of the equity interests in an entity and transfers a subordinate equity interest in the entity to a family member, while retaining an applicable retained interest, Section 2701 applies. If the applicable retained interest is a qualified payment right and Transferor also has a liquidation participation right triggering the "lower of" rule,[307] it is possible that the amount of the Section 2701 transfer computed under the "lower of" rule, and therefore the value of the transferred subordinate equity interest, may be minimal. However, since Section 2701 applies to the transfer, under the minimum value rule, the amount of the transfer is at least equal to 10 percent of the value of the sum of the Transferor's total equity interests prior to the transfer, including the amount of any indebtedness of the entity owed to the transferor and applicable family members.[308]

[5] Special Rules Under Section 2701

[a] Section 2701(d)

[i] **In general.** The amount of a Section 2701 transfer to a family member is reduced if there is a "qualified payment interest"[309] because an applica-

---

[304] Reg. § 25.2701-3(c)(3)(i)(B).

[305] Reg. § 25.2701-3(c)(3)(i)(C).

[306] Reg. § 25.2701-3(c)(3)(ii). Lease payments are considered full and adequate consideration if a good-faith effort is made to determine the fair rental value under the lease and the lease terms conform to such value. Id. However, an arrearage with respect to such a lease is an indebtedness. Id.

[307] See IRC § 2701(a)(3)(B); supra ¶ 19.02[4][c][ii].

[308] If, in the example in the text, Transferor had transferred only 60 percent of the subordinate equity interest, the amount of the transfer under the minimum valuation rule would be 60 percent of the amount determined in the example.

[309] A "qualified payment interest" is any interest that is valued as a qualified payment right under Section 2701. Reg. § 25.2701-4(a). See supra ¶¶ 19.02[4][c][i], 19.02[4][c][ii]. The term includes a qualified payment right held by a transferor to the extent the transferor makes no election to treat the qualified payment right as an unqualified payment right IRC § 2701(c)(3)(C)(i); see infra text accompanying note 320); a nonqualified payment right held by a transferor to the extent the transferor elects to treat it as a qualified payment right (IRC § 2701(c)(3)(C)(ii); see infra text accompanying note 316); and a qualified or nonqualified payment right held by an applicable family member to the extent

ble retained interest is valued at greater than zero if it has a distribution right that is a qualified payment interest.[310] Generally, if there is a deficiency in the amount of the qualified payments made by the entity with respect to a qualified payment interest, the transferor or applicable family member to whom such payments should have been made is subsequently going to be treated as having made an estate or gift tax transfer under Section 2701(d).[311] The assumption is that the qualified payments that are not paid are shifting value in the entity to the benefit of the subordinate interest holders without (absent the application of Section 2701(d)) subjecting that value to transfer taxation. Upon expiration of a four-year grace period,[312] Section 2701(d) imposes a transfer tax on the amount of any delinquent qualified payments with respect to a qualified payment interest, and it essentially increases the delinquent amount by adding compound interest to it for the period of the delinquency, subject to a ceiling discussed later in this section.[313] The compounding rule is an enforcement mechanism that essentially encourages the controlled entity to make scheduled payments equal to the amounts used in the valuation of the qualified payment interest at the time of the Section 2701 transfer. The compounding rule should be considered both in making the initial determination of the rate

---

that the applicable family member elects to treat it as a qualified payment right. IRC §§ 2701(c)(3)(C)(i), 2701(c)(3)(C)(ii). See infra text accompanying notes 316, 321–322.

[310] See IRC §§ 2701(a)(3), 2701(c)(3).

[311] See infra ¶ 19.02[5][a][iii]. However, there generally is a four-year grace period for the entity to make sufficient payments. IRC § 2701(d)(2)(C). See infra text accompanying notes 343–350. The Section 6501(c)(9) open statute of limitations rule applies to any taxable gifts under Section 2701(d) if they are not adequately disclosed on a gift tax return. See infra ¶ 19.02[5][d].

In addition, if the application of the Section 2701(d) compounding rule (see infra ¶ 19.02[5][a][iv]) results in double taxation of an amount under the transfer taxes, the Treasury has authority to promulgate regulations to alleviate such double taxation. IRC § 2701(e)(6). Cf. infra ¶ 19.02[5][c].

[312] IRC § 2701(d)(2)(C).

[313] The compounding rule adds to the amount of any delinquent qualified payment an amount that assumes that any such delinquent amount was received on its due date and was reinvested at a yield equal to its discount rate, the rate used in valuing the applicable retained interest at the time of the original Section 2701 transfer. IRC § 2701(d)(2)(A)(i)(II). See infra text accompanying notes 371–385. The ceiling rule is discussed infra text accompanying notes 386–392.

From a planning perspective, Section 2701(d) is one of the most important players in the Section 2701 arena. See Zaritsky & Aucutt, Structuring Estate Freezes Under Chapter 14 ¶ 2.04[2][a] (Warren, Gorham & Lamont 1993); Harrison "Using a Multi-Class Corporation to Achieve Estate and Gift Tax Savings—Does It Work After Chapter 14?" 44 Syracuse L. Rev. 1153 (1993).

of return on a qualified payment interest[314] and an election regarding qualified payment treatment.[315]

[ii] Qualified payment elections. A transferor or an applicable family member may elect to treat a nonqualified payment right as a qualified payment interest.[316] Elective qualified payment status applies only to the extent that the amounts and times of payments assumed under the election are permissible under the legal instrument giving rise to the payment right and are consistent with the legal right of the entity to make the payment.[317] An election cannot cause the value of the applicable retained interest to exceed its fair market value determined without regard to Section 2701.[318] For example, a transferor cannot elect to value a noncumulative right to dividends of $100 per year on the assumption that dividends of $110 per year will be paid.[319] In the alternative, a transferor can elect to have a qualified payment right treated as unqualified under Section 2701.[320] If distribution payments that satisfy the qualified payment right requirements are to be made to an applicable family member, the applicable family member must affirmatively elect to treat the payment interest as a qualified payment interest.[321] Without an election, the applicable family member's payment right is treated as nonqualified.[322] If a payment right of either a transferor or an applicable family member is treated as nonqualified, the payment right is valued at zero under Section 2701[323] and the holder of the right avoids any application of Section 2701(d).

---

[314] The rate of return affects the fair market value of the qualified payment interest. See supra ¶ 19.02[4][c].

[315] See infra ¶ 19.02[5][a][ii].

[316] IRC § 2701(c)(3)(C)(ii). The election is made by attaching a statement to the Form 709, United States Gift (and Generation-Skipping Transfer) Tax Return, filed by the transferor on which the transfer is reported. Reg. § 25.2701-2(c)(5).

[317] IRC § 2701(c)(3)(C)(ii); Reg. § 25.2701-2(c)(2)(ii).

[318] Reg. § 25.2701-2(c)(2). See Reg. § 25.2701-2(d) Ex. 5.

[319] HR Conf. Rep. No. 964, 101st Cong., 2d Sess. 1134 (Ex. 1) (1990), reprinted in 1991-2 CB 560, 605.

[320] IRC § 2701(c)(3)(C)(i).

[321] IRC § 2701(c)(3)(C)(i). See Reg. § 25.2701-2(c)(4). This requirement puts an applicable family member who did not make the Section 2701 transfer on notice of Section 2701(d) and the consequences if there are payment deficiencies.

[322] IRC § 2701(c)(3)(C)(i). See Reg. § 25.2701-2(c)(4).

Of course, since the applicable family member is not the transferor, this presumption does not have any current transfer tax consequences to the applicable family member.

[323] IRC § 2701(a)(3)(A). See supra ¶ 19.02[4][c] text accompanying note 206.

An election either into or out of qualified payment status may be made with respect to a portion of the payment right.[324] Once made, any qualified payment election is revocable only with the consent of the Commissioner.[325]

In the discussion that follows, the term "transferor of a qualified payment interest" generally includes an applicable family member who makes an election to treat a qualified payment right as a qualified payment interest.

[iii] Taxable events under Section 2701(d). If a distribution right is a qualified payment interest[326] and if the scheduled payments are not made, the taxable estate or taxable gifts of the transferor will be increased to compensate for any deficiencies in the amount of qualified payments.[327] The increase in the transfer tax base may occur at the death of the transferor,[328] at the time of an inter vivos transfer of the qualified payment interest,[329] or, at the election of the transferor, upon receipt of any qualified payment more than four years beyond its due date.[330]

Death of the Transferor. If an applicable retained interest with a distribution right that is a qualified payment interest on which inadequate payments have been made[331] is includible in the transferor's gross estate,[332] the transferor's death is the taxable event triggering an increase[333] in the transferor's "taxable estate."[334] The transferor in essence has a receivable that is included in the transferor's gross estate and is transferred to the transferee family member at the time of the transferor's death.[335] The amount should be included as

---

[324] Reg. §§ 25.2701-2(c)(1), 25.2701-2(c)(2), 25.2701-2(c)(4).

[325] IRC § 2701(c)(3)(iii); Reg. § 25.2701-2(c)(3).

[326] See supra note 309.

[327] See IRC §§ 2701(d)(1), 2701(d)(3)(A). Section 2701(d)(4)(A) also applies the Section 2701(d) rules to any applicable family member who has retained an applicable retained interest conferring a right to qualified payments and who elects to have the payments so treated. See Reg. § 25.2701-2(c)(4); supra text accompanying notes 321–322.

[328] IRC § 2701(d)(3)(A)(i).

[329] IRC § 2701(d)(3)(A)(ii).

[330] IRC § 2701(d)(3)(A)(iii). See supra note 311. There are also two special sets of rules applicable to transfers to applicable family members. See infra text accompanying notes 351–363, 364–366.

[331] The four-year grace period is disregarded in determining whether there are delinquent payments. Reg. § 25.2701-4(c)(5) (last sentence).

[332] This includes an applicable retained interest that is held directly or one that was transferred inter vivos but is included in the transferor's gross estate. See infra text accompanying note 339.

[333] The amount of the increase is discussed infra ¶ 9.02[5][a][iv].

[334] IRC §§ 2701(d)(1)(A), 2701(d)(3)(A)(i).

[335] The amount of the delinquent payments would be a phantom asset included in the gross estate under Section 2033 as an account receivable. It likely receives no stepped-up basis under Section 1014, because when paid it would be an item of income in respect of

an increase in the value of the qualified payment interest that is included in the transferor's gross estate.

Inter Vivos Transfer of an Applicable Retained Interest Providing a Qualified Payment Interest. If the transferor makes an inter vivos transfer of an applicable retained interest with a distribution right that is a qualified payment interest on which inadequate payments have been made[336] during the transferor's lifetime, the transferor's "taxable gifts" are increased for the calendar year of the transfer.[337] The statute requires an increase in the taxable gifts of the transferor, thus precluding the allowance of an annual exclusion with respect to any increase,[338] but not precluding use of the unified credit.

If an inter vivos transfer of the qualified payment interest is made and the interest is potentially includible in the transferor's gross estate (other than under Section 2035), no deficiency transfer occurs until gross estate inclusion occurs or the possibility of gross estate inclusion (other than under Section 2035) no longer exists.[339]

Any termination of a right to a qualified payment is a taxable event under Section 2701(d).[340] Thus, a Section 2701(d) taxable event occurs (either inter vivos or at death) if an individual is treated as indirectly holding a qualified payment interest held by a trust on the earlier of the termination of the individual's interest in the trust (either inter vivos or at death) or the termination of the trust's interest in the qualified payment interest (whether by disposition or otherwise).[341] For example, assume Transferor transfers a qualified payment interest to a trust retaining a life estate and thereafter a deficiency occurs in the

---

a decedent. See IRC §§ 691, 1014(c); Comm'r v. American Light and Traction, 156 F2d 398 (7th Cir. 1946) (placing all taxpayers on the cash method of accounting with respect to the receipt of dividends).

[336] The four-year grace period is disregarded in determining whether there are delinquent payments. Reg. § 25.2701-4(c)(5) (last sentence).

[337] IRC §§ 2701(d)(1)(B), 2701(d)(3)(A)(ii). The amount of the transfer is discussed infra ¶ 19.02[5][a][iv].

[338] The Section 2503(b) annual exclusion reduces the total amount of gifts in arriving at "taxable gifts" and since only "taxable gifts" under Section 2503(a) are increased here, the increase does not qualify for an annual exclusion.

It is questionable how any gift tax paid on the taxable gift should be used to adjust the basis of the previously transferred subordinate equity interest under Section 1015(d). Cf. infra ¶ 19.02[5][f][ii], especially note 514.

[339] Reg. § 25.2701-4(b)(2). If there is no delinquency transfer prior to the transferor's death, there is an increase in the amount of the transferor's taxable estate. Reg. § 25.2701-4(b)(2)(ii). See supra text accompanying notes 331–335. Comparison can be made to the estate tax inclusion period rules that apply to generation skipping transfers. See IRC §§ 2642(f)(1), 2642(f)(3) discussed at ¶ 16.02[7]. See especially ¶ 16.02[7][c] text accompanying note 485, discussing the interrelationship of Sections 2035 and 2038.

[340] IRC § 2701(d)(5).

[341] IRC § 2701(d)(5); Reg. § 25.2701-4(b)(1).

qualified payments. There is an increase in Transferor's taxable gifts if the trust sells the qualified payment interest or if Transferor gifts or sells the income interest. There is an increase in Transferor's taxable estate if Transferor dies holding the income interest of the trust containing the qualified payment interest.[342]

Elective Transfer. There is a four-year grace period under Section 2701(d).[343] If a qualified payment is made within four years of its due date, it is treated as being paid on its due date.[344] If a qualified payment is made at any time after the four-year grace period[345] and before any testamentary or inter vivos transfer of the qualified payment interest, the transferor may elect to treat the receipt of the qualified payment as a taxable event.[346] The election can be made only with respect to qualified payments that are currently, or were previously, received.[347] When an election occurs, the taxable gifts[348] of the transferor are increased for the year in which the election is made,[349] but the amount of the increase does not include the late qualified payment itself.[350] Generally an election is made to mitigate the effect of the compounding rules.

---

[342] Reg. § 25.2701-4(b)(1). See supra text accompanying notes 331–335.

[343] IRC § 2701(d)(2)(C). The four-year grace period is inapplicable if the transferor dies or transfers the qualified payment interest prior to such payment. Reg. § 25.2701-4(c)(5) (last sentence).

[344] IRC § 2701(d)(2)(C).

[345] IRC § 2701(d)(2)(C). This is a date four years subsequent to the due date of the payment. See Reg. § 25.2701-4(c)(2).

[346] IRC §§ 2701(d)(1)(B), 2701(d)(3)(A)(iii). The election must include a statement meeting certain requirements specified in the regulations. See Reg. § 25.2701-4(d)(3)(iii). The election is revocable only with the consent of the Commissioner. Reg. § 25.2701-4(d)(1).

[347] Reg. § 25.2701-4(d)(1). See Reg. § 25.2701-4(c)(4). Payments for which an election is made are treated as having been made on their due dates for purposes of subsequent taxable events. Reg. § 25.2701-1(d)(1). See Reg. § 25.2701-4(d)(4) Ex.

[348] Since taxable gifts are increased, the amount of the increase does not qualify for the annual exclusion. It is questionable how any gift tax paid on the taxable gift should be used to adjust the basis of the previously transferred subordinate equity interest under Section 1015(d). Cf. infra ¶ 19.02[5][f][ii], especially note 514.

[349] Reg. § 25.2701-4(d)(3). If the election is made for the year in which the payment is received on a timely filed return for the year, the taxable event is deemed to occur on the date the qualified payment is received. Reg. § 25.2701-4(d)(3)(i). If the election is for a payment received in a prior year or if a return for the year of payment is not timely filed, the taxable gifts are generally increased on the first day of the month preceding the month in which the return is filed, unless the transferor dies prior to the election, in which case the taxable gift occurs on the later of the date of death or the first day of the month immediately preceding the month in which the return is filed. Reg. § 25.2701-4(d)(3)(ii). The Section 2701(d)(2)(B) ceiling limitation on the value of the transfer is not applicable to elective transfers under Section 2701(d)(3)(A)(iii). Reg. § 25.2701-4(d)(2). See infra text accompanying notes 369–392, 393–399.

[350] See infra text accompanying notes 393–399.

Transfer to Spouse. If an inter vivos or testamentary transfer of a qualified payment interest qualifies for a marital deduction, an inter vivos transfer to a spouse qualifies for an annual exclusion, or to the extent an inter vivos transfer is made to a spouse for consideration, the transfer is not a Section 2701(d) taxable event[351] and the spouse steps into the shoes of the transferor for purposes of Section 2701(d).[352] If a transferor dies while holding a qualified payment interest for which a Section 2056 or a Section 2106(a)(3) estate tax marital deduction is allowed,[353] there is no taxable event under Section 2701(d) at the transferor's death.[354] The surviving spouse is treated as the holder of the interest from the date of the transferor's original Section 2701 transfer and the spouse is subject to the Section 2701(d) rules with respect to any deficiencies on the qualified payment interest.[355] A purchase of a qualified payment interest from the transferor's estate either by a spouse or by a Section 2056(b)(7) trust may be treated[356] as a transfer qualifying for an estate tax marital deduction to the extent that the funds used to make the purchase qualified for an estate tax marital deduction.[357] If an executor is given discretion to satisfy a marital bequest[358] with a qualified payment interest, the transfer generally is not a taxable event to the extent that the qualified payment interest is used to satisfy the bequest.[359] Either a purchase using marital deduction funds or a discretionary funding of the marital bequest must generally occur before the due date for filing the transferor's federal estate tax return (including extensions).[360]

---

[351] IRC §§ 2701(d)(3)(B)(i), 2701(d)(3)(B)(ii).

[352] IRC § 2701(d)(3)(B)(iii). See Reg. § 25.2701-4(b)(3)(ii).

[353] If a partial marital deduction is allowed under Section 2056(b)(8) relating to a charitable remainder trust, the surviving spouse is treated as the holder of the entire interest passing to the trust. Reg. § 25.2701-4(b)(3)(ii)(A) (last sentence).

[354] IRC § 2701(d)(3)(B)(i).

[355] IRC § 2701(d)(3)(B)(iii). If a surviving spouse transfers the interest to his or her subsequent spouse, the rule also applies.

[356] See infra text accompanying note 360.

[357] Reg. § 25.2701-4(b)(3)(ii)(C). For example, if a $300,000 qualified payment interest is purchased with $100,000 of cash that qualified for a Section 2056 or a Section 2106(a)(3) marital deduction, the deficiency on the one third of the qualified payment interest is considered as transferred in a Section 2056 or Section 2106(a)(3) bequest. Id. The deficiency on the remaining two-thirds interest would increase the transferor's taxable estate. IRC § 2701(d)(3)(A)(i). See supra text accompanying notes 331–334.

A purchase by a Section 2056(b)(5) trust or a Section 2056(b)(6) trust or an estate trust arrangement should qualify for this rule and the omission of reference to them by the regulations seems inappropriate.

[358] See infra text accompanying note 360.

[359] Reg. § 25.2701-4(b)(3)(ii)(B).

[360] Reg. §§ 25.2701-4(b)(3)(ii)(B)(1), 25.2701-4(b)(3)(ii)(C). A taxable event is avoided when the purchase or funding occurs after the due date of the transferor's federal

If the transferor makes an inter vivos transfer of the qualified payment interest to a spouse, the spouse again steps into the shoes of the transferor if a deduction is allowed under Section 2523, an exclusion is allowed under Section 2503(b) for the transfer,[361] or to the extent that the spouse provides consideration for the transfer.[362] There are no Section 2701(d) consequences to the transferor; the spouse is treated as the holder of the interest from the date of the transferor's original Section 2701 transfer[363] and is taxed on any deficiencies on the qualified payment interest.

Transfer to Any Other Applicable Family Member or to the Section 2701 Transferor. If there is a transfer of a qualified payment interest to an applicable family member of the Section 2701 transferor (other than the transferor's spouse) or to a Section 2701 transferor from an applicable family member,[364] all deficiencies in the qualified payments up to the time of the transfer are included in the tax base of the person making the transfer.[365] However, the transferee of either such transfer is treated in the same manner as the person making the transfer would have been treated with respect to late or unpaid qualified payments occurring after the taxable event.[366] Thus, the deficiency rules continue to apply to the transferee and Section 2701(d) may not be avoided by means of a transfer to an applicable family member transferee or to

---

estate tax return if the executor files a statement with the return indicating the qualified payment interests to be purchased or the extent to which bequest will be funded with the qualified payment interest, and before the date one year prior to the running of the statute of limitations on assessment of additional estate tax, the executor notifies the District Director that: such purchase or satisfaction has occurred; or, in the case of a purchase, that funds have been permanently set aside for such purchase; or, in the case of a satisfaction, that the qualified payment interest has been permanently set aside for that purpose. Reg. §§ 25.2701-4(b)(3)(ii)(B)(2), 25.2701-4(b)(3)(ii)(C).

[361] Cf. IRC § 2524. If a partial marital deduction is allowable under Section 2523(g) relating to charitable remainder trusts, the spouse is treated as the holder of the entire interest passing to the trust. Reg. § 25.2701-4(b)(3)(ii)(A) (last sentence).

[362] IRC §§ 2701(d)(3)(B)(ii), 2701(d)(3)(B)(iii). Cf. IRC § 2524. For example, if there is purchase of a transferor's interest for full consideration, there are no Section 2701(d) consequences to the transferor and the spouse steps into the transferor's shoes for purposes of Section 2701(d).

[363] IRC §§ 2701(d)(3)(B), 2701(d)(3)(B)(ii).

[364] The transfer may be made either by the interest holder or an individual treated as the interest holder, i.e., the Section 2701 transferor's spouse or an applicable family member of the Section 2701 transferor. Reg. § 25.2701-4(b)(3)(i).

[365] IRC §§ 2701(d)(1)(B), 2701(d)(3)(A)(ii), 2701(d)(4)(B), 2701(d)(4)(C); Reg. § 25.2701-4(b)(3)(i). As with all inter vivos transfers, the four-year grace period is not applicable in determining the deficiency amount. Reg. § 25.2701-4(c)(5) (last sentence). See supra text following note 325 and accompanying notes 336, 337.

[366] IRC §§ 2701(d)(4)(B), 2701(d)(4)(C).

the Section 2701 transferor.[367] It is unclear whether this set of rules applies only to inter vivos transfers or to both inter vivos and testamentary transfers.[368]

[iv] The amount of the Section 2701(d) transfer. The computation of the amount of the Section 2701(d) increase in the transfer tax base for any deficiency on a qualified payment interest employs a compounding rule,[369] making the application of Section 2701(d) potentially expensive. The computational rules are consistent with the basic philosophy of Section 2701 in that any Section 2701(d) increase in the transfer tax base inures to the economic benefit of the family members to whom the subordinate equity interest was originally transferred. There is generally a ceiling on the amount of the Section 2701(d) increase in the transfer tax base, which, in effect, limits the increase to the amount of the appreciation in the value of the transferee's subordinate equity interest.[370]

The Computation. If there is an actual inter vivos transfer or a gross estate inclusion of a qualified payment interest,[371] there is a two-part computation of the amount of the Section 2701(d) transfer tax base increase. The amount[372] of the qualified payments that should have been paid[373] during the period[374] is increased by an amount equal to the earnings such payments would have

---

[367] If the transfer were to one other than an applicable family member or the Section 2701 transferor, the deficiency rules would no longer apply.

[368] The Sections 2701(d)(4)(B) and 2701(d)(4)(C) statutory language applies only to a Section 2701(d)(3)(A)(ii) transfer of an applicable retained interest. While this could involve either an inter vivos or a testamentary transfer, a Section 2701(d)(3)(A)(ii) transfer results in only increased taxable gifts under Section 2701(d)(1)(B). This implies that these rules apply only to inter vivos transfers. The regulations imply that the transfer could involve a testamentary transfer as well as an inter vivos transfer because the introductory clause of the regulations does not limit the transfer to an inter vivos transfer. See Reg. § 25.2701-4(b)(3)(i).

[369] IRC § 2701(d)(2)(A).

[370] IRC § 2701(d)(2)(B). See infra text accompanying notes 386–392, but see infra text accompanying note 398.

[371] IRC §§ 2701(d)(3)(A)(i), 2701(d)(3)(A)(ii). See supra ¶ 19.02[5][a] text accompanying notes 331–335, 336–342. The computation for an elective transfer appears infra text accompanying notes 393–399.

[372] While Section 2701(d)(2)(A) speaks in terms of the "value" of the payments, the regulations appropriately refer to the "amount" of the payments that should have been paid. Reg. § 25.2701-4(c)(1).

[373] This includes all payments; there is no four-year grace period. Reg. § 25.2701-4(c)(5) (last sentence).

[374] If an applicable family member other than a spouse is the taxpayer as a result of Section 2701(d)(4)(B), the period commences on the date the interest of the original transferor was terminated. Reg. § 25.2701-4(c)(1)(i)(A) (parenthetical). See supra text accompanying notes 364–366.

earned if the payments had been paid when due[375] and had been reinvested on that date at the appropriate discount rate.[376] The appropriate discount rate is the discount rate that was employed in valuing the right to the qualified payment at the time of the original Section 2701 transfer.[377] That amount is reduced by the amount of qualified payments actually received between the time of the original Section 2701 transfer and the current taxable event, increased by the amount of earnings that the actual payments would have generated had they been reinvested on the date paid at the appropriate discount rate.[378] In computing the reduction, any qualified payment made within four years after its due date and prior to the inter vivos or testamentary transfer is treated as having been paid on its due date.[379] Any payment with respect to a qualified payment interest is applied toward the earliest unpaid qualified payment.[380] A payment made in the form of a debt obligation paying compound interest at a rate at least equal to the appropriate discount rate is treated as a qualified payment if the term of the obligation (including extensions) does not exceed four years from the date it is issued.[381]

The amount of the reduction is increased to the extent necessary to prevent double taxation[382] by (1) the portion of the fair market value of the qualified payment interest solely attributable to any right to receive unpaid qualified payments determined as of the date of the taxable event;[383] (2) the fair market value of any equity interest in the entity received in lieu of qualified payments and held at the time of the taxable event;[384] and (3) the amount that the trans-

---

[375] The due date is the date specified in the governing instrument. If no due date is stated, the due date is the last day of each calendar year. Reg. § 25.2701-4(c)(2).

[376] IRC § 2701(d)(2)(A)(i). See Reg. § 25.2701-4(c)(1)(i).

[377] IRC § 2701(d)(2)(A)(i)(II); Reg. § 25.2701-4(c)(3).

[378] IRC § 2701(d)(2)(A)(ii); Reg. § 25.2701-4(c)(1)(ii). There is no additional reduction if the payments were reinvested at a yield higher than the appropriate discount rate. Id.

[379] Reg. § 25.2701-4(c)(5). Cf. IRC § 2701(d)(2)(C). Earnings on payments made later than the four-year window are calculated using the actual date of the payment.

[380] Reg. § 25.2701-4(c)(4). See Reg. § 25.2701-4(d)(4) Ex.

[381] Reg. § 25.2701-4(c)(5). A payment in the form of an equity interest in the entity is not a qualified payment and does not terminate the compounding of interest at the appropriate discount rate. Id. However, the fair market value of the equity interest is used to reduce the Section 2701(d) amount. See infra text accompanying note 384. Cf. IRC § 2701(d)(2)(A)(ii). See Reg. § 25.2701-4(c)(1)(ii)(C)(2).

[382] See Reg. § 25.2701-4(c)(1)(ii)(C).

[383] Reg. § 25.2701-4(c)(1)(ii)(C)(1). This adjustment would include a right to receive the qualified payment that was included as a receivable in transferor's gross estate under Section 2033. See supra text accompanying note 335.

[384] Reg. § 25.2701-4(c)(1)(ii)(C)(2). See supra note 381.

feror's prior taxable gifts were increased as a result of transferor's failure to enforce the right to receive such qualified payments.[385]

The Ceiling Rule. A ceiling is generally imposed on the amount of the transfer tax base increase under Section 2701(d).[386] Since the entity's failure to make qualified payments should inure to the economic benefit of the subordinate equity interests, the amount of the transfer tax base increase should not exceed the appreciation in the value of the subordinate equity interests occurring subsequent to the original Section 2701 transfer.

The amount of the ceiling is determined by first computing the fair market value of all of the equity interests subordinate to the qualified payment interest at the date of the Section 2701(d) taxable event.[387] The value of the subordinate equity interests at the time of the taxable event is increased by any amount used by the entity to acquire any subordinate equity interest between the time of the original Section 2701 transfer and the taxable event.[388] Because the ceiling limits the Section 2701(d) increase to the appreciation in the value of the subordinate equity interest subsequent to the original Section 2701 transfer, the ceiling is determined by reducing the adjusted fair market value of the subordinate equity interests at the time of the taxable event by the fair market value of all the subordinate equity interests at the time of the original Section 2701 transfer.[389] Finally, the transferor's proportionate share of appreciation of the subordinate equity interest is determined by multiplying the total appreciation by an "applicable percentage."[390] The applicable percentage is the number of shares or units of the applicable retained interest held by the transferor on the date of the Section 2701(d) taxable event divided by the total number of shares or units of the same class outstanding on that date.[391] If the

---

[385] Reg. § 25.2701-4(c)(1)(ii)(C)(3). Payments treated as paid as a result of a transferor's Section 2701(d)(3)(A)(iii) election are treated as having been paid on their due dates. Reg. § 25.2701-4(d)(1). See also Reg. § 25.2701-4(d)(4) Ex.

[386] IRC § 2701(d)(2)(B). The ceiling rule is not applicable where a Section 2701(d)(3)(A)(iii) election has been made. Reg. § 25.2701-4(d)(2).

[387] IRC § 2701(d)(2)(B)(i)(I). The amount of any accrued liability with respect to the qualified payment right is disregarded in computing the fair market value. Reg. § 25.2701-4(c)(6)(i)(A)(1). The Section 2701(a)(4) minimum value junior equity interest rule is also disregarded in making the computation. Reg. § 25.2701-4(c)(6)(ii). See supra ¶ 19.02[4][f].

[388] Reg. § 25.2701-4(c)(6)(i)(A)(2). This increase is reduced by any amounts received on the resale or issuance of any such subordinate interest during the period. Id.

[389] IRC § 2701(d)(2)(B)(i)(II). See Reg. § 25.2701-4(c)(6)(i)(B). If the transfer involves a subsequent interest holder as a result of the application of Section 2701(d)(4)(B) (see supra text accompanying notes 364–366), the first two amounts are determined from the date the interest of the prior interest holder terminated. Reg. § 25.2701-4(c)(6)(i) (parentheticals).

[390] IRC § 2701(d)(2)(B)(i).

[391] IRC § 2701(d)(2)(B)(ii); Reg. § 25.2701-4(c)(6)(iii).

transferor has two or more classes of applicable retained interests, the applicable percentage is the largest applicable percentage of any class.[392]

The Computation in an Elective Situation. If the taxable event occurs as a result of an election by the transferor on the actual but untimely[393] receipt of a qualified payment,[394] the amount of the increase in taxable gifts involves only the compounded hypothetical earnings with respect to that payment and all previously received payments for which an election is available but has not been made.[395] Any qualified payments received are treated as though paid with respect to the earliest unpaid qualified payment.[396] The election results in a taxable gift in an amount equal to the earnings the payments would have generated if the payments had been paid and reinvested at a yield equal to the appropriate discount rate from the timely payment date to the date of the election.[397] The increase in the transfer tax base determined under this computation is not subject to the ceiling rule.[398] Payments for which an election is

---

[392] Reg. § 25.2701-4(c)(6)(iii). The legislative history of Section 2701 contains the following example to illustrate the rules relating to the amount of the transfer and the ceiling rule:

> A corporation has four classes of stock. Class A is entitled to the first $10 of dividends each year; Class B is entitled to the second $10 of dividends each year; Class C is entitled to the third $10 of dividends each year; and Class D is entitled to all dividends in excess of those paid to classes A, B, and C. Classes A, B, and C all have cumulative rights to dividends. In a transaction to which the provision applies, Father gives Daughter stock in classes A and C while retaining stock in class B. Class D is owned by an unrelated party. Dividends are not paid on the class C stock and several years later Father dies holding the class B stock. The cap on future amounts subject to transfer tax equals the excess of the fair market value of stock in classes C and D at the date of Father's death over such value at the date of the gift multiplied by a fraction equal to the percentage of class B stock held by Father.

HR Conf. Rep. No. 964, 101st Cong., 2d Sess. 1135 (Ex. 5) (1990), reprinted in 1991-2 CB 560, 605.

[393] See IRC § 2701(d)(2)(C); Reg. § 25.2701-4(d)(1).

[394] IRC § 2701(d)(3)(A)(iii). See IRC § 2701(d)(1)(B); supra text accompanying notes 343–350.

[395] Reg. § 25.2701-4(d)(1). See Reg. § 25.2701-4(d)(4) Ex.

[396] Reg. § 25.2701-4(c)(4). See Reg. § 25.2701-4(d)(4) Ex.

[397] IRC § 2701(d)(2)(A)(i); Reg. § 25.2701-4(c)(1)(i)(B). The following example is based on Regulations Section 25.2701-4(d)(4) Ex. Assume Taxpayer should have received a $500 dividend at the end of each year, but receives none until the end of year five when $500 is received. Assume Taxpayer also makes a Section 2701(d)(3)(A)(iii) election with respect to the $500 receipt in year five. If the appropriate discount rule is 10 percent, Taxpayer would be treated as making a gift of $232, $732 ($500 plus 10 percent of $500 compounded annually for four years) minus $500, the dividend treated as received at the end of year one.

[398] Reg. § 25.2701-4(d)(2).

made are also treated as having been paid on the earliest due dates for purposes of any subsequent taxable events.[399]

[b] The Section 2701(e)(7) Separate Interest Rule

The Secretary has authority to determine that any applicable retained interest shall be treated as two or more separate interests for purposes of Section 2701 valuation.[400] As an example of the separate interest rule, assume grantor G holds two classes of stock; G retains the first class and transfers the second class to child C. The first class is entitled to the first $100 of dividends payable each year and 50 percent of any additional dividends payable for the year. The second class is entitled to the other 50 percent of additional dividends. The Secretary may prescribe regulations that treat the first class of stock as two separate interests—a right to preferred dividends of $100 and a right to 50 percent of the dividends in excess of $100. In such case, the right to 50 percent of the excess dividends would be treated as a right that is of the same class as the right transferred, and would not be subject to valuation under Section 2701.[401]

[c] The Section 2701(e)(6) Relief Rule

[i] **Introduction** When an increase in the value of a transferred subordinate equity interest occurs[402] as a result of Section 2701, the same value may be subject to subsequent taxation under the gift tax or the estate tax.[403] For example, if an applicable retained interest is assigned a zero value under Section 2701 and the same interest is the subject matter of a subsequent gift

---

[399] Reg. § 25.2701-4(d)(1). See Reg. § 25.2701-4(d)(4) Ex.

[400] IRC § 2701(e)(7). The determination may be by regulations, revenue rulings, notices, or other documents of general application. Reg. § 25.2701-7. In addition, if separation is deemed necessary and appropriate to carry out the purposes of Section 2701, the Commissioner may so provide by ruling issued to a taxpayer upon request. Id.

[401] See HR Conf. Rep. No. 964, 101st Cong., 2d Sess. 1135 (Ex. 3) (1990), reprinted in 1991-2 CB 560, 605; IRC § 2701(a)(2)(B), discussed supra ¶ 19.02[3][b], especially text accompanying notes 177–178.

[402] Technically, there is no gift of a separate interest, but an increased valuation of the amount of gift on interests actually transferred. However, the zero valuation rule in effect results in an immediate indirect gift of the interests valued at zero or assigned some other below fair market valuation, or a partial gift of such interests.

[403] Such "double taxation" may also occur as a result of the application of Section 2701(d). In such a circumstance, the Treasury is authorized to provide regulatory relief. IRC § 2701(e)(6). See supra ¶ 19.02[5][a] text accompanying note 311.

The interrelationship of Section 2701 to the income tax and the generation-skipping transfer tax is considered infra ¶¶ 19.02[5][f][ii], 19.02[5][f][iii].

by the transferor, the value of such interest in essence is subject to taxation twice, once at the time of the transfer subject to Section 2701 and again at the time of the actual transfer. Alternatively, if the applicable retained interest is subsequently included in the transferor's gross estate,[404] the value of such applicable retained interest is essentially being taxed twice, once under the gift tax and again under the Section 2001(b) estate tax unified transfer tax mechanism.[405] Section 2701 prescribes the promulgation of regulations[406] that have been adopted to provide relief from such double taxation.[407] Several requirements must be met in order to trigger the regulatory relief rules. Those requirements, the amount of relief, and the form of relief, as well as a series of special rules related to split Section 2701 gifts, are considered later in this section.

In applying the relief rules, two new terms are added to the list of the Section 2701 tax vocabulary. The first term is "*the initial transferor*," who is the individual who made the transfer that triggered the application of Section 2701 and who (other than the transferor's spouse in the case of a Section 2513

---

[404] Inclusion would generally occur under Section 2033, although it could occur under many of the gross estate inclusion provisions.

[405] Although it can be argued that the "gift" of the applicable retained interest is included in the decedent's gross estate and thus, because of the flush language of Section 2001(b), that it should not be included in the amount of "adjusted taxable gifts" under Section 2001(b)(1)(B), this is an unlikely interpretation of Section 2001(b). The prior gift was a gift of the subordinate equity interest whose value was increased as a result of the application of Section 2701; it was not a gift of the applicable retained interest that is included in the gross estate. Even though, in effect, double taxation occurs as a result of inclusion of the value of the interest under both Section 2001(b)(1)(A) and Section 2001(b)(1)(B), in all likelihood relief is not provided by that section. However, the government hedges its bet by precluding any double benefit under the Section 2701(e)(6) regulatory relief rule, just in case there is a Section 2001(b)(1)(B) reduction as a result of the Section 2001(b) flush language or in case such a similar double benefit occurs under Section 2101. Reg. § 25.2701-5(g)(1). Similar bet-hedging occurs under Reg. § 25.2701-5(g)(2).

[406] IRC § 2701(e)(6).

[407] Reg. § 25.2701-5. The regulations are effective for transfers of Section 2701 interests after May 4, 1994. Reg. § 25.2701-5(h). If the subsequent inter vivos transfer or estate tax inclusion occurred on or before May 4, 1994, the initial transferor may use the current regulatory rules under Regulations Section 25.2701-5, the rules provided in two prior sets of proposed regulations, or any other reasonable interpretation of the statute. Id. The proposed regulations immediately prior to the adoption of the final regulations allowed only a reduction in the amount of "adjusted taxable gifts" under Section 2001(b)(1)(B). Prop. Reg. § 25.2701-5(a), 1992-1 CB 1239, 1241. The prior (original) proposed regulations generally provided for a nonrefundable estate tax credit as the remedy for adjusting the taxes due. Prop. Reg. § 25.2701-5, 1991-2 CB 1118, 1122. However, after a number of commentators criticized both approaches, the government withdrew them and enacted the current regulations. See King, "Final Estate Tax Freeze Rules 'Simplify' Subtraction Method," 70 Taxes 460, 489 (July 1992).

split gift)⁴⁰⁸ is the only person to whom relief from subsequent double taxation is granted.⁴⁰⁹ The initial transferor is the individual who transferred the subordinate equity interest to a family member in a situation where either the transferor or an applicable family member of the transferor held an applicable retained interest that was accorded special valuation under the Section 2701 rules.⁴¹⁰ The specially valued applicable retained interest is generally *"a Section 2701 interest,"* the second new term found in the relief rules.⁴¹¹ However, an applicable retained interest is treated as a Section 2701 interest only to the extent that the transfer of such interest (which triggers the relief rules) effectively reduces the combined amount of ownership of such applicable retained interests held by the initial transferor and applicable family members below the combined ownership level of such interests by such persons at the time of the initial transfer.⁴¹² For example, assume the initial transferor (or an applicable family member) acquires more of the applicable retained interest than the initial transferor and applicable family members held at the time of the original transfer, and assume the initial transferor subsequently transfers a portion of the applicable retained interest that does not exceed the additional acquired amount. The transferred interest is not "a Section 2701 interest," and no relief is allowed with respect to the transfer.⁴¹³

Relief is available to the initial transferor upon the transfer of a Section 2701 interest under both the gift tax and the estate tax. Gift tax relief is provided if, during the initial transferor's lifetime, the holder of the Section 2701 interest (either the initial transferor or an applicable family member) transfers a Section 2701 interest to or for the benefit of an individual other than the initial transferor or an applicable family member of the initial transferor in a transfer that is subject to federal estate⁴¹⁴ or gift taxation.⁴¹⁵ The gift tax relief takes the form of a reduction in the initial transferor's taxable gifts under Section 2502(a).⁴¹⁶ Estate tax relief is provided in several circumstances in the form of

---

⁴⁰⁸ See infra ¶ 19.02[5][c][v].

⁴⁰⁹ Reg. § 25.2701-5(a)(1).

⁴¹⁰ Reg. § 25.2701-5(a)(1).

⁴¹¹ Reg. § 25.2701-5(a)(4).

⁴¹² Reg. § 25.2701-5(a)(4). If a portion of a Section 2701 interest previously has been granted relief under the rules, the limitation applies to the remaining portion. Id.

⁴¹³ Reg. § 25.2701-5(d) Ex. 3 (involving a transfer of a senior equity interest acquired after a Section 2701 transfer). Thus, only transferred interests in excess of the excess amount constitute Section 2701 interests.

⁴¹⁴ See infra text accompanying note 435.

⁴¹⁵ Reg. § 25.2701-5(a)(2). See infra ¶ 19.02[5][c][iii]; Reg. §§ 25.2701-5(d) Exs. 1, 4, 5. If a transfer is made for consideration, see infra text accompanying notes 444–451.

⁴¹⁶ Reg. §§ 25.2701-5(a)(1), 25.2701-5(a)(2).

a reduction of the initial transferor's adjusted taxable gifts[417] in the computation of estate tax liability[418] at the initial transferor's death.[419]

[ii] **The amount of the reduction.** Since the purpose of the relief rules is to mitigate double taxation, the reduction relief is limited to the extent that the value of the Section 2701 interest is included twice in the transfer tax base. In general,[420] the amount of the reduction of either taxable gifts under the gift tax[421] or adjusted taxable gifts under the estate tax[422] is the *lesser* of: (1) the amount by which the initial transferor's taxable gifts were increased as a result of the application of Section 2701 to the initial transfer[423] or (2) an amount referred to as the duplicated amount.[424] The duplicated amount is essentially the excess of the transfer tax value[425] of the Section 2701 interest determined at the time of the subsequent estate or gift tax transfer over its Section 2701 value at the time of the initial transfer.[426]

If only a portion of the amount of the subordinate equity interest was initially transferred and valued under Section 2701,[427] on a subsequent transfer of the entire Section 2701 interest, the duplicated amount[428] is multiplied by a fraction equal to the portion of subordinate equity interest that was originally

---

[417] See Reg. §§ 25.2701-5(a)(1), 25.2701-5(a)(3).

[418] IRC §§ 2001(b), 2101(b).

[419] Reg. § 25.2701-5(a)(3). See infra ¶ 19.02[5][c][iv]; Reg. § 25.2701-5(d) Ex. 2.

[420] There are special rules related to transfers of partial interests (see Reg. § 25.2701-5(c)(3)(iv)) discussed infra text accompanying notes 452, 453) and Section 2701 transfers that are split gifts under Section 2513 (see Reg. §§ 25.2701-5(e), 25.2701-5(f) discussed infra ¶ 19.02[5][c][v]).

[421] IRC § 2502(a).

[422] IRC §§ 2001(b)(1)(B), 2101(b)(1)(B).

[423] Reg. § 25.2701-5(b)(1).

[424] Reg. § 25.2701-5(b)(2). If more than one class of Section 2701 interest exists, the amount of relief under the reduction rule is determined separately with respect to each class of Section 2701 interest. Reg. § 25.2701-5(c)(3)(v).

[425] In general, the "transfer tax value" is the value of the Section 2701 interest as finally determined under Chapter 11 or Chapter 12 (including the right to receive any distribution thereon other than qualified payments) reduced by deductions directly related to the Section 2701 interest. Reg. § 25.2701-5(c)(2). Cf. IRC § 691(c)(2)(C).

[426] Reg. § 25.2701-5(c)(1). See, e.g., Reg. § 25.2701-5(d) Ex. 1(ii).

[427] This refers to a portion of the subtraction method Step 2 amount of subordinate equity interests held by the transferor, applicable family members, and family members of the transferor at the time of the original Section 2701 transfer. Step 2 of the subtraction method is discussed supra ¶ 19.02[4][d][ii].

[428] This limitation applies only to the duplicated amount under the second part of the reduction computation, not the initial increase in the transferor's taxable gifts due to Section 2701 under the first part of the computation. That is because the computation of the initial increase would itself reflect the transfer of only a portion of the subordinate equity interest. See supra ¶ 19.02[4][d][iii].

transferred.[429] If the initial transferor subsequently transferred an additional portion of the subordinate equity interest in another initial transfer, the amount of the reduction with respect to any subsequent transfer of a Section 2701 interest is the sum of the reductions computed with respect to each initial transfer.[430] For example, if Transferor owned all of the applicable retained interests and the subordinate equity interests of an entity and made a Section 2701 transfer of one third of the subordinate equity interest and subsequently transferred all of the applicable retained interest, the duplicated amount would be only one third of the excess of the total value of the applicable retained interests at the time of the subsequent transfer over their value under Section 2701 at the time of the initial transfer.[431] If after the first transfer of one third of the subordinate equity interest, Transferor later transferred another one third of the subordinate equity interest in a second transfer subject to Section 2701 and subsequently transferred all of the applicable retained interests, there would be a second proportionate computation of the duplicated amount, and the two separate computations of reductions would be combined in determining the total duplicate amount.[432]

[iii] **Gift tax relief.** During the initial transferor's lifetime, the holder of a Section 2701 interest (the initial transferor or an applicable family member)

---

[429] Reg. § 25.2701-5(c)(1). The fraction is equal to the subtraction method Step 3 (transferred) amount over the subtraction method Step 2 (total) amount. Id. See supra ¶¶ 19.02[4][d][ii], 19.02[4][d][iii]; Reg. § 25.2701-5(d) Ex. 4 (where the portion was one half because only one half of initial transferor's subordinate equity interest was transferred in the initial transfer).

[430] Reg. § 25.2701-5(c)(3)(vi).

[431] See supra text accompanying notes 427–429.

[432] See supra text accompanying note 430. For example, assume a corporate entity is worth $700,000 in year one, $500,000 in year two, and $600,000 in year three, and Transferor held applicable retained interests in the entity worth $700,000, $500,000, and $600,000 respectively in the three years and subordinate equity interests worth zero in each year. Further assume that under Section 2701 all of the value was allocated to subordinate equity interests. In year one, Transferor gives one third of the subordinate interests to Child (a Section 2701 transfer of $233,333) and in year two, Transferor gives a second one third of the subordinate interests to Child (a Section 2701 transfer of $166,667), and in year three, Transferor gives all of the applicable retained interests to Child (a Section 2511 transfer of $600,000). Transferor's remedial relief would be a total of:

(1)	The first ⅓:	
	the lesser of $233,333 or ⅓ of $600,000	
	(the duplicated amount of $600,000 – zero) =	$200,000
(2)	The second ⅓:	
	the lesser of $166,667 or ⅓ of $600,000	
	(the duplicated amount of $600,000 – zero) =	$166,667
(3)	There is no duplication as to the retained ⅓ of	
	the subordinate equity interest	–0–
	Total	$366,667

may transfer that Section 2701 interest to or for the benefit of an individual other than the initial transferor or an applicable family member of the initial transferor[433] in a transfer[434] that is subject to federal estate[435] or gift taxation.[436] Upon such a transfer, there is a reduction in the initial transferor's Section 2502(a) taxable gifts.[437] For example, assume an initial transferor *T* was the sole owner of an entity and that *T* transferred all of the subordinate equity interests in the entity to a family member. Further assume *T* subsequently made an inter vivos gift transfer of all of the Section 2701 interest to an unrelated individual. *T*'s taxable gifts for the calendar year in which the Section 2701

---

[433] See infra text accompanying notes 449–451.

[434] The entity attribution rules of Regulations Section 25.2701-6 apply to determine the extent to which such a transfer occurs. Reg. § 25.2701-5(a)(2). See supra ¶ 19.02[2][d].

[435] The testamentary transfer here occurs where the Section 2701 interest is included in an applicable family member's gross estate. See infra text accompanying note 439.

[436] Any inclusion in a decedent's gross estate and any inter vivos transfer without adequate consideration other than a Section 2503(e) transfer should be treated as "subject to" the federal estate or gift taxation. Cf. ¶ 13.02[4][b][i]. If Section 2503(e) applies to a transfer, it is not treated as a transfer of property by gift and not "subject to" gift tax. The remedial relief rules are inapplicable, because no double taxation occurs.

Although property that qualifies for a Section 2503(b) annual exclusion is "subject to" the gift tax, the annual exclusion is disregarded in making the relief computation. Cf. ¶ 13.02[4][b][i]. For example, assume Transferor, who has made no previous transfers in any year, makes a transfer of a subordinate equity interest worth zero and retains an applicable retained interest worth $11,000 but valued at zero under Section 2701. A transfer of property by gift of $11,000 is made after the application of Section 2701, but the annual exclusion eliminates any taxable gift. If Transferor subsequently transfers the applicable retained interest to an unrelated person when it is still worth $11,000, no taxable gift results. Although the second transfer is "subject to" the gift tax, there is no relief because there was no "taxable gift" as a result of Section 2701 applying to the initial transfer. See Reg. § 25.2701-5(b)(1). The initial taxable gift was zero. Alternatively, if the applicable retained interest had a fair market value of $15,000 at the time of the initial transfer, was valued at zero under Section 2701, and was worth $11,000 at the time of the subsequent transfer, Transferor would be entitled to $4,000 of relief (the lesser of: (1) $15,000 less $11,000 or (2) $11,000). If Section 2701 had not been enacted, Transferor would not have made a taxable gift on either transfer. The first transfer would be valued at zero and the second transfer of $11,000 would be excluded from taxable gifts by the annual exclusion. After the application of Section 2701, Transferor makes a $4,000 taxable gift on the initial transfer, and Transferor is entitled to $4,000 of relief after the second transfer. A transfer qualifying in its entirety for the annual exclusion is "subject to" the gift tax even though it does not generate any gift tax liability. If these are the only gifts made, the $4,000 of relief provides Transferor with no benefit in the year of the subsequent transfer because of the annual exclusion. However, the relief is carried over. See infra text accompanying note 442. Cf. Reg. § 25.2702-6(b)(2) (providing preferential treatment to the annual exclusion under the Section 2702 relief rules discussed at ¶ 19.03[4][c][i]).

For the consequences if the transfer is made for consideration, see infra text accompanying notes 444–451.

[437] Reg. § 25.2701-5(a)(2). See Reg. § 25.2701-5(d) Exs. 1, 4, 5.

---

interest is transferred qualify for relief. They would be reduced by the lesser of the increase in gifts in the prior year as a result of the application of Section 2701 or the duplicated amount, the current transfer tax value of the Section 2701 interest reduced by its prior Section 2701 value.[438] If an initial transferor makes an original Section 2701 transfer of a subordinate equity interest and an applicable family member holds a Section 2701 interest, reduction relief is provided to the initial transferor when the applicable family member makes an inter vivos gift of or bequeaths a Section 2701 interest to someone other than the initial transferor or an applicable family member of the initial transferor.[439] The amount of the reduction[440] first reduces the initial transferor's taxable gifts for the year of the applicable family member's transfer or death.[441] If the amount of the reduction exceeds the initial transferor's taxable gifts for the year, the excess reduction amount is carried forward and applied against the initial transferor's taxable gifts in each succeeding year until the excess is exhausted.[442] Any excess reduction amount remaining at the initial transferor's death reduces the initial transferor's adjusted taxable gifts in computing the initial transferor's estate tax liability.[443]

The gift tax relief is unavailable to the extent[444] that the initial transferor or an applicable family member makes an inter vivos transfer of the Section

---

[438] See Reg. §§25.2701-5(d) Exs. 1(i), 1(ii) (Section 2701 interests declined in value after the initial Section 2701 transfer and thus their value on the subsequent transfer constituted the lesser duplicated amount under the reduction rules. As a result, in the year of the Section 2701 transfer, there were no taxable gifts with respect to the transfer of the Section 2701 interest). Double taxation may also occur if there is a simultaneous transfer of the interests. See supra ¶ 19.02[2][b] note 83. In such circumstances, after applying the relief rules, only 100 percent of the value of the interests is taxed.

[439] Reg. § 25.2701-5(a)(2). For the consequences if the transfer is made for consideration, see infra text accompanying notes 444–451.

[440] See supra ¶ 19.02[5][c][ii].

[441] Reg. § 25.2701-5(a)(2). See Reg. § 25.2701-5(d) Ex. 1(iii).

[442] Reg. § 25.2701-5(a)(2). See Reg. § 25.2701-5(d) Ex. 1(iii).

[443] Reg. §§ 25.2701-5(a)(1), 25.2701-5(a)(2), 25.2701-5(a)(3). The amount of reduction may reduce the initial transferor's federal estate tax liability to only zero. Reg. § 25.2701-5(a)(3).

Whenever, as here, there is a carryover of excess reduction amount with a reduction in the adjusted taxable gifts at a transferor's death (see infra text accompanying note 471), adjusted taxable gifts are not only reduced directly by the carryover but indirectly by the prior reductions in taxable gifts. See IRC §§ 2001(b) (flush language), 2001(b)(1)(B), 2101(b)(1)(B), 2101(c)(1). Thus, the total amount of reduction relief is reflected in a direct or indirect reduction of adjusted taxable gifts.

[444] If a transfer is for partial consideration (a part-gift, part-sale), the gift portion of the transfer should be treated as a transfer of a portion of the Section 2701 interest (see Reg. § 25.2701-5(c)(3)(iv) and infra text accompanying notes 452–453), and the consideration sale portion should be subject to the consideration rules discussed here. Regulations Section 25.2701-5(c)(3)(i) implies that if any consideration is received, this rule applies;

2701 interest to one other than the initial transferor or an applicable family member of the initial transferor for consideration in money or money's worth.[445] To the extent that a transfer for consideration occurs, relief is generally provided only at the initial transferor's death when there is a reduction of adjusted taxable gifts in the computation of the initial transferor's estate tax liability.[446] However, if an equity interest is received in an exchange of a Section 2701 interest in a nonrecognition transaction, the transaction is not treated as an inter vivos transfer,[447] and the equity interest that is received in the non-recognition exchange is substituted for the initial Section 2701 interest under the relief rules.[448]

Gift tax relief is postponed if the Section 2701 interest is transferred to or for the benefit of the initial transferor or an applicable family member of the initial transferor regardless of whether the transfer is for consideration.[449] The postponement lasts until the initial transferor or the applicable family member makes a transfer to or for the benefit of an individual other than the initial transferor or an applicable family member of the initial transferor,[450] or until the initial transferor's death,[451] whichever occurs earlier.

If, after an initial Section 2701 transfer, the initial transferor or the applicable family member makes a transfer of only a portion of the entire Section 2701 interest, the amount of the relief is proportionate to the interest transferred.[452] Thus, if the initial transferor transfers one third of the Section 2701

---

however, the relief allowed in such circumstances (see infra text accompanying notes 457–460) is inadequate if the transfer is not separated into separate gift and sale transactions as suggested previously.

[445] Reg. § 25.2701-5(c)(3)(i). This includes a transfer that is *treated* as a transfer for consideration in money's worth. Cf. IRC § 2516. For example, if the Transferor transfers an applicable retained interest to Child to satisfy a support obligation and the requirements of Section 2516 are met, there is a transfer that is treated as if consideration was received.

[446] See infra text accompanying notes 457–460.

[447] Reg. § 25.2701-5(c)(3)(iii). See IRC § 7701(a)(45). See also, IRC §§ 351, 368, 721.

[448] Reg. § 25.2701-5(c)(3)(iii).

[449] See Reg. § 25.2701-5(a)(2). An intervivos transfer by the initial transferor or an applicable family member or an inclusion of the Section 2701 interest in the applicable family member's gross estate may result in postponement.

[450] Reg. § 25.2701-5(a)(2).

[451] See Reg. § 25.2701-5(c)(3)(i). See infra text accompanying notes 461–464.

[452] Reg. § 25.2701-5(c)(3)(iv).

interest, the reduction amount is one third of the amount of the reduction re-lief.[453]

[iv] **Estate tax relief.** Estate tax relief in the form of a reduction in the initial transferor's adjusted taxable gifts[454] is provided in four different situations. First, if a Section 2701 interest is included in the initial transferor's gross estate at death, the initial transferor's adjusted taxable gifts are reduced by the amount of the reduction relief.[455] If the initial transferor holds only a portion of the Section 2701 interest at death, having made a prior inter vivos transfer of the other portion of the Section 2701 interest, the amount of reduction is the total reduction amount multiplied by the portion of the Section 2701 interest transferred at death.[456]

Estate tax relief is granted in a second situation to the extent that there is an inter vivos transfer of a Section 2701 interest by either the initial transferor or an applicable family member for consideration in money or money's worth[457] to a person other than the initial transferor or an applicable family member of the initial transferor.[458] The Section 2701 interest transfer is

---

[453] Reg. § 25.2701-5(c)(3)(iv). See supra ¶ 19.02[5][c][ii]. The computation is made as if all of the Section 2701 interest was transferred and the amount of reduction is then multiplied by the one-third transferred portion. Cf. Reg. § 25.2701-5(d) Ex. 5 (where there was an initial transfer of only a portion of the subordinate equity interest (one half) and a subsequent transfer of only a portion of the senior equity interest (one fourth), the reduction amount is computed on the one-half interest and that amount is multiplied by one fourth, the portion subsequently transferred). See supra text accompanying notes 427–429.

[454] See Reg. § 25.2701-5(a)(1); IRC §§ 2001(b)(1)(B), 2101(b)(1)(B). The reduction in adjusted taxable gifts reduces the top marginal rate of tax imposed on the initial transferor's taxable estate.

[455] Reg. § 25.2701-5(a)(3). See supra ¶ 19.02[5][c][ii]. See also Reg. § 25.2701-5(d) Ex. 2(i) (involving a Section 2701 transfer followed by an inclusion of the applicable retained interest in the initial transferor's gross estate, resulting in a reduction in initial transferor's adjusted taxable gifts equal to the lesser of the Section 2701 increase in the initial transfer or the duplicated amount).

[456] Reg. § 25.2701-5(c)(3)(iv). See supra text accompanying notes 452, 453. If the initial transferor had made an inter vivos gift of one third of the Section 2701 interest triggering reduction relief on that one-third (see supra note 453), and held the other two-thirds at death, a determination of the total reduction is made as if decedent owned all of the Section 2701 interest at death and that amount is multiplied by the fraction (here two-thirds) of such interest held at death. Overall, the initial transferor will receive a reduction for the entire Section 2701 interest. The amount of reduction relief with respect to the previous one-third gift will either reduce the lifetime taxable gifts or, if unused, will also reduce the adjusted taxable gifts at death.

[457] The Regulations Section 25.2701-5(a)(2) rule is inapplicable to the transfer. See supra text accompanying note 445. This does not include a nonrecognition transaction. See supra text accompanying notes 447, 448.

[458] Reg. § 25.2701-5(c)(3)(i). See supra text accompanying notes 444, 445.

deemed to occur at the death of the initial transferor.[459] The initial transferor's adjusted taxable gifts are reduced in the same manner as if the initial transferor's gross estate included a Section 2701 interest having an estate tax value equal to the consideration in money or money's worth received in the exchange valued at the time of the exchange.[460]

Estate tax relief is granted in a third situation if a Section 2701 interest is held by an applicable family member at the time of the initial transferor's death. If such an interest[461] is not included in the initial transferor's gross estate,[462] it is deemed transferred to a person other than the initial transferor or an applicable family member at the time of the initial transferor's death. As a result, there is a reduction in the initial transferor's adjusted taxable gifts.[463] The fair market value of the deemed transferred Section 2701 interest immediately prior to the initial transferor's death is used to determine the amount of the reduction.[464]

Estate tax relief is granted in a fourth situation where there is a carryover of unused gift tax reduction to the initial transferor's estate.[465] The carryover reduction is used to reduce the adjusted taxable gifts in computing the initial transferor's estate tax liability.[466]

[v] **Special rules for split gifts.** If the initial transfer subject to Section 2701 is a split gift under Section 2513,[467] a series of special rules apply to provide relief.[468]

---

[459] Reg. § 25.2701-5(c)(3)(i).

[460] Reg. § 25.2701-5(c)(3)(i). See Reg. § 25.2701-5(d) Ex. 2(ii). This rule applies regardless of whether adequate and full consideration in money or money's worth is received. If less than adequate consideration was received, the initial transferor would have had a partial gift relief reduction adjustment, since the transaction would have been a part-gift, part-sale. See supra note 444.

The reduction can reduce the initial transferor's federal estate tax liability only to zero. Reg. §§ 25.2701-5(a)(3), 25.2701-5(d) Ex. 2(ii).

[461] Reg. § 25.2701-5(c)(3)(ii).

[462] Cf. Reg. § 25.2701-5(g). See supra text accompanying notes 449–451.

[463] Reg. § 25.2701-5(c)(3)(ii). See Reg. § 25.2701-5(d) Ex. 2(iii).

[464] Reg. § 25.2701-5(c)(3)(ii). The initial transferor's executor has the burden of proof with respect to the valuation of the Section 2701 interest. Id. The reduction can reduce the initial transferor's federal estate tax liability only to zero. Reg. § 25.2701-5(a)(3).

[465] This can occur either as a result of an inter vivos or testamentary transfer by an applicable family member (see supra text accompanying notes 439–443, 450), or as a result of an initial Section 2513 split gift Section 2701 transfer where the Section 2701 interest is subsequently transferred during the spouses' joint lifetimes and the donor spouse is treated as the initial transferor. (See infra text accompanying note 471.)

[466] Reg. §§ 25.2701-5(a)(1), 25.2701-5(a)(2), 25.2701-5(a)(3). The reduction can reduce the initial transferor's federal estate tax liability only to zero. Reg. § 25.2701-5(a)(3).

[467] See ¶ 10.03.

[468] Reg. § 25.2701-5(e).

If the Section 2701 interest is transferred during the joint lives of the donor and the spouse in a transfer qualifying for gift tax reduction relief, the gift tax reduction relief is split equally between the spouses.[469]

If the amount of relief reduction allocated to either spouse exceeds that spouse's taxable gifts for the calendar year, there is a carryover of that spouse's unused reduction to subsequent years.[470] At death, any still unused reduction reduces adjusted taxable gifts in the computation of that spouse's estate tax liability.[471]

If all or part of the Section 2701 interest is not transferred during the joint lives of the spouses, the reduction relief remaining[472] is allocated solely to the donor.[473] If either spouse dies, the donor spouse is treated as the initial transferor of any remaining Section 2701 interest.[474] Therefore, in computing the reduction, any reduction relief not previously allocated to the nondonor spouse is assigned to the donor.[475] The assigned reduction relief is subject to any limitations that would be applicable to the spouse if the spouse survived the donor.[476] If the spouse survives, the spouse is no longer treated as an initial transferor except to the extent of any carryovers related to a Section 2701 transfer during the spouses' joint lives.[477] As a result, the surviving spouse is permitted to reduce the aggregate sum of taxable gifts for purposes of both any

---

[469] Reg. § 25.2701-5(e)(2). See Reg. § 25.2701-5(f) Ex. 1. The relief would occur when a Section 2701 interest is transferred by the initial transferor or an applicable family member in a transfer subject to federal gift taxation or is included in an applicable family member's gross estate, and it passes to a person other than the initial transferor or a family member of the initial transferor. See supra ¶ 19.02[5][c][iii] especially text accompanying notes 433–436. On a transfer of only a portion of the Section 2701 interest during their joint lives, that portion of the remedial relief is similarly split. See Reg. §§ 25.2701-5(c)(3)(iv), 25.2701-5(f) Ex. 2.

[470] See Reg. § 25.2701-5(f) Ex. 1. Cf. Reg. § 25.2701-5(a)(2). The carryover of relief is identical to the carryover rules where an applicable family member's transfer is attributed to the initial transferor. See supra text accompanying notes 439–443.

[471] See Reg. § 25.2701-5(f) Ex. 1. Cf. Reg. § 25.2701-5(a)(2). See supra note 443.

[472] The spouse is allowed reduction relief with respect to reduction carryovers generated by Section 2701 during the spouses' joint lives. See supra text accompanying notes 469–471 and infra text accompanying notes 477, 482.

[473] Reg. § 25.2701-5(e)(3)(i). Thus, to the extent that the transfer of the Section 2701 interest occurs at or after the death of the first spouse to die, the remaining remedial relief applies only to the donor to the exclusion of the spouse. Id.

[474] Reg. § 25.2701-5(e)(3)(i). See Reg. §§ 25.2701-5(f) Exs. 3, 4, 5. Cf. IRC § 2001(d), discussed at ¶ 2.01[2] note 59, allowing similar relief to a donor where split gifts are subsequently included in the donor's gross estate.

[475] See supra note 469.

[476] Reg. § 25.2701-5(e)(3)(iv). The amount of assigned reduction is limited to the amount of the increase in the spouse's gift tax incurred by reason of the original transfer of the Section 2701 interest. Id. See Reg. §§ 25.2701-5(f) Exs. 3, 5(ii).

[477] Reg. § 25.2701-5(e)(3)(ii)(B). See supra text accompanying notes 469–471.

subsequent gift tax[478] and estate tax computations,[479] as well as to reduce the amount of tax payable on prior taxable gifts in computing the spouse's estate tax[480] by the amount of the surviving spouse's remaining relief that is transferred to the predeceasing donor.[481]

If the spouse predeceases the donor, only the carryover related to a Section 2701 transfer during the joint spouses' lives[482] is available to reduce the adjusted taxable gifts in the computation of the estate tax imposed on the spouse's estate.[483] This is so even if the Section 2701 interest is included in the spouse's gross estate.[484] No other reduction relief is available to the spouse, either in computing the spouse's adjusted taxable gifts[485] or gift tax payable[486] in determining the spouse's federal estate tax liability.[487]

[d] Open Statute of Limitations

When Congress originally enacted Section 2701 in 1990, it enacted an open statute of limitations rule that applied to both Section 2701(a) and Section 2701(d)[488] transfers if such transfers were not adequately disclosed on a gift tax return or in a statement attached to the return.[489] In 1997, the open statute of limitations rule was extended to apply to all gift transfers.[490] However, the adequate disclosure requirements for Section 2701 and Section 2701(d) transfers are not as broad as the adequate disclosure requirements for

---

[478] IRC § 2502(a).

[479] The reduction would result in a corresponding reduction in adjusted taxable gifts under Section 2001(b)(1)(B) or Section 2101(b)(1)(B).

[480] IRC §§ 2001(b)(2), 2101(b)(2).

[481] Reg. § 25.2701-5(e)(3)(ii)(A). See Reg. § 25.2701-5(f) Ex. 4. Cf. IRC § 2001(e) discussed at ¶ 2.01[2] note 59 (applying similar relief to a spouse where a split gift is subsequently included in the donor's gross estate under Section 2035).

[482] See supra text accompanying notes 469–471.

[483] Reg. § 25.2701-5(e)(3)(iii).

[484] Reg. § 25.2701-5(e)(3)(iii).

[485] IRC §§ 2001(b)(1)(B), 2101(b)(1)(B).

[486] IRC §§ 2001(b)(2), 2101(b)(2).

[487] Reg. § 25.2701-5(e)(3)(iii). But see supra text accompanying note 474.

[488] See supra ¶ 19.02[5][a], especially note 311.

[489] IRC § 6501(c)(9). Under the rule if any gift of property is not adequately disclosed on a gift tax return, the gift tax may be assessed or court collection proceedings commenced without assessment at any time. IRC § 6501(c)(9). The rule does not apply if the gift is disclosed on the return or in a statement attached to the return in a manner adequate to apprise the Service of the nature of the item. Id.
The open statute of limitations rule was also applicable to Section 2702 transfers made after 1990. See ¶ 19.03[4][d].

[490] The rule that applies to transfers after December 31, 1996, is discussed in detail at ¶ 9.04[10].

other gift transfers.[491] Under the rules applicable to such transfers,[492] the gift tax return (or seemingly a statement attached to the return) must provide: (1) a description of the transactions, including a description of the transferred and retained interests and the methods used in valuing each;[493] (2) the identity of, and relationship between all of the parties (including related parties holding equity interests);[494] and (3) a detailed description (including all actuarial factors and discount rates) used to determine the amount of the gift.[495]

[e] The Relationship of Section 2701 to Other Gift Tax Provisions

When applicable, Section 2701(a) increases the gift tax value of a subordinate equity interest transferred to family member. As there is a gift transfer, other gift tax provisions are applicable to a gift whose valuation has been increased by Section 2701.[496] Transfers of property subject to Section 2701(a) may qualify for Section 2513 gift splitting[497] and the Section 2503(b) annual exclusion. Thus, a Section 2701(a) increase in valuation of a transfer of a present interest in a subordinate equity interest qualifies for the annual exclusion. If a transfer subject to Section 2701(a) qualifies for a marital deduction,[498] any Section 2701 increase in the value of the transfer also qualifies for the marital deduction.[499] Any increase in gift tax resulting from the application

---

[491] Compare Reg. § 301.6501(c)-1(e)(2) (applicable to Sections 2701 and 2701(d)) with Reg. §§ 301.6501(c)-1(f)(2), 301.6501(c)-1(f)(3) (general adequate disclosure rules). See IRC § 6501(c)(9); ¶ 9.04[10].

Regulations Section 301.6501(c)-1(e) is applicable to transfers on or after January 28, 1992. Reg. § 301.6501(c)-1(f)(3).

[492] A transfer includes the entire transaction or series of transactions (including any transaction that affected the transferred interest) of which the transfer (or taxable event) was a part. Reg. § 301.6501(c)-1(e)(2).

[493] Reg. § 301.6501(c)-1(e)(2)(i).

[494] Reg. § 301.6501(c)-1(e)(2)(ii).

[495] Reg. § 301.6501(c)-1(e)(2)(iii). For entity interests that are not actively traded, this includes financial and other data used in determining value, such as balance sheets and earnings statements. Id.

[496] The following discussion in the text is inapplicable to an increase in "taxable gifts" that occurs as a result of the application of Section 2701(d). See supra ¶ 19.02[5][a] text accompanying note 338.

[497] Cf. supra ¶ 19.02[5][c][v].

[498] Cf. IRC § 2701(e)(1)(A).

[499] IRC § 2523. Cf. IRC § 2701(d)(3)(B).

If a subordinate equity interest is transferred to a charitable remainder or a charitable lead trust with a family member holding another interest in the trust, the amount of the noncharitable and charitable interests (and the resulting charitable deduction) are increased proportionately to reflect the increase in the value of the corpus of the trust as a result of the application of Section 2701. See IRC § 2522(c)(2). See also supra ¶ 19.02[2][a] note 76. Cf. ¶ 19.03[2][c] note 93. An outright transfer of a subordinate equity interest to char-

of Section 2701 may be offset by the Section 2505 unified credit. If the transfer of the subordinate equity interest subject to Section 2701 (or a portion of that interest) is disclaimed and the disclaimer is a qualified disclaimer under Section 2518,[500] Section 2701 may not apply. For example, if Transferor transfers a subordinate equity interest to Child and, as a result of Child's qualified disclaimer, the subordinate equity interest passes to an unrelated person, the disclaimer will prevent the application of Section 2701 to the original transfer.[501]

[f] The Relationship of Section 2701 Transfers to Other Taxes

The relationship of Section 2701 to the estate, income, and the generation-skipping transfer taxes is unclear.[502] It is clear that a Section 2701 "transfer" is a transfer only for purposes of the gift tax and not for the other taxes.[503] However, it is unclear whether the value of a transfer as determined under Section 2701 establishes value only for the gift tax, for other transfer taxes, or for all taxes.[504] The legislative history and the regulations are virtually silent in resolving this issue.[505] The relationship of Section 2701 to each of the three taxes is considered separately in the following section.

[i] The estate tax. A Section 2701 "transfer" is not a transfer for purposes of the estate tax.[506] The relationship of Section 2701 to the estate tax is generally not complex because the typical freeze generally involves an outright

---

ity is not subject to Section 2701 because the transfer is not to a family member. IRC § 2701(a)(1).

[500] IRC § 2518(b).

[501] A disclaimer of a portion of the subordinate equity interest to an unrelated person would make Section 2701 inapplicable to that portion of the property. If the disclaimer resulted in another member of transferor's family, as defined in Section 2701(e)(1), acquiring the subordinate equity interest, Section 2701 would remain applicable.

[502] Similar issues arise with respect to the relationship of Section 2702 to the other taxes. See ¶ 19.03[4][e].

[503] Section 2701(a)(1) provides that "[s]olely for urposes of determining whether a transfer . . . is a gift . . . " (emphasis added).

[504] Section 2701(a)(1) provides "[s]olely for purposes of determining whether a transfer . . . is a gift (and the value of such transfer). . . . " The parenthetical clause "the value of such transfer" may be modified by the term "gift" and be read "the value of such transfer *by gift*" with the result that Section 2701 value would apply only for purposes of the Chapter 12 gift tax. In the alternative, the clause "value of such transfer" may be read more broadly to establish value for all other taxes. Cf. IRC § 7806(b). It is also arguable that Section 2701 value applies only for other *transfer* tax purposes. See infra note 516.

[505] See infra notes 512, 516.

[506] See supra note 503. Cf. IRC §§ 2035, 2036, 2037, 2038.

transfer of the subordinate equity interest[507] and the inclusion of any applicable retained interest in the transferor's gross estate.[508] Valuation of the transfer under the gift tax is irrelevant to valuation under the estate tax because the estate tax has its own separate valuation mechanism.[509] The principal relationship between Section 2701 valuation and the estate tax valuation is found in Section 2701(e)(6), which provides for adjustments to mitigate double taxation resulting from the application of Section 2701 and the estate tax provisions.[510]

[ii] **The income tax.** The relationship between Section 2701 and the income tax is minimal.[511] There is an issue whether the retained interest valued under Section 2701 is taken into consideration in determining the Section 1015 basis of the subordinate equity interest and in making a part-gift, part-sale computation. The Service seemingly takes the position that the retained interest valued under Section 2701 is disregarded under the income tax.[512] If so, and if there is a transfer for no consideration to which Section 2701 applies, the basis of the applicable retained interest is disregarded in determining the Section 1015 basis of the subordinate equity interest.[513] Further, the income tax basis adjustments to the transferred subordinate equity interest under Section 1015(d) may be made without taking into consideration any appreciation in the subordinate equity interest as a result of the Section 2701 increase in the

---

[507] Even if an interest is in a trust, the ordering rules under the attribution rules generally treat the transfer as an outright transfer. See Reg. § 25.2701-6(a)(5)(ii); supra ¶ 19.02[4][d] text accompanying note 267.

[508] IRC § 2033.

[509] See IRC §§ 2031, 2032, 2032A. Cf. IRC § 1014.

[510] See supra ¶ 19.02[5][c]. Section 2701(a) essentially accelerates the transferor's transfer taxes (see supra ¶ 19.02[1][c] note 23) with relief from double taxation provided by Section 2701(e)(6). The relief is often deferred until the transferor's death when the amount of relief is dependent upon the valuations under the two separate mechanisms. See supra ¶¶ 19.02[5][c][ii], 19.02[5][c][iv].

[511] The relationship of Section 2701(d) to the income tax is discussed supra ¶ 19.02[5][a] notes 335, 338, 348. Nonrecognition transactions within the meaning of Section 7701(a)(45) of the income tax are accorded nonrecognition under the Section 2701(e)(6) rules. See supra ¶ 19.02[5][c] text accompanying notes 447–448. See also supra ¶ 19.02[5][e] note 499 for a potential relationship of Section 2701 and the Section 170 charitable deduction.

[512] The Service seemingly rejects the argument that "the amount of a gift under section 2701 necessarily affects the results under other provisions of the Internal Revenue Code (such as the determination of basis under Section 1015) that are based on the value of the transferred property." TD 8395 Supplementary Information (Effect on Other Internal Revenue Code Sections) (Jan. 29, 1992), 1992-1 CB 316, 318. There is no actual discussion of the relationship in the final regulations.

[513] IRC § 1015(a).

amount of the gift.[514] Similarly, if there is a sale of a subordinate equity interest to a family member for its fair market value, with a Section 2701 transfer converting the transaction into a part-gift for gift tax purposes, there is only a sale of the subordinate equity interest for income tax purposes.[515]

[iii] **The generation-skipping transfer tax.** The relationship of Section 2701 valuation to the generation-skipping transfer tax is also unclear.[516] It is

---

[514] See IRC §§ 1015(d)(1), 1015(d)(6). For example, assume Transferor gives a subordinate equity interest with a fair market value of $100 and a basis of $50 to Child and retains an applicable retained interest with a fair market value of $500, a basis of $250, which is valued under Section 2701 valuation at zero, resulting in a $600 gift tax value being placed on the transferred subordinate equity interest and the imposition of $300 in gift tax on the transfer. If the conclusion reached in the text is correct, Child's Section 1015 income tax basis in the subordinate equity interest would be $100, the total of the basis of the subordinate equity interest under Section 1015(a) of $50 plus $150, one half (the Section 1015(d)(6) net appreciation on the subordinate equity interest of $50/ $100) times $300 (the gift tax attributable to the transfer), but limited by Section 1015(d)(1) to the $100 fair market value of the property.

In the alternative, if full regard were given to the applicable retained interest in measuring the basis, there would be a Section 1015(a) basis of $300 increased under Section 1015(d) by the net appreciation of $300/$600 times the gift tax of $300 or Section 1015(d)(6) adjustment of $150 to $450. However, if Section 2701 valuation applies in making the Section 1015 computation, it seems likely that the $250 adjusted basis of the applicable retained interest should not be considered a part of the adjusted basis of the subordinate equity interest to be transferred under Section 1015(a) and the carryover basis prior to the Section 1015 adjustment should be only $50. If so, in determining the Section 1015(d) adjustment, other issues arise with a variety of possible solutions: (1) whether in measuring the Section 1015(d)(6)(B) net appreciation of the transferred property only the basis of the subordinate equity interest is used resulting in net appreciation of $600 – $50 or $550; (2) whether the Section 1015(d)(1) fair market value of the transferred interest is $100, the fair market value of the subordinate equity interest, or the gift tax value of the interest, after applying Section 2701, $600.

[515] Under the income tax part-gift, part-sale regulations (see Reg. §§ 1.1001-1(e), 1.1015-4), the basis of the applicable retained interest should be disregarded (see supra text accompanying note 513) and in the example at supra note 514, if Child paid $100 for the transfer of the subordinate equity interest, Transferor would recognize $50 of gain and under Section 1012, Child's basis in the subordinate equity interest would be $100. If the subordinate equity interest were transferred for less than its fair market value, there would be an income tax part-gift, part-sale with respect to the subordinate equity interest. If the subordinate equity interest in the example at supra note 513 were transferred for $75 of consideration, Transferor would recognize a gain of $25 and Child's basis would be $75 increased by a Section 1015(d) adjustment for the gift tax paid. See Reg. §§ 1.1001-1(e), 1.1015-4(a)(1), 1.1015-4(a)(2); supra note 514.

[516] See supra text accompanying note 505. The Senate Report and the Conference Committee Report discuss the implications of Chapter 14 for "transfer tax" purposes, specifically mentioning the estate tax and the gift tax, but failing to mention the generation-skipping transfer tax. See HR Conf. Rep. No. 964, 101st Cong., 2d Sess., 1130–1138 (1990), reprinted in 1991-2 CB 560, 603–607, and Explanatory Material Concerning Committee on Finance 1990 Reconciliation Submission Pursuant to House Concurrent

arguable that Section 2701 merely establishes value solely for gift tax purposes and does not apply to the generation-skipping transfer tax.[517] Alternatively, it can be asserted that Section 2701 is applicable in establishing the value of property transferred for the purposes of both taxes.[518] A third, middle ground is that the valuation of the transferred interest after application of Section 2701 applies to the generation-skipping transfer tax only where Chapter 13 specifically refers to Chapter 12 value.[519]

A simple example illustrates the issues. Assume Transferor owns an entity worth $1 million with an applicable retained interest with a fair market value of $900,000 and a subordinate equity interest with a fair market value of $100,000. If Transferor transfers the subordinate equity interest to Grandchild and the retained interest is valued at zero under Section 2701, there is a $1 million Chapter 12 gift. If the generation-skipping transfer tax consequences

---

Resolution 310, 136 Cong. Rec. S15629, S15679–15683 (Oct. 18, 1990). See ¶ 19.03[1] note 5.

In the explanation of proposed regulations under Chapter 14, the Service stated:

Although these two sections [i.e., Sections 2701 and 2702] apply to determine the amount of the gift, they do not change the value of the transferred property for other tax purposes. Thus, *in general*, sections 2701 and 2702 do not apply for purposes of the generation-skipping transfer tax.

PS-92-90, Supplementary Information (Explanation of Provision *Overview*), 1991-1 CB 998, 999 (emphasis added). The use of the phrase "in general" implies a general rule and begs the question of what exceptions exist. Neither the proposed regulations nor the final regulations, which both are silent on the issue, offer an answer.

Although Section 2701 valuation arguably should be read into all other Code sections to the same extent (see IRC § 7806(b)), it would not be unreasonable for the Service to argue that the valuation could be read into only the other transfer tax provisions and not the income tax provisions. See supra note 512.

[517] See supra notes 504, 512; Zaritsky & Aucutt, Structuring Estate Freezes Under Chapter 14 ¶ 2.03[4][a] (Warren, Gorham & Lamont, 1993) taking this position.

[518] See supra note 504.

[519] See IRC § 2642(b)(1)(A). This position may explain the "in general" language in the proposed regulations. See supra note 517. Section 2642(b)(1)(A) first appeared in the Code in 1986, prior to the enactment of Section 2701 in 1990. See Tax Reform Act of 1986, Pub. L. No. 99-514, § 1431(a), 100 Stat. 2085, 2723 (1986), reprinted in 1986-3 CB (Vol. 1) 1, 640, and Omnibus Budget Reconciliation Act of 1990, Pub. L. No. 101-508, § 11602(a), 104 Stat. § 1388-1, 1388-491 (1990), reprinted in 1991-2 CB 481, 525. The retention of the reference to Chapter 12 value in Section 2642(b)(1)(A) may have been an oversight and, if so, Section 2642(b)(1)(A) should be read without consideration of Chapter 14. The proposed regulations under Section 2642 seemed to take that approach by referring only to fair market value. Prop. Reg. § 26.2642-2(a)(1), 1993-1 CB 867, 877. However, the final regulations incorporate the reference to Chapter 12 value, stating that, in the case of a timely election to avoid the automatic allocation of GST exemption, the value used is the "fair market value of the property as finally determined for purposes of Chapter 12." Reg. § 26.2642-2(a)(1). The final regulations post-date the enactment of Chapter 14 implying that Chapter 14 valuation is incorporated into Section 2642(b)(1)(A).

are determined without regard to Section 2701, there is a $100,000 direct skip and the estate freeze is still a planning technique for avoiding the generation-skipping transfer tax.[520] At the other extreme, if the Chapter 12 value of the transfer establishes the Chapter 13 value of the transfer, there is a $1 million direct skip.[521] If the middle ground is adopted, there is a $100,000 direct skip,[522] but the $1 million Chapter 12 valuation is used in allocating GST exemption under Section 2642(b)(1)(A).[523] As a result of Section 2642(b)(1)(A), Transferor must allocate $1 million of GST exemption to the transfer to avert Chapter 13 taxation on the transfer or Transferor must elect out of an automatic $1 million allocation of GST exemption to avoid use of the $1 million of GST exemption[524] with the result that there would be Chapter 13 tax on a $89,000 direct skip transfer.[525]

It is surprising that the Service has been virtually silent with respect to the relationship of Section 2701 to the income and generation-skipping transfer taxes. One hopes that the Service will not read Section 2701 value into the other taxes, so as to avoid even more complexity in an already complex area.[526] The ball is in the Service's court.

---

[520] This position would seem to be consistent with Sections 2612(c)(1) and 2623 which values a direct skip at "the value of the property received by the transferee." Additionally, a subsequent transfer of the applicable retained interest to a skip person would constitute a direct skip generation-skipping transfer of that interest.

[521] If the Service takes this position, the regulations under Section 2701(e), a section that specifically refers to a Chapter 13 generation-skipping transfer tax adjustment that avoids double taxation, will have to be expanded to avoid double generation-skipping transfer taxation as well as double estate and gift taxation. See Reg. § 25.2701-5; supra ¶ 19.02[5][c].

[522] See supra text accompanying note 520.

[523] IRC § 2642(b)(1)(A); Reg. § 26.2642-2(a)(1). See supra note 519.

[524] The burden falls upon the transferor to elect out of the automatic allocation of GST exemption and avoid an overallocation of GST exemption. IRC §§ 2632(b)(3), 2642(b)(1)(A). The transferor must affirmatively and irrevocably elect out of the automatic allocation by timely filing a Form 709 and paying the generation-skipping transfer tax. IRC § 2632(b)(3); Reg. § 26.2632-1(b)(1). See ¶ 15.03[3][c].

[525] There would be a zero inclusion ratio on the first $11,000 of the transfer and a tax imposed on the remaining $89,000 of the transfer at the highest estate tax rate. IRC §§ 2001(c)(1), 2001(c)(2)(B), 2641(a), 2642(c).

[526] See supra notes 514, 515, 521.

[g] Effective Dates

Section 2701 is applicable to transfers made after October 8, 1990.[527] The regulations under Section 2701 (other than Regulation Section 25.2701-5)[528] are effective as of January 28, 1992.[529]

¶ 19.03 SECTION 2702: SPECIAL VALUATION RULES FOR TRANSFERS OF INTERESTS IN TRUSTS

[1] Introduction

In measuring the amount of a gift of an interest in property, the fair market value of the entire property is normally reduced by the fair market value of any interest retained by the transferor.[1] The transferor has the burden of establishing the value of the retained interest,[2] and typically uses actuarial principles and federally determined interest rates to meet that burden.[3] Congress concluded that normal valuation principles should not apply to intrafamily transfers, and it enacted Section 2702.[4] It was concerned that in making a gift of a remainder to a family member, the donor using normal valuation methods could overvalue the retained income interest and thereby depress the value of the remainder; or, in the alternative, the donor could inflate the value of a retained remainder and reduce the value of a gifted income interest.[5] Accord-

---

[527] Omnibus Budget Reconciliation Act of 1990, Pub. L. No. 101-508, § 11602(e)(1), 104 Stat. 1388-1, 1388-500, reprinted in 1991-2 CB 481, 529.

[528] Reg. § 25.2701-5 is effective for transfers after May 4, 1994. Reg. § 25.2701-5(h). For consequences under Section 2701(e)(6) prior to that date, see supra ¶ 19.02[5][c] note 407.

[529] Reg. § 25.2701-8. For periods between October 8, 1990, and January 28, 1992, taxpayers may rely on any reasonable interpretation of the statutory provisions, including the proposed regulations and final regulations. Id.

[1] Smith v. Shaughnessy, 318 US 176 (1943); Reg. § 25.2511-1(e); IRC § 7520. See infra note 3.

[2] Robinette v. Helvering, 318 US 184 (1943).

[3] See IRC § 7520. See also ¶¶ 4.02[5], 10.02[2][f].

[4] Omnibus Budget Reconciliation Act of 1990, Pub. L. No. 101-508, § 11602(a), 104 Stat. 1388-1, 1388-491 (1990), reprinted in 1991-2 CB 481, 527. Section 2702 is discussed in detail in Begleiter, "Estate Planning in the Nineties: Friday the Thirteenth, Chapter 14: Jason Goes to Washington—Part II," 47 De Paul L. Rev. 1 (1997).

[5] Explanatory Materials Concerning Committee on Finance 1990 Reconciliation Submission Pursuant to House Concurrent Resolution 310, 136 Cong. Rec. S15629, S15680 (Oct. 18, 1990). This cite deserves further comments. The Omnibus Budget Reconciliation Act of 1990 was prepared under a very short deadline. In order to avoid delay, the bill

ingly, in connection with family transfers, Section 2702(a) generally values any retained interests at zero, thereby increasing the value of the interest transferred.

Section 2702 is aimed primarily at averting two types of estate freezing techniques. The first technique is a grantor retained income trust, GRIT. Under a typical GRIT, Grantor would transfer property to a trust, retain the trust income for a term of years generally intended to be somewhat shorter than Grantor's life expectancy,[6] and provide for a remainder to Children. The value of the gifted remainder would equal only a small portion of the value of the property making up the corpus of the trust,[7] and assuming Grantor outlived the term of years, post-transfer appreciation in the value of the corpus would escape the transfer tax imposed by Chapters 11 and 12.[8] Thus, if Grantor survived the retained income period, transfer tax would be avoided on both a significant portion of the value of the transferred corpus and the post-transfer appreciation on the corpus.[9] During the mid-1980s, two factors made such arrangements particularly enticing. The increases in the unified credit and in the interest rates used in valuing temporal interests provided enhanced leveraging opportunities.[10] Under the more generous unified credit, more property could be transferred without current transfer tax imposition. Moreover, a 10 percent assumed rate of return (up from 6 percent) for valuing temporal interests was often a higher rate of return than most trusts actually earned. The combination of these factors allowed a transferor to make a transfer in trust and use the government-prescribed 10 percent interest rate to overstate the value of the retained interest, thereby reducing the value of the gift, and to use the unified credit to avoid current transfer taxation. In a similar vein, the value of the assets placed in trust might actually increase at a rate greater than 10 percent per

---

was brought to the floor of the Senate without the printing of a formal report. In an effort to complete the legislative record, the report language was merely printed in the Congressional Record at the beginning of the debate on the Reconciliation Bill.

Congressional concern here was similar to its concern in situations involving improper valuation of gifts of partial interests to charity that resulted in the enactment of restrictions on deductions of partial interests to charity. See ¶¶ 5.05[4]–5.05[8].

[6] The shorter than life expectancy period is used in an attempt to escape the clutches of Section 2036(a)(1).

[7] Assuming a 10 percent interest rate and a fifteen-year income interest retained by Grantor, the amount of the gift to Children would be equal to only 23.9392 percent of the value of the corpus.

[8] If the remainder passed to skip persons, the appreciation would not necessarily avoid generation-skipping transfer taxation imposed by Chapter 13. See IRC § 2642(f)(2) discussed at ¶ 16.02[7][b].

[9] Any income distributed from the trust that was held by the Grantor at death would be included in Grantor's gross estate under Section 2033.

[10] See IRC § 2505, discussed at ¶ 9.06; Reg. §§ 20.2031-7A(d)(6), 25.2512-5A(d)(1), 25.2512-5A(d)(6).

year, while producing only a small amount of ordinary income to be paid to Grantor under the trust terms.

The transaction had little or no downside risk other than transactional costs and lost alternative opportunities. If Grantor outlived the term of the trust, then the assets would be distributed to the remainderpersons for the cost of the gift tax on the depressed value of the gift of the remainder. However, if Grantor died during the term of the trust, the property would be included in Grantor's gross estate under Section 2036, generally providing the same ultimate result as if the transaction had never been undertaken. Furthermore, under Section 2001(b), the property would be excluded from adjusted taxable gifts.[11] In other words, if Grantor died too soon, it would be as if the gift had never been made. Grantor had everything to gain and nothing to lose, except the loss of the income from any amount of gift tax paid on creation of the GRIT,[12] the transactional costs, and the opportunity to use any unified credit consumed in the transaction to make gifts that would not be brought back into Grantor's gross estate.

Grantor frequently would also retain a contingent reversionary interest in or a general power of appointment over the corpus of a GRIT[13] that would come into play only if Grantor died within the income period, since, in any event, there would be gross estate inclusion of the corpus in the event of Grantor's death before the end of the income period. The retention of the contingent interest or power further reduced the gift tax value of the remainder gift to the family member. Assuming a set term of years, the older the grantor, the more valuable the contingent interest or power, because of the increased risk of death during the term of the trust.[14] In addition, the contingent interest or power restored control over the disposition of the property to Grantor, in whose gross estate it would be included, adding the option of qualifying the property for the marital deduction if Grantor had a surviving spouse.

Section 2702(a) applies[15] to intra-family GRITs, generally placing a zero value on the retained interest thereby increasing the value of transferred inter-

---

[11] See IRC § 2001(b) (flush language).

[12] Assuming the amount of the gift did not exceed the Grantor's remaining Section 2505 credit, no gift tax was paid and there was minimal downside risk.

[13] The retention of a general power of appointment by a grantor over the corpus of a trust transferred by Grantor results in inclusion in Grantor's gross estate under Section 2038, not Section 2041. Reg. § 20.2041-1(b)(2).

[14] See, e.g., TAM 8546001 (July 1985) (contingent principal interest was valued using the L N Table). Cf. Table S at Reg. § 20.2031-7(d)(7).

[15] Until its retroactive repeal, Section 2036(c) applied to GRITs. Omnibus Budget Reconciliation Act, Pub. L. No. 101-508, § 601(a), 104 Stat. 1388-1, 1388-490, reprinted in 1991-2 CB 481, 524. See Stephens, Maxfield, Lind & Calfee, Federal Estate and Gift Taxation, ¶ 4.08[9], especially ¶ 4.08[9][e][i] (Warren, Gorham & Lamont, 6th ed. 1991).

ests.[16] Section 2702 also applies to the valuation of retained secondary life estates, reversions, and retained powers over such interests,[17] whether retained by the grantor or by applicable family members.[18]

Section 2702 also applies to a joint purchase, a second type of estate freeze technique. Prior to the enactment of Section 2702, if Grantor purchased an income interest for life in property for its fair market value and Grantor's Child purchased a remainder interest in the same property also for its fair market value, Grantor made no gift at the time of the purchase and the property avoided inclusion in Grantor's gross estate at Grantor's death.[19] For gift tax purposes,[20] Section 2702 essentially treats this type of joint purchase by family members as though the term income interest purchaser had owned and transferred the *entire* property in return for any consideration paid by the family member remainderperson in purchasing the property.[21] Assuming the remainderperson paid fair market value for the remainder, the joint purchase in effect results in a gift by the term interest holder of an amount equal to the cost of the term holder's income interest.[22]

The ensuing discussion considers the general rules of Section 2702,[23] specifically defining the terms used by the statute. It then considers the exceptions

---

[16] See Priv. Ltr. Rul. 9109033 (Nov. 30, 1990) (Section 2702 applied to a typical GRIT). If a grantor outlives the term of the income interest, GRITs are still successful in freezing value, even where Section 2702 increases the amount of the gift transfer from the value of the remainder to the full value of the corpus.

[17] See infra ¶ 19.03[2][a][iv].

[18] See infra ¶ 19.03[2][a][iv]. The propriety of the result under Section 2702 (an increased valuation of a gift by the amount of the value that is retained by the term interest-holder) can be questioned when the transfer involves a retained reversion. A retained reversion generally does not result in a freeze; the reversionary interest in the trust (including any appreciation on the property) will be subject to a subsequent transfer tax either on a subsequent gift by the transferor or by inclusion in the transferor's gross estate under Section 2033 or under Section 2037. If, because of the valuation method used, there was undervaluation of the income interest on the original transfer resulting in an overvaluation of the reversion, such overvaluation should also be used with respect to any subsequent transfer of the reversion.

[19] Cf. IRC §§ 2033, 2036, neither of which was applicable.

[20] The Section 2702(c)(2) joint purchase rule is inapplicable to the estate tax and the generation-skipping transfer tax. See Reg. § 25.2702-4(c); infra ¶¶ 19.03[4][e][i], 19.03[4][e][iii].

[21] IRC § 2702(c)(2).

[22] IRC § 2702(c)(2). Technically, unless the term interest is a qualified interest, the term interest holder's transfer is treated as a transfer of the interests after the term interest to a family member, triggering zero valuation of the term interest under Section 2702(a)(2)(A). See infra ¶ 19.03[4][a].

[23] See infra ¶ 19.03[2]. Section 2702 is critiqued in McCouch, "Rethinking Section 2702," 2 Fla. Tax Rev. 99 (1994). For other articles discussing Section 2702, see Blattmachr & Painter, "Planning for Split-Interest Transfers Under the Section 2702 Final

for incomplete transfers,[24] for transfers of qualified interests,[25] for some regulatory exceptions,[26] and for personal residence trusts.[27] Finally, special rules applicable to Section 2702 are considered.[28]

[2] The General Rule

[a] The Requirements of Section 2702

There are two principal requirements under Section 2702(a)(1) to bring the Section 2702 valuation rule into play. First, there must be a *transfer* of an interest *in trust* to (or for the benefit of) a *member of* the transferor's *family*. Second, an *interest* in the trust must be *retained* by the transferor or an *applicable family member*. If the two requirements are met, then any retained interest that is not essentially covered by an exception is valued at zero. Some simple examples will illustrate the rule: If Grantor creates a GRIT providing income to Grantor for fifteen years and a remainder to Grantor's Children, there is a transfer in trust of the remainder to a family member and a retention of an income interest by Grantor. Section 2702 values the retained income interest at zero, with the result that the transferred remainder is treated as having a value equal to the full value of corpus.[29] Even if Children pay adequate and full consideration for the remainder interest, Section 2702 still applies to value the Grantor's retained interest at zero and the result is a gift of the entire corpus reduced by the consideration received by Grantor, the value of Grantor's income interest.[30] Similarly, if Grantor creates a trust with income to Spouse for life, then income to Grantor for life, and a remainder to Children,

---

Regulations," 77 J. Tax'n 18 (1992); Gans, "GRITs, GRATs and GRUTs: Planning and Policy," 11 Va. Tax Rev. 761 (1992); Dees, "The Slaying of Frankenstein's Monster: The Repeal and Replacement of Section 2036(c)," 69 Taxes 151 (1991).

[24] IRC § 2702(a)(3)(A)(i). See infra ¶ 19.03[3][a].

[25] IRC § 2702(b). See infra ¶ 19.03[3][b].

[26] IRC § 2702(a)(3)(A)(iii). See infra ¶ 19.03[3][c].

[27] IRC § 2702(a)(3)(A)(ii). See infra ¶ 19.03[3][d].

[28] See infra ¶ 19.03[4].

[29] Cf. Reg. § 25.2702-2(d) Ex. 1. If Grantor outlives the fifteen-year period, post-transfer appreciation of the corpus is still excluded from Grantor's gross estate.

If during the first ten years Grantor subsequently transfers the last five years of the fifteen-year income interest to Children, the gift of the last five years income interest to the Children has a value equal to the entire value of the remaining income interest because the requirements of Section 2702 are again met and Grantor's retained income interest is again valued at zero. Cf. Reg. § 25.2702-6(a), which averts double gift taxation and is discussed infra ¶ 19.03[4][c][i].

[30] Reg. § 25.2702-4(d) Ex. 2. See IRC §§ 2512(b), 2702(a)(3)(B).

Section 2702 values Grantor's retained secondary life estate at zero, and there is a transfer of the entire value of the corpus.[31] Alternatively, if Grantor creates a trust with income to Grantor's Parent for life and a reversion to Grantor, the two requirements of Section 2702 again are met. A zero valuation is assigned to Grantor's retained reversionary interest, and there is a gift of an income interest having a value equal to the entire value of corpus of the trust. Similar to the prior example, if Parent paid adequate and full consideration for the income interest, Grantor would still make a gift equal to the value of the reversionary interest.[32]

In determining whether the two requirements of Section 2702 are met, an examination of the Section 2702 statutory terms must be made. The first requirement is that there must be a *transfer* of an interest *in trust* to (or for the benefit of) a *member of* the transferor's *family*.

[i] A transfer in trust. A transfer in trust may be a transfer to a new trust, an existing trust, or an assignment of an interest in an existing trust.[33] A Section 2702 transfer includes an exercise of a pre-1942 general power of appointment and an exercise, release, and a lifetime lapse to the extent the lapse is considered a release[34] of a post-1942 general power of appointment, all of which are transfers under the gift tax.[35] However, a Section 2702 transfer does

---

[31] Cf. IRC §§ 2503(b), 2523(h)(1), 2524. See infra ¶ 19.03[2][c] text accompanying notes 83, 93.

[32] Cf. IRC §§ 2503(b), 2523(h)(1), 2524. See infra ¶ 19.03[2][c] text accompanying notes 83, 93.

[33] Reg. § 25.2702-2(a)(2). See Reg. § 25.2702-1(c)(8), discussed infra ¶ 19.03[3][c] note 154.

[34] A release includes a lifetime lapse that is not excepted from release status under the five-or-five rule. See IRC § 2514(e), discussed ¶ 10.04[4][c].

[35] Priv. Ltr. Rul. 9804047 (Oct. 28, 1997). For example, assume Taxpayer is the income beneficiary of a trust established by Taxpayer's Parent that provides income to Taxpayer for life, and a remainder to Taxpayer's Children. Parent transfers $11,000 to the trust in the year and gives Taxpayer a *Crummey* power to remove the $11,000 from the trust within a limited period. See ¶ 9.04[3][f]. On a lapse of Taxpayer's power, after applying the Section 2514(e) exception, see ¶ 10.04[4][c], there is a $6,000 release of the power by Taxpayer resulting in a transfer by Taxpayer to the trust. Since the two requirements of Section 2702 are met with respect to that transfer, Section 2702 values Taxpayer's income interest at zero and there is a transfer to Children by Taxpayer valued at the full $6,000 amount. In the absence of the application of Section 2702, e.g., where a nonrelated person was the remainderperson of the trust, Taxpayer would make a transfer of only the value of a remainder interest in the $6,000 amount. Priv. Ltr. Rul. 9804047 (Oct. 28, 1997).

not include the exercise, release or lapse of a power of appointment that is not a transfer under the gift tax[36] or the execution of a Section 2518 disclaimer.[37]

The transfer does not have to be a transfer to an actual trust. Section 2702 imputes a trust if there is a transfer of an interest in property with respect to which there is one or more "term interests."[38] Term interests include both a life interest in property or an interest in property for a term of years.[39] Thus, if Grantor transfers a legal remainder interest in Grantor's farm to a family member and retains either a life estate or a right to income for a term of years, the transfer is treated as a transfer in trust.[40] A term interest includes one in a series of successive interests, but it does not include contemporaneous interests.[41] Thus, the creation of a tenancy in common with a family member, a joint tenancy with a right of survivorship with a family member, or a tenancy by the entirety is not a term interest to which a trust is imputed or to which Section 2702 is applicable.[42]

An arm's-length lease of property to a family member with a reversion to lessor is technically the creation of a term interest that could be treated as an imputed transfer in trust meeting the requirements of Section 2702.[43] If Section 2702 were applied in such a situation,[44] the reversion would have a zero value and the owner of the property would make a transfer to the extent of the value of the entire property less the present value of the rent to be received under the lease.[45] However, the regulations provide that if a leasehold is transferred for adequate and full consideration, the leasehold is not treated as a term inter-

---

[36] Reg. § 25.2702-2(a)(2)(i). See IRC § 2514. This encompasses an exercise, release or lapse of a nongeneral power, the release or lapse of a pre-1942 general power of appointment (see Section 2514(a)), and a lapse of a post-1942 general power to the extent that it is within the Section 2514(e) five-or-five exception.

[37] Reg. § 25.2702-2(a)(2)(ii).

[38] IRC § 2702(c)(1).

[39] IRC § 2702(c)(3).

[40] IRC §§ 2702(c)(1), 2702(c)(3). Since the other Section 2702 requirements are met, the income interest is valued at zero and, as a result, there is a gift transfer equal to the entire value of the farm.

If the nontrust property was Grantor's principal residence rather than the farm, this might be treated as a transfer to a personal residence trust making Section 2702 inapplicable because of the personal residence trust exception. IRC §§ 2702(a)(3)(A)(ii), 2702(c)(1). However, it is questionable whether a trust would be imputed in such circumstances. See infra ¶¶ 19.03[3][d] text accompanying note 210, 19.03[3][d][ii], ¶ 19.03[4][a] note 282. But see also infra ¶ 19.03[3][d] note 168.

[41] Reg. § 25.2702-4(a).

[42] Reg. § 25.2702-4(a).

[43] IRC §§ 2702(c)(1), 2702(c)(3).

[44] The incomplete transfer exception would not apply even if adequate consideration was received for the leasehold. IRC §§ 2702(a)(3)(A)(i), 2702(a)(3)(B).

[45] IRC §§ 2702(a)(1), 2702(a)(2)(A).

est, no trust is imputed, and Section 2702 is inapplicable.[46] A lease is treated as transferred for adequate and full consideration if, at the time the lease is entered into or extended, a good-faith effort is made to determine the fair rental value of the property and the terms of the lease conform to that value.[47]

A joint purchase of property with at least one person holding a term interest in the property should be treated as an imputed transfer to a trust.[48] The ramifications of such a transfer are considered in the discussion of the joint purchase rule with the other special rules in the following section.[49]

[ii] Family members. The term "member of the transferor's family" is defined broadly under Section 2702. It encompasses the transferor's spouse, ancestors and lineal descendants of the transferor and the transferor's spouse, brothers or sisters of the transferor, and the spouses of any of these persons.[50] Therefore, Section 2702 is inapplicable to transfers to nieces and nephews, aunts and uncles, or more remote relatives.[51]

Section 2702 requires only a transfer of an interest in the property to a family member. If another interest in the same property is simultaneously transferred to a non-family member, Section 2702 still applies. For example, assume Grantor transfers property to a trust providing for income to Grantor for life, then income to Grantor's Brother for life and a remainder to Grantor's Niece. Even though Niece is not a family member, because Brother is a family member, Section 2702 applies. As a result, Grantor's retained income interest is valued at zero and there is a gift transfer equal to the entire fair market value of the property.[52] If Grantor had simply provided income to Grantor for life and a remainder to Grantor's Niece, Section 2702 would not apply, because there would be no transfer to a family member, and Grantor would make a transfer of property by gift of only the actuarial value of the remainder interest.

---

[46] Reg. § 25.2702-4(b). Seemingly, a lease at fair market value is similar to an annuity interest because a set bona fide amount is to be paid and the transaction is difficult to manipulate making the exception appropriate.

[47] Reg. § 25.2702-4(b).

[48] IRC § 2702(c)(2). Cf. IRC §§ 2702(c)(1), 2702(c)(3).

[49] See infra ¶ 19.03[4][a].

[50] IRC §§ 2702(e), 2704(c)(2). Compare the limited definition of "family members" used under Section 2701 that includes only spouses and descendants and their spouses but does not apply to family members in higher generations, siblings, or spouses of such persons. IRC § 2701(e)(1). See ¶ 19.02[2][a][iii].

[51] However, if Grantor transfers a remainder interest in a trust to Grantor's Niece or Nephew (Grantor's Sibling's child) retaining an income interest in Grantor, and Sibling transfers a remainder interest in a trust to Sibling's Niece or Nephew (Grantor's Child), the Service should apply the reciprocal trust doctrine and apply Section 2702 to the transfers. Cf. supra ¶ 4.08[7][d].

[52] See infra ¶ 19.03[2][c] note 93.

Although a spouse is a family member under Section 2702,[53] a former spouse is not. A spouse is treated as a former spouse (causing Section 2702 to be inapplicable to a transfer) if there is a Section 2516[54] transfer prior to a divorce of an interest in property held in trust and the transferor spouse retains all other interests in the trust.[55] For example, assume that pursuant to a written agreement relative to marital property rights, Grantor transfers property in trust to pay income to Spouse for fifteen years with a reversion to Grantor, and assume that the transfer of the income interest to Spouse meets the requirements of Section 2516. Section 2702 does not apply,[56] and Grantor makes no gift.[57] As a result of the imputed trust rule, the exception applies regardless of whether the property is held in a trust.[58]

This rule excepting certain property settlements has the effect of putting most pre-divorce and post-divorce property settlement transfers on an equal footing. However, the rule does not apply if there is a completed transfer of an interest in the same property to a third person.[59] This limits the exception too

---

[53] IRC §§ 2702(e), 2704(c)(2)(A).

[54] Section 2516 applies not only to post-divorce transfers, but also to transfers within a possible maximum period of two years between the date a written property settlement agreement is entered into and the date of a final divorce decree. See ¶ 10.06.

[55] Reg. § 25.2702-1(c)(7). See IRC § 2702(a)(3)(A)(iii). Although the regulations simply state that Section 2702 is inapplicable to such a transfer, in essence, it is treating a current spouse as a former spouse. See Kasner, "Avoiding Transfer Tax Problems in Divorce Settlements," 58 Tax Notes 594 (Feb. 1, 1993).

[56] Under Section 2702, it is as though the transfer occurred after the divorce. See Reg. § 25.2702-4(d) Ex. 5.

[57] See IRC § 2512. If this exception to the application of Section 2702 did not apply, Grantor would have made a transfer of the value of the reversion, i.e., the corpus less the value of the Section 2516 consideration received for the income interest. See infra note 59.

[58] IRC § 2702(c)(1).

[59] Reg. § 25.2702-1(c)(7). For example, if Grantor transfers an income interest in trust to Spouse for life (in a transfer to which Section 2516 applies creating consideration for the transfer) and Grantor retains a reversion upon Spouse's death, but on Grantor's failure to survive Spouse, the property passes to their Children, the exception does not apply and Grantor makes a transfer of the full value of the corpus less the amount of Section 2516 consideration received. See Reg. § 25.2702-4(d) Ex. 5. If Grantor had retained a power to allocate the remainder interest among the Children, Grantor would have retained an interest in all of the non–Section 2516 interests in the property (see Reg. § 25.2702-2(a)(4)) and the regulatory exception would apply. As a practical matter, since the corpus will in all likelihood be included in Grantor's gross estate under Section 2037 in any event, Grantor is ill-advised to name the Children as alternative remainderpersons and should simply provide for them by will to avert a gift on creation of the trust. If in the divorce negotiations Spouse insists that the Children be named as remainderpersons, as seen previously, the application of Section 2702 could be avoided by allowing Grantor to retain a power of appointment among the Children, thereby avoiding current gift tax consequences.

Section 2702

narrowly; it should apply to a situation in which a Section 2516 transfer is made to a spouse and no other transfer is made to a member of the transferor's family. For example, if Grantor transfers property to a trust with income to current Spouse for fifteen years (and Spouse's interest falls within Section 2516), then a reversion to Grantor if living and, if not, a remainder to Niece, the exception should apply because there really has not been a transfer to a family member. Instead, the exception is inapplicable, Spouse is treated as a family member, Section 2702 applies, and Grantor has made a gift of the corpus less the value of Spouse's income interest, rather than a mere gift of the value of Niece's contingent remainder interest.

[iii] **Applicable family member.** Under the second requirement of Section 2702, an *interest* in the trust must be *retained* by the transferor or an *applicable family member.* The term applicable family member includes only the transferor's spouse, ancestors of the transferor or the transferor's spouse, and the spouses of any ancestors.[60]

[iv] **A retained interest.** An interest is retained under Section 2702 only if it is held by the same individual *both* before and after the transfer in trust.[61] If Grantor makes a transfer of an income interest to Spouse for life and a remainder to Children, even though an applicable family member (Spouse) holds an interest after the transfer, Spouse did not hold the interest before the transfer and Spouse does not "retain" an interest; thus, Section 2702 is inapplicable.[62] Since Grantor transfers all interests in the property resulting in a transfer of the entire value of the property, there is no need for Section 2702 because there is no retained interest.

Appropriately, if a term interest is created on the transfer, any interest in the property held by the transferor immediately after the transfer is treated as an interest retained by the transferor.[63] For example, if Grantor creates a trust with income to Mother for life and a reversion to Grantor, Grantor's reversion is a retained interest, Section 2702 applies, the reversion is valued at zero, and the transferred income interest has a value for gift tax purposes equal to the value of the entire corpus of the trust.

The retained interest may be held either by the transferor or an applicable family member.[64] If an applicable family member retains an interest, Section 2702 applies and values the applicable family member's interest at zero in de-

---

[60] IRC §§ 2701(e)(2), 2702(a)(1). The Section 2701 definition of "applicable family member" is employed under Section 2702. See ¶ 19.02[2][b][i].

[61] Reg. § 25.2702-2(a)(3).

[62] Reg. § 25.2702-2(d)(1) Ex. 3. Even if a Section 2523(f) QTIP election is made by Grantor, there is still no retention of an interest. Id.

[63] Reg. § 25.2702-2(a)(3).

[64] IRC § 2702(a)(1).

termining the amount of the transfer by the *transferor* to a family member. For example, if Parent holds a life estate in a trust and Child holds the remainder interest[65] and Child assigns the remainder interest to Grandchild, Child makes a transfer in trust to a member of Child's family (Grandchild), an applicable family member (Parent) retains an income interest, Section 2702 values Parent's interest at zero, and Child's transfer is an amount equal to the entire value of the corpus. Furthermore, if Child sold the remainder to Grandchild, Section 2702 would still apply[66] and there would be a gift of the full value of the corpus less the value of the consideration received, the value of Parent's income interest.[67]

In determining whether there is a retained interest, the term "interest" is broadly defined. It includes either a successive equitable interest in trust property or a successive legal interest in nontrust property.[68] However, the term refers only to temporal interests and interests following temporal interests; it does not include contemporaneous interests such as a tenancy in common, a tenancy by the entirety, or a joint tenancy with a right of survivorship.[69]

A retained interest also includes a mere power held with respect to any interest that makes the interest incomplete for gift tax purposes.[70] Thus, if Grantor creates a trust with income to any of Grantor's Children that Grantor selects and a remainder equally to Grantor's Grandchildren or, in the alternative, if Grantor creates a trust with income equally to Children and a remainder to any of Grandchildren Grantor selects, the interest over which Grantor retains a power is an incomplete interest for gift tax purposes, but it is a re-

---

[65] It is irrelevant who created the trust. For example, it may have been created by Parent's Parent or by Parent's Spouse. If Parent's Spouse created the trust, the transfer to the trust may have marital deduction if a QTIP election was made under Section 2056(b)(7) or a Section 2523(f).

[66] Cf. IRC § 2702(a)(3)(B).

[67] Cf. IRC § 2702(a)(3)(B); Reg. § 25.2702-4(d) Ex. 2.

[68] See IRC § 2702(c)(1); supra text accompanying notes 38, 39.

[69] Cf. IRC § 2702(c)(3); Reg. § 25.2702-4(a). See supra text accompanying notes 41, 42.

[70] Reg. § 25.2702-2(a)(4). See Reg. § 25.2702-2(d) Ex. 6. Cf. Reg. § 25.2702-2(d) Ex. 7. It does not include a nongeneral power created by a third person. Thus, Section 2702 does not apply where a trust beneficiary holding a variety of interests in trust transfers all those interests other than a non-general power of appointment conferred by the grantor of the trust. Priv. Ltr. Ruls. 9908022 (Nov. 25, 1998), 9918006 (Nov. 28, 1998).

The term "interest" as used here should also apply for purposes of the first requirement of Section 2702 and, if this type of interest is retained by Grantor, it should not be treated as transferred under the first requirement of Section 2702. Thus, if Grantor creates a trust with income to any of Grantor's Children that Grantor selects for fifteen years and a remainder to an unrelated person, there would be a retained interest in Grantor, but no transfer to a family member. Section 2702 would not apply to the transfer, with the result that there would only be a gift of the remainder interest to be valued under Section 7520. See infra ¶ 19.03[3][a] text accompanying note 99.

tained interest for purposes of Section 2702. After applying the Section 2702 valuation rules in either situation previously stated, Grantor is treated as making a transfer of the entire value of the corpus of the trust.[71]

A retained interest does not include an interest of a transferor or an applicable family member as the permissible recipient of distributions of income in the sole discretion of an independent trustee[72] when there is an assignment of a remainder interest.[73] Assume Parent had previously created a trust with income to Child *A* for life and a remainder to Child *B* at Child *A*'s death, but Parent also granted an independent trustee the power to sprinkle income to Parent for the shorter of Parent or Child *A*'s life.[74] If Child *B* assigns the remainder interest to Grandchild, Parent's[75] retained interest as a possible distributee is disregarded.[76] As a result of this rule, Section 2702 is inapplicable, because there is no retained interest held by an applicable family member; therefore Child *B* makes a transfer of only the value of the remainder interest.[77]

If a transferor makes an installment sale of property or transfers property for a private annuity, the right to the installment payments or to the annuity

---

[71] See Reg. § 25.2702-6(c) Ex. 6. The regulations' broad definition of "interest" treats a transferor as owning an interest in property even though the Transferor can derive no personal benefit from the property. This concept is not new to income, estate, or gift taxation. See IRC §§ 671, 674, 675, 2036(a)(2), 2038, 2511; Reg. § 25.2511-2(c). Cf. Helvering v. Clifford, 309 US 331 (1940). The definition will undoubtedly be judicially upheld; however, the definition may go beyond the notion of a retained interest as that term is used in the language of Section 2702 and it may be viewed as an unwarranted extension of the statutory language, because subsequent gift or estate tax consequences will occur with respect to the incomplete transfer in any event. See IRC §§ 2036–2038, 2511; Reg. § 25.2511-2(f).

[72] The term "independent trustee" is defined by Section 674(c) to constitute one who is not the grantor nor more than one half of whom are related or subservient parties who are subservient to the wishes of the grantor. See IRC § 672(c) for the definition of "related or subservient parties."

[73] Reg. § 25.2702-1(c)(6). See IRC § 2702(a)(3)(A)(iii).

[74] In these circumstances, Parent makes a transfer of the full value of the corpus. Rev. Rul. 77-378, 1977-2 CB 347.

[75] Parent is an applicable family member, but Child *A* is not. IRC §§ 2701(e)(2), 2702(a)(1). See supra text accompanying note 60.

[76] The rationale for this exception is likely the difficulty in valuing Parent's interest and hence in valuing Child *A*'s interest.

[77] If the income interest were held by an applicable family member of Child *B* (Child *A*, who is Child *B*'s sibling, is not an applicable family member of Child *B*), any disregard of the sprinkling power would be insignificant because the entire income interest would be a retained interest valued at zero and there would be a gift by Child *B* of the entire corpus.

payments should not be treated as a retained interest in the property,[78] and Section 2702 should not apply to either type of transaction.

[b] A Transfer of a Portion of an Interest in a Trust

Section 2702 applies to a transfer of a portion of an income or a remainder interest in a trust.[79] In effect, portions of a trust are treated as separate trusts. For example, if Grantor retains an income interest in all of the corpus of a trust for ten years and at the end of the ten years, two thirds of the corpus passes to Grantor's Child and one third passes to Grantor's Niece, the statute treats this as two transfers to two trusts. The first trust with two thirds of the corpus is subject to Section 2702, but the second trust is not. As a result, there is a transfer of the entire value of two thirds of the original corpus of the trust and a transfer of only a remainder interest in one third of the original corpus of the trust.[80]

[c] The Relationship of Section 2702 to Other Gift Tax Provisions

When applicable, Section 2702 may determine whether there is a gift and may increase the value of a gift transfer. Because there is an actual transfer that is treated as a gift under Chapter 12, other gift tax provisions are applicable to the gift valued pursuant to Section 2702. When Section 2513 gift-splitting is elected on a transfer subject to Section 2702,[81] the value of the gift transfer determined under Section 2702 qualifies for gift-splitting.[82] If there is a transfer to the transferor's spouse that qualifies for a marital deduction, the value of the gift after the application of Section 2702 qualifies for a marital

---

[78] A retained interest requires the transferor to hold the interest both before and after the transfer. Reg. § 25.2702-2(a)(3). An installment sale and a private annuity are transfers with a right to receive proceeds unrelated to the transferred property. Thus, no interest is retained (held both before and after the transfer). Cf. IRC §§ 2702(b)(1), 2702(b)(2). See ¶¶ 4.08[4], 4.08[5], 4.11[5].

[79] IRC § 2702(d).

[80] Similarly, if Grantor creates a trust with two thirds of the income to Child and one-third to be divided between Grantor's Nieces in any portion Grantor decides, with a remainder to an unrelated person, a division of the corpus is made under Section 2702(d) and as to two thirds of the original trust, there is a completed transfer of all of the corpus (without applying Section 2702), and as to one third of the original trust, there is no transfer to a family member and a gift of only the value of the remainder.

[81] See supra ¶ 10.03.

[82] Cf. Reg. § 25.2702-6(c) Ex. 5.

deduction.[83] The increased value of the transfer can also be shielded by the Section 2505 unified credit.

The Section 2702 gift or increase in the value of the gift is not an "interest in property" that qualifies for a Section 2518 disclaimer. Section 2518 will apply only if the interest that triggered the application of Section 2702 (or a portion of that interest) is effectively disclaimed to a non-family member. For example, if Transferor creates a GRIT with a remainder to Child and, as a result of Child's valid disclaimer, the remainder passes to an unrelated person, the disclaimer will make Section 2702 inapplicable to the transfer.[84]

Section 2512(b) and Section 2516, both of which deal with consideration for transfers, should be applicable in measuring the amount of a Section 2702 transfer.[85] The amount of Section 2512 consideration received should be measured in relation to the amount of the Section 2702 transfer. Assume, for example, that in consideration for each other's transfer, *C* and *GC* each transfer $5,000 to a trust that provides income to *C* for life and a remainder to *GC*. Under Section 2702, *C* makes a joint purchase transfer of $10,000 to *GC* and *GC* under the zero valuation rule makes a $5,000 transfer to *C*.[86] As the transfers are in consideration for one another, Section 2512(b) applies and uses the Section 2702 transfer amount of consideration with the result that *GC* receives $10,000 of consideration for *GC* transfer and *GC* makes no gift, while *C* re-

---

[83] IRC § 2523. For example, if Grantor transfers property with a retained income interest for a term of years and a remainder to Spouse, the full value of the corpus is transferred as a result of Section 2702 and the full value qualifies for a marital deduction. But see Zaritsky & Aucutt, Structuring Estate Freezes Under Chapter 14 ¶ 2.03[4][c] (Warren, Gorham & Lamont, 1993). The authors suggest that use of the term "amount" throughout the regulations (see, e.g., Reg. §§ 25.2701-1(a)(1), 25.2702-1(a)) as opposed to the term "value" may limit Section 2702's application to the transferred amount but that actual fair market value of an interest (not its Section 2702 value) may be used in determining the marital deduction and annual exclusion amounts. The authors agree that while such an analysis is "intuitively wrong," it may be the rationale for the semantic distinction in the regulations.

If Grantor places property in trust with income to Spouse until the earlier of Spouse's death, divorce, or remarriage, with a reversion to Grantor, the transfer should not qualify for the marital deduction even though Section 2702 causes the transfer to be valued as a transfer of the entire property, because Spouse's interest is a terminable interest. IRC § 2523(b).

[84] If the disclaimer resulted in a family member of Transferor acquiring the remainder, i.e., if Child disclaimed and as a result the property passed to Grandchild, Section 2702 would remain applicable. A disclaimer of a portion of the remainder to an unrelated person would make Section 2702 inapplicable to that portion of the property. IRC § 2702(d). See supra ¶ 19.03[2][b].

[85] However, consideration received will not cause a transfer to be incomplete under the incomplete transfer exception. IRC § 2702(a)(3)(B).

[86] See IRC §§ 2702(c)(2) (see infra ¶ 19.03[4][a]) and 2702(a)(2)(a) (see supra ¶ 19.03[2][a]), respectively.

ceives $5,000 of consideration for *C*'s transfer and makes a $5,000 gift.[87] Where Section 2516 applies to a transfer to a spouse and there is no transfer to any third party, Section 2702 is inapplicable,[88] because of an exception that essentially equates a spouse to a former spouse (who is unrelated) and a pre-divorce property settlement transfer to a post-divorce property settlement transfer.[89]

The Section 2503(b) annual exclusion may apply to a transfer whose value is enhanced by the application of Section 2702. A gift of an income interest to a family member with a reversion retained by the grantor, where the reversionary interest is valued at zero and the value of the gift of the income interest as a result of Section 2702 equals the full value of the corpus[90] is a gift of a present interest that qualifies for an annual exclusion.[91] Seemingly, the value of the gift resulting from the application of Section 2702 should qualify for an annual exclusion.[92] If so, and if $11,000 was transferred to the trust, the full $11,000 value of the corpus should qualify for an annual exclusion, even though the actuarial value of the family member's income interest is equal to an amount less than $11,000.[93]

Assume a grantor creates a trust retaining the income for a term of years or for life and transfers a remainder to a family member and that the zero valuation rule applies to result in a gift equal in value to the entire value of the corpus to the family member.[94] Since the value of the transfer equals the entire

---

[87] In the absence of Section 2702, the amount of the gifts would depend upon the values of the parties' relative interests. If *C*'s income interest were worth 70 percent of the corpus and *GC*'s remainder were worth 30 percent of the corpus, *C* would make no gift because *C* would transfer $1,500 to *GC*, but *C* would receive $3,500 of consideration from *GC*, and *GC* would make a gift of $2,000 or the amount of *GC*'s transfer of $3,500 reduced by the $1,500 of consideration from *C*.

[88] Reg. § 25.2702-1(c)(7). See IRC § 2702(a)(3)(A)(iii).

[89] See supra ¶ 19.03[2][a] text accompanying notes 53–59.

[90] See supra ¶ 19.03[2][a] text following note 31.

[91] IRC § 2503(b). See Reg. § 25.2503-3(b).

[92] But see supra note 83.

[93] If there is a Section 2702 transfer that involves both gifts to income beneficiaries and remainderpersons, the effect of the Section 2702 increase in value on the various interests is unclear. For example, if Grantor provides income to Child for a term of years with a reversion to Grantor if living and, if not, remainder to Grandchild, does the Section 2702 increase, as a result of valuing the reversion as zero, pass to Child, to Grandchild, or to Child and Grandchild according to the proportionate values of their interests? Seemingly, the latter result is appropriate. Would it make a difference if the remainder were to an unrelated person? The Code and regulations provide no guidance with respect to the results in such circumstances. However, the Supplementary Information accompanying Proposed Regulations Section 25.2702-1(c)(3) at 62 Fed. Reg. 19,072 (Apr. 18, 1997) implies that the entire increase in the transfer is to the related person. Cf. ¶¶ 19.02[2][a] note 76, 19.02[5][f] note 498.

[94] See supra ¶ 19.03[2][a]; Reg. § 25.2702-2(d)(1) Ex. 1.

value of the corpus, it might be argued that the transfer qualifies for an annual exclusion.[95] However, Section 2702 is a valuation provision and although the value of the remainder for gift tax purposes equals the full value of the corpus, the remainder is not a present interest and the transfer does not qualify for an annual exclusion.[96]

[3] Exceptions

There are several situations in which the zero valuation rule of Section 2702 is inapplicable, either because Section 2702 does not apply or because Section 2702 applies but the normal valuation rules come into play.[97] When an exception applies, Section 7520 valuation is generally used in valuing any transferred interest.[98]

[a] Incomplete Gifts

Section 2702 is inapplicable if there is no complete gift of any interest in the property to a family member.[99] For example, if Grantor creates a trust retaining a life estate and holding a power to appoint the remainder among family members, there is no completed gift of the remainder or of any transferred interest and Section 2702 does not apply.[100] However, if the transfer of an interest in property to a family member is complete, Section 2702 applies regardless of whether other interests in the property transferred are complete. This rule, coupled with the rule that a retained power that prevents a transfer from being a completed gift is a retained interest for Section 2702 purposes,[101] can produce some interesting results. For example, if Grantor retains a life estate, then provides a secondary life estate to Child, and Grantor holds a power to appoint the remainder, there is a completed transfer of the entire value of the corpus; the life estate and the power to appoint the remainder are treated as retained interests and, because the gift of the secondary life estate prevents the entire gift from being incomplete, both the primary life estate and the remainder are assigned a zero valuation under Section 2702 with the result that there

---

[95] IRC § 2503(b).

[96] See Reg. § 25.2503-3(a).

[97] Some of the exceptions continue to allow for estate planning opportunities with benefits similar to prior law. See supra ¶ 19.03[1].

[98] See supra ¶ 19.03[1] text accompanying note 3, infra ¶ 19.03[3][b] text accompanying note 112; IRC § 2702(c)(4), discussed infra ¶ 19.03[4][b].

[99] IRC § 2702(a)(3)(A)(i); Reg. § 25.2702-1(c)(1). This exception seems unnecessary because the first requirement of Section 2702 is not satisfied. See supra ¶ 19.03[2][a].

[100] Cf. Reg. § 25.2702-2(d)(1) Ex. 4.

[101] Reg. § 25.2702-2(a)(4). See supra ¶ 19.03[2][a] text accompanying note 70.

is a transfer of the entire value of the corpus to Child.[102] However, if in this example, Grantor had also retained a power to revoke Child's interest, the incomplete gift exception would apply.[103]

If an undivided proportionate share of a transfer is an incomplete gift, the proportionate-share rule applies and Section 2702 is inapplicable to that portion of the transfer.[104] For example, if Grantor creates a trust with income to Grantor for life and one half of the remainder to Daughter and one half of the remainder to Grandchildren, but Grantor retains a power to appoint among the Grandchildren, Section 2702(d) divides the trust equally into two trusts. Section 2702 applies to the first trust and, as a result, there is a transfer of the value of the entire corpus of that trust because the zero value rule applies. As to the second trust, there is no gift of the remainder, Section 2702 is inapplicable because the incomplete gift exception applies, and there is no transfer of any property by gift.[105] Overall, there is a gift of one half of the value of the original corpus.

There must be a completed gift of an interest to a *family member* to trigger Section 2702. For example, if Grantor creates a trust with income to Grantor for ten years, then income to any of Grantor's children whom Grantor selects[106] and a remainder to a non-family member, there is a completed gift of an interest in the property and the incomplete gift exception does not apply. Nevertheless, the first requirement of Section 2702 is not met because there is no transfer to a member of Grantor's family.[107] Thus, Section 2702 is inapplicable, and there is a gift of only the value of the remainder.

Consideration received by a transferor is disregarded in determining whether a gift is incomplete under the incomplete gift rule.[108] Thus, if Grantor retains a life estate in a trust and sells a remainder for its fair market value to Child, the consideration is disregarded, in determining whether a gift is made, there is a completed transfer of the remainder to a family member, and Section 2702 applies. As a result, the retained life estate is valued at zero and there is a gift of corpus less the consideration received, or a gift equal to the value of Grantor's income interest.[109]

---

[102] Reg. § 25.2702-2(a)(4). See Reg. § 25.2702-2(d)(1) Ex. 6.

[103] See Reg. § 25.2702-2(d)(1) Ex. 4.

[104] Reg. §§ 25.2702-1(c)(1), 25.2702-2(d)(1) Ex. 5. See IRC § 2702(d).

[105] IRC § 2702(a)(3)(A)(i). Cf. Reg. § 25.2701-2(d)(1) Ex. 4.

[106] Cf. Reg. § 25.2702-2(a)(4), which treats Grantor as owning such interest.

[107] IRC § 2702(a)(1).

[108] IRC § 2702(a)(3)(B); Reg. § 25.2702-1(c)(1).

[109] Cf. Reg. § 25.2702-4(d) Ex. 2. Technically, this transaction constitutes a joint purchase. See infra ¶ 19.03[4][a] text accompanying note 268, ¶ 19.03[2][a] text accompanying note 30.

[b] Qualified Interests

If a retained interest is a "qualified interest," the zero valuation rule is inapplicable and the regular valuation rules apply.[110] Statutorily, this is not an exception to the application of Section 2702 to the transfer. In fact, Section 2702 applies;[111] however, the statute applies Section 7520 to value the retained qualified interest.[112] With one exception, the end result of the application of Section 7520 valuation to a retained qualified interest is as if Section 2702 had not been enacted. There is an exception, however, if the transferor retains any additional interests in conjunction with an otherwise qualified interest, such as a contingent reversion on premature death, or a power to appoint on the transferor's premature death. In such a case, Section 2702 remains applicable and assigns a zero value to the *additional* interest or power (but not the accompanying qualified interest).[113]

The congressional purpose for the enactment of Section 2702 is to assure proper valuation of retained interests;[114] if the interests are qualified interests, that concern of Congress is alleviated and regular valuation methods are appropriate. The qualified interest valuation rules are patterned after the rules for transfers of partial interests to charity[115] and generally apply to valuation of both qualified income interests and qualified remainder interests under Section 2702.[116]

[i] **Qualified income interests.** A qualified income interest can be created by transferring property to a trust and either retaining a qualified annuity interest,[117] which is commonly referred to as a GRAT (a grantor retained annu-

---

[110] IRC § 2702(a)(2)(B).

[111] IRC § 2702(a)(2)(B).

[112] IRC § 2702(a)(2)(B). Section 7520 is used to value a qualified annuity interest or a remainder after a qualified annuity interest and Section 664 is used to value a qualified unitrust interest or a remainder following a qualified unitrust interest. Reg. § 25.2702-2(b)(2). See Reg. §§ 1.664-2(c), 1.664-4, 20.2055-2(f)(2) for detailed rules on valuing annuity trust and unitrust interests.

[113] See supra ¶ 19.03[1] text following note 13and infra text accompanying notes 147–149. Compare the result with respect to other exceptions, such as the personal residence trust exception. See infra ¶ 19.03[3][d] note 162. Many transferors retain powers or interests to facilitate control over who receives the remainder if death occurs before their term interest expires.

[114] See supra ¶ 19.03[1] text accompanying note 5.

[115] See ¶¶ 5.05[4]–5.05[6], 11.02[2], 11.02[3].

[116] See also infra ¶ 19.03[3][c] for other regulatory exceptions related to qualified interests.

[117] Reg. §§ 25.2702-3(b), 25.2702-3(d). See Melcher & Arend, "Grappling With GRATs," 72 Taxes 661 (1994).

ity trust), or retaining a qualified unitrust interest,[118] which is commonly referred to as a GRUT (a grantor retained unitrust).[119] These qualified income interests are patterned after the income interests given to a charity in a charitable lead trust.[120]

A qualified annuity interest is an irrevocable right to receive at least as frequently as annually a fixed amount, either a set dollar amount or a set fraction or set percentage of the initial fair market value of the property transferred.[121] A qualified unitrust interest is an irrevocable right to receive at least annually a set fraction or percentage of the net fair market value of the trust corpus[122] determined on an annual basis.[123] The annuity amount or the unitrust

---

[118] Reg. §§ 25.2702-3(c), 25.2702-3(d).

[119] An excellent in-depth article on the use of qualified interests is Gans, "GRITs, GRATs and GRUTs: Planning and Policy," 11 Va. Tax Rev. 761 (1992). The uses of GRATs and GRUTs are also discussed in Zaritsky & Aucutt, Structuring Estate Freezes Under Chapter 14, ¶¶ 11.01–11.11 (Warren, Gorham & Lamont, 1993).

[120] See ¶ 5.05[6]. Cf. ¶¶ 5.05[5][a], 5.05[5][b].

If the transferor dies during the term of a GRAT or a GRUT, the Service will likely assert that Section 2036 is, to some extent, applicable. Cf. Rev. Ruls. 76-273, 1976-2 CB 268, 82-105, 1982-1 CB 133, involving a charitable remainder unitrust and an annuity trust, respectively, and an interest retained by the transferor where the government not only applied Section 2036 but also computed the portions of the corpus to be included in the transferor's gross estate. See Priv. Ltr. Rul. 9412036 (Dec. 23, 1993) (Section 2036 applied to a GRUT citing Rev. Rul. 76-273, 1976 CB 268 as authority). The Service may also argue that Section 2039 applies in such circumstances. See FSA 200036012 (May 25, 2000). See ¶ 4.11 note 3. But see infra ¶ 19.03[4][e] text accompanying note 367.

[121] IRC § 2702(b)(1); Reg. §§ 25.2702-3(b)(1)(i), 25.2702-3(b)(1)(ii). See TAMs 200010010 (Nov. 23, 1999), 200011005 (Nov. 23, 1999) (both holding that if liability incurred to pay annuity amount, then there is an income tax event to grantor on termination of trust to extent liability exceeds adjusted basis in trust property relying on Rev. Rul. 85-13, 1985-1 CB 184).

[122] See Reg. § 25.2522(c)-3(c)(2)(vii).

[123] IRC § 2702(b)(2); Reg. § 25.2702-3(c)(1)(i). Both an annuity trust and a unitrust must contain a provision meeting the requirements of Regulations Sections 1.664-2(a)(1)(iii) and 1.664-3(a)(1)(v), respectively (relating to adjustments for any incorrect determinations of the value of the property in the trust). Reg. §§ 25.2702-3(b)(2), 25.2702-3(c)(2).

An annuity amount or a unitrust amount must be payable based on either the anniversary date of the creation of the trust or the taxable year of the trust. In either situation, the amount must be paid at least annually, but may be paid more frequently. If the payment is based on the anniversary date, proration of the annuity amount is required only if the last period during which the annuity is payable to the grantor is a period of less than twelve months. If the payment is made based on the taxable year, proration of the annuity amount is required for each short taxable year of the trust during the grantor's term. The prorated amount is stated to be the annual annuity amount multiplied by a fraction, the numerator of which is the number of days in the short period and the denominator of which is 365. An annuity amount payable based on the taxable year of the trust may be paid after the close of the taxable year, provided the payment is made no later than the

factor is not required to be the same amount or factor in each year. The regulations permit a decrease in the amount or factor,[124] and they also permit an increase to the extent that the increase does not exceed 120 percent of the amount or factor paid in the preceding year.[125] Thus, the annuity trust or unitrust factor could increase from 10 percent to 12 percent to 14.4 percent in each of two successive years.[126] The allowance of an increase represents a reasonable compromise between the government's concern of taxpayers' zeroing out of a gift through use of a balloon payment in the final year of the term and taxpayers' desire for flexibility as to the amount.[127]

Neither type of retained income interest is disqualified if actual income in excess of the designated amounts is payable to the term interest holder; however, such excess income is not taken into account in valuing the qualified annuity trust or unitrust interests.[128] Appropriately, an interest is not a qualified interest if it is equal to the *lesser* of either (1) the qualified amount (whether an annuity or unitrust) or (2) the actual income amount.[129] A trust providing for a combination of a qualified annuity trust and a qualified unitrust interest is a qualified interest if the term interest holder is to receive the *greater* of the

---

date by which the trustee is required to file the federal income tax return of the trust for the taxable year (determined without regard to extensions). An annuity amount payable on the anniversary date may be paid at any time within 105 days after the anniversary date. Reg. §§ 25.2702-3(b)(3), 25.2702-3(b)(4), 25.2702-3(c)(3), 25.2702-3(c)(4).

[124] See Reg. § 25.2702-3(e) Ex. 3.

[125] Reg. §§ 25.2702-3(b)(1)(ii), 25.2702-3(c)(1)(ii).

[126] Reg. §§ 25.2702-3(b)(1)(ii), 25.2702-3(c)(1)(ii). See Reg. § 25.2702-3(e) Ex. 2, noting especially the result in year seven (where a greater than 20 percent increase is not prohibited, but is not considered in valuing the annuity *amount*) and in years eight through ten.

[127] In providing this result, the Supplementary Information accompanying comments the final regulations state (TD 8395, 1992-1 CB 316, 319):

> [T]he final regulations provide flexibility to taxpayers by permitting the annuity or unitrust amount to be 120 percent of the annuity or unitrust amount paid for the preceding year. The proposed regulations prohibited increases to prevent transferors from "zeroing out" a gift while still effectively transferring the appreciation on all the property during the term to the remainder beneficiary (e.g., by providing for a balloon payment in the final year of the term). The Treasury Department and the Service believe that such a result would be inconsistent with the principles of section 2702. The final regulations, with minimal complexity, strike a balance between the government's policy concerns and taxpayers' desire for planning flexibility.

[128] Reg. §§ 25.2702-3(b)(1)(iii), 25.2702-3(c)(1)(iii), 25.2702-3(e) Ex. 1. See Priv. Ltr. Ruls. 9345035 (Aug. 13, 1993), 9441031 (July 12, 1994), Priv. Ltr. Ruls. 9444033 (Aug. 5, 1994), 200001013 (Sept. 30, 1999) (all applying these excess payment rules).

[129] Reg. § 25.2702-3(e) Ex. 4. This is appropriate because there would be no right to receive a fixed amount during each year of the term interest.

two amounts each year;[130] however, it does not qualify if the term interest holder is to receive the *lesser* of the two amounts.[131]

The term of the qualified interest must be fixed for the term holder's life, for a term of years, or for the shorter (but not the longer) of the two periods.[132] If the period is for a term of years, the regulations inappropriately reduce the value of the term of years by the value of the actuarial possibility that the term holder will die within the term of years, effectively shortening the period of the term of years.[133] Retention of a power to revoke a qualified annuity interest

---

[130] Reg. § 25.2702-3(d)(1). If there is a combination of the greater of the two amounts, that interest is valued at the greater of the two values at the time of creation of the trust. Id.

[131] Reg. § 25.2702-3(d)(1).

[132] Reg. § 25.2702-3(d)(3). Successive term interests for the benefit of the same individual are treated as the same interest. Id.

[133] See Reg. §§ 25.2702-3(e) Exs. 5, 6; TAM 9707001 (Oct. 25, 1996). This result seemingly was rationalized by the thought that if the term holder dies within the term of years and the remaining term interest is paid to the term holder's estate (either expressly or by operation of law), under the general rules of Section 2702, the term holder is deemed to have retained a contingent reversionary income interest that is valued at zero. See also infra text accompanying note 146; Reg. § 25.2702-3(e) Ex. 1.

The Tax Court has declared the regulatory position in Regulations Section 25.2702-3(e) Ex. 5 invalid. Walton v Comm'r, 115 TC 589 (2000). In a unanimous reviewed opinion, the court recognized that a retained contingent reversion to one's estate is consistently treated under other estate and gift tax areas as an interest held by the term holder. See ¶¶ 4.05[5][b], 10.01[3][d]. No reduction in the value of the term of years should be made by the regulations with respect to such a contingent reversion. See McCaffrey, Plaine and Schneider, "The Aftermath of Walton; The Rehabilitation of the Fixed-Term, Zeroed-Out GRAT," 95 J. Tax'n 325 (2001); McCaffrey and Schneider, "The Flaw in Example 5; Did the Section 2702 Regs. Try to Extend the Repeal of the Doctrine of Worthier Title?" 93 J. Tax'n 219 (2000); and Gans, "GRITs GRATs and GRUTs," 11 Va. Tax. Rev. 761, 799 (1992), which also reach this conclusion.

For example, if Term Holder transfers property retaining a term interest for ten years and a remainder to Child after ten years and further provides that the remainder to Child accelerates if Term Holder predeceases the ten-year period, then the term holder has retained an income interest for ten years or life, whichever is shorter and the value of the transfer to Child should reflect the possibility of Term Holder predeceasing Child. If, instead, either expressly or by operation of law, Term Holder's estate has the right to the term interest if term holder dies within the ten-year period, the value of Child's interest is not affected by the potential reversion, but the value of Term Holder's gross estate is affected. IRC § 2033. Thus, the government's interest in subjecting to transfer tax the full value of what is transferred is not undermined and the timing of the imposition of transfer tax is also appropriate. However, under the examples in the Section 2702 regulations, Child's interest is increased in either event, and even though the qualified retained interest is a term of years, it is valued for a period less than the term of years.

Seemingly, the result in Reg. § 25.2702-3(e) Ex. 6 would also be altered to treat the full ten-year term (but not the alternative thirty-five-year term) as a qualified interest. The ten-year term is a definitive term as of the creation of the trust. The alternative term is a mere contingent term that does not qualify as a qualified interest.

or a qualified unitrust interest transferred to a transferor's spouse is treated as the retention of the qualified annuity or unitrust interest by the transferor.[134]

The qualified income interest must be paid from the creation of the trust.[135] During the term of the qualified interest, the governing instrument must prohibit payments to anyone other than the term interest holder; a failure to do so disqualifies the entire interest.[136] The qualified income interest must be paid to the term interest holder and must not constitute a mere right of the term holder to withdraw the qualified amount.[137] The payment may be made after the close of the taxable year, provided it is made no later than the time for filing the trust's income tax return (without regard to extensions).[138] The issuance of a note, other debt instrument, option, or similar financial arrangement, either directly or indirectly, does not constitute payment of the annuity or unitrust amount because the issuance of such instruments effectively delays

---

[134] Reg. § 25.2702-2(a)(5). For example, assume Transferor creates a retained qualified annuity or unitrust term interest for ten years followed by a qualified annuity or unitrust interest in Transferor's Spouse for an additional ten years, if Spouse is then living, and a remainder to Transferor's Child and, in addition, Transferor retains the power to revoke Spouse's interest, the amount of Transferor's gift is the fair market value of the property transferred reduced by the value of both Transferor's and Spouse's qualified interests. The interests of both Transferor and Spouse at the creation of the trust are fixed and ascertainable and Transferor is deemed to have retained the interests for twenty years. Reg. § 25.2702-2(d)(1) Ex. 7.

However, if the spouse's revocable interest arose only if donor died during donor's term interest, the revocable transfer to the spouse is a contingent revocable qualified interest and it is not a qualified interest because the Regulations Section 25.2702-3(d)(3) requirement is not met. Cook v. Comm'r, 269 F3d 854 (7th Cir. 2001), aff'g 115 TC 15 (2000) (the court in the *Walton* case (Walton v. Comm'r, 269 F3d 854 (7th Cir. 2001) aff'g 115 TC 589 (2000)) noted that the result in *Walton* invalidating Regulations Section 25.2702-3(e) Ex. 5 does not change the *Cook* result); Schott v. Comm'r, TCM 2001-110 (2001) (following *Cook* and distinguishing *Walton*); TAM 9741001 (June 18, 1997); Priv. Ltr. Rul. 199951032 (Sept. 28, 1999). See supra text accompanying notes 132, 133.

Seemingly, any power over an otherwise qualified interest that would cause the interest to be treated as an incomplete gift under Chapter 12 (see Reg. § 25.2702-2(a)(4)) should result in the otherwise qualified interest being treated as a qualified interest, although the regulations specifically limit this rule to only a power to revoke and only a spouse's interest.

[135] Reg. § 25.2702-3(d)(1).

[136] Reg. § 25.2702-3(d)(2). See Reg. § 25.2702-3(e) Ex. 7.

[137] Reg. §§ 25.2702-3(b)(1)(i), 25.2702-3(c)(1)(i).

[138] Reg. §§ 25.2702-3(b)(1)(i), 25.2702-3(c)(1)(i). If there is a short taxable year or the last taxable year of the term, the trust must meet the requirements of Regulations Section 1.664-2(a)(1)(iv) in the case of an annuity trust and Regulations Section 1.664-3(a)(1)(v) in the case of unitrust. Reg. §§ 25.2702-3(b)(3), 25.2702-3(c)(3). Cf. TAM 9506001 (Sept. 28, 1994) (additional contributions not prohibited prior to enactment of the final regulations).

payment.[139] Further, for trusts created after September 20, 1999, the trust instrument must prohibit the trustee from issuing a note or other instrument in satisfaction of the payment.[140]

Appropriately, the governing instrument of an annuity trust must prohibit any additional contributions to the annuity trust.[141] Because the amount of payment under a unitrust is based on the amount of the trust corpus, there is no similar restriction on additional contributions to a unitrust. The governing instrument of either type of qualifying income interest must prohibit commutation (prepayment of the interest for its actuarial value)[142] of the term holder's interest.[143]

[ii] **Qualified remainder interests.** Where the retained interest is a remainder interest (which includes a reversion),[144] it is a qualified remainder interest only if (1) at all times after creation of the trust[145] all other interests in

---

[139] Reg. §§ 25.2702-3(b)(1)(i), 25.2702-3(c)(1)(i). Thus, borrowing from an unrelated person to make the payment does not violate the regulations. However, the step transaction doctrine will be applied if a series of transactions result in consequences that are inconsistent with the regulations. See Supplementary Information to the Regulations (Sept. 5, 2000).

See also TAM 9604005 (Oct. 17, 1995) (non-interest-bearing notes did not qualify as annuity payments). The TAM is discussed in Pompilio, "Revisiting Promissory Notes to Pay a GRAT's Annuity Amount," 27 Tax Advisor 465 (1996) (written prior to the regulations).

[140] Reg. § 25.2702-3(d)(5)(i). A transitional rule is provided under which trusts created prior to September 21, 1999, will be treated as complying with the regulation if no notes or other instruments are issued after September 20, 1999 to satisfy such payments and if any such notes or payments issued prior to September 21, 1999, are paid in full by December 31, 1999. Reg. § 25.2702-3(d)(5)(ii).

[141] Reg. § 25.2702-3(b)(4).

[142] Commutation occurs on an early termination of a trust with a distribution of proceeds based on the actuarial values of the respective interests. Thus, it is in the nature of a prepayment.

[143] Reg. § 25.2702-3(d)(4). The rationale for this rule was explained in the Supplementary Information accompanying the final regulations as follows (TD 8395, 1992-1 CB 316, 319):

> Commutation (i.e., the prepayment of the term holder's interest) shifts the risk of a decline in interest rates from the remainder beneficiaries to the term holder. Therefore, a commuted term interest may not ultimately yield the same value to the term holder as the annuity or unitrust interest originally retained by the transferor. Congress intended in enacting Section 2702, that a term interest would be valued at an amount greater than zero, only if the form of the term interest insures that the holder *actually* receives the value attributed to the interest. Allowing commutation would be inconsistent with this intent.

[144] Reg. § 25.2702-3(f)(2).

[145] Reg. § 25.2702-3(f)(1)(ii).

the trust are qualified annuity interests or qualified unitrust interests;[146] (2) the remainder interest receives all or a fractional share of the property (which includes the post-transfer appreciation on such property);[147] and (3) the remainder is a noncontingent remainder.[148] A remainder is noncontingent only if it is to be paid to the beneficiary or the beneficiary's estate in all events.[149] Thus, if Transferor creates a valid qualified income interest to Parent for life with a reversion to Transferor if living and a remainder to Children if not, the qualified remainder exception is inapplicable because the remainder is a contingent remainder. As a result, the reversion is valued at zero[150] and there is a gift of the entire corpus.[151] Finally, the trust must specifically prohibit payment to the term interest holders of any trust income in excess of the qualifying annuity trust or qualifying unitrust amount.[152] Thus, if the greater of the trust's actual income or the qualified annuity or unitrust amount may be paid to the holders of the term interests, the remainder interest is not a qualified remainder.[153]

[c] Other Regulatory Exceptions

Section 2702(a)(3)(iii) provides the Treasury with regulatory authority to provide additional exceptions to the application of Section 2702 if the exceptions are not inconsistent with the purposes of the section. The exceptions are not limited to charitable transfers,[154] although several additional exceptions do

---

[146] Reg. § 25.2702-3(f)(1)(iv). See supra ¶ 19.03[3][b][i]; Reg. § 25.2702-3(f)(3) Ex. 1.

[147] See Reg. §§ 25.2702-3(f)(2), 25.2702-3(f)(3) Ex. 3. Thus, a right to receive a stated or pecuniary amount is not a qualified remainder interest. See Vogel "Estate Planning for Cash-Poor Millionaires: A New Look at Retained Interests in Trust," 91 J. Tax'n 143 (1999) (critical of this requirement found in the last two sentences of Regulations Section 25.2702-3(f)(2)). Cf. IRC § 2702(d).

[148] IRC § 2702(b)(3); Reg. § 25.2702-3(f)(1)(iii).

[149] IRC § 2702(b)(3); Reg. § 25.2702-3(f)(1)(iii).

[150] IRC § 2702(a)(2)(A).

[151] Reg. § 25.2702-3(f)(3) Ex. 4. Compare the result where Transferor retains a contingent reversion of the retained qualified income interest. See supra note 133. If Transferor created a valid qualified income interest to Parent for life with a remainder to whichever of Transferor's Children Transferor selected, Transferor should be deemed to have retained a reversion. See Reg. § 25.2702-2(a)(4). Thus, it would not be a contingent remainder interest and there would be a gift of the value of Parent's interest, not a gift equal to the entire value of the corpus.

[152] Reg. § 25.2702-3(f)(1)(iv).

[153] Reg. § 25.2702-3(f)(3) Ex. 2.

[154] There are three noncharity current regulatory exceptions to the application of Section 2702: Regulations Section 25.2702-1(c)(6) discussed supra ¶ 19.03[2][a] text accompanying notes 72–77; Regulations Section 25.2702-1(c)(7) discussed supra ¶ 19.03[2][a] text accompanying notes 53–59; Regulations Section 25.2702-1(c)(8). Regulations Section

apply to some charitable transfers. Seemingly because of the similarity to the split-interest charitable deduction rules and the inability to create inappropriate valuations under those rules, the regulations make Section 2702 inapplicable:[155] (1) to a transfer to a charitable remainder trust if it is (a) a pooled income fund,[156] (b) a charitable remainder annuity trust,[157] (c) a charitable remainder unitrust paying only the unitrust amount,[158] or (d) a charitable remainder unitrust with a net income clause[159] but only where either (i) there are only two consecutive noncharitable beneficial interests and the transferor holds the second of such interests or (ii) the only permissible recipients of the unitrust amount are the transferor, the transferor's U.S. citizen spouse, or both the transferor and the transferor's U.S. citizen spouse;[160] and (2) to a charitable lead trust if the only interests in the charitable lead trust other than the remainder interest or a qualified annuity or unitrust interest is an interest that qualifies for a charitable deduction under Section 2522.[161] These exceptions become important where in addition to the transfer to a charity, there is a transfer to a family member and either the transferor or an applicable family member have retained interests in the trust. In these circumstances, if there were no exception, Section 2702 would increase the value of the transfer to the family member by the value of the retained interest. For example, assume Grantor transfers property to a pooled income fund with income to Grantor for life, then income to Child for life, and a remainder to Charity. If Grantor's interest is worth 20 percent of the corpus and Child's interest is worth 50 percent of the corpus, under the exception Grantor makes an 80 percent gift of the corpus (a portion of which is a gift to charity). In the absence of the exception, Grantor would make a gift of 100 percent of the corpus.

25.2701-1(c)(8) adds an exception where a surviving spouse transfers property received from a decedent spouse to a QDOT pursuant to Section 2056A. See ¶ 5.07[2][b]. In such circumstances, the decedent spouse is essentially treated as the transferor, and even though surviving spouse retains an income interest with a remainder to a family member, Section 2702 is inapplicable. See ¶ 5.07[2][b] text accompanying notes 25, 26.

[155] Note that Section 2702 is made inapplicable here as compared to qualified interests that are subject to Section 2702 but are valued under general Section 7520 and Section 664 valuation rules. See IRC § 2702(a)(2)(B).

[156] IRC § 642(c)(5). See ¶ 5.05[5][c].

[157] IRC § 664(d)(1). See ¶ 5.05[5][a].

[158] IRC § 664(d)(2) especially IRC § 664(d)(2)(A). See ¶ 5.05[5][b].

[159] IRC §§ 664(d)(2), 664(d)(3). See ¶ 5.05[5][b] text accompanying notes 223–228.

[160] Reg. § 25.2702-1(c)(3)(i). The rule is applicable only to transfers on or after May 19, 1997. Prior to that date, any transfer in trust where the remainder qualifies for a charitable deduction under Section 2522 qualified for the exception. Reg. § 25.2702-1(c)(3)(ii). See ¶ 5.05[5][b].

[161] Reg. § 25.2702-1(c)(5). See ¶¶ 5.05[6], 11.02[3].

[d] Personal Residence Trusts

Section 2702 is inapplicable (and regular Section 7520 valuation rules apply)[162] if the transfer is of an interest in a trust whose corpus is a residence used as a personal residence by the term interest holders.[163] This type of trust is referred to as a personal residence trust.[164] The Treasury has stated the following rationale for the exception:[165]

> Congress recognized that many people desire to maintain the family ownership of their home and pass ownership on to future generations, while retaining its use for a period of time. The annuity and unitrust requirements are not, however, conducive to the transfer of a residence. Accordingly, section 2702(a)(3)(A)(ii) provides an exception to the annuity and unitrust requirements. Under this limited exception, the grantor's retained interest need not be in one of these forms, but rather can take the form of a right to the use and occupancy of the residence.

The exception should apply regardless of whether the interest transferred to a family member is a remainder interest or a term interest.[166]

The regulations provide for two different types of personal residence trusts, a regular personal residence trust and a qualified personal residence trust.[167] The rules for a qualified personal residence trust are more flexible than

---

[162] Since Section 2702 is inapplicable, the amount of the gift transfer will be determined by reducing the fair market value of the residence transferred by the value of the term interest retained as well as the value of a retained contingent reversion or a power to appoint the remainder interest in the event the grantor dies prior to the end of the term interest. See PS-4-96 Supplementary Information, 61 Fed. Reg. 16,623 (1996). See supra ¶ 19.03[1] text following note 13; Priv. Ltr. Rul. 9447036 (Aug. 29, 1994). Compare the results with respect to a contingent reversion following a GRAT or GRUT considered supra ¶ 19.03[3][b] text accompanying note 113.

See Harrison, "Calculating the Potential for Transfer Tax Savings in Personal Residence GRITS," 81 J. Tax'n 232 (1994).

[163] However, if the grantor of a personal residence trust dies during the term of the trust during which the residence is being held for the use of the grantor, the trust assets generally are includible in the grantor's gross estate under Section 2036. Cf. supra ¶ 19.03[3][b] note 120. But see infra ¶ 19.03[4][e] text accompanying note 367.

[164] IRC § 2702(a)(3)(A)(ii); Reg. § 25.2702-5(a)(1). The Clinton administration has proposed a repeal of Section 2702(a)(3)(A)(ii). See Dept. of Treasury, "General Explanation of the Administration's Revenue Proposals," 131 (Feb. 1998); Jt. Comm. Tax'n "Description of Revenue Provisions Contained in the President's Fiscal Year 2000 Budget Proposal" 294 (Feb. 22, 1999).

[165] PS-4-96 Supplementary Information, 61 Fed. Reg. 16,623 (1996). Since this is the purpose of the exception, it can be suggested that the exception should be subject to a ten-year recapture rule if the family members dispose of the residence within that period. Cf. IRC §§ 2032A(c), 2057(f) discussed at ¶¶ 4.04[7], 5.08[5].

[166] But see infra ¶ 19.03[3][d] note 237.

[167] IRC § 2702(a)(3)(A)(ii). See Reg. §§ 25.2702-5(b), 25.2702-5(c).

those applicable to a regular personal residence trust and reformation rules are allowed with respect to both types of trusts.[168]

[i] Requirements applicable to both types of personal residence trusts. There are several requirements common to both regular and qualified personal residence trusts.

Personal Residence. The transfer of an interest in a trust that consists of a residence is exempted from the clutches of Section 2702 only if the residence is used as a personal residence by the term interest holder. The term "personal residence" is defined to include the principal residence of the term holder,[169] one other residence that is treated as "used" by the term holder within the meaning of Section 280A(d)(1),[170] or an undivided fractional interest in either residence.[171]

The term personal residence is interpreted broadly and may include a houseboat, a house trailer, or stock in a cooperative housing unit.[172] A personal residence includes appurtenant structures used for residential purposes (such as a garage) and adjacent land not in excess of an amount of land reasonably appropriate for residential purposes (taking into account the residence's size and location).[173] A personal residence does not include any personal property held

---

[168] Compare infra ¶¶ 19.03[3][d][ii], 19.03[3][d][iii]. Qualified personal residence trusts are discussed in the following articles: Melcher & Rosenbloom "How Well Do QPRTs Really Work?" 77 Taxes 27 (Feb. 1999); Fox, Hodgman & Van Meter, "Qualified Personal Residence Trusts Yield Tax Savings," 22 Est. Plan. 206 (July & Aug. 1995).

If a trust does not comply with one or more of the regulatory requirements for qualification as a regular personal residence trust or a qualified personal residence trust, the trust may be reformed by judicial reformation or a nonjudicial reformation that is effective under state law. The reformation must be commenced within ninety days after the due date (including extensions) for filing the gift tax return reporting the transfer to the trust and must be completed within a reasonable time. If the reformation is not completed by the due date of the gift tax return, a statement must be attached to the gift tax return indicating that the reformation has been or will be commenced within the ninety-day period. In the case of a pre-1997 trust, the reformation must be commenced within ninety days after December 23, 1997, and completed within a reasonable period. Reg. § 25.2702-5(a)(2).

[169] Reg. §§ 25.2702-5(b)(2)(i)(A), 25.2702-5(c)(2)(i)(A). See IRC § 121.

[170] Reg. §§ 25.2702-5(b)(2)(i)(B), 25.2702-5(c)(2)(i)(B). Cf. IRC § 163(h)(4)(A)(i)(II). The term "use" is defined later in this section. See infra text accompanying notes 177–187.

[171] Reg. §§ 25.2702-5(b)(2)(i)(C), 25.2702-5(c)(2)(i)(C). See Priv. Ltr. Ruls. 9606003 (Nov. 7, 1995) (community property interest), 9626041 (Apr. 2, 1996) (tenancy in common interest).

[172] Cf. Reg. § 1.1034-1(c)(3)(i); Prop. Reg. § 1.121-1(c). See Priv. Ltr. Rul. 9448035 (Sept. 2, 1994) (stock in cooperative housing corporation).

[173] Reg. §§ 25.2702-5(b)(2)(ii), 25.2702-5(c)(2)(ii)). See Reg. § 25.2702-5(d) Ex. 3; Priv. Ltr. Ruls. 9001046 (Oct. 11, 1989) (five parcels of land), 9442019 (July 19, 1994) (ten acres of land surrounding residence), 9503025 (Oct. 27, 1994) (two parcels of vacant land across the street from residence), 9645010 (Aug. 2, 1996) (16.6 acres with guest

in conjunction with the residences (e.g., household furnishings).[174] Thus, if both a residence and the furnishings for the residence are held in a trust, the trust will not qualify as a personal residence trust. A personal residence is not disqualified if it is subject to a mortgage.[175] If mortgage payments are made by a transferor who holds an interest in the trust, the payments should qualify for the personal residence trust exception and result in a gift by the transferor equal to the actuarial value of the gifted interest.[176]

Use of the Residence. A residence is treated as a personal residence only if its primary use when occupied by the term holder or third parties is as a residence.[177] When a personal residence is rented, the rental use must be as a personal residence.[178] A residence is not used primarily as a residence if it is used to provide transient lodging and substantial services are provided in connection with the lodging.[179]

If the residence is the term holder's principal residence, it may have a secondary business use that would qualify a portion of it for an income tax business expense deduction.[180] The business portion of the principal residence must meet the requirements of Section 280A(c)(1) or Section 280A(c)(4). The allocable business portion must be used exclusively and on a regular basis as the term holder's principal place of business,[181] as a place of business frequented by customers, clients, or patients in the normal course of the term holder's business, as the locale for the provision of day care services, or as a

---

houses), 9705017 (Nov. 1, 1996) (three parcels with two guest houses), 9741004 (July 3, 1997) (two parcels of land). Cf. Bennett v. United States, 61-2 USTC ¶ 9697 (DC No. Ga. 1961).

[174] Reg. §§ 25.2702-5(b)(2)(ii), 25.2702-5(c)(2)(ii).

[175] Reg. §§ 25.2702-5(b)(2)(ii), 25.2702-5(c)(2)(ii). In the case of a regular personal residence trust, the mortgage payments would have to be made directly by transferor (or some other person), while a qualified personal residence trust may hold cash for the purpose of making mortgage payments. See infra text accompanying notes 191, 212.

[176] If a residence is subject to a mortgage, there are also potential income tax consequences to the transferor. Cf. Malone v. United States, 326 F. Supp. 106 (ND Miss. 1971), aff'd per curiam, 455 F2d 502 (5th Cir. 1972); Johnson v. Comm'r, 495 F2d 1079 (6th Cir. 1974).

[177] Reg. §§ 25.2702-5(b)(2)(iii), 25.2702-5(c)(2)(iii). A provision in the trust allowing the grantor of the trust to rent the residence at its fair rental value upon termination of the trust does not disqualify the trust from the exception. Priv. Ltr. Rul. 9448035 (Sept. 2, 1994).

[178] Reg. §§ 25.2702-5(b)(2)(iii) (last sentence), 25.2702-5(c)(2)(iii) (last sentence).

[179] Reg. §§ 25.2702-5(b)(2)(iii) (last sentence), 25.2702-5(c)(2)(iii) (last sentence). This eliminates a hotel or bed and breakfast from qualifying for the personal residence trust exception.

[180] Reg. §§ 25.2702-5(b)(2)(iii), 25.2702-5(c)(2)(iii). See Reg. § 25.2702-5(d) Ex. 1; Priv. Ltr. Ruls. 9609015 (Nov. 22, 1995) (rental unit), 9741004 (July 3, 1997) (same).

[181] See Comm'r v. Soliman, 506 US 168 (1993); IRC § 280A(c)(1) last sentence.

separate structure used in connection with the term holder's trade or business that is not attached to the dwelling unit.[182]

If the residence is not the term holder's principal residence, it must be treated as "used" by the term holder within the meaning of Section 280A(d)(1).[183] Such a residence may be rented, but if rented at any time during the year, the term holder is required to use the residence personally in excess of the greater of fourteen days or 10 percent of the number of days during the year that the residence is rented.[184] Generally, when the regulations determine use by the term holder, they require actual physical occupancy by the term holder.[185] However, if a residence is not rented during the year, it is treated as used by the term holder if it is "held for use" by the term holder.[186] A residence is held for use by the term holder if it is unoccupied or it is occupied only by a spouse or a Section 152 dependent of the term holder, and it is available at all times for use by the term holder as a personal residence, because it is not rented to any third party.[187]

[ii] A regular personal residence trust.

In General. A regular personal residence trust is a trust whose governing instrument[188] permits the trust for the original duration of the term interest to hold as its only assets one residence used or held for use as a personal resi-

---

[182] IRC §§ 280A(c)(1), 280A(c)(4).

[183] Reg. §§ 25.2702-5(b)(2)(i)(B), 25.2702-5(c)(2)(i)(B).

[184] IRC § 280A(d)(1). See Reg. § 25.2702-5(d) Ex. 2; Priv. Ltr. Rul. 200117021 (Jan. 25, 2001). Although the regulations do not specifically so provide, the Section 280A(d)(1) use requirement is not required if the property is not rented at any time during the year. Cf. IRC § 163(h)(4)(A)(iii). In such circumstances, the taxpayer can satisfy the "held for use" test, which is discussed infra text accompanying note 186.

In making the previously mentioned determination, the Section 280A(d)(2) definition of "personal use" is disregarded. Reg. §§ 25.2702-5(b)(2)(i)(B), 25.2702-5(c)(2)(i)(B). Section 280A(d)(2) treats an owner as using a residence if it is used by relatives, the owner uses another's property in an exchange of use with its owner, or the owner rents the property at less than its fair rental value. It also provides that some personal use (time spent on maintenance and repairs) by the term holder is not treated as personal use.

Seemingly, a principal residence may also be rented if it otherwise meets the requirements of being the taxpayer's "principal" residence.

[185] Reg. §§ 25.2702-5(b)(2)(iii), 25.2702-5(c)(2)(iii).

[186] Reg. §§ 25.2702-5(b)(1), 25.2702-5(c)(7)(i).

[187] Reg. §§ 25.2702-5(b)(1), 25.2702-5(c)(7)(i). See Reg. § 25.2702-5(d) Ex. 5. The "held for use" test should apply to either a principal or secondary residence as long as neither is rented during the year. See also supra note 184.

The held for use exception would apply in a situation where the term holder is in a convalescent home or some similar type of housing. See Reg. § 25.2702-5(d) Ex. 5.

[188] A governing instrument is the instrument or instruments creating and governing the operation of the trust arrangement. Reg. § 25.2702-2(a)(9). See infra text accompanying notes 200–202.

dence of the term holder[189] and qualified proceeds.[190] Because a regular personal residence trust may not hold any other assets, expenses of the trust, including mortgage payments, must be paid from nontrust funds and any rents generated by the property must be paid to the term holder and may not be paid to the trust.[191] The governing instrument of a regular personal residence trust must prohibit the residence from being sold or otherwise transferred during the original duration of the term interest of the trust.[192] Furthermore, at any time after the original term interest while the trust is a grantor trust, the governing interest of the trust must also prohibit the sale or transfer of the residence directly or indirectly to the grantor of the trust, the grantor's spouse, an entity controlled by the grantor, or another grantor trust of the grantor or the grantor's spouse.[193] However, a distribution of the residence, for no consideration, upon or after the expiration of the retained term interest to another grantor trust of either the grantor or of the grantor's spouse, or directly to the grantor's spouse is not prohibited.[194] A regular personal residence trust is substantially restricted as to the content and use of its corpus as compared to the more flexible qualified personal residence trust, considered subsequentlyin the following paragraphs.[195]

Qualified Proceeds. A regular personal residence trust generally may not hold any asset other than one residence and qualified proceeds.[196] "Qualified proceeds" are defined as proceeds payable to the trust as a result of damage to or the destruction or involuntary conversion[197] of the personal residence.[198] The

---

[189] The terms "use" or "held for use" are defined supra ¶ 19.03[3][d][i].

[190] Reg. § 25.2702-5(b)(1). See infra text accompanying notes 196–199.

[191] Reg. § 25.2702-5(b)(1). Expenses or income relating to the residence would normally be paid by or to the term holder. If expenses are paid by a person other than the term holder, there is a gift to the term holder, and if income is paid to a person other than the term holder, there is a gift by the term holder.

[192] Reg. § 25.2702-5(b)(1).

[193] Reg. § 25.2702-5(b)(1). See infra text accompanying notes 224–228 for a discussion of the rule and the terms used here.

[194] Reg. § 25.2702-5(b)(1). See infra text accompanying note 229.

[195] See infra ¶ 19.03[3][d][iii].

[196] Reg. § 25.2702-5(b)(1).

[197] See IRC § 1033.

[198] Even though the qualified proceeds may be paid to the trust, the trust may not hold an insurance policy as an asset of the trust corpus. Cf. Reg. §§ 25.2702-5(b)(1), 25.2702-5(b)(3). The regulations are silent as to the consequences if the terms of the trust are violated by the proceeds not timely being reinvested or if there is some other violation of the regular personal residence trust requirements. While this would constitute a breach of the trustee's duty, it is also possible that a commutation of the trust could occur. In such circumstances, the regulations should parallel the rules for a qualified personal residence trust (see Reg. § 25.2702-5(c)(4)) and require the trust corpus to be returned to the transferor. The regulations do not contain any such specific requirement and thus commu-

proceeds are qualified only if the trust instrument requires reinvestment of the proceeds and any income generated by them in a personal residence within two years of receipt.[199]

Trust Imputation. If a person transfers a legal remainder interest in a personal residence outright (not in trust) to a family member and retains use of the property for a term interest (either a term of years or for life), the transfer of the legal interest is likely not treated as a transfer to a regular personal residence trust under the imputed trust rule of Section 2702(c)(1).[200] Although a trust could be imputed, it would fail to have a governing instrument that would satisfy the specific requirements considered previously.[201] Imputation of such a trust could lead to abuse of the personal residence trust exception if the residence were subsequently sold and the proceeds were commuted, split according to the relative actuarial interests of the parties. Thus, the imputation rules likely do not apply to create a regular personal residence trust, although it is possible that the reformation rules might be used in conjunction with the imputation rules to create a regular personal residence trust.[202]

[iii] A qualified personal residence trust. The Section 2702 personal residence trust exception also applies to a "qualified" personal residence trust.[203] A qualified personal residence trust must satisfy the general requirements applicable to a regular personal residence trust,[204] but it is permitted (1) to hold cash and other assets that are related to the residence;[205] (2) to sell the

---

tation might be allowed although this would seem inappropriate for the same reasons expressed infra text accompanying notes 235–237. See also Covey, "GRITs (Including Personal Residence Trusts), GRATs, and GRUTs," Nat'l Law Found. 57 (Dec. 7, 1992).

[199] Reg. § 25.2702-5(b)(3).

[200] See supra ¶ 19.03[2][a][i]. If a trust is imputed, the imputed trust rule should also be applied where a person transfers a legal term interest to a family member and retains a reversion in the property after the term interest.

[201] See supra text accompanying notes 188–199; Reg. §§ 25.2702-5(b), 25.2702-5(c)(1), especially 25.2702-5(b)(1). Note that all statements and examples in the regulations refer to property actually held in trust and the regulations speak of the governing instrument of the trust. Reg. §§ 25.2702-5, especially 25.2702-5(b)(1).

[202] It is possible that a trust imputed by Section 2702(c)(1) could be timely reformed to satisfy the regular personal residence trust requirements and thereby qualify as a regular personal residence trust. See Reg. § 25.2702-5(a)(2) and supra note 168. Seemingly no policy would be violated if an imputed trust were reformed to qualify for the exception. Similar imputation should also occur under the joint purchase rule and possibly to an imputed qualified personal residence trust. See infra text accompanying note 220 and infra ¶ 19.03[4][a] text accompanying note 282.

[203] Reg. §§ 25.2702-5(a)(1), 25.2702-5(c).

[204] Compare Reg. § 25.2702-5(c) with Reg. § 25.2702-5(b).

[205] Reg. § 25.2702-5(c)(5).

residence and reinvest the proceeds in another residence;[206] (3) to receive or make improvements to the residence;[207] and (4) to be converted into a qualified annuity trust.[208] As a result of its flexibility, a qualified personal residence trust, rather than a regular personal residence trust, generally will be used by taxpayers wishing to avoid Section 2702.

Other than the exceptions noted previously, the governing instrument of a qualified personal residence trust must contain provisions satisfying all of the regulatory requirements applicable to a qualified personal residence trust.[209] There is likely no imputation of a qualified personal residence trust under Section 2702(c)(1), because all of the specific requirements applicable to a qualified personal residence trust must be contained in the governing instrument of the trust, although such a trust might be imputed under the reformation rules.[210]

Cash and Other Assets. The governing instrument of a qualified personal residence trust may permit additions of cash to the trust and the trust to hold cash in a separate account.[211] The amount of cash held may not exceed the amount needed to pay trust costs related to the residence reasonably expected to be incurred within the succeeding six months for expenses, such as insurance and repairs, mortgage payments, or improvements.[212] The governing instrument may also permit cash contributions to the trust to acquire the initial personal residence within three months of the creation of the trust if the trustee has previously entered into a contract to purchase the initial residence or to acquire a replacement residence within three months of the trustee entering into a contract to make the replacement.[213] The instrument may also permit the transfer to the trust of improvements to the residence (in lieu of cash to make such

---

[206] Reg. §§ 25.2702-5(c)(5)(ii)(C), 25.2702-5(c)(7). But see Reg. §§ 25.2702-5(c)(5)(ii)(C), 25.2702-5(c)(9).

[207] Reg. § 25.2702-5(c)(5)(ii)(B).

[208] Reg. § 25.2702-5(c)(8)(i)(B).

[209] Reg. § 25.2702-5(c)(1). A governing instrument is the instrument or instruments creating and governing the operation of the trust arrangement. Reg. § 25.2702-2(a)(9).

[210] See the discussion of the imputation of a regular personal residence trust, supra text accompanying notes 200–202. Arguably, an imputed trust could be reformed to satisfy the qualified personal residence trust requirements. See Reg. § 25.2702-5(a)(2) supra notes 168, 202.

[211] Reg. § 25.2702-5(c)(5)(ii)(A)(1).

[212] Reg. §§ 25.2702-5(c)(5)(ii)(A)(1)(i), 25.2702-5(c)(5)(ii)(A)(1)(ii). Such cash contributions may themselves constitute gifts in part at the time mortgage payment or improvement is made. See infra note 214.

[213] Reg. §§ 25.2702-5(c)(5)(ii)(A)(1)(iii), 25.2702-5(c)(5)(ii)(A)(1)(iv).

improvements).[214] The trust may also hold policies of insurance on the residence.[215]

The governing instrument must require that the trustee at least quarterly determine whether there is any cash held in the trust in excess of that permitted and require, once the determination is made, the immediate distribution of any excess cash to the term holder.[216] In addition, the trust instrument must require that within thirty days of termination of the term holder's interest, any amounts of cash held by the trust not used to pay expenses must be distributed to the term holder.[217] The instrument must also require that any income of the trust be distributed to the term holder not less frequently than annually.[218]

The governing instrument must prohibit distribution of corpus to any beneficiary other than the transferor prior to the termination of the retained term interest.[219] This rule protects the government from any commutation of the trust corpus.[220]

Sale and Insurance Proceeds. The governing instrument of a qualified personal residence trust generally may permit the trust to sell the personal residence and to hold the proceeds from the sale in a separate account.[221] If the governing instrument permits the holding of proceeds, it must provide that the trust ceases to be a qualified personal residence trust with respect to the proceeds held by the trust unless, within a period of two years of the sale, the proceeds are reinvested in a replacement personal residence held in the trust.[222] If the governing instrument does not permit the trust to hold the proceeds of

---

[214] Reg. § 25.2702-5(c)(5)(ii)(B). The improved residence must meet the requirements of a personal residence. Id. The value of the improvement added (like a mortgage payment) or the infusion of cash also qualifies for the qualified personal residence trust exception to the application of Section 2702. Both the improvement and the cash infusion should be treated as a partial gift at the time the improvement is made.

[215] Reg. § 25.2702-5(c)(5)(iv)(D).

[216] Reg. § 25.2702-5(c)(5)(ii)(A)(2).

[217] Reg. § 25.2702-5(c)(5)(ii)(A)(2). Expenses must be due and payable at the termination or directly related to the termination.

[218] Reg. § 25.2702-5(c)(3). The income may result from rental of the residence or income earned from the cash added to the trust.

[219] Reg. § 25.2702-5(c)(4).

[220] See infra text accompanying note 236. Cf. supra ¶ 19.03[3][b] note 143.

[221] Reg. § 25.2702-5(c)(5)(ii)(C). But see infra text accompanying notes 224–228. Seemingly, there is substantial flexibility with respect to the investment of the proceeds.

[222] Reg. § 25.2702-5(c)(7)(ii). Cf. Reg. § 25.2702-5(c)(5)(ii)(C); IRC § 1034 (repealed by Taxpayer Relief Act of 1997, Pub. L. No. 105-34, § 312(b), 111 Stat. 788, 839 (1997), reprinted in 1997 in 1997-4 CB (Vol. 1) 1, 53). The period is shortened and the trust is terminated on the termination of the term holder's interest during the period. Reg. § 25.2702-5(c)(7)(ii)(B). In such circumstances, the trust corpus generally would be included in the transferor's gross estate under Section 2036 and the trust corpus should be paid to the successor beneficiaries. But see supra text accompanying note 219.

the sale of the residence, it must provide that the trust ceases to be a qualified personal residence trust at the time of the sale of the residence.[223]

There are some restrictions on the sale of the residence in a qualified personal residence trust. The governing instrument of the qualified personal residence trust must prohibit the trust from selling or transferring the residence, directly or indirectly, to the grantor, the grantor's spouse, an entity controlled[224] by the grantor or the grantor's spouse, or another grantor trust[225] of the grantor or the grantor's spouse during the original term of the trust or at any time after the original term interest while the trust is a grantor trust.[226] The restrictions, which apply both to a regular personal residence trust and a qualified personal residence trust, are imposed to preclude a grantor from using the qualified personal residence trust exception with the intent of purchasing the residence from the trust just prior to the expiration of a grantor trust in a sale or exchange that is free from any income tax[227] and transferring cash or other assets to the remainderpersons in place of the residence.[228] However, a distribution of the residence, for no consideration, upon or after the expiration of the retained term interest to another grantor trust of either the grantor or the grantor's spouse or directly to the grantor's spouse is not prohibited.[229] And the Service has allowed a grantor upon the creation of a qualified personal residence trust to enter into an agreement to rent the property for its fair rental value after the trust term expires.[230]

The governing instrument may permit the trust to hold one or more insurance policies on the property[231] and to hold, in a separate account, the proceeds of the insurance payable to the trust as a result of damage to or destruction of

---

[223] Reg. § 25.2702-5(c)(7)(ii).

[224] Reg. §§ 25.2701-2(b)(5)(ii), 25.2701-2(b)(5)(iii) (generally imposing a 50 percent control test). See ¶ 19.02[2][b] text accompanying notes 94–102.

[225] For purposes of the regulations, a grantor trust is a trust treated as owned by the grantor or the grantor's spouse under Sections 671–677. Reg. § 25.2702-5(c)(9).

[226] Reg. §§ 25.2702-5(c)(5)(ii)(C), 25.2702-5(c)(9). The regulations permit a distribution of the residence, for no consideration, upon or after the expiration of the retained term interest to another grantor trust of either the grantor or of the grantor's spouse, or directly to the grantor's spouse. This rule applies to trusts created after May 16, 1996.

[227] Rev. Rul. 85-13, 1985-1 CB 184.

[228] PS-4-96 Supplementary Information, 61 Fed. Reg. 16,623 (1996). See supra text accompanying notes 192, 193. Such transactions are referred to as bait and switch techniques where the residence is a temporary "stand-in" for other assets. Id.

[229] Reg. §§ 25.2702-5(c)(5)(ii)(C), 25.2702-5(c)(9).

[230] Priv. Ltr. Rul. 9916030 (Jan. 22, 1999). Seemingly, this ruling would also apply to a regular personal residence trust.

[231] Cash may also be transferred to the trust to fund insurance premiums due within the succeeding six months. Reg. § 25.2702-5(c)(5)(ii)(A)(1)(i).

the residence.[232] If the trust instrument permits the trust to hold the insurance proceeds, rules similar to those applicable when a trust holds the proceeds of the sale of a personal residence apply[233] generally requiring replacement or repair of the residence within a two-year period.[234]

Cessation of the Trust. The final requirements for a qualified personal residence trust relate to the cessation of the trust prior to termination of the term interest. The governing instrument of a qualified personal residence trust must prohibit commutation.[235] On premature termination of the term interest, the trust must provide that the full corpus of the trust be paid to the transferor.[236] This requirement precludes any indirect circumvention of Section 2702 by terminating the qualified personal residence trust prior to its stated term and dividing the proceeds actuarially between interest holders.[237]

The governing instrument must also provide for a cessation of the trust if the residence ceases to be used or held for use as a personal residence of the term holder.[238] Exceptions are provided in certain instances where there is a sale and reinvestment of the proceeds in a new residence or the involuntary or compulsory conversion and replacement of the residence.[239] Cessation rules ap-

---

[232] Reg. § 25.2702-5(c)(5)(ii)(D). Any amounts received as a result of involuntary conversion of the property are treated as insurance proceeds. Id. See IRC § 1033.

[233] See supra text accompanying notes 221–223.

[234] Reg. § 25.2702-5(c)(7)(iii)(B). Although the regulations speak in terms of a date two years from the date of the damage or destruction, the period should be two years from the receipt of insurance proceeds. See Reg. § 25.2702-5(c)(7)(iii)(B). Cf. IRC § 1033(a)(2)(B); Reg. § 25.2702-5(b)(3). The two-year period is irrelevant if the trust terminates at an earlier date. See Reg. §§ 25.2702-5(c)(7)(ii), especially 25.2702-5(c)(7)(ii)(B), 25.2702-5(c)(7)(iii)(B).

[235] Reg. § 25.2702-5(c)(6). Commutation results in prepayment to the term holder of the actuarial value of the remaining term interest prior to the time for termination of that interest under the trust document, resulting in an acceleration of the remainder and termination of the trust. Cf. supra ¶ 19.03[3][b] text accompanying notes 142, 143.

[236] Reg. § 25.2702-5(c)(4).

[237] This specific restriction on commutation seems to be superfluous in view of the requirement that the governing instrument must preclude distributions of corpus to any beneficiary other than the transferor prior to the expiration of the retained term interest. Reg. § 25.2702-5(c)(4). The regulations do not make the commutation restriction specifically applicable to a regular personal residence trust. See supra note 198. Under the stringent limitations on the sale and transfer of a residence in a regular personal residence trust, a commutation of the term interest would generally be impossible. However, there is the possible but unlikely imputation of a personal residence trust even without a reformation of the trust. See supra text accompanying notes 200–202. Thus, commutation (an indirect circumvention of Section 2702) of a regular personal residence trust should also be precluded.

[238] Reg. § 25.2702-5(c)(7)(i). The requirements for use or held for use as a personal residence are discussed supra text accompanying notes 177–187.

[239] Reg. § 25.2702-5(c)(8).

ply where there is a failure to reinvest the proceeds within the prescribed periods after a sale or involuntary or compulsory conversion of the residence.[240] On cessation of the qualified personal residence trust, the trust instrument must provide that within thirty days of the cessation[241] the trust is either to terminate and the corpus be distributed to the transferor[242] or, alternatively, the assets or the assets may be rolled over into a qualified annuity trust for the balance of the term holder's term.[243] The trustee may be given discretion as to which of these alternative courses of action to take.[244]

To the extent that the assets are rolled over into a qualified annuity trust, the governing instrument of the qualified annuity interest trust must meet the regular requirements applicable to a qualifying annuity interest.[245] The right to receive the annuity must commence on the date of the sale, damage, or destruction of the residence or the failure to use the property as a residence.[246] The governing instrument must set a floor on the annuity amount, the floor being an amount that is not less than the amount that the annuity would have been if the trust had originally been created as a GRAT.[247] The floor amount

---

[240] See supra text accompanying notes 222, 234.

[241] Reg. § 25.2702-5(c)(8)(i).

[242] Reg. § 25.2702-5(c)(8)(i)(A). The regulation specifically provides for the trust corpus to be distributed to the *term holder*. However, this regulation may contradict Regulations Section 25.2702-5(c)(4), which requires the governing instrument to prohibit distributions of corpus to any beneficiary other than the transferor prior to the expiration of the term interest. Seemingly, Regulations Section 25.2702-5(c)(8)(i)(A) assumes that the transferor is always the term interest holder, but this should not necessarily be so. See supra text accompanying note 166. If the qualified personal residence trust has a family member term interest holder with a reversion to the transferor, there is a conflict between Regulations Sections 25.2702-5(c)(8)(i)(A) and 25.2702-5(c)(4). Regulations Section 25.2702-5(c)(4) should control.

[243] Reg. § 25.2702-5(c)(8)(i)(B). See Priv. Ltr. Ruls. 9441039 (July 15, 1994), 9447036 (Aug. 29, 1994) (both involving trusts with rollover provisions). A rollover into a qualified unitrust is not permitted. See also Reg. § 25.2702-5(c)(8)(i)(B).

[244] Reg. § 25.2702-5(c)(8)(i)(C).

[245] Reg. § 25.2702-5(c)(8)(ii)(A). See Reg. § 25.2702-3; supra ¶ 19.03[3][b][i].

[246] Reg. § 25.2702-5(c)(8)(ii)(B). The purpose of this requirement is to ensure that the corpus is not inflated by any earnings on the proceeds between the relevant sale, damage, or destruction date and the date the trust ceases to be a qualified personal residence trust. See supra text accompanying note 221 with respect to investments of such proceeds. The governing instrument may provide that payment of the annuity may be deferred until thirty days after the assets are converted to a qualified annuity provided that the deferred payment bears interest at the Section 7520 interest rate in effect on the cessation date. Reg. § 25.2702-5(c)(8)(ii)(B). The governing instrument may permit the trustee to reduce the aggregate deferred annuity payments (and therefore the interest therein) by the amount of any income actually paid to the annuitant during the deferral period. Id.

[247] Reg. § 25.2702-5(c)(8)(ii)(C)(1). See infra note 248. If only a portion of the trust ceases, the annuity is appropriately reduced to reflect the fact that the term holder is still receiving a portion of the value of the term interest in the form of an interest in a personal

depends upon whether the entire trust ceases to be a qualified personal residence trust[248] or whether only a portion of the trust ceases to be a qualified personal residence trust.[249]

[iv] The two personal residence trusts limitation. At the time of the transfer by the term holder to either a personal residence trust or a qualified personal residence trust, the Section 2702(a)(3)(A)(ii) exception does not apply if the term holder already is the grantor of two trusts in which the *grantor currently* holds term interests in personal residences.[250] Furthermore, if there is more than one such trust, the corpus of one of the trusts must consist of the

---

residence. Thus, it is not possible artificially to allocate a portion of the value of the term interest to the remainder interest by decreasing the amount of the annuity. If a reduced annuity were allowed, the result could circumvent Section 2702 in much the same manner as would a commutation of the term interest. See supra ¶ 19.03[3][b] note 143.

[248] Reg. § 25.2702-5(c)(8)(ii)(C)(2). The annuity may not be less than an amount determined by dividing the lesser of (1) the value of all interests retained by the term holder (as of the original transfer date or dates that should reflect the valuation suggested supra ¶ 19.03[3][b] text accompanying note 133); or (2) the value of all the trust assets (on the conversion date) by an annuity factor. The annuity factor is determined using the original term of the term holder's interest at the rate used in valuing the retained interest at the time of the original transfer. Id.

For example, if the initial value of the term holder's retained interest was $100,000 on the date the trust was created, the trust assets are worth $250,000 upon the conversion date, no part of the trust continues as a qualified personal residence trust, the original term of the trust was for ten years, and the rate used in valuing the interest at the time of the original transfer was 6 percent, the annuity cannot be less than $100,000 divided by an annuity factor determined using ten years as the term and 6 percent as the rate of interest. This results in an annuity of $13,586.77.

[249] Reg. § 25.2702-5(c)(8)(ii)(C)(3). If only a portion of the trust ceases to be a qualified personal residence trust, the annuity cannot be less than the amount determined supra note 248 (the annuity floor for a trust that completely ceases) multiplied by a fraction: (1) the numerator of which is the fair market value of all the trust assets on the conversion date less the fair market value of the trust assets as to which the trust continues as a qualified residence trust and (2) the denominator of the fraction is the fair market value of the trust assets on the conversion date. Id. For example, if the trust referred to supra note 248 reinvested $150,000 in a personal residence and the total value of the trust on the date of conversion was $250,000, the annuity of $13,586.77, determined supra note 248, would be multiplied by two-fifths ($250,000-$150,000 divided by $250,000) to determine the floor. Thus the annuity floor is $5,434.71. See Reg. § 25.2702-5(d) Ex. 6.

[250] Reg. § 25.2702-5(a)(1). The two-trust limitation is not found in the statute, but is imposed by the regulations. Cf. IRC § 163(h)(4)(A)(i). Residences provide an opportunity for valuation abuse under Sections 2702 and 2702 should allow only a narrow exception for transfers of residences to family members. See the Supplementary Information accompanying the final regulations. See TD 8395, Supplementary Information (Personal Residence Trusts), 1992-1 CB 316, 319. This rationale is given for the use of the Section 163(h) definition of "personal residences," which is limited to only two such residences, one of which must be a principal residence.

transferor's principal residence.[251] It is possible for a grantor to have retained interests in more than two personal residence trusts, but only as long as no more than two retained interests are held concurrently. If an individual holds a term interest in a trust holding a personal residence, but that individual is not the grantor of the trust, the trust is not counted under that individual's two trust limitation.[252] Thus, if a term interest holder, in addition to creating two trusts, each of which holds a personal residence, also holds a term interest in a trust holding another personal residence created by a related person who retains a reversion in the corpus of that trust, the term interest holder's two trust limitation is not violated.[253] Further, if a grantor creates a trust giving an income interest to a family member with a reversion in the grantor, the trust is not counted in determining the two trust limitation because the grantor does not retain a term interest.[254]

Trusts holding fractional interests in the same residence are treated as a single trust.[255] Thus, it is possible for a grantor to hold term interests simultaneously in more than two personal residence trusts and have all the trusts qualify for the personal residence exception, as long as no more than two residences are involved and one is the transferor's principal residence. For example, if Parent retains a term interest in two trusts, transferring one half of a single residence to each, with the remainder in one trust passing to Son and the other remainder passing to Daughter, the trusts count as only one personal residence trust under the two trust limitation.[256]

If spouses own interests in the same residence,[257] they may transfer their interests to the same personal residence trust, retaining term interests therein, as long as the governing instrument prohibits any other person from holding a term interest in the trust concurrently with either of them.[258] Under the two trust limitation, this single trust would count as a personal residence trust for each spouse.

---

[251] Reg. §§ 25.2702-5(b)(2)(i), 25.2702-5(c)(2)(i).

[252] Reg. § 25.2702-5(a)(1).

[253] Reg. § 25.2702-5(a)(1).

[254] Cf. Reg. §§ 25.2702-5(a)(1), 25.2702-5(b)(2)(i), 25.2702-5(c)(2)(i).

[255] Reg. § 25.2702-5(a)(1) (last sentence). If fractional interests are combined and the transferor holds interests in two personal residence trusts, the corpus of one trust must hold the transferor's principal residence. See supra text accompanying note 251.

[256] Reg. § 25.2702-5(a)(1) (last sentence).

[257] This includes ownership as community property, as well as joint tenants, tenants by the entirety, or tenants in common. Reg. §§ 25.2702-5(b)(2)(iv), 25.2702-5(c)(2)(iv).

[258] Reg. §§ 25.2702-5(b)(2)(iv), 25.2702-5(c)(2)(iv).

[4] Special Rules Under Section 2702

[a] The Joint Purchase Rule

An indirect application of Section 2702 occurs under the joint purchase rule.[259] If in a single transaction or series of related transactions, two or more members of the same family[260] acquire noncontemporaneous interests in property, the transaction is recast by the statute. The person (or persons) acquiring the term interest (or interests) in the property is treated as acquiring the entire property and then transferring to the other purchasers the interests acquired by the other purchasers in the transaction.[261] This imputed transfer to the other purchasers is treated as made in exchange for any consideration paid by the other purchasers for the interests they acquired in the property.[262] For example, if Parent purchases a life estate worth $100,000 (as computed under Section 7520) for $100,000, and Child purchases for $50,000 a remainder interest worth $50,000 in the same property, Parent is treated as acquiring the entire property and transferring the remainder interest to Child (a family member) while retaining an income interest. Section 2702 causes Parent's retained income interest to be valued at zero.[263] For gift tax purposes, Parent is treated as transferring the entire $150,000 property in return for $50,000 of consideration from Child, and, as a result of the imputed transfer, Parent makes a gift transfer of $100,000.[264] The effect of this rule in a normal joint purchase situation is to treat Parent as making a gift equal to the $100,000 value of the interest Parent purchased.

A joint purchase may involve more than two family members. For example, assume Father, Mother, and Child pay fair market value of $300,000, $100,000, and $200,000, respectively, for a life estate, a secondary life estate, and a remainder interest in property worth $600,000. Under the Section 2702(c) joint purchase rule, Father is deemed to make a transfer of $300,000 ($600,000 less $300,000 of consideration), and Mother is deemed to make a transfer of $100,000 ($600,000 less $500,000 of consideration). The statute in-

---

[259] See Kasner, "Reassessing the Joint Purchase as an Estate Planning Technique," 55 Tax Notes 665 (May 4, 1992).

[260] IRC §§ 2702(e), 2704(c)(2). The term "members of the same family" under Section 2702(c)(2) should be interpreted the same as the term "member of the family" in Section 2702(e). See supra ¶ 19.03[2][a][ii].

[261] IRC § 2702(c)(2).

[262] IRC § 2702(c)(2). Cf. IRC § 2512(b).

[263] IRC § 2702(a)(2)(A).

[264] See Reg. § 25.2702-4(d) Ex. 1.

dicates that the transfer is to the other persons, but does not indicate specifically to whom or in what amounts the transfers are made.[265]

The joint purchase rule does not apply to a joint purchase of contemporaneous interests such as a tenancy in common, a joint tenancy with a right of survivorship, or a tenancy by the entirety,[266] because such contemporaneous interests are not term interests under Section 2702.[267] However, a purchase of a remainder interest from a family member who owned the fee simple is treated as a joint purchase resulting in a transfer (and gift) by the fee owner.[268] Similarly, a purchase of a life estate from a family member who owned the fee simple interest should be treated as a joint purchase resulting in a transfer (and gift) by the purchaser of the life estate in the amount of the purchase price.[269]

In order to trigger an imputed transfer, the statutory language of the Section 2702(c)(2) joint purchase rule requires only the acquisition of the interests, not their purchase. However, the regulations require a purchase to trigger an imputed transfer by limiting the amount of the imputed transfer to the amount of consideration actually furnished by the imputed transferor for all interests in the property.[270] Thus, under the statutory language alone, if Parent transfers a life estate to Child and a remainder to Grandchild, technically there is a joint acquisition in a single transaction by Child and Grandchild, and Child is deemed to transfer the entire property to Grandchild. This absurd result is precluded by the regulations' adoption of the consideration limitation, and Child is treated as making a transfer only to the extent that Child provides consideration to Parent for Child's interest.[271]

---

[265] This creates numerous issues. For example, seemingly each transferor makes a transfer to the other persons in proportion to the relative fair market values of their interests. See supra ¶ 19.03[2][c] note 93. Father's transfer to Mother is a terminable interest that does not qualify for a marital deduction. No QTIP election is available because Mother does not have the right to all of the income for life. IRC §§ 2056(b)(7)(B)(ii)(I), 2523(f)(2)(B). See Reg. § 25.2523(f)-1(c)(1)(i). Mother's transfer to Father is also a terminable interest that should qualify for a marital deduction under Section 2523(f) if a QTIP election is made, because Father has a qualifying income interest for life. IRC § 2523(f)(2)(B).

Similar allocation problems arise if Father pays $400,000 for his interest (worth $300,000) and Mother pays $200,000 for her interest (worth $100,000) and Child pays nothing. Now Father makes a gift of $400,000 and Mother a gift of $200,000, but to whom are the gift transfers allocated? See supra ¶ 19.03[2][c] note 93.

[266] Reg. § 25.2702-4(d) Ex. 3.

[267] Reg. § 25.2702-4(a). See supra ¶ 19.03[2][a] text accompanying notes 41, 42.

[268] Reg. § 25.2702-4(d) Ex. 2. See supra ¶ 19.03[2][a] text accompanying note 30.

[269] Cf. Reg. § 25.2702-4(d) Ex. 2; infra text accompanying notes 270, 271.

[270] Reg. § 25.2702-4(c).

[271] Reg. § 25.2702-4(d) Ex. 4.

The joint purchase rule incorporates all of the rules of Section 2702 applicable to outright transfers.[272] Even though the property involved in the joint purchase of noncontemporaneous interests is not held in a trust, a trust is imputed, triggering the application of the Section 2702(a) rules.[273]

The joint purchase rule is applicable whether the property is acquired in a single transaction or a series of related transactions.[274] The regulations are silent on the meaning of "series of related transactions."[275] Normal step transaction doctrine tests should be used to determine whether the transfers are related.[276]

As a result of the separate portion rule, the joint purchase rule may apply to an acquisition of only a portion of property.[277] Thus, if Transferor purchases a life estate in a piece of commercial property and Child purchases a one-third remainder interest in the property with a Niece and Nephew acquiring the other two thirds with all parties providing adequate consideration for their interests, the joint purchase rule would apply to create a gift transfer by Transferor of only one third of the value of the income interest in the property.

The Section 2702 valuation rules and exceptions to the application of Section 2702[278] also apply to joint purchases. Consequently, when there is a purchase for full and adequate consideration of a term interest in an annuity trust or unitrust and the Section 2702(c)(2) joint purchase rule applies, the retained interest is valued under the Section 7520 valuation rules because it is a qualified annuity or unitrust interest; consequently, no gift occurs.[279] The personal residence trust exception also applies to joint purchases.[280] A joint purchase by a trust of a residence that the term holder uses as a personal residence[281] is not subject to Section 2702, assuming all trust interest holders provide adequate consideration for their interests in the trust and the trust is a

---

[272] The introductory clause of Regulations Section 25.2702-4(c) states that there is a transfer "[s]olely for purposes of Section 2702." As with regular Section 2702 transfers, the joint purchase rule creates a transfer only for purposes of the gift tax, and its imputed transfer is not a transfer for income, estate, or generation-skipping transfer tax purposes. Reg. § 25.2702-4(c). See infra ¶ 19.03[4][e] text accompanying note 360.

[273] See IRC § 2702(c)(1); Reg. § 25.2702-6(c) Ex. 8 (in essence treating jointly purchased property as held in a trust).

[274] IRC § 2702(c)(2).

[275] See Reg. § 25.2702-4(c).

[276] See, e.g., McDonald's Restaurants of Ill., Inc. v. Comm'r, 688 F2d 520 (7th Cir. 1982).

[277] IRC § 2702(d). See supra ¶ 19.03[2][b].

[278] See supra ¶ 19.03[3].

[279] See Reg. §§ 25.2702-4(c), 25.2702-4(d) Ex. 1 (last sentence); supra ¶ 19.03[3][b] note 112. Cf. IRC §§ 2702(a)(2)(B), 2702(b).

[280] See supra ¶ 19.03[3][d].

[281] See Reg. § 25.2702-5(b)(2).

qualified personal residence trust.[282] In addition, a joint purchase of certain tangible property[283] is subject to the special valuation rules that are considered in the following section[284] and are applicable to such property.[285]

[b] Transfers of Certain Tangible Property

Section 2702 provides a special valuation rule for a term interest retained by the transferor in nonwasting[286] tangible property, if the term interest holder's failure to assert rights with respect to the property would not have a substantial effect upon the value of the remainder interest in the property.[287] The value of the term interest is the amount that the transferor establishes that an unrelated third party would pay for the term interest.[288] That value replaces the normal Section 2702 zero valuation for the retained term interest.[289] For example, assume Transferor transfers a remainder interest in a painting worth $1 million to Child retaining an interest for a term of years. Also assume that the term interest is actuarially worth $400,000 under Section 7520, but a willing buyer would pay only $200,000 for the term use of the property. Under the

---

[282] Priv. Ltr. Ruls. 9841017 (Oct. 9, 1998), 200112023 (Dec. 18, 2000). Seemingly such a purchase by a regular personal residence trust will not satisfy the requirements of a regular personal residence trust. See supra ¶ 19.03[3][d] text accompanying note 191, supra ¶ 19.03[3][d] text accompanying notes 200–202. But, see ¶ 19.03[3][d] note 202 suggesting that an imputation may be possible especially if the imputed trust is timely reformed. See also supra ¶ 19.03[3][d] note 168.

The joint purchase of a personal residence by a qualified personal residence trust is a significant estate planning vehicle even after the enactment of Section 2702. See supra ¶ 19.03[1] note 20. No gift occurs on the joint purchase. Priv. Ltr. Ruls. 9841017 (Oct. 9, 1998), 200112023 (Dec. 18, 2000). Compare the results in the hypothetical supra text accompanying notes 263–264. In addition, the residence likely is not included in the term holder's gross estate. See infra ¶ 19.03[4][e] text accompanying notes 367–369. Note that neither Priv. Ltr. Rul. 9841017 nor Priv. Ltr. Rul. 200112023 discussed the potential application of Section 2036, although Priv. Ltr. Rul. 200112023 held that neither Section 2033 nor Section 2039 would be applicable. See also Blattmachr, "Split Purchase Trusts v. Qualified Personal Residence Trusts," 138 Tr. & Est. 56 (Feb. 1999).

[283] IRC § 2702(c)(4).

[284] See infra ¶ 19.03[4][b].

[285] See Reg. § 25.2702-2(d)(2) Ex. 8.

[286] The special valuation rule generally is limited to property for which no depreciation or depletion would be allowed if the property were used in a trade or business or held for the production of income, i.e., property without an ascertainable useful life. Reg. § 25.2702-2(c)(2)(i)(A). Under a de minimis exception, any depreciable improvements to the property that do not exceed 5 percent of the fair market value of the entire property are disregarded. Reg. § 25.2702-2(c)(2)(ii).

[287] IRC § 2702(c)(4).

[288] IRC § 2702(c)(4).

[289] IRC § 2702(c)(4).

special rule, Transferor makes a transfer of $800,000 ($1 million less $200,000), rather than the $1 million transfer that would occur if the zero valuation rule applied.[290] The special valuation rule applies to a situation where there is no possibility of shifting value from the income interest holder to the remainderperson as a result of nonuse of the property.[291] Paintings, antiques, and jewelry qualify for the special rule,[292] as does most raw land.[293] A joint purchase (as opposed to an outright transfer) of tangible property should be a gift only to the extent that the excess of the value of the consideration provided by the purchaser of the term interest exceeds the value a willing buyer would pay for such interest.[294]

Under the special valuation rule, the transferor has the burden of establishing the amount that an unrelated third party would pay for the term interest.[295] Actual sales or rentals of term interests in property that are comparable to the transferor's both in the nature and character of the property and in the duration of the term interest may satisfy that burden of proof. However, little weight is given to mere appraisals of the amount.[296] Failure to establish the value of an interest generally will result in a zero valuation of that interest.[297] However, if the property is a qualified interest in an annuity trust or a unitrust, the special valuation rule gives way to the qualified interest rule and regular Section 7520 valuation is used.[298]

If property that qualifies under this special rule is subsequently converted to nonqualifying property, the conversion is generally treated as a transfer of the unexpired portion of the term interest for zero consideration.[299] The conver-

---

[290] See Reg. § 25.2702-2(d)(2) Ex. 8.

[291] See Reg. § 25.2702-2(c)(2).

[292] See Reg. §§ 25.2702-2(d)(2) Exs. 8–10.

[293] If the land holds depletable interests qualifying for a depletion allowance if held for business or for the production of income, the exception does not apply. See supra note 286.

[294] See Explanatory Materials Concerning Committee on Finance 1990 Reconciliation Submission Pursuant to House Concurrent Resolution 310, 136 Cong. Rec. S15629, S15682 (Oct. 18, 1990). Thus, in the hypothetical supra text, if Transferor paid $400,000 and Child $600,000 for their respective interests, Transferor would make a gift of $200,000 ($400,000 less $200,000).

[295] Reg. § 25.2702-2(c)(1).

[296] Reg. § 25.2702-2(c)(3). Amounts determined under Section 7520 are not evidence of what a willing buyer would pay for the interest. Id.

[297] Reg. § 25.2702-2(c)(1). But see Reg. § 25.2702-2(d)(2) Ex. 9 (where an inadequate valuation at least established a floor on valuation).

[298] Reg. § 25.2702-2(c)(1). See IRC §§ 2702(a)(2)(B), 2704(c)(4); supra ¶ 19.03[3][b] note 112.

[299] Reg. § 25.2702-2(c)(4)(i). The value of the unexpired portion of the term interest is determined by a ratio. The ratio is the amount that bears the same relation to the value of the term interest on the date of the conversion (determined under Section 7520 using

sion transfer rule does not apply if the conversion is into a qualified annuity trust.[300] If the property that previously qualified for this special rule is added to or improved in a way that affects the nature of the property so that it would no longer qualify for the special rule, the entire property is treated as converted on the date the addition or improvement is commenced.[301] If the addition or improvement does not affect the nature of the property, the addition or improvement is treated as a transfer potentially subject to Section 2702.[302]

[c] The Double Taxation Regulation[303]

If a retained interest in property is assigned a special valuation under Section 2702,[304] the gift value of the transferred interest is increased to reflect the special value of the retained interest. The retained interest may be subsequently transferred inter vivos by the transferor or subsequently included in the transferor's gross estate. When a subsequent transfer occurs, the value of the retained interest is possibly included twice in the transfer tax base. Although the statute does not provide for remedial relief in these circumstances,[305] the

---

both the rate in effect and the fair market value of the property on the date of the original transfer) as the value of the term interest on the original transfer date, determined under the willing-buyer, willing-seller test, bears to the Section 7520 value of the term interest as of that date. Reg. § 25.2702-2(c)(4)(ii). For example, using the hypothetical supra text following note 289, the term interest was worth $400,000 under Section 7520 and a willing buyer would pay $200,000 for it. Assume that on the conversion the Section 7520 value of the term interest is $300,000. On conversion, Transferor would make a transfer of $150,000 ($300,000 times $200,000/$400,000). See Reg. § 25.2702-2(d)(2) Ex. 10.

[300] Reg. § 25.2702-2(c)(4)(iii). See Reg. § 25.2702-5(c)(8) for rules that apply in determining the amount of the annuity payment required and the requirements (including provision for such a conversion in the original governing instrument) of the qualified annuity trust. Id. The rules (borrowed from those applicable to a personal residence trust) are discussed supra ¶ 19.03[3][b] text accompanying notes 242–249.

[301] Reg. § 25.2702-2(c)(5)(i). See supra note 286.

[302] Reg. § 25.2702-2(c)(5)(ii). The transfer is made as of the date the addition or improvement is commenced. Id. See supra text accompanying note 294. The addition or improvement may also qualify for valuation pursuant to Section 2702(c)(4). Reg. §§ 25.2702-2(b)(1) (introductory clause), 25.2702-2(c)(5)(ii).

[303] This subject, as well as all of Section 2702, is critiqued in McCouch, "Rethinking Section 2702," 2 Fla. Tax Rev. 99 (1994).

[304] This includes both a zero valuation and a special Section 2702(c)(4) valuation.

[305] Compare IRC § 2701(e)(6), discussed ¶ 19.02[5][c].

regulations do provide relief from double transfer taxation in appropriate circumstances.[306]

[i] **Double taxation under the gift tax.** If a transferor places property in a trust and retains an income interest and if Section 2702 applies and values the retained interest at zero, the interest transferred by gift is valued by including the value of the retained interest. If the transferor subsequently transfers the retained income interest in an inter vivos gift transfer, the value of the income interest is effectively subject to the gift tax on two occasions: it is essentially subject to gift tax upon creation of the trust (as a result of Section 2702 valuation) and, again, on the subsequent inter vivos gift transfer. Remedial relief is provided to eliminate double gift taxation.[307] Remedial relief is also available where the transferor makes a Section 2702 transfer and retains a reversion and the transferor subsequently transfers the reversionary interest with the result that the value of the reversionary interest is essentially subject to gift tax twice.[308]

On the subsequent inter vivos transfer by gift of either type of interest, the relief afforded is a reduction in "the aggregate sum of taxable gifts" for the year under Section 2502(a)(1). The reduction amount is the lesser of: (1) the increase in the valuation of the gift resulting from the application of Section 2702 on the prior transfer[309] or (2) the amount of the increase in taxable gifts that results from the subsequent transfer.[310] Accordingly, after this reduction is made, the taxable gift attributable to the subsequent transfer is only the excess, if any, of the current value of the interest over the prior Section 2702 increase

---

[306] Reg. § 25.2702-6. See Randall, Gardner & Stewart, "Using the Rationale of Reg. § 25.2702-6 in Other Estate Tax Computations," 70 Taxes 615 (1992).

[307] Reg. §§ 25.2702-6(a)(1), 25.2702-6(b). The regulation applicable to double gift taxation also applies where valuation is determined under the Section 2702(c)(4) valuation rule. Reg. § 25.2702-6(a)(1). The relief should apply to a subsequent transfer of the retained interest.

However, it should not apply to a conversion of the property into a qualified annuity interest because with respect to such a conversion there is no double gift taxation. See Reg. § 25.2702-2(c)(4)(iii); supra ¶ 19.03[4][b] text accompanying note 300. Remedial relief is inappropriate on the conversion of a personal residence trust, since no double taxation occurs. See Reg. § 25.2702-5(c)(8).

[308] Reg. §§ 25.2702-6(a)(1), 25.2702-6(b)(1). If Section 2702 applies to a transfer of a remainder because an applicable family member retained the income interest in the trust (see supra ¶ 19.03[2][a] text accompanying notes 64–67), no relief is provided to the applicable family member upon the subsequent transfer of the retained income interest. The applicable family member has not been subjected twice to gift tax on the value of the income interest.

[309] This is the difference between the value of the Section 2702 interest determined without regard to the Section 2702 special valuation rules and the value under the special rules. Reg. § 25.2702-6(b)(1)(i).

[310] Reg. §§ 25.2702-6(b)(1), 25.2702-6(c) Exs. 1–3.

in valuation.[311] In computing the amount of the increase in taxable gifts attributable to the subsequent transfer, the annual exclusion[312] is first applied to any other non–Section 2702 transfers made by the transferor to the transferee in the same year even if those non–Section 2702 transfers were made later in the calendar year.[313]

To illustrate the previously mentioned rules, assume that Grantor creates a GRIT for Grantor's life and, that under the zero value rule, the amount of the Section 2702 increase in the valuation of the interest transferred is $40,000. Assume also that Grantor subsequently gives the retained life estate then worth $45,000[314] to Grantee and makes no other gifts to Grantee in the year, and the subsequent transfer, after the $11,000 annual exclusion, is $34,000. Since the $34,000 amount is less than the Section 2702 increase in the original transfer to the GRIT of $40,000, the aggregate amount of taxable gifts is reduced by $34,000 in the year in which the subsequent transfer was made, with the result that there is no increase in taxable gifts in the year of the subsequent transfer.[315] Alternatively, if the prior Section 2702 valuation increase had been only $20,000 and the subsequent gift (after an annual exclusion) was $34,000, the reduction in the subsequent year would be $20,000.[316]

The regulations do not indicate whether a subsequent transfer by gift of only a portion of the retained interest qualifies for the regulatory relief.[317] Re-

---

[311] Reg. § 25.2702-6(b)(1).

[312] This rule is inapplicable to a transfer of a reversionary interest that is a future interest. Reg. § 25.2503-3(a).

[313] Reg. § 25.2702-6(b)(2). See Reg. § 25.2702-6(c) Ex. 2.

[314] Assume that, although the actuarial factor has declined over time, the corpus has increased in value, or the assumed rate of return has increased.

[315] The Regulations Section 25.2702-6(b)(1)(i) amount is $40,000, the Regulations Section 25.2702-6(b)(ii) amount is $34,000, and the Section 2502(a)(1) aggregate sum of taxable gifts is reduced by the smaller, $34,000, amount. Since the current $34,000 aggregate sum of gifts is reduced by $34,000, there is a wash and no gift tax liability arises with respect to the subsequent transfer.

If there were another gift of $11,000 of cash by Grantor to Grantee at any time during the year of the subsequent gift, the $11,000 cash transfer would qualify for an annual exclusion. The amount of the remedial reduction of the $45,000 gift would be the lesser of $40,000 or $45,000 (no reduction for an annual exclusion), and the aggregate sum of taxable gifts in the subsequent year would be $5,000 ($45,000 (after the annual exclusion) less the $40,000 amount of the prior transfer). See Reg. § 25.2702-6(c) Ex. 2.

[316] Thus, $14,000 of the subsequent year's gift (after an annual exclusion) would be included in the aggregate sum of taxable gifts for that year. See Reg. § 25.2702-6(c) Ex. 3.

[317] The regulations require a transfer by gift of the interest previously valued under Section 2702 in order to trigger remedial relief. If, for example, the retained interest is an interest to designate among income beneficiaries and a designation is made for a single year, there is no transfer of the retained interest in the trust. See Reg. § 25.2702-6(c) Ex. 6. Alternatively, if the transferor relinquishes the power to designate or specifically

lief should be available to a transfer of either a fractional share or a co-termi-nous portion of the retained interest. In computing the relief reduction, the amount of the current transfer should be compared to an appropriate portion of the Section 2702 increase in the valuation of the gift on the prior transfer. For example, in the first hypothetical mentioned previously, if Grantor transferred one half of the retained income interest (worth $22,500) to Grantee, the reduc-tion should be the lesser of $20,000 (one half of the original transfer) or $11,500 (the current transfer of $22,500 after the $11,000 annual exclusion).[318]

Similarly, if Grantor assigned the right to the future income interest for Grantor's life[319] to an unrelated person, but retained the right to the income for the next ten years,[320] relief should apply to the transfer. The relief should be calculated using a portion of the Section 2702 increase equal to the portion of Grantor's retained ten-year income interest in relation to the right to the in-come for entire Grantor's life expectancy as the Section 2702 increase in amount.[321]

If the subsequent transfer (whether of a retained income interest or a re-versionary interest) is the subject of Section 2513 gift-splitting, the transferor who made the prior transfer may assign one half of the remedial relief to the

---

designates a beneficiary for the entire income term, then there is a transfer of the retained interest and the remedial relief applies. See Reg. § 25.2702-6(c) Ex. 7. While technically these examples track the requirements of the regulations, one can question whether the regulations are too stringent. In the first situation, if Grantor never relinquished the power to designate, there would have been (except to the extent of any annual exclusions al-lowed) a double taxation of the value of the retained interest. The regulations could treat each year's designation as a transfer of a portion of the retained interest and prorate the Section 2702 amount over the life of the payments in granting relief.

[318] As before, there would be no increase in taxable gifts for the year with respect to the subsequent year's transfer. See supra note 315.

Similarly, if Grantor makes a part-gift, part-sale of the interest, the gift portion should qualify for regulatory relief with the same portion of the total amount of Section 2702 increase used to compute the amount of the appropriate reduction. However, with re-spect to the portion of the transfer that involves a sale of Grantor's interest (or, for that matter on a sale of the entire interest), no relief should be provided for a subsequent gift of the sales proceeds because of the potential difficulty in tracing such proceeds.

[319] Grantor's motive would likely be to try to avoid Section 2036, but still retain some income.

[320] If the income after ten years were assigned to Child or some other family mem-ber, then Section 2702 would again apply to the retained income interest and Grantor would have made a gift of the entire income interest (and of the remainder if it is held by a person who is an applicable family member). See supra ¶ 19.03[2][a] text accompanying notes 64–67. In such circumstances, Regulations Section 25.2702-6(a) would definitely apply.

[321] Reg. § 25.2702-6(b)(1)(i). If Grantor then died within the ten-year period (trigger-ing Section 2036), the adjustment to the aggregate sum of taxable gifts under Section 2502(a)(1) should be taken into account in determining the amount of adjusted taxable gifts in the Section 2001(b) estate tax computation.

consenting spouse.[322] If an assignment is made, one half of the Section 2702 increase in amount[323] on the prior transfer is assigned to the consenting spouse in computing the consenting spouse's reduction relief.[324] The reduction applies only when gift-splitting is elected on the subsequent transfer, but not on the initial transfer.[325] If gift-splitting occurs on both transfers, the reduction relief is automatically split between the spouses and no assignment is necessary.[326] If the original transfer was subject to gift-splitting and the subsequent transfer was not, potential reduction relief with respect to the one half of the Section 2702 increase amount assigned to the consenting spouse on the original transfer is lost.

[ii] **Double taxation as a result of the estate tax.** An interest valued under Section 2702 for gift tax purposes may also be subject to the estate tax. However, the relief from double taxation is more limited under the estate tax because when property transferred inter vivos is subjected to the estate tax, adequate relief is frequently provided by the Section 2001(b) estate tax computation mechanism. Returning to the example stated previously involving GRIT property,[327] if the life estate is not subsequently gifted and the transferor dies,

---

[322] Reg. § 25.2702-6(a)(3). See Reg. § 25.2702-6(c) Ex. 4. The assignment must be attached to the Form 709, United States Gift (and Generation-Skipping Transfer) Tax Return, on which the consenting spouse reports the split gift. Reg. § 25.2702-6(a)(3). In the event of the transferor's death prior to the return, the transferor's executor or legal representative should be permitted to make the assignment. Cf. Reg. § 25.2513-2(c).

[323] Reg. § 25.2702-6(b)(1)(i). Assignment of one half of the reduction is an all-or-nothing choice, and an assignment of a portion or less than 50 percent of the relief likely is not allowed. See Reg. § 25.2702-6(a)(3).

[324] See Reg. § 25.2702-6(c) Ex. 4. For example, if Grantor transfers an income interest to Parent and retains a reversionary interest, and subsequently transfers the reversionary interest to a third party and gift-splitting is elected on the subsequent transfer, Grantor may use all of the Section 2702 increase or may assign one half of it to the consenting spouse. Reg. § 25.2702-6(a)(3).

If no gift-splitting occurred on the prior transfer and if the Section 2702 increase in the prior transfer amount exceeds the total subsequent transfer amount, the assignment should be made. See Reg. §§ 25.2702-6(b)(1)(i), 25.2702-6(b)(1)(ii). If the total subsequent transfer exceeds the Section 2702 increase amount (i.e., the retained interest increases in value), the decision whether the assignment should be made involves a consideration of the amount of the excess, the use of annual exclusions, and the relative transfer tax rates of each spouse.

[325] Reg. § 25.2702-6(a)(3).

[326] When the subsequent transfer is subject to gift-splitting, technically an assignment of the transferring spouse's one half of the one half of the Section 2702 increase amount is permitted under the regulations. See Reg. § 25.2702-6(a)(3). Theoretically, such an assignment is inappropriate because each spouse should be viewed as a separate transferor of one half of the property on each of the transfers. Practically, the assignment would rarely be beneficial to the spouses.

[327] See supra text accompanying note 314.

the property generating the income interest would be pulled into the transferor's gross estate under Section 2036.[328] In this situation, no special remedial relief is needed and, indeed, none is provided, because under the Section 2001(b) estate taxing mechanism the transfer whose value is enhanced by Section 2702 is not subject to double taxation. Although the property will be included under Section 2001(b)(1)(A) in the estate tax computation because it is included in the transferor's taxable estate, the prior inter vivos gift will not be included as an adjusted taxable gift under Section 2001(b)(1)(B).[329] Thus, the property will be included only once in the amount subject to estate tax, Section 2001(b)(2) will essentially allow a credit against the estate tax for gift taxes paid,[330] and there will not be double taxation.

For example, assume there is an inter vivos transfer of a remainder worth $200,000 to a family member with a retained life estate in Grantor worth $100,000. The value of the life estate is zero and is included in the gift transfer as a result of the application of Section 2702 and there is a gift transfer valued at $300,000. If the corpus is subsequently included in Grantor's gross estate under Section 2036 when it is worth $400,000, there is no double taxation. The $400,000 is included in the amount of the taxable estate under Section 2001(b)(1)(A), but the $300,000 gift (which includes $100,000 of increased valuation under Section 2702) is not included in adjusted taxable gifts under Section 2001(b)(1)(B) because of the flush language of Section 2001(b) that excludes amounts included in the taxable estate from adjusted taxable gifts. In addition, the gift tax incurred on the full $300,000 gift is credited against the estate tax liability under Section 2001(b)(2).[331]

Special estate tax relief for property transferred by gift is warranted in limited circumstances where the transferred interest (whose value is increased by Section 2702) is not itself included in the transferor's gross estate, but the retained interest is included.[332] In this circumstance, there is a reduction in the *adjusted taxable gifts* under Section 2001(b)(1)(B) by the lesser of: (1) the Section 2702 increase in the valuation of the gift in the prior year or (2) the increase in the transferor's gross estate resulting from the inclusion of the retained interest valued earlier under Section 2702 in the transferor's gross es-

---

[328] Similar consequences generally would occur with respect to gross estate inclusion under Section 2035, Section 2037, or Section 2038. But see infra note 336.

[329] See IRC § 2001(b) (flush language).

[330] See ¶ 2.01[2].

[331] This overall result occurs when gifted property is subsequently included in the gross estate of the transferor, regardless of whether Section 2702 applied to the original transfer.

[332] In such circumstances, adjusted taxable gifts under Section 2001(b)(1)(B) are not reduced as a result of the flush language of Section 2001(b).

tate.[333] This reduction, along with the Section 2001(b)(2) credit reduction for gift taxes incurred, avoids any double inclusion and taxation.

This special estate tax relief reduction is only needed in two situations.[334] The first situation is where a remainder interest in a trust is included in a transferor's gross estate and the included interest was previously valued (when held by the transferor) under the Section 2702 zero valuation rule.[335] Where a Section 2702 transfer involved a zero valuation of a remainder (or reversionary) interest, and the remainder (or reversion) is subsequently included in the transferor's gross estate (generally under Section 2033),[336] the Section 2001(b) estate taxing mechanism generally does not prevent double taxation.[337] The prior gift was a gift of only an income interest, which is a different interest than the remainder interest that is included in the transferor's gross estate. Accordingly, the flush language of Section 2001(b) does not apply and the value of the remainder (or reversion) is included in both the gift tax and estate tax

---

[333] Reg. § 25.2702-6(b)(1). This interpretation of the regulation takes some liberty with the language of Regulations Section 25.2702-6(b)(1)(ii).

[334] See Reg. § 25.2702-6(a)(2).

[335] Reg. § 25.2702-6(a)(2)(ii). This rule does not apply to a Section 2702(c)(4) valuation because Section 2702(c)(4) applies only to a retained term interest, not a retained reversionary interest. See supra ¶ 19.03[4][b] text accompanying note 286. The flush language of Regulations Section 25.2702-6(a)(2) referring to valuation under the Section 2704(c)(4) rule (Reg. § 25.2702-2(c)) should apply only in conjunction with Regulations Section 25.2702-6(a)(2)(i).

[336] This first situation can involve circumstances in which the remainder interest is included in the transferor's gross estate under sections other than Section 2033. For example, assume that Grantor transfers an income interest to Child for Child's life and a remainder to whomever of Grantor's Grandchildren Grantor selects. Under Section 2702, the trust remainder is treated as a retained interest (Reg. § 25.2702-2(a)(4)) and is given a zero valuation (IRC § 2702(a)(2)(A)) increasing the value of the income interest to the full value of the corpus. See supra ¶ 19.03[2][a] note 71. If Child predeceases Grantor, there is a second gift transfer when Grantor selects the recipient Grandchild and reduction relief is available. See Reg. § 25.2702-6(a). If Grantor predeceases Child, the remainder interest (which was previously included in the value of the gift due to Section 2702) is included in Grantor's gross estate under Section 2038 because Grantor had a power to alter the remainderpersons of the trust. Technically, Section 2036(a)(2) also would apply to include the remainder interest because Grantor immediately prior to Grantor's death could have altered the income during Grantor's life among the Grandchildren had Child predeceased Grantor. It is also possible to create a scenario where there would have been inclusion under Section 2035 or Section 2037 and where Regulations Section 25.2702-6(a)(2)(ii) would then apply. If in the previous example, Grantor had relinquished the power over the remainder within three years before Grantor's death, Section 2035 would have applied to include the remainder. If the income interest to Child had been for Grantor's life (rather than Child's life), Section 2037 would have applied to the remainder. See IRC § 2037(b)(2). In all of these situations, the regulations provide for a reduction in adjusted taxable gifts under Section 2001(b)(1)(B). Reg. §§ 25.2702-6(a)(2)(ii), 25.2702-6(b)(1).

[337] Cf. Reg. § 25.2702-6(b)(3); infra text accompanying notes 346–349.

Section 2702

transfer base and is essentially taxed twice.[338] In these circumstances, reduction relief is appropriately granted by reducing the adjusted taxable gifts under Section 2001(b)(1)(B). For example, assume that Grantor makes a $200,000 gift transfer (after an annual exclusion) of an income interest to a family member retaining a reversion worth $100,000. Section 2702 increases the value of the transferred income interest to $300,000. Assume further that the reversion is subsequently included in Grantor's gross estate under Section 2033 when it is worth $400,000.[339] The amount of adjusted taxable gifts under Section 2001(b)(1)(B) is reduced by the lesser of: (1) the $100,000 prior increase in the gift under Section 2702 or (2) the $400,000 inclusion in the gross estate.[340]

The estate tax reduction rule is also warranted where a term interest in a trust previously valued under Section 2702[341] is subsequently included in a transferor's gross estate *solely* by reason of Section 2033. Adjusted taxable gifts are again reduced.[342] This situation usually[343] occurs where a term interest holder purchases an interest for a term of years in a joint purchase that is taxed under Section 2702(c)(2)[344] and the term interest holder subsequently dies before expiration of the term of years. Double taxation occurs because the purchased term of years interest is essentially transferred by gift as a result of Section 2702(a)(2) and subsequently the value of the remaining term of years is included in the term interest holder's gross estate under Section 2033.[345]

In the two estate tax relief reduction situations stated previously, it is arguable (although likely not successfully arguable) that the Section 2001(b)(1)(B) adjusted taxable gifts are reduced as a result of the flush lan-

---

[338] It is included in the estate tax computation, both in the Section 2001(b)(1)(A) taxable estate and Section 2001(b)(1)(B) adjusted taxable gift amount.

[339] The $400,000 amount is included in the estate tax computation under Section 2001(b)(1)(A) taxable estate amount.

[340] Reg. § 25.2702-6(b)(1). As a result, the Section 2001(b)(1)(B) adjusted taxable gifts include only the $200,000 actual gift of the income interest on the original transfer without any valuation enhancement by valuation of the retained interest under Section 2702.

[341] The term interest could previously have been valued under the zero valuation rule or the Section 2702(c)(4) rule. See Reg. § 25.2702-6(a)(2).

[342] Reg. § 25.2702-6(a)(2)(i).

[343] If Estate of D'Ambrosio v. Comm'r, 101 F3d 309 (3d Cir. 1996), and the cases which follow it are properly decided (see ¶¶ 4.08[1][a], 4.08[7][c] text accompanying notes 140–146 and infra note 367) and Grantor sells a remainder (for its fair market value) to a family member, and retains the income for a term of years, Section 2036 does not apply when Grantor predeceases the term of years, but Section 2033 does apply to include the value of the income for the remaining term of years in Grantor's gross estate. In that situation, Regulations Section 25.2702-6(a)(2)(i) would again be applicable.

[344] See supra ¶ 19.03[4][a].

[345] See Reg. § 25.2702-6(c) Ex. 8.

guage in Section 2001(b).[346] If so, relief is provided by the Section 2001(b) mechanism and, if a reduction is also provided by the regulations, there would be a double reduction of adjusted taxable gifts.[347] In part to preclude such an inappropriate double reduction, any regulatory reduction relief[348] is reduced by any reduction in the adjusted taxable gifts under Section 2001(b)(1)(B).[349]

[d] The Open Statute of Limitations

If a transfer occurring as a result of the application of Section 2702 is not adequately disclosed on a gift tax return,[350] the statute of limitations remains open for an unlimited period.[351] The open statute of limitations parallels a similar rule originally applicable to transfers subject only to Sections 2701(a) and 2701(d),[352] and Section 2702, but now applicable to all gift tax transfers.[353] However, the adequate disclosure requirements for Sections 2702 (as well as Sections 2701 and 2701(d)) transfers are not as broad as the adequate disclosure requirements for other gift transfers.[354] Under the rules applicable to such transfers,[355] the gift tax return (or seemingly a statement attached to the return) must provide: (1) a description of the transactions, including a description of the transferred and retained interests and the methods used in valuing each;[356] (2) the identity of, and relationship between all of the parties (including related

---

[346] This seems unlikely, because the gifts whose value the operation of Section 2702 increased are not includible in the gross estate of the decedent.

[347] Both the flush language of Section 2001(b) and Regulations Section 25.2702-6(b)(1) would apply.

[348] Reg. § 25.2702-6(b)(1).

[349] Reg. § 25.2702-6(b)(3). This special reduction rule applies in a situation in which a reduction in adjusted taxable gifts occurs as a result of the operation of Section 2001(e). See Reg. § 25.2702-6(c) Ex. 5.

[350] See ¶ 9.04[10].

[351] IRC § 6501(c)(9).

[352] See ¶ 19.02[5][d].

[353] The original rule was applicable to Sections 2701 and 2702 transfers made after 1990.

[354] Compare Reg. § 301.6501(c)-1(e)(2) (applicable to Section 2702) with Reg. §§ 301.6501(c)-1(f)(2), 301.6501(c)-1(f)(3) (general adequate disclosure rules). See IRC § 6501(c)(9); ¶ 9.04[10]. Regulations Section 301.6501(c)-1(e) is applicable to transfers on or after January 28, 1992. Reg. § 301.6501(c)-1(f)(3).

[355] A transfer includes the entire transaction or series of transactions (including any transaction that affected the transferred interest) of which the transfer (or taxable event) was a part. Reg. § 301.6501(c)-1(e)(2).

[356] Reg. § 301.6501(c)-1(e)(2)(i).

parties holding equity interests);[357] and (3) a detailed description (including all actuarial factors and discount rates) used to determine the amount of the gift.[358]

[e] The Relationship of Section 2702 to Other Taxes

The relationship of Section 2702 to the estate, income, and generation-skipping transfer taxes is relatively clear.[359] A Section 2702 "transfer" is a transfer only for purposes of the gift tax and not for the other taxes.[360] However, it is unclear whether the value of a transfer as determined under Section 2702 establishes value only for the gift tax, only for the other transfer taxes, or for all taxes,[361] although as is seen in the following discussion, this issue is not as significant in the Section 2702 context as it is under Section 2701.[362] The relationship of Section 2702 to each of the three taxes is considered separately in the following.

[i] **The estate tax.** When Section 2702 increases the value of a gift transfer, the increase is generally disregarded for estate tax purposes,[363] regardless of whether the Section 2702 transfer involves a direct transfer with a retained interest[364] or the transfer involves a joint purchase.[365] Gift transfers and their valuation are irrelevant for estate tax purposes because the estate tax has its own transfer and valuation rules independent of the gift tax provisions.[366] Fur-

---

[357] Reg. § 301.6501(c)-1(e)(2)(ii).

[358] Reg. § 301.6501(c)-1(e)(2)(iii). For entity interests that are not actively traded, this includes financial and other data used in determining value, such as balance sheets and earnings statements. Id.

[359] Compare the unclear relationship of Section 2701 to the other taxes. See ¶ 19.02[5][f].

[360] Section 2702(a)(1) provides that "*[s]olely* for purposes of determining whether a transfer . . . is a gift. . . . " (emphasis added).

[361] Section 2702(a)(1) provides "[s]olely for purposes of determining whether a transfer . . . is a gift (and the value of such transfer). . . . " The clause "the value of such transfer" may be modified by the term "gift" and be read "the value of such transfer *by gift*" with the result that the Section 2702 value would apply only for purposes of the Chapter 12 gift tax. In the alternative, the clause "value of such transfer" may be read more broadly to establish value for all other taxes (cf. IRC § 7806(b)) or only for other *transfer* taxes.

[362] Compare the relationship of valuation under Section 2701 to valuation under the other taxes. See ¶¶ 19.02[5][f][i]–¶ 19.02[5][f][iii].

[363] This statement disregards the administratively provided relief in Regulations Sections 25.2702-6(a)(1) and 25.2702-6(b)(1).

[364] This statement disregards the administratively provided relief in Regulations Sections 25.2702-6(a)(1) and 25.2702-6(b)(1).

[365] Reg. § 25.2702-4(c).

[366] See IRC §§ 2031, 2032, 2032A. Cf. IRC § 1014.

thermore, if there is a direct transfer with a retained life estate or a retained income interest that has not expired at the transferor's death, the question of adequate and full consideration for Section 2036 purposes is resolved under Section 2036, without regard to the amount of the Section 2702 transfer.[367] If there is a joint purchase with adequate consideration paid by all parties, the Section 2702 "transfer"[368] is not a transfer for Section 2036 purposes.[369]

[ii] **The income tax.** If property is transferred and Section 2702 applies to increase the amount of the gift transfer resulting in an increase in the gift taxes paid on the transfer, the increased gift taxes paid are used in computing the Section 1015(d) adjustment to basis for gift taxes paid. For example, if Transferor transfers property with an adjusted basis of $200,000 and fair market value of $500,000 to a trust retaining an income interest for a term of years with a family member remainderperson, the Section 2702 amount of the transfer is $500,000. Assuming the transfer generates $200,000 in gift taxes, the trust's adjusted basis in the property is $320,000, $200,000 under Section 1015(a) plus $120,000 ($300,000/$500,000 times $200,000) under Section 1015(d).[370] In the event of a joint purchase, the acquired property would generally have a Section 1012 cost basis equalling the fair market value of the property acquired jointly. Even though Section 2702 would possibly create a gift

---

[367] Even without regard to Section 2702, there is controversy over what amount is adequate and full consideration for Section 2036 purposes. One line of cases requires consideration equal to the full value of the transferred corpus in order to avoid Section 2036. See, e.g., Estate of Gradow v. United States, 897 F2d 516 (Fed. Cir. 1990). The other line of cases requires consideration equal only to the value of the remainder interest. See Estate of D'Ambrosio v. Comm'r, 101 F3d 309 (3d Cir. 1996); Wheeler v.United States, 116 F3d 749 (5th Cir. 1997); Estate of Magnin v. Comm'r, 184 F3d 1074 (9th Cir. 1999). See ¶¶ 4.08[1][a], ¶ 4.08[7][c] text accompanying notes 140–146. The cases may be reconcilable. See ¶ 4.08[7][c] text accompanying notes 145-146. The enactment of Section 2702 does not alter the outcome of the controversy. Assuming the D'Ambrosio line of cases is correct, the joint purchase of an interest in a GRAT, GRUT, or QPRT in a bona fide transaction with adequate and full consideration should avoid a gift (see Priv. Ltr. Rul. 9841017 (Oct. 9, 1998)) and any inclusion of the property in the term interest holder's gross estate. See also Jordan "Sale of Remainder Interests: Reconciling Gradow v. United States and Section 2702," 14 Va. Tax. Rev. 672 (1995); Jensen, "Estate and Gift Effects of Selling a Remainder: Have D'Ambrosio, Wheeler, and Magnin Changed the Rules?" 4 Fla. Tax Rev. 537 (1999).

[368] IRC § 2702(c)(2).

[369] As a result, there is no transfer of underlying property by the owner of the term interest to trigger Section 2036. Thus, no Estate of Gradow, Estate of D'Ambrosio issue is raised. See supra note 367, supra text accompanying note 360. Cf. supra ¶ 19.03[4][a] note 282.

[370] IRC §§ 1015(d)(1), 1015(d)(6). An identical $320,000 income tax basis would result if the property worth $500,000 with an adjusted basis of $200,000 were transferred to a trust with income to transferor's Parent for life and a reversion to Transferor and, as a result, the Section 2702 transfer generated $200,000 in gift taxes.

and its valuation enhancement of the transfer generates additional gift taxes, there would be no Section 1015 adjustment because of the lack of net appreciation in the value of the gift, assuming the interest deemed gifted by Section 2702 was purchased at its fair market value.[371]

The same result would occur even if the joint purchase involved a purchase of a remainder interest by a family member from the outright owner of the property resulting in a Section 2702 transfer.[372]

[iii] **The generation-skipping transfer tax.** Section 2702 will not affect any consequences under the generation-skipping transfer tax. A Section 2702 transfer is not a transfer for purposes of Chapter 13.[373] While Section 2702 can create a gift transfer, in addition to enhancing the value of property actually transferred, it is tempting to conclude that Section 2702 can create a direct skip transfer as well. A Section 2702 gift transfer, although a transfer subject to a tax imposed by Chapter 12, is not a transfer of "an interest in property" under Section 2612(c)(1) because of the definition of "an interest in property" under Section 2652(c).[374] For example, if Transferor creates a trust with a retained income interest for a term of years with a remainder to Grandchild and Section 2702 applies to increase the amount of the transfer, it might be argued that there is a direct skip of the entire value of the property to Grandchild.[375] However, the transfer to Grandchild is not of an interest in property as required by Section 2612(c) and there is no direct skip.[376] Similarly, if a transferor makes a joint purchase with a skip person,[377] the skip person does not have a Section 2652(c) interest in the property and there is no direct skip.[378]

---

[371] See IRC § 1015(d)(6). Additionally, even though a gift is concocted under Section 2702 generating gift taxes, Section 1015(d)(1) limits any increase for gift taxes paid to the fair market value of the property acquired by gift.

[372] See supra ¶ 19.03[4][a] text accompanying notes 268, 269. For example, if Transferor sold a remainder worth $100,000 to Child in property that Transferor owned outright and that had a $200,000 adjusted basis with a $500,000 fair market value and the remainder interest had an adjusted basis of $40,000, Transferor would recognize a $60,000 gain on the sale and there would be a $400,000 gift as a result of Section 2702. If the gift generated $160,000 in gift taxes, Child's basis for the property acquired would be its $100,000 cost.

[373] See supra text accompanying note 360. Nevertheless, the two taxes interrelate for estate planning purposes. See Garner "Planning With Chapter 14 and GST Interaction," 21 Est. Plan. 147 (May & June 1994).

[374] See IRC § 2652(c)(1)(A) (parenthetical).

[375] See IRC § 2612(c).

[376] See IRC § 2652(c)(1)(A) (parenthetical). Section 2642(f) would postpone the occurrence of the direct skip until the end of the estate tax inclusion period when the property is valued. In addition, see ¶ 16.02[7][a].

[377] See IRC § 2613(a).

[378] IRC §§ 2612(c), 2652(c)(1)(A).

Furthermore, a transfer by Child of a remainder interest in a trust in which Parent held the income interest to Child's Grandchild would be a transfer of the entire trust corpus under Section 2702.[379] However, the transfer would not be a direct skip because Child has not transferred a Section 2652(c) interest in property to Child's Grandchild.[380]

Section 2702 valuation is not used for any generation-skipping transfer tax purposes.[381] Under the generation-skipping transfer tax provisions, it is the fair market value of the property actually transferred, not its Section 2702 enhanced value, which is used in measuring the amount of a direct skip, taxable termination, or taxable distribution.[382] In the determination of the applicable fraction, it is the fair market value of all the property held in the trust that is considered, not the value of the separate individuals' interests in the trust that may be shifted from one individual to another by Section 2702.[383] Shifting the value of one person's interest in property held in the trust to another person does not matter, because in the determination of the denominator of the applicable fraction the fair market value of all interests in the trust is considered, regardless of the value of the separate interests under Section 2702.[384]

[f] Effective Dates

Section 2702 is applicable to transfers after October 8, 1990.[385]

---

[379] See supra ¶ 19.03[2][a] text following note 64.

[380] IRC § 2652(c)(1)(A) (parenthetical).

[381] Compare the more complex valuation issues involved in the interrelationship of Section 2701 to the generation-skipping transfer tax. See ¶ 19.02[5][f][iii].

[382] IRC §§ 2621, 2622, 2623.

[383] IRC § 2642(b).

[384] IRC § 2642(b).

[385] Omnibus Budget Reconciliation Act of 1990, Pub. L. No. 101-508, § 11602(e)(1), 104 Stat. 1388-1, 1388-500, reprinted in 1991-2 CB 481, 529. The final regulations are effective as of January 28, 1992. Reg. § 25.2702-7. For transfers between October 8, 1990, and January 28, 1992, taxpayers may rely on any reasonable interpretation of the statute, which includes both the proposed and final regulations. Id. Proposed Regulations Sections 25.2702-5(b)(1), 25.2702-5(c)(1), and 25.2702-5(c)(9) are effective with respect to trusts created after May 16, 1996. Prop. Reg. § 25.2702-7.

¶ 19.04 SECTION 2703. CERTAIN RIGHTS AND RESTRICTIONS DISREGARDED

[1] Introduction

[a] General Principles

For purposes of the estate, gift, and generation-skipping transfer taxes, the valuation of any property may be affected by agreements such as options, buy-sell agreements, or restrictions on the sale of such property. It would be a bonanza for a taxpayer or a taxpayer's estate if the taxpayer could enter into an agreement with a family member, which was not binding as to third parties, to sell property inter vivos or at taxpayer's death for a price equal to a small portion of the property's fair market value and to have that sale price establish valuation for transfer tax purposes. Permitting such agreements to establish valuation could lead to an annihilation of the entire federal transfer tax system.

At the other end of the spectrum, arm's-length agreements, even if among family members, should be respected for transfer tax purposes if they are bona fide fair market value business arrangements. The effect on valuation of agreements falling in between these two dichotomies has led to continuous controversy between the government and taxpayers. Bridging the gap between these dichotomies to provide some certainty has been an ongoing process for the courts and Congress. Section 2703 adds a degree more of certainty to the area, but many questions remain.

[b] Background

Historically, much of the case law in this area involves buy-sell agreements with respect to businesses,[1] but the principles established apply to almost any type of property that lacks easily measurable valuation. In 1958, the Treasury promulgated Regulations Section 20.2031-2(h),[2] which encompassed prior case law[3] and essentially permitted an agreement to establish value if:

---

[1] See St. Louis County Bank v. United States, 674 F2d 1207 (8th Cir. 1982); Carpenter v. Comm'r, 64 TCM (CCH) 1274 (1992); Estate of Lauder v. Comm'r, 64 TCM (CCH) 1643 (1992); Seltzer v. Comm'r, 50 TCM (CCH) 1250 (1985); Rudolph v. United States, 93-1 USTC ¶ 60,130 (SD Ind. 1993); Reg. § 20.2031-2(h) (providing rules specifically related to "securities").

[2] See TD 6296, 23 Fed. Reg. 4529 (June 23, 1958).

[3] See Bensel v. Comm'r, 36 BTA 246 (1937), nonacq. sub nom. 1937-2 CB 36, aff'd, 100 F2d 639 (3d Cir. 1938); Estate of Salt v. Comm'r, 17 TC 92 (1951), acq. 1952-1 CB 4; Estate of Weil v. Comm'r, 22 TC 1267 (1954), acq. 1955-2 CB 10; Estate of Lit-

1. The price of the property was readily determinable under the terms of the agreement;

2. The agreement restricted the taxpayer's lifetime disposition of the property;

3. The decedent's estate was obligated to some extent to sell the property; and

4. The agreement represented "a bona fide business arrangement and not a device to pass the decedent's [property] to the natural objects of decedent's bounty for less than adequate and full consideration in money or money's worth."[4]

A substantial body of case law interpreting the regulation subsequently developed, much of which is discussed in the following text. One of the most significant cases was *St. Louis County Bank v. United States*,[5] which involved a family buy-sell arrangement relating to the closely held stock of a family corporation. The court held that while there was a valid business purpose for the agreement (a desire to maintain family control of the stock),[6] "a reasonable inference could be drawn that the agreement was testamentary in nature and a device for the avoidance of estate tax."[7] Thus, the court split the business purpose and device language of the regulation into two separate requirements both of which had to be satisfied to establish valuation.

[c] Enactment of Section 2703

When Congress introduced Chapter 14 in its attack on estate freezes,[8] it enacted Section 2703 as one weapon in that attack.[9] Section 2703 codifies

---

tick v. Comm'r, 31 TC 181 (1958), acq. 1959-2 CB 5, acq. and withdrawn in part, 1984-2 CB 1.

[4] Reg. § 20.2031-2(h). The specific requirements of the regulation are considered infra ¶ 19.04[3].

[5] St. Louis County Bank v. United States, 674 F2d 1207 (8th Cir. 1982), rev'g and remanding Roth v. United States, 511 F. Supp. 653 (ED Mo. 1981). See infra ¶ 19.04[3][b] text accompanying notes 62–72.

[6] See Estate of Bischoff v. Comm'r, 69 TC 32 (1977); Estate of Reynolds v. Comm'r, 55 TC 172 (1970), acq. 1971-2 CB 2, 3; Slocum v. United States, 256 F. Supp. 753 (SDNY 1966); infra ¶ 19.04[3][a].

[7] St. Louis County Bank v. United States, 674 F2d 1207, 1210 (8th Cir. 1982). The court stated that the decedent was in poor health at the time of the agreement, the agreement had not been used at another family member's death, and the property had zero valuation under the formula in the agreement.

[8] See ¶ 19.01[1].

[9] Omnibus Budget Reconciliation Act of 1990, Pub. L. No. 101-508, § 11602(a), 104 Stat. 1388-1, 1388-498 (1990), reprinted in 1991-2 CB 481, 524.

some of the current law,[10] adds a new requirement that generally must be met in order for an agreement to be taken into consideration in valuation,[11] and is intended to merely supplement rather than replace prior law.[12]

Section 2703(a) provides that for purposes of the estate, gift, and generation-skipping transfer taxes,[13] the value of any property is determined without regard to any option, agreement, or other right to acquire or use the property at less than the fair market value (without regard to such option, agreement, or right) or to any restriction on the right to sell or use such property.[14] Section 2703(b) creates an exception and allows such rights or restrictions to be considered in valuing property if three separate requirements, two of which are extracted from Regulations Section 20.2031-2(h), are met.[15] However, even if a right or restriction is not swept aside under the Section 2703(a) rule, the Section 2703(b) exception just opens the door to look at the right or restriction as a factor in valuing the property. Further requirements must be satisfied for the rights or restrictions to be effective in establishing valuation.[16]

[2] The General Rule of Section 2703

The general rule, as set forth in Section 2703(a), states that the fair market value of property is to be determined without regard to any option, agreement, or other right to acquire or use the property at a price less than the fair market

---

[10] IRC §§ 2703(b)(1), 2703(b)(2).

[11] IRC § 2703(b)(3).

[12] Congress did not intend the enactment of Section 2703 to alter the requirements for giving weight to a buy-sell agreement. Explanatory Material Concerning Committee on Finance 1990 Reconciliation Submission Pursuant to House Concurrent Resolution 310, 136 Cong. Rec. S15683 (Oct. 18, 1990). This cite to "Explanatory Material" deserves further comment. The Omnibus Budget Reconciliation Act of 1990 was prepared under a very short deadline. In order to avoid delay, the bill was brought to the floor of the Senate without the printing of a formal report. In an effort to complete the legislative record, the report language was merely printed in the *Record* at the beginning of the debate on the reconciliation bill.

[13] See Reg. § 25.2703-1(a)(1).

[14] IRC § 2703(a). See Reg. § 25.2703-1(a)(2); Priv. Ltr. Rul. 9622036 (Mar. 4, 1996) (Section 2703 inapplicable because shareholders required to buy stock at its fair market value). See also Dees, "The Slaying of Frankenstein's Monster: The Repeal and Replacement of Section 2036(c)," 69 Taxes 151, 163 (1991); Adams, Herpe, & Carey, "Buy-Sell Agreements After Chapter 14" 132 Tr. & Est. 22 (May 1993). For a comprehensive discussion of all forms of estate freezing techniques, see Zaritsky & Aucutt, Structuring Estate Freezes Under Chapter 14, Warren, Gorham & Lamont (1993).

[15] See Reg. § 25.2703-1(b)(3) in essence conclusively presuming the requirements are met in limited circumstances. See infra ¶ 19.04[4].

[16] See infra ¶ 19.04[6].

value[17] or to any restriction on the right to sell or use such property.[18] The rule applies regardless of the source of the right or restriction. The option, agreement, right, or restriction that is to be disregarded may be found in the articles or bylaws of a corporation, a shareholders' agreement, a partnership agreement, an agreement among partners, or any other agreement; in addition, it may merely be implicit in the capital structure of an entity.[19]

Although the implication of the language of Section 2703(a) is that it applies only to buy-sell agreements,[20] a broad reading of the statutory language could extend the scope of the section to apply to an entire partnership agreement to disregard an entire partnership entity.[21]

---

[17] IRC § 2703(a)(1). While a literal reading of the statute would appear to permit a right to acquire property at greater than its fair market value in valuing the property to be taken into consideration, seemingly any such right, even though it is not subject to Section 2703(a), should be given the same degree of analysis as any other right. For example, if Decedent's gross estate is worth less than the Section 2010(c) applicable exclusion amount (say $800,000) and Decedent entered into a binding buy-sell agreement with the sole heir of Decedent's estate to acquire the property for the applicable exclusion amount, the agreement should not establish value. Cf. IRC § 1014. Even though Section 2703(a) would seem in such circumstances to disregard the Section 2703(b)(2) device requirement growing out of Regulations Section § 20.2031-2(h) (as expanded in St. Louis County Bank v. United States, 674 F2d 1207 (8th Cir. 1982) and infra ¶ 19.04[3][b] text accompanying notes 62–72), the device language of the regulation should be used to disregard this agreement.

[18] IRC § 2703(a)(2). See Reg. § 25.2703-1(d) Ex. 1 (a lease on property whose terms were not comparable to leases entered into among unrelated parties is a restriction disregarded under Section 2703(a)).

[19] Reg. § 25.2703-1(a)(3). See Explanatory Material Concerning Committee on Finance 1990 Reconciliation Submission Pursuant to House Concurrent Resolution 310, 136 Cong. Rec. S15683 (daily ed. Oct. 18, 1990); supra ¶ 19.04[1][c] note 12.

[20] See IRC §§ 2703(a)(1) (which applies to "any option, agreement or other right to acquire or use the property . . . "), 2703(a)(2) (which applies to "any restriction on the right to sell or use such property").

[21] This broad interpretation of the section has been expounded by the Service in a series of rulings. TAMs 9719006 (Jan. 14, 1997), 9723009 (Feb. 24, 1997), 9725002 (Mar. 3, 1997), 9735003 (May 8, 1997); Priv. Ltr. Ruls. 9730004 (Apr. 3, 1997), 9842003 (July 2, 1998); TAM 9736004 (June 6, 1997) (the latter TAM involving a limited liability company). In each of the situations, shortly before the decedent's death, assets of the decedent were contributed to a limited partnership in which the other partners were exclusively or primarily, the members of the decedent's family. In several, the decedent's intended, testamentary beneficiaries, acting as agents of the decedent, transferred the decedent's assets to the partnership. In all of the situations, the Service concluded that the assets transferred at the decedent's death were the underlying assets contributed to the partnership (and not the partnership interests). In each of the situations, the Service also concluded that the exception of Section 2703(b) was inapplicable because all of its requirements were not met. See infra ¶ 19.04[3].

[T]he series of transactions (the creation and funding of the partnership, and the transfer of the partnership interests) is properly characterized as one integrated transaction, i.e., the transfer at the decedent's death of the underlying assets, subject to the partnership agreement, by the decedent.[22]

The argument that has been advanced by the Service to disregard the partnership entity is that the entire partnership structure is a "restriction" on the assets inside of the partnership that should not affect valuation. The argument interprets the term "property" as used in the introductory clause of Section 2703(a) to refer to the assets contained in the partnership.[23] After docketing several cases for trial but subsequently dropping or settling them,[24] the Service finally litigated two cases,[25] in which the courts failed to adopt either of the two arguments and apply Section 2703(a).[26]

One type of right or restriction is not disregarded under Section 2703(a):[27] a perpetual restriction[28] on the use of real property that on a prior transfer

---

[22] TAM 9719006 (Jan. 14, 1997).

[23] An article providing a detailed discussion of the arguments on each side of the issue is Bray, "Does Section 2703 Apply to the Valuation of Family Limited Partnership?" 75 Taxes 198 (1997). See also FSA 200143004 (July 5, 2001) (expounding the Service's argument); Kasner, Tax Notes Today 50-47 (1997) (asserting that the Service's position is wrong).

[24] The cases are discussed in Eastland, "The Art of Making Uncle Sam Your Assignee Instead of Your Senior Partner: The Use of Partnership in Estate Planning," ALI-ABA Cont. Legal Ed. 892 (Nov. 16, 1998).

[25] Church v. United States, 85 AFTR2d 2000-804 (WD Tex. 2000), aff'd without opinion, 88 AFTR2d 2001-5352 (5th Cir. 2001), Estate of Strangi v Comm'r, 115 TC 478 (2000) (reviewed by the court).

[26] The court in Church v. United States, 85 AFTR2d 2000-804 (WD Tex. 2000), aff'd without opinion, 88 AFTR2d 2001-5352 (5th Cir. 2001), also refused to adopt a *Murphy* case approach of disregard transfers of the entity (see Estate of Murphy v. Comm'r, 60 TCM (CCH) 73 (1990); ¶ 4.02[4][b] note 163) and to find a gift or creation of the entity on a disappearing value theory (see ¶ 10.01[2][b] text accompanying note 25). The court in Estate of Strangi v Comm'r, 115 TC 478 (2000), considered only the "property" argument, but also held that the partnership had economic substance even though it was skeptical of the nontax business purposes offered by the taxpayer.
It is likely that in the future the Service will attempt to use Section 2703(a) to disregard various provisions or restrictions in a partnership agreement or imposed by state law, rather than to disregard the partnership itself, although no cases have yet been decided. See FSA 200143004 (July 5, 2001) (where the Service made such an argument with respect to an S corporation).

[27] Reg. § 25.2703-1(a)(4).

[28] Although such easements in gross are problematic, state legislatures sometimes come to the rescue. See Fla. Stat. § 704.06 (2001).

qualified[29] for a gift tax charitable deduction under Section 2522(d)[30] or for an estate tax charitable deduction under Section 2055(f).[31] Instead, such a qualified easement is taken into consideration in valuing the real property for federal transfer tax purposes, generally decreasing the value of the property. For an easement to qualify under those sections, the easement need not be for conservation purposes.[32] Although common types of such easements include a facade easement where the owner of historic real property permanently relinquishes the right to alter or demolish the property, a scenic easement, or an open space easement,[33] an easement in perpetuity for any purpose will qualify.[34]

[3] The Section 2703(b) Statutory Exception

In order for any option, agreement, right, or restriction to be taken into consideration in valuing the property to which they relate, Section 2703(b) lists three separate requirements[35] that generally[36] must be satisfied:

    1. The option, right, agreement, or restriction must be a bona fide business arrangement;[37]

---

[29] If the transfers were concurrent (for example, at death) either a Section 2055(f) deduction or a Section 2703 reduction should be allowed, but to allow both would result in a double deduction. Cf. IRC § 2055(d). Since the regulation uses the term "qualified," it applies only where there was a previous qualification and deduction. On a concurrent transfer at death, the property should be included in the gross estate at its full fair market value and a Section 2055(f) deduction should be allowed. Similarly, on a concurrent inter vivos transfer there would be a single Section 2522 deduction from the fair market value of the property.

[30] IRC § 2522(d) allows a deduction for the value of a restriction granted in perpetuity on the use that may be made of real property that is given to a qualified organization. See IRC §§ 170(h)(2)(c), 170(h)(3), 170(h)(5)(A); ¶ 11.02[4].

[31] Section 2055(f) allows a deduction for the value of a restriction granted in perpetuity on the use that may be made of real property to a qualified organization. See IRC §§ 170(h)(2)(C), 170(h)(3), 170(h)(5)(A); ¶ 5.05[7][c].

[32] IRC §§ 2055(f), 2522(d) (second parentheticals). See ¶¶ 5.05[7][c] note 348, 11.02[2][d] note 100.

[33] See IRC § 170(h)(4)(A); Symington v. Comm'r, 87 TC 892 (1986); Hilborn v. Comm'r, 85 TC 677 (1985); Fannon v. Comm'r, 56 TCM (CCH) 1587 (1989).

[34] See supra note 31.

[35] IRC § 2703(b); Reg. § 25.2703-1(b)(2). See TAM 9550002 (Aug. 31, 1955) (none of the requirements met).

[36] But see another exception provided by Regulations Section 25.2703-1(b)(3), discussed infra ¶ 19.04[4].

[37] IRC § 2703(b)(1). See also Reg. § 25.2703-1(b)(1)(i).

2. The option, agreement, right, or restriction must not be a device to transfer property to members of the decedent's family for less than full and adequate consideration in money or money's worth;[38] and

3. The terms of the option, right, agreement, or restriction must be comparable to similar arrangements entered into by persons in an arm's-length transaction.[39]

The first two requirements (the bona fide business arrangement and no device requirements) seemingly are identical to two of the requirements under pre–Section 2703 law,[40] although the legislative history of Section 2703 states that these requirements are merely "*similar* to those contained in the present Treasury regulations."[41] The third requirement appears to be new.[42] Because of the obvious similarity between the exception under Section 2703(b) and the exception created under Regulations Section 20.2031-2(h), much of the case law under Regulations Section 20.2031-2(h) is applicable as well to Section 2703(b). Each of the requirements will be considered separately here.

Although the statute and regulations under Section 2703 provide the elements required for the exception to apply, they fail to provide the applicable time for evaluation. The taxpayer will desire to have an agreement examined when entered, but the Service is more likely to examine the agreement when the agreement's limitations are applied. At this later time, it is more likely that the agreement will fail to approximate fair market value, the agreement will look more testamentary in nature, and any valid business purpose for the agreement's inception will be clouded by the fact that family members have received property for less than its fair market value and the estate has been able to support a valuation that also does not approximate that figure. In general, under Regulations Section 20.2031-2(h), the Service has been unsuccessful in its argument for evaluation of the applicable elements at the later time.[43] This is not true, however, in the case where provisions of the agreement have been modified following their initial adoption. If modification occurs, both the

---

[38] IRC § 2703(b)(2). See also Reg. § 25.2703-1(b)(1)(ii).

[39] IRC § 2703(b)(3). See also Reg. § 25.2703-1(b)(1)(iii).

[40] IRC §§ 2703(b)(1), 2703(b)(2). See Reg. § 20.2031-2(h); supra ¶ 19.04[1][b] text accompanying note 4.

[41] See Explanatory Material Concerning Committee on Finance 1990 Reconciliation Submission Pursuant to House Concurrent Resolution 310, 136 Cong. Rec. S15683 (Oct. 18, 1990) (emphasis added.) The requirements appear to be identical, not merely similar. See supra ¶ 19.04[1][c] note 12.

[42] IRC § 2703(b)(3). See infra ¶ 19.04[3][c] especially text accompanying notes 97, 98.

[43] Rudolph v. United States, 93-1 USTC ¶ 60,130 (SD Ind. 1993). See also St. Louis County Bank v. United States, 674 F2d 1207 (8th Cir. 1982); Slocum v. United States, 256 F. Supp. 753 (SDNY 1966); Estate of Littick v. Comm'r, 31 TC 181 (1958), acq. 1959-2 CB 5, acq. and withdrawn in part 1984-2 CB 1.

courts and the Service are willing to reexamine the elements at the time the modification takes place.[44] In such cases, the exception requirements will be more difficult for the taxpayer to prove.

[a] Bona Fide Business Arrangement

The first requirement is that the option, agreement, right, or restriction placed on the property is a "bona fide business arrangement."[45] The term "bona fide business arrangement" is not defined in either the Code or the regulations.[46] However, prior case law and the legislative history of Section 2703 provide a wide range of legitimate business reasons for such agreement.[47] An arrangement to facilitate the maintenance of family ownership and control of a business is a bona fide business arrangement,[48] even if the business is a passive trade or business.[49] Arrangements to facilitate the retention of key employees,[50] to provide incentives to managers to increase efficiency,[51] to maintain a tenant,[52] or to ensure the continued employment of stockholders who are key employees[53] all qualify as bona fide business arrangements. Additionally, arrangements to avoid expensive appraisals in determining the purchase price, to plan for future liquidity needs, to create markets for equity interests, and to

---

[44] See, e.g., St. Louis County Bank v. United States, 674 F2d 1207 (8th Cir. 1982); Rudolph v. United States, 93-1 USTC ¶ 60,130 (SD Ind. 1993). See also Reg. § 25.2703-1(c), under which a right or restriction that is substantially modified is treated as a right or restriction created on the date of the modification. In a similar vein, see Estate of True v. Comm'r, 82 TCM (CCH) 27 (2001), stating that "[i]n exceptional circumstances, courts [have] examined the adequacy of consideration and conduct of parties *after* the buy-sell agreement if intervening events within the parties' control caused a wide disparity between the buy-sell agreement's formal price and fair market value." Id. at notes 51–52.

[45] IRC § 2703(b)(1).

[46] See Reg. § 25.2703-1(b).

[47] See Explanatory Material Concerning Committee on Finance 1990 Reconciliation Submission Pursuant to House Concurrent Resolution 310, 136 Cong. Rec. S15683 (Oct. 18, 1990); supra ¶ 19.04[1][c] note 12.

[48] St. Louis County Bank v.United States, 674 F2d 1207 (8th Cir. 1982); Estate of Reynolds v. Comm'r, 55 TC 172 (1970), acq. 1971-2 CB 2, 3; Estate of Fiorito v. Comm'r, 33 TC 440 (1959), acq. 1960-2 CB 4; Estate of Bischoff v. Comm'r, 69 TC 32 (1977), Church v. United States, 85 AFTR2d 2000-804 (WD Tex. 2000), aff'd without opinion, 88 AFTR2d 2001-5352 (5th Cir. 2001).

[49] Estate of Bischoff v. Comm'r, 69 TC 32, 40 (1977). However, in a series of recent technical advice memoranda and private letter rulings, no such business purpose was found. See supra ¶ 19.04[2] note 21.

[50] Bensel v. Comm'r, 36 BTA 246 (1937), nonacq. sub. nom. 1937-2 CB 36, aff'd, 100 F2d 639 (3d Cir. 1938).

[51] Cobb v. Comm'r, 49 TCM (CCH) 1364 (1985).

[52] Cobb v. Comm'r, 49 TCM (CCH) 1364 (1985).

[53] Priv. Ltr. Rul. 8541005 (June 21, 1985).

prevent the transfer of assets to unwanted parties constitute bona fide business arrangements.[54]

[b] Not a Device to Transfer Property to Members of Decedent's Family for Less Than Full and Adequate Consideration

The second requirement is that the option, agreement, right, or restriction must not be a device to transfer property to members of the decedent's[55] family for less than adequate consideration in money or money's worth.[56]

[i] Not a family device. The existence of the family relationship requirement is more ambiguous than it appears on the face of the statute. The confusion derives from two sources. First, there is no definition of "members of the decedent's family"[57] contained in the statute. Additionally, while the statute uses the term "members of the decedent's family," the regulations substitute the term "the natural objects of the transferor's bounty."[58] Natural objects of a transferor's bounty, although an elusive term to define, generally includes individuals beyond members of a transferor's family, although one court has nar-

----

[54] See Explanatory Material Concerning Committee on Finance 1990 Reconciliation Submission Pursuant to House Concurrent Resolution 310, 136 Cong. Rec. S15681 (Oct. 18, 1990); supra ¶ 19.04[1][c] note 12.

[55] Since Section 2703 is applicable to all three transfer taxes, the statute should have used the term taxpayer's family rather than the decedent's family.

[56] IRC § 2703(b)(2). In a series of recent technical advice memoranda and private letter rulings, Section 2703(b) was inapplicable because such a device was found. TAMs 9719006 (Jan. 14, 1997), 9723009 (Feb. 24, 1997), 9725002 (Mar. 3, 1997), 9735003 (May 8, 1997), 9736004 (June 6, 1997); Priv. Ltr. Rul. 9730004 (Apr. 3, 1997), 9842003 (July 2, 1998).

[57] The regulations define the term "members of the transferor's family" for purposes of the regulatory exception providing deemed satisfaction of the Section 2703(b) requirements (see infra ¶ 19.04[4]) by employing the Regulations Section 25.2701-2(b)(5) broad definition of "members of a family." See infra ¶ 19.04[4] text accompanying notes 103–105. This definition is considered at ¶ 19.02[2][b] notes 98–102. However, this definition should not be employed under Section 2703(b)(2) because its use is specifically limited to the deemed satisfaction rule. See Regulations Section 25.2703-1(b)(3) limiting the definition to "this section" referring only to the deemed satisfaction rule. Applying the broad definition of "members of a family" borrowed from Regulations Section 25.2701-2(b)(5), the Service ruled in TAM 9841005 (Oct. 9, 1998) that the transferor's stepchildren were members of the family of the transferor for purposes of determining whether restrictions on the transfer of certain partnership interests were a means of transferring interests to the transferor's family members for less than full and adequate consideration.

[58] Reg. § 25.2703-1(b)(1)(ii). There have been legislative attempts to amend Section 2703(b)(2) to conform it to the regulations. To date no such legislation has been enacted. See the House version of the Technical Corrections Bill of 1991, HR Conf. Rep. 1555, 102d Cong., 1st Sess. (1991); The Revenue Bill of 1992, HR Conf. Rep. 11, 102d Cong., 2d Sess. (1992).

rowly limited it to a situation where an unrelated party shares a relationship with a decedent such as to effectively be considered a member of the decedent's family.[59] At least one case has held that in situations of family discord, the natural objects of the testator's bounty may not include discordant related family members.[60]

The confusion here should be corrected by legislation, perhaps to include both family members and natural objects of one's bounty and to define the term family members. Notwithstanding the discrepancy in the statute and regulations over family members, it is obvious that one of Congress's primary concerns was the passage of wealth to younger generations through a device that was testamentary in nature. In the absence of a close familial relationship between the decedent and the remaining parties to a buy-sell arrangement, the regulations under Section 2703 provide a safe harbor.[61]

A sense of the family transfer device requirement is gained from a review of two significant cases evaluating the requirement.[62] In *St. Louis County Bank v. United States*, family members entered into an agreement restricting the transfer of the stock in a family moving and storage business.[63] The agreement provided that the company, or family members retain an option to purchase stock at the death of a shareholder and a right of first refusal whenever shares were offered for sale.[64] The option included a formula price of ten times the average annual net earnings per share for the preceding five years, excluding real estate gains and losses.[65] Seven years after the shareholders' agreement was executed, the business was changed to a real estate investment company. Because all of the company's gains and losses then came from real estate, the formula price generated a per share value of zero.[66] At the death of the controlling shareholder, the company exercised its option and acquired the decedent's interest for no consideration.[67]

The court found that the option agreement, while valid at inception, had become unreasonable because of the voluntary choice of changing the nature

---

[59] Estate of Gloeckner v. Comm'r, 152 F3d 208, 215 (2d Cir. 1998) (defining a natural object under Reg. § 20.2031-2(h)).

[60] Estate of Bischoff v. Comm'r, 69 TC 32 (1977).

[61] See infra ¶ 19.04[4].

[62] These cases were decided under Regulations Section 20.2031-2(h); however, the requirement is the same under Section 2703(b)(2). See supra ¶ 19.04[3] text accompanying notes 40, 41. A third pre–Section 2703 case contains an extensive discussion of the device requirement. See Estate of True v. Comm'r, 82 TCM (CCH) 27 (2001).

[63] St. Louis County Bank v. United States, 674 F2d 1207, 1208 (8th Cir. 1982).

[64] St. Louis County Bank v. United States, 674 F2d 1207, 1208 (8th Cir. 1982).

[65] St. Louis County Bank v. United States, 674 F2d 1207, 1209 (8th Cir. 1982).

[66] St. Louis County Bank v. United States, 674 F2d 1207, 1209 (8th Cir. 1982).

[67] St. Louis County Bank v. United States, 674 F2d 1207, 1209 (8th Cir. 1982).

of the business.[68] The court was also bothered by the state of the decedent's health on the date of execution of the agreement. He had suffered two heart attacks within a few years before execution.[69] Moreover, upon the prior death of decedent's brother, brother had transferred his shares to his wife and assigned a value of $850 per share for estate tax purposes in conflict with the option price.[70] The court noted that the price set in an option agreement generally would be respected, despite a significant disparity between the formula price and actual value at the date of transfer.[71] However, the court found that the facts of this case showed that the agreement had become unreasonable and a testamentary tax avoidance device.[72]

In *Estate of Lauder*,[73] family members entered agreements under which shares in their well-known cosmetic enterprises could only be transferred among the companies or family members at a formula price consisting of book value, excluding intangible assets.[74] Because intangible assets, such as trademarks and goodwill, are significant assets of cosmetics firms, the book value price was a substantial bargain.[75] The proper value of the transferor's shares for estate tax purposes became a battle of experts, with the testimony of four experts discussed in the opinion.[76] The court concluded that the agreements violated the testamentary device requirement because the formula price significantly undervalued the stock at the date of inception,[77] was arbitrarily chosen,[78] and was adopted without negotiation.[79]

As these two cases illustrate, the device requirement is violated when the right of restriction is entered into between the parties as a tax avoidance device. Whether such a device exists may involve an inquiry into the intent of

---

[68] St. Louis County Bank v. United States, 674 F2d 1207, 1211 (8th Cir. 1982).

[69] St. Louis County Bank v. United States, 674 F2d 1207, 1210 (8th Cir. 1982).

[70] St. Louis County Bank v. United States, 674 F2d 1207, 1211 (8th Cir. 1982).

[71] St. Louis County Bank v. United States, 674 F2d 1207, 1211 (8th Cir. 1982).

[72] St. Louis County Bank v. United States, 674 F2d 1207, 1211 (8th Cir. 1982).

[73] Estate of Lauder v. Comm'r, 64 TCM (CCH) 1643 (1992), supplementing 60 TCM (CCH) 977 (1990).

[74] Estate of Lauder v. Comm'r, 64 TCM (CCH) 1643, 1648–1651 (1992).

[75] Estate of Lauder v. Comm'r, 64 TCM (CCH) 1643, 1659 (1992). The Service estimated a deficiency of $42,702,597.67. Id. at 1644.

[76] Estate of Lauder v. Comm'r, 64 TCM (CCH) 1643, 1651–1656, 1660–1661 (1992).

[77] Estate of Lauder v. Comm'r, 64 TCM (CCH) 1643, 1651–1656, 1660–1661 (1992).

[78] Estate of Lauder v. Comm'r, 64 TCM (CCH) 1643, 1651–1656, 1660–1661 (1992).

[79] Estate of Lauder v. Comm'r, 64 TCM (CCH) 1643, 1658–1659 (1992).

the parties to the agreement.[80] Some factors that are considered in determining whether the device requirement is violated include: the transferor's health,[81] changes in a business subject to a right or restriction,[82] selective enforcement of the agreement,[83] the pattern of the negotiations (whether the price was negotiated or established in an arbitrary manner),[84] and lack of an appropriate appraisal.[85]

Generally, a determination of the necessary relationship of the parties, the presence of an avoidance device, and the adequacy of consideration is fixed by circumstances at inception of the agreement.[86] However, the courts are not precluded from looking at postinception events, especially where those events are the result of voluntary action by the parties involved.[87] In sum, a device will be found if the overall aroma of the transferred right or restriction discloses a tax avoidance motive.

[ii] **Full and adequate consideration.** The term "full and adequate consideration" is contained both in the statute and the regulations describing the exception to Section 2703.[88] At first glance, it appears that anything less than fair market value cannot constitute "full and adequate consideration." However, if this were the case, the exception would be consumed by the general rule. As a result, courts have noted that the term is not described in the regulations and have assumed that "a formula price may reflect adequate and full consideration notwithstanding the fact that the price falls below fair market value."[89] Tying full and adequate consideration into the requirement of arm's-length comparables, the term is best defined as a price not lower than that

---

[80] Rudolph v. United States, 93-1 USTC ¶ 60,130 (SD Ind. 1993) (discussing use of intent in Dom v. United States, 828 F2d 177, 182 (3d Cir. 1987)).

[81] St. Louis County Bank v. Comm'r, 674 F2d 1207, 1210 (8th Cir. 1982). This was a factor in a series of recent technical advice memoranda and private letter rulings. See TAMs 9719006 (Jan. 14, 1997), 9723009 (Feb. 24, 1997), 9725002 (Mar. 3, 1997), 9735003 (May 8, 1997), 9736004 (June 6, 1997); Priv. Ltr. Rul. 9730004 (Apr. 3, 1997), 9842003 (July 2, 1998).

[82] St. Louis County Bank v. Comm'r, 674 F2d 1207, 1211 (8th Cir. 1982).

[83] St. Louis County Bank v. Comm'r, 674 F2d 1207, 1211 (8th Cir. 1982).

[84] Estate of Lauder v. Comm'r, 64 TCM (CCH) 1643, 1658 (1992).

[85] Estate of Lauder v. Comm'r, 64 TCM (CCH) 1643, 1658 (1992).

[86] See supra ¶ 19.04[3] text accompanying notes 43, 44. This would be the time of modification if an agreement were substantially modified. See infra ¶ 19.04[7].

[87] See St. Louis County Bank v. United States, 674 F2d 1207 (8th Cir. 1982), where there was a voluntary change by the parties of the nature of the business resulting in an unreasonable price for the shares under the agreement.

[88] See IRC § 2703(b)(2); Reg. § 25.2703-1(b)(1)(ii).

[89] Estate of Lauder v. Comm'r, 64 TCM (CCH) 1643, 1660 (1992). See also Estate of Reynolds v. Comm'r, 55 TC 172 (1970), acq. 1971-2 CB 2, 3.

reached by parties with adverse interests.[90] Consequently, the determination of full and adequate consideration will often be solved only through a battle between the taxpayer and the Service's expert witnesses.

[c] Similar Arrangement Test

The third requirement is that the option, agreement, right, or restriction must be comparable to similar arrangements entered into by persons in an arm's-length transaction.[91] The taxpayer is required to show that, when the agreement was made, it was one that could have been obtained in a fair bargain among unrelated parties in the same business dealing at arm's length.[92] A right or restriction meets that test if it conforms with the general business practice of unrelated parties in the same business under negotiated agreements.[93] General business practice may be established by expert testimony. Generally, a showing of isolated comparables will not suffice; however, if the business is a unique business, comparables from similar businesses may be used.[94]

In determining whether an agreement conforms to general business practice, the taxpayer will generally be expected to compare the anticipated term of the agreement, the present value of the property, the expected value of the property at the time of exercise, and the adequacy of the consideration.[95] If more than one valuation method is commonly used in similar agreements, a right or restriction does not fail to evidence a general business practice merely because it uses only one of the recognized methods.[96] The similar arrangements test is the real unknown under Section 2703. Since the requirement is new, case law is lacking and the regulations are, to say the least, vague. It will be difficult in most situations to establish an applicable comparable. Few arrangements limiting the transfer of interests are public record and there will be some businesses that, because of the nature of their assets (i.e., businesses that are heavily laden with intangibles), simply do not have a comparable. The burden of proof rests with the taxpayer. The bottom line is that much depends

---

[90] Estate of Lauder v. Comm'r, 64 TCM (CCH) 1643, 1660 (1992). See also Estate of Reynolds v. Comm'r, 55 TC 172 (1970), acq. 1971-2 CB 2, 3; Estate of True v. Comm'r, 82 TCM (CCH) 27 (2001).

[91] IRC § 2703(b)(3). See Reg. § 25.2703-1(d) Ex. 1 where this requirement was not met.

[92] Reg. § 25.2703-1(b)(4)(i).

[93] Reg. § 25.2703-1(b)(4)(i). It is not necessary that the terms of a right or restriction parallel the terms of a particular agreement. Reg. § 25.2703-1(b)(4)(ii).

[94] Reg. § 25.2703-1(b)(4)(ii).

[95] Reg. § 25.2703-1(b)(4)(i).

[96] Reg. § 25.2703-1(b)(4)(ii).

upon how the Service intends to apply the test: is it essentially a restatement of historic requirements,[97] or is it an additional stringent requirement?[98]

[4] Deemed Satisfaction

A right or restriction is treated as satisfying each of the three requirements of Section 2703(b), and, therefore, is excepted from Section 2703(a) and will be considered in the valuation of property if two requirements are met.[99] The first requirement is that more than one half of the value of the property subject to the right or restriction is owned directly or indirectly by individuals who are not "members of the transferor's family."[100] The second requirement is that the property owned by non-family members must be subject to the right or restriction to the same extent as the property owned by the transferor.[101] Such an agreement predominantly involving non-family members is taken into consideration in the valuation of the property.[102] In determining whether the deemed exception applies, the principal difficulty is in defining members of the transferor's family. For purposes of this rule, natural objects of one's bounty are treated as family members.[103] Defining the term "natural objects of one's bounty" involves the same issues and problems that were previously discussed with the device requirement.[104] For purposes of this exception, members of the transferor's family are the transferor's spouse, any ancestor of the transferor or the transferor's spouse, any spouse of such ancestor, and any lineal descendants of the parents of the transferor or the transferor's spouse (but seemingly not the spouses of such descendants).[105] Determination of ownership becomes even more complicated because ownership includes not only direct ownership,

---

[97] See Reg. § 20.2031-2(h). Estate of True v. Comm'r, 82 TCM (CCH) 27 (2001) suggests that this requirement was part of the historic requirements. Id. at 65.

[98] In one private letter ruling, the Service flatly accepted that the stock option agreement described was comparable to similar arrangements. However, the option described was of the plain vanilla variety. Priv. Ltr. Rul. 9350016 (Sept. 16, 1993).

[99] Reg. § 25.2703-1(b)(3).

[100] Reg. § 25.2703-1(b)(3). Cf. United States v. Parker, 376 F2d 402 (5th Cir. 1967) (the "value" of one's shares does not necessarily correspond to the percentage of one's ownership of the outstanding shares).

[101] Reg. § 25.2703-1(b)(3).

[102] The requirements of Regulations Section 20.2031-2(h) must still be considered if the agreement is to fix valuation. See infra ¶ 19.04[6].

[103] Reg. § 25.2703-1(b)(3).

[104] See supra ¶ 19.04[3][b] text accompanying notes 57–60.

[105] Reg. §§ 25.2703-1(b)(3), 25.2701-2(b)(5)(i). The Section 2703 regulation curiously borrows from the Section 2701(e)(2) definition of "applicable family members," but not the Section 2701(e)(1) member of the family definition (which would include the spouses of descendants). See ¶ 19.02[2][b][ii]; Priv. Ltr. Rul. 9222043 (Feb. 28, 1992)

but indirect ownership by attribution from entities. Three entity attribution rules apply: (1) a person is deemed to own any interest owned by a corporation proportionate to the relative fair market value of their interest in the corporation;[106] (2) a person is deemed to own any interest owned by a partnership proportionate to the relative fair market value of the greater of their capital interest or profits interest in the partnership;[107] and (3) any equity interest held by an estate, trust, or other entity is attributed to a person to the extent that the person's beneficial interest in the entity may be satisfied by the equity using the maximum exercise of discretion in the person's favor.[108] Under these rules, if the same interest is attributed to both a family and a non-family member, the interest is deemed owned by the family member.[109]

In determining whether the exception applies, the regulations do not state whether the 50 percent test is to be satisfied at the time the agreement is made or at the time the property is valued. Because the exception replaces requirements that seemingly must be satisfied at the time the agreement is made,[110] it is assumed that the exception is also tested at that time, although it would not be unreasonable to require the test to be met at both points in time.[111]

[5] Multiple Rights and Restrictions

There will be instances where a business has instituted several different restrictions on the sale of interests. Where multiple restrictions are present, a finding that one restriction has not met the requirements for the exception in Section 2703(b) is not dispositive of a similar finding on other restrictions. Each independent restriction will be judged under the requirements of Section 2703(b)

(holding that the definition includes nephews and nieces of the transferor). Cf. TAM 9841005 (Oct. 9, 1998) (transferor's stepchildren are family members).

[106] Reg. §§ 25.2701-6(a)(2), 25.2703-1(b)(3).

[107] Reg. §§ 25.2701-6(a)(3), 25.2703-1(b)(3).

[108] Reg. §§ 25.2701-6(a)(4), 25.2703-1(b)(3). The Regulations Section 25.2701-6 attribution rules are discussed in greater detail at ¶ 19.02[2][d].

[109] Regulations Section 25.2703-1(b)(3) (last sentence) provides that if an interest is attributed to a family member it is treated as held only by a family member. The regulation also appropriately disregards the Regulations Section 25.2701-6(a)(5) multiple attribution rules. Reg. § 5.2703-1(b)(3) (last sentence).

[110] See supra ¶ 19.04[3] text accompanying notes 43, 44.

[111] Consideration should be given to whether the addition of a family member to an agreement results in a substantial modification of the agreement in effect altering the time the agreement is entered into. See infra ¶ 19.04[7] text accompanying notes 150, 151.

on its separate merits.[112] The facts and circumstances, however, determine whether or not restrictions are independent of one another.[113]

[6] Establishing Valuation When a Right or Restriction Is Excepted From Section 2703

The fact that a right or restriction is not disregarded under Section 2703(a) (because either Section 2703(b) or the regulatory exception applies),[114] does not mean that the right or restriction establishes value for transfer tax purposes. It means only that the right or restriction can be taken into consideration in determining the value of the property. Section 2703 merely supplements prior law; it does not replace it.[115] Thus, prior law must be examined to determine the weight that a right or restriction is given in establishing valuation, rather than merely being considered as a factor in the property's valuation.

[a] Estate Tax Valuation

The rules for establishing valuation for estate tax purposes are well developed. The regulations provide a number of additional requirements that must be satisfied to establish estate tax value, each of which are described in the following section.[116] Although the regulation speaks of agreements with respect to securities, it should be equally applicable to agreements with respect to all types of property.

[i] Restrictions on lifetime dispositions. The agreement must restrict lifetime dispositions by the owner.[117] The regulations provide: "Little weight

---

[112] Reg. § 25.2703-1(b)(5).

[113] Reg. § 25.2703-1(b)(5).

[114] Reg. § 25.2703-1(b)(3). See supra ¶¶ 19.04[3], 19.04[4].

[115] See supra ¶ 19.04[1][c] text accompanying note 12.

[116] Reg. § 20.2031-2(h). Although the regulation requires that there be both a bona fide business arrangement and that the right or restriction not be a device to transfer property for inadequate consideration, both those requirements had to be met to satisfy Section 2703(b) or should be conclusively presumed to be met if Regulations Section 25.2703-1(b)(3) is satisfied. See supra ¶ 19.04[4]. Thus, although they are requirements of Regulations Section 20.2031-2(h), they are already satisfied or are deemed satisfied and they are not further considered here.

[117] Estate of Gannon v. Comm'r, 21 TC 1073 (1954), acq. 1954-2 CB 4; Estate of Matthews v. Comm'r, 3 TC 525 (1944); Hoffman v. Comm'r, 2 TC 1160, 1179 (1943), acq. 1944-2 CB 11, 13, aff'd on other grounds, 148 F2d 285 (9th Cir. 1945), cert. denied, 326 U.S. 730 (1945); Estate of Caplan v. Comm'r, 33 TCM (CCH) 189 (1974); Rev. Rul. 59-60, 1959-1 CB 237; Rev. Rul. 53-157, 1953-2 CB 255.

will be accorded a price contained in an option or contract under which the decedent is free to dispose of the underlying [property] at any price he chooses during his lifetime."[118] The rationale seems obvious. If the decedent is at liberty to dispose of the property up to the time of death, the failure to take action is in the nature of a testamentary disposition and certainly not a sale in accordance with the agreement.[119]

A problem arises when the agreement is silent on the question of lifetime dispositions. In one case,[120] no specific mention was made of lifetime transfers. However, the agreement did provide that "the rights and interest of the several partners shall not be transferable or assignable."[121] In construing this clause in a way most favorable to the taxpayer, the court concluded that the parties intended the agreement to act as a lifetime, as well as a post-death, restriction on alienability.[122]

[ii] Obligation of the estate to sell. The second requirement is that the estate be obligated to sell the decedent's interest in the property.[123] If the estate is merely required by the agreement to offer the interest at a fixed price if it decides to sell, the agreement will not fix valuation.[124] The rationale behind this requirement is that the estate, if not obligated to sell, may choose never to offer the interest for sale. In such a situation, the interest has a "retention value," a value that is based on participation in the future growth of the property.[125] The offer to sell, as distinguished from the obligation to sell, is called the right of first refusal. It is not definitive for estate tax valuation purposes.[126]

---

[118] Reg. § 20.2031-2(h).

[119] In the following cases the agreement was treated as a bequest rather than a sale: Estate of Matthews v. Comm'r, 3 TC 525 (1944); Estate of Caplan v. Comm'r, 33 TCM (CCH) 189 (1974); Estate of Hammond v. Comm'r, 13 TCM (CCH) 903 (1954), modified in part, 14 TCM (CCH) 83 (1955).

[120] Estate of Fiorito v. Comm'r, 33 TC 440 (1959), acq. 1960-2 CB 4.

[121] Estate of Fiorito v. Comm'r, 33 TC 440, 445 (1959), acq. 1960-2 CB 4.

[122] Estate of Fiorito v. Comm'r, 33 TC 440, 445 (1959), acq. 1960-2 CB 4.

[123] See, e.g., Estate of Littick v. Comm'r, 31 TC 181 (1958), acq. 1959-2 CB 5, acq. and withdrawn in part 1948-2 CB 1; Estate of Salt v. Comm'r, 17 TC 92 (1951), acq. 1952-1 CB 4; Estate of Anderson v. Comm'r, 36 TCM (CCH) 972 (1977), aff'd, 619 F2d 587 (6th Cir. 1980).

[124] Worcester County Trust Co. v. Comm'r, 134 F2d 578 (1st Cir. 1943); Lomb v. Sugden, 82 F2d 166 (2d Cir. 1936), rev'g 11 F. Supp. 472 (WDNY 1935); Mathews v. United States, 226 F. Supp. 1003 (EDNY 1964); Baltimore Nat'l Bank v. United States, 136 F. Supp. 642 (M. Md. 1955); Koch v. Comm'r, 28 BTA 363 (1933); Michigan Trust Co. v. Comm'r, 27 BTA 556 (1933).

[125] See Corneel, "Valuation Techniques, in Buy-Sell Agreements: Effect on Gift and Estate Taxes," 24 NYU Inst. on Fed. Tax'n 631, 660 (1966), and cases cited therein.

[126] Worcester County Trust Co. v. Comm'r, 134 F2d 578 (1st Cir. 1943); James v. Comm'r, 148 F2d 236 (2d Cir. 1945), aff'g 3 TC 1260 (1944); Berzon v. Comm'r, 63 TC

However, it has been recognized as possibly having a depressing effect on the value of the interest.[127]

While the estate must be obligated to sell, the business or its owners need not be under an identical obligation to buy in order for the agreement to fix valuation. Two alternative arrangements exist. The "mandatory" buy-sell arrangement provides that the estate must sell, and the business or its owners must buy, at the value stated in the agreement. Because it is recognized that the interest can never be sold for more than the price contained in the agreement, that price, in effect, is the market price and will have great weight, if not actually fix the value, for estate tax purposes.[128]

In the second arrangement, while the estate must still be obligated to sell, or at least obligated to offer the interest for sale, the business or its owners need only have the right (but not an obligation) to buy at a fixed or determinable price within a reasonable time after the death of the deceased owner. This alternative has been described as a "buyer's option" or "call." The buyer's option should place a ceiling on the estate tax valuation if it is an enforceable agreement under state law. A problem exists with the buyer's option that is not present in the mandatory buy-sell agreement. In the case of the mandatory buy-sell agreement, mutual promises to sell and to buy serve to furnish the necessary consideration to support the agreement. In the buyer's option situation, where the agreement provides merely that the seller must sell, additional consideration must be recited or the agreement may not be respected.[129] For example, in one case, the would-be buyers' agreement to forgo compensation for services as directors of the company was held to be the necessary consideration.[130] The Service has argued against the buyer's option as a value determinant on the ground that the holder may not have the means necessary to

---

601 (1975), acq. 1975-2 CB 1, aff'd, 534 F2d 528 (2d Cir. 1976); Estate of Reynolds v. Comm'r, 55 TC 172 (1970), acq. 1971-2 CB 2, 3.

[127] See supra text accompanying note 119. See also Estate of Reynolds, 55 TC 172 (1970), acq. 1971-2 CB 2, 3; Alexander, "Current Valuation Problems," 1963 USC Tax Inst. 685; "Estate Planning Through Family Bargaining," 8 Real Prop. Prob. & Tr. J. 223 (1973).

[128] Brodrick v. Gore, 224 F2d 892 (10th Cir. 1955); Estate of Littick v. Comm'r, 31 TC 181 (1958), acq. 1959-2 CB 5, acq. and withdrawn in part 1984-2 CB 1.

[129] Bensel v. Comm'r, 36 BTA 246 (1937), nonacq. sub nom. 1937-2 CB 36, aff'd, 100 F2d 639 (3d Cir. 1938); Estate of Armstrong v. Comm'r, 146 F2d 457 (7th Cir. 1944).

[130] Citizens Fidelity Bank & Trust Co. v. United States, 209 F. Supp. 254 (WD Ky. 1962). It should be noted that other elements of the contract were also scrutinized to ensure that it was enforceable under state law.

exercise it. This argument has been rejected by the courts,[131] and unexercised options have fixed estate tax valuation.[132]

[iii] **Method prescribed by agreement.** The final requirement is that valuation must be specified or readily ascertainable according to the terms of the agreement and that value must have been reasonable when the agreement was made.[133] To date, there seems to be no case holding against the taxpayer on the grounds of unreasonable valuation.[134] Rather, the focus is on whether the value is sufficiently fixed by agreement. When the price is specified in a dollar amount, clearly no problem exists.[135] On the other hand, if the value of the interest as stated in the agreement is substantially greater than fair market value at death but was reasonable when the agreement was made, the estate should nonetheless be forced to abide by that high valuation.[136] If the price is not for a cash amount, it must either be an ascertainable amount under some formula related to factors that are determinable or it may allow for a determination of value by independent appraisers.

[b] Gift Tax Valuation

Seemingly, the factors that can fix valuation for estate taxes (a determinable amount, as well as lifetime and death restrictions that in essence box the taxpayer in) would also fix gift tax value. Nevertheless, the courts have rejected such an assumption.[137] However, the courts do deem it appropriate to take the agreement into account in determining fair market value. On close analysis, the different treatment seems appropriately to turn on the question of whether at the crucial time of valuation (gift or death) a valid agreement exists under which the property can then be purchased at the asserted price. If a living donor is free to retain corporate shares for their investment value, that

---

[131] Wilson v. Bowers, 57 F2d 682 (2d Cir. 1932), aff'g 51 F2d 261.

[132] Wilson v. Bowers, 57 F2d 682 (2d Cir. 1932), aff'g 51 F2d 261; Child's Estate v. Comm'r, 2 TCM (CCH) 388 (1943), rev'd on other grounds, 147 F2d 368 (3d Cir. 1945).

[133] Baltimore Nat'l Bank v. United States, 136 F. Supp. 642 (D. Md. 1955). But see St. Louis Co. Bank v. United States, 674 F2d 1207 (8th Cir. 1982).

[134] Child's Estate v. Comm'r, 2 TCM (CCH) 388 (1943), rev'd on other grounds, 147 F2d 368 (3d Cir. 1945), the option price of $10 per share was held to govern estate tax valuation despite evidence that the fair market value at the time of decedent's death would have been $100 per share had there been no agreement.

[135] If the agreement's stated value is greatly below fair market value, even though it was close when the agreement was made, the Service may argue that it was not bona fide. Stem, "Buy-Sell Agreements," 19 NYU Inst. on Fed. Tax'n 653, 666 (1961).

[136] See generally Casner, Estate Planning 944 (Little Brown & Co., 4th ed. 1980).

[137] Spitzer v. Comm'r, 153 F2d 967 (8th Cir. 1946), aff'g 4 TCM (CCH) 562 (1945); Comm'r v. McCann, 146 F2d 385 (2d Cir. 1944); Berzon v. Comm'r, 63 TC 601 (1975), acq. 1975-2 CB 1, aff'd, 534 F2d 528 (2d Cir. 1976).

value may well exceed a price the donor is required to accept only if the donor makes a voluntary decision to sell or otherwise takes some action, such as retiring, which activates a sleeping option. Not surprisingly, the Service seems to agree.[138]

[c] Generation-Skipping Transfer Tax Valuation

If an agreement relates to valuation of property involved in a generation-skipping transfer, the rules for estate or gift tax valuation discussed previously respectively should be applied depending upon whether the generation-skipping transfer occurs at death or in an inter vivos transfer situation.[139]

[7] Effective Dates and Substantial Modification

Section 2703 applies to agreements, options, rights, or restrictions entered into or granted after October 8, 1990, and to preexisting agreements, options, rights, or restrictions that are "substantially modified" after October 8, 1990.[140] A substantial modification of an agreement is treated as the creation of a new agreement on the date of modification.[141] Thus, the substantial modification rule plays a role both in determining whether an agreement is subject to Section 2703 and, assuming Section 2703 applies, the specific agreement that is to

---

[138] Compare Rev. Rul. 53-189, 1953-2 CB 294 (option price did not fix gift tax valuation even though donor was not free to dispose of shares at negotiated price during life, citing Spitzer v. Comm'r, 153 F2d 967 (8th Cir. 1946), aff'g 4 TCM (CCH) 562 (1945) and other cases) with Reg. § 20.2031-2(h) (indicating when an option price will control for estate tax purposes).

[139] Cf. Reg. §§ 26.2642-2(a)(1), 26.2642-2(b)(1).

[140] Omnibus Budget Reconciliation Act of 1990, Pub. L. No. 101-508, §§ 11602(e)(1)(A)(ii)(I), 11602(e)(1)(A)(ii)(II), 104 Stat. 1388-1, 1388-500 (1990), reprinted in 1991-2 CB 481, 529. See Reg. §§ 25.2703-1(c), 25.2703-2.

Section 2703 is an initial threshold that must be satisfied if an agreement is to be considered in any way in the valuation of the transferor's property. After Section 2703 is satisfied, the weight the agreement is given in valuing property will be determined under the requirements of Regulations Section 20.2031-2(h). And, all property subject to an option or contract to purchase to which Section 2703 does not apply (e.g., pre–October 8, 1990 agreements that are not substantially modified after that date) remain subject to Regulations Section 20.2031-2(h). For a discussion of the requirements of Regulations Section 20.2031-2(h), see supra ¶¶ 19.04[1][c] text accompanying note 15, 19.04[3][a], 19.04[3][b], 19.04[6].

[141] If a substantial modification of an agreement occurs after the date of the transfer, then the substantial modification is disregarded for purposes of applying Section 2703 to the transfer. Hence, a modification of an agreement subsequent to a decedent's death did not cause Section 2703 to apply for purposes of valuing stock on the date of the decedent's death. Estate of Gloeckner v. Comm'r, 152 F3d 208 (2d Cir. 1998).

be tested under Section 2703. An agreement that originally satisfied the requirements of Section 2703(b) when executed may no longer withstand such scrutiny after a substantial modification.

The regulations provide some guidance as to what constitutes a substantial modification.[142] They define a substantial modification as "any discretionary modification of a right or restriction, whether or not authorized by the terms of the agreement, that results in other than a de minimis change to the quality, value, or timing of the rights of any party with respect to the property that is subject to the right or restriction."[143] A mandatory modification required by the terms of a right or restriction is not a substantial modification;[144] however, the failure to make a mandatory modification is presumed to be a substantial modification unless it can be shown that the modification would not have resulted in a substantial modification.[145] A discretionary modification of an agreement conferring a right or restriction that does not change the right or restriction,[146] or that only results in a de minimis change to the right or restriction is not a substantial modification.[147] Neither the modification of an option

---

[142] Reg. § 25.2703-1(c). The final regulations were effective January 28, 1992. In determining whether a modification made after October 8, 1990, and before January 28, 1992, is substantial, taxpayers are to rely on any reasonable interpretation of the statutory language. Reg. § 25.2703-2. Reliance on the temporary or final regulations constitutes a reasonable interpretation of the statutory language. Id.

[143] Reg. § 25.2703-1(c)(1).

[144] Reg. § 25.2703-1(c)(2)(i).

[145] Reg. § 25.2703-1(c)(1).

[146] Reg. § 25.2703-1(c)(2)(ii). Thus, the amendment of an agreement providing rights or restrictions to reflect a change in a company's name or registered agent is not a substantial modification of the agreement because the rights or restrictions contained in the agreement have not changed. Reg. § 25.2703-1(d) Ex. 3. See also Priv. Ltr. Ruls. 9141043 (Oct. 11, 1991) (change in number of directors and split of shares), 9152031 (Sept. 30, 1991) (reorganization of investment partnership), 9218074 (Jan. 31, 1992) (changes in stock ownership to bring in younger generation ownership to persons who are active in the business and modification to reflect shift in voting rights), 9226051 (Mar. 30, 1992) (amendment related to life insurance policies under partnership buy-sell agreement), 9241014 (July 8, 1992) (amendment to reflect stock split and proposed change in voting rights), 9248026 (Sept. 1, 1992) (substitution of unrelated parties), 9451050 (Sept. 22, 1994) (changes in real estate partnership were substantially identical to those in original partnership agreement), 9711017 (Dec. 11, 1996) (extension of terms as a result of corporate reorganization), 200010015 (Nov. 30, 1999) (plan for stock options and stock appreciation rights to key employees who did not include current shareholders or family members), 200122024 (Feb. 27, 2001) (various amendments to articles of incorporation, including transfer restrictions and right-of-first-refusal provisions constituted only a de minimis change).

[147] Reg. § 25.2703-1(c)(1). See Priv. Ltr. Rul. 9417007 (Apr. 29, 1994); Priv. Ltr. Rul. 9449017 (Sept. 13, 1994) (amendment granting surviving shareholders the option to purchase decedent's stock before the corporation redeemed the stock in decedent's estate); Priv. Ltr. Rul. 9507208 (Nov. 18, 1994) (minor de minimis amendments); Priv. Ltr. Rul.

price to more closely approximate fair market value[148] nor modification of a capitalization rate in a fixed relationship to a specified market interest rate[149] constitutes a substantial modification triggering the application of or reconsideration under Section 2703. The addition of a family member as a party to an agreement[150] is considered a substantial modification, unless the addition is mandatory under the terms of the right or restrictions, or, if discretionary, the added family member is not in a generation lower than the lowest generation of individuals already party to the right or restriction.[151]

¶ 19.05 SECTION 2704: TREATMENT OF CERTAIN LAPSING RIGHTS AND RESTRICTIONS

[1] Introduction

Section 2704[1] provides rules for determining the effect of certain lapsing rights and restrictions on the value of interests in corporations and partnerships.[2] The

---

9719014 (Feb. 3, 1997) (exemption from agreement of certain transfers); Priv. Ltr. Rul. 9924015 (Mar. 16, 1999) (limited partnership substituted for revocable trust as party to buy-sell agreement).

[148] Reg. § 25.2703-1(c)(2)(iv). Priv. Ltr. Rul. 9152031 (Sept. 30, 1991) (modification of interest rates satisfied this test); Priv. Ltr. Rul. 9322035 (June 4, 1992) (similar facts), 9432017 (May 16, 1994) (modifications made to more closely reflect fair market value), 9652010 (Sept. 26, 1996) (modification of option price), 9719014 (Feb. 3, 1997) (right of first refusal price changed to 100 percent of fair market value for some parties), 200015012 (Jan. 5, 2000) (similar facts).

[149] Reg. § 25.2703-1(c)(2)(iii).

[150] This includes an addition as a result of a transfer of property that subjects the transferee family member to an agreement with respect to the transferred property. Reg. § 25.2703-1(c)(1).

[151] Reg. §§ 25.2703-1(c)(1), 25.2703-1(d) Ex. 2. See also Priv. Ltr. Ruls. 9248026 (Sept. 1, 1992), 9310003 (Dec. 4, 1992), 9324018 (Mar. 19, 1993), 9620017 (Feb. 15, 1996) (mandatory transfer to unrelated individuals); IRC § 2651, discussed ¶ 17.01.

[1] Section 2704 is discussed in Darby & Brier, "The Impact of Code Sec. 2704 on Family Limited Partnerships," 134 Tr. & Est. 79 (Sept. 1995), 134 Tr. & Est. 76 (Oct. 1995); August, "Planning for Lapsing Rights and Restrictions: The Impact of Section 2704 on Valuation," 82 J. Tax'n 342 (1995); Hausman, "Family Limited Partnerships," 78 Tax Notes 95 (1998).

[2] A partnership under Section 2704 includes a limited liability company. See TAM 9736004 (June 6, 1997).

section contains two separate sets of rules[3] that apply with respect to all transfer taxes—the estate tax, the gift tax, and the generation-skipping transfer tax.[4]

The first set of rules was enacted to overturn the holding of *Estate of Harrison v. Commissioner*.[5] In *Harrison*, decedent held both a limited and a general partnership interest in a partnership. The general partnership interest contained the right to liquidate the partnership, but the limited partnership interest did not. Because of the right to liquidate contained in the general partnership interest, decedent's limited partnership interest was worth $59 million if held with the general partnership interest, but worth only $33 million if held without it. Pursuant to a buy-sell agreement at decedent's death, the general partnership interest was required to be sold to the decedent's sons for $750,000.[6] The Tax Court held that the limited partnership interest was includible in decedent's gross estate at a value of $33 million, not at a value of $59 million as argued by the Service, because the decedent's right to liquidate the partnership effectively lapsed at death because of the obligation to sell the general partnership interest to the decedent's sons. In overturning the *Harrison* case, Section 2704(a) provides that certain lapses in voting, liquidation, or similar rights are treated as transfers of those rights by the person holding the rights.[7]

The second set of rules in Section 2704 was enacted to reduce the valuation discounts[8] that would otherwise be allowed with respect to a transfer of an interest in an entity within a family where there are restrictions on the liquidation of the entity or an interest in the entity and where the entity is controlled by the family immediately before the transfer.[9] If the restrictions on the liquidation of the entity or an interest in the entity are more stringent than those provided by the federal or state law applicable to the entity, Section 2704(b) generally disregards such restrictions in valuing the transferred interest.[10] Congress has essentially concluded that such restrictions are imposed primarily to reduce the value of the transfers for transfer tax purposes, without causing a

---

[3] See IRC §§ 2704(a), 2704(b).

[4] IRC §§ 2704(a)(1), 2704(b)(1).

[5] Estate of Harrison v. Comm'r, 52 TCM (CCH) 1306 (1987). See HR Conf. Rep. No. 964, 101st Cong., 2d Sess. 1028, 1137 (1990), reprinted in 1991-2 CB 560, 606.

[6] In the *Harrison* case, Judge Shields concluded that the decedent's limited partnership interest was to be valued without reference to the decedent's power to liquidate the partnership since such power was extinguished at death. Estate of Harrison v. Comm'r, 52 TCM (CCH) 1306, 1310 (1987).

[7] See Reg. § 25.2704-1(a)(1).

[8] See ¶¶ 4.02[4], 10.02[2][c].

[9] See Estate of Watts v. Comm'r, 51 TCM (CCH) 60 (1985), aff'd, 823 F2d 483 (11th Cir. 1987), which was essentially overturned by Section 2704(b). See also infra ¶ 19.05[3][b] note 53.

[10] See Reg. § 25.2704-2(a).

genuine reduction in the economic value of the transferred interest.[11] While Section 2704(b) results in a reduction of the discount for lack of marketability because of the lack of ability to liquidate, the subsection does not reduce the amount of any minority interest discount with respect to the transfer.[12]

[2] Section 2704(a): Lapsed Voting or Liquidation Rights

[a] General Rule

Section 2704(a) treats certain lapses in voting or liquidation rights as transfers by the person holding the right for purposes of the estate, gift, and generation-skipping transfer taxes.[13] Section 2704(a) applies if (1) there is a lapse[14] in a voting or liquidation right[15] in a corporation or partnership and (2) the holder of the right at the time of the lapse, and members of the holder's family,[16] control[17] the entity before and after the lapse.[18] If the lapse occurs during the holder's lifetime, the lapse is treated as a transfer by gift.[19] If the lapse occurs upon the holder's death, the lapse is treated as a transfer includible in the gross estate of the holder.[20] Both inter vivos and testamentary lapses are treated as transfers for the generation-skipping transfer tax.[21]

[b] Definitions

There are various terms used under Section 2704(a), some of which are synonymous with terms employed by Sections 2701 and 2702, and some of

---

[11] See HR Conf. Rep. No. 964, 101st Cong., 2d Sess. 1028, 1137–1138 (1990), reprinted in 1991-2 CB 560, 606–607.

[12] HR Conf. Rep. No. 964, 101st Cong., 2d Sess. 1028, 1137 (1990), reprinted in 1991-2 CB 560, 606.

[13] An interest subject to the right may be held directly or indirectly. Reg. § 25.2704-1(a). An interest is indirectly held to the extent that the value of the interest would have been includible in an individual's gross estate if the individual had died immediately prior to the lapse. Reg. § 25.2704-1(a)(2)(iii).

[14] See infra ¶ 19.05[2][b][ii].

[15] See infra ¶ 19.05[2][b][i].

[16] See infra ¶ 19.05[2][b][iii].

[17] See infra ¶ 19.05[2][b][iv].

[18] IRC § 2704(a)(1). See Reg. § 25.2704-1(f) Ex. 2 (Section 2704(a)(1) inapplicable because family members did not control the entity after the lapse).

[19] IRC § 2704(a)(1).

[20] IRC § 2704(a)(1).

[21] IRC § 2704(a)(1).

which are also used under Section 2704(b). The terms are discussed in the following sections.

[i] **Voting and liquidation rights.** A voting right is the right to vote with respect to any matter of the entity.[22] Thus, a right to vote only for members of the Board of Directors of a corporation is a voting right. The right of a general partner to participate in partnership management is also a voting right.[23] A liquidation right is a right or ability to compel the entity to acquire all or a portion of the holder's equity interest in the entity.[24] Thus, a liquidation right need not result in the complete liquidation of the entity.[25] A voting right or liquidation right may be conferred in a variety of ways, such as by means of a state law, a corporate charter, a partnership agreement, or any other similar means.[26] The Treasury is authorized to provide regulations applying Section 2704(a) to rights similar to voting and liquidation rights.[27]

[ii] **Lapses.** A lapse must occur to trigger Section 2704(a). A lapse does not occur unless the voting or liquidation rights with respect to the transferred interest are restricted or eliminated.[28] Thus, if the voting or liquidation rights are simply transferred to other persons, no lapse occurs.[29] However, if the transfer of an interest results in the loss of the power to control the liquidation of an interest retained by the transferor that is subordinate[30] to the transferred interest, the transfer results in the lapse of the liquidation right with respect to the subordinate interest.[31] A lapse of a voting or liquidation right may occur in

---

[22] Reg. § 25.2704-1(a)(2)(iv).

[23] Reg. § 25.2704-1(a)(2)(iv). See Priv. Ltr. Rul. 9710021 (Dec. 6, 1996) (voting rights in business trust treated as such rights in a partnership).

[24] Reg. § 25.2704-1(a)(2)(v). If as a result of aggregate voting power there is a liquidation right, the right is treated as a liquidation right and not a voting right. See Reg. § 25.2704-1(a)(2)(iv).

[25] Reg. § 25.2704-1(a)(2)(v).

[26] Reg. § 25.2704-1(a)(4).

[27] IRC § 2704(a)(3). Regulations applying Section 2704(a) to similar rights have been reserved. See Reg. § 25.2704-1(e).

[28] Reg. §§ 25.2704-1(b), 25.2704-1(c)(1). See Priv. Ltr. Ruls. 9309018 (Dec. 3, 1992) (no lapse where each shareholder had same voting and liquidation rights after a recapitalization of a corporation), 9451050 (Sept. 22, 1994) (no lapse where partners had same voting and liquidation rights after a family partnership recapitalization).

[29] Reg. § 25.2704-1(c)(1). See Reg. §§ 25.2704-1(f) Exs. 4 (no lapse of voting or liquidation rights even though gift of stock reduced transferor's stock ownership below a level to control liquidation), 7 (same as to liquidation rights).

[30] "Subordinate" is defined in Regulations Section 25.2701-3(a)(2)(iii). Reg. § 25.2704-1(a)(2)(vi). See ¶ 19.02[2] note 24.

[31] Reg. § 25.2704-1(c)(1). See Reg. § 25.2704-1(f) Ex. 7 (rule not applicable because the retained interest was not a subordinate interest); Priv. Ltr. Rul. 9352001 (Sept. 3,

the same manner as the creation of such rights[32]—by reason of a state law, a corporate charter, a partnership agreement, or other means.[33]

The lapse of a voting or liquidation right occurs at the time a presently exercisable voting or liquidation right is restricted or eliminated.[34] If a lapse is only temporary and the right may be restored upon the occurrence of an event beyond the control of both the holder and the holder's family, no lapse occurs until the lapse becomes permanent with respect to the holder.[35]

[iii] **Members of the family.** The members of an individual's family include the individual's spouse, any ancestor or lineal descendant of the individual or the individual's spouse, brothers and sisters of the individual, and the spouses of any of these persons.[36]

[iv] **Control.** For purposes of Section 2704, "control" is defined by employing the Section 2701 definition.[37] "Control of a corporation" is defined as the holding of 50 percent or more (by vote or value) of the stock of a corporation.[38] "Control of a partnership" is defined as the holding of (1) 50 percent or more of the capital or profits interests in the partnership or (2) any interest as a general partner in a limited partnership.[39] Entity attribution rules apply with the result that any interest in a corporation or partnership held by an individual indirectly through another corporation, another partnership, a trust, or any other entity is treated as held by the individual directly in proportion to the individual's ownership in the intervening entity.[40]

1993) (recapitalization of corporation with taxpayer receiving nonvoting stock for voting stock resulted in a lapse of a liquidation right).

[32] See supra text accompanying note 26.

[33] Reg. § 25.2704-1(a)(4). Priv. Ltr. Rul. 9804001 (Sept. 30, 1997) (lapse occurred under agreement and state law).

[34] Reg. §§ 25.2704-1(b), 25.2704-1(c)(1).

[35] Reg. § 25.2704-1(a)(3). See Reg. §§ 25.2704-1(f) Exs. 3 (lapse for a set period was not a temporary lapse because it was not beyond control of the holder and the holder's family), 9 (under partnership agreement, incompetency of general partner did not constitute a lapse).

[36] IRC § 2704(c)(2); Reg. § 25.2704-1(a)(2)(ii). This is the same definition that is employed under Section 2702. See IRC § 2702(e); Reg. § 25.2702-2(a)(1); ¶ 19.03[2][a][ii].

[37] IRC §§ 2701(b)(2), 2704(c)(1). See ¶ 19.02[2][b] text accompanying notes 94–102; IRC § 2701(e)(3).

[38] IRC §§ 2701(b)(2)(A), 2704(c)(1); Reg. §§ 25.2704-1(a)(2)(i), 25.2701-2(b)(5)(ii)(A).

[39] IRC §§ 2701(b)(2)(B), 2704(c)(1); Reg. §§ 25.2704-1(a)(2)(i), 25.2701-2(b)(5)(iii).

[40] IRC §§ 2701(e)(3)(A), 2704(c)(3). See ¶ 19.02[2][d]. In measuring control, the entity attribution rules apply to both the taxpayer and members of the taxpayer's family. Id.

[c] Exceptions for Certain Lapses of Liquidation Rights

Even though there is a lapse of a liquidation right, several statutory and regulatory exceptions make Section 2704(a) inapplicable. Section 2704(a) does not apply if the holder of an interest (or the holder's estate) and the members of the holder's family cannot, immediately after the lapse, liquidate an interest that the holder could have liquidated prior to the lapse.[41] To the extent necessary to avoid double taxation, the lapse of a liquidation right previously valued to the holder[42] under Section 2701 is not treated as a Section 2704(a) lapse.[43] Finally, Section 2704(a) does not apply to the lapse of a liquidation right if the lapse occurs solely by reason of a change in state law.[44]

[d] Amount of the Transfer

The amount of the transfer is the excess (if any) of the value of all interests in the entity held by the holder of the lapsed right immediately before the lapse (determined as if the voting and liquidation rights were non-lapsing), over the value of such rights immediately after the lapse (determined as if all such rights were held by one individual).[45] For example, assume that D and D's two children each own both general partnership and limited partnership interests in Partnership X. State law provides that a general partner has a right to participate in partnership management. Pursuant to the partnership agreement, upon the death or withdrawal of a general partner, X must redeem the general partnership interest for its liquidation value. The partnership agreement also provides that only a general partner can liquidate the partnership. A limited partner's capital interest will not be redeemed until the partnership liquidates.

The value of a limited partnership interest is greater when held with a general partnership interest that gives the partner the right to liquidate the part-

---

[41] Reg. § 25.2704-1(c)(2)(i)(A). See IRC § 2704(a)(1)(B). In determining whether an interest can be liquidated immediately after the lapse, reference is made to state law and to the governing instruments of the entity, but any applicable restriction described in Section 2704(b) is disregarded. Reg. § 25.2704-1(c)(2)(i)(B). See infra ¶ 19.05[3][b]; Reg. § 25.2704-1(f) Ex. 6 (applicable restriction disregarded with the result that a lapse occurred). If after an applicable restriction is disregarded the governing instrument is less restrictive than state law, the ability to liquidate is determined by the governing instrument disregarding the applicable restriction. Reg. § 25.2704-1(c)(2)(i)(B). Cf. Reg. § 25.2704-2(d) Ex. 3.

[42] See Reg. § 25.2704-1(f) Ex. 8 (exception was inapplicable because the lapse did not occur with respect to the "holder" under Section 2701).

[43] Reg. § 25.2704-1(c)(2)(ii). See ¶ 19.02[4].

[44] Reg. § 25.2704-1(c)(2)(iii).

[45] IRC § 2704(a)(2); Reg. § 25.2704-1(d). The amount of the Section 2704(a) transfer is determined only after determining the effect of the transferor's transfer or death upon the valuation of the interest. See Reg. § 25.2704-1(f) Ex. 1.

nership. Upon *D*'s death, *D*'s limited partnership interest is left to *D*'s spouse and, as required by the partnership agreement, *D*'s general partnership interest is redeemed. Section 2704(a) will apply to the lapse of *D*'s liquidation right because, immediately after the lapse, *D*'s family has the right to liquidate *D*'s limited partnership interest. Therefore, *D*'s gross estate includes an amount equal to the excess of the value of *D*'s interests in *X* held immediately prior to death (determined immediately after *D*'s death but as though the liquidation right had not and would not lapse), over the fair market value of *D*'s interests in *X* immediately after death.[46]

[3] Section 2704(b): Restrictions on Liquidation

[a] General Rule

For purposes of the estate, gift, and generation-skipping transfer tax, Section 2704(b) provides that an "applicable restriction"[47] on the ability of a corporation or partnership to liquidate is disregarded in determining the value of an interest in the entity[48] if (1) there is a transfer of the interest[49] in a corporation or partnership to, or for the benefit of, a member of the transferor's family[50] and (2) the transferor and members of the transferor's family control[51] the entity immediately before the transfer. Thus, when Section 2704(b) applies, the value of the interest in the entity is determined as if the right to liquidate were currently exercisable and as if the rights of the transferor were determined under the state law that would apply but for the restriction.[52]

---

[46] Reg. § 25.2704-1(f) Ex. 5. This example reverses the result of Estate of Harrison v. Comm'r, 52 TCM (CCH) 1306 (1987).

[47] See infra ¶ 19.05[3][b].

[48] Section 2704(b) applies in measuring the amount of a Section 2701 transfer. Reg. §§ 25.2704-2(c), 25.2704-2(d) Ex. 5.

[49] In Kerr v. Comm'r, 113 TC 449, 463 (1999) (taxpayers attempted to avoid this statutory requirement by arguing that recipients of limited partnership interests were, under state law, mere assignees and not holders of limited partnership interests, but the court concluded that under the specific facts the recipients were limited partners).

[50] See supra ¶ 19.05[2][b][iii].

[51] See supra ¶ 19.05[2][b][iv].

[52] Reg. § 25.2704-2(c). See Reg. §§ 25.2704-2(d) Exs. 1–4. If, after an applicable restriction is disregarded, the governing instrument is less restrictive than state law, the ability to liquidate is determined by the governing instrument disregarding the applicable restriction. Reg. § 25.2704-2(d) Ex. 3.

[b] Applicable Restrictions

An applicable restriction is any restriction on an interest in a corporation or partnership that (1) limits the ability to liquidate the entity in whole or in part;[53] (2) is more restrictive than state law;[54] and (3) either lapses, in whole or in part, after the transfer[55] *or* can be removed, in whole or in part, by the transferor or any member of the transferor's family, either alone or collectively.[56]

At the heart of Section 2704 (b) is a determination whether an entity's restriction on liquidation is more restrictive than federal or state law.[57] It is the

---

[53] IRC § 2704(b)(2)(A); Reg. §§ 25.2704-2(b) (first sentence), 25.2704-2(d) Ex. 5; FSA 9919009 (Jan. 13, 1999).

The language of Regulations Section 25.2704-2(b) (first sentence) refers to "the ability to liquidate the entity (in whole or in part). . . . " By itself, this language could be read to refer to a complete liquidation or to a partial liquidation (i.e., a pro rata distribution of more than the current and accumulated earnings of the entity), and not to include the ability to liquidate one owner's equity interest in a non–pro rata liquidation. The failure of Regulations Section 25.2704-2(b) to refer back to the definition of "liquidation right" in Regulations Section 25.2704-1(a)(2)(v), which expressly refers to the right to compel the entity to acquire all or part of an owner's equity interest, could be construed to support this interpretation. However, the Service contends that the provision applies to the non–pro rata liquidation of an owner's equity interest. Reg. § 25.2704-2(d) Ex. 5.

Case law has concluded that Section 2704(b) does not apply to the non–pro rata liquidation of only one owner's equity interest. See Kerr v. Comm'r, 113 TC 449, 473 (1999); Knight v. Comm'r, 115 TC 506 (2000); Estate of Jones v. Comm'r, 116 TC 121 (2001).

[54] IRC § 2704(b)(3)(B); Reg. § 25.2704-2(b) (first sentence). See Priv. Ltr. Ruls. 9730004 (Apr. 3, 1997), 9842003 (July 2, 1998); TAMs 9723009 (Feb. 24, 1997), 9725002 (Mar. 3, 1997), 9735003 (May 8, 1997), 9736004 (June 6, 1997) (all involving limitations on ability to liquidate a partner's interest that were more restrictive than default provisions under state law). Compare Priv. Ltr. Rul. 9710021 (Dec. 6, 1996) (liquidation on set dates or other events not more restrictive than state law); FSA 200143004 (July 5, 2001) (no restrictions on liquidation of an S corporation other than state law.

[55] IRC § 2704(b)(2)(B)(i).

[56] IRC § 2704(b)(2)(B)(ii). See Reg. § 25.2704-2(d) Ex. (1), which effectively overturns the decision reached in Estate of Watts v. Comm'r, 51 TCM (CCH) 60 (1985), aff'd, 823 F2d 483 (11th Cir. 1987).

Ability to remove a restriction is determined by state law that would apply but for a more restrictive rule in the governing instrument. When this rule applies, de facto control of the entity is implicitly required after the transfer so that transferor or transferor's family members have the right to remove an otherwise nonlapsing restriction. See Reg. § 25.2704-2(d) Exs. 2, 3.

In TAM 9723009 (Feb. 24, 1997) (a de minimis interest of a non-family shareholder of a corporate general partner disregarded in determining whether the transferee's family could remove a restriction because the non-family shareholder was added for the purpose of avoiding Section 2704). See Kerr v. Comm'r, 113 TC 449, 470 (1999) (resolution of a similar issue unnecessary in the determination of the case).

[57] Thus, an applicable restriction excludes any restriction imposed by federal or state law. IRC § 2704(b)(3)(B).

Service's position that if there is a default provision under state law, any restriction that is more restrictive than the default provision (even though the restriction is permitted by state law) is an applicable restriction.[58] The Service has been unsuccessful in the cases considering the issue.[59]

There are exceptions to the applicable restriction definition. It does not include any commercially reasonable restrictions that arise out of any financing by the entity from a person who is not related[60] to the transferor, transferee, or a member of the family of either.[61] Any option, right to the property, or agreement that is subject to Section 2703 and that is disregarded under that section[62] is not an applicable restriction.[63]

The Secretary has authority to issue regulations, providing that other restrictions that have the effect of reducing the value of a transferred interest for purposes of the transfer taxes but that do not ultimately reduce the value of such interest to the transferee, are to be disregarded for purposes of applying Section 2704(b).[64]

Some states have amended their state laws to place greater restrictions on liquidation rights. See, e.g., Colo. Rev. Stat. Ann. § 7-62-603 (West 2001); 6 Del. Code Ann. § 17-603 (2001); Tex. Rev. Civ. Stat. Ann. art. 6132 a-1-6.03 (West 2002). Such amendments will likely result in forum shopping. See Mezzullo, "State Law Changes Affect FLP & FLLC Valuation Issues." 1 Pass-Through Entities 7 (Sept.–Oct. 1998).

[58] See supra note 54. See also Stephanson, "How to Establish a Successful Family Limited Partnership," 44 Prac. Law. 41, 51–53 (Sept. 1998); Owen "Valuation Discounts and Family Limited Partnerships: This Could Be the Last Time . . . ," 1 Pass-Through Entities 19, 21–22 (May–June 1998); Hausman, "Family Limited Partnerships" 78 Tax Notes 95, 104–108 (1998); Darby & Brier, "The Impact of Code Sec. 2704 on Family Limited Partnerships, 134 Tr. & Est. 79, 82–84 (Sept. 1995).

[59] In Kerr v. Comm'r, 113 TC 449, 469 (1999), the court held that a partnership agreement that provided for liquidation on the earlier of a fifty-year term or a dissolution by agreement of all the partners was not more restrictive than the limitations that would apply under Texas law. TRLPA ¶ 8.01. Id. at 472. The *Kerr* case has been followed in Knight v. Comm'r, 115 TC 506 (2000) (Texas law); Estate of Jones v. Comm'r, 116 TC 121 (2001) (Texas law); Estate of Harper v. Comm'r, 79 TCM (CCH) 2232 (2000) (same result under California law). Cf. supra note 53.

[60] The term "not related" is defined by the regulations to include any person whose relationship to the transferor, transferee, or any member of the family of either is not described in Section 267(b). Reg. § 25.2704-2(b). For purposes of this definition, the term "fiduciary of a trust" as used in Section 267(b) excludes banks as defined in Section 581. Id.

[61] IRC § 2704(b)(3)(A). See Reg. § 25.2704-2(d) Ex. 4, which would apply the exception if the lender were not a related person.

[62] See ¶ 19.04.

[63] Reg. § 25.2704-2(b).

[64] IRC § 2704(b)(4).

[4] Effective Dates

Section 2704(a) applies to lapses occurring after January 28, 1992, of rights created after October 8, 1990.[65] Section 2704(b) applies to transfers occurring after January 28, 1992, of property subject to an applicable restriction created after October 8, 1990.[66] For lapses and transfers after October 8, 1990 (the date of the enactment of Section 2704), and prior to January 28, 1992 (the date of the finalized regulations), any reasonable interpretation of the statutory provisions may be used.[67]

---

[65] Omnibus Budget Reconciliation Act of 1990, Pub. L. No. 101-508, § 11602(e)(1)(A)(iii), 104 Stat. 1388-1, 1388-500 (1990), reprinted in 1991-2 CB 481, 529; Reg. § 25.2704-3. See Priv. Ltr. Ruls. 9229028 (Apr. 21, 1992); 9352012 (Sept. 29, 1993) (rights created prior to Oct. 9, 1990 not altered in post-Oct. 8, 1990 tax-free reorganization), 9802004 (Sept. 30, 1997) (rights in entities created prior to Oct. 9, 1990). With respect to property transferred prior to October 8, 1990, any failure to pay dividends and a failure to exercise any other rights shall not be treated as a subsequent transfer. Omnibus Budget Reconciliation Act of 1990, Pub. L. No. 101-508, § 602(e)(i)(B), 104 Stat. 1388-1, 1388-501 (1990), reprinted in 1991-2 CB 481, 529.

[66] Omnibus Budget Reconciliation Act of 1990, Pub. L. No. 101-508, § 11602(e)(1)(A)(iii), 104 Stat. 1388-1, 1388-500 (1990), reprinted in 1991-2 CB 481, 529; Reg. § 25.2704-3. See Priv. Ltr. Rul. 9711017 (Dec. 11, 1996) (restrictions imposed prior to Oct. 9, 1990 not altered in post–October 8, 1990, tax-free reorganization).

[67] Reg. § 25.2704-3. The provisions of any proposed or final regulations are considered a reasonable interpretation. Id.

Table of IRC Sections

[Text references are to paragraphs and notes ("n.").]

[Text references are to paragraphs and notes ("n.").]

[Text references are to paragraphs and notes ("n.").]

[Text references are to paragraphs and notes ("n.").]

[Text references are to paragraphs and notes ("n.").]

[Text references are to paragraphs and notes ("n.").]

[Text references are to paragraphs and notes ("n.").]

[Text references are to paragraphs and notes ("n.").]

[Text references are to paragraphs and notes ("n.").]

[Text references are to paragraphs and notes ("n.").]

[Text references are to paragraphs and notes ("n.").]

[Text references are to paragraphs and notes ("n.").]

[Text references are to paragraphs and notes ("n.").]

[Text references are to paragraphs and notes ("n.").]

[Text references are to paragraphs and notes ("n.").]

[Text references are to paragraphs and notes ("n.").]

[Text references are to paragraphs and notes ("n.").]

[Text references are to paragraphs and notes ("n.").]

[Text references are to paragraphs and notes ("n.").]

[Text references are to paragraphs and notes ("n.").]

[Text references are to paragraphs and notes ("n.").]

[Text references are to paragraphs and notes ("n.").]

[Text references are to paragraphs and notes ("n.").]

[Text references are to paragraphs and notes ("n.").]

[Text references are to paragraphs and notes ("n.").]

[Text references are to paragraphs and notes ("n.").]

[Text references are to paragraphs and notes ("n.").]

[Text references are to paragraphs and notes ("n.").]

[Text references are to paragraphs and notes ("n.").]

[Text references are to paragraphs and notes ("n.").]

[Text references are to paragraphs and notes ("n.").]

[Text references are to paragraphs and notes ("n.").]

[Text references are to paragraphs and notes ("n.").]

[Text references are to paragraphs and notes ("n.").]

[Text references are to paragraphs and notes ("n.").]

[Text references are to paragraphs and notes ("n.").]

[Text references are to paragraphs and notes ("n.").]

[Text references are to paragraphs and notes ("n.").]

[Text references are to paragraphs and notes ("n.").]

[Text references are to paragraphs and notes ("n.").]

[Text references are to paragraphs and notes ("n.").]

Table of
Treasury Regulations

[Text references are to paragraphs and notes ("n.").]

[Text references are to paragraphs and notes ("n.").]

[Text references are to paragraphs and notes ("n.").]

[Text references are to paragraphs and notes ("n.").]

[Text references are to paragraphs and notes ("n.").]

[Text references are to paragraphs and notes ("n.").]

[Text references are to paragraphs and notes ("n.").]

[Text references are to paragraphs and notes ("n.").]

[Text references are to paragraphs and notes ("n.").]

[Text references are to paragraphs and notes ("n.").]

[Text references are to paragraphs and notes ("n.").]

[Text references are to paragraphs and notes ("n.").]

[Text references are to paragraphs and notes ("n.").]

[Text references are to paragraphs and notes ("n.").]

[Text references are to paragraphs and notes ("n.").]

[Text references are to paragraphs and notes ("n.").]

[Text references are to paragraphs and notes ("n.").]

[Text references are to paragraphs and notes ("n.").]

[Text references are to paragraphs and notes ("n.").]

TEMPORARY REGULATIONS

[Text references are to paragraphs and notes ("n.").]

[Text references are to paragraphs and notes ("n.").]

[Text references are to paragraphs and notes ("n.").]

Table
of Revenue Rulings,
Revenue Procedures,
and Other IRS Releases

[Text references are to paragraphs and notes ("n.").]

REVENUE RULINGS

[Text references are to paragraphs and notes ("n.").]

[Text references are to paragraphs and notes ("n.").]

[Text references are to paragraphs and notes ("n.").]

[Text references are to paragraphs and notes ("n.").]

[Text references are to paragraphs and notes ("n.").]

[Text references are to paragraphs and notes ("n.").]

[*Text references are to paragraphs and notes ("n.").*]

[Text references are to paragraphs and notes ("n.").]

[Text references are to paragraphs and notes ("n.").]

ANNOUNCEMENTS

FIELD SERVICE ADVICE

GENERAL COUNSEL'S MEMORANDA

INCOME TAX UNIT RULINGS

IRS LEGAL MEMORANDA

[Text references are to paragraphs and notes ("n.").]

NOTICES

Notice

89-24 . . . . 4.02[5] n.244; 10.02[2][b][iii] n.57;
16.02[6] n.409
89-60 . . . . 4.02[5] n.244
94-78 . . . . 5.05[5][a][i] n.169
96-34 . . . . 8.01[1][a][iii] ns. 26, 27
97-19 . . . . . 6.07[1] ns. 12, 14, 15; 9.02[1] n.7
97-63 . . . . 5.05[3][b][ii] n.115
98-34 . . . . 6.07[1] n.15
99-31 . . . . 5.05[5][b][i] n.228
2000-37 . . . . . . 5.05[5][a] n.158; 1 5.05[5][b]
n.214; 1.02[2][b][i] n.56; 11.02[2][b][ii]
n.67
2001-50 . . . 16.02[4][a] n.225; 16.02[9][a] n.575
2001-62 . . . . 10.07[2][b] n.30

TECHNICAL ADVICE MEMORANDA

TAM

8137027 . . . . 6.01[3][b] n.32
8512004 . . . . 3.05[3][b] n.46
8546001 . . . . 19.03[1] n.14
8727003 . . . . 9.04[3][f] n.104
9005001 . . . . 4.05[2][a] n.6
9005002 . . . . 5.06[8][d][ii] n.355
9008003 . . . . 5.06[3][g] n.69
9010004 . . . . 4.07[2][b][ii] n.49
9010005 . . . . 4.07[2][b][ii] n.49
9013001 . . . . 4.04[6] n.218
9015001 . . . . 4.07[2][b][ii] n.49
9016002 . . . . 4.07[2][b][ii] n.49
9017002 . . . . 4.07[2][b][ii] n.49
9018002 . . . . 4.05[2][a] n.6
9021002 . . . . 5.06[8][b][iii] n.250
9023004 . . . . 5.06[8][b][iii] n.250
9027004 . . . . 4.04[6] n.226
9033004 . . . . 5.06[8][d][ii] n.334
9038002 . . . . 4.04[6] ns. 224, 235
9040001 . . . . 5.06[8][d][ii] n.334
9040003 . . . . 6.06[2] n.28
9045002 . . . . 9.04[3][f] n.104
9049002 . . . . 4.07[2][b][ii] n.49
9050004 . . . . 5.06[5] n.93
9051002 . . . . 5.03[3][c] n.71
9113028 . . . . 4.04[7][b][i] n.277
9127008 . . . . 10.01[5] n.146
9128001 . . . . 6.04[1] n.6
9128009 . . . . 10.03[2] n.23
9131006 . . . . 9.04[3][e] n.87
9133001 . . . . 10.01[3][e] n.106
9135003 . . . . 6.06[2] n.22
9141008 . . . . 9.04[3][f] n.110
9145004 . . . . 3.05[3][b] n.46
9145005 . . . . 5.05[1][a] n.7

TAM

9207004 . . . . 5.03[5][a] n.101
9212001 . . . . 4.04[3][b][iii] n.53; 4.04[7][b][ii]
n.282
9217004 . . . . . . 10.01[3] n.77; 10.02[4] n.139
9220007 . . . . 5.06[8][d][ii] n.328
9225002 . . . . 4.04[6] n.235
9226007 . . . . 4.07[2][b][ii] n.49
9228001 . . . . 5.07[2][b] n.21
9228004 . . . . 5.06[3][h] n.82
9228005 . . . . 4.04[6] n.235
9229004 . . . . 5.06[8][d][ii] n.334
9230002 . . . . 4.04[6] n.220
9231003 . . . . 10.01[5] n.150
9232002 . . . . 10.01[3][c] n.96
9237009 . . . . 5.06[8][d][ii] n.325
9240003 . . . . 4.02[3][g] n.129
9244001 . . . . 5.06[8][e] n.413
9245002 . . . . 4.04[6] n.235
9301005 . . . . 5.06[3][h] n.82
9307001 . . . . 5.06[8][d][iii] n.383
9309001 . . . . 10.01[3][e] n.106
9315005 . . . . 10.01[2] n.13
9321046 . . . . 19.02[2][a][i] n.55
9326002 . . . . 8.04[2] n.16
9326003 . . . . 5.05[8][b] n.363
9327005 . . . . 5.06[8][d][iii] n.375
9327006 . . . . 5.05[8][b] ns. 364, 365
9328004 . . . . 4.04[5][a] n.180
9333002 . . . . 4.04[7][b][i] ns. 270, 274
9333004 . . . . 5.03[3][c] n.71
9346003 . . . . 4.04[6] n.235
9349003 . . . . 4.03[2] n.16
9403002 . . . . 4.02[4][b][ii] n.155
9409018 . . . . 5.06[5][b][i] n.103; 10.01[3][h]
n.124
9411010 . . . . 5.06[8][d][iii] n.383
9414019 . . . . 5.06[8][d][iii] n.383
9419006 . . . . 5.05[3][b][i] n.111
9428002 . . . . 4.04[3][c][ii] n.127
9432001 . . . . 4.02[4][b][ii] n.151
9434004 . . . . 8.04[2] n.16
9436005 . . . . 10.02[2][c][i] n.79
9441003 . . . . 4.04[6] n.220
9443003 . . . . 4.04[3][b][vi] n.74
9447004 . . . . 19.02[2][b][ii] n.103; 19.02[4][d]
n.217; 19.02[4][d][iv] n.263
9449001 . . . 4.02[4][b][ii] n.151; 4.02[4][b][iv]
n.168; 10.02[2][c][i] n.78
9506001 . . . . 19.03[3][b][i] n.138
9507044 . . . . 6.04[2] n.17
9508002 . . . . 4.04[6] n.220
9509003 . . . . 10.07[2][d] n.78
9511002 . . . . 5.06[8][b][iv] n.26
9533001 . . . . 11.03[5] n.110
9534001 . . . 13.02[4][b][ii] n.285; 16.02[9][b]
n.583
9550002 . . . . 19.04[3] n.35
9604002 . . . . 5.03[3][c] n.69
9604005 . . . . 19.03[3][b][i] n.139
9610005 . . . . 10.07[2] n.12
9628004 . . . . 9.04[3][f] n.110
9642001 . . . . 2.01[2] n.46

[Text references are to paragraphs and notes ("n.").]

TREASURY DECISIONS

Table of Cases

[Text references are to paragraphs and notes ("n.").]

[Text references are to paragraphs and notes ("n.").]

[Text references are to paragraphs and notes ("n.").]

[Text references are to paragraphs and notes ("n.").]

Busch, Estate of v. Comm'r . . . . . 4.02[3][b]
n.64; 4.02[4][e][i] n.203
Bush v. US . . . . . .5.03[8] n.161; 5.05[3][b][i]
n.104
Byram, Estate of v. Comm'r 4.06 n.13

C

Cafaro, Estate of v. Comm'r . . . . . 5.03[5][b]
n.125
Calder v. Comm'r . . . . .9.04[3][b] n.62
California Trust Co. v. Riddell . . . . . 4.05[6]
n.72; 5.06[8][a] n.205
Camp v. Comm'r   10.01[8] & ns. 193, 194;
10.01[10][e] n.231
Campbell, Universal Oil Prods. Co. v. . . . . .
. . . . .5.05[1][b] n.23
Campbell, Estate of v. Comm'r (TCM 1991)
. . . . 2.02[1] n.14
Campbell, Estate of v. Comm'r (TC 1972)
. . . . 10.02[4] n.141; 10.04[3][a] n.13
Caplan, Estate of v. Comm'r   19.04[6][a][i]
ns. 117, 119
Cardeza, Estate of v. Comm'r . . . . 4.05[5][b]
n.57; 5.03[2][a] n.20; 5.03[2][b] n.23
Carli v. Comm'r . . . . 4.05[3] n.23; 5.03[5][e]
n.140
Carlson v. Patterson . . . . . . 11.03[4][b] n.52
Carpenter v. Comm'r . . . . . . 19.04[1][b] n.1
Carpenter v. US . . . . 10.01[4] n.142
Carpenter, Estate of v. Comm'r   5.05[2][b]
n.68; 5.06[3][a] n.30; 5.06[8][b][iii]
n.245
Carr v. Comm'r . . . . 10.02[2][c][ii] n.89
Carrieres v. Comm'r . . . . 5.06[3][b] n.42
Carson v. Comm'r . . . . 9.02[2] n.12
Carson, Estate of v. Comm'r . . . . 5.03[3][b]
n.58
Carter v. US . . . . 5.03[2][a] n.20
Carter, Estate of v. US . . . . . . 3.05[3][b] n.37
Cartwright v. US . . . . 4.02[2][c] n.50;
4.02[3][d] & n.94
Cary, Estate of v. Comm'r . . . . 4.02[3][b] ns.
66, 72
Casey, Estate of v. Comm'r . . . 4.02[4][c][iii]
n.184
Cass v. Tomlinson . . . . . 5.06[8][b][iii] n.250
Cassidy, Estate of v. Comm'r . . . . 5.05[7][a]
n.330
Cavenaugh, Estate of v. Comm'r . . . .
. . . . 5.06[8][d][ii] n.329
Cavett, Estate of v. Comm'r . . . . . . 10.02[3]
n.131
Central Nat'l Bank, McDougall v. . . . 8.04[3]
ns. 18, 19
Central Trust of Cincinnati v. Welch . . . . . .
. . . . 5.03[4][a] n.91
Cerf v. Comm'r . . . . . . 10.01[8] ns. 199, 201;
10.01[9] n.207; 12.01[1] n.10
Cervi v. US . . . . 10.01[4] n.139
Cervin, Estate of v. Comm'r . . . . 4.02[4][e][i]
n.201

Chagra, Estate of v. Comm'r . . . .
. . . . 2.02[1] n.15
Chamberlain, Estate of v. Comm'r . . . .
. . . . . 10.07[2] n.27; 10.07[2][a] n.28
Champlin v. Comm'r . . . . 8.03[1] n.6
Chanin v. US . . . . 9.04[1][b] ns. 27, 28;
9.04[3][e] n.90; 10.01[2][b][i] ns. 19, 21;
10.02[6][a] n.173
Chapman, Estate of v. Comm'r . . . . . 3.04[2]
n.24
Charles v. Hassett . . . . 9.04[3][a] n.52
Chase Manhattan Bank, Comm'r v. . . . .
. . . . 10.01[5][d] n.172
Chase Nat'l Bank v. Comm'r . . . . . 10.02[4]
n.140
Chase Nat'l Bank of NY v. Comm'r . . . . . .
. . . . 6.03[2][b] n.35
Chastain v. Comm'r . . . . . 5.05[3][b][i] n.110;
8.04[1] n.12
Chenoweth, Estate of v. Comm'r . . . .
. . . 4.02[2][a] n.26; 5.05[5][a][ii] n.205;
5.05[5][b][ii] n.262; 5.05[5][c][i] n.288;
5.06[5] n.93
Cherokee Tobacco . . . . 7.06 ns. 6, 7
Chesterton, Estate of v. US . . . . . . 5.03[5][b]
n.120
Chew Heong v. US 7.06 n.9
Child v. US . . . . 5.05[1][b] n.36
Childress v. US . . . . 5.03[5][e] n.136
Child's Estate v Comm'r . . . . 19.04[6][a][ii]
n.132; 19.04[6][a][iii] n.134
Chiles v. US . . . . 5.06[5][a] n.95
Chown, Estate of v. Comm'r . . . 4.05[6] n.70
Christiernin v. Manning . . . . . 4.05[5][b] n.56
Christmas, Estate of v. Comm'r   5.06[6][b]
n.157
Church v. US (5th Cir.) . . . . 4.02[4][g] n.238
Church v. US (EDNY) . . . . 2.02[3][b][ii] n.45
Church v. US (WD Tex.) . . . . 10.01[2][b][ii]
n.25; 10.02[2][c][v] n.122; 19.04[2] ns.
25, 26; 19.04[3][a] n.48
Churchhill v. US . . . . 5.05[2][a] n.58
Cidulka, Estate of v. Comm'r . . . . 9.04[1][b]
n.34; 10.01[2] n.13; 10.01[2][d] n.31
Citizens & S. Nat'l Bank v. US . . . 5.06[3][a]
n.29
Citizens Bank & Trust Co. v. Comm'r . . . . .
. . . . 4.02[2][c] n.53
Citizens Bank & Trust Co. of Bloomington,
Pearcy v. . . . . 8.05[4] n.13
Citizens Fidelity Bank & Trust Co. v. US . . .
. . . . 19.04[6][a][ii] n.130
Citizens Nat'l Bank of Evansville v. US . . . .
. . . . 5.06[8][b][i] n.229
Citizens' Nat'l Bank of Waco v. US . . . .
. . . . 10.02[2][b][i] n.44
City Bank Farmers Trust Co., Helvering v.
. . . 10.01[10][e] n.232; 11.03[3][b] n.35
City Bank Farmers Trust Co. v. US . . . .
. . . . 6.05[2][a][i] n.16
Clack, Estate of v. Comm'r . . . 5.06[8][d][ii]
n.319
Clark v. Comm'r . . . . 9.04[3][a] n.58; 9.05[1]
n.5; 10.03[3][b] n.44

[Text references are to paragraphs and notes ("n.").]

[Text references are to paragraphs and notes ("n.").]

[Text references are to paragraphs and notes ("n.").]

[Text references are to paragraphs and notes ("n.").]

G

[Text references are to paragraphs and notes ("n.").]

[Text references are to paragraphs and notes ("n.").]

[Text references are to paragraphs and notes ("n.").]

[Text references are to paragraphs and notes ("n.").]

[Text references are to paragraphs and notes ("n.").]

[Text references are to paragraphs and notes ("n.").]

[Text references are to paragraphs and notes ("n.").]

Mergott, Estate of v. US . . . . 5.06[3][a] n.30;
5.06[3][b] n.38
Meriano, Estate of v. Comm'r . . . . 5.03[3][a]
n.41; 5.04[3] n.15
Merriam, US v. . . . . 5.03[3][a] n.50
Merrill v. Fahs . . . . . 4.06 n.16; 10.02[5][d]
n.167; 10.06[1] n.4; 10.06[3] n.33
Merwin, Estate of v. Comm'r . . . 4.04[6] ns.
233, 237
Messing v. Comm'r . . . . 4.02[2][a] n.8;
4.02[3][f] n.113
Metcalf, Estate of v. Comm'r . . . . 5.03[5][b]
n.124
Metzger, Estate of v. Comm'r . . . . . . 4.05[3]
n.28; 10.01[3][h] n.122
Meyer, Estate of v. Comm'r . . . . . 3.05[4][a]
n.58; 3.05[4][b] n.59
Meyer v. US . . . . 5.06[8][c] & n.292
Michigan Trust Co. v. Comm'r . . . .
. . . . 19.04[6][a][ii] n.124
Miglionico v. US . . . . 4.05[2] n.4
Miller v. Comm'r (9th Cir.) . . . 10.01[1] n.9;
10.01[4] n.143
Miller v. Comm'r (TC) . . . . . . 5.04[3] n.18
Miller v. US . . . . 4.04[3][c] n.104
Miller, Estate of v. Comm'r . . . . . 4.05[5][b]
n.53
Miller, Estate of v. US . . . 5.06[8][d][ii] n.331
Millikin, Estate of v. Comm'r . . . .
. . . . 5.03[3] n.38
Mills, Comm'r v. . . . . 10.02[6][b] n.174
Mill's Will, In re . . . . 8.04[2] n.17
Mimnaugh v. US . . . . 4.05[6] n.67
Minotto, Estate of v. Comm'r . . . .
. . . . 4.05[6] n.73
Minskoff v. US . . . . 4.05[7][b] n.85
Minter v. US . . . . 4.04[3][b][v] n.68;
4.04[7][b][ii] n.286
Mitchell, Estate of v. Comm'r (9th Cir.) . . . .
. . . 4.02[2][a] ns. 13, 31, 37; 4.02[3][b]
n.69; 4.02[4][e][vi] n.224; 4.02[4][e][vii]
n.225; 4.02[4][f] n.231
Mitchell, Estate of v. Comm'r (TCM 1981)
. . . . 4.05[5][b] n.52
Mitchell, Estate of v. Comm'r (TCM 1968)
. . . . 4.02[3][b] n.60
Mittelman, Estate of v. Comm'r . . . .
. . . . 5.06[8][b][i] n.218
Mladinich, Estate of v. Comm'r . . 4.05[5][a]
n.46
Moir v. US . . . . 5.03[3][a] n.44
Molter v. US . . . . 4.05[8] n.105
Monroe v. US . . . . 10.04[3][e] n.27
Monroe, Estate of v. Comm'r . . . 10.07[2][c]
n.73
Mooneyham v. Comm'r . . . .
. . . . 10.02[2][c][ii] n.89
Moor, Estate of v. Comm'r . . . . . . 5.05[4][a]
n.128
Moore v. Comm'r (2d Cir.) . . . . 10.02[6][d]
n.185
Moore v. Comm'r (TCM) . . . 4.02[3][f] n.115;
4.02[4][c][ii] n.174
Moore, Knowlton v. . . . . 12.01[1] n.1

Moore v. US (WD Ky.) . . . . 5.06[7][b] n.179
Moore v. US (ND Ohio) . . . . 5.06[8][c] n.286
Moore, Estate of v. Comm'r . . . . . 5.03[5][b]
n.128
Morgan v. Comm'r . . . . 4.05[2][a] n.5
Morris v. Comm'r . . . . 4.02[3][b] n.70
Morrissey v. Comm'r . . . . . . 4.02[2][a] n.28
Morse, Estate of v. Comm'r . . . . . 5.03[5][e]
n.140
Morton v. Comm'r . . . . 4.02[2][a] n.29
Morton, Taylor v. . . . . 7.06 ns. 6, 8
Morton, Estate of v. Comm'r . . . .
. . . . 4.05[6] n.73
Motter, Beeler v. . . . . 4.07[3][b] n.87
Mosher v. US . . . . 5.05[3][b][i] n.109
Moss, Estate of v. Comm'r (TCM 1982) . . . .
. . . . 5.06[3][a] n.31
Moss, Estate of v. Comm'r (TC 1980) . . . . .
. . . . 4.05[3] n.32
Mudry v. US . . . . 7.02[3] & ns. 77, 79
Mueller v. US . . . . 9.04[5][a] n.147
Mueller, Estate of v. Comm'r . . . . 4.02[2][a]
ns. 27, 33, 35; 4.02[4][e][vii] n.226
Mulliken v. Magruder . . . 4.02[3][g] ns. 126,
135, 136
Murchie, Delaney v. . . . . 6.03[2][a] ns. 22, 23;
6.04[2] ns. 13, 14
Murphy, Estate of v. Comm'r 4.02[4][b][i]
n.150; 4.02[4][b][iii] n.163; 4.02[4][g]
n.237; 19.04[2] n.26
Murrah v. Wiseman . . . . 4.05[5][a] n.47
Murray v. US . . . . 5.06[5][b][iii] n.134
Muserlian v. Comm'r . . . . 10.01[1] n.11
Musgrove, Estate of v. Comm'r . . . . . 4.05[3]
n.32; 4.07[2][b][i] n.40

N

National Sav. Trust Co. v. US . . . . 5.05[1][b]
n.41
National Taxpayers Union v. US . . . . 2.01[3]
n.67
National Westminster Bank, PLC v. US . . . .
. . . . 7.06 n.10
Nationsbank of Tex., NA v. US . . . . . 2.01[3]
n.67
Naumoff v. Comm'r . . . . 9.04[4] n.142
Neal v. US . . . . 10.01[5] ns. 150, 153
Necastro, Estate of v. Comm'r . . . 4.02[2][a]
ns. 27, 37; 4.02[3][b] n.71; 4.02[4][e][v]
ns. 222, 223
Neisen, Estate of v. Comm'r . . . . . 5.06[6][b]
n.157
Neilson, Foster v. 7.06 n.6
Nelson v. Comm'r . . . . 5.06[7][b] n.187
Nelson, Estate of v. Comm'r (TCM 1983) . . .
. . . . 5.06[8][b][iii] n.245
Nelson, Estate of v. Comm'r (TCM 1980) . . .
. . . . 4.02[2][a] n.10
Nemerov, Estate of v. Comm'r . . . . . 4.05[4]
n.39
Nettz v. Phillips . . . . 5.06[8][d][iv] n.400

[Text references are to paragraphs and notes ("n.").]

[Text references are to paragraphs and notes ("n.").]

Q

R

[Text references are to paragraphs and notes ("n.").]

[Text references are to paragraphs and notes ("n.").]

[Text references are to paragraphs and notes ("n.").]

[Text references are to paragraphs and notes ("n.").]

[Text references are to paragraphs and notes ("n.").]

[Text references are to paragraphs and notes ("n.").]

Y

Z

Index

[References are to paragraphs.]

M